October 24–28, 2016
Indianapolis, IN, USA

Association for
Computing Machinery

Advancing Computing as a Science & Profession

CIKM'16

Proceedings of the 2016 ACM
Conference on Information and Knowledge Management

Sponsored by:

ACM SIGIR & ACM SIGWEB

Supported by:

Alibaba Group, Baidu, Huawei, Data-Centric Alliance, Google, Yahoo! Research, Prof. Ram Kumar Memorial Foundation, Whova, AMiner, Techpoint, Walmart, IUPUI, & Universtiy of Illinois at Urbana-Champaign

Association for
Computing Machinery

Advancing Computing as a Science & Profession

The Association for Computing Machinery
2 Penn Plaza, Suite 701
New York, New York 10121-0701

Notice to Past Authors of ACM-Published Articles
ACM intends to create a complete electronic archive of all articles and/or other material previously published by ACM. If you have written a work that has been previously published by ACM in any journal or conference proceedings prior to 1978, or any SIG Newsletter at any time, and you do NOT want this work to appear in the ACM Digital Library, please inform permissions@acm.org, stating the title of the work, the author(s), and where and when published.

ISBN: 978-1-4503-4073-1 (Digital)

ISBN: 978-1-4503-4719-8 (Print)

Additional copies may be ordered prepaid from:

ACM Order Department
PO Box 30777
New York, NY 10087-0777, USA

Phone: 1-800-342-6626 (USA and Canada)
+1-212-626-0500 (Global)
Fax: +1-212-944-1318
E-mail: acmhelp@acm.org
Hours of Operation: 8:30 am – 4:30 pm ET

Printed in the USA

CIKM 2016 General Chairs' Welcome

Warm welcome to the 2016 ACM International Conference on Information and Knowledge Management (CIKM 2016)! CIKM is held annually at locations all over the world. The last two years it has been in Australia and China. In 2016 it returns to the United States in Indianapolis and is held Oct. 24-28.

CIKM 2016 will be the 25th running of the conference, which remains the only conference that inherently focuses on the need for users to have unified systems that access structured and unstructured data. With a new theme on Frontier and Applications of Big Data Science, CIKM 2016 further broadens the scope of topics of CIKM to include all topics in the general area of data science, including both foundational work and applications and encouraging interdisciplinary topics across multiple relevant communities such as information retrieval, databases, data mining, and knowledge management. CIKM has traditionally emphasized on relevance to industry and government applications; CIKM 2016 continues this tradition and further increases this emphasis by including a CIKM Cup Workshop and expanding its Industry Track to include a variety of submissions including long papers, short papers, and software system demonstrations in addition to its invited talks. Furthermore, to facilitate recruiting and encourage interactions between students and industry recruiters, CIKM 2016 introduced a new Career Day event. The conference also has a special session "CIKM at its 25th Anniversary" to celebrate its growth and success. The whole conference program includes eight tutorials, eight workshops, 182 oral presentations of full papers, 116 poster presentations of short papers, 20 system demonstrations, and three keynote talks. We are honored and grateful to have three outstanding members of National Academy of Engineering as our keynote speakers, Rakesh Agrawal, Andrei Broder, and Susan Dumais.

Organizing a conference such as CIKM requires the dedication and effort of many volunteers. We are grateful to an outstanding group of colleagues for serving on the organization team and for generously contributing their time and energy, including especially our Local Organization Chair and Treasurer, Mohammad Al Hasan; Research Track Program Chairs, Elisa Bertino, Fabio Crestani, Javed Mostafa, Jie Tang, Luo Si, and Xiaofang Zhou; Industry Track Program Chairs, Yi Chang, Yunyao Li, and Parikshit Sondhi; Tutorial Chairs, Hui Fang, Latifur Khan, and Charles Nicholas; Workshop Chairs, Iadh Ounis, Huawei Shen, and Min Song; CIKM Cup Chairs, Pavel Izhutov and Nikita Spirin; Sponsorship Chairs, Sarath Janga (who also Co-Chaired the Career Day with Snehasis), Dou Shen, and Yi Zhang; Publication Chairs, Kavita Ganesan, Chase Geigle, and Xia Ning; Publicity Chairs, David Grossman, Yan Qu, and Hongning Wang; and Event Coordinator, Maureen Bowling who has taken care of most logistics of the conference. The conference would be impossible to organize without their volunteer spirit. Throughout the entire period of conference organization, we have also benefited from advice and mentoring from the CIKM Steering Committee, especially the past chair David Grossman and the current chair Jimi Shanahan, past CIKM Chairs Alistair Moffat, James Bailey, and Qi He, and other conference chairs, James Allan, Ricardo Baeza-Yates, Charles Clarke, Bruce Croft, Hang Li, Mark Sanderson, and Marianne Winslett. We want to thank all of them, especially Jimi and Alistair who not only provided mentoring but also offered detailed help for the conference budget and multiple planning decisions. Finally, we want to thank the two hosting universities, IUPUI and UIUC, ACM sponsors, SIGIR and SIGWEB, special sponsors, Professor Ram Kumar Memorial Foundation, AMiner and Whova, and all our corporate sponsors, especially our Platinum

Sponsor Alibaba, Gold Sponsor Baidu, Silver Sponsor Huawei, and Bronze (CIKM Cup) Sponsor DCA for their generous support for CIKM 2016.

We hope that you will enjoy the conference and the opportunity to share and discuss ideas in Big Data Science with other researchers and practitioners around the world.

Snehasis Mukhopadhyay
CIKM'16 General CoChair
Indiana University Purdue University Indianapolis, USA

ChengXiang Zhai
CIKM'16 General CoChair
University of Illinois at Urbana-Champaign, USA

CIKM 2016 Industry Track Program Chairs' Preface

It is our great pleasure to welcome you to industry track of the 25th ACM International Conference on Information and Knowledge Management (CIKM 2016). Our primary emphasis is on papers that advance the understanding of, and show how to deal with, practical issues related to the deployment of information and knowledge management systems that address the need for integration of structured and unstructured data in real-world applications.

CIKM 2016 Industry Track attracted a significant number of submissions from countries all over the world: 111 long paper (10-page) submissions, 22 accepted (19.8% acceptance rate); 26 short paper (4-page) submissions, 7 accepted (26.9% acceptance rate). CIKM being a premier conference in information retrieval, data mining and databases, the acceptance rates historically tend to be low.

Each paper was first independently reviewed by at least three program committee members, and then discussed among them in a discussion moderated by a program chair. Borderline papers were thoroughly reviewed by the program chairs before final decisions were made.

All accepted long papers will be presented at the talk sessions and all short papers at the poster sessions. We have invited outstanding keynotes to be given by internationally renowned, distinguished scientists and practitioners: Rong Jin (Alibaba), Marc Nojork (Google), Shivakumar Vaithyanathan (IBM Research), and Haifeng Wang (Baidu).

We hope that you will find this program interesting, and that this industry track will provide you with a valuable opportunity to learn and exchange ideas with other researchers and practitioners from academia, industry and governments around the world.

Yi Chang
Yahoo Research

Yunyao Li
IBM Research - Almaden

Parikshit Sondhi
WalmartLabs

PC Chairs' Welcome

It is our great pleasure to welcome you to the 25th ACM International Conference on Information and Knowledge Management (CIKM 2016), held in Indianapolis, USA from October 24–28, 2016. CIKM is a top-tier ACM conference in the areas of information retrieval, knowledge management and databases. Since 1992, it has successfully brought together leading researchers and developers from the three communities, with the purpose of identifying challenging problems facing the development of advanced knowledge and information systems, and shaping future research directions through the publication of high quality, applied and theoretical research findings. CIKM 2016 continues to create an outstanding technical program including research paper presentations; poster presentations for extended short papers and short papers; and industry track presentations arranged by Industry Track Chairs. In total, we have received 701 full paper (10 pages) submissions and 234 short paper (4 pages) submissions reviewed by a group of 60 senior program committee members and 464 program committee members. The research track accepted 160 full papers with acceptance rate as 23%. 54 full paper submissions were accepted as extended short papers (6 pages) and 55 short submissions were accepted as short papers (4 pages) with acceptance rate as 24%.

We are grateful to everyone who made this technical program possible. First of all, we would like to thank all the contributing authors who submitted their excellent work. The conference would not exist without your contributions. Second, we would in particular like to recognize the immense efforts of the senior program committee members, program committee members, and external reviewers, who selected the technical program with their great expertise. Finally, we hope to thank all our corporate sponsors for their generous support.

We hope you enjoy the program and the opportunity to interact and collaborate with friends and colleagues from around the world.

CIKM 2016 PC Chairs

Elisa Bertino
Purdue University

Fabio Crestani
University of Lugano

Javed Mostafa
University of North Carolina

Jie Tang
Tsinghua University

Luo Si
Alibaba Group Inc
& Purdue University

Xiaofang Zhou
University of Queensland

Table of Contents

Session 1d: Better Queries

Session 1e: Better Search

Session 1f: Industry Session I

Session 2a: Learning to Rank

Session 2b: Question Answering

Session 2c: Wikipedia

Session 2d: Clustering

Session 2e: Understanding Text

Keynote Address 2

Session 4a: Information Retrieval

Session 4b: User Behavior and Interfaces

Session 4c: Documents

Session 4d: Knowledge Mining and Management

Session 4e: Truth Discovery

Session 4f: Industry Session IV

Session 5a: Sentiment and Opinion Mining

Session 5b: Time Series

Session 5c: Learning for Classification and Prediction

Session 5d: Social Media

Session 5e: Queries and Search

Session 5f: Industry Session V

Session 6e: Entity Detection and Analysis

Session 6f: Industry Session VI

Session 7a: Advertising and Ranking

Session 7b: Query Analytics

Session 7c: Information Retrieval III

Session 7d: Data Mining

Session 7e: Network Analytics

Session 8d: Algorithms

Session 8e: High Performance Big Data

Session 8f: Industry Session VIII

Poster Session I: Short Papers

Poster Session II: Extended Short Papers

Industry Track Short Papers

Industry Track Demo Papers

Workshops

CIKM 2016 Organization

General Chairs: Snehasis Mukhopadhyay (Indiana University Purdue University Indianapolis, USA)
ChengXiang Zhai (University of Illinois at Urbana-Champaign, USA)

Local Organization Chair and Treasurer: Mohammad Al Hasan (Indiana University – Purdue University Indianapolis, USA)

Research Track Program Chairs: Elisa Bertino (Purdue University, USA)
Fabio Crestani (University of Lugano, Switzerland)
Javed Mostafa (University of North Carolina, USA)
Luo Si (Alibaba Group Inc and Purdue University, USA)
Jie Tang (Tsinghua University, China)
Xiaofang Zhou (University of Queensland, Australia)

Industry Track Program Chairs: Yi Chang (Yahoo Research, USA)
Yunyao Li (IBM Almaden Research Center, USA)
Parikshit Sondhi (WalmartLabs, USA)

Proceedings Chairs: Kavita Ganesan, (Github Inc., USA)
Chase Geigle (University of Illinois at Urbana-Champaign, USA)
Xia Ning (Indiana University – Purdue University Indianapolis, USA)

Tutorial Chairs: Hui Fang (University of Delaware, USA)
Latifur Khan (University of Texas at Dallas, USA)
Charles Nicholas (University of Maryland, Baltimore County, USA)

Workshop Chairs: Iadh Ounis (University of Glasgow, UK)
Huawei Shen (Chinese Academy of Sciences , China)
Min Song (Yonsei University, Korea)

Publicity Chairs: David Grossman (Georgetown University, USA)
Yan Qu (eBay Inc, USA)
Hongning Wang (University of Virginia, USA)

Sponsorship Chairs: Sarath Janga (Indiana University – Purdue University Indianapolism USA)
Dou Shen (Baidu, China)
Yi Zhang (University of California, Santa Cruz, USA)

CIKM Cup Chairs: Pavel Izhutov (Stanford University, USA)
Nik Spirin (University of Illinois at Urbana-Champaign, USA)

CIKM Career Day Chairs: Sarath Janga (Indiana University – Purdue University Indianapolis)
Snehasis Mukhopadhyay (Indiana University – Purdue University Indianapolis)

Steering Committee:
James G. Shanahan (University of California Berkeley & Church and Duncan Group Inc, USA)
Ricardo Baeza-Yates, (Universidad de Chile, Chile)
Nick Craswell (Microsoft Bing, USA)
Marianne Winslett (University of Illinois at Urbana–Champaign, USA)
Phillip Yu (University of Illinois at Chicago, USA)
Rakesh Agrawal (Data Insights Laboratories, USA)

Senior Program Committee:
James Allan (UMass Amherst, USA)
Gionis Aristides (Aalto University, Finland)
Ira Assent (Aarhus University, Denmark)
Leif Azzopardi (University of Glasgow, United Kingdom)
Michael Bendersky (Google, Inc., USA)
Klaus Berberich (Max Planck Institute for Informatics, Germany)
Francesco Bonchi (The ISI Foundation, Turin, Italy)
Fazli Can (Bilkent University, Turkey)
K. Selcuk Candan (Arizona State University, USA)
Robert G Capra (University of North Carolina, USA)
Benjamin Carterette (University of Delaware, USA)
Carlos Castillo (Eurecat, Spain)
James Caverlee (Texas A&M University, USA)
Lei Chen (Hong Kong University of Science and Technology, Hong Kong)
Bruce Croft (University of Massachusetts Amherst, USA)
J. Shane Culpepper (RMIT University, Australia)
Maarten de Rijke (University of Amsterdam, Netherlands)
Gianluca Demartini (University of Sheffield, United Kingdom)
Debora Donato (StumbleUpon Inc, USA)
Eduard Dragut (Temple University, USA)
Yi Fang (Santa Clara University, USA)
Zhu Feida (Singapore Management University, Singapore)
Nicola Ferro (University of Padua, Italy)
Rayid Ghani (University of Chicago, USA)
Mohammad Hasan (Indiana University Purdue University, USA)
Claudia Hauff (Delft University of Technology, Netherlands)
Jimmy Huang (York University, Canada)
Yoshiharu Ishikawa (Nagoya University, Japan)
Shen Jialie (Singapore Management University, Singapore)
Hideo Joho (University of Tsukuba, Japan)
Gareth Jones (Dublin City University, Ireland)
Jaap Kamps (University of Amsterdam, Netherlands)
Murat Kantarcioglu (University of Texas at Dallas, USA)
Diane Kelly (University of Tennessee, USA)
Nick Koudas (University of Toronto, Canada)
Oren Kurland (Technion, Israel Institute of Technology, Israel)
Wai Lam (The Chinese University of Hong Kong, Hong Kong)
Guoliang Li (Tsinghua University, China)
Sebastian Link (The University of Auckland, New Zealand)

Senior Program Committee (continued):

Christina Lioma (University of Copenhagen, Denmark)
Donato Malerba (Università degli Studi di Bari Aldo Moro, Italy)
Don Metzler (Google, USA)
Jian-Yun Nie (Universit, de Montr,al, Canada)
Andreas Nuernberger (Otto-von-Guericke University of Magdeburg, Germany)
Iadh Ounis (University of Glasgow, United Kingdom)
Gabriella Pasi (Università degli Studi di Milano Bicocca, Italy)
Wen-Chih Peng (National Chiao Tung University, Taiwan)
Raffaele Perego (ISTI-CNR, Italy)
Mark Sanderson (RMIT University, Australia)
Jaideep Srivastava (University of Minnesota, USA)
Jimeng Sun (Georgia Tech, USA)
Yizhou Sun (Northeastern University, USA)
Hanghang Tong (City College, CUNY, USA)
Suresh Venkatasubramanian (University of Utah, USA)
Jun Wang (Alibaba Group Inc, USA)
Wei Wang (UCLA, USA)
Ryen White (Microsoft Research, USA)
Xintao Wu (University of Arkansas, USA)
Emine Yilmaz (University College London, United Kingdom)
Aidong Zhang (State University of New York at Buffalo, USA)

Research Track PC:

Foto Afrati (National Technical University of Athens, Greece)
Mikhail Ageev (Moscow State University, Russia)
Maristella Agosti (University of Padua, Italy)
Dirk Ahlers (NTNU, Norway)
Gail-Joon Ahn (Arizona State University, USA)
Ahmet Aker (University of Sheffield, United Kingdom)
Elif Aktolga (University of Massachusetts Amherst, USA)
M-Dyaa Albakour (Signal Media, United Kingdom)
Alex Alejandro (Aicure, USA)
Jussara Almeida (UFMG, Brazil)
Omar Alonso (Microsoft, USA)
Ismail Sengor Altingovde (Middle East Technical University, Turkey)
Giambattista Amati (Fondazione Ugo Bordoni, Italy)
Aijun An (York University, Canada)
Aris Anagnostopoulos (Sapienza University of Rome, Italy)
David Anastasiu (University of Minnesota, USA)
Linda Andersson (Vienna University of Technology, Austria)
Annalisa Appice (University Aldo Moro of Bari, Italy)
Avi Arampatzis (Democritus University of Thrace, Greece)
Walid Aref (Purdue University, USA)
Azin Ashkan (Technicolor Labs, USA)
Medha Atre (IIT Kanpur, India)
Bahman Bahmani (Stanford University, USA)
Zhifeng Bao (RMIT University, Australia)

Research Track PC (continued):

Pierpaolo Basile (University of Bari, Italy)
Roberto Basili (Univ. of Roma Tor Vergata, Italy)
Senjuti Basu Roy (University of Washington Tacoma, USA)
Srikanta Bedathur (IBM Research, India)
Behshad Behzadi (Google Inc., Switzerland)
Nicholas Belkin (Rutgers University, USA)
Patrice Bellot (LSIS - Univ. Marseille, France)
Fabricio Benevenuto (Federal University of Minas Gerais (UFMG), Brazil)
Michele Berlingerio (IBM Research, Ireland)
Catherine Berrut (LIG, Université Joseph Fourier Grenoble I, France)
Kanishka Bhaduri (Netflix Inc, USA)
Arnab Bhattacharya (Indian Institute of Technology, Kanpur, India)
Marco Bianchi (CNIPA, Italy)
Ralf Bierig (Vienna University of Technology, Austria)
Albert Bifet (Telecom ParisTech, France)
Petko Bogdanov (University at albany SUNY, USA)
Paolo Boldi (Università degli Studi di Milano, Italy)
Gloria Bordogna (National Research Council of Italy - CNR, Italy)
Mohamed Bouguessa (Université du Québec à Montréal - UQAM, Canada)
Panagiotis Bouros (Aarhus University, Denmark)
Christos Boutsidis (Goldman Sachs, USA)
Mateusz Budnik (University of Grenoble, France)
Paul Buitelaar (Insight - National University of Ireland, Galway, Ireland)
Wray Lindsay Buntine (Monash University, Australia)
David Buttler (Lawrence Livermore National Laboratory, USA)
Klemens Böhm (Karlsruhe Institute of Technology (KIT), Germany)
Fidel Cacheda (Universidad de A Coruña, Spain)
Pável Calado (INESC-ID, Universidade de Lisboa, Portugal)
B. Barla Cambazoglu (Independent researcher, Spain)
Huiping Cao (New Mexico State University, USA)
Mark Carman (Monash University, Australia)
David Carmel (Yahoo! Research, Israel)
Claudio Carpineto (Fondazione Ugo Bordoni, Italy)
Marc Cartright (Google Inc., USA)
Pablo Castells (Universidad Autónoma de Madrid, Spain)
Bogdan Cautis (ENST Paris - UMR CNRS 5141, France)
Varun Chandola (State University of New York at Buffalo, USA)
Kevin Chang (University of Illinois at Urbana-Champaign, USA)
Lijun Chang (University of New South Wales, Australia)
Nitesh Chawla (University of Notre Dame, USA)
Muhammad Cheema (Monash University, Australia, Australia)
Enhong Chen (University of Science & Technology of China, China)
Hsin-Hsi Chen (National Taiwan University, Taiwan)
Ming-Syan Chen (National Taiwan University, Taiwan)
Zhiyuan Chen (Google, USA)
Hong Cheng (The Chinese University of Hong Kong, Hong Kong)
Reynold Cheng (The University of Hong Kong, Hong Kong)

Research Track PC (continued):

Shiwen Cheng (UCR, USA)
Xueqi Cheng (Institute of Computing Technology, CAS, P. R. China)
Jean-Pierre Chevallet (Grenoble Alpes University, France)
Ed H. Chi (Google, Inc., USA)
Jaegul Choo (Korea University, Korea)
Jason Chou (HTC Research, USA)
Vassilis Christophides (INRIA Paris, France)
Kun-Ta Chuang (National Cheng Kung University, Taiwan)
Aleksandr Chuklin (University of Amsterdam, Netherlands)
Stephane Clinchant (Xerox Research Centre Europe, France)
Gao Cong (Nanyang Technological University, Singapore)
Paolo Cremonesi (Politecnico di Milano, Italy)
Bin Cui (Peking University, China)
Peng Cui (Tsinghua University, China)
Alfredo Cuzzocrea (ICAR-CNR and University of Calabria, Italy)
Eva D'Hondt (LIMSI, France)
Theodore Dalamagas (Imis Institute, "Athena" R.C., Greece)
Anirban Dasgupta (IIT Gandhinagar, India)
Brian Davison (Lehigh University, USA)
Martine De Cock (University of Washington Tacoma, USA)
Marco De Gemmis (University of Bari, Italy)
Pablo de La Fuente (Universidad de Valladolid, Spain)
Antonios Deligiannakis (Technical University of Crete, Greece)
Ke Deng (RMIT University, Australia)
Prasad Deshpande (IQLect, India)
Emanuele Di Buccio (University of Padua, Italy)
Giorgio Maria Di Nunzio (University of Padua, Italy)
Laura Dietz (Mannheim University, Germany)
Wei Ding (University of Massachusetts Boston, USA)
Chaabane Djeraba (CRISTAL, University Lille1, France)
Gill Dobbie (University of Auckland, New Zealand)
Vladimir Dobrynin (Saint-Petersburg State University, Russia)
Josep Domingo-Ferrer (Universitat Rovira i Virgili, Spain)
Yuxiao Dong (University of Notre Dame, USA)
Christos Doulkeridis (University of Piraeus, Greece)
Huizhong Duan (Airbnb Inc., USA)
Murat Dundar (Indiana University Purdue University Indianapolis, USA)
Koji Eguchi (Kobe University, Japan)
Carsten Eickhoff (ETH Zurich, Switzerland)
Markus Endres (University of Augsburg, Germany)
Dora Erdos (Boston University, USA)
Liana Ermakova (PSU, IRIT, Russia)
Yuan Fang (Institute for Infocomm Research, Singapore)
Farkas Csilla (USC, USA)
Yansong Feng (University of Edinburgh, China)
Juan M. Fernández-Luna (University of Granada, Spain)
Elena Ferrari (University of Insubria, Italy)

Research Track PC (continued):

Marcus Fontoura (Microsoft Corporation, USA)
Eibe Frank (University of Waikato, New Zealand)
Karin Friberg Heppin (University of Gothenburg, Sweden)
Ingo Frommholz (University of Bedfordshire, United Kingdom)
Ariel Fuxman (Google, USA)
Ricardo José Gabrielli Barreto Campello (University of São Paulo, Brazil)
Esther Galbrun (Inria Nancy – Grand Est, France)
Jing Gao (University at Buffalo, USA)
Anastasia Giachanou (University of Lugano, Switzerland)
Giorgos Giannopoulos (Imis Institute, "Athena" R.C., Greece)
Aris Gkoulalas-Divanis (IBM Dublin Research Lab, Ireland)
Nadav Glbandi (Yahoo! Research Israel, Israel)
Lorraine Goeuriot (Laboratoire d'informatique de Grenoble, France)
Ayse Goker (Robert Gordon University, United Kingdom)
Zhiguo Gong (Universify of Macau, Macao)
Thomas Gottron (Innovation Lab, SCHUFA Holding AG, Germany)
Guillaume Gravier (CNRS, IRISA, France)
Antonino Gulli (Elsevier, United Kingdom)
Francesco Gullo (UniCredit R&D, Italy)
Jiafeng Guo (Institute of Computing Technology, China)
Sunil Gupta (Deakin University, Australia)
Claudio Gutierrez (Universidad de Chile, Chile)
Ido Guy (Yahoo Labs, Israel)
Stephan Günnemann (Technical University of Munich, Germany)
Maria Halkidi (University of Piraeus, Greece)
Shuguang Han (University of Pittsburgh, USA)
Wook-Shin Han (POSTECH, Korea)
Allan Hanbury (Vienna University of Technology, Austria)
Preben Hansen (Stockholm University, Sweden)
Sanda Harabagiu (Human Language Technology Research Institute, University of Texas at Dallas, USA)
Jer Hayes (IBM, Ireland)
Ben He (University of Chinese Academy of Sciences, China)
Daqing He (University of Pittsburgh, USA)
Jingrui He (Arizona State University, USA)
Jiyin He (CWI, Netherlands)
Yeye He (Microsoft Research, USA)
Raquel Hill (Indiana University, USA)
Alexander Hinneburg (Martin-Luther-University Halle-Wittenberg, Germany)
Hongbo Xu (Chinese Academy of Sciences, China)
Huiqi Hu (East China Normal University, China)
Luke Huan (Univ. of Kansas, USA)
Hong Huang (UGoe, Germany)
Hongzhao Huang (Rensselaer Polytechnic Institute, USA)
Xuanjing Huang (Fudan University, China)

Research Track PC (continued):

Zi Huang (The University of Queensland, Australia)
Gilles Hubert (IRIT, France)
Pan Hui (Hong Kong University of Science and Technology, Hong Kong)
Theo Huibers (University of Twente, Netherlands)
Seung-Won Hwang (Yonsei University, Korea)
Dmitry Ignatov (National Research University Higher School of Economics, Russia)
Ekaterini Ioannou (Technical University of Crete, Greece)
Mizuho Iwaihara (Waseda University, Japan)
Szymon Jaroszewicz (Polish Academy of Sciences, Poland)
Jiepu Jiang (University of Massachusetts Amherst, USA)
Lili Jiang (Tsinghua University, China)
Xiaoming Jin (Tsinghua University, China)
Joemon Jose (University of Glasgow, United Kingdom)
Amruta Joshi (UCLA, USA)
James Joshi (University of Pittsburgh, USA)
Panos Kalnis (King Abdullah University of Science and Technology, Saudi Arabia)
Bhargav Kanagal (Google, USA)
Nattiya Kanhabua (Aalborg University, Denmark)
Panagiotis Karras (Skoltech, Russia)
Gabriella Kazai (Lumi.do, United Kingdom)
Yiping Ke (Nanyang Technological University, Singapore)
Liadh Kelly (Trinity College Dublin, Ireland)
Anastasios Kementsietsidis (Google Research, USA)
Arijit Khan (NTU, Singapore)
Latifur Khan (UTD, USA)
Evgeny Kharitonov (Moscow Institute of Physics and Technology, Russia)
Xiangnan Kong (WPI, USA)
Alexander Kotov (Wayne State University, USA)
Donald Kraft (Louisiana State University, USA)
Udo Kruschwitz (University of Essex, United Kingdom)
Ashish Kundu (IBM T.J. Watson Research Center, USA)
Monica Landoni (University of Lugano (USI), Switzerland)
Ni Lao (Google Inc., USA)
Theodoros Lappas (Stevens Institute of Technology, USA)
Raymond Y.K. Lau (City University of Hong Kong, Hong Kong)
Hady Lauw (Singapore Management University, Singapore)
Julien Leblay (AIST, Japan)
Kyumin Lee (Utah State University, USA)
Wang-Chien Lee (The Pennsylvania State University, USA)
Johannes Leveling (Elsevier, Netherlands)
Chengkai Li (University of Texas at Arlington, USA)
Fangtao Li (Google, USA)
Hao Li (Rensselaer Polytechnic Institute, USA)
Ping Li (Rutgers University, USA)
Sujian Li (Peking University, China)

Research Track PC (continued):

Research Track PC (continued):

Sebastian Michel (University of Kaiserslautern, Germany)
Peter Mika (Yahoo! Research, Spain)
Taiki Miyanishi (Kobe University, Japan)
Dunja Mladenic (Jozef Stefan Institute, Slovenia)
Marie-Francine Moens (KU Leuven, Belgium)
Boughanem Mohand (IRIT University Paul Sabatier Toulouse, France)
Alessandro Moschitti (Qatar Computing Research Institute, Italy)
Josiane Mothe (Institut de Recherche en Informatique de Toulouse, France)
Abdullah Mueen (University of New Mexico, USA)
Philippe Mulhem (LIG-CNRS, France)
Hannes Mühleisen (Centrum Wiskunde & Informatica (CWI), Netherlands)
Emmanuel Müller (Hasso-Plattner-Institute, Germany)
Henning Müller (HES-SO, Switzerland)
Roberto Navigli (Sapienza Universita' di Roma, Italy)
Wolfgang Nejdl (L3S and University of Hannover, Germany)
Mahmood Neshati (Shahid behesti University, Iran)
Dong Nguyen (University of Twente, Netherlands)
Hung Nguyen (UQ, Australia)
Xia Ning (IUPUI, USA)
Eirini Ntoutsi (Leibniz Universitaet Hannover, Germany)
Werner Nutt (Free University of Bozen-Bolzano, Italy)
Neil O'Hare (Yahoo! Research, Spain)
Michael O'Mahony (University College Dublin, Ireland)
Douglas Oard (University of Maryland, USA)
Salvatore Orlando (Università Ca' Foscari Venezia, Italy)
Balaji Palanisamy (University of Pittsburgh, USA)
Weike Pan (Shenzhen University, China)
Spiros Papadimitriou (Rutgers University, USA)
Stavros Papadopoulos (MIT & Intel Labs, USA)
Evangelos Papalexakis (Carnegie Mellon University, USA)
Douglass Parker (UCLA, USA)
Virgil Pavlu (Northeastern Univ, USA)
Konstantinos Pelechrinis (University of Pittsburgh, USA)
Zhiyong Peng (State Key Lab. of Software Engineeering, China)
Milan Petkovic (Philips Research Laboratories, Netherlands)
Vivien Petras (HU Berlin, Germany)
Ali Pinar (Sandia National Laboratories, USA)
Karen Pinel-Sauvagnat (IRIT, France)
Florina Piroi (Vienna University of Technology, ISIS, IFS, Austria)
Emily Pitler (Google, Inc., USA)
Vassilis Plachouras (Thomson Reuters, United Kingdom)
Dimitris Plexousakis (Institute of Computer Science, FORTH, Greece)
Tieyun Qian (Wuhan University, China)
Weining Qian (East China Normal University, China)
Lu Qin (University of Technology, Australia)
Georges Quénot (Laboratoire d'Informatique de Grenoble, CNRS, France)

Research Track PC (continued):

Davood Rafiei (University of Alberta, Canada)
Chotirat Ratanamahatana (Chulalongkorn University, Thailand)
Chandan K. Reddy (Wayne State University, USA)
Chiara Renso (KDDLAB, ISTI-CNR, Pisa, Italy, Italy)
Matteo Riondato (Two Sigma Investments, USA)
Thomas Roelleke (Queen Mary University of London, United Kingdom)
Oleg Rokhlenko (Yahoo! Research, Israel)
Paolo Rosso (Technical University of Valencia, Spain)
Francois Rousseau (École Polytechnique, France)
Dmitri Roussinov (The University of Strathclyde, United Kingdom)
Dimitris Sacharidis (TU Wien, Austria)
Alan Said (Recorded Future, Sweden)
Saeed Salem (North Dakota State University, USA)
Vasilis Samoladas (Technical University of Crete, Greece)
Rodrygo Santos (Universidade Federal de Minas Gerais, Brazil)
Mohamed Sarwat (Arizona State University, USA)
Saket Sathe (IBM Research Australia, Australia)
Ralf Schenkel (Universitaet Passau, Germany)
Uri Schonfeld (Yahoo, USA)
Erich Schubert (Ludwig-Maximilians-Universität München, Germany)
Matthias Schubert (Ludwig-Maximilians-University Munich, Germany)
Russell Sears (Pure Storage, USA)
Florence Sedes (I.R.I.T. Univ. P. Sabatier, France)
Giovanni Semeraro (University of Bari, Italy)
Hua Sha (UC Berkeley, USA)
Azadeh Shakery (University of Tehran, Iran)
Bin Shao (Microsoft Research Asia, China)
Mohamed Sharaf (University of Queensland, Australia)
Huawei Shen (Chinese Academy of Sciences, China)
Shuming Shi (Microsoft Research Asia, China)
Xiaolin Shi (Microsoft Research, USA)
Kyuseok Shim (Seoul National University, Korea)
Fabrizio Silvestri (Yahoo Labs, Italy)
Alkis Simitsis (HP Labs, USA)
Kevin Small (Amazon, USA)
Jan Snajder (University of Zagreb, TakeLab FER, Croatia)
Parikshit Sondhi (Walmart Labs, USA)
Yang Song (Microsoft Research, USA)
Sucheta Soundarajan (Syracuse University, USA)
Anna Squicciarini (The Pennsylvania State University, USA)
Nisheeth Srivastava (UCSD, USA)
Kostas Stefanidis (ICS-FORTH, Greece)
Markus Strohmaier (University of Koblenz-Landau, Germany)
Simone Stumpf (City University London, United Kingdom)
Karthik Subbian (Facebook, USA)
L. Venkata Subramaniam (IBM Research - India, India)
Fabian M. Suchanek (Télécom ParisTech University, France)

Research Track PC (continued):

Torsten Suel (New York University, USA)
Aixin Sun (Nanyang Technological University, Singapore)
Huan Sun (University of California, Santa Barbara, USA)
Neel Sundaresan (eBay, USA)
Einoshin Suzuki (Kyushu University, Japan)
Pascale Sébillot (IRISA, France)
Lynda Tamine (IRIT, France)
Chenhao Tan (Cornell University, USA)
Pang-Ning Tan (Michigan State University, USA)
Cynthia Tang
Jiliang Tang (Michigan State University, USA)
Egemen Tanin (University of Melbourne, Australia)
Shirish Tatikonda (IBM Almaden Research Center, USA)
Manolis Terrovitis (Imis Institute, "Athena" R.C., Greece)
Amin Teymorian (Georgetown University, USA)
Dimitri Theodoratos (NJIT, USA)
Paul Thomas (Microsoft, Australia)
Brian Thompson (U.S. Army Research Lab, USA)
Ilya Tikhomirov (Federal Research Center, Russian Academy of Sciences, Russia)
Marko Tkalcic (Free University of Bolzano, Italy)
Anastasios Tombros (Queen Mary University of London, United Kingdom)
Nicola Tonellotto (ISTI-CNR, Italy)
Goce Trajcevski (Northwestern University, USA)
Truyen Tran (Deakin University, Australia)
Dolf Trieschnigg (Mydatafactory, Netherlands)
Christos Tryfonopoulos (University of Peloponnese, Greece)
Ming-Feng Tsai (National Chengchi University, Taiwan)
Panayiotis Tsaparas (University of Ioannina, Greece)
Vincent S. Tseng (National Chiao Tung University, Taiwan)
Theodora Tsikrika (Information Technologies Institute, CERTH, Greece)
Deepak Turaga (IBM Research, USA)
Denis Turdakov (Institute for System Programming RAS, Russia)
Ata Turk (Boston University, USA)
Yannis Tzitzikas (University of Crete and FORTH-ICS, Greece)
Leong Hou U (University of Macau, Macao)
Antti Ukkonen (Finnish Institute of Occupational Health, Finland)
Theo van der Weide (Radboud University Nijmegen, Netherlands)
Jacco van Ossenbruggen (CWI & VU University Amsterdam, Netherlands)
Aparna Varde (Montclair State University, USA)
Vasilis Vassalos (Athens University of Economics and Business, Greece)
Natalia Vassilieva (Hewlett Packard Labs, USA)
Michalis Vazirgiannis (AUEB, Greece)
Olga Vechtomova (University of Waterloo, Canada)
Sumithra Velupillai (KTH Royal Institute of Technology, Sweden)
Suzan Verberne (Institute for Computing and Information Sciences, Radboud University Nijmegen, Netherlands)

Research Track PC (continued):

Stratis Viglas (University of Edinburgh, United Kingdom)
Michail Vlachos (IBM Research, Switzerland)
Akrivi Vlachou (Norwegian University of Science and Technology, Norway)
Stefanos Vrochidis (Information Technologies Institute, Greece)
Slobodan Vucetic (Temple University, USA)
Ivan Vulić (University of Cambridge, United Kingdom)
Anil Kumar Vullikanti (Virginia Tech, USA)
Jeroen Vuurens (Delft University of Technology, Netherlands)
V.G.Vinod Vydiswaran (University of Michigan, USA)
Huaiyu Wan (Beijing Jiaotong University, China)
Xiaojun Wan (Peking University, China)
Chi Wang (Microsoft Research, USA)
Houfeng Wang (Peking University, China)
Jason Wang (New Jersey Institute of Technology, USA)
Jianyong Wang (Tsinghua University, China)
Jingang Wang (Alibaba Inc, China)
Shengrui Wang (University of Sherbrooke, Canada)
Wei Wang (UNSW, Australia)
William Yang Wang (Carnegie Mellon University, USA)
Wouter Weerkamp (904Labs, Netherlands)
Michael Wiegand (Spoken Language Systems, Saarland University, Germany)
Anthony Wirth (The University of Melbourne, Australia)
Christa Womser-Hacker (University Hildesheim, Germany)
Kam-Fai Wong (The Chinese University of Hong Kong, Hong Kong)
Raymond Chi-Wing Wong (The Hong Kong University of Science and Technology, Hong Kong)
Dingming Wu (The University of Hong Kong, Hong Kong)
Junjie Wu (Beihang University, China)
Sen Wu (Stanford University, USA)
Yinghui Wu (University of California Santa Barbara, USA)
Xiaokui Xiao (Nanyang Technological University, Singapore)
Yanghua Xiao (Fudan University, China)
Li Xiaoli (Nanyang Technological University, Singapore)
Xu Xinshun (Shandong University, China)
Li Xiong (Emory University, USA)
Makoto Yamada (Yahoo! Labs, USA)
De-Nian Yang (Academia Sinica, Taiwan)
Shengqi Yang (UCSB, USA)
Tao Yang (Ask.com & UCSB, USA)
Xiaochun Yang (Northeastern University, China)
Yang Yang (Tsinghua University, China)
Zi Yang (Language Technologies Institute, USA)
Hengshuai Yao (University of Alberta, Canada)
Mi-Yen Yeh (Institute of Information Science, Academia Sinica, Taiwan)
Man Lung Yiu (Hong Kong Polytechnic University, Hong Kong)

Research Track PC (continued):

Hwanjo Yu (POSTECH, Korea)
Philip Yu (University of Illinois at Chicago, USA)
Carlo Zaniolo (UCLA, USA)
Fabio Massimo Zanzotto (DISP, University of Rome "Tor Vergata", Italy)
David Zellhoefer (Berlin State Library - Staatsbibliothek zu Berlin, Germany)
Ji Zhang (The University of Southern Queensland, Australia)
Jing Zhang (Tsinghua, China)
Lanbo Zhang (University of California, Santa Cruz, USA)
Mi Zhang (Fudan University, China)
Min-Ling Zhang (Southeast University, China)
Nan Zhang (The George Washington University, USA)
Qin Zhang (Indiana University Bloomington, USA)
Qiong Zhang (Alibaba, USA)
Ruofei Zhang (Microsoft Inc., USA)
Weinan Zhang (University College London, United Kingdom)
Ying Zhang (UTS, Australia)
Jun Zhao (National Laboratory of Pattern Recognition, Institute of Automation, Chinese Academy of Sciences, China)
Paul Zhao (Institute of Computer Science & Technology of Peking University, China)
Xin Zhao (Renmin University of China, School of Information, China)
Zhe Zhao (University of Michigan, Ann Arbor, USA)
Guodong Zhou (Soochow University, China)
Ke Zhou (University of Glasgow, United Kingdom)
Xiangdong Zhou (Fudan University, China)
Yongluan Zhou (University of Southern Denmark, Denmark)
Honglei Zhuang (University of Illinois, USA)
Imed Zitouni (Microsoft, USA)
Chengqing Zong (Institute of Automation, Chinese Academy of Sciences, China)
Lei Zou (Peking University, China)
Guido Zuccon (Queensland University of Technology, Australia)

Industry Track PC: Vineet Abhishek (Walmart Labs, USA)
Kavita Ganesan (Github Inc., USA)
Xiao Bai (Yahoo! Research, Spain)
Iyad Batal (GE Global Research, USA)
Bin Bi (Microsoft Research, USA)
Jiang Bian (Microsoft Research, China)
Rui Cai (Microsoft Research, Asia, China)
Suleyman Cetintas (Yahoo Labs, USA)
Jianhui Chen (Yahoo Research, USA)
Lin Chen (Snapchat Inc., USA)
Marina Danilevsky (IBM Research, USA)
Hongbo Deng (Google, USA)
Pavel Dmitriev (Cornell University, USA)
Dejing Dou (University of Oregon, USA)
Zhicheng Dou (Renmin University of China, China)
Huizhong Duan (Airbnb Inc., USA)
Ravikant Dvs (Facebook, USA)
Shima Gerani (Freelancer.com, Canada)
Sonal Gupta (Stanford, USA)
Wei Han (WalmartLabs, USA)
Liangjie Hong (Etsy, USA)
Xia Hu (Texas A&M University, USA)
Jiepu Jiang (University of Massachusetts Amherst, USA)
Maryam Karimzadehgan (Google, USA)
Sergey Kirshner (Walmart Labs, USA)
Pranam Kolari (Walmart Labs, USA)
Deguang Kong (Samsung Research America, USA)
Weize Kong (Center for Intelligence Information Retrieval, USA)
Dongryeol Lee (Faraday Future, USA)
Liangda Li (Yahoo Research, USA, USA)
Qi Li (Twitter Inc., USA)
Xin Li (Beijing Institute of Technology, China)
Ciya Liao (Microsoft, USA)
Fei Liu (University of Central Florida, USA)
Lei Liu (HP Labs (USA), USA)
Yandong Liu (Uber, USA)
Zitao Liu (Pinterest, USA)
Ziyang Liu (Arizona State University, USA)
Roger Luo (Snapchat Inc., USA)
Manish Marwah (HP Labs, USA)
Sameep Mehta (IBM, India Research Lab, India)
Chikashi Nobata (Apple Inc., USA)
Hua Ouyang (Apple Inc., USA)
Shimei Pan (UMBC, USA)
Daehoon Park (University of Illinois at Urbana-Champaign, USA)
Manas Pathak (Walmartlabs, USA)
B. Aditya Prakash (Virginia Tech, USA)

Industry Track PC (continued):

Mingjie Qian (Yahoo Research, USA)
Altaf Rahman (Yahoo Labs, USA)
Pankaj Rajan (Walmart Labs, USA)
Avishek Saha (Yahoo Labs, USA)
Prithviraj Sen (IBM Corporation, USA)
Aneesh Sharma (Twitter Inc, USA)
Xiaolin Shi (Snapchat Inc., USA)
Yue Shi (Facebook, USA)
Yang Song (IBM, USA)
L. Venkata Subramaniam (IBM Research - India, India)
Jian-Tao Sun (Microsoft Research Asia, China)
Wei Sun (Purdue University, USA)
Idan Szpektor (Yahoo Research, Israel)
Jiliang Tang (MSU, China)
Hanghang Tong (City College, CUNY, USA)
Vinod Vydiswaran (University of Michigan, USA)
Chenguang Wang (Peking University, China)
Pengyuan Wang (University of Georgia, USA)
Xuanhui Wang (Google, USA)
Yingfei Wang (Princeton University, USA)
Jian Xu (TouchPal, USA)
Jun Xu (Institute of Computing Technology, Chinese Academy of Sciences, China)
Makoto Yamada (Kyoto University, USA)
Hengshuai Yao (University of Alberta, Canada)
Dawei Yin (JD Inc., USA)
Ke Zhai (Microsoft, USA)
Aston Zhang (University of Illinois at Urbana-Champaign, USA)
Jiawei Zhang (University of Illinois at Chicago, USA)

Demo Track PC:

Alan Akbik (IBM Research, USA)
Liang Gou (Visa Research, USA)
Sairam Gurajada (Max-Planck Institute for Informatics, Germany)
Yeye He (Microsoft Research, USA)
Hongxia Jin (IBM Almaden Research Center, USA)
U Kang (Seoul National University, Korea)
Benny Kimelfeld (Technion - Israel Institute of Technology, Israel)
Shamanth Kumar (Arizona State University, USA)
Jae-Gil Lee (KAIST, Korea)
Vincent Leroy (University of Grenoble - CNRS, France)
Chengkai Li (University of Texas at Arlington, USA)
Rui Li (Google, USA)
Behrooz Omidvar-Tehrani (Ohio State University, USA)
Nikita Spirin (UIUC, USA)
Katerina Tzompanaki (Telecom ParisTech, France)
Marilyn Walker (UCSC, USA)
Peifeng Yin (IBM, USA)
Qi Zhang (Fudan University, China)
Mianwei Zhou (Yahoo Lab, USA)
Huaiyu Zhu (IBM Research - Almaden, USA)

CIKM 2016 Sponsors & Supporters

Sponsors

acm Association for Computing Machinery

SIGIR Special Interest Group on Information Retrieval

sigweb

Platinum Supporter

Alibaba Group 阿里巴巴集团

Gold Supporter

Baidu 百度

Silver Supporter

HUAWEI

Bronze Supporter

General Supporters

CIKM Cup Supporter

Career Day Supporter

Academic Supporters

Skipping Word: A Character-Sequential Representation based Framework for Question Answering

Lingxun Meng
Sogou Inc
Beijing, 100084, China.
menglingxun@sogou-inc.com

Yan Li, Mengyi Liu
Key Lab of Intelligent Information Processing of CAS, ICT, Beijing, 100190, China.
{yan.li, mengyi.liu}@vipl.ict.ac.cn

Peng Shu
Sogou Inc
Beijing, 100084, China.
shupeng203672@sogou-inc.com

ABSTRACT

Recent works using artificial neural networks based on word distributed representation greatly boost the performance of various natural language learning tasks, especially question answering. Though, they also carry along with some attendant problems, such as corpus selection for embedding learning, dictionary transformation for different learning tasks, etc. In this paper, we propose to straightforwardly model sentences by means of character sequences, and then utilize convolutional neural networks to integrate character embedding learning together with point-wise answer selection training. Compared with deep models pre-trained on word embedding (WE) strategy, our character-sequential representation (CSR) based method shows a much simpler procedure and more stable performance across different benchmarks. Extensive experiments on two benchmark answer selection datasets exhibit the competitive performance compared with the state-of-the-art methods.

Keywords

semantic matching; deep learning; convolutional neural networks; word embeddings;

1. INTRODUCTION

Inspired by the achievements of convolutional networks (a.k.a, ConvNets) in the field of computer vision, more and more researchers constitute ConvNets for kinds of natural language processing tasks, e.g., text classification [5], short text pair re-ranking [14, 11], e.t.c. Nearly all of them pointed out that ConvNets could successfully capture local syntactic structure to boost performance. In addition to the appropriate use of ConvNets, researchers also owed their success to recent distributed representation of words, like *word2vec* [9]. No doubt perfect word embedding (WE) could greatly boost the performance, but there are so many English word embedding systems available online, trained with different corpus, algorithms and preprocessing methods. Thus, evaluating the effectiveness of different word embedding systems becomes a laborious job. Moreover, for other languages, like Chinese, there exists few word embedding systems available, so this further makes the selection of right corpus, right word segmentation tools and even right algorithms more expensive and difficult.

Recently, some researchers start to use character representation to constitute different natural language models based on the fact that character embedding model not only alleviates the parametric burden significantly, but also brings more ability of handling morphologically rich language and out-of-vocabulary words [6]. Besides, character-level representation has also been successfully investigated for text classification [16], where one-hot representation is feed into Deep ConvNets. No matter what algorithms are used to construct task-specific semantic learning framework, the same concept is shared that characters make words, and then words construct whole sentences. In fact of reality, we believe that root word is the primary lexical unit of comprehension, so direct construction from characters to sentences is reasonable and enough for semantic learning which forms our original motivation.

In this paper, we take the first attempt to construct text matching based on character-sequential representation (CSR). Different from previous works, we first directly model sentences as sequences of characters, skipping the traditional word-level comprehension, and then utilize shallow weight-sharing ConvNets to learn the matching task. Experiments on two popular question answering benchmarks show the competitive performance compared with the other state-of-the-art methods.

2. SEMANTIC MATCH LEARNING

Text matching is generally believed as the key of many natural language processing tasks, such as question answering, information retrieval and relevance classification. The majority of previous works formulated sentence, phrase or text using semantic parsing methods, which require experts to handcraft grammars and knowledge base schema [1]. Recently, lots of works spring up by using ConvNets to constitute text based on word representation [11]. Our method follows this constitution, but replaces the word look-up table with more fundamental character look-up table, and the look-up table, convolutional filters and normalization parameters are shared between question-answer pairs (see Fig. 1 for better understanding).

CIKM'16, October 24-28, 2016, Indianapolis, IN, USA
© 2016 ACM. ISBN 978-1-4503-4073-1/16/10...$15.00
DOI: http://dx.doi.org/10.1145/2983323.2983861

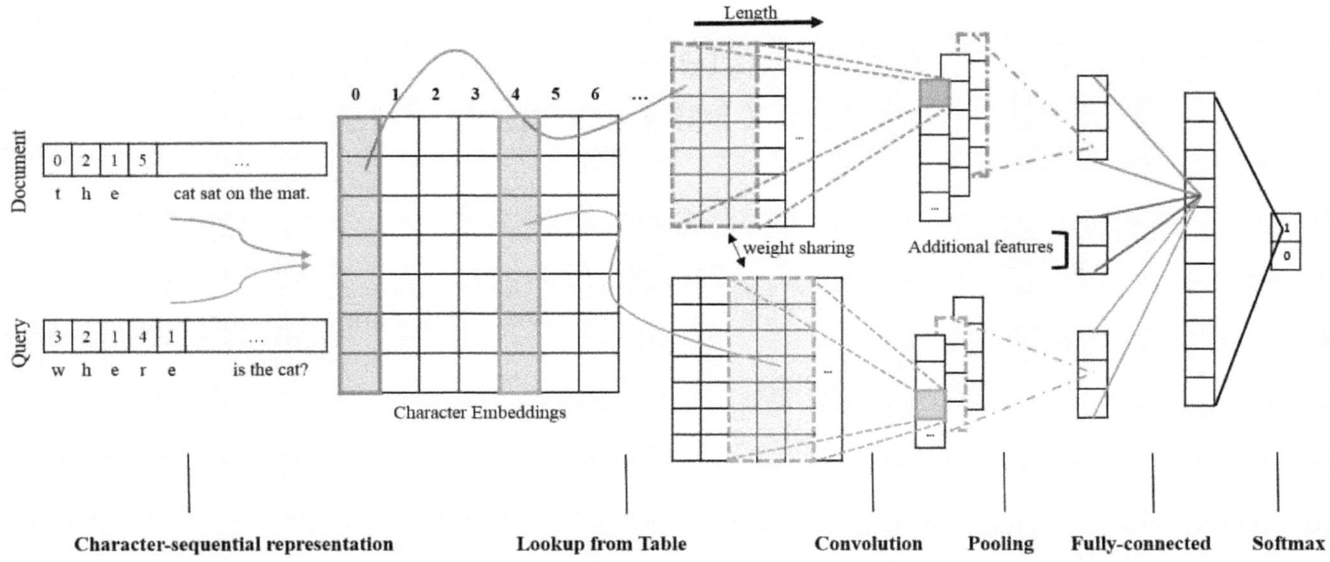

Figure 1: Our framework for sentence-pair matching.

2.1 Character-Sequential Representation

The sentence in this paper is represented as a sequence of characters: $[c_0, ..., c_{|s|-1}]$, where c_i is drawn from the character set C. Each character is represented by its corresponding index in the character set C, namely $\{0, \cdots, |C|-1\}$. To learn the character representation, we design the first layer of our model as a look-up table, i.e., character embedding matrix $\boldsymbol{W} \in \mathbb{R}^{d \times |\boldsymbol{C}|}$, where each column represents a character embedding $\mathbf{c}$ which is d-dimensional. Forwarding from this layer, we get our sentence represented as follow:

$$\boldsymbol{S} = [\boldsymbol{c}_0 \quad \boldsymbol{c}_1 \quad \cdots \quad \boldsymbol{c}_{|s|-1}]. \tag{1}$$

Different from previous character embedding methods, we construct sentences directly from characters, skipping the transitional step of modeling word-level comprehension (i.e., character-sentence rather than character-word-sentence). We think the comprehension unit is radical, so semantic learning from character representation is feasible.

2.2 Convolution and Pooling

The convolution layer consists of a filter bank $\boldsymbol{F} \in \mathbb{R}^{n \times c \times w}$, along with filter biases $\boldsymbol{b} \in \mathbb{R}^n$, where n and w refer to the number and width of filters respectively, and c denotes the channels of data from the lower layer. More specifically, for the first convolution layer, c equals to the embedding dimension d, which means to convolve across the characters to learn the pattern. In our construction, all the convolution operation is one-dimensional one. Formally, the output of the convolution with filter bank $\boldsymbol{F}$ over sentence $\boldsymbol{S}$ is computed as follow:

$$\boldsymbol{T} = [t_{i,j}] = \boldsymbol{F} * \boldsymbol{S} + \boldsymbol{b} = [\boldsymbol{F}_i^T \boldsymbol{S}_{j-w+1:j} + b_i] \tag{2}$$

where i indexes the number of filter bank F, $F_i \in \mathbb{R}^{(d*w)}$ is the vectorization of each filter map, $S_{j-w+1:j}$ vectorizes a sliding window matrix covering embeddings from the index $(j-w+1)^{th}$ to j^{th}.

The above equation formulates two types of convolution: *wide* and *narrow* . The previous works [4] pointed out that using *wide* type of convolution was able to better and more frequently reach boundaries of sentences than the *narrow* type. More importantly, the *wide* convolution operation could ignore the requisition of the *narrow* type that filter width must be smaller than input data width to guarantee a valid non-empty result. In our implementation, we use *narrow* type since our character based sequence is not sensitive to boundary information that much. However, we consist that using *wild* type may always guarantee a better performance. In this way, we get the output $\boldsymbol{T} \in \mathbb{R}^{n \times (|s|-w+1)}$.

Pooling operation is often used to eliminate the differences in length for sentence representation, and it is also benefit to filter out unimportant or noisy characters and words. Technically, there exist two types of pooling strategy, i.e., *average* pooling and *max* pooling, and *max* pooling is more widely used due to its fast convergence and less computational complexity. Recently, *k-max* pooling strategy [4] was proposed to extract k large activation values rather than the topmost one, and this could construct a deeper architecture with several convolutional layers. For simplification, we adopt the normal *max* pooling strategy in this work. We get our result, pool($\boldsymbol{T}$): $\mathbb{R}^{n \times (|s|-w+1)} \to \mathbb{R}^n$.

2.3 Batch Normalization

Batch Normalization (BN) [2] was originally proposed to reduce the changes in distribution of each layers input during training, which was called *internal covariance shift* . As an important component of deep networks, it allows us to use much higher learning rates and be less careful about initial data preprocessing and weights initialization. Furthermore, it can also act as a regularization, in some cases eliminating the use of dropout.

Specifically, for the given output $\boldsymbol{T}$ after the convolution operation, we will normalize each $\boldsymbol{t}_i$ along the filter number axis as follow:

$$\hat{\boldsymbol{t}_i} = \frac{\boldsymbol{t}_i - \mathrm{E}[\boldsymbol{t}_i]}{\sqrt{\mathrm{Var}[\boldsymbol{t}_i]}}, \tag{3}$$

Dataset	Set	#Question	#QApairs	%Corect
TrecQA	Train	94	4,718	7.4%
	Dev	65	1,117	18.4%
	Test	68	1,442	17.2%
WikiQA	Train	2,118	20,360	5.11%
	Dev	296	2,733	5.12%
	Test	633	6,165	4.75%

Table 1: Statistics of the answer selection datasets.

where the expectation and variance are computed over the whole training data set. A pair of parameters $\boldsymbol{\gamma}_i$ and $\boldsymbol{\beta}_i$ (with the same dimension with $\boldsymbol{t}_i$) are further used to scale and shift the normalized value as follow:

$$\mathrm{BN}(\boldsymbol{T}) = [\boldsymbol{\gamma}_i \cdot \hat{\boldsymbol{t}_i} + \boldsymbol{\beta}_i]. \tag{4}$$

Above parameters are learnt along with the whole model training, and it usually suggests that Batch Normalization should better be used before nonlinearity activation and covers both fully connected layers and convolutional layers.

2.4 *Pointwise* Learning to Rank

Since our character-sequential model focuses on binary classification task, e.g., question answering, we deploy the cross-entropy loss to discriminatively train our framework as follow:

$$L_\theta = -\frac{1}{N}\sum_{i=1}^{N}\sum_{j=1}^{M}(y_j^{(i)} \log p_j^{(i)}) + \lambda \|\boldsymbol{F}\|^2 \tag{5}$$

where $p_j^{(i)}$ is the jth probability output of sample i^{th} through our networks, $y_j^{(i)}$ is the corresponding ground truth, θ contains all the parameters, i.e., $\theta = \{\boldsymbol{W}, \boldsymbol{F}, \boldsymbol{b}, \boldsymbol{\gamma}, \boldsymbol{\beta}\}$, λ is set to be $5e^{-4}$.

We use Stochastic Gradient Descent (SGD) to optimize our network, and AdaDelta is used to automatically adapt the learning rate during the training procedure. For higher performance, hyper-parameter selection is conducted on the development set, and BN layer after each convolution layer is also added to speed up the network optimization. In addition, dropout is applied after the first hidden layer for regularization, and early stopping is used to prevent over fitting with a patience of 5 epochs.

3. EXPERIMENTS

We evaluate the proposed method on two benchmarks of answer selection problem, i.e., TrecQA [12] and WikiQA [13].

3.1 Datasets

TrecQA[1] was collected from Text Retrieval Conference (TREC) QA track (8-13) data, and the correctness of the selected answer was guaranteed by manual judgment for parts of the dataset.

WikiQA[2] is another open domain question-answer dataset, collected from real queries of Bing search engine without human editorial revision. Table 1 summarizes the statistics on the two datasets.

[1]http://cs.stanford.edu/people/mengqiu/data/qg-emnlp07-data.tgz

[2]http://research.microsoft.com/en-us/downloads/4495da01-db8c-4041-a7f6-7984a4f6a905/

NetConfig	WE	CSR
Embedding dim	50, 300	50
CNN filter width	5	3, 5
CNN num. of filters	100	128, 32
Dropout rate	0.5	0
Batch Norm	w	w, w/o
Sim Matrix	w	w/o
Pooling	*average*	*max*

Table 2: The configuration of networks used for WE and CSR based networks in the TrecQA and WikiQA dataset, respectively.

3.2 Experimental Setup

We set the maximum word length of questions and answers to be 30/80 for TrecQA dataset, and 50/50 for WikiQA dataset respectively. Alike, we set the maximum character length of questions and answers to be 192/386 for TrecQA dataset, and 125/386 for WikiQA dataset respectively. All the words can not be found in the pre-trained word look-up table indexed by an extra index named *UNK_IND*.

Following [16], our character set C also consists of 71 characters, including 26 english lower letters, 10 digits, 33 other characters, the new line character, the padding symbol and the unknown symbol. The characters are as follows:

abcdefghijklmnopqrstuvwxyz0123456789
,;.!?:'"/\|_@#$%˜ˆ'&*+-=<>()[]{}

4. RESULTS AND DISCUSSIONS

The configuration parameters of both word embedding (WE) and character-sequential representation (CSR) based networks are listed in Table 2 (we carefully implemented WE based network architecture according to [11]). Additionally, similarity weight matrix ($sim(x, y) = x^T \mathbf{M} y$, where $\mathbf{M}$ is the similarity matrix) between question answer pairs is learnt along with WE models training, that is mentioned in [11] to perform a better matching. For fair comparison, the simple word-level overlap feature and IDF-weighted word overlap feature are used in both WE and CSR based models.

We use the open deep learning framework Caffe [3] to complete our implementation. Due to the randomness caused by *max*-pooling implementation in Caffe, we run 10 times the training and report the mean and variance value as our final result.

For quantitative evaluation, we use two classic measurements, i.e., Mean Average Precision (MAP) and Mean Reciprocal Rank (MRR), which are consistent with previous works. Specifically, the official *trec_eval* scorer tool is used to compute the above measurements[3].

We use three sets of word embedding for WE based models: (i) **word2vec**[4] [9] is trained on part of Google News dataset, containing 100 billion words; (ii) **GloVe-twitter** [10] is trained on 2 billion tweets, containing 27 billion tokens; (iii) **GloVe-6B**[5] is trained on Wikipedia data and the

[3]http://trec.nist.gov/trec_eval/

[4]https://code.google.com/archive/p/word2vec/

[5]http://nlp.stanford.edu/projects/glove/

Model	TrecQA		WikiQA	
	MAP	MRR	MAP	MRR
WE(glv-t)	.6719	.7702	.6445	.6583
WE(glv-6)	.6999	.8048	.6430	.6542
WE(w2v)	.5898	.6804	.6533	.6693
CSR	**.7295** ± .0036	**.8232** ± .0031	**.6608** ± .0099	**.6811** ± .0101

Table 3: Results of WE models based on different pre-trained WE and CSR models. w2v: word2vec. glv-t: GloVe-twitter. glv-6: GloVe-6B.

Model	TrecQA		Model	WikiQA	
	MAP	MRR		MAP	MRR
Jeopardy[12]	.6029	.6852	PV[7]	.5976	.6058
LCLR[14]	.7092	.7700	Bigram[15]	.5993	.6086
Bigram[15]	.7113	.7846	LCLR[14]	.6190	.6190
NASM [8]	**.7339**	.8117	CNN[13]	.6520	.6652
CSR	.7295 ± .0036	**.8232** ± .0031	CSR	**.6608** ± .0099	**.6811** ± .0101

Table 4: Results of our models and other methods from the literature.

fifth English Gigawords with totally 6 Billion tokens. The dimension of our character embedding for both datasets is set to 50, and standard setup is adopted of considering questions that have both correct and negative answers for evaluation. Table 3 shows the results of three versions of WE models, and please kindly note that our WE based model implementations are all slightly better than the original paper reports. We can also see that different pre-trained WE model results in unstable performance even in the same dataset, especially TrecQA, and the same embedding tool shows totally different performance on different datasets. Although our CSR based model adopts end-to-end strategy to learn the representation directly from the data without extra corpus, it exhibits competitive result in both datasets.

Table 4 compares the proposed model with the previous state-of-the-art methods. Different from the comparative methods using noisy sampled TRAIN-ALL as training set, we report our final results trained on the TRAIN set, which is much smaller than TRAIN-ALL. It is obvious that the proposed CSR exhibits its effectiveness, even without any extra-corpus for embedding pre-training.

5. CONCLUSION

In this paper, we address the problem of word embedding (WE) based answer selection that extra-corpus are needed for perfect word embedding. To solve this problem, we propose an end-to-end character-sequential representation (CSR) based ConvNets for answer selection, which simply models sentences by character sequences, and then integrates character embedding learning with point-wise answer ranking training. Extensive experiments provide further evidence that construction directly from characters to sentences works as well as or even better than the character-word-sentence hierarchical formula. We hope this work can bring some insights to the research and industrial communities that corpus-free and skip-word representation from character directly to sentence as an end-to-end strategy could play its role on various languages with its advantages of simplification and concise body.

6. ACKNOWLEDGMENTS

We thank all the co-workers in wireless sponsored search advertising (ADWR) team for details discussion and consummation. The authors also thank Dingding Qian and Kai Chen for the paper submission suggestion. This paper is partially supported by Natural Science Foundation of Zhejiang Province, P.R.China under contract No.LQ15F020005.

7. REFERENCES

[1] J. Berant, A. Chou, R. Frostig, and P. Liang. Semantic parsing on freebase from question-answer pairs. In *EMNLP*, 2013.

[2] S. Ioffe and C. Szegedy. Batch normalization: Accelerating deep network training by reducing internal covariate shift. *CoRR*, 2015.

[3] Y. Jia, E. Shelhamer, J. Donahue, S. Karayev, J. Long, R. Girshick, S. Guadarrama, and T. Darrell. Caffe: Convolutional architecture for fast feature embedding. *CoRR*, 2014.

[4] N. Kalchbrenner, E. Grefenstette, and P. Blunsom. A convolutional neural network for modelling sentences. In *ACL*, pages 655–665, 2014.

[5] Y. Kim. Convolutional neural networks for sentence classification. *EMNLP*, 2014.

[6] Y. Kim, Y. Jernite, D. Sontag, and A. M. Rush. Character-aware neural language models. *AAAI*, 2016.

[7] Q. V. Le and T. Mikolov. Distributed representations of sentences and documents. *CoRR*, 2014.

[8] Y. Miao, L. Yu, and P. Blunsom. Neural variational inference for text processing. *CoRR*, 2015.

[9] T. Mikolov, I. Sutskever, K. Chen, G. S. Corrado, and J. Dean. Distributed representations of words and phrases and their compositionality. In *NIPS*, pages 3111–3119, 2013.

[10] J. Pennington, R. Socher, and C. D. Manning. Glove: Global vectors for word representation. In *EMNLP*, pages 1532–1543, 2014.

[11] A. Severyn and A. Moschitti. Learning to rank short text pairs with convolutional deep neural networks. In *Proceedings of SIGIR*, pages 373–382. ACM, 2015.

[12] M. Wang, N. A. Smith, and T. Mitamura. What is the jeopardy model? a quasi-synchronous grammar for qa. In *EMNLP-CoNLL*, volume 7, pages 22–32, 2007.

[13] Y. Yang, W.-t. Yih, and C. Meek. Wikiqa: A challenge dataset for open-domain question answering. In *EMNLP*, pages 2013–2018. Citeseer, 2015.

[14] W.-t. Yih, M.-W. Chang, C. Meek, and A. Pastusiak. Question answering using enhanced lexical semantic models. *ACL*, 2013.

[15] L. Yu, K. M. Hermann, P. Blunsom, and S. Pulman. Deep learning for answer sentence selection. *NIPS Deep Learning and Representation Learning Workshop*, 2014.

[16] X. Zhang, J. Zhao, and Y. LeCun. Character-level convolutional networks for text classification. In *NIPS*, pages 649–657, 2015.

Towards Time-Discounted Influence Maximization

Arijit Khan
School of Computer Science and Engineering
Nanyang Technological University, Singapore
arijit.khan@ntu.edu.sg

ABSTRACT

The classical influence maximization (IM) problem in social networks does not distinguish between whether a campaign gets viral in a week or in a year. From the practical standpoint, however, campaigns for a new technology or an upcoming movie must be spread as quickly as possible, otherwise they will be obsolete. To this end, we formulate and investigate the novel problem of maximizing the time-discounted influence spread in a social network, that is, the campaigner is interested in both *"when"* and *"how likely"* a user would be influenced. In particular, we assume that the campaigner has a utility function which monotonically decreases with the time required for a user to get influenced, since the activation of the seed nodes. The problem that we solve in this paper is to maximize the expected aggregated value of this utility function over all network users. This is a novel and relevant problem that, surprisingly, has not been studied before.

Time-discounted influence maximization (TDIM), being a generalization of the classical IM, still remains **NP**-hard. However, our main contribution is to prove the sub-modularity of the objective function for *any* monotonically decreasing function of time, under a variety of influence cascading models, e.g., the independent cascade, linear threshold, and maximum influence arborescence models, thereby designing approximate algorithms with theoretical performance guarantees. We also illustrate that the existing optimization techniques (e.g., CELF) for influence maximization are more efficient over TDIM. Our experimental results demonstrate the effectiveness of our solutions over several baselines including the classical influence maximization algorithms.

1. INTRODUCTION

In influence maximization (IM), whenever a social network user buys a product or endorses an action (e.g., sharing photos, re-tweeting hash tags), she is viewed as being influenced or activated. The classical influence maximization problem [5, 10] identifies the top-k seed users in a social network such that the expected number of influenced users in the network, starting from those seed users and following some influence cascading model, is maximized. The budget k on the seed-set size usually depends on how many initial users the campaigner can directly influence to buy her product by advertisements, giving free samples, and discounted prices.

CIKM'16 , October 24-28, 2016, Indianapolis, IN, USA

 ISBN 978-1-4503-4073-1/16/10... $15.00
DOI: http://dx.doi.org/10.1145/2983323.2983862

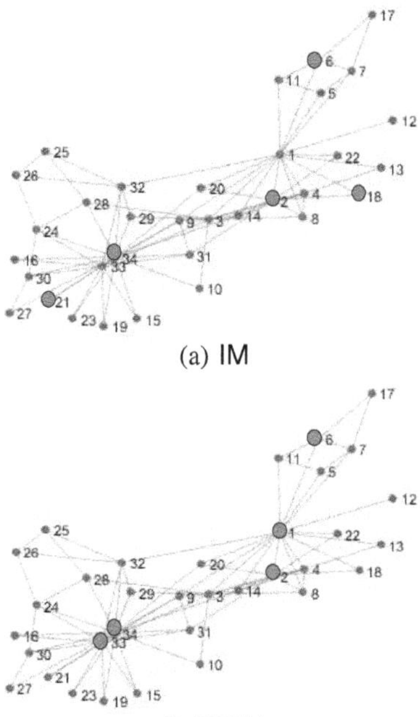

(a) IM

(b) TDIM

Figure 1: Top-5 Seeds (in Bold), *Zachary's Karate Club* Dataset

In their seminal paper [10], Kempe et al. left the time required for influence maximization unconstrained. However, in most cases, the campaigner is also interested in when a user would be influenced – the sooner, the better. For example, multiple competing companies launch comparable products around the same time (e.g., Nintendo's Wii vs. Sony's Playstation vs. Microsoft's X-Box; Microsoft's Surface vs. Apple's iPad vs. Samsung Note 3) [12]. Thus, a campaigner would like to inform the maximum number of people about her latest products as quickly as possible. In the domain of movies, the success of a film depends on public interests, and with the general attention span being far shorter, most films stay in theatres only in their first week or two [1].

In the aforementioned temporal context of information diffusion, we design a novel influence maximization problem, called the time-discounted influence maximization (TDIM). The campaigner provides a utility function $U(\delta t(u, S))$ that monotonically decreases with the time $\delta t(u, S)$ required to influence a user u, since the activation of the seed set S. As information diffusion is a probabilistic process, we aim at finding the optimal seed set that maximizes the campaigner's aggregated expected utility considering all users.

[1] http://www.boxofficemojo.com/yearly/chart/?yr=2015

TDIM is a non-trivial problem because U can be *any* arbitrary monotonically decreasing function; and therefore, the top-k seed set could be very different than those for the classical influence maximization. We illustrate this with the well-known Zachary's karate club dataset [15], which is a karate club social network of 34 members, documenting 78 pairwise links between these members who interacted outside the club from 1970 to 1972. Edge probabilities are assigned in proportion to the number of interactions, and we consider the IC model of influence cascade. In Figure 1, we show the top-5 seed nodes both for IM and TDIM, with a utility function exponentially decreasing over time. As one may observe, the seed nodes are more centrally located (i.e., closeness centrality) in case of TDIM, which facilitates a rapid dissemination of information to a large number of users. Clearly, this is the problem of interest for most practical scenarios.

Related Research and Novelty of Our Work. The temporal aspect of information diffusion has been explored in statistical physics [9]. Prior works [2, 6] considered influence maximization within a given time deadline, i.e., a finite time window must be considered. Our work TDIM is different because the campaigner assigns a utility score based on when a node gets influenced – the earlier, the better. This is often more useful than prior works where every node activation is treated equally if that happens within the specified time window. In fact, TDIM is a generalization of these prior works, because the time deadline can be simulated by properly selecting the utility function. A few other works [7, 13] aimed at finding the seed set such that a predefined coverage is achieved in the minimum time. Recently, Chang et. al. studied influence sustainability [1], that is, to maximize the count of those time steps when more than a threshold number of new users get activated. Clearly, the notion of influence sustainability is also different from ours.

2. PRELIMINARIES

A social network $\mathcal{G} = (V, E, P)$ consists of a set of n nodes V, $E \subseteq V \times V$ is a set of e directed edges, and $P : E \to (0, 1)$ is a probability function that assigns a probability to each edge. The probability p_{uv} on a directed edge $(u, v) \in E$ represents the probability that node v adopts a product due to the influence of node u, because u adopted that product before. When v adopts the product, it automatically becomes eligible to influence its neighbors. We shall discuss various influence cascading models in Section 2.1.

We denote by S the seed set for the campaigner. As influence cascade is a probabilistic process, let us denote by $\Delta T(u, S)$ the random variable corresponding to the time required for influencing a user u, since the activation of the seed set S. Let $\delta t(u, S)$ be a realization of $\Delta T(u, S)$. Next, we assume that the campaigner has a utility function $U(\delta t(u, S))$, where U can be *any* monotonically decreasing function of δt. We are now ready to define our problem.

PROBLEM 1 (TDIM). *Given a network $\mathcal{G} = (V, E, P)$, a budget on the seed set size k, and the campaigner's utility function U which decreases monotonically with time, find the seed set S of size k such that the campaigner's expected aggregated utility considering all network users is maximized. Formally,*

$$\arg\max_{S} \sum_{u \in V} \mathbb{E}[U(\Delta T(u, S))]$$
$$\textit{such that} \quad |S| = k \tag{1}$$

We denote by $\mathbb{E}$ the expectation in the above equation. TDIM, being a generalization of the influence maximization (IM) problem, is also **NP**-hard. Therefore, the question that remains is whether our new objective function in Equation 1 still retains some of the other properties, such as monotonicity and sub-modularity, of the classical IM. We shall discuss them in the context of three widely-used influence diffusion models – independent cascade (IC) [10], linear threshold (LT) [10], and maximum influence arborescence (MIA) [3], which are introduced below.

2.1 Influence Diffusion Models

In all our models, the campaign spreads from an initially active set of seed nodes in discrete steps. By following [7, 10], we consider one time step as one attempt of a node to influence its users.

Independent Cascade Model. In the IC model, when some node u first becomes active at step t, it gets a single chance to activate each of its currently inactive out-neighbors v; it succeeds with probability $p_{u,v}$. If u succeeds, then v will become active at step $t + 1$. Whether or not u succeeds at step t, it cannot make any further attempts in the subsequent rounds. If a node v has incoming edges from multiple newly activated nodes, their attempts are sequenced in an arbitrary order. Also, each node can be activated only once and it stays active until the end. The campaigning process runs until no more activations are possible.

Linear Threshold Model. In the LT model, each node v has an activation threshold θ_v, selected uniformly from $(0, 1)$. In addition, there is a constraint that the sum of the probabilities of all incoming edges for every node must be at most 1. If the sum of the probabilities of the incoming edges from all active nodes is greater than or equal to the activation threshold of an inactive node, then the node gets activated in the next round. Each node can only be activated once and stays active until the end.

Maximum Influence Arborescence. This model assumes that the influence from the seed nodes propagates only via the *maximum influence paths*. A path from a source to a destination node is called the maximum influence path if this has the highest probability compared to all other paths between the same pair of nodes. Ties are broken in a predetermined and consistent way, such that the maximum influence path between a pair of nodes is always unique.

2.2 Properties of TDIM

Let us denote $F(S) = \sum_{u \in V} \mathbb{E}[U(\Delta T(u, S))]$. A function F is sub-modular if it satisfies the following. $F(S_1 \cup \{v\}) - F(S_1) \geq F(S_2 \cup \{v\}) - F(S_2)$, for all elements v and all pairs of sets $S_1 \subseteq S_2$. We prove sub-modularity and monotonicity of our objective function $F(S)$ below.

THEOREM 1. TDIM *objective function is sub-modular under the* IC *model.*

PROOF. Our proof follows by constructing an equivalent view of the IC model with the notion of *possible worlds* [10]. Each possible world is a certain instance of the uncertain graph, and obtained by independent sampling of the edges. Every possible world X is associated with a probability of existence $prob(X)$. Let us consider the campaigner's aggregated utility in the possible world X, i.e., $F_X(S) = \sum_{u \in V} U(\delta t_X(u, S))$. The following holds.

$$F(S) = \sum_{\text{all possible world } X} [F_X(S) \times prob(X)] \tag{2}$$

Our proof follows by showing that $F_X(S)$ is sub-modular. As the non-negative linear combination of sub-modular functions is also sub-modular, then $F(S)$ would be sub-modular. However, in an analogous argument, $F_X(S)$ is the summation of $U(\delta t_X(u, S))$ for all $u \in V$. Therefore, we show the sub-modularity of $U(\delta t_X(u, S))$ in order to illustrate the sub-modularity of $F(S)$. In other words, for all $S_1 \subseteq S_2$, we prove the following.

$$U(\delta t_X(u, S_1 \cup \{v\})) - U(\delta t_X(u, S_1))$$
$$\geq U(\delta t_X(u, S_2 \cup \{v\})) - U(\delta t_X(u, S_2)) \tag{3}$$

Note that X is a deterministic graph and the IC model follows discrete time steps. Therefore, $\delta t_X(u, S)$ can be measured as the shortest path distance in X from any seed node in S to u. Formally, $\delta t_X(u, S) = \min_{s \in S} l_X(s, u)$, where $l_X(s, u)$ is the shortest path distance from s to u in X. Now consider two distinct cases.

Case 1. $\delta t_X(u, S_2) > \delta t_X(u, \{v\})$. It immediately follows that $\delta t_X(u, S_1) > \delta t_X(u, \{v\})$. This is because $S_1 \subseteq S_2$. Hence, the left-hand and right-hand sides of Equation 3 become $U(\delta t_X(u, \{v\})) - U(\delta t_X(u, S_1))$ and $U(\delta t_X(u, \{v\})) - U(\delta t_X(u, S_2))$, respectively. Next, one can verify that $\delta t_X(u, S_1) \geq \delta t_X(u, S_2)$, and $U(\delta t_X(u, S_1)) \leq U(\delta t_X(u, S_2))$. This is because U is monotonically decreasing. Therefore, Equation 3 holds.

Case 2. $\delta t_X(u, S_2) \leq \delta t_X(u, \{v\})$. In this case, the right-hand side of Equation 3 becomes zero. However, the left-hand side is always no less than zero, because $\delta t_X(u, S_1 \cup \{v\}) \leq \delta t_X(u, S_1)$. Since U is monotonically decreasing, $U(\delta t_X(u, S_1 \cup \{v\})) \geq U(\delta t_X(u, S_1))$. Therefore, Equation 3 also holds in this case. This completes the proof. □

THEOREM 2. TDIM *objective function is sub-modular under the* LT *model.*

PROOF. The proof follows by considering the *live-edge* model, which is shown to be equivalent to the LT model in [10]. In the live-edge model, each node v picks at most one of its incoming edges at random, that is, it selects the incoming edge from u with probability $p_{u,v}$, and it does not select any incoming edge with probability $1 - \sum_{u \in V} p_{u,v}$. Let X be one possible world with probability $Prob(X)$ under the live-edge model, and $F_X(S)$ be the campaigner's aggregated utility in X. Analogous to the proof of Theorem 1, one can show that $F_X(S)$ is sub-modular. Now, our objective function $F(S)$ can be expressed as follows.

$$F(S) = \sum_{\text{all possible world } X} [F_X(S) \times prob(X)] \tag{4}$$

As the non-negative linear combination of sub-modular functions is sub-modular, $F(S)$ is sub-modular. □

It is easy to verify that $F(S)$ is monotonic under the IC and the LT model. Below, we prove its monotonicity and sub-modularity under the MIA model, which are not immediately realized.

THEOREM 3. TDIM *objective function is monotonic under the* MIA *model.*

PROOF. Let us denote by $F_u(S) = \mathbb{E}[U(\Delta T(u, S))]$, and therefore, $F(S) = \sum_{u \in V} F_u$. We will show that $F_u(S)$ increases monotonically with S, thereby proving the monotonicity of $F(S)$.

We consider the uncertain sub-graph with the maximum influence paths from S to u. We denote by X one possible world of this uncertain sub-graph, having probability $prob(X)$, and shortest-path length of $\delta t_X(u, S)$ from S to u. Therefore, we get:

$$F_u(S) = \sum_{\text{all possible world } X} [U(\delta t_X(u, S)) \times prob(X)] \tag{5}$$

Next, consider a node $v \notin S$. With the possible worlds for the seed set S, we show how one can derive the possible worlds for the seed set $S \cup \{v\}$. Let us denote by E_1 the set of edges that are in the maximum influence path from v to u, but not in the maximum influence paths from S to u. For a specific possible world X (corresponding to seed set S), if we start sampling the edges in E_1, we get a set of new possible worlds $Y_1, Y_2, \ldots, Y_r$, where $r = 2^{|E_1|}$, such that $prob(X) = prob(Y_1) + prob(Y_2) + \ldots + prob(Y_r)$. Note that if we initially started with two different possible worlds $X_1 \neq X_2$, all the new possible worlds generated from X_1 and X_2 will be pairwise independent. In fact, the set of new possible worlds generated as above will correspond to all the possible worlds for the seed set $S \cup \{v\}$. Next, we observe that if Y is a new possible world generated from X, $\delta t_X(u, S) \geq \delta t_Y(u, S \cup \{v\})$. Therefore, U being monotonically decreasing, $U(\delta t_X(u, S)) \leq U(\delta t_Y(u, S \cup \{v\}))$. Finally, by applying Equation 5 on the new possible worlds, which correspond to the seed set $S \cup \{v\}$, we get $F_u(S) \leq F_u(S \cup \{v\})$. Hence, the theorem. □

THEOREM 4. TDIM *objective function is sub-modular under the* MIA *model.*

PROOF. We first show that $F_u(S) = \mathbb{E}[U(\Delta T(u, S))]$ is sub-modular under the MIA model. Since $F(S) = \sum_{u \in V} F_u$, the sub-modularity of $F(S)$ will automatically hold.

Consider any two seed sets S_1, S_2 such that $S_1 \subseteq S_2$, and any other node v. Let us consider the uncertain sub-graph consisting of the maximum influence paths from $S_2 \cup \{v\}$ to u. Let X be one possible world of this uncertain sub-graph, with probability $prob(X)$. Then, for any node set $S \subseteq S_2 \cup \{v\}$, we have:

$$F_u(S) = \sum_{\text{all possible world } X} [U(\delta t_X(u, S)) \times prob(X)] \tag{6}$$

By following an argument similar to the proof of Theorem 1, one can show that:

$$\begin{aligned} &U(\delta t_X(u, S_1 \cup \{v\})) - U(\delta t_X(u, S_1)) \\ &\geq U(\delta t_X(u, S_2 \cup \{v\})) - U(\delta t_X(u, S_2)) \end{aligned} \tag{7}$$

By combining Equations 6 and 7, we get the following.

$$F_u(S_1 \cup \{v\}) - F_u(S_1) \geq F_u(S_2 \cup \{v\}) - F_u(S_2) \tag{8}$$

Therefore, $F_u(S)$ is sub-modular. Hence, the result follows. □

Finally, given a specific seed set, computing the campaigner's expected aggregated utility is #**P**-hard for IC, LT, and MIA models. This directly follows from the fact that TDIM is a generalization of the IM, and computation of the expected spread, given a seed set, is #**P**-hard under IC, LT, and MIA models [3,7].

3. ALGORITHMS

As the TDIM objective function is non-negative, monotone, and sub-modular, an iterative hill-climbing approach that greedily maximizes the marginal gain at every iteration provides a solution with an approximation guarantee $(1 - \frac{1}{e}) \approx 0.63$ of the optimal solution [10]. Here, e is the base of the natural logarithm. We describe our greedy algorithm below.

Greedy Algorithm. We perform k iterations to identify the top-k seed nodes. At each iteration, we add the seed node s^* to S_1 that maximizes the marginal gain in the campaigner's expected aggregated utility. Here, S_1 denotes the partial seed set which was already computed in previous iterations. Formally,

$$s^* = \arg\max_{s \in V \setminus S_1} [F(S_1 \cup \{s\}) - F(S_1)] \tag{9}$$

We denote by $F(S)$ the campaigner's expected aggregated utility for the seed set S. As stated earlier, unfortunately there is no efficient way to compute $F(S)$ for a given S. Therefore, we employ Monte Carlo (MC) sampling to estimate it. Thus, in essence, our greedy algorithm produces a solution within $(1 - \frac{1}{e} - \epsilon)$ of the optimal influence spread, where ϵ depends on the accuracy of the MC estimate for expected utility given a seed set.

Table 1: Graph Dataset Characteristics

Dataset	# Node	# Edge	Edge Prob: Mean, SD, Quartiles
DBLP	684 911	4 569 982	0.008±0.007, {0.005, 0.005, 0.010}
NetHEPT	15 235	62 776	0.010±0.000, {0.010, 0.010, 0.010}

Time Complexity. The time complexity of each iteration of our greedy algorithm is $\mathcal{O}(nK(n+e))$, where K is the number of MC samples to get a good estimate. Since, we require k iterations, the overall complexity of our greedy algorithm is $\mathcal{O}(nkK(n+e))$.

Optimization Techniques. The greedy algorithm, as described above, is not very efficient because at every iteration, it recomputes the marginal gains for all remaining nodes. Leskovec et. al. earlier proposed the CELF optimization [11] based on the idea of sub-modularity. The main intuition is that the marginal gain provided by a node in the current iteration cannot be better than the marginal gain provided by the node in previous iterations. Hence, we may not require to compute the marginal gains for all remaining nodes in every iteration. As the TDIM objective function is also sub-modular, we apply the CELF optimization.

4. EXPERIMENTS

Datasets. We involve two real-world datasets, *DBLP* [8] and *NetHEPT* [4], each representing a directed uncertain graph (Table 1). For *DBLP*, as in [8], the edge probabilities are proportional to an exponential cdf of mean $\mu = 10$ to the number of collaborations, i.e., if two authors collaborated c times, the corresponding edge probability is proportional to: $1 - \exp^{-c/10}$. The *NetHEPT* dataset was used in [4] for the influence-maximization task with constant edge probabilities (0.01).

Campaigner's Utility Function. We consider three utility functions that decays differently over time.

Exponential: $U(\delta t) = \alpha^{\delta t}$

Multiplicative: $U(\delta t) = \frac{1}{\delta t + 1}$

Linear: $U(\delta t) = \max\{1 - \beta \times \delta t, 0\}$

In our experiments, we set $\alpha = 0.9$ and $\beta = 0.2$. We selected the above functions in a way such that the campaigner's utility per user varies on a scale from 0 to 1.

Comparing Methods. We compare our TDIM greedy algorithm with two baselines. First, we compare against the classical IM greedy algorithm. Second, as the utility function monotonically decreases with time, we consider a variation of the classical IM, that selects seed nodes only considering the influence within its 1-hop. We refer to our two baselines as IM and IM1, respectively. In all cases, we apply the CELF optimization [11] for efficiency.

The code is implemented in C++ and the experiments were performed on a single core of a 100GB, 2.40GHz Xeon server. In all our experiments, the number of MC samples is fixed as $K = 1000$ [8]. Due to limitation of space, we only demonstrate our results with IC model and top-$k = 50$ seed nodes.

Effectiveness and Efficiency. As illustrated in Table 2, TDIM usually outperforms both the baselines in terms of the campaigner's expected utility. This is because the TDIM greedy algorithm directly optimizes the campaigner's utility at every iteration. We recall that our designed utility functions assign a utility per user in the scale from 0 to 1. Therefore, the improvement by TDIM over baselines would be even higher if we consider utility functions having larger ranges. We found that IM1 often outperforms IM, which is due to the monotonically decreasing nature of our utility functions.

Table 3 presents the seed set finding times. As it is expected, IM1 requires the least amount of time because it computes influence only within 1-hop of every node. However, we also found that TDIM is always faster than classical IM, which indicates that the CELF optimization is more effective for TDIM. As demonstrated in Figure 1, the TDIM seed nodes are more centrally located based on closeness centrality. Therefore, if a node (e.g., a peripheral node) is not close to a large number of other nodes in the network, that node will never be considered as one of the top candidates in any iteration of TDIM greedy algorithm. However, such a node, if reachable to many other nodes in the graph, could still be considered as a top candidate in the subsequent iterations of IM greedy method. Thus, the number of re-computations required for TDIM is usually smaller than that for IM. This makes the CELF optimization more effective in case of TDIM. We also demonstrate this fact in our experimental results. This is evident from the less number of recomputations required for TDIM, as shown in Table 3.

Table 2: Effectiveness of Top-50 Seed Nodes

	Utility Function	Expected Utility		
		IM	IM1	TDIM
NetHEPT	Linear	235.74	935.31	**968.31**
	Multiplicative	397.66	654.61	**681.32**
	Exponential	1205.09	1558.60	**1672.34**
DBLP	Linear	230.22	**255.62**	254.51
	Multiplicative	165.68	179.72	**181.47**
	Exponential	303.17	322.44	**323.75**

Table 3: Efficiency of Finding Top-50 Seed Nodes

	Utility Function	Seeds Finding Time (sec)			# Recomputation		
		IM	IM1	TDIM	IM	IM1	TDIM
NetHEPT	Linear			4037.49			3261
	Multiplicative	13252.50	74.07	7942.96	15744	332	8850
	Exponential			12705.30			12141
DBLP	Linear			5949.23			379
	Multiplicative	6138.41	6006.54	5589.80	1476	178	425
	Exponential			6131.49			754

5. CONCLUSIONS

We formulate and study the novel problem of maximizing a campaigner's time-discounted utility via influence maximization. We show that the problem is sub-modular and monotonic under various influence diffusion models, and propose approximate algorithms with theoretical performance guarantees. We also demonstrate that the existing optimization techniques for the classical influence maximization could be more effective in our current setting. In future work, we shall consider the problem with more advanced optimization techniques, e.g., TIM [14] that was employed for the classical influence maximization.

6. REFERENCES

[1] C. Chang, P. Yang, M. Lyu, and K. Chuang. Influential Sustainability on Social Networks. In *ICDM*, 2015.

[2] W. Chen, W. Lu, and N. Zhang. Time-Critical Influence Maximization in Social Networks with Time-Delayed Diffusion Process. In *AAAI*, 2012.

[3] W. Chen, C. Wang, and Y. Wang. Scalable Influence Maximization for Prevalent Viral Marketing in Large-Scale Social Networks. In *KDD*, 2010.

[4] W. Chen, Y. Wang, and S. Yang. Efficient Influence Maximization in Social Networks. In *KDD*, 2009.

[5] P. Domingos and M. Richardson. Mining the Network Value Customers. In *KDD*, 2001.

[6] M. Gomez-Rodriguez, L. Song, N. Du, H. Zha, and B. Schölkopf. Influence Estimation and Maximization in Continuous-Time Diffusion Networks. *ACM Trans. Inf. Syst.*, 34(2):9:1–9:33, 2016.

[7] A. Goyal, F. Bonchi, L. V. S. Lakshmanan, and S. Venkatasubramanian. On Minimizing Budget and Time in Influence Propagation over Social Networks. *Social Netw. Analys. Mining*, 3(2):179–192, 2013.

[8] R. Jin, L. Liu, B. Ding, and H. Wang. Distance-Constraint Reachability Computation in Uncertain Graphs. *PVLDB*, 2011.

[9] M. Karsai, M. Kivelä, R. K. Pan, K. Kaski, J. Kertész, A.-L. Barabási, and J. Saramäki. Small but Slow World: How Network Topology and Burstiness Slow Down Spreading. *Phys. Rev. E*, 83:025102, 2011.

[10] D. Kempe, J. M. Kleinberg, and E. Tardos. Maximizing the Spread of Influence through a Social Network. In *KDD*, 2003.

[11] J. Leskovec, A. Krause, C. Guestrin, C. Faloutsos, J. VanBriesen, and N. Glance. Cost-effective Outbreak Detection in Networks. In *KDD*, 2007.

[12] W. Lu, F. Bonchi, A. Goyal, and L. V. S. Lakshmanan. The Bang for the Buck: Fair Competitive Viral Marketing from the Host Perspective. In *KDD*, 2013.

[13] Z. Lu, Y. Wen, and G. Cao. Information Diffusion in Mobile Social Networks: The Speed Perspective. In *INFOCOM*, 2014.

[14] Y. Tang, X. Xiao, and Y. Shi. Influence Maximization: Near-optimal Time Complexity Meets Practical Efficiency. In *SIGMOD*, 2014.

[15] W. W. Zachary. An Information Flow Model for Conflict and Fission in Small Groups. *J. Anthropological Research*, 33:452–473, 1977.

Quantifying Query Ambiguity with Topic Distributions

Yuki Yano
Yahoo Japan Corporation
yuyano@yahoo-corp.jp

Yukihiro Tagami
Yahoo Japan Corporation
yutagami@yahoo-corp.jp

Akira Tajima
Yahoo Japan Corporation
atajima@yahoo-corp.jp

ABSTRACT

Query ambiguity is a useful metric for search engines to understand users' intents. Existing methods quantify query ambiguity by calculating an entropy of clicks. These methods assign each click to a one-hot vector corresponding to some mutually exclusive groups. However, they cannot incorporate non-obvious structures such as similarity among documents. In this paper, we propose a new approach for quantifying query ambiguity using topic distributions. We show that it is a natural extension of an existing entropy-based method. Further, we use our approach to achieve topic-based extensions of major existing entropy-based methods. Through an evaluation using e-commerce search logs combined with human judgments, our approach successfully extended existing entropy-based methods and improved the quality of query ambiguity measurements.

Keywords

Query Ambiguity, Search Intent, Topic Distribution

1. INTRODUCTION

Understanding users' intents is important for search engines to fulfill users' needs. To measure these intents, query ambiguity is a commonly used criterion that quantifies how ambiguous or clear users' intents are for each query. Knowing query ambiguity is beneficial for search engines, for example, in controlling a trade-off between relevancy and diversity [11], in deciding whether to personalize or not [5], and in using as ranking features [2]. Query ambiguity can be classified into three levels [12]: *ambiguous*, *broad*, and *clear*. An *ambiguous* query, such as "giant", has several meanings and is hard to detect the user's intents. A *broad*, query, such as "songs", has one main topic but has several subtopics. A *clear* query, such as "University of Tokyo", has a specific meaning. Therefore, the difference in these levels is the extent of candidate topics that users can be thought to consider.

CIKM'16 , October 24 - 28, 2016, Indianapolis, IN, USA

ISBN 978-1-4503-4073-1/16/10. . . $15.00

DOI: http://dx.doi.org/10.1145/2983323.2983863

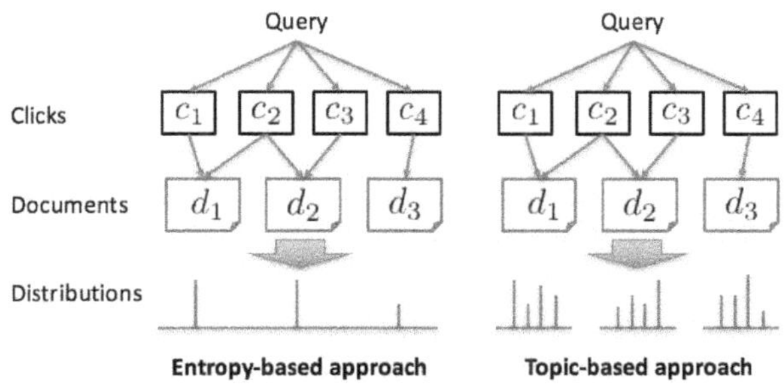

Figure 1: Difference between existing (left) and proposed (right) approaches in the expression of click distributions. Existing approach regards each document as exclusive, while proposed one considers topic similarity of documents.

In general, query ambiguity is calculated by using the past clicks of users [5, 13, 6]. For example, *click entropy* [5] quantifies query ambiguity by calculating an entropy of click distributions. A key aspect of this approach is that it assigns each click to a one-hot vector corresponding to each document (or other mutually exclusive groups such as domains, categories, and click patterns) and calculates the entropy using this distribution. The left side of Figure 1 depicts this approach. However, it cannot incorporate non-obvious structures such as similarity among documents. Considering the taxonomy of query ambiguity described above, it is intuitively obvious that this information can play an important part in quantifying query ambiguity.

In this paper, we propose a new approach for quantifying query ambiguity by using topic distributions. The right side of Figure 1 depicts our approach. It expresses each document (or other mutually exclusive groups) as a topic distribution, and quantifies query ambiguity by evaluating the similarity of each distribution. We show that our proposed approach is a natural extension of an existing entropy-based method. Further, we use our approach to achieve topic-based extensions of major existing entropy-based methods: *click entropy*, *user entropy* [13], and *pattern entropy* [6]. Through an evaluation using e-commerce search logs combined with human judgments, our approach successfully extended existing entropy-based methods and improved the quality of query ambiguity measurements.

Our work makes two major contributions.

- We propose a topic-based approach for quantifying query ambiguity and use it to achieve topic-based extensions of existing methods.

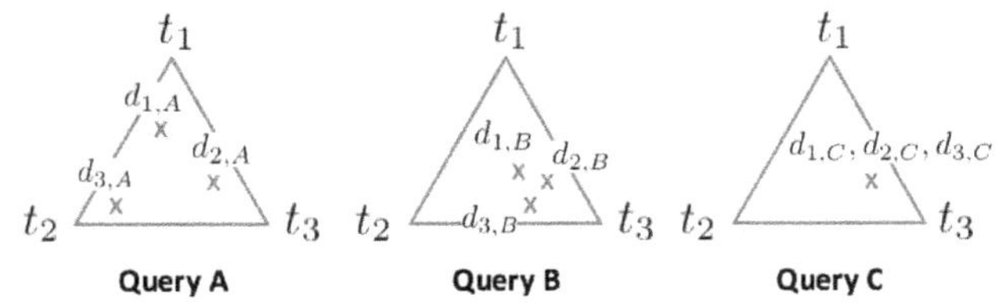

Figure 2: Examples of topic distributions of clicked documents with three topics. Order of query ambiguity is most likely $QueryA > QueryB > QueryC$.

- We reveal the effectiveness of utilizing topic distributions for quantifying query ambiguity by evaluating our extensions with a real-world e-commerce data set.

2. METHODOLOGY

In this section, we provide the details of our proposed approach. We first show the overview of our proposed approach, then define the problem that it is intended to solve, and finally formulate proposed extensions of existing methods.

2.1 Overview of Approach

We evaluate query ambiguity by incorporating topic distributions of clicks. The key idea of our approach is that if a query becomes more ambiguous, topic distributions of clicks become more different. In other words, we define query ambiguity as the extent of clicks in a topic space. For example, if we have three clicked documents like in Figure 1, our proposed approach places these documents onto the topic space like in Figure 2. Figure 2 shows examples that have different topic distributions of clicked documents. Intuitively, because the extent of topic distributions of each document is different, the order of query ambiguity is most likely $QueryA > QueryB > QueryC$.

2.2 Problem Definition and Existing Methods

Given a query q, a clicked document $d \in \mathcal{D}$, and a topic $t \in \mathcal{T}$, we assume $p(d|q)$ to be a click distribution of document d with a query q, and $p(t|d)$ to be a topic distribution of topic t with a document d. Our goal is to calculate query ambiguity with a query q, click-through document set $\mathcal{D}_q$, click distributions $\{p(d|q); d \in \mathcal{D}_q\}$, and topic distributions $\{p(t|d); d \in \mathcal{D}_q, t \in \mathcal{T}\}$. Note that we can also assume other mutually exclusive groups such as domains, categories, and patterns instead of documents.

With these notations, *click entropy* [5] is defined as (1)[1].

$$click\_ent(q, \mathcal{D}_q) = \sum_{d \in \mathcal{D}_q} -p(d|q) \log (p(d|q)). \quad (1)$$

Similarly, *user entropy* [13] is defined as (2).

$$user\_ent(q, U_q, \mathcal{D}_q) = \frac{\sum_{u \in U_q} click\_ent(q, \mathcal{D}_{u,q})}{|U_q|}, \quad (2)$$

where U_q is the set of users who input the query q and $\mathcal{D}_{u,d}$ is the set of documents that the user u clicked. Furthermore, *pattern entropy* [6] is defined as (3).

$$pattern\_ent(q, \Gamma_q) = \sum_{\tau \in \Gamma_q} -p(\tau|q) \log (p(\tau|q)), \quad (3)$$

where $\tau = \{(d, p(d)); d \in \mathcal{D}_\tau\}$ is a click pattern and Γ_q is the set of click patterns associated with the query q.

2.3 Proposed Approach

As mentioned in Section 2.1, we quantify query ambiguity as the extent of topic distributions. This extent is calculated in two steps. First, we calculate the average topic distribution of clicked documents by (4), that is, the topic distribution of the query q.

$$p(t|q) = \sum_{d \in \mathcal{D}_q} p(t|d)p(d|q). \quad (4)$$

Then, we quantify query ambiguity by calculating the average Kullback-Leibler divergence between $p(t|q)$ and $p(t|d)$ of each document d. In other words, we calculate the average distance of each document from a gravity given as (4).

$$\begin{aligned} topic\_ent(q, \mathcal{D}_q) &= \sum_{d \in \mathcal{D}_q} p(d|q) D_{KL}(p(t|d)||p(t|q)) \\ &= \sum_{d \in \mathcal{D}_q} p(d|q) \sum_{t \in \mathcal{T}} p(t|d) \log \left(\frac{p(t|d)}{p(t|q)} \right). \quad (5) \end{aligned}$$

As (5), $topic\_ent(q, \mathcal{D}_q)$ is non-negative: it is zero for queries that are completely clear and has a larger value for queries that are more ambiguous.

Note that our approach does not depend on methods to generate topic distributions. In our experiments, we used Bag-of-Words (BoW) and Latent Dirichlet Allocation (LDA) [3] for calculating topic distributions.

2.4 Topic-based Extensions of Existing Methods using Proposed Approach

Considering the problem described in Section 2.2, we can say that an existing entropy-based method is a special case in which each document is assumed to correspond to an unique topic (i.e., $p(t|d) = 1$ and $d_i \neq d_j \Rightarrow t_{d_i} \neq t_{d_j}$). With these conditions, (5) can be reduced to (6), which is the same as *click entropy* given as (1).

$$\begin{aligned} \sum_{d \in \mathcal{D}_q} p(d|q) \sum_{t \in \mathcal{T}} p(t|d) \log \left(\frac{p(t|d)}{p(t|q)} \right) &= \sum_{d \in \mathcal{D}_q} p(d|q) \log \left(\frac{p(t_d|d)}{p(t_d|q)} \right) \\ &= \sum_{d \in \mathcal{D}_q} -p(d|q) \log (p(d|q)). \end{aligned} \quad (6)$$

Thus, we can say that our proposed approach is a natural extension of *click entropy*.

Because of this relationship, our approach can be easily applied to other existing entropy-based methods. We can extend *user entropy* (2) as (7) by using (5) instead of *click entropy*.

$$topic\_user\_ent(q, U_q, \mathcal{D}_q) = \frac{\sum_{u \in U_q} topic\_ent(q, \mathcal{D}_{u,q})}{|U_q|}. \quad (7)$$

Furthermore, *pattern entropy* (3) can be expressed as (8) by using the topic distribution of each click pattern.

$$\begin{aligned} p(t|\tau) = \sum_{d \in \mathcal{D}_\tau} p(t|d)p(d|\tau), \quad p(t|q) = \sum_{\tau \in \Gamma_q} p(t|\tau)p(\tau|q), \\ topic\_pattern\_ent(q, \Gamma_q) = \sum_{\tau \in \Gamma_q} p(\tau|q) D_{KL}(p(t|\tau)||p(t|q)). \end{aligned} \quad (8)$$

[1]We write *entropy* as *ent* in each formula.

Table 1: Number of labels with ambiguity levels (rows) and query frequencies (columns).

	Low	Medium	High	Total
Ambiguous	8	26	30	64
Broad	44	50	70	164
Clear	140	119	95	354

Table 2: Statistics of corpora with each data type.

Data type	#docs	#tokens	avg-len
ItemClick	1,000,000	9,426,323	9.43
CategoryClick	23,869	825,284,382	34575.57

3. EXPERIMENTS

In this section, we show the results of our experiments. We first describe details of our experiments and then evaluate each approach by using an ordinal scale with human labels.

3.1 Data Description

We evaluated our proposed approach by using search logs of Yahoo! JAPAN's shopping site[2]. The target site is a mall-type e-commerce site that has more than 300 thousand stores and over 100 million items. Our proposed approach needs contents of clicked documents for the calculation, however the data set that previous researchers [13, 6] used does not have these contents. Thus, we used these e-commerce search logs that fully contain clicks and contents in this experiment. Note that these search logs were generated by the search engine of the e-commerce site. This search engine used attributes of each item and matching scores between a query and contents for the ranking, but it did not use any query features such as query ambiguity.

We used search logs from October 1 to November 31, 2015 and divided queries into three groups by their frequencies in the same manner as [13]. From each group, we drew a random sample of 200 queries and classified them into three ambiguity levels [12]: *ambiguous*, *broad*, and *clear*. Queries were labeled by three annotators (employees of the shopping site), and we selected queries for which at least two annotators made the same judgments. Krippendorff's α of our annotation was 0.42, which meant moderate agreement among the three annotators [1]. Table 1 shows the details of the labels. We used these labels for calculating Kendall's τ of each approach, which is a measure of an ordinal scale, and a larger value means more correlated[3]. Further, we checked statistically significant of each result by using bootstrapping with 1,000 bootstrap samples.

For evaluations, we used two kinds of data sets, ItemClick and CategoryClick, which construct click distributions differently. ItemClick simply uses clicked items (i.e., documents) for click distributions. On the other hand, CategoryClick uses human-labeled categories provided by the site instead of items themselves. The e-commerce site has 23,869 categories, and each item is tagged as belonging to one of these categories. Using Figure 1 as an example, CategoryClick uses those categories as "Documents".

3.2 Comparison Methods

We compared our proposed extensions described in Section 2 with *click entropy*, *user entropy*, and *pattern entropy*.

[2]http://shopping.yahoo.co.jp/

[3]We used SciPy [7] to calculate Kendall's τ in experiments.

Table 3: Kendall's τ between ambiguity scores and human labels over ItemClick. * denotes statistically significant at $p \leq 0.05$ against the corresponding existing method.

Method	τ_{all}	$\tau_{amb\text{-}brd}$	$\tau_{brd\text{-}clr}$
click entropy	0.243	0.175	0.180
topic entropy (BoW)	0.328*	0.280	0.233
topic entropy (LDA)	0.320*	0.295*	0.215
user entropy	-0.103	-0.017	-0.097
topic user entropy (BoW)	-0.027*	0.043	-0.043
topic user entropy (LDA)	0.022*	0.063	-0.002*
pattern entropy	0.281	0.157	0.230
topic pattern entropy (BoW)	0.350*	0.274	0.259
topic pattern entropy (LDA)	**0.383***	**0.331***	**0.278**

As mentioned in Section 2.3, we used BoW and LDA for calculating topic distributions. Using BoW, we divided each document of clicked items into terms and assumed the term distribution to be the topic distribution. We used BoW only for ItemClick because CategoryClick integrates items by using categories. Using LDA, we trained models by gensim [10] and used a different strategy for each data type. For ItemClick, we drew a random sample of 1,000,000 items from all items for constructing LDA models and inferred topic distributions at run time using these models. For CategoryClick, on the other hand, we pre-computed the topic distribution of each category by using LDA. Because the number of categories is small, we used all items and summed up documents for each category. Table 2 shows the details of the corpora. Note that we used the title of each item as one document and tokenized by using MeCab [8]. Furthermore, we only used nouns (except numerals) and restricted vocabulary to the 100,000 most frequent tokens (except overly frequent tokens that appeared in over 10% of all documents).

In experiments, we tried 9 similarity thresholds σ (0.1, 0.2, ..., 0.9) for *pattern entropy* and *topic pattern entropy*, and 10 kinds of *#topics* (100, 200, ..., 1000) for LDA. Then, we chose the one with the best performance for the result.

3.3 Results

Table 3 shows Kendall's τ of each method over ItemClick. In Table 3, τ_{all} is Kendall's τ with all labels, $\tau_{amb\text{-}brd}$ is Kendall's τ with *ambiguous* and *broad*, and $\tau_{brd\text{-}clr}$ is Kendall's τ with *broad* and *clear*. The results show that the proposed extensions outperformed the existing methods in all cases. In more detail, it seems the improvement of $\tau_{amb\text{-}brd}$ contributed more than that of $\tau_{brd\text{-}clr}$. *Ambiguous* and *broad* differ in the depth of users' intents, and the similarity between clicks needs to be considered to distinguish these two labels correctly. Consequently, this result indicates the effectiveness of utilizing topic distributions, which is the key point of our approach. Of the three existing methods, *pattern entropy* had the best results while *user entropy* had the worst. Because users can be expected to have their own purchase intents, we think query ambiguity of each user is relatively small in an e-commerce search, resulting in poor *user entropy*. Among the proposed extensions, LDA-extensions obtained better results than BoW-extensions in almost all cases. Since LDA is assumed to provide richer topics than BoW, this result shows that the performance of the proposed extensions and the quality of topics are correlated. Furthermore, BoW-extensions also outperformed the

Table 4: Kendall's τ between ambiguity scores and human labels over CategoryClick. * denotes statistically significant at $p \leq 0.05$ against the corresponding existing method.

Method	τ_{all}	$\tau_{amb\text{-}brd}$	$\tau_{brd\text{-}clr}$
click entropy	0.364	0.271	0.280
topic entropy (LDA)	0.398	0.368	0.288
user entropy	-0.008	-0.130	0.043
topic user entropy (LDA)	0.127*	-0.035	0.142*
pattern entropy	0.475	0.379	0.337
topic pattern entropy (LDA)	**0.487**	**0.420**	**0.341**

existing methods, while they simply used the terms of documents without any domain knowledge. Therefore, BoW can be a suitable choice to use if there is no prior information.

Table 4 shows Kendall's τ of each method over CategoryClick. As with results in Table 3, the proposed extensions improved the correlation in all cases; however, the improvement was smaller than for ItemClick. This is natural because the merit of introducing topics is small when clicks are summarized by well-designed groups like in CategoryClick. Still, consistently showing positive results regardless of the quality or granularity of groups is a good property. Focusing on the correlation of label pairs, the proposed extensions still outperformed the existing methods by $\tau_{amb\text{-}brd}$ just like for ItemClick. On the other hand, the improvement of $\tau_{brd\text{-}clr}$ was very small with *click entropy* and *pattern entropy*. While the categories are somewhat rough classifications, we think that almost all clicks of *clear* were grouped in the same category, and thus the results of each method were close.

4. RELATED WORK

Query ambiguity is an important part of query intent, and it can improve the performance of retrieval [11, 5, 2]. Song et al. [12] proposed a taxonomy of query ambiguity as three types: *ambiguous*, *broad*, and *clear*. They found that these types are different in an extent of topic distributions of queries. Cronen-Townsend and Croft [4] proposed *clarity score* for quantifying query ambiguity. They calculated *clarity score* by measuring KL divergence between a query language model and a collection language model and showed that the score strongly correlated with the average precision of TREC test collections. Qiu et al. [9] used topics of queries' terms for measuring query ambiguity. They used ODP taxonomy as topics and showed that topic intersections of each term were suitable criteria for query ambiguity.

For click-based measures, the most basic method is *click entropy*, which Dou et al. [5] proposed. *Click entropy* quantifies query ambiguity by calculating an entropy of click distribution. They used *click entropy* for measuring whether or not a query should be personalized, and they found that personalization is insufficient with small *click entropy*. Wang and Agichtein [13] proposed *user entropy*, which averages *click entropy* by each user. They showed that *user entropy* is useful for low-frequency queries. Duan et al. [6] proposed *pattern entropy*, which utilizes users' click patterns for calculating the entropy instead of utilizing simple clicks. They argued that click patterns provide a richer representation of query intents, such as multi-click intents.

Compared with *click entropy* and other derived methods, which quantify query ambiguity as the entropy of a single distribution generated from clicks, our proposed approach differs in that it considers topic distributions rather than a single distribution for quantifying query ambiguity.

5. CONCLUSIONS AND FUTURE WORK

In this paper, we proposed a new approach for quantifying query ambiguity by using topic distributions. We showed that our proposed approach is a natural extension of the existing entropy-based method. Further, we used our method to achieve topic-based extensions of major existing entropy-based methods. Through an evaluation using e-commerce search logs combined with human judgments, our approach successfully extended existing entropy-based methods and improved the quality of query ambiguity measurements.

Query ambiguity could be used to improve various search tasks such as ranking, diversification, and query suggestions, and we will all evaluate our approach in those settings. Furthermore, we will also consider applying it to actual services.

6. REFERENCES

[1] R. Artstein and M. Poesio. Inter-coder agreement for computational linguistics. *Comput. Linguist.*, 34(4):555–596, 2008.

[2] P. N. Bennett, K. Svore, and S. T. Dumais. Classification-enhanced ranking. In *Proceedings of WWW '10*, pages 111–120, 2010.

[3] D. M. Blei, A. Y. Ng, and M. I. Jordan. Latent dirichlet allocation. *J. Mach. Learn. Res.*, 3:993–1022, 2003.

[4] S. Cronen-Townsend and W. B. Croft. Quantifying query ambiguity. In *Proceedings of HLT '02*, pages 104–109, 2002.

[5] Z. Dou, R. Song, and J.-R. Wen. A large-scale evaluation and analysis of personalized search strategies. In *Proceedings of WWW '07*, pages 581–590, 2007.

[6] H. Duan, E. Kiciman, and C. Zhai. Click patterns: An empirical representation of complex query intents. In *Proceedings of CIKM '12*, pages 1035–1044, 2012.

[7] E. Jones, T. Oliphant, P. Peterson, et al. SciPy: Open source scientific tools for Python, 2001–. [Online; accessed 2016-04-25].

[8] T. Kudo, K. Yamamoto, and Y. Matsumoto. Applying conditional random fields to japanese morphological analysis. In *Proceedings of EMNLP '04*, pages 230–237, 2004.

[9] G. Qiu, K. Liu, J. Bu, C. Chen, and Z. Kang. Quantify query ambiguity using odp metadata. In *Proceedings of SIGIR '07*, pages 697–698, 2007.

[10] R. Řehůřek and P. Sojka. Software Framework for Topic Modelling with Large Corpora. In *Proceedings of the LREC 2010 Workshop on New Challenges for NLP Frameworks*, pages 45–50, 2010.

[11] R. L. Santos, C. Macdonald, and I. Ounis. Selectively diversifying web search results. In *Proceedings of CIKM '10*, pages 1179–1188, 2010.

[12] R. Song, Z. Luo, J.-R. Wen, Y. Yu, and H.-W. Hon. Identifying ambiguous queries in web search. In *Proceedings of WWW '07*, pages 1169–1170, 2007.

[13] Y. Wang and E. Agichtein. Query ambiguity revisited: clickthrough measures for distinguishing informational and ambiguous queries. In *Proceedings of HLT '10*, pages 361–364, 2010.

ASNets : A Benchmark Dataset of Aligned Social Networks for Cross-Platform User Modeling

Xuezhi Cao , Yong Yu
Apex Data and Knowledge Management Lab
Dept. of Computer Science and Engineering,
Shanghai Jiao Tong University
cxz,yyu@apex.sjtu.edu.cn

ABSTRACT

Aligning heterogeneous online social networks is a highly beneficial task proposed in recent years. It targets at automatically aligning accounts from multiple networks by whether they are held by the same natural person. Aligning the networks can improve personalized services by cross-platform user modeling, and is the prerequisite for cross-network analysis. However, there is currently no public benchmark dataset available due to its recency. As performances of this task depend highly on the dataset, experiments using different private datasets are not directly comparable. Therefore, in this paper we propose ASNets, a benchmark dataset with two sets of aligned social networks. With this dataset, we can now properly evaluate different approaches and compare them fairly. The two sets of aligned networks have 328,224 and 141,614 aligned users respectively, covering multilingual usage (Chinese and English) and various types of social networks including general purposed networks, review sites and microblogging sites. We describe the collecting methodology and statistics in details, and evaluate several state-of-the-art network aligning approaches. Beside introducing the dataset, we further propose several potential research directions that benefit from ASNets.

Keywords

Benchmark Dataset, Network Alignment, User Modeling

1. INTRODUCTION

As online social networks (OSNs) develops, people launch different kinds of OSNs for various needs. For example, we have Facebook for friendship, LinkedIn for professional relations and Pinterest for content discovery. To maintain all kinds of social relations and to discover different types of contents, normally people participate in more than one OSN. However, the networks work separately and the alignment indicating which accounts are held by the same natural person usually remains unrevealed.

CIKM'16 , October 24-28, 2016, Indianapolis, IN, USA

DOI: http://dx.doi.org/10.1145/2983323.2983864

Aligning the social networks is beneficial for users, service providers and also researchers:

- **For users:** We may provide integrated environment to keep up-to-date with friends' activities [10]. Also, we can achieve better user preferences modeling by aggregating action histories from multiple networks, leading to the improvement of all kinds personalized services [12].
- **For providers:** Research showed that users tend to copy links from associated out-site accounts, resulting in quick community growth [13]. With the alignment, we can extend such growth to users who have not yet manually associate their out-site accounts.
- **For researchers:** The alignment is the prerequisite knowledge for research topics such as cross-platform recommendation and user behavior analysis [4].

Therefore, we consider this topic as a highly valuable one.

Service providers as well as researchers have made plenty attempts to recover the alignment. One direct way is to let the users manually associate their accounts. For example, social networks now allow "log in with Twitter accounts" and etc. There are also specifically designed third-party platforms, e.g. About.Me[1]. However, not all users associate their cross-platform accounts due to the tedious manually work. Besides, not all networks enable cross-platform account associations. Therefore, automatically aligning is required. Researchers employ various kinds of user information for this task, including usernames [6], user profile (email, location, education) [2, 7, 10] and social relationship [9]. Experiments show that recovering the alignment automatically is a promising direction.

However, there is still no public benchmark dataset available for this task. It has become an implicit obstacle for further development. Most existing experiments use private dataset crawled by the authors. Such datasets vary a lot in terms of quality, network type, use scenario and scale. We summarize most of the datasets used in existing works in Table 1. Furthermore, due to the specialty of the task, performance depends highly on the dataset. Results using different datasets are not numerically comparable. For example, exact name match method has a precision of 52.58% and 77.00% on datasets used in [9] and [11] respectively.

Therefore, we assemble and publish ASNets for the community. ASNets has several advantages comparing to existing private datasets in terms of alignment scale, coverage

[1]http://about.me/

Table 1: Summary of Datasets Used in Existing Works

Data Set	MOBIUS [11]	MNA [3]	MAH [9]	**ASNets (This Paper)**	
Data Source	32 Sites	Twitter Foursquare	Twitter BlogCatalog	Facebook Twitter	Weibo Douban
# Aligned Users	100,179	500	2,710	328,224	141,614
Avg Network Degree	×	10.68/5.87	Unknown	8.79/19.05	44.35/19.07
# UGCs per User	×	1563.46/15.00	×	×	286.55/120.41

and generality. Besides explaining the dataset and collecting methodologies in details, we also evaluate several state-of-the-art network aligning approaches using ASNets. We further propose several potential research directions that benefit from ASNets.

2. DATASET

The ASNets dataset can be freely accessed online[2]. All data (including the alignment) are collected from public available information in target social networks, thus it would not cause any privacy leak. Still, for privacy concerns we anonymize the sensitive information such as user handle, username and user generated contents by id or hashing. Ideas for extending the dataset are welcomed (please contact the first author).

Due to the variety of OSNs, we include two sets of alignments in our dataset: one between Facebook and Twitter and the other between Douban and Weibo.

2.1 F-T Set : Facebook-Twitter

We collect the alignment between Facebook and Twitter from About.Me, a third party platform specifically designed for associating user's online accounts. The alignment is explicitly revealed through About.Me's profile page. We conduct the collection by starting from several randomly selected About.Me accounts as seeds and expanding by their social links. In total, we collect 1,107,695 accounts, among which 422,291 accounts are associated with Facebook and 669,198 with Twitter. For alignment, we have 328,224 aligned (common) users. We also collect social relations (follows) in both Facebook and Twitter among those users.

2.2 W-D Set : Weibo-Douban

Weibo[3] and Douban[4] are China's largest microblog site and movie-rating site respectively. For this dataset, the alignment is revealed explicitly in user's Douban homepage. Therefore, we start the collection from Douban. We go through all users in Douban by user id and result in 1,694,399 active users (with at least 10 actions). Among those users, 141,614 users are associated with Weibo account. Besides social relations in both networks, we also collect user generated contents (UGCs). Specifically, we collect user's movie rating histories in Douban and microblog histories in Weibo. On average we have around 287 microblogs and 120 rating histories per user.

2.3 Statistics & Summary

We show the basic statistics of ASNets in Table 1.

Comparing to datasets used in existing works, ASNets has several advantages. First of all, it is freely available to the community thus can be used as benchmark for proper comparison between approaches. Secondly, ASNets has a wide coverage on use scenarios. The two sets of aligned networks cover multiple types of social networks including general purposed (Facebook), microblogging (Twitter & Weibo) and movie-rating (Douban) networks. ASNets also covers multilingual scenarios (English-focused and Chinese-focused networks). Thirdly, the scale of ASNets is significantly larger than existing ones. Finally, we include item-based and text-based UGCs in W-D set. As most user actions in OSNs can be categorized into item-based or text-based UGCs, so ASNets characterizes most scenarios. By including UGCs, ASNets enables researches to leverage UGCs for network aligning, and also supports the cross-platform recommendation task. Due to the complexity of UGCs in general-purposed OSN (Facebook), we exclude them in the F-T set for now.

We also decide to exclude user profiles from ASNets intentionally due to the following reasons. User profile information such as email, location, affiliation and etc., with no doubts provide strong signals for recovering the alignment. However, such information varies between networks. Special handling is required for different scenarios, a general approach may not be applicable [6]. Heavy engineering work is required instead of scientific research. The accessibility of such information is also questionable. With user's raising awareness of online privacy protection, such information's accessibility will be further limited in the future [5]. In addition, most approaches can easily integrate such information with the learning process. So, excluding user profiles from ASNets does not limit future usage of such information for real applications.

3. CONSISTENCY ANALYSIS

In this section, we show the consistency across networks. Specifically, we analyze whether and to what extent are username, social ties and UGCs consistent with the alignment.

We employ edit distance to measure similarity between usernames. Define $P_{ed}(d)$ to be the set of account pairs with edit distance at most d, precision and recall by

$$Prec@d = \frac{|R \cap P_{ed}(d)|}{|P_{ed}(d)|}, Rec@d = \frac{|R \cap P_{ed}(d)|}{|R|} \quad (1)$$

where R is the ground truth alignment. Figure 1 (a) shows the result. As we can notice, most pairs with edit distance less than 3 are actually true alignments. However, the coverage is rather low.

To model social tie, we employ Jaccard Similarity Coefficient. We further normalize the coefficient as we only focus on the ranking instead of absolute value. Results showed in Figure 1 (b) prove the existence of social tie consistency. However, even when all the alignments are given except for the target user, highest Jaccard coefficient does not always indicate true alignment.

[2]http://dataset.apexlab.org/asnets
[3]http://www.weibo.com/
[4]http://www.douban.com/

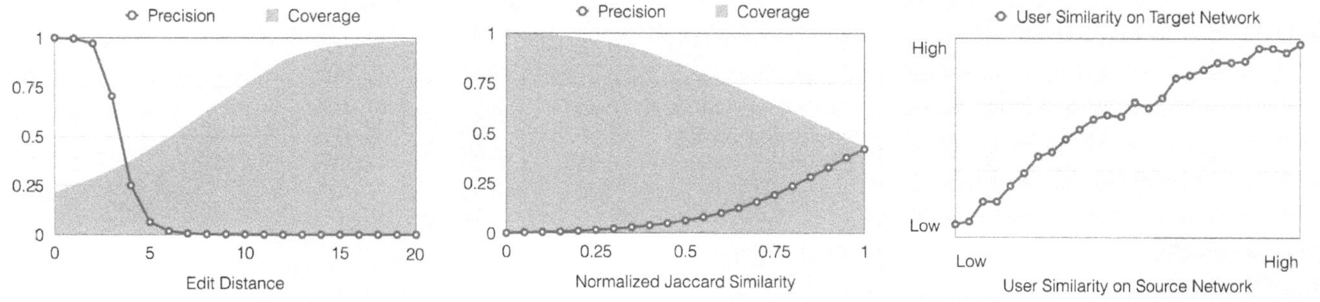

(a) Username Consistency (b) Social Tie Consistency (c) User Preference Consistency

Figure 1: Consistency across Social Networks. Results are according to W-D set.

For user generated contents, we analyze whether users with similar activities in one network are still similar in the other network. We employ topic model (Latent Dirichlet Allocation [1]) for modeling text-based UGCs and Jaccard Similarity Coefficient for item-based UGCs. We group user pairs by similarity on the source network, and evaluate the averaged similarity on the target network. Results showed in Figure 1 (c) support the assumption and prove the existence of UGC consistency across networks. Note that UGC consistency alone can not be used to pin-point the corresponding account as the username or social tie consistency.

4. NETWORK ALIGNING - EVALUATION

In this section we evaluate several state-of-the-art approaches for aligning social networks using our dataset ASNets.

4.1 Task Definition & Evaluation Metric

The task's formal definition and corresponding evaluation metrics also vary in existing works due to different focus and underlying assumptions. Here we summarize a rather general one as the following.

The task is: given two social networks A, B over user sets U_A, U_B, with username, social relations and user generated contents as side information, recover the alignment $\hat{R} \subset U_A \times U_B$ where $(u, v) \in \hat{R}$ indicates accounts u, v belong to same natural person according to the algorithm.

The aligning task is actually a retrieval task that finds the required pairs of accounts. Therefore we employ F1-Score as the evaluation metric. Assuming the ground truth alignment is R, then we have $Prec(\hat{R}) = \frac{|\hat{R} \cap R|}{|\hat{R}|}$ and $Recall(\hat{R}) = \frac{|\hat{R} \cap R|}{|R|}$.

The benefit of this definition and metric is its generality. It breaks several assumptions in existing works. It does not force users to have only one account in each network, and also allows users to participate in only one network.

4.2 Comparing Algorithms

We compare the following algorithms in our experiments.

- **MNA [3]** : Focuses on social relations and UGCs, and then employ stable marriage for alignment.
- **MAH [9]** : Captures social relations information (hypergraph) by low-dimension latent space.
- **MOBIUS [11]** : Focuses on user's behavior pattern when choosing usernames.
- **NAME** : Directly aligns accounts with same username, which provides an upper-bound for works that focuses only on alias-disambiguation [6].

We do not compare between approaches focusing on user profiles as ASNets is not designed for user profile based modelings. Reasons are stated in previous section.

4.3 Evaluation Results

Because most existing works are based on the full mapping assumption (assuming all users participate in both networks), we also conduct the experiment under this setting. Therefore, we select only the aligned users in ASNets for the experiment. 30% of the alignment is given as training data. We show the results in Table 2. We also list the performance reported in the original paper for each of the algorithms as 'Reported F1-Score' in the table. As we can see, performance evaluated using ASNets is noticeable different with the original reported performance. The reasons are as follows.

For **MAH** and **MOBIUS**, their original datasets have 52% and 77% alignments with exactly the same username respectively while in ASNets we have only around 20%. The differences may due to the collecting methodology and the data source used. For example, people tend to use real name in Facebook while nickname in Twitter, so the usernames are more likely to be different. Also note that the relative improvements of these approaches comparing to username match method are mostly consistent when using both ASNets and the original datasets. For **MNA**, different UGCs might be the reason as they originally targeted at text-to-text modeling while in ASNets we provide heterogeneous actions between text-based and item-based sites.

Another major issue causing the performance drop is the data scale. **MAH** and **MNA** are originally evaluated using dataset with only 2,710 and 500 aligned users respectively, while in ASNets we have 328,224 and 141,614 for the two subsets. The difficulty to find corresponding accounts from hundreds of accounts and from hundreds of thousands of accounts must be significantly different.

5. FUTURE DIRECTIONS

Besides aligning networks, we may as well employ ASNets for other research topics that rely on aligned social network. We propose three potential directions in this section.

5.1 Cross-Platform User Modeling

Most current recommender systems are within-site systems, e.g. recommending movies based on one's movie rating history or ranking tweets according to one's retweeting history. With no doubts these recommender systems succeed in improving user's online experience. However, they

Table 2: Experimental Results with 30% Training Data

Approach	Reported F1-Score	Facebook-Twitter			Weibo-Douban		
		Precison	Recall	F1-Score	Precison	Recall	F1-Score
MAH	0.7668	42.82%	42.82%	0.4282	41.74%	41.74%	0.4174
MNA	0.8960	67.64%	62.21%	0.6481	64.39%	61.41%	0.6287
MOBIUS	0.9138	55.48%	55.48%	0.5548	51.37%	51.37%	0.5137
NAME	-	100.00%	21.52%	0.3541	100.00%	14.70%	0.2562

still face the cold-start problem [8]: recommender system fails on new users who do not have enough action histories.

With aligned OSNs, we may model user's preferences jointly over multiple networks simultaneously. The goal is to model user's general preferences instead of only movie/tweet preferences. Following this, we can directly borrow action histories from other aligned networks for the target user to alleviate the cold-start problem. Also, comprehensiveness of user modeling can be boosted.

This task is similar with cross-domain recommendation. However, due to lack of actual cross-domain dataset, most works use generated pseudo-cross-domain data, e.g. partition movie rating logs by movie genres (action/romance/etc.). There are also works transfer from movies to books within same site. These domains still have lots in common and are of homogenous format. On the other hand, our dataset provides aligned social networks with heterogenous user actions covering item-based movie rating logs and text-based tweeting histories, thus is also suitable for this topic.

5.2 Anonymity-Protecting Strategy

Despite the benefits of aligning social networks, there are still users who want to keep their anonymity online. Note that aligning social networks does not result in privacy leak as we conduct the aligning only based on public available information. In other word, user's online action histories have already jeopardized their anonymity.

There are service providers trying to protect user's online anonymity, mostly by showing only partial of the user's actions or friends list. These strategies do help, however also limit the usage of the social network. One future direction is to find a better strategy to protect user's online anonymity with minimum negative effects on the social network usage. For example, making minimum alternation to user's social relation (e.g. adding/hiding least number of fake relations).

5.3 Multi-Network Analysis

There are plenty of research works on various aspects of social network analysis, including community detection, link prediction, measuring user influence and etc. With the aligned OSNs, researchers could extend such analysis to multi-network scenario. Such extensions are not trival because the task definition as well as the underlying objective functions might be fundamentally different.

Further, as OSNs are all based on user's real friendship, work relations or interests, the following question is can we recover the underlying networks in real world? Ultimately, the goal is to align the online world with the real world.

6. CONCLUSION

As social networks develop, aligning the current fragmented social networks has been proposed as a novel topic recently. Although there exist several research works in this direction, there is still no public dataset available. In this paper, we propose a benchmark dataset (ASNets), containing two sets of large-scale aligned social networks. With the dataset, different approaches can be properly evaluated and fairly compared. We evaluate and compare several state-of-the-art approaches using ASNets. We further propose several potential research topics that can also benefit from the dataset. We will keep maintaining and updating the coverage of the dataset for wider usage in this direction.

7. REFERENCES

[1] D. M. Blei, A. Y. Ng, and M. I. Jordan. Latent dirichlet allocation. *the Journal of machine Learning research*, 3:993–1022, 2003.

[2] F. Carmagnola and F. Cena. User identification for cross-system personalisation. *Information Sciences*, 179(1):16–32, 2009.

[3] X. Kong, J. Zhang, and P. S. Yu. Inferring anchor links across multiple heterogeneous social networks. In *CIKM*, pages 179–188. ACM, 2013.

[4] S. Kumar, R. Zafarani, and H. Liu. Understanding user migration patterns in social media. In *AAAI*, 2011.

[5] S. Labitzke, I. Taranu, and H. Hartenstein. What your friends tell others about you: Low cost linkability of social network profiles. In *SNA-KDD*, 2011.

[6] J. Liu, F. Zhang, X. Song, Y.-I. Song, C.-Y. Lin, and H.-W. Hon. What's in a name?: an unsupervised approach to link users across communities. In *WSDM*, pages 495–504. ACM, 2013.

[7] A. Nunes, P. Calado, and B. Martins. Resolving user identities over social networks through supervised learning and rich similarity features. In *SAC*, pages 728–729. ACM, 2012.

[8] A. I. Schein, A. Popescul, L. H. Ungar, and D. M. Pennock. Methods and metrics for cold-start recommendations. In *SIGIR*. ACM, 2002.

[9] S. Tan, Z. Guan, D. Cai, X. Qin, J. Bu, and C. Chen. Mapping users across networks by manifold alignment on hypergraph. In *AAAI*, 2014.

[10] J. Vosecky, D. Hong, and V. Y. Shen. User identification across multiple social networks. In *NDT*, pages 360–365. IEEE, 2009.

[11] R. Zafarani and H. Liu. Connecting users across social media sites: a behavioral-modeling approach. In *SIGKDD*. ACM, 2013.

[12] J. Zhang, X. Kong, and P. S. Yu. Transferring heterogeneous links across location-based social networks. In *WSDM*. ACM, 2014.

[13] C. Zhong, M. Salehi, S. Shah, M. Cobzarenco, N. Sastry, and M. Cha. Social bootstrapping: how pinterest and last. fm social communities benefit by borrowing links from facebook. In *WWW*. ACM, 2014.

Data Locality in Graph Engines: Implications and Preliminary Experimental Results

Yong-Yeon Jo, Jiwon Hong, Myung-Hwan Jang,
Jae-Geun Bang, and Sang-Wook Kim*
Dept. of Computer and Software,
Hanyang University,
Seoul, Korea.
{jyy0430, nowiz, sugichiin, worms710, wook}@hanyang.ac.kr

ABSTRACT

The size of graphs has dramatically increased. Graph engines for a single machine have been emerged to process these graphs efficiently. However, existing engines have overlooked a data locality which is an imperative factor to improve the performance of these engines in the previous literature. In this paper, we show the importance of data locality with graph algorithms by running on graph engines based on a single machine.

CCS Concepts

•**Information systems → Data layout;** *Graph-based database models;*

Keywords

Data layout; data locality; graph engines; single machine

1. INTRODUCTION

A number of datasets used in various applications are represented as a graph composed of nodes and edges. To process those data for analysis, a variety of graph algorithms have been proposed in the literature. These algorithms have some difficulty in terms of their processing performance because the size of graphs has been increasing dramatically. Recently, *graph engines* have been proposed to help implement these graph algorithms efficiently and also conveniently [4][5][9]. These engines can be classified into two categories according to their design philosophy. One is aimed for running itself in a distributed environment [2][6] and the other for running itself in a single machine [3][11].

A large graph was difficult to be processed/analyzed in a single machine due to the low processing power and large storage access latency. This caused significant research efforts to make the large graph processed/analyzed with a large number of machines distributed over a network. We call this the *scale-out approach* [2][6].

*Corresponding author

CIKM'16, October 24-28, 2016, Indianapolis, IN, USA
© 2016 ACM. ISBN 978-1-4503-4073-1/16/10...$15.00
DOI: http://dx.doi.org/10.1145/2983323.2983865

These days, however, recent researches have started to take the *scale-up approach* in a single machine, thanks to the advance of memories having significantly increased bandwidth & capacity and the emergence of secondary storage having significantly increased bandwidth such as SSDs [4][9][11]. This advanced hardware technology enables graph engines based on a single machine to process/analyze large graphs. Some recent researches claim that an engine on a single machine might outperform an engine based on the distributed environment composed of tens (or hundreds) of machines [3][11].

The studies on a single machine based engines have mainly focused on optimizing IO performance by using two strategies: (1) to induce sequential IOs rather than random IOs [4][9] and (2) to reduce the number of IOs by selective accesses [3][11]. Their results reveal that these two strategies help increase the overall performance significantly.

We note, however, existing engines overlook the *data locality*, a property that the data entities accessed together are stored in a storage unit (e.g., cache blocks in main memory or pages in secondary storage) or adjacent units [7]. In this paper, we claim that data locality is an important key factor that has a potential to improve the performance of graph algorithms significantly.

If multiple data entities requested by a graph algorithm exist within a single or adjacency physical storage unit, their processing/analysis can be done with only a *single access or sequential access* to the storage. Otherwise, multiple (random) accesses to different storage units are required. In summary, the improved data locality *decreases the number of data accesses and/or increases the degree of sequential accesses*, which subsequently leads to considerable performance improvement of graph algorithms running on a single machine.

The degree of data locality is determined by access patterns of a given graph algorithm. Thus, we can improve the data locality of the same graph algorithm by determining the *data layout* in storage when storing data entities, in such a way that the data entities accessed together by the graph algorithm are stored within the same storage unit or in (physically) adjacent units.

This paper aims to demonstrate the importance of data locality in performing graph algorithms. For this demonstration, we employ a quite simple data layout, optimized for a specific graph algorithm. We realize three different versions of the graph algorithm on top of three representative graph engines (i.e., GraphChi [4], X-Stream [9], and FlashGraph [11]), execute the three versions of the algorithm on a single machine with different data layouts with/without considering data locality, and finally analyze their performance.

The results show that the execution time of the graph algorithm is reduced with the data layout that takes the data locality into consideration. Specifically, the execution time is reduced up to 60% when data locality is considered in determining layout.

2. MOTIVATION: DATA LOCALITY

Data locality is an important factor to affect the performance of graph algorithms considerably, but it has been overlooked in the literature. In this section, we present the notion of data locality and its significance that motivates our research.

Data locality is a property that data accessed together by a given algorithm are located on the same or adjacently located storage unit(s) (e.g., blocks in cache and main memory or pages in the secondary storage) [7]. Higher data locality indicates that the physical order of data entities located in storage (i.e., data placement) is well matched to that of data entities accessed by a given algorithm, which subsequently would make the performance better.

Good data locality improves performance in two aspects. The first one is *the high degree of sequential data accesses.* If some data entities are located in neighboring storage units, they may produce sequential accesses when accessed together. It has been known that sequential accesses are much faster than random accesses. In the SSD, the sequential IOs show performance much better than the random IOs [1]. In the memory, sequential access is faster than random access [1].

Figure 1 shows the change in data locality according to different data layouts. A data layout has nine storage units represented by rectangles. A circle represents a data entity in a storage unit. The numbers in circles indicate the order of access requests by the given algorithm. The storage units surrounded by dotted lines are those required to access in processing the given algorithm because they have the data entities requested. When data layout A (resp. C) is changed to data layout B (resp. D), all required units can be accessed sequentially rather than randomly, which leads to significant performance gain in performing the given graph algorithm.

The second one is *a small number of storage units accessed.* If the required data entities are located in a smaller number of storage units, the number of IO requests to secondary storage and the number of cache misses in the main memory would be both reduced, which subsequently provides significant performance improvement in processing the algorithm. In Figure 1, data layout C (resp. D) requires a less number of IO requests than data layout A (resp. B).

As shown in Figure 1, the degree of data locality in data layouts B and C are higher than that of data layout A, which will show the worst data locality, for the given graph algorithm. Ultimately, with data layout D, most data can be accessed in a sequential fashion with the minimized number of IO requests. As a result, data layout D may provide significantly reduced execution time for the given algorithm compared with other ones (i.e., data layouts A, B, and C).

The primary goal of this paper is to examine carefully how much improvement in performance can be achieved by changing just the data layout into the one *taking data locality into account,* more importantly, with the same data structures, same graph engines, and same graph algorithms.

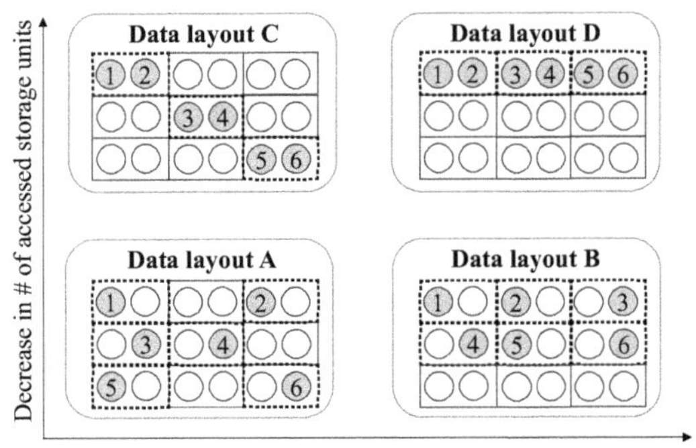

Figure 1: Changes in data locality with different data layouts.

3. DATA LAYOUT FOR GOOD DATA LOCALITY: A CASE OF BFS

Data locality could be different depending on the graph data to be processed and the data access pattern of the graph algorithm to be performed. Moreover, data locality of the same data processed by the same graph algorithm could also be different depending on input parameters (e.g., the starting node in the case of BFS). Therefore, it is very difficult to find out the data layout for given graph data that provides the optimal data locality for all the graph algorithms in the target application. However, it seems feasible to find out the layout that provides a good data locality for a *single* target algorithm by considering its data access pattern.

We employ the breadth-first search (BFS), a widely used algorithm for graph traversal, as our target [10]. Given a graph, we build the data layout that provides the best data locality for BFS by analyzing its data access pattern. Then, we investigate how much the change of a layout affects the performance in executing the given algorithm.

From the starting node given initially, BFS traverses a graph recursively in a level-by-level basis. It explores *all the direct neighbors* of its visiting node first, prior to visiting its other indirect neighbors (i.e., those nodes reachable but not directly). In a BFS level, it re-starts with each node visited in the previous level as a new starting node. BFS ends when there does not exist any node that is unvisited but reachable from the starting node given initially.

If we construct a data layout for BFS, a graph data, and a starting node given initially by mimicking its data access pattern by BFS (i.e., by following the order of the nodes visited during BFS), the resulting layout should give the highest data locality in that execution. Specifically, we determine the data layout as follows: (1) run BFS with the graph data and record the order nodes visited; (2) make all the nodes physically placed in the layout in such a way that their order is exactly same as that recorded in step (1); (3) finally make each edge physically placed within the same storage unit of the layout together with its source node.

Figure 2 shows the data layout, for BFS, the graph, and starting node a, built by the process above. We know that BFS visits nodes in the order of 'a-b-c-d-e-f'[1]. We observe that nodes in the node list of the layout are placed in this order and that edges are placed in the edge list following the order of their source node. The layout guarantees all the nodes and edges are accessed sequentially for BFS with the given graph and the starting node.

[1]The alphabetical order is employed for siblings.

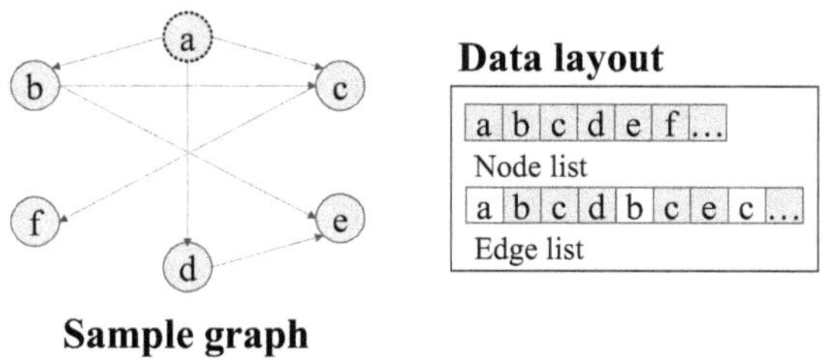

Figure 2: Data layout for BFS.

It is true that the optimal data layout aimed for a starting node may not be optimal any longer for other starting nodes. However, it is apparent that BFS performs better with the layout for different starting nodes than with other layouts not taking data locality into consideration. This is because, even if the starting node is changed, neighboring nodes and their adjacent edges are placed together in the same or adjacent storage unit(s).

Because a node could have multiple neighboring nodes, we need a tie-break strategy in building the BFS-based data layout. We simply employ the *high-degree strategy* that uses the node degree when a tie-break is necessary. We denote the layout built with the high-degree strategy as DL(BFS_degree). For comparison, we also use another BFS-based layout, denoted as DL(BFS_random), which uses random selection for tie-break. In Section 4, we compare the performances obtained with the two different layouts.

The BFS-based data layout could be beneficial to other graph algorithms that access a node and its neighbors together as in BFS. PageRank [8] and weakly connected component (WCC) [10] are typical examples. Thus, we verify the effectiveness of the BFS-based layout for these algorithms in comparison with the baseline in Section 4.

4. PERFORMANCE EVALUATION

In this section, we show that data locality has significant impact on the performance of graph algorithms, via extensive experiments with three different graph engines.

4.1 Experimental Settings

We conducted our experiments on a PC equipped with Intel i7 3.4GHz and a 1TB Samsung SSD 850 Pro. We assigned 8GB of main memory solely for graph engines to perform graph algorithms. In the experiments, we used three kinds of real-world datasets, which are widely used in this research community. Table 1 shows the characteristics of the datasets[2]. We used three graph algorithms for the evaluation: BFS [10], PageRank [8], and WCC [10].

Table 1: Real-world datasets used

Graph datasets	#nodes	#edges
Twitter	42M	1.5B
sk-2005	51M	1.9B
Friendster	66M	1.8B

Graph engines on a single machine are categorized by two criteria: programming models and memory models. In our experiments, we used three representative graph engines: GraphChi [4], X-Stream [9], and FlashGraph [11]. In the aspect of memory models, GraphChi and X-Stream employ an *external memory model* while FlashGraph does a *semi-external memory model*. In the aspect of programming models, GraphChi and FlashGraph adopt a *vertex-centric model* while X-Stream does an *edge-centric model*.

We utilized three different data layouts: (1) DL(Baseline): layout where nodes and edges are randomly rearranged from the original; (2) DL(BFS_degree): as mentioned in Section 3; (3) DL(BFS_random): as mentioned in Section 3. We carefully evaluated these layouts with different graph algorithms running on different graph engines.

The data layout to consider data locality requires extra time for rearranging nodes and edges in storage. For the datasets used in our evaluation, however, it took around 30 minutes on average, which is four times higher than the time to perform a single BFS (in the case with GraphChi).

Once the data layout is rearranged, however, it could be used efficiently for the same graph algorithm with different parameter values and for different graph algorithms having similar access patterns. Thus, the conversion time is acceptable. For instance, let us consider a situation to run a BFS starting from every node. In this case, the rearranging time can be considered negligible, considering the total number nodes in a graph.

Also, notice that most graph engines require preprocessing to convert the input graph into their own data structure before processing a graph algorithm. This requires at least one read and one write for every storage unit. Around 90% of the time required in creating a new data layout for high data locality is spent in handling read/write requests. If we incorporate the process of creating a layout into the preprocessing step in a graph engine, the extra time for employing a new layout will be greatly reduced.

4.2 Effect of data locality: Results & analyses

4.2.1 *Case of the BFS on GraphChi*

Table 2: Performance result of BFS on GraphChi

Data layouts	IO time	#Shard	Trans. time	Comp. time	Total time
BFS_degree	11.59	63	263.86	9.00	294.39
BFS_random	11.56	63	266.55	9.20	297.56
Baseline	20.47	131	539.04	16.62	595.59

Time unit: seconds

In this experiment, we show the effect of data locality by executing the same BFS with three different data layouts on GraphChi. We selected 20 nodes randomly and ran a BFS starting with every selected node identically in all the three layouts.

GraphChi uses a pair of a shard and an interval. A shard consists of an edge list, each of which has the same number of edges. An interval consists of a list of nodes corresponding to the edges in its paired shard. GraphChi loads each pair <interval, shard> one by one and its corresponding sub-pairs into main memory which are transformed to a data structure for execution, and then executes them [4].

Table 2 shows the average time to execute a BFS starting with 20 nodes on GraphChi. The total time is composed of four components: *IO time* denotes the total IO time; *#Shard* does the number of <interval, shard> pairs required in execution; *Trans. time* denotes the time for transforming a pair and some sub-pairs to the data structure; *Comp. time* denotes the time for performing BFSs on the data loaded into main memory.

[2]Twitter: an.kaist.ac.kr/traces/WWW2010
sk-2005: cise.ufl.edu/research/sparse/matrices/LAW
Friendster: snap.stanford.edu/data

The results show that the total time is reduced by about 50% with the BFS-based data layout compared with all time components with DL(Baseline). The difference in performance between the two BFS-based layouts is insignificant. After all, we understand the layout considering the access patterns of the BFS could improve data locality in doing a BFS, which subsequently decreases the execution time.

Let us examine the results in each component. We confirmed that *IO time* and *#Shard* decrease as data locality gets improved. *Trans. time*, which is proportional to *#Shard*, also gets reduced as *#Shard* decreases. We also observed that *Comp. time* decreases with the BFS-based layout. Regardless of layouts, the number of neighboring nodes visited by a BFS from the same starting node is identical. This indicates the amount of computations is not changed with different layouts. Thus, we conjecture that the improvement comes from the cache hit rate improved along with data locality.

4.2.2 *Effects of data locality with different graph algorithms running on different graph engines*

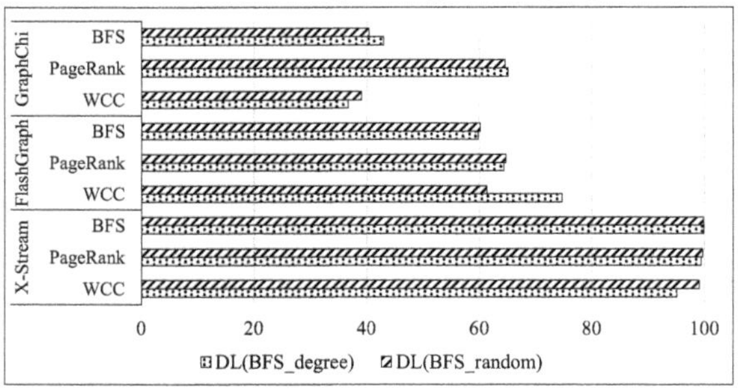

Figure 3: Ratio of execution times with BFS-based layouts to that with the baseline.

We ran the three graph algorithms (i.e., BFS, PageRank, and WCC) on three different engines (i.e., GraphChi, FlashGraph, and X-Stream) with three different layouts (i.e., DL(BFS_degree), DL(BFS_random), and DL(baseline)). Figure 3 shows the result. Each bar indicates the ratio of execution times with BFS-based layouts (i.e., DL(BFS_degree) and DL(BFS_random)) to that with the baseline (i.e., DL(baseline)). A bar represents the average of the ratios obtained with three datasets shown in Table 1.

We observe that the performance of graph algorithms is much better (up to 60% decrease) with BFS-based layouts than with the baseline on GraphChi and FlashGraph while those with the three layouts on X-Stream are not that different from one another. GraphChi and FlashGraph, based on a vertex-centric model, access and process only those nodes and edges required by a graph algorithm while X-Stream, based on an edge-centric model, access and process all the nodes and edges regardless of the requests from a graph algorithm. Thus, the graph algorithms running on X-Stream never benefit from the BFS-based layouts that consider data locality[3].

We notice that BFS-based layouts help improve the performance of PageRank and WCC as well as that of BFS. This is because their data access patterns are not so different from that of BFS (i.e., after accessing a node, they access its neighboring nodes again as in BFS). This indicates a layout designed for a graph algorithm could help other algorithms that have similar access patterns.

[3]Due to space limitations, we do not present in detail the performance of the original layout given in the source of datasets. However, we confirmed via extra experiments that BFS-based layouts again outperform the original ones up to 40% on GraphChi and 30% on FlashGraph.

5. CONCLUSIONS

In this paper, we addressed the issue of data locality, overlooked in previous researches on graph engines based on a single machine.

We summarize our contributions as follows: (1) to point out the significance of data locality on the performance of graph algorithms; (2) to identify the two aspects with which good data locality helps performance improvement (i.e., sequential data accesses and storage unit accesses); (3) to conduct extensive evaluation with all combinations of three graph algorithms, three graph engines, three data layouts, and three datasets. The results show that the layouts considering data locality significantly helps improve the performance of graph algorithms (up to 60% decrease over the baseline).

We plan to perform research on how to design the optimal layout in case multiple graph algorithms of different data access patterns coexist, which can be seen as the problem of *physical database design.*

6. ACKNOWLEDGMENTS

Dr. Chanik Park and Dr. Hyungsoo Jung gave us the insight towards the importance of the notion of data locality in developing high-performance graph engines.

This work was supported by (1) Semiconductor Industry Collaborative Project between Hanyang University and Samsung Electronics Co. Ltd., (2) the National Research Foundation of Korea (NRF) grant funded by the Korea government (No. NRF-2014R1A2A1A10054151), and (3) the MSIP (Ministry of Science, ICT and Future Planning), Korea, under the ITRC (Information Technology Research Center) support program (IITP-2015-H8501-15-1013) supervised by the IITP (Institute for Information and communication Technology Promotion).

7. REFERENCES

[1] J. Adam. The pathologies of big data. *Communications of the ACM*, 52(8):36–44, 2009.

[2] J. E. Gonzalez et al. Graphx: Graph processing in a distributed dataflow framework. In *USENIX OSDI*, pages 599–613, 2014.

[3] W.-S. Han et al. Turbograph: a fast parallel graph engine handling billion-scale graphs in a single pc. In *ACM SIGKDD*, pages 77–85, 2013.

[4] A. Kyrola, G. Blelloch, and C. Guestrin. Graphchi: Large-scale graph computation on just a pc. In *USENIX OSDI*, pages 31–46, 2012.

[5] Y. Low et al. Distributed graphlab: a framework for machine learning and data mining in the cloud. *Proceedings of the VLDB Endowment*, 5(8):716–727, 2012.

[6] G. Malewicz et al. Pregel: a system for large-scale graph processing. In *ACM SIGMOD*, pages 135–146, 2010.

[7] K. S. McKinley, S. Carr, and C.-W. Tseng. Improving data locality with loop transformations. *ACM Transactions on Programming Languages and Systems*, 18(4):424–453, 1996.

[8] L. Page et al. The pagerank citation ranking: bringing order to the web. Stanford InfoLab, 1999.

[9] A. Roy, I. Mihailovic, and W. Zwaenepoel. X-stream: Edge-centric graph processing using streaming partitions. In *ACM SOSP*, pages 472–488, 2013.

[10] R. Sedgewick and K. Wayne. Algorithms 4th edition, 2011.

[11] D. Zheng et al. Flashgraph: Processing billion-node graphs on an array of commodity ssds. In *USENIX FAST*, pages 45–58, 2015.

Active Zero-Shot Learning

Sihong Xie¶ Shaoxiong Wang§ Philip S. Yu†
†Department of Computer Science, University of Illinois at Chicago, Chicago, IL, USA
§Department of Computer Science, Tsinghua University, Beijing, China
¶Department of Computer Science and Engineering, Lehigh University, Bethlehem, PA, USA

ABSTRACT

In multi-label classification in the big data age, the number of classes can be in thousands, and obtaining sufficient training data for each class is infeasible. Zero-shot learning aims at predicting a large number of unseen classes using only labeled data from a small set of classes and external knowledge about class relations. However, previous zero-shot learning models passively accept labeled data collected beforehand, relinquishing the opportunity to select the proper set of classes to inquire labeled data and optimize the performance of unseen class prediction. To resolve this issue, we propose an active class selection strategy to intelligently query labeled data for a parsimonious set of informative classes. We demonstrate two desirable probabilistic properties of the proposed method that can facilitate unseen classes prediction. Experiments on 4 text datasets demonstrate that the active zero-shot learning algorithm is superior to a wide spectrum of baselines. We indicate promising future directions at the end of this paper.

INTRODUCTION

In some real world applications such as image, text and video classification, it is not uncommon to have tens of thousands of classes to predict. It becomes extremely difficult for traditional classification methods to learn the mapping from data and each and every class, as collecting training data for all classes is simply infeasible. For example, when one wants to identify many potentially useful tags for online contents like blogs, videos and images, it is markedly laborious to exhaust *all* possible tags and assign each piece of content to its relevant classes. Therefore, many classes will not have labeled data and traditional classification models will fail. Zero-shot learning utilizes external knowledge bases describing class relations to predict classes that do not have any training data (the "unseen classes") [5, 7, 9]. Usually, zero-shot learning algorithms first map instances to intermediate attributes, which can be seen classes (those with labeled data), human-specified or data-dependent attributes. Then the predicted attributes are mapped to a large number of unseen classes through the knowledge bases. In this way, prediction of unseen classes become possible and no training data is necessary for those classes.

Zero-shot learning has been studied for more than a decade [1] from various aspects. Two fundamental zero-shot paradigms, direct attribute prediction (DAP) and indirect attribute prediction (IAP) are given in [5]. More sophisticated zero-shot models are proposed, such as max-margin semi-supervised learning to exploit the unlabeled data [6], and multi-view zero-shot learning utilizing multiple data sources [3]. Multiple knowledge bases such as WordNet [7, 12], Wikipedia [2, 9], web search logs [8] and human-annotated images [5] are compared. The authors in [2, 9, 13] propose to learn the intermediate attributes using deep learning.

Although the zero-shot learning literature has addressed some of the crucial issues, most existing works assume that a zero-shot model can only passively learn from labeled data collected for a pre-determined and fixed subset of classes [6, 9]. However, given the ever-increasing amount of online contents, potentially hundreds of thousands of classes can be identified. It is infeasible to tag large amoutn of relevant contents for each class, while which classes have higher priority to be tagged is a question. Instead, one has to actively decide which classes are the most useful to collect labeled data to train a zero-shot model to predict the remaining classes. The key is that complex dependencies exist among classes such that some classes provide more global information about the other classes, and unseen class predictions can benefit from the "properly" selected seen classes. The work [10] proposed a representative class selection strategy. Our experiments shows that representativeness is not a proper metric for seen class selection.

To solve the above challenges, we propose to actively select a parsimonious set of informative classes to collect labeled data, and keep the large number of remaining classes unseen to save labeling efforts. Traditional active learning strategies query labels of instances for *all* instead of *some* classes [11], and the effectiveness of the learning methods is not related to the seen-unseen class connections, which we study here. We formulate zero-shot learning as a two-phase procedure, corresponding to which the informativeness of a seen class can be characterized by its discriminative power (accuracy) and the information it provides for the unseen classes (connectivity) via the external knowledge base. The proposed strategy exploits the entropy of inter-class similarities to measure the above two aspects of a class. We discover that the inter-class similarity follows a beta distribution, based on which we further reveal the relationship between the entropy and the probability that an unseen class is sufficiently connected to the seen ones. Extensive experiments on 4 text classification datasets with up to thousands of classes show that by obtaining labeled data for a small number of classes, we are able to significantly improve the unseen class prediction, compared with other active class selection strategies.

CIKM'16, October 24-28, 2016, Indianapolis, IN, USA

DOI: http://dx.doi.org/10.1145/2983323.2983866

THE PROPOSED APPROACH

Let the set of d seen classes be denoted by $\mathcal{S}$ and the set of k unseen ones be denoted by $\mathcal{U}$. Without loss of generality, assume that the seen classes are indexed by $\{1,\ldots,d\}$, and the remaining unseen classes are indexed by $\{d+1,\ldots,d+k\}$. Training data is given by $\mathcal{D}_0 = \{(\mathbf{x}_1,\mathbf{y}_1),\ldots,(\mathbf{x}_n,\mathbf{y}_n)\}$, where $\mathbf{x}_i \in \mathcal{X} = \mathbb{R}^p$ is the feature vector of the i-th instance and $\mathbf{y}_i \in \mathcal{Y} = \{0,1\}^d$ is the corresponding seen class vector. Zero-shot learning aims at predicting the ground truth of the k unseen classes $\mathbf{z} \in \mathcal{Z} = \{0,1\}^k$ for any test data $\mathbf{x} \in \mathcal{X}$. The above procedure can be captured by two mappings: $f : \mathcal{X} \to \mathcal{Y}$ and $g : \mathcal{Y} \to \mathcal{Z}$ such that the composed predictive model $g \circ f : \mathcal{X} \to \mathcal{Z}$ has good performance.

We focus on the intelligent selection of d classes to form the attribute space $\mathcal{Y}$, such that d is small to minimize labeling efforts, and the prediction in the unseen class space $\mathcal{Z}$ is optimized. Since we focus on the effects brought by class split, we fix the other components: the mapping $f{:}\mathcal{X} \mapsto \mathcal{Y}$ consists of multiple logistic regression models, each of which predicts one and only one seen class; a class similarity matrix K is derived from a related corpus as the knowledge base. Given two index sets $\mathcal{I}$ and $\mathcal{J}$, let $K^{\mathcal{I}\mathcal{J}}$ be the sub-matrix of K that consists of the rows indexed by $\mathcal{I}$ and columns indexed by $\mathcal{J}$. Then $K^{\mathcal{U}\mathcal{U}}$ is the similarity matrix for the unseen classes, and $K^{\mathcal{U}\mathcal{S}}_{ij}$ being the similarity between the i-th unseen class and the j-th seen class. One can view K as the adjacent matrix of the graph $\mathcal{G} = (\mathcal{V},\mathcal{E})$, where $\mathcal{V}$ is the set of all classes and the edge weights are the class similarities. Given the above notations, with $\hat{\mathbf{y}} \in \mathbb{R}^d$ being the predicted seen classes, the mapping g is defined by $g : \hat{\mathbf{y}} \mapsto K^{\mathcal{U}\mathcal{S}}\hat{\mathbf{y}}$.

Methodology

Intuitively, we want to select an unseen class that can convery more information about the remaining unseen ones, and make it a seen class. The connectivity between the i-th unseen class and the remaining ones can be a measurement of the amount of information conveyed. Such connectivity can be calculated by various centrality metrics of the i-th node on the sub-graph of $\mathcal{G}$ consisting of all the curent unseen classes. The degree centrality of the i-th unseen class is one such measures and can be calculated as $\sum_{j=1}^{k} K^{\mathcal{U}\mathcal{U}}_{ij}$, where k is the current number of unseen classes. We then select the unseen class with the largest degree centrality as the next seen class (this selection strategy is called "*max-deg-uu*"). One possible drawback is that, the i-th class can be connected to only a small number of unseen classes with high weights $K^{\mathcal{U}\mathcal{U}}_{ij}$, but not connected to others. Selecting this class will not add much information about the unseen classes that are not well connected to this class.

We take a probabilistic perspective and use entropy to characterize the distribution of the significant connections between a class and the others. First, the similarities between each unseen class and the other unseen ones are normalized to a probability distribution:

$$P^{\mathcal{U}\mathcal{U}} = \text{diag}(\mathbb{1}^\top K^{\mathcal{U}\mathcal{U}})^{-1} K^{\mathcal{U}\mathcal{U}}, \tag{1}$$

where $\text{diag}(\mathbf{v})$ denotes the diagonal matrix with diagonal elements being the entries of $\mathbf{v} \in \mathbb{R}^u$, and $\mathbb{1}$ is the all-one vector. Then we calculate the entropy of the connections between the i-th unseen class and others, $i = 1,\ldots,k$:

$$H(i) = -\sum_{j=1}^{u} P^{\mathcal{U}\mathcal{U}}_{ij} \log P^{\mathcal{U}\mathcal{U}}_{ij}. \tag{2}$$

We select the class that have the highest entropy, acquire labeled data for that class, and move it from $\mathcal{U}$ to $\mathcal{S}$. The labeled instances for the selected classes are used to train a prediction model, which is added to the mapping f. This selection procedure is repeated until the labeling budget runs out. Lastly, we obtain the zero-shot model consisting of f and g. The algorithm is shown in Algorithm 1. Intuitively, the larger the $H(i)$, the more classes in the pool of unseen classes are connected to the i-th unseen class, which shall have the highest utility to be added to the pool of seen classes. An extreme case is that there is only one unseen class connected to the i-th unseen class (not counting self connection), then the i-th unseen class is not providing information to the remaining unseen classes and shall not be selected. Formally, we want to minimize $\mathsf{Pr}(j \notin C_j(s), \forall s \in \mathcal{S}))$, the probability that j-th unseen class that is not well connected to any seen class. Let $C_j(s)$ be the event that the j-th unseen class is well connected to the s-th seen class.

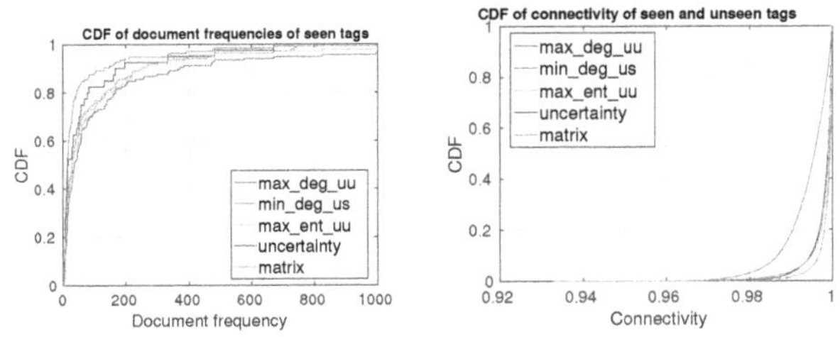

(a) CDF of document frequency of selected classes

(b) CDF of the seen-unseen classes connectivities

Figure 1: Analysis of seen-unseen tag split resulting from the proposed selection method

$$\mathsf{Pr}(j \notin C_j(s), \forall s \in \mathcal{S}) = \prod_{s\in\mathcal{S}} \mathsf{Pr}(j \notin C_j(s)), \tag{3}$$

by assuming that the entries in $P^{\mathcal{S}\mathcal{U}}_{sj}, s \in \mathcal{S}$ are independently distributed conditioned on j. With a higher $H(s)$, $P^{\mathcal{S}\mathcal{U}}_{sj}, j = 1,\ldots,u$ are more evenly distributed (over the unseen classes) and more of the probabilities $\mathsf{Pr}(j \notin C_j(s)), s \in \mathcal{S}$ will be small, leading to a smaller $\mathsf{Pr}(j \notin C_j(s), \forall s \in \mathcal{S}))$.

Algorithm 1 Active Zero-shot Learning

Input: Unlabeled training data $\{\mathbf{x}_1,\ldots,\mathbf{x}_n\}$, class similarity matrix K, budget b.
Output: Zero-shot prediction model $g \circ f$.
Randomly select seeding classes to form $\mathcal{S}$, and the remaining classes go to $\mathcal{U} = \{1,\ldots,d+k\} \setminus \mathcal{S}$.
while $b > 0$ **do**
  Normalize the sub-matrix $K^{\mathcal{U}\mathcal{S}}$ by Eq. (1).
  Calculate the entropies using Eq. (2).
  Select the class (denoted by t) that have the largest entropies.
  Query the labels of the training instances for the class t.
  $\mathcal{S} = \mathcal{S} \cup \{t\}, \mathcal{U} = \mathcal{U} \setminus \{t\}, b = b - 1$.
end while

EXPERIMENTS

StackExchange is a QA (questions and answers) system where members can ask and answer questions. The predictions of zero-shot learning can be used to prompt users to associate their questions with tags that have not used by any user (unseen tags), and thus facilitate question organization and retrieval. We adopt 3 sites from StackExchange: askubuntu, dba and unix (see Table 1). Bag-of-words representation with TF-IDF transformation is used as the feature vectors of the questions. Each tag is treated as a class, and a question can have multiple tags, so the tasks can be formulated as multi-label classification problems. Only those tags that appear in at least 10 questions are kept. Tags provided by the users for

Table 1: Datasets

	askubuntu	dba	unix
# Training	55684	12070	23069
# Test	55883	12211	23025
# Tags	1003	345	775

the questions are used as ground truth. Each selection strategy is tested on 20 randomly picked seeding seen classes, and we report the averaged performances over 20 runs. Questions are randomly split into disjoint training and test sets. The training data is used to train classification models (Liblinear with default settings), each of which maps from features to a seen tag. Then we map the predicted seen classes on the test data to unseen classes via a knowledge base, which is an embedding of the tags in a low dimensional space via restricted Boltzmann machine trained on the text corpus of questions. Tag similarity is calculated through a kernel function: $K(\mathbf{t}_1, \mathbf{t}_2) = \exp(\|\mathbf{t}_1 - \mathbf{t}_2\|^2/\sigma^2)$ where $\mathbf{t}_1$ and $\mathbf{t}_2$ are the low dimensional representations of two tags, and $\sigma = 10$ throughout the experiments.

We adopt 3 common metrics (precision@5, NDCG@5 and micro-AUC) to evaluate the performance of tag retrieval. Since there is no previous study on active zero-shot learning, we compare *max-ent-uu* with the following baselines that capture different aspects of seen-unseen class splits.

- *max-deg-uu*: as mentioned in the methodology section, this method labels data for the classes that have the highest degree centrality.
- *min-deg-us*: we take the row sums of the matrix $K^{\mathcal{US}}$, which captures the total similarity between unseen tags and seen tags. The unseen class with smallest row sum is picked. The intuition is that unseen tags that are farthest away from the current seen classes can provide complementary information to the current seen ones.
- *uncertainty*: uncertainty-based sampling queries the labels of the top unseen classes that has the highest entropy in their predictions on the training data, according to the current class split. This baseline runs in an incremental manner as *max-ent-uu* and *min-deg-us*.
- *matrix*: in [4] the author proposed a matrix partition algorithm to split a set of instances into two such that the mutual information between the distributions of the two sets is maximized. This method is considered to be a representativeness-based active learning method. We adapt their model and treat classes as instances. This algorithm runs in batch-mode and we only report its performance when 100 additional classes are selected.

We set the number of unseen classes selected in each iteration to 2 ($c = 2$) in Algorithm 1 and the other iterative baselines. We test other values for this parameter ($c = 5$ and $c = 10$), and find out that $c = 2$ gives the best results.

Results In Figure 2, we show how the zero-shot prediction performances of 4 iterative algorithms evolve as more seen classes are added, plus the batch-mode method *matrix*. Each row in Figure 2 consists of 3 sub-figures showing the performance in precision@5, ndcg@5 and micro AUC, respectively. In each sub-figure, the performance of *max-ent-uu* (shown in green solid lines), is compared with those of the 4 baselines. From the figures, we can see that across all datasets and all metrics, except that in Figures 2(c), *max-ent-uu* consistently outperforms all the baselines. In some cases, *max-ent-uu* ends up with performance two times better than the runner-up (Figures 2(g) and 2(b)). The baselines *min-deg-us, uncertainty* and *matrix* consistently have performance between those of *max-ent-uu* and *max-deg-uu* in 8 out of 9 cases.

Surprisingly, the seemingly naive method *min-deg-us* can gradually pick up its performance and ends up with similar or better performance with the more sophisticated methods *matrix* in the dba and unix datasets, although its performance at the beginning is not very impressive. Our explanation is that by selecting the classes that are least similar to the already picked ones, more information can be revealed. However, this baseline fails to consider unseen class coverage information, and the selected classes may not be well-connected to the large clusters of unseen classes (as we will see next), leading to less effective seen-to-unseen class mapping. Furthermore, the performance of *matrix* is quite close to *uncertainty* in all cases. Our conjecture is that by picking the current unseen classes that do not have confident predictions, *uncertainty* is able to explore the class space that has not been explored before, and ends up with a seen class space that represent the whole class space quite well, which is what *matrix* aims for.

Analyzing the seen-unseen classes relations Here we empirically shows why the proposed method works via the analysis of the resulting seen-unseen connection matrix $K^{\mathcal{US}}$. In Figure 1(a), we plot the CDFs of the frequencies of the selected classes that appear in the training instances (namely document frequencies) on one dataset (best viewed in color). We can see that among the 5 strategies, the *max-deg-uu* tends to select classes that have higher document frequencies than those selected by *max-ent-uu*, as the CDF of *max-deg-uu* is more shifted to the right. It has been shown in text classification that, the more frequent a word appears in the corpus, the less informative it is, as evidenced by the commonly used tf-idf transformation. A frequent seen class is likely to be predicted more often by predictive models that takes into account of the class prior distribution. Such seen class become a less discriminative feature when used as features for the mapping g. This partly explains why the baseline *max-deg-uu* has the worst performance in 10 out of 12 cases among all methods.

From Figure 1(a), we see that the baseline *min-deg-us* also tends to select classes that are less frequent than those selected by *max-ent-uu*, then why hasn't *min-deg-us* outperformed *max-ent-uu*? In Figure 1(b), we plot the CDF of the seen-unseen class connectivities on the same dataset, where connectivities are the row sums of $K^{\mathcal{SU}}$. We see that *max-ent-uu* produces connectivities as strong as those produced by *max-deg-uu*. The seen classes selected by *min-deg-us* tend to have low connectivities with unseen classes, and the baselines *uncertainty* and *matrix* produces medium connectivities. If the connectivities are strong, then the seen classes can provide significant information about the unseen classes. We have similar observations on the other datasets, and we conclude that *max-ent-uu* is more likely to find seen classes that simultaneously possess the following properties: 1) discriminative about the test data (low document frequency) and 2) informative about the unseen classes (high coverage). The unique combination of these two properties helps *max-ent-uu* outperform the baselines.

CONCLUSIONS AND FUTURE WORK

We study active learning in the zero-shot prediction setting for the purpose of finding a small number of informative seen classes to facilitate unseen class predictions. We propose an entropy-based selection method, which is demonstrated to be able to capture the desirable distribution of seen-unseen similarity. Experiments show that the proposed method outperform both representativeness and uncertainty based active learning methods. In the future, we plan to

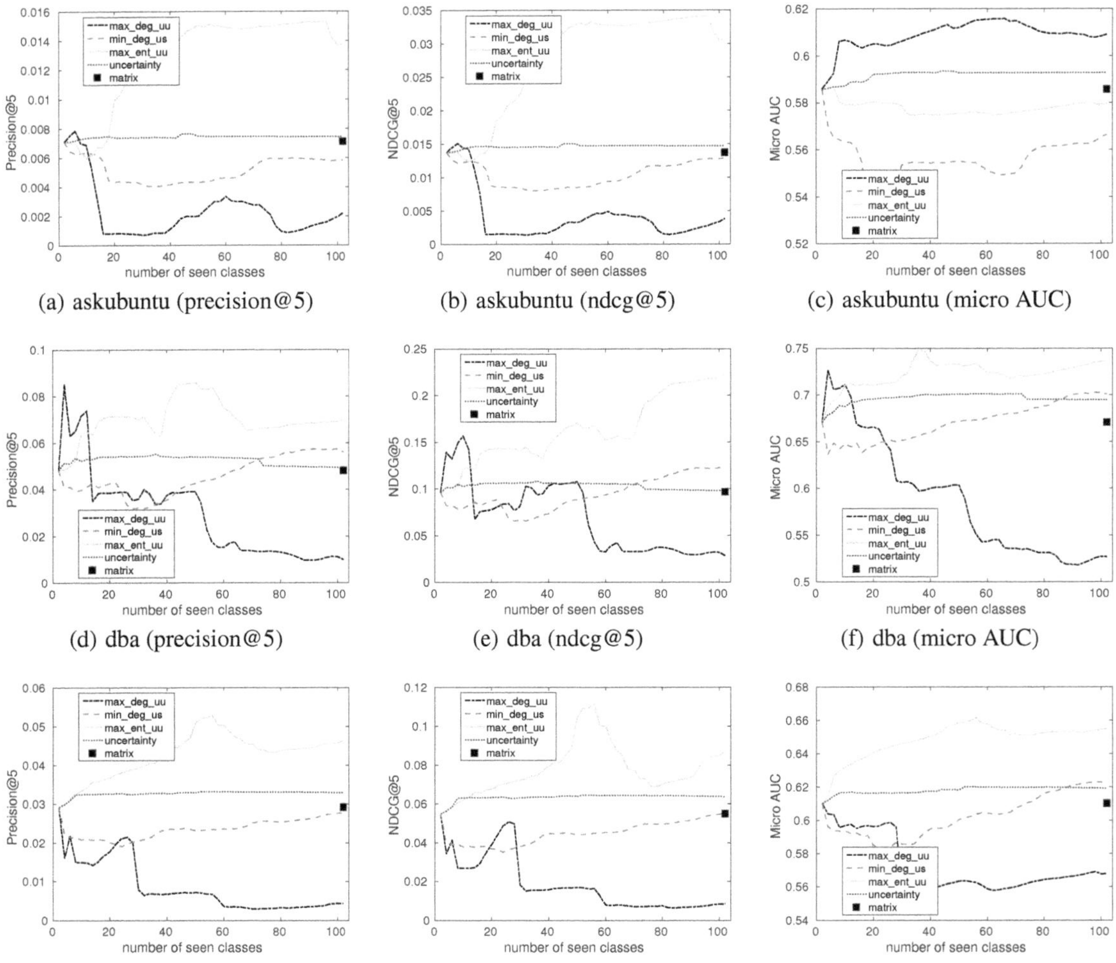

(a) askubuntu (precision@5) (b) askubuntu (ndcg@5) (c) askubuntu (micro AUC)

(d) dba (precision@5) (e) dba (ndcg@5) (f) dba (micro AUC)

(g) unix (precision@5) (h) unix (ndcg@5) (i) unix (micro AUC)

Figure 2: Comparisons of the proposed method and the baselines

explore more selection strategies based on other zero-shot learning properties. Further reducing the labeling efforts by instance selecting is also a promising direction.

Acknowledgment

This work is supported in part by NSF Award III-1526499, and NVIDIA Corporation with the donation of the Titan X GPU.

REFERENCES

[1] T. G. Dietterich and G. Bakiri. Solving multiclass learning problems via error-correcting output codes. *J. Artif. Int. Res.*, 1995.

[2] A. Frome, G. S. Corrado, J. Shlens, S. Bengio, J. Dean, M. Ranzato, and T. Mikolov. DeViSE: A Deep Visual-Semantic Embedding Model. In *NIPS*. 2013.

[3] Y. Fu, T. Hospedales, T. Xiang, Z. Fu, and S. Gong. Transductive multi-view embedding for zero-shot recognition and annotation. In *ECCV*. 2014.

[4] Y. Guo. Active instance sampling via matrix partition. In *NIPS*. 2010.

[5] C. Lampert, H. Nickisch, and S. Harmeling. Learning to detect unseen object classes by between-class attribute transfer. In *CVPR*, 2009.

[6] X. Li and Y. Guo. Max-margin zero-shot learning for multi-class classification. In *AISTAT*, 2015.

[7] X. Li, S. Liao, W. Lan, X. Du, and G. Yang. Zero-shot Image Tagging by Hierarchical Semantic Embedding. In *SIGIR*, 2015.

[8] T. Mensink, E. Gavves, and C. G. M. Snoek. COSTA: Co-Occurrence Statistics for Zero-Shot Classification. In *CVPR*, 2014.

[9] M. Norouzi, T. Mikolov, S. Bengio, Y. Singer, J. Shlens, A. Frome, G. Corrado, and J. Dean. Zero-Shot Learning by Convex Combination of Semantic Embeddings. *CoRR*, 2013.

[10] A. Pentina and C. H. Lampert. Active task selection for multi-task learning. 2016.

[11] G.-J. Qi, X.-S. Hua, Y. Rui, J. Tang, and H.-J. Zhang. Two-dimensional active learning for image classification. In *CVPR*, 2008.

[12] M. Rohrbach, M. Stark, and B. Schiele. Evaluating knowledge transfer and zero-shot learning in a large-scale setting. In *CVPR*, 2011.

[13] R. Socher, M. Ganjoo, C. D. Manning, and A. Ng. Zero-shot learning through cross-modal transfer. In *NIPS*. 2013.

Learning to Account for Good Abandonment in Search Success Metrics

Madian Khabsa[1], Aidan Crook[1], Ahmed Hassan Awadallah[1], Imed Zitouni[1], Tasos Anastasakos[1], Kyle Williams[2]
[1]Microsoft
[2]The Pennsylvania State University
{madian.khabsa, aidan.crook, hassanam, izitouni, tasoanas}@microsoft.com
kwilliams@psu.edu

ABSTRACT

Abandonment in web search has been widely used as a proxy to measure user satisfaction. Initially it was considered a signal of dissatisfaction, however with search engines moving towards providing answer-like results, a new category of abandonment was introduced and referred to as *Good Abandonment.* Predicting good abandonment is a hard problem and it was the subject of several previous studies. All those studies have focused, though, on predicting good abandonment in offline settings using manually labeled data. Thus, it remained a challenge how to have an online metric that accounts for good abandonment. In this work we describe how a search success metric can be augmented to account for good abandonment sessions using a machine learned metric that depends on user's viewport information. We use real user traffic from millions of users to evaluate the proposed metric in an A/B experiment. We show that taking good abandonment into consideration has a significant effect on the overall performance of the online metric.

1. INTRODUCTION

In traditional web search, a search engine responds to user queries by returning a list of relevant links from which the user is assumed to click on the most relevant one . In the case when the user leaves the search engine result page (SERP) without clicking on any result, it is typically referred to as query *abandonment.* Abandonment has long been assumed to indicate that the user has failed to find what he is looking for, therefore it became an indication of dissatisfaction [5, 3]. However, search engines have evolved beyond just returning 10 blue links to presenting direct answers and rich results that can satisfy the users information needs without clicks. Examples of these scenarios include: weather information, business hours and phone numbers, package tracking, and many others. In these scenarios, it is rather desired for the query to be abandoned, and such type of abandonment is referred to as *Good abandonment.*

CIKM'16 , October 24-November 28, 2016, Indianapolis, IN, USA

DOI: http://dx.doi.org/10.1145/2983323.2983867

With the growing share of mobile search among all web search, users on mobile devices are more likely to issue queries that can result in good abandonment [12]. In fact, it was estimated that 27% of of searches were performed with predetermined goal of having the search satisfied by the content on the SERP itself without the intention to click on any results [14].

Good abandonment presents a challenge for search engine metrics that rely heavily on user clicks to detect satisfaction. That is mainly because the users are less likely to leave traces that may be interpreted as explicit signals of satisfaction. On the other hand, when a user clicks in a scenario that is supposed to be answered by a direct answer, this click may be used as a signal of dissatisfaction, or at least an incomplete satisfaction of the user's need. Nevertheless, satisfaction is rather hard to capture in this scenario.

The problem is further exacerbated on mobile devices where 54.8% of the queries could potentially lead to good abandonment [12]. More recently, the surge in mobile search usage was culminated as the volume of queries originating from mobile devices exceeded those originating from desktops [1]. Thus, the sheer volume of abandoned queries is larger than ever. This presents a challenge for commercial search engines to identify queries with abandonment intent, and later populate a SERP with the desired information need, for failing to present the required information will risk degrading the user experience that may translate into dissatisfaction.

Previous work on good abandonment has mainly focused on either identifying queries with potential good abandonment [12] or detecting good abandonment on offline data that was manually labeled by judges [15, 12]. However, in real scenarios of web search engines, online evaluation on real traffic is imperative to identify improvements of the system. In this realm, we describe the challenges associated with devising a good abandonment aware metric, and show how a machine learned metric can be built using viewport information.

Our main contribution in this work is the introduction of a method to modify a standard search engine success metric to account for good abandonment. The resulting augmented metric is shown to be more sensitive than current state-of-the-art click based counterparts. The metric is validated using online data of millions of users through A/B experiments. Furthermore, our proposed metric relies on attention modeling to identify sources of success, which was shown to be a good indicator of satisfaction [7, 11].

The remainder of this paper is organized as follows. Section 2 describes related work. In Section 3 we describe the good abandonment model. While online evaluation is presented in Section 4. We then conclude the paper in Section 5.

2. RELATED WORK

Good abandonment was formally introduced by Li et al. in [12] where they studied queries for which the information need is potentially satisfied by the content of the SERP itself. They analyzed abandonment across devices, and across different market segments. In the study they found that good abandonment is far more prevalent on mobile devices. In a different study, it was estimated that at least one quarter of web search queries were issued with predetermined intention of finding the information need on the SERP page itself, instead of following any link [14]. There has also been an effort to understand the underlying reason behind abandonment [6], with factoid queries being one class of queries that highly correlate with good abandonment [3].

Chuklin and Serdukov devised a set of features to build an SVM based classifier to detect bad abandonment using topical and linguistic features in conjunction with historical data[4]. The approach was evaluated on a manually labeled offline data. Koumpouri and Simaki conducted a user study to identify classes of queries that lead to good abandonment, and later constructed a decision tree using implicit measures to predict good abandonment[10]. Arkhipova and Grauer's work is the closest to our work where they devised a metric based on Dynamic Bayesian Network with its parameters being estimated on data from a user study. The metric was later tested on a small sample of mobile query sessions after introducing degradation to multiple parts of the system to show that the new metric is more sensitive to degradation [2]. However, they make the limiting assumption that users scan the results sequentially, whereas we make no assumptions about the browsing model. In addition, their dataset consists of multiple tasks that do not necessarily lead to good abandonment, with some of the parameters in their model being manually chosen. In our approach, all the parameters are learned from the data.

3. DETECTING GOOD ABANDONMENT

We propose to extend the search engine success metric to handle good abandonment as follows. Assume the function F to be the current success metric of a search engine, where F does not reward good abandonment. We introduce a function G that will be learned in Section 3.2, which evaluates *an abandoned query impression*, q_i, in order to distinguish good abandonment from bad abandonment. G only returns success when the impression q_i resulted in good abandonment. Using F and G we construct a new success metric S, such that for a given query impression q_j:

$$S(q_j) = \begin{cases} G(q_j) & \text{if } q_j \text{ is abandoned and not reformulated} \\ F(q_j) & \text{otherwise} \end{cases}$$

The query q_j is considered reformulated iff its edit distance with query q_{j+1} is below a given threshold.

Metrics are devised to quantify the performance of a given aspect of the search engine. System designers benchmark improvements by how much gain they attain on a given metric. Furthermore, success metrics become the function for which ranking algorithms are trained to maximize. Hence, there are many constraints imposed on devising new metrics. One such constraint is that metrics are only allowed to utilize *exogenous* signals, those that the system has no direct control over. On the other hand, *endogenous* signals are not allowed, since the system has direct control over them. For example, designing a feature based on whether a certain answer or vertical was shown on the SERP is an *endogenous* signal because the system has control on which verticals to show. A machine learned ranker will eventually learn that the presence of a certain vertical leads to gains in the metric, thus it would show that vertical whether it is relevant to the query or not. In addition to the constraint on the signals, metrics need to be interpretable, and should not be black boxes that merely output numbers. This stems from the need to understand the causes of success and failure in order to debug the system.

Given the aforementioned constraints, the good abandonment part of the metric G is learned through machine learning using the dataset describe in Section 3.1. Whereas we use a standard click based model [8] for the metric F, although it can be replaced with another metric without loss of generality.

3.1 Dataset

The source of the offline data in this study comes from randomly sampled abandoned queries in the mobile logs of a major search engine. Each query, along with the presented results were crowd sourced to 3 judges who were asked to provide satisfaction level on a 5 points scale. The judges were also shown the previous and next query in the session to provide them with the context. Majority voting was used to determine the final label of each query, and later the labels were binarized by considering ratings of 4 and 5 as satisfaction (SAT), similar to the trend in the literature. Overall, we collected a total of 3,895 labeled queries, of which we retained 1,565 queries that were labeled as SAT and 1,924 queries that were labeled DSAT.

3.2 Approach

To compensate for the lack of clicks, user attention can be used as an implicit signal to detect satisfaction. Previous work has shown that user attention, as measured by gaze tracking, is a good predictor of good abandonment [13]. The problem with gaze tracking, however, is that it is not feasible in an A/B setting since it requires special instrumentation that is not available to users at large scale.

Viewport information (information about the visible portion of the screen) was shown to be useful for understanding user intent on mobile devices [7], and it also correlates with gaze time [11]. Furthermore, it can scale with the large number of users whereas more accurate instrumentation such as eye tracking is not scalable.

Our approach relies on viewport information to record implicit interactions of the user with the SERP, such as scrolls, the part of the screen that is visible to the user, how long was each element of the SERP visible to the user, etc. The data from the viewport is processed and features are extracted to capture the main events. We use the same set of features that was described in [15], which was previously introduced in [11].

Given the constraints, we treat the problem as binary classification where the the goal is to classify *abandoned queries*

Table 1: The list of features used building the good abandonment metric G

Id	Feature Description
1	The total distance swiped in pixels
2	Attributed reading time (RT) of the first visible answer
3-5	Max, Min, StdDev attributed RT for answers
6-7	Max, StdDev attributed RT per pixel for answers
8	StdDev attributed RT for organic results
9-10	Max, StdDev shown fraction of organic results

into good and bad classes. First, we perform feature selection by choosing the top K most informative features ranked by information gain from the list of features proposed in [15]. Table 1 lists the choosen featues. Later, these features are used to build a shallow decision tree classifier. Decision tree is chosen because it is easily interpretable, yet effective. The obtained model achieves 66% F1 score on the offline judged data using 10 fold cross validation. Our model achieves a relatively competitive accuracy when considering that a boosted tree model trained using hundreds of features, and trees achieves 75% F1 score on the same dataset [15]. Recall that the goal is not to build the most accurate classifier on the labeled data, although it is desired, rather we seek to devise a satisfaction metric within the given *constraints*, and validate it on online data.

4. EXPERIMENTAL EVALUATION

Our evaluation relies on controlled experimentation, specifically A/B testing [9]. In designing the experiment it is important to keep in mind that certain *answers*, or *verticals* are more likely to appear on good abandoned queries [10]. The more likely the answer to be triggered in good abandonment scenario, the more sensitive the metric should be when degradation in that answer are introduced.

On the other hand, since clicks combined with dwell time remain a desired interaction from the system stand point, the metric should be careful not to over reward abandonment, especially in scenarios where the user is expected to click on results. A desired metric should be able to show sensitivity for good abandonment cases, while at the same time not change the signal when click through is expected.

Based on the discussions above we use an A/B experiment in which the user experience is degraded in the treatment pool by randomly modifying the position of the answer on the SERP. For example, assuming the search engine determined that the weather answer should be shown for a given query with the optimal position being at the top, then the treatment effect would move the answer to a random position on the SERP. It's possible that the final position of the answer remains the same as the one determined by the ranking algorithm. Clearly this is a degradation experiment since it presents a rather random ordering of answers instead of the optimal one.

The new metric is evaluated based on its performance when a given answer was present on the SERP. There are two set of answers that are chosen. The first list of answers is carefully chosen to represent impressions with high likelihood of good abandonment. Whereas the second list is a list of answers for which high click through was previously observed in the search engine logs. Ideally, the metric is expected to show improvements on the first list, while not introducing new significant changes on the second list of answers (some times this is referred to as A/A experiment where the metric is expected not to change). The following answers are chosen to capture potential good abandonment scenarios:

- **Weather answer**: this answer is shown when the query is believed to be weather related
- **Dictionary answer**: an answer that returns the definition of the query word
- **Finance answer**: shows finance related information such as stock and index prices

On the other hand, the following answers were chosen to represent the high click through scenarios:

- **Tracking answer**: an answer that shows tracking information when the query is a package tracking number. Users tend to track on the link in the answer to go to the courier's website.
- **Navigational Queries**: an answer that identifies navigational queries and returns the expected Url.
- **Showtimes**: this answer returns information about movies and theaters showing times. Users typically click on links to multiple movies and theaters when interacting with this answer

For comparison we employ a baseline metric that is common in the literature wherein satisfactions are observed whenever a user clicks on a result and spends at least t seconds on it [8]. Such approaches has already been shown to correlate with satisfaction, but it fails to capture cases with good abandonment. The baseline is appropriate in this experiment as it can show the improvements introduced by a good abandonment sensitive metric, while at the same time serve as guard against aggressive abandonment rewarding by ensuring that both metrics do not deviate when clicks are expected.

In Table 2, the results of running both the baseline and the new good abandonment sensitive metric on one week of traffic to the mobile segment of a commercial search engine are presented. As mentioned earlier, the experiment introduced a degradation to the user experience, therefore negative delta is expected. The top part of the table shows the answers for which the new metric is expected to show improvement (that is, the new metric should be able to find a negative delta). Whereas the bottom part contains answers for which the delta from both metrics should not differ. In addition to computing the delta between the treatment and the control for each metric, the deltas of both the baseline and the new model are tested to check if their difference is statistically significant at $\alpha = 0.05$, which is denoted in the last column. From the table we find that the new metric is able to detect degradation for both weather and dictionary answers by showing negative delta, whereas the baseline results in a positive delta (that is, the randomization result is better than the optimal result). The behavior of the baseline can be explained by the fact that the randomization is leading to more clicks on SERP results instead of answer-lead abandonment, thus the success metric would increase. While both the baseline and the model fail to detect a degradation

Table 2: **The performance of the new metric, S, (under model) compared to the baseline metric, F, categorized by answer types. In the top part of the table, the expected delta is negative, while in the bottom part the new metric should not deviate from the baseline. Pairwise sig denote whether the delta of the baseline is statistically significant from the delta of the new metric**

Answer	Baseline		Model		Pairwise Sig
	delta	pValue	delta	pValue	
Weather	0.0423	1.21E-06	-0.0181	6.58E-5	Yes
Dictionary	0.0228	4.55E-07	-0.0111	3.80E-06	Yes
Finance	0.0851	0	0.0355	0	Yes
Tracking	-0.04422	0.3505	-0.0481	0.2829	No
Navigational Query	-0.0001	0.8984	-0.0005	0.4562	No
Showtimes	-0.002	0.698	0.007	0.057	No

for the finance answer, the new proposed metric reduces the delta suggesting it is moving in the right direction.

On the other hand, for the cases where high CTR is expected, we find that the new metric conforms with the baseline in terms of delta signal. Furthermore, the resulting deltas from both metrics can not be considered different at $\alpha = 0.05$. It is worth noting that the insignificance is not due to the size of the data.

5. CONCLUSIONS AND FUTURE WORK

In this work we introduced a new success metric that is capable of detecting good abandonment in mobile search. The metric is used as an extension to click based models, and is based on machine learned classifier. We utilize attention modeling through viewport information of the user to come up with signals of satisfaction. Our metric is evaluated on online data of millions of users of a commercial search engine through A/B experiment where its effectiveness is shown.

In the future, we plan to study good abandonment in desktop search where viewport is of limited value since the SERP can be rendered without the need for scrolling.

6. REFERENCES

[1] Google mobile numbers. http://adwords.blogspot.com/2015/05/building-for-next-moment.html, 2015. Last accessed 2-2-2016.

[2] O. Arkhipova and L. Grauer. Evaluating mobile web search performance by taking good abandonment into account. In *Proceedings of the 37th international ACM SIGIR conference on Research & development in information retrieval*, pages 1043–1046. ACM, 2014.

[3] A. Chuklin and P. Serdyukov. Good abandonments in factoid queries. In *Proceedings of the 21st international conference companion on World Wide Web*, pages 483–484. ACM, 2012.

[4] A. Chuklin and P. Serdyukov. Potential good abandonment prediction. In *Proceedings of the 21st international conference companion on World Wide Web*, pages 485–486. ACM, 2012.

[5] A. Das Sarma, S. Gollapudi, and S. Ieong. Bypass rates: reducing query abandonment using negative inferences. In *Proceedings of the 14th ACM SIGKDD international conference on Knowledge discovery and data mining*, pages 177–185. ACM, 2008.

[6] A. Diriye, R. White, G. Buscher, and S. Dumais. Leaving so soon?: understanding and predicting web search abandonment rationales. In *Proceedings of the 21st ACM international conference on Information and knowledge management*, pages 1025–1034. ACM, 2012.

[7] Q. Guo, H. Jin, D. Lagun, S. Yuan, and E. Agichtein. Mining touch interaction data on mobile devices to predict web search result relevance. In *Proceedings of the 36th international ACM SIGIR conference on Research and development in information retrieval*, pages 153–162. ACM, 2013.

[8] Y. Kim, A. Hassan, R. W. White, and I. Zitouni. Modeling dwell time to predict click-level satisfaction. In *Proceedings of the 7th ACM international conference on Web search and data mining*, pages 193–202. ACM, 2014.

[9] R. Kohavi, R. Longbotham, D. Sommerfield, and R. M. Henne. Controlled experiments on the web: survey and practical guide. *Data mining and knowledge discovery*, 18(1):140–181, 2009.

[10] A. Koumpouri and V. Simaki. Queries without clicks: Evaluating retrieval effectiveness based on user feedback. In *Proceedings of the 35th international ACM SIGIR conference on Research and development in information retrieval*, pages 1133–1134. ACM, 2012.

[11] D. Lagun, C.-H. Hsieh, D. Webster, and V. Navalpakkam. Towards better measurement of attention and satisfaction in mobile search. In *Proceedings of the 37th International ACM SIGIR Conference on Research & Development in Information Retrieval*, SIGIR '14, pages 113–122, New York, NY, USA, 2014. ACM.

[12] J. Li, S. Huffman, and A. Tokuda. Good abandonment in mobile and pc internet search. In *Proceedings of the 32nd international ACM SIGIR conference on Research and development in information retrieval*, pages 43–50. ACM, 2009.

[13] W. Lu and Y. Jia. Inferring user preference in good abandonment from eye movements. In *Web-Age Information Management*, pages 457–460. Springer, 2015.

[14] S. Stamou and E. N. Efthimiadis. Interpreting user inactivity on search results. In *Advances in Information Retrieval*, pages 100–113. Springer, 2010.

[15] K. Williams, J. Kiseleva, A. C. Crook, I. Zitouni, A. Hassan Awadallah, and M. Khabsa. Detecting good abandonment in mobile search. In *Proceedings of the 25th International Conference on World Wide Web*, 2016.

Modeling and Predicting Popularity Dynamics via an Influence-based Self-Excited Hawkes Process

Peng Bao
School of Software Engineering
Beijing Jiaotong University
Beijing, China
baopeng@bjtu.edu.cn

ABSTRACT

Modeling and predicting the popularity dynamics of *individual* user generated items on online social networks has important implications in a wide range of areas. The challenge of this problem comes from the inequality of the popularity of content and the numerous complex factors. Existing works mainly focus on exploring relevant factors for prediction and fitting the time series of popularity dynamics into certain class of functions, while ignoring the underlying arrival process of attentions. Also, the exogenous effect of user activity variation on the platform has been neglected. In this paper, we propose a probabilistic model using an influence-based self-excited Hawkes process (*ISEHP*) to characterize the process through which individual microblogs gain their popularity. This model explicitly captures three ingredients: the intrinsic attractiveness of a microblog with exponential time decay, the user-specific triggering effect of each forwardings based on the endogenous influence among users, and the exogenous effect from the platform. We validate the ISEHP model by applying it on Sina Weibo, the most popular microblogging network in China. Experimental results demonstrate that our proposed model consistently outperforms existing prediction models.

Keywords

popularity dynamics; microblogs; survival theory; self-excited Hawkes process; influence; periodicity

1. INTRODUCTION

With the explosive growth of User Generated Contents (UGC) on online social networks, it becomes an important issue to predict the popularity of UGC items, including microblogs, tweets, videos, to name a few. Popularity prediction has important implications in a wide range of domains, including viral marketing, public opinion monitoring, etc. However, popularity prediction is challenging since numerous factors can affect the popularity of online content. Moreover, popularity is very asymmetric and broadly-distributed. Early studies devote to characterizing the distribution of the popularity over an aggregation of UGC items [1] and making prediction on the final popularity by exploiting temporal correlations [2].

Recently, researchers began to model the popularity dynamics of individual UGC items [3, 4, 5, 6]. In general, current models fall into two main paradigms, each with known strengths and limitations. One focuses on making predictions by exploring relevant factors and applying standard regression or classification methods [7, 8]. These models reveal many effective factors for prediction. However, there are still numerous factors to be investigated and they lack predictive power for the popularity dynamics of individual items. The other line of enquiry, in contrast, treats the popularity dynamics as time series, making predictions by fitting these time series into certain class of functions [9, 10]. Despite their initial success in certain domains, these models are deterministic and ignore the underlying arrival process of attentions. In order to directly model the process that a piece of information gains its popularity, Shen et al. employed reinforced Poisson process (RPP) to model the arriving process of paper citations [11]. The RPP assumes that information spreading is an arriving process of attention to a particular piece of information, simply using the total count of citations as the sole indicator of triggering effect of all citations, which fails to model the triggering effect of forwarding dynamics. Subsequently, Bao et al. proposed a self-excited Hawkes process (SEHP) to model the popularity dynamics of microblogs, which treats the triggering strength of each forwardings equally [12]. This is impractical due to the inhomogeneous influence between individuals. Moreover, both of the RPP and SEHP do not consider the exogenous effect, such as the user activity variation on the platform. Therefore, we still lack an effective method to predict the popularity dynamics.

In this paper, we propose a probabilistic model using an *Influence-based Self-Excited Hawkes Process (ISEHP)* to model the process through which individual microblogs gain their popularity. This model explicitly captures the intrinsic attractiveness of a microblog with exponential time decay, the user-specific triggering effect of each forwardings based on the endogenous social influence, and the exogenous effect from the platform. We validate the proposed model by applying it on Sina Weibo[1], the most popular microblogging network in China. Experimental results demonstrate that our proposed model consistently outperforms the existing models.

CIKM'16, October 24-28, 2016, Indianapolis, IN, USA
© 2016 ACM. ISBN 978-1-4503-4073-1/16/10...$15.00
DOI: http://dx.doi.org/10.1145/2983323.2983868

[1] http://t.cn

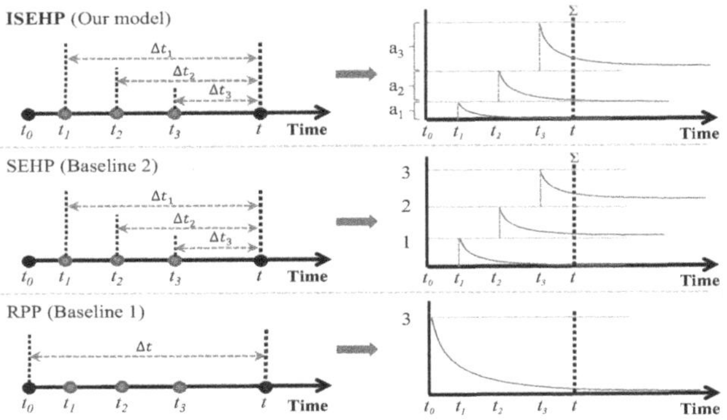

Figure 1: Differences among RPP, SEHP, and ISEHP

2. PROBLEM STATEMENT

On microblogging networks, microblogs gain their popularity as being forwarded. In this paper, we aim to model and predict the popularity dynamics of an individual microblog in the early stages and predict its popularity in the future. Here, the popularity of a given microblog is measured by the number of its forwadings. We call *indicator time* T_i as the time at which we observe the forwarding history of a microblog and the *reference time* T_r as the time at which we intent to predict its popularity. Intuitively, T_i refer to the length of the training period. The popularity dynamics of microblog m up to T_i is characterized by a set of time stamps $\{t_i\}$ $(1 \le i \le N)$, where N is the observed number of forwardings.

Formally, the prediction problem can be described as: for a microblog m, given its popularity dynamics $\{t_i\}$ up to the indicator time T_i, predicting its popularity at any reference time T_r.

3. MODELING POPULARITY DYNAMICS

We now present our model for microblogs. We show in this section that its popularity dynamics can be modeled by considering three ingredients via an influence-based self-exciting Hawkes process.

3.1 Model Formulation

When a microblog spreads, it creates a *cascade* on the microblogging network. The popularity dynamics of each microblog during observed time period $[0, T]$ can be characterized by a set of time stamps $\{t_i\}$ $(1 \le i \le N)$ which denote the occurrence time of each forwardings. Here, N is the total number of forwardings. Without loss of generality, we have $0 = t_0 \le t_1 \le t_2 \le ... \le t_i \le ... \le t_N \le T$. For a microblog, we model its popularity dynamics using an ISEHP, which consists of three time-varying terms: the intrinsic attractiveness $\lambda_{int}(t)$ of the microblog itself, the endogenous self-excitation $\lambda_{endo}(t)$ of each forwardings, and the exogenous effect $\lambda_{exo}(t)$ from the platform. Then, the rate function is defined by a linear combination of them as

$$\lambda(t) = \lambda_{int}(t) + \lambda_{endo}(t) + \lambda_{exo}(t), \quad (1)$$

where detailed specifications for each term are listed below:

- $\lambda_{int}(t)$: It is characterized by a variable with *exponential time decay*.
- $\lambda_{endo}(t)$: We employ a self-excited Hawkes process [13] with *different triggering strength* of each forwardings to model the endogenous self-excitation, taking account of the inhomogeneous social influence among users (as illustrated in Figure 1).
- $\lambda_{exo}(t)$: A *periodical sin function* is adopted to model the exogenous effect for simplicity, based on the empirical finding that the overall user activity on the platform exhibits a diurnal rise and fall pattern[16].

Table 1: Symbols and definitions in the ISEHP model

Symbol	Definition
N	total number of forwardings for a microblog
T	the observed time
t_i	the occurrence time each forwardings
$j_{max}(t)$	the index of the last forwarding before time t
v	initial triggering strength
a_j	triggering strength of the jth forwarding
β	exponent of the decaying function
γ	strength of periodicity
p	period
s	phase shift of periodicity

Therefore, the ISEHP is expressed with the following rate function

$$\lambda(t) = ve^{-\beta t} + \sum_{j=1}^{j_{max}(t)} a_j e^{-\beta(t-t_j)} + \gamma \sin\left(\frac{2\pi}{p}(t+s)\right), \quad (2)$$

where v is the initial triggering strength that reflects the attractiveness of the microblog, a_j is the triggering strength of each subsequent forwarding, and $j_{max}(t)$ is the index of the last forwarding before time t. We set an exponential decaying function with exponent β for simplicity. There are many metrics to quantify the influence of a user on social network[14, 15]. Here, we simply employ the logarithmic of the number of its followers in the follow-ship network to denote a_j. We will try other metrics in the future extension. As for the last term, p stands for the period of the cycle, s stands for the phase shift of periodicity, and γ denotes the strength of periodicity. More specifically, from [16], we can observe a daily periodicity of 24 hours and a peak activity in the noon. Therefore, we set $p = 24$ and $s = 18$ in this paper. To summarize, there are three uncertain parameters v, β, γ in this rate function. All of the symbols and definitions in the ISEHP model could be found in Table 1. Next, we will model the dynamical process in detail.

According to the survival theory, given that the $(i-1)$-th forwarding arrives at t_{i-1}, the probability that the i-th forwarding arrives at t_i follows

$$p(t_i|t_{i-1}) = e^{-\int_{t_{i-1}}^{t_i} \lambda(t)dt} \lambda(t_i), \quad (3)$$

and the probability that no forwarding arrives between t_N and T is

$$p(T|t_N) = e^{-\int_{t_N}^{T} \lambda(t)dt}. \quad (4)$$

Assuming that forwardings during different time intervals are statistically independent, the likelihood of observing a cascade of a microblog and its subsequent forwardings during time interval $[0, T]$ follows

$$\ell(v, \beta, \gamma) = p(T|t_N) \prod_{i=1}^{N} p(t_i|t_{i-1}). \quad (5)$$

By substituting Eqs. (2), (3), and (4) in Eq. (5), we obtain the logarithmic likelihood

$$\ell(v,\beta,\gamma) = \frac{v}{\beta}\left(e^{-\beta T}-1\right)+\sum_{j=1}^{j_{max}(T)}\left(\frac{a_j}{\beta}e^{-\beta(T-t_j)}-1\right)+ \gamma\cos\left(\frac{2\pi}{p}(T+s)\right)+\sum_{i=1}^{N}\log\left(ve^{-\beta t_i}+A(i)+B(i)\right), \tag{6}$$

where $A(i)=\sum_{j=1}^{j_{max}(t_i)}a_je^{-\beta(t_i-t_j)}$ and $B(i)=\gamma\sin\left(\frac{2\pi}{p}(t_i+s)\right)$.

3.2 Parameter Estimation and Prediction

Given cascade data from Weibo, we utilize maximum likelihood estimation methods to estimate the parameters in the ISEHP model. For parameter v,β,γ, the optimal values can be found by maximizing the log-likelihood ℓ in Eq. (6) using the gradient ascent method. The gradients for each parameter are

$$\frac{\partial\ell}{\partial v}=\frac{1}{\beta}\left(e^{-\beta T}-1\right)+\sum_{i=1}^{N}\log\left(\frac{e^{-\beta t_i}}{ve^{-\beta t_i}+A(i)+B(i)}\right)$$

$$\frac{\partial\ell}{\partial\beta}=-\sum_{i=1}^{N}\left(\frac{vt_ie^{-\beta t_i}+\sum_{j=1}^{j_{max}(t_i)}\left((t_i-t_j)\,a_je^{-\beta(t_i-t_j)}\right)}{ve^{-\beta t_i}+A(i)+B(i)}\right)+ \frac{1-(\beta T-1)\,ve^{-\beta T}-\sum_{j=1}^{j_{max}(T)}a_j\left(\beta\left(T-t_j\right)-1\right)e^{-\beta(T-t_j)}}{\beta^2}$$

$$\frac{\partial\ell}{\partial\gamma}=\cos\left(\frac{2\pi}{p}(T+s)\right)+\sum_{i=1}^{N}\log\left(\frac{\sin\left(\frac{2\pi}{p}(t_i+s)\right)}{ve^{-\beta t_i}+A(i)+B(i)}\right).$$

According to the standard gradient ascent method, update rules at the nth iteration are shown as follows.

$$v^{(n+1)}=v^{(n)}+\eta_1\cdot\frac{\partial\ell}{\partial v}$$
$$\beta^{(n+1)}=\beta^{(n)}+\eta_2\cdot\frac{\partial\ell}{\partial\beta}$$
$$\gamma^{(n+1)}=\gamma^{(n)}+\eta_3\cdot\frac{\partial\ell}{\partial\gamma}$$

where η_1,η_2 and η_3 are the learning rate at each iteration. The algorithm stops when the change in an iteration is small enough.

Next we show that, with the estimated v^*,β^* and γ^*, the model can be used to predict the expected number of forwardings $c(t)$ up to any given time t. Indeed, according to Eq. (2), for $t\geq T$, this prediction task is equivalent to the following differential equation

$$\frac{\mathrm{d}c(t)}{\mathrm{d}t}=ve^{-\beta t}+\sum_{j=1}^{j_{max}(t)}a_je^{-\beta(t-t_j)}+\gamma\sin\left(\frac{2\pi}{p}(t+s)\right) \tag{7}$$

with the boundary condition $c(T)=N$. Solving this differential equation, we obtain the prediction function

$$c(t)=X-\frac{v^*}{\beta^*}e^{-\beta^*t}-\frac{1}{\beta^*}\sum_{j=1}^{j_{max}(t)}a_je^{-\beta^*(t-t_j)}-\frac{\gamma^*p}{2\pi}\cos\left(\frac{2\pi}{p}(t+s)\right), \tag{8}$$

where

$$X=N+\frac{v^*}{\beta^*}e^{-\beta^*T}+\frac{1}{\beta^*}\sum_{j=1}^{j_{max}(t)}a_je^{-\beta^*(T-t_j)}+\frac{\gamma^*p}{2\pi}\cos\left(\frac{2\pi}{p}(T+s)\right).$$

4. EXPERIMENTS

In this section, we demonstrate the effectiveness of the proposed ISEHP model.

4.1 Dataset

Experiments are conducted on a dataset from Sina Weibo, published by the WISE 2012 Challenge[2]. We select microblogs that were submitted during July 1-31, 2011 and have more than 10 forwardings during the first hour and more than 100 forwardings during forty-eight hours after submission. This resulting dataset consists of 5670 microblogs and their cascades.

In addition, the dataset also contains a snapshot of the social network recording the followships among users. The social network contains 58.6 million users and 265.5 million followships among them.

4.2 Baseline Models and Evaluation Metrics

To compare the predictive power of the ISEHP model against other models, we introduce two models that have been used or can be used to model and predict popularity dynamics. Specifically, the comparison methods in our experiments are listed as follows:

- **RPP** [11]: RPP incorporates three key ingredients: the intrinsic attractiveness, the aging effect, and the reinforcement mechanism using a reinforced Poisson process. Here, we employ the version with prior.
- **SEHP** [12]: SEHP captures the triggering effect of each forwardings with equal strength, distinguishing itself from the RPP where all previous forwardings are simply aggregated as a single triggering effect.

In order to validate the prediction performance of the ISEHP model, we compare it with the existing prediction models, in terms of two metrics: Mean Absolute Percentage Error ($MAPE$) and $Accuracy$. Let $c_m(t)$ be the observed popularity for a microblog m up to time t, and $\hat{c}_m(t)$ be the predicted popularity. The $MAPE$ measures the average deviation between the predicted and observed popularity over all microblogs. For a dataset of M microblogs, the $MAPE$ is defined as

$$MAPE=\frac{1}{M}\sum_{m=1}^{M}\left|\frac{\hat{c}_m(t)-c_m(t)}{c_m(t)}\right|.$$

$Accuracy$ measures the fraction of microblogs, correctly predicted under a given error tolerance ϵ. Specifically, the $Accuracy$ of popularity prediction over M microblogs is defined as

$$Accuracy=\frac{1}{M}\sum_{m=1}^{M}\mathrm{I}\left[\left|\frac{\hat{c}_m(t)-c_m(t)}{c_m(t)}\right|\leq\epsilon\right].$$

where $\mathrm{I}[X]$ is an indicator function which return 1 if the statement X is true and 0 otherwise. In this paper, the threshold ϵ is set as 0.1.

4.3 Experimental Results

We set the training period, i.e., T, as 6 hours and then predict the popularity for each microblog from the 1st to 42nd hour after the training period.

[2]http://www.wise2012.cs.ucy.ac.cy/challenge.html

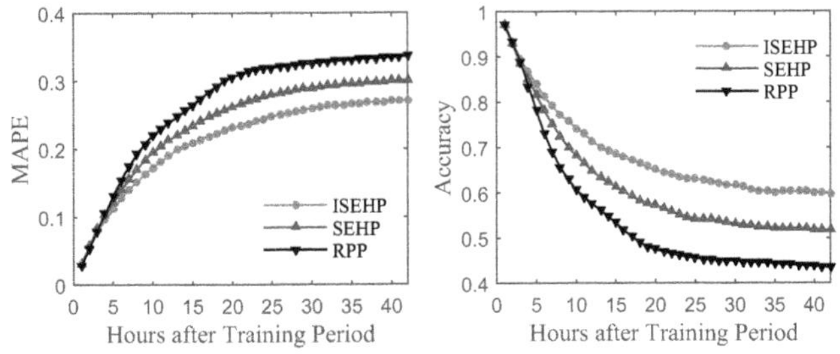

Figure 2: Prediction performance

We find the ISEHP model, proposed in this paper, achieves lower error and higher accuracy than the RPP and SEHP methods, as shown in Figure 2.

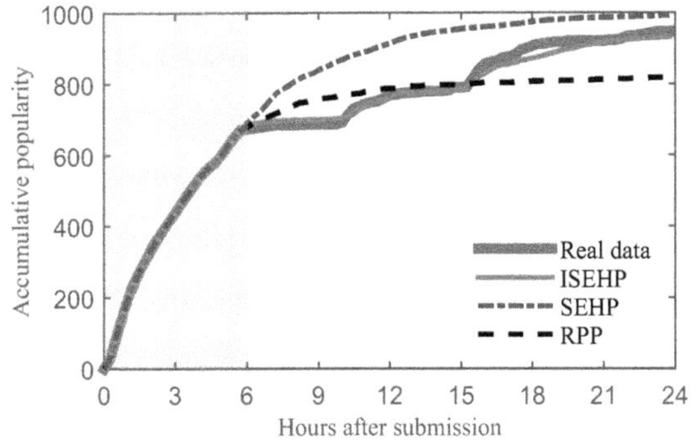

Figure 3: A case study

To offer some intuitions about the comparison, we also give a case study, as shown in Figure 3. Here, the shadowed area indicates the training period for this microblog, which is 6 hours. We can observe that our proposed model not only has a more desirable prediction accuracy, but also possesses the ability to capture the multimodal property of complex contagions.

5. CONCLUSIONS AND DISCUSSIONS

In this paper, we proposed a probabilistic model to characterize and predict the popularity dynamics of microblogs via an influence-based self-excited Hawkes process. It is consists of three parts: the intrinsic attractiveness with exponential time decay, the endogenous self-excitation among individuals with user-specific social influence, and the exogenous effect from the platform. In addition, the proposed model is efficient to be trained using only the popularity dynamics of individual microblog. Experiments on a Sina Weibo dataset demonstrate that our proposed model consistently outperforms the existing prediction models.

More importantly, it provides us great insights in understanding the fundamental mechanism of information diffusion and sheds light on the collective attention on online social networks. We will further study the various roles played by individuals and the structural factors from the underlying user network. Besides, one is also encouraged to discover a universal law of human dynamics.

Acknowledgments

This work was funded by the Fundamental Research Funds for the Central Universities under grant number 2015R-C031 and the State Visiting Scholar Funds from the China Scholarship Council under grant number 201607095027. The authors would like to thank Prof. ChengXiang Zhai for valuable discussions and suggestions.

6. REFERENCES

[1] R. Crane and D. Sornette. Robust Dynamic Classes Revealed by Measuring the Response Function of a Social System. *Proc. Natl. Acad. Sci.*, 105(41): 15649-15653, 2008.

[2] G. Szabo and B. A. Huberman. Predicting the Popularity of Online Content. *Commun. ACM*, 53(8): 80-88, 2010.

[3] K. Lerman and T. Hogg. Using a Model of Social Dynamics to Predict Popularity of News. In *Proc. of WWW '10*, pp. 621–630, USA.

[4] D. Wang, C. Song, and A.-L. Barabási. Quantifying Long-Term Scientific Impact. *Science*, 342: 127-132, 2013.

[5] S. Gao, J. Ma, and Z. Chen. Modeling and Predicting Retweeting Dynamics on Microblogging Platforms. In *Proc. of WSDM '15*, pp. 107-116, China.

[6] Q. Zhao, M. A. Erdogdu, H. Y. He, A. Rajaraman, and J. Leskovec. SEISMIC: A Self-Exciting Point Process Model for Predicting Tweet Popularity. In *Proc. of KDD '15*, pp. 1513-1522, Australia.

[7] L. Hong, O. Dan, and B. D. Davison. Predicting Popular Messages in Twitter. In *Proc. of WWW '11*, pp. 57-58, India.

[8] P. Bao, H. W. Shen, J. Huang, and X. Q. Cheng. Popularity Prediction in Microblogging Network: a Case Study on Sina Weibo. In *Proc. of WWW '13*, pp. 177-178, Brazil.

[9] Y. Matsubara, Y. Sakurai, B. A. Prakash, L. Li, and C. Faloutsos. Rise and Fall Patterns of Information Diffusion: Model and Implications. In *Proc. of KDD '12*, pp. 6-14, China.

[10] M. Gomez-Rodriguez, J. Leskovec, and B. Schölkopf. Modeling Information Propagation with Survival Theory. In *Proc. of ICML '13*, pp. 666–674, USA.

[11] H. W. Shen, D. Wang, C. Song, and A.-L. Barabási. Modeling and Predicting Popularity Dynamics via Reinforced Poisson Processes. In *Proc. of AAAI '14*, pp. 291-297, Canada.

[12] P. Bao, H. W. Shen, X. Jin, and X. Q. Cheng. Modeling and Predicting Popularity Dynamics of Microblogs using Self-Excited Hawkes Processes. In *Proc. of WWW '15*, pp. 9-10, Italy.

[13] A.G. Hawkes. Spectra of Some Self-exciting and Mutually Exciting Point Processes. *Biometrika*, 58(1): 83-90, 1971.

[14] A. Anagnostopoulos, R. Kumar, and M. Mahdian. Inuence and Correlation in Social Networks. In *Proc. of KDD '08*, pp. 7-15, USA.

[15] L. Liu, J. Tang, J. Han, M. Jiang, and S. Yang. Mining Topic-level Inuence in Heterogeneous Networks. In *Proc. of CIKM '10*, pp. 199-208, Canada.

[16] P. Bao, H. W. Shen, W. Chen, and X. Q. Cheng. Cumulative Effect in Information Diffusion: Empirical Study on a Microblogging Network. PLoS ONE, 8(10):e76027.

Incorporate Group Information to Enhance Network Embedding

Jifan Chen, Qi Zhang, Xuanjing Huang
Shanghai Key Laboratory of Data Science
School of Computer Science, Fudan University
825 Zhangheng Road, Shanghai, P.R.China
{jfchen14, qz, xjhuang}@fudan.edu.cn

ABSTRACT

The problem of representing large-scale networks with low-dimensional vectors has received considerable attention in recent years. Except the networks that include only vertices and edges, a variety of networks contain information about groups or communities. For example, on Facebook, in addition to users and the follower-followee relations between them, users can also create and join groups. However, previous studies have rarely utilized this valuable information to generate embeddings of vertices. In this paper, we investigate a novel method for learning the network embeddings with valuable group information for large-scale networks. The proposed methods take both the inner structures of the groups and the information across groups into consideration. Experimental results demonstrate that the embeddings generated by the proposed methods significantly outperform state-of-the-art network embedding methods on two different scale real-world networks.

Keywords

Network Embedding; Group Information; Large Scale

1. INTRODUCTION

Many types of relations and processes in physical, social, and information systems can be naturally modelled by networks, such as communication, citation, and social information. However, in real-world applications, the size of many networks is extremely large. For example, Twitter has 316 million monthly active users [1] in 2015. Methods that process these networks directly through vertices and edges may encounter efficiency issues when solving practical real-world problems. Hence, network embedding, which is used to represent each vertex of a network with a low-dimensional vector that can preserve the similarities between them, has attracted continuous attention and has been successfully used in various applications, including image processing, knowledge graph, recommendation, etc.

[1]https://about.twitter.com/company

CIKM'16 , October 24-28, 2016, Indianapolis, IN, USA

DOI: http://dx.doi.org/10.1145/2983323.2983869

Along with the increasing requirements, a variety of researchers have studied the network embedding construction problem from different aspects [10, 3, 7, 9, 8]. Classical methods (e.g., IsoMap [10] and Laplacian eigenmaps [1]) usually transform this task into a constrained optimization problem. Hence, the usefulness of these methods may be heavily impacted by the computation consumption of processing hundreds of millions of nodes. To process large-scale networks, DeepWalk [7] uses a shallow neural network architecture. LINE [9] uses both first-order and second-order proximity to train the embedding, and negative sampling methods to reduce the computational requirement. However, most of the previous studies focused on a classical network and took only vertices and edges into consideration.

In practical tasks, in addition to vertices and edges, many networks contain groups or communities. For example, in social media (e.g., Youtube and Facebook), users can create groups that other users can join. Previous literatures [11] also show that this kind of network is common in real-world social, collaboration, information, and many other kinds of networks. More than 200 different kinds of large real-world networks where nodes explicitly state their group memberships were studied in the work done by Yang and Leskovec [11]. Although communities or groups in networks can provide valuable information, previous network embedding studies rarely took this information into consideration.

In this paper, we study the problem of incorporating group information for network embedding generation. We think that the generated embedding of vertices should be placed closely in low dimensional space if they share similar neighbours or the group they joined are similar. In order to meet the requirements, we then propose a novel method to achieve the task. First, a random walk cross groups is adopted to gain the information between vertices. Then the inner structures of groups are obtained by random sample vertices in that group. Finally, we propose to use a group vector to preserve the information between vertices as well as the information of groups.

2. THE PROPOSED METHODS

Inspired by the work of DeepWalk [7] and the idea of modelling document [4, 2] in natural language processing, our model contains two main stages, sampling and training. We will then illustrate the two steps in details.

In the sampling stage, we uniformly take a random vertex v_i as the root of a random walk W_{v_i}, then from the root we sample the neighbors of the last vertex visited until we reach the maximum length L. After this step, we can get $W_{v_i} = v_i, v_{i+1}, v_{i+2}, ..., v_L$, where v_{i+n} is one of the neighbours of v_{i+n-1}. In our experiment, we set the length L to be fixed, but there is no restriction for these walks to be the same length. Then, for each generated random walk

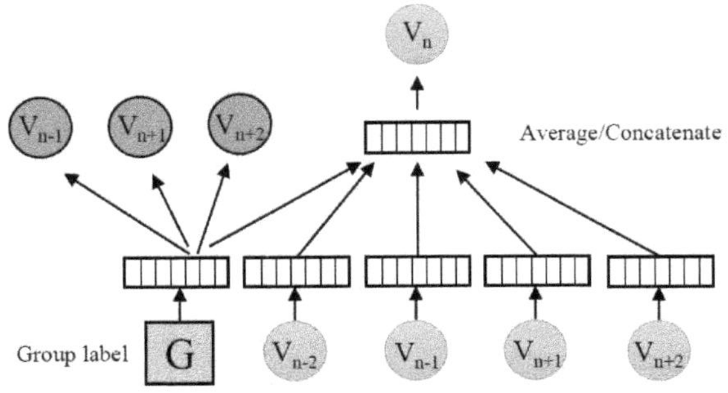

Figure 1: The architecture of the proposed model, the blue circles represent the vertices sampled by random walk and labeled by group G, the orange circles represent the vertices random sampled in group G, and the green square represents the group label.

W_{v_i}, we randomly sample a group label g_j from the groups v_i belongs to and assign it to W_{v_i}, those labeled walks are then used for training.

The framework of our training model is shown in Figure 1, as we can see, every group label and vertex is mapped to a unique vector and all the vertex embeddings are shared among different groups. The group vector and the vertex vectors are averaged or concatenated to predict the center vertex in a sliding window over a random walk. We also use the group vector to predict the vertices randomly sampled in that group. More formally, the objective of our proposed model is defined to maximize the following log probability:

$$\mathscr{L} = \sum_{g_i \in C} (\alpha \sum_{W \in W_{g_i}} \sum_{v_j \in W} \log p(v_j | v_{j-k}, ..., v_{j+k}, g_i) + \beta \sum_{\hat{v_j} \in \hat{W}_{g_i}} \log p(\hat{v_j} | g_i)), \quad (1)$$

where C is the set of different groups and g_i is the label of the ith group, W_{g_i} contains random walks W labeled with g_i, $\hat{W}_{g_i}$ contains vertices randomly sampled from group g_i, α and β are the weights that specifies a trade-off between the information cross groups and the information in that group, the probability $\log p(v_j|v_{j-k}, ..., v_{j+k}, g_i)$ and $\log p(\hat{v_j}|g_i)$ are respectively defined as:

$$\log p(v_j | v_{j-k}, ..., v_{j+k}, g_i) = \frac{\exp(\bar{u}^T u'_j)}{\sum_{n=1}^{M} \exp(\bar{u}^T u'_n)}, \quad (2)$$

$$\log p(\hat{v_j} | g_i) = \frac{\exp(u_{g_i}^T \hat{u_j})}{\sum_{n=1}^{M} \exp({u_{g_i}}^T \hat{u_n})}, \quad (3)$$

where M is the number of vertices in the network, u' and u are respectively the output and input vector representation of v, and $\bar{u}$ is the averaged vector representation of the context and label g_i, defined as follows,

$$\bar{u} = \frac{1}{2k}(u_{g_i} + \sum_{-k \le p \le k, p \ne 0} u_{j+p}), \quad (4)$$

where k is the size of sliding window and u is the input representation of vertex v.

The computation of gradient $\nabla \log p(v_j|v_{j-k}, ..., v_{j+k}, g_i)$, $\nabla \log p(\hat{v_j}|g_i)$, is proportion to the number of vertices in the network G, and in real-world networks, there can be hundreds of millions of vertices, so it is impractical to compute these gradients directly. To address this problem, we adopt the approach of negative sampling proposed in [5] to reduce the computational requirement.

We then give a brief explanation to our proposed model. Since we adopt random walks starting from different vertices in the network, and there should be similar walks for the vertices sharing similar neighbours, thus, those vertices will be placed closely. Also, as we use the group vector to predict the vertices randomly sampled in that group, vertices in that group will be placed closely. Moreover, because of the special form of assigning group labels to random walks, vertices from different groups may be assigned with the same group label, the group vector acts as a memory cell that contains both the information of vertieces in that group and across groups, resulting in a closer distance between some vertices in same groups. We name our proposed model **GENE**, which means group enhanced network embedding.

3. EXPERIMENT

In this section, we report the experimental results of our methods on two large scale real-world networks. We use two different group recommendation tasks to evaluate the quality of the generated embeddings.

3.1 Datasets

We use two large real world datasets for evaluating the proposed methods[2].

- **Amazon:** This network is provided by Yang [11] and collected by crawling Amazon website. In this network, if a product i is frequently co-purchased with product j, the graph contains an undirected edge from i to j. Each product category provided by Amazon defines each ground-truth community.

- **Youtube:** This network is provided by Alan Mislove [6]. Youtube is a video-sharing web site that includes a social network. In the Youtube social network, users form friendship each other and users can create groups which other users can join. Such user-defined groups are considered as ground-truth communities.

3.2 Baseline Methods

We compare our proposed methods with some of the state-of-art existing network embedding methods to validate the performance.

- **DeepWalk [7]:** It uses information obtained from truncated random walks to learn latent representations by treating walks as the equivalent of sentences.

- **LINE [9]:** It is a network embedding method, which tries to preserve both the local and global network structures.

- **GroupWalk:** It only takes the labeled random walks cross groups mentioned above into consideration. The group vector and the vertex vectors are averaged or concatenated to predict the centre vertex in a sliding window over a random walk.

- **GroupOnly:** It only uses the group vector to predict the vertices sampled in a specific group.

[2]They are publicly available. http://snap.stanford.edu/data/

Table 1: Results of recommendation Task1 on Amazon

	percentage	10%	20%	30%	40%	50%	60%	70%	80%	90%
MAP@5	DeepWalk	52.52%	58.93%	65.80%	69.60%	73.65%	74.64%	76.41%	77.61%	79.01%
	LINE	46.22%	53.26%	60.02%	64.22%	68.38%	70.22%	72.08%	73.12%	74.79%
	GroupWalk	58.85%	66.67%	73.09%	77.26%	81.25%	82.65%	84.17%	85.22%	**87.25%**
	GroupOnly	56.90%	61.03%	63.23%	68.94%	72.98%	74.59%	74.95%	74.26%	70.86%
	GENE	**63.64%**	**70.65%**	**76.25%**	**80.50%**	**84.13%**	**84.79%**	**85.63%**	**85.41%**	84.41%

Table 2: Results of recommendation Task2 on Amazon

	Percentage	5%	10%	15%	20%	25%	30%
MAP@5	DeepWalk	33.94%	51.57%	55.29%	58.53%	62.00%	64.85%
	LINE	30.27%	46.38%	49.88%	53.21%	56.70%	59.64%
	GroupWalk	37.67%	61.61%	63.05%	66.60%	70.07%	72.88%
	GroupOnly	34.86%	58.15%	61.75%	64.85%	64.88%	72.80%
	GENE	**42.48%**	**62.32%**	**67.01%**	**70.07%**	**72.91%**	**75.56%**

3.3 Experiment Protocols

We evaluate the proposed methods on two tasks of recommendation, the ground-truth communities in the datasets are treated as the groups mentioned above.

- **Task 1:** We randomly sample 10% nodes in the network and then remove their communities by the ratio increasing from 10% to 90%. The randomly removed communities are used as the ground-truth for evaluation. The performance of recommendation can be evaluated with them. It is a simulation for the following situation: There are several new nodes joined the network, they have formed the relationship with other nodes but with few communities, then we have to recommend new communities for them.

- **Task 2:** For all of the nodes in the network, we remove their communities by the ratio increasing from 5% to 30%. The randomly removed communities are used as the ground-truth for evaluation. It is a simulation for such situation: The whole network has been well formed and is relatively stable, then we have to recommend new communities for the nodes in the network to join.

The recommend protocol is described as follows: First, for each node n, we find its most similar points set S by computing the cosine similarity between its embedding and other nodes' embedding. Second, for each node r in the set S, find all the communities r belongs to, if there are any group that dose not belong to n, we recommend this group to n.

3.3.1 Parameters Setting

In the random walk phase, we iterate over the network for 10 times. At each iteration, we sample one random walk per node and we set the walk length to be fixed to 15 for both of the networks. For the GENE model, we simply set $\alpha = \beta = 1$. For the negative sampling part in the proposed method, the number of negative samples is set to 5. The number of vertices randomly sampled from groups is also set to 5.

3.4 Results and Analysis on Amazon

The results on Task 1 are shown in Table 1, it is obvious that the MAP@5 of all the methods improve as we increase the ratio of removing communities. It is because when the ratio increases, the number of ground-truth answers also increases, causing a higher precision of top ones.

Another observation from the table is that by adding group vertices, GroupWalk achieves consistently better performance than DeepWalk, and GroupOnly also achieves a fairly good performance. GENE outperforms all of the other methods and achieves the best performance. It not only proves the group information is useful but also shows the way we proposed to incorporate those inner-group and cross-group information is actually useful.

From Table 1, we can also find that the performance of the GroupOnly model improves at first as we remove more communities. But when we remove more than 70% communities, its performance begins to decrease. This is mainly because when we remove a large amount of community relationships from some vertices, then those vertices can only appear in a small set of communities, causing a lower probability to be sampled in sampling stage and thus they can be trained with less communities. So there is no surprise for the decreased performance, and this also explains why there is a drop of performance of the GENE model when we remove the communities by 90%.

Then we compare the GroupWalk and the GroupOnly model, the GroupWalk performs much better than the GroupOnly consistently. The result states that there are more groups recommended by finding nodes sharing the same neighbors than the nodes in the same community on Amazon network.

The GENE model achieves the best performance except the 90% remove of communities, it proves our assumption that both inner-group and cross-group information are helpful for network embedding construction, and they act like a supplement to each other. GENE model has taken both of the information into consideration, so it performs better than the GroupWalk and GroupOnly model alone. The performance of the GENE decreases as the GroupOnly model, but in a much small range, showing this model is also stable.

The results for Task 2 are shown in Table 2, the results are almost in the same patterns as what shows in Table 1. The GENE model outperforms all of the other methods, and in general, GroupWalk and GroupOnly also achieve better results than DeepWalk and LINE. It proves that our proposed method can do better in recommendation for the stable vertices in a network as well as the vertices which join the network recently.

Table 3: Results of recommendation Task1 on Youtube

	percentage	10%	20%	30%	40%	50%	60%	70%	80%	90%
MAP@5	DeepWalk	11.71%	14.39%	21.32%	27.96%	32.48%	34.61%	36.75%	39.10%	40.25%
	LINE	7.34%	7.88%	14.52%	17.56%	20.92%	22.46%	23.56%	25.72%	29.31%
	GroupWalk	13.79%	19.15%	22.68%	31.55%	33.54%	38.46%	40.93%	44.21%	**49.71%**
	GroupOnly	16.50%	21.56%	29.39%	33.48%	37.37%	42.65%	38.30%	37.43%	36.27%
	GENE	**23.31%**	**24.92%**	**32.00%**	**39.52%**	**42.21%**	**45.31%**	**49.99%**	**51.93%**	48.23%

Table 4: Results of recommendation Task2 on Youtube

	percentage	5%	10%	15%	20%	25%	30%
MAP@5	DeepWalk	7.74%	11.51%	13.44%	15.78%	18.79%	21.75%
	LINE	4.02%	5.96%	8.41%	9.35%	10.88%	12.91%
	GroupWalk	9.57%	12.67%	15.09%	18.69%	21.53%	24.87%
	GroupOnly	12.88%	16.77%	18.65%	21.88%	25.57%	27.85%
	GENE	**13.56%**	**18.62%**	**20.92%**	**24.51%**	**28.20%**	**32.08%**

3.5 Results and Analysis on Youtube

The Youtube network is quite different from Amazon especially for its sparse group membership. Facing such situation, let's look at our results in Table 3 and Table 4.

The results in Table 3 are much worse than the results of Amazon network shown in Table 1, but it is reasonable since the group membership per node decreases a lot, it is harder for recommendation. Once again, GENE achieves the best performance, and incorporating group information significantly improves the performance.

Take a comparison between the GroupWalk and GroupOnly model, things go to the opposite side of what shows in Amazon network. The GroupOnly model generally performs better than GroupWalk model, except for the cases when we remove more than 70% of communities. Such results show that there are more groups recommended by finding nodes in the same community than the nodes sharing the same neighbours on Youtube network. From this result, we can also see the difference between the two networks. The best performance of GENE model once again proves it can preserve both the inner-group and cross-group information. The results shown in Table 4 are consistent with the results in Table 3.

Overall, from these results, we conclude that with the test under two different networks, our network embedding trained with group information is more effective on the task of recommendation than the previous methods for training network embedding.

4. CONCLUSIONS

In this work, we study the problem of enhancing network embeddings using group information for the networks which explicitly contain groups or communities. We assume that a good network embedding with group information should take the inner-group information as well as the cross-group information into consideration. Hence, we propose a model which incorporates both the inner structure within a group and the information cross groups to train the network embedding. Experimental results demonstrate that the embeddings generated by the proposed method outperforms state-of-the-art network embedding methods on two different scale real-world networks.

5. ACKNOWLEDGEMENT

The authors wish to thank the anonymous reviewers for their helpful comments. This work was partially funded by National Natural Science Foundation of China (No. 61532011, 61473092, and 61472088), the National High Technology Research and Development Program of China (No. 2015AA015408).

6. REFERENCES

[1] M. Belkin and P. Niyogi. Laplacian eigenmaps and spectral techniques for embedding and clustering. In *NIPS*, volume 14, pages 585–591, 2001.

[2] N. Djuric, H. Wu, V. Radosavljevic, M. Grbovic, and N. Bhamidipati. Hierarchical neural language models for joint representation of streaming documents and their content. In *Proceedings of the 24th International Conference on World Wide Web*, pages 248–255. International World Wide Web Conferences Steering Committee, 2015.

[3] Y. Jacob, L. Denoyer, and P. Gallinari. Learning latent representations of nodes for classifying in heterogeneous social networks. In *Proceedings of the 7th ACM international conference on Web search and data mining*, pages 373–382. ACM, 2014.

[4] Q. Le and T. Mikolov. Distributed representations of sentences and documents. In *Proceedings of The 31st International Conference on Machine Learning*, pages 1188–1196, 2014.

[5] T. Mikolov, I. Sutskever, K. Chen, G. S. Corrado, and J. Dean. Distributed representations of words and phrases and their compositionality. In *Advances in neural information processing systems*, pages 3111–3119, 2013.

[6] A. Mislove, M. Marcon, K. P. Gummadi, P. Druschel, and B. Bhattacharjee. Measurement and analysis of online social networks. In *Proceedings of the 7th ACM SIGCOMM conference on Internet measurement*, pages 29–42. ACM, 2007.

[7] B. Perozzi, R. Al-Rfou, and S. Skiena. Deepwalk: Online learning of social representations. In *Proceedings of the 20th ACM SIGKDD international conference on Knowledge discovery and data mining*, pages 701–710. ACM, 2014.

[8] J. Tang, M. Qu, and Q. Mei. Pte: Predictive text embedding through large-scale heterogeneous text networks. In *Proceedings of the 21th ACM SIGKDD International Conference on Knowledge Discovery and Data Mining*, pages 1165–1174. ACM, 2015.

[9] J. Tang, M. Qu, M. Wang, M. Zhang, J. Yan, and Q. Mei. Line: Large-scale information network embedding. In *Proceedings of the 24th International Conference on World Wide Web*, pages 1067–1077. International World Wide Web Conferences Steering Committee, 2015.

[10] J. B. Tenenbaum, V. De Silva, and J. C. Langford. A global geometric framework for nonlinear dimensionality reduction. *Science*, 290(5500):2319–2323, 2000.

[11] J. Yang and J. Leskovec. Defining and evaluating network communities based on ground-truth. In *2012 IEEE 12th International Conference on Data Mining*, pages 745–754. IEEE, 2012.

Exploiting Cluster-based Meta Paths for Link Prediction in Signed Networks

Jiangfeng Zeng, Ke Zhou, Xiao Ma✉, Fuhao Zou, Hua Wang
Huazhong University of Science and Technology
Wuhan China, 430074
{jfzeng, k.zhou, cindyma, fuhao_zou, hwang}@hust.edu.cn

ABSTRACT

Many online social networks can be described by signed networks, where positive links signify friendships, trust and like; while negative links indicate enmity, distrust and dislike. Predicting the sign of the links in these networks has attracted a great deal of attentions in the areas of friendship recommendation and trust relationship prediction. Existing methods for sign prediction tend to rely on path-based features which are somehow limited to the sparsity problem of the network. In order to solve this issue, in this paper, we introduce a novel sign prediction model by exploiting cluster-based meta paths, which can take advantage of both local and global information of the input networks. First, cluster-based meta paths based features are constructed by incorporating the newly generated clusters through hierarchically clustering the input networks. Then, the logistic regression classifier is employed to train the model and predict the hidden signs of the links. Extensive experiments on Epinions and Slashdot datasets demonstrate the efficiency of our proposed method in terms of Accuracy and Coverage.

Categories and Subject Descriptors

H.3.3 [**Information Search Retrieval**]: Information Filtering; J.4 [**Computer Applications**]: Social and Behavioral Sciences

Keywords

Signed Networks; Link prediction; Cluster-based Meta Path

1. INTRODUCTION

The increasing popularity of social networks allows online users to participate in online activities conveniently. Users can form positive links with others through friendships in social network websites, e.g., Facebook, Twitter, LinkedIn, etc, as well as establish negative relationships, e.g., distrust, foes, in websites like Epinions, Slashdot, etc.

CIKM'16 , October 24-28, 2016, Indianapolis, IN, USA

DOI: http://dx.doi.org/10.1145/2983323.2983870

In order to help users better connect to others, a set of link prediction methods have been explored to detect the latent relationship in the networks which may link two users together in the future[6, 7, 9]. Existing link prediction algorithms can be roughly divided into two groups, which correspond to supervised and unsupervised methods. Supervised methods consider the link prediction problem as a classification problem by using the existence of links as labels, while unsupervised methods make use of the topological properties of the snapshot of the network[7, 11].

Typically, link prediction methods only consider the presence/absence of a connection between two nodes, and ignore the possible sign of the connection. However, in signed networks, not only the link prediction problem is important, but also correctly predicting the sign of the links matters. Existing sign prediction algorithms mainly rely on path-based features, and the effectiveness of these models depend on the number of paths between the target nodes[1, 5, 8]. That is to say, the accuracy of prediction is higher for edges with larger values of embeddedness (embeddedness is the number of paths with length two between the target nodes). However, the sparsity problem is serious in real networks. As a result, it will be quite difficult to find such kind of paths connecting arbitrary nodes in such sparse networks.

Our proposed method for the problem is motivated by the meta paths based relationship prediction model proposed in heterogeneous information networks[10]. Different meta paths capture different semantics between any two vertices in the networks, which consider not only the regular paths between nodes, but also the structural information of the networks. It has been verified by Sun et al.[10] that the prediction accuracy of meta paths based models are usually higher than other traditional path based models, e.g., Personalized-PageRank[2], SimRank[3]. By extending their intuition into the homogeneous networks, we assume that two nodes are more likely to be similar in the networks if their neighbors belong to the same clusters. Based on this intuition, we introduce the cluster-based meta paths, which can efficiently alleviate the sparsity problem appeared in pure path based sign prediction models by employing not only the local information of nodes, but also the global structural information of the networks.

The contributions of our work can be summarized as follows. **First**, we propose a novel cluster-based meta path which incorporates meaningful network structural information into path-based features for link prediction in signed networks. **Second**, we show the effectiveness of cluster-based meta path features by thoroughly comparing the prediction results generated by pure path-based features and cluster-based meta path features of different cluster layers.

The rest of the paper is organized as follows: the notations are defined in Section 2. Section 3 introduces the proposed sign prediction model. The experiment results and analysis are presented in Section 4. Finally, Section 5 concludes this study with future work.

2. PRELIMINARY

A signed network can be denoted as a graph $G = (V, E, \Sigma)$ where $V = \{1, 2, ..., |V|\}$ is a finite set of nodes of the graph. For $\forall u_i, u_j \in V$, E consists a set of directed or undirected edges $e_{i,j}$ between two nodes. The third component of the graph is a mapping $\Sigma : s_{e_{i,j}} \rightarrow \{+1, -1\}$ giving a sign to each edge, where $s_{e_{i,j}} = 1$ represents that positive relationship exists between node u_i and node u_j, while $s_{e_{i,j}} = -1$ means that these two nodes share a negative relationship in the graph.

3. THE APPROACH

3.1 Problem definition

Formally, given a graph $G = (V, E, \Sigma)$, and a test edge $e_{i,j} \in E$ whose sign is hidden, the problem is to infer the disappeared sign of the edge $e_{i,j}$ based on the information extracted from the rest of the graph.

3.2 Meta Paths

In a heterogeneous information network schema, two entities can be connected via different paths, which usually carry different semantic meanings. In this paper, we use the meta path definition from [10] in a network schema as follows:

Definition 1. **Meta Path(MP)**

A meta path $P = A_0 \xrightarrow{R_1} A_1 \xrightarrow{R_2} ... \xrightarrow{R_l} A_l$ is a path defined on the graph of network schema $T_G = (\mathcal{A}, \mathcal{R})$, and defines a new composite relation $R_1 R_2 ... R_l$ between type A_0 and A_l, where $A_i \in \mathcal{A}$ and $R_i \in \mathcal{R}$ for $i = 0, ..., l$. $A_0 = dom(R_1)$, $A_l = range(R_l)$, and $A_i = range(R_i) = dom(R_{i+1})$ for $i = 1, ..., l-1$.

Different meta paths usually contain different semantics in a heterogeneous graph. The following examples are two representative meta paths in the DBLP network schema:

$P_1 : paper \xrightarrow{PublishedIn} venue \xrightarrow{PublishedIn^{-1}} paper$

$P_2 :\ paper \xrightarrow{Contains} term \xrightarrow{Contains^{-1}} paper$

Meta path P_1 defines the relationship of publishing in the same venue for two papers. Intuitively, if two papers published in the same venues, these two papers seem to belong to the same research area. P_2 captures the relationship of sharing similar research topics between two papers. It can be seen that meta paths can capture different relationships hidden in the network, which are extremely helpful to capture the structural information embedded in a heterogeneous graph.

Now let's think about the role of entity 'venue' in the above meta paths. Many papers are published in the same venues, therefore, 'venue' can be considered as hubs which have the attribute of attracting large volume of other types of entities in the networks. Inspired by this phenomenon, we begin to think that whether it is possible to introduce a type of entities which can be considered as hubs in homogeneous networks. Intuitively, a cluster containing multiple nodes is exactly qualified for this requirement. Therefore, in the setting of homogeneous networks, we first introduce the definition of node-based meta paths as follows, and the cluster-based meta paths will be discussed in the next section.

Definition 2. **Node-based Meta Path(NBMP)**

A node-based meta path is defined as $U \xrightarrow{R} U \xrightarrow{R^{-1}} U$, where $U \in V$, R represents composite relations between any pair of nodes in the networks, and the link type R^{-1} is the inverse of relation R. Simplest instances of node-based meta paths are the paths with length two, which can be denoted by $p : u_i - u_k - u_j$, where $u_i, u_k, u_j \in V$, and $e_{i,k}$, $e_{k,j} \in E$.

3.3 Cluster-based Meta Paths based Sign Prediction Model

The proposed model can be executed in three steps. **First,** in order to investigate how the network structure influence the quality of meta-paths, we hierarchically clustering the input network and adding a set of new entities into the input network based on the newly obtained clusters of different layers. **Second,** defining features based on meta-paths which include the entities of clusters. **Third,** predicting the signs of links using the logistic regression classifier.

Note that, in the first step, plenty of algorithms can be used for the hierarchical clustering task. In this paper, we employ the InfoMap clustering algorithm proposed in [4], where the input is the signed networks with both positive and negative links, and the output is the hierarchical clusters. Based on the newly obtained clusters, we introduce the definition of cluster-based meta paths as follows:

Definition 3. **Cluster-based Meta Path(CBMP)**

A cluster-based meta path is defined as $U \xrightarrow{R} U \xrightarrow{B} C_x \xrightarrow{B^{-1}} U \xrightarrow{R^{-1}} U$, where $U \in V$, R represents composite relations between two arbitrary nodes. C_x signifies the clusters in the xth layer. B denotes a node belongs to cluster C_x, and B^{-1} is the inverse of relation B. $C_{x,y} (C_{x,y} \in C_x)$ means the yth cluster in layer x.

Figure 1 is a simple example describing how cluster-based entities can be added to the input network. As we can see that, 3 first-layer clusters $C_{1,1}$, $C_{1,2}$,$C_{1,3}$, as well as 2 second-layer clusters $C_{2,1}$, $C_{2,2}$ are obtained through clustering and added to the network as some super nodes. For example, nodes u_1, u_2, u_3, u_i belong to the first-layer cluster $C_{1,1}$; and nodes u_9, u_{11} belong to the first-layer cluster $C_{1,3}$ and second-layer cluster $C_{2,1}$. The solid links represent the relationships with known labels between nodes in the input network, and the dotted links denote edges with hidden signs (For simplicity, the directions and signs of links are omitted.).

Suppose the nodes u_i and u_j are two target nodes, the neighbors of node u_i are u_1 and u_9, and the neighbors of node u_j are u_2, u_5, u_7, u_8 and u_{11}. According to Definition 2, only 2 instances of node-based meta paths exists in this graph, that is, $p_1 : u_i - u_1 - u_2 - u_j$; $p_2 : u_i - u_9 - u_{11} - u_j$. However, according to Definition 3, there are 4 instances of the cluster-based meta paths existing in the first layer, and 1 instance in the second layer: $p_{11} : u_i - u_1 - C_{1,1} - u_2 - u_j$; $p_{12} : u_i - u_9 - C_{1,3} - u_7 - u_j$; $p_{13} : u_i - u_9 - C_{1,3} - u_8 - u_j$; $p_{14} : u_i - u_9 - C_{1,3} - u_{11} - u_j$; $p_{21} : u_i - u_9 - C_{2,1} - u_{11} - u_j$.

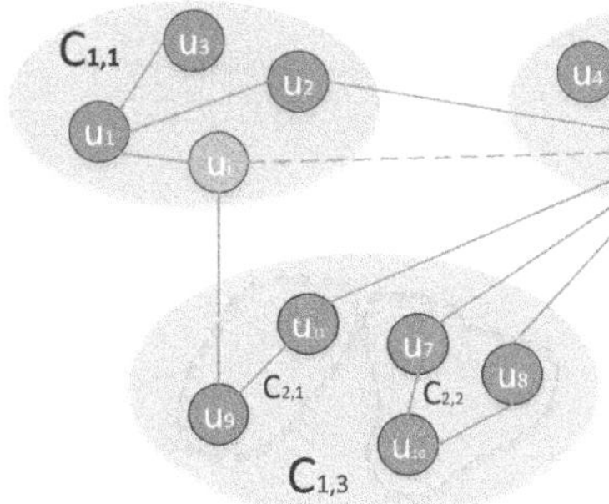

Figure 1: A toy example describing the relations between nodes and clusters.

In fact, paths p_{11}, p_{14} and p_{21} are equivalent to node-based meta paths p_1 and p_2. However, there are two more cluster-based meta paths, e.g., p_{12}, p_{13}, which include the structural information of the network by exploiting clustering. In other words, our proposed cluster-based meta paths can guarantee having sufficient number of paths between nodes, which will effectively alleviate the sparsity problem.

Feature computation. The values of CBMP features can be computed by the number of path instances following meta paths of different cluster layers between the target nodes u_i and u_j. For example, the feature vector for edge $e_{i,j}$ in Figure 1 can be denoted as $f_{i,j} = \{f_1, f_2\}$, where $f_1 : 1 \times 1 + 0 + 1 \times 3 = 4$, $f_2 : 1 \times 1 + 0 = 1$.

Note that, it is more efficient to employ matrix multiplication to find the path instances than directly searching paths in the whole dataset. Two types of matrices are essential for the multiplication in our setting: one is the *Node-Node Adjacency Matrix*; the other is the *Node-Cluster Belong-ship Matrix* representing the relationships between each node and each cluster of different cluster layers. Due to limited space, we will not discuss it further. Please refer to [10] for more detail.

Learning methodology. Following the method in [5, 8], we apply the logistic regression classifier to do edge sign prediction based on both the node-based meta paths features and cluster-based meta paths features. Logistic regression learns a model as follows:

$$p^{+}(s_{e_{i,j}}) = \frac{1}{1+e^{-(a_0+\sum_{m=1}^{k} a_m f_{i,j}^{m})}} \tag{1}$$

The coefficients $\{a_0, ..., a_k\}$ are learned from the training data using maximum likelihood estimation, and k is the number of features. If $p^{+}(s_{e_{i,j}}) \geq 0.5$, there exists a positive relationship between nodes u_i and u_j, else negative results are obtained.

4. EXPERIMENTS AND ANALYSIS

4.1 Datasets Description

Two real-world online social networks are used in the experiments, namely Epinions and Slashdot downloaded from *http://snap.stanford.edu/data/*. Both the networks have explicit sign labels on the links. By preprocessing the datasets, we filter out the nodes which only exist in positive links or negative links. The statistics of datasets we used in our experiment are shown in Table 1. From this table we can conclude that both the datasets are quite sparse and imbalanced, i.e., more positive links exist than negative links.

Table 1: Statistics of the datasets

	Epinions	*Slashdot*
# of nodes	114,476	75,144
# of links	807,894	537,665
Fraction of + links	88.83%	79.06 %
Fraction of - links	11.17%	20.96%
Sparsity	99.38%	99.04%

4.2 Methodology and Metrics

We evaluate the proposed method using a *leave-one-out* methodology: each edge in the testing network is successively removed and the methods try to predict the sign of that edge using the rest of the network. In order to avoid over-fitting, we adopt 10-*fold cross-validation*. We randomly created 10 disjoint test folds each consisting of 10% of the whole number of edges in the networks. For each test fold, the remaining 90% of the links serve as the training set. Then the accuracy and coverage are generated by averaging them over the 10 folds.

Since the datasets are quite imbalanced, we follow the methodology of [5] and create a balanced dataset with equal numbers of positive and negative edges, so that random guessing yields a 50% accuracy. In order to assess the performance of the methods, we computed the accuracy of the prediction results as $Accuracy = \frac{CE}{|E|}$, where CE and $|E|$ represent the number of edges for which the sign is correctly predicted and the total number of edges in the network, respectively. Another evaluation metrics we are interested in is the prediction coverage: $Coverage = \frac{PE}{|E|}$, where PE is number of predictable edges. The coverage metric measures the degree to which the missing data can be predicted and covered relative to the whole dataset.

4.3 Results Analysis

In this study, 5 groups of meta paths based features have been used when implementing the proposed model:

$p_1 : U \xrightarrow{R} U \xrightarrow{-R} U$, $p_2 : U \xrightarrow{R} U \xrightarrow{B} C \xrightarrow{B^{-1}} U \xrightarrow{R^{-1}} U$,

$p_{3(4,5)} : U \xrightarrow{R} U \xrightarrow{B} C_{1(2,3)} \xrightarrow{B^{-1}} U \xrightarrow{R^{-1}} U$

In order to decrease the complexity, we treat the composite relations R as the adjacency relations, therefore, p_1 is degraded to the simplest path-based feature with length two; p_2 is a special type of cluster-based meta path where the whole dataset is considered as a super cluster; p_3, p_4 and p_5 are cluster-based meta paths of the first cluster layer, second cluster layer and third cluster layer, respectively. The reason for selecting the first three cluster layers can be found in Section 4.4. Note that each R can have two directions (inlink, outlink) and two signs (positive, negative), that is to say, each type of meta paths feature is composed of 16 sub-features. Thus we have $16 \times 5 = 80$ features in all.

In order to demonstrate the efficiency of our proposed cluster-based meta paths features, we compare the prediction accuracy and coverage metrics of the sign prediction models based on different features. SBP represents social balance based features which are proposed in [5], and AllMP denotes a combination of node-based meta paths features and cluster-based meta paths features.

From Figure 2 we can observe that, pure path-based features, e.g., SBP and NBMP, perform a little bit better than

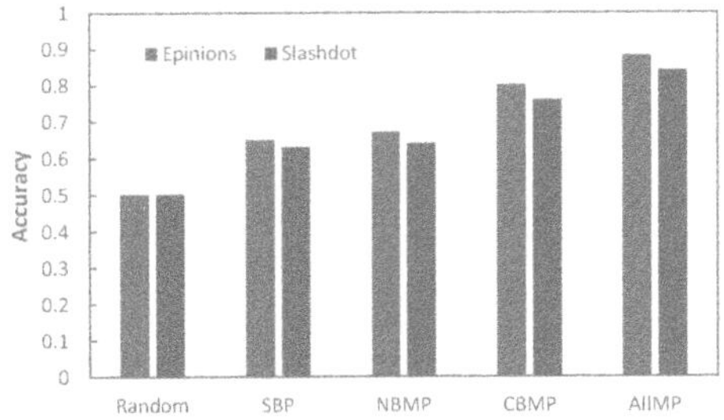

Figure 2: Accuracy of the predictor based on different meta paths features.

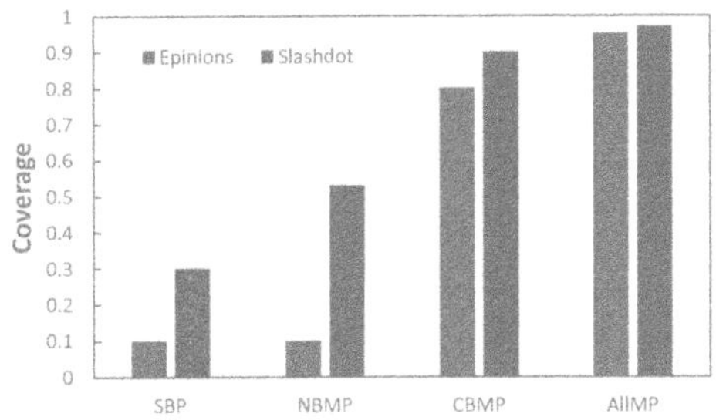

Figure 3: Coverage of the predictor based on different meta paths features.

random guessing, which is consistent with the results reported in [5]. In our consideration, this is mainly caused by the sparsity problem of networks. Not enough balanced triads or node-based paths can be found in such sparse datasets, which largely influence the accuracy of the prediction results. CBMP achieves better results than NBMP. The reason is that CBMP captures not only the local information, but also the global topological features by graph clustering as we have discussed in Section 3.3. In addition, consistent with our intuition, the best prediction accuracy is achieved by AllMP features, which verifies the fact that any one type of features cannot singly produce the best result.

Figure 3 shows the coverage. CBMP and AllMP yield better coverage rate than SBP and NBMP, which demonstrate that our proposed cluster-based meta paths features can effectively alleviate the sparsity problem in real networks.

4.4 Effect of hierarchical clustering layers

Figure 4 describes how the prediction accuracy is influenced by cluster-based meta paths of different cluster layers. When the clustering layer is 0, the whole dataset is considered as one big cluster, substantial meta paths can be found, which makes the final result inaccurate. When the clustering becomes fine-grained, the results get better. This can be explained as informative network structures are generated with the fine-grained clustering. As we can see that, the results are getting stable when the cluster layer reaches 3. This is because the sparsity problem is serious in much too fine-grained clusters, therefore, few cluster-based meta paths exist in these cluster layers.

5. CONCLUSION

In this paper, we have introduced the cluster-based meta paths based model which can effectively alleviate the sparsity problem in sign prediction tasks. By hierarchically clustering the input networks, newly generated clusters are added

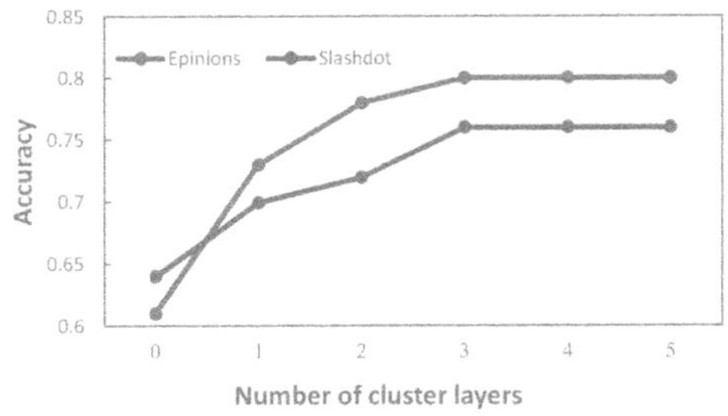

Figure 4: Accuracy of the predictor based on CBMP of different cluster layers.

to the networks and incorporated into cluster-based meta paths. The logistic regression classifier is employed to predict the hidden signs of links based on the proposed meta paths features of different cluster layers. Extensive comparative experiments demonstrate the efficiency of our model.

One of the main issues in defining meta paths is how to set the length of meta-paths, in this paper, we set the composite relations R as the adjacency relations for simplicity. In the future, we will find out how to set a proper length of cluster-based meta paths. Besides, it is interesting to see how the accuracy will be like if different kinds of clustering methods are applied.

6. ACKNOWLEDGMENTS

This research is funded by the National Natural Science Foundation of China under grants No.61232004 and No.61502189, and the Fundamental Research Funds for the Central Universities, HUST:2016YXMS088.

7. REFERENCES

[1] K.-Y. Chiang, N. Natarajan, A. Tewari, and I. S. Dhillon. Exploiting longer cycles for link prediction in signed networks. In *CIKM 2011*.

[2] D. Fogaras, B. Rácz, K. Csalogány, and T. Sarlós. Towards scaling fully personalized pagerank: Algorithms, lower bounds, and experiments. *Internet Mathematics*, 2(3):333–358, 2005.

[3] G. Jeh and J. Widom. Simrank: a measure of structural-context similarity. In *KDD 2002*.

[4] A. Lancichinetti and S. Fortunato. Community detection algorithms: a comparative analysis. *Physical review E*, 80(5):056117, 2009.

[5] J. Leskovec, D. Huttenlocher, and J. Kleinberg. Predicting positive and negative links in online social networks. In *WWW 2010*.

[6] D. Liben-Nowell and J. Kleinberg. The link-prediction problem for social networks. *JASIST*, 58(7):1019–1031, 2007.

[7] L. Lü and T. Zhou. Link prediction in complex networks: A survey. *Physica A*, 390(6):1150–1170, 2011.

[8] X. Ma, H. Lu, and Z. Gan. Implicit trust and distrust prediction for recommender systems. In *WISE 2015*, pages 185–199. Springer, 2015.

[9] T. Murata and S. Moriyasu. Link prediction based on structural properties of online social networks. *New Generation Computing*, 26(3):245–257, 2008.

[10] Y. Sun, J. Han, X. Yan, P. S. Yu, and T. Wu. Pathsim: Meta path-based top-k similarity search in heterogeneous information networks. *VLDB*, 2011.

[11] J. Tang, Y. Chang, C. Aggarwal, and H. Liu. A survey of signed network mining in social media. *arXiv preprint arXiv:1511.07569*, 2015.

Predicting Importance of Historical Persons using Wikipedia

Adam Jatowt, Daisuke Kawai and Katsumi Tanaka

Kyoto University
Yoshida-Honmachi, Sakyo-ku
606-8501 Kyoto, Japan
{adam, tanaka}@dl.kuis.kyoto-u.ac.jp
daisuke@gauge.scphys.kyoto-u.ac.jp

ABSTRACT
Wikipedia contains a lot of contemporary as well as history-related information, and given its vast coverage and richness, it can be used to rank entities in a variety of different ways. In this work, we are interested in utilizing Wikipedia for judging historical person's importance. Based on the two well-known lists of the most important people in the last millennium, we look closely into factors that determine significance of historical persons. We predict person's importance using six classifiers equipped with features derived from link structure, visit logs and article content.

Keywords
Wikipedia, historical analysis, person influence

1. INTRODUCTION
Wikipedia provides the wealth of information about the present as well as about the past. It contains numerous biographies of historical persons, descriptions of past events, histories of places and so on. It is not surprising that Wikipedia is an important source of history-related knowledge for many Web users. For example, the study of search tactics in the context of temporal information retrieval elucidated that users tend to primarily rely on Wikipedia when looking for past-related information [10].

Given its large coverage and reasonable quality [4], it is possible to utilize Wikipedia for automatically extracting or deriving history-related knowledge (e.g., [13,14,15]). In this work, we study the significance of persons described in Wikipedia articles. Studies of persons' importance and influence help to understand their role in history and allow comparing them with others. *Comparative history* [6] is especially relevant in this regard as a branch of historical studies concerned with contrastive exploration of events and entities from different times and places. Motivated by a broad objective of supporting and complementing historical studies by computational approaches, we propose to estimate person's importance using Wikipedia-derived features, especially, features based on the link structure of Wikipedia. In particular, we are interested in two research questions in this study:

Q1. *Can we predict historical person's importance using data derived from Wikipedia?*

Q2. *What are the features that make a person significant?*

We utilize two well-known lists of the most important persons in the past that were compiled by professionals [3,7]. Based on these data we investigate whether it is possible to successfully use Wikipedia for historical significance prediction and we look into the components that make a person important and memorable. Specifically, we study which features of Wikipedia articles about a historical person are predictive for considering the person as one of the top most influential individuals in the history using range of different classifiers.

2. RELATED WORK
Wikipedia with its huge amount of collectively created content remains an attractive data source for researchers who increasingly utilize it for numerous knowledge intensive tasks (e.g., [1,8,9,13,14,15]). In this work we focus on a particular subset of such researches, that is, on works devoted to the derivation of history-related knowledge such as comparative analysis of historical persons' significance. Eom *et al.* [2] analyzed the hyperlink networks of 24 Wikipedia language editions and automatically extracted the top 100 historical figures for each language edition. Thanks to this, they could investigate spatial, temporal, and gender distributions of persons with respect to their cultural origins. Skiena and Ward [13] proposed ranking historical people using *PageRank* algorithm applied on the hyperlink graph of Wikipedia, where nodes represent person-related articles. To complement their analysis they also looked into the occurrences of person names in Google Books dataset [11][1]. Takahashi *et al.* [14] measured the historical influence of persons in Wikipedia through the spatio-temporal analysis based on the modified PageRank algorithm [12].

Although, in this work we also predict the importance of persons, our methodology is different than ones used in [2,13,14]. Unlike those researches, we employ a classification approach based on the data compiled by professionals. In addition, we also try to understand which particular features are useful to determine the historical significance in the context of Wikipedia.

CIKM'16 , October 24-28, 2016, Indianapolis, IN, USA
© 2016 ACM. ISBN 978-1-4503-4073-1/16/10…$15.00
DOI: http://dx.doi.org/10.1145/2983323.2983871

[1] https://books.google.com/ngrams/datasets

3. DATASET CREATION

For creating the dataset to be used for feature construction we have downloaded the English Wikipedia dump provided by Wikimedia foundation[2]. DBpedia ontology datasets (PersonData ontology class) [1] were used for selecting Wikipedia articles about persons. We next extracted the core content of articles with BeautifulSoup library[3] excluding lists and common footers.

We then collected hyperlinks using *Yago2* [8] and merged redirecting nodes as well as we removed self-links by excluding links with identical origin and destination. Birth and death dates of persons were also obtained from Yago2. Every date was converted to the decade-level granularity for simplifying computations. In case when a person lacked her birth or death date, the missing date was substituted by the most probable birth or death decade following the procedure used in [9]. In particular, the most probable decade was estimated based on all the persons who were born or who died at the same decade as the one of the target person. Persons without both the dates recorded were necessarily removed. After retaining only people born in and after the 11th century, the final dataset contained 459,991 persons.

4. PREDICTING INFLUENCE

In this section we describe features used for classification and the motivation behind their choice.

4.1 Features

4.1.1 Time-Invariant Importance

A common way to measure person importance is to analyze how it is connected with others. We thus create a directed graph, $G(V,E)$, where V is the set of nodes (or Wikipedia articles) representing persons and E is the set of linking them edges. An edge e_{ij} ($e_{ij} \in E$) from a node v_i to a node v_j ($v_i, v_j \in V$) indicates the presence of a hypertext link in v_i that leads to v_j. We next estimate a node's prestige in G by applying a centrality measure based on the iterative score computation using the random walk theory [11]:

$$\boldsymbol{R} = (1-\alpha)\boldsymbol{M}\times\boldsymbol{R} + \alpha\left[\frac{1}{|V|}\right]_{|V|\times 1} \quad (1)$$

$\boldsymbol{R}$ is a vector containing node scores, $\boldsymbol{M}$ is an aperiodic transition matrix, while α is a decay factor equal to 0.15. Note that since G contains all the nodes (persons) in our dataset, the importance of each node is computed involving persons who lived at different time periods. Hence, we call this measure the *time-invariant person importance*.

4.1.2 Contemporary Importance

We hypothesize that important persons should not only be in general well-connected with other people, but, in many cases, they should have also high prestige within the "social networks" of their times. To measure such *contemporary importance* we simulate a historical social network in a unit time period t_l as a graph, $G^l(V^l,E^l)$. G^l is composed of the set of nodes V^l denoting Wikipedia articles about persons who lived at t_l, and of the edge set E^l including the hypertext links between these articles. Using the century granularity, t_l represents a single century. Eleven *temporal social networks* are then created for the entire time period of analysis, $T=(t_1,\ldots,t_l,\ldots,t_{11})$. Note that a person v_i with its lifespan denoted by $\tau(v_i)$ is assigned to a given century t_l if the midpoint of her life is contained in this century ($2|\tau(v_i) \cap t_l| > |\tau(v_i)|$). In other words, a person belongs to the social network of a given century t_l if the larger part of her life was at t_l.

We compute the node importance using Eq. 1 calculated this time however on each historical social network, G^l. Note that the computed score indicates how prominent a person was among the people of her century, while the score described in Sec. 4.1.1 measures person's prestige among all the people in the dataset, irrespectively of time.

To ensure the across-century comparability, the score of each node in a given century is normalized by dividing it by the total sum of the scores of all the people assigned to that century.

4.1.3 Current Importance

Many influential historical persons are still remembered and are often referred to due to their legacy and perceived significance. We thus quantify to what extent a given historical person is connected with the present times. In particular, following [9], we approximate such connection by estimating the connectivity of historical persons with the "present" persons. As present persons we consider people who were alive during any year included in the period Θ = [1970s, 2000s]. Note that this period can be arbitrarily extended or shortened to represent the notion of the present time.

The past-to-present connectivity measure we want to compute should reflect the closeness of nodes denoting historical persons to the nodes which correspond to the present persons. To compute it, we bias the random walk on G using the static score distribution vector $\boldsymbol{d}$ (see Eq. 2) in a similar way to the one employed in *TrustRank* [5] algorithm used for filtering spam Web pages. We call it the *current importance of persons*.

$$\boldsymbol{R} = (1-\alpha)\boldsymbol{M}\times\boldsymbol{R} + \alpha\boldsymbol{d}$$
$$\boldsymbol{d} = \begin{cases} 1/|d| & if\ \tau(v_i)\cap\Theta \neq \emptyset \\ 0 & if\ \tau(v_i)\cap\Theta = \emptyset \end{cases} \quad (2)$$

4.1.4 Popularity

We consider the view frequency of an article as an effective measure of attention and interest of public in the person described by this article. It is reasonable to assume that many important historical persons are quite well-known and the information on them is often checked and referred to. To quantify the popularity of past persons, we utilize access logs made available by the Wikipedia Foundation[4]. Specifically, we use the number of accesses to all the Wikipedia articles within our dataset that took place during 5 years from January 2009 to December 2013.

4.1.5 Consistency of Popularity

The fact that a person-related article has been viewed continuously with a stable frequency, or, rather, some rare events (e.g., anniversaries, commemorations) triggered sudden rises of its popularity over brief time periods could help to tell if a person is "continuously important" or not. We then measure the consistency of person's popularity using the article view distribution:

$$C(v_i) = -\sum_{j=1}^{m} P_j(v_i)logP_j(v_i) \quad (3)$$

$C(v_i)$ is the entropy of view distribution where $P_j(v_i)$ denotes the normalized access count of an article v_i during j-th month based on the total access data of the article from Jan. 2009 to Dec. 2013.

[2] https://dumps.wikimedia.org/enwiki

[3] https://pypi.python.org/pypi/beautifulsoup4

[4] https://dumps.wikimedia.org/other/pagecounts-raw/

4.1.6 Content Features

We next include few simple features based on articles and their content.

4.1.6.1 Article Length

We hypothesize that articles about significant persons should have on average more content than ones on less significant individuals. Indeed, the content of articles on salient persons often includes persons' detailed biographies, circumstances of their lives, descriptions of achievements, contributions and relations to other people or to contemporary events, as based on multiple studies by historians, and other professionals. We then use the length of the article content measured in bytes as another feature.

4.1.6.2 In-degree

The number of links pointing to a person is also considered as a simple measure of node importance.

4.1.6.3 Out-degree

Correspondingly, it is reasonable to assume that important persons could have many outgoing links to other persons, similarly to the above assumption regarding the content's length. We use then both the in- and out-degrees as additional classification features.

4.1.7 Distance from Present

We suspect a potential effect of time such as "*the longer time ago a person lived, the more probable is that she or he is considered influential*". This could be supported by the reasoning that the person's importance could arise due to its memory being cherished and, perhaps, also gradually strengthened over long time (e.g., few centuries). To capture the influence of time, we then calculate the number of decades that passed from the decade representing the mid-life point of a person until now.

4.2 Classification Setup

We make use of the two well-known lists of the 100 most influential persons in history: one by M.H. Hart and one compiled by the Life magazine [3]. The former was originally constructed in 1992 forming the basis of the book "*The 100: A Ranking of the Most Influential Persons in History*" [7] which was translated into 15 languages and sold in over half a million copies. The list by the Life magazine was created in 1988 and is available online[5]. After removing persons born before the 11th century we had 55 persons for the Hart's list and 80 for the Life list.

We employ several classifiers using Scikit-learn[6] library with 10-fold cross validation for determining whether a given person belongs or not to the aforementioned lists of important persons. All the classification features listed in Sec. 4.1 have been standardized by subtracting their means and dividing by their standard deviations.

To create instances of the negative class we decided not to select persons randomly as it would overestimate the classification results due to the inherent bias towards more recent decades. That is, randomly selected persons would likely be the ones from the last two centuries due to the present-related bias of the distribution of person-related articles in Wikipedia [9,13,14]. In addition, the random selection would result in picking many less famous persons due to the power low characteristics of Wikipedia articles (e.g., *In-degree*, *Time-Invariant Importance*) making then the classification task relatively easy. Instead, we have selected instances of the negative class by employing the following procedure. For each classification feature (except for the *Distance from Present*) we have selected from each century 100 persons having the top value of this feature, making sure they are not present in either of the above-mentioned lists of the important historical persons. We then removed duplicate persons. The resulting set contains 3,553 people who are likely to be somehow important and famous due to the high values of at least one of their classification features. Note that this set is also balanced over time. We then randomly selected the negative instances for training and testing, repeating each time during the 10-fold cross validation procedure.

5. Results

Table 1 presents the classification results using different classifiers: SVM [15] with linear kernel (SVM Lin.), SVM with RBF kernel (SVM RBF), Naïve Bayes (NB), Nearest Neighbors (NN), Decision Tree (Dec. Tree) and Random Forrest (Ran. Forr.). We can see that, in general, the prediction task is quite successful and it is possible to determine with a reasonably good precision whether a person is or is not in the lists of top influential people. It is also easier to successfully classify instances based on the Life's than based on the Hart's list (likely, due to more persons in the former). An additional observation is that Decision Tree performs best on the later, while the Nearest Neighbors method is the top-performing one on the former.

In Tables 2-3 we show the classification results obtained by using SVM with linear kernel when a given feature is used alone. Additionally, in Tables 4-5 we include the results when a given feature is removed. Due to space limitation we could not show the results by all the classifiers, and, instead, we chose ones given by SVM equipped with linear kernel for its popularity and the frequent usage in text classification research.

Looking at the results we can observe that, somewhat unsurprisingly, *Popularity* used alone is quite a strong predictor of significance (F_1-score of 0.727 and 0.731 for the Hart's and Life's list, respectively). However, it is not sufficient as evidenced by contrasting the results of Tables 2 and 3 with the overall performance shown in Table 1. The entropy of the view distribution (*Consistency of Popularity*) has however much smaller impact (F_1-score of 0.286 and 0.558, respectively), which means that the consistency of the access over time matters less than the total sum of views. Interestingly, the ablation of this feature results in the largest performance drop for the Life list. Also, notably, just only the knowledge of the *Article Length* or *Out-degree* helps to classify persons from the Hart's list with reasonably good success.

When it comes to the link-related metrics such as *Time-Invariant, Contemporary* and *Current Importance* we can observe that *Current Importance* achieves on average better results than the other two link structure dependent measures. This suggests that the connectivity with the present may be a stronger discriminative signal for ranking historical persons than the overall connectivity measure within the whole social graph (*Time-Invariant Importance*) or the one within the people living at the same century (*Contemporary Importance*). The last feature seems to perform worse than the other two which implies that some important historical persons may not be well-known or "connected" within their times. Alternatively, perhaps, our memory and knowledge of their lives might be insufficient.

Overall, the results indicate that to a good extent it is possible to recreate professional judgments by employing automatic means based only on the Wikipedia-derived data. We also notice that using *Time-Invariant Importance* alone, as suggested in the prior literature, is generally insufficient. Finally, while many

[5]http://www.tostepharmd.net/hissoc/top100people.html

[6]http://scikit-learn.org/stable/index.html

observations are consistent for both the used lists, still some results are different (e.g., the effect of *Article Length* and *Distance from Present*) suggesting that it is not easy to definitely reject or accept some of the features.

Table 1 Classification results of precision (P), recall (R) and F1-score (F_1) using the Hart's (H) and Life's (L) lists.

Classifier	P (H)	R (H)	F_1 (H)	P (L)	R (L)	F_1(L)
SVM Lin.	*0.816*	*0.804*	*0.803*	*0.879*	*0.863*	*0.860*
SVM RBF	0.714	0.688	0.685	0.850	0.798	0.788
NB	0.735	0.693	0.683	0.743	0.676	0.653
NN	0.804	0.789	0.784	**0.932**	**0.931**	**0.931**
Dec. Tree	**0.818**	**0.813**	**0.815**	0.901	0.897	0.898
Ran. Forr.	0.810	0.799	0.801	0.915	0.912	0.912

Table 2 Classification results on the Hart's list with SVM (linear kernel) for each feature used alone.

Feature used	Precision	Recall	F_1
Time-Invariant Importance	0.593	0.520	0.437
Current Importance	0.635	0.543	0.476
Contemporary Importance	0.361	0.457	0.300
Article length	0.749	0.710	0.701
In-degree	0.714	0.608	0.572
Out-degree	0.702	0.658	0.644
Popularity	**0.802**	**0.741**	**0.727**
Consistency of Popularity	0.237	0.449	0.286
Dist. from Present	0.648	0.635	0.629

Table 3 Classification results on the Life's list with SVM (linear kernel) for each feature used alone.

Feature used	Precision	Recall	F_1
Time-Invariant Importance	0.685	0.602	0.558
Current Importance	0.738	0.604	0.539
Contemporary Importance	0.531	0.484	0.336
Article length	0.633	0.551	0.489
In-degree	0.731	0.661	0.636
Out-degree	0.550	0.512	0.440
Popularity	**0.812**	**0.744**	**0.731**
Consistency of Popularity	0.685	0.602	0.558
Dist. from Present	0.669	0.646	0.637

Table 4 Classification results on the Hart's list using SVM (linear kernel) with a given feature ablated.

Feature removed	Precision	Recall	F_1
Time-Invariant Importance	0.821	0.812	0.812
Current Importance	0.817	0.806	0.806
Contemporary Importance	0.835	0.824	0.825
Article length	0.788	0.764	0.763
In-degree	0.795	0.781	0.781
Out-degree	0.767	0.726	**0.718**
Popularity	**0.741**	**0.724**	0.724
Consistency of Popularity	0.816	0.803	0.804
Dist. from Present	0.830	0.819	0.818

Table 5 Classification results on the Life's list using SVM (linear kernel) with a given feature ablated.

Feature removed	Precision	Recall	F_1
Time-Invariant Importance	0.882	0.867	0.864
Current Importance	0.878	0.861	0.857
Contemporary Importance	0.881	0.865	0.862
Article length	0.875	0.858	0.856
In-degree	0.872	0.849	0.845
Out-degree	0.875	0.859	0.855
Popularity	0.847	0.830	0.825
Consistency of Popularity	**0.844**	**0.814**	**0.809**
Dist. from Present	0.857	0.822	0.817

6. CONCLUSIONS & FUTURE WORK

Data mining approaches for historical studies have recently gained much interest. In this paper we harness Wikipedia for measuring historical person's significance. In particular, we investigate methods for across-time comparison of personal importance. Based on the two popular lists of significant persons compiled by professionals we study to what extent it is possible to determine person's importance and what are its decisive factors.

In future, we plan to use textual features of articles and include different data sources than Wikipedia. We also want to focus on other entities besides persons such as events or places and on measuring influence with richer set of constraints. The latter could involve (a) **topics** such as science, literature, art (e.g., the most important persons in physics), (b) **spatial areas** such as Asia, Germany, Paris (e.g., the most important persons in Europe) and (c) **time frames** such as middle ages, 1980s, 2013 (e.g., the most important persons in the 19th century), as well as **their combinations** (e.g., the most important persons in physics in Europe in the 19th century).

7. ACKNOWLEDGMENTS

This research was supported in part by MEXT Grants-in-Aid for Scientific Research (15K12158, 15H01718) and by the Japan Science and Technology Agency (JST) research promotion program Presto/Sakigake: "Analyzing Collective Memory and Developing Methods for Knowledge Extraction from Historical Documents".

8. REFERENCES

[1] S. Auer, C. Bizer, G. Kobilarov, J. Lehmann, R. Cyganiak, and Z. Ives. DBpedia: A Nucleus for a Web of Open Data. In *ISWC'07/ASWC'07*, Springer, 722–735, 2007

[2] Y.-H. Eom, P. Aragón, D. Laniado, A. Kaltenbrunner, S. Vigna, D. L. Shepelyansky. Interactions of Cultures and Top People of Wikipedia from Ranking of 24 Language Editions, *PLoS ONE* 10(3), 2014

[3] R. Friedman. *The Life Millennium: The 100 Most Important Events and People of the Past 1000 Years*, Bulfinch P., 1998

[4] J. Giles. Internet Encyclopaedias Go Head to Head, *Nature* 438, 900-901, 2005

[5] Z. Gyöngyi, H. Garcia-Molina, and J. Pedersen. Combating Web Spam with Trustrank. In *VLDB2004*, 576-587

[6] C. J. Halperin *et al.* Comparative History in Theory and Practice: A discussion. *The American Historical Review*, 87(1):123–143, 1982

[7] M. H. Hart. *The 100: A Ranking of the Most Influential Persons in History*. Citadel; Revised edition (June 1, 2000)

[8] J. Hoffart *et al.* YAGO2: Exploring and Querying World Knowledge in Time, Space, Context, and Many Languages. In *WWW '11*, 229-232

[9] A. Jatowt, D. Kawai, K. Tanaka: Digital History Meets Wikipedia: Analyzing Historical Persons in Wikipedia. In *JCDL2016*, 17-26

[10] H. Joho, A. Jatowt and R. Blanco. Temporal Information Searching Behaviour and Strategies. *Inf. Process. Manag.* 51(6): 834-850, 2015

[11] J.-B. Michel *et al.* Quantitative Analysis of Culture Using Millions of Digitized Books. *Science*, 331(6014), 176-182, 2011

[12] L. Page, S. Brin, R. Motwani, and T. Winograd. The PageRank Citation Ranking: Bringing Order to the Web. *Technical Report, Stanford University*, January 29, 1998

[13] S. Skiena and C. B. Ward. *Who's Bigger, Where Historical Figures Really Rank*. Cambridge University Press, 2014

[14] Y. Takahashi, H. Ohshima, M. Yamamoto, H. Iwasaki, S. Oyama, and K. Tanaka. Evaluating Significance of Historical Entities based on Tempo-spatial Impacts Analysis using Wikipedia Link Structure. In *HT '11*. ACM, New York, NY, USA, 83-92

[15] S. Whiting, J.M. Jose and O. Alonso. Wikipedia as a Time Machine. In *TempWeb'14 Workshop at WWW2014*, 857-861

[16] V. Vapnik. *The Nature of Statistical Learning Theory*, Springer-Verlag, 1995

Noise-Contrastive Estimation for Answer Selection with Deep Neural Networks

Jinfeng Rao[1], Hua He[1], and Jimmy Lin[2]

[1] Department of Computer Science, University of Maryland, College Park
[2] David R. Cheriton School of Computer Science, University of Waterloo

jinfeng@cs.umd.edu, huah@umd.edu, jimmylin@uwaterloo.ca

ABSTRACT

We study answer selection for question answering, in which given a question and a set of candidate answer sentences, the goal is to identify the subset that contains the answer. Unlike previous work which treats this task as a straightforward *pointwise* classification problem, we model this problem as a ranking task and propose a *pairwise* ranking approach that can directly exploit existing pointwise neural network models as base components. We extend the Noise-Contrastive Estimation approach with a triplet ranking loss function to exploit interactions in triplet inputs over the question paired with positive and negative examples. Experiments on TrecQA and WikiQA datasets show that our approach achieves state-of-the-art effectiveness without the need for external knowledge sources or feature engineering.

1. INTRODUCTION

Answer selection is an important component of an overall question answering system: given a question q and a candidate set of sentences $\{c_1, c_2, \ldots c_n\}$, the task is to identify sentences that contain the answer. In a standard pipeline architecture [11], answer selection is applied to the output of a module that performs textual retrieval or lightweight term-based matching. Selected sentences can then be directly presented to users or serve as input to subsequent stages that identify "exact" answers [12].

Although answer selection is formally considered a *pointwise* classification problem, in reality candidate sentences are ranked in decreasing probability of containing the answer, and results are evaluated using similarity measurement metrics on ranked lists. The nature of the task inspired us to formalize it as a ranking problem.

In this work, we develop a novel *pairwise* ranking approach to learn the relative order of answer pairs. Given a question sentence, our approach takes a pair of candidate answer sentences as input and learns to predict which answer is more relevant to the question. We use Noise-Contrastive Estimation to learn joint representations of the triplet input (question, positive answer, negative answer) directly, then stack a triplet ranking loss function on top to learn nonlinear feature correlations from the joint representations. The objective is to minimize the total number of inversions in the rankings.

Our approach is flexible in that it can take advantage of existing pointwise models as base components. We use two recent pointwise neural networks that perform either sentence-level [3] or word-level modeling [4], both of which are competitive in various text processing tasks. We demonstrate the effectiveness of our approach against competitive pointwise baselines [4, 3, 20, 22, 10, 6, 16, 9] for the answer selection task. We show that joint representation learning from triplets comprising the question and both positive and negative answers is superior than learning a pointwise representation on (question, positive answer) pairs. Experiments on both TrecQA and WikiQA datasets show that our approach achieves state-of-the-art effectiveness without using sparse features, syntactic parsers, or external knowledge sources like WordNet.

CIKM'16 , October 24 - 28, 2016, Indianapolis, IN, USA

ISBN 978-1-4503-4073-1/16/10...$15.00

DOI: http://dx.doi.org/10.1145/2983323.2983872

2. RELATED WORK

There has been much recent work on applying neural networks to answer selection [3, 4, 5, 22, 14, 13, 10]. Previous work has been based on pointwise neural network models. For example, He et al. [3] developed a multi-perspective convolutional neural network model that incorporates fine-grained sentence representations. He and Lin [4] developed a 19-layer deep convolutional neural network model and a similarity focus layer to encourage comparisons between word contexts across sentences. Other researchers [5, 21] have also adopted attention mechanisms for convolutional neural networks to better model interactions between input sentences. Another research direction is the use of extra sparse features (e.g., BM25) [10, 14].

In contrast to previous work, we propose a pairwise ranking approach that takes advantage of Noise-Contrastive Estimation (NCE) for model training. The basic idea behind NCE is that a good model should be able to discriminate a good sample from its neighboring bad samples. Given pairs of positive and negative samples, the model should learn differentiable representations to distinguish positive and negative samples. This idea has been studied for word representation learning [7].

3. MODEL ARCHITECTURE

We show the overall architecture of our pairwise ranking model in Figure 1, consisting of two major components.

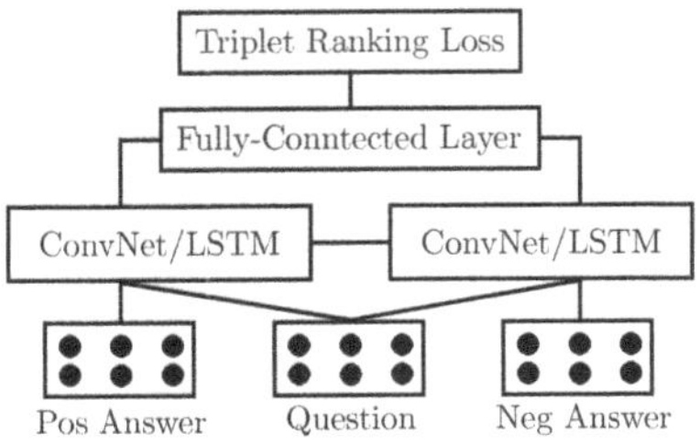

Figure 1: Architecture of our pairwise ranking model, which is trained on triplets comprised of (question, positive answer, negative answer).

The base component is comprised of two pointwise neural network models, each of which takes a pair of (question, answer) sentences and produces a similarity score to represent the semantic distance of the pair. Our pairwise ranking model is expected to output a larger similarity score given the positive pair and a smaller score given the negative pair. On top, we evaluate a triplet ranking loss function (see below) to learn the joint representation of answer pairs.

Our model has a "Siamese" structure [2], which consists of two parallel pointwise models, each processing a pair of question and answer sentences. Parameters of the two base models are shared during training. In testing, we take one of the two base models to produce the feature representation of a (question, answer) pair, and then feed those features into the fully-connected layer for computing a relevance score. Although many previous pointwise models also use the "Siamese" structure, there are important differences: each base component of a typical pointwise model only takes one input sentence, whereas each base component of our pairwise model takes a (question, answer) pair as input and explores features interactions between the sentence pairs.

In this work we use existing published work [3, 4] as the base pointwise models; these have achieved state-of-the-art effectiveness on multiple tasks, i.e., paraphrase identification, semantic textual similarity measurements, and question answering. More importantly, these two models represent different approaches to model design. He et al. [3] focus on *sentence-level* modeling, which tries to capture semantic similarities from multiple perspectives by applying different types of similarity metrics, convolutional filters, poolings, and window sizes on input sentences. This model also incorporates a structured similarity layer over sentence representations for fine-grained comparisons. He and Lin [4] propose a *word-level* model and develop a pairwise word interaction layer to explicitly identify word pairs across input sentences, a similarity focus layer to guide model attention onto important word pairs, and a 19-layer deep ConvNet for classification. Due to limited space, we elide technical details of both and refer readers to the original papers.

Experimental results in Section 4 show that our pairwise ranking approach, when paired with each as the base component, is able to make further effectiveness improvements for both types of models.

3.1 Triplet Ranking Loss Function

Both word-level and sentence-level base components take input sentence pairs of (question, answer) and produce a score through a representation function $f(\cdot)$. This score captures how semantically similar the two input sentences are. Our goal is to learn a representation function $f(\cdot)$ such that given some question q, positive pairs (q, p^+) are assigned larger similarity scores than negative pairs (q, p^-):

$$f(q, p^+) > f(q, p^-), \forall q, p^+, p^-$$

where q, p^+, p^- denote the question, positive answer, and negative answer, respectively. We then use a triplet ranking loss, which minimizes the distance between the question q and a positive answer p^+, and maximizes the distance between the q and a negative answer p^-, summed over positive pairs (q, p^+) and the corresponding negative pool $p^- \in N(q, p^+)$:

$$\min_W \sum_{(q,p^+)} \sum_{p^- \in N} max(0, 1 - (f(q, p^+) - f(q, p^-)) + \lambda \|W\|^2$$

where λ is a regularization parameter, and W is the parameters of neural network model $f(\cdot)$.

3.2 Sampling Strategy

To counter overfitting, it is common practice to train a model with a large variety of samples. However, due to its pairwise nature, our pairwise ranking model requires $O(N^2)$ time complexity to enumerate all pairs, which is computationally impractical. Therefore, it is essential to balance the coverage of training samples and limit computational resources. We use three negative sampling strategies to select the most informative negative samples.

Random Sampling. We randomly select a number of negative samples for each positive answer.

Max Sampling. We select the most difficult negative samples. In each epoch, we compute the similarities between all (p^+, p^-) pairs using the trained model from the previous training epoch. Then we select the negative answers by maximizing their similarities to the positive answer:

$$maxNeg^i(p^-) = \arg\max_{p^-} sim(f^{i-1}(q, p^+), f^{i-1}(q, p^-))$$

where $maxNeg^i(p^-)$ is the selected negative sample in epoch i, $f^{i-1}(\cdot, \cdot)$ is the trained model in epoch $i-1$, and sim is the *cosine* distance. In the first epoch, we randomly select negative samples.

Mix Sampling. We take advantages of both random sampling and max sampling by selecting half of the samples from each strategy.

4. EXPERIMENTAL SETUP

We evaluated our ranking model on two question answering datasets. Relevant statistics are shown in Table 1.

TrecQA. The TrecQA dataset [15] is a widely-used benchmark for question answering, collected from the TREC Question Answering tracks and packaged by Yao et al. [19]. In the literature [20, 22, 10, 6, 16, 9], we observe two versions of TrecQA: both have the same training set but their development and test sets differ due to different pre-processing.

Previous work [22, 10, 6, 4] used the version that has 82 questions in the development set and 100 questions in the test set (what we call "Raw TrecQA"). However, there exists questions that have no answer sentences.[1] More recent work [16, 9] further cleaned the dataset by removing

[1]MAP and MRR scores computed with the official `trec_eval` scorer do not change if questions with empty answer sets are removed, since the scorer will ignore questions with empty answer set.

Dataset	Split	#Questions	#Pairs	%PosRate
Raw TrecQA	TRAIN	1229	53417	12.0
	DEV	82	1148	19.3
	TEST	100	1517	18.7
Clean TrecQA	DEV	65	1117	18.4
	TEST	68	1442	17.2
WikiQA	TRAIN	873	8672	12.0
	DEV	126	1130	12.4
	TEST	243	2351	12.5

Table 1: Statistics of TrecQA and WikiQA datasets

questions that have only positive/negative answers or no answers, resulting in only 65 questions in the development set and 68 questions in the test set (what we call "Clean TrecQA"). We evaluated our model on both versions for a fair comparison against previous work, and we show that the MAP/MRR scores reported on both TrecQA versions are *not* comparable.

WikiQA. The open domain question-answering WikiQA data was collected from Bing query logs [18]. For each question, the authors selected Wikipedia pages and used sentences in the summary paragraph as candidates, which were then annotated on a crowdsourcing platform. We follow the same pre-processing steps as Yang et al. [18], where questions with no correct candidate answers are excluded and answer sentences are truncated to 40 tokens.

We conducted experiments with two base components, each with its own settings. We used the GloVe word embeddings [8] for the sentence-level model [3] and PARAGRAM-PHRASE word embeddings [17] for the word-level model [4]. Both word embeddings have 300 dimensions. Words not found in the vocabulary were initialized randomly with values uniformly sampled from $[-.05, .05]$. We did not update word embeddings in all experiments. SGD with a learning rate of 10^{-3} for the sentence-level base component and RMSPROP with a learning rate of 10^{-4} for the word-level base component were used for training. We chose these different word embeddings and optimizers in order to keep experimental settings the same as in previous work [3, 4]. We used the tanh function as the non-linear activation function and a dropout layer ($p = 0.5$) in the fully-connected layer, plus parameter regularization ($\lambda = 10^{-4}$). Our code and data are available online.[2]

Effectiveness is measured in terms of Mean Average Precision (MAP) and Mean Reciprocal Rank (MRR). In all experiments, we selected training models that obtain the best MRR scores on the development set for testing.

5. RESULTS

The results of our experiments on the three different test sets are shown in Table 2. SentLevel denotes the multi-perspective model [3] and WordLevel denotes the pairwise word interaction model [4]. The rows with PairwiseRank show our pairwise ranking approach with the use of the two different base components (either the WordLevel or SentLevel model). We compare our results to others reported in the literature on an ACL wiki site [1].

Our best results for all the three datasets in Table 2 were obtained from max sampling. On both the raw and clean

[2]https://github.com/Jeffyrao/pairwise-neural-network

Reference	MAP	MRR
Wang et al. [14] s(2015)	0.713	0.791
Miao et al. [6] (2015)	0.734	0.812
Severyn et al. [10] (2015)	0.746	0.808
SentLevel [3] (2015)	0.762	0.830
WordLevel [4] (2016)	0.755	0.825
PairwiseRank+SentLevel	**0.780**	**0.834**
PairwiseRank+WordLevel	0.764	0.827

(a) Raw TrecQA

Reference	MAP	MRR
Santos et al. [9] (2016)	0.753	0.851
Wang et al. [16] (2016)	0.771	0.845
SentLevel [3] (2015)	0.777	0.836
WordLevel [4] (2016)	0.738	0.827
PairwiseRank+SentLevel	**0.801**	**0.877**
PairwiseRank+WordLevel	0.762	0.854

(b) Clean TrecQA

Reference	MAP	MRR
Miao et al. [6] (2015)	0.689	0.707
Santos et al. [9] (2016)	0.689	0.696
Wang et al. [16] (2016)	0.706	0.723
SentLevel [3] (2015)	0.693	0.709
WordLevel [4] (2016)	**0.709**	**0.723**
PairwiseRank+SentLevel	0.701	0.718
PairwiseRank+WordLevel	0.693	0.710

(c) WikiQA

Table 2: Results on TrecQA and WikiQA.

versions of the TrecQA data, our PairwiseRank+SentLevel model achieves MAP and MRR scores that are among the best reported in the literature. The models achieve better effectiveness on clean TrecQA than on raw TrecQA. This is because the clean version removes questions with only negative answers: these questions will always have zero values when computing MAP and MRR scores, thereby degrading the overall effectiveness. Thus, numbers reported on raw and clean TrecQA data should not be compared.

In terms of the comparison between the original models and our pairwise ranking models, the two original base models (WordLevel and SentLevel) achieve competitive effectiveness, while our pairwise ranking models (PairwiseRank +SentLevel/WordLevel) can still improve on them in most cases. On the clean TrecQA data, this improvement is quite large. On the WikiQA data, the WordLevel model remains the best, but PairwiseRank+SentLevel improves over the base SentLevel model, bringing its effectiveness up to being on par with our best model.

Overall, these empirical results show that the joint representations learned from the triplet inputs are effective, and that our pairwise ranking approach is able to exploit such joint information.

We also studied the effects of the three different sampling strategies. Figures 2 and 3 show the effectiveness of different sampling strategies with the PairwiseRank+SentLevel and PairwiseRank+WordLevel models. We set the number of negative samples to six and eight. We only show the MAP figures here due to space limitations, but the patterns for MRR scores are generally similar. For the PairwiseRank+SentLevel and PairwiseRank+WordLevel mod-

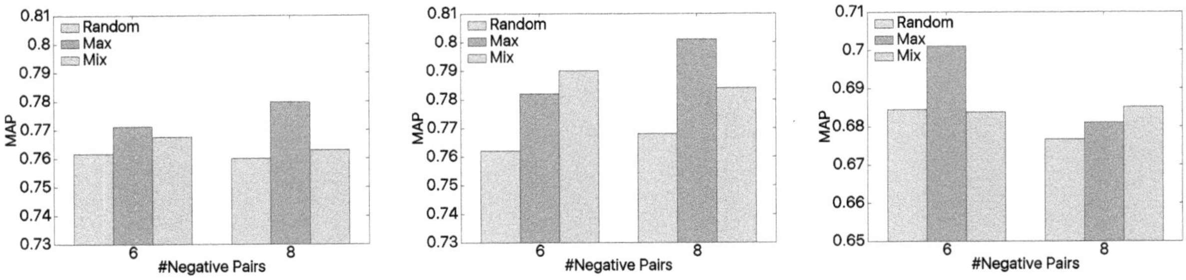

(a) Raw TrecQA (b) Clean TrecQA (c) WikiQA

Figure 2: Comparison of sampling strategies for PairwiseRank+SentLevel.

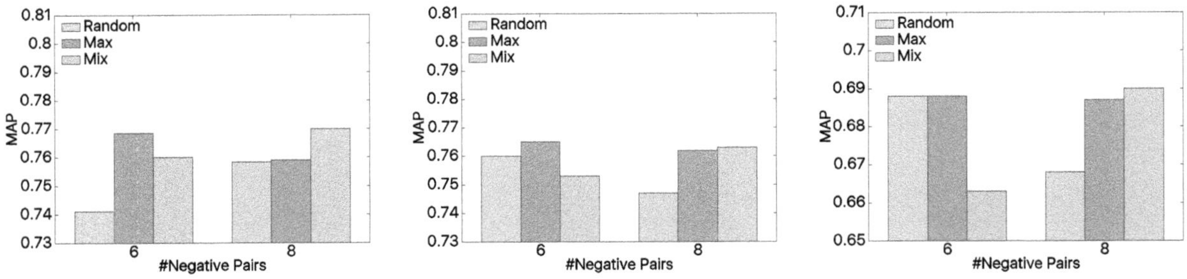

(a) Raw TrecQA (b) Clean TrecQA (c) WikiQA

Figure 3: Comparison of sampling strategies for PairwiseRank+WordLevel.

els, max and mix sampling consistently outperforms random sampling. In most settings, max sampling obtains the best performance. This shows that more "challenging" negative training samples are beneficial for training a better model in our pairwise ranking approach.

6. CONCLUSION

In this work, we proposed and evaluated a novel contrastive learning approach to answer selection that can use existing deep neural network models as plug-in components. Experiments show that our contrastive learning approach can improve upon the component models under competitive settings on standard QA datasets. We present three strategies for selecting negative samples and demonstrate the effectiveness of selecting the most "difficult" training examples to distinguish between good and bad answers.

Acknowledgments. This work was supported by the U.S. National Science Foundation (NSF) under IIS-1218043 and CNS-1405688 and the Natural Sciences and Engineering Research Council of Canada (NSERC). Any opinions, findings, conclusions, or recommendations expressed are solely those of the authors.

7. REFERENCES

[1] ACL. Question answering (state of the art), http://aclweb.org/aclwiki/index.php?title=Question_Answering_(State_of_the_art), accessed Aug., 18, 2016.
[2] J. Bromley, J. W. Bentz, L. Bottou, I. Guyon, Y. LeCun, C. Moore, E. Säckinger, and R. Shah. Signature verification using a "siamese" time delay neural network. *IJPRAI*, 1993.
[3] H. He, K. Gimpel, and J. Lin. Multi-perspective sentence similarity modeling with convolutional neural networks. *EMNLP*, 2015.
[4] H. He and J. Lin. Pairwise word interaction modeling with deep neural networks for semantic similarity measurement. *NAACL*, 2016.
[5] H. He, J. Wieting, K. Gimpel, J. Rao, and J. Lin. UMD-TTIC-UW at SemEval-2016 task 1: Attention-based multi-perspective convolutional neural networks for textual similarity measurement. *SemEval*, 2016.
[6] Y. Miao, L. Yu, and P. Blunsom. Neural variational inference for text processing. *arXiv:1511.06038*, 2015.
[7] T. Mikolov and J. Dean. Distributed representations of words and phrases and their compositionality. *NIPS*, 2013.
[8] J. Pennington, R. Socher, and C. D. Manning. GloVe: Global vectors for word representation. *EMNLP*, 2014.
[9] C. d. Santos, M. Tan, B. Xiang, and B. Zhou. Attentive pooling networks. *arXiv:1602.03609*, 2016.
[10] A. Severyn and A. Moschitti. Learning to rank short text pairs with convolutional deep neural networks. *SIGIR*, 2015.
[11] S. Tellex, B. Katz, J. Lin, G. Marton, and A. Fernandes. Quantitative evaluation of passage retrieval algorithms for question answering. *SIGIR*, 2003.
[12] E. M. Voorhees. Overview of the TREC 2002 question answering track. *TREC*, 2002.
[13] D. Wang and E. Nyberg. CMU OAQA at TREC 2015 LiveQA: Discovering the right answer with clues. *TREC*, 2015.
[14] D. Wang and E. Nyberg. A long short-term memory model for answer sentence selection in question answering. *ACL*, 2015.
[15] M. Wang, N. A. Smith, and T. Mitamura. What is the Jeopardy model? A quasi-synchronous grammar for QA. *EMNLP-CoNLL*, 2007.
[16] Z. Wang, H. Mi, and A. Ittycheriah. Sentence similarity learning by lexical decomposition and composition. *arXiv:1602.07019*, 2016.
[17] J. Wieting, M. Bansal, K. Gimpel, and K. Livescu. Towards universal paraphrastic sentence embeddings. *ICLR*, 2016.
[18] Y. Yang, W.-t. Yih, and C. Meek. WikiQA: A challenge dataset for open-domain question answering. *EMNLP*, 2015.
[19] X. Yao, B. Van Durme, C. Callison-Burch, and P. Clark. Answer extraction as sequence tagging with tree edit distance. *HLT-NAACL*, 2013.
[20] W.-t. Yih, M.-W. Chang, C. Meek, and A. Pastusiak. Question answering using enhanced lexical semantic models. *ACL*, 2013.
[21] W. Yin, H. Schütze, B. Xiang, and B. Zhou. ABCNN: Attention-based convolutional neural network for modeling sentence pairs. *arXiv:1512.05193*, 2015.
[22] L. Yu, K. M. Hermann, P. Blunsom, and S. Pulman. Deep learning for answer sentence selection. *NIPS deep learning workshop*, 2014.

Global and Local Influence-based Social Recommendation

Qinzhe Zhang*, Jia Wu*, Hong Yang§, Weixue Lu†, Guodong Long*, Chengqi Zhang*
* Centre for Quantum Computation and Intelligent Systems (QCIS),
University of Technology Sydney, NSW 2007, Australia
§ MathWorks, Beijing, 100190, China
† Academy of Mathematics and Systems Science,
Chinese Academy of Sciences, Beijing, 100090, China
qinzhe.zhang@student.uts.edu.au; jia.wu@uts.edu.au; hong.yang@mathworks.cn;
wxlu@amss.ac.cn; guodong.long@uts.edu.au; chengqi.zhang@uts.edu.au

ABSTRACT

Social recommendation has been widely studied in recent years. Existing social recommendation models use various explicit pieces of social information as regularization terms, *e.g.,* social links are considered as new constraints. However, social influence, an implicit source of information in social networks, is seldomly considered, even though it often drives recommendations in social networks. In this paper, we introduce a new global and local influence-based social recommendation model. Based on the observation that user purchase behaviour is influenced by both global influential nodes and the local influential nodes of the user, we formulate the global and local influence as an regularization terms, and incorporate them into a matrix factorization-based recommendation model. Experimental results on large data sets demonstrate the performance of the proposed method.

Keywords

Social Recommendation, Dual Social Influence.

1. INTRODUCTION

The advent of *social media* provides us with the opportunity to use social information to enhance the performance of traditional recommender systems. This practice, termed *Social Recommendation*, has resulted in a sizable number of studies in recent years. The *friendship* or *trust relationship*, successfully incorporated in most existing strategies [1, 9, 11, 12, 15], is explicit social information which can improve the quality of recommendations. For instance, the empirical studies by [18] have shown that a correlation exists between trust and user similarity when a community's trust network is bound to a specific application. Lu [12] adopted author identity and social connections to design regularization constraints for integration with a text-based predictor. In [14], social network analysis is fused with topic modeling, and this method can be used in many text mining problems,

CIKM'16, October 24-28, 2016, Indianapolis, IN, USA

DOI: http://dx.doi.org/10.1145/2983323.2983873

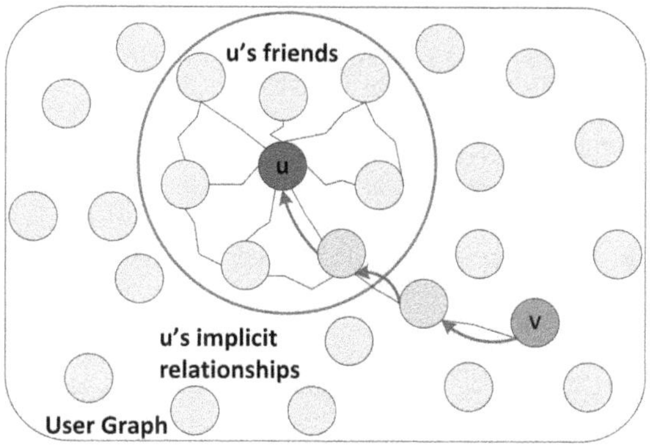

Fig. 1: A toy example of explicit and implicit social relationships for a user u in a social network.

such as community discovery, spatial text mining, etc. An outstanding work [13] focuses on using friendship in social data to improve recommendation performance. It explores two classical measures to evaluate the similarity between all socially connected friends as regularization terms which can be incorporated with recommender systems to constrain matrix factorization. The authors compare several classical baselines and their results demonstrate that the proposed model enhances the performance when predicting missing ratings in the User-Item rating matrix.

Relying on such explicit social information may not be effective in a recommendation scenario, however, because of the inherent limitations summarized below:

- **Scenario-Sensitive** Trust is a complicated concept that can be interpreted in various ways according to the context. Moreover, trust is a minority relationship category in the social world, thus its impact in the social information context may vary.

- **Sparsity** In ratings-oriented websites, the user-user social graph is also very sparse, as is the user-item rating matrix. This is understandable, since people can get in touch with others by social-oriented applications, rather than via rating communities online.

- **Unavailability** Trust or friendship data may be hidden due to privacy concerns. And a friendship is normally a binary value which indicates whether a pair of nodes constitute friendship, rather than providing a numeric value to represent the strength of the link.

We are thus motivated to mine the implicit social relationships in social networks. Fig. 1 illustrates the relationships between a user's explicit social information and their implicit social information. The nodes inside the blue solid circle represent the explicit social connections of u, e.g., u's friends, while nodes outside the circle symbolize implicit social information, such as social influence. The social influence of v can be spread through several traceable edges to u. Intuitively, we discern that users tend to be affected by implicit social connections when making purchasing decisions rather than by explicit relationships such as friendship. On the basis of this observation, we aim to adopt implicit social influence, as a new category of social information in recommendation, to improve recommendation quality.

2. GLOBAL AND LOCAL INFLUENCES

Social influence has been successfully used in marketing and innovation propagation [2,5–7,17], and many works focus on finding the most influential nodes in a network. Wang et al. [16] discovered the most influential vertexes on the basis of community detection and selection, while Guo in [8] proposed a new perspective which aims to find the most influential nodes for each user (target user) in the network. Barbieri et al. [3] proposed a social influence model based on topic modeling.

These above works explain well how social influence is exerted on an entire network or on individuals. For example, a "Web Celebrity", such as Steve Jobs, can exert much broader influence over innovation, new products or digital devices in our society than an unknown reviewer. The recent phenomenon of "Community Stars" has also become widespread. Anyone using social media may now find real life information about, say, books or restaurants, from people who have become "famous" within a certain domain, rather than obtaining this information from their friends. We therefore develop two terms, global influential nodes and local influence nodes, to represent "Web Celebrities" and "Community Stars" respectively. We aim to exploit both global and local social influence model (short for GIM and LIM respectively) information to formulate the social model in social recommender systems. The challenge is to design a new model to incorporate the information from both global influential nodes and local influence nodes. To this end, we propose a dual social influence embedded framework for social recommendation. Our contributions are summarized as follows:

- We first study a global and local social influence-based social recommendation problem.
- We develop the Global Influential Model (GIM) and Local Influential Model (LIM) to find the global/local influential nodes.
- We incorporate the GIM and LIM as an regularization term to constrain the matrix factorization for social recommendation.

3. PROBLEM DEFINITION

Given a user-item rating matrix $R = (U, V)$, U is the set of nodes representing users in the rating dataset and $G = (U, E, w_e), e \in E$ is the users' social network graph. E is the set of edges with a numerical value $w_e \in$[0,1] that represents how large the effect is on a specific edge. Using our GIM and LIM, a set of local and global nodes can be found on each target user u in the network, respectively. This mimics our real life observation that purchasing decisions or preferences tend to affected by the most influential nodes. Furthermore, we believe that the top-k global influence nodes represent the effect on a person's general life perspective while the top-k local influence maximization result represents the influence exerted on aspects of an individual's personal life. Combining these two types of influence can comprehensively model how social influence exerts an effect on behaviours in different granularity.

In summary, we study the problem of how effectively and efficiently implicit social influence information can improve the accuracy of missing value prediction in a rating matrix.

4. METHODOLOGY

We first discuss the implementation of GIM (Sec. 4.1) and LIM (Sec. 4.2), and then introduce the Monte Carlo simulation (Sec. 4.3) used in global/local influence model. After that we describe our overall framework and the corresponding objective function (Sec. 4.4).

4.1 GIM: Global Influence Model

The purpose of the GIM is to find the seed set S^* that spreads the maximum influence on the entire network,

$$S^* = \arg\max_{S \subseteq V, |S|=k} \sigma(S), \tag{1}$$

where $\sigma(S)$ is the expected influence spread by the seed set S and is defined as,

$$\sigma(S) = E[I(S)] = \sum\nolimits_j jp(I(S) = j), \tag{2}$$

where $I(S)$ represents the number of nodes influenced by current seed set S.

4.2 LIM: Local Influence Model

The LIM aims to find the set of nodes $S^*(i)$ that most influence the target node i. The corresponding optimization function is defined as:

$$S^*(i) = \arg\max_{S \subseteq V, |S|=k} w_{S \to i}, \tag{3}$$

where $w_{S \to i}$ represents the influence that the seed nodes in S can reach the node i.

4.3 Monte Carlo Simulation

When handling large-scale networks, the computation of either $\sigma(S)$ in Eq. (1) or $w_{S(i) \to i}$ in Eq. (3) becomes a #P-hard problem [8]. To address this issue, we adopt Monte Carlo simulation to obtain the approximate result.

Monte Carlo simulation is a widely adopted computational algorithm that depends on repeatedly conducting random sampling to obtain numerical results [4]. In general, Monte Carlo methods can be employed to solve any problem that has a probabilistic interpretation. Here, we exploit independent cascade model [10] to simulate the influence spread in the network. This method observes nodes activated situation in the entire network and starts from an randomly picked seed set. Each node in the seed set will try to activate its neighbours with a certain probability determined by the influence value. Such process continuously repeats until there are no more nodes can be activated through this neighbour-driven diffusion process. By doing so, we can

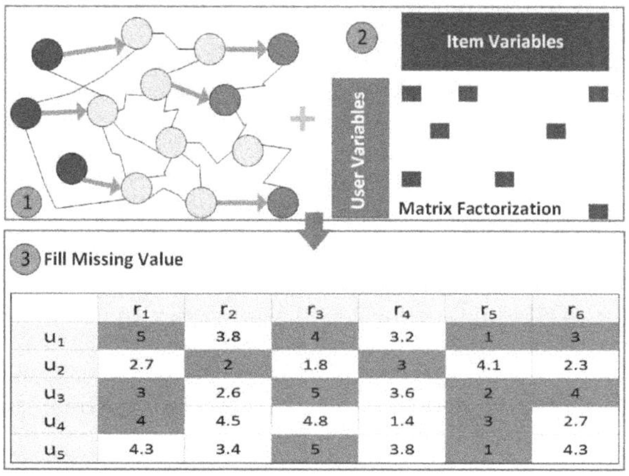

Fig. 2: GLSIR framework: we utilize implicit social influence information from our GIM and LIM models, embedded in the matrix factorization process, for improving the accuracy of missing value prediction in original user-item rating matrix.

observe the overall nodes activation result. To sum up, by exploiting independent cascade model in each round in the entire Monte Carlo simulation process, we can obtain the approximate social influence maximization results for both GIM and LIM.

4.4 Social Influence-based Recommendation

In this section, we present our global and local social influence-based recommendation model - GLSIR for short. Fig. 2 illustrates the overall framework of GLSIR. We formulate the objective function by embedding the results from GIM and LIM with a classical low-rank matrix factorization, shown below,

$$\begin{aligned}\min F(U,V,S,D) &= \frac{1}{2}\sum_{i=1}^{m}\sum_{j=1}^{n} I_{ij}(R_{ij} - U_i^t V_j)^2 \\ &+ \frac{\beta}{2}\sum_{i=1}^{m}\sum_{k\in S^*\cup S^*(i)} w_{k\to i}\|U_i - U_k\|_F^2 \\ &+ \frac{\lambda_1}{2}\|U\|_F^2 + \frac{\lambda_2}{2}\|V\|_F^2,\end{aligned} \tag{4}$$

where V_j represents the set of items rated by user U_i and I_{ij} is an indicator function (*i.e.,* $I_{ij} = 1$ *if user* u_i *rates item* v_j *and 0 otherwise*). The overall top-k influential nodes $k \in S^* \cup S^*(i)$ are discovered by combining the results of GIM and LIM. $w_{k\to i}$ indicates the influence weight node u_k can exert on node u_i, whether the pair of nodes connect directly or indirectly. Here, parameter β aims to balance the mutual effect of the dual social influence embedded model (the second term) and the collaborative filtering model used by many recommender systems (the first term) while λ_1 and λ_2 prevent the problem of over-fitting. We integrate the implicit social influence information model, as a regularization term, to constrain the matrix factorization and achieve more accurate prediction in R. As U_k is a fixed node set to the target nodes in the network, a local minimum of the objective function given by Eq. (4) can be calculated by performing gradient descent with respect to the feature vector U_i and

Algorithm 1 GLSIR Algorithm.

Input: A positive number k, a target node i, a graph G, the number of simulation times D, the rating matrix R, the iteration step-size λ, parameters λ_1, λ_2, β.

Output: U,V.

```
1: Initialize U_0, V_0
2: S* <— GIM
3: S*(i) <— LIM
4: while Not convergent do
5:    Update U with fixed V, S :
         U_i^{t+1} = U_i^t − λ * ∂F/∂U_i in Eq. (5) with S* ∪ S*(i)
6:    Update V with fixed U, S :
         V_j^{t+1} = V_j^t − λ * ∂F/∂V_j in Eq. (6) with R
7: end while
8: return U and V.
```

V_j in Eq. (5) and Eq. (6) respectively,

$$\begin{aligned}\frac{\partial F}{\partial U_i} &= \sum_{j=1}^{n} I_{ij}(U_i^T V_j - R_{ij})V_j + \lambda_1 U_i \\ &+ \beta\sum_{k\in S^*\cup S^*(i)} w_{k\to i}(U_i - U_k) \\ &+ \beta\sum_{j\neq i} I(i\in S^*\cup S^*(i))w_{k\to i}(U_i - U_j)\end{aligned} \tag{5}$$

$$\frac{\partial F}{\partial V_j} = \sum_{i=1}^{m} I_{ij}(U_i^T V_j - R_{ij})U_i + \lambda_2 V_j \tag{6}$$

5. ALGORITHM

As seen in Algorithm 1, we integrate the global and local social influence maximization results, which represent the most influential nodes for individuals in the social network, with a basic matrix factorization techniques as the constraint, for the purpose of predicting the missing value in the rating matrix. We then use the gradient descent strategy to solve the optimal problem for our objective function.

6. EXPERIMENTS

6.1 Experimental Settings

Benchmark data. The data MFW is collected from Mafengwo[1], launched in 2006, which is one of the most popular website for sharing tourism details, reviews and ratings of local highlights (e.g., restaurants and bars). It is also one of the largest online travel websites offering comprehensive tourism guidance, tips, travel diaries and beautiful images. It has Facebook-like social network functions which encourage users to connect with each other. Unlike friendship-based social recommendation, connected individuals in Mafengwo may not be aware of their offline connections, thus although it is not easy to calculate the similarity between pairs of users, it is suitable for us to conduct influence analysis across the whole network.

Our dataset comprises 11,498 unique user ratings on 1,582 travel locations with 475,900 edges. We mark at least 40% of each user's items as the training set to evaluate recommendation performance.

Metric. A classic metric is used to measure recommendation performance - mean absolute error (MAE) - which is

[1]http://www.mafengwo.cn/

Table 1: Results *w.r.t* MAE

DataSet	UMean	IMean	NMF	SRPCC	GLSIR
MFW 80%	0.7012	0.6354	0.5830	0.5619	**0.5129**
MFW 60%	0.7088	0.6385	0.5880	0.5679	**0.5234**
MFW 40%	0.7195	0.6401	0.5936	0.5752	**0.5297**

defined mathematically below:

$$MAE = 1/T \sum_{i,j} \left| R_{ij} - \overline{R}_{ij} \right| \quad (7)$$

where R_{ij} represents the rating score user i gives to item j while $\overline{R}_{ij}$ means the predicted value by one specific method.

Baselines. We implement the following four methods for comparison. These methods are briefly introduced below:

- **UserMean** uses the mean value of every user's rating score for prediction.
- **ItemMean**, is similar to UserMean, but uses the mean value of every item to predict the unassigned items.
- **NMF**, only considers user-item, is generally used in collaborative filtering for recommendation.
- **SRPCC** [13] is a representative method in social-based recommender systems which uses average-based social regularization with Pearson Correlation Coefficient as the similarity function.

Parameter Settings. The iteration step-size λ is set to 0.01. λ_1 and λ_2 are set to 0.001. We analyze the parameters β and k, searched from $\{0.0001, 0.001, 0.01, 0.1, 1\}$ and $\{10, 30, 50, 70, 90\}$ respectively.

The proposed GLSIR model achieves the best performance by setting $\beta = 0.01, k = 50$ on Mafengwo data.

6.2 Experimental Results

As shown in Table 1, our GLSIR method significantly outperforms other baselines in terms of MAE and RMSE measures with various proportions of data training. The proposed GLSIR is typically 5% to 15% more accurate than the baseline methods. Compared to the SRPCC [13] which adopts direct friendship similarity information for recommendation, a remarkable improvement can be observed from our model. This also demonstrates that implicit social relationships, e.g., social influence, are more effective for predicting individuals' purchasing decisions or common tastes.

7. CONCLUSIONS

In this paper, we modelled social influence information to address social recommendations by embedding global and local influence nodes as regularization terms into a matrix factorization recommendation model. Experiments and comparisons on the large, real-world dataset show the proposed global and local influence-based social recommendation approach significantly outperforms current baselines.

ACKNOWLEDGEMENTS

This work was supported by Australia Discovery Projects (Nos. DP140102206 and DP140100545) and Australia Linkage Projects (Nos. LP150100671 and LP160100630), and China Scholarship Council Foundation (No. 201206410056). J. Wu is the corresponding author.

8. REFERENCES

[1] V. Agarwal and K. Bharadwaj. A collaborative filtering framework for friends recommendation in social networks based on interaction intensity and adaptive user similarity. *Social Network Analysis and Mining*, 3(3):359–379, 2013.

[2] E. Bakshy, J. M. Hofman, W. A. Mason, and D. J. Watts. Everyone's an influencer: quantifying influence on twitter. In *WSDM*, pages 65–74, 2011.

[3] N. Barbieri, F. Bonchi, and G. Manco. Topic-aware social influence propagation models. *Knowledge and information systems*, 37(3):555–584, 2013.

[4] E. Cashwell and C. Everett. Monte carlo method. *New York*, 1959.

[5] W. Chen, C. Wang, and Y. Wang. Scalable influence maximization for prevalent viral marketing in large-scale social networks. In *SIGKDD*, pages 1029–1038. ACM, 2010.

[6] W. Chen, Y. Wang, and S. Yang. Efficient influence maximization in social networks. In *SIGKDD*, pages 199–208, 2009.

[7] W. Chen, Y. Yuan, and L. Zhang. Scalable influence maximization in social networks under the linear threshold model. In *ICDM*, pages 88–97. IEEE, 2010.

[8] J. Guo, P. Zhang, C. Zhou, Y. Cao, and L. Guo. Personalized influence maximization on social networks. In *CIKM*, pages 199–208, 2013.

[9] I. Guy, N. Zwerdling, D. Carmel, I. Ronen, E. Uziel, S. Yogev, and S. Ofek-Koifman. Personalized recommendation of social software items based on social relations. In *RecSys*, pages 53–60, 2009.

[10] D. Kempe, J. Kleinberg, and É. Tardos. Maximizing the spread of influence through a social network. In *KDD*, pages 137–146, 2003.

[11] F. Liu and H. J. Lee. Use of social network information to enhance collaborative filtering performance. *Expert systems with applications*, 37(7):4772–4778, 2010.

[12] Y. Lu, P. Tsaparas, A. Ntoulas, and L. Polanyi. Exploiting social context for review quality prediction. In *WWW*, pages 691–700, 2010.

[13] H. Ma, D. Zhou, C. Liu, M. R. Lyu, and I. King. Recommender systems with social regularization. In *WSDM*, pages 287–296, 2011.

[14] Q. Mei, D. Cai, D. Zhang, and C. Zhai. Topic modeling with network regularization. In *WWW*, pages 101–110, 2008.

[15] B. Sigurbjörnsson and R. Van Zwol. Flickr tag recommendation based on collective knowledge. In *WWW*, pages 327–336, 2008.

[16] Y. Wang, G. Cong, G. Song, and K. Xie. Community-based greedy algorithm for mining top-k influential nodes in mobile social networks. In *KDD*, pages 1039–1048, 2010.

[17] J. Weng, E.-P. Lim, J. Jiang, and Q. He. Twitterrank: finding topic-sensitive influential twitterers. In *WSDM*, pages 261–270, 2010.

[18] C.-N. Ziegler and G. Lausen. Analyzing correlation between trust and user similarity in online communities. In *IFIPTM*, pages 251–265, 2004.

Tag-Aware Personalized Recommendation Using a Deep-Semantic Similarity Model with Negative Sampling

Zhenghua Xu* Cheng Chen† Thomas Lukasiewicz* Yishu Miao* Xiangwu Meng†

*Department of Computer Science, University of Oxford, United Kingdom
{zhenghua.xu, thomas.lukasiewicz, yishu.miao}@cs.ox.ac.uk
†School of Computer Science, Beijing University of Posts and Telecommunications, China
{ccbupt,mengxw}@bupt.edu.cn

ABSTRACT

With the rapid growth of social tagging systems, many efforts have been put on tag-aware personalized recommendation. However, due to uncontrolled vocabularies, social tags are usually redundant, sparse, and ambiguous. In this paper, we propose a deep neural network approach to solve this problem by mapping both the tag-based user and item profiles to an abstract deep feature space, where the deep-semantic similarities between users and their target items (resp., irrelevant items) are maximized (resp., minimized). Due to huge numbers of online items, the training of this model is usually computationally expensive in the real-world context. Therefore, we introduce negative sampling, which significantly increases the model's training efficiency (109.6 times quicker) and ensures the scalability in practice. Experimental results show that our model can significantly outperform the state-of-the-art baselines in tag-aware personalized recommendation: e.g., its mean reciprocal rank is between 5.7 and 16.5 times better than the baselines.

Keywords

Tag-Aware Personalized Recommendation; Deep Neural Network; Deep-Semantic Similarity; Negative Sampling

1. INTRODUCTION

In the era of Web 2.0, social tagging systems are introduced by many websites, where users can freely annotate online items using arbitrary tags (commonly known as *folksonomy* [5]). Since social tags are good summaries of the relevant items and the users' preferences, and also contain little sensitive information about their creators, they are valuable information for privacy-enhanced personalized recommendation. Consequently, many efforts have been put on tag-aware personalized recommendation using *content-based filtering* [2, 8] or *collaborative filtering* [1, 9]. However, as users can freely choose their own vocabulary, social tags may contain many uncontrolled vocabularies, such as homonyms, synonyms, words in arbitrary languages, or even user-created words. This results in very sparse, redundant, and ambiguous tag information, which greatly degrades the performance of the tag-aware recommendation systems.

A solution to this problem is to apply clustering in the tag space [8]; however, clustering requests to compute the similarity between tags which is usually very time-consuming (or even intractable). Another solution is to use autoencoders; in [10], abstract representations for tag-based user profiles are first modeled by autoencoders and then used as inputs of user-based collaborative filtering to generate recommendation. Although this method is reported to achieve better performance than the clustering-based collaborative filtering method [10], it still suffers from two drawbacks: (i) the model's learning signal comes from the reconstruction error, which is not the objective of personalized recommendation, i.e., distinguishing the user's target items from the irrelevant ones; (ii) the recommendation is solely based on user profiles, so the relevance between users and items is indirectly inferred from other similar users. So its performance in personalized recommendation is damaged to a great extent.

In this paper, motivated by the above observations, we propose to address the uncontrolled vocabulary problem by using deep neural networks to map both the tag-based user and item profiles to an abstract deep feature space, where the similarities between users and their target items (resp., irrelevant items) are maximized (resp., minimized). We call the similarities on the deep feature space *deep-semantic similarities* and this model *deep-semantic similarity based personalized recommendation* (DSPR) model. DSPR has the following advantages: (i) The training objective is directly correlated with differentiating the user's target items from the irrelevant ones, so the resulting abstract features for user and item profiles are very effective representations for personalized recommendation. (ii) The relevance between users and items is directly computed using the similarities between the abstract user and item profiles.

However, to train DSPR, the deep-semantic similarities between the user in each training sample and all the candidate items have to be computed in each training run. As the number of candidate items for a recommendation system is usually very large (millions), and training deep neural networks often requires numerous training samples and many

CIKM'16, October 24–28, 2016, Indianapolis, IN, USA.
© 2016 ACM. ISBN 978-1-4503-4073-1/16/10...$15.00
DOI: http://dx.doi.org/10.1145/2983323.2983874

training runs, training the DSPR model is computationally expensive in practice, which results in scalability problem. To address this problem, we propose to use *negative sampling* [7], to significantly enhance DSPR's training efficiency, while maintaining almost the same training effectiveness.

The contributions of this paper are threefold: (i) We propose a tag-aware personalized recommendation system that uses deep-semantic similarity-based neural networks to extract abstract and recommendation-oriented representations for tag-based user and item profiles so as to achieve a superior personalized recommendation. (ii) For scalability in practice, we use negative sampling to increase the model's training efficiency (109.6 times quicker). (iii) We provide experimental results, which show that our model can significantly outperform the state-of-the-art baselines in tag-aware personalized recommendation: e.g., its mean reciprocal rank is between 5.7 and 16.5 times better than the baselines.

2. RELATED WORK

Many systems have been proposed for tag-aware personalized recommendation on the Social Web. Content-based systems [2, 8] aim at recommending items that are similar to those that a user liked previously. Collaborative systems recommend to users items liked by similar users using machine learning techniques, such as nearest neighbor modeling [9] and matrix factorization [1]. Due to uncontrolled vocabularies, social tags are usually redundant, sparse, and ambiguous. A solution is to apply clustering in the tag space to aggregate redundant tags and reduce ambiguities [8]. But tag clustering is usually time-consuming in practise, so another solution is to use autoencoders [10].

Deep learning has been successfully applied in many search and recommendation applications, such as item recommendation [4] and Web search [6]. Similarly to our work, [4] and [6] use deep-semantic similarity models with a ranking-oriented training objective. However, these models are very different from DSPR: (i) they are not tag-aware systems and not designed to solve the redundancy, sparsity, and ambiguity problems in tag space; (ii) instead of using negative sampling, these two works intentionally assume the number of candidate items to be very small (5 in [6] and 10 in [4]) to make the model trainable. Obviously, this assumption is unreasonable in real-world situations. Negative sampling was first introduced in the NLP community to learn word representation more efficiently [7]. To our knowledge, our work is the first that applies negative sampling to enhance the training efficiency of deep-semantic similarity-based models.

3. PRELIMINARIES

A *folksonomy* is a tuple $\mathcal{F} = (U, T, I, A)$, where U, T, and I are sets of *users*, *tags*, and *items*, respectively, and $A \subseteq U \times T \times I$ is a set of assignments (u, t, i) of a tag t to an item i by a user u [5].

A *user profile* is a feature vector $x_u = (g_1^u, \ldots, g_M^u)$, where $M = |T|$ is the tag vocabulary's size, and $g_j^u = |\{(u, t_j, i) \in A \mid i \in I\}|$ is the number of times that user u annotates items with tag t_j. Similarly, an *item profile* is a vector $x_i = (g_1^i, \ldots, g_M^i)$, where $g_j^i = |\{(u, t_j, i) \in A \mid u \in U\}|$ is the number of times that item i is annotated with tag t_j [2].

Personalized recommendation is then defined as follows. For a user u, the system produces a ranked recommendation list $\tau = [i_1 \geq i_2 \geq \cdots \geq i_n]$ for all items s.t. $i_a \geq i_b$ iff $Recom(u, i_a) \geq Recom(u, i_b)$, where $Recom(u, i)$ is a recommendation function measuring how relevant item i is to u.

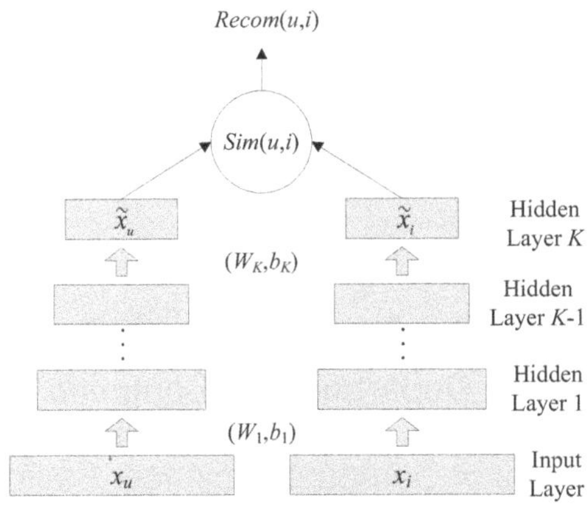

Figure 1: Overview of DSPR

4. DSPR WITH NEGATIVE SAMPLING

Figure 1 shows an overview of our *deep-semantic similarity-based personalized recommendation* (*DSPR*) model. Generally, DSPR takes the tag-based user and item profiles x_u and x_i (as defined in Section 3) as inputs of two deep neural networks with shared parameters. These inputs are then passed through multiple hidden layers and projected into an abstract deep feature space on the final hidden layer, where the similarities between the abstract representations of user and item profiles are computed. Finally, a recommendation function is used to rank items by applying the softmax function on the resulting similarities.

The motivation of sharing parameters is as follows: (i) Since both user and item profiles are modeled from the same folksonomy, they share the same tag space and same value range in each dimension; so it is reasonable to use shared parameters to reduce computational and memory costs in model training. (ii) Shared parameters make two neural networks use the same abstract feature space to describe users and items, which is beneficial for measuring their relevancy.

Formally, given the user profile x_u, the item profile x_i, a weight matrix W_1, and a bias vector b_1, the intermediate output h_1 of the first hidden layer is defined as follows:

$$h_1(u) = \tanh(W_1 x_u + b_1), \quad (1)$$
$$h_1(i) = \tanh(W_1 x_i + b_1), \quad (2)$$

where tanh is used as the activation function. Similarly, the intermediate output of the jth hidden layer h_j, $j \in \{2, \ldots, K\}$, is defined as:

$$h_j(u) = \tanh(W_j h_{j-1}(u) + b_j), \quad (3)$$
$$h_j(i) = \tanh(W_j h_{j-1}(i) + b_j), \quad (4)$$

where W_j and b_j are the weight matrix and the bias vector for the jth hidden layer, and K is the total number of hidden layers. The outputs of Kth hidden layer are the abstract feature representations of user and item profiles, denoted $\widetilde{x}_u$ and $\widetilde{x}_i$, respectively. Formally,

$$\widetilde{x}_u = h_K(u), \qquad \widetilde{x}_i = h_K(i). \quad (5)$$

Then, the similarity between a user u and an item i is measured using the cosine similarity between the abstract representations of their profiles, formally defined as

$$Sim(u, i) = \frac{\widetilde{x}_u \cdot \widetilde{x}_i}{||\widetilde{x}_u|| ||\widetilde{x}_i||}, \quad (6)$$

and called *deep-semantic similarity*.

Finally, to generate personalized recommendations, a recommendation function is used to measure the relevance of an item i to a user u by applying the softmax function on the resulting deep-semantic similarities; formally,

$$Recom(u,i) = \frac{e^{Sim(u,i)}}{\sum_{i' \in I} e^{Sim(u,i')}}. \quad (7)$$

As we assume that the target items of a given user are those annotated by this user, to achieve good personalized recommendations, these items should have higher recommendation scores than others. We thus conduct the model training with an objective to maximize the recommendation scores of target items; equivalently, it is to maximize the deep-semantic similarities between users and their target items and minimize those with irrelevant ones. Formally, it is equivalent to minimizing the following loss function:

$$L(\Theta) = -\sum_{(u,i^*)} \log(Recom(u,i^*))$$
$$= -\sum_{(u,i^*)} [\log(e^{Sim(u,i^*)}) - \log(\sum_{i' \in I} e^{Sim(u,i')})], \quad (8)$$

where Θ represents the parameters W_j and b_j in the neural network; (u,i^*) are training samples, which are pairs of a user u and his/her target item i^*, generated from assignments (u,t,i^*) in a training dataset.

In training, we first initialize the weight matrices W_j, using the random normal distribution, and initialize the biases b_j to be zero vectors; the model is then trained by back-propagation using mini-batch gradient descent; finally, the training stops when the model converges or reaches the maximum training runs. As for regularization, validation-based early stopping is used to avoid overfitting.

4.1 Negative Sampling

Although the loss function in Equation (8) is computable, it is computationally very expensive. This is because, for each training sample (u,i^*) in each training run, the second term requests to compute and sum the deep-semantic similarities between u and all candidate items in I. In the real-world context, the number of candidate items for an online recommendation system is usually very large (millions), and training a deep neural network often requires numerous training samples (millions) and many (thousands) training runs; the training of the DSPR model is thus very time-consuming in practice. However, this term is important: with its help, minimizing the loss function not only maximizes the deep-semantic similarities between the given user and his/her target items, but also minimizes those with irrelevant items. Consequently, it helps to distinguish the target item from the irrelevant ones.

To tackle this dilemma, we use *negative sampling* [7] to greatly reduce the time needed to process each training sample, and to ensure the scalability of DSPR. In negative sampling, instead of using all irrelevant items, for each training sample, we randomly sample only a small portion of irrelevant items from the set of candidate items as *negative examples* to approximate the noise and to differentiate target items from irrelevant ones. Consequently, the negative-sampling-based loss function is formally defined as follows:

$$L^{NS}(\Theta) = -\sum_{(u,i^*)} [\log(e^{Sim(u,i^*)}) - \log(\sum_{(u,i^-) \in D^-} e^{Sim(u,i^-)})],$$

where (u,i^-) are negative samples, which are contained in a negative dataset D^- and generated by randomly sampling S negative examples i^- for each training sample (u,i^*).

Table 1: Dataset Information

Users (u)	Tags (t)	Items (i)	Assignments ((u,t,i^*))
1 843	3 508	65 877	339 744

5. EXPERIMENTS

To show the strength of the DSPR with negative sampling (DSPR-NS) model in solving the uncontrolled vocabulary problem and offering superior personalized recommendation performance, we use three models based on state-of-the-art solutions, clustering [8] and autoencoders [10], as the baselines: (i) Clustering-based cosine similarity (**CCS**): hierarchical clustering [8] is used to model the users and items as cluster-based feature vectors, upon which content-based filtering using cosine similarity is applied for recommendations. (ii) Clustering-based collaborative filtering (**CCF**): CCF is similar to CCS but applies user-based collaborative filtering for recommendations. (iii) Autoencoder-based collaborative filtering (**ACF**) [10]: an autoencoder is used to obtain abstract representations of user profiles, upon which collaborative filtering is applied for recommendations.

The experiments are performed on the same public real-world dataset as used in [10], which is gathered from the Delicious bookmarking system and released in HetRec 2011 [3]. After using the same pre-processing to remove the infrequent tags that are used less than 15 times, the resulting dataset is as shown in Table 1. As we assume that the target items of a given user are the ones annotated by this user, we randomly select 80% of the assignment data as training set, 5% as validation set, and 15% as test set. The assignments (u,t,i^*) in the training set are used to construct user and item profiles and to extract the user-item pairs (u,i^*) as training samples. We also extract user-item pairs from the assignments in the validation set as validation samples, which are used to avoid over-fitting by early stopping. Finally, user-item pairs extracted from the assignments in the test set are used as test samples to evaluate the recommendation performance. Specifically, for each test sample (u,i^*), we first pass the profiles of u and all candidate items in I through the well-trained neural networks; then the relevance between u and all candidate items are computed based on Equation (7); finally, a recommendation list is generated where all candidate items are ranked according to their relevancy to u.

All models are implemented using Python and Theano and run on a GPU server with an NVIDIA Tesla K20 GPU and 8GB GPU memory. The parameters of DSPR-NS are set as follows: (i) # of hidden layers (i.e., K): 3; (ii) # of neurons in the first, second, and third hidden layers: 3 000, 300, and 128, respectively; (iii) training batch size: 128; (iv) # of negative examples for each training sample (i.e., S): 127; (v) # of maximum training runs: 10 000; and (vi) learning rate for model training: 0.001.

Since users usually only browse the topmost recommended items, we apply the *precision at k (P@k)*, *recall at k (R@k)*, and *F1-score at k (F@k)* as evaluation metrics. To take into account the order of items, we also employ the *mean average precision (MAP)* and *mean reciprocal rank (MRR)* as metrics to give greater importance to items ranked higher.

5.1 Main Results

Table 2 shows in detail the personalized recommendation performance of DSPR-NS and the three baselines in terms of $P@k$, $R@k$, $F@k$, MAP, and MRR, where four cut-off ranks k = 1, 5, 10, and 20 are selected.

Table 2: Recommendation Performance of Different Models (in %)

Models	$P@1$	$P@5$	$P@10$	$P@20$	$R@1$	$R@5$	$R@10$	$R@20$	$F@1$	$F@5$	$F@10$	$F@20$	MAP	MRR
CCF	1.194	0.868	0.814	0.667	0.089	0.417	0.765	1.158	0.165	0.564	0.789	0.847	0.416	0.200
ACF	1.465	1.139	0.950	0.798	0.194	0.561	0.891	1.370	0.342	0.752	0.919	1.008	0.606	0.252
CCS	3.527	2.279	1.970	1.712	0.263	0.892	1.637	2.741	0.490	1.282	1.788	2.108	1.254	0.523
DSPR-NS	**22.68**	**17.41**	**14.86**	**11.43**	**1.750**	**5.772**	**9.219**	**13.21**	**3.250**	**8.669**	**11.38**	**12.26**	**8.097**	**3.517**

Table 3: Training Efficiency and Effectiveness

	DSPR-O	DSPR-NS		
# of runs	500	500	1 000	10 000
time (hrs)	124.0	1.121	2.243	22.42
MRR-VS	0.02172	0.02157	0.02367	0.03555

The results in Table 2 show that our DSPR-NS model achieves the best personalized recommendation performance. It significantly outperforms the three other baselines in all metrics; e.g., the MRR of DSPR-NS is roughly 5.7, 13, and 16.5 times better than the ones of CCS, ACF, and CCF, respectively; also, the comparison results in $P@k$, $R@k$, $F@k$, and MAP are similar. The superior performance of DSPR-NS mainly has the following two reasons: (i) the training objective of DSPR-NS is directly correlated with distinguishing the user's target items from the irrelevant ones; so, the resulting abstract features for user and item profiles are much more effective representations for personalized recommendation than those generated by clustering and autoencoders; (ii) the relevance between users and items in DSPR-NS is directly computed using the deep-semantic similarities between user and item profiles; so, it can achieve more accurate recommendations than CCF and ACF, where the recommendations are only based on user profiles, so the relevance has to be inferred indirectly from other similar users.

5.2 Efficiency and Scalability

To investigate the training efficiency and scalability of DSPR, besides DSPR with negative sampling (DSPR-NS), we construct another model (DSPR-O) which is identical to DSPR-NS, except using the original loss function in Equation (8) for model training. The training time is recorded to compare the training efficiency of two models. But the standard training loss is not suitable for evaluating training effectiveness, as DSPR-O and DSPR-NS use different loss functions. Here, we use MRR on validation samples (MRR-VS) to measure the training quality, it is because (i) both training objectives are to get better personalized recommendations, so the higher the MRR-VS the better the model; (ii) MRR-VS is monitored during the training process to avoid over-fitting, so using it will not increase the training time.

As shown in Table 3, it costs DSPR-O 124.0 hours to finish the training of 500 runs, but DSPR-NS only takes 1.121 hours (i.e., 109.6 times quicker); meanwhile, the MRR-VS of two models are almost the same (0.02172 vs. 0.02157). This indicates that negative sampling can significantly enhance the training efficiency of DSPR, while maintaining almost the same training effectiveness. In addition, training 500 runs is usually not enough; more runs are required to train a good recommendation model. As shown in Table 3, it takes only 22.42 hours for DSPR-NS to finish the training of 10 000 runs and enhance MRR-VS up to 0.03555. However, without negative sampling, such training will cost DSPR-O 103.3 days, which is very impractical. So negative sampling greatly increases the scalability of DSPR and makes it possible to properly train DSPR in real-world situations.

6. SUMMARY AND OUTLOOK

We have proposed a tag-aware personalized recommendation system using a deep-semantic similarity model, DSPR, to extract recommendation-oriented representations for social tags, to address the uncontrolled vocabulary problem and to achieve superior personalized recommendations. We have also proposed to use negative sampling to greatly reduce the system's training time and to ensure a good scalability in practice. Experiments show that DSPR significantly outperforms the state-of-the-art baselines in personalized recommendation in terms of all selected metrics.

In the future, more extensive experiments will be conducted to further evaluate the performance of DSPR on different parameter settings and additional folksonomy datasets, e.g., Last.fm. Also, we plan to use hybrid learning signals or more sophisticated neural networks, e.g., convolutional network or LSTM, to learn more effective abstract tag representations for tag-aware personalized recommendations.

Acknowledgments

This work was partially supported by the UK EPSRC grants EP/J008346/1, EP/L012138/1, and EP/M025268/1. We acknowledge the use of Oxford University's ARC resources.

7. REFERENCES

[1] M. R. Bouadjenek, H. Hacid, M. Bouzeghoub, and A. Vakali. Using social annotations to enhance document representation for personalized search. In *SIGIR*, 2013.

[2] I. Cantador, A. Bellogín, and D. Vallet. Content-based recommendation in social tagging systems. In *RecSys*, 2010.

[3] I. Cantador, P. Brusilovsky, and T. Kuflik. Second Workshop on Information Heterogeneity and Fusion in Recommender Systems (HetRec2011). In *RecSys*, 2011.

[4] A. M. Elkahky, Y. Song, and X. He. A multi-view deep learning approach for cross domain user modeling in recommendation systems. In *WWW*, 2015.

[5] A. Hotho, R. Jäschke, C. Schmitz, and G. Stumme. Information retrieval in folksonomies: Search and ranking. In *ESWC*, 2006.

[6] P.-S. Huang, X. He, J. Gao, L. Deng, A. Acero, and L. Heck. Learning deep structured semantic models for web search using clickthrough data. In *CIKM*, 2013.

[7] T. Mikolov, I. Sutskever, K. Chen, G. S. Corrado, and J. Dean. Distributed representations of words and phrases and their compositionality. In *NIPS*, 2013.

[8] A. Shepitsen, J. Gemmell, B. Mobasher, and R. Burke. Personalized recommendation in social tagging systems using hierarchical clustering. In *RecSys*, 2008.

[9] K. H. Tso-Sutter, L. B. Marinho, and L. Schmidt-Thieme. Tag-aware recommender systems by fusion of collaborative filtering algorithms. In *SAC*, 2008.

[10] Y. Zuo, J. Zeng, M. Gong, and L. Jiao. Tag-aware recommender systems based on deep neural networks. *Neurocomputing*, 2016.

Personalized Semantic Word Vectors

Javid Ebrahimi
University of Oregon
Eugene, Oregon 97403, USA
javid@cs.uoregon.edu

Dejing Dou
University of Oregon
Eugene, Oregon 97403, USA
dou@cs.uoregon.edu

ABSTRACT

Distributed word representations are able to capture syntactic and semantic regularities in text. In this paper, we present a word representation scheme that incorporates authorship information. While maintaining similarity among related words in the induced distributed space, our word vectors can be effectively used for some text classification tasks too. We build on a log-bilinear document model (lbDm), which extracts document features, and word vectors based on word co-occurrence counts. First, we propose a log-bilinear author model (lbAm), which contains an additional author matrix. We show that by directly learning author feature vectors, as opposed to document vectors, we can learn better word representations for the authorship attribution task. Furthermore, authorship information has been found to be useful for sentiment classification. We enrich the author model with a sentiment tensor, and demonstrate the effectiveness of this hybrid model (lbHm) through our experiments on a movie review-classification dataset.

Keywords

word vectors; document model; author model

1. INTRODUCTION

Distributed word representations are now ubiquitous in the NLP community. Neural models [3] map words to an n-dimensional space through language modeling. This allows learning multiple dimensions of similarity that encode the syntactic, semantic [12] features of words in a compressed, numerical format. These models generally do not utilize the statistics of the document, nor the corpus, because they are trained on local context windows [17]. However, the learned vectors can be fine-tuned by discriminative neural networks and can be used for text classification tasks [20, 8]. Perhaps Le and Mikolov's Paragraph Vector [9] can be distinguished from others since they have extended the `word2vec` [12] to allow for word, sentence and document vectors in a unified framework.

Log-bilinear document model (lbDm) [11] uses term-document data to learn semantic word vectors. It derives a probabilistic model with a log-bilinear energy function to model the document, as opposed to sequences of word windows. The lbDm uses the bag-of-words assumption and its formulation is similar to LDA [4]. However, it defines a novel energy function and the learned document features are not confined to the topic simplex. Despite the simplicity of the model, it works well in text classification tasks. It has been applied to sentiment classification [10], document classification [7], and information retrieval [23].

We extend lbDm in two ways. First, we show that by sharing the document features, based on authorship, we can find personalized semantic word vectors that perform significantly better in the authorship attribution task. Second, combined with sentiment matrices, these new author-sentiment-biased word vectors can improve the results of sentiment classification. In our hybrid model, the negative energy of a word, given the document, its author, and its sentiment, is proportional to the dot product of the word vector and its sentiment-transformed author vector. Our idea in employing authorship information could be applied to other document or word embedding models as well.

2. RELATED WORK

This work is based on a log-bilinear language model proposed in [13, 14]. They used Restricted Boltzmann Machines for language modeling. That model was later modified by [11, 10] to develop a log-bilinear document model (lbDm) for sentiment classification and subjectivity recognition. The lbDm is based on the bag-of-words assumption, and the probability of a word, given the document features, can be defined by a softmax function. Introducing the document feature vector helped their model to go beyond a window of words, to learn word representations in the context of the whole document.

Our work is also related to personalization, which has been investigated in different tasks, including language modeling [26, 6], author topic modeling [18], authorship attribution [19], and sentiment classification [1, 21]. For instance, Wachsmuth et al. [25] use an argumentation model for each reviewer to classify the sentiment in the movies. In [15] an author-specific generative model of a movie review is employed, in order to take author preferences and writing style into account, so as to improve sentiment classification. Results in [21] show improved word embedding after taking the user and the product evidence into account. Similarly, Hovy [5] shows that sentiment analysis can be improved by the inclusion of author demographics, such as age and gender.

3. LOG-BILINEAR AUTHOR MODEL

In the log-bilinear Document model (lbDm) [11], a document is represented using a continuous mixture distribution over words indexed by a document-specific random variable θ. Based on the

CIKM'16, October 24-28, 2016, Indianapolis, IN, USA
© 2016 ACM. ISBN 978-1-4503-4073-1/16/10...$15.00
DOI: http://dx.doi.org/10.1145/2983323.2983875

bag-of-words assumption, words in a document are conditionally independent given the independent mixture variable θ. Thus, the probability of a document is,

$$p(d) = \int p(d,\theta)d\theta = \int p(\theta)\prod_{i=1}^{N} p(w_i|\theta)d\theta$$

where N is the number of words in d and w_i is the i_{th} word in d.

In the log-bilinear author model (lbAm), we have an author representation matrix $U \in \mathbb{R}^{\beta\times|A|}$ where each author a (represented as a one-hot vector) in the author set A, has a β dimensional vector representation $Ua = \psi_a$, corresponding to that author's column in U. Thus, the probability of a document given its author is,

$$p(d,a) = \int p(d,\psi_a)d\psi = \int p(\psi)\prod_{i=1}^{N} p(w_i|\psi,a)d\psi \quad (1)$$

We define the following energy function,

$$E(w;\psi,\phi,a,b) = -\psi_a^T\phi_w - b_w$$

The energy function uses a word embedding matrix $R \in \mathbb{R}^{\beta\times|V|}$, where each word w (represented as a one-hot vector) in the vocabulary V, has a β dimensional vector representation $\phi_w = Rw$, corresponding to that word's column in R. A bias b_w for each word to capture differences in overall word frequencies is also added. For the distribution $p(w|a)$, we use a standard softmax function,

$$p(w|a;U,R,b) = \frac{\exp(\psi_a^T\phi_w + b_w)}{\sum_{w'\in V}\exp(\psi_a^T\phi_{w'} + b_{w'})}$$

Unlike lbDm, we do not have any document-specific features and are only interested in authors' vectors. This model is more useful in applications such as authorship attribution or author topic modeling, which address problems such as: *Who are likely to have written documents similar to an observed document?* and *Which authors produce similar papers?* [18].

4. LOG-BILINEAR HYBRID MODEL

Authorship information can also improve sentiment classification. Different people use different diction to describe similar views. Thus, a sentiment classifier that uses authorship can perform better. Hybrid model (lbHm) aims to take both authorship and sentiment information into account. One way to do this is to use linear additions of sentiment-shared and authorship-shared vectors. This might result in problems of scaling and of tuning. Instead, we represent sentiments by a tensor γ, and use the following energy function,

$$E(w;\psi,\gamma,\phi,a,s,b) = -\psi_a^T\gamma^{[s]}\phi_w - b_w$$

where $\gamma^{[s]} \in \mathbb{R}^{\beta\times\beta}$ is a slice in the sentiment tensor that denotes the transformation matrix associated with the sentiment s. This representation realizes more complex interactions between sentiment and authorship. In addition, the transformation of the author vector, based on sentiment, helps capture the features of the sentiment-bearing words that a specific author uses.

5. LEARNING

Here, we discuss the learning algorithm for lbHm, which is more general than lbAm. Given an i.i.d document collection D, let d_k denote the k_{th} document, with author a, and sentiment s. We aim to learn model parameters R and b. Using MAP estimates for ψ and γ, we can approximate this learning problem as,

$$L(D) = \prod_{d_k\in D} p(\hat{\psi_a})p(\hat{\gamma})\prod_{i=1}^{N_k} p(w_i|\hat{\psi_a},\hat{\gamma},s;R,b)$$

where $\hat{\psi_a}$ denotes the MAP estimate of author vector ψ_a, and $\hat{\gamma}$ is the MAP estimate of the sentiment tensor γ. Adding the regularization terms, the final log-likelihood learning problem is,

$$\max_{R,b} \lambda \parallel R \parallel_F + \lambda \parallel \hat{\gamma} \parallel_F + \lambda \parallel U \parallel_F + \sum_{d_k\in D}\sum_{i=1}^{N_k} \log p(w_i|\hat{\psi_a},\hat{\gamma},s;R,b) \quad (2)$$

To optimize this non-convex objective function, we use coordinate ascent. First, we optimize the word representations (R and b) while leaving the MAP estimates $\hat{\psi_a}$ and $\hat{\gamma}$ fixed. Then we find $\hat{\psi_a}$ while leaving the R, b, and $\hat{\gamma}$ fixed, and finally, we do the same for $\hat{\gamma}$. We continue this process until no further improvement is gained.

The contributions made by a document d_k from D to the derivatives of $L(D)$ with regard to the slice s of the tensor γ are given by,

$$\sum_{i=1}^{N_k} \frac{\partial \log p(w_i|\hat{\psi_a},\hat{\gamma},s)}{\partial\gamma^{[s]}} = N_k\left\langle \hat{\psi_a}\phi_{w_i}^T \right\rangle_D - N_k\left\langle \hat{\psi_a}\phi_{w_i}^T \right\rangle_M \quad (3)$$

where N_k is the length of the document and $\langle.\rangle_D$ and $\langle.\rangle_M$ denote expectations w.r.t. word count distribution and $p(w_i|\hat{\psi_a},\hat{\gamma},s)$, respectively. Partial derivatives with regard to $\hat{\psi_a}$, R and b can be computed similarly. Computation of these derivatives can be performed linearly, in the size of the vocabulary, and we use LBFGS for optimization.

6. EXPERIMENTS

In this section we discuss our experiments, in which we use two datasets for sentiment classification [16] and authorship attribution [2]. We make comparisons with some other word representation schemes. After learning the word embeddings, we use the mean representation vector as the document features, i.e., the average vector of all the words present in the document. For all the methods in the experiments, we used SVM trained with both polynomial and linear kernels and report the best of the two. In both experiments, we could add extra features to improve the accuracy and compete with state-of-the-art results. The focus of our work, however is to show the superiority of the word representation model compared with other schemes.

We set the regularization parameter λ to 10^{-4} and the number of the dimensions of the word vectors β to 50. Following [24], we control the standard deviation of the embeddings, and set the scaling hyper-parameter to 0.1.

6.1 Authorship Attribution

Authorship attribution deals with identifying the authors of documents. We follow the setup of the PAN'11 competition (Argamon and Juola, 2011): We train the models on the training subset, tune the parameters according to the given validation subset, and run the tuned models on the given testing subset. The training dataset consists of 9337 documents and 72 authors, while the validation and test sets contain 1298 and 1300 documents respectively.

For our baselines, we use the word topic distributions from the Author Topic model (AT) [18], bag-of-words, lbDm [11], and continuous bag-of-words (CBOW) [12]. We also compare our results with the Paragraph Vector model (PV) [9], which can be used for joint word representation learning and supervised learning.

For classification purposes in PV, the paragraph vector for instances with similar labels can be shared. We used the `gensim` implementation [1] of PV.

Method	Test	Validation
lbDm	25.64	27.48
AT	30.50	33.15
BOW	38.43	39.68
CBOW	13.89	14.66
PV	33.38	32.04
lbAm	**41.41**	**42.46**

Table 1: Accuracy on PAN'11 Dataset

The poor performance of lbDm can be attributed to the large number of classes and the inability of the model to differentiate among authors' interests by treating every document independently of the others. Moreover, compared with AT, distributed representation of lbAm is not confined to the topic simplex, and it can better capture semantic similarities. While the representations produced by CBOW have high quality (Table 2), they perform poorly on the classification task. Similarly, PV yields a low accuracy on authorship attribution. The reason for this is that PV would perform better when it has access to a large amount of labeled/unlabeled data. This becomes even more challenging for PV in a problem with many classes (72 in this dataset).

A qualitative assessment, based on cosine similarity of the words, and some query words can be seen in Table 2. We compare lbAm with AT, and CBOW using the `word2vec` tool[2].

	lbAm	AT	CBOW
	person	forward	owned
	send	notice	recently
company	business	asap	industry
	products	referencing	consultant
	texas	spend	marketplace
	affiliates	havoc	general
	locate	proposed	president
counsel	courts	portions	vice
	merged	courts	litigation
	attorneys	affadavit	attorney
	discussions	purpose	netting
	agreement	replacing	master
agreements	assist	portions	employment
	standard	trail	brokerage
	provisions	finalized	confidentiality
	version	conform	perform
	agreed	exelon	states
parties	prices	llc	attorneys
	discussed	legal	provisions
	benefit	locational	context

Table 2: Similarity of learned word vectors by lbAm, AT, and CBOW. Each query word is listed with its 5 most similar words, based on the cosine similarity of the vectors.

6.2 Sentiment Classification

To evaluate our hybrid model (lbHm), we use the well-known movie review dataset [16], which contains 2000 reviews and 312 authors. In order to have sufficient data per author, we created two datasets, wherein only the authors with at least five (dataset-5), and at least ten (dataset-10) reviews of each polarity are considered. This reduces the number of reviews in the first dataset to 1239 (552 positive, and 687 negative) with 48 authors, and the number in the second dataset to 788 (332 positive and 456 negative) with 25 authors. Results of 10-fold cross validation are reported in Table 3.

Method	dataset-5	dataset-10
LDA	74.98	75.10
lbDm	81.09	80.83
BOW	87.49	85.40
CBOW	79.82	80.58
PV	83.53	81.77
lbSm	86.70	85.94
lbHm	**88.05**	**86.59**

Table 3: Accuracy of sentiment classification

We compare our results with LDA [4], lbDm, CBOW, PV, and bag-of-words. The lbSm is similar to lbAm, where the document features are shared based on the sentiment, instead of authorship. Our lbHm takes both sentiment and authorship into account, and it achieves the best results.

It is interesting to see the relatively poor performance of PV on these datasets. It had achieved impressive performance on another movie review dataset [10], in a transductive setting, with a large number of labeled and unlabeled training instances. Whereas here, we have a relatively small dataset with no unlabeled training instances. As another contributing factor which was also demonstrated in [22], the average length of the reviews in that dataset (i.e., 227) is a almost a third of the average length of the dataset that we used (i.e., 646)

As a qualitative evaluation of the variables in the lbHm model, we visualize the author vector, before (ψ_a), and after applying the positive and negative sentiment matrices ($\psi_a^T \gamma^{[s]}$) in Table 4. Authors are represented by the words that have the highest cosine similarity with the author vectors.

The words in bold font are the sentiment-bearing words that rise up, among the top words, as most similar to the author vector, in the sentiment transformed space. The words that are underlined are sentiment-bearing words that are among the words most similar to the original author vector, which might or might not remain among the top-ranked words after the transformation. IbHm captures relationships between authorship and sentiment variables, and it produces word vectors that are also suitable for a sentiment classification task.

7. CONCLUSIONS

In this paper, we presented two extensions of a previous log-bilinear document model (lbDm) to induce semantic word representations. This bilinear model can be efficiently modified, using parameter sharing or linear operations for improved document classification. Log-bilinear author model (lbAm) learns personalized word representations by sharing the document features based on authorship. Knowing the author of a document can also improve sentiment classification. Log-bilinear hybrid model (lbHm), in addition to author vectors, uses a sentiment tensor to enrich the model based on the sentiment of the document. The advantage of our models is that while they produce high-quality word vectors, they also can be readily fed to standard classifiers.

A natural extension to this work is to apply similar formulations to other document modeling techniques. For example, the Para-

[1]http://radimrehurek.com/gensim/

[2]https://code.google.com/archive/p/word2vec/

	auth	auth-pos	auth-neg
	killing	killing	mixture
	mixture	**transcend**	cringed
	cringed	mixture	hairstylist
	personal	pleasant	stinker
	galoshes	hairstylist	distract
	community	sex-driven	believable
Reviewer-12	pleasant	terrifying	stalwart
	hairstylist	ferris	**unscrupulous**
	hot	thoroughly	railway
	terrifying	confrontations	recognizable
	ferris	recognizable	non-cynics
	stinker	psychopath	ultra-low
	sharing	**competent**	faucet
	distract	arabs	**ludicrous**
	drives	pleasant	tracy
	parody	sex-driven	screenwriters
	vancouver	simple	deeds
	pleasant	merely	sitcom
	number	performance	**decrepit**
	sex-driven	**intricately**	kravitz
Reviewer-16	terrifying	molly	carving
	london's	**scrumptious**	**vicious**
	late	cuteness	attacks
	june	story	publique
	merely	play's	performance
	mushy	herb	unique
	dinosaurs	**moralistic**	**horribly**
	attacks	surroundings	realistic

Table 4: The author vector, for two reviewers in the movie-review polarity dataset, before (ψ_a), and after applying the positive and negative sentiment matrices ($\psi_a^T \gamma^{[s]}$). In all columns, words that have the highest cosine similarity with the vector are shown. The bold and underlined words bear sentiment.

graph Vector [9], or the Predictive Text Embedding [22] could also be extended to allow for a combination of authorship and sentiment features. In addition, employing external features sets for the tasks could improve the results presented in this paper.

8. ACKNOWLEDGMENT

This work was partially supported by the NIH grant R01GM103309.

9. REFERENCES

[1] M. Al Boni, K. Zhou, H. Wang, and M. S. Gerber. Model adaptation for personalized opinion analysis. In *Proceedings of ACL-IJCNLP*, pages 769–774, 2015.

[2] S. Argamon and P. Juola. Overview of the international authorship identification competition at PAN-2011. In *CLEF (Notebook Papers/Labs/Workshop)*, 2011.

[3] Y. Bengio, R. Ducharme, P. Vincent, and C. Janvin. A neural probabilistic language model. *Journal of Machine Learning Research*, 3:1137–1155, 2003.

[4] D. M. Blei, A. Y. Ng, and M. I. Jordan. Latent Dirichlet Allocation. *Journal of Machine Learning Research*, 3:993–1022, 2003.

[5] D. Hovy. Demographic factors improve classification performance. In *Proceedings of ACL-IJCNLP*, pages 752–762, 2015.

[6] Y.-Y. Huang, R. Yan, T.-T. Kuo, and S.-D. Lin. Enriching cold start personalized language model using social network information. In *Proceedings of ACL*, pages 611–617, 2014.

[7] H. Jing, Y. Tsao, K.-Y. Chen, and H.-M. Wang. Semantic naïve Bayes classifier for document classification. In *Proceedings of the IJCNLP*, pages 1117–1123, 2013.

[8] N. Kalchbrenner, E. Grefenstette, and P. Blunsom. A convolutional neural network for modelling sentences. In *Proceedings of ACL*, pages 655–665, 2014.

[9] Q. Le and T. Mikolov. Distributed representations of sentences and documents. In T. Jebara and E. P. Xing, editors, *Proceedings of ICML*, pages 1188–1196, 2014.

[10] A. L. Maas, R. E. Daly, P. T. Pham, D. Huang, A. Y. Ng, and C. Potts. Learning word vectors for sentiment analysis. In *Proceedings of ACL*, pages 142–150, 2011.

[11] A. L. Maas and A. Y. Ng. A probabilistic model for semantic word vectors. In *Workshop on Deep Learning and Unsupervised Feature Learning, NIPS*, 2010.

[12] T. Mikolov, I. Sutskever, K. Chen, G. S. Corrado, and J. Dean. Distributed representations of words and phrases and their compositionality. In *Proceedings of NIPS*, pages 3111–3119. 2013.

[13] A. Mnih and G. Hinton. Three new graphical models for statistical language modelling. In *Proceedings of ICML*, pages 641–648, 2007.

[14] A. Mnih and Y. W. Teh. A fast and simple algorithm for training neural probabilistic language models. In *Proceedings of ICML*, pages 1751–1758, 2012.

[15] S. Mukherjee, G. Basu, and S. Joshi. Joint author sentiment topic model. In *Proceedings of SDM*, pages 370–378, 2014.

[16] B. Pang, L. Lee, and S. Vaithyanathan. Thumbs up?: Sentiment classification using machine learning techniques. In *Proceedings of EMNLP*, pages 79–86, 2002.

[17] J. Pennington, R. Socher, and C. Manning. Glove: Global vectors for word representation. In *Proceedings of EMNLP*, pages 1532–1543, 2014.

[18] M. Rosen-Zvi, T. Griffiths, M. Steyvers, and P. Smyth. The author-topic model for authors and documents. In *Proceedings of UAI*, pages 487–494, 2004.

[19] Y. Seroussi, F. Bohnert, and I. Zukerman. Authorship attribution with author-aware topic models. In *Proceedings of ACL*, pages 264–269, 2012.

[20] R. Socher, A. Perelygin, J. Wu, J. Chuang, C. D. Manning, A. Y. Ng, and C. Potts. Recursive deep models for semantic compositionality over a sentiment treebank. In *Proceedings of EMNLP*, pages 1631–1642, 2013.

[21] D. Tang, B. Qin, and T. Liu. Learning semantic representations of users and products for document level sentiment classification. In *Proceedings of ACL-IJCNLP*, pages 1014–1023, 2015.

[22] J. Tang, M. Qu, and Q. Mei. Pte: Predictive text embedding through large-scale heterogeneous text networks. In *Proceedings of SIGKDD*, pages 1165–1174, 2015.

[23] X. Tu, J. Luo, B. Li, and T. He. Log-bilinear document language model for ad-hoc information retrieval. In *Proceedings of CIKM*, pages 1895–1898, 2014.

[24] J. Turian, L. Ratinov, and Y. Bengio. Word representations: A simple and general method for semi-supervised learning. In *Proceedings of ACL*, pages 384–394, 2010.

[25] H. Wachsmuth, M. Trenkmann, B. Stein, and G. Engels. Modeling review argumentation for robust sentiment analysis. In *Proceedings of COLING*, pages 553–564, 2014.

[26] G.-R. Xue, J. Han, Y. Yu, and Q. Yang. User language model for collaborative personalized search. *ACM Transactions on Information Systems*, 27(2):11:1–11:28, 2009.

Query Expansion Using Word Embeddings

Saar Kuzi
saarkuzi@campus.technion.ac.il

Anna Shtok
annabel@tx.technion.ac.il

Oren Kurland
kurland@ie.technion.ac.il

Technion — Israel Institute of Technology

ABSTRACT

We present a suite of query expansion methods that are based on *word embeddings*. Using Word2Vec's CBOW embedding approach, applied over the entire corpus on which search is performed, we select terms that are semantically related to the query. Our methods either use the terms to expand the original query or integrate them with the effective pseudo-feedback-based relevance model. In the former case, retrieval performance is significantly better than that of using only the query, and in the latter case the performance is significantly better than that of the relevance model.

1. INTRODUCTION

Query expansion approaches are intended to ameliorate the vocabulary mismatch between the short query and relevant documents [4]. We present query expansion methods that rely on global, query-independent, analysis of the corpus using *word embeddings*. Specifically, we use Word2Vec's Continuous Bag-of-Words (CBOW) approach [11] that represents terms in a vector space based on their co-occurrence in windows of text. Similarities between the term vectors were shown to correspond to semantic similarities [11].

We use the Word2Vec term embeddings to select terms that are similar to the query as a whole or to its constituent terms. The selected terms are used to expand the query in a unigram language model framework. The resultant retrieval performance is significantly better than using the query alone, and a recently proposed translation model based on Word2Vec [21]. In addition, we present an approach to integrating the terms selected using word embeddings with an effective pseudo-feedback-based method: the relevance model [10]. The resultant performance significantly transcends that of the relevance model.

2. QUERY EXPANSION MODELS

Our goal is to expand a query q using semantically related terms. To that end, we train offline the Word2Vec Continuous Bag-of-Words (CBOW) model [11] using the entire document corpus D on which search is performed. The model's goal is to estimate the probability that a term will appear in a position in a text based on terms that appear in a window around this position. As a result, each term in the corpus is represented by a vector embedded in a vector space. Similarities between these vectors were shown to correspond to semantic similarities between the terms [11]. Accordingly, we select terms similar to the query in this vector space.

Our query expansion methods operate in a unigram language model framework. The methods use term scoring functions presented in Section 2.1. Section 2.2 presents a method of using the terms with the highest scores for query expansion. In Section 2.3 we present an approach for integrating the terms selected by our methods with a pseudo-feedback-based relevance model [10].

2.1 Term scoring methods

2.1.1 *The centroid method*

Adding Word2Vec vectors representing terms that constitute an expression often yields a vector that semantically corresponds to the expression [11]. We leverage this observation to score terms for expansion. Herein, $\vec{t}$ denotes the L_2-normalized Word2Vec vector representing term t.

We represent q by $\vec{q}_{Cent} \stackrel{def}{=} \sum_{q_i \in q} \vec{q_i}$, where q_i is a query term; this is the (query-length) scaled centroid of the query terms' vectors. The score of term t in the collection is:

$$S_{Cent}(t; q) \stackrel{def}{=} \exp(\cos(\vec{t}, \vec{q}_{Cent})). \tag{1}$$

2.1.2 *Fusion-based methods*

The Cent approach scores terms by their semantic similarity with the query as a whole. As an alternative, we create for each query term, q_i, a list L_{q_i} of its n most similar terms t in the corpus according to $\cos(\vec{q_i}, \vec{t})$ (cf., [3, 13]); n is a free parameter. These n similarities are softmax-normalized to yield probabilities: $p(t|q_i) \stackrel{def}{=} \frac{\exp(\cos(\vec{q_i},\vec{t}))}{\sum_{t' \in L_{q_i}} \exp(\cos(\vec{q_i},\vec{t'}))}$ for $t \in L_{q_i}$; $p(t|q_i) \stackrel{def}{=} 0$ for $t \notin L_{q_i}$. We fuse the resulting term lists using CombSUM, CombMNZ and CombMAX [7]:

$$S_{CombSUM}(t; q) \stackrel{def}{=} \sum_{q_i \in q} p(t|q_i); \tag{2}$$

$$S_{CombMNZ}(t; q) \stackrel{def}{=} |\{q_i \in q : p(t|q_i) \neq 0\}| \sum_{q_i \in q} p(t|q_i); \tag{3}$$

$$S_{CombMAX}(t; q) \stackrel{def}{=} \max_{q_i \in q} p(t|q_i). \tag{4}$$

CIKM'16 , October 24-28, 2016, Indianapolis, IN, USA

DOI: http://dx.doi.org/10.1145/2983323.2983876

2.2 Expanding the query

The ν terms assigned the highest score by a method $\mathcal{M}$ ($\in$ {Cent, CombSUM, CombMNZ, CombMAX}) are used for query expansion; ν is a free parameter. We sum-normalize these terms' scores, $S_{\mathcal{M}}(t;q)$, to obtain a probability distribution, $p(\cdot|\mathcal{M})$, that constitutes a unigram language model defined over the vocabulary. (Terms not among the ν with the highest scores are assigned zero probability.) We integrate this language model with a language model induced from q. Formally, the maximum likelihood estimate (MLE) of term t with respect to q is: $p_{MLE}(t|q) \stackrel{def}{=} \frac{\text{tf}(t\in q)}{|q|}$, where $\text{tf}(t \in q)$ is the count of t in q and $|q|$ is the query length. The resulting model, **Q-$\mathcal{M}$**, uses the interpolation parameter λ:

$$p(t|\mathcal{M},q) \stackrel{def}{=} (1-\lambda)p(t|\mathcal{M}) + \lambda p_{MLE}(t|q). \quad (5)$$

2.3 Integration with the relevance model

Our premise is that pseudo-feedback-based query expansion approaches are of complementary nature to our global expansion methods that use Word2Vec for corpus analysis. Hence, we now turn to integrate an effective pseudo feedback approach, the relevance model [10], with our methods.

The probability assigned to term t by RM1 is [10]:

$$p(t|RM1) \stackrel{def}{=} \sum_{d\in\mathcal{D}_{\text{init}}} p(t|d)p(d|q); \quad (6)$$

$\mathcal{D}_{\text{init}}$ is an initial document list described below; $p(t|d)$ is the probability assigned to t by d's Dirichlet smoothed language model [19]; $p(d|q)$ is d's normalized query likelihood.

Clipping RM1 by setting to zero the probability of all but the c terms that yield the highest $p(t|RM1)$, and sum-normalizing their probabilities, yields $p_{clip}(t|RM1)$ [1]. Similarly, we use the c terms assigned the highest $S_{\mathcal{M}}(t;q)$, where $\mathcal{M} \in$ {Cent, CombSUM, CombMNZ, CombMAX}, to induce the language model $p(\cdot|\mathcal{M})$ as described above. The language models are integrated using a parameter α:

$$p(t|RM,\mathcal{M}) \stackrel{def}{=} \alpha p(t|\mathcal{M}) + (1-\alpha)p_{clip}(t|RM1). \quad (7)$$

We clip this language model to use the ν terms (ν is a free parameter) assigned the highest $p(t|RM,\mathcal{M})$, yielding $p_{clip}(\cdot|RM,\mathcal{M})$ which is integrated with q:

$$p(t|RM,\mathcal{M},q) \stackrel{def}{=} (1-\lambda)p_{clip}(t|RM,\mathcal{M}) + \lambda p_{MLE}(t|q). \quad (8)$$

These methods are denoted **RM-$\mathcal{M}$** where $\mathcal{M} \in$ {Cent, CombSUM, CombMNZ, CombMAX}. If α is set to 0 in Eq. 7, i.e., Word2Vec-based expansion is not used, then Eq. 8 is the relevance model RM3 [1].

2.4 Document ranking

Documents are ranked by the cross entropy between a query model and their Dirichlet smoothed language models [19]. We use a few query language models. Using $p_{MLE}(\cdot|q)$ results in an initial (standard language-model-based) ranking (denoted **init**) from which the result list $\mathcal{D}_{\text{init}}$, used for relevance model construction, is derived. We also use the (query) language models from Eq. 5 and 8, Q-$\mathcal{M}$ and RM-$\mathcal{M}$, respectively. Relevance model RM3 [1], which is a special case of Equation 8 as noted above, is used for reference.

3. EXPERIMENTAL SETUP

The TREC datasets specified in Table 1 were used for experiments. Titles of TREC topics serve for queries. Krovetz stemming and stopword removal (using the INQUERY list) were applied to documents and queries. The Indri toolkit (www.lemurproject.org) was used for experiments.

Table 1: TREC datasets used for experiments.

Collection	TREC disks	# of Docs	Topics
WSJ	Disks 1&2	173,252	51-200
AP	Disks 1&3	242,918	51-200
ROBUST	Disks 4,5-CR	528,155	301-450, 601-700
WT10G	WT10g	1,692,096	451-550
GOV2	GOV2	25,205,179	701-850

MAP (@1000), precision of the top five documents (p@5), and the reliability of improvement (RI) [14] are used as evaluation measures. RI is: $\frac{|Q_+|-|Q_-|}{|Q|}$; Q is the set of queries; Q_+ and Q_- are the sets queries for which the average precision (AP) is higher and lower, respectively, than that of the initial ranking. RI is a measure of the robustness of a query expansion method. Statistically significant differences of performance are determined using the two-tailed paired t-test at a 95% confidence level.

We train the CBOW model of Word2Vec[1] using all documents in each corpus, except for GOV2. For GOV2, due to vocabulary size scale issues, we used the Word2Vec models trained over WT10G[2]. Documents were processed as described above except that terms longer than 50 characters were excluded due to Word2Vec limitations. Word2Vec incorporates several free parameters: the dimension of the term vectors was set to values in $\{100, 500\}$, the number of negative examples is in $\{5, 10\}$, and the window size is in $\{8, 16, 64\}$; sub-sampling of frequent terms was not performed. All other parameters were set to default values.

The Dirichlet smoothing parameter for document language models is set to 1000 unless otherwise specified. The query weight λ in *all* expansion models is in $\{0, 0.2, \ldots, 1\}$. The number of terms, ν, used by *all* query expansion models, is in $\{10, 25\}$. The number of terms similar to a single query term, n (see Section 2.1.2), is selected from $\{50, 100\}$. For the methods described in Section 2.2, the values of the aforementioned free parameters (including those of Word2Vec) are set using leave-one-out cross validation performed over queries, where MAP serves as the optimization criterion.

The free parameters of the RM-$\mathcal{M}$ models (Section 2.3) are set as follows. First, we set the parameters of RM1 per value of c ($\in \{50, 100\}$) terms. The other parameters of RM1 are set using leave-one-out cross validation where the maximization criterion is the resultant RM3's MAP: (1) the Dirichlet smoothing parameter used for document language models for constructing RM1 is in $\{0, 1000\}$; (2) the number of documents in $\mathcal{D}_{\text{init}}$ from which RM1 is constructed is in $\{10, 25, 50\}$; (3) the original query weight λ ($\in \{0, 0.2, \ldots, 1\}$). The values of all remaining parameters are set using leave-one-out cross validation; here, the MAP of the resultant query expansion method is optimized. The parameters are those of the CBOW model, α ($\in \{0, 0.2, \ldots, 1\}$), λ ($\in \{0, 0.2, \ldots, 1\}$), n and c; the latter two are coupled to the same values in the RM-Comb methods.

For RM3, which serves as a baseline, the ranges of the number of expansion terms, the query weight λ, the Dirich-

[1]www.code.google.com/p/word2vec

[2]Applying Word2Vec models trained using one corpus on another corpus was shown to be effective for query expansion [17] and translation models [21].

Table 2: **Expanding the original query. The best and second best results in each column are boldfaced. The best result in a column is underlined. Statistically significant differences with the initial ranking (init), RM3, NTLM, Q-Cent, Q-CombSUM and Q-CombMNZ are marked with 'i', 'r', 't', 'c', 's' and 'm', respectively.**

	WSJ			AP			ROBUST			WT10G			GOV2		
	MAP	p@5	RI	MAP	p@5	RI	MAP	p@5	RI	MAP	p@5	RI	MAP	p@5	RI
init	.272	.489	–	.216	.413	–	.249	.476	–	.198	.355	–	.299	.588	–
RM3	$\underline{\mathbf{.324^{i}}}$	$.520^{i}$	$\underline{\mathbf{.355}}$	$\underline{\mathbf{.274^{i}}}$	.435	$\underline{\mathbf{.443}}$	$\underline{\mathbf{.282^{i}}}$	.483	$\underline{\mathbf{.293}}$	$\underline{\mathbf{.234^{i}}}$	$\underline{\mathbf{.390}}$	.082	$\underline{\mathbf{.331^{i}}}$	.596	$\underline{\mathbf{.392}}$
NTLM	$.277^{r}$	.504	−.073	$.226^{i,r}$	.442	.094	$.241^{r}$	.481	−.241	$.201^{r}$	.344	−.031	$.280^{i,r}$	.574	−.311
Q-Cent	$.294^{i,r,t}$	$.519^{i}$	.187	$\mathbf{.243^{i,r,t}}$	.432	.289	$\mathbf{.256^{i,r,t}}$	**.488**	**.241**	$.201^{r}$	.348	.052	$.300^{r,t}$	$\mathbf{.622^{i,t}}$	−.041
Q-CombSUM	$\mathbf{.295^{i,r,t}}$	$.520^{i}$	.227	$.235^{i,r}_{c}$	$.447^{i}$	.221	$.253^{r,t}$	.487	.137	$\mathbf{.205^{r}}$	**.359**	**.134**	$.301^{r,t}$	$.615^{i,t}$	−.014
Q-CombMNZ	$.291^{i,r,t}$	$\underline{\mathbf{.524^{i}}}$	.273	$.234^{i,r}_{c}$	$\underline{\mathbf{.451^{i}}}$	**.383**	$.252^{i,r,t}_{c}$	.476	.205	$.203^{r}$	.353	$\underline{\mathbf{.155}}$	$.297^{r,t}_{s}$	$.616^{i,t}$	−.095
Q-CombMAX	$.294^{i,r,t}$	$\mathbf{.521^{i}}$	**.313**	$.237^{i,r,t}$	$\mathbf{.448^{i}}$	.282	$.253^{i,r,t}$	$\underline{\mathbf{.491^{i}_{m}}}$	.237	$.203^{r}$	.351	.124	$\mathbf{.305^{i,r,t}_{c,s,m}}$	$\underline{\mathbf{.631^{i,r,t}}}$	**.074**

Table 3: **Integration with the relevance model. The best result in a column is boldfaced. Statistically significant differences with the initial ranking (init), RM3, RM-Cent, RM-CombSUM and RM-CombMNZ are marked with 'i', 'r', 'c', 's' and 'm', respectively.**

	WSJ			AP			ROBUST			WT10G			GOV2		
	MAP	p@5	RI	MAP	p@5	RI	MAP	p@5	RI	MAP	p@5	RI	MAP	p@5	RI
init	.272	.489	–	.216	.413	–	.249	.476	–	.198	.355	–	.299	.588	–
RM3	$.324^{i}$	$.520^{i}$	.355	$.274^{i}$	.435	.443	$.282^{i}$	.483	**.293**	$.234^{i}$	.390	.082	$.331^{i}$	.596	**.432**
RM-Cent	$\mathbf{.332^{i,r}}$	$\mathbf{.548^{i,r}}$	**.387**	$\mathbf{.282^{i,r}}$	$\mathbf{.464^{i,r}}$	.416	$\mathbf{.291^{i,r}}$	.495	.261	$\mathbf{.240^{i,r}}$	.396	**.155**	$.335^{i,r}$	$\mathbf{.623^{r}}$	.392
RM-CombSUM	$.325^{i}_{c}$	$.533^{i}$	.320	$.279^{i,r}$	.447	**.483**	$\mathbf{.291^{i,r}}$	.492	.245	$.236^{i}$	$\mathbf{.402^{i}}$	.113	$.335^{i,r}$	$.618^{r}$	.405
RM-CombMNZ	$.318^{i,r}_{c,s}$	$.523^{i}_{c}$	.247	$.278^{i,r}$	$.432_{c}$	.456	$.289^{i,r}$	.483	.249	$.231^{i}$	$.396^{i}$	.093	$.335^{i,r}$	$.614^{r}_{c}$	**.432**
RM-CombMAX	$.330^{i,r}_{s,m}$	$.541^{i,r}$	.373	$.278^{i}$	$.439_{c}$	**.483**	$.290^{i,r}$	$\mathbf{.496_{m}}$	.245	$.237^{i}$	$\mathbf{.402^{i}}$	.113	$\mathbf{.336^{i,r}}$	$.622^{r}$	.297

let smoothing parameter used to construct the model, and the number of documents in $\mathcal{D}_{\text{init}}$ from which RM3 is constructed, are as specified above for the RM-$\mathcal{M}$ models. Leave-one-out cross validation was applied to set parameter values.

The NTLM translation model serves as an additional baseline [21]. The 10 terms most similar to each query term, based on Word2Vec, were considered as translation terms. Translation probabilities were computed using sum-normalized cosine similarity between a query term and a translation term. The top 1000 documents in the initial ranking were re-ranked using NTLM as we found that ranking all documents in the corpus that contain at least one query term often resulted in inferior performance in four out of five corpora. Following the source code of [21], very frequent or very rare query terms were assigned a 1.0 translation probability[3]. The free parameters of NTLM, namely those of Word2Vec, were set using leave-one-out cross validation.

4. EXPERIMENTAL RESULTS

4.1 Expanding the query

Table 2 presents the performance of the Q-$\mathcal{M}$ methods from Section 2.2; these expand the original query with semantically related terms. All these methods outperform, in terms of MAP and p@5, both the initial retrieval and NTLM in the vast majority of cases; the majority of MAP improvements are statistically significant; the Q-$\mathcal{M}$ methods are also more robust (RI) than NTLM. In all corpora except for WT10G, the Q-$\mathcal{M}$ methods often outperform RM3 in terms of p@5, however rarely statistically significantly. Although RM3 is the best MAP performing expansion method in most cases, the Q-$\mathcal{M}$ methods yield effective performance and do not require initial retrieval as RM3.

We also see in Table 2 that no Q-$\mathcal{M}$ method dominates the others. The MAP and p@5 of Q-Cent, which performs expansion based on the query as a whole, is almost always statistically indistinguishable from that of the Q-Comb models that use expansions based on individual query terms.

Table 2 shows that NTLM, which uses Word2Vec-based translation probabilities, is almost always outperformed by RM3. Therefore, below we focus on RM3 as a baseline.

4.2 Integration with the relevance model

Table 3 presents the performance of the RM-$\mathcal{M}$ methods from Section 2.3 which integrate the Word2Vec-based expansion terms with the relevance model. RM-Cent, which integrates terms semantically similar to the query as a whole with the relevance model, performs best in most cases. RM-Cent always outperforms RM3 in terms of MAP and p@5; all MAP improvements are statistically significant. Among the models that utilize expansions based on individual query terms, RM-CombSUM and RM-CombMAX are the most effective: they always outperform RM3 for MAP and p@5. Finally, the robustness (RI) of each of our methods is higher than that of RM3 over at least two out of the five corpora.

4.3 Further analysis

We use query #546, "recycle cans", from WT10G to shed some light on the advantages of embedding-based query expansion. The 10 terms assigned the highest probability by RM1, Q-Cent and RM-Cent are: {**recycle**, **can**, paint, **plastic**, paper, accept, steel, contain, material, **bottle**}, {**can**, **recycle**, styrofoam, scrap, postconsumer, compost, **plastic**, trash, cardboard, **bottle**} and {**recycle**, **can**, **plastic**, **bottle**, paint, styrofoam, scrap, postconsumer, compost, trash}, respectively. (Boldfaced terms appear in all three lists.) Free parameters were fixed to effective values,

[3]The exact criteria for frequency-based term filtering is provided in the source code of [21]; applying the method without this filter or applying the filter on translation terms as well resulted in inferior retrieval effectiveness.

and no integration with the query was performed so as to focus on the effectiveness of the expansion terms.

The average precision (AP) of RM1, Q-Cent and RM-Cent for the query is 0.084, 0.096 and 0.107, respectively, showing again the merits of integrating Word2Vec-based expansion terms with the relevance model. The three models share 4 out of 10 terms. Among the RM1 terms we find general verbs ("accept", "contain") which could cause query drift as is common in pseudo-feedback-based methods. In contrast, all the terms in the Q-Cent list are topical ("scrap", "styrofoam" and "bottle" are all recycled materials/items). This difference translates to a higher AP of Q-Cent than RM1. Naturally, word-embeddings-based expansion can cause query drift, as is the case for other global expansion methods. Indeed, it was shown that local training of word embeddings using retrieved documents can improve expansion effectiveness [6].

We also found that the top terms of the Word2Vec-based expansion and the relevance model often differ. This further attests to the complementary nature of these expansion approaches leveraged by the RM-$\mathcal{M}$ methods.

5. RELATED WORK

Word embeddings were used to re-weight the query terms [20] and to compare a query directly with a document [16, 12]. Document embeddings [5, 2] and word-embeddings-based translation models [8, 21] were also used for retrieval. We focused on query expansion and showed that our methods outperform an embedding-based translation model [21].

Embedding-based query expansion was also used in the medical domain [9], but did not outperform retrieval using only the query. Supervised concept-based embedding of n-grams was used for document retrieval [15]. Our methods utilize unsupervised unigram embeddings.

Recently, query expansion approaches conceptually similar to our Q-CombSUM method were proposed [3, 6, 13]: expansion terms are scored using the (weighted) sum of their embedding-based similarities with query terms. We used additional approaches to integrate these similarities, and combined them with pseudo-feedback-based expansion.

Work on embedding a query language model for query expansion [18] provides formal grounds to using a centroid-based representation of the embedding vectors of the query terms as in our Q-Cent and RM-Cent methods. Our RM-Cent method which integrates the expanded query with a relevance model is different than that which uses an embedding of a relevance model to expand the query [18].

In work to be presented closely in time to ours [17], expansion terms are scored, in spirit, by the arithmetic (similarly to our Q-CombSUM method) and geometric mean of their embedding-based similarities to the query terms; our Q-Cent method was also used; our Q-CombMNZ and Q-CombMAX methods (and their RM-$\mathcal{M}$ counterparts) were not presented. The merits of integrating embedding-based query expansion with a relevance model were demonstrated as in our work; and, the merits of using embeddings for relevance model construction were also shown [17].

6. CONCLUSIONS

We demonstrated the merits of query expansion methods that utilize word embeddings induced in a query-independent manner from the entire document corpus. Specifically, our methods utilize the embeddings to expand the query with terms that are semantically related to the query as a whole or to its terms. In addition, we showed the effectiveness of an approach for integrating our query expansion methods with a pseudo-feedback-based query expansion approach; namely, the relevance model.

Acknowledgments. We thank the reviewers for their comments. This work was supported in part by the Israel Science Foundation (grant no. 433/12), the Technion-Microsoft Electronic Commerce Research Center, and by the Irwin and Joan Jacobs Fellowship for graduate students.

7. REFERENCES

[1] N. Abdul-Jaleel, J. Allan, W. B. Croft, F. Diaz, L. Larkey, X. Li, M. D. Smucker, and C. Wade. UMASS at TREC 2004 — novelty and hard. In *Proc. of TREC-13*, 2004.

[2] Q. Ai, L. Yang, J. Guo, and W. B. Croft. Improving language estimation with the paragraph vector model for ad-hoc retrieval. In *Proc. of SIGIR*, pages 869–872. ACM, 2016.

[3] M. Almasri, C. Berrut, and J. Chevallet. A comparison of deep learning based query expansion with pseudo-relevance feedback and mutual information. In *Proc. of ECIR*, pages 709–715, 2016.

[4] C. Carpineto and G. Romano. A survey of automatic query expansion in information retrieval. *ACM Computing Surveys*, 44(1):1, 2012.

[5] S. Clinchant and F. Perronnin. Aggregating continuous word embeddings for information retrieval. In *Proc. of the Workshop on Continuous Vector Space Models and their Compositionality*, pages 100–109. ACL, 2013.

[6] F. Diaz, B. Mitra, and N. Craswell. Query expansion with locally-trained word embeddings. *CoRR*, 2016.

[7] E. A. Fox and J. A. Shaw. Combination of multiple searches. In *Proc. of TREC-2*, 1994.

[8] D. Ganguly, D. Roy, M. Mitra, and G. J. Jones. Word embedding based generalized language model for information retrieval. In *Proc. of SIGIR*, pages 795–798, 2015.

[9] T. Goodwin and S. M. Harabagiu. UTD at TREC 2014: Query expansion for clinical decision support. In *Proc. of TREC*, 2014.

[10] V. Lavrenko and W. B. Croft. Relevance-based language models. In *Proc. of SIGIR*, pages 120–127, 2001.

[11] T. Mikolov, K. Chen, G. Corrado, and J. Dean. Efficient estimation of word representations in vector space. *CoRR*, abs/1301.3781, 2013.

[12] E. Nalisnick, B. Mitra, N. Craswell, and R. Caruana. Improving document ranking with dual word embeddings. In *Proc. of WWW*, pages 83–84, 2016.

[13] D. Roy, D. Paul, M. Mitra, and U. Garain. Using word embeddings for automatic query expansion. In *Proc. of the ACM SIGIR 2016 Workshop on Neural Information Retrieval (Neu-IR 2016)*, 2016.

[14] T. Sakai, T. Manabe, and M. Koyama. Flexible pseudo-relevance feedback via selective sampling. *ACM Transactions on Asian Language Information Processing (TALIP)*, 4(2):111–135, 2005.

[15] A. Sordoni, Y. Bengio, and J.-Y. Nie. Learning concept embeddings for query expansion by quantum entropy minimization. In *Proc. of AAAI*, pages 1586–1592, 2014.

[16] I. Vulić and M.-F. Moens. Monolingual and cross-lingual information retrieval models based on (bilingual) word embeddings. In *Proc. of SIGIR*, pages 363–372, 2015.

[17] H. Zamani and W. B. Croft. Embedding-based query language models. In *Proc. of ICTIR*, 2016.

[18] H. Zamani and W. B. Croft. Estimating embedding vectors for queries. In *Proc. of ICTIR*, 2016.

[19] C. Zhai and J. D. Lafferty. A study of smoothing methods for language models applied to ad hoc information retrieval. In *Proc. of SIGIR*, pages 334–342, 2001.

[20] G. Zheng and J. Callan. Learning to reweight terms with distributed representations. In *Proc. of SIGIR*, pages 575–584, 2015.

[21] G. Zuccon, B. Koopman, P. Bruza, and L. Azzopardi. Integrating and evaluating neural word embeddings in information retrieval. In *Proc. of ADCS*, pages 12:1–12:8, 2015.

Efficient Distributed Regular Path Queries on RDF Graphs Using Partial Evaluation*

Xin Wang[†§¶], Junhu Wang[‡], Xiaowang Zhang[†§]
[†]School of Computer Science and Technology, Tianjin University, P.R. China
[‡]School of Information and Communication Technology, Griffith University, Australia
[§]Tianjin Key Lab. of Cognitive Computing and Application, P.R. China
[¶]State Key Lab. for Novel Software Technology, Nanjing University, P.R. China
wangx@tju.edu.cn, j.wang@griffith.edu.au, xiaowangzhang@tju.edu.cn

ABSTRACT

We propose an efficient distributed method for answering regular path queries (RPQs) on large-scale RDF graphs using partial evaluation. In local computation, we devise a dynamic programming approach to evaluate local and partial answers of an RPQ on each computing site in parallel. In the assembly phase, an automata-based algorithm is proposed to assemble the partial answers of the RPQ into the final results. The experiments on benchmark RDF graphs show that our method outperforms the state-of-the-art message passing methods by up to an order of magnitude.

Keywords

regular path query; RDF graph; partial evaluation

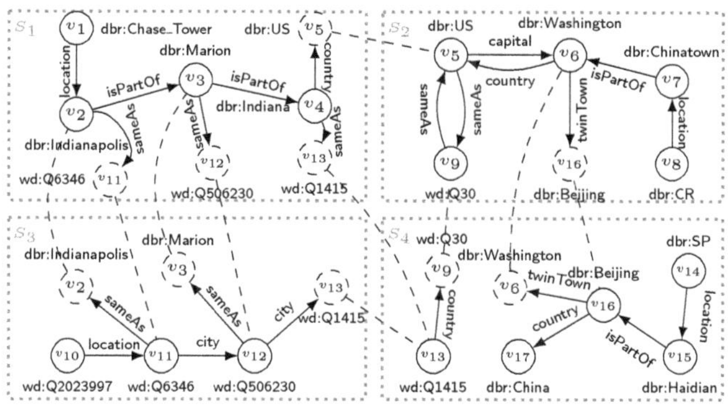

Figure 1: A distributed RDF graph T_1

1. INTRODUCTION

Let U and L be disjoint sets of URIs and literals, respectively. An RDF graph T is a set of triples. Each *triple* $(s, p, o) \in U \times U \times (U \cup L)$ states the fact that the resource s has the relationship p to the resource $o \in U$, or the resource s has the property p with the value $o \in L$, where s is called the subject, p the predicate (or property), and o the object. In recent years, driven by the Linked Data campaign, increasingly large amounts of RDF graph data from various domains have been published on the Web. It has become essential to develop scalable distributed techniques to efficiently manage large-scale RDF graphs with millions or even billions of triples in the Linked Data cloud. Fig. 1 shows a distributed RDF graph T_1, excerpted from the Linked Data, which is stored on a 4-site cluster.

As one of the key functionalities provided by most query languages for graph data, *regular path queries*, or RPQs, are widely recognized as a requisite tool for querying large graphs in a navigational manner. For this reason, the latest version of standard RDF query language, SPARQL 1.1, has introduced the *property path* feature that includes RPQs at its core. An RPQ $Q = (x, r, y)$ on an RDF graph T asks for a set of pairs of resources (s, o) such that there exists a path ρ in T from s to o with the label of ρ satisfying the regular expression r in Q. For example, the RPQ

$$Q_1 = (x, \mathsf{location}/(\mathsf{sameAs}^*/(\mathsf{isPartOf}|\mathsf{city}))^+/\mathsf{country}, y)$$

on T_1 asks to find pairs of resources (s, o) such that o is the country where s is located in. Although theoretical aspects of RPQs have been well studied [4, 1, 3], practical techniques, such as efficient RPQ evaluation and optimization, have been largely overlooked, especially distributed/parallel approaches for RPQs over large-scale RDF graphs.

The canonical method for evaluating an RPQ is to run the *product automaton* constructed from the NFA that is equivalent to the graph data and the NFA that is equivalent to the RPQ [4]. Thus far, [6] is the most representative work that is dedicated to RPQ evaluation in distributed settings by using message passing mechanism to parallelize the product automaton method. However, the drawback of this approach is that it may incur excessive communication cost when dealing with big RDF graphs due to the large number of messages passed between different sites in a cluster.

In this paper, we propose an efficient method for answering RPQs over large-scale distributed RDF graphs using *partial evaluation*. The basic idea of partial evaluation is as follows: given a function $\mathsf{f}(s, d)$ where s is the known input and d is the as yet unavailable input, (1) we partially evaluate $\mathsf{f}(s, d)$ only w.r.t. s and obtain a partial answer that is

*This work was done while the first author was a visiting scholar at Griffith University.

CIKM'16, October 24-28, 2016, Indianapolis, IN, USA
© 2016 ACM. ISBN 978-1-4503-4073-1/16/10...$15.00
DOI: http://dx.doi.org/10.1145/2983323.2983877

a residual function $f'(d)$ depending only on d; (2) the complete answer of f can be generated by evaluating $f'(d)$ w.r.t. d. This idea can be naturally employed to evaluate queries in a distributed manner, where a query Q is treated as f, a fragment of data F_i on each site S_i is treated as the known input s, and data fragments on other sites are considered as the unavailable input d. Obviously, in this setting, (1) first we can locally compute $f(s, d)$ on each site *in parallel* to get partial answers to Q, (2) then send all the partial answers to a coordinator site, and (3) lastly assemble these partial answers into the final answers to Q via $f'(d)$.

More recently, partial evaluation has been applied in distributed query processing on graph data [2, 5]. Algorithms for evaluating reachability, bounded reachability, and regular reachability queries on distributed graphs have been developed based on partial evaluation in [2]. In fact, a regular reachability query $Q = (s, r, t)$, which merely asks *whether* there exists a path ρ from the *given* resource s to t such that ρ satisfies r, is just a special form of a RPQ. Since the answers to a regular reachability query are *Boolean values*, the method of solving a set of Boolean equations can be used in [2]. However, such an approach cannot be trivially adapted to evaluate RPQs that have a more rich semantics (i.e., a set of *pairs* of resources), which is also the main challenge we address in this paper. In [5], a partial-evaluation-based method is proposed to deal with SPARQL BGP queries on distributed RDF graphs, which is another type of graph queries that is mostly orthogonal to RPQs studied in this paper. Thus far, we are not aware of any distributed algorithm that answers RPQs under its standard semantics using partial evaluation.

Contributions. Our main contributions include: (1) for the local computation phase of partial evaluation, we propose a novel dynamic programming algorithm that can evaluate RPQs over distributed RDF graphs to obtain local and partial answers in parallel; (2) for the assembly phase of partial evaluation, we devise an automata-based algorithm that can efficiently assemble partial answers into crossing answers to RPQs. (3) Experiments are conducted to verify the efficiency and scalability of our proposed algorithms.

2. LOCAL COMPUTATION

2.1 Distributed RPQs

Given an RDF graph T, we use $S(T)$, $P(T)$, and $O(T)$ to denote the set of subjects, predicates, and objects in T, respectively. We define the set of *resources* in T as $Res(T) = S(T) \cup (O(T) \cap U)$. A path in T from resource x to y is a sequence $\rho = v_0e_0v_1 \cdots v_{n-1}e_{n-1}v_n$, where $v_0 = x$, $v_n = y$, $(v_i, e_i, v_{i+1}) \in T$ for every $i \in \{0, \ldots, n-1\}$. Obviously, a path ρ can also be viewed as a set of triples in T, i.e., $\rho = \{(v_i, e_i, v_{i+1}) \in T \mid i \in \{0, \ldots, n-1\}\}$. Let $\Sigma = P(T)$ be a finite alphabet. The label of a path ρ, denoted by $\lambda(\rho)$, is the string $e_0 \cdots e_{n-1} \in \Sigma^*$.

A RPQ on T is denoted by $Q = (x, r, y)$, where x, y are variables, and r is a regular expression over Σ. In accordance with the SPARQL property path syntax, r is recursively defined as $r ::= \varepsilon \mid p \mid r/r \mid r|r \mid r^*$, where $p \in \Sigma$ and /, |, and * are concatenation, alternation, and the Kleene closure, respectively. The shorthands r^+ for r/r^* and $r?$ for $\varepsilon|r$ are also allowed. We use $r[i]$ to denote the i-th symbol in r. $L(r)$ is the language expressed by r. The answer set of an RPQ Q on T, denoted by $[\![Q]\!]_T$, is defined as a set of all pairs of resources (s, o) such that there exists a path ρ in T from s to o satisfying $\lambda(\rho) \in L(r)$.

For a certain subject $s_i \in S(T)$, we refer to the triples with the same subject s_i collectively as the *entity* s_i, denoted by $Ent(s_i)$. The set of all entities occurred in T is denoted by $\mathcal{E}(T) = \{Ent(s) \mid s \in S(T)\}$. Given a partition $\{\mathcal{E}_1, \ldots, \mathcal{E}_n\}$ of $\mathcal{E}(T)$, $\mathcal{F} = \{F_1, \ldots, F_n\}$ is a *fragmentation* of T, where *fragment* $F_i = \bigcup_{Ent(s) \in \mathcal{E}_i} Ent(s)$ for $i \in \{1, \ldots, n\}$. T is considered as a *distributed RDF graph* w.r.t. $\mathcal{F}$. The function $\mathsf{frag}(s)$ returns the subscript i of F_i that s belongs to, i.e., $Ent(s) \in \mathcal{E}_i$. For a fragment F_i, we also identify the set of incoming resources $F_i.I = \{s \mid \exists\, (s', p, s) \in F_j \wedge \mathsf{frag}(s) = i \wedge i \neq j\}$ and the set of outgoing resources $F_i.O = \{s \mid \exists\, (s', p, s) \in F_i \wedge \mathsf{frag}(s) = j \wedge i \neq j\}$. $\mathcal{S} = \{S_0, S_1, \ldots, S_n\}$ is a set of $(n+1)$ computing nodes, i.e., *sites*, in a computer cluster. S_0 is designated as the *coordinator site*. W.l.o.g., each F_i is stored at S_i for $i \in \{1, \ldots, n\}$.

Let T be a distributed RDF graph w.r.t. a fragmentation $\mathcal{F}$, and Q be an RPQ on T. The problem that we address in this paper is to evaluate the answer set $[\![Q]\!]_T$. (1) The *local answer set* of Q w.r.t. F_i is $[\![Q]\!]_{F_i} = \{(s, o) \mid$ there exists a *local path* $\rho \subseteq F_i$ from s to o s.t. $\lambda(\rho) \in L(r)\}$, and local answer set of Q on T is $[\![Q]\!]^l_T = \bigcup_{i=1}^n [\![Q]\!]_{F_i}$. (2) The *crossing answer set* of Q is $[\![Q]\!]^c_T = \{(s, o) \mid$ there exists a *crossing path* ρ in T from s to o s.t. $\lambda(\rho) \in L(r)\}$, where a crossing path crosses at least two fragments. Obviously, we have $[\![Q]\!]^l_T \cup [\![Q]\!]^c_T = [\![Q]\!]_T$ and $[\![Q]\!]^l_T \cap [\![Q]\!]^c_T = \emptyset$.

2.2 Local Computation Algorithm

Our local computation algorithm, in partial evaluation for distributed RPQs, is to find not only the local answer set w.r.t. F_i, but also the *partial answer set*, i.e., the set of paths in F_i that may *possibly* be connected with partial answers in other fragments to form crossing answers.

The algorithm, named evalET, is shown in Algorithm 1, whose process is based upon the depth-first traversal of the *expression tree* ET_Q of an RPQ $Q = (x, r, y)$. In fact, ET_Q is a parse tree of r. Each node v of ET_Q has its label $v.re$ where re is a subexpression of r. Recursively, (1) if v is the root of ET_Q, $v.re = r$; (2) if $v.re = r_1^*$, then v has only one child v_1 and $v_1.re = r_1$; (3) if $v.re = r_1/\ldots/r_n$ (resp. $r_1|\ldots|r_n$), v has n children $v_1, \ldots, v_n$ and $v_i.re = r_i$ for $i \in \{1, \ldots, n\}$; (4) if $v.re = p$ (resp. ε), v is a leaf node. Meanwhile, $v.op$ denotes the outermost operation on $v.re$.

Upon receiving an RPQ Q from the coordinator site S_0, evalET is invoked on the *root* v of ET_Q on each site, *in parallel*. Then, evalET recursively visits each child of v (line 2), and calculates a quadruple relation $v.R$ (line 3) for v depending on $v.op$ (lines 4-9). For each tuple $(s, o, a, b) \in v.R$, (s, o) is a local answer and/or a partial answer (together with (a, b)) of the RPQ $(x, v.re, y)$.

For $v.op = \varepsilon$, p, $*$, and |, the calculations of $v.R$ are self-explanatory (lines 5-8), while more efforts are needed for the case $v.op = /$ by calling the function evalCat (line 9). Actually, evalCat implements an extended version of a multi-way nested loop join. That is, for a tuple (s, o, a, b) in the current intermediate result set R_t, if o is an outgoing resource, i.e., $o \in F_i.O$, then the tuple is directly put in $v.R$ without further joining (lines 16-17); for a tuple (s', o', a', b') in the k-th child's relation $v_k.R$ ($k \in \{2, \ldots, n\}$), if s' is an incoming resource, i.e., $s' \in F_i.I$, then the tuple is put in the next intermediate result set R' to participate in further joining without being joined by R_t (lines 18-19).

Algorithm 1: evalET // executed at each site S_i

1 **Function** evalET
  Input : A node v in the expression tree ET_Q.
  Output: The quadruple relation $v.R$ associated with v.
2 Let $(v_1, \ldots, v_n)$ be the sequence of child nodes of v;
3 $R \leftarrow \emptyset$;
4 **switch** $v.op$ **do**
5   **case** ε **do** $v.R \leftarrow \{(s, s, 0, 0) \mid s \in S(F_i)\}$;
6   **case** $p = r[a]$ **do** $v.R \leftarrow \{(s, o, a, a) \mid (s, p, o) \in F_i\}$;
7   **case** $*$ **do** $v.R \leftarrow$ evalET$(v_1)^*$; // * closure operation
8   **case** $\mid$ **do** $v.R \leftarrow \bigcup_{i=1}^{n}$ evalET(v_i);
9   **case** $/$ **do** $v.R \leftarrow$ evalCat$((v_1, \ldots, v_n))$;
10 **return** $v.R$;
11 **Function** evalCat
  Input : The sequence of child nodes $(v_1, \ldots, v_n)$ of v.
  Output: The quadruple relation $v.R$ for $v.op = /$.
12 $R_t \leftarrow$ evalET(v_1); // the current intermediate result set
13 **for** $k \leftarrow 2$ **to** n **do**
14   $R' \leftarrow \emptyset$; // the next intermediate result set
15   $v_k.R \leftarrow$ evalET(v_k);
16   **foreach** $(s, o, a, b) \in R_t$ **do**
17   **if** $o \in F_i.O$ **then** $R \leftarrow R \cup \{(s, o, a, b)\}$;
18   **foreach** $(s', o', a', b') \in v_k.R$ **do**
19   **if** $s' \in F_i.I$ **then** $R' \leftarrow R' \cup \{(s', o', a', b')\}$;
20   **if** $o = s'$ **then** $R' \leftarrow R' \cup \{(s, o', a, b')\}$;
21   $R_t \leftarrow R'$;
22 $R \leftarrow R \cup R_t$;
23 **return** R;

It can be observed that the time complexity of evalET is $O(|r||R_m|^2)$, where $|r|$ is the length of the regular expression r in Q, and $|R_m|$ is the size of the largest $v.R$ in ET_Q on all sites. It seems that $|R_m|^2$ makes the algorithm unfeasible for a large input. However, the nested loop here (lines 16-20) is just used to help understand the idea of our algorithm; in our implementation, we have employed optimized hash indexes to obtain a significantly fast evalCat procedure.

In fact, Algorithm 1 follows a dynamic programming approach, which is inspired by [3]. In particular, we have adapted the algorithm in [3] for the distributed setting.

2.3 Automata of RPQs and Partial Answers

We define the *automaton of an RPQ* $Q = (x, r, y)$ as an NFA A_Q converted from r by using the Thompson's construction algorithm. Formally, $A_Q = (S, \Sigma_\varepsilon, \delta, q_0, q_f)$, where S is a finite set of states, $\Sigma_\varepsilon = \Sigma \cup \{\varepsilon\}$ is the alphabet ($\Sigma = P(T)$), $\delta : S \times \Sigma_\varepsilon \rightarrow 2^S$ is the transition function, q_0 is the initial state, and q_f is the final state. It is obvious to see that there exists a *bijective* function between the i-th predicate $r[i]$ in r and the corresponding $\delta(q, r[i])$. We define the *ε-closure transition function* $\delta_\varepsilon(q, r[i]) = \{q' \mid \exists\ j \text{ s.t. } \delta(q', r[j]) \neq \emptyset \wedge q'$ is reachable from some state in $\delta(q, r[i])$ via 0 or more ε-edge(s) in $G_{A_Q}\}$, where G_{A_Q} is the *transition graph* of A_Q. For a symbol $r[i]$ in r, the set of *successors* of i, denoted by suc(i), is $\{j \mid \delta(q', r[j]) \neq \emptyset \wedge q' \in \delta_\varepsilon(q, r[i])\}$.

For a distributed RDF graph T with its fragmentation $\mathcal{F}$, we identify three types of the *partial answer sets* of an RPQ $Q = (x, r, y)$ w.r.t. a fragment $F_i \in \mathcal{F}$ as follows: (1) the *prefix partial answer set* $[\![Q]\!]_{F_i}^{pre} = \{(s, o, a, b) \mid o \in F_i.O \wedge \exists$ a path ρ in F_i from s to $o \wedge \exists$ a path ρ' in G_{A_Q} from q_0 to $q \wedge \lambda(\rho) = \lambda(\rho')\}$; (2) the *infix partial answer set* $[\![Q]\!]_{F_i}^{inf} = \{(s, o, a, b) \mid s \in F_i.I \wedge o \in F_i.O \wedge \exists$ a path ρ in F_i from s to $o \wedge \exists$ a path ρ' in G_{A_Q} from q to $q' \wedge \lambda(\rho) = \lambda(\rho')\}$; and (3) the *suffix partial answer set* $[\![Q]\!]_{F_i}^{suf} = \{(s, o, a, b) \mid s \in F_i.I \wedge \exists$ a path ρ in F_i from s to $o \wedge \exists$ a path ρ' in G_{A_Q} from q to $q_f \wedge \lambda(\rho) = \lambda(\rho')\}$. In the above definitions, let $\rho = v_0e_0v_1 \cdots v_{n-1}e_{n-1}v_n$, a and b are the indexes of e_0 and e_{n-1} in r, respectively. Let w be a string whose length is k, we define first$(r) = \{i \mid \exists\ w \in L(r) \wedge r[i]$ matches $w[1]\}$ and last$(r) = \{i \mid \exists\ w \in L(r) \wedge r[i]$ matches $w[k]\}$.

For the post-processing step of local computation (not shown in Algorithm 1), each site S_i in parallel refines the quadruple relation $R =$ evalET$(ET_Q.root)$ into four subsets, i.e., $[\![Q]\!]_{F_i}$, $[\![Q]\!]_{F_i}^{pre}$, $[\![Q]\!]_{F_i}^{inf}$, and $[\![Q]\!]_{F_i}^{suf}$, as follows: for each $(s, o, a, b) \in R$, (1) if $a \in$ first$(r) \wedge b \in$ last(r), put it into $[\![Q]\!]_{F_i}$; (2) if $a \in$ first$(r) \wedge o \in F_i.O$, put it into $[\![Q]\!]_{F_i}^{pre}$; (3) if $s \in F_i.I \wedge o \in F_i.O$, put it into $[\![Q]\!]_{F_i}^{inf}$; and (4) if $s \in F_i.I \wedge b \in$ last(r), put it into $[\![Q]\!]_{F_i}^{suf}$. Note that each (s, o, a, b) may be put into more than one subset.

3. ASSEMBLY

In the assembly phase, upon receiving all the local and partial answer sets, i.e., $[\![Q]\!]_{F_i}$, $[\![Q]\!]_{F_i}^{pre}$, $[\![Q]\!]_{F_i}^{inf}$, and $[\![Q]\!]_{F_i}^{suf}$, from every site S_i, the coordinator site S_0 can easily obtain $[\![Q]\!]_T^{l} = \bigcup_{i=1}^{n}[\![Q]\!]_{F_i}$, $[\![Q]\!]_T^{pre} = \bigcup_{i=1}^{n}[\![Q]\!]_{F_i}^{pre}$, $[\![Q]\!]_T^{inf} = \bigcup_{i=1}^{n}[\![Q]\!]_{F_i}^{inf}$, and $[\![Q]\!]_T^{suf} = \bigcup_{i=1}^{n}[\![Q]\!]_{F_i}^{suf}$. Finally, S_0 invokes Algorithm 2, called assemble, to weave the three types of the partial answer sets into the final crossing answer set $[\![Q]\!]_T^{c}$.

Algorithm 2: assemble // executed at the coordinator site S_0

  Input : $[\![Q]\!]_T^{pre}$, $[\![Q]\!]_T^{inf}$, and $[\![Q]\!]_T^{suf}$.
  Output: The crossing answer set $[\![Q]\!]_T^{c}$.
1 $Map_{inf} \leftarrow \emptyset$, $Map_{suf} \leftarrow \emptyset$; // hash tables
2 **foreach** $(s, o, a, b) \in [\![Q]\!]_T^{inf}$ **do** // initialise
3   $Map_{inf}[(s, a)] \leftarrow Map_{inf}[(s, a)] \cup \{(o, b)\}$;
4 **foreach** $(s, o, a, b) \in [\![Q]\!]_T^{suf}$ **do**
5   $Map_{suf}[(s, a)] \leftarrow Map_{suf}[(s, a)] \cup \{(o, b)\}$
6 $R \leftarrow [\![Q]\!]_T^{pre}$; // the current intermediate result set
7 **while** $R \neq \emptyset$ **do**
8   $R_t \leftarrow \emptyset$; // the next intermediate result set
9   **foreach** $(s, o, a, b) \in R$ **do**
10   **foreach** $i \in$ suc(b) **do** // advance A_Q to $\delta(q, r[i])$
11       $R_{suf} \leftarrow Map_{suf}[(o, i)]$;
12   **foreach** $(o', b') \in R_{suf}$ **do** // crossing answers
13         $[\![Q]\!]_T^{c} \leftarrow [\![Q]\!]_T^{c} \cup \{(s, o')\}$;
14       $R_{inf} \leftarrow Map_{inf}[(o, i)]$;
15   **foreach** $(o', b') \in R_{inf}$ **do** // extend paths
16         $R_t \leftarrow R_t \cup \{(s, o', a, b')\}$;
17   $R \leftarrow R_t$;
18 **return** $[\![Q]\!]_T^{c}$;

The assemble algorithm, starting with $R = [\![Q]\!]_T^{pre}$ (line 6), extends potential paths in R by connecting them to partial answers in $[\![Q]\!]_T^{inf}$ and/or $[\![Q]\!]_T^{suf}$, repeatedly (lines 7-17). If a potential path $(s, o, a, b) \in R$ can be successfully (i.e., $\exists\ i \in$ suc(b) and $Map_{suf}[(o, i)] \neq \emptyset$) connected to a partial answer in $[\![Q]\!]_T^{suf}$, then a crossing answer forms (lines 10-13); otherwise, a potential path may also be extended by a partial answer in $[\![Q]\!]_T^{inf}$ under the same condition (lines 10, 14-16). Note that the cycle avoiding logic is omitted in the algorithm due to lack of space. In our implementation, we do have a mechanism to detect and avoid cycle answers. The following theorem ensures the correctness of assemble.

THEOREM 1. *Given a distributed RDF graph T with its fragmentation $\mathcal{F} = \{F_1, \ldots, F_n\}$ and an RPQ $Q = (x, r, y)$*

on T, let $\{F_{m_1}, \ldots, F_{m_k}\}$ be a subset of $\mathcal{F}$, and w.l.o.g. assume $(v_{l_0}, v_{l_1}, a_1, b_1) \in [\![Q]\!]^{pre}_{F_{m_1}}$, $(v_{l_{i-1}}, v_{l_i}, a_i, b_i) \in [\![Q]\!]^{inf}_{F_{m_i}}$ for $i \in \{2, \ldots, k-1\}$, and $(v_{l_{k-1}}, v_{l_k}, a_k, b_k) \in [\![Q]\!]^{suf}_{F_{m_k}}$. If $a_{i+1} \in \mathsf{suc}(b_i)$ for $i \in \{1, \ldots, k-1\}$, then (v_{l_0}, v_{l_k}) is a crossing answer of Q on T, i.e., $(v_{l_0}, v_{l_k}) \in [\![Q]\!]^{c}_{T}$.

PROOF. (Sketch) (1) Since $(v_{l_0}, v_{l_1}, a_1, b_1) \in [\![Q]\!]^{pre}_{F_{m_1}}$, $\exists$ a path ρ_1 in F_{m_1} from v_{l_0} to v_{l_1} and $\exists$ a path ρ'_1 in G_{A_Q} from q_0 to q_{b_1} and $\lambda(\rho_1) = \lambda(\rho'_1)$; (2) since $(v_{l_{i-1}}, v_{l_i}, a_i, b_i) \in [\![Q]\!]^{inf}_{F_{m_i}}$, $\exists$ a path ρ_i in F_{m_i} from $v_{l_{i-1}}$ to v_{l_i} and $\exists$ a path ρ'_i in G_{A_Q} from q_{a_i} to q_{b_i} and $\lambda(\rho_i) = \lambda(\rho'_i)$, for $i \in \{2, \ldots, k-1\}$; and (3) since $(v_{l_{k-1}}, v_{l_k}, a_k, b_k) \in [\![Q]\!]^{suf}_{F_{m_k}}$, $\exists$ a path ρ_k in F_{m_k} from $v_{l_{k-1}}$ to v_{l_k} and $\exists$ a path ρ'_k in G_{A_Q} from q_{a_k} to q_f and $\lambda(\rho_k) = \lambda(\rho'_k)$. Because $a_{i+1} \in \mathsf{suc}(b_i)$, we have $q_{a_{i+1}} \in \delta_\varepsilon(q_{b_i}, r[b_i])$ for $i \in \{1, \ldots, k-1\}$, thus, there exist both a path $\rho = \rho_1 \cdots \rho_k$ in T from v_{l_0} to v_{l_k} and a path $\rho' = \rho'_1 \cdots \rho'_k$ in G_{A_Q} from q_0 to q_f. $\square$

It can be observed that the time complexity of assemble is bounded by $O(|\rho_m||r||R_m|(|[\![Q]\!]^{inf}_T| + |[\![Q]\!]^{suf}_T|))$, where ρ_m is longest simple path in T and R_m is the largest possible R in the evaluation process of assemble.

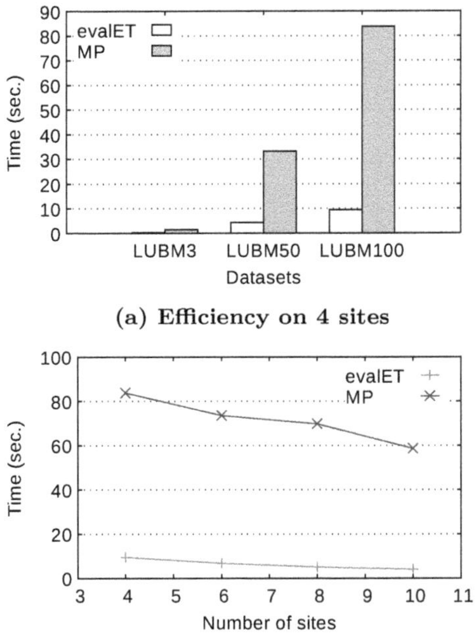

(a) **Efficiency on 4 sites**

(b) **Scalability varying the number of sites**

Figure 2: Experimental results

4. EXPERIMENTS

We conducted preliminary experiments to verify the efficiency and scalability of our algorithms. The prototype, which implemented the proposed algorithms, is deployed on a 10-site cluster connected by a gigabit Ethernet swith. Each node has one CPU with 4 cores of 3.1 GHz, 4 GB memory, and 500GB disk. For comparison, the message passing algorithms in [6], denoted by MP, were also implemented. All programs were implemented in Java.

We generated 3 datasets, LUBM3 (337K triples), LUBM50 (6.9M triples), and LUBM100 (13.9M triples), using the LUBM benchmark, and randomly partitioned these RDF graphs by hashing each entity $Ent(s_i)$ to a site in the cluster. We also selected 10 representative RPQs that cover all combinations of /, |, and * operators and whose answer sets are not empty on the LUBM RDF graphs. The time in our experiments is the average running time of these RPQs.

Experiment 1: Efficiency. We tested the RPQ evaluation time over 3 datasets on a 4-site cluster. The results are shown in Fig. 2(a). It can be observed that evalET outperforms MP by up to an order of magnitude. The reason is that, as the size of RDF graphs increases, the communication cost of MP significantly increases due to the growing volume of messages passed, whereas, in evalET, sites only need to pass the partial results once to the coordinator.

Experiment 2: Scalability. The scalability of evalET was tested on LUBM100 by varying the number of sites from 4 to 10, as shown in Fig. 2(b). Although, with the number of sites increasing, the absolute time reduction of MP is larger than evalET, the speedup ratio evalET is about 1.61 times of MP. This is mainly because the increased number of messages passed, when the cluster grows, partly offsets the speedup of parallelization for MP.

5. CONCLUSIONS

In this paper, we have presented a distributed method for efficiently evaluating RPQs under its standard semantics on large RDF graphs based on partial evaluation. The proposed dynamic programming algorithm can find partial answers, in parallel, which are then assembled by the automata-based assembly algorithm to obtain the final crossing answers. The experiments have verified that the scalability and efficiency of our method outperform the state-of-the-art message passing methods by a large margin. We are currently working on the optimization for the algorithms and the experimental study on larger synthetic and real-world RDF graphs.

6. ACKNOWLEDGMENTS

This work is supported by the National Natural Science Foundation of China (61572353), the Australian Research Council (ARC) Discovery Project (DP130103051), and the Open Fund Project of State Key Lab. for Novel Software Technology (Nanjing University) (KFKT2015B20).

7. REFERENCES

[1] D. Calvanese, G. De Giacomo, M. Lenzerini, and M. Y. Vardi. Answering regular path queries using views. In *IDCE*, pages 389–398. IEEE, 2000.

[2] W. Fan, X. Wang, and Y. Wu. Performance guarantees for distributed reachability queries. *VLDB*, 5(11):1304–1316, 2012.

[3] K. Losemann and W. Martens. The complexity of evaluating path expressions in sparql. In *PODS*, pages 101–112. ACM, 2012.

[4] A. O. Mendelzon and P. T. Wood. Finding regular simple paths in graph databases. *SIAM Journal on Computing*, 24(6):1235–1258, 1995.

[5] P. Peng, L. Zou, M. T. Özsu, L. Chen, and D. Zhao. Processing sparql queries over distributed rdf graphs. *The VLDB Journal*, 25(2):243–268, 2016.

[6] M. Shoaran and A. Thomo. Fault-tolerant computation of distributed regular path queries. *Theoretical Computer Science*, 410(1):62–77, 2009.

Webpage Depth-level Dwell Time Prediction

Chong Wang
Information Systems Dept.
New Jersey Institute of Technology
Newark, NJ 07102, USA
cw87@njit.edu

Achir Kalra*
Forbes Media
499 Washington Blvd
Jersey City, NJ 07310
akalra@forbes.com

Cristian Borcea
Computer Science Dept.
New Jersey Institute of Technology
Newark, NJ 07102, USA
borcea@njit.edu

Yi Chen†
Martin Tuchman School of Management
New Jersey Institute of Technology
Newark, NJ 07102, USA
yi.chen@njit.edu

ABSTRACT

The amount of time spent by users at specific page depths within webpages, called dwell time, can be used by web publishers to decide where to place online ads and what type of ads to place at different depths within a webpage. This paper presents a model to predict the dwell time for a given <user, webpage, depth> triplet based on historic data collected by publishers. Dwell time prediction is difficult due to user behavior variability and data sparsity. We adopt the Factorization Machines model because it is able to capture the interaction between users and webpages, overcome the data sparsity issue, and provide flexibility to add auxiliary information such as the visible area of a user's browser. Experimental results using data from a large web publisher demonstrate that our model outperforms deterministic and regression-based comparison models.

Keywords

Computational Advertising; User Behavior; Data Mining

1. INTRODUCTION

Online display advertising provides many benefits that traditional marketing channels do not, such as fast brand building and effective targeting. In display advertising, an advertiser pays a publisher for space on webpages to display a banner during page views in order to attract visitors that are interested in its products. A *page view* happens each time a webpage is requested by a user and displayed in a browser. One display of an ad in a page view is called an *ad impression*, the basic unit of ad delivery.

Currently, there are two main ad pricing models, pay-by-action and pay-by-impression. In pay-by-action, advertisers are charged when the impressions are clicked or converted. But the rate of click or conversion are often very low. Also, some advertisers, e.g. car vendors, do not expect users to purchase their products through ads. They just want to increase their brand awareness and make more users be aware of their logos or products. In pay-by-impression, advertisers have to pay for the impressions served (i.e., sent to the users' browsers) but not *viewed* by users who do not spend time at the page depth where the ads are placed [1]. To solve this issue, a new model is emerging: pricing ads by the number of impressions viewed by users, instead of just being served. This is attractive for advertisers, who want to prevent investment waste. The Interactive Advertising Bureau (IAB) defines a *viewable impression* as one that is at least 50% shown on the screen for at least one second. Advertisers may require various visible ad areas and/or time durations. They can thus specify viewability requirements in guaranteed delivery contracts with publishers. Predicting the likelihood of an ad being viewed can be very helpful in many applications: In guaranteed delivery, according to different viewability requirements, publishers can determine which ad to be served by predicting its viewability, in order to maximize the revenue. In real-time bidding, advertisers can decide bidding price based on the predicted viewability. Therefore, ad viewability prediction is essential to fulfill the marketing requirements and thus maximize the return on investment for advertisers as well as boost the advertising revenue for publishers.

However, the only existing work on viewability prediction is done by Wang et al. [6]. They propose a probabilistic latent class model that predicts the probability that a user scrolls to a page depth where an ad may be placed, but not the dwell time. Also, all existing studies on dwell time prediction focus on the time a user spends on an entire page, not a specific page depth. Liu et al. [4] predict the Weibull distributions of page-level dwell time using regression trees with features, e.g., keywords, page size. Yi et al. [8] use

*The author is also with the Computer Science Department, New Jersey Institute of Technology, USA.
†Corresponding Author.

CIKM'16, October 24-28, 2016, Indianapolis, IN, USA
© 2016 ACM. ISBN 978-1-4503-4073-1/16/10...$15.00
DOI: http://dx.doi.org/10.1145/2983323.2983878

support vector regression to predict page-level dwell time with features such as content length, topical category, and device. Kim et al. [2] present a regression model to estimate the Gamma distributions of the time that a user spends on a clicked result. Xu et al. [7] propose a webpage re-ranking algorithm by estimating page-level dwell time. Yin et al. [9] state that viewing textual items is such a casual behavior that people may terminate the viewing process at any time. The authors develop a model to estimate user preferences according to the item-level (page-level) dwell time.

In contrast, our work is the first to predict dwell time at a specific depth in a page view. Working at a finer granularity, depth-level dwell time prediction is more challenging than page-level dwell time prediction. This open problem is non-trivial due to the variability of user behavior and data sparsity, i.e., most users read only a few webpages, while a webpage is visited by a small subset of users. It is also difficult to explicitly model user interests as well as the characteristics of entire pages and depths. Thus, we explore a machine learning model to predict the dwell time at a page depth where an ad is placed, i.e., the time that the ad is shown on screen. The proposed method can also be applied to predict the dwell time of any items on a page. We adopt the Factorization Machines (FM) model because it is able to capture the interaction between input features, overcome the data sparsity issue, and provide flexibility to add auxiliary information. Our FM models consider basic factors (i.e., user, page, and page depth) and auxiliary information such as context features. We determined experimentally that viewport (i.e., the visible area of a user browser) is the most important context feature. We evaluated our model using real-data from a Forbes Media, a large web publisher. The experimental results demonstrate that our model outperforms the comparison models.

2. DEPTH DWELL TIME PREDICTION

Problem Definition. *Given a page view, i.e., a user u and a webpage a, the goal is to predict the dwell time of a given page depth X, i.e., the time duration that X is shown on the screen. The dwell time of X is denoted as T_{uaX}.*

2.1 Dataset

A large web publisher (i.e., Forbes Media) provides user browsing logs collected from real website visits in one week and webpage metadata. The dataset contains 2 million page views. For each page view, it records the user id, page url, state-level user geo location, user agent, and browsing events, e.g. the user opened/left/read the page. Each event stores the event time stamp and the page depths where the top and bottom of the user screen are. Once a user scrolls to a page depth and stays for one second, an event is recorded. The page depth is represented as the percentage of the page. The reason that we adopted page percentage rather than pixels is because it provides a relative measure independent of device screen size. If a user reads 50% of a page on a mobile device, while another user reads 50% of the same page on a desktop, it is assumed that they read the same content.

Each event has a time stamp so that the time that a user spent on a part of a page can be calculated. To infer the current part of a page that a user is looking at, the user log also records the page depths at which the first and the last rows of pixels of the screen are. Thus, we are able to infer the part of the page to which the user scrolls and how long the user stayed at that part of the page. Therefore, the dwell time at a page depth can be easily calculated from the information provided by the user log.

2.2 Model

It is intuitive that the dwell time of a page depth is highly related to the user's interests and reading habits, the topic of the article in the page, the design at that page depth, etc. For instance, some users tend to stay longer on pages, while some are less patient. A viral content may attract most users to scroll deep on the page and spend a long time on the whole page. Page depths with important topic sentences may keep most users longer on them. Thus, the characteristics of individual users, webpages, and page depths should be taken into account for depth-level dwell time prediction. More importantly, the interactions of these three factors must be modeled so that their joint effect is captured: 1) The interaction of users and pages captures a user's interest in a page. 2) The interaction of users and page depths can reflect individual users' browsing habits. For example, some users read entire pages carefully, but some only read the upper half. 3) The interaction of pages and depths models the design of individual pages at individual page depths. For example, pages that have a picture at a depth may receive relatively short dwell time at that depth because people usually can understand a picture more quickly than text. However, it is non-trivial to explicitly model user interests, page characteristics, the attractiveness of page depths, and their interactions. Also, although implicit feedback, e.g. reading dwell time, is more abundant than explicit feedback, e.g. ratings, it often has higher variability [9], which makes prediction more challenging.

We adopt Factorization machines (FM) [5], which are a generic approach that combines the high-prediction accuracy of factorization models with the flexibility of feature engineering. The reason that we adopt the FM model is that it can capture the interaction of multiple inter-related factors, overcome the data sparsity, and provide the flexibility to add auxiliary information.

According to the problem definition, the basic FM model requires three factors: user, page, and page depth. The input is derived from the user-page-depth matrix built from the user logs: In the basic form of depth-level dwell time prediction, we have a 3-dimensional cube containing n_u users, n_a pages, and n_d page depths. Thus, each dwell time is associated with a unique triplet <user, page, depth>. Such a 3D matrix can be converted into a list of $(n_u + n_a + n_d)$ rows. The target variable for each row corresponds to an observed dwell time represented by the triplet. N training page views lead to $N \cdot 100$ rows, as each page view contains 100 observed dwell time values (one for each percent from 1% to 100% page depth). This input is similar to what is prepared for regressions. However, regressions would not work well because the data is very sparse and they are unable to capture the interaction between the input variables.

The basic idea of FM is to model each target variable as a linear combination of interactions between input variables. Formally, it is defined as following.

$$\hat{y}(\mathbf{x}) = w_0 + \sum_{i=1}^{n} w_i x_i + \sum_{i=1}^{n-1} \sum_{j=i+1}^{n} \langle \mathbf{v_i}, \mathbf{v_j} \rangle x_i x_j \quad (1)$$

where, $\hat{y}(\mathbf{x})$ is the prediction outcome given an input $\mathbf{x}$. w_0 is a global bias, i.e., the overall average depth-level dwell time. $\sum_{i=1}^{n} w_i x_i$ is the bias of individual input variables. For example, some users would like to read more carefully than others; some pages can attract users to spend more time on them; some page depths, e.g., very bottom of a page, usually receive little dwell time. The first two terms are the same as in linear regression. The third term captures the sparse interaction between each pair of input variables.

Unlike standard regression models which model the weight of each interaction by a real number w_{ij}, the FM model uses a factorized parametrization to capture the interaction effect (Eq. 2). Such low-rank interaction allows the FM model to estimate reliable parameters even in sparse data.

$$\langle \mathbf{v_i}, \mathbf{v_j} \rangle = \sum_{k=1}^{K} v_{ik} v_{jk} \tag{2}$$

The basic FM model works with only three factors: user, page, and depth. However, context information can also help improve the prediction performance. Thus, we identify two context features, *viewport* (i.e., the part of a user browser visible on the screen) and *local day of the week*, which are intuitively related to user reading behavior. The viewport indicates the device utilized by the user (e.g., a mobile device usually have a much smaller visible browser area than a desktop) and can directly determine the user experience. Specifically, one viewport value consists of the height and the width of a browser, e.g., 1855×1107. To reduce sparsity, both heights and widths are put into buckets with size 100 pixels. For instance, 1855×1107 can be discretized into 18×11. The local day of the week, expected to reflect if users are working, is inferred from the GMT time and user geo provided in the user log.

In addition, although in theory user demographics and page attributes are already considered in the latent user and page dimensions, incorporating these additional sources of information as features may further improve the prediction accuracy in some applications [3]. For user demographics, we consider user geo locations because this is the only explicit feature about users that can be easily obtained by publishers. User geo, inferred from IPs, may reflect a user's interests and education, and it may determine the user's network condition. Specifically, geo is the country name if the user is outside USA or a state name if she is within USA. For page attributes, we consider article length and channel. Article length is represented by the word count of the article in the page, and it has been proven to be a significant factor impacting page-level dwell time [8]. Article lengths are put into buckets so that there are a limited number of possible states. The channel of the article in a page is its topical category on the publisher's website, e.g., finance and lifestyle. A channel can be a high-level topic label of a page.

Context and auxiliary features, i.e., user geo and page attributes, can be used to extend the basic FM model. In Section 3.4, we compare the prediction performance of different combinations of auxiliary features.

3. EXPERIMENTAL EVALUATION

3.1 Experiment Datasets

A one-week user log, collected as described in Section 2.1, is split into three sets of training and testing data. The experimental results are reported by taking the average over the sets. On average, the training and test data contain 150K+ and 20K+ page views, respectively. The training/test data consist of all depths of all training/test page views.

3.2 Comparison Models

GlobalAverage: This model is used in two ways. In Section 3.5, it computes the average dwell time of each page depth X in all training page views. If a user did not scroll to X, its dwell time in the page view is zero. In Section 3.6, it computes the fraction of training page depths whose dwell time is no less than the required dwell time. The 100 constant numbers obtained are used to make a deterministic prediction for the page depth.

ChannelAverage: It is similar to GlobalAverage, but it computes the average dwell time of each depth X of the same page channel (rather than all training page views).

Regression: We built two regression models. 1) *Regress_bc* is developed based on an existing work on page dwell time prediction [8]. To apply it to depth-level prediction, one more feature, i.e., page depth, is added. 2) *Regress_view+dep* is developed based on the finding in Section 3.4 that shows the viewport to be the best feature for improving prediction. Thus, it has only two input features: viewport and depth. In the viewability prediction test, logistic regression with the same features is adopted. They outputs the probability that the dwell time of X is at least a certain seconds.

3.3 Metrics

The metrics we adopt are Root-Mean-Square Deviation (RMSD) and Logistic Loss. Both serve to aggregate the magnitudes of the errors in predictions for various times into a single measure of the predictive power of a method. Thus, for both metrics, lower values are better.

RMSD: $RMSD = \sqrt{\frac{\sum_{j=1}^{N}\sum_{i=1}^{100}(\hat{y}_{ij}-y_{ij})^2}{N \cdot 100}}$ measures the differences between the values predicted, $\hat{y}_i$, and the values observed, y_i. N is the number of test page views. The second sum accumulates the errors at all 100 page depths in the ith page view. y_{ij} is the actual dwell time at the jth page depth in the ith page view.

Logistic Loss: It is widely used in probabilistic classification. Compared to the RMSD, it penalizes a method more for being both confident and wrong.

$$logloss = -\frac{1}{N \cdot 100}\sum_{i=1}^{N}\sum_{j=1}^{100}[y_{ij}\log(\hat{y}_{ij}) + (1 - y_{ij})\log(1 - \hat{y}_{ij})]$$

3.4 Comparison of Feature Combinations

Table 1: RMSD Comparison of Auxiliary Features

Approaches	K=10	K=20	K=30
FM	11.4667	11.5501	11.5925
FM (viewport)	11.141	**11.0309**	11.172
FM (dow)	11.4655	11.5331	11.5728
FM (geo)	11.5563	11.6735	11.7201
FM (length)	11.7064	11.727	11.8084
FM (channel)	11.7502	11.8827	11.9211
FM (viewport+dow)	11.5152	11.3235	11.3763
FM (viewport+geo)	11.0318	11.0767	11.2299
FM (viewport+length)	11.3026	11.5273	11.5666
FM (viewport+channel)	11.5319	11.3474	11.5725
FM (all five)	11.4084	11.7641	11.7385

We add context and auxiliary features into the basic FM model in order to evaluate the effect of different combinations. The results are presented in Table 1. The first row is the basic FM model. We vary the dimension of the 2-way interactions, K, which is the length of the latent vector v for each variable (Eq. 2).

The results show that viewport is the most significant context feature. Intuitively, viewport indicates the type of device, which influences reading experience and thus the way users engage with webpages. Local day of the week, denoted as "dow", does not improve the basic FM as much as viewport does. The three explicit user and page attributes do not enhance the performance of the basic FM. The possible reason is that the granularities of user geo and channels are too coarse. Learning latent features for each channel and geo cannot specifically capture the characteristics of individual users and pages. Article length may not play a key role at depth-level, as the text length in a screen is determined by the viewport size, not the length of the article. Also, increasing K does not always lead to performance improvement. Longer latent feature vectors may fit the data better, while they may cause overfitting. As the Bias-Variance trade-off, the optimal K can be obtained by cross-validation.

3.5 Depth-level Dwell Time Prediction

Table 2: Depth Dwell Time Prediction Comparison

Approaches	RMSD
GlobalAverage	13.8346
ChannelAverage	13.8219
Regress_bc	14.1009
Regress_view+dep	13.8301
FM (viewport;K=20)	11.0309

We compare the best model obtained from the previous experiment, i.e., FM (viewport) with K=20, with the baselines. All models are applied to predict the exact dwell time of each page depth in test page views. The results in Table 2 demonstrate that the FM model significantly outperforms the baselines. This is because it is able to overcome sparsity and capture pairwise interactions between users and pages. The RMSDs of GlobalAverage and ChannelAverage are similar. This suggests that controlling the channel variable does not help with performance. Regress_bc has the highest RMSD, which indicates that methods for page-level dwell time prediction cannot be easily applied to depth-level prediction. With only the combined viewport/depth feature, Regress_view+dep does not obtain a better prediction outcome than simple averaging.

3.6 Viewability Prediction

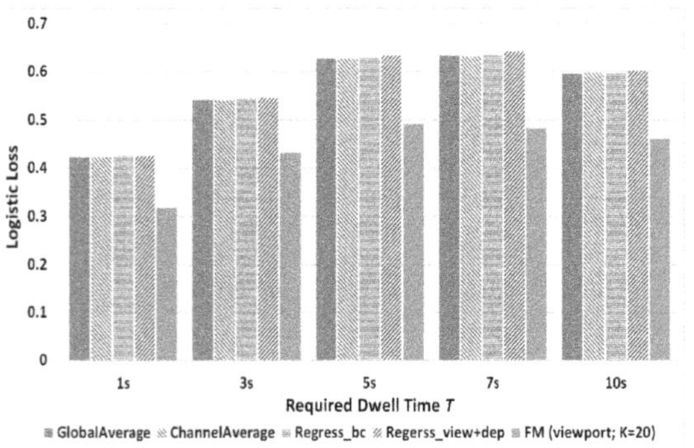

Figure 1: Viewability Prediction Comparison

We vary the dwell time threshold of a viewable impression from 1s (IAB standard) to 10s. For each page depth in the dataset, its target variable is 1 if its dwell time is at least T seconds; otherwise 0. In this way, the prediction problem is converted from regression to classification. The prediction outcome of each test page depth is the probability that its dwell time is at least T seconds.

Figure 1 shows that the FM model clearly outperforms the baselines. We also notice that the FM model achieves the best performance at the two ends (1s and 10s). Given a page depth, it is more challenging to predict if the dwell time is at least 5s. The reason is that the number of page depths with dwell time at least 5s and the number of page depths with dwell time less than 5s are very close (about 50%). In contrast, there are about 70% page depths whose dwell time is at least 1s. Similar to the depth-level dwell time prediction, GlobelAverage and ChannelAverage have very similar performance. Also, the Regress_bc and the Regress_view+dep are slightly worse than simple averaging.

4. CONCLUSIONS

Web publishers and advertisers are interested to predict how much time a user spends at different places in a webpage in order to maximize their profit and return on investment. This paper presents a model based on Factorization Machines to predict webpage depth-level dwell time for a page view. Using real-world data, both page depth-level dwell time and viewability prediction experiments consistently show our model outperforms the comparison models.

Acknowledgement

This work is partially supported by NSF under grants No. CAREER IIS-1322406, CNS 1409523, and DGE 1565478, by a Google Research Award, and by an endowment from the Leir Charitable Foundations. Any opinions, findings, and conclusions expressed in this material are those of the authors and do not necessarily reflect the views of the funding agencies.

5. REFERENCES

[1] Google. The importance of being seen. https://think.storage.googleapis.com/docs/the-importance-of-being-seen_study.pdf,2014.

[2] Y. Kim, A. Hassan, R. W. White, and I. Zitouni. Modeling dwell time to predict click-level satisfaction. In *WSDM'14*, pages 193–202. ACM, 2014.

[3] Y. Koren, R. Bell, and C. Volinsky. Matrix factorization techniques for recommender systems. *Computer*, (8):30–37, 2009.

[4] C. Liu, R. W. White, and S. Dumais. Understanding web browsing behaviors through weibull analysis of dwell time. In *SIGIR'10*, pages 379–386. ACM, 2010.

[5] S. Rendle. Factorization machines with libfm. *TIST*, 3(3):57, 2012.

[6] C. Wang, A. Kalra, C. Borcea, and Y. Chen. Viewability prediction for online display ads. In *CIKM'15*, pages 413–422. ACM, 2015.

[7] S. Xu, H. Jiang, and F. C.-M. Lau. Mining user dwell time for personalized web search re-ranking. In *IJCAI'11*, volume 22, page 2367, 2011.

[8] X. Yi, L. Hong, E. Zhong, N. N. Liu, and S. Rajan. Beyond clicks: dwell time for personalization. In *RecSys'14*, pages 113–120. ACM, 2014.

[9] P. Yin, P. Luo, W.-C. Lee, and M. Wang. Silence is also evidence: interpreting dwell time for recommendation from psychological perspective. In *KDD'13*, pages 989–997. ACM, 2013.

Collaborative Social Group Influence for Event Recommendation

Li Gao[†], Jia Wu[⋆], Zhi Qiao[‡], Chuan Zhou[†], Hong Yang[§], Yue Hu[†]
[†] Institute of Information Engineering, Chinese Academy of Sciences, Beijing, 100093, China
[⋆] Centre for Quantum Computation and Intelligent Systems (QCIS),
University of Technology Sydney, NSW 2007, Australia
[‡] IBM Research - China, Beijing, 100193, China
[§] MathWorks, Beijing, 100190, China
{gaoli, huyue, zhouchuan}@iie.ac.cn; jia.wu@uts.edu.au;
qzbj@cn.ibm.com; hong.yang@mathworks.cn

ABSTRACT

In event-based social networks, such as *Meetup*, social groups refer to self-organized communities that consist of users who share the same interests. In many real-world scenarios, users usually have social group preference and join interested social groups to attend events. It is therefore necessary to consider the influence of social groups to improve the event recommendation performance; however, existing event recommendation models generally consider users' individual preferences and neglect the influence of social groups. To this end, we propose a new Bayesian latent factor model *SogBmf* that combines *social group influence* and *individual preference* for event recommendation. Experiments on real-world data sets demonstrate the effectiveness of the proposed method.

CCS Concepts

•Information systems → Data mining; •Human-centered computing → *Social recommendation;*

Keywords

Event recommendation; Social group influence

1. INTRODUCTION

Recent years have witnessed the rapid growth and popularity of event-based social networks (EBSNs), which are convenient tools with which users can organize and participate in social events, *e.g.*, cocktail parties, playing sports and attending technical conferences. To enhance user experience, given the sheer volume of available events in EBSNs, event recommender systems [2, 6, 10] have been developed to suggest the events that users are most likely to attend.

A typical event-based social network, such as *Meetup*, integrates a new module called *social groups* which refer to self-organized communities that consist of users who share the same interests. By categorizing users' social relationships into several distinct social groups, social events can be promoted within related social groups to attract more users. Users of EBSNs join social groups and often share comments to promote events, which indicates that social groups are necessary tools for connecting users and events. Based on this observation, it is clearly necessary to consider the influence of social groups when attempting to improve the performance of event recommender systems.

The recent work in [5] presents a group preference-based Bayesian personalized ranking method for recommendation; however, the formulated social groups in this method depend on the interactions and collaborations between users who give positive feedback on a specific item. The study in [3] presents a context-aware approach, in which the information from social groups is used to regularize the user and event latent factor matrices. In deed, the group-collaborative event recommendation encounters the following challenges: 1) how to properly formulate the social group influence, and 2) how to strategically embed social group influence to achieve accurate event rating scores.

Motivated by the above observations, our work aims to build a more realistic model of social group influence on the rating scores generated by the interactions between user-group preferences and group-event correlation, where user-group preference is regarded as latent factor (Challenge #1). We propose a Bayesian latent factor model (denoted as *SogBmf*) for event recommendation, based on the matrix factorization framework, to integrate social group influence with individual preference (Challenge #2). A gradient descent algorithm is applied to learn the parameters. Experimental results on real-world data sets empirically demonstrate that our method consistently achieves an improvement in accuracy.

2. PROBLEM STATEMENT

The problem of event recommendation is formulated as follows: suppose that we have a set of users, $S = \{u_1, u_2, \ldots, u_n\}$ with the ith user denoted as u_i, and a set of events, $I = \{v_1, v_2, \ldots, v_m\}$ with the jth event denoted as v_j. We denote the user-event interaction matrix as $R \in \{0,1\}^{n\times m}$. If user u_i joins event v_j, the entry R_{ij} is 1; otherwise, it is 0. Then, the problem turns to predict the unobserved entries in R and rank the event v_j for each user u_i by score $r(u_i, v_j)$ which indicates user u_i's preference for event v_j.

Predicting the rating score $r(u_i, v_j)$ plays a key role. In this work, there are three types of entities: users, groups and events, and their relationships, including 1) user/group relationships where users join the social groups, 2) group/event relationships where social groups post events, and 3) user/event relationships where users participate in events. We **aim** to embed the influence of the so-

CIKM'16, October 24-28, 2016, Indianapolis, IN, USA

DOI: http://dx.doi.org/10.1145/2983323.2983879

cial groups into the matrix factorization framework [4] for event recommendation, based on these data.

3. METHODOLOGY

We propose a Bayesian latent factor model, denoted as *SogBmf*, which embeds social group influence for event recommendation.

3.1 Mixture Rating for Recommendation

As shown in Figure 1, we propose a mixture rating framework for the score $r(u_i, v_j)$ for event recommendation, which factorizes the user-event interaction/rating matrix into the social group influence rating and individual preference rating matrices. The matrices given in Figure 1 are defined as follows.

DEFINITION 1. *(User-group preference matrix). $F \in \mathbb{R}^{g\times n}$ denotes the user-group preference matrix, where each entry F_{ij} denotes the degree of preference for the jth user toward the ith group. Generally, $F_{ij} > 0$ if the jth user joins the ith group.*

DEFINITION 2. *(Group-event matrix). The group-event matrix is denoted by $C \in \{0,1\}^{g\times m}$. $C_{ij} = 1$ means that the jth event is posted in the ith social group.*

DEFINITION 3. *(Latent factor matrix). The user latent factor matrix is denoted by $U \in \mathbb{R}^{k\times n}$, where user i is determined by a latent factor vector $U_i \in R^k$. Similarly, the event latent factor matrix is denoted by $V \in \mathbb{R}^{k\times m}$, where event j is described by a latent factor vector $V_j \in R^k$.*

Thus, the rating score $r(u_i, v_j)$ is calculated as:

$$r(u_i, v_j) = r_{sg}(u_i, v_j) \oplus r_{ip}(u_i, v_j) \qquad (1)$$

where $r(u_i, v_j)$ is the ultimate rating score by combining the social group influence rating $r_{sg}(u_i, v_j)$ and the individual preference rating $r_{ip}(u_i, v_j)$, where the new operator $r_1 \oplus r_2 = \alpha r_1 + (1-\alpha) r_2$ with $0 \le \alpha \le 1$ is a tradeoff parameter.

Social group influence rating. Let F_i be a social group preference vector of user u_i, C_j be an event v_j vector posted by groups. Then $r_{sg}(u_i, v_j)$ is denoted as:

$$r_{sg}(u_i, v_j) = F_i^T C_j \qquad (2)$$

Individual preference rating [1]. Let $U_i \in R^k$ be user u_i's latent factor vector, $V_j \in R^k$ be event v_j's latent factor vector. $r_{ip}(u_i, v_j)$ can be denoted as:

$$r_{ip}(u_i, v_j) = U_i^T V_j \qquad (3)$$

Thus, the problem of event recommendation needs to solve **F**, **U** and **V**, so that the mixture rating can be calculated as follows:

$$R = \alpha F^T C + (1-\alpha) U^T V \qquad (4)$$

3.2 Our SogBmf Model

The conditional distribution with Gaussian observation noise over the observed entries in R is defined as:

$$P(R|F, U, V, \sigma_R^2) = \prod_{i=1}^{n}\prod_{j=1}^{m}[\mathcal{N}(R_{ij}|\alpha F_i^T C_j + (1-\alpha)U_i^T V_j, \sigma_R^2)]^{I_{ij}} \qquad (5)$$

where I_{ij} is the indicator function that is equal to 1 if user u_i joins event v_j and equal to 0 otherwise.

Generally, users' feedback scores on events are implicit [6], thus Bayesian personalized ranking (BPR) [8] can be used to effectively

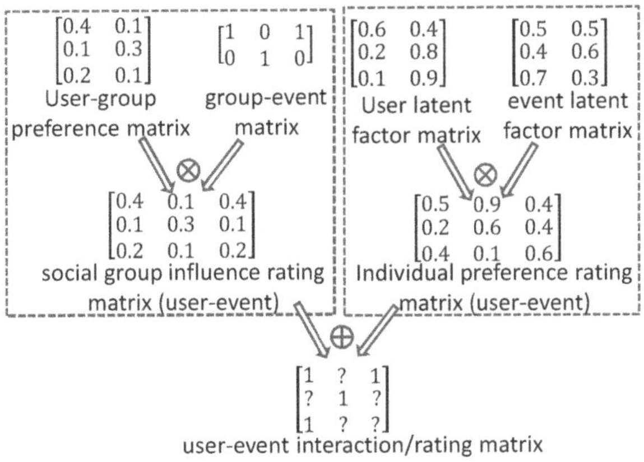

Figure 1: The mixture rating for event recommendation, which incorporates social group influence and individual preference to factorize the user-event interaction/rating matrix into a social group influence rating matrix and an individual preference rating matrix.

solve the implicit feedback recommendation problem. Let P_u^I be the positive event set for which the entry gets positive feedback from user u, and let N_u^I denote the negative event set for which the entry gets negative feedback. Based on the BPR optimization criterion [8], Eq. (5) can be extended as Eq. (6), where $R_>$ denotes that events in P_u^I are ranked higher than events in N_u^I.

$$P(R_>|F, U, V) = \prod_{(u_i, v_j, v_k)\in(S, P_u^I, N_u^I)} P(r(u_i, v_j) > r(u_i, v_k)|F, U, V) \qquad (6)$$

In EBSNs, users join social groups and often share comments to promote social events. Social groups reflect social relationships. We use $H \in \mathbb{R}^{n\times n}$ to denote social relationships between users that are defined as follows:

$$H_{ij} = \frac{|G(u_i) \cap G(u_j)|}{|G(u_i) \cup G(u_j)|} \qquad (7)$$

where $G(u_i)$ denotes the social groups joined by user u_i, and $|\mathcal{X}|$ denotes the cardinality of the set $\mathcal{X}$.

In terms of events v_k, if users u_i and u_j co-participate in v_k, they share the same interest. We use $Q \in \mathbb{R}^{n\times n}$ to represent the interest similarity between users

$$Q_{ij} = \frac{|E(u_i) \cap E(u_j)|}{|E(u_i) \cup E(u_j)|} \qquad (8)$$

where $E(u_i)$ denotes the social events attended by user u_i.

We hypothesize that the similarity in the observed space is consistent with the latent space. Thus, we regularize the latent space by the observed matrices H and Q in that:

- Users that are similar in the user latent space U have similar event preferences which can be derived from the interest similarity matrix Q;

- Users that are similar in the social group preference latent space F have tight social connections which can be derived from the social relations matrix H.

The posterior distribution is formulated as follows:

$$
\begin{aligned}
&P(F,U,V|R_>,C,Q,H,\Omega) \\
&= \frac{P(R_>,C,Q,H|F,U,V,\Omega)P(F,U,V|\Omega)}{P(R_>,C,Q,H,\Omega)} \\
&\propto P(R_>|F,U,V)P(Q|U,\Omega)P(H|F,\Omega)P(F|\Omega)P(U|\Omega)P(V|\Omega) \\
&= \prod_{(u_i,v_j,v_k)\in(S,P_u^I,N_u^I)} P(r(u_i,v_j)>r(u_i,v_k)|F,U,V) \\
&\quad \prod_{s,t}\mathcal{N}(Q_{st}|U_s^TU_t,\sigma_Q^2)\prod_{p,q}\mathcal{N}(H_{pq}|F_p^TF_q,\sigma_H^2) \\
&\prod_x\mathcal{N}(F_x|0,\sigma_F^2)\prod_y\mathcal{N}(U_y|0,\sigma_U^2)\prod_z\mathcal{N}(V_z|0,\sigma_V^2) \qquad (9)
\end{aligned}
$$

where Ω denotes that the zero-mean spherical Gaussian prior is placed on latent factor vectors and observed matrices.

Based on the BPR optimization criterion [8], we set $P(r(u_i,v_j)>r(u_i,v_k)|F,U,V)=l(r(u_i,v_j)-r(u_i,v_k))$, where $l(x)=\frac{1}{1+e^{-x}}$ is the logistic function. We expect to maximize the log-posterior distribution $\ln P(F,U,V|R_>,C,Q,H,\Omega)$, which can be converted to find F, U and V to minimize the function with hybrid quadratic regularization terms as follows:

$$
\begin{aligned}
\min_{F,U,V}\ \mathcal{O} = &\sum_{(u_i,v_j,v_k)\in(S,P_u^I,N_u^I)} \ln(1+e^{r(u_i,v_k)-r(u_i,v_j)}) \\
&+\lambda_Q\|Q-U^TU\|_F^2+\lambda_H\|H-F^TF\|_F^2 \\
&+\lambda_F\|F\|_F^2+\lambda_U\|U\|_F^2+\lambda_V\|V\|_F^2 \qquad (10)
\end{aligned}
$$

where λ_Q, λ_H, λ_F, λ_U and λ_V are non-negative regularization parameters, and $\|\cdot\|_F$ is the Frobenius norm.

3.3 Parameter Learning

Let the function $I(v_j\in P_{u_i}^I, v_k\in N_{u_i}^I)$ ($I(i,j,k)$ for short) denote the indicator function, which equals 1 if both $v_j\in P_{u_i}^I$ and $v_k\in N_{u_i}^I$ stand; otherwise, it equals 0. Let function $J(i,j,k)=\frac{e^{r(u_i,v_k)-r(u_i,v_j)}}{1+e^{r(u_i,v_k)-r(u_i,v_j)}}$. We can then obtain the gradient descent of the optimization function given in Eq. (10) with respect to the latent parameters F, U and V as follows:

$$
\begin{aligned}
\frac{\partial\mathcal{O}}{\partial U_i} = &\sum_{v_j\in P_{u_i}^I}\sum_{v_k\in N_{u_i}^I}(1-\alpha)J(i,j,k)I(i,j,k)(V_k-V_j) \\
&-2\lambda_Q\sum_{s=1}^n U_s(Q_{is}-U_i^TU_s)+2\lambda_UU_i \qquad (11)
\end{aligned}
$$

$$
\begin{aligned}
\frac{\partial\mathcal{O}}{\partial V_p} = &\sum_{u_i\in S}\sum_{q=1}^m -(1-\alpha)\{J(i,p,q)I(i,p,q)U_i-J(i,q,p) \\
&I(i,q,p)U_i\}+2\lambda_VV_p \qquad (12)
\end{aligned}
$$

$$
\begin{aligned}
\frac{\partial\mathcal{O}}{\partial F_i} = &\sum_{v_j\in P_{u_i}^I}\sum_{v_k\in N_{u_i}^I}\alpha J(i,j,k)I(i,j,k)(C_k-C_j) \\
&-2\lambda_H\sum_{t=1}^n F_t(H_{it}-F_i^TF_t)+2\lambda_FF_i \qquad (13)
\end{aligned}
$$

The parameters update rules are thus as follows:

$$
U_i=U_i-\gamma_u\frac{\partial\mathcal{O}}{\partial U_i},\ V_j=V_j-\gamma_v\frac{\partial\mathcal{O}}{\partial V_j},\ F_i=F_i-\gamma_f\frac{\partial\mathcal{O}}{\partial F_i} \qquad (14)
$$

Algorithm 1 shows *SogBmf* model for event recommendation.

Algorithm 1 The *SogBmf* algorithm.

Input: User-event interaction R, group-event matrix C, users social relations H, users interest similarity Q. Parameters α, γ_u, γ_v, γ_f, ξ and the regularization parameters.
Output: User-group preference F, latent factor matrices U, V.
Initialize U, V and F with randomly generated values
Set index $b=0$
Compute the objective function $\mathcal{O}^b=\mathcal{O}(U,V,F)$
repeat
  Compute the gradients as in Eq. (11), Eq. (12), Eq. (13)
  Update the parameters U, V and F as in Eq. (14)
  $b=b+1$
  Compute the objective function $\mathcal{O}^b=\mathcal{O}(U,V,F)$
until $\frac{|\mathcal{O}^{b-1}-\mathcal{O}^b|}{\mathcal{O}^{b-1}}\le\xi$
return the parameters F, U and V.

4. EXPERIMENTS

4.1 Experimental Settings

4.1.1 Data Sets

We select the data from Chicago, Los Angeles, and New York City from *Meetup* for analysis, as these cities have a large number of group/event pairs. The data sets are extracted from the work [2]. Details of the data sets are summarized in Table 1.

Table 1: Data set statistics

	Chicago	Los Angeles	New York
#users	59504	89201	205592
#events	86988	167254	234160
#groups	8007	14657	21155

4.1.2 Setups

We randomly partition each of the three data sets into two non-overlapping sets for training and testing. For each user u_i, 70% of the historical events P_u^I are randomly sampled as the training data, and the remaining 30% are used for testing. We then randomly take one historical event of each user from the training data to construct the validation data. A similar setup was used in the previous work [5].

We repeat the above steps for five times and thus receive five copies of training data and test data. The reported experimental results are the average of the five runs.

4.1.3 Metrics

We use two metrics to evaluate the event recommendation performance, namely, AUC and NDCG@n. AUC in the evaluation can be formulated as

$$
AUC=\frac{1}{|S|}\sum_{u\in S}\frac{1}{|P_u^I|}\sum_{v_j\in P_u^I}\frac{1}{|N_u^I|}\sum_{v_k\in N_u^I}I(r(u,v_j)>r(u,v_k)),
$$

and NDCG@n is used to compare the top-n recommendation performance [5].

4.1.4 Benchmark Methods

We implement the following methods for comparison, including 1) *PMF* [4], a probabilistic matrix factorization method for recommendation; 2) *BPR-MF* [8], the recommendation model dealing with implicit feedback in event recommendation; 3) *GBPR* [5].

Table 2: Experimental results of the compared methods *w.r.t.* AUC and NDCG@5.

Data sets	Metrics	*PMF*	*BPR-MF*	*GBPR*	*SogBmf*
Chicago	AUC	0.7142$\pm$0.0004	0.8453$\pm$0.0009	0.8645$\pm$0.0011	**0.8894**$\pm$0.0005
	NDCG@5	0.1711$\pm$0.0009	0.2194$\pm$0.0003	0.2308$\pm$0.0004	**0.2723**$\pm$0.0013
Los Angeles	AUC	0.7611$\pm$0.0010	0.8521$\pm$0.0005	0.8724$\pm$0.0004	**0.8948**$\pm$0.0004
	NDCG@5	0.1916$\pm$0.0010	0.2231$\pm$0.0005	0.2417$\pm$0.0005	**0.2744**$\pm$0.0005
New York	AUC	0.7384$\pm$0.0005	0.8536$\pm$0.0017	0.8713$\pm$0.0005	**0.8967**$\pm$0.0007
	NDCG@5	0.1842$\pm$0.0005	0.2128$\pm$0.0005	0.2421$\pm$0.0012	**0.2931**$\pm$0.0006

We adapt *GBPR* for event recommendation, based on group preferences that indicate the interaction and collaboration between users.

4.1.5 *Parameters Setting*

The parameter α is searched from $\alpha \in \{0.2, 0.4, 0.6, 0.8, 1\}$ and the regularization parameters in Eq. (10) are selected from $\lambda_Q = \lambda_H = \lambda_F = \lambda_U = \lambda_V \in \{0.001, 0.01, 0.1\}$. The learning rate for the gradient descent method is selected from $\gamma_u = \gamma_v = \gamma_f \in \{0.001, 0.01, 0.1\}$. The AUC performance on the validation data for the three data sets is used to select the best parameters. As a result, parameter α is set to $\alpha = 0.2$, the regularization parameters are set to 0.1, and the learning rate for the gradient descent is set to 0.01. The dimension of the latent factor matrix is set to $k = 100$. We use the above tuned parameters for evaluation.

4.2 Experimental Results

The experimental results are shown in Table 2, from which we make the following observations: 1) On all three data sets, the proposed *SogBmf* method always obtains better results than the other baseline methods, measured by the evaluation metrics. The improvements over the baselines are statistically significant with $p < 0.005$ using the Wilcoxon signed rank significance test. 2) *SogBmf* and *GBPR* obtain better performance than *PMF* and *BPR-MF*, demonstrating that embedding social group information can improve the performance of event recommendation. 3) *SogBmf* obtains better results than *GBPR*. The social groups in *GBPR* are virtual, while the groups in EBSNs are self-organized communities consisting of users who share the same interests, which demonstrates the greater effect of social group influence on event recommendation.

5. RELATED WORK

Several recommendation methods based on social group information and users' preferences for social groups [7, 9] have been proposed, but they do not target event recommendation. In contrast, this paper focuses on applying the influence of social groups to event recommender systems.

The work [2] proposed to use online and offline patterns of interaction for recommending new events. Later studies [6, 10] extended this work to improve recommendation performance, but they did not incorporate the effects of social group influence on event recommendation. Based on the interactions and collaborations between users who give positive feedback on a specific item, [5] proposed a recommendation method that used group preferences. The literature [3] exploited social-aware group information for event recommendation, in which group information was used to regularize the user and event latent factor matrices. However, they have not properly formulated social group influence on the event rating scores. In this paper, we embed social group influence into the matrix factorization framework to further reflect the interactions between users and events.

6. CONCLUSIONS

In this paper, we study a new problem of event recommendation embedding with social group influence in EBSNs. We present a new Bayesian latent factor model *SogBmf* to consider social group influence and individual preference for improving the performance of event recommender systems. Experiments on real-world data demonstrate the effectiveness of the proposed method.

Acknowledgements

This work was supported by the 973 Program (No. 2013CB329605), NSFC (No. 61502479 and 61370025), Strategic Leading Science and Technology Projects of CAS (No. XDA06030200), Xinjiang Uygur Autonomous Region Science and Technology Project (No. 201230123), Australian Research Council (ARC) Discovery Projects (No. DP140100545), and China Scholarship Council Foundation (No. 201206410056). C. Zhou is the corresponding author.

7. REFERENCES

[1] M. Jiang, P. Cui, F. Wang, W. Zhu, and S. Yang. Scalable recommendation with social contextual information. *IEEE Trans. Knowl. Data Eng.*, 26(11):2789–2802, 2014.

[2] X. Liu, Q. He, Y. Tian, W.-C. Lee, J. McPherson, and J. Han. Event-based social networks: linking the online and offline social worlds. In *SIGKDD*, pages 1032–1040, 2012.

[3] A. Q. Macedo, L. B. Marinho, and R. L. Santos. Context-aware event recommendation in event-based social networks. In *RecSys*, pages 123–130, 2015.

[4] A. Mnih and R. Salakhutdinov. Probabilistic matrix factorization. In *NIPS*, pages 1257–1264, 2007.

[5] W. Pan and L. Chen. GBPR: Group preference based Bayesian personalized ranking for one-class collaborative filtering. In *IJCAI*, pages 2691–2697, 2013.

[6] Z. Qiao, P. Zhang, Y. Cao, C. Zhou, L. Guo, and B. Fang. Combining heterogenous social and geographical information for event recommendation. In *AAAI*, pages 145–151, 2014.

[7] L. Quijano-Sanchez, J. A. Recio-Garcia, B. Diaz-Agudo, and G. Jimenez-Diaz. Social factors in group recommender systems. *ACM Trans. Intell. Syst. Technol.*, 4(1):1–30, 2013.

[8] S. Rendle, C. Freudenthaler, Z. Gantner, and L. Schmidt-Thieme. BPR: Bayesian personalized ranking from implicit feedback. In *UAI*, pages 452–461, 2009.

[9] A. Salehi-Abari and C. Boutilier. Preference-oriented social networks: Group recommendation and inference. In *RecSys*, pages 35–42, 2015.

[10] W. Zhang and J. Wang. A collective Bayesian poisson factorization model for cold-start local event recommendation. In *SIGKDD*, pages 1455–1464, 2015.

Graph-Based Multi-Modality Learning for Clinical Decision Support

Ziwei Zheng and Xiaojun Wan
Institute of Computer Science and Technology, Peking University, Beijing 100871, China
Key Laboratory of Computational Linguistics (Peking University), MOE, China
{micheal_zzw, wanxiaojun}@pku.edu.cn

ABSTRACT
The task of clinical decision support (CDS) involves retrieval and ranking of medical journal articles for medical records of diagnosis, test or treatment. Previous studies on this task are based on bag-of-words representations of document texts and general retrieval models. In this paper, we propose to use the paragraph vector technique to learn the latent semantic representation of texts and treat the latent semantic representations and the original bag-of-words representations as two different modalities. We then propose to use the graph-based multi-modality learning algorithm for document re-ranking. Experimental results on two TREC-CDS benchmark datasets demonstrate the excellent performance of our proposed approach.

Keywords
Clinical Decision Support; Paragraph Vector; Graph-based Multi-Modality Learning; TREC.

1. INTRODUCTION
The task of Clinical Decision Support (CDS) is designed to assess the ability of search engines to retrieve biomedical journal articles relevant for answering generic clinical questions about medical records[7][8]. Each topic in this track consists of a sentence-long summary and a paragraph-long description of a patient case, along with one of three types of clinical information: diagnosis (i.e., "*What is this patient's diagnosis?*"), test ("*What diagnostic test is appropriate for this patient?*") or treatment ("*What treatment is appropriate for this patient?*"), which is likely to support physicians and other health professionals with clinical decision-making tasks by medical records such as a list of symptom, a treatment plan and a particular test. The CDS task aims to retrieve articles to particular case based on the summary, description, or both. The task has become one important evaluation track on TREC 2014 and TREC 2015.

CDS is a newly established task and it is considered a special kind of document retrieval task. Most previous studies adopted existing popular retrieval models for addressing this task [7][8]. In many retrieval models, texts are required to be represented as a feature vector and one of the most common representation is bag-of-words (BOW). Despite its popularity, BOW model casts off the order of words and thus cannot reflect the genuine semantics of word sequences. Moreover, BOW model cannot deal with synonymy or polysemy. There is a big semantic gap between topic and document based on the BOW model, and there is also a big document-to-document semantic gap.

CIKM'16, October 24-28, 2016, Indianapolis, IN, USA
© 2016 ACM. ISBN 978-1-4503-4073-1/16/10…$15.00
DOI: http://dx.doi.org/10.1145/2983323.2983880

In recent years, a variety of neural network methods [9][10] have been proposed to map words, paragraphs or documents to dense vectors which are considered to embody their latent semantics. In this study, we investigate leveraging the Paragraph Vector model [10] to map texts into latent semantic representations. After that, we have two different representations (i.e., BOW representations and latent semantic representations) for each topic and each document. We then propose to use the graph-based multi-modality learning algorithm for document re-ranking by considering the two different representations as two modalities.

Evaluation results on two benchmark datasets (TREC CDS 2014 and TREC CDS 2015) show that our proposed method can significantly improve the retrieval performance, and the overall performance is very competitive as compared with the TREC participating systems.

The contributions of this paper are summarized as follows:

1) We proposed a new method consisting of three steps for addressing the CDS task.

2) We proposed to leverage Paragraph Vector to learn the latent semantics of biomedical journal articles.

3) We proposed to use the graph-based multi-modality learning algorithm for document re-ranking in the CDS task.

4) We achieved the state-of-the-art performance on two benchmark datasets.

2. OUR PROPOSED METHOD
2.1 Overview
Our proposed method for the CDS task consists of three steps: initial document retrieval, latent semantic learning and multi-modality re-ranking. The first step aims to retrieve a small set of candidate documents from the large corpus by using typical retrieval models. The second step aims to learn the latent semantic representations of the documents and paragraphs. The last step aims to re-rank the candidate documents by using the graph-based multi-modality learning algorithm. We can see that the first step helps to largely reduce the document set to be re-ranked, and thus it can improve the efficiency of the re-ranking process. Moreover, the candidate document set retrieved in the first step contain less noisy documents and thus it is beneficial to the graph-based re-ranking results. The second step is used to obtain another different representation of each document or paragraph, besides the conventional BOW representation. After that, we have two representations for each document or paragraph, and these two representations can be considered two modalities, which are then used in the third step. The details of the three steps will be described in next sections, respectively.

2.2 Initial Document Retrieval

For initial document retrieval, we use the LemurTFIDF model [2] as retrieval model. In this model, a word's TF score is computed with the Okapi TF formula and then a document or topic description is represented by a TFIDF-based term vector. Note that we use the concatenation of the summary and description of a topic to represent the topic and simply use the term "topic description" to denote the concatenated text in this paper. As a preprocessing step for our approach, each word was stemmed using Porter's stemmer. The rank scores of documents are computed as the cosine similarity between the TFIDF vectors of documents and the topic description for each topic.

What's more, we used MeSH[1] [6] to enrich topic description. MeSH is the National Library of Medicine's (NLM) controlled vocabulary thesaurus. It consists of sets of terms naming descriptors in a hierarchical structure that permits searching at various levels of specificity. We simply increase the occurrence number of a word in the topic description by one if the word is a MeSH word, and then compute the TF score of this word using the Okapi TF formula for topic enrichment.

In order to obtain a better candidate document set, we further apply the pseudo relevance feedback technique. First, we apply the LemurTFIDF model implemented in Terrier [5], an open source retrieval system, to get prior ranking results. Then, we select Top-*K* documents in the prior ranking results, choose 20 words from each Top-*K* document with highest LemurTFIDF scores, and then add these items to the topic description representation as feedback model. Finally, we rank all documents according to their cosine similarity with the new topic representation. We simply set *K* to 5.

After initial document retrieval, we keep and use only Top-2000 documents of each topic for multi-modality re-ranking.

2.3 Latent Semantic Learning with Paragraph Vector

Paragraph vector [10], which was inspired by word embedding [9] and has been proved to be one of the state-of-the-art methods for document modeling, is an unsupervised framework to learn continuous distributed vector representations for pieces of variable-length texts. In the paragraph vector framework, both documents and words are mapped to unique vectors. Each document is treated as a unique token which is the context of all the words in the document.

More formally, given a sequence of training word $w_1, w_2, \ldots, w_T$ and the paragraph p, the aim is to maximize the average log probability

$$\frac{1}{T}\sum_{t=k}^{T-k} log\, p(w_t | w_{t-k}, \ldots, w_{t+k}, p)$$

In paragraph vector model, the objective can be typically achieved by the softmax function, a generalization of the logistic function. It has the form as follows:

$$p(w_t | w_{t-k}, \ldots, w_{t+k}, p) = \frac{e^{y_{w_t}}}{\sum_i e^{y_i}}$$

Each of y_i is un-normalized log-probability for each output word i, computed as

$$y = b + Uh(w_{t-k}, \ldots, w_{t+k}, p; W, D)$$

where U, b are the softmax parameters. h is constructed by a concatenation or average of word vectors and paragraph vector looked up from matrices *W* and *D*.

The paragraph vector model considers the order of word and represents paragraph as a vector in lower-dimension space compared with the BOW vector. Intuitively, the paragraph vector contains latent semantic information and we believe considering this latent vector can improve document ranking results.

In our study, the open source toolkit *word2vec* is used to generate paragraph vectors. This toolkit was firstly developed to implement the word vector model and then modified to obtain paragraph vector. The vector dimension is simply set to 100 and the window size of words is set to 10. The negative sampling method is used and the number of negative samples is set to 5 and the sampling threshold is set to 1e-3. The iteration time is set to 20. All the above parameter values were suggested by Quoc Le.

In our study, we segment each document into paragraphs by paragraph breaks (i.e. <p> tags) and map each paragraph to a unique vector. Document vectors are generated by simple addition of vectors of paragraphs with normalization. Note that we will use "paragraph vector" to denote the document vector of a document in subsequent sections.

2.4 Graph-Based Multi-Modality Re-Ranking

2.4.1 Basic Manifold-Ranking Algorithm

The manifold-ranking method [3] is a universal ranking algorithm and it is initially used to rank data points by their graph-based relationships with the prior assumption that nearby points and points on the same structure (typically referred to as a cluster or a manifold) are likely to have the same ranking scores. In our study, we use the manifold-ranking method to re-rank the initially retrieved documents. In other words, the data points refer to the topic description and all documents in the candidate set. The manifold-ranking process of the document re-ranking task can be formalized as follows:

Given a set of vectors $\chi = \{x_0, x_1, x_2, \ldots, x_n\} \subset R^m$ and these vectors can be either BOW vectors or paragraph vectors. The BOW vectors are generated in the same way of the initial document retrieval process. The only change is that BOW vectors of topics are enriched on the basis of Top-*K* documents of initial retrieval results instead of the ranking results by Terrier. The paragraph vectors are generated by the method we introduce in Section 2.3. The first point x_0 represents the topic description and the rest n points represent all the initially retrieved documents (data point to be ranked).

The ranking scores are expressed as a vector $f = [f_0, f_1, \ldots, f_n]^T$ and the initial values are expressed as a vector $y = [y_0, y_1, \ldots, y_n]^T$ with $y_0 = 1, y_i = 0\ (i \neq 0)$. The similarity relationship is constructed as a matrix $W = (W_{ij})_{(n+1)\times(n+1)}$, in which each W_{ij} corresponds to the cosine similarity between x_i and x_j and $W_{ii} = 0$. $S = D^{-1/2} W D^{-1/2}$ denotes the normalization of matrix W and $D = (D_{ij})_{(n+1)\times(n+1)}$ where $D_{ii} = \sum_{j=0}^{n} W_{ij}$ is a diagonal matrix.

According to Zhou et al.'s work, f can be optimized by iterating process $f^{t+1} = \alpha S f^t + (1-\alpha) y$ where $0 < \alpha < 1$. After convergence, $f^* = lim_{t\to\infty} f^t$, and f_i^* stands for the final ranking score of document i.

[1] https://www.nlm.nih.gov/mesh/MBrowser.html

2.4.2 Multi-Modality Learning Algorithm

The basic manifold-ranking algorithm makes use of the similarity relationships based on uniform vectors. In our study, we expect to take into account not only statistical features but also semantic features during our re-ranking process. Specifically, we wish to use both traditional BOW vectors and paragraph vectors to improve ranking results. The two modalities are very different and they have unique characteristics. Therefore, it would be more appropriate to consider both the two modalities and the multi-modality manifold-ranking algorithm [4] is thus applied for document re-ranking.

In our multi-modality re-ranking process, we construct two matrices W^a and W^b to represent the similarity relationships of documents based on the BOW vectors and the paragraph vectors, respectively. The definitions of W^a and W^b are the same with W in the basic manifold-ranking algorithm. In particular, W^a is built from BOW vectors and W^b is built from paragraph vectors. S^a and S^b are the normalization of W^a and W^b in the same way. By the work of [4], there are three iterating schemes for fusing two modalities: linear fusion scheme, sequential scheme and score combination scheme.

Linear fusion scheme:

$$f^{t+1} = \mu S^a f^t + \eta S^b f^t + (1-\mu-\eta)y$$

where $0 < \mu, \eta$ and $\mu + \eta < 1$

$$f^* = lim_{t\to\infty} f^t$$

Sequential fusion scheme:

$$f^{t+1} = \mu S^a f^t + \eta S^b f^t - \mu\eta S^b S^a f^t + (1-\mu)(1-\eta)y$$

where $0 < \mu, \eta < 1$

$$f^* = lim_{t\to\infty} f^t$$

Score combination scheme:

$$f_a{}^{t+1} = \mu S^a f_a{}^t + (1-\mu)y$$

$$f_b{}^{t+1} = \eta S^b f_b{}^t + (1-\eta)y$$

$$f_a{}^* = lim_{t\to\infty} f_a{}^t$$

$$f_b{}^* = lim_{t\to\infty} f_b{}^t$$

$$f^* = \lambda f_a{}^* + (1-\lambda) f_b{}^* \text{ where } 0 < \lambda < 1$$

By using the three schemes above, we obtain the re-ranking results by considering both statistical and semantic characteristics.

3. EVALUATION

3.1 Data Set and Evaluation Metrics

In 2014 and 2015, the TREC-CDS track was designed to assess the ability of search engines to retrieve biomedical journal articles relevant for answering generic clinical questions about medical records. There are 30 topics in the track of each year and each topic within this track consists of a sentence-long summary and a paragraph-long description of a patient case, along with one of three types of clinical information: diagnosis, test or treatment. The top 100 documents in the retrieval results are used for evaluation by evaluation toolkits. We used the two TREC-CDS datasets for evaluation in this study. In TREC-CDS 2015, there are two tasks (Task A and Task B) and in Task B a diagnosis field is provided for the treatment and test topics. In order to keep the consistency of two datasets, we only experimented with Task A in TREC-CDS 2015.

We used *trec_eval* and *sample_eval* toolkits for evaluation, which was officially adopted by TREC-CDS. As in TREC-CDS, infNDCG is used as the main metric and we also provided results of infAP, Precision@10 and R-Prec measures.

3.2 Evaluation Results

In the experiments, the proposed multi-modality re-ranking methods with the three fusion schemes introduced in Section 2.4 are denoted as "DoubleM(SEQ)", "DoubleM(LIN)" and "DoubleM(COM)", respectively. The basic manifold-ranking methods based on BOW vectors and paragraph vectors are denoted as "SingleM(BOW)" and "SingleM(P2V)", and the baseline corresponds to the initial document retrieval results. In the experiments, the regularization parameter μ for the BOW modality is fixed at 0.65 and parameter η for the paragraph vector modality is fixed at 0.15. Therefore, we set $\alpha = 0.65$ for "SingleM(BOW)", $\alpha = 0.15$ for "SingleM(P2V)", $\mu = 0.65$ and $\eta = 0.15$ for all multi-modality re-ranking methods. The combination weight parameter λ is simply set to 0.5 for the score combination scheme. To compare with state-of-the-art methods, we also list the two best results of automatic participants [7][8]. In 2014, they are SNUMedinfo [12] and NovaSearch [6]. In 2015, they are wsu_ir [11] and LIST_LUX [1]. NovaSearch and LIST_LUX generate a variety of ranking results with different retrieval models and use RRF as the fusion algorithm to fuse these results. SUNMedinfo trains a classifier to predict document types and improves ranking results with classification scores. Wsu_ir purposes a retrieval model to accumulate retrieval scores in diverse sources (e.g. topic summary, topic description, UMLS). MeSH is used by these groups for query extraction and simplification.

Table 1 shows the comparison results (infNDCG) of different re-ranking schemes. We can see that the basic manifold-ranking algorithm (SingleM) with either BOW or paragraph vectors can improve the initial retrieval results, and the results validate the effectiveness of the re-ranking process. Moreover, the proposed multi-modality algorithms (DoubleM) can significantly outperform the basic manifold-ranking methods due to the use of both the two representations. The two representations are two different views of each document and they can complement each other in the re-ranking process. We can also see that the sequential fusion scheme (SEQ) in the multi-modality learning algorithm performs better than the linear fusion scheme (LIN) and the score combination (COM) scheme on both datasets.

Tables 2 and 3 compare the results of our best method (DoubleM(SEQ)) and the best results of automatic participants in 2014 and 2015, respectively. We also provide the median and average results across all submitted automatic runs. We can see that our method performs better than all automatic participants in TREC-CDS over the main metric (i.e., infNDCG). Particularly, the performance of our method on the main metric is much better than that of the best participant (i.e., SNUMedinfo) in TREC-CDS 2014 and slightly better than that of the best participant (i.e., wsu_ir) in TREC-CDS 2015. In addition to the main metric, our method can achieve the best performance of infAP and R-Prec in TREC-CDS 2014, and achieve the best performance of Prec10 in TREC-CDS 2015. We can also see that the performance of our method on different metrics is much higher than the median and average performance of all submitted automatic runs. In all, our method achieves the state-of-the-art performance in both TREC-CDS 2014 and 2015, and the results validate the efficacy of our method.

In order to investigate the influence of parameters in multi-modality re-ranking, the parameter μ is varied from 0.61 to 0.7 and the parameter η is varied from 0.11 to 0.2 in "DoubleM(SEQ)" on the two datasets. Figures 1 and 2 show the surface charts on the two datasets and the BOW axis stands for μ and the P2V axis stands for η. We can see from the figures that both two modalities contribute to the improvement of the results, and our proposed method can achieve very good performance over a relatively wide range of parameter values, which demonstrates the robustness of our proposed method.

Table 1. Comparison results of different re-ranking schemes

	TREC-CDS 2014	TREC-CDS 2015
Baseline	0.2357	0.2350
SingleM(BOW)	0.2786	0.2703
SingleM(P2V)	0.2675	0.2450
DoubleM(LIN)	0.2790	0.2689
DoubleM(COM)	0.2950	0.2903
DoubleM(SEQ)	**0.2967**	**0.2957**

Table 2. Comparison results between our results and best automatic participants' results in 2014 ("n/a" means the performance value has not been reported in literatures)

	infNDCG	infAP	Prec10	R-Prec
SNUMedinfo	0.2674	0.0659	0.3633	n/a
NovaSearch	0.2631	0.0757	**0.3900**	0.2165
DoubleM(SEQ)	**0.2967**	**0.0934**	0.3633	**0.2275**
Median	0.1723	0.0418	0.2567	0.1426
Average	0.1575	0.0388	0.2365	0.1262

Table 3. Comparison results between our results and best automatic participants' results in 2015

	infNDCG	infAP	Prec10	R-Prec
wsu_ir	0.2939	**0.0842**	0.4667	**0.2306**
LIST_LUX	0.2894	0.0787	0.4533	0.2299
DoubleM(SEQ)	**0.2957**	0.0713	**0.4800**	0.2162
Median	0.2120	0.0441	0.3650	0.1751
Average	0.1973	0.0434	0.3308	0.1538

4. CONCLUSIONS

In this paper, we proposed to use the paragraph vector technique and the multi-modality ranking algorithm for addressing the task of clinical decision support. We achieved the state-of-the-art performance on two benchmark datasets. In future work, we will explore to make use of more advanced deep learning techniques (e.g. LSTMs) for learning semantic representations and further improve the re-ranking performance.

5. ACKNOWLEDGMENTS

The work was supported by NSFC (61331011), National Hi-Tech Research and Development Program of China (2015AA015403) and IBM Global Faculty Award Program. Xiaojun Wan is the corresponding author.

6. REFERENCES

[1] Asma Ben Abacha and Saoussen Khelifi. LIST at TREC 2015 Clinical Decision Support Track: Question Analysis and Unsupervised Result Fusion. In Proceedings of TREC 2015.

[2] Chengxiang Zhai. Notes on the Lemur TFIDF model. http://www.cs.cmu.edu/~lemur/1.0/tfidf.ps

[3] D. Zhou, J. Weston, A. Gretton, O. Bousquet and B. SchÖlkopf. Ranking on data manifolds. In Proceedings of NIPS-03.

[4] Hanghang Tong, Jingrui He, Mingjing Li, Changshui Zhang, Wei-Ying Ma. Graph Based Multi-Modality Learning. In MM'05, November 6–11, 2005, Singapore.

[5] I. Ounis, G. Amati, V. Plachouras, B. He, C. Macdonald, et al. Terrier: A High Performance and Scalable Information Retrieval Platform. In Proceedings of OSIR 2006.

[6] J. Gobeill, A. Gaudinat, E. Pasche, P. Ruch. Full-texts representation with Medical Subject Headings, and co-citations network reranking strategies forTREC 2014 Clinical Decision Support Track. In Proceedings of TREC 2014.

[7] Kirk Roberts, Matthew S. Simpson, Ellen Voorhees, William R. Hersh. Overview of the TREC 2015 Clinical Decision Support Track. In Proceedings of TREC 2015.

[8] Matthew S. Simpson, Ellen M. Voorhees, William Hersh. Overview of the TREC 2014 Clinical Decision Support Track. In Proceedings of TREC 2014.

[9] Mikolov, Tomas, Sutskever, Ilya, Chen, Kai, Corrado, Greg, and Dean, Jeffrey. Distributed representations of phrases and their compositionality. In Advances on Neural Information Processing Systems, 2013.

[10] Quoc Le and Tomas Mikolov. Distributed Representations of Sentences and Documents. In Proceedings of the 31st International Conference on Machine Learning, Beijing, China, 2014.

[11] Saeid Balaneshin-kordan, Alexander Kotov and Railan Xisto. WSU-IR at TREC 2015 Clinical Decision Support Track: Joint Weighting of Explicit and Latent Medical Query Concepts from Diverse Sources. In Proceedings of TREC 2015.

[12] Sungbin Choi, Jinwook Choi. SNUMedinfo at TREC CDS track 2014: Medical case-based retrieval task. In Proceedings of TREC 2014.

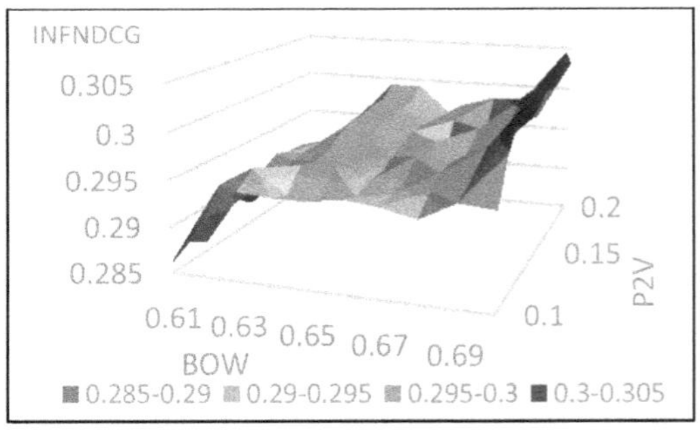

Figure 1. InfNDCG vs. μ and η for "DoubleM(SEQ)" in 2014

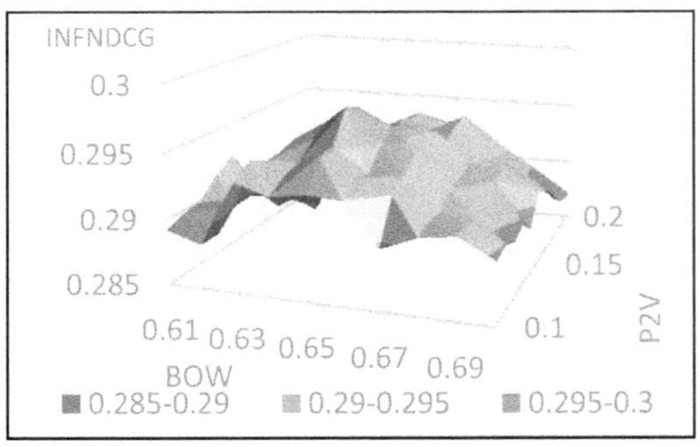

Figure 2. InfNDCG vs. μ and η for "DoubleM(SEQ)" in 2015

Where are You Tweeting? A Context and User Movement Based Approach

Zhi Liu
Computer Science and Engineering
University of North Texas
Denton, TX 76207
zhiliu@my.unt.edu

Yan Huang
Computer Science and Engineering
University of North Texas
Denton, TX 76207
Yan.Huang@unt.edu

ABSTRACT

Geotagged tweets allow one to extract geo-information-trend, search local events, and identify natural disasters. In this paper, we propose a Hidden-Markov-based model to integrate tweet contents and user movements for geotagging. A language model is obtained for different locations from training datasets and movements of users among cities are analyzed. Home cities of users are considered in modeling the patterns of user movements. Evaluation on a large Twitter dataset shows that our method can significantly improve geotagging accuracy by 55% for home cities and 2% for other non-home cities as well as reduce error distances by orders of magnitude compared with pure text-based methods.

Keywords

Geotagging, Tweet, Hidden Markov Model

1. INTRODUCTION

Social media and mobile devices provide users platforms to share their thoughts, opinions, interests, and whereabouts. With 310 millions monthly active users[1], Twitter is one of the busiest microblogs worldwide. Geotagged tweets allow one to extract geo-information-trend [3], search local events [16], and identify natural disasters [13]. However, geotags are not consistently available due to privacy concerns and other reasons. In fact, only less than 1% of tweets contain a geotag [1] and nearly 90% of Twitter users do not have geo-location enabled[2]. Geotagging is the process of assigning a location to a tweet indicating where it is published. Accurate geotagging, the focus of this work, will provide added values to social media contents for applications such as emergency response, event search, trend detection, and smart transportation.

The availability of user geotagged tweets allows one to profile the geographic distributions of terms in tweets and these distributions have been used in several existing work for geotagging. Bayesian based method generates a language model for a location and calculates the probability of a tweet belonging to different locations based on the Bayesian model [7]. Given the local language model θ_L, the probability of a tweet T belonging to a location L can be calculated as: $P(L|T) = \frac{P(T|\theta_L)P(L)}{P(T)}$ and $P(T|\theta_L) = \prod_i P(t_i|\theta_L)$. The location with the maximal probability is assigned to a tweet as its geotag. In [4], the authors also propose a similar method to estimate the locations of tweets based on the distributions of words. Kullback-Leibler (KL) divergence based method measures the difference between a tweet and the local language model [7, 12]. The location with minimal KL value is assigned to the tweet. Gaussian model or Gaussian Mixture Model (GMM) fits geotags of n-grams in tweets into Gaussian distributions. The center of the Gaussian distribution [6] or a weighted sum of GMMs [11] is assigned as the geotag of tweets.

Another line of work uses location relevant words from contents as an important clue. In [2], local geo-parsing is considered to suggest locations . Geotagging is done through classification. Location indicative words (LIWs) in the content are detected mainly by three measurements: term frequency, inverse city frequency, and information gain. These LIWs are used as features to classify tweets into cities. In [15], the authors combine different indicators including content information, user profile, and time zone in estimating the locations of tweets.

All of the above approaches rely solely on social media content for geotagging. However, pure content-based methods leave out the movement patterns of a user. The sequence of geotags of tweets published by a user is aligned with the location sequence of the same user. The movement of a user is affected by various factors such as home location, travel distance, recent activities, and the characteristics of cities. Using user movement patterns can potentially help improve the geotagging accuracy.

Thus in this work, we propose a framework that integrates content and user movement to achieve better geotagging performance. Specifically, this paper makes the following contributions: 1) We introduce movement patterns of users into geotagging; 2) We propose a Hidden Markov Model to integrate language model and user movements for geotagging; 3) The evaluation on a large Twitter dataset shows that our model increases geotagging geotagging accuracy by 2% for non-home cities and 55% for home cities as well as reduce

[1]https://investor.twitterinc.com/results.cfm
[2]http://www.beevolve.com/twitter-statistics/

CIKM'16 , October 24-November 28, 2016, Indianapolis, IN, USA

DOI: http://dx.doi.org/10.1145/2983323.2983881

error distances by orders of magnitude compared with pure text-based methods discussed above.

2. INTEGRATING MOVEMENT PATTERN IN GEOTAGGING

The problem of geotagging tweets is equivalent to estimating the locations of users where they publish the tweets. Locations of users are not only revealed by tweet content but also by a user's previous and next locations because traveling preferences have a great influence on the next locations of users. In this section, we propose a Hidden-Markov-based model to integrate user movement and tweet content in geotagging. The model also considers the home location of a user to better represent the transition probability for users of different home cities.

In our model, the states of the Hidden Markov Model are the city level locations of users and the state observations are tweets. The state (city) is not directly visible but the observation (tweet) is visible. Therefore, the sequence of tweets generated gives some information about the sequence of cities. Each tweet corresponds to a state which represents the city where the user publishes the tweet. The transition probabilities of the HMM are observed from large number of user movement records.

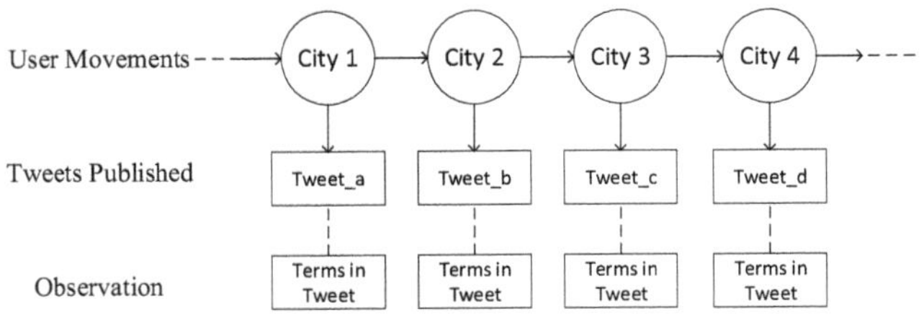

Figure 1: Estimating geotags of tweets by Hidden Markov Model

More specifically, as it is shown in Figure 1, for each user with N published tweets, he/she will have N corresponding states. Each state represents the location of the user where he/she publishes the tweet. The discrete states of the HMM are the set of all the cities. The goal is to predict a series of states (cities) from a series of observations (tweets) of the user.

Transition Probabilities: Transition probabilities are observed from a large number of user traveling records. For each user u with a list of published tweets $T^u = \langle T_1^u, T_2^u, \dots \rangle$, we obtain the list of cities where he has visited through the geotags of his tweets: $\mathcal{C}^u = \langle \mathcal{C}_1^u, \mathcal{C}_2^u, \mathcal{C}_3^u \dots \rangle$. Given a city $\mathcal{C}_i$, the transition probability from $\mathcal{C}_i$ to city $\mathcal{C}_j$, $P(\mathcal{C}_j|\mathcal{C}_i)$, is defined as:

$$P(\mathcal{C}_j|\mathcal{C}_i) = \frac{\sum_u \mathcal{C}_i^u \to \mathcal{C}_j^u}{\sum_u \mathcal{C}_i^u \to \mathcal{C}^u} \quad (1)$$

where $\mathcal{C}_i^u \to \mathcal{C}_j^u$ denotes a pair of consecutive cities in the sequence $\mathcal{C}^u$. So $\sum_u \mathcal{C}_i^u \to \mathcal{C}_j^u$ is the total frequency of users traveling from city $\mathcal{C}_i$ to $\mathcal{C}_j$, and $\sum_u \mathcal{C}_i^u \to \mathcal{C}^u$ is the frequency of users traveling from city $\mathcal{C}_i$ to any other city. So this probability can be explained as: for the users who publish a tweet in city $\mathcal{C}_i$, they have a chance of $P(\mathcal{C}_j|\mathcal{C}_i)$ to publish next tweet in city $\mathcal{C}_j$, which is also the transition probability in our model.

Home City Influence on Transition Probabilities: The home location of a user has a great influence on the transition probability. For two users u_1 and u_2 in the same city C where u_1's home location is in C and u_2 is a visitor, the probability of u_1 to stay in C is much higher than u_2 and the probability of u_2 to return to his home city is very high as well. So, home city greatly influences the transition probability between two cities.

To address this issue, we train transition probabilities separately based on home cities of users. We use U to denote all users in the dataset and $U_{\mathcal{C}_i}$ is the users with home city $\mathcal{C}_i$. For a user u with home city $\mathcal{C}_i$: 1) When u moves between city $\mathcal{C}_i$ and $\mathcal{C}_j$ (includes $j = i$), $P(\mathcal{C}_j|\mathcal{C}_i)$ are observed from all the users in $U_{\mathcal{C}_i}$; 2) When u moves from city $\mathcal{C}_j$ to city $\mathcal{C}_k$, $i \neq j$ & $i \neq k$, the training data are from users in $\{U - U_{\mathcal{C}_j}\}$. For the second case, we combine all the users whose home city is not $\mathcal{C}_j$ together due to the lack of enough training data for users in every city.

Observation Probabilities: The observation probability gives the likelihood of an observation from a given state. For geotagging, given a tweet T, there is an observation probability $P(T|\mathcal{C})$ for each city $\mathcal{C}$. From the geotagged tweets, we build the language model $\theta_\mathcal{C}$ for each city. The probability of term t from a tweet which published in city $\mathcal{C}$ can be estimated as: $p(t|\theta_\mathcal{C}) = tf_{(t,\mathcal{C})}/dl_\mathcal{C}$, where $tf_{(t,\mathcal{C})}$ is the frequency of term t in city $\mathcal{C}$ and $dl_\mathcal{C}$ is the total frequencies of all terms in city $\mathcal{C}$[10]. Then given the state of city C, the observation probability $P(T|\mathcal{C})$ is defined as:

$$P(T|\mathcal{C}) = \prod_{t_i \in T} P(t_i|\theta_\mathcal{C}) \quad (2)$$

In this work, we smooth the probability of $P(t_i|\theta_\mathcal{C})$ by using the Dirichlet smoothing [17]. The stop words[3] are removed before calculating the observation probabilities.

Inference: The probability of the initial state, $P(S_0 = \mathcal{C}_j)$, is given by the transition probability of $P(\mathcal{C}_j|\mathcal{C}_i)$, where $\mathcal{C}_i$ is the home city of the user. This is based on the observation that a user is likely to travel to any city from his home city and the first tweet observation is not necessarily from his home city. Then based on the Viterbi algorithm, we find the city sequence which can maximize the product of the observation probabilities and transition probabilities as the geotags of tweets. Assuming the total number of tweets of a user is N, the number of cities is $|\mathcal{C}|$, and each tweet contains $|T|$ terms, the time complexity of estimating the location of these N tweets is $O(N \times |\mathcal{C}|^2 + N \times |\mathcal{C}| \times |T|)$.

3. GEOTAGGED TWITTER DATASET

We collected tweets published from May 21 to July 6, 2015 using Twitter Streaming API[4] with the spatial bounding box $[24°3'N, 127°7'W, 48°8'N, 65°5'W]$, which covers U.S. mainland. The dataset consists of over 60 million geotagged tweets from 2,200,402 Twitter users.

Knowing a user's home helps to understand user movement patterns. Users are bound by travel distance from his home and the types of outbound cities from home affect visiting possibility. However, only 16% users register their city

[3]http://xpo6.com/list-of-english-stop-words/
[4]https://dev.twitter.com/streaming/overview

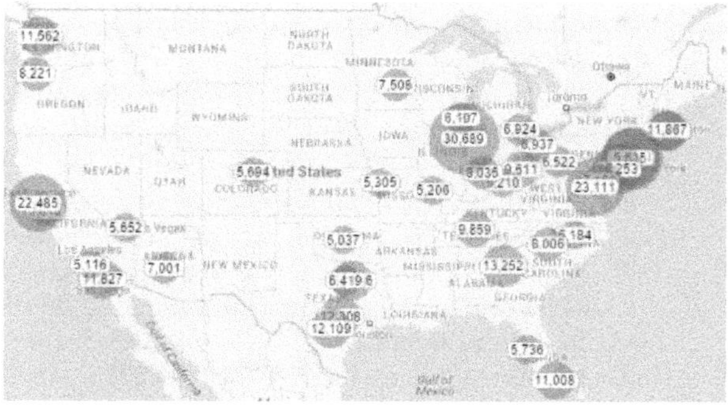

(a) The distribution of number of users in 40 selected U.S. cities.

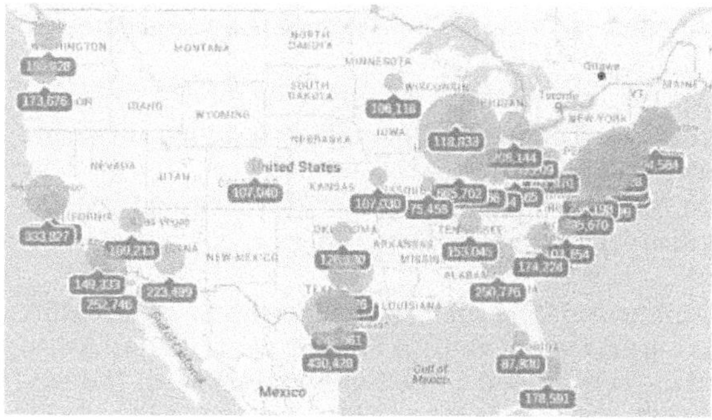

(b) The distribution of number of tweets in 40 selected U.S. cities.

Figure 2: The distributions of users and tweets in the dataset.

	Overall			Non-Home City			Home City		
Methods	Mean	Med.	Acc.	Mean	Med.	Acc.	Mean	Med.	Acc.
Random	2847	2450	3.86	2252	2334	4.9	2845	2439	3.8
Bayesian	1402	1022	36.7	1245	765	31.8	1375	994	36.8
KL divergence	1318	954	38.8	1191	741	32.8	1301	944	38.9
HMM-based	**52.6**	**1.82**	**95.1**	**997**	**181**	**34.6**	**52.4**	**1.82**	**96.3**

Table 1: Mean Error Distance (km), Median Error Distance (km), and Accuracy(%) of the geotag estimation results.

level home locations [8] and collecting the home location from user profile is strictly limited by the rules of Twitter API.

Previous work has provided different methods for estimating the home locations of users [9] based on analyzing content information or geographic distribution of friends. In this work, we assign home location following the method used in [14, 5]. A set of tweets of each Twitter user is selected to estimate the home location (this set will not be used for building and testing geotagging models). These tweets are assigned into different cities according to their geotags. We use city boundaries from the United States Census Bureau[5] to decide which city a geotagged tweet belongs to. Then we assign the city with the most number of tweets as a user's home. In [14], the authors show that the home location obtained in this way has an 85 percent accuracy.

We then select all cities with more than 5,000 users. There are 40 cities C in our dataset. We only keep the tweets: (1) tweeted by users in C; (2) published in C. Figure 2 shows the number of users and the number of geotagged tweets in these 40 cities. The top three cities with the most number of users and tweets are Los Angeles (46,508 users;1,183,634 tweets), Chicago(30,689 users; 634,665 tweets), and New York(30,689 users; 419,130 tweets).

4. EXPERIMENT

We implement four algorithms and compare their performances under different cases. To reduce the impact of spammers and robots, we only keep users with number of geo-tagged tweets between 5 and 500 in our dataset [12]. The first quarter of tweets (sorted by published time) of users are used to estimate home cities. We then run a 10 fold cross validation on the rest of the datatset. Here it should be noted that all the tweets from the same user will be assigned to the same fold.

Methods: We use the random selection method as the baseline method and select two methods proposed by the related works to compare with our algorithm.

- **Random selection (Random):** Select a city as the geotag location of tweet randomly.
- **Bayesian:** The Bayesian-based method described in introduction [7].
- **Kullback-Leibler divergence (KL divergence):** The KL divergence between tweet T and city C is calculated as equation 3 and the geotag is based on the ranking of the KL divergence [7, 12].

$$KL(\theta_T|\theta_C) = \sum_t p(t|\theta_T) log \frac{p(t|\theta_T)}{p(t|\theta_C)} \quad (3)$$

- **HMM-based:** The method proposed in this paper.

Measurements: A tweet is assigned to a city as its geotag. We then assign the coordinate of the city center as the predicated location of the tweet. The city center we used is listed in Wikipedia [6]. We use three measures:

- **Accuracy (Acc).** The percent of tweets which are predicted in the same city where they are published.
- **Mean Error Distance (km):** The average error distance between predicted location and actual location.
- **Median Error Distance (km):** The median error distance between predicted location and actual location.

[5]http://www.census.gov/en.html

[6]https://en.wikipedia.org/wiki/List_of_United_States_cities_by_population

In this paper, we define the distance as the geographic distance.

Table 1 shows that our HMM-based methods can significantly improve the performance of geotagging compared with related works. The overall accuracy is improved by more than 55%; and the mean error distance and median error distance of our method are orders of magnitude better.

We are interested in learning if the improvement is mainly due to the reason that more than 90% of tweets are published in home cities which tend to be easier to estimate. We separate the performance for home cities and non-home cities. Since more than 90% tweets are published in home cities of users, all of these algorithms achieve similar performances in the home cities with the overall case. For the difficult case of non-home cities, the two algorithms from related work, the Bayesian-based method and the KL divergence method, perform better than they do in home cities. This illustrates that when users travel to non-home cities, they may tend to use terms with local characteristics. By contrast, when users stay in home cities, their words are more commonly used with less regional information. However, for the tweets published in these non-home cities, our HMM-based model still outperforms other two methods by nearly 2% in accuracy and the error distances are significantly smaller at the same time. Compared with related works, the improvement on error distances demonstrates that even for the incorrectly estimated cases, our model can locate the tweet with a closer city from the real location of the tweet due to the benefits from the usage of patterns of user movements. In general, the results demonstrate that integrating home city and movement will benefit geotagging in both home and non-home cities.

5. CONCLUSION

In this paper, we propose an HMM-based algorithm for geotagging by integrating a local language model and user movements. We evaluate our model on a large Twitter dataset under different cases. The results show that our method can improve the accuracy by more than 55% percent compared with the baseline algorithms. Even for the tweets published in non-home cities, our method still achieves better results on accuracy and error distances.

6. REFERENCES

[1] H. Abdelhaq, C. Sengstock, and M. Gertz. Eventweet: Online localized event detection from twitter. *Proceedings of the VLDB Endowment*, 6(12):1326–1329, 2013.

[2] H. Bo and P. C. T. BALDWIN. Geolocation prediction in social media data by finding location indicative words. *Proceedings of COLING 2012: Technical Papers*, pages 1045–1062, 2012.

[3] C. Budak, T. Georgiou, D. Agrawal, and A. El Abbadi. Geoscope: Online detection of geo-correlated information trends in social networks. *Proceedings of the VLDB Endowment*, 7(4):229–240, 2013.

[4] Z. Cheng, J. Caverlee, and K. Lee. You are where you tweet: a content-based approach to geo-locating twitter users. In *Proceedings of the 19th ACM international conference on Information and knowledge management*, pages 759–768. ACM, 2010.

[5] E. Cho, S. A. Myers, and J. Leskovec. Friendship and mobility: user movement in location-based social networks. In *Proceedings of the 17th ACM SIGKDD*, pages 1082–1090. ACM, 2011.

[6] D. Flatow, M. Naaman, K. E. Xie, Y. Volkovich, and Y. Kanza. On the accuracy of hyper-local geotagging of social media content. In *Proceedings of the Eighth ACM International Conference on Web Search and Data Mining*, pages 127–136. ACM, 2015.

[7] S. Kinsella, V. Murdock, and N. O'Hare. I'm eating a sandwich in glasgow: modeling locations with tweets. In *Proceedings of the 3rd international workshop on Search and mining user-generated contents*, pages 61–68. ACM, 2011.

[8] R. Li, S. Wang, H. Deng, R. Wang, and K. C.-C. Chang. Towards social user profiling: unified and discriminative influence model for inferring home locations. In *Proceedings of the 18th ACM SIGKDD*, pages 1023–1031. ACM, 2012.

[9] Z. Liu and Y. Huang. Closeness and structure of friends help to estimate user locations. In *International Conference on Database Systems for Advanced Applications*, pages 33–48. Springer, 2016.

[10] J. M. Ponte and W. B. Croft. A language modeling approach to information retrieval. In *Proceedings of the 21st annual international conference on Research and development in information retrieval*, pages 275–281. ACM, 1998.

[11] R. Priedhorsky, A. Culotta, and S. Y. Del Valle. Inferring the origin locations of tweets with quantitative confidence. In *Proceedings of the 17th ACM conference on Computer supported cooperative work and social computing*, pages 1523–1536. ACM, 2014.

[12] S. Roller, M. Speriosu, S. Rallapalli, B. Wing, and J. Baldridge. Supervised text-based geolocation using language models on an adaptive grid. In *Proceedings of the 2012 Joint Conference on Empirical Methods in Natural Language Processing and Computational Natural Language Learning*, pages 1500–1510. Association for Computational Linguistics, 2012.

[13] T. Sakaki, M. Okazaki, and Y. Matsuo. Earthquake shakes twitter users: real-time event detection by social sensors. In *Proceedings of the 19th international conference on World wide web*, pages 851–860. ACM, 2010.

[14] S. Scellato, A. Noulas, R. Lambiotte, and C. Mascolo. Socio-spatial properties of online location-based social networks. *ICWSM*, 11:329–336, 2011.

[15] A. Schulz, A. Hadjakos, H. Paulheim, J. Nachtwey, and M. Mühlhäuser. A multi-indicator approach for geolocalization of tweets. In *ICWSM*, 2013.

[16] J. Weng and B.-S. Lee. Event detection in twitter. *ICWSM*, 11:401–408, 2011.

[17] C. Zhai and J. Lafferty. A study of smoothing methods for language models applied to ad hoc information retrieval. In *Proceedings of the 24th annual international ACM SIGIR conference on Research and development in information retrieval*, pages 334–342. ACM, 2001.

Ensemble Learned Vaccination Uptake Prediction using Web Search Queries

Niels Dalum Hansen
University of Copenhagen
IBM Denmark
nhansen@di.ku.dk

Christina Lioma
University of Copenhagen
c.lioma@di.ku.dk

Kåre Mølbak
Statens Serum Institut
KRM@ssi.dk

ABSTRACT

We present a method that uses ensemble learning to combine clinical and web-mined time-series data in order to predict future vaccination uptake. The clinical data is official vaccination registries, and the web data is query frequencies collected from Google Trends. Experiments with official vaccine records show that our method predicts vaccination uptake effectively (4.7 Root Mean Squared Error). Whereas performance is best when combining clinical and web data, using solely web data yields comparative performance. To our knowledge, this is the first study to predict vaccination uptake using web data (with and without clinical data).

1. INTRODUCTION AND RELATED WORK

Predicting public health events, e.g. how many people may get vaccinated in the near future, can reduce the reaction time of public health professionals, resulting in more efficient services and improved public health. Traditionally, public health event prediction relied on *clinical data* (e.g. microbiological results or patient registries) that was collected from designated bodies. In the last decade however, non-clinical *web data* (e.g. search engine queries or microblog messages), has been shown useful to the task of predicting public health events. Clinical and web data are complementary sources of evidence: Whereas clinical data contributes expert and curated information to the prediction, web data contributes near real-time information on a large scale about e.g. symptoms or health concerns that may go undetected or unreported by the official clinical channels.

We present a method for predicting vaccination uptake by combining clinical and web data using ensemble learning. Combining such clinical and web search data for vaccination uptake prediction is novel. So far, research on vaccination uptake has focused on the effect of physician recommendations on vaccination uptake [4]; how combined sources of information (e.g. physician, television, friends) influence people's decisions about vaccination [5]; and the effects of media coverage on vaccination uptake with respect to influenza vaccination [11], HPV vaccination [8], and MMR vaccination [17]. To our knowledge, our study is the first to predict vaccination uptake using web data (with and without clinical data).

Web and/or clinical data have been used before for other types of health event predictions, e.g. influenza activity [6, 12, 13, 14, 16, 19], dengue fever [1] and cholera [3]. How the different types of data should be handled has evolved from using a unified model for both web and clinical data [9, 18], to using ensemble methods that model separately clinical and web data and then combine the outputs [15]. When web search query frequencies are used for prediction [15, 16, 18], a single linear model is used to combine the query frequencies into a prediction. Methods using query frequencies select queries either by (i) timely correlation between query search frequency and the health event [6, 15, 16, 18], or by (ii) expert selection of queries [1, 14, 19]. Both approaches have disadvantages. Approach (i) relies on calculating the correlation between the health event time-series and all queries, which is computationally expensive. It also assumes that historic correlation equals predictive power in the future, which may not always be the case. Approach (ii) relies on human experts, which is costly and does not scale well. In this work we propose a third approach: We select queries based on web descriptions of the health event, in our case of the vaccine in question, and we use an ensemble learning approach, specifically stacking, to predict vaccination uptake.

CIKM'16, October 24-28, 2016, Indianapolis, IN, USA

DOI: http://dx.doi.org/10.1145/2983323.2983882

2. ENSEMBLE LEARNING PREDICTION

Vaccination uptake prediction with time-series data can be formulated as: $\hat{E}(t) \approx E(t-1)$, where $\hat{E}(t)$ is the predicted vaccination uptake at time t, and $E(t-1)$ is the observed vaccination uptake at time $t-1$. We compute $\hat{E}(t)$ using ensemble learning by combining separate predictions on vaccination uptake based on clinical and web data into one prediction. Ensemble learning combines predictions from an ensemble of level-0 models into one prediction using a level-1 meta model. We use an ensemble method called *stacking*. First, all level-0 models are trained. Then, a level-1 model is trained to make a final prediction using all the predictions of the level-0 models as input. We experiment with three different types of level-1 models: a linear model, support vector regression (SVR) with a linear kernel, and SVR with a Gaussian kernel. Both our clinical and web data are time-series, i.e. each data point has a temporal reference.

2.1 Level-1 models

Stacking with linear model. We define a linear model with two explanatory variables: $\hat{E}(t) = \mu + \beta_1 \hat{E}_c(t) + \beta_2 \hat{E}_w(t)$, where $\hat{E}_c(t)$ is the prediction based on clinical data at time t, $\hat{E}_w(t)$ is the prediction based on web data at time t, and μ, β_1 and β_2 denote the coefficients that need to be optimized. We use ordinary least squares to find the coefficients that minimize: $\min_{\mu,\beta_1,\beta_2} \sum_t \left(E(t) - \mu - \beta_1 \hat{E}_c(t) - \beta_2 \hat{E}_w(t)\right)^2$.

Stacking with SVR. SVR solves the same problem as the linear model presented above, but with the possibility of using kernels to transform the input into another feature space. In addition μ, β_1 and β_2 are selected to minimize the following: $\min_{\mu,\beta_1,\beta_2} \sum_t V(E(t) - \mu - \beta_1 \hat{E}_c(t) - \beta_2 \hat{E}_w(t)) + \frac{\lambda}{2}(\mu^2 + \beta_1^2 + \beta_2^2)$, where λ is a hyperparameter controlling the penalty for large coefficients, and $V(r)$ is defined as 0 if $|r| < \epsilon$ and otherwise $|r| - \epsilon$. The parameter ϵ controls how precise the prediction has to be before it is treated as correct.

We experiment with an SVR with linear kernel and with a Gaussian kernel defined as: $K(x, x') = \exp(-\gamma||x - x'||^2)$, where γ is a hyperparameter.

2.2 Level-0 models

Prediction with clinical data. As level-0 models we use three well-known time-series methods: autoregressive (AR) models [18, 9], ARIMA and Holt Winters (HW).

AR models estimate $\hat{E}(t)$ as: $\hat{E}(t) = \mu + \sum_{i=1}^{m} \beta_i E(t-i)$ where m is the number of autoregressive terms, μ is the intercept, and the βs control the weight that each past observation has on the prediction. AR models assume that future values of E can be predicted by a linear combination of the m most recently observed values of E. With enough autoregressive terms AR models can handle seasonal changes, but not general upwards or downwards trends.

An extension of the AR models are the ARIMA (AutoRegressive Integrated Moving Average) models. In addition to the autoregressive terms, these models also include a moving average, which is a weighted sum of the q most recent forecasting errors. Let m denote the number of autoregressive terms and q the number of moving averages; then: $\hat{E}(t) = \mu + \sum_{i=1}^{m} \beta_i E(t-i) + \sum_{j=1}^{q} \phi_j \epsilon_{t-j} + \epsilon_t$, where $\epsilon_t = E(t) - \hat{E}(t)$. To handle trend, the original signal E can be differentiated one or more times [2].

HW forecasting is defined by three recursive equations controlling: level, trend and seasonality. HW can forecast time-series with both trend and seasonal changes. Each equation is defined as a weighted sum in which the weight of historic observations decreases exponentially with time. HW forecasting with level, trend and seasonality is recursively defined as:

$$\begin{aligned} \text{level} \quad & a_t = \alpha(E(t) - s_{t-l}) + (1-\alpha)(a_{t-1} + b_{t-1}) \\ \text{trend} \quad & b_t = \beta(a_t - a_{t-1}) + (1-\beta)b_{t-1} \\ \text{seasonality} \quad & s_t = \gamma(E(t) - a_t) + (1-\gamma)s_{t-l} \end{aligned} \tag{1}$$

where l is the length of the season and α, β and γ are the smoothing parameters which control the influence of the historic level, trend and seasonality. Predictions are made by combining level, trend and seasonality: $\hat{E}(t) = a_{t-1} + b_{t-1} + s_{t-l+1}$.

Prediction with web data. As level-0 models we use a linear model, bagging and weighted majority. Our web data consists of time-stamped query frequencies (described in Section 3).

Linear model. Given a collection of n query frequency time-series, denoted Q, we define a simple linear model as: $\hat{E}(t) = \mu + \sum_{i=1}^{n} \alpha_i Q_i(t)$, where μ and α are coefficients to be estimated. Such a model can be fitted using any of several methods, the most common being ordinary least squares. Another approach is to use LASSO regularization which is commonly used for making predictions using query frequencies [15, 16, 18]. This approach adds an additional constraint to the optimization, namely that the sum of the coefficients should also be minimized. The weight of this sum is controlled by the hyperparameter λ. This approach can be used to avoid overfitting and to reduce the coefficients of non-informative features to zero and thereby induce a sparse model. This is a useful property in this context because the collection of queries might contain non-informative terms.

Bagging. With bagging, we consider the average of the predictions made on subsets of the training data. This helps to reduce variance and overfitting. We generate subsets of the training data by uniformly sampling with replacement n datasets of size m. For each dataset a linear model, as defined above, is fitted using LASSO regularization, where the parameter λ is found using 3-fold cross-validation. The prediction of the ensemble is the average of the n predictions.

Weighted Majority. We extend the bagging approach to a boosting approach using a weighted majority (WM) algorithm [10]. The WM algorithm works by combining predictions from a collection of models using a weighted average. Each model is associated with its own weight related to its previous predictive performance. If the overall prediction is wrong by a constant ϵ, the weights are updated. The updating works as follows: if the individual prediction of a model has an error $> \epsilon$, a new weight is calculated as $w_i = w_i \exp(-\eta)$, where w_i is the weight for model i and η is a hyperparameter controlling the penalty for making wrong predictions. Our collection of models is identical to the models used for the bagging approach described above.

3. EXPERIMENTAL EVALUATION

Data[1]**.** We evaluate the effectiveness of our approach in predicting vaccination uptake in Denmark for all official children vaccines: DiTeKiPol-1, DiTeKiPol-2, DiTeKiPol-3, DiTeKiPol-4, PCV-1, PCV-2, PCV-3, MMR-1, MMR-2(4), MMR-2(12), HPV-1, HPV-2 and HPV-3. We use as clinical data the actual vaccination uptake recorded by the country's official body, the State Serum Institut. Specifically, the vaccination uptake is the total number of vaccines given in a month divided by the number of people expected to be vaccinated that month (based on the size of the monthly birth cohorts published by Statistics Denmark).

We use as web data web search queries that are related to each vaccine. We generate these queries from descriptions of each vaccine in: *www.ssi.dk*, *www.patienthåndbogen.dk*, and *www.min.medicin.dk* (authoritative medical health portals). We remove stopwords and collect terms that occur in at least two different descriptions of each vaccine. We treat each term as a query (i.e. we use only single term queries)

[1]All our data is freely available at: https://sid.erda.dk/share_redirect/c7j6MdrscL

Vaccine	Terms in Danish (English)
MMR	levende (alive), mæslinger (measles), vaccine, vaccinen (the vaccine), udbrud (outbreak), alvorlige (serious), fåresyge (mumps), måneders (months), undersøgelser (examinations) beskyttelse (protection), voksne (adults), gravid (pregnant), kombineret (combined), dosis, hunde (dogs), alderen (the age), hjernebetændelse (inflammation of the brain) lungebetændelse (pneumonia), gives (is given), mfr (mmr), røde (red)
DiTeKiPol	mæslinger (measles), vaccinen (the vaccine), alvorlige (serious), beskyttelse (protection), kombineret (combined), vaccination, indeholder (contains), type, beskytter (protects) sygdomme (illness), meningitis, forårsaget (caused), dræbte (killed), b, kighoste (whooping cough), vare (lasts), polio, difteri (diphtheria), mindst (least), stivkrampe (tetanus)
PCV	vaccinen (the vaccine), alvorlige (serious), alderen (the age), lungebetændelse (pneumonia), vaccination, infektioner (infections), sygdomme (illness), forebygger (prevents) meningitis, forårsaget (caused), antal (number), blodforgiftning (blood poisoning)
HPV	beskyttelse (protection), gives (is given), vaccination, tilbuddet (the offer), kondylomer (condyloma), doser (doses), kønsvorter (genital warts), tilbydes (is offered), piger (girls) livmoderhalskræft (cervical cancer), forventes (is expected), indeholder (contains), januar (january), langvarig (long term), indført (introduced), tilbud (offer), type, human beskytter (protects), effekten (the effect), skyldes (caused by), hpv, pigerne (the girls)

Table 1: Our 58 queries.

and we submit it to Google Trends using Denmark as the geographical region and with the time period set to January 2011 - September 2015 (only limited coverage of Denmark is available prior to 2011). Only 58 out of 85 queries had enough coverage in Google Trends to return a result. We use these 58 queries for our predictions (shown in Table 1).

Training. We use as training data all data which is available prior to the data point being predicted. Hence if we are predicting the vaccination uptake in February 2014 we train on data from January 2011 – January 2014. All models are refitted for each time step. We use monthly time steps. To allow for inference of seasonality, the level-0 models are initialized with 24 months of available data (January 2011 – December 2012) as training data. For the level-1 models we start by using 12 months of data (January 2013 – December 2013). We evaluate our predictions using the root mean squared error (RMSE), which penalizes large errors more than small.

Our prediction methods are fitted using R packages with default settings at all times, except for the starting point for HW, where we manually select a starting point of the optimization if it cannot be completed with the default value. The AR model is trained using 12 autoregressive terms to capture seasonal variations. For bagging and weighted majority we use as many subsets as there are queries, each subset contains 10 randomly sampled queries. For the weighted majority we use $\eta = 5$ and $\epsilon = 2$ for all experiments.

Results. Table 2 shows the results when predicting vaccination uptake using either clinical or web data only (with the methods presented in Section 2). "Naive" refers to our naive baseline $\hat{E}(t) = E(t-1)$. Our methods outperform the naive baseline except for the HPV vaccines. This might be due to an intense debate in Denmark regarding the safety of this particular vaccine. Such a debate is likely to boost query frequencies but not necessarily vaccination uptake (the fact that many more people talk about HPV does not mean that many more HPV vaccines are given). We see that methods using clinical data outperform the methods using web data for the majority of the vaccines. But interestingly this difference is not very big and for the vaccines DiTeKiPol-3 and DiTeKiPol-4 the methods based on web data perform best. DiTeKiPol-4 is especially interesting since a shortage in 2013 resulted in unusual vaccination behaviour for a few months. When making predictions from web data our two new approaches (bagging and WM) perform best for 9 of the 13 vaccines.

Table 3 shows the results for the ensemble predictions using clinical and web data. Except for the three HPV vaccines, the ensemble approaches outperform all other methods using only one data source. We see that when using an SVR with a Gaussian kernel as level-1 model we obtain the best results, i.e. 7/13 lowest RMSE. When comparing within the methods using an SVR with a Gaussian kernel, the HW+WM is the best performing method. The most improvements are obtained when combining predictions based on web data with either predictions from HW or AR12.

		Clinical data			Web data			
	Naive	HW	AR12	ARIMA	WM	B	L	O
MMR-1	20.704	**18.149**	**18.606**	**15.574**	**16.609**	**16.597**	**16.605**	30.387
MMR-2 (4)	20.582	**13.110**	**16.566**	**16.284**	**15.841**	**15.635**	**15.500**	29.288
MMR-2 (12)	20.637	**19.592**	**20.600**	**18.726**	21.631	20.815	**21.112**	31.897
HPV-1	8.080	11.291	11.192	9.871	13.474	14.320	12.701	11.547
HPV-2	8.704	12.522	12.806	11.276	18.154	18.025	18.423	15.404
HPV-3	6.579	9.161	13.958	9.418	24.239	23.494	23.074	17.317
DiTeKiPol-1	14.091	**6.700**	**5.185**	**5.097**	**8.067**	**8.058**	**8.069**	15.913
DiTeKiPol-2	17.693	**7.520**	**8.030**	**8.064**	**10.003**	**9.941**	**9.951**	20.082
DiTeKiPol-3	17.884	**17.596**	20.936	19.459	**17.160**	**17.160**	**17.158**	30.424
DiTeKiPol-4	21.676	26.103	21.676	23.385	**15.414**	**15.535**	**15.934**	33.888
PCV-1	13.323	**6.897**	**6.394**	**6.623**	**7.745**	**7.797**	**7.845**	14.014
PCV-2	17.533	**7.266**	**8.845**	**8.353**	**9.679**	**9.796**	**9.770**	**16.027**
PCV-3	18.405	**7.877**	**7.781**	**7.634**	**10.410**	**10.364**	**10.368**	**15.582**

Table 2: RMSE of predictions with only clinical or web data. WM: weighted majority, B: Bagging, L: linear model w. LASSO and O: linear model w. OLS. Blue: lowest RMSE per vaccine. Bold: better than naive.

4. CONCLUSIONS

We presented a method that uses ensemble learning to combine clinical and web-mined time-series data to make predictions about future vaccination uptake. As clinical data we used official registries of vaccines in Denmark. As web data we used query frequencies collected from Google Trends. We created those queries by extracting terms from publicly available descriptions of the vaccines on the web. Experiments using all officially recommended children vaccines in Denmark for the period January 2011 – September 2015 showed that for 10/13 vaccines our ensemble learning methods that combined clinical with web data for prediction outperformed predictions using either clinical or web data alone. Though this combination yields the lowest overall error, using only web data gives predictions with an error only slightly worse than for the predictions made using only clinical data. This indicates the potential usefulness of web data, such as query frequencies, to predict vaccination uptake in countries where there is no national vaccination registry. This work complements wider efforts in tackling medical and health problems computationally with machine learning or retrieval [20, 21].

5. REFERENCES

[1] E. H. Chan, V. Sahai, C. Conrad, and J. S. Brownstein. Using web search query data to monitor dengue epidemics: A new model for neglected tropical disease surveillance. *PLoS Negl Trop Dis*, 5(5):e1206, 2011.

[2] C. Chatfield. *The analysis of time series: An introduction.* CRC press, 2013.

[3] R. Chunara, J. R. Andrews, and J. S. Brownstein. Social and news media enable estimation of epidemiological patterns early

OLS

	HW+WM	HW+B	HW+L	HW+O	AR12+WM	AR12+B	AR12+L	AR12+O	ARIMA+WM	ARIMA+B	ARIMA+L	ARIMA+O
MMR-1	**15.190**	**15.476**	**15.187**	**16.842**	**17.697**	17.572	17.457	**18.151**	16.296	16.492	15.968	17.877
MMR-2 (4)	**12.875**	13.497	13.349	13.121	16.305	16.108	16.195	**16.032**	18.872	16.220	21.085	**15.871**
MMR-2 (12)	**18.082**	**17.650**	**17.541**	**17.221**	**18.711**	**19.523**	**18.762**	**18.909**	**18.469**	19.409	18.961	**18.693**
HPV-1	**10.552**	**10.435**	**10.960**	11.516	**9.377**	**9.690**	**10.130**	**10.281**	10.348	10.080	9.992	10.080
HPV-2	12.743	**12.923**	14.384	**12.191**	**11.883**	**12.201**	13.240	**10.503**	**10.708**	**10.655**	**10.279**	**9.220**
HPV-3	**8.743**	**8.771**	10.231	9.987	**11.321**	**11.063**	**12.110**	**12.151**	9.893	**9.237**	9.818	9.918
DiTeKiPol-1	**6.416**	**6.875**	**6.477**	**5.498**	**4.835**	**4.831**	**4.829**	**5.082**	6.072	5.690	5.625	5.584
DiTeKiPol-2	9.094	8.216	8.967	7.956	**7.686**	**7.343**	8.116	**8.019**	9.461	8.989	15.485	9.057
DiTeKiPol-3	18.478	17.891	18.410	**16.662**	17.529	18.225	17.550	**18.439**	17.168	17.227	**17.137**	**19.076**
DiTeKiPol-4	15.812	17.977	17.495	**19.860**	17.290	19.891	16.537	**19.849**	24.391	45.079	36.403	24.220
PCV-1	7.042	**5.783**	**5.716**	**5.391**	**6.201**	**5.950**	**5.830**	**5.973**	10.785	**6.569**	9.174	**6.169**
PCV-2	**8.317**	8.236	9.283	7.553	10.135	**8.670**	10.401	**8.284**	8.395	8.399	9.681	**8.330**
PCV-3	**7.345**	**7.436**	8.199	**7.759**	**6.825**	**7.014**	**7.108**	**6.736**	7.931	8.364	8.240	7.670

SVR linear

	HW+WM	HW+B	HW+L	HW+O	AR12+WM	AR12+B	AR12+L	AR12+O	ARIMA+WM	ARIMA+B	ARIMA+L	ARIMA+O
MMR-1	**16.541**	**15.969**	**15.478**	**16.905**	17.298	17.252	17.399	**18.496**	19.406	16.793	16.857	**18.204**
MMR-2 (4)	**12.648**	**12.981**	**12.388**	**12.952**	16.148	**15.373**	16.663	**15.095**	**14.969**	16.101	**15.419**	**15.620**
MMR-2 (12)	**17.906**	**18.054**	**17.872**	**17.374**	**19.302**	**19.020**	**18.248**	**19.075**	**19.123**	**18.193**	19.195	**17.731**
HPV-1	**10.530**	**10.649**	**10.922**	**11.146**	**10.486**	**10.494**	**10.688**	**10.657**	10.331	10.789	10.810	10.448
HPV-2	13.489	**12.344**	**12.130**	**12.425**	**10.147**	**10.467**	**11.984**	**11.062**	**9.738**	**9.906**	**10.482**	**8.727**
HPV-3	**8.903**	**8.260**	**8.501**	10.674	**11.732**	**11.718**	**13.049**	**12.617**	9.806	10.001	9.484	10.411
DiTeKiPol-1	6.926	**5.993**	**5.739**	**6.500**	**4.740**	**4.758**	**4.626**	**5.077**	**5.090**	5.354	5.287	5.507
DiTeKiPol-2	9.808	9.476	9.006	9.100	8.476	8.563	10.503	**7.734**	9.938	8.480	9.872	9.591
DiTeKiPol-3	22.546	22.599	22.546	**17.433**	21.402	21.925	21.154	**19.003**	22.244	21.319	22.104	**19.568**
DiTeKiPol-4	16.694	37.909	17.357	**14.461**	15.922	16.405	16.124	**16.164**	22.072	26.591	18.984	**17.609**
PCV-1	7.351	7.186	**6.175**	**6.198**	**5.282**	**6.143**	**6.335**	**5.510**	6.765	7.413	6.840	6.830
PCV-2	**7.689**	7.946	15.613	7.955	9.029	8.879	9.104	**8.823**	8.794	11.662	14.559	9.024
PCV-3	**7.648**	8.261	8.388	**7.784**	**6.904**	**6.758**	**6.994**	**6.633**	9.649	9.384	9.058	8.491

SVR Gaussian

	HW+WM	HW+B	HW+L	HW+O	AR12+WM	AR12+B	AR12+L	AR12+O	ARIMA+WM	ARIMA+B	ARIMA+L	ARIMA+O
MMR-1	**14.928**	16.694	**16.355**	**16.198**	17.770	18.207	18.117	**16.927**	16.703	17.490	17.569	17.560
MMR-2 (4)	14.377	**12.870**	14.094	13.122	**15.709**	**14.780**	**15.024**	**15.468**	**14.973**	**15.109**	16.625	**15.838**
MMR-2 (12)	**18.007**	**17.446**	**18.972**	**16.530**	**17.945**	**19.115**	**18.406**	**18.176**	**18.385**	**18.553**	19.625	19.041
HPV-1	**10.748**	11.606	11.918	**11.289**	**11.002**	**10.902**	11.403	**9.130**	11.664	10.684	11.505	9.987
HPV-2	13.513	**11.958**	**12.304**	**12.097**	**10.789**	**12.376**	9.964	**12.483**	**10.537**	**11.249**	11.715	**10.961**
HPV-3	12.889	13.784	14.775	13.352	**13.016**	14.521	15.222	14.374	12.818	12.172	12.147	12.682
DiTeKiPol-1	**5.204**	**5.008**	**5.098**	**5.331**	5.486	5.467	5.486	6.227	5.725	6.393	5.577	6.615
DiTeKiPol-2	7.927	8.017	8.172	9.661	**7.149**	**7.443**	**7.818**	8.078	9.009	9.870	9.848	8.721
DiTeKiPol-3	**16.639**	**16.448**	**16.433**	**17.275**	18.650	18.442	19.009	**18.355**	18.380	17.545	18.298	**18.962**
DiTeKiPol-4	15.616	**14.877**	**15.246**	**16.543**	16.865	16.038	16.687	**15.653**	15.938	15.647	**15.923**	**15.932**
PCV-1	**5.256**	**5.808**	**5.769**	**5.664**	**5.450**	**6.358**	**6.363**	**6.614**	**6.724**	7.160	**6.611**	7.091
PCV-2	**6.463**	7.665	7.366	7.470	**8.811**	**7.450**	**6.952**	9.026	8.672	9.062	8.991	9.148
PCV-3	**7.121**	**7.665**	8.396	**7.798**	9.022	9.556	**10.008**	7.871	8.616	8.148	9.527	8.176

Table 3: RMSE of ensemble predictions (clinical and web data). Blue: lowest RMSE per vaccine. Bold: lower RMSE than for the individual ensemble components in Table 1.

in the 2010 Haitian cholera outbreak. *The American Journal of Tropical Medicine and Hygiene*, 86(1):39–45, 2012.

[4] L. M. Gargano, N. L. Herbert, J. E. Painter, J. M. Sales, C. Morfaw, K. Rask, D. Murray, R. DiClemente, and J. M. Hughes. Impact of a physician recommendation and parental immunization attitudes on receipt or intention to receive adolescent vaccines. *Human vaccines & immunotherapeutics*, 9(12):2627–2633, 2013.

[5] L. M. Gargano, N. L. Underwood, J. M. Sales, K. Seib, C. Morfaw, D. Murray, R. J. DiClemente, and J. M. Hughes. Influence of sources of information about influenza vaccine on parental attitudes and adolescent vaccine receipt. *Human vaccines & immunotherapeutics*, 2015.

[6] J. Ginsberg, M. H. Mohebbi, R. S. Patel, L. Brammer, M. S. Smolinski, and L. Brilliant. Detecting influenza epidemics using search engine query data. *Nature*, 457(7232):1012–1014, 2009.

[7] R. J. Hyndman and Y. Khandakar. Automatic time series for forecasting: The forecast package for R. Technical report, Monash University, Department of Econometrics and Business Statistics, 2007.

[8] B. J. Kelly, A. E. Leader, D. J. Mittermaier, R. C. Hornik, and J. N. Cappella. The HPV vaccine and the media: How has the topic been covered and what are the effects on knowledge about the virus and cervical cancer? *Patient education and counseling*, 77(2):308–313, 2009.

[9] D. Lazer, R. Kennedy, G. King, and A. Vespignani. The parable of Google flu: Traps in big data analysis. *Science*, 343(14 March), 2014.

[10] N. Littlestone and M. K. Warmuth. The weighted majority algorithm. *Information and computation*, 108(2):212–261, 1994.

[11] K. Ma, W. Schaffner, C. Colmenares, J. Howser, J. Jones, and K. Poehling. Influenza vaccinations of young children increased with media coverage in 2003. *Pediatrics*, 117(2):e157–e163, 2006.

[12] D. J. McIver and J. S. Brownstein. Wikipedia usage estimates prevalence of influenza-like illness in the United States in near real-time. *PLoS Comput Biol*, 10(4):e1003581, 2014.

[13] M. J. Paul, M. Dredze, and D. Broniatowski. Twitter improves influenza forecasting. *PLoS currents*, 6, 2014.

[14] P. M. Polgreen, Y. Chen, D. M. Pennock, F. D. Nelson, and R. A. Weinstein. Using internet searches for influenza surveillance. *Clinical infectious diseases*, 47(11):1443–1448, 2008.

[15] M. Santillana, A. T. Nguyen, M. Dredze, M. J. Paul, E. O. Nsoesie, and J. S. Brownstein. Combining search, social media, and traditional data sources to improve influenza surveillance. *PLoS Comput Biol*, 11(10):e1004513, 2015.

[16] M. Santillana, E. O. Nsoesie, S. R. Mekaru, D. Scales, and J. S. Brownstein. Using clinicians' search query data to monitor influenza epidemics. *Clinical Infectious Diseases*, 59(10):1446–1450, 2014.

[17] M. J. Smith, S. S. Ellenberg, L. M. Bell, and D. M. Rubin. Media coverage of the measles-mumps-rubella vaccine and autism controversy and its relationship to MMR immunization rates in the United States. *Pediatrics*, 121(4):e836–e843, 2008.

[18] S. Yang, M. Santillana, and S. Kou. Accurate estimation of influenza epidemics using Google search data via ARGO. *Proceedings of the National Academy of Sciences*, 112(47):14473–14478, 2015.

[19] Q. Yuan, E. O. Nsoesie, B. Lv, G. Peng, R. Chunara, and J. S. Brownstein. Monitoring influenza epidemics in China with search query from Baidu. *PloS one*, 8(5):e64323, 2013.

[20] R. Dragusin, P. Petcu, C. Lioma, B. Larsen, H. Jørgensen and O. Winther. Rare Disease Diagnosis as an Information Retrieval Task. *ICTIR*, 356–359, 2011.

[21] R. Dragusin, P. Petcu, C. Lioma, B. Larsen, H. L. Jørgensen, I. J. Cox, L. K. Hansen P. Ingwersen and O. Winther. Specialized tools are needed when searching the web for rare disease diagnoses. *Rare Diseases*, 1(1):e25001, 2013.

Location-aware Friend Recommendation in Event-based Social Networks: A Bayesian Latent Factor Approach

Yao Lu
Institute of Information Engineering,
Chinese Academy of Sciences
luyao9023@iie.ac.cn

Zhi Qiao
IBM Research - China
Beijing, China
qzbj@cn.ibm.com

Chuan Zhou
Institute of Information Engineering,
Chinese Academy of Sciences
zhouchuan@iie.ac.cn

Yue Hu
Institute of Information Engineering,
Chinese Academy of Sciences
huyue@iie.ac.cn

Li Guo
Institute of Information Engineering,
Chinese Academy of Sciences
guoli@iie.ac.cn

ABSTRACT

In this paper we study the friend recommendation problem in event-based social networks (EBSNs). Effective friend recommendation is of benefit to EBSNs, since it can promote user interaction and accelerate information diffusion for promoted events. Different from usual friend recommendations, the aim of making friends in EBSNs is to better participate offline events and enhance user experience. Meanwhile friend recommendation in EBSNs encounters three types of data, i.e. geographical information, implicate user rating, and user behavior. These differences imply that existing friend recommendation approaches are not adequate any more for EBSNs. Under this background, in this paper we propose a Bayesian latent factor model, which can jointly formulate above three types of data, for friend recommendation with better event promotion and user experience. Results on real-world datasets show the efficacy of our approach.

Keywords

Friend recommendation, event-based social network, Bayesian latent factor model

1. INTRODUCTION

Event-based social networks (EBSNs), like Meetup and Plancast, become more and more popular recently, where users can create, promote and share upcoming events of any kind [4]. Effective friend recommendation plays an important role in EBSNs, since it can enrich user interaction, accelerate information diffusion, and help event promotion.

Different from existing friend recommendation problems, the aim of making friends in EBSNs is to better participate offline events and enhance user experience [2]. Our data analysis in Section 2 shows that users in EBSNs are more likely to follow people with the similar area preference. Meanwhile EBSNs meets three type information, i.e. implicate user rating, geographical information and user behavior. All these differences imply that existing friend recommendation approaches are not adequate any more for ESBNs. Therefore, an interesting problem is how to make friend recommendation in EBSNs for better event promotion and user experience. We call this problem as *Event-oriented Friend Recommendation* hereafter.

To this end, we present a Bayesian latent factor model, which combines **G**eographical information, **I**mplicate user ratings and user **B**ehaviors for accurate **F**riend **R**ecommendation (GIB-FR for short). The main contributions of this paper are threefold:

(i) We propose the event-oriented friend recommendation problem, which aims to enhance event promotion and user experience.

(ii) As a solution, we propose a Bayesian latent factor model, which can jointly formulate geographical information, implicate user ratings and user behaviors.

(iii) We evaluate the proposed recommendation method over five real-world datasets collected from Plancast. Experimental results show that the proposed method performs better against existing methods.

CIKM'16 , October 24-28, 2016, Indianapolis, IN, USA
© 2016 ACM. ISBN 978-1-4503-4073-1/16/10... $15.00
DOI: http://dx.doi.org/10.1145/2983323.2983883

2. PRELIMINARY

In this section, we first describe the datasets and analyze the geographical influence on user's online connections. Then we formally define the target problem.

2.1 Data Sets

We collect data from Plancast, one of the most popular EBSNs, and select for analysis the data from New York City (NYC), Los Angeles (LA), Chicago (Chi.), Washington (Was.) and San Francisco (SF), as these cities have a large number of users. The data sets are extracted from the work [4]. Table 1 summarizes the detailed information of datasets, such as users number, events number, the ratio of present edges to absent edges in online social network, and the average degree.

2.2 Observations

We engage in some high-level investigation of how geographical information influence the user online connections. (1) *Event distribution.*: how events are located in a city? (2) *Area homophily*: Do users with similar location history tend to have online connections?

Table 1: Statistics of the data sets.

City	Users	Events	+ve:-ve	Average degree
NYC	3,155	5149	1:127	49.192
SF	7,402	10868	1:240	61.319
LA	1,501	1843	1:65	45.316
Chi.	529	736	1:41	25.078
Was.	596	954	1:43	27.064

Event distribution. Based on the data statistics, we find that most events were located around centers and concentration areas. For example, we use the Chicago data and perform k-Means clustering to find these concentration areas. Here we assign 20 to k. Figure 1(a) shows the results. Each node represents an event's location, a node with same color represent a geographical cluster.

Area homophily. The principle of homophily [3] suggests that users with similar characteristics tend to associate with each other. In particular, we study area homophily, we test weather users who share common areas when they participate social events will have a tendency to associate with each other. Figure 1(b) clearly shows that the probability of two users following each other increase with the number of their common areas. The x-axis is the number of common areas and the y-axis is the probability of the two users follow each other.

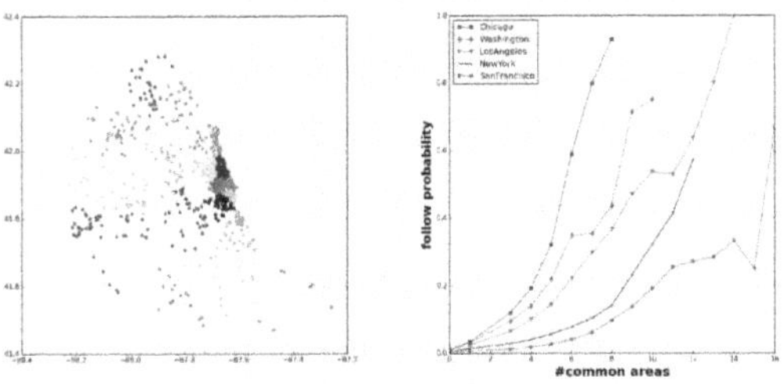

(a) Event distribution (b) Area homophily

Figure 1: Geographical influence

In summary, according to the analysis above, we can observe that (a) events in EBSNs are located around concentration areas, and (b) users with the common concentration areas have a tendency to follow each other.

2.3 Problem Definition

Let $U = \{u_1, u_2, ..., u_n\}$ denote the set of users and R denotes user ratings where $R_{ij} = 1$ indicates user u_i follows user u_j and 0 otherwise. For the friend recommendation task, the dyadic rating 1/0 is implicit which brings the implicit feedback challenge.

In the EBSNs, we also have another two types of entities: E (event) and L (event location). Let the set of events be $E = \{e_1, e_2, ..., e_n\}$. For each event $e_i \in E$, it has a location $l_i \in L$.

Formally, the friend recommendation problem is defined as ranking all candidate users for each user, according to the dyadic rating score R_{ij}. Hence predicting the rating R_{ij} plays a central role in friend recommendation.

Bayesian latent factor model is practical and flexible here: it can incorporating topological and side information and scale to large networks. Hence we propose Bayesian latent factor based GIB-FR model which can combine geographical information and user behaviors for personal recommendation. Moreover, for the implicit feedback challenge and pair-wise ranking, a Bayesian personal ranking (BPR) [8] framework is introduced.

3. MODEL FRAMEWORK

In this section, we introduce GIB-FR model which incorporates all the information within a single model to better predicting the follow relationships. We use matrix factorization to derive latent feature space from the data, and we use a BPR framework to learn the parameters.

3.1 The Proposed Model

3.1.1 User Rating

We use the latent factor model to predict the user rating, which is widely used in recommendation tasks. For user i, we embody it with two low-dimensional latent factor vectors $U_i \in R^k$ and $V_i \in R^k$, where U_i indicates user $i's$ personal preference as follower, and V_i indicates his personal preference as followee. Thus the dyadic rating R_{ij} of user u_i to user u_j is approximated as follows.

$$\hat{R_{ij}} = U_i^T V_j \tag{1}$$

3.1.2 GIB-FR Model

In order to settle down the implicit feedback challenge, we use the Bayesian personal ranking (BPR) framework, which emphases on predicting the dyadic ratings R_{ij} and top ranking items with high scores. Based on the BPR optimization criterion, we regard user followed by user u as a positive set denoted as S_u^P, while the remaining users as the negative set denoted as S_u^N. Then we expect to rank the positive set S_u^p higher than the negative set S_u^N, we denote the rank as M. We define the likelihood function as

$$P(M|\Theta) = \prod_{(u_i, u_j, u_k) \in (U, S_{u_i}^P, S_{u_i}^N)} P(R_{ij} > R_{ik}|\Theta) \tag{2}$$

where Θ is the parameter set in the model, $P(R_{ij} > R_{ik}) := L(R_{ij} - R_{ik})$ and function L is the logistics function.

Geographical and behavioral information. As referred above, the geographical and behavioral information can help us better learn the user preference. There actually exist two important interactions: the location interactions M^l and the offline interactions M^e, where each element $M_{ij}^l \in M^l$ represents whether user u_i visited region l_j and each element $M_{ij}^e \in M^e$ represents whether user u_i participated into event e_j. By using the two sources of interactions conjointly, we may discover that user is prone to follow people who attend the similar events or visit similar areas.

For the geographical information, the location interactions M_{ij}^l of user u_i with region l_j can be approximated as follows.

$$\hat{M_{ij}^l} = U_i^T C_j \tag{3}$$

where U_i is the user latent factor vector and C_j is the location latent factor vector. To capture area homophily, we use the K-Means algorithm to cluster all the events to k regions, where each region can be present as a latent factor vector.

For the behavioral information, the offline interactions M_{ij}^e of user u_i with event e_j can be approximated as follows.

$$\hat{M_{ij}^e} = U_i^T B_j \tag{4}$$

where U_i is the user latent factor vector and B_j is the event latent factor vector.

Now we integrate both the geographical and behavioral information into a unified model. And the likelihood is given by

$$\begin{aligned} &P(M, M^e, M^L|\Theta) \\ &= P(M|U,V) \cdot P(M^e|U,B,\sigma_e^2) \cdot P(M^l|U,C,\sigma_l^2) \end{aligned} \tag{5}$$

For the user behavior matrix M^e and user location matrix M^l, we adopt a probabilistic linear model with Gaussian observation noise. We define the conditional distribution over the observed rating as

$$P(M^e|U,B,\sigma_e^2) = \prod_{j=1}^{M}\prod_{i=1}^{N}[N(M_{ij}^e|U_i^T B_j, \sigma_e^2)]^{I_{ij}^e} \quad (6)$$

$$P(M^l|U,C,\sigma_l^2) = \prod_{j=1}^{K}\prod_{i=1}^{N}[N(M_{ij}^l|U_i^T C_j, \sigma_l^2)]^{I_{ij}^l} \quad (7)$$

where $N(x|\mu, \sigma^2)$ is the probability density function of the Gaussian distribution with mean μ and variance σ^2, and I_{ij}^e and I_{ij}^l are the indicator functions. I_{ij}^e equals to 1 if user u_i participated event e_j and equals to 0 otherwise, and I_{ij}^l equals to 1 if user u_i participated event located in location l_j and equals to 0 otherwise. We also place zero-mean spherical Gaussian priors on user, event and location feature vectors respectively.

Now we can get the posterior distribution from the likelihood and priors. As it is known to all, maximizing the log-posterior is equivalent to minimizing the loss function with quadratic regularization terms:

$$E = \sum_{(u_i,u_j,u_k)\in(U,S_{u_i}^P,S_{u_i}^N)} ln(1+e^{-u_i(v_j-v_k)})$$
$$+\frac{\lambda_e}{2}\sum_{j=1}^{M}\sum_{i=1}^{N} I_{ij}^e(M_{ij}^e - U_i^T B_j)^2 + \frac{\lambda_l}{2}\sum_{j=1}^{K}\sum_{i=1}^{N} I_{ij}^l(M_{ij}^l - U_i^T C_j)^2$$
$$+\sum_{i=1}^{N}(\frac{\lambda_U}{2}\|U_i\|^2 + \frac{\lambda_V}{2}\|V_i\|^2) + \frac{\lambda_B}{2}\sum_{i=1}^{M}\|B_i\|^2 + \frac{\lambda_C}{2}\sum_{i=1}^{K}\|C_i\|^2 \quad (8)$$

where λ_U, λ_V, λ_B and λ_C are regularization parameters.

3.2 Parameter Learning

The parameter can be learned by minimizing the above objective function E by using stochastic gradient descent (SGD) algorithm. SGD has fast speed to convergence and high scalability in large-scale data sets.

We first choose the triples (u_i, u_j, u_k) from $(U, S_{u_i}^P, S_{u_i}^k)$ randomly with replacement. Then based on the objective function in Eq. (9), we have the following gradients:

$$\frac{\partial E}{\partial U_i} = \frac{-e^{-U_i(V_j-V_k)}}{1+e^{-U_i(V_j-V_k)}}(V_j - V_k) - \lambda_e\sum_{j=1}^{M}(M_{ij}^e - U_i^T B_j)B_j I_{ij}^e$$
$$- \lambda_l\sum_{j=1}^{K}(M_{ij}^l - U_i^T C_j)C_j I_{ij}^l + \lambda_U\|U_i\| \quad (9)$$

$$\frac{\partial E}{\partial V_j} = \frac{-e^{-U_i(V_j-V_k)}}{1+e^{-U_i(V_j-V_k)}}U_i + \lambda_V\|V_j\| \quad (10)$$

$$\frac{\partial E}{\partial V_k} = \frac{e^{-U_i(V_j-V_k)}}{1+e^{U_i(V_j-V_k)}}U_i + \lambda_V\|V_k\| \quad (11)$$

$$\frac{\partial E}{\partial B_j} = \lambda_e\sum_{i=1}^{M}(U_i^T B_j - M_{ij}^e)U_i I_{ij} + \lambda_B\|B_j\| \quad (12)$$

$$\frac{\partial E}{\partial C_j} = \lambda_l\sum_{i=1}^{M}(U_i^T C_j - M_{ij}^l)U_i I_{ij} + \lambda_C\|C_j\| \quad (13)$$

We thus have the update rules used in the SGD algorithm framework:

$$U_i = U_i - \gamma\frac{\partial E}{\partial U_i};\ V_j = V_j - \gamma\frac{\partial E}{\partial V_j}$$
$$V_k = V_k - \gamma\frac{\partial E}{\partial V_k};\ B_j = B_j - \gamma\frac{\partial E}{\partial B_j} \quad (14)$$
$$C_j = C_j - \gamma\frac{\partial E}{\partial C_j}$$

where $\gamma > 0$ is the learning rate.

The complete steps to learn the model parameters are depicted in Algorithm 1.

Algorithm 1 The algorithm to learn the model parameters.

Input: user online social matrix M^{on}, user behavior matrix M^e, user location matrix M^l, and parameter ϵ.
Output: user latent factor U, V, event latent factor B and location latent factor C

```
Initialize U, V, B and C with randomly generated vectors
Generate (U, S_u^P, S_u^N) from M^on
Draw (u_i, v_j, v_k) from(U, S_u^P, S_u^N)
Initialize parameter pQ = 0
Compute AUC value Q for train data
repeat
   pQ = Q
   Calculate the gradients as in Eqs.(9~13)
   Update the parameters as in Eq. (14)
   Compute AUC value Q for train data
until Q - pQ > ε
return the parameters U, V, B and C.
```

4. EXPERIMENT AND RESULTS

4.1 Experimental Setup

We use the data described in Sec. 2 in our experiments. To quantitatively evaluate the effectiveness of the proposed model and compare with other baseline methods, we randomly sample twenty percent of the user-user pairs as test data, and the rest as training data. We randomly divide the training data into 5 parts to do cross validation. We repeat the above procedure for three times, so we have three copies of training data and test data. The experimental results are averaged over the performance on those copies of test data.

Evaluation Measures. We evaluate the performance of different approaches in terms of AUC, P@k (Precision at Position k), and MAP (Mean Average Precision). AUC measures the overall results of classification, and is suitable for highly imbalanced datasets. P@k and MAP measure the performance in ranking problem.

Baselines and Parameter Settings. We compare the results of different methods on our datasets, including KNN, weight regularized matrix factorization (WR-MF), Bayesian personal ranking matrix factorization (BPR-MF), adamic adar index (AA), resource allocation index (RAI), preferential attachment (PA) and factor-rank (FR) [6].

The AUC performance on the validation data is used to select the best parameters. The learning rate γ is selected from $\gamma \in \{0.001, 0.01, 0.1\}$, and the regularization parameters are selected form $\lambda_e = \lambda_l = \lambda_U = \lambda_V \in \{0.001, 0.01, 0.1\}$. We perform a grid search for parameters and as a result the learning rate is set to 0.01, the regularization parameters are set to 0.001. The dimension of latent factor K affect the model complexity. We carefully tune K by evaluating the AUC performance. As the results shown in Figure 3, we get the best performance when $K = 8$, so we set $K = 8$.

4.2 Experimental Results

Classification Performance. Table 2 shows the results on AUC in different datasets. It can be clearly seen that our proposed GIB-FR model significantly outperforms the seven comparison methods. The reason here is that GIB-FR can capture user behavior and geographical information.

Prediction Performance. Because users usually only check a few top-ranked friends, we use P@3 and MAP to study the prediction performance. As the results shown in Figure 2, GIB-FR generally achieves the best results in all datasets. Thus, we can conclude that the proposed model can obtain better recommendation results.

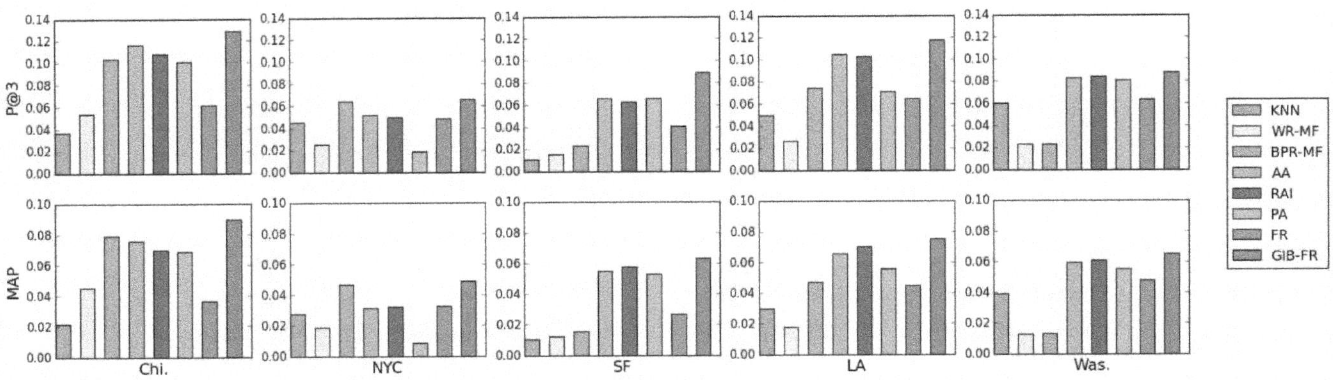

Figure 2: Results on P@3 and MAP

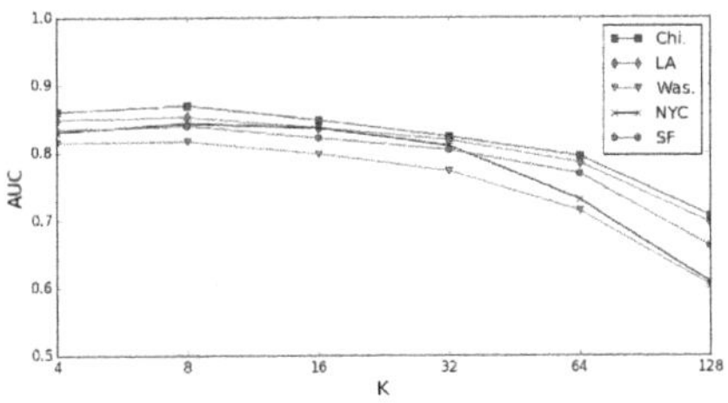

Figure 3: Test on parameter K

Table 2: AUC Results

Methods	Chi.	NYC	SF	LA	Was.
KNN	0.7238	0.6419	0.5895	0.6943	0.6809
WR-MF	0.8061	0.8068	0.7957	0.8142	0.7607
BPR-MF	0.8373	0.8122	0.7971	0.8151	0.7927
AA	0.8364	0.8215	0.8031	0.8354	0.8049
RAI	0.8453	0.8270	0.8033	0.8349	0.8050
PA	0.8162	0.7554	0.7552	0.7837	0.7519
FR	0.8455	0.8244	0.8158	0.8430	0.8123
GIB-FR	**0.8691**	**0.8428**	**0.8391**	**0.8523**	**0.8161**

5. RELATED WORK

User recommendation with geographical information. In recent years, user recommendation with geographical information has been extensively studied. [1] revealed that user social connections are highly related to their geographical distance. [9] proposed a link prediction model that considers the user geographical history. However, these methods do not consider the correlation between geographical information and user preference in friend recommendation problem.

Recommendation on EBSNs. Several studies have been conducted for recommendation tasks on EBSNs. [10] proposed a factorization model that exploits social and location features for group recommendation. Event recommendation has been extensively studied [5, 7]. However, event-oriented friend recommendation is still an untouched problem.

6. CONCLUSIONS

In this paper, we put forward the event-oriented friend recommendation problem, which aims at enhancing event promotion and user experience. To address this problem, we presented the GIB-FR model to integrate geographical information, implicate user ratings and user behaviors. The SGD algorithm was employed to learn the GIB-FR model. Results on real-world datasets shown the efficacy of our method.

Acknowledgements

This work was supported by the 973 Program (No. 2013CB329605), NSFC (No. 61502479), Strategic Leading Science and Technology Projects of CAS (No. XDA06030200), and Xinjiang Uygur Autonomous Region Science and Technology Project (No. 201230123). C. Zhou is the corresponding author.

7. REFERENCES

[1] P. DeScioli, R. Kurzban, E. N. Koch, and D. Liben-Nowell. Best friends alliances, friend ranking, and the myspace social network. *Perspectives on Psychological Science*, 6(1):6–8, 2011.

[2] J. Hannon, M. Bennett, and B. Smyth. Recommending twitter users to follow using content and collaborative filtering approaches. In *RecSys*, pages 199–206, 2010.

[3] P. F. Lazarsfeld, R. K. Merton, et al. Friendship as a social process: A substantive and methodological analysis. *Freedom and control in modern society*, 18(1):18–66, 1954.

[4] X. Liu, Q. He, Y. Tian, W.-C. Lee, J. McPherson, and J. Han. Event-based social networks: linking the online and offline social worlds. In *SIGKDD*, pages 1032–1040, 2012.

[5] A. Q. Macedo, L. B. Marinho, and R. L. Santos. Context-aware event recommendation in event-based social networks. In *RecSys*, pages 123–130, 2015.

[6] A. K. Menon and C. Elkan. Link prediction via matrix factorization. In *Machine Learning and Knowledge Discovery in Databases*, pages 437–452. 2011.

[7] Z. Qiao, P. Zhang, Y. Cao, C. Zhou, L. Guo, and B. Fang. Combining heterogenous social and geographical information for event recommendation. In *AAAI*, 2014.

[8] S. Rendle, C. Freudenthaler, Z. Gantner, and L. Schmidt-Thieme. Bpr: Bayesian personalized ranking from implicit feedback. In *UAI*, pages 452–461, 2009.

[9] S. Scellato, A. Noulas, and C. Mascolo. Exploiting place features in link prediction on location-based social networks. In *SIGKDD*, pages 1046–1054, 2011.

[10] W. Zhang, J. Wang, and W. Feng. Combining latent factor model with location features for event-based group recommendation. In *SIGKDD*, pages 910–918, 2013.

Extracting Skill Endorsements from Personal Communication Data

Darshan M. ShankaraLingappa*
Helsinki Institute for Information Technology and Dept. of Computer Science
Aalto University, Finland

Gianmarco De Fransicsi Morales*
Qatar Computing Research Institute
Doha, Qatar

Aristides Gionis*
Helsinki Institute for Information Technology and Dept. of Computer Science
Aalto University, Finland

ABSTRACT

People are increasingly communicating and collaborating via digital platforms, such as email and messaging applications. Data exchanged on these digital communication platforms can be a treasure trove of information on people who participate in the discussions: who they are collaborating with, what they are working on, what their expertise is, and so on. Yet, personal communication data is very rarely analyzed due to the sensitivity of the information it contains.

In this paper, we mine personal communication data with the goal of generating *skill endorsements* of the type *"person A endorses person B on skill X."* To address privacy concerns, we consider that each person has access only to their own data (i.e., conversations with their peers). By using our method, they can generate endorsements for their peers, which they can inspect and opt to publish.

To identify meaningful skills we use a knowledge base created from the StackExchange Q&A forum. We study two different approaches, one based on building a *skill graph*, and one based on *information retrieval* techniques. We find that the latter approach outperforms the graph-based algorithms when tested on a dataset of user profiles from StackOverflow. We also conduct a user study on email data and find that the information retrieval-based approach achieves a MAP@10 score of 0.617.

Keywords

personal data; skill endorsements; e-mail mining

1. INTRODUCTION

The ability to identify individuals who are experts on certain skills is an essential element for organizational effectiveness. Finding experts an important ingredient in a modern digital economy, where employers use online platforms to outsource tasks to experts.

Traditionally, finding experts is facilitated by professional social networks or knowledge bases. In these systems, individuals self-declare their areas of expertise. For example, users in LinkedIn[1] build their profile by reporting their skills and expertise. However, such systems suffer from noisy and incomplete data, as well as user biases.

In this paper we introduce a new approach to build a *skill endorsement graph*, which can be used for finding experts. Our goal is to generate *skill endorsements* of the type *"person A endorses person B on skill X."* An important feature of our approach is that it leverages personal communication data, such as email, messaging applications, or discussion fora. Our assumption is that data collected from such platforms can used to generate accurate skill profiles based on what people actually do during their working days: which projects they work on, which topics they discuss, which tools they use, and so on.

On the other hand, communication data may contain private information, so it is important to develop methods that extract skills in a privacy-preserving manner. To address these privacy concerns, we consider that each person has access only to their own data (i.e., conversations with their peers). Thus, users can generate endorsements for their peers, which they can inspect and opt to publish. The skill-endorsement graph for a set of individuals can then be constructed by aggregating all individual-level skill endorsements.

A major challenge to any skill-extraction method is to identify a set of tokens that can be considered as skills. To address this challenge, we build a knowledge base of skills by processing the StackExchange Q&A forum. Our underlying assumption is that tags that appear in StackExchange posts are considered to be skills. Given the knowledge base extracted from StackExchange and individual-level communication data (such as email conversation or messaging), we study two different approaches for extracting skill endorsements between a person and their peers. The first approach is based on matching a set of keywords extracted from the communication data of a person to an underlying *skill graph* and finding the most representative skills via *personalized PageRank* (PPR). The second approach is based on *information retrieval* techniques, in particular, on similarity in a vector space model. A vector built from a person's commu-

*Emails: darshan.mallenahallishankaralingappa@aalto.fi; gdfm@acm.org; aristides.gionis@aalto.fi

CIKM'16, October 24-28, 2016, Indianapolis, IN, USA
© 2016 ACM. ISBN 978-1-4503-4073-1/16/10...$15.00
DOI: http://dx.doi.org/10.1145/2983323.2983884

[1]http://www.linkedin.com

nication text is used as a query against the StackExchange discussions to retrieve the most relevant associated skills.

We evaluate the proposed methods by using StackOverflow users for which ground-truth skills are known, as well as by conducting a user study on real email data. Our results show that the information retrieval approach outperforms significantly the graph-based approach.

2. RELATED WORK

Literature on email mining is quite sparse, mostly due to the sensitive nature of the data, and the privacy concerns of the users. Here we review the few studies that have tackled the problem of extracting skills from email data.

Campbell et al. [5] are the first to consider the problem of finding expertise via email communications. Their proposed system runs on the server of an organization having access to the emails of all the employees. First, their system collects all the emails associated with a given query. Then, it builds a graph by considering all pairs of users who have an email exchange within the email collection. Finally, it uses the HITS algorithm Kleinberg [7] to extract authoritative sources from the graph. In a similar fashion, Balog and de Rijke [1] use a probabilistic approach to model associations between individuals for a given query topic.

Both previous methods find experts with respect to a given query. The scenario envisioned in this paper is different, as we extract skill endorsements for each person participating in email or online forum communication without requiring any input query. Furthermore, these methods require access to all the emails within the organization, while our method assumes access only to the communication data of a single person, in order to alleviate privacy concerns. Thus, our method is not directly comparable with these previous works.

On the other hand, Kivimäki et al. [6] consider the problem of extracting skills from a text document. First they build a skill graph from LinkedIn and Wikipedia. Then, for a given input document, they identify the most similar Wikipedia pages. These pages are used as seed nodes in a random walk that provides skill summarization. Our method is similar in spirit, but we use a different knowledge base.

3. BUILDING A KNOWLEDGE BASE

A central concept to our approach is the *skill knowledge base*, which is used to model the relationship among skills, and relate skills with other keywords found in the personal communication data. To build a high-quality skill knowledge base we formulate the following desiderata:

Coverage: represent a wide range of skills as comprehensively as possible;

Quality: accurately reflect the relationship among skills, and the relationship among skills and other keywords;

Automation: it should be built and updated automatically.

As a starting point for our skill knowledge base we use StackExchange,[2] a Q&A platform that encompasses 155 different topics, such as math, computer science, finance, law, and history. The platform hosts about 13 million questions, 21 million answers, and has more than 8 million users across all its sites. These websites cover a wide range of skills, and the data is publicly available.[3]

[2]https://stackexchange.com

[3]https://archive.org/details/stackexchange

The users of StackExchange *tag* their questions to categorize their posts. Our main idea is to use these tags as skills, and our skill knowledge base relies heavily on these tags. In this paper we explore two alternatives: a graph-based approach, where we only model relationships between tags/skills, and a vector space-based approach, where we index the whole Q&A repository annotated by tags/skills.

In the graph-based approach, we form a *skill graph* where vertices represent tags and edges represent co-occurring tags. Edge weights are co-occurrence counts. More formally, let $\mathcal{D}$ be the set of all posts in StackExchange and $\mathcal{T}$ the set of unique tags. Let $D(B,T) \in \mathcal{D}$ be a single post, where B is the body of the post and $T \subseteq \mathcal{T}$ is the set of tags. The skill graph is a weighted graph $G(V, E, w)$ with $V = \mathcal{T}$. An edge between two vertices i and j exists if and only if there exists a post $D(B,T) \in \mathcal{D}$ such that $i \in T \wedge j \in T$. The weight of the edge is $w_{ij} = |\{D \in \mathcal{D} \mid i \in T \wedge j \in T\}|$.

In our preliminary experiments, we found that the quality of results improves when ignoring tags that appear fewer than 100 times. These low-frequency tags represent niche and uncommon skills. The final graph G has approximately $|V| = 38\,\text{k}$ vertices and $|E| = 3.4\,\text{M}$ edges.

Our second approach uses information retrieval techniques and indexes the whole Q&A repository annotated by the associated tags. In particular, we build an inverted index $\mathcal{I}$ on the body B of the posts $D \in \mathcal{D}$, and the tags associated with each post are retained to create a *tagged vector space*. After pre-processing the whole StackExchange dataset, the resulting index contains about 22 M posts.

4. EMAIL PROCESSING

In our email-processing pipeline, we consider that users are executing our algorithms on their own emails, and they produce skill endorsements for their peers. The emails are extracted and then, the text is cleaned and finally we identify and extract entities (noun phrases) via standard NLP tools.

Let us call *user* the individual whose emails are being analyzed (i.e., the source of the endorsements), and *peers* the other individuals that user has communicated with (i.e., the targets of the endorsements). We identify the email threads (set of emails having the same subject) associated with a peer. By using the process described above, we extract a list of entities for each email thread, which summarizes the thread, and which the algorithms described next can use to infer the endorsements.

Note that our method can also be used to other types of personal communication data, such as online fora. In such cases an appropriate data-processing pipeline should be established.

5. SKILL EXTRACTION ALGORITHMS

In this section we describe the two proposed approaches for extracting skill endorsements from email data, a graph-based algorithm and an index-based algorithm.

5.1 Graph-based algorithm

This algorithm uses the skill graph described in Section 4. Given the entities extracted from the emails between a *user* and a *peer*, the goal is to match the entities to the vertices of the skill graph and summarize all matched entities with the most important skills. This is achieved in three steps,

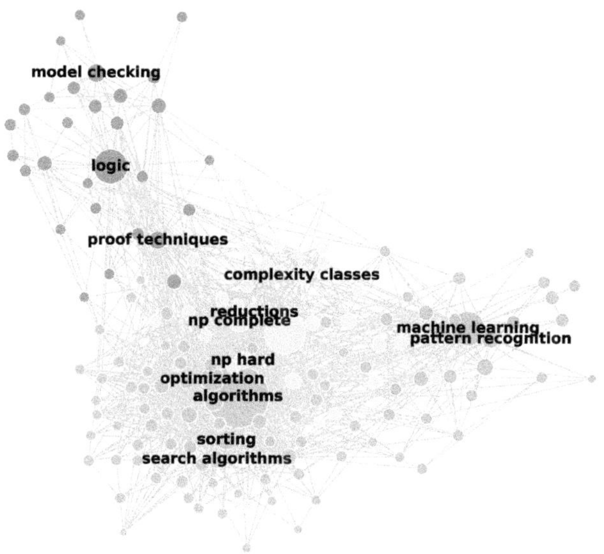

Figure 1: Graph clusters in the computer science part of the skill graph.

described next. We refer to this algorithm as GSE (graph-based skill endorsements).

Graph clustering. As a preprocessing step, we partition the skill graph into topical clusters. We use the Louvain algorithm [2], a hierarchical agglomerative method that optimizes modularity. Figure 1 illustrates the output of the clustering algorithm when considering the skill graph created on the *computer science* part of StackExchange. The clusters are very homogeneous and well defined, for instance, it is possible to recognize the theoretical computer science cluster in the middle in yellow, and the data mining and machine learning cluster on the right in grey.

Entity matching. In the next step we consider the email thread between a *user* and a *peer*, for whom we want to generate skill endorsements. Applying the processing pipeline described before, we extract entities from the email thread, and we match those entities and terms on the skill graph. When an entity is found in the skill graph, we say that the corresponding vertex is *matched.* The matching of entities induces a subgraph on the skill graph, which represents a set of candidate skills that can be used to infer the skill endorsements. In most cases an email thread is related to a small number of topics, so the matched skills of the thread will be located in a small number of clusters of the skill graph. To improve the relevance of the extracted skills, we focus our attention on the subgraph formed by taking the union of all the clusters that contain at least one matched skill.

Skill ranking. Let G' be the subgraph formed in the previous step (either the whole skill graph or the subgraph of the matching clusters), and let M be the set of matched skills in G'. In the final step, we summarize the skills M by considering the global structure of G'. For example, if the skills *'decision trees'* and *'nearest neighbor algorithm'* have been matched, we can summarize them with the skill *'supervised learning'*, which is highly connected with the former two, even though the latter skill has not been matched.

This task is achieved by centrality-based techniques, used to find important vertices in the graph G' with respect to the matched vertices M. There is a plethora of such centrality measures. In our experiments, we surveyed a number of these, including PageRank (PR), personalized PageRank (PPR), normalized personalized PageRank (NPPR = $^{\text{PPR}}/_{\text{PR}}$), effective importance (EI = $^{\text{PPR}}/_{w(v)}$) [3], and harmonic centrality [4]. We write GSE(X), where X = PR, PPR, NPPR, ..., to refer to algorithm GSE with centrality measure X. Our results show that the variants of PageRank perform similarly, with PPR being the best variant, while harmonic centrality performs the worst. Therefore, for sake of brevity, in some cases we restrict our attention to GSE(PPR).

5.2 Index-based algorithm

The second algorithm, referred to as ISE (index-based skill endorsements), uses the tagged vector space version of the knowledge base. Given an email thread for which we want to infer skill endorsements, ISE uses the thread as a query, and considers the tags of the retrieved posts as candidate skills.

Equivalently, ISE can be described as a k-NN multi-label classification method. In more detail, given a query, the algorithm retrieves top-k closest vectors according to a BM25-like similarity function. The algorithm then assigns a score $r(t)$ to each tag as the sum of the similarity of the vectors in which it appears

$$r(t) = \sum_{v \in R} \begin{cases} \text{sim}(q, v) & \text{if } t \in \ell(v) \\ 0 & \text{otherwise,} \end{cases} \tag{1}$$

where R is the set of top-k nearest neighbor vectors. The ranking of the skills is the one induced by $r(t)$.

6. EXPERIMENTAL EVALUATION

We evaluate our methods on several different tasks. First, we consider a prediction task on StackOverflow users. Then we report the results of a user study involving email data. We provide further evidence by running our algorithms on Apache Spark mailing list. Finally we test our algorithms on the public emails of Hillary Clinton.

StackOverflow users. We consider predicting the tags used by a given StackOverflow user given their posts. We use the body of the posts as the input to our text-mining pipeline. The ground truth is the set of tags associated with the user, while we assume that these tags are the skills of the user. Due to sparsity in the model, it is likely that the prediction performance depends on the number of posts of a user. That is, we hypothesize that the prediction task becomes easier for users with more data. To test this hypothesis, we draw a random set of 150 StackOverflow users by performing stratified sampling according to the quantile of the number of their posts across the whole population. The posts by these 150 users are excluded from the knowledge base.

We compare two different versions of the GSE algorithm (the global skill graph vs. clustered graph), and the ISE algorithm. We use *mean average precision* (MAP). as the evaluation metric. The results shown in Figures 2 and 3 indicate that ISE outperforms GSE by a large margin. We also see that in most cases MAP does not increases significantly with the number of the posts of a user, indicating that a few posts suffice for making a good prediction.

User Study. We perform a user study on nine users, most of whom have a computer science background. We ask the users to specify three peers they communicate frequently.

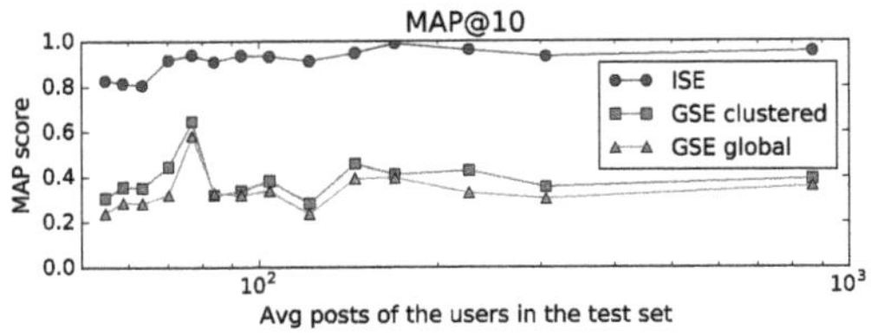

Figure 2: MAP@10 for different Algorithms

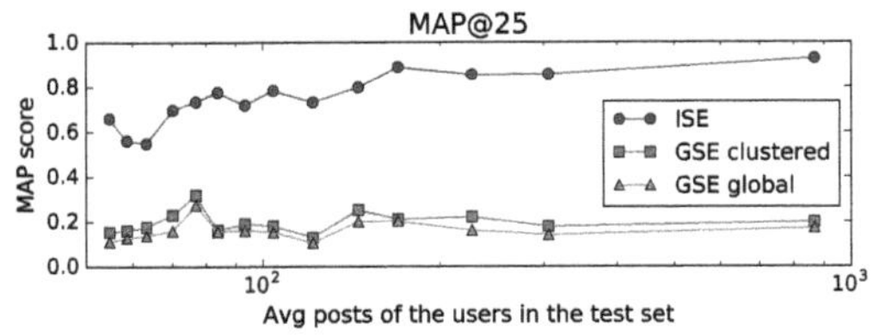

Figure 3: MAP@25 for different Algorithms

Table 1: Results from the user study on nine volunteers.

Algorithm	MAP@10	MAP@25	Average rating
ISE	0.617	0.557	3.74
GSE(PPR)	0.201	0.200	1.52
GSE(NPPR)	0.178	0.196	1.88
GSE(EI)	0.194	0.173	1.75
GSE(Harmonic)	0.238	0.198	1.71

Then, the users run our system on their email to infer skill endorsements are inferred for these peers. For each algorithm, we show a ranked list of the top 25 skills of each peer, and ask the users to indicate whether each skill is relevant. We also ask users to assess the list as a whole on a 5-point Likert scale (with 5 being more relevant). In the survey, we define a relevant skill for a peer as: *"the peer has done some work in the area, or could provide advice about it."* We compare ISE to 4 variants of GSE (the clustered version, which performs slightly better than the global one), namely, PPR, NPPR, EI, and Harmonic. For comparison we use the same MAP metric, as well as the average rating on the Likert scale.

The results, shown in Table 1, indicate again that ISE outperforms all GSE variants by a wide margin, irrespective of the centrality measure used.

Use cases. Next we apply our best-performing algorithm, ISE, on different publicly-available datasets. First, we use the Apache Spark mailing lists and we infer the skills of the most frequent users. In this case we treat the mailing list address as the user, and the people posting on the mailing list as the peers. The results are shown in Table 2. We see that one of the top skills for two of the users is 'Apache Spark,' as expected. Judging from the inferred skills, it is not surprising that Joseph Bradley is a developer of the MLlib project at Databricks.[4] Note that 'git@git.apache.org' is the email id of the bot named CodingCat which reports on merging of the code and compilation of the project.

Finally, we apply our algorithm on Hillary Clinton's emails. Her peers' skills are summarized in Table 3. Since Hillary Clinton was the Secretary of State at the time of the email collection, her discussions usually include foreign relationships, and hence different countries are reported as skills.

[4]http://www.cs.cmu.edu/~jkbradle

Table 2: Skills for users of the Apache Spark mailing list.

Email	Skills
sowen@cloudera.com	apache spark, hadoop, java, scala, spark
joseph@databricks.com	machine learning, apache spark, gradient descent, flex, random forest
git@git.apache.org	github, git, jira, infrastructure, bugzilla

Table 3: Skills inferred for Hillary Clinton.

israel, palestine, united states, nuclear weapons, politics

7. CONCLUSIONS

We proposed a novel approach for inferring an individual's skills by analyzing their personal communication data. Our approach makes use of a public knowledge base from the StackExchange Q&A forum. We found that ISE, an index-based approach, outperforms all version of GSE, a graph-based algorithm, when tested on the users of StackOverflow. The results from the user study confirmed the superiority of ISE, as its rating on a 5-points Likert scale is close to 4. We also collected open-ended feedback from the users taking the survey. We found that some of the top skills extracted by our algorithms were soft skills such as *group meetings*, *phd advisor*, and *grading*. However, the users were expecting, and suggested, hard skills such as *graph mining* or *machine learning*. This result might be a bias caused by the background of the users, and deserves further investigation. Finally we note that results on the enron email dataset were not as good. This can be attributed to the fact that stackexchange knowledge base is not well defined for all the available professions. To overcome this problem, one can use a more appropriate user-generated content for building the skill knowledge base.

Acknowledgements. This work has been supported by the Finnish Funding Agency for Innovation (project "Re:Know"), and by EU H2020 Program (project "SoBigData").

8. REFERENCES

[1] K. Balog and M. de Rijke. Finding experts and their details in e-mail corpora. In *WWW*, 2006.
[2] V. D. Blondel, J.-L. Guillaume, R. Lambiotte, and E. Lefebvre. Fast unfolding of communities in large networks. *J. Stat. Mech-Theory E*, 2008(10):P10008, 2008.
[3] P. Bogdanov and A. Singh. Accurate and scalable nearest neighbors in large networks based on effective importance. In *CIKM*, pages 1009–1018, 2013.
[4] P. Boldi and S. Vigna. Axioms for centrality. *Internet Mathematics*, 10(3-4):222–262, 2014.
[5] C. S. Campbell, P. P. Maglio, A. Cozzi, and B. Dom. Expertise identification using email communications. In *CIKM*, 2003.
[6] I. Kivimäki, A. Panchenko, D. V. Adrien Dessy, P. Francq, C. Fairon, H. Bersini, and M. Saerens. A graph-based approach to skill extraction from text. In *TextGraphs-8*, 2013.
[7] J. M. Kleinberg. Authoritative sources in a hyperlinked environment. *JACM*, 46(5):604–632, 1999.

A Self-Organizing Map for Identifying Influential Communities in Speech-based Networks

Sameen Mansha
Information Technology
University of Punjab, Lahore
sameen.mansha@itu.edu.pk

Faisal Kamiran
Information Technology
University of Punjab, Lahore
faisal.kamiran@itu.edu.pk

Asim Karim
Lahore University of
Management Sciences, Lahore
akarim@lums.edu.pk

Aizaz Anwar
Information Technology
University of Punjab, Lahore
aa364@itu.edu.pk

ABSTRACT

Low-literate people are unable to use many mainstream social networks due to their text-based interfaces even though they constitute a major portion of the world population. Specialized speech-based networks (SBNs) are more accessible to low-literate users through their simple speech-based interfaces. While SBNs have the potential for providing value-adding services to a large segment of society they have been hampered by the need to operate in low-income segments on low budgets. The knowledge of influential users and communities in such networks can help in optimizing their operations. In this paper, we present a self-organizing map (SOM) for discovering and visualizing influential communities of users in SBNs. We demonstrate how a friendship graph is formed from call data records and present a method for estimating influences between users. Subsequently, we develop a SOM to cluster users based on their influence, thus identifying community-level influences and their roles in information propagation. We test our approach on Polly, a SBN developed for job ads dissemination among low-literate users. For comparison, we identify influential users with the benchmark greedy algorithm and relate them to the discovered communities. The results show that influential users are concentrated in influential communities and community-level information propagation provides a ready summary of influential users.

Keywords

Speech-based social networks, Influential users and communities, self organizing maps.

1. INTRODUCTION

With the inception of high speed internet and fast computing resources, online social networking has become an essential tool for connecting various offline communities all across the globe. Despite the popularity of social networks a large portion of the world's population is still unable to be part of online social networks. The prime reasons for this situation are rooted in low-literacy, poverty, and in some places, lack of internet connectivity. Recently, it has been demonstrated that speech-based and non-textual systems are favored by low-literate users over text-based ones [11]. For this reason, some speech-based networks (SBNs) have been introduced to cater to the needs of low-literate users by providing speech-based interfaces for communication [16, 13, 14].

SBNs often face scalability and sustainability challenges in practice. A major reason for this is that most users of SBNs have low buying power and they cannot pay charges for the services. This hurdle in the widespread use of SBNs can be overcome by devising mechanisms for optimizing the utilization of resources. One way to maximize information propagation and hence reduce operation costs is by taking advantage of influential users and communities in the network. However, identification of influential communities has not been reported for SBNs, and methods developed for other social networks are not directly applicable to SBNs because of differences in characteristics.

In this work, we develop a self-organizing map (SOM) for discovering influential communities in SBNs. A SOM is a powerful information clustering and visualization technique that not only finds groups of related objects but also displays the relationships among the groups in two-dimensions for easy interpretation. We adapt SOM to the clustering of users based on their inter-user influences. The resulting communities (clusters) are related to others thus exposing the community-level structure of information propagation in the network. We demonstrate how a social network graph is constructed from an SBN's call data records (CDR). We also present a method for estimating the influence of a user on another based on the information in the CDR. We apply our SOM on a real-world SBN named Polly. The results are validated by identifying influential users using the general greedy algorithm [8] in each community.

CIKM'16, October 24-28, 2016, Indianapolis, IN, USA
© 2016 ACM. ISBN 978-1-4503-4073-1/16/10...$15.00
DOI: http://dx.doi.org/10.1145/2983323.2983885

2. MOTIVATION AND RELATED WORK

Typical speech-based social networks provide telephone-based voice manipulation and forwarding system for communication and dissemination of development-related information, e.g., provision of job ads, group messaging facility, etc. For example, Polly is a telephone-based entertainment service that allows any caller to record a short message, modify it using a choice of funny sound effects, and forward the modified recording to their friends by phone numbers. Users can also browse a list of audio recorded job ads that can be forwarded to their friends [1]. Polly was first tested in 2011 among low skilled office workers in Lahore, Pakistan. Within 3 weeks, Polly spread to 2,032 users, engaging them in 10,629 calls. However, it was shutdown due to unsustainable cellular airtime cost and insufficient telephone capacity [14]. After a year of rebuilding and capacity enhancement, Polly was launched again in May 2012 [15]. Keeping in view the demands for sustainability of SBNs such as Polly, social influence of users and communities in the network can be used as a criterion for the allocation of resources. Influence maximization aims to identify users in social networks that can lead to greatest influence (e.g., spread of information). This task has been studied extensively for conventional social networks for applications like viral marketing. The greedy algorithm, which is considered a benchmark algorithm for this task, finds top-k influential users [8]. Influence propagation patterns have been studied in Polly [10] and the task of influence maximization has been addressed [3]. More recently, the idea of influential communities in social networks has been introduced to expose the community-level structure of users and their roles in information propagation [4, 12]. We focus on community-level influence but target SBNs with their unique features encoded in call data records. In the area of social network analysis, some works have reported characterization of individual users by applying self-organizing maps (SOM) [5, 6] but none have applied it for identification of influential communities in SBNs.

3. METHODOLOGY

First, we discuss the construction of social network graph from a SBN's call data records (CDR), including a method for estimating influence between users. Then, we develop a SOM for finding and visualizing influential communities.

3.1 Social Network Graph

We process the CDR of the SBN to construct the social network graph. Typically, the CDR contain information about users, their interactions (Short Message Service (SMS) and audio/voice messages), and usage of the network.

A social network graph $N_G = \{V, E\}$ is constructed from the CDR where V is the set of vertices, E is the set of edges and N_G is a weighted directed graph. Each vertex $\mu \in V$ in N_G corresponds a unique user in the CDR. An edge $(\mu, \nu) \in E$ from vertex $\mu \in V$ to vertex $\nu \in V$ exists in N_G when user μ sends voice/text messages to user ν. Every edge is associated with a weight that is the influence of the source user upon the target user (calculation discussed below). The in-degree of vertex μ is the number of other users (vertices) that send messages to (link to) user μ, while the out-degree of vertex μ is the number of other users that user μ sends messages to. In general, N_G can contain disconnected components when a subset of vertices in N_G have no edges to other vertices.

Calculating Influence: Determining influence probability between users in a social network accurately is crucial to the influence maximization problem. Although previous work (e.g., [7]) has discussed estimation of influence probabilities in social networks. We introduce two different parameters to assign edge weights (influence) based on available information in the CDR of SBN.

1. Interaction Indicator ($r(\mu, \nu) \in \{0, 1\}$): This interaction indicator is equal to 1 when user μ sends one or more voice messages to user ν; otherwise, it is equal to zero.

2. Spread Factor ($s(\mu, \nu)$): Equation 1 gives the influence spread of user μ over user ν where F is the number of voice messages that user μ has forwarded to user ν and M is the number of voice messages from user μ that user ν has received and forwarded to other users.

$$s(\mu, \nu) = \frac{M}{F} \tag{1}$$

Suppose a user μ forwards 3 voice messages (m_1, m_2, m_3), such as job ads, to user ν who then forwards m_3 to other users, then $s(\mu, \nu) = 1/3 = 0.33$.

The influence of user μ on user ν in N_G is defined as

$$INF(\mu, \nu) = s(\mu, \nu) + r(\mu, \nu) \tag{2}$$

$INF(\mu, \nu)$ can range in the interval [0,2] with higher values signifying greater influence (i.e., capability to spread information) in the network. Notice that $INF(\mu, \nu) \geq 1$ whenever user μ interacts with user ν but this influence will increase with the number of messages of μ forwarded by ν. Moreover, in general, $INF(\mu, \nu) \neq INF(\nu, \mu)$ as each user can behave differently. We set the influence of a user on itself equal to 2, i.e., $INF(\mu, \mu) = 2$.

All inter-user influences in N_G can be captured in an adjacency matrix X of size $N \times N$ where $N = |V|$ is the number of vertices in N_G. That is, each element of X , $x_{\mu\nu}$, is set equal to $INF(\mu, \nu)$. Note that X will not be a symmetric matrix in general. This matrix is used for identifying influential communities as discussed next.

3.2 SOM for Identifying Influential Communities

A self-organizing map (SOM) is a powerful unsupervised information processing and pattern recognition method [9]. It is a type of artificial neural network used to convert complex nonlinear statistical relationships between high dimensional data into simple geometric relationships on a low-dimensional display. Generally SOM consists of a layer of units or neurons that adapt themselves to input patterns such they are activated for similar patterns only. The adaption is done through an iterative procedure which processes input patterns repeatedly. Upon presentation of each input pattern, neuron closer to it and all its neighbors are moved closer to input pattern. After a significant number of iterations all neurons move into the area of high concentration of input patterns.

To find influential communities and the relationships among them in N_G, we cluster $X = [x_1, x_2, \ldots, x_N]$ using a SOM. The ith user is represented by a feature vector x_i comprising of its influences (INF) on other users and corresponding to the ith row of X. Two users that influence the same set of users strongly are likely to fall in one cluster, and a collection of such users will form a community of users that influence each other strongly. In a SOM, each community is represented by a neuron, and the geometric closeness of

Algorithm 1 SOM for Influential Community Discovery in SBNs

Input: Adjacency matrix $X = [x_1, \ldots, x_N]$ of N_G
Output: A topology of influential communities, $Y = \{y_1, \ldots, y_K\}$
begin
  Initialize weight matrix randomly, $W = \{w_1, \ldots, w_K\}$
  repeat select $x \in X$ randomly
    determine winning neuron y' such that
    $y = \arg\min_{y \in Y} d(x, w_y)$
    for all $y \in h(y') \subset Y$
      $w_y = w_y + \eta(t)(x - w_y)g(y, y)$
    decrease η by a small amount
  until termination condition is true
end

two neurons show the relative strength of influence between the respective communities. Let $Y = \{y_1, y_2, \ldots, y_K\}$ be the set of neurons corresponding to the communities to be discovered. We consider a 2-D $\sqrt{K} \times \sqrt{K}$ arrangement for the neurons; thus $\sqrt{K}$ has to be an integer and each neuron $y_i = (a, b)$ is identified by its coordinates in the 2-D grid where a and b can be integers from 0 to $\sqrt{K} - 1$. The weight matrix of the SOM is given by $W = [w_1, w_2, \ldots, w_K]$ where w_i is the weight vector of size N of the ith neuron.

Algorithm 1 shows the steps required in training a SOM for identifying influential communities in an SBN (N_G). The SOM is initialized by randomly assigning weights in the interval $[-1, +1]$. Subsequently, features vectors $x \in X$ are fed randomly and repeatedly through the SOM. For each input x the 'winning' neuron y is found. This is the neuron whose weight w_y is closest to input x. This is determined via the distance function $d(x, w_y)$. We use the Euclidean distance for this purpose. The neighborhood function $h(y)$ returns the neurons neighboring y. In our case, the immediate neighbors of y in the 2-D grid are considered. For each neighboring neuron y, the corresponding weight w_y is updated such that it is brought closer to x. The learning rate parameter $\eta > 0$ controls the amount of update in each iteration. Furthermore, the update for the winning neuron is stronger than that for its neighbors. This is defined by the Gaussian function $g(y, y)$ centered on y. The learning rate is reduced with the number of iterations to smooth out the convergence of the SOM. Convergence occurs when change in the weight matrix W from one iteration to the next becomes acceptably small.

After the SOM is trained, each user is assigned to the neuron whose weight is closest to the feature vector of the user. In this way, a clustering of users is obtained based on influence. Each cluster is actually a community of users and the relative position of the communities in the 2-D grid indicates their relationship w.r.t. influence and information propagation.

4. EXPERIMENTAL RESULTS

In this section, we discuss the results of our experiments on a real-world speech-based network.

Dataset Description: We evaluate our methodology on Polly which is a telephone-based social network developed for providing services to low-literate users in South Asia [1]. The CDR that we use contains 213,196 users with 2,522,981 interactions among them recorded in more than 700 MB of log data and 200 GB of audio data.From this information we construct the social network graph N_G whose vertices represent unique users and its edges are labeled with influence values (INF). Influences are calculated by considering number of calls, job ads listened, and job ads forwarded. Table 1 shows key characteristics of CDR and (N_G) used.

Table 1: Description of Call Data Records (CDR) and Social Network Graph (N_G)

Key Statistics of Polly's CDR	
No. of users	213196
No. of calls made	2522981
No. of requests for calls	1051669
No. of requests for job delivery	33597
No. of times job ads listened	386199
Key Characteristics of N_G	
No. of edges	13694
No. of connected components	3272
Vertices in biggest connected component	2407
Edges in biggest connected component	3332
Diameter of biggest connected component	10

Community-level Social Influence Analysis: Figure 1 shows the output of our SOM when applied to Polly. We discover 25 communities (clusters of users) that are arranged in a 5×5 grid of cells. Each cell in the grid is identified by its 2-D coordinates with values starting from 0. For example, the bottom left and top right cells (communities) are identified as (0, 0) and (4, 4) respectively. The background color of each cell indicates the normalized sum of the distances between the corresponding neuron's weight and those of its neighbors. A darker background color of a cell signifies that the corresponding community is closer to its neighbors w.r.t. influence, i.e., their influence potential are similar. We also find influential users in the network by using greedy algorithm [8]. The top 50 influential users are shown by yellow dots in their respective communities. Our implementation of SOM for finding influential communities is based on the MiniSom tool [2].

It is observed from Figure 1 that the greedy algorithm finds 5 users from the community (4,4), 4 users each from (2,1), (4,0) and (4,1), and 3 users each from communities (0,4), (1,3), (2,2), (3,1), (3,3) and (4,2). On the other end, communities (0,1), (1,2), (2,3), (3,0), and (3,2) do not contain any top-50 influential users. Thus, top-50 influential users appear in only a few communities. These are therefore the influential communities in Polly. It is also seen from the background colors that influential communities lie closer to each other. For example, communities (2,1), (2,2), (3,1), (4,0),(4,1), (4,2) and (4,4) contain 26 top-50 influential users (i.e., 52% of influential users lie in 7 communities) and they are placed closer to each other on the grid. On the other hand communities that contain less number of any top-50 influential users are also closer to each other, e.g., (0,0), (1,0), (2,0), (3,0) and (1,2). The closeness of influential communities on the grid provide a clearer idea of community-level information propagation. After spreading within an influential community, information introduced in it is more likely to spread to neighboring communities on the grid than to other communities.

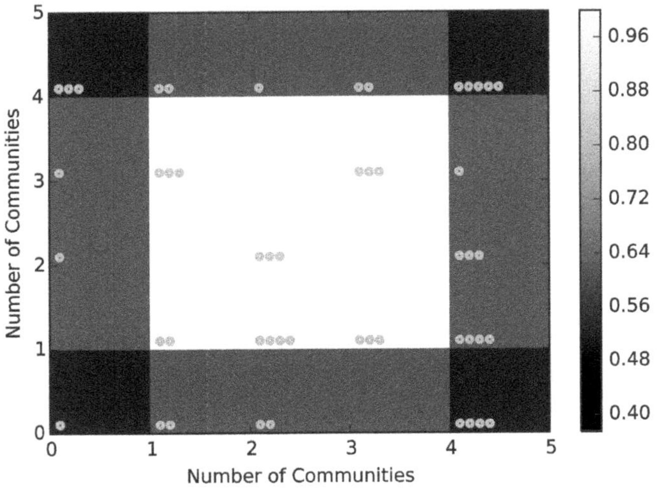

Figure 1: Community-level influence analysis: 5×5 communities with top-50 influential users identified by yellow dots

5. CONCLUSION

In this paper, we present a self-organizing map (SOM) for finding influential communities and exposing the community-level structure of influence in a speech-based network (SBN). A SBN differs from conventional social networks in that it provides voice-based interactions among users for services aimed towards low-literate people in low income regions. We discuss the construction of a social network graph from an SBN's database including the important aspect of determining influence between users. Our SOM not only identifies important communities based on influence but also displays their relationships. As such, the SOM summarizes information propagation in a social network that can help in optimizing its operations for scalability and sustainability. We demonstrate our methodology on a real-world SBN operated for disseminating job ads among low-literate users.

As future work, it would be interesting to evaluate SOM for community-level influence analysis in conventional social networks. For SBNs, further studies are needed to understand its dynamics such as growth, attrition, influence, and societal impact.

Acknowledgment

We would like to show our gratitude to Dr. Agha Ali Raza (Information Technology University, Pakistan) and Prof. Roni Rosenfeld(Carnegie Mellon University, Pittsburgh, USA) for their cooperation and providing us access to Polly's Call Data Records and log files.

6. REFERENCES

[1] https://www.cs.cmu.edu/~./Polly/. [Online; accessed 2016-22-08].

[2] https://github.com/JustGlowing/minisom. [Online; accessed 2016-22-08].

[3] A. Anwar, S. Mansha, F. Kamiran, and A. Karim. Identification of influential users in speech-based networks. In *Pacific Asia Conference on Information Systems (PACIS) Proceedings*, 2016.

[4] N. Barbieri, F. Bonchi, and G. Manco. Cascade-based community detection. In *International Conference on Web search and Data Mining Proceedings*, pages 33–42. ACM, 2013.

[5] R. Boulet, B. Jouve, F. Rossi, and N. Villa. Batch kernel som and related laplacian methods for social network analysis. *Neurocomputing*, 71(7):1257–1273, 2008.

[6] A. Bruggmann, M. M. Salvini, and S. Fabrikant. Cartograms of self-organizing maps to explore user generated content. In *International Cartographic Conference Proceedings*, pages 25–30, 2013.

[7] A. Goyal, F. Bonchi, and L. V. Lakshmanan. Learning influence probabilities in social networks. In *International Conference on Web search and Data Mining Proceedings*, pages 241–250. ACM, 2010.

[8] D. Kempe, J. Kleinberg, and É. Tardos. Maximizing the spread of influence through a social network. In *International Conference on Knowledge Discovery and Data Mining Proceedings*, pages 137–146. ACM, 2003.

[9] T. Kohonen, editor. *Self-organizing Maps*. Springer Verlag New York, Inc., Secaucus, NJ, USA, 1997.

[10] Y. Lin, A. A. Raza, J.-Y. Lee, D. Koutra, R. Rosenfeld, and C. Faloutsos. Influence propagation: Patterns, model and a case study. In *Pacific-Asia Conference on Knowledge Discovery and Data Mining Proceedings*, pages 386–397. Springer, 2014.

[11] I. Medhi, A. Sagar, and K. Toyama. Text-free user interfaces for illiterate and semi-literate users. In *International Conference on Information and Communication Technologies and Development Proceedings*, pages 72–82. IEEE, 2006.

[12] Y. Mehmood, N. Barbieri, F. Bonchi, and A. Ukkonen. Csi: Community-level social influence analysis. In *Machine learning and Knowledge Discovery in Databases Proceedings*, pages 48–63. Springer, 2013.

[13] N. Patel, D. Chittamuru, A. Jain, P. Dave, and T. S. Parikh. Avaaj otalo: a field study of an interactive voice forum for small farmers in rural india. In *Human Factors in Computing Systems Conference Proceedings*, pages 733–742. ACM, 2010.

[14] A. A. Raza, M. Pervaiz, C. Milo, S. Razaq, G. Alster, J. Sherwani, U. Saif, and R. Rosenfeld. Viral entertainment as a vehicle for disseminating speech-based services to low-literate users. In *International Conference on Information and Communication Technologies and Development Proceedings*, pages 350–359. ACM, 2012.

[15] A. A. Raza, F. Ul Haq, Z. Tariq, M. Pervaiz, S. Razaq, U. Saif, and R. Rosenfeld. Job opportunities through entertainment: virally spread speech-based services for low-literate users. In *Human Factors in Computing Systems Conference Proceedings*, pages 2803–2812. ACM, 2013.

[16] J. Sherwani, N. Ali, S. Mirza, A. Fatma, Y. Memon, M. Karim, R. Tongia, and R. Rosenfeld. Healthline: Speech-based access to health information by low-literate users. In *ICTD Conference Proceedings*, pages 1–9. IEEE, 2007.

Crowdsourcing-based Urban Anomaly Prediction System for Smart Cities

Chao Huang, Xian Wu and Dong Wang
Department of Computer Science and Engineering
University of Notre Dame
Notre Dame, IN, USA
chuang7@nd.edu, xwu9@nd.edu, dwang5@nd.edu

ABSTRACT

Crowdsourcing has become an emerging data collection paradigm for smart city applications. A new category of crowdsourcing-based urban anomaly reporting systems have been developed to enable pervasive and real-time reporting of anomalies in cities (e.g., noise, illegal use of public facilities, urban infrastructure malfunctions). An interesting challenge in these applications is how to accurately predict an anomaly in a given region of the city before it happens. Prior works have made significant progress in anomaly detection. However, they can only *detect* anomalies after they happen, which may lead to significant information delay and lack of preparedness to handle the anomalies in an efficient way. In this paper, we develop a *Crowdsourcing-based Urban Anomaly Prediction Scheme (CUAPS)* to accurately *predict* the anomalies of a city by exploring both spatial and temporal information embedded in the crowdsourcing data. We evaluated the performance of our scheme and compared it to the state-of-the-art baselines using four real world datasets collected from 311 service in the city of New York. The results showed that our scheme can predict different categories of anomalies in a city more accurately than the baselines.

Keywords

Crowdsourcing, Anomaly Prediction, Bayesian Inference, Smart Cities

1. INTRODUCTION

This paper presents a new Crowdsourcing-based Urban Anomaly Prediction Scheme (CUAPS) to address the urban anomaly prediction problem for smart cities. Urban environment (e.g., air, noise, river) and infrastructures (e.g., buildings, roads, parking lots) are essential parts of a well-functioning city and monitoring their conditions has recently received a significant amount of attentions [3, 9–11]. With the ubiquity of Internet connectivity and the proliferation of smartphones, crowdsourcing has become an emerging data collection paradigm for smart city applications (e.g., location-based services, environment monitoring, information distillation) [3–6]. Along this trend, a new category of crowdsourcing-based urban anomaly reporting systems have been developed to allow common citizens to report, track, and comment on the urban anomalies they encountered in their daily lives (e.g., noise, illegal use of public facilities, urban infrastructure malfunctions). An interesting challenge in these applications is how to accurately predict an anomaly in a given region of the city before it happens. Accurate prediction of anomalies can help the governments and communities to effectively prevent anomalies from happening or handle them efficiently if they happen [7].

Several technical challenges exist in order to solve the anomaly prediction problem by exploring the crowdsourcing data from common citizens in a city. First, *Sparse Crowdsourcing Data*: the crowdsourcing reports are often sparse and incomplete since people may not report anomalies all the time at all places in a city. Furthermore, some of their reports miss important information (e.g., time, location, description of the anomaly) and hence are less useful. Thus, it is difficult to predict the anomaly of a given region from the crowdsourcing data from that region alone. Second, *Uncertain Geographic Dynamics*: anomalies in different geographic regions of the city often have very different probability distributions (e.g., the distribution of noise reports in a downtown subdivision is likely to be different from the one of a quiet subdivision in the suburb). Therefore, it is also not a trivial task to use crowdsourcing reports from one region of the city to predict the anomaly of another.

To address the above challenges, we develop a new Crowdsourcing-based Urban Anomaly Prediction Scheme (CUAPS) to predict the anomaly in a given region of a city by exploring both spatial and temporal information embedded in the crowdsourcing data. In particular, we first develop a Bayesian inference model to identify dependent regions in terms of their anomaly distributions. Then we derive an optimal abnormal state prediction scheme that predicts the anomaly in a region from both its own historical data using a Markov model and the data from its dependent regions. Finally, we evaluate the CUAPS approach using four real-world 311 service datasets collected from the city of New York. The evaluation results showed that our scheme can predict different categories of anomalies in a city more accurately than the state-of-the-art baselines.

In summary, our contributions are as follows:

- This paper addresses the problem of urban anomaly prediction using crowdsourcing data that is publicly available. (Section 2)

CIKM '16, October 24–28, 2016, Indianapolis, IN, USA.

DOI: http://dx.doi.org/10.1145/2983323.2983886

- We develop a principled framework (i.e., CUAPS scheme) that allows us to derive an *optimal* solution to accurately predict the anomaly of each region in a city by exploring the dependency of anomaly occurrence between different regions and the historical anomaly distribution of an individual region. (Section 3)

- We perform experiments to compare the performance of our CUAPS scheme with the-sate-of-the-art baselines using real-world data sets collected from 311 service in New York. Experimental results demonstrate that the proposed approach outperforms existing methods in terms of prediction accuracy. (Section 4)

2. PROBLEM FORMULATION

In this section, we formulate the problem of urban anomaly prediction using crowdsourcing data. In particular, we consider a set of X geographic regions of a city, which are indexed by $i = 1, ..., X$ and each region has Y_i anomalies till time slot K (i.e., the time slot before the predicted slot). We further define the following inputs to our model.

- *Definition 1.* **Anomaly Trajectory**. A trajectory Tr_i of region i is an anomaly trace reported by the crowd in chronological order, e.g., $Tr = l_1 \rightarrow ... \rightarrow l_z \rightarrow ... \rightarrow l_Z$, where each reported anomaly consists of a geospatial coordinates and a timestamp, i.e., $l_z = (latitude, longitude, timestamp)$.

- *Definition 2.* **Abnormal State Vector**. We define the abnormal state vector $AS_{X \times K}$ to represent if there exists reported anomaly of each region in K time slots. In particular, $AS_{i,k} = 1$ denotes that there exists a reported anomaly in kth time slot and $AS_{i,k} = 0$ otherwise.

- *Definition 3.* **Temporal Vector**. For each region, we define the temporal vector t_{Δ_i} as the time difference of consecutive anomalies in that region. This feature has also been considered in [2].

For each region, we consider two features (i.e., the number of anomalies Y_i and temporal vector t_{Δ_i}) in a Bayesian inference model. In our model, the anomaly distribution of each region belongs to one of C clusters (which are indexed by $c = 1, ...C$). Each cluster consists of regions with similar anomaly distributions. We assumes the Multinomial distribution for each cluster and use a common Dirichlet prior to accommodate the possible difference in anomaly distributions between regions within the same cluster.

The problem of inferring the urban anomaly prediction using crowdsourcing data is formulated as follows: given the anomaly trajectory Tr_i till time slot K ($Tr_{i,K}$) of each region in a city, the goal is to predict the unknown abnormal state of all regions in the next time slot $K+1$. Formally, we compute:

$$\forall i, 1 \leq i \leq X : P(AS_{i,(K+1)} | Tr_{i,K}) \tag{1}$$

3. CROWDSOURCING-BASED URBAN ANOMALY PREDICTION

The developed CUAPS consists of three components: Clustering Dependent Regions, Markov Trajectory Estimation and Optimal Anomaly Prediction. We will discuss each component in detail in this section. Figure 1 shows an overview of the CUAPS.

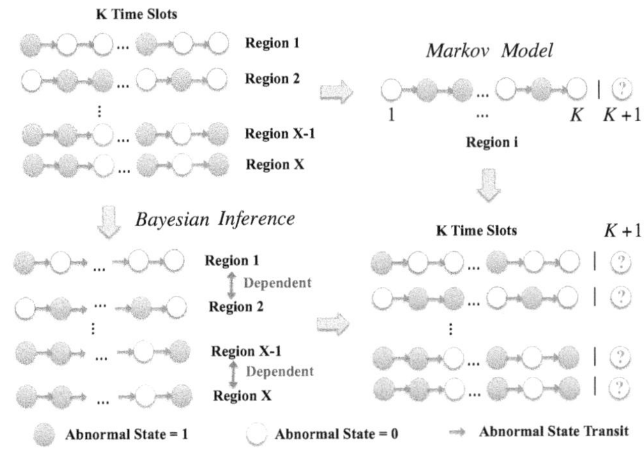

Figure 1: Crowdsourcing-based Urban Anomaly Prediction

3.1 Clustering Dependent Regions

We first cluster similar regions based on the number of anomalies and temporal vector features discussed in the previous section. In particular, we iteratively update hyperparameters of each cluster distribution (i.e., γ and η) and the cluster assignment (i.e., e) in the Bayesian inference model until convergence.

3.1.1 Updating Cluster Hyperparameters

To update cluster hyperparameters, we maximize the likelihood function $\Pr(Y, t_\Delta | \gamma, \eta, e)$ with respect to γ and η respectively. Note that adjusting γ_c only affects the likelihood with respect to Y_i of regions in cth cluster. Therefore, we are equivalently maximizing $\prod_{i,e_i=c} \Pr(Y_i|\gamma_c, e)$ and compute the maximum likelihood update for γ_c given the anomalies distribution Y_i of regions in cth cluster. Similarly, we are equivalently maximizing $\prod_{i,e_i=c} \Pr(t_{\Delta_i}|\eta_c, e)$ and compute the maximum likelihood update for η_c given the temporal distribution t_{Δ_i} of regions in cth cluster. Formally, the step of updating cluster hyperparameters can be written as follows:

$$\gamma_c^* = \arg\max_{\gamma_c} \Pr(Y|\gamma_c, e), \quad \eta_c^* = \arg\max_{\eta_c} \Pr(t_\Delta|\eta_c, e) \tag{2}$$

Finding the maximum likelihood updates for γ_c can be derived from the two-step process from a Dirichlet-multinomial distribution [8].

3.1.2 Updating Cluster Assignments

Based on the updates of cluster hyperparamters, we adjust the cluster assignment e_i by maximizing the likelihood function. Note that varying e_i only affects the likelihood with respect to region i. Thus, maximizing the likelihood function $\Pr(Y, t_\Delta | e_i = c)$ is equivalent as:

$$e_i^* = \arg\max_c \Pr(Y_i | e_i = c) \Pr(t\_\Delta_i | e_i = c) \quad (3)$$

To compute $\Pr(Y_i | e_i = c)$, note that it is the probability of drawing Y_i from a Dirichlet-Multinomial distribution with know parameters γ_c and η_c. [8] provides the solutions for cluster assignments.

3.2 Markov Trajectory Estimation

We consider a the abnormal state transition of each region follows a Markov model. For simplicity, we assume the state in the predicted slot ($AS_{i,k+1}$) only depends on its previous state ($AS_{i,k}$) in this paper. We noted that we could also consider multiple previous states to predict the current state.

In a Markov model with binary variables (i.e., the value of $AS_{i,k}$ are binary), two transition probabilities are enough to describe the system dynamics: (i) $P_{0,1}$: the probability that $AS_{i,k}$ changes its state from 0 to 1 and (ii) $P_{1,0}$: the probability that $AS_{i,k}$ changes its state from 1 to 0. The probability $P_{0,0}$ that $AS_{i,k}$ remains in the 0 state in the next time-slot can be easily computed as $P_{0,0} = 1 - P_{0,1}$. Similarity, $P_{1,1} = 1 - P_{1,0}$.

Given a state trajectory, and the probability of its initial 0 state P_0^0 or 1 state P_1^0, we can compute its probability. For example, if the state trajectory is 1, 0, 1, the joint probability of the state sequence is $P_1^0 \cdot P_{1,0} \cdot P_{0,1}$, where $P_{1,0}$ and $P_{0,1}$ are the transition probabilities. Then we use the transitional probabilities we learned from the last K time-slots to predict the state of time slot $K + 1$.

3.3 Optimal Anomaly Prediction

We define regions within the same cluster as dependent regions. For each region, we use Ne_i to represent the set of its dependent regions. Using the Markov model discussed above, we can estimate the next state (i.e., $K + 1$th time slot) of each region (i.e., $AK_{i,(K+1)}$). Based on the outputs of the above two components, we can estimate an optimized state value of each region by leveraging its dependency with other regions and its individual abnormal state trajectory. In particular, we define the objective function of our problem as follows:

$$f = \sum_{i=1}^{X} \sum_{i' \in Ne_i} |AK_{i,(K+1)}{}^* - AK_{i',(K+1)}|, \; AK_{i',(K+1)} \in [0,1] \quad (4)$$

where i' is the index for the dependent regions of region i and $AK_{i,(K+1)}{}^*$ is the optimized inference of $(K+1)$th state of region i. $AK_{i',(K+1)}$ is the state inference from Markov model. Here, the goal is to find the $AK_{i,(K+1)}{}^*$ for every region that minimizes the defined objective function. This optimization problem can be solved in linear time using weighted median algorithm.

4. EVALUATION

In this section, we conduct experiments to evaluate the performance of the *Crowdsourcing-based Urban Anomaly Prediction Scheme (CUAPS)* scheme on four real world datasets we collected from 311 service in New York City (NYC). We demonstrate the effectiveness of our proposed scheme on this dataset and compare the performance of our scheme to the state-of-the-art baselines. In the rest of this section: (i) we present the experiment settings and evaluation metrics we used in our experiments. (ii) We introduce the state-of-the-art baselines and present the evaluation results that demonstrate the *CUPAS* scheme can predict different categories of anomalies in a city more accurately than the compared baselines.

4.1 Experiment Setups and Evaluation Metrics

4.1.1 Dataset Statistics

311 is NYC's non-emergency service platform. This platform allows people to complain things happened around them by texting, phone call or mobile app. Each complaint record is formatted as: (complaint category, latitude, longitude, timestamp). The complaint categories in our four collected datasets are *Noise*, *Blocked Driveway*, *Illegal Conversion Of Residential Building (ICRB)* and *Illegal Parking* respectively. The time duration of the collected 311 complaints from Jan 2014 to Mar 2015. In NYC, we use road segments with a level from L_1 to L_5 as major roads to partition the entire city, which resulting in 862 regions [12]. Then each 311 complaint can be mapped to one of these regions. We note that the data is very sparse in an individual region, which makes the anomaly prediction problem a very challenging task. The statistics of these datasets are summarized in Table 1.

Table 1: Data Traces Statistics

Complain Category	Noise	Blocked Driveway	ICRB	Illegal Parking
Number of Instances	151174	92335	27724	69100

4.1.2 Evaluation Metric

In our evaluation, we use the following metrics to evaluate the estimation performance of the *CUAPS* scheme: *Precision*, *Recall*, *F1-measure* and *Accuracy*. Their definitions are given in Table 2.

Table 2: Metric Definitions

Metric	Definition
Precison	$\frac{TP}{TP+FP}$
Recall	$\frac{TP}{TP+FN}$
$F1-measure$	$\frac{2 \times Precison \times Recall}{Precison + Recall}$
Accuracy	$\frac{TP+TN}{TP+TN+FP+FN}$

4.2 Evaluation of Our Scheme

In this subsection, we evaluate the performance of the proposed *CUAPS* scheme and compare it to the state-of-the-art techniques as follows:

- *Bayesian Inference with Ground Truth (BIGT)*: it uses Bayesian model to cluster dependent regions and applies ground truth information of dependent regions to predict anomaly in a given region.
- *Markov Model (MM)*: it uses the Markov model to predict current state of the system from the transitional probabilities learned from the state trajectory of a region.

Table 3: Prediction Results on NY 311 Service Datasets

	Noise				Blocked Driveway			
Algorithm	Accuracy	Precision	Recall	F1	Accuracy	Precision	Recall	F1
CUAPS	**0.712**	**0.760**	**0.730**	**0.745**	**0.651**	**0.719**	**0.640**	**0.677**
BIGT	0.594	0.630	0.711	0.668	0.571	0.629	0.609	0.619
MM	0.645	0.738	0.596	0.659	0.589	0.645	0.625	0.634
GP	0.505	0.582	0.500	0.537	0.535	0.600	0.562	0.580
Random	0.461	0.536	0.467	0.500	0.446	0.517	0.468	0.491
	ICRB				Illegal Parking			
Algorithm	Accuracy	Precision	Recall	F1	Accuracy	Precision	Recall	F1
CUAPS	**0.655**	**0.667**	**0.823**	**0.736**	**0.627**	**0.644**	**0.906**	**0.753**
BIGT	0.586	0.666	0.588	0.625	0.549	0.595	0.875	0.708
MM	0.517	0.800	0.235	0.363	0.622	0.750	0.617	0.677
GP	0.482	0.550	0.647	0.594	0.603	0.782	0.529	0.631
Random	0.448	0.529	0.529	0.529	0.431	0.560	0.437	0.491

- *Gaussian Processing (GP)*: it is a nonparametric approach to predict the abnormal state of each region by exploring temporal features [1].
- *Random*: it randomly guesses the next abnormal state of each region.

4.2.1 Evaluation Results

In our evaluation, we evaluated the above schemes using the data from Jan 2014 to Sep 2014 to training data to predict the abnormal state of next day. To accommodate some baselines that need a small fraction of ground truth labels as inputs, we set the percent of ground to be used as 20%. The evaluation results of Noise, Blocked Driveway, Illegal Conversion Of Residential Building (ICRB) and Illegal Parking in Table 3. We observe that *CUAPS* outperforms the compared baselines in most of the evaluation metrics: it predicts correctly the most number of next abnormal states while keeping the falsely reported one the least.

5. CONCLUSION

In this paper, we developed a *Crowdsourcing-based Urban Anomaly Prediction Scheme (CUAPS)* to accurately predict urban anomalies for smart city applications. The CUAPS allows us to derive an *optimal* solution to accurately predict different categories of anomaly at different regions in a city. It explores both the dependency of anomaly occurrence between different regions and the historical anomaly distribution of an individual region. We evaluate our new scheme on four real-world datasets collected from 311 service in the city of New York. The results showed that our scheme outperforms state-of-the-art baselines in terms of prediction accuracy.

Acknowledgment

This material is based upon work supported by the National Science Foundation under Grant No. CBET-1637251, CNS-1566465 and IIS-1447795 and Army Research Office under Grant W911NF-16-1-0388. The views and conclusions contained in this document are those of the authors and should not be interpreted as representing the official policies, either expressed or implied, of the Army Research Office or the U.S. Government. The U.S. Government is authorized to reproduce and distribute reprints for Government purposes notwithstanding any copyright notation here on.

6. REFERENCES

[1] P. Esling and C. Agon. Time-series data mining. *ACM Computing Surveys (CSUR)*, page 12, 2012.

[2] A. Ferraz Costa, Y. Yamaguchi, A. Juci Machado Traina, C. Traina Jr, and C. Faloutsos. Rsc: Mining and modeling temporal activity in social media. In *KDD*, pages 269–278. ACM, 2015.

[3] H.-P. Hsieh, S.-D. Lin, and Y. Zheng. Inferring air quality for station location recommendation based on urban big data. In *KDD*, pages 437–446. ACM, 2015.

[4] C. Huang and D. Wang. Exploiting spatial-temporal-social constraints for localness inference using online social media. In *ASONAM*. ACM/IEEE, 2016.

[5] C. Huang and D. Wang. Topic-aware social sensing with arbitrary source dependency graphs. In *IPSN*. ACM/IEEE, 2016.

[6] C. Huang and D. Wang. Unsupervised interesting places discovery in location-based social sensing. In *DCOSS*, pages 67–74. IEEE, 2016.

[7] J. Y. Lee, U. Kang, D. Koutra, and C. Faloutsos. Fast anomaly detection despite the duplicates. In *WWW*, pages 195–196. ACM, 2013.

[8] T. Minka. Estimating a dirichlet distribution, 2000.

[9] D. Wang, T. Abdelzaher, and L. Kaplan. Surrogate mobile sensing. *IEEE Communications Magazine*, 52(8):36–41, 2014.

[10] D. Wang and C. Huang. Confidence-aware truth estimation in social sensing applications. In *Sensing, Communication, and Networking (SECON), 2015 12th Annual IEEE International Conference on*, pages 336–344. IEEE, 2015.

[11] J. Wang, Y. Zhao, and D. Wang. A novel fast anti-collision algorithm for rfid systems. In *Wireless Communications, Networking and Mobile Computing, 2007. WiCom 2007. International Conference on*, pages 2044–2047. IEEE, 2007.

[12] Y. Zheng, H. Zhang, and Y. Yu. Detecting collective anomalies from multiple spatio-temporal datasets across different domains. *SIGSPATIAL*, 2015.

Near Real-time Geolocation Prediction in Twitter Streams via Matrix Factorization Based Regression

Nghia Duong-Trung
Information Systems and Machine Learning Lab
Universitätsplatz 1
31141 Hildesheim, Germany
duongn@ismll.uni-hildesheim.de

Nicolas Schilling
Information Systems and Machine Learning Lab
Universitätsplatz 1
31141 Hildesheim, Germany
schilling@ismll.uni-hildesheim.de

Lars Schmidt-Thieme
Information Systems and Machine Learning Lab
Universitätsplatz 1
31141 Hildesheim, Germany
schmidt-thieme@ismll.uni-hildesheim.de

ABSTRACT

Previous research on content-based geolocation in general has developed prediction methods via conducting pre-partitioning and applying classification methods. The input of these methods is the concatenation of individual tweets during a period of time. But unfortunately, these methods have some drawbacks. They discard the natural real-values properties of latitude and longitude as well as fail to capture geolocation in near real-time. In this work, we develop a novel generative content-based regression model via a matrix factorization technique to tackle the near real-time geolocation prediction problem. With this model, we aim to address a couple of un-answered questions. First, we prove that near real-time geolocation prediction can be accomplished if we leave out the concatenation. Second, we account the real-values properties of physical coordinates within a regression solution. We apply our model on Twitter datasets as an example to prove the effectiveness and generality. Our experimental results show that the proposed model, in the best scenario, outperforms a set of state-of-the-art regression models including Support Vector Machines and Factorization Machines by a reduction of the median localization error up to 79%.

CCS Concepts

•Information systems → Blogs; Social networking sites; Geographic information systems; **•Theory of computation** → Models of learning;

Keywords

Geolocation; Matrix Factorization; Regression; Twitter

1. INTRODUCTION

One of the early pioneer papers about geolocation in Twitter streams was published back in 2010 [3]. In this work, the authors concatenate all user's tweets during a specified duration into one single representative document. A geographical variable was introduced to model the topic distribution across different geographical regions. Hence, the observed user locations are generated from geographical regions and the region variable in topic models is associated with the user's geographical location. Previous works have been developed to solve the classification task to predict user location. Based on these initial ideas, a wide range of follow-up research focuses on solving this type of prediction problem.

Prerequisites to these methods are how the earth's surface is represented. Geolocations can be visualized as points or clusters based on a pre-partitioning of regions into discrete sub-regions using city locations, location indicative words as well as vernacular expressions with the aid of comprehensive gazetteers. But unfortunately, the text of tweets are usually banal and ad hoc where named location words might not exist. To solve this problem, using an invisible grid to partition the earth's surface then got attention in many state-of-the-art models. One can develop the simplest uniform rectangular grid with cells of equal-sized degrees [11]. Furthermore, many research directions focus on more advanced grids by using either an adaptive grid based on k-d trees [9] or a hierarchical structure [10].

As being discussed, these approaches have some drawbacks due to some reasons. First of all, as being classification methods, they heavily depend on pre-partitioning or a framing architecture that is used to split the regions into discrete sub-regions. Thus, they discard the natural properties of real physical coordinates. Moreover, concatenating tweets into one representative document requires a time-consuming collection as well as data abundance. In addition, concatenation of tweets during a particular duration, e.g. a month, leads to failure of capturing geolocation in near real-time situations. Effective geolocation of a user while posting a single short tweet based purely on its content is a direction worth-investigating and also constitutes a more difficult task.

In this work, in contrast to these aforementioned approaches and to the best of our knowledge, we firstly investigate a generative content-based regression model to predict exact latitude and longitude. Furthermore, we also analyze the near real-time geolocation in general.

2. PROBLEM STATEMENT

The problem we study in this paper is to predict the near real-time geolocation, e.g. the geolocation of a user at a particular tweet's posting time, using content information only. Consider a dataset D containing a set of tweets where each tweet is described by n many features. The dataset will be split into a training D^{train},

CIKM'16 , October 24-28, 2016, Indianapolis, IN, USA

DOI: http://dx.doi.org/10.1145/2983323.2983887

a test D^{test} and a validation D^{valid} set. The D^{valid} will be used for hyperparameter optimization later. We denote m, l and v as the number of tweets in D^{train}, D^{test} and D^{valid} respectively. The tweet features are mapped from a dictionary that comprises all words/tokens/unigrams in the dataset. We denote the vocabulary size by $|V| = n$.

Each tweet is annotated with a ground-truth coordinate pair $\mathbf{y} \in \mathbb{R}^2$, $\mathbf{y} = (y^{lat}, y^{lon})$ where $y^{lat} \in \mathbb{R}$ is the latitude and $y^{lon} \in \mathbb{R}$ is the longitude of the associated tweet. By $\bar{\mathbf{y}}_{u_i} = (\bar{y}^{lat}_{u_i}, \bar{y}^{lon}_{u_i})$ we denote the average geolocation of a user i in the training set, where $\bar{y}^{lat}_{u_i} \in \mathbb{R}$ is the average latitude and $\bar{y}^{lon}_{u_i} \in \mathbb{R}$ is the average longitude. Furthermore, we denote the average geolocation of all users in the training set as $\bar{\mathbf{y}}_U = (\bar{y}^{lat}_U, \bar{y}^{lon}_U)$. Given some training data $X^{train} \in \mathbb{R}^{m \times n}$, and the respective labels $Y^{train} \in \mathbb{R}^{m \times 2}$, we seek to learn a prediction model $f : \mathbb{R}^n \rightarrow \mathbb{R}^2$ which maps tweets to geolocations such that for some test data $X^{test} \in \mathbb{R}^{v \times n}$, the sum of localization errors

$$\sum_{i=1}^{v} d(f(X_i^{test}), Y_i^{test}) \tag{1}$$

is minimal. We denote the set of ground-truth labels for the test data as $Y^{test} \in \mathbb{R}^{v \times 2}$.

3. METHODOLOGY

In this section, we demonstrate our matrix factorization based regression model. We also present a learning algorithm for our approach which is based on stochastic gradient descent.

3.1 The Matrix Factorization Based Regression Model

Instead of using the highly sparse word counts as features in a linear regression, we firstly factorize the input space by learning a matrix $T \in \mathbb{R}^{m \times k}$ for tweets and $W \in \mathbb{R}^{k \times n}$ for words of each tweet to reconstruct X as:

$$X \approx TW, \tag{2}$$

where the number of latent features k is usually much smaller than the number of words n, such that through this approach, tweets are projected into a lower dimensional latent feature space. This latent representation of a tweet is then used within a linear combination to predict the geolocation of a user at a posting time:

$$\begin{aligned} \hat{y}_l^{lat} &= \bar{y}_{u_l}^{lat} + \phi_0 + \sum_{k=1}^{K} \phi_k T_{lk}^{lat} \\ \hat{y}_l^{lon} &= \bar{y}_{u_l}^{lon} + \theta_0 + \sum_{k=1}^{K} \theta_k T_{lk}^{lon} \end{aligned} \tag{3}$$

where $\phi \in \mathbb{R}^{k+1}$ and $\theta \in \mathbb{R}^{k+1}$ are weight coefficients vectors for learning latitude and longitude respectively. Notice that we also actually perform two factorizations of X, one for latitude which yields T^{lat}, this is done for longitude as well.

3.2 Learning from Training Data

We have to learn parameters T^{lat}, T^{lon}, W^{lat}, W^{lon}, θ, ϕ, where the W matrices are only used for reconstructing X and the T matrices are used to predict the actual geolocation. We optimize the prediction of the gelocation as well as the factorization of X for the absolute error. In order to avoid overfitting to the training data, we apply a Tikhonov regularization on the regression parameters θ and ϕ, the latent feature matrices are regularized using the Frobenius norm. The overall loss term for learning the parameters associated to predicting latitude then looks like:

$$\begin{aligned} \mathcal{L}^{lat}(\hat{y}^{lat}, y^{lat}) &= \frac{1}{|X^{train}|}\left|\hat{y}^{lat} - y^{lat}\right| + \lambda_\phi \left\|\phi\right\|^2 \\ &+ \left\|X^{train} - T^{lat}W^{lat}\right\|_F^2 + \lambda_T \left\|T^{lat}\right\|_F^2 + \lambda_W \left\|W^{lat}\right\|_F^2 , \end{aligned} \tag{4}$$

where the overall loss term associated to longitude $\mathcal{L}^{lon}(\hat{y}^{lon}, y^{lon})$ is similar. The only difference is that it involves θ, T^{lon} and W^{lon}. In Equation 4, the term $\left\|X^{train} - T^{lat}W^{lat}\right\|_F^2$ is the residual error of transforming X into T^{lat}, W^{lat}. The regularization terms $\lambda_\phi \left\|\phi\right\|^2$, $\lambda_T \left\|T^{lat}\right\|_F^2$ and $\lambda_W \left\|W^{lat}\right\|_F^2$ are multiplied by regularization parameters λ_ϕ, λ_T, and λ_W that control the amount of regularization. To solve the above optimization tasks, we apply the Stochastic Gradient Descent together with Adaptive Subgradient Method to control the learning rate.

3.3 Prediction of Test Data

By optimizing the respective loss terms for the training data, we learn the latent representation T of all training tweets as well as the linear regression parameters θ and ϕ for predicting the final geolocation. However, as we want to predict geolocations of unseen test tweets, the latent representations T for the individual training tweets cannot be employed. Out of this reason, we perform a fold-in, where we factorize the feature matrix X^{test} of the test data, using the latent representation W of the word tokens that was learned on the training data. We denote the latent tweet representations for the test tweets by T'^{lat} and T'^{lon} for latitude and longitude respectively and factorize X^{test} as

$$X^{test} \approx T'^{lat} W^{lat} \tag{5}$$

as well as the respective term for longitude.

As we can see in Equation 5, we reuse W^{lat} from the learning phase. Subsequently, in the fold-in, we define the objective function that we need to minimize for T'^{lat} as follows:

$$\begin{aligned} \mathcal{L}^{lat}\left(X^{test}, T'^{lat}W^{lat}\right) &= \frac{1}{|X^{test}|} \\ \left(\left\|X^{test} - T'^{lat}W^{lat}\right\|_F^2 + \lambda_{test}\left\|T'^{lat}\right\|_F^2\right) \end{aligned} \tag{6}$$

where the objective function that we need to minimize for T'^{lon} is similar. Finally, we can perform predictions for the test users using Equation 3. However, not all users that appear in the test data necessarily have to appear in the training data, hence we cannot use their average geolocation for the final prediction. In this situation, we use the median geolocation of all users of the training data as:

$$\bar{\mathbf{y}}_{u_l} = \begin{cases} \bar{\mathbf{y}}_{u_l}, & \text{if } u_l \in D^{train} \\ \bar{\mathbf{y}}_U, & \text{otherwise} \end{cases} \tag{7}$$

Algorithm 1 illustrates how our proposed model works. In order to obtain a good predictive performance, we also need to carefully tune the hyperparameters in our model. We tune the hyperparameters by assessing the validation performance of our model and choosing the hyperparameter configuration which performs best. The hyperparameter configuration that achieves the smallest error on the validation set is then used by the model to evaluate on the test set.

Algorithm 1 The matrix factorization based regression model

Require: $X^{train} \in \mathbb{R}^{m \times n}, X^{test} \in \mathbb{R}^{l \times n}, Y \in \mathbb{R}^{m \times 2}$
Ensure: $T \in \mathbb{R}^{m \times k}$, $T' \in \mathbb{R}^{l \times k}$, $W \in \mathbb{R}^{k \times n}$, $\phi \in \mathbb{R}^{k+1}$, $\theta \in \mathbb{R}^{k+1}$

Initialize $T^{lat}, T^{lon}, W^{lat}, W^{lon}, \phi, \theta, T'^{lat}, T'^{lon}$
// *Learning*
for *epoch* $\in 1, \ldots, max\_epoch$ **do**
  for *iteration* $\in 1, \ldots, M$ **do**
    Pick m randomly
    Pick X^{train}_{mn} randomly
    for $k \in 1, \ldots, K$ **do**
      Learning $T^{lat}_{mk}, T^{lon}_{mk}, W^{lat}_{kn}, W^{lon}_{kn}, \phi_{Tmk}, \theta_{Tmk}$
    end for
    Update ϕ_0, θ_0
  end for
end for
// *Fold-in*
for *epoch* $\in 1, \ldots, max\_epoch'$ **do**
  for *iteration* $\in 1, \ldots, L$ **do**
    Pick l randomly
    if X^{test}_{ln} exists **then**
      for $k \in 1, \ldots, K$ **do**
        Learning $T'^{lat}_{lk}, T'^{lon}_{lk}$
      end for
    end if
  end for
end for
for $l \in 1, \ldots, L$ **do**
  $\hat{y}^{lat}_l \leftarrow \bar{y}^{lat}_{u_l} + \phi_0 + \phi_{lk} T'^{lat}_{lk}$
  $\hat{y}^{lon}_l \leftarrow \bar{y}^{lon}_{u_l} + \theta_0 + \theta_{lk} T'^{lon}_{lk}$
end for
return $d(\mathbf{y}, \hat{\mathbf{y}})$

4. EXPERIMENTS

In this section, we describe the datasets that we use as well as the data preprocessing procedure. Due to performing a regression task instead of a classification task we compare our model directly with other state-of-the-art regression models, namely linear regression model (LReg) [4], Support Vector Machines (SVM) [1] and Factorization Machines (FM) [8].

4.1 Dataset

We have worked with three publicly available tweet datasets containing geolocation information and compiled them to fit the near real-time scenario. The first dataset comprises the tweets posted within the United States, the second dataset contains tweets localized to north America and the last one comprises the tweets from all over the world. Through this, we evaluate our model's effectiveness and generality within different geographical scopes from a country to the whole world. We randomly split *all tweets of each user* by a 60/20/20 scheme, denoted as LocalRandom (LR). Moreover, we also investigate how our model works in case of a user appearing in the test set might not exist in the training data by splitting *all tweets* using the 60/20/20 scheme, called GlobalRandom (GR).

US. This dataset is originally collected by [3], and was later also used in [2, 11, 7]. The dataset comprises tweets gathered from the "Gardenhose" sample stream in the first week of March, 2010. In this dataset, the authors already provide geotagged tweets that we simply reuse. The resulting dataset contains 377,616 tweets posted by 9,475 users.

NA. The second dataset was collected by [9] and later used by [10, 6]. This dataset contains tweets within north America, including the United States, parts of Canada and Mexico from September 4th to November 29th, 2011. Because the NA dataset only contains user IDs and tweet IDs, we have to fetch the tweets from Twitter using its official API to check whether the tweets are available as well as their availability of embedded coordinates. Only 226,595 tweets out of 38 million posted by 10,950 users have geotags available and therefore are considered for the final dataset.

WORLD. The last dataset was compiled by [5] and later used by [10, 6]. The dataset comprises tweets from all over the world. As being described above with the NA dataset, we also apply the same retrieving procedure. The resulting dataset then contains 121,327 tweets posted by 80,179 users. In the WORLD dataset, 70% of users has only one tweet, so that we only apply the GR 60/20/20 splitting scheme to it.

4.2 Data Preprocessing

In addition to length restriction, tweets are also characterized by the use of terms that are not found in natural language, including hashtags, abbreviations, emoticons and URLs. Through this, we propose a data preprocessing procedure as follows.

Tokenization. We apply a uni-gram tokenization procedure that preserves hashtags, @-replies, abbreviations, blocks of punctuation, emoticons and unicode glyphs and other symbols as tokens. We remove URL tokens to prevent the tweets where bots are posting information such as advertisement to enter our dataset.

Bag-of-words representation. After all tweets are tokenized, they are converted from sparse vectors of token counts into sparse vectors of bag-of-words representations using term frequency - inverse document frequency (TF.IDF) scores. By using the TF.IDF scores, we discard language and grammar structure, the token's order, semantics and meaning as well as part-of-speech. The TF.IDF weights reflect how important a token is to an instance. The more common a token is to many instances, the more penalization it gets. The tokens with the highest TF.IDF weight are often the tokens that best characterize the instance.

4.3 Evaluation Metrics

Given the ellipsoidal shape of the earth's surface, we apply the Haversine distance to calculate the distance of two points represented by their latitude in range of $\{-90, 90\}$ and longitude in range of $\{-180, 180\}$. The Haversine distance $d : \mathbb{R}^2 \times \mathbb{R}^2 \to \mathbb{R}$ is the great circle distance between two geographical coordinate pairs. The Haversine distance can be calculated by:

$$d(\mathbf{y}, \hat{\mathbf{y}}) = 2r \arcsin\left(\left(\sin^2\left(\frac{|\hat{y}^{lat} - y^{lat}|}{2}\right) + \cos(y^{lat})\cos(\hat{y}^{lat})\sin^2\left(\frac{|\hat{y}^{lon} - y^{lon}|}{2}\right)\right)^{\frac{1}{2}}\right) \quad (8)$$

where r is the radius of the earth. Because of the ellipsoidal shape of the earth, its radius varies from the equator to the poles. We take the mean of the earth's radius which amounts to $r = 6371$ km. Finally, the evaluation metrics are the mean and median Haversine localization error d in kilometers between the ground-truth geolocation $\mathbf{y}$ and the predicted geolocation $\hat{\mathbf{y}}$.

4.4 Results and Comparison

We compare our models to the user average location (AL), and a couple of state-of-the-art regression models. We report the results both in mean and median localization errors in Table 1.

Table 1: The mean and median Haversine distance error in km of all models. The best distances are in bold.

Corpus	LR_US		LR_NA		GR_US		GR_NA		GR_WORLD	
Model	mean	median	mean	median	mean	median	mean	median	mean	median
User average location	29.64	0.67	164.45	7.20	27.07	0.66	177.51	7.24	3195.64	2668.71
Linear regression [4]	56.47	16.61	220.29	66.73	54.37	16.40	233.88	68.40	3196.94	2645.66
SVM with RBF kernel [1]	34.63	7.81	157.81	8.42	32.29	8.22	171.72	10.23	3179.57	2654.17
Factorization machines [8]	29.67	0.68	164.51	7.27	27.09	0.66	177.53	7.26	3219.16	2650.48
Our model	**29.15**	**0.66**	**157.22**	**6.95**	**26.44**	**0.65**	**170.08**	**7.19**	**2524.66**	**553.24**

Table 2: Statistics of the US, NA and WORLD datasets.

	US	NA	WORLD
#tweets	377,616	226,595	121,327
#users	9,475	10,950	80,179
$\|V\|$	5216	5292	5145
average tweet's length	12	5	5

In the AL model, the model discards all the content of tweets and only accounts for physical coordinates. If a user appears in both training and test sets, the predicted geolocation is the average of his geolocation in the training set. Otherwise, if a user only exists in the test set, the average geolocation of the whole training set is then used as prediction. For the LReg, SVM and FM, we run them separately to predict latitude and longitude. Subsequently, we combine the predicted latitude and longitude to conduct a final localization error. We also apply a grid-search mechanism applying on a validation set to find the best hyperparameter configurations for each prediction of latitude and longitude.

For our proposed model, we optimize it for the absolute error loss. On each dataset, we repeat running the models 10 times and take the average results. We can see that all other regression models on average do not perform that well, mainly because of using the extremely sparse $5,200$ TF.IDF scores. Our model, however, maps each tweet individually into an eight-dimensional latent feature space and uses those features for prediction.

The results show that our model outperforms all competitors with the smallest mean and median localization errors. Thus, we can reduce the error in comparison to the AL model on the LR_US dataset by 1.7% and 1.5%, whereas the reduction amounts to 2.3% and 1.5% on the GR_US dataset. For the LR_NA and GR_NA datasets, the reduction amounts account for 4.4%, 3.5%, 4.2% and 0.7% for the mean and median respectively. For the GR_WORLD dataset, we notice the significant improvement where the error is reduced by approximately 21% and 79% for the mean and median. We conclude that optimizing for the median localization error yields a bigger improvement as the region gets larger and therefore the average location does not work that well.

5. CONCLUSIONS

In our work, we propose an effective matrix factorization based regression approach to entail an early attempt to solve the task of near real-time geolocation prediction using publicly available datasets that were originally exploited for classification models. We apply our model on Twitter datasets to prove its potential of effectiveness and the generalization abilities. Starting from the model's significant performance especially when applying it in a wide geoscope, we can develop a generative regression approach for this type of geolocation prediction scenario where as the input might be generalized to textual descriptions of images or any types of text in social media. Through this, our model can further predict the user trajectory as he continues posting tweets along a path. Moreover, we can further investigate on the affection of tweet concatenation or the number of tweets needed to achieve an acceptable distance error and time span.

6. REFERENCES

[1] C.-C. Chang and C.-J. Lin. LIBSVM: A library for support vector machines. *ACM Transactions on Intelligent Systems and Technology*, 2:27:1–27:27, 2011.

[2] J. Eisenstein, A. Ahmed, and E. P. Xing. Sparse additive generative models of text. In *Proceedings of the 28th International Conference on Machine Learning (ICML-11)*, pages 1041–1048, 2011.

[3] J. Eisenstein, B. O'Connor, N. A. Smith, and E. P. Xing. A latent variable model for geographic lexical variation. In *Proceedings of the 2010 Conference on Empirical Methods in Natural Language Processing*, pages 1277–1287. Association for Computational Linguistics, 2010.

[4] R.-E. Fan, K.-W. Chang, C.-J. Hsieh, X.-R. Wang, and C.-J. Lin. Liblinear: A library for large linear classification. *The Journal of Machine Learning Research*, 9:1871–1874, 2008.

[5] B. Han, P. Cook, and T. Baldwin. Geolocation prediction in social media data by finding location indicative words. *Proceedings of COLING 2012: Technical Papers*, pages 1045–1062, 2012.

[6] B. Han, P. Cook, and T. Baldwin. Text-based twitter user geolocation prediction. *Journal of Artificial Intelligence Research*, pages 451–500, 2014.

[7] L. Hong, A. Ahmed, S. Gurumurthy, A. J. Smola, and K. Tsioutsiouliklis. Discovering geographical topics in the twitter stream. In *Proceedings of the 21st international conference on World Wide Web*, pages 769–778. ACM, 2012.

[8] S. Rendle. Factorization machines with libfm. *ACM Transactions on Intelligent Systems and Technology (TIST)*, 3(3):57, 2012.

[9] S. Roller, M. Speriosu, S. Rallapalli, B. Wing, and J. Baldridge. Supervised text-based geolocation using language models on an adaptive grid. In *Proceedings of the 2012 Joint Conference on Empirical Methods in Natural Language Processing and Computational Natural Language Learning*, pages 1500–1510. Association for Computational Linguistics, 2012.

[10] B. Wing and J. Baldridge. Hierarchical discriminative classification for text-based geolocation. In *Proceedings of the 2014 Conference on Empirical Methods in Natural Language Processing*, pages 336–348, 2014.

[11] B. P. Wing and J. Baldridge. Simple supervised document geolocation with geodesic grids. In *Proceedings of the 49th Annual Meeting of the Association for Computational Linguistics: Human Language Technologies-Volume 1*, pages 955–964. Association for Computational Linguistics, 2011.

Distilling Word Embeddings: An Encoding Approach

Lili Mou, Ran Jia, Yan Xu, Ge Li,* Lu Zhang, Zhi Jin*
Key Laboratory of High Condence Software Technologies (Peking University), MoE, China
Institute of Software, Peking University, China *Corresponding authors
{doublepower.mou, jiaran1994}@gmail.com
{xuyan14, lige, zhanglu, zhijin}@sei.pku.edu.cn

ABSTRACT

Distilling knowledge from a well-trained cumbersome network to a small one has recently become a new research topic, as lightweight neural networks with high performance are particularly in need in various resource-restricted systems. This paper addresses the problem of distilling word embeddings for NLP tasks. We propose an encoding approach to distill task-specific knowledge from a set of high-dimensional embeddings, so that we can reduce model complexity by a large margin as well as retain high accuracy, achieving a good compromise between efficiency and performance. Experiments reveal the phenomenon that distilling knowledge from cumbersome embeddings is better than directly training neural networks with small embeddings.

Keywords

Model compression; neural networks; word embeddings

1. INTRODUCTION

Distilling knowledge from a neural network—that is, transferring valuable knowledge from a cumbersome network to a lightweight one—is pioneered by Buciluǎ et al. [3]; it has attracted increasing attention over the last two years [7, 5].

As addressed by Hinton et al. [7], the objective of training networks is probably different from deploying networks: during training we focus on extracting as much knowledge as possible from a large dataset, whereas deploying networks takes into consideration multiple aspects, including accuracy, memory, time, and energy consumption. It would be appealing if we can first well train a cumbersome network offline, and then distill its knowledge to a small one for deployment. The aim of knowledge distillation is thus to reduce model complexity as well as to retain high performance, which is particularly important to neural networks' applications in resource-restricted scenarios, e.g., real-time systems, mobile devices, and large ensembles of models.

Much evidence in the literature shows the feasibility of transferring knowledge from one neural network to another, for instance, from shallow networks to deep ones [11], from feed-forward networks to recurrent ones [12], or vice versa [1, 4]. The main idea of the above studies is to train a *teacher model* first, and then use the teacher model's output (estimated probabilities by softmax, say, in a classification problem) to guide a *student model*. Several variants of training objectives include applying regression over the input of softmax [1] and softening the teacher model's probabilities [7]. We call such approaches "matching softmax" (Figure 1a). It is also argued that the estimated probabilities by a teacher model convey more information than one-hot represented ground truth; hence knowledge distillation is feasible and beneficial [7].

Despite the above generic approach, this paper focuses on distilling word embeddings in NLP applications. Particularly, we find the specificity of embeddings brings new opportunities for knowledge distillation.

As word embeddings map discrete words to distributed, real-valued vectors, it can be viewed that a word is first represented as a one-hot vector and then the vector is multiplied by a large embedding matrix, known as a look-up table. During the matrix-vector multiplication, one and only one column in the look-up table is verbatim retrieved for a particular word. Thus, we may build an interlayer—sandwiched between the high-dimensional embeddings and the ensuing network—to squash embeddings to a low-dimensional space (Figure 1b). The standard cross-entropy loss can then be applied to train the encoding layer and other parameters in the network. In such a supervised manner, task-specific knowledge in the original cumbersome embeddings can be distilled to low-dimensional ones.

In summary, the main contributions of this paper are three-fold: (1) We address the problem of distilling word embeddings in NLP applications. (2) We propose a supervised encoding approach to distill task-specific knowledge from cumbersome word embeddings. (3) Our experimental results in sentiment analysis and relation classification tasks reveal a phenomenon that distilling low-dimensional embeddings from large ones is better than directly training a network with small embeddings. It should also be noticed that the proposed encoding approach does not rely on a teacher model; our method is complementary to existing matching softmax for knowledge distillation.

2. BACKGROUND OF MATCHING SOFTMAX

As said, existing approaches to knowledge transfer between two neural networks mainly follow a two-step strat-

CIKM'16 , October 24-28, 2016, Indianapolis, IN, USA

DOI: http://dx.doi.org/10.1145/2983323.2983888

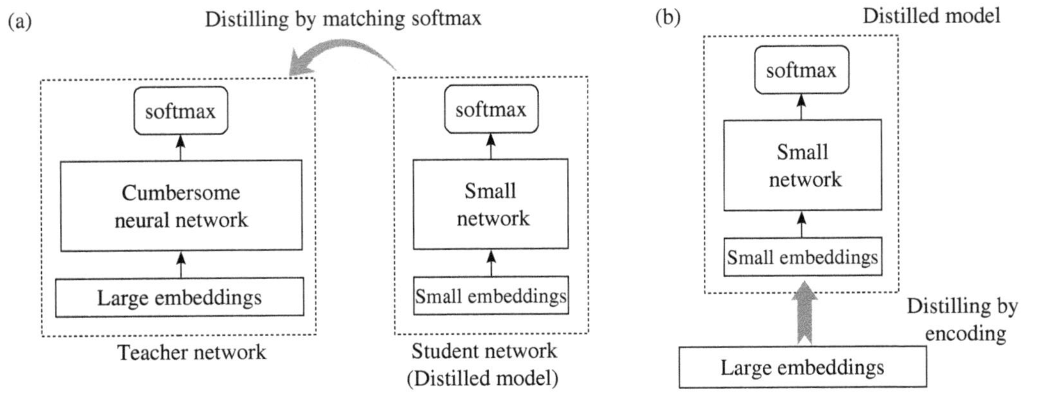

Figure 1: Distilling knowledge by (a) matching softmax, and (b) encoding embeddings.

egy: first training a teacher network; then using the teacher network to guide a student model by matching softmax, depicted in Figure 1a.

For a classification problem, softmax is typically used as the output layer's activation function. Let $\boldsymbol{z} \in \mathbb{R}^{n_c}$ be the input of softmax. (n_c is the number of classes.) The output of softmax is

$$y_i = \frac{e^{z_i/T}}{\sum_{j=1}^{n_c} e^{z_j/T}}$$

where T is a relaxation variable (used later), called *temperature*. $T = 1$ for standard softmax.

Take a 3-way classification problem as an example. If a teacher model estimates $\boldsymbol{y} = (0.95, 0.04, 0.01)^\top$ for three classes, it is valuable information to the student model that Class 2 is more similar to Class 1 than Class 3 to Class 1.

However, directly imposing constraints on the output of softmax may be ineffective: the difference between 0.04 and 0.01 is too small. Ba et al. [1] match the input of softmax, $\boldsymbol{z}$, rather than $\boldsymbol{y}$. Hinton et al. [7] raise the temperature T during training, which makes the estimated probabilities softer over different classes. The temperature of 3, for instance, softens the above $\boldsymbol{y}$ to $(0.64, 0.22, 0.14)^\top$. Matching softmax can also be applied along with standard cross-entropy loss (with one-hot ground truth), or more elaborately, the teacher model's effect declines in an annealing fashion when the student model is more aware of data [11].

3. THE PROPOSED ENCODING APPROACH FOR DISTILLING EMBEDDINGS

This section introduces in detail our proposed method for word embedding distillation (Figure 1b). We also analyze the neural network's model capacity with distilled embeddings, and discuss the rationale for distilling small embeddings from large ones in a supervised manner, instead of directly training with small embeddings.

Word embeddings are a standard component for neural natural language processing. As feeding word indexes directly to neural networks is somewhat nonsensical, words are mapped to a real-valued vector, called *embeddings*, where each dimension captures a certain aspect of underlying word semantics. Usually, they are trained in an unsupervised fashion, e.g., maximizing the probability of a large corpus [2, 9], or maximizing a scoring function [6, 8]. The learned embeddings can be fed to standard neural networks for supervised learning, e.g., POS tagging, named entity recognition, and semantic role labeling [6].

To formalize word embeddings in algebraic notations, we let $\boldsymbol{x}_i \in \mathbb{R}^{|\mathscr{V}|}$ be one-hot representation of the i-th word x_i in the vocabulary $\mathscr{V}$; the i-th element in the vector $\boldsymbol{x}_i$ is on, with other elements being 0. Let $\Phi_c \in \mathbb{R}^{n_\text{embed} \times |\mathscr{V}|}$ be a (cumbersome) embedding matrix (look-up table). Then the vector representation of the word is exactly the i-th column of the matrix, given by $\Phi_c \cdot \boldsymbol{x}_i$.

Now we consider distilling, from cumbersome embeddings $\Phi_c \cdot \boldsymbol{x}_i$, an n_distill-dimensional vector for the word, where n_distill is smaller than n_embed. It is accomplished by encoding with a non-linear neural layer, i.e.,

$$\text{vec}(x_i) = f(W_\text{encode} \cdot \Phi_c \boldsymbol{x}_i + \boldsymbol{b}_\text{encode}) \quad (1)$$

where $W_\text{encode} \in \mathbb{R}^{n_\text{distill} \times n_\text{embed}}$ and $\boldsymbol{b}_\text{encode} \in \mathbb{R}^{n_\text{distill}}$ are parameters of the encoding layer; vec($\cdot$) denotes the distilled vector representation of a word.

These distilled embeddings can then be fed to a neural network (with parameters Θ) for further processing. Let m be the number of data samples and n_c be the number of target classes; suppose further $\boldsymbol{y}^{(j)}$ is the output of softmax for the j-th data sample and $\boldsymbol{t}^{(j)}$ the one-hot represented ground truth. Our training objective is the standard cross-entropy loss, given by

$$\underset{W_\text{encode}, \boldsymbol{b}_\text{encode}, \Theta, \Phi}{\text{minimize}} \quad -\sum_{j=1}^{m}\sum_{i=1}^{n_c} t_i^{(j)} \log y_i^{(j)}$$

We would like to point out that distilling embeddings does not increase, or in fact may reduce, model capacity vis-à-vis directly training with small embeddings, despite the large number of parameters in cumbersome embeddings and the coding layer's weights.

Theorem 1. *The model capacity of a neural network with distilled embeddings is less than or equal to that of a neural network trained directly with small embeddings.*

Proof. The intuition is straightforward: small embeddings are free parameters which are not constrained, whereas the distilled embeddings are subject to the form in Equation 1. Formally, let $\mathcal{H}_d, \mathcal{H}_s$ be the hypothesis classes of networks with distilled/small embeddings, respectively. For each $h_d \in \mathcal{H}_d$ with cumbersome embeddings Φ_c and encoding parameters $W_{\text{encode}}, \boldsymbol{b}_{\text{encode}}$, there exists a hypothesis $h_s \in \mathcal{H}_s$, satisfying that $h_s = h_d$ with small embeddings Φ_s, whose i^{th} column (the small embedding for i^{th} word) is $f(W_{\text{encode}}\Phi_c \boldsymbol{x}_i + \boldsymbol{b}_{\text{encode}})$. Hence, $\mathcal{H}_d \subseteq \mathcal{H}_s$. ◄

A curious question is then why distilling embeddings may help, compared with directly training the neural network with small embeddings. We provide an intuitive explanation as follows.

Since word embeddings are typically learned from a large corpus in an unsupervised manner, the knowledge in embeddings is restrained by dimensionality. For example, the sentiment of a word is of secondary importance compared with its syntactic functionality in a sentence. Hence, sentiment information might be lost in low-dimensional embeddings, which is unfavorable in a sentiment analysis task. On the contrary, large embeddings have the capacity to capture different aspects of word semantics. The proposed supervised encoding approach may then distill task-specific (e.g., sentiment) knowledge to a small space, while eliminating irrelevant information. Therefore, we may reasonably expect that distilling embeddings would outperform direct use of small ones.

Deployment Issues

Before deploying the model, we shall precompute the distilled embeddings, vec(·), according to Equation 1 after training all parameters. The original embeddings $\Phi_c \boldsymbol{x}$ and encoding parameters (W_{encode} and b_{encode}) can then be safely discarded, and we obtain a small model (dashed rectangle in Figure 1b) with a set of small embeddings, which are distilled from large ones.

As we shall see in the experiments, the small model will be very computational efficient because we have reduced a large number of parameters.

4. EVALUATION

In this section, we present our experimental results. We first describe the testbed and protocol of our experiments in Subsection 4.1. Then we analyze in Subsection 4.2 the performance of our approach regarding several aspects, namely accuracy, memory, and time consumption.

4.1 Tasks, Models, and Protocols

We tested our distilling approach in two tasks: sentiment analysis and relation classification.

The sentiment analysis task aims to classify a sentence into 5 categories according to its sentiment: strongly/weakly positive/negative and neural. We used Stanford Sentiment Treebank[1] as our dataset, which contains 8544/1101/221 sentences for training, validation, and testing. Phrases (subsentences) in the training set are also labeled with sentiment, enriching the training set to more than 150k samples. For validation and testing, only the sentiment of a whole sentence was considered.

The second task is to classify the relation between two tagged entities in a sentence. The SemEval 2010 dataset,[2] we used, comprises 8000 training samples, from which we split 10% for validation; there are additional 3000 samples for testing. Target labels include 9 directed relations (e.g. Component-Whole) plus a default Other; in total, we have 19 classes. The official F_1-score was applied as our measurement.

To set up our experiments, we leveraged two state-of-the-art neural models: a tree-based convolutional neural network (TBCNN) for sentiment analysis [10], and a long short term memory-based recurrent network along shortest dependency path (SDP-LSTM)[3] between two entities for relation classification [13].

For each task, we evaluated our proposed methods by distilling 300-dimensional embeddings to 50 dimensions, further processed by a thin network (also 50d). In comparison, we trained the 50d network directly with small 50d embeddings. All models were trained by mini-batch gradient descent with back-propagation. For both settings of distilling and non-distilling, we tried extensive configurations of hyperparameters, mainly following the original papers.[4] After choosing the setting with the highest validation accuracy, we ran each model 5 times for smoothing with different random initializations, and report the average test accuracy or F_1-score.

Task	Method	Acc.	#Param	Time
Sentiment analysis by TBCNN	Cumbersome embed.	51.6	6.9M	1x
	Small embed.	46.4	0.94M (0.14x)	0.04x
	Distilled embed.	47.5		
	Matching softmax	45.8		

Table 1: Comparison between cumbersome embeddings, small embeddings, matching softmax, and distilled embeddings. The official measure is accuracy (acc.) in percentage.

Task	Method	F_1	#Param	Time
Relation classification by SDP-LSTM	Cumbersome embed.	82.1	8.8M	1x
	Small embed.	79.0	1.3M (0.15x)	0.04x
	Distilled embed.	79.4		
	Matching softmax	80.1		
	Hybrid	80.2		

Table 2: Comparison between cumbersome embeddings, small embeddings, matching softmax, and distilled embeddings. We further made an attempt to combine matching softmax and distilling embeddings (denoted as "Hybrid"). The official measure for relation classification is the F_1-score.

4.2 Results

Tables 1 and 2 presents the results of our proposed model as well as two competing settings: training a wider network with cumbersome embeddings, and directly training a thin network with small embeddings.

In both experiments, cumbersome embeddings yield the highest performance, the distilled embeddings rank second, and small embeddings are worst. Basically, our method outperforms direct training of a small network by a margin of approximately one standard deviation (std = 1.1 and 0.6, re-

[1]http://nlp.stanford.edu/sentiment/

[2]http://semeval2.fbk.eu/semeval2.php?location=data

[3]We only used word embeddings, and ignored other features like hyponymy, dependency types, which were used in [13]. In this way, we focus on the problem of embedding distillation itself.

[4]Due to the limitation of space, we list candidate configurations on our website:
https://sites.google.com/site/distillembeddings/

spectively). As the results were obtained by averaging over 5 initializations, we deem the improvement is fair.

Regarding model complexity, our distilled embeddings reduce memory and time to a large extent to 14–15% and 4%, respectively (C++ implementation on a single CPU). Therefore, the resulting network is significantly more lightweight, which is helpful to deployment in neural networks' applications.

To further test our method under extreme conditions, we distilled word embeddings to 10d and 30d. We chose to conduct the experiments in the second task, because it is of lower variance. As demonstrated in Figure 2, our method consistently outperforms direct training with small embeddings in all scenarios; moreover, the margin increases when the dimension becomes small. Such result is consistent with our human intuition, and verifies the conjecture in Section 3—small embeddings contain less knowledge specific to the task of interest; the proposed supervised encoding approach can distill task-specific knowledge from large embeddings.

We also notice that our approach is, in fact, complementary to existing matching softmax methods: the encoding layer distills task-specific knowledge from large embeddings in a bottom-up fashion, whereas matching softmax distills generic knowledge in a top-down fashion.

In both tasks, we also tried the matching softmax approach, whose settings and hyperparameters are mainly derived from [7], i.e., $T = 2$ and a 1 : 1 mixture of ground truth and the teacher model's output. Its performance is not consistent: in the sentiment analysis task, matching softmax hurts the performance by 0.6%, whereas it improves the relation classification task by 1.1%. (See Tables 1 and 2 again.) One plausible explanation is that the teacher model itself has not achieved remarkable accuracy (only about 50%) in the 5-way sentiment classification task. Using a teacher model introduces additional knowledge as well as errors. If the latter dominates, matching softmax may hurt the student model. However, our encoding approach to embedding distillation does not reply on a teacher model. Combined with matching softmax, it improves another 0.1% (although may not be large) in the second experiment, showing that the two methods can be potentially combined, as they are complementary to each other.

5. CONCLUSION

In this paper, we addressed the problem of distilling embeddings for NLP, which is important when deploying a neural network in resource-restricted scenarios. We proposed an encoding approach that distills cumbersome word embeddings to a low dimensional space. Experimental results have shown the superiority of our proposed distilling method to training neural networks directly with small embeddings; that the performance gain increases significantly especially when the dimension becomes small. Moreover, our approach does not reply on a teacher model, which is complementary to matching softmax; these two methods of knowledge distillation could also be combined.

6. ACKNOWLEDGMENTS

We thank all reviewers for their insightful comments and Rui Yan for discussion of the manuscript. This research is supported by the National Basic Research Program of China (the 973 Program) under Grant No. 2015CB352201 and the National Natural Science Foundation of China under Grant Nos. 61232015, 91318301, 61421091, and 61502014.

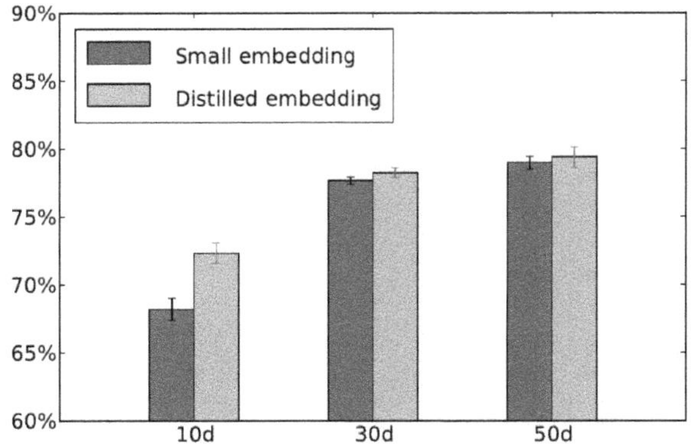

Figure 2: Accuracy versus dimension in the experiment of relation classification.

7. REFERENCES

[1] J. Ba and R. Caruana. Do deep nets really need to be deep? In *NIPS*, pages 2654–2662, 2014.

[2] Y. Bengio, R. Ducharme, P. Vincent, and C. Janvin. A neural probabilistic language model. *JMLR*, 3:1137–1155, 2003.

[3] C. Buciluǎ, R. Caruana, and A. Niculescu-Mizil. Model compression. In *SIGKDD*, pages 535–541, 2006.

[4] W. Chan, N. R. Ke, and I. Lane. Transferring knowledge from a RNN to a DNN. *arXiv:1504.01483*, 2015.

[5] W. Chen, J. T. Wilson, S. Tyree, K. Q. Weinberger, and Y. Chen. Compressing neural networks with the hashing trick. In *ICML*, pages 2285–2294, 2015.

[6] R. Collobert and J. Weston. A unified architecture for natural language processing: Deep neural networks with multitask learning. In *ICML*, pages 160–167, 2008.

[7] G. Hinton, O. Vinyals, and J. Dean. Distilling the knowledge in a neural network. *arXiv:1503.02531*, 2014.

[8] T. Mikolov, I. Sutskever, K. Chen, G. Corrado, and J. Dean. Distributed representations of words and phrases and their compositionality. In *NIPS*, pages 3111–3119, 2013.

[9] F. Morin and Y. Bengio. Hierarchical probabilistic neural network language model. In *AISTAT*, pages 246–252, 2005.

[10] L. Mou, H. Peng, G. Li, Y. Xu, L. Zhang, and Z. Jin. Discriminative neural sentence modeling by tree-based convolution. In *EMNLP*, pages 2315–2325, 2015.

[11] A. Romero, N. Ballas, S. E. Kahou, A. Chassang, C. Gatta, and Y. Bengio. FitNets: Hints for thin deep nets. In *ICLR*, 2014.

[12] D. Wang, C. Liu, Z. Tang, Z. Zhang, and M. Zhao. Recurrent neural network training with dark knowledge transfer. *arXiv:1505.04630*, 2015.

[13] Y. Xu, L. Mou, G. Li, Y. Chen, H. Peng, and Z. Jin. Classifying relations via long short term memory networks along shortest dependency paths. In *EMNLP*, pages 1785–1794, 2015.

Regularising Factorised Models for Venue Recommendation using Friends and their Comments

Jarana Manotumruksa[1] Craig Macdonald[2] Iadh Ounis[2]

University of Glasgow, UK
[1]j.manotumruksa.1@research.gla.ac.uk, [2]{firstname.lastname}@glasgow.ac.uk

ABSTRACT

Venue recommendation is an important capability of Location-Based Social Networks such as Yelp and Foursquare. Matrix Factorisation (MF) is a collaborative filtering-based approach that can effectively recommend venues that are relevant to the users' preferences, by training upon either implicit or explicit feedbacks (e.g. check-ins or venue ratings) that these users express about venues. However, MF suffers in that users may only have rated very few venues. To alleviate this problem, recent literature have leveraged additional sources of evidence, e.g. using users' social friendships to reduce the complexity of – or regularise – the MF model, or identifying similar venues based on their comments. This paper argues for a combined regularisation model, where the venues suggested for a user are influenced by friends with similar tastes (as defined by their comments). We propose a MF regularisation technique that seamlessly incorporates both social network information and textual comments, by exploiting word embeddings to estimate a semantic similarity of friends based on their explicit textual feedback, to regularise the complexity of the factorised model. Experiments on a large existing dataset demonstrate that our proposed regularisation model is promising, and can enhance the prediction accuracy of several state-of-the-art matrix factorisation-based approaches.

1. INTRODUCTION

With an overwhelming amount of data in Location-Based Social Networks, recommending venues that are relevant to the users' preferences is challenging. Traditional Matrix Factorisation [9] (MF) is a collaborative filtering-based approach widely used to predict ratings that users give to venues. A regularisation technique is commonly used to ensure that the MF models simple and to avoid over-fitting. MF treats all users equally, i.e. the predicted rating of a *target* user for a venue can be influenced by any other user, as long as they share similar preferences, and regardless of their relationship. However, when the users' rating data are sparse in nature, i.e. users/venues have very few ratings, the rating prediction accuracy of traditional MF approaches can be significantly degraded. To alleviate this problem, previous works [4, 10] have incorporated social network information (e.g. the user's friendships) to enhance the prediction accuracy. In particular, Ma *et al.* [10] proposed a MF approach called SoReg, where a social regularisation component assumes that users are likely to be influenced by their friends who rate similar venues with similar scores.

Apart from social network information, the textual comments left by users are another form of explicit preference information. Indeed, comments can be leveraged to enhance the prediction accuracy and provide useful insights about user's preferences. For instance, Hu *et al.* [5] showed that by incorporating the comments left by the users on venues (along with the geographical proximity of venues), a more effective rating prediction model can be achieved. Similarly, Huang *et al.* [6] showed that a representation of user's preferences extracted from comments provides useful insights for restaurant owners. They argued that users' ratings are influenced by a variety of aspects. For example, assuming the widely used rating scale range from 1 to 5 (where 1 denotes user does not like a venue and 5 is the most positive rating), the reason that a user rated a restaurant 4 rather than 5 could be that he/she liked the food and price but was disappointed by the service. Typically, comments are represented as a Bag-of-Words (BoW). However, we argue that BoW is not effective at capturing the semantic properties of comments because they ignore the ordering and the semantics of the words. An example of two comments about a venue that are semantically similar are *delicious sushi bar in Illinois* and *best Japanese restaurant in Chicago*. While these two comments have no words in common, their semantic properties are similar, however a similarity measured based upon BoW would fail to capture these properties. Recently, Mikolov *et al.* [11, 12] proposed a word embedding technique that represents a word within a multi-dimensional vector space based on the contexts surrounding the word. Previous work [1] has shown that using word embeddings to analyse comments not only captures the semantic properties but also the sentiment expressed in the comments. With such benefits, various literature [1, 13, 14] have proposed to apply word embeddings to recommendation tasks. For instance, Musto *et al.* [13] proposed a collaborative filtering technique that applies word embeddings to the textual content of items obtained from their Wikipedia pages, in order to recommend items to users. In contrast, we propose a model that models the comments of each user using word embeddings.

Although the previous venue recommendation literature have shown that both social network [4, 10] and comments [5] are important sources of evidence to enhance the quality of recommendations, a model that seamlessly incorporate

CIKM'16 , October 24-28, 2016, Indianapolis, IN, USA

DOI: http://dx.doi.org/10.1145/2983323.2983889

these two factors has not been previously studied. In addition, unlike the approach proposed by Hu *et al.* [5], we aim to leverage comments at the user-level, rather than at the venue-level (i.e. to represent user's preferences). Moreover, we do not consider the geographical locations of venues in this model. Table 1 summarises user-venue prediction approaches and their intuitions. Inspired by the previous studies mentioned above, we argue that by considering score of rating and comments both target user and his friends left for venues, a more accurate user-venue rating prediction model can be achieved. To address these challenges, we propose a regularisation model that enables traditional MF models to incorporate additional informations. Our contributions in this paper are the following: (1) we propose a regularisation model that incorporates social and textual information, which exploits word embeddings to model friends' preferences based on the comments they have left on venues, (2) we conduct experiments on a large publicly available dataset and demonstrate that our proposed regularisation model is promising, and can enhance the prediction accuracy of several state-of-the-art rating prediction approaches.

2. MATRIX FACTORISATION WITH SOCIAL & TEXTUAL REGULARISATION

In this section, we first outline the traditional Matrix Factorisation (MF) and the social regularisation model proposed by Ma *et al.* [10] in details. Next we explain how we exploit word embeddings to model friends' preferences from their comments and describe our proposed social-textual regularisation model (Section 2.3). The intuitions for each model are highlighted in Table 1. Later, in Section 4, we demonstrate the usefulness of our proposed model in enhancing the prediction accuracy of several state-of-the-art MF rating prediction approaches.

2.1 Traditional Matrix Factorisation

Traditional Matrix factorisation-based approaches assume that users can influence each others if they share similar preferences, i.e. who rate venues similarly (see Table 1). Traditionally, user-venue ratings are represented as a matrix $R^{m\times n}$ where m and n are a number of users and venues, respectively, and $R_{i,j}$ indicates the 1-5 scale rating feedback by user i on venue j. Traditional MF techniques aim to approximate the matrix R by finding a decomposition of R, i.e. a dot product of latent factors of users $U \in \mathbb{R}^{m\times d}$ and venues $V \in \mathbb{R}^{n\times d}$ where d is the number of latent dimensions:

$$R \approx U^T V$$

Next, the two latent factor matrices U and V are optimised by minimising the regularised square error on a set of observed ratings using decomposition technique such as singular value decomposition. Hence, a loss function is defined as:

$$L(U,V) = \min_{U,V} \frac{1}{2}\sum_{i=1}^{m}\sum_{j=1}^{n} I_{i,j} \cdot (R_{i,j} - U_i^T V_j)^2 \qquad (1)$$

where $I_{i,j}$ is an indicator variable that is 1 if user i rated venue j, otherwise 0. To avoid overfitting, i.e. $U^T V = R$, a traditional regularisation technique is added into Eq. (1):

$$\underset{MF}{L(U,V)} = L(U,V) + \frac{\lambda}{2}(\|U\|_F^2 + \|V\|_F^2) \qquad (2)$$

where λ is a regularisation parameter and $\|.\|_F^2$ denotes the Frobenius norm. Finally, Stochastic Gradient Descent (SGD) is applied to find a local minimum of the loss function, by optimising each of the latent factor matrices U, V, while fixing the other, until convergence.

$$\begin{aligned} \frac{\partial \underset{MF}{L(U,V)}}{\partial U_i} &= \sum_{j=1}^{n} I_{i,j}(R_{i,j} - U_i^T V_j)V_j + \lambda U_i \\ \frac{\partial \underset{MF}{L(U,V)}}{\partial V_j} &= \sum_{i=1}^{m} I_{i,j}(R_{i,j} - U_i^T V_j)U_i + \lambda V_j \end{aligned} \qquad (3)$$

2.2 Social Regularisation

Based on an assumption that friends who have similar preferences are likely to rate venues similarly (see Table 1), Ma *et al.* [10] proposed a social regularisation model, denoted SoReg, which aims to minimise the distance between latent factors of target user U_i, and his/her friends, U_f, by incorporating friendship information from the social network as:

$$\underset{SoReg}{L(U,V)} = \underset{MF}{L(U,V)} + \frac{\alpha}{2}\sum_{i=1}^{m}\sum_{f\in\mathcal{F}(i)} pcc(i,f)\|U_i - U_f\|_F^2 \quad (4)$$

where $\mathcal{F}(.)$ is the set of friends of user i, α is a parameter that controls social influences. *pcc*() estimates the similarity between the ratings of two users using the Pearson Correlation Coefficient (PCC), calculated as follows:

$$pcc(i,f) = \frac{\sum_{j\in V_r(i)\cap V_r(f)} (R_{ij}-\overline{R}_i)\cdot(R_{fj}-\overline{R}_f)}{\sqrt{\sum_{j\in V_r(i)\cap V_r(f)} (R_{ij}-\overline{R}_i)}\cdot\sqrt{\sum_{j\in V_r(i)\cap V_r(f)} (R_{fj}-\overline{R}_f)}} \quad (5)$$

where $V_r(i)$ are the venues that user i has rated and $\overline{R}_i$ is their average rating. This regularisation ensures that friends who have rated venues similarly (e.g. $pcc(i,f) = 0.9$) are predicted to give similar ratings to other venues, $U_i^T V \approx U_f^T V$.

2.3 Social Regularisation using Word Embeddings

As mentioned in Section 1, we argue that users are not only influenced by their friends who visit similar venues and provide similar ratings to that venues, but are also influenced by friends who share similar tastes, which can be extracted from the explicit textual feedback in the form of comments they have left for each venue (Table 1). An intuitive scenario for this assumption could be that u_i, u_j and u_k are friends who all enjoy a visit to a restaurant. u_i and u_j are impressed by the service at the restaurant and food, but u_k is only impressed by the setting of the restaurant. Estimating user similarity using PCC exploited by Ma's approach [10] (Eq. (4)) can only capture the similarity of the users based on their ratings, which in this case are all positive. However, the taste of u_k is quite different from the others. To tackle this problem, we propose to examine the comments left by friends, to identify those that share similar interests. In particular, instead of measuring the comment similarity using a traditional bag-of-words representation, we propose to exploit word embeddings, a popular technique that can capture semantic regularities of text [11, 12], to effectively model a user's tastes over a venue. For a comment c_{ij} left by user i on venue j, we obtain a word embedding representation by summing the vectors of the terms that occurred in the user's comment on the venue as follows:

$$w2v(c_{ij}) = \sum_{t\in c_{ij}} \vec{\nu}_t \qquad (6)$$

Table 1: Overview of user-rating prediction approaches.

Models	Social	Comments	Params	Intuition
MF, MF_N [9], MF_P [15], SVD [7]	×	×	λ	Users are likely to prefer venues rated that other similar users rate highly.
VMF [5]	×	✓	λ	+ Users are likely to prefer venues that share similar characteristics (according to textually similar comments).
SoReg [10], TrustSVD [4]	✓	×	λ, α	+ Users are likely to prefer venues that their friends rate highly.
BoWReg	✓	✓	λ, α	+ Users are likely to prefer venues visited by their friends who have similar tastes (based on textually similar comments).
DeepReg	✓	✓	λ, α	+ Users are likely to prefer venues visited by their friends who have similar tastes (based on semantically similar comments).

where t is a term that occurs in the comment c_{ij} and $\vec{v}_t \in \mathbb{R}^k$ is a vector representation of term t obtained from word embeddings. k is the number of dimensions in the word embedding space. Thereafter, the similarity between two users based on their comments about venues they have both visited is estimated as:

$$sim_{w2v}(i,f) = \frac{\sum_{j \in V_c(i) \cap V_c(f)} sim(w2v(c_{ij}), w2v(c_{fj}))}{|V_c(i) \cap V_c(f)|} \quad (7)$$

where $sim()$ denotes the cosine similarity between two vectors and $V_c(i)$ is the set of venues for which user i has left a comment. Next, inspired by Ma *et al.* [10], we integrate the social and textual information into MF as a component of the regularisation (but using comments rather than ratings to identify similar friends):

$$\frac{\alpha}{2} \sum_{i=1}^{m} \sum_{f \in \mathcal{F}(i)} sim_{w2v}(i,f) \|U_i - U_f\|_F^2 \quad (8)$$

Similar to the traditional Frobenius norm regularisation technique in Eq. (1), our proposed social-textual regularisation model can be easily added to various matrix factorisation-based approaches. We add our proposed social regularisation model (Eq. (8)) to Eq. (2) and perform SGD on latent factors U_i to obtain a local minimum of objective function (denoted as DeepReg) while SGD on the latent factor V_j remains the same as in Eq. (3):

$$\frac{\partial \underset{DeepReg}{L(U,V)}}{\partial U_i} = \frac{\partial \underset{MF}{L(U,V)}}{\partial U_i} + \alpha \sum_{f \in \mathcal{F}(i)} sim_{w2v}(i,f)(U_i - U_f) \quad (9)$$

3. EXPERIMENTAL SETUP

This section describes the experimental setup used to evaluate the usefulness of our proposed regularisation model in enhancing the rating prediction accuracy of traditional MF, in comparison with various state-of-the-art rating prediction approaches. All experiments are conducted using the publicly available Yelp dataset.[1] The dataset consists of 2,225,213 ratings by 552,339 users for 77,079 venues. It contains social network information, with ~3.5M friend links. Following Hu *et al.* [5], we perform stemming and remove standard stopwords from comments in the dataset. We report the user-rating prediction accuracy in term of Mean Absolute Error (MAE) and Root Mean Square Error (RMSE) (for both metrics, lower is better), which are widely used in previous literature [4, 5, 10]. We compare our proposed approach, called DeepReg (Eq. (9)), with a number of baselines, which can be grouped into 4 categories: traditional Matrix Factorisation (MF), social-based MF, textual-based MF and a baseline social-textual-based MF that does not consider word embeddings. The baselines are summarised below, while their parameters and sources of evidence are highlighted in Table 1.

[1] https://www.yelp.com/dataset_challenge

MF, MF_N, MF_P and SVD: Four matrix factorisation baselines that consider only the user-venue matrix to predict the ratings. We use traditional MF (denoted MF) as described in Section 2.1, Non-negative MF (MF_N) [9], Probabilistic MF (MF_P) [15] and Singular Value Decomposition (SVD) [7], a state-of-the-art MF that considers user and venue biases (e.g. low or high average ratings R_i). These are widely used baselines in recommendation systems [4, 5, 10].
SoReg and TrustSVD: Both consider the user-venue ratings matrix R and friendship $\mathcal{F}(.)$ to predict ratings. SoReg, discussed above, is a state-of-the-art regularisation model (Eq. (4)), while TrustSVD [4] is a state-of-the-art social-based MF that considers social information, built upon SVD.
VMF: is a state-of-the-art textual-based MF approach that considers textual information (i.e. comments about a venue) proposed by Hu *et al.* [5]. To permit a fair evaluation, we have re-implemented the approach to consider only textual information, and ignore the geographical location properties of venues, in common with our own proposed approach that does not consider the location of venues.
BoWReg: Building upon SoReg, this represents the user's comments using BoW similarity, and hence considers both social friends and comments. In particular, this model is similar to our proposed model but instead the similarity between two users is estimated using an average of the cosine similarity of the user's comment BoW vectors as follows:

$$sim_{bow}(i,f) = \frac{\sum_{j \in V_c(i) \cap V_c(f)} sim(bow(c_{ij}), bow(c_{fj}))}{|V_c(i) \cap V_c(f)|} \quad (10)$$

where $bow(c_{ij})$ returns a vector that represents the term frequency of terms occurring in comment c_{ij}. We use **BoWReg** as a baseline that considers both social network and textual information without using word embeddings.

We implement and conduct all experiments using LibRec [2], a Java library for recommender systems. Following previous works [4, 10], we set the latent factor dimension d to 10 and $\lambda = 0.001$. Our experiments are conducted in a 5-fold cross-validation, split by user, where each fold has 60% training, 20% validation and 20% testing. We use the validation set to determine the social parameter, α. An experiment conducted by Ma *et al.* [10] showed that the value of α has a marked impact on the prediction accuracy. Setting α extremely high can degrade the prediction accuracy as users are fully influenced by their friends (i.e. users are predicted to prefer every venue that their friends like). Following [10], we vary $0.000001 \leq \alpha \leq 1$, multiplying α by 10 at each iteration. For each fold, the α that minimised RMSE on the validation set is used for testing. For word embeddings, we use the Word2Vec tool[2], training a skip-gram model [11] using the default settings (window size 5 and $k = 100$ dimensions[3]) on the Yelp dataset. We choose the skip-gram model over the continuous-bag-of-words (CBOW) model as Mikolov *et al.* [12] reported that the skip-gram model performs better than or equally to the CBOW model.

[2] https://code.google.com/archive/p/word2vec/ [3] Initial experiments showed no marked change in prediction accuracy for larger k.

Table 2: Prediction accuracy in terms of MAE and RMSE of various approaches. Percentage differences of prediction accuracy are calculated with respect to the best performing result, which is highlighted in bold.

Metrics	MF_N	MF_P	MF	VMF	SoReg	BoWReg	$DeepReg_{MF}$	SVD	TrustSVD	$DeepReg_{SVD}$
MAE	1.3881	1.5924	1.1640	1.2198	1.1260	1.1004	**1.0781**	1.1067	1.0292	**1.0077**
Δ	22.34%	32.30%	7.39%	11.62%	4.26%	2.03%		8.94%	2.09%	
RMSE	1.8994	2.0643	1.5243	1.5006	1.3870	1.4354	**1.3456**	1.4357	1.3034	**1.2504**
Δ	29.16%	34.82%	11.72%	10.33%	2.99%	6.26%		12.90%	4.06%	

4. EXPERIMENTAL RESULTS

Table 2 reports the rating prediction accuracy, in terms of MAE and RMSE, of our proposed DeepReg and other baselines. The left hand side of the table compares systems based upon MF, while the right-hand side contains SVD-based approaches; as explained below, DeepReg can be implemented upon both MF and SVD, which we denote with subscripts, i.e. $DeepReg_{MF}$. Firstly, we note that the relative prediction accuracy of the baselines on the Yelp dataset are consistent with the results reported by Ma *et al.* [10] and Guo *et al.* [4], namely that SoReg outperforms MF_N and MF_P, and TrustSVD outperforms SVD, respectively.

Next, from the left portion of Table 2, we observe that $DeepReg_{MF}$, our proposed social-textual regularisation model using word embeddings, outperforms all MF baselines for both MAE and RMSE. In particular, our proposed regularisation model can enhance the prediction accuracy of the traditional MF (MF) by 7% for MAE and 11% for RMSE. These imply that social information and textual content of comments are useful in enhancing the accuracy of rating prediction. Moreover, by comparing $DeepReg_{MF}$ and SoReg, the MAE and RMSE results show that minimising the distance between latent factors of friends based on the semantic similarity of their comments is more effective than estimating user similarity solely based upon similar ratings (i.e. PCC, as per Eq. (5)). Comparing $DeepReg_{MF}$ with BoWReg, we find that the prediction accuracy is again enhanced (2% for MAE and 6% for RMSE). This shows that the word embeddings offer a more useful, semantic space for modelling comments by users upon venues, which results in a more effective regularisation. Although the improvements in Table 2 are relatively small, we note that small improvements in MAE and RMSE can lead to marked improvements in the quality of recommendations in practice [8]. Moreover, the observed performances are evaluated over 2.2M ratings. Naturally, we believe that refined word embedding models (e.g. obtained by varying window size or background training dataset) may provide further improvements.

Finally, the right hand side of Table 2 reports the application of our proposed regularisation model to an approach based upon SVD. This allows comparison with TrustSVD [3], a state-of-the-art MF that considers social information built upon SVD. We note that DeepReg can be easily applied to SVD by just replacing the loss function of MF in Eq. (9) with the loss function of SVD[4]. On analysing the right hand side of Table 2, we find that these implementations are consistent with results reported by Guo *et al.* [4], as TrustSVD outperforms SVD by ~7-10% on both metrics. Moreover, SVD with our proposed regularisation model outperforms TrustSVD by 2% and 4% on MAE and RMSE, respectively. These results imply that not only friends can influence each others, but that the semantic properties of comments left by friends also play an important role in generating more effective matrix factorisation models.

[4] For more details of SVD's loss function, see [7].

5. CONCLUSIONS

In this paper, we explored whether social network information and textual content of comments can be leveraged to enhance the accuracy of rating prediction. We proposed a social-textual regularisation model that seamlessly incorporates both the user's social network and comments as a source of evidence, to minimise the latent factors of friends based on their semantic similarity. Our comprehensive experiments on a public dataset of 500k users and 2.2M ratings demonstrated the usefulness of our proposed regularisation model in enhancing the prediction accuracy of several MF-based approaches, and can outperform the state-of-the-art for social regularisation (SoReg) by 3-4%, and the state-of-the-art for social matrix factorisation (TrustSVD) by 2-4%.

6. REFERENCES

[1] X. Fu and X. Li. From movie reviews to restaurants recommendation. Technical report, Stanford University, 2015. http://stanford.io/2aB0T0f.

[2] G. Guo, J. Zhang, Z. Sun, and N. Yorke-Smith. LibRec: A Java library for recommender systems. In *Proc. of UMAP*, 2015.

[3] G. Guo, J. Zhang, and N. Yorke-Smith. A novel Bayesian similarity measure for recommender systems. In *Proc. of IJCAI*, 2013.

[4] G. Guo, J. Zhang, and N. Yorke-Smith. TrustSVD: Collaborative filtering with both the explicit and implicit influence of user trust and of item ratings. In *Proc. of AAAI*, 2015.

[5] L. Hu, A. Sun, and Y. Liu. Your neighbors affect your ratings: on geographical neighborhood influence to rating prediction. In *Proc. of SIGIR*, 2014.

[6] J. Huang, S. Rogers, and E. Joo. Improving restaurants by extracting subtopics from Yelp reviews. *iConference (Social Media Expo)*, 2014.

[7] Y. Koren. Factorization meets the neighborhood: a multifaceted collaborative filtering model. In *Proc. of SIGKDD*, 2008.

[8] Y. Koren. Factor in the neighbors: Scalable and accurate collaborative filtering. *Transactions on Knowledge Discovery from Data (TKDD)*, 4(1), 2010.

[9] D. D. Lee and H. S. Seung. Learning the parts of objects by non-negative matrix factorization. *Nature*, 401(6755), 1999.

[10] H. Ma, D. Zhou, C. Liu, M. R. Lyu, and I. King. Recommender systems with social regularization. In *Proc. of WSDM*, 2011.

[11] T. Mikolov, K. Chen, G. Corrado, and J. Dean. Efficient estimation of word representations in vector space. *arXiv:1301.3781*, 2013.

[12] T. Mikolov, I. Sutskever, K. Chen, G. S. Corrado, and J. Dean. Distributed representations of words and phrases and their compositionality. In *Proc. of NIPS*, 2013.

[13] C. Musto, G. Semeraro, M. De Gemmis, and P. Lops. Word embedding techniques for content-based recommender systems: an empirical evaluation. In *Proc. of RecSys*, 2015.

[14] M. G. Ozsoy. From word embeddings to item recommendation. *arXiv:1601.01356*, 2016.

[15] R. Salakhutdinov and A. Mnih. Bayesian probabilistic matrix factorization using Markov chain Monte Carlo. In *Proc. of ICML*, 2008.

Improving Search Results with Prior Similar Queries

Yashar Moshfeghi
School of Computing Science
University of Glasgow
Glasgow, UK
Yashar.Moshfeghi@glasgow.ac.uk

Kristiyan Velinov
School of Computing Science
University of Glasgow
Glasgow, UK
Kristiyan.Velinov@glasgow.ac.uk

Peter Triantafillou
School of Computing Science
University of Glasgow
Glasgow, UK
Peter.Triantafillou@glasgow.ac.uk

ABSTRACT

This paper describes a novel approach to re-ranking search engine result pages (SERP): Its fundamental principle is to re-rank results to a given query, based on exploiting evidence gathered from past similar search queries. Our approach is inspired by collaborative filtering, with the main challenge being to find the set of similar queries, while also taking efficiency into account. In particular, our approach aims to address this challenge by proposing a combination of a similarity graph and a locality sensitive hashing scheme. We construct a set of features from our similarity graph and build a prediction model using the Hoeffding decision tree algorithm. We have evaluated the effectiveness of our model in terms of P@1, MAP@10, and nDCG@10, using the Yandex Data Challenge data set. We have compared the performance of our model against two baselines, namely, the Yandex initial ranking and the decision tree model learnt on the same set of features when extracted based on query repetition (i.e. excluding the evidence of similar queries in our approach). Our results reveal that the proposed approach consistently and (statistically) significantly outperforms both baselines.

Keywords: SERP, Collaborative Filtering, Graph

1. INTRODUCTION

Nowadays, a key challenge faced by search engines is to re-rank the results presented to searchers according to their current and long-term interactions with the system. The reward can be a significantly improved search engine result page (SERP) that could better satisfy searchers' information needs (IN). There are multiple approaches to provide custom tailored search results to users relying on training complex ranking models [15, 20] or relying on training classifiers [16]. In addition to these important steps towards improving the ranking of a SERP, we offer a new key insight, namely that, first, the above approaches only use a small subset of the available information in the log data, i.e. the information that pertains to a given query and its repetitions, (e.g. the work by Volkovs [18]). Secondly, that by focusing only on query repetitions, such approaches miss valuable information, which can be accumulated from *similar* queries. This issue is even more important when we are facing a cold start problem, i.e. a given query has not been issued before. In this paper, we propose to construct our feature set not only from the information available for a given query and its past repeated instances, but also from the information available for its similar queries, which in turn can alleviate the cold start problem described above.

The use of log analysis in particular past queries for better satisfying searchers' IN has been widely studied and there have been numerous proposals in the literature on how to utilise them effectively [17]. For instance, the uses of past query log analysis on user search behaviour and the analysis of short-term session based logs has been shown to successfully recommend queries to searchers, as illustrated by Baeza-Yates et al. [2]. Craswell and Szummer [7] show the effectiveness of using random walks on the query-click graph [3] to provide query recommendations. Others have looked at using the query rewrites observed in a query log [19] or using searchers' history by preferring recent queries over older ones [4] or considering both short- and long-term interests of searchers [12] for query recommendation. In this paper, our aim is to optimise re-ranking the search results by analysing the log information available not only about a query, but also about other similar queries, utilising query graph structure.

In a query graph structure, nodes are queries, and edges represents an association between two queries. The information used to construct the edges defines the type of the graph [1] which can be a word graph (queries having the same words), session graph (queries belonging to the same session) [5], URL cover graph (the same URLs in the list of queries results being clicked), URL link graph (the two clicked URLs having a link between themselves), or link graph (the two URLs having a set of common terms in their content) [1, 4]. In contrast to the above, in our approach, an edge is constructed between two queries purely based on the overlap of the documents in their SERPs, regardless of documents' content, link or user's click-action. This approach relies on the observation that highly similar queries have highly overlapping document sets. In this way, we can also deal with datasets where query terms are anonymised and synonym detection is impossible. Therefore, the following research question emerges: *can the use of our query graph, referred to as similarity graph, in feature generation improve the performance of re-ranking models and how?* The rest of the paper is organised as follows: the approach is described in Section

CIKM'16 , October 24-28, 2016, Indianapolis, IN, USA

DOI: http://dx.doi.org/10.1145/2983323.2983890

2, Section 3 and 4 discuss our experimental methodology and results respectively, and we conclude in Section 5.

2. EXPLOITING PRIOR SIMILAR QUERIES

In order to construct our similarity graph, we first present every node in the graph with two attributes: (i) a query used for comparison and (ii) a list of all queries which contain the same list of documents as the one used for comparison, i.e. repeated queries. We then compute the similarity between two queries based on the number of common documents between them. Therefore, a key task of our proposed approach is to identify similar queries for a given query. Our proposed method rests on two pillars. The first pillar, is a *similarity query graph* $G = (V, E)$, over all previously issued queries from the log data; specifically, $V = \{q_1^s, q_2^s, .., q_n^s\}$ and $\{q_i^s, q_j^s\} \in E \Leftrightarrow sim(q_i^i, q_j^i) >= \theta$, where q_i^s is a *query super-node tuple*, which intuitively embodies all query instances/repetitions, formally, such that $q_i^s = (q_i^i, R_i)$ and q_i^i is an instance of the query, and R_i is the set of all repeating instances of q_i^i. The second pillar is an algorithm which, for a given instance q_i^i, walks/searches over the graph to find the set S of all instances q_k^i, such that $S = \{q_k^i | sim(q_i^i, q_k^i) >= \theta)\}$. Given this set we proceed with generating our feature set. Given that we compare queries based on their sets of documents on SERP we use the MinHash signature on those to find all highly similar queries and build the graph. We use the same approach for finding a starting point of the graph search.

2.1 MinHash Signature

Once constructed, the graph offers the benefit of quickly finding all similar nodes given a starting point q_k^s. However, the creation of the similarity graph is associated with $O(n^2)$ computational complexity, which is high. Furthermore, finding the search starting point has a worst case complexity of $O(n)$, which defeats the purpose of the graph as one could use the iteration to find all similar nodes. The solution to these issues was inspired by the work presented by Das et al. [8] where the authors cluster users based on the Jaccard similarity [11] between their click action sets by applying a min-wise independent permutations locality sensitive hashing scheme or MinHash [6]. The MinHash scheme can be seen as a probabilistic clustering technique, as the probability to produce the same hash for two sets is equal to the Jaccard similarity between the two.

Using such a technique, for a given query a signature is generated by concatenating several min-hashes. Each MinHash band, stores a list of potentially similar nodes for a given signature. These MinHash bands are populated and used while building the graph. As pointed by Das et al. [8] multiple bands increase the recall of a search because every single one presents a new chance to find a match. In this way the precision of a search is increased because the chance of producing several identical hashes for very different sets becomes very low.

When a new query arrives, its signature is computed for band one and if the band contains an exact match this node is used for the beginning of the graph search. If there is no exact match, the most similar node is kept and the same process repeats for the next band until no other bands remain. If there is no exact match by the end of the list of maps, then the most similar node is used for the search.

Prediction Model: In order to re-rank the SERPs, we extent the approach proposed in Volkovs [18] by constructing our feature set not only from the information available for a given query and its past repeated instances, but also from the information available for its similar queries extracted from similarity graph (see Section 2.1). The list of created features are as follows: (1) total/average/maximum/minimum relevance for a document; (2) maximum/average Jaccard similarity for a document between queries for the scenarios where it was clicked/missed/shown/ skipped; (3) the number of times a document was clicked/ missed/shown/ skipped; (4) the number of times a document was clicked/ missed/shown/skipped discounted by rank; and (5) initial document's position on SERP. Given the final generated set of features, we then predict the ranking of the SERP, using the standard machine learning technique of Hoeffding decision tree algorithm [9][1].

3. EXPERIMENTAL SET-UP

Test Collection & Evaluation Protocols: In order to investigate our research question, we partition and preprocess the Yandex log file[2] to create the training and test data sets. The training set for all experiments consists of the queries from the first four days of the Yandex log file. For testing the effectiveness our approach, we created three test collections each of which contains queries for one of the next three days of the same log file, i.e. day five, six and seven of the Yandex logs. The aim is to investigate how the predictive power of our model would be affected as a function of time passed after the training period. Each of these three test collections then was further divided into two test groups: the first test group contained only those queries, which existed in our training set (i.e. the similarity graph). The second test group contained all queries including those queries, which did not exist in the training set. The aim is to investigate how the predictive power of our model would be affected when the model is facing the cold start problem.

Queries that did not have click-through action were removed since they would not contribute to our experiment. We then calculated the document relevance score[3] in the range of 0 to 2 depending on the dwell time for a given document as described in Yandex 2013 Re-ranking Challenge (i.e. 0 if less than 50 units, 1 if between 50 and 399, and 2 if above 399 or the click action is the last for the session).

Evaluation Metrics: To measure the performance of the models, we used three different metrics. First, we report a measure of the Normalized Discounted Cumulative Gain at cut off 10 (NDCG@10) [13] for a list of sessions, since this metric was suggested by the Yandex data challenge. We also report Precision at cut off 1 (P@1) [13] for a list of sessions, since the accuracy of the first rank position in SERP is very important. We finally report Mean Average Precision at cut off 10 (MAP@10) [13] for a list of sessions.

Evaluation Methodology: In order to investigate the research questions, we tested the effect of two parameters that have great influence on the performance of the proposed approach, i.e. similarity threshold and graph node capacity (maximum number of queries per node). In this

[1] Implemented in the Weka machine learning tool kit (http://www.cs.waikato.ac.nz/ml/weka/)

[2] https://www.kaggle.com/c/yandex-personalized-web-search-challenge/data

[3] https://www.kaggle.com/c/yandex-personalized-web-search-challenge/details/evaluation

	Day Five Test Collection			Day Six Test Collection			Day Seven Test Collection		
Experiment	P@1	MAP@10	nDCG@10	P@1	MAP@10	nDCG@10	P@1	MAP@10	nDCG@10
Yandex	0.7001	0.0790	0.8198	0.7044	0.0799	0.8234	0.7218	0.0801	0.8327
S.9-C1	0.7204 (2.89%)‡	0.0811 (2.65%)‡	0.8294 (1.17%)‡	0.7182 (1.95%)‡	0.0814 (1.87%)‡	0.8298 (0.77%)‡	0.7383 (2.28%)‡	0.0818 (2.12%)‡	0.8407 (0.96%)‡
S.7-C1000	**0.7307 (4.37%)‡**	**0.0821 (3.92%)‡**	**0.8343 (1.76%)‡**	**0.7303 (3.67%)‡**	**0.0827 (3.5%)‡**	**0.8356 (1.48%)‡**	**0.7477 (3.58%)‡**	**0.0829 (3.49%)‡**	**0.8451 (1.48%)‡**

Table 1: P@1, MAP@10, and nDCG@10 for all queries in the similarity graph.

	Day Five Test Collection			Day Six Test Collection			Day Seven Test Collection		
Experiment	P@1	MAP@10	nDCG@10	P@1	MAP@10	nDCG@10	P@1	MAP@10	nDCG@10
Yandex	0.5933	0.0748	0.7527	0.5922	0.0750	0.7509	0.6028	0.0751	0.7574
S.9-C1	0.5994 (1.02%)‡	0.0754 (0.8%)‡	0.7556 (0.38%)‡	0.5961 (0.65%)‡	0.0754 (0.53%)‡	0.7527 (0.23%)‡	0.6072 (0.72%)‡	0.0756 (0.66%)‡	0.7595 (0.27%)‡
S.7-C1000	**0.6025 (1.55%)‡**	**0.0757 (1.2%)‡**	**0.7571 (0.58%)‡**	**0.5997 (1.26%)‡**	**0.0758 (1.06%)‡**	**0.7544 (0.46%)‡**	**0.6098 (1.16%)‡**	**0.0758 (0.93%)‡**	**0.7607 (0.43%)‡**

Table 2: P@1, MAP@10, and nDCG@10 for all queries including cold start ones.

paper, for each dataset, we tried several different quantities of graph node capacity, namely 1, 10, 100, and 1000. The maximum number of graph node capacity was set to 1000 for computational reasons. We also tried several different quantities for the similarity threshold, varying from 0.6 to 1.0 with the step of 0.1. While graph search depth could also contribute to the end results, it was fixed to 10, a value at which it is bound to return all similar nodes. That way we can isolate the contribution of the novel aspects of the system. We tested the performance of our models with different combinations of the parameters mentioned above on our test collections.

Each run is denoted by concatenating its corresponding parameter setting, i.e. SyCz. Sy indicates the similarity threshold, i.e. S stands for similarity threshold to associate a link between two nodes and y defines its value. Cz represents the graph node capacity, i.e. C stands for node capacity (the maximum number of queries stored per node) and z stands for the respective value. Due to limited space, we do not include the complete results, but instead report the best performing scenarios.

Baseline Models: We used two different baselines. First, for comparison we report the performance of the original Yandex ranking (identified as Yandex) along with our model depending on the combination scenario (identified as SyCz). Second, as a stronger baseline, we report the performance of a decision tree model over the Volkovs [18] features (identified as Volkovs) extracted by excluding our proposed similarity graph. This was achieved by setting the similarity threshold to 1.0 meaning that the queries would be linked if and only if they are identical, i.e. the graph would have no edges which in turn results in excluding the information regarding similar queries when generating features. The following section discusses our experimental results.

4. RESULTS

Tables 1 and 2 show the effectiveness of our models compared to initial Yandex rankings for the P@1, MAP@10, and nDCG@10 measures, for the three test collections (Day Five, Six and Seven) and two different levels of sparsity (excluding and including the cold start problem). Every result line in these tables is associated with an experiment scenario whose parameters are encoded in the *Experiment* column. We performed a paired t-test between measures obtained for each user to check the significance of the difference with the baseline (Yandex in Table 1 and 2). We use (†) and (‡) to denote the fact that a model had results different from that of the baseline with the confidence levels ($p < 0.05$) and ($p < 0.01$) respectively.

Main Results: With respect to models based on features generated over highly similar queries, we observed that the proposed model consistently and significantly outperformed original ranking provided by Yandex (shown in Table 1). In particular our approach has the most impact on the top rank position of the SERP (i.e. P@1) shown to be favoured by searchers [10]. This shows that substantial performance improvements can be achieved by integrating evidences gathered from highly similar queries for re-ranking SERP.

Our findings indicate that by increasing the capacity of each node for keeping repeated queries information, we achieve higher effectiveness in terms of our evaluation metrics. However, this can have a negative effect on the efficiency of the building the MinHash signature (described in Section 2.1). Since MinHash signature process can be performed off-line, this effect of building the MinHash signatures in the efficiency of the model can be reduced. As future work, we aim to estimate such an effect.

In addition, we can see that the model considering lower node capacity, require queries to be highly similar (i.e. the best performing model was when the similarity threshold was set to 0.9) and as the node capacity increases, the best consistently performing scenario is the one that considers lower similarity threshold (i.e. 0.7). We finally observed that while the performance of our model gradually decreases as a function of time, the model consistently and significantly outperformed original ranking provided by Yandex (Column "Day Seven Test Collection" in Table 1). This means that while it is still significant, as the time passes the effectiveness of the predicted ranking decreases.

Cold start. In Table 2 we present how our proposed model performs in the case of the cold start problem. There is a consistent and significant increase of effectiveness in in the ranking of SERP over the baseline (original ranking provided by Yandex) and this holds for all our evaluation metrics. While the improvement is smaller when we also consider cold start scenario, we observed similar performance behaviour in terms of varying node capacity and similarity threshold. We also observed that time had a similar effect on the predictive power of our model.

Comparison to Volkovs Model. Figure 1 shows the effectiveness of our models compared to a harder baseline i.e. Volkovs model. All result values in the figures are in comparison to their improvements over original ranking provided by Yandex for the P@1, MAP@10, and nDCG@10 measures, for the two test collections (Day Five and Seven) and two different levels of sparsity (excluding and including cold start problem). We denote this difference with Δ, e.g. ΔP@1, ΔMAP@3, etc. We performed a paired t-test between the Δ obtained over the metrics for our model to check the significance of this difference with the Δ obtained from Volkovs model. Our results indicate that the use of features generated over highly similar queries consistently and (statistically) significantly outperforms the models based on query repetitions, i.e. Volkovs model (with $p < 0.01$). In particular, we observed that the decision tree model consistently favoured features, which are generated over similar queries, especially in the node capacity range between 1 and 100, while when at capacity 1000 in some cases the decision tree model also favoured features based on repeating queries. These results suggest that models based on repeated queries require enough previous evidences (i.e. repetition of queries) to be effective.

Figure 1: Differences of P@1, MAP@10, and nDCG@10 to Yandex Baseline

All queries in the similarity graph

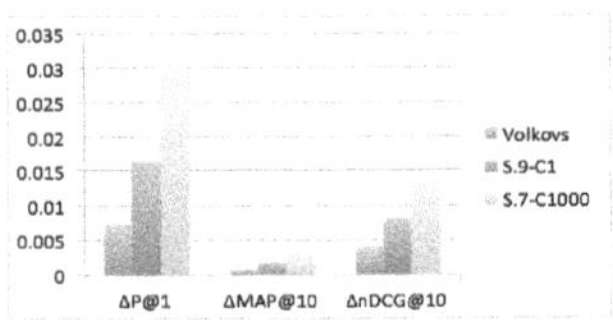

(a) Day Five Test Collection

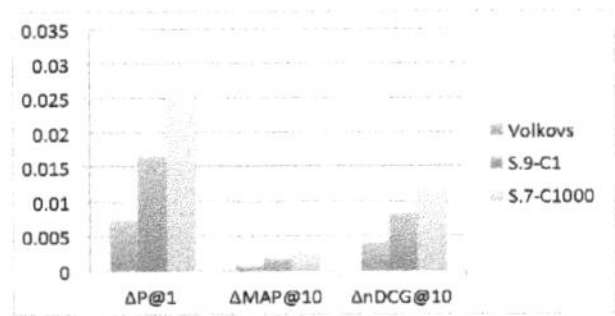

(b) Day Seven Test Collection

All queries including cold start ones.

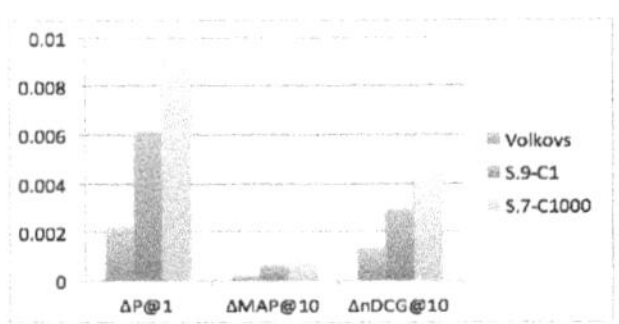

(c) Day Five Test Collection

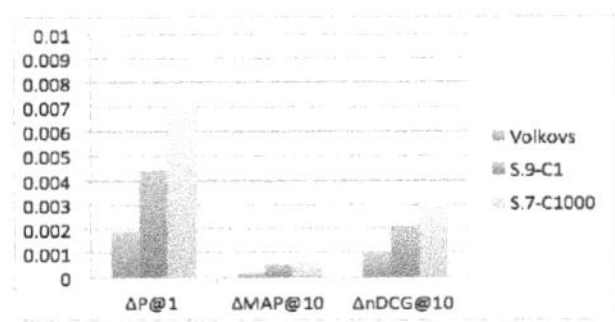

(d) Day Seven Test Collection

5. CONCLUSIONS

This paper described a novel approach to re-rank search engine result page (SERP) by taking into account evidences gathered from prior search queries which are similar to a given query. Our proposed approach is inspired by collaborative filtering, where we re-ranked SERP for a given query by taking into account evidences gathered from prior similar queries. The main challenge was to find the set of similar queries while also taking into account the effectiveness/efficiency of the proposed approach. We tackled this problem by proposing a combination of a similarity graph and a locality sensitive hashing scheme. We then generated features described in Volkovs [18] from our similarity graph and evaluated the gains of such features by using Hoeffding decision tree algorithm. Using the Yandex Data Challenge data set, we extensively evaluated our proposed model, pitted against two baselines, namely the Yandex initial ranking and a decision tree model learnt on Volkovs [18] features extracted based on query repetitions only. The effectiveness of our model was evaluated in terms of P@1, MAP@10, and nDCG@10. The preliminary results of our experiments showed that we were able to (statistically) significantly improve the effectiveness of the mature Yandex SERP, with up to 4.37% for P@1 shown to be favoured by searchers [10] and with up to 1.76% for nDCG@10. While the improvement may appear low, please keep in mind that the results presented for the first [14] and third [18] best performing group participating in the challenge introduce a 1.99% and 1.69% improvement over Yandex initial ranking for nDCG@10 metric using the entire training set. Our approach managed to achieve a 1.76% improvement for nDCG@10 while using only the first four days of the training set. Our results also show that despite a gradual decrease in the performance, the learned model was still able to outperform Yandex initial ranking as time passes. In addition, similar performance improvement was observed over the more advanced baseline (i.e. Volkovs model). Finally, our positive results encourage us to further explore models that utilise features extracted from highly similar prior queries to improve re-ranking performance and the potential of our proposed approach.

Acknowledgement: This work was supported by the Economic and Social Research Council [grant number ES/L011921/1].

6. REFERENCES

[1] R. Baeza-Yates. Graphs from Search Engine Queries. In *SOFSEM '07*, pages 1–8, 2007.

[2] R. Baeza-Yates, C. Hurtado, and M. Mendoza. Query Recommendation using Query Logs in Search Engines. In *Current Trends in Database Technology-EDBT' 04 Workshops*, pages 588–596, 2004.

[3] D. Beeferman and A. Berger. Agglomerative Clustering of a Search Engine Query Log. In *KDD '00*, pages 407–416, 2000.

[4] P. Boldi, F. Bonchi, C. Castillo, D. Donato, and S. Vigna. Query Suggestions Using Query-flow Graphs. In *WSCD '09*, pages 56–63, 2009.

[5] P. Boldi, F. Bonchi, C. Castillo, and S. Vigna. From "Dango" to "Japanese Cakes": Query Reformulation Models and Patterns. In *Web Intelligence*, pages 183–190, 2009.

[6] A. Z. Broder, M. Charikar, A. M. Frieze, and M. Mitzenmacher. Min-Wise Independent Permutations. *Journal of Computer and System Sciences*, 60(3):630–659, 2000.

[7] N. Craswell and M. Szummer. Random Walks on the Click Graph. In *SIGIR '07*, pages 239–246, 2007.

[8] A. S. Das, M. Datar, A. Garg, and S. Rajaram. Google News Personalization: Scalable Online Collaborative Filtering. In *WWW'07*, pages 271–280. ACM, 2007.

[9] G. Hulten, L. Spencer, and P. Domingos. Mining Time-Changing Data Streams. In *SIGKDD'01*, pages 97–106. ACM Press, 2001.

[10] T. Joachims, L. Granka, B. Pan, H. Hembrooke, F. Radlinski, and G. Gay. Evaluating the Accuracy of Implicit Feedback from Clicks and Query Reformulations in Web Search. *ACM Trans. Inf. Syst.*, 25(2), apr 2007.

[11] J. Leskovec, A. Rajaraman, and J. D. Ullman. *Mining of Massive Datasets*. Cambridge University Press, 2 edition, 2014.

[12] J. Luxenburger, S. Elbassuoni, and G. Weikum. Matching Task Profiles and User Needs in Personalized Web Search. In *CIKM '08*, pages 689–698, 2008.

[13] C. D. Manning, P. Raghavan, H. Schütze, et al. *Introduction to Information Retrieval*, volume 1. Cambridge university press Cambridge, 2008.

[14] P. Masurel, K. Lefévre-Hasegawa, C. Bourguignat, and M. Scordia. Dataiku's Solution to Yandex's Personalized Web Search Challenge. In *WSDM' 14 Workshop on Log-based Personalization*, 2014.

[15] M. Shokouhi, R. W. White, P. Bennett, and F. Radlinski. Fighting Search Engine Amnesia: Reranking Repeated Results. In *SIGIR'13*, pages 273–282. ACM, 2013.

[16] G. Song. Point-Wise Approach for Yandex Personalized Web Search Challenge. Technical report, IEEE, 2014.

[17] S.-K. Song and S. H. Myaeng. A Novel Term Weighting Scheme Based on Discrimination Power Obtained from Past Retrieval Results. *IPM*, 48(5):919–930, Sept. 2012.

[18] M. Volkovs. Context Models For Web Search Personalization. In *WSDM' 14 Workshop on Log-based Personalization*, 2014.

[19] R. W. White, M. Bilenko, and S. Cucerzan. Leveraging Popular Destinations to Enhance Web Search Interaction. *ACM Trans. Web*, 2(3):16:1–16:30, July 2008.

[20] R. W. White, W. Chu, A. Hassan, X. He, Y. Song, and H. Wang. Enhancing Personalized Search by Mining and Modeling Task Behavior. In *WWW'13*, pages 1411–1420, 2013.

The Solitude of Relevant Documents in the Pool

Aldo Lipani[1] Mihai Lupu[1] Evangelos Kanoulas[2] Allan Hanbury[1]

[1]Inst. of Software Technology & Interactive Systems, Vienna University of Technology, Vienna, Austria
{lipani, lupu, hanbury}@ifs.tuwien.ac.at

[2]Informatics Institute, University of Amsterdam, Amsterdam, The Netherlands
e.kanoulas@uva.nl

ABSTRACT

Pool bias is a well understood problem of test-collection based benchmarking in information retrieval. The pooling method itself is designed to identify all relevant documents. In practice, 'all' translates to 'as many as possible given some budgetary constraints' and the problem persists, albeit mitigated. Recently, methods to address this pool bias for previously created test collections have been proposed, for the evaluation measure precision at cut-off ($P@n$). Analyzing previous methods, we make the empirical observation that the distribution of the probability of providing new *relevant* documents to the pool, over the runs, is log-normal (when the pooling strategy is fixed depth at cut-off). We use this observation to calculate a prior probability of providing new relevant documents, which we then use in a pool bias estimator that improves upon previous estimates of precision at cut-off. Through extensive experimental results, covering 15 test collections, we show that the proposed bias correction method is the new state of the art, providing the closest estimates yet when compared to the original pool.

Keywords

Pool bias, $P@n$, test collections, TREC

1. INTRODUCTION

The pool bias refers to an undesirable side effect caused by the use of the *pooling method*. This bias manifests itself by the discounting of Information Retrieval (IR) systems when tested on previously built test collections, due to the retrieval of potentially relevant but non-judged documents [4].

An IR test collection is composed of: a collection of documents, a set of topics, and ideally a complete set of paired relations between topics and documents called relevance assessments, which indicate whether a document is either relevant or non-relevant for a given topic. Soon in the history of IR, with the explosion in size of the document collections and therefore of the number of relevance assessments required, the building of such test collections became impractical; to address this issue, the pooling method was introduced [9].

CIKM'16 , October 24-28, 2016, Indianapolis, IN, USA

© 2016 ACM. ISBN 978-1-4503-4073-1/16/10... $15.00

DOI: http://dx.doi.org/10.1145/2983323.2983891

The main advantage of the pooling method is to limit the number of relevance assessments through the use of previously collected search results provided by various retrieval systems. The first introduced and most commonly used pooling strategy is the *fixed-depth at n*. This strategy consists in selecting the top n documents retrieved by each retrieval system, then collecting them in a set, called the pool, which later will be fully judged. Although its main limitation is due the introduced incompleteness of the relevance assessments, as pointed out by Spärck Jones [3], the aim of the pooling method is not to find all the relevant documents but an unbiased sample of them. However, this is not an easy problem because, in the absence of full evaluation, and in the presence of millions of potentially relevant documents, there is no guarantee that a future retrieval method will not retrieve completely different yet relevant documents.

There are three ways to mitigate the pool bias: 1) increasing the depth of the pool, 2) increasing the number of topics, which would reduce the variance and, 3) increasing the number of pooled runs, which should increase the diversity of the pooled documents. Each of them has as effect an increment on the number of judgments to be performed. However, only the first two solutions are directly controllable by the test collection builder, leaving the third to the participation of the IR community in solving the challenge for which the test collection is going to be built.

To tackle the pool bias issue, the IR community has pursued two research paths, one developing pooling strategies aimed at mitigating the pool bias when creating new test collections [2, 8, 7] and the other, developing pool bias estimators aimed at correcting the observed pool bias on existing test collections. Witnessing an explosion in the number of test collections developed each year that use the pooling method with fixed-depth at n pooling strategy and an increasing bias due to an increasing trend in the creation of test collections for niche domain-specific IR, where a required minimal participation is usually not met, in this paper we extend the work done on the latter research path. We develop a new pool bias estimator for the metric Precision at cut-off ($P@n$) based on empirical observations. There are two reasons for working with such a simple metric: there is an increasing demand from practitioners for metrics that make 'sense' [1], and it is a corner stone for other more complex metrics.

2. BACKGROUND

Webber and Park [10] introduced a method to correct the pool bias, which they tested on Rank-Biased-Precision at cut-off but claimed to work also with $P@n$. This method adds to the score of a new run a coefficient equal to the mean difference, indicated with $\delta P@n$, between the score obtained when a run, initially part of the pool

R_p, is pooled and not-pooled:

$$\delta P@n(r_p) = P@n(r_p, Q^{R_p}) - P@n(r_p, Q^{R_p \setminus \{r_p\}}) \quad (1)$$

The correction coefficient for a run ($r_u \notin R_p$) is the expectation:

$$\operatorname*{E}_{r_p \in R_p} [\delta P@n(r_p)] \quad (2)$$

where Q^{R_p} is the set of judged documents created using the set of pooled runs R_p. This approach assumes that any given new run is sampled from the same distribution as the pooled ones. This is of course not always true, because runs are selected based on their performance by human intervention. A limitation of this approach is that it computes a coefficient that is constant and therefore does not depend on the actual status of the biased run. Another limitation of this approach is that the correction is not bounded by the tested run, thereby we may have a score that may exceed the upper limit of the $P@n$ co-domain, which is defined as $[0, 1]$.

Lipani et al. [5] presented a more sophisticated method for correcting $P@n$ that outperforms the Webber approach. It is based on measuring the effect of the new run on the pooled runs in terms of $P@n$, and anti-precision at cut-off ($\overline{P}@n$, the ratio of non relevant document over the cut-off n). The effects are observed via the application of a merging function between the new run and the pooled runs, where the function changes the rank of the documents in the pooled runs based on the shared documents with the new run. After having computed these quantities, an indicator is calculated based on them, and used to trigger or not the correction method. If triggered, the correction is equal to the ratio between the non-judged documents over n times the maximum likelihood estimator for the probability of relevance of the non-judged documents in the run.

3. ANALYSIS

In this section we analyze empirically the assumptions about the Webber approach [10]. The mean in Eq. (2) is valid under the assumption that the distribution of $\delta P@n$, as defined in Eq. (1), is normal. This assumption implies that runs are similar to each other, which is of course not true. To empirically demonstrate the groundlessness of this hypothesis, we observe in Fig. 1, on the top, that the distribution of the $\delta P@n$ is not normally distributed. This makes the estimate for the correction biased for a new run because the distribution of runs is not centered on the calculated mean.

To find a better estimate, we look at the ratio between the number of uniquely identified relevant documents discovered by pooling the run r_p and the number of non-judged documents that the run would have if it had not been pooled. This quantity may be interpreted as the probability of the non-judged documents of the run to be relevant:

$$\begin{aligned} &P(d \in [r_p]_1^n \setminus Q^{R_p \setminus \{r_p\}}, d \in Q_+^{R_p}) = \\ &= \frac{P@n(r_p, Q^{R_p}) - P@n(r_p, Q^{R_p \setminus \{r_p\}})}{1 - \left(P@n(r_p, Q^{R_p \setminus \{r_p\}}) + \overline{P}@n(r_p, Q^{R_p \setminus \{r_p\}})\right)} = \\ &= \frac{\delta P@n(r_p)}{\bar{k}'@n(r_p)} \end{aligned} \quad (3)$$

where we use the notation introduced by Lipani et al. [5]: $\bar{k}'@n$ is the ratio between the number of non-judged documents and n when r_p is not in the pool; $\overline{P}@n$ is the anti-precision at cut-off, also known in statistics as the false discovery rate, the ratio between the number of non-relevant documents and n; and $Q_+^{R_p}$ is the set of pooled documents that are relevant. We observe empirically that its distribution is log-normal. Indicating with X this distribution and with Y its log-transformation $Y = \ln(X)$, Y is

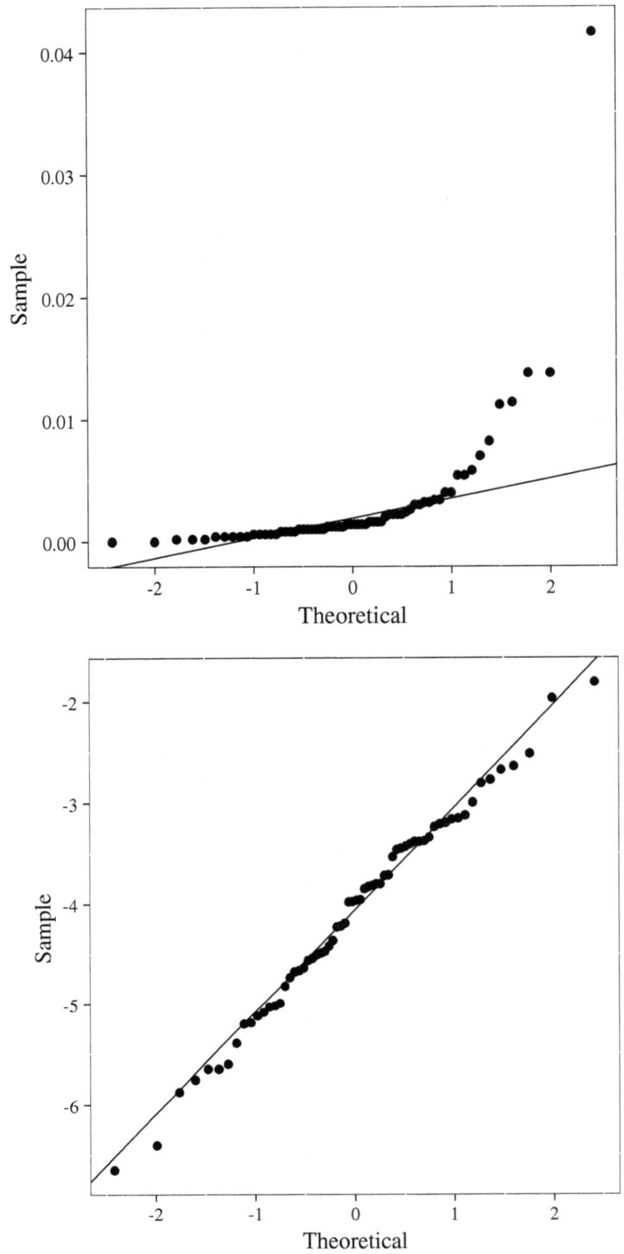

Figure 1: Q-Q Plots of a normal distribution against, on the top, the distribution of δP, as defined in Eq. (1) and, on the bottom, the log transformation of the distribution of the probability of providing new relevant documents to the pool $\delta P/\bar{k}$, as defined in Eq. (3), for the test collection Ad Hoc 8.

normally distributed. In the Q-Q plot in Fig. 1 on the bottom, we observe how the theoretical normal distribution correlates with the sample distribution. To calculate the mean of the new estimate, we compute the mean of the distribution Y and then transform it back to the domain of the distribution X, which leads to the geometric mean of the X:

$$e^{\mathrm{E}[\ln(X)]} = e^{\mathrm{E}[Y]} = \sqrt[|Y|]{\prod_{y \in Y} y} = \mathrm{GM}[X] \quad (4)$$

where GM is the geometric mean. Thereby, the correction coeffi-

Algorithm 1 Revised estimator based on the Webber approach

$r_u \leftarrow$ unpooled run
$R_p \leftarrow$ set of pooled runs
$T \leftarrow$ set of topics
$Q \leftarrow$ qrels on T derived from R_p
$s_{r_u} \leftarrow P@n(r_u, Q)$
$\bar{k}_{r_u} \leftarrow 1 - (s_{r_u} + \overline{P}@n(r_u, Q))$
for all $r_p \in R_p$ **do**
  $R'_p \leftarrow R_p \setminus \{r_p\}$
  $Q' \leftarrow$ qrels on T derived from R'_p
  $s'_{r_p} \leftarrow P@n(r_p, Q')$
  $\delta P_{r_p} \leftarrow P@n(r_p, Q) - s'_{r_p}$
  $\bar{k}'_{r_p} \leftarrow 1 - (s'_{r_p} + \overline{P}@n(r_p, Q'))$
end for
$a \leftarrow \bar{k}_{r_u} \cdot \mathrm{GM}_{r_p \in \{r \in R_p \,:\, \delta P_r \neq 0\}} \left[\delta P_r / \bar{k}'_{r_p}\right]$
return $s_{r_u} + a$

cient for a run ($r_u \notin R_p$) is the following function:

$$\bar{k}@n(r_u) \cdot \underset{r_p \in R_p}{\mathrm{GM}} \left[\delta P@n(r_p)/\bar{k}'@n(r_p)\right] \tag{5}$$

Comparing Eq. (2) and Eq. (5) we notice that the numerator of this last equation is the same, but with the difference that now, every $\delta P@n$ gets divided by the number of uniquely identified documents provided to the pool, and then multiplied by the same but for r_u, and the arithmetic mean has been substituted by the geometric mean.

However, Eq. (4) is only valid when X is well behaved in the sense of not having zero values. Considering this, in Eq. (5) it mandates the removal of those runs for which δP_{r_p} is zero. This is reasonable because: first, if $\delta P_{r_p} \neq 0$ it can be shown that $\bar{k}'_{r_p} \neq 0$ and consequently the fraction in Eq. (5) is well defined. Second, such zero values bring no information to our estimate of the contribution of the run. In fact, one could generate an unbounded number of runs with $\delta P_{r_p} = 0$.

In Alg. 1 we make use of Eq. (5), filtering out 0 values, and redefining the previous Webber approach. Two benefits of this modification are that no longer every correction is based on a prior probability of the run to find relevant documents among its non-judged ones, and that it is not a constant number as it was before. Also, comparing the algorithm of the Lipani approach [5], we observe here some similarities, such as the use of $\bar{k}'@n$ and of $\overline{P}@n$.

4. EXPERIMENTS & RESULTS

In this section, we present the experimental setup and the material used. It follows the methodology previously used by the already mentioned studies [10, 5, 6]. In the second part, we discuss the results.

4.1 Material & Experimental Set up

To test the effectiveness of the new algorithm, we tested[1] the method on 15 test collections sampled from the TREC evaluation campaign: 7 from the Ad Hoc track, 3 from the Web track, and 1 from each of the Genomics, Robust, Legal, Medical, and Microblog tracks. This sample allowed us to also explore more specific IR domains, where a different behavior may be expected. The experiments consist in running repeated simulations, where a run at each iteration is taken out of the pool with all the runs submitted by the same organization, and a synthetic pool is generated, in a leave-one organization-out fashion. This is done to better simulate the absence of any similar run added to the pool by the same organization. Moreover, to avoid the presence of runs produced by buggy implementations of IR search engines, the bottom 25% of poorly performing runs are filtered out.

To measure the effectiveness of the different approaches, three measures are used: Mean Absolute Error (MAE), System Rank Error (SRE) and System Rank Error with statistical significance (SRE*). MAE measures the mean of the absolute difference of runs' scores when in the pool and when not. SRE measures the difference in ranks between the true ranking and new ranking with using the corrections. Finally, SRE* is similar to SRE, but counts the difference only if statistically significant (paired t-test, $p < 0.05$).

We compared the new approach with the previously mentioned Webber and Lipani approaches, and the baseline, which is the Reduced Pool. The Reduced Pool measures the bias we get if no correction is provided.

4.2 Results

In Tab. 1 the full results are presented. We observe that our approach is top performer in the majority of the cases (45 for MAE, 37 for SRE and 9 for SRE*), with some worst results (15 for MAE, 16 for SRE and, 6 for SRE*) mostly obtained on Ad Hoc 7 and Ad Hoc 8, where the Lipani approach performs better. The Lipani approach, although in general it is not as good as our approach, which has a more stable behavior, collecting fewer worst results (9 for MAE, 6 for SRE and, 1 for SRE*). The Webber approach and the Reduced Pool are the ones that get the majority of the worst results, as also demonstrated in previous work [5].

When our approach is applied to the test collections: Ad Hoc 3, Ad Hoc 5, Ad Hoc 7, Ad Hoc 8, Web 9, Web 2002, Genomics 2005 and Microblog 2011 we can observe that the MAE for the correction applied to $P@5$ gets the worst score (8 of the 15 worst performer cases mentioned above). Here, after an empirical analysis, we have two hypotheses for why this happens, and we claim that it happens for a combination of both. The first hypothesis relies on the observation that for such test collections, the ratio between the number of pooled runs and the number of organizations is much greater than 1. This means that multiple runs from the same organization have been pooled and therefore contribute a very similar set of documents to the pool. Thereby, it nullifies the leave-one run-out approach embedded in our and the Webber methods, as shown in Eq. (2) and (5), looking inside E in the first and GM in the second equation, when the run r_p, originally in the pool Q^{R_p} is removed from the pool ($Q^{R_p \setminus \{r_p\}}$). Note that this leave-one run-out happens inside the algorithm and is different from the leave-one organization-out testing procedure that happens before the algorithm is triggered. However, for Legal 2006 and Medical 2011, although the ratio is also large, we may not observe the same effect due the more shallow pool depth. The second hypothesis is that when we want to count the top number of relevant documents of a run and we have such large number of relevance judgments, there is a high likelihood that the top documents of every run have been already pooled by other runs. This means that, as for the first hypothesis, the effect of the leave-one run-out embedded in the method is nullified. We split these two hypotheses because they have a different nature, although they have the same effect that can be mitigated by the same solution.

In general, these two hypotheses cause a significant error due to the fact that the number of points collected in order to compute an unbiased estimate of the geometric mean is insufficient. When these sets are small, it means that either there are no non-judged documents, or the ones that exist bring no new information in terms

[1]The software is available on the website of the first author.

Table 1: **Summary of the results per test collection generated through a leave-one organization-out using the top 75% of the best performing pooled runs. With: $|R|$ number of runs submitted, $|O|$ number of organizations involved, $|R_p|$ number of pooled runs, d depth of the pool and $|T|$ number of topics. Last row counts how many times each approach per metric performed best or worst, tie not included.**

Track		P@n	Our			Lipani			Webber			Reduced Pool		
			MAE	SRE	SRE*	MAE	SRE	SRE*	MAE	SRE	SRE*	MAE	SRE	SRE*
Ad Hoc 2	$\|R\|$: 38	5	0.0029	13	1	0.0041	13	1	0.0049	14	1	0.0047	13	1
	$\|O\|$: 22	10	0.0046	12	0	0.0093	18	0	0.0102	16	0	0.0095	18	0
	$\|R_p\|$: 30	20	0.0043	11	0	0.0108	27	0	0.0112	25	0	0.0122	30	0
	d : 100	30	0.0053	7	0	0.0134	30	0	0.0124	19	0	0.0153	32	0
	$\|T\|$: 50	100	0.0069	14	0	0.0226	66	0	0.0163	42	1	0.0307	94	1
Ad Hoc 3	$\|R\|$: 40	5	0.0061	2	0	0.0024	1	0	0.0032	1	0	0.0024	1	0
	$\|O\|$: 22	10	0.0036	3	0	0.0022	2	0	0.0023	0	0	0.0023	2	0
	$\|R_p\|$: 21	20	0.0029	1	0	0.0028	1	0	0.0027	2	0	0.0030	1	0
	d : 200	30	0.0035	4	0	0.0038	7	0	0.0039	8	0	0.0041	7	0
	$\|T\|$: 50	100	0.0047	13	0	0.0065	13	0	0.0060	15	0	0.0085	14	0
Ad Hoc 4	$\|R\|$: 33	5	0.0082	13	0	0.0084	13	0	0.0104	16	0	0.0098	14	0
	$\|O\|$: 19	10	0.0092	12	0	0.0104	14	0	0.0114	15	0	0.0119	16	0
	$\|R_p\|$: 24	20	0.0090	10	0	0.0111	14	0	0.0124	18	0	0.0132	20	0
	d : 100	30	0.0103	10	0	0.0116	13	0	0.0128	17	0	0.0144	20	0
	$\|T\|$: 50	100	0.0127	21	0	0.0128	20	0	0.0144	28	0	0.0218	38	3
Ad Hoc 5	$\|R\|$: 61	5	0.0139	60	1	0.0073	37	3	0.0083	38	3	0.0076	38	3
	$\|O\|$: 21	10	0.0077	43	0	0.0073	40	0	0.0080	42	0	0.0079	45	0
	$\|R_p\|$: 53	20	0.0075	60	0	0.0068	41	0	0.0079	55	0	0.0077	49	0
	d : 100	30	0.0067	59	0	0.0068	41	0	0.0081	57	0	0.0083	54	0
	$\|T\|$: 50	100	0.0069	84	0	0.0053	61	0	0.0084	107	0	0.0102	114	1
Ad Hoc 6	$\|R\|$: 74	5	0.0089	7	0	0.0102	9	5	0.0158	14	5	0.0118	9	5
	$\|O\|$: 29	10	0.0068	4	0	0.0057	6	0	0.0084	6	0	0.0063	6	0
	$\|R_p\|$: 25	20	0.0050	2	0	0.0058	4	0	0.0072	8	0	0.0071	4	0
	d : 100	30	0.0048	3	0	0.0062	1	0	0.0068	3	0	0.0079	2	0
	$\|T\|$: 50	100	0.0051	9	0	0.0068	17	0	0.0073	13	0	0.0116	16	0
Ad Hoc 7	$\|R\|$: 103	5	0.0085	44	5	0.0024	8	2	0.0032	8	2	0.0025	8	2
	$\|O\|$: 42	10	0.0063	47	0	0.0024	7	0	0.0030	7	0	0.0025	7	0
	$\|R_p\|$: 63	20	0.0037	25	0	0.0023	12	0	0.0027	16	0	0.0025	14	0
	d : 100	30	0.0034	28	0	0.0024	28	0	0.0029	26	0	0.0028	29	0
	$\|T\|$: 50	100	0.0035	43	0	0.0028	34	0	0.0035	42	0	0.0043	54	0
Ad Hoc 8	$\|R\|$: 129	5	0.0050	22	2	0.0020	3	0	0.0035	3	0	0.0021	3	0
	$\|O\|$: 41	10	0.0050	29	4	0.0021	3	0	0.0033	3	0	0.0022	3	0
	$\|R_p\|$: 66	20	0.0034	19	2	0.0020	5	0	0.0031	11	0	0.0022	5	0
	d : 100	30	0.0030	15	2	0.0021	8	0	0.0031	15	0	0.0024	10	0
	$\|T\|$: 50	100	0.0024	21	3	0.0022	22	1	0.0032	32	7	0.0036	48	10
Web 9	$\|R\|$: 104	5	0.0030	10	0	0.0024	9	0	0.0023	9	0	0.0022	9	0
	$\|O\|$: 23	10	0.0022	9	0	0.0020	13	0	0.0022	13	0	0.0021	13	0
	$\|R_p\|$: 39	20	0.0019	8	0	0.0035	17	0	0.0036	20	0	0.0039	20	0
	d : 100	30	0.0023	12	0	0.0035	27	0	0.0041	35	0	0.0047	37	0
	$\|T\|$: 50	100	0.0035	23	0	0.0067	67	0	0.0059	66	0	0.0079	82	0
Web 2001	$\|R\|$: 97	5	0.0008	2	0	0.0011	2	0	0.0009	2	0	0.0009	2	0
	$\|O\|$: 29	10	0.0027	11	0	0.0020	11	0	0.0020	11	0	0.0018	11	0
	$\|R_p\|$: 35	20	0.0028	12	0	0.0030	12	0	0.0026	13	0	0.0028	17	0
	d : 100	30	0.0028	37	0	0.0036	44	0	0.0024	28	0	0.0034	34	0
	$\|T\|$: 50	100	0.0039	42	0	0.0082	89	0	0.0037	40	0	0.0070	73	0
Web 2002	$\|R\|$: 69	5	0.0075	88	0	0.0044	52	0	0.0043	53	0	0.0043	53	0
	$\|O\|$: 16	10	0.0038	41	0	0.0047	50	0	0.0043	50	0	0.0052	56	0
	$\|R_p\|$: 60	20	0.0048	78	0	0.0046	74	0	0.0036	49	0	0.0048	73	0
	d : 50	30	0.0041	60	0	0.0055	90	0	0.0035	53	0	0.0054	76	0
	$\|T\|$: 50	100	0.0010	35	0	0.0048	126	0	0.0019	52	0	0.0034	95	0
Genomics 2005	$\|R\|$: 62	5	0.0113	99	0	0.0056	70	0	0.0055	72	0	0.0061	72	0
	$\|O\|$: 32	10	0.0045	71	0	0.0072	122	0	0.0068	118	0	0.0082	129	0
	$\|R_p\|$: 46	20	0.0034	55	0	0.0074	82	0	0.0070	85	0	0.0091	101	0
	d : 60	30	0.0040	69	0	0.0077	90	0	0.0074	103	0	0.0106	148	0
	$\|T\|$: 49	100	0.0041	87	0	0.0052	97	0	0.0054	115	0	0.0094	176	0
Robust 2005	$\|R\|$: 74	5	0.0107	3	0	0.0189	15	2	0.0334	26	4	0.0249	18	4
	$\|O\|$: 17	10	0.0123	6	0	0.0239	14	6	0.0381	25	7	0.0303	19	10
	$\|R_p\|$: 18	20	0.0137	9	2	0.0269	17	6	0.0383	31	11	0.0361	29	11
	d : 55	30	0.0160	8	1	0.0284	18	5	0.0394	33	10	0.0417	30	10
	$\|T\|$: 50	100	0.0121	19	4	0.0154	26	0	0.0210	30	4	0.0300	35	4
Legal 2006	$\|R\|$: 34	5	0.0336	21	2	0.1355	41	3	0.1123	44	4	0.1533	45	4
	$\|O\|$: 8	10	0.0343	27	0	0.1557	22	0	0.1131	44	6	0.1757	47	9
	$\|R_p\|$: 14	20	0.0438	37	3	0.1126	34	7	0.0566	40	6	0.0878	46	10
	d : 10	30	0.0327	39	2	0.0707	26	0	0.0377	41	4	0.0585	44	5
	$\|T\|$: 39	100	0.0107	26	13	0.0215	40	16	0.0113	27	13	0.0176	37	19
Medical 2011	$\|R\|$: 127	5	0.0243	112	0	0.0300	130	0	0.0366	141	0	0.0552	209	0
	$\|O\|$: 29	10	0.0270	118	0	0.0283	113	1	0.0414	157	4	0.0688	263	12
	$\|R_p\|$: 46	20	0.0144	57	0	0.0201	89	0	0.0216	87	0	0.0351	167	0
	d : 10	30	0.0103	78	0	0.0151	82	0	0.0144	88	0	0.0234	117	0
	$\|T\|$: 34	100	0.0035	56	0	0.0063	94	1	0.0042	61	0	0.0069	103	0
Microblog 2011	$\|R\|$: 184	5	0.0211	95	3	0.0112	23	0	0.0120	23	0	0.0115	23	0
	$\|O\|$: 58	10	0.0076	47	0	0.0125	51	0	0.0129	48	0	0.0130	51	0
	$\|R_p\|$: 49	20	0.0087	42	0	0.0139	67	0	0.0137	50	0	0.0150	70	0
	d : 30	30	0.0102	70	0	0.0162	90	0	0.0159	79	0	0.0180	96	0
	$\|T\|$: 49	100	0.0044	53	0	0.0047	58	0	0.0044	48	0	0.0048	58	0
	top performer		45	37	9	18	16	3	7	7	0	2	0	0
	worst performer		15	16	6	9	6	1	12	11	0	37	32	9

of being or not being in the pool. Thereby, the error introduced is bigger than the one we would have observed if we had not corrected the run at all. In fact we can observe that the second best result, but for Genomics 2005, excluding the Lipani approach, is obtained by the Reduced Pool. Therefore to mitigate this effect, it is necessary to introduce a trigger that checks if the number of data points collected are sufficient to compute the estimate and perform the correction, and if not, to fall back to the Reduced Pool error.

5. CONCLUSION

We have presented a new approach, empirically justified, to correct the pool bias for the evaluation measure $P@n$. The method is based on new insights on the fixed-depth at n pooling strategy, namely the observation of a relation between the probability of a run to provide uniquely identified relevant documents to the pool and the log-normal distribution. The proposed method largely outperformed the previous approaches, although for two test collections, Ad Hoc 7 and Ad Hoc 8, where the Lipani estimator works better. We identified two hypotheses that would explain the worst performing cases, both of which tracing their source to situations where, for the metric at hand, the vast majority of runs have all of their documents judged in the reduced pool. A cross comparison between the algorithm of the Lipani estimator and the algorithm presented here shows some similarities which may inspire a new improvement on the correction of the pool bias.

Acknowledgments

This research was partially supported by the Austrian Science Fund (FWF) project number P25905-N23 (ADmIRE), and by the Google Faculty Research Award scheme. All content represents the opinion of the authors, which is not necessarily shared or endorsed by their respective employers and/or sponsors.

6. REFERENCES

[1] Charles L. A. Clarke and Mark D. Smucker. Time well spent. In *Proc. of IIiX*, 2014.

[2] Gordon V. Cormack, Christopher R. Palmer, and Charles L. A. Clarke. Efficient construction of large test collections. In *Proc. of SIGIR*, 1998.

[3] Karen Sparck Jones. Letter to the editor. *Information Processing & Management*, 39(1), 2003.

[4] Aldo Lipani. Fairness in information retrieval. In *Proc. of SIGIR*, 2016.

[5] Aldo Lipani, Mihai Lupu, and Allan Hanbury. Splitting water: Precision and anti-precision to reduce pool bias. In *Proc. of SIGIR*, 2015.

[6] Aldo Lipani, Mihai Lupu, and Allan Hanbury. The curious incidence of bias corrections in the pool. In *Proc. of ECIR*, 2016.

[7] Aldo Lipani, Guido Zuccon, Mihai Lupu, Bevan Koopman, and Hanbury Allan. The impact of fixed-cost pooling strategies on test collection bias. In *Proc. of ICTIR*, 2016.

[8] Alistair Moffat, William Webber, and Justin Zobel. Strategic system comparisons via targeted relevance judgments. In *Proc. of SIGIR*, 2007.

[9] K. Spärck Jones and C. J. van Rijsbergen. Report on the need for and provision of an "ideal" information retrieval test collection. *British Library Research and Development Report No. 5266*, 1975.

[10] William Webber and Laurence A. F. Park. Score adjustment for correction of pooling bias. In *Proc. of SIGIR*, 2009.

Scarce Feature Topic Mining for Video Recommendation

Wei Lu
Department of Computing
Hong Kong Polytechnic University
Kowloon, Hong Kong
cswlu@comp.polyu.edu.hk

Fu-lai Chung
Department of Computing
Hong Kong Polytechnic University
Kowloon, Hong Kong
korris.chung@polyu.edu.hk

Kunfeng Lai
Tencent
Nanshan Technique Park
Shenzhen, China
calvinlai@tencent.com

ABSTRACT

Recommendation for user generated content sites has gained significant attention. To satisfy the niche tastes of users, product recommendation poses more challenges due to the data sparsity issue. This work is motivated by a real world online video recommendation problem, where the click records database suffers from sparseness of video inventory and video tags. Targeting the long tail phenomena of user behavior and sparsity of item features, we propose a personalized compound recommendation framework for online video recommendation called Dirichlet mixture probit model for information scarcity (DPIS). Assuming that each record is generated from a representation of user preferences, DPIS is a probit classifier utilizing record topical clustering on the user part for recommendation. As demonstrated by the real-world application, the proposed DPIS achieves better performance than traditional methods.

Keywords

recommender system; topic model; Bayesian approach

1. INTRODUCTION

Recommender systems have changed the way people discover items on the web. How to suggest new items based on their needs and interests is an important task. To model the interaction between users and items, we must understand the hidden facets and the high level topics of their favors. This kind of topics can be obtained collaboratively from diverse sources, such as clicking history, rating scores or objective reviews, and often have comprehensive characteristics. For example, two users may have similar preferences towards detective films, but different viewing records of action movies due to their different preferences of actors. Hence, how to model these hidden factors is a key to obtaining satisfactory recommendation performance [3].

As to online video recommendation, a typical database stores the historical viewing records of active users, with each record referring to one video clicked. Many past researches relying on human feedbacks are typically in a text review form, with the goal of predicting rating scores for unseen items [2]. However, this kind of holistic information for contents is not always available. Fortunately, with increasing availability of e-commerce sources, new recommender tasks are not only based on traditional aspects regarding contents and users, but also different kinds of meta knowledge such as tags. Taking the records from Tencent QQ Browser as an example, there are four categories of information provided as video word tag (in Chinese), namely, type, region, director and actor (Figure 1). As understanding the topic factors is helpful for justifying user preference, the challenge hence lies in discovering both user-item correlation and user preference topics represented by this tag-form text in a single learning stage.

CIKM'16 , October 24-28, 2016, Indianapolis, IN, USA

DOI: http://dx.doi.org/10.1145/2983323.2983892

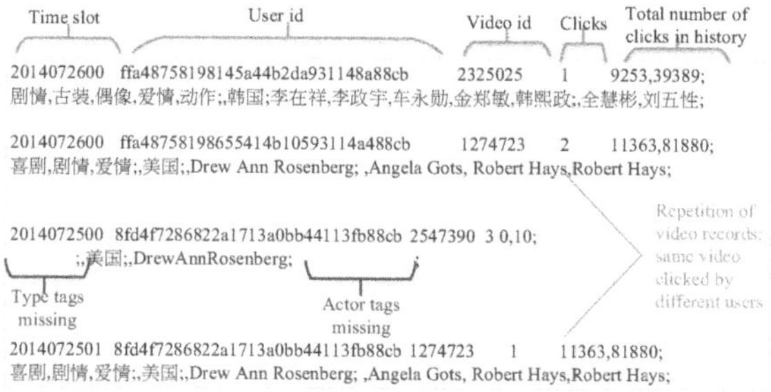

Figure 1: Sample records obtained from Tencent QQ browser.

The topical modeling based recommender system encounters two aspects of sparseness. First, users concentrate on a relatively small number of items comparing to the large inventory [1]. Due to the huge volume of users, videos clicked everyday have features of being extremely dynamic and long tailed. When videos are sorted from the most popular to the least ones, with normalized rank between 0 and 100, 18% of the top popular videos account for about 80% of the user clicking records. Second, the item features are scarce. Since the textual features are extracted from product descriptions, no attributes with well-defined values could be found due to the unstructured nature of the data [5]. Thus, it is a difficult task to categorize each item with just one- or two-keyword based string matching. For topic model based filtering, one common practice is to treat item feature as bag-of-word. In our application, since the tag length for each video is not long, treating each record as a single document indicates a considerably large vocabulary size but a relatively small amount of context per document. Such an information scarcity (IS) problem poses challenges for conventional text mining topic model such as Latent Dirichlet Allocation (LDA), which depends on co-occurring words for topic discovery.

In this paper, we address the aforementioned challenges by proposing a unified Dirichlet mixture probit model for information scarcity (DPIS). It learns topics over scarce information by directly modeling the generation of records. Specifically, the clicking history of a user is assumed to consist of a mixture of topics, and each

Table 1: An illustrative example of user record

user	video	tag words	clicks
u_1	v_1	horror suspense	10
	v_2	comedy romance drama	1
	v_3	action comedy drama	1
u_2	v_2	comedy romance drama	2
	v_3	action comedy drama	1

record sample as a whole is assigned a specific topic with certain probability, from which its corresponding tags are generated. In the generative model, the words describing each item are drawn from the vocabulary of the record. The topic proportions, formulated as a multinomial vector, are also used as an *item vector* to describe whether a user viewing the item or not. Although DPIS does not model the user-level generative process, the link between active users and video pools can be learned through a probit model, with a Laplacian prior enforced on the sparse parameters. Hence, our work differs from standard approaches, as the *item vectors* now serve two roles: explaining both the words that tag the video record; and capturing the collaborative component. In this way, the overall model can not only cluster the semantic topics of the video records based on aggregated item features for active users, but can also combine the observed features and generates topics for newly synthesized data. Here, we employ a collapsed Gibbs sampling inference to find the posterior solution to the topic discovery and the probit parameters, which is convenient to implement, and conduct experiments on real-world data collections.

2. PROBLEM FORMULATION

Our aim is to incorporate user preference into the sparse feature based semantic learning. The first straight forward approach is to extend two-level, document-word hierarchy into a three-level, author-document-word hierarchy. The following analogies can be made for video recommender system: user to author, record to document, and tag to word. Specifically, a video tag count matrix $W \in \mathbb{Z}_+^{S\times V}$ can be obtained, where $\mathbb{Z}_+$indicates positive integer, S is the record sample size, V is the size of word tag vocabulary. There is also a binary user-record matrix $Y \in \{0,1\}^{D\times S}$, indicating which user each record belongs to, where D is the number of active users. With an averaged four million records coming in daily and a total of over $500,000$ evolving tag words, the following statistics are reported. The tag word length is usually less than 30, leaving the word count matrix W with a sparsity of 99.2%. Moreover, 94% of the users have fewer than 20 clicking records, so the word expressions and video sets are extremely vibrant comparing to its library. In such case, when attempting to incorporate the item attribute (tag word) into finding the shared latent low-dimensional space between users and items, how to appropriately explore the hidden interactions behind the scarce item features becomes a key challenge.

As each record belongs to only one user, in the DPIS metaphor, behaviors of each user can be regarded as a document, while each record is the sentence constructed by tag words. Thus, the *author (document)-sentence-word* hierarchy not only builds linkage between user and video, but also preserves the correlations among tags belonging to the same video. To further elaborate our intuition for the proposed hierarchical model, we start with some exploratory analysis of the data to illustrate why traditional topic models like LDA would tend to fail in this scarce application scenario. Consider a set of two users $U = \{u_1, u_2\}$ and a set of three videos $V = \{v_1, v_2, v_3\}$ in Table 1. Each video has its corresponding tags W_{v_i} (to make the table clear, only 2-3 words are included). Inferred from the last column of Table 1, the highest frequency of word-pair is dominated by the ones from v_1. Even though $\{v_2, v_3\}$ would be a common topic intersection, the recommendation would still bias towards the suspense type, and overlooks users' interest in the other type, i.e. comedic drama.

In comparison, if a clicking record is treated as a whole, it is obvious that $\{v_1, v_2\}$ and $\{v_1, v_3\}$ will each co-occur once, while $\{v_2, v_3\}$ will appear twice. Through this kind of aggregation, the biased co-occurrence frequencies are equilibrated and the correlation among tags in the same record are maintained. Using the record-level co-occurrence frequency as the corresponding tag co-occurrence frequency will hence enhance the latent topic discovery for items and user preferences representation. A preliminary 10-factor Pareto test justifies the advantage of concatenating records of each active user, where the percentage of the data expressed by the first factor increases from 10 to 78 when records from the same user are concatenated, which means that this approach indeed improves the interpretation of the data.

3. APPROACH: A COMPOUND DIRICHLET MIXTURE MODEL

Our compound model, which is a probabilistic generative model, as graphically shown in Figure 2, combines both user-item information and item-feature level clustering in the representation process. There are three assumptions for the generative process of the model: (1) user collection is generated by a topic mixture model; (2) there exists one-to-one correspondence between mixture components and clusters; (3) tag words for each record are generated simultaneously according to the probability of record-level topic assignment. Its hierarchical Bayesian structure is characterized by hyper-parameters$\{\gamma, \alpha, \beta\}$ and column vector sets $\{\boldsymbol{\theta}_s, \mathbf{t}_d, \boldsymbol{\omega}_d\}$. The shaded nodes denote two observations. The key difference comparing to other topic model is that, each record of individual user, instead of each word, is generated from a mixture component, topic k, according to the weights of topics.

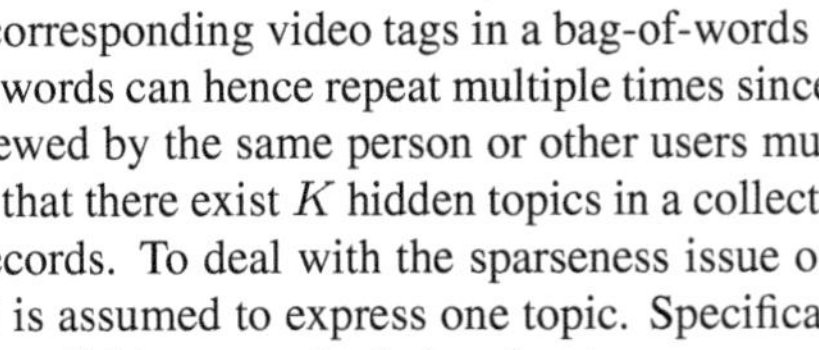

Figure 2: Generative process of the DPIS model.

The observed data are the viewing records collection of active users with corresponding video tags in a bag-of-words format. The same set of words can hence repeat multiple times since each video could be viewed by the same person or other users multiple times. We assume that there exist K hidden topics in a collection of video watching records. To deal with the sparseness issue of word tags, each record is assumed to express one topic. Specifically, we consider that the clicking samples belonging to one user as a mixture of topics, where each record as a collection of tags is drawn from a topic capturing one type of user preference independently. And the tag word in each record is drawn with the same probability from the topic independently. With this approach, DPIS is capable of capturing the strong correlations of tag words in the same record, and hence represents the latent semantics of a record as a whole.

The generative process for the model is summarized as follows:

1. For each record s,
   - Draw topic proportions $\boldsymbol{\theta}_s \sim Dir(\alpha)$

- Draw topic assignment $\mathbf{z}_s \sim Multinomial(\boldsymbol{\theta}_s)$
- For each word in the sample s,
  - Draw word $\mathbf{w}_s \sim Multinomial(\Phi_{\mathbf{z}_s})$

2. For each user d,
   - Draw the parameters $[\boldsymbol{\omega}_d]_{K\times 1}$ by

$$\omega_{\mathbf{d}} \sim \mathcal{N}(0, \gamma^{-1}\mathbf{I}_K) \tag{1}$$

where $\mathbf{I}_K$ represents the $K \times K$ identity matrix.

3. For each user-record tuple $y_{d,s}$, draw the indicator by

$$y_{d,s} = \begin{cases} +1, \; if \; t_{d,s} \geq 0, \\ -1, \; otherwise, \end{cases}$$

$$t_{d,s} \sim \mathcal{N}(\omega_d \theta_s^T, 1) \tag{2}$$

Based on the assumption that tag words in a record are generated independently when the topic assignment for the record is known, we can write the probability for sentence generation as:

$$p(s|z = k) = \prod_{w \in s} p(w|z = k) \tag{3}$$

The response matrix Y is represented by a latent matrix $T \in \mathbb{R}_{D\times S}$. θ acts as a shared matrix between topical clustering and response classification. Thus the latent matrix T and the probit link can be generated according to equation (2). This kind of prior together with the probit link combines with semantic topic modeling and is utilised for recommendation.

Given the inferred latent topics θ_s, which represents a K-dim discrete set of topic assignment given $p(\boldsymbol{\Theta}|\mathbf{W})$, the missing entries in the user-record set Y can be inferred as

$$P(Y_{ds}|-) = \iint p(\theta_s, \omega_d|\mathbf{W}, \alpha)p(Y_{ds}|\theta_s, \omega_d)\mathrm{d}\theta_s \mathrm{d}\omega_d \tag{4}$$

with $p(Y_{ds}|\theta_s, \omega_d)$ being defined as the probit link and $\mathbf{W}$ represents the observed part of record-tag interactions. $p(\theta_s, \omega_d|\mathbf{W}, \alpha)$ is directly approximated with the MAP solution of (θ_s^*, ω_d^*). Based on the posterior probability of $P(Y_{ds}|-)$, which is used as a probability ranking for recommendation, the candidate items are ranked accordingly.

4. EXPERIMENTS

To provide recommendation evaluation in a formal and rigorous way, we examine the quality of the generated category and prediction using DPIS model in both warm-start and cold-start situations. We consider assessing our model comparing to direct tag match, traditional topic model and topic model for short texts. We use records in three consecutive weeks at the same time slot from Tencent QQ browser. There are $4,071,811$ samples in total with $137,465$ unique users, and $9,393$ unique videos they clicked. So, baseline methods including tagommender [6], and five other probabilistic model: Latent Dirichlet Allocation (LDA), Author Topic (AT) Model, labeled LDA (LaLDA) [4], fast discriminant LDA(DLDA)[7] and collapsed Gibbs Sampling algorithm for the Dirichlet Multinomial Mixture model (GSDMM) [9] are considered.

For each of the recommendation scenarios, we generated the test data sets for both warm-start and cold-start experiments in a 5-fold cross-validation way similar to the work of Wang et. al [8].

4.1 Prediction Performance Evaluation

We start with the warm-start cases, where both video and users in the testing set have been appeared in the training sets. To evaluate the model quantitatively, we investigate the influence of topic number K on the performance of recommendation. The common metrics for recommendation evaluation used here are precision, recall and average hit rate. Figure 3(a) – (c) show these three metrics of the four algorithms respectively when n equals to 3 with varying cluster number K from 15 to 150. The graphs illustrate that DPIS for topic number larger than 15 outperforms the other recommendation algorithms in terms of every quality measure. As we increase the topic number, the three measures have an overall trend of improving, stabilized around topic number equalling to 80. This can also be utilized as a way of determining the appropriate topic number for this dataset. From a user perspective, the averaged hit rate counts is a more important factor for judging recommender system, since it indicates whether the recommended items would fit users' interest at earlier order. Although DPIS resembles to AT model most, due to the different way of placing the topic probabilistic distribution, the single topic assumption for each record estimates the sparse data better and hence generate better results comparing to AT which relies on the co-occurrence of tag words. Furthermore, as AT does not model the direct relation between user and record, but only clusters user and tag topics separately, the hit rate does not change much with increasing number topics. This is due to a lack of efficient ranking mechanism to differentiate the priority of preferences within similar user groups.

The influence of how many videos should be recommended is also worth discussing. Usually for the browser interface, 5 to 10 videos are listed as a guessing of user interest. The values for all three metrics mentioned in the previous subsection are illustrated in Figure 3(d) – (f). The increase of pool number will enhance the probability to recommend the favored video. Thus, recall and average hit-rank grows gradually and stabilizes. DPIS has outstanding performance comparing to other methods on precision when the recommendation candidate number is small. The prediction precision decreases below the average performances of other methods when the candidate video number is larger than seven. Both the recall values and average hit rates for DPIS are more consistent comparing to other methods. All these phenomena indicate that DPIS can hit the correct preferences of users at an earlier stage of recommendation which makes it more suitable for short list of video recommendation.

For the cold-start case as stated, we examine the case where new videos are added for recommendation. The precision and recall with recommended item size ranging from one to five are illustrated in Figure 3(g) and (h). The overall trend is similar to the warm-start case, GSDMM does better comparing to LDA and Tagomender, which supports our choice of targeting the scarceness of information. However, its performance is limited due to the restriction of single topic assignment for each user, which is usually not the case. As a contrary, although DPIS assigns only one topic to each record for the purpose of solving tag sparsity issue, each video can appear multiple times, which indicates that there is still probability that the video could be assigned to multiple topics based on the high-level semantic clustering of user preference. Hence, the overall performance of DPIS is better than GSDMM, when both methods are targeting at the short-length of text features.

4.2 Topic Examination

Considering the topic-modeling component part of the DPIS model alone, we compare the perplexity of LDA with and without data expansion, fast DLDA and GSDMM. Each of the models were initialized with the same hyper-parameters and topic number, if required, to impose a fair comparison. The perplexity is defined as $Perplexity = exp(-\frac{\sum_i \log p(\hat{w}_i)}{\sum_i N_i})$, where N_i is the number of observed features, i sums from 1 to the number of entities and

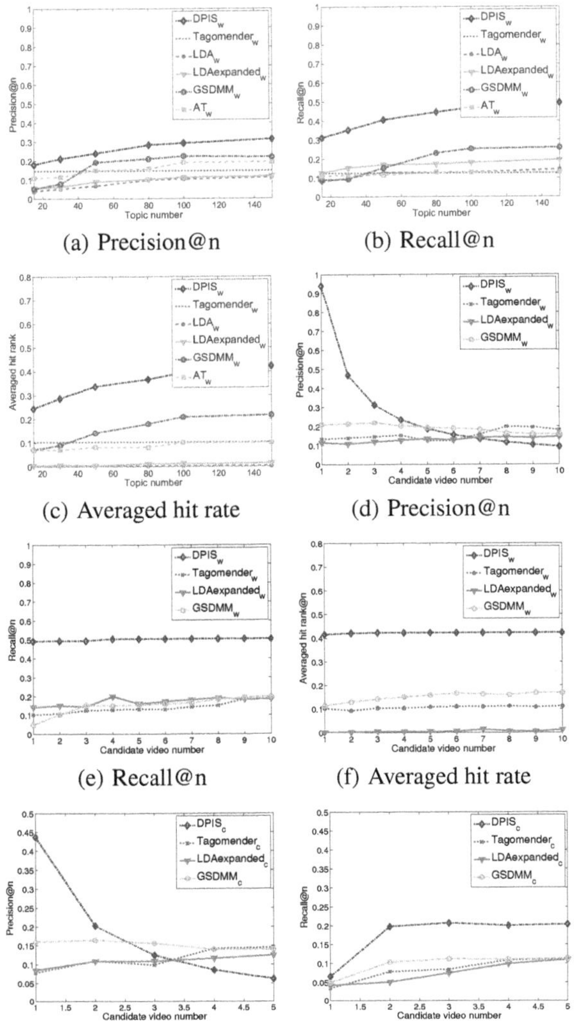

(a) Precision@n (b) Recall@n

(c) Averaged hit rate (d) Precision@n

(e) Recall@n (f) Averaged hit rate

(g) Precision@n (h) Recall@n

Figure 3: Warm-start: Vary topic number K from 15 to 150 with n equal to 3 ((a) – (c)) and vary candidates number n from 1 to 10 with topic number equal to 150 ((d) – (f)). Cold-start: Vary candidates number n from 1 to 5 with topic number equal to 150 ((g) – (h)). The error bar is too small to show.

$\log p(\hat{w}_i)$ is the log-likelihood of the term w as per the learned model. Since larger likelihoods imply better chances of observing the true value, with a monotonically decreasing function applied on it, a lower perplexity would indicate a better model explanation. Table 2 summarizes the perplexities using each of the methods. The degradation of using expanded words for LDA suggests that simple augmentation will not improve the co-occurrence pattern, but worsens the topic interpretation due to a destruction of the original data structure and an overlook of the latent relations between the word combinations. We can see that although supervised fast DLDA method outperforms DPIS in prediction accuracy, its performance on perplexity is not as competitive as DPIS. This might be benefited from the record level modeling of topics, which makes DPIS more suitable for scarce information exploration.

Table 2: Perplexity Comparison

Method	LDA	LDA expand	fast DLDA	GSDMM	DPIS
Perp.	1432	1627	1982	1074	**1035**

5. CONCLUSIONS

With the exponential growth in online video usage, predicting the potential interest of user is a typical recommendation application. Large-scale video databases and user click logs from Tencent browser have long-tailed and sparse features, which presents challenges to traditional recommender systems. Targeting this two-aspect information scarcity, we present DPIS, a novel probit topic model for video recommendation. Through concatenating viewing records for maintaining tag word correlation, the probabilistic generating processes for record-level topic representation of user preferences is described and the Gibbs sampling algorithm for inference and parameter learning is realized. Experiments prove that the proposed model can improve the quality of recommendation based on semantical topics of user preference.

6. ACKNOWLEDGMENTS

This research was partly supported by UGC, GRF Project PolyU 152039/14E. We would also like to thank Yu Xu and the Mobile Internet group at Tencent, Shenzhen for data provision.

7. REFERENCES

[1] M. Grčar, D. Mladenič, B. Fortuna, and M. Grobelnik. Data sparsity issues in the collaborative filtering framework. *Advances in Web Mining and Web Usage Analysis*, pages 58–76, 2006.

[2] Y. Koren, R. Bell, and C. Volinsky. Matrix factorization techniques for recommender systems. *Computer*, 42(8):30–37, Aug. 2009.

[3] J. McAuley and J. Leskovec. Hidden factors and hidden topics: Understanding rating dimensions with review text. In *Proceedings of the 7th ACM conference on Recommender Systems*, pages 165–172. ACM, 2013.

[4] D. Ramage, D. Hall, R. Nallapati, and C. D. Manning. Labeled lda: A supervised topic model for credit attribution in multi-labeled corpora. In *Proceedings of the 2009 Conference on Empirical Methods in Natural Language Processing: Volume 1 - Volume 1*, EMNLP '09, pages 248–256, Stroudsburg, PA, USA, 2009. Association for Computational Linguistics.

[5] F. Ricci, L. Rokach, and B. Shapira. *Recommender Systems Handbook*. Springer US, 2015.

[6] S. Sen, J. Vig, and J. Riedl. Tagommenders: Connecting users to items through tags. In *Proceedings of the 18th International Conference on World Wide Web*, WWW '09, pages 671–680, New York, NY, USA, 2009. ACM.

[7] H. Shan and A. Banerjee. Mixed-membership naive Bayes models. *Data Mining and Knowledge Discovery*, 23(1):1–62, 2011.

[8] C. Wang and D. M. Blei. Collaborative topic modeling for recommending scientific articles. In *Proceedings of the 17th ACM SIGKDD International Conference on Knowledge Discovery and Data Mining*, KDD '11, pages 448–456, New York, NY, USA, 2011. ACM.

[9] J. Yin and J. Wang. A Dirichlet multinomial mixture model-based approach for short text clustering. In *Proceedings of the 20th ACM SIGKDD International Conference on Knowledge Discovery and Data Mining*, KDD '14, pages 233–242, New York, NY, USA, 2014. ACM.

Learning to Re-Rank Questions in Community Question Answering Using Advanced Features

Giovanni Da San Martino†, Alberto Barrón-Cedeño†, Salvatore Romeo†, Antonio Uva‡, Alessandro Moschitti†
†Qatar Computing Research Institute, Hamad bin Khalifa University, Doha, Qatar
‡Department of Computer Science and Information Engineering, University of Trento, Trento, Italy
†{gmartino, albarron, sromeo, amoschitti}@qf.org.qa, ‡antono.uva@unitn.it

ABSTRACT

We study the impact of different types of features for question ranking in community Question Answering: bag-of-words models (BoW), syntactic tree kernels (TKs) and rank features. It should be noted that structural kernels have never been applied to the question reranking task, i.e., question to question similarity, where they have to model paraphrase relations. Additionally, the informal text, typically present in forums, poses new challenges to the use of TKs. We compare our learning to rank (L2R) algorithms against a strong baseline given by the Google rank (GR). The results show that (i) our shallow structures used in TKs are robust enough to noisy data and (ii) improving GR requires effective BoW features and TKs along with an accurate model of GR features in the used L2R algorithm.

Keywords

Community Question Answering; Learning to Rank; Syntactic Structures

1. INTRODUCTION

In recent years, there has been a renewed interest in IR for Community Question Answering (cQA). This combines traditional Question Answering with a modern Web scenario, where users pose questions expecting to receive answers from other users. The most critical problem arises when an original question, asked by a user, has not been asked before. In this case the retrieval system will search for relevant comments to other questions in order to find an appropriate answer. In this noisy and complex setting, powerful search engines (e.g., Google), have a hard time to retrieve comments that can correctly answer the original question. We approach this problem by searching similar questions rather than directly retrieving comments. Indeed, if an original user question q_o is similar to a sought question q_s, which has been answered before, we can just return the answers associated with q_s.

The automatic retrieval of relevant questions requires models different from typical search engines. Firstly, both queries and documents are short texts: questions may include descriptions or subquestions but they are not typically larger than one or two paragraphs. Thus, on one hand, word similarities are needed for dealing with data sparseness; on the other hand, representations based on parse-tree can be easily modeled. Secondly, the syntactic structure of the questions is rather important for learning to recognize paraphrases and thus selecting the right candidates. For instance, the corpus question, *How do I get a visa for Qatar to visit my wife?*, has roughly the same BoW representation as question *How do I get a visa for my wife to have her visit Qatar?*, but their answers are totally different. The structure of the questions can be exploited to detect the difference between these difficult cases.

The study of cQA models for question–question similarity has typically relied on annotations provided by users, which could imply low reliability. Recently, a new resource has been released for cQA for the shared task at SemEval 2016 on Answer Selection in cQA [10].[1] Task B of the challenge provides a dataset of questions, each associated with ten candidate similar questions. The candidates were (i) retrieved and ranked with the Google search engine, using the question as input in their Web API and (ii) manually labelled by human annotators. Thus, this dataset enables a reliable testing of the most advanced methods for question reranking on top of the baseline rank generated by the currently most powerful search engine.

In this paper, we provide insights on reranking the output of a Web search engine using advanced features. In particular, we use (i) text similarity features, derived from the classical BoW representations, e.g., n-grams, skip-grams; (ii) syntactic/structural relational features injected by tree kernels (TKs), which have been shown to achieve the state of the art on the related task of answer sentence reranking [12]; and (iii) features for modeling the initial rank provided by the search engine, which represents a strong baseline.

Our extensive experimentation produced the following results: (i) the BoW features based on similarity measures alone do not improve GR. (ii) Our TKs applied to questions alone outperform the models based on similarity measures and when jointly used with the rank features improve all the models. In particular, they outperform GR by 1.72 with respect to MAP (95% of statistical confidence).

2. RELATED WORK

The first step to automatically answer questions on cQA sites is to retrieve a set of questions similar to the user's

CIKM '16, October 24–28, 2016, Indianapolis, IN, USA.

DOI: http://dx.doi.org/10.1145/2983323.2983893

[1] http://alt.qcri.org/semeval2016/task3/

Table 1: **A reranking example. For each candidate the Google rank (GR), the binary gold standard (GS) relevance, and our rank (R) are reported.**

q_o: What are the tourist places in Qatar? I'm likely to travel in the month of June. Just wanna know some good places to visit.

GR	*GS*	*R*	*Question Text*
1	-1	8	The Qatar banana island will be transfered by the end of 2013 to 5 stars resort called Anantara. Has anyone seen this island? Where is it? Is it near to Corniche?
2	+1	2	Is there a good place here where I can spend some quality time with my friends?
3	-1	7	Where is the best beach in Qatar? Maybe a silent and romantic bay? Where to go for it?
4	-1	9	Any suggestions on what are the happenings in Qatar on Holidays? Something new and exciting suggestions please?
5	-1	3	Where in Qatar is the best place for Snorkeling? I'm planning to go out next friday but don't know where to go.
6	-1	6	Can you give me some nice places to go or fun things to do in Doha for children 17-18 years old? Where can we do some watersports (just for once, not as a member), or some quad driving? Let me know please. Thanks.
7	+1	1	Which all places are there for tourists to Qatar? My nephew 18 years on visit.
8	-1	10	Could you suggest the best holiday destination in the world?
9	-1	5	I really would like to know where the best place to catch fish here in Qatar is. But of course from the beach. I go every week to Umsaeed but rerly i catch somthing! So experianced people your reply will be appreciated.

input. The set of similar questions is later used to extract possible answers for the input question. However, determining question similarity remains one of the main challenges in cQA due to problems such as the "lexical gap". Different approaches have been proposed to overcome this problem. Early methods used statistical machine translation techniques to compute semantic similarity between two questions. For instance, [15] applied a phrase-based translation model. Their experiments on Yahoo! Answers showed that models based on phrases are more effective than those using words, as they are able to capture contextual information. However, approaches based on SMT have the problem of requiring lots of data in order to estimate parameters.

Algorithms that try to go beyond simple text representation are presented in [3] and [4]. In [3] a similarity between two questions on Yahoo! Answers is computed by using a language model with a smoothing method based on the category structure of Yahoo! Answers. In [4], the authors search for semantically-similar questions identifying the question topic and focus. More specifically, they compute a similarity between the questions' topics, which represent general users interests, and the questions' focus. Here, the authors use LDA topic modeling to learn the latent semantic topics that generate question/answer pairs and use the learned topics distribution to retrieve similar questions. The quality of the ranking returned by all these systems was measured on a set of test questions from Yahoo! Answers, with question relevancy judgment annotated by users, sometimes assigned automatically based on heuristics.

The methods above only exploited language models or general knowledge given by Yahoo! categories or LDA topics, whereas we model the syntactic/semantic relations between pairs of questions using shallow syntactic parsing and lexical matching. Thus the most similar work to ours is [13], where the authors found semantically related questions by computing the similarity between the syntactic trees of the two questions. They used a tree similarity computed in terms

Table 2: **Class distribution in the training, development, and test partitions.**

Class	train	dev	test	overall
Relevant	1,083	214	233	1,530
Irrelevant	1,586	286	467	2,339
Total	2,669	500	700	3,869

Table 3: **Distribution of Relevant and Irrelevant questions at different R ranking positions of GR.**

R	train	dev	test	overall
1	0.21 ± 0.05	0.24 ± 0.07	0.40 ± 0.11	0.25 ± 0.07
2	0.14 ± 0.03	0.18 ± 0.02	0.12 ± 0.02	0.14 ± 0.03
3	0.11 ± 0.02	0.10 ± 0.01	0.08 ± 0.01	0.10 ± 0.02
4	0.12 ± 0.03	0.08 ± 0.01	0.10 ± 0.03	0.11 ± 0.03
5	0.09 ± 0.02	0.09 ± 0.01	0.08 ± 0.02	0.09 ± 0.02
6	0.08 ± 0.02	0.09 ± 0.02	0.05 ± 0.01	0.08 ± 0.02
7	0.08 ± 0.02	0.07 ± 0.01	0.05 ± 0.01	0.07 ± 0.02
8	0.06 ± 0.01	0.04 ± 0.01	0.03 ± 0.00	0.05 ± 0.01
9	0.07 ± 0.02	0.06 ± 0.01	0.04 ± 0.01	0.07 ± 0.02
10	0.05 ± 0.01	0.05 ± 0.01	0.04 ± 0.01	0.05 ± 0.01

of the number of substructures shared between two trees and the results derived on an annotated dataset showed the effectiveness of this approach.

Different from such approach, we use pairs of questions, (q_o, q_s), as learning instances, thus defining relational models connecting the syntactic trees of q_o and q_s. This way, the learning algorithms learn transformations that suggest if questions constituted by similar words have similar (paraphrases) or different semantics.

3. PROBLEM DESCRIPTION

Conceptually, question retrieval is not much different from a standard retrieval task. Given the asked (original) question q_o, a search engine seeks the Web (or a specific Web forum) for relevant webpages. In cQA, webpages are threads containing the questions q_s, with their user comments, where the latter can provide information for answering q_o. For example, Table 1 shows an original question followed by some questions retrieved by the search engine. The main difference with standard document retrieval is the document scoring function. Indeed, although both question and comments are part of the candidate webpage (thread), the question's text provides more synthetic and precise information for inferring if the candidate thread is relevant for q_o or not.

Table 2 gives class-distribution statistics of the SemEval cQA corpus we used [10]. The corpus is composed of 387 user questions, each of which includes 10 potentially-related questions. The task organizers used the Google search engine, which represents also the strong baseline for the task, to select potentially relevant forum questions. Table 3 shows the distribution of relevant/irrelevant forum questions per ranking position. Although relevant questions tend to be concentrated towards the top of the GR, they are fairly spread over the entire ranking.

4. L2R WITH ADVANCED FEATURES

The ranking function can be implemented by a scoring function $r : Q \times Q \rightarrow \mathbb{R}$, where Q is the set of questions. Function r can be implemented by a linear function $r(q_o, q_s) = \vec{w} \cdot \phi(q_o, q_s)$, where $\vec{w}$ is a linear model and $\phi()$ provides a feature vector representation of pair (q_o, q_s).

We adopt binary SVMs to learn r from examples. Even if SVMrank has been proposed specifically for ranking tasks, we ran several experiments to compare them and observed similar results. We model $\phi(q_o, q_s)$ with three different fea-

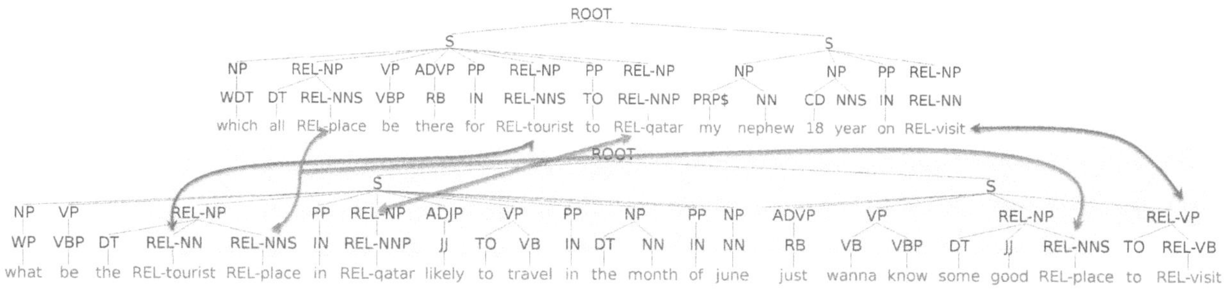

Figure 1: Our representation based on syntactic trees for the q_o–q_s pairs enriched with REL links.

ture sets: (i) tree kernels applied to the syntactic structures of question pairs, (ii) similarity features computed between q_o and q_s, and (iii) rank features, i.e., kernels over the question position in the rank produced by the search engine.

4.1 Tree Kernel Models

Tree kernels are functions that measure the similarity between tree structures. We essentially used the model proposed in [11], originally proposed for ranking passages. Different from [11], our questions may contain multiple subquestions, a subject, greetings, and elaborations; thus they are composed of several sentences. We merge the whole question text in a macro-tree using a fake root node connecting the parse trees of all the sentences. Since we represent pairs of questions, we connect the constituents of two macro-trees corresponding to (q_o, q_s), respectively. For example, given the original question q_o in Table 1 along with the seventh candidate, q_s^7, we build the graph in Figure 1. We link the two macro-trees by connecting phrases, e.g., NP, VP, PP, when there is at least lexical match between the phrases of q_o and q_s. Note that such links are marked with the presence of a REL tag. Finally, we apply a partial tree kernel (PTK) [9] and obtain the following kernel:

$$K((q_o, q_s^i), (q_o, q_s^j)) = TK(t(q_o, q_s^i), t(q_o, q_s^j)) + TK(t(q_s^i, q_o), t(q_s^j, q_o)),$$

where $t(x, y)$ extracts the syntactic tree from text x, enriching it with REL tags computed with respect to y. Thus t is an asymmetric function.

4.2 Feature Vectors

Our L2R approach relies on three subsets of features to derive the relationship between the original and the forum questions: text similarities, PTK similarity, and Google rank.

Text Similarity Features. We compute a total of 20 similarities, $sim(q_o, q_j)$, using word n-grams ($n = [1, \ldots, 4]$), after stopword removal, using greedy string tiling [14], longest common subsequences [1], Jaccard coefficient, word containment [8], and cosine similarity.

PTK Features. Another similarity is obtained by comparing syntactic trees with PTK, i.e., $TK(t(q_o, q_s^i), t(q_s^i, q_o))$. Note that, different from the model in Section 4.1, PTK here is applied to the questions of the same pair and thus only produces one feature.

Ranking-based Features. Our ranking feature is based on the ranking generated by Google. Each forum question is located in one position in the range $[1, \ldots, 10]$. We try to exploit this information in two ways "as-is" (pos) or the inverse (pos^{-1}).[2]

[2]In the dataset, the ten associated forum questions do not corresponds to the top-10, ranked according to GR as some of them were filtered out. We only report our findings with rank features projected into the range $[0, \ldots, 10]$ for brevity.

Table 4: Performance of models using ranking-based features combined with linear and RBF kernels. † shows statistically different results (at 95%) wrt. GR.

	DEV			TEST		
Model	MAP	AvgRec	MRR	MAP	AvgRec	MRR
GR baseline	71.35†	86.11	76.67†	74.75†	88.30	83.79
Sim.	64.80	82.52	73.73	70.70	85.78	80.58
TK	69.97	86.86	77.73	73.98	88.90	82.55
TK + Sim	71.07	87.72	78.14	73.81	89.21	82.86
Linear Kernel						
Sim + pos	68.04	85.07	76.00	71.99	87.92	81.19
Sim + pos^{-1}	70.17	85.98	78.17	75.15	89.19	84.29
TK + pos	71.77	88.46	78.12	75.34	90.67	83.19
TK + pos^{-1}	72.64	87.69	75.58	76.18†	90.62	84.62
RBF Kernel						
Sim. + pos	70.42	86.38	78.50	74.61	89.10	83.81
Sim. + pos^{-1}	69.82	85.91	77.17	74.58	89.09	83.57
TK + pos	72.93	87.95	77.54	75.72	90.80	83.86
TK + pos^{-1}	73.65†	88.78	79.58†	76.41†	91.14	84.62

5. EXPERIMENTS

We use the evaluation framework of SemEval 2016 Task 3 [10]. It consists in reranking questions based on their similarity with the one provided by a user. The data enables a comparison between our models and the systems of the challenge. In a set of preliminary experiments, we compared a reranker, SVMrank [7] with a standard binary SVMs. As the results were comparable, we employed SVMs using the KeLP toolkit[3], which enables to combine our three subsets of features within different kernels; namely RBF for the similarity features, tree kernels for the parse trees, and either linear or RBF kernels for the ranking-based feature. We set the C parameter of SVMs to 1 in all the experiments and the parameters of the TKs and RBF kernel to default values.

We conducted three experiments with growing complexity for assessing the effectiveness of our different feature sets (see Section 4), with respect to GR. In agreement, with the SemEval challenge, we evaluate our rankings with Mean Average Precision (MAP), average Recall (AvgRec), and Mean Reciprocal Rank (MRR).

We tested the performance of each of the feature sets in isolation and pair-wise. Table 4 reports the obtained performance both on the development and test sets. The strong baseline is computed on GR —a product of the Google technology and its associated knowledge bases. We have two advantages over Google: (i) it is not tuned up on the specific Web data we use and (ii) it does not probably use syntactic structures in powerful algorithms such as TKs.

[3]`https://github.com/SAG-KeLP`

Table 5: **Performance of different rank features (all models include RBF kernel on similarities and tree kernel). † shows statistically different results (at 95%) with respect to GR. The best SemEval systems are included for comparison.**

	DEV			TEST		
Model	MAP	AvgRec	MRR	MAP	AvgRec	MRR
GR baseline	71.35†	86.11	76.67	74.75†	88.30	83.79
Linear Kernel						
pos	72.18	88.41	78.00	75.67	90.77	83.38
pos^{-1}	73.28†	88.47	80.00	76.28†	90.72	84.62
RBF Kernel						
pos	73.24†	88.37	78.40	76.47†	90.78	84.21
pos^{-1}	73.60†	88.85	79.67	75.89	90.57	84.14
SemEval top-3						
UH-PRHLT [6]	–	–	–	76.70	90.31	83.02
ConvKN [2]	–	–	–	76.02	90.70	84.64
Kelp [5]	–	–	–	75.83	91.02	82.71

Our results support the hypotheses above. Indeed, the MAP of the models derived by Similarities, TK, and their combinations is below GR: without accessing to the Google resources, our models can just approach the search engine's performance. However, when using the Position feature, our best model outperforms the MAP of GR by 2.30 and 1.66 absolute percent points on the development and test sets, respectively. The RBF kernel on the Position feature produces a larger improvement as it can more effectively express higher similarity values when the positions of questions are close. This cannot be done with a linear kernel.

To better study the results above, Table 5 reports the combinations between the kernel function (Linear or RBF) and the representation of the Position feature (the position itself or its inverse). While all combinations improve above the baseline, there is no clear indication on the best choice between pos or pos^{-1}. However, the use of the RBF kernel results in the highest performance.

Our best configuration obtains a MAP of 76.47, which is not statistically different from the best system of the competition, i.e., UH-PRHLT [6]. Still the latter makes heavy use of knowledge bases, such as BabelNet and FrameNet.

6. CONCLUSIONS

Establishing question–question similarity is a key component of real-world cQA systems. In this paper, we showed that the combination of similarity features, syntactic structures based on tree kernels and features based on the ranking of search engines is able to boost the reranking performance on a real-world cQA dataset. In particular, our results suggest that Google uses general models that can be on par with specific models trained on specific domains. However, if we also use advanced syntactic/semantic representations for modeling the structural relations between questions, we can achieve higher results. In particular, for the first time, we modeled and tested relational tree kernels for cQA, which are robust to noise and can thus boost Google's ranking.

In the future, we would like to better structure the representation of the questions. Indeed, as mentioned before, there are several different sections of the question text, e.g., subquestions, subject, elaborations. These could be used to improve our shallow representation, which, at the moment, merges all the question trees in a flat macro-tree.

Acknowledgments

This work is part of the QCRI, HKBU project, Interactive sYstems for Answer Search (IYAS).

References

[1] L. Allison and T. Dix. A bit-string longest-common-subsequence algorithm. *Inf. Process. Lett.*, 23(6):305–310, Dec. 1986.

[2] A. Barrón-Cedeño, G. Da San Martino, S. Joty, A. Moschitti, F. Al-Obaidli, S. Romeo, K. Tymoshenko, and A. Uva. ConvKN at SemEval-2016 Task 3: Answer and question selection for question answering on arabic and english fora. In *Proceedings of SemEval '16*, pages 896–903, San Diego, California, June 2016. ACL.

[3] X. Cao, G. Cong, B. Cui, C. S. Jensen, and C. Zhang. The use of categorization information in language models for question retrieval. In *CIKM*, pages 265–274, 2009.

[4] H. Duan, Y. Cao, C.-Y. Lin, and Y. Yu. Searching questions by identifying question topic and question focus. In *ACL*, pages 156–164, 2008.

[5] S. Filice, D. Croce, A. Moschitti, and R. Basili. Kelp at semeval-2016 task 3: Learning semantic relations between questions and answers. In *Proceedings of SemEval '16*, pages 1116–1123, San Diego, California, June 2016. ACL.

[6] M. Franco-Salvador, S. Kar, T. Solorio, and P. Rosso. UH-PRHLT at SemEval-2016 Task 3: Combining lexical and semantic-based features for community question answering. In *Proceedings of SemEval '16*, pages 814–821, San Diego, California, June 2016. ACL.

[7] T. Joachims. Optimizing search engines using clickthrough data. KDD, pages 133–142, 2002.

[8] C. Lyon, J. Malcolm, and B. Dickerson. Detecting short passages of similar text in large document collections. EMNLP, pages 118–125, 2001.

[9] A. Moschitti. Efficient Convolution Kernels for Dependency and Constituent Syntactic Trees. In *ECML*, pages 318–329. 2006.

[10] P. Nakov, L. Màrquez, A. Moschitti, W. Magdy, H. Mubarak, A. A. Freihat, J. Glass, and B. Randeree. SemEval-2016 task 3: Community question answering. In *Proceedings of SemEval '16*. ACL, 2016.

[11] A. Severyn and A. Moschitti. Structural relationships for large-scale learning of answer re-ranking. SIGIR, pages 741–750, 2012.

[12] K. Tymoshenko and A. Moschitti. Assessing the impact of syntactic and semantic structures for answer passages reranking. In *Proceedings of CIKM '15*, pages 1451–1460, New York, NY, USA, 2015. ACM.

[13] K. Wang, Z. Ming, and T.-S. Chua. A syntactic tree matching approach to finding similar questions in community-based qa services. In *SIGIR*, pages 187–194, 2009.

[14] M. Wise. Yap3: Improved detection of similarities in computer program and other texts. In *SIGCSE*, pages 130–134, 1996.

[15] G. Zhou, L. Cai, J. Zhao, and K. Liu. Phrase-based translation model for question retrieval in community question answer archives. In *ACL*, pages 653–662, 2011.

Learning to Rank System Configurations

Romain Deveaud Josiane Mothe
IRIT UMR5505, Université de Toulouse, France
firstname.lastname@irit.fr

Jian-Yun Nie
DIRO, Université de Montréal, Québec
nie@iro.umontreal.ca

ABSTRACT

Information Retrieval (IR) systems heavily rely on a large number of parameters, such as the retrieval model or various query expansion parameters, whose values greatly influence the overall retrieval effectiveness. However, setting all these parameters individually can often be a tedious task, since they can all affect one another, while also vary for different queries. We propose to tackle this problem by dealing with entire *system configurations* (i.e. a set of parameters representing an IR system) instead of single parameters, and to apply state-of-the-art Learning to Rank techniques to select the most appropriate configuration for a given query. The experiments we conducted on two TREC AdHoc collections show that this approach is feasible and significantly outperforms the traditional way to configure a system, as well as the top performing systems of the TREC tracks. We also show an analysis on the impact of different features on the model's learning capability.

Categories and Subject Descriptors

H.3.3 [**Information Storage & Retrieval**]: Information Search & Retrieval

Keywords

Information retrieval; learning to rank; retrieval system parameters

1. INTRODUCTION

The effectiveness of Information Retrieval (IR) systems heavily relies on a large number of parameters, ranging from the choice of stemmer, the smoothing technique to the number of terms that are added to the query when performing automatic query expansion. Over the years, and through the evaluation forums such as TREC, the IR community has produced abundant field knowledge, scattered in the literature, on setting the appropriate values of these parameters, in order to optimise the performance of the retrieval systems. The parameters are usually studied in isolation: one attempts to set the value for only one or a few parameters at a time, without taking into account the influence of the setting of other parameters. This makes it difficult to configure a globally optimised set of parameters, as modern IR systems involve a quite large number of parameters that are mutually dependent. There has been no systemic study trying to set the best values for all the parameters of a system.

In this paper, we treat a complete set of parameters of a system as a *system configuration*. We cast the problem of selecting the most appropriate system configuration as a configuration ranking problem using a learning to rank (L2R) [8] approach. The candidate space is formed of tens of thousands of possible system configurations, each of which sets a specific value for each of the system parameters. L2R models are trained to rank them with respect to a performance measure. This approach has the advantage of taking all the system parameters into account at the same time, thus allowing them to influence each other. Moreover, our approach can make a query-dependent choice of system configuration, i.e. different search strategies could be selected for different types of query.

To our knowledge, this is the first study using L2R to rank system configurations. The most similar work to ours is [2], which aims to predict system performance using regression models. While the predicted system performance could be used to select the best system configuration, our study is broader, and the regression method is a special case of the L2R techniques we examine.

The main contribution of this paper is that we propose a new way based on L2R to set system parameters and show its feasibility and competitive or superior retrieval effectiveness to the state of the art on two TREC collections.

2. LEARNING TO RANK SYSTEM CONFIGURATIONS

Our method is based on L2R approaches for IR [8]. However, instead of ranking documents for a query, we rank system configurations. The problem is formulated below.

We assume that an IR system involves a set $\mathbf{P}$ of parameters. Each parameter $p_i \in \mathbf{P}$ can take a value from its domain D_i. Therefore, we have $\prod_i |D_i|$ possible configurations (without considering the fact that some configurations are impossible). This number could be very large, given the quite large number of system parameters used in modern systems and their possible values. We also assume that we have a set $\mathbf{Q}$ of queries for which we have relevance judg-

CIKM'16, October 24-28, 2016, Indianapolis, IN, USA

DOI: http://dx.doi.org/10.1145/2983323.2983894

ments on a document collection, which can be used to generate training examples for L2R models: for each possible configuration $c_j \in \mathbf{C}$, where $\mathbf{C}$ is the space of all configurations, we generate a measure in the IR performance metric (such as MAP, P@n, etc.) for the pair (q_k, c_j). Our goal is to rank the possible configurations for a new query q such that the best ranked system configuration could lead to the best performance.

A L2R model is based on a set of features defined on (q_k, c_j). Usually, in L2R approaches, the features are related to the query, the document (and sometimes the document collection), as well as the relationships between them. In this work, we define features in a similar way, by computing features related to the query q_k and to the configuration c_j. Our primary goal in this paper is to test the feasibility of L2R approaches for setting system configurations.

We consider a set of common system parameters (see Table 1): 1 parameter for retrieval model and 4 parameters for pseudo-relevance feedback. Notice that these parameters are all for retrieval (not for indexing) and can be set for a query on the fly. For each of the possible configuration[1], we run the Terrier IR system [11] to obtain the corresponding performance measures. This amounts to more than 10,000 different configurations for each training query.

Table 1: Description of the system parameters that we use to build our dataset

Parameter	Description & values[2]
Retrieval model	21 different retrieval models: DirichletLM, JsKLs, BB2, PL2, DFRee, DFI0, XSqrAM, DLH13, HiemstraLM, InL2, DLH, DPH, IFB2, TFIDF, InB2, InexpB2 , DFRBM25 , BM25, LGD, LemurTFIDF, InexpC2.
Expansion model	7 query expansion models: nil, Rocchio, KL, Bo1, Bo2, KLCorrect, Information, KLComplete.
Expansion documents	Number of documents used for query expansion: 2, 5, 10, 20, 50, 100.
Expansion terms	Number of expansion terms: 2, 5, 10, 15, 20.
Expansion min-docs	Minimal number of documents an expansion term should appear in: 2, 5, 10, 20, 50.

We define a set of 65 features for L2R models on a pair (q_k, c_j) that can be divided into four different groups: 43 features computed using query word statistics (QuerySTATS), 16 features describing the linguistic properties of the query (QueryLing), 1 feature describing the retrieval model (RetModel), and 4 features related to query expansion parameters (Expansion). The two last groups of features are the same as shown in Table 1. We provide a brief description of QueryStats and QueryLing features.

QueryStats: These features are query-dependent statistical features that were previously used in both query difficulty prediction [4, 6] and learning to rank [9] settings. These features include query terms statistics such as variations of their IDF in the collection (min, max, avg, and sum IDF over the query terms), Query Feedback [14] (min, max, etc.) calculated using various numbers of feedback documents and several default retrieval models such as QL and Bo2, or variant of the NQC which is based on the standard deviation of retrieved documents scores [12].

QueryLing: These are also query-dependent features, but they focus on modelling the linguistic properties of the query. We implemented the features defined in [10], such as the number of WordNet synsets for query terms, the number of prepositions in the query, and so on.

Query-dependent features aim to inform the L2R technique about the characteristics of the query, thus allowing to select different system configuration on a per query basis. As a first investigation, we use all the reasonable features at our disposal without performing any feature selection, leaving this aspect for future work. While the study of the influence of the intrinsic parameters of retrieval models, such as Language Models or BM25, is out of the scope of this paper, we plan to explore it in future experiments. In the following experiments, we used the default parameters provided by Terrier for all the retrieval models.

We use three common performance metrics to rank system configurations: MAP, P@100, and Rprec. These metrics are chosen because they were found to be the least correlated [1].

Three types of L2R techniques have been proposed in the literature based on point-wise, pair-wise and list-wise principles [8]. The point-wise approaches aim at learning to predict a relevance score or class for each document, while the pair-wise approaches learn to predict if one document is more relevant than another. Finally, the list-wise models consider the whole list of documents and optimise a ranking measure. All the L2R models could be suitable to our task: they can rank system configurations in such a way that the best configuration will be ranked first. This is the configuration that we want to select. Notice, however, that the relative positions of the elements at lower positions are also important in L2R models, in particular in pair-wise and list-wise models. The optimisation related to this part of ranking may not be crucial or necessary for our task. Our learning objective could be different. However, we do not examine this question in this paper.

We experimented with a large selection of the existing L2R techniques made available by the RankLib[3] and the SVM^{rank} [4] toolkits. The performance varies largely among the models. Due to space limit, we only report the results with the following representative models: Gradient Boosted Regression Trees (GBRT) [5], Random Forests [3], LambdaMART [13], and SVM^{rank} [7], since we found that these techniques were the most effective for our task. Our selection of L2R techniques covers all the three categories: GBRT and Random Forests are point-wise techniques, SVM^{rank} is pair-wise, and LambdaMART is classified as both pair-wise and list-wise. We trained the three techniques implemented in RankLib to optimise the nDCG@10 of the ranked list of configurations, in which the effectiveness of a configuration is used *in lieu* of the relevance grade of the original L2R algorithms. SVM^{rank} has its own optimisation criteria.

3. EXPERIMENTAL RESULTS

We carried out experiments on two TREC AdHoc test collections: TREC-7 (queries 351-400) and TREC-8 (queries

[1]Impossible configurations, such as using nil expansion method but a number of expansion documents and terms, are excluded.

[2]Details can be found at terrier.org/docs/v4.0/javadoc.

[3]sourceforge.net/p/lemur/wiki/RankLib/

[4]www.cs.cornell.edu/people/tj/svm_light/svm_rank.html

Table 2: **Results with different L2R models and feature ablations. △ indicates statistically significant improvements over the Grid Search baseline, according to a paired t-test ($p < 0.05$). ▼ indicates statistically significant decreases induced by a feature ablation with respect to the corresponding (All) models.**

	MAP		P@100		RPrec	
BM25	0.1942		0.1719		0.2330	
Grid Search	0.2480		0.2213		0.2835	
Random Forests (All)	0.3319 △		0.2785 △		0.3439 △	
- QUERYSTATS	0.3180 △	(-4.17%)	0.2947 △	(+5.80%)	0.3658 △	(+6.35%)
- QUERYLING	0.3367 △	(+1.43%)	0.2835 △	(+1.80%)	0.3507 △	(+1.96%)
- RETMODEL	0.3210 △	(-3.28%)	0.2746	(-1.44%)	0.3462 △	(+0.65%)
- EXPANSION	0.2201▼	(-33.68%)	0.1843▼	(-33.84%)	0.2384▼	(-30.69%)
SVM^{rank} (All)	0.3073 △		0.2529		0.3204	
- QUERYSTATS	0.2820 △	(-8.23%)	0.2667 △	(+5.48%)	0.3304 △	(+3.12%)
- QUERYLING	0.2918 △	(-5.03%)	0.2501	(-1.11%)	0.3498 △	(+9.19%)
- RETMODEL	0.3118 △	(+1.48%)	0.2628 △	(+3.91%)	0.3400 △	(+6.10%)
- EXPANSION	0.1723▼	(-43.92%)	0.1203▼	(-52.43%)	0.1914▼	(-40.28%)
GBRT (All)	0.3338 △		0.2803 △		0.3400 △	
- QUERYSTATS	0.3375 △	(+1.11%)	0.2699	(-3.71%)	0.3275 △	(-3.71%)
- QUERYLING	0.2982 △	(-10.68%)	0.2908	(+3.75%)	0.3288 △	(-3.31%)
- RETMODEL	0.3299 △	(-1.17%)	0.2702	(-3.62%)	0.3581 △	(+5.32%)
- EXPANSION	0.2345▼	(-29.75%)	0.1775▼	(-36.66%)	0.2505▼	(-26.32%)
LambdaMART (All)	0.3271 △		0.2772 △		0.2873	
- QUERYSTATS	0.3272 △	(+0.03%)	0.2705 △	(-2.42%)	0.2692	(-6.28%)
- QUERYLING	0.3324 △	(+1.62%)	0.2695 △	(-2.78%)	0.3486 △	(+21.34%)
- RETMODEL	0.3144 △	(-3.87%)	0.2713 △	(-2.13%)	0.3528 △	(+22.78%)
- EXPANSION	0.2188▼	(-33.11%)	0.1456▼	(-47.49%)	0.2078▼	(-27.67%)
Upper bound (oracle performance)	0.4136		0.3434		0.4490	

401-450) for which we merged the queries into one set since the document collection is the same. We used a 5-fold cross validation, where each fold has separate training (3/5), validation (1/5), and test sets (1/5). The training queries are used to train L2R models, the validation queries are used to minimise over-fitting, and the test queries are used to evaluate the learned models. We report the average performance on the test queries in Table 2. For each test query, we use the system configuration that has been ranked first by the learned models.

In order to evaluate the effect of each group of features presented in Section 2 (QUERYSTATS, QUERYLING, RETMODEL, EXPANSION) for selecting the configuration, we perform the following abalation analysis: we remove one group of features at a time, and perform again the learning and testing without the ablated features in order to see the change in retrieval effectiveness. A large decrease in retrieval effectiveness would indicate that the ablated features are deemed important for the learner.

The rows with (All) mean that the models have been learned using the full set of 65 features, while the other rows exhibit results without the ablated group of features. We compare the results of our approach to two baselines: a Grid Search method, which selects the best configuration on a set of training queries (we used both the training and the validation queries here) and uses it on the test queries. This corresponds to the common practice in IR for setting multiple parameters at once. Notice that this configuration is query-independent. For an easy comparison, we also provide the performance of a standard BM25 run (without query expansion), using the default configuration provided by Terrier. We also report in Table 2 the Upper bound of our method, which uses the best possible system configuration for each query (i.e. the oracle performance).

On analysing Table 2, we can make three main observations. Firstly, and most importantly, we see that all L2R techniques can effectively learn to rank reasonable system configurations. All the L2R models can produce much better results than the traditional way (Grid Search) to set system parameters. This result clearly indicates the benefit of using a L2R model to select an appropriate system configuration for a query, rather than setting a unique configuration globally. Among the L2R models, Random Forest, GBRT and LambdaMART produce equivalent performances, while SVM^{rank} performs slightly lower. The superiority of pair-wise and list-wise models over point-wise models cannot be concluded. This observation differs slightly from the traditional use of L2R models where pair-wise and list-wise models are found to perform better than point-wise models [8]. The difference can be explained by the fact that the relative positions of configurations at lower ranks have important impact in pair-wise and list-wise L2R models, while this is not important for our task. The L2R models also compare favorably to the best performing systems of the TREC-7 and TREC-8 AdHoc tracks. The best systems at TREC-7 and TREC-8 achieved 0.3032 and 0.3303 in MAP, while the LambdaMART (All) model can produce 0.3148 and 0.3396 in MAP on the two separate sets of queries.

Secondly, we observe that ablating the EXPANSION group of features always significantly decreases the performance of the learned models, hinting the huge importance of these features for learning an effective model. A possible explanation is that the best parameters for query expansion vary a lot across queries, and the other features are unable to make differences among them. Therefore, in absence of the expansion features, the L2R models cannot make an informed choice on system configuration.

The ablation of the other groups of features has less impact. When we remove the RETMODEL feature, the performances can increase or decrease slightly. This highlights the fact that our approach is able to effectively rank system configuration even without using the retrieval model as a feature. A possible explanation is that the other features are often sufficient to determine the best configuration, or the selections of retrieval model across queries are usually consistent so that the feature about the retrieval model does not provide much additional help. Similar observation also holds on the query-dependent features. However, this does not mean that query-dependent features are useless. There could be more questions about the specific features in this group : some of the features could be redundant, while some others do not seem to be strongly informative. Notice also that we have two groups of query features. When we remove one of them in our ablation analysis, it is possible that the other group can still provide similar information about the query. We will perform more analyses on the features and their effects in future work.

Finally, the results demonstrate the importance of making query-dependent configuration selections. The low impact of query-dependent features in configuration selection does not mean that the final selection of configuration is not query-dependent. For each query, a L2R model always makes a different selection based on the available features. The benefit of query-dependent selection can be best seen by contrasting the L2R models with Grid search, which sets the best query-independent configuration: We can see tat all the query-dependent configuration selections by L2R models are better than Grid search. However, compared to the Oracle performance, we also see that the selections by L2R models are not always the best for each query. There is much room for improvements on this in the future.

4. CONCLUSION

In this paper, we proposed a new approach to set system configuration using learning-to-rank methods. We showed that this is a feasible approach, and it can produce superior performance to the state of the art. Our experiments also showed the importance and benefits to make query-dependent configuration setting. The feature ablation analysis showed various impact of different features. In particular, query features showed lower impact than we expected. More investigations are needed to fully understand the reason. In this study, we did not make a selection of the features to be used and simply used all the features proposed in the literature that sound relevant. However, we observe that the relevance of some of the features to our task may be low. The features can also be redundant, providing similar information. It will be useful to perform feature selection in the future.

This study is a first investigation in the new direction of learning to set system configurations. Many underlying questions remain to be addressed in the future. For example, should the learning objective be different from those used in the L2R algorithms? How can we define a different learning algorithm specifically for ranking configurations?

Acknowledgments

This work is partly supported by the French Agency for Scientific Research (Agence Nationale de la Recherche) under the CAAS project (ANR 2010 CORD 001 01), and partly by an NSERC-Discovery grant.

5. REFERENCES

[1] A. Baccini, S. Déjean, L. Lafage, and J. Mothe. How many performance measures to evaluate information retrieval systems? *Knowledge and Information Systems*, 30(3), 2012.

[2] A. Bigot, S. Déjean, and J. Mothe. Learning to Choose the Best System Configuration in Information Retrieval: the Case of Repeated Queries. *Journal of Universal Computer Science*, 21(13):1726–1745, 2015.

[3] L. Breiman. Random forests. *Machine Learning*, 45(1):5–32, Oct. 2001.

[4] D. Carmel and E. Yom-Tov. Estimating the query difficulty for information retrieval. *Synthesis Lectures on Information Concepts, Retrieval, and Services*, 2(1):1–89, 2010.

[5] J. H. Friedman. Greedy function approximation: A gradient boosting machine. *Annals of Statistics*, 29:1189–1232, 2000.

[6] C. Hauff, D. Hiemstra, and F. de Jong. A survey of pre-retrieval query performance predictors. In *Proc. of CIKM*, 2008.

[7] T. Joachims. Optimizing search engines using clickthrough data. In *Proc. of KDD*, 2002.

[8] T.-Y. Liu. Learning to rank for information retrieval. *Foundations and Trends in Information Retrieval*, 3(3):225–331, 2009.

[9] C. Macdonald, R. L. Santos, I. Ounis, and B. He. About learning models with multiple query-dependent features. *ACM Transations on Information Systems*, 31(3), 2013.

[10] J. Mothe and L. Tanguy. Linguistic features to predict query difficulty. In *Proc. of SIGIR*, 2005.

[11] I. Ounis, G. Amati, V. Plachouras, B. He, C. Macdonald, and C. Lioma. Terrier: A High Performance and Scalable Information Retrieval Platform. In *Proc. of OSIR*, 2006.

[12] A. Shtok, O. Kurland, D. Carmel, F. Raiber, and G. Markovits. Predicting query performance by query-drift estimation. *ACM Transactions on Information Systems*, 30(2):11:1–11:35, 2012.

[13] Q. Wu, C. J. Burges, K. M. Svore, and J. Gao. Adapting boosting for information retrieval measures. *Information Retrieval*, 13(3):254–270, 2010.

[14] Y. Zhou and W. B. Croft. Query performance prediction in web search environments. In *Proc. of SIGIR*, 2007.

Adaptive Distributional Extensions to DFR Ranking

Casper Petersen
University of Copenhagen
cazz@di.ku.dk

Jakob Grue Simonsen
University of Copenhagen
simonsen@di.ku.dk

Kalervo Järvelin
University of Tampere
Kalervo.Jarvelin@staff.uta.fi

Christina Lioma
University of Copenhagen
c.lioma@di.ku.dk

ABSTRACT

Divergence From Randomness (DFR) ranking models assume that informative terms are distributed in a corpus differently than non-informative terms. Different statistical models (e.g. Poisson, geometric) are used to model the distribution of non-informative terms, producing different DFR models. An informative term is then detected by measuring the divergence of its distribution from the distribution of non-informative terms. However, there is little empirical evidence that the distributions of non-informative terms used in DFR actually fit current datasets. Practically this risks providing a poor separation between informative and non-informative terms, thus compromising the discriminative power of the ranking model. We present a novel extension to DFR, which first detects the best-fitting distribution of non-informative terms in a collection, and then adapts the ranking computation to this best-fitting distribution. We call this model Adaptive Distributional Ranking (ADR) because it adapts the ranking to the statistics of the specific dataset being processed each time. Experiments on TREC data show ADR to outperform DFR models (and their extensions) and be comparable in performance to a query likelihood language model (LM).

CCS Concepts

•Information systems → Retrieval models and ranking;

1. INTRODUCTION

Early work on automatic indexing [3, 8, 9] observed that *informative* words, e.g. those belonging to a technical vocabulary, are distributed in a document collection differently than *non-informative* words, e.g. those usually treated as stopwords. Specifically, the difference in the distributions of these two different types of words was that informative words were observed to appear more densely in few so-called *elite* documents. Based on this, non-informative words were modelled by a Poisson distribution, and it was hypothesised that an informative word can be detected by measuring the extent to which its distribution deviates from a Poisson distribution, or, in other words, by testing the hypothesis that the word distribution on the whole document collection does not fit the Poisson model [2]. This so-called 2-Poisson model has led to well-known ranking models such as BM25 [18] or Divergence from Randomness (DFR) [2, 14].

For DFR ranking models in particular (presented in Section 2), the idea that non-informative terms tend to follow a specific distribution is central. Different distributions (e.g. the Poisson or geometric distribution) can be used to obtain different DFR ranking models. The goal is to choose a distribution that provides a good fit to the empirical distribution of non-informative terms in C. However, there is little empirical evidence that the distributions used in DFR actually fit current datasets. Practically this risks providing a poor separation between informative and non-informative terms, thus compromising the discriminative power of the ranking model.

Motivated by this, we present a novel extension to DFR, which first detects the best-fitting distribution (among a candidate set of distributions) of non-informative terms in a collection, and then adapts the ranking computation to this "best-fitting" distribution. We call this model Adaptive Distributional Ranking (ADR, presented in Section 3) because it adapts the ranking to the statistics of the specific dataset being processed each time. With our approach, only one ranking model is obtained per collection: the one that provides the best fit to the distribution of non-informative terms in that collection. Evaluation on TREC datasets (Section 4) shows that our ADR models outperform the original DFR models, as well as more recent DFR extensions and perform on a par with a query likelihood LM [17].

2. DIVERGENCE FROM RANDOMNESS

Given a query q and a document d, a DFR ranking model estimates the relevance $R(q,d)$ of d to q as [2]:

$$R(q,d)=\sum_{t\in q} f_{t,q}\cdot(-\log_2 P_1)\cdot(1-P_2) \qquad (1)$$

where t is a term, $f_{t,q}$ is the frequency of t in q, $-\log_2 P_1$ is the information content of t in d, and $(1-P_2)$ is the risk of accepting t as a descriptor of d's topic. We explain each of these two components next.

The information content P_1 measures the divergence of $f_{t,d}$ from $f_{t,C}$, where a higher divergence means more information is carried by t in d. The assumption is that terms that bring little information are distributed over all documents in a certain way across the entire corpus; different distributions (called "models of randomness" in DFR) give rise to different DFR ranking models. For example, using a Poisson distribution, P_1 is:

$$P_1(t,\lambda,d)=e^{-\lambda}\lambda^{\hat{f}_{t,d}}/\hat{f}_{t,d}! \qquad (2)$$

where $\lambda=f_{t,C}/|C|$ is the parameter of the Poisson distribution, and $\hat{f}_{t,d}=f_{t,d}\cdot\log_2(1+c\cdot \text{avg\_l}/|d|)$ is a logarithmic term fre-

CIKM'16, October 24-28, 2016, Indianapolis, IN, USA

DOI: http://dx.doi.org/10.1145/2983323.2983895

quency normalisation where c is a free parameter, avg_l is the average document length in the collection, and $|d|$ is the length of d (the number of terms). Eqn. 2 returns the probability of seeing $\hat{f}_{t,d}$ occurrences of t in d and effectively tests whether t's distribution on C fits the Poisson distribution. If the probability of obtaining $\hat{f}_{t,d}$ occurrences of t is low, then t carries a high amount of information [2]. In addition to the Poisson distribution used in this example, DFR models can be instantiated also with the geometric, tf-idf (I_n), tf-itf (I_F) and tf-expected-idf (I_n^e) [2].

The second component of Eqn. 1, the information gain, P_2, is the conditional probability of encountering $f_{t,d}+1$ occurrences of t in d. If P_2 is high, the risk $(1-P_2)$ associated with accepting t as a descriptor of d is low. Such "after-effect" sampling was taken [2] to be normalised either with Laplace: $P_2 = f_{t,d}/(f_{t,d}+1)$ or Bernoulli normalisation: $P_2 = (f_{t,C}+1)/(n_t \cdot f_{t,d}+1)$ where n_t is the number of documents where t occurs.

3. ADAPTIVE DISTRIBUTIONAL RANKING

Our ADR models follow the basic DFR rationale presented above, but adapt the computation of P_1 in Eqn. 1 to the best-fitting distribution of non-informative term collection frequencies for each collection. The ADR algorithm is shown below.

Algorithm *ADR(C)*
Input: Collection C; $\mathbb{Y}$ = {parameterised statistical models}
1. **for** the set T of non-informative terms in C
2. **for** each model $\mathcal{M} \in \mathbb{Y}$
3. find $\mathcal{M}$'s best parameters for fitting T
4. find $\hat{\mathcal{M}}$ that fits T best
5. replace P_1 in Eqn. 1 by $\hat{\mathcal{M}}$
6. **return** an ADR model derived for C

Given some collection C and a set $\mathbb{Y}$ of candidate parameterised statistical models, we determine for each candidate model the optimal parameter values (if any) that make it fit how non-informative terms are distributed in C (step 3 in the algorithm), select the best-fitting distribution (step 4), and plug it in the place of P_1 in Eqn. 1 (step 5). The output is an ADR model adapted specifically to C (i.e. a collection-specific ranking model). In this work, we use as candidate parameterised statistical distributions all the discrete models in [16], namely the geometric, negative Binomial, Poisson, power law and Yule–Simon. However, any other set of candidate distributions can be used in step 2. We explain steps 3 – 5 next.

3.1 Step 3. Optimal parameter fitting

A parameterised statistical distribution $\mathcal{M} = \{g(T|\theta) : \theta \in \Theta\}$ where $\theta \in \Theta$ is a real or integer-valued vector, is a family of probability density or mass functions $g(T|\theta)$. *Parameter estimation* is then the problem of finding, among all the probability density/mass functions of $\mathcal{M}$, the $\hat{\theta}$ that most likely generated T. We estimate $\hat{\theta}$ with maximum likelihood estimation as follows: We seek the density/mass function that makes the observed term frequencies "most likely" [13] using a likelihood function, $\mathcal{L}(\theta|T)$, that specifies the likelihood of θ given T. $\hat{\theta}$ is then obtained by maximising the average likelihood $\hat{\theta} = \text{argmax}_{\theta \in \Theta} \mathcal{L}(\theta|T)/|T|$ where $\mathcal{L}(\theta|T) = \sum_{i=1}^{|T|} \log g(f_{t,C}^i|\theta)$, and $f_{t,C}^i$ is the collection frequency of the ith term $t \in T$.

3.2 Step 4: Best-fitting distribution

In step 4 of the ADR algorithm we select, from the set of candidate statistical distributions, the one that best quantifies the distribution of term frequencies for non-informative terms in C. We do this using Vuong's Closeness Test [20] and Akaike's Information Criterion [1], both of which are among the least controversial and widely used statistical tests for model selection [5]. Both tests are based on the Kullback–Leibler divergence and will favour the same model in the limit of large sample sizes, i.e. the model that minimises the information loss w.r.t. the unknown but "true" model.

3.3 Step 5: Distribution–adapted ranking

Let $\hat{\mathcal{M}}$ be the best-fitting distribution to the collection term frequencies of the non-informative terms. Then, in step 5, we replace the distribution P_1 in Eqn. 1 by $\hat{\mathcal{M}}$, yielding:

$$R(q,d) = \sum_{t \in q} f_{t,q} \cdot (-\log_2 \hat{\mathcal{M}}) \cdot (1-P_2) \quad (3)$$

$\hat{\mathcal{M}}$ captures the same assumption as all DFR models: that non-informative terms are distributed in a certain way. However, whereas in DFR this assumption is not tested, ADR empirically validates the choice of $\hat{\mathcal{M}}$ per collection.

4. EVALUATION

We next evaluate the retrieval performance of our ADR models. As ADR can produce different ranking models for different datasets, we split this section into two parts. Section 4.1 presents our datasets and the ADR models instantiated for these datasets. Section 4.2 compares the retrieval performance of these ADR models against relevant baselines.

4.1 Deriving ADR Models

We use TREC disks 4 and 5 (TREC-d45) with queries 301-450 and 601-700 and ClueWeb cat. B. (CWEB09) with queries 1 - 200, minus query 20 for which no documents are judged relevant as datasets. All datasets are indexed without stop word removal and without stemming using Indri 5.10. For our ADR models, we must identify non-informative terms in each collection and the best fitting distribution of $f_{t,C}$ of the non-informative terms in the collection. We detect non-informative terms using SVM classification, as follows. Given an initial list of 40 informative and non-informative terms (manually compiled by three humans with complete agreement, see Table 1), we compute the term weight of these terms (using IDF [11], x^I [3], residual-IDF (RIDF) [4], gain [15] and z-measure [8] - see [12] for an overview of term weighting), and use these term weights as features to train a binary SVM classifier using 10-fold cross-validation on all feature combinations. We use an SVM approach instead of any of the above term-weighting approaches, as the latter ones require (manual) setting some ad hoc threshold above/below which terms are considered informative/non-informative. In contrast, the best classifier correctly classifies $\propto 86\%$ of the terms using RIDF and gain term weights as features. We use this classifier to classify each term in TREC-d45 and CWEB09 as informative or non-informative.

Next, using steps 3 – 4 of the ADR algorithm we find that the best-fitting statistical model to the distribution of non-informative term frequencies in both datasets is the discrete Yule–Simon (YS) with parameter $p = 1.804$ (TREC-d45) and $p = 1.627$ (CWEB09).

The YS distribution is defined for $x \in \mathbb{Z}^+, x \geq 1$ [19]:

$$\text{P}(x|p+1) = (p+1) \cdot \frac{\Gamma(x) \cdot \Gamma(p+1)}{\Gamma(x+p+1)} \quad (4)$$

where $p > 0$ is the distribution parameter and Γ is the gamma

Informative terms		Non-informative terms	
hypothermia	intercepted	welcome	awesome
congolese	furloughs	beginner	jolly
outpaced	randomization	spade	out
anthropocentric	existentialist	delete	temp
iridescence	canvass	quit	feels
archdiocesan	colonisation	least	loss
nonconformist	airbrushed	silly	clear
overclocking	leviathans	cent	off
nominalization	inflammation	jar	test
translucent	handmade	chat	fork
shortwave	monasticism	yards	move
crystallography	aperitif	fast	pair
expressionist	pathologize	view	stop
cephalopod	abolishment	fold	colour
paparazzi	bookcase	roll	sit
presided	hydraulic	follow	back
beneficiary	vested	pen	hello
convection	floods	day	stair
custodian	chivalry	flash	best
populist	constrained	money	considerable

Table 1: Informative and non-informative terms.

function. Replacing x with $\hat{f}_{t,d}$ (see Section 2), we obtain:

$$P_1^{YS}(\hat{f}_{t,d}|p+1) = (p+1) \cdot \frac{\Gamma(\hat{f}_{t,d}) \cdot \Gamma(p+1)}{\Gamma(\hat{f}_{t,d}+p+1)} \quad (5)$$

which, for a term t, returns the probability of having $\hat{f}_{t,d}$ occurrences of t. Identically to the original Poisson model [2], Eqn. 5 is theoretically dubious as it is a discrete distribution whose input is a real number. Consequently, we use Lanczo's method to approximate the Γ function identical to [2]. Plugging Eqn. 5 into Eqn. 1 gives:

$$R(q,d) = \sum_{t \in q} f_{t,q} \cdot (-\log_2 P_1^{YS}) \cdot (1-P_2) \quad (6)$$

We refer to Eqn. 6 as our YS ADR model, or YS for short.

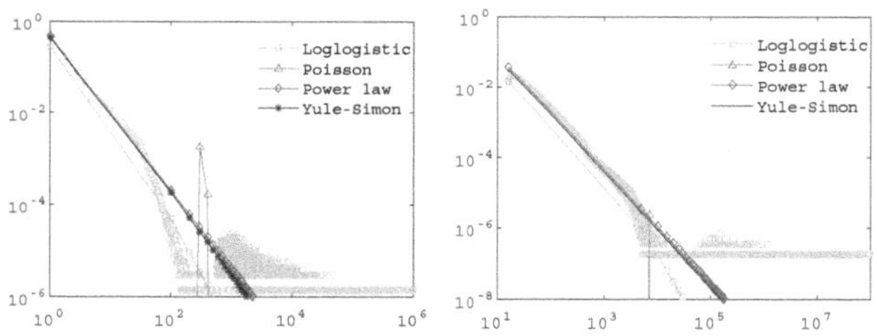

(a) TREC Disks 4 & 5 (b) CWEB09

Figure 1: Collection term frequencies for non-informative terms (grey) in CWEB09, and TREC-d45. Superimposed on each figure are MLE fitted log-logistic, Poisson, power law and Yule–Simon distributions as references.

4.2 Retrieval Experiments

Baselines and Tuning. We compare our ADR ranking model (YS) to a Poisson (P), tf-idf (I_n), log-logistic (LL), smoothed power law (SPL) and query-likelihood unigram LM with Dirichlet smoothing (LMDir). P and I_n are original DFR models [2]; LL [6] and SPL [7] are information models that extend the original DFR models. All DFR/ADR models are postfixed with L2 meaning that Laplace and logarithmic term normalisation (see Section 2) are used. Following previous work [2, 7], the parameter values of the distributions used in DFR/ADR (e.g. Poisoon or Yule–Simon) are induced from the collection statistics in two ways (we experiment with both): $T_{tc} = f_{t,C}/|C|$, or $T_{dc} = n_t/|C|$. E.g., PL2-T_{tc} is a Poisson model using Laplace and logarithmic term normalisation, where Poisson's $\lambda = T_{tc} = f_{t,C}/|C|$

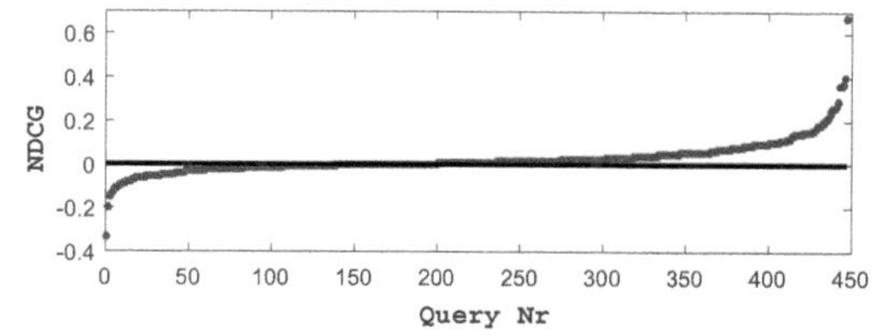

Figure 2: Per query difference in nDCG between YSL2 and LMDir for all queries. Horizontal line indicates no difference. Points above zero favour YSL2 over LMDir.

(see Eqn. 2), and YSL2-T_{dc} is a Yule–Simon ADR model using Laplace and logarithmic term normalisation, where Yule–Simon's $p = T_{dc} = n_t/|C|$ (see Eqn. 4). We retrieve the top-1000 documents according to each ranking model using title-only queries, and measure performance using P@10, Bpref, ERR@20, nDCG@10 and nDCG. All models are tuned using 3-fold cross-validation and we report the average over all three test folds. We vary c (the free parameter in the logarithmic term normalisation - see Section 2) in the range $\{0.5,1,2,4,6,8\}$ [7], and μ of LMDir in the range $\{100,500,800,1000,2000,3000,4000,5000,8000,10000\}$.
Findings. The results are shown in Table 2. For CWEB09, our YSL2 models obtain the best performance at all times. For TREC-d45, our YSL2 models obtain the best performance on early precision retrieval (P@10, ERR@20 and nDCG@10), while the SPLL2 models perform best on nDCG and Bpref (with YSL2 following closely). As Fig. 1 shows, the power law (used in SPLL2) and Yule–Simon (used in YSL2) have very similar fits, which explains their similar scores in Table 2. In Fig. 1 we also see that the log-logistic, power law and Yule–Simon all approximate the head of the distribution (collection term frequencies up to ≈ 100), though all fail to model the "noisy" tail (collection term frequencies > 1000) well. In contrast, the Poisson distribution fails to model the empirical data in any range, possibly explaining the overall low retrieval performance in Table 2. That the Yule–Simon distribution gives the highest retrieval performance indicates the merit of using the best-fitting distribution for DFR ranking models. Fig. 2 shows the per-query difference in nDCG between the YSL2 and LMDir baseline for all queries. We see that the number of queries that benefit from YSL2 is substantially higher (270 queries) than for the LMDir (163 queries), confirming the scores in Table 2.

5. RELATED WORK

Our work can be seen as a refinement of DFR ranking models. Several other approaches attempt such refinements. For example, Clinchant and Gaussier [6] formulated heuristic retrieval constraints to assess the validity of DFR ranking models, and found that several DFR ranking models do not conform to these heuristics. On this basis, a simplified DFR model based on a log-logistic (LL) statistical distribution was proposed, which adheres to all heuristic retrieval constraints. Experimental evaluation showed that the LL model improved MAP on several collections. In a follow-up study, Clinchant and Gaussier [7] introduced *information models* which are simplified DFR models that do not rely on so-called after-effect normalisation. They instantiated the LL and a "smoothed power law" (SPL) ranking model, and showed that both models tend to outperform a LM, BM25, but not two original DFR models on smaller TREC and CLEF collections. Closest to ours is the work by Hui et al. [10] who developed DFR extensions where the distributions of $f_{t,C}$

	TREC disks 4& 5					ClueWeb09 cat. B.				
Model	nDCG	P@10	Bpref	ERR@20	nDCG@10	nDCG	P@10	Bpref	ERR@20	nDCG@10
LMDir	.4643	.3845	.2239	.1043	.3968	.2973	.2586	.2209	.0973	.1769
PL2-T_{tc} [2]	.2524*	.1273*	.1009*	.0359*	.1332*	.1448*	.0712*	.1258*	.0211*	.0472*
PL2-T_{dc} [2]	.2487*	.1217*	.0960*	.0347*	.1273*	.1444*	.0709*	.1252*	.0314*	.0471*
I_nL2-T_{tc} [2]	.2917*	.1627*	.1114*	.0478*	.1742*	.1596*	.0782*	.1405*	.0352*	.0511*
I_nL2-T_{dc} [2]	.2818*	.1626*	.1088*	.0481*	.1745*	.1596*	.0783*	.1407*	.0352*	.0512*
LLL2-T_{tc} [6]	.4812	.4049	.2341	.1072	.4142	.3184	.2542	.2349	.0926	.1706
LLL2-T_{dc} [6]	.4810	.3982	.2329	.1069	.4097	.3180	.2542	.2349	.0928	.1707
SPLL2-T_{tc} [7]	.4863	.4144	.2375	.1103	.4276	.3207	.2529	.2357	.0945	.1720
SPLL2-T_{dc} [7]	**.4876**	.4176	**.2387**	.1107	.4299	.3224	.2586	.2370	.0958	.1752
YSL2-T_{tc} (ADR)	.4644	.3982	.2280	.1048	.4069	.3197	.2601	.2359	.0951	.1752
YSL2-T_{dc} (ADR)	.4860	**.4182**	.2381	**.1113**	**.4312**	**.3240**	**.2666**	**.2376**	**.0985**	**.1810**

Table 2: Retrieval performance. Grey denotes larger than the LMDir baseline. Bold marks the best results. * marks statistically significant difference from the LMDir baseline using a t-test at the .05% level.

are modelled using multiple statistical distributions. However, (i) no justification or empirical validation of the choice of statistical distributions used was given, and (ii) the distribution of all terms, rather than only the non-informative terms, was used. Finally, Hui et al's models also removed e.g. collection-wide term frequencies from the ranking component, hence effectively removing the notion of divergence from the DFR framework.

6. CONCLUSION

Divergence From Randomness (DFR) ranking models assume that informative terms in a collection are distributed differently than non-informative terms. Different DFR models are produced depending on the statistical model (e.g. Poisson, geometric) used to quantify the distribution of non-informative terms, where an informative term is detected by measuring the divergence of its distribution from the distribution of non-informative terms. However, there is little evidence that the distributions used in DFR actually fit the the distribution of non-informative terms. To address this, we presented a novel DFR extension called Adaptive Distributional Ranking (ADR), which adapts the ranking computation to the statistics of the specific collection being processed each time. Our ADR models first determine the best-fitting distribution of non-informative terms, and then integrate this distribution into ranking. Experiments on TREC data showed that our ADR models outperformed DFR models (and their extensions), and achieved performance comparable to a query likelihood LM. In future work we plan to experiment with additional collections. We will also study automatically deriving ad hoc distributions suited for the collection data in ADR instead of selecting among a list of standard distributions.

7. ACKNOWLEDGMENTS

Work partially funded by C. Lioma's FREJA research excellence fellowship (grant no. 790095).

8. REFERENCES

[1] H. Akaike. A new look at the statistical model identification. *IEEE TAC*, 19(6):716–723, 1974.

[2] G. Amati and C. J. Rijsbergen. Probabilistic models of information retrieval based on measuring the divergence from randomness. *ACM TOIS*, 20(4):357–389, 2002.

[3] A. Bookstein and D. R. Swanson. Probabilistic models for automatic indexing. *JASIS*, 25(5):312–316, 1974.

[4] K. Church and W. Gale. Inverse document frequency (idf): A measure of deviations from Poisson. In *NLP-VLC*, pages 283–295. Springer, 1999.

[5] K. A. Clarke. Nonparametric model discrimination in international relations. *JCR*, 47(1):72–93, 2003.

[6] S. Clinchant and É. Gaussier. Bridging language modeling and divergence from randomness models: A log-logistic model for IR. In *ICTIR*, pages 54–65, 2009.

[7] S. Clinchant and E. Gaussier. Information-based models for Ad Hoc IR. In *SIGIR*, pages 234–241. ACM, 2010.

[8] S. P. Harter. A probabilistic approach to automatic keyword indexing. part I. on the distribution of specialty words in a technical literature. *JASIS*, 26(4):197–206, 1975.

[9] S. P. Harter. A probabilistic approach to automatic keyword indexing. part II. an algorithm for probabilistic indexing. *JASIS*, 26(5):280–289, 1975.

[10] K. Hui, B. He, T. Luo, and B. Wang. Relevance weighting using within-document term statistics. In *CIKM*, pages 99–104. ACM, 2011.

[11] K. S. Jones. A statistical interpretation of term specificity and its application in retrieval. *JD*, 28(1):11–21, 1972.

[12] C. Lioma and R. Blanco. Part of speech based term weighting for information retrieval. In M. Boughanem, C. Berrut, J. Mothe, and C. Soulé-Dupuy, editors, *ECIR*, volume 5478 of *LNCS*, pages 412–423. Springer, 2009.

[13] I. J. Myung. Tutorial on maximum likelihood estimation. *JMP*, 47(1):90–100, 2003.

[14] I. Ounis, C. Lioma, C. Macdonald, and V. Plachouras. Research directions in terrier: a search engine for advanced retrieval on the web. *Novatica*, VIII(1):49–56, 2007.

[15] K. Papineni. Why inverse document frequency? In *ACL*, pages 1–8. ACL, 2001.

[16] C. Petersen, J. G. Simonsen, and C. Lioma. Power law distributions in information retrieval. *ACM TOIS*, 21(4):1–36, 2015.

[17] J. M. Ponte and W. B. Croft. A language modeling approach to information retrieval. In *SIGIR*, pages 275–281. ACM, 1998.

[18] S. E. Robertson and S. Walker. Some simple effective approximations to the 2-Poisson model for probabilistic weighted retrieval. In *SIGIR*, pages 232–241. Springer, 1994.

[19] H. A. Simon. On a class of skew distribution functions. *Biometrika*, pages 425–440, 1955.

[20] Q. H. Vuong. Likelihood ratio tests for model selection & non-nested hypotheses. *Econometrica*, 57:307–333, 1989.

CyberRank- Knowledge Elicitation for Risk Assessment of Database Security

Hagit Grushka-Cohen,
Department of Software and Information Systems Engineering, Ben-Gurion University of the Negev
hgrushka@post.bgu.ac.il

Oded Sofer, Ofer Biller
IBM Security Division, IBM Cyber Security Center of Excellence, Beer Sheva
{odedso, ofer.biller}@il.ibm.com

Bracha Shapira, Lior Rokach
Department of Software and Information Systems Engineering, Ben-Gurion University of the Negev
{bshapira,liorrk}@bgu.ac.il

ABSTRACT

Security systems for databases produce numerous alerts about anomalous activities and policy rule violations. Prioritizing these alerts will help security personnel focus their efforts on the most urgent alerts. Currently, this is done manually by security experts that rank the alerts or define static risk scoring rules. Existing solutions are expensive, consume valuable expert time, and do not dynamically adapt to changes in policy.

Adopting a learning approach for ranking alerts is complex due to the efforts required by security experts to initially train such a model. The more features used, the more accurate the model is likely to be, but this will require the collection of a greater amount of user feedback and prolong the calibration process. In this paper, we propose CyberRank, a novel algorithm for automatic preference elicitation that is effective for situations with limited experts' time and outperforms other algorithms for initial training of the system. We generate synthetic examples and annotate them using a model produced by Analytic Hierarchical Processing (AHP) to bootstrap a preference learning algorithm. We evaluate different approaches with a new dataset of expert ranked pairs of database transactions, in terms of their risk to the organization. We evaluated using manual risk assessments of transaction pairs, CyberRank outperforms all other methods for cold start scenario with error reduction of 20%.

Keywords

Risk assessment; Preference elicitation; Ranking; Cold Start; Semi Supervised; Cyber Security

1. INTRODUCTION

Security information and event management (SIEM) systems are widely used by organizations to implement security policies and detect attacks and data abuse. Known security risks include abuse of an organization's sensitive information and violation of personal privacy. Various solutions based on anomaly detection identify risks such as data leakage, data misuse, and attacks in database systems [1,2,3,4,5,6]. These systems produce alerts when policy rules are violated or anomalous activities are performed [3,6]. Each alert demands the attention of a security officer [3] who must decide whether an alert represents a risk which should be investigated or dismissed. Some alerts, such as those that pertain to sensitive data, are more urgent than others. Security officers are inundated with data due to the large volume of alerts, and they could easily miss an urgent alert or only become aware of an important alert after it is too late, while handling alerts which pose less risk to the organization. Moreover, an excessive number of irrelevant alerts can cause the user to lose confidence in the security system and abandon it. This challenge is not unique to cyber security systems and represents a hurdle for the adoption of AI alert systems in other environments such as healthcare [8].

Our objective is to develop a prioritization method that automatically rank alerts by the risk a transaction poses, enabling security experts to focus their time and efforts on the most important alerts. Some studies [1,9] have tried to tackle this problem by elevating the threshold of anomaly detection algorithms, however this has resulted in lower recall thereby missing important alerts.

The determination of the level of risk associated with an alert (or activity) is based on the security officer's (SO) knowledge and understanding of each individual case presented to her. The alert is associated with metadata that is used by the SO to determine the risk. Such metadata features may include: User Group, Database Accessed or User OS Vulnerabilities (has the user installed all latest security patches). The definition of risk varies depending on the domain and organization. Given this, most currently used systems must first learn organizational preferences by interrogating the system officer. For example, an organization may prefer to focus their security efforts on protecting trade secrets in their engineering database while being less concerned with the integrity of their corporate wiki.

The security domain is very dynamic: attacks evolve over time, with more sophisticated attacks being created all of the time, and new rules and regulations are established (e.g., regulations related to maintaining customers' privacy). As a result, the risk associated with an activity may change accordingly.

The state-of-the-art approaches for ranking use learning algorithms such as recommender systems to learn user's preferences [10]. Supervised learning algorithms such as Ranking SVM [11,12] or Learning to Rank [13,14] require datasets with annotated examples in order to learn user preferences. Our problem presents a constant cold start situation as features and preferences vary between organizations, and only domain experts are able to accurately annotate the data; therefore, the creation of such datasets is expensive, a fact which often prevents organizations from adopting In addition, even when organizations are willing to invest expert time, most existing methods for ranking alerts generate a long list of customized rules to weigh features, or they use preference elicitation heuristics such as analytic hierarchical processing (AHP) that transform questionnaire answers to features weights. Being rule-based these solutions are static and do not improve with users'

CIKM'16, October 24-28, 2016, Indianapolis, IN, USA
 ISBN 978-1-4503-4073-1/16/10…$15.00
DOI: http://dx.doi.org/10.1145/ 2983323.2983896

feedback; thus they cannot effectively handle the dynamic nature of the risks.

In this paper, we present CyberRank, a novel algorithm for bootstrapping cold start ranking with preference elicitation in the domain of the security of database transactions. It is a method for automatic preference elicitation that is effective in situations with little data availability or requiring minimal user feedback. We generate synthetic examples and annotate them using a model produced by the AHP heuristic, and we use this dataset to bootstrap a preference learning algorithm. Over time the model can be retrained by combining the synthetic data with feedback data gathered from the user. This enables the learning model to provide meaningful results with little or no training examples and keep improving as feedback is gathered. CyberRank, the proposed algorithm provides several advantages: (i) it provides useful results out of the box, (ii) it improves over time, (iii) it is explainable as the SVM model provides linear weights that can be explained to the user, and (iv) can be calibrated by users as needed (e.g., upon policy change).

2. RELATED WORK

Estimating the riskiness of objects can be accomplished by mimicking the ways in which experts rank activities or by defining policy rules. Customized rules are static and their creation is time consuming, in contrast to learning algorithms for ranking which can model the expert knowledge dynamically.

2.1 Ranking Algorithms

Ranking algorithms serve as the base of recommender systems which are often used for document retrieval in a variety of settings [10, 15]. The ranking function assigns a score to each of the ranked entities. The ranking order represents the entities' preference with respect to the question asked. There are two main approaches for the task of ranking (or two main types of ranking algorithms): the pairwise approach and the listwise approach.

2.1.1 *Pairwise approach*

This approach formulizes the problem as a classification problem by collecting pairs of instances, for example, database (DB) activities, and assigning a label representing the relative riskiness of the two activities to the pair. It then trains a supervised classification model such as ranking SVM [11,12] RankBoost, and RankNet [16]. For this, we form the difference of all comparable elements such that our data is transformed into $(x'_k, y'_k) = \left(x_i - x_j, sign(y_i - y_j)\right)$ for all comparable pairs. The task is to separate positive samples from negative ones.

2.1.2 *Listwise approach*

Instead of using object pairs as instances, this approach uses a list of objects as instances in learning and trains a learning function through the minimization of a listwise loss function defined on the predicted list and the ground truth list. Listwise approaches include RankCosine, ListNet, or ListMLE algorithms [13,14].

2.2 AHP

Analytic hierarchy process (AHP) [17] is a heuristic for quickly eliciting preferences, which requires the expert to answer questions about pairs of features and their values (e.g., *"What is more risky: (a) accessing a sensitive object or (b) a user with system vulnerability?"*). In our setting, the result is a weighted model that can be used to grade DB records based on the given value of each feature. In the case of [18], AHP scores were found to be correlated to user perception of risk.

The AHP method has the advantage that it provides measures of judgement consistency, meaning if value *a* is better than value *b*, and value *b* is better than value *c*, then value *a* should be better than value *c*. This allows estimating how consistent the rankings are.

However, this is a static solution that does not enable ongoing learning and therefore needs to be repeated when additional policies are implemented or new hazards are identified.

2.3 Semi-Supervised Learning for Ranking

In the semi-supervised approach, the lack of annotated training data is addressed by leveraging unannotated examples [15]. Zhang and Ben He [19] created pseudo labels for learning a ranking model in the domain of information retrieval (IR). They chose training examples from query results which were easily divided into two clusters, based on the level of relevance, and labeled the documents in the more relevant cluster as positive.

2.4 Alerting Methods in the Security Domain

Several methods, such as [2,3,4], have been proposed and applied for the detection of data leakage, data misuse, and attacks in database systems. The main approach focuses on using machine learning, mostly unsupervised, to detect anomalous patterns or outliers [3,5]. The focus is on reducing false positive rates due to class imbalance (most activities are legitimate). In this work we are not attempting to detect misuse or anomalous activities but to prioritize the alerts produced by anomaly detection systems.

3. Ranking by Risk

We examined three approaches for prioritization: a baseline approach for preference elicitation using AHP, a supervised pairwise learning approach, and a hybrid approach (described below) which bootstraps the learning algorithm using the preference elicitation model.

3.1 CyberRank Hybrid Approach

Our objective is to develop a system that allows easy initial calibration in order to circumvent the cold start (similar to AHP), while being capable of learning from feedback. We present CyberRank, a method for bootstrapping learning algorithms for ranking based on preference elicitation.

CyberRank consists of two stages: setup and learning (see Figure 1). The setup stage includes preference elicitation with AHP and the generation of synthetic training data annotated with the AHP model. During the learning stage a supervised model is trained from the data, and this model is used for ranking alerts. The user can provide feedback as well, and when feedback is provided, the model is retrained on a training set comprised of both the synthetic and feedback data.

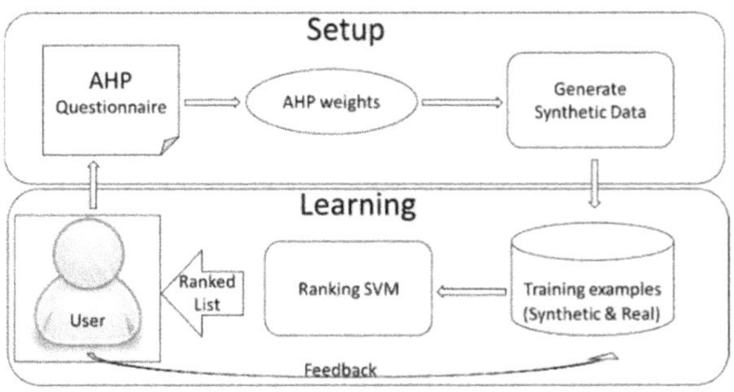

Figure 1 CyberRank Process Breakdown: Setup Stage and Learning Stage

3.1.1 *Preference Elicitation with AHP*

The SO identifies relevant features for the ranking task. For each pair of features, the SO answers which feature is more risky (see section 2.2). The answers are then combined using the AHP heuristic to provide a weighted model for producing a score between 0 and 1 for each transaction.

3.1.2 Generating a Synthetic training set

Synthetic data is generated by sampling values for each feature from a uniform distribution. The result is a vector of categorical values for each feature. Each vector is scored using the weighted model produced in 3.1.1. The score represents the transaction risk according to the questionnaire model (a higher score suggests higher risk).

Pairs of synthetic data points are chosen for training pairwise ranking. In order to make the samples more separable (provide the model with clear cut training examples) we choose pairs with AHP scores difference higher than 0.3 (this difference was chosen empirically based on the pair distance distribution).

3.1.3 Training a Ranking SVM Model

Using the synthetic data generated in step 3.1.2 we train a two class linear SVM model for pairs of transactions.

3.1.4 Incorporating New Training Data (user feedback)

As user feedback is gathered, the new data points are added to the synthetic dataset for training, and the model is retrained. To compensate for the imbalance due to initially small amount of data gathered, we are oversampling the real user generated data. Real transactions are given higher weight during training so that the model assigns 50% of the decision according to the synthetic samples and 50% according to the synthetic dataset (when enough user feedback is gathered the synthetic model can be discarded).

4. EXPERIMENTAL SETTING

The experiments are designed to evaluate CyberRank, based on the accuracy of the pairwise ranking as a function of the size of the training sets. We compared CyberRank with other methods in terms of the number of training examples required to reach a satisfactory level of accuracy. The following is a description of the dataset collected, the compared methods, and the results.

4.1 Datasets

Our dataset is made of two types of data: synthetic annotated examples and manually annotated examples provided by security experts.

4.1.1 SO annotated dataset

The user annotation is based on categorized data within each feature: users were better able to understand and consider categorized data rather than numerical values. For example, referring to the user's IP as external or internal is more informative than the IP itself. Therefore, when constructing the examples to be annotated by expert users we categorized all of the values.

We randomly created possible scenarios using combinations of possible categories for each feature. Each vector was scored using the weighted model created with the AHP (based on the questionnaire filled by the SO).

The dataset annotated by the SO was comprised as follows: one third of the pairs had a low difference in AHP score, another third of the pairs were significantly different based on AHP, and the remaining third fell in between in this regard.

We gathered 170 pairs of examples. For each pair, the SO indicated which transaction is riskier (first or second).

4.1.2 Synthetically annotated data set:

We generated 100 pairs with scores with an AHP score difference higher than 0.3 as described in section 3.1.2. The labels for these pairs were determined using the AHP weighted model. Each pair was represented by the deduction of the values of the features of the second example from the values of the features of the first example. The labels were the sign of the deduction of the AHP scores.

4.2 Experiments

We conducted experiments to test the performance of our approach compared to four models, all of which are briefly introduced below:
1) Pure AHP – defined the risk score based on the AHP weights, no training was involved (simply applying to the test dataset).

2) Vanilla Ranking SVM – trained only on the SO annotated samples.

3) CyberRank no oversampling – Ranking SVM trained on both: (i) user samples and (ii) synthetic data produced with the AHP model (from step 1). No oversampling as described in 3.1.4.

4) CyberRank without pair distance criteria – using Ranking SVM to train the model over randomly chosen synthetic pairs. (we do not require a difference in AHP score as described in 3.1.2).

5) CyberRank – trained on a weighted combination of user generated data and synthetic data produced with the AHP model.

We compared the models' performances for different sized SO annotated datasets. We started with 10 examples and increased the number of samples by five each time, up to 80 samples. Given that we have only 12 features, we were able to apply the models over 10 samples annotated by end users. For less than 10 samples we could not apply model 2 as the model failed to converge.

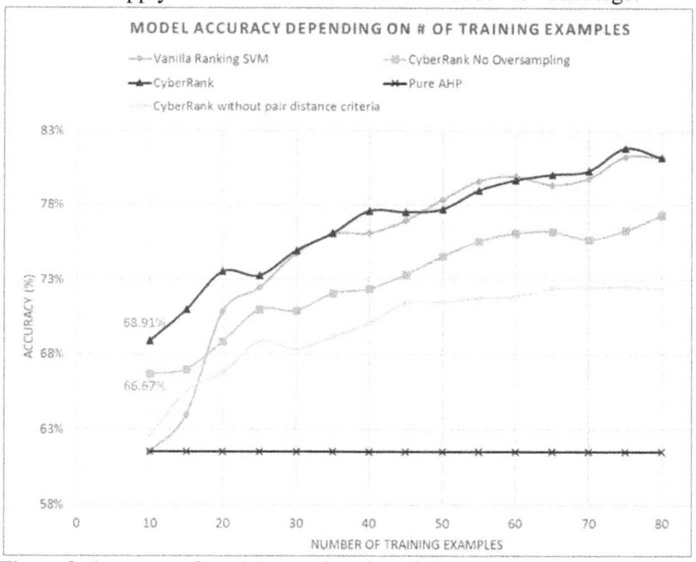

Figure 2. Accuracy of models as a function of the number of training examples

4.3 Evaluation Metric

We conducted 30-fold cross-validation experiments on training datasets, and evaluated the accuracy of our model over the testing dataset, made of 30 percent of the original annotated by SO dataset.

5. Results

5.1 Ranking Accuracy

Figure 2 summarizes the performance of all compared models: AHP, Vanilla Ranking SVM, Ranking SVM with Synthetic Data, and CyberRank. As demonstrated from the results, CyberRank approach outperforms baseline learning algorithms in the cold start scenario: trained only on synthetic data it achieves 61.5% accuracy and 71% accuracy when trained on 15 samples, significantly surpassing the 64% achieved by Ranking SVM on the same sample size (error reduction of 20%). We performed a paired t-test for sample sizes of 10 and 15 examples and found that the means of the Vanilla Ranking SVM and CyberRank are significantly different at $p < 0.05$.

At no point did the Ranking SVM model outperform CyberRank, even when ample data was available: with 70-80 annotated examples both models achieved ~81% accuracy. For a small number of training examples (10 and 20) there was high standard deviation in the accuracy of the Vanilla learning approach (0.12 and 0.11, see Table 1), suggesting high dependency on the examples sampled. Using CyberRank the standard deviation is much lower, reducing that dependency.

The CyberRank variants: (i) no oversampling, and (ii) no distance criteria for synthetic data, both underperformed compared to CyberRank and Ranking SVM.

6. Conclusions

In this paper, we presented and analyzed CyberRank, a novel algorithm for bootstrapping cold start ranking with preference elicitation in the domain of the security of database transactions.

Our proposed algorithm, CyberRank, enables bootstrapping a pairwise preference learning algorithm, such as Ranking SVM, using synthetic examples annotated with a model created using AHP. CyberRank overcomes the need for a minimal number of samples when using supervised learning with a large number of features. It shortens the time before the model becomes useful in cold start scenarios. Our experiments show that the Vanilla Ranking SVM model does not outperform CyberRank at any point. Moreover, CyberRank may be modified to replace the AHP step by annotating synthetic examples using existing policy weights rules, which is useful if a customized model is already available.

We conclude from the experiment that AHP provides a non-trivial baseline for capturing expert knowledge but not accurately enough alone. For generating synthetic data to train on, AHP performed well when using the distance criteria for choosing pairs – when the score difference in AHP was small the pairs confused the Ranking SVM yielding significantly worse results. During the human tagging phase, the security experts expressed a similar intuition that deciding on similar pairs was harder. Oversampling the human annotated examples provided faster improvement of the model, this is especially important in cold start when gathering examples is the most expensive.

The underlying preference model (AHP) is flexible, and in the case of policy changes or changes in the security landscape the preference questionnaire answers may be changed and new synthetic data introduced to the training for reflecting the change. For example, if it is discovered that there are many cyber-attacks from a specific country, the SO can remake the AHP model and produce synthetic samples according to the new preferences. Our proposed approach is not limited to Ranking SVM – other algorithms may be plugged in (we had similar results using decision trees).

Although CyberRank algorithmic framework was originally designed for the domain of the security of database transactions preference learning, it could be used in solving general cold start ranking problems.

All the data and code discussed in the paper are made available[1].

---

[1] https://github.com/hagitGC/CyberRank

7. Acknowledgments

This work has been partially supported by the IBM Cyber Security Center of Excellence, Beer Sheva and by IBM Security Division. Many thanks to Dario Kramer and Rosa Miroshnikov of IBM USA and IBM Canada for their fruitful contribution to the experiments process.

8. REFERENCES

[1] Sallam, A., Bertino, E., Hussain, S.R., Landers, D., Lefler, R.M. and Steiner, D., 2015. DBSAFE—An Anomaly Detection System to Protect Databases From Exfiltration Attempts. *IEEE SYSTEMS JOURNAL*.

[2] Kim, G., Lee, S. and Kim, S., 2014. A novel hybrid intrusion detection method integrating anomaly detection with misuse detection. *Expert Systems with Applications*, 41(4), pp.1690-1700.

[3] Chandola, V., Banerjee, A. and Kumar, V., 2009. Anomaly detection: A survey. In *ACM computing surveys* (CSUR), 41(3), p.15.

[4] Veeramachaneni, K. and Arnaldo, I., AI2: Training a big data machine to defend.

[5] Hodge, V.J. and Austin, J., 2004. A survey of outlier detection methodologies.In *Artificial Intelligence Review*, 22(2), pp.85-126.

[6] Niu, Z., Shi, S., Sun, J. and He, X., 2011. A survey of outlier detection methodologies and their applications. In *Artificial intelligence and computational intelligence* (pp. 380-387). Springer Berlin Heidelberg.

[7] Costante, E., Vavilis, S., Etalle, S., den Hartog, J., Petkovic, M. and Zannone, N., 2013, July. Database anomalous activities detection and quantification. In *Security and Cryptography (SECRYPT), 2013 International Conference* (pp. 1-6). IEEE.

[8] Pecht, M. and Jaai, R., 2010. A prognostics and health management roadmap for information and electronics-rich systems. *Microelectronics Reliability*, 50(3), pp.317-323.

[9] Geng, J., Ye, D., Luo, P. and Lv, P., 2015. A Novel Clustering Algorithm for Database Anomaly Detection. In *Security and Privacy in Communication Networks* (pp. 682-696). Springer International Publishing

[10] Ricci, F., Rokach, L. and Shapira, B., 2011. *Introduction to recommender systems handbook* (pp. 1-35). Springer US

[11] Joachims, T., 2002, July. Optimizing search engines using clickthrough data. In *SIGKDD* (pp. 133-142). ACM.

[12] Zhang, Y., Xu, J., Lan, Y., Guo, J., Xie, M., Huang, Y. and Cheng, X., 2015, October. Modeling Parameter Interactions in Ranking SVM. In *Proceedings of the 24th ACM International on Conference on Information and Knowledge Management* (pp. 1799-1802). ACM.

[13] Cao, Z., Qin, T., Liu, T.Y., Tsai, M.F. and Li, H., 2007, June. Learning to rank: from pairwise approach to listwise approach. In *ICML* (pp. 129-136). ACM.

[14] Xia, F., Liu, T.Y., Wang, J., Zhang, W. and Li, H., 2008, July. Listwise approach to learning to rank: theory and algorithm. In *ICML* (pp. 1192-1199). ACM.

[15] Liu, T.Y.,2009. Learning to rank for information retrieval. *Foundations and Trends in Information Retrieval*, 3(3), pp.225-331

[16] Burges, C., Shaked, T., Renshaw, E., Lazier, A., Deeds, M., Hamilton, N. and Hullender, G., 2005, August. Learning to rank using gradient descent. *ICML* (pp. 89-96). ACM.

[17] Saaty, T.L., 2008. Decision making with the analytic hierarchy process. International journal of services sciences, 1(1), pp.83-98.

[18] Harel, A., Shabtai, A., Rokach, L. and Elovici, Y., 2012. M-score: A misuseability weight measure. *Dependable and Secure Computing, IEEE Transactions* on, 9(3), pp.414-428.

[19] Zhang, X., He, B., Luo, T., Li, D. and Xu, J., 2013, October. Clustering-based transduction for learning a ranking model with limited human labels. CIKM (pp. 1777-1782).

Online Food Recipe Title Semantics: Combining Nutrient Facts and Topics

Tomasz Kusmierczyk
NTNU, Trondheim, Norway
tomaszku@idi.ntnu.no

Kjetil Nørvåg
NTNU, Trondheim, Norway
noervaag@idi.ntnu.no

ABSTRACT

Dietary pattern analysis is an important research area, and recently the availability of rich resources in food-focused social networks has enabled new opportunities in that field. However, there is a little understanding of how online textual content is related to actual health factors, e.g., nutritional values. To contribute to this lack of knowledge, we present a novel approach to mine and model online food content by combining text topics with related nutrient facts. Our empirical analysis reveals a strong correlation between them and our experiments show the extent to which it is possible to predict nutrient facts from meal name.

Keywords

LDA, text regression, social media mining, online food recipe

1. INTRODUCTION

As fundamental concepts in our daily lives, food and dietary patterns are important research topics. However traditional ways of studying them are limited in scope and reach; the access to resources generated in social media have enabled new opportunities and research directions. In recent years online food-oriented communities have gained immense popularity and have moved this sphere of our lives on-line. Thus designing appropriate, specialized mining techniques may benefit not only in better understanding of online patterns but also in enabling new possibilities for practical applications.

The primary form of information that online users interact with is text. However in the context of food studies other factors play an equally important role. Key recipe characteristics that influence our health are nutrient facts, among which the most popular and important are food energy and quantities of fat, proteins, sugars, carbohydrates, cholesterol and sodium. Although several works studying those factors in the context of social media recently appeared, only few take into account textual content, and, moreover, mostly using external, predefined databases. One of the reasons for that is the lack of appropriate tools and techniques for effectively exploring these combined data dimensions. In our paper we address this gap.

CIKM'16 , October 24-28, 2016, Indianapolis, IN, USA

 ISBN 978-1-4503-4073-1/16/10...$15.00

DOI: http://dx.doi.org/10.1145/2983323.2983897

Our first objective is to gain a deeper *understanding of associations between words and nutritional values*. Thus, the analytical part of our paper is devoted to studying correlations between them. In contrast to previous works, we rely only on short, free-form textual food titles provided by inexperienced social media users and do not require additional meta data such as a list of ingredients.

Another challenge this paper targets is to design and develop a model that would be helpful in mining online food content. Empirical observations provide useful hints that motivate design choices of such a model. We expect that using text in conjunction with additional information, i.e., nutrients, should provide noticeable improvement in many practical applications.

Two practical problems that we are particularly interested in are *identifying compact and meaningful food topics* and *predicting nutrient fact values* in various settings. One common setting in the context of online food platforms is when only some subset of nutrients is known. Another is when no nutritional values are known at all. For example we imagine a mobile application that can scan a meal name in a restaurant and then provide approximate nutritional values to help select food appropriately.

Our main contributions are: (i) a study of a large-scale online food community in terms of relations between nutritional values and textual descriptions (recipe names), (ii) the introduction of a new topic model combining text with several outputs (nutrient facts) regression, and (iii) an evaluation of our approach's efficacy in discovering recipe topics and predicting nutritional values.

2. RELATED WORK

Studying social media contents in order to discover food and dietary patterns and correlations is a relatively new research direction; so, few related studies exist in this context.

Some recent works study dietary preferences in social media from a geographic and temporal perspective. In the influential work by West et al. [11], recipe access logs were analyzed in order to observe seasonal and weekly trends in people's preferences towards nutritional values in different US regions. Similar observations were made by Said and Bellogin [8] when studying user rating behavior. Wagner et al. [9], recently investigated the dynamics of online food consumption. Finally, Kusmierczyk et al. [4] observed differences in nutrient value preferences from the perspective of both online recipe consumption and creation.

Recently, several researchers tried to exploit connections between textual content and dietary patterns. Abbar et al. [1] managed to build a model predicting county-wide obesity and diabetes statistics using food mentions in Twitter. Muller et al. [5] designed a system that calculates recipe nutritional values. In the proposed approach, the authors first match recipe ingredients and based on them then infer nutrient facts. A similar approach was taken by

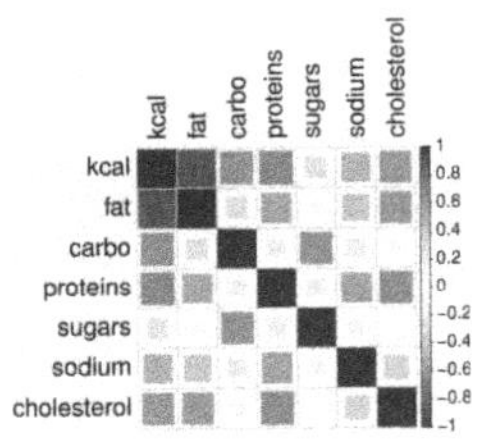

Figure 1: Correlations between recipe nutrients.

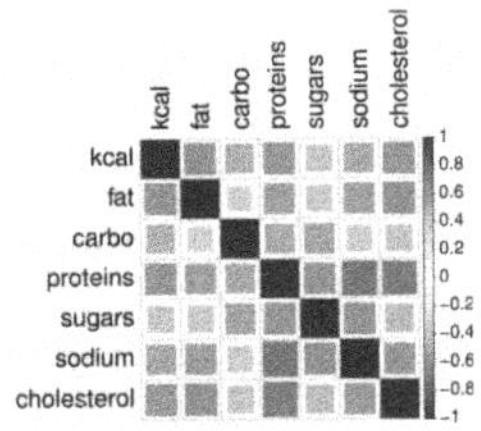

Figure 2: Correlations over words between info-gains corresponding to nutritional values.

De Choudhury et al. [2], who used the US Department of Agriculture National Nutrient Database to obtain nutritional and calorific information from Instagram food posts.

When the focus is on understanding social media patterns, LDA and topic models are the standard approach to identify textual clusters of interest, e.g., when studying topics around patterns in diet [2], relations between tweets and public health [7], or life satisfaction [3]. Although the method is popular not only in our context, out-of-the-box solutions are not always sufficient and proposing variants adjusted to specific domain is often necessary, as in [10]. For example, existing models extending LDA, e.g. [6], attach regression component to words whereas we link it on topic level.

3. DATA SET

Our study relies on the data retrieved from the largest English online food recipe platform, namely *allrecipes.com*.[1] The web site was crawled and archived in July 2015, and the data set contains more than 240 thousand recipes.

For each recipe, metadata with title and information about nutritional facts (per 100 g) are provided. Unfortunately, some nutrient values were missing for the majority of recipes, and all seven of the most important facts (i.e., kilocalories (denote *kcal*), *fat*, carbohydrates (denote *carbo*), *proteins*, *sugars*, *sodium*, *cholesterol*) were present in only 58 thousand recipes. Thus, our experiments focused on this subset.

Initially, recipe titles were arbitrary strings defined as free-form text by the users. Several standard text pre-processing, data cleaning steps were necessary. First, we filtered out punctuation, special characters, numbers and stop-words. Then, using a Porter stemmer, word forms were unified. Finally, we filtered out all words occurring less than 2 times in the corpus. This procedure resulted in a vocabulary containing of 4,679 unique words. However, only 1,578 words were used more than 10 times. The most popular words are 'chicken', appearing in 5,230 (9%) of titles, and 'salad', found in 3,728 (6%) of titles.

4. NUTRIENT FACTS AND TEXT CORRELATIONS

In our study we focus on relations between nutrient facts and associated textual content as one of our goals is to extend the understanding of how they depend on each other.

[1]http://allrecipes.com

Table 1: Top 5 words with the highest information gain for nutrient facts.

Nutrient Fact	Important Words
kcal	chicken, cooki, pie, dip, pasta
fat	cooki, pie, chicken, casserol, sausag
carbos	cake, pie, dip, pasta, cooki
proteins	chicken, cooki, cake, chocol, pork
sugars	cake, chocol, pie, cooki, appl
sodium	cooki, chicken, cake, chocol, casserol
cholesterol	chicken, cooki, shrimp, pork, egg

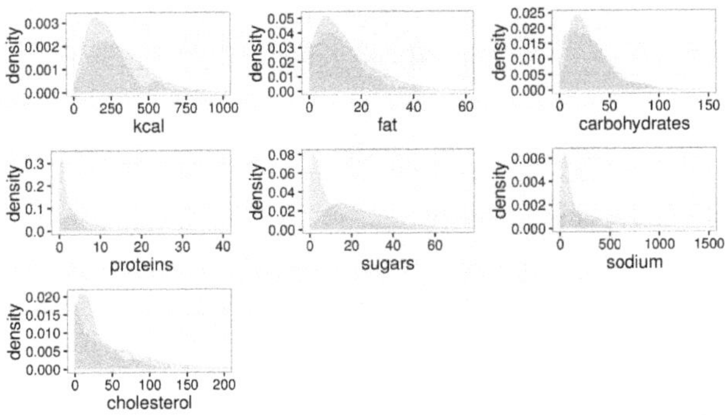

Figure 3: Comparison of nutrient fact distributions in recipes with (green) and without (red) a word 'frost' in the title.

First, we were interested in associations between nutrition values in the context of recipes produced by the studied online community. Figure 1 presents a Pearson correlation matrix between all 7 nutrient facts. We observe a cluster of strongly positively correlated values composed of almost all facts. The only two nutrition values that behave differently are sugars and carbohydrates. Sugars have almost no correlation to fat and cholesterol and are negatively correlated to proteins and sodium. Furthermore, the correlations between carbohydrates and fat, proteins and cholesterol are significantly weaker than for other nutrients. Some of these discoveries are surprising and demonstrate that online food content may be biased in an unexpected way: studies like ours are needed to gain better understanding of these online communities.

To measure the influence of words on nutritional values we applied information gain. As an attribute feature we used either a presence or an absence of the word in the recipe title. Table 1 presents the most influential words. We noticed a high overlap between top correlated words, e.g., the word 'cooki' (cookie) is important for all nutrients. Furthermore, we observed that information gains of words were similar between nutrient facts. Figure 2 presents the info-gain correlation measured over words. For each word we calculated information gain to all nutrient values. Then we measured Spearman correlation over words between info-gains corresponding respectively to kcal, fat etc. Observed correlations are very high, showing that the same words are important for all nutrient facts. For example, we found 13 words that are present in top-100 lists of all nutrients. Some of these words are meal names (e.g., 'lasagna'), some represent ingredients (e.g., 'cranberries') but also more surprising observations were made. For example, the word 'frost' was identified as having a very high information gain. Figure 3 compares nutrient value distributions in recipes with and without 'frost' in the title. We observe, for example, that sugars are biased towards higher and proteins towards lower values.

5. COMBINING NUTRIENT FACTS AND TEXT TOPICS

The empirical analysis in Section 4 revealed a strong correlation among nutritional values and between nutritional values and particular words. Furthermore, we noticed that similar words are

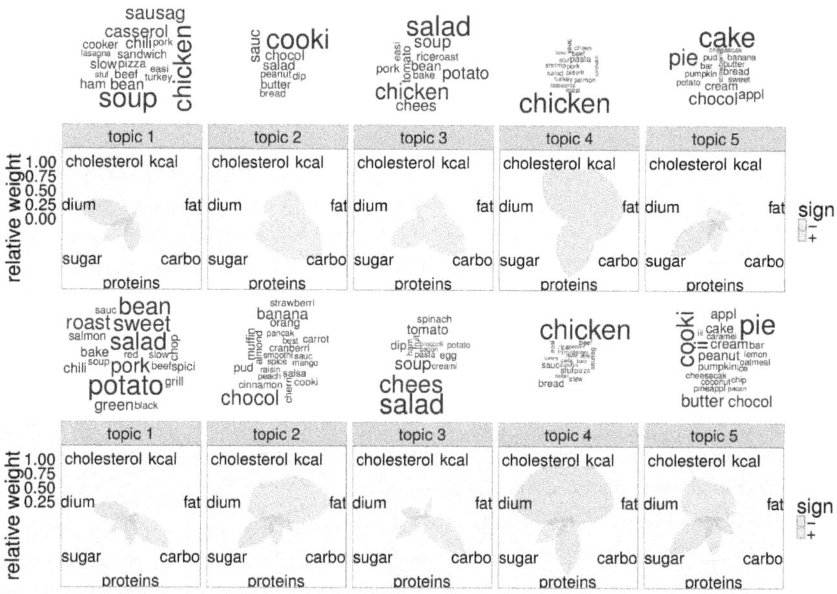

Figure 5: Comparison of topics found by standard LDA (bottom) and our model (top).

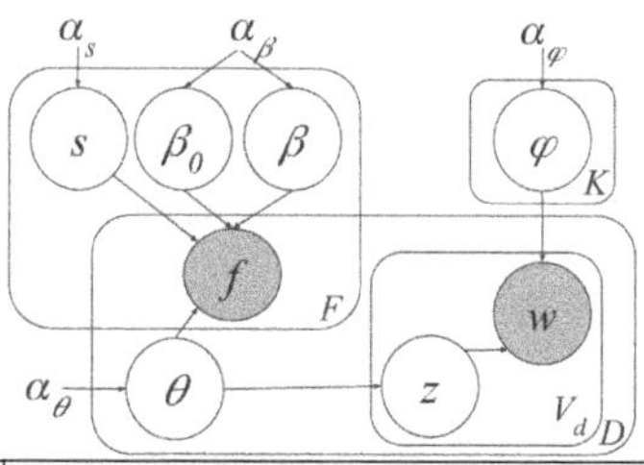

K	number of topics
D	number of documents (recipes)
F	number of outputs (nutrients)
V	number of unique words
V_d	number of words in document (recipe) d
θ	the multinomial distribution of topics for recipe d
φ	word distributions for topics
z	topic assignment for word w in document d
w	observed word from document d
f_{id}	observed i-th nutrient for document (recipe) d
β_i	i-th nutrient vector of topic weights
β_0^i	i-th nutrient bias
s_i	i-th nutrient standard deviation

Figure 4: LDA with built-in multi-output linear regression extension.

associated with all nutrient facts. Taking those observations together we can conclude that it is possible to model text topics in conjunction with related nutrient facts to provide an interpretable and low-dimensional representation of such content. Our approach to combining nutrients and topic modeling is to propose a model that uses the latent topic space to explain both observed words and nutritional values.

Among latent topic models, the most popular is *latent dirichlet allocation* (LDA). Unlike simple clustering methods, LDA allows text documents to exhibit multiple topics, i.e., each document is assigned a distribution of topics from which word topics and words are later drawn. We adopt LDA by extending it with multiple linear regression components.

Linear regression is a well established statistical technique where dependent variables are modeled as a weighted sum of explanatory variables and bias. Each input is assigned a weight that measures its influence on the output, e.g., close to 0 weight means no influence. In our case dependent variables are nutritional values and regression is repeated as many times as there are outputs. Explanatory variables are LDA topic distributions per document (recipe). In contrast to a standard approach where LDA clustering is done before and separated from regression, our approach combines both models and learns topic distributions in a way that they express both text clusters and all nutrient facts well.

The detailed graphical representation of our approach is presented in Figure 4. LDA is extended by adding F regressions (top left corner) where the i-th output ($i \in 1..F$) for the d-th ($d \in 1..D$) recipe is drawn from the normal distribution: $f_{id} \sim \mathcal{N}(\beta_i^T \theta_d + \beta_0^i, s_i)$, where β_i is a K-dimensional vector of topic weights for the i-th output, β_0^i is a bias and the output's error is modeled by the standard deviation s_i. The model has several parameters. α_θ and α_φ parameterize respectively the document topic distributions (Dirichlet) and the topic word distributions (Dirichlet). In both cases we used popular heuristics, i.e., $\alpha_\theta = 0.1$ and $\alpha_\varphi = 0.1$. Linear regression weights were assigned the following priors: $\beta \sim \mathcal{N}(0, \alpha_\beta)$ where we used uninformative parametrization with standard deviation $\alpha_\beta = 100$. Similarly for $s = \frac{1}{\sqrt{\tau}}$ where precision $\tau \sim gamma(\alpha_s^{shape}, \alpha_s^{rate})$ we used $\alpha_s^{shape} = 3$, $\alpha_s^{rate} = 3$.

6. EXPERIMENTAL EVALUATION

We prototyped our model using a black box Gibbs sampler, namely *JAGS*.[2] To study its behavior and performance we compare it to standard LDA using the popular *gensim*[3] implementation. First, we examine the clustering results for recipe topics identification. Then, we observe performance for the nutritional values prediction task.

6.1 Recipe Topics Identification

Figure 5 compares recipe title topics found by our model (top) and by standard LDA (bottom) along with associated nutrient facts weights. For visualization purposes we chose $K = 5$. For each topic we present 7 weights coupled to respective nutrients. In the first case (for our model) we simply present empirical expected values of β_i obtained for each of topics. However, standard LDA provides only textual topics and to obtain nutritional value weights in the second case, we applied linear regression separately. In the figure positive values are represented with a green and negative with

[2]http://mcmc-jags.sourceforge.net/
[3]https://radimrehurek.com/gensim/

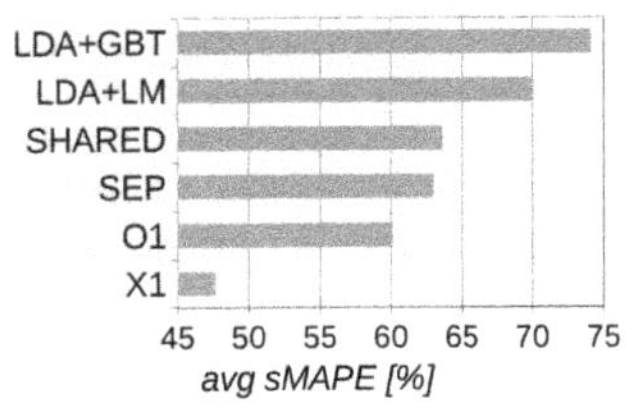

Figure 6: Nutrients prediction average performance.

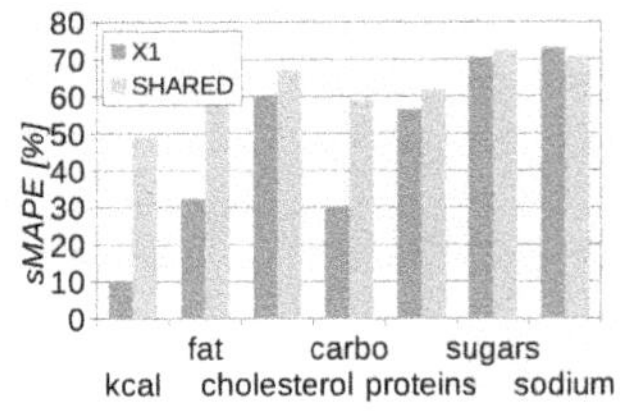

Figure 7: Prediction improvement when additional outputs values are included.

a red color. Although absolute values are not very informative and only relative proportions between topics are interpretable, weights were scaled, i.e., each weight was divided by the (absolute) maximum over topics (per nutrient fact).

The topics obtained by the two models differ noticeably both in terms of text and nutrient fact weights. Topics obtained by our model more consistently influence nutritional values, i.e., they either add or subtract from all outputs (for example topics 2 and 3 have only negative and topic 4 only positive weights), whereas standard LDA topics mix more often positive and negative influences. Furthermore, topics presented in the first row (our model) are more discriminative in selecting which nutrient facts they influence, i.e., they have more zeros. For example, only topic 1 contributes significantly to the output value of sodium. In Section 4 we observed that this nutrient correlates differently from the others and therefore our model separated it to a devoted topic. On the other hand, in the second row (standard LDA) almost all topics influence all outputs.

Topics discovered by our method differ also in terms of textual content. In general the first row in Figure 5 contains slightly more focused topics. For example, topic 1 is focused only on 'chicken' and 'soup' whereas in topic 1 in the second row there are 6 words of almost equal importance. Furthermore, we observe some differences in selecting and combining words. For example, our model combined 'cake' with 'pie', while the standard LDA combined 'pie' with 'cooki' (cookie) and 'cake' is not important for any topic.

6.2 Nutritional Values Prediction

Predicting nutritional values of an unknown recipe can be helpful and applied in various settings depending on circumstances. We simulate three of them: when we have no information about the recipe (apart from its title), when one of the nutrients is known (denote O1) and when all but one nutrient are known (denote X1). Furthermore, in the first setting we consider two variants: with latent representation shared between all outputs (denote SHARED) and with a separate model for each of outputs (denote SEP). In all cases we set $K = 30$, as it is a popular heuristic value. Our model we compare to LDA with *linear regression* (LDA+LM) and with *gradient boosted regression trees*[4] (LDA+GBT).

For evaluation purposes we split the data set randomly into training (80%) and test (20%) subsets. Predictions $\hat{f_{id}}$ for unseen recipes we obtained by taking empirical expected values of samples from the model with fixed (from the training phase) word distribution φ, weights β and deviations s (precisions τ). Prediction quality we measure using *symmetric Mean Absolute Percentage Error*: $sMAPE_i = \frac{2}{|test|}\sum_{d \in test}\frac{|f_{id} - \hat{f_{id}}|}{|f_{id}| + |\hat{f_{id}}|}$, a measure that has much better statistical properties than *MAPE*. Using percentage error allows us to compare results for different outputs and to average over outputs $i \in 1..F$ without favoring any of them: $avg\ sMAPE = \frac{1}{F}\sum_i sMAPE_i$.

Figure 6 compares prediction performance of our model (in several variants) to the baselines. We observe a significant improvement over LDA+GBT and LDA+LM for our approaches. Surprisingly there is not much difference between the model with the latent representation shared between outputs (SHARED) and using the separate representation for each of the outputs (SEP), showing that the same topics can be successfully used for many outputs. On the other hand, we observe a huge improvement when outputs are known additionally to the title (O1 and X1). However the boost is different for different outputs. Figure 7 presents the performance results split by nutrients. For fat, sugars and sodium, differences are negligible, but when other nutritional values are known, energy value (kcal) can be determined almost with no error. Although this result is not surprising it shows that our model makes proper use of additional information if provided.

[4]https://cran.r-project.org/web/packages/gbm/gbm.pdf

7. CONCLUSIONS

In this paper, we extended our understanding of the relation between textual content and associated nutritional values in the context of online food communities. Exploiting observations from the analytical part we designed a novel topic model that exploits both correlations between outputs and words. The performance of our method we evaluated in two practical tasks, i.e., compact topics identification and multiple outputs prediction. Furthermore we exhibited the extent to which including regression information in the training process helps in selecting the appropriate compact representation.

Acknowledgments. We thank Christoph Trattner for creating the *allrecipes.com* dataset and sharing it with us.

8. REFERENCES

[1] S. Abbar, Y. Mejova, and I. Weber. You tweet what you eat: Studying food consumption through Twitter. In *Proc. of CHI*, 2015.
[2] M. De Choudhury and S. S. Sharma. Characterizing dietary choices, nutrition, and language in food deserts via social media. In *Proc. of CSCW*, 2016.
[3] H. A. Schwartz et al. Characterizing geographic variation in well-being using tweets. In *Proc. of ICWSM*, 2013.
[4] T. Kusmierczyk, C. Trattner, and K. Nørvåg. Temporality in online food recipe consumption and production. In *Proc. of WWW*, 2015.
[5] M. Muller et al. Ingredient matching to determine the nutritional properties of internet-sourced recipes. In *Proc. of PervasiveHealth*, 2012.
[6] D. M. Mimno and A. McCallum. Topic models conditioned on arbitrary features with dirichlet-multinomial regression. In *Proc. of UAI*, 2008.
[7] M. J. Paul and M. Dredze. You are what you tweet: Analyzing Twitter for public health. In *Proc. of ICWSM*, 2011.
[8] A. Said and A. Bellogín. You are what you eat! Tracking health through recipe interactions. In *Proc. of RSWeb*, 2014.
[9] C. Wagner, P. Singer, and M. Strohmaier. The nature and evolution of online food preferences. *EPJ Data Science*, 3(1):1–22, 2014.
[10] C. Wang and D. M. Blei. Collaborative topic modeling for recommending scientific articles. In *Proc. of SIGKDD*, 2011.
[11] R. West et al. From cookies to cooks: Insights on dietary patterns via analysis of web usage logs. In *Proc. of WWW*, 2013.

A Non-Parametric Topic Model for Short Texts Incorporating Word Coherence Knowledge

Yuhao Zhang[1] Wenji Mao[1,2] Daniel Zeng[1,2]

[1]State Key Laboratory of Management and Control for Complex Systems, Institute of Automation, Chinese Academy of Sciences

[2]School of Computer and Control Engineering, University of Chinese Academy of Sciences

{zhangyuhao2012, wenji.mao, dajun.zeng}@ia.ac.cn

ABSTRACT

Mining topics in short texts (e.g. tweets, instant messages) can help people grasp essential information and understand key contents, and is widely used in many applications related to social media and text analysis. The sparsity and noise of short texts often restrict the performance of traditional topic models like LDA. Recently proposed Biterm Topic Model (BTM) which models word co-occurrence patterns directly, is revealed effective for topic detection in short texts. However, BTM has two main drawbacks. It needs to manually specify topic number, which is difficult to accurately determine when facing new corpora. Besides, BTM assumes that two words in same term should belong to the same topic, which is often too strong as it does not differentiate two types of words (i.e. general words and topical words). To tackle these problems, in this paper, we propose a non-parametric topic model npCTM with the above distinction. Our model incorporates the Chinese restaurant process (CRP) into the BTM model to determine topic number automatically. Our model also distinguishes general words from topical words by jointly considering the distribution of these two word types for each word as well as word coherence information as prior knowledge. We carry out experimental studies on real-world twitter dataset. The results demonstrate the effectiveness of our method to discover coherent topics compared with the baseline methods.

Keywords

Text Mining; Topic Model; Bayesian Nonparametric Model.

1. INTRODUCTION

Short texts such as tweets, instant messages and advertisements, are widespread in Web environment. Mining topics in these texts can help us understand the key contents implied and facilitate many applications like user profiling [8], recommendation [1, 10], information diffusion and influence analysis [13, 16] and so on. It is more challenging to mining topics in short texts than that in normal long documents as the data is sparse and usually noisy as well. Traditional topic models like PLSI [5], LDA [2] and HDP [6] represent documents as a mixtures of topics and capture the document-level word co-occurrence patterns to reveal topics. These methods often suffer from data sparsity when facing short texts.

CIKM'16 , October 24-28, 2016, Indianapolis, IN, USA

© 2016 ACM. ISBN 978-1-4503-4073-1/16/10…$15.00

DOI: http://dx.doi.org/10.1145/2983323.2983898

Several models have been proposed specifically for mining topics in short texts. Traditional methods [9, 16] adopt the "aggregation strategies" which combine short texts together as pseudo documents and then use conventional topic model like LDA for topic detection. These strategies make conventional topic models perform better than using them directly in short texts. As these methods did not really model the short texts, their performances vary with datasets and aggregation strategies. To model short texts, non-negative matrix factorization is used to exploit global word co-occurrence, which is proved useful in practice [18]. The Biterm Topic Model (BTM) [17] further extends it to a more principle approach by modeling the generative process of word co-occurrence patterns in corpus, which avoids the problem of data sparsity at document-level. The BTM model performs well in both short and normal texts. There are also some other models designed specifically for tweets. Twitter-LDA [19] and Twitter-BTM [4] incorporate user information into a LDA variation and the BTM respectively. However, all the above models need to specify the topic number manually, which is difficult to accurately determine when facing new corpora.

As one of the state of the art methods focusing on general-domain short texts modeling, BTM lacks the ability to differentiate general words and topical words, which may affect the detection of true topical words. The distinction is both important and effective in practice for topic modeling [4, 19]. Twitter-BTM attempts to address this issue by considering user's preference between the two word types in twitter environment. However, it models the two words within same biterm separately without considering their coherence information. Twitter-LDA only differentiates the two word types at the corpus level, and lacks a more fine-grained distinction of them for different words. Besides, both Twiter-LDA and Twitter-BTM are not applicable to topic detection in short texts without user information.

To tackle the above issues in topic mining for short texts, in this paper we propose a non-parametric coherent topic model (npCTM) that differentiates general words and topical words at the word level and incorporates word coherence information as prior knowledge for differentiation. On the basis of the BTM model, we first incorporate the Chinese restaurant process (CRP) [7] to determine topic number automatically in our model. As different words may prefer different word types, we directly model the distribution of the word types for each word. We also incorporate the word coherence information at the corpus level using point mutual information (PMI). We then distinguish general words from topical words by jointly considering the distribution of the two word types for each word and using word coherence information as prior knowledge. Experimental results on real world twitter dataset demonstrate that our method performs better in discovering coherent topics than the baseline methods.

2. Proposed Method

In this section, we first give a brief introduction of the non-parametric statistical method CRP. Then we propose how to acquire word coherence knowledge from corpus. Finally, we present our non-parametric topic model npCTM and the parameters inference of the model.

2.1 Chinese Restaurant Process

The Chinese restaurant process is a distribution on partitions of integers. The CRP works according to the following metaphor: imagine a sequence of customers entering a restaurant with infinite tables. When the nth costumer enters, she sits at an occupied table with probability proportional to the number of previous customers sitting there, and at an unoccupied table with probability proportional to α. The cluster assignments under the CRP distribution are exchangeable, which means the probability of a particular seating configuration does not depend on the customers' arriving order.

Let z_i be the index of the table where the ith customer sits and z_{-i} be all the other customers' seats. Let m_k denotes the number of customers sitting at table k and m be the total number of customers. Let K be the number of tables where $m_k > 0$ and α be the parameter of CRP. The probability of customer i sitting at each table is represented as follows:

$$p(z_i = k \mid z_{-i}, \alpha) = \begin{cases} \dfrac{m_k}{m-1+\alpha} & k \le K \\ \dfrac{\alpha}{m-1+\alpha} & k = K+1 \end{cases} \quad (1)$$

2.2 Acquiring Word Coherence Knowledge

We follow the idea of BTM [17] which models the word co-occurrence patterns directly by turning original texts into biterms, and represents biterms as unordered word-pairs co-occurring in the same context. In addition, to differentiate general words (G) and topical words (T) in biterms, we extract word coherence information from corpus, use this information as prior knowledge and incorporate it into our model.

A document containing n words will be converted into C_n^2 biterms. There are three types of biterms G-G, G-T (or T-G), and T-T in our method. Intuitively, the representative words of each topic tend to co-occur more frequently, indicating that biterms of the T-T type could have higher coherence values than those of the G-T, T-G and G-G types. For two words w_a and w_b in a biterm, we use PMI as the coherence measure and compute their PMI value from the corpus as follows:

$$PMI(w_a, w_b) = \log \frac{P(w_a, w_b)}{P(w_a)P(w_b)} \quad (2)$$

where $P(w_a, w_b)$ is the probability of w_a and w_b co-occurring in the corpus, and $P(w_a)$ and $P(w_b)$ are probabilities of w_a and w_b occurring in the corpus respectively.

Then we use sigmoid function to convert the PMI of words within each biterm into a probability value which reflects the word coherence in our method. For biterm b_i containing words w_a and w_b, this probability η_{b_i} can be acquired as follows:

$$\eta_{b_i} = \frac{1}{1+e^{-PMI(w_a,w_b)}} = \frac{1}{1+\dfrac{P(w_a)P(w_b)}{P(w_a,w_b)}} \quad (3)$$

2.3 The npCTM Model

We now present our non-parametric topic model npCTM. Our method uses CRP as a non-parametric prior to determine the topic number. To distinguish general words from topical words, our model captures both the global coherence information of a biterm and the distributions of the word type information within the biterm. For each biterm b_i, we consider both the probability η_{b_i} and the distribution of the word types for each word in b_i. Each word in b_i either belongs to a certain topic or the background topic reflecting the distribution of general words. Specifically, given a biterm b_i ,we choose its topic z_i based on CRP. As η_{b_i} reflects the coherence of words within b_i and higher value of η_{b_i} indicates b_i is more likely to belong to the T-T type. So with probability η_{b_i} we set the topic of the words in b_i to z_i. With probability $1-\eta_{b_i}$, we determine the word types of words in b_i separately. We use the word type distribution $Bernoulli(\mu_{w_{i,j}})$ to determine whether a word in b_i belong to the topic z_i or to the background topic. The generative process of our model is as follows:

1. Draw background word distribution $\phi_B \sim Dirichlet(\beta)$
2. For each word w, draw $\mu_w \sim Beta(\lambda_1, \lambda_2)$
3. For each biterm b_i, $i \in [1, N]$
   a) Draw topic $z_i \sim CRP(\alpha)$
   b) If z_i is a new topic,
      - draw topic word distribution $\phi_{z_i} \sim Dirichlet(\beta)$
   c) Draw $\rho_i \sim Bernoulli(\eta_{b_i})$
   d) If $\rho_i = 1$,
      - draw $w_{i,1}$, $w_{i,2} \sim Multinomial(\phi_{z_i})$

      If $\rho_i = 0$,
      - For each word $w_{i,j}$, $j = 1,2$
        i. $\kappa_{w_{i,j}} \sim Bernoulli(\mu_{w_{i,j}})$
        ii. If $\kappa_{w_{i,j}} = 1$, draw $w_{i,j} \sim Multinomial(\phi_{z_i})$
            If $\kappa_{w_{i,j}} = 0$, draw $w_{i,j} \sim Multinomial(\phi_B)$

2.4 Parameters Inference

We adopt collapsed Gibbs Sampling, a widely used inference method based on Markov chain Monte Carlo algorithm, to estimate the parameters of our model. Gibbs sampling cycles through the variables and estimates them alternatively. Each time the method replaces the value of one variable by a value drawn from the distribution of that variable conditioned on the values of the remaining variables. As conjugate prior is used in our model, we adopt collapsed Gibbs sampling to integrate out some variables which can simplify the sampling procedure.

In our model, we need to sample topics $z = \{z_1, \ldots, z_N\}$ for each biterm $b_1, \ldots, b_N$. The topic-word distributions ϕ and word type parameter μ can be updated based on the sampling results. To perform Gibbs sampling, we first initialize these variables for the Markov chain randomly. For simplicity, let Θ be the variables except z and m_{z_i} be the number of biterms belonging to z_i. We can sample z as follows:

$$P(z_i = t \mid b_i, z_{-i}, \Theta) \propto \begin{cases} m_{z_i} P(b_i \mid z_i, z_{-i}, \Theta) & (t \text{ is an existing topic}) \\ \alpha P(b_i \mid z_i, z_{-i}, \Theta) & (t \text{ is a new topic}) \end{cases} \quad (4)$$

Based on the generative process of our model, $P(b_i \mid z_i, z_{-i}, \Theta)$ can be split into four parts, with each part listing in one line below:

$$P(b_i \mid z_i, z_{-i}, \Theta) \propto \eta_{b_i}\phi_{w_{i,1}|z_i}\phi_{w_{i,2}|z_i} + (1-\eta_{b_i})\mu_{w_{i,1}}\phi_{w_{i,1}|z_i}\mu_{w_{i,2}}\phi_{w_{i,2}|z_i} + (1-\eta_{b_i})\mu_{w_{i,1}}\phi_{w_{i,1}|z_i}(1-\mu_{w_{i,2}})\phi_{w_{i,2}|B} + (1-\eta_{b_i})(1-\mu_{w_{i,1}})\phi_{w_{i,1}|B}\mu_{w_{i,2}}\phi_{w_{i,2}|z_i} + (1-\eta_{b_i})(1-\mu_{w_{i,1}})\phi_{w_{i,1}|B}(1-\mu_{w_{i,2}})\phi_{w_{i,2}|B} \quad (5)$$

The four parts correspond to the four word type combinations T-T, T-G, G-T and G-G respectively. To simplify the computation, the above formula (5) can be represented as:

$$P(b_i \mid z_i, z_{-i}, \Theta) \propto \{\eta_{b_i}\phi_{w_{i,1}|z_i}\phi_{w_{i,2}|z_i} + (1-\eta_{b_i})[\mu_{w_{i,1}}\phi_{w_{i,1}|z_i} + (1-\mu_{w_{i,1}})\phi_{w_{i,1}|B}][\mu_{w_{i,2}}\phi_{w_{i,2}|z_i} + (1-\mu_{w_{i,2}})\phi_{w_{i,2}|B}]\} \quad (6)$$

So we can sample the corresponding topic of each biterm according to formula (4) and (6). Then based on the values of the four parts in formula (5), we can sample the word type information for each biterm. With the word type information and the topic information of each biterm, we can update ϕ and μ as follows:

$$\phi_{w_{i,j}|z_i} = \frac{n_{w_{i,j}|z_i} + \beta}{\sum_w n_{w_{i,j}|z_i} + V\beta} \quad (7)$$

$$\phi_{w_{i,j}|B} = \frac{n_{w_{i,j}|B} + \beta}{\sum_w n_{w_{i,j}|B} + V\beta} \quad (8)$$

$$\mu_{w_{i,j}} = \frac{l_{w_{i,j},1} + \lambda_1}{l_{w_{i,j},1} + l_{w_{i,j},2} + \lambda_1 + \lambda_2} \quad (9)$$

where $n_{w_{i,j}|z_i}$ and $n_{w_{i,j}|B}$ denote the numbers of $w_{i,j}$ in topic z_i and background B respectively, and V denotes the vocabulary size, and $l_{w_{i,j},1}$ and $l_{w_{i,j},2}$ denote the numbers of $w_{i,j}$ belong to the topical word type and general word type respectively.

3. EXPERIMENTS

We evaluate the performance of our proposed model for short texts.by comparing it with the baseline methods under the typical topic coherence measures.

3.1 Experimental Setup

Dataset. We use a public twitter dataset collected in June 2011 through twitter API [14]. We only keep English tweets. We remove stop words as well as words with extremely high frequency, since similar to stop words, these words will influence the performance of topic models. We also remove words occurring less than 20 times as they can hardly represent the topic information. We then filter out tweets with one or two words and convert the letters of all tweets into lower case. We randomly sample 300,000 tweets used for training topic models and use 3,101,271 tweets left as reference dataset for the topic coherence evaluation task .

Baseline Methods. We compare our npCTM model with four baseline methods. They are LDA, BTM, HDP, and npCTM-UB. LDA is a classic topic model which has been widely used. BTM is a representative topic mining method for short texts. HDP is a widely used non-parametric topic model based on Dirichlet process. We also compare our model with npCTM-UB, which is a simplified version of our npCTM model without the background topic.

Parameter Setting. In our model, we set the parameter values $\alpha = 10$, $\beta = 1$ and $\lambda_1 = \lambda_2 = 1$. For npCTM-UB, we use $\alpha = 10$ and $\beta = 1$. The initial topic number of both models is set to 300. We choose a relative large initial topic number and the model will change it to a proper value by the sampling process. As LDA and BTM could not determine the topic number automatically, we choose three topic numbers for them. Their topic numbers K are set to 20, 50 and 80 standing for relatively small, medium and large topic numbers respectively. For LDA, we set $\alpha = 1/K$ and $\beta = 1/K$. For BTM, we use the settings in [17], that is $\alpha = 50/K$ and $\beta = 0.01$. For each model above, we run Gibbs sampling 300 times. We use the HDP model with a variational inference algorithm. We set the first level concentration $\alpha = 1$ and the truncation number K=150. We set the second level concentration $\beta = 1$ the second level truncation T = 15.

3.2 Evaluation of Topic Quality

A traditional way to evaluate topic models is comparing the perplexity or marginal likelihood on a held-out test [2, 15]. Recent study [3] shows that these evaluation metrics could not test the interpretability of topics very well. Besides, our model optimizes the likelihood of word occurrences directly, which is different from models like LDA. Recent work [11, 12] shows that topic coherence measures could assess topic quality very well. Thus we evaluate the quality of topics t based on PMI and LCP as mentioned in [12].

$$PMI(t) = \sum_{j=2}^{N}\sum_{i=1}^{j-1}\log\frac{P(w_i, w_j)}{P(w_j)P(w_i)} \quad (10)$$

$$LCP(t) = \sum_{j=2}^{N}\sum_{i=1}^{j-1}\log\frac{P(w_i, w_j)}{P(w_i)} \quad (11)$$

We evaluate our method and the baseline methods using the average PMI score and LCP score of the detected topics. For each topic, we use the top L words for topic coherence evaluation. In our experiment, L is set to 5 and 10. After the sampling process, we omit topics with less than 10 biterms, as these topics contain too limited information to form any meaningful topics in practice.

Our model finally discovers 53 topics in this experiment. The results on the comparison of topic coherence for each method are shown in Table 1. We can see that both LDA and HDP did not perform well because these two models were not designed for short texts and their model performances were affected by the sparsity of data. BTM performs better, but its topic coherence score varies with the predefined topic numbers. We can see that our npCTM-UB performs slightly better than BTM. Our npCTM model achieves the best results among all the models under the PMI measure and LCP measure when L=5, demonstrating the advantage of differentiating general and topical information. Generally, the experimental results demonstrate that our model performs better than the baseline methods and produces more coherent topics. The results also reveal that our model can automatically determine a proper topic number through the sampling process.

Table 2 illustrates the top 10 words of the football topic produced by our model and BTM. The non-representative topic words are marked bold. The example shows that our model derives relatively more coherent topics than BTM with different settings.

4. CONCLUSIONS

Mining topics in short texts is an important technique for information retrieval and text processing, and has been widely used in many applications. Existing methods either suffer from the data sparsity problem or need to specify a fixed topic number in advance. In this paper, we propose a non-parametric topic model

Table 1. Results on the comparison of topic coherence for each method

Method		LDA				BTM				HDP	npCTM -UB	npCTM
Topic Number		20	50	80	Average	20	50	80	Average	150	44	53
PMI	L=5	-5.74	-4.97	-5.76	-5.49	4.01	6.07	3.93	4.67	-3.77	6.54	**9.65**
	L=10	-32.22	-36.85	-43.10	-37.39	6.39	13.85	9.67	9.97	-24.48	14.46	**20.61**
LCP	L=5	-43.88	-46.24	-47.79	-45.97	-35.68	-36.42	-37.66	-36.59	-40.68	-34.84	**-33.49**
	L=10	-269.64	-288.75	-301.65	-286.68	-235.67	-236.74	-240.02	-237.48	-246.32	**-233.82**	-234.48

Table 2. Illustration of top 10 words of the football topic

BTM	npCTM
football season win team play state nfl college **open top** (k=20) football team nfl win season play sports fans **fantasy top** (k=50) football season nfl team college play state win sports **fantasy** (k=80)	football season team college nfl sports fans beat tickets games

which can distinguish general words from topical words by jointly considering the distribution of these two word types for each word as well as using word coherence information as prior knowledge. We carry out empirical studies on real-world twitter dataset. The experimental results show that our model can automatically determine a proper topic number and discover coherent topics more effectively compared with the baseline methods.

5. ACKNOWLEDGMENTS

This work is supported by the National Science Foundation of China under Grant No. 71621002, No. 91224008 and No. 71472175.

6. REFERENCES

[1] Belém, F., Santos, R., Almeida, J. and Gonçalves, M. 2013. Topic Diversity in Tag Recommendation. *Proceedings of the 7th ACM Conference on Recommender Systems*, 141–148.

[2] Blei, D.M., Ng, A.Y. and Jordan, M.I. 2003. Latent dirichlet allocation. *The Journal of Machine Learning Research*. 3, 993–1022.

[3] Chang, J., Gerrish, S., Wang, C., Boyd-graber, J.L. and Blei, D.M. 2009. Reading Tea Leaves: How Humans Interpret Topic Models. *Advances in Neural Information Processing Systems 22*, 288–296.

[4] Chen, W., Wang, J., Zhang, Y., Yan, H. and Li, X. 2015. User Based Aggregation for Biterm Topic Model. 489–494.

[5] Ding, C., Li, T. and Peng, W. 2008. On the Equivalence Between Non-negative Matrix Factorization and Probabilistic Latent Semantic Indexing. *Comput. Stat. Data Anal.* 52, 8, 3913–3927.

[6] Gao, Z., Song, Y., Liu, S., Wang, H., Wei, H., Chen, Y. and Cui, W. 2011. Tracking and Connecting Topics via Incremental Hierarchical Dirichlet Processes. *2011 IEEE 11th International Conference on Data Mining*, 1056–1061.

[7] Gershman, S.J. and Blei, D.M. 2012. A tutorial on Bayesian nonparametric models. *Journal of Mathematical Psychology*, 56, 1, 1–12.

[8] Harvey, M., Crestani, F. and Carman, M.J. 2013. Building user profiles from topic models for personalised search. *Proceedings of the 22nd ACM international conference on Conference on information and knowledge management*, 2309–2314.

[9] Hong, L. and Davison, B.D. 2010. Empirical study of topic modeling in twitter. *Proceedings of the First Workshop on Social Media Analytics*, 80–88.

[10] Hu, B. and Ester, M. 2013. Spatial Topic Modeling in Online Social Media for Location Recommendation. *Proceedings of the 7th ACM Conference on Recommender Systems*, 25–32.

[11] Lau, J.H., Baldwin, T, and Newman, D. 2013. On Collocations and Topic Models. *ACM Transactions on Speech and Language Processing*, 10, no. 3 (2013): 10:1–10:14.

[12] Lau, J.H., Newman, D. and Baldwin, T. 2014. Machine Reading Tea Leaves: Automatically Evaluating Topic Coherence and Topic Model Quality. *Proceedings of the 14th Conference of the European Chapter of the Association for Computational Linguistics*, 530–539.

[13] Li, D., Shuai, X., Sun, G., Tang, J., Ding, Y. and Luo, Z. 2012. Mining topic-level opinion influence in microblog. *Proceedings of the 21st ACM international conference on Information and knowledge management*, 1562–1566.

[14] Li, R., Wang, S. and Chang, K.C.-C. Towards Social Data Platform: Automatic Topic-focused Monitor for Twitter Stream. *Proc. VLDB Endow.* 6, 14 (2013), 1966–1977.

[15] Wallach, H.M., Murray, I., Salakhutdinov, R. and Mimno, D. 2009. Evaluation Methods for Topic Models. *Proceedings of the 26th Annual International Conference on Machine Learning*, 1105–1112.

[16] Weng, J., Lim, E.-P., Jiang, J. and He, Q. 2010. TwitterRank: finding topic-sensitive influential twitters. *Proceedings of the third ACM international conference on Web search and data mining*, 261–270.

[17] Yan, X., Guo, J., Lan, Y. and Cheng, X. 2013. A Biterm Topic Model for Short Texts. *Proceedings of the 22Nd International Conference on World Wide Web*, 1445–1456.

[18] Yan, X., Guo, J., Liu, S., Cheng, X. and Wang, Y. 2013. Learning Topics in Short Texts by Non-negative Matrix Factorization on Term Correlation Matrix. *Proceedings of the 2013 SIAM International Conference on Data Mining*. Society for Industrial and Applied Mathematics. 749–757.

[19] Zhao, W.X., Jiang, J., Weng, J., He, J., Lim, E.-P., Yan, H. and Li, X. 2011. Comparing Twitter and Traditional Media Using Topic Models. *Advances in Information Retrieval*, 338–349.

Forecasting Seasonal Time Series Using Weighted Gradient RBF Network based Autoregressive Model

Wenjie Ruan
School of Computer Science
The University of Adelaide
Adelaide, Australia
wenjie.ruan@adelaide.edu.au

Quan Z. Sheng
School of Computer Science
The University of Adelaide
Adelaide, Australia
qsheng@cs.adelaide.edu.au

Peipei Xu
School of Electronic Engineering, UESTC
Chengdu, China
peipei.xu6@gmail.com

Nguyen Khoi Tran, Nickolas J.G. Falkner
School of Computer Science
The University of Adelaide
nguyen.tran@adelaide.edu.au

Xue Li
School of IT and EE
The University of Queensland
Brisbane, Australia
xueli@itee.uq.edu.au

Wei Emma Zhang
School of Computer Science
The University of Adelaide
Adelaide, Australia
wei.zhang01@adelaide.edu.au

ABSTRACT

How to accurately forecast seasonal time series is very important for many business area such as marketing decision, planning production and profit estimation. In this paper, we propose a weighted gradient Radial Basis Function Network based AutoRegressive (WGRBF-AR) model for modeling and predicting the nonlinear and non-stationary seasonal time series. This WGRBF-AR model is a synthesis of the weighted gradient RBF network and the functional-coefficient autoregressive (FAR) model through using the WGRBF networks to approximate varying coefficients of FAR model. It not only takes the advantages of the FAR model in nonlinear dynamics description but also inherits the capability of the WGRBF network to deal with non-stationarity. We test our model using ten-years retail sales data on five different commodity in US. The results demonstrate that the proposed WGRBF-AR model can achieve competitive prediction accuracy compared with the state-of-the-art.

1. INTRODUCTION

A time series is a sequence of data points made of successive measurements across a continuous time intervals, such as ocean tides data, counts of sunspots data, and the daily closing value of the Dow-Jones Industrial Average. The seasonal and trend patterns are usually served as basic components in many time series, especially in economic and business areas [1]. This paper proposes a novel model structure to accurately model the time series that exhibits seasonal, highly nonlinear and non-stationary features. Figure 1 shows examples of typical seasonal time series - monthly retail sale data of department, hardware and clothing in US from the year 1992 to 2001. We observe that these seasonal time series data reflects *i)* strong nonlinearity that cannot be well handled by linear models, *ii)* significant seasonal patterns which repeat a similar fluctuation pattern but with a stable increase each year.

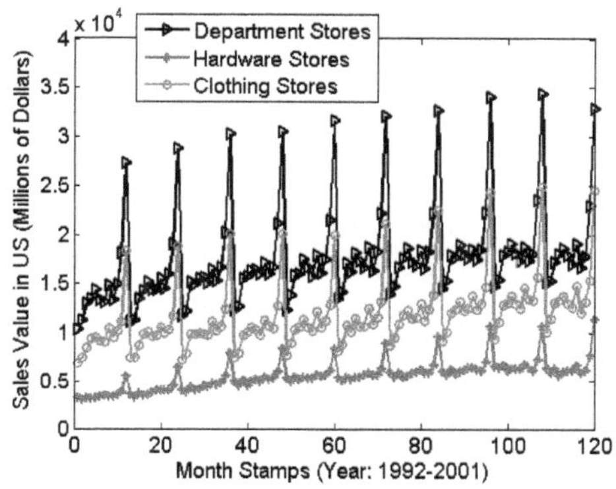

Figure 1: Three sales time-series data from USA

To accurately model this type of time-series data, many remarkable approaches are proposed over last decades [1, 20]. The most straightforward technique is to decompose the series into different components (such as seasonal part, trend part and cyclical components) by using some seasonal adjustment methods [20]. However, such decomposition may lose some valuable information among the data [12]. Another classical solution is built upon the famous Box-Jenkins model [13] that first derives a stationary time series by the time-series differencing, then the traditional Auto Regressive Moving Average (ARMA) model is applied, which is called Autoregressive Integrated Moving Average (ARIMA) [1]. However, this technique assumes that the main component of the time series is linear, thus being difficult to capture the nonlinearity in seasonal time series [2].

Recently, Artificial Neural Networks (ANNs) have attracted huge attentions and become one of the most favorable methods for time series modeling and prediction [6, 18]. Because of their remarkable universal approximation capability, various types of ANNs are also investigated to forecast the seasonal time series. For example, Zhang *et al.* [20] for the first time utilize three-layer feed-forward ANNs to model the time

CIKM'16 , October 24-28, 2016, Indianapolis, IN, USA
© 2016 ACM. ISBN 978-1-4503-4073-1/16/10...$15.00
DOI: http://dx.doi.org/10.1145/2983323.2983899

series with seasonal and trend patterns. In [19], they further systematically investigate which factors in feed-forward ANNs have impact on the performance of quarterly time-series prediction. Nevertheless, to achieve satisfied performance, ANNs normally require a large model size (*i.e.*, many parameters) and thus need more training data.

As a result, another technique that combines both merits of ANNs and ARMA has been emerged recently for time series prediction - the neural network based functional varying-coefficient models [2, 5]. One of the modeling methods is the radial basis function network based autoregressive (RBF-AR) model [9, 16]. The RBF-AR model adopts a set of RBF networks to approximate the coefficients of a state-dependent AR model [14]. As such, RBF-AR model inherits both advances of the state-dependent AR model in the description of nonlinear dynamics and the merit of the RBF networks in functional approximation. However, applying RBF-AR into seasonal time-series prediction still requires to derive a stationary time series beforehand, leading to latent information loss thus fail to capture the fine-grained fluctuations in seasonal time series [7].

To fill this gap, this paper proposes a weighted gradient RBF network-based AR model to predict the seasonal time series. Specifically, instead of using RBF network, we design a gradient RBF (GRBF) network with regression weights to approximate the vary-coefficients in FAR. The GRBF network is a powerful ANN that can well quantify the non-stationarity in seasonal time series [4]. To further enhance its approximation capacity, we augment a linear regression function as the connection weights between the hidden layer units and the output in traditional GRBF networks instead of constants. In summary, the main contributions of this paper are as follows:

- We propose to approximate the vary-coefficients in functional autoregressive model using a wighted gradient RBF networks, called WGRBF-AR model that can model a class of nonlinear and non-stationary time series with a high accuracy. To the best of our knowledge, this paper is the first one to do so.
- We apply our model to forecast real seasonal time series. The results on five ten-year real retail sales data in US demonstrate that, with a same or smaller model size, WGRBF-AR model outperforms other similar models in terms of prediction accuracy.

2. THE PROPOSED SOLUTION

2.1 Weighted Gradient RBF Network

The traditional GRBF network is a three-layer feed-forward network, which includes an input layer, a hidden layer and an output layer [4]. The input vector of GRBF network is the gradient of the time series modeled, thus the hidden layer can respond to the gradient changes of data efficiently. Among others, the output of each hidden node is also revised with a term which is to accelerate the performance of the one-step prediction [6]. Assuming the time series under study is $\{y_t : t = 1, 2, ..., N\}$, the traditional gradient RBF network is defined as:

$$\hat{y}_i = \sum_{k=1}^{m} w_k \exp\{-\lambda \|\mathbf{x}_i - \mathbf{c}_k\|^2\} \times (y_{i-1} + \delta_k) \qquad (1)$$

where m represents the node number in the hidden layer, δ_k is a constant value associated with the center, w_k means the network weight, $\mathbf{x}_i = [y_{i-1} - y_{i-2}, y_{i-2} - y_{i-3}, \cdots, y_{i-d} - y_{i-d-1}]^T$ represents d- dimensional input vector, $\mathbf{c}_k$ is the center vector, λ is a scaling number ($\lambda > 0$) that measures the width of the symmetric response in the hidden node, and $\|\cdot\|$ is the vector 2-norm. The centers $\mathbf{c}_k$ and scalars $\delta_k (1 \leq k \leq m)$ are chosen from the training data $\{\mathbf{x}_i\}$. If $\{\mathbf{x}_j\}$ is selected as the center $\mathbf{c}_k$, the corresponding $\delta_k = y_j - y_{j-1}$. We use the Orthogonal Least Squares (OLS) algorithm [3] to select the subset $\mathbf{c}_k$.

In this paper, to further accelerate its approximation capability, we use a regression-type weight, which is a function of the input variables, to replace the constant weights in the traditional GRBF network, *i.e.*, $w_k = v_{k0} + v_{k1}(y_{i-1} - y_{i-2}) + ... + v_{kd}(y_{i-d} - y_{i-d-1})$. Fig 2 illustrates the structure of our WGRBF model. As we can see, each input node contributes to the network weights. This direct link between the weights and the input gradient variables makes the WGRBF network more efficient and thus produces a more parsimonious network.

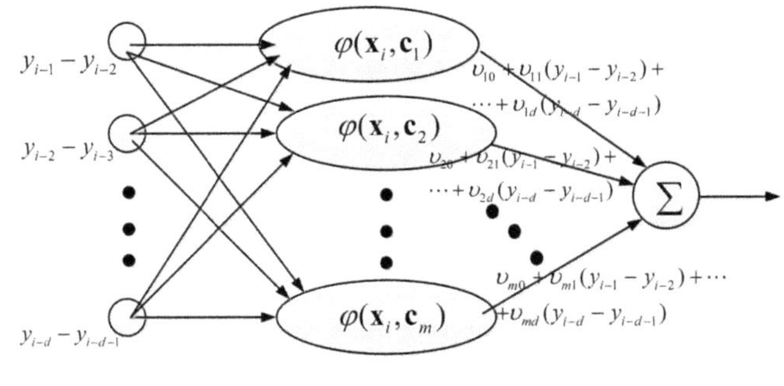

Figure 2: Structure of the WGRBF networks

2.2 WGRBF-AR Model

As aforementioned, the functional AR model is a flexible structure with strong capability of modeling nonlinear time series. We intend to enable the FAR model to model the non-stationary time series. To achieve this goal, we approximate the functional coefficients in the FAR model by using the proposed WGRBF networks. The traditional FAR model has following structures.

$$y_t = \phi_0(\mathbf{X}_t^*) + \sum_{i=1}^{p} \phi_i(\mathbf{X}_t^*) y_{t-i} + \varepsilon_t \qquad (2)$$

where $\mathbf{X}_t^*$ means the state vector consisted by lagged values of y_t, p is the model order and ε_t represents a sequence of *i.i.d.* random variables which is independent of the observations $y_{t-i} > 0$; $\phi_0(\mathbf{X}_t^*), \cdots, \phi_p(\mathbf{X}_t^*)$ indicates the functional coefficients.

In reality, most of the seasonal time series not only exhibits a trend and a local level pattern but also reveals some homogeneous features, such as some parts in the time series are very similar to other parts (see the yearly repeated pattern of sales time series in Fig. 1). We assume that the modeled time series generally have those properties. Thus we derive the WGRBF-AR model by specifying functional coefficients of the FAR model using the weighted GRBF networks. Specifically, the proposed WGRBF-AR model has a structure (without loss of generality, the first-order

WGRBFs are used) as follows.

$$\begin{cases} y_t = \phi_0(\mathbf{X}_t^*) + \sum_{i=1}^{p} \phi_i(\mathbf{X}_t^*) y_{t-i} + \varepsilon_t \\ \phi_0(\mathbf{X}_t^*) = w_0 + \sum_{k=1}^{m} w_k \exp\{-\lambda \|\mathbf{X}_t^* - \mathbf{Z}_k\|^2\} \\ \phi_i(\mathbf{X}_t^*) = w_{i,0} + \sum_{k=1}^{m} w_{i,k} \exp\{-\lambda \|\mathbf{X}_t^* - \mathbf{Z}_k\|^2\} \\ \mathbf{X}_t^* = [y_{t-1} - y_{t-2}, y_{t-2} - y_{t-3}, \cdots, y_{t-d} - y_{t-d-1}]^T \\ w_{i,k} = v_{i0,k} + v_{i1,k}(y_{t-1} - y_{t-2}) + v_{i2,k}(y_{t-2} - y_{t-3}) \\ \qquad + \ldots + v_{id,k}(y_{t-d} - y_{t-d-1}) \end{cases} \tag{3}$$

where $\phi_0(\mathbf{X}_t^*), \cdots, \phi_p(\mathbf{X}_t^*)$ are all composed of WGRBFs, $\mathbf{X}_t^*$ indicates input vector of WGRBF and $\mathbf{Z}_k = (z_{k,1}, \ldots, z_{k,d})$ means the center vector. The term $\phi_0(\mathbf{X}_t^*)$ is an offset that can grasp the time-varying local level. This term plays an important role to capture non-stationary processes with fluctuations of local mean and trend. The $\phi_0(\mathbf{X}_t^*), \cdots, \phi_p(\mathbf{X}_t^*)$ are varying coefficients that enable the model adopt to the nonlinear features [6]. In Eqn. 3, we can observe that the WGRBF-AR model actually contains the weighted GRBF network as one of its components. From the perspective of neural network, the WGRBF-AR model can be seen as a certain generalization of the WGRBF network [6]. It draws upon both advantages of the FAR model in nonlinear dynamics and the WGRBF network in dealing nonstationarity. Note that, although we only describe the first-order WGRBF-AR model as in Eqn. 3, a higher order form can be easily extended without involving any new ideas.

2.3 Identification of WGRBF-AR Model

Intuitively, we can categorize the parameters in WGRBF-AR model into a linear part and a nonlinear part, thus the model can be reformed as a linear combination of nonlinear functions. Parameter identification of our model can be viewed as a separable nonlinear least squares problem [10]. In this paper, we adopt the Variable Projection (VP) algorithm to solve the optimization problem [11]. In details, it projects the linear parameters out of the problem, leaving the nonlinear least squares problems involving only the non-linear parameters. From Eqn. 3, we observe that there are more linear parameters than nonlinear parameters. As a result, applying VP optimization method is substantially efficient since only the nonlinear parameters consume more searching resource [11]. Specifically, we represent the set of linear parameters in Eqn. 3 as:

$$\theta_L \triangleq \{w_0, w_{i,0}, v_{ij,k} \mid$$
$$i = 0, 1, \ldots, p; j = 1, 2, \ldots, d; k = 1, 2, \ldots, m\} \in \mathbb{R}^{(p+1)(m \times d+2)}. \tag{4}$$

Similarly, the set of nonlinear parameters in Eqn. 3 is formulated as

$$\theta_N \triangleq (\lambda, \mathbf{Z}_1^T, \cdots, \mathbf{Z}_m^T)^T \in \mathbb{R}^{1+m \times d}. \tag{5}$$

Thus, the model can be rewritten in the following regression form of linear parameters:

$$y_t = \varphi(\theta_N; \mathbf{X}_t^*)^T \theta_L + \varepsilon_t \tag{6}$$

As a result, the optimal parameters θ_L, θ_N can be determined by minimizing the following nonlinear function:

$$\min_{\theta_L, \theta_N} \|\mathbf{y} - \Psi(\theta_N)\theta_L\|^2 \tag{7}$$

where the component of $\mathbf{y}$ is $y(i)$; the rows of the matrix of $\Psi(\theta_N)$ correspond to the vector $\varphi(\theta_N; \mathbf{X}_t^*)^T$.

As such, we observe that Eqn. 7 has the same solution:

$$* \min_{\theta_N} \|\mathbf{y} - \Psi(\theta_N)\Psi(\theta_N)^+ \mathbf{y}\|^2 = \|(\mathbf{I} - \Psi(\theta_N)\Psi(\theta_N)^+)\mathbf{y}\|^2 \tag{8}$$

where $\Psi(\theta_N)^+$ indicates the *Moore-Penrose inverse* of $\Psi(\theta_N)$ [8]. We first optimize objective function with respect to the nonlinear parameters θ_N, shown as Eqn. 8. Then we utilize very efficient linear least-squares method to optimize linear parameters $\hat{\theta_L}$ [1]. We calculate the *Jacobian matrix* of residuals analytically or using finite differences [8]. The nonlinear least squares algorithms can be applied to solve the nonlinear parameters θ_N, *e.g.,* Gauss-Newton or Levenberg-Marquardt method [9]. We choose the orders of the WGRBF-AR model by the cross-validation.

3. EXPERIMENTS

Seasonal Time-series Data: Retail sale data is a typical time series data that exhibits strong nonlinear, non-stationary and seasonal pattens. Thus many researchers utilize the monthly retail sales data to evaluate the performance of models [20, 17]. In this paper, five different ten-year retail-sales data are used to test our performance[1]. The five retail-sale datasets are retail sales amounts in department stores, book stores, clothing stores, furniture stores and hardware stores during 1992 to 2001. These series are collected in month and without seasonal adjustment, thus they all exhibit stronger seasonality (shown in Fig. 1). Similar to other works [20, 17], we adopt the *Root Mean Square Error* (RMSE) to evaluate the modeling performance.

Comparison Methods: We compare our method with the following five baseline works: *i) ANN-DSDT* [20] first utilizes trend and seasonal adjustment (*i.e.,* de-treding and de-seasonalization) to the targeted time series then adopt a 3-layer feed-forward NNs to perform the prediction; *ii) TDNN-* [17] means time-delay neural network which is well-known NN for temporal data modeling; *iii) ARIMA* [1] is the most famous time series model that can handle non-stationary time-series data; *iv) SVR* [1] means support vector regression which is an extension from *support vector machine* (SVM); *v) RBF-AR* [7] is a typical quasi-linear autoregressive model which its autoregressive coefficients are constructed by radial basis function networks. It is very successful in stationary time series modeling.

Parameter Settings: In our model, we consider 12 variables $\{y_{(t-1)} - y_{(t-2)}, y_{(t-2)} - y_{(t-3)}, \ldots, y_{(t-12)} - y_{(t-13)}\}$ to be the candidate input that affects y_t. We set the dimension of state vector $\mathbf{X}_t^*$ as 1 for simplicity. And the number of hidden nodes m is chosen as 0 or 1. We select the state vector $\mathbf{X}_t^*$ from input candidates. For the baseline methods, we first apply differencing to obtain a stationary time series, and we set the parameters as described in the papers [15, 17, 20]. All the experiments are conducted in MATLAB-2015b by using a 2.5GHz i7, RAM 16GB laptop with WIN10 OS.

Similar to the baseline works [20, 17, 7], for each of the series, we divide the data set into three parts: the data of the year 2000 and 2001 are used for validation and testing receptively, and the rest are adopt to train the model. We choose a model that produces the smallest RMSE in both the training and validation. We run the experiments 30 times to get the average RMSE.

Table 1 presents the prediction performance of compared

[1]https://www.usa.gov/statistics

Table 1: **The RMSE of sales prediction for five commodities in 2001 using different methods**

Methods	Department	Hardware	Closing	Furniture	Book
ANN-DSDT	975.55	49.17	315.43	99.45	88.74
TDNN	628.78	35.74	372.52	173.11	91.51
ARIMA	1005.41	100.71	519.6	124.44	98.17
SVR	602.35	39.47	802.79	266.47	97.98
RBF-AR	411.84	23.53	337.72	191.54	96.81
Our method	321.21	15.53	283.31	171.54	83.83

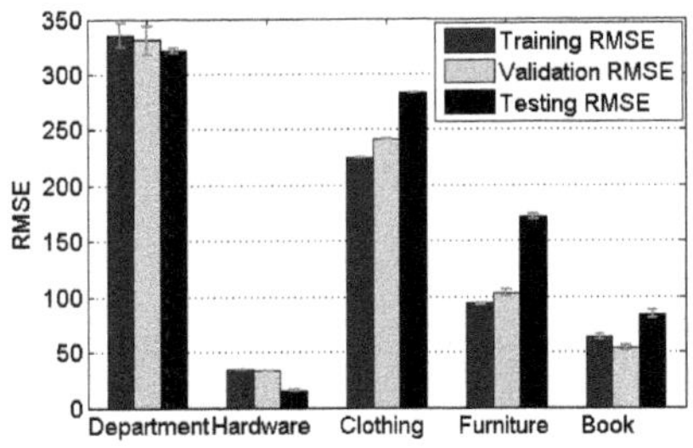

Figure 3: Mean and standard deviation of RMSE for training, validation and testing using our method

methods on five different one-year retail sales time series. The results show that our method achieves better result on four out of five datasets. Especially, for predicting the sales in the hardware and book stores, the proposed weighted gradient RBF network based AR model gets an average 15.53 and 83.83 RMSE. It is worth to mention that ANN-DSDT also reveals very competitive results on the predictions of hardware, furniture and book sales, especially for the furniture dataset, achieving 99.45 RMSE.

Fig. 3 shows the mean values and standard deviations (STD) of RMSE in training, validation and testing in the experiments by using our method. We can observed that the RMSE in training and testing is very close, which exhibits the good scalability of our model. The STD of 30 experiments are also very small, reflecting that the model identification algorithm is capable of performing a robust and stable search. In summary, the proposed WGRBF-AR model achieves competitive results to other state-of-the-art techniques, providing a promising alternative for seasonal and trend time series modeling.

4. CONCLUSION

In this paer, a weighted gradient RBF network based AR model is designed to model and predict the trend and seasonal time series. The proposed model draws upon both recent advances in gradient RBF network and functional autoregressive model that can accurately model the nonlinear, non-stationary and seasonal time series. The experiments on five retail sales datasets show that our model achieves very competitive results comparing to the state-of-the-art.

5. REFERENCES

[1] C. Chatfield. *Time-series forecasting.* CRC Press, 2000.

[2] R. Chen and R. S. Tsay. Functional-coefficient autoregressive models. *Journal of the American Statistical Association*, 88(421):298–308, 1993.

[3] S. Chen, C. F. Cowan, and P. M. Grant. Orthogonal least squares learning algorithm for radial basis function networks. *Neural Networks, IEEE Transactions on*, 2(2):302–309, 1991.

[4] E. Chng, S. Chen, and B. Mulgrew. Gradient radial basis function networks for nonlinear and nonstationary time series prediction. *Neural Networks, IEEE Transactions on*, 7(1):190–194, 1996.

[5] J. Fan and W. Zhang. Statistical methods with varying coefficient models. *Statistics and its Interface*, 1(1):179, 2008.

[6] M. Gan, C. P. Chen, H.-X. Li, and L. Chen. Gradient radial basis function based varying-coefficient autoregressive model for nonlinear and nonstationary time series. *Signal Processing Letters, IEEE*, 22(7):809–812, 2015.

[7] M. Gan, Y. Cheng, K. Liu, and G.-l. Zhang. Seasonal and trend time series forecasting based on a quasi-linear autoregressive model. *Applied Soft Computing*, 24:13–18, 2014.

[8] M. Gan, H.-X. Li, and H. Peng. A variable projection approach for efficient estimation of rbf-arx model. *Cybernetics, IEEE Transactions on*, 45(3):462–471, 2015.

[9] M. Gan, H. Peng, X. Peng, X. Chen, and G. Inoussa. A locally linear rbf network-based state-dependent ar model for nonlinear time series modeling. *Information Sciences*, 180(22):4370–4383, 2010.

[10] G. Golub and V. Pereyra. Separable nonlinear least squares: the variable projection method and its applications. *Inverse problems*, 19(2):R1, 2003.

[11] G. H. Golub and V. Pereyra. The differentiation of pseudo-inverses and nonlinear least squares problems whose variables separate. *SIAM Journal on numerical analysis*, 10(2):413–432, 1973.

[12] P. T. Ittig. A seasonal index for business. *Decision Sciences*, 28(2):335, 1997.

[13] A. Pankratz. *Forecasting with univariate Box-Jenkins models: Concepts and cases*, volume 224. John Wiley & Sons, 2009.

[14] M. Priestley. State-dependent models: A general approach to non-linear time series analysis. *Journal of Time Series Analysis*, 1(1):47–71, 1980.

[15] M. Qi and G. P. Zhang. Trend time–series modeling and forecasting with neural networks. *Neural Networks, IEEE Transactions on*, 19(5):808–816, 2008.

[16] Y. Qin, H. Peng, W. Ruan, J. Wu, and J. Gao. A modeling and control approach to magnetic levitation system based on state-dependent arx model. *Journal of Process Control*, 24(1):93–112, 2014.

[17] T. Taskaya-Temizel and M. C. Casey. A comparative study of autoregressive neural network hybrids. *Neural Networks*, 18(5):781–789, 2005.

[18] G. Zhang, B. E. Patuwo, and M. Y. Hu. Forecasting with artificial neural networks:: The state of the art. *International journal of forecasting*, 14(1):35–62, 1998.

[19] G. P. Zhang and D. M. Kline. Quarterly time-series forecasting with neural networks. *Neural Networks, IEEE Transactions on*, 18(6):1800–1814, 2007.

[20] G. P. Zhang and M. Qi. Neural network forecasting for seasonal and trend time series. *European journal of operational research*, 160(2):501–514, 2005.

When Sensor Meets Tensor: Filling Missing Sensor Values Through a Tensor Approach

Wenjie Ruan
School of Computer Science
The University of Adelaide
Adelaide, Australia
wenjie.ruan@adelaide.edu.au

Peipei Xu
School of Electronic Engineering, UESTC
Chengdu, China
peipei.xu6@gmail.com

Quan Z. Sheng
School of Computer Science
The University of Adelaide
Adelaide, Australia
michael.sheng@adelaide.edu.au

Nguyen Khoi Tran,
Nickolas J.G. Falkner
School of Computer Science
The University of Adelaide
nguyen.tran@adelaide.edu.au

Xue Li
School of IT and EE
The University of Queensland
Brisbane, Australia
xueli@itee.uq.edu.au

Wei Emma Zhang
School of Computer Science
The University of Adelaide
Adelaide, Australia
wei.zhang01@adelaide.edu.au

ABSTRACT

In the era of the *Internet of Things*, enormous number of sensors have been deployed in different locations, generating massive time-series sensory data with geo-tags. However, such sensory readings are easily missing due to various reasons such as the hardware malfunction, connection errors, and data corruption. This paper focuses on this challenge—how to accurately yet efficiently recover the missing values for corrupted time-series sensor data with geo-stamps. In this paper, we formulate the time-series sensor data as a 3-order *tensor* that naturally preserves sensors' temporal and spatial dependencies. Then we exploit its low-rank and sparse-noise structures by drawing upon recent advances in Robust Principal Component Analysis (RPCA) and tensor completion theory. The main novelty of this paper lies in that, we design a highly efficient optimization method that combines the alternating direction method of multipliers and accelerated proximal gradient to recover the data tensor. Besides testing our method using the synthetic data, we also design a real-world testbed by passive RFID (Radio-Frequency IDentification) sensors. The results demonstrate the effectiveness and accuracy of our approach.

1. INTRODUCTION

With rapid development of the IoT (Internet of Things) and constant growth of accessibility of sensors, the amount of sensory data increases exponentially [3]. Such sensor data normally are collected as time-series in an on-line and parallel manner [12]. However, in practice, sensor readings are usually missing due to the unexpected hardware failures (*e.g.,* power outages) or communication conflicts [6]. The missing data will not only greatly decrease the real-time monitoring performance, but also compromise the accuracy of back-end data analysis such as data predication, inference and visualization. Besides the data loss, the observed sensory data are also easily affected by the environment, making the accurate data recovery even more challenging [6].

The core problem of the missing value recovery lies on how to model the relationship between the known entries and the unknown ones. The most widely used and straightforward technique is filtering or regression algorithms that estimates the missing values according to their local temporal/spatial interdependence, such as Median Filter, Exponential Moving Average [7], Kalman Filtering [5], or regression methods with various complexities [10]. However, such intuitive approaches unavoidably ignore the global correlations of data (*e.g.,* in some circumstances, the missing value may depend on the entries that are far away), leading to inaccurate estimation in some circumstances.

To solve this issue, some researchers treat the sensory data as a matrix and propose various matrix completion/recovery methods to estimate the missing values by capturing their inherent low-rank structure [2, 8]. Those methods usually model time-dependent sensory data as a matrix $S = [s_1, s_2, ..., s_T]$ where vector $s_k \in \mathbb{R}^N$ represents the N-dimension sensor data at timestamp k, and only partial values in S can be observed, represented by $S_{i,j}$ where $(i, j) \in \Omega$ is the subset of known entries. So matrix completion based methods are, in principle, to recover the unknown entries by solving $\min_X\{\text{rank}(X)|\mathcal{P}_\Omega(X) = \mathcal{P}_\Omega(S)\}$ [8], where $X \in \mathbb{R}^{N\times T}$ indicates recovered data matrix and $\mathcal{P}_\Omega$ is the project operator that means only entries in Ω are observed. Because it is a *NP-hard* problem (untraceable), many researchers have proposed various convex relaxation approaches trying to solve the problem [2, 8]. Also, several robust low-rank matrix completion methods are recently proposed to deal with the case that the observed data matrix S are corrupted by noise [1]. Though promising, matrix completion based models regard geo/time-dependent sensor data as a 2-D matrix that still takes advantage of the temporal information.

Recently, tensor completion/recovery has been emerged as an active research topic since Liu *et al.* first proposed a tensor completion method for estimating missing visual data [9]. Many pioneering similar works appear, such as low-

CIKM'16 , October 24-28, 2016, Indianapolis, IN, USA

DOI: http://dx.doi.org/10.1145/2983323.2983900

rank tensor completion via convex optimization [15], tensor completion based on Tucker rank [13], *etc.* However, most of the related works are mainly attempted in computer vision and machine learning community, and they are mostly based on an assumption that the known entries in the data tensor are accurate without noise [13, 15]. This gap strongly motivates us to answer the question—*can we recover the missing values from noisy sensory data using tensor completion theory?* To the best of our knowledge, this paper is one of the first few works to do so. Comparing to the matrix formulation that only preserves the time-series information, tensor-based model naturally captures both temporal and spatial interdependent relationships of sensory readings.

Nevertheless, applying this high-level idea into practical geo-sensory data requires addressing several challenges. Similar to the robust matrix recovery formulation [1], *robust tensor completion* can be formulated to solve the problem[1] $\min_{\mathcal{X},\mathcal{E}}\{\text{rank}(\mathcal{X})+\lambda\|\mathcal{E}\|_0 \mid \mathcal{P}_\Omega(\mathcal{X}+\mathcal{E})=\mathcal{P}_\Omega(\mathcal{S})\}$. As a result, the first challenge is that, the above optimization problem is NP-hard and thus untraceable [9]. For the matrix version, we can replace rank($\mathcal{X}$) and L_0-norm by its tightest convex surrogate (*i.e.,* trace norm) and L_1-norm accordingly, making it traceable (convex optimization problem). But how to define the rank's convex surrogate for a tensor is a challenging issue. Secondly, even we can define an effective convex surrogate and make the problem traceable, how to efficiently solve the convex optimization problem while guaranteeing its convergence needs careful design.

To address above issues, we generalize the idea of adopting trace norm in matrix completion into the tensor, replacing the rank regularization term by the sum of the trace norm of each tensor-mode unfolding (see details in Sec. 3). Furthermore, to optimize the objective function, we first apply a variable-splitting trick by introducing auxiliary tensor variables to decouple the interdependency of different tensor-modes, then we design an efficient yet convergence-guaranteed optimization method by drawing upon recent advances of ADMM (Alternating Direction Method of Multipliers) [15] and accelerate proximal gradient[14] (see details in Sec. 3 and Algorithm 1). In a nutshell, our main contributions are summarized as follows:

- We develop a robust tensor completion method to recover the missing values for geo-dependent noisy time-series sensor data. To the best of our knowledge, this paper is a very first few attempts to do so.
- We design an efficient ADMM based optimization scheme to solve the robust tensor completion problem with a guarantee of convergence to optimal solution.

2. PROBLEM FORMULATION AND NOTATIONS

First, we mathematically define our target problem. Assuming that we have $M \times N$ sensors deployed in different spatial areas and collect (noisy) sensor readings[2] for T timestamps, we then can formulate it as a 3-order tensor $\mathcal{S} \in \mathbb{R}^{M\times N\times T}$ and $\mathcal{S}=\mathcal{X}+\mathcal{E}$ where X represent the true sensor readings (without noise) and $\mathcal{E}$ means the added noise. We use the projection operator $\mathcal{P}_\Omega(\mathcal{S}):\mathbb{R}^{M\times N\times T}\to\mathbb{R}^K$ that indicates the K observed sensor readings $s_{i,j,k}$ where the index $(i,j,k)\in\Omega$,mapping a tensor to a vector. Formally, this paper therefore aims to solve the following *Corrupted Sensor Value Recovery* problem:

PROBLEM 1 (CORRUPTED SENSOR VALUE RECOVERY). *To accurately recover the true sensor readings $\mathcal{X}$ and additive noise $\mathcal{E}$ given a partially observed data tensor $\mathcal{S}_\Omega$.*

Throughout this paper, we represent scalars, vectors and matrices by lowercase letters *e.g.,* a, bold lowercase letters such as $\mathbf{a}$, and upper letters A. Tensors of d-order/dimension are written by calligraphic letters like $\mathcal{A}\in\mathbb{R}^{I_1\times I_2\times\cdots\times I_d}$, whose elements are represented by $a_{i_1\cdots i_k\cdots i_d}\in\mathbb{R}$ and $1\le i_k\le I_k, 1\le k\le d$. Thus a vector can be seen as a 1-order tensor and a matrix can be seen as a 2-order tensor.

The unfolding (matricization or flattening) is the operation that transforms a tensor into a matrix. The mode-k unfolding of $\mathcal{A}$ is denoted by $unfold(\mathcal{A},k)=A_{(k)}\in\mathbb{R}^{I_k\times\prod_{i\neq k}I_i}$, *i.e.,* the row of the matrix $A_{(k)}$ are determined by the k-th component of the tensor $\mathcal{A}$, whereas all the remaining components form its column. The opposite operation "*folding*" is defined as $fold(A_{(k)},k)=\mathcal{A}$. The inner product of two tensors with identical size is computed by $<\mathcal{A},\mathcal{B}>:=\sum_{i_1,i_2,\cdots,i_d}a_{i_1i_2\cdots i_d}b_{i_1i_2\cdots i_d}$. The Frobenius norm of $\mathcal{A}$ is defined as $\|\mathcal{A}\|_F:=(\sum_{i_1,i_2,\cdots,i_d}|a_{i_1i_2\cdots i_d}|^2)^{\frac{1}{2}}$. The multiplication of a tensor $\mathcal{A}\in\mathbb{R}^{I_1\times I_2\times\cdots\times I_d}$ with a matrix $U\in\mathbb{R}^{J\times I_k}$ in mode-k is denoted by $\mathcal{A}\times_k U\in\mathbb{R}^{I_1\times\cdots\times I_{k-1}\times J\times I_{k+1}\times\cdots\times I_d}$.

3. ROBUST TENSOR COMPLETION

Being similar to matrix completion, Problem 1 can be formulated as solving a low-rank minimization problem.

$$\min_{\mathcal{X},\mathcal{E}} \ \text{rank}_{Tucker}(\mathcal{X})+\lambda\|\mathcal{E}\|_0 \quad \text{s.t. } \mathcal{P}_\Omega(\mathcal{X}+\mathcal{E})=\mathcal{P}_\Omega(\mathcal{S}) \tag{1}$$

where $\text{rank}_{Tucker}(\mathcal{S})$ is the Tucker-rank of a tensor[4]. Similar to matrix completion, this problem is NP-hard. Thus, to make it tractable, we replace Tucker rank by its *convex surrogate* and use L_1-norm instead of L_0-norm as an optimization problem: $\min_{\mathcal{X},\mathcal{E}}\{\text{ConSurro}(\mathcal{X})+\lambda\|\mathcal{E}\|_1 \mid \text{s.t. } \mathcal{P}_\Omega(\mathcal{X}+\mathcal{E})=\mathcal{P}_\Omega(\mathcal{S})\}$.

Then the first issue is how to define the convex surrogate of a tensor. For a matrix, the trace norm $\|.\|_*$ is the tightest convex envelop of its rank, used as the convex surrogate. Thus, the idea can be generalized into the high-order tensor, defining its trace norm as the sum of the trace norms [9] of the mode-i unfolding in tensor $\mathcal{X}$, *i.e.,* $\sum_i\|X_{(i)}\|_*$. Equation 1 can be therefore transformed into a convex problem:

$$\begin{aligned}\min_{\mathcal{X},\mathcal{E}} \ & \sum_{i=1}^{3}\|X_{(i)}\|_*+\lambda\|\mathcal{E}\|_1 \\ \text{s.t. } & \mathcal{P}_\Omega(\mathcal{X}+\mathcal{E})=\mathcal{P}_\Omega(\mathcal{S})\end{aligned} \tag{2}$$

To solve Eqn. 2, we introduce an Alternating Direction Method of Multipliers [15] that is very efficient in dealing with convex optimization problems by breaking them into smaller pieces, each of which are then easier to handle. However, the trace norm of each mode unfolding $\|X_{(i)}\|_*,(i=1,2,3)$ shares the same values in data tensor $\mathcal{S}$ and cannot be optimized independently so that existing ADMM cannot directly be applied to our problem. Hence, we split these interdependent terms by introducing auxiliary variables $\mathcal{X}_1,\mathcal{X}_2,\mathcal{X}_3$, so that they can be solved independently. Specifically, we reformulate Eqn. 2 as

$$\begin{aligned}\min_{\mathcal{X}_1,\mathcal{X}_2,\mathcal{X}_3,\mathcal{E}} \ & \sum_{i=1}^{3}\|X_{i,(i)}\|_*+\lambda\|\mathcal{E}\|_1 \\ \text{s.t. } & \mathcal{P}_\Omega(\mathcal{X}_i+\mathcal{E})=\mathcal{P}_\Omega(\mathcal{S}), \ \ i=1,2,3.\end{aligned} \tag{3}$$

[1] $\mathcal{X},\mathcal{E},\mathcal{S}$ are the recovered data tensor, additive noise tensor and observed data tensor, $\mathcal{P}_\Omega$ means the known entries of tensor

[2] we assume the additive noises are sufficiently sparse relative to the data tensor S

We hence define its *augmented Lagrangian function* $L_{\mu,\Lambda_i} = \sum_{i=1}^{3}(\frac{1}{2\mu}\|\mathcal{P}_\Omega(\mathcal{X}_i+\mathcal{E})-\mathcal{P}_\Omega(\mathcal{S})\|^2 - \langle\Lambda_i, \mathcal{P}_\Omega(\mathcal{X}_i+\mathcal{E})-\mathcal{P}_\Omega(\mathcal{S})\rangle) + \sum_{i=1}^{3}\|\mathbf{X}_{\mathbf{i},(\mathbf{i})}\|_* + \lambda\|\mathcal{E}\|_1$. According to ADMM, we first fix $\mathcal{E}$ to optimize $\mathcal{X}_i$ $(i=1,2,3)$ by solving

$$\min_{\mathcal{X}_1,\mathcal{X}_2,\mathcal{X}_3} \sum_{i=1}^{3}(\frac{1}{2\mu}\|\mathcal{P}_\Omega(\mathcal{X}_i+\mathcal{E})-\mathcal{P}_\Omega(\mathcal{S})\|^2 - \langle\Lambda_i, \mathcal{P}_\Omega(\mathcal{X}_i+\mathcal{E})-\mathcal{P}_\Omega(\mathcal{S})\rangle$$
$$+\|X_{i,(i)}\|_*) \equiv \sum_{i=1}^{3}(\mu\|X_{i,(i)}\|_* + \frac{1}{2}\|\mathcal{P}_\Omega(\mathcal{X}_i)-\mathcal{D}_i\|^2) \quad (4)$$

where $\mathcal{D}_i = \mathcal{P}_\Omega(\mathcal{S}) - \mathcal{P}_\Omega(\mathcal{E}) + \mu\Lambda_i$. We define the function $f(\mathcal{X}_i) = \frac{1}{2}\|\mathcal{P}_\Omega(\mathcal{X}_i)-\mathcal{D}_i\|^2$ and calculate the gradient $\nabla f(\mathcal{X}_i) = \mathcal{P}_\Omega^*(\mathcal{P}_\Omega(\mathcal{X}_i)-\mathcal{D}_i)$, where $\mathcal{P}_\Omega^*(\cdot)$ means the adjoint operation of $\mathcal{P}_\Omega(\cdot)$ such as $\mathcal{P}_\Omega^*(\mathcal{S}) : \mathbb{R}^K \to \mathbb{R}^{M\times N\times T}$. According to Accelerated Proximal Gradient (APG) method [14], we can independently minimize $\mathcal{X}_i$ through iterative optimization to make the final sum minimal. Specifically, we get optimal $\mathcal{X}_i^{(k+1)}$ given $\mathcal{X}_i^{(k)}$ until it converges by solving

$$\min_{\mathcal{X}_i^{(k+1)}} f(\mathcal{X}_i^{(k)}) + \nabla f(\mathcal{X}_i^{(k)})(\mathcal{X}_i^{(k+1)} - \mathcal{X}_i^{(k)}) + \frac{1}{2\eta}\|\mathcal{X}_i^{(k+1)} - \mathcal{X}_i^{(k)}\|^2$$
$$+\mu\|X_{i,(i)}^{(k+1)}\|_* = \frac{1}{2\eta}\|\mathcal{X}_i^{(k+1)} - \mathcal{X}_i^{(k)} + \eta\nabla f(\mathcal{X}_i^{(k)})\|^2 + \mu\|X_{i,(i)}^{(k+1)}\|_*$$
$$\propto \frac{1}{2}\|\mathcal{X}_i^{(k+1)} - \mathcal{X}_i^{(k)} + \eta\nabla f(\mathcal{X}_i^{(k)})\|^2 + \eta\mu\|X_{i,(i)}^{(k+1)}\|_* \quad (5)$$

To solve Eqn. 5, we first need to define *singular value thresholding operator* for tensor. For matrix, the singular value threshold operator is defined as $\mathcal{T}_\mu(X) := U diag(\bar{\sigma})V^\intercal$, where $X = U diag(\sigma)V^T$ is the singular value decomposition (SVD) and $\bar{\sigma} := max(\sigma-\mu, 0)$. Similarly, we define the singular value threshold operator for tensor as $\mathcal{T}_{i,\mu}(\mathcal{X}) := \text{fold}(\mathcal{T}_\mu(X_{(i)}), i)$. We thus can calculate the closed-form solution of Eqn. 5 as follows:

$$\mathcal{X}_i^{(k+1)} = \mathcal{T}_{i,\eta\mu}(\mathcal{X}_i^{(k)} - \eta\nabla f(\mathcal{X}_i^{(k)})) \quad (6)$$

In the next, we will optimize $\mathcal{E}$ when fixed $\mathcal{X}_i$ by solving following problem:

$$\min_{\mathcal{E}} \lambda\|\mathcal{E}\|_1 + \sum_{i=1}^{3}(\frac{1}{2\mu}\|\mathcal{P}_\Omega(\mathcal{X}_i+\mathcal{E}) - \mathcal{P}_\Omega(\mathcal{S}) - \mu\Lambda_i\|^2)$$
$$\propto \mu\lambda\|\mathcal{E}\|_1 + \frac{1}{2}\sum_{i=1}^{3}\|\mathcal{P}_\Omega(\mathcal{E}) - \mathcal{M}_i\|^2 \quad (7)$$

where $\mathcal{M}_i = \mathcal{P}_\Omega(\mathcal{S}) + \mu\Lambda_i - \mathcal{P}_\Omega(\mathcal{X}_i)$.

To solve the Eqn. 7, we introduce *Homogeneous Tensor Array* [4] by stacking a set of component tensors of the same size along the first mode as follows:

$$\bar{\mathcal{X}} := (\mathcal{X}_1, \mathcal{X}_2, \mathcal{X}_3)^\intercal \in \mathbb{R}^{3M\times N\times T}, \quad (8)$$

and its corresponding linear operator $\mathcal{C} : \mathbb{R}^{M\times N\times T} \to \mathbb{R}^{3M\times N\times T}$, *i.e.*, $\bar{\mathcal{X}} = \mathcal{C}(\mathcal{X}) \in \mathbb{R}^{3M\times N\times T}$ Then its adjoint operator can be defined as $\mathcal{C}^* : \mathbb{R}^{3M\times N\times T} \to \mathbb{R}^{M\times N\times T}$, such that $\mathcal{X} = \mathcal{C}^*(\bar{\mathcal{X}}) = \sum_{i=1}^{3}\mathcal{X}_i$. As a result, we can rewrite the Eqn. 7 as

$$\min_{\mathcal{E}} \mu\lambda\|\mathcal{E}\|_1 + \frac{1}{2}\|\mathcal{C}(\mathcal{P}_\Omega(\mathcal{E})) - \bar{\mathcal{M}}\|^2 \propto \frac{\mu\lambda}{3}\|\mathcal{E}\|_1 + \frac{1}{2}\|\mathcal{P}_\Omega(\mathcal{E}) - \frac{\mathcal{C}^*(\bar{\mathcal{M}})}{3}\|^2$$
$$= \frac{\mu\lambda}{3}\|\mathcal{E}\|_1 + \frac{1}{2}\|\mathcal{P}_\Omega(\mathcal{E}) - \frac{1}{N}\sum_{i=1}^{N}(\mathcal{P}_\Omega(\mathcal{S}) + \mu\Lambda_i - \mathcal{P}_\Omega(\mathcal{X}_i))\|^2 \quad (9)$$

where $\bar{\mathcal{M}} = (\mathcal{M}_1, \mathcal{M}_2, \mathcal{M}_3)^\intercal$, $\mathcal{C}(\mathcal{P}_\Omega(\mathcal{E})) = (\mathcal{P}_\Omega(\mathcal{E}), \mathcal{P}_\Omega(\mathcal{E}), \mathcal{P}_\Omega(\mathcal{E}))^\intercal$.

According to the Iterative Shrinkage Thresholding (IST) algorithm that $\min_{\mathbf{y}}\{\frac{1}{2}\|\mathbf{y}-\mathbf{x}\|_2^2 + \mu\|\mathbf{y}\|_1\}$ has a closed form solution $\mathbf{y} = \mathcal{S}_\mu(\mathbf{x}) := sign(\mathbf{x})max(|\mathbf{x}| - \mu, 0)$, we can solve Eqn. 9 to get $\mathcal{E} = \mathcal{S}_{\frac{\mu\lambda}{3}}(\frac{1}{3}\sum_{i=1}^{3}(\mathcal{P}_\Omega(\mathcal{S}) + \mu\Lambda_i - \mathcal{P}_\Omega(\mathcal{X}_i)))$.

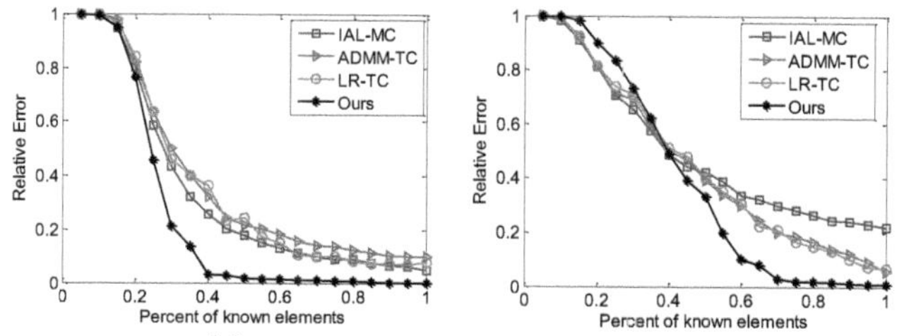

(a) (b)

Figure 1: (a) Relative errors for different observation percentages ($\rho_n = 0.1$, $a = 1$); (b) Relative errors for different observation percentages under noise ($\rho_n = 0.25$, $a = 1$)

Finally, given $\mathcal{X}_i^{(k+1)}$ and $\mathcal{E}_i^{(k+1)}$, we update the Lagrangian multiplier parameter by $\mathbf{\Lambda}_i^{(k+1)} = \mathbf{\Lambda}_i^{(k)} - \frac{1}{\mu}(\mathcal{P}_\Omega(\mathcal{X}_i^{(k+1)} + \mathcal{E}^{(k+1)}) - \mathcal{P}_\Omega(\mathcal{S})$. Note that the above solution is based on the form of 3-order tensor. Extension to higher-order tensor involves fundamentally no new ideas.

4. EXPERIMENTS

We conducted the experiments in MATLAB R2015b on a laptop with a CORE i7 2.40GHz CPU and 8GB RAM. We used the Tensor Toolbox[3] for tensor operations and decompositions. We first conducted a simulation experiment using synthetic data to compare with the state-of-the-art data recovery methods under different data loss percentages and additive noise ratios. Then we designed a real-world experimental testbed using passive Radio-frequency Identification hardware to evaluate the performance of our method. Similar to other data recovery works [9, 8], we adopted the *relative error* $\frac{\|\mathcal{X}-\mathcal{X}_0\|}{\|\mathcal{X}_0\|}$, where $\mathcal{X}, \mathcal{X}_0$ denote the recovered and original data tensor respectively, to evaluate the recovery performance.

We compared our method with four typical methods: *i) M-AF* means the moving averaging interpolation that is the most widely-used method to fill in missing values in time series data; *ii) IAL-MC* is the inexact augmented Lagrangian method that can recover a data matrix of being arbitrarily corrupted [8], it is a matrix-based robust completion method and greatly motivates our work; *iii) LR-TC* is the earliest yet very effective tensor completion method using block coordinate descent optimization [9]; *iv) ADMM-TC* also utilizes ADMM for solving the tensor completion problem under no noise assumption [15].

4.1 Synthetic Data

Similar to the works in [9, 15], we generated a $50\times50\times20$ data tensor with Tucker rank-$(5,5,5)$. We randomly chose a fraction ρ_n of the tensor entries that were polluted by an additive i.i.d. (*i.e.*, independent and identically distributed) noise following uniform distribution $\mathcal{U}(-a, a)$. Then a fraction ρ_o of the corrupted tensor elements were randomly picked as observed values in $\mathcal{S}_\Omega$. In the experiments, we set μ and η as constants for simplicity.

In Fig. 1, we can see that our method has a significantly higher recovery accuracy than the other three algorithms. In our method, there appears to be a phase transition threshold in ρ_o where the relative error of the algorithm improves drastically. This threshold increases with ρ_n: it is about 40% for $\rho_n = 10\%$, and it increases to 70% for $\rho_n = 25\%$.

[3]http://www.sandia.gov/~tgkolda/TensorToolbox/index-2.6.html

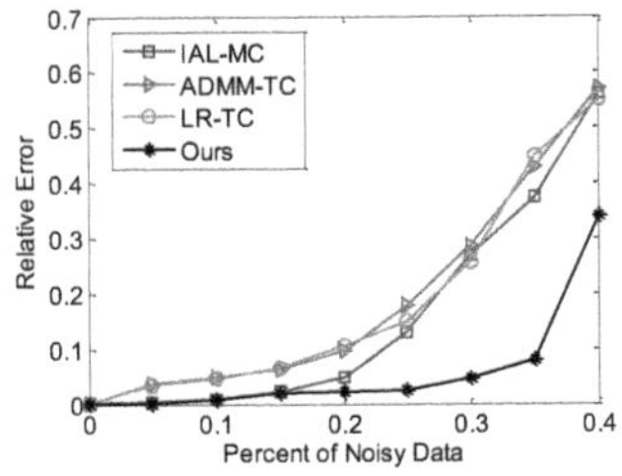

Figure 2: Relative errors for different corruption percentages ($\rho_o = 1$, $a = 1$)

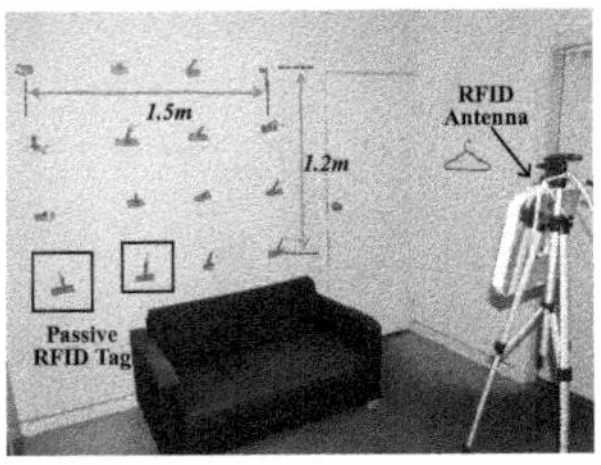

Figure 3: Experimental testbed of RFID sensors

Next, we fixed ρ_o at 100% and varied ρ_n from 1% to 40%. The same set of metrics was reported and plotted in the left graph of Fig 2. Again, our model works better than the other models, which appears to be very susceptible to increasing ρ_n's. There is also a threshold in ρ_n(15% in this case) below, other methods recover the data with higher relative error. The experimental results on the synthetic data suggest that our method can achieve better recovery with partial observations.

4.2 RFID Sensory Data

Passive RFID tags are one of the most frequently-used sensors due to its cheap price and battery-free character [11]. It is widely used to identify and track objects through remotely accessing the electronically stored data. However, since passive RFID tags are powered by radio signals and deliver the data via the weak backscatter signal, they experience severe RSSI reading loss, especially with a high sampling rate or when tag/reader is moving. As a result, how to accurately recover missing RSSI readings is still a challenge, especially for a large-scale RFID usage. To deal with this practical issue as well as test our method, we designed a testbed consisting geo-tagged 4×4 RFID sensor array (see Fig. 3) and collected overall 115,200 RSSIs (Received Signal Strength Indicators) readings (one hour's data). We formulated it into a data tensor with different sizes to simulate various using scenarios (*e.g.*, 4×4, 20×20, 20×40 and 40×40 sensor arrays).

Table 1: Relative errors for different tag-array size under 20% missing values

Sensor Array Size	4×4	20×20	20×40	40×40
MAF	0.2431	0.2462	0.2505	0.257
Our method	0.2481	0.187	0.126	0.091

Table 1 shows the recovery results of our method and MAF (most frequently used in practical RFID system). For small-scaled deployment (*i.e.*, 4×4 sensor array), our method achieves similar performance to MAF. However, our tensor-based method performs significantly better than MAF in a large-scale deployment (*e.g.*, 20×20 sensor array). The lack of performance improvement in 4×4 sensor array mainly lies in the fact that the low-rank structure only exists in mode-3 of data tensor which conflicts our assumption that requires tensor low-rank in all modes. This problem will leave for our future work.

5. CONCLUSION

In this paper, we propose a method for recovering the missing data by using the robust tensor completion. The proposed method can accurately recover the missing values given partial observed corrupted data. Our method assumes that the data tensor is low rank in all unfolding modes, however this maybe not the case in certain applications. We will study this issue in our future work.

6. REFERENCES

[1] E. J. Candès, X. Li, Y. Ma, and J. Wright. Robust principal component analysis? *Journal of the ACM (JACM)*, 58(3):11, 2011.

[2] E. J. Candès and B. Recht. Exact matrix completion via convex optimization. *Foundations of Computational mathematics*, 9(6):717–772, 2009.

[3] L. Da Xu, W. He, and S. Li. Internet of things in industries: a survey. *Industrial Informatics, IEEE Transactions on*, 10(4):2233–2243, 2014.

[4] D. Goldfarb and Z. Qin. Robust low-rank tensor recovery: Models and algorithms. *SIAM Journal on Matrix Analysis and Applications*, 35(1):225–253, 2014.

[5] M. S. Grewal. *Kalman filtering*. Springer, 2011.

[6] H.-P. Hsieh, S.-D. Lin, and Y. Zheng. Inferring air quality for station location recommendation based on urban big data. In *Proc. of the 21th ACM SIGKDD Intl. Conference on Knowledge Discovery and Data Mining*, pages 437–446, 2015.

[7] A. Lawrance and P. Lewis. An exponential moving-average sequence and point process. *Journal of Applied Probability*, pages 98–113, 1977.

[8] Z. Lin, M. Chen, and Y. Ma. The augmented lagrange multiplier method for exact recovery of corrupted low-rank matrices. *arXiv:1009.5055*, 2010.

[9] J. Liu, P. Musialski, P. Wonka, and J. Ye. Tensor completion for estimating missing values in visual data. In *Computer Vision, 2009 IEEE 12th Intl. Conference on*, pages 2114–2121, 2009.

[10] A. M. Norcia, M. Clarke, and C. W. Tyler. Digital filtering and robust regression techniques for estimating sensory thresholds from the evoked potential. *IEEE Engineering in Medicine and Biology Magazine*, 4(4):26–32, 1985.

[11] W. Ruan. Unobtrusive human localization and activity recognition for supporting independent living of the elderly. In *Proceedings of 2016 IEEE International Conference on Pervasive Computing and Communication Workshops (PerCom Workshops)*, pages 1–3, 2016.

[12] Y. Sakurai, Y. Matsubara, and C. Faloutsos. Mining and forecasting of big time-series data. In *Proceedings of the 2015 ACM SIGMOD International Conference on Management of Data*, pages 919–922. ACM, 2015.

[13] M. Signoretto, R. Van de Plas, B. De Moor, and J. A. Suykens. Tensor versus matrix completion: a comparison with application to spectral data. *Signal Processing Letters, IEEE*, 18(7):403–406, 2011.

[14] K.-C. Toh and S. Yun. An accelerated proximal gradient algorithm for nuclear norm regularized linear least squares problems. *Pacific Journal of Optimization*, 6(615-640):15, 2010.

[15] R. Tomioka, K. Hayashi, and H. Kashima. Estimation of low-rank tensors via convex optimization. *arXiv preprint arXiv:1010.0789*, 2010.

PEQ : An Explainable, Specification-based, Aspect-oriented Product Comparator for E-commerce

Abhishek Sikchi
Indian Institute of Technology
Kharagpur, India
sikchi70@gmail.com

Pawan Goyal
Indian Institute of Technology
Kharagpur, India
pawang.iitk@gmail.com

Samik Datta
Flipkart
India
samik.datta@flipkart.com

ABSTRACT

While purchasing a product, consumers often rely on specifications as well as online reviews of the product for decision-making. While comparing, one often has in mind a specific aspect or a set of aspects which are of interest to them. Previous work has used comparative sentences, where two entities are compared directly in a single sentence by the review author, towards the comparison task. In this paper, we extend the existing model by incorporating the feature specifications of the products, which are easily available, and learn the importance to be associated with each of them. To test the validity of these product ranking measures, we comprehensively test it on a digital camera dataset from Amazon.com and the results show good empirical outperformance over the state-of-the-art baselines.

Keywords

Comparison mining; Decision support systems

1. INTRODUCTION

Being able to compare among alternative product models has a direct role to play in decision making by potential buyers. However, it is often hard to arrive at a conclusion of a good choice due to the huge number of brands and models. Websites such as PriceGrabber[1] compare prices of products whereas DPReview[2], CameraDecision[3], etc. give comparative tables of feature specifications as documented by the manufacturer but they do not provide insight into how those features translate into usefulness during the actual use, which can be very specific. On the other hand, user reviews often describe first-hand experiences of using the product but the major drawbacks are the need to read many reviews to get an estimate of agreement between users and the need to manually compare different products. The goal of our work is to fill-in this space and provide a means of comparing products of the same type (e.g., competing cameras). Some of the previous works have focused on comparative sentences in the reviews. While Kessler and Kuhn [3, 4] use approaches such as semantic role labeling and structure alignment to detect product comparison sentences, they do not provide a model to use these for actual comparison. Tkachenko and Lauw [6], on the other hand, takes the product comparison sentences as input and gives a generative model for product comparisons.

However, relying on the language alone can be inapt. For instance, sentences shown in Table 1 differ a lot from other sentences used to compare the same aspects of digital cameras due to the unique choice of words by their reviewers or simply because of typing errors, as in the sentence s_2. On the other hand, one can well hypothesize that in an ideal situation, a rational consumer would opt for a product which has a better set of specifications – a theory supported by psychologists and economists alike. These specifications or attribute values do play a role in determining the intrinsic quality of the product. Specifications have earlier successfully been used along with the product reviews to generate augmented specifications [5].

We propose a model, *PEQ*, that integrates the language along with the products' attributes in order to model comparisons made on the basis of comparative sentences about two entities. Understanding such comparisons have several applications. From the manufacturers' perspective, they could better understand the relative strength or weakness of their products, and hence develop better products. From the consumers' perspective, they could exercise better, informed purchasing decisions by comparing the various features of certain kind of products.

2. THE EXPLAINABLE CHOICE MODEL

The *psychological* theory of choices, as illustrated in [1] and the references therein, posits that the outcome of a product comparison (e.g., digital cameras), hinged on an aspect (e.g., ergonomics), is arrived at by inspecting the products' features. The *economic* theory of choices, as presented in [7] and the references therein, additionally assumes *rational* decision making on the part of the buyer, manifested in the form of *utility* maximization – a buyer and aspect dependent comparison of products' features vis-à-vis prices.

In recent times, with the proliferation of user-generated online product review corpora documenting outcomes of thousands of product comparisons along with accompanying explanatory text, one further wishes to augment the tradi-

[1]https://www.pricegrabber.com
[2]https://www.dpreview.com/products/compare/cameras
[3]https://www.cameradecision.com

CIKM'16 , October 24-28, 2016, Indianapolis, IN, USA
 ISBN 978-1-4503-4073-1/16/10. . . $15.00
DOI: http://dx.doi.org/10.1145/2983323.2983901

Aspect	Sample sentences
Functionality	s_1 : There's a reason nikon d7000 has almost twice as many buttons/knobs/what-have-you than the D5000: you are meant to use them!
Form factor	s_2 : The TL225 also wieghs a half-ounce more then the TL220 due to the choice of displays.
Image quality	s_3 : Then I bought Canon 40D, and I got the same problem, I even tried Nikon D90, the red dots were reduced, but still very noticeable. s_4: I'm still experimenting, but my gut feeling is that if you were to compare a 16MP DX crop from the center of the D800e frame versus the 16MP D7000 DX at very slow shutter speeds, that the D7000 would have less blur from mirror slap.

Table 1: Sample Comparative Sentences about Digital Cameras

tional choice models with language models for the explanatory text. This greatly aids the interpretability of such comparisons and enables novel decision support systems for e-commerce. Herein, we extend the work presented in [6].

Given a corpus of sentences containing pairwise product comparisons hinged on a specific aspect, our task is twofold: first, we seek to recover the partial order inducing comparative relations on the universe of cited products, with respect to the aspect under consideration, and, second, we infer the outcome of the comparison for every sentence in the corpus. In addition to the above mentioned corpus, we also make use of corpora containing product specifications.

Formally, the review corpus, $\mathcal{S}$, consists of sentences S that compare a pair of products each, $h(S) \in \mathcal{P}$ and $t(S) \in \mathcal{P}$, where $h(S)$ is the product appearing first in S, and $t(S)$ is the product appearing later. The subset of $\mathcal{S}$ involving the pair of products, P_i and P_j, is denoted by S_{ij}. For pairs that are *never* compared in any sentence, $S_{ij} = \phi$.

In what follows, we first model the outcome of product comparisons, relying solely on their specifications, and then model the language one would use to explain those comparisons.

2.1 Intrinsic Goodness

For every pair of products, $(P_i, P_j) \in \mathcal{P} \times \mathcal{P}$, we intend to infer their comparative relationship, with respect to an aspect $A \in \mathcal{A}$, *solely* based on their specifications. To this end, we endow each product $P \in \mathcal{P}$ with an intrinsic *goodness* score, $G_P \in \mathbb{R}$. The outcome of the aforementioned comparison, thus, reduces to the relative values of G_{P_i} and G_{P_j}, modulo an uncertainty that models lack of consensus. In other words, for every sentence $S \in \mathcal{S}$ the outcome of the comparsion is influenced by the relative values of $G_{h(S)}$ and $G_{t(S)}$.

We model the intrinsic goodness to closely resemble the utility, sans an explicit negative coefficient on the price. As an example, while selecting the best digital camera with respect to picture quality, a rational buyer would emphasize relevant specifications like number of megapixels, size of the sensor etc. over and above less relevant features like weight, weather proofing etc. We model this as a linear combination of the specifications including price, with an aspect-dependent weight vector W_A. The intrinsic goodness of each product is thus measured by:

$$G_P = W_A^T X_P \tag{1}$$

where $X_P \in \mathcal{X}$ is the vector encoding the product's specifications. Although we do not explicitly constrain the corresponding component for price in W_A to be negative, in our experiments it often turns out to be so, giving the intrinsic goodness score an utility-theoretic interpretation. An extension that models the non-linearity is discussed in 3.1.

2.2 Rational Choice

For every sentence, $S \in \mathcal{S}$, we let the binary random variable $C_S \in \{0, 1\}$ denote the direction of the comparison, with $C_S = 0$ implying that $h(S)$ is favored over $t(S)$, and vice-versa. The random variable C_S is further assumed to depend on the relative values of the intrinsic goodnesses of the products involved, $G_{h(S)}$ and $G_{t(S)}$. This leads to the *rational* choice model:

$$\begin{aligned} \Pr\{C_S = 0; X_{h(S)}, X_{t(S)}\} &= \Pr\{h(S) \succ_A t(S)\} \\ &= \sigma(\vartheta \times (G_{h(S)} - G_{t(S)})) \end{aligned} \tag{2}$$

Where $\succ_A \subset \mathcal{P} \times \mathcal{P}$ is the partial order induced by the comparison with respect to the aspect $A \in \mathcal{A}$, and ϑ is a tunable parameter.

2.3 Language Model

The outcome of the comparison between $h(S) \in \mathcal{P}$ and $t(S) \in \mathcal{P}$, as embodied in C_S, influences the *language* of the sentence S that we endeavour to model in this section.

We follow the conventions introduced in [6], and posit *two* language models, θ_0 and θ_1, that models the aspect specific sentiment conveying words. We emphasise that our language models are not distributions over words. They are, instead, distributions over *features*, words anchored with respect to $h(S)$ and $t(S)$. We refer the reader to [6] for a detailed exposition.

3. THE *PEQ* GENERATIVE PROCESS

We now describe the generative process that underlies PEQ.

Choice Model. For every comparative sentence, $S \in \mathcal{S}$, that compares two products $h(S)$ and $t(S)$, we first sample the outcome, C_S, according to the choice model $C_S \sim \texttt{Bernoulli}(\sigma(\vartheta \times (G_{h(S)} - G_{t(S)}))$.

Language Model. Depending on the orientation of the choice, we next pick one of $\theta_0, \theta_1 \sim \texttt{Dir}(\alpha)$, from whence the lingustic features, f, is sampled: $f \sim \texttt{Mult}(\theta_{C_S})$.

In line with [6], the joint probability is expressed as follows:

$$\Pr\{F(S) \mid C_S = c\} = \prod_{f \in F(S)} \Pr\{f \mid \theta_c\} \tag{3}$$

Where $F(S)$ enumerates the features present in S.

Armed with the generative process, the comparison outcome for each sentence S, thus, can be obtained as the posterior distribution of C_S, and the partial order among the products can be recovered by comparing the values of G_P. We illustrate the learning algorithm in the next section. The aspect-specific weight vector, W_A, comparison outcomes $C_S, \forall S \in \mathcal{S}$ and the language models $\theta_c, \forall c \in \{0,1\}$ constitute the hidden variables. The observables comprise of the features $F(S), \forall S \in \mathcal{S}$ and the product specifications $X_P, \forall P \in \mathcal{P}$.

3.1 Learning W_A

Given an assignment of $C_S, \forall S \in \mathcal{S}$, we employ RankSVM, as introduced in [2], to recover W_A. It is a variant of the celebrated Support Vector Machine that learns W_A and respects the pairwise preference constraints posed by $C_S, \forall S \in \mathcal{S}$ in a large-margin setting. The input to this phase are the product specifications, X_P, and the orientation of choices, C_S. Note that extension to the non-linear setting is trivial via kernels. We leave the possibility of augmenting RankSVM to handle chance-constraints, such as those specified by $\Pr\{C_S\}$, to a future work. Once W_A is learnt, we appeal to Equation 1 for deriving the intrinsic goodness of each product.

3.2 Learning C_S

For learning $C_S, \forall S \in \mathcal{S}$, we resort to Gibbs sampling. Following [6], we employ a *collapsed* Gibbs sampler that integrates out θ_0, θ_1 analytically. Letting $\{\mathcal{S}_c \mid \forall c \in \{0,1\}\}$ denote a partition of $\mathcal{S}$, the conditional probabilities can be expressed as:

$$\Pr\{\mathcal{S}_c \mid c; \alpha\} = \frac{\Gamma(\alpha F)}{\Gamma^F(\alpha)} \frac{\prod_{f=1}^{F} \Gamma(\alpha + n(f,c))}{\Gamma(\alpha F + \sum_{f=1}^{F} n(f,c))} \tag{4}$$

Where $n(f,c)$ denotes the frequency of the feature f in $\mathcal{S}_c$, and F denotes the size of the feature vocabulary. We refer the reader to [6] for a detailed derivation.

Fixing $G_P, \forall P \in \mathcal{P}$ (i.e., by fixing W_A), and $C_{S'}$ for every sentence in $\mathcal{S}$ other than S itself, we sample C_S from the following posterior distribution:

$$\begin{aligned} &\Pr\{C_S = c \mid \mathcal{C}_{\neg S}, \cdots\} \\ &\propto \Pr\{C_S \mid G_{h(S)}, G_{t(S)}) \times \prod_{c \in \{0,1\}} P(\mathcal{S}_c \mid c; \alpha) \\ &\propto \exp\{-C_S \vartheta W_A^T (X_{h(S)} - X_{t(S)})\} \times \prod_{c \in \{0,1\}} P(\mathcal{S}_c \mid c; \alpha) \end{aligned} \tag{5}$$

We repeat the process until convergence.

4. EXPERIMENTS

We obtain the corpus of comparative sentences $\mathcal{S}$ from Tkachenko and Lauw [6] which contains reviews from the Digital Cameras category of Amazon. The dataset has comparative sentences extracted from reviews, in which each sentence is annotated with three key information: whether a sentence is comparative, the entities being compared, and the aspect of interest. In total, the number of products being compared within extracted sentences is 180. The four aspects used are functionality, form factor, image quality and price, and they respectively have 457, 78, 129, and 165 comparative sentences. Each aspect is a distinct instance of the problem. The distributions between the two classes (whether the head entity or the tail entity is favored) are relatively well-balanced. We used 500 iterations of the Gibbs sampler to stablize the *PEQ* model. The results are reported in 10-fold cross-validation settings.

4.1 Results

We perform experiments under both supervised and unsupervised settings. Where in the unsupervised setting, only the f's are observed, in the supervised setting, we would consider some C_s variables (corresponding to a subset of labeled sentences) to also have known outcomes. This effects in grouping together sentences of the same label, which would then influence the respective feature distributions, θ_0 and θ_1.

Supervised Configuration. In supervised setting, all the competing algorithms are given a set of labeled (training) data, which is 50% of the total dataset, and the rest as unlabeled (test) data. For sentence-level classification accuracy, each algorithm is required to identify the favored entity for each comparative sentence in the test data, which is essentially a binary classification problem. To measure the performance of an algorithm, we calculate the fraction of correctly classified sentences (over the total number of sentences in the test set). We measure our results against RankSVM model and the CompareGem model formulated in [6] as baseline.

Aspect	CompareGem	RankSVM	PEQ
Functionality	86.8	87.5	**90.2**
Form Factor	72.5	**88.6**	85.7
Image Quality	**68.8**	67.2	64.7
Price	66.7	67.6	**70.5**

Table 2: Classification accuracy for supervised model

For entity ranking accuracy, the majority vote, considering all the sentences that mention a pair is used as crowdsourced benchmark. Therefore, this benchmark reflects how users in general rank these entities.

Tables 2 and 3 show the classification and ranking accuracies for all the competing models in the supervised settings. We see that *PEQ* always performs better than CompareGem in terms of ranking accuracy. For classification accuracy, it performs better than CompreGem in 3 out of 4 aspects. For form-factor, RankSVM outperforms PEQ in both classification and ranking accuracy with a slight margin, and CompareGem by a huge margin. This might be indicative of the fact that specifications are very good indicative for product ranking for the 'Form-factor'.

Aspect	CompareGem	RankSVM	PEQ
Functionality	87.4	88.2	**88.3**
Form Factor	82.7	**90.2**	89.3
Image Quality	75.5	74.4	**76.6**
Price	74.0	66.3	**74.5**

Table 3: Ranking accuracy for supervised model

Unsupervised Configuration. In the unsupervised configuration, no labeled data is used as input. The task resembles clustering into two clusters, rather than classification. We can still use the labels to evaluate this clustering, by computing purity instead. As a baseline, we compare against CompareGem only, since RankSVM cannot be used in the absence of any labels. CompareGem has already been compared to existing methods for both clustering and ranking tasks and found to be superior in most cases. Our model outperforms CompareGem in almost all cases except for the aspect 'price' as shown in Tables 4 and 5.

Aspect	CompareGem	PEQ
Functionality	70.2	73.6
Form-factor	65.6	65.8
Image-quality	62.5	63.7
Price	57.0	56.4

Table 4: Classification accuracy (purity) for unsupervised model

Aspect	CompareGem	PEQ
Functionality	64.6	68.2
Form-factor	64.4	67.4
Image-quality	59.6	61.7
Price	56.0	54.7

Table 5: Ranking accuracy for unsupervised model

4.2 Feature Analysis

We study the features which are the most discriminative between the two classes, and play important role in the supervised model. A discriminative feature f is one whose conditional probability $\Pr\{c|f\} > 0.8$.

We notice that for functionality, the top feature for $c = 0$, is "h(S)_from_t(S)", while that for $c = 1$ is "from_h(S)_t(S)". Although it involves the same word "from", the different relative positions with respect to the entities make a difference and this underlines the importance of the bag-of-features model. Example sentences with these features are shown below.

- ($c = 0$) On my *D5100*, LiveView autofocus typically took half a second in lower-light conditions, which is no match for the viewfinder, but a huge improvement from the *D5000*.
- ($c = 1$) I like the consistency in the controls as far as moving from a *D7000* to a *D600*.

Other than their relative positions, the actual words that help make up a feature also matter. In Figure 1, we present the most frequently found words in sentences assigned to each class, for the aspect 'Form factor'. Interestingly, we see contrasting features such as "lighter" (for $c = 0$) vs. "heavier" (for $c = 1$). Similarly, for price, we find "less" (for $c = 0$) vs. "more" (for c = 1).

For the specifications which were used as features in the RankSVM model, it was observed that attributes like 'resolution' and 'maximum shutter priority' had more weight for the aspect 'Image quality' whereas 'dimensions' had more relative weight for aspect 'Form factor'.

5. CONCLUSION

In summary, we study the problem of comparative review mining and propose *PEQ*, a new integrated model that learns the products being favored by modelling the intrinsic goodness of the entity as well as the comparative relations at the level of entity pairs. We use Gibbs sampling to infer the sentence-level preferences and RankSVM model to

Figure 1: Word Clouds showing different distributions for the aspect Form factor

learn the intrinsic goodness in terms of weighted sum of the product specifications. We validate our model on Amazon reviews and compare against existing models and baselines. The model performs better in most cases than the baselines CompareGem and RankSVM. We conclude that the use of the specifications of an entity, which are easily available on the internet leads to a better understanding in comparison of products. This validates the fact that the intrinsic goodness of products is, to a great extent, determined by the values of its attributes. The experiments convincingly show the helpfulness of our model in both supervised and unsupervised configurations.

6. REFERENCES

[1] D. Görür, F. Jäkel, and C. E. Rasmussen. A choice model with infinitely many latent features. In *Proceedings of the 23rd international conference on Machine learning*, pages 361–368. ACM, 2006.

[2] T. Joachims. Optimizing search engines using clickthrough data. In *Proceedings of the eighth ACM SIGKDD international conference on Knowledge discovery and data mining*, pages 133–142. ACM, 2002.

[3] W. Kessler and J. Kuhn. Detection of product comparisons – how far does an out-of-the-box semantic role labeling system take you? In *Proceedings of the 2013 Conference on Empirical Methods in Natural Language Processing (EMNLP 2013)*, pages 1892–1897, Seattle, USA, October 2013. Association for Computational Linguistics.

[4] W. Kessler and J. Kuhn. Structural alignment for comparison detection. In *Proceedings of the 10th Conference on Recent Advances in Natural Language Processing (RANLP 2015)*, pages 275–281, Hissar, Bulgaria, September 2015.

[5] D. H. Park, C. Zhai, and L. Guo. Speclda: Modeling product reviews and specifications to generate augmented specifications. In *Proceedings of the 2015 SIAM International Conference on Data Mining, Vancouver, BC, Canada, April 30 - May 2, 2015*, pages 837–845, 2015.

[6] M. Tkachenko and H. W. Lauw. Generative modeling of entity comparisons in text. In *Proceedings of the 23rd ACM International Conference on Conference on Information and Knowledge Management*, pages 859–868. ACM, 2014.

[7] G. Zhao, M. L. Lee, W. Hsu, and W. Chen. Increasing temporal diversity with purchase intervals. In *Proceedings of the 35th international ACM SIGIR conference on Research and development in information retrieval*, pages 165–174. ACM, 2012.

Forecasting Geo-sensor Data with Participatory Sensing Based on Dropout Neural Network

Jyun-Yu Jiang
Department of Computer Science
University of California, Los Angeles
jyunyu.jiang@gmail.com

Cheng-Te Li
Department of Statistics
National Cheng Kung University
chengte@mail.ncku.edu.tw

ABSTRACT

Nowadays, geosensor data, such as air quality and traffic flow, have become more and more essential in people's daily life. However, installing geosensors or hiring volunteers at every location and every time is so expensive. Some organizations may have only few facilities or limited budget to sense these data. Moreover, people usually tend to know the forecast instead of ongoing observations, but the number of sensors (or volunteers) will be a hurdle to make precise prediction. In this paper, we propose a novel concept to forecast geosensor data with participatory sensing. Given a limited number of sensors or volunteers, participatory sensing assumes each of them can observe and collect data at different locations and at different time. By aggregating these sparse data observations in the past time, we propose a neural network based approach to forecast the future geosensor data in any location of an urban area. The extensive experiments have been conducted with large-scale datasets of the air quality in three cities and the traffic of bike sharing systems in two cities. Experimental results show that our predictive model can precisely forecast the air quality and the bike rentle traffic as geosensor data.

CCS Concepts

•**Information systems** → **Geographic information systems;** •**Mathematics of computing** → *Time series analysis;* •**Computing methodologies** → Neural networks;

Keywords

Geo-sensor data forecasting; Participatory sensing; Urban computing

1. INTRODUCTION

Participatory sensing [6] is a well-known concept to collect various kinds of environmental informatics, such as air quality, traffic, and human mobility. In the typical setting of participatory sensing, the originator pays a set of participants, and asks them to carry some geosensors (e.g. mobile devices or air-quality sensors) and move in the targeted geographical area within a certain time period. To collect sufficient data in terms of geography and time, the participants are required to avoid either staying at a location too long or moving to other places that had been sensored by other participants. The government or some organizations can take advantage of geosenor data to predict future environmental informatics.

However, the environmental informatics may change rapidly, and nearby locations could have significantly different geosensor values. For example, air quality highly depends on the weather condition and human behaviors. The air quality may be quite different in the morning and noon. Moreover, a location with unhealthy air quality may be only one mile away from a healthy place [11]. Hence, forecasting environmental informatics based on the geosensor data collected from the paradigm of participatory sensing may lead to unsatisfying results. In addition, while the targeted area to be sensed is too large, it is unrealistic to assume that we can recruit a large number of participants. Therefore, the geosensor data collected from participatory sensing is supposed to be very sparse in both spatial and temporal aspects.

In this paper, we attempt to solve the data sparsity problem of participatory sensing for forecasting environmental informatics. Given a small set of participants carrying sensors, based on the concept of participatory sensing, we assume that they randomly appear at different locations at different time point to collect geosensor data. Our goal is to exploit such sparse and incomplete geosensor data to forecast the future environmental informatics (i.e., the air quality and the rental traffic of bike sharing in this paper) for all the locations in the targeted geo-spatial area. We propose a neural network-based approach with several useful features, including statistical, temporal and spatial features. However, participatory sensing may lead to several unsensed features. To solve this problem, we present an approach inspired by *dropout neural network* [7], which is a method to prevent overfitting. In the end, we also conduct extensive experiments to demonstrate that our approach can precisely forecast geosensor data with sparse and incomplete geosensor data.

In the literature, there are two relevant studies [3,12]. The work [12] assumes that the air quality values of all the monitoring stations are known, and uses such *complete* geosensor data to predict the future air quality. The other work [3] aims at inferring the *past* air quality values for arbitrary locations using *complete* geosensor data. It is apparent that our forcasting based on participatory sensing is more challenging due to spatio-temporal data sparsity. In addition,

CIKM'16, October 24-28, 2016, Indianapolis, IN, USA
© 2016 ACM. ISBN 978-1-4503-4073-1/16/10...$15.00
DOI: http://dx.doi.org/10.1145/2983323.2983902

(a) Traditional Approach

(b) Participatory Sensing

Figure 1: The scenarios of forecasting geosensor data with traditional approach and participatory sensing.

our setting is more realistic and general since not all kinds of environmental informatics can have monitoring stations to obtain observed data.

2. PROBLEM STATEMENT

In this section, we introduce the problem statement of forecasting geosensor data with participatory sensing.

Motivation. Figure 1 illustrates the forecasting of geosensor data based on traditional approach and participatory sensing. To forecast geosensor data, most of previous work tend to set up a sensor at every location so that the model can have sufficient historical data monitored to predict the future data. However, it is too expensive to afford sensors at all locations. Furthermore, setting up additional sensors for new locations will be an extra cost. Hence, we propose to forecast geosensor data with participatory sensing.

Consider that we have hired k participants carrying sensors (with a limited budget), at every time point, each of them will randomly bound for a location (which is different from destinations of other participants) and utilize the sensor to record the geosensor data. Through participatory sensing, we can have geosensor data of k locations at every time point. The goal of this paper is to aggregate the data from participatory sensing and contextual information (e.g. meteorology data) to predict the future geosensor data.

Problem Definition. We formally define the problem of forecasting geosensor data with participatory sensing. Let C be the set of locations for forecasting. For each location $c \in C$, $L(c) = (lo(c), la(c))$ shows its longitude and latitude. The geosensor data of location $c \in C$ at the time $t \in \mathbb{Z}$ is denoted as $r(c,t)$, where each time point represents a one-hour duration. $M(c,t)$ represents the meteorology information of the location $c \in C$ at the time $t \in \mathbb{Z}$, including weather, temperature, pressure, humidity, wind speed and direction. Given the number of participants (or the budget) k $(1 \leq k \leq |C|)$, $S(t)$ denotes the set of k observed locations. For each location c and each time t, our goal is to predict the geosensor data $r(c,t)$ with the observed data $\{r(c',t') \mid c' \in S(t'), t' < t\}$ and meteorology information $\{M(c',t') \mid c' \in S(t'), t' < t\}$.

3. PROPOSED APPROACH

In this section, we propose a neural network based approach with various useful features. To handle some missing features due to participatory sensing, the concept of dropout neural network is borrowed to solve the problem. We also conducted the theoretical analysis to show the reasonableness of our approach.

3.1 Feature Extraction

To train the model, we extract several useful features from the observed data and meteorology information.

3.1.1 Statistical Features

The statistical information, derived from the historical data, is important to understand the knowledge of the targeted informatics Hence, we extract some statistical features from the observed data.

Overall Statistics. The geosensor data of a location may be consistent, so the statistics of past observations should be meaningful. Here we calculate the mean and median of data observed at the target location c before time t as two numerical features.

Hour-based Statistics. Although the data of a location may be consistent in day-level, there still may be dissimilar patterns for different hours. Hence, we compute the statistical values of observed data at the target location c by 24 hours as 2 numerical features.

3.1.2 Temporal Features

To predict time-series data, temporal information is much more important. Therefore, features about time and data observed in past are extracted as the temporal features.

Current Time. The time t itself may be important since it can represent the stage of a day or a year. Intuitively the time stage can also be helpful to make the prediction more precise. Therefore, the hour of t is treated as a 24-dimensional categorical feature.

Past Observed Data. The geosensor data may be dependent upon historical data. Many previous work [1,8,9,12] also consider the past sensed data as time series data, such as forecast air quality and ozone level. Here we take the data observed at the target location c in past 48 hours $\{r(c,t-i) | 1 \leq i \leq 48, c \in S(t-i)\}$ as 48 numerical features. Note that there will be several missing features because of participatory sensing. The solution to handle this problem will be introduced in Sec. 3.2.

3.1.3 Spatial Features

The geosensor data are all correlated with a geographical location, so the spatial information may be essential to forecast the future data.

Neighbor Observed Data. The geosensor data may be similar at close locations. In other words, the data at near locations may be a good indicator for geosensor data forecasting. Furthermore, the data from near locations can to some degree solve the problem of unsensed features.

To encode the information from other locations, we group

Figure 2: The illustration of our solution inspired by dropout neural network to handle the unsensed features. Note that x_1^u and x_2^u are features possible to be unsensed, and x_1^n is the feature always available. z_j^1 denotes the input into the first hidden layer, and f is the activation function.

them into 24 neighbor groups G_i^c by the distance (3 levels) and the bearing (8 levels) to the location c. For each group G_i^c, the median of observed data at locations in the group at the last time point $\{r(c', t-1) \mid c' \in G_i^c, c' \in S(t-1)\}$ is calculated as a numerical feature. Hence, the geosensor data around the target location can be encoded in the model. Another benefit of grouping locations is that there may be multiple locations in each group. Compared to observing each location separately, the probability of missing features will be lower from p to $p^{|G_i^c|}$, where p is the missing rate of a single location $1 - k/|C|$.

Meteorology Information. The meteorology information is also an important factor reflecting the geosensor data. For example, temperature can significantly affects air quality. Wind directions affect the transportation of air pollution materials. Here we apply the meteorology data $M(c', t-1)$ of the target location c and neighbor groups G_i^c at time $t-1$ as features. For numerical information like temperature and wind speed, we encode them as numerical features, and calculate the median for each neighbor group. For discrete information like weather and wind directions, we encode them as categorical features, and compute the mode for each neighbor group. In this paper, we adopt weather, temperature, pressure, humidity, wind speed and direction as the meteorology information, including $4 \times (1+24)$ numerical features and $2 \times (1+24)$ categorical features.

Note that even though gathering locations into neighboring groups can reduce the missing features, there may be still several spatial features unsensed by participatory sensing. Moreover, the missing rate of meteorology data at the target location c may not be reduced. Therefore, we also apply the solution mentioned in Sec. 3.2 to solve this problem.

3.2 Training with Unsensed Features

In this paper, we utilize the artificial neural network to train a model with features mentioned in Sec. 3.1. Note that the number of hidden layers can be any number. We simply assign one hidden layer for evaluating the idea.

As mentioned in Sec. 3.1, a problem of participatory sensing is that some features will be unsensed and missing. However, the case in participatory sensing is different from other scenarios of missing data. Because the participants carry sensors choose the locations randomly, the distribution of missing should also correspond with the same distribution. In other words, from the other aspect, the phenomenon of unsensed features can be treated as the results that we randomly ignore or remove them. Dropout [7] is an approach to randomly drop units from neural networks and thereby dealing with overfitting. Inspired by dropout, we consider that the input units of unsensed features are dropped during training. Figure 2 further demonstrates the illustration of our solution. We first divide features into two sets, including a set X^u that might be unsensed and X^n that might not. For each feature $x_i^u \in X^u$, we set a flag g_i to record whether x_i^u is sensed. Based on the number of participants and the number of locations in the neighbor groups, the probability of being sensed can be computed as p_i for the feature x_i. Therefore, from the viewpoint of all data points, the input into the first hidden layer can be treated as follows:

$$z_j^1 = \sum_{x_i^u \in X^u} (x_i^u \cdot g_i \cdot w_i^u) + \sum_{x_i^n \in X^n} (x_i^n \cdot w_i^n) + b,$$

where $g_i \sim \text{Bernoulli}(p_i)$, and b is the bias term. Through this approach, these unsensed features will no longer be a defect. The model can utilize them to prevent overfitting. Finally, we can learn an artificial neural network model with unsensed features.

4. EXPERIMENTS

Datasets. We conduct experiments on five datasets to forecast the air quality (AQ) [11, 12] and the rentle traffic of bike sharing (BS) [5, 10] respectively. For the AQ task, datasets covering three major Chinese cities, including Beijing (BJ), Tianjin (TJ) and Guangzhou (GZ), are applied. The AQ task aims to forecast the $PM_{2.5}$, which is an important air quality index (AQI). Note that although some previous work utilize data from stations near the target city as additional information, we apply only the stations in the city because participatory sensing is based on a limited budget. For the BS task, the experiments are conducted on datasets of two US cities, including Washington D.C. (DC) and New York City (NYC). The BS task is to forecast the rentle traffic in a bike sharing system, which is the number of users who rentle bikes in each time duration. Datasets in both tasks contain the meteorology information. For hours with multiple meteorology records, we compute the values of median and mode for aggregating numerical and categorical information. Table 1 further provides detailed data statistics.

Table 1: Data statistics of five datasets in two tasks.

Dataset	Air Quality (AQ)			Bike Sharing (BS)	
	BJ	TJ	GZ	DC	NYC
Time span	2014/05/01-2015/04/30			2014/04/01-2014/04/30	
# Stations	36	27	42	351	325
# Records	278,085	191,167	283,735	5,359,995	1,886,144
# Meteorology Records	116,867	106,614	30,305	683	449

Experimental Settings. For each dataset, every station is treated as a location to sense so that the ground truth can be guaranteed. We equally divide the time span of each dataset as training and testing periods for evaluation. For every time t, k locations are randomly sampled as the set $S(t)$. Basically, we set k as 50% of locations in each dataset. For analysis, we also evaluate the performance of the BJ dataset with different k.

Table 2: **The overall performance of five methods in five datasets for air quality (AQ) and bike sharing (BS) tasks. Note that k is set as 50% of locations. All improvements of our method are significant differences at 95% level in a paired t-test.**

Dataset		Metric	ARMA	SKNN	SVR	ANN	Ours
AQ	BJ	RMSE	61.9305	48.0565	64.5315	41.5409	**36.6724**
		MAE	29.7170	26.2598	41.6494	24.4895	**22.6632**
	TJ	RMSE	49.3223	34.8156	54.7269	37.1958	**31.6178**
		MAE	26.1218	20.8746	37.1335	23.5406	**20.6767**
	GZ	RMSE	17.5112	16.1787	23.7665	13.8771	**13.4062**
		MAE	9.4470	10.6069	16.5019	9.3448	**9.2335**
BS	DC	RMSE	2.8287	2.6056	2.0471	2.0138	**1.8594**
		MAE	1.2328	1.4400	0.9726	0.9546	**0.8955**
	NYC	RMSE	5.9696	4.9828	4.4075	4.1515	**3.8225**
		MAE	3.4115	2.9644	2.5854	2.4919	**2.1987**

Competitive Baselines. Our approach is compared with four baselines: (1) Auto-Regression-Moving-Average (ARMA): ARMA [2] is a well-known model for time-series data prediction. It predicts the geosensor data only by previously sensed data. For the data unsensed by participatory sensing, we directly ignore them and concatenate the sensed data as the input of ARMA. (2) Spatial k-Nearest Neighbors (SKNN): SKNN forecasts the geosensor data by aggregating the sensed data of k spatially closest locations at time $t-1$. (3) Support Vector Regression (SVR): SVR is a variation of support vector machine (SVM) for regression. We utilize the past observed data as features, and set unsensed features as 0. (4) Artificial Neural Network (ANN): We also feed only the past observed data into ANN. Note that it is applied to our approach mentioned in Sec. 3.2 as well.

Experimental results. Root-mean-square error (RMSE) and mean absolute error (MAE) [4] are adopted as the evaluation metrics in our experiments. Table 2 shows the overall performance of five methods. For the AQ task, SVR and ARMA perform the worst among the baseline methods. The reason might be the disappearance and discontinuity of data. Conversely, SKNN performs better because there are always k locations sampled to be the neighbors. ANN performs the best. It also indicates that our approach to handle unsensed features is effective. For the BS task, SKNN performs worse because the rentle traffic may not be relevant to neighbor locations. Besides, ANN still achieves the best performance among the baseline methods. Our approach outperforms all baseline methods in all datasets. It shows that the features in the model and the method to handle unsensed features are so effective. Figure 3 shows that the performance in the BJ dataset with different observed percentages (i.e., the number of participants or sensed locations). It is obvious that all methods perform better when the percentage increases. In addition, our approach performs best among all methods. We also evaluate our approach with different number of the hidden layer as shown in Table 3. With more neurons in the hidden layer, the model is able to achieve better performance.

5. CONCLUSIONS

In this paper, we propose a novel idea of forecasting geosensor data with participatory sensing. Through a small set of participants carrying sensors, we attempt to exploit the sparse and incomplete data to predict the future environmental informatics. A neural network-based solution with features in several aspects is proposed to solve the problem. We also provide a concept inspired by dropout neural network to handle the problem of unsensed features. Experiments conducted on five real-world datasets exhibit the promising effectiveness of our approach. The ongoing future work is to consider the sequential properties of time series data into the model.

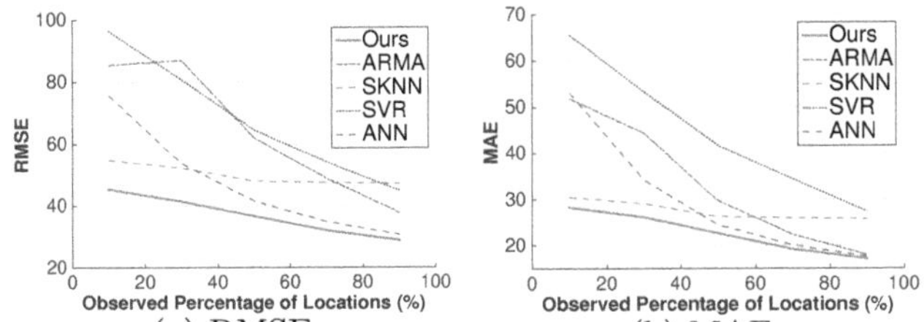

(a) RMSE (b) MAE

Figure 3: The performance in the Beijing (BJ) dataset of the air quality (AQ) task with different observed percentage of locations (i.e., the number of participants).

Table 3: The performance of our approach in the Beijing (BJ) dataset of the air quality (AQ) task with different sizes of the hidden layer.

Size	32	64	128	256	512	1024
RMSE	42.5288	39.5373	37.7825	36.6724	36.0191	35.7773
MAE	27.3475	25.1453	23.4175	22.6632	21.8336	20.9201

6. ACKNOWLEDGMENTS

This work was sponsored by Ministry of Science and Technology of Taiwan under grant 104-2221-E-001-027-MY2.

7. REFERENCES

[1] T. Dye, C. MacDonald, and C. Anderson. Guideline for developing an ozone forecasting program. Technical report, Environmental Protection Agency, 1999.

[2] E. J. Hannan. *Multiple time series*, volume 38. John Wiley & Sons, 2009.

[3] H.-P. Hsieh, S.-D. Lin, and Y. Zheng. Inferring air quality for station location recommendation based on urban big data. In *KDD '15*, pages 437–446. ACM, 2015.

[4] R. J. Hyndman and A. B. Koehler. Another look at measures of forecast accuracy. *International journal of forecasting*, 22(4):679–688, 2006.

[5] Y. Li, Y. Zheng, H. Zhang, and L. Chen. Traffic prediction in a bike-sharing system. In *SIGSPATIAL GIS '15*. ACM, 2015.

[6] F. Restuccia, S. K. Das, and J. Payton. Incentive mechanisms for participatory sensing: Survey and research challenges. *TOSN*, 12(2):13:1–13:40, 2016.

[7] N. Srivastava, G. Hinton, A. Krizhevsky, I. Sutskever, and R. Salakhutdinov. Dropout: A simple way to prevent neural networks from overfitting. *JMLR*, 15(1):1929–1958, 2014.

[8] Y. Zhang, M. Bocquet, V. Mallet, C. Seigneur, and A. Baklanov. Real-time air quality forecasting, part i: History, techniques, and current status. *Atmospheric Environment*, 60:632–655, 2012.

[9] Y. Zhang, M. Bocquet, V. Mallet, C. Seigneur, and A. Baklanov. Real-time air quality forecasting, part ii: State of the science, current research needs, and future prospects. *Atmospheric Environment*, 60:656–676, 2012.

[10] Y. Zheng, L. Capra, O. Wolfson, and H. Yang. Urban computing: concepts, methodologies, and applications. *TIST*, 5(3):38, 2014.

[11] Y. Zheng, F. Liu, and H.-P. Hsieh. U-air: When urban air quality inference meets big data. In *KDD '13*, pages 1436–1444. ACM, 2013.

[12] Y. Zheng, X. Yi, M. Li, R. Li, Z. Shan, E. Chang, and T. Li. Forecasting fine-grained air quality based on big data. In *KDD '15*, pages 2267–2276. ACM, 2015.

Iterative Search using Query Aspects

Manmeet Singh, W. Bruce Croft
Center for Intelligent Information Retrieval
College of Information and Computer Sciences
University of Massachusetts,
Amherst, MA
(msingh, croft)@cs.umass.edu

ABSTRACT

Pseudo-relevance feedback (PRF) via query expansion has proven to be effective in many information retrieval tasks. In most existing work, the top-ranked documents from an initial search are assumed to be relevant and used for feedback. There are some drawbacks to this approach. One limitation is that there might be other relevant documents which were not retrieved or considered for the the feedback process. Another issue is one or more of the top retrieved documents may be non-relevant, which can introduce noise into the feedback mechanism. Term-level diversification, on the other hand, uses an effective technique for identifying terms associated with query aspects or subtopics. We propose a new iterative feedback method that combines PRF with aspect generation to improve feedback effectiveness. In our experiments, we discovered a new property of convergence of feedback terms that was incorporated into the PRF process. We show that the resulting method significantly outperforms the baseline relevance model.

CCS Concepts

•**H.3.3 Information Search and Retrieval** → Retrieval Models, Relevance Feedback;

Keywords

pseudo-relevance feedback, search diversification, iterative search

1. INTRODUCTION

Local feedback techniques such as pseudo-relevance feedback (PRF) have been used to improve retrieval performance without user interaction[18, 12, 15, 6, 13, 14]. They have been shown to work better than global context analysis[17]. PRF uses the top retrieved documents to extract expansion terms and weights those terms according to some model, such as tf.idf. Although this approach has generally proven to be effective, there are limitations. Non-relevant documents may be retrieved, introducing noise into the term selection and weighting process. Other relevant documents containing important terms may not be retrieved at high ranks. One way to address these limitations is to improve the existing pseudo-relevance feedback techniques [8, 4, 11]. Another is to change the assumptions behind PRF. Term-level diversification uses an effective technique to discover terms that describe different aspects or subtopics related to a query [1]. By using this technique to select terms for PRF, we change the assumption that the top-ranked documents are relevant and instead assume the top-ranked documents describe the important aspects. Another assumption we change is that a single iteration of feedback will be the most effective. In the orginal implementations of relevance feedback, multiple iterations were used and not found to be effective. These experiments were, however, done on small collections and using manual relevance assessments [15]. We propose an automatic iterative method for PRF that incorporates the aspect generation technique from term-level diversification. Specifically, we use the DSPApprox method to discover aspects and compare this to a simple tf.idf term selection method. In our experiments, we show that feedback terms do in fact converge over multiple iterations and that the aspects generated produce significant improvements compared to the well-known RM3 baseline and a single iteration of PRF.

The rest of the paper is organized as follows. Sec. 2 details the related work. In Sec. 3 we explain the methodology and then Sec. 4 details the experimental setup. Sec. 5 shows the results and in Sec. 6 we discuss and analyze the findings. Finally, Sec. 7 concludes the paper.

CIKM '16, October 24–28, 2016, Indianpolis, IN, USA.
© 2016 ACM. ISBN 123-4567-24-567/08/06...$15.00
DOI: http://dx.doi.org/10.1145/2983323.2983903

2. RELATED WORK

A variety of approaches to automatic query expansion for improving the performance of retrieval queries have been previously studied. Pseudo-relevance feedback has proven to be a successful technique for query expansion [9, 6]. It has also been shown to be effective for query classification [18], query translation, and spelling corrections.

Lavrenko and Croft's relevance model (RM3) algorithm [6] is a pseudo-relevance feedback method developed for the language modeling framework. The standard formulation of this method involves submitting an original query (LM), using the resulting ranked list to perform weighted query expansion, and performing a second round of retrieval. We compare our results to this method. Lv and Zhai used a boosting approach-FeedbackBoost [8] that iteratively selects and combines basis feedback methods. In each iteration, a basis feedback method is selected to improve those queries on which the already selected basis feedback methods perform poorly in terms of both effectiveness and robustness. It uses a linear combination of these basis feedback methods as its final feedback model. Kurland and Lee proposed an iterative pseudo-feedback approach to ad hoc information retrieval using cluster-based language models [5]. In this method, an initial set of documents are retrieved based on vector space model. Then the retrieved documents are analyzed based on the context of all terms in a document and query using clustering. Li and He used a pseudo relevance feedback method [3] named iterative probabilistic one-class SVMs to re-rank the retrieved images; but their intended application is not a direct scoring of potential retrieval candidates.

Aspect based-retrieval approach has been studied in retrieval and diversification tasks [1, 16]. An aspect representation determines how the information needs underlying a query are represented as multiple aspects of the query. Generating these aspects automatically is not as well understood. A topic term extraction algorithm named DSPApprox was proposed by Lawrie and Croft [6, 7] for hierarchical multi-document summarization. This method was also incorporated in term level diversification by Dang and Croft using the vocabulary of the retrieved documents for automatic aspect or topic generation [1]. Harman and Buckley recognized that weak aspect coverage [2] in the resulting feedback model or final expansion model is something algorithms must detect and remedy to avoid query drift. Our technique also addresses this issue by covering various aspects and then using the most important ones for the feedback process.

3. METHODOLOGY

Our method identifies the possible aspects iteratively and uses the most important ones for PRF. To generate these aspects, we compare the DSPApprox method and a simple tf.idf term selection method. Let S be the set of possible aspects that could be generated by a query Q. Let K be the number of aspects generated per query in every pass. Let N be the number of documents we use to generate these aspects. Here K, N are free parameters whose values need to be determined. Let the feedback terms generated using the top N documents on query Q in the intermediate step by aspect generation method be $t_1, t_2, t_3 ..., t_K$. Now we have generated K new queries- $Q \cup t_1, Q \cup t_2, ..., Q \cup t_K$ and our set S contains maximum K aspects. We repeat the process with each of the generated K queries until no new terms are found. We discard duplicate terms generated in any of the iterations. For preprocessing, we removed stop-words, used stemming and case folding before applying the algorithm.

The problem formulated above can be represented as a k-ary tree data-structure, where root node represents the base query. The K possible child-nodes, represent the intermediate queries $Q \cup t_1, Q \cup t_2, ..., Q \cup t_K$. Each of these child nodes can further have K child nodes making maximum of K^2 nodes (possible queries) at level two and the process goes on the same way for every level. There was considerable overlap in the aspects generated, and as duplicate aspects are discarded, there were never K^2 nodes at level 2 or higher. Let $S_0, S_1, S_2, ...$ be the aspect sets generated at each level. Our final aspect set S is $\{S_0 \cup S_1 \cup S_2, ...\}$. Algorithmically, this problem could be solved by breadth first search using a queue data-structure. This approach is what we use in our iterative search method. Though we had put thresholds on the maximum number of feedback terms to be considered and on the number of levels the algorithm should search iteratively, we never reach any of the threshold conditions as terms converged before reaching these thresholds.

Our research shows a new property of convergence in the application of multi-level PRF (i.e., there are no new terms after a certain level). This convergence was achieved on all the queries of the dataset with the DSPApprox method as well as tf.idf weighting. This happened due to the overlap of aspects with every feedback query. From the converged set, we then selected the best terms for PRF.

One might argue that the above algorithm may be slow and hence not good for an online setting even if it produces good results. This concern is addressed by the fact that the above algorithm could easily be parallelized by distributing the feedback queries on multiple servers while maintaining a shared set for the aspects generated across systems. Our analysis section also shows that the algorithm runs fast even without parallelism because the convergence is achieved quite quickly.

3.1 Aspect Generation

Aspects denote the multiple possible intents, interpretations, or subtopics associated with a given query. It is an explicit idea expressed within a query. For example, in the query "painting on wood" there is a "painting" aspect and a "wood" aspect. Logically, documents covering both of these aspects would be considered relevant. More generally, a document will have a higher degree of relevance the more query aspects it includes.

Automatic construction of these query aspects has been difficult and the techniques have generally relied on manually created descriptions of the aspects. Term-level diversification is also an explicit approach which uses terms without grouping. We use a greedy algorithm named DSPApprox to generate these aspects. The algorithm [10] iteratively selects terms from the candidate topic term set T. The utility of each term is the product of its topicality and predictive ability. At each step, the algorithm selects the topic term $t^* \in T$ with maximum utility. Then, it decreases the predictive ability of other topic terms that predict the same vocabulary. This ensures that topic terms from the uncovered part of the vocabulary will emerge for selection in the next iteration. The algorithm stops once the utility of all candidate topic terms reaches zero, indicating that all vocabulary has been covered and we get the list of top feedback terms. In the tf.idf based selection method top terms with the highest weights are used and added to the aspect set. In the end, top terms with highest tf.idf weighing are selected from the final set (after conver- gence) as aspects. As the DSPApprox approach covers more diverse topics [1] the set of terms generated after convergence are different than the tf.idf term selection method.

4. EXPERIMENTAL SETUP

4.1 Dataset

We experimented with the Robust Track of TREC 2004 which has 528,155 news articles. We use all the 250 queries in this set for our experiments. The Robust Track data is a standard ad hoc retrieval testbed with an emphasis on the overall reliability of IR systems and it contains difficult queries for a heterogeneous data set. This data set is called "Robust04" in the following discussion.

4.2 Baselines

In order to evaluate the effectiveness of our technique, we used two methods as baselines for comparison. The first baseline (RM3) is one of the most effective and robust pseudo feedback methods under language modeling framework. It uses the query likelihood score of a feedback document as the weight and estimates a query language model (for feedback) based on weighted aggregation of term counts in the feedback documents. The second baseline uses the terms generated by single iteration of PRF. This baseline helps us evaluate whether the top terms we chose from the converged set are better than the terms chosen from the set obtained after level one, highlighting the importance of the convergence property.

4.3 Parameter Settings

Our technique needs to choose optimal values for the following hyperparameters in order to get maximum prediction accuracy:

K: # of aspects requested per query
N: # of top documents considered to generate aspects
r: # of feedback terms added to original query
fborigWt: weight(importance) to base query terms vs feedback terms

We used grid search method to determine the best values for these parameters. The best combination we obtained was K = 50, N = 10, r = 10, fborigWt = 0.8. The tuning of other free paramters- maximum # of aspects to be considered and maximum # of levels to explore was not required as we quickly obtained convergence for all 250 queries.

5. RESULTS

The results were evaluated on various standard metrics. The first and second columns in the table shown below are the baseline results obtained using the RM3 and one-level of PRF respectively. The next two columns presents the results obtained by our iterative search method which uses query aspects generated via tf.idf weighting and the DSPApprox technique respectively.

Table 1: Results on Robust04. † indicates significantly better than baseline for 0.05 as threshold for p value

Metrics vs Method	RM3	Baseline-2	Using TF-IDF	Using DSPApprox
MAP	0.250	0.256	0.267 †	0.277 †
P@10	0.425	0.427	0.442 †	0.445 †
P@20	0.362	0.366	0.376	0.375
NDCG@10	0.425	0.417	0.432	0.436 †
NDCG@20	0.412	0.409	0.421 †	0.424 †
R@10	0.139	0.140	0.149 †	0.147 †
R@20	0.210	0.217	0.221 †	0.221 †

The mean average precision (MAP) improved by 6.8% and 10.8% respectively compared to the relevance model (RM3). Our method also does a better job on ranking the top 10 and 20 documents. The results confirm that our method significantly outperforms the baseline methods.

Figure 1. shows the number of aspects which were generated for each query after the convergence was achieved. The average # of aspects generated by tf-idf weighing and DSPApprox method were 188 and 148 respectively. Hence, on an average iterative search using DSPApprox method converges faster.

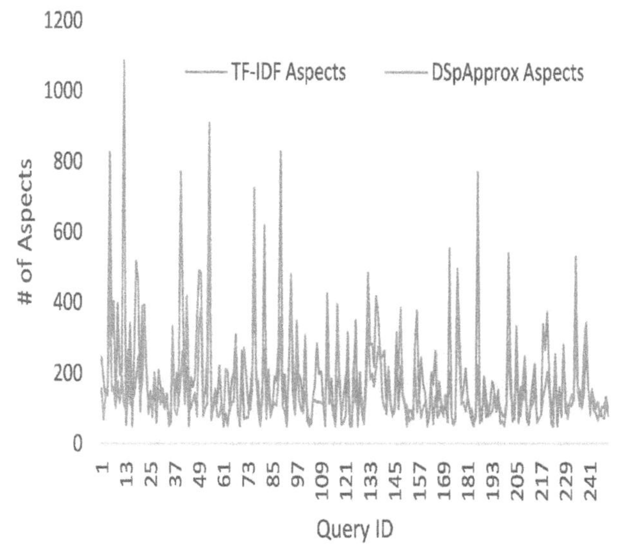

Figure 1: # of aspects generated for each query after convergence

6. DISCUSSION

Our experimental results clearly show that the quality of aspects generated through the iterative process were much better as it led to significant improvement in the accuracy. Our method covered most of the aspects and then used the top ones as feedback terms while the baseline methods were choosing highest tf.idf weighing terms from the top N documents. Iteratively, our algorithm explores relevant documents which in turn gives us more effective feedback terms. To further strengthen our argument, we tried using feedback terms from a much larger pool of documents and the accuracy declined compared to the baseline results. Thus, the iterative process retrieves higher numbers of relevant documents that we couldn't get through RM3 based pseudo-relevance feedback.

There are several other questions that need to be addressed. In first place, why does convergence even happen? Intuitively, generation of similar aspects led to the convergence. Our algorithm converged by level 2 and 3 for K values 50, 25 respectively. Another question which arises from our work is whether the DSPApprox method and tf.idf selection method generated the same set of terms after convergence? The answer to this question is no as neither are the terms generated by both the methods the same nor is any of them subset of the other. DSPApprox tries to identify terms based on topics, hence it would try not to retrieve a term which is already covered in terms of topicality. This seems to be the most appropriate reason why the average number of aspects retrieved by this algorithm are less compared to the other technique we used. There is a high overlap, however, in the terms generated by both the algorithms.

One might argue that more number of non-relevant documents could be generated as we are doing multiple passes. Even if one or more of the top retrieved documents is non-relevant (which could introduce noise in feedback process), our method doesn't just use these documents as it iteratively explores them and the final set of feedback terms are taken from the converged set. Our experiments with the tf.idf selection method also proved this hypothesis. P@10 tells us how many in the top 10 retrieved documents are relevant and nDCG@10 tells how close we did compared to the ideal ranking if we consider the top 10 documents. We used the top N (= 10) documents for feedback in every pass and as P@10, nDCG@10 have improved, this shows that our method generates fewer non-relevant documents and less noisy feedback terms. Our assumption was that top-ranked documents describe the important aspects instead of being relevant when we used term-level diversification. This hypothesis is also supported by the improvement in the MAP values.

7. CONCLUSIONS

In this paper, we presented an iterative algorithm which does multiple passes of PRF. We experimentally discovered a new property of convergence that helped us to select better feedback terms, thereby improving the retrieval effectiveness. We also conclude that the knowledge of initial set of top documents is not necessarily sufficient to generate high quality feedback terms. The technique also proved effective to avoid noisy terms which is a drawback in PRF. Our approach is efficient and can be easily parallelized to make it more useful for online setting.

There are several possible avenues along which our work could be extended in future. We can cluster the terms from the converged set and then use it for diversification. Our technique may prove effective for query classification tasks. We are also interested in using other families of feedback methods in our iterative search.

8. ACKNOWLEDGMENTS

This work was supported in part by the Center for Intelligent Information Retrieval and in part by NSF IIS-1160894. Any opinions, findings and conclusions or recommendations expressed in this material are those of the authors and do not necessarily reflect those of the sponsor.

9. REFERENCES

[1] V. Dang and W. B. Croft. Diversity by proportionality: An election-based approach to search result diversification. In *35th International ACM SIGIR Conference on Research and Development in IR*, SIGIR '12, pages 65–74, NY, USA, 2012. ACM.

[2] D. Harman and C. Buckley. The nrrc reliable information access (ria) workshop. In *ACM SIGIR Conference*, '04, pages 528–529, NY, USA, 2004. ACM.

[3] J. He, M. Li, Z. Li, H.-J. Zhang, H. Tong, and C. Zhang. *Advances in Multimedia Information Processing - PCM 2004, Part II*, chapter PRF Based on Iterative Probabilistic One-Class SVMs in Web Image Retrieval, pages 213–220. Springer Berlin Heidelberg, Berlin, Heidelberg, 2005.

[4] G. Kumaran and J. Allan. Simple questions to improve pseudo-relevance feedback results. In *29th Annual International ACM SIGIR Conference on Research and Development in IR*, SIGIR '06, pages 661–662, NY, USA, 2006. ACM.

[5] O. Kurland, L. Lee, and C. Domshlak. Better than the real thing? iterative pseudo-query processing using cluster-based language models. *CoRR*, abs/cs/0601046, 2006.

[6] V. Lavrenko and W. B. Croft. Relevance based language models. In *24th Annual International ACM SIGIR Conference on Research and Development in IR*, SIGIR '01, pages 120–127, NY, USA, 2001. ACM.

[7] D. Lawrie, W. B. Croft, and A. Rosenberg. Finding topic words for hierarchical summarization. In *Proceedings of SIGIR 01*, pages 349–357, 2001.

[8] Y. Lv, C. Zhai, and W. Chen. A boosting approach to improving pseudo-relevance feedback. In *34th International ACM SIGIR Conference on Research and Development in IR*, SIGIR '11, pages 165–174, NY, USA, 2011. ACM.

[9] M. Mitra, A. Singhal, and C. Buckley. Improving automatic query expansion. In *21st Annual International ACM SIGIR Conference on Research and Development in IR*, SIGIR '98, pages 206–214, New York, NY, USA, 1998. ACM.

[10] D. Petkova and W. B. Croft. Hierarchical language models for expert finding in enterprise corpora. In *18th International Conference on Tools with AI*, pages 599–606, 2006.

[11] K. Raman, R. Udupa, P. Bhattacharya, and A. Bhole. On improving pseudo-relevance feedback using pseudo-irrelevant documents. In *ECIR 2010*, 2010.

[12] S. E. Robertson and K. S. Jones. Relevance weighting of search terms. *JASIS*, 27(3):129–146, 1976.

[13] S. E. Robertson, S. Walker, S. Jones, M. Hancock-beaulieu, and M. Gatford. Okapi at TREC3. In *Text REtrieval Conference*, 1994.

[14] G. Salton, J. Allan, and A. Singhal. Automatic text decomposition and structuring. *Information Processing & Management*, 32(2):127–138, 1996.

[15] G. Salton and C. Buckley. Improving retrieval performance by relevance feedback. *Journal of the American Society for Information Science*, 41:288–297, 1990.

[16] R. L. Santos, C. Macdonald, and I. Ounis. Exploiting query reformulations for web search result diversification. In *19th International Conference*, WWW '10, pages 881–890, NY, USA, 2010. ACM.

[17] J. Xu and W. B. Croft. Query expansion using local and global document analysis. In *19th Annual International ACM SIGIR Conference on Research and Development in IR*, SIGIR '96, pages 4–11, NY, USA, 1996. ACM.

[18] C. Zhai and J. Lafferty. Model-based feedback in the language modeling approach to information retrieval. In *Tenth International Conference*, CIKM '01, pages 403–410, NY, USA, 2001. ACM.

A Preference Approach to Reputation in Sponsored Search

Aritra Ghosh
Microsoft
Bangalore, India
arghosh@microsoft.com

Dinesh Gaurav
Microsoft
Bangalore, India
digaurav@microsoft.com

Rahul Agrawal
Microsoft
Bangalore, India
rahulagr@microsoft.com

ABSTRACT

Determining reputation of an advertiser in sponsored search is a recent important problem with direct impact on revenue for web publishers and relevance of ads. Individual performance of advertisers is usually expressed through observed click through rate, which depends on advertiser reputation, ad relevance and position. However, advertiser reputation has not been explicitly modeled in click prediction literature. Using traditional approaches in web page popularity for organic search in this context is not reasonable as the notion of link-structure in web is not directly applicable to sponsored search. In this study, we motivate and propose a pairwise preference relation model to study the advertiser reputation problem. Pairwise comparisons of advertisers give information over and above the information available in their individual historical performances. We relate the notion of preference among the advertisers to the spectral properties of the preference graph. We provide empirical evidence of the existence of reputation bias in click behavior. Consequently, we experiment with this signal to improve click prediction.

Keywords

Sponsored Search; Advertiser Reputation; Click Prediction

1. INTRODUCTION

Sponsored search is becoming the dominant advertising medium for advertisers and de-facto revenue stream for search engines. In a typical sponsored search scenario, search engines display ads, among other organic search results, by matching user's queries to the advertiser's keywords. When the user clicks on an ad, search engine charges the advertiser an amount proportional to the latter's bid. To maximize revenue, ads are shown based on a ranking obtained from a measure dependent on their Click-through-rate (CTR) and bid. CTR for an ad can be viewed as the probability of click for a given ad for a query.

In literature, there has been a lot of work around query-ad CTR prediction [3, 9]. In the tail queries, insufficient ad impression data makes it hard. CTR prediction for tail queries is an interesting research problem, and usually employs semantic properties of the query and ad content [9]. Another interesting aspect of CTR prediction is the externalities introduced by surrounding ads [11, 12]. Textual similarities of surroundings ads and the impact on CTR have been also studied [10]. We observe that, CTR of an advertiser decreases when appearing with a reputed advertiser. Although, for the same query, the advertiser gets preferred more when appearing with a lesser known advertiser. An important challenge is to differentiate among advertisers whose ads are semantically similar with the query based on reputation. The impact of advertiser reputation influencing the observed CTR has not been explored in sponsored search to the best of our knowledge.

In organic search, reputation of web pages have been studied extensively. Ubiquitous algorithms like PageRank and HITS exploit the implicit referral-linkage structure inherent in web [1, 8]. This, however, is absent among advertisers in sponsored search. In this paper, we propose a framework to address this issue from the pair-wise comparisons of advertisers which are explicitly constructed from the historical co-impressions in ad-slates (We define ad-slate as the set of ads displayed when a query is searched by the user). Risk minimization framework, from pairwise data for ranking [5], is not suitable as the only feature vector is Advertiser-Id (one-hot representation where dimension is huge). In particular, our problem is related to rank aggregation from pairwise data.

We summarize our contributions as follows. We model advertiser reputation in sponsored search as a rank aggregation problem by explicitly constructing pair-wise comparison among advertisers from search logs. We show that advertiser reputation is related to the spectral properties of the user preference matrix constructed from the pair-wise data. Through experiments on real-world data from a popular search engine, we show the existence of reputation bias in sponsored search. Further, we show that using advertiser reputation as an externality, improves click prediction.

2. PRELIMINARIES AND BACKGROUND

We denote $[n] = \{1, \cdots, n\}$ as the n items (or alternatives) that have to be ranked. The set of observed pair-wise comparisons, is given as $\mathcal{S} = \{(i, j, a_{ji}, a_{ij})\,;\, i < j,\ i, j \in [n]\,;\, a_{ij} \in \mathbb{R}_+\}$. Here a_{ij} denotes the number of times item j was preferred over item i. We define μ_{ij} as the probability to pick a pair (i, j) for comparison across all such pairs. We define the matrix entries $\mathbf{P}_{ij}$ as the probability with which

CIKM'16, October 24 - 28, 2016, Indianapolis, IN, USA

ISBN 978-1-4503-4073-1/16/10...$15.00

DOI: http://dx.doi.org/10.1145/2983323.2983904

item j is preferred over i. Clearly, $\mathbf{P}_{ij} = 1 - \mathbf{P}_{ji}$ and we set $\mathbf{P}_{ii} = 0$. Given distributions $(\{\mu_{ij}\}, \mathbf{P})$, a fundamental problem is to find a ranking by optimizing a measure that reflects the inherent quality of each item. In practice, most often, we observe only a finite set of comparisons $\mathcal{S}$ which maybe uneven across pairs. A standard approach is to define the pairwise comparison matrix from the empirical observation $\mathcal{S}$ which approximates the pair-wise preference matrix $\mathbf{P}$. A particularly popular model is the **Bradley-Terry-Luce (BTL)** This is a parametric model which assumes that there exists a n-dimensional weight vector $\mathbf{w} = [w_1, \ldots, w_n]$ that abstractly measures the quality of each item. Pair-wise preference probabilities $\mathbf{P}_{ij}$ are then modeled as

$$\mathbf{P}_{ij} = \frac{w_j}{w_i + w_j} \tag{1}$$

From a practical perspective, there exists several algorithms which work on the pairwise-comparison matrix $\hat{\mathbf{P}}$ to find an approximate ranking under BTL condition. Popular algorithms like MC3 [2] and Rank Centrality [7], are in fact similar. Our proposed approach to determine the advertiser ranking is closer in spirit to these algorithms.

3. ADVERTISER REPUTATION IN SPONSORED SEARCH

To motivate the usage of rank aggregation in advertiser reputation, we start with an idealistic model which assumes that a strict total ordering among the advertisers $(A_1, \ldots, A_n)$ is given. We define $A_i \succ A_j$ as advertiser A_i is preferred to A_j. We define the $n \times n$ preference matrix $\mathbf{P}$ for this strict ordering as

$$\mathbf{P}_{ij} = \begin{cases} 1 & \text{if } A_j \succ A_i \\ 0 & \text{otherwise} \end{cases} \tag{2}$$

Thus, when $\mathbf{P}_{ij} = 1$, it means that advertiser j was preferred over advertiser i with probability 1. For illustration purpose, we assume that $\mathbf{P}$ is such that the alternatives are arranged in the decreasing order of preference $(A_1 \succ \cdots \succ A_n)$.

We try to associate a random walk with the advertiser preference matrix. We define the transition matrix $\mathbf{Q}$ of the Markov chain as,

$$\mathbf{Q}_{ij} = \begin{cases} \frac{\mathbf{P}_{ij}}{n} & \text{if } i \neq j \\ 1 - \sum_{k \neq i} \frac{\mathbf{P}_{ik}}{n} & \text{otherwise} \end{cases} \tag{3}$$

We observe that $\mathbf{Q}$ is a lower triangular matrix. Thus $\mathbf{Q}$ is a reducible matrix and may not have a so-called unique perron vector, the eigenvector corresponding to the largest eigenvalue of $\mathbf{Q}$. To get around this issue, we add a small perturbation to $\mathbf{Q}$ to form the matrix

$$\mathbf{Q}_\alpha = (1-\alpha)\mathbf{Q} + \frac{\alpha}{n}\mathbf{J}, \quad \alpha \in (0,1) \tag{4}$$

where $\mathbf{J}$ is the all-ones matrix. Thus, effectively we are changing $\mathbf{Q}$ to an irreducible matrix by adding small perturbation to all the entries. In the following, we make the claim.

Claim 0.1 *The eigenvector $\mathbf{x} = [x_1, \ldots, x_n]$ corresponding to the largest eigenvalue of $\mathbf{Q}_\alpha$ is such that $x_i > x_{i+1}$ $\forall i$ and thus preserves the ordering among the advertisers.*

PROOF. Let $\mathbf{x}$ be the Perron vector of $\mathbf{Q}_\alpha$ and let λ be the corresponding perron root (or the largest eigenvalue which is 1). Then, we have the relation $\mathbf{Q}_\alpha^T \mathbf{x} = \lambda \mathbf{x}$. Here in matrix $\mathbf{Q}_\alpha$, we have $x_{n-1} - x_n = \frac{2}{n}(1-\alpha)x_{n-1} > 0$. This is because x is a strictly positive perron vector. Thus, $x_{n-1} > x_n$. After some algebraic manipulations, we have

$$x_{k+1} - x_k = \frac{1-\alpha}{n}[(n-k)x_{k+1} - (n-k+1)x_k] \tag{5}$$

Thus by induction, it is evident that, $x_1 > x_2 > \cdots > x_n$ which implies that the order of preference among advertisers is indeed preserved by the principal eigenvector.

In the example constructed above, we made the idealistic assumption that if $i \succ j$, then i will be chosen with probability 1 when compared with j. We relax this condition and assume that our advertiser preference matrix follows a general BTL condition. Simply stated, this means that entries $\mathbf{P}_{ij}$ of true advertiser preference matrix $\mathbf{P}$ are in $[0, 1]$ and is not restricted to $\{0, 1\}$. However in practice, preference matrix $\mathbf{P}$ is never available and the pair-wise comparison matrix $\hat{\mathbf{P}}$ is used as a surrogate. We define $\hat{\mathbf{P}}_{ij}$ as the fraction of times advertiser j was preferred to advertiser i, when both of them were compared. In particular, we have $\hat{\mathbf{P}}$ as

$$\hat{\mathbf{P}}_{ij} = \begin{cases} 0 & \text{if } a_{ij} + a_{ji} = 0 \\ \frac{a_{ij}}{a_{ij}+a_{ji}} & \text{otherwise} \end{cases} \tag{6}$$

As the number of comparisons across pairs grows larger, estimated $\hat{\mathbf{P}}_{ij}$ tends to the true $\mathbf{P}_{ij}$. We are interested in the true ranking or reputation vector $\mathbf{w}$. Towards this, we construct $\hat{\mathbf{Q}}_\alpha$ as defined in (4) using comparison matrix $\hat{\mathbf{P}}$ defined in (6). We hope to approximate $\mathbf{w}$ with $\hat{\mathbf{w}}$, the stationary distribution of $\hat{\mathbf{Q}}_\alpha$. Thus, we are interested in the normalized error $\frac{||\hat{\mathbf{w}} - \mathbf{w}||_2}{||\mathbf{w}||_2}$. It is easy to apply proof techniques used in rank centrality [7], to prove that this error (with high probability) is bounded by $\mathcal{O}\left(\sqrt{\log n/k}\right)$, k being the minimum number of comparisons made for compared pairs. Interestingly, the number of comparisons in the context of sponsored search increases as more and more logs are available, thus improving the correctness of ranking over time.

3.1 Proposed Approach

In sponsored search, for a given query ($\mathbf{q}$), few selected advertisers ($A = \{A_1, \cdots, A_M\}$) are shown. Suppose a user clicks A_2 when presented together with A_1, we consider that the user preferred advertiser A_2 to advertiser A_1 in that ad-slate. Aggregation of all the signals from click logs allows us to compute the preference comparison matrix as defined in (6) among the advertisers.

In sponsored search, advertisers are shown to users in a sequential manner. It is well-known that this ordering does have a huge impact on the click behavior of the user. We compensate for this using conventional approach of position correction [6]. While more accurate ways of incorporating position bias have been studied, for the purpose of studying advertiser reputation we restrict ourselves in this simple settings. Let $g(i)$ be the factor by which probability decreases if shown from first position to i^{th} position. Clearly, $g(1) = 1$.

Thus, the click log for a given ad-slate x can be succinctly expressed in the form $\mathcal{T}_x(A, K) = (a_i, \cdots, a_m, K_1, \cdots, K_m)$ where ad a_i was shown at position i as well as one of the ad was clicked ($K_i \in \{0,1\}$, $\sum K_i = 1$). In practice, multiple clicks can happen in an ad-slate. Our formulation can be easily extended to address this. Let x is an index that runs over all ad slates. Then, over the set of all valid pairs (i,j) in slate x, we define

$$Y_{ij}^x = \begin{cases} \min\{\frac{g(i)}{g(j)}, 1\} & \text{if } a_j \text{ was clicked and } a_i \text{ was not} \\ 0 & \text{otherwise} \end{cases} \tag{7}$$

Given this, we define the estimated preference matrix as

$$\hat{\mathbf{Q}}_{ij} = \begin{cases} \frac{\sum_x Y_{ij}^x}{\sum_x Y_{ij}^x + \sum_x Y_{ji}^x} & \text{if } \sum_x Y_{ij}^x + \sum_x Y_{ji}^x > 0 \\ 0 & \text{otherwise} \end{cases} \tag{8}$$

Effectively, $\hat{\mathbf{P}}_{ij}$ is equivalent the fraction of clicks a_j got when it was shown with a_i after position correction. The transition matrix $\hat{\mathbf{Q}}$, is,

$$\hat{\mathbf{Q}}_{ij} = \begin{cases} \frac{1}{d_i}\hat{\mathbf{P}}_{ij} & \text{if } i \neq j \\ 1 - \sum \frac{1}{d_i}\hat{\mathbf{P}}_{ij} & \text{if } i = j \end{cases} \tag{9}$$

where d_i is the number of advertisers i was compared to. The corpus of advertisers is typically large and several of them are never shown together since their mutual interests may not intersect, causing transition matrix $\hat{\mathbf{Q}}$ to be sparse. To get around this, we add a small teleportation probability similar to pagerank. Thus our estimated transition matrix becomes

$$\hat{\mathbf{Q}}_\alpha = (1-\alpha)\hat{\mathbf{Q}} + \frac{\alpha}{n}\mathbf{J} \tag{10}$$

From $\hat{\mathbf{Q}}_\alpha$, computed using the transformations above, it is straight forward to compute stationary distribution. We note that finding the stationary distribution of $\hat{\mathbf{Q}}_\alpha$ is a well-studied problem.

It is interesting to note that advertiser ranking for each query topic is much more effective than a global ranking. Similar to topic sensitive pagerank [4], our proposed approach can be easily extended to address this and we skip the same for sake of space.

Remark (Comparison with CTR Based Ranking) We observe that ranking based on advertiser CTR does not necessarily represent reputation of advertisers. The pitfall in this approach is that it does not take into account how spread out the interest of an advertiser is and also the commercial intent of queries bidded upon by the advertisers. For example, a CTR based ranking would position popular advertisers like Amazon.com, Walmart.com within only top 5 percentile, whereas relatively lesser known advertisers will be in in top 0.01 percentile because of their highly commercial, specific query segment. For sake of brevity, we skip details of this experiment. Moreover, we used Advertiser CTR as one of the baseline feature in click prediction experiment which we discuss in Section. 4.

3.2 Reputation Bias in Sponsored Search

Reputation of an advertiser is an important factor in determining a click. In the following, we study how reputation impacts click-behavior empirically. We consider an ad-slate with advertisers $A_1, \ldots, A_m$ where one of them was clicked. Let $[w_1, \ldots, w_m]$ denote their true weight vector. We denote the event of a click in a slate as $\mathbf{c}$. If advertiser reputation

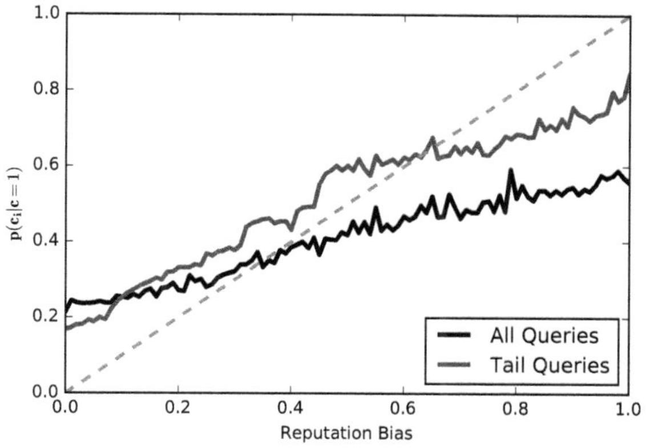

Figure 1: $\Pr(c_i|c = 1)$ is plotted against reputation bias for all queries and tail queries.

was the sole factor in determining this click ($\mathbf{c}$), then the probability A_i was clicked (denoted as c_i) should be proportional to w_i. In particular, the probability that advertiser i is clicked, given a click, is

$$\Pr(c_i|\mathbf{c} = 1) = \frac{w_i}{\sum_{k=1}^m w_k} \tag{11}$$

We define $\frac{w_i}{\sum_{k=1}^m w_k}$ as the reputation Bias (RB) for advertiser A_i. To study the dependence of $\Pr(c_i|\mathbf{c})$ on RB, we study the correlation between them.

We find the approximation $\hat{\mathbf{w}}$ to the true weight vector using our proposed approach. When reputation effect is the sole factor, $\Pr(c_i|\mathbf{c})$ is equal to RB under BTL condition. We compute the reputation bias for each ad in all ad-slates after position correction. To get $\Pr(c_i|\mathbf{c})$, we empirically estimate from their fraction of clicks. We considered two sets of data for this, one comprising the entire set of queries and the other containing only tail queries (In search engines, tail correspond to infrequent queries). We plot the correlation between them in Figure 1. For the entire set of queries, we observe that although $\Pr(c_i|\mathbf{c})$ is not completely governed (closer to ideal line) by reputation bias, they indeed have very high positive correlation. Interestingly in the tail queries, it is much more closer to the ideal line. For tail queries, often syntactic, semantic and frequency features do not work well. Consequently, clicks are mostly driven by reputation of the advertiser. We also observe that RB tends to underestimate/overestimate closer to boundaries. This can be attributed to the fact that predicted $\Pr(c_i|\mathbf{c})$ concentrates on a particular advertiser independent of syntactic and semantic information in the presence of a highly reputed advertiser.

4. EMPIRICAL ILLUSTRATIONS

In this section, we describe the experimental setup to evaluate the impact of advertiser reputation in click prediction.

4.1 Click Prediction

CTR for a query($\mathbf{q}$)-ad($\mathbf{a}$) pair is generally computed as the fraction of time ad($\mathbf{a}$) gets clicked when shown for the query($\mathbf{q}$). Most query-ad pairs appear relatively infrequently because of large number of queries and ads. Thus, syntactic

Dataset	Model	AUC change	Log-loss change
Dataset 1	Baseline+ RB (LR)	0.15%	-0.10%
	Baseline+ RB (GBDT)	0.58%	-18.80%
Dataset 2	Baseline+ RB (LR)	0.18%	-0.20%
	Baseline+ RB (GBDT)	1.20%	-20.50%
Dataset 3	Baseline+ RB (LR)	0.27%	-0.20%
	Baseline+ RB (GBDT)	1.50%	-2.90%

Table 1: Improvements in search engine click prediction model when using reputation bias.

and semantic features are used in addition to prior information to predict CTR [9]. Prediction task can be defined as $\Pr(\text{Click}|\mathbf{q}, \mathbf{a})$. Most often, contextual effects are assumed to be minimal. However, it is known that CTR is a combined function of semantics of the query, ad content as well as other external factors. External ($\mathbf{E}$) factor includes textual similarity among ads, depth of the slate, effects of organic search [10, 12, 11]. We define conditional CTR prediction in the presence of externalities as $\Pr(\text{Click}|\mathbf{q}, \mathbf{a}, \mathbf{E})$.

We provided empirical evidence of reputation bias in ad-slates which implies it acts as an external factor. We are interested in estimating conditional CTR, $\Pr(\text{Click}|\mathbf{q}, \mathbf{a}, \mathbf{E})$, where $\mathbf{E}$ denotes the effect of reputation of competing advertisers. In the following, we discuss experimental results using this contextual information.

4.2 Baselines and Datasets

Existing search engine click prediction (including syntactic, semantic and frequency based features) is used as the baseline model. Historical advertiser CTR (which can be a reasonable proxy for reputation), query CTR, query-ad CTR are included in the baseline model. Reputation bias is used as an additional feature along with the baseline CTR model to improve the prediction.

We measure the performance of reputation bias signal based on Area-Under-Curve (AUC) of the ROC curve and Log-loss which are often used as measure of performance in click prediction. For training/testing, we took a random sampled set from 30/10 days of logs from Bing search engine. We note that, historical count based features can be predominant for queries which appear frequently. This motivates us to study the impact of reputation bias on different segments of queries. In first dataset, we used all the queries. In second dataset, head queries (with sufficient volume) were not used. In the third dataset, we used tail queries only. Number of queries and logs were 11 (3.3) million and 30.2 (10) million in training (testing) data. For dataset 2 (3) number of queries and logs were approximately 70% (20%) and 40% (10%) of Dataset 1. We compared using 2 basic models, namely, linear logistic regression (LR) and gradient boosted decision trees (GBDT).

4.3 Results and Discussion

We tabulate the observations related to Log-loss per instance and AUC performance in Table 1. We present relative changes from the baseline model which we are comparing against in each experiment. We observe that AUC improvement from reputation effect, although small for linear classifier, is significant for non-linear classifiers. Also, the AUC improvement is highest in tail queries (dataset 3) where prior information is mostly absent. We note that this is in line with our previous analysis in figure 1. We can see, using reputation bias increases AUC by 1.50% on tail queries whereas in the whole dataset, it is 0.60%. When the frequency of query-ad pair is large, the empirical CTR captures the impact of all features as well as the contextual factors. However gains come in the absence of frequency effect.

5. CONCLUSION

In this paper, we study the advertiser reputation problem in sponsored search. We show how this can be related to the spectral properties of the preference graph. Through experiments, we show that advertiser reputation is a significant information when combined with other traditional features. In addition, for cold start problem in tail, we observe that reputation can play a substantial role. An interesting future direction would be studying applications of rank aggregation models apart from BTL in sponsored search.

6. ACKNOWLEDGMENTS

We would like to thank our colleagues Vishwa Kumbalimutt and Pradeep Shenoy for providing us with valuable comments.

7. REFERENCES

[1] C. H. Ding, H. Zha, X. He, P. Husbands, and H. D. Simon. Link analysis: hubs and authorities on the world wide web. *SIAM review*, pages 256–268, 2004.

[2] C. Dwork, R. Kumar, M. Naor, and D. Sivakumar. Rank aggregation methods for the web. In *Proc. WWW*, pages 613–622. ACM, 2001.

[3] T. Graepel, J. Q. Candela, T. Borchert, and R. Herbrich. Web-scale bayesian click-through rate prediction for sponsored search advertising in microsoft's bing search engine. In *Proc. ICML*, 2010.

[4] T. H. Haveliwala. Topic-sensitive pagerank. In *Proc. WWW*, pages 517–526. ACM, 2002.

[5] T. Joachims. Optimizing search engines using clickthrough data. In *Proc. SIGKDD*. ACM, 2002.

[6] D. Kempe and M. Mahdian. A cascade model for externalities in sponsored search. In *Internet and Network Economics*, pages 585–596. Springer, 2008.

[7] S. Negahban, S. Oh, and D. Shah. Iterative ranking from pair-wise comparisons. In *Proc. NIPS*, 2012.

[8] L. Page, S. Brin, R. Motwani, and T. Winograd. The pagerank citation ranking: bringing order to the web. 1999.

[9] M. Richardson, E. Dominowska, and R. Ragno. Predicting clicks: estimating the click-through rate for new ads. In *Proc. WWW*, pages 521–530. ACM, 2007.

[10] C. Xiong, T. Wang, W. Ding, Y. Shen, and T.-Y. Liu. Relational click prediction for sponsored search. In *Proc. WSDM*, pages 493–502. ACM, 2012.

[11] D. Yin, B. Cao, J.-T. Sun, and B. D. Davison. Estimating ad group performance in sponsored search. In *Proc. WSDM*, pages 143–152. ACM, 2014.

[12] D. Yin, S. Mei, B. Cao, J.-T. Sun, and B. D. Davison. Exploiting contextual factors for click modeling in sponsored search. In *Proc. WSDM*. ACM, 2014.

Clustering Speed in Multi-lane Traffic Networks

Bing Zhang*
bing@u.northwestern.edu

Goce Trajcevski†
goce@eecs.northwestern.edu

Feiying Liu
feiying@u.northwestern.edu

Northwestern University
2145 Sheridan Road
Evanston, IL, 60201

ABSTRACT

We address the problem of efficient spatio-temporal clustering of speed data in road segments with multiple lanes. We postulate that the navigation/route plans typically reported by different providers as a single-value need not be accurate in multi-lane networks. Our methodology generates lane-aware distribution of speed from GPS data and agglomerates the basic space and time units into larger clusters. Thus, we achieve a compact description of speed variations which can be subsequently used for more accurate trips planning. We provide experiments that demonstrate the benefits of our proposed approaches.

Keywords

Speed Clustering, Trajectories, Multi-lane Roads

1. INTRODUCTION

Routing and navigation have been popular applications relying on traffic data since 1980s [6]. Techniques for efficiently determining driving directions in terms of shortest travelled distance or shortest travel-time, or even eco-routes (i.e., in terms of optimizing the fuel consumption and/or CO emission) have been investigated by many researchers, both in databases [12] and transportation communities [9], and implemented by various map services providers (e.g., Google, HERE, etc.). Algorithmic calculations rely on certain estimated values of the traffic flow – equivalently, average speed along the segments of the underlying road-networks – a value that changes dynamically [12, 13] within a certain period (e.g., a day) and may depend on several factors, such as: time of day, capacity (lanes), road surface, etc. Traditionally, traffic speed estimation is based on an averaged speed among all observed vehicles as a "characteristic value", for which there are two main approaches: (1) Speed samples from each vehicle at different timestamps (averaged within road segment) [8]; (2) Total travel distance divided by the total travel time along a particular/targeted road segment [12]. Existing route-planning methodologies and tools share one

Figure 1: Belmont Ave. exit on Lake Shore Drive

basic assumption: on any road segment, at a certain time-period, vehicles have only one kind of motion. However, the existence of multiple lanes may yield significantly different speeds on the same road-segment and at same time-intervals. Thus, using the average speed as a descriptor may not be good enough for many routing applications. As an illustration, consider an actual picture from Chicago's Lake Shore Drive, near Belmont Avenue exit, shown in Figure 1. The cars back up at the rightmost lane by Belmont Avenue exit – used when accessing Wrigley Field baseball stadium, while the rest of the 3 lanes on northbound Lake Shore have very low densities. This situation occurs quite frequently during non-rush hours throughout the baseball season. Thus, averaging the observations from particular (groups of) vehicles, could produce an inaccurate picture about the traffic distribution – and, yet, most of the popular traffic speed estimation methods are based on averaging the samples from vehicles over a period of time or area — e.g., *Time Mean Speed* and *Space Mean Speed* [4].

At the heart of the motivation for this work is the observation that – to the best of our knowledge – the state of the art approaches have not incorporated multi-lane information when designing traffic speed profiles to be used for routes planning. We note that the research on map-matching GPS points from moving objects [2] has not fully exploited the settings of multiple lanes.

As mentioned, route planning is a foundational task for many Location-Based Services but traditional methods [8, 12] can only vary a single (average) speed value throughout: (a) different time intervals; and (b) along different (portions

*Research Supported by the NSF III 1213038 grant
†Research Supported by the NSF grants CNS 0910952 and III 1213038, and ONR grant N00014-14-10215

CIKM'16, October 24-28, 2016, Indianapolis, IN, USA
© 2016 ACM. ISBN 978-1-4503-4073-1/16/10...$15.00
DOI: http://dx.doi.org/10.1145/2983323.2983905

of) road segments. In the context of the example in Figure 1, this would mean that a request for a route-plan between Navy Pier and Lawrence Avenue would use the average speed around Belmont Ave. exit, yielding incorrect time-estimate for the targeted trip planning. To tackle such issues, our main contributions are:

- We achieve a compact description of speed variations in multi-lane road networks that can be used for more accurate trips planning.
- We propose an agglomerative speed clustering algorithm to represent the distribution in a more compact manner.
- We present experimental observations based on real data from highways around Rome to demonstrate the benefits of our proposed method.

2. PRELIMINARIES

We now present a brief overview of the related background and introduce the terminology. Traditionally, in Moving Objects Databases (MOD) [5], the motion of an object with a distinct ID (*oID*) is represented as a *trajectory* $Tr_{oID} = [p_1, p_2 ... p_n]$, where each p_i is a triplet $p_i = (x_i, y_i, t_i)$; t_i being the time that the object was at location (x_i, y_i).

In this work, a road-network is a collection of multi-lane road segments. A *road segment* r is a octuple $r = (r_{ID}, r_{Dir}, r_s, r_e, r_{type}, r_{length}, r_{speed}, r_{lane})$, where: r_{ID} is its unique identifier; r_{Dir} is a binary value indicating whether r is one-way or two-way segment; r_s and r_e are k-tuples (k = number of lanes) representing the starting and ending points of each lane (centroids); r_{type} indicates the type of the road to which the segment belongs (e.g., urban, rural, etc...); r_{length} is its length; r_{speed} is the maximum speed; and r_{lane} is an integer specifying the number of lanes in each direction. A *road network* is an (augmented) graph $G_{RN} = (V_{RN}, E_{RN})$ where V_{RN} is the set of nodes representing the terminal points of road segments, and E_{RN} is the collection of road segments.

We note that in traditional traffic-stream studies there are different measures characterizing the motion along road segments [4], often coupled with the available technology. For example, inductive sensors are good for estimating the flow, however, they cannot characterize the speed. On-board GPS devices are good at obtaining an average speed of individual moving objects, however, they are error-prone in terms of location, and cannot capture fluctuations in-between samples. In this work, we assume that motion-relevant data is obtained from (a sequence of) GPS points via a suitable map-matching algorithm.

3. SPATIAL-TEMPORAL PARTITIONING AND MERGING

Partition-and-merge framework for clustering trajectories has been proposed in [7] – however, the work did not consider the time-dimension (i.e., the speed) and was dealing with free 2D motion, not constrained to road networks. Models have been proposed based on trajectories' geographical information (including moving objects' heading and trajectory density) and semantic information. Compared with conventional trajectory clustering framework, in our problem of mining traffic speed clusters, GPS sample points are constrained by road-network. However, map-matching with uncertain location poses other challenges.

There are three steps for data partitioning: a) map-matching GPS points to corresponding road segments. b) Identifying lane information within augmented road-network. c) Spatial-temporal partitioning to divide road segments and associated GPS points into basic units for further merging.

3.1 Map-matching and Lane Labeling

Map-matching algorithms use information generated from positioning technologies and supplement it with data from a high resolution road-network map to provide an enhanced positioning output. They identify the correct road on which vehicles travel and determine vehicles' location on that segment – and can be categorized into four groups: geometric, topological, probabilistic, and other advanced techniques [10]. In this work, we extend the most commonly used geometric map-matching algorithm called "point-based matching" (or point-to-curve matching).

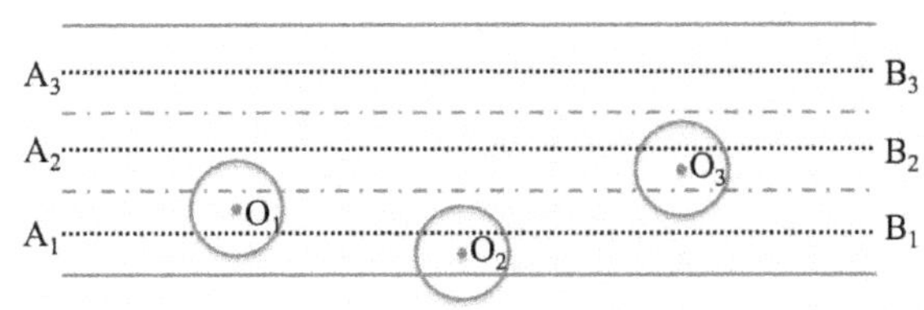

Figure 2: Lane labeling

An augmented road segment and three GPS sample points are shown in figure 2. Traditional road segment without width is merely the central line $\overline{A_2B_2}$. We augment it with lane width – yielding $\overline{A_1B_1}$ and $\overline{A_3B_3}$ as central line of inner lane and outer lane accordingly.

The uncertainty area of each GPS sample point is modeled by a horizontal disk with radius r centered at (x, y, t), where (x, y) is the expected location at time $t \in (t_i, t_{i+1})$ [11]. Let $D_p(x, y, t, r)$ denote the disk centered at point $P(x, y, t)$ with radius r, and A_i denote the area of lane i, approximated by a rectangle. Assuming an uniform distribution of the location inside D_p, the probability of one GPS point located within the area of certain lane can be estimated by: $P_{lane} = \frac{D_p(x,y,t,r) \cap A}{D_p(x,y,t,r)}$. Then, GPS points are matched to the lane ID which has the highest probability.

3.2 Partitioning and Merging

The philosophy of clustering traffic speed data is to group those GPS points that are spatially and temporally close to each other *and* with similar speed. Thus, based on a suitable minimum unit, larger clusters can be formed through merging and reorganizing. We define the Unit Cell (UC) as:
Unit Cell: A Unit Cell $UC_{kl} = (\Delta^S_{kl}, \Delta^T_{kl}, V_{kl}, D_{kl})$ in the lth lane of a given road segment is the minimal partition in spatial and temporal dimension, characterized by a spatial range $\Delta^S_{kl} = d^+_{kl} - d^-_{kl}$, temporal interval $\Delta^T_{kl} = t^+_{kl} - t^-_{kl}$, and a set of trajectories $D_{kl} = [Tr_1, Tr_2, ... Tr_n]$ that belong to it. The set D_{kl} determines the speed-value V_{kl} associated with UC_{kl} – i.e., it is a set of trajectories such that they all have values of their speed that is within $[v^{min}_{k,l}, v^{max}_{k,l}]$ throughout the spatial and temporal boundaries of UC_{kl}. More importantly, $v^{max}_{k,l} - v^{min}_{k,l} \leq \delta'_v$ – tolerance threshold – and $V_{kl} = (v^{max}_{k,l} + v^{min}_{k,l})/2$. We note that the spatial range uses only "1D interval" – i.e., $d^+_{kl} - d^-_{kl}$ because the

"conventional" 2-D space is restructured as 1-D along the driving direction. However, this is only representing the distance(s) from starting point of the road segment (i.e., the corresponding lane) until the beginning of the k-th unit cell and the width is pre-determined by the width of the lanes for a given road-type. Figure 3 shows a scenario of six such unit cells distributed in two lanes, splitting each lane in 3 components, and with one temporal component.

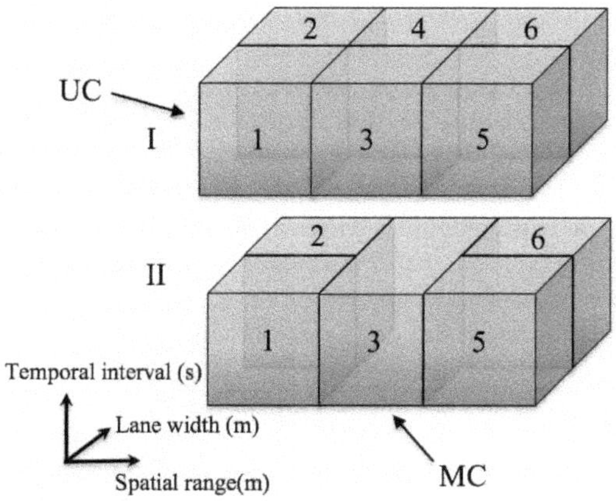

Figure 3: Merging mechanism

Merged Cell: Intuitively, a Merged Cell (MC) is a union of multiple neighboring unit cells $MC_j = UC_1 \cup UC_2 \cup ... \cup UC_n$. Its spatial range is defined as $R_{MC} = \cup_i \Delta_i^S$ and its temporal interval $T_{MC} = \cup_i \Delta_i^T$.

However, the more important criteria that we require for merging two neighboring unit cells, inspired by [3, 7], are:
(1) $V_{(k+1)l} - V_{kl} \leq \delta_v''$ – i.e., the speed-values in the cells are close enough to each other, and
(2) $||D_{(k+1)l}| - |D_{kl}|| \leq \tau$ – i.e., the cells need to have close enough number of trajectories in their support-set.

An illustration of a merging cell MC formed by two neighboring UCs is shown in figure 3, in the *(space, time, lane#)* dimensionality. We constrain the union to consist of neighboring UC's in order to keep the spatial and temporal continuity. The first observation that, depending on the merging order chosen, a given collection of *UCs* need not yield a unique (collection of) *MCs*. A slight generalization of the scenario illustrated in Figure 3 can easily demonstrate that a particular cell can participate in as many as six different mergings, provided that there are ≥ 3 lanes. One can envision cells as being nodes in a graph and edges existing between neighboring cells. Upon merging, two nodes coalesce into one – and, to select a criterion for merging, a priority needs to be assigned among the adjacent vertices. Figure 3 illustrates merging of two neighboring edges from two lanes, sharing the same time-interval and distance from the start of the road-segment. However, in the current implementation, this is the 3rd criterion:
(3.1) First we check whether cells can be merged along the spatial dimension within the same lane.
(3.2) If not, we check next whether two cells with the same spatial extent can be merged along the temporal dimension.
(3.3) Lastly, we check whether two cells can be merged along neighboring lanes.

For every iteration of merging process there are three basic steps that are followed when processing each node.

I If there are no neighbors along the merging direction, the current cell is skipped and marked as visited.

II We check the cross-section coordinates between current cell and its neighbor in the order of preferences of merging directions. If cross-section coordinates are aligned and they satisfy the merging criteria, a merged cell is formed to replace them. One example is shown in figure 3–I. When we merge UC_3 with UC_4 along lane width dimension, their cross-section are aligned and a new MC_3 is formed. If we try to merge MC_3 with UC_5 along spatial range dimension in figure 3–II, their cross-section cannot match, and the cell will be skipped.

III Newly merged cell inherits all the neighboring relationship from merged cells. At the same time, all neighbors of two merged cells update their neighbor lists, by replacing original cells with the new one.

Speed Cluster: When the merging process for a particular (unit or merged) cell can no longer continue, we call that cell a *Speed Clusters* (SC)

Algorithm 1 formalizes the above description.

Algorithm 1 Cluster Mining (CellSets, DirectionSets)

```
ClusterID = NextID(NULL);
for Merging Direction MD IN DirectionList do
    while Cell in CellSets is unvisited do
        Neighbor = Cell.Neighbors(i) along MD;
        if Neighbor.size() == 0 then
            Cell.visited = True;
            Continue;
        else if Align(Cell, Neighbor) == True AND CanMerge(Cell, Neighbor) == True then
            NewCell = merge(Cell, Neighbor);
            NewCell.Neighbors = mergeNeighbor(Cell, Neighbor);
            updateNeighbor(Cell, Neighbor, NewCell);
            delete Cell, Neighbor;
        else
            Cell.visited = True;
        end if
    end while
    CellSets.visited = False;
end for
Return CellSets;
```

Assume that there are a total of n GPS points in the database, and (on the average) a road segment is composed of $O(K)$ spatial intervals in each lane and $O(M)$ intervals in the temporal dimension, defining the unit cells. Under a uniform distribution, each unit cell will consist of $O(n/(KM))$ GPS points from various trajectories. Calculating the merged cells and clusters along a road segment can have an upper bound of $O((KM)^2)$ provided each one of the $K \cdot M$ cells is taken as a starting point to obtain the best possible clustering in terms of the minimal final number of clusters.

4. EXPERIMENTS AND CONCLUDING REMARKS

Dataset: The Grande Raccordo Anulare (GRA) is a toll-free, ring-shaped orbital motorway that encircles Rome. It is one of the most important roads with heavy traffic for the most of the day. The dataset contains GPS trace of 320 taxi cabs in Rome, collected over 30 days in the Rome area, from February 1 to March 2 of 2014 [1]. The cardinality of the dataset is 8,368,858.

Baseline: The baseline approach we compared with is a traditional traffic speed estimation method (cf. Section 1), by calculating the average speed among all speed samples. In order to incorporate the variation along temporal dimension, we divide speed samples into 24 subsets, which represent 24 hours in a day. Average speed within each hour is calculated accordingly.

Evaluation: The data was divided into four folds according to sample time, each containing GPS points within one week. We used three weeks data to train our model, and we randomly pick trajectories from the remaining set to estimate the travel time, by using both baseline method and traffic speed clustering model.

The experiment was repeated 15 times and the average of all the runs is shown in Figure 4. The x-axis represents the aggregated travel distance, and y-axis stands for average estimated travel. On average, the travel time by using speed clustering method is reduced by 20%, compared with baseline approach. For the entire road networks, there are 8,328,960 UCs before merging, and 414,982 MCs after merging, which is a 95% reduction.

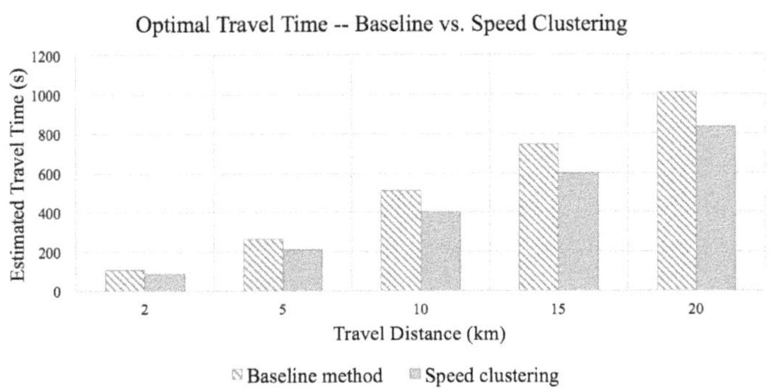

Figure 4: Travel time estimation using baseline approach and agglomerative method

We proposed a speed clustering approach that incorporate multi-lane information with partitioning and merging. We postulate that incorporating such information will yield a more precise calculation for route planning. We use Rome taxi data to demonstrate that, compared with baseline approach, our method yields faster trajectories for longer routes.

There are multiple extensions to our work. Firstly, we need to investigate the trade-offs in terms of complexity overheads (both space and time). Secondly, we note that partitioning and merging requires a choice of (fixed) merging rule. Even if this choice can be determined through experiment, additional computation is made. We plan to consider other kinds of learning approaches in conjunction with different clustering techniques. We also plan for a more thorough treatment of the (impact of the) GPS uncertainty/error [14] to the speed cluster mining algorithm. During the lane labeling process, large GPS errors will incur potential mislabeling, which later lead to noise points in the merging phase. One possible direction is to soft allocate the weight of GPS points to different lanes based on certain probabilities.

5. REFERENCES

[1] L. Bracciale, M. Bonola, P. Loreti, G. Bianchi, R. Amici, and A. Rabuffi. CRAWDAD dataset roma/taxi (v. 2014-07-17). Downloaded from http://crawdad.org/roma/taxi/20140717, July 2014.

[2] R. Dalumpines and D. M. Scott. Gis-based map-matching: Development and demonstration of a postprocessing map-matching algorithm for transportation research. In *Advancing geoinformation science for a changing world*, pages 101–120. Springer, 2011.

[3] C. H. Q. Ding, X. He, H. Zha, M. Gu, and H. D. Simon. A min-max cut algorithm for graph partitioning and data clustering. In *Proceedings of the 2001 IEEE ICDM*, pages 107–114, 2001.

[4] N. H. Gartner, C. J. Messer, and A. K. Rathi. *Monograph on traffic flow theory*. Federal Highway Administration, 1997.

[5] R. H. Güting and M. Schneider. *Moving Objects Databases*. Morgan Kaufmann, 2005.

[6] G. Laporte. The vehicle routing problem: An overview of exact and approximate algorithms. *European Journal of Operational Research*, 59(3):345–358, 1992.

[7] J.-G. Lee, J. Han, X. Li, and H. Gonzalez. Traclass: trajectory classification using hierarchical region-based and trajectory-based clustering. *Proceedings of the VLDB Endowment*, 1(1):1081–1094, 2008.

[8] A. Pascale, F. Deflorio, M. Nicoli, B. Dalla Chiara, and M. Pedroli. Motorway speed pattern identification from floating vehicle data for freight applications. *Transportation Research Part C: Emerging Technologies*, 51:104–119, 2015.

[9] V. Pillac, M. Gendreau, C. Guéret, and A. L. Medaglia. A review of dynamic vehicle routing problems. *European Journal of Operational Research*, 225(1):1–11, 2013.

[10] M. a. Quddus, W. Y. Ochieng, and R. B. Noland. Current map-matching algorithms for transport applications: State-of-the art and future research directions. *Transportation Research Part C: Emerging Technologies*, 15:312–328, 2007.

[11] G. Trajcevski, O. Wolfson, K. Hinrichs, and S. Chamberlain. Managing uncertainty in moving objects databases. *ACM Trans. Database Syst.*, 29(3):463–507, Sept. 2004.

[12] Y. Wang, Y. Zheng, and Y. Xue. Travel time estimation of a path using sparse trajectories. In *Proceedings of the 20th ACM SIGKDD*, pages 25–34. ACM, 2014.

[13] J. Yuan, Y. Zheng, X. Xie, and G. Sun. T-drive: enhancing driving directions with taxi drivers' intelligence. *Knowledge and Data Engineering, IEEE Transactions on*, 25(1):220–232, 2013.

[14] B. Zhang, G. Trajcevski, and L. Liu. Towards fusing uncertain location data from heterogeneous sources. *GeoInformatica*, 20(2):179–212, 2016.

Learning to Rank Non-Factoid Answers: Comment Selection in Web Forums

Kateryna Tymoshenko
University of Trento
Povo (Trento), Italy
kateryna.tymoshenko@unitn.it

Daniele Bonadiman
University of Trento
Povo (Trento), Italy
d.bonadiman@unitn.it

Alessandro Moschitti*
Qatar Computing Research Institute
HBKU, Doha, Qatar
amoschitti@qf.org.qa

ABSTRACT

Recent initiatives in IR community have shown the importance of going beyond factoid Question Answering (QA) in order to design useful real-world applications. Questions asking for descriptions or explanations are much more difficult to be solved, e.g., the machine learning models cannot focus on specific answer words or their lexical type. Thus, researchers have started to explore powerful methods for feature engineering. Two of the most promising methods are convolution tree kernels (CTKs) and convolutional neural networks (CNNs) as they have been shown to obtain high performance in the task of answer sentence selection in factoid QA. In this paper, we design state-of-the-art models for non-factoid QA also carried out on noisy data. In particular, we study and compare models for comment selection in a community QA (cQA) scenario, where the majority of questions regard descriptions or explanations. To deal with such complex task, we incorporate relational information holding between questions and comments as well as domain-specific features into both convolutional models above. Our experiments on a cQA corpus show that both CTK and CNN achieve the state of the art, also according to a direct comparison with the results obtained by the best systems of the SemEval cQA challenge.

1. INTRODUCTION

Community Question Answering (cQA) enables users to freely ask questions in web forums and expect some good answers in the form of comments from other users. However, many comments are typically not pertinent to the user question, thus automatic approaches for selecting those useful are very valuable.

Previous work for automatic answer sentence selection, e.g., [22, 23, 18], has inspired recent international competitions on cQA, where answer sentences are replaced by entire comments of forum users. For example, SemEval-2016 Task 3[1] in Subtask A asks to rank the posts in comment threads that answer the question *well* before those that are just *bad* or *potentially useful*. Tab. 1 describes an example: the participants are given a question, its author's ID, a set of comments along with the IDs of the users who wrote them, and their systems have to rerank the comments so that the good ones are pushed to the top. All the comments are manually annotated with their relevance with respect to the question and thus can be used for training and testing learning to rank (L2R) algorithms.

Question		
Author:	princess_naila	
Subject:	Psychiatrist in DOHA	
Body:	Could someone advise the best psychiatrist/psycologist in DOHA?	
Comments		
Author	**Comment**	**Label**
feba mariyam	i heard a good doctor in doha clinic...	**potentially useful**
princess _naila	ok..shall check that out..thank you :)	**Bad**
Equin0x	"Visit Psychiatrist clinic of Hamad Hospital located opposite ""The Center"" exactly facing KFC."	**Good**

Table 1: Qatar Living question and comments examples

The overall setting of this task is similar to that of the answer sentence selection in the factoid QA, therefore an intuitive approach would be to employ state-of-the-art answer sentence selection models. However, it should be noted that the cQA questions are typically non-factoid, e.g., asking for opinions or advice. Moreover, the text involved in this scenario is rather noisy, making it difficult to outperform simple bag-of-word models.

To tackle such complexity, we rely on state-of-the-art machine learning methods such as CTKs and CNNs . Thus, we design L2R models for comment selection using (i) CTKs based on our previous successful CTK models for factoid QA [18, 20, 21], and (ii) new CNNs. In particular, we improve the CTK models using some basic filtering strategies for building robust tree structures that can deal with the noisy and relatively larger size of forum comments. At the same time, we deal with the more challenging nature of non-factoid questions by encoding relational information in both CTKs and CNNs. The experiments with the official data of SemEval cQA challenge [14] show that CNNs are on par with CTKs: we attain state-of-the-art accuracy using two completely different models, although we also needed to define some task specific features. In particular, our models evaluated on the official test set produce a MAP of 78.80, just 0.4 less than the best system (79.19), and would have ranked second[2].

2. STRUCTURES FOR CTKs

Severyn et al. [18] built a reranker for QA applying CTKs to a shallow structural representation of question and answer sentences, called **SH**. This is constituted by two trees with lemmas, at leaf level and their part-of-speech (POS) tags at the preterminal level.

*Professor at University of Trento, DISI.

[1] http://alt.qcri.org/semeval2016/task3/

[2] http://alt.qcri.org/semeval2016/task3/index.php?id=results

CIKM'16 , October 24 - 28, 2016, Indianapolis, IN, USA

ISBN 978-1-4503-4073-1/16/10... $15.00

DOI: http://dx.doi.org/10.1145/2983323.2983906

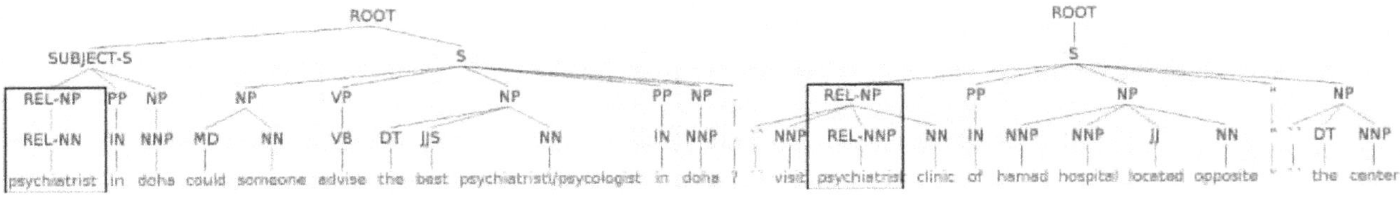

Figure 1: SH tree for the Q/Comment pair.

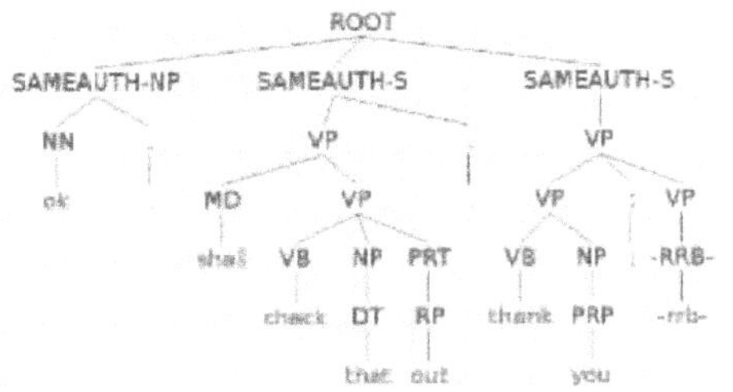

Figure 2: CONST tree enriched with question author information

The authors mark the lemmas that occur in both question and answer passage by prepending the **REL** tag to the labels of the corresponding POS-tag nodes and their parents, thus encoding information about their relatedness.

In our work, we adjust their representation to fit the cQA task, i.e., we enrich the structures with additional relational information and cQA-specific thread knowledge. Additionally, we found that using a constituency structure **CONST** is more effective than SH. Moreover, differently from [18], we do not remove the punctuation marks from the trees, as, for example, the comments that ask additional questions and thus contain a question mark are unlikely to answer the original question.

Most importantly, we encode the following cQA-related information: (i) the question subject is a separate subtree under the **SUBJECT-S** root in the question tree; (ii) following the intuition that the question author unlikely will correctly answer his/her own question, we add the **SAMEAUTH** label to the sentence nodes in the comment tree. Additionally, when constructing the CONST representation of the question tree, we do not use the question body, but only its subject[3]. Figure 1 provides an example of the **REL-** encoding in the SH tree with lemma *psychiatrist* marked with REL- in both trees and question subject separated from its body. Fig. 2 illustrates a CONST representation of the author's comment to her own question.

3. RELATIONAL NNs FOR cQA

We propose a NN for matching sentence pairs on the same research line of answer selection [17, 9, 5, 23]. The general architecture is depicted in Fig. 3. It includes two main components (i) two sentence encoders that map input documents i into fixed size m-dimensional vectors x_{s_i}, and (ii) a feed forward NN that computes the similarity between the two sentences in the input.

Let d be the size of the word embeddings, the sentence encoders are composed of (i) a sentence matrix $\mathbf{s}_i \in \mathbb{R}^{d \times |i|}$ obtained by concatenating the word vector of the corresponding word in the input sentence $\mathbf{w}_j \in \mathbf{s}_i$, and (ii) a sentence model $f : \mathbb{R}^{d \times |i|} \rightarrow \mathbb{R}^m$, which maps the sentence matrix to a fixed size sentence embedding $x_{s_i} \in \mathbb{R}^m$. The choice of the sentence model plays a crucial role as the resulting representation of the input sentences affects the successive steps of computing their similarity. Previous work uses different types of sentence models for matching sentence pairs such as LSTM, distributional sentence model, and convolutional sentence model. In particular, the latter is composed of a sequence of convolution-pooling feature maps and has achieved the state of the art in various NLP tasks [7, 8].

Here, we implement a sentence model with a convolutional operation followed by a k-max pooling layer with $k = 1$. This choice has been proved successful for factoid QA [17]. The sentence vectors, x_{s_i}, are concatenated together and given as input to standard NN layers, which are constituted by a non-linear hidden layer and a sigmoid output layer. The sentence encoder, $x_{s_i} = f(s_i)$, outputs a fixed-size vector representation of the input sentence s_i. In the remainder of the paper, we will refer to the question and the comment representations as the question embedding (QE) and the comment embedding (CE). Similarly the output of the penultimate layer of the network (the hidden layer whose output feeds the final classification layer) is a compact representation of the input question and comment pair, which we call Joint Embedding (JE).

3.1 Injecting Relational features

Despite the fact that NNs can automatically generate embeddings from raw inputs, adding manually engineered features can be useful for solving complex tasks such as cQA. In particular, we can add any discrete features to the model, as described in [2], i.e., use an additional lookup layer for every feature, $feat$. Word features can be added to the model by augmenting the word embedding with the corresponding feature embedding. Given a word, w_j, its final word embedding is defined as $\mathbf{w}_j \in \mathbb{R}^d$, where $d = d_w + d_{feat}$. Specific cQA features, $\mathbf{x}_{feat}$, can be inserted into the join layer using feature embedding; the resulting vector is $\mathbf{x}_{s_1+s_2+x_{feat}} \in \mathbb{R}^t$, where $t = 2m + d_{feat}$.

Sec. 2 shows that establishing relational links (REL nodes) between a question (Q) and comment (C) is very important for solving the cQA tasks. We enable our NNs to capture the connections between words shared by Q and C by encoding relational links as binary word features. In particular, we associate each word w in the input sentences with a *word overlap* feature $o \in \{0, 1\}$, where $o = 1$ means that w is shared by both Q and C, i.e., overlaps, $o = 0$ otherwise. Basically the word-overlap vector plays the role of the REL tag added to the CTK structures (see Sec 2).

Nicosia et al. [15] describe other important features for cQA, including whether (i) the author of the comment is the same of the question (SAMEAUTH); and (ii) the comment in consideration is followed by another comment from the author of the question (SAMEAUTH^{+}). These two sentence features are binarized and added to the network at the join layer.

4. EXPERIMENTS

In these experiments, we compare CTKs and CNNs, also combining them with traditional feature vector representations.

4.1 Experimental setup

Experimental dataset. We use the Subtask A *Question-Comment Similarity* subset of the Semeval-2016 Task 3 English cQA dataset[4]. This enables a direct comparison with results of challenge. The dataset of questions and comments was extracted from the *Qatar*

[3]Our preliminary experiments showed that adding question body to the CONST representation does not affect the performance.

[4]http://alt.qcri.org/semeval2016/task3/index.php?id=description-of-tasks

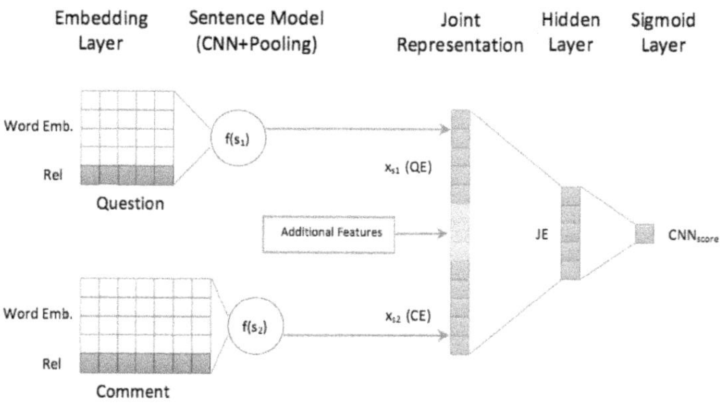

Figure 3: Neural Network model

Living forum[5]. For each question, the first ten comments were collected and manually annotated as good, i.e., answering the question, and potentially useful or bad. The Potentially useful class was relabeled as bad during the challenge evaluation. The train, development and test sets contain 1790, 244 and 327 questions.
QA metrics. We employ Mean Average Precision (MAP), the official Subtask A metric, and Mean Reciprocal Rank (MRR).
CTKs. We trained our models with SVM-light-TK[6]. It enables the use of CTKs [13] in SVM-light [6]. We used the partial and the subset tree kernels (PTK and STK) with their default parameters and the polynomial kernel (P) of degree 3 on all feature vectors[7].
Preprocessing We truncate all the comments to 2000 symbols and all the sentences to 70 words. When generating the structural representations described in Section 2, we used the first three sentences of a question or a comment. We used the Illinois chunker [16] and the Stanford CoreNLP [10] toolkit for the needed preprocessing.
Signatures. If a specific user always signs their posts with the same phrase, e.g., "*The tough gets going..*", we consider this phrase irrelevant and remove it. More specifically, we delete all the strings with length exceeding 20 characters that occur at the end of more than one comment by the same user.
cQA-relevant features vectors (QF). We used the thread-level features by one of the top-performing SemEval-2015 systems [15]. Among others, they include the features encoding whether the comment (c) is authored by the question (q) author, whether c contains a question, an acknowledgment word or a URL, and other intuitions.

4.2 Neural Network experiments

We pre-initialize the word embeddings with skipgram embedding of dimensionality 50 trained on the English Wikipedia dump [12]. The input sentences are encoded with fixed-sized vectors using a convolutional operation of size 5 and a k-max pooling operation with $k = 1$. We use a single non-linear hidden layer (with hyperbolic tangent activation, Tanh), whose size is equal to the size of the sentence embeddings, i.e., 200. The network is trained using SGD with shuffled mini-batches using the Rmsprop update rule. The model is trained until the validation loss stops improving.

For computational reasons, we decided to limit the size of the input sentences to 100 words. This did not degrade the observed performance. To improve learning generalization and avoid co-adaptation of features (which negatively impact the transfer capabilities of the sentence embeddings), we opted for adding dropout [19] between the layers of the network. Table 2 reports the results of our NNs on the development set. The first sentence model is a word embedding averaging model (W2V), where the sentence embeddings are calculated by averaging the word vectors. Then, two strong baseline sentence models are presented, a Long-Short Term Memory (LSTM) sentence model [4] and our vanilla CNN, presented in Section 3. Our CNN, without any additional features, outperforms W2V, obtaining similar accuracy than LSTM. Thus, we decided to use the convolutional sentence model mainly for computational reasons. The second part of the table shows CNN incrementally enhanced by the *overlap*, SAMEAUTH and SAMEAUTH$^+$ features (see Sec. 3.1) for further improving its performance.

Encoders	MAP	MRR	Features	MAP	MRR
W2V	0.6284	68.53	CNN	0.6496	71.26
LSTM	0.6477	**71.78**	+*overlap*	0.6648	73.46
CNN	**0.6496**	71.26	+SAMEAUTH	0.6684	72.56
			+SAMEAUTH$^+$	**0.6741**	**73.64**

Table 2: NNs results on the development dataset

4.3 Results and Discussion

Table 3 reports the performance of our systems and compares it to the state of the art. Its first four lines report the performance of the top systems in the Semeval-2016 Subtask A competition[8]. The participants were allowed to submit one primary and two contrastive runs. The teams were ranked according to the MAP score obtained by their primary system (the official rank is reported in parentheses). The remainder of the table describes the performance of our systems on the development (DEV) and on the test (TEST) sets. We did not use DEV to tune any parameters.

The *Kernel* column reports the name of the kernel used in SVMs. V_{QF} is an SVM using a polynomial kernel over the QF feature vector. CNN is the convolution neural network described in Sec. 3. CTK_{SH} and CTK_C are the CTK-based SVMs trained on the SH and CONST representations described in Sec. 2, respectivelyĊTK+V denotes the composite kernel that is a sum of two kernels.

Notably, both CTK models that encode only one cQA task-specific intuition (i.e., whether the question and the comment have the same author) are only slightly outperformed by CNNs and achieve an MAP only one point lower than ConvKN-primary, the second best-ranking system in official ranking of the competition.

Additionally, we observe that CTK_{SH} with the PTK and CTK_C with STK obtain almost the same performance. This is important, as PTK generates a richer feature space but STK has a lower computational complexity. Training an SVM with PTK and STK on CTK_C took 4213.93 and 1006.58 cpu-seconds, respectively. Next, the CTK and V combinations, CTK_C+V_{QF} (STK) and CTK_{SH}+ V_{QF} (PTK), obtained the MAPs of 78.78 and 78.80 on TEST, respectively. They would have ranked second in the competition.

Finally, since both CNNs and CTKs achieve the state of the art on cQA, and since our earlier work [21] showed that combining CNNs and CTKs improves factoid QA, we experimented with combining the two approaches for cQA. We used the question, comment and joint embeddings learned by CNNs as feature vectors in V and combined them with QF and CTK_C. We have experimented with all possible combinations: Sec. 3 of Table 3 lists the best ones. The subscripts QE and CE indicate the use of the question and comment embeddings (Sec. 3) as the feature vector, whereas | denotes that the respective vectors were concatenated into a single vector.

None of the combinations improved over the CTKs models with QF features, however, an interesting finding is that, in general, V

[5] http://www.qatarliving.com/forum

[6] http://disi.unitn.it/moschitti/Tree-Kernel.htm We use classification setting and use the distance to the decision hyperplane as a ranking score.

[7] We employ a composite CTK that is a sum ot two CTKs applied to the question and comment trees separately.

[8] http://alt.qcri.org/semeval2016/task3/data/uploads/semeval2016_task3_submissions_and_scores.zip

Models	Kernel	DEV		TEST	
		MAP	MRR	MAP	MRR
1. Baseline models					
Kelp-primary [3] (#1)	n/a	n/a	n/a	79.19	86.42
ConvKN-contrastive1 [1]	n/a	n/a	n/a	78.71	86.15
SUper team-contrastive1 [11]	n/a	n/a	n/a	77.68	84.76
ConvKN-primary [1] (#2)	n/a	n/a	n/a	77.66	84.93
2. CNN and CTK models					
V_{QF}	P	63.45	70.51	73.50	82.98
CNN	n/a	67.41	73.64	77.13	83.85
CTK_{SH}	PTK	64.10	71.97	76.67	83.53
CTK_C	STK	65.30	73.24	75.42	82.35
CTK_C	PTK	63.82	70.53	76.39	82.94
CTK_{SH}+V_{QF}	PTK, P	68.45	74.49	**78.80**	86.16
CTK_C+V_{QF}	STK, P	67.26	74.07	**78.78**	86.26
3. Combining CTK and CNN models					
$V_{QE\|CE}$	P	65.63	72.69	75.15	82.37
$V_{QE\|CE\|QF}$	P	68.17	75.32	**77.22**	83.98
CTK_C+$V_{QE\|CE}$	STK,P	66.71	75.18	76.25	83.33
CTK_C+$V_{QE\|CE\|QF}$	STK,P	**68.92**	**76.61**	**77.25**	**84.16**

Table 3: Performance of CTK, CNN and QF models on the development (DEV) and test (TEST)

systems, which use only embeddings as features outperform V_{QF}. Concatenating the QE, CE and QF into a single feature vector results in a further improvement, e.g., $V_{QE|CE|QF}$ achieves an MAP of 77.22 on the TEST, which is only 0.44 points lower than the MAP of the **#2** ranked system. CTK_C+$V_{QE|CE}$, a combination of QE and CE with CTK_C (without QF) slightly improves over CTK_C (using STK) on both DEV and TEST sets. However, the CTK_C+$V_{QE|CE|QF}$, a combination of CTKs, CNN and QF, scores lower than $CTK_C + V_{QF}$, thus additional investigation is needed to understand how to successfully combine CTK and CNN.

5. CONCLUSION

In this paper, we studied state-of-the-art QA methods and applied them to cQA. Several challenges have to be tackled in this kind of real-world applications: the questions are mainly non-factoid and the text is typically informal and noisy. We provided two solutions based on tree kernels applied to robust syntactic structures and applied them to comment reranking tasks in cQA. Additionally, we designed new CNNs for comment reranking, which exploit cQA features as well as important relational information between questions and comments. The results show that tree kernels and CNNs can achieve the state of the art. The high quality of our solutions is also confirmed by the official results of a cQA challenge, among which our best system would have achieved the second position. The most important aspect of our future work will be to investigate ways of successfully combining CTKs and CNNs.

Acknowledgements

This work has been partially supported by the EC project CogNet, 671625 (H2020-ICT-2014-2, Research and Innovation action) and by an IBM Faculty Award.

References

[1] A. Barrón-Cedeño, G. Da San Martino, S. Joty, A. Moschitti, F. Al-Obaidli, S. Romeo, K. Tymoshenko, and A. Uva. ConvKN at SemEval-2016 task 3: Answer and question selection for question answering on Arabic and English fora. In *SemEval-2016*. ACL, 2016.

[2] R. Collobert, J. Weston, L. Bottou, M. Karlen, K. Kavukcuoglu, and P. Kuksa. Natural language processing (almost) from scratch. *The Journal of Machine Learning Research*, 12:2493–2537, 2011.

[3] S. Filice, D. Croce, A. Moschitti, and R. Basili. KeLP at SemEval-2016 Task 3: Learning Semantic Relations between Questions and Answers. In *SemEval-2016*. ACL, 2016.

[4] S. Hochreiter and J. Schmidhuber. Long short-term memory. *Neural computation*, 9(8):1735–1780, 1997.

[5] B. Hu, Z. Lu, H. Li, and Q. Chen. Convolutional neural network architectures for matching natural language sentences. In *NIPS*. 2014.

[6] T. Joachims. Optimizing search engines using clickthrough data. In *KDD*. ACM, 2002.

[7] N. Kalchbrenner, E. Grefenstette, and P. Blunsom. A convolutional neural network for modelling sentences. *ACL*, 2014.

[8] Y. Kim. Convolutional neural networks for sentence classification. In *EMNLP*, 2014.

[9] Z. Lu and H. Li. A deep architecture for matching short texts. In *NIPS*, 2013.

[10] C. D. Manning, M. Surdeanu, J. Bauer, J. Finkel, S. J. Bethard, and D. McClosky. The Stanford CoreNLP natural language processing toolkit. In *Proceedings of ACL: System Demonstrations*, 2014.

[11] T. Mihaylova, P. Gencheva, M. Boyanov, I. Yovcheva, T. Mihaylov, M. Hardalov, Y. Kiprov, D. Balchev, I. Koychev, P. Nakov, I. Nikolova, and G. Angelova. Super team at semeval-2016 task 3: Building a feature-rich system for community question answering. In *SemEval-2016*. ACL, 2016.

[12] T. Mikolov, I. Sutskever, K. Chen, G. S Corrado, and J. Dean. Distributed representations of words and phrases and their compositionality. In *Advances in NIPS 26*, 2013.

[13] A. Moschitti. Efficient convolution kernels for dependency and constituent syntactic trees. In *ECML*. Springer, 2006.

[14] P. Nakov, L. Màrquez, A. Moschitti, W. Magdy, H. Mubarak, A. A. Freihat, J. Glass, and B. Randeree. SemEval-2016 task 3: Community question answering. In *SemEval*. ACL, 2016.

[15] M. Nicosia, S. Filice, A. Barrón-Cedeño, I. Saleh, H. Mubarak, W. Gao, P. Nakov, G. Da San Martino, A. Moschitti, K. Darwish, L. Màrquez, S. Joty, and W. Magdy. QCRI: Answer selection for community question answering - experiments for Arabic and English. In *SemEval*, 2015.

[16] V. Punyakanok and D. Roth. The use of classifiers in sequential inference. In *NIPS*, 2001.

[17] A. Severyn and A. Moschitti. Learning to rank short text pairs with convolutional deep neural networks. In *SIGIR*. ACM, 2015.

[18] A. Severyn, M. Nicosia, and A. Moschitti. Learning adaptable patterns for passage reranking. *CoNLL-2013*, 2013.

[19] N. Srivastava, G. Hinton, A. Krizhevsky, I. Sutskever, and R. Salakhutdinov. Dropout: A simple way to prevent neural networks from overfitting. *The Journal of Machine Learning Research*, 15(1):1929–1958, 2014.

[20] K. Tymoshenko and A. Moschitti. Assessing the impact of syntactic and semantic structures for answer passages reranking. In *CIKM*. ACM, 2015.

[21] K. Tymoshenko, D. Bonadiman, and A. Moschitti. Convolutional neural networks vs. convolution kernels: Feature engineering for answer sentence reranking. In *NAACL-HLT*. ACL, 2016.

[22] M. Wang and C. D. Manning. Probabilistic tree-edit models with structured latent variables for textual entailment and question answering. In *ACL*, 2010.

[23] L. Yu, K. M. Hermann, P. Blunsom, and S. Pulman. Deep learning for answer sentence selection. *CoRR*, 2014.

A Theoretical Framework on the Ideal Number of Classifiers for Online Ensembles in Data Streams

Hamed R. Bonab*
Bilkent Information Retrieval Group
Computer Engineering Department
Bilkent University, 06800, Ankara, Turkey
hamed@bilkent.edu.tr

Fazli Can
Bilkent Information Retrieval Group
Computer Engineering Department
Bilkent University, 06800, Ankara, Turkey
canf@cs.bilkent.edu.tr

ABSTRACT

A priori determining the ideal number of component classifiers of an ensemble is an important problem. The volume and velocity of big data streams make this even more crucial in terms of prediction accuracies and resource requirements. There is a limited number of studies addressing this problem for batch mode and none for online environments. Our theoretical framework shows that using the same number of independent component classifiers as class labels gives the highest accuracy. We prove the existence of an ideal number of classifiers for an ensemble, using the weighted majority voting aggregation rule. In our experiments, we use two state-of-the-art online ensemble classifiers with six synthetic and six real-world data streams. The violation of providing independent component classifiers for our theoretical framework makes determining the exact ideal number of classifiers nearly impossible. We suggest upper bounds for the number of classifiers that gives the highest accuracy. An important implication of our study is that comparing online ensemble classifiers should be done based on these ideal values, since comparing based on a fixed number of classifiers can be misleading.

Keywords

Big data stream; ensemble size; weighted majority voting

1. INTRODUCTION

Online ensembles for data stream classification has gained a great importance over the past few years in big data research. Extensive empirical results show that combining a suitable number of classifiers improves the accuracy of predictions, versus a single classifier [3, 4, 5, 14]. However, increasing the number of component classifiers of an ensemble results in greater computational resource requirements in terms of time and memory. The high volume and velocity of big data streams make this even more crucial in online environments.

There is a limited number of studies for batch mode ensembles. Latinne et al. [12] propose a simple empirical procedure for limiting the number of classifiers based on the McNemar non-parametric test of significance. Similar approaches [2, 8], suggest a range of 10 to 20 base classifiers for bagging depending on its particular base classifier and dataset. Oshiro et al. [13] cast the idea that, there is an ideal number of component classifiers within an ensemble, which exploiting more base classifiers would bring no significant performance gain and would only increase computational costs, using the weighted average area under the ROC curve (AUC) and some dataset density metrics. Fumera et al. [7, 8] apply an existing analytical framework for the analysis of linearly combined classifiers of bagging, using misclassification probability. Hernández-Lobato et al. [10] suggest a statistical algorithm for determining the size of an ensemble, by estimating required number of classifiers for obtaining stable aggregated predictions, using majority voting.

The contributions of our work are the following: (a) To the best of our knowledge, we are first to study the number of component classifiers of online ensembles using weighted majority voting; (b) We theoretically model online ensembles for data streams using a geometric framework and prove that for the highest prediction accuracy, the number of classifiers should be the same as the number of class labels; (c) We experimentally examine our hypothesis, using two state-of-the-art ensemble classifiers and several synthetic and real-world data streams. We show the existence of the ideal number of classifiers; however, the violation of providing independent component classifiers makes exactly determining the ideal number of classifiers nearly impossible; and (d) We suggest an upper bound for the number of classifiers that gives the highest accuracy. Our study also shows that comparing online ensemble classifiers should be done based on these ideal values, as comparing based on a fixed number of classifiers can be misleading.

2. A GEOMETRIC FRAMEWORK

Motivation. We propose a framework for studying the theoretical side of online ensemble classifiers over data streams, based on [6]. Its general schema is presented in Fig. 1. Individual scores of component classifiers are modeled in a spatial environment as vectors for establishing a relationship between geometric features of vectors, and their corresponding effectiveness. Euclidean norm is used as the loss function for optimization purposes. According to [9], there are clear

*Present e-mail address: hamed.bonab@stonybrook.edu

CIKM'16 , October 24-28, 2016, Indianapolis, IN, USA
© 2016 ACM. ISBN 978-1-4503-4073-1/16/10... $15.00
DOI: http://dx.doi.org/10.1145/2983323.2983907

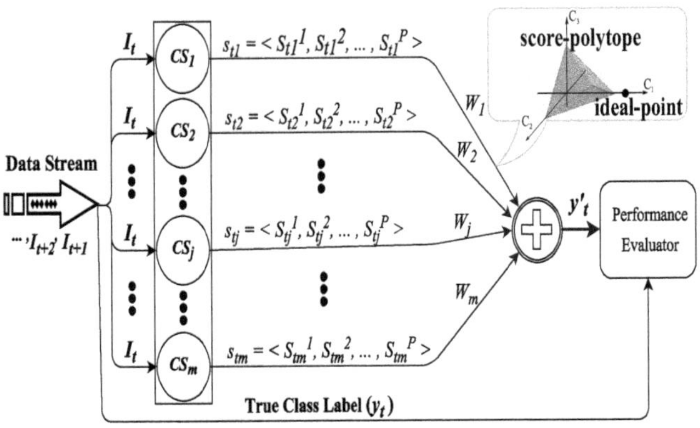

Figure 1: Schema of our geometric framework.

advantages of using the Euclidean norm for the LSQ solution. For aggregation, we use the weighted majority voting rule.

Optimum Weight Assignment. As shown in Fig. 1, we have an ensemble of component classifiers $\xi = \{CS_1, CS_2, \cdots, CS_m\}$. We assume that all $CS_j (1 \leq j \leq m)$ are independent of each other. For continual updates of the weights, we use the n latest instances $I = \{I_1, I_2, \cdots, I_n\}$, as an instance window, where I_n is the latest instance and all of the true class labels are available, $C = \{C_1, C_2, \cdots, C_p\}$. For each instance $I_i (1 \leq i \leq n)$, each component classifier $CS_j (1 \leq j \leq m)$ has a score-vector of $s_{ij} =< S_{ij}^1, S_{ij}^2, \cdots, S_{ij}^p >$. Mapping all score-vectors of I_i into a p-dimensional space, builds a polytope which we call the *score-polytope* of I_i. For the true class label of I_i we have $o_i =< O_i^1, O_i^2, \cdots, O_i^p >$ as the ideal-point. We aim to find the optimum weight vector $w =< W_1, W_2, \cdots, W_m >$, to minimize the distance between the score-polytope and ideal-point. Using the squared Euclidean norm as our measure of closeness for the linear least squares problem (LSQ) results

$$\min_{w} ||o - Sw||_2^2 \tag{1}$$

Where for each instance I_i, $S \in \mathbb{R}^{m \times p}$ is the matrix with relevance scores s_{ij} in each row, w is the vector of weights to be determined, and o is the vector of the ideal-point [9]. Since we have n instances in our window, we use the following function for our optimization solution.

$$f(W_1, W_2, \cdots, W_m) = \sum_{i=1}^{n} \sum_{k=1}^{p} (\sum_{j=1}^{m} (W_j S_{ij}^k) - O_i^k)^2 \tag{2}$$

Taking a partial derivation over $W_q (1 \leq q \leq m)$, setting the gradient to zero $\nabla f = 0$, and finding optimum points give us the optimum weight vector. Letting the following summations as a_{qj} and d_q

$$a_{qj} = \sum_{i=1}^{n} \sum_{k=1}^{p} S_{iq}^k S_{ij}^k, \quad (1 \leq q, j \leq m) \tag{3}$$

$$d_q = \sum_{i=1}^{n} \sum_{k=1}^{p} O_i^k S_{iq}^k, \quad (1 \leq q \leq m) \tag{4}$$

lead to m linear equations with m variables (weights). The proper weights in the following matrix equation are our intended optimum weight vector. Briefly, $Aw = d$, where A is the coefficients matrix and d is the remainder vector.

$$\begin{bmatrix} a_{11} & a_{12} & \cdots & a_{1m} \\ a_{21} & a_{22} & \cdots & a_{2m} \\ \vdots & \vdots & \ddots & \vdots \\ a_{m1} & a_{m2} & \cdots & a_{mm} \end{bmatrix} \times \begin{bmatrix} W_1 \\ W_2 \\ \vdots \\ W_m \end{bmatrix} = \begin{bmatrix} d_1 \\ d_2 \\ \vdots \\ d_m \end{bmatrix} \tag{5}$$

Discussion. According to Eq. 3, A is a symmetric square matrix. If A has full rank, our problem has a unique solution. On the other hand, in the sense of a least squares solution [9], it is probable that A is rank-deficient, and we may not have a unique solution. Studying the properties of this matrix lead us to the following theorem.

THEOREM 1. *If the number of component classifiers is not equal to the number of class labels, $m \neq p$, then the coefficient matrix would be rank-deficient,* $\det A = 0$.

PROOF. Since we have p dimensions in our Euclidean space, p independent score vectors would be needed for the basis spanning set. Any number of vectors, m, more than p is dependent on the basis spanning set, and any number of vectors, m, less than p is insufficient for constructing the basis spanning set. □

The above theorem excludes some cases in which we cannot find optimum weights for aggregating votes. In addition, for cases where $m = p$, letting $\det A = 0$ for the parametric coefficient matrix results in some conditions that we have vote agreement, and cannot find a unique optimum weight vector. As an example, suppose that we have 2 component classifiers for a binary classification task, $m = p = 2$. Letting $\det A = 0$, will result in following equations; $S_{11}^1 + S_{12}^2 = 1$ or $S_{11}^2 + S_{12}^1 = 1$, meaning the agreement of component classifiers. This gives better insight for the commonly agreed upon idea that "the classifiers should be different from each other, otherwise the overall decision will not be better than the individual decisions" [11]. Optimum weights can be reached when we have the same number of independent and diverse component classifiers as class labels.

Conclusion. This theorem supports the idea that there is an ideal number of component classifiers for an ensemble, with which we can reach the most accurate results. Increasing or decreasing the number of classifiers from this ideal point would deteriorate predictions. We refer to this situation as "the law of diminishing returns in ensemble construction." Our framework suggests the number of class labels of a dataset as the ideal number of component classifiers, with the premise that they generate independent scores. However, real-world datasets and existing ensemble classifiers do not guarantee this premise most of the time. Determining the exact value of this ideal point for a given ensemble classifier, over a real-world data stream, is still a challenging problem.

3. EXPERIMENTAL SETUP

In our experiments, we show the relationship between the number of classifiers and number of class labels for 12 different data streams and 2 online ensembles. We conduct our experiments on Accuracy Updated Ensemble (AUE)[5] and Leverage Bagging (LevBag)[3] ensembles using synthetic and real-world data streams. For implementation, we used the MOA framework; for evaluation, we used the Interleaved Test-Then-Train approach [4].

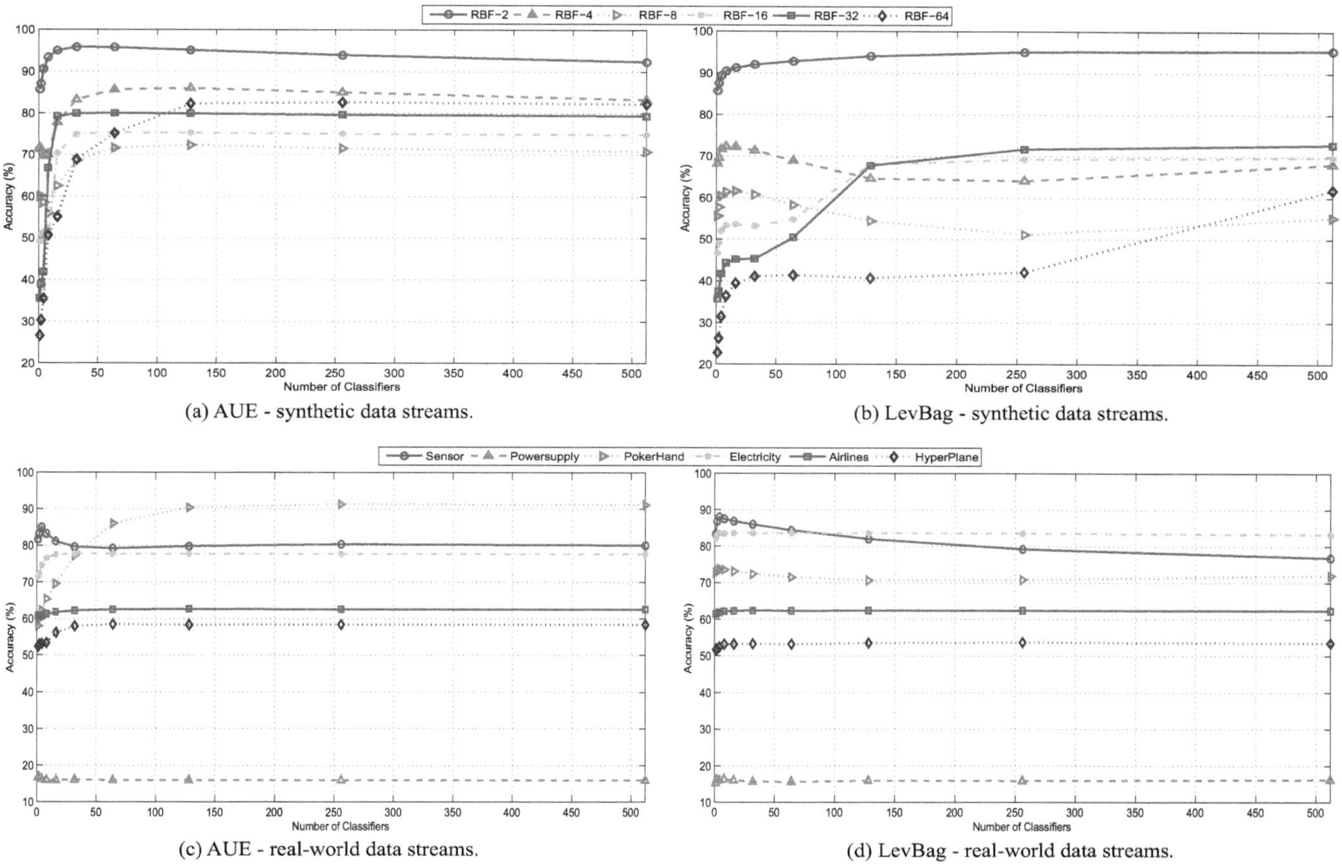

(a) AUE - synthetic data streams.

(b) LevBag - synthetic data streams.

(c) AUE - real-world data streams.

(d) LevBag - real-world data streams.

Figure 2: Prediction behavior of AUE and LevBag ensembles, in terms of accuracy, with different number of classifiers ranging from 2^0 to 2^9 by doubling at each step, for synthetic and real-world data streams.

Table 1: Summary of Real-world Data Streams

Dataset	#Instances	#Attr.	#Class Labels
Sensor [1]	2,219,803	5	54
Powersupply [1]	29,928	2	24
PokerHand [4]	1×10^7	10	10
Electricity [4]	45,312	8	2
Airlines [4]	539,383	7	2
HyperPlane [1]	1×10^7	10	5

3.1 Data Streams

There are a few real-world data streams in the literature. Finding proper data streams, where the number of class labels is the only variant, is nearly impossible.

Synthetic Data Streams. We chose the popular Random RBF generator, since it is capable of generating data streams with an arbitrary number of features and class labels [4]. Using this generator implemented in the MOA framework, we prepared 6 different datasets, each containing 1 million instances with 20 attributes. The number of class labels is chosen as 2, 4, 8, 16, 32, and 64. We reflect these in the naming of our RBF data streams (RBF-2, RBF-4, etc.).

Real-world Data Streams. We selected 6 different real-world datasets used as data streams in the literature—they all are available online for downloading [1, 4]. Table 1 gives a summary of these data streams.

3.2 Ensemble Methods

We used 2 state-of-the-art ensemble classifiers: AUE and LevBag that use the weighted majority voting and majority voting aggregation rules, respectively, and have different component classifier training strategies. We exploited Hoeffding trees as base component classifiers for both ensembles [4]. Ensemble sizes in terms of the number of base classifiers grow exponentially from 2^0 to 2^9, by doubling at each step. This range is chosen to show the behavior in a large-scale of possibilities.

4. RESULTS AND DISCUSSION

Observations. Fig. 2 shows the impact of doubling the ensemble sizes on the accuracy of predictions. We plot the experimental results with the real numerical scale rather than the logarithmic, since it provides a better exposition of the results. In each plot, the existence of a peak point in which an online ensemble reaches its maximum accuracy is well-illustrated. For the ever-increasing cases, we believe that there is a peak point out of our range. Computational requirements, in term of CPU time and memory usage, are roughly doubled with doubling ensemble size.

Following our theoretical expectations, AUE provides higher consistency compared to LevBag, as seen in Fig. 2-(a) vs. (b) and (c) vs. (d). Since synthetic data streams have a large number of attributes, 20, the possibility of training independent and diverse component classifiers is high [11,

Table 2: Highest/Peak Accuracy Values in Percentage and the Corresponding Number of Component Classifiers of Ensembles for Different Data Streams

	AUE		LevBag	
Dataset	Acc.	#Classifiers	Acc.	#Classifiers
RBF-2	95.80	32	95.44	512
RBF-4	86.05	128	72.27	8
RBF-8	72.33	128	61.58	16
RBF-16	75.33	64	69.76	512
RBF-32	79.80	64	72.77	512
RBF-64	82.64	256	61.91	512
Sensor	84.99	4	87.99	4
Powersupply	16.74	1	16.34	8
PokerHand	91.30	256	73.82	4
Electricity	77.73	32	83.66	16
Airlines	62.63	128	62.43	256
HyperPlane	58.47	64	53.68	256

13]. For example, Fig. 2-(a) shows that for a lower number of class labels (RBF-2, -4, and -8) the results are highly consistent with our theoretical expectations. On the other hand, for larger number of class labels (RBF-16, -32, and -64) we observe lower consistency. The impact of the number of attributes and class labels is also true for real-world data streams: PokerHand, HyperPlane, and Electricity provides higher consistency than those of Sensor, Powersupply, and Airlines.

Statistical Analysis. Table 2 shows the highest/peak accuracy values and corresponding number of classifiers for both ensembles. We conducted the Wilcoxon signed-ranks test for further analysis of our results, with $\alpha = 0.05$. Comparing the accuracy peaks of AUE and LevBag results in 10 positive and 2 negative differences. The two-tailed probability value, $P = 0.027$, is less than 0.05; it can be accepted that the accuracy peaks of AUE are statistically significantly higher than those of LevBag. Comparing the number of component classifiers on these peak values results in 4 positive and 7 negative differences, with two-tailed probability value, $P = 0.147$. While there is no statistically significant difference between the numbers of component classifiers for the two algorithms, AUE reaches higher peaks compared to LevBag. Hence, comparing ensembles based on a fixed number of component classifiers can be misleading. However, studies based on a fixed number of classifiers can be acceptable since in such cases all ensemble methods can be equally disadvantaged. For example, without ensuring fairness, comparing the accuracy of AUE and LevBag ensembles each with 8 or 16 base classifiers, which are in the range of conventional comparisons [5, 14], results in no statistically significant difference in our experiments.

We compared the observed peak accuracy values of both ensembles using the non-parametric Friedman statistical test with $\alpha = 0.05$ and $F(2, 22)$. The resulting two-tailed probability value, $P = 0.032$, rejects the null-hypothesis. The multiple comparisons show that the theoretical number of classifiers are statistically significantly different from the practical peak accuracy values of both algorithms. However, multiplying these theoretical number of classifiers by a constant value, in our case 2, makes the differences statistically insignificant. This can be used for obtaining upper-bounds of the ideal number of classifiers for a given data stream and ensemble classifier.

5. CONCLUSION AND FUTURE WORK

Our model showed that: (1) Theoretically, using the same number of independent component classifiers as class labels gives the highest prediction accuracy; (2) Practically, due to the violation of independency of component classifiers, determining these peak values is nearly impossible. However, upper bounds can be considered for this problem and that needs further investigation. An important implication of our study is that comparing online ensemble classifiers should be done based on these peak values, since comparing based on a fixed number of classifiers can be misleading.

6. ACKNOWLEDGEMENTS

We appreciate Jon M. Patton from Miami Univ. of OH, and Alper Can for their valuable comments on this work.

7. REFERENCES

[1] X. Zhu, Stream Data Mining Repository, http://www.cse.fau.edu/ xqzhu/stream.html, 2010.
[2] E. Bauer and R. Kohavi. An empirical comparison of voting classification algorithms: Bagging, boosting, and variants. *Mach. Learn.*, 36(1-2):105–139, 1999.
[3] A. Bifet, G. Holmes, and B. Pfahringer. Leveraging bagging for evolving data streams. In *ECML PKDD*, pages 135–150, 2010.
[4] A. Bifet, G. Holmes, B. Pfahringer, R. Kirkby, and R. Gavaldà. New ensemble methods for evolving data streams. In *ACM SIGKDD*, pages 139–148, 2009.
[5] D. Brzezinski and J. Stefanowski. Reacting to different types of concept drift: The accuracy updated ensemble algorithm. *IEEE TNNLS*, 25(1):81–94, 2014.
[6] L.-W. Chan. Weighted least square ensemble networks. In *IJCNN*, volume 2, pages 1393–1396, 1999.
[7] G. Fumera and F. Roli. A theoretical and experimental analysis of linear combiners for multiple classifier systems. *IEEE TPAMI*, 27(6):942–956, 2005.
[8] G. Fumera, F. Roli, and A. Serrau. A theoretical analysis of bagging as a linear combination of classifiers. *IEEE TPAMI*, 30(7):1293–1299, 2008.
[9] P. C. Hansen, V. Pereyra, and G. Scherer. *Least Squares Data Fitting with Applications.* JHU Press, 2013.
[10] D. Hernández-Lobato, G. Martínez-Muñoz, and A. Suárez. How large should ensembles of classifiers be? *Patt. Recog.*, 46(5):1323–1336, 2013.
[11] L. I. Kuncheva and C. J. Whitaker. Measures of diversity in classifier ensembles and their relationship with the ensemble accuracy. *Mach. Learn.*, 51(2):181–207, 2003.
[12] P. Latinne, O. Debeir, and C. Decaestecker. Limiting the number of trees in random forests. In *MCS*, pages 178–187, 2001.
[13] T. M. Oshiro, P. S. Perez, and J. A. Baranauskas. How many trees in a random forest? In *MLDM*, pages 154–168, 2012.
[14] N. C. Oza and S. J. Russell. Experimental comparisons of online and batch versions of bagging and boosting. In *ACM SIGKDD*, pages 359–364, 2001.

User Modeling on Twitter with WordNet Synsets and DBpedia Concepts for Personalized Recommendations

Guangyuan Piao
Insight Centre for Data Analytics, NUI Galway
IDA Business Park, Galway, Ireland
guangyuan.piao@insight-centre.org

John G. Breslin
Insight Centre for Data Analytics, NUI Galway
IDA Business Park, Galway, Ireland
john.breslin@nuigalway.ie

ABSTRACT

User modeling of individual users on the Social Web platforms such as Twitter plays a significant role in providing personalized recommendations and filtering interesting information from social streams. Recently, researchers proposed the use of concepts (e.g., DBpedia entities) for representing user interests instead of word-based approaches, since Knowledge Bases such as DBpedia provide cross-domain background knowledge about concepts, and thus can be used for extending user interest profiles. Even so, not all concepts can be covered by a Knowledge Base, especially in the case of microblogging platforms such as Twitter where new concepts/topics emerge everyday.

In this short paper, instead of using concepts alone, we propose using *synsets* from WordNet and *concepts* from DBpedia for representing user interests. We evaluate our proposed user modeling strategies by comparing them with other bag-of-concepts approaches. The results show that using synsets and concepts together for representing user interests improves the quality of user modeling significantly in the context of link recommendations on Twitter.

Keywords

User Modeling; Personalization; User Interest Profiles

1. INTRODUCTION

User modeling on Social Web platforms such as Twitter, which aims at building user interest profiles, has been proven to be an important way for capturing user interests from User-Generated Content (UGC). The generated user interest profiles then can be used for dealing with the *information overload* problem for providing personalized recommendations. Defining a way of representing user interests is an essential step in building user interest profiles. Previous work either used *bag-of-words*, *topic modeling* or *bag-of-concepts* approach to represent user interests. Bag-of-concepts approach uses concepts for representing user interests. For example, given the first sample tweet posted by a user named `Bob` in Table 1, we know that the user is interested in *entities* such as `dbpedia`[1]`:The_Black_Keys` and `dbpedia:The_Wombats`. The *bag-of-concepts* approach has been preferred in recent studies [10] so as to exploit background knowledge of concepts from a Knowledge Base (KB) (defined as the combination of an ontology and instances of the classes in the ontology) for extending user interests. For instance, based on the background knowledge from DBpedia, we can further infer that `Bob` is interested in `dbpedia:Indie_rock` as both `dbpedia:The_Wombats` and `dbpedia:The_Black_Keys` are pointing to `dbpedia:Indie_rock` via the property `dbpedia-owl`[2]`:genre`. In what follows, by a *concept* we mean an *entity* or *category* from a KB (e.g., DBpedia[3]) for representing user interests.

Table 1: Two sample tweets posted by Bob

#1	*My Top 3 #lastfm Artists: Eagles of Death Metal(14), The Black Keys(6) & The Wombats(6)*
#2	*Just completed a 3.89 km ride. We're gonna need more...*

Although Knowledge Bases such as DBpedia provide rich semantics from background knowledge for representing and propagating user interests, they cannot cover all existing and emerging concepts. In addition, Knowledge Bases lack full coverage for the lexicographic senses of lemmas, which can be provided by WordNet instead. For example, in the case of the second tweet posted by `Bob`, we cannot extract any concept from the tweet. To circumvent this drawback, we propose using WordNet[4] synsets and DBpedia concepts together for representing user interests. Synsets in WordNet are unordered sets of synonyms - words that denote the same concept and are interchangeable in many contexts. By doing so, from the second tweet, we can extract synsets such as: s_1=[*kilometer, kilometre, km, klick (a metric unit of length equal to 1000 meters (or 0.621371 miles))*] and s_2 = [*drive, ride (a journey in a vehicle (usually an automobile))*], which denote the user interests that would be missed if a concepts-alone approach was used.

Therefore, the goal of the study is to investigate the effectiveness of using WordNet synsets and DBpedia concepts

CIKM'16, October 24-28, 2016, Indianapolis, IN, USA

DOI: http://dx.doi.org/10.1145/2983323.2983908

[1]The prefix `dbpedia` denotes http://dbpedia.org/resource/
[2]The prefix `dbpedia-owl` denotes http://dbpedia.org/ontology/
[3]http://wiki.dbpedia.org
[4]https://wordnet.princeton.edu

together for representing user interests. Proposed user modeling strategies are evaluated in the context of link recommendations on Twitter, by comparing our strategies and bag-of-concepts approaches using concepts alone for user modeling.

2. RELATED WORK

A line of work has been proposed to use *concept-based* representations of user interests using a KB from Linked Data (e.g., Freebase, DBpedia) [2,8,10]. This line of work goes beyond other approaches, such as *bag-of-words* [7] and *topic modeling* [4] which focus on words and cannot provide semantic information and relationships among these words. Abel et al. [1] showed that *entity-based* user interest profiles perform better than other user modeling strategies such as *hashtag-* and *topic-based* user profiles on Twitter in the context of news recommendations. Orlandi et al. [8] investigated *entity-based* user profiles and *category-based* user profiles based on the category information of entities from DBpedia. Besides a straightforward extension that gives equal weight to each extended category with respect to an entity, they also proposed a discounting strategy for those extended categories. The results based on a user study showed that *category-based* user profiles have similar performance to the *entity-based* ones and both of them outperform the *word-based* approach as a baseline. On top of that, Piao et al. [10] proposed a mixed approach using *entity-* and *category-based* user profiles and presented its effectiveness compared to other user modeling strategies. Our work differs in that we represent user interests using WordNet synsets and DBpedia concepts together instead of using concepts alone. However, as we are using synsets in addition to concepts for representing user interests, interest propagation methods that were developed for concept-based user interests profiles can be applied to our interest profiles in the same way.

3. CONTENT-BASED USER MODELING

Interest Representation. In this work, we use synsets from WordNet and concepts from DBpedia for representing the interests of users. The generic model for interest profiles representing users is specified in Definition 1.

Definition 1. The interest profile of a user $u \in U$ is a set of weighted WordNet synsets or DBpedia concepts where with respect to the given user u for an interest $i \in I$ its weight $w(u,i)$ is computed by a certain function w.

$$P_u = \{(i, w(u,i)) \mid i \in I, u \in U\} \quad (1)$$

Here, $I = \{s_1, \ldots, s_k\} \cup \{c_1, \ldots, c_m\} = \{i_1, \ldots, i_n\}$ denotes the set of synsets in WordNet and concepts in DBpedia, and U denotes users.

The process of building user interest profiles using our user modeling framework is presented in Figure 1. It consists of three main steps as follows.

Interest Extraction. As we use WordNet synsets and DBpedia concepts for representing user interests, the first step is to extract synsets and concepts from UGC. In the same way from other bag-of-concept approaches, the concepts are extracted using NLP APIs such as the Aylien API[5]. To

[5]http://aylien.com/

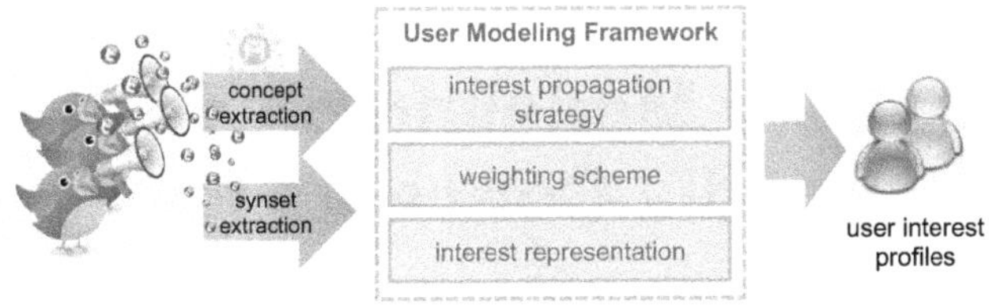

Figure 1: The process of generating user interest profiles

Algorithm 1: The WordNet-based WSD algorithm for tweets

input : a polysemous word w in a tweet t
output: the proper synset of w

```
1  C ← {w_1, ..., w_n}; // C is the context of w,
       i.e., other words in t with w
2  X ← {s_1, ..., s_k}; // X is the set of candidate
       synsets for w returned by WordNet
3  s ← null; // s is the synset to be returned
4  score ← 0; // score is the similarity score
       assigned to s regarding the context C
5  T ← ∅; // T is the set of all candidate
       synsets for all words in C
6  for w_j ∈ C do
7      if POS(w_j) = POS(w) then
8          X_j ← {s_j1, ..., s_jm};
9          T ← T ∪ X_j;
10 for s_i ∈ X do
11     for s_h ∈ T do
12         score_ih ← SINSIM(s_i, s_h); // computing
               similarity scores between s_i and
               every synset s_h ∈ T
13         if score_ih ≥ score then
14             score ← score_ih;
15             s ← s_i; // s is the synset s_i ∈ X
                   having the highest similarity
                   score regarding the synsets T
16 return s
```

extract WordNet synsets, a WordNet-based Word Sense Disambiguation (WSD) algorithm [3] (see Algorithm 1), which was developed in the context of movie recommendations, has been adapted. This method extracts the WordNet synset for a word in terms of a context. In our scenario, the context of a word w is the set of words appearing in the same tweet with w (line 1) and having the same Part-Of-Speech (POS) as w. For a given tweet, our user modeling framework preprocesses with tokenization, POS tagging and lemmatization, and then uses Algorithm 1 for extracting all synsets for words based on their context. The similarity between any two synsets in Algorithm 1 (line 12) is measured as follows [5]:

$$SIMSIM(s_a, s_b) = -\log(N_p/2D) \quad (2)$$

where N_p is the number of nodes in the shortest path p from s_a and s_b, and D is the maximum depth of the taxonomy.

Weighting Scheme. We use the Term Frequency - Inverse Document Frequency (TF-IDF) as the weighting scheme for synsets and concepts: $w(u,i) = f(u,i) \times \log \frac{M}{m_i}$, where

$f(u,i)$ denotes the frequency of a synset or concept i in a user's tweets, M is the total number of users, and m_i is the number of users interested in i (i.e., who mentioned i in their tweets). Finally, we further normalize user interest profiles so that the sum of all weights in a profile is equal to 1: $\sum_{i \in I} w(u,i) = 1$.

Interest Propagation. As we are using both WordNet synsets and DBpedia concepts for user modeling, we can exploit background knowledge from DBpedia with respect to the extracted concepts for propagating user interests using existing methods. We use an extension strategy using category information from DBpedia for concepts with a discounting strategy for the extended interests as follows [10]:

$$CategoryDiscount = \frac{1}{\alpha} \times \frac{1}{\log(SP)} \times \frac{1}{\log(SC)} \quad (3)$$

where: *SP = Set of Pages belonging to the Category, SC = Set of Sub-Categories. SP* and *SC* discount the category in the context of DBpedia. Thus, an extended category is discounted more heavily if it is a general one (i.e., the category has a great number of pages or sub-categories). In addition, α is a parameter for discounting the extension from original user interest profiles (we set $\alpha = 2$ as in [10]).

4. EXPERIMENTAL EVALUATION

Our main goal here is to analyze and compare the different user modeling strategies in the context of link recommendations. We do not aim to optimize the recommendation quality, but are interested in comparing the quality achieved by the same recommendation algorithm when inputting user profiles based on different user modeling strategies. In the same way as in existing literature, we adopt a lightweight content-based algorithm where the recommendation algorithm recommends links according to their *cosine* similarity with a given user profile [1, 10].

Definition 2. Recommendation Algorithm: given a user profile P_u and a set of candidate links N = $\{P_{i1}, ..., P_{in}\}$, which are represented via profiles using the same vector representation, the recommendation algorithm ranks the candidate items according to their cosine similarity to the user profile.

Dataset. The dataset used in this experiment is from [10]. The Twitter dataset includes all tweets published by 480 *active* users on Twitter (a user is *active* if the user published at least 100 posts [6,10]). The main details of the dataset are presented in Table 2. We further selected users who shared at least one link (URL) in their tweets during the last two weeks. We only consider links having at least four topics (concepts) to filter out non-topical links (e.g., links sharing current location via Swarm[6]). 322 out of 480 users met the criteria who published 247,676 tweets in total.

4.1 Evaluation methodology

The ground truth of links, which we consider as *relevant* for a specific user, was given by links shared via the user's tweets within the last two weeks. We used the ground truth links from 322 users, as well as the links shared by other users but not shared by 322 users in the dataset, for constructing candidate links. In total, the ground truth of links consists of 3,959 links, and the candidate set of links consists of 15,440 distinct links. Tweets older than two weeks (i.e., excluding those from the last two weeks, as used for ground truth), were used for constructing user profiles.

[6]https://www.swarmapp.com

Table 2: Dataset statistics

# of users	480
total # of tweets	348,554
average time span of tweets per user (days)	471
average # of tweets per user	726
average # of tweets per user per day	7.2

Given the ground truth and the candidate set of links, we applied different user modeling strategies together with the recommendation algorithm (see Definition 2) to provide personalized link recommendations. The quality of the top-N recommendations was measured via the following metrics, which have been used in previous studies [1, 2, 8].

- **MRR** The *MRR* (Mean Reciprocal Rank) indicates at which rank the first item *relevant* to the user occurs on average.
- **S@N** The Success at rank N (S@N) stands for the mean probability that a relevant item occurs within the top-N of the ranking.
- **R@N** The Recall at rank N (R@N) represents the mean probability that *relevant* items are successfully retrieved within the top-N recommendations.
- **P@N** The Precision at rank N (P@N) represents the mean probability that retrieved items within the top-N recommendations are *relevant* to the user.

We will focus on the top-10 list of recommendations for success, recall and precision as our recommendation system will list 10 link recommendations to a user. The *bootstrapped paired t-test*, which is an alternative to the paired t-test when the assumption of normality of the method is in doubt, is used for testing the significance where the significance level was set to 0.05 unless otherwise noted.

4.2 Results

To evaluate whether our new synset & concept-based user interest profiles outperform concept-based profiles, we use the concept-based user interest profiles (`P(concept)`) [1] and extended `P(concept)` using background knowledge from DBpedia (`P(concept+category)`) [10] as two baselines. Our approach is represented as `P(synset&concept)`, which uses synset and concepts for representing user interests. In addition, the synset & concept-based user interest profiles extended with background knowledge are denoted as `P(synset&concept+category)`.

The results of link recommendations based on different user modeling strategies in terms of aforementioned four different evaluation metrics are presented in Figure 2. As we can see from the figure, there is a significant improvement for `P(synset&concept)` and `P(synset&concept+category)` compared to the concept-based approaches (`P(concept)` and `P(concept+category)`, $p < 0.05$). For example, the quality of recommendations is improved by `P(synset&concept)`

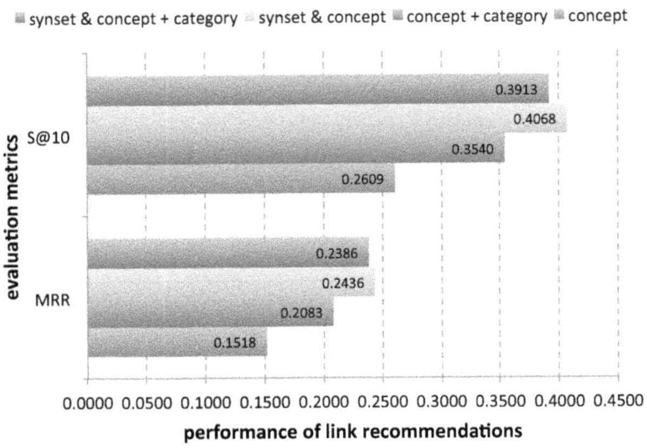

(a) MRR and success rate

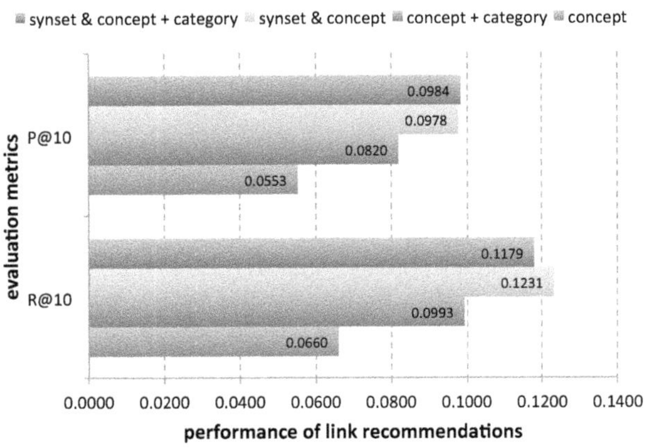

(b) Precision and recall

Figure 2: Performance of link recommendations based on different user modeling strategies

56% and 61% in terms of S@10 and MRR, 77% and 87% in terms of P@10 and R@10, compared to using `P(concept)`. Similarly, using `P(synset&concept+category)` improves the recommendation performance 11% and 15% in terms of S@10 and MRR, 20% and 19% in terms of P@10 and R@10 compared to using `P(concept+category)`. This indicates that using synsets and concepts together is beneficial for user modeling on Twitter instead of using concepts alone.

It is also interesting to observe that `P(synset&concept)`, which uses synsets and concepts together without any interest propagation, has competitive performance compared to the one using the same interest representation and propagating interests with background knowledge (`P(synset&concept+category)`).

5. CONCLUSIONS

In this paper, we were interested in examining if using synsets from WordNet and concepts from DBpedia for representing user interests can improve the quality of user modeling on Twitter. We presented our user modeling strategies using both synsets and concepts and evaluated them by comparing to other concept-based strategies in the context of link recommendations on Twitter. The study results showed that using synsets and concepts together for representing user interests improves the quality of user modeling significantly. In addition, user profiles with a rich interest representation without any interest propagation (`P(synset&concept)`) can provide competitive performance compared to `P(synset&concept+category)`. Future studies will focus on investigating user modeling strategies considering other dimensions (e.g., temporal dynamics of user interests) together [9].

6. ACKNOWLEDGMENTS

This publication has emanated from research conducted with the financial support of Science Foundation Ireland (SFI) under Grant Number SFI/12/RC/2289 (Insight Centre for Data Analytics).

7. REFERENCES

[1] F. Abel, Q. Gao, G.-J. Houben, and K. Tao. Analyzing user modeling on twitter for personalized news recommendations. In *User Modeling, Adaption and Personalization*, pages 1–12. Springer, 2011.

[2] F. Abel, C. Hauff, G.-J. Houben, and K. Tao. Leveraging User Modeling on the Social Web with Linked Data. In *Web Engineering SE - 31*, pages 378–385. Springer, 2012.

[3] M. Degemmis, P. Lops, and G. Semeraro. A content-collaborative recommender that exploits WordNet-based user profiles for neighborhood formation. *User Modeling and User-Adapted Interaction*, 17(3):217–255, 2007.

[4] M. Harvey, F. Crestani, and M. J. Carman. Building User Profiles from Topic Models for Personalised Search. In *Proceedings of the 22nd ACM international conference on Information & Knowledge Management*, pages 2309–2314, 2013.

[5] C. Leacock and M. Chodorow. Combining Local Context and WordNet Similarity for Word Sense Identification. *An Electronic Lexical Database*, pages 265–283, 1998.

[6] C. Lu, W. Lam, and Y. Zhang. Twitter user modeling and tweets recommendation based on Wikipedia concept graph. In *Workshops at the Twenty-Sixth AAAI Conference on Artificial Intelligence*, 2012.

[7] A. Mislove, B. Viswanath, K. P. Gummadi, and P. Druschel. You are who you know: inferring user profiles in online social networks. In *Proceedings of the third ACM international conference on Web search and data mining*, pages 251–260. ACM, 2010.

[8] F. Orlandi, J. Breslin, and A. Passant. Aggregated, interoperable and multi-domain user profiles for the social web. In *Proceedings of the 8th International Conference on Semantic Systems*, pages 41–48. ACM, 2012.

[9] G. Piao. Towards Comprehensive User Modeling on the Social Web for Personalized Link Recommendations. In *Proceedings of the 2016 Conference on User Modeling Adaptation and Personalization*, UMAP '16, pages 333–336, New York, NY, USA, 2016. ACM.

[10] G. Piao and J. G. Breslin. Analyzing Aggregated Semantics-enabled User Modeling on Google+ and Twitter for Personalized Link Recommendations. In *User Modeling, Adaptation, and Personalization*, pages 105–109. ACM, 2016.

Improving Entity Ranking for Keyword Queries

John Foley, Brendan O'Connor & James Allan
Center for Intelligent Information Retrieval
College of Information and Computer Sciences
University of Massachusetts Amherst
{jfoley, brenocon, allan}@cs.umass.edu

ABSTRACT

Knowledge bases about entities are an important part of modern information retrieval systems. A strong ranking of entities can be used to enhance query understanding and document retrieval or can be presented as another vertical to the user.

Given a keyword query, our task is to provide a ranking of the entities present in the collection of interest. We are particularly interested in approaches to this problem that generalize to different knowledge bases and different collections. In the past, this kind of problem has been explored in the enterprise domain through Expert Search. Recently, a dataset was introduced for entity ranking from news and web queries from more general TREC collections.

Approaches from prior work leverage a wide variety of lexical resources: e.g., natural language processing and relations in the knowledge base. We address the question of whether we can achieve competitive performance with minimal linguistic resources.

We propose a set of features that do not require index-time entity linking, and demonstrate competitive performance on the new dataset. As this paper is the first non-introductory work to leverage this new dataset, we also find and correct certain aspects of the benchmark. To support a fair evaluation, we collect 38% more judgments and contribute annotator agreement information.

1. INTRODUCTION

Entities are the people, places, and concepts that exist in the world and in a growing variety of knowledge bases (e.g., YAGO [17], DBPedia [1]). These entities are often naturally related to users' information needs. Some queries that are more factual in nature (e.g., "how tall is Dilma Rousseff", or "what is Petrobras?") can even be answered directly from these knowledge bases. In contrast, queries that still focus on entities but that have a deeper information need, (e.g., "politicians implicated in operation lava jato") could possibly be answered by a very rich knowledge base, but could also be satisfied by understanding the relevant entities within a target collection, such as a news or web corpora.

In this work, we explore methods for ranking general-knowledge entities in a target collection in response to a short keyword query. Because we are interested in alternate domains and languages, we focus on developing a strong, simple approach to this problem that reduces the amount of linguistic resources needed for system development.

There is a large amount of recent work that automates the search and ranking of collection and query-relevant entities, particularly to support search tasks [9, 16, 26, 28, 21]. Even earlier, in the TREC Enterprise track, a similar problem was explored: finding people within a corpus that would be best to answer a particular question [7, 24, 3, 2].

Until recently, there was no dataset to explore this problem intrinsically on general web entities. Schuhmacher et al. introduced a new dataset based on the TREC Robust04 and Web13/14 data [25], and evaluated a learning-to-rank approach based upon features of entities linked in pseudo-relevant documents. These entity links could be compared to the sort of document-person co-occurrence or authorship information used in expert search.

The approach presented in Schuhmacher et al. is based around document-entity links and is quite successful [25]. We found that running the recommended entity linker was computationally prohibitive for our needs. While other entity linkers might be more efficient, generalizing to new languages is an open research area [18, 19, 15]. In particular: the organizers of TAC-KBP observe that a 90% linking accuracy requires that about 20,000 query mentions be labeled for training [19].

Two questions motivate our work:

1. Can we build a competitive entity ranking approach with only dictionary-based entity recognition [5] and then resolve ambiguity at query-time?

2. Can we minimize the linguistic, lexical, and knowledge-base resources needed to implement such an approach?

In this work, we describe an approach that does not rely upon entity linking, yet performs remarkably well. We believe this indicates that we can create entity ranking systems in less-studied domains: especially on private data (e.g., expert search, a corporation's email, e-Discovery) and on low-resource languages (e.g., the Cherokee language Wikipedia has only 720 articles[1].

[1] http://wikipedia.org/wiki/List_of_Wikipedias

CIKM'16, October 24-28, 2016, Indianapolis, IN, USA
© 2016 ACM. ISBN 978-1-4503-4073-1/16/10...$15.00
DOI: http://dx.doi.org/10.1145/2983323.2983909

2. ENTITY-TAGGING

We describe a simple tagging procedure that allows us to build up document-entity relationships without actually performing entity linking. This is important because although there has been substantial research on entity linking [23, 13], constructing an entity linker for novel types of entities or novel languages still requires non-trivial engineering and research effort [19, 15].

To give a further sense of the inherent ambiguity of our approach, and to demonstrate that this is not an alternative to entity-linking in the general case, we present the results of our system's tagger on the headline from a news article within the Robust04 corpus in Figure 1.

Figure 1: Actual output created by our tagging system. The number on each brace represents the number of entries in DBPedia with that title (before disambiguation terms). "HEAT" links to 26 possible articles, including albums, songs, and temperature but "HEAT WAVE" links to only 9 such articles.

We hypothesize that this dictionary-based *tagging* is sufficient for use in entity ranking since other documents that are related to the query (e.g., "el nino") can help us determine in what sense these mentions were intended ("HEAT" is temperature, not music), and ultimately, what entities are actually relevant to the query. Our approach does not actually need to know which entity was in any single document.

Compared to the output of a traditional entity linking system, which generates a single link for each candidate span, the output of our tagging approach is a bipartite graph of "title mentions" and entities. Our scoring models operate over these bipartite graphs in top ranked documents. An advantage of our approach is that despite having a high false-positive rate, it is not limited to entities of types supported by existing entity linkers.

2.1 Performance Implications

As a simple demonstration, we observed that our method is capable of tagging the half-million news documents in the Robust04 corpus in six minutes on a single core desktop computer, whereas the processing of a popular NER [22] toolkit on that corpus took more than 20 hours. These numbers, while anecdotal, at least suggest that our method would likely be more efficient than any existing solutions.

We believe that efficiency is necessary to an approach that generalizes to an evolving knowledge base: if the knowledge base is changing, you want it to be efficient to re-tag documents to incorporate recent changes.

3. ENTITY SCORING MODELS

In this section, we develop features for a model that will help us relate a users' query q, the pseudo-relevant documents in a target collection, and the entities in a "knowledge-base". Because we are interested in generalizing to evolving or private domains, we model our knowledge base as a collection of textual records, rather than a large collection of relations, where each record refers to an entity e.

Having previously tagged our documents to reflect all the possibly mentioned entities e, we can now derive scores that reflect their importance based on their occurrence in the knowledge base $K(e,q)$, and in the top-relevant documents D_q. Our features each make an assumption that some sort of similarity can be created between an entity record e, and the user's query q. In the case that this is not possible, we briefly explore our features under the assumption that our knowledge base similarity function is equal to a constant, the no-KB case: $K_{\text{NONE}}(e,q) = 1$. Obviously this is weaker than assuming we have a language model similarity between our query and its knowledge-base entry. We further explore $K_{\text{ABS}}(e,q)$ and $K_{\text{WIKI}}(e,q)$ which correspond to only abstracts and full wikipedia pages.

Now we focus on leveraging the information in D_q, or the set of top documents under the retrieval model score $S(d,q)$ where d is an individual document, and q is our query.

We additionally have some other sources of information: the bag of entities probability for a document $M(e,d) = freq(e,d)/freq(*,d)$, and the collection-discounted version of the above: $M_D(e,d) = M(e,d)/(freq(e,*)/freq(*,*))$. M captures if the entity is frequent within a document, normalized for length, and M_D captures whether an entity is frequently in a document normalized to the collection. The latter naturally captures the idea of stop-entities, such as "The".

Note that we base our features loosely on the term-weighting function Relevance Modeling [20], with entities substituted for terms in the top relevant documents, and with additional discounting, or alternate combinations of cross-document importances.

First we have a comparison between giving importance to high-frequency entity occurrences $M(e,d)$, and entity occurrences that occur proportionally more locally than globally: $M_D(e,d)$. Both formulations capture important information.

$$f_1(e,q) = \sum_{d \in D_q} K(e,q)S(d,q)M(e,d) \tag{1}$$

$$f_2(e,q) = \sum_{d \in D_q} K(e,q)S(d,q)M_D(e,d) \tag{2}$$

Then we have our "product" features, which discount entities that do not occur in many documents much more strongly; one that mixes in the document score, and one that assumes all top documents are equally helpful. We actually calculate these products in log space in order to avoid numerical underflow.

$$f_3(e,q) = \prod_{d \in D_q} K(e,q)S(d,q)M_D(e,d) \tag{3}$$

$$f_4(e,q) = \prod_{d \in D_q} K(e,q)M_D(e,d) \tag{4}$$

We also include a document-independent feature, which is simply the knowledge-base similarity itself.

$$f_5(e,q) = K(e,q) \tag{5}$$

Given each of these five features, we can substitute our knowledge-base similarity function for our three separate cases $K_{\text{NONE}}, K_{\text{ABS}}, K_{\text{WIKI}}$. Surprisingly, we do not find that the K_{WIKI} features dominate, all different levels of query-knowledge-base similarity are important.

3.1 Static Features

Unlike previous work, we find that static, popularity priors are helpful - perhaps because we forego such features in an entity-linking step. The first static prior we add is a PageRank($\lambda = 0.15, \tau = 0.001$) feature calculated from the Wikipedia graph as specified in the textbook by Croft et al. [8]. The second feature is a popularity score derived from the FACC entity links provided for ClueWeb09 [14] (the chance a random entity is that entity).

4. EXPERIMENTAL SETUP

In these experiments, we use titles and abstracts from DBPedia[2], as reproducible preprocessing of Wikipedia.

4.1 Corrections in Evaluation Measures

In Schuhmacher et al. [25], the evaluation numbers are miscalculated because non-relevant documents were given a weight of 1, instead of 0. The measures presented in prior work are therefore inflated by 10-20%, due to this miscalculation. Numbers presented in this work are lower still due to the increased number of true relevant labels collected, as discussed in the next subsection. We re-evaluate all measures based upon ranking files.

Instead of NDCG, we choose to evaluate with mean average precision (MAP) because only one of the datasets has multilevel relevance judgments. Although our models are trained on MAP, we additionally show P@5, because we collected judgments to that depth, and the ability to use our entity ranking for an extrinsic task is likely to be dependent on high early precision.

4.2 Entity Judgment extension

We pooled our best non-learning-to-rank models (along with runs from prior work [25]) and evaluated all methods fully to a depth of five. We did this in two stages.

Initially, we created an evaluation set as a pilot evaluation: following the methodology of Schuhmacher et al. [25], we had graduate students in our lab create additional judgments while initially testing our new techniques, labeling only those documents that were entirely new to our approach, as nearly all of our top-5 documents were unjudged.

In order to obtain diversity in annotators, we had workers on Amazon's Mechanical Turk judge the (query, document) pairs from pooled runs. We limited workers to those having achieved Master's qualification, and offered $0.08 per label.

Information about the collected data is available in Table 1. The final relevance set we used involved majority-voting, where ties were broken toward relevance. We make our enhanced entity judgments available to future work[3].

5. RESULTS

We derive train/test splits using five-fold cross validation as split by the RankLib learning-to-rank software package [10]. We use the non-linear Random Forests algorithm from this package.

Surprisingly, we find acceptable performance on news even without a knowledge base using a single feature, which suggests that an approach can be somewhat successful even without rich resources. We even see quite good performance

[2]http://wiki.dbpedia.org/Downloads2015-04

[3]http://cs.umass.edu/~jfoley/cikm2016

Table 1: Analysis of judgments collected locally and on Mechanical Turk

	Robust04	ClueWeb12
Queries	25	22
Original Judgments [25]	1250	3306
Pilot Judgments	322	609
MTurk Judgments	730	1085
MTurk-MTurk agreement	75% of 48	92% of 64
Original-MTurk agreement	76% of 213	80% of 334
Pilot-MTurk agreement	78% of 309	80% of 427
Final Judgments	1946	4353

Table 2: Presentation of Results: (*) represents a statistical improvement over the previous row $p < 0.05$ with a one-tailed pairwise randomization test. All unsupervised approaches are presented above the dividing line.

	Robust04		ClueWeb12	
Model	MAP	P@5	MAP	P@5
Best K_{NONE} (f_3)	0.152	0.536	0.062	0.317
Best K_{ABS} (f_2)	0.201*	0.648*	0.142*	0.411*
Best K_{WIKI} (f_2)	0.229*	0.752*	0.246*	0.654*
RankLib	0.299*	0.712	0.249	0.764*
RankLib+Static	0.370*	0.816*	0.304*	0.782
REWQ [25]	0.406	0.792	0.300	0.845*
Fusion	0.570*	0.856*	0.391*	0.818

using only one of our features with a knowledge base similarity based on the article text (f_2), which suggests that even without any annotations or entity links, an entity ranking system of reasonable quality is possible. Going to a machine learned model and then incorporating static features both yield statistically significant improvements.

On both datasets, there is no statistical difference between our run with static features and the best run from prior work [25]. We retrained the proposed model with our expanded set of judgments, expecting some improvement, but we were unable to match the run files they provided, possibly due to the non-determinism of the algorithms in RankLib, so we compare to the most optimistic scores.

A promising result for our simpler approach is that not only are we able to tie results from prior work (RankLib+Static $\approx$ REWQ), we are able to achieve statistically significant improvements over prior work when we include both sets of features into a "Fusion" model.

6. RELATED WORK

In the past, entity search, linking, and ranking have been thoroughly studied in TREC and TAC challenges [11, 4, 12, 6]. However, Schuhmacher et al. are the first to expand this problem to modern ad-hoc retrieval queries and test collections [25]. We note that entity retrieval over the knowledge-base graphs is less relevant to our work, since we consider a well-linked knowledge base to be a lexical resource, but research in this area is ongoing [27].

Similar problems have been explored in the enterprise domain through Expert Search [7, 24, 3], however, the presence of a strong authorship relation between entities and documents makes expert finding different. Moreover, we note that our validation of non-linking approaches motivates further study of expert search approaches to our task, something that prior work [25] dismissed out of hand. We note that our models are most similar to Balog et al.'s Model 2 [2], but applied with less linking certainty (emails are unambiguous) and on a much larger knowledge base.

While there is much modern work on entity linking, constructing an entity linker for novel types of entities or novel languages still requires non-trivial engineering and research effort [19, 15]. In particular, although recent TAC entity linking work has focused on multilingual efforts, the organizers of this challenge observe that a 90% linking accuracy requires that about 20,000 query mentions are labeled for training. Although there is work on new techniques that require less supervision and are more robust, these techniques still require substantial resources: name translation dictionaries, similarity scores, and surface forms [18]. It is for this reason that we are interested in approaches to this entity ranking problem that don't require entity linking. We wish to highlight that dictionary-based entity recognition is not novel [5], but we are the first to use it on a modern test collection for entity ranking.

7. CONCLUSION

In this work, we focus on the task of entity ranking in the context of exploring a target corpus. We substantially improve a recent dataset for this problem by adding annotator agreement and more labels. For the task itself, we propose an approach that does not rely upon entity linking for performance, freeing our approach from requiring linguistic resources typically annotated by experts. The only labels used by our system were acquired inexpensively at high quality through crowd sourcing, suggesting that our approach is likely to be a strong, simple, and useful approach in new domains, such as private data and low resource languages.

Although our approach is straightforward, we find that it is competitive to the work which introduced this modern dataset. We hope that our expansion of the truth data and revisiting of this task will encourage others to explore more interesting approaches to this task in the future.

8. ACKNOWLEDGMENTS

This work was supported in part by the Center for Intelligent Information Retrieval and in part by NSF grant #IIS-0910884 and NSF grant #IIS-1617408. Any opinions, findings and conclusions or recommendations expressed in this material are those of the authors and do not necessarily reflect those of the sponsor.

We would like to especially thank Michael Schuhmacher and Laura Dietz for their help to reproduce their results [25].

9. REFERENCES

[1] S. Auer, C. Bizer, G. Kobilarov, J. Lehmann, R. Cyganiak, and Z. Ives. *Dbpedia: A nucleus for a web of open data.* Springer, 2007.

[2] K. Balog, L. Azzopardi, and M. De Rijke. Formal models for expert finding in enterprise corpora. In *SIGIR'06*, pages 43–50.

[3] K. Balog, Y. Fang, M. de Rijke, P. Serdyukov, and L. Si. Expertise retrieval. *Foundations and Trends in Information Retrieval*, 6(2–3):127–256, 2012.

[4] K. Balog, P. Serdyukov, and A. P. d. Vries. Overview of the trec 2010 entity track. Technical report, DTIC Document, 2010.

[5] A. Boldyrev, G. Weikum, and M. Theobald. *Dictionary-Based Named Entity Recognition.* PhD thesis, Universität des Saarlandes Saarbrücken, 2013.

[6] D. Carmel, M.-W. Chang, E. Gabrilovich, B.-J. P. Hsu, and K. Wang. ERD'14: entity recognition and disambiguation challenge. In *ACM SIGIR Forum, 2014.*

[7] N. Craswell, A. P. de Vries, and I. Soboroff. Overview of the trec 2005 enterprise track. In *TREC*, pages 199–205, 2005.

[8] W. B. Croft, D. Metzler, and T. Strohman. *Search engines: Information retrieval in practice.* Addison-Wesley Reading, 2010.

[9] J. Dalton, L. Dietz, and J. Allan. Entity query feature expansion using knowledge base links. In *SIGIR'14*, pages 365–374.

[10] V. Dang. Ranklib. https://sourceforge.net/p/lemur/wiki/RankLib, 2015.

[11] G. Demartini, T. Iofciu, and A. P. De Vries. Overview of the INEX 2009 entity ranking track. In *Focused Retrieval and Evaluation*, pages 254–264. Springer, 2010.

[12] J. Dunietz and D. Gillick. A new entity salience task with millions of training examples. *EACL'14*, page 205.

[13] P. Ferragina and U. Scaiella. Tagme: on-the-fly annotation of short text fragments (by wikipedia entities). In *CIKM'10*, pages 1625–1628.

[14] E. Gabrilovich, M. Ringgaard, and A. Subramanya. Freebase annotation of clueweb corpora. http://lemurproject.org/clueweb09/FACC1/, June 2013.

[15] F. Hasibi, K. Balog, and S. E. Bratsberg. On the reproducibility of the tagme entity linking system. In *ECIR'16*, pages 436–449.

[16] J. Hoffart, D. Milchevski, and G. Weikum. Stics: searching with strings, things, and cats. In *SIGIR'14*, pages 1247–1248.

[17] J. Hoffart, F. M. Suchanek, K. Berberich, and G. Weikum. Yago2: A spatially and temporally enhanced knowledge base from wikipedia. *Artificial Intelligence*, 194:28–61, 2013.

[18] Y. Hong, D. Lu, D. Yu, X. Pan, X. Wang, Y. Chen, L. Huang, and H. Ji. RPI Blender TAC-KBP2015 system description. In *Text Analysis Conference*, 2015.

[19] H. Ji, J. Nothman, B. Hachey, and R. Florian. Overview of TAC-KBP2015 Tri-lingual Entity Discovery and Linking. 2015.

[20] V. Lavrenko and W. B. Croft. Relevance based language models. In *SIGIR 2001*, pages 120–127, New York, NY, USA, 2001. ACM.

[21] X. Liu and H. Fang. Latent entity space: a novel retrieval approach for entity-bearing queries. *Information Retrieval Journal*, 18(6):473–503, 2015.

[22] C. D. Manning, M. Surdeanu, J. Bauer, J. Finkel, S. J. Bethard, and D. McClosky. The Stanford CoreNLP natural language processing toolkit. In *ACL'14 Demo.*

[23] P. McNamee and H. T. Dang. Overview of the TAC 2009 knowledge base population track. In *TAC'09*, volume 17, pages 111–113, 2009.

[24] D. Petkova and W. B. Croft. Proximity-based document representation for named entity retrieval. In *CIKM'07*, pages 731–740.

[25] M. Schuhmacher, L. Dietz, and S. Ponzetto. Ranking entities for web queries through text and knowledge. In *CIKM'15.*

[26] C. Xiong and J. Callan. EsdRank: Connecting Query and Documents through External Semi-Structured Data. In *CIKM'15.*

[27] N. Zhiltsov, A. Kotov, and F. Nikolaev. Fielded sequential dependence model for ad-hoc entity retrieval in the web of data. In *SIGIR'15*, pages 253–262.

[28] G. Zuccon, B. Koopman, and P. Bruza. Exploiting inference from semantic annotations for information retrieval: Reflections from medical IR. In *ESAIR'14*, pages 43–45, 2014.

The Healing Power of Poison: Helpful Non-relevant Documents in Feedback

Mostafa Dehghani Samira Abnar Jaap Kamps
Institute for Logic, Language and Computation, University of Amsterdam, The Netherlands
{dehghani,s.abnar,kamps}@uva.nl

ABSTRACT

The use of feedback information is an effective approach to address the vocabulary gap between a user's query and the relevant documents. It has been shown that some relevant documents act like "poison pills," i.e. they hurt the performance of feedback systems despite the fact that they are relevant. In this paper, we study the positive counterpart of this by investigating the helpfulness of non-relevant documents in feedback. In general, we find that although documents that are explicitly judged as non-relevant are normally assumed to be poisonous for feedback systems, sometimes considering high-scored non-relevant documents as a positive feedback helps to improve the performance of retrieval. In our experimental data, we observe a considerable fraction of non-relevant documents in higher ranked positions of the initial retrieval run, for most of the topics. Hence, by ignoring the potential value of non-relevant documents, we may loose a lot of useful information.

We investigate the potential contribution of non-relevant documents using existing state-of-the-art feedback methods. Our main findings are the following. First, we find that some of the non-relevant documents are *exclusively helpful*, they improve retrieval on their own, and others are *complementary helpful*, they lead to further improvement when added to a set of relevant documents. Second, we discover that, on average, exclusively helpful non-relevant documents have a higher contribution to the performance improvement, compared to the complementary ones. Third, we show that non-relevant documents in topics with poor average precision in the initial retrieval are more likely to help in the feedback.

Keywords: Relevance Feedback, Helpful Non-relevant Documents

1. INTRODUCTION

Often, the only difference between a medicine and a poison is the dose. Some substances are extremely toxic, and therefore, are primarily known as a poison. Yet, even poisons can have medicinal value.

`Paracelsus, Father of Toxicology`

Query expansion based on feedback information is one of the classic approaches for improving the performance of information retrieval systems, especially when the user information need are complex to express precisely in a few keywords. True Relevance Feedback (TRF) systems try to enrich the user query using a set of judged documents, that their relevance is assessed either explicitly by the user or implicitly inferred from the user behavior. However, this information is not always available. Alternatively, Pseudo Relevance Feedback (PRF) methods, also called blind relevance feedback, assumes that the top-ranked documents in the initial retrieved results are all relevant and use them for the feedback model.

CIKM'16 , October 24 - 28, 2016, Indianapolis, IN, USA

ISBN 978-1-4503-4073-1/16/10...$15.00
DOI: http://dx.doi.org/10.1145/2983323.2983910

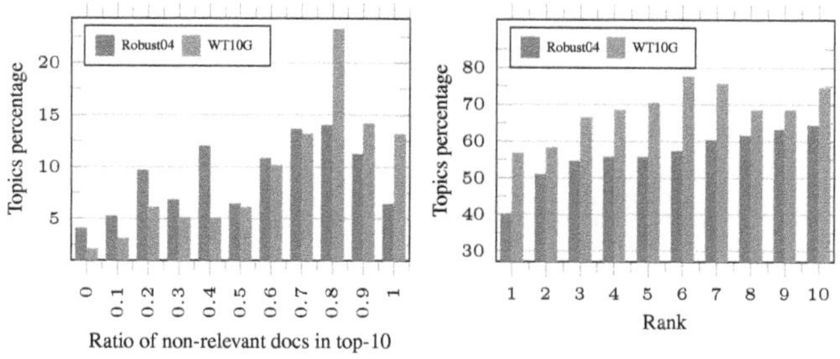

(a) Percentage of topics with different ratio of non-relevant docs in top-10 results **(b)** Percentage of topics with non-relevant docs at different ranks

Figure 1: Prevalence of non-relevant documents in top ranked positions.

Normally feedback documents that are annotated as relevant are considered to be beneficial for feedback and feedback documents that are annotated as non-relevant are expected to be poisonous, i.e. they supposedly decrease the performance of the feedback systems if they are used as positive feedback. Based on this assumption, some of the TRF methods, use non-relevant documents as negative feedback [14, 15] and some PRF methods try to avoid using these documents. For example, some PRF methods attempt on detecting non-relevant documents in order for being robust against their noises [5, 6], or they manage to partially use their content in the feedback procedure, like some of their passages [8, 10]. Although PRF methods use non-relevant documents, they do not directly intend to take advantage of them as helpful documents. In other words, most of the time, removing non-relevant documents from the feedback set of PRF methods leads to a better performance. However, it has been shown that the assumption that all relevant documents improve the performance of feedback systems as positive feedback documents is not always true and sometimes even the relevant documents act like "poison pills" and decrease the performance [13]. As a counterpart fact, we speculate that non-relevant documents might sometimes be helpful as positive feedback [4]. Thus, in this paper, we are investigating the potential healing power of poisonous documents.

Do we really need to think of dealing with non-relevant documents when we are only taking top-scored documents into consideration for the feedback? Based on an analysis of standard test collections, the answer is: yes we do; because they are very prevalent in the top rank positions. Figure 1a depicts the percentage of topics with different ratio of non-relevant documents in top-10 results retrieved using the KL-Divergence model, in the two standard TREC

Table 1: Number of helpful non-relevant documents in different rank levels in the initial run.

level	Robust			WT10G		
	NR	BHNR	CHNR	NR	BHNR	CHNR
5	641	55 (%8.6)	106 (%16.5)	314	32 (%10.2)	45 (%14.3)
10	1404	82 (%5.8)	205 (%16.5)	671	58 (%8.6)	88 (%13.1)
15	2212	86 (%3.9)	219 (%9.9)	1050	66 (%6.3)	96 (%9.14)
20	3083	91 (%2.9)	232 (%7.5)	1423	71 (%5.0)	103 (%0.72)
50	8872	112 (%1.3)	241 (%2.7)	3862	74 (%1.9)	107 (%2.8)
100	18630	124 (%0.7)	250 (%1.3)	14040	79 (%0.6)	112 (%0.8)
500	66269	129 (%0.2)	257 (%0.4)	30827	84 (%0.3)	119 (%0.4)

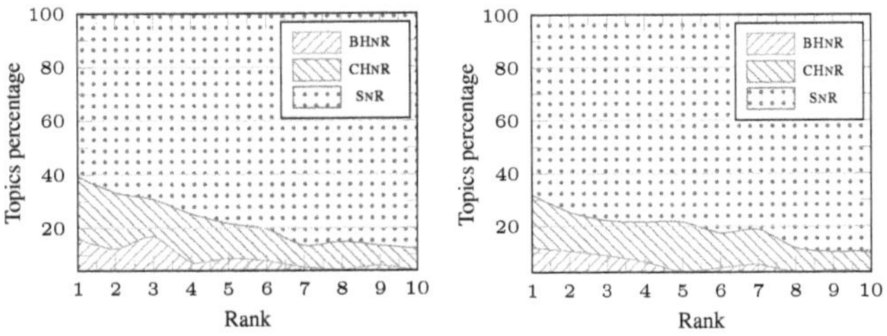

(a) Robust04 dataset (b) WT10G dataset

Figure 2: Percentage of topics with different types of non-relevant documents in different rank positions.

datasets: Robust04 and WT10G. It shows that for instance, about 30% of topics have seven or eight explicitly judged non-relevant document in their top-10 results for both datasets. Figure 1b also demonstrates the percentage of topics with non-relevant documents at different ranks. For instance, in WT10G, in more than 50% of topics, the top rank document is non-relevant or in more than 50% of topics, the document at rank two is non-relevant in both datasets. So, in general, there is a high probability of hitting a non-relevant document in top rank positions and ignoring their potential helpfulness is turning a blind eye to a lot of useful information.

We believe that every high-scored retrieved document, either judged as relevant or non-relevant, may contain information that can be a clue for understanding the complex information need of the user. Hence, if an ideal system is able to perfectly control the amount and the way each document contributes to the feedback model for each topic, not only it will not be hurt by a non-relevant document, but it will even be able to take advantage of its information to further improve the performance.

Generally, the main aim of this paper is to investigate the helpfulness of highly ranked non-relevant documents for improving further results by being used in the feedback methods. We break this down into the following research questions:

RQ1 *How can a non-relevant document help to improve retrieval performance?*

RQ2 *How large is the contribution of helpful non-relevant feedback documents?*

RQ3 *Does the helpfulness of the non-relevant documents depend on the quality of the initial retrieved results?*

For the sake of this study, we try to select the clearest and most explicit examples of helpful non-relevant documents (HNR), i.e. retrieved documents that are judged as non-relevant but considering them in the feedback set leads to improvement in the performance of retrieval, utilising the existing state-of-the-art feedback methods. Based on our observations, we divide HNR into two groups: Bridge Helpful Non-relevant (BHNR) documents that are able to improve the performance individually, and Complementary Helpful Non-relevant (CHNR) that further improve the performance if they are employed together with a set of relevant documents.

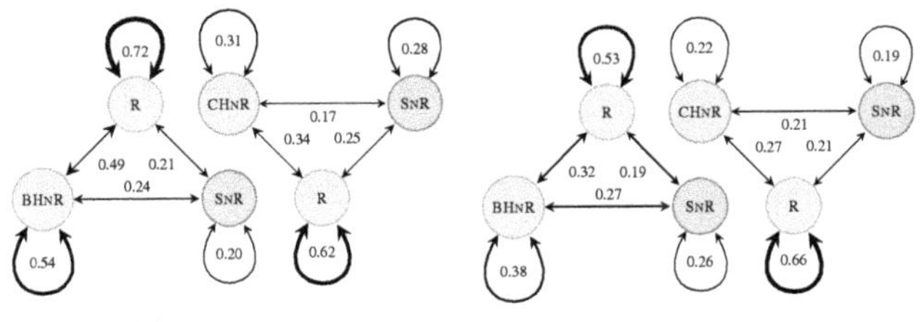

(a) Robust04 (b) WT10G

Figure 3: Intra and inter similarity of relevant (R), SNR, BHNR, and CHNR documents.

We use the Robust04 with 528,155 newswire documents and 249 topics, as well as WT10G with 1,692,096 web documents and 99 topics as the test collections, which are different in terms of both size and genre of documents. We use the KL-Divergence model, with Dirichlet smoothing as the retrieval model in all of the experiments. We employ three state-of-the-art feedback methods, relevance model (RM3) [1], MEDMM [11], and SWLM [2, 3]. It is important to note that we investigate only documents that are explicitly judged as non-relevant, and ignore unjudged documents.

2. HELPFUL NON-RELEVANT DOCUMENTS

In this section, we address our first research question: "How can a non-relevant document help to improve retrieval performance?" Typically, it is expected that using a non-relevant document as positive feedback would cause a decrease in the average precision (AP). However, we show that some non-relevant documents not only do not hurt the feedback performance but they will even improve it.

Some hypothesis may be explanatory to this kind of documents. The first thing that comes to mind is that this is the effect of judgement noises and these documents are relevant but they have been misjudged. The second argument is that these documents are marginally relevant to the topic but with a focus on an aspect of the topic which is not related to the user information need or these documents are generally relevant to the topic but have no new valuable information to satisfy the user and because of using *binary* relevance judgments, they are annotated as non-relevant. In this case, they might contain terms that are helpful for query expansion. There is a discussion in linguistics that every utterance has two basic parts, *theme*, which indicates the topic of discourse, and *rheme*, which gives new information about the theme. In the retrieval problem, in rather crude terms, we may say that the theme of a document states what it is about, and the rheme of a document expresses what the searcher wishes to find in it [7]. So, for the searcher, relevance is a function of both theme and rheme of the document based on her current interests and his personal state of knowledge, while for the feedback method relevance is a function of the place of the document in the current state of knowledge as a whole. Thus, the mere annotation of a document as non-relevant for a topic does not imply that the document is not useful as positive feedback for that topic.

2.1 Bridge HNR

To understand the properties and behavior of HNR documents, we are attempting to extract the most explicit instances of HNR in our test collection and study their characteristics. To this end, for each of the feedback methods we use a single non-relevant document appearing in top-k retrieved documents per topic as the only feedback document and keep the track of change in AP of the corresponding topic. If the document makes the AP increase in all the systems, we mark that document as a HNR document.

We looked into several instances and found that regardless of the judgement noise, most of the times a non-relevant document improves the performance in single document feedback in two different situations: First, when the topic is a specific topic and the

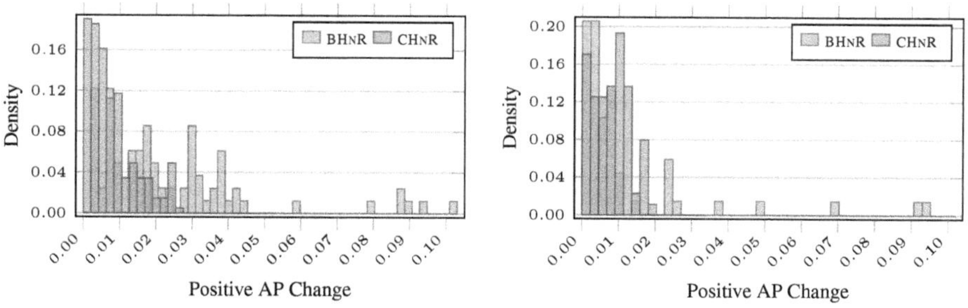

(a) Robust04 dataset

(b) WT10G dataset

Figure 4: Distribution of HNR documents based on the amount of average change in the AP.

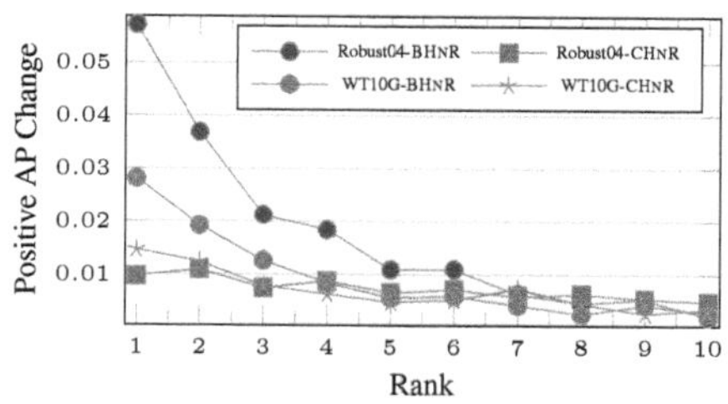

Figure 5: Average AP change caused by HNR documents in different rank positions.

HNR document is a broad topic document, which does not address directly the topic in a particular way, but some general frequent words in the language usage of the document help to retrieve more specific documents in the next feedback run. For example, in Robust04 dataset, topic 311 is "Industrial Espionage", and one of the HNR documents is about "counter-espionage services for combating organised crime, terrorism and foreign operations", and expanding query with generally related terms like terrorism, foreign, etc. boost the score of some relevant documents in the feedback run. Second, when the topic is a topic which the user is able to articulate it in different ways and the helpful non-relevant document does not address the user information need, but some of its frequent words express the topic in other ways. For instance, in Robust04 dataset,topic 348 is "creativity", which based on the description of the topic, relevant documents are supposed to be about the definition of creativity, and one of the HNR documents is about "the founder of a company in Singapore, named Creative Technology", which contains terms like "original thinkers","smart", "innovation", and these terms are related to the main concept of creativity. In both of these cases, the HNR document is not directly related to the topic, but it plays the role of a bridge to non-retrieved relevant documents. We refer to these documents as Bridge Helpful Non-relevant (BHNR) documents.

2.2 Complementary HNR

In a second experiment, we give one more chance to the remaining non-relevant documents to be helpful. To do this, for each topic, we check if adding the non-relevant document to the true relevance feedback set will further improve its performance. Thus, we examine the possibility of each individual non-relevant document to be helpful when it is used along with a set of relevant documents. We mark the documents that have a positive effect on the AP of the corresponding topic, in all the systems as a HNR document.

We explored different cases where a non-relevant document helps together with a set of relevant documents and discovered that this happens mostly in the situations where the HNR document is a multi-topic document, and technically it is partially relevant. This document is not able to be helpful in single-document feedback since its non-relevant part causes topic drift [6, 12]. However, together with other relevant documents, not only the effect of its non-relevant part is neutralised and compensated by the relevant documents, but its relevant part even reinforces the feedback models. We refer to these documents as Complementary Helpful Non-relevant (CHNR) documents. We examined the BHNR documents in our second experiment and observed that all of them are CHNR as well. So, we exclude them from CHNR documents to better analyse properties of each type. In Table 1, the rate of BHNR and CHNR documents are listed in different rank levels of the initial run in two datasets. As it is expected, in both datasets and in both types, HNR documents occur in a higher percentage in the early rankings. Moreover, an inspection of the various depth levels shows that from all HNR documents in top 500, a high percentage of them (60%-75%) take place in top-10. This might be one of the reasons that most of the pseudo relevance feedback methods work well with ten feedback documents [9]. We will restrict our analysis on the helpfulness of non-relevant documents to this level, i.e. up to rank ten. We also looked into the agreement of the three feedback methods in our experiments and observed that they behave quite differently. So, as a pragmatic choice, we study only the clear cases where all the methods agree on their helpfulness.

As it is pointed out in the introduction, we think that every high-scored retrieved document, either judged as relevant or non-relevant, can help feedback systems improve the performance. However, in this paper, we are not able to reveal the healing power of some of them, maybe because of the design of our experiments or due to the shortcoming of the existing feedback methods. Hence, we do not call them "bad" relevant document, and instead, we call them, Stubborn Non-relevant (SNR) documents. Figure 2 shows how likely a non-relevant document can be helpful in different top 10 rank positions. As expected, the percentages of the topics with HNR documents are higher in the higher ranks and generally, non-relevant documents are more likely to help along with a set of relevant documents, as CHNR, than individually as BHNR.

In order to understand the relation between HNR, SNR, and relevant documents, for each type of HNR documents, we select topics with at least two HNR, two SNR, and two relevant documents in their top ten results and calculate the intra and inter similarity of these groups of documents based on the average similarity of all document pairs, using JS-Divergence of their smoothed language models. Figure 3 shows the intra and inter similarity of relevant, SNR, BHNR, and CHNR documents in two datasets. As it is expected, in both datasets, the similarity of BHNR to the relevant documents and CHNR to the relevant documents is relatively higher than the similarity of SNR documents to the relevant documents. However, the intra similarity of BHNR documents is higher than CHNR documents. This observation is in accordance with the assumption that the BHNR documents are related to the topic (hence similar to the relevant documents) in general but they do not have the particular information which satisfies the searcher to be annotated as relevant. Also, CHNR documents are mostly multi-topic documents that have a part related to the query, but their non-relevant parts could be quite diverse, which leads to a low intra similarity.

3. IMPACT OF HNR DOCUMENTS

We now investigate our second research question: "How large is the contribution of helpful non-relevant feedback documents?" In order to evaluate the impact of HNR documents on the performance of feedback, we calculate the average of change of AP they make over all the employed feedback systems. For BHNR documents, we consider the amount of AP change compared to the initial run, and for CHNR, we consider the AP change compared to the feedback run without their presence in the feedback set. Figure 4 depicts the distribution of BHNR and CHNR documents based on the amount

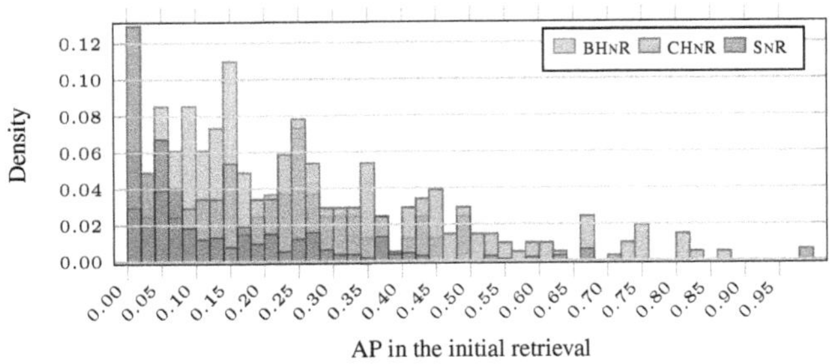

(a) Robust04 dataset

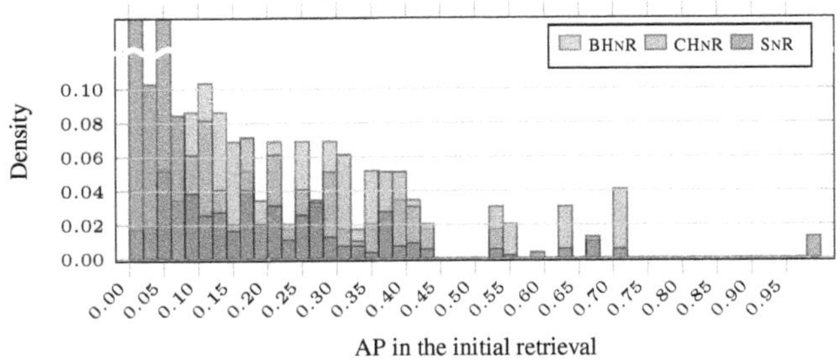

(b) WT10G dataset

Figure 6: Distribution of different types of non-relevant documents based on the amount of AP in the initial retrieval.

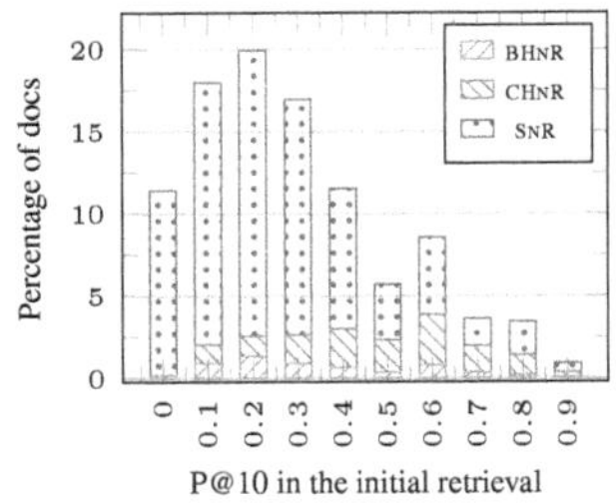

(a) Robust04 dataset

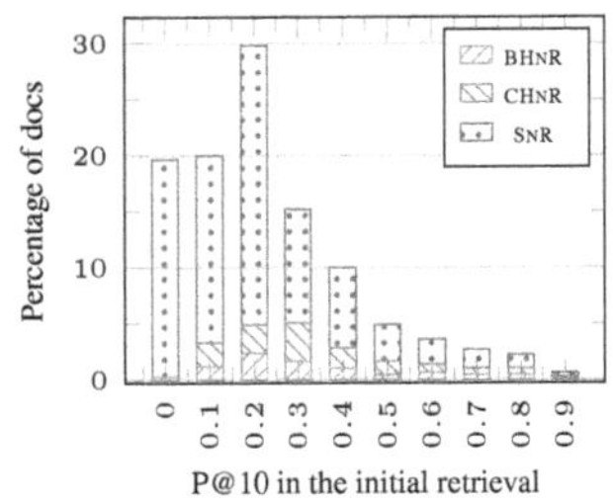

(b) WT10G dataset

Figure 7: Percentage of different types of non-relevant documents (out of all retrieved documents) in topics with different P@10 in initial retrieval.

of average change in the AP in the two datasets, which shows that most of the HNR documents have a rather small contribution in AP. Figure 5 demonstrates the average AP change caused by the HNR documents in different rank positions. From the BHNR documents, in average, top rank documents have a greater contribution. However, based on the plots in this figure, the average amount of the positive contribution of the CHNR documents seems independent of the rank of the document. We have examined the contribution of all the BHNR documents in different ranks as CHNR and saw a roughly uniform plot as well. This reveals that since in CHNR experiments, involved relevant documents in the feedback can be from any rank, the feedback set is a mixture of documents from different ranks, hence the rank effect is disappeared.

4. IMPACT OF INITIAL PERFORMANCE

This section discusses our third research question: "Does the helpfulness of the non-relevant documents depend on the quality of the initial retrieved results?" In order to understand the relation between the quality of the initial retrieval and the helpfulness of the non-relevant documents, in Figure 6, we plot the distribution of BHNR, CHNR, and SNR documents based on the AP of the topic that these documents are retrieved for, in the initial run. Apparently, HNR documents occur mostly when the AP of the initial run is not too high. This is natural since when your baseline is not too good, it is easier to improve it, while when the performance of the baseline is high, it is easy to destroy it. In both datasets, CHNR documents are most likely to occur when both the AP of the initial run and the number of SNR in top-10 results are low. These properties are in accordance with the observations from Figure 7, where the percentages of BHNR, CHNR, and SNR in topics with different P@10 in the initial retrieval are presented. The more relevant documents exist in the feedback set, the greater the chance that a non-relevant document helps as a CHNR, and for low performing topics in terms of P@10, it is easier for a non-relevant document to improve the performance individually as a BHNR.

5. CONCLUSIONS

The main goal of this paper was to investigate the helpfulness of highly ranked non-relevant documents for improving further results by being used in the feedback methods. We designed some experiments based on the existing state-of-the-art feedback methods to assess the possibility of helpfulness of non-relevant documents. We found that some of the non-relevant documents can be helpful exclusively, and some others may help when they are employed as a complement to a set of relevant documents. We also discovered that in average compared to complementary ones, exclusively helpful non-relevant documents have a higher contribution to the improvement in performance . In addition, we showed that the non-relevant documents in topics with poor average precision in the initial retrieval are more likely to help in the feedback.

This research is a primary step and further analysis is necessary to understand the nature of helpful non-relevant documents and how we can change feedback methods to be able to better take advantage of them. Also, as a direction from which this research is extendable, we are going to build a classifier to characterise the helpfulness of non-relevant documents based on the existing feedback methods.

Acknowledgments This research is funded in part by Netherlands Organization for Scientific Research through the *Exploratory Political Search* project (ExPoSe, NWO CI # 314.99.108), and by the Digging into Data Challenge through the *Digging Into Linked Parliamentary Data* project (DiLiPaD, NWO Digging into Data # 600.006.014).

REFERENCES

[1] N. Abdul-jaleel, J. Allan, W. B. Croft, O. Diaz, L. Larkey, X. Li, M. D. Smucker, and C. Wade. Umass at trec 2004: Novelty and hard. In *TREC-13*, 2004.

[2] M. Dehghani. Significant words representations of entities. In *SIGIR '16*, pages 1183–1183, 2016.

[3] M. Dehghani, H. Azarbonyad, J. Kamps, D. Hiemstra, and M. Marx. Luhn revisited: Significant words language models. In *CIKM '16*, 2016.

[4] M. D. Dunlop. The effect of accessing nonmatching documents on relevance feedback. *ACM Trans. Inf. Syst.*, 15(2):137–153, 1997.

[5] B. He and I. Ounis. Finding good feedback documents. In *CIKM '09*, pages 2011–2014, 2009.

[6] B. He and I. Ounis. Studying query expansion effectiveness. In *ECIR'09*, pages 611–619, 2009.

[7] W. J. Hutchins. On the problem of "aboutness" in document analysis. *Journal of informatics*, 1(1):17–35, 1977.

[8] X. Li and Z. Zhu. Enhancing relevance models with adaptive passage retrieval. In *ECIR'08*, pages 463–471, 2008.

[9] Y. Lv and C. Zhai. A comparative study of methods for estimating query language models with pseudo feedback. In *CIKM '09*, pages 1895–1898, 2009.

[10] Y. Lv and C. Zhai. Positional relevance model for pseudo-relevance feedback. In *SIGIR '10*, pages 579–586, 2010.

[11] Y. Lv and C. Zhai. Revisiting the divergence minimization feedback model. In *CIKM '14*, pages 1863–1866, 2014.

[12] C. Macdonald and I. Ounis. Expertise drift and query expansion in expert search. In *CIKM '07*, pages 341–350, 2007.

[13] E. Terra and R. Warren. Poison pills: Harmful relevant documents in feedback. In *CIKM '05*, pages 319–320, 2005.

[14] X. Wang, H. Fang, and C. Zhai. Improve retrieval accuracy for difficult queries using negative feedback. In *CIKM '07*, pages 991–994, 2007.

[15] X. Wang, H. Fang, and C. Zhai. A study of methods for negative relevance feedback. In *SIGIR '08*, pages 219–226, 2008.

Probabilistic Approaches to Controversy Detection

Myungha Jang, John Foley, Shiri Dori-Hacohen, and James Allan
Center for Intelligent Information Retrieval
College of Information and Computer Sciences
University of Massachusetts
{mhjang, jfoley, shiri, allan}@cs.umass.edu

ABSTRACT

Recently, the problem of automated controversy detection has attracted a lot of interest in the information retrieval community. Existing approaches to this problem have set forth a number of detection algorithms, but there has been little effort to model the probability of controversy in a document directly.

In this paper, we propose a probabilistic framework to detect controversy on the web, and investigate two models. We first recast a state-of-the-art controversy detection algorithm into a model in our framework. Based on insights from social science research, we also introduce a language modeling approach to this problem. We evaluate different methods of creating *controversy language models* based on a diverse set of public datasets including Wikipedia, Web and News corpora.

Our automatically derived language models show a significant relative improvement of 18% in AUC over prior work, and 23% over two manually curated lexicons.

1. INTRODUCTION

The power of search is inherently coupled to the trustworthiness and reliability of the dataset the user is searching. Web search can be both helpful and troubling in this regard. In medicine, one may find misinformation that professionals consider incorrect, whether it is fraudulent treatments or side-effects that simply do not exist, such as the link between vaccines and autism. In the political domain, increasing polarization of sources and viewpoints leads to "Filter Bubbles" [15], where users are only able to find results that agree with them or the way they formulated their query. In these domains and more, the ability to reliably detect the presence of controversy in search results could aid critical literacy and the ability to make real-life decisions. Our task is to determine if a given Web document discusses controversial topics.

However, existing search engines are unlikely to reveal controversial topics to users unless they already know about the controversies [10]. There is an increasing call for search engines to detect these queries and address them appropriately [9, 12]. Previous work [8, 11] presented an algorithm for classifying controversy in Web documents using Wikipedia; this reliance introduces efficiency concerns, and limits the classifier's potential scope to topics covered in Wikipedia. Additionally, to date, little effort has been made to formulate a probabilistic model to detect controversy.

In this work, we investigate probabilistic models for automated controversy detection and thus provide theoretic modeling of the problem. First, we develop a probabilistic framework for the controversy detection problem and re-cast the state-of-the-art algorithm in that probabilistic perspective. We use this new perspective to extend prior work from a binary classification model to a probabilistic model that can be used for ranking. We then introduce the *controversy language model*, a new approach to address the controversy detection problem. We develop this language-modeling approach based on a recent qualitative analysis of controversy [5], which is more efficient and easier to compute than the more expensive Wikipedia-based controversy detection algorithm. Finally, we empirically validate our controversy language models and find that our approach significantly outperforms the state-of-the-art algorithm for controversy detection [8].

CIKM'16, October 24-28, 2016, Indianapolis, IN, USA

DOI: http://dx.doi.org/10.1145/2983323.2983911

2. RELATED WORK AND BACKGROUND

Controversy detection studies often focus on certain genres or data sources, such as news [3, 14], Twitter [16], and Wikipedia [13, 17, 21]. Since these studies frequently use data-source-specific features such as Wikipedia's edit history features or Twitter's social graph information, it seems unlikely that existing work can be easily generalized to controversy detection on arbitrary webpages.

While some past work uses sentiment as a signal when researching controversy [2, 3], others have argued that opinion and controversy are distinct and non-overlapping concepts [1]. Researchers have shown that using sentiment for controversy detection performs poorly on webpages [8] and that controversy and sentiment are not directly related [14].

Choi et al. attempt to identify controversy and controversial subtopics using various features, particularly a mixture model of topic and sentiment [3]. We depart from their work by directly modeling the probability of controversy.

There also have been a few attempts to detect controversial content with lexicons. Roitman et al. retrieve Wikipedia articles with claims about controversial query topics [18], and Mejova et al. use crowdsourcing to label controversial words [14].

In the social sciences, Cramer explains that the term "controversy" tends to be metadiscursive. Writers label something as "the controversy" by using their writing to categorize others' writings and speakings about a topic. Hence, the phrase "the controversy" is indexical of controversial events because it is a linguistic way of pointing at a particular event. Cramer's work suggests that language could be a key feature in identifying controversy.

2.1 Wikipedia Controversy Features

Previous work studied algorithms that generate scores that signal controversy in Wikipedia [13, 7, 21]. We refer to these scores as Wikipedia Controversy Features (WCF). The scores use various information extracted from Wikipedia pages, meta-data, talk pages, and the page's edit history.

We use the following features to reimplement the kNN-WC algorithm (see §2.2) which relies on them, as well as to collect highly controversial documents for our new language modeling approach:

D Score The presence of the `{dispute}` tag placed on an article by editors. Only 0.03% of articles contain this tag.

C Score is generated by a regression-based method [7, 13] that trains on revisions that are labeled with `{controversial}` tags.

M Score is generated by Yasseri et al. based on features of edits to predict the ferocity of an "edit war" [21].

2.2 kNN-WC Algorithm

Dori-Hacohen and Allan [8] presented an algorithm for identifying whether a given Web document discusses controversial topics. To the best of our knowledge, this work is the first and only attempt to extend the controversy detection problem to general web pages in open domain [8], and build upon past work that investigated controversy detection on Wikipedia. We will refer to their work as k Nearest Neighbors of Wikipedia Controversy (kNN-WC).

The kNN-WC algorithm assumed that the controversy in a web document can be detected from the levels of controversy of related topics. The algorithm modeled related topics as related Wikipedia articles, and existing controversy labels on the Wikipedia neighbors [13, 21] were used to derive a final judgment on the original document (see §2.1).

Overview of kNN-WC Algorithm: kNN-WC [8] consists of four steps: (1) Find k Wikipedia neighbors given a webpage, (2) compute the three WCF scores (D, C, and M) for each neighbor, (3) aggregate the k values of each WCF score and turn them into three binary labels using thresholds, and (4) vote the labels and make a final decision.

Limitations: kNN-WC is constrained by its dependency on Wikipedia controversy indicators, which are sourced solely from Wikipedia-specific features such as mutual reverts of editors. Search of k-NN for each document is a non-trivial operation, which raises practical efficiency issues. In addition, topical coverage in Wikipedia is necessitated.

In our work, we first contribute a generalization of this algorithm to a probabilistic framework, grounding it in a theoretical conception. We then depart from it by presenting a new language model for controversy.

3. PROBABILISTIC MODELING OF THE kNN-WC ALGORITHM

In this section, we formulate the controversy detection problem with a probabilistic perspective and recast the kNN-WC algorithm as obtaining a probability of controversy for binary classification. We then extend the kNN-WC *algorithm* for binary classification and derive the kNN-WC *model*, a probabilistic model that can be used for ranking.

We formulate the controversy detection problem as obtaining the following probabilities: Let D be a document. We define $P(C|D)$ as the probability that D is controversial, and $P(NC|D)$ as the opposite (i.e., non-controversial), such that the two probabilities sum to 1.

$P(C|D)$ can be represented by two components: $P(C, D)$, a joint probability of the presence of controversy and D; and $P(D)$, a prior probability of D. For binary classification, we are interested in whether $P(C|D) > P(NC|D)$. However, $P(D)$ is the same for $P(C|D)$ and $P(NC|D)$, and we can thus ignore it in comparison. We model the approach of the kNN-WC algorithm by assuming that $P(C|D)$ can be estimated from the joint probability $P(C, D)$ by the following equation. We then assume that a document and its topics, denoted as T_D are interchangeable.

$$P(C|D) = \frac{P(C,D)}{P(D)} \approx \frac{P(C,T_D)}{P(D)} \quad (1)$$

In the context of kNN-WC, we interpret Wikipedia neighbors as a set of "latent topics" in the document. We denote a set of similar Wikipedia articles to the document (i.e., neighbors) as W_D. W_D was obtained by matching the query generated from the D to the Wikipedia index.

$$P(C,T_D) \approx P(C,W_D) \quad (2)$$

By treating the Wikipedia neighbors as topics, we are able to model $P(C, W_D)$ via WCF (see §2.1). By construction, a WCF reflects some estimate of the co-occurrence of controversy and the topic.

Likewise, the kNN-WC algorithm used a binary indicator function $P(C, W_D) \approx c(W_D)$ that outputs 1 (controversial) or 0 (non-controversial). One of the best performing settings of this algorithm [8]:

$$c(W_D) = \mathbb{1}[\max(WCF_M(W_D)) > \theta_M] \quad (3)$$

where $WCF_M(W_D)$ is a set of M scores for W_D, θ_M is a threshold, and $\mathbb{1}$ converts true to 1 and false to 0.

To support further evaluation of the kNN-WC model, we extend the indicator function to a numeric scoring function by removing the threshold so that the model can produce a ranking instead of binary classes. Let $f(W_D)$ be a function that returns an aggregated value of the given neighbors' WCF scores.

$$f(W_D) = \mathrm{agg}(WCF_{\{M,C,D\}}(W_D)) \quad (4)$$

We then convert this aggregation function to a probability by normalizing over all possible document neighbors W_D, represented here by a normalization factor Z. Eq. (5) shows the finally derived kNN-WC model.

$$P(C|D) \approx \frac{1}{Z} f(W_D) \quad (5)$$

4. CONTROVERSY LANGUAGE MODELS

Cramer [5] manually studies patterns of text surrounding specific terms as **controversy**, **dispute**, **scandal**, and **saga** within the Reuters corpus [19], as being indicative of controversy. Motivated by Cramer's research, we propose a new probabilistic model of controversy that considers how similar the document's language is to the one that discusses a range of controversial topics.

Since we are only interested if $P(C|D) > P(NC|D)$ holds, rather than the actual probabilities, we can use rank-safe approximations.

Each $P(C|D)$ and $P(NC|D)$ can be represented using Bayes theorem, which allows us to consider the following odds-ratio:

$$\frac{P(C|D)}{P(NC|D)} = \frac{P(D|C)}{P(D|NC)} \cdot \frac{P(C)}{P(NC)} > 1 \tag{6}$$

Now our test condition can be expressed as:

$$\frac{P(D|C)}{P(D|NC)} > \frac{P(NC)}{P(C)} \tag{7}$$

where for our purposes, we can treat the right hand side as a constant cutoff (since it is independent of the document D), which can be learned with training data. To avoid underflow, we actually calculate the log of this ratio.

$$\log P(D|C) - \log P(D|NC) > \alpha \tag{8}$$

Therefore, we only have to estimate the probabilities $P(D|C)$ and $P(D|NC)$, which we do using the language modeling framework, construction of a language model of controversy L_C, and a non-controversial language model L_{NC}. We make the standard term independence assumption for each word (w) in our document (D), and avoid zero probabilities with linear smoothing. In practice, we estimate both the global language model (L_G) [6] and the non-controversial language model (L_{NC}) as the same by constructing them from the set of all documents.

$$P(D\ C) \approx P(D|L_C) = \prod_{w \in D} (\lambda P(w|L_C) + (1-\lambda)P(w|L_G))$$

$$P(D|NC) \approx P(D|L_{NC}) \approx P(D|L_G) = \prod_{w \in D} P(w|L_G)$$

Here, D_C is a set of controversial documents, and D_{NC} is a set of non-controversial documents, which we estimate in our collections as the background collection, D_{BG}.

$$P(w|L_C) = \frac{\sum_{d \in D_C} tf(w,d)}{\sum_{d \in D_C} |d|}, P(w|L_{NC}) = \frac{\sum_{d \in D_{BG}} tf(w,d)}{\sum_{d \in D_{BG}} |d|}$$

Therefore, to build a language model of controversy, we need to find D_C. We explore WCF features and Cramer-inspired query based models to construct D_C as following:

WCF: Top K Wikipedia articles that have high WCF (e.g, M, C, D) values.

Controversy-indicative terms: Documents that are retrieved by a query believed to indicate controversy. We explore Cramer's terms [5] as well as manual lexicons from past work [14, 18].

5. EVALUATION

We leverage the dataset introduced in prior work [8] that consists of judgments for 303 webpages[1] from the ClueWeb09 collection[2]. We perform 5-fold cross-validation and report measures on the reconstructed test set.

We implement our probabilistic model based on kNN-WC, the state-of-the-art approach. Rather than use the full text of the web pages, we follow the kNN-WC algorithm and use the "TF10" query, where the document is approximated by the ten most frequent terms (excluding the 571-word SMART stopword list).

Prior work reported accuracy; we note that 65% of the 303 documents were non-controversial, so that accuracy does not provide the best view of this dataset. In this work, we primarily present results using the Area Under the Curve (AUC) measure, as we can compare performance without tuning thresholds. Since accuracy was used in prior work, we report it as well. Compared to kNN-WC algorithm, we improve from 0.72 accuracy (as presented in [8]) and 0.737 accuracy (as reproduced) to 0.779 ($p < 0.001$). For our statistical significance tests, we follow in the footsteps of the `pROC`[3], and obtain confidence intervals from bootstrap resamples of the predictions.

For each fold, we trained two parameters by grid search: K, the number of top documents to choose, and λ, the smoothing parameter (Table 1). For example, to create our M-score-based language model, we ranked the documents in our Wikipedia collection by their M score, and derived a language model based on the concatenation of the top K documents.

For building Cramer language models, where the relevant document sets were not created by WCF, we used the Galago search engine to rank documents using a query-likelihood retrieval. We explore 6 different corpora as document sources (Table 2). The K highest-scoring documents were then used as our controversial document set: D_C.

Table 1: Wikipedia-Based Controversy Detection Approaches. All LM approaches have significant improvements over their respective kNN-WC counterpart at the $p < 0.05$ level.

Method	WCF	AUC
kNN-WC model §3	M	0.733
kNN-WC model	C	0.743
kNN-WC model	D	0.500†
LM §4	M	0.801
LM	C	0.835
LM	D	0.795

† In the kNN-WC-D approach, no neighbors were found with dispute tags, so it is equivalent to the weak baseline performance of the *NO* classifier.

6. RESULTS

In Table 1, we present results of our models built around WCF, as introduced in §2.1. All our language modeling approaches are significantly stronger than the k-NN derived approaches. We only report results of WCF features independently because methods of aggregating these features did not improve significantly over the best feature, and these methods were not quite comparable across kNN-WC and LM approaches.

In Table 2, we present an initial exploration of Cramer's hypothesis that news is able to name and define controversy. While Cramer defined four keywords to be indicative of controversy, we find that "`controversy`" dominates effectiveness on this dataset. We explore these keywords as queries into an expansion corpus, and construct a language model from

[1]http://ciir.cs.umass.edu/downloads

[2]http://lemurproject.org/clueweb09/

[3]http://cran.r-project.org/web/packages/pROC

Table 2: Language Models built from documents relevant to Cramer's controversial terms [5]. Collection size $|C|$ in millions of documents and type shown for comparison of results. We found that our wiki dataset was significantly better than all others, which had no pairwise differences otherwise.

Expansion Dataset	Type	$\|C\|$	AUC
DBPedia	Wiki	4.6M	0.853
ClueWeb09B (Spam60)	Web	33.8M	0.741
Reuters	News	0.8M	0.745
NYT-LDC	News	1.8M	0.710
Robust04	News	0.5M	0.711
Signal-1M	News	1M	0.710

Table 3: Language Models built from Cramer's terms and existing lexicons on DBPedia. We find that "controversy" is the most indicative term, and that "saga" is no better than random. Combining terms led to no improvement over "controversy" alone.

Query to build D_C	AUC
`controversy`	0.856
Roitman [18]	0.823
`dispute`	0.740
`scandal`	0.721
Mejova [14]	0.698
`saga`	0.500

the highest scoring documents for the given query. That language model is then used for classification.

While we were pleasantly surprised by the efficacy of this simple approach, we did not see the best performance in the news corpora [19] used by Cramer, but rather in using DBPedia as the expansion set. We also explored this approach on other news datasets (Robust04, NYT-LDC [20], and Signal1M [4]) but results were statistically equivalent on all news corpora we tried.

Roitman et al. [18] and Mejova et al. [14] present manually-curated lexicons for controversy tasks. We explore their use intrinsically, with Jaccard Similarity between the lexicon and the document terms in Table 4 and as queries to build a language model in Table 3.

Table 4: A comparison of lexicons built manually and through crowd-sourcing in prior work to our automatically derived language models A (*) indicates significant improvement over the best lexicon approach.

Method	Document	AUC
Roitman Lexicon [18]	TF10	0.543
Mejova Lexicon [14]	TF10	0.562
Mejova Lexicon [14]	Full	0.615
Roitman Lexicon [18]	Full	0.695
Cramer Language Model	Full	0.783
WCF Language Model	Full	0.823*
WCF Language Model	TF10	0.835*
Cramer Language Model	TF10	0.856*

7. CONCLUSION

We introduce probabilistic approaches to modeling controversy, by both recasting prior work into a theoretical framework, as well as introducing a new model. Using insights from recent social science research, we motivate and explore the first language modeling approach to detecting controversy. We find that our new approach is statistically better than prior work, while simultaneously being more efficient. We demonstrate that strongly indicative terms are as helpful for this problem as complicated Wikipedia-based controversy features and more effective than existing lexicons.

8. ACKNOWLEDGMENTS

This work was supported in part by the Center for Intelligent Information Retrieval, in part by NSF grant IIS-0910884, and in part by NSF grant IIS-1217281. Any opinions, findings and conclusions or recommendations expressed in this material are those of the authors and do not necessarily reflect those of the sponsor. We thank Peter Cramer, Guy Campos and Gonen Dori-Hacohen for thoughtful discussions.

9. REFERENCES

[1] R. Awadallah, M. Ramanath, and G. Weikum. Harmony and dissonance: Organizing the people's voices on political controversies. In *WSDM'12*.

[2] M.-A. Cartright, E. Aktolga, and J. Dalton. Characterizing the subjectivity of topics. In *SIGIR'09*.

[3] Y. Choi, Y. Jung, and S.-H. Myaeng. Identifying controversial issues and their sub-topics in news articles. In *Intelligence and Security Informatics*. Springer, 2010.

[4] D. Corney, D. Albakour, M. Martinez, and S. Moussa. What do a million news articles look like? In *Workshop on Recent Trends in News IR, ECIR'16*.

[5] P. A. Cramer. *Controversy as news discourse*, volume 19. Springer Science & Business Media, 2011.

[6] W. B. Croft, D. Metzler, and T. Strohman. *Search engines: Information retrieval in practice*, volume 283. Addison-Wesley Reading, 2010.

[7] S. Das, A. Lavoie, and M. Magdon-Ismail. Manipulation among the arbiters of collective intelligence: how wikipedia administrators mold public opinion. In *CIKM'13*.

[8] S. Dori-Hacohen and J. Allan. Automated controversy detection on the web. In *ECIR'15*.

[9] S. Dori-Hacohen, E. Yom-Tov, and J. Allan. Navigating Controversy as a Complex Search Task. In *Supporting Complex Search Tasks, at ECIR'15*.

[10] S. L. Gerhart. Do Web search engines suppress controversy? *First Monday*, 9, 2004.

[11] M. Jang and J. Allan. Improving automated controversy detection on the web. In *SIGIR'16*.

[12] M. Kacimi and J. Gamper. Diversifying search results of controversial queries. In *CIKM'11*.

[13] A. Kittur, B. Suh, B. A. Pendleton, and E. H. Chi. He says, she says: conflict and coordination in wikipedia. In *SIGCHI'07*.

[14] Y. Mejova, A. X. Zhang, N. Diakopoulos, and C. Castillo. Controversy and sentiment in online news. *arXiv preprint arXiv:1409.8152*, 2014.

[15] E. Pariser. *The Filter Bubble: What the Internet Is Hiding from You.* 2011.

[16] A.-M. Popescu and M. Pennacchiotti. Detecting controversial events from twitter. In *CIKM'10*.

[17] H. S. Rad and D. Barbosa. Identifying controversial articles in wikipedia: A comparative study. In *WikiSym 2012*.

[18] H. Roitman, S. Hummel, E. Rabinovich, B. Sznajder, N. Slonim, and E. Aharoni. On the Retrieval of Wikipedia Articles Containing Claims on Controversial Topics. In *WWW'16*.

[19] T. Rose, M. Stevenson, and M. Whitehead. The Reuters Corpus Volume 1. In *LREC 2002*.

[20] E. Sandhaus. The New York Times annotated corpus. *LDC*, 6(12):e26752, 2008.

[21] T. Yasseri, R. Sumi, A. Rung, A. Kornai, and J. Kertész. Dynamics of conflicts in wikipedia. *PloS one*, 7(6):e38869, 2012.

Evaluating Document Retrieval Methods for Resource Selection in Clustered P2P IR

Rami S. Alkhawaldeh
University of Glasgow
University Avenue, G12 8QQ
Glasgow, United Kingdom
r.alkhawaldeh85@gmail.com

Joemon M. Jose
University of Glasgow
University Avenue, G12 8QQ
Glasgow, United Kingdom
Joemon.Jose@glasgow.ac.uk

Deepak P
Queen's University
University Road, BT7 1NN
Belfast, United Kingdom
deepakp7@gmail.com

ABSTRACT

Resource Selection (or Query Routing) is an important step in P2P IR. Though analogous to document retrieval in the sense of choosing a relevant subset of resources, resource selection methods have evolved independently from those for document retrieval. Among the reasons for such divergence is that document retrieval targets scenarios where underlying resources are semantically homogeneous, whereas peers would manage diverse content. We observe that semantic heterogeneity is mitigated in the clustered 2-tier P2P IR architecture resource selection layer by way of usage of clustering, and posit that this necessitates a re-look at the applicability of document retrieval methods for resource selection within such a framework. This paper empirically benchmarks document retrieval models against the state-of-the-art resource selection models for the problem of resource selection in the clustered P2P IR architecture, using classical IR evaluation metrics. Our benchmarking study illustrates that document retrieval models significantly outperform other methods for the task of resource selection in the clustered P2P IR architecture. This indicates that clustered P2P IR framework can exploit advancements in document retrieval methods to deliver corresponding improvements in resource selection, indicating potential convergence of these fields for the clustered P2P IR architecture.

Categories and Subject Descriptors

H.4.2 [**Information Systems Applications**]: P2P Information Retrieval

Keywords

Document Retrieval Methods; Resource Selection; Information Retrieval; Peer-to-Peer; Clustering Peers; Content-based; Evaluation

1. INTRODUCTION

Federated search provides a uniform interface across plurality of searchable resources by way of a broker. P2P IR systems do federated search over multiple peers, each of which manages a subset of the full dataset. In cooperative P2P IR environments, the brokers acquire content information from their resources beforehand and could potentially build indexes upon such information; these are then used to make a decision regarding routing a given query to those peers that are most likely to contain relevant documents [5, 8]. This contrasts with un-cooperative environments, where the resources provide only the search API. Resource selection (i.e., Query routing) is the problem of selecting a subset of relevant peers for a given query in P2P IR systems [18]. Following resource selection, the query is sent to the selected resources which would then process it and send results back to the broker. The broker would merge results from across peers providing a single ranked list of results to the user. Resource selection is a critical component in P2P IR; low-quality resource selection, the case where the relevant peers get excluded would inevitably lead to less effective IR results. In this paper, we consider the applicability of document retrieval methods for resource selection in a well-studied co-operative P2P IR environment that uses text clustering to structure content within peers [10].

There has been a large amount of work on resource selection mechanisms for general co-operative P2P IR where the broker operates on a set of resources, each of which manage a subset of the dataset. In a sense, the problem of resource selection may be seen as analogous to the problem of selection of relevant documents in conventional IR systems. In a federated P2P IR based scholarly article search system, the allocation of documents to resources could be dependent on factors such as the publication venue and publisher, which are typically completely orthogonal to the content in the documents. Thus, each resource could comprise documents that are semantically as diverse as the corpus itself. This diversity of topics at the level of each resource breaks the analogy between resource selection and document retrieval, since documents are typically focused on topic or a small number of topics and are thus limited in their heterogeneity. This, among other factors, has led to divergence between the techniques for resource selection and document retrieval, with each stream evolving independently. For example, popular resource selection methods such as CVV [20] and Taily [2] use information about word distributions across peers, whereas popular document retrieval models rely more on simpler term weighting (e.g., tf-idf) and divergence from randomness (e.g., BB2 [3]).

There has been renewed interest in the clustered P2P IR architecture [10, 1, 13] that employs text clustering to build a two-tier structure. The usage of text clustering in the architecture ensues that routing decisions be made at the level of resource groups that are internally homogeneous. This property of the clustered P2P IR architecture also brings resources conceptually closer to documents in the sense of not being very divergent topically. In this paper, we posit that the clustered P2P IR architecture necessitates a re-look at

CIKM'16, October 24-28, 2016, Indianapolis, IN, USA
© 2016 ACM. ISBN 978-1-4503-4073-1/16/10...$15.00
DOI: http://dx.doi.org/10.1145/2983323.2983912

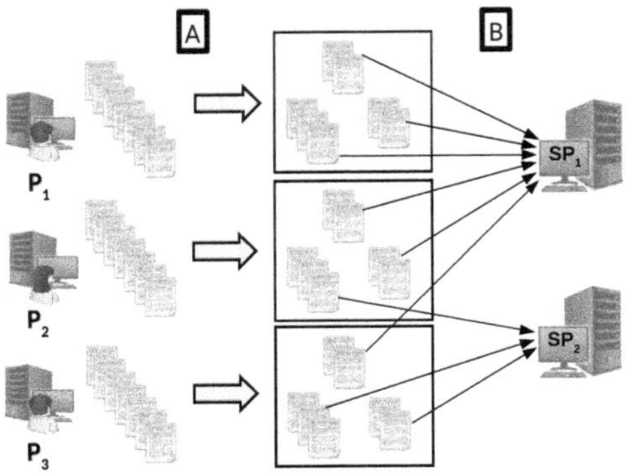

Figure 1: Clustered 2-Tier Architecture

the applicability of document retrieval methods for resource selection. Our main contributions are as follows:

- We consider the applicability of document retrieval methods for resource selection in the context of clustered P2P IR where routing decisions are to be made among semantically coherent resources.
- We do an empirical benchmarking of document retrieval methods against state-of-the-art resource selection methods, on the clustered P2P IR architecture. Our results across many testbeds establish that document retrieval methods are able to deliver consistently superior accuracies in resource selection.

We start by describing the clustered P2P architecture, our target environment, and outline reasons as to why we think that would be a friendly environment for document retrieval methods. We then summarize the document retrieval and resource selection methods that we benchmark in this study, followed by our empirical analysis and conclusions.

2. CLUSTERED 2-TIER ARCHITECTURE

Figure 1 illustrates the construction of the clustered 2-tier architecture. Each of the peers maintain a subset of documents, as shown by the different P_is in the left side of the figure. The subset of documents within each peer are subjected to a clustering process, illustrated in the figure as Step **A**; we will call this as *intra-peer clustering.* Though the figure shows 3 clusters consistently for every peer, there could in general be any number of clusters. Phase **B** clusters these intra-peer clusters, across peers, into a specified number (two, in the figure) of clusters. Each such cluster is managed by a super-peer (SP_i). Due to the clustering, not every super-peer necessarily would have representation from each peer; in our example, SP_2 does not have representation from P_1. The super-peer level, as may be noted, is an additional layer giving the framework the name 2-tier. Every query to the P2P IR system is sent to *each* of the super-peers, which would then use the information from the intra-peer clusters it manages, to route the query to one or more peers to which it is connected.

For a news search engine where different peers manage content from separate news agencies, sports related news articles may be separated out from others within each peer in the intra-peer clustering phase. Due to the second-level clustering, the sports clusters from separate peers are expected to be collected into a super-peer. Thus, the 2-stage clustering process ensures that routing decisions can be made at the level of super-peers that manage coherent content internally as well as among each other, while not disturbing the document assignment to peers; this likens the scenario to a domain-specific search at each super-peer.

Type	Technique	Remarks
Vector Space	TF-IDF	TF-IDF Cosine similarity b/w Query and Document Vectors
Document Relevance	Okapi.BM25	Combination of binary independence model with term frequency saturation.
Query Relevance	LM	Language Model based assessment of query relevance
Divergence from Randomness	BB2	Bose-Einstein Model
	In_expB2	Inv Exp. Doc. Freq. Model
	In_expC2	Inv Exp. Doc. Freq. Model
	InL2	Inv Doc. Freq. Model

Table 1: Document Retrieval Models

Motivation: In general P2P IR without any intra-peer clustering, different resources at the resource selection level could potentially have widely varying content; this makes it infeasible to consider resources as analogous to documents, since document processing techniques often are built with the assumption that only a few topics are touched upon, in each document. An example is the concentration parameter in LDA that enforces topic sparsity at the document level. As another example, two large documents comprising text segments from across domains could achieve a high tf-idf cosine value due to a lot of small similarities adding up and end up being competitive with a pair of documents from the same domain; thus, tf-idf cosine is better applicable in cases where documents exhibit a good amount of lexical skew (akin to topical focus). In short, the absence of content coherence in general P2P IR architectures has made it infeasible to exploit the advances in document processing directly for resource selection, resulting in a divergent evolution of techniques for the tasks, as discussed earlier. Our central hypothesis is that the clustered P2P architecture, by virtue of clustering, helps bring back the analogy between documents and resources, thus recalling document relevance methods into contention for resource selection.

3. DOCUMENT RETRIEVAL METHODS

Table 2 summarizes the document retrieval methods that we will use in our benchmarking study. The vector space model-based tf-idf scheme [4] quantifies the cosine similarity between tf-idf vectors, without treating the query and the documents differently. We also employ probabilistic retrieval models such as Okapi.BM25 [15] and Language Modeling (LM [9]) in our analysis. These differ in terms of the conceptualization of the model they create; BM25 models relevant documents given a query, whereas LM models query relevance using the document as a reference. The third type of models quantify divergence from randomness, based on the idea that the informativeness of a term may be measured by examining how much the term frequency distribution departs from a benchmark distribution generated by a random process. The different techniques in this family differ in terms of the randomness model they employ (listed in the table), and the formulation used in the after-effect and normalization steps. The details of these divergence models appear in [3]; a webpage[1] summarizes them succinctly.

Usage for Resource Selection: The above techniques, with the exception of TF-IDF (e.g., [14] aggregates TF-IDF across documents in a peer), have not been exploited much for resource selection in hierarchical P2P IR, such as our setting. Since these techniques are specialized to ranking documents, i.e., sets of words, resources under each super-peer need to be modelled as documents. We do this by simply using the *big document* model [17]. Under this model, one big document is created for each resource managed by the super-peer; as a toy example, $SP2$ in Figure 1 would

[1]http://terrier.org/docs/v3.5/dfr_description.html

Method	Resource Score Computation
CVV	$\propto \sum_q CVV(q) \times DF_P(q)$ where $CVV(q)$ is the variance of q across peers and $DF_P(q)$ is the total frequency of q in the peer P
CORI	$\propto \sum_q \frac{DF_P(q)}{DF_P(q)+\alpha+\beta\times\#words\_in\_P}$, $DF_P(Q)$ defined as for CVV
vGlOSS	Estimate of #docs the peer would return assuming query words co-occur in docs
KL	LDA-based topic-wise PDFs over words from each peer compared against topic dist from Q using KL-divergence
Taily	Approximates distribution of document scores in each resource using a gamma dist. and scores resources based on the estimate of high-scored documents from the distribution

Table 2: Resource Selection Models for Co-operative P2P IR (Q stands for query)

be searching over two documents, one built by collating the documents it manages from P3 and the other formed by the document subset of P2. Having defined the big documents, resource selection is just about ranking the big documents using the chosen model and routing the query to the resources corresponding to the top-ranked big documents.

4. CO-OPERATIVE P2P IR RESOURCE SELECTION METHODS

We now summarize the co-operative P2P IR resource selection methods used in our study, in Table 3. CVV [20] scores resources by preferring those that have a high concentration of unevenly distributed (across resources) query terms; it may be noted that in scenarios such as our news search example, term occurrences are expected to not vary much across resources. CORI [5] generalizes Okapi.BM25 to arrive at a resource level probabilistic scoring. vGlOSS [8] scores resources using an estimate of the number of relevant documents in them making use of a query word co-occurrence assumption. KL [19] makes use of topic distributions learnt using intra-peer clustering, and scores resources using the KL-divergence of the query topic distribution from that of each resource. Taily [2], the most recent technique, fits a gamma distribution over the scores for documents (wrt the query) within each resource. This, along with the size of the resource, is used to estimate the number of top-scored documents for each query within the resource. We do not use the decision-theoretic framework [7] in our analysis since it requires (as noted in [16]) extra information such as relevance judgements not presumed in other methods.

Usage in Clustered P2P IR: Each of these resource selection methods are used at each super-peer, the resource selection point, in the clustered 2-tier architecture.

5. EVALUATION FRAMEWORK

For a given testbed, comprising a document corpus split into peer-level collections (with or without replication), we first do the two-level clustering to instantiate the clustered 2-tier architecture. We use repeated bi-sect k-means for intra-peer clustering upto a cluster size threshold of 5. This is followed by a K-means clustering in the second phase with $k = 50$ so that the intra-peer clusters are distributed among 50 super-peers [1]. Our query set is a set of 100 simulated queries generated from TREC topics 451-550[2]. Having setup the framework, we use each method chosen for the study to do resource selection on each super-peer in response to each query; for a fixed choice of the selectivity parameter (say, 5%), that much of peers are selected within each super-peer. The query is then sent to the chosen resources (across super-peers) who in turn perform document retrieval using the Okapi.BM25 model; their results are collected and merged using the well-known COMBMNZ merging strategy [12]. The final merged result set is evaluated against classical IR parameters such as precision and MAP, as well as recall since labelled relevance information is available for the query-testbed combination we use. In addition to popular P2P IR testbeds comprising ≈1.6 million documents listed from [11], we also evaluate our approach on a meta-search task on the FedWeb 2013 dataset [6] (13k documents, 200 queries) consisting of results across 157 search engines, each of which are modeled as a separate peer. Since the result trends across methods were found to be consistent across varying values of pre-specified percentages of peers to be selected at each super-peer, we will report the average of results from 10 settings with the selectivity parameter varying from 5% to 50% in increments of 5%.

[2]http://trec.nist.gov/data/webmain.html

6. EXPERIMENTAL RESULTS

P2P IR Testbeds: Table 3 summarizes the results on the IR testbeds viz., DLWOR, DLWR, ASISWOR and ASISWR (details in [11]); DL* and ASIS* simulate digital library and file-sharing scenarios respectively. We report precision, recall and MAP figures evaluated over the top-1000 documents, for each technique-testbed combination. While top-1000 is usually realistic for getting a subset of relevant documents in P2P IR, fewer documents are usually expected to be utilized in scenarios involving manual perusal of results; we thus report the Precision at top-10 results too, in the table. The top and bottom parts of the table illustrate the document retrieval and standard resource selection methods respectively; each value that is seen to be better than the best value for the [metric,testbed] combination in the other category is boldfaced. Additionally, the best value across categories is underlined as well. We performed bootstrap 2-paired t-tests to analyze whether the performance improvements of document retrieval methods were statistically significant; results of such tests are also indicated in the table. It may be seen from the table that the document retrieval methods perform better in every testbed and evaluation metric, barring one case where Taily is seen to outperform others. The last row counts the number of document retrieval methods (out of the 7 being studied) that perform either equally or better than the best performing general resource selection method under study, on the corresponding evaluation metric. As may be seen, on an average, roughly 40% of document retrieval methods are seen to outperform the best performing resource selection methods, across metrics. This establishes that document retrieval methods are very effective for resource selection in the clustered P2P IR architecture, and should be preferred to classical resource selection methods designed for general P2P IR.

Federated Web Search Testbed: Table 4 summarizes the corresponding results on the federated web search testbed, in the same format as for P2P IR testbeds. The results on this testbed also confirm the superior performance of the document retrieval methods for resource selection in the clustered P2P IR architecture in the meta-search environments. It is notable that five of seven document retrieval methods outperform the best performing general resource selection method, on each metric.

7. CONCLUSIONS AND FUTURE WORK

We considered the problem of resource selection in the clustered P2P IR architecture. We postulated an enhanced applicability of document retrieval methods for resource se-

Table 3: Results on P2P IR Testbeds (○ & • indicate statistical significance at $p < 0.05$ and $p < 0.01$ respectively)

Method	DLWOR				DLWR				ASISWOR				ASISWR			
	Prec	Recall	MAP	Pr@10	Prec	Recall	MAP	Pr@10	Prec	Recall	MAP	Pr@10	Prec	Recall	MAP	Pr@10
TF-IDF	**0.0293•**	**0.5244**	**0.0911**	**0.1792**	**0.0256**	**0.4740**	**0.0307•**	0.0253	0.0189	0.3391	0.0531	0.1342	0.0191	0.3741	0.0194	0.0150
BM25	0.0177	0.2878	0.0559	0.1108	0.0170	0.3019	0.0241	0.0267	0.0253	0.4516	0.0719	0.1602	**0.0199**	**0.3919**	0.0195	0.0143
LM	0.0281	0.4889	**0.0896**	**0.1805**	**0.0259**	0.4591	**0.0349•**	**0.0357°**	0.0256	0.4427	**0.0742**	**0.1727°**	**0.0217°**	**0.4009°**	**0.0232**	**0.0157**
BB2	**0.0290°**	**0.5238**	**0.0925**	**0.1765**	0.0250	0.4721	**0.0300°**	0.0242	**0.0263**	**0.4689**	**0.0757°**	**0.1703°**	0.0188	0.3713	0.0194	0.0150
Inexp_B2	**0.0286**	0.5150	0.0884	0.1740	0.0247	0.4625	**0.0289**	0.0242	0.0257	0.4563	**0.0742**	**0.1703°**	0.0190	0.3693	0.0198	0.0152
Inexp_C2	**0.0286**	0.5136	**0.0895**	0.1740	0.0247	0.4638	**0.0288**	0.0245	0.0256	0.4537	**0.0741**	**0.1710°**	0.0191	0.3686	0.0199	0.0153
InL2	**0.0291•**	0.5130	0.0887	**0.1775**	**0.0255**	0.4658	**0.0307•**	0.0257	**0.0260**	0.4628	**0.0741**	**0.1680**	0.0192	0.3771	0.0196	0.0150
CVV	0.0266	0.4961	0.0842	**0.1757**	0.0216	0.4254	0.0236	0.0198	0.0252	0.4594	0.0714	0.1635	0.0191	**0.3846**	0.0188	0.0147
CORI	0.0280	0.4983	0.0845	0.1697	0.0243	0.4532	**0.0282**	0.0242	**0.0260**	**0.4645**	**0.0737**	**0.1640**	0.0186	0.3694	0.0188	0.0143
vGlOSS	0.0245	0.4510	0.0777	0.1643	0.0212	0.3970	0.0275	**0.0288**	0.0226	0.4089	0.0705	0.1593	**0.0197**	0.3820	**0.0215**	0.0152
KL	0.0172	0.2727	0.0453	0.1323	0.0155	0.2461	0.0175	0.0275	0.0188	0.3368	0.0530	0.1347	0.0170	0.3221	0.0175	0.0155
Taily	**0.0282**	**0.5216**	**0.0894**	0.1605	**0.0251**	**0.4777**	0.0277	0.0238	0.0258	0.4606	0.0705	0.1583	0.0193	0.3783	0.0204	**0.0173**
	5	**2**	**4**	**4**	**3**	**-**	**6**	**1**	**2**	**1**	**5**	**5**	**2**	**2**	**1**	**-**

Table 4: Results on FedWeb2013 Testbed

Method	Prec	Recall	MAP	Pr@10	nDCG@10
TF-IDF	**0.0626•**	**0.5858•**	**0.2526•**	**0.4285•**	**0.2721•**
BM25	0.0178	0.2223	0.1161	0.1842	0.1159
LM	0.0475	0.4260	0.1552	0.3036	0.1951
BB2	**0.0641•**	**0.6047•**	**0.2610•**	**0.4430•**	**0.2886•**
Inexp_B2	**0.0622•**	**0.5835•**	**0.2490•**	**0.4117°**	**0.2657•**
Inexp_C2	**0.0622•**	**0.5835•**	**0.2490•**	**0.4113°**	**0.2655•**
InL2	**0.0615•**	**0.5692•**	**0.2458•**	**0.4203•**	**0.2680•**
CVV	0.0496	0.4627	0.1566	0.3184	0.2010
CORI	0.0431	0.3953	0.1389	0.2922	0.1656
vGlOSS	0.0340	0.3155	0.1050	0.2381	0.1454
KL	0.0234	0.2071	0.0508	0.1599	0.1225
Taily	**0.0580**	**0.5419**	**0.2228**	**0.3808**	**0.2198**
	5	**5**	**5**	**5**	**5**

lection in the target architecture, given the content homogeneity among intra-peer clusters at the resource selection layer. We empirically benchmarked well-known document retrieval methods against the state-of-the-art resource selection methods designed for general P2P IR. An extensive analysis of retrieval effectiveness over P2P IR and federated-search testbeds using classical IR evaluation metrics validate our hypothesis convincingly, with document retrieval methods consistently outperforming others. This establishes that document retrieval methods ought to be the preferred choice for resource selection in clustered P2P IR environments. Our empirical analysis indicates that the language modeling approach (LM) should be the preferred resource selection method for both P2P IR and Federated Web Search scenarios; further, BB2 is seen to be competitive in P2P IR.

From a future work perspective, our results indicate a potential convergence of the document retrieval and resource selection tasks in the clustered P2P IR architecture so that future advancements in document retrieval may be effectively leveraged to achieve corresponding gains in resource selection on the target framework. With the improved accuracy of document retrieval techniques being apparent from our study, their indexing overhead and messaging costs need to be analyzed for fast uptake.

8. ACKNOWLEDGEMENT

We would like to thank the University of Jordan for supporting this study.

9. REFERENCES

[1] R. S. Alkhawaldeh and J. M. Jose. Experimental study on semi-structured peer-to-peer information retrieval network. In *In CLEF 2015, Toulouse, France, September 8-11, 2015, Proceedings*, pages 3–14. 2015.

[2] R. Aly, D. Hiemstra, and T. Demeester. Taily: Shard selection using the tail of score distributions. In *SIGIR*, 2013.

[3] G. Amati and C. J. Van Rijsbergen. Probabilistic models of information retrieval based on measuring the divergence from randomness. *ACM TOIS*, 20(4):357–389, 2002.

[4] R. Baeza-Yates, B. Ribeiro-Neto, et al. *Modern information retrieval*, volume 463. ACM press New York, 1999.

[5] J. P. Callan, Z. Lu, and W. B. Croft. Searching distributed collections with inference networks. In *SIGIR*, 1995.

[6] T. Demeester, D. Trieschnigg, D. Nguyen, and D. Hiemstra. Overview of the trec 2013 federated web search track. In *Proceedings of the TREC*, pages 1–11, 2013.

[7] N. Fuhr. A decision-theoretic approach to database selection in networked ir. *ACM TOIS*, 17(3):229–249, 1999.

[8] L. Gravano, H. García-Molina, and A. Tomasic. Gloss: Text-source discovery over the internet. *ACM Trans. Database Syst.*, 24(2):229–264, June 1999.

[9] D. Hiemstra. *Using language models for information retrieval.* Taaluitgeverij Neslia Paniculata, 2001.

[10] I. A. Klampanos and J. M. Jose. An evaluation of a cluster-based architecture for peer-to-peer information retrieval. In *DEXA*, pages 380–391, 2007.

[11] I. A. Klampanos, V. Poznański, J. M. Jose, P. Dickman, and E. H. Road. A suite of testbeds for the realistic evaluation of peer-to-peer information retrieval systems. In *ECIR*, 2005.

[12] J. H. Lee. Analyses of multiple evidence combination. *SIGIR Forum*, 31(SI):267–276, July 1997.

[13] J. Lu and J. Callan. Federated search of text-based digital libraries in hierarchical peer-to-peer networks. In *Proceedings of ECIR'05*, pages 52–66, Berlin, Heidelberg, 2005. Springer-Verlag.

[14] M. Melucci and A. Poggiani. A study of a weighting scheme for information retrieval in hierarchical peer-to-peer networks. In *Proceedings of ECIR*, pages 136–147, 2007.

[15] S. E. Robertson, S. Walker, S. Jones, M. M. Hancock-Beaulieu, M. Gatford, et al. Okapi at trec-3. *NIST*, 109:109, 1995.

[16] L. Si and J. Callan. Unified utility maximization framework for resource selection. In *CIKM*, pages 32–41. ACM, 2004.

[17] L. Si, R. Jin, J. Callan, and P. Ogilvie. A language modeling framework for resource selection and results merging. In *CIKM*, pages 391–397. ACM, 2002.

[18] A. S. Tigelaar, D. Hiemstra, and D. Trieschnigg. Peer-to-peer information retrieval: An overview. *ACM TOIS*, 2012.

[19] J. Xu and W. B. Croft. Cluster-based language models for distributed retrieval. In *SIGIR*, 1999.

[20] B. Yuwono and D. L. Lee. Server ranking for distributed text retrieval systems on the internet. In *DASFAA*, 1997.

Detecting and Ranking Conceptual Links between Texts Using a Knowledge Base

Martin Tutek[1], Goran Glavaš[1,2], Jan Šnajder[1],
Nataša Milić-Frayling[3], Bojana Dalbelo Bašić[1]
[1] Faculty of Electrical Engineering and Computing, University of Zagreb, Croatia
[2] Data and Web Science Group, University of Mannheim, Germany
[3] School of Computer Science, University of Nottingham, United Kingdom
{martin.tutek, goran.glavas, jan.snajder, bojana.dalbelo}@fer.hr
natasa.milic-frayling@nottingham.ac.uk

ABSTRACT

Recent research has explored the use of Knowledge Bases (KBs) to represent documents as subgraphs of a KB concept graph and define metrics to characterize *semantic relatedness* of documents in terms of properties of the document concept graphs. However, none of the studies so far have examined to what degree such metrics capture a *user-perceived* relatedness of documents. Considering the users' explanations of how pairs of documents are related, the aim is to identify concepts in a KB graph that express the same notion of document relatedness. Our algorithm generates paths through the KB graph that originate from the terms in two documents. KB concepts where these paths intersect capture the semantic relatedness of the two starting terms and therefore the two documents. We consider how such intersecting concepts relate to the concepts in the users' explanations. The higher the users' concepts appear in the ranked list of intersecting concepts, the better the method in capturing the users' notion of document relatedness. Our experiments show that our approach outperforms a simpler graph method that uses properties of the concept nodes alone.

Keywords

Content analysis; semantic relatedness, knowledge base graph

1. INTRODUCTION

Typical information retrieval (IR) tasks, such as search, query expansion, and recommendation, rely upon techniques that involve (1) a representation of document content and (2) operators applied to that representation to measure document relevance to a user's query or similarity of compared documents. Most traditional IR approaches use a 'bag-of-words' document representation and relevance metrics based on lexical overlap [9, 7, 8]. As such, they are not well equipped to support more complex information needs requiring generalization or enumeration of specific information items. For example, the following two text snippets have no lexical overlap but are both relevant to the query "recent natural disasters in Asia":

> *"In July 2013, much of southwest China experienced heavy rainfall that led to widespread flooding..."*

> *"It was the most powerful earthquake ever recorded to have hit Japan..."*

Methods such as Latent Semantic Indexing [2] and Latent Dirichlet Allocation [1] aim to capture the underlying semantic meaning and establish relatedness of documents beyond lexical overlap. Unfortunately, they cannot easily provide a user-interpretable explanation of uncovered semantic relations.

Recently we have seen efforts to explicate the semantic relation among documents by using knowledge bases (KBs) to characterize relations among document terms. By mapping document terms onto KB concepts, each document is represented as a *concept subgraph* of a KB graph [10, 6]. This representation presents opportunities for formalizing retrieval operations as operators over graphs that leverage both explicit concept links and statistical properties of terms in the document corpus. An essential step in using KB representations is to define metrics to characterize *relatedness* of two documents. That can be achieved by first defining *pairwise relatedness of terms* and then deriving *relatedness of documents* containing the terms.

While there are many principled ways of using the concept graphs to define semantic similarity of documents, there is a fundamental question of whether the relatedness metrics agree with the users' notion of document relatedness. To the best of our knowledge, there have been no empirical studies of how users' characterization of related documents, expressed in natural language (NL) statements, maps onto the concept graphs and how the users' notion of relatedness compares with the metrics of KB-based algorithms. The former is particularly important to generate a NL explanation of relevance metrics and search results. Our research aims to fill that gap.

Starting with the users' explanations of how pairs of documents are related, we aim to devise methods that can identify concepts in a KB graph that express the same notion of document relatedness. Our algorithm first maps document terms onto KB concepts and then generates paths through the KB graph that originate from document concepts. For a pair of documents we can then identify all concept paths that intersect and therefore have a KB concept in common. Such KB concepts capture the semantic relatedness of document terms and the corresponding documents. We score and rank common concepts and use them to characterize the document relatedness.

That brings us to the final step of verifying how common document concepts relate to the users' explanations of document relatedness. We map the users' expressions onto the KB concepts and observe how high they appear in the ranked list of intersecting concepts. The higher they rank, the better the method captures the users'

CIKM '16, October 24–28, 2016, Indianapolis, IN, USA.

DOI: http://dx.doi.org/10.1145/2983323.2983913

notion of document relatedness. Findings of our experiments show that the algorithm that fully exploits KB structure by considering KB concept links performs significantly better than a method that relies upon concept statistics only.

2. RELATED WORK

Definition and implementation of document similarity is intrinsically related to the underlying IR approach and varies significantly with the adopted document representation, as can be seen from research in vector-space and probabilistic models [9, 8], latent semantic indexing [2], and KB-supported models [10, 6].

Use of KB-based document representations presents new opportunities to tackle two important retrieval challenges: (1) capture concepts that are common to two documents but not explicitly mentioned in the documents and (2) communicate to the user the rationale behind the document relatedness in a user-interpretable form through concepts linked to the document terms.

Recent work with KB-based document similarity[10, 6] focuses on entity linking to a specific KB (e.g., DBPedia or BabelNet), with the aim of producing a document similarity score. For example, Schuhmacher and Ponzetto [10] measure similarity in terms of a graph edit distance between respective document subgraphs using weighted concept edges. They do not explore in detail the conceptual links between documents and the relative importance of linked KB concepts within documents.

Ni et al. [6] extend the model from [10] by assigning different weights to linked concepts and allowing for inexact node matching by a means of comparing their *embedding vectors*. They derive concept weights from concept properties in the KB without taking into account term mentions in the document (e.g., term frequency). Since concepts are compared within an embedding space, the potential for generating user-understandable explanations of document relatedness is lost.

None of the above methods relate document similarity metrics to the users' notion of document relatedness. We argue that this is important in order to maximize the benefits of semantically rich representations that KBs offer. To this end, we explore ways to incorporate users' expressions of relatedness into the KB representations and similarity operators. We use BabelNet [5] to generate document concept graphs and identify shared concepts on the connecting paths that capture document relatedness. We analyze the set of shared concepts with regards to the concepts in the users' explanations of document relatedness to see to what degree our algorithms capture the users' notion of semantic similarity.

3. METHODOLOGY

In this section we describe the algorithm for recognizing and ranking conceptual links between the documents. Although in our experiments we use BabelNet as the KB and Babelfy [4] as the concept linker, the algorithm itself is KB and linker independent.

3.1 Concept Intersection Graph

The first step in creating a document concept graph is linking the terms mentioned in the document with concepts in the KB. Let d be an input document and $B = (V_B, E_B)$ the KB graph in which nodes denote the concepts contained in the KB and edges capture semantic relations between concepts. Let $V_d \subset V_B$ be the set of KB concepts to which the linker connects document terms.

In order to relate two documents, we consider paths in B that connect any concept linked in the first document with any concept in the second document. Due to the size and density of KBs, such exhaustive search for concept paths is computationally intractable. Thus, we reduce the search space by limiting the path length, starting with the set of document concepts V_d of linked entities and creating a *concept front*, i.e., a subgraph of B that contains all nodes that are up to n edges distant from the nodes in V_d.

Let $B_i = (V_{B_i}, E_{B_i})$ and $B_j = (V_{B_j}, E_{B_j})$ be the concept fronts of size n for documents d_i and d_j, respectively. We merge the two concept fronts into a single graph, $B_{ij} = (V_{B_i} \cup V_{B_j}, E_{B_i} \cup E_{B_j})$ and examine the *candidate concepts* from the intersection of the two concept fronts, $V_F = V_{B_i} \cap V_{B_j}$. Since we use breadth-first-search strategy to build the concept fronts, each candidate concept node, $v_f \in V_F$, must have at least one path to at least one concept linked from each of the input documents. By merging these two paths on the shared node $v_f \in V_F$, we obtain an *inter-document path* from the concept $v_i \in V_{d_i}$ to the concept $v_j \in V_{d_j}$. After collecting all such document connecting paths, we proceed by assigning a *relatedness score* to each of them. In fact, we consider several characteristic of documents and concepts to define the score.

3.2 Scoring Paths and Concepts

Our objective is to characterize the concepts $v_f \in V_F$ found in the intersection of the two concept fronts and, as an intermediate step, we score directional inter-document paths through the concepts, $p = \{(v_1, v_2), \ldots, (v_k, v_{k+1}), \ldots (v_{n-1}, v_n)\}$. The starting node of the path $v_1 \in V_i$ denotes the concept linked from the first input document d_i, the ending node $v_n \in V_j$ denotes the concept linked from the second document d_j, and an intersecting node $v_k \in V_F$ is one of the candidate concepts that reflects the relatedness of the concepts v_1 and v_n. For each such path p, we compute several features with which we aim to capture the relevance of the path for the explanation of commonalities between the documents.

Salience of linked entities (SAL). SAL aims to capture prominence of KB concepts within documents. For the sake of simplicity, we adopt document term frequency as a measure of SAL. Thus, for each directional path from the document d_i to the document d_j, we compute the SAL score for the concept $v_1 \in V_{d_i}$ at the start and the concept $v_n \in V_{d_j}$ at the end of the document connecting path.

Linking confidence (LC). LC is a measure of confidence that a term mentioned in a document is linked to the correct concept in the KB. For each document connecting path $\{(v_1, v_2), \ldots, (v_{n-1}, v_n)\}$, we compute LC scores for nodes v_1 and v_n, with the aim of reducing the contribution of paths that connect document terms that are more likely to be incorrectly linked to the KB concepts.

Specificity of path relations (SR). We adopt the assumption from [10] that more specific relations between concepts are more informative and thus more effective in supporting IR tasks. Let $r(v_k, v_{k+1})$ be the semantic relation of an edge (v_k, v_{k+1}) and R the set of all KB relations. We compute the relation relevance score of path p as the average of information contents of individual relations along p:

$$spec(p) = \frac{1}{|p|} \sum_{(v_k, v_{k+1}) \in p} -\log \frac{freq(r(v_k, v_{k+1})) + 1}{|R| + \sum_{r' \in R} freq(r')}$$

where $freq(r)$ is the number of occurrences of relation r in the KB.

Specificity of path concepts (SC). For each node v along the path, we compute the specificity of the corresponding concept c in terms of the relative frequency of c in a large corpus D:

$$ic(c, D) = -\log \frac{freq(c, D) + 1}{|D| + \sum_{c' \in D} freq(c', D)}$$

This is motivated by the assumption that terms that occur rarely in the corpus better describe the document and are better indicators of document relatedness. We used the Google Book Ngrams [3] as a large corpus D to estimate term specificity. The feature score for the whole path is the average of SC of individual nodes.

Path symmetry (SYM). Another assumption we make is that an explanatory path in the KB is more relevant for a given pair of documents if it is more symmetric with respect to some candidate concept node $v_f \in V_F$. A symmetric explanatory path means that the same set of semantic relations are required to traverse (1) from a concept linked from the first document (denoted by v_1) to the candidate concept v_f and (2) from a concept linked from the second document (denoted by v_n) to the candidate concept v_f. Let $p_1 = \{(v_1, v_2), \dots, (v_{k-1}, v_k)\}$ and $p_2 = \{(v_k, v_{k+1}), \dots, (v_{n-1}, v_n)\}$ (with $v_k \in V_F$) be the two subpaths of the inter-document path p and let $r(p)$ denote the set of KB relations on the path p. We then quantify the symmetry of the path as follows:

$$sym(p) = \frac{|r(p_1) \cap r(p_2)|}{|p|}$$

Ranking common concepts. Because the scores of above features are on different scales, we standardize the scores for each feature (z-score) before combining them into a single score for a path. We compute the final relatedness score of the path p by averaging all the feature scores assigned to that path. Finally, we compute the score for each node v_f in the front intersection V_F by summing the scores of all the paths that contain v_f. The algorithm outputs the ranked list of the KB concepts in V_F. In cases when the same concept has been found in both documents (i.e., $v_1 = v_n$), the connecting path p degenerates to an empty sequence, and the *path symmetry* and *specificity of path relations* are assigned the maximum z-score.

Complexity. The time complexity of the algorithm, stemming from the breadth-first search for the front concepts V_F, is $O(|V_d|b^{n+1})$, where b is the branching factor of nodes in the KB and n the distance in edges from the starting node. The branching factor is not constant. We estimate $b = 10$ by averaging out-degrees of all nodes traversed in BabelNet. In our experimental setting, we used $n = 5$ and the average number of concepts in the intersection was $\hat{V}_F = 10000$.

4. EVALUATION

As noted in the introduction, research efforts in KB-based representation of documents have primarily focussed on characterizing document relatedness through computing a semantic similarity score. Evaluations were thus conducted by measuring correlation between user- and method-assigned scores. In contrast, we score and rank concepts from a KB that connect paths originating from compared documents, thus reflecting the document relatedness. In our evaluations, we observe how they relate to the concepts expressed by the users when articulating their views about document relatedness.

4.1 Dataset Preparation

The dataset used in our experiments consists of pairs of news articles for which connecting concepts need to be identified by the users and the algorithms, and compared. In order to ensure that there are conceptual links between documents, we guided the news pairing process. However, as the procedure below shows, we have not introduced any bias in favor of our algorithm:

1. We asked three annotators to come up with short lists of concepts for three types of notions – general (e.g., *"shark attack"*), named entities (e.g., *"Elon Musk"*), and events (e.g., *"FA Cup final"*);
2. We used the provided concepts as queries for online web search engines and obtained a collection of 25 news stories;
3. We computed cosine similarity between term vectors of the retrieved news articles. We then randomly paired each news story d_i with two other stories d_j and d_k, so that the probability of randomly selecting d_j and d_k was proportional to their cosine similarity with d_i. In other words, documents with larger cosine similarity were more likely to be paired.

Table 1: Annotation example

Story #1. *"A pet shop owner has survived an attack by a deadly, 20ft python after police wrestled the snake back into its cage. Terry Wilkins was cleaning the reptile's cage at his store in Kentucky, on Monday when it bit him, wrapped itself round his head and started crushing his neck. The snake had covered Mr Wilkins' face and was moving in for the kill when two nearby police officers intervened and saved his life."*
Story #2 *"A 9-year-old Northern California boy was mauled to death by his sister's pit bulls while she was at her job Sunday morning, police said. Investigators believe the three pit bulls Alexandria Griffin-Heady calls her "wolfpack" attacked Tyler Griffin-Huston during his 24-year-old sister's approved weekend custody of him at her Linda residence, KHTK-TV reported."*
Raw annotations: Both stories recount animal attacks on humans; In both cases, the victim is male; Both incidents happened in the US; In both cases, the police were involved;
BabelNet codifications: animal (bn:00004222n), attack/assault (bn:00006467n), human (bn:00044576n); male/man (bn:00001533n); United States (bn:00003341n); police (bn:00022026n);

Following the above steps, we obtained a dataset comprising 50 pairs of news and instructed seven annotators to (1) indicate how two texts are related, i.e., what common aspects link them, (2) describe the common aspects in their own words, and (3) rank the aspects in the decreasing order of importance. We intentionally left the annotation task underspecified in order to elicit all types of connections between two articles that the users may find and articulate. We made sure that each article pair was processed by two annotators so that we can determine the annotators' agreement.

To compare the relatedness of news stories based on users' assessment and based on our algorithm, we manually mapped the annotators' NL descriptions to BabelNet concepts. This step was carried out by a single annotator to ensure that the same users' notions were consistently linked to the same BabelNet concepts. The annotation is exemplified in Table 1. As expected, not all aspects identified by the annotators could be directly mapped onto BabelNet concepts, including statements such as *"Both news stories are written in a negative tone"* or *"Chances of events happening are relatively small"*. We labelled such explanations as *not-codifiable* and penalized our approach in the experimental evaluation as not being able to generate KB based representation of users' explanations. We measured the inter-annotator agreement in terms of the (rank-agnostic) F_1 measure and observed a very low score of 11.4%. This confirms the highly subjective nature of the task. Thus we chose not to resolve annotators' disagreements but, rather, evaluate the methods against each annotator's input and then compute the average performance for each document pair.

4.2 Experiments Design and Findings

We designed our experiments to compare (1) KB concepts used by the annotator to describe pairwise document relatedness against (2) KB concepts identified and ranked by several algorithms. We observe where the annotators' concepts can be found in the ranked lists of concepts returned by the algorithms.

Evaluation metrics. We initially applied the mean average precision (MAP) by averaging precision scores at the rank positions where the annotators' concepts are observed. However, (1) MAP scores are not informative when there is a large imbalance between the size of the ranked list and the number of relevant items, as in

Table 2: Algorithm performance

Algorithm	MAP (%)	MWAR
N-gram overlap	8.65	4012.3
Concept overlap	10.46	3789.4
KB ranker	**10.94**	**3020.4**

our case where algorithms return thousands of ranked KB concepts while annotators provide only a handful, and (2) MAP metrics cannot take into account the concept ranking provided by the annotators. For these reasons we introduced the *mean weighted average rank* (MWAR) metric. For a given document pair, let G be the ranked list of concepts provided by an annotator and let A be the list of concepts produced by an algorithm (typically $|A| \gg |G|$). With $a(G_i)$ being the rank in A of the i-th concept from the annotator's list, the *weighted average rank* (WAR) is computed as follows:

$$WAR(G, A) = \frac{\sum_{i=1}^{|G|} (|G| - i + 1) \cdot a(G_i)}{\sum_{i=1}^{|G|} i}$$

The MWAR is simply the mean of WAR scores over all document pairs (lower is better). The annotators' concepts that are not present in the concept lists produced by the algorithm are assigned rank $|A| + 1$. The two baselines that we use produce significantly shorter rankings than our KB-based algorithm. To allow for fair comparison, we also assign rank $|A| + 1$ to gold concepts when they are missing from the baseline ranking.

Parameter optimization. We split the dataset of 50 article pairs into the development set (10 pairs) and test set (40 pairs). We use the development set to determine the optimal value for the path lengths, i.e., front distance; we set it to $n = 4$ (cf. Section 3.1).

Baselines. We compare the performance of our KB-based algorithm with two baseline algorithms. The first algorithm is the *n-gram overlap*, which identifies term n-grams that occur in both documents and ranks them in decreasing order of frequencies. The second baseline, *concept overlap*, considers KB concepts that literally appear in the document. It ranks the common concepts based on their frequency in the two texts. These baselines are selected to contrast our approach with one algorithm that does not utilize KB in any way and another that considers only KB concept nodes that appear in the texts while it does not utilize KB links and relatedness to other concepts.

Results. Table 2 shows the performance of our KB-based algorithm (*KB ranker*) and the two baselines. The KB-based algorithm outperforms both baselines, for MWAR significantly ($p < 0.05$, Student's t-test). This justifies the use of KB to explain document relatedness by (1) seeking conceptual links as opposed to simple term overlap, and (2) identifying concept paths and common frontal concepts.

5. CONCLUSION

One of key benefits of the KB based document representations is the availability of explicit semantic links among concepts that can be used to describe the relation between documents in a user-interpretable form. Similarly, a user could describe, in natural language, desired properties and relatedness of relevant documents. Such a specification would be then expressed in terms of KB concepts and links and used to identify documents that fit the users' criteria. In both instances, it is critical to compare users' expressions with those KB concepts that algorithms use to characterize semantic relevance of documents.

We presented a method and experiment results of comparing users' expressions of document relatedness with several algorithms designed to work with document concept graphs to measure semantic similarity. Our initial results show that algorithms that exploit full KB structure lead to a better matching of users' expressions than those relying upon simple lexical overlap or concept statistics only.

Our further research will include systematic evaluation and optimization of algorithm components and improvements of concept rankings. That will include larger datasets and more intuitive and versatile annotation schemes.

6. ACKNOWLEDGMENTS

This work has been funded by the Unity Through Knowledge Fund of the Croatian Science Foundation, under the grant 19/15: "EVEnt Retrieval Based on semantically Enriched Structures for Interactive user Tasks (EVERBEST)". The research has been carried out within the activities of the Centre of Research Excellence for Data Science and Cooperative Systems supported by the Ministry of Science, Education and Sports of the Republic of Croatia. We thank the annotators for their efforts and the reviewers for their comments.

7. REFERENCES

[1] D. M. Blei, A. Y. Ng, and M. I. Jordan. Latent Dirichlet allocation. *Journal of machine Learning research*, 3(Jan):993–1022, 2003.

[2] S. Deerwester, S. T. Dumais, G. W. Furnas, T. K. Landauer, and R. Harshman. Indexing by latent semantic analysis. *Journal of the American society for information science*, 41(6):391, 1990.

[3] J.-B. Michel, Y. K. Shen, A. P. Aiden, A. Veres, M. K. Gray, J. P. Pickett, D. Hoiberg, D. Clancy, P. Norvig, J. Orwant, et al. Quantitative analysis of culture using millions of digitized books. *Science*, 331(6014):176–182, 2011.

[4] A. Moro, A. Raganato, and R. Navigli. Entity linking meets word sense disambiguation: a unified approach. *Transactions of the ACL*, 2:231–244, 2014.

[5] R. Navigli and S. P. Ponzetto. BabelNet: The automatic construction, evaluation and application of a wide-coverage multilingual semantic network. *Artificial Intelligence*, 193:217–250, 2012.

[6] Y. Ni, Q. K. Xu, F. Cao, Y. Mass, D. Sheinwald, H. J. Zhu, and S. S. Cao. Semantic documents relatedness using concept graph representation. In *Proceedings of ACM WSDM '16*, pages 635–644. ACM, 2016.

[7] J. M. Ponte and W. B. Croft. A language modeling approach to information retrieval. In *Proceedings of ACM SIGIR '98*, pages 275–281. ACM, 1998.

[8] S. Robertson and H. Zaragoza. *The probabilistic relevance framework: BM25 and beyond*. Now Publishers Inc, 2009.

[9] G. Salton, A. Wong, and C.-S. Yang. A vector space model for automatic indexing. *Communications of the ACM*, 18(11):613–620, 1975.

[10] M. Schuhmacher and S. P. Ponzetto. Knowledge-based graph document modeling. In *Proceedings of the ACM WSDM '14*, pages 543–552. ACM, 2014.

DePP: A System for Detecting Pages to Protect in Wikipedia

Kelsey Suyehira
Computer Science Department
Boise State University
Boise, ID 83725 USA
kelseysuyehira@u.boisestate.edu

Francesca Spezzano
Computer Science Department
Boise State University
Boise, ID 83725 USA
francescaspezzano@boisestate.edu

ABSTRACT

Wikipedia is based on the idea that anyone can make edits to the website in order to create reliable and crowd-sourced content. Yet with the cover of internet anonymity, some users make changes to the website that do not align with Wikipedia's intended uses. For this reason, Wikipedia allows for some pages of the website to become protected, where only certain users can make revisions to the page. This allows administrators to protect pages from vandalism, libel, and edit wars. However, with over five million pages on Wikipedia, it is impossible for administrators to monitor all pages and *manually* enforce page protection. In this paper we consider for the *first* time the problem of deciding whether a page should be protected or not in a collaborative environment such as Wikipedia. We formulate the problem as a binary classification task and propose a novel set of features to decide which pages to protect based on (i) users page revision behavior and (ii) page categories. We tested our system, called DePP, on a new dataset we built consisting of 13.6K pages (half protected and half unprotected) and 1.9M edits. Experimental results show that DePP reaches 93.24% classification accuracy and significantly improves over baselines.

1. INTRODUCTION

In order to create reliable and crowd-sourced content, Wikipedia is based on the idea that anyone can make edits to the website. Although in certain circumstances, this is not the case. Some restrictions may be placed on pages because of an identified likelihood of damage if the page is left open for editing by anyone. Placing these restrictions is known as *page protection*[1]. There are different levels of page protection for which different levels of users can make edits (or, in general, perform actions on the page): fully protected pages can be edited (or moved) only by administrators, semi-protected pages can be edited only by autoconfirmed users, while move protection does not allow pages to be moved to a new title, except by an administrator. Page protections can also be set for different amounts of time, including 24 or 36 hours, or indefinitely. Examples of protected pages on English Wikipedia are *Drug* and *Bigfoot*. Users can recognize these kind of pages by the image of a lock in the upper right hand corner of the page.

Common motivations that an administrative user may have in protecting a page include consistent vandalism or libel from one or more users. A page protection can also be applied if edit wars are occurring. According to Wikipedia, an edit war is when two users cannot agree on the content of an article and one user repeatedly reverts the other's edits[2]. If a page becomes protected, this forces the users to go to the article's talk page in order to settle the conflict or to find help in resolving the dispute.

Currently, English Wikipedia contains over five million pages. Only a small percentage of those pages are currently protected, about 0.2 percent. Since many of the protected pages can be templates or user pages, the amount of protected article pages is even smaller. However, around 17 pages become protected every day[3]. This ratio makes it difficult for administrative users to monitor over all Wikipedia pages to determine if any need to be protected. Users can request pages to be protected or unprotected but an administrative user would have to analyze the page to determine if it should be protected, what level of protection to give, and for how long the protection should last, if not indefinitely. All this work is currently *manually* done by administrators.

In this paper we study for the *first* time the problem of deciding whether a page should be protected or not in a collaborative environment such as Wikipedia. Our contributions are the following. (1) We formulate the *new* problem as a binary classification task and propose a novel set of features to identify pages to protect based on (i) users behavior in editing page revisions and (ii) page categories. (2) We built a new dataset consisting of 13.6K pages (half protected and half unprotected) and 1.9M edits to test our approach. (3) We tested our features with different classification algorithms and we show that we are able to classify if a given article should be protected with an accuracy of 93.24%, significantly outperforming over baselines.

2. RELATED WORK

To the best of our knowledge, little research has been done

[1]https://en.wikipedia.org/wiki/Wikipedia:Protection_policy

[2]https://en.wikipedia.org/wiki/Wikipedia:Edit_warring

[3]We have observed the number of protected pages that are listed on the Wikipedia website from May 6, 2016 through Aug 6, 2016.

CIKM'16, October 24-28, 2016, Indianapolis, IN, USA
© 2016 ACM. ISBN 978-1-4503-4073-1/16/10...$15.00
DOI: http://dx.doi.org/10.1145/2983323.2983914

on the topic of page protection in Wikipedia. Page protection is a form of organizational "wiki-work". A few papers have researched different forms of wiki-work, including the featured article process [10], or mining editors' activity to automatically assign Barnstars [7]. Hill and Shaw [4] studied the impact of page protection on user patterns of editing. They also created a dataset (they admit it may not be complete) of protected pages to perform their analysis.

One of the main reasons to apply page protection is to prevent edit warring. This often happens on pages about controversial topics. Roitman et al. [9] proposed an algorithm to retrieve relevant articles containing claims for a given controversial topic. However, their algorithm requires the list of controversial topics as input, and no study has been done between retrieved pages and page protection.

Beside edit warring, another reason why pages are protected is to avoid or block vandalism from occurring. The problem of vandalism detection on Wikipedia has been heavily studied. Many works have attempted to predict which pages have been vandalized (see [3] for a survey) or when certain acts of damage have occurred [8, 6], while other recent research proposes an early warning system to detect vandal users [5]. Currently, ClueBot NG [1] and STiki [2] are the state-of-the-art tools used by Wikipedia to detect vandalism. ClueBot NG is a bot based on an artificial neural network which scores edits and reverts the worst-scoring edits. STiki is an intelligent routing tool which suggests potential vandalism to humans for definitive classification. It works by scoring edits on the basis of metadata and reverts, and computing a reputation score for each user.

There are not currently bots on Wikipedia that can search for pages that may need to be protected. WikiMedia does have a script[4] available in which administrative users can protect a set of pages all at once. However, this program requires that the user supply the pages, or the category of pages to be protected and is only intended for protecting a large group of pages at once. There are some bots on Wikipedia that can help with some of the wiki-work that goes along with protecting or removing page protection. This includes adding or removing a template to a page that is marked as protected or no longer marked as protected. These bots can automatically update templates if a page protection has expired. We believe the work done in this paper would be helpful to detect pages to protect by reducing the time many administrators have to spend checking and marking pages as protected and updating the page template, or the time other users have to spend watching pages instead of creating quality content.

3. DATASET

Wikipedia has different types of pages that may need to be protected, besides article pages. These include user pages, talk pages, and templates. Moreover, it has different mechanisms to protect a page as edit protection, move protection, or upload protection. As also stated in [4], building a dataset of protected pages is challenging because of inconsistencies in the Wikipedia data in reporting protection events. Thus, in this paper we concentrated on articles pages because these are more likely to have changes to the protection, and we consider the (semi and full) edit protection level as edit protection times can be easily retrieved from Wikipedia API.

[4] https://www.mediawiki.org/wiki/Manual:Pywikibot/protect.py

As the percentage of protected pages, out of the total number of articles on Wikipedia is very small, we built a balanced dataset of protected/unprotected pages as follows.

We first collected the entire list of edit protected articles up to April 7, 2016 resulting in 6,799 pages. Then, we gather a list of unprotected pages of almost the same size by requesting random article pages from the Wikipedia API (we double checked if the random page was protected, and if so, we discarded the page). We collected a total of 6,824 unprotected pages.

For each protected/unprotected selected page, we then gathered up to the last 500 most recent revisions, if there were that many. However, if the page was protected, we only gathered the revisions up until the most recent protection. If there was more than one recent protection, we gathered the revision information between the two protections. This allowed us to focus on the revisions leading up to the most recent page protection. Revision information that we collected included the user who made the revision, the timestamp of the revision, the size of the revision, the categories of the page, and any comments, tags or flags associated with the revision.

Our final dataset[5] consists of a total of 13.6K (half protected and half unprotected) pages and 1.9M edits.

4. THE DEPP SYSTEM

In this section we describe the set of features we define to develop our DePP system. These features take into account the page revision history and the page categories.

The first group of six features is computed, for each page, on the whole edit history we have in our dataset (up to 500 edits per page) and looks at how Wikipedia users contribute to a particular page:

[E1] *Total average time between revisions*: pages that have very few edits over a long period of time are less likely to become protected (as their content is more stable) than pages with many edits that happen with little time between them.

[E2] *Total number of users making 5 or more revisions*: this feature counts the number of users who make more than five edits to a page.

[E3] *Total average number of revisions per user*: if there are many users making a few changes to a page, it is less likely to become protected than if a few users are making a lot of changes to a page.

[E4] *Total number of revisions by non-registered users*: this feature measures the number of changes made to a page from non-registered users. If a user has not spent the time to set up an account, it is less likely that they are a proficient user and more likely to be a spammer or vandal. Therefore, the more non-registered users that are editing a page, the more likely it is that the page may need to be protected.

[E5] *Total number of revisions made from mobile device*: similar to feature E4, this feature looks at the number of revisions that are tagged as coming from a mobile device. This is a useful feature because users making changes from a mobile device are not likely to be sitting down to spend time making revisions to a page that would add a lot of value. It is possible that a user making a change from a mobile device is only adding non-useful information, vandalizing a page, or reverting vandalism that needs to be removed immediately.

[5] The dataset is available at https://sites.google.com/site/francescaspezzano/publications/depp

[E6] *Total average size of revisions*: it is possible that users vandalizing a page, or adding non-useful information would make an edit that is smaller in size. This is opposed to a proficient user who may be adding a large amount of new content to a page. For this reason, we measure the average size of an edit. Small edits to a page may lead to a page becoming protected more than large edits would.

In the second group of features we take into account the page editing pattern over the time. We define these features by leveraging the features E1-E6 as follows. For each page we consider the edits made in the latest 10 weeks and we split this time interval into time frames of two weeks (last two weeks, second last two weeks, etc.). Then, we compute features E1 to E6 within each time frame. This produces a total of 30 new features: 6 features times 5 time intervals. These features are denoted as Ei-j^{th} where $1 \leq i \leq 6$ identifies the feature and $1 \leq j \leq 5$ refers to the time interval. For instance E2-4th represents the feature E2 computed in the 4th last two weeks. The idea of these features is to monitor features E1-E6 over time to see if some anomaly starts to happen at some point. For instance, if a page is new we may observe a lot of edits of larger size in a short time after the page is created as users are building the content of the page. Later when the content is stable, we may observe fewer edits of smaller size representing small changes in the page. On the other hand, if the content of the page was stable and suddenly we observe a lot of edits from many users, it may indicate the page topic became controversial and the page may need protection.

The next features we propose use information about page categories[6]:

[NC] *Number of categories*: this feature counts the number of categories that a page is marked under. Pages that are classified under many different categories are likely to be more complex than pages that are grouped into fewer categories. They are therefore more likely to become protected.

[PC] *Probability of protecting the page given its categories*: given all the pages in the training set T and a page category c, we compute the probability $\mathtt{pr}(c)$ that pages in category c are protected as the number of protected pages in T divided by the total number of pages in T having category c. Then, given a page p having categories $c_1, \ldots, c_n$, we compute this feature as the probability that the page is in at least one category whose pages have a high probability to be protected as

$$PC(p) = 1 - \prod_{i=1}^{n}(1 - \mathtt{pr}(c_i))$$

In addition to the above two features, we define another group of features that shows how much features E1-E6 vary for a page p w.r.t. the average of these values among all the pages in the same categories as p. Specifically, given the set of pages in the training set T, we computed the set C of the top-100 most frequent categories. Additionally, for each category $c \in C$, we averaged the features E1-E6 among all the pages (denoted by T_c) having category c in the training set. Then, for each page p we computed 600 features (6 times 100), one for each feature Ei ($1 \leq i \leq 6$) and for each category $c \in C$ as follows:

[6] Wikipedia has special categories to group protected pages according to the protection type. We excluded these categories in the computation of the category-based features.

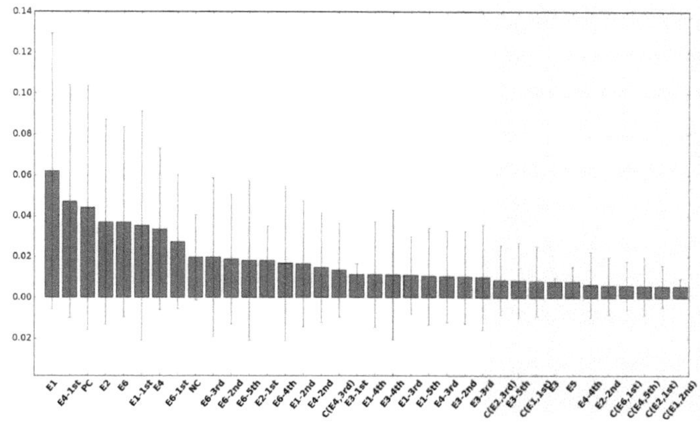

Figure 1: Feature importance (top-36 features).

$$C(Ei, c) = \begin{cases} |Ei(p) - \mathtt{avg}_{p' \in T_c}(Ei(p'))| & \text{if } p \text{ is in category } c \\ 0 & \text{otherwise} \end{cases}$$

where $Ei(p)$ is the value of the feature Ei for the page p. The aim of this group of features is to understand if a page is anomalous w.r.t. other pages in the same category.

In summary, in this paper we propose a total of 638 features for `DePP`, out of which 36 consider the page revision history, 2 consider the page categories only, and 600 consider the variation w.r.t. the page revision features within each category.

5. EXPERIMENTS

We implemented the proposed features and tested their accuracy in the prediction task with 10-fold cross validation by using different classification algorithms, namely logistic regression, support vector machine, k-nearest neighbor, and random forest.

The accuracy achieved by each of these classifiers is shown in Table 1. As we can see, random forest achieves the highest mean accuracy value of 93.24% over 10-folds of the cross validation. This shows that `DePP` is able to classify pages to protect from pages that do not need protection, very efficiently.

Features Importance. In order to better understand our features, we used forests of 250 randomized trees to determine feature importance. The relative importance (for the classification task) of a feature f in a set of features is given by the depth of f when it is used as a decision node in a tree. Features used at the top of the tree contribute to the final prediction decision of a larger fraction of the input samples. The expected fraction of the samples they contribute to can thus be used as an estimate of the relative importance of the features. Figure 1 shows the importance of the top-36 features for the classification task. The green bars in the plot show the feature importance using the whole forest, while the blue bars represent the variability across the trees. The top-3 most important features are:

- Total average time between revisions (E1): we observe, in our dataset, that the mean average time between revisions is 5.8 days for protected pages and 2.9 months for unprotected ones.

- Total number of revisions by non-registered users in the latest two weeks (E4-1st): in the most recent two weeks, non-registered users make more edits on protected pages (10 edits on average) than on unprotected ones (0.25 edits on average).
- Probability of protecting the page given its categories (PC): a protected page is more likely to be in categories that have other protected pages than an unprotected page (a probability of 0.84 on average vs. 0.52).

Overall, in the top-36 most important features we have all our basic features E1-E6, 9 category-based features, and the majority of the features E1-E6 computed in different time intervals.

Comparison with Baselines. To the best of our knowledge, there is no automated tool in Wikipedia detecting which page to protect, but all the work is manually done by administrators. One of the main reasons for protecting a page on Wikipedia is to stop edit wars, vandalism or libel from happening, or continuing to happen on a page. Thus, we compare DePP with the following baselines:

[B1] *Number of revisions tagged as "Possible libel or vandalism"*: These tags are added automatically without human interference by checking for certain words that might be likely to be vandalism. If a match is found, the tag is added.

[B2] *Number of revisions that Cluebot NG or STiki reverted as possible vandalism*: number of reverted edits in the page made by each one of these two tools.

[B3] *Number of edit wars between two users in the page*: Edit warring occurs when two users do not agree on the content of a page or revision. Therefore, we count the number of edit wars within the revision history of a page as another baseline. We define an edit war as one user making a revision to a page, followed by another user reverting that revision, and this pattern happens 2 or 3 consecutive times.

The performances of the above baselines are shown in Table 1. By considering the best classifier (random forest), baselines based on number of vandalism edits in a page (B1 and B2) present very poor accuracy performances (55.96% and 65.55% resp.). As studied in [5], vandals surf Wikipedia pages link-wise, category wise, or randomly. So, even if they start vandalizing a page that then becomes protected, they can successively move to any other arbitrary page, so B1 and B2 seem not to be good indicators of page protection.

Baseline B3, based on edit wars, performs better than the other two with an accuracy of 73.36%, confirming the fact that at least one edit war happens in pages that end up protected[7]. All baselines together reach an accuracy of 78.09% and are significantly beaten by DePP. By combining DePP with all the three baselines, the accuracy does not improve (93.327% with random forest).

6. CONCLUSIONS

In this paper we proposed DePP, the first system detecting pages to protect in Wikipedia. DePP leverages features based on users page revision behavior and page categories. We built a new dataset to test our system containing 13.6K protected and unprotected pages and 1.9M edits. We showed that DePP performs very well with an accuracy of 93.24% and significantly beats baselines.

As future work we plan to implement and test DePP directly on Wikipedia. DePP does not look at edit content, so it can work with all the different language versions of Wikipedia. Moreover, we would like to extend our data classification task to not just consider which pages require protection versus do not require protection, but attempt to classify the type of protection, including semi-protected or fully protected, and for how long a page my need to be protected, such as a short period of time or indefinitely.

[7]Average number of edit wars in protected pages is 1.37 while the same number for unprotected pages is 0.06.

	Baselines
B1	55.964%
B2	65.617%
B3	73.361%
B1+B2+B3	78.089%
	DePP
SVM	89.275%
Logistic Regression	90.816%
K Nearest Neighbor	88.225%
Random Forest	**93.237%**

Table 1: DePP accuracy results and comparison with baselines. Baselines are computed with random forest.

7. REFERENCES

[1] http://en.wikipedia.org/wiki/User:ClueBot_NG.
[2] http://en.wikipedia.org/wiki/Wikipedia:STiki.
[3] B. T. Adler, L. de Alfaro, S. M. Mola-Velasco, P. Rosso, and A. G. West. Wikipedia vandalism detection: Combining natural language, metadata, and reputation features. In *CICLing*, pages 277–288, 2011.
[4] B. M. Hill and A. D. Shaw. Page protection: another missing dimension of wikipedia research. In *OpenSym*, pages 15:1–15:4, 2015.
[5] S. Kumar, F. Spezzano, and V. S. Subrahmanian. VEWS: A wikipedia vandal early warning system. In *SIGKDD*, pages 607–616, 2015.
[6] S. Kumar, R. West, and J. Leskovec. Disinformation on the web: Impact, characteristics, and detection of wikipedia hoaxes. In *WWW*, pages 591–602, 2016.
[7] D. W. McDonald, S. Javanmardi, and M. Zachry. Finding patterns in behavioral observations by automatically labeling forms of wikiwork in barnstars. In *OpenSym*, pages 15–24, 2011.
[8] R. Priedhorsky, J. Chen, S. T. K. Lam, K. Panciera, L. Terveen, and J. Riedl. Creating, destroying, and restoring value in wikipedia. In *GROUP*, pages 259–268, 2007.
[9] H. Roitman, S. Hummel, E. Rabinovich, B. Sznajder, N. Slonim, and E. Aharoni. On the retrieval of wikipedia articles containing claims on controversial topics. In *WWW Companion*, pages 991–996, 2016.
[10] F. B. Viégas, M. Wattenberg, and M. M. McKeon. The hidden order of wikipedia. In *OCSC*, pages 445–454, 2007.

Hashtag Recommendation Based on Topic Enhanced Embedding, Tweet Entity Data and Learning to Rank

Quanzhi Li, Sameena Shah, Armineh Nourbakhsh, Xiaomo Liu, Rui Fang
Research and Development
Thomson Reuters
3 Times Square, NYC, NY 10036
{quanzhi.li, sameena.shah, armineh.nourbakhsh, xiaomo.liu, rui.fang}@thomsonreuters.com

ABSTRACT
In this paper, we present a new approach of recommending hashtags for tweets. It uses Learning to Rank algorithm to incorporate features built from topic enhanced word embeddings, tweet entity data, hashtag frequency, hashtag temporal data and tweet URL domain information. The experiments using millions of tweets and hashtags show that the proposed approach outperforms the three baseline methods – the LDA topic, the tf.idf based and the general word embedding approaches.

Keywords
Hashtag recommendation; topic enhanced word embedding; learning to rank; tweet; social media

1. INTRODUCTION
In Twitter, a hashtag is a string of characters proceeded by the # character, and is used to build a topic community or as a descriptive label [16]. Usually a hashtag consists of short, often abbreviated terms. Previous studies have shown that hashtags can be used for various purposes. Despite the importance of hashtag, only 20% of the tweets have a hashtag. This paper focuses on the problem of recommending hashtags for a given tweet. Previous studies on tag recommendation have mainly focused on content similarity-based approaches and user preferences [18, 11]. For example, Kyne et al. [4] recommend hashtags by combining hashtags obtained from similar tweets, using the cosine similarity measure, as well as hashtags from similar users. In this study, we try to address this problem by exploring the features and integration method different from previous studies. We briefly describe these features in the following paragraphs.

A word embedding is a dense, low-dimensional and real-valued vector for a word. Word embeddings help learning algorithms achieve better performance in natural language processing tasks by grouping similar words together, and have been used in many NLP applications, such as sentiment analysis and text classification [7, 8, 9]. However, most existing word embedding models assume only one vector for each word, which ignores polysemy and therefore may affect the performance of applications using them. In order to enhance discriminativeness, one approach is to exploit latent topic models to assign topics for each word, and learn topical word embeddings based on both words and their topics. The basic idea is that we allow each word to have different embeddings under different topics. In this study, we will use topic enhanced word embedding (TEWE) for the tag recommendation task.

Named entities (called entity thereafter) contained in a tweet are important topic indicators of this tweet, and they usually have close relationship with hashtags appearing in this tweet. Therefore, we also include entity and hashtag co-occurrence information in the proposed approach. During the process of analyzing hashtags, we observed that sometimes an entity name is used as part of or the whole of a hashtag name in this tweet, so we also use the entity-hashtag matching information to choose candidate hashtags for a tweet. Another observation is that, for tweets containing links, some hashtags are just the domain name of the link, such as #nbc and www.nbc.com. So this domain-hashtag matching information is also used in our method.

For the hashtag candidate list generated based on TEWE or entity hashtag co-occurrence, we generate two new lists by applying two factors to re-rank the list: hashtag popularity (frequency) and hashtag temporal information (time).

Each of the above methods (features) can be used stand-alone to generate a candidate list. In this study, we exploit the learning to rank algorithm to integrate them together to create a final hashtag recommendation list. TEWE reflects both the syntactic structure and semantics of words. Entity data adds another type of information based on hashtag's composition and relationship with entities. URL domain matching is another different type of information. These various types of information complement each other to some degree, and we expect integrating them together will improve the recommendation performance. Learning to rank helps find the best weights for different features, especially for this type of task, which tries to rank the results, instead of just giving a yes/no binary decision. To evaluate our proposed approach, we use the hashtags in a tweet as the gold standard. If the hashtag appears in our recommended list, then it is a hit. We use hit rate as performance metric [11, 14].

2. RELATED STUDIES
For recommending hashtags for tweets, previous works have focused on a couple of directions [20, 21, 19, 14, 11]. The first is to recommend hashtags based on content similarity, as mentioned in the previous section. Fewer focused on the abstracted topics of tweets, mainly using LDA topics. LDA has been used in previous studies for text classification. It is unsupervised, and it needs to associate tweets with hashtags. Godin et al. [3] exploited LDA to recommend hashtags, but they actually recommend words and then ask evaluators to evaluate if the recommended words are good candidates for using as hashtag. An unsupervised model, Twitter- LDA, is proposed in [19], but it is not used for any

CIKM'16 , October 24-28, 2016, Indianapolis, IN, USA
© 2016 ACM. ISBN 978-1-4503-4073-1/16/10…$15.00
DOI: http://dx.doi.org/10.1145/2983323.2983915

recommendation task. She and Chen [14] propose a supervised recommendation (TOMOHA) solution. They assume that each tweet is about one local topic and there is a global background topic for the corpus, and treat hashtags as labels of local topics. Based on the trained model, they infer the possibility that a hashtag will be contained in a new tweet and recommend the most probable ones. Sedhai and Sun [11] focus on recommending hashtags for hyperlinked tweets, exploiting web pages linking from tweets. In order to understand user interest, posting time and tweet content, Ma et al propose two topic models to model the hashtag annotation behavior [6]. Gong et al. [16] take the types of hashtags into consideration; they incorporate hashtag type as a hidden variable in their nonparametric Bayesian method using Dirichlet Process Mixture Models.

Word embedding and its variations have been researched in previous studies [1, 8, 9, 13]. Collobert et al. [1] introduce C&W model to learn word embedding based on the syntactic contexts of words. Another implementation is the word2vec from Mikolov et al. [9]. Previous studies have used word embedding on Twitter related tasks [15], but they are not used for predicting hashtags existing in tweets.

3. RESEARCH OVERVIEW

In this section we describe the features used in our proposed approach, the learning to rank algorithm, and the evaluation method.

3.1 Topic Enhanced Word Embedding

TEWE tries to exploit latent topic models to assign topics for each word, and learn topical word embeddings based on both the word and its topic, so that the same word in different contexts with different meanings will have different embeddings. In this study, LDA and Gibbs sampling are used to iteratively assign latent topics for each word. After all, each word will be discriminated into a specific topic t_i, forming a word-topic pair (w_i, t_i), which can be used to learn TEWE embeddings. The Skip-Gram word embedding model is extended to implement the TEWE model [8, 13]. For each target word w_i with its topic t_i, the objective is defined to maximize the following average log probability:

$$L(D) = \frac{1}{M}\sum_{i=1}^{M} \sum_{-k \le c \le k, c \ne 0} \log \Pr(w_{i+c} \mid w_i) + \log \Pr(w_{i+c} \mid t_i) \quad (1)$$

Compared to only using the target word w_i to predict context words in Skip-Gram, TEWE also uses the topic t_i of target word to predict the context words. Here we consider each topic as a pseudo word that occurs in all the positions of words assigned with this topic. The topic vector will represent the collective semantics of words under this topic. A word's TEWE embedding is the concatenation of its word embedding and topic embedding. If a word appears at different locations of a text, it will have different TEWEs if it has different topics at these locations.

A tweet has multiple words, and its length varies. There are different ways to obtain tweet representation from word embeddings. We explore four types of convolutional layers: min, average (ave), max, and the concatenation of max, min and ave. Our experiment using a separate development data set shows that the concatenation approach gives the best result, and so it is used in this study. After we have the TEWE embeddings for a tweet, the relevant hashtags are recommended based on the cosine similarity between this tweet's embedding and the embeddings of tweets in the training data. The hashtags from the most similar tweets are returned as the candidate hashtags. This computation can be done distributed, so finding a list of candidate hashtags is very quick. In our experiments, it takes less than 0.1 second.

In study [14], a hashtag is treated as the label of a topic and is directly used in their recommendation model. In our study, we use the LDA topics instead of directly using hashtags as the topic labels. The amount of hashtags is huge and directly using them in the TEWE model will make it unmanageable. In our experiments, the number of topics is set as 200, a value based on our preliminary experiment. Usually a larger training corpus will help improve the quality of an embedding model. In this study, 20 million tweets which contain hashtags are used to learn the embeddings for words.

3.2 Entity Data

Entity Hashtag Co-occurrence: For a given tweet, the score of a hashtag H_i is calculated by a probabilistic model as follow:

$$S(H_i) = \sum_{E_j \in N} P(H_i \mid E_j) \quad (2)$$

Where N is the set of entities in this tweet, E_j is an entity. $P(H_i|E_j)$ is the proportion that E_j co-occurred with H_i, given all the hashtags considered for this tweet. The co-occurrence frequency is calculated based on the training date set. The candidate hashtags are then generated based on the ranking of $S(H_i)$ scores.

Entity Matching: We observed that many hashtags directly use a proper noun or noun as part of or the whole of their names, e.g. #neverTrump and #nba. Based on this observation, we design a feature which will check if an entity (or part of the entity if it has multiple tokens) in the tweet appears in a hashtag. And this information is used to find relevant hashtags. If this tweet has no entity, then there is no hashtags recommended based on this feature.

3.3 URL Domain Matching

We also observe that, for tweets containing links, some hashtags are just the domain name of the link, or part of the hashtag name is the domain name. In the experiment, the real link address is obtained by following the short URL and redirections. The URL domain matching and the entity matching features are based on the nature of the hashtag composition, and they exploit different type of information from features based on TEWE or entity hashtag co-occurrence.

3.4 Hashtag Popularity and Temporal Data

In addition to the features mentioned above, we also use two other factors to generate new features: hashtag popularity rank and temporal-based rank. **Rank by Popularity:** it will take the frequency of a hashtag in the data set as a factor when ranking the candidates. More popular ones will have a higher rank. **Rank by Time**: it will consider how recently the tag is used. The closer to the test tweet, the higher rank the tag will get.

These two factors will apply after we get the top N tag candidates based on other methods. For example, after we return the top 30 candidates based on TEWE, we apply the popularity ranking approach to re-rank these 30 candidates based on their popularity. And this will generate a new list with different order. The temporal-based ranking act similarly.

3.5 Learning to Rank (RankLearning)

The features described above convey different types of information: syntactic, semantics, co-occurrence, popularity, time, and hashtag composition. We hypothesize that integrating them together will improve the recommendation performance, since they complement each other to certain degree.

Because of the nature of this task, which is to give an ordered list of recommended items, we design this integration as a learning to rank question. Learning to rank can rank the candidates according to their relevance or other factors to the query, which is a tweet in our case, and it has been used in many recommendation tasks, and also in some tweet related task [17]. Putting all the features and factors together, we will have multiple candidate lists with different candidates or orders. A learning to rank algorithm is used to build a ranking model based on 16,000 training tweets, and this model is used on the test data set. The algorithm used in this study is extended from LibLinear [5]. This extension efficiently trains L2-regularized L2-loss linear rankSVM by trust region Newton method and selection trees.

3.6 Evaluation method

In our experiments, we compare the proposed approach with the method using just TEWE, and three other baseline methods: the approach using just word embedding and two important approaches from previous studies, the tf.idf method [18, 4] and the LDA topic method [3]. She and Chen [14] reported their approach, TOMOHA, performed very closely to the tf.idf method. So in this study we just compare our methods to tf.idf, without comparing to TOMOHA again. Ma et al [6] propose a novel approach for hashtag annotation, but their experiment shows that their approach is not better than the tf.idf method, so we do not compare our approach to theirs in this study. The performance metric is Hit Rate, which has been used in previous study [11, 14]. Hit rate@1 means the percentage of hits we get when just recommending one hashtag. Hit rate@10 means the hit percentage when we return 10 hashtags.

4. EXPERIMENTS

We first describe the data set and the preprocessing steps for generating embeddings, and then we report the experiment result.

Table 1. Data Set Statistics

Total number of tweets	98 million
Tweets having hashtag	19.4 million
% of tweets having hashtag	20.6%
Total number of hashtags	39.7 million
Number of unique hashtags	2.45 million
Average occurrences per hashtag	16.2
% of occurrences by the top 1% most frequent hashtags	66.7%
% of occurrences by the top 10% most frequent hashtags	78.1%

4.1 Data Set and TEWE Generation

The training tweets used in this study are from September and October 2015. They were acquired through Twitter's public 1% streaming API and Twitter's Decahose data (10% of Twitter streaming data) granted to us by Twitter for research purpose. Only English tweets are used in this study. In total, there are 98 million English tweets acquired. Table 1 shows some statistics of the data set. Among the 98 million tweets, about 20.6% of them contain one or more hashtags. This shows an increase on using hashtag in tweets; previous study [4] reported that only 14% of tweets have hashtags in 2012. The total number of hashtags in the data set is nearly 40 million. There are 2.45 million unique hashtags. Although, on average, the frequency of a hashtags' occurrences is about 16, the data shows that hashtag usage is much skewed. Very few hashtags enjoy high popularity in tweets and users, while the vast majority of them are used in only a few tweets or by only several users. This observation is consistent with earlier studies [4]. Table 1 show that the top 1% most frequent hashtags account for 66.7% of the occurrences of all hashtags in this data set.

We collected 8,000 tweets as test data. They are not included in the training data set used for generating embeddings or calculating idf values for the tf.idf approach. And these tweets are randomly chosen from the first week of November of 2015, whose time period is after the data used for generating embeddings and other features. Some tweets have multiple hashtags. In this case, we randomly take one of them as the label of the tweet. All hashtags are removed from the tweet text before the text is used to generate features. The 16,000 tweets used for training the learning to rank model are drawn from the same time period.

Word Embedding and TEWE Generation Preprocessing Steps: Each tweet used in the training process is preprocessed to get a clean version. The preprocess steps are as follows: All URLs are removed; All mentions are removed. This includes the mentions appearing in a regular tweet and the user handles at the beginning of a retweet, e.g. RE: @abc; Dates and years are converted to two symbols representing date and year, respectively; All numbers are normalized to special symbol; All special characters, except #, are removed.

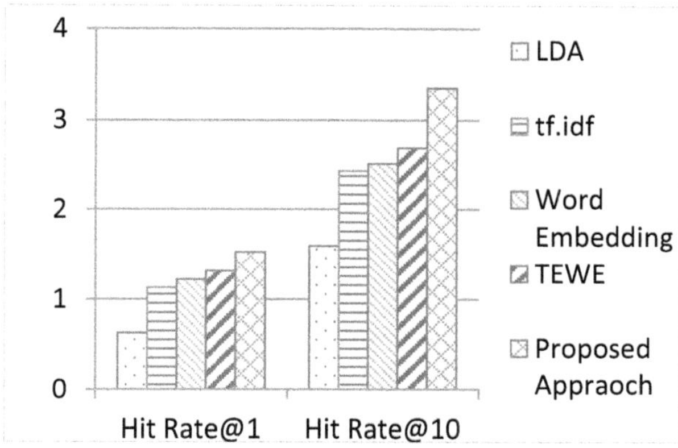

Figure 1: Experiment results based on Hit Rate

These preprocessing steps are necessary, since most of the tokens removed or normalized are not useful, such as mentions and URLs. Keeping them will increase the vector space size and computing cost. Stop words are not removed from building embedding model, since they provide important context in which other words are used.

For the tf.idf method, the pre-processing steps for tweets are similar to the steps used for building embedding model: all URLs and mentions are removed; dates and numbers are replaced by a special symbol. All special characters are removed; stop words are removed, which is different from embedding methods.

Embedding Model Parameter Setting: for generating word embeddings, the term frequency threshold is set as 3. The word embedding dimension is set to 300. The size of 300 is chosen based on our preliminary experiment of this task, and also experiments on other types of tasks, such as tweet sentiment analysis and topic classification. For the TEWE model, we use LDA to learn topic models. The number of topics is set as 200. Both the word embedding size and topic embedding size are 300. So a TEWE embedding size is 600. These numbers are chosen based on preliminary tests.

4.2 Results

Figure 1 shows the comparison result for the five approaches described before. In the proposed approach, for each feature (also listed in Table 2), the top 20 hashtags are returned as the candidate hashtags for that feature. Then all the candidate hashtags are aggregated and ranked by the learning to rank model learned from training data.

Figure 1 shows that the LDA method has the lowest performance, and this is consistent with results from previous studies. The word embedding method performs slightly better than tf.idf. TEWE performs relatively better than all the previous three. Our proposed approach, which integrates all the features using learning to rank, is the best performer. This is due to the integration of different types of information which complement each other, and also due to the learning to rank algorithm, which is suitable for this type of task. All these differences are statistically significant at p=0.01 using t-test, partially because our test data set is large. The hit rates showing in this figure may not be as high as one may have expected. One reason is that some hashtags in the test data are new ones, which means they did not appear in the training data. Another factor, which is more important, is that many hashtags are not really closely related to the content of the tweet containing these hashtags, and so it is hard to predict them based on tweet text. Some hashtags, such as #news, can appear in tweets that are about totally different topics.

Table 2. Features ranked by their importance. *By xxx, yyy* means hashtags are ranked first by *xxx* and then by *yyy*.

Method to select candidate hashtags
TEWE, by similarity, frequency
TEWE, by similarity
TEWE, by similarity, time
Entity, by co-occurrence
Entity, by co-occurrence, frequency
Entity, by co-occurrence, time
Entity, by matching
URL domain, by matching

Table 2 shows the order of importance of these features learned from learning to rank algorithm. It shows that the TEWE features are the most important ones, and the entity matching and URL domain matching features are the least important ones. This is partially because only a small portion of the tweets have URLs or entity matched with hashtags.

5. CONCLUSION

A new approach for recommending hashtags for tweets is proposed in this paper. It uses Learning to Rank algorithm to incorporate features built from topic enhanced word embeddings, tweet entity data, hashtag frequency, hashtag temporal data and tweet URL domain information. The data used for generating features in our proposed approach also exist in other types of social media, such as Facebook. Therefore, potentially this approach can also be used in those social media platform.

REFERENCES

[1] Collobert, Ronan, Jason Weston, Leon Bottou, et al., Natural language processing (almost) from scratch. *Journal of Machine Learning Research*, 12:2493–2537, 2011.

[2] Fan, R.-E., K.-W. Chang, C.-J. Hsieh, X.-R. Wang, and C.-J. Lin. LIBLINEAR: A Library for Large Linear Classification, *Journal of Machine Learning Research* 9 (2008), 1871-1874

[3] F. Godin, V. Slavkovikj, W. De Neve, B. Schrauwen, and R. Van de Walle. Using topic models for twitter hashtag recommendation. In *WWW'13*

[4] S. M. Kywe, T.-A. Hoang, E.-P. Lim, and F. Zhu. On recommending hashtags in twitter networks. In *Social Informatics,* pages 337–350, 2012.

[5] Hing-Pei Lee and Chih-Jen Lin. Large-scale linear rankSVM. *Neural Computation*, 26(2014), 781-817.

[6] Ma, Z., Sun, A., Yuan Q., Cong, G., Tagging your tweets: a probabilistic modeling of hashtag annotation in Twitter. *CIKM 2014.*

[7] Matt, T., Document Classification by Inversion of Distributed Language Representations. *53th ACL conference*, page 45-49, July 26-31, Beijing, 2015

[8] Mikolov, T.; Chen, K.; Corrado, G. and Dean J., 2013. Efficient Estimation of Word Representations in Vector Space. *In Proceedings of Workshop at ICLR.*

[9] Mikolov, T., Sutskever, I.; Chen, K.; Corrado, G. and Dean J., 2013. Distributed Representations of Words and Phrases and their Compositionality. *In Proceedings of NIPS*

[10] Jeff Mitchell and Mirella Lapata, Vector-based Models of Semantic Composition, *Proceedings of ACL 2008*.

[11] Surendra Sedhai, Aixin Sun, Hashtag Recommendation for Hyperlinked Tweets, *SIGIR 2014*.

[12] Socher, R.; Perelygin, A.; Wu, J.; Chuang, J.; Manning, C.; Ng, A. et al. Recursive Deep Models for Semantic Compositionality Over a Sentiment Treebank, *EMNLP 2014*

[13] Yang Liu, Zhiyuan Liu, Tat-Seng Chua, Maosong Sun, Topical Word Embeddings, *AAAI 2015*

[14] Jieying She, Lei Chen, TOMOHA: TOpic MOdel-based HAshtag Recommendation on Twitter. *WWW 2014*

[15] A. Tomar, F. Godin, B.Vandersmissen, W. D. Neve , Towards Twitter hashtag recommendation using distributed word representations and a deep feed forward neural network. *ICACCI, 2014*

[16] Tsur, O. and Rappoport, A. 2012. What's in a hashtag: content based prediction of the spread of ideas in microblogging communities. *WSDM 2012*, New York, NY

[17] T.-Y. Liu. Learning to rank for information retrieval, 2009.

[18] E. Zangerle, W. Gassler, and G. Specht. On the impact of text similarity functions on hashtag recommendations in microblogging environments. *Social Network. Analysis Mining*, 3(4):889–898, 2013.

[19] Z. Ding, X. Qiu, Q. Zhang, X. Huang. Learning topical, translation model for microblog hashtag suggestion. *IJCAI 2013*.

[20] Paolo Ferragina, Francesco Piccinno, Roberto Santoro, On Analyzing Hashtags in Twitter, *ICWSM 2015*

[21] Su Mon Kywe, Ee-Peng Lim and Feida Zhu, A Survey of Recommender Systems in Twitter, *Social Informatics, 2012.*

[22] Y. Gong, Q. Zhang, X. Huang, Hashtag Recommendation Using Dirichlet Process Mixture Models, *EMNLP 2015*.

An Experimental Comparison of Iterative MapReduce Frameworks

Haejoon Lee[†] Minseo Kang[‡] Sun-Bum Youn[§] Jae-Gil Lee[‡*] YongChul Kwon[¶]

[†]School of Computing, KAIST, Korea

[‡]Graduate School of Knowledge Service Engineering, KAIST, Korea

[§]Netmarble Games, Korea

[¶]Microsoft Corp., USA

{philjjoon, minseo, jaegil}@kaist.ac.kr sbyoun@netmarble.com yongchul.kwon@microsoft.com

ABSTRACT

MapReduce has become a dominant framework in big data analysis, and thus there have been significant efforts to implement various data analysis algorithms in MapReduce. Many data analysis algorithms are inherently *iterative*, repeating the same set of tasks until a convergence. To efficiently support iterative algorithms at scale, a few variants of Hadoop and new platforms have been proposed and actively developed in both academia and industry. Representative systems include HaLoop, iMapReduce, Twister, and Spark. In this paper, we experimentally compare Hadoop and the aforementioned systems using various workloads and metrics. The *five* systems are compared through four iterative algorithms—PageRank, recursive query, k-means, and logistic regression—on 50 Amazon EC2 machines (200 cores in total). We thoroughly explore the effectiveness of their new caching, communication, and scheduling mechanisms in support of iterative computation. Our evaluation also shows the performance depending on data skewness and memory residency. Overall, we believe that our evaluation and interpretation will be useful for designing a new framework or improving the existing ones.

Keywords

Iterative algorithms; MapReduce; Hadoop; Spark; Benchmark

1. INTRODUCTION

MapReduce [5] has become the most popular framework for large-scale processing and big data analysis. It allows us to easily develop distributed, parallel applications running in a cluster of commodity machines, without tedious detail of distributed execution such as scheduling and fault-tolerance. Its sweet spot is known to be batch processing of data-intensive tasks [6]. Thus, many data-intensive database and data mining operations, such as similarity join and decision tree classification, have been successfully translated to the MapReduce framework [15]. As a result, we have witnessed remarkable performance improvements compared to original implementations. Moreover, Hadoop [1], an open-source implementation of MapReduce, has contributed to the huge success of the framework.

Despite its popularity, MapReduce has faced criticisms for its performance limitations in several advanced applications [6, 12]. One of such criticisms is the inefficiency of handling *iterative* algorithms [2, 3, 4, 7, 17, 18]. Many data analysis algorithms, such as PageRank, recursive query, k-means, and logistic regression, require iterative computation, repeatedly executing the same set of tasks until a stopping condition is satisfied. MapReduce does not directly support such iterative computation, but users could handcraft a chain of MapReduce jobs by writing a driver program [14]. Although this naïve implementation can scale beyond capacity of a single machine, it may incur severe performance penalty because the framework is not aware of the iteration. For example, the data sets invariant while running an algorithm must be loaded and processed repeatedly for each iteration, thereby wasting disk I/O, network bandwidth, and CPU resources.

To alleviate the inefficiency for iterative algorithms, some variants of Hadoop and new platforms have been developed in research and open-source communities. Representative systems include HaLoop [2, 3], Twister [7], iMapReduce [18], MapReduce Online [4], and Spark [17]. HaLoop, iMapReduce, and MapReduce Online are implemented by modifying the MapReduce component of Hadoop, whereas Twister and Spark are implemented independently from Hadoop. Various techniques such as disk caches and distributed shared memory have been incorporated into those systems in support of efficient iterative computation.

To the best of our knowledge, those systems have not been systematically compared with one another, though each system was compared against Hadoop only. Therefore, to examine a broad range of techniques, we choose five systems—Hadoop, HaLoop, Twister, iMapReduce, and Spark—for our comparison. Hadoop is the baseline which lacks the capability of handling iterative computation. HaLoop, Twister, and iMapReduce are research prototypes, which all of them are being actively cited. MapReduce Online is not explicitly included since iMapReduce is built on top of it. Apache Spark is included mainly because of its popularity in recent days even though it does not strictly conform to the MapReduce paradigm. However, we do not include graph processing systems [8] such as Pregel and GraphLab in our comparison, because the scope of this paper is comparison of "MapReduce-like" general purpose systems rather than graph processing systems.

In this paper, we experimentally compare the *five* systems, seeking for in-depth understanding of the performance of iterative computation. Since three of them are just research prototypes and are not optimized to production level, we do *not* concentrate on the absolute performance of each system but on the intrinsic capabilities and the techniques to support iteration in each system.

*Jae-Gil Lee is the corresponding author.

CIKM'16 , October 24-28, 2016, Indianapolis, IN, USA

© 2016 ACM. ISBN 978-1-4503-4073-1/16/10... $15.00

DOI: http://dx.doi.org/10.1145/2983323.2983647

Specifically, the contributions of this paper include:

1. We investigate the impacts of such techniques on performance through systematic and fair comparison of the systems. To precisely explain the impacts, we use various evaluation metrics as well as various workloads generated by running diverse algorithms on both real-world and synthetic data sets (Section 3).
2. We discuss the advantages and disadvantages of the systems with regard to iterative computation such that users and developers can exploit our lessons in the use and development of such systems (Section 4).

We found that all systems are scalable but some of the key techniques such as input data caching may have diminishing return depending on data sets and algorithms. The primary factors on the performance are shown to be the size of input and intermediate data, invariability of the keys of intermediate data, efficiency of network communication, flexibility of task scheduling, and so on. Also, we observed that memory-based engines generally perform better than disk-based engines but the performance rapidly degrades when the data does not fit in memory.

The full (10 page) version of this paper is available at http://dm.kaist.ac.kr/lab/papers/cikm16_expr_full.pdf. The source code is available at https://github.com/IterativeExperimentsMapReduce.

2. EVALUATION METHODOLOGY

2.1 Cluster and System Setup

We conduct experiments on an Amazon EC2 cluster (Sections 3.1–3.3) or on a local cluster (Section 3.4), as described below.

- *Amazon EC2 cluster*: The cluster consists of 50 m1.xlarge Amazon EC2 spot instances, located in US West (Oregon). Each instance has four virtual CPUs, 4×420 GB of local storage, and 15 GB of main memory. All instances run on Ubuntu 14.04.1 LTS.
- *Local cluster*: The cluster consists of 4 commodity servers. A server has two Intel Core i7-4790 CPUs, each equipped with four cores, 1 TB of local storage, and 32 GB of main memory. Thus, this cluster has 32 cores in total. All servers run on Ubuntu 14.01 LTS.

We use Hadoop 1.2.1, HaLoop 0.20.2, Twister 0.9, iMapReduce 0.1, and Spark 1.2.0. HaLoop and iMapReduce are implemented using Hadoop 0.8 and 0.19.2 respectively. Twister is configured to use ActiveMQ [16] 5.4.3 for its message broker. Spark runs with Scala 2.10.0 and Hadoop 1.2.1. JDK 1.8.0 is used for running the systems. The maximum per-machine Java heap size is configured to be 12 GB.

2.2 Data Sets

2.2.1 *Real-World Data Sets*

We use the real-world data sets in Table 1, which are characterized into graph data and row data. The two *graph* data sets are used for both PageRank and recursive query, and the two *row* data sets are used for k-means and logistic regression respectively.

As for graph data, *LiveJournal* is a social network data set available at the SNAP repository [13]. *ClueWeb* is a web graph data set, and we use TREC Category B[1]. ClueWeb has much more vertices and edges than LiveJournal. LiveJournal is more densely-connected than ClueWeb, in that the average degree (i.e., the ratio of the number of vertices to that of edges) of the former is about ten times higher than that of the latter. We substitute all vertex identifiers in LiveJournal with longer strings to increase its size without changing its network structure, just like Bu et al. [2, 3] did. As a result, the data set was extended from 1 GB to 10 GB.

As for row data, *Cosmo-Gas* and *Cosmo-All* are scientific simulation data sets, where each row represents the information of a particle. Cosmo-All has all particles of the *cosmo50* data set [10], whereas Cosmo-Gas contains only the gas particles. For k-means clustering, the three variables for x, y, and z positions are kept with Cosmo-Gas. For logistic regression, a binary variable that indicates if a row is a star particle is added to Cosmo-All as a *dependent* variable, and other variables are used as *independent* variables.

Table 1: Real-world data sets used for all algorithms.

Graph Data	Algorithms	# of Vertices	# of Edges
LiveJournal	PageRank,	4,847,571	68,993,773
ClueWeb	Recursive	428,136,613	454,075,638
Row Data	Algorithm	# of Points	# of Dims
Cosmo-Gas	k-means	147,251,521	3
Cosmo-All	Logistic	315,086,245	10

With these base data sets in Table 1, we generate various sizes of data sets to test the scalability of the systems. In the next section, "1X"∼"5X" indicate the variations of a data set having proportional sizes. For LiveJournal, ClueWeb, and Cosmo-Gas, the base data set becomes "1X", and larger ones are generated by replicating it by 2, 3, 4, and 5 times. When replicating Cosmo-Gas, Gaussian noises are added in order to avoid the exactly same values. For Cosmo-All, the base data set becomes "5X" since it is sufficiently large, and smaller ones are obtained by randomly sampling 20%, 40%, 60%, and 80% of the base data set.

2.2.2 *Synthetic Data Sets*

We use also synthetic data sets in order to investigate the response of each system to the *skewness* of the input data. The performance of PageRank is sensitive to skewness since the algorithm sends PageRank contributions to more neighbors on higher-degree vertices. The LFR benchmark [11] generates graph data sets for use in PageRank, which are summarized in Table 2. They are generated according to the following parameters: N is the number of vertices, $\langle k \rangle$ is the average degree, max_k is the maximum degree, and $t1$ is the exponent part of the power-law distribution of degrees. Here, max_k exponentially increases while N and $\langle k \rangle$ are fixed. As max_k gets larger, the degree values should disperse to a larger range to keep $\langle k \rangle$ the same; that is, the skewness of degrees gets higher. Consequently, some tasks will transfer much larger number of PageRank contributions than others. In this way, we control the skewness between the tasks.

Table 2: Synthetic graph data sets used for PageRank.

Data Set	N	$\langle k \rangle$	max_k	$t1$
LFR1	200,000	1,000	$1,000 \times 1.6^0$	2
LFR2			$1,000 \times 1.6^1$	
LFR3			$1,000 \times 1.6^2$	
LFR4			$1,000 \times 1.6^3$	
LFR5			$1,000 \times 1.6^4$	

2.3 Evaluation Metrics

Total elapsed time is the time spent for running an algorithm against a data set on a specific system. Total elapsed time is determined to be the interval between the job finish time and the job start time included in system log files. On the other hand, some systems require reformatting or full duplication of input data before run-

[1]http://lemurproject.org/clueweb09/

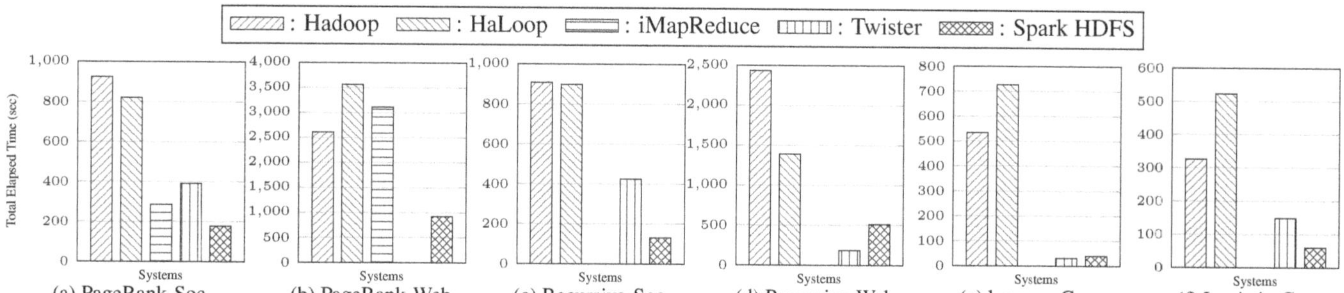

(a) PageRank-Soc. (b) PageRank-Web. (c) Recursive-Soc. (d) Recursive-Web. (e) kmeans-Cosmo. (f) Logistic-Cosmo.

Figure 1: Total elapsed time of the five systems (50 machines).

Table 3: Total HDFS read in Figure 1 (Unit: **GB**).

Systems	1a	1b	1c	1d	1e	1f
Hadoop	134.052	213.045	100.732	82.037	65.433	82.027
HaLoop	44.173	143.668	11.300	7.179	51.934	74.526
iMapReduce	6.240	30.534	-	-	-	-
Spark	9.900	7.600	9.900	7.600	6.500	8.200

Table 4: Reduce shuffle I/O in Figure 1 (Unit: **MB**).

Systems	1a	1b	1c	1d	1e	1f
Hadoop	30,593	241,205	14,943	98,227	0.847	0.241
HaLoop	16,912	141,951	2,979	9,642	0.818	0.739
iMapReduce	970	16,842	-	-	-	-
Spark	8,500	34,600	2,883	2.601	1.988	0

ning a main job, and this preprocessing time is *not* included in total elapsed time since it is a one-time cost.

Normalized time is the ratio of the total elapsed time of a certain configuration to that of the base configuration. For example, in scalability tests, normalized time is the ratio of the total elapsed time for a certain data set to that for the smallest data set. Consequently, normalized time always starts from 1. It shows sensitivity of the total elapsed time to the change of a parameter value. The intention of this normalization is to mitigate the difference in maturity of each system.

Total HDFS read is the total amount of the data read *from the HDFS*—not from the local file system—during the entire execution of an algorithm. This metric assesses how effectively each system reduces *remote* disk I/O. It is the sum of the outputs of the counter "HDFS_BYTES_READ" for Hadoop, HaLoop, and iMapReduce; and it is the first output of the counter "Input" for Spark since the subsequent outputs of that counter indicate the accesses to the RDD which is typically stored in main memory.

Reduce shuffle I/O is the total amount of the data shuffled from mappers to reducers during the entire execution of an algorithm. This metric assesses how effectively each system reduces network communication for the shuffle. It is the sum of the outputs of the counter "Reduce Shuffle Bytes" for Hadoop and HaLoop, a custom counter added by the authors for iMapReduce, and the counter "Shuffle Read" for Spark.

We measure those metrics mostly twice and choose one measurement after confirming that the two measurements do not vary significantly, since it is too expensive to repeat many times on Amazon EC2. If an execution does not finish within two hours, we terminate the execution and give up obtaining the corresponding result.

3. EVALUATION RESULTS

3.1 Overall Comparison

Figure 1 shows the total elapsed time of the five systems for the six combinations of algorithms and data sets. More importantly, we would like to figure out the overall performance characteristics of the five systems. Overall, Hadoop showed the worst performance as expected; HaLoop showed a little improvements over Hadoop; iMapReduce and Twister showed more improvements than HaLoop; and Spark in general achieved the best performance. Since Spark is maintained and tuned by a vibrant open-source community, this commercial-quality tuning in addition to the advantage of its framework seems to contribute to the highest performance.

To facilitate this comparison of the overall performances, we present the results for *total HDFS read* and *reduce shuffle I/O*[2] of Figure 1 since these two metrics impact greatly on the total elapsed time. As for the former in Table 3, because the cache of each system converts remote disk I/O to local disk I/O, a value represents how much such a caching mechanism effectively reduces remote disk I/O. Roughly speaking, the difference between Hadoop and another system indicates the amount of disk I/O saved by the caching mechanism. As for the latter in Table 4, a value represents the amount of the data transferred from mappers to reducers, which incurs network communication. PageRank has high values owing to the PageRank contributions of *all* vertices, recursive query has moderate values since it carries only reachable vertices, and both k-means and logistic regression have low values since they need only the centroid or parameter information. In both tables, the smaller a value is, the higher the performance is. These values are highly correlated to the total elapsed time except HaLoop (owing to a configuration issue which will be explained later).

Before going into the details, we would like to address a few points that will be referenced for the interpretation of the results.

- **Remark 1**: The communication efficiency (network utilization) is higher in Spark than in Twister since Twister performs broadcasting via a broker network. In other words, Twister requires significant effort in tuning the broker network to achieve high performance.
- **Remark 2**: Removing duplicates in recursive query tends to be more efficient in Twister than in Spark. Spark processes it at once globally according to *lazy evaluation* [9], whereas Twister is *originally designed* to do it in two steps—locally on each worker and then globally on the combiner.
- **Remark 3**: The amount of the data shuffled tends to be larger in PageRank than in recursive query because of the characteristics of the algorithms, as shown in Table 4.
- **Remark 4**: The amount of the data shuffled in recursive query is larger for LiveJournal than for ClueWeb since the former is much more densely-connected than the latter. See the entries of Spark in Table 4 where the static data is completely cached.

Twister vs. Spark

Spark and Twister are similar in that both are memory-based engines. Since the results of recursive query were available for two

[2]The results are not available for Twister since it does not provide counters.

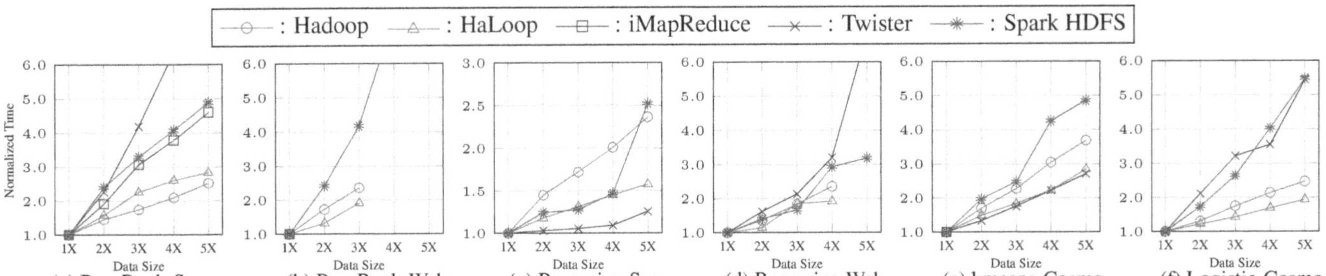

(a) PageRank-Soc. (b) PageRank-Web. (c) Recursive-Soc. (d) Recursive-Web. (e) kmeans-Cosmo. (f) Logistic-Cosmo.

Figure 2: Normalized time of the five systems with varying the data size (50 machines).

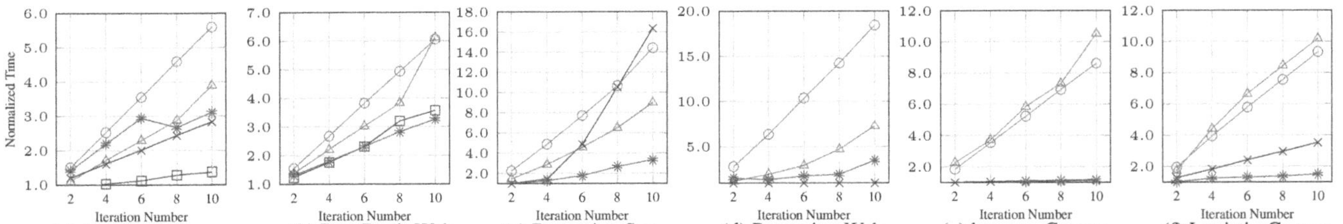

(a) PageRank-Soc. (b) PageRank-Web. (c) Recursive-Soc. (d) Recursive-Web. (e) kmeans-Cosmo. (f) Logistic-Cosmo.

Figure 3: Normalized time of the five systems with varying the iteration number (50 machines).

different data sets, we compared the relative performance between these systems using Figures 1c and 1d. Twister showed lower performance than Spark in Figure 1c by **Remark 1** and **Remark 4** since the higher shuffle cost was managed well in Spark but not in Twister. On the other hand, Spark showed lower performance than Twister in Figure 1d by **Remark 2**. In Figure 1c, duplicate removal was done entirely on main memory in both systems. In Figure 1d, however, Spark spilled intermediate results to local disk owing a larger size of ClueWeb whereas Twister did not. Twister needed less memory than Spark because of its two-step approach.

We note that this difference is attributed to the *architectural choices* made in Twister and Spark: two-step and lazy evaluations. Spark adopts lazy evaluation to avoid unnecessary computation, but its benefit was hidden because Spark had to spill intermediate results. We did *not* inject the two-step approach into Spark even though we could do it. Again, please recall that our strategy is to follow the conventional style for each system.

Hadoop vs. HaLoop

Hadoop and HaLoop are similar in that HaLoop is a direct extension of Hadoop. The performance improvement in HaLoop is mostly achieved by the reducer input cache which converts HDFS I/O to local disk I/O [2]. The size of static data that can benefit from the reducer input cache is much larger for ClueWeb than for LiveJournal. Thus, the difference between Hadoop and HaLoop became more prominent in Figures 1b and 1d with ClueWeb than in Figures 1a and 1c with LiveJournal.

The effect of the reducer input cache can be marginal depending on the algorithms. In PageRank, recursive query, and logistic regression, the keys of the intermediate results that determine the reducer to be sent do *not* change across iterations. In contrast, in k-means, the keys of the intermediate results are determined by the current set of centroids, changing per iteration. Thus, the hit ratio of the reducer input cache cannot be very high. On the other hand, the mapper input cache is more important for k-means than the reducer input cache. Not surprisingly, Hadoop manages this issue by observing data locality, as shown by Figure 1e.

The reducer input cache is also less effective when intermediate data is small. With regard to logistic regression in Figure 1f, the size of the intermediate results to be shuffled is tiny as in Table 4, because they are partial sums of the parameter values. Also, they do not need to be joined with the static data.

iMapReduce

iMapReduce showed the best performance among the disk-based engines but showed worse performance than the memory-based engines. The performance gain is mostly achieved by the persistent connections between each pair of a map task and a reduce task. Its effect was verified by the smaller amounts of the total HDFS read and the reduce shuffle I/O in Tables 3 and 4. However, it was difficult to draw meaningful conclusions about iMapReduce since we could not complete many experiments due to its instability.

3.2 Effect of Data Size

Figure 2 shows the normalized time of the five systems for the same six combinations of algorithms and data sets as the data size increases from the data set **1X** to the data set **5X**. (1) In general, the disk-based engines showed sub-linear scalability as the data size increased. This high scalability is a little misleading because the elapsed time of a disk-based engine with 1X was much longer than that of a memory-based engine. Thus, the *normalized* elapsed time even for the same elapsed time was shown to be lower in Hadoop or HaLoop. (2) On the other hand, we observed that the elapsed time of a memory-based engine sometimes rapidly increased as the data size increased when the systems start using disk as well because a data set did not fit in main memory.

A few interesting observations in Figure 2 with regard to the memory-based engines are as follows.

- In Figures 2a and 2d, the elapsed time of Twister started to increase *rapidly* at 3X or 4X. ActiveMQ, the broker service, was configured to use 5 GB of main memory. When we measured the size of the data transferred from the master to each worker in Figure 2a, it amounted to 2.32 GB for 1X, 4.66 GB for 2X, and 7.86 GB for 3X. Thus, ActiveMQ used disk from 3X, causing the slow down in broadcasting.
- Since all the implementations are in Java, garbage collection has significant impact on the performance of the memory-based engines. A *major (or full) garbage collection* is triggered when the amount of available memory falls below a certain threshold. It is costly but occurs quite infrequently. We found that major garbage collection occurred for Twister with 4X and 5X in Figure 2d, contributed to the increase of the execution time.
- In comparison between Figure 2a and Figure 2b, the elapsed time of Spark increased more rapidly as the data size increased

with ClueWeb than with LiveJournal. The main difference between the two cases is whether disk was used for the shuffle. While no disk was used with LiveJournal, 34 GB (1X) to 484 GB (5X) of disk space was used with ClueWeb.

3.3 Effect of Iteration Number

Figure 3 shows the normalized time of the five systems for the same six combinations of algorithms and data sets as the number of iterations increases from 2 to 10. All five systems showed reasonable increases as the number of iterations increased. That is, the elapsed time for each iteration was nearly constant or even became a little smaller as an algorithm proceeded.

The disk-based engines in general showed constant elapsed time per iteration as shown in the close-to linear slope of Hadoop or HaLoop except in Figure 3d. The memory-based engines typically showed gentle slopes, meaning that the time added after the first iteration was relatively small. This is because after Twister or Spark load static data from the local disk or HDFS, as long as main memory is sufficient to hold static and variable data, they do not have to access disk anymore.

A few noticeable observations in Figure 3 are as follows.

- In Figure 3d, the slope of Hadoop was much steeper than those of the other systems, partially because of generally higher slopes for recursive query than for the other algorithms. Since there is no previous result to check duplicates at the beginning, the proportion of the *first* iteration is not very significant in recursive query compared with the other algorithms.
- The slope of Twister was lower in Figures 3d, 3e, and 3f than in Figures 3a and 3c. This trend can be explained by the amounts of reducer shuffle I/O, i.e., by **Remark 3** and **Remark 4**. The size of the static data mainly affects the elapsed time of the first iteration, whereas the size of the shuffled data mainly affects that of a subsequent iteration. Nevertheless, in Figure 3c, Spark showed higher efficiency than Twister by virtue of **Remark 1**.
- The slope of Spark was very low in Figures 3e and 3f for the same reason as above. While the slope of Spark was kept to be low in other figures, it became steeper in Figures 3c and 3d owing to **Remark 2** as well as in Figures 3a and 3b owing to **Remark 3**.

3.4 Effect of Data Skew

This experiment was conducted by running three reducers on our local cluster. Since the vertices in a LFR network were sorted in the order of their degrees, we divided the network into input splits by *range partitioning* to maximize data skew across input splits.

Figure 4 shows the elapsed time of the five systems. The elapsed time of Hadoop, HaLoop, and iMapReduce all increased as the skewness became higher. Comparing the increase rate, Hadoop and HaLoop did not show a significant difference—in both systems by 1.5 times from LFR1 to LFR5. iMapReduce showed a little higher rate (1.7 times) than the two systems. This higher rate was mainly caused by the one-to-one correspondence between mappers and reducers, which hindered the flexibility of scheduling.

Interestingly, Twister and Spark showed almost constant execution time regardless of the skewness. (1) Twister, because of its characteristics of relying on the combiner, typically does not use the vertex id as the key unlike other systems, but uses the index of the map task and pads the PageRank contributions to the value part of a key-value pair. In this way, each reducer will receive almost the same number of PageRank contributions since the keys are evenly distributed irrelevant to the skewness. Partial sums are obtained in each reducer, and these partial sums are aggregated in

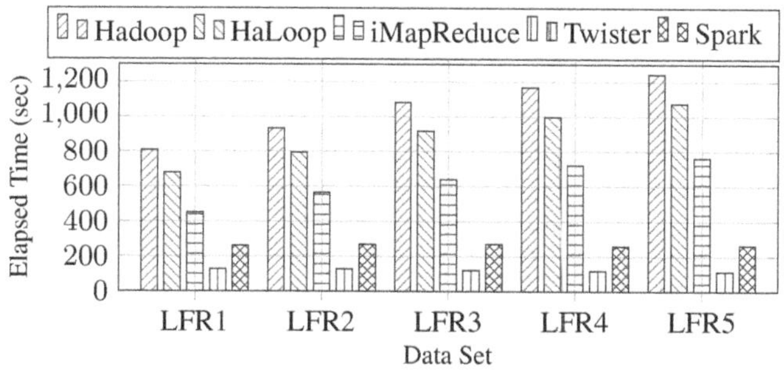

Figure 4: Elapsed time with varying skewness (4 machines).

the combiner. (2) Spark calculates partial sums by using the function `reduceByKey` [9]. Thus, even though a partition contains the vertices of high degrees, the PageRank contributions emitted from that partition to the same destination can be summed up locally. As a result, this function manages the amount of the data shuffled to other workers, just like the combiner of Hadoop. On the other hand, the implementations provided by the authors for Hadoop, HaLoop, and iMapReduce did not use the combiner for PageRank.

4. LESSONS LEARNED

In this section, we discuss the lessons learned from the experiments and identify missing opportunities.

Caching Mechanism, Memory Management

- The reducer input cache of HaLoop is effective especially when the static data is large. The cache is also sensitive to the characteristics of an algorithm as we observed in the k-means experiments. In a nut shell, memory-based engines are also effectively implementing the same technique by caching the static data in memory. To maximize its benefit, the algorithm developers should be aware of such static data partitioning. From the system perspective, an efficient indexing mechanism to quickly retrieve a cached entry would be useful for the developers.
- Memory-based engines are much more efficient than disk-based engines. Thus, the system and algorithm developers should pay more attention to memory management as it is a more critical resource in memory-based engines than in disk-based engines. Selectively storing static or variable data on main memory, just like the function `persist` of the RDD in Spark, is helpful to reduce the overall usage of main memory. Also, the performance of memory-based engines significantly degrades under low-memory condition. Smooth transition from memory to disk using faster storage (e.g., SSD) and efficient spilling would be challenging but interesting.

Programming Model, High-Level Interface

- An iteration may consist of complex data flows, and MapReduce may not be the best way to express such algorithms. For example, the map phase is always required before repartition even though no transformation is necessary. A flexible programming model in Spark allows users to express more generic data flows beyond the strict MapReduce API.
- It is promising to have a declarative language like SQL with *iterative construct* that can be translated into a well-understood set of operators and data structures so that let users focus on "what" rather than "how" as well. Spark is the closest in this direction among the systems evaluated in this paper by providing a set of well-understood operations such as map, filter, and joins. Optimizing the iterative data flow with these oprations is another interesting area of research.

Data Transfer, Network Communication

- It is *not* always beneficial to force all reduce outputs to be collected by the combiner in Twister. Checking a convergence condition sometimes can be omitted since one may want to terminate an iterative algorithm after a fixed number of iterations. The combiner necessarily becomes a bottleneck and at the same time a single point of failure.
- Efficient data transfer is crucial to achieve high performance. Twister delegates data transfer to the broker network, which requires significant expertise in tuning. Although the feature-rich communication layer may greatly simplify a distributed system, it adds more cost and complexity to the setup and maintenance of the whole system.
- We found that a broadcast is a frequent communication pattern in iterative algorithms. Also, hierarchical aggregation, e.g., which aggregates locally in the reducers and then again in the combiner as in recursive query of Twister, is beneficial for scalability and robust to data skew. Optimizing such common communication patterns is critical to achieve high performance.

Data Skew, Persistent & Asynchronous Execution

- Data skew in iterative algorithms can be mitigated by key reassignment and/or hierarchical (partial) aggregation, as shown in Twister and Spark.
- The benefit of persistent socket connection in iMapReduce is *not* verified in our experiments. Although the reduce shuffle I/O is reduced dramatically, the gain in total elapsed time is not as significant. In addition, persistent connection hinders flexible task scheduling, being susceptible to data skew.

Based on our evaluation and experience, the rule-of-thumb choice for a system is suggested in Figure 5.

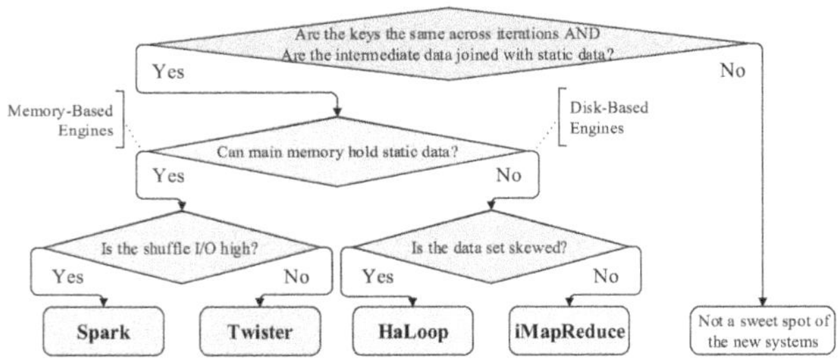

Figure 5: Choice of the systems depending on the environments.

5. CONCLUSION

We conducted extensive experiments on the five MapReduce-like systems, Hadoop, HaLoop, iMapReduce, Twister, and Spark, by running four different algorithms against various real-world and synthetic data sets. We ran these systems on 50 Amazon EC2 x-large instances (200 cores), measuring elapsed time, remote disk I/O, and reduce shuffle I/O, in order to capture their performance characteristics. The new systems were shown to improve the performance of iterative algorithms mainly by reducing the disk I/O for static data. We found that Spark in general achieved the best performance when the operations were executed entirely in main memory. Through our evaluation and interpretation, we discovered the primary factors that impact on the performance: invariability of the keys of variable data, availability of main memory especially in memory-based engines, amount of variable (intermediate) data transferred together with network utilization, and flexibility of task scheduling. The sweet spots of each system were identified using these factors. Since the resources (CPU cores and main memory) of a cluster node become more powerful, we expect that memory-based engines such as Spark will become more prevalent in the near future. Automatic tuning of granularity of tasks, graceful transition between memory and disk, and optimization of common operations are yet to be solved and still have room for improvement.

Acknowledgments

This research, "Geospatial Big Data Management, Analysis and Service Platform Technology Development," was supported by the MOLIT (The Ministry of Land, Infrastructure and Transport), Korea, under the national spatial information research program supervised by the KAIA (Korea Agency for Infrastructure Technology Advancement) (16NSIP-B081011-03).

6. REFERENCES

[1] Apache. Apache Hadoop. https://hadoop.apache.org/.

[2] Y. Bu, B. Howe, M. Balazinska, and M. D. Ernst. HaLoop: Efficient iterative data processing on large clusters. *PVLDB*, 3(1):285–296, 2010.

[3] Y. Bu, B. Howe, M. Balazinska, and M. D. Ernst. The HaLoop approach to large-scale iterative data analysis. *VLDB J.*, 21(2):169–190, 2012.

[4] T. Condie, N. Conway, P. Alvaro, J. M. Hellerstein, K. Elmeleegy, and R. Sears. MapReduce online. In *NSDI*, pages 313–328, 2010.

[5] J. Dean and S. Ghemawat. MapReduce: Simplified data processing on large clusters. In *OSDI*, pages 137–150, 2004.

[6] C. Doulkeridis and K. Nørvåg. A survey of large-scale analytical query processing in MapReduce. *VLDB J.*, 23(3):355–380, 2014.

[7] J. Ekanayake, H. Li, B. Zhang, T. Gunarathne, S. Bae, J. Qiu, and G. Fox. Twister: A runtime for iterative MapReduce. In *HPDC*, pages 810–818, 2010.

[8] M. Han, K. Daudjee, K. Ammar, M. T. Özsu, X. Wang, and T. Jin. An experimental comparison of Pregel-like graph processing systems. *PVLDB*, 7(12):1047–1058, 2014.

[9] H. Karau, A. Konwinski, P. Wendell, and M. Zaharia. *Learning Spark*. O'Reilly Media, 2015.

[10] Y. Kwon, D. Nunley, J. P. Gardner, M. Balazinska, B. Howe, and S. Loebman. Scalable clustering algorithm for n-body simulations in a shared-nothing cluster. In *SSDBM*, pages 132–150, 2010.

[11] A. Lancichinetti and S. Fortunato. Community detection algorithms: A comparative analysis. *Phys. Rev. E*, 80(5):056117, 2009.

[12] K. Lee, Y. Lee, H. Choi, Y. D. Chung, and B. Moon. Parallel data processing with MapReduce: A survey. *SIGMOD Record*, 40(4):11–20, 2011.

[13] J. Leskovec and A. Krevl. SNAP Datasets: Stanford large network dataset collection. http://snap.stanford.edu/data, June 2014.

[14] D. Miner and A. Shook. *MapReduce Design Patterns*. O'Reilly Media, 2012.

[15] K. Shim. MapReduce algorithms for big data analysis. *PVLDB*, 5(12):2016–2017, 2012. Tutorial.

[16] B. Snyder and D. Bosanac. *ActiveMQ in Action*. Manning Publications, 2011.

[17] M. Zaharia, M. Chowdhury, M. J. Franklin, S. Shenker, and I. Stoica. Spark: Cluster computing with working sets. In *HotCloud*, 2010.

[18] Y. Zhang, Q. Gao, L. Gao, and C. Wang. iMapReduce: A distributed computing framework for iterative computation. *J. Grid Comput.*, 10(1):47–68, 2012.

A Density-Based Approach to the Retrieval of Top-K Spatial Textual Clusters*

Dingming Wu
College of Computer Science & Software Engineering, Shenzhen University
Shenzhen, China
dingming@szu.edu.cn

Christian S. Jensen
Department of Computer Science
Aalborg University
Aalborg, Denmark
csj@cs.aau.dk

ABSTRACT

Spatial keyword queries retrieve spatial textual objects that are near a query location and are relevant to query keywords. The paper defines the top-k spatial textual clusters (k-STC) query that returns the top-k clusters that are located close to a given query location, contain relevant objects with regard to given query keywords, and have an object density that exceeds a given threshold. This query aims to support users who wish to explore nearby regions with many relevant objects. To compute this query, the paper proposes a basic and an advanced algorithm that rely on on-line density-based clustering. An empirical study offers insight into the performance properties of the proposed algorithms.

1. INTRODUCTION

Spatial keyword queries [8, 11, 21, 23] allow users to find nearby objects that are relevant to given keywords. For instance, Figure 1(a) illustrates a spatial keyword query q (located at the dot, in London) with keywords 'outdoor seating' that requests the top-5 restaurants (denoted by squares) from TripAdvisor.

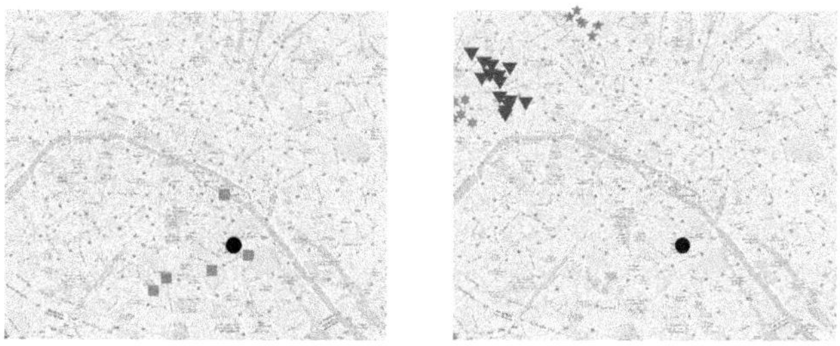

(a) Top-5 Objects (b) Top-5 Clusters

Figure 1: Top-k Objects vs. Top-k Clusters

While most variants of the spatial keyword query retrieve results with a single-object granularity, we focus on the retrieval of sets of spatially close objects in order to support browsing, or exploratory, user behavior. We view the retrieved sets of objects as spatial textual clusters and propose and study a new type of query, namely the top-k **Spatial Textual Cluster** (k-STC) query that returns the top-k clusters such that (i) each cluster contains relevant objects with regard to query keywords, (ii) the density of each cluster satisfies a query constraint, and (iii) the clusters are ranked based on both their spatial distance and text relevance with regards to the query arguments. Figure 1(b) shows an example 5-STC query (black dot) with the same keywords ('outdoor seating') and location as the query in Figure 1(a). The top-5 spatial textual clusters (again restaurants in London) are shown.

We use density-based clustering for finding clusters. The two basic steps to computex the top-k STC query are to obtain the objects that are relevant to the query keywords and to apply clustering to these objects. We consider a cluster scoring function that favors clusters close to the query location and that contain objects with high relevance with regard to the query keywords.

The query keywords are only known when a query arrives, and pre-computing the clusters for all possible sets of query keywords is infeasible. The challenge is then to develop an efficient algorithm that is able to find top-k clusters with a response time that supports interactive search. More specifically, we propose a basic algorithm that combines on-line density-based clustering with an early stop condition. This algorithm applies DBSCAN [9] to objects indexed by an IR-tree [21] to find top-k clusters. In addition, we propose an advanced approach that includes three novel techniques. First, to retrieve clusters, the neighborhood of each object has to be checked in the basic algorithm. We design a skipping rule that reduces the number of objects to be examined. Second, a result cluster consists of dense neighborhoods. However, determining whether a neighborhood is dense in the basic algorithm involves an expansive range query. We design Spatially Gridded Posting Lists (SGPL) to estimate the selectivity of range queries, thus enabling the pruning of sparse neighborhoods. Third, we show how to use the SGPL to gain better range query performance for the range queries that cannot be avoided. An empirical study with real data demonstrates that the paper's proposals offer scalability and are capable of excellent performance.

Section 2 defines the setting. The basic and advanced algorithms are presented in Sections 3 and 4. We report on the empirical performance study in Section 5, and Sections 6 and 7 cover related work and offer conclusions and research directions.

2. PROBLEM DEFINITION

We consider a data set $\mathcal{D}$ in which each object $p \in \mathcal{D}$ is a pair $\langle \lambda, \psi \rangle$ of a point location $p.\lambda$ and a text description, or document, $p.\psi$ (e.g., the facilities and menu of a restaurant). Document $p.\psi$ is represented by a vector $(w_1, w_2, \cdots, w_i)$ in which each dimension

*This research was supported in part by project 61502310 from National Natural Science Foundation of China and a grant from the Obel Family Foundation.

CIKM'16, October 24-28, 2016, Indianapolis, IN, USA
© 2016 ACM. ISBN 978-1-4503-4073-1/16/10...$15.00
DOI: http://dx.doi.org/10.1145/2983323.2983648

corresponds to a distinct term t_i in the document. The weight w_i of a term in the vector can be computed in several different ways, e.g., using tf-idf weighting [16] or language models [15].

We adopt the density-based clustering model [9], and clusters are query-dependent. We revisit key concepts in the context of the top-k spatial textual cluster query.

First, given a set of keywords ψ, the **relevant object set** D_ψ satisfies (i) $D_\psi \subseteq \mathcal{D}$ and (ii) $\forall p \in D_\psi (\psi \cap p.\psi \neq \emptyset)$. The **$\epsilon$-neighborhood** of a relevant object $p \in D_\psi$, denoted by $N_\epsilon(p)$, is defined as $N_\epsilon(p) = \{p_i \in D_\psi \mid \|p\, p_i\| \leq \epsilon\}$. An **$\epsilon$-neighborhood** of a relevant object $N_\epsilon(p)$ is **dense** if it contains at least $minpts$ objects, i.e., $|N_\epsilon(p)| \geq minpts$.

Next, several concepts relate to connectedness. A relevant object p is a **core** if its ϵ-neighborhood is dense, and a relevant object p_i is **directly reachable** from a relevant object p_j with regard to ϵ and $minpts$ if $p_i \in N_\epsilon(p_j)$ and $|N_\epsilon(p_j)| \geq minpts$. A relevant object p_i is **reachable** from a relevant object p_j with regard to ϵ and $minpts$ if there is a chain of relevant objects $p_1, \cdots, p_n$, where $p_i = p_1$, $p_j = p_n$, such that p_m is directly reachable from p_{m+1} for $1 \leq m < n$. A relevant object p_i is **connected** to a relevant object p_j with regard to ϵ and $minpts$ if there is a relevant object p_m such that both p_i and p_j are reachable from p_m with regard to ϵ and $minpts$.

A **spatial textual cluster** R with regard to ψ, ϵ, and $minpts$ is a subset of D_ψ and is a maximal set such that $\forall p_i, p_j \in R$, p_i and p_j are connected through dense ϵ-neighborhoods when considering only objects in D_ψ.

A **top-k Spatial Textual Cluster** (k-STC) query $q = \langle \lambda, \psi, k, \epsilon, minpts \rangle$ takes five arguments: a point location λ, a set of keywords ψ, a number of requested object sets k, a distance constraint ϵ on neighborhoods, and the minimum number of objects $minpts$ in a dense ϵ-neighborhood. It returns a list of k spatial textual clusters that minimize a scoring function and that are in ascending order of their scores. The maximality of each cluster implies that the top-k clusters do not overlap. The density requirement parameters ϵ and $minpts$ are able to capture how far the user is willing to move before reaching another object.

Intuitively, a cluster with high text relevance and that is located close to the query location should be given a high ranking in the result. We thus use the following scoring function.

$$score_q(R) = \alpha \cdot d_{q.\lambda}(R) + (1 - \alpha) \cdot (1 - tr_{q.\psi}(R)), \quad (1)$$

where $d_{q.\lambda}(R)$ is the minimum spatial distance between the query location and the objects in R and $tr_{q.\psi}(R)$ is the maximum text relevance in R. The approaches we present are applicable to scoring functions that are monotone with respect to both spatial distance and text relevance. Parameter α is used to balance the spatial proximity and the text relevance of the retrieved clusters. All spatial distances and text relevances are normalized to $[0, 1]$.

Example 2.1: Consider the example k-STC query q with location $q.\lambda$ and $q.\epsilon$ as shown in Figure 2) and with $q.\psi = \{coffee, tea\}$, $q.k = 1$, and $q.minpts = 2$. The data set contains the 7 objects $p_1, p_2, \cdots, p_7$. The figure also shows the document vector and the Euclidean distance to the query location for each object. Let $\alpha = 0.5$ and $tr_{q.\psi}(p.\psi) = \sum_{t \in q.\psi \cap p.\psi} w_t$. The top-1 cluster is $R = \{p_3, p_5\}$ that has score 0.315 (= $0.5 \times (0.11 + 0.15)/2 + (1 - 0.5) \times (1 - (0.5 + 0.5)/2)$). □

3. BASIC APPROACH

We adopt the IR-tree [21] and inverted file [24] index structures to organize objects. An inverted file index has two main components: (i) A vocabulary of all distinct words appearing in the text descriptions of the objects in the data set and (ii) a posting list for each word t, i.e., a sequence of pairs (id, w), where id is the identifier of an object whose text description contains t and w is the word's weight in the object.

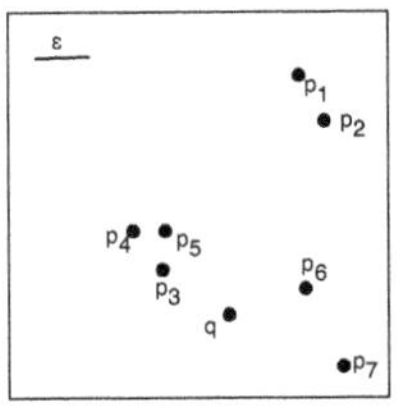

	coffee	tea	pizza	$d_{q.\lambda}(p_i.\lambda)$
p_1	(0.2,	0.2,	0)	0.25
p_2	(0.2,	0.2,	0)	0.2
p_3	(0.5,	0,	0)	0.11
p_4	(0,	0,	0.5)	0.18
p_5	(0,	0.5,	0)	0.15
p_6	(0.5,	0,	0)	0.1
p_7	(0.5,	0.5,	0)	0.19

Figure 2: Example k-STC Query

The IR-tree extends the R-tree with inverted files. Each leaf node contains entries of the form $e_O = (id, \Lambda)$, where $e_O.id$ refers to an object identifier and $e_O.\Lambda$ is a minimum bounding rectangle (MBR) of the location of the object. Each leaf node also contains a pointer to an inverted file indexing the text descriptions of all objects stored in the node. Each non-leaf node N contains entries of the form $e = (id, \Lambda)$, where $e.id$ points to a child node of N and $e.\Lambda$ is the MBR of all rectangles in entries of the child node. Each non-leaf node also contains a pointer to an inverted file indexing the pseudo text descriptions of the entries stored in the node. A pseudo text description of an entry e is a summary of all (pseudo) text descriptions in the entries of the child node pointed to by e. This enables derivation of an upper bound on the text relevance to a query of any object contained in the subtree rooted at e.

Given a query, the top-k spatial textual clusters are the top-k density-based clusters found from the relevant object set D_ψ with regard to the query keywords. A straightforward solution is (i) to obtain the object set D_ψ, (ii) to find all density-based clusters in D_ψ, (iii) to sort these according to the scoring function, and (iv) to return the top-k clusters. This solution is inefficient, since finding all clusters is expensive. The basic algorithm avoids finding all clusters. Specifically, some candidate clusters are first obtained, and a threshold is set according to the score of the k-th candidate cluster. The basic algorithm estimates a bound on the scores of all unfound clusters. If the bound is worse than the threshold, the currently found top-k clusters are the result.

As shown in Algorithm 1, the basic algorithm first obtains the relevant object set D_ψ with regard to the query keywords by taking the union of the posting lists of the query terms in the inverted index (line 1). Next, it sorts the objects in D_ψ in ascending order of their Euclidean distances to the query location, i.e., $d_{q.\lambda}(p.\lambda)$, and keeps the sorted copy i *slist* (line 2). In addition, the objects in D_ψ are sorted in ascending order of their converted text relevance with regard to the query keywords, i.e., $1 - tr_{q.\psi}(p.\psi)$, and the sorted copy is kept in *tlist* (line 3).

The candidate list *rlist* is initialized as empty (line 4). The threshold is set to infinity (line 5). The algorithm does sorted access in parallel on the sorted lists *slist* and *tlist* (line 7). As an object p is obtained from one of the lists, function **GetCluster** (Algorithm 2) tries to retrieve the cluster containing p as a core object (line 8). Meanwhile, the objects contained in the cluster are removed from both *slist* and *tlist*. If the retrieved cluster is not empty, it is added to the candidate list *rlist*, and the threshold τ is updated to the score of the k-th candidate in *rlist* (lines 9–11). The algorithm estimates a lower bound on the scores of all unfound clusters by using the minimal Euclidean distance sb and minimal converted text relevance tb of all objects left in *slist* and *tlist*, i.e., $bound = \alpha \cdot sb + (1 - \alpha) \cdot tb$ (lines 12–14). The result is guaranteed to be found when $bound \geq \tau$ or *slist* is exhausted (indicating that *tlist* is also exhausted) (line 15). The top-k candidate clusters in *rlist* are the result.

LEMMA 1. *The stop condition (line 15) in Algorithm 1 guarantees the correct result.*

PROOF. Omitted. □

Algorithm 1 **Basic**(Query q, IR-tree $irtree$, InvertedIndex $iindex$, Integer k)

1: $D_\psi \leftarrow$ **LoadRelevantObjects**$(q.\psi, iindex)$;
2: $slist \leftarrow$ sort objects in D_ψ in ascending order of $d_{q.\lambda}(p.\lambda)$;
3: $tlist \leftarrow$ sort objects in D_ψ in ascending order of $1 - tr_{q.\psi}(p.\psi)$;
4: $rlist \leftarrow \emptyset$;
5: $\tau \leftarrow \infty$;
6: **repeat**
7:     Object $p \leftarrow$ sorted access in parallel to $slist$ and $tlist$;
8:     $c \leftarrow$ **GetCluster**$(p, q, irtree, tlist, slist)$;
9:     **if** $c \neq \emptyset$ **then**
10:         Add c to $rlist$;
11:         $\tau \leftarrow$ score of the k-th cluster in $rlist$;
12:     $sb \leftarrow$ **First**$(slist)$;
13:     $tb \leftarrow$ **First**$(tlist)$;
14:     $bound \leftarrow \alpha \cdot sb + (1 - \alpha) \cdot tb$;
15: **until** $bound \geq \tau \vee slist = \emptyset$
16: Return $rlist$;

To retrieve a cluster R containing p as a core object, function **GetCluster** (Algorithm 2) issues a range query centered at p with radius $q.\epsilon$ on the IR-tree (line 2). The goal is to check whether the ϵ-neighborhood of p is dense. If $neighbors$ contains fewer than $q.minpts$ objects, object p is marked as noise, and an empty set is returned (lines 3–6). Otherwise, $neighbors$ is considered as a temporary cluster (line 8) that is expanded by checking the ϵ-neighborhood of each object p_i in $neighbors$ except p (lines 12 and 13). If the ϵ-neighborhood of p_i is dense (line 14), the objects inside and previously labeled as noise are added to the temporary cluster (lines 16 and 17). Next, the objects inside and not belonging to the temporary cluster are added to both the temporary cluster and to $neighbors$ in preparation for further expansion in subsequent iterations (lines 18–21). To avoid duplicate operations, the objects that are marked as noise or are added to the temporary cluster are removed from $tlist$ and $slist$ (lines 4, 9, 20). The temporary cluster R is finalized and returned if no more object can be added.

Function **RangeQuery** (Algorithm 3) is used to find the objects in the ϵ-neighborhood of an object p using an IR-tree on the objects. A priority queue organizes the IR-tree nodes to be visited using the minimum Euclidean distance between nodes and the query as the key. First, the root node of the IR-tree is added to the queue (line 3). The algorithm iteratively visits and removes the first node in the queue (lines 5 and 6). If the node is a leaf node, the objects in it that are relevant to the query keywords and that are located in range $q.\epsilon$ are added to $neighbors$ (lines 7–10). Otherwise, the node is a non-leaf node. Its child nodes that are relevant to the query keywords and that are located in range $q.\epsilon$ are inserted into the priority queue (lines 12–14). The process terminates when the queue is exhausted.

4. ADVANCED APPROACH

The basic approach is inefficient because it checks the neighborhoods of all relevant objects with regard to the query keywords and because checking a neighborhood involves a time-consuming range query. The advanced approach includes three techniques that address these inefficiencies.

4.1 Object Skipping

Function **GetCluster** tries to find a cluster R containing a relevant object p as a core object. It first determines whether the ϵ-neighborhood of p is dense. If so, cluster R is initialized as the relevant objects inside the$p$'s ϵ-neighborhood. An object is examined if its neighborhood has been checked. Next, the relevant objects other than p in the ϵ-neighborhood of p are examined in turn. If a neighborhood under consideration is dense, the newly found relevant objects in it are added to R. This way, R is finalized when each relevant object has been examined. However, it is possible to get a cluster R by examining only a portion of the relevant objects. Consider Figure 3, where the neighborhoods of objects p_1, p_2, p_3, and p_4 are given as dashed and solid circles. The neighborhood of p_4 (solid circle) is covered by the union of the neighborhoods of p_1, p_2, and p_3 (dashed circles), making it unnecessary to check the neighborhood of p_4 after having examined p_1, p_2, and p_3. Based on this observation, we define a skipping rule that reduces the number of relevant objects to be examined, and we design an algorithm **OS** that implements the rule.

Algorithm 2 **GetCluster**(Object p, Query q, IR-tree $irtree$, List $tlist$, List $slist$)

1: $R \leftarrow \emptyset$;
2: $neighbors \leftarrow irtree.$**RangeQuery**$(q, p)$;
3: **if** $neighbors.size < q.minpts$ **then**
4:     Remove p from $tlist$ and $slist$;
5:     Mark p as a noise;
6:     Return R;
7: **else**   ▷ p is a core;
8:     Add $neighbors$ to R;
9:     Remove $neighbors$ from $tlist$ and $slist$;
10:     Remove p from $neighbors$;
11:     **while** $neighbors$ is not empty **do**
12:         Object $p_i \leftarrow$ remove an object from $neighbors$;
13:         $neighbors_i \leftarrow irtree.$**RangeQuery**$(q, p_i)$;
14:         **if** $neighbors_i.size \geq q.minpts$ **then**
15:             **for** each object p_j in $neighbors_i$ **do**
16:                 **if** p_j is a noise **then**
17:                     Add p_j to R;
18:                 **else if** $p_j \notin R$ **then**
19:                     Add p_j to R;
20:                     Remove p_j from $tlist$ and $slist$;
21:                     Add p_j to $neighbors$;
22:     Return R;

Algorithm 3 **RangeQuery**(Query q, Object p)

1: $neighbors \leftarrow \emptyset$;
2: PriorityQueue $queue \leftarrow \emptyset$;
3: $queue.$**Enqueue**$(root)$;
4: **while** $queue$ is not empty **do**
5:     $e \leftarrow queue.$**Dequeue**$()$;
6:     $N \leftarrow$ **ReadNode**(e);
7:     **if** N is a leaf node **then**
8:         **for** each object o in N **do**
9:             **if** o is relevant to $q.\psi$ and $\|p\ o\|_{min} \leq q.\epsilon$ **then**
10:                 $neighbors.$**Add**(o);
11:     **else**
12:         **for** each entry e' in N **do**
13:             **if** e' is relevant to $q.\psi$ and $\|p\ e'\|_{min} \leq q.\epsilon$ **then**
14:                 $queue.$**Enqueue**(e');
15: Return $neighbors$;

SKIPPING RULE 1. *Let $S = (p_1, p_2, \cdots, p_n)$ be the order in which a set of objects is examined. Object p_i $(i > 1)$ can be skipped if the neighborhood of p_i is fully covered by the union of the neighborhoods of the objects examined before p_i, i.e., if $N_\epsilon(p_i) \subset \cup_{1 \le j < i} N_\epsilon(p_j)$, where $N_\epsilon(p_i)$ is represented as a circular region centered at p_i and with radius ϵ.*

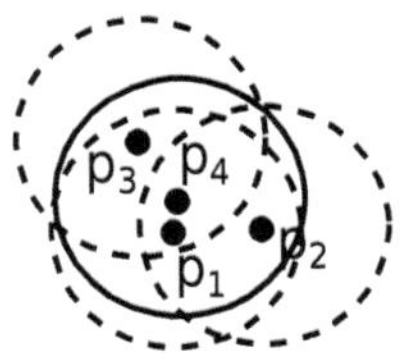

Figure 3: Neighborhoods

The skipping rule is effective when given a good ordering S. In Figure 3, if $S = (p_1, p_2, p_4, p_3)$, no object can be skipped. However, if $S = (p_1, p_2, p_3, p_4)$, object p_4 can be skipped. Intuitively, if the union of the neighborhoods of the objects that have been examined covers a large area, the probability of skipping the next object is high.

To achieve an algorithm **OS** that implements the skipping rule, Algorithm 2 is modified in two ways. First, given an object p, the objects in p's neighborhood are sorted in descending order of their distance to p. The idea is that the farther the objects are from p, the larger the area covered by their neighborhoods is. Referring to lines 2 and 13 in Algorithm 2, the objects returned from **RangeQuery** are sorted in descending order of their distances. Let $S(p)$ be the sorted list of the objects in the neighborhood of p. List *neighbors* (line 2 in Algorithm 2) maintains the objects to be examined. It is initialized as the sorted list $S(p)$. For each object p_i in $S(p)$, the sorted list $S(p_i)$ of p_i is appended to $S(p)$. The algorithm terminates when $S(p)$ is exhausted. Second, each time, when about to check the neighborhood of an object (line 13 in Algorithm 2), the skipping rule is considered. If the rule applies, the algorithm continues to process the next object. The skipping rule involves the testing of whether a circle is covered by the union of several circles. This can be accomplished using a recursive subdivision of the circle by non-overlapping squares.

4.2 Spatially Gridded Posting Lists

We proceed to design **spatially gridded posting lists** (SGPL) to estimate the selectivity of a range query on the IR-tree, such that sparse neighborhoods can be pruned without issuing expensive range queries.

An $n \times n$ grid is created on the data set. For each word w, a spatially gridded posting list is constructed covering all the objects that contain w. Let D_{w_i} be the set of objects containing word w_i. The SGPL of w_i is a sorted list of entries, where each entry takes the form (c_j, S_{w_i,c_j}), where c_j (sorting key) is the index value of a grid cell C_{c_j} and S_{w_i,c_j} is a set of objects that belong to D_{w_i} and that are located in grid cell C_{c_j}, i.e., $\forall p \in S_{w_i,c_j} (p \in D_{w_i} \wedge p.\lambda \in C_{c_j})$. Grid cells are indexed using a space filling curve, e.g., a Hilbert curve or a Z-order curve. The SGPLs of all distinct words in the data set are organized similarly to the inverted file. Empty cells are not stored. Given a word, its SGPL can be retrieved straightforwardly.

Example 4.1: Figure 4(a) illustrates a 4×4 grid on the 7 objects in Example 2.1. Grid cells are indexed using a 2-order Z-curve. Numbers in italics are the Z-order derived keys for the cells. Figure 4(c) shows the SGPLs for words 'coffee' and 'tea'. For example, the entry for 'coffee' tells that the document of p_3 contains 'coffee' and that p_3 is located in the cell with index value 3. □

Given a set $q.\psi$ containing m query keywords, the corresponding m SGPLs are merged to estimate the selectivity of the query. We define a merging operator $\bigoplus$ on SGPLs that produces a count for each non-empty cell. The count for cell C is the cardinality of the union of the sets of objects located in C from different SGPLs, i.e.,

$$\bigoplus_{w_i \in q.\psi} SGPL_{w_i} = \{(c_j, |\bigcup_{w_i \in q.\psi} S_{w_i,c_j}|\}. \quad (2)$$

Example 4.2: The third row in Figure 4(c) is the result of merging the SGPLs of words 'coffee' and 'tea'. For example, the entry $(3, 2)$ tells that the cell with index value 3 contains 2 objects after merging. □

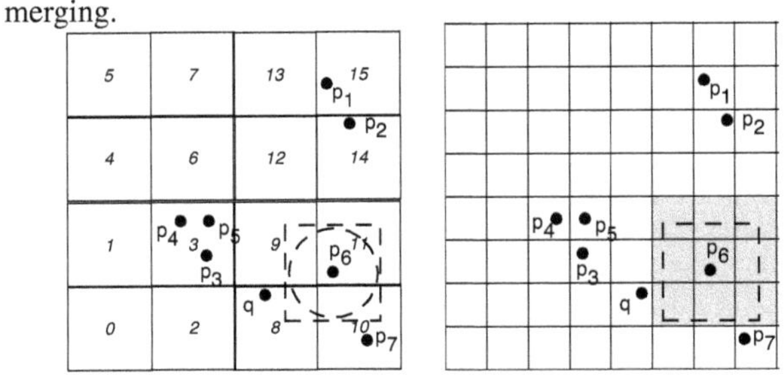

(a) 4×4 Grid (b) 8×8 Grid

coffee	$(3, \{p_3\}), (10, \{p_7\}), (11, \{p_6\}), (14, \{p_2\}), (15, \{p_1\})$
tea	$(3, \{p_5\}), (10, \{p_7\}), (14, \{p_2\}), (15, \{p_1\})$
coffee $\bigoplus$ tea	$(3, 2), (10, 1), (11, 1), (14, 1), (15, 1)$

(c) SGPL

Figure 4: Example Spatially Gridded Posting Lists

The merged result of the SGPLs of the query keywords is used to estimate the selectivity of the circular range query q_c centered at an object p with radius ϵ (e.g., the dashed circle in Figure 4(a)). We approximate the circle q_c as its circumscribed square q_s (e.g., the dashed square in Figure 4(a)). The sum of the counts of the grid cells that intersect square q_s in the merged SGPLs of the query keywords is returned as the selectivity. It is not necessary to merge the whole SGPL of each query keyword—only the cells that intersect q_s need to be considered. We thus define a parameterized merging operator $\bigoplus(q_s)$ as follows.

$$\bigoplus_{w_i \in q.\psi} (q_s) SGPL_{w_i} = \{(c_j, |\bigcup_{w_i \in q.\psi} S_{w_i,c_j}| \mid C_{c_j} \cap q_s \neq \emptyset\} \quad (3)$$

In Figure 4, where q_s is the dashed square, *coffee* $\bigoplus(q_s)$*tea* $= \{(10, 1), (11, 1)\}$. Based on the coding scheme of the space-filling curve, we adopt an efficient existing algorithm [10] to retrieve the cells that intersect the query range q_s.

The derived selectivity serves as an upper bound on the number of objects falling inside circle q_c. If the selectivity (upper bound) is less than $q.minpts$, the ϵ-neighborhood of object p is guaranteed to be sparse. Otherwise, function **RangeQuery** is called to compute the exact number of objects in the ϵ-neighborhood of object p. Hence, some sparse ϵ-neighborhoods can be found efficiently. However, it is not guaranteed that all sparse relevant ϵ-neighborhoods can be found using the SGPLs of query keywords, since the selectivity is not always a tight upper bound due to the granularity of the grid and the use of the circumscribed square of the circular range.

Example 4.3: Let $q.minpts = 2$objects. In Figure 4(a), the dashed square q_s approximates the ϵ-neighborhood of p_6. Since q_s intersects grid cells 8, 9, 10, and 11 in the merged result of the SGPLs of words 'coffee' and 'tea', the selectivity is 2, i.e., the number of objects covered by the four grid cells. Hence, the ϵ-neighborhoods of p_6 is conservatively assessed as not sparse, and **RangeQuery** is called to compute the exact number of objects in the ϵ-neighborhood. However, if using the finer grid in Figure 4(b), the selectivity is 1 ($< q.minpts$). Only the gray cells intersect the query range. Thus, the ϵ-neighborhood of p_6 is guaranteed to be sparse, with no need to call function **RangeQuery**. □

We observe that using a finer grid may help avoid expensive **RangeQuery** operations. However, the cost of the selectivity estimation increases when using a finer grid. The empirical study covers the effects of the grid granularity.

4.3 FastRange

SGPLs can also be used to support the processing of range queries on the IR-tree. We propose an algorithm **FastRange** that handles range queries on SGPLs. We first override the merging operator $\bigoplus(q_s)$ as $\overline{\bigoplus}(q_s)$.

$$\overline{\bigoplus_{w_i \in q.\psi}}(q_s)SGPL_{w_i} = \{(c_j, \bigcup_{w_i \in q.\psi} S_{w_i,c_j} \mid C_{c_j} \cap q_s \neq \emptyset\} \quad (4)$$

Operator $\bigoplus(q_s)$ computes the *number* of objects inside each cell intersecting query range q_s, while operator $\overline{\bigoplus}(q_s)$ computes the *set of the identifiers* of the objects inside each such cell. As shown in Algorithm 4, **FastRange** takes two arguments: *list*, the result of operator $\overline{\bigoplus}(q_s)$, and q_c, the circular region centered at an object p and with radius ϵ. If a cell c from *list* is contained in the query range q_c, all the objects in c are added to the result (lines 3 and 4). If a cell c intersects q_c, only objects in c that have distance to p no greater than ϵ are added to the result (lines 6–8).

Algorithm 4 FastRange(SGPL *list*, Range q_c)

```
1: result ← ∅;
2: for each cell c ∈ list do
3:     if c is completely inside the query range q_c then
4:         All the objects inside c are added to result
5:     else                              ▷ c intersects the query range
6:         for each object o inside c do
7:             if ||o p|| ≤ ε then
8:                 Add o to result;
```

5. EMPIRICAL STUDIES

Experimental Setup. We use a real data set from TripAdvisor that contains 100,789 restaurants. Each restaurant has a text description of length 3 words on average. The total number of distinct words is 202. The data set is small. But as we are not aware of other public real data sets that match our problem motivation, we generate larger data sets for scalability evaluation. Specifically, we generate data sets of size 200K, 400K, 600K, 800K, and 1M. For a randomly picked object p in TripAdvisor, we generate a new object whose location is obtained by slightly shifting the location of p and whose text description is the same as that of p.

We generate 4 query sets with 1, 2, 3, and 4 keywords, respectively. Each set comprises 100 queries. No query has an empty result. To generate a query, we randomly pick an object in the dataset and use its location as the query location, and we randomly choose words from the object as the query keywords.

We evaluate the performance of the basic approach (Basic), the advanced approach with object skipping (Adv1), the advanced approach with object skipping and selectivity estimation (Adv2), and the advanced approach with object skipping, selectivity estimation, and FastRange (Adv3), under different parameter settings. Table 1 shows the parameter values used in the experiments, where the bold values are default values. All algorithms were implemented in Java, and an Intel(R) Core(TM) i7-3770 CPU @ 3.40GHz with 16GB main memory was used for the experiments. All the data structures are memory resident.

Table 1: Parameter Values

Interpretation	Parameter	Values
# of clusters	k	5, **10**, 15, 20
# of query keywords	$\|q.\psi\|$	1, **2**, 3, 4
	ϵ	0.0001, 0.0005, **0.001**, 0.005, 0.01
Density requirements	$minpts$	10, 20, **50**, 100, 200
Z-curve order, SGPL	h	3, 4, 5, **6**, 7, 8, 9, 10
Spatial/textual weight	α	0.1, 0.3, **0.5**, 0.7, 0.9
Data set size	$\|\mathcal{D}\|$	**100K**, 200K, 400K, 600K, 800K, 1M

Varying the Number of Keywords $|q.\psi|$. Figure 5 shows how the four approaches are affected by the number of query keywords. The advanced algorithms exhibits the best performance. The number of range queries issued and the elapsed time are aligned. In subsequent experiments, we do not show the number of range queries.

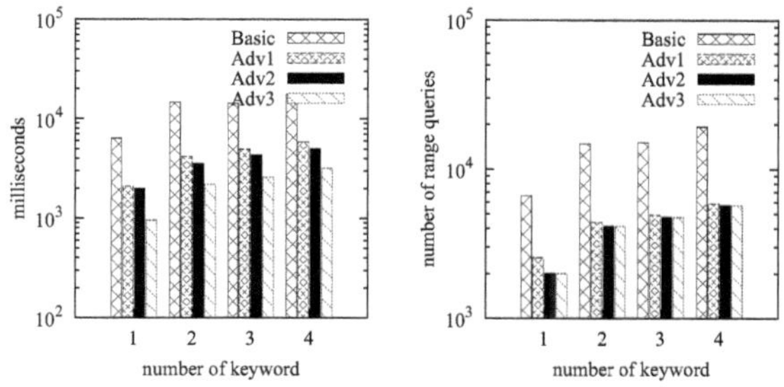

Figure 5: Varying the Number of Keywords

Varying Density Requirement. Figure 6 shows the effects of varying ϵ and $minpts$. As ϵ increases, more object neighborhoods become dense, and if the ϵ-neighborhood of a relevant object satisfies the density requirement, we need to examine the relevant objects inside the ϵ-neighborhood to expand the cluster. Hence, the cost increases. However, the performance is not sensitive to $minpts$ in range $[10, 200]$ given that $\epsilon = 0.001$.

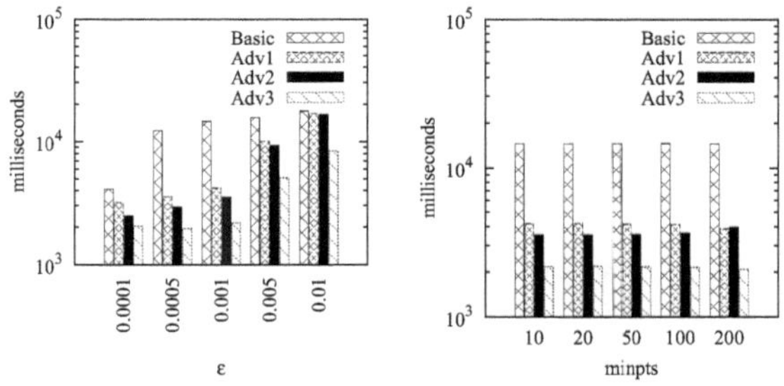

Figure 6: Varying ϵ and $minpts$

Varying α and the Number k of Requested Clusters. The four approaches are insensitive to varying α in the range 0.1 to 0.9 and to varying the number k of requested clusters in the range 5 to 20.

Scalability. Figure 7 shows the effect of varying the data set size. We observe that the algorithms scale linearly and that the advanced algorithm is affected the least by an increasing data set size.

Varying the Order of Z-Curve h in SGPL. SGPL uses a grid indexed by a Z-curve. The order h of the Z-curve defines the granularity of the grid: a larger h yields a finer grid. A finer grid improves the ability to estimate the selectivity of range queries and the ability to detect sparse ϵ-neighborhoods. Figure 7 shows that as h increases, the performance improves. When h exceeds 6, the performance of SGPL becomes stable, suggesting that the selectivity estimation ability is close to optimal at this point.

Summary. Overall, the best advanced approach outperforms the basic approach by an order of magnitude. The elapsed time and the number of range queries are proportional to each other, which indicates that the time consuming part of the k-STC queries is the range

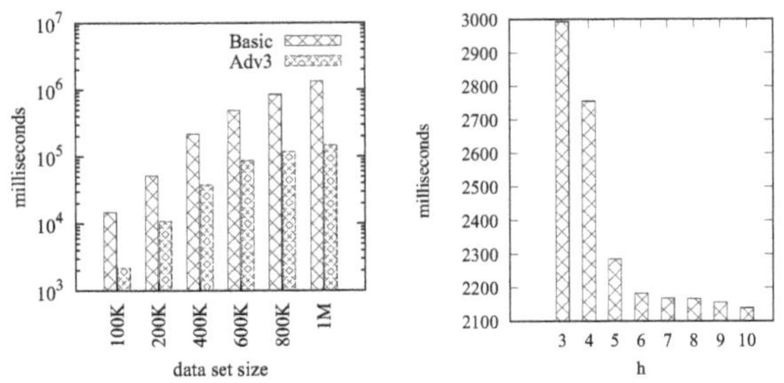

Figure 7: Varying Data Size and the Order h in SGPL

queries. The proposed advanced approach significantly reduce the cost incurred by the range queries.

6. RELATED WORK

Several studies consider queries that are similar to that of this study. One study [2, 18] targets the case where the user wishes to find nearby groups of relevant objects. Considering the co-location relationship between objects, other studies [7, 12, 19] consider the retrieval of regions so that the total weights of objects inside the regions are maximized. In these studies, result regions are either fixed-sized rectangles or circles. A recent study [6] computes a maximum-sum region where the road network distance between objects is less than a query constraint and the sum of the scores of the objects inside the region is maximized. This kind of query may retrieve a region containing many objects with low scores and ignore a promising region with few objects with high scores. The collective spatial keyword query [3, 5, 14] finds a group of objects that are close to a query point and that collectively cover a set of query keywords. Another query [4] uses prestige-based relevance for ranking. None of the above studies use clustering techniques, and we believe that the paper's study is the first to attempt to use clustering for spatial keyword querying.

Next, the most popular density based clustering method is DBSCAN [9]. Its "density-reachability" connects objects within a certain distance threshold of each other, and a cluster consists of all density-connected objects together with all objects that are within the threshold distance of these objects. Such clusters can have arbitrary shapes. OPTICS [1] generalizes DBSCAN, removing the need to choose a value for the distance threshold. DBRS [20] improves DBSCAN by repeatedly picking an unclassified point at random and examining its neighborhood. VDBSCAN [13] aims for varied-density dataset analysis. GDBSCAN [17] clusters objects according to their spatial and their non-spatial attributes. While the paper's study uses DBSCAN, it is possible to also use other density-based clustering models that are based on DBSCAN.

An extended version of this paper is available [22].

7. CONCLUSIONS AND FUTURE WORK

This paper proposes a new type of query, namely the top-k spatial textual clusters (k-STC) query that returns the top-k clusters that (i) are located the closest to the query location, that (ii) contain the objects whose text descriptions are the most relevant to the query keywords, and that (iii) have densities that exceed a threshold. Qualifying clusters are ranked according to a scoring function that takes into account the distance to the query location and the relevance to the query keywords. We propose a basic algorithm that is an on-line clustering method. To improve performance, we propose an advanced approach that includes three techniques: (i) a skipping rule that is used to reduce the number of objects to be examined, (ii) spatially gridded posting lists (SGPL) that are used to estimate the selectivity of the range queries so that sparse neighborhoods can be pruned at low cost, and (iii) a fast range query algorithm that leverages the SGPL. Empirical studies on a real data set indicate that the paper's proposals are capable of excellent performance.

This work opens to a number of interesting research directions. For example, the density requirements ϵ and $minpts$ in the query define the form of the clusters to be retrieved. However, a density requirement good for a city center may not work for the countryside. Thus, it is of interest to enable parameters to vary according to the local data density.

8. REFERENCES

[1] M. Ankerst, M. M. Breunig, H.-P. Kriegel, and J. Sander. OPTICS: ordering points to identify the clustering structure. In *SIGMOD*, pages 49–60, 1999.

[2] K. Bøgh, A. Skovsgaard, and C. S. Jensen. Groupfinder: A new approach to top-k point-of-interest group retrieval. *PVLDB*, 6(12):1226–1229, 2013.

[3] X. Cao, G. Cong, T. Guo, C. S. Jensen, and B. C. Ooi. Efficient processing of spatial group keyword queries. *ACM TODS*, 40(2):13, 2015.

[4] X. Cao, G. Cong, and C. S. Jensen. Retrieving top-k prestige-based relevant spatial web objects. *PVLDB*, 3(1):373–384, 2010.

[5] X. Cao, G. Cong, C. S. Jensen, and B. C. Ooi. Collective spatial keyword querying. In *SIGMOD*, pages 373–384, 2011.

[6] X. Cao, G. Cong, C. S. Jensen, and M. L. Yiu. Retrieving regions of interest for user exploration. *PVLDB*, 7(9):733–744, 2014.

[7] D.-W. Choi, C.-W. Chung, and Y. Tao. A scalable algorithm for maximizing range sum in spatial databases. *PVLDB*, 5(11):1088–1099, 2012.

[8] G. Cong, C. S. Jensen, and D. Wu. Efficient retrieval of the top-k most relevant spatial web objects. *PVLDB*, 2(1):337–348, 2009.

[9] M. Ester, H.-P. Kriegel, J. Sander, and X. Xu. A density-based algorithm for discovering clusters in large spatial databases with noise. In *KDD*, pages 226–231, 1996.

[10] J. K. Lawder and P. J. H. King. Using space-filling curves for multi-dimensional indexing. In *BNCOD*, pages 20–35, 2000.

[11] Z. Li, K. C. K. Lee, B. Zheng, W.-C. Lee, D. L. Lee, and X. Wang. IR-tree: an efficient index for geographic document search. *IEEE TKDE*, 23(4):585–599, 2011.

[12] J. Liu, G. Yu, and H. Sun. Subject-oriented top-k hot region queries in spatial dataset. In *CIKM*, pages 2409–2412, 2011.

[13] P. Liu, D. Zhou, and N. Wu. VDBSCAN: Varied density based spatial clustering of applications with noise. In *Service Systems and Service Management*, pages 1–4, 2007.

[14] C. Long, R. C.-W. Wong, K. Wang, and A. W.-C. Fu. Collective spatial keyword queries: a distance owner-driven approach. In *SIGMOD*, pages 689–700, 2013.

[15] J. M. Ponte and W. B. Croft. A language modeling approach to information retrieval. In *SIGIR*, pages 275–281, 1998.

[16] G. Salton, A. Wong, and C. S. Yang. A vector space model for automatic indexing. *Commun. ACM*, 18:613–620, 1975.

[17] J. Sander, M. Ester, H.-P. Kriegel, and X. Xu. Density-based clustering in spatial databases: The algorithm GDBSCAN and its applications. *Data Min. Knowl. Discov.*, 2(2):169–194, 1998.

[18] A. Skovsgaard and C. S. Jensen. Finding top-*k* relevant groups of spatial web objects. *VLDB J.*, 24(4):537–555, 2015.

[19] Y. Tao, X. Hu, D.-W. Choi, and C.-W. Chung. Approximate maxrs in spatial databases. *PVLDB*, 6(13):1546–1557, 2013.

[20] X. Wang and H. J. Hamilton. DBRS: A density-based spatial clustering method with random sampling. In *PAKDD*, pages 563–575, 2003.

[21] D. Wu, G. Cong, and C. S. Jensen. A framework for efficient spatial web object retrieval. *VLDB J.*, 21(6):797–822, 2012.

[22] D. Wu and C. S. Jensen. A density-based approach to the retrieval of top-k spatial textual clusters. *CoRR*, abs/1607.08681, 2016.

[23] D. Wu, M. L. Yiu, G. Cong, and C. S. Jensen. Joint top-k spatial keyword query processing. *IEEE TKDE*, 24(10):1889–1903, 2012.

[24] J. Zobel and A. Moffat. Inverted files for text search engines. In *ACM Comput. Surv.*, volume 38, article 6, 2006.

Top-N Recommendation on Graphs

Zhao Kang, Chong Peng, Ming Yang, Qiang Cheng
Department of Computer Science, Southern Illinois University, Carbondale, IL, USA
{Zhao.Kang, pchong, ming.yang, qcheng}@siu.edu

ABSTRACT

Recommender systems play an increasingly important role in online applications to help users find what they need or prefer. Collaborative filtering algorithms that generate predictions by analyzing the user-item rating matrix perform poorly when the matrix is sparse. To alleviate this problem, this paper proposes a simple recommendation algorithm that fully exploits the similarity information among users and items and intrinsic structural information of the user-item matrix. The proposed method constructs a new representation which preserves affinity and structure information in the user-item rating matrix and then performs recommendation task. To capture proximity information about users and items, two graphs are constructed. Manifold learning idea is used to constrain the new representation to be smooth on these graphs, so as to enforce users and item proximities. Our model is formulated as a convex optimization problem, for which we need to solve the well known Sylvester equation only. We carry out extensive empirical evaluations on six benchmark datasets to show the effectiveness of this approach.

Keywords

top-N recommendation; laplacian graph; collaborative filtering

1. INTRODUCTION

Recommender systems have become increasingly indispensable in many applications [1]. Collaborative filtering (CF) based methods are a fundamental building block in many recommender systems. CF based recommender systems predict the ratings of items to be given by a user based on the ratings of the items previously rated by other users who are most similar to the target user.

CF based methods can be classified into memory-based methods [21] and model-based methods [14, 15]. The former includes two popular methods, user-oriented [9] and item-oriented, e.g., ItemKNN [6], depending on whether the neighborhood information is derived from similar users or items. First they compute similarities between the active item and other items, or between the active user and other users. Then they predict the unknown rating by combining the known rating of top k neighbors. Due to the simplicity of memory-based CF, it has been successfully applied in industry. However, it suffers from several problems, including data sparsity, cold start and data correlation [3], as users typically rate only a small portion of the available items, and they also tend to rate similar items closely. Therefore, the similarities between users or items cannot be accurately obtained with the existing similarity measures such as cosine and Pearson correlation, which in turn compromises the recommendation accuracy.

To alleviate the problems of memory-based methods, many model-based methods have been proposed, which use observed ratings to learn a predictive model. Among them, matrix factorization (MF) based models, e.g., PureSVD [5] and weighted regularized MF (WRMF) [10], are very popular due to their capability of capturing the implicit relationships among items and their outstanding performance. Nevertheless, it introduces high computational complexity and also faces the problem of uninterpretable recommendations. Because the rating matrix is sparse, the factorization of the user-item matrix may lead to inferior solutions [7]. By learning an aggregation coefficient matrix [13], recently, sparse linear method (SLIM) [17] has been proposed and shown to be effective. However, it just captures relations between items that have been co-purchased/co-rated by at least one user [12]. Moreover, it only explores the linear relations between items. Another class of methods use Bayesian personalized ranking (BPR) criterion to measure the difference between the rankings of user-purchased items and the remaining items. For instance, BPRMF and BPRKNN [19] have been demonstrated to be effective for implicit feedback datasets.

In this paper, we propose a novel Top-N recommendation model based on graphs. This method not only takes into account the neighborhood information, which is encoded by our user graph and item graph, but also reveals hidden structure in the data by deploying graph regularization. In the real world, data often reside on low-dimensional manifolds embedded in a high-dimensional ambient space. Like the Netflix Prize problem, where the size of the user-item matrix can be huge, there exist relationships between users (such as their age, hobbies, education, etc.) and movies (such as their genre, release year, actors, origin country, etc.). Moreover, people sharing the same tastes for a class of movies

CIKM'16 , October 24 - 28, 2016, Indianapolis, IN, USA

ISBN 978-1-4503-4073-1/16/10...$15.00

DOI: http://dx.doi.org/10.1145/2983323.2983649

are likely to rate them similarly. As a result, the rows and columns of the user-item matrix possess important structural information, which should be taken advantage of in actual applications.

To preserve local geometric and discriminating structures embedded in a high-dimensional space, numerous manifold learning methods, such as locally linear embedding (LLE) [20], locality preserving projection (LPP) [18], have been proposed. In recent years, graph regularization based nonnegative matrix factorization [4] of data representation has been developed to remedy the failure in representing geometric structures in data. Inspired by this observation, to comprehensively consider the associations between the users and items and the local manifold structures of the user-item data space, we propose to apply both user and item graph regularizations. Unlike many existing recommendation algorithms, we first establish a new representation which is infused with the above information. It turns out that this new representation is not sparse anymore. Therefore, we perform recommendation task with this novel representation.

2. DEFINITIONS AND NOTATIONS

Let $U = \{u_1, u_2, ..., u_m\}$ and $T = \{t_1, t_2, ..., t_n\}$ represent the sets of all users and all items, respectively. The whole set of user-item purchases/ratings are represented by the user-item matrix X of size $m \times n$. Element x_{ij} is 1 or a positive value if user u_i has ever purchased/rated item t_j, otherwise it is marked as 0. The i-th row of X denotes the purchase/rating history of user u_i on all items. The j-th column of X is the purchase/rating history of all users on item t_j. $\|X\|_F^2 = \sum_i \sum_j x_{ij}^2$ is the squared Frobenius norm of X. $\mathrm{Tr}(\cdot)$ stands for the trace operator. I denotes the identity matrix. $\odot$ is the Hadamard product.

3. PROPOSED MODEL

3.1 User and Item Graphs

User-item rating matrix is an overfit representation of user tastes and item descriptions. This leads to problems of synonymy, computational complexity, and potentially poorer results. Therefore, a more compact representation of user tastes and item descriptions is preferred. Graph regularization is effective in preserving local geometric and discriminating structures embedded in a high-dimensional space. It is based on the well known manifold assumption [18]: If two data points such as $\mathbf{x}_i$ and $\mathbf{x}_j$ are close in the geodesic distance on the data manifold, then their corresponding representations $\mathbf{y}_i$ and $\mathbf{y}_j$ are also close to each other. In practice, it is difficult to accurately estimate the global manifold structure of the data due to the insufficient number of samples and the high dimensionality of the ambient space. Therefore, many methods resort to local manifold structures. Much effort on manifold learning [18] has shown that local geometric structures of the data manifold can be effectively modeled through a nearest neighbor graph on sampled data points.

We adopt graph regularization to incorporate user and item proximities. In this paper, we construct two graphs: the user graph and the item graph. We assume that users having similar tastes for items form communities in the user graph, while items having similar appeals to users form communities in the item graph. Since "birds of a feather flock together", this assumption is plausible and turns out to indeed benefit recommender systems substantially in our experiment results. As an example for movie recommendation, the users are the vertices of a "social graph" whose edges represent relations induced by similar tastes.

More formally, we construct an undirected weighted graph $G_c = (V_c, E_c; S_c)$ on items, called the item graph. The vertex set V_c corresponds to items $\{t_1, \cdots, t_n\}$ with each node t_i corresponding to a data point $\mathbf{x}_i$ which is the i-th column of X. Symmetric adjacency matrix S_c encodes the inter-item information, in which s_{ij} is the weight of the edge joining vertices t_i and t_j and represents how strong the relationship or similarity items t_i and t_j have. $E_c = \{e_{ij}\}$ is the edge set with each edge e_{ij} between nodes t_i and t_j associated with a weight s_{ij}. The graph regularization on the item graph is formulated as

$$\begin{aligned}&\frac{1}{2}\sum_{i,j=1}^{n}\|\mathbf{y}_i - \mathbf{y}_j\|_2^2 s_{ij} = \sum_{i=1}^{n}\mathbf{y}_i^T\mathbf{y}_i d_{ii} - \sum_{i,j=1}^{n}\mathbf{y}_i^T\mathbf{y}_j s_{ij}\\ &=\mathrm{Tr}(YD_cY^T) - \mathrm{Tr}(YS_cY^T) = \mathrm{Tr}(YL_cY^T),\end{aligned} \tag{1}$$

where D_c is a diagonal matrix with $d_{ii} = \sum_{j=1}^{n} s_{ij}$, and $L_c = D_c - S_c$ is the graph Laplacian. To preserve the structural information of the manifold, we want (1) to be as small as possible. It is apparent that minimizing (1) imposes the smoothness of the representation coefficients; i.e., if items t_i and t_j are similar (with a relatively bigger s_{ij}), their low-dimensional representations $\mathbf{y}_i$ and $\mathbf{y}_j$ are also close to each other. Therefore, optimizing (1) is an attempt to ensure the manifold assumption.

The crucial part of graph regularization is the definition of the adjacency matrix S_c. There exist a number of different similarity metrics in the literature [21], e.g., cosine similarity, Pearson correlation coefficient, and adjusted cosine similarity. For simplicity, in our experiment, we use cosine similarity for explicit rating datasets and Jaccard coefficient for implicit feedback datesets. For binary variables, the Jaccard coefficient is a more appropriate similarity metric than cosine because it is insensitive to the amplitudes of ratings. It measures the fraction of users who have interactions with both items over the number of users who have interacted either of them. Formally, according to cosine definition, the similarity s_{ij} between two items t_i and t_j is defined as $s_{ij} = \frac{\mathbf{x}_i \cdot \mathbf{x}_j}{\|\mathbf{x}_i\|_2 \|\mathbf{x}_j\|_2}$, where '$\cdot$' denotes the vector dot-product operation. For Jaccard coefficient, $s_{ij} = \frac{|\mathbf{x}_i \cap \mathbf{x}_j|}{|\mathbf{x}_i \cup \mathbf{x}_j|}$, where $\cap$ and $\cup$ represent intersection and union operations, respectively. Likewise, by defining the user graph $G_r = (V_r, E_r; S_r)$ whose vertex set V_r corresponds to users $\{u_1, \cdots, u_m\}$, we get a corresponding expression $\mathrm{Tr}(Y^T L_r Y)$. Here L_r denotes the Laplacian of G_r, which is similarly obtained from the data points corresponding to the users, that is, the rows of X.

3.2 Model

By exploiting both user and item graphs, our proposed model can be written as

$$\min_{Y} \|X - Y\|_F^2 + \alpha\mathrm{Tr}(YL_cY^T) + \beta\mathrm{Tr}(Y^T L_r Y). \tag{2}$$

The first term of (2) penalizes large deviations of the predictions from the given ratings. The last two terms measure the smoothness of the predicted ratings on the graph structures and encourage the ratings of nodes with affinity to be similar. They can alleviate the data sparsity issue to some extent. When the item neighborhood information is not available, user neighborhood information might exist, vice versa. The parameters α and β adjust the balance between the reconstruction error and graph regularizations.

By setting the derivative of the objective function of (2) with respect to Y to zero, we have

$$(\beta L_r + I)Y + \alpha Y L_c = X. \tag{3}$$

Equation (3) is the well known Sylvester equation, which costs $O(m^3)$ or $O(n^3)$ with a general solver. But in our situation, X is usually extremely sparse, and L_r and L_c can also be sparse, especially for large m and n, so the cost can be $O(m^2)$ or $O(n^2)$, or sometimes even as low as $O(m)$ or $O(n)$ [2]. Many packages or programs are available to solve (3).

To use the reconstructed matrix Y to make recommendations for user u_i, we just sort u_i's non-purchased/non-rated items based on their scores in non-increasing order and recommend the top N items.

4. CONNECTION TO EXISTING WORK

To the best of our knowledge, there are very few studies on graph Laplacian in the context of recommendation task. Graph regularized weighted nonnegative matrix factorization (GWNMF) [7] was proposed to incorporate the neighborhood information in a MF approach. It solves the following problem

$$\begin{aligned} &\min_{U,V} \|M \odot (X - UV^T)\|_F^2 + \alpha Tr(U^T L_r U) + \beta Tr(V^T L_c V) \\ &s.t. \quad U \geq 0, V \geq 0, \end{aligned} \tag{4}$$

where M is an indicator matrix. U and V^T are in latent spaces, whose dimensionality is usually specified with an additional parameter. The latent factors are generally not obvious and might not necessarily be interpretable or intuitively understandable. Here (4) has to learn both user and item representations in the latent spaces. In our approach, we just need to learn one representation and thus the learning process is simplified. On the other hand, U and V^T are supposed to be of low dimensionality, and thus useful information can be lost during the low-rank approximation of X from U and V^T. The encoding of graph Laplacian on U and V^T might be not accurate any more. On the contrary, our method can better preserve the information in X, so it can potentially give better recommendations than GWNMF. Moreover, it is well known that several drawbacks exist in the MF approach, e.g., low convergence rate, many local optimums of U and V^T due to the non-convexity of (4). In contrast, our model (2) is strongly convex, admitting a unique, globally optimal solution.

Table 1: The datasets used in evaluation

dataset	#users	#items	#trns	rsize	csize	density	ratings
Delicious	1300	4516	17550	13.50	3.89	0.29%	-
lastfm	8813	6038	332486	37.7	55.07	0.62%	-
BX	4186	7733	182057	43.49	23.54	0.56%	-
Filmtrust	1508	2071	35497	23.54	17.14	1.14%	0.5-4
Netflix	6769	7026	116537	17.21	16.59	0.24%	1-5
Yahoo	7635	5252	212772	27.87	40.51	0.53%	1-5

In this table, the "#users", "#items", "#trns" columns represent the number of users, number of items and number of transactions, respectively, in each dataset. The "rsize" and "csize" columns show the average number of ratings of each user and of each item, respectively, in each dataset. Column corresponding to "density" shows the density of each dataset (i.e., density=#trns/(#users×#items)). The "ratings" column is the rating range of each dataset . The ratings in FilmTrust are real values with step 0.5, while in the other datasets are integers.

5. EXPERIMENTAL EVALUATION

5.1 Datasets

Table 1 shows the characteristics of the datasets. Delicious, lastfm and BX have only implicit feedback. In particular, Delicious was from the bookmarking and tagging information[1], in which each URL was bookmarked by at least 3 users. Lastfm represents music artist listening information[2], in which each music artist was listened to by at least 10 users and each user listened to at least 5 artists. BX is derived from the Book-Crossing dataset[3] such that only implicit interactions were contained and each book was read by at least 10 users.

FilmTrust, Netflix and Yahoo contain multi-value ratings. Specifically, FilmTrust is a dataset crawled from the entire FilmTrust website[4]. The Netflix is derived from Netflix Prize dataset[5] and each user rated at least 10 movies. The Yahoo dataset is a subset obtained from Yahoo!Movies user ratings[6]. In this dataset, each user rated at least 5 movies and each movie was rated by at least 3 users.

5.2 Evaluation Methodology

For fair comparison, we follow the dataset preparation approach used by SLIM [17] and adopt the 5-fold cross validation. For each fold, a dataset is split into training and test sets by randomly selecting one non-zero entry for each user and putting it in the test set, while using the rest of the data for training. Then a ranked list of size-N items for each user is produced. We subsequently evaluate the method by comparing the ranked list of recommended items with the item in the test set. In the following results presented in this paper, N is equal to 10 by default.

For Top-N recommendation, the most direct and meaningful metrics are hit-rate (HR) and the average reciprocal hit-rank (ARHR) [6], since the users only care if a short recommendation list contains the items of interest or not rather than a very long recommendation list. HR is defined as $HR = \frac{\#\text{hits}}{\#\text{users}}$, where #hits is the number of users whose item in the testing set is contained (i.e., hit) in the size-N recommendation list, and #users is the total number of users. ARHR is defined as: $ARHR = \frac{1}{\#\text{users}} \sum_{i=1}^{\#\text{hits}} \frac{1}{p_i}$, where p_i is the position of the i-th hit in the ranked Top-N list. In this metric, hits that occur earlier in the ranked list are weighted higher than those occur later, and thus ARHR indicates how strongly an item is recommended.

6. EXPERIMENTAL RESULTS

6.1 Top-N Recommendation Performance

We use 5-fold cross-validation to choose parameters for all competing methods and report their best performance in Table 2. It can be seen that the HR improvements achieved by our method against the next best performing scheme (i.e., SLIM) are quite substantial on lastfm, Yahoo, BX, FilmTrust datasets[7]. For Delicious and Netflix datasets, our

[1]http://www.delicious.com
[2]http://www.last.fm
[3]http://www.informatik.uni-freiburg.de/ cziegler/BX/
[4]http://www.librec.net/datasets.html
[5]http://www.netflixprize.com/
[6]http://webscope.sandbox.yahoo.com/catalog.php?datatype=r
[7]Code is available at https://github.com/sckangz/CIKM16

Table 2: Comparison of Top-N recommendation algorithms

method	Delicious params				HR	ARHR	lastfm params				HR	ARHR
ItemKNN	300	-	-	-	0.300	0.179	100	-	-	-	0.125	0.075
PureSVD	1000	10	-	-	0.285	0.172	200	10	-	-	0.134	0.078
WRMF	250	5	-	-	0.330	0.198	100	3	-	-	0.138	0.078
BPRKNN	1e-4	0.01	-	-	0.326	0.187	1e-4	0.01	-	-	0.145	0.083
BPRMF	300	0.1	-	-	0.335	0.183	100	0.1	-	-	0.129	0.073
GWNMF	10	5	10	-	0.340	0.211	20	50	10	-	0.137	0.077
SLIM	10	1	-	-	0.343	**0.213**	5	0.5	-	-	0.141	0.082
Our	0.01	0.001	-	-	**0.345**	0.194	40	10	-	-	**0.198**	**0.085**
method	**BX params**				**HR**	**ARHR**	**FilmTrust params**				**HR**	**ARHR**
ItemKNN	400	-	-	-	0.045	0.026	5	-	-	-	0.583	0.352
PureSVD	3000	10	-	-	0.043	0.023	20	10	-	-	0.601	0.369
WRMF	400	5	-	-	0.047	0.027	30	2	-	-	0.604	0.371
BPRKNN	1e-3	0.01	-	-	0.047	0.028	4e-3	1e-3	-	-	0.625	0.391
BPRMF	400	0.1	-	-	0.048	0.027	100	0.5	-	-	0.610	0.375
GWNMF	10	100	5	-	0.049	0.027	15	5	2	-	0.615	0.380
SLIM	20	0.5	-	-	0.050	0.029	10	15	-	-	0.628	0.397
Our	0.01	0.01	-	-	**0.060**	**0.030**	1e-4	1e-5	-	-	**0.651**	**0.405**
method	**Netflix params**				**HR**	**ARHR**	**Yahoo params**				**HR**	**ARHR**
ItemKNN	200	-	-	-	0.156	0.085	300	-	-	-	0.318	0.185
PureSVD	500	10	-	-	0.158	0.089	2000	10	-	-	0.210	0.118
WRMF	300	5	-	-	0.172	0.095	100	4	-	-	0.250	0.128
BPRKNN	2e-3	0.01	-	-	0.165	0.090	0.02	1e-3	-	-	0.310	0.182
BPRMF	300	0.1	-	-	0.140	0.072	300	0.1	-	-	0.308	0.180
GWNMF	5	30	50	-	0.169	0.080	20	200	50	-	0.313	0.183
SLIM	5	1.0	-	-	**0.173**	**0.098**	10	1	-	-	0.320	0.187
Our	0.02	0.01	-	-	0.166	0.078	5e-3	5e-6	-	-	**0.379**	**0.194**

[1] The parameters for each method in the table are as follows: ItemKNN: the number of neighbors k; PureSVD: the number of singular values and the number of SVD; WRMF: the latent space's dimension and the weight on purchases; BPRKNN: its learning rate and regularization parameter λ; BPRMF: the latent space's dimension and learning rate; GWNMF: dimension of the latent space, λ, and μ; SLIM: the l_2-norm regularization coefficient β and the l_1-norm regularization parameter λ. Our: item graph regularization parameter α and user graph regularization parameter β.

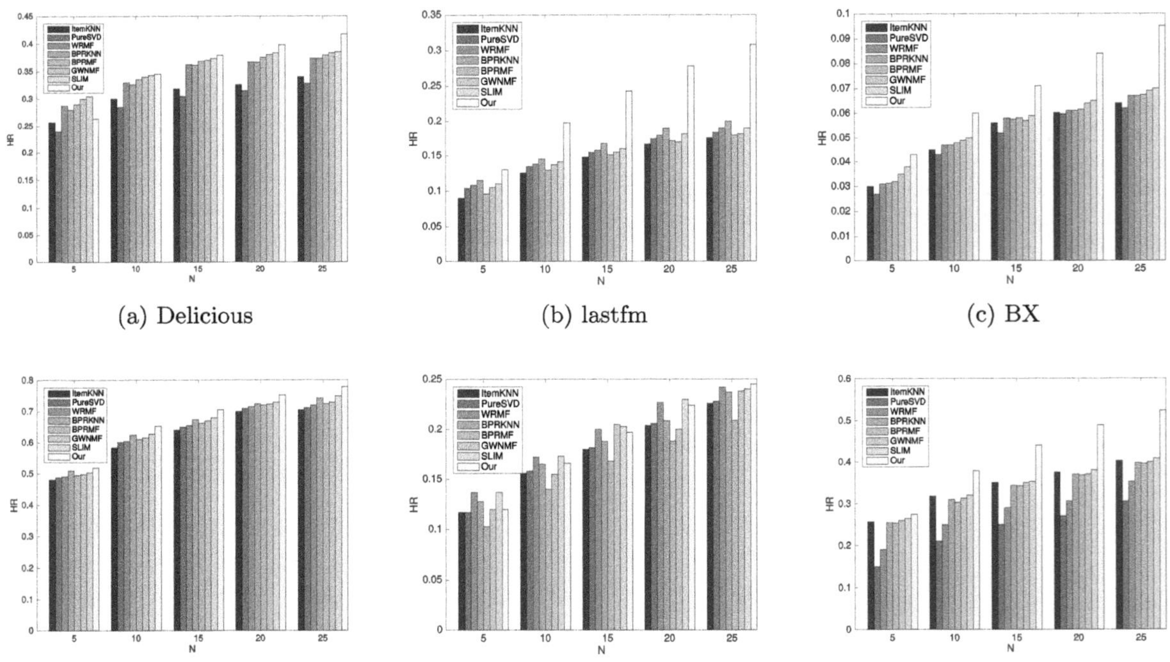

(a) Delicious (b) lastfm (c) BX

(d) FilmTrust (e) Netflix (f) Yahoo

Figure 1: Performance versus Different Values of N.

performance is close to the best performance of other methods. In most cases, there is no much difference among other state-of-the-art methods in terms of HR. Figure 1 shows the performance in HR of various methods for different values of N(i.e., 5, 10, 15, 20 and 25) on all six datasets. Our method works the best in most cases.

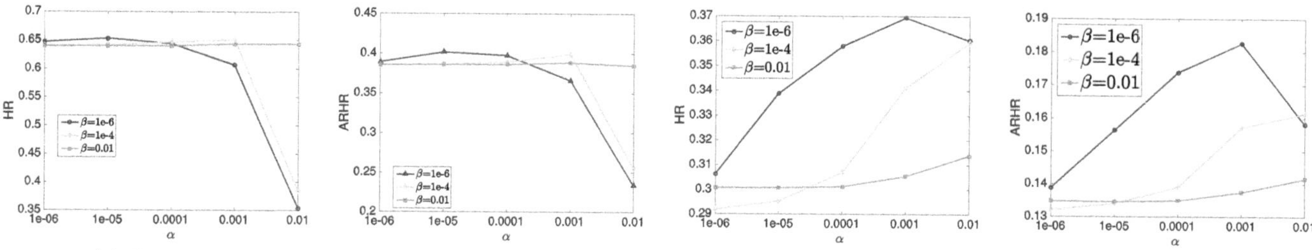

(a) FilmTrust (b) FilmTrust (c) Yahoo (d) Yahoo

Figure 2: Influence of α and β on HR and ARHR.

6.2 Parameter Effects

Our model involves two trade-off parameters α and β, which dictate how strongly item and user neighborhoods and structure information contribute to the objective and performance. In Figure 2, we depict the effects of different α and β values on HR and ARHR for dataset FilmTrust and Yahoo. The search for α ranges from 1e-6 to 1e-2 with points from {1e-6, 1e-5, 1e-4, 1e-3, 1e-2}, the search points for β are from {1e-6, 1e-4, 1e-2}. As can be seen from all figures, our algorithm performs well over a wide range of α and β values. HR and ARHR share the same trend with varying α and β. Specifically, when α is small, HR and ARHR both increase with α. After a certain point, they begin to decrease. For FilmTrust, the performance with $\beta = 0.01$ is very stable with respect to α. This suggests that user-user similarity dominates the FilmTrust dataset.

6.3 Matrix Reconstruction

To show how our method reconstructs the user-item matrix, we compare it with the method of next best performance, SLIM, on FilmTrust. The density of FilmTrust is 1.14% and the mean for those non-zero elements is 2.998. The reconstructed matrix $\hat{X}_{SLIM}$ from SLIM has a density of 83.21%. For those 1.14% non-zero entries in X, $\hat{X}_{SLIM}$ recovers 99.69% of them and their mean value is 1.686. In contrast, the reconstructed matrix by our proposed algorithm has a density of 91.7%. For those 1.14% non-zero entries in X, our method recovers all of them with a mean of 2.975. These facts suggest that our method better recovers X than SLIM. In other words, SLIM loses too much information. This appears to explain the superior performance of our method.

In fact, above analysis is equivalent to the two widely used prediction accuracy metrics: Mean Absolute Error (MAE) and Root Mean Squared Error (RMSE). Since our method can recover the original ratings much better than SLIM, our algorithm gives lower MAE and RMSE. This conclusion is consistent with our HR and ARHR evaluation.

Table 3: Results with Different Similarity Metrics

Datasets	HR		ARHR	
	Jaccard	Cosine	Jaccard	Cosine
Delicious	**0.345**	0.330	0.194	**0.202**
lastfm	0.198	**0.204**	0.085	**0.087**
BX	**0.060**	0.057	**0.030**	0.024

Table 4: Results by using different graphs

	User Graph	Item Graph	User-Item Graph
FilmTrust	0.638	0.625	0.651
Yahoo	0.303	0.379	0.379

6.4 Graph Construction

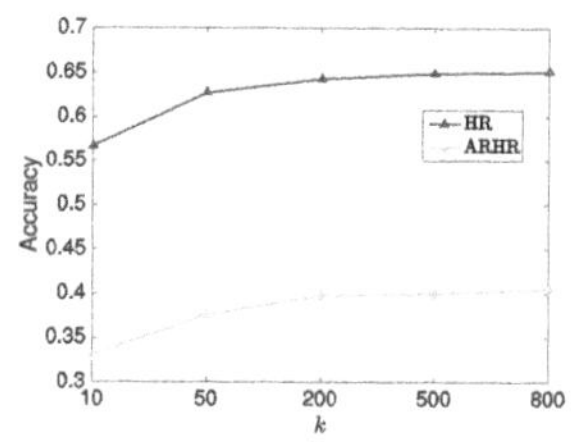

Figure 3: Influence of neighborhood size k on recommendation accuracy for FilmTrust dataset.

As we discussed previously, similarity is an important ingredient of graph construction. In many recommendation algorithms, the similarity computation is crucial to the recommendation quality [8]. To demonstrate the importance of similarity metric, we use the cosine measure rather than the Jaccard coefficient to measure the similarity in binary datasets. We compare the results in Table 3. As demonstrated, for lastfm dataset, HR and ARHR increase after we adopt the cosine similarity. However, for Delicious and BX dataset, the Jaccard coefficient works better. Therefore, the difference of final results can be big for certain datasets with different similarity measures. We expect that the experimental results in Table 2 can be further enhanced if one performs a more careful analysis of L_r and L_c. For example, it has been reported that normalizing the similarity scores can improve the performance [6]. Also, a number of new similarity metrics have recently been proposed, e.g., [16], which may be also exploited.

Another important parameter is the neighborhood size k, which cannot be known a priori [11]. For some small datasets, setting a small k may not include all useful neighbors and would infer incomplete relationships. In practice, a large number of ratings from similar users or similar items are not available, due to the sparsity inherent to rating data. We just use the fully connected graph in our experiments. To demonstrate this, we test the effects of neighborhood size k with values $\{10, 50, 200, 500, 800\}$ on FilmTrust data. As can be seen from Figure 3, the neighborhood size indeed influences the performance of our proposed recommendation method. Specifically, the performance keeps increasing as k increases when k is small compared to the size of dataset, then the performance keeps almost the same as the final accuracy obtained in Table 2 as k it becomes larger. This conforms that a small neighborhood size can not capture all similarity information.

6.5 Effects of User and Item Graphs

While the overall improvements are impressive, it would be interesting to see more fine-grained analysis of the impact of user-user and item-item similarity graphs. We use FilmTrust and Yahoo datasets as examples to show the effects of user and item graphs. Table 4 summarizes the HR values obtained with user graph, item graph, and both user and item graph. It demonstrates that we are able to obtain the best performance when we combine user and item graph. Thus neighborhood information of users and items can alleviate the problem of data sparsity by taking advantage of structural information more extensively, which in turn benefits the recommendation accuracy.

7. CONCLUSION

In this paper, we address the demands for high-quality recommendation on both implicit and explicit feedback datasets. We reconstruct the user-item matrix by fully exploiting the similarity information between users and items concurrently. Moreover, the reconstructed data matrix also respects the manifold structure of the user-item matrix. We conduct a comprehensive set of experiments and compare our method with other state-of-the-art Top-N recommendation algorithms. The results demonstrate that the proposed algorithm works effectively. Due to the simplicity of our model, there is much room to improve. For instance, our model can be easily extended to include side information (e.g., user demographic information, item's genre, social trust network) by utilizing the graph representation. In some cases, external information is more informative than the neighborhood information.

8. ACKNOWLEDGMENTS

This work is supported by the U.S. National Science Foundation under Grant IIS 1218712, National Natural Science Foundation of China under grant 11241005, and Shanxi Scholarship Council of China 2015-093. Q. Cheng is the corresponding author.

9. REFERENCES

[1] G. Adomavicius and A. Tuzhilin. Toward the next generation of recommender systems: A survey of the state-of-the-art and possible extensions. *Knowledge and Data Engineering, IEEE Transactions on*, 17(6):734–749, 2005.

[2] P. Benner, R.-C. Li, and N. Truhar. On the adi method for sylvester equations. *Journal of Computational and Applied Mathematics*, 233(4):1035–1045, 2009.

[3] F. Cacheda, V. Carneiro, D. Fernández, and V. Formoso. Comparison of collaborative filtering algorithms: Limitations of current techniques and proposals for scalable, high-performance recommender systems. *ACM Transactions on the Web*, 5(1):2, 2011.

[4] D. Cai, X. He, J. Han, and T. S. Huang. Graph regularized nonnegative matrix factorization for data representation. *Pattern Analysis and Machine Intelligence, IEEE Transactions on*, 33(8):1548–1560, 2011.

[5] P. Cremonesi, Y. Koren, and R. Turrin. Performance of recommender algorithms on top-n recommendation tasks. In *RecSys*, pages 39–46. ACM, 2010.

[6] M. Deshpande and G. Karypis. Item-based top-n recommendation algorithms. *ACM Transactions on Information Systems (TOIS)*, 22(1):143–177, 2004.

[7] Q. Gu, J. Zhou, and C. H. Ding. Collaborative filtering: Weighted nonnegative matrix factorization incorporating user and item graphs. In *SDM*, pages 199–210. SIAM, 2010.

[8] G. Guo, J. Zhang, and N. Yorke-Smith. A novel bayesian similarity measure for recommender systems. In *IJCAI*, pages 2619–2625. AAAI Press, 2013.

[9] J. L. Herlocker, J. A. Konstan, A. Borchers, and J. Riedl. An algorithmic framework for performing collaborative filtering. In *SIGIR*, pages 230–237. ACM, 1999.

[10] Y. Hu, Y. Koren, and C. Volinsky. Collaborative filtering for implicit feedback datasets. In *ICDM*, pages 263–272. IEEE, 2008.

[11] J. Huang, F. Nie, and H. Huang. A new simplex sparse learning model to measure data similarity for clustering. In *Proceedings of the 24th International Conference on Artificial Intelligence*, pages 3569–3575. AAAI Press, 2015.

[12] Z. Kang and Q. Cheng. Top-n recommendation with novel rank approximation. In *SDM*, pages 126–134. SIAM, 2016.

[13] Z. Kang, C. Peng, and Q. Cheng. Robust subspace clustering via tighter rank approximation. In *CIKM*, pages 393–401. ACM, 2015.

[14] Z. Kang, C. Peng, and Q. Cheng. Top-n recommender system via matrix completion. In *Thirtieth AAAI Conference on Artificial Intelligence*, 2016.

[15] N. Koenigstein, P. Ram, and Y. Shavitt. Efficient retrieval of recommendations in a matrix factorization framework. In *CIKM*, pages 535–544. ACM, 2012.

[16] H. Liu, Z. Hu, A. Mian, H. Tian, and X. Zhu. A new user similarity model to improve the accuracy of collaborative filtering. *Knowledge-Based Systems*, 56:156–166, 2014.

[17] X. Ning and G. Karypis. Slim: Sparse linear methods for top-n recommender systems. In *ICDM*, pages 497–506. IEEE, 2011.

[18] X. Niyogi. Locality preserving projections. In *NIPS*, volume 16, page 153. MIT, 2004.

[19] S. Rendle, C. Freudenthaler, Z. Gantner, and L. Schmidt-Thieme. Bpr: Bayesian personalized ranking from implicit feedback. In *UAI*, pages 452–461. AUAI Press, 2009.

[20] S. T. Roweis and L. K. Saul. Nonlinear dimensionality reduction by locally linear embedding. *Science*, 290(5500):2323–2326, 2000.

[21] B. Sarwar, G. Karypis, J. Konstan, and J. Riedl. Item-based collaborative filtering recommendation algorithms. In *WWW*, pages 285–295. ACM, 2001.

KB-Enabled Query Recommendation for Long-Tail Queries

Zhipeng Huang, Bogdan Cautis †, Reynold Cheng, Yudian Zheng
The University of Hong Kong, †Huawei Noah's Ark Lab, Hong Kong
{zphuang, ckcheng, ydzheng2}@cs.hku.hk, †cautis.bogdan@huawei.com

ABSTRACT

In recent years, query recommendation algorithms have been designed to provide related queries for search engine users. Most of these solutions, which perform extensive analysis of users' search history (or *query logs*), are largely insufficient for *long-tail queries* that rarely appear in query logs. To handle such queries, we study a new solution, which makes use of a knowledge base (or *KB*), such as YAGO and Freebase. A KB is a rich information source that describes how real-world entities are connected. We extract entities from a query, and use these entities to explore new ones in the KB. Those discovered entities are then used to suggest new queries to the user. As shown in our experiments, our approach provides better recommendation results for long-tail queries than existing solutions.

1. INTRODUCTION

Keyword search, which allows a user to express her query with a number of keywords, has become a fundamental tool in Web search engines. In the last decade, significant improvements have been made to improve the accuracy of keyword search [10]. Recently, the topic of *query recommendation*, which is closely related to keyword search, has attracted a lot of interest from research and industry communities. Besides displaying the "*classic ten blue result links*" from her keyword search, a search engine may suggest alternative formulations of the query, which can be more articulated, focused, and interesting to the user. Providing accurate query recommendations while the user is typing her query, almost instantaneously, can be extremely beneficial, in terms of enhancing the user experience and providing guidance to the retrieval process [11].

Existing work on query recommendation often involves the analysis of *query logs*, which contain a variety of information about previous keyword search activities (e.g., the query contents, the webpages selected by users, and click-through rates) [1, 2, 23]. These query logs are often used to construct a graph, which represents the relationship among queries, terms, and webpages; often, an importance weight for each edge is also computed. For example, in [4], the weight between two query nodes is proportional to the number of times the two queries appear in the same session. While these works have been shown to be useful for query recommendation, most of them do not focus on *long-tail queries*, i.e., queries that rarely appear in query logs. The fact is that long-tail queries exist in abundance, and they cannot be ignored. In our experiments, 32% of 20 million queries appear three or fewer times in an extended query log from a commercial search engine. Because a long-tail query has a low occurrence frequency (and statistical significance), the accuracy of query recommendation solutions can be affected. We have tested the query-flow graph (QFG) method [4] and the term-query-flow graph (TQGRAPH) one [6], two well-known query recommendation algorithms, on long-tail queries. As we will discuss in our experimental results, they are far from accurate, reflecting that there is room for improvement in the recommendation process.

CIKM'16 , October 24-28, 2016, Indianapolis, IN, USA
 ISBN 978-1-4503-4073-1/16/10. . . $15.00
DOI: http://dx.doi.org/10.1145/2983323.2983650

In this paper, we propose an effective recommendation algorithm, called KB-QREC, for long-tail queries. Its main idea is to utilize a *knowledge base* (or *KB*) in the query suggestion process. A KB, such as YAGO [19] and Freebase [5], is a rich information source that describes the intricate relationships among real-world entities. Our solution uses a KB to assist the query recommendation process, alleviating the low-frequency problem of long-tail queries. Let us consider the following query:

q_1: *akira kurosawa influence george lucas*

Through an entity-linking process [22], *Akira_Kurosawa* and *George _Lucas* are identified to be the entities in the KB. Then, KB-QREC explores entities in the KB that are conceptually related to them. For example, *Hidden_Fortress* is a film directed by *Akira_Kurosawa*, and *Star_Wars* is one directed by *George_Lucas*. The relationships among these entities can be expressed by a *meta path* [16]:

$$P_1 : director \xrightarrow{directed} film,$$

where *director*, *film*, and *directed* are the types of nodes and links, respectively, in a KB. Correspondingly, the *meta path instance* *Akira_Kurosawa* $\xrightarrow{directed}$ *Hidden_Fortress* exists in the KB. The meta-path P_1 can also describe the relationship between entities *George_Lucas* and *Star_Wars*.

Next, KB-QREC uses the two discovered entities to suggest for q_1 the following alternative query:

q_2: *hidden fortress star wars comparison*

In other words, KB-QREC extracts the entities of a query, discovers more entities from the underlying KB, and uses those found entities to suggest queries to a user.

Challenges and solutions. In the process illustrated above, we have to address a few challenges. First, given the entities found in a query (e.g., *Akira_Kurosawa* and *George_Lucas* in q_1), how do we find other entities from the KB? As discussed before, *meta* *paths*, such as P_1, can be used in this process. However, there can be a huge number of meta paths connecting two KB nodes [16], hence we need to identify the useful ones given a large number of entity pairs. Second, after these entities are discovered, we need to perform query recommendation based on them. We examine how KB-QREC can be designed to tackle these challenges, giving fast and accurate query recommendation. We have also tested our solutions on real datasets. We found that KB-QREC can rightly suggest queries that are otherwise absent from other existing approaches.

The paper is organized as follows. We discuss related works in Section 2. Some preliminary information is given in Section 3. We present KB-QREC in Section 4. Our experimental results are discussed in Section 5. We conclude in Section 6.

2. RELATED WORKS

There is a rich body of research on mining the query terms, click-through data, and the logical user sessions in order to extract useful patterns and similarity measures – be it syntactical, semantical, or behavioral – for alternative query formulations in Web search engines. At their core, the techniques boil down to computing similarity between query instances, often using as an intermediary step various graphs involving queries, pages, users, and terms.

The short paper of [25] was among the first to suggest mining from query logs the sequential search behavior, and to combine it with content-based similarity. In [2], the authors introduce the concept of *cover-graph*, a bipartite graph between queries and Web pages, where links indicate corresponding clicks. In [8], another method using search *short cuts* was proposed.

The studies of [4, 6] present similar style graph-based methods, in which the flow patterns are exploited for query recommendation, using the *query-flow graph* and the *term-query-flow graph*, respectively. The former technique builds a graph over queries, in which links model the transition likelihood in query sessions. The latter technique extends this idea by adding to the graph also the query terms, in this way being able to recommend even for queries that may not explicitly appear in the graph (are not "covered"). In both works, the selection of the top-k query recommendations is done by performing random walks in the graph. In [9], the authors rely on a click-through bipartite graph but also consider the context of the query, its immediately preceding queries, in order to better identify suggestions at query time via suffix-trees.

Besides accuracy, two significant challenges for all these works are *efficiency* and *coverage*. Regarding efficiency, naturally, query recommendation in a Web search engine should trigger within *typing latency*, in order to disrupt as little as possible the user experience; one well-accepted upper-bound on the recommendation latency is $100ms$ and this threshold may be hardly met by techniques that must perform random walks in a large graph. This is why a lot of effort has been put into smart indexing and pre-fetching policies, the approximation of random walks, etc. Regarding coverage, which captures how often the recommendation engine can provide meaningful query suggestions, the existing techniques still under-perform on the so called *long-tail* queries, those which are not very frequent and have scarce support for recommendations. Indeed, long-tail queries are generally handled poorly by the state-of-the-art approaches, such as the ones of [4, 6], simply because little to no evidence is available in the historical records for them.

Very few works have considered the integration of semantics, in its most common and rich form, the one of a KB, as the means for a deeper understanding of the query intents and of the relationships that may support suggestions. Among them, [21] proposed to enhance the query-flow graph with templates over a hierarchy of entity types (the sort of hierarchy that Wordnet or the *isA* projection of a knowledge base could provide). In [18], the authors considered the mining, ranking, and recommending of so called "entity aspects" (query segments that represent subtopics) in keyword search. Their approach combines several metrics and methods for computing similarity or compatibility, including semantics via word2vec [17] descriptions. Finally, in [7], the authors consider a slightly different query suggestion scenario, in which the focus is on anticipating the user's information need (say, the next query, i.e., a related but not so obvious query suggestion), in the context of a Web page that is currently visited (represents the current query) and of the entities this page may contain (Wikipedia entities); once again, this is done by extending the query-flow graph to an entity-query flow graph.

In our view, these works take only a partial approach in the quest to provide more accurate query suggestions, especially for long-tail queries, based on semantics. They only make use of limited semantic-relatedness measures, such as the entity type hierarchy or word2vec [17]. Our thesis is that better results can be obtained by a broader exploration of the relationships between entities. This can only be done by adopting the meta paths, the direct or composite relationships among entities, as a key ingredient in the process of reasoning for relatedness and of building suggestions. As we show in this paper, this introduces new opportunities, in particular for providing suggestions that are less obvious, but raises also new technical challenges: for instance, the space of meta paths can be very large in general and must be explored and filtered very efficiently in order to support online query suggestions.

The importance of rare queries is emphasized in [11], arguing that search engines are less effective on long-tail queries, and that reformulations are much more common for them.

Finally, entity linking, the problem of identifying entities from a KB in a given piece of text, is also a well-known problem for which most recent efforts focused on how to optimize the latency of generic approaches, which have good precision; see [3] and the references therein. We assume similar overhead in our query processing pipeline as in [3].

3. PRELIMINARIES

In this section, we first revisit query logs in keyword search in Section 3.1, and the well-established notion of query-flow graph in Section 3.2, which conceptually captures the behavior of users when reformulating queries. Then, we introduce necessary terminology and concepts for the knowledge base and the meta paths therein in Section 3.3.

3.1 Query Logs

A typical model for the log of a keyword search engine is a set of records (q_i, u_i, t_i, C_i), where q_i is a query submitted by user u_i at time t_i, and C_i is the set of clicked URLs during this query process.

Following common practice, we partition a query log into task-oriented sessions, where each one is a contiguous sequence of query records from the same user, assuming a fixed maximal separation time t_θ (a typical t_θ value is 30 minutes). Within the same session, we can assume that the user's search intent remains unchanged.

3.2 Query-Flow Graph

One of the most studied directions for the problem of top-k query recommendation we revisit in this paper relies on the extraction of behavioral patterns in query reformulation, from extensive collections of historical search and click records (the query logs). The query-flow graph (QFG in short) [4] is a graph representation of query logs, capturing the "flow" between query units. Intuitively, a QFG is a directed graph of queries, in which an edge (q_i, q_j) with weight w indicates that the query q_j follows query q_i in the same session with probability w in the query log.

More formally, the QFG is defined as a directed graph $G_{qf} = (Q, E, W)$, where Q is the set of nodes, with each node representing a unique query in the log, $E \subseteq Q \times Q$ is the set of edges, and W is a weighting function assigning a weight $w(q_i, q_j)$ to each edge $(q_i, q_j) \in E$. In G_{qf}, two queries q_i and q_j are connected if and only if there exists a session in the query log where q_j follows q_i.

The main application of QFG is to perform query recommendation. Given a graph $G_{qf} = (Q, E, W)$ and a query $q \in Q$, the top-k recommendations for q could be obtained in this graph by some kind of proximity-based top-k node retrieval, be it neighborhood-based (e.g., the queries q' to which q connects with the largest weights $w(q, q')$) or path-based (e.g., by Personalized PageRank w.r.t. node q). No matter what kind of proximity we choose, QFG can only perform well on those popular queries, which appear very frequently in the query log. For those long-tail queries, about which the query log has little information, as shown in our experiments, QFG has very poor recommendation performance. This is why we resort to knowledge bases to address these long-tail queries.

3.3 Knowledge Base and Meta Paths

A knowledge base, or Heterogeneous Information Network (HIN), such as YAGO [15] or DBPedia [24], can be viewed as a set of facts (a.k.a. triples), where each fact describes a relationship between two entities. Different models for knowledge bases have been studied in the literature. One of the most common formalizations of knowledge relies on the *RDF model*, which models triples (s, p, o) to denote a subject, property, and respectively, object. Alternatively, *property graphs* model this type of information by labeled edges and nodes, with labels indicating the edge types and node classes, respectively; additionally, in this model, nodes can carry various property-value pairs.

Independently of syntactic formalization flavors, for the purposes of this work, given a set of entity types (or classes) $\mathcal{L}$ and a set of link types (or relationships) $\mathcal{R}$, we see a knowledge base simply as a directed graph $K = (V_e, E_{ee})$ with an entity type mapping function $\phi : V_e \rightarrow 2^{\mathcal{L}}$ and a relationship mapping function $\psi : E_{ee} \rightarrow \mathcal{R}$. Each node in K represents an *entity* $e \in V_e$, and belongs to some entity types $\phi(v) \subseteq 2^{\mathcal{L}}$; this can be seen as a form of resource typing. Each link $e \in E$ has a relationship label $\psi(e) \in \mathcal{R}$. In a knowledge base K, two entities e_1, e_2 may be connected via multiple edges and paths. Conceptually, each of these paths represents a specific direct or composite relationship between them. We model all these direct and composite relationships by *meta paths* [20]. Specifically, a meta path P in the knowledge base is a sequence of entity types $t_1, \ldots, t_n$ connected by link types $l_1, \ldots, l_{n-1}$, and will be represented as $P = t_1 \xrightarrow{l_1} t_2 \ldots t_{n-1} \xrightarrow{l_{n-1}} t_n$. For example, a meta path $person \xrightarrow{marryTo} person$ represents the direct relationship between entities of the type $person$.

4. METHOD

We now introduce our knowledge-enabled query recommendation approach, denoted in short KB-QREC, which can make use of the rich information in a KB to improve the performance of the query recommendation task for long-tail queries. In Section 4.1, we give an overview to our method, then in Section 4.2 we describe the details for building offline the necessary data structures, from the input query log and the knowledge base. Finally, in Section 4.3 we describe the online phase for recommendation using KB-QREC.

4.1 Overview

Intuitively, KB-QREC is a combination of the query-flow graph G_{qf} with a knowledge base K, the two being bridged by entity-to-query links between entity nodes in K and query nodes in G_{qf}. After we perform entity linking on the queries in G_{qf}, we can further analyze the entities within K. With the rich information in KB, we can better understand the rationale behind the flow of queries.

Formally, the KB-QREC underlying data structure is a quadruple $(G_{qf}, K, t_{\mathcal{EQ}}, \mathcal{P})$, where we have (1) $G_{qf} = (Q, E_{\mathcal{QQ}}, W)$ is a query-flow graph (Section 3.2); (2) $K = (V_{\mathcal{E}}, E_{\mathcal{EE}})$ is a KB (Section 3.3); (3) $t_{\mathcal{EQ}}$ is a transition probability matrix associating to each linked entity-query pair (e, q) a probability $t_{\mathcal{EQ}}(e, q)$ in $(0, 1)$; (4) $\mathcal{P}$ is a set of meta paths over the entity types in K. Specifically, $\mathcal{P}[t]$ is a set of meta paths, each having an associated importance score, for entity type $t \in \mathcal{L}$. We denote by $\mathcal{P}[t][p]$ the weight of meta path p for entity type t.

Intuitively, with the knowledge base K enhancing the original query-flow graph, we can better grasp the behavior of the search engine users, by analyzing the flow among entities. For example, suppose the two queries q_1 *"george lucas"* and q_2 *"star wars"* appear in sequence in the same session, and thus we have $(q_1, q_2) \in E_{\mathcal{QQ}}$. If we can detect the two entities e_1 *George_Lucas* and e_2 *Star_Wars*, we also have $(e_1, q_1), (e_2, q_2) \in t_{\mathcal{EQ}}$. Then we can analyze the flow from e_1 to e_2 in our knowledge base K, in addition to the flow from q_1 to q_2 in the query-flow graph. For example, we can find that in the knowledge base e_1 and e_2 are connected by the meta path $director \xrightarrow{directed} film$, and this is one piece of evidence for the fact that users may tend to search for these two queries jointly. We can exploit such evidence when answering queries w.r.t. directors.

4.2 Offline Steps in KB-QREC

Before detailing how we perform recommendations with KB-QREC, we first describe how to build the necessary data structures from a query log offline. Section 4.2.1 recalls the query-flow graph G_{qf} approach, Section 4.2.2 shows how to construct an entity-query transition matrix $t_{\mathcal{EQ}}$, and Section 4.2.3 shows how to build the meta path collection $\mathcal{P}$.

4.2.1 Building the Query-Flow Graph G_{qf}

We adopt the approach of [4] to build the query flow graph G_{qf}. Specifically, we perform a linear scan on the query log. For each query pair (q, q') that appears within the same session, in this order timewise, we have $(q, q') \in E_{\mathcal{QQ}}$. We set $w(q, q')$ to be $f(q, q')/f(q)$, where $f(q, q')$ is the frequency of co-occurrences of q and q' in sessions, and $f(q)$ is the frequency of q itself.

4.2.2 Computing $t_{\mathcal{EQ}}$

For each query $q \in Q$, we perform entity linking on it, and denote by $\theta(q)$ the set of entities found in q. Note that, by definition, each entity e detected in a query instance has also a corresponding entity node in the knowledge base K. $t_{\mathcal{EQ}}(e, q)$ measures how relevant an entity e is to the query q. It is defined proportional to the frequency of q in the query log divided by the total frequency of all the queries containing e. Formally, $t_{\mathcal{EQ}}(e, q) = \frac{f(q)}{\sum_{q' \mid e \in \theta(q')} f(q')}$. Note that $\sum_q t_{\mathcal{EQ}}(e, q) = 1$ holds for all e.

4.2.3 Constructing the meta path collection $\mathcal{P}$

If we view $\theta(q)$ as a representation of the query q, we can extract the entity-to-entity transitions within sessions. For example, a query *"star wars"* after query *"geoge lucas"* accounts for a transition from entity *Geoge_Lucas* to entity *Star_Wars*. In our knowledge base, these entities have their corresponding nodes connected via multiple paths, and each such path stands for a specific relationship between the two entities. To capture these relationships, we construct a set of outgoing meta paths in $\mathcal{P}$ for each entity type $t \in \mathcal{L}$ appearing in the query log, as follows.

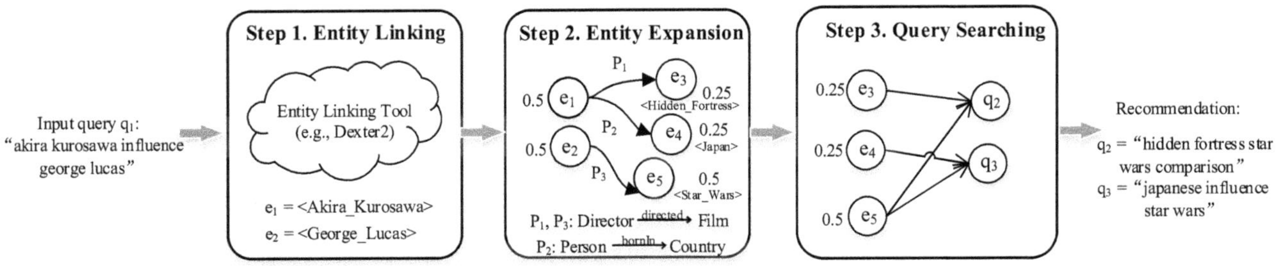

Figure 1: Three steps to generate query recommendations with KB-QREC.

Algorithm 1: KB-QREC recommendation engine

Input: $(G_{qf}, K, t_{\mathcal{EQ}}, \mathcal{P})$, a query q, k
Output: top k recommendation list Rec for q

```
1  Rec ← ∅
2  θ(q) ← entityLinking(K, q)
3  RelatedEntities ← ∅
4  for e ∈ θ(q) do
5      for t ∈ φ(e) do
6          for p ∈ P[t] do
7              entities ← getNeighbor(K, e, p)
8              for e' ∈ entities do
9                  RelatedEntities[e'] ←
                   RelatedEntities[e'] + 1/(|θ(q)|·|entities|)
10 queryWeight ← ∅
11 for e ∈ RelatedEntities do
12     distribution ← PPR(G_qk, e, RelatedEntities[e])
13     queryWeight ← queryWeight + distribution
14 Rec ← topK(queryWeight)
15 return Rec
```

As in [7], we denote by $t_{q\to q'}(e \to e')$ the transition probability from entity e to entity e' via a pair of queries q and q'. If $(q,q') \in E_{\mathcal{QQ}}$ and $(e,q),(e'q') \in t_{\mathcal{EQ}}$, then we have $t_{q\to q'}(e \to e') = w(q,q')/(|\theta(q)| \cdot |\theta(q')|)$. Then, the transition probability from entity e to entity e' can be defined as:

$$t_{\mathcal{EE}}(e,e') = 1 - \prod\nolimits_{(q,q')\in E_{\mathcal{QQ}}} (1 - t_{q\to q'}(e \to e')).$$

So far, we have defined the transition probability among entities derived from a query log. Suppose now we receive a query q containing entity e: if e has already been encountered in the query logs, we can directly use the information on e to perform recommendations for q. For example, we can directly return the queries q' with largest entity-to-query transition probability $t_{\mathcal{EQ}}(e,q')$, or we can perform Personalized PageRank to retrieve queries with high probability. However, this works only if e has been seen in the query log, and this can be rarely the case for long-tail queries.

To address this problem, we want to share the information between the short-tail and the long-tail queries. One solution is to find a meta path in K to represent the relationship between entity pairs. Then, for a new entity e' that has not been encountered in the query log, we can use this meta path to derive related entities in K. We now describe how to select from the knowledge base K the meta paths that will be used in this way for query suggestion.

Given two entities e and e', most often, there can be a large number of distinct paths in K connecting them. Each of these paths potentially represents a relationship between them. However, not all these paths are equally meaningful. Unsurprisingly, a very long path between e and e' may have a "diluted" meaning, as pointed out also in [20]; therefore a natural approach, and the one we follow here, is to select the shortest paths between e and e' to represent their relationships. Then, for each entity type $t \in \phi(e)$, we bookkeep the meta paths in $\mathcal{P}[t]$ and accumulate the weight $t_{\mathcal{EE}}(e,e')$.

4.3 Online steps in KB-QREC

We are now ready to detail in this section how to generate query recommendations for a given query q, using the KB-QREC method. The overview is given in Algorithm 1, and a runtime example is shown in Figure 1. Generally, there are three steps:

Step 1. Entity Linking. (line 2) We firstly need to perform entity linking on the input query q, and get the set of entities $\theta(q)$ contained in it. Note that each of these entities have corresponding nodes in the knowledge base K. For example in Figure 1, given an input query q_1 *"akira kurosawa influence george lucas"*, we perform entity linking on it and get the entities e_1 and e_2.

Step 2. Entity Expansion. (lines 3-9) for each $e \in \theta(q_1)$, we look at its entity types $\phi(e)$ in the knowledge base K. Then, for each $t \in \phi(e)$, we perform a path-constrained random walk [14] on K with each meta path $p \in \mathcal{P}[t]$, and get the related entities for q_1. To each of these related entities, we assign a weight as defined in line 9 of Algorithm 1. For example, e_1 has the type *Director* and *Person* in K. Then, we use the pre-recorded meta path $Director \xrightarrow{directed} Film$ and $Person \xrightarrow{bornIn} Country$, to find related entities e_3 and e_4. Finally, these related entities, e_3 and e_4, are assigned each a weight of $1.0/(2 \times 2) = 0.25$.

Step 3. Query Searching. (lines 10-14) Last but not least, we need to find out the most relevant queries w.r.t. the set of related entities. One commonly-used way is to perform Personalized PageRank (PPR). Specifically, for each related entity e, we perform a PPR on $G_{qf} \cup t_{\mathcal{EQ}}$, starting from e, with initial probability $RelatedEntities[e]$. We sum up the stable probability distribution for each PPR to obtain the aggregated per-query result. The k queries with the largest aggregated probability should be our recommendations. In our example, we perform PPR computations starting from e_3, e_4, and e_5, respectively, with the corresponding probability. Finally, we sum up the probability distribution over queries to get the top-2 recommendations, q_2 and q_3.

Note that the recommendation process only considers the entities $\theta(q)$, without considering the unique information about query q itself. In other words, the recommendation results are the *same* for all queries containing the *same* entities, i.e., $Rec(q) = Rec(q')$ if $\theta(q) = \theta(q')$. While this interpretation already proves to be effective for long-tail queries containing entities, it may also harm the results in certain cases. We intend to study how to combine the KB-QREC method with an existing one, to get a best-of-both-worlds approach, in the future.

5. EXPERIMENTS

We compare the performance of three configurations: the query-flow graph (denoted as QFG), the term-query-flow graph (denoted as TQGRAPH), and the knowledge-enable method (denoted as KB-QREC), focusing on their performance on long-tail queries.

5.1 Implementation

For QFG, we re-implemented the query-flow graph as described in [4]. We adopt the typical recommendation approach by maximum weight, i.e., for an input query q, the query q' with largest value of $w(q,q')$ will be the one recommended. An advantage of this approach is that it can provide very locally related recommendations with high efficiency.

For TQGRAPH, we directly used a Scala implementation published by the authors of [12]. We used the default parameters, i.e., a restart probability for the random walk $\alpha_{re} = 0.9$ and the convergence distance $\epsilon = 0.005$.

For KB-QREC, we used YAGO [13] as our KB. YAGO is a large-scale knowledge graph derived from Wikipedia, WordNet, and GeoNames. We use its "Core Facts", i.e., YAGO-Core [16], which contains $4M$ facts (edges) of 125 types, over $2.1M$ entities. These entities have $365K$ entity types, organized in a hierarchy with 5 layers. We follow the procedure in Section 4.2.3 to select the meta paths, and use the approach in Section 4.3 to provide recommendations.

5.2 Dataset

We used in all our experiments a well-known public dataset from a major commercial search engine, which consists of web queries collected from $657k$ users over a two months period. This dataset is sorted by anonymous user ID and sequentially arranged, containing $20M$ query instances corresponding to around $9M$ distinct queries. After we sessionized the query log with $\theta_t = 30min$, we obtained a total of $12M$ sessions. As the focus of this paper is not on entity linking, we directly used Dexter2 [22] to tag the entities from queries. After entity linking, we obtained a total of $0.4M$ distinct entities in our dataset.

5.3 Methodology

We adopt the automatic evaluation process described in [21], to assess the performance of the five configurations as predictors of the next query in a session. Basically, we make use of part of the query logs (training data) to predict the user's behavior over a kept-apart query log (the test data). In the test query log, we denote by $q_{i,j}$ the j_{th} query in the session s_i. We assume that $\{q_{i,j} \mid j > 1\}$ is a good recommendations for query $q_{i,1}$ which, as argued in previous literature, is a reasonable assumption for scalable evaluation.

To assess the performance of each method, we simply count their "hits" in the test data, i..e., for each session thereof, how many times one of the recommended top-k queries for $q_{i,1}$ is in $\{q_{i,j} \mid j > 1\}$. While the objective of this evaluation approach may not necessarily be aligned with what a good recommendation may be on particular instances, by being entirely unsupervised and used on a large number of sessions, it becomes a strong indicator of the techniques' performance. For a more complete assessment, we also intend to perform a complementary user study in the future.

In order to test how robust each method is, we used 90%, 50% and 10% of the query logs to train the recommendation systems. We denote them as D_{90}, D_{50}, and D_{10}. Note that the smaller the query log, the less historical information we have on queries. The statistics of these datasets are shown in Table 1. We can see that the number of sessions and the number of distinct queries drops almost linearly with the size of query log, but the number of distinct entities is more stable. This means that we can still rely on the information on entities, even when we have a very small query log.

Table 1: Statistics about the datasets

	$\#sessions$	$\#queries$	$\#entities$
$Dataset$	$12M$	$9.2M$	$0.40M$
D_{90}	$11M$	$8.4M$	$0.39M$
D_{50}	$5.9M$	$4.9M$	$0.30M$
D_{10}	$1.2M$	$1.1M$	$0.13M$

We used the remaining 10% of the query log to generate the test sessions. We first extracted those sessions with at least two queries, and obtained 467473 such sessions. As explained before, we then took the first query of each session as input and the following queries as the ground truth recommendations. Formally, the ground truth for input query $q_{i,1}$ is $\{q_{i,j} \mid j > 1\}$, where $q_{i,j}$ is the j_{th} query appearing in the i_{th} session.

We further extracted the long-tail queries from the test sessions: if the frequency of a query in the whole query log is no more than a threshold θ_f, we refer to it as belonging to the long-tail. Then, we form our test sessions by those whose first query $q_{i,1}$ belongs to the long-tail. By setting θ_f to be 10, 5, and 3, respectively, we have three different testing dataset L_{10}, L_5, and L_3. Note that these three test datasets contain only long-tail queries w.r.t. the frequency threshold θ_f, but they include both entity-bearing queries and queries without entities. As our knowledge-enabled method can only apply to entity-bearing queries, we further filter our all sessions where the first query is not of this kind, i.e., $|\theta(q_{i,1})| = 0$. This leads to the three test datasets L'_{10}, L'_5, and L'_3, which contain only sessions starting by long-tail queries with entities.

We stress here that the feature of containing entities or not is not really affected by the frequency; head, torso, or tail queries alike have a ratio of approximately 60% entity-bearing queries. We measured the following two metrics to evaluate the performance of each configuration:

- $Coverage$. Percentage of input queries that can be answered with at least one recommendation.
- $Precision@5$. Percentage of recommended queries in the top-5 lists that are in the ground truth, as described previously. Formally, $Precision@5 = \frac{\#HIT}{5 \cdot \#query}$, where $\#HIT$ is the number of recommended queries that are part of the ground truth, and $\#query$ is the number of input queries.

5.4 Results and Analysis

Figure 2 presents the coverage results on L'_{10}, L'_5, and L'_3. We can see that (i) all the configurations show a decrease in coverage when we use a smaller query log, but the knowledge-enabled methods remain relatively stable. In particular: KB-QREC still has the same coverage even when we use 10% of query log. (ii) KB-QREC holds a stable coverage on queries with different frequencies, while QFG and TQGRAPH have a lower coverage as the queries have lower frequency. (iii) When we use 10% of query log, KB-QREC has higher coverage than QFG and TQGRAPH.

Figure 3 presents the precision@5 results on L'_{10}, L'_5 and L'_3. We can see that: (i) KB-QREC has the highest precision@5 on all the three datasets, (ii) QFG has extremely low precision@5, because of its low coverage, and (iii) similar to the results of coverage, all the three configurations show a decrease in precison@5 when we use a smaller query log, but KB-QREC remains relatively stable.

If we compare the precision@5 results across the three data configurations, we can see that (i) performance for QFG drops when we test on a longer tail (queries with lower frequency), and (ii) KB-QREC has a rather stable performance even when we test on queries with lower frequency. This is because the KB-QREC method only considers the entities $\theta(q)$ in q. Even when the query q does not appear frequently in the query log, KB-QREC can still make use of the flow recorded for other queries q', containing the same entities. This property makes KB-QREC suitable for long-tail queries, and even for those that were not seen before in the query log.

The extra information in the knowledge base can account for all these improvements on both coverage and precision@5. It is natural that more information leads to better performance. An advantage of our KB-QREC method is that the amount of information in the knowledge base remains the same, no matter how large is the

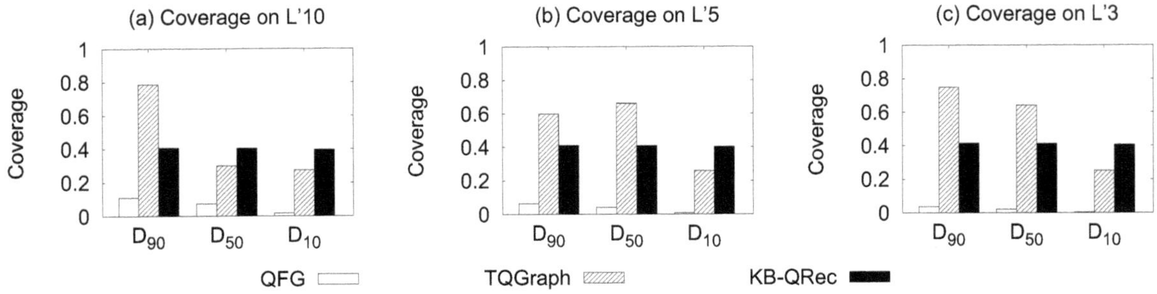

Figure 2: Coverage results on long-tail queries with entities.

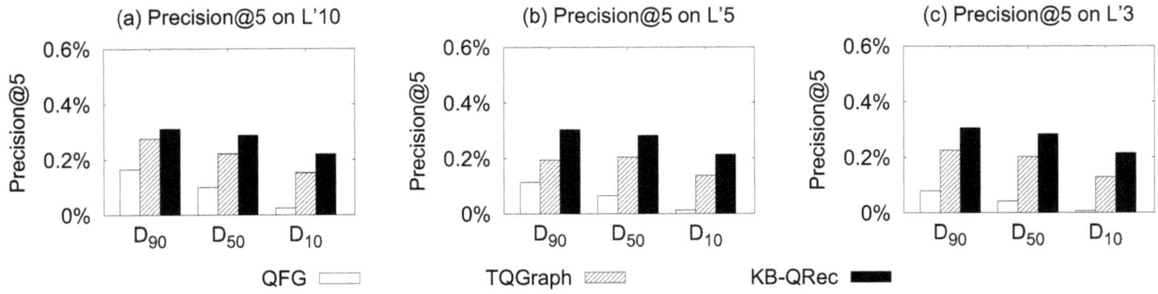

Figure 3: Precision@5 results on long-tail queries with entities.

query log trained upon. This can explain why the performance of KB-QREC remains stable even with a relatively small query log, as when we test on queries with very low frequency.

6. CONCLUSION

In this paper, we propose a knowledge-enabled approach for query recommendation, one of the most visible features in Web search. Its performance for long-tail queries significantly overpasses that of state-of-the-art methods. This is important, as it is well-known that most queries are rare and it is precisely for them that query recommendations are most useful. Using a real-world dataset from a major commercial Web search engine, our automatic evaluation shows that the knowledge-enabled method can bring significant improvements, in terms of both coverage and precision.

Acknowledgements

Zhipeng Huang, Yudian Zheng, and Reynold Cheng were supported by the Research Grants Council of Hong Kong (RGC Projects HKU 17229116 and 17205115) and the University of Hong Kong (Projects 102009508 and 104004129). We would like to thank the reviewers for their insightful comments.

7. REFERENCES

[1] R. A. Baeza-Yates, C. A. Hurtado, and M. Mendoza. Query recommendation using query logs in search engines. In *Current Trends in Database Technology - EDBT Workshops*, 2004.

[2] R. A. Baeza-Yates and A. Tiberi. Extracting semantic relations from query logs. In *KDD*, 2007.

[3] R. Blanco, G. Ottaviano, and E. Meij. Fast and space-efficient entity linking for queries. In *WSDM*, 2015.

[4] P. Boldi, F. Bonchi, C. Castillo, D. Donato, A. Gionis, and S. Vigna. The query-flow graph: model and applications. In *CIKM*, 2008.

[5] K. Bollacker, C. Evans, P. Paritosh, T. Sturge, and J. Taylor. Freebase: a collaboratively created graph database for structuring human knowledge. In *SIGMOD*. ACM, 2008.

[6] F. Bonchi, R. Perego, F. Silvestri, H. Vahabi, and R. Venturini. Efficient query recommendations in the long tail via center-piece subgraphs. In *SIGIR*, 2012.

[7] I. Bordino, G. D. F. Morales, I. Weber, and F. Bonchi. From machu_picchu to "rafting the urubamba river": anticipating information needs via the entity-query graph. In *WSDM*, 2013.

[8] D. Broccolo, L. Marcon, F. M. Nardini, R. Perego, and F. Silvestri. Generating suggestions for queries in the long tail with an inverted index. *Inf. Process. Manage.*, 2012.

[9] H. Cao, D. Jiang, J. Pei, Q. He, Z. Liao, E. Chen, and H. Li. Context-aware query suggestion by mining click-through and session data. In *KDD*, 2008.

[10] W. B. Croft, D. Metzler, and T. Strohman. *Search Engines - Information Retrieval in Practice*. Pearson Ed., 2009.

[11] D. Downey, S. T. Dumais, and E. Horvitz. Heads and tails: studies of web search with common and rare queries. In *SIGIR*, 2007.

[12] H. Feild and J. Allan. Task-aware query recommendation. In *SIGIR*, 2013.

[13] Z. Huang, Y. Zheng, R. Cheng, Y. Sun, N. Mamoulis, and X. Li. Meta structure: Computing relevance in large heterogeneous information networks. In *SIGKDD*, 2016.

[14] N. Lao and W. W. Cohen. Relational retrieval using a combination of path-constrained random walks. *Machine learning*, 2010.

[15] F. Mahdisoltani, J. Biega, and F. M. Suchanek. YAGO3: A knowledge base from multilingual Wikipedias. In *CIDR*, 2015.

[16] C. Meng, R. Cheng, S. Maniu, P. Senellart, and W. Zhang. Discovering meta-paths in large heterogeneous information networks. In *WWW*, 2015.

[17] T. Mikolov, I. Sutskever, K. Chen, G. Corrado, and J. Dean. Distributed representations of words and phrases and their compositionality. *CoRR*, abs/1310.4546, 2013.

[18] R. Reinanda, E. Meij, and M. de Rijke. Mining, ranking and recommending entity aspects. In *SIGIR*, 2015.

[19] F. M. Suchanek, G. Kasneci, and G. Weikum. Yago: a core of semantic knowledge. In *WWW*, 2007.

[20] Y. Sun, J. Han, X. Yan, P. S. Yu, and T. Wu. Pathsim: Meta path-based top-k similarity search in heterogeneous information networks. *VLDB*, 2011.

[21] I. Szpektor, A. Gionis, and Y. Maarek. Improving recommendation for long-tail queries via templates. In *WWW*, 2011.

[22] S. Trani, D. Ceccarelli, C. Lucchese, S. Orlando, and R. Perego. Dexter 2.0: an open source tool for semantically enriching data. In *ISWC*, 2014.

[23] J.-R. Wen, J.-Y. Nie, and H.-J. Zhang. Clustering user queries of a search engine. In *WWW*, 2001.

[24] DBpedia 3.7. http://wiki.dbpedia.org/Downloads37.

[25] Z. Zhang and O. Nasraoui. Mining search engine query logs for query recommendation. In *WWW*, 2006.

RAP: Scalable RPCA for Low-rank Matrix Recovery

Chong Peng, Zhao Kang, Ming Yang, and Qiang Cheng
Southern Illinois University
Carbondale, IL, USA, 62901
{pchong, zhao.kang, ming.yang, qcheng}@siu.edu

ABSTRACT

Recovering low-rank matrices is a problem common in many applications of data mining and machine learning, such as matrix completion and image denoising. Robust Principal Component Analysis (RPCA) has emerged for handling such kinds of problems; however, the existing RPCA approaches are usually computationally expensive, due to the fact that they need to obtain the singular value decomposition (SVD) of large matrices. In this paper, we propose a novel RPCA approach that eliminates the need for SVD of large matrices. Scalable algorithms are designed for several variants of our approach, which are crucial for real world applications on large scale data. Extensive experimental results confirm the effectiveness of our approach both quantitatively and visually.

Keywords

RPCA, fixed rank, scabality, low-rank recovery

1. INTRODUCTION

High-dimensional data have been ubiquitously used in numerous tasks of machine learning and data mining, which is often challenging in real world applications. To alleviate this challenge and to explore putative, low-dimensional structures of such high-dimensional data, dimension reduction techniques have been studied extensively, among which principal component analysis (PCA) is widely used for unsupervised learning [6, 9, 10]. Classic PCA seeks the best rank-r estimate Z of a matrix M by solving $\min_{rank(Z)\leq r} \|M-Z\|$, with $\|\cdot\|$ denoting the spectral norm of a matrix. However, it suffers from poor estimation of Z when there are grossly corrupted entries in the data. As real world applications often encounter gross errors, it is highly desirable to design more robust PCA (RPCA) approaches. In the past decade, a number of methods have been proposed including, for example, alternating minimization [13], random sampling techniques [15], multivariate trimming, and so on [4].

CIKM'16 , October 24 - 28, 2016, Indianapolis, IN, USA

ISBN 978-1-4503-4073-1/16/10... $15.00

DOI: http://dx.doi.org/10.1145/2983323.2983651

More recently, a new type of RPCA method has emerged and become popular for many tasks [3, 20] with a general form:

$$\min_{Z,S} \operatorname{rank}(Z) + \lambda\|S\|_0, \quad s.t. \quad X = Z + S, \tag{1}$$

where $\|\cdot\|_0$ is the ℓ_0 (pseudo) norm that counts the number of nonzero elements, and λ is a trade-off parameter that balances the rank of Z and the sparsity of S. It is assumed that the data matrix $X \in \mathcal{R}^{d\times n}$ can be decomposed into a low-rank component Z and a sparse one S, which is natural for many scenarios. For example, for images containing the same scene taken under different illuminating conditions, the scene is the low-rank component while shadows on these images represent the sparse components [1]. However, the optimization problem in (1) is NP-hard due to the minimization of the rank function and the ℓ_0 norm. In practice, their convex relaxations are often used with which (1) becomes

$$\min_{Z,S} \|Z\|_* + \lambda\|S\|_1, \quad s.t. \quad X = Z + S, \tag{2}$$

where $\|\cdot\|_*$ represents the nuclear norm defined as the summation of all singular values of a matrix, and $\|\cdot\|_1$ is the ℓ_1 norm that adds the absolute values of all elements of a matrix. It has been theoretically shown that Z and S can be exactly recovered by (2) with high probability, when nonzero entries of S are uniformly distributed in locations while Z and S satisfy some mild conditions [3]. Despite the convexity and ease of optimization, (2) may suffer from inaccurately recovering Z and S if the data are grossly corrupted or the underlying matrix does not have the incoherence property [3]. Another drawback of (2) [11] is that the nuclear norm is a biased estimator of the rank due to its similar behavior to ℓ_1 norm of a vector [7, 23]. It has been shown that some newly developed non-convex approximations to ℓ_0 norm [7, 21] can provide better estimation accuracy and variable selection consistency [19], and thus these approximations have drawn increasing attention in such applications as subspace clustering [12, 17, 18]. Recently, non-convex RPCA has been proposed by using a non-convex rank approximation [11]. However, it still has two potential limitations: First, to accurately separate the low-rank and sparse components, its model parameters need to be carefully tuned, which considers little prior knowledge on the desired rank of Z. Second, the singular value decomposition (SVD) of large matrices needs to be computed, which hinders the applications of RPCA to large-scale data due to the associated high complexity.

In this paper, to alleviate the above mentioned limitations, we propose a novel RPCA approach, named Robust scalable (Ascendable) PCA (RAP), based on a factorization model which fixes the rank of Z by exploiting prior knowledge and avoids computing SVD of large matrices. Essentially important for real world applications, our method is scalable.

2. RELATED WORK

The convex approach to RPCA in (2) has been studied thoroughly in the literature. To incorporate the spatial connection information of the sparse elements, $\ell_{2,1}$ norm is introduced in (2) as follows [22]:

$$\min_{Z,S} \|Z\|_* + \lambda\|S\|_{2,1}, \quad s.t. \quad X = Z + S, \tag{3}$$

where $\|\cdot\|_{2,1}$ is defined to be the summation of ℓ_2 norms of all column vectors of a matrix. To overcome the above mentioned drawback of the nuclear norm, a non-convex RPCA model is proposed by replacing the nuclear norm in (3) with $\|Z\|_\gamma = \sum_i \frac{(1+\gamma)\sigma_i(Z)}{\gamma+\sigma_i(Z)}$ with $\gamma > 0$ and $\sigma_i(Z)$ being the i-th largest singular value of Z [11]. Both the non-convex and convex models in (2) and (3) need to tune some balancing parameters to accurately recover the low-rank component, which is time consuming and tedious, making these methods less systematic and automatic. Although an optimal choice of this parameter has been theoretically found for (2) [3], the conditions are not often satisfied in reality, and as a result Z with an exceedingly high rank may be obtained.

3. PROPOSED METHOD

Assume that X can be separated into a low-rank component Z and a sparse one S, i.e., $X = Z + S \in \mathcal{R}^{d\times n}$, then Z can be represented as $Z = LW$, where $L \in \mathcal{R}^{d\times r}$ is a basis matrix, $W \in \mathcal{R}^{r\times n}$ is a weight matrix, and r is the desired rank of Z. Therefore, each column of Z can be constructed as a linear combination of the basis vectors. Inspired by (1), we formulate the following model:

$$\min_{L,S,W} \|S\|_1 \quad s.t. \quad X = LW + S. \tag{4}$$

With this formulation, we can see that the rank of the low-rank component is at most r by matrix factorization and no balancing parameter is needed. (4) may lead to different variants for various applications. To derive these variants, we consider a specific application of RPCA, background-foreground separation. In general, there are three cases: single background, multiple suddenly changing backgrounds, and multiple gradually changing backgrounds. For these cases, we discuss the corresponding variants of (4) in the following.

In the case of a single background, we have $r = 1$, and (4) can be reformulated as

$$\min_{L,S} \|S\|_1, \quad s.t. \quad X_i = L + S_i, \tag{5}$$

where M_i is the i-th column of M with $M = X$ or S. With (5) we assume that all images can be separated as combinations of one common background and the varying foregrounds.

In the case of multiple backgrounds with sudden changes, we have $r > 1$, and (4) can be expressed as

$$\begin{aligned} &\min_{L,S,W} \|S\|_1 \\ &s.t. \quad X = LW + S, W \in \{0,1\}^{n\times r}, \sum_{j=1}^{r} W_{ij} = 1, \end{aligned} \tag{6}$$

by which we assume that each frame can be separated as a combination of one background and one foreground. It is noted that (5) is a special case of (6), where W in the former is an all-1 row vector of length n.

In the case that there are gradual changes in the backgrounds, (4) can be formulated as

$$\min_{L,S,W} \|S\|_1 \quad s.t. \quad X = LW + S, W_{ij} \geq 0, \sum_{i=1}^{r} W_{ij} = 1, \tag{7}$$

where W takes continuous rather than binary values as in (6). The optimization of (5), (6), and (7) will be developed in Section 4. It is noted that models (5) and (6) are special cases of (7) by restricting W values.

4. OPTIMIZATION

Because (5) and (6) are special cases of (7), for clarity of presentation, we will firstly derive the optimization of the general model (7), then we will specialize the optimization procedures of the other models based on that of (7).

4.1 Optimization of model (7)

The augmented Lagrange function of (7) is

$$\begin{aligned} &\mathcal{L}(L,S,W,\Theta,\rho) = \|S\|_1 + Tr(\Theta^T(X - LW - S)) \\ &+ \frac{\rho}{2}\|X - LW - S\|_F^2, \quad s.t. \quad W \geq 0, \sum_{i=1}^{r} W_{ij} = 1. \end{aligned} \tag{8}$$

First, the subproblem for optimizing W is

$$\begin{aligned} &\min_W Tr(\Theta^T(X - LW - S)) + \frac{\rho}{2}\|X - LW - S\|_F^2, \\ &s.t. \quad W \geq 0, \sum_{i=1}^{r} W_{ij} = 1, \end{aligned} \tag{9}$$

The above optimization problem is equivalent to solving the following optimization problems for each column of W:

$$\min_w \frac{1}{2}w^TQw - y^Tw, \quad s.t. \quad w_j \geq 0, \sum_{j=1}^{r} w_j = 1, \tag{10}$$

where $Q := L^TL$, $y := L^T(X_i - S_i + \Theta_i/\rho)$, and $w := W_i$. (10) is a standard quadratic programming (QP) problem and has been studied extensively. We directly make use of the 'quadprog' function in Matlab with the default interior point method to solve for w. Then L, S, Θ, and ρ are updated as follows:

$$L = (X - S + \Theta/\rho)W(WW^T)^{-1}, \tag{11}$$

$$S = \mathcal{T}_{\frac{1}{\rho}}(X - LW - S + \Theta/\rho), \tag{12}$$

$$\Theta = \Theta + \rho(X - LW - S), \quad \rho = \rho\kappa, \tag{13}$$

where $[\mathcal{T}_\alpha(D)]_{ij} = \max(|D_{ij}| - \alpha, 0)\text{sign}(D_{ij})$, and $\kappa > 1$ controls the increasing speed of ρ.

It is noted that, due to the nonnegative constraints on W in (9), there is no analytic solution of W for this subproblem, which requires higher computational cost because inner iterations are needed. To speed it up, we propose a relaxed formulation of (7), where we drop the nonnegative constraints on W as follows:

$$\min_{L,S,W} \|S\|_1 \quad s.t. \quad X = LW + S, \quad \sum_{i=1}^{r} W_{ij} = 1. \tag{14}$$

We express (14) in a column manner as follows:

$$\min_{w} \frac{1}{2} w^T Q w - y^T w, \quad s.t. \sum_{j=1}^{r} w_j = 1. \tag{15}$$

The Lagrange function of (15) is

$$J(w, \lambda) = \frac{1}{2} w^T Q w - y^T w + \lambda(\sum_{j=1}^{r} w_j - 1), \tag{16}$$

where λ is the Lagrange multiplier. The optimal solution is obtained by setting $\nabla J(w, \lambda) = 0$. Therefore, we have

$$\begin{bmatrix} w \\ \lambda \end{bmatrix} = \begin{bmatrix} 2Q & \mathbf{1}_r \\ \mathbf{1}_r^T & 0 \end{bmatrix}^{-1} \begin{bmatrix} y \\ 1 \end{bmatrix}, \tag{17}$$

where $\mathbf{1}_r$ is an all-1 column vector of length r. Therefore, the optimal W can be obtained as

$$W = \left[\begin{bmatrix} 2Q & \mathbf{1}_r \\ \mathbf{1}_r^T & 0 \end{bmatrix}^{-1} \begin{bmatrix} L^T(X - S + \frac{1}{\rho}\Theta) \\ \mathbf{1}_n^T \end{bmatrix} \right]_{1:r}, \tag{18}$$

where $[\cdot]_{1:r}$ denotes the first r rows of a matrix. For L, S, Θ and ρ, the updating rules follow the updating of (7).

4.2 Optimization of model (5) / (6)

As special cases of (7), the optimization of (5) and (6) may follow the above subsection. To be more efficient, we consider the special constraints and update W as follows:

$$[W]_{ij} = \begin{cases} 1, & \text{if } i = \operatorname{argmin}_{1 \le t \le r} \|[X - S + \frac{\Theta}{\rho}]_j - L_t\|_2^2 \\ 0, & \text{otherwise.} \end{cases} \tag{19}$$

By simple algebra, due to the special structure of W, L is equivalently updated column-wisely as

$$L_i = \frac{1}{\sum_j W_{ij}} \sum_{(i,j) \in \{(i,j) | W_{ij} = 1\}} (X_j - S_j + \Theta_j / \rho), \tag{20}$$

for $i = 1, 2, \cdots, r$. It is noted that, for (5), calculating W and L is more straightforward with the following updating:

$$W = \mathbf{1}_n, \quad L = \frac{1}{n} \sum_{i=1}^{n} (X_i - S_i + \Theta_i / \rho). \tag{21}$$

For notational convenience, we call the optimization procedures corresponding to (5), (6), (7), and (14) as RAP-S, RAP-MS, RAP-MG, and RAP-MGR, respectively.

4.3 Complexity

Given that r is fixed, it is straightforward to verify that RAP-S, RAP-MS, and RAP-MGR all have a complexity of $O(dn)$. For RAP-MG, each sub-QP problem has a constant cost; hence, solving (9) has a complexity of $O(n)$. Therefore the total complexity of RAP-MG is $O(dn)$.

5. EXPERIMENTS

Three important practical applications are used to evaluate our method: foreground-background separation on surveillance video, shadow removal from human face images, and anomaly detection. We compare our method with some state-of-the-art methods, including convex RPCA [3], and AltProj [16][1]. Specifically, we use inexact ALM (IALM)[2] [3, 14] to solve convex RPCA. IALM and AltProj make use of the PROPACK package [5] to solve SVDs.

5.1 Foreground-background separation

It is a popular way to detecting moving objects or interesting activities in a scene by removing background(s) from a video sequence. In this test, we choose a set of video datasets including Escalator Airport, Hall Airport, Bootstrap, Campus, Fountain, Water Surface, Shopping Mall, Curtain, Office, PETS2006, Pedestrian, Highway, Lobby, Camera Parameter, Light Switch-1, Light Switch-2, and Time Of Day. These data sets can be divided into two scenarios: with a single background (the first 12) and with multiple backgrounds (the last five)[3]. For all these datasets, $X \in \mathcal{R}^{d \times n}$ are constructed by reshaping each frame into a column vector.

In the single-background case, we compare RAP-S with IALM and AltProj on the first 12 datasets. For RAP-S, we fix $\rho = 0.001$, $\kappa = 1.5$, and $r = 1$ for all the datasets. In a way similar to AltProj, we vanish those small values in $(-0.001, 0.001)$ for S. For IALM, we use the default balancing parameter given in the corresponding paper. Besides, we fix $\rho = 10^{-4}$ and $\kappa = 1.5$ for IALM, which results in a good visual quality and faster convergence. For AltProj, we fix $r = 1$ and use the other default parameters. For all these methods, we terminate the iteration when $\frac{\|X-Z-S\|_F}{\|X\|_F} \le 10^{-3}$ is satisfied as in [16]. We compare these methods in terms of the rank of Z, the density of S defined to be ratio of nonzero elements in S, the relative fitting error $\frac{\|X-Z-S\|_F}{\|X\|_F}$, total number of iterations as well as that of (partial) SVDs[4], and computational time. The results are shown in Table 1, which are all obtained on a dual-core Intel Xeon E3-1240 V2 3.40 GHz Linux Server with 8 GB memory. It is observed that IALM has the best performance in sparsity of S. However, it results in higher ranks of Z and takes much longer time than both AltProj and RAP-S. AltProj results in Z with the desired rank and has generally smaller fitting errors. However, AltProj needs more iterations than IALM and RAP-S, and the latter two can achieve lower fitting errors given the same number of iterations. Both IALM and AltProj need to solve SVDs at each iteration, which are computationally expensive. For RAP-S, it results in the desired rank for Z[5]; it has comparable or more sparsity on S than AltProj, and has comparable fitting error to IALM. The most important is that RAP-S does not need to solve

[1] available at http://www.personal.psu.edu/nsa10/codes.html.

[2] available at http://perception.csl.illinois.edu/matrix-rank/sample_code.html#RPCA.

[3] All datasets used in this subsection are available at:
http://perception.i2r.a-star.edu.sg/bk_model/bk_index.html
http://limu.ait.kyushu-u.ac.jp/dataset/en/
http://wordpress-jodoin.dmi.usherb.ca/dataset2012/
http://research.microsoft.com/en-us/um/people/jckrumm/wallflower/testimages.htm.

[4] The reported number is the number of partial SVDs, because IALM and AltProj solve partial SVDs with PROPACK package.

[5] For RAP, we use Z to denote LW.

Table 1: Results over Datasets with Single Background

Data	Method	Rank(Z)	$\|S\|_0/(d \times n)$	$\frac{\|X-L-S\|_F}{\|X\|_F}$	Iterations	# of SVDs	Time
Hall Airport	AltProj	1	0.9806	5.16e-5	46	47	113.98
	IALM	556	0.8500	8.15e-4	11	12	408.03
	RAP-S	1	0.9194	6.93e-4	17	0	28.54
Highway	AltProj	1	0.9331	2.96e-4	37	38	49.65
	IALM	539	0.8175	6.02e-4	12	13	269.10
	RAP-S	1	0.9242	8.34e-4	17	0	15.70
Office	AltProj	1	0.8018	9.40e-4	51	52	84.43
	IALM	374	0.7582	9.46e-4	11	12	230.53
	RAP-S	1	0.8702	1.00e-3	17	0	20.89
PETS2006	AltProj	1	0.8590	5.20e-4	35	36	44.64
	IALM	293	0.8649	5.63e-4	12	13	144.26
	RAP-S	1	0.8655	6.06e-4	18	0	16.11
Shopping Mall	AltProj	1	0.9853	3.91e-5	45	46	45.35
	IALM	328	0.8158	9.37e-4	11	12	123.99
	RAP-S	1	0.9084	9.24e-4	17	0'	12.80
Pedes-trian	AltProj	1	0.5869	9.32e-4	41	42	37.90
	IALM	35	0.8910	5.69e-4	11	12	36.18
	RAP-S	1	0.6490	7.01e-4	17	0	11.36
Bootstrap	AltProj	1	0.9747	1.17e-4	44	45	107.15
	IALM	1146	0.8095	6.27e-4	12	13	1182.92
	RAP-S	1	0.9284	9.09e-4	17	0	27.82
Water Surface	AltProj	1	0.8890	3.97e-4	47	48	27.27
	IALM	224	0.7861	5.32e-4	12	13	51.00
	RAP-S	1	0.9021	4.69e-4	18	0	6.71
Campus	AltProj	1	0.9790	9.50e-5	41	42	54.1
	IALM	488	0.8136	9.30e-4	11	12	242.59
	RAP-S	1	0.9353	7.35e-4	17	0	14.30
Curtain	AltProj	1	0.8280	7.46e-4	40	41	102.41
	IALM	834	0.7398	6.84e-4	12	13	747.36
	RAP-S	1	0.8968	5.9e-4	18	0	30.57
Fountain	AltProj	1	0.9113	2.91e-4	50	51	23.90
	IALM	102	0.8272	4.91e-4	12	13	25.62
	RAP-S	1	0.8589	5.19e-4	18	0	5.44
Escalator Airport	AltProj	1	0.9152	2.29e-4	40	41	110.75
	IALM	957	0.7744	7.76e-4	11	12	1,040.91
	RAP-S	1	0.8817	6.82e-4	17	0	33.94

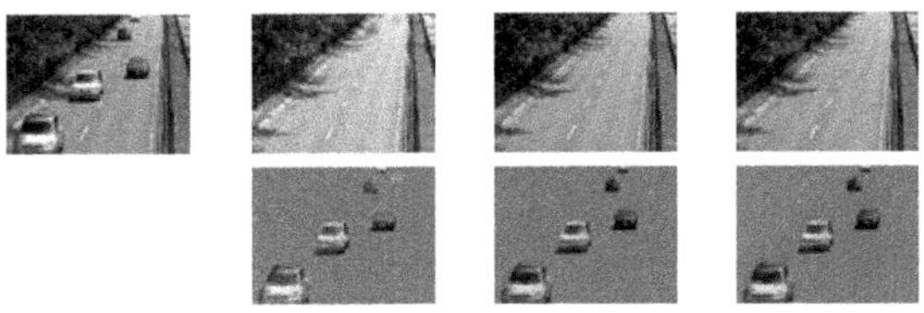

(a) Original (b) IALM (c) AltProj (d) RAP-S

Figure 1: Foreground-background separation in the Highway video. The top left is the original frame and the rest are extracted background (top) and foreground (bottom).

any SVD and the speed is around 4 times faster than AltProj and at least 10 times faster than IALM on most of the datasets. At the same time, RAP-S also has good visual quality. To illustrate this, we show some sample frames and resultant Z and S in Fig. 1 of Highway. It is observed that AltProj and RAP-S have comparable performance visually, where the foregrounds are well separated from the background. However, the low rank component by IALM still contains artifacts from the sparse component. For example, in Fig. 1, two cars are not completely removed from the background in the upper part of the image.

In the case of multiple backgrounds, we compare RAP-MS, RAP-MG, and RAP-MGR with AltProj and IALM, following the same parameter settings discussed above. We show the quantitative results and sample visual results of Light Switch-2 dataset in Table 2 and Fig. 2, respectively, which are all obtained on a six-core Intel Xeon E5-2620 V3 2.40 GHz Windows Server with 32 GB memory. We have similar observations to the single-background case. For RAP-MG, we parallel the computation of W at each iteration using 4 cores; however, RAP-MGR has almost the same

Table 2: Results over Datasets with Multiple Backgrounds

Data	Method	Rank(Z)	$\|S\|_0/(d \times n)$	$\frac{\|X-Z-S\|_F}{\|X\|_F}$	Iterations	# of SVDs	Time
Lobby	AltProj	2	0.9243	1.88e-4	39	41	68.53
	IALM	223	0.8346	6.19e-4	12	13	205.83
	RAP-MS	2	0.8597	6.54e-4	18	0	30.27
	RAP-MG	2	0.8523	7.28e-4	18	0	48.03
	RAP-MGR	2	0.8521	7.28e-4	18	0	27.77
Light Switch-1	AltProj	2	0.9600	1.12e-4	55	57	180.28
	IALM	499	0.6737	9.99e-4	11	12	497.41
	RAP-MS	2	0.9649	6.21e-4	17	0	43.93
	RAP-MG	2	0.9156	9.35e-4	17	0	77.07
	RAP-MGR	2	0.9158	9.31e-4	17	0	43.88
Light Switch-2	AltProj	2	0.9050	2.24e-4	47	49	129.31
	IALM	591	0.7921	7.93e-4	12	13	926.97
	RAP-MS	2	0.8319	7.81e-4	18	0	49.19
	RAP-MG	2	0.8213	9.21e-4	18	0	80.73
	RAP-MGR	2	0.8216	9.22e-4	18	0	45.86
Camera Parameter	AltProj	2	0.8806	5.34e-4	47	49	129.20
	IALM	607	0.7750	6.86e-4	12	13	647.85
	RAP-MS	2	0.8170	5.48e-4	18	0	45.77
	RAP-MG	2	0.8460	7.61e-4	18	0	73.39
	RAP-MGR	2	0.8460	7.61e-4	18	0	42.05
Time Of Day	AltProj	2	0.8646	4.72e-4	44	46	90.02
	IALM	351	0.6990	6.12e-4	13	14	384.61
	RAP-MS	2	0.8132	7.40e-4	18	0	35.04
	RAP-MG	2	0.8383	6.47e-4	19	0	61.12
	RAP-MGR	2	0.8383	6.47e-4	19	0	34.92

RAP-MG needs to solve SVD (matrix inverse) of size $(r+1) \times (r+1)$, which in our experiments is 3×3 and can be ignored compared to AltProj and IALM.

Table 3: Recovery Results of Face Data

Data	Method	Rank(Z)	$\|S\|_0/(d \times n)$	$\frac{\|X-Z-S\|_F}{\|X\|_F}$	Iterations	# of SVDs	Time
Subject 1	AltProj	1	0.9553	8.18e-4	50	51	4.20
	IALM	32	0.7745	6.28e-4	25	26	2.39
	RAP-S	1	0.9898	9.78e-4	8	0	0.40
Subject 2	AltProj	1	0.9755	2.34e-4	49	50	5.00
	IALM	31	0.7656	6.47e-4	25	26	2.66
	RAP-S	1	0.9918	5.72e-4	9	0	0.45

performance as RAP-MG only with a much faster speed. Additionally, to investigate the recovery performance with the gradually changing backgrounds, we show two original frames of Time Of Day video and the recovery results in Fig. 3. It is observed that AltProj and RAP-MS fail to recover the correct background for the first frame while RAP-MG and -MGR succeed. All methods produce visually good results on the second frame.

5.2 Shadow removal from face images

Face recognition is an important task in pattern recognition and computer vision, but it is usually challenging when face images are taken under varying lighting conditions [2]. It is crucial to handle shadows, peculiarities and saturations on face images, which can be achieved by applying RPCA. Extended Yale B (EYaleB) dataset [8] contains face images of 38 persons, each of whom has 64 heavily corrupted images taken under different lighting conditions. We choose two of the subjects (subject 1 and subject 2) and convert all face images of size 192×168 to 32,256-dimensional vectors. For each subject, a data matrix $X \in \mathcal{R}^{32,256 \times 64}$ is constructed. It is natural to assume that the face images reside in a rank one space, hence we set $r = 1$. The quantitative and visual results are given in Table 3 and Fig. 4, respectively. Fig. 4 demonstrates that the low-rank component recovered by IALM still has heavy shadows, whereas those by AltProj and RAP-S do not. $\rho = 10$ and $\kappa = 1.5$ are used for RAP-S.

5.3 Anomaly Detection

Another important application of RPCA is anomaly detection. If we inject several images of one subject into a dominating set of images of another subject, then the newly

(a) Original (b) IALM (c) AltProj (d) RAP-MS (e) RAP-MG (f) RAP-MGR

Figure 2: Foreground-background separation in the Light Switch-2 video. From top to bottom are two frames and extracted results. For each method, from left to right are the extracted background and dynamic foreground, respectively.

(a) Original (b) IALM (c) AltProj (d) RAP-MS (e) RAP-MG (f) RAP-MGR

Figure 3: Foreground-background separation in the Time Of Day video. From top to bottom are two frames and extracted results. For each method, from left to right are the extracted background and dynamic foreground, respectively.

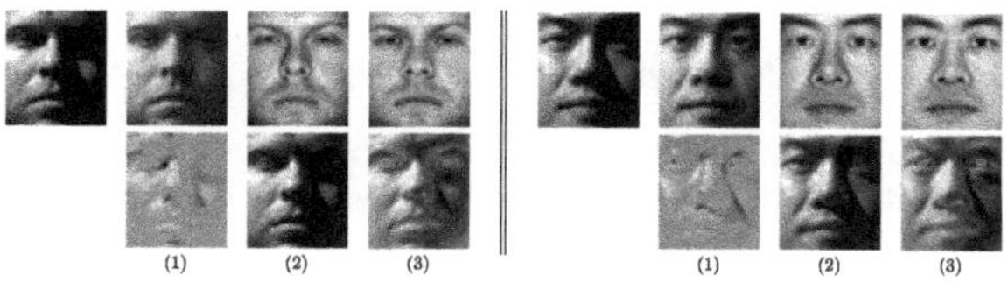

Figure 4: Shadow removal results on EYaleB data. For each of the two parts, from left to right are original data, results of (1) IALM, (2) AltProj, and (3) RAP-S, respectively. The top panel are the original image and low rank components, while the bottom are the sparse components.

Figure 5: Selected '1's and '7's from USPS dataset.

Figure 6: Anomaly identified by RAP-S, including written '1's and outliers '7's.

added images are outliers, or anomaly, and the dominant images form a low-dimensional subspace. The task is to detect all anomalies. USPS dataset contains 9,298 images of hand-written digits 0-9 with size 16×16. We choose the first 190 images of '1' and the last 10 images of '7' as shown in Fig. 5 and align the vectorized images into the data matrix. In this case, '1' is the dominant digit and '7's are outliers. Anomaly detection is not only to detect the '7's, but also the anomaly of hand-written '1's. For the anomaly in '1' images or outliers '7', the corresponding columns in S contain relatively larger values. We simply use ℓ_2 norm as a measure of these values, then identify the outliers by finding the columns of S with the largest values of ℓ_2 norms [11]. Fig. 7 shows the ℓ_2 norms of the columns of S. For ease of visualization, values that are smaller than 4 are made zeros. Totally, seven anomalies in '1's and all '7's are detected. The identified anomalies or outliers are shown in Fig. 6. $r = 1$, $\rho = 0.001$ and $\kappa = 1.5$ are used for RAP-S.

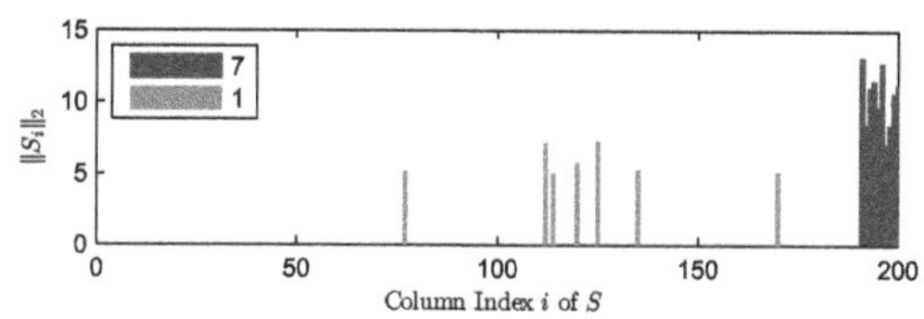

Figure 7: ℓ_2-norms of each row of S.

5.4 Scalability

To numerically illustrate the scalability of RAP algorithms[6], we show the time cost versus the values of n and d, respectively, in Fig. 8. For all these algorithms, we temporarily ignore the terminating tolerance and terminate them within 50 iterations with $\rho = 0.001$ and $\kappa = 1.5$. The figures empirically verify that RAP algorithms have a linear complexity in n or d and desirable scalability.

6. CONCLUSION

This paper proposes a scalable RPCA method (RAP) as well as its several variants for specific applications. The proposed method and all variants have linear complexity in both data size and dimension, which renders it possible to have RPCA applications on large scale data. Besides, the desired low rank of Z can be guaranteed, which is more systematic than other approaches that need to carefully tune balancing parameters. Quantitatively, RAP not only has the fastest speed but also comparable performance in other measures. Visually, RAP demonstrates better quality than other state-of-the-art methods under various conditions.

Acknowledgment

Qiang Cheng is the corresponding author. This work is supported by National Science Foundation under grant IIS-1218712, National Natural Science Foundation of China, under grant 11241005, and Shanxi Scholarship Council of China 2015-093, Fund Program for the Scientific Activi-

[6]It is suggested to use RAP-MGR instead of RAP-MG in Section 5.1, therefore, we only show the results of RAP-S, RAP-MS, and RAP-MGR.

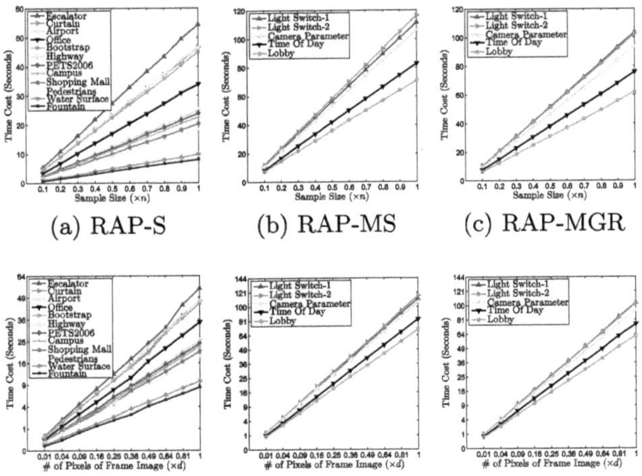

(a) RAP-S (b) RAP-MS (c) RAP-MGR

(d) RAP-S (e) RAP-MS (f) RAP-MGR

Figure 8: Plots of time cost of RAP-S, RAP-MS, and RAP-MGR as functions of data size in (a)-(c) and dimension in (d)-(f), respectively.

ties of Selected Returned Overseas Professionals in Shanxi Province.

References

[1] N. S. Aybat, D. Goldfarb, and G. Iyengar. Fast first-order methods for stable principal component pursuit. *arXiv preprint arXiv:1105.2126*, 2011.

[2] R. Basri and D. W. Jacobs. Lambertian reflectance and linear subspaces. *Pattern Analysis and Machine Intelligence, IEEE Transactions on*, 25(2):218–233, 2003.

[3] E. J. Candès, X. Li, Y. Ma, and J. Wright. Robust principal component analysis? *Journal of the ACM (JACM)*, 58(3):11, 2011.

[4] C. Croux and G. Haesbroeck. Principal component analysis based on robust estimators of the covariance or correlation matrix: influence functions and efficiencies. *Biometrika*, 87(3):603–618, 2000.

[5] X. Ding, L. He, and L. Carin. Bayesian robust principal component analysis. *Image Processing, IEEE Transactions on*, 20(12):3419–3430, 2011.

[6] C. Eckart and G. Young. The approximation of one matrix by another of lower rank. *Psychometrika*, 1(3):211–218, 1936.

[7] J. Fan and R. Li. Variable selection via nonconcave penalized likelihood and its oracle properties. *Journal of the American statistical Association*, 96(456):1348–1360, 2001.

[8] A. S. Georghiades, P. N. Belhumeur, and D. J. Kriegman. From few to many: Illumination cone models for face recognition under variable lighting and pose. *Pattern Analysis and Machine Intelligence, IEEE Transactions on*, 23(6):643–660, 2001.

[9] H. Hotelling. Analysis of a complex of statistical variables into principal components. *Journal of educational psychology*, 24(6):417, 1933.

[10] I. Jolliffe. *Principal component analysis.* Wiley Online Library, 2002.

[11] Z. Kang, C. Peng, and Q. Cheng. Robust pca via nonconvex rank approximation. In *Data Mining (ICDM), 2015 IEEE International Conference on*, pages 211–220. IEEE, 2015.

[12] Z. Kang, C. Peng, and Q. Cheng. Robust subspace clustering via tighter rank approximation. In *Proceedings of the 24th ACM International on Conference on Information and Knowledge Management*, pages 393–401. ACM, 2015.

[13] Q. Ke and T. Kanade. Robust l_1 norm factorization in the presence of outliers and missing data by alternative convex programming. In *Computer Vision and Pattern Recognition, 2005. CVPR 2005. IEEE Computer Society Conference on*, volume 1, pages 739–746. IEEE, 2005.

[14] Z. Lin, M. Chen, and Y. Ma. The augmented lagrange multiplier method for exact recovery of corrupted low-rank matrices. *arXiv preprint arXiv:1009.5055*, 2010.

[15] R. Maronna, D. Martin, and V. Yohai. *Robust statistics.* John Wiley & Sons, Chichester. ISBN, 2006.

[16] P. Netrapalli, U. Niranjan, S. Sanghavi, A. Anandkumar, and P. Jain. Non-convex robust pca. In *Advances in Neural Information Processing Systems*, pages 1107–1115, 2014.

[17] C. Peng, Z. Kang, H. Li, and Q. Cheng. Subspace clustering using log-determinant rank approximation. In *Proceedings of the 21th ACM SIGKDD International Conference on Knowledge Discovery and Data Mining*, pages 925–934. ACM, 2015.

[18] C. Peng, Z. Kang, M. Yang, and Q. Cheng. Feature selection embedded subspace clustering. *IEEE Signal Processing Letters*, 23(7):1018–1022, July 2016.

[19] Z. Wang, H. Liu, and T. Zhang. Optimal computational and statistical rates of convergence for sparse nonconvex learning problems. *Annals of statistics*, 42(6):2164, 2014.

[20] J. Wright, A. Ganesh, S. Rao, Y. Peng, and Y. Ma. Robust principal component analysis: Exact recovery of corrupted low-rank matrices via convex optimization. In *Advances in neural information processing systems*, pages 2080–2088, 2009.

[21] S. Xiang, X. Tong, and J. Ye. Efficient sparse group feature selection via nonconvex optimization. In *ICML (1)*, pages 284–292, 2013.

[22] H. Xu, C. Caramanis, and S. Sanghavi. Robust pca via outlier pursuit. In *Advances in Neural Information Processing Systems*, pages 2496–2504, 2010.

[23] C.-H. Zhang. Nearly unbiased variable selection under minimax concave penalty. *The Annals of Statistics*, pages 894–942, 2010.

Query Answering Efficiency in Expert Networks Under Decentralized Search

Liang Ma
IBM T. J. Watson Research
Yorktown, NY, USA
maliang@us.ibm.com

Mudhakar Srivatsa
IBM T. J. Watson Research
Yorktown, NY, USA
msrivats@us.ibm.com

Derya Cansever
Army CERDEC
Aberdeen, MD, USA
derya.h.cansever.civ@mail.mil

Xifeng Yan
University of California
Santa Barbara, CA, USA
xyan@cs.ucsb.edu

Sue Kase
Army Research Laboratory
Adelphi, MD, USA
sue.e.kase.civ@mail.mil

Michelle Vanni
Army Research Laboratory
Adelphi, MD, USA
michelle.t.vanni.civ@mail.mil

Abstract

Expert networks are formed by a group of expert-professionals with different specialties to collaboratively resolve specific queries. In such networks, when a query reaches an expert who does not have sufficient expertise, this query needs to be routed to other experts for further processing until it is completely solved; therefore, query answering efficiency is sensitive to the underlying query routing mechanism being used. Among all possible query routing mechanisms, decentralized search, operating purely on each expert's local information without any knowledge of network global structure, represents the most basic and scalable routing mechanism. However, there is still a lack of fundamental understanding of the efficiency of decentralized search in expert networks. In this regard, we investigate decentralized search by quantifying its performance under a variety of network settings. Our key findings reveal the existence of network conditions, under which decentralized search can achieve significantly short query routing paths (i.e., between $O(\log n)$ and $O(\log^2 n)$ hops, n: total number of experts in the network). Based on such theoretical foundation, we then study how the unique properties of decentralized search in expert networks is related to the anecdotal small-world phenomenon. To the best of our knowledge, this is the first work studying fundamental behaviors of decentralized search in expert networks. The developed performance bounds, confirmed by real datasets, can assist in predicting network performance and designing complex expert networks.

Keywords

Expert Networks; Query Answering; Decentralized Search; Performance Bounds

1. INTRODUCTION

Expert networks are composed of a group of expert-professionals, who cooperate with each other to solve specific queries (e.g., reported by clients) using their professional knowledge in a variety of related subjects. The collaboration among experts is knowledge-driven, manifesting in the process of expert searching: Upon receiving a query by an expert, she first attempts to solve the problem specified in the query; if she fails, then this query is routed to another expert for further processing. This process continues until the query is resolved. Such expert networks are abundant in real life. One canonical example is the enterprise call center, where if a query ticket cannot be solved by the first responding agent, then a series of processing/forwarding attempts are triggered until qualified agents are found. The fundamental goal regarding expert networks is to route each query to experts with sufficient expertise in a timely and accurate manner. This is a challenging issue as efficient query routing mechanisms depend on the professional knowledge of each individual expert as well as the social knowledge of other experts' specialties possessed at each expert. When the expert profiles (e.g., expertise) are not properly maintained in expert networks, finding the most knowledgeable experts with high probability while minimizing the number of routing steps is explored in [1,2]. On the other hand, even if each expert's profile is accurately exposed to all of her contacts, this routing issue remains challenging. In particular, under the assumption that each expert has connections to only a limited number of other experts, a series of routing rules are proposed in [3, 4] for improving the resolution efficiency in specific tasks (e.g., IT services). Under the same assumption, generative models [5] are developed for making global expert recommendations by estimating all possible routes to potential resolvers. The efficacy of these mechanisms, however, relies heavily on the broad knowledge of network global structure; in addition, these mechanisms, requiring non-negligible training periods, are generally complicated and sensitive to operational scenarios, thus not applicable to large-scale or dynamic networks (e.g., with experts joining/leaving the network). All these limitations, therefore, motivate us to consider if there exist simple yet efficient query routing solutions that function with only basic network information and are robust against network variations.

Among all possible query routing mechanisms, *decentralized search*, operating purely on each expert's local information, represents the most basic and adaptive routing mechanism in expert networks. Specifically, under decentralized search, before reaching experts with sufficient expertise for a given query, each intermediate expert forwards this query to one of her contacts with the highest problem solving abil-

CIKM'16, October 24-28, 2016, Indianapolis, IN, USA

DOI: http://dx.doi.org/10.1145/2983323.2983652

ities, which therefore forms a pure local-information-based forwarding rule. Since no historical training data or network global structure is required for routing decision making, decentralized search can be broadly adopted by any network scenarios for query routing. However, decentralized search, greedy in nature at each routing step, is generally ignored in the research community mainly for the following reason: When an expert forwards a query to one of her contacts via decentralized search, she has no clue whether this decision would successfully lead to a short path through the entire network, and thus the efficiency of decentralized search is uncertain. We note, however, without fundamental understanding of such simple decentralized search, we can never justify the value/necessity of designing other complicated query routing mechanisms for expert networks. Therefore, in this paper, we consider this unsolved fundamental problem: What is the efficiency of decentralized search in expert networks? We study this problem by quantifying the performance of decentralized search under various network settings so as to understand under what conditions decentralized search can achieve efficiency/inefficiency in query routing.

In this paper, the basic approach we employ to study the performance of decentralized search is to establish its performance bounds in generic expert network models. Such models should capture two main connection properties among experts: (i) experts are rich in connections to peer experts with similar expertise; (ii) each expert also tends to connect to a few experts with fairly dissimilar expertise. Integrating these two properties that characterize expert social connections, we propose one expert network model. In this model, local expert connections (experts with similar expertise) enable the formation of the basic network structure, on top of which long-range expert connections (experts with fairly dissimilar expertise) determine to what extent the expert inter-connections do not respect such basic network structure. We prove that the natural superposition of these two properties in expert networks can lead to high efficiency of decentralized search without any centralized guidance under a range of network settings. Accordingly, if an expert network is verified to satisfy such conditions that guarantee efficient decentralized search, then there is no need to design complicated query routing mechanisms as the light-weighted decentralized search will suffice. Furthermore, by a case study of real datasets, we demonstrate how commercial expert networks may take proactive actions to train their constituent experts, which equivalently approaches the efficient query routing conditions discussed in this paper.

1.1 Further Discussions on Related Work

Regarding expert networks, most existing works [1–4] seek to develop/improve query routing mechanisms, where different levels of network global knowledge are required. With network historical data, [6] develops a Markov Decision Process (MDP) model to optimize routing policies. However, the correlation between successful query answering probability and each expert's expertise level is ignored in the proposed model. Employing game theory, [7] proposes query incentive networks to understand agent collaborations and interactions in on-line communities. In addition, routing efficiency improvement is investigated in [8] when additional expert contacts are carefully chosen. Our work belongs to a different but closely related line of work that focuses on the fundamental understanding of the most basic query routing mechanism in expert networks. Our work shares similar goals with [9] in that [9] tries to build models to understand routing behaviors in expert networks, particularly in human factors that influence routing tendencies. However, [9] does not show how the efficiency of such routing behaviors are affected by network properties. By contrast, we not only present deep insights into decentralized search in expert networks, but also show how its efficacy is related to network's structural and social properties.

For the underlying influence of network properties on the routing efficiency, [10] show that every pair of nodes are joined by a path of length $O(\log n)$ (n: total number of nodes in the network) in a randomly generated graph. The existence of such short paths is maintained even when the network demonstrates certain structural properties [11]. Further, more complicated statistical models are considered in [12] for node inter-connections (e.g., Poisson distributions). When the number of links incident to nodes follows the power-law distribution, [13] explores how such distribution may affect routing preference. In addition, with special network properties, networks may exhibit small-world phenomenon [11, 14–18]. However, [18] proves that there exists one and only one network setting that enables efficient searching for a unique target.

1.2 Summary of Contributions

We study, for the first time, decentralized search in expert networks from the perspective of fundamental performance quantifications. Our contributions are five-fold:

1) We propose the *diversified model* to model expert inter-connections and expertise distributions.

2) We prove that decentralized search is highly efficient under a wide range of network settings in the diversified model; the corresponding average routing path length is between $O(\log n)$ and $O(\log^2 n)$ (n: total number of experts).

3) We further establish conditions for the case when decentralized search is ineffective, and develop the corresponding lower bounds to quantify its performance.

4) We discuss how above theoretical results are related to the special characteristics of small-world phenomenon in expert networks.

5) We show that the theoretical bounds can also approximate the routing performance in real datasets, thus providing guidance in planning practical complex expert networks.

The remainder of the paper is organized as follows. Section 2 formulates the problem. The expert network model is proposed in Section 3. Main results of decentralized search in expert networks are presented and analyzed in Section 4. Experiments are conducted under both synthetic networks and real datasets in Section 5. Section 6 concludes the paper.

2. PROBLEM FORMULATION

In this section, we propose mathematical models to capture expert inter-connections, and then formally present decentralized search and state our research objective.

2.1 Expert Inter-Connections

We assume that in an expert network with n experts, experts can collectively solve problems in up to m different areas. For all experts, we assume that their expertise in different areas are quantifiable to non-negative integers, and thereby each expert is associated with an expertise vector defined as follows: The *expertise vector* of expert u, denoted by $\mathbf{e}^{(u)}$, is an $m \times 1$ column vector with the value in entry i (i.e., $e_i^{(u)}$) indicating u's skill in area i (larger value corresponds to superior skill); $e_j^{(u)} = 0$ if u does not have any skill in area j. We call $||\mathbf{e}^{(u)}||_1 := \sum_i |e_i^{(u)}|$ the *total ability* of expert u. Using this concept, we can compare the expertise levels in different areas for one individual expert or in the same area across multiple experts. Furthermore, we define the *expertise distance* from expert u to expert w as $d(u \rightarrow w) := \sum_i \max(e_i^{(w)} - e_i^{(u)}, 0)$. Intuitively, expertise distance characterizes the superior skills of one expert against another, and it implies that generally $d(u \rightarrow w) \neq d(w \rightarrow u)$. With all these concepts, we are ready to model homophily and heterophily of expert inter-connections.

Homophily refers to the tendency that each expert is rich in connections to peer experts with similar expertise. To characterize such expertise similarity, both inferior and superior skills should be considered when comparing two experts, i.e., expertise difference in all areas between two experts must be within a threshold. Therefore, a natural way to model homophily is: For a universal constant integer $\delta \geq 1$, called *similarity degree*, each expert (denoted by u) connects to all experts in set $R := \{w \in V \setminus \{u\} : ||\mathbf{e}^{(w)} - \mathbf{e}^{(u)}||_1 \leq \delta\}$, where V is the set of experts in the entire network and "\" is set minus. All experts in set R are called *local contacts* of expert u. When experts are connected by the homophily rule (adding local contacts for each expert), an expert network basis, called *network substrate*, is formed. The network substrate is determined purely by the constant parameter δ, and thus the network substrate does not exhibit any randomness (assuming that the expertise vectors of all experts are fixed).

Heterophily refers to the phenomenon that each expert has a few connections to experts with fairly dissimilar expertise. These dissimilar experts are called *long-range contacts*, which are crucial in determining the network diameter (average length of the shortest path connecting each pair of nodes). However, unlike homophily, there exists randomness in observing which two dissimilar experts are connected. Therefore, we use a statistical model to capture heterophily, which consists of two steps: (i) for expert u, compute the set of candidates C_u that can be long-range contacts of u by $C_u := \{w \in V \setminus \{u\} : \mathbf{e}^{(w)} \not\preceq \mathbf{e}^{(u)}\}$; (ii) for a universal constant integer $k \geq 1$ and constant $r \geq 0$, expert u has k out-going edges to connect to long-range contacts with independent probabilities. Specifically, for the k out-going edges from u, each edge terminates at expert w ($w \in C_u$) with probability, denoted by $\Pr(u \rightarrow w)$, proportional to $[d(u \rightarrow w)]^{-r}$. In other words, $\Pr(u \rightarrow w) = [d(u \rightarrow w)]^{-r} / \sum_{v \in C_u} [d(u \rightarrow v)]^{-r}$, called the *inverse r-th power distribution*.

This heterophily model captures that in practical expert networks, expert u connecting to a long-range expert w is because w has superior skills in certain areas compared to u, instead of how inferior skills that w exhibits in other areas; therefore, we use expertise distance $d(u \rightarrow w)$ to capture such expertise dissimilarity. Note that the long-range contact construction rule indicates that the i-th and j-th edges from u may terminate at the same expert (may even be one of u's local contacts); therefore, k is the maximum number of long-range contacts for each expert. Moreover, r serves as a structural parameter that controls the scale of long-range contacts for each individual expert. In particular, when $r = 0$, all experts in the candidate set C_u are equally likely to be long-range contacts of u, which corresponds to a purely random case; when r increases, long-range contacts of an expert tend to only exist within her vicinity (measured by the expertise distance); when r approaches $+\infty$, all long-range contacts disappear, i.e., there is no heterophily in the expert network. In this paper, we study how these parameters relate to the efficiency of decentralized search.

2.2 Decentralized Search

We now formally present decentralized search for query routing. In an expert network, its constituent experts can generally resolve queries in more than one problem area; however, for the queries posted to the network, the most frequent case is that each of them belongs to one and only one problem area[1]. In this regard, we model each query as a 2-tuple (i, τ), where i is the problem area to which this query belongs and τ ($\tau > 0$) indicates the corresponding difficulty level, i.e., query (i, τ) is solvable by experts with expertise level in area i being at least τ. We assume that there is no ambiguity in determining the problem areas of queries, and there exist qualified experts in the network to solve each query, i.e., for any query (i, τ), $\exists$ expert w with expertise in area i and $e_i^{(w)} \geq \tau$. In this paper, the most crucial assumption is that for each query holder, besides knowing the expertise vector and (local and long-range) contacts of herself, she also knows the expertise vectors of all her (local and long-range) contacts; however, she does not have knowledge of expertise vectors or contacts of other experts, i.e., no experts have the global view[2] of the network. Under these assumptions, decentralized search is detailed in Algorithm 1. In Algorithm 1, for a given query, if the current query holder u cannot solve this query, then line 3 searches for the best expert from all u's contacts (with ties broken arbitrarily) as the next routing step. This process continues until a qualified expert is found.

Remark: In decentralized search, if a query holder's contacts cannot solve the received query, then this query holder has no knowledge of where the qualified experts are. Therefore, one may concern that the condition in line 2 may never be satisfied for some queries, thus resulting in endless loops. We will show in Section 3 that the structural properties of the network model abstracted from real networks ensure that at least one expert satisfying the condition in line 2 can be found by Algorithm 1 (although the resulting routing path may be long).

2.3 Objective

Suppose that the problem area and the difficulty level in each query are independently and uniformly distributed (subject to the maximum problem solving ability in the network) and the first query holder is also randomly chosen. Our goal is to understand decentralized search in expert networks by computing its upper/lower bound of the *average routing path length* (measured by the number of hops) under different network structures and expert inter-connections.

3. EXPERT NETWORK MODEL

Based on expert inter-connection models in Section 2, we now present an expert network model, called *diversified model*. In this model, both the total abilities and specialties may vary for different experts. Moreover, this model naturally captures the Gaussian-like distribution of expert total abilities in real expert networks. Suppose that up to m ($m \geq 1$) specific areas can be solved in the expert network. Let λ denote the maximum expertise level in each area (i.e., the maximum value for every entry in any expertise vector), then the diversified model is structured as follows:

[1]If a query contains problems in p ($p > 1$) areas, then this query can be treated as p separate queries.

[2]If the global picture of the network is fully known to each expert, then simple breadth-first search will suffice to find the shortest query routing path, which is not of interest to this paper.

Algorithm 1: Decentralized Search

input : Expert network, query (i, τ), first query holder u
output: Routing path $\mathcal{P}$ for resolving query (i, τ)

$\mathcal{P} \leftarrow u$; `// "←":assignment operation`
while $e_i^{(u)} - \tau < 0$ **do**
  $u = \arg\max_{w \in \mathcal{N}(u)} \left(\min(e_i^{(w)} - \tau, 0) \right)$; `// N(u): set of all (local and long-range) contacts of u`
  $\mathcal{P} \leftarrow \mathcal{P} + u$; `// append u to P`
end

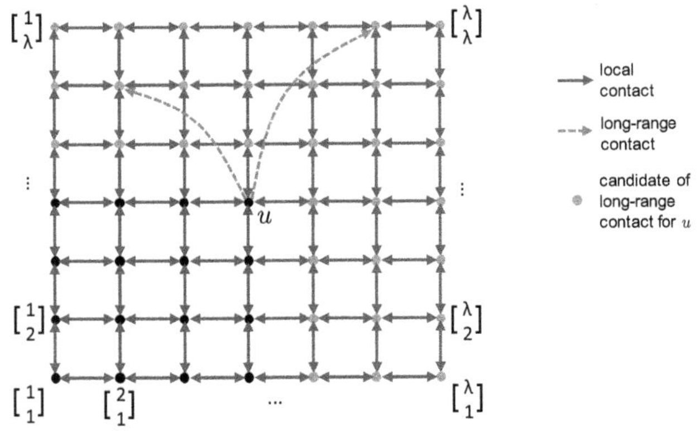

Figure 1: Diversified model ($\delta = 1$, $m = 2$, $k = 2$, $[\cdot]$: expertise vector).

1. suppose for any expertise vector $\mathbf{e}$, $\forall i$, e_i is an integer between 1 and λ (i.e., $[1, 1, \ldots, 1]^T \preceq \mathbf{e} \preceq [\lambda, \lambda, \ldots, \lambda]^T$), and each possible value of $\mathbf{e}$ corresponds to one expert. Hence, the total number of experts is $n = \lambda^m$;
2. each expert only has the most similar experts (i.e., similarity degree $\delta = 1$) as local contacts, thus forming an m-dimensional grid (Fig. 1 illustrates a sample 2-dimensional grid). As Fig. 1 shows, if an expert is not at the boundary, she has $2m$ local contacts; otherwise, the number of local contacts is between m and $2m$.

Then based on the above network substrate, long-range contacts are constructed following the inverse r-th power distribution for each expert (see the example in Fig. 1).

Discussions: In this model, the number of experts with the total ability ϕ is $\sum_{q=0}^{\min(m,(\phi-m)/\lambda)} [(-1)^q \binom{m}{q} \binom{\phi-1-q\lambda}{m-1}]$, and the expected value of total ability is $(m + m \sqrt[m]{n})/2$. By these numerical expressions, the distribution of total abilities is reported in Fig. 2 under different values of m. The most important property of the diversified model revealed by Fig. 2 is that the expert total ability follows a Gaussian-like distribution as m increases. Therefore, the diversified model ($m > 2$) represents a real expert network that is abundant in experts with average problem solving abilities, while lacks experts with significantly superior/inferior total abilities.

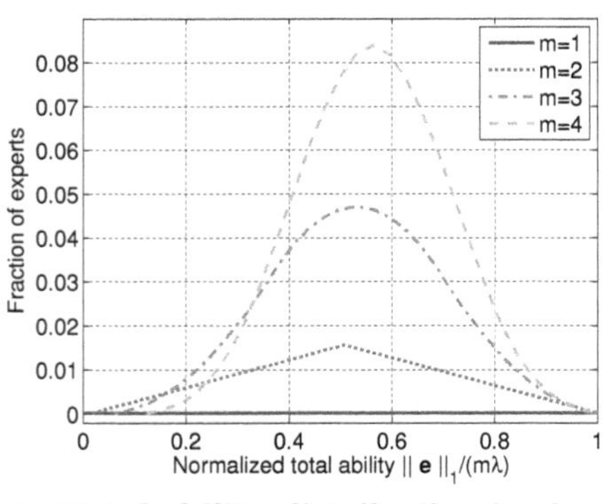

Figure 2: Total ability distribution in the diversified model ($n = 4096$).

Remark: The theoretical results in this paper are based on the network model proposed in this section, where specific expertise distributions over experts are required. Nevertheless, we point out that even if such requirement is not strictly satisfied, our theoretical results still demonstrate high accuracy in predicting query routing performance (see the case study of real datasets in Section 5), thus making contributions from both theoretical and practical perspectives.

4. EFFICIENCY OF DECENTRALIZED SEARCH IN EXPERT NETWORKS

Recall that we assume (in Section 2) that the problem area and the difficulty level in queries are generated uniformly (up to the maximum problem solving ability per area in the expert network) at random, and the first query holder is also arbitrarily chosen. We now present the corresponding quantitative performance bounds and analysis of decentralized search under the diversified model. We then discuss how the small-world phenomenon is related to decentralized search in expert networks.

4.1 Statement of Main Results

Under the diversified model, we have the performance bounds of decentralized search stated as below, where $\ln(\cdot)$ denotes natural logarithm. In these results, we assume that n is sufficiently large such that $\sqrt[m]{n} > 8$ and $n >> k$. Complete theoretical proofs are presented in [19].

THEOREM 1. *The average routing path length generated by decentralized search is monotonically increasing with r.*

THEOREM 2. *The average routing path length generated by decentralized search is upper bounded by*

$$O\Big(\frac{1}{m^r} \cdot \big(\ln n\big)^{r+1}\Big) \quad \text{for } 0 \le r \le 1.$$

THEOREM 3. *The average routing path length generated by decentralized search is lower bounded by*

$$\Omega\left(\frac{1}{k^{1/r}} \cdot n^{\frac{r-1}{mr}}\right) \quad \text{for } r > 1.$$

COROLLARY 4. *Any routing path length generated by decentralized search is upper bounded by $\sqrt[m]{n}$.*

4.2 Performance of Decentralized Search in Expert Networks

1) $0 \le r \le 1$. Theorem 2 shows that when $0 \le r \le 1$, the average routing path length using decentralized search is upper bounded by a polylogarithmic function, i.e., a polynomial function of $\ln n$. Therefore, decentralized search is highly efficient in expert searching when $0 \le r \le 1$. Such high efficiency occurs mainly for the following two reasons: (i) In expert networks, experts exhibit a certain level of randomness in inter-connections, which causes the formation of a network gradient that drives the query to the destination via decentralized search. (ii) Qualified experts for a given query may not be unique, i.e., query routing terminates at any expert who is capable of resolving this query; therefore, the query routing problem in expert networks is an *anycast* problem. Hence, if a query is routed to an over-qualified expert, then this query does not need to be further routed to the expert with the exact required knowledge level as the problem is already solvable. Another significant insight revealed by Theorem 2 is that decentralized search is most effective when $r = 0$ (i.e., long-range contacts are randomly selected) as the number of experts n is sufficiently large according to our assumption; the corresponding routing path length is only logarithmic in the network size.

2) $r > 1$. When r increases, Theorem 1 shows that the average routing path length also rises. When $r > 1$, as shown in Theorem 3, the average routing path length can no longer be expressed as a polylogarithmic function, which indicates the ineffectiveness of decentralized search. Nevertheless, Corollary 4 proves that for any values of r, there is always an upper bound, which is determined by the network size. Therefore, the worst performance of decentralized search happens when r approaches $+\infty$, for which the lower bound is $\Omega(\sqrt[m]{n})$. Comparing to Corollary 4, this result suggests that the performance bound in Theorems 3 is tight when r is large. On the other hand, Theorem 3 also shows that although a larger k may increase the probability of connecting to qualified experts, the impact of k in reducing the average routing path length is weakened when $r > 1$. This is because when r is large, long-range contacts tend to only exist in the vicinity of each expert or even overlap with local contacts, and thus the contribution of a large k diminishes.

4.3 Uniqueness of Small-World Phenomenon in Expert Networks

As shown in [10,20], the basic standard for justifying networks with the small-world phenomenon is that the associated network diameters can be expressed as a polylogarithmic function of n. Thus, by Theorem 2, we conclude that not only does the small-world phenomenon *exist* when $0 \leq r \leq 1$, but also decentralized search is able to find these short paths. This is in sharp contrast with the unicast problem in prior works on the small-world phenomenon. Specifically, assuming that individual connections also follow the inverse r-th power distribution (constructed based on their lattice distances) in the unicast problem, [18] shows that though the small-world phenomenon is pervasive for a range of r, decentralized search is *only* efficient under a unique value of r. This is because in a unicast problem with the destination being t, along the way from the current message holder to t, if one intermediate node routes this message to a long-distant node (corresponding to one over-qualified expert in expert networks) that is beyond t, then this message needs to be routed back to t, thus resulting in long routing paths.

5. EXPERIMENTS

In this section, we evaluate the performance of decentralized search by computing its average routing path length under the diversified model and explaining the corresponding observations using the performance bounds in Section 4. Then, we compare the predicted query routing time using the performance bounds to the actual routing time in a case study of real datasets for justifying the applicability of the performance bounds to real networks.

Performance Under the Diversified Model: To evaluate the performance of decentralized search, we select $n = 729$ and $m = 1, 2, 3$ for the diversified model under $k = 1, 2, 3$. We generate queries by randomly selecting the corresponding problem area and the required expertise level; moreover, the first query holders are also randomly chosen. For each network parameter setting, 100 random network realizations are generated, and 500 Monte Carlo runs (each run corresponds to a newly generated query) are conducted on each network realization. Using decentralized search, the resulting routing path length averaged over all network realizations and Monte Carlo runs are reported in Fig. 3.

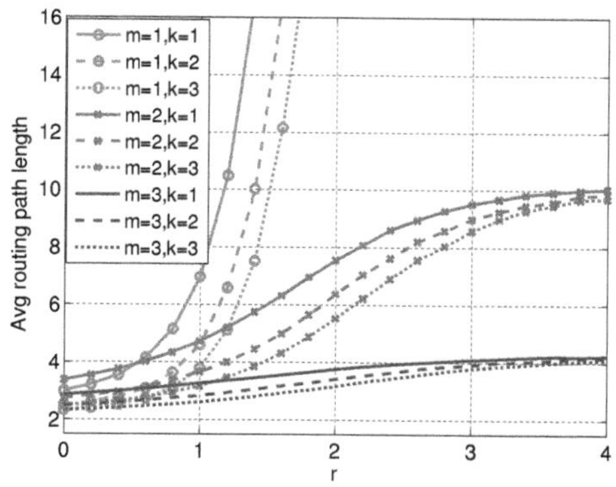

Figure 3: Average routing path length ($n = 729$).

In Fig. 3, as expected, we first observe that the average routing path length increases with r (supported by Theorem 1). The most significant conclusion we can draw from Fig. 3 is that they confirm the high efficiency of decentralized search when $0 \leq r \leq 1$ (as proved in Theorem 2). Specifically, compared to the network size (729 experts), decentralized search achieves extremely small routing path length, i.e., between 2 to 4 when $r = 0$. When r increases ($r > 1$), the performance under different parameters begins to depart, and the performance under small m degrades significantly, for which Theorem 3 provides a quantitative bound to capture such performance deterioration. Nevertheless, such performance degradation converges when r is large, because all routing path lengths are constrained by the upper bound (independent of r) established in Corollary 4.

Case Study of Real Datasets: Next, using our theoretical results, we analyze real-world query routing data collected from the IBM IT service department throughout 2006. Depending on query contents, these datasets are categorized into four independent classes: Operating System 1 (OS-1), Operating System 2 (OS-2), Database, and Web Service. Table 1 lists the network parameters in these datasets. For these datasets, we first observe that their network structures can be characterized by the diversified model[3] for the case of $m = 2$ and $k = 1$. In Table 1, two values of r (i.e., r_1 and r_2) are derived from these datasets based on expert inter-connections, where r_2 corresponds to new connections after applying a *mentoring program* to the original expert networks (associated with r_1). In this mentoring program, some less-skilled experts are mentored by experienced experts, which equivalently reduces the value of r. In order to justify application of our theoretical results in Section 4, we still need to determine whether or not the query routing behaviors in these real datasets share any similarities with decentralized search. To this end, we define relative expertise difference as $||\mathbf{e}^{(w)} - \mathbf{e}^{(u)}||_1 / ||\mathbf{e}^{(u)}||_1$, where w is the next hop expert selected by expert u. The query forwarding probability versus relative expertise difference averaged over all queries received in the four networks of the datasets is shown in Fig. 4 (a). As comparison, we also compute the same metric based on decentralized search in the diversified model as reported in Fig. 4 (b), where three networks of similar network sizes and similar values of r_1 and r_2 as those in the real datasets are evaluated. We note that Fig. 4 (a) and (b) have similar shapes, i.e., the expert

[3]Note that in Table 1, the expert network associated with each dataset is not as strictly structured as that in Fig. 1, i.e., some experts in Fig. 1 may be missing; however, the performance prediction remains accurate.

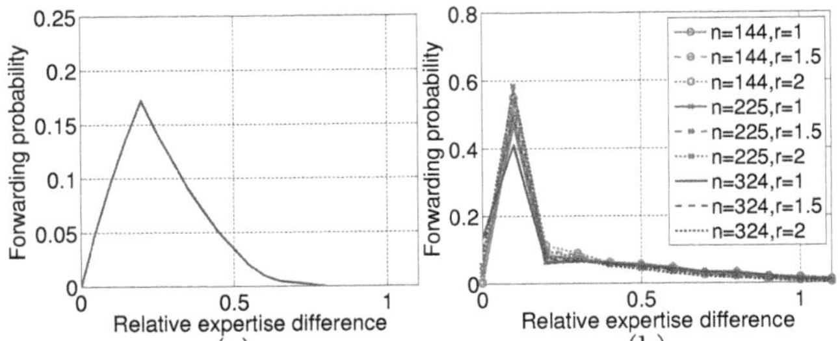

(a) (b)

Figure 4: (a) Query routing behavior in IBM datasets; (b) query routing behavior of decentralized search in the diversified model ($m = 2$, $k = 1$).

Table 1: Performance in Real Expert Networks

Datasets	n	r_1	r_2	real $\overline{L}_1/\overline{L}_2$	predicted $\overline{L}_1/\overline{L}_2$
OS-1	184	1.98	1.44	1.44	1.63
OS-2	122	1.24	1.04	1.31	1.45
Database	305	1.61	1.01	2.37	2.87
Web Service	266	1.14	1.04	1.19	1.26

with neither too similar nor too different expertise is selected with high probability as the next hop; therefore, the routing behaviors in these datasets do exhibit a certain level of decentralized search. Hence, we can use our results in Section 4 on decentralized search to predict the routing performance in these real datasets. Let $\overline{L}_i$ denote the average query routing path length under r_i ($i = 1, 2$). We compare the real $\overline{L}_1/\overline{L}_2$ with the predicted $\overline{L}_1/\overline{L}_2$ using Theorem 3 (as $r_1, r_2 > 1$ for all datasets). The comparison in Table 1 shows that using the theoretical performance bounds, the predicted routing path length is accurate (the error is 21.1% for Database, and 5.9% $\sim$ 13.2% for other datasets); therefore, the theoretical results in this paper can naturally serve as an efficient tool for analyzing/predicting behaviors in real expert networks. Moreover, these datasets also suggest that to achieve high routing efficiency, network owners can take proactive actions to adjust the expert connections such that the resulting network condition (r_2 is close to 1) approaches the high efficiency region (i.e., $0 \leq r \leq 1$).

6. CONCLUSION

We investigated the efficiency of local-information-based decentralized search for query answering in expert networks, focusing on quantifying the performance of decentralized search under various network settings. Under the proposed network model, we established fundamental theories demonstrating when decentralized search is exceptionally effective in finding short query routing paths. In cases where decentralized search is ineffective, we also quantified how the performance deterioration is correlated to network structures. Evaluations and comparisons of these theoretical results in both synthetic networks and real datasets confirm the efficiency of decentralized search in expert networks as well as the significance of the developed performance bounds in guiding real network design.

7. ACKNOWLEDGEMENTS

Research was sponsored by the Army Research Laboratory and was accomplished under Cooperative Agreement Number W911NF-09-2-0053 (the ARL Network Science CTA). The views and conclusions contained in this document are those of the authors and should not be interpreted as representing the official policies, either expressed or implied, of the Army Research Laboratory or the U.S. Government. The U.S. Government is authorized to reproduce and distribute reprints for Government purposes notwithstanding any copyright notation here on.

8. REFERENCES

[1] K. Balog, L. Azzopardi, and M. De Rijke, "Formal models for expert finding in enterprise corpora," in *ACM SIGIR*, 2006.

[2] P. Serdyukov, H. Rode, and D. Hiemstra, "Modeling multi-step relevance propagation for expert finding," in *ACM CIKM*, 2008.

[3] Q. Shao, Y. Chen, S. Tao, X. Yan, and N. Anerousis, "Efficient ticket routing by resolution sequence mining," in *ACM SIGKDD*, 2008.

[4] H. Zhang, E. Horvitz, Y. Chen, and D. C. Parkes, "Task routing for prediction tasks," in *AAMAS*, 2012.

[5] G. Miao, L. E. Moser, X. Yan, S. Tao, Y. Chen, and N. Anerousis, "Generative models for ticket resolution in expert networks," in *ACM SIGKDD*, 2010.

[6] A. Banerjee and S. Basu, "A social query model for decentralized search," in *ACM SNAKDD*, 2008.

[7] J. Kleinberg and P. Raghavan, "Query incentive networks," in *IEEE FOCS*, 2005.

[8] J. Zeng and W. Hsu, "Optimal routing in a small-world network," *Journal of Computer Science & Technology*, vol. 21, pp. 476–481, 2006.

[9] H. Sun, M. Srivatsa, S. Tan, Y. Li, L. M. Kaplan, S. Tao, and X. Yan, "Analyzing expert behaviors in collaborative networks," in *ACM SIGKDD*, 2014.

[10] B. Bollobás and F. D. L. Vega, "The diameter of random regular graphs," *Combinatorica*, vol. 2, pp. 125–134, 1982.

[11] D. J. Watts and S. H. Strogatz, "Collective dynamics of 'small-world' networks," *Nature*, vol. 393, pp. 440–442, 1998.

[12] M. Draief and A. Ganesh, "Efficient routeing in poisson small-world networks," *Journal of Applied Probability*, pp. 678–686, 2006.

[13] L. A. Adamic, R. M. Lukose, A. R. Puniyani, and B. A. Huberman, "Search in power-law networks," *Phys. Rev. E*, vol. 64, p. 046135, 2001.

[14] S. Milgram, "The small world problem," *Psychology Today*, vol. 67, pp. 61–67, 1967.

[15] J. Travers and S. Milgram, "An experimental study of the small world problem," *Sociometry*, vol. 32, pp. 425–443, 1969.

[16] C. Korte and S. Milgram, "Acquaintance networks between racial groups: Application of the small world method," *Journal of Personality and Social Psychology*, vol. 15, pp. 101–108, 1970.

[17] J. Guare, *Six Degrees of Separation: A Play.* Vintage Books, 1990.

[18] J. Kleinberg, "The small-world phenomenon: An algorithmic perspective," in *ACM STOC*, 2000.

[19] L. Ma, "Query answering via decentralized search," Technical Report, IBM T. J. Watson Research Center, Yorktown, NY, USA, Jul 2016. [Online]. Available: http://researcher.ibm.com/researcher/files/us-maliang/QueryRoutingTR.pdf

[20] J. Kleinberg, "Complex networks and decentralized search algorithms," in *International Congress of Mathematicians*, 2006.

A Study of Realtime Summarization Metrics

Matthew Ekstrand-Abueg
mattea@ccs.neu.edu
Northeastern University

Richard McCreadie
richard.mccreadie@glasgow.ac.uk
University of Glasgow

Virgil Pavlu
vip@ccs.neu.edu
Northeastern University

Fernando Diaz
fdiaz@microsoft.com
Microsoft Research

ABSTRACT

Unexpected news events, such as natural disasters or other human tragedies, create a large volume of dynamic text data from official news media as well as less formal social media. Automatic real-time text summarization has become an important tool for quickly transforming this overabundance of text into clear, useful information for end-users including affected individuals, crisis responders, and interested third parties. Despite the importance of real-time summarization systems, their evaluation is not well understood as classic methods for text summarization are inappropriate for real-time and streaming conditions.

The TREC 2013-2015 Temporal Summarization (TREC-TS) track was one of the first evaluation campaigns to tackle the challenges of real-time summarization evaluation, introducing new metrics, ground-truth generation methodology and dataset. In this paper, we present a study of TREC-TS track evaluation methodology, with the aim of documenting its design, analyzing its effectiveness, as well as identifying improvements and best practices for the evaluation of temporal summarization systems.

1. INTRODUCTION

Crisis events such as natural disasters or other human tragedies often precipitate massive interest from a wide variety of users [10]. Furthermore, the rise in popularity of e-newspapers and social media has resulted in vast quantities of event-related information being generated and consumed online. On the other hand, much of this published information is redundant, of poor quality, out-of-date or inaccurate [6]. Hence, the general public is increasingly relying on real-time summarization services to get a concise overview of an event, such as the BBC live news timeline, the CNN mobile application, or a government emergency alert system.

The aim of real-time summarization is to generate an updating summary for an event over time, containing all of the important information that the user might want to know, while avoiding information redundancy and latency in reporting. Because of the wide variety of information sources and the large volume of content, manually generating such summaries is costly. As such, there has been a recent upsurge in research into how to build such updating summaries automatically. Indeed, evaluation campaigns such as NTCIR's Temporal Information Access task[1] and the TREC Temporal Summarization[2] and Real-time Summarization[3] tracks are dedicated to supporting research in this area.

However, one of the key takeaway messages that has emerged from these evaluation campaigns is that robust evaluation of real-time summarization systems is difficult, and there is not yet a consensus on the best way to achieve it. In particular, although real-time summarization bears similarities to tasks such as information filtering [14] and topic tracking [1], the evaluation methods used in these other domains are not suitable for real-time summarization, since they do not consider content redundancy. Meanwhile, the text summarization community [16] has primarily focused on multi-document summarization (MDS). However, MDS evaluation makes three key assumptions that do not hold in the real-time summarization scenario: 1) input documents are processed offline as a batch (instead of as a stream); 2) input documents are known to be relevant to the topic; and 3) summaries are of fixed length. As a result, new evaluation methodologies and metrics are needed to effectively evaluate and compare real-time summarization systems.

The main evaluation campaign for real-time summarization was the TREC Temporal Summarization Track, which ran for three years between 2013 and 2015. This track introduced new evaluation metrics, a novel two-stage ground-truth generation methodology, and a new dataset, all with the aim of better enabling the evaluation of real-time summarization systems. However, to-date, the evaluation methodology used within the track has not been analyzed or empirically validated.

The contributions of this study are four-fold. First, we document the design of the evaluation methodology and the reasoning behind this design. Second, we analyze the effectiveness of this evaluation methodology in terms of agreement with user preferences and reusability. Third, based on the reusability analysis we propose and evaluate an enhancement to the methodology. Fourth, we discuss best practices for temporal summarization evaluation.

CIKM'16 , October 24 - 28, 2016, Indianapolis, IN, USA

ISBN 978-1-4503-4073-1/16/10...$15.00

DOI: http://dx.doi.org/10.1145/2983323.2983653

[1] https://sites.google.com/site/ntcirtemporalia/
[2] http://www.trec-ts.org/
[3] https://github.com/trecrts/trecrts-eval

2. RELATED WORK

Realtime summarization has been previously attempted, but generally on a smaller scale. For instance, early work attempting to summarize an event used that event's Wikipedia page as a gold standard summary [9]. Our work extends this methodology, but uses manual extraction of time-stamped *nuggets*, or key facts, from the entire Wikipedia edit stream rather than the final page created. In addition to this previous work, we will briefly review prior work in evaluation of summarization and discuss why realtime summarization requires novel evaluation metrics.

Multidocument summarization (MDS) refers to the batch summarization of document sets. MDS approaches take as input a set of (clean) documents about a topic to be summarized and generates a fixed length summary, normally by extracting sentences from those documents [16]. The MDS task was originally proposed as an evaluation task at the Document Understanding Conference (DUC)[4]. The evaluation of MDS approaches was later continued at the Text Analysis Conference (TAC) [7]. MDS performance is usually evaluated using the ROUGE [12] suite of metrics, and we will compare to multiple popular variants [13]. While MDS experimentation can evaluate batch summarization, it is less suited to realtime summarization. First, realtime summarization considers a stream of documents instead of a batch; thus the single gold standard summary looks more like a timeline than a paragraph. Second, MDS considers a fixed length summary, whereas realtime summarization cannot know *a priori* anything about the length of the best summary. These first two points mean that ROUGE is inappropriate for realtime summarization. Third, MDS assumes that the input documents are relevant whereas realtime summarization considers a stream of arbitrarily relevant content.

Our evaluation methodology is related to work studying *retrospective MDS*, where systems process the entire stream–or batch extracts from the stream–at once, instead of incrementally. The work of Allan *et al.* [2] studies extracting sentences from a large batch of news documents. Like our methodology, this work uses an idealized summary for evaluation. However, this prior work assumes complete judgments of all updates in the stream, something that is impossible in our scenario. Tweet timeline generation considers retrospective summarization of a stream of tweets for a given topic [18]. This methodology is driven more by a semi-automatic clustering of tweets and, as a result, is subject implicit biases in the corpus, which we attempt to mitigate using a canonical record such as a Wikipedia page.

As mentioned earlier, information filtering [14] can be considered a document level version of our task. The evaluation methodology used in that work, however, considers a simple notion of relevance, not capturing subtopic/factual structure or novelty. Although some work has studied novelty in the context of filtering [20], it does not have an explicit representation of subtopics. As such, evaluation criterion cannot estimate notions like subtopic recall, which is captured in out methodology by the nuggets contained within a document/stream. Topic Tracking [1] focuses on the same document level decision with single-level relevance.

3. EVALUATION METHODOLOGY

In this section, we describe our proposed methodology for evaluating realtime summarization systems. In particular, our methodology has three parts: Stream Simulation, Information Nuggets, and Performance Metrics.

3.1 Stream Simulation

Given an archive of timestamped documents, we can simulate a realtime summarization environment by providing documents to the system in temporal order. Given a query at time t, a system then emits zero or more sentences as updates as it receives each document after time t, the set of which we call a summary. Simulation provides a controlled, reproducible environment in which to assess how realtime summarization systems behave. Our evaluation metrics use this stream to grade the extent to which a summary's updates are relevant, comprehensive, and novel to the query.

3.2 Information Nuggets

The second part of our evaluation methodology requires the construction of a gold standard for each event, against which we can evaluate system-produced summaries. In MDS, the gold standard is represented by one or more textual summaries written by human assessors about each event. A system-generated summary can then be evaluated in terms of how similar it is to these gold-standard summaries, where the assumption is that good system summaries will be similar to the gold standard.

The gold standard in realtime summarization is a manually constructed timeline, consisting of a set of timestamped subtopics or *information nuggets* representing the unique pieces of information that a user following the event would like to know. For example, for the query 'hurricane sandy,' may include nuggets such as 'Sandy made direct hit on Jamaica,' '41 killed in the Caribbean and one in Bahamas,' and other nuggets related to landfall in New York and its aftermath. We will discuss one method for creating the set of nuggets in Section 4.

Given a query, we evaluate a summary by manually matching its updates with these information nuggets. While the nugget curation process scales with the size of the event, the matching process requires km manual comparisons for k updates and m nuggets. We will revisit this issue in Section 6.

3.3 Performance Metrics

Our design of metrics covers different aspects of evaluation: precision, comprehensiveness (recall), novelty, brevity and latency. We present results testing the appropriateness and robustness of the first four metrics. Factors like latency are very important to realtime summarization evaluation but estimating parameters such as latency penalties raises issues beyond the scope of this paper.

We believe that during and immediately following events, the most broadly useful summaries follow push notification alerts, although deciding exactly what is critical new information is a difficult task. As such, while we proposed a set of metrics for the task to cover all aspects independently, the cumulative metric targets this model.

Our precision metric, referred to as *gain*, is the sum of the relevance of each matching nugget. For a summarization system producing an update stream $\mathcal{S}$, gain is computed as:

$$\mathbf{G}(\mathcal{S}) = \frac{1}{|\mathcal{S}|} \sum_{u \in \mathcal{S}} \sum_{n \in \mathbf{M}(u)} \mathbf{g}(u, n) \quad (1)$$

where $\mathbf{M}(u)$ is the set of nuggets matching u and $\mathbf{g}(u, n)$ measures the utility of matching u with n. We adopt a gain-based metric that can integrate costs such as latency.

[4]http://www-nlpir.nist.gov/projects/duc/

year	runs	events	nuggets/event
2013	28	10	119.667
2014	24	15	92.9333
2015	45	21	47.4286

Table 1: TREC Temporal Summarization track statistics.

Our comprehensiveness metric, referred to as *comprehensiveness*, is the proportion of all nuggets matched by the system updates,

$$\mathbf{C}(\mathcal{S}) = \frac{1}{|\mathcal{N}|} \sum_{u \in \mathcal{S}} \sum_{n \in \mathbf{M}(u)} \mathbf{g}(u, n) \quad (2)$$

where $\mathcal{N}$ is our set of nuggets. Like the F-measure, our combined metric, $\mathcal{H}$, is the harmonic mean of $\mathbf{G}$ and $\mathbf{C}$,

$$\mathcal{H}(\mathcal{S}) = 2 * \frac{\mathbf{C}(\mathcal{S}) * \mathbf{G}(\mathcal{S})}{\mathbf{C}(\mathcal{S}) + \mathbf{G}(\mathcal{S})} \quad (3)$$

In order to reward novelty, we only allow each nugget to be matched by at most one update in the system's summary. We ignore later matches to updates in the summary for computing Equations 1 and 2, considering redundant content nonrelevant. We do not account explicitly for brevity in our metrics; we enforce it in our experimentation by constraining updates to be selected from segmented sentences from the stream documents.

4. DATA

We collected data from three years of the TREC Temporal Summarization track.[5] Each year's data consists of three components. The first component includes the evaluation events from 2012-2014 with Wikipedia entries providing fine-grained documentation of the event progression [11] and having substantial representation in the target corpus, the KBA Stream Corpus.[6] Assessors at NIST used the revision history of these pages to construct each topic's nugget set (Section 3.2), forming the ideal summaries. The second component of the data consists of participant runs. For three years, track participants designed summarization systems and generated summaries following the protocol described in Section 3.1. Participants provided confidence values for individual updates which allows for selective evaluation and analysis. We present summary statistics for this data in Table 1. The final component of our data consists of a manual matching between the nuggets in the ideal summary and the systems' output. Because the union of all submitted runs still resulted in an enormous set of updates, the set of updates inspected and matched by assessors was sampled from this union. Specifically, each run was guaranteed to have its top 60 updates (as determined by the system's confidence values) judged by assessors. The system updates were then pooled for matching. NIST assessors matched these pooled updates to the previously created nuggets. We conservatively expanded the set of matches using near duplicate detection [4].

5. USER EVALUATION

While Section 3 presented the track metrics and their desired properties, here we demonstrate that these metrics reflect what users consider to be a high quality event summary.

[5]http://www.trec-ts.org/

[6]http://trec-kba.org/

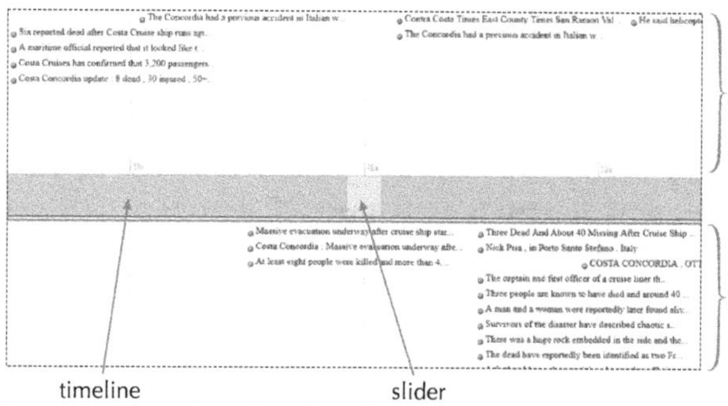

Figure 1: Pairwise visualization of event summary extracts.

To this end, we conducted a controlled experiment measuring the correlation of system ordering by human judges and our metrics for the 2014 track data. Our approach elicits pairwise judgments from assessors, as has previously been done for retrieval evaluation [17]. Under this approach, assessors were shown pairs of summaries (or rather summary extracts–as discussed further below), and were asked to state a preference for one summary or the other.

5.1 Experimental Setup

We sampled 1,000 summary pairs of systems such that each system appeared in the same number of pairs for each event. Duplicate summary pairs were omitted. Because full system summaries could include hundreds or thousands of updates, they were truncated to ease the cognitive load during assessment. Specifically, we truncated summaries so that they included the top thirty updates as sorted by the system's confidence value.

An assessor was presented with instructions describing the task followed by a short overview of the current event. The assessor then opened a webpage that visualized the two timelines and was instructed to scroll the timeline until they had read all 30 updates in each summary (Figure 1). The placement of each timeline in the 'A' vs 'B' slot was randomly selected. Afterward, the assessor was asked to state which of the two summaries they preferred or that they had no preference. Furthermore, we asked assessors to select one or more explanations for the decision.These explanations included: topicality, coverage, quality, redundancy, and timeliness.

We recruited assessors through the CrowdFlower[7] crowdsourcing marketplace, which aggregates multiple existing marketplaces. Assessors were provided with a single page containing six summary pairs for assessment, as prior research has indicated that larger batch sizes can result in better quality work [15]. In order to address unreliability in judgments, we employed the following quality assurance techniques. First, following best practices [3], three individual crowd workers provided preferences for each pair of summaries. The final assessment produced was the majority vote across the three assessors. Summary pairs for which no majority agreement was reached were dropped from the evaluation. Second, work submitted was subject to a speed trap of 60 seconds per page. This detected automatic bots and assessors that were simply randomly selecting labels. Assessors that submitted a page in under 60 seconds were flagged and removed from the evaluation. Third, to avoid over-reliance on individual assessors, the maximum number of assessments that any one assessor could contribute was set to 100. Fourth, as summaries were in English, we restricted the geographic regions that could participate in the

[7]http://www.crowdflower.com/

labeling task to only those from the United States, Canada and the United Kingdom. Finally, upon attempting the job, workers were subject to a 1 page test (summary 6 pairs), for which their accuracy was compared against a manually created gold standard (comprised of 32 examples). Workers were required to answer 4 or more of these test questions correctly to continue. We paid US $0.15 for each set of 6 summary pairs assessed. In total, 3,000 assessments were collected (1,000 summary pairs * 3 unique assessors).

5.2 Results

One hundred unique workers attempted the task, of which 77 passed the 1 page test. Approximately 40% of the crowd workers completed the maximum number of judgments (96 pairs/16 pages of work), followed by a 'tail' of workers who completed fewer assessments, which is typical behavior in crowdsourced tasks [3]. The average time it took the workers to assess a pair of summaries was 25 seconds, or 2 minutes 32 seconds per page. Out of these impressions, assessors made a preference judgment (stated a preference for either summary A or summary B) 67.1% of the time and preferred neither in the remaining 32.9% of cases. Inter-worker agreement over the preferences was 81.25%, which indicates that the labels were of high quality and the task was of appropriate difficulty. The most frequently selected reason for the preference was 'coverage' (40.7%) followed by, 'quality' (19.4%), 'topical' (15.4%), timeliness (10.5%), and redundancy (10.2%), with 3.7% of preference judgments providing no reason.

We counted the number of times a system was preferred in pairwise impressions. We refer to this as the system's win rate. In Figure 2, we compare each system's win rate with the metrics discussed in Section 3. The results in Figure 2 show a significant correlation between our comprehensiveness metric and assessor preference. This is understandable, as an assessor is likely to be able to judge some amount of coverage when our pool is limited to the top 30 updates per team. Although we *were* somewhat surprised that assessors were able to estimate a recall-oriented metric better than the precision-oriented metric, this phenomenon is consistent with previous literature [8]. Gain shows a weaker, but still reasonable correlation, and our combined metric shows significant correlation, supporting its use for our evaluation as an effective single measure for system performance.

Although we observed good response rates of assessors providing reasons for preferences, we found that only 'redundancy' was correlated with our metrics. We found a statistically significant correlation with comprehensiveness ($\tau: 0.42, \rho: 0.56, r = 0.62$ with $p < 0.05$ for all measures). Assessors claimed that coverage was important, but we did not find that they were actually able to detect differences. It seems that assessors appear averse to redundant content, whose presence can degrade comprehensiveness.

Additionally, we compare our results to a baseline using the ROUGE evaluation framework. As we do not have traditional summaries, we concatenate all nuggets into a summary to serve as the gold standard, and concatenate all updates per system into a single summary to serve as the participant summary. While this is may not be optimal, to our knowledge there do not exist other established evaluation frameworks for such types of summaries; indeed one of the purposes of the TREC Track was to establish such a method. As shown in Table 2, correlation with track metrics was lower for the ROUGE than it was for the win-rate described earlier. This was true for all popular ROUGE variants tested, including ROUGE 2, 4 and SU-4 P, R, and F metrics, except ROUGE-4P having reasonable kendall correlation, but poorer pearson and spearman.

Metric	Kendall	Pearson	Spearman
ROUGE-2P	0.30	**0.54**	0.43
ROUGE-2R	-0.11	0.36	-0.13
ROUGE-2F	0.13	**0.58**	0.21
ROUGE-4P	**0.35**	**0.48**	0.43
ROUGE-4R	0.13	0.18	0.16
ROUGE-4F	0.22	0.42	0.33
ROUGE-SU4P	0.05	0.02	0.12
ROUGE-SU4R	-0.15	0.41	-0.16
ROUGE-SU4F	0.18	**0.64**	0.29

Table 2: Correlation values for ROUGE metrics vs user study winRate using kendall, pearson, and spearman coefficients.

5.3 Pair-preference case analysis

To better understand the disagreement between study assessors and the primary track $\mathcal{H}$ metric, we identified 80 cases with strong disagreement out of the 946 pairs assessed and manually analyzed them. We observed that in all of these cases, a recall-orientated system (that produces a verbose summary containing thousands of updates) was being compared to a precision-oriented summary (that typically produced 40-100 updates). In these cases, the human assessors preferred the summaries produced by the recall-orientated systems, while the metric $\mathcal{H}$(gain, comprehensiveness) prefers the precision-orientated one. This can be explained by the fact that the user study truncates summaries to the 30 with the highest score, and hence the user will not penalize these systems for returning excessive content (since it is not shown). In contrast, the $\mathcal{H}$ metric contains a gain component that will penalize large numbers of redundant or off-topic updates.

Furthermore, we observed that users prefer timelines which concentrated the updates in the first few hours of an event, the initial view of the assessment interface. For this reason, precision-orientated summarization systems that delayed returning content until later in the event (typically systems that returned updates on end-of-hour boundaries) were penalized by the user study. This is a source of disagreement between the user study and the track $\mathcal{H}$ metric, since the latency decay used within the $\mathcal{H}$ metric was quite forgiving, in that it allowed for multiple hours to pass before late reporting of information was penalized significantly. Our metrics, without redesign, can made far more sensitive of latency, if so desired. In general, from this study, we can draw two main conclusions. First, verbose summaries are difficult to evaluate with users since they need to be truncated to display, which is a source of evaluation error. Second, users of this timeline interface tend to prefer to see updates near the beginning of the event, indicating that for evaluating timeline summaries, the latency discount function used should more strongly penalize systems that return information late.

6. REUSABILITY

Our user study demonstrates that the method described in Section 3 provides a good metric for systems participating in the manual nugget matching process. However, in order for our simulation to be of value for future research, it must be reusable after the initial experiments and evaluation have been completed [5]. In particular, the data and associated metrics should ideally be able to accurately determine the

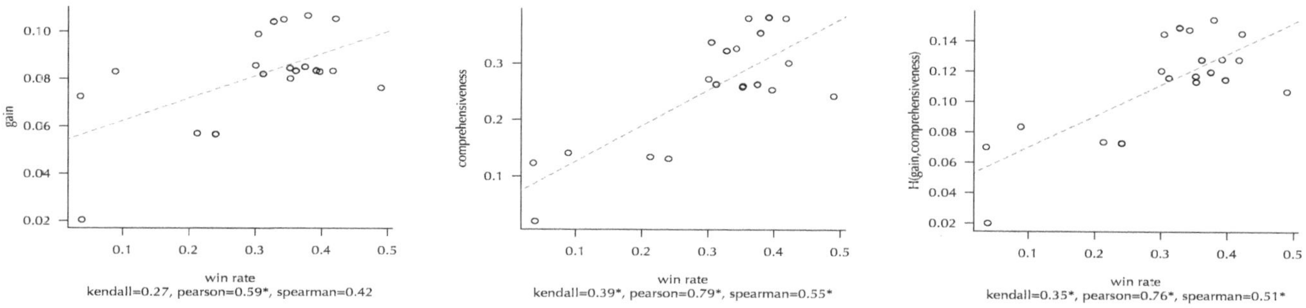

(a) gain (b) comprehensiveness (c) H(gain,comprehensiveness)

Figure 2: Performance for all participating systems scored by the three primary track metrics vs the controlled experiment win rate for the 2014 track. Starred correlations have $p < 0.05$.

performance of novel systems compared to systems which participated in the original manual assessment without requiring additional manual effort.

In this section, we explore the robustness of our metrics in the presence of new runs with potentially missing judgments. We quantify the robustness of the metrics when entire sets of runs are suppressed from contributing to the pool. This simulates the behavior of a new system being developed using preexisting data.

	Holdout τ (τ_{AP})	
Year	**System**	**Team**
2013	0.97 (0.85)	0.95 (0.82)
2014	0.97 (0.87)	0.82 (0.75)
2015	0.95 (0.89)	0.90 (0.93)

Table 3: Kendall's τ (τ_{AP}) values comparing the track scores vs scores holding out individual/all systems for each team.

6.1 Evaluation with Missing Judgments

To analyze reusability, we perform two procedures which mimic the addition of new systems. In the first, we remove from the pool all updates submitted by a system which were not submitted by any other system. We perform the standard evaluation procedure for that system, report its score using the primary track metric $\mathcal{H}$, and repeat for each submitted system. This method simulates a new system to be evaluated without ability to collect and match additional updates. Therefore, it provides a good representation of whether or not we can accurately determine the relative performance of this new system compared to the systems submitted to the track. It is actually more difficult than simply having future systems, as we artificially shrink the test collection size to perform this analysis.

Next, we repeat the same procedure, instead removing all unique updates for all systems submitted by the same team rather than for a single system. This corrects for systems which are simply small variations of a single system submitted by the same group, a common practice in these track settings and analogous to having a new team submit systems after the track evaluation is complete. Again we compare the system rankings to the original ranks.

As a standard method of comparing the similarity of two ranked lists, we compute the Kendall's τ values to compare the original system rankings to each of the two holdout methodologies. Kendall's τ measures the proportion of pairs of items which are ranked identically across two different rankings. However, τ gives equal weight in the metric to pairs at the bottom of the list as to pairs at the top. But when evaluating system performance, it is usually more important if one high-performing system outperforms another than is it for two low-performing systems. As such, we also compute τ_{AP} values, as this method better describes the correlation between the top ranks in the list, or top performing systems in our setting [19]. This is important, as the goal of a new system is to outperform existing systems, and the evaluation methodology should be able to accurately assess this case.

The Kendall's τ and τ_{AP} results for our holdout experiments are reported in Table 3 for all tracks. We also plot the results to more fully analyze the concordance of the methods, as both τ and τ_{AP} can hide subtle, yet important swaps. The holdout results data are shown in Figure 3, holding out individual systems on TS15 track (left), and holding out teams (middle TS14, right TS15). Overall, there is high concordance between the original results and the holdout results, suggesting the utility of the dataset for additional experiments. Concordance at top ranks was much higher for the 2013 and 2014 tracks, with the exception of 2014 team holdouts, which is why we show the remaining three plots here. In the 2015 track, we note two or three high-performing systems which stand as outliers to the general consistency, and cause the generally lower τ_{AP} numbers, although they remain in an acceptable range. This is often found in TREC datasets, where one or two teams submit systems trying to retrieve particularly unique results. In fact it was true in this case as well, as the top 2015 team outperformed others primarily due to high recall and having a high proportion of unique updates than the other submissions.

Looking more closely at the systems and scores for the 2014 team holdouts, we see that the Comprehensiveness is fairly high for all systems (Figure 2), but the Gain is low, and in particular, this means that a small proportion of submitted updates were relevant. This is primarily due to the large number of updates provided by many teams. As such, if even a small number of those previously relevant updates are found not relevant, the scores can fluctuate wildly. In the 2015 track, teams had better estimated the number of updates needed, so the scores are better overall and are less sensitive to small variations in the dataset. The 2013 track had more nuggets per event than the other two, also improving its resilience to lost matches in the holdout process.

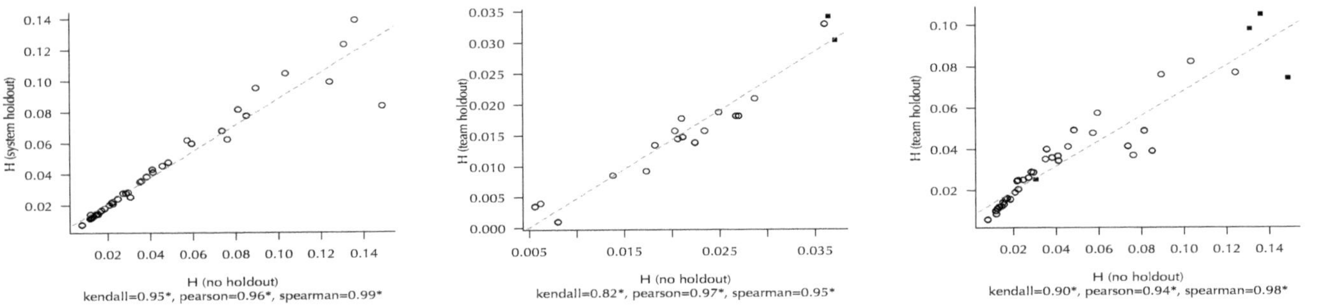

(a) system holdout (2015) (b) team holdout (2014) (c) team holdout (2015)

Figure 3: Reusability analysis comparing the scores for each system as reported by the track versus removing from the pool unique updates submitted by that system for the left plot for the 2015 track, and for that entire team for middle and right plots for the 2014 and 2015 tracks respectively.

7. DISCUSSION

The results of our controlled experiment demonstrated a correlation between our metrics and human judges. We were surprised by the lack of strong correlation with gain, since differences in precision would be more recognizable given our high precision presentation (only the top 30 updates were displayed). This may result from assessors' difficulty in distinguishing between systems with very minute differences in gain. At the same time, our experiment could be improved by conducting an evaluation of system performance in real-time. Indeed, this is one of the motivations for the TREC 2016 Realtime Summarization track.

Although the datasets differed in terms of number of participating teams and systems submitted, number of topics, size of those topics, and number of nuggets and matches found, the evaluation methodology resulted in reusable data with strong correlations to the original sets despite the challenging task of holding out a significant portion of the systems involved in the pooling. This robustness strongly suggests that the data and metrics are correlated to users across track years, and that the same methodology could be used in future stream summarization tasks that want to simultaneously optimize for the diverse criteria here, such as microblog summarization, social media news feeds, news outlet information aggregation, and crisis responder information feeds.

Additionally, while our simulation-based evaluation method measures the effectiveness of systems ignoring efficiency concerns, much like the Cranfield approach, this system could be easily adapted to rate efficiency as well by running in real-time and processing updates when they are provided to the evaluation system. This could allow for on-line training of these systems in conjunction with crowd worker annotations. Again, these ideas are being explored by the TREC 2016 Realtime Summarization track.

In closing, our studies provide strong evidence supporting the methodology used in the TREC Temporal Summarization track. While this track has run for three years, our experiments are the first to demonstrate the validity and utility of the methodology. The results provide evidence that the collection is reusable for future research and we provide a novel algorithm able to improve the robustness when judgments are incomplete. Our results, taken together, provide strong support for using this methodology for realtime summarization tasks in the future.

8. REFERENCES

[1] J. Allan, editor. *Topic Detection and Tracking: Event-based Information Organization*. Inf. Retrieval. 2002.

[2] J. Allan, R. Gupta, and V. Khandelwal. Temporal summaries of new topics. In *Proc of SIGIR*, 2001.

[3] O. Alonso and R. Baeza-Yates. Design and implementation of relevance assessments using crowdsourcing. In *Proc. of ECIR*, 2011.

[4] G. Baruah, A. Roegiest, and M. D. Smucker. The effect of expanding relevance judgements with duplicates. In *Proc. of SIGIR*, 2014.

[5] B. Carterette, E. Gabrilovich, V. Josifovski, and D. Metzler. Measuring the reusability of test collections. In *Proc. of WSDM*, 2010.

[6] Y. Chen, N. J. Conroy, and V. L. Rubin. News in an online world: the need for an automatic crap detector. In *Proc. of ASIS&T*, 2015.

[7] H. T. Dang and K. Owczarzak. Overview of the TAC 2008 update summarization task. In *Proc. of TAC*, 2008.

[8] M. Dostert and D. Kelly. Users' stopping behaviors and estimates of recall. In *Proc. of SIGIR*, 2009.

[9] Q. Guo, F. Diaz, and E. Yom-Tov. Updating users about time critical events. In *Inf. Retrieval*. Springer, 2013.

[10] M. Imran, C. Castillo, F. Diaz, and S. Vieweg. Processing social media messages in mass emergency: A survey. *ACM Comput. Surv.*, July 2015.

[11] B. Keegan, D. Gergle, and N. Contractor. Hot off the wiki: Structures and dynamics of wikipedia's coverage of breaking news events. *American Behavioral Scientist*, 2013.

[12] C.-Y. Lin. ROUGE: a Package for Automatic Evaluation of Summaries. In *Proc. of ACL*, 2004.

[13] C.-Y. Lin and F. Och. Looking for a few good metrics: Rouge and its evaluation. In *NTCIR Workshop*, 2004.

[14] H. P. Luhn. A business intelligence system. *IBM J. Res. Dev.*, 1958.

[15] R. Mccreadie, C. Macdonald, and I. Ounis. Identifying top news using crowdsourcing. *Inf. Retrieval*, 2013.

[16] A. Nenkova and K. McKeown. Automatic summarization. *Foundations and Trends in Information Retrieval*, 2011.

[17] P. Thomas and D. Hawking. Evaluation by comparing result sets in context. In *Proc. of CIKM*, 2006.

[18] Y. Wang, G. Sherman, J. Lin, and M. Efron. Assessor differences and user preferences in tweet timeline generation. In *Proc. of SIGIR*, 2015.

[19] E. Yilmaz, J. A. Aslam, and S. Robertson. A new rank correlation coefficient for information retrieval. In *Proc. of SIGIR*, 2008.

[20] Y. Zhang, J. Callan, and T. Minka. Novelty and redundancy detection in adaptive filtering. In *Proc. of SIGIR*, 2002.

Framing Mobile Information Needs: An Investigation of Hierarchical Query Sequence Structure

Shuguang Han[1], Xing Yi[2], Zhen Yue[2], Zhigeng Geng[2], Alyssa Glass[2]
[1] University of Pittsburgh, 135 N Bellefield Ave., Pittsburgh, PA, USA
[2] Yahoo! Research, 701 First Ave., Sunnyvale, CA, USA
shh69@pitt.edu, {xingyi,zhenyue,zgeng,alyssag}@yahoo-inc.com

ABSTRACT

When using search engines, people often issue multiple related queries to accomplish a complex search task. A simple query-task structure may not fully capture the complexity of query relations since people may divide a task into multiple subtasks. As a result, this paper applies a three-level hierarchical structure with query, goal and mission - a mission includes several goals, and a goal consists of multiple queries. Particularly, we focus on analyzing query-goal-mission structure for mobile web search because of its increasing popularity and lack of investigation in the literature. This study has three main contributions: (1) we study the query-goal-mission structure for mobile web search, which was not studied before. (2) We identify several differences between mobile and desktop search patterns in terms of goal/mission length, duration and interleaving. (3) We demonstrate that the query-goal-mission structure can be applied to design better user satisfaction metrics. Specifically, goal-based search success rate and mission-based abandonment rate are better aligned with users' long-term engagement than query and session based metrics.

Keywords

Mobile web search, search goal, search mission, query structure, user engagement

1. INTRODUCTION

Modern search engines are experiencing several important changes - the involvement of more complex search tasks and an increasing usage on mobile devices. Complex search tasks often require users to issue multiple related queries while traditional search analysis seldom considers the query relations [10]. This drives researchers to investigate users' search behaviors at the session level [2, 3, 8], assuming that two queries in the same session should share the same goal. A search session is often defined as the 30-minute timeout for user inactivity [16]. However, as many studies pointed out, under this definition, a search session frequently involves queries from multiple unrelated tasks [10, 15]. As a result, recent research has started focusing on the task-level analysis for web search [2, 16]. To the best of our knowledge, existing findings on this topic are mainly drawn from the analysis of desktop search logs. Due to the apparent differences between mobile and desktop search behaviors [19], it is critical to understand how people organize their search tasks in mobile sessions and how it differs from desktop search.

Consider a query sequence – "goggle ski, goggle for men, ski pants, ski pants size, ski pants price, restaurants, restaurant near me". The first two queries belong to the same task since the user was searching for "ski goggle"; the middle three queries also belong to the same task because the user was looking for "ski pants". However, it is unclear whether "ski goggle" and "ski pants" should be treated as the same task. To capture this complex query structure, we adopt a three-level hierarchical structure that organizes a query sequence into query, goal and mission, as proposed by Jones and Klinkner [10]. Following the definitions in [10], a search goal is an atomic information need that includes one or more related queries, and a search mission consists of one or more related search goals. Under these definitions, the above query sequence can be seen as having three search goals: buying ski goggles, buying ski pants, and finding a nearby restaurant. The first two goals are associated with the same mission (buying ski equipment) and the third goal is associated with a different mission.

Therefore, we adopt the query-goal-mission structure for analyzing mobile search sequences. Our study is based on a web-scale search log sampled from Yahoo! search engine, which involves millions of search sessions. To obtain a more comprehensive result, we also examine the desktop query-goal-mission structure for comparison. The first step of conducting the study is to develop an algorithm that automatically constructs such complex structure in a scalable way. We employ the approach adopted in both Jones and Klinkner [10] and Lucchese et al. [16], and improve the algorithm by incorporating several novel query log features. The details of our method is provided in §3.

After obtaining a large-scale, segmented search query sequence, our next task is to understand the mobile query-goal-mission structure: (1) how it differs from desktop query structure, and (2) how to apply the query structure information for supporting real-world mobile searches. To answer the first question, we compare several goal and mission measurements, including goal/mission duration and goal/mission length, between mobile and desktop searches. For the second question, prior studies have shown that the query-task

CIKM'16, October 24 - 28, 2016, Indianapolis, IN, USA

ISBN 978-1-4503-4073-1/16/10...$15.00

DOI: http://dx.doi.org/10.1145/2983323.2983654

structure (a task resembles to a search goal in our study) can be applied in many applications, including recommending better queries [2], improving search results ranking [21] and designing better user satisfaction metrics [15]. In this paper, we study how the three-level query structure is applied for designing better user satisfaction metrics since it is the least-studied application in literature and an important topic for search evaluation [12, 15].

This paper has three key contributions: (1) we develop a novel two-step approach, adapting the methods developed in [10] and [16], to automatically construct the query-goal-mission structure for a search sequence (§3). Our method employs a more comprehensive and larger set of features to achieve improved performance (§4). More importantly, (2) we perform a large-scale query-goal-mission structure analysis with millions of search sessions, and identify important differences between mobile and desktop search patterns (§5). (3) We discover that the query-goal-mission structure can be used to design better user satisfaction metrics - goal is better in determining search success while mission is better for understanding search abandonment (§6). These are not investigated in prior studies.

2. RELATED WORK

Studies [10, 15, 16] based on large-scale search log analysis identified that search queries are not independent. To discover the connections among different queries, researchers have been long investigating the ways of segmenting query sequences into meaningful search units. Queries from the same unit are assumed to have tighter relations than those from different units [2, 7, 16]. Search session is one type of unit, and it is often determined by a fixed timeout cutoff [7, 16]. However, under this definition, a session may include multiple unrelated tasks [2, 10]. This work resulted in recent studies [2, 16] focused on more fine-grained analysis at the task level. Although there have been several attempts [10, 14, 16] to identify search tasks within a search session, accurate task extraction remains a challenge due to the complexity of the task definition - a task can involve sub-tasks, and several tasks may share the same mission. Therefore, Jones and Klinkner [10] proposed a three-level hierarchical structure containing query, goal and mission. Following this study, our work is built on top of the three-level query structure, but differs in terms of: 1) we propose several novel features for goal/mission identification, which are shown to be more effective; and 2) we provide a large-scale analysis of such complex structure and explore its potential applications in mobile search.

Rich query structure information can be applied in various applications. First, task and session information were often adopted to enrich users' search contexts and further improve their search experience [2, 21]. Feild and Allan [2] found that the task information can help improve query recommendation performance. White et al. [21] enhanced personalized search by mining users' search behaviors within the same task. Second, task and session information were also applied to design better user satisfaction metrics [11, 15]. For instance, Liao et al. [15] found that sessions and queries are not as precise as tasks in determining user satisfaction. Since the query-task structure cannot capture the complex structure as in a query-goal-mission schema, we expect that the query-goal-mission structure can provide additional value and define better user satisfaction metrics.

The above studies were mostly performed using desktop search logs, while the study of mobile search is rare. With the increasing popularity of mobile devices, dedicated research on mobile search patterns is needed. Indeed, Song et al. [19] found significant differences between mobile and desktop search patterns in query and click patterns. Other researchers [4, 5, 20] discovered that mobile users are frequently involved in complex search tasks, yet a fine-grained analysis of mobile search sequence structure is missing. Thus, we focus our investigation on these mobile query structures.

3. FRAMING SEARCH SEQUENCES

The first task of our study is to build a hierarchical query-goal-mission structure for each mobile query sequence. In this paper, a query sequence refers to a mobile search session. Following [19], we use 30-minute user inactivity as the timeout cutoff to determine a session. The search goal and mission are defined the same as [10] - a **search goal** is an atomic information need resulting in one or more queries, and a **search mission** is a related set of information needs, resulting in one or more search goals.

Problem definition. We formalize our search sequence structure identification problem as following: suppose that we have an m-query mobile session $\mathcal{S} = (q_1, q_2, q_3, ..., q_m)$. We want to partition it into a set of goals ($\mathcal{G}$) and missions ($\mathcal{M}$). To achieve this, we propose a two-step approach. In the first step, we determine if a query pair belongs to the same goal or mission through the Logistic Regression (LR) classifier as did in Jones and Klinkner [10], for which we need manually-labeled ground-truth datasets (§4.1) and classification features (Table 1). The model output is the probability of a query pair belonging to the same goal/mission.

In the second step, we group queries into goals and missions, where we adopt the average-linkage hierarchical clustering algorithm. The goal clustering starts with initializing each query as a goal. Then, we loop through all goal pairs and merge the two most similar goals into one (the similarity is defined as the probability of a query pair belonging to the same goal, as computed in the goal classifier). We repeat this process until the similarities of all goal pairs are smaller than a threshold $\mathcal{T}_G$. For mission clustering, we apply the same approach, except: (1) we compute with the mission similarity (i.e., the probability of a query pair belongs to the same mission); (2) the clustering process stops when reaching the mission pair similarity threshold $\mathcal{T}_M$; and (3) the initialized missions are the identified goal clusters.

Features. The logistic regression classifiers employ four groups of features for each query pair (q_i, q_j), in which i and j $(i < j)$ denote the sequential positions of the two queries in the session $\mathcal{S}$. The four feature groups are provided in Table 1. The first two groups are directly adopted from [10, 16], and the mobile query global features are computed based on a large-scale search log with millions of search sessions (§4.1). However, when computing the mobile query pair global features, we must also properly handle data sparsity – we find that only 3% of mobile query pairs occur in two consecutive weeks. To resolve this problem, we propose an additional feature group that calculates query pair features based on the aggregation of query term pairs. A term pair global feature is calculated in the similar manner as the query pair global feature, except the statistics are based on terms rather than queries. The extracted term-pair based features form our third feature group. Furthermore, we consider a fourth

Table 1: Features for query pair classification. Feature groups with ‡ indicates the new features we proposed.

Mobile query pair local feature (local)	
jaccard, edit distance and time interval	Same as [10].
Mobile query pair global feature (queryglobal)	
pmi and pq12	$\frac{p(q_i \to q_j)}{p(q_i \to *)p(* \to q_j)}$ and $\frac{p(q_i \to q_j)}{max_{q_m} p(q_i \to q_m)}$, [10].
llr and χ^2	Log-likelihood ratio and χ^2 for the query pair (q_i, q_j) [17].
entropy_x_q1 and entropy_q1_x	$\sum_x p(q_i \vert q_x) \log_2 p(q_i \vert q_x)$ and $\sum_x p(q_x \vert q_j) \log_2 p(q_x \vert q_i)$ [10].
Mobile query term pair global feature (termglobal.mobile) ‡	
t_pmi	$\frac{1}{N} \sum_{t_m \in q_i, t_n \in q_j} \frac{p(q_i \to q_j)}{p(q_i \to *)p(* \to q_j)}$.
t_pq12, t_llr, t_χ^2, t_entropy_x_q1, t_entropy_q1_x are computed using the same method as t_pmi.	
Desktop query term pair global feature (termglobal.desktop) ‡	
dt_pmi, dt_pq12, dt_llr, dt_χ^2, dt_entropy_x_q1 and dt_entropy_q1_x are computed using desktop search logs with the above process.	

feature group that obtains term-based features from desktop search logs, enriching the feature set with additional search queries. The last two groups are our proposed new features (highlighted by ‡ in Table 1).

4. SEGMENTATION EXPERIMENTS

4.1 Data Collection

Our experiments are performed on a large-scale search log sample from the Yahoo search engine on both mobile and desktop devices during a three-week period (2/23 to 3/15 in 2015), covering millions of search queries and sessions. To train and evaluate the goal and mission classification and clustering models, we need a ground-truth dataset. This paper constructs three ground-truth data sets, i.e., D_0, D_1 and D_2 as shown in Figure 1. Each dataset consists of approximately 1,000 query pairs randomly sampled from the search log. D_0 is extracted from mobile search logs in Week 2 and it is used to train our goal classifier and mission classifier. D_1 and D_2 are two testing data sets for mobile search and desktop search, respectively. Note that we do not collect a desktop training dataset because the model trained on the mobile training dataset can be effectively applied for desktop testing dataset and achieves reasonably good performance.

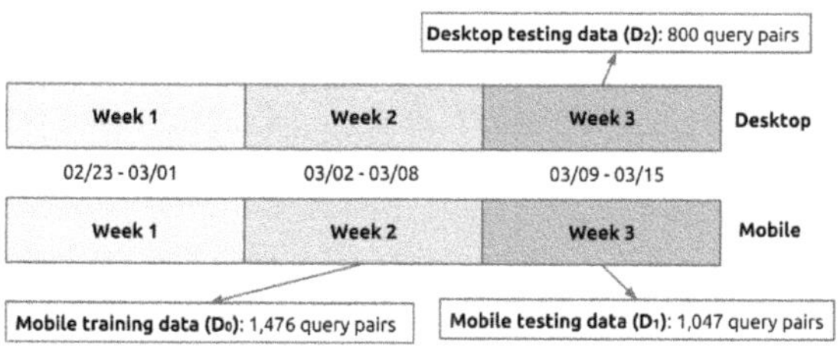

Figure 1: An illustration of data corpus and sampled training and testing datasets

For each of the ground-truth datasets, we collect editorial judgments from two independent paid editors. We observed more than 80% agreements for both goal and mission judgments (85.80% for goal and 83.21% for mission in D_0, 91.31% for goal and 87.39% for mission in D_1, and 91.70% for goal and 82.57% for D_2), indicating high precision quality labels for our data sets. The conflicts were resolved by a third editor. The following experiments in this paper are performed on the conflict-resolved datasets.

4.2 Query Pair Classification Performance

Our experiment begins with training a goal classifier and a mission classifier using D_0. Here, we report the performances of these two classifiers on the testing dataset D_1 (we do not provide results for D_2 as the findings were the same). The results are provided in Table 2. We use the classification algorithm in [10] as the baseline, for which they use the combination of *local + queryglobal* features (the italic row in Table 2). We adopt F1 score for the same goal/mission to measure the classification performance. We note multiple findings from the data in Table 2.

Table 2: Search goal and mission classification performances on D_1. The row in italics denotes the baseline. Rows with ‡ denote the new features.

Feature groups	F1(goal)	F1(mission)
local	**0.6574**	0.8038
queryglobal	0.3384	0.7903
termglobal.mobile ‡	0.5444	0.8165
termglobal.desktop ‡	0.5937	0.8206
local + queryglobal	*0.6485*	*0.8128*
local + termglobal.mobile ‡	0.6099	0.8505
local + termglobal.desktop ‡	0.6339	**0.8622**

First, the query local feature is the strongest signal for both search goal and search mission classification. In particular, in goal classification, the query local feature achieves the best performance, while adding global features does not result in much improvement. The results show a different trend for mission classification, for which query global features do provide a positive contribution. This reflects the inherent difference between a goal and a mission - a mission defines the connection between two queries at a more abstract level and thus requires external knowledge for understanding the query relation. Such knowledge can be learned from both query pair and term-pair co-occurrence statistics and is consistent across different device types.

Second, compared to the baseline, our proposed term-pair based features (both local + termglobal.mobile and local + termglobal.desktop) generate better performance in mission classification while having no difference for goal classification. In particular, the term-based query pair features obtained from desktop search logs achieve the best performance. We believe this result is because the desktop search logs contain richer information, and thus produces more robust global features and resolves the data sparseness for tail query pairs. This indicates the possibility of transferring desktop knowledge into mobile search when mobile search information is missing or sparse.

4.3 Goal/Mission Clustering Performance

Outputs of the best performing classifiers are then used in the second step for goal and mission clustering. We evaluate the clustering performance using the following procedure. Suppose that we have m human-labeled query pairs from n search sessions. We first run the clustering algorithm on all n sessions. Then, based on the clustering outputs, we evaluate the labeled query pairs on how accurately they are clustered, i.e., whether the same-goal queries are in the same goal cluster, and whether the same-mission queries are in the same mission cluster. We employ three evaluation measurements - overall accuracy, accuracy for the same goal/mission and accuracy for different goals/missions.

The clustering algorithm requires specifying the stopping thresholds $\mathcal{T}_G$ and $\mathcal{T}_M$ (see §3). Here, they are tuned based on the training dataset D_0 with a 10-fold cross validation. We set $\mathcal{T}_G = 0.35$ for goal clustering and $\mathcal{T}_M = 0.50$ for mission clustering as they produce the best performances. The clustering performances are presented in Table 3. We find that our algorithm achieves reasonably high accuracy. We further examine the algorithm performance for desktop testing dataset (i.e., D_2). In Table 3, the overall accuracy seems to be even better for both goal and mission identification (comparing to D_1). This confirms that our classifiers are robust in identifying search goals and search missions.

Table 3: Clustering performance on D_1 and D_2

	Goal/mission	Acc.	Acc. same	Acc. diff.
D_1	Goal	0.8700	0.7117	0.9017
	Mission	0.8424	0.8160	0.8747
D_2	Goal	0.9122	0.7484	0.9816
	Mission	0.8586	0.7724	0.9715

5. CHARACTERIZING MOBILE SEARCH SEQUENCE STRUCTURE

This section provides a large-scale analysis of search sequence structures with millions of mobile and desktop search sessions randomly sampled from one-week search log of the Yahoo search engine (i.e., Week 3 in Figure 1). In particular, we focus on analyzing how mobile search goals/missions differ from desktop search goals/missions. Note that the following statistical significance is reported based on Wilcoxon singed-rank test since data is not normally distributed.

Goal/Mission/Session Length. Table 4 reports a list of descriptive statistics about the metric difference between mobile and desktop for the query-goal-mission structure. The difference is computed in the following way. First, we calculate the mean values of each metric in Table 4 for both mobile and desktop. Then, the mobile metric value is subtracted by the desktop metric value for computing the difference. We find that #goals/mission is relatively stable across different devices, meaning that people tend to frame their information needs with a steady hierarchical structure. However, a desktop session contains more queries, goals and missions, which may indicate that people on desktop are more likely to arrange a continuous time slot (i.e., a session) to complete more goals and missions, while people may need multiple discrete time periods on mobile devices to complete the same number of goals and missions.

Regarding the goal and mission lengths, we find that a search goal/mission contains more queries on mobile than on desktop. This finding may be because mobile search goals/missions are more complex than desktop, and thus require more queries to complete; or because mobile search queries are more likely to fail, requiring more frequent query refinement for each goal. In analyzing the first scenario, we find no substantial difference for #goals/mission between mobile and desktop (on the contrary, this number is slightly larger on desktop). For the second hypothesis, goal/mission duration analysis provides more insights; however, further experiments are needed to test this hypothesis in the future.

Table 4: The differences of goal/mission/session metrics between mobile and desktop.

Measurements	Δ = desktop - mobile	Sig.
Δ(#queries/goal)	-0.1913	p<0.001
Δ(#queries/mission)	-0.2172	p<0.001
Δ(#queries/session)	0.2461	p<0.001
Δ(#goals/session)	0.4082	p<0.001
Δ(#missions/session)	0.3251	p<0.001
Δ(#goals/mission)	0.0012	p<0.001

Goal/Mission Duration. Following [10], we define the goal/mission duration as the time difference between the first query and the last query within the search goal/mission. Same as the above analysis, we also compute the goal/mission duration difference between desktop and mobile. The above analysis indicates that a mobile search goal/mission contains more queries than desktop. Thus, we expect that a goal/mission lasts longer on mobile. We do find that mobile search goals are longer (4.8 seconds longer on mobile than desktop); however, mobile search missions are actually significantly shorter (30.6 seconds longer on desktop than mobile). This indicates that people spent less time on mobile for each query. It is possible that users do not spend as much time exploring search results associated with failed queries, and quickly refine and resubmit another query.

Goal/Mission Interleaving. Multitasking is a common behavior on search engines. Our findings support that search goals and missions are sometimes interleaved with other goals and missions. Therefore, we compute the percentages of interleaved goals and missions on both desktop and mobile devices and provide the results in Table 5. We find that the overall interleaving percentage is relatively small since most of the search sequences only have one goal and one mission. Besides, search missions are more likely to be interleaved than search goals since a search goal usually refers to a simple easy-to-achieve sub-task while a search mission may last for a longer time. More interestingly, compared to mobile search, desktop search has more interleaved goals and missions. This may either indicate that people tend to be more focused on mobile or suggest that the current support for mobile multitasking search is still insufficient. We expect that this situation may change as mobile search interfaces continue to evolve. Our goal/mission interleaving analysis will similarly need to evolve as these supportive interfaces change.

Table 5: Goal/mission interleaving percentages. A number in bold (italics) indicates a significance comparing goal and mission (mobile and desktop).

	mobile		desktop	
measurements	goal	mission	goal	mission
Mean	0.0299	**0.0319**	*0.0321*	***0.0481***

Summary. The above analysis provides several interesting findings for mobile search sequence structures. First, comparing to desktop search, we find that people are likely to search for simpler missions on mobile devices. However, we still observe that people tend to issue more queries on mobile. This suggests that mobile search requires further improvement on effectiveness. Second, we find that mobile search tends to have fewer goal/mission interleaving, which might be related to a lack of effective support for mobile multitasking. Future studies may focus on developing proper techniques/interfaces for search task switching. Third, observing the differences among search goals/missions/sessions, we believe that session-based search analysis in prior studies should be re-examined at a more fine-grained level such as on top of search goals and missions.

6. MOBILE SEARCH EVALUATION WITH GOALS AND MISSIONS

To understand the usefulness of the hierarchical query sequence structure, this section explores its application in defining better user satisfaction metrics (e.g., search success and search abandonment). Existing user satisfaction metrics are mostly measured at the query or session level. With the identified goals and missions, we are able to measure user satisfaction at four different levels (query, goal, mission and session) and make comparisons. Here, we focus on metrics for mobile search in particular.

6.1 Experiment Setup

To understand the effectiveness of a user satisfaction metric, the canonical method is to manually label a large set of search queries with user satisfaction levels [6, 9]. A better user satisfaction metric should be highly correlated with the labeled data. However, this is hard to scale. Our paper adopts an alternative approach by correlating the defined user satisfaction metrics with users' long-term engagement metric [1]. The underlying assumption is that if users are satisfied with the search in the short term, they are more likely to engage with the search system in the long run. Therefore, a strong correlation with the long-term engagement indicates a good user satisfaction measurement.

A typical metric that measures long term engagement is number of sessions per day per user. This metric is not very sensitive and usually needs to be tracked for a long term. To conduct the experiment, we tracked individual users in a stable, controlled experimentation environment for five weeks in the Yahoo search engine. We then used the first week as the qualifying period to compute the short-term user satisfaction metrics such as query success rate and query abandonment rate for each user. The subsequent four weeks were used to compute the long-term engagement metric - number of sessions per day per user. We then looked at the correlation between the short-term and long-term metrics, which is indicated by the goodness-of-fit (we use R^2) in the regression model. Higher R^2 indicates a stronger correlation thus better predictive power. Through this study, we can compare the goal/mission level user satisfaction metrics against the query/session level user satisfaction metrics to find out if they can predict long-term engagement more accurately.

6.2 Measuring Search Success

A widely used signal for measuring search success is click with dwell time longer than 30 seconds (i.e., long-dwell click). Although this cutoff is derived from desktop search logs, it is widely used in mobile search as well [18]. Thus, we set 30 seconds as the cutoff for long dwell click in our experiments. We consider the following four metrics to measure search success at the query, goal, mission and session levels, respectively. Then, we compare the R^2 of each search success metric in predicting the long term engagement metric (Table 6).

- query success rate: #queries with long-dwell clicks divided by total #queries.
- goal success rate: #goals for which the last query has long-dwell clicks divided by total #goals.
- mission success rate: #missions for which the last query has long-dwell clicks divided by total #missions.
- session success rate: #sessions for which the last query has long-dwell clicks divided by total #sessions.

According to Table 6, all of the four search success metrics have significant correlations with the long term engagement metric. Among the four metrics, goal success rate achieves the best performance for the long term engagement. The relatively low performance of query success rate is likely due to the unmeasured presence of query reformulations. Researchers have found that query reformulation can indicate satisfaction more accurately than pure clicks [6]. If a following query is a similar query submitted within a short time interval, even though the current query has a long dwell click, it may still indicate dissatisfaction because the user has not completed the task. Therefore, measuring goal success rate using the last query in a goal has the best correlation with the long term metric. The mission and session success rate also show strong correlations with long-term engagement. However, they do not provide any further benefits compared to the goal success rate.

Table 6: Correlation analysis of different success and abandonment metrics for predicting long term engagement. $*/\diamond/\dagger$ denotes a significant increase comparing to query/session/mission success rate (or session/query/goal abandonment rate).

Level	R^2 **(success rate)**	R^2**(abandonment rate)**
query	*0.6738*	0.7404 $\diamond$
session	0.7338 $*$	*0.6949*
goal	0.7485 $* \diamond \dagger$	0.7627 $* \diamond$
mission	0.7473 $* \diamond$	0.7845 $* \diamond \dagger$

6.3 Measuring Search Abandonment

Search queries without any result clicks, called search abandonment, is often viewed as an important behavior signal for measuring user dissatisfaction. However, not all abandonment is bad. When users are able to get direct answers from a search result page, they may be satisfied without the need to click on any results [13]. When defining search abandonment for user dissatisfaction, we remove all the queries with good abandonment by examining the direct answer on the search result page. As in our analysis of search success, we define four search abandonment metrics at the query, goal, mission and session level respectively. We then examine the R^2 of each search abandonment metric with the long term engagement metric. The search abandonment metrics we investigated:

- query abandonment rate: #queries with no click divided by total #queries.
- goal abandonment rate: #goals for which the last query has no click divided by total #goals.
- mission abandonment rate: #missions for which the last query has no click divided by total #missions.
- session abandonment rate: #sessions for which the last query has no click divided by total #sessions.

The results are shown in Table 6. All four abandonment metrics show significant correlations with long-term engagement. Among the four metrics, we observe that the session abandonment rate has the lowest correlation with long term engagement. This finding might be because the traditional session definition does not measure task boundaries accurately. When segmenting query sequences more precisely with goals or missions, we do find significant improvements. In addition, if a no-click query is the last query in a goal, but not the last query in a mission, it's possible that users may still get some information from the search results which inspires the next search goal in the same mission. When the last query in a mission has no click, it's very likely that the user has given up searching for related information. Thus, the mission abandonment rate is better aligned with users' search satisfaction, and thus their long term engagement with the search engine.

7. CONCLUSION AND FUTURE WORK

This paper developed an automatic algorithm to identify query-goal-mission structures from mobile query sequences. The algorithm can effectively extract and incorporate features derived from both mobile and desktop search logs, and produced good performance on multiple datasets. We further applied this algorithm in a web-scale search logs, and found several significant differences in goal/mission length, goal/mission duration and goal/mission interleaving behaviors between mobile and desktop. Compared to desktop search, mobile users tend to handle fewer and simpler search missions within a session, issue more queries within a goal and a mission, and exhibit decreased goal/mission interleaving behaviors. We also examined the utility of the identified hierarchical query sequence structure by applying it to define user satisfaction metrics. We find that the goal-based search success rate and mission-based abandonment rate can predict the long-term user engagement more accurately than the query and session-based metrics.

Defining user satisfaction metrics is only one application of the hierarchical structure. The hierarchical query structure can also be applied to other problems, such as re-ranking relevant search results, recommending and suggesting search queries. We would like to explore these topics in the future. We additionally plan to study this same query structure in a cross-session, rather than within-session, context.

8. REFERENCES

[1] A. Drutsa, G. Gusev, and P. Serdyukov. Future user engagement prediction and its application to improve the sensitivity of online experiments. In *WWW*, pages 256–266, 2015.

[2] H. Feild and J. Allan. Task-aware query recommendation. In *SIGIR*, pages 83–92, 2013.

[3] D. Guan, S. Zhang, and H. Yang. Utilizing query change for session search. In *SIGIR*, pages 453–462, 2013.

[4] S. Han, D. He, Z. Yue, and P. Brusilovsky. Supporting cross-device web search with social navigation-based mobile touch interactions. In *UMAP*, pages 143–155, 2015.

[5] S. Han, Z. Yue, and D. He. Understanding and supporting cross-device web search for exploratory tasks with mobile touch interactions. *TOIS*, 33(4):16, 2015.

[6] A. Hassan, X. Shi, N. Craswell, and B. Ramsey. Beyond clicks: Query reformulation as a predictor of search satisfaction. In *CIKM*, pages 2019–2028, 2013.

[7] D. He, A. Göker, and D. J. Harper. Combining evidence for automatic web session identification. *IP&M*, 38(5):727–742, 2002.

[8] J. Jiang, S. Han, J. Wu, and D. He. Pitt at trec 2011 session track. In *TREC*, 2011.

[9] J. Jiang, A. Hassan Awadallah, X. Shi, and R. W. White. Understanding and predicting graded search satisfaction. In *WSDM*, pages 57–66, 2015.

[10] R. Jones and K. L. Klinkner. Beyond the session timeout: automatic hierarchical segmentation of search topics in query logs. In *CIKM*, pages 699–708, 2008.

[11] E. Kanoulas, B. Carterette, P. D. Clough, and M. Sanderson. Evaluating multi-query sessions. In *SIGIR*, pages 1053–1062, 2011.

[12] D. Lagun, C.-H. Hsieh, D. Webster, and V. Navalpakkam. Towards better measurement of attention and satisfaction in mobile search. In *SIGIR*, pages 113–122. ACM, 2014.

[13] J. Li, S. Huffman, and A. Tokuda. Good abandonment in mobile and pc internet search. In *SIGIR*, pages 43–50, 2009.

[14] L. Li, H. Deng, Y. He, A. Dong, Y. Chang, and H. Zha. Behavior driven topic transition for search task identification. In *WWW*, pages 555–565, 2016.

[15] Z. Liao, Y. Song, L.-w. He, and Y. Huang. Evaluating the effectiveness of search task trails. In *WWW*, pages 489–498, 2012.

[16] C. Lucchese, S. Orlando, R. Perego, F. Silvestri, and G. Tolomei. Discovering tasks from search engine query logs. *TOIS*, 31(3):14, 2013.

[17] C. D. Manning and H. Schütze. *Foundations of statistical natural language processing*. MIT press, 1999.

[18] M. Shokouhi and Q. Guo. From queries to cards: Re-ranking proactive card recommendations based on reactive search history. In *SIGIR*, pages 695–704. ACM, 2015.

[19] Y. Song, H. Ma, H. Wang, and K. Wang. Exploring and exploiting user search behavior on mobile and tablet devices to improve search relevance. In *WWW*, pages 1201–1212, 2013.

[20] Y. Wang, X. Huang, and R. W. White. Characterizing and supporting cross-device search tasks. In *WSDM*, pages 707–716. ACM, 2013.

[21] R. W. White, W. Chu, A. Hassan, X. He, Y. Song, and H. Wang. Enhancing personalized search by mining and modeling task behavior. In *WWW*, pages 1411–1420, 2013.

Combining Powers of Two Predictors in Optimizing Real-Time Bidding Strategy under Constrained Budget

Chi-Chun Lin[†*] Kun-Ta Chuang[‡§] Wush Chi-Hsuan Wu[†*] Ming-Syan Chen[†¶]
Department of Electrical Engineering, National Taiwan University, Taiwan, R.O.C.[†]
Department of Computer Science and Information Engineering, National Cheng Kung University, Taiwan, R.O.C.[‡]
{megaacc.lin, wush978}@gmail.com[*] ktchuang@mail.ncku.edu.tw[§] mschen@ntu.edu.tw[¶]

ABSTRACT

We address the bidding strategy design problem faced by a Demand-Side Platform (DSP) in Real-Time Bidding (RTB) advertising. A RTB campaign consists of various parameters and usually a predefined budget. Under the budget constraint of a campaign, designing an optimal strategy for bidding on each impression to acquire as many clicks as possible is a main job of a DSP. State-of-the-art bidding algorithms rely on a single predictor, namely the clickthrough rate (CTR) predictor, to calculate the bidding value for each impression. This provides reasonable performance if the predictor has appropriate accuracy in predicting the probability of user clicking. However when the predictor gives only moderate accuracy, classical algorithms fail to capture optimal results. We improve the situation by accomplishing an additional winning price predictor in the bidding process. In this paper, a method combining powers of two prediction models is proposed, and experiments with real world RTB datasets from benchmarking the new algorithm with a classic CTR-only method are presented. The proposed algorithm performs better with regard to both number of clicks achieved and effective cost per click in many different settings of budget constraints.

1. INTRODUCTION

Online display advertisement (AD) is the main source of revenue for Internet business. After years of evolution, the mechanism of display AD has changed from the pre-allocated style to keyword-based matching of sponsored search, and recently advanced to the per-impression manner of Real-Time Bidding (RTB) paradigm [2]. Via real-time auctions, the RTB solution enables automatic AD impressions selling and purchasing between advertisers and publishers. According to Google's white paper [2], RTB has been promisingly recognized as the leading mechanism for online AD markets. Participants in the RTB ecosystem include publishers, Supply-Side Platforms (SSPs), advertisers, Demand-Side Platforms (DSPs), AD exchanges and networks, and users surfing on the Internet. While a user visits a Web page or activates a mobile app of a publisher with an AD slot available, the attributes of this user and the AD slot are sent via the AD exchange to the DSP. DSP will determine whether the pair, consisting of the user and the slot, conforms to the targeting rules of its customers (advertisers), and decide whether to acquire this impression to display the AD provided by the advertisers in real time. If this impression is of interest, a bidding value is calculated and sent to the AD exchange for auction. Typically, a *second price auction* is held to select the winner. That is, the auction winner, who sent the highest bidding price, will pay the second highest bidding value among all bidders in the auction to the publisher and get her AD displayed. This amount paid by the advertiser is regarded as the *winning price* (WP) of the impression in the auction. Refer to Figure 1 for an illustration of the RTB auction flow. Details of the RTB mechanism can be found in [7].

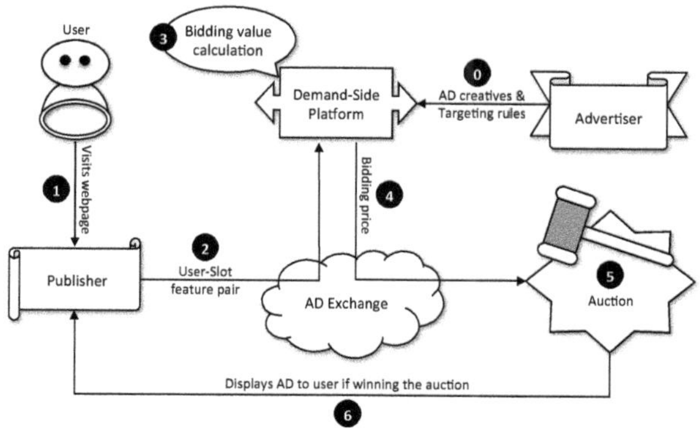

Figure 1: An illustration of the RTB auction flow.

DSP plays an important role on behalf of advertisers in the RTB ecosystem. Its primary task is to determine the bidding price for each incoming AD impression opportunity in real time where the price has to reflect the value of the impression. Typically an impression's value is evaluated by key performance indicators (KPIs) such as clickthrough rate (CTR) or conversion rate (CVR). An impression with a higher expected KPI will be assigned a greater bidding value. There have been works in the literature studying strategies that help the DSP to calculate the bidding price from the expected KPI of an impression. State-of-the-art optimal bidding algorithms rely on a single input, namely the CTR or CVR predictor, to calculate the bidding value. The optimal performance will result from a predictor that correctly estimates the related KPI. If the predictor can merely acquire moderate accuracy, however, it is expected that this kind of solutions will fail to capture optimal results.

In the literature, there have been works regarding the prediction of an impression's winning price from its features. With the winning price becoming directly predictable under reasonable accuracy, we are able to improve the quality of the bidding strategy. Specifically, if an additional winning price predictor is accomplished in the bidding process, the computed bidding value will be able to reflect the true value of an impression more precisely and enhance the overall efficiency for the bidding process of the AD campaign. This sort of framework could provide better results than

CIKM'16, October 24-28, 2016, Indianapolis, IN, USA
 ISBN 978-1-4503-4073-1/16/10...$15.00
DOI: http://dx.doi.org/10.1145/2983323.2983656

previous models relying on a single KPI predictor. We propose in this paper a new method combining powers of two prediction models, namely CTR and WP predictors. We first describe shortcomings of classical single predictor methods, and then develop our new algorithm. The efficiency of the algorithm is shown by analogy to the well known online stochastic knapsack problem. We also perform experiments to benchmark the proposed method with one of the classic strategies. The experimental results show that our method, when applied on real world RTB datasets, performs better with regard to both number of clicks achieved and effective cost per click in many different settings of budget constraints.

The contributions of this work are multi-fold. (1) We describe the shortcomings of classical bidding schemes and address their non-optimality. (2) We develop a new algorithm that utilizes two prediction models and discuss its optimality. (3) To the best of our knowledge, we are the first to combine two predictors in designing a bidding strategy for RTB. (4) Experiments with real world datasets are performed to assess the efficiency of the new method. We also set up a formal procedure for benchmarking RTB bidding algorithms by adopting the competitive analysis.

2. PRELIMINARIES

2.1 Related Work

Online computational AD is a rapid evolving area with a number of sub-disciplines. Among them, RTB has attracted more and more research interests in recent years. Works in RTB concern various aspects including *bid landscape forecasting* [1], *bid winning price prediction* [8], and *bidding strategy design* [10, 5, 9]. Interested readers can refer to [7] for the comprehensive review.

Two state-of-the-art bidding strategies are discussed in [5, 10] both with the performance measured in terms of number of clicks achieved in the campaign lifetime under a certain budget constraint. In [5], the bidding value is determined by a linear function of the predicted CTR of an impression. The work [10] develops a new function which is in a concave instead of linear relationship with the predicted CTR. It is supposed that the algorithm named ORTB in [10] be optimal if only one prediction model, namely the CTR predictor, can be used. We propose to further increase the performance of the bidding function if one additional estimator, the WP predictor, is incorporated into the bidding value calculation.

The work [4] employs the similar idea of incorporating winning price prediction into the bidding value computation. However, it considers only the winning price predictor while we take into account CTR and WP predictors simultaneously. To sum up, there have been works concerning bidding strategy design on top of the CTR predictor or the WP predictor, but existing ones design their algorithms with either one of the two. We are the first, to the best of our knowledge, who incorporate both of the two predictors in developing an optimal RTB bidding algorithm.

2.2 Problem Formulation

We start by formally stating the problem to be addressed. Note that there are various pricing schemes in RTB and we limit our discussion to CPM (cost per mille) pricing. In light of CPM, the price of winning an auction is immediately charged by the publisher after the advertiser's AD creative is displayed, regardless of whatever the user's action after seeing the AD. Also, the second price auction mechanism is assumed. Given the set of impression opportunities $\psi : \{\vec{x}_1, \vec{x}_2, ..., \vec{x}_n\}$ of a campaign with each impression represented by its *feature vector* $\vec{x}_i | 1 \leq i \leq n$, and the campaign budget B, we wish to obtain as many clicks as possible by bidding on these impressions while keeping the total expense under the budget constraint. We have to decide 1) Whether to place a bid on each $\vec{x}_i$ or not, and 2) If it is to bid, what is the bidding value? We denote the outcome (click or not) of winning $\vec{x}_i$ by an indicator variable $I(\vec{x}_i)$ where $I(\vec{x}_i)$ equals 1 if winning $\vec{x}_i$ leads to a click and 0 otherwise. The exact cost of $\vec{x}_i$ is denoted by $P(\vec{x}_i)$, which means the actual amount to be paid for winning $\vec{x}_i$. That is, $P(\vec{x}_i)$ is the winning price of $\vec{x}_i$. If bidding with $b(\vec{x}_i)$ does not win the auction for $\vec{x}_i$, $I(\vec{x}_i)$ and $P(\vec{x}_i)$ will be both 0. Now the *Bidding Strategy Design* (BSD) problem is defined as follows.

DEFINITION **BSD**: Determine the bidding value $b(\vec{x}_i)$ for each $\vec{x}_i \in \psi$ to maximize $\sum_{i=1}^{n} I(\vec{x}_i)$, subject to $\sum_{i=1}^{n} P(\vec{x}_i) \leq B$.

Note that we answer both questions aforementioned by a single function $b(\cdot)$. Specifically, for the first question, if $b(\vec{x}_i)$ equals 0, we skip this impression and the corresponding $I(\vec{x}_i)$ and $P(\vec{x}_i)$ equal 0 consequently. Also keep in mind that $P(\vec{x}_i)$ is always less than $b(\vec{x}_i)$ since the auction is in a second price manner.

2.3 Challenges in Classical Algorithms

With the BSD problem formally formulated, we present a brief review on two classical algorithms, LIN [5] and ORTB [10], that rely on a single CTR predictor to determine the bidding value for an impression. LIN models an impression's bidding value as a linear function of its predicted CTR (denoted as $pCTR$ hereafter) by

$$b_{LIN}(\vec{x}_i) = \lambda_{LIN} \cdot pCTR(\vec{x}_i). \quad (1)$$

ORTB calculates the bidding value for an impression from a concave-shaped function of its $pCTR$ as[1]

$$b_{ORTB}(\vec{x}_i) = \sqrt{\frac{c}{\lambda_{ORTB}} \cdot pCTR(\vec{x}_i) + c^2} - c. \quad (2)$$

In these two equations, λ_{LIN}, λ_{ORTB} and c are tunable parameters of the corresponding algorithms. Clearly, they both produce the bidding value for an impression from the predicted CTR. LIN is a so-called *truth telling* strategy emphasizing that an impression's bidding value should be linearly proportional to its expected usefulness, while ORTB is also truth telling except that it models the bidding value by a slightly complicated yet still monotonically increasing function of the worth expectation of an impression.

While the corresponding works of LIN and ORTB demonstrated their effectiveness, we now claim and prove that these classical algorithms cannot lead to the optimal result.

THEOREM 1. *Classical BSD algorithms relying on merely a single CTR predictor cannot be optimal.*

PROOF. We prove by giving a counterexample. Consider a campaign with $B = 130$ and 4 impressions shown in the right of Figure 2 (ignore the pWP and bid-eff. columns for now). Clearly, an optimal algorithm should place a bid on $\vec{W}$ and a bid on $\vec{Y}$ with $b(\vec{W}) > 80$ and $b(\vec{Y}) > 40$ while bidding on $\vec{X}$ and $\vec{Z}$ with $b(\vec{X}) < 60$ and $b(\vec{Z}) < 20$ if impressions can arrive in any order. Such a bidding scheme wins $\vec{W}$ and $\vec{Y}$ with total cost $120 < 130$ and obtains 2 clicks without wasting the budget on the non-clicking impressions $\vec{X}$ and $\vec{Z}$. However, neither ORTB nor LIN can achieve this no matter how their parameters are tuned. We plot the bidding/winning price – pCTR relationship for these impressions at the left part of Figure 2. The dotted curve conforms to the optimal bidding strategy, which is in a shape that none of the two algorithms' bidding function can possibly be. It is because the dotted curve corresponds

[1]There is another variant with a more complicated model in [10], but it performs similarly to the one presented here. As such, we omit the discussion of that alternative.

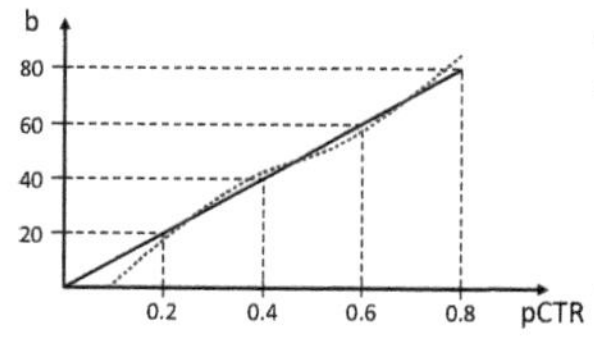

Imp.	Click	pCTR	WP	pWP	bid-eff.
$\vec{W}$	1	0.8	80	82	0.009756
$\vec{X}$	0	0.6	60	62	0.009677
$\vec{Y}$	1	0.4	40	41	0.009756
$\vec{Z}$	0	0.2	20	21	0.009524

Figure 2: An illustrative sample scenario of RTB campaign.

to a polynomial of degree 3, while the degree of ORTB's function is only 2, not to speak of the degree-1 (linear) function of LIN. □

It might be argued that, however, one is able to design a bidding function with a polynomial of degree 3 or greater. But please note that the sample campaign is just an over-simplified scenario consisting of only 4 impressions. If the similar pattern of impressions such as $\vec{Z}, \vec{Y}, \vec{X}$ (ordered by increasing pCTR first, and then the click pattern happens to be $0, 1, 0$) or $\vec{Y}, \vec{X}, \vec{W}$ (click pattern $1, 0, 1$) occurs repeatedly in a campaign (this is inevitable since the CTR predictor has limited accuracy), one will need to design a bidding function of an unrealistic high degree, which sounds meaningless and whose relationship of bidding value versus predicted CTR is difficult to be explained. Hence, we emphasis that in addition to the predicted CTR, other factors should also be considered in designing the bidding strategy in order to deal with the stochastic relationship of the actual click behavior versus the predicted CTR.

2.4 Dataset Overview and Intuition

We use the iPinYou dataset[2] to develop our algorithm and perform experiments. The dataset is a collection of real world RTB DSP logs used in a bidding algorithm competition held in 2013[3]. It consists of 3 seasons' data. For each season, the competition officer released to participants a training set for algorithm development and parameter tuning, as well as a testing set for validation and offline leaderboard benchmarking. A thorough analysis report on this dataset can be found in [11].

According to the argument of [1], the winning bid prices of auctions in RTB follow the log-normal distribution. A trivial extension can be made as: in RTB, the winning bid prices of auctions for impressions *with user clickthrough* also follow the log-normal distribution. Moreover, inspired by [8] that proposed a method for predicting individual impression's winning price directly from its feature vector, we are able to develop a BSD solution utilizing the characteristic of the winning price distribution of a campaign as well as the predicted winning price of each impression in the campaign. The algorithms will be described in the next section.

3. METHODOLOGY

In this section, our BSD algorithms are presented. The algorithms are divided into two phases. The first phase inputs the training dataset and trains the models required in the second phase while the latter phase determines the actual bidding price for each impression in the online bidding process with the testing dataset. We discuss algorithms in two cases: one with perfect CTR and WP prediction, and the other with imperfect prediction. Though the perfect prediction can not possibly be realistic, we still deliberate it because it helps us gain some insight into the development of an algorithm under the condition of imperfect prediction.

3.1 Perfect Prediction: Algorithm PERF

When the CTR and WP predictors are flawless (in other words, having 100% prediction accuracy), what we are concerned about is to spend the budget in the most efficient way so that we can acquire the most clicks with the lowest budget consumption. The algorithm is called PERF and its two phases are described below.

Phase 1 (model training)
Input:
Impression logs
Output:
I - Click predictor
P - Winning price (cost) predictor
Ω - Campaign's PDF of winning prices with click
N_{tr}, N_{te} - Number of impressions with click

The click predictor I is used to forecast whether an impression opportunity will have clickthrough or not. The impression is represented by a feature vector $\vec{x}$ consisting of user attributes (e.g., age, gender, location), AD attributes (e.g., dimension, visibility, title) and attributes from the publisher side (e.g., URL/App name, content category). For some $\vec{x}$, we are sure that $I(\vec{x})$ is either 1 or 0 because it is predicted perfectly. The winning price predictor P reveals the winning price (i.e., cost) $P(\vec{x})$ for $\vec{x}$. For approximation in practice, I can be trained by some well known binary classification methods (e.g., SVM, random forest), and P can be learned by the censored regression proposed in [8]. The distribution PDF Ω can be obtained by simply calculating the average and standard deviation of winning prices from impression logs with clickthrough since we know it conforms to the log-normal distribution, or alternatively by the more sophisticated method described in [1]. The number of impressions with click serves as a basis for estimating the number of clicking impressions from the testing campaign under the assumption that both training and testing sets exhibit similar distributions. We just count the number of impressions with click from the training set, and multiply it by the ratio of campaign lifetime to produce the expected number of clicking impressions of the testing campaign. That is, $N_{te} = N_{tr} \times \frac{T_{te}}{T_{tr}}$ where T_{tr} and T_{te} is the campaign lifetime of training and testing sets respectively. I, P, Ω and N_{te} will be used in the online bidding phase as follows.

Phase 2 (online bidding)
Input:
B - Campaign budget
$\vec{x}$ - Individual impression feature vector
State variable:
B_{cur} - Current budget available, initialized as B
Output:
$b(\vec{x})$ - Bid value for $\vec{x}$ (0 means don't bid on $\vec{x}$)
Procedure:

1. Solve $\int_0^{\beta} p\, N_{te}\, \Omega(p)\, \mathrm{d}p = B$ for β to obtain the value p_{bound}.
2. Input an impression $\vec{x}$. Check if $I(\vec{x}) = 1$. If yes, go to Step 3. Otherwise return 0 and continue with the next impression. Stop if there is no impression left.
3. Use $P(\vec{x})$ to obtain the expected cost for $\vec{x}$.
4. If $P(\vec{x}) \leq B_{cur}$ and $P(\vec{x}) \leq p_{bound}$, return $P(\vec{x}) + \delta$ where δ is a small amount (can be the minimum unit of currency accepted in the auction) and update B_{cur} accordingly as Step 5. Otherwise return 0 and go back to Step 2.
5. $B_{cur} := B_{cur} - P(\vec{x})$ if bidding with $P(\vec{x}) + \delta$ on $\vec{x}$ wins the auction. If B_{cur} becomes 0, or there is no impression left, then stop. Otherwise go back to Step 2.

Here are details of the design. With the perfect click predictor, we know whether an impression will lead to a click or not, thus we skip all impressions with $I(\vec{x}) = 0$ and proceed further only with

[2] Downloaded from http://data.computational-advertising.org
[3] See http://contest.ipinyou.com

those having $I(\vec{x}) = 1$ in Step 2. For each clicking impressions, we know its exact cost by the perfect WP predictor $P(\vec{x})$. To allocate the budget to acquire as many clicks as possible, we begin spending on impressions with the cheapest price and proceed to those with higher prices gradually until all budget is consumed, or until the campaign has passed all over. The integral in Step 1 and the comparison of $P(\vec{x})$ with p_{bound} in Step 3 reflects this strategy.

3.2 Imperfect Prediction: Algorithm PRUD

In this subsection we discuss the case when the CTR and WP predictions are imperfect since it is impossible to have perfect predictors in reality. The algorithm is called PRUD (naming inspired by "a *prudent* bidder") and also consists of two phases.

Phase 1 (model training)
Input:
Impression logs
Output:
$pCTR$ - CTR predictor
pWP - Winning price (cost) predictor
ρ_{cut} - bid efficiency cutoff value

The training phase has three outputs, two of which are CTR predictor and WP predictor. To train the CTR predictor, we refer to the logistic regression proposed in [6]. The censored regression [8] is used in WP model training. In addition, a *bid efficiency cutoff* value is produced. The bid efficiency ρ of an impression $\vec{x}$ is defined as:

$$\rho(\vec{x}) = pCTR(\vec{x}) \,/\, pWP(\vec{x}). \quad (3)$$

The bid efficiency corresponds to the following argument. When an impression is with a high CTR, we would have a strong intention to bid on it because the expected revenue is high due to the high clickthrough rate (i.e., probability of click). However, when an impression has a relatively low CTR but is accompanied with a low predicted WP, it could still be reasonable to "invest" on this impression since even if it ends up with no clickthrough eventually, the loss of investment is insignificant due to the low price (cost). That is, we use the predicted CTR and WP simultaneously to determine whether an impression is worthy of spending our budget. The *higher CTR* and *lower WP* an impression has (thus *bigger* ρ), the more valuable it appears. Therefore, we define the bid efficiency as dividing CTR by WP to reflect this intuition.

After defining the bid efficiency for an impression, we now face a problem: to or not to bid on an impression with a certain bid efficiency value? To remedy it, we use the training dataset to perform a search for a *cutoff* value, that is, the lowest ρ value acceptable for this campaign under a predefined budget constraint. When an impression has a ρ higher than or equal to the cutoff value, we bid on it with the predicted WP plus a small lift-up value (since it is a second price auction). Otherwise the impression is skipped. We find the cutoff value that results in the most clicks achieved in a campaign's training period under some budget constraint. And then, the same cutoff value is used as the threshold in the same campaign's testing period with the same condition of budget constraint.

We now present the online bidding algorithm as follows.

Phase 2 (online bidding)
Input:
B - Campaign budget
$\vec{x}$ - Individual impression feature vector
State variable:
B_{cur} - Current budget available, initialized as B
Output:
$b(\vec{x})$ - Bid value for $\vec{x}$ (0 means don't bid on $\vec{x}$)
Procedure:

1. Input an impression $\vec{x}$. Check if $\rho(\vec{x}) \geq \rho_{cut}$. If yes, go to Step 2. Otherwise return 0 and continue with the next impression. Stop if there is no impression left.
2. If $pWP(\vec{x}) \leq B_{cur}$, return $pWP(\vec{x}) + \delta$ where δ is a small amount (can be the minimum unit of currency accepted in the auction) and update B_{cur} accordingly as Step 3. Otherwise return 0 and go back to Step 1.
3. $B_{cur} := B_{cur} - P(\vec{x})$ if bidding with $pWP(\vec{x}) + \delta$ on $\vec{x}$ wins the auction and its exact winning price is $P(\vec{x})$. If B_{cur} becomes 0, or there is no impression left, then stop. Otherwise go back to Step 1.

An illustrative example for PRUD. Recall the sample campaign in Figure 2. The predicted winning prices for the four impressions and their corresponding bid efficiencies are listed at the pWP and bid-eff. columns respectively. Setting ρ_{cut} to 0.0097, PRUD picks up $\vec{W}$ and $\vec{Y}$, discards $\vec{X}$ and $\vec{Z}$, and produces the optimal result of 2 clicks with budget consumption 120.

3.3 PRUD and Knapsack Problem

It is worth noting that we can relate BSD to the well known *knapsack problem* (KP). We regard each bidding impression opportunity $\vec{x}_i$ as a stone with value v_i and weight w_i. We have a knapsack capable of holding stones and its capacity is W. Our goal is to load the knapsack with as valuable stones as possible while keeping the total weight under the knapsack capacity. For the analogy of PRUD to KP, the value v_i of a stone $\vec{x}_i$ is the corresponding CTR prediction $pCTR(\vec{x}_i)$ and the stone's weight w_i is the associated predicted cost $pWP(\vec{x}_i)$. The campaign budget B is considered as the knapsack capacity W. There are many forms of KP and here we are dealing with the *online stochastic* variant. Specifically, we do not know the characteristic portfolio of all stones in advance. Instead, the stones are coming one after another thus we can inspect a stone's value and weight only after receiving one, and then decide whether to pack it or not immediately on the fly. Once a stone has been packed, we are unable to discard it afterwards. Nor can we reconsider a previously unpacked stone later again. The book [3] provides excellent discussion and algorithms for various types of KP problems. For the online stochastic one, an algorithm named *THRESHOLD* is given as follows. First, an *efficiency threshold* T is defined. Then upon receiving a stone $\vec{x}_i$, its efficiency is calculated by v_i/w_i and compared with T. If the efficiency is greater than or equal to T, the stone is packed. Otherwise the stone is discarded. Each stone is handled sequentially in the coming order until finally the knapsack capacity is exhausted or all stones have been processed. Unfortunately there is no guaranteed optimal solution for the online stochastic KP. The THRESHOLD algorithm is a semi-optimal one if the threshold value T is carefully determined. In our BSD context, algorithm PRUD learns the best threshold value by tuning the bid efficiency cutoff value with the training dataset. Provided the testing dataset has a distribution of impressions similar to the training dataset, and the budget is set to a fixed percentage of the sum of all impressions' cost (say, 1/16 of $\sum P(\vec{x}_i)$), the same cutoff value learned from the training phase can be used in the online bidding phase to produce the same level of semi-optimal result.

4. EXPERIMENTS AND BENCHMARKING

We depict in this section our experiments for benchmarking the two algorithms PRUD and ORTB. We use the 9 campaigns in seasons 2 and 3 of the iPinYou dataset for the experiments because

Season	Cpg.	CTR AUC	WP_{pred} Avg.	WP_{real} Avg.	WP_{pred} RMSE	WP_{real} Stdev.	1/64 ORTB	1/64 PRUD	1/32 ORTB	1/32 PRUD	1/16 ORTB	1/16 PRUD	1/8 ORTB	1/8 PRUD	1/4 ORTB	1/4 PRUD	1/2 ORTB	1/2 PRUD
3	2259	0.8870	102.81	126.64	77.16	79.44	16.67	30.21	29.17	38.54	42.71	51.04	55.21	65.63	69.79	78.13	88.54	95.83
3	2261	0.8756	94.53	123.74	78.79	83.53	28.05	32.93	31.71	42.68	42.68	53.66	53.66	65.85	74.39	79.27	90.24	95.12
3	2821	0.8195	99.39	120.90	66.40	80.29	20.00	21.72	24.14	28.28	33.79	38.62	45.86	51.72	62.76	70.00	81.03	86.21
3	2997	0.7440	69.96	87.36	62.16	75.18	17.04	17.71	23.32	22.65	31.84	31.39	43.72	42.38	57.85	58.52	76.91	78.03
2	1458	0.9257	81.83	91.23	53.18	62.55	72.08	72.30	73.97	73.41	77.42	76.53	80.76	80.53	86.76	85.54	92.66	92.66
2	3358	0.9286	121.54	134.07	50.83	65.42	62.75	66.97	67.34	69.72	72.29	74.13	79.45	80.37	87.16	87.52	92.66	93.03
2	3386	0.8094	111.45	122.46	58.57	69.97	24.78	25.65	29.37	29.12	35.81	36.06	45.85	46.84	59.98	65.18	79.93	80.67
2	3427	0.9025	106.01	116.10	51.44	62.73	59.49	60.70	62.74	63.41	70.73	71.54	75.75	76.02	82.38	81.30	90.65	90.24
2	3476	0.8671	95.69	108.84	53.28	62.97	43.63	47.03	51.27	53.54	60.91	62.61	66.57	68.56	79.60	79.04	88.39	88.39

Table 1: Leftmost: Statistics of CTR and WP predictors. Rightmost: Benchmark results of ORTB versus PRUD in competitive ratio.

they provide a more comprehensive set of features than season 1. We first introduce the preparation of data, followed by some issues of predictor model training and algorithm tuning. Finally, the benchmark results are presented.

4.1 Implementation and Tuning

Data Preparation. It is known that PRUD performs best when training and testing sets express similar impression distributions. ORTB also tunes its parameters with the training set and operates in the testing phase with what learned, so that the same argument (best performance under similar training/testing distributions) holds naturally. Hence, we want to benchmark them under this condition. As such, we randomly sample 2/3 of impressions from the original iPinYou training set for each of the 9 campaigns to produce 9 new data collections which serve as our new training sets, and 1/3 of original training impressions to form the 9 new testing sets.

Feature Extraction. The predictor training requires a feature set as input. The iPinYou dataset provides 24 features and we select 17 of them. All features are extracted and converted to binary by dummy encoding. The number of converted features ranges from 87,845 for the smallest campaign to 510,357 for the largest one.

Predictor Quality. After feature extraction, CTR and WP predictors are trained respectively with L2-regularized logistic regression and censored regression. We list AUC (area under ROC curve) of CTR predictor and RMSE (root mean squared error) of WP predictor in the left of Table 1. The standard deviations of real winning prices and the average values for both predicted and real winning prices are depicted as well. These WP-related statistics are measured from impressions with click, excluding non-clicking ones. From the table, we see that CTR predictor performs well on season 2 but somewhat unsatisfactorily on season 3. Meanwhile, the RMSE values of WP predictor all fall within one standard deviation of real winning prices. It can be observed that the predictor has acceptable (but far from perfect) accuracy in predicting winning prices. Note that predicting an individual impression's winning price from its feature vector under RTB context is still a pioneer subject in the literature, and what we can do best currently is the model proposed by [8] which produces the moderate performance shown here. We will demonstrate that, however, incorporating such an ordinary predictor into algorithm PRUD adds considerable power in optimizing the bidding efficiency.

WP Predictor Lift Value. From Table 1, we see that WP predictor tends to underestimate[4] hence a proper *lift* value has to be added. Otherwise we will lose too many impressions if we just bid according to the original predicted prices. What follows is, how should the lift value be determined? It is difficult to be derived theoretically and after some experiments we decide to find the value empirically by a heuristic procedure. Specifically, we find the smallest L with the training data by the following inequality[5] for each campaign:

$$pWP(\vec{x}) + L > P(\vec{x}) \quad \text{for 95\% of} \quad \{\vec{x} \mid I(\vec{x}) = 1\}. \tag{4}$$

After L is determined, we use $pWP'(\vec{x}) = pWP(\vec{x}) + L$ as the new predicted WP for each $\vec{x}$ of the campaign. The lift value not only serves as a compensation to the underestimated winning price, but also acts as the δ value described in the online bidding phase of algorithm PRUD in Section 3.2. We regard L as another parameter of PRUD in addition to the bid efficiency cutoff value ρ_{cut}.

Tuning for ORTB. ORTB has two parameters: c and λ. We follow the ORTB work to tune them. Please refer to [10] for details.

Tuning for PRUD. PRUD also has two parameters. We have explained how the lift value L is determined. What remains is the bid efficiency cutoff value ρ_{cut}. Following the same scenario in [10], we set the budget as 1/64, 1/32, 1/16, 1/8, 1/4 and 1/2 respectively of the total cost of all impressions for each campaign. Since there are 9 campaigns, we have thus a total of $9 \times 6 = 54$ test cases. We use the training set to find the optimal ρ_{cut} that produces the largest number of clicks for each test case.

Tuning for PERF. Though PERF is not realizable in practice, we are still able to implement it because we have the complete testing data on hand. Recall the model training phase from Section 3.1. The click predictor, cost predictor and campaign PDF of winning prices with click (actually we use the exact composition of clicking impressions instead of the probability distribution) are readily revealed by scanning the whole testing data. We implement PERF and use it as the basis for comparing the relative performance of ORTB with PRUD to be discussed in the next subsection.

4.2 Benchmark Results

The results collected from applying each of the three algorithms on the prepared dataset are depicted in the right of Table 1. We follow the convention of *competitive analysis* and present the *competitive ratio* (CR) in the table. For each campaign-budget setting, we run PERF, ORTB and PRUD separately and then calculate the competitive ratio by dividing the number of clicks that ORTB or PRUD delivers by the number of clicks achieved by PERF:

$$CR = \frac{\#Click_{ORTB|PRUD}}{\#Click_{PERF}} \times 100\%. \tag{5}$$

PERF provides the upper-bound a bidding algorithm is able to reach and the competitive ratio indicates how well ORTB or PRUD can do compared to PERF. It can be observed that PRUD wins ORTB in 41 cases, loses to ORTB in 11 cases and ties with ORTB in 2 cases out of the total 54 cases. To ease the assessment, we also draw the CR chart by bar plot in Figure 3.

[4] This is expected as what has been discussed in [8].

[5] The percentage 95% is selected because it performs best among several values tested. 100% is not used because it will result in an extremely large lift value.

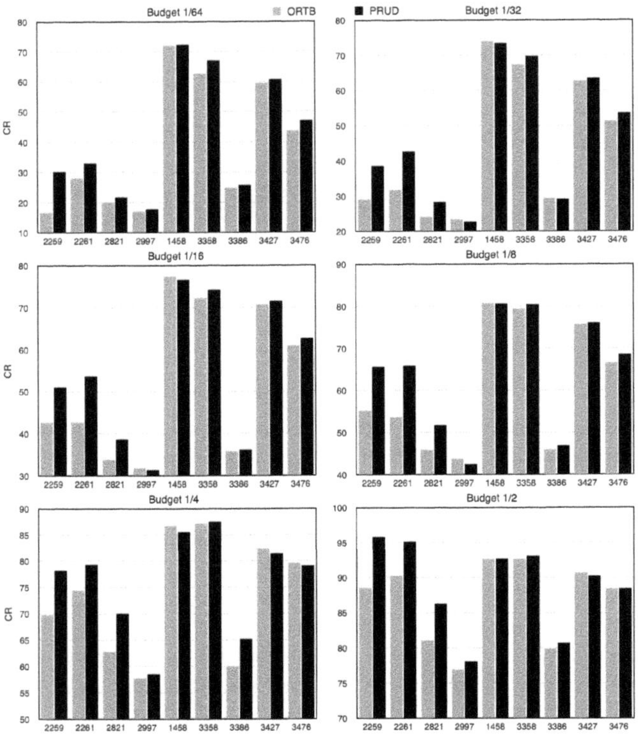

Figure 3: ORTB versus PRUD measured in competitive ratio.

Relation of AUC to algorithm performance. We find in general that, the lower AUC the CTR predictor for a campaign, the more improvement PRUD provides over ORTB. It is because that ORTB relies on merely the CTR predictor and thus a better prediction performance directly results in the delicacy of the final outcome of ORTB. On the other hand, PRUD incorporates additionally the WP predictor, and the WP predictor in some manner compensates the defect of the CTR predictor.

A plus in addition to clicks. We also show the performance comparison by *effective cost per click* (eCPC) in Figure 4. The eCPC is calculated by dividing the total cost of a campaign by the number of clicks obtained. The lower the eCPC is, the more cost-efficiency an algorithm provides. It can be seen that PRUD exhibits lower eCPC than ORTB in almost all cases (51 of 54, or 94%). Even for many cases that PRUD loses to ORTB in terms of number of clicks, PRUD still performs better if measured by eCPC. This is not surprising, though. Since we develop PRUD by starting from pursuing impressions with high bid efficiency while the efficiency is determined by dividing the predicted CTR (related to number of clicks) by the predicted winning price (related to cost), and this formula is in the reciprocal form of eCPC, PRUD favors eCPC (higher efficiency implying lower eCPC) naturally.

5. CONCLUDING REMARKS

In this paper, we develop a new bidding strategy based on two predictors, the CTR and WP predictors, to serve as the bidding value generator for a DSP running its real time auction in the RTB context. The algorithm, named PRUD, is expected to be optimal by analogy to the well known online stochastic knapsack problem. We perform experiments with real world RTB datasets and use a formal competitive analysis benchmarking flow to compare PRUD with the state-of-the-art single-predictor ORTB bidding algorithm. Our results show the outstanding bidding efficiency of PRUD in terms of not only a greater number of clicks achieved, but also a lower effective cost per click for an advertising campaign. By combining powers of the two predictors, PRUD provides a new cost-efficient strategy for a DSP competing in the rapid emerging RTB market.

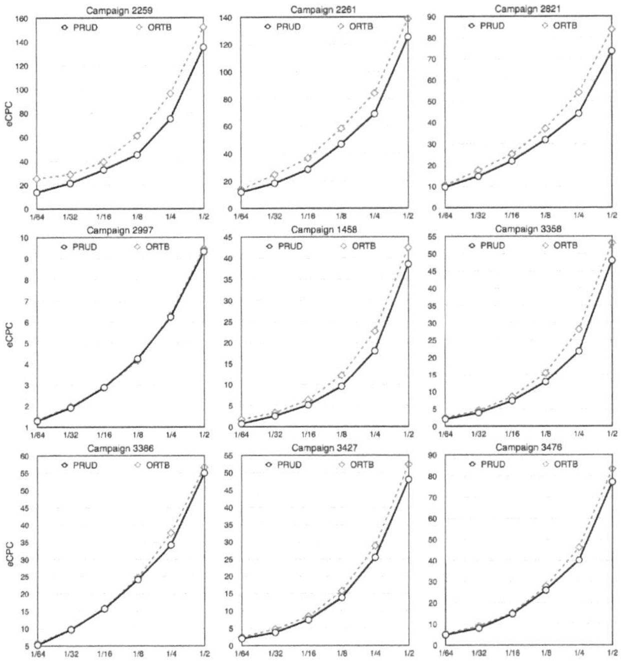

Figure 4: ORTB versus PRUD measured in effective cost per click.

Acknowledgments

This paper was supported in part by Ministry of Science and Technology, R.O.C., under Contract 105-2221-E-006-140-MY2, 105-2634-B-006-001, and 104-2221-E-002-214-MY3. The authors also thank Bridgewell for providing their RTB logs for a preliminary analysis in this work.

6. REFERENCES

[1] Y. Cui, R. Zhang, W. Li, and J. Mao. Bid landscape forecasting in online ad exchange marketplace. In *KDD*, 2011.

[2] Google. *The arrival of real-time bidding and what it means for media buyers*. Google, 2011.

[3] H. Kellerer, U. Pferschy, and D. Pisinger. *Knapsack problems*. Springer, 2004.

[4] X. Li and D. Guan. Programmatic buying bidding strategies with win rate and winning price estimation in real time mobile advertising. In *PAKDD*. Springer, 2014.

[5] C. Perlich, B. Dalessandro, R. Hook, O. Stitelman, T. Raeder, and F. Provost. Bid optimizing and inventory scoring in targeted online advertising. In *KDD*, 2012.

[6] M. Richardson, E. Dominowska, and R. Ragno. Predicting clicks: estimating the click-through rate for new ads. In *WWW*, 2007.

[7] J. Wang and S. Yuan. Real-time bidding: A new frontier of computational advertising research. In *WSDM*, 2015.

[8] W. C.-H. Wu, M.-Y. Yeh, and M.-S. Chen. Predicting winning price in real time bidding with censored data. In *KDD*, 2015.

[9] W. Zhang, Y. Rong, J. Wang, T. Zhu, and X. Wang. Feedback control of real-time display advertising. In *WSDM*, 2016.

[10] W. Zhang, S. Yuan, and J. Wang. Optimal real-time bidding for display advertising. In *KDD*, 2014.

[11] W. Zhang, S. Yuan, J. Wang, and X. Shen. Real-time bidding benchmarking with ipinyou dataset. *arXiv:1407.7073*, 2014.

Attractiveness versus Competition: Towards an Unified Model for User Visitation

Thanh-Nam Doan
School of Information Systems
Singapore Management University
tndoan.2012@phdis.smu.edu.sg

Ee-Peng Lim
School of Information Systems
Singapore Management University
eplim@smu.edu.sg

ABSTRACT

Modeling user check-in behavior provides useful insights about venues as well as the users visiting them. These insights can be used in urban planning and recommender system applications. Unlike previous works that focus on modeling distance effect on user's choice of check-in venues, this paper studies check-in behaviors affected by two venue-related factors, namely, *area attractiveness* and *neighborhood competitiveness*. The former refers to the ability of an area with multiple venues to collectively attract check-ins from users, while the latter represents the ability of a venue to compete with its neighbors in the same area for check-ins. We first embark on a data science study to ascertain the two factors using two Foursquare datasets gathered from users and venues in Singapore and Jakarta, two major cities in Asia. We then propose the VAN model incorporating user-venue distance, area attractiveness and neighborhood competitiveness factors. The results from real datasets show that VAN model outperforms the various baselines in two tasks: home location prediction and check-in prediction.

Keywords

Neighborhood Competition, Area attractiveness, location-based social network

1. INTRODUCTION

Motivation. The popularity of smartphones and wearable devices in recent years has helped to create new location based social networking (LBSN) applications for users to publish their visits (or check-ins) to different venues. By analyzing these check-in data, one may derive useful insights for urban planning, business recommendation, and other applications.

Previous works on LBSN data have shown that users prefer to visit venues near their home locations[7, 5]. This is also known as the *distance effect*. It underscores the importance of home location of users when analyzing their movement. Other than the distance effect which is specific to a user-venue pair, there are other venue factors that have not yet been studied and modeled.

In this paper, we introduce *area attractiveness* and *neighborhood competitiveness* as two new venue factors for analyzing and modeling check-in behavior. Area attractiveness refers to the ability of an area with multiple venues to collectively attract check-ins from users. Neighborhood competitiveness specifies the ability of a venue to compete with its neighbors in the same area for check-ins. We hypothesize that when a user decides a venue to visit, she will first select an area before finalizing the venue in the area. This two stage process suggests that some areas attract more visitors than others. The choice of area will reduce the cognitive load on the user as she has fewer candidate venues in the area to choose from.

CIKM'16 , October 24-28, 2016, Indianapolis, IN, USA

DOI: http://dx.doi.org/10.1145/2983323.2983657

Learning the area attractiveness and neighborhood competitiveness factors from check-in data gives rise to several useful applications. Urban planners can redesign a city's transportation network by making attractive areas more accessible. Businesses need to know both area attractiveness and neighborhood competitiveness in order to decide the new store locations. A personalized store recommendation app can also leverage on the two factors when making suggestions to its users.

Research Objectives. In this research, we therefore aim to incorporate area attractiveness and neighborhood competition into a new unified model for analyzing user-venue check-in behavior. This model should also include the distance effect which has already been used in the earlier models.

There are however several research challenges. Firstly, area attractiveness and neighborhood competitiveness are new concepts that have not been formally studied earlier. It is not easy to illustrate the effects of these two factors using real data. Hence, there is a need to conduct data science research on the factors. Secondly, the check-ins from users to venues are the results of multiple user and venue factors interacting with one another. Exactly how the interaction takes place is unclear. The challenge is therefore to create some generative stories to describe this interaction. Finally, there is no obvious ground truth in real datasets for evaluation of proposed models. We will need to adopt an indirect approach to conduct model evaluation.

Our results and findings of this research are as follows:

- We carefully gather Foursquare check-in data of users and venues from two cities, Singapore and Jakarta. Next, we determine the exact home locations of a subset of users through some stringent criteria. This gives us good datasets to embark on this research.
- We conduct an empirical analysis of the gathered check-in data and demonstrate the existence of neighborhood competitiveness, area attractiveness factors and also distance effect.
- We propose a probabilistic model called **VAN** to capture the check-in behavior of users incorporating these above effects.
- The performance of our proposed model is evaluated on real

datasets so as to demonstrate its superior accuracy. Specifically, we apply our proposed model and other baselines to two crucial tasks: home location prediction and check-in prediction. We show that our proposed model outperforms the baselines with reasonable results.

2. RELATED WORKS

Check-in prediction research: Chen *et al.* [4] surveyed the performance of matrix factorization in check-in prediction. Then, they proposed a model to combine matrix factorization and multi-center Gaussian model to predict the check-ins in LBSN with social information as the regularization. However, the work does not consider distance from users to areas and the neighborhood competition among venues. Cho *et al.* [5] viewed check-in locations of users as the mixture of check-ins near *home* and *work*. Our differences are that we assume only one home location for each user and the size of area in our model is predefined as parameter.

Home location identification: There are some works [10, 1] tackling home location identification problem but they predict the home locations of users at city level instead of giving exact locations.

Neighborhood Competition: Hu *et al.* [8] showed that there is weak correlation in rating between venue and its neighbors. Moreover, this correlation is *independent* of venue category. However, their model does not give the exact home location of users nor the ranking of venues. Doan *et al.* [6] proposed a new model named *Competitive Rank* based on *PageRank* to mine the competition between venues and their neighbors. The drawback of this model is that it considers every check-in to be the same but ignores the distance from the user to the check-in venue. To the best of our knowledge, the Huff model [9] measures the competitiveness of a store by its size but size information is not available in practice. Qu *et al.* [13] incorporates information from social network into Huff model. This extended model also replace users' home location by users' activity centers but not using the home location of users can reduce the performance in check-in prediction[7].

3. EMPIRICAL ANALYSIS OF CHECK-IN BEHAVIORAL DATA

In this section, we describe the two datasets as well as preprocessing methods to clean the data. We then use them to conduct empirical analysis on the check-in behavior to find the evidence of *distance effect*, *area attractiveness* and *neighborhood competition*.

3.1 Datasets

To study user check-in behavior and how it is affected by user and venue characteristics, we need Foursquare datasets that capture complete check-in data of both users and venues. We thus decided to crawl check-in data of users and venues in two cities, Singapore and Jakarta. Due to Foursquare's crawling restrictions, we could only crawl the publicly visible check-in data via Twitter APIs.

SG Dataset. This dataset consists of 1.11 millions check-ins by 55,891 Singapore Foursquare users on 75,346 venues between August 15, 2012 and June 3, 2013 (see Table 1). The users and venues are determined to be located in Singapore based on their profile declared location and venue's geo-location respectively.

JK Dataset. Similarly, we crawled another Foursquare dataset for the users and venues in Jakarta the largest city in Indonesia from July 2014 to May 2015. There are 119,618 check-ins performed by 14,974 users on 38,183 venues. The numbers are generally smaller than those of **SG** dataset.

Users with home locations. Among the users in the **SG** (or **JK**) datasets, we identify a subset of users whose home locations can be determined using the method described in Section 3.2. We then construct another dataset to include users with home locations and the venues that they perform check-ins on. This leads us to the **H_SG** and **H_JK** datasets. The number of users with home location in **H_SG** and **H_JK** are 856 and 455 respectively. Compared with **SG** and **JK** users, the users in **H_SG** and **H_JK** are relatively more active in performing check-ins. For example, **SG** has about 20 check-ins per user while **H_SG** has about 74 check-ins per user.

Table 1: Dataset Statistics

	SG	H_SG	JK	H_JK
# users	55,891	856	14,974	455
# venues	75,346	12,020	38,183	4,380
# check-in's	1.11M	63,777	119,618	9,557
# user-venue pairs with $>$ 0 check-ins	541,588	28,298	81,188	5,422

3.2 Home Location Identification

We selected a subset of users whose home locations can be clearly identified using both their check-ins and check-in messages. The following are the detailed steps:

- We selected a subset of venues under the "home (private)" category which is in turn a sub-category of the "residence" category. We found 8447 and 1985 venues satisfying this criteria in the **SG** and **JK** datasets respectively.
- We further identified 3276 and 891 users who performed check-ins at only one "home (private)" venue each in the **SG** and **JK** datasets respectively. This rules out users who performed check-ins at multiple "home (private)" venues.
- We finally selected an even smaller set of users who also shouted some home relevant messages during their check-ins to their "home (private)" venues. These messages have to include some "home" related key phrases, e.g., "back home", "home finally", etc.. For the **JK** dataset, we use the matching Malay key phrases like "Tidur dulu" (sleep first), "Rumah" (House), "Pondok"(cottage), "sampai di rumah" (arrived to home), "bobo"(sleep).

We finally obtained 856 users with home locations among (1.5% of all **SG** users) those users in the **SG** dataset. We denote the Foursquare dataset of these users and their check-in venues by **H_SG**. These users have 63,777 check-ins on 12,020 venues as shown in Table 1. Note that this represents 1.5% of all users and 5.7% of all check-ins in **SG**. Similarly, we obtained the **H_JK** dataset for 455 Jakarta users (3% of all **JK** users) with home locations. These dataset covers 4380 venues and 9557 check-ins.

3.3 Distance Effect

Using **H_SG** and **H_JK** datasets with exact users' home locations, we are able to study distance effect within a city, i.e., distance between the geo-coordinates of user's home location and venue location. We derive the probability of users performing check-ins on venues that are within a distance bin away from users' reported home locations. Specifically, for each user, we divide the city into several circular rings with the user's home location at the center. Every ring has a width of 1 kilometer. In other words, the first ring covers distance range [0,1km), the second ring covers distance range [1km, 2km), and so on. As the large distance rings involve the check-ins of very few users, we exclude rings with distance larger than 25 km. Next, we compute the probability of the user performing check-ins on venues within each distance ring. We finally compute for each distance ring the average probability of all users performing check-ins on venues within that distance ring.

We plot the average probability for different distance rings in Figure 1(a) and observe that: (a) users are more likely to visit or check into venues nearer to their home locations; (b) the decreasing probability trend appears in both **H_SG** and **H_JK** datasets; (c) the probability becomes more stable for venues within the distance rings 10 to 15 km away from users in both datasets.

3.4 Area Attractiveness

Despite the distance effect, some venues may still attract check-ins from users far away. Li *et. al.* [10] developed an influence scope model for measuring the attractiveness of venues to their followers. In this paper, instead of examining attractiveness at the venue level, we model attractiveness at the area level. There are three significant advantages of doing so. Firstly, it reduces the number of parameters in modeling which in turn reduces the learning time. Secondly, we address data sparsity issue at the venue level. Finally, we believe that the area a venue belongs to has a major influence over its ability to attract users. Due to space limitations, we are going to illustrate this by the following empirical analysis on only **H_SG** dataset.

We empirically select three well known fast food chains, i.e., McDonald, KFC and Starbucks, with many branches. We expect branches of the same chain to be very similar to one another by food variety, food quality, ambience and service. Hence, at the venue level, we should not expect any difference among their abilities to attract users from other locations. We now divide the city into square areas of width equals to 0.05 degree (equivalent to about 5.55 km on the equator) and assign every venue to exactly one area. The location of each area is its center of the mass derived from the locations of its venues. The detail of area construction is in Section 4. We call the top five areas with most number of venues the *dense areas* while the areas from ranks 10 to 15 the *sparse areas*. We exclude other lower ranked areas as they do not contain any of the three fast food venues.

For each fast food chain, we examine the distances between each dense area (represented by its center of mass) and the home locations of users who perform check-ins to its venues inside the area. We then generate a boxplot for the user-area distance of all dense areas. We perform the same procedure for sparse areas. Figure 1(b) shows that for each fast food chain, branches within the *dense areas* attract users farther than branches in the *sparse areas*. This suggests that the attractiveness of area plays an important role bringing far away users to the venues in the area.

3.5 Neighborhood Competition Effect

To show competition among venues within the same area, we adopt the method originally proposed by Weng *et al.*[14] to study competition among memes. We divide the check-in history into weeks. We then measure the following entropies for each week.

- **System entropy (E_s):** $E_s(t) = -\sum_v f_v(t) \log f_v(t)$ where $f_v(t)$ is the fraction of check-ins in week t performed on venue v, i.e., $f_v(t) = \frac{\#cks(v,t)}{\sum_v \#cks(v,t)}$. The system entropy essentially measures the degree to which the distribution of check-ins concentrates on a small fraction of venues.

- **Average area entropy (E_A):** We first define the entropy of an area a to be $E_a(t) = -\sum_{v\in a} f_{v,a}(t) \log f_{v,a}(t)$ and $f_{v,a}(t) = \frac{\#cks(v,t)}{\sum_{v\in a} \#cks(v,t)}$. We then take the average of all area entropies, i.e., $E_A(t) = Avg_a E_a(t)$. We divide the city into square cells of 0.05 degree width. The construction of areas is discussed further in Section 4. Similar to system entropy, average area entropy captures the degree to which the distribution of check-ins of an area concentrates on a small fraction of venues (in the area).

- **Average user entropy (E_U):** We next define the average user entropy as $E_U(t) = Avg_{u\in U} E_u(t)$ where entropy of user u is $E_u(t) = -\sum_v f_{u,v}(t) \log f_{u,v}(t)$ and $f_{u,v}(t) = \frac{\#cks(u,v,t)}{\#cks(u,t)}$. This entropy quantifies the concentration of users' attention on the venues they perform check-ins on.

Figure 1(c) shows the three entropies over weeks in both **H_SG** and **H_JK** datasets. The first important observation is that the average user entropy is much smaller than system entropy. It clearly suggests that each user's attention is limited to very small fraction of venues in the entire city. Venues therefore have to compete to gain attraction from users. Secondly, we observed from Figure 1(c) that system entropy is much larger than average area entropy in both datasets. This implies that check-ins within an area concentrated on smaller fraction of venues than the fraction of venues in the entire city receiving check-ins from the whole user population.

The above empirical analysis concludes that venues compete more with their nearby neighbors than those farther away. Thus, grouping venues into areas and modeling competition among venues in each area is an appropriate modeling approach.

4. VISITATION BY ATTRACTIVENESS AND NEIGHBORHOOD COMPETITION MODEL

In this section, we propose the *Visitation by Attractiveness and Neighborhood competition* (VAN) model and study its parameter learning process.

4.1 Model Description

Let U and V denote the set of users and venues in a city respectively. We divide the city into mutually exclusive square cells of width s. We use a_v to denote the square or *area* which contains v. More notations and their meanings are shown in Table 2.

The **VAN** model makes the following assumptions for each check-in between user and venue:

- First of all, every user chooses an area to perform a check-in based on its attractiveness and the distance between the user and the area.

- Secondly, every venue must compete against their neighboring venues in order to gain a check-in.

We assign each venue v a **competitiveness** value σ_v to measure its ability to compete with its neighbors. The value of σ_v is positive, and the larger the σ_v the more competitive the venue v.

The **neighbors** of a venue v, $N(v)$, are venues within a_v and the areas adjacent to a_v denoted by $Adj(a_v)$. That is, $N(v) = \{v'|v' \in Adj(a_v)\} \cup \{v'|v' \in a_v\} \setminus \{v\}$. We consider the venues in $Adj(a_v)$ as neighbors because we want to include venues in these nearby area as competitors of v. Otherwise, the competing neighbors of some venues near the border of a_v might not be included.

The **center** of area a is defined as the center of the mass location of venues inside a. The **attractiveness** of area σ_a is defined by the root mean square of the **competitiveness** scores of venues in a. That is, $\sigma_a = \sqrt{\sum_{v\in a} \sigma_v^2}$. It means that the venues inside the area contribute their competitiveness together to attract user check-ins.

Every check-in of user i to venue v follows a two-step process. Firstly, user i must select the area a_v. Secondly, the venue v in area a_v must win over all other neighboring venues in $N(v)$ to gain a check-in from user i.

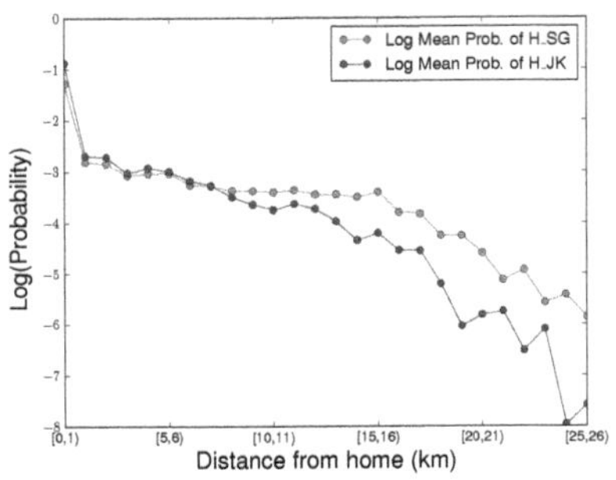

(a) Fraction of check-ins as a function of distance from home in **H_SG** and **H_JK** datasets in log scale.

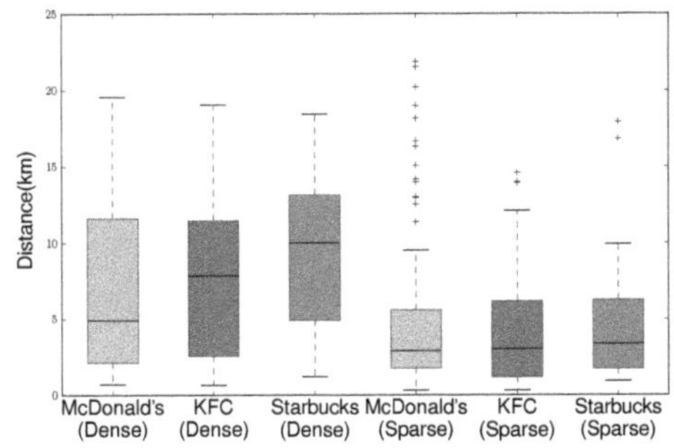

(b) Boxplot of distance from areas containing fast food chain to their check-ins users in **H_SG**

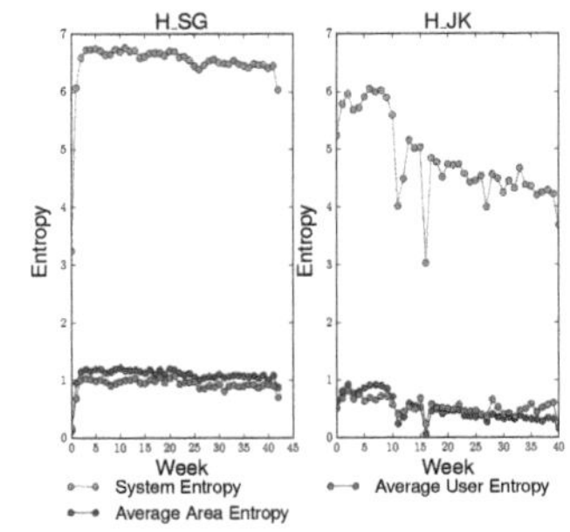

(c) Weakly entropy in **H_SG** and **H_JK** datasets.

Figure 1: The plots of empirical studies.

Table 2: Table of Notations.

Notations	Meaning
U / V / C	set of all users/venues/check-ins
w_{iv}	number of check-in of user i to venue v
w_v	total number of check-in of venue v
a_v	area a_v containing venue v
s	the width of area
σ_v	competitiveness score of venue v
σ_{a_v}	attractiveness of area a_v
$N(v)$	set of neighbor venues of v
$CDF(\cdot)$	cumulative density function of standard normal distribution
$S(\cdot)$	Sigmoid function
$p(i \rightarrow a_v)$	probability of user i visiting area a_v

- User i selects the area a_v under the effect of attractiveness of area a_v. Moreover, if the distance between i and a_v increases, the probability of user i choose area a_v decreases. We model this by zero-mean Gaussian distribution whose variance is σ_{a_v}. The Euclidean distance between user i and a_v is the random variable generated from the distribution. In other words, the home location of user i is generated from the Gaussian distance whose mean is the location of area a_v and variance is σ_{a_v}.
- To model the winning of venue v over its neighbors, we need to model the difference of competitiveness of v and that of one of its neighbor, say v' . We propose two options: *cumulative distribution function (CDF)* of standard Gaussian distribution i.e. $CDF(\sigma_v - \sigma_{v'}; 0, 1)$ and *Sigmoid function* of $\sigma_v - \sigma_{v'}$, i.e. $S(\sigma_v - \sigma_{v'})$. Both functions map differences between the competitiveness values of two venues into the range $[0, 1]$. If venue v is more competitive than its neighbor v' i.e. $\sigma_v > \sigma_{v'}$, the two functions will return a higher probability of v winning the check-in over v'.

Example: Figure 2 depicts two check-ins at venue v by user i i.e. $w_{iv} = 2$. To perform each check-in at venue v, user i has to select area (b, 3)(enclosed by red box) considering the distance from his home location to the center of area (b, 3) and the attractiveness of area (b, 3). Moreover, the venue v needs to *win* over all of its neighbors in the adjacent areas (i.e. venues within the green box).

4.2 Formalization & Inference

The probability p_{iv} of a check-in from user i to venue v is:

$$p_{iv} = p(i \rightarrow a_v) \prod_{v' \in N(v)} p(v > v') \tag{1}$$

Equation 1 says that p_{iv} depends on two components: $p(i \rightarrow a_v)$ denoting the probability of user i selecting area a_v and $p(v > v')$ denoting the probability of venue v winning over its neighbor v'.

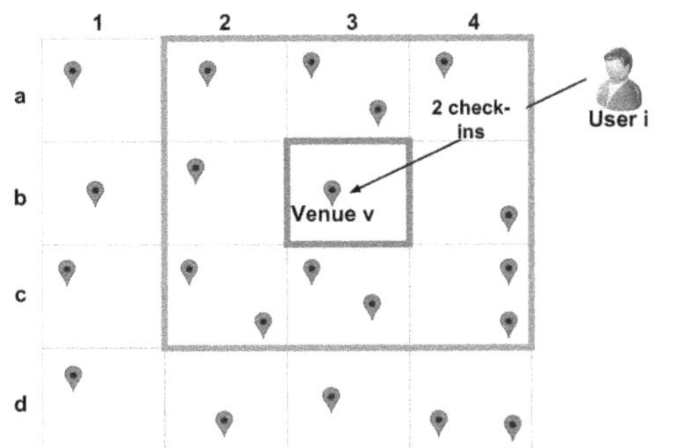

Figure 2: Example of Check-in graph.

Let (x_i, y_i) and (x_{a_v}, y_{a_v}) denote the location of user i and center of area a_v respectively. The probability $p(i \rightarrow a_v)$ is defined:

$$p(i \rightarrow a_v) = \mathcal{N}((x_i, y_i); (x_{a_v}, y_{a_v}), \sigma^2_{a_v}) \tag{2}$$

We model the attractiveness of each area a_v by a bivariate Gaussian distribution with center of area as mean and covariance matrix representing the attractiveness of a_v, i.e., σ_{a_v}. The larger Euclidean distance between user i and center of area a_v, the smaller the $p(i \rightarrow a_v)$. The covariance matrix is diagonal and has same value σ_{a_v} because we assume that the attractiveness of area a_v in *x-axis* is similar to its attractiveness in *y-axis*.

The log-likelihood of a set of check-ins C from users from U on venues from V is then defined.

$$\begin{aligned}
&\mathcal{L}(C|\{\sigma_v\}_{v \in V}) = \sum_{(i,v) \in C} w_{iv} \log p_{iv} \\
&= \sum_{(i,v) \in C} w_{iv} \log p(i \rightarrow a_v) + \sum_{v} w_v \sum_{v' \in N(v)} \log p(v > v') \\
&= \sum_{(i,v) \in C} w_{iv} \left(-2 \log \sigma_{a_v} - \frac{1}{2\sigma^2_{a_v}} ((x_i - x_{a_v})^2 + (y_i - y_{a_v})^2) \right) \\
&+ \sum_{v} w_v \sum_{v' \in N(v)} \log p(v > v') + const
\end{aligned} \tag{3}$$

As shown in Table 2, w_{iv} denotes the number of check-ins between user i and venue v, and w_v denotes the total number of check-ins on venue v. We consider two options to model the probability $p(v > v')$, i.e., Sigmoid function and cumulative density function of standard Gaussian distribution. Depending on the choice of the above options, we derive two variants of VAN models denoted by $\textbf{VAN}_{Sigmoid}$ and $\textbf{VAN}_{CDF}$.

Inference of user home locations: Taking derivative *w.r.t.* the

x-coordinate of user i's home location and set it to 0 gives us:

$$\frac{\partial \mathcal{L}}{\partial x_i} = \sum_v w_{iv}\left(-\frac{1}{2\sigma_{a_v}^2} 2(x_i - x_{a_v})\right) = 0$$
$$x_i = \frac{\sum_v \frac{w_{iv}}{\sigma_{a_v}^2} x_{a_v}}{\sum_v \frac{w_{iv}}{\sigma_{a_v}^2}} \text{ and } y_i = \frac{\sum_v \frac{w_{iv}}{\sigma_{a_v}^2} y_{a_v}}{\sum_v \frac{w_{iv}}{\sigma_{a_v}^2}} \quad (4)$$

Based on Equations 4, we derive some interesting observations about the home location of user i.

- The home location of user i is the *weighted average* of centers of area of venues checked in by i.
- The weight associated to each area has two components: the number of check-ins of user i to venue in the area and the attractiveness of the area. The former helps to predict the home location close to the check-in area due to distance effect. However, area attractiveness has an inverse effect on the importance of area. That is, more attractive areas should contribute less to identifying the home location of user i.
- Suppose the maximum and minimum of x-coordinate (i.e. latitude) of city are x_{max} and x_{min} respectively so we have $\forall a_v : x_{min} \leq x_{a_v} \leq x_{max}$. Thus, $\forall i \in U : x_{min} \leq x_i \leq x_{max}$. Similarly, $\forall i \in U : y_{min} \leq y_i \leq y_{max}$ for y-coordinate. Hence, the weighted average of centers of check-in areas ensures that the home location of user i to be within the city boundary.

Inference of competitiveness of venues: To maximize $\mathcal{L}$ with respect to σ_v and the constraint $\sigma_v > 0$, we add the regularization term $\sum_{v\in V} \log \sigma_v$ and use *gradient descent* with *back-tracking*[3] to find the optimal values of σ_v. The regularization term $\sum_{v\in V} \log \sigma_v$ helps us to keep all σ_v positive because if $\exists v \in V : \sigma_v \to 0$, then $\log \sigma_v$ and $\sum_{v\in V} \log \sigma_v$ will become $-\infty$.

5. EVALUATION USING REAL DATA

We evaluate the VAN models on real dataset in two separate tasks: home location prediction task and check-in prediction task. The geography degree is chosen as the unit of parameter s.

5.1 Home location prediction

Description: In this task, we aim to predict the home locations of users using our VAN models and some baselines. Among the baseline methods for comparison, Periodic Mobility Model (PMM) [5] is the state-of-the-art home location prediction method.

Setup: In total, we have the exact home location of 856 users in **H_SG** dataset. However, there are 341 of them whose home location cannot be predicted by PMM model as these users have too few check-ins or too few venues not giving PMM enough data to learn their home locations. Hence, we will conduct the experiment on the remaining 515 users. In the experiment, we randomly separate 515 users into five equal folds. For each run, we hide the home location of users in one fold and use all check-in data from all five folds and home location of users from the remaining four folds as input. Each model will then predict the home location of users in the hidden fold. For PMM, only the check-in data of users is used to predict their home locations. Hence, each time, we select one fold and predict home location of users in that fold by their check-in data. Similar to **H_SG**, there are 154 out of 455 users in **H_JK** whose home locations could be predicted by PMM. We therefore also divide them into five folds in the experiment.

Note: Our model could perform over the entire dataset but to guarantee the fairness, we only conduct experiment over the subset of users in which PMM could perform in both datasets.

Baselines: We consider several baselines below in this task.

- Center of the mass *COM*: This model returns the center of the mass of all check-ins of a user as his/her home location.
- Most check-in venue *MCV*: This model selects the most frequent check-in venue of a user as his/her home location.
- Periodic Mixture Model *PMM* [5]: It groups check-ins of a user into two clusters named *home* and *work*. The *home* cluster represents non-working hours check-ins and the center of this cluster is the predicted home location of the user.

The two simple baselines *COM* and *MCV* are used for comparison because they appear in previous research works [5, 7, 13].

Performance Measure: We measure the *distance* between the predicted home venue p_i and the actual home location h_i of user i. The overall performance is thus defined by the **average error** ($error_m$) between all predicted home locations and actual home locations. Moreover, we define another metric $prec@k$ is ratio of users whose distance from their predicted home location to actual home is less than k. Formally, $error_m = \frac{\sum_{i\in U} dist(p_i,h_i)}{|U|}$; $prec@k = \frac{|\{i: dist(p_i,h_i)<k\}|}{|U|}$ where $dist(\cdot,\cdot)$ returns the physical distance between two locations. In our experiment, we choose $k = 5km$.

Table 3: Home prediction result of H_SG and H_JK. The unit of average error in this table is meter. The best result of each dataset is highlighted.

	s	Average Error($prec@5km$) H_SG	Average Error($prec@5km$) H_JK
COM	-	6570.3 (46.2%)	5564.4 (43.4%)
MCV	-	7117.7 (40.3%)	5547.2 (45.5%)
PMM	-	6126.3 (49.3%)	4823.2 (60.8%)
$VAN_{Sigmoid}$	0.1	5561.8 (50.7%)	5623.8 (53.3%)
	0.05	**5046.4** (59.8%)	5125.2 (60.4%)
	0.025	5475.2 (56.7%)	4757.8 (64.4%)
VAN_{CDF}	0.1	5564.6 (51.46%)	5331.1 (56.1%)
	0.05	5181.6 (**60.4%**)	4866.1 (59.1%)
	0.025	5213.8 (56.9%)	**4357.2** (**68.2%**)

Result: Table 3 depicts the performance of baselines and our models with different s parameter values in **H_SG** and **H_JK**.

In the case of **H_SG** dataset, our **VAN**$_{Sigmoid}$ and **VAN**$_{CDF}$ model outperform *PMM* model by 12.34% and 13.16% in term of average error, respectively. Compared with other baselines, the VAN models yield accuracy of average error with up to 28% improvement. Both variants of VAN model also perform better in $prec@5km$ metric. The superior performance of VAN models is not affected by the s parameter.

For **H_JK**, we observe that the performance of our VAN models is affected by the s parameter setting. The optimal s value is 0.025. Under this setting, our VAN models outperform PMM and other baselines. The reason for the poorer performance of other settings may be due to the sparsity of check-ins in this dataset.

5.2 Check-in prediction task

In this section, we evaluate our model in check-in prediction task. This task predicts check-ins between users and venues.

Setup: We sort check-ins in the **H_SG** and **H_JK** datasets by time and then divide each dataset into 10 folds. For each run of experiment, we hide one fold as test set and use the remaining nine folds as training set.

Baselines: For comparison, we use some baselines below

- Probabilistic Matrix Factorization *PMF*[12]: It factorizes check-in matrix into user-latent factor and venue-latent factor matrix alone. We use the number of latent factors $K = 10$.

Table 4: **The $recall@k$ of H_SG and H_JK datasets in check-in prediction task. We highlight the best result for each value of k.**

		VAN_{CDF}			$VAN_{Sigmoid}$			PMF	MGM	PMF-MGM	N-MF		Expo-MF
	k \ s	0.1	0.05	0.025	0.1	0.05	0.025				100m	200m	
H_SG	20	**4.4%**	1.9%	1.1%	4.2 %	1.95%	0.48%	1.4%	0.36%	1.35%	0.3%	0.29%	1.5%
	50	**8.7%**	4.2%	3.1%	8.67%	4.62%	1.67%	2.6%	0.61%	2.5 %	0.8%	0.75%	1.6%
	100	12.1%	6.6%	6 %	**12.26%**	10.53%	5.65%	3.8%	1.11%	3.7 %	1.4%	1.35%	2.3%
H_JK	20	0.38%	0.56%	0.8%	0.36%	0.74%	**0.96%**	0.14%	0.24%	0.14%	0.57%	0.7%	0.3%
	50	**2.2%**	1.9 %	1.6%	1.73%	1.74%	1.51%	0.29%	0.7 %	0.3 %	0.96%	1.2%	1.1%
	100	**4.3%**	4 %	3.2%	3.8%	3.49%	3 %	1.12%	1.8 %	1.1 %	1.4%	1.7%	2.5%

- Multi-center Gaussian Model *MGM*[4]: It proposed a check-in prediction method using multiple Gaussian distributions as the activity centers of users. We automatically detect the clusters of *MGM* by applying the non-parametric method from Blei *et. al.* [2]. The α parameter of *MGM* which controls the impact of high frequent check-ins venues is set to default value $\alpha = 0.2$.

- Fusion Framework *PMF-MGM*[4]: It combines matrix factorization and *MGM*. It is reported to outperform *PMF* and *MGM* models. We implemented this combined method using *PMF* and *MGM* as its components.

- Matrix Factorization with Neighborhood Influence *N-MF*[8]: It studies the characteristics of geographical neighbors based on the matrix factorization framework. We use the number of latent features $K = 20$ and two venues are neighbors if their distance is less then a predefined threshold d. In our experiment, we set d to 100 meters and 200 meters.

- Exposure Matrix Factorization *Expo-MF*[11]: It incorporates the location of venues and user exposure to increase the performance of check-in prediction under matrix factorization framework. Similar to their experiment, we apply K-Means to cluster venues, the location vector of each venue is its probability to each cluster. We use $K = 100$ for the number of latent factors and the number of clusters in K-Means.

We have different values of latent factors K for *PMF*, *N-MF* and *Expo-MF* because we choose K that produces the best prediction performance for each model in the pool of values 10, 20, 100. These values are default setting reported in the original papers.

Performance Measure: After training, for each user, we select the top k venues predicted by each method and compare against all the venues checked in by the users in the test data.We use $recall@k$ as the metric to compare the performance of our model and the baselines. Finally, we report the average $recall@k$ over all folds. We do not use $precision@k$ because we cannot distinguish between a user disliking a venue and a user not knowing the venue. Formally, $recall@k = \frac{1}{|U|}\sum_{u \in U} \frac{|\mathcal{L}(u,k) \cap \mathcal{L}^t(u)|}{|\mathcal{L}^t(u)|}$ where $\mathcal{L}(u,k)$ is the top k venues of each user u of each predictive method; $\mathcal{L}^t(u)$ represents set of venues of user u in test set and $|\cdot|$ returns the number of elements of set.

Result: The result of check-in prediction task for two datasets **H_SG** and **H_JK** are shown in Table 4 . In our experiment, our model with Sigmoid or CDF function always outperforms all baselines in both datasets. For instance, in **H_SG**, our model could achieve recall up to three times better than PMF and 10 times better than MGM. Overall, in both datasets, if we reduce the area width, the performance of VAN model decreases. Specifically, the performance of area width of 0.05 is usually better than the one of area width of 0.025 but worse than that of area width 0.1. Additionally, the result of VAN_{CDF} usually outperforms $VAN_{Sigmoid}$. *Expo-MF* only considers the location of venues while *N-MF* uses the information of neighbor alone. However, these two baselines do not enjoy better result than both variants of VAN model. Thus, the results suggest that neighborhood competition and area attractiveness are useful factors to be modeled. Between two baselines, *MGM* performans better than *PMF* in **H_JK** dataset but not in **H_SG**. *PMF-MGM* is the hybrid of *MGM* and *PMF* so its performance is in the middle of both models.

6. CONCLUSION

In this paper, we model user visitation by using two new factors: neighborhood competition and area attractiveness. Our experiments show that our model outperforms several baselines in *check-in prediction* and *home location prediction* tasks.

7. ACKNOWLEDGMENT

This research is supported by the Singapore National Research Foundation under its International Research Centre@ Singapore Funding Initiative and administered by the IDM Programme Office, Media Development Authority (MDA).

8. REFERENCES

[1] L. Backstrom, E. Sun, and C. Marlow. Find me if you can: improving geographical prediction with social and spatial proximity. In *WWW*, 2010.

[2] D. M. Blei and M. I. Jordan. Variational inference for dirichlet process mixtures. *Bayesian analysis*, 2006.

[3] S. Boyd and L. Vandenberghe. *Convex Optimization.* Cambridge University Press, New York, NY, USA, 2004.

[4] C. Cheng, H. Yang, I. King, and M. R. Lyu. Fused matrix factorization with geographical and social influence in location-based social networks. In *AAAI*, volume 12, 2012.

[5] E. Cho, S. A. Myers, and J. Leskovec. Friendship and mobility: User movement in location-based social networks. KDD, 2011.

[6] T. Doan, F. C. T. Chua, and E. Lim. Mining business competitiveness from user visitation data. In *SBP*, 2015.

[7] T. Doan, F. C. T. Chua, and E. Lim. On neighborhood effects in location-based social networks. In *WI-IAT*, 2015.

[8] L. Hu, A. Sun, and Y. Liu. Your neighbors affect your ratings: On geographical neighborhood influence to rating prediction. In *SIGIR*, 2014.

[9] D. L. Huff. A probabilistic analysis of shopping center trade areas. *Land Economics*, pages 81–90, 1963.

[10] R. Li, S. Wang, H. Deng, R. Wang, and K. C.-C. Chang. Towards social user profiling: unified and discriminative influence model for inferring home locations. In *KDD*, 2012.

[11] D. Liang, L. Charlin, J. McInerney, and D. M. Blei. Modeling user exposure in recommendation. In *WWW*, 2016.

[12] A. Mnih and R. Salakhutdinov. Probabilistic matrix factorization. In *NIPS*, 2007.

[13] Y. Qu and J. Zhang. Trade area analysis using user generated mobile location data. In *WWW*, 2013.

[14] L. Weng, A. Flammini, A. Vespignani, and F. Menczer. Competition among memes in a world with limited attention. *Scientific Reports*, 2012.

OptMark: A Toolkit for Benchmarking Query Optimizers

Zhan Li, Olga Papaemmanouil and Mitch Cherniack
Brandeis University, Waltham, MA, USA
{zhanli,olga, mfc}@cs.brandeis.edu

ABSTRACT

Query optimizers have long been considered as among the most complex components of a database engine, while the assessment of an optimizer's quality remains a challenging task. Indeed, existing performance benchmarks for database engines (like TPC benchmarks) produce a performance assessment of the query runtime system rather than its query optimizer. To address this challenge, this paper introduces *OptMark*, a toolkit for evaluating the quality of a query optimizer. OptMark is designed to offer a number of desirable properties. First, it decouples the quality of an optimizer from the quality of its underlying execution engine. Second it evaluates independently both the effectiveness of an optimizer (i.e., quality of the chosen plans) and its efficiency (i.e., optimization time). OptMark includes also a generic benchmarking toolkit that is minimum invasive to the DBMS that wishes to use it. Any DBMS can provide a system-specific implementation of a simple API that allows OptMark to run and generate benchmark scores for the specific system. This paper discusses the metrics we propose for evaluating an optimizer's quality, the benchmark's design and the toolkit's API and functionality. We have implemented OptMark on the open-source MySQL engine as well as two commercial database systems. Using these implementations we are able to assess the quality of the optimizers on these three systems based on the TPC-DS benchmark queries.

1. INTRODUCTION

Query optimizers have been recognized as among the most complex components of a DBMS. Among the myriad of optimizer design choices are whether they are top-down or bottom-up [8], how (or if) they constrain the search space of possible plans [9], or whether or not plans are modified dynamically [3]. Despite the wide variety in approaches to query optimization, the assessment of an optimizer's *quality* remains highly subjective. Indeed, DBMS performance benchmarks (e.g., the TPC benchmarks) conflate query optimization and query execution, producing a performance assessment that reflects upon the DBMS' query runtime system as much as (and arguably more than) its query optimizer.

Undoubtedly, a major reason that no query optimizer benchmark exists is because such a benchmark is extremely difficult to design and implement[20]. We have identified the following three key challenges in the design of an effective optimizer benchmark:

(1) Dual Assessment Measures: Optimizers should be evaluated for both their *effectiveness* and *efficiency* in generating plans for a given suite of queries. An optimizer benchmark must hence measure the effectiveness, i.e., the quality of plans generated for queries in a given query suite. But in comparing the optimizers of two different DBMSs, it is insufficient to compare the execution times of plans chosen by the optimizers for the same query, even if both DBMSs are implemented on the same platform. To illustrate, a plan generated by the MySQL optimizer [1] may fare poorly compared to that of commercial DBMS for a join-heavy query because joins in MySQL queries can only be executed as *nested-loop joins*. This does not necessarily reflect the effectiveness of the MySQL optimizer which might consistently generate the highest-performing plans possible that exclusively use nested-loop joins. Thus, optimizer effectiveness must be assessed evaluating generated plans relative to other plans the DBMS' query execution engine is capable of running.

An optimizer benchmark must also measure the efficiency, i.e., the resources (i.e., time and space) required by an optimizer to generate plans. A given optimizer could be very effective if it combines *exhaustive search* (thus considering all possible plans for a given query) with an extremely accurate cost model. But in practice, it is infeasible to exhaustively consider all possible plans, especially for the most complex and expensive queries (e.g., queries involving large numbers of tables) where optimization is needed most.[1] Thus, efficiency is a measure of how well a query optimizer can scale to process the most complex of queries.

(2) Benchmark Generality: An optimizer benchmark should be runnable over any DBMS regardless of the (hardware and OS) platforms over which it runs, and benchmark scores for different optimizers should be comparable even when run on differing platforms. This implies that (1) the benchmark code should be configurable to any DBMS (but ideally requiring minimal DBMS-specific code to do so), and (2) time-based metrics of effectiveness (runtime of generated plan for given query) and efficiency (time spent optimizing given query) should be avoided as they are incomparable for systems running on different platforms.

(3) Isolated Assessment: A DBMS optimizer's performance must be decoupled from that of the DBMS' query execution engine. Thus, end-to-end benchmarks such as the TPC-H and TPC-DS benchmarks [2] are not good query optimizer benchmarks because they report query execution times which depend not only on

[1] This is the reason that most optimizers have timeout settings that allow optimization to be curtailed prior to consideration of all plans.

CIKM'16 , October 24-28, 2016, Indianapolis, IN, USA

DOI: http://dx.doi.org/10.1145/2983323.2983658

the plan chosen by an optimizer but (even more so) on the capabilities of the DBMS query execution engine.

In this paper, we introduce *Opt-Mark*: a Query [Opt]imizer Bench[Mark] with the following key features:

1. *Effectiveness metrics* that assess the performance of optimizer-chosen plans relative to other plans that can be run by the same DBMS.
2. *Efficiency metrics* that are not based on optimization timing but instead on the size of the search space that an optimizer considers (thus measuring both space and time).
3. *A Toolkit* consisting of generic benchmark code together with a concise API that must be implemented for a benchmarked DBMS in a system-specific way.

This paper is structured as follows. We present the benchmark design, including effectiveness and efficiency measures in Section 2, and describe the toolkit code, including the API requiring DBMS-specific implementation in Section 3. We present benchmark results for 3 systems: MySQL and two well-known commercial DBMSs (which we refer to as Systems X and Y respectively) in Section 4. We describe related work in Section 5 and conclude with our final remarks in Section 6.

2. BENCHMARK DESIGN

In this section we present the design of OptMark, its *effectiveness* and *efficiency* measures and techniques used for determining them.

2.1 Optimizer Effectiveness

The *effectiveness* of a DBMS' optimizer reflects the quality of the plans it generates. The main challenge here is isolating the effectiveness of the optimizer from the underlying DBMS's query execution engine. We argue that effectiveness should be evaluated relatively to the capabilities of the underlying query (runtime) engine so as to decouple the effectiveness assessment of this component. In other words, an optimizer should not be penalized for not considering query operations (i.e., join algorithms, access methods, etc) that are not supported by the runtime engine of the DBMS.

The necessity of decoupling the optimizer from the query engine is illustrated in the case of MySQL [1] whose query engine supports *nested-loop joins* (NLJ) as the sole means of evaluating joins. Especially for join-heavy queries, MySQL will frequently be outperformed by DBMSs that also support other join operations such as *sort-merge* and *hash* joins. However, the MySQL optimizer should be considered effective if it consistently identifies the best NLJ plan for a given query, even though the MySQL query engine is less effective than those that can perform other types of joins.

Driven from the above discussion, we introduce the concept of a *relative optimal plan* of a query in a given DBMS. The relative optimal plan refers to the best plan the DBMS can run for that query. This plan might be different across different DBMSs.

Effectiveness Metrics OptMark measures optimizer effectiveness using two metrics that both compare the plans that an optimizer chooses for a given query suite Q with the plans it could have chosen for the same query engine:

1. *Performance Factor:* For any query $q \in Q$ and optimizer O_D for DBMS D, the *Performance Factor* of O_D relative to q, $\mathbf{PF}(O_D, q)$, measures the proportion of plans in the search space that are worse than the optimizer-chosen plan, which is defined as

$$\mathbf{PF}(O_D, q) = \frac{|\{p | p \in P_D(q), \mathtt{r}(D,p) \geq \mathtt{r}(D, O_D(q))\}|}{|P_D(q)|} \quad (1)$$

such that $O_D(q)$ is the plan O_D generates for q, $P_D(q)$ is the set of all plans that could be executed by D to evaluate q, $\mathtt{r}(D,p)$ is the measured runtime of plan p over D and $\mathtt{r}(D, O_D(q))$ is the runtime of the plan O_D generates for q over D. We note here that the timing of $\mathtt{r}(D,p)$ is subject to numerous environment conditions (e.g., empty DB and OS buffers, no contention) and one should control these factors (e.g., by executing the queries in isolation and using a cold cache every time). Thus, the best possible score for this metric is 1 (indicating that an optimizer chooses the optimal plan for the query q) and the closer the score is to 0, the poorer is the optimizer-chosen plan.

2. *Optimality Frequency:* Optimizer O_D finds a relative optimal plan for query $q \in Q$ if $\mathbf{PF}(O_D, q) = 1$. Thus, the optimality frequency of O_D, $\mathbf{OF}(O_D, Q)$, is the percentage of queries in the query set Q for which O_D chooses the relative optimal plan.

The two metrics described above can be leveraged to provide insight on (a) the quality of the optimizer-chosen plan, (b) the quality of the cost model and (c) the quality of the plan enumeration process of a given optimizer. First, the performance factor reflects the quality of the optimizer-chosen plan compared to other plans the DBMS is capable of running relative to a given query. A performance factor of 1 indicates that the optimizer-chosen plan is better than *all* plans while the lower the performance factor the more plans are better than the chosen one. Second, the quality of the cost model can be measured by determining how many of the plans that did better than the optimizer-chosen plan were considered by the optimizer. Third, the quality of the plan enumeration can be measured by the number of plans that did better than the optimizer-chosen plan and were not considered by the optimizer. For the plans that were considered by the optimizer, the optimizer did not choose them because of an inaccurate cost model. For the plans that were not considered by the optimizer, the optimizer did not include them in its search space due to poor plan enumeration.

2.1.1 *Plan Space Generation*

Evaluating the effectiveness requires the enumeration and execution of *all* possible plans the optimizer could execute for a given query. This process is unfeasible, especially for complex queries due to the exponential number of queries to be executed. Alternatively, one could collect those plans that optimizer considered (i.e., costed) in the process of choosing a plan. We can then compare these plans with the optimizer-chosen plan and calculate the above effectiveness metrics. However, this approach ignores flaws that might exist in the optimizer's enumeration strategy that might have resulted in an optimizer not considering a plan that it should have. For example an optimizer that only considers poor plans but costs them correctly would be considered effective (i.e., with performance factor of 1) despite choosing poor plans.

OptMark takes an alternative approach and generates a set of comparable plans for a given query by generating a random sample set of candidate execution plans that may or may not have been considered by the optimizer. Our approach assesses the quality of the optimizer-chosen plan relative to the plans that the runtime engine is capable of executing. The challenge here is to estimate the proportion of plans that perform worse than the optimizer's chosen plan (i.e., the performance factor) without having any prior knowledge of the performance distribution of the candidate plans. In the following section we describe how to identify the size of the sample set required to estimate the performance factor with a given confidence and precision. We then proceed to describe how we generate these sample plans.

2.1.2 Sample Size

To calculate the sample size required to estimate (with a specified level of confidence and precision) the performance factor of O_D relative to a query q, $\mathbf{PF}(O_D, q)$, we use the formula from [7]:

$$n = \frac{Z^2 p(1-p)}{e^2} \tag{2}$$

such that, e is the desired level of precision (aka sampling error), Z is the value from the standard normal distribution that corresponds to the desired confidence level (e.g., $Z = 1.96$ for a a confidence interval of 95%) and p is an estimate of the proportion of plans that will be worse than the optimizer's plan or 0.5 when this estimate is unknown. Equation 2 assumes that our candidate plan set size (i.e., population size) is large compared with the sample size while for smaller populations a modified formula can be used that reduces slightly the required sample size.

It follows that if the user desires to estimate the performance factor of a query with a 95% confidence level and 5% precision, it needs to generate at least 385 random sample plans. Hence, if we randomly generate 385 plans and found that 80% of the plans perform worse the optimizer's chosen plan, we can conclude with 95% confidence that the optimizer's plan is better than 75% - 85% possible plans, i.e., the performance factor is 0.75 - 0.85.

2.1.3 Random Plan Generation

Given a number of random plans to generate, OptMark generates these plans by exploring the three main features that characterize query plans: the *join ordering*, the *physical join algorithm* used for each join and *table access methods*. Our process first produces a random join ordering for a given query and then expands this plan with randomly selected physical join operations and access methods. Next we describe this process starting with the random join ordering generation for a given query.

Random Join Orderings Traditionally, join orderings are represented as binary trees (aka join trees) where internal nodes represent join operations and the leaf nodes represent tables. Our join ordering generation process generates an unbiased random binary join tree and then generates a random sequence of tables to populate the leaves of the join tree. Every join ordering of a query joining n tables can be encoded as a pair (s, p) such that:

1. s is a bit sequence that represents the preorder traversal of the ordering's binary tree such that each successive bit denotes the next node of the tree visited in the traversal and is a '1' if that node is an internal node (join) and a '0' if that node is a leaf node (table). Hence, the bit sequence has length $(2n-1)$ consisting of $(n-1)$ '1's and n '0's.
2. p represents the sequence of tables to populate the leaf nodes in the binary tree. Specifically, p is some permutation of the tables in the query. The permutation sequence then specifies the leaves of the join tree from left to right.

OptMark generates random join orderings by generating random encodings of join trees (s, p). The random generation of the bit sequence s involves flipping a biased coin for each bit in the sequence (going from left-to-right) to decide if the "next" bit should be a '0' or an '1' [4]. Because the last bit in the bit sequence must be a '0', given that the last visited node in a preorder traversal must be a leaf node, we use the algorithm in [4] to generate $2(n-1)$ bits at random and add a '0' at the end. To ensure that every tree is enumerated with equal probability, one must use a biased coin when deciding between a '1' and a '0' and the degree of bias depends on what has been generated thus far. For each bit in the sequence s, we determine the probability that the bit should be filled with a '0', which is expressed as $P(r, k)$ such that r is the number of '1's in the bit sequence thus far minus the number of '0's in the bit sequence thus far and k is the number of bits that have yet to be assigned. The formula to calculate $P(r, k)$ as written in [4] is:

$$P(r,k) = \frac{r(k+r+2)}{2k(r+1)} \tag{3}$$

Given a query that joins n tables, OptMark uses the above formula to estimate the probability of each bit in a $2(n-1)$ bit sequence and create a random sequence s. It then generates a random permutation p of the tables and outputs a random join ordering (s, p).

Given the join ordering, we then replace all join operators with randomly selected physical join operators to generate a physical plan to include in the sample. Specifically, for each join node in the join tree, if its inputs have no corresponding join predicate in the query, we force a cross join. Otherwise, we randomly select one of the physical join operators supported by the execution engine. We then add random access methods for each input table by randomly selecting an applicable index or, if one does not exist, a sequential scan as the table access method. The above process is repeated until we generate as many plans as specified by the sample size determined as described in Section 2.1.2.

2.2 Optimizer Efficiency

The *efficiency* of a DBMS' optimizer reflects the resource requirements (i.e., time and memory) necessary for the optimizer to choose a query plan. In theory, a DBMS could consider all possible candidate plans for a query (*exhaustive enumeration*) regardless of the time and space that this requires[2], and provided it was armed with an accurate cardinality and cost model, would always choose an optimal plan. In practice, exhaustive enumeration is infeasible for complex, join-heavy queries and most optimizers "time-out" prior to consideration of all plans for such queries.

One possible approach to measure optimizer efficiency is to calculate the average time that an optimizer spends optimizing queries in the benchmark query suite. However, this metric has two notable deficiencies: 1) optimizer times recorded for DBMSs running on different platforms are incomparable, and 2) this metric only measures time and not memory. The OptMark benchmark instead measures efficiency using four metrics that specify the size of the search space processed during the optimization of a query:

1. **#LP**: the number of logical plans enumerated,
2. **#JO**: the number of join orderings enumerated,
3. **#PP**: the number of physical plans costed, and
4. **#PJ**: the number of physical join plans costed.

It is clear that each of these metrics is a measure of the size of the search space explored for a given query. But as we show in Table 1, these metrics are also strongly correlated with optimization time. This table shows the degree of correlation between each metric and the time spent by four different DBMSs optimizing averaged over the 93 join queries from the TPC-DS benchmark. Correlation is demonstrated with r^2 values that show the goodness-of-fit of the linear regression, and that fall between 0.0 and 1.0 with higher values indicating higher correlation. Note that the most highly correlated metric (shown for each DBMS in boldface) varies from system to system, demonstrating that there is no single "best" metric for all systems. However, all metrics have very strong correlations (over 0.7 in all cases) with the optimization time and therefore can be used as predictors of an optimizer's optimization time. An interesting observation is that the r^2 value of **#PP** and **#PJ**, and that of **#LP** and **#JO** are very close to, or even identical to each other on all the DBMSs. The reason is that non-join plans (e.g., table

[2]The time and space required by an optimizer will always impact ad hoc queries however.

System	#LP	#JO	#PP	#PJ
MySQL	0.92	0.93	**0.94**	**0.94**
PostgreSQL	0.72	0.72	**0.97**	**0.97**
System X	**0.81**	**0.81**	0.71	0.72
System Y	0.77	0.75	**0.85**	**0.85**

Table 1: Correlation of efficiency metrics and optimization times

scan plans and index scan plans) are typically much fewer than join plans, and thus take much less optimization time[13].

To benchmark a given DBMS one must be able to extract at *least one* and as many of the four metrics as possible, so that efficiency results can be compared to as many other DBMSs as possible.

Linear Regression Results To collect the results of Table 1, we processed an optimization structure exposed by System X, added instrumentation to the open source code of PostgreSQL and parsed trace files of MySQL and System Y. These techniques allowed us to count the physical plans that were costed by each DBMS during optimization, and from these results we were able to determine the values of the other metrics: determining physical join plans by removing all non-join physical plans (e.g., group-by plans and index plans) from the physical plans, determining logical plans by converting each physical operator in the physical plan to its logical equivalent and ignoring duplicates, and determining join orderings on the basis of physical join structures.

MySQL shows a quite strong correlation of the logical plans: almost as high as the correlation of the physical plans. MySQL resolves all joins to nested-loop joins and when mapping logical plans to physical ones it only needs to convert selection operators to table access methods (e.g., table scan, index scan). Hence, in this engine we are able to reconstruct almost the majority of the logical plans, as very few logical ones are pruned before converting to physical ones. On the other hand, **#LP** and **#JO** seems to be a stronger predictors of optimization time than the physical plan metrics **#PP** and **#PJ** for System X. For this engine we were able to collect *all* logical plans and join orderings considered by the optimizer and hence the correlation is high. However, the data structure offered by this specific engine only reports the physical plans that the optimizer considered to be "promising" plans. A high percentage of the pruned plans are not reported although they do add an overhead to the optimization process (since the optimizer examined them). Hence our experiments used a reduced set of physical plans and the regression results thus show a lower correlation of **#PP** compared with **#LP**.

3. THE OPTMARK TOOLKIT

We next introduce OptMark, a query optimizer benchmark toolkit that assists developers measure optimizer effectiveness and efficiency. Any DBMS for which benchmark results are desired can use our toolkit by implementing a small, simple set of API functions. These functions extract all the optimization metadata and statistics we need to evaluate the effectiveness metrics and efficiency predictors we discussed in the Sections 2.1-2.2. OptMark is minimum invasive to the underlying database engine. It is executed as a stand-alone tool and runs against a given target database using a standard JDBC interface. It could be extended to any schema and query set, but we expect it to be used on queries that stress the performance of an optimizer. Typically, these are queries with non-trivia number of joins.

Benchmark Requirements For a given DBMS to run the benchmark, it must satisfy the following requirements. First, it must support JDBC. The benchmark compares the runtime of the optimizer-chosen plan with the sample set of plans it generates, so OptMark must be able to connect to DBMS through JDBC to execute specific query plans. Second, it must support query hints (or directives) to force the optimizer to consider only plans that adhere to a specific join ordering and/or use specific join operations and access methods. This allows us to to generate a sample set of physical plans with which to compare optimizer generated plan and use it to evaluate the optimizer's effectiveness. Finally, it must expose at least one of the four predictors we describe in Section 2.2. These allow us to quantify the time and space used by optimizer in generating a plan for a query and determine the optimizer's efficiency. Note that not every optimizer exposes each of these indicators, but any two optimizers can be compared if they expose a *common* indicator.

3.1 Effectiveness Assessment & API

In Section 2.1 we discussed our technique for evaluating the effectiveness of an optimizer. A building block of our approach is enumerating a sample set of physical join plans for a given join query and processing them to collect their execution time. This indicates two requirements for our toolkit. First, it must be aware of the physical join algorithms supported by the underlying DBMS it is executed on (e.g., MySQL supports only nested-loop join, while DBMSs X and Y support also hash join and merge-sort join). Second, OptMark must be able to enforce the execution of a query using a given physical plan. This plan will specify the join ordering, the physical join operators to be used as well as table access methods. The latter could be either an index-based scan, if an index is available, or a sequential scan.

Our approach to execute a given physical plan relies on a standard feature in modern databases: query hints that affect the plan choice by the query optimizer. As the syntax of query hints varies for different systems, OptMark users need to implement a set of API functions which return the exact syntax of query hints on the system OptMark is running against. This API allows our toolkit to be independent of the underlying DBMS.

Effectiveness API Our effectiveness API consists of three main functions which return (a) the supported physical join operators, (b) the syntax for hinting the use of a given index and (c) the syntax for hinting a specific join method. Next we provide the formal signatures of these API functions.

1. `Set{String} joinTypes()`
   This method returns a list of physical join methods the system supports in the syntax of join hints.
2. `String indexHint(String t, String ind)`
   Given the table name, `t`, and an applicable index on it, `ind`, the method returns the hint syntax for forcing an index scan on `t` using the index `ind`.
3. `String joinHint(String t1, String al1, String index1, String t2, String al2, String index2, String join, String clause)`
   Given the name, alias and the indexes of two joining tables, the method returns the hint syntax to force a two-way join using the specific indexes on each table. The alias and index parameters are optional. The above API function can also support nested queries. Specifically, the table parameters `t1` and `t2` could be a base table, or a sub-query. If the table parameter is a subquery then the alias parameter is used as a reference of that query. The index parameters `ind1` and `ind2` are the output of the method `indexHint()`, i.e., they are the hint syntax for using an index-based table scan. The parameter `join` is the output of the method `joinTypes()`, i.e., it is the syntax for forcing the optimizer to use a specific physical join operator for executing

the query. The parameter `clause` is a string representation of the join conditions to be used.

OptMark also needs to determine which indexes exist on which tables and over which attributes, this information can be got by a JDBC function `getIndexInfo()`.

Benchmarking Effectiveness Next we describe OptMark's approach for assessing the effectiveness of an optimizer. Given a set of queries to execute the benchmark on and an implementation of the effectiveness API for the DBMS OptMark is running on, our toolkit generates a sample set of physical plans against which the optimizer chosen plan is compared with based on the execution time. As discussed in Section 2.1.2 the size of the sample set is determined by the user-defined confidence level and margin of error.

For a given query, the random plans with which the optimizer-chosen plan is compared with are generated as follows:

1. First it generates random join orderings as discussed in Section 2.1.3.
2. For each of joins in a given join ordering, if there is no join predicate between two tables it forces a cross join. Otherwise, it randomly selects one physical join operation from all physical join operations returned by `joinType()`.
3. For every table in the query we identify if there are any indexes on a predicate attribute (all index information is returned by `getIndexInfo()`) and we randomly select to use an index or sequential scan to access each table.
4. Steps 1 - 3 generate a single random plan. We repeat this process until we collect the desired sample size.

For each plan in our sample set we create a SQL query that enforces the specified join ordering, join algorithm and access method. The join orderings of step 2 and the choice of join operations in step 3 are enforced according to directives specified in `joinHint()` while the access method is enforced by adding the SQL directive specified by `indexHint()`. The output hint-based SQL query is executed and OptMark collects its runtime and evaluates the query's performance factor. The process is repeated for all queries in a given benchmarking query suite and the optimality frequency of the query set is reported.

3.2 Efficiency Assessment & API

In Section 2.2 we introduce our four efficiency predictors used by OptMark, namely the number of logical and physical plans as well as the number of join orderings and physical join plans. Given a set of benchmark queries, OptMark will report the predictors the DBMS exposes for each of the queries in this query set.

Efficiency API The API that must be implemented in a DBMS specific way to support efficiency assessment of its optimizer should include a function that returns for any given query at *least one* of our four efficiency indicators: (1) number of logical plans, (2) number of logical join plans, (3) number of physical plans and (4) number of physical join plans. All numbers refer to the plans the optimizer considers for the given query.

4. BENCHMARK RESULTS

We have implemented OptMark's effectiveness and efficiency APIs over three DB systems: MySQL, a commercial system with a top-down optimizer that we refer to as System X, and a commercial system with a bottom-up optimizer that we refer to as System Y. Our implementations are illustrated in [15].

We run our toolkit on a server equipped with a 3.06 GHz Octa CPU and 32 GB of memory. We use the TPC-DS benchmark [2] for generating our benchmarking dataset and query suite. The workload consists of 24 queries with a minimum of 5 tables in each query. The benchmark toolkit runs on a dataset of 100GB.

System	#LP	#JO	#PP	#PJ
MySQL	N/A	N/A	48	40
PostgreSQL	N/A	N/A	810	778
System X	146	123	N/A	N/A
System Y	N/A	N/A	540	514

Table 2: Values of efficiency predictors

4.1 Efficiency Results

We use four metrics, **#LP**, **#JO**, **#PP**, **#PJ**, to measure the efficiency of an optimizer (Section 2.2). Since all metrics have high correlation with optimization time, any one of them can be used as a metric for efficiency evaluation. The metrics can be used to compare the efficiency of different versions of an optimizer. For example, if one introduces a new enumeration strategy, we can use the metrics to check if the new strategy makes the optimizer more efficient. However, one needs to be careful using them to compare different optimizers. For example, the efficiency metrics of MySQL should be less than those of optimizers which supports more physical join operators than just nested loop join which is the only physical join operation MySQL supports. But the comparison between them does not make much sense because they support different join operations.

We are not able to implement OptMark on PostgreSQL because it doesn't support query hints. But as PostgreSQL exposes ways to extract physical plans and physical join plans, we can still do efficiency evaluation for PostgreSQL. Table 2 shows the values of the four efficiency predictors for the four DBMSs we used. For each predictor, we take the average number over all queries in the workload. Some efficiency predictors are not applicable for some DBMSs because they are not exposed by the DBMSs. From the result we can observe MySQL has the least number of physical plans and physical join plans, which makes sense because MySQL resolves all joins to nested-loop join, its search space is far smaller than the other systems.

4.2 Effectiveness Results

We used OptMark to collect effectiveness results on System X. Similar results for System Y and MySQL can be found in [15]. For each of our 24 TPC-DS queries we generated a random sample set of 385 plans, allowing us to estimate the performance factor of the optimizer with 95% confidence and 5% margin of error.

Effectiveness metrics Table 3 shows the performance factor of each query for System X. The optimality frequency of System X is 0.5, and hence one can conclude that the optimizer of System X chose the relative optimal plan in no more than 50% of the queries. The average performance factor for the queries that do not find the relative optimal plan is 0.927. Furthermore, we can say with 95% confidence that System X finds a plan that is better than 80% of the generated sample plans (PF$\pm$ 5% > 80%) for 96% of the queries.

Quality of optimizer-chosen plan For System X at most 50% of the queries used the best plan (these are the queries in Table 3 with a performance factor of 1). For the remaining of the queries one should interpret the results along with 95% confidence and 5% margin of error we used to generate our sample set of plans. For example, the performance factor of query 13 is 0.88, hence, with 95% confidence we can say that the optimizer-chosen plan is better than 88% $\pm$ 5% plans in the search space.

An interesting observation is that while the optimality frequency (0.5) of System X shows that in half of the queries the chosen plan was not the best, in 96% of the queries the chosen plan was better than 80% of the plans in the sample set. Our results indicate that while the chosen plan by the optimizer of System X might not be the best in half of the cases, it is one of the top plans, which is a good enough plan for an optimizer with limited resources.

query	q6	q7	q13	q17	q18	q19	q24	q25	q26	q27	q29	q40	q46	q48	q50	q54	q61	q62	q66	q68	q73	q79	q84	q85
PF	1	1	0.88	0.917	0.854	1	1	1	0.899	0.989	0.825	0.979	0.94	1	0.969	1	1	0.977	0.982	1	1	1	1	0.912

Table 3: Performance Factor (PF) for System X

Quality of Cost Model and Plan Enumeration For the queries with performance factor less than 1 one can examine the plans that perform better than the optimizer-chosen plan and get some insight of the quality of the cost model and plan enumeration approach. We examined query 29 which has the lowest performance factor and we discovered that there are 71 plans in the sample that did better than the optimizer-chosen plan. Among them there are 54 plans that were considered by the optimizer, while 17 plans were not considered by the optimizer. As discussed in Section 2.2, we were not able to extract all physical plans the optimizer considered for System X, the number of plans considered here serves as a lower bound. This indicates the cost model fails to estimate accurately the cost of at least 54/71 (76%) of these better plans. The enumeration quality was however high as the optimizer did not consider only at most 17/71 (24%) of the better plans.

For query 18 which also has a low performance factor, we discovered 56 plans that did better than optimizer-chosen plan. Out of these, 24 plans were considered by the optimizer, while 32 plans were not. So the cost model fails to accurately estimate the cost of at least 43% of these plans while the enumeration approach did not even consider 57% of these plans.

Finally, to evaluate the efficiency of the optimizer for these queries we collected the number of logical plans. For query 29, the optimizer considers 93 logical plans, while for query 18, the optimizer considers 74 logical plans, indicating the optimizer was more efficient in coming up with a plan for query 18.

5. RELATED WORK

Despite of the importance of optimizer benchmarks to date no end-to-end optimizer benchmark is available. [19] offers a set of tools that support the design and generation of custom testbeds for optimizers but does not provide any measures to evaluate the quality of the produced optimizers. In [11] they provide a high-level overview of the unique challenges in testing a query optimizer. Our work covers two of the metrics they discussed: optimization time (i.e., efficiency), and query performance (i.e., effectiveness). A number of papers present tools to assist optimizer benchmarking. [21] presents algorithms to generate either a whole space of alternative plans, or a uniform random sample. But their research was specific to one system while the way we generate our sample set of plans is applicable to any DBMS.

There has also been work on testing different components of the query optimizer. [18] introduces a toolkit to visualize the plan space to facilitate the analysis of the cost model and behavior of a plan. In [22] and [12] they focus on the accuracy of cost model. The impact of I/O cost estimation on quality of query optimizers has been studied in [17]. In [14] they present ways to quantify the contributions of cardinality estimation, the cost model and the plan enumeration algorithm and provide guidelines for the complete design of a query optimizer.A number of papers addressed the problem of testing cardinality estimation models. [10] describes the replacement and validation of a new cardinality estimation model in Microsoft SQL Server. [16] defines a metric to measure deviations of size estimations from actual sizes. [6] presents a set of techniques that make exact cardinality query optimization a viable option. The effectiveness of transformation rules are studied in [5]. All of the above work focuses only on testing specific components of the query optimizer, while OptMark provides an end-to-end optimizer benchmark, aiming to reveal overall deficiencies and strengths of the benchmarked optimizer.

6. CONCLUSIONS

This paper introduces OptMark, a toolkit for evaluating the quality of database optimizers. OptMark offers a set of desirable features to support the assessment of optimizer quality. First, it provides methods for assessing both effectiveness (i.e., quality of the optimizer's chosen plan) *and* efficiency (i.e., optimization time) of an optimizer. Second OptMark decouples the evaluation of the optimizer performance from the performance of its underlying DBMSs execution engine, which distinguishs it from existing DBMS benchmarks (like TPC). Finally, it is minimum invasive to the underlying engine in that any DBMS for which benchmark results are desired can use our toolkit by implementing a simple set of API functions.

7. ACKNOWLEDGMENT

This research was funded by NSF IIS 1217952.

8. REFERENCES

[1] MySQL: An open source relational database, http://www.mysql.com/.

[2] TPC-DS Benchmark, http://www.tpc.org/tpcds/.

[3] Adaptive query optimization. In *Encyclopedia of Database Systems*, page 50. 2009.

[4] M. Atkinson and J. Sack. Generating binary tree at random. *Information Processing Letters*, 1992.

[5] S. Chaudhuri, L. Giakoumakis, V. R. Narasayya, and R. Ramamurthy. Rule profiling for query optimizers and their implications. In *ICDE*, 2010.

[6] S. Chaudhuri, V. R. Narasayya, and R. Ramamurthy. Exact cardinality query optimization for optimizer testing. *VLDB*, 2009.

[7] W. G. Cochran. *Sampling Techniques, 2nd Ed.* New York: John Wiley and Sons, Inc., 1963.

[8] D. DeHaan and F. W. Tompa. Optimal top-down join enumeration. In *SIGMOD*, 2007.

[9] P. Fender, G. Moerkotte, T. Neumann, and V. Leis. Effective and robust pruning for top-down join enumeration algorithms. In *ICDE*, 2012.

[10] C. Fraser, L. Giakoumakis, V. Hamine, and K. F. Moore-Smith. Testing cardinality estimation models in SQL server. In *DBTest*, 2012.

[11] L. Giakoumakis and C. A. Galindo-Legaria. Testing SQL server's query optimizer: Challenges, techniques and experiences. *IEEE Data Eng. Bull.*, 2008.

[12] Z. Gu, M. A. Soliman, and F. M. Waas. Testing the accuracy of query optimizers. In *DBTest*, 2012.

[13] I. F. Ilyas, J. Rao, G. M. Lohman, D. Gao, and E. T. Lin. Estimating compilation time of a query optimizer. In *SIGMOD*, 2003.

[14] V. Leis, A. Gubichev, A. Mirchev, P. Boncz, A. Kemper, and T. Neumann. How good are query optimizers, really? In *VLDB*, 2016.

[15] Z. Li, O. Papaemmanouil, and M. Cherniack. Optmark: A toolkit for benchmarking query optimizers. *arXiv:1608.02611 [cs.DB]*.

[16] G. Moerkotte, T. Neumann, and G. Steidl. Preventing bad plans by bounding the impact of cardinality estimation errors. *VLDB*, 2009.

[17] Y. Qin, K. Salem, and A. K. Goel. Towards adaptive costing of database access methods. In *ICDE*, 2007.

[18] N. Reddy and J. R. Haritsa. Analyzing plan diagrams of database query optimizers. In *VLDB*, 2005.

[19] M. Stillger and J. C. Freytag. Testing the quality of a query optimizer. *IEEE Data Eng. Bull.*, 18(3):41–48, 1995.

[20] F. Waas. benchmarking query optimizers, http://database-research.com/2011/04/19/benchmarking-query-optimizers/.

[21] F. Waas and C. A. Galindo-Legaria. Counting, enumerating, and sampling of execution plans in a cost-based query optimizer. In *SIGMOD*, 2000.

[22] F. M. Waas, L. Giakoumakis, and S. Zhang. Plan space analysis: an early warning system to detect plan regressions in cost-based optimizers. In *DBTest*, 2011.

Multi-Dueling Bandits and Their Application to Online Ranker Evaluation

Brian Brost[1] Yevgeny Seldin[1] Ingemar J. Cox[1,2] Christina Lioma[1]
[1] University of Copenhagen [2] University College London
brian.brost@di.ku.dk seldin@di.ku.dk ingemar@ieee.org c.lioma@di.ku.dk

ABSTRACT

Online ranker evaluation focuses on the challenge of efficiently determining, from implicit user feedback, which ranker out of a finite set of rankers is the best. It can be modeled by *dueling bandits*, a mathematical model for online learning under limited feedback from pairwise comparisons. Comparisons of pairs of rankers is performed by *interleaving* their result sets and examining which documents users click on. The dueling bandits model addresses the key issue of which pair of rankers to compare at each iteration.

Methods for simultaneously comparing more than two rankers have recently been developed. However, the question of which rankers to compare at each iteration was left open. We address this question by proposing a generalization of the dueling bandits model that uses simultaneous comparisons of an unrestricted number of rankers.

We evaluate our algorithm on standard large-scale online ranker evaluation datasets. Our experimentals show that the algorithm yields orders of magnitude gains in performance compared to state-of-the-art dueling bandit algorithms.

1. INTRODUCTION

Evaluation of rankers can be done online by presenting the ranked lists produced by rankers to users and then inferring the quality of the rankers by analyzing users' clicks. Online evaluation of rankers has become increasingly popular, partly because user behaviour can be easily logged. This provides online evaluation methods with inexpensive access to large amounts of training data [5]. One of the key drawbacks of online evaluation methods is that the outputs of new, potentially poor, rankers need to be presented to actual users. If a new ranker turns out to be poor, then users will be presented with poor results and, in the worst case, might abandon the service [7]. Conversely, if new rankers are not presented there is a risk of overlooking better rankers in the pool of rankers.

In online evaluation, it is usually easier for users to make relative judgements, rather than absolute judgements. Rankers can be compared by *interleaving* their result lists and examining which documents a user clicks on. Interleaving methods were found to require 1-2 orders of magnitude less data than absolute metrics to detect even small differences in retrieval quality [5].

When using interleaving to compare pairs of rankers, it is critical to determine which two rankers to interleave at each comparison, i.e. to resolve the exploration-exploitation tradeoff. *Dueling bandits* is an elegant mathematical framework for solving this [15, 18, 19, 17].

Recently, interleaving has been generalized to *multileaving* which permits more than two rankers to be compared in a single comparison [12, 13, 2]. Prior work on multileaving has shown that repetitive simultaneous comparison of fixed sets of rankers through multileaving is similarly accurate in identifying the best ranker in the set and faster than sequential comparisons of pairs of rankers through interleaving. However, prior work focused only on the comparisons themselves, and did not address the key issue of selecting subsets of rankers for each comparison. This approach has disadvantages. Firstly, since poor rankers are participating on all the comparisons the quality of the multileaved lists throughout the evaluation process is poor. Secondly, very poor rankers that could potentially be eliminated early in the process continue being evaluated, which does not allow the comparisons to focus on rankers whose quality is harder to distinguish.

We extend the dueling bandit framework and propose a *Multi-Dueling Bandit* algorithm that provides an intelligent selection of rankers for simultaneous comparisons and improves the trade-off between exploration and exploitation. Our experimental evaluations of the new algorithm on real web search learning-to-rank datasets show that our algorithm yields orders of magnitude improvement in performance compared to state-of-the-art dueling bandit algorithms.

2. BACKGROUND AND RELATED WORK

Our work builds on two main bodies of literature. The first is concerned with *selecting* promising rankers from a pool of rankers and the second is concerned with *combining* their ranked lists and *evaluating* their relative quality. The corresponding prior work is discussed next.

2.1 Dueling Bandits

Learning from limited relative feedback from pairwise comparisons can be modeled as a K-armed *dueling* bandit problem [15]. The goal is to select pairs of rankers, so that a

CIKM'16, October 24 - 28, 2016, Indianapolis, IN, USA

ISBN 978-1-4503-4073-1/16/10...$15.00

DOI: http://dx.doi.org/10.1145/2983323.2983659

mix of their rankings will be almost as good as the ranking of the best ranker in the pool. There are several possible definitions of the best ranker for pairwise comparisons. The most common definition is the *Condorcet winner*, which is a ranker that is (pairwise) better that any other ranker in the pool. Note that a Condorcet winner is not guaranteed to exist. Nevertheless, many dueling bandit algorithms assume the existence of a Condorcet winner and we follow suit.

Zoghi *et al.* [18] proposed an algorithm for the dueling bandit setting based on the idea of *relative upper confidence bounds* (RUCB). The algorithm maintains a relative upper confidence bound on the probability that a given arm i is better than another arm j. The algorithm then selects an arm i that might be the best, based on its upper confidence bounds relative to all other arms, and then selects the challenger with the highest upper confidence bound relative to i. Zoghi *et al.* [17] subsequently proposed a divide-and-conquer algorithm, *MergeRUCB*, extending their earlier work in [18]. Experiments by Zoghi *et al.* suggest that for large numbers of arms it outperforms RUCB.

Komiyama *et al.* [10] proposed an algorithm, *Relative Minimum Empirical Divergence* (RMED), which draws arms based on whether an arm has not been compared with other arms sufficiently often, or if it is not substantially beaten by many other arms. To decide if an arm has been sufficiently explored it uses bounds based on the KL-divergence. They showed that this algorithm outperformed RUCB and MergeRUCB. To the best of our knowledge this is currently the best performing dueling bandit algorithm.

All algorithms listed above are limited to pairwise comparisons, whereas our proposed algorithm is based on simultaneous comparisons of multiple rankers.

2.2 Comparison Methods

Combining ranked lists and evaluating chosen rankers is based on click-through information obtained by *interleaving* (for two rankers) or *multileaving* (for two or more rankers) methods.

Interleaving has been generalised to simultaneous comparison of more than two rankers. The proposed multileaving methods include Team Draft Multileave (TDM) [12], Optimised Multileave (OM) [12], Probabilistic Multileave (PM) [13], and Sample Only Scored Multileave (SOSM) [2]. SOSM was found to outperform the other multileaving methods, which can either be less accurate, or fail to scale well with the number of rankers [2]. We used SOSM to multileave rankers for our multi-dueling bandit algorithm.

3. THE MULTI-DUELING BANDIT PROBLEM

In multi-dueling bandits, at each iteration, t, an algorithm selects a subset, S_t, of K arms and observes outcomes of noisy pairwise comparisons (duels) between all pairs of arms in S_t. In the ranking scenario this corresponds to multileaving the ranked lists of the subset, S_t, of rankers and then inferring the relative quality of the lists (and the corresponding rankers) from user clicks. When the size of S_t is limited to 2 the problem reduces to standard dueling bandits.

Let $P = [p_{ij}]$ be a matrix of probabilities that arm i wins in a pairwise comparison with arm j (it satisfies $p_{ij} = 1 - p_{ji}$ and we define $p_{ii} = \frac{1}{2}$). In pairwise comparisons the best arm is not always well-defined. We follow the assumption in most dueling bandit literature that there exists a Condorcet winner, which is a unique arm $*$ satisfying $p_{*j} > \frac{1}{2}$ for all $j \neq *$. That is, the Condorcet winner $*$ is pairwise better than any other arm j. The quality of all arms is then defined by their *regret*, $r(j) = p_{*j} - \frac{1}{2}$, which is a shifted probability of losing to the best arm (this definition also coincides with dueling bandits). Smaller regret corresponds to better quality and the regret of playing the best arm is zero. The quality of a set of arms S_t is defined by the average quality of the constituent arms (the average regret)

$$r(S_t) = \frac{\sum_{j \in S_t} p_{*j}}{|S_t|} - \frac{1}{2}. \tag{1}$$

The goal of a multi-dueling bandit algorithm is to select subsets of arms $S_1, S_2, \dots,$ so that the cumulative regret $\sum_{t=1}^{T} r(S_t)$ is minimized. All arms have to be selected a small number of times in order to be explored, but the goal of the algorithm is to minimize the number of times when suboptimal arms are selected.

Simultaneous comparison of more than two arms may affect their pairwise winning probabilities. For example, in ranking, the effective length of a multileaved ranked list is typically limited by 10 items, since users rarely go beyond the first page of results. Therefore, the simultaneous comparison of more than 10 rankers means that some rankers may be compared based on a merged list that does not include their top suggestions. This may affect the estimates of their relative quality. This effect, which we refer to as *distortion* may also occur when less than 10 rankers are compared, since the limited length of the merged list does not allow perfect representation of every ranker. The exact level of distortion depends on the data, ranker, and method used for multileaving. The level of distortion of estimates of the pairwise winning probabilities made by SOSM, which was used in our experiments, is evaluated in Section 4.2.4. It is important to emphasize that in all our experimental comparisons, except one pathological case, the advantage of parallel exploration outweighed the disadvantage due to distortion in estimates.

3.1 Multi-Dueling Bandit Algorithm

The proposed multi-dueling bandit algorithm maintains optimistic estimates of pairwise winning probabilities p_{ij} and plays arms that, according to these optimistic estimates, have a chance of being the Condorcet winner. When there is a single candidate, the algorithm *exploits* this knowledge and plays only that candidate. When there are multiple candidates the algorithm *explores* by comparing them all. We increase parallel exploration by adding additional arms to such comparisons, as described below.

Our estimates of pairwise winning probabilities are based on empirical counts of wins/losses. In order for these estimates to be meaningful the algorithm has to assume that pairwise winning probabilities are *consistent* with the pairwise winning probability matrix P, irrespective of the composition of the set S_t (meaning that they are not distorted). More precisely, since correct identification of the Condorcet winner depends on correct estimation of the probabilities p_{*j}, it is important that they remain at a certain margin above $\frac{1}{2}$ irrespective of the composition of S_t. Incorrect estimation of p_{ij}-s for $i, j \neq *$ does not influence identification of the Condorcet winner and, therefore, their distortion does not disturb the operation of the algorithm.

We now describe our algorithm, which is provided in the Algorithm 1 box. We denote by $n_{ij}(t)$ the number of times up to round t that i and j were compared with each other. Let $w_{ij}(t)$ denote the number of times when arm i beat arm j. We break ties randomly, so that $n_{ij}(t) = w_{ij}(t) + w_{ji}(t)$. We compute upper confidence bounds $u_{ij}(t)$ on the probabilities p_{ij}:

$$u_{ij}(t) = \frac{w_{ij}(t)}{n_{ij}(t)} + \sqrt{\frac{\alpha \ln t}{n_{ij}(t)}} \tag{2}$$

(u_{ij}-s are the optimistic estimates of p_{ij}-s and they are analogous to those used in [18] for pairwise comparisons). The first term in $u_{ij}(t)$ is an empirical estimate of p_{ij} and the second term bounds the fluctuations of this estimate with high probability, see [1, 18]. The α parameter in the second term controls the width of the upper confidence bound.

Additionally, we maintain a second wider upper bound $v_{ij}(t)$, which we use to increase parallel exploration. We define $v_{ij}(t)$ by

$$v_{ij}(t) = \frac{w_{ij}(t)}{n_{ij}(t)} + \sqrt{\frac{\beta\alpha \ln t}{n_{ij}(t)}}, \tag{3}$$

where the parameter $\beta \geq 1$ controls how much wider it is than the upper confidence bound of Equation 2. When there is more than one candidate for a Condorcet winner according to the "narrow" confidence bounds in Equation 2 an exploration round is triggered and arms that could be Condorcet winner candidates according to the "wide" confidence bounds are compared. This leads to some arms being explored preemptively and decreases the overall number of exploration rounds by increasing parallel exploration.

Given K arms, we define $U_i(t) = \min_{j \in K, j \neq i}\{u_{ij}(t)\}$, i.e. $U_i(t)$ is the smallest upper confidence bound of i. Let E denote the set of potential Condorcet winners, which contains all arms i for which $U_i(t) \geq 1/2$. Additionally, we define $V_i(t) = \min_{j \in K, j \neq i}\{v_{ij}(t)\}$ and F to be the set of potential Condorcet winners according to the wider upper bounds, that is, all arms for which $V_i(t) \geq 1/2$.

At each iteration of Algorithm 1, if there is only a single potential Condorcet winner in E, we choose this arm. If there are several potential Condorcet winners, we select all arms in the larger set F. In the unlikely event that there are no potential Condorcet winners, we select all arms.

$W = [w_{ij}] := 0_{K \times K}$
Play all arms and update the corresponding entries in W
for $t = 2, \ldots, T$ **do**
  $U := [u_{ij}(t)] = \frac{w_{ij}(t)}{n_{ij}(t)} + \sqrt{\frac{\alpha \ln t}{n_{ij}(t)}}$, $u_{ii}(t) = 1/2$
  $V := [v_{ij}(t)] = \frac{w_{ij}(t)}{n_{ij}(t)} + \sqrt{\frac{\beta\alpha \ln t}{n_{ij}(t)}}$, $v_{ii}(t) = 1/2$
  E $= \{i \text{ s.t. } U_i(t) \geq 1/2\}$ (The set of potential champions according to U)
  F $= \{i \text{ s.t. } V_i(t) \geq 1/2\}$ (The set of potential champions according to V)
  if $|E| > 1$ **then**
    Choose all arms $f \in F$ for comparison and update the corresponding entries in W
  else if $|E| = 1$ **then**
    Choose the arm $e \in E$
  else
    Choose all arms for comparison and update the corresponding entries in W
end

Algorithm 1: Multi-Dueling Bandit (MDB) Algorithm.

Table 1: Datasets. Each dataset consists of a number of query-document pairs, together with a relevance judgement for the pair. Each document is represented by a feature vector.

Datasets	Queries	URLs	Features
MSLR-WEB30K [2]	31,531	3,771,125	136
YLR Set 1 [4]	19,944	473,134	700
YLR Set 2 [4]	1,266	34,815	700
Yandex [3]	9,124	97,290	245

4. EXPERIMENTAL EVALUATION

We next present the experimental evaluation of our Multi-Dueling Bandits (MDB) algorithm.

4.1 Experimental Setup

We begin by describing our experimental setup.

4.1.1 *Baselines*

We compare our MDB algorithm to three state-of-the-art dueling bandit algorithms, namely RUCB and MergeRUCB, both implemented in the freely available software package Lerot [11], and RMED1 [10]. As per [17], we set the α parameter of Equation 2 for RUCB to 0.51, and to 1.01 for MergeRUCB. For RMED1 we use the same parameter setting as [10]: $f(K) = 0.3K^{1.01}$. To select the parameters for MDB, we carried out a grid search on the grid $\{0.5, 1, 1.5\} \times \{1.25, 1.5, 2, 4\}$ on a separate dataset, specifically the validation set of the YLR1 dataset, and found the best parameters to be $\alpha = 0.5$ and $\beta = 1.5$. We used these as our parameter settings for MDB for all other experiments.

4.1.2 *Datasets*

We compare the algorithms on four large-scale evaluation datasets summarised in Table 1[1]. Since there was no Condorcet winner for the Yandex dataset, we randomly sampled subsets of 200 rankers from the Yandex dataset, selecting the first subset with a Condorcet winner.

4.1.3 *Ranker Construction*

Following [17], for each dataset we choose the rankers to be the features of the dataset. That is, for a given feature, we construct a ranker which ranks documents only according to the score of that feature. As noted in [17] this is a somewhat artificial setup from a learning-to-rank perspective, however from the point of view of *evaluating* dueling and multi-dueling bandit algorithms, the difficulty of a problem instance is affected by the relative performance of the rankers, not their absolute performance. Using the feature rankers is therefore useful for assessing the performance of dueling and multi-dueling bandit algorithms since many of

[1]Only 519 features are non-zero for YLR Set 1 and only 596 features are non-zero for YLR Set 2. The remaining features are zero for all query-document pairs.

the features perform similarly and are therefore difficult to distinguish using interleaved or multileaved comparisons.

4.1.4 Simulated User Model

All experiments are conducted using a simulated user model. For each iteration we randomly sample with replacement one query from the pool of queries of the dataset. The dueling or multi-dueling bandit algorithms choose rankers, whose results are then interleaved or multileaved respectively, and presented to a simulated user. For the dueling bandit algorithms, we compare pairs of rankers using probabilistic interleaving [8]. For MDB, we use SOSM [2]. Both probabilistic interleaving and SOSM only present the top-10 documents to users. Clicks are then generated from a probabilistic user model [9]. The interleaving or multileaving algorithm scores the chosen rankers using the clicks generated by the user.

The click model used for these experiments was the navigational user model from [9], unless otherwise stated. This click model has been used as a standard click model for dueling bandit algorithm evaluation in [17].

4.2 Results

Below we summarize the experimental results for the various experiments. For all figures, the error bars show the standard deviation of cumulative regret across runs for each algorithm at the given time step.

4.2.1 Dependence of Cumulative Regret on Number of Iterations

Figure 1 shows how the cumulative regret increases with each iteration using the real learning to rank dataset YLR1. It shows that MDB substantially outperforms the baselines. It outperforms the best dueling bandit algorithm, RMED1, by almost 2 orders of magnitude. RMED1 outperforms RUCB and MergeRUCB, as expected from the results of [10]. The results for the other datasets are similar, and can be seen in the extended version [3], with MDB outperforming the best dueling bandit algorithm, RMED1, by a factor of 3 in the dataset with the smallest number of features, and orders of magnitude for the other datasets.

Note that for the Yandex dataset, since there was no Condorcet winner, we randomly sampled 200 of the 245 feature rankers to obtain a dataset with a Condorcet winner. Results using the full Yandex dataset with no Condorcet winner are described in the extended version [3].

4.2.2 Dependence on Click Model

To test the robustness of our approach to the choice of click model, we also investigated performance using the perfect and informational click models [9]. Figure 2 shows the cumulative regret for the informational click model, using randomly selected subsets of size 200 of the rankers from the YLR1 dataset. We chose to use subsets of the full dataset for these experiments due to the computational costs of running RMED1 on the full YLR1 dataset. For all click models MDB outperforms the best dueling bandit algorithm by between 1 and 2 orders of magnitude, and the results for the other click models are included in the extended version [3].

For MDB, the regret doubles when going from the perfect to the navigational click model, but does not increase further for the informational click model. In contrast, for the dueling bandit algorithms, regret for the informational click model is approximately double that for the navigational

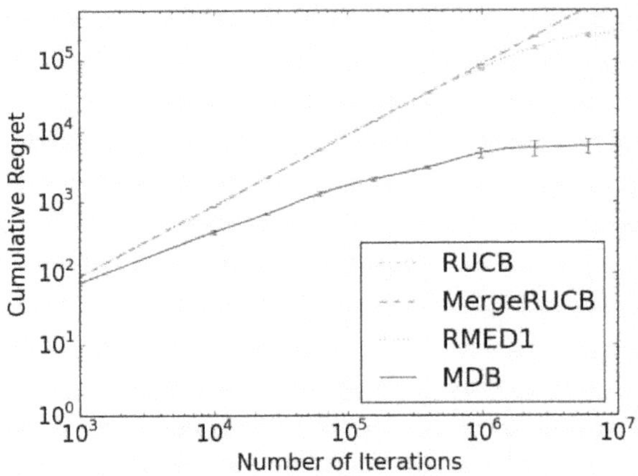

Figure 1: Cumulative regret averaged over 10 runs against number of iterations for the 4 algorithms on the YLR1 dataset with the navigational click model.

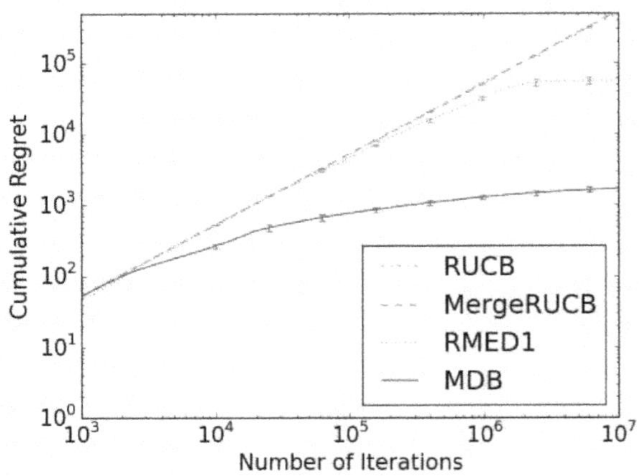

Figure 2: Cumulative regret averaged over 10 runs against number of iterations for the 4 algorithms on the YLR1 dataset using the informational click model.

click model, which is approximately double that of the perfect click model. MDB is therefore least affected by varying the click model in our experiments.

4.2.3 Dependence on Number of Rankers

To isolate the impact of the number of rankers being compared on the real datasets involving multileaving, we investigate how regret scales with the number of rankers being compared using the YLR1 dataset. We randomly sampled subsets of rankers of sizes $\{10, 25, 40, 55, 70, 85, 100, 115, 130, 145\}$ from the YLR1 dataset. Note that we randomly sampled different subsets of rankers for each run. For each of these subsets we then carried out 10 runs of each algorithm over 5,000,000 iterations and recorded the average cumulative regret.

Figure 3 shows how the performance of the 4 algorithms varies as a function of the number of rankers. Additionally we have shown the performance of a random policy which simply selects a random subset of the rankers for multileav-

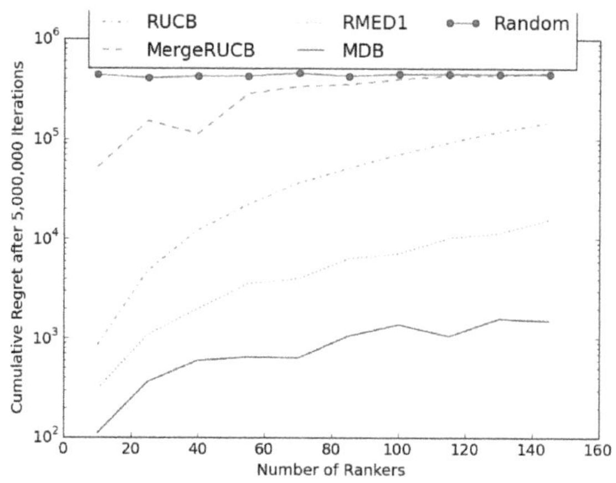

Figure 3: Cumulative regret averaged over 10 runs after 5,000,000 iterations against number of rankers for the 4 algorithms, and a random policy, on subsets with M rankers of the YLR1 dataset with navigational click model.

ing at each iteration. We observe that as the number of rankers increases the cumulative regret increases most for RUCB and MergeRUCB, while it increases more slowly for RMED1. Regret appears to be almost independent of the number of rankers for MDB.

These experiments were also carried out for the perfect and informational click models, and the results were very similar but have been omitted due to page restrictions.

For the MDB algorithm, the regret associated with having to explore suboptimal rankers does not appear to be additionally compounded by the number of rankers being explored. This is an important characteristic of the MDB algorithm, since if we can explore additional rankers with no substantial additional cost, the risks associated with large-scale online ranker evaluation are substantially mitigated.

Note that it may appear that regret levels off for MergeRUCB as we increase the number of rankers. This is due to the fact that for 5,000,000 iterations there is a limit to how much regret can be incurred just by making random choices in 5,000,000 iterations. For larger problem sizes and for a time frame of 5,000,000 iterations, MergeRUCB begins to perform no better than a random policy. This does not imply that MergeRUCB performs as badly as a random policy in general, but for these problem instances it has not yet begun to eliminate suboptimal arms after 5,000,000 iterations. Further iterations would be needed to show improvements relative to the random policy.

4.2.4 *Distortion of probability estimates due to multileaving*

As discussed earlier, simultaneous comparison of more than two arms may affect their pairwise winning probabilities. We called this effect *distortion.* We can quantify this effect by first randomly sampling a fixed size subset of rankers that includes a Condorcet winner, and then measuring, after some fixed number of multileavings, the fraction of rankers that beat the Condorcet winner more than 50% of the time. If there is no distortion, and the number of multileavings is sufficient, we expect this fraction to be zero.

In these experiments we test the level of distortion in the multileaving method SOSM, and examine how robust our MDB algorithm is to distortions in the multileaving method.

For each dataset, and each click model, we randomly sample subsets of rankers of sizes 3, 10, and 100 that include a Condorcet winner. We examine the probabilities of the rankers beating the Condorcet winner after 3,000 multileavings. Note that this is likely to be an overestimate of the distortion of the multileaving method, since, for rankers of very similar quality, 3,000 iterations may not be sufficient to reliably distinguish rankers. Table 2 shows the average, over 30 runs, of the percentage of rankers that beat the Condorcet winner. Note that we have only included the results for the informational click model, the results for the remaining click models are shown in the extended version [3].

We observe that the distortion problem is almost unique to the MSLR dataset, and is exacerbated by the noisiest click model, the informational click model. The distortion problem is exclusively related to the feature ranker 133 in the MSLR dataset. Feature ranker 133 scores documents solely based on the query-document clicks, i.e. a document was clicked on in response to a query. This feature is very good at identifying 1 or 2 documents that are very likely to be relevant. However, when asked to rank documents in a multileaved set, most of the documents, even though they might be relevant, have not been previously clicked on. As such, ranker 133 is unable to distinguish between the vast majority of documents. Thus, even though ranker 133 performs well in pairwise comparisons, where it has contributed half of the documents in the results list, it performs very poorly when multileaved with many other rankers. Table 2 also includes results for the MSLR dataset, when feature ranker 133 is excluded. This is denoted by MSLR*. When ranker 133 is excluded, no substantial distortion is observed.

The moderate levels of distortion observed for the Yandex and MSLR dataset (excluding feature ranker 133) are likely to be mostly caused by the fact that there are many rankers that are very similar in quality, and so 3,000 comparisons are not sufficient to differentiate these similar rankers.

Table 2: Percentage of rankers beating the Condorcet winner (distortion), averaged over 30 runs, after 3,000 iterations for 3, 10, and 100 rankers being multileaved for each dataset and click model. The dataset denoted MSLR* is the MSLR dataset with feature ranker 133 removed.

	Distortion		
Num. Rankers	3	10	100
MSLR Informational	0.0%	6.8%	41.3%
MSLR* Informational	0.0%	2.9%	2.7%
YLR1 Informational	0.0%	0.0%	0.3%
YLR2 Informational	0.0%	1.0%	0.9%
Yandex Informational	3.3%	3.9%	3.4%

The only problem setting where our MDB algorithm did not substantially outperform the best baseline dueling bandit algorithm, RMED1, was for the MSLR dataset with all 136 feature rankers with the informational click model. The results for this problem setting are shown in Figure 4. This is due specifically to the feature ranker 133 in the MSLR dataset. In the extended version [3], we show that there was

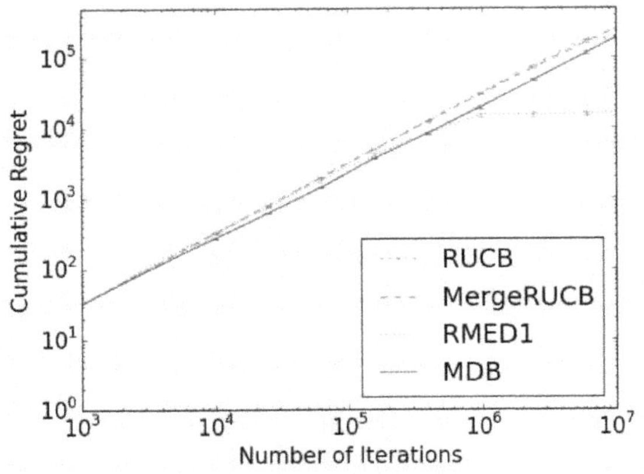

Figure 4: Average cumulative regret over 10 runs against number of iterations for the 4 algorithms on the MSLR dataset using the informational click model.

some distortion for all click models for the MSLR dataset. However, it is with the informational click model that the distortion is greatest, reaching 41.3% for 100 rankers. This is a very high percentage. The MDB algorithm appears to be robust to more reasonable levels of distortion, suffering substantially less regret than the baselines for the MSLR dataset with the navigational click model, and with the perfect click model (this result is omitted due to the page restriction). Additionally, for the MSLR dataset with feature ranker 133 removed, MDB substantially outperformed all baselines for all click models. Results are omitted due to the page restriction.

5. CONCLUSIONS AND FUTURE WORK

This paper proposes a generalisation of the K-armed dueling bandits termed multi-dueling bandits (MDB). We have applied MDB in online ranker evaluation to leverage the power of simultaneous comparisons through multileaving and improve the exploration-exploitation trade-off. Our experimental results on data from 4 standard datasets demonstrated up to 1 to 2 orders of magnitude reduction in regret compared to state-of-the-art dueling bandit algorithms, RUCB [18], MergeRUCB [17], and RMED1 [10] in all except one pathological case discussed below. Generally, relative benefits compared to dueling bandits increased with the number of rankers being compared. For MDB, the incurred regret did not increase substantially as the number of rankers increased. As such, the risks associated with large-scale online ranker evaluation are substantially mitigated. Further experiments showed that MDB was robust to various user click models.

Experiments were also conducted to examine the behaviour of MDB in the absence of a Condorcet winner, which is the case for the full Yandex dataset. In this case, the regret was approximated by measuring the NDGC@10 score. In this case MDB outperformed the best dueling bandit algorithm, RMED1, by approximately an order of magnitude after 5,000,000 iterations.

We also investigated the level of distortion of pairwise winning probabilities in multileaving using SOSM. For the MSLR dataset using a navigational click model, the distortion reached 41.3%. In this case MDB was inferior to RMED1. The high level of distortion was due to the peculiarities of ranker 133. If ranker 133 is removed, the distortion of pairwise winning probabilities is significantly reduced and MDB outperforms all other algorithms.

There are a number of avenues for future work. The distortion of pairwise winning probabilities in multileaving needs further investigation. All existing multileaving algorithms exhibit this behaviour. It remains an open question as to whether a new multileaving algorithm can be designed to avoid this problem, or at least minimize it. Furthermore, a theoretical analysis of our algorithm needs to be developed to better understand its power and limitations. Additionally, since a Condorcet winner is not guaranteed to exist, it may be useful to explore other concepts of winners, such as the Copeland [16], Borda [14] and von Neumann [6] criteria. Finally, we note that the proposed multi-dueling bandit algorithm can be applied to a broad class of problems and applications in other domains, e.g. recommender systems.

6. REFERENCES

[1] P. Auer, N. Cesa-Bianchi, and P. Fischer. Finite-time analysis of the multiarmed bandit problem. *Machine learning*, 47(2-3):235–256, 2002.

[2] B. Brost, I. J. Cox, Y. Seldin, and C. Lioma. An improved multileaving algorithm for online ranker evaluation. SIGIR, 2016.

[3] B. Brost, Y. Seldin, I. J. Cox, and C. Lioma. Multi-dueling bandits and their application to online ranker evaluation - extended version. *arXiv preprint arXiv:1608.06253*, 2016.

[4] O. Chapelle and Y. Chang. Yahoo! learning to rank challenge overview. In *Yahoo! Learning to Rank Challenge*, 2011.

[5] O. Chapelle, T. Joachims, F. Radlinski, and Y. Yue. Large-scale validation and analysis of interleaved search evaluation. *TOIS*, 30(1), 2012.

[6] M. Dudík, K. Hofmann, R. E. Schapire, A. Slivkins, and M. Zoghi. Contextual dueling bandits. *arXiv preprint arXiv:1502.06362*, 2015.

[7] K. Hofmann, S. Whiteson, and M. de Rijke. Balancing exploration and exploitation in learning to rank online. pages 251–263. Springer, 2011.

[8] K. Hofmann, S. Whiteson, and M. de Rijke. A probabilistic method for inferring preferences from clicks. In *CIKM*, pages 249–258. ACM, 2011.

[9] K. Hofmann, S. Whiteson, and M. D. Rijke. Fidelity, soundness, and efficiency of interleaved comparison methods. *TOIS*, 31(4):17, 2013.

[10] J. Komiyama, J. Honda, H. Kashima, and H. Nakagawa. Regret lower bound and optimal algorithm in dueling bandit problem. *arXiv preprint arXiv:1506.02550*, 2015.

[11] A. Schuth, K. Hofmann, S. Whiteson, and M. de Rijke. Lerot: An online learning to rank framework. In *Proceedings of the 2013 workshop on Living labs for information retrieval evaluation*, pages 23–26. ACM, 2013.

[12] A. Schuth, F. Sietsma, S. Whiteson, D. Lefortier, and M. de Rijke. Multileaved comparisons for fast online evaluation. In *CIKM*. ACM, 2014.

[13] A. Schuth et al. Probabilistic multileave for online retrieval evaluation. SIGIR, 2015.

[14] T. Urvoy, F. Clerot, R. Féraud, and S. Naamane. Generic exploration and k-armed voting bandits. In *ICML*, 2013.

[15] Y. Yue, J. Broder, R. Kleinberg, and T. Joachims. The k-armed dueling bandits problem. *Journal of Computer and System Sciences*, 78(5):1538–1556, 2012.

[16] M. Zoghi, Z. Karnin, S. Whiteson, and M. de Rijke. Copeland dueling bandits. *arXiv preprint arXiv:1506.00312*, 2015.

[17] M. Zoghi, S. Whiteson, and M. de Rijke. Mergerucb: A method for large-scale online ranker evaluation. In *WSDM*, 2015.

[18] M. Zoghi, S. Whiteson, R. Munos, M. d. Rijke, et al. Relative upper confidence bound for the k-armed dueling bandit problem. In *JMLR Workshop and Conference Proceedings*, number 32. JMLR, 2014.

[19] M. Zoghi, S. A. Whiteson, M. de Rijke, and R. Munos. Relative confidence sampling for efficient on-line ranker evaluation. In *WSDM*. ACM, 2014.

Robust Contextual Outlier Detection: Where Context Meets Sparsity

Jiongqian Liang and Srinivasan Parthasarathy
Computer Science and Engineering, The Ohio State University, Columbus, OH, USA
{liangji,srini}@cse.ohio-state.edu

ABSTRACT

Outlier detection is a fundamental data science task with applications ranging from data cleaning to network security. Recently, a new class of outlier detection algorithms has emerged, called *contextual outlier detection*, and has shown improved performance when studying anomalous behavior in a specific context. However, as we point out in this article, such approaches have limited applicability in situations where the context is sparse (i.e., lacking a suitable frame of reference). Moreover, approaches developed to date do not scale to large datasets. To address these problems, here we propose a novel and robust approach alternative to the state-of-the-art called RObust Contextual Outlier Detection (ROCOD). We utilize a local and global behavioral model based on the relevant contexts, which is then integrated in a natural and robust fashion. We run ROCOD on both synthetic and real-world datasets and demonstrate that it outperforms other competitive baselines on the axes of efficacy and efficiency. We also drill down and perform a fine-grained analysis to shed light on the rationale for the performance gains of ROCOD and reveal its effectiveness when handling objects with sparse contexts.

1. INTRODUCTION

"An *outlier* is an observation that deviates so much from other observations as to arouse suspicion that it was generated by a different mechanism" [6]. Detecting outliers finds applications in a wide range of domains including cyber-intrusion detection, epidemiology studies, fraud detection, and data cleaning. A number of efforts in this space have treated all attributes, associated with a data point, in an egalitarian fashion. However, in many domains, some attributes are usually highly related to the outlier behavior, called *behavioral attributes* or *indicator attributes*, while other attributes only provide contexts of the behavior, termed *contextual attributes*. It has been demonstrated recently that by distinguishing contextual attributes from behavioral attributes, the precision of outlier detection can be increased [4, 13, 14, 17, 5]. Formally, *contextual outlier* or *conditional anomaly* is defined as an object with behavior deviating from other objects with similar contextual information [4, 13, 14]. Contextual attributes are used to define the contexts, and objects sharing similar contexts with an object form its *reference group*. Behavior attributes, on the other hand, are used for examining outlierness in a specific context, compared to the reference group.

One pitfall of existing contextual outlier detection methods is that they might fail to examine the outlierness of objects with sparse contexts. To intuitively show this, we use a toy example of credit card fraud detection. For simplicity, suppose we intend to detect suspicious transactions and only monitor two variables, the annual income of cardholders and the amount of each transaction (shown in Figure 1).

The Importance of Contextual Attributes: Though contextual attributes are not directly related to the anomalous behavior, they provide useful information on contexts for outlier detection. In the example of Figure 1, transaction amount and annual income can be respectively regarded as the behavioral attribute and contextual attribute. If we merely consider the behavioral attribute, then points G, E and F will not be flagged as outliers, which is not reasonable. Therefore, we need auxiliary information from the contextual attributes to pinpoint the outliers.

Incorporating Contextual Attributes: One conventional way to incorporate contextual attributes is treating them similarly with behavioral attributes by concatenating the two. In the example above, all the boundary points (A, B, ..., G) will be reported as outliers. Another way is to use existing contextual outlier detection techniques.Following the definition of the contextual outlier, we can examine the difference of behavioral attribute between a point and other points with the similar contextual attribute. One will then report point C and D as outliers since their behavior values (y values) are quite different from other points with similar contextual values (x values).

Limitations of Existing Approaches: These two methods have limitations on addressing objects with sparse contexts (A, B, E, F and G). The former approach tends to overestimate the outlierness of objects with unusual contexts because the outlierness score can be directly contributed by contextual attributes. Moreover, the latter approach fails to properly examine the outlierness of objects with sparse contexts. In fact, applying state-of-the-art contextual outlier detection algorithm [13] for the toy example, we obtain outlierness score ranking of $B > D > C > A \gg G, E, F$. However, a close look at our example reveals that A and B

CIKM'16 , October 24-28, 2016, Indianapolis, IN, USA
 ISBN 978-1-4503-4073-1/16/10... $15.00
http://dx.doi.org/10.1145/2983323.2983660

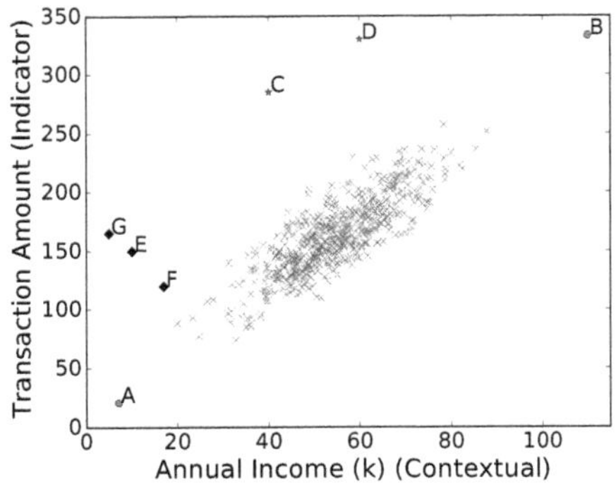

Figure 1: Toy example of contextual outliers.

should ideally not be flagged as outliers since they follow the normal pattern between the two attributes that a lower value in contextual attribute corresponds to a lower value in behavioral attribute and vice versa. Therefore, we need a more robust approach for outlier detection to distinguish E, F, G with A and B, giving A and B lower outlierness scores. To the best of our knowledge, this paper is the first piece of work attempting to rectify this problem.

To this end, we propose a refined approach, called RObust Contextual Outlier Detection (ROCOD), to better exploit contextual attributes to assist outlier detection, ROCOD can particularly address the problems caused by the contextual sparsity, making it more robust towards broad outlier detection tasks. Specifically, we propose *local expected behavior* and *global expected behavior* models that seek to understand the dependence structure between behavioral attributes and contextual attributes. Local expected behavior models are designed to predict the behavior by referring to the objects with similar context, called *contextual neighbors*. Global expected behavior models learn the dependence structure between contextual attributes and behavioral attributes from the data, and infer the behavior in a holistic sense. We then propose a regularized integration function to naturally couple both types of behavior models based on the number of contextual neighbors, which naturally accommodates objects with sparse contexts. We run ROCOD on both synthetic and real-world datasets and compare it with *five* state-of-the-art outlier detection techniques. Our experimental results show that ROCOD outperforms all the baselines on both effectiveness (measured by different metrics) and efficiency.

2. ROCOD

To the best of our knowledge, none of the existing works addresses the problem caused by the sparsity of contexts in contextual outlier detection (see our extended paper [7] for a detailed review of related work). In this section, we introduce our RObust Contextual Outlier Detection (ROCOD) approach to tackle this problem in detail.

2.1 Problem Formulation

Given a series of objects, the i-th object can be represented as

$$z^{(i)} = \binom{x^{(i)}}{y^{(i)}} = (x_1^{(i)}, x_2^{(i)}, ..., x_C^{(i)}, y_1^{(i)}, y_2^{(i)}, ..., y_B^{(i)})^T \quad (1)$$

where $z^{(i)}$ is the whole attribute vector, $x^{(i)}$ is contextual attribute vector and $y^{(i)}$ is behavioral attribute vector. Without loss of generality, we assume $x^{(i)}$ has C dimensions and $y^{(i)}$ has B dimensions. Following this, the whole dataset can be denoted as $Z = \langle z^{(1)}, z^{(2)}, ..., z^{(N)} \rangle$, where N is the total number of objects. Among them, we denote O as the set of outliers. Given the dataset Z, our goal is to assign each object i with an outlierness score S_i so that outliers in O have much higher values than other objects.

Conforming to the definition of the contextual outlier, the outlierness of an object arises from the abnormal behavioral attributes in its particular context. In other words, provided the contextual attributes, there is underlying pattern restricting the behavioral attributes to some expected values, beyond which one object will be considered as an outlier. We here call it the *dependent pattern* and define the expected behavior as follows.

DEFINITION 1. ***Expected Behavior.*** *For object i, the expected behavior is the values of its behavioral attributes predicted by the underpinning dependent pattern, given its contextual attributes $x^{(i)}$.*

Formally, denote the underpinning dependent pattern as a function $f(\cdot)$, then the expected behavior is

$$\hat{y}^{(i)} = f(x^{(i)}) \quad (2)$$

Following the definition, a contextual outlier is the object with behavioral attributes violating the dependent pattern under its contextual attributes. We can gauge the outlierness score of object i by measuring the difference of $\hat{y}^{(i)}$ and $y^{(i)}$. Therefore, revealing the expected behavior of each object is a crucial part of flagging contextual outliers.

However, it is nontrivial to find out the pattern function $f(\cdot)$ and the expected behavior since the data distribution is usually unknown and the data is inherently noisy. We next discuss how we approach this problem from both a local and global perspective and how to combine them.

2.2 Local Expected Behavior Modeling

We first study the dependent pattern and expected behavior from the local aspect. We define *contextual neighbors*:

DEFINITION 2. ***Contextual Neighbors.*** *Contextual neighbors of an object are the objects that are similar to it on contextual attributes.*

Formally, the set of contextual neighbors of object i is

$$CN_i = \left\{ j : j \in D \wedge j \neq i \wedge sim(x^{(i)}, x^{(j)}) \geq \alpha \right\} \quad (3)$$

where α is a preset similarity threshold and $sim(\cdot)$ is a similarity function of two vectors. $D = \{1, 2, ..., N\}$ denotes the set of objects indexes. While $sim(\cdot)$ can be any reasonable similarity function, we choose cosine similarity here.

We then define *local expected behavior* as follows.

DEFINITION 3. ***Local Expected Behavior.*** *The local expected behavior of an object is the average values of behavioral attributes among all its contextual neighbors.*

This definition hinges on the underlying assumption of contextual outlier detection that objects with similar contextual attributes share similar behavioral attributes [4, 13, 14] and is also a natural extension of Tobler's first law of geography [16]. To formalize it, the expected behavior of object i given contextual attributes $x^{(i)}$ is

$$\hat{y}^{(i)} = \Phi(x^{(i)}) = \frac{\sum_{j \in CN_i} y^{(j)}}{|CN_i|} \quad (4)$$

where $\Phi(\cdot)$ denotes local behavior pattern.

The local behavior pattern is tightly tied to the definition of contextual outlier detection and is supposed to directly reflect the dependent relationship between behavioral attributes and contextual attributes. Moreover, it does not make any assumption on the distribution of data. While this local property has been widely used in spatial and temporal outlier detection [19, 8], we generalize it to a broader range of applications with arbitrarily defined contexts. However, since the local expected behavior relies on the contextual neighbors, it will be inapplicable if one object does not have contextual neighbors. Therefore, the local expected behavior cannot be inferred for all the objects and we need a more robust way to compute the expected behavior.

2.3 Global Expected Behavior Modeling

We now introduce a global approach to capture the underlying dependent pattern in the data and infer the expected behavior, called *global expected behavior.* A natural way of capturing the global dependent relationship between behavioral attributes and contextual attributes is to adopt regression models. For each behavioral attribute, we can learn a regression model considering contextual attributes as features and the behavioral attributes as the target values. In total, we learn B regressors from the dataset with B behavioral attributes. With the regression models, we hereby define global expected behavior.

DEFINITION 4. ***Global Expected Behavior.*** *The global expected behavior of an object is the values of behavioral attributes predicted by the regression models taking its contextual attributes as input.*

Formally, the global expected behavior of object i is

$$\hat{y}^{(i)} = \Psi(x^{(i)}) \tag{5}$$

where $\Psi(\cdot)$ incorporates the regression models learned from the whole dataset using contextual attributes as independent variables and behavioral attributes as dependent variables. $\Psi(\cdot)$ takes the contextual attributes $x^{(i)}$ as input and outputs the expected behavior attribute vector $\hat{y}^{(i)}$. Note that we can adopt any regression model here, either linear or non-linear. Obviously, this manner of behavior modeling is a holistic approach since the regression models are learned from the whole dataset.

2.4 Ensemble Expected Behavior

So far we have introduced two different perspectives to depict the underpinning relationship between behavioral attributes and contextual attributes, and used them to compute local and global expected behavior. Local expected behavior adopts the contextual neighbors as the reference frame while global expected behavior is predicted by adopting the regression models learned from the whole dataset.

These two ways of inferring expected behavior offer complementary benefits. Local expected behavior is a model-free approach and should have a lower bias when the number of contextual neighbors is large. However, local expected behavior contains larger variance in general and is prone to noise, especially when the number of contextual neighbors is small. In fact, it cannot be applied at all when there is no contextual neighbor. On the other hand, global expected behavior infers the values considering the dependent relationship between the two categories of attributes in a holistic way. Therefore, it is expected to contain smaller variance and is more robust against noise. However, its bias tends to be larger since it cannot capture the fine-grained local pattern for each object.

Considering the different advantages of the two approaches, we intend to find an appropriate manner to integrate them. One possible method is to simply take a weighted sum of them with pre-defined weights. However, it is not trivial to determine reasonable weights and the issue of zero contextual neighbors still remains.

To resolve these issues, we propose an adaptive weighted sum to integrate these two methods. Instead of fixing the weights for all objects, we adjust the weights according to the number of contextual neighbors of each object. Given an object i, we define the ensemble expected behavior as

$$\hat{y}^{(i)} = \lambda_i \cdot \Phi(x^{(i)}) + (1 - \lambda_i) \cdot \Psi(x^{(i)}) \tag{6}$$

where

$$\lambda_i = \frac{\sqrt{|CN_i|}}{\max\limits_{1 \leq j \leq N} \sqrt{|CN_j|}}. \tag{7}$$

Here, $\Phi(x^{(i)})$ and $\Psi(x^{(i)})$ are respectively local expected behavior and global expected behavior as defined in Equation 4 and Equation 5. The intuition behind this weighted combination is that if an object has a sufficient number of contextual neighbors, we believe the contextual neighbors are a reliable reference frame and place more weight on local expected behavior. Otherwise, we put more weight on the global metric. In addition, we take the square root transformation on $|CN_i|$ to improve the normality of $\lambda_i \cdot \Phi(x^{(i)})$ [2].

By setting weight on local expected behavior proportional to the square root of the number of contextual neighbors, the model is more robust and can appropriately deal with context sparsity. In particular, it properly solves the problem of zero contextual neighbors by naturally setting the weight of local expected behavior to zero when $|CN_i| = 0$.

With the ensemble expected behavior for each object, we measure the outlierness score of object i by the difference of expected behavior $\hat{y}^{(i)}$ and real behavior $y^{(i)}$, specifically by the L2-norm $\left\| y^{(i)} - \hat{y}^{(i)} \right\|_2$. Here, the L2-norm of the difference assumes each behavioral attribute contributes equally to the outlierness score. However, this might not be true since the attributes can have different credibility at flagging the outlier. For example, if the real values of one behavioral attribute are highly consistent with the expected ones, indicating the pattern is well captured by our approach as a whole, then a slight difference of real value and expected value should be a strong sign of outlierness. Following this intuition, we weight each behavioral attribute based on how good the expected behavior on capturing the real behavior values. For each behavioral attribute, we use the coefficient of determination [9] to measure consistency between the real behavior and the expected one. For j-th behavioral attribute, the coefficient of determination is calculated by

$$R^2(y_j, \hat{y}_j) = 1 - \frac{\sum\limits_{1 \leq i \leq N} ({y_j}^{(i)} - \hat{y}_j^{(i)})^2}{\sum\limits_{1 \leq i \leq N} ({y_j}^{(i)} - \bar{y}_j)^2} \tag{8}$$

where $\bar{y}_j = \frac{1}{N} \sum\limits_{1 \leq i \leq N} {y_j}^{(i)}$, ${y_j}^{(i)}$ is the value of j-th behavioral attribute for object i, and $\hat{y}_j^{(i)}$ is the expected value of it using our approach. We define the weight of j-th behavioral attribute as $w_j = \max(R^2(y_j, \hat{y}_j), 0)$ and therefore the range of w_j is $[0, 1]$. We now can calculate the outlierness score of object i using

$$S_i = \left\| W^T(y^{(i)} - \hat{y}^{(i)}) \right\|_2 \tag{9}$$

where $W = (w_1, w_2, ..., w_B)^T$.

`ROCOD` detects outliers using Equation 9. Specifically, `ROCOD` uses it to capture the outlierness score for each object and the n objects with highest outlierness scores are selected as outliers, where n is the number of outliers defined by users.

Furthermore, we scale up our algorithm by leveraging Locality Sensitive Hashing (LSH) to efficiently find the contextual neighbors and parallelizing the computation. See more details in the extended version of this paper [7].

3. EXPERIMENTS AND ANALYSIS

In this section, we run `ROCOD` on several datasets and compare the performance with a series of baselines. For more details about experiment setup and analysis, see the extended paper [7].

3.1 Experimental Setup

3.1.1 Dataset and Data Preprocessing

Evaluating contextual outlier detection algorithms is challenging due to the lack of ground truth. In this paper, we employ six datasets to evaluate the performance of our algorithm, two of which contain labeled ground-truth outliers. For the four datasets without ground-truth outliers, we inject contextual outliers using the perturbation scheme described by Song *et al.* [13] – a de-facto standard for evaluating contextual outlier detection techniques. This scheme works as follows. To inject one outlier into a dataset with N objects, we uniformly select an object $z^{(i)} = (x^{(i)}, y^{(i)})^T$ at random. We then randomly select $p = \min(50, \frac{N}{4})$ objects from the dataset, among which we pick the object $z^{(j)} = (x^{(j)}, y^{(j)})^T$ such that the Euclidean distance between $y^{(i)}$ and $y^{(j)}$ is maximized. We add a new object $z' = (x^{(i)}, y^{(j)})^T$ into the dataset as a contextual outlier [1].

The basic information of the six datasets is shown in Table 1. It includes: 1) **Synthetic** dataset, which is generated using the CAD model [13]. 2) **Bodyfat** dataset from CMU statlib [2], where attributes on body fat percentage are treated as behavioral attributes and other physical features are considered as contextual attributes. 3) **ElNino** dataset from UCI ML repository [3], where we use the temporal and spatial attributes as contextual attributes and regard attributes on winds, humidity and temperature as behavioral attributes. 4) **Houses** dataset from CMU statlib, where we use the house price as the behavioral attributes and other attributes as contextual attributes (such as median income). 5) **YouTube-Twitter** dataset from previous work [1], where attributes from Twitter are adopted as contextual attributes while the attributes from YouTube are regarded as behavioral attributes. 6) **Kddcup99** dataset adapted from KDD Cup 1999 [4], where we only retain *u2r* and *r2l* attacks and treat them as outliers while removing other attacks [10]. Moreover, considering that *service*, *duration*, *src_bytes* and *dst_bytes* are most essential attributes for intrusion behavior [20], we use them as behavioral attributes and the rest of attributes are treated as contextual attributes.

[1]In total, we inject $1\% * N$ outliers into the dataset (except for Bodyfat due to the small size of the dataset).

[2]ftp://rcom.univie.ac.at/mirrors/lib.stat.cmu.edu/

[3]https://archive.ics.uci.edu/ml/datasets/El+Nino

[4]http://kdd.ics.uci.edu/databases/kddcup99/task.html

3.1.2 Baselines and Evaluation Metrics

We compare `ROCOD` to the state-of-the-art approaches on outlier detection. They contain 1) Conditional Anomaly Detection (**CAD**) proposed by Song *et al.* [13]. 2) Locality Sensitive Outlier Detection (**LSOD**) [18], which is a representative of distance-based anomaly detection algorithm leveraging locality-sensitive hashing and other techniques [11] for efficiency optimization. 3) Local Outlier Factor (**LOF**) [3], which is a local method comparing the local reachability density of each node to its neighbors. 4) Connectivity-based Outlier Factor (**COF**) [15], an extension of LOF differentiating low density from isolation. 5) Gaussian Mixture Model (**GMM**) [12] measuring the outlierness score by probability density.

These approaches output a full list of objects ranked by their outlierness scores with higher ones on the top, and return the first n objects as outliers. To comprehensively evaluate the performance of outlier detection, we use three different metrics: 1) AUC of Precision-Recall Curve. 2) Top-n Precision, defined as the precision of the objects ranked among top-n, which is also called *precision at n*. 3) Top-n normalized Discounted Cumulative Gain (nDCG), measuring the effectiveness of ranking for the first n objects.

3.2 Experiment Results and Analysis

We run the experiments on a Linux Machine with two Intel Xeon x5650 2.67GHz CPUs. It contains 12 cores and 48GB of RAM. All the algorithms are implemented in `C++` and compiled using Intel compiler. `OpenMP` is used to exploit the parallelism. Also, we have the following settings for the outlier detection methods: 1) For CAD and GMM, we set the number of Gaussian components as 30 and the maximum number of EM iterations as 100. 2) For LSOD, we use the distance to the 30-th nearest neighborhood as the outlier score. 3) For COF and LOF, we set the range of size of neighborhoods from 10 to 100 as suggested by the authors. 4) For `ROCOD`, the cosine similarity threshold α is chosen by looking at the distribution of randomly sampled pairs of objects (more details in [7]). We choose Ridge regression for the linear model and tree regression for the nonlinear model, denoted as `ROCOD_1` and `ROCOD_2` respectively. As comparisons, we also use only local expected behavior and global expected behavior to flag outliers, denoted as **LEB** and **GEB**. Results are shown in Table 2, which presents the performance of each approach on detecting outliers in all the datasets, measured by three different metrics. We highlight some observations below.

1) We can see that `ROCOD` (either `ROCOD_1` or `ROCOD_2`) performs the best at almost all the datasets. In some datasets, especially Synthetic, Houses and KDDcup99, `ROCOD` significantly outperforms other baselines on all three evaluation metrics. For example, the top-100 precision of `ROCOD_2` on KDDcup99 is twice as much as the best of baselines (CAD). The advantage of `ROCOD` is more pronounced in terms of top-n metrics, indicating our method is able to show outliers at the top more precisely. In Synthetic and ElNino dataset, the top-100 precision and nDCG of our approach is almost

Datasets	Outliers	# Objects N	# Outliers	Contextual Attributes	Behavior Attributes
Synthetic	Injected by perturbation scheme.	50,500	500	20	20
Bodyfat	Injected by perturbation scheme.	277	25	13	2
ElNino	Injected by perturbation scheme.	94,874	939	6	5
Houses	Injected by perturbation scheme.	20,846	206	8	1
YouTube-Twitter	Promotional users.	62,458	2,974	48	41
Kddcup99	u2r and r2l attacks.	98,372	1,094	47	69

Table 1: Basic information of the datasets. Outliers are injected by perturbation scheme for datasets without ground truth.

Synthetic									
Metrics	ROCOD_1	ROCOD_2	**LEB**	**GEB**	**CAD**	**GMM**	**LSOD**	**LOF**	**COF**
PRC (AUC)	0.392	**0.913**	0.781	0.679	0.628	0.055	0.265	0.384	0.135
Top-100 Precision	0.740	**0.950**	0.890	0.860	0.880	0.150	0.450	0.710	0.230
Top-100 nDCG	0.749	**0.960**	0.867	0.877	0.891	0.192	0.431	0.730	0.280
Bodyfat									
Metrics	ROCOD_1	ROCOD_2	**LEB**	**GEB**	**CAD**	**GMM**	**LSOD**	**LOF**	**COF**
PRC (AUC)	**0.750**	**0.750**	0.614	**0.750**	**0.750**	0.430	0.644	0.725	0.667
Top-10 Precision	0.900	**1.000**	0.800	0.900	0.900	0.400	0.300	0.400	0.300
Top-10 nDCG	0.936	**1.000**	0.875	0.933	0.936	0.287	0.206	0.305	0.215
ElNino									
Metrics	ROCOD_1	ROCOD_2	**LEB**	**GEB**	**CAD**	**GMM**	**LSOD**	**LOF**	**COF**
PRC (AUC)	0.670	**0.990**	0.964	0.883	0.220	0.461	0.806	0.797	0.767
Top-100 Precision	0.960	**1.000**	0.990	**1.000**	0.400	0.790	**1.000**	0.950	**1.000**
Top-100 nDCG	0.970	**1.000**	0.968	**1.000**	0.404	0.825	**1.000**	0.947	**1.000**
Houses									
Metrics	ROCOD_1	ROCOD_2	**LEB**	**GEB**	**CAD**	**GMM**	**LSOD**	**LOF**	**COF**
PRC (AUC)	0.656	**0.766**	0.312	0.634	0.232	0.135	0.101	0.116	0.119
Top-100 Precision	0.740	**0.840**	0.300	0.650	0.350	0.210	0.080	0.260	0.250
Top-100 nDCG	0.694	**0.860**	0.226	0.717	0.461	0.222	0.067	0.247	0.245
YouTube-Twitter									
Metrics	ROCOD_1	ROCOD_2	**LEB**	**GEB**	**CAD**	**GMM**	**LSOD**	**LOF**	**COF**
PRC (AUC)	0.141	**0.146**	0.136	0.124	0.125	0.131	0.124	0.105	0.106
Top-100 Precision	**0.530**	0.470	0.440	0.360	0.370	0.180	0.280	0.230	0.260
Top-100 nDCG	**0.605**	0.440	0.426	0.413	0.362	0.168	0.272	0.223	0.240
KDDcup99									
Metrics	ROCOD_1	ROCOD_2	**LEB**	**GEB**	**CAD**	**GMM**	**LSOD**	**LOF**	**COF**
PRC (AUC)	0.137	**0.143**	0.071	0.051	0.027	0.128	0.027	0.019	0.014
Top-100 Precision	0.390	**0.600**	0.070	0.020	0.300	0.000	0.070	0.020	0.000
Top-100 nDCG	0.293	**0.518**	0.129	0.031	0.316	0.000	0.085	0.015	0.000

Table 2: Performance comparisons of baselines on 6 datasets. ROCOD_1 uses the linear model in the global expected behavior while ROCOD_2 adopts the non-linear model. LEB and GEB are the approaches utilizing only local expected behavior and global expected behavior (with non-linear model) respectively. Three metrics are used to evaluate the performance (higher is better). Best performances w.r.t. each metric are shown in bold.

perfect (very close to 1.0).
2) Without separating contextual and behavioral attributes, general outlier detection approaches (e.g., LSOD, LOF and COF), perform poorly on the datasets. This issue is more evident on Bodyfat and Houses dataset, which contain more contextual attributes than behavioral attributes. The main reason is that these approaches simply combine contextual attributes with behavioral attributes and the effect of contextual attributes on outlierness score may obfuscate the role of behavioral attributes. This phenomenon is obvious on the dataset of Houses and Kddcup99, where contextual outlier detection techniques CAD and ROCOD achieve much higher top-100 precision than other methods.

3) ROCOD with the non-linear model for global expected behavior (ROCOD_2) outperforms the one with the linear model (ROCOD_1). This is not surprising and consistent with our intuition that the non-linear model is more capable of modeling the complex relationship among attributes. In fact, ROCOD_2 obtains the best performance in all the datasets except YouTube-Twitter, where ROCOD_1 performs the best on top-100 precision and nDCG while ROCOD_2 is better in terms of AUC of the precision-recall curve.

We also measure the wall-clock running time of all the methods and find out that ROCOD is more efficient than other baselines. Refer to the extended paper for more experimental results on the scalability of ROCOD [7].

3.3 Drilling Down on Efficacy Gains

Here, we drill-down to distil the performance gains of ROCOD. We take Kddcup99 dataset as an example and visualize outliers flagged by different methods among all other objects in 2-D coordinates. In order to visualize high-dimensional data, we extract the largest component from the contextual attributes space and behavioral attributes space respectively and plot the data points directly in the 2-D coordinate. Figure 2 shows the visualization of all the objects. Green diamonds are outliers correctly identified while black diamonds are normal objects but flagged incorrectly as outliers by the approaches. We show the top-100 outliers detected by each method and the precision is shown at the upper right corner of each plot. We include the results from LSOD, CAD and ROCOD, which are the three best approaches in this dataset. Moreover, we also identify 100 objects with sparsest contexts, i.e., their contextual attributes are very different from others (marked as red dots in Figure 2d).

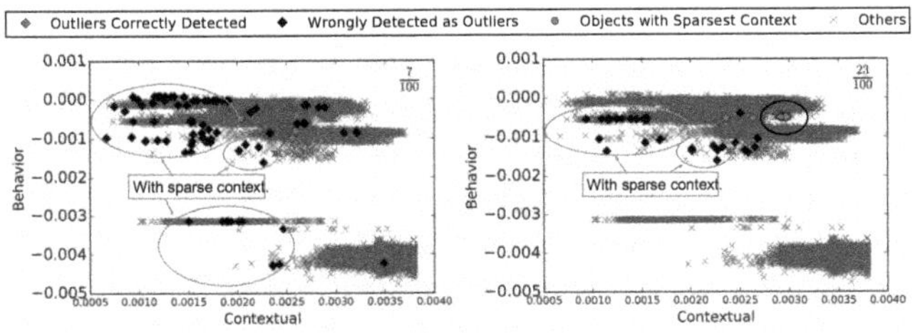

(a) Top 100 outliers using LSOD (b) Top 100 outliers using CAD

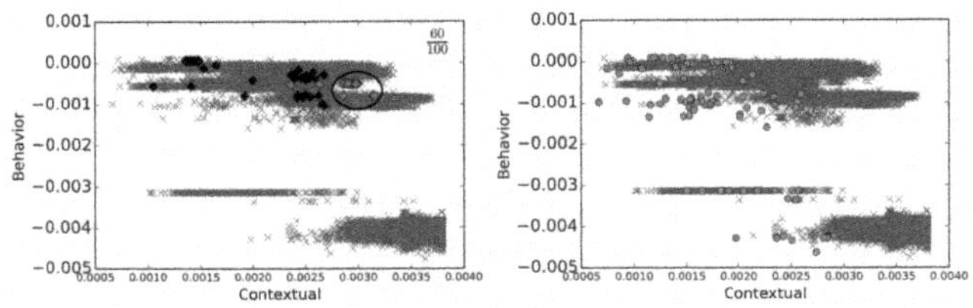

(c) Top 100 outliers using ROCOD (d) Objects with Sparsest Context

Figure 2: Visualization of Kddcup99 dataset in the 2-D coordinate. (a)-(c) show outliers detected by different approaches. Red round circles in (a) and (b) highlight objects with sparsest contexts. Black round circles in (b) and (c) highlight the same clusters of outliers correctly detected by CAD and ROCOD. (d) shows 100 objects with the sparsest contextual attributes, indicated by red dots.

Comparing Figure 2c with Figure 2a and Figure 2b, we notice that LSOD and CAD tend to mistakenly detect similar groups of normal objects as outliers, which are highlighted in red circles in the plots (Figure 2a and Figure 2b), while ROCOD avoids similar mistakes. To understand the reason for this observation, we look at these groups of objects in Figure 2d and find out that most of them are show in red dots and therefore are objects containing sparse contextual attributes. This strongly supports our statement that existing outlier detection techniques (such as LSOD and CAD) tend to assign higher outlierness scores to objects with anomalous contextual attributes though they are normal considering their behavioral attributes. Even state-of-the-art approach CAD cannot properly resolve this issue. ROCOD, however, is not affected much by these objects and is able to impartially measure the outlierness scores of them. Moreover, it is also interesting to observe that though ROCOD and CAD are two totally different approaches, they correctly detect the same group of outliers, circled by black bold rectangles in Figure 2b and 2c. In general, ROCOD is much better than CAD at correctly identifying outliers in this dataset.

4. CONCLUSION

We propose ROCOD to exploit contextual attributes for detecting outliers, particularly dealing with the sparsity of context. We introduce local expected behavior and global expected behavior models to infer the behavioral attributes and describe a natural algorithm to fuse them. Experimental results show that ROCOD detects outliers more accurately and efficiently than prior approaches.

Acknowledgements. This work is supported by NSF Award NSF-EAR-1520870 and NSF-DMS-1418265.

5. REFERENCES

[1] A. Abisheva *et al.* Who watches (and shares) what on youtube? and when?: using twitter to understand youtube viewership. In *WSDM*. ACM, 2014.

[2] M. Bartlett. The square root transformation in analysis of variance. *JASA*, pages 68–78, 1936.

[3] M. M. Breunig *et al.* Lof: identifying density-based local outliers. In *SIGMOD*. ACM, 2000.

[4] V. Chandola, A. Banerjee, and V. Kumar. Anomaly detection: A survey. *CSUR'09*, 41(3):15, 2009.

[5] M. Hauskrecht et al. Conditional outlier approach for detection of unusual patient care actions. In *AAAI'13*.

[6] D. M. Hawkins. *Identification of outliers*, volume 11. Springer, 1980.

[7] J. Liang and S. Parthasarathy. Robust contextual outlier detection: Where context meets sparsity. *arXiv preprint arXiv:1607.08329*, 2016.

[8] C.-T. Lu, D. Chen, and Y. Kou. Algorithms for spatial outlier detection. In *ICDM'03*. IEEE, 2003.

[9] N. J. Nagelkerke. A note on a general definition of the coefficient of determination. *Biometrika*, 1991.

[10] H. V. Nguyen *et al.* Mining outliers with ensemble of heterogeneous detectors on random subspaces. In *DSFAA*. Springer, 2010.

[11] G. H. Orair *et al.* Distance-based outlier detection: consolidation and renewed bearing. *VLDB*, 2010.

[12] S. Roberts and L. Tarassenko. A probabilistic resource allocating network for novelty detection. *Neural Computation*, 6(2):270–284, 1994.

[13] X. Song *et al.* Conditional anomaly detection. *TKDE*, 19(5):631–645, 2007.

[14] G. Tang *et al.* Mining multidimensional contextual outliers from categorical relational data. In *SSDBM*, page 43. ACM, 2013.

[15] J. Tang *et al.* Enhancing effectiveness of outlier detections for low density patterns. In *PAKDD*, pages 535–548. Springer, 2002.

[16] W. R. Tobler. A computer movie simulating urban growth in the detroit region. *Economic geography*, 46:234–240, 1970.

[17] M. Valko *et al.* Conditional anomaly detection with soft harmonic functions. In *ICDM*, 2011.

[18] Y. Wang *et al.* Locality sensitive outlier detection: A ranking driven approach. In *ICDE*, 2011.

[19] A. S. Weigend, M. Mangeas, and A. N. Srivastava. Nonlinear gated experts for time series: Discovering regimes and avoiding overfitting. *IJNS*, 1995.

[20] K. Yamanishi *et al.* On-line unsupervised outlier detection using finite mixtures with discounting learning algorithms. *DMKD*, 2004.

Credibility Assessment of Textual Claims on the Web

Kashyap Popat Subhabrata Mukherjee Jannik Strötgen Gerhard Weikum
Max Planck Institute for Informatics
Saarbrücken, Germany
{kpopat,smukherjee,jstroetge,weikum}@mpi-inf.mpg.de

ABSTRACT

There is an increasing amount of false claims in news, social media, and other web sources. While prior work on truth discovery has focused on the case of checking factual statements, this paper addresses the novel task of assessing the credibility of arbitrary claims made in natural-language text — in an open-domain setting without any assumptions about the structure of the claim, or the community where it is made. Our solution is based on automatically finding sources in news and social media, and feeding these into a distantly supervised classifier for assessing the credibility of a claim (i.e., true or fake). For inference, our method leverages the joint interaction between the language of articles about the claim and the reliability of the underlying web sources. Experiments with claims from the popular website *snopes.com* and from reported cases of Wikipedia hoaxes demonstrate the viability of our methods and their superior accuracy over various baselines.

Keywords

Credibility Analysis; Rumor and Hoax Detection;
Text Mining

1. INTRODUCTION

Motivation: With the explosive growth of the Web, online news, and social media, there is also a large amount of false claims. This issue is present in many domains, ranging from fake reviews on product websites, erroneous stock prices, manipulative statements about companies, celebrities, and politicians, all the way to disseminating false news [4, 7]. Determining the credibility of a claim is a challenging task. As reported in [5], even humans sometimes cannot easily distinguish hoax articles in Wikipedia from authentic ones, and quite a few people have mistaken satirical articles (e.g., from *theonion.com*) as truthful news.

With the increasing number of hoaxes and rumors, fact-checking websites like *snopes.com*, *politifact.com*, *truthorfiction.com* and others have become popular. These websites compile articles written by experts who manually investigate contentious claims by determining their provenance and authenticity from various sources; and provide a verdict (*true* or *fake*) with supporting evidence. The work in this paper aims to replace this manual verification/falsification with an automated system.

State of the Art and its Limitations: Prior work on credibility analysis (see [9] for a survey) has focused on factual claims (e.g., [7, 8, 10]) and/or online communities with specific characteristics like user metadata, who-replied-to-whom, who-edited-what, etc. (e.g., [5, 12]). Truth-finding methods of this kind, starting with the seminal work of [19], assume that claims follow a structured template with clear identification of the questionable values [7, 8], or correspond to subject-predicate-object triples obtained by information extraction [13]. A classic example is *"Obama is born in Kenya"* viewed as a triple ⟨*Obama, born in, Kenya*⟩ where *"Kenya"* is the critical value. The assumption of such a structure is crucial in order to identify alternative values for the questionable slot (e.g., *"Hawaii"*, *"USA"*, *"Africa"*), and is appropriate when checking facts for tasks like knowledge base curation. However, these approaches are limited in their coverage and cannot handle many kinds of claims found on news and social media, which are often in the form of long sentences or entire paragraphs.

Novel Problem: The work in this paper aims to overcome these limitations by addressing the case of arbitrary *textual claims* that are expressed freely in an *open-domain* setting, without making any assumptions on the structure of the claim, or characteristics of the community or website where the claim is made.

Example: Consider the following claim[1] from the fake news website *thenochill.com*: *"15 Year Old Killed Trespassing While Playing Pokemon Go"*. Our objective is to assess the credibility of this statement as *true* or *fake*. For instance, our model classifies this claim as *fake*. Another example of such a claim is the statement *"I want to share this shocking news: Obama care will require all Americans to be implanted with RFID chips. This chip serves no purpose but a sinister agenda."* which appeared in a social media site a few years ago.

Our Approach: We present a novel approach to identify fake *textual claims*, in an *open-domain* setting, where we do not assume any community-specific characteristics or structure in the input data. Given a claim in the form of a sentence or paragraph, we first use a search engine to identify documents from multiple web-sources, which refer to

[1]http://thenochill.com/teen-killed-while-playing-pokemon-go/

CIKM'16 , October 24-28, 2016, Indianapolis, IN, USA
© 2016 ACM. ISBN 978-1-4503-4073-1/16/10... $15.00
DOI: http://dx.doi.org/10.1145/2983323.2983661

the claim. We refer to these documents as *reporting articles* in this paper. Then, we analyze the interplay between the *language* (e.g., bias, subjectivity, etc.) of the retrieved articles, and the *reliability* of the web-sources where the articles appeared. Finally, we propose a *Distant Supervision* based classifier which uses these factors to assess the credibility of the claim reported by multiple sources (*cf.* Section 2, 3).

We perform experiments with claims from the fact-checking website *snopes.com* and with data about hoaxes and fictitious persons in Wikipedia. The performance of our approach demonstrates major improvements in accuracy over various baselines (*cf.* Section 4, 5).

2. OVERVIEW OF OUR APPROACH

We capture the following factors that help in determining the credibility of a claim:

i) How is the claim reported? The *writing style* of the articles reporting the claim gives important clues about the credibility of the claim. For example, related work in detecting biased language [17] and credibility analysis in closed communities [12, 11] leverage linguistic features like discourse, subjectivity, and modality.

ii) Who is reporting the claim? The *provenance* of the claim coupled with the *reliability* of the source plays a key role in understanding its credibility. For instance, *theonion.com* is known to publish satirical articles, whereas *wikipedia.org* usually provides objective information according to its *Neutral Point of View* policy.

Consider a set of textual claims $\langle C \rangle$ in the form of sentences or short paragraphs, and a set of web-sources $\langle WS \rangle$ containing articles $\langle A \rangle$ that report on the claims. Let $a_{ij} \in A$ denote an article of web-source $ws_j \in WS$ about claim $c_i \in C$. Each claim c_i is associated with a binary random variable y_i that depicts its credibility label, where $y_i \in \{T, F\}$ (T stands for *True*, whereas F stands for *Fake*). Each article a_{ij} is associated with a random variable y_{ij} that depicts the credibility opinion (*True* or *Fake*) of the article a_{ij} (from ws_j) regarding c_i – when considering only this article. Figure 1 illustrates this model. Given the labels of a subset of the claims (e.g., y_1 for c_1, and y_3 for c_3), our objective is to predict the credibility label of the remaining claims (e.g., y_2 for c_2).

To learn the parameters in our credibility assessment model, we use *Distant Supervision* to attach observed true/fake labels of claims to corresponding reporting articles, and learn a *Credibility Classifier*. In this process, we need to (a) understand the language of the article, and (b) consider the *reliability* of the underlying web sources reporting the articles. Thereafter, we (c) compute the credibility opinion scores of individual articles, and finally, (d) *aggregate* these scores from all articles to obtain the overall credibility label of target claims.

3. CREDIBILITY ASSESSMENT

The following sections describe the features used in our model and how we learn the parameters.

3.1 Language Stylistic Features

The style in which a claim is reported in an article plays a critical role in understanding its credibility. A true claim is assumed to be reported in an objective and unbiased language. On the other hand, if a claim is reported in a highly

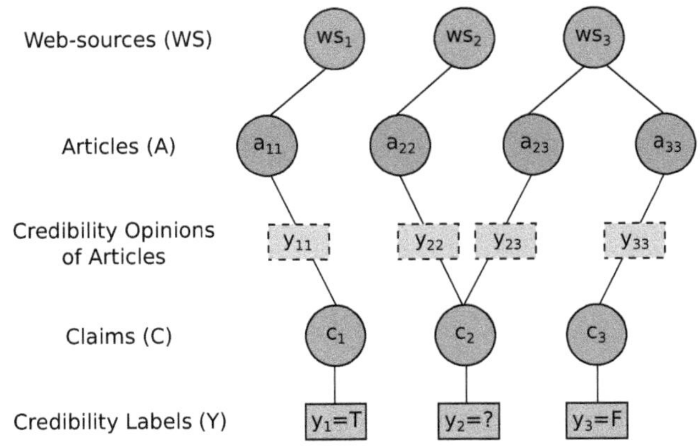

Figure 1: Factors for credibility analysis.

subjective or a sensationalized style, then it is likely to be less credible. This hypothesis is validated in [13] through an experiment using Amazon Mechanical Turk.

In order to capture the linguistic style of the reporting articles to model the above hypothesis, we use the set of lexicons from [11], in particular the following types of stylistic features:

Assertive verbs: capture the degree of certainty to which a proposition holds,

Factive verbs: presuppose the truth of a proposition in a sentence,

Hedges: soften the degree of commitment to a proposition,

Implicatives: trigger presupposition in an utterance,

Report verbs: emphasize the attitude towards the source of the information,

Discourse markers: capture the degree of confidence, perspective, and certainty in the set of propositions made,

Subjectivity and bias: a list of positive and negative opinionated words, and an affective lexicon to capture the state of mind (like attitude and emotions) of the writer while writing an article,

Feature vector construction: For each article a_{ij}, we compute the normalized frequency of all the linguistic features $\langle f_k \rangle$. Given all the stylistic language features, we compute

$$F^L(a_{ij}) = \langle freq^{f_k}_{a_{ij}} = n^{f_k}_{a_{ij}} / length(a_{ij}) \rangle$$

where, $n^{f_k}_{a_{ij}}$ = *number of times* f_k *occur in* a_{ij}.

3.2 Source Reliability

Apart from the reporting style of the article, the reliability of the web-source hosting the article also has a significant impact on the credibility of the claim. For instance, one should not believe a claim reported by an article from the "The UnRreal Times" website[2], as opposed to a claim on the "World Health Organization" website.

To capture the reliability of the web-source for each web article, we determine the AlexaRank and PageRank of its source and use them as proxies for the source reliability. AlexaRank [3] is based on a combined measure of unique visitors and page views of the website. PageRank determines importance of the website by counting the number and qual-

[2]A satire, spoof, parody and humour portal: http://www.theunrealtimes.com/

[3]https://support.alexa.com/hc/en-us/articles/200449744-How-are-Alexa-s-traffic-rankings-determined-

Type of Feature	Number of Features
Linguistic	
Assertive Verbs	66
Factive Verbs	27
Hedges	100
Implicatives	32
Report Verbs	181
Discourse Markers	13
Subjectivity and Bias	8770
Reliability	
Source Identity	#web-sources
PageRank	1
AlexaRank	1

Table 1: Statistics of features used in our model.

ity of links to and from the website. To avoid modeling from sparse observations, we combine all the web-sources having less than 10 articles in the dataset to a single web-source.
Feature vector construction: For each article a_{ij}, we capture the identity of its web-source ws_j using a one-hot vector of dimension *cardinality*($< WS >$) (after collapsing the "long-tail" sources to a single source) by setting the jth element in the vector to 1, and the remaining ones to 0. We also use the AlexaRank and PageRank of the web-source as additional features capturing the source reliability.

$F^{SR}(a_{ij}) = \langle 0\ldots, ws_j = 1, 0\ldots, \log PR_{ws_j}, \log AR_{ws_j}\rangle$ where, PR and AR represent the PageRank, and the Alexa-Rank, respectively.

3.3 Credibility Classification using Distant Supervision

Credibility labels are available *per-claim*, and not per-reporting-article. Thus, in our approach for credibility aggregation from multiple sources, we use *Distant Supervision* for *training* — whereby we attach the (observed) label y_i of each claim c_i to each article a_{ij} reporting the claim (i.e., setting labels $y_{ij} = y_i$). For instance, in Figure 1, $y_{11} = y_1 = T, y_{33} = y_3 = F$. Using these $\langle y_{ij}\rangle$ as the corresponding training labels for $\langle a_{ij}\rangle$, with the corresponding feature vectors $\langle F^L(a_{ij}) \cup F^{SR}(a_{ij})\rangle$, we train an L_1-regularized logistic regression model on the training data. Statistics of features used in our model are given in Table 1.

For any *test* claim c_i whose credibility label is unknown, and its corresponding reporting articles $\langle a_{ij}\rangle$, we use this *Credibility Classifier* to obtain the corresponding credibility opinions $\langle y_{ij}\rangle$ of the articles. We determine the overall credibility label y_i of c_i by considering a sum of *per-article* credibility probabilities:

$$y_i = \underset{l\in\{T,F\}}{\arg\max} \sum_{a_{ij}} Prob(y_{ij} = l) \quad (1)$$

4. CASE STUDIES

4.1 Snopes

We performed experiments with data from a typical fact checking website: *snopes.com*. *Snopes* covers Internet rumors, hoaxes, urban legends, e-mail forwards, and other stories of unknown or questionable origin. It is a well-known resource for validating and debunking such stories, receiving around 300,000 visits a day [15]. They typically collect rumors and claims from *Facebook*, *Twitter*, *Reddit*, news websites, e-mails by users, etc.

Total claims	4856
True claims	1277 (26.3%)
Fake claims	3579 (73.7%)
Web articles	133272
Avg. articles per claim	27.44

Table 2: *Snopes* data statistics.

Each article verifies a single claim, e.g., *"North Carolina no longer considers the $20 bill to be legal tender"*. The Snopes editors assign a *manual* credibility verdict to each such claim: *True* or *False*. Few of the claims have labels like *Mostly True* or *Mostly False*. We map *Mostly True* labels to *True*, and *Mostly False* labels to *False* — thereby considering only *binary* credibility labels for this work. Claims having labels like *Partially True* or *Partially False* are ignored. The credibility verdict is accompanied by a description how the editor(s) came across the claim (e.g., it was collected from a Facebook post, or received by an email etc.), an *Origin* section describing the origin of the claim, and an *Analysis* section justifying the verdict. Our model is agnostic of the structure of Snopes as we use only the claim and its credibility verdict, ignoring all other related information.

We collected data from *Snopes* published until February 2016. For each claim c_i, we fired the *claim text* as a *query* to the Google search engine and extracted the first three result pages (i.e., up to 30 articles) as a set of reporting articles $\langle a_{ij}\rangle$. We ignore the ranking information in the set of collected articles to have minimal dependency on the search engine. Other search engines, or other means of evidence gathering can easily be used. We then crawled all these articles from their corresponding web-sources $\langle ws_j\rangle$. We removed search results from the *snopes.com* domain to avoid any kind of bias. Statistics of the data crawled from *snopes.com* is given in Table 2.

4.2 Wikipedia

We collected a set of 100 proven hoaxes reported on Wikipedia[4], e.g., *"Alien autopsy film by Ray Santilli"*, *"Disappearing blonde gene"* etc. All these hoaxes can be mapped to claims of types: "*<ENTITY> exists*", "*<ENTITY> is genuine*" or "*<EVENT> occurred*". While collecting the data, hoaxes not falling under these categories were ignored. Words related to hoaxes, e.g., *fake*, *fictional*, *nonexistent*, etc., were removed from the claim description to avoid any kind of search bias while retrieving articles using a search engine. Since the dataset contains only hoaxes, the ground-truth label for all of these claims is *Fake*.

In addition, we also collected a set of 57 fictitious people as reported on the Wikipedia page[5], e.g., *"Ern Malley, an Australian poet"*, *"P. D. Q. Bach, a composer"* etc. All these entities can be mapped to claims of type: "*<ENTITY> exists*". The ground-truth label for all of these claims is *Fake* as the dataset contains only fictitious people.

[4]https://en.wikipedia.org/wiki/List_of_hoaxes#Proven_hoaxes
[5]https://en.wikipedia.org/wiki/List_of_fictitious_people

	Hoaxes	Fictitious People
Total Claims	100	57
Web articles	2813	1552
Avg. articles per claim	28.13	27.22

Table 3: Wikipedia data statistics.

Table 3 reports the statistics of the dataset. As described earlier, we used a search engine to get a set of reporting articles for these claims. Similar to the previous case, we removed results from the *wikipedia.org* domain. Note that we trained our *Credibility Classifier* on *Snopes* data, and tested it on this data from *Wikipedia* — thereby demonstrating that our model generalizes and can be easily applied to data from other domains.

5. EXPERIMENTS

We conducted a set of experiments using data from *Snopes* and *Wikipedia* to test the performance of our methods.

Evaluation Measures: We train our models with *Snopes* data, and report standard 10-fold cross-validation accuracy on all datasets. *Snopes*, primarily being a hoax debunking website, is biased towards (refuting) the *Fake* claims. Therefore, we also report the per-class accuracy, and the *macro-averaged accuracy* which is the average of *per-class* accuracy — giving equal weight to both classes irrespective of the data imbalance. We also report the Area-under-Curve (AUC) values of the ROC (Receiver Operating Characteristic) curve. To highlight the effectiveness of our model in identifying fake claims (i.e., hoaxes, rumors etc.), we also report the precision, recall and F1 score for the *Fake* claim class.

5.1 Credibility Assessment: *Snopes*

While performing 10-fold cross-validation on the claims, we trained on any 9-folds of the data — where the algorithm learned the *Credibility Classifier* and web-source reliabilities from the reporting articles and their corresponding sources present in the training split. In order to remove any training bias, we ignored all *Snopes*-specific references from the data and the search engine results.

For addressing the data imbalance issue, we adjust the classifier's loss function. We place a large penalty for misclassifying instances from the *true* class which boosts certain features from that class. The overall effect is that the classifier makes fewer mistakes for *true* instances, leading to balanced classification. We set the penalty for the *true* class to 2.8 — given by the ratio of the number of *fake* claims to *true* claims in the *Snopes* data.

We compare to the following baselines:

ZeroR[6]**:** This is a trivial baseline, designed for imbalanced data, that always labels a claim as the class with the largest proportion, i.e., *fake* in our case. The overall accuracy of this baseline is **73.69%**, and the macro-averaged accuracy is **50%**.

FactChecker: Recent work on fact checking [13] relies on the hypothesis that claims reported by objective articles are more likely to be true than those reported in subjective articles. The authors extracted *alternative* fact candidates for the given claim, and used the hypothesis to rank all candidates. This approach works well in their use case of knowledge base curation, as all the claims are factual and have the form of Subject-Predicate-Object (SPO) triples. On the other hand, the claims in our case are textual snippets without any explicit alternative candidates. Therefore, we could only implement this method as a baseline "in spirit". To this end, we used the code[7] of [11] to construct an "Objectivity Detector". Given a claim and a set of reporting articles, the target claim was labeled *true* if the sum of the objectivity scores of its reporting articles — as determined by the Objectivity Detector — was higher than the sum of the subjective scores, and *fake* otherwise. This approach resulted in **55.29%** overall accuracy and **56.27%** macro-averaged accuracy for credibility classification.

[6]https://weka.wikispaces.com/ZeroR

Along with the above baselines, we also report the results of our model with different feature configurations for linguistic style and web-source reliability:

- Model using only *language* (LG) features,
- Model using only *web-source reliability* (SR) features,
- Aggregated model with the combination of, *language* and *source reliability* (LG + SR) features.

Table 4 shows the 10-fold cross-validation accuracy of various baselines against different configurations of our model, with the ROC curves plotted in Figure 2. From the results, we observe that using only language stylistic features (LG) is not sufficient; it is important to understand the source reliability (SR) of the article as well. High precision score for the *Fake* claim class shows the strength of our model in detecting *Fake* claims.

5.2 Credibility Assessment: *Wikipedia*

To demonstrate the generality of our approach, the model trained on the *Snopes* dataset was tested on the *Wikipedia* dataset of hoaxes and fictitious persons. The results are shown in Table 5. Similar to the *Snopes* setting, we removed all references to Wikipedia from the data and the search engine results. As we can see from the results, our system is able to detect hoaxes and fictitious people with high accuracy, although the claim descriptions here are stylistically quite different from those of *Snopes*.

6. ERROR ANALYSIS AND DISCUSSION

Poor performance on detecting fake claims: As we see from the results, the system accuracy for detecting fake claims is low compared to that for the true claims. While performing an error analysis of the results, we observed that many of the well written articles from reputed web-sources refer to the fake claims in *negated* form such as "... the company's spokesperson *denied* that ...". Our model does not capture these finer linguistic aspects like implicit or explicit negation, and, therefore, commits mistakes. In future, we would like to propose features which capture these finer semantics of the article text so that we can have a more accurate system.

[7]Code and data available from: http://www.mpi-inf.mpg.de/departments/databases-and-information-systems/research/impact/credibilityanalysis/

Configuration	Overall Accuracy (%)	*True* Claims Accuracy (%)	*Fake* Claims Accuracy (%)	Macro-averaged Accuracy (%)	AUC	*Fake* Claims Precision	*Fake* Claims Recall	*Fake* Claims F1-Score
LG + SR	71.96	75.43	70.77	**73.10**	**0.80**	0.89	0.71	0.79
LG	69.43	66.47	70.55	68.51	0.75	0.85	0.71	0.77
SR	66.52	68.56	65.90	67.23	0.73	0.85	0.66	0.74
FactChecking	55.29	58.34	54.21	56.27	0.58	0.78	0.54	0.64
ZeroR	73.69	00.00	100	50.00	0.50	0.74	1.00	0.85

Table 4: Performance comparison of our model vs. related baselines with 10-fold cross-validation on Snopes data. LG: language stylistic features, SR: web-source reliability.

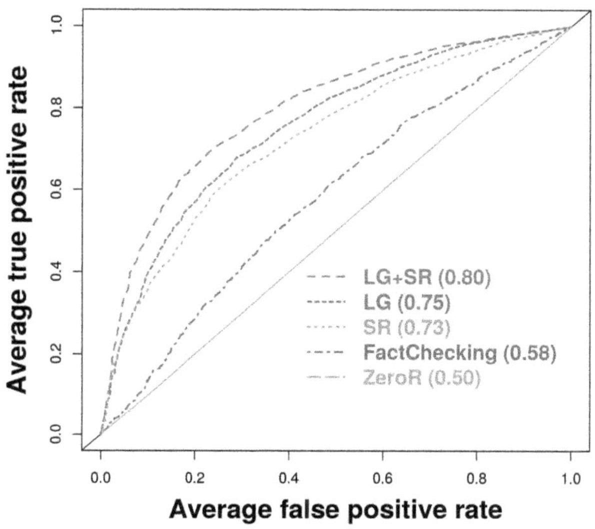

Figure 2: ROC curves for different model configurations.

Marginal contribution of web-source reliability: Results also indicate that the performance of the full model configuration (LG+SR) achieves only slight improvement over the configuration LG. This can be attributed to the fact that these rank measures (PageRank and AlexaRank) capture the authority and popularity of the web-sources, but not their reliability from the credibility point of view. For example, the PageRank of the satirical news website *The Onion* is very high (7 out of 10). However, this does not indicate anything about its reliability. Hence, as future work, it would be interesting to design an algorithm which automatically captures the ranking of web-sources based on their credibility.

Understanding the credibility assessment output: While performing error analysis, we observed that the probability scores do not help in understanding the output. This is also true for related truth finding approaches. It would thus be nice to have interpretable evidence as an additional output of the system which can explain the credibility assessment. Table 6 gives a snapshot of claims with the credibility assessment given by our system, along with manual annotation of snippets that can be used as evidence. As future work, we want to automate this process of generating evidence.

Test Data	#Claims	Accuracy (%)
Wiki Hoaxes	100	84.00
Wiki Fictitious People	57	66.07

Table 5: Accuracy of credibility classification on *Wikipedia* data.

7. RELATED WORK

Our work draws motivation from the following areas:

Truth discovery: In approaches to truth discovery [2, 3, 7, 10, 14, 19], the goal is to resolve conflicts in multi-source data. Input data is assumed to have a structured representation: an entity of interest along with its potential values provided by different sources. It is assumed that the conflicting values are already available.

Work in [13] goes a step further by proposing a method to generate conflicting *values* or *fact candidates* from Web contents. However, this work still operates on structured input in the form of Subject-Predicate-Object (SPO) triples for the fact candidates, obtained by applying Open Information Extraction to Web pages. The method proposed in [8] supports credibility assessment of statements but it relies on the *user* providing the *doubtful* portion of the input statement.

All the above approaches are limited to resolving conflicts amongst alternative fact candidates (or, multi-source data) in structured datasets. In our work, we address these limitations and propose a general approach to process unstructured natural-language claims without requiring any alternative claims.

Credibility analysis within communities and social media: An approach for credibility analysis within online health communities is proposed in [12], based on a probabilistic graphical model to jointly infer user trustworthiness, language objectivity, and statement credibility. A similar approach is used to identify credible news articles, trustworthy news sources, and expert users in [11]. Wikipedia hoaxes are studied in [5].

Prior research on credibility assessment of social media posts exploits *community-specific* features for detecting rumors, fake, and deceptive content [1, 16, 18]. Temporal, structural, and linguistic features were used to detect rumors on Twitter in [6]. Detecting fake images in Twitter based on influence patterns and social reputation is addressed in [4].

Claim	Verdict & Evidence
A woman stabbed her boyfriend with a sharpened selfie stick because he didn't like her newest Instagram selfie quickly enough.	**[Verdict]:** False **[Evidence]:** A weird kind of story in heavy circulation online states ... No, the claim is not a fact.
90% of people in the U.S. marry their high school sweethearts.	**[Verdict]:** False **[Evidence]:** The school category resulted in only 14% of total respondent base. In analyzing these surveys, one must realize that potential biases in survey methods exist, such as ... It seems absolutely clear that these and other surveys conducted in early 1990s represent nowhere nearly close to 90% ...
A Facebook coupon offering 50% off at Target stores is real.	**[Verdict]:** False **[Evidence]:** The newest questionable offer to take hold of Facebook newsfeeds involves the false promise of a coupon ... A rep for Target HQ confirms to Consumerist that there is no such coupon and this is a fake.
Two Maryland sheriff's deputies were fatally shot and a suspect killed on Wednesday in a shootout at a Baltimore-area Panera restaurant.	**[Verdict]:** True **[Evidence]:** Two Maryland sheriff's deputies were fatally shot and a suspect killed Wednesday in a shootout at a Baltimore-area Panera restaurant filled with lunchtime customers. (Reuters) Authorities found a semiautomatic handgun in Evans's vehicle, which he might have been living in.
A dying child was made an honorary fireman by the Phoenix Fire Department.	**[Verdict]:** True **[Evidence]:** We'll make him an honorary Fireman for the day. He can come down to the fire station, eat with us, go out on all the fire calls, the whole nine yards! The Fire Chief decided that the Phoenix Fire Department should make sure the dying boy had an experience truly befitting a fireman.
A declared-dead jockey returned to the track and shocked the grandstand crowd.	**[Verdict]:** True **[Evidence]:** When the crowd realized that the shirtless, bloodied, toe-tagged man who was staggering across the grandstand area was the jockey who had been declared dead about a half hour earlier, the crowd and the race officials rushed towards Neves, as shock turned to celebration.

Table 6: Snapshot of claims with assessment from Credibility Classifier, and manually annotated snippets as evidence.

All these approaches are limited to online communities and social media, relying heavily on community-specific characteristics. In contrast, we study credibility in an open domain setting without relying on such explicit signals.

8. CONCLUSIONS

In this paper, we proposed a general approach for credibility analysis of unstructured textual claims in an open-domain setting. We make use of the language style and source reliability of articles reporting the claim to assess its credibility. Experiments on analyzing the credibility of real-world claims, from the fact-checking website *Snopes*, and on hoaxes and fictitious persons listed on *Wikipedia*, demonstrate the effectiveness of our approach. As future work, we want to investigate the role of attribution or speaker information, refined linguistic aspects like negation, and understanding the article's perspective about the claim.

9. REFERENCES

[1] C. Castillo, M. Mendoza, and B. Poblete. Information credibility on twitter. In *WWW 2011*.

[2] X. L. Dong, L. Berti-Equille, and D. Srivastava. Integrating conflicting data: The role of source dependence. *Proc. VLDB Endow.*, 2(1):550–561, 2009.

[3] A. Galland, S. Abiteboul, A. Marian, and P. Senellart. Corroborating information from disagreeing views. In *WSDM 2010*.

[4] A. Gupta, H. Lamba, P. Kumaraguru, and A. Joshi. Faking sandy: characterizing and identifying fake images on twitter during hurricane sandy. In *WWW Companion 2013*.

[5] S. Kumar, R. West, and J. Leskovec. Disinformation on the web: Impact, characteristics, and detection of wikipedia hoaxes. In *WWW 2016*.

[6] S. Kwon, M. Cha, K. Jung, W. Chen, and Y. Wang. Prominent features of rumor propagation in online social media. In *ICDM 2013*.

[7] X. Li, X. L. Dong, K. Lyons, W. Meng, and D. Srivastava. Truth finding on the deep web: Is the problem solved? *PVLDB*, 6(2):97–108, 2012.

[8] X. Li, W. Meng, and C. Yu. T-verifier: Verifying truthfulness of fact statements. In *ICDE 2011*.

[9] Y. Li, J. Gao, C. Meng, Q. Li, L. Su, B. Zhao, W. Fan, and J. Han. A survey on truth discovery. *SIGKDD Explorations*, 17(2):1–16, 2015.

[10] Y. Li, Q. Li, J. Gao, L. Su, B. Zhao, W. Fan, and J. Han. On the discovery of evolving truth. In *KDD 2015*.

[11] S. Mukherjee and G. Weikum. Leveraging joint interactions for credibility analysis in news communities. In *CIKM 2015*.

[12] S. Mukherjee, G. Weikum, and C. Danescu-Niculescu-Mizil. People on drugs: Credibility of user statements in health communities. In *KDD 2014*.

[13] N. Nakashole and T. M. Mitchell. Language-aware truth assessment of fact candidates. In *ACL 2014*.

[14] J. Pasternack and D. Roth. Knowing what to believe (when you already know something). In *COLING 2010*.

[15] D. Pogue. At snopes.com, rumors are held up to the light. http://www.nytimes.com/2010/07/15/technology/personaltech/15pogue-email.html, July 15, 2010. [Online; accessed 26-Apr-2016].

[16] V. Qazvinian, E. Rosengren, D. R. Radev, and Q. Mei. Rumor has it: Identifying misinformation in microblogs. In *EMNLP 2011*.

[17] M. Recasens, C. Danescu-Niculescu-Mizil, and D. Jurafsky. Linguistic models for analyzing and detecting biased language. In *ACL 2013*.

[18] Q. Xu and H. Zhao. Using deep linguistic features for finding deceptive opinion spam. In *COLING 2012*.

[19] X. Yin, J. Han, and P. S. Yu. Truth discovery with multiple conflicting information providers on the web. *IEEE Trans. on Knowl. and Data Eng.*, 20(6):796–808, June 2008.

Collective Traffic Prediction with Partially Observed Traffic History using Location-Based Social Media

Xinyue Liu
Dept. of Computer Science
Worcester Polytechnic Insitute
Worcester, MA, USA
xliu4@wpi.edu

Xiangnan Kong
Dept. of Computer Science
Worcester Polytechnic Insitute
Worcester, MA. USA
xkong@v

Yanhua Li
Dept. of Computer Science
Worcester Polytechnic Insitute
Worcester. MA. USA

ABSTRACT

Traffic prediction has become an important and active research topic in the last decade. Existing solutions mainly focus on exploiting the past and current traffic data, collected from various kinds of sensors, such as loop detectors, GPS devices, *etc.* In real-world road systems, only a small fraction of the road segments are deployed with sensors. For all the other road segments without sensors or historical traffic data, previous methods may no longer work. In this paper, we propose to use location-based social media, which captures a much larger area of the road systems than deployed sensors, to predict the traffic conditions. A simple but effective method called CTP is proposed to incorporate location-based social media semantics into the learning process. CTP also exploits complex dependencies among different regions to improve the prediction performances through collective inference. Empirical studies using traffic data and tweets collected in Los Angeles area demonstrate the effectiveness of CTP.

Keywords

Traffic Prediction; Collective Inference; Social Media; Data Mining

1. INTRODUCTION

With ever-increasing urban population and the slow development of transport infrastructure, traffic congestion has become a major issue in many cities. Excessive traffic congestion can cause serious problems for road users, such as travel delays, resource wasting, and pollution. In 2011, traffic congestion costs urban Americans 5.5 billion hours of travel delay, 2.9 billion gallons of extra fuel, for a total congestion cost of 121 billion dollars [7]. To alleviate these issues, there is a great need for building models to accurately predict traffic conditions in the near future.

Traffic prediction problem has been extensively studied [2,3,9]. Previous research mainly focus on exploiting historical traffic data, which are collected from sensors deployed

CIKM'16 , October 24-28, 2016, Indianapolis, IN, USA

DOI: http://dx.doi.org/10.1145/2983323.2983662

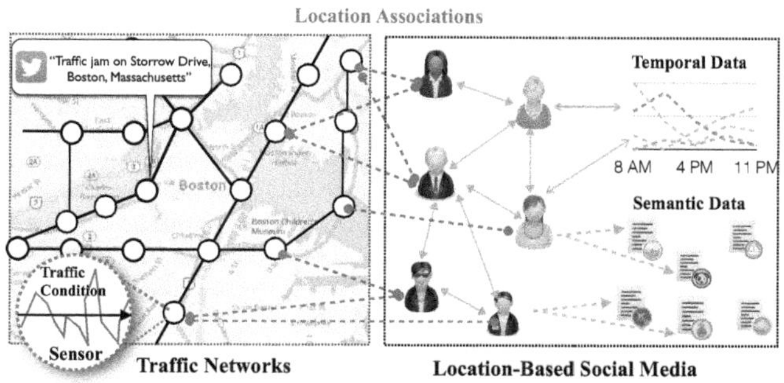

Figure 1: An illustration of using location-based social media to predict traffic conditions.

on the roads [9]. It is usually assumed that all the historical traffic data are given beforehand, or all road segments to be predicted are deployed with sensors. However, in many real-world tasks, only a small fraction of the regions, such as the major highways, are deployed with sensors. While for all the other regions, historical and current traffic conditions are usually unknown, due to the lack of road sensors. *Location-based social media* (LBSM), such as Twitter and Foursquare, has become popular in the last decade. LBSM can provide abundant information about the road users in real-time, covering a wide range of geographic areas. For example, many car drivers can tweet through the dictation systems in smart phones (such as Siri) or through the modern car consoles. Passengers in the cars can also tweet using mobile devices, especially when being stuck in traffic. In LBSM, these messages are often associated with location tags, indicating the geolocations of the users. The contents of these messages may also be related to current traffic conditions, accidents or future events. In the left part of Fig. 1, we show an example of a user writing a tweet "Traffic jam on Storrow Drive, Boston, Massachusetts" tagged with his/her geolocation. By mining the *semantic* and *spatial* information from LBSM, we can effectively infer the future traffic conditions on a wide range of regions, including the road segments without sensors.

In this paper, we propose to use LBSM data to facilitate the traffic prediction process with partially observed traffic history. The problem of traffic prediction has not been studied in this context so far. Unlike prior works on traffic prediction [9] and social media sensing [1, 10], we assume that some geographical regions in the road system are not deployed with sensors, where the historical traffic data is not observed. The major research challenges of this paper are summarized as follows: **(a) Lack of Historical Traffic Data in Partial Regions:** One fundamental problem of

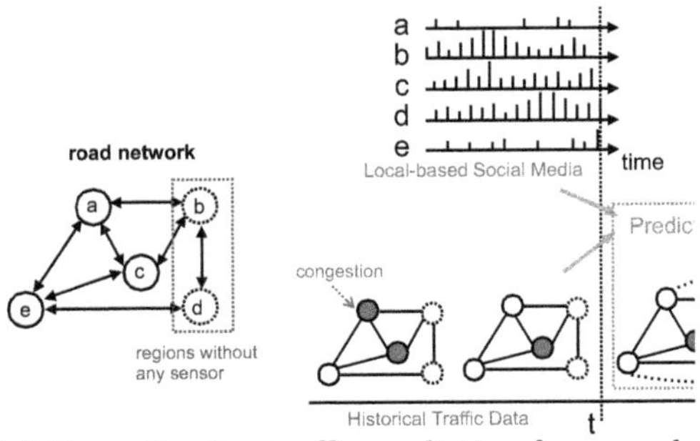

(a) Our collective traffic prediction framework based social media

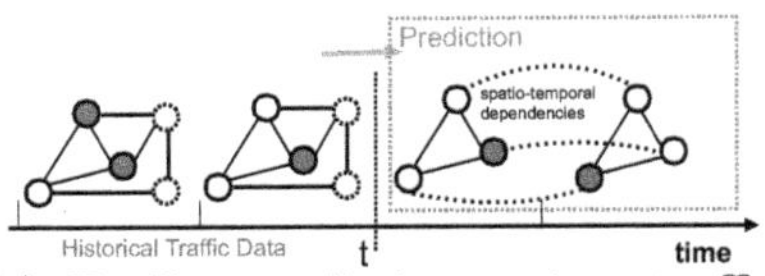

(c) Traffic prediction using traffic data only [8]

Figure 2: Comparison of the different settings for traffic prediction. Each node of the road network represents a region, and the edges represent the spatial connections between different regions.

traffic prediction problem lies in the fact that many regions of the road network are not deployed with sensors. Most existing traffic prediction methods, as shown in Figure 2(c), mainly rely on historical traffic data to make predictions on future traffic conditions. For regions without sensors, these methods cannot be applied to predict future traffic. **(b) Sparsity of LBSM Information at Fine Granularities:** One problem of traffic prediction using LBSM is the sparsity of information with the required granularity of spatiotemporal resolution. Existing traffic prediction methods using social media mainly target on large spatial granularity, such as states of a country [10], or large temporal granularity, such as days or hours [1]. This is because usually only a small amount of LBSM content is generated in a small region during a small time window, as shown in Tab. 1. However, for traffic prediction tasks, we often need to target on small temporal granularity (60 minutes or less), as well as on small spatial granularity (a few square miles). At such granularity, we usually can only collect a small number of LBSM content. The features extracted from such less content are highly sparse, which may result in weak performance.

To alleviate the aforementioned issues, we introduce CTP (Collective Traffic Prediction) framework, as illustrated in Fig. 2(a), to predict the future traffic condition on a set of regions collectively by exploiting their spatial and temporal relationships. Unlike the conventional traffic prediction methods, CTP uses both LBSM data and partially observed traffic data in prediction. Fig. 1 shows the idea of using LBSM data to help predicting traffic conditions for different road segments and time. Furthermore, CTP also exploits three types of dependencies among spatiotemporal regions: (1) *intra-region temporal dependency*; (2) *inter-region temporal dependency*. (3) *inter-region spatial dependency*. By exploiting these dependencies, CTP can effectively predict traffic conditions for a set of inter-related regions collectively.

2. PROBLEM FORMULATION

In this section, we first introduce the notations that will be used throughout this paper. then we define the problem.

2.1 LBSM-augmented Traffic Network

Suppose we are given a LBSM-augmented traffic network, which can be represent as $G(\mathcal{R}, \mathcal{E}, \mathcal{X}, \mathcal{V})$. $\mathcal{R}$ and $\mathcal{E}$ are the set of regions and the set of edges in the network respectively. We define $\mathcal{R} = \{r_1, \ldots, r_n\}$, each $r_i \in \mathcal{R}$ represents a geographical region on the map. $\mathcal{E} \subset \mathcal{R} \times \mathcal{R}$ denotes the set of spatial connections among these regions through the traffic network. To tackle the problem of the lack of traffic history for partial regions, we extract information from LBSM data to improve our predictions. For each regions $r_i \in \mathcal{R}$, we have a set of feature vectors $\mathcal{X}_i = \{\boldsymbol{x}_i^{(1)}, \ldots, \boldsymbol{x}_i^{(m)}\}$, in which the superscripts with parentheses are called *temporal indices* and the subscripts are called *spatial indices*. Specifically, $\boldsymbol{x}_i^{(j)} \in \mathbb{R}^d$ denotes the LBSM feature vector collected in the region r_i in the time window j, where $j \in \{1, \cdots, m\}$. The details of how the LBSM feature vectors are extracted will be discussed in Sec. 4.2. Let $\mathcal{X} = \{\mathcal{X}_1, \ldots, \mathcal{X}_n\}$ represent the set of LBSM-augmented features on all regions. For each region $r_i \in \mathcal{R}$, we also have a set of target variables $\mathcal{V}_i = \{v_i^{(1)}, \ldots, v_i^{(m)}\} \in \mathbb{R}^m$ indicating the traffic conditions, where $v_i^{(j)} \in \mathbb{R}$ denotes the average speed of all vehicles traveling in the region r_i within the time window j. $\mathcal{V} = \{\mathcal{V}_1, \ldots, \mathcal{V}_n\}$ represents sets of targets in all regions.

Table 1: Average # of tweets in each region under different spatiotemporal resolutions in our dataset.

Temporal Resolution	Spatial Resolution	Ave. #Tweets
12 hours	1×1	47,113
1 hour	1×1	3,926
1 hour	2×2	1,306
1 hour	3×3	554
1 hour	4×4	389
1 hour	30×30	15

2.2 Traffic Prediction with Fully Observed Traffic History

Most existing traffic prediction methods mainly rely on historical traffic data to make predictions on future traffic conditions. Suppose $\mathcal{V}^{(t)} = \{v_1^{(t)}, \cdots, v_n^{(t)}\}$ and $\mathcal{X}^{(t)} = \{\boldsymbol{x}_1^{(t)}, \cdots, \boldsymbol{x}_n^{(t)}\}$ denote the set of all traffic conditions and the set of LBSM feature vectors for all regions in time window t respectively. Hence, the prediction task is to predict $\mathcal{V}^{(t)}$ given the traffic history $(\mathcal{V}^{(t-l_1)}, \ldots, \mathcal{V}^{(t-1)})$, where $l_1 \in \mathbb{N}^+$ is called *traffic time lag* that specifies how many time slices of historical traffic data are used in the prediction. Suppose we set $l_1 = 2$, auto regression [8] learning a regression model that predicts each $v_g^{(t)}$ independently as

$$v_g^{(t)} = \alpha + \beta_1 v_g^{(t-1)} + \beta_2 v_g^{(t-2)} \quad (1)$$

As stated before, this model is limited since it requires fully observed historical traffic data.

2.3 Traffic Prediction with Partially Observed Traffic History

In real-world traffic prediction, the traffic history can only be observed in partial regions. Our goal is to predict future traffic conditions of different regions (under fine granularity) in the road network based upon the partially observed historical traffic data. $U \subset \{1, \cdots n\}$ is the set of spatial indices for unobserved regions, $O = \{1, \cdots n\} - U$ is the set of spatial indices for observed regions. $\mathcal{R}_U \subset \mathcal{R}$ represents the set of regions, where the traffic history data are unobserved, $\mathcal{R}_O = \mathcal{R} - \mathcal{R}_U$ represents the set of regions where the traffic history data are observed. Suppose $\mathcal{V}_O^{(t)} = \{v_i^{(t)} | i \in O\}$ to denote the set of all traffic conditions of observed regions in time window t. Hence, the prediction task is to predict $\mathcal{V}^{(t)}$ given the partially observed traffic history $\{\mathcal{V}_O^{(t-l_1)}, \ldots, \mathcal{V}_O^{(t-1)}\}$. LBSM-aided approaches also consider the historical LBSM features $\{\mathcal{X}^{(t-l_2)}, \ldots, \mathcal{X}^{(t-1)}\}$ to predict the traffic conditions $\mathcal{V}^{(t)}$, where $l_2 \in \mathbb{N}^+$ is called the *LBSM time lag*. Note that the historical LBSM contents originate in unobserved regions $\mathcal{R}_U$ are available. Previous empirical studies [1,6] typically suggest optimal values for l_1 ranging from 2 to 6 and $l_2 = 2$. In this paper, we simply use $l_1 = 2$ and $l_2 = 2$. Thus, the inference problem in LBSM-aided traffic prediction is to estimate $v_g^{(t)}$ using $v_g^{(t-2)}$, $v_g^{(t-1)}$, $\boldsymbol{x}_g^{(t-2)}$ and $\boldsymbol{x}_g^{(t-1)}$ when $g \in O$, but using $\boldsymbol{x}_g^{(t-2)}$ and $\boldsymbol{x}_g^{(t-1)}$ only when $g \in U$. Previous approaches [1] require *i.i.d.* assumptions, in which each $v_g^{(t)}$ that has observed history is estimated independently as follows

$$v_g^{(t)} = \alpha + \beta_1 v_g^{(t-1)} + \beta_2 v_g^{(t-2)} + \gamma_1 \boldsymbol{x}_g^{(t-1)} \boldsymbol{m} + \gamma_2 \boldsymbol{x}_g^{(t-2)} \boldsymbol{m} \quad (2)$$

where $\boldsymbol{m} = \mathbb{R}^d$ is the transformation vector. As to the situation of $g \in U$, no historical traffic data is available, so $v_g^{(t)}$ can only be estimated independently as follows

$$v_g^{(t)} = \alpha + \gamma_1 \boldsymbol{x}_g^{(t-1)} \boldsymbol{m} + \gamma_2 \boldsymbol{x}_g^{(t-2)} \boldsymbol{m} \quad (3)$$

The only dependency that is considered in Eq. 2 is the dependency between the prediction target $v_g^{(t)}$ and its historical traffic conditions $v_g^{(t-1)}$ and $v_g^{(t-2)}$. However, in the real-world traffic networks, there are other types of dependencies exist between regions, which cannot be ignored. We consider other types of dependencies in Sec. 3.

We also note that the model proposed in [1] can only perform predictions under temporal resolution of 12 hours and spatial resolution of 1×1 (consider the target area as a single region). However, much finer spatiotemporal resolution is desired in real world traffic prediction application. As the spatiotemporal resolution goes finer, the amount of information can be extracted from LBSM data becomes sparser and sparser. From Tab. 1, we can see that under the resolution setting in [1], about 47,113 tweets can be collected in each time window. But when the spatial resolution increases to 30×30, only about 15 tweets can be collected for each region in each time window. It is challenging to build effective prediction models with such sparse LBSM information.

3. THE PROPOSED METHOD

To make better predictions given the sparsity of LBSM information, in Sec. 3.1-3.3, we explicitly consider three types of dependencies in the traffic networks, which address challenge (b) in Sec. 1. In Sec. 3.4, we describe how CTP simultaneously predict traffic conditions of multiple regions, which tackles challenge (a) in Sec. 1.

3.1 Intra-Region Temporal Dependency

The first type of dependency we consider is called *intra-region temporal dependency*, in which we discover the dependencies between the traffic conditions of the same region across different time slices. In traffic prediction, historical data are always considered as the primary factor since the traffic conditions across the timeline are not independent for any given location. For example, in the road networks, the probability of traffic congestion in region r_i in time window t should be high if we know that r_i was congested in $t-1$, and r_i is unlikely to be congested in t if we know r_i was not congested in $t-1$. So given a region r_g in a road network, by considering the *intra-region temporal dependency* alone, we will have the following prediction model

$$v_g^{(t)} = \alpha + \sum_{k=1}^{l_1} \beta_k v_g^{(t-k)} \quad (4)$$

where $v_g^{(t-k)}$ is the traffic history feature of $v_g^{(t)}$.

3.2 Inter-Region Temporal Dependency

Another type of dependency we consider is called *inter-region temporal dependency*, in which we discover the dependencies between the traffic conditions of the spatial related regions across different time windows. In other words, the traffic condition of any given region in time window t is correlated with the traffic conditions of its neighbors at the previous time windows $\{t-l_1, \ldots, t-1\}$. For example, the probability of traffic congestion in region r_i in time window t should be high if we know that most of its neighboring regions were congested in the previous time window $t-1$. And r_i is unlikely to be congested in time window t if we know most of r_i's neighboring regions are not congested in time window $t-1$.

We define overall traffic condition of neighboring regions of r_i in time window $t-l$ as follows

$$\mathcal{N}(v_i^{(t)}, l) = \frac{\sum_{(r_i, r_j) \in \mathcal{E}, r_j \in \mathcal{R}_O} v_j^{(t-l)}}{|\{r_j | (r_i, r_j) \in \mathcal{E}, r_j \in \mathcal{R}_O\}|} \quad (5)$$

where $\mathcal{E}$ is the set of edges we discussed in Sec. 2, and $|\{\cdot\}|$ denotes the number of elements in the set.

Hence, by considering *inter-region temporal dependency* alone, we have

$$v_g^{(t)} = \alpha + \sum_{k=1}^{l_1} \beta_k \mathcal{N}(v_g^{(t)}, k) \quad (6)$$

where $\mathcal{N}(v_g^{(t)}, k)$ is the inter-region temporal feature of $v_g^{(t)}$.

3.3 Inter-Region Spatial Dependency

The third type of dependency we consider is called *inter-region spatial dependency*, in which we discover the dependencies between the traffic conditions of spatially related regions within the same time window. For example, in the traffic networks, the probability of traffic congestion in region r_i within the time window t should be high if we know that most of its neighboring regions are congested in the same time window t , and r_i is unlikely to be congested within t if we know most of its neighboring regions are not congested in t. Formally, we define the overall traffic condition of neighboring regions of r_i in the same time window t as follows

$$\tilde{\mathcal{N}}(v_i^{(t)}) = \frac{\sum_{(r_i,r_j)\in\mathcal{E}} v_j^{(t)}}{|\{r_j|(r_i,r_j)\in\mathcal{E}\}|} \tag{7}$$

Note that $\tilde{\mathcal{N}}(\cdot)$ averages all neighboring traffic conditions predicted by our iterative algorithm, even some regions are unobserved. This is because that CTP makes initial predictions of the traffic conditions in unobserved regions using LBSM features only, then update these predictions iteratively by considering the overall traffic condition of neighboring regions within the same time window. More details of our proposed framework will be discussed in Sec. 3.4. Hence, by considering *inter-region spatial dependency* alone, we have

$$v_g^{(t)} = \alpha + \beta\tilde{\mathcal{N}}(v_g^{(t)}) \tag{8}$$

where $\tilde{\mathcal{N}}(v_g^{(t)})$ is the inter-region spatial feature of $v_g^{(t)}$. For collective traffic prediction, we aim at inferring the traffic conditions of correlated regions simultaneously. Thus, when three types of dependencies are considered together with the LBSM feature vectors, for $g \in O$ we have

$$v_g^{(t)} = \alpha + \sum_{k=1}^{l_1}\beta_k v_g^{(t-k)} + \sum_{k=1}^{l_1}\gamma_k\mathcal{N}(v_g^{(t)},k) + \eta\tilde{\mathcal{N}}(v_g^{(t)}) + \sum_{k=1}^{l_2}\epsilon_k \boldsymbol{x}_g^{(t-k)}\boldsymbol{m}_{gk} \tag{9}$$

As to the case that $g \in U$, we have

$$v_g^{(t)} = \alpha+\sum_{k=1}^{l_1}\gamma_k\mathcal{N}(v_g^{(t)},k)+\eta\tilde{\mathcal{N}}(v_g^{(t)})+\sum_{k=1}^{l_2}\epsilon_k\boldsymbol{x}_g^{(t-k)}\boldsymbol{m}_{gk} \tag{10}$$

Other than considering the two more types of dependencies, our method is also different from [1] by learning separate transformation vectors $\boldsymbol{m}_k$ for each $\boldsymbol{x}_g^{(t-k)}$.

3.4 Iterative Framework

With the dependencies described above, we now present the CTP algorithm, which is inspired by ICA (Iterative Classification Algorithm) [5]. CTP algorithm is also summarized in Tab. 2. It contains the following key steps:

Training: The traffic history features, inter-region temporal features and inter-region spatial features are extracted from the traffic dataset and appended to the LBSM features to form the extended training set. Note that the inter-region spatial features are extracted using $\mathcal{N}(\cdot)$ instead of $\tilde{\mathcal{N}}(\cdot)$. This is because part of regions in traffic network is unobserved, so the traffic history in these regions is still unknown. $\mathcal{N}(\cdot)$ retrieves the overall neighboring traffic condition from observed regions. After the extended training set is built, we can apply the base learner on the data to obtain a local model f.

Input:

$\{\mathcal{X}^{(1)},\ldots,\mathcal{X}^{(t-1)}\}$: set of attribute vectors
$\{\mathcal{V}_O^{(1)},\ldots,\mathcal{V}_O^{(t-1)}\}$: set of traffic conditions of observed regions
$\mathcal{R}_O$: set of observed regions
$\mathcal{R}_U$: set of unobserved regions
$\mathcal{E}$: set of edges connecting all neighboring regions
Max_It: maximum # of iteration
A: a base learner for the local model

Training:

- Learn the local model:
  1. Extended training set $\mathcal{D} = \left\{(\bar{\boldsymbol{x}}_i^{(j)}, v_i^{(j)})\right\}$
     for all $2 \le j \le t-1$ and $i \in \{k|r_k \in \mathcal{R}_O\}$ where
     $\bar{\boldsymbol{x}}_i^{(j)} = \left(\boldsymbol{x}_i^{(j-2)}, \boldsymbol{x}_i^{(j-1)}, v_i^{(j-2)}, v_i^{(j-1)}, \mathcal{N}(v_i^{(j)},2), \mathcal{N}(v_i^{(j)},1), \mathcal{N}(v_i^{(j)},0)\right)$
  2. Let $f = A(\mathcal{D})$ be the local model

Bootstrap:

- Estimate the label sets:
  1. Produce an estimated value $\hat{v}_i^{(t)}$ for $v_i^{(t)}$ as follow:
     for $r_i \in \mathcal{R}_O$:
     $\hat{v}_i^{(t)} = f\left((\boldsymbol{x}_i^{(t-2)}, \boldsymbol{x}_i^{(t-1)}, v_i^{(t-2)}, v_i^{(t-1)}, \mathcal{N}(v_i^{(t)},2), \mathcal{N}(v_i^{(t)},1), 0)\right)$
     for $r_i \in \mathcal{R}_U$:
     $\hat{v}_i^{(t)} = f\left((\boldsymbol{x}_i^{(t-2)}, \boldsymbol{x}_i^{(t-1)}, 0, 0, \mathcal{N}(v_i^{(t)},2), \mathcal{N}(v_i^{(t)},1), 0)\right)$

Iterative Inference:

- Repeat until convergence or #iteration> Max_It
  1. Construct the extended testing instance:
     for $r_i \in \mathcal{R}_O$:
     $\bar{\boldsymbol{x}}_i^{(t)} = \left(\boldsymbol{x}_i^{(t-2)}, \boldsymbol{x}_i^{(t-1)}, v_i^{(t-2)}, v_i^{(t-1)}, \mathcal{N}(v_i^{(t)},2), \mathcal{N}(v_i^{(t)},1), \tilde{\mathcal{N}}(v_i^{(t)})\right)$
     for $r_i \in \mathcal{R}_U$
     $\bar{\boldsymbol{x}}_i^{(t)} = \left(\boldsymbol{x}_i^{(t-2)}, \boldsymbol{x}_i^{(t-1)}, 0, 0, \mathcal{N}(v_i^{(t)},2), \mathcal{N}(v_i^{(t)},1), \tilde{\mathcal{N}}(v_i^{(t)})\right)$
  2. Update the estimated values $\hat{v}_i^{(t)}$ for $v_i^{(t)}$ on each testing instance:
     $\hat{v}_i^{(t)} = f(\bar{\boldsymbol{x}}_i^{(t)})$

Output:

$\hat{\mathcal{V}}^{(t)} = \{\hat{v}_i^{(t)}|r_i \in \mathcal{R}_O \text{ and } r_i \in \mathcal{R}_U\}$

Table 2: The CTP algorithm

Bootstrap: Two problems are raised before CTP infers the future traffic conditions. The first one is that how to initialize the inter-region spatial features while all traffic conditions in the future time window t are still unknown. CTP uses *bootstrap* to tackles this problem, in which it initializes all the inter-region spatial features as zeros [4]. The second problem is that how to initialize the traffic history features for unobserved regions, *i.e.* $v_i^{(t-1)}$ where $i \in U$. CTP also initializes these unknown traffic history features as zeros (*i.e.* the universal average value of traffic condition in the de-trended dataset). Then the local model f can be applied to make the initial predictions on all regions in the future time window t.

Iterative Inference: In this step, we first update the inter-region spatial features based upon the initial predictions, then we apply f on the extended feature vectors with updated inter-region spatial features, which updates the predictions. Again, we can use these updated predictions to further update the inter-region spatial features. This iterative procedure continues until the predictions converge or a maximum number of iteration has been reached.

4. EXPERIMENTS

4.1 Data Collection

We collected the traffic data set from traffic detectors in the Greater Los Angeles area between October 19, 2014 and November 28, 2014 using the California Performance Measurement System(PeMS[1]). This collection results in a total number of 31,102,272 entries of traffic records. We also collected tweets from the same area during the same time range

[1]http://pems.dot.ca.gov

using the Twitter streaming API[2] with a geolocation filter defining the bounding box of the Greater Los Angeles area. For each tweet, we store all meta-data and post content. This collection results in a total number of 2,648,446 tweets.

4.2 Data Preparation

In the PeMS traffic dataset, each data entry has the format $(t, lat, long, v)$, which keeps track of the average speed v of all vehicles passing by the detector located at coordinates $(lat, long)$ within the 1-hour time window t. Different from [1], which was designed for a lower spatial resolution by treating the target area as a single region, our experiments aim at a much finer spatial granularity. We evenly divide the target area into $r \times r$ grids, where r is the spatial resolution parameter. Then we transform the dataset into the format $(t, r_g, v_g^{(t)})$, which keeps track of the average speed $v_g^{(t)}$ of all vehicles traveling in region (grid) r_g in time window t. To exclude the periodic fluctuations in the traffic data, we follow the approach in [1] to de-trend each $v_g^{(t)}$.

As to the Twitter dataset, for each time window t and region g, we put the contents of all tweets originate in t and from g together and cast them into the space of stemmed words (stop-words removed), which generates a non-negative sparse vector $\boldsymbol{x}_g^{(t)}$. These vectors are used as the LBSM semantic features. Stacking all such vectors in time window t together, we obtain a semantic feature matrix $\mathbf{F}^{(t)} \in \mathbb{R}^{n \times d}$, where n is the number of regions in the graph, and d is the number of stemmed words.

4.3 Compared Methods

We compare the proposed CTP with following methods:

- **Tweets Semantics Only (TwSeO)** [1]: TwSeO uses the semantic feature matrices $\mathbf{F}^{(t-1)}$ and $\mathbf{F}^{(t-2)}$ to predict the average speed of each region in time window t. The model used by TwSeO is shown in Eq. 3. The original method proposed in [1] requires both tweet semantic data and historical traffic data. However, in our experiments, the historical data is not available in some regions. Thus, we compare CTP with TwSeO method which can be considered as a degenerated version of the method proposed in [1].

- **Traffic Data Only (TDO)** [8]: Due to the lack of historical traffic data, TDO always take the universal average speed of the entire traffic network, which is 0 in our de-trended traffic dataset, as the prediction for the unobserved regions. As to the observed regions, TDO uses the auto-regression model [8] shown in Eq. 1.

- **Traffic Data Only with Complete Traffic History(TDO-floor)** [8]: TDO-floor predicts future traffic condition by using the auto regression model proposed in [8] with fully observed historical traffic data. TDO-floor serves as a lower-bound baseline since it assumes all historical traffic data in the road network is observed.

The maximum number of iteration in the inference procedure of CTP are all set as 20.

[2]https://dev.twitter.com/streaming/overview

4.4 Experimental Settings

We partition the data into two parts, with the beginning $(u-1)/u$ $(u = 3, \ldots, 7)$ as the training set and the remaining as the test set. Moreover, k-fold cross-validation is used to randomly sample $1/k$ regions as unobserved, *i.e.* regions without historical traffic data. Note that all models are required to make predictions on all regions in test set, including the unobserved ones. Various spatial resolutions ($r \times r$, where $r = 5, 10, \ldots, 30$) and different fractions of unobserved regions($1/k$, where $k = 2, 3, 4, 5$) are tested respectively.

4.5 Evaluation Metrics

Root Mean Square Error (RMSE) and Mean Absolute Error (MAE) are used to evaluate the performance of compared methods, the definitions are as follows

$$\text{RMSE} = \sqrt{\frac{1}{m-l} \sum_{t=l+1}^{m} \sum_{g=1}^{n} (\hat{v}_g^{(t)} - v_g^{(t)})^2}$$

$$\text{MAE} = \frac{1}{m-l} \sum_{t=l+1}^{m} \sum_{g=1}^{n} |\hat{v}_g^{(t)} - v_g^{(t)}|$$

, where $l = \max(l_1, l_2)$ and $\hat{v}_g^{(t)}$ is the estimated value of $v_g^{(t)}$.

4.6 Results

We first study the effectiveness of our proposed CTP method on traffic prediction. Fig. 3 shows the comparison of CTP and other methods in terms of RMSE and MAE, where we set $r = 5$ and $k = 2$. The results under other spatial resolutions and ratio of unobserved regions are similar and will be discussed in Sec. 4.7. We can observe that the TDO-floor method outperforms other three methods in terms of both metrics for all training/test ratios. This is because TDO-floor uses the complete traffic history data while other compared methods only have traffic history of 50% regions. Among all three methods using only partially observed traffic history, our proposed CTP method performs the best in terms of both metrics. This improvement can be explained by the fact that CTP leverages the semantic features extracted from LBSM data as well as exploits the spatiotemporal dependencies between regions. Due to the novel experimental setting used in this work, the method proposed in [1] no longer works as it relies on complete traffic history. A degenerated version of their method, TwSeO, which only uses LBSM semantic features is compared here. We can observe that TwSeO is outperformed by all compared methods, which indicates that using tweets semantics alone can not achieve satisfying performance at fine spatiotemporal granularity. This observation shows the limitation of [1] under the assumption that historical traffic data of some regions is not available.

4.7 Parameter Study

We now study the effect of the spatial resolution parameter in our experimental setting. Fig. 4 compares the performance of all four methods at different spatial resolutions. Each figure in Fig. 4 shows the results under different ratios of test data and we set $k = 2$ for all of them. Specifically, we set the spatial resolution parameter r to $\{5, 10, \ldots, 30\}$ and show the RMSE of each method (MAE scores are similar and we omit them due to the page limitation). The higher spatial

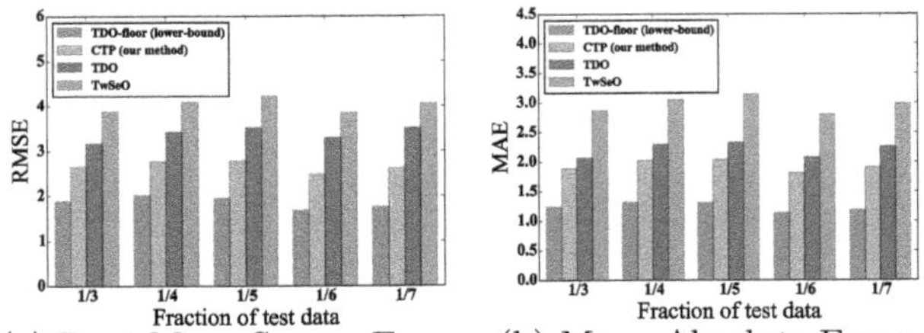

(a) Root Mean Square Error (b) Mean Absolute Error

Figure 3: Comparison of different methods

resolution (larger r) produces smaller region, which results in sparser LBSM data in each region. We observe that CTP achieves the best performance consistently under different spatial resolutions compared to other methods using only partially observed traffic history. Even under large r, where the LBSM information is extremely sparse (about 15 tweets per region in a time window), CTP can reduce the prediction errors compared to TDO. Meanwhile, TwSeO is consistently outperformed by TDO and the gap between them becomes larger when r increases. This observation demonstrates the effectiveness of exploiting the spatiotemporal dependencies.

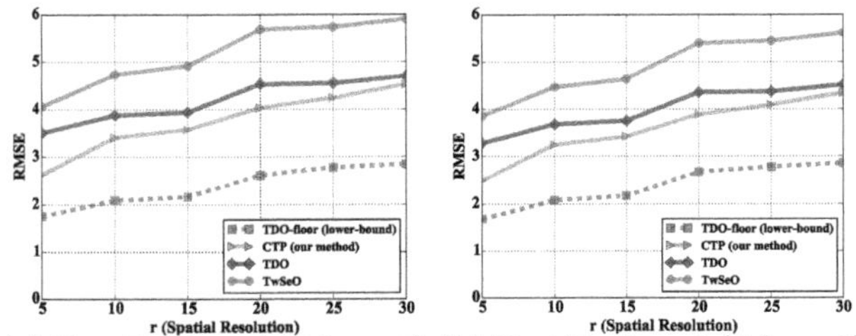

(a) Test Ratio = 1/7 ($u = 7$) (b) Test Ratio = 1/6 ($u = 6$)

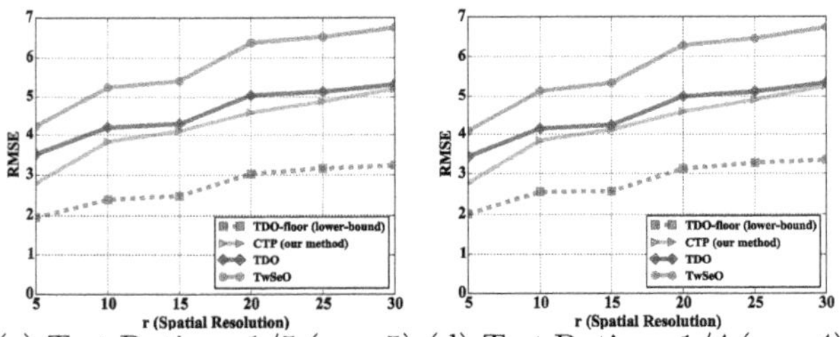

(c) Test Ratio = 1/5 ($u = 5$) (d) Test Ratio = 1/4 ($u = 4$)

Figure 4: Different spatial resolutions

We also study the effect of parameter k, which indicates the ratio of unobserved regions in our experiments. To do this, we set k equals to $\{2, 3, 4, 5\}$ respectively, which is equivalent to set 50%, 33.3%, 25%, and 20% of all regions in the target area as unobserved (with no historical traffic data). The results in Fig. 5 show that CTP achieves better performance compared to TwSeO and TDO consistently under different values of k. We note that the performances of TwSeO and TDO-floor do not change under different values of k. This is because TwSeO only use the LBSM semantic feature matrices $\mathbf{F}^{(t-1)}$ and $\mathbf{F}^{(t-2)}$ that are not affected by k, and TDO-floor uses the complete traffic history regardless of the value of k.

5. CONCLUSION

In this paper, we studied the problem of collective traffic prediction with LBSM information. Our work is different from the conventional traffic prediction methods in several aspects. The proposed CTP method extracts and exploits the semantic and spatial information in LBSM. Besides, CTP also makes use of the complex dependencies exist in the road traffic networks to tickle the sparsity problem in LBSM data. With these novelties, CTP can even make predictions in the regions without historical traffic data under much finer temporal and spatial granularity. Experimental results on traffic data and Twitter data collected from the Los Angeles area of California demonstrate that CTP improves the performance of traffic prediction.

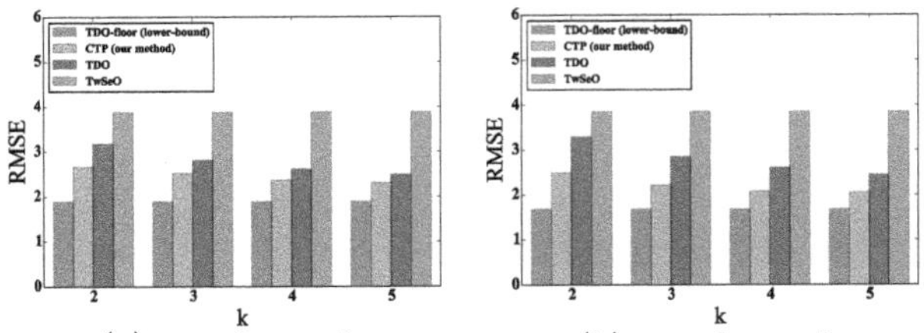

(a) $u = 3, r = 5$ (b) $u = 6, r = 5$

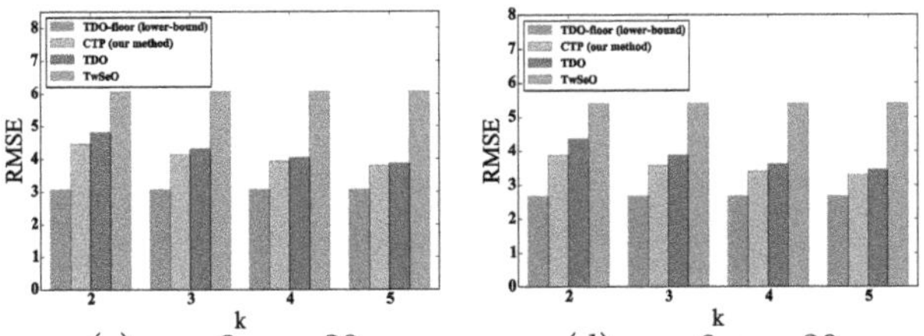

(c) $u = 3, r = 20$ (d) $u = 6, r = 20$

Figure 5: Different ratios of unobserved regions

6. ACKNOWLEDGEMENTS

This material is based upon work supported by the National Science Foundation through grant CNS-1626236.

7. REFERENCES

[1] J. He, W. Shen, P. Divakaruni, L.Wynter, and R. Lawrence. Improving traffic prediction with tweet semantics. In *IJCAI*, pages 1387–1393, 2013.
[2] E. Horvitz, J. Apacible, R. Sarin, and L. Liao. Prediction, expectation, and surprise: Methods, designs, and study of a deployed traffic forecasting service. In *UAI*, 2005.
[3] A. Khosravi, E. Mazloumi, S. Nahavandi, D. Creighton, and J. Van Lint. A genetic algorithm-based method for improving quality of travel time prediction intervals. *Transportation Research Part C: Emerging Technologies*, 19(6):1364–1376, 2011.
[4] X. Kong, X. Shi, and P.S. Yu. Multi-label collective classification. In *SDM*, pages 618–629. SIAM, 2011.
[5] Q. Lu and L. Getoor. Link-based classification. In *ICML*, pages 496–503, Washington, DC, 2003.
[6] W. Min and L. Wynter. Real-time road traffic prediction with spatio-temporal correlations. *Transportation Research Part C: Emerging Technologies*, 19(4):606–616, 2011.
[7] D. Schrank, B. Eisele, and T.Lomax. TTI's 2012 urban mobility report. *Texas A&M Transportation Institute. The Texas A&M University System*, 2012.
[8] B.L. Smith and M.J. Demetsky. Traffic flow forecasting: comparison of modeling approaches. *Journal of transportation engineering*, 123(4):261–266, 1997.
[9] B.L. Smith, B.M. Williams, and R.K. Oswald. Comparison of parametric and nonparametric models for traffic flow forecasting. *Transportation Research Part C: Emerging Technologies*, 10(4):303–321, 2002.
[10] J. Xu, A. Bhargava, R. Nowak, and X. Zhu. Socioscope: Spatio-temporal signal recovery from social media. In *Machine Learning and Knowledge Discovery in Databases*, pages 644–659. Springer, 2012.

Recommendations For Streaming Data

Karthik Subbian
University of Minnesota
Minneapolis, MN
karthik@cs.umn.edu

Charu Aggarwal
IBM Watson Research Center
Yorktown Heights, NY
charu@us.ibm.com

Kshiteesh Hegde
University of Minnesota
Minneapolis, MN
hegde@cs.umn.edu

ABSTRACT

Recommender systems have become increasingly popular in recent years because of the broader popularity of many web-enabled electronic commerce applications. However, most recommender systems today are designed in the context of an offline setting. The online setting is, however, much more challenging because the existing methods do not work very effectively for very large-scale systems. In many applications, it is desirable to provide real-time recommendations in large-scale scenarios. The main problem in applying streaming algorithms for recommendations is that the in-core storage space for memory-resident operations is quite limited. In this paper, we present a probabilistic neighborhood-based algorithm for performing recommendations in real-time. We present experimental results, which show the effectiveness of our approach in comparison to state-of-the-art methods.

1. INTRODUCTION

The increasing importance of web-enabled e-commerce applications has led to a greater popularity of recommender systems. In collaborative filtering applications, users provide ratings for various products, and the collective intelligence stored in these ratings is used in order to make recommendations. Many such systems have seen an increasing volume of transactions and ratings, which has led to numerous *computational and scalability challenges*. This increased volume of ratings has been driven by the larger number of users at these sites, and numerous ways in which implicit feedback is received from user activities.

In many social applications, such as *Facebook*, items are highly transient, and new items can appear with time. As the underlying user patterns change, the recommendations can also vary significantly with time. The increasing size of such data necessitates the use of real-time streaming algorithms. The two most commonly used classes of algorithms, namely latent factor models and neighborhood-based methods, are computationally challenging. In particular, the main challenges in scaling up recommender systems to the real-time scenario with the aforementioned algorithms are as follows:

- Neighborhood-based recommender systems require an offline phase, which is generally computationally intensive. It is often difficult to perform the underlying computations in real time. Furthermore, with dynamic ratings, it becomes challenging to scale up such systems, particularly when the amount of available memory is limited. It is crucial to be able to perform all the computations in core because disk access is often not practical in such settings.
- Latent factor models require the factorization of a large matrix of entries. In cases where the matrix changes rapidly over time, it becomes difficult to perform the factorization in limited space.
- The temporal nature of recommender systems is such that all ratings for a particular user are not received simultaneously. This makes the problem more difficult because the sets of both the specified (observed) and unspecified (unobserved) entries change dynamically with time. Clearly, the streaming model needs to keep up with these changes in real time.

In this paper, we present a probabilistic neighborhood-based algorithm for performing recommendations in real-time. Our approach uses a min-hash based scheme to construct the underlying recommendation system. To handle the large volume of streaming data, we propose a probabilistic data structure for approximate and efficient model maintenance. We also establish theoretical bounds on the approximation error of our online model and show that the error reduces exponentially with available memory.

1.1 Related Work

Recommender systems became increasingly popular in the mid-nineties, as new systems such as GroupLens [11] were proposed for recommendation. The user-based collaborative filtering models were one of the earliest models [11]. User-based methods utilize the ratings of *similar* users on the *same* item in order to make predictions. While such methods were initially quite popular, they are not easily scalable and sometimes inaccurate. Subsequently, item-based methods [3, 4] were proposed, which compute predicted ratings as a function of the ratings of the *same* user on *similar* items. More recently personalization of recommendation with collaborative filtering using *offline* min-hash clustering was proposed [21]. There are recent attempts to characterize user, item, and topic relationships for recommendation

CIKM'16 , October 24-28, 2016, Indianapolis, IN, USA

DOI: http://dx.doi.org/10.1145/2983323.2983663

using stochastic process models in a streaming setting [8]. In another related work a similarity search approximation for neighborhood-based model is proposed [17]. A detailed discussion of neighborhood-based methods for recommender systems may be found in [5, 2]. Latent factor models have become popular in the context recommender systems [6, 10] and some of them have been used in combination with neighborhood methods [7]. Matrix factorization is another popular approach for learning latent factors and online updates for factorization is another trend in this direction [15, 16]. A detailed discussion of recent advances in collaborative filtering, with a specific emphasis on latent factor models, may be found in [9, 2]. A significant amount of work has been devoted to mining algorithms for streaming data [1]. In this paper we directly approach the problem of recommendation in a streaming setting using a probabilistic neighborhood model with a min-hash technique.

2. RECOMMENDATION FRAMEWORK

In this section, we will introduce the framework for the streaming recommendation problem. A major assumption in streaming recommendation applications is that all the ratings of a particular user or all the ratings of a particular item are not received at the same time. This is different from multidimensional streaming applications in which all dimensions of the same record are always received simultaneously. In recommendation applications, a user may specify a rating for a particular item at any given time. Furthermore, a new user or a new item may enter the system at any given time. In general, since ratings are never deleted, the number of users and items may only increase over time, but they may never decrease. Therefore, we make the assumption that the number of users at time t is given by $m(t)$ and items at time t as $n(t)$. Clearly, $m(t)$ and $n(t)$ can non-decreasing with time t. Therefore, at any given time t, the size of the ratings matrix is $m(t) \times n(t)$.

The ratings are received in the format $\langle UserId, ItemId, Rating \rangle$, as users enter ratings over time. While it is reasonable to assume that users will specify a rating only once for an item, it is possible to handle duplicate ratings by retaining only the latest rating entered by a user for a particular item. Let us assume that ratings have binary values, which are drawn from $\{-1, +1\}$. However, non-binary ratings can also be handled in a relatively straightforward generalization of our technique. A value of $+1$ indicates a liking of an item, whereas a value of -1 indicates a dislike.

In the online setting, it may be desirable to query the system at any given time for recommendations. Typical examples of queries are as follows: (a) determine the top-k recommended items given a user, and (b) determine the top-k relevant users given an item. The first form of recommendation is common more in web-centric applications, while the second form is more useful for targeted marketing scenarios. Despite their application centric differences, the two formulations are similar from a conceptual point of view and minor variations of the same approach can be used to solve both of them.

In this paper, we study a neighborhood-based approach to perform the recommendations. The main problem of the neighborhood-based approach is that it requires an offline phase, in which the similarity between every pair of item is computed. This is particularly difficult in the stream setting because the update of a single rating may require the re-computation of the distance between the item and all other items. Furthermore, one cannot assume that the entire ratings matrix is held in main memory. In such cases, the approach may require several passes over the disk just to compute the pairwise item similarity. While it is reasonable to assume that the ratings matrix will be stored on disk, it is important to be able to maintain memory-resident summaries so that *most* of the computations can be performed in main memory. As we will see later, we will design an approach which requires mostly memory-resident operations and limited access to disk.

2.1 Offline Neighborhood-based Model

Before discussing the streaming model in detail, we will first introduce an offline neighborhood-based model. We will focus on item-based models because they are generally more accurate and also particularly well suited to the streaming scenario.

Consider two items i and j, for which only a subset of the users have specified ratings at time t. As discussed earlier, each rating is drawn from $\{-1, +1\}$. Let the set of users who have specified a positive rating of $+1$ for item i be denoted by $P(i,t)$, and let the set of users who have specified negative rating of -1 of item i till time t be denoted by $N(i,t)$. In order to compute the neighborhood distance between the two items, we will compute the distance separately on the basis of their positive ratings and on the basis of their negative ratings. The similarity $S^+(i,j,t)$ between items i and j at time t on the basis of their positively specified ratings is as follows:

$$S^+(i,j,t) = \frac{P(i,t) \cap P(j,t)}{P(i,t) \cup P(j,t)} \quad (1)$$

In other words, the similarity on the basis of only the positive rating is equal to the Jaccard coefficient between the two sets. A corresponding notion can be defined on the basis of the negative ratings $N(i,t)$ and $N(j,t)$ as $S^-(i,j,t)$.

The overall similarity between the two items is then obtained by combining the positive similarity results $S^+(i,j,t)$ and the negative similarity results $S^-(i,j,t)$. However, this combination must appropriately weight the number of positive and the number of negative ratings. Therefore, the combined similarity $S(i,j,t)$ is as follows:

$$S(i,j,t) = \frac{\alpha \cdot S^+(i,j,t) + \beta \cdot S^-(i,j,t)}{\alpha + \beta}, \quad (2)$$

where, $\alpha = |P(i,t)| + |P(j,t)|$ and $\beta = |N(i,t)| + |N(j,t)|$. Here α and β are the weights of the positive and the negative ratings, respectively, for an item-pair combination (i,j) at time t. These similarities are used to define the groups of most similar items.

2.2 Predicting Ratings with Similar Items

The peer groups can be used to predict the specific ratings of particular user-item combinations. The first step is to compute the similarity of a given item with all the other items. The weighted average of the ratings of the most similar items to a particular item i is predicted as the user rating for that item. Let $I_i(u)$ be the set of items most similar to item i, for which the user u has specified ratings. Furthermore, let the specified rating of user u for item j be r_{uj} (assuming that a rating has indeed been specified). Then, the overall neighborhood-based *prediction* $p_{ui}(t)$ of user u for item i at time t is as follows:

$$p_{ui}(t) = \frac{\sum_{j \in I_i(u)} (S(i,j,t) \cdot r_{uj})}{\sum_{j \in I_i(u)} S(i,j,t)} \quad (3)$$

Note that this computation requires the determination of the most similar items to a given item. This can require disk-resident offline computation. Clearly, this is not a feasible option for resolving online queries. In the static offline setting, the most similar items to a given item are pre-computed a priori, which are used to provide query responses. Therefore, it is crucial to set up both disk-resident and memory-resident data structures, which can be leveraged effectively at query time. Although a limited amount of access to the disk-resident ratings matrix continues to be required, most of our approach uses probabilistic data structures, such as the min-hash index, which can be maintained in an online fashion.

3. STREAMING RECOMMENDATIONS

In this section, we will propose a min-hash technique to perform recommendations in a space-constrained setting. The idea in the min-hash approach is to use a probabilistic data structure, which can approximately compute the similarity between the items.

The similarity can be approximately computed by tracking the relevant users for each item in a min-hash index. Let us consider two items i and j. As before, assume that the set of users who have rated item i positively at time t is denoted by $P(i,t)$ and the set of users who have rated item j positively at time t is denoted by $P(j,t)$. The basic idea is to impose a sort order on the users with the help of a hash function. What is the probability that the first user with a positive rating for item i in this sort order is the same as the first user with a positive rating for item j in the sort order? This is equal to the probability that both columns i and j take on the value of +1, when at least one of the columns takes on the value of +1. This probability is equal to $\frac{P(i,t) \cap P(j,t)}{P(i,t) \cup P(j,t)}$, which is exactly the same as the Jaccard coefficient between $P(i,t)$ and $P(j,t)$. This is, therefore, equal to the similarity $S^+(i,j,t)$ between items i and j. This basic principle can be used to estimate the Jaccard coefficient by using multiple sort orders to repeat the process and determine the fraction of cases in which the first positive rating for both items is provided by the same user. A similar approach can be used to compute the Jaccard coefficient on the negative ratings. Therefore, the two can be combined in order to compute the similarity between the items. Note that the combination of the similarity on the positive items and the negative items requires the tracking of $|N(i,t)|$ and $|P(i,t)|$, which is performed separately. For each item, we always separately maintain the number of positive and negative ratings of that item. This can easily be maintained in streaming fashion.

How are these random sort orders implemented? The sort orders are implemented with the use of a hash function. In order to implement d mutually independent sort orders, we use d mutually independent hash functions denoted by $f_1(\cdot) \dots f_d(\cdot)$. The argument of each such hash function is the identifier of a user, and the hash function value is a random number which is uniformly distributed in $(0,1)$. For each item j in the data, the following two pieces of information are maintained:

1. The hash functions $f_1(\cdot) \dots f_d(\cdot)$ are applied to the user-indices that have rated item j positively. For each hash function $f_s(\cdot)$, the least hash value among these positive users is maintained. Furthermore, the user-index which maps to the least hash value is also maintained. The former is referred to as the *min-hash value*, and the latter is referred to as the *min-hash index*. Because there are d hash functions, a total of d hash function-hash value pairs are maintained for each item. Thus, the sth pair is of the form $(f_s(u), u)$, where u is the index of a user. Overall for $n(t)$ items, a total of $d \cdot n(t)$ pairs are maintained. This data structure maintained over the positively rated items is denoted by $\mathcal{M}^+$.

2. The hash functions $f_1(\cdot) \dots f_d(\cdot)$ are applied to the user-indices that have rated item j negatively. For each hash function $f_s(\cdot)$, the least hash value among the negative users are maintained. As the previous case, both the hash index and hash value are maintained. This portion of the data structure maintained over the negatively rated items is denoted by $\mathcal{M}^-$.

It is noteworthy that the size of these data structures is much smaller than the size of the ratings matrix, when the value of d is small. Therefore, this data structure can be maintained in main memory.

Furthermore, the data structure can be updated efficiently. Consider an incoming rating r_{ui} that is positive. The first step is to apply the d hash functions to the user u to result in the d hash values $f_1(u) \dots f_d(u)$. For the ith item, its d different hash value/hash index pairs are retrieved from $\mathcal{M}^+$ because the rating r_{ui} is positive. The sth current hash value (where $s \in \{1 \dots d\}$) for item i in $\mathcal{M}^+$ is compared to $f_s(u)$. If $f_s(u)$ is smaller than the sth current hash value in $\mathcal{M}^+$, then the corresponding pair in $\mathcal{M}^+$ is replaced with the new pair $(f_s(u), u)$. Otherwise, no change is made to the sth value in $\mathcal{M}^+$ for item i. This process is repeated for each value of $s \in \{1 \dots d\}$. If the rating r_{ui} is negative, then exactly the same steps are used, except that the changes are made to $\mathcal{M}^-$ rather than $\mathcal{M}^+$.

Note that it is easy to compute the similarity between two item pairs with the use of the min-hash index. For example, the value of $S^+(i,j,t)$ is equal to fraction of the d min-hash indices in $\mathcal{M}^+$, which are the same. In other words, if $i_1 \dots i_d$ be the top-d min-hash indices of item i in $\mathcal{M}^+$, and $j_1 \dots j_d$ be the top-d min-hash indices of item j in $\mathcal{M}^+$, then the similarity between items i and j can be estimated as follows:

$$S^+(i,j,t) \approx R^+(i,j,t) = \frac{\sum_{s=1}^{d} \delta(i_s = j_s)}{d} \quad (4)$$

Here $\delta(\cdot)$ is an indicator function, which takes on the value of 1 when i_s and j_s are the same, and 0, otherwise. The value if $S^-(i,j,t)$ can be computed in a similar way, except that the data structure $\mathcal{M}^-$ is used to compute the similarity rather than $\mathcal{M}^+$. In order to combine the similarity measures $S^+(i,j,t)$ and $S^-(i,j,t)$ into a single similarity measure $S(i,j,t)$, the number of positive and negative ratings of the items i and j are required. These can be dynamically tracked in online fashion by incrementing counters tracking the number of positive or negative ratings for each item, as they are received. In addition, the number of specified ratings $N(i,t)$ for each item i is maintained separately.

3.1 Quality of Recommendations

The quality of the recommendation is highly dependent on the quality of similarity computed. Therefore, in the following, we will bound the quality of the similarity, which is computed using the min-hash approach. This is an important result because it ensures a high fidelity for the quality of recommendations.

LEMMA 1 (LOWER TAIL BOUND). *For any $\epsilon \in (0,1)$, Equation 4 provides an approximated value $R^+(i,j,t)$ of the Jaccard coefficient, which lies outside a factor $(1-\epsilon)$ of the true value $S^+(i,j,t)$ with the following probability.*

$$P(R^+(i,j,t) < (1-\epsilon)\cdot S^+(i,j,t)) \leq exp(-d\cdot S^+(i,j,t)\cdot \epsilon^2/2) \quad (5)$$

PROOF. We restate Equation 4 here:

$$S^+(i,j,t) \approx R^+(i,j,t) = \frac{\sum_{r=1}^{d} \delta(i_r = j_r)}{d}$$

$$d \cdot S^+(i,j,t) \approx d \cdot R^+(i,j,t) = \sum_{r=1}^{d} \delta(i_r = j_r)$$

Note that we are summing up d i.i.d. Bernoulli variables in the aforementioned equation. This particular form of the summation can be directly used in conjunction with the Chernoff bound. Each element $\delta(i_r = j_r)$ in the summation is a Bernoulli random variable. Furthermore, this Bernoulli random variable is equal to 1 with probability $S^+(i,j,t)$. In such a case, the lower-tail Chernoff bound applies to the summation. By applying the lower tail Chernoff bound, we obtain the following:

$$P(d \cdot R^+(i,j,t) < (1-\epsilon) \cdot d \cdot S^+(i,j,t)) \leq \exp(-d \cdot S^+(i,j,t) \cdot \epsilon^2/2)$$

$$P(R^+(i,j,t) < (1-\epsilon) \cdot S^+(i,j,t)) \leq \exp(-d \cdot S^+(i,j,t) \cdot \epsilon^2/2)$$

This completes the proof. □

LEMMA 2 (UPPER TAIL BOUND). *For any $\epsilon \in (0, 2 \cdot e-1)$, the approximated value $R^+(i,j,t)$ of the Jaccard coefficient lies outside a factor $(1+\epsilon)$ of the true value $S^+(i,j,t)$ with the following probability.*

$$P(R^+(i,j,t) > (1+\epsilon)\cdot S^+(i,j,t)) \leq exp(-d\cdot S^+(i,j,t)\cdot \epsilon^2/4)$$

Due to shortage of space, we have omitted the proof for Lemma 2. However, it is straightforward to establish the upper tail bound, with a similar argument to Lemma 1. Thus, the probability of errors in the overall similarity computation reduces exponentially with increasing number of hash functions. This ensures that the approximate approach will yield similar results to the exact approach.

Note that whenever a rating has to be predicted for an user and item pair, it is straight forward to compute the predicted rating using (4), (2), and (3) (in that order). We refer to our proposed approach as STREAMREC in our experiments.

4. EXPERIMENTAL RESULTS

We evaluate our approach in terms of its effectiveness on prediction errors, efficiency using running time and sensitivity to change in model parameters.

4.1 Dataset

We chose two real-world public datasets to cover a different stream lengths, number of items/users, domain diversity, and rating scale.

Book Crossing: A four-week crawl from August to September 2004 from the Book-Crossing community is available at [18]. It contains 278,858 users providing 1,149,780 ratings about 271,379 books. The rating scale in this dataset ranges from 0 to 10.

Dating: This is an online dating website[1], where 17,359,346 ratings of 168,791 profiles are provided by 135,359 website users. All users are anonymized and this data set is publicly available [19]. Online dating website ratings are in the scale of 1 to 10.

These public datasets are stored offline and therefore, we had to simulate the streaming nature. In streaming settings, the user and items pairs mostly arrive in some random order. However, in our data sets the ratings were sorted by users and we account for this by randomizing the order of ratings.

4.2 Baselines

We used several important well-established baselines, which encompass both the neighborhood-based and latent-factor models. The two most popular baselines used in evaluating recommender systems are: Alternating Least Squares (ALS) [12] and Stochastic Gradient Descent (SGD) [10]. Probabilistic Matrix Factorization (PMF) [13] is a Bayesian approach for matrix factorization, in which the model capacity is controlled automatically by integrating over all model parameters and hyper-parameters. SVDPP [7] is another baseline that combines the latent factor models nicely in to the neighborhood based models as an optimization. A gradient descent approach is used to solve the optimization problem. We also evaluated a two-layer undirected graphical model, Restricted Boltzmann Machines (RBM), for collaborative filtering process as another baseline. The parameters for all baselines were tuned using a 5% validation set from the tail end of each data set.

4.3 Evaluation Measure

We have used Root Mean Squared Error (RMSE) and Mean Absolute Error (MAE) to quantify the effectiveness of our approach compared to baselines. RMSE penalizes prediction errors quadratically and the measure is affected more significantly by larger errors. For different applications, the importance of these measure may vary. Hence, we evaluate all approaches on both measures.

4.4 Efficiency Analysis

The most important part of a streaming algorithm is its ability to perform model maintenance in online fashion [1]. The basic idea is to be able to deal effectively with high-velocity data sets, by being able to efficiently perform model updates. In this section, we will show the efficiency of maintaining the streaming recommendation model.

We compare the running time of our approach against various baselines in Fig. 1(a) and (d). Our approach is extremely fast in terms of the running time compared to all the baselines. As we progress along the stream, we see newer items or users and more ratings have to be processed. Therefore, as time progresses, all algorithms generally have a larger computational burden. While all baselines take more time to process this, our approach consistently processes 100K records in fraction of a second. This is because of the fast probabilistic approach used for creating the summarized representation in a fixed number of operations. The updates

[1] *http://libimseti.cz/*

used in the probabilistic approach are straightforward, linear, and additive. This makes it ideal for the streaming scenario.

Among the baselines, PMF and ALS were the slowest in terms of the overall efficiency and also in terms of the rate of increase along the progression of stream. This is because PMF uses Markov Chain Monte Carlo (MCMC) approximation to learn the MAP estimate. The use of the MCMC technique is extremely inefficient, particularly in the streaming setting. Both SGD and SVDPP use stochastic gradient updates and are hence relatively fast in term of running time, at least compared to PMF and ALS. Despite their speed, they still have larger running times when they have to process a very large dataset.

Each approach also has an offline querying time, that is the time taken to query the rating for an unseen user-item pair. This time is primarily for offline testing purposes. Our approach took 1.41 milliseconds for bookcrossing and 2.91 milliseconds for the dating datasets. While the fastest baselines SVDPP and SGD required less than 1 millisecond and slowest PMF was about 4 milliseconds on all datasets. In general, these numbers are not distinguishable from a querying latency perspective, because most of the work is really focused in the *streaming* setting of updating the model in an efficient way. All the numbers reported here are using a single CPU. However, testing using our approach is trivially distributable across multiple machines or cores, as long as the M^+ and M^- data structures are available across all machines or in a shared memory.

4.5 Effectiveness Analysis

We used 5% of each dataset for validation and parameter tuning. Of the remaining 95% we use the first 20% of the dataset purely for training our model. We split the remaining data into 20 equal parts (of 3.8%) to check the effectiveness of our approach at those points. The results are shown in Fig. 1(b,c,e,f). To evaluate each of the baselines, we simulate a continuous stream of the training data until a certain point of the stream and test on the next 3.8% of the stream data. Some baselines are of course not incremental in nature. Therefore, to obtain the complete benefit of their approach, they were re-trained from scratch at each evaluation point. In this context, it needs to be pointed out that our approach was evaluated in a far more *restricted setting* compared to the baselines, where such non-streaming "fixes" were not allowed. We chose an arbitrarily small number of hash functions ($d = 20$) for evaluating our approach. As we show later, the effectiveness of our technique increases with increasing the number of hash functions.

As we progress along the stream, all methods clearly benefit from the increasing amount of training data. However, the rate of decrease in RMSE is different for each method as seen in Fig. 1(b,e). When large amounts of training data are available, the decrease is very minimal and the methods are quite stable. This is because the latent factor models do not gain much in terms of additional 3.8% training data. However, our method is quite stable as the similarity values computed do not change until a significant number of new users rate the item.

Another significant benefit of our approach is the much larger change in MAE, while having a stable downward trend in RMSE. Remember that the RMSE values are more affected by a few larger errors. These trends show that the proposed approach does not make increasing number of larger errors, along the stream, while constantly reducing large numbers of smaller errors. While other methods like PMF have stable RMSE, but increasing trend in MAE. These approaches, in a sense, make increasing number of smaller errors while keeping the RMSE under control (which is often their objective).

However, note that our approach works in a restricted streaming setting, whereas the baseline methods are allowed offline retraining from scratch where needed. In spite of this fact, the slightly better performance of a single baseline approach is not very significant.

4.6 Sensitivity Analysis

Our approach is sensitive to the number of hash functions d used in the min-hash approach. Due to lack of space, we have shown the results for only Dating dataset. However, we note that the results were similar for Book-crossing dataset.

As we discussed in Section 3, the reduction in approximation error in computing similarities exponentially falls off with increasing number of hash functions. This is very evident from Fig. 2 (a) for RMSE and (b) for MAE. Thus, a reasonable number of hash function is sufficient in practice to achieve a good performance in terms of RMSE and MAE.

The running time, for our approach, increases linearly with d and this is can be easily seen by looking at the cross-section of plots in Fig. 2(c). It is clear that using smaller number of hash functions is ideal both in terms of effectiveness and efficiency. But this does not mean that a use of $d = 1$ is ideal. In practice, we found that having around 10 to 20 hash functions is reasonable on various datasets.

5. CONCLUSIONS

With the increasing ease in ability to collect implicit and explicit ratings through various manual and automated mechanisms, the importance of streaming recommendations has increased considerably in recent years. In this paper, we propose an efficient algorithm to perform streaming recommendations by using efficient probabilistic data structures. These data structures allow compact representations of the ratings matrix, which can be efficiently leveraged to provide recommendations in online time. Our approach may be considered the first truly online method for performing recommendations in real time settings. Our experimental results validate the effectiveness and efficiency of our approach over existing methods.

6. REFERENCES

[1] C. Aggarwal. Data Streams: Models and Algorithms, *Springer*, 2007.

[2] C. Aggarwal. Recommender Systems: The Textbook, *Springer*, 2016.

[3] M. Deshpande, and G. Karypis. Item-based top-n recommendation algorithms. *ACM TOIS*, 22(1), pp. 143–177, 2004.

[4] B. Sarwar, G. Karypis, J. Konstan, and J. Riedl. Item-based collaborative filtering recommendation algorithms. *WWW*, pp. 285–295, 2001.

[5] C. Desrosiers and G. Karypis. A comprehensive survey of neighborhood-based recommendation methods. *Recommender Systems Handbook*, pp. 107–144, 2011.

[6] T. Hofmann. Latent semantic models for collaborative filtering. *ACM TOIS*, 22(1), pp. 89–114, 2004.

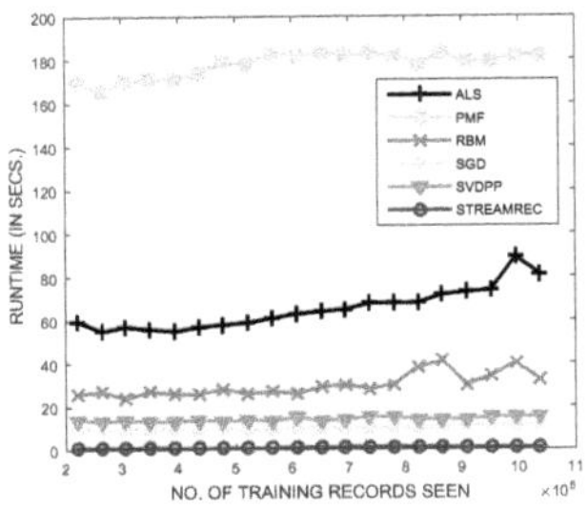

(a) Book Crossing Runtime

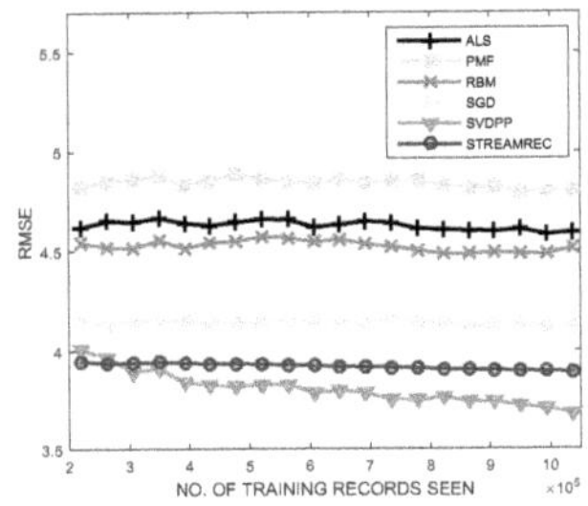

(b) Book Crossing RMSE

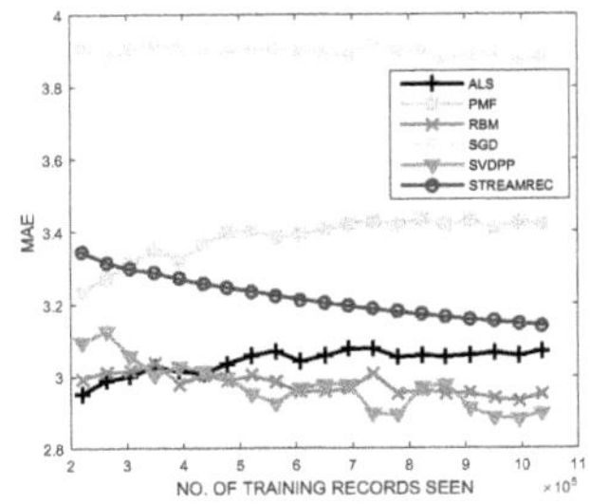

(c) Book Crossing MAE

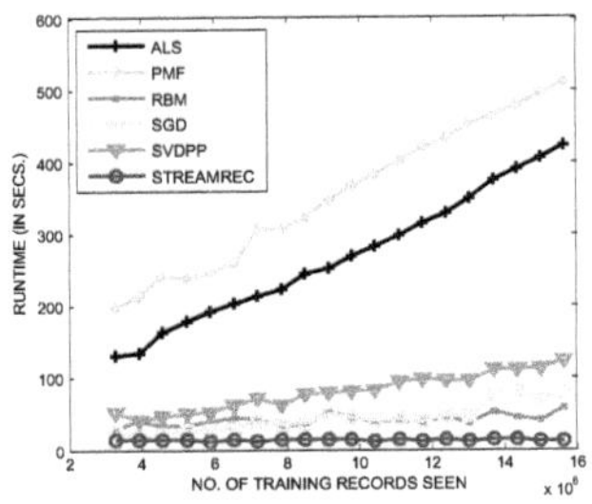

(d) Dating Runtime

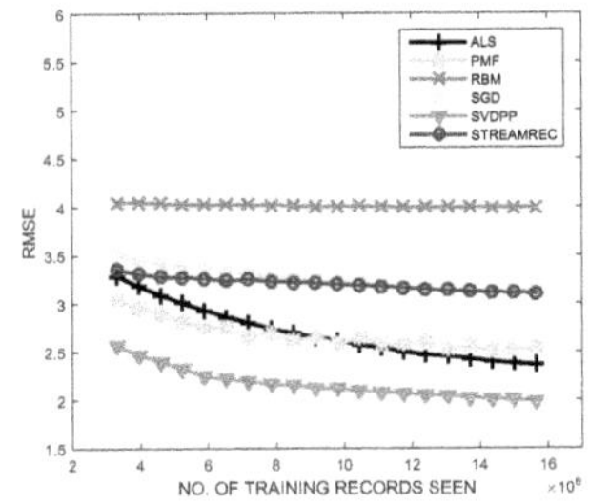

(e) Dating RMSE

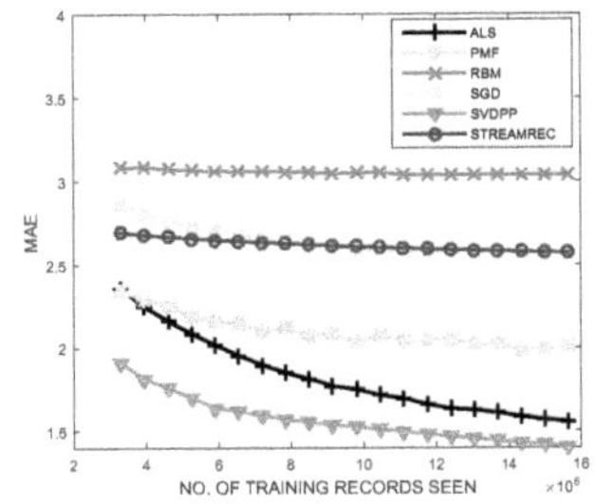

(f) Dating MAE

Figure 1: Efficiency and effectiveness plots for Book Crossing and Dating datasets.

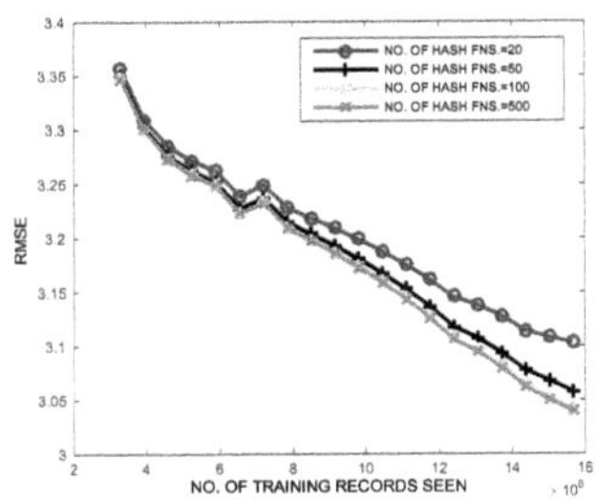

(a) Dating RMSE

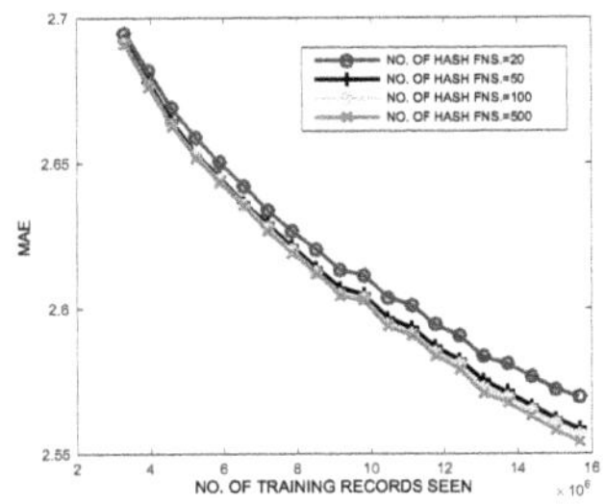

(b) Dating MAE

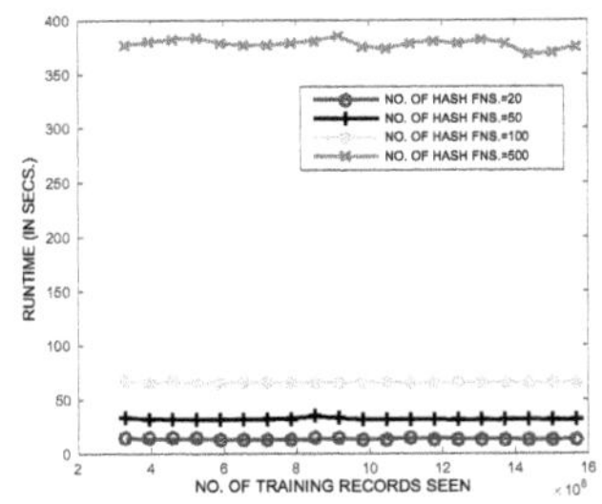

(c) Dating Runtime

Figure 2: Sensitivity plots for Dating dataset.

[7] Y. Koren. Factorization meets the neighborhood: a multifaceted collaborative filtering model. *KDD*, pp. 426–434, 2008.

[8] S. Chang, Y. Zhang, J. Tang, D. Yin , Y. Chang, M. H-Johnson, and T. S. Huang. Streaming Recommender Systems, *https://arxiv.org/pdf/1607.06182v1.pdf*, 2016.

[9] Y. Koren and R. Bell. Advances in collaborative filtering. *Recommender Systems Handbook*, Springer, pp. 145–186, 2011.

[10] Y. Koren, R. Bell, and C. Volinsky. Matrix factorization techniques for recommender systems. *Computer*, 42(8), pp. 30–37, 2009.

[11] P. Resnick, N. Iacovou, M. Suchak, P. Bergstrom, and J. Riedl. GroupLens: an open architecture for collaborative filtering of netnews. *CSCW*, pp. 175–186, 1994.

[12] Y. Zhou, D. Wilkinson, R. Schreiber and R. Pan. Large-Scale Parallel Collaborative Filtering for the Netflix Prize. *Algorithmic Aspects in Information and Management*. Shanghai, China. pp. 337-348, 2008.

[13] R. Salakhutdinov and A. Mnih. Bayesian Probabilistic Matrix Factorization using Markov Chain Monte Carlo. *ICML*, 2008.

[14] G. Hinton. A Practical Guide to Training Restricted Boltzmann Machines. University of Toronto, *Tech report UTML TR 2010-003*, 2010.

[15] A. Karatzoglou, A. J. Smola, and M. Weimer. Collaborative Filtering on a Budget, *AISTATS*, pp. 389–396, 2010.

[16] J. Z. Sun, K. R. Varshney, K. Subbian. Dynamic matrix factorization: A state space approach. *ICASSP*, pp. 1897–1900, 2012.

[17] Y. Huang, B. Cui, W. Zhang, J. Jiang, and Y Xu. Tencentrec: Real-time stream recommendation in practice, *SIGMOD*, pp. 227–238, 2015.

[18] www2.informatik.uni-freiburg.de/~cziegler/BX/

[19] www.occamslab.com/petricek/data/

[20] E. Diaz-Aviles, L. Drumond, L. Schmidt-Thieme, and W. Nejdl. Real-time top-n recommendation in social streams. *RecSys*, 2012.

[21] A. S. Das, M. Datar, A. Garg, and S. Rajaram. Google News Personalization: Scalable Online Collaborative Filtering. *WWW*, 2007.

PRO: Preference-Aware Recurring Query Optimization

Zhongfang Zhuang*, Chuan Lei†, Elke Rundensteiner*, Mohamed Eltabakh*
*{zzhuang, rundenst, meltabakh}@cs.wpi.edu, †chuan@nec-labs.com

*Computer Science Department
Worcester Polytechnic Institute
Worcester MA, 01609 USA

†NEC Labs. America
10080 N. Wolfe Road, SW3-350
Cupertino CA, 95014 USA

ABSTRACT

While recurring queries over evolving data are the bedrock of the analytical applications, resources demanded to process a large amount of data for each recurring execution can be a fatal bottleneck in cost-sensitive cloud computing environments. It is thus imperative to design a system responsive to users' preferences regarding how resources should be utilized. In this work, we propose PRO, a preference-aware recurring query processing system that optimizes recurring query executions complying with user preferences. First, we show that finding an optimal execution configuration is an NP-complete problem due to the cost interdependencies between consecutive executions. We propose an execution relation graph (ERG) model that effectively incorporates these dependencies between executions. This model enables us to transform our problem into a well-known graph problem. We then design a graph-based approach (called PRO-OPT) leveraging dynamic programming and pruning techniques with pseudo-polynomial complexity. Our experiments confirm that PRO consistently outperforms state-of-the-art solutions by 9 fold in processing time under a rich variety of circumstances on the Wikipedia datasets.

Keywords

Recurring Query; Preference-Aware; Execution Selection;

1. INTRODUCTION

Applications ranging from clickstreams analysis for online advertisement recommendations, log analysis for intrusion detection, to user sentiment inference on products are all recurring complex analytical tasks. These applications execute periodically on data subsets that arrive within the last hour(s), day(s), week(s), or even month(s) depending on the applications' scope of interest. Companies like Facebook, LinkedIn, and Twitter dominantly utilize in-house clusters with open source infrastructures to perform these tasks as recurring queries over massive evolving datasets [14, 15].

CIKM'16 , October 24-October 28, 2016, Indianapolis, IN, USA

DOI: http://dx.doi.org/10.1145/2983323.2983664

One key question for such in-house computing clusters is "*how to handle system overload?*" A system overload may incur severe delays in response time or even a failure in producing meaningful results when processing recurring queries with large amounts of evolving data. Thus, if a recurring query processing system cannot process every query execution within a reasonable latency, one feasible solution is to drop certain recurring query executions to assure success of all critical executions.

Dropping at the execution level produces exact results for a subset of executions, whereas tuple-based sampling techniques [2, 16] produce approximate results which are typically acceptable only for aggregation queries. Therefore, depending on the queries semantics and complexity, execution dropping can be the preferred solution.

However, execution dropping must consider users' preference as well as the integrity of results for analytical workloads. Thus, it is imperative to design a system that (1) allows data scientists to specify their execution selection preferences as part of the recurring query submitted to the system; (2) supports efficient recurring query processing with limited resources based on user preference functions; and (3) provides a proactive execution strategy for data fluctuations based on runtime statistics.

State-of-the-Art Techniques. Some prior work [10, 11] focused on supporting recurring queries. However, their solutions do not provide any system-level optimizations for application-driven preference requirements, nor do they skip executions to minimize the resource utilization.

Other systems [6, 12, 2, 16] minimize resource utilization by providing approximate or partial results for large scale analytical queries. More precisely, ApproxHadoop [6] explores input data sampling for workloads, while iMR [12] proposes to sample and load-shed at the data origination (i.e., where the data is generated). BlinkDB [2] aims to balance between result accuracy and response time requirements specifically for aggregation queries. G-OLA [16] supports tuple-based incremental online aggregation by partitioning data into smaller trunks of identical size on Spark.

None of these techniques target in particular recurring queries where future periodic executions of a query can be anticipated. Instead, their focus is limited to reduce the input size of *one individual execution* to manageable size of work. That is, their approximation techniques are designed to reduce the execution time at the tuple or data block granularity [6, 12, 2, 16]. In contrast, the preference-aware recurring query processing, in this work, requires a system to choose a subset of executions to complete (i.e., sampling at the execution granularity) instead of sampling individual tuples/blocks from the data source. Such a system guarantees that all delivered results are a subset of the exact answer with consideration of user-specified preferences. This property is important since it allows the recurring application to rely on the results received to be correct.

Challenges. To achieve the design goals of preference-aware recurring query processing illustrated above, the following key challenges must be tackled.

Intractable Search Space of Execution Selection. Finding a subset of executions from all executions with the maximum satisfaction of user-specified preferences requires considering all possible combinations of query executions. This is a NP-complete combinatorial problem [13]. Plus, adding application preferences introduces additional dimensions to the problem.

Stochastic Execution Costs. Consecutive executions of a recurring query may share large segments of overlapping input data. Hence, a decision about one particular execution of a query may affect the costs of its subsequent executions and thus the final configuration. This *stochastic cost* nature of recurring query executions complicates our execution selection problem with uncertainties. Effective selection strategies must be designed to reduce the execution costs.

Contributions. Our contributions include:

- We establish a preference-aware recurring query model. This model incorporates the preference specification into PRO's optimization problem to ensure the maximum satisfaction of application preferences across the selected query executions (Sections 2 and 3).
- We show that our problem of finding a subset of executions that maximally satisfy user-specified preferences is NP-complete. Our platform-independent PRO optimizer is designed to utilize a dynamic programming strategy to generate an optimal execution plan for a given period of time with a pseudo-polynomial time complexity. Platform independence enables the PRO optimizer to be employed in any batch processing system, such as Hadoop, Spark, etc (Sections 4 and 5).
- Our experimental study on real-world datasets shows PRO consistently outperforms the state-of-the-art solution in processing time by 9 fold for various scenarios (Section 7).

2. PRELIMINARY

Recurring Query Parameters. A recurring query has three parameters, namely a window w, a slide s and a preference specification *pref*. The scope of data to be processed in each *execution* E_i of a recurring query Q is specified by the time window w on the dataset, while the slide s specifies the frequency of execution. Namely, two consecutive executions E_i and E_{i+1} apply the query Q to the data within time ranges $[t-w, t]$ and $[t+s-w, t+s]$ respectively, where t is the current timestamp. Lastly, $pref$ denotes the preference specification associated with the query Q.

The preference specification $pref$ has three parameters, including (1) a period of time in the form of m consecutive executions for a recurring query, (2) the number of executions k out of those m executions required by a user, and (3) a preference function $\mathcal{U}$ given by the user indicating the relative importance of each individual execution among the m executions for the application. We further explain the preference function in Section 3.1.

The system must guarantee that the number of executions dropped never exceeds the value of $m-k$. Given the limited available resources, we will drop executions such that the delivered answer is a subset of the original answer. Choosing the appropriate values for these three preference parameters requires domain knowledge from the users. For example, one way to determine k is to leverage the knowledge from domain experts on the freshness or significance of results. In this case, if the results slowly become stale, then a relatively small k can be chosen [5].

Under heavy workload, it may not be possible to remove excess load while still meeting the bound on k. In this case, we apply "admission control" on recurring queries, where the most costly queries whose preference specification cannot be met are suspended.

Recurring Query Processing. In recurring systems [10, 11], a recurring query Q is registered, where w and s are defined as configuration parameters. Once registered, the system periodically triggers the execution of Q according to its w and s parameters. Given a recurring query Q, the recurring system [10] pre-processes the input data and subdivides the input files into smaller segments, called panes, with a refined granularity. Each pane is an individual file F_j on HDFS.

An execution E_i processes a sequence of files (F_{x+1} to F_{x+n}), where n is the number of files contained in the window w. When the window of interest w slides by s, any overlapping data files between the two consecutive executions, E_i and E_{i+1}, do not need to be processed again. Therefore, the pane-based partitioning divides a single query execution into a sequence of subtasks over non-overlapping pane inputs, each producing partial results. These partial results are then combined to generate the final desired results. This execution strategy reduces the **unnecessary I/O and CPU costs** otherwise associated with repeated work across overlapping windows [10].

Although the state-of-the-art recurring query system [10] avoids repetitive data processing caused by window and slide semantics, it still strictly processes all recurring query executions to completion in isolation without supporting the preferences specified by the users. In this work, we extended their model to also accept a preference function $pref$ as part of a recurring query.

3. PRO PROBLEM FORMULATION

In this section, we further describe the preference functions specified in the recurring query. Based on these preference functions, we design a metric called *penalty score* (*ps*) that indicates how preferable each execution is. We then utilize this metric to formulate our optimization goal.

3.1 PRO Preferences

The *penalty score* is defined based on the preference function $\mathcal{U}$ in the PRO query model.

DEFINITION 1 (PENALTY SCORE). *For a query Q and its execution E_i, one preference function $\mathcal{U}$ maps the cost of an execution E_i to a penalty score ps with ps between 0 (maximal preference) and 1 (minimal preference).*

EXAMPLE 1. *A user may be asked to minimize the resource to process a recurring query due to the limited availability of resources of an in-house cluster. In such case, the execution with the lowest cost is the most preferred. This preference function can be expressed as:*

$$\mathcal{U}(E_i) = 1 - \frac{cost_{min}}{cost(E_i)} \quad (1)$$

where $cost_{min}$ denotes the execution with the lowest estimated processing cost, and $cost(E_i)$ denotes the estimated cost of the execution E_i.

EXAMPLE 2. *A user may favor to update a recommendation model at night (from 8pm to 2am) due to higher user engagements. Thus the executions at night are considered to be the most important, whereas the executions during the day (from 2am - 8pm) are less important. Equation 2 shows such a preference function $\mathcal{U}(\cdot)$ for all E_i (i = 1,...n):*

$$\mathcal{U}(E_i) = \begin{cases} 0.5 & for \quad 8pm < T_i < 2am \\ 1 & for \quad 2am < T_i < 8pm \end{cases} \quad (2)$$

Note that although the executions during the day (from 2am - 8pm) are less important, they can still be processed when the in-house cluster has extra resources.

PRO Hybrid Preference Function. Our preference function $\mathcal{U}$ can also be a combination of multiple preference functions. For ease of elaboration, here we assume that these preference functions are independent. The users thus can specify the relative importance of each function by assigning relative weights. Each user may provide as many preference functions as desired along with the associated weight factors to express their importance. The hybrid penalty score of *one execution* E_i thus becomes:

$$\mathcal{U}(E_i) = \sum_{j=1}^{n} \alpha_j \mathcal{U}_j(E_i) \quad (3)$$

where $\sum_{j=1}^{n} \alpha_j = 1$ and $\alpha_j \geq 0, \forall j \in [1, n]$. For example, having $\alpha_1 = \alpha_2 = 0.5$ means that both preference functions $\mathcal{U}_1(\cdot)$ and $\mathcal{U}_2(\cdot)$ are equally important for E_i to the user.

3.2 Problem Definition

DEFINITION 2 (PROBLEM DEFINITION). *Given a recurring query $Q(w, s, pref)$ with window w, slide s and a preference specification $pref$ (i.e., $pref(m, k, \mathcal{U})$), the* ***preference-aware recurring query optimization problem*** *is to find an execution configuration ε with the size $|\varepsilon| = k$, selected from the total number of m executions that minimizes the penalty score of a recurring query Q. That is,*

$$Minimize\text{: } ps(Q) = \sum_{E_i \in \varepsilon} \mathcal{U}(E_i)$$

where $\mathcal{U}(E_i)$ is the total penalty score of each execution $E_i \in \varepsilon$ as per Equation 3.

Finding the optimal solution for this problem requires enumerating all possible combinations of query executions for Q, which is prohibitively expensive. Consecutive executions of a recurring query may share one or more overlapping input files. This overlap among recurring executions causes the cost of one execution to depend on its preceding executions included in the execution configuration. Any solution to our execution selection problem would need to tackle this *stochastic cost* nature of recurring queries. In the following sections, we will first describe our proposed solutions to the above problem with a fixed value of k. Then, we will discuss a relaxed problem in which the value of k can vary.

4. PRO PROBLEM ANALYSIS

4.1 Modeling Transition Costs

As described in Section 2, an execution E_i processes a sequence of files (F_{x+1} to F_{x+n}), where n is the number of files contained in a window w. To avoid repetitive data loading among consecutive executions, the intermediate results generated from previous executions are cached for subsequent reuse. Hence, the unnecessary I/O costs and the corresponding execution time resulting from overlapping windows for a query can be eliminated.

Due to the caching of intermediate results, the cost of a query execution E_i on a file F_x can differ significantly on whether some preceding executions have already processed F_x. Therefore, the cost model now should account for the caching mechanism as follows.

$$cost(F_x) = \begin{cases} cost_L + cost_P & F_x \text{ is new} \\ cost_P & F_x'\text{s cache is available} \end{cases} \quad (4)$$

where $cost_L$ and $cost_P$ denote the cost of data loading and computation of an execution E_i, respectively. The *cost of an execution E_i* is thus defined below.

DEFINITION 3 (EXECUTION COST). *Given a recurring query Q, E_i is one query execution of Q over n input files $\mathbb{F}_i = \{F_{x+1}, F_{x+2}, ..., F_{x+n}\}$. The cost of this execution $cost(E_i)$ is defined as:*

$$cost(E_i) = cost(\mathbb{F}_i) = \sum_{l=1}^{n} cost(F_{x+l}) \quad (5)$$

where $cost(F_{x+l})$ is defined in Equation 4.

Given that the consecutive executions are interdependent and the cost of processing one execution may be affected by its preceding executions, we define the notion of a *transition cost* to model this unique characteristic of the recurring query execution.

DEFINITION 4 (TRANSITION COST). *Given two executions E_i and E_j $(1 \leq i < j)$ of a recurring query Q, and the file sets $\mathbb{F}_i$ and $\mathbb{F}_j$ processed by E_i and E_j respectively, the costs of processing these two executions independently are $cost(E_i)$ and $cost(E_j)$, respectively. Then the* ***transition cost*** *(denoted as $cost(E_{i,j})$) from E_i to E_j is defined as follows:*

$$cost(E_{i,j}) = cost(\mathbb{F}_j \backslash \mathbb{F}_i) \quad (6)$$

where $\mathbb{F}_j \backslash \mathbb{F}_i$ denotes the files associated only with E_j but not with E_i.

Note that this *transition cost* can be utilized to calculate the penalty score *ps* if a cost-based preference function is provided as part of the *pref* parameter. For example, assuming execution E_i had previously been chosen to be processed, then the penalty score *ps* of E_j is $\left(1 - \frac{cost_{min}}{cost(E_{i,j})}\right)$.

4.2 Modeling the PRO Optimization Problem

With this notion of *transition cost*, the uncertainty in the execution cost can be eradicated by modeling our problem of selecting execution configurations with a weighted directed acyclic graph $\mathcal{G} = (\mathcal{V}, \mathcal{E})$. Each vertex in graph $\mathcal{G}$ represents an execution (e.g., $v_i \in \mathcal{V}$ represents execution E_i), and the weight of each directed edge $e_{i,j} \in \mathcal{E}$ from vertex v_i to vertex v_j ($\forall v_i, v_j \in \mathcal{V}$ and $i < j$) represents the penalty score *ps* (Definition 1) of choosing $E_j \in \mathcal{E}$ right after E_i.

Definition 5. *Given a time period consisting of m executions $\{E_1, E_2, ..., E_m\}$, a directed acyclic graph ERG $\mathcal{G} = (\mathcal{V}, \mathcal{E})$, called **Execution Relation Graph** is defined as*

1. *$v_0 \in \mathcal{V}$ denotes the root node (v_0 leads to the first selected execution),*
2. *$\forall i \in [1, m]$, $v_i \in \mathcal{V}, i \in [1, m]$ represents execution E_i,*
3. *a directed edge $e_{i,j} = (v_i, v_j) \in \mathcal{E}$ exists only if $v_i, v_j \in \mathcal{V}$ and $i < j$. This directed edge denotes the decision of choosing E_j directly after choosing E_i. The weight of $e_{i,j}$ denotes its penalty score (Definition 1), which is always positive.*

Definition 6. *Given a ERG graph $\mathcal{G}$ by Definition 5, a **directed length-k path** $\mathcal{P}_i$ in $\mathcal{G}$ is defined as follows:*

1. *$\mathcal{P}_i$ starts at the root node v_0,*
2. *$\mathcal{P}_i$ is composed of k edges (denoted as $|\mathcal{P}_i| = k$).*

5. PRO OPTIMIZER

To solve the core preference-aware recurring query optimization problem defined in Section 4.2, we have transformed it into a minimum weight length-k path graph problem. We now propose the PRO optimizer consisting of a family of algorithms for finding a length-k path with minimum weight, taking **both** the *length of a path* and the *weight of a path* into consideration. First, we present an exhaustive search-based solution with pruning. Thereafter, we propose a lightweight dynamic programming approach (PRO-OPT) to produce an optimal solution. The PRO-OPT is extensible to execution configurations with varying numbers of executions. Lastly, we design an adaptive methodology to tackle fluctuations in the data rates.

5.1 Enhanced Exhaustive Search

To find minimum weight length-k paths as per Definition 6 in an ERG graph $\mathcal{G}$, the PRO optimizer needs to enumerate all possible length-k paths and to select the one with the minimum weight. Unfortunately, the search space can be shown to be exponentially huge [7]. There is not one unique solution, i.e., there can be more than one length-k path with the identical minimum weight.

A basic search algorithm would approach this problem by traversing the graph $\mathcal{G}$ in a breadth-first search manner from root v_0. In the i-th iteration, it forms all possible length-i paths. After k iterations, it produces all length-k solutions. It then selects the one with minimal weight. If more than one length-k path with equal minimal weight exist, then this approach randomly selects one of them to be the final execution configuration. The exhaustive search solution is exponentially expensive as there are $\binom{m}{k}$ length-k paths in an ERG $\mathcal{G}$.

While the search space is intractable, one key observation is that certain subset of vertices in $\mathcal{G}$ do not need to be considered any further as part of the final solution at each iteration without losing optimality (see Lemma 1).

Lemma 1 (Vertex Pruning). *Given an ERG $\mathcal{G} = (\mathcal{V}, \mathcal{E})$ and a desired path length k, then the out degree of $v_a \in \mathcal{V}$ is denoted as $deg^+(v_a)$. In order to be considered fo r a length-k path at the **i-th iteration**, the vertex v_a must satisfy:*

$$deg^+(v_a) \geq k - i. \quad (7)$$

5.2 Dynamic Programming-Based Approach

We now propose a dynamic programming-based PRO-OPT approach that reduces search complexity. The key idea of PRO-OPT is to exploit tabulation by building a series of reusable *sub-paths* to form a length-k solution. An important result is that PRO-OPT guarantees to produce an **optimal** solution with a *pseudo-polynomial* time complexity.

Definition 7 (Minimum Weight Sub-paths). *Let $\mathcal{P}_i^{(h)}$ denote the set of all length-h paths starting at vertex v_i and ending at any other vertex in a ERG $\mathcal{G}$. Then we define $p_{i,min}^{(h)}$ as the minimum weight length-h path in $\mathcal{P}_i^{(h)}$.*

Next we show that we can form a minimum weight length-h path by adding one new edge to the current minimum weight sub-path of length $h-1$.

Definition 8 (Extension of Paths). *Given an ERG $\mathcal{G} = (\mathcal{V}, \mathcal{E})$ by Definition 5 and an integer k as the desired path length. All sub-paths with length h less than k can be extended according to the following equation:*

$$w(p_{i,min}^{(h)}) = \begin{cases} min\{w(e_{i,j})\}, & h = 1 \\ min\{w(e_{i,j}) + w(p_{j,min}^{(h-1)})\}, & h \in [2:k] \end{cases} \quad (8)$$

where $i \in [0, m]$, $j \in [i+1, m-h+1]$. $w(e_{i,j})$ and $w(p_{j,min}^{(h-1)})$ represent the weight of edge $e_{i,j}$ and the minimum weight of length-$(h-1)$ sub-path starting from v_j, respectively.

For a given vertex v_i, only edges starting at v_i and of length less than or equal to $m-h$ (i.e., $e_{i,i+1}, e_{i,i+2}, ..., e_{i,m-h}$) are considered to form the minimum weight length-h sub-path $p_{i,min}^{(h)}$. Multiple sub-paths starting from one vertex can have the same minimum weight. Hence, all minimum weight sub-paths $p_{i,min}^{(h)}$ from one vertex and their respective associated minimum weight are stored in the Dynamic Search Table (DST) to assure re-computations are avoided.

PRO-OPT Pruning Strategy. Similar to Lemma 1, not all minimum weight sub-paths need to be considered. Instead, some sub-paths can never form a length-k path. Therefore, we now reduce the Dynamic Search Table (DST) by pruning these useless sub-paths.

Our formal PRO-OPT algorithm given in Algorithm 1 exploits both the sub-path extension method (Definition 8) and dynamic pruning strategy to produce a minimum weight length-k path.

The proposed dynamic pruning strategy does not affect the correctness of PRO-OPT as it prunes sub-paths if and only if they cannot be used to produce any length-k paths. We now state the correctness of PRO-OPT in Lemma 2.

Lemma 2 (Optimality of PRO-OPT). *Given an ERG $\mathcal{G} = (\mathcal{V}, \mathcal{E})$, the length-k path produced by PRO-OPT has the minimal weight among all possible length-k paths.*

5.3 Discussion

Problem Relaxation. As mentioned in Section 3.2, the expected number of executions k can vary due to different reasons. For example, domain experts may want to increase k due to the change of their applications. The number of executions k can also decrease when resources become less available. Thus, PRO optimizer should have the ability to generate a *new* execution configuration ε' with a different

Algorithm 1 PRO-OPT Algorithm

```
INPUT: Directed graph G = (V, E) and integer k
OUTPUT: A minimum weight simple k-path within G
for h = 1, h ≤ k, h ← h + 1 do
    for i = k − h + 1, i < |V| − k, i ← i + 1 do
        for l = i + 1, l < |V| − 2, l ← l + 1 do
            if h = 1 then
                w(p^h_{i,min}) = min{w(e_{i,i+l})}
                store w(p^h_{i,min}) and p^h_{i,min}
            else if 2 ≤ h < k then
                w(p^h_{i,min}) = min{w(e_{i,i+l}) + w(p^{(h−1)}_{i+l,min})}
                store w(p^h_{i,min}) and p^h_{i,min}
            else if h = k then
                w(p^h_{0,min}) = min{w(e_{0,l}) + w(p^{(h−1)}_{l,min})}
                store w(p^h_{0,min}) and p^h_{0,min}
                break
            end if
        end for
    end for
end for
```

number of executions based on the *old* one as needed. Fortunately, our PRO-OPT is designed to build longer sub-paths incrementally based on existing sub-paths stored in DST. Therefore, a smaller size execution configuration ε' is existed in DST. In addition, the minimum weight length-$k+i$ path can be extended from existing length-$k+i-1$ paths with a linear time complexity. Thereafter, if more than k executions are feasible for the new time period based on the cost estimation (Equation 1) and the available resources, our PRO optimizer will produce an optimal execution configuration (i.e., the minimum weight length-$k+i$ path) for the new time period.

Overlapping m Executions. Another issue concerns that consecutive time periods of m executions may overlap with each other. For example, if we have two consecutive overlapping time periods B_i and B_j $(i < j)$ of m executions each, for any execution $E_i \notin \mathbb{E}_i \bigcap \mathbb{E}_j$, the execution cost of E_i does not need to be changed. However, the costs of all executions that belong to both periods (i.e., $\mathbb{E}_i \bigcap \mathbb{E}_j$) need to be adjusted to account for the fact that repetitive computations are eliminated in the PRO system. Consequently, the edge weights that represent penalty scores in an ERG graph are updated as well. Thereafter, we can simply apply the above discussed adaptive technique to determine whether a re-optimization is needed for the new time period.

6. EXPERIMENTAL EVALUATION

6.1 Experimental Setup & Methodology

Experimental Infrastructure. We conduct all experiments on a shared-nothing cluster with one master node and 39 slave nodes.* Each node has a configuration of 16 core AMD 3.0GHz processors, 32GB RAM, 250GB disk, and these 40 nodes are interconnected with 1Gbps ethernet. Each node runs CentOS of version 6.5, Java 1.7 and Hadoop 1.2.1. Each node is configured to concurrently run up to 8 map and 8 reduce tasks. The sort buffer size is set to 512MB. We keep the default replication factor to 3.

*This cluster is supported by NSF Grant CNS-1305258.

Datasets and Queries. We use two real world datasets for our experiments. The Wikipedia page editing log (400GB), and the current version of all article pages from Wikipedia (54GB) [1] being modified and updated continuously. We focus on operations that are critical for emerging data analytical tasks, such as aggregation queries and top-k queries.

Algorithms and Systems. We implemented our PRO optimizer with the proposed algorithms, PRO-EES and PRO-OPT on top of a distributed platform, in this case Apache Hadoop [3]. In addition, we implemented a depth first search algorithm PRO-DFS for the purpose of comparison. Native Redoop [10] is used in runtime performance experiments. Since there is no support for preference-aware optimization in native Redoop, we also configure a variation of Redoop as k-Redoop, to only process first k executions in each time period to make a fair competitor in robustness experiments.

Metrics & Methodology. We evaluate *PRO runtime* performance by varying the input data volume and the number of machines in the cluster and we measure the execution time- a common metric for data management systems [11]. We evaluate the *result quality* using ranking quality measurement methods, namely Kendall's tau [9], Normalized Discounted Cumulative Gain (NDCG) [8] and Expected Reciprocal Rank [4]. Each method produces a precision result pr and we define our error rate er to be $er = 1-pr$. Thereafter, we compare error rates of PRO-OPT with native Redoop (i.e., all executions are being executed). We utilize the preference function $\mathcal{U}_1$ in Table 1 for the above experiments. We verify the robustness of PRO optimizer with various preference functions in optimizer robustness experiments.

#	Preference Functions
$\mathcal{U}_1(E_i)$	$1 - \frac{cost_{min}}{cost(E_i)}$
$\mathcal{U}_2(E_i)$	$\begin{cases} 0.5 & E_i.priority = high \\ 1 & E_i.priority = low \end{cases}$
$\mathcal{U}_3(E_i)$	$\sum_{j=1}^{n} \alpha_j \mathcal{U}_j(E_i)$

Table 1: Preference Functions Used in the Experiments

6.2 PRO Runtime Performance

Varying the cluster size. Figure 1(a) demonstrates the scalability of PRO by varying the number of nodes in the computing cluster. Compared to native Redoop, PRO-OPT shows an average of 323% savings in processing time from cluster size of 10 to 40 and up to 840% savings in processing time when the number of nodes in the cluster is 10 and execution selection ratio is 0.1.

Varying the data size. Figure 1(b) illustrates the execution times of PRO-OPT solution with different data sizes ranging from 40GB to 400GB per a time period of m executions. PRO-OPT resource utilization significantly drops compared to processing all executions. For example, PRO-OPT saves up to 9 fold in execution time when the data size is 400GB compared to native Redoop processing all executions. The execution time of PRO grows much slower than native Redoop system for increased data sizes. For instance, we observe the increasing rate of execution time from native Redoop is 35% higher than PRO. The reason is that since we use resource-driven preference function, PRO-OPT always selects executions that will use the least resources.

6.3 Result Quality

We use PRO-OPT with execution selection ratios ranging from [0.1, 0.9] to compute two lists of frequent items, i.e.,

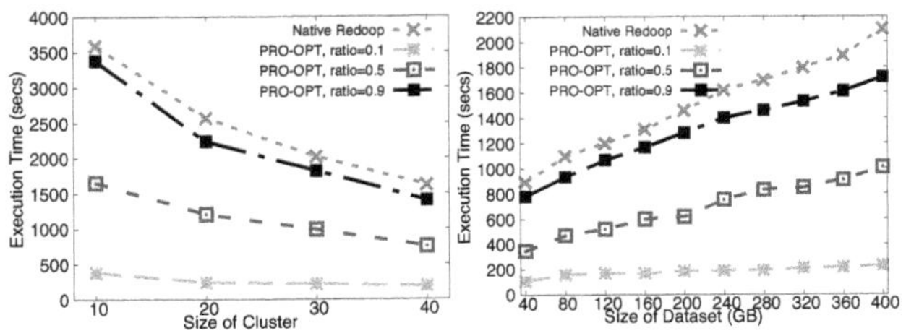

(a) Vary Cluster Size (b) Vary Quality Method

Figure 1: PRO Runtime Performance

top-n frequent words (List #1) and the most frequent editors in Wikipedia articles (List #2). We then compare error rates between the results from PRO-OPT and Redoop. In Figure

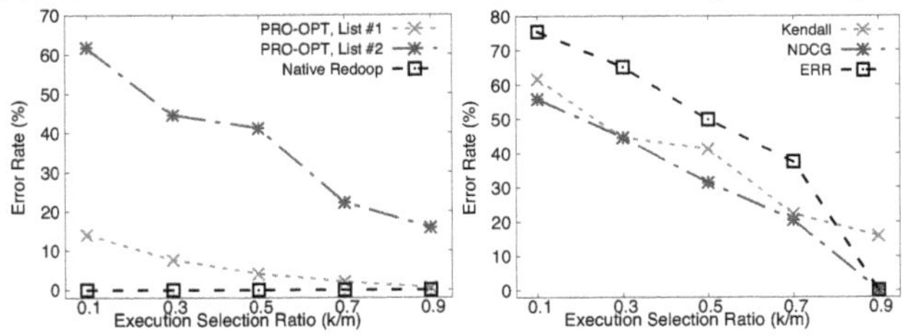

(a) Vary Item List (b) Vary Quality Method

Figure 2: PRO Error Rate

2(a), we notice the error rate is much higher for List #2 than List #1. For List #1, the error rate ranges from 14% to 0.5% when execution selection ratio is between 0.1 and 0.9, respectively. For List #2, the error rate is 61.8% when there is 10% of all executions within one time period are processed and 15.8% when 90% of all executions within one time period are processed. The reason is the ranking of frequent words is more stable than the list of most frequent editors. In the best case, we have an error rate of 0.06% when the execution selection ratio is 0.9 with NDCG in Figure 2(b). In the worst case, when execution selection ratio is 0.1 with ERR method, we have an error rate of 75%. We observe that the error rate of all three ranking measurement methods show the same significantly decreasing trend as the execution selection ratio increasing from 0.1 to 0.9 as a result of processing more input data. The trade-off is that PRO uses far less resources compared to native Redoop, yet still is able to produce high quality results.

6.4 Robustness of PRO Optimizer

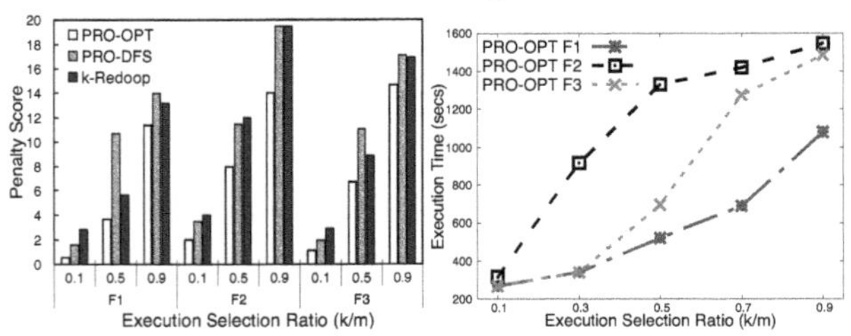

(a) Penalty Score (b) Execution Time

Figure 3: Varying Preference Functions

Next, we examine the effect of varying preference functions from Table 1 on the penalty scores and execution times. For that, we vary the execution selection ratio from [0.1, 0.9] on the x-axis. The number of executions in each time period is set to 30 and input data size is 240GB for one time period. We randomly select 15 out of 30 executions as "low priority" (penalty score is 1). The rest are set to "high priority" (penalty score is 0.5) in preference function $\mathcal{U}_2$. We combine functions $\mathcal{U}_1$ and $\mathcal{U}_2$ using function $\mathcal{U}_3$ with relative importance of each function ($\mathcal{U}_1$ and $\mathcal{U}_2$) equally to 0.5. Figure 3(a) shows that PRO-OPT always produces execution configurations with minimum penalty scores compared to PRO-DFS and k-Redoop for all three preference functions. Figure 3(b) shows that the processing times of execution configurations generated by PRO-OPT with different preference functions can differ drastically. For example, when execution selection ratio is 0.5, the execution configuration produced by PRO-OPT with the function $\mathcal{U}_2$ takes 61% longer time to process than PRO-OPT with the function $\mathcal{U}_1$ and 47% longer compared to PRO-OPT with function $\mathcal{U}_3$. The reason is the execution configurations actually have different sets of executions according to different preferences.

7. CONCLUSION

This paper presents the first preference-aware recurring query processing solution. Our PRO system offers 3 key innovations. (1) The preference-aware recurring query model established for PRO integrates recurring query processing with various preferences specified by application developers. (2) The proposed execution relation graph models the interdependencies and stochastic execution costs among executions. (3) Our novel PRO-OPT algorithm effectively produces an optimal execution configuration with a pseudo-polynomial time complexity. Its efficiency enables PRO to adaptively re-optimize when faced with data fluctuations. Lastly, our experimental results demonstrate that our PRO solution consistently outperforms state-of-the-art technologies by 9 fold in a large range of scenarios.

8. REFERENCES

[1] Wikimedia downloads. https://dumps.wikimedia.org.

[2] S. Agarwal, B. Mozafari, et al. Blinkdb: queries with bounded errors and bounded response times on very large data. In *EuroSys*, pages 29–42, 2013.

[3] Apache. Hadoop. http://hadoop.apache.org.

[4] O. Chapelle, D. Metlzer, Y. Zhang, and P. Grinspan. Expected reciprocal rank for graded relevance. In *CIKM*, pages 621–630, 2009.

[5] J. Gama, R. Sebastião, et al. Issues in evaluation of stream learning algorithms. In *SIGKDD*, pages 329–338, 2009.

[6] Í. Goiri, R. Bianchini, S. Nagarakatte, et al. Approxhadoop: Bringing approximations to mapreduce frameworks. In *ASPLOS*, pages 383–397, 2015.

[7] A. Hassidim, O. Keller, et al. Finding the minimum-weight k-path. In *Algorithms and Data Structures*, pages 390–401. Springer, 2013.

[8] K. Järvelin and J. Kekäläinen. Cumulated gain-based evaluation of ir techniques. *ACM TODS*, 20(4):422–446, 2002.

[9] M. G. Kendall. A new measure of rank correlation. *Biometrika*, pages 81–93, 1938.

[10] C. Lei, E. A. Rundensteiner, and M. Y. Eltabakh. Redoop: Supporting recurring queries in hadoop. In *EDBT*, pages 25–36, 2014.

[11] C. Lei, Z. Zhuang, E. A. Rundensteiner, and M. Eltabakh. Shared execution of recurring workloads in mapreduce. *PVLDB*, 8(7):714–725, 2015.

[12] D. Logothetis, C. Trezzo, K. C. Webb, et al. In-situ mapreduce for log processing. In *USENIXATC*, pages 9–9, 2011.

[13] H. Ryser. Combinatorial mathematics. *The Carus Mathematical Monographs, No. 14*, 1963.

[14] J. Sarma. Hadoop at facebook. https://www.facebook.com/notes/facebook-engineering/hadoop/16121578919.

[15] R. Sumbaly, J. Kreps, and S. Shah. The big data ecosystem at linkedin. In *SIGMOD*, pages 1125–1134, 2013.

[16] K. Zeng, S. Agarwal, A. Dave, M. Armbrust, and I. Stoica. G-ola: Generalized on-line aggregation for interactive analysis on big data. In *SIGMOD*, pages 913–918, 2015.

Discovering Temporal Purchase Patterns with Different Responses to Promotions

Ling Luo
School of IT,
University of Sydney,
Sydney, NSW2006, Australia
ling.luo@sydney.edu.au

Bin Li
Data61, CSIRO, Eveleigh,
NSW2015, Australia
bin.li@data61.csiro.au

Irena Koprinska
School of IT,
University of Sydney,
Sydney, NSW2006, Australia
irena.koprinska@sydney.edu.au

Shlomo Berkovsky
Data61, CSIRO, Eveleigh,
NSW2015, Australia

Fang Chen
Data61, CSIRO, Eveleigh,
NSW2015, Australia

{shlomo.berkovsky,fang.chen}@data61.csiro.au

ABSTRACT

The supermarkets often use sales promotions to attract customers and create brand loyalty. They would often like to know if their promotions are effective for various customers, so that better timing and more suitable rate can be planned in the future. Given a transaction data set collected by an Australian national supermarket chain, in this paper we conduct a case study aimed at discovering customers' long-term purchase patterns, which may be induced by preference changes, as well as short-term purchase patterns, which may be induced by promotions. Since purchase events of individual customers may be too sparse to model, we propose to discover a number of latent purchase patterns from the data. The latent purchase patterns are modeled via a mixture of non-homogeneous Poisson processes where each Poisson intensity function is composed by long-term and short-term components. Through the case study, 1) we validate that our model can accurately estimate the occurrences of purchase events; 2) we discover easy-to-interpret long-term gradual changes and short-term periodic changes in different customer groups; 3) we identify the customers who are receptive to promotions through the correlation between behavior patterns and the promotions, which is particularly worthwhile for target marketing.

Keywords

customer segmentation; customer behaviors; temporal modeling; non-homogeneous Poisson process

1. INTRODUCTION

Behavior analytics has been recognized as an indispensable part of business intelligence [15]. Understanding customer behaviors is of a great interest to marketing researchers and business analysts, as this information can help them communicate better with the customers and develop appropriate strategies. Thus, the purchase behavior modeling facilitates effective marketing resource management. For example, the purchase behavior model enables the stakeholders to know their customer needs, identify the customer segments that are most likely to buy their products, and reach target customers in a cost- and time-efficient way [14].

We are interested in the purchase timing – when customers buy the products, as it supports the companies in finding the right time to promote products or communicate with customers [9]. Various factors could impact the purchase timing, ranging from personal necessity, preference and seasonal effects, to marketing variables such as promotions. The stakeholders often also desire to know who are receptive to their promotions. Therefore, besides the aggregated behaviors of all customers, it is also important to understand the differences among individual customers. However, for a certain product, the individual purchase events may be too sparse to analyze the behavior patterns and check whether they have been stimulated by promotions. We resort to discovering latent types of the behavior patterns through a soft-membership customer segmentation.

We propose a mixture of Non-Homogeneous Poisson Processes (NHPP) to discover the latent customer groups and conduct the soft-membership customer segmentation based on the dynamically observed purchase behavior. The purchase behavior pattern of each group is modeled by the intensity function of NHPP, which integrates: 1) a polynomial component for the long-term patterns due to preference drifts or seasonal effects and 2) a periodic component for the short-term patterns driven by customer needs and promotions. We adopt the Expectation Maximization (EM) algorithm to find the latent groups as well as estimate the coefficients of the intensity functions.

From the case study on the supermarket transaction data: 1) we validate that the NHPP model can estimate the purchase events accurately, significantly outperforming the baseline method; 2) we discover the representative long-term and short-term purchase behavior patterns of customer groups, which captures dynamics in the purchase behavior and helps to understand different customers and products; 3) we explore the effectiveness of promotions on different customers and find the customers who are receptive to price reductions.

CIKM'16, October 24-28, 2016, Indianapolis, IN, USA

DOI: http://dx.doi.org/10.1145/2983323.2983665

Our proposed approach to discovering temporal patterns of purchase behaviors with different responses to promotions can act as a backbone of a more effective target marketing.

2. RELATED WORK

Extensive research on customer behavior has been carried out to provide decision support for business management. Following the classical negative binomial model proposed in [6], the extensions [4, 13] concentrated on modeling the number of products sold over the whole observation period of all customers. They focused on estimating the overall number of purchase events, and did not support customer segmentation based on the heterogeneity of customers. To segment customers, previous work used demographic information such as gender, age, occupation to examine the differences among groups, such as the number of purchases, response to price reduction [5]. However, it was found that it is not helpful to segment customers based on demographic and psychographic variables for the frequently purchased products, and that using the behavioral variable is a sensible approach to building customer segments [10]. The behavioral segmentation groups customers according to their usage rate, loyalty status and response to a product. For instance, Bucklin et al. [3] proposed a mixture of logit models to segment customers based on their purchase timing, quantity and brand choice, but their work did not consider the dynamics of purchase behaviors.

Recent models took behavior changes into account while conducting customer segmentation, as it allows stakeholders to monitor dynamic business environment and evaluate their marketing campaigns [1, 2, 11, 12]. Iwata et al. [7] adapted the topic model to track the changes of customer interests and item trends. However, their model could not provide specific behavior patterns regarding the marketing variables for each latent group, making the results difficult to interpret. The hierarchical time-rescaling model proposed in [8] could identify different purchase patterns such as periodic, bursty and sale-effect patterns via point processes, but it was only modeled at the individual level.

In summary, to the best of our knowledge, there are no reported methods that could discover long-term and short-term purchase behavior patterns from a collection of sparse transaction records and analyze the responses of customers to the dynamic marketing variables like sales promotions.

3. METHODOLOGY

As shown in Figure 1, there are three modules in our method: 1) we build the mixture of NHPP model for the customer purchase behavior based on the transaction records; 2) we adopt the EM algorithm to infer the group membership of individual customer for each product and estimate the coefficients of the NHPP intensity functions; 3) we conduct a comprehensive segment analysis to reveal long-term and short-term temporal patterns of the non-stationary behavior and provide insights of how customers from different segments respond to promotions.

3.1 Poisson Process for Purchase Behavior

The Poisson process is a simple yet powerful stochastic process that describes the number of random points in a temporal or spatial space, such as the occurrences of incidents at an intersection and arrivals of customers to a service center. The Poisson process can be equivalently represented by the counting process $\{N(t), t \geq 0\}$, where $N(t)$ is a random variable for the number of arrivals in the interval $[0, t)$. The counting variable $N(t)$ has a Poisson distribution with parameter Λ, so that we have $P(N(t) = n) = e^{-\Lambda}\frac{\Lambda^n}{n!}$ and $E(N(t)) = \Lambda$. If the intensity λ of the Poisson process is a constant, it is called a *homogeneous* Poisson process (HomoPP), and $\Lambda = \lambda t$. However, if λ changes over time, the Poisson process is a *non-homogeneous* Poisson process (NHPP). The varying intensity can be described by a function $\lambda(x)$, and $\Lambda = \int_0^t \lambda(x)dx$.

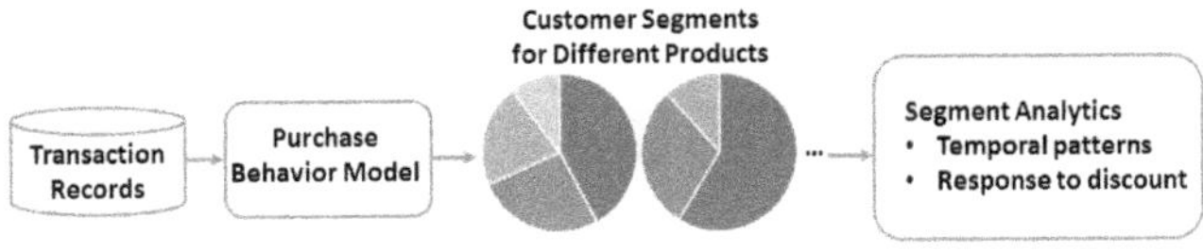

Figure 1: Flowchart of the model

As for the customer purchase behavior analysis, the purchase events for a product could be described by an NHPP. The number of purchase events up to t is a counting process $\{N(t)\}$, which could be affected by various contextual factors. We use $\lambda(x)$ to capture the temporal dynamics over long-term and short-term observations:

1) The long-term patterns can be influenced by the factors such as customer preference changes and seasonal effects. We select the polynomial function to model the gradual long-term changes, considering the trade-off between tractability and flexibility of the model. As the main challenge in the estimation procedure is the integral $\int_0^t \lambda(x)dx$ [8], using the polynomial function could generate the closed-form solution efficiently, and it is capable of capturing typical long-term dynamics of the behavior.

2) The short-term patterns are used to describe periodic purchase behaviors, which are mainly driven by the customer needs or attractiveness of promotions. In the context of supermarket, the personal needs and the promotions of a product are generally periodic, so we use a sine function as the short-term component of the purchase behavior.

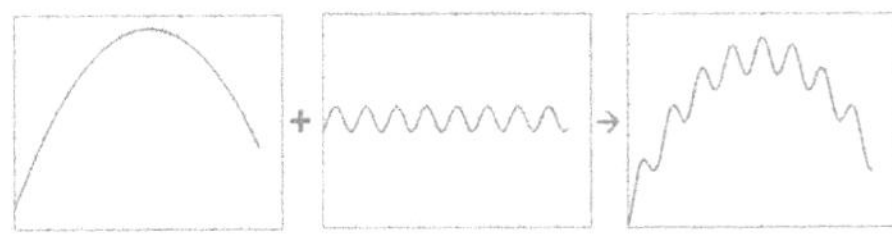

Figure 2: Integrate the polynomial component (left) and the periodic component (middle) to get the intensity curve (right).

Therefore, the intensity function would be an integration of a polynomial component and a periodic component as illustrated in Figure 2. Formally, the definition of $\lambda(x)$ is,

$$\lambda(x) = \sum_{d=0}^{D} w_d x^d + a\sin(bx + c) \quad (1)$$

with the restriction that $\lambda(x) \geq 0$ for any x. $\lambda(x)$ acts like a density function for purchase events, so higher $\lambda(x)$ values correspond to more frequent purchase events, and vice versa. The polynomial component fits the trend of the purchase intensity fluctuations, including typical patterns such as increase, decrease, U-shape or inverse U-shape, depending on w_d. The parameter D is the degree of the polynomial component, which is tuned to the data set (usually $D = 2$ suffices). For the sine component, a, b, c are the amplitude, frequency and phase of the short-term patterns. If $w_d = 0$ for $d > 0$ (i.e., the polynomial component is a constant w_0), the purchase intensity only has periodic patterns; if $a = 0$, the purchase intensity only has long-term trends; if both are true, the purchase behavior is a HomoPP with $\lambda = w_0$.

As we are interested in the daily purchase behavior, the granularity of our analysis is set to 1 day. If $N(t)$ denotes the number of purchase events up to day t, then $\{\Delta N(t) = N(t) - N(t-1), t \geq 1\}$ ($\Delta N(t) \geq 0$) are the daily purchase events. The expectation of $\Delta N(t+\delta)$ for a small time interval δ is $\int_t^{t+\delta} \lambda(x)dx$. For a small δ, the value of $\lambda(t+\delta)$ represents the instantaneous purchase rate at $t+\delta$. Assuming the intensity is constant during $(t, t+\delta]$, the unbiased estimation of $\lambda(t+\delta)$ is $E(\Delta N(t+\delta))/\delta$. As the granularity level of our model is 1 day, the underlying NHPP intensity $\lambda(x)$ can be viewed as a piece-wise step function with constant intensity within each day. Thus, we can estimate coefficients θ (w_d, a, b, c in Equation 1) of $\lambda(x)$ by maximizing the log likelihood over the number of purchase events for each day $\Delta N(t), t \in \{1, ..., T\}$.

3.2 Segment Customers with Mixture Model

The purchase events of an individual may be too sparse for an analysis of behavior patterns and response to promotions. Moreover, the supermarkets often desire to get higher-level information such as different types of behavior patterns of all customers and the proportion of customers with a certain type of behavior. A mixture model of NHPP is applied to segment customers based on the purchase behavior patterns characterized by the above intensity functions.

Formally, our problem is: given a transaction data set with U customers and M products, for a target product m, 1) extract all customers $\{u_i\}_m$ ($i \in \{1, 2, ..., U\}$), who bought m, 2) identify K latent groups of $\{u_i\}_m$, based on the individual customer u_i's $N_{im}(T)$ purchase decisions during the observation period $[0, T]$, where $N_{im}(T)$ is the total number of purchase of m by u_i. As the following description is all in the context of the purchase behavior of a certain product m, we omit the subscript m.

The purchase behavior of customers in the latent group k share the same $\lambda_k(x)$, and the behavior of a customer could be a combination of $\lambda_k(x)$ of multiple groups, so u_i has soft membership π_{ik} in group k, and $\sum_{k=1}^{K} \pi_{ik} = 1$. Our task is to discover the K latent groups, and estimate the following parameters:

1) Θ: coefficients of $\lambda_k(x)$ for K groups. The coefficient θ_k for group k includes $\{w_{dk}\ (d \in \{1, 2, ..., D\}), a_k, b_k, c_k\}$.

2) $\Phi \in [0, 1]^{K\times 1}$: relative sizes of K groups, where ϕ_k is the relative size of mixture component k, $\sum_{k=1}^{K} \phi_k = 1$.

3) $\Pi \in [0, 1]^{U\times K}$: soft memberships over K groups for all customers, where $\sum_{k=1}^{K} \pi_{ik} = 1$.

Given the observations of u_i's $N_i(T)$ purchase events $\mathbf{x}_i \in (0, T]^{1\times N_i(T)}$, the element x_{ij} is the time of u_i's j^{th} purchase. The log likelihood of the observations is,

$$\ell(\Theta, \Phi) = \sum_{i=1}^{U} \log \sum_{z_i=1}^{K} p(\mathbf{x}_i | z_i; \Theta) p(z_i; \Phi) \qquad (2)$$

where $z_i \in \{1, ..., K\}$ is the latent group variable for u_i, $p(z_i = k) = \pi_{ik}$, and $\mathbf{x}_i$ has been generated by NHPP with the intensity function $\lambda_k(x)$.

To estimate the customer membership and coefficients for each group, we use the EM algorithm to construct a mixture of NHPPs for the observations and infer the parameters iteratively. The input of the algorithm includes the number of groups K, the parametric form of $\lambda_k(x)$, and the purchase records $\{\mathbf{x}_i\}, i \in \{1, 2, .., U\}$. Then the algorithm starts from the E-step and iterates between the E-step and M-step until convergence.

In the **E-step**, if it is the first iteration, we assign u_i to a group randomly or based on a predefined initialization rule. From the second iteration, we use the estimation of Θ and Φ from the M-step of the previous iteration to infer new Π. The posterior probability of u_i in the latent group k is,

$$p(z_i = k | \mathbf{x}_i, \Theta, \Phi) = \frac{p(\mathbf{x}_i | z_i = k, \Theta) p(z_i = k, \Phi)}{\sum_{s=1}^{K} p(\mathbf{x}_i | z_i = s, \Theta) p(z_i = s, \Phi)} \qquad (3)$$

In detail, given n ordered ($0 < x_{i1} < ... < x_{in} \leq T$) and independent observations at $\{x_{ij}\}$ ($j \in \{1, ..., n\}$), the likelihood of these observations is,

$$p(\mathbf{x}_i | z_i = k, \Theta) = \Big(\prod_{j=1}^{n} \lambda_k(x_{ij})\Big) e^{-\int_0^T \lambda_k(x)dx} \qquad (4)$$

Particularly, the posterior probability $p(z_i = k | \mathbf{x}_i, \Theta, \Phi)$ in Equation 3 is u_i's soft membership in group k, which is also denoted by π_{ik}. Thus far, the group membership for all customers would be successfully updated for this iteration and the M-step is ready to start.

In the **M-step**, we estimate the values of Θ and Φ based on daily purchase event $\{\Delta N(t)\}$ ($t \in \{1, ..., T\}$) and Π obtained in the E-step.

For group k, the daily purchase event $\{\Delta N_k(t)\}$ in T days aggregates the purchase events of all customers in k. It is computed by $\Delta N_k(t) = \sum_{i=1}^{U} \pi_{ik} \Delta N_i(t)$, which considers the purchase event increment $\Delta N_i(t)$ of u_i on day t, and u_i's soft membership π_{ik} in k. The $\{\Delta N_k(t)\}$ is used to estimate θ_k by maximizing the likelihood of $\lambda_k(x)$.

Finally, we update the relative size of group k by summing individual soft memberships of group k, $\phi_k = \sum_{i=1}^{U} \pi_{ik}$.

The algorithm iterates between the E-step and the M-step until convergence or for a manually defined number of iterations. The final output is the estimations of Φ, Π and Θ in the final iteration.

3.3 Analyze Customer Segments

Based on Φ, Π and Θ of mixture NHPP models and soft customer segmentation result, we analyze the purchase behavior and compare the differences among segments with respect to the following features: 1) segment size ϕ_k; 2) number of purchase events $\int_0^T \lambda(x)dx$; 3) long-term patterns such as increase or decrease of purchase intensity, determined by w_d of the polynomial component; 4) cycle length of the periodic short-term patterns, computed by $2\pi/b$.

More importantly, we are interested in discovering whether the purchase intensity of a customer segment is influenced by promotions. We compute the correlation r_k between $\lambda_k(x)$ of each segment and the price curve. If r_k is negative, segment k is receptive to promotions, and customers purchase more frequently when the price is lower. Otherwise, segment k is not receptive to promotions, which means the customers would keep buying regardless of price reductions.

4. CASE STUDY

We conduct a case study on the transaction records of 931 customers, collected by an Australian national supermarket chain through the loyalty cards between January 1st and December 31st, 2014 [12]. From the case study, we aim to: 1) evaluate the capability of the proposed method for modeling the purchase events of individual customers, 2) discover long-term and short-term purchase patterns of latent customer segments and understand the differences among the segments, 3) identify customer segments that are receptive to product promotions.

4.1 Data Preprocessing

In our data set, each transaction record includes customer ID, product ID, timestamp, product metadata, purchased quantity and cost. We notice that supermarket promotions generally involve a series of products from the same brand, so we choose "brand" as the granularity level of our analysis and aggregate the purchase records of the same brand to model the customer behavior. We select 27 brands from 7 categories (as listed in Table 1) based on the popularity. The name "own brand" refers to the supermarket's self-owned production brand. For each brand, the active customers are chosen based on whether they bought products from that brand more than 10 times in one year.

To explore the customer response to promotions, we use the price of each brand. We first normalize the daily product price to $(0, 1]$, using the ratio of the daily price to the maximal price of the product. This step can eliminate the differences of magnitude among prices of various products. Then, we compute the brand price as a weighted average of prices of all products from the brand. The daily brand price can reflect the promotion time and the discount rate.

For the other parameters, the number of segments for each brand is configured empirically based on the data fitness; the degree of polynomial component of Equation 1 is set to 2, which is adequate to capture the long-term patterns within the one-year observation period for our study.

4.2 Purchase Behavior Analysis

Table 1 lists the results obtained using the soft-membership customer segmentation method. For each brand, as customers have a mixed membership over multiple segments, the columns under "Size of Segment" are the relative sizes of all segments. For the brand with fewer than 4 segments, the cells are empty for the non-existing segments.

4.2.1 *Evaluate Fitness of Purchase Events*

To quantitatively evaluate the behavior model, we first compute the absolute difference between the estimated and actual number of purchase events on day t. Then we average the differences over T days, $\sum_{t=0}^{T} |\int_0^t \lambda(x)dx - N(t)|/T$, to compute the Mean Absolute Error (MAE). Based on the segment-wise MAE, we compute the weighted MAE across all the segments of a brand, taking the segment sizes in Table 1 into consideration. Figure 3 shows that the NHPP model has lower MAE than the HomoPP model for all the brands. The average MAE across brands for HomoPP is 0.61, while for NHPP it is 0.19 (t-test result: $p < 0.001$). For some brands, e.g., Brands 1, 6 and 22, the MAE of HomoPP is particularly high, indicating that the HomoPP cannot reliably model the dynamic purchase behavior of these brands.

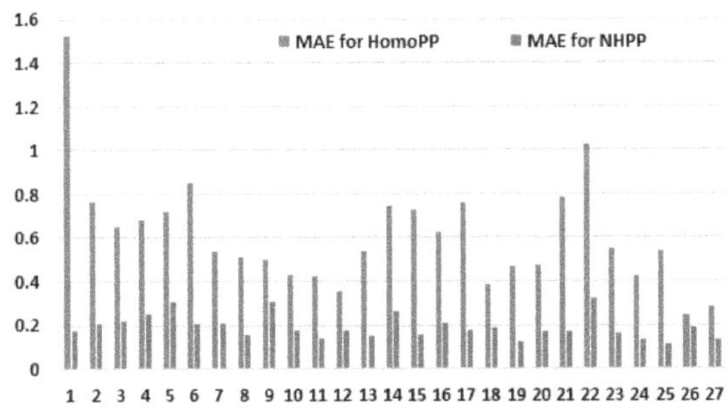

Figure 3: Weighted MAE of HomoPP (blue) and NHPP (red) models on all brands.

4.2.2 *Long-term and Short-term Behavior Patterns*

We notice that customer segments with similar number of purchase events may have significantly different long-term and short-term patterns. For example, in Figure 4, segments 1 and 2 of Brand 8 have different long-term patterns, but their numbers of purchase events are 19.2 and 19.3.

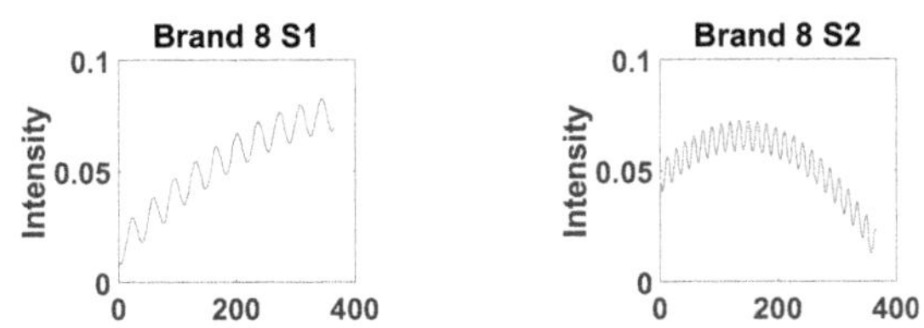

Figure 4: The segments with similar number of purchase events but different temporal patterns.

For the coefficients of the quadratic component in Equation 1, $\sum_{d=0}^{D} w_d x^d$ $(d = 2)$, we mainly check 1) whether the parabola opens upward ($w_2 > 0$) or downward ($w_2 < 0$); 2) the location of the turning point x_{tp} $(-w_1/2w_2)$. There are 5 major long-term patterns – *increase*, *decrease*, *U-shape*, *inverse U-shape*, and *stable*.

In the left part of Table 2, we summarize the proportion of each long-term pattern to explore the trends shared at the category level. To compute this proportion, we first get the distribution and the weight of the 5 long-term patterns in each brand. For the category, we average the distributions over all relevant brands.

We first notice that Ice Cream and Soft Drinks have large proportions of U-shape patterns, 42.67% and 65.67%, respectively. The third category with the U-shape pattern is Snacks (21.50%), which has a large gap from the top two. It is reasonable that customers buy fewer ice cream and soft drinks during winter (in the mid-year in Australia) than summer, which leads to the U-shape purchase intensity curve. As for the inverse U-shape pattern, the Confectionery Category ranks first, comprising 93% segments with inverse U-shape patterns. Then the Biscuits & Cookies Category has 89.33% inverse U-shape patterns. The results indicate that a large portion of customers tend to purchase more energy-rich foods like confectionery and cookies in winter rather than in summer. For the other three types of long-term patterns, the proportions are lower than 30%, without clearly dominant patterns. The Ice Cream, Snacks and Ce-

Table 1: Customer response to price reduction and mean discount rate for all brands

Brand	Category	Brand Name	Size of Segment				Correlation with Price				Receptive to Promotions	Mean Discount Rate
			1	2	3	4	1	2	3	4		
1	Ice Cream	own brand	0.56	0.28	0.16		**-0.2**	0.35	-0.14		0.72	0.12
2		Peters	0.72	0.21	0.07		-0.06	**-0.2**	-0.11		**1.00**	0.25
3		Streets	0.77	0.23			-0.01	**-0.2**			**1.00**	0.24
4	Soft Drinks	Coca-Cola	0.29	0.56	0.08	0.07	0.41	-0.12	**-0.28**	0.08	0.64	0.23
5		own brand	0.37	0.25	0.33	0.05	0.26	**-0.62**	0.54	0.26	0.25	0.16
6		Schweppes	0.48	0.15	0.27	0.1	**-0.31**	**-0.23**	-0.17	-0.06	**1.00**	0.27
7	Biscuits & Cookies	Arnotts	0.51	0.3	0.17	0.02	-0.03	-0.09	-0.08	-0.1	**1.00**	0.22
8		own brand	0.31	0.5	0.18	0.02	-0.19	0.25	0.02	0.18	0.31	0.09
9		Fantastic	0.45	0.42	0.13		0.15	-0.08	0.26		0.42	0.28
10	Snacks	Smiths	0.25	0.45	0.25	0.04	0.32	**-0.38**	0.26	0.08	0.45	0.23
11		own brand	0.31	0.47	0.16	0.05	0.16	**-0.37**	0.47	-0.04	0.52	0.09
12		Red Deli	0.84	0.16			0.11	0.05			0.00	0.25
13		Doritos	0.5	0.04	0.45	0.01	-0.14	-0.03	0.03	0	0.55	0.25
14	Confectionery	Cadbury	0.67	0.13	0.14	0.06	0.12	-0.02	**-0.2**	-0.06	0.33	0.29
15		own brand	0.21	0.73	0.06		0.09	-0.12	-0.04		0.79	0.08
16		Mars	0.14	0.27	0.37	0.22	-0.03	-0.08	-0.06	-0.04	**1.00**	0.29
17		Lindt	0.75	0.25			-0.12	**-0.2**			**1.00**	0.27
18		Allens	0.9	0.1			-0.01	0.21			0.90	0.22
19	Chilled Desserts	own brand	0.2	0.48	0.3	0.02	0.16	0	0.1	0.08	0.48	0.11
20		Yoplait	0.33	0.21	0.29	0.17	-0.15	0.19	0.15	-0.03	0.50	0.17
21		Vaalia	0.25	0.21	0.41	0.12	0.18	0.05	-0.17	-0.01	0.54	0.15
22		Chobani	0.2	0.64	0.16		-0.11	0.1	-0.07		0.36	0.19
23		Jalna	0.32	0.56	0.13		**-0.52**	0.39	0.18		0.32	0.12
24	Cereal	Kelloggs	0.09	0.24	0.51	0.16	**-0.2**	0.13	-0.19	-0.18	0.76	0.16
25		Uncle Toby	0.36	0.36	0.18	0.1	**-0.34**	-0.12	0.06	**-0.27**	0.82	0.14
26		Sanitarium	0.6	0.31	0.09		-0.07	-0.03	-0.03		**1.00**	0.18
27		own brand	0.7	0.3			0.02	0.26			0.00	0.07

Table 2: Distributions of 5 long-term patterns and the cycle lengths of short-term periodic behavior for various categories

Category	Long-term Patterns					Short-term Patterns		
	Increase	Decrease	U-shape	Inverse U	Stable	Mean	Max	Min
Ice Cream	18.67%	0%	42.67%	14.67%	24.00%	14.35	30.18	9.66
Soft Drinks	11.67%	9.00%	65.67%	13.67%	0%	14.91	29.03	6.38
Biscuits & Cookies	10.00%	0.67%	0%	89.33%	0%	13.19	33.54	6.49
Snacks	24.50%	0%	21.50%	33.00%	21.00%	15.87	27.81	6.69
Confectionery	7.00%	0%	0%	93.00%	0%	12.86	56.91	6.47
Chilled Desserts	17.80%	29.60%	0%	52.60%	0%	14.65	34.48	6.28
Cereal	0%	21.25%	2.25%	59.00%	17.50%	25.43	62.83	7.00

real have about 20% of stable patterns. This means that these customer segments have relatively stationary purchase intensities and the customers purchase them regularly, less sensitive to seasonal effects.

As for the short-term periodic patterns (listed in the right part of Table 2), the mean cycle length across all categories is about 16 days. The mean value for each category is the average of segment-wise cycle lengths, weighted by the segment sizes. The weighted mean cycle length for Cereal is 25.43, almost double the cycle lengths of the other categories. The main reason for this is that cereals are often sold in large packs (e.g., 1kg), which take longer to consume. For the other categories, the mean cycle lengths are between 12.86 and 15.87 days, which are all about 2 weeks.

4.2.3 Customer Response to Promotions

To analyze how a customer segment responds to the promotions of a brand, we compute the correlation between the purchase intensity of each segment and the daily brand price, as reported in columns under "Correlation with Price" in Table 1. The negative correlations are expected if the customer behavior in that segment is receptive to the price reduction. The second last column lists the proportion of customers who are receptive to price reductions, which sums the sizes of all the segments with negative correlations. The Mean Discount Rate (MDR) in the last column is computed by averaging (1−daily price).

The results show that Brands 2, 3, 6, 7, 16, 17, 18 and 26, have negative correlations for all their customer segments. These brands also have higher average MDR, which is 0.25, while the average MDR for all brands is 0.19. This means that these brands have relatively larger or more frequent sales promotions than the other brands. Therefore, having more customers receptive to the price reductions in these brands is beneficial for the supermarket.

There are 7 supermarket own brands (Brands 1, 5, 8, 11, 15, 19 and 27), one for each category. The MDR of all these brands are the lowest in their corresponding category. The average MDR for these supermarket brands is 0.1, which is half of the average MDR for all the other brands, 0.22. For the supermarket own brands, the average proportion who are receptive to promotions is 43.8%, while for the other brands it is 70.1%. The substantial difference observed between these two proportions confirms that fewer customers of supermarket own brands are receptive to price reductions, compared to the customers of other brands.

From the category level, Ice Cream and Confectionery have larger proportions of customers who are receptive to price change, which are 91% and 89%, respectively. Snacks and Chilled Desserts only have 38% and 44% of customers who are receptive to promotions, respectively. There are two possible reasons: 1) the average MDR of Ice Cream and Confectionery are 0.2 and 0.23, which are higher than Chilled Desserts, 0.148; 2) products of Snacks (e.g., potato chips and nuts in small packs) are generally cheaper than Ice Cream and Confectionery (e.g., chocolates).

4.3 Key Results and Discussion

Most long-term patterns are mainly caused by seasonal effects and personal preference changes. If the demand for a category tends to be influenced by season, the category will have more U-shape and inverse U-shape patterns. If the purchase behavior is mainly driven by the preference, the different types of long-term patterns are more evenly distributed for the category, which reflects the preference drifts of different customers. The short-term patterns are mainly determined by regular promotions, shopping habits and the necessity of the products. Another influential factor is whether it is easy to stockpile the product at home.

As for the responsiveness of customer segments to the price changes, if there are regular attractive promotions, the purchase intensity is negatively correlated with the price. Higher proportions of customers have been motivated by the larger price reductions, and there are 8 brands with all segments receptive to promotions. The supermarket own brands do not have frequent promotions and have lower prices than their branded counterparts, so there are fewer negative correlations for these brands.

5. CONCLUSIONS

In this paper, we propose to use a mixture of NHPP models to segment customers in terms of latent long-term and short-term purchase behavior patterns. Our contribution is three-fold: 1) we validate the significant advantages of using our NHPP model to estimate the non-stationary occurrence of purchase events; 2) we decompose the dynamic behavior patterns into long-term trends related to factors such as seasonal effects and preference drifts, and short-term periodic purchases driven by personal needs and promotions; 3) we explore customer response to promotions using the correlation between purchase intensity and price, and identify customers who are receptive to price reductions.

From the practical viewpoint, the analysis of behavior patterns and customer response to promotions could help the business management to select good timing and suitable rate of promotions. In addition, our method could compare the differences of the distribution of long-term patterns and the cycle lengths of the periodic behavior from the category level, which provides a guide to optimizing the promotion strategies for different categories. In future work, we will consider how a promoted product influences similar products by simultaneously considering multiple Poisson processes and their interactions.

6. REFERENCES

[1] P. Adamopoulos and V. Todri. The effectiveness of marketing strategies in social media: Evidence from promotional events. In *Proceedings of the 21th ACM SIGKDD Int'l Conf. on Knowledge Discovery and Data Mining*, pages 1641–1650. ACM, 2015.

[2] G. M. Allenby, R. P. Leone, and L. Jen. A dynamic model of purchase timing with application to direct marketing. *Journal of the American Statistical Association*, 94(446):365–374, 1999.

[3] R. E. Bucklin, S. Gupta, and S. Siddarth. Determining segmentation in sales response across consumer purchase behaviors. *Journal of Marketing Research*, pages 189–197, 1998.

[4] C. Chatfield and G. J. Goodhardt. A consumer purchasing model with erlang inter-purchase times. *Journal of the American Statistical Association*, 68(344):828–835, 1973.

[5] D. Dong and H. M. Kaiser. Studying household purchasing and nonpurchasing behaviour for a frequently consumed commodity: two models. *Applied Economics*, 40(15):1941–1951, 2008.

[6] A. S. Ehrenberg. The pattern of consumer purchases. *Applied Statistics*, pages 26–41, 1959.

[7] T. Iwata, S. Watanabe, T. Yamada, and N. Ueda. Topic tracking model for analyzing consumer purchase behavior. In *Proc. of the 22nd Int'l Joint Conf. on Artificial Intelligence*, pages 1427–143. AAAI Press, 2009.

[8] H. Kim, N. Takaya, and H. Sawada. Tracking temporal dynamics of purchase decisions via hierarchical time-rescaling model. In *Proc. of the 23rd ACM Int'l Conf. on Information and Knowledge Management*, pages 1389–1398. ACM, 2014.

[9] K. Kopperschmidt and W. Stute. Purchase timing models in marketing: a review. *AStA Advances in Statistical Analysis*, 93(2):123–149, 2009.

[10] P. Kotler and G. Armstrong. *Principles of marketing.* pearson education, 2010.

[11] B. Li, X. Zhu, R. Li, C. Zhang, X. Xue, and X. Wu. Cross-domain collaborative filtering over time. In *Proc. of the 22nd Int'l Joint Conf. on Artificial Intelligence*, pages 2293–2298. AAAI Press, 2011.

[12] L. Luo, B. Li, I. Koprinska, S. Berkovsky, and F. Chen. Who will be affected by supermarket health programs? Tracking customer behavior changes via preference modeling. In *Pacific Asia Conference on Knowledge Discovery and Data Mining*, volume 9651, pages 527–539. Springer, 2016.

[13] D. G. Morrison and D. C. Schmittlein. Generalizing the NBD model for customer purchases: What are the implications and is it worth the effort? *Journal of Business & Economic Statistics*, 6(2):145–159, 1988.

[14] P. E. Rossi, R. E. McCulloch, and G. M. Allenby. The value of purchase history data in target marketing. *Marketing Science*, 15(4):321–340, 1996.

[15] J. N. Sheth, B. Mittal, and B. I. Newman. *Customer behavior: consumer behavior and beyond.* Dryden Press Fort Worth, TX., 1999.

ZEST: a Hybrid Model on Predicting Passenger Demand for Chauffeured Car Service

Hua Wei[†], Yuandong Wang[†], Tianyu Wo[†], Yaxiao Liu[‡], Jie Xu[†,§]
[†]State Key Laboratory of Software Development Environment, Beihang University, China;
[‡]Department of Computer Science and Technology, Tsinghua University, China;
[§]School of Computing, University of Leeds, UK
{weihua, wangyd, woty}@act.buaa.edu.cn; liuyaxiao12@mails.tsinghua.edu.cn;
J.Xu@leeds.ac.uk

ABSTRACT

Chauffeured car service based on mobile applications like Uber or Didi suffers from supply-demand disequilibrium, which can be alleviated by proper prediction on the distribution of passenger demand. In this paper, we propose a **Z**ero-Grid **E**nsemble **S**patio**T**emporal model (*ZEST*) to predict passenger demand with four predictors: a temporal predictor and a spatial predictor to model the influences of local and spatial factors separately, an ensemble predictor to combine the results of former two predictors comprehensively and a Zero-Grid predictor to predict zero demand areas specifically since any cruising within these areas costs extra waste on energy and time of driver. We demonstrate the performance of ZEST on actual operational data from ride-hailing applications with more than 6 million order records and 500 million GPS points. Experimental results indicate our model outperforms 5 other baseline models by over 10% both in MAE and sMAPE on the three-month datasets.

Keywords

Spatiotemporal Data Mining; Demand Prediction; Chauffeured Car Service

1. INTRODUCTION

Chauffeured car service based on ride-hailing applications like Uber and Didi serves as an important transportation to provide passengers with convenient and professional services. However, in metropolises like Beijing or New York, it is common to see passengers seeking for taxicabs roadside either in downtown or in suburbs while some taxi drivers are cruising idly on the street.

This contradiction reveals the supply-demand disequilibrium with the following two scenarios: *Scenario 1*, demand exceeds supply, where passengers' needs would not be met in a timely response. As is shown in the Figure 1(a), 90% passengers who withdrew their requests canceled their orders in the first 10 minutes and specifically, 80% canceled in their first 5 minutes. *Scenario 2*, supply exceeds demand, where drivers would spend overly long time in seeking for passengers. Figure 1(b) indicates that over 20% chauffeured drivers spend over 2 hours seeking for their next customers while only 40% drivers can pick up their next passengers within 30 minutes. In particular, areas that are highly possible of having zero demand in the next time period should be more concerned because any cruising within may be a waste in energy and time. Besides, after knowing some areas are very likely to be zero-demand area, the drivers can avoid driving to those areas, while dispatching centers of car companies can dispatch their cars and set their prices ahead of time dynamically, which can successively alleviates the disequilibrium of both Scenario-1 and Scenario-2 areas.

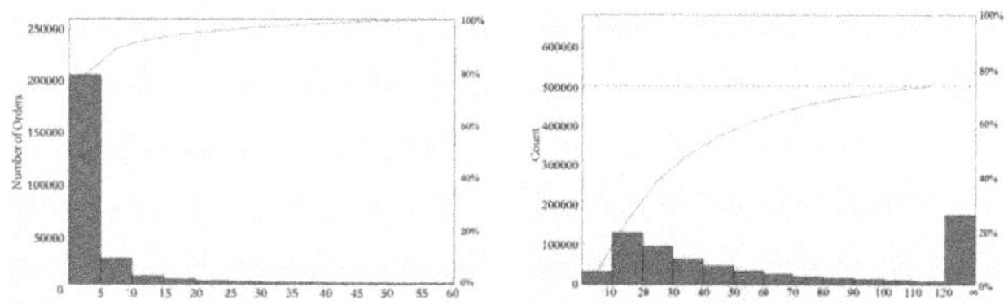

(a) Waiting time (min) (b) Cruising time (min)

Figure 1: Distribution of passengers' waiting time before canceling order and drivers' cruising time in Beijing during September 2015

To solve the problem of disequilibrium, an overall prediction for passenger demand provides a global distribution of passengers, upon which we can dispatch in supply and adjust prices dynamically in advance. Although there are plenty of methods for prediction like Linear Regression and Multiple Additive Regression Tree, particularly, the pattern of demand for road transportation can be modeled as Poisson Process [5]. Li et al. [4] and Moreira-Matias et al. [6] both took advantage of Auto-Regression Moving Average method in time series analysis, which predicted the number of passengers in certain region based on historical pick-up data. However, aforementioned studies have assumed that the quantity of demanding passengers is equal to the pick-up counts recorded by taxi. But in countries where roadside taxi hailing is permissible, there are still plenty of people who manage but fail to take taxis.

Thus, there is a bias between the pick-up records and passenger demand. Zhang et al. [7] noticed this bias and ob-

CIKM'16 , October 24-28, 2016, Indianapolis, IN, USA

DOI: http://dx.doi.org/10.1145/2983323.2983667

served online hidden context to infer the passenger demand. Instead of inferring the unpicked-up passengers, Jiang et al. [3] utilized the order data generated by demanding passengers through ride-hailing applications, which properly settled the bias since passengers in demand can only make requests through mobile applications. Therefore, the demand of passengers can be considered equal to the amount of orders recorded by applications. But the model they utilized was based on Linear Regression, which oversimplified the temporal and spatial influences. Moreover, as their model is based on regression, they cannot provide information on the possibility of areas having zero demand in the next time period.

In this manner, this paper focuses on the prediction of passengers in demand of chauffeured car service and how possible one region will have zero demand in certain periods. The major contributions of this paper can be summarized as follows: a) Based on the local data, a simple yet novel parameter named *FluctuationRate* is proposed in the temporal predictor to filter out irrelevant historical records; b) the influences of neighborhoods are modeled using different kinds of datasets, while most of the existing researches are based on onefold data; c) a specified model named *Zero-Grid Predictor* is presented to predicted areas with zero demand, along with an ensemble predictor combining the results of temporal and spatial model. The integration keeps the advantages of temporal and spatial model and provides the possibility of zero demand area, which is not covered by many state-of-art prediction models on passenger demand. Evaluations on real operational datasets with over 6 million order records and 500 million GPS points show that compared to ground truth, our model achieves 0.68 in MAE and 12.6% in sMAPE on average, which outperforms other five baseline models.

2. METHODOLOGY

In this section, we clarify some definitions and present the prediction model, including the framework and detailed design of each component.

2.1 Preliminary

Definition 1: *Time Period, Hour of Day and Day of Week.* We divide one day into several time periods while in experiment, the length of one period is 60 minutes and one day is divided into 24 periods. For example, when the length of each time period is one hour, "2015-06-01 16:03:22" at Monday's hour of day (HOD) and day of week (DOW) will be 16 and 0 accordingly.

Definition 2: *Grid, Row, Col.* We divide one city into mutually disjoint grids, where each point in the records can be mapped into one grid by locating the index of row number *row* and column number *col*. In experiments, the distance from one grid to another is approximately equal to the driving distance within 10 minutes in the city.

Definition 3: *Order.* Given the time period t and grid r, the amount of order records requested from passengers within t and r are denoted as $Order_t^r$.

Definition 4: *Zero-Grid.* When a grid r has zero order in time period t, i.e $Order_t^r = 0$, we call r is a Zero-Grid. From the perspective of saving energy and time, Zero-Grids should be given close attention in dispatching to meet the need of demanded areas.

2.2 Framework of Model

As is shown in Figure 2, the construction of our model is mainly based on the offline learning on historical data, online data preprocessing and online prediction. For order data and GPS data stream, we firstly partition and aggregate them into certain grids and time periods as *Order*. Then in the offline learning process, preprocessed data is separately fed into predictors to re-train our models every week. Upon the model, online predictions can be generated with preprocessed input data.

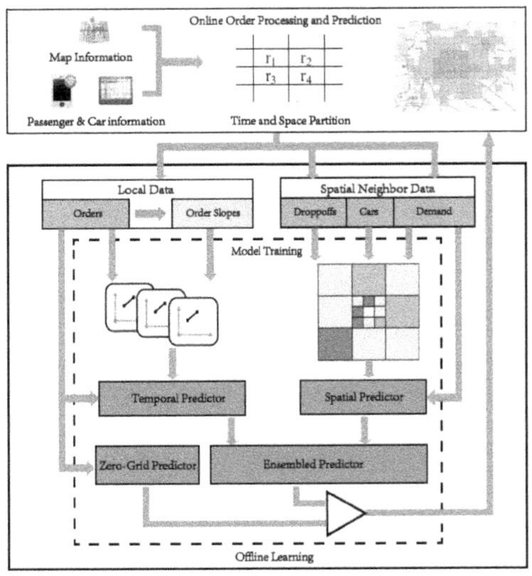

Figure 2: Framework of the prediction model

As is shown in Figure 2, our prediction model includes a temporal predictor (TP), a spatial predictor (SP), an ensemble predictor (EP) that combines former two predictors and a Zero-Grid predictor (ZP) which provides the possibilities of a grid r being a Zero Grid. When a grid has a high possibility of having zero demand in the next time period, the final prediction will be zero.

2.3 Temporal Predictor

Intuitively, given a region, its demand at certain period could be roughly deduced from demand at comparable periods, like same time of the day or same day of the week. However, the passenger demand is sometimes irregularly variant at same time of the day and may lead to bias if all historical periods are taken into prediction.

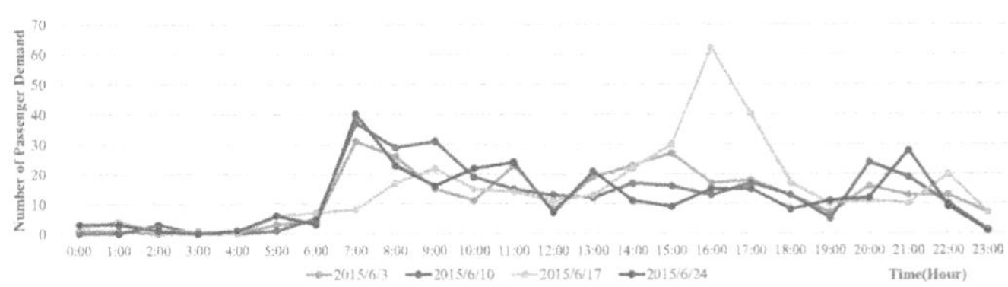

Figure 3: Passenger demand near Renmin University of Wednesdays in June 2015

Figure 3 gives an example of the passenger demand in Renmin Univerisity area at Wednesdays in July where the passenger demand did fluctuate in different days. When we were predicting for the passenger demand in 16:00 of

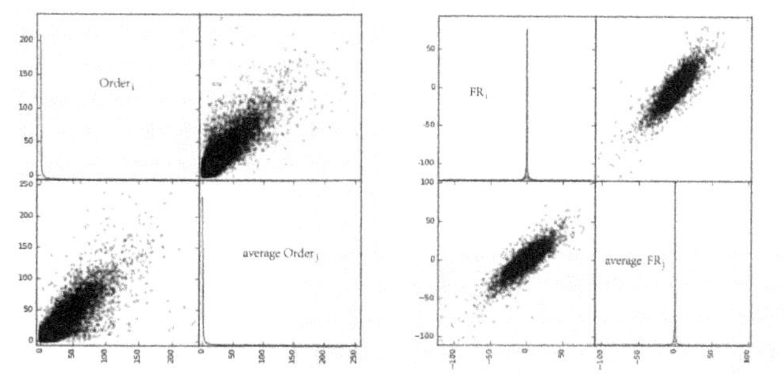

(a) $Order_i$ of average $Order_j$ (b) FR_i of average FR_j

Figure 4: Correlations of *Orders* and *FRs*

July 24th, the prediction value was $\frac{17+13+67}{3} \approx 30$ using all historical data. If we found out that patterns in July 3rd and 10th are more similar with 24th than 17th based on the change of demands, we would get the inference of $\frac{17+13}{2} = 15$ using more relevant data, which is closer to the actual value (16 in this case).

Therefore, we define a parameter *FluctuationRate* to reflect the similarities between demand fluctuation in different time periods. Given grid r at time i, *FluctuationRate* is defined as Equation 1:

$$FluctuationRate_i^r = \frac{Order_i^r - Order_{i-1}^r}{\Delta t} \tag{1}$$

where Δt is the length of time slots. In the following sections of this paper, we abbreviate $FluctuationRate_i^r$ as FR_i^r. As is shown in Figure 4, the correlations between FR_i and the average value of FR_j is more apparent than the correlations between $Order_i$ and the average $Order_j$ for every j, where $i-4 \leq j < i$.

In temporal predictor, FR is employed to filter out less related period in past three months. The inputs of the *TP* are : a) the order number of grid r of last time slot t_{cur}, $Order_{t_{cur}}^r$; b) the set of historical $Order_i^r$ in last three months; c) the set of historical FR_i^r in last three months; and d) the similarity error ε where we say $FR_{t_m}^r$ and $FR_{t_n}^r$ are similar when $|FR_{t_m}^r - FR_{t_n}^r| < \varepsilon$.

The details of the algorithm are presented as follows: Firstly, we calculate the parameter $FR_{t_{cur}}^r$ for current time t_{cur}. Secondly, we select all the time slot t_i whose FR is similar with $FR_{t_{cur}}^r$. Then we select t_i's next time slot and its corresponding FR, upon which we can predict the order number of grid r of next time slot t_{cur+1} through the average of FRs and $Order_{t_{cur}}$. Note that unless the data after filtering is null, a traditional time-varying poisson model will not be used.

2.4 Spatial Predictor

Spatial predictor makes use of target grid's neighborhood data to predict its future demand, including passenger demand and drop-off data, along with the vehicle data of the target grid.

Intuitively, passenger demand is related to each other in different regions as the passengers and vehicles are moving around the city. Passengers may take public transportation to the nearest subway or bus station and then orders chauffeured service to their destination. Therefore, it's inferred that passenger demand $Order_t^r$ in grid r at time t is related with the drop-off passengers in r's neighborhood before t, $Dropoff_{t_{before}}^{r_{neighbor}}$. Besides, it's also speculated that since passengers who had left grid r just before t was unlikely to show up again in r at t, passenger demand $Order_t^r$ is related with the demand in r before t, $Order_{t_{before}}^r$. What's more, drivers also have their own experience in pick-up points, which could be referred by the number of vehicle (*Cars*) in target region.

For a target grid to predict, we divide and aggregate its neighborhood into uneven grids as is shown in Figure 5(a) considering range-based influence, feature quality and dimension. For grids with larger size, the final value of each feature will be an average value of corresponding features regarding all included grids. Note that the overall neighborhood area in Figure 5(a) contains 79 grids, which would increase the feature dimension dramatically if there was no aggregation.

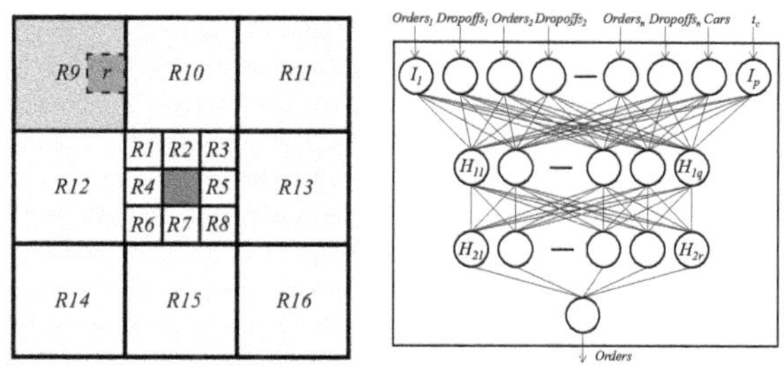

(a) Dividing scheme (b) Features for SP

Figure 5: Framework of spatial predictor

As is shown in Figure 5(b), for a target grid to predict, we use four types of features: time t_c to predict; the number of passenger demand in grid r_i, $Orders^{r_i}$; the number of drop-off passengers, $Dropoffs^{r_i}$; the number of vehicles, $Cars^i$. Firstly, passenger demand features are generated from the demand data of target's surrounding three-circle areas (containing 24 grids) in past three time periods (1 hour ago, 2 to 3 hours ago and 4 to 6 hours ago), one average value per period and grid. Secondly, passenger drop-off features are generated from the drop-off data of target's surrounding first circle with 8 grids in past three time periods (1 hour ago, 2 to 3 hours ago and 4 to 6 hours ago). Thirdly, the vehicle feature are generated from the quantity of vehicles within target grid in past one hour.

After generating features, an artificial neural network is trained to model the correlations in demands at different grids where the number of layers and the number of nodes in hidden layers are related with the input data.

2.5 Ensemble Predictor

In ensemble predictor, we aggregate the result of temporal predictor and spatial predictor. Although the idea of modeling temporally and spatially is intuitive yet widely used in spatiotemporal prediction [1] [8] [9], it is still flexible when confronted with different objectives. Note that the temporal predictor makes use of local data and spatial predictor mainly make use of its neighborhood data, which are non-repetitive and can provide not only local but relatively overall information in predicting target grid's passenger demand.

In practice, we train Gradient Boosting Decision Trees (GBDT) to combine the results of different predictors. To train such trees, we transform the time into two features:

HOD and DOW, along with the location of grids and other two features: the results of temporal and spatial predictor.

2.6 Zero-Grid Predictor

Based on historical records, a zero-grid predictor can provide possibilities of zero-demand areas for drivers and chauffeured car services. Before training *ZP*, we select features correlated to the zero demand including location, time period and this grid's historical records. For a given grid r at time t to predict, features are generated from r's average demand of past one and two hours and past demand at the same *DOW* and *HOD* of past one and two weeks. Besides, we use r's relative position (*row* and *col*) in a city, along with the time t's *DOW* and *HOD*. Specifically, considering that the location features *row* and *col* are non-linearly related, a Gradient Boosting Classifier is trained to predict the possibility of Zero Grid. Upon a zero-grid predictor, we utilize the ensemble predictor to infer regions where the demand has a low possibility of being zero.

3. EXPERIMENT

In this section, we introduce the datasets, baselines and results of our experiment.

3.1 Datasets

In this paper, we generate three kind of data, including the demand and drop-off data and the vehicle data through two benchmark datasets: the order dataset collected from mobile phone applications and GPS dataset collected from onboard GPS devices in real operating cars. These real operational datasets are sampled and provided by one of China's largest car rental and car-hailing service providers. The details are summarized in Table 1.

Table 1: Summary of datasets

Data Source	Domain	Entities
Order	Orders with estimated on-board location	6,792,756 orders
	Orders with actual drop-off location	4,206,832 drop-offs
GPS	GPS points of cars	512,658,480 GPS points
Urban Size	Area in 6th Ring Road of Beijing, 64×67 km	30×24 grids

3.2 Baselines

In experiments, we compare our model with 5 different baselines methods in total. In each experiment, the comparison of model performance is under the same temporal and spatial conditions for fair. The first three methods are classical and widely used techniques for prediction while the next two methods have been applied to passenger demand prediction in most recent studies:

Classical Poisson Process (TVP_C) was firstly proposed in [2] and the model assumes that the demand of passengers obeys a Non-homogeneous Poisson process with a time-dependent arriving rate function $\lambda(t)$.

Weighted Time-Varying Poisson Process (TVP_W) is a model modified from TVP_C, which adds weights for latest demand pattern [6].

Multiple Additive Regression Tree ($MART\_C$) is a widely-used machine learning technique for regression problems, which produces a prediction model and improves the quality of each base learner.

Classical Linear Regression (LR_C) is an approach for modeling the relationship between target variable and independent variables, which has been applied in studies in demand prediction [3].

Auto-Regression Moving Average ($ARMA$) provides a description of a stationary stochastic process in terms of two polynomials in the statistical analysis of time series, one for the auto-regression and the second for the moving average [6].

3.3 Ground Truth and Metrics

Since the actual value of orders (including the canceled ones) in grid r at time t, a_t^r can directly reflect the passenger demands, we take it as **ground truth**. In the predicting process, we compare the result of prediction p_t^r with the actual value a_t^r in the following metrics:

Regression Metrics. In the evaluation of regression problem, the MAE and sMAPE are utilized to reflect the accuracy of prediction on the number of passenger demand.

$$MAE = \frac{1}{n}\sum |p_t^r - a_t^r|, sMAPE = \frac{1}{n}\sum \frac{|p_t^r - a_t^r|}{\delta_t^r} \quad (2)$$

$$\delta_t^r = \begin{cases} c & p_t^r = a_t^r = 0, c \neq 0 \\ p_t^r + a_t^r & otherwise \end{cases} \quad (3)$$

Classification Metrics. The measures precision (*prec*) and recall (*rec*) defined as Equation 4 are popular metrics used to evaluate the quality of a classification system:

$$prec = \frac{tp}{tp+fn}, rec = \frac{tp}{tp+fp} \quad (4)$$

where tp is the number of true positive predictions, fn is the number of false negative predictions and fp is the number of false positive predictions.

3.4 Experimental Results

3.4.1 Results of Temporal Predictor

For temporal predictor, we reveal the effectiveness of using *FluctuationRate* as a filter on the selection of historical data. All the methods in comparison are conducted on the dataset of Beijing in July, August and September, 2015. And the results of MAE and sMAPE are an overall average for every month.

As is shown in Figure 6, while the MAEs of the three models are about the same, after adding FluctuationRate (T_FR), the performance on the metrics of sMAPE is greatly improved than traditional Poisson Process (TVP_C) and Weighted Time-Varying Poisson Process Model (TVP_W).

3.4.2 Results of Spatial Predictor

As we mentioned in Section 2.4, feature dimensions would be much higher without aggregation and might have great impact on the training of model. Thus, we firstly verify

Table 2: Results of spatial predictors with different features

	Feature Types			Orders' Time Range			Orders' Distance Range			Dropoffs' Distance Range		
	F_t+F_o	F_t+F_o +F_d	F_t+F_o +F_d+F_c	1h	3h	6h	1c	2c	3c	1c	2c	3c
MAE	3.1637	1.3664	**1.0339**	1.2309	1.0972	**1.0861**	1.1827	1.1031	**1.0331**	1.9564	1.8140	**1.0339**
sMAPE	0.2334	0.2329	**0.2316**	0.2428	0.2312	**0.2308**	0.2611	0.2371	**0.2313**	0.2394	0.2343	**0.2316**

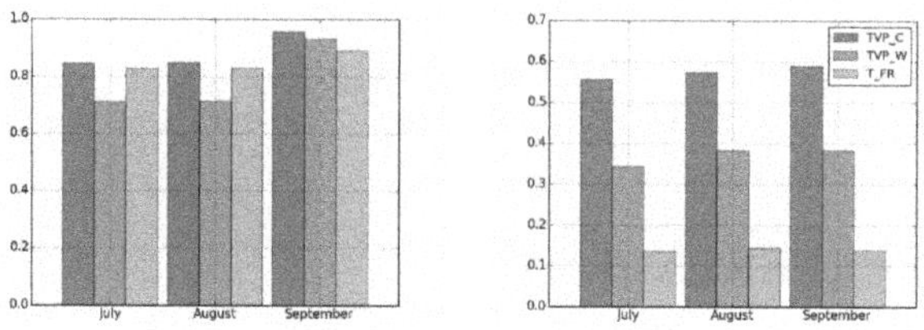

(a) MAE (b) sMAPE

Figure 6: Results of temporal predictor

the significance of division and aggregation, upon which we clarify the effectiveness of the features that we use in the spatial predictor in every month.

Effects of Division and Aggregation In this experiment, features are extracted from the order and GPS datasets of Beijing in July, August and September, 2015. Then we feed the original and aggregated features into *ANN_NonAgg* and *ANN_Agg* respectively. Results in the Figure 7 show that the process of division and aggregation has remarkably improved the performance of learning by over 50% in both MAE and sMAPE for all three months.

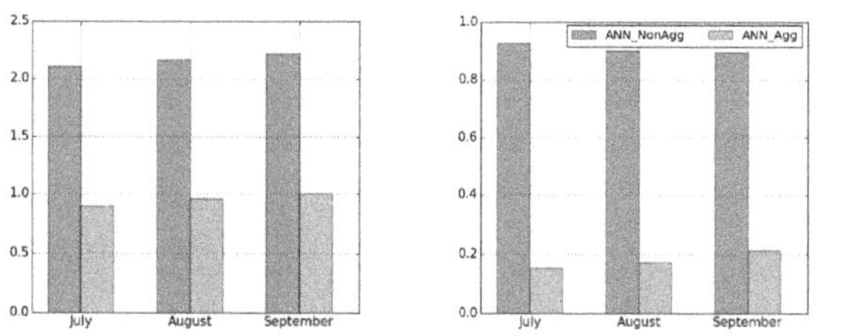

(a) MAE (b) sMAPE

Figure 7: Results of models with and without aggregation

Effects of Different Features. In this experiment, stochastic continuous data in two weeks between June and September 2015 are chosen as training data, and the models are validated on the data of the next week accordingly.

Comparison between feature types. Results in Table 2 illustrate that the increase in relevant feature types we select leads to the improvements on both MAP and sMAPE, where F_t stands for *time*, F_o for *Orders*, F_d for *dropoffs* and F_c for *Cars*.

Range selection for $Orders_{t_j}^{r_i}$. As is shown in Table 2, by extending the time period of passenger demand from 1 hour before t_i (*1h*) to 3 hour (*3h*) and 6 hour (*6h*) step by step, there is a reduction in both MAE and sMAPE. So does with the expanding of grids inside the first circle (*1c*), the second (*2c*) and the third circle (*3c*).

Range selection for $Dropoffs_{t_j}^{r_i}$. The results in Table 2 indicate that adding time periods into features increases the performances of the prediction step by step (*1c, 3c, 6c*). Hence, it's helpful to feed the drop-offs in past 1 hour in surrounding three circle regions into the spatial predictor.

3.4.3 Results of Ensemble Predictor

Table 3 presents that the performance is reached in prediction when combining TP and SP into EP (called EST). In Table 3, the ensemble predictor not only outperforms the individual TP and SP by over 15% in MAE and over 6% in sMAPE, but also has a lower MAP and sMAPE than feeding all the features into baseline methods (*LR_C* and *MART_C*). This is mainly because ensemble predictor keeps the advantages of temporal predictor and spatial predictior which utilizes both local and global information through linear and non-linear models.

Table 3: Results of ensemble predictors

Model	All Samples		Zero Samples	
	MAE	sMAPE	MAE	sMAPE
TP	0.8591	0.1407	0.1601	0.6082
SP	1.0339	0.2316	0.1687	**0.2611**
LR_C	1.2927	0.1445	6.3438	1.0000
MART_C	0.8081	0.1394	8.9117	1.0000
EST	**0.7037**	**0.1321**	**0.0012**	1.0000

Specifically, the sMAPEs for samples whose actual demand is zero provided by *LR_C*, *MART_C* and $TP + SP$ are all 1.0000, which indicates the ineffectiveness of these predictors for zero samples. Therefore, a Zero-Grid Predictor is necessary for performance improvements.

3.4.4 Results of Zero-Grid Predictor

As mentioned in Section 2.6, we train a Zero-Grid Predictor (ZP) to provide information for driver chauffeured car service. The performances of ZP on different months when possibility threshold of positive is 0.5, where *prec* and *rec* of prediction are nearly 93% and 75% on average and the AUC of ZP reaches 95.8%.

3.4.5 Overall Results

The comparison between different methods are shown in Figure 8 adding *ARMA_8* and the combination of our **Z**ero-Grid **E**nsemble **S**patio**T**emporal model ($ZEST$). *ARMA_8* is an ARMA model taking past eight hours as a moving average. The results in Figure 8 show that $ZEST$ outperforms *ARMA_8*, *LR_C* and *MART_C* by over 10% in the prediction for every month. What's more, the integration of ZP also improves the overall performances of *EP+TP+SP*.

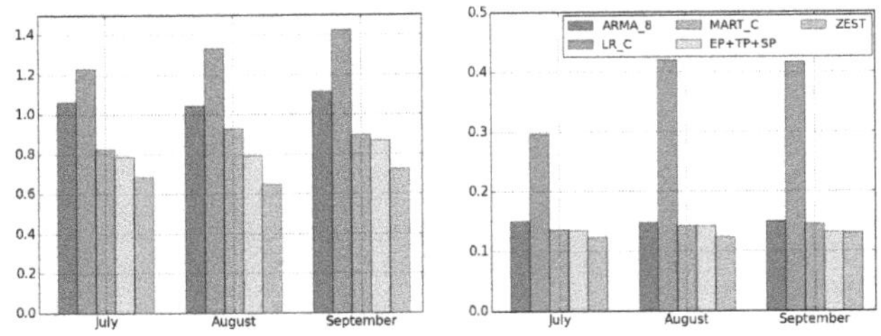

(a) MAE (b) sMAPE

Figure 8: Overall results of predictors

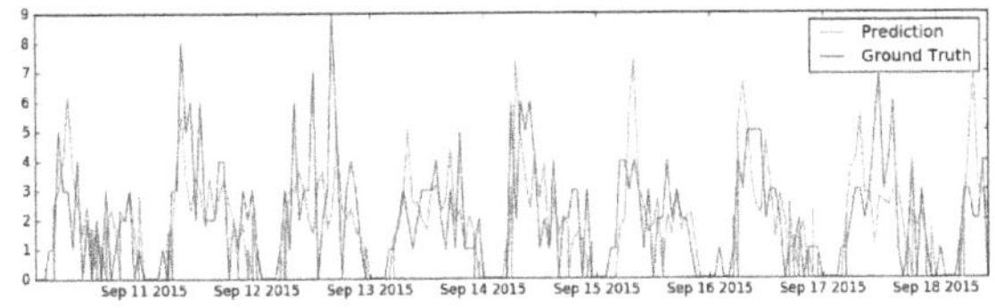

(a) Prediction of Yizhuang area

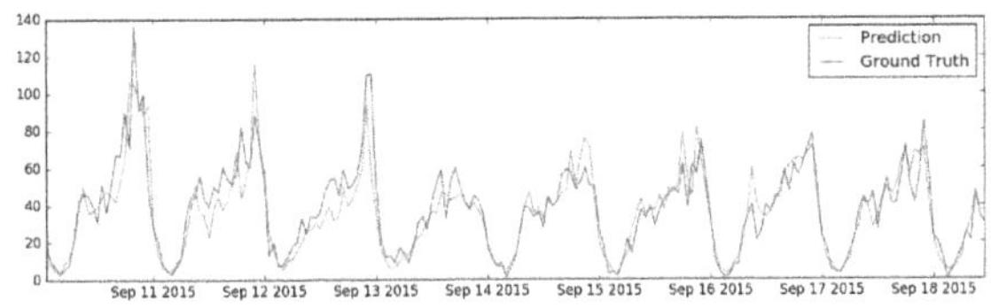

(b) Prediction of Sanlitun area

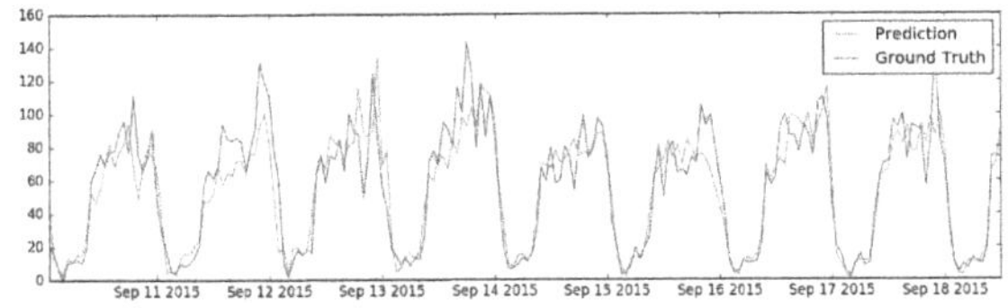

(c) Prediction of Beijing Capital International Airport

Figure 9: Results of *ZEST* against ground truth

Specifically, several areas are displayed as examples of our model's results against the ground truth from September 10 to September 18 in Beijing in Figure 9. Figure 9(a) illustrates the prediction in Yizhuang Area, one of Beijing's biggest residential areas, and Figure 9(b) shows the prediction in Sanlitun Area, Beijing's business and entertainment district. It can be conveyed that Yizhuang suffers from morning rush-hour in a small extent while Sanlitun suffers from evening and late-night peaks, where in general, our model catches these peaks and deals with off-peaks properly, especially the time periods with zero demand. Besides, Figure 9(c) shows the performances of *ZEST* in Beijing's traffic zones, where our model can accurately forecast the demand in these districts.

4. CONCLUSION

In this paper, we develop a hybrid model in predicting the passenger demand which makes use of different kinds of datasets from chauffeured cars. The effectiveness of *FluctuationRate* is confirmed to select similar historical records in temporal prediction. Then we model the influences of neighborhood regions to the target region through features like demands, drop-offs and vehicle numbers in a spatial predictor and then combine the temporal and spatial predictor all together. What's more, to improve the working efficiency for chauffeured car drivers and alleviate supply-demand imbalance, we train a Zero-Grid predictor to predict the possibility of an area being a zero demand area. The integration of Zero-Grid predictor, ensemble predictor, spatial predictor and temporal predictor outperforms five baseline methods.

Acknowledgment

This work is supported by the 863 Program (2015AA01A202), China Key R&D Program (2016YFB1000103), NSFC (61421003) and Beijing Municipal Science and Technology Commission (Z151100003615002). Tianyu Wo is the corresponding author of this paper.

5. REFERENCES

[1] T. Cheng, J. Haworth, B. Anbaroglu, G. Tanaksaranond, and J. Wang. Spatiotemporal data mining. In *Handbook of Regional Science*, pages 1173–1193. Springer, 2014.

[2] A. Ihler, J. Hutchins, and P. Smyth. Adaptive event detection with time-varying poisson processes. In *Proceedings of the 12th ACM SIGKDD international conference on Knowledge discovery and data mining*, pages 207–216. ACM, 2006.

[3] W. Jiang, T. Wo, M. Zhang, R. Yang, and J. Xu. *A Method for Private Car Transportation Dispatching Based on a Passenger Demand Model.* Springer International Publishing, 2015.

[4] X. Li, G. Pan, Z. Wu, G. Qi, S. Li, D. Zhang, W. Zhang, and Z. Wang. Prediction of urban human mobility using large-scale taxi traces and its applications. *Frontiers of Computer Science*, 6(1):111–121, 2012.

[5] L. Matias, J. Gama, J. Mendes-Moreira, and J. Freire, de Sousa. Validation of both number and coverage of bus schedules using avl data. In *International IEEE Conference on Intelligent Transportation Systems*, pages 131–136, 2010.

[6] L. Moreira-Matias, J. Gama, M. Ferreira, J. Mendes-Moreira, and L. Damas. Predicting taxi–passenger demand using streaming data. *Intelligent Transportation Systems, IEEE Transactions on*, 14(3):1393–1402, 2013.

[7] D. Zhang, T. He, S. Lin, S. Munir, J. Stankovic, et al. Dmodel: Online taxicab demand model from big sensor data in a roving sensor network. In *Big Data (BigData Congress), 2014 IEEE International Congress on*, pages 152–159. IEEE, 2014.

[8] Y. Zheng, F. Liu, and H. P. Hsieh. U-air: when urban air quality inference meets big data. In *Proceedings of the 19th ACM SIGKDD international conference on Knowledge discovery and data mining*, pages 1436–1444, 2013.

[9] Y. Zheng, X. Yi, M. Li, R. Li, Z. Shan, E. Chang, and T. Li. Forecasting fine-grained air quality based on big data. In *ACM SIGKDD International Conference on Knowledge Discovery and Data Mining*, pages 2267–2276, 2015.

A Filtering-based Clustering Algorithm for Improving Spatio-temporal Kriging Interpolation Accuracy

Qiao Kang, Wei-keng Liao, Ankit Agrawal, and Alok Choudhary
{qiao.kang, wkliao, ankitag, choudhar}@eecs.northwestern.edu
Electrical Engineering and Computer Science Department
Northwestern University, Evanston, Illinois, United States

ABSTRACT

Geostatistical interpolation is the process that uses existing data and statistical models as inputs to predict data in unobserved spatio-temporal contexts as output. Kriging is a well-known geostatistical interpolation method that minimizes mean square error of prediction. The result interpolated by Kriging is accurate when consistency of statistical properties in data is assumed. However, without this assumption, Kriging interpolation has poor accuracy. To address this problem, this paper presents a new filtering-based clustering algorithm that partitions data into clusters such that the interpolation error within each cluster is significantly reduced, which in turn improves the overall accuracy. Comparisons to traditional Kriging are made with two real-world datasets using two error criteria: normalized mean square error(NMSE) and χ^2 test statistics for normalized deviation measurement. Our method has reduced NMSE by more than 50% for both datasets over traditional Kriging. Moreover, χ^2 tests have also shown significant improvements of our approach over traditional Kriging.

Keywords

Kriging; Spatio-temporal interpolation; Spatio-temporal clustering;

1. INTRODUCTION

Geostatistical interpolation is the process that uses existing data and statistical models as inputs to predict data in unobserved spatio-temporal contexts as output. Kriging[7] is a well-known geostatistical interpolation method that minimizes mean square prediction error. Everyday weather forecasting, environmental hazard prediction and mineral mining are all its application domains. For example, Holdaway[5] has modelled variogram for predicting monthly U.S temperature. Noel[11] has modelled Piezometric-Head data in the Wolfccamp Aquifer for predicting heavy metal pollution level.

Kriging interpolation algorithm requires statistical assumptions about data. Firstly, Kriging interpolation assumes intrinsic stationarity in data. It means that semivariogram, a function of covariance between two points, depends on the displacement vector between them rather than their absolute coordinates. If data is not intrinsic stationary, Kriging interpolation will have poor accuracy.[14] Another commonly used assumption for Kriging is isotropy. Isotropic data implies that covariance functions with respect to distance between data points in all directions are the same, which in turn simplifies computation of Kriging interpolation. Unfortunately, real-world datasets usually do not obey these two assumptions, so Kriging interpolation accuracy is poor if these two properties are blindly assumed. A strategy that improves Kriging interpolation accuracy is to apply non-parametric analysis of data using randomized subsampling[3] when a dataset does not hold these two properties. However, this approach requires human interaction. Moreover, because non-parametric analyses with subsampling use only a subset of data, there are still concerns for final Kriging interpolation accuracy.

In this paper, we present a filtering-based data clustering algorithm that is designed to improve Kriging interpolation accuracy when data does not obey essential statistical properties. Input data points are divided into clusters based on the similarity function of Kriging interpolation error with respect to semivariogram models specified by users. Because only data within the same cluster are used to interpolate results, Kriging interpolation accuracy does not suffer from invalid statistical assumptions for the overall dataset. Our clustering algorithm will find the number of clusters without user interaction. The algorithm has two phases: filtering and reinforcement. Clusters are formed by minimizing clustering-based Kriging interpolation accuracy, while maximizing number of points in individual cluster. Maximizing individual cluster size not only prevents the algorithm from producing trivial results, but also ensures that clustering-based Kriging uses as much data as possible for interpolation.

We use two real world datasets to evaluate our algorithm. Comparisons to traditional Kriging are made using two error criteria: normalized mean square error(NMSE) and χ^2 test statistics for normalized deviation measurement. Our clustering-based Kriging has reduced NMSE by more than 50% for both datasets compared to NMSE produced Kriging without clustering. Moreover, only our clustering-based

CIKM'16 , October 24-28, 2016, Indianapolis, IN, USA
© 2016 ACM. ISBN 978-1-4503-4073-1/16/10...$15.00
DOI: http://dx.doi.org/10.1145/2983323.2983668

Kriging has χ^2 test statistics less than 1% significance level while Kriging without clustering has the χ^2 test statistics at least greater than 10% significance level.

The rest of this paper is arranged as the follows. Firstly, we present the ordinary Kriging interpolation algorithm in section 2. Secondly, we illustrate the design of our proposed filter-based clustering algorithm in section 3. Thirdly, we discuss the implementation of proposed algorithm using both caching and heuristics for improving computational performance in section 4. Finally, we demonstrate evaluations of the proposed algorithm with two real world datasets using two error measurements in section 5.

2. KRIGING ALGORITHM

There are three variants of Kriging: Simple Kriging, ordinary Kriging and universal Kriging.[12] The type of Kriging used in this paper is ordinary Kriging. In this section, we describe ordinary Kriging presented in [14] based on variogram function.

Given n input data points consist of k dimensional coordinates $S = \{s_1, ..., s_n\}$, their associated physical attributes $\{z_1, ..., z_n\}$, a variogram model γ for covariance between data points, Kriging algorithm is a mapping $Z : \mathbb{R}^k \to \mathbb{R}$ that predicts the physical attribute $Z(s_0)$ by $\sum_{i=1}^{n} w_i Z(s_i)$ at a new location s_0, whereas $Z(s_i) = z_i \forall s_i \in S$ by input definition. Weights $W = \{w_1, ..., w_n\}$ are assigned such that the mean square error (MSE) of $\hat{Z}(s_0)$ is minimized subject to constraint $\sum_{i=1}^{n} w_i = 1$. With intrinsic stationarity assumption, semivariogram function has the property $\gamma(h) = \frac{1}{2}E(Z(s+h) - Z(s)) \forall h \in \mathbb{R}^k$. As a result, we can formulate a dual optimization problem with the following Lagrange function.

$$\begin{aligned}L(S, W, \lambda) &= MSE(\hat{Z}(s_0)) - \lambda(\sum_{i=1}^{n} w_i - 1) \\ &= 2\sum_{i=1}^{n} w_i \gamma(s_0 - s_i) - \lambda(\sum_{i=1}^{n} w_i - 1) \\ &- \sum_{i=1}^{n}\sum_{j=1}^{n} w_i w_j \gamma(s_i - s_j)\end{aligned}$$

Solving the Lagrange function with first order condition, we can have the following linear system.

$$\frac{dL}{dw_i} = 2w_i\gamma(s_0 - s_i) - 2\sum_{j=1}^{n} w_i \gamma(s_j - s_i) - \lambda$$

$$\frac{dL}{d\lambda} = 1 - \sum_{i=1}^{n} w_i$$

Setting the derivatives equal to zero, we can obtain a linear system of $n+1$ equations. Let Γ be an $(n+1) \times (n+1)$ dimension matrix, where $\Gamma[i,j] = \gamma(s_i - s_j)\ \forall i, j \in [n]$, $\Gamma[n+1, n+1] = 0$, and the rest of entries are 1. Let m be an $n \times 1$ dimensional column vector with $m[i] = \gamma(s_0 - s_i) \forall i \in [n]$ and $m[n+1] = 1$. Let $w = (w_1, ..., w_n, \frac{\lambda}{2})^T$. Sherman[14] formulates the linear system as $\Gamma w = m$, so assigning Kriging interpolation weights is reduced to solving the linear system and retrieving weights w. The variance of Kriging is $w^T m$.

2.1 Spatio-temporal Kriging

Although Kriging was originally formulated for the purpose of predicting physical attributes of spatial data, spatio-temporal data interpolation such as weather forecast can also apply Kriging. For example, in [5], a spatio-temporal variogram model is formulated to interpolate future temperatures in St. Paul metropolitan area using recent temperatures of all cities in Minnesota State by Kriging. The inputs are spatio-temporal coordinates of cities in Minnesota State $\{s_i = (x_i, y_i, t_i)\}$ for location (x_i, y_i) and time stamp t_i, next day's time stamp, and the spatial coordinates of St. Paul metropolitan area. Moreover, each s_i is associated with an attribute z_i, representing temperature at location (x_i, y_i) and time stamp t_i. The output is the estimated next day's temperature in St. Paul metropolitan area. An efficient implementation of real-time spatio-temporal Kriging for solving this type of problem is in [15].

2.2 Clustering-based Kriging

Abedini, Nasseri and Ansari exploit data preprocessing using K-means clustering algorithm for Kriging interpolation.[1] Firstly, the algorithm separates data points into clusters by using K-means clustering. Then, the prediction for physical attribute $\hat{Z}(s_i)$ of a data point s_i is interpolated via other members in the same cluster. Finally, the accuracy of the algorithm is evaluated by using normalized mean square error (NMSE), which is defined as the following equation.

$$\frac{1}{s^2 n}\sum_{i=1}^{n}(\hat{Z}(s_i) - Z(s_i))^2.$$

s^2 is the sample variance. NMSE not only measures the actual square error, but also takes the sample variance into account.

K-means clustering-based Kriging has two challenges to be addressed. Firstly, the algorithm requires the number of clusters to be determined in advance. For large spatio-temporal datasets, trying a large number of parameter k is expensive. Human effort is also required to compare different types of error measurements for choosing an optimal k. Secondly, the algorithm only considers distance between pair-wise data points without taking the covariance of physical attributes into account. Thus, the algorithm may not necessarily minimize the Kriging interpolation error.

3. DESIGN

We propose a top-down based clustering algorithm that improves Kriging interpolation accuracy within each output cluster. A cluster that does not violate an error constraint specified by users is called consistent cluster, which is formally defined in definition 3.1. The algorithm is an optimization problem that maximizes the size of individual clusters without violating consistent constraint for clusters. Maximizing size of clusters avoids trivial output, which means that one data point corresponds to one cluster. Moreover, it ensures that clustering-based Kriging uses as much consistent data as possible for interpolation, which in turn maintains precision for Kriging interpolation.

Kriging requires fitted variogram model to be specified in advance. In [2], it has been shown that weighted least square

Algorithm 1: Filtering-based clustering algorithm

```
Data: s_1, ..., s_n, Z(s_1), ..., Z(s_n), a threshold, and a
      variogram model M
Result: A queue of clusters Q, each point s_i belongs
        to a unique cluster.
1  C ←{s_1, ..., s_n};
2  Q ←{C};
3  while (C ⟵ next_element(Q)) ≠ ∅ do
4      C' ⟵new cluster;
5      converge ⟵ false;
6      while converge == False do
7          converge ⟵ true;
8          for s ∈ C do
9              converge ⟵
               converge ∧ Filter(s,C,C',threshold,M);
10         end
11     end
12     converge ⟵ false;
13     while converge == False do
14         converge ⟵ true;
15         for s ∈ C do
16             converge ⟵ converge ∧
               Reinforce(s,C,C',threshold,M);
17         end
18     end
19     Remove all elements in C' from C;
20     if !is_empty(C') then
21         Insert(Q, C');
22     end
23 end
```

Algorithm 2: Filtering

```
Data: point s, cluster C, where s ∈ C, C', a
      threshold, and a variogram model M
Result: if the point is consistent to the cluster
Remove(s, C);
t ⟵ normalized_kriging_error(s,C,M);
if |t| > threshold then
    Add(s, C');
    Return False;
else
    Add(s, C);
    Return True;
end
```

(WLS) is feasible for most common models such as exponential model and spherical model. The algorithm assumes that a predefined variogram model remains invariant.

Initially all data points are inserted into a single cluster. Starting from line 3, the algorithm iteratively separates data points into clusters with two phases: filtering phase and reinforcement phase. Points that are inconsistent to the rest of points in the same cluster are filtered out at filtering phase. A new cluster will be initialized to hold the filtered points. Because the algorithm checks consistency by using all remaining data point in the original cluster, it may remove points that are consistent to the original cluster at the end of filtering phase. Therefore, it has to reinforce the cluster by adding falsely removed points back at reinforcement phase. Figure 1 illustrates the two phases.

Algorithm 3: Reinforcement

```
Data: point s, cluster C, where s ∈ C, C', a
      threshold, and a variogram model M
Result: if the cluster is consistent
Add(s, C);
if consistent(C,threshold,M) then
    Remove(s, C');
    Return False;
else
    Remove(s, C);
    Return True;
end
```

3.1 Filtering Phase

The first inner while loop from line 6 to line 11 of algorithm 1 iteratively filters out any point that have large discrepancy between its Kriging interpolated physical attribute based on other points in the same cluster and its actual physical attribute. Points are removed from the cluster in a Gauss-Seidel style, which iterates through cluster and removes points without taking previously removed points into account.

Algorithm 2 (filter function) returns a Boolean. It calls the function *normalized_kriging_error*. This function uses other elements in C to predict the physical attribute of s by the Kriging interpolation described in section 2. Then the difference between the predicted value and the actual value of $Z(s)$ is normalized by dividing Kriging variance. The result is referred as normalized Kriging error. Consequently, the threshold can be chosen from a significance value in standard normal distribution. Selecting threshold from a standard distribution has the advantage of controlling the degree of confidence that a user requires for clustering-based Kriging interpolation accuracy. If the threshold is exceeded, the algorithm will return false and the convergence variable is set to be false. In this case, another round of filtering for cluster C will be triggered because the cluster has not converged yet.

3.2 Reinforcement Phase

In the second inner while loop from line 13 to line 18 of algorithm 1, the algorithm iteratively attempts to add removed points back to the original cluster if the consistency constraint is not violated. Hence the size of the cluster is maximized subject to the Kriging consistency constraint. Kriging cluster consistency, defined in definition 3.1, states that the normalized Kriging error should be less than the threshold for every point in all clusters explicitly.

Algorithm 3 (reinforce function) returns a Boolean. It inserts a point s back to a cluster C and test the Kriging consistency of C. This process computes the normalized kriging error for all points in C. If any of the points has normalized Kriging error exceeding the threshold, the consistency test fails and the point is rejected to be inserted back to the cluster C for current round of reinforcement.

3.3 Convergence Analysis

Clustering is defined to be a partition of objects into

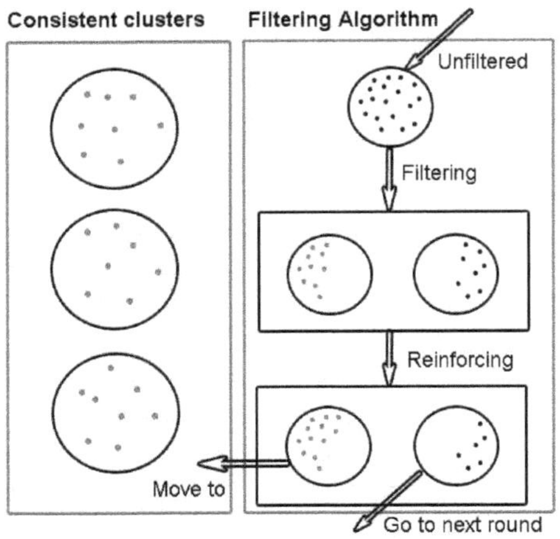

Figure 1: An illustration of filter algorithm. The left side contains clusters that are filtered and reinforced. The right side shows how a cluster is filtered and reinforced. The remaining points at the end of the process enter the next round.

groups such that objects within every group are as correlated as possible and objects between groups are as less correlated as possible. The term correlation defined for our clustering algorithm is based on Kriging interpolation accuracy: Any point within a cluster should be estimated by Kriging interpolation using other points in the same cluster with low normalized Kriging error.

Definition 3.1. *A cluster C is consistent if and only if the Kriging interpolation of any element in C using the rest of elements in C does not have a normalized Kriging error greater than the threshold.*

Definition 3.2. *A converged set of clusters $Q = \{C_1, ..., C_k\}$ satisfies: For any $2 \leq j \leq k$ and $C_i \in Q$ such that $j > i$, C_i is not consistent if any of points in C_j is inserted into C_i.*

Proposition 3.3. *The output of algorithm 1 is a converged set of clusters.*

Proof. It is possible to prove this statement by induction on the number of iterations for the loop at line 3.

Base case: At the end of first iteration, C has been filtered and reinforced. $\forall s \in C'$, because reinforcement phase is finished, it is impossible to put s back to C, which is the only element in Q.

Inductive assumption: Suppose that at the end of kth step, $\forall s \in C'$, $\nexists A \in Q$ such that A is consistent after s is inserted into it.

Inductive step: Consider the $(k+1)^{th}$ step, C is the cluster created in the last iteration. Because we cannot filter more number of elements than the number of elements in C, C' at the end of this iteration strictly contained in the input C. By inductive assumption, $s \in C'$ is inconsistent with rest of the clusters in Q. However, because the way how the algorithm reinforces the cluster C, any element in C' must not be consistent with C in the end. Otherwise they would have been put back to C. As a result, the inductive assumption is true at $(k+1)^{th}$ step. □

Despite the fact that we have shown the final result is a stable solution for maximizing cluster size subject to threshold constraint, a question remains is that how the order of data affects rate of convergence. The strategy used in our implementation is to shuffle data in advance. However, in the future, it is interesting to find out how to align data so that filtering and reinforcement are faster.

3.4 Complexity Analysis

Kriging interpolation algorithm is the core of filtering and reinforcement phases. In section 2, we have shown that Kriging interpolation algorithm can be reduced to solving a linear system of equations. In our implementation, we use lower upper permutation (LUP) approach to solve the linear system. The solution is exact, but the complexity is bounded by $O(n^3)$. However, other solvers can speed up performance. For example, in [10] and [9], there are Kriging solvers that solve the linear system reduced from Kriging interpolation algorithm efficiently. In the following analysis, we treat this computation as Kernel function and focus on analysing the complexity of Algorithm 1 at high level, namely the number of calls to the kernel functions *normalized_kriging_error* and *consistent*.

A round of filtering and reinforcement at least reduces the size of data to be filtered by 1. Otherwise the outer loop at line 3 breaks, so the outer loop is executed at most by $n-1$ times. Consider filtering phase, the worst case is that we filter 1 point per round from C to C', which costs $O(n^2)$. For reinforcement phase, it is also possible that points are reinforced back to the C 1 point per round. which costs $O(n^2)$. Therefore, the overall complexity is $O(n^3)$.

4. IMPLEMENTATION

We designed two approaches for improving computational performance: Caching and Heuristics. These two approaches do not change the result of experiments. Hence there is no accuracy loss. The entire algorithm was implemented in C language.

4.1 Caching for Kriging Interpolation

When the filtering phase is converging, only a few points in the cluster are filtered out per round. Therefore, many points in the cluster still have the same neighbours as before. Thus, there is no need to compute normalized Kriging error again during the next round of filtering for those points if we can store the result of *normalized_kriging_error* for each data point. If no neighbours have been filtered out in the previous round by checking the number of neighbours, the algorithm can simply read out the result of *normalized_kriging_error* without computing it again.

Similarly for reinforcement, when a point is put back into C, which is the cluster it has been filtered out from, the algorithm can check consistency of the cluster using cached results for points that have the same neighbours as before. In addition, if reinforcement succeeds for a point, the cached result can be used for next round of reinforcement. Otherwise the caches of points that belongs to the neighbour of the reinforced point should be poisoned for correctness.

4.2 Heuristics for Reinforcement

During reinforcement, the algorithm checks if C is consistent after adding a point from C' to C. Checking consistency requires computing normalized Kriging error for each point in the cluster, which is equivalent to a Jacobi style filtering phase. A trick can be used to report inconsistency faster. We can check the consistency of points that are more likely to violate the threshold constraint first. If they violated the constraint, there is no need to check the rest of points.

Firstly, a point that violates the threshold constraint is likely to be the point that is reinforced because it has been filtered out in the filtering phase at current iteration. We can treat this point as a special case and revise its consistency to the cluster before all other points. Secondly, we can wisely use the caching information in the previous round. For those points that already have high errors, their errors are likely to exceed threshold than points with low errors when a new point is inserted to the cluster that they belong to. This estimation is a heuristic because the cached result may not be correct due to cache poisoning. However, it provides a raw approximation for normalized Kriging errors cheaply given the cluster size is large. We can sort the order of reinforcement in descending order based on cached normalized Kriging error and check consistency of points in this order. The extra cost is $O(nlogn)$ on average for quick sort. However, it may save many $O(n^3)$ operations for solving linear systems.

5. EXPERIMENTAL RESULTS

We used two datasets in different applications to evaluate our algorithm. The first SOCR dataset is a classical dataset for testing Kriging interpolation accuracy. We will compare our filtering-based Kriging to K-means clustering-based Kriging and Kriging without clustering in terms of accuracy. The second IGRA dataset is a spatio-temporal dataset with regular time interval. We will fit a variogram model step by step and justify that our clustering-based Kriging produces lower errors.

5.1 Quality Measurements

There are two measurements for evaluating the quality of spatio-temporal clusters in the following experiments. The first measurement is NMSE value, which is defined in section 2.2. It is a ratio between sum of squared leave-one-out cross-validation error and sample variance. The second measurement is χ^2 test statistics. We compute the normalized Kriging error $\frac{(\hat{s_i}-s_i)}{\sigma}$ using leave-one out cross-validation for all points in every cluster. The sum of squares of these errors is the χ^2 test statistics. For both measurements, the smaller the values, the better the quality of clusters.

5.2 SOCR Data

SOCR dataset [1] contains 85 data points, distributed near the south border of United States. Each data point has a 2 dimensional coordinate and a physical attribute that describes the water pollution level at the location. Because the dataset contains strong anisotropy[11], it is a challenging spatial dataset for Kriging. The dataset also contains nugget effect, which indicates that the covariance of two points that are very close to each other is a constant greater than 0.

Noel[11] fitted the parameters for NE-SW direction and NW-SE direction with geometrical anisotropy model derived by Journel and Huijbregts[6]as the following.

$$\gamma(h,\phi) = 14000 + 38h^2\cos^2(\frac{\pi}{4}-\phi) + 15h^2\cos^2(\frac{\pi}{4}+\phi)$$

The output of algorithm 1 successfully divided the data points into 5 clusters. The last two clusters contain only three points, so they are treated as noise. The experimental results are shown in Table 1. The t-test p-value is a paired sample t-test for absolute Kriging errors between each of Kriging interpolation methods and Kriging interpolation without clustering at every data point. We reproduced K-means clustering-based Kriging with k=6 in [1], which is the best result they claimed, using K-means implementation in [8]. Our filter algorithm reduced NMSE more than the K-means algorithm presented in [1]. Furthermore, although K-means clustering-based Kriging reduced NMSE, there is no significant improvement for both absolute errors and normalized errors by observing t-test p-value column and χ^2 column respectively. In addition, the 1% lower tile of χ^2 distribution with degree of freedom 85 is 57.63. As a result, only our filtering-based clustering algorithm has reduced errors that pass both χ^2 test and paired sample t-test with high confidence level.

Table 1: SOCR Dataset Results

Method	cluster size	NMSE	χ^2	t-test p-value
Unclustered	1	0.24	197.75	0.5
K-means	6	0.11	161.88	0.3252
Filtering	5	0.048	22.53	$9.541E^{-9}$

5.3 IGRA Data

IGRA dataset [2] contains sensor data collected by 67 NOAA stations across United States in real time. Every data point contains two dimensional spatial coordinates for longitude and latitude, a physical attribute for atmosphere temperature, and a time stamp. The update interval for atmosphere temperature between two time stamps is 12 hours for all stations. This dataset is challenging because of anisotropy. An illustration of anisotropy with maximum Kriging range equals 30 is shown in Figure 2a. The variogram in East direction appears to be different from other directions.

Similar to [5], we consider the monthly temperature of all stations. The semi-variance plot for average of all stations in January 2014 with 4620 data points is shown in Figure 2b.

In Figure 2b, when $h > 30$, the variogram oscillates as h increases. This oscillation indicates that the atmosphere temperatures between two locations that are far from each other are weakly correlated. Similar to [4], which uses nearest neighbors for Kriging interpolation, we apply local Kriging based on spatial range. The limit for maximum distance is set to be 30. There is also a sign of nugget effect for semivariance, starting from approximately 50. Using geoR [13], we fitted an exponential variogram model illustrated in Figure 2c.

$$\gamma(h) = 54.84102 + 153.71639exp(-0.05462576\|h\|)$$

Setting threshold to be 0.6, which is the threshold that gives reasonable size and number of clusters by several trials, we apply our clustering algorithm to IGRA atmosphere data at 67 stations in January 2014. The result is compared with Kriging without clustering. At every time stamp, the number of clusters is at most 6, with the last one or two clusters containing noise filtered in the end. Therefore, the results are reasonable because the algorithm does not reduce errors by dividing stations into trivial partitions.

[1] http://wiki.stat.ucla.edu/socr/index.php/SOCR_061708_NC_Data_Aquifer

[2] http://www.ncdc.noaa.gov/data-access/weather-balloon-data

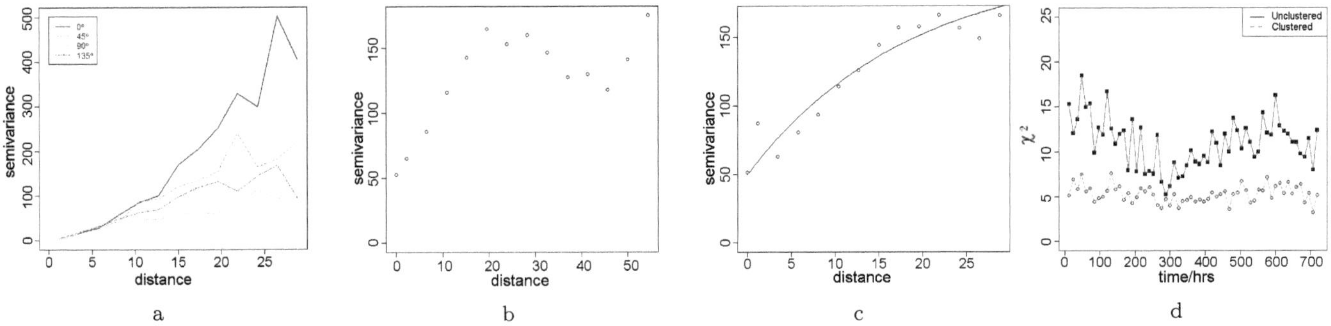

Figure 2: (a) IGRA data variogram in four directions. The vertical axis shows the averaged covariance between points at a particular distance. Different lines show the variograms in different directions. (b) January IGRA data variogram. The vertical axis shows the averaged covariance between points at a particular distance. (c) Fitted model of the variogram curve bounded by distance 30. (d) Horizontal axis represents time in hours. Vertical axis shows the χ^2 IGRA Kriging error for Kriging with clustering and Kriging without clustering. The χ^2 statistics of clustering-based Kriging is lower than Kriging without clustering across all time stamps.

In Figure 2d, the χ^2 test statistics for both filtering-based clustering and Kriging without clustering are illustrated. For any given time stamp, Kriging with clustering has χ^2 test statistics much smaller than Kriging without clustering. Moreover, the NMSEs span from 0.08 to 3.8. However, the high NMSEs are resulted from noisy clusters filtered in the end. If we do not consider clusters with size less than 5, the NMSE is on average 0.27, with some outstanding time stamps at 1 or 2 for small clusters. Kriging without clustering has NMSE spanning from 6 to 18. These results indicate that Kriging interpolation accuracy based on clusters produced by our algorithm is better than Kriging interpolation accuracy without clustering.

6. SUMMARY AND FUTURE WORK

In this paper, we propose a filtering-based clustering algorithm that improves Kriging interpolation accuracy. Theoretical proofs have shown that the final clusters have consistency and convergence characteristics. We have proposed two implementation techniques, caching and heuristics, that help to improve the performance of proposed algorithm. Furthermore, experimental results have shown that the filtering-based clustering algorithm has significantly improved Kriging interpolation accuracy compared to traditional Kriging approach and K-means clustering-based Kriging.

The future work consists of at least two directions. The first direction is to derive theorems that can bound the rate of convergence of algorithm 1 given ground truth about data. The second direction is to speed up the performance of filter algorithm by using parallel programming.

7. ACKNOWLEDGEMENTS

This work is supported in part by the following grants: NSF awards CCF-1029166, IIS-1343639, CCF-1409601; DOE awards DE-SC0007456, DE-SC0014330; AFOSR award FA9550-12-1-0458; NIST award 70NANB14H012; DARPA award N66001-15-C-4036.

8. REFERENCES

[1] Abedini, M., Nasseri, M., and Ansari, A. Cluster-based ordinary kriging of piezometric head in west texas/new mexico – testing of hypothesis. *Journal of Hydrology 351* (2008), 360–367.

[2] Brunell, R. M. An automatic procedure for fitting variograms by cressie's approximate weighted least squares criterion. http://www.smu.edu/-/media/Site/Dedman/Departments/Statistics/TechReports/TR259.ashx?la=en, 1992.

[3] Guan, Y., Sherman, M., and Calvin, J. A. Non-parametric test for spatial isotrophy using subsampling. *Journal of the American Statistical Association 99*, 467 (2004), 810–821.

[4] Guccione, P., Appice, A., Ciampi, A., and Malerba, D. Trend cluster based kriging interpolation in sensor data networks. In *Proceedings of the 2011 international conference on Modeling and Mining Ubiquitous Social Media* (2011), pp. 118–137.

[5] Holdaway, M. R. Spatial modeling and interpolation of monthly temperature using kriging. *Climate Research 6* (1996), 215–225.

[6] Journel, A., and Huijbregts, C. *Mining statistics.* American Press, New York, 1978.

[7] Krige, D. A statistical approach to some basic mine valuation problems on the witwatersrand. *Journal of the Chemical* (1952), 119–139.

[8] Liao, W. Parallel k-means data clustering. http://users.eecs.northwestern.edu~wkliao/Kmeans/, 2005.

[9] Memarsadeghi, N., Raykar, V. C., Duraiswami, R., and Mount, D. M. Efficient kriging via fast matrix-vector products. In *Aerospace Conference IEEE* (2008).

[10] Mou, S., Liu, J., and Morse, A. S. A distributed algorithm for solving a linear algebraic equation. In *transactions on automatic control IEEE* (2015).

[11] Noel, C. *Statistics for Spatial Data.* John Wiley & Sons Inc., 2015.

[12] Noel, C., and Wikle, C. K. *Statistics for Spatio-temporal Data.* John Wiley & Sons Inc., 2010.

[13] Ribeiro Jr., P. J., and Diggle, P. J. Analysis of geostatistical data. https://cran.r-project.org/web/packages/geoR/geoR.pdf, 2015.

[14] Sherman, M. *Spatial Statistics and Spatio-Temporal Data.* John Wiley & Sons Inc., 2010.

[15] Srinivasan, B. V., Duraiswami, R., and Murtugudde, R. Efficient kriging for real-time spatio-temporal interpolation. In *20th Conference on Probability and Statistics in the Atmospheric Sciences* (2010), p. 228.

Reuse-based Optimization for Pig Latin

Jesús Camacho-Rodríguez
Hortonworks
Santa Clara, CA, USA

Dario Colazzo
Université Paris-Dauphine,
PSL Research University,
CNRS, LAMSADE
Paris, France

Melanie Herschel
IPVS, University of Stuttgart
Stuttgart, Germany

Ioana Manolescu
INRIA & LIX, École
Polytechnique, CNRS
Palaiseau, France

Soudip Roy Chowdhury
Fractal Analytics
Mumbai, India

ABSTRACT

Pig Latin is a popular language which is widely used for parallel processing of massive data sets. Currently, subexpressions occurring repeatedly in Pig Latin scripts are executed as many times as they appear, and the current Pig Latin optimizer does not identify reuse opportunities.

We present a novel optimization approach aiming at identifying and reusing repeated subexpressions in Pig Latin scripts. Our optimization algorithm, named *PigReuse*, identifies subexpression merging opportunities, selects the best ones to execute based on a cost function, and reuses their results as needed in order to compute exactly the same output as the original scripts. Our experiments demonstrate the effectiveness of our approach.

Keywords

Reuse-based Optimization; Linear Programming; PigLatin

1. INTRODUCTION

The efficient processing of very large volumes of data has lately relied on massively parallel processing models, of which MapReduce is the most well known. However, the simplicity of these models leads to relatively complex programs to express even moderately complex tasks. Thus, to facilitate the specification of data processing tasks to be executed in a massively parallel fashion, several higher-level query languages have been introduced.

In this work, we consider Pig Latin [18], which has raised significant interest from the application developers as well as the research community. Pig Latin provides dataflow-style primitives for expressing complex analytical data processing tasks. Pig Latin programs (also named *scripts*) are automatically optimized and compiled into parallel processing jobs by the Apache Pig system [19], which is included in all leading Hadoop distributions e.g., HDP [10], CDH [4].

Part of this work was performed while the authors were with Université Paris-Sud and INRIA.

CIKM'16 , October 24-28, 2016, Indianapolis, IN, USA
© 2016 ACM. ISBN 978-1-4503-4073-1/16/10... $15.00
DOI: http://dx.doi.org/10.1145/2983323.2983669

In a typical batch of Pig Latin scripts, there may be many identical (or equivalent) sub-expressions, that is: script fragments applying the same processing on the same inputs, but appearing in distinct places within the same (or several) scripts. While the Pig Latin engine includes a query optimizer, it is currently not capable of recognizing such repeated subexpressions. As a consequence, they are executed as many times as they appear in the script batch, whereas there is obviously an opportunity for enhancing performance by identifying common subexpressions, executing them only once, and reusing the results in every script needing them.

Identifying and reusing common subexpressions occurring in Pig Latin scripts automatically is the target of the present work. The problem bears obvious similarities with the known multi-query optimization and workflow reuse problems; however, as we discuss in Section 6, the Pig Latin primitives lead to several novel aspects of the problem, which lead us to propose dedicated, new algorithms to solve them.

Motivating example. A Pig Latin script consists of a set of *binding expressions* and *store expressions*. Each binding expression <u>var</u> = op means that the expression op is evaluated, and the resulting bag of tuples is bound to the variable <u>var</u>, which can be used by follow-up expressions in a script.

Consider the following Pig Latin script a_1:

```
1 A = LOAD 'page_views' AS (user, time, www);
2 B = LOAD 'users' AS (name, zip);
3 R = JOIN A BY user, B BY name;
4 S = FOREACH R GENERATE user, time, zip;
5 STORE S INTO 'a1out1';
6 T = JOIN A BY user LEFT, B BY name;
7 STORE T INTO 'a1out2';
```

Line 1 loads data from a file page_views and creates a bag of tuples that is bound to variable A. Each of these tuples consists of three attributes (user,time,www). Line 2 loads data from a second file, and binds the resulting tuple bag to B. Line 3 joins the tuples of A and B based on the equality of the values bound to attributes user and name. The next line uses the Pig Latin operator FOREACH, that applies a function on every tuple of the input bag. In this case, line 4 projects the attributes user, time and zip of every tuple in R. Then the result is stored in the file a1out1. In turn, line 6 executes a left outer join over the tuples of A and B based on the equality of the values bound to the same attributes user and name, and the result is stored in a1out2.

The following script a_2 only executes a left outer join over the same inputs:

```
A = LOAD 'page_views' AS (user, time, www);
B = LOAD 'users' AS (name, zip);
R = JOIN A BY user LEFT, B BY name;
STORE R INTO 'a2out';
```

The script b that we introduce next produces the same outputs as a_1 and a_2:

```
1  A = LOAD 'page_views' AS (user, time, www);
2  B = LOAD 'users' AS (name, zip);
3  R = COGROUP A BY user, B BY name;
4  S = FOREACH R GENERATE flatten(A), flatten(B);
5  T = FOREACH S GENERATE user, time, zip;
6  STORE T INTO 'a1out1';
7  U = FOREACH R GENERATE flatten(A),
8                 flatten (isEmpty(B) ? {(null,null,null)} : B);
9  STORE U INTO 'a1out2';
10 STORE U INTO 'a2out';
```

However, *b's execution time is 45% of the combined running time of a_1 and a_2.* The reason is twofold. First, observe that the joins are rewritten into a `COGROUP`[1] operation (line 3) and `FOREACH` operations (lines 4 and 7-8). The interest of cogroup is that through some simple restructuring, one can carve out of the cogroup output various flavors of joins (natural, outer, nested, semijoin etc.) This restructuring operation differs depending on whether we want to generate the join between `A` and `B` needed for script a_1 (line 4), or the left outer join between `A` and `B` for scripts a_1 and a_2 (lines 7-8). The detailed semantics of these restructuring operations will become clear in Section 4. Thus, the first reason for the speedup of b w.r.t. a_1 and a_2 is that the `COGROUP` output is reused to generate the result for both joins. The second reason is that in b, the left outer join is computed only once, and its result is used to produce the desired output of scripts a_1 (line 9) and a_2 (line 10).

A typical feature of our optimizer is that it works on the algebraic representation of Pig Latin scripts. Thus, it is orthogonal to the Pig Latin query evaluation and execution process. This allows our approach (*i*) to benefit from the Pig Latin optimizer, and (*ii*) to apply our optimization independently of the underlying Pig Latin query compilation and execution engines.

Contributions. The technical contributions of this work are the following.

- We propose PigReuse, a multi-query optimization algorithm that merges equivalent subexpressions it identifies in Directed Acyclic Graph of algebraic representation of a batch of Pig Latin scripts. PigReuse produces then an optimal merged plan where redundant computations have been eliminated, by relying on Binary Integer Linear Programming in order to select the best plan based on the provided cost function.
- We present techniques to improve *effectiveness* of our baseline PigReuse optimization approach.
- We have implemented PigReuse as an extension module within the Apache Pig system. We present an experimental evaluation of our techniques using two different cost functions to select the best plan.

Outline. Section 2 is dedicated to preliminaries. Section 3 presents the main techniques over which PigReuse relies on, while Section 4 presents strategies to enhance it. Section 5 describes our experimental evaluation. Finally, Section 6 discusses related work, and then we conclude.

[1] `COGROUP` is a generalization of the *group-by* operation on two or more relations: for every distinct value of the grouping key occurring in any of the inputs, it outputs a tuple that includes an attribute *group* bound to the grouping key, and a bag of tuples for each input R_i such that the bag R_i includes all tuples in R_i that contain the value of the grouping key.

s_1
```
A = LOAD 'page_views' AS (user, time, www);
B = LOAD 'users' AS (name, zip);
R = JOIN A BY user, B BY name;
S = FOREACH R GENERATE user, time, zip;
STORE S INTO 's1out';
```

s_2
```
A = LOAD 'page_views' AS (user, time, www);
B = LOAD 'users' AS (name, zip);
C = LOAD 'power_users' AS (id, phone);
R = JOIN A by user, B BY name;
S = FOREACH R GENERATE user, time, zip;
T = JOIN S BY user, C by id;
STORE T INTO 's2out';
```

s_3
```
A = LOAD 'page_views' AS (user, time, www);
B = LOAD 'users' AS (name, zip);
R = FOREACH A GENERATE user, time;
S = JOIN R by user LEFT, B by name;
STORE S INTO 's3out';
```

s_4
```
A = LOAD 'page_views' AS (user, time, www);
B = LOAD 'users' AS (name, zip);
C = LOAD 'power_users' AS (id, phone);
R = JOIN A BY user, B by name, C by id;
S = FOREACH R GENERATE user, www, zip, id, phone;
STORE S INTO 's4out';
```

(a)

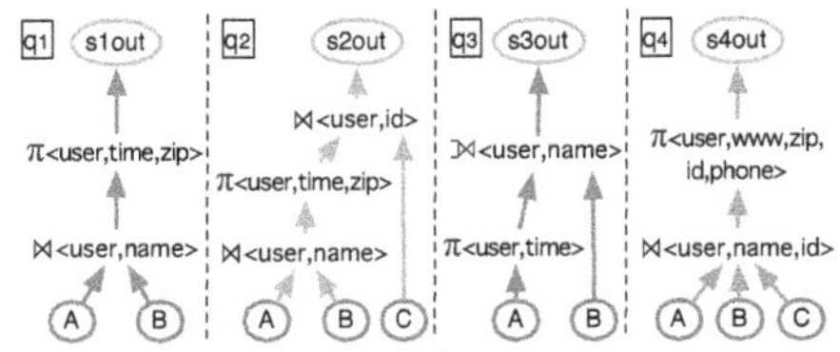

(b)

Figure 1: Sample Pig Latin scripts (a) and their corresponding algebraic DAG representation (b).

2. PRELIMINARIES

Since our approach strictly depends on rewriting Pig Latin expressions into equivalent ones, we rely on algebraic representation of Pig Latin scripts. Actually, the Pig Latin data model features complex data types (e.g., tuple, map etc.) and nested relations with duplicates (bags). Thus, we rely on the Nested Relational Algebra for Bags [8] (NRAB, for short) to represent Pig Latin scripts. We consider a subset of the NRAB algebra and extend it with other operators, such as *cogroup*. In turn, we have formalized (and implemented) the entire Pig Latin-to-NRAB translation process. Formal details of the translation are presented in [3].

We represent a set of NRAB binding expressions obtained from a Pig Latin program as a Directed Acyclic Graph (DAG); each binding is represented as a node, while edges represent the data flow among nodes.

To illustrate, Figure 1.a introduces four different Pig Latin scripts s_1-s_4; we will reuse them throughout the paper. The scripts read data from the three input relations `page_views`, `users`, and `power_users`; from now on, we denote these relations as `A`, `B`, and `C`.

After connecting the different algebraic expressions generated from s_1, we obtain the DAG query q_1 shown in Figure 1.b, also including the DAG-based representations of s_2-s_4. We denote the NRAB projection operator as π, while the selection operation is denoted as σ. In turn, inner join is denoted as $\bowtie$, while left outer join is denoted as ⟕.

3. REUSE-BASED OPTIMIZATION

Based on the previously introduced representation of Pig Latin scripts as NRAB DAGs, we now introduce our PigReuse algorithm that optimizes the query plans corresponding to a batch of scripts by reusing results of repeated subexpressions. More specifically, given a collection of NRAB DAG queries Q, PigReuse proceeds in two steps:

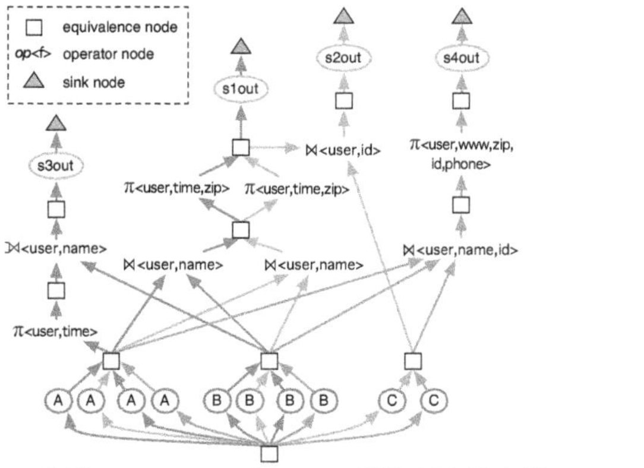

Figure 2: EG corresponding to NRAB DAGs q_1-q_4.

Step (1). *Identify and merge all the equivalent subexpressions in Q.* To this end, we use an AND-OR DAG, in which an AND-node (or operator node) corresponds to an algebraic operation in Q, while an OR-node (or equivalence node) represents a set of subexpressions that generate the same result.
Step (2). *Find the optimal plan from the AND-OR DAG.* Based on a cost model, we make a globally optimal choice of the set of operator nodes to be evaluated. Our approach is independent of the particular cost function chosen.

The final output of PigReuse is an optimized plan that contains (*i*) the operator nodes leading to *minimizing the cummulated cost* of all the queries in Q, while *producing, together, the same set of outputs* as the original Q, and (*ii*) equivalence nodes that represent *result sharing* of an operator node with other operators in Q. In the following sections, we describe each step of our reuse-based optimization algorithm in detail.

3.1 Equivalence-based merging

To join all detected equivalent expressions in Q, we build an AND-OR DAG, which we term *equivalence graph* (EG, in short); the construction is carried out in the spirit of previous optimization works [7, 21]. In the EG, an AND-node corresponds to an algebraic operation (e.g., selection, projection etc.). An OR-node o is introduced whenever a set of expressions $e_1, e_2, \ldots, e_k$ have been identified as equivalent; in the EG, the children of o are the algebraic nodes at the roots of the expressions $e_1, e_2, \ldots, e_k$. In the following, we refer to AND-nodes as *operator nodes*, and OR-nodes as *equivalence nodes*. Formally, we define an EG as follows.

DEFINITION 1. An equivalence graph (EG) is a DAG, defined by the pair $(O \cup A \cup T_o, E)$, with O, A, and T_o disjoint sets of nodes, and:

- O is the set of equivalence nodes, A is the set of operator nodes, T_o is the set of sink nodes.
- $E \subseteq (O \times A) \cup (A \times O) \cup (A \times T_o)$ is a set of directed edges such that: each node $a \in A$ has an in-degree of at least one, and an out-degree equal to one; each node $o \in O$ has an in-degree of at least one, and an out-degree of at least one; each node $t_o \in T_o$ has an in-degree of at least one. ◇

Observe that in an EG, O nodes can only point to A nodes, while A nodes can point to O or T_o nodes.

Building the equivalence graph. To build the equivalence graph, we need to identify equivalent expressions within the input NRAB query set Q. We rely on the standard notion of query equivalence, i.e., two expressions are *equivalent* iff their result is provably the same regardless of the data on which they are computed. Our equivalence search algorithm is sound but not complete; see [3] for a detailed discussion.

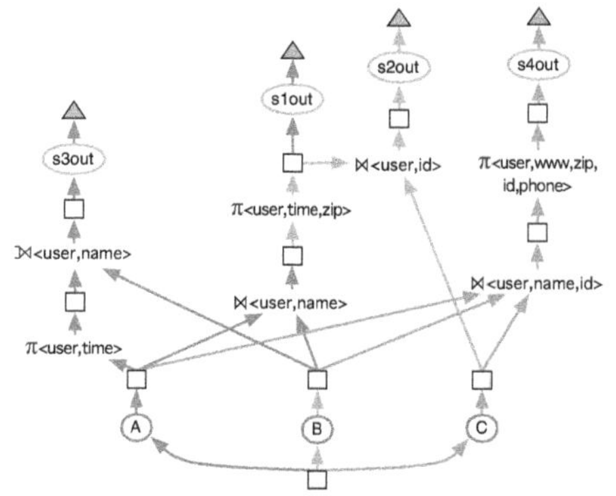

Figure 3: Possible REG for the EG in Figure 2.

Figure 2 depicts the EG corresponding to the NRAB DAGs q_1 to q_4 in Figure 1.b. In Figure 2, all the leaf nodes in the NRAB DAGs that correspond to the same *scan* operation (namely, nodes A, B, and C) feed the same equivalence node. The equi-joins coming from DAGs q_1 and q_2 on relations A and B over attributes *user* and *name* are also inputs to the same equivalence node.

3.2 Cost-based plan selection

Once an EG has been generated from a set of NRAB queries, our goal is to find the best alternative plan (having the smallest possible cost) computing the same outputs as the original scripts. We call the output plan a *result equivalence graph* (or REG, in short).

DEFINITION 2. A result equivalence graph (REG) with respect to an EG defined by $(O \cup A \cup T_O, E)$ is itself a DAG, defined by the pair $(O^* \cup A^* \cup T_O, E^*)$ such that:

- $O^* \subseteq O$, $A^* \subseteq A$, $E^* \subseteq E$.
- The set of sink nodes T_o is identical in EG and REG. Each sink node has an in-degree of exactly one.
- Each operator node in-degree in EG and REG is equal. Each equivalence node has an in-degree of exactly one, and an out-degree of at least one. ◇

In the REG, we choose exactly one among the alternatives provided by each EG equivalence nodes; the REG produces the same outputs as the original EG, as all sink nodes are preserved. Further, each REG can be straightforwardly translated into a NRAB DAG which is basically an executable Pig Latin expression. The latter expression is the one we turn to Pig for execution.

The choice of which alternative to pick for each equivalence node is guided by a *cost function*, the overall goal being to minimize the global cost of the plan. We assign a cost (weight) to each edge $n_1 \rightarrow n_2$ in the EG, representing all the processing cost (or effort) required to fully build the result of n_2 out of the result of n_1.

Figure 3 shows a possible REG produced for the EG depicted in Figure 2. This REG can be obtained by using a cost function based on counting the operator nodes in the optimized script. In Section 5, we consider different cost functions and compare them experimentally.

3.3 Cost minimization

We model the problem of finding the minimum-cost REG relying on *Binary Integer Programming* (BIP), that has

$$\text{Minimize } \mathcal{C} = \sum_{e \in E} \mathcal{C}_e x_e \quad \text{subject to:}$$

$$x_e \in \{0,1\} \qquad \forall e \in E \qquad (1)$$

$$\textstyle\sum_{e \in E_{t_o}^{in}} x_e = 1 \qquad \forall t_o \in T_o \qquad (2)$$

$$\textstyle\sum_{e \in E_a^{in}} x_e = x_{E_a^{out}} \times |E_a^{in}| \qquad \forall a \in A \qquad (3)$$

$$\textstyle\sum_{e \in E_o^{in}} x_e = \max_{e \in E_o^{out}} x_e \qquad \forall o \in O \qquad (4)$$

Figure 4: BIP reduction of the problem.

already been used to solve database optimization problems [12, 25]. Broadly speaking, a linear programming problem can be expressed as: **given** a set of linear inequality constraints over a set of variables **find** value assignments for the variables **such that** the value of an objective function depending on these variables is minimized. Many years of research and development efforts have led to the implementation of extremely efficient BIP solvers.

Generating the result equivalence graph. Given an input EG, for each node $n \in O \cup A \cup T_o$, we denote by E_n^{in} and E_n^{out} the sets of incoming and outgoing edges for n, respectively. For each edge $e \in E$, we introduce a variable x_e, denoting whether or not e is part of the REG. Since in our specific problem formulation any x_e takes values in $\{0,1\}$, our problem is formulated as a BIP problem. Further, for each edge $e \in E$, we denote by $\mathcal{C}_e$ the cost assigned to e by some cost function $\mathcal{C}$. Importantly, the model we present next is independent of the chosen cost function.

Our optimization problem is stated in BIP terms in Figure 4. Equation (1) states that each x_e variable takes values in $\{0,1\}$. (2) ensures that every output is generated exactly once. (3) states that if the (only) outgoing edge of an operator node is selected, all of its inputs are selected as well. This is required in order for the algebraic operator to be capable of correctly computing its results. Finally, (4) states that if an equivalence node is generated, it should be used at least once, which is modeled by means of a *max* expression (details about its BIP encoding can be found in [3]).

4. EFFECTIVE PIGREUSE

In the following, we present three extensions to the basic PigReuse algorithm which allow for identifying and exploiting additional factorization opportunities (formal details can be found in [3]).

Normalization of the input NRAB DAGs is carried out by *reordering* π operator nodes as follows: we push them away from *scan* operators or closer to *store* operators. We do this by visiting all operator nodes in a NRAB DAG, starting from a *scan*, and by moving each π operator up one level at a time if possible. Although pushing projections up through a plan is counterintuitive from the classical optimization point of view, *it increases the chances to find equivalent subexpressions*, as we will shortly illustrate. Further, after our reuse-based algorithm produces the optimized REG, we push the π operators back down to avoid the performance loss incurred by manipulating many attributes at all levels.

Since *cogroup* nests the input relations, reordering π with this operator requires complex rewriting. Specifically, we use the NRAB restructuring operator in the rewriting, denoted as $map\langle\varphi\rangle$, which applies a function φ to all tuples in the input. Thus, we rewrite the project π into a *map* that applies π on the corresponding bag of tuples in the input relation.

To illustrate the advantages of this phase, Figure 5.a shows the EG generated by PigReuse over the *normalized* NRAB DAGs q_1 to q_4. Comparing this EG with the one shown in Figure 2, we see that due to the swapping of the π operator corresponding to q_2, our algorithm can identify an additional common subexpression between q_2 and q_4, by determining the equivalence between the joins over A, B, and C; the corresponding equivalence node is highlighted.

Join decomposition. The semantics of Pig Latin's join operators e.g., ⋈, ⟕, ⟖, or ⟗ allow rewriting these operators into combinations of *cogroup* and *map* operators. The advantage of decomposing the joins in this way is that the result of the *cogroup* operation, which does the heavy-lifting of assembling groups of tuples from which the *map* will then build join results, can be shared across different kinds of joins. The *map* will be different in each case depending on the join type, but the most expensive component of computing the join, namely the *cogroup*, will be factorized.

Figure 5.b shows the EG generated by PigReuse after applying *normalization and decomposition* to the NRAB DAGs q_1 to q_4. One can observe that the decomposition of the ⋈ operators from q_1 and q_2, and the ⟕ operator from q_3 leads to an additional sharing opportunity, as the result of the *cogroup* on attributes *user* and *name* can be shared by the subsequent *map* operations (highlighted equivalence node).

Observe that ⋈ operators were rewritten into two operators. The first one is a *cogroup* on the attributes used by the join predicate. The second one is a *map* that does the following for each input tuple: (*i*) project each bag of tuples corresponding to the *cogroup* input relations; (*ii*) apply a NRAB bag destroy operation, denoted as δ, which unnests one level those bags; and (*iii*) perform a cartesian product $\times$ among the tuples resulting from unnesting those bags. If a bag is empty, e.g., the input relation did not contain any value for the given grouping value, the δ operator does not produce any tuple, and thus the tuples from the other bags for the given tuple are discarded. Thus, the rewriting produces the exact same result as the original operator.

For the left outer join ⟕ rewriting, *cogroup* is followed by a *map* operator that (*i*) unnests the bag associated to the left input of the *cogroup*; (*ii*) if the bag associated to the right input ($\underline{\mathsf{var}_2}$) is empty, it replaces it with a bag with a null tuple, otherwise it keeps the bag as it is; (*iii*) unnests the bag resulting from the previous operation; and (*iv*) performs a cartesian product on the tuples resulting from the δ operations in order to generate the ⟕ result.

Aggressive merge is based on the observation that it is possible to derive the results of a join or *cogroup* operator from the results of a *cogroup'* operator, as long as the former relies on *a subset* of the input relations and attributes of *cogroup'*. This means that these rewritings rely on the notion of *cogroup containment*. In particular, this entails checking the containment relationship between respective sets of input relations and attributes. Then, in order to generate the result of the original ⋈ or *cogroup* operator, we add the appropriate operator on top of *cogroup'*. Differently from previous extensions, *aggressive merge* is applied while creating the EG.

Figure 5.c depicts the new EG produced by PigReuse using aggressive merge; the new connections are highlighted. The figure shows how the results for the *cogroup*, ⋈, and ⟕ operators on A and B relations are derived from the *cogroup* operator on A, B, and C.

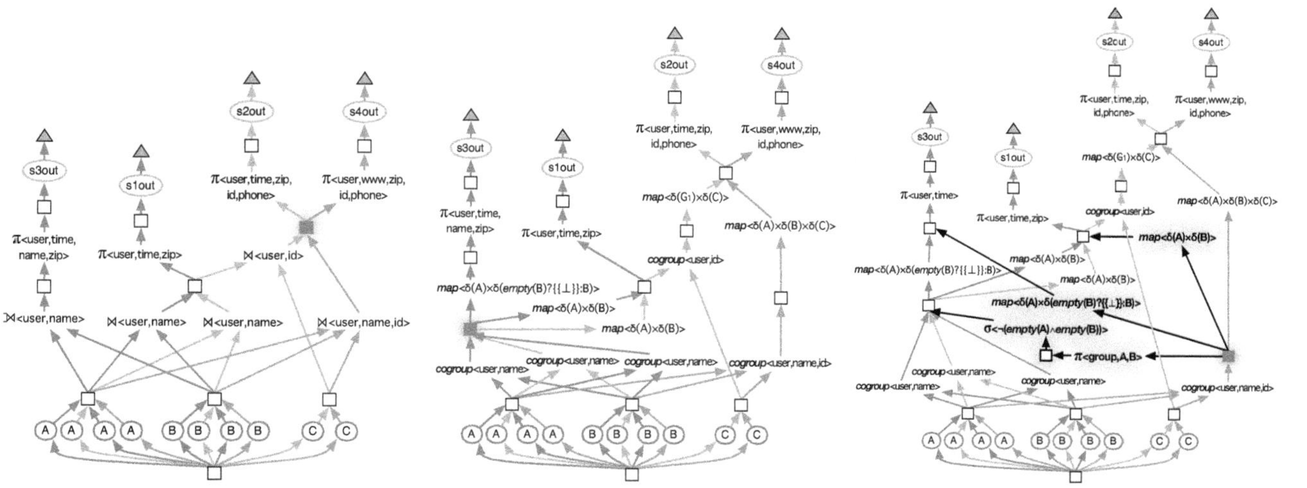

(a) (b) (c)

Figure 5: EG generated by PigReuse on (a) the *normalized* DAGs q_1-q_4, (b) the *normalized* and *decomposed* DAGs q_1-q_4, and (c) applying *aggressive merge* on the *normalized* and *decomposed* DAGs q_1-q_4.

5. EXPERIMENTAL EVALUATION

We have implemented PigReuse in Java 1.6. The source code amounts to about 8000 lines and 50 classes. It works on top of Apache Pig 0.12.1 [19], which relied on the Hadoop platform 1.1.2 [9]. The cost-based plan selection algorithm uses the Gurobi BIP solver 5.6.2 (www.gurobi.com).

Deployment. All our experiments run in a cluster of 8 nodes connected by a 1GB Ethernet. Each node has a 2.93GHz Quad Core Xeon processor and 16GB RAM, runs Linux CentOS 6.4, and has two 600GB SATA hard disks where HDFS is mounted.

Setup. For validation, we used data sets and scripts provided by the PigMix [20] PigLatin performance benchmark. We created a `page_views` input file of 250 million rows; the benchmark includes other input files, which are based on the `page_views` file, and are much smaller than this one. The total size of the data set amounted to approximately **400 GB** before the 3-way replication applied by HDFS.

We run our algorithm with two different workloads, denoted W_1 and W_2, containing 12 and 20 Pig Latin scripts, respectively. Details about these workloads are given in [3].

Cost functions and experiment metrics. Currently we have implemented two cost functions in PigReuse, focusing on reducing the number of logical operators, and the number of MapReduce jobs, respectively. Beyond these two cost functions used by our PigReuse algorithm, we also quantify the performance of executing a PigLatin workload through the following standard metrics: the **Execution time** is the wall-clock time measured from the moment when the scripts are submitted to the Pig engine, until the moment their execution is completely finished; the **Total work** is the sum of the effort made on all the nodes, i.e., the total CPU time as returned by logs of the MapReduce execution engine.

Experimental results. We now study the benefits brought by the optimizations proposed in this work. The reported results are averaged over three runs.

Figure 6 shows the effectiveness of our baseline PigReuse algorithm (PR), PigReuse with *normalization* (PR+N), PigReuse with *normalization* and *decomposition* (PR+ND), and PigReuse applying all our extensions including *aggressive merge* (PR+NDA). The figure shows relative values for the execution time and total work metrics. The cost function that minimizes the total number of operators in the EG is denoted by *minop*, while the cost function that minimizes the total number of MapReduce jobs is denoted by *minmr*.

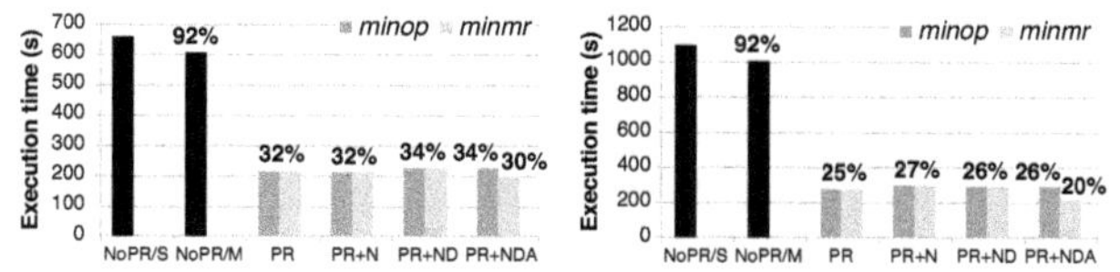

(a) Execution time

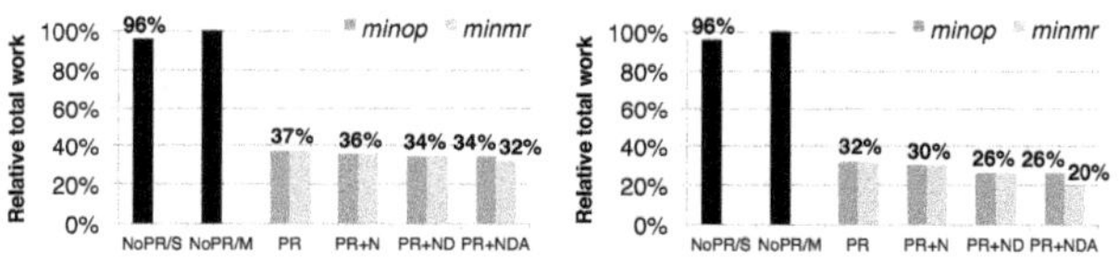

(b) Total work

Figure 6: PigReuse evaluation using workload W_1 (left) and W_2 (right).

In Figure 6.a, we notice that the total execution time is reduced by more than 70% on average among our PigReuse algorithms. Two alternative executions without PigReuse are shown. In the first one (NoPR/S), we execute *sequentially* every script in each workload using a single Pig client. In the second one (NoPR/M), we use multiple Pig clients that send *concurrently* the jobs resulting from the scripts to MapReduce. As it can be seen, the execution time for the second variant is lower as jobs resulting from multiple scripts are scheduled together, and thus the cluster usage is maximized. However, observe that the total work (Figure 6.b) increases for the multi-client alternative. The reason is that the scheduler cannot overlap significantly the map phases of multiple queries since there are too many map tasks. Thus, their execution remains quite sequential.

For the workloads we considered, our extensions reduced the total work over the baseline PigReuse algorithm (Figure 6.b). However, this was not always the case for the execution time (Figure 6.a). The reason is that some of the resulting plans requiring more effort had less sequential execution steps, thus they could be parallelized easier by the MapReduce engine. When *aggressive merge* was applied, the execution time and the total work decreased only if the *minmr* cost function was used. The reason is that if the *minop* function is used, PigReuse generates the same REG for PR+ND and PR+NDA, namely, the REG with the minimum number of operators. However, with *minmr*, PigReuse chooses a plan with more operators but that runs faster.

6. RELATED WORK

Relational multi-query optimization. Our work directly relates to multi-query optimization (MQO). The early works [11, 22] proposed exhaustive, expensive algorithms which were not integrated with existing system optimizers. The technique presented in [21] was the first to integrate MQO into a Volcano-style optimizer, while [26] presents a completely integrated MQO solution accounting also for the usage and maintenance of materialized views. The approach of [23] takes into account the physical requirements of the consumers of common sub-expressions in order to propose globally optimal execution plans. While all of these works deals with the relational algebra, our approach optimizes workloads expressed in terms of the richer NRAB algebra including nesting. Further, differently from these approaches, ours can be directly applied to alternative implementations of Pig Latin or of any other language based on NRAB.

The above considerations still hold for the approach proposed in [6], which relies on sharing *physical* operators in large SQL workloads. The approach presented in [15] also addresses both global optimization and sharing possibilities at once, but it aims at optimizing a single query, while extensions to multi-query are not trivial and not explored so far. As pointed out in [6], the global optimization plus sharing problem can not be expressed by a linear program and thus a branch-and-bound heuristic solution is proposed, whereas our sharing problem can be solved optimally through BIP.

[14] optimizes SQL workloads at runtime and tries to maximize recycling opportunities of intermediary results. Due to the complexity constraints of considering multiple rewritings for each query, [14] only considers the optimized plan for each of them, in contrast to PigReuse. This design choice comes at the price of missing sharing opportunities.

Reuse-based optimizations on MapReduce. Recent works have sought to avoid redundant processing for a batch of MapReduce jobs by sharing their scans or intermediary results. Since the semantics of the computation is not visible at the level of MapReduce programs, these works are either limited to detecting identical inputs and outputs of MapReduce tasks (without being able to reason on task equivalence) [1, 16, 24], or need some annotations to the jobs to inform about sharing opportunities [5, 13]. Our PigReuse algorithm works on the higher-level semantic representation of Pig Latin scripts. This enables more complex reuse-based optimizations, e.g., through algebraic expression rewriting.

MQO for higher-level languages based on MapReduce has been considered in [2, 17]. For Hive workloads, [2] shows by example that improving replication of frequently used data, re-ordering queries in a workload, and scheduling queries in parallel can improve performance. In turn, [17] studies how to schedule Pig Latin programs in order to best profit from the shared computations. The core of our work, instead, is concerned with identifying common sub-expression of a workload, and examining the global sharing problem, which are not addressed in [17].

7. CONCLUSIONS

We have presented a novel reuse-based optimization approach for Pig Latin scripts. Our PigReuse algorithm identifies sub-expression merging opportunities, and selects the best ones to merge based on a cost-based search process implemented with the help of a linear program solver. PigReuse allows plugging any cost function and its output is a merged script reducing its value. Our experimental results demonstrate the effectiveness of our optimization strategies.

8. REFERENCES

[1] P. Agrawal, D. Kifer, and C. Olston. Scheduling shared scans of large data files. *PVLDB*, 2008.

[2] P. Alvaro, N. Conway, and A. Krioukov. Multi-query optimization for parallel dataflow systems, 2009.

[3] J. Camacho-Rodríguez, D. Colazzo, M. Herschel, I. Manolescu, and S. R. Chowdhury. PigReuse: A Reuse-based Optimizer for Pig Latin. Technical report, 2016. https://hal.inria.fr/hal-01353891.

[4] CDH. http://www.cloudera.com/.

[5] I. Elghandour and A. Aboulnaga. ReStore: reusing results of MapReduce jobs. *PVLDB*, 2012.

[6] G. Giannikis, D. Makreshanski, G. Alonso, and D. Kossmann. Shared workload optimization. *PVLDB*, 2014.

[7] G. Graefe. The Volcano optimizer generator: Extensibility and efficient search. In *ICDE*, 1993.

[8] S. Grumbach and T. Milo. Towards Tractable Algebras for Bags. In *PODS*, 1993.

[9] Apache Hadoop. http://hadoop.apache.org/.

[10] HDP. http://www.hortonworks.com/.

[11] M. Jarke. Common subexpression isolation in multiple query optimization. In *Query Processing in Database Systems*. Springer, 1985.

[12] K. Karanasos, A. Katsifodimos, and I. Manolescu. Delta: Scalable data dissemination under capacity constraints. *PVLDB*, 2013.

[13] J. LeFevre, J. Sankaranarayanan, H. Hacigumus, J. Tatemura, N. Polyzotis, and M. J. Carey. Opportunistic Physical Design for Big Data Analytics. In *SIGMOD*, 2014.

[14] F. Nagel, P. Boncz, and S. D. Viglas. Recycling in pipelined query evaluation. In *ICDE*, 2013.

[15] T. Neumann and G. Moerkotte. Generating optimal dag-structured query evaluation plans. *Computer Science-Research and Development*, 24(3):103–117, 2009.

[16] T. Nykiel, M. Potamias, C. Mishra, G. Kollios, and N. Koudas. MRShare: sharing across multiple queries in MapReduce. *PVLDB*, 2010.

[17] C. Olston, B. Reed, A. Silberstein, and U. Srivastava. Automatic optimization of parallel dataflow programs. In *USENIX*, 2008.

[18] C. Olston, B. Reed, U. Srivastava, R. Kumar, and A. Tomkins. Pig latin: a not-so-foreign language for data processing. In *SIGMOD*, 2008.

[19] Apache Pig. http://pig.apache.org/.

[20] http://cwiki.apache.org/confluence/display/PIG/PigMix.

[21] P. Roy, S. Seshadri, S. Sudarshan, and S. Bhobe. Efficient and Extensible Algorithms for Multi Query Optimization. In *SIGMOD*, 2000.

[22] T. K. Sellis. Multiple-query optimization. *ACM Trans. Database Syst.*, 13(1):23–52, Mar. 1988.

[23] Y. N. Silva, P.-A. Larson, and J. Zhou. Exploiting Common Subexpressions for Cloud Query Processing. In *ICDE*, 2012.

[24] G. Wang and C.-Y. Chan. Multi-Query Optimization in MapReduce Framework. *PVLDB*, 2013.

[25] J. Yang. Algorithms for materialized view design in data warehousing environment. *PVLDB*, 1997.

[26] J. Zhou, P.-A. Larson, J.-C. Freytag, and W. Lehner. Efficient exploitation of similar subexpressions for query processing. In *SIGMOD*, 2007.

Discriminative View Learning for Single View Co-Training

Joseph St.Amand, Jun Huan
Electrical Engineering & Computer Science
University of Kansas
1450 Jayhawk Blvd
Lawrence, KS 66045
{j817s517, jhuan}@ittc.ku.edu

ABSTRACT

Co-training, a popular semi-supervised learning technique, is severely limited as it applicable only to datasets which have a natural division of the feature space into two or more distinct views. In this paper, we investigate techniques to apply co-training to single-view data sets. We develop a view learning technique which takes a single view dataset and learns multiple views. These learned views balance the available discriminatory information in the dataset, while still meeting Blum's co-training criteria. In addition, we constrain the views such that pairs of learned view embedding functions exhibit sparsity in a complementary pattern, which aid in increasing diversity. Finally, we demonstrate the efficacy of our approach via experimental means on several real-world datasets from different domains.

Keywords

Semi-supervised Learning, Single-view Co-training, Discriminative Features, Multi-View Learning

1. INTRODUCTION

Co-training, a multi-view learning technique in which classifiers leverage complementary information between views, has been applied across many domains with great success [5, 7, 9, 10, 16, 17, 18]. An exciting recent direction is single-view co-training, where multiple view are generated from a single-view dataset in order to apply co-training style algorithms, often times increasing classification performance beyond that of single-view techniques [5, 6, 23, 26].

A critical limitation of state of the art co-training methods is that they focus almost exclusively on partitioning the feature space [5, 6, 26]. We hypothesize that considering more complex transformations of the feature space could produce views which are more compatible with the underlying classification algorithm. In applications where the best feature representation is not known, methods which can learn more complex transformations of the data have achieved state of the art performance on many problems [12, 14, 15, 21].

CIKM'16 , October 24-28, 2016, Indianapolis, IN, USA

DOI: http://dx.doi.org/10.1145/2983323.2983671

In this paper, we propose a view generation technique which uses discriminative power as a proxy for view sufficiency. We hypothesize that evenly embedding the available discriminative information between the views could satisfy the view sufficiency assumption of [3], which is not often formalized in the literature. Additionally, we satisfy the independence of views assumption by constraining our view embedding functions to exhibit complementary sparsity, which fosters diversity between views and could overcome any view insufficiency [28].

Our contributions in this paper are as follows; 1) We develop a new view generation technique for single-view co-training, in which the data has no naturally occurring partition of the feature space. 2) We prove that pairs of embeddings that are learned together are independent. This fosters diversity between views, an exciting property which could allow co-training to succeed, even in the presence of view insufficiency. 3) To demonstrate the efficacy and utility of our method, we provide an empirical evaluation with current state of the art method on several real-world datasets from different domains.

2. RELATED WORK

A variety of algorithms have been proposed to extend co-training to single-view datasets[5, 6, 23, 26]. A common general strategy is to create artificial views of the data which meet the co-training assumptions, while integrating some other assumptions about the data. The original co-training assumptions proposed by [3] are:

1. *Conditional Independence of Views* – The views of the data must be independent when conditioned on the label value.
2. *View Sufficiency* – Each view must be sufficient for learning a classifier with relatively low error.

Some consider the view independence assumption to be prohibitively strong. As an alternative, [2] made a much weaker "ϵ-expansion" assumption, and proved that given an appropriately strong PAC-learning algorithm on each view, then ϵ-expandability is sufficient for co-training to succeed. Intuitively, co-training can succeed if one of the classifiers is never "confident but wrong". An analysis by [28] places more emphasis on the view sufficiency assumption, which proves that if the diversity between the two views is large enough, co-training could output a near-good hypothesis, even in the presence of insufficient views.

The goal of [5] is to predict if an email is spam when given the body and subject of the email. Interestingly enough, they found that randomly splitting the feature space can produce more accurate predictions than training on the naturally occurring views. One possible explanation is that random splitting could result in more diverse features, demonstrating the results of [28] in action.

[6] introduces an algorithm called Pseudo Multi-View Co-Training(PMC) which learns a partition of the feature space. PMC improves on random feature splitting by introducing the $\epsilon-$ expandability property of [2] as a constraint. They apply their method on a specially prepared version of the USPS handwritten digits dataset [8], where each sample consists of two digits. In their implementation, they meet the $\epsilon-$ expandability condition, but only on average. Despite this, they demonstrate that their method is capable of learning a division of the feature space which separates one digit from another.

The Two-view Subspace Feature Splitting(TSFS) algorithm of [29] proposes a two-step approach, they first learn an orthogonal subspace, and then perform multi-view feature selection. To accomplish this, TSFS learns an orthogonal subspace via Principal Component Analysis(PCA) [13] on the covariance matrix, and then partitions the subspace between the views. However, there is no reason to believe that the PCA directions are specific to any class. Furthermore, PCA is sensitive to pre-processing and normalization steps, which could lead to disastrously different results. Finally, in practice the algorithm shares features, violating the conditional independence of views assumption.

On another note, we would like to highlight the work of [14], which proposed to use higher-order tensors to learn discriminative directions for use as feature detectors. These have several nice properties, including independence and invariance to scaling and linear transformations. We take inspiration from the discriminative formulation of [14]. Note that they do not address the co-training problem and our contributions differ significantly, this will be made clear in the follow section.

3. METHOD

We first introduce our notation and scenario. In the single-view semi-supervised learning scenario we are given a labeled data matrix $X \in \mathbb{R}^{d \times p}$ which consists of d samples, each with p features. Each sample $\vec{x}$ is associated with a label vector $\vec{y} \in \{0,1\}$. In addition, we also have a set of n unlabeled samples given as $U \in \mathbb{R}^{n \times p}$, where $n >> d$. In our method development, we may partition samples conditioned on a label value (e.g. $X^1 = \{\vec{x}_i | y_i = 1\}$).

Our overall goal is to learn matrix-valued view embedding functions A, B with which to generate views of both the labeled and unlabeled datasets(i.e. $X^A = XA$, $X^B = XB$, $U^A = UA$, $U^B = UB$). At this point we have arrived at the typical co-training scenario and may train classifiers in the normal fashion.

Taking inspiration from [14], we begin by partitioning the labeled samples into the two matrices X^1, X^0 to form the class conditional second moment matrices $C^0 = \frac{1}{N} X^0 \cdot (X^0)^T$ and $C^1 = \frac{1}{N} X^1 \cdot (X^1)^T$. Maximizing the ratio in equation 1 is a generalized eigenvalue problem, the solution of which is the eigenvector a, associated with the eigenvalue λ. We can expect that the 2-norm of a data sample projected along a to be close to either λ or 1 on average, depending on the value of its assigned label.

$$\frac{\mathbb{E}[(\vec{a}^T \vec{x_i})^2 | y_i = 1]}{\mathbb{E}[(\vec{a}^T \vec{x_i})^2 | y_i = 0]} = \frac{\vec{a}^T\ C^1 \vec{a}}{\vec{a}^T\ C^0 \vec{a}} \tag{1}$$

We now diverge from [14] and extend this concept to multiple views. To ensure each view is composed from equally discriminative directions, we minimize the ratio in equation 2 with the maximum value.

$$\min_{\vec{a},\vec{b}} \max \left\{ -\frac{\vec{a}^T\ C^1 \vec{a}}{\vec{a}^T\ C^0 \vec{a}}, -\frac{\vec{b}^T\ C^1 \vec{b}}{\vec{b}^T\ C^0 \vec{b}} \right\} \tag{2}$$

To address the view independence assumption, we introduce a penalty to enforce that both directions $(\vec{a}, \vec{b})$ have a *complementary sparsity* pattern (i.e. $a_i = 0 \implies b_i \neq 0$ and $b_i = 0 \implies a_i \neq 0$). This penalty ensures that each pair of features is uncorrelated, with the intention to increase the diversity between views.

To ensure the problem is bounded, we further constrain the vectors $\vec{a}$ and $\vec{b}$ to unit length. For smoothness of the objective function, we replace the *max* function with the *softmax* function, defined as $softmax(x,y) = ln(e^{-x} + e^{-y})$. This results in the complete non-linearly constrained optimization problem of equation 3.

$$\begin{aligned} \min_{\vec{a},\vec{b}} \quad & softmax \left[-\frac{\vec{a}^T\ C_1 \vec{a}}{\vec{a}^T\ C_0 \vec{a}}, -\frac{\vec{b}^T\ C_1 \vec{b}}{\vec{b}^T\ C_0 \vec{b}} \right] \\ \text{subject to} \quad & \sum_{i=0}^{p} \vec{a}_i^2 \vec{b}_i^2 = 0 \\ & \vec{a}^T \vec{a} = 1 \\ & \vec{b}^T \vec{b} = 1 \end{aligned} \tag{3}$$

3.1 Optimization

The optimization objective (eq. 3) is subject to some non-linear constraints, making global optimization difficult. Before beginning, we simplify the problem by making the substitution $C = (C^0)^{-1}\ C^1$. The problem is then to minimize the simpler cost function $softmax(-\vec{a}^T\ C\vec{a}, -\vec{b}^T\ C\vec{b})$ under the same constraints. We optimize this using a non-convex Alternating Direction Method of Multipliers(ADMM) [4, 25], the implementation of which is shown as Algorithm 1. Here, the function Π is a projection onto the constraints defined in equation 3. We terminate the optimization process when a solution $\vec{x}$ is found which meets primal feasibility, or if the procedure exceeds a predetermined maximum number of iterations. Due to the non-convexity of the constraints, the algorithm is not guaranteed to converge on a global solution. To alleviate this, we utilize random restarts and take the solution with the lowest objective function value.

3.2 Algorithm

In our survey of the co-training literature, we found that there are several different styles for implementing the co-training algorithm. In the spirit of reproducible research, we provide the pseudo-code for our specific implementation of co-training as Algorithm 2.

We begin by sorting the labeled samples into two sets by their respective label values, these are in turn used to estimate the class-conditional second moment matrices C^0 and C^1. In step 1 of Algorithm 3 we invert C^0. If the

Algorithm 1 ADMM to solve equation 3

Input: $\vec{a}, \vec{b}$
Input: C^1, C^0 ▷ Class-Conditional Matrices
Let $\vec{x} = [\vec{a}; \vec{b}]$ ▷ Stacked to form a vector
$C = (C^0)^{-1}\, C^1$ ▷ Ensure C^0 is full rank
while iter < max_iter AND primal feasibility > 1e-05 **do**
    $\vec{x}^{k+1} = \underset{\vec{x}}{\text{argmin}} \left(f(\vec{x}) + (\rho/2)\|\vec{x} - \vec{z}^k + \vec{u}^k\|_2^2 \right)$
    $\vec{z}^{k+1} = \Pi(\vec{x}^{k+1} + \vec{u}^k)$ ▷ Nonlinear projection onto the feasible set
    $\vec{u}^{k+1} = \vec{u}^k + \vec{x}^{k+1} - \vec{z}^{k+1}$
end while
Output: $[\vec{a}; \vec{b}]$ ▷ from $[\vec{a}; \vec{b}] = \vec{x}$

number of labeled samples used to form C^0 is less than the feature dimensionality of the matrix, then C^0 will be rank-deficient. To alleviate this, we use a common technique [24] of adding the identity matrix multiplied by a small number to C^0 (i.e $C^0 = C^0 + \alpha\, I$). In our implementation we arbitrarily choose $\alpha = 1e-4$.

The matrix valued view-embedding functions A and B are iteratively constructed. At each iteration, we use algorithm 1 extract a pair of embedding functions $\vec{a}, \vec{b}$ and append them to the view embedding matrices A, B. After each round we use a deflation technique to remove the influence of $\vec{a}, \vec{b}$ from C.

Recall that $C = (C^0)^{-1}\, C^1$ and is symmetric positive semi-definite. Note that $\vec{a}$ and $\vec{b}$ are not true eigenvectors of C, thus Hotelling deflation may not preserve the positive semi-definiteness of C. For this reason, we elect to use Schur complement deflation [20]

$$A_t = A_{t-1} - \frac{A_{t-1}\vec{x}_t\vec{x}^T\, A_{t-1}}{\vec{x}^T\, A_{t-1}\vec{x}}$$

which preserves the positive semi-definiteness of C.

This leads to algorithm 3, a straightforward method with which to form a set of view embedding matrices A and B, these transform the single-view data to two discriminative views. To capture additional information we take each feature embedding $\vec{a}$ and add an additional embedding $\vec{a}^2$. Note that simultaneously learned embedding functions $(\vec{a_i}^2, \vec{b_i}^2)$ are still independent due to their complementary sparsity patterns. The complete pseudo-code for our implementations are shown in Algorithms 1, 2 & 3.

3.3 Diversity of View Embeddings

The feature embeddings $\vec{a}$ and $\vec{b}$ possess several attractive properties which make them desirable for use as view generation functions.

Property 3.1. *Embedding functions $\vec{a_i}, \vec{b_i}$ extracted from C_i are orthogonal.*

Proof. By design, $\vec{a_i}$ and $\vec{b_i}$ are constrained in equation 3 such that $\vec{a_i}^T\vec{b_i} = 0$. □

Property 3.2. *Let $\vec{x}$ be a vector of i.i.d standard normal random variables, then the two embeddings $(\vec{a_i}^T\vec{x}), (\vec{b_i}^T\vec{x})$ learned from C_i are uncorrelated.*

Algorithm 2 Co-training Implementation

Input: X^A, X^B ▷ Labeled View Samples
Input: U^A, U^B ▷ Unlabeled View Samples
Input: m ▷ max. # co-training iterations
Input: k ▷ # labels to exchange
Input: r ▷ # labels to sample
Input:
iter ← 0
while iter < max iter **do**
    Train classifier h_A on X^A
    Train classifier h_B on X^B
    Make prediction on unlabeled set.
    $\{y_A\} \leftarrow h_A(U^A)$
    $\{y_B\} \leftarrow h_B(U^B)$
    Sample & sort predictions.
    $\{p_A\} \leftarrow r$ pos. labeled samples from $\{y_A\}$
    $\{n_A\} \leftarrow r$ neg. labeled samples from $\{y_A\}$
    $\{p_B\} \leftarrow r$ pos. labeled samples from $\{y_B\}$
    $\{n_B\} \leftarrow r$ neg. labeled samples from $\{y_B\}$
    $\{p_A\}$ retains top k, sorted by confidence.
    $\{n_A\}$ retains top k, sorted by confidence.
    $\{p_B\}$ retains top k, sorted by confidence.
    $\{n_B\}$ retains top k, sorted by confidence.
    $\{s_A\} \leftarrow \{p_A\} \cup \{n_A\}$
    $\{s_B\} \leftarrow \{p_B\} \cup \{n_B\}$
    Exchange labeled samples.
    $X^A \leftarrow X^A \cup \{s_B\}$
    $X^B \leftarrow X^B \cup \{s_A\}$
    iter ← iter + 1
end while
Train final classifier.
$X \leftarrow [X^A;\, X^B]$
Train classifier h_{final} on X
Output: h_{final}

Proof. Let $\vec{x}$ be a vector of i.i.d standard normal random variables.
Let $\vec{a_i}, \vec{b_i}$ be embedding functions learned from C_i.

$$\begin{aligned}
\mathbb{E}[\vec{a_i}^T\vec{x} \cdot \vec{b_i}^T\vec{x}] &= \mathbb{E}[\vec{a_i}^T\vec{x} \cdot \vec{x}^T\vec{b_i}] \\
&= \vec{a_i}^T\mathbb{E}[\vec{x}\vec{x}^T]\vec{b_i} \\
&= \vec{a_i}^T\text{Cov}(\vec{x})\vec{b_i} \\
&= \vec{a_i}^T\, I\vec{b_i} \\
&= \vec{a_i}^T\vec{b_i} = 0
\end{aligned}$$

□

Property 3.2 is particularly attractive and demonstrates that simultaneously found feature embeddings are uncorrelated, which could increase the diversity between views. The work of [28] proves that if a view is insufficient for learning, diversity between views could be enough to overcome the insufficiency, making it an extremely desirable property.

4. EXPERIMENTS

In our experiments we compare our algorithm with the following methods on three real-world datasets.

1. **SVL** – Single-view logistic regression for classification,

Algorithm 3 Discriminative View Learning

Input: C^1, C^0 ▷ Class-Conditional Matrices
Input: X, U ▷ Labeled & Unlabeled Data
Input: k ▷ # Feature Detectors to Extract
$C = (C^0)^{-1}\, C^1$
$A \leftarrow [\,]$ ▷ Empty Matrix
$B \leftarrow [\,]$ ▷ Empty Matrix
for $i = 1, ..., k$ **do**
  Solve Eq. 3 for $\vec{a}, \vec{b}$ via ADMM
  $A \leftarrow [A\vec{a}]$
  $B \leftarrow [B\vec{b}]$
  $C_i \leftarrow C_i - \frac{C_i \vec{a}\vec{a}^T\, C_i}{\vec{a}^T\, C_i \vec{a}}$ ▷ Schur complement deflation
  $C_{i+1} \leftarrow C_i - \frac{C_i \vec{b}\vec{b}^T\, Ci}{\vec{b}^T\, C_i \vec{b}}$ ▷ Schur complement deflation
end for
$X^A \leftarrow X[A, A^2]$
$X^B \leftarrow X[B, B^2]$
$U^A \leftarrow U[A, A^2]$
$U^B \leftarrow U[B, B^2]$
Output: X^A, X^B ▷ Labeled Views A & B
Output: U^A, U^B ▷ Unlabeled Views A & B

to be used as a baseline in measuring the performance of the co-training based methods.

2. **RFS** – Random Feature Splitting, a co-training approach where the feature space is randomly partitioned into 2-views. We use this method as a second baseline for co-training.

3. **TSFS** – The Two-view Subspace Feature Splitting algorithm of [29], which operates by projecting the data onto a learned subspace and then greedily selects the best projection directions which are used as a basis for the learned views.

4. **PMC** – The Pseudo Multi-View Co-Training of [6], which automatically learns a partition of the feature space to form two views.

5. **DVL** – The Discriminate View Learning method proposed in this paper.

Due to differences in function and implementation, executing a fair and balanced comparison is challenging. We implement the SVL, RFS, TSFS and DVL algorithms using the Matlab[22] programming language. We obtained an implementation(also in Matlab) of the PMC algorithm from the author's website[1]. All algorithms use logistic regression as the base classifier and tune for the best performing $\lambda \in \{1e-4, 1e-3, 1e-2, 1e-1, 1e1, 1e2, 1e3\}$. In our experiments the widely used F1-score is our metric of choice, as obtaining a high F1-score requires both high precision and recall. All reported F1-scores are the result of using standard 5-fold cross validation.

4.1 Mice Protein Expression

In our first experiment, we use a dataset from a study on mice exposed to context fear conditioning, a task used to assess associative learning in the study of Down syndrome [1, 11]. The dataset contains the levels of 77 proteins measured in the cerebral cortex of mice. Mice are labeled as belonging to one of eight different categories, depending on whether the mouse was part of the control or trisomy group, injected with saline or Memantine, and whether it underwent behavioral conditioning. We remove this 8-way label and instead adopt the goal to predict the binary valued "Behavior" label, which indicates whether the mouse underwent context fear conditioning.

We preprocess the data by removing the transforming the nominally valued binary features to have the numerical values $\{-1, 1\}$. We remove the mouse IDs as they are unique to the sample and normalize all samples to have unit length. We randomly select 525 of each positive and negative samples to form a balanced dataset. During each round of cross-validation, we retain the labels of 20 positive and negative samples, the rest are discarded. During each co-training iteration we move 20 samples from the unlabeled training set to the labeled training set, we terminate all algorithm after 20 rounds of co-training. The results of this experiment are shown in Figure 1.

[1]http://www.cse.wustl.edu/ mchen/code/pmc.tar

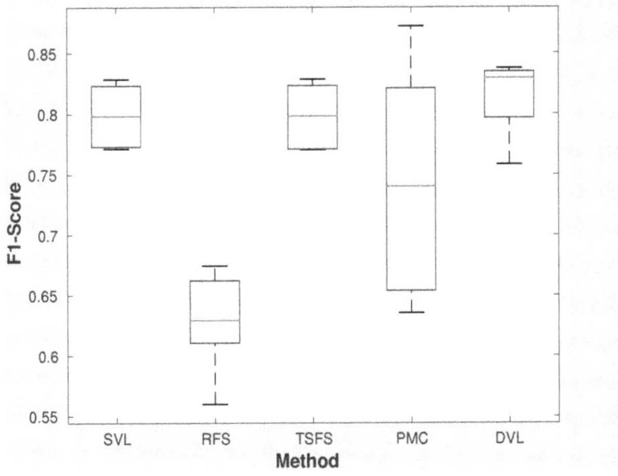

Figure 1: F1-scores resulting from 5 folds of cross validation on the Mice Protein Expression data set.

4.2 Ionosphere

We run our second experiment using the Ionosphere [27] dataset, where the goal is to classify radar samples from a phased array of 16 high-frequency antennas. Each sample consists of the recorded data from a pulse radar return. The positive returns are those which reflect off electrons in the atmosphere, while the negative returns pass mostly through the atmosphere and escape out to space. We obtained this dataset from the UCI data repository[19][2]. We take 125 of both positive and negative samples to form a balanced set, then preprocess the data by normalizing each samples to unit length. We run 10 iterations of co-training, during each iteration we move 20 samples to the unlabeled set. We display the results of this experiment in Figure 2.

4.3 Gamma Particle Detection

We apply our developed algorithm to the Major Atmospheric Gamma Imaging Cherenkov (MAGIC) Telescope Project

[2]https://archive.ics.uci.edu/ml/datasets/Ionosphere

Table 1: **Compiled results from the three run experiments are the mean of the F1 Score from 5 folds of cross validation. Results marked with $*$ are significant at the 5% level as determined by a two sided t-test.**

	Method				
Dataset	**SVL**	**RFS**	**TSFS**	**PMC**	**DVL**
Mice	0.7987	0.6298	0.7981	0.7423	**0.8238**
Ionosphere	0.7931	0.7152	0.7866	0.7007	**0.8400****
MAGIC	0.7415	0.6675	0.7415	0.0164	**0.7497****

dataset[3]. This data was generated by the MAGIC Telescope Project for the registration of high energy gamma particles using imaging techniques in the ground-based Cherenkov gamma telescope. The binary classification task is to predict if a detected particle group originates from a gamma ray.

We take 6,000 samples each with both positive and negative labels, for a total of 12,000 samples. We remove all the labels, save for 20 of the positive and 20 of the negative. During each co-training iteration we allow up to 40 samples to be moved from the unlabeled to the labeled set. We limit the amount of co-training iterations to 125. The results of which are shown in Figure 3.

4.4 Results

We found that the DVL method performed(as measured by F1-Score) similar to or better than the state-of-the-art methods. We calculated the average performance for each method for all experiments and compiled this information in Table 1. For each experiment, we used a two-sided t-test to compare the two highest average results. In the ionosphere and gamma particle detection experiments, the DVL method yielded the best performance on the 5% significance level.

[3]Obtained from https://archive.ics.uci.edu/ml/machine-learning-databases/magic/

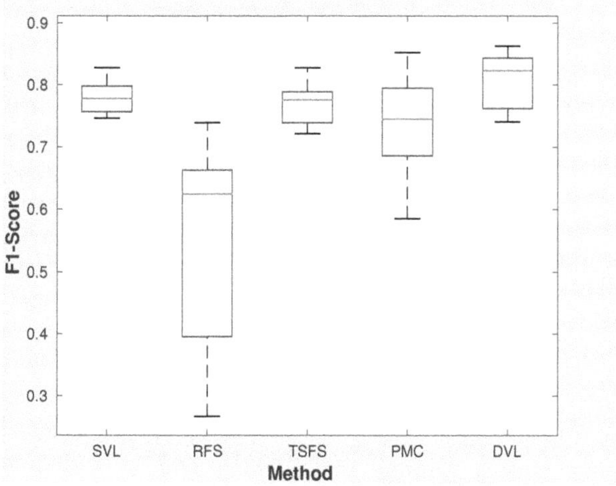

Figure 2: F1-scores resulting from 5 folds of cross validation on the Ionosphere data set. DVL method statistically significant(via 2-sided t-test) with $p =$ 0.041.

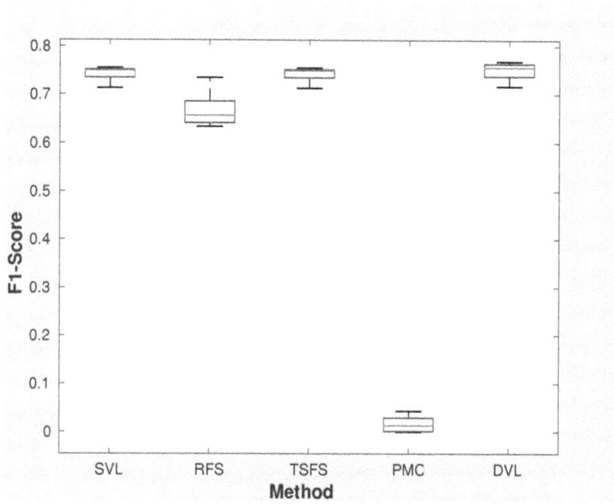

Figure 3: F1-Scores of experiments on the MAGIC Gamma dataset. All classification results displayed result from the algorithms optimal logistic regression parameter λ. DVL method statistically significant(via 2-sided t-test) with $p = 0.048$.

4.5 Discussion

In DVL, the view embedding functions depend on estimating the class conditional covariance matrices to a reasonably high accuracy. The performance of our method could suffer if the dimension of the feature space is too high, and the number of labels present is low. A solution that may alleviate this could be to update the view embedding functions U and V as part of the co-training procedure.

A question yet to be answered is how to extend the presented work to handle the multi-class scenario? An obvious approach could be to calculate a set of class conditional covariance matrices for each label value in either a one-vs-all or one-vs-one fashion. Unfortunately, this will cause the number of views to be on the order of $\frac{K!}{2(N-2)!}$, where K is the number of classes.

5. CONCLUSION

In this paper we proposed a novel method that when presented with a single-view dataset learns two view embedding functions with approximately equal amounts of discriminative features. We provided a simple proof that our view embeddings contain diversity with respect to pairs of simultaneously found feature embeddings, which could alleviate learning in the presence of insufficient views. Our experimental results demonstrate the performance of our algorithm for the semi-supervised binary classification scenario on several real-world dataset from different domains.

6. REFERENCES

[1] M. M. Ahmed, A. R. Dhanasekaran, A. Block, S. Tong, A. C. S. Costa, M. Stasko, and K. J. Gardiner. Protein dynamics associated with failed and rescued learning in the ts65dn mouse model of down syndrome. *PLoS ONE*, 10(3):e0119491, 03 2015.

[2] M. Balcan, A. Blum, and K. Yang. Co-training and expansion: Towards bridging theory and practice. In *Advances in Neural Information Processing Systems 17 [Neural Information Processing Systems, NIPS*

2004, December 13-18, 2004, Vancouver, British Columbia, Canada], pages 89–96, 2004.

[3] A. Blum and T. Mitchell. Combining labeled and unlabeled data with co-training. In *Proceedings of the Eleventh Annual Conference on Computational Learning Theory*, COLT' 98, pages 92–100, New York, NY, USA, 1998. ACM.

[4] S. Boyd, N. Parikh, E. Chu, B. Peleato, and J. Eckstein. Distributed optimization and statistical learning via the alternating direction method of multipliers. *Found. Trends Mach. Learn.*, 3(1):1–122, Jan. 2011.

[5] J. Chan, I. Koprinska, and J. Poon. Co-training with a single natural feature set applied to email classification. In *Proceedings of the 2004 IEEE/WIC/ACM International Conference on Web Intelligence*, WI '04, pages 586–589, Washington, DC, USA, 2004. IEEE Computer Society.

[6] M. Chen, K. Weinberger, and Y. Chen. Automatic feature decomposition for single view co-training. In L. Getoor and T. Scheffer, editors, *Proceedings of the 28th International Conference on Machine Learning (ICML-11)*, ICML '11, pages 953–960, New York, NY, USA, June 2011. ACM.

[7] M. Collins and Y. Singer. Unsupervised models for named entity classification. In *In Proceedings of the Joint SIGDAT Conference on Empirical Methods in Natural Language Processing and Very Large Corpora*, pages 100–110, 1999.

[8] Y. L. Cun, B. Boser, J. S. Denker, R. E. Howard, W. Habbard, L. D. Jackel, and D. Henderson. Advances in neural information processing systems 2. chapter Handwritten Digit Recognition with a Back-propagation Network, pages 396–404. Morgan Kaufmann Publishers Inc., San Francisco, CA, USA, 1990.

[9] R. Ghani. Combining labeled and unlabeled data for text classification with a large number of categories. In *In Proceedings of the IEEE International Conference on Data Mining*, 2001.

[10] R. Ghani. Combining labeled and unlabeled data for multiclass text categorization. In *In Proceedings of the International Conference on Machine Learning*, pages 187–194, 2002.

[11] C. Higuera, K. J. Gardiner, and K. J. Cios. Self-organizing feature maps identify proteins critical to learning in a mouse model of down syndrome. *PLoS ONE*, 10(6):e0129126, 06 2015.

[12] G. E. Hinton, N. Srivastava, A. Krizhevsky, I. Sutskever, and R. Salakhutdinov. Improving neural networks by preventing co-adaptation of feature detectors. *CoRR*, abs/1207.0580, 2012.

[13] I. Jolliffe. *Principal Component Analysis*. Springer Verlag, 1986.

[14] N. Karampatziakis and P. Mineiro. Discriminative features via generalized eigenvectors. In *Proceedings of the 31th International Conference on Machine Learning, ICML 2014, Beijing, China, 21-26 June 2014*, pages 494–502, 2014.

[15] A. Krizhevsky, I. Sutskever, and G. E. Hinton. Imagenet classification with deep convolutional neural networks. In F. Pereira, C. Burges, L. Bottou, and K. Weinberger, editors, *Advances in Neural Information Processing Systems 25*, pages 1097–1105. Curran Associates, Inc., 2012.

[16] A. Kumar and H. D. III. A co-training approach for multi-view spectral clustering. In *Proceedings of the 28th International Conference on Machine Learning, ICML 2011, Bellevue, Washington, USA, June 28 - July 2, 2011*, pages 393–400, 2011.

[17] A. Levin. Unsupervised improvement of visual detectors using co-training. In *In ICCV*, pages 626–633, 2003.

[18] Y. Li, W. Liu, and Y. Wang. Laplacian regularized co-training. In *Signal Processing (ICSP), 2014 12th International Conference on*, pages 1408–1412, Oct 2014.

[19] M. Lichman. UCI machine learning repository, 2013.

[20] L. W. Mackey. Deflation methods for sparse pca. In D. Koller, D. Schuurmans, Y. Bengio, and L. Bottou, editors, *NIPS*, pages 1017–1024. Curran Associates, Inc., 2008.

[21] J. Mairal, F. R. Bach, J. Ponce, G. Sapiro, and A. Zisserman. Supervised dictionary learning. In *Advances in Neural Information Processing Systems 21, Proceedings of the Twenty-Second Annual Conference on Neural Information Processing Systems, Vancouver, British Columbia, Canada, December 8-11, 2008*, pages 1033–1040, 2008.

[22] MATLAB. *version 8.5.1 (R2015a)*. The MathWorks Inc., Natick, Massachusetts, 2015.

[23] K. Nigam and R. Ghani. Analyzing the effectiveness and applicability of co-training. In *Proceedings of the Ninth International Conference on Information and Knowledge Management*, CIKM '00, pages 86–93, New York, NY, USA, 2000. ACM.

[24] J. C. Platt, K. Toutanova, and W.-t. Yih. Translingual document representations from discriminative projections. In *Proceedings of the 2010 Conference on Empirical Methods in Natural Language Processing*, EMNLP '10, pages 251–261, Stroudsburg, PA, USA, 2010. Association for Computational Linguistics.

[25] A. P. RuszczyÅĎski. *Nonlinear optimization.* Princeton, N.J. Princeton University Press, 2006.

[26] A. Salaheldin and N. El-Gayar. Complementary feature splits for co-training. In *Information Science, Signal Processing and their Applications (ISSPA), 2012 11th International Conference on*, pages 1303–1308, July 2012.

[27] V. G. Sigillito, S. P. Wing, L. V. Hutton, and K. B. Baker. Classification of radar returns from the ionosphere using neural networks. *Johns Hopkins APL Tech. Dig*, vol. 10:262–266, 1989. in.

[28] W. Wang and Z.-H. Zhou. Co-training with insufficient views. In C. S. Ong and T. B. Ho, editors, *ACML*, volume 29 of *JMLR Proceedings*, pages 467–482. JMLR.org, 2013.

[29] W. Zhang and Q. Zheng. Tsfs: A novel algorithm for single view co-training. In *Computational Sciences and Optimization, 2009. CSO 2009. International Joint Conference on*, volume 1, pages 492–496, April 2009.

Learning Points and Routes to Recommend Trajectories

Dawei Chen*† Cheng Soon Ong†* Lexing Xie*†

*The Australian National University, †Data 61, CSIRO, Australia
{u5708856, chengsoon.ong, lexing.xie}@anu.edu.au

ABSTRACT

The problem of recommending tours to travellers is an important and broadly studied area. Suggested solutions include various approaches of points-of-interest (POI) recommendation and route planning. We consider the task of recommending a sequence of POIs, that simultaneously uses information about POIs and routes. Our approach unifies the treatment of various sources of information by representing them as features in machine learning algorithms, enabling us to learn from past behaviour. Information about POIs are used to learn a POI ranking model that accounts for the start and end points of tours. Data about previous trajectories are used for learning transition patterns between POIs that enable us to recommend probable routes. In addition, a probabilistic model is proposed to combine the results of POI ranking and the POI to POI transitions. We propose a new F_1 score on pairs of POIs that capture the order of visits. Empirical results show that our approach improves on recent methods, and demonstrate that combining points and routes enables better trajectory recommendations.

Keywords

Trajectory recommendation; learning to rank; planning

1. INTRODUCTION

This paper proposes a novel solution to recommend travel routes in cities. A large amount of location traces are becoming available from ubiquitous location tracking devices. For example, FourSquare has 50 million monthly users who have made 8 billion check-ins [7], and Flickr hosts over 2 billion geo-tagged public photos [6]. This growing trend in rich geolocation data provide new opportunities for better travel planning traditionally done with written travel guides. Good solutions to these problems will in turn lead to better urban experiences for residents and visitors alike, and foster sharing of even more location-based behavioural data.

There are several settings of recommendation problems for locations and routes, as illustrated in Figure 1. We summarise recent work most related to formulating and solving learning problems on assembling routes from POIs, and refer the reader to a number of recent surveys [1, 27, 28] for general overviews of the area. The first setting can be called POI recommendation (Figure 1(a)). Each location (A to E) is scored with geographic and behavioural information such as category, reviews, popularity, spatial information such as distance, and temporal information such as travel time uncertainty, time of the day or day of the week. A popular approach is to recommend POIs with a collaborative filtering model on user-location affinity [21], with additional ways to incorporate spatial [13, 16], temporal [24, 11, 8], or spatial-temporal [25] information.

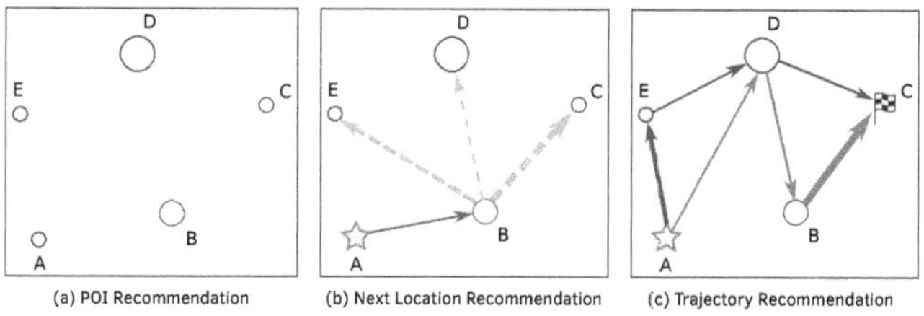

Figure 1: Three settings of trajectory recommendation problems. Node size: POI score; edge width: transition score between pairs of POIs; grey: observed; star: starting location; flag: ending location. See Section 1 for details.

Figure 1(b) illustrates the second setting: next location recommendation. Here the input is a partial trajectory (e.g. started at point A and currently at point B), the task of the algorithm is to score the next candidate location (e.g, C, D and E) based on the perceived POI score and transition compatibility with input $A \to B$. It is a variant of POI recommendation except both the user and locations travelled to date are given. The solutions to this problem include incorporating Markov chains into collaborative filtering [20, 4, 26], quantifying tourist traffic flow between points-of-interest [29], formulating a binary decision or ranking problem [2], and predict the next location with sequence models such as recurrent neural networks [15].

This paper considers the final setting: trajectory recommendation (Figure 1(c)). Here the input are some factors about the desired route, e.g. starting point A and end point C, along with auxiliary information such as the desired length of trip. The algorithm needs to take into account location desirability (as indicated by node size) and transition compatibility (as indicated by edge width), and compare route hypotheses such as A-D-B-C and A-E-D-C. Existing work in this area either uses heuristic combination of loca-

CIKM'16 , October 24-28, 2016, Indianapolis, IN, USA
© 2016 ACM. ISBN 978-1-4503-4073-1/16/10...$15.00
DOI: http://dx.doi.org/10.1145/2983323.2983672

tions and routes [18, 14, 17], or formulates an optimisation problem that is not informed or evaluated by behaviour history [9, 3]. We note, however, that two desired qualities are still missing from the current solutions to trajectory recommendation. The first is a principled method to jointly learn POI ranking (a prediction problem) and optimise for route creation (a planning problem). The second is a unified way to incorporate various features such as location, time, distance, user profile and social interactions, as they tend to get specialised and separate treatments. This work aims to address both challenges. We propose a novel way to learn point preferences and routes jointly. In Section 2, we describe the features that are used to ranking points, and POI to POI transitions that are factorised along different types of location properties. Section 3 details a number of our proposed approaches to recommend trajectories. We evaluate the proposed algorithms on trajectories from five different cities in Section 4. The main contributions of this work are:

- We propose a novel algorithm to jointly optimise point preferences and routes. We find that learning-based approaches generally outperform heuristic route recommendation [14]. Incorporating transitions to POI ranking results in a better sequence of POIs, and avoiding sub-tours further improves performance of classical Markov chain methods.
- Our approach is feature-driven and learns from past behaviour without having to design specialised treatment for spatial, temporal or social information. It incorporates information about location, POI categories and behaviour history, and can use additional time, user, or social information if available.
- We show good performance compared to recent results [14], and also quantify the contributions from different components, such as ranking points, scoring transitions, and routing.
- We propose a new metric to evaluate trajectories, pairs-F_1, to capture the order in which POIs are visited. Pairs-F_1 lies between 0 and 1, and achieves 1 if and only if the recommended trajectory is exactly the same as the ground truth.

Supplemental material, benchmark data and results are available online at https://bitbucket.org/d-chen/tour-cikm16 .

2. POI, QUERY AND TRANSITION

The goal of tour recommendation is to suggest a sequence of POIs, $(p_1, \dots, p_L)$, of length L such that the user's utility is maximised. The user provides the desired start ($p_1 = p_s$) and end point ($p_L = p_e$), as well as the number L of POIs desired, from which we propose a trajectory through the city. The training data consists of a set of tours of varying length in a particular city. We consider only POIs that have been visited by at least one user in the past, and construct a graph with POIs as nodes and directed edges representing the observed transitions between pairs of POIs in tours.

We extract the category, popularity (number of distinct visitors) [5], total number of visits and average visit duration for each POI. POIs are grouped into 5 clusters using K-means according to their geographical locations to reflect their neighbourhood. Furthermore, since we are constrained by the fact that trajectories have to be of length L and start and end at certain points, we hope to improve the

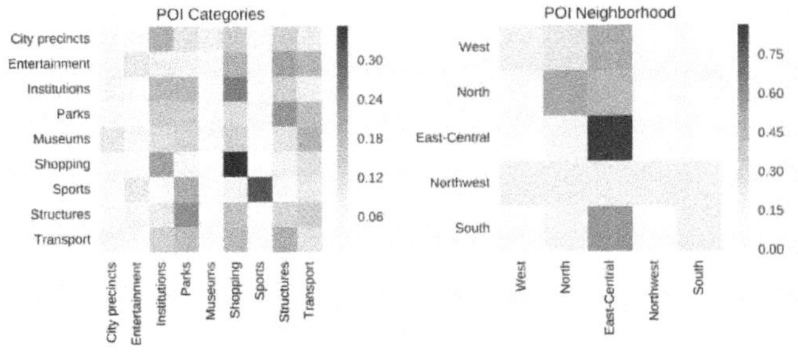

Figure 2: Transition matrices for two POI features from Melbourne: POI category and neighbourhood.

recommendation by using this information. In other words, we use the *query* $q = (p_s, p_e, L)$ to construct new features by contrasting candidate POIs with p_s and p_e. For each of the POI features (category, neighbourhood, popularity, total visits and average duration), we construct two new features by taking the difference of the feature in POI p with p_s and p_e respectively. For the category (and neighbourhood), we set the feature to 1 when their categories (and cluster identities) are the same and -1 otherwise. For popularity, total visits and average duration, we take the real valued difference. Lastly, we compute the distance from POI p to p_s (and p_e) using the Haversine formula [22], and also include the required length L.

In addition to information about each individual POI, a tour recommendation system would benefit from capturing the likelihood of going from one POI to another different POI. One option would be to directly model the probability of going from any POI to any other POI, but this has several weaknesses: Such a model would be unable to handle a new POI (one that has not yet been visited), or pairs of existing POIs that do not have an observed transition. Furthermore, even if we restrict ourselves to known POIs and transitions, there may be locations which are rarely visited, leading to significant challenges in estimating the probabilities from empirical data.

We model POI transitions using a Markov chain with discrete states by factorising the transition probability (p_i to p_j) as a product of transition probabilities between pairs of individual POI features, assuming independence between these feature-wise transitions. The popularity, total visits and average duration are discretised by binning them uniformly into 5 intervals on the log scale. These feature-to-feature transitions are estimated from data using maximum likelihood principle. The POI-POI transition probabilities can be efficiently computed by taking the Kronecker product of transition matrices for the individual features, and then updating it based on three additional constraints as well as appropriate normalisation. First we disallow self-loops by setting the probability of (p_i to p_i) to zero. Secondly, when multiple POIs have identical (discretised) features, we distribute the probability uniformly among POIs in the group. Third, we remove feature combinations that has no POI in dataset. Figure 2 visualises the transition matrices for two POI features, category and neighbourhood, in Melbourne.

3. TOUR RECOMMENDATION

In this section, we first describe the recommendation of points and routes, then we discuss how to combine them, and finally we propose a method to avoid sub-tours.

3.1 POI Ranking and Route Planning

A naive approach would be to recommend trajectories based on the popularity of POIs only, that is we always suggest the top-k most popular POIs for all visitors given the start and end location. We call this baseline approach POIPOPULARITY, and its only adaptation to a particular query is to adjust k to match the desired length.

On the other hand, we can leverage the whole set of POI features described in Section 2 to learn a ranking of POIs using rankSVM, with linear kernel and L2 loss [12],

$$\min_{\mathbf{w}} \frac{1}{2}\mathbf{w}^T\mathbf{w} + \quad C \sum_{p_i, p_j \in \mathcal{P},\ q \in \mathcal{Q}} \max\left(0,\ 1 - \mathbf{w}^T(\phi_{i,q} - \phi_{j,q})\right)^2,$$

where $\mathbf{w}$ is the parameter vector, $C > 0$ is a regularisation constant, $\mathcal{P}$ is the set of POIs to rank, $\mathcal{Q}$ denotes the queries corresponding to trajectories in training set, and $\phi_{i,q}$ is the feature vector for POI p_i with respect to query q. The ranking score of p_i given query q is computed as $R_{i,q} = \mathbf{w}^T\phi_{i,q}$.

For training the rankSVM, the labels are generated using the number of occurrences of POI p in trajectories grouped by query (p_s, p_e, L), without counting the occurrence of p when it is the origin or destination of a trajectory. Our algorithm, POIRANK, recommends a trajectory for a particular query by first ranking POIs then takes the top ranked $L-2$ POIs and connects them according to the ranks.

In addition to recommend trajectory by ranking POIs, we can leverage the POI-POI transition probabilities and recommend a trajectory (with respect to a query) by maximising the transition likelihood. The maximum likelihood of the Markov chain of transitions is found using a variant of the Viterbi algorithm (with uniform emission probabilities). We call this approach that only uses the transition probabilities between POIs as MARKOV.

3.2 Combine Ranking and Transition

We would like to leverage both point ranking and transitions, i.e., recommending a trajectory that maximises the points ranking of its POIs as well as its transition likelihood at the same time. To begin with, we transform the ranking scores $R_{j,q}$ of POI p_j with respect to query q to a probability distribution using the softmax function,

$$P_R(p_j|q) = \frac{\exp(R_{j,q})}{\sum_i \exp(R_{i,q})}, \tag{1}$$

One option to find a trajectory that simultaneously maximises the ranking probabilities of its POIs and its transition likelihood is to optimise the following objective:

$$\operatorname*{argmax}_{\mathcal{T} \in \mathcal{P}^L} \alpha \sum_{k=2}^{L} \log P_R(p_k|q) + (1-\alpha) \sum_{k=1}^{L-1} \log P(p_{k+1}|p_k),$$

such that $p_1 = p_s$, $p_L = p_e$ and $p_k \in \mathcal{P}$, $1 \le k \le L$. The first term captures the POI ranking, and the second one incorporates the transition probabilities. $\mathcal{T} = (p_1, \dots, p_L)$ is any possible trajectory, $\alpha \in [0,1]$ is a parameter to trade-off the importance between point ranking and transition, and can be tuned using cross validation in practice. Let $S(p; p', q)$ be a convex combination of point ranking and transition,

$$S(p; p', q) = \alpha \log P_R(p|q) + (1-\alpha) \log P(p|p'), \tag{2}$$

then the best path (or walk) can be found using the Viterbi algorithm. We call this approach that uses both the point ranking and transitions RANK+MARKOV, with pseudo code

Algorithm 1 RANK+MARKOV: recommend trajectory with POI ranking and transition

Input: $\mathcal{P}, p_s, p_e, L$
Output: Trajectory $\mathcal{T} = (p_s, \cdots, p_e)$ with L POIs
Initialise score matrix A and backtracking pointers B
for $p \in \mathcal{P}$ **do**
    $A[2,p] = S(p; p_s, q)$
    $B[2,p] = p_s$
end for
for $l = 2$ to $L-1$ **do**
    for $p \in \mathcal{P}$ **do**
        $A[l+1,p] = \max_{p' \in \mathcal{P}}\{A[l,p'] + S(p;p',q)\}$
        $B[l+1,p] = \operatorname{argmax}_{p' \in \mathcal{P}}\{A[l,p'] + S(p;p',q)\}$
    end for
end for
$\mathcal{T} = \{p_e\}$, $l = L$, $p = p_e$
repeat
    Prepend $B[l,p]$ to $\mathcal{T}$
    $l = l-1$, $p = B[l,p]$
until $l < 2$
return $\mathcal{T}$

shown in Algorithm 1, where A is the score matrix, and entry $A[l,p]$ stores the maximum value associated with the (partial) trajectory that starts at p_s and ends at p with l POI visits; B is the backtracking-point matrix, and entry $B[l,p]$ stores the predecessor of p in that (partial) trajectory. The maximum objective value is $A[L, p_e]$, and the corresponding trajectory can be found by tracing back from $B[L, p_e]$.

3.3 Avoiding sub-tours

Trajectories recommended by MARKOV (Section 3.1) and RANK+MARKOV (Section 3.2) are found using the maximum likelihood approach, and may contain multiple visits to the same POI. This is because the best solution from Viterbi decoding may have circular sub-tours (where a POI already visited earlier in the tour is visited again). We propose a method for eliminating sub-tours by finding the best path using an integer linear program (ILP), with sub-tour elimination constraints adapted from the Travelling Salesman Problem [19]. In particular, given a set of POIs $\mathcal{P}$, the POI-POI transition matrix and a query $q = (p_s, p_e, L)$, we recommend a trajectory by solving the following ILP:

$$\max_{x,u} \sum_{i=1}^{N-1}\sum_{j=2}^{N} x_{ij}\ \log P(p_j|p_i)$$

$$s.t.\quad x_{ij} \in \{0,1\},\ x_{ii} = 0,\ u_i \in \mathbf{Z},\ \forall i,j = 1,\cdots,N \tag{3}$$

$$\sum_{j=2}^{N} x_{1j} = \sum_{i=1}^{N-1} x_{iN} = 1,\ \sum_{i=2}^{N} x_{i1} = \sum_{j=1}^{N-1} x_{Nj} = 0 \tag{4}$$

$$\sum_{i=1}^{N-1} x_{ik} = \sum_{j=2}^{N} x_{kj} \le 1,\ \forall k = 2,\cdots,N-1 \tag{5}$$

$$\sum_{i=1}^{N-1}\sum_{j=2}^{N} x_{ij} = L-1, \tag{6}$$

$$u_i - u_j + 1 \le (N-1)(1-x_{ij}), \forall i,j = 2,\cdots,N \tag{7}$$

where $N = |\mathcal{P}|$ is the number of available POIs and x_{ij} is a binary decision variable that determines whether the transition from p_i to p_j is in the resulting trajectory. For brevity, we arrange the POIs such that $p_1 = p_s$ and $p_N = p_e$.

Table 1: Statistics of trajectory dataset

Dataset	#Photos	#Visits	#Traj.	#Users
Edinburgh	82,060	33,944	5,028	1,454
Glasgow	29,019	11,434	2,227	601
Melbourne	94,142	23,995	5,106	1,000
Osaka	392,420	7,747	1,115	450
Toronto	157,505	39,419	6,057	1,395

Firstly, the desired trajectory should start from p_s and end at p_e (Constraint 4). In addition, any POI could be visited at most once (Constraint 5). Moreover, only $L-1$ transitions between POIs are permitted (Constraint 6), i.e., the number of POI visits should be exactly L (including p_s and p_e). The last constraint, where u_i is an auxiliary variable, enforces that only a single sequence of POIs without sub-tours is permitted in the trajectory. We solve this ILP using the Gurobi optimisation package [10], and the resulting trajectory is constructed by tracing the non-zeros in x. We call our method that uses the POI-POI transition matrix to recommend paths without circular sub-tours MARKOVPATH.

Sub-tours in trajectories recommended by RANK+MARKOV can be eliminated in a similar manner, we solve an ILP by optimising the following objective with the same constraints described above,

$$\max_{x,u} \sum_{i=1}^{N-1} \sum_{j=2}^{N} x_{ij} \; S(p_j; p_i, q), \tag{8}$$

where $S(p_j; p_i, q)$ incorporates both point ranking and transition, as defined in Equation (2). This algorithm is called RANK+MARKOVPATH in the experiments.

4. EXPERIMENT ON FLICKR PHOTOS

We evaluate the algorithms above on datasets with trajectories extracted from Flickr photos [23] in five cities, namely, Edinburgh, Glasgow, Melbourne, Osaka and Toronto, with statistics shown in Table 1. The Melbourne dataset is built using approaches proposed in earlier work [5, 14], and the other four datasets are provided by Lim et al. [14].

We use leave-one-out cross validation to evaluate different trajectory recommendation algorithms, i.e., when testing on a trajectory, all other trajectories are used for training. We compare with a number of baseline approaches such as RANDOM, which naively chooses POIs uniformly at random (without replacement) from the set $\mathcal{P} \setminus \{p_s, p_e\}$ to form a trajectory, and POIPOPULARITY (Section 3.1), which recommends trajectories based on the popularity of POIs only. Among the related approaches from recent literature, PERSTOUR [14] explores POI features as well as the sub-tour elimination constraints (Section 3.3), with an additional time budget, and its variant PERSTOUR-L, which replaces the time budget with a constraint of trajectory length. Variants of point-ranking and route-planning approaches including POIRANK and MARKOV (Section 3.1), which utilises either POI features or POI-POI transitions, and RANK+MARKOV (Section 3.2) that captures both types of information. Variants that employ additional sub-tour elimination constraints (MARKOVPATH and RANK+MARKOVPATH, Section 3.3) are also included. A summary of the various trajectory recommendation approaches can be found in Table 2.

4.1 Performance metrics

A commonly used metric for evaluating POI and trajectory recommendation is the F_1 score on points, which is the harmonic mean of precision and recall of POIs in trajectory [14]. While being good at measuring whether POIs are correctly recommended, F_1 score on points ignores the visiting order between POIs. We propose a new metric pairs-F_1 that considers both POI identity and visiting order, by measuring the F_1 score of every pair of POIs, whether they are adjacent or not in trajectory,

$$\text{pairs-F}_1 = \frac{2 P_{\text{PAIR}} R_{\text{PAIR}}}{P_{\text{PAIR}} + R_{\text{PAIR}}},$$

where P_{PAIR} and R_{PAIR} are the precision and recall of ordered POI pairs respectively. Pairs-F_1 takes values between 0 and 1 (higher is better). A perfect pairs-F_1 is achieved *if and only if* both the POIs and their visiting order in the recommended trajectory are exactly the same as those in the ground truth. On the other hand, pairs-$F_1 = 0$ means none of the recommended POI pairs was actually visited (in the designated order) in the real trajectory. An illustration is shown in Figure 3, the solid grey lines represent the ground truth transitions that actually visited by travellers, and the dashed blue lines are the recommended trajectory by one of the approaches described in Section 3. Both examples have a perfect F_1 score, but not a perfect pairs-F_1 score due to the difference in POI sequencing.

Table 2: Summary of information captured by different trajectory recommendation algorithms

	Query	POI	Trans.	No sub-tours
RANDOM	×	×	×	×
PERSTOUR[14]	×	√	×	√
PERSTOUR-L	×	√	×	√
POIPOPULARITY	×	√	×	×
POIRANK	√	√	×	×
MARKOV	×	√	√	×
MARKOVPATH	×	√	√	√
RANK+MARKOV	√	√	√	×
RANK+MARKOVPATH	√	√	√	√

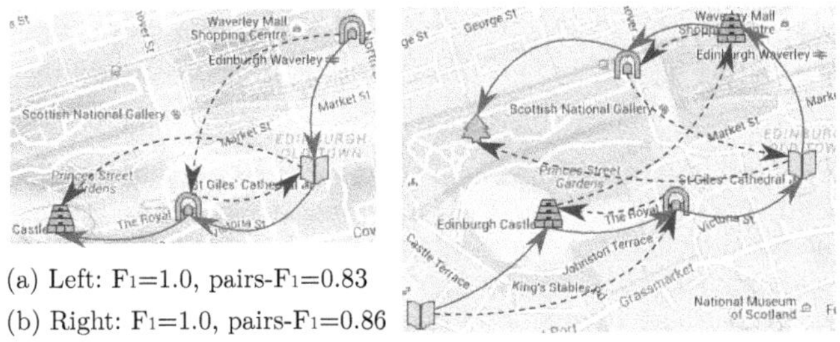

(a) Left: F_1=1.0, pairs-F_1=0.83
(b) Right: F_1=1.0, pairs-F_1=0.86

Figure 3: Examples for F_1 vs pairs-F_1 as evaluation metric. Solid grey: ground truth; dashed blue: recommended trajectories. See Section 4.1 for details.

4.2 Results

The performance of various trajectory recommendation approaches are summarised in Table 3 and Table 4, in terms of F_1 and pairs-F_1 scores respectively. It is apparent that algorithms captured information about the problem (Table 2) outperform the RANDOM baseline in terms of both metrics on all five datasets.

Algorithms based on POI ranking yield strong performance, in terms of both metrics, by exploring POI and query specific features. POIRANK improves notably upon POIPOPULARITY and PERSTOUR by leveraging more fea-

Table 3: Performance comparison on five datasets in terms of F_1 score. The best method for each dataset (i.e., a column) is shown in bold, the second best is shown in *italic*.

	Edinburgh	Glasgow	Melbourne	Osaka	Toronto
RANDOM	0.570 ± 0.139	0.632 ± 0.123	0.558 ± 0.149	0.621 ± 0.115	0.621 ± 0.129
PERSTOUR[14]	0.656 ± 0.223	$\mathbf{0.801 \pm 0.213}$	0.483 ± 0.208	0.686 ± 0.231	0.720 ± 0.215
PERSTOUR-L	0.651 ± 0.143	0.660 ± 0.102	0.576 ± 0.141	0.686 ± 0.137	0.643 ± 0.113
POIPOPULARITY	$\mathbf{0.701 \pm 0.160}$	0.745 ± 0.166	0.620 ± 0.136	0.663 ± 0.125	0.678 ± 0.121
POIRANK	$\mathit{0.700 \pm 0.155}$	$\mathit{0.768 \pm 0.171}$	$\mathit{0.637 \pm 0.142}$	$\mathbf{0.745 \pm 0.173}$	$\mathbf{0.754 \pm 0.170}$
MARKOV	0.645 ± 0.169	0.725 ± 0.167	0.577 ± 0.168	0.697 ± 0.150	0.669 ± 0.151
MARKOVPATH	0.678 ± 0.149	0.732 ± 0.168	0.595 ± 0.148	0.706 ± 0.150	0.688 ± 0.138
RANK+MARKOV	0.659 ± 0.174	0.754 ± 0.173	0.613 ± 0.166	0.715 ± 0.164	0.723 ± 0.185
RANK+MARKOVPATH	0.697 ± 0.152	0.762 ± 0.167	$\mathbf{0.639 \pm 0.146}$	$\mathit{0.732 \pm 0.162}$	$\mathit{0.751 \pm 0.170}$

Table 4: Performance comparison on five datasets in terms of pairs-F_1 score. The best method for each dataset (i.e., a column) is shown in bold, the second best is shown in *italic*.

	Edinburgh	Glasgow	Melbourne	Osaka	Toronto
RANDOM	0.261 ± 0.155	0.320 ± 0.168	0.248 ± 0.147	0.304 ± 0.142	0.310 ± 0.167
PERSTOUR[14]	0.417 ± 0.343	$\mathbf{0.643 \pm 0.366}$	0.216 ± 0.265	0.468 ± 0.376	0.504 ± 0.354
PERSTOUR-L	0.359 ± 0.207	0.352 ± 0.162	0.266 ± 0.140	0.406 ± 0.238	0.333 ± 0.163
POIPOPULARITY	$\mathit{0.436 \pm 0.259}$	0.507 ± 0.298	0.316 ± 0.178	0.365 ± 0.190	0.384 ± 0.201
POIRANK	0.432 ± 0.251	$\mathit{0.548 \pm 0.311}$	0.339 ± 0.203	$\mathbf{0.511 \pm 0.309}$	$\mathbf{0.518 \pm 0.296}$
MARKOV	0.417 ± 0.248	0.495 ± 0.296	0.288 ± 0.195	0.445 ± 0.266	0.407 ± 0.241
MARKOVPATH	0.400 ± 0.235	0.485 ± 0.293	0.294 ± 0.187	0.442 ± 0.260	0.405 ± 0.231
RANK+MARKOV	$\mathbf{0.444 \pm 0.263}$	0.545 ± 0.306	$\mathbf{0.351 \pm 0.220}$	0.486 ± 0.288	0.512 ± 0.303
RANK+MARKOVPATH	0.428 ± 0.245	0.533 ± 0.303	$\mathit{0.344 \pm 0.206}$	$\mathit{0.489 \pm 0.287}$	$\mathit{0.514 \pm 0.297}$

tures. In contrast, MARKOV which leverages only POI transitions does not perform as well. Algorithms with ranking information (RANK+MARKOV and RANK+MARKOVPATH) always outperform their respective variants with transition information alone (MARKOV and MARKOVPATH).

We can see from Table 3 that, in terms of F_1, MARKOVPATH and RANK+MARKOVPATH outperform their corresponding variants MARKOV and RANK+MARKOV without the path constraints, which demonstrates that eliminating sub-tours improves point recommendation. This is not unexpected, as sub-tours worsen the proportion of correctly recommended POIs since a length constraint is used. In contrast, most Markov chain entries have better performance in terms of pairs-F_1 (Table 4), which indicates Markov chain approaches generally respect the transition patterns between POIs.

PERSTOUR [14] always performs better than its variant PERSTOUR-L, in terms of both metrics, especially on Glasgow and Toronto datasets. This indicates the time budget constraint is more helpful than length constraint for recommending trajectories. Surprisingly, we observed that PERSTOUR is outperformed by RANDOM baseline on Melbourne dataset. It turns out that on this dataset, many of the ILP problems which PERSTOUR needs to solve to get the recommendations are difficult ILP instances. In the leave-one-out evaluation, although we utilised a large scale computing cluster with modern hardware, 12% of evaluations failed as the ILP solver was unable to find a feasible solution after 2 hours. Furthermore, a lot of recommendations were suboptimal solutions of the corresponding ILPs due to the time limit. These factors lead to the inconsistent performance of PERSTOUR on Melbourne dataset.

4.3 An Illustrative Example

Figure 4 illustrates an example from Edinburgh. The ground truth is a trajectory of length 4 that starts at a POI of category *Structures*, visits two intermediate POIs of category *Structures* and *Cultural* and terminates at a POI of category *Structures*. The trajectory recommended by PERSTOUR is a tour with 11 POIs, as shown in Figure 4(a), with none of the desired intermediate POIs visited. POIRANK (Figure 4(b)) recommended a tour with correct POIs, but with completely different routes. On the other hand, MARKOV (Figure 4(c)) missed one POI but one of the intermediate routes is consistent with the ground truth. The best recommendation, as shown in Figure 4(d), with exactly the same points and routes as the ground truth, which in this case is achieved by RANK+MARKOVPATH.

5. DISCUSSION AND CONCLUSION

In this paper, we propose an approach to recommend trajectories by jointly optimising point preferences and routes. This is in contrast to related work which looks at only POI or next location recommendation. Point preferences are learned by ranking according to POI and query features, and factorised transition probabilities between POIs are learned from previous trajectories extracted from social media. We investigate the maximum likelihood sequence approach (which may recommend sub-tours) and propose an improved sequence recommendation method. Our feature driven approach naturally allows learning the combination of POI ranks and routes.

We argue that one should measure performance with respect to the visiting order of POIs, and suggest a new pairs-F_1 metric. We empirically evaluate our tour recommendation approaches on five datasets extracted from Flickr photos, and demonstrate that our method improves on prior work, in terms of both the traditional F_1 metric and our proposed performance measure. Our promising results from learning points and routes for trajectory recommendation suggests that research in this domain should consider both information sources simultaneously.

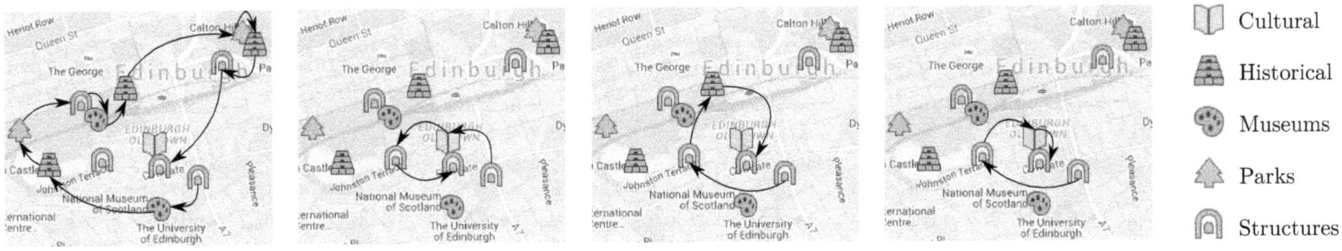

(a) PERSTOUR (b) POIRANK (c) MARKOV (d) Best

Figure 4: Different recommendations from algorithm variants. See the main text in Section 4.3 for description.

Acknowledgements. We thank Kwan Hui Lim for kindly providing his R code to reproduce his experiments. This work is supported in part by the Australian Research Council via the Discovery Project program DP140102185.

6. REFERENCES

[1] J. Bao, Y. Zheng, D. Wilkie, and M. Mokbel. Recommendations in location-based social networks: a survey. *GeoInformatica*, 19(3):525–565, 2015.

[2] R. Baraglia, C. I. Muntean, F. M. Nardini, and F. Silvestri. LearNext: learning to predict tourists movements. CIKM '13, pages 751–756. ACM, 2013.

[3] C. Chen, D. Zhang, B. Guo, X. Ma, G. Pan, and Z. Wu. TRIPPLANNER: Personalized trip planning leveraging heterogeneous crowdsourced digital footprints. *IEEE Transactions on Intelligent Transportation Systems*, 16(3):1259–1273, 2015.

[4] C. Cheng, H. Yang, M. R. Lyu, and I. King. Where you like to go next: Successive point-of-interest recommendation. IJCAI '13, pages 2605–2611. AAAI Press, 2013.

[5] M. De Choudhury, M. Feldman, S. Amer-Yahia, N. Golbandi, R. Lempel, and C. Yu. Automatic construction of travel itineraries using social breadcrumbs. HT '10, pages 35–44. ACM, 2010.

[6] Flickr. Flickr photos on the map. https://www.flickr.com/map , retrieved May 2016.

[7] Foursquare. FourSquare: about us. https://foursquare.com/about , retrieved May 2016.

[8] H. Gao, J. Tang, X. Hu, and H. Liu. Exploring temporal effects for location recommendation on location-based social networks. RecSys '13, pages 93–100. ACM, 2013.

[9] A. Gionis, T. Lappas, K. Pelechrinis, and E. Terzi. Customized tour recommendations in urban areas. WSDM '14, pages 313–322. ACM, 2014.

[10] Gurobi. Gurobi Optimization. http://www.gurobi.com , retrieved May 2016.

[11] H.-P. Hsieh and C.-T. Li. Mining and planning time-aware routes from check-in data. CIKM '14, pages 481–490. ACM, 2014.

[12] C.-P. Lee and C.-b. Lin. Large-scale linear rankSVM. *Neural computation*, 26(4):781–817, 2014.

[13] D. Lian, C. Zhao, X. Xie, G. Sun, E. Chen, and Y. Rui. GeoMF: Joint geographical modeling and matrix factorization for point-of-interest recommendation. KDD '14, pages 831–840. ACM, 2014.

[14] K. H. Lim, J. Chan, C. Leckie, and S. Karunasekera. Personalized tour recommendation based on user interests and points of interest visit durations. IJCAI '15, 2015.

[15] Q. Liu, S. Wu, L. Wang, and T. Tan. Predicting the next location: A recurrent model with spatial and temporal contexts. AAAI '16, 2016.

[16] Y. Liu, W. Wei, A. Sun, and C. Miao. Exploiting geographical neighborhood characteristics for location recommendation. CIKM '14, pages 739–748. ACM, 2014.

[17] E. H.-C. Lu, C.-Y. Chen, and V. S. Tseng. Personalized trip recommendation with multiple constraints by mining user check-in behaviors. SIGSPATIAL '12, pages 209–218. ACM, 2012.

[18] X. Lu, C. Wang, J.-M. Yang, Y. Pang, and L. Zhang. Photo2Trip: Generating travel routes from geo-tagged photos for trip planning. MM '10, pages 143–152. ACM, 2010.

[19] C. H. Papadimitriou and K. Steiglitz. *Combinatorial optimization: algorithms and complexity.* Dover Publications, 1998.

[20] S. Rendle, C. Freudenthaler, and L. Schmidt-Thieme. Factorizing personalized Markov chains for next-basket recommendation. WWW '10, pages 811–820. ACM, 2010.

[21] Y. Shi, P. Serdyukov, A. Hanjalic, and M. Larson. Personalized landmark recommendation based on geotags from photo sharing sites. ICWSM '11, 2011.

[22] R. W. Sinnott. Virtues of the haversine. *Sky and telescope*, 68(2):159, 1984.

[23] B. Thomee, B. Elizalde, D. A. Shamma, K. Ni, G. Friedland, D. Poland, D. Borth, and L.-J. Li. YFCC100M: The new data in multimedia research. *Communications of the ACM*, 59(2):64–73, 2016.

[24] Q. Yuan, G. Cong, Z. Ma, A. Sun, and N. M. Thalmann. Time-aware point-of-interest recommendation. SIGIR '13, pages 363–372. ACM, 2013.

[25] Q. Yuan, G. Cong, and A. Sun. Graph-based point-of-interest recommendation with geographical and temporal influences. CIKM '14, pages 659–668. ACM, 2014.

[26] W. Zhang and J. Wang. Location and time aware social collaborative retrieval for new successive point-of-interest recommendation. CIKM '15, pages 1221–1230. ACM, 2015.

[27] Y. Zheng. Trajectory data mining: an overview. *ACM Transactions on Intelligent Systems and Technology*, 6(3):29, 2015.

[28] Y. Zheng, L. Capra, O. Wolfson, and H. Yang. Urban computing: concepts, methodologies, and applications. *ACM Transactions on Intelligent Systems and Technology*, 5(3):38, 2014.

[29] Y.-T. Zheng, Z.-J. Zha, and T.-S. Chua. Mining travel patterns from geotagged photos. *ACM Transactions on Intelligent Systems and Technology*, 3(3):56:1–56:18, May 2012.

Towards Representation Independent Similarity Search Over Graph Databases

Yodsawalai Chodpathumwan, Amirhossein Aleyasen
University of Illinois
{ychodpa2,aleyase2}@illinois.edu

Arash Termehchy
Oregon State University
termehca@oregonstate.edu

Yizhou Sun
Northeastern University
yzsun@ccs.neu.edu

ABSTRACT

Finding similar entities is a fundamental problem in graph data analysis. Similarity search algorithms usually leverage the structural properties of the database to quantify the degree of similarity between entities. However, the same information can be represented in different structures and the structural properties observed over particular representations may not hold for the alternatives. These algorithms are effective on some representations and ineffective on others. We define the property of representation independence for similarity search algorithms as their robustness against transformations that modify the structure of databases but preserve the information content. We introduce a widespread group of such transformations called *relationship reorganizing*. We propose an algorithm called **R-PathSim**, which is provably robust under relationship reorganizing. Our empirical results show that current algorithms except R-PathSim are highly sensitive to the data representation and R-PathSim is as efficient and effective as other algorithms.

Keywords

Structural similarity search; Database transformation; Representation independence

1. INTRODUCTION

Finding similar or strongly related entities is a fundamental problem in graph data management [5, 6, 9]. It is a building block of algorithms for various important problems, such as similarity query processing and community detection [5, 8]. Since the properties of *similar* or *related* entities cannot be precisely defined, current similarity search algorithms use intuitively appealing heuristics that leverage information about the links between entities. For instance, *Random Walk with Restart* (RWR) quantifies the degree of similarity between two entities as the likelihood that a random surfer visits one of the entities in the database given it starts and keeps re-starting from the other entity [9]. *SimRank* evaluates the similarity between two entities according to how likely two random surfers will meet each other if they start from the two entities [5]. Figure 1a shows fragments of IMDb (*imdb.com*), which contains information about movies, actors, and characters. IMDb represents relationship between a character, its movie, and the actor who played the character by connecting these entities through some edges. Assume that a user asks for the most similar movie to *Star Wars III* in Figure 1a. RWR and SimRank find *Star Wars III* more similar to *Star Wars V* (RWR-score = 0.061, SimRank-score = 0.213) than to *Jumper* (RWR-score = 0.060, SimRank-score = 0.185) which is arguably an effective answer.

Generally, there is no canonical representation for a particular set of content and people often represent the same information in different, i.e., non-isomorphic, structures [1, 3]. Database designers may represent the same information in one form or another for reasons such as improving the running time of queries and reducing redundancy [1]. The choice of representation may unintentionally influence the output of current similarity search algorithms. Consider the excerpts of Freebase (*freebase.com*) in Figure 1b which contains the same information as Figure 1a. It differs with Figure 1a only in how it represents the relationships between a character, its movie, and its actor: it connects them to a common node labeled *starring*. As opposed to their results over Figure 1a, RWR and SimRank find *Star Wars III* more similar to *Jumper* (RWR-score = 0.014, SimRank-score = 0.076) than to *Star Wars V* (RWR-score = 0.011, SimRank-Score = 0.074) in Figure 1b.

The power of similarity search algorithms, however, remains out of the reach of most users as the algorithms are usable only by trained data analysts who can predict which algorithms are likely to be effective for particular representation of the dataset. Since these algorithms do not normally offer any clear description of their desired representations, users have to rely on their own expertise and use trial and error to find the representations in which the algorithm returns effective results. However, we want our algorithms to be used by ordinary users, not just experts who know the internals of these algorithms and can restructure the data. Furthermore, the structures of databases constantly evolve and users may have to repeat the process of finding the right representation and restructuring their data accordingly.

One approach to solve the problem is to run a similarity search algorithm over all possible representations of a dataset and select the representation(s) with the most accurate answers. However, it is undecidable to compute all possible representations of a graph database [3]. Thus, it is infeasible to generate and run algorithms over them. Researchers have proposed the idea of *universal relation* to

CIKM'16, October 24-28, 2016, Indianapolis, IN, USA

DOI: http://dx.doi.org/10.1145/2983323.2983673

achieve some level of schema independence for SQL queries over relational databases [1]. One may extend this idea and define a universal representation in which all graph databases can be represented and develop similarity search algorithms that are effective over this representation. Nevertheless, the experience gained from the idea of universal relation, indicates that such representation may not always exist [1]. Furthermore, it may not be practical to force developers to organize their data in and create their algorithms for a particular style of representation.

In this paper, we propose the property of *representation independence* for similarity search algorithms, i.e., the ability to deliver the same answers regardless of the choices of structure for organizing the data. To the best of our knowledge, the property of representation independence has not previously been explored for similarity search algorithms and/or graph databases. We believe that the key to the success of building representation independent analytics in general and similarity search algorithms in particular is to modify current algorithms to become representation independent instead of developing completely new algorithms. Current algorithms are being used in industry and it is easier for organizations to modify these algorithms rather than using new algorithms. Our contributions are as follows.

- We formally define the representation independence of a similarity search algorithm as its robustness under transformations that modify the structure of database but preserve its information content.
- We introduce a group of content-preserving transformations called *relationship reorganizing.* We show that current similarity search algorithms are not representation independent. We extend a current similarity search algorithm called PathSim and develop an algorithm, namely Robust-PathSim (*R-PathSim*), that is representation independent under relationship reorganizing.
- We empirically study the representation independence of well-known similarity search algorithms under relationship-reorganizing using real-world databases. Our results indicate that relationship-reorganizing transformation considerably affects the output of all algorithms but R-PathSim. Our results show that R-PathSim is as effective and as efficient as current algorithms.

The full proofs for our theorems can be found at [2].

2. BACKGROUND

2.1 Related Work

The architects of relational model envisioned the desirable property of *logical data independence.* Oversimplifying a bit, this meant that an exact query should return the same answers no matter which schema is chosen for the data [1]. Developers usually achieve logical data independence by creating a set of views over the database, which keeps the application unaffected from modifications in the database schema [1]. However, characteristics of the ideal representations for similarity search are not clearly defined. Hence, it takes far more time and much deeper expertise to find and maintain the proper representation for the data. Moreover, our goal is to achieve representation independent without making users create and tune data representations.

Researchers have proposed query interfaces over tree-shaped XML data that return the same answers to a keyword query

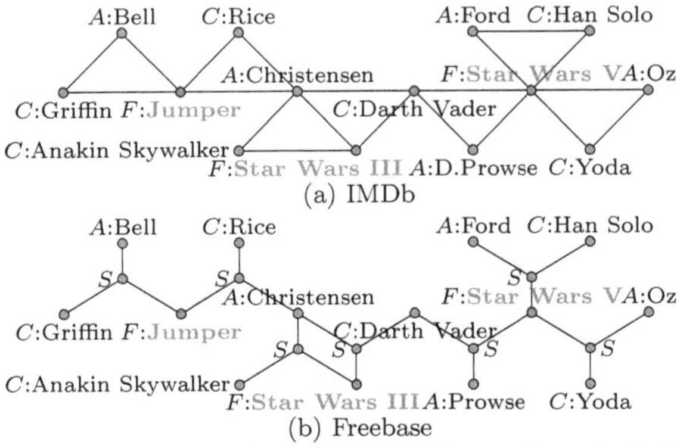

Figure 1: Fragments of IMDb and Freebase, where A, C, F, and S refer to *actor*, *character*, *film* and *starring*, respectively.

over databases with equivalent content but different choices of structure [7]. We, however, introduce and study the concept of representation independence for a different problem and data model. The task of similarity search has a different semantic than keyword search and requires different types of algorithms. Further, graph databases are more complex than tree-shaped XML databases and offer novel challenges in defining the concept of representation independence and developing representation independent algorithms.

2.2 Data Model

Let *dom* be a fixed and countably infinite set of values. To simplify our definitions, we assume the members of *dom* are strings. Let L be a finite set of labels. Each member of L denotes a *semantic type* in a domain of interest, e.g. *actor* in movie domain. A database D defined over L is a graph $D = (V, E, \mathcal{L}, \mathcal{A})$, where V is the set of nodes, $E \subseteq V \times V$ is the set of edges, $\mathcal{L}$ is a total function from V to L that assigns a label to each node, and $\mathcal{A}$ is a function from V to *dom* that assigns values to nodes in V. We denote the set of all databases whose labels belong to L as $\mathbf{L}$. Real-world databases often contain nodes without any value to represent relationships between or categorize entities [4]. Figure 1b is an example of using nodes without values to represent relationships between entities. About 30% of 1.23 billion RDF triples collected from the Web contain nodes without values [4]. We call the nodes with values *entities* [5, 6]. We assume that each label in L denotes a semantic type for entities or for nodes without values, but not for both.

We denote a similarity query q, query for short, over database D as (v), where v is an entity in D. Query $q = (v)$ seeks for entity nodes other than v in D that are similar to v [6, 5, 9, 8]. For example, query ($film$:Star Wars III) over Figure 1b asks for other entities similar to the node $film$:Star Wars III in this database. A similarity search algorithm returns a ranked list of entities as the result of query q. We denote the result of query q over database D using algorithm S by $q_S(D)$. If S is clear from the context, we denote $q_S(D)$ as $q(D)$.

3. REPRESENTATION INDEPENDENCE

Intuitively, a representation independent similarity search algorithm should return the same list of entities for the same query across databases that represent the same information. Researchers have defined the conditions under which relational or XML schemas represent the same information [3, 1, 7]. Graph databases, however, do not generally follow strict schemas. Hence, we extend the ideas on comparing information contents of databases for graph data model.

Transformation T is a function from a set of databases $\mathbf{L}$ to a set of databases $\mathbf{K}$, denoted as $T : \mathbf{L} \rightarrow \mathbf{K}$. For instance, consider the set of labels $L_1 = \{actor, film, char\}$ and $L_2 = \{actor, film, char, starring\}$. The databases in Figures 1a and 1b belong to $\mathbf{L_1}$ and $\mathbf{L_2}$, respectively. One may define transformation $T_{IMDb2Freebase} : \mathbf{L_1} \rightarrow \mathbf{L_2}$, which replaces every triangle between nodes of labels *film*, *character*, and *actor* with a subgraph whose nodes have the same labels and values of the nodes in the triangle and are connected to a single new node with label *starring*. $T_{IMDb2Freebase}$ maps the database in Figure 1a to the one in Figure 1b.

Intuitively, transformation T is invertible if one can reconstruct database D from the information in $T(D)$. For example, transformation $T_{IMDb2Freebase}$ is invertible as one can reconstruct the original database, e.g., Figure 1a, using the information in its transformed one, e.g., Figure 1b. More formally, $T : \mathbf{L} \rightarrow \mathbf{K}$ is *invertible* iff there is a transformation $T^{-1} : \mathbf{K} \rightarrow \mathbf{L}$ such that for all $D \in \mathbf{L}$ we have $T^{-1}(T(D)) = D$. Because the transformed database of an invertible transformation contain sufficient information to build the original database, the original and transformed databases contain essentially the same information [1, 3].

To precisely define representation independence over a transformation T, we should make sure that users can pose the same set of queries over databases D and $T(D)$. Similarity search queries over a database D are entities of D, thus, D and $T(D)$ should contain the same set of entities. Moreover, similarity search algorithms generally view the labels of nodes as their semantic types [6]. For example, they assume that the nodes with label *film* in Figure 1a represent entities from the same semantic type, while the entities of labels *film* and *actor* belong to different semantic types. Thus, for these algorithms to return the same results over a transformation T, T should map entities of the same label in the original database D to entities with the same label in the transformed database $T(D)$. We consider two data values equal iff they are lexicographically equal. Our approach also supports other definitions of equality between data values.

DEFINITION 1. *Transformation* $T : \mathbf{L} \rightarrow \mathbf{K}$ *that transforms database* $D = (V, E, \mathcal{L}, \mathcal{A})$ *to* $T(D) = (V_T, E_T, \mathcal{K}, \mathcal{A}_T)$ *is entity preserving iff there is a bijective mapping* M *between entities in* V *and* V_T *such that*

- $\forall v \in V$, $\mathcal{A}(v) = \mathcal{A}_T(M(v))$
- $\forall v_1, v_2 \in V$, $\mathcal{L}(v_1) = \mathcal{L}(v_2)$ *iff* $\mathcal{K}(M(v_1)) = \mathcal{K}(M(v_2))$.

For example, transformation $T_{IMDb2Freebase}$ is entity preserving. By the abuse of notation, we denote the entity in database $T(D)$ that is mapped to the entity v in database D, as $T(v)$. To simplify our definitions, we assume that transformations do not rename the labels in databases. Our results extend for the transformations that rename labels.

If a transformation is both invertible and entity preserving, it is *similarity preserving*. Each similarity preserving transformation T maps a databases D to a database $T(D)$ that has the same information and the same set of possible queries as D. Hence, it is possible to design a similarity search algorithm that returns essentially the same answers for every query over D and $T(D)$.

DEFINITION 2. *Similarity search algorithm* S *is representation independent under similarity preserving transformation* $T : \mathbf{L} \rightarrow \mathbf{K}$ *iff for each database* $D \in \mathbf{L}$ *and* $T(D) \in \mathbf{K}$ *and every query* q *over* D*, there is a bijective mapping* N *between* $q(D)$ *and* $T(q)(T(D))$ *such that*

- $\forall v \in q(D)$ *and* $N(v) \in T(q)(T(D))$, $N(v) = T(v)$
- $\forall u, v \in q(D)$, v *appears before* u *iff* $N(v)$ *appears before* $N(u)$ *in* $T(q)(T(D))$.

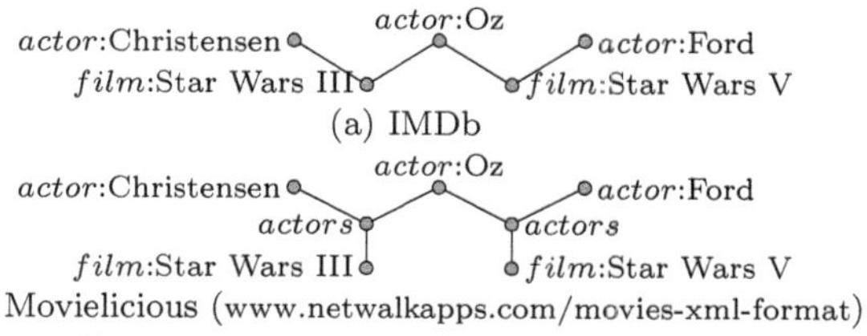

Figure 2: Fragments of movie databases.

The first condition in Definition 2 guarantees that the answers to q over D and $T(q)$ over $T(D)$ contain the same set of entities. Its second condition ensures that these entities appear at the same order in results of q over D and $T(q)$ over $T(D)$. According to Definition 2, if answers v and u are placed at the same position, in $q(D)$, $T(v)$ and $T(u)$ must also appear at the same position in $T(q)(T(D))$.

The result of a query is a list of entities, where each entity is shown by its semantic type and value. A database may have several entities with equal values from of the same semantic type. Hence, it may not be possible to check the first condition of Definition 2 using only the semantic types and values of the entities in the results of a query. One may assign a unique (printable) id to each entity in the database to address this problem. [3]. To simplify our framework and definitions, we assume that databases do not contain entities that belong to the same semantic type and have equal values. Our results extend for other cases.

4. RELATIONSHIP REORGANIZATION

4.1 Relationship-Reorganizing Transformations

Generally speaking, a relationship-reorganizing transformation T maps database D to database $T(D)$ such that D and $T(D)$ contain the same set of entities and relationships, but they may represent these relationships in different forms. More specifically, D and $T(D)$ may express the same relationship between the same set of entities using some edges or some nodes without values. For example, Figure 2b uses a set of edges to represent the relationship between a movie and its actors. However, Figure 2a expresses the same relationship between the same set of entities by a node without value, i.e., *actors*. In this section, we formally define this type of representational variation. First, we find patterns that represent relationships between entities in a database. Then, we define the conditions under which two patterns represent the same information. Finally, we define a relationship-reorganizing transformation as a bijective mapping between patterns that represent the same information in the original and transformed databases.

A **walk** in database is a sequence of nodes and edges where each edge's endpoints are the preceding and following nodes in the sequence. We show a walk in database D as a sequence of nodes $[v_0, \ldots, v_n]$, such that v_i are nodes and (v_{i-1}, v_i) ,$0 \leq i \leq n$, are edges in D. Intuitively, a walk represents some relationship between its entities. For example, walk [*actor*:Ford, *actors*, *film*:Star Wars V] in Figure 2a shows that actor *Ford* has played in movie *Star Wars V*. To simplify our framework, we assume that each database is a simple graph: it has at most one edge between each two nodes and does not have any loop at each node. Our framework extends for other cases. We are interested in walks that express relationships between entities. Hence, we consider only walks that start and end with entities.

Some walks contain consecutive forward and backward traverses from an entity to a node without value. For example, walk [*actor*:Ford, *actors*, *film*:Star Wars V, *actors*, *film*:Star Wars V] in Figure 2b expresses the relationship between actor *Ford* and movie *Star Wars V*. It contains consecutive forward and backward traverses from entity *film*:Star Wars V to the node without value *actors*. The information expressed by this walk can be represented using a shorter walk [*actor*:Ford, *actors*, *film*:Star Wars V], which does not contain any consecutive forward and backward traverses from *film*:Star Wars V to *actors*. Hence, unless otherwise noted, we consider only walks that does *not* have any consecutive forward and backward traverses from an entity to a node without value because they do not contain any information regarding the relationship between entities or their information can be expressed by shorter walks.

The **meta-walk** of a walk $[v_1, \cdots, v_n]$ in database $D = (V, E, \mathcal{L}, \mathcal{A})$ is a sequence of labels $[\mathcal{L}(v_1), \cdots, \mathcal{L}(v_n)]$. For example, the meta-walk of walk [*actor*:Ford, *actors*, *film*:Star Wars V] in Figure 2b is [*actor*, *actors*, *film*]. Each meta-walk represents a pattern of relationship between entities of certain semantic types. Some meta-walks represent basically the same relationships between the same sets of semantic types. For instance, meta-walk [*actor*, *film*] in Figure 2a and meta-walk [*actor*, *actors*, *film*] in Figure 2b represent the relationship of starring in movies between the same set of actors and movies. Next, we define the conditions under which two meta-walks represent the same relationship between the same set of entities. Given database $D = (V, E, \mathcal{L}, \mathcal{A})$, the value of an entity node $e \in V$ is the pair $\mathcal{L}(v) : \mathcal{A}(v)$. The value of a walk $w = [v_0, \ldots, v_n]$ is the tuple $[a_0, \ldots, a_m]$, $m \leq n$ such that a_0 and a_m are the values of v_0 and v_n, respectively, and for all $0 \leq i < j \leq n$ and $0 \leq i', j' \leq m$ if $a_{i'}$ and $a_{j'}$ are the values of entity nodes v_i and v_j, respectively, then $i' < j'$. For instance, the value of walk [*actor*:Ford, *actors*, *film*:Star Wars V] is [*actor*:Ford, *film*:Star Wars V]. Values of two walks are **equal** iff they have equal arities and their corresponding positions contain the same label and equal values. Two walks are **content equivalent** iff their values are equal. We show content-equivalent walks w and x as $w \equiv x$. We denote the set of walks in database D whose meta-walks are p as $p(D)$. Meta-walks p_1 in database D_1 and p_2 in database D_2 are **content equivalent** iff there is a bijection $M : p_1(D_1) \to p_2(D_2)$ where for all $w \in p_1(D_1)$, $w \equiv M(w)$. For instance, meta-walks [*actor*, *film*] in Figure 2b and [*actor*, *actors*, *film*] in Figure 2a are content equivalent. We denote content-equivalent meta-walks p_1 and p_2 as $p_1 \equiv p_2$.

Naturally, content-equivalent meta-walks represent the same sets of relationships between the same sets of entities. Thus, if a transformation bijectively maps each meta-walk in database D_1 to its content-equivalent meta-walk in database D_2, D_1 and D_2 represent the same information. We formally prove this intuition later in the section. However, this straightforward definition ignores some interesting transformations. For example, intuitively the databases in Figure 2a and Figure 2b contain the same information. But, there is not any meta-walk in Figure 2a that is content equivalent to meta-walk p_3=[*actor*, *actors*, *actor*] in Figure 2b. By looking closely at the Figure 2b and original Movielicious data, we observe that the node *actors* always groups actors that play in the same movie. Thus, each walk of p_3 is a part of a walk of meta-walk p_4= [*actor*, *actors*, *film*, *actors*, *actor*] in Figure 2b. Hence, if a transformation maps p_4 to a content-equivalent meta-walk in Figure 2a, it also preserves the information of p_3. Generally, some meta-walks contain other meta-walks. If a transformation preserves the information of a meta-walk, it will preserve the information of its contained meta-walks. Let us formalize this relationship between meta-walks. A walk w is a **subwalk** of walk x, shown as $w \sqsubseteq x$, iff w is a subsequence of x. For example, walk $[v_1, v_2, v_3]$ is a subwalk of walk $x_1 = [v_1, v_2, v_4, v_2, v_3]$, but walk $[v_1, v_3]$ is not a subwalk of x_1. Meta-walk p is a subwalk of meta-walk r, denoted as $p \sqsubseteq r$, iff a walk of p is a subwalk of a walk of r. For example, [*actor*, *actors*, *actor*] is a subwalk of [*actor*, *actors*, *film*, *actors*, *actor*] in Figure 2b.

DEFINITION 3. *Given meta-walks p and p' in database D, p'* **includes** *p iff*

- *there is a bijection M between $p(D)$ and $p'(D)$ such that for every walk $w \in p(D)$, we have $w \sqsubseteq M(w)$ and w and $M(w)$ start at the same node and end at the same node.*
- *there exists an entity label l whose occurrence in p' is more than in p, and the closest entity labels to the left and to the right of l in p' are not l.*

For example, meta-walk [*actor*, *actors*, *film*, *actors*, *actor*] includes [*actor*, *actors*, *actor*] in Figure 2b. A meta-walk p in database D is **maximal** iff it has a walk in D and it is not included in any other meta-walk. For instance, [*actor*, *actors*, *film*, *actors*, *actor*] is maximal in Figure 2a. Maximal meta-walks subsume the information of non-maximal meta-walks. Thus, if a transformation preserves only the information of maximal meta-walks in a database, it will preserve the information content of the database. Let $\mathcal{P}(\mathbf{L})$ denote the set of all meta-walks in the set of databases $\mathbf{L}$. We denote the set of all maximal meta-walks in $\mathbf{L}$ as $\mathcal{P}_{\max}(\mathbf{L})$.

DEFINITION 4. *Transformation $T : \boldsymbol{L} \to \boldsymbol{K}$ is* **relationship reorganizing** *iff there is a bijective mapping $M : \mathcal{P}_{\max}(\boldsymbol{L}) \to \mathcal{P}_{\max}(\boldsymbol{K})$ such that $p \equiv M(p)$.*

The transformations that map Figure 2b to Figure 2a and Figure 1a to Figure 1b are relationship-reorganizing. Using Definitions 3 and 4, we have the following theorem.

THEOREM 1. *Every relationship-reorganizing transformation is similarity preserving.*

4.2 Toward Robust Similarity Algorithms

To the best of our knowledge, the most frequently used methods for similarity search on graph database are based on random walk, e.g., RWR [9], pairwise random walk, e.g., SimRank [5], or relationship-constrained framework, e.g., PathSim [6]. There are other similarity measures, such as common neighbors, $Katz_\beta$ measure, hitting time, and commute time, which can be considered as special cases of aforementioned heuristics. Hence, we discuss similarity search methods based on these three frameworks.

Methods that use random walk and pairwise random walks leverage the topology of a graph database to measure the degree of similarities between entities. A relationship-reorganizing transformation may remove many edges from and add many

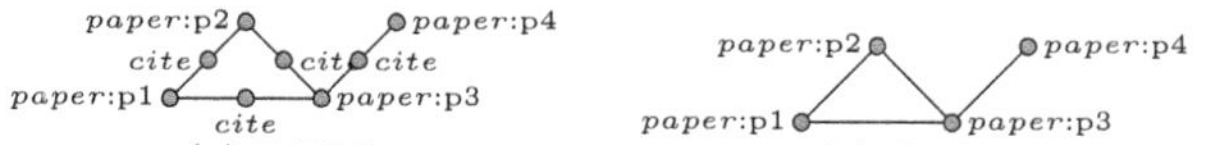

(a) DBLP (b) SNAP

Figure 3: Fragments of two citation databases

new nodes and edges to a database. Thus, it may radically modify the database topology. For example, a relationship-reorganizing transformations may drastically change the degree of a node and modify the probability that random surfers visit the node. Hence, these methods cannot always return the same answers over the original and the transformed database for the same query. In Section 1, we have shown that RWR and SimRank return different results over a database and its relationship reorganization in Figure 1.

PathSim measures the similarity between entities over a given relationship [6]. PathSim uses meta-walks to represent relationships between entities. For instance, the relationship between two movies in Figure 1b based on their common actors is expressed by *[film,actors,actor,actors,film]*. Let $p(e,f,d)$ be a set of walks of meta-walk p from entity e to entity f in database D. PathSim measures the similarity between e and f according to the input meta-walk p as $s(e,f) = \frac{2\times|p(e,f,D)|}{|p(e,e,D)|+|p(f,f,D)|}$. PathSim considers walks with and without consecutive forward and backward traverses from an entity to a node without value when it computes $s(e,f)$.

PathSim may return different answers for the same queries over the same relationship on a database and its relationship reorganizations. Figure 3 shows fragments of DBLP from *dblp.uni-trier.de*, and SNAP from *snap.stanford.edu* that contain information about citations. Consider the meta-walk s = *[paper, cite, paper, cite, paper]* in Figure 3a, and its corresponding meta-walk s' = *[paper, paper, paper]* in Figure 3b. s has a walk between entities $p3$ and $p4$, x = [*paper*:p3, *cite*, *paper*:p4, *cite*, *paper*:p4]. But, there is no walk of meta-walk s' between $p3$ and $p4$ in Figure 3b. Hence, PathSim reports $p1$ to be more similar to $p2$ than $p3$ in Figure 3a, but considers $p1$ to be more similar to $p3$ than $p2$ in Figure 3b. PathSim returns different answers because it considers walks with consecutive forward and backward traverses from an entity to a node without value, such as x.

From here onward, we call a walk without consecutive forward and backward traverses from an entity to a node without value **informative**, and **non-informative** otherwise. As discussed in Section 4.1, non-informative walk either do not provide any information about the relationship between entities or their information can be represented by a shorter walk. Figure 3a and Figure 3b show that non-informative walks may be present in a database but be absent from its relationship-reorganizing transformations. Hence, if we modify PathSim so that it computes similarity scores using only informative walks, it will be representation independent under relationship-reorganizing transformations. Using Definition 3 and 4, we have the following theorem.

THEOREM 2. *Let* $T : \boldsymbol{L} \rightarrow \boldsymbol{K}$ *be a relationship-reorganizing transformation and* p *be a meta-walk in* $D \in \boldsymbol{L}$. *There is a meta-walk* r *in* $T(D)$ *such that for each pair of entities* e *and* f *in* D, *we have* $|p(e,f,D)| = |r(T(e),T(f),T(D))|$.

Given entities e and f and a meta-walk p in database D and their corresponding entities and meta-walk in $T(D)$, $T(e)$, $T(f)$, and r, the numerator and denominator of $s(e,f)$ will be respectively equal to the numerator and denominator of $s(T(e),T(f))$. Hence, the modification of PathSim will return equal similarity scores for queries over a database and its relationship-reorganizing transformation. We call this extension of PathSim, *Robust-PathSim* (*R-PathSim*).

The computation of R-PathSim is similar to that of PathSim [6] with extra steps of detecting and ignoring non-informative walks. The *commuting matrix* of meta-walk $p = [l_1, \cdots, l_k]$ in database D is $M_p = A_{l_1 l_2} A_{l_2 l_3} \cdots A_{l_{k-1} l_k}$, where $A_{l_i l_j}$ is the adjacency matrix between nodes of labels l_i and l_j in D. Each entry $M_p(i,j)$ represents the the number of walks between entities $i \in l_i(D)$ and $j \in l_j(D)$. Given commuting matrix M_p, we can compute the PathSim score between i and j as $\frac{2M_p(i,j)}{M_p(i,i)+M_p(j,j)}$. However, R-PathSim uses only the informative walks. A meta-walk whose walks may not be informative is in the form of $p = [l_1, \cdots, l_i, x_{n_i}, \cdots, x_{m_i}, l_i, \ldots, l_k]$, $1 \leq i \leq k$ where l_i's are entity labels and $x_{n_i}, \cdots, x_{m_i}$ are labels of nodes without values. Meta-walk p may have non-informative walks because it contains meta-walks $s_i = [l_i, x_{n_i}, \ldots, x_{m_i}, l_i]$. Let M_{s_i} be the commuting matrix of s_i. The diagonal entries in M_{s_i} contain the number of non-informative walks of s_i. Let $M^d_{s_i}$ denote a diagonal matrix of M_{s_i}. Matrix $M_{s_i} - M^d_{s_i}$ contains the number of informative walks of s_i. To compute the number of informative walks of meta-walk p, we first find subwalks of p that start and end with same entity label and their remaining labels are non-entity labels. We call this set of meta-walks S and denote the rest of the subwalks of p R. The number of informative walks of p between each pair of entities in D is $M_p = \prod_{s \in S}(M_s - M^d_s) \prod_{r \in R} M_r$.

It may take a long time to compute the commuting matrix of a relatively long meta-walk in query time. Also, it is not feasible to precompute and store the commuting matrices for every possible meta-walk. PathSim precomputes commuting matrices for relatively short meta-walks. Then, PathSim concatenates them in the query time to get the commuting matrix of a longer meta-walk. This approach efficiently computes PathSim scores [6]. We follow the same method to compute R-PathSim scores efficiently.

5. EMPIRICAL EVALUATION

Datasets & Setting: We use 3 datasets in our experiments. We use Arxiv High Energy Physics paper citation graph from SNAP with 34,536 nodes and 42,158 edges whose fragments are shown in Figure 3b. We use a subset of IMDb data with 2,409,252 nodes and 7,525,281 edges whose fragments are shown in Figure 4a. We also use a subset of Microsoft Academic Search data with 44,068 nodes and 44,220 edges whose fragments are shown Figure 5. We implement our and other algorithms using MATLAB 8.5 on a Linux server with 64GB memory and two quad core processors.

Robustness: We use normalized Kendall's tau to compare ranked lists. The value of normalized Kendall's tau varies between 0 and 1 where 0 means the two lists are identical and 1 means one list is the reverse of the other. As users are interested in the highly ranked answers, we compare top 5 and 10 answers. Because it takes too long to run SimRank and RWR over full IMDb dataset, we use the largest subset of IMDb with 47,835 nodes and 130,916 edges over which we can run SimRank and RWR reasonably fast to evaluate their robustness. We set the restart probability of RWR to 0.2 and the damping factor of SimRank to 0.8. We reorganize IMDb database to the structures of Freebase (FB), Movielicious (MVL) and a structure from

		IM2MV	IM2AS	IM2FB
Top 5	RWR	0.444	0.459	0.158
	SimRank	0.365	0.392	0.337
Top 10	RWR	0.404	0.415	0.155
	SimRank	0.343	0.348	0.322

Table 1: Average ranking differences for all transformations.

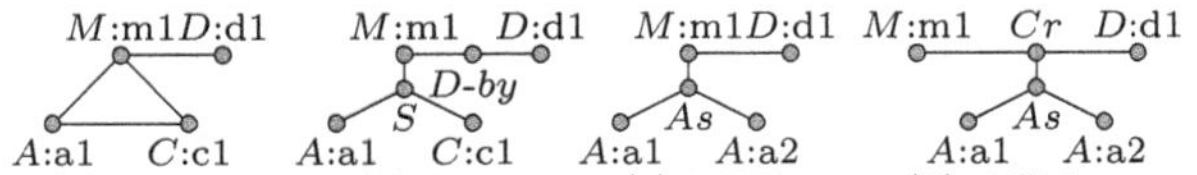

(a) IMDb (b) FB (c) MVL (d) ASM

Figure 4: Fragments of movies databases where A, M, C, D, S, As, Cr and $D\text{-}by$ denote *actor*, *movie*, *character*, *director*, *starring*, *actors*, *credit* and *directed-by*.

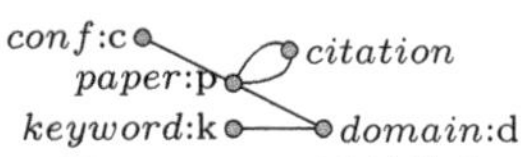

Figure 5: Fragments of MAS databases.

evc-cit.info/cit041x/assignment_css.html (ASM) whose fragments are shown in Figure 4. We denote the transformations from IMDb to Freebase as IM2FB, from IMDb to Movielicious as IM2MV, and from IMDb to ASM as IM2AS. Since MVL and ASM structures do not have any *character*, we remove character nodes in IMDb when applying IM2MV and IM2AS transformations. For query workload, we randomly sample 50 movies in IMDb database based on their degrees. Table 1 shows the average ranking differences for top 5 and 10 answers returned by RWR and SimRank over IM2MV, IM2AS, and IM2FB transformations. Because R-PathSim delivers the same rankings over these transformations, we have omitted the results for R-PathSim. Since each entity label and its consecutive entity labels in every meta-walk over IMDb are different, all walks used in the computation of PathSim are informative. Corresponding meta-walks in FB, MVL and ASM to those meta-walks in IMDb also follow the same properties. Similar to R-PathSim, PathSim is robust over these transformations. Thus, we omit the results of PathSim from the table. According to Table 1, the rankings produced by RWR and SimRank varies considerably over relationship-reorganizing transformations. We have shown in Section 4 that PathSim is not robust under certain relationship-reorganizing transformations. We use SNAP dataset and reorganize it to the structure of DBLP as depicted in Figure 3a. We randomly sample 50 papers from SNAP based on their degrees for query workload. We use [*paper, paper, paper*] on SNAP and [*paper, citation, paper, citation, paper*] on DBLP for PathSim. The average ranking differences for top 5 and 10 answers of PathSim are 0.522 and 0.495, respectively. Hence, the output of PathSim varies significantly over relationship-reorganizing transformations.

Efficiency: We evaluate the efficiency of R-PathSim and PathSim over full IMDb dataset. We transform IMDb to Movielicious (MVL) structure that contains both informative walks and non-informative walks to evaluate the impact of detecting informative walks in R-PathSim. This results in a database of 1,272,253 nodes and 2,886,494 edges. We precompute and store commuting matrices for meta-walks of size, i.e., number of labels, up to 3 to be used in query processing as done in PathSim [6]. MVL has 16 meta-walks with sizes less or equal to 3, respectively. It takes 49.5 seconds for R-PathSim to precompute and store the commuting matrices of these meta-walk which are reasonable for a preprocessing step. We have executed PathSim over the same datasets and get almost equal running times as the ones of R-PathSim. We randomly select 100 movies from MVL based on their degrees and use them as our query workloads. Given that commuting matrices up to size 3 are materialized, the average query processing time in second per query per meta-walk for meta-walks of size 5 and 7 are .033 and .023 for R-PathSim, and .029 and .021 for PathSim. Efficiency evaluation over other datasets can be found at [2].

Effectiveness: We evaluate the effectiveness of R-PathSim over the Microsoft Academic Search (MAS) dataset. For query workload, we randomly sample 50 conferences based on their degrees from the dataset. To provide the ground truth, given a conference q, we manually group all other conferences in three categories: *similar*, which contains all conferences that have the same domain as q; *quite-similar*, which includes the conferences in the domains that are closely related to the domain of q; and *least-similar* that contain conferences in the domains that are not strongly related to the domain of q. We use Normalized DCG (nDCG) to compare the effectiveness of R-PathSim and PathSim. The value of nDCG ranges between 0 and 1 where higher values show more effective ranking. We report the values of nDCG for top 5 (nDCG@5) and top 10 (nDCG@10) answers. We use meta-walk [*conf, paper, citation, paper, citation, paper, conf*] to find similar conferences based on their papers' citations. The average nDCG@5 (nDCG@10) for R-PathSim and PathSim are .264 (.315) and .261 (.313), respectively.

6. CONCLUSION

We postulated that a similarity search algorithm should return essentially the same answers for the same query over different representations of a database. We introduced a family of widespread representational shift over graph databases called relationship-reorganizing transformation. We showed that current similarity search algorithms are not representation independent and proposed a new algorithm that is representation independent under this transformation.

7. ACKNOWLEDGMENTS

This work is supported by NSF grant number 1421247.

8. REFERENCES

[1] S. Abiteboul, R. Hull, and V. Vianu. *Foundations of Databases: The Logical Level.* Addison-Wesley, 1994.

[2] Y. Chodpathumwan, A. Aleyasin, A. Termehchy, and Y. Sun. Representation Independent Proximity and Similarity Search. 2015, arXiv:1508.03763 [cs.DB].

[3] W. Fan and P. Bohannon. Information Preserving XML Schema Embedding. *TODS*, 33(1), 2008.

[4] A. Hogana, M. Arenas, A. Mallea, and A. Polleres. Everything you always wanted to know about blank nodes. *Web Semantics*, 2014.

[5] G. Jeh and J. Widom. SimRank: A Measure of Structural-context Similarity. In *KDD*, 2002.

[6] Y. Sun, J. Han, X. Yan, S. P. Yu, and T. Wu. PathSim: MetaPath-Based Top-K Similarity Search in Heterogeneous Information Networks. In *VLDB*, 2011.

[7] A. Termehchy, M. Winslett, Y. Chodpathumwan, and A. Gibbons. Design Independent Query Interfaces. *TKDE*, 2012.

[8] H. Tong and C. Faloutsos. Center-Piece Subgraphs: Problem Definition and Fast Solutions. In *KDD*, 2006.

[9] H. Tong, C. Faloutsos, and J. Pan. Fast Random Walk with Restart and its Applications. In *ICDM*, 2006.

Why Did You Cover That Song?: Modeling N-th Order Derivative Creation with Content Popularity

Kosetsu Tsukuda, Masahiro Hamasaki, and Masataka Goto
National Institute of Advanced Industrial Science and Technology (AIST), Japan
{k.tsukuda, masahiro.hamasaki, m.goto}@aist.go.jp

ABSTRACT

Many amateur creators now create derivative works and put them on the web. Although there are several factors that inspire the creation of derivative works, such factors cannot usually be observed on the web. In this paper, we propose a model for inferring latent factors from sequences of derivative work posting events. We assume a sequence to be a stochastic process incorporating the following three factors: (1) the original work's attractiveness, (2) the original work's popularity, and (3) the derivative work's popularity. To characterize content popularity, we use content ranking data and incorporate rank-biased popularity based on the creators' browsing behavior. Our main contributions are three-fold: (1) to the best of our knowledge, this is the first study modeling derivative creation activity, (2) by using a real-world dataset of music-related derivative work creation to evaluate our model, we showed the effectiveness of adopting all three factors to model derivative creation activity and considering creators' browsing behavior, and (3) we carried out qualitative experiments and showed that our model is useful in analyzing derivative creation activity in terms of category characteristics, temporal development of factors that trigger derivative work posting events, etc.

Keywords

Derivative creation; latent variable model; user generated content

1. INTRODUCTION

The era when only professional creators were able to create and provide content on the web has passed; now amateur creators who used to be just consumers can also easily create and provide content. Such content is known as user generated content (UGC). Since not all amateur creators can create new content from scratch, it is popular to use existing original (1st generation) work as the basis for new content; such content is called *derivative work* [5] or 2nd generation work. For example, on YouTube[1], there are many videos in which amateur creators dance to an existing song or perform a cover of it. On Thingiverse[2], which is a web service where amateur creators can share 3D model data intended for a 3D printer, it is popular for creators to download original 3D model data created by others, modify it, and upload their new version. In this kind of derivative work creation activity, a creator influenced by 2nd generation content can create 3rd generation content. Similarly, N-th generation content can be transformed into N+1-th generation content. Such derivative work creation activity is called "N-th order derivative creation [4]."

We know that derivative creation is popular, but *why* are individual derivative works created? There are various factors that inspire the creation of derivative works. However, since the factors that trigger derivative creation cannot usually be observed on the web, they are difficult to detect. To get around this problem, we assume that when a creator creates a derivative work, there are three triggering factors: (1) original work's attractiveness, (2) original work's popularity, and (3) derivative work's popularity. Based on this assumption, we propose a model to estimate the factors that triggered derivative work creation. Since the relative influence of the three factors varies among creators, our model also incorporates the latent relationships between creators and each of the three factors. Moreover, our model uses content ranking information to take into account the popularity of original and derivative works. By referring to the examination model of a web search result [7], we model popularity based on the hypothesis that higher ranked content has a larger influence because such content is, with high probability, viewed by many creators. By using efficient Bayesian inference based on the stochastic expectation-maximization (EM) algorithm [6], we can obtain the latent triggers for derivative work posts.

Our main contributions in this paper are as follows. First, to the best of our knowledge, this is the first study modeling derivative creation activity. Our model can simultaneously take into account the influences of three factors: (1) original work attractiveness, (2) original work popularity, and (3) derivative work popularity. Second, we quantitatively evaluated our model by using derivative creation data of the music content. Our experimental results show that the model adopting all three factors achieves the best result in terms of the log likelihood computed by using test data. We also show that when we consider the content popularity based on popularity ranking, the method reflecting creators' browsing behavior is the most effective to model derivative creation activity. Third, we carried out qualitative experiments in terms of (1) category characteristics, (2) temporal development of factors that trigger the derivative work posting events, and (3) N-th order derivative creation process and showed that our model can be used to analyze derivative work creation activity.

2. RELATED WORK

[Analysis of Derivative Creation Activity] A limited number of studies have investigated derivative creation activity. Eto *et al.* [3] developed a 3D modeling application and a model sharing web service called Modulobe, which allows users to create 3D models from scratch or based on the work of other creators. They reported that 10.4% of models were parents of other models and the chains of creation reached four generations. Cheliotic and Yew [1] examined

[1]http://www.youtube.com
[2]http://www.thingiverse.com

CIKM'16 , October 24 - 28, 2016, Indianapolis, IN, USA

ISBN 978-1-4503-4073-1/16/10...$15.00
DOI: http://dx.doi.org/10.1145/2983323.2983674

the remixing activity in the ccMixter online music community[3]. They reported that derivative creation greatly boosted the output of a community as well as increased the diversity of the output. Hamasaki *et al.* [ ] analyzed derivative creation activity on a video sharing web service called Niconico[4]. They used explicit citation information between an original work and its derivative works and discussed certain statistics (*e.g.*, the number of works derived from an original work). All the studies mentioned above analyzed *how* derivative works had been created by using a network based on the relationships between the original content and derivative works. In this work, we focus on *why* derivative works were created and propose a model to estimate the factors and their influences.

[Modeling Influences in Social Communities] Since estimating influences among users in social activities is useful for various applications, such as influential user detection [ ] and personalized recommendation [ ], many methods for estimating such influences have been proposed. One major approach is to use an information diffusion model such as the independent cascade model [ ]. Although discrete time is assumed with this model, Saito *et al.* [ ] proposed a model based on Poisson processes that allows for continuous time modeling. However, their model requires a network of users in which a node corresponds to a user and an edge between users represents the existence of influence. To overcome this limitation, Iwata *et al.* [ ] proposed a model that discovers latent influences between users without a network. Although the cascade Poisson process [ ] models a sequence of cascading events, the model proposed by Iwata *et al.*, which is called the shared cascade Poisson process (SCPP), can handle multiple sequences of adoption events for multiple items by sharing parameters. Tanaka *et al.* [ ] extended the SCPP to estimate the factors that trigger item purchase events. They considered the users' view histories for TV advertisements in addition to influences between users and showed that the SCPP is also effective in modeling purchase events. Our model extends the SCPP and the model proposed by Tanaka *et al.* [ ], differing from them in the following two respects. First, in the other models, there is no need to consider the effect of adopted items such as purchased items. However, in derivative creation activity, adopted items (*i.e.*, derivative works) also influence other creators' creation activity. Therefore, we extended the SCPP so that we can handle the effect of both original works and derivative works. Second, although the other models assume that the popularity of items is constant regardless of time, we assume that content popularity depends on time. Hence, our model incorporates the time-dependent popularity of both original works and derivative works by considering content ranking data and the creators' ranking browsing behavior.

3. MODEL

In an online social activity model, it is common to consider user preference for content (we refer to the factor as original work attractiveness) and influences among users [,]. However, in derivative creation activity, the existence of user influence is unlikely because no obvious influences among creators (users) have been observed in derivative creation activity analysis [, ,]. Instead, it seemed that the *rich-get-richer* phenomenon exists in the activity [ ]. Hence, we assume that the popularity of original and derivative works is an important factor in modeling derivative creation activity. Note that although we describe the *complete* model as incorporating four factors (original work attractiveness, creator influence, original work popularity, and derivative work popularity) in this section, our proposed model incorporates three of these (setting aside the creator influence factor).

3.1 Notations

Given a category (*e.g.*, "3D models of chairs" or "music videos covering songs") and observation time period T, let $\mathcal{I}$ be a set of original works posted to a web service (*e.g.*, Thingiverse or YouTube) between time 0 and time T. Let (t^p_{ij}, u^p_{ij}) denote the jth derivative work posting event of original work i. More specifically, creator $u^p_{ij} \in \mathcal{U}$ posts i's derivative work at time t^p_{ij}. Here, $\mathcal{U}$ is the set of creators. Without loss of generality, we assume that derivative work posting events are sorted in ascending order of their timestamps: $t^p_{ij} \leq t^p_{ij'}$ for $j < j'$. When J_i represents the total number of i's derivative works posted during the observation time period, a set of derivative work posting events of i is given by $\mathcal{D}_i = \{(t^p_{ij}, u^p_{ij})\}_{j=1}^{J_i}$. Hence, a set of derivative work posting events of all original works is given by $\mathcal{D} = \{\mathcal{D}_i\}_{i \in \mathcal{I}}$.

Suppose creators can see the ranking of original works on the web service, where original works are ranked based on the popularity computed using statistics such as view count. Let (t^o_{ik}, r^o_{ik}) denote the kth ranked event of $i \in \mathcal{I}$. That is, i is ranked at the r^o_{ik}th place at time t^o_{ik}. We also assume that the events are sorted in ascending order of their timestamps without loss of generality: $t^o_{ik} \leq t^o_{ik'}$ for $k < k'$. Let K^o_i be the total number of i's ranked events between time 0 and time T, then a set of ranked events of i is given by $\mathcal{O}_i = \{(t^o_{ik}, r^o_{ik})\}_{k=1}^{K^o_i}$. Therefore, a set of ranked events of all original works is given by $\mathcal{O} = \{\mathcal{O}_i\}_{i \in \mathcal{I}}$.

Similarly, suppose creators can also see the ranking of derivative works. In the same manner as with the ranked event of the original work, let (t^c_{ik}, r^c_{ik}) denote the kth ranked event of i's derivative work. Let K^c_i be the total number of ranked events of i's derivative works between time 0 and time T; then a set of ranked events of i's derivative works is given by $\mathcal{C}_i = \{(t^c_{ik}, r^c_{ik})\}_{k=1}^{K^c_i}$. Note that $\mathcal{C}_i$ includes ranked events of all i's derivative works. Finally, a set of ranked events of all derivative works of all original works is given by $\mathcal{C} = \{\mathcal{C}_i\}_{i \in \mathcal{I}}$.

3.2 Factors

3.2.1 *Original Work Attractiveness (Oatt)*

A creator may create original work i's derivative work because he/she thinks that i is attractive even if it is not popular. The attractiveness of i can be due to i's various features; in the case of a song, the features can be the melody, beat, lyrics, etc. We assume that each creator has a different preference for original content attractiveness. We also assume that the post rate based on original work attractiveness is constant in the time period from 0 to T as described in Figure 1(a). Here, the rate at time t represents the instantaneous probability of a creator posting i's derivative work at t. This kind of constant rate is known as the "background rate" in the point process framework [ ]. Based on these assumptions, we model the rate at which creator u posts i's derivative work triggered by i's attractiveness as follows: $f_i(u) = \alpha_i \theta_{Ou}$, where $\alpha_i \geq 0$ is the original work attractiveness. The $\theta_{Ou} \geq 0$ represents the probability that u is influenced by original work attractiveness when he/she creates a derivative work, and $\sum_{u \in \mathcal{U}} \theta_{Ou} = 1$. If u puts a higher priority on original work attractiveness than other factors, θ_{Ou} becomes large. In Figure 1(a), the height of the blue line corresponds to $\alpha_i \theta_{Ou}$.

3.2.2 *Creator Influence (Cinf)*

Creator u may create original work i's derivative work because creator u' posted i's derivative work; in other words, u is influenced by u'. We assume that the influences of u' on other creators are different from one creator to another. For example, if u is a

[3]http://ccmixter.org

[4]http://www.nicovideo.jp

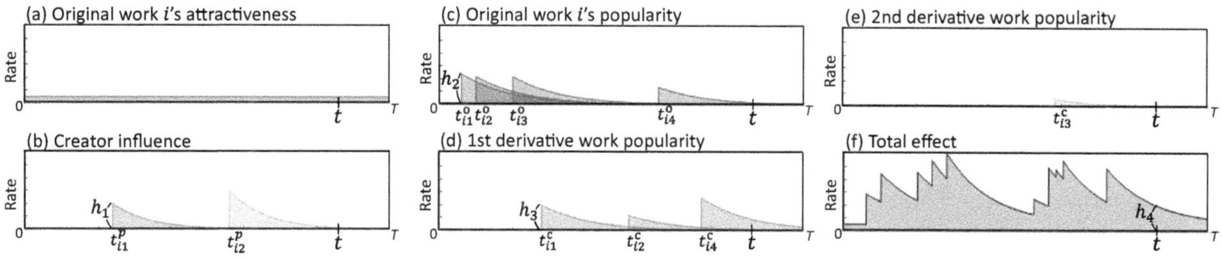

Figure 1: Rate at which creator u posts original work i's derivative work at time t.

fan of u', u' has a larger influence on u than on other creators. We also assume that a creator's influence on another creator decays over time. This assumption is often used to model information diffusion processes between users [10]. Based on these assumptions, we model the rate at which u posts i's derivative work at time t based on the influence of u' who posted i's derivative work at time t' as follows. $g_{(i,t',u')}(t,u) = \alpha_{u'}\theta_{u'u}\mathrm{e}^{-\gamma_p(t-t')}$ if $t' < t$, and 0 otherwise, where $\alpha_{u'} \geq 0$ is the influence of u' on other creators, $\theta_{u'u} \geq 0$ represents the strength of the relation between u' and u, and $\sum_{u \in \mathcal{U} \setminus u'} \theta_{u'u} = 1$, where $\mathcal{U} \setminus u'$ is the set of creators excluding u'. Hence, $\alpha_{u'}\theta_{u'u}$ means the influence of u' on u. Finally, $\mathrm{e}^{-\gamma_p(t-t')}$ models the decay of influence over time with decay parameter $\gamma_p \geq 0$. Note that if u' posts i's derivative work after u, u' does not influence u: $g_{(i,t',u')}(t,u) = 0$ if $t' \geq t$.

In Figure 1(b), two creators post original work i's derivative works. Let the first creator (shown in red) be u'. The influence of u' is $\alpha_{u'}\theta_{u'u}$, which corresponds to h_1 in the figure, when u' posts the derivative work. The influence decreases as time proceeds.

3.2.3 Original Work Popularity (Opop)

If original work i is popular among consumers, creator u may create i's derivative work because his/her derivative work might also become popular. As mentioned in Section 3.1, we assume creators can see the popularity ranking of original works. When two original works are ranked, we hypothesize that the higher ranked one has a larger influence than the lower ranked one. This hypothesis comes from the position bias in the web search: it has been proved that higher ranked results receive more user attention and have larger probabilities of being examined during search sessions [7]. In addition, we assume that each creator has a different preference for original work popularity. As is the case with creator influences, we also assume that the influence of original work popularity on a creator decays over time. Based on these assumptions, we model the rate at which u posts i's derivative work at time t based on the influence of i's popularity as follows: $h_{o(i,t',r')}(t,u) = rb(r')\omega_i\theta_{-1u}\mathrm{e}^{-\gamma_o(t-t')}$ if $t' < t$, and 0 otherwise, where r' represents the rank of i at time t', and function rb computes the rank bias. As reported in studies on behavior analysis of search result examination, the probability that each ranked item is viewed dramatically decreases as the rank drops [7]. Based on the examination behavior, we compute the rank bias as $rb(r') = \frac{1}{r'}$. In Section 5.3, we evaluate the usefulness of rank bias. The term $\omega_i \geq 0$ represents the influence of i's popularity, $\theta_{-1u} \geq 0$ represents the probability that u is influenced by original work popularity when he/she creates a derivative work, and $\sum_{u \in \mathcal{U}} \theta_{-1u} = 1$. Finally, $\mathrm{e}^{-\gamma_o(t-t')}$ models the decay of influence over time with decay parameter $\gamma_o \geq 0$.

In Figure 1(c), the original work i appears four times in the popularity ranking. Let r' be the rank of the first ranked event. The influence of the event is $rb(r')\omega_i\theta_{-1u}$, which corresponds to h_2 in Figure 1(c) at t^o_{i1}. Then, the influence decreases as time proceeds.

3.2.4 Derivative Work Popularity (Dpop)

If original work i's derivative work created by creator u' is popular among consumers, creator u may also create i's derivative work because his/her derivative work might also become popular even if u is not a fan of u'. Based on similar assumptions and the hypothesis described in Section 3.2.3, when i's derivative work was ranked r'th at time t', we model the rate at which u posts i's derivative work at time t based on the influence of i's derivative work popularity as follows. $h_{d(i,t',r')}(t,u) = rb(r')\sigma_i\theta_{-2u}\mathrm{e}^{-\gamma_d(t-t')}$ if $t' < t$, and 0 otherwise, where $\sigma_i \geq 0$ represents the influence of the popularity of i's derivative work, $\theta_{-2u} \geq 0$ represents the probability that u is influenced by derivative work popularity when he/she creates a derivative work, and $\sum_{u \in \mathcal{U}} \theta_{-2u} = 1$. Finally, $\mathrm{e}^{-\gamma_d(t-t')}$ models the decay of influence over time with decay parameter $\gamma_d \geq 0$.

Figure 1(d) and (e) show the influences of i's first and second derivative work popularity, respectively. Let r' be the rank of the first ranked event in Figure 1(d). The influence of the first ranked event is $rb(r')\sigma_i\theta_{-2u}$, which corresponds to h_3 in Figure 1(d) at t^c_{i1}. Then, the influence decreases as time proceeds.

3.3 Derivative Work Post Rate

Based on the factors described in Sections 3.2.1 to 3.2.4, the rate at which u posts i's derivative work at t is given by:

$$\lambda_i(t,u) = f_i(u) + \sum_{(t',u') \in \mathcal{D}_{it \setminus u}} g_{(i,t',u')}(t,u) + \sum_{(t',r') \in \mathcal{O}_{it}} h_{o(i,t',r')}(t,u) + \sum_{(t',r') \in \mathcal{C}_{it}} h_{d(i,t',r')}(t,u), \quad (1)$$

where $\mathcal{D}_{it \setminus u} = \{(t',u') | (t',u') \in \mathcal{D}_i \text{ and } t' < t \wedge u' \neq u\}$, $\mathcal{O}_{it} = \{(t',r') | (t',r') \in \mathcal{O}_i \text{ and } t' < t\}$, and $\mathcal{C}_{it} = \{(t',r') | (t',r') \in \mathcal{C}_i \text{ and } t' < t\}$. Here, $\lambda_i(t,u)$ corresponds to h_4 in Figure 1(f).

4. INFERENCE

Given $\mathcal{D}$, $\mathcal{O}$, and $\mathcal{C}$, we infer the model parameters by using the stochastic EM algorithm. Following Iwata *et al.* [6], we assume that a set of i's derivative work posting events $\mathcal{D}_i$ is generated from a marked point process [9] at a rate of $\lambda_i(t,u)$. Based on this assumption, the likelihood of the function of $\mathcal{D}$ is given by:

$$P(\mathcal{D}|\mathcal{O},\mathcal{C},\boldsymbol{\alpha},\boldsymbol{\omega},\boldsymbol{\sigma},\boldsymbol{\Theta},\boldsymbol{\gamma}) = \prod_{i \in \mathcal{I}} \exp\left(-\int_0^T \sum_{u \in \mathcal{U}} \lambda_i(t,u)dt\right) \prod_{j=1}^{J_i} \lambda_i(t^p_{ij}, t^p_{ij}), \quad (2)$$

where $\boldsymbol{\alpha} = \{\alpha_l\}_{l \in \mathcal{I} \cup \mathcal{U}}$, $\boldsymbol{\omega} = \{\omega_i\}_{i \in \mathcal{I}}$, $\boldsymbol{\sigma} = \{\sigma_i\}_{i \in \mathcal{I}}$, $\boldsymbol{\Theta} = \{\boldsymbol{\theta}_u\}_{u \in \mathcal{U}_+}$, $\boldsymbol{\theta}_u = \{\theta_{uu'}\}_{u' \in \mathcal{U} \setminus u}$, and $\boldsymbol{\gamma} = \{\gamma_p, \gamma_o, \gamma_d\}$. Here, $\mathcal{U}_+$ denotes $\mathcal{U} \cup \{0, -1, -2\}$, where 0, -1, and -2 represent virtual creators for Oatt, Opop, and Dpop, respectively. The term $\exp\left(-\int_0^T \sum_{u \in \mathcal{U}} \lambda_i(t,u)dt\right)$ represents the probability that no creator posts i's derivative work between time 0 and time T.

Following Iwata *et al.* [ ], we introduce latent variables $z_{ij} \in \{0, 1, \cdots, |\mathcal{D}_{it\backslash u}| + |\mathcal{O}_{it}| + |\mathcal{C}_{it}|\}$ to indicate the index of the latent trigger of the jth derivative work posting event of original work i. The terms $z_{ij} = 0$, $|\mathcal{D}_{it\backslash u}| + 1 \leq z_{ij} \leq |\mathcal{D}_{it\backslash u}| + |\mathcal{O}_{it}|$, $|\mathcal{D}_{it\backslash u}| + |\mathcal{O}_{it}| + 1 \leq z_{ij} \leq |\mathcal{D}_{it\backslash u}| + |\mathcal{O}_{it}| + |\mathcal{C}_{it}|$ indicate that the event was triggered due to the influence of Oatt, Opop, and Dpop, respectively. $z_{ij} = j'$ $(1 \leq j' \leq |\mathcal{D}_{it\backslash u}|)$ indicates that the event was triggered due to the influence of the creator who posted the j'th derivative work of i. By using the latent variables, the derivative work post rate in Equation (1) can be written as $\lambda_i(t, u) = \sum_z \lambda_i(t, u, z)$, where $\lambda_i(t, u, z) = f_i(u)$ if $z = 0$, $g_{(i, t^p_{iz}, u^p_{iz})}(t, u)$ if $1 \leq z \leq |\mathcal{D}_{it\backslash u}|$, $h_{o(i, t^o_{iz'}, r^o_{iz'})}(t, u)$ if $|\mathcal{D}_{it\backslash u}| + 1 \leq z \leq |\mathcal{D}_{it\backslash u}| + |\mathcal{O}_{it}|$, and $h_{d(i, t^c_{iz''}, r^c_{iz''})}(t, u)$ if $|\mathcal{D}_{it\backslash u}| + |\mathcal{O}_{it}| + 1 \leq z$. Here, $z' = z - |\mathcal{D}_{it\backslash u}|$ and $z'' = z - |\mathcal{D}_{it\backslash u}| - |\mathcal{O}_{it}|$.

Since the integral part in Equation (2) can be analytically calculated, by combining the above equations, the joint distribution of $\mathcal{D}$ and latent variables $\mathcal{Z} = \{\{z_{ij}\}_{j=1}^{J_i}\}_{i \in \mathcal{I}}$ is given by:

$$P(\mathcal{D}, \mathcal{Z}|\mathcal{O}, \mathcal{C}, \boldsymbol{\alpha}, \boldsymbol{\omega}, \boldsymbol{\sigma}, \boldsymbol{\Theta}, \boldsymbol{\gamma})$$
$$= \prod_{i \in \mathcal{I}} \exp\left[\alpha_i T + \frac{1}{\gamma_p} \sum_{j=1}^{J_i} \alpha_{u_{ij}} \left(1 - \mathrm{e}^{-\gamma_p (T - t^p_{ij})}\right)\right.$$
$$+ \frac{\omega_i}{\gamma_o} \sum_{k=1}^{K^o_i} rb(r^o_{ik}) \left(1 - \mathrm{e}^{-\gamma_o (T - t^o_{ik})}\right)$$
$$\left. + \frac{\sigma_i}{\gamma_d} \sum_{k=1}^{K^c_i} rb(r^c_{ik}) \left(1 - \mathrm{e}^{-\gamma_d (T - t^c_{ik})}\right)\right] \prod_{j=1}^{J_i} \lambda_i(t^p_{ij}, t^p_{ij}, z_{ij}). \quad (3)$$

We assume a Gamma prior for each of the original work attractiveness scores α_i as $P(\alpha_i|a, b) \propto \alpha_i^{a-1} \exp(-b\alpha_i)$, where a and b are hyperparameters. In this study, following Iwata *et al.* [ ], we set $a = b = 1$. We also assume a Gamma prior for each creator influence α_u, influence of original work popularity ω_i, and influence of derivative work popularity σ_i. In addition, we assume a Dirichlet prior over $\boldsymbol{\theta}_u$, $u \in \mathcal{U}_+$ as $P(\boldsymbol{\theta}_u|\beta) \propto \prod_{u' \in \mathcal{U}\backslash u} \theta_{uu'}^{\beta-1}$. We use a Gamma prior for $\boldsymbol{\alpha}$, $\boldsymbol{\omega}$, and $\boldsymbol{\sigma}$ and a Dirichlet prior for $\boldsymbol{\Theta}$ to analytically calculate the marginalization over the parameters. The marginalized joint distribution is computed by integrating out those parameters:

$$P(\mathcal{D}, \mathcal{Z}|\mathcal{O}, \mathcal{C}, \boldsymbol{\gamma}, \beta, a, b)$$
$$= \iiiint P(\mathcal{D}, \mathcal{Z}|\mathcal{O}, \mathcal{C}, \boldsymbol{\alpha}, \boldsymbol{\omega}, \boldsymbol{\sigma}, \boldsymbol{\Theta}, \boldsymbol{\gamma}) P(\boldsymbol{\alpha}|a, b)$$
$$\times P(\boldsymbol{\omega}|a, b) P(\boldsymbol{\sigma}|a, b) P(\boldsymbol{\Theta}|\beta) d\boldsymbol{\alpha} d\boldsymbol{\omega} d\boldsymbol{\sigma} d\boldsymbol{\Theta}. \quad (4)$$

Based on the marginalized joint distribution, we developed a stochastic EM procedure for the iteration. In the E-step, given the current state of all but one variable z_{ij}, the new latent assignment of z_{ij} is sampled from the following probability:

$$P(z_{ij} = y|\mathcal{D}, \mathcal{Z}_{\backslash ij}, \mathcal{O}, \mathcal{C}, \boldsymbol{\gamma}, \beta, a, b)$$
$$\propto \frac{P\left(\mathcal{D}, \mathcal{Z}_{\backslash ij}, z_{ij} = y|\mathcal{O}, \mathcal{C}, \boldsymbol{\gamma}, \beta, a, b\right)}{P\left(\mathcal{D}_{\backslash ij}, \mathcal{Z}_{\backslash ij}|\mathcal{O}, \mathcal{C}, \boldsymbol{\gamma}, \beta, a, b\right)}, \quad (5)$$

where $y \in \{0, 1, \cdots, |\mathcal{D}_{it\backslash u}| + |\mathcal{O}_{it}| + |\mathcal{C}_{it}|\}$, and $\backslash ij$ represents the procedure excluding the jth derivative work posting event of i. In the M-step, we estimate the decay parameters $\boldsymbol{\gamma}$ and Dirichlet parameter β by maximizing the logarithm of the joint likelihood in Equation (4). Following Iwata *et al.* [ ], $\boldsymbol{\gamma}$ is estimated using Newton's method and β is estimated using the fixed point iteration method [ ]. Finally, we can make the point estimates of the integrated out parameters α_i, α_u, ω_i, σ_i, and $\theta_{uu'}$.

Table 1: Statistics of our dataset.

Category	$\lvert\mathcal{I}\rvert$	$\lvert\mathcal{O}\rvert$	$\lvert\mathcal{D}\rvert$	$\lvert\mathcal{C}\rvert$	$\lvert\mathcal{U}\rvert$
Sing	4,035	64,973	199,320	67,627	18,715
Dance	396	30,925	9,420	22,954	1,153
Play	583	38,726	5,526	20,492	692

5. QUANTITATIVE EXPERIMENTS

In this section, we answer the following two research questions: (1) is adopting three factors (Oatt, Opop, and Dpop) effective to model derivative creation activity? (Section 5.2) and (2) what kinds of ranking bias methods are effective to model derivative creation activity? (Section 5.3)

5.1 Dataset

We used derivative creation activity data of music content on Niconico, which is one of the most popular video sharing web services in Japan. On Niconico, any user can upload and view videos, and derivative creation activity of music content occurs frequently: as of the end of April 2016, more than 140,000 original song videos and more than 590,000 derivative videos had been uploaded to Niconico. Most original songs are created using singing synthesizer software called VOCALOID; we restricted ourselves to original song videos of this type. Niconico maintains three categories of derivative works: (1) sing: covering an original song, (2) dance: dancing to an original song, and (3) play: playing an original song on a musical instrument such as a guitar or piano. We crawled original songs (*i.e.*, original works) posted between 1/1/2010 and 3/31/2013 and their derivative works posted between 1/1/2010 and 6/30/2013. Data between 1/1/2010 and 3/31/2013 were used as training data and data between 4/1/2013 and 6/30/2013 were used as test data. In each category, we eliminated original works that had fewer than two derivative works and creators who posted fewer than three derivative works during the training period.

We also collected ranking data. On Niconico, users can see the top 100 daily ranking of original songs and the top 100 daily rankings for derivatives in each of the sing, dance, and play categories. Ranking data on one day is created based on several statistics of the previous day (*e.g.*, view count and comment count) so that the ranking data represent the work's aggregated popularity. We crawled the top 100 ranking data in each of the original song and three derivative content categories between 1/1/2010 and 6/30/2013. Since only daily ranking data is available on Niconico, the timestamp in all our experiments is measured in days.

Table 1 lists the statistics of the dataset used in the experiments.

5.2 Combination of Factors

[Comparison Models] As mentioned in Section 3, we hypothesize that a model adopting Oatt, Opop, and Dpop is the most effective. To evaluate this hypothesis, the following six models were compared: (1) Oatt, (2) Oatt+Cinf, (3) Oatt+Cinf+Opop+Dpop, (4) Oatt+Opop, (5) Oatt+Dpop, and (6) Oatt+Opop+Dpop, where Oatt+Cinf, for example, represents the model that combines the factors of Oatt and Cinf. Among the six models, (2) corresponds to SCPP [ ] and (6) is our proposed model.

[Evaluation Metric] Predictive performance is one of the most commonly used metrics to evaluate the appropriateness of a learned model [,]. Predictive performance is computed using the negative logarithm of the likelihood for posting events (t, u) during the test period from T to T'. The logarithm of the likelihood is given by $L = \sum_{i \in \mathcal{I}} \left(-\int_T^{T'} \sum_{u \in \mathcal{U}} \lambda_i(t, u) dt\right) \sum_{(t,u) \in \mathcal{D}_i^{\text{test}}} \log \lambda_i(t, u)$, where $\mathcal{D}_i^{\text{test}}$ is the test data for i. When the value of $-L$ is small, the predictive performance is high. To examine the influence of the length of the test period on our results, we examined spans of test

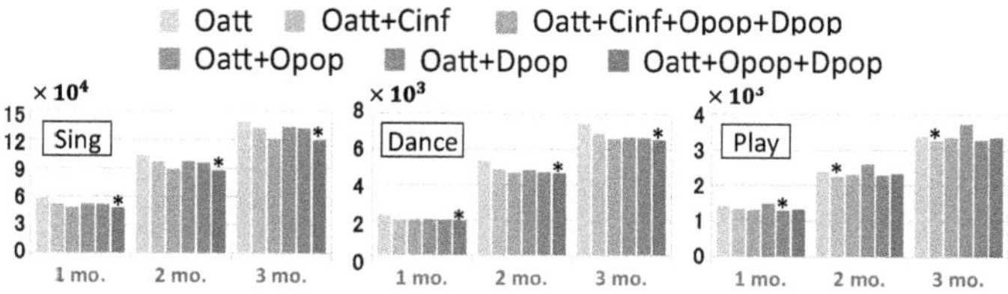

Figure 2: Negative logarithm of likelihood of each model. Vertical axis and horizontal axis represent negative log-likelihood and test periods (*e.g.*, "1 mo." is first set of test data), respectively.

data from one month (4/1/2013 to 4/30/2013) up to three months (4/1/2013 to 6/30/2013).

[Results] Figure 2 shows the negative log-likelihood during each test period in each category. The model that achieved the best performance is marked with "*". In the "sing" and "dance" categories, Oatt–Opop+Dpop exhibited the best result for all test periods. In the "play" category, it did not perform the best, but it stably exhibited high performance in all categories during all test periods. Although other models exhibited the best results in the "play" category, they were unstable because their average ranks in both the "sing" and "dance" categories were low. From these results, we conclude that our proposed model adopting Oatt, Opop, and Dpop is the most effective to model derivative creation activity.

5.3 Ranking Bias Method Comparison

[Settings] As mentioned in Section 3.2.3, our model uses the reciprocal rank method to bias the content ranking based on the creators' browsing behavior of a ranked list (hereafter, "Reciprocal"). To evaluate its effectiveness, we compared it with the following two methods. The first method, "Linear," linearly decreases the ranking bias, $rb(r^o_{ik}) = \frac{101-r^o_{ik}}{100}$. Here, $rb(r^c_{ik})$ is also computed in the same manner. With this method, it is assumed that content influence does not dramatically decrease when the content position in the ranking decreases compared to Reciprocal. The second method, "Uniform," does not take into account the ranking bias: $rb(r^o_{ik}) = rb(r^c_{ik}) = 1$ regardless of the content rank. With this method, it is assumed that all ranked content has equal influence. We used the negative logarithm of the likelihood as an evaluation metric, as in Section 5.2.

[Results] Figure 3 shows the results of the three ranking bias methods. Reciprocal outperformed the other two methods for all test periods in all categories. In addition, Linear always outperformed Uniform: this result indicates the usefulness in considering the rank position of content. Based on these results, we conclude that Reciprocal, which reflects the creators' browsing behavior, is the most effective for modeling derivative creation activity.

6. QUALTITATIVE EXPERIMENTS

In this section, we report on the qualitative analysis results in terms of (1) category characteristics, (2) temporal development of factors that trigger derivative work posting events, and (3) N-th order derivative creation process.

6.1 Category Characteristics

By using the posterior distribution of latent variables in Equation (5), we can analyze the impact of each of the three factors (Oatt, Opop, and Dpop) that trigger derivative work posting events in a category. Algorithm 1 shows the pseudo-code for computing the strengths of the three factors for the jth derivative work posting event of i. In the pseudo-code, E_f, E_{h_o}, and E_{h_d} correspond to the strength of Oatt, Opop, and Dpop, respectively, where $E_f + E_{h_o} + E_{h_d} = 1$. By summing E_f of all derivative works of all original works in a category, we can obtain the strength of Oatt in the category. In the same manner, we can obtain the strength of E_{h_o} and E_{h_d} in a category.

Table 2 lists the ratios of the three factors during the training period. The ratios of the three factors vastly differed from one category to another. In the "sing" category, the ratios of Opop and Dpop were both high, while that of Oatt was low. These results indicate that the creators in this category are susceptible to fads and put a high priority on content popularity. In the "dance" category, the ratio of Dpop was high. In this category, not all creators can compose their own choreography. Hence, a creator often posts a derivative work in which the creator dances to the original song with the original choreography. After that, other creators also post derivative works in which they imitate the choreography. The results show that our model described this category's characteristics well. In the "play" category, the ratio of Oatt was high. This indicates that creators in this category often play their favorite original songs without being affected by fads.

6.2 Temporal Development of Factors

By using Algorithm 1, we can also analyze the temporal development of factors that trigger the derivative work posting events of each original work. This section reports the temporal development of factors per month. Given original work i, we computed the sum of E_f for each i's derivative work posting event every month. Similarly, we computed the sum of E_{h_o} and E_{h_d} every month.

Figure 4 shows example results for the three original songs that we selected for this evaluation. In each category, we show the temporal development of factors for one original work. The horizontal axis represents months in the training period, and the vertical axis represents the number of derivative works posted in a month. The first month on the horizontal axis is the month when the original work's first derivative work was posted. The blue, orange, and red bars indicate the number of posting events caused by Oatt, Opop, and Dpop, respectively. Again, we can observe the characteristics

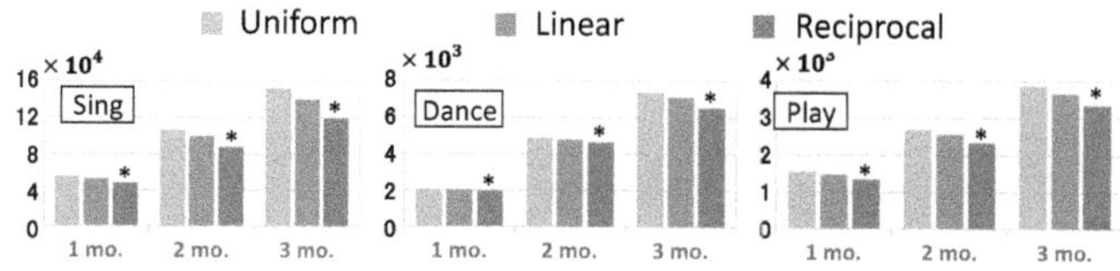

Figure 3: Negative logarithm of likelihood of each ranking bias method.

Algorithm 1 Calculate degree of three factors for jth derivative work posting event of i

Require: $P(z_{ij}|\mathcal{D}, \mathcal{Z}_{\backslash ij}, \mathcal{O}, \mathcal{C}, \gamma, \beta, a, b)$

$E_f \Leftarrow P(z_{ij} = 0|\mathcal{D}, \mathcal{Z}_{\backslash ij}, \mathcal{O}, \mathcal{C}, \gamma, \beta, a, b)$, $E_{h_o} \Leftarrow 0$, $E_{h_d} \Leftarrow 0$, $y \Leftarrow 1$
while $y \leq |\mathcal{O}_{it}| + |\mathcal{C}_{it}|$ **do**
  if $y \leq |\mathcal{O}_{it}|$ **then**
    $E_{h_o} \Leftarrow E_{h_o} + P(z_{ij} = y|\mathcal{D}, \mathcal{Z}_{\backslash ij}, \mathcal{O}, \mathcal{C}, \gamma, \beta, a, b)$
  else
    $E_{h_d} \Leftarrow E_{h_d} + P(z_{ij} = y|\mathcal{D}, \mathcal{Z}_{\backslash ij}, \mathcal{O}, \mathcal{C}, \gamma, \beta, a, b)$
  end if
  $y \Leftarrow y + 1$
end while
return E_f, E_{h_o}, E_{h_d}

Table 2: Ratios of estimated factors (%).

Factor	Sing	Dance	Play
Original work attractiveness (Oatt)	14.6	17.3	42.5
Original work popularity (Opop)	40.0	21.7	40.0
Derivative work popularity (Dpop)	45.4	61.0	17.5

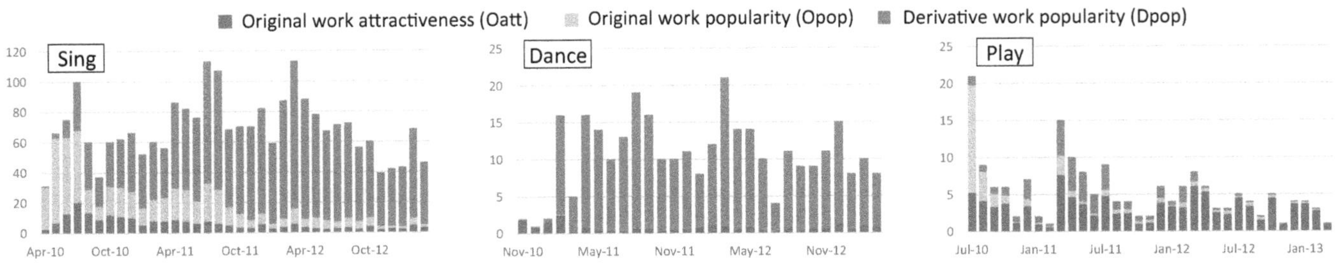

Figure 4: Estimated number of derivative work posting events triggered by each of three factors per month. Vertical axis represents the number of derivative works posted in a month.

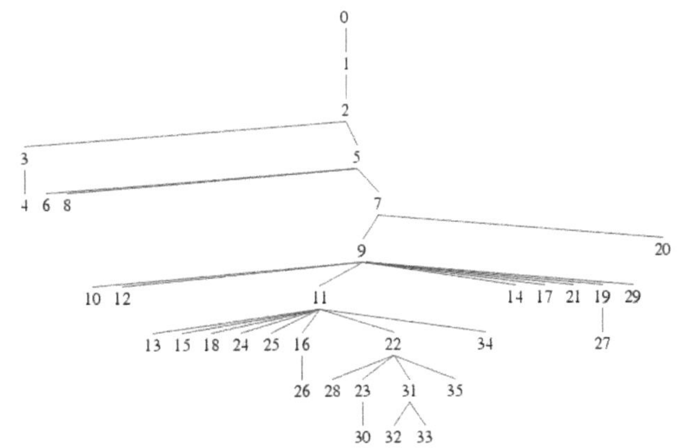

Figure 5: Derivative work creation process of an original work in "dance" category. 0 represents the original work, and $j \geq 1$ represents the jth derivative work.

of each category. In the "sing" category, in the early period of the derivative creation activity, Oatt and Opop had a large influence. We estimate that some derivative works created in the period became popular; after that, other creators who put a high priority on Dpop also posted the original work's derivative work. This is why the influence of Dpop increased as time proceeded. We also observed that Oatt had some influence even at the end period of the graph. This indicates the possibility that some creators happened to find the original song (*e.g.*, by keyword search) and covered the song. In the "dance" category, a limited number of creators who can compose original choreography posted derivative works in the early period (see the blue bars in the first two months). After that, many other creators were influenced by such derivative works and posted new derivative works. In the first half of the test period in the "play" category, many creators who put a high priority on Opop or Dpop posted this original work's derivative works; while in the last half, creators who put a high priority on Oatt kept posting derivative works.

6.3 N-th Order Derivative Creation Process

By using the posterior distribution of latent variables, we can visualize the derivative creation process of an original work. To visualize the process, for each derivative work, we detected y, which is the maximum value in Equation (5). When y was equal to 0 or indicated the index of the original work's ranked event, derivative work creation was triggered by the original work; when y indicated the index of the ranked event of the j'th derivative work, derivative work creation was triggered by the j'th derivative work.

Figure 5 shows the derivative creation process of an original work in the "dance" category. In the figure, 0 represents an original work, and $j \geq 1$ represents the jth derivative work. An edge between numbers indicates that the lower content creation was triggered by the upper one. In this derivative creation process, the 9th and 11th derivative works played an important role because they triggered many derivative creations. We also observed that 10th order derivative creation (30th, 32nd, and 33rd derivative works) occurred in this process.

7. CONCLUSION

We proposed a model for inferring latent factors and their influences in derivative creation activity. For future work, we are interested in applying our model to other derivative creation data such as data on Thingiverse. We are also interested in extending our model by considering additional factors. For example, some original works may be often used to create derivative works during Christmas. Considering such seasonality is one possible way to extend our model.

Acknowledgements

This work was partly supported by MEXT KAKENHI Grant Number (15H06887) and CREST, JST.

8. REFERENCES

[1] G. Cheliotis and J. Yew. An analysis of the social structure of remix culture. In *C&T*, pages 165–174, 2009.

[2] L. S. Donald and I. M. Michael. *Random Point Processes in Time and Space*. Springer, 1991.

[3] K. Eto *et al.* Modulobe: A creation and sharing platform for articulated models with complex motion. In *ACE*, pages 305–308, 2008.

[4] M. Goto. Grand challenges in music information research. *Dagstuhl Follow-Ups: Multimodal Music Processing*, 3:217–225, 2012.

[5] M. Hamasaki *et al.* Network analysis of massively collaborative creation of multimedia contents: Case study of hatsune miku videos on nico nico douga. In *UXTV*, pages 165–168, 2008.

[6] T. Iwata *et al.* Discovering latent influence in online social activities via shared cascade poisson processes. In *KDD*, pages 266–274, 2013.

[7] T. Joachims *et al.* Accurately interpreting clickthrough data as implicit feedback. In *SIGIR*, pages 154–161, 2005.

[8] A. Karatzoglou *et al.* Multiverse recommendation: N-dimensional tensor factorization for context-aware collaborative filtering.

[9] G. Last and A. Brandt. *Marked point processes on the real line : the dynamic approach*. Springer, 1995.

[10] S. Myers and J. Leskovec. On the convexity of latent social network inference. In *Advances in Neural Information Processing Systems 23*, pages 1741–1749. 2010.

[11] K. Saito *et al.* Learning continuous-time information diffusion model for social behavioral data analysis. In *ACML*, pages 322–337, 2009.

[12] A. Simma and M. I. Jordan. Modeling events with cascades of poisson processes. In *UAI*, pages 546–555, 2010.

[13] X. Song *et al.* Personalized recommendation driven by information flow. In *SIGIR*, pages 509–516, 2006.

[14] X. Song *et al.* Information flow modeling based on diffusion rate for prediction and ranking. In *WWW*, pages 191–200, 2007.

[15] Y. Tanaka *et al.* Inferring latent triggers of purchases with consideration of social effects and media advertisements. In *WSDM*, pages 543–552, 2016.

[16] J. Yang and J. Leskovec. Modeling information diffusion in implicit networks. In *ICDM*, pages 599–608, 2010.

Anomalies in the Peer-review System: A Case Study of the Journal of High Energy Physics

Sandipan Sikdar
Dept. of CSE
IIT Kharagpur
West Bengal, India – 721302
sandipansikdar@cse.iitkgp.ernet.in

Matteo Marsili
ICTP
Strada Costiera
34014 Trieste, Italy
marsili@ictp.it

Niloy Ganguly
Dept. of CSE
IIT Kharagpur
West Bengal, India – 721302
niloy@cse.iitkgp.ernet.in

Animesh Mukherjee
Dept. of CSE
IIT Kharagpur
West Bengal, India – 721302
animeshm@cse.iitkgp.ernet.in

ABSTRACT

Peer-review system has long been relied upon for bringing quality research to the notice of the scientific community and also preventing flawed research from entering into the literature. The need for the peer-review system has often been debated as in numerous cases it has failed in its task and in most of these cases editors and the reviewers were thought to be responsible for not being able to correctly judge the quality of the work. This raises a question "Can the peer-review system be improved?" Since editors and reviewers are the most important pillars of a reviewing system, we in this work, attempt to address a related question - given the editing/reviewing history of the editors or reviewers "can we identify the under-performing ones?", with citations received by the edited/reviewed papers being used as proxy for quantifying performance. We term such reviewers and editors as anomalous and we believe identifying and removing them shall improve the performance of the peer-review system. Using a massive dataset of Journal of High Energy Physics (JHEP) consisting of $29k$ papers submitted between 1997 and 2015 with 95 editors and 4035 reviewers and their review history, we identify several factors which point to anomalous behavior of referees and editors. In fact the anomalous editors and reviewers account for 26.8% and 14.5% of the total editors and reviewers respectively and for most of these anomalous reviewers the performance degrades alarmingly over time.

Keywords

Peer-review system; Editor; Reviewer; Citation

CIKM'16 , October 24-November 28, 2016, Indianapolis, IN, USA

© 2016 ACM. ISBN 978-1-4503-4073-1/16/10. . . $15.00

DOI: http://dx.doi.org/10.1145/2983323.2983675

1. INTRODUCTION

Before the contributions of a paper are brought to the notice of the research community, it has to usually pass through a peer-review process, whereby, the correctness and the novelty of the paper is judged by a set of knowledgeable peers. The primary intent of which is to prevent flawed research from getting into mainstream literature [10].

Debates on peer-review system: The effectiveness of this system has been put to question in numerous cases ([9, 12, 13]) with flawed research being added to literature while significantly novel contributions being rejected. That the reviewers often fail to reach consensus ([5]) and that rejected papers are often cited more in the long run ([2]), have already been pointed out. Although there have been several proposals to make it more effective ([3, 7, 11]), the research community is coming to a conclusion that although peer-review system is indispensable it is nonetheless flawed [1].

Entities in the peer-review system: The effectiveness of the peer-review system is dependent directly on the knowledge and training of the editors and reviewers. The editor is responsible for identifying the correct set of referees who can give expert comments on the submission and also for taking the final decision whether a particular paper should be accepted or rejected. The assisting reviewers send their views on the paper in the form of a report. This report is an important part of the whole process as it not only forms the basis of the acceptance/rejection decision but is also sent to the authors for further improvement of the paper.

Anomalous behavior: Ideally impactful papers should be accepted for publication while flawed works should be rejected. We quantify the impact of a paper by the citations it garnered. Thus, a paper getting accepted but managing to garner very less or no citation should be attributed to the anomaly of the system; similarly, a paper getting rejected by the peer-review-system but garnering large number of citations in the long run is also an anomaly. We in this paper investigate the reasons behind the anomalous behaviors ([4]) of the reviewers and editors as they are the most important entities of the peer-review system. Note that although the number of such anomalous editors or referees might be small compared to the number of normal editors or reviewers (as is usually the case with any anomalous set), the damage they can cause to the peer-review system could be irreparable and therefore a thorough investigation of this set is extremely necessary.

Characterizing anomalous editors and reviewers: A thorough investigation of the behavior of the **editors** shows that those editors who (i) are assigned papers more frequently, (ii) select reviewers from a very small set, (iii) assign themselves as reviewers more often (rather than assigning other reviewers) are often under-performers and hence anomalous. Similarly, for **reviewers** we observe the following behaviors to be anomalous - (i) frequent assignments, (ii) very small or very large delay in sending reports, (iii) reviewing papers in very specific topics, (iv) assignments from a very small set of editors or in some cases a single editor, (v) very high or very low proportion of acceptance, (vi) large delay in informing the editor about inability to review and (vii) often declining to review. Papers accepted by reviewers with such behaviors are often low cited while those rejected by them are often highly cited.

Identifying anomalous editors and reviewers: All the above observations lead us to believe that anomalous editors and reviewers can be differentiated from the genuine contributors. To this aim we use these observations as features and by leveraging anomaly detection techniques we are indeed able to filter out the anomalous editors and reviewers. In specific we use k-means clustering [8] to classify normal and anomalous editors and reviewers. We find 26.8% of the editors and 14.5% of the reviewers to be anomalous. We further observe that the papers accepted by these anomalous reviewers are on average cited less while those rejected by them are cited more.

Organization of the paper: The rest of the paper is organized as follows. In section 2 we describe in detail the dataset we used for our analysis and point out certain important features. In section 3 we identify several factors which help in characterizing anomalous editors and referees. In section 4 we identify anomalous editors and reviewers. We further assess the performance of the anomalous reviewers in section 5. We finally conclude in section 6 by highlighting our main contributions and pointing to certain future directions.

2. DATASET

As mentioned earlier, the main aim of this work is to understand the anomalous behaviors of the peer-review system. For this purpose, we use the dataset provided to us by the Journal of High Energy Physics (JHEP)[1]. JHEP is one of the leading journals with an impact factor of 6.1 [2] (2014) and publishes theoretical, experimental and phenomenological papers.

The dataset consists of **28871** papers that were submitted between 1997 (year of inception) and 2015 of which **20384** were accepted and **7073** were rejected. The rest of the papers were either withdrawn by the authors or the final decisions were not available. The meta information available for each paper are (i) title, (ii) name of the contributing authors, (iii) abstract, (iv) date of publication and (v) number of citations till 2015. More importantly, we have for each paper full action history from the date of submission to the date of publication including the editor(s) and the reviewer(s) involved for the review of the paper, the report provided by the reviewer and the report sent to the authors by the editor. We further queried the *Inspire* [3] database to obtain the meta information of the papers (not published/rejected in JHEP). Using this information we created a citation profile for each paper i.e., citations received by the paper per year from the year of its publication. Garfield et. al. [6] had noted that most papers receive the bulk of their citations within the first three years of publication. Moreover it is known that old papers generally have more citations, as the paper had more time to accumulate the citations. Thus to account for this effect, we calculated total citations received by each paper in the first three years from its year of publication (e.g., for a paper published in 2007 we consider the citations received by it till 2010). For the rest of this article, by citation of a paper we refer to the number of citations it received in the first three years from the year of its publication and we only consider the papers published between 1997 to 2012 for our experiments. Some general properties of the whole dataset are summarized below -

(i) Number of unique editors in the dataset is 95 while the number of reviewers is 4035.

(ii) There are 15127 unique authors in the dataset and of those 12434 have at least one accepted paper.

(iii) Average number of submissions per author is 5.18 while the average number of authors per paper is 2.87.

(iv) Average number of reviews for accepted and rejected are 1.76 and 1.35 respectively.

(v) Average number of assignments per editor is 298.28 while per reviewer it is 7.52.

3. ANOMALOUS BEHAVIOR

In the peer-review process each submission is assigned to an editor who in turn assigns one or more reviewers with the task of judging the quality of the contributions of the submitted paper. The reviewer submits a report to the editor who in turn takes the final decision as to accept or reject the paper based on the report. Therefore, the editors and the reviewers are the two important entities of the peer-review system and they are mainly responsible for ensuring that flawed research does not get into the literature while at the same time correctly identify impactful contributions for publication. So in our setting we define the following two cases to be anomalous -

(i) Accepted papers having low citation (research wrongly judged as impactful).

(ii) Rejected papers having high citation (quality research wrongly judged as flawed).

In this section we look into the anomalous behavior of the two important entities of the peer-review process: (i) the editors and (ii) the reviewers.

3.1 Editor

We begin by analyzing the anomalous behavior of the editors. We define the behavior of an editor to be anomalous if the papers assigned to her are on average cited less when accepted or are cited more when rejected. In specific, we in-

[1] jhep.sissa.it/jhep

[2] http://www.springer.com/physics/particleandnuclear physics/journal/13130

[3] https://inspirehep.net/

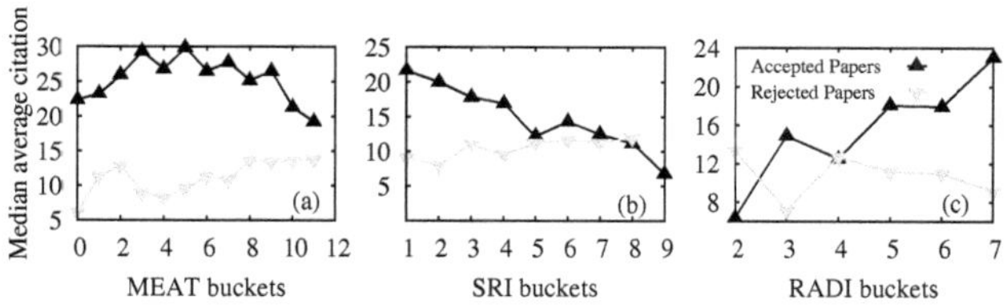

Figure 1: (a) Median Average citation (MAC) versus $MEAT$. $MEAT$ values are bucketed into 12 bins of equal size with range(1, 498.8).(b) MAC versus SRI and (c) MAC versus $RADI$. For both (b) and (c), the x-axis values are bucketed by values corresponding to ($\geq$ 0 and $<$ 0.1), ($\geq$ 0.1 and $<$ 0.2) and so on.

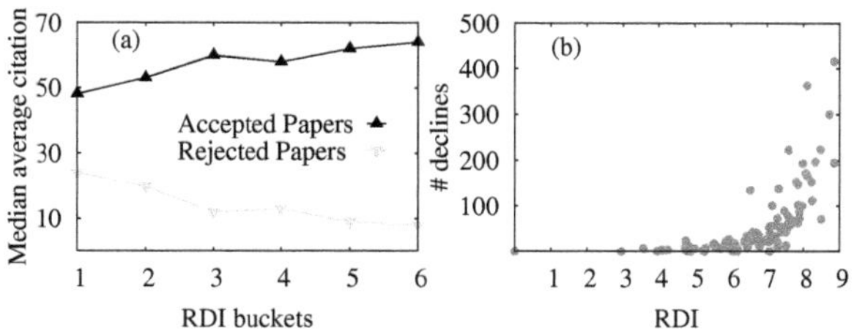

Figure 2: (a) Median Average citation versus SRI. SRI values are bucketed by values corresponding to ($\geq$ 0 and $<$ 0.1), ($\geq$ 0.1 and $<$ 0.2) and so on. (b) RDI versus number of declines. Increasing trend indicates higher the RDI, higher is the number of declines.

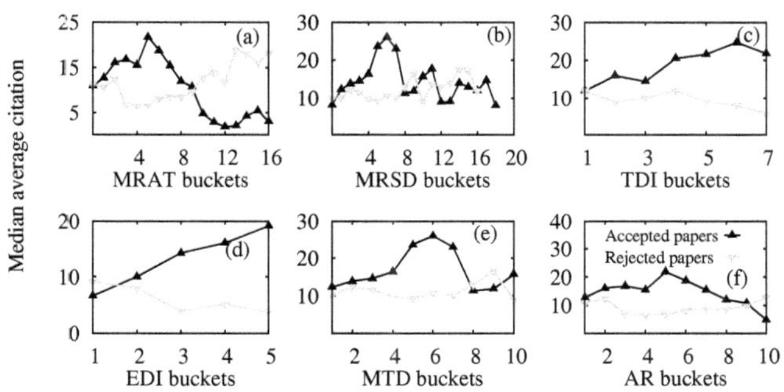

Figure 3: (a) Median Average citation (MAC) versus $MRAT$. $MRAT$ values are bucketed into 20 buckets of equal size with range(1,498.8),(b) MAC versus $MRSD$ (c) MAC versus TDI, (d) MAC versus EDI, (e) MAC versus MTD and (f) MAC versus AR. For both (c),(d) and (e), the x-axis values are bucketed by values corresponding to ($\geq$ 0 and $<$ 0.1), ($\geq$ 0.1 and $<$ 0.2) and so on. For (b) and (f) values (x-axis) are divided into 10 buckets of equal size.

vestigate different factors related to the editor that can lead to such anomaly.

3.1.1 Mean Editor Assignment Time (MEAT)

For each editor we obtain the time span (in days) between any two consecutive assignments and calculate the average time span between the two assignments. Formally, we define for editor i, $MEAT_i$ as

$$MEAT_i = \frac{1}{n-1}\sum(\delta_{j+1} - \delta_j)$$

where n is the total number of assignments to the editor i and δ_j is the date of the jth assignment. In figure 1(a) we bin the editors based on the $MEAT$ and calculate the median average citation of the papers assigned to the editors in each bin. We observe that for accepted papers very low or very high $MEAT$ values lead to lower citations. An exact opposite behavior is observed for rejected papers. This indicates that editors who are assigned time and again (low $MEAT$) or rarely (high $MEAT$) often fail to judge the quality of the papers assigned to them.

3.1.2 Self Review Index (SRI)

Self Review Index (SRI) measures the fraction of papers for which the editor assigned herself as the reviewer. Formally, for an editor i, we define SRI_i as

$$SRI_i = \frac{\varrho_i}{\rho_i}$$

where ρ_i is the number of papers i was assigned as editor while ϱ_i is the number of papers i assigned herself as reviewer. We observe that with increasing values of SRI the median average citation for accepted papers decreases while that for rejected papers increases (refer to figure 1(b)).

3.1.3 Referee-Author pair Diversity Index (RADI)

We observe that editors in numerous cases assign papers from a certain author to only a certain reviewer. To investigate whether this allows for less impactful research from this author getting accepted, we define a metric which we call **Referee-Author pair Diversity Index (RADI)**. Formally we define for editor i, the $RADI_i$ score as

$$RADI_i = -\sum_{j,k} p_{j,k} \log p_{j,k}$$

where $p_{j,k}$ denotes the proportion of times a paper from author k was assigned to reviewer j by the editor i. In figure 1(c) we bin the editors based on the $RADI$ and calculate the median average citation of the papers assigned to the editors in each bin. We observe that more the diversity score higher is the citation of the accepted papers and correspondingly lower is the citation of the rejected papers.

3.1.4 Referee Diversity Index (RDI)

As a following step, we check whether an editor always chooses from a fixed set of reviewers or a diverse set of reviewers while making a paper assignment and, more importantly, does this influence the performance of the editor in terms of the impact of the reviewed paper. We define for each editor(i) a metric called **Referee Diversity Index** (RDI_i) as -

$$RDI_i = -\sum_{j} p_j \log p_j$$

where p_j denotes the proportion of times reviewer j was assigned a paper by editor i. More diverse the set of reviewers higher is the score. In figure 1(b) we bin the editors based on the RDI and calculate the median average citation of the papers assigned to the editors in each bin. We observe that more the diversity score, higher is the citation of the accepted papers and correspondingly lower is the citation of the rejected papers.

A summary statistic of all the above factors that may be used to identify anomalous editors are noted in Table 1.

The dataset allows us to find out the cases when the reviewer declined to review a paper on being assigned by an editor. We observe that editors with high RDI are also declined more often. In figure 2(b) we plot RDI value and the number of declines for each editor. An increasing trend indicates that more diversely the editor tries to select reviewers more she gets declined by the reviewers. This in many cases may force the editor to be less proactive and always select from a specific set of 'reliable' referees.

3.2 Reviewer

In this section, we investigate anomalous behavior of the referees. Recall that we define the behavior of a reviewer to be anomalous if the papers accepted by her are low cited or the papers rejected by her are highly cited. As in case of the editors, here also we investigate different factors that could be indicative of such anomalous behavior.

3.2.1 *Mean Reviewer Assignment Time (MRAT)*

This is essentially same as MEAT. For a reviewer i, we define $MRAT_i$ as

$$MRAT_i = \frac{1}{n-1} \sum (\delta_{j+1} - \delta_j)$$

where n is the total number of assignments of reviewer i and δ_j is the date of the jth assignment. In figure 3(a) we plot $MRAT$ (binned) and median average citation of the papers reviewed for each reviewer. We observe that papers reviewed by reviewers with low $MRAT$ (high frequency of assignment) tend to be cited less and increases as $MRAT$ increases. This is followed by again a steep decrease in citation. This indicates that the reviewers assigned very frequently are often less reliable while those assigned only occasionally are also not likely to correctly judge the quality of the paper.

3.2.2 *Mean Report Sending Delay (MRSD)*

We argue that the time taken by a reviewer to send back the review report could be an indicator of his performance. If a reviewer on average sends back the review very quickly it is highly likely that the review was done in a hurry. Similarly, if the report was sent after being reminded by the editor numerous times, it is also highly likely the review report could be anomalous. For a reviewer we calculate the time delay between the date of her assignment and the date she sent back the report for each of her assignments. To measure $MRSD$ we calculate the mean value of all the delays. Note that we do not consider the assignments which the reviewer declined. Formally, for a reviewer i, we define $MRSD_i$ as

$$MRSD_i = \frac{1}{n} \sum (\delta_i - \Delta_i)$$

where n is the total number of assignments, Δ_i is the date of assignment and δ_i is the date when the report was received by the editor. On plotting against median average citation we observe a similar trend as was observed in case of $MRAT$ (refer to figure 3(b)). Papers reviewed by reviewers with low $MRSD$ value are often less cited, indicating that reviewers sending back their report very quickly often do it in a hurry and fail to correctly judge the quality of the paper while those taking very long to send report are prone to failure as well.

3.2.3 *Topic Diversity Index (TDI)*

JHEP associates with each submission a set of keywords which roughly indicates the domain of the work. We use these associated keywords as a proxy for topic. For each reviewer, we segregate all the keywords of the papers reviewed by her which we call the keyword corpus for the reviewer. Formally for a reviewer i, we define TDI_i as

$$TDI_i = -\sum_j p_j \log p_j$$

where p_j is the proportion of keyword j in the keyword corpus for reviewer i. We segregate the reviewers based on the diversity score and calculate the median average citation of the papers reviewed by them. We observe that the median average citation for reviewers with low TDI are low mainly because the number of papers reviewed by them are also less. The value increases with increasing TDI (refer to figure 3(c)). The reviewers with low TDI are often the ones who have reviewed a very small number of papers while the reviewers with high TDI are mostly assigned papers by a large number of editors.

3.2.4 *Editor Diversity Index (EDI)*

Reviewers could be selected for review by a large set of editors or could only be selected by a single or a small set of editors. We check whether a reviewer selected by many editors is more reliable compared to one who is selected by a single or a very small set of editors. To this aim we assign each reviewer a score called Editor Diversity Index, EDI_i which is defined as

$$EDI_i = -\sum_j p_j \log p_j$$

where p_j represents the proportion of times reviewer i was assigned by editor j. We segregate the reviewers based on EDI and calculate the median average citation of the papers reviewed by them. We observe that as EDI increases median average citation also increases (refer to figure 3(d)) indicating that reviewers assigned by multiple editors are often more reliable.

Table 1: Features used for detecting anomalies.

	Factor	Mean	Median	Max	Min	St. Dev
Editor	$MEAT$	35.06	29.1	108.25	3.28	23.19
	RDI	6.57	6.79	8.85	0.0	1.44
	$RADI$	8.86	9.21	11.94	0.0	1.87
	SRI	0.28	0.25	0.85	0.0	0.19
Reviewer	$MRAT$	363.3	193.7	5389	26.9	508.9
	$MRSD$	19.28	17.50	122	16.5	11.45
	TDI	4.07	3.96	8.10	1.0	1.44
	EDI	1.12	0.91	4.58	0.0	1.19
	AR	0.65	0.71	1.0	0.0	0.2
	MTD	3.86	3.12	69.0	1.0	4.96
	DFI	0.19	0.12	1.0	0.0	0.30

3.2.5 *Mean Time to Decline (MTD)*

We further investigated the cases where the reviewer declined the assignment. In specific, we calculated the time delay (in days) between the date she was assigned and the date she conveyed her decision of declining to review. For each reviewer we define **Mean Time to Delay**, MTD_i as

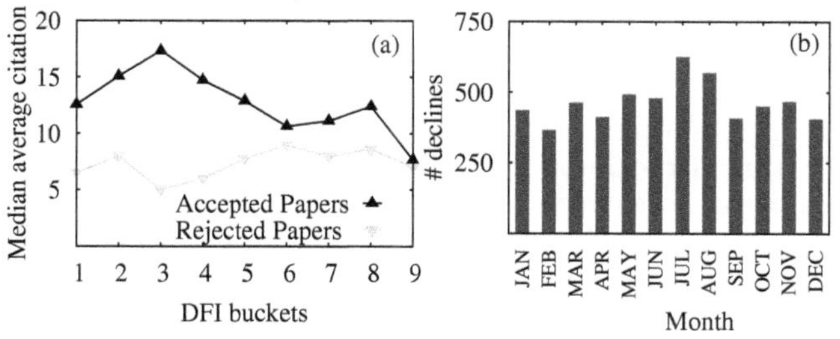

Figure 4: (a) Median Average citation versus DFI. DFI values are bucketed by values corresponding to (≥ 0 and < 0.1), (≥ 0.1 and < 0.2) and so on. (b) Number of declines versus the month of the year.

$$MTD_i = \frac{1}{d}\sum_j(\mu_j - \Delta_j)$$

where d is the number of assignments that reviewer i declined and μ_j and Δ_j are respectively the date of assignments and date of reply for paper j by reviewer i. We segregate the reviewers based on their MTD values and calculate the median average citation. We observe that the reviewers who delay often in reporting their decision to the editor of being unable to review usually tend to fail in judging a paper quality when they do review (refer to figure 3(f)).

3.2.6 *Acceptance Ratio (AR)*

Acceptance Ratio (AR) of a reviewer is defined as the proportion of papers accepted by the reviewer. For a reviewer i, AR_i is formally defined as

$$AR_i = \frac{a_i}{a_i + r_i}$$

where a_i and r_i respectively denote the number of papers accepted and rejected by reviewer i. We observe that reviewers with high AR often accept less impactful papers while reviewers with very low AR often fail to identify quality research (refer to figure 3(e)). Note that the reviewers are segregated based on their respective AR values while the median average citation is calculated. They are segregated into bins based on the AR values where typically the bins are (≥ 0 and < 0.1), (≥ 0.1 and < 0.2) and so on.

3.2.7 *Decline Fraction Index (DFI)*

Decline Fraction Index (DFI) for a reviewer is the fraction of times she declined to review. For a reviewer i, we define DFI_i as

$$DFI_i = \frac{\vartheta_i}{\theta_i}$$

where θ_i is the total number of assignments while ϑ_i is the number of times i declined to review. In figure 4(a) we plot median average citation versus DFI. We observe that for accepted papers the citation is higher for lower DFI values and it drops as DFI increases indicating that reviewers declining too frequently often fail to judge the quality of the paper assigned to them.

A summary statistics of all the above factors that may be used to identify anomalous referees are noted in Table 1.

We further looked into the data and made some interesting observations which are summarized below -

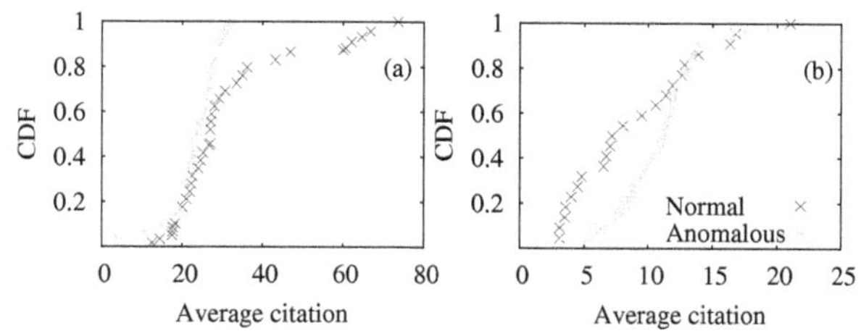

Figure 5: Cumulative distribution function of the average citations for the two sets of editors (anomalous and normal).

(i) A bulk of the instances where a reviewer declined to review occurred in the month of July and August. This is represented in figure 4(b). This probably relates to the vacation time in the Europe and the US. (ii) Of the 4035 reviewers 756 of the reviewers have not been assigned a paper for the last two years. On further investigation we observed that among these there are 505 such reviewers who in their immediate last review assignment agreed to review but did not send back the report.

4. IDENTIFYING ANOMALOUS EDITORS AND REVIEWERS

In the previous sections we discussed how different factors indicate anomalous behavior of referees and editors. In this section, we check whether we can use them to automatically differentiate between normal and anomalous editors and referees. We propose separate unsupervised models for editors and reviewers.

4.1 Editors

For each editor i, we measure $MEAT_i$, RDI_i, $RADI_i$ and SRI_i which form a feature vector. We also consider the editors who were assigned at least 5 papers and accepted at least 1 paper before 2013. To detect anomalies we use the $k-means$ clustering setting with $k = 2$. The two clusters are of sizes 25 and 68 respectively. Clearly this set of 25 editors are the anomalous ones. In figure 5 we plot the cumulative distribution of average citation of accepted (figure 5(a)) and rejected (figure 5(b)) papers. We observe that citation of accepted papers assigned to anomalous editors are significantly lower while citation of rejected papers are significantly higher compared to those assigned to normal editors.

4.2 Reviewers

Similarly for each reviewer i we associate a feature vector of size seven consisting of $MRAT_i$, $MRSD_i$, TDI_i, EDI_i, AR_i, MTD_i and DFI_i. We filter out reviewers who have reviewed at least 5 papers and accepted at least 1 before 2013. This reduces our set of reviewers to 2328. By using $k-means$ clustering ($k = 2$), we obtain two clusters of size 339 and 1999. On plotting cumulative distribution of the average citation for accepted (refer to figure 6(a)) and rejected papers (refer to figure 6(b)), we observe that the papers accepted by anomalous reviewers are cited significantly lesser while those rejected by them are cited significantly higher compared to the normal referees.

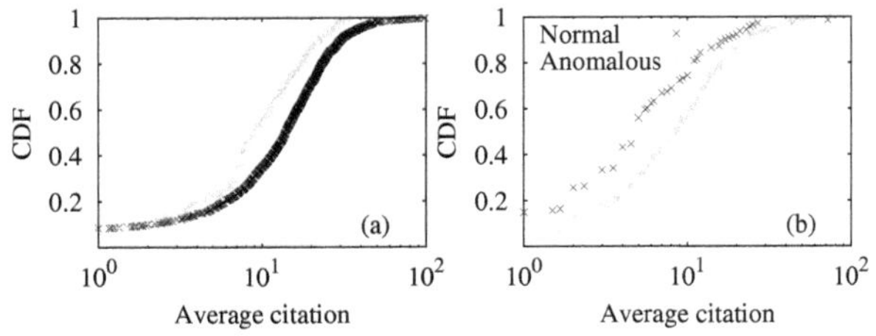

Figure 6: Cumulative distribution function of the average citations for the two sets of reviewers (anomalous and normal).

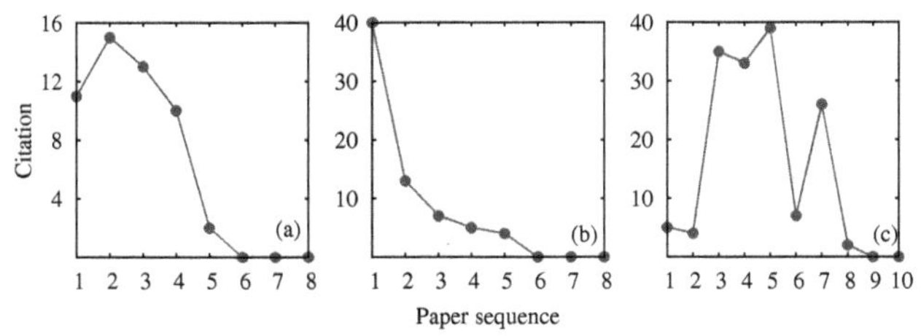

Figure 7: Mean citation profile of the reviewers in the three categories.

5. PROFILING ANOMALOUS REVIEWERS

In this section we analyze in more details the performance of the anomalous reviewers. To this aim, we consider for each reviewer, the sequence of papers accepted by her and the citation accrued (within the first three years from publication) by each of these papers. A decreasing trend would suggest decline in performance of the reviewer. Depending on the trend we observe three broad categories within the set of anomalous reviewers
(i) performance deteriorates constantly over time (proportion = 42.5%, figure 7(a)).
(ii) performance is good for initial few papers but deteriorates in the long run (proportion = 22.6%, figure 7(b)).
(iii) performance fluctuates but has a deteriorating trend in the long run (proportion = 34.9%, figure 7(c)).

6. CONCLUSION

In this paper we provided a framework for identifying anomalous reviewers and editors based on their review history considering Journal of High Energy Physics as a case study. We identified several factors that are indicative of anomalous behavior of the editors as well as reviewers. In specific for editors we observed that - (i) high frequency of assignment, (ii) selecting from a very small set of referees for reviewing, (iii) assigning same reviewer to papers of same author and (iv) assigning herself as reviewer instead of assigning someone else could be indicative of anomalous behavior of the editor.

Similarly for reviewers we observe that - (i) high frequency of assignment, (ii) delay in sending report, (iii) assignment from only a single editor or a very small set of editors (iv) very high or very low acceptance ratio and (vi) delay in notifying the editor about her decision to decline are also indicative of anomalous behavior and often leads to under-performance. Based on these factors we were able to identify anomalous referees and editors using an unsupervised clustering approach.

Future directions: We believe our findings could be useful in better assignment of editors and reviewers and thereby improve the performance of the peer-review system. Assigning good reviewers is an important part of the peer-review process and our findings allow for identifying under-performing referees. This could be a first step towards developing a reviewer-recommendation system whereby the editors are recommended a set of reviewers based on their performance. We plan to come up with such a system in subsequent works.

Acknowledgment

We would like to thank publication team of Journal of High Energy Physics (JHEP) for providing us the necessary data and they were the only ones willing to provide it.

7. REFERENCES

[1] P. Bacchetti. Peer review of statistics in medical research: the other problem. *British Medical Journal*, 324(7348):1271, 2002.
[2] R. D. Braatz. Papers receive more citations after rejection [publication activities]. *Control Systems, IEEE*, 34(4):22–23, 2014.
[3] H. Caswell. Improving peer review.
[4] V. Chandola, A. Banerjee, and V. Kumar. Anomaly detection: A survey. *ACM computing surveys (CSUR)*, 41(3):15, 2009.
[5] S. Cole, G. A. Simon, et al. Chance and consensus in peer review. *Science*, 214(4523):881–886, 1981.
[6] E. Garfield. Journal impact factor: a brief review. *Canadian Medical Association Journal*, 161(8):979–980, 1999.
[7] J. Graffy, R. Bryar, S. Kendall, and D. Crook. Improving peer review. *Primary Health Care Research and Development*, 7(01):1–2, 2006.
[8] J. A. Hartigan and M. A. Wong. Algorithm as 136: A k-means clustering algorithm. *Journal of the Royal Statistical Society. Series C (Applied Statistics)*, 28(1):100–108, 1979.
[9] F. J. Ingelfinger. Peer review in biomedical publication. *The American journal of medicine*, 56(5):686–692, 1974.
[10] J. P. Kassirer and E. W. Campion. Peer review: crude and understudied, but indispensable. *JAMA*, 272(2):96–97, 1994.
[11] R. A. McNutt, A. T. Evans, R. H. Fletcher, and S. W. Fletcher. The effects of blinding on the quality of peer review: a randomized trial. *JAMA*, 263(10):1371–1376, 1990.
[12] A. S. Relman and M. Angell. How good is peer review? *The New England journal of medicine*, 321(12):827–829, 1989.
[13] R. Smith. Peer review: a flawed process at the heart of science and journals. *Journal of the royal society of medicine*, 99(4):178–182, 2006.

Multi-source Hierarchical Prediction Consolidation

Chenwei Zhang[†] Sihong Xie[♯] Yaliang Li[‡] Jing Gao[‡] Wei Fan[♮] Philip S. Yu[†§]
[†]Department of Computer Science, University of Illinois at Chicago, Chicago, IL, USA
[♯]Computer Science and Engineering Department, Lehigh University, Bethlehem, PA, USA
[‡]SUNY Buffalo, Buffalo, NY, USA
[♮]Baidu Research Big Data Lab, Sunnyvale, CA, USA
[§]Institute for Data Science, Tsinghua University, Beijing, China
[†]{czhang99,psyu}@uic.edu, [♯]sxie@cse.lehigh.edu, [‡]{yaliangl,jing}@buffalo.edu, [♮]fanwei03@baidu.com

ABSTRACT

In big data applications such as healthcare data mining, due to privacy concerns, it is necessary to collect predictions from multiple information sources for the same instance, with raw features being discarded or withheld when aggregating multiple predictions. Besides, crowd-sourced labels need to be aggregated to estimate the ground truth of the data. Due to the imperfection caused by predictive models or human crowdsourcing workers, noisy and conflicting information is ubiquitous and inevitable. Although state-of-the-art aggregation methods have been proposed to handle label spaces with flat structures, as the label space is becoming more and more complicated, aggregation under a label hierarchical structure becomes necessary but has been largely ignored. These label hierarchies can be quite informative as they are usually created by domain experts to make sense of highly complex label correlations such as protein functionality interactions or disease relationships.

We propose a novel multi-source hierarchical prediction consolidation method to effectively exploits the complicated hierarchical label structures to resolve the noisy and conflicting information that inherently originates from multiple imperfect sources. We formulate the problem as an optimization problem with a closed-form solution. The consolidation result is inferred in a totally unsupervised, iterative fashion. Experimental results on both synthetic and real-world data sets show the effectiveness of the proposed method over existing alternatives.

Keywords

Ensemble; Unsupervised Learning; Hierarchy; Crowdsourcing

1. INTRODUCTION

For various tasks such as crowdsourcing, healthcare data mining in big data applications, multiple information sources may provide labeling information on the same instance simultaneously. Once we obtained the labeling information from multiple information sources or human beings, it is necessary to consolidate the collected information to infer the ground truth labels. Since the imperfect information from a single information source exists ubiquitously, it is also important that labeling information from multiple sources need to be consolidated to resolve noises and conflicts. Moreover, due to privacy concerns, raw features of instances are often discarded or withheld and only labels are available for aggregation purposes. For example in online healthcare forums, the raw features of a patient need to be discarded for privacy concerns and only diseases names collected from multiple doctors are consolidated to infer the ground truth.

In those applications, instead of assigning a single label for each instance, it is usually more informative to associate an instance with more than one labels to characterize multiple properties an instance has. For example, an image instance can be described by multiple tags such as "monarda", "bird" and hence belongs to multiple categories. A protein can be associated with more than one functions, denoting various functionalities. A patient may be associated with several candidate diseases, each of them diagnosed by a doctor.

Typically, those tasks consider all the labels on the same "flat" level. However, it is still insufficient to measure the value of the informativeness of labels when we isolate labels with each other and ignore the correlations between them. A better way is to organize labels in a hierarchical taxonomy. In this way, besides correlations such as co-occurrences among "flat" labels, a label hierarchy contains rich information to make sense of highly complex label correlations.

Problem Studied: In this paper, we want to incorporate the label hierarchy into the prediction consolidation process when only the labeling information from multiple information sources are available, which is formally defined as the Multi-source Hierarchical Prediction Consolidation(MHPC) problem, illustrated in Figure 1.

Informative label hierarchies are prevalently observed in various applications. For example, in crowdsourcing for protein functionality annotation, the functional labels of a protein are in a hierarchy, representing the functional relations. In healthcare data mining, disease labels can be also constructed with a tree-like disease taxonomy, denoting the pathology structure of human diseases. Current works in the literature [1, 2] try to consolidate predictions from multiple information sources. However, those works have access to raw features of the data and they totally ignore the hierarchical information , which may lead to potential loss of valuable information [3].

CIKM'16 , October 24-28, 2016, Indianapolis, IN, USA
© 2016 ACM. ISBN 978-1-4503-4073-1/16/10... $15.00
DOI: http://dx.doi.org/10.1145/2983323.2983676

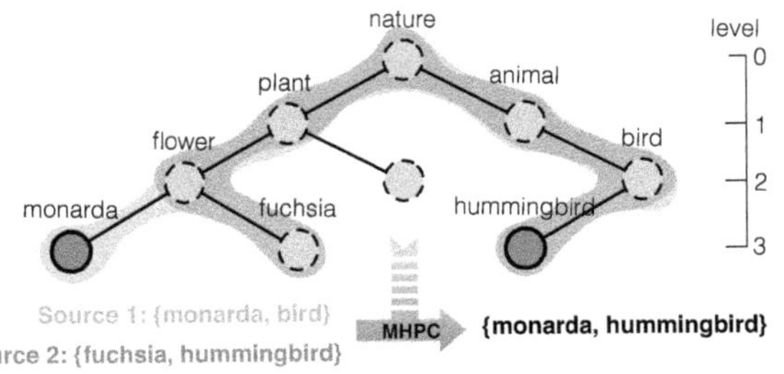

Figure 1: An illustrative example of the multi-source hierarchical prediction consolidation problem. Two individual information sources give label predictions to an image and MHPC tries to find a consolidated label prediction that maximizes the consensus among these predictions while preserving the structures of the label hierarchy.

With a number of approaches proposed to exploit the label hierarchy for various tasks [4] such as classification or clustering, it is reasonable to believe that informative label hierarchies, which inherently come with many prediction consolidation tasks, are also able to offer auxiliary and valuable information for the MHPC problem. For example, the conflicts between two label predictions in Figure 1 can be resolved by mapping label predictions to level 2, where we have {flower, bird} for both label predictions. Moreover, the label hierarchy may provide some constraints so that label predictions which violate the hierarchical structure will be less useful.

Given the importance of incorporating the label hierarchy, the MHPC problem itself is a novel problem which is rarely studied. Various learning problems are summarized in Figure 2, where model-level ensemble learning [5, 6, 7] tries to aggregate labels at the output level and hierarchical multi-label learning exploits the label hierarchy to improve the model performance on a wide range of multi-label learning tasks [3, 4]. The multi-source hierarchical prediction consolidation problem is an unsupervised ensemble learning problem that aggregates hierarchical multi-label predictions on the model-level, where very few work has been done.

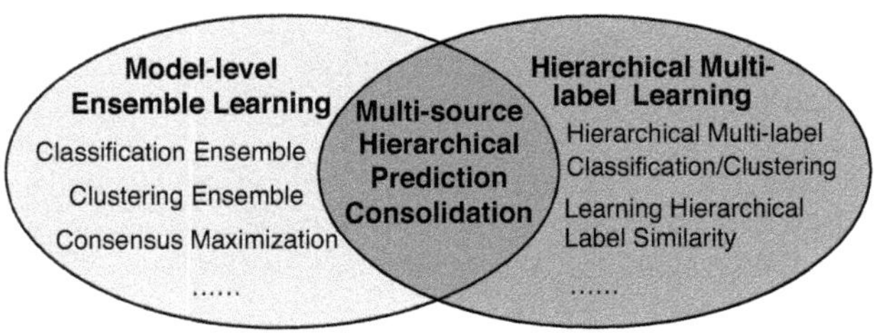

Figure 2: Position of the multi-source hierarchical prediction consolidation problem.

In this paper, we try to solve the MHPC problem by formulating it as an optimization task. The objective function for optimization favors the smoothness over all information sources as well as penalizing any two instances which have high hierarchical instance similarity but conflict with each other in the consolidation result. We derive a closed-form solution for this optimization problem. After that, the MPHC algorithm is introduced where two phases, namely estimating hierarchical similarities and minimizing consensus cost, are conducted in an iterative, totally unsupervised fashion to get the consolidated label prediction for each instance.

2. PROBLEM STATEMENT

Before introducing the proposed method, we will give the definitions of some important concepts and formulation of the MHPC problem first in this section.

2.1 Terminology Definition

Suppose we are given label matrices $\mathbf{Y}_1$, $\mathbf{Y}_2$,...,$\mathbf{Y}_M$ provided by M information sources and a hierarchical adjacency matrix $\mathbf{H}$. An label matrix $\mathbf{Y}_m$ is an N by K matrix indicating the labeling information on all N instances and K labels provided by the information source m. Within $\mathbf{Y}_m$, the i-th row $\mathbf{Y}_{m(i)}$ is a label vector of instance i provided by information source m, where $\mathbf{Y}^k_{m(i)} = 1$ if the information source m associates the instance i with label k. A hierarchical adjacency matrix $\mathbf{H}$ embodies the hierarchical structure for all K labels where $\mathbf{H}_{kk'} = 1$ if and only if when label k is the direct descendant of label k'. Other terminologies are introduced further when they are used.

2.2 Problem Statement

Based on the terminologies defined above, the **Multi-source Hierarchical Prediction Consolidation** problem is formally defined as: given label matrices $\{\mathbf{Y}_1, \mathbf{Y}_2, \ldots, \mathbf{Y}_m\}$ and a hierarchical adjacency matrix $\mathbf{H}$, the MHPC problem tries to incorporate the label hierarchy into finding a consolidated label matrix $\hat{\mathbf{Y}}$ that maximizes the consensus among all label matrices. The maximum consensus is achieved by minimizing the consensus cost in prediction consolidation.

3. MODELING HIERARCHICAL CONSENSUS

This section describes how we come up with a consolidation agreement from multiple information sources by incorporating the label hierarchy into the minimization of consensus cost. Section 3.1 describes the objective function for minimizing the consensus cost as well as its closed-form solution. Section 3.2 integrates the hierarchical information into the objective function when estimating instance similarities.

3.1 Minimizing the Consensus Cost

We formulate the following objective function:

$$\min_{\hat{\mathbf{Y}}} \frac{1}{M}\sum_{m=1}^{M}\left\|\hat{\mathbf{Y}}-\mathbf{Y}_m\right\|_F^2+\lambda\sum_{i=1}^{N}\sum_{j=1}^{N}\mathbf{W}_{ij}\left\|\hat{\mathbf{Y}}_{(i)}-\hat{\mathbf{Y}}_{(j)}\right\|_2^2 \quad s.t. \quad \lambda \geqslant 0, \quad (1)$$

where $\|\ .\ \|$ denotes the $\ell 2$-norm for matrices and vectors. The first term favors the smoothness of the consolidation result over label predictions from all the information sources. The second term serves as a regularization term which ensures that label vectors of any two instances in the consolidation result(the i-th and the j-th instance in $\hat{\mathbf{Y}}$) do not differentiate themselves from each other very much if they share a high hierarchical instance similarity $\mathbf{W}_{ij}$. Estimation for $\mathbf{W}$ will be further explained in Section 3.2. λ serves as a regularization coefficient to penalize violation for the hierarchical similarity constraints.

Note that the objective function in Equation 1 can be rewritten in a matrix form as:

$$\mathrm{J}(\hat{\mathbf{Y}}) = \frac{1}{M}\sum_{m=1}^{M}\Big(\mathrm{Tr}(\hat{\mathbf{Y}}^{\mathrm{T}}\hat{\mathbf{Y}}) - 2\,\mathrm{Tr}(\mathbf{Y}_m{}^{\mathrm{T}}\hat{\mathbf{Y}}) + \mathrm{Tr}(\mathbf{Y}_m{}^{\mathrm{T}}\mathbf{Y}_m)\Big) + \lambda\,\mathrm{Tr}(\hat{\mathbf{Y}}^{\mathrm{T}}\mathbf{L}\hat{\mathbf{Y}}) \quad s.t. \quad \lambda \geqslant 0 \tag{2}$$

where $\mathbf{L}$ is the symmetric normalized Laplacian matrix

$$\mathbf{L} = \mathbf{D}^{-\frac{1}{2}}(\mathbf{D}-\mathbf{W})\mathbf{D}^{-\frac{1}{2}} \tag{3}$$

and $\mathbf{D}$ is the degree matrix of $\mathbf{W}$.

To find a $\hat{\mathbf{Y}}$ that gives the minimum value of $\mathrm{J}(\hat{\mathbf{Y}})$, we first prove the convexity of $\mathrm{J}(\hat{\mathbf{Y}})$ by showing the positive definite property of the Hessian matrix of $\mathrm{J}(\hat{\mathbf{Y}})$ with respect to $\hat{\mathbf{Y}}$.

$$\frac{\partial^2\,\mathrm{J}(\hat{\mathbf{Y}})}{\partial\hat{\mathbf{Y}}^2} = 2\,(\mathbf{I}+\lambda\mathbf{L}) \quad s.t. \quad \lambda \geqslant 0. \tag{4}$$

The Hessian matrix shown in Equation 4 is positive definite because $\lambda\mathbf{L}$ is positive-semidefinite [8] and adding an identity matrix to it makes the resulting Hessian matrix positive definite [9]. Therefore, setting the derivative of $\mathrm{J}(\hat{\mathbf{Y}})$ with respect to $\hat{\mathbf{Y}}$ to zero

$$\frac{\partial\,\mathrm{J}(\hat{\mathbf{Y}})}{\partial\hat{\mathbf{Y}}} = \frac{1}{M}\sum_{m=1}^{M}\Big(2\hat{\mathbf{Y}} - 2\mathbf{Y}_m\Big) + 2\lambda\mathbf{L}\hat{\mathbf{Y}} = 0 \tag{5}$$

leads to a global minimized consensus cost $\mathrm{J}(\hat{\mathbf{Y}})$ given $\mathbf{W}$.

A closed-form solution can be obtained by solving the Equation 5:

$$\hat{\mathbf{Y}} = \Big(1+\lambda(\mathbf{D}^{-\frac{1}{2}}(\mathbf{D}-\mathbf{W})\mathbf{D}^{-\frac{1}{2}})\Big)^{-1}\frac{1}{M}\sum_{m=1}^{M}\mathbf{Y}_m = (\mathbf{I}+\lambda\cdot\mathbf{L}))^{-1}\bar{\mathbf{Y}}, \tag{6}$$

where $\bar{\mathbf{Y}} = \frac{1}{M}\sum_{m=1}^{M}\mathbf{Y}_m$ and $\mathbf{I}$ is the identity matrix.

From Equation 6, we can see that hierarchical similarity constraints are not introduced when $\lambda = 0$. In this case, the consolidation result degrades to the simple averaging of all the label prediction we obtained. While $\lambda > 0$, the Laplacian matrix $\mathbf{L}$ regularizes the simple averaging result and guides the $\bar{\mathbf{Y}}$ towards a global consensus $\hat{\mathbf{Y}}$ with label hierarchies being considered.

3.2 Estimating the Hierarchical Similarity

Given any two label vectors, each of which denotes a label prediction for an instance, an instance similarity matrix $\mathbf{W}$ in Equation 1 is inferred from the consolidation result to measure the similarities between label vectors. We assume that each label has a unique degree of support, asserting that such label belongs to an instance. Then, the instance similarity value $\mathbf{W}_{ij}$ of any two instance i and instance j can be calculated by the following Equation:

$$\mathbf{W}_{ij} = \exp\left(-\frac{1}{\sigma}\sqrt{\sum_{k=1}^{K}\vec{S}_k(\hat{\mathbf{Y}}^k_{(i)} - \hat{\mathbf{Y}}^k_{(j)})^2}\right), \tag{7}$$

where $\sqrt{\sum_{k=1}^{K}\vec{S}_k(\hat{\mathbf{Y}}^k_{(i)} - \hat{\mathbf{Y}}^k_{(j)})^2}$ in Equation 7 measures the weighted Euclidean distance between label vectors of two consolidated instances in $\hat{\mathbf{Y}}$, namely $\hat{\mathbf{Y}}_{(i)}$ and $\hat{\mathbf{Y}}_{(j)}$. $\vec{S}$ is a support label vector that serves as weights for distance measurement where each entry $\vec{S}_k$ of $\vec{S}$ indicates the degree of support of the label k to the distance estimation. σ is a constant factor and the exponential function exp (.) converts the distance measurement to a similarity measurement.

Usually, we assume that each label has an individual degree of support to the overall similarity estimation. However, as the label space is becoming more and more complicated, such simplified assumption totally ignores correlations among labels and therefore will lead to an inaccurate similarity estimation due to the label sparsity. For example, there can be thousands of labels for flower names such as "monarda", "fuchsia" and so on. However, it is very unlikely that label predictions provided by various information sources cover all of those flower names. Although these labels share the same general idea (the "flower"), if the support value is calculated on each label separately, none of those labels is able to contribute to the support value of label "flower" which they share the general idea with. Also, different information sources may have preferences in providing certain labels so remaining labels may be rarely used.

The label hierarchy organizes labels in a tree-like structure in which general labels are the ancestors of specific labels. With a label hierarchy being incorporated, labels are no longer independent of each other: the general idea is that when an information source assigns the label k to an instance, the existence of that label reflects a direct occurrence of this label to support the instance. Moreover, such label assignment on label k also indicates indirect occurrences, although not explicitly labeled, from its ancestor labels on the label hierarchy. Therefore, we would like to let the occurrence of each label contributes not only to itself but also to all its ancestor labels in a label hierarchy.

To make this happen, we first apply the label augmentation algorithm to convert each label vector $\mathbf{Y}_{\mathbf{m}(i)}$ to an augmented label vector $\mathbf{Y}^*_{m(i)}$, as shown in Algorithm 1.

Algorithm 1 Label Augmentation

Input: A label vector $\mathbf{Y}_{m(i)}$
A hierarchical adjacency matrix $\mathbf{H}$
Output: An augmented label vector $\mathbf{Y}^{k*}_{m(i)}$.

function LABELAUGMENTATION($\mathbf{Y}_{m(i)}$, $\mathbf{H}$)
    Initialize $\mathbf{Y}^*_{m(i)}$ as a zero vector
    for each k with $\mathbf{Y}^k_{m(i)} = 1$ **do**
        $t \leftarrow k$
        while $t \neq ROOT$ **do**
            $\mathbf{Y}^{t*}_{m(i)} \leftarrow 1$
            $t \leftarrow t'$ where $\mathbf{H}_{tt'} = 1$
return $\mathbf{Y}^*_{m(i)}$

By augmentation, the direct occurrence of a label in the label vector contributes not only to itself, but also to its ancestor labels in the hierarchy. We propose to use the occurrence value $\vec{C}_k = \sum_{m=1}^{M}\sum_{i=1}^{N}\mathbf{Y}^{k*}_{m(i)}$ of a label k in all augmented label vectors to estimate the support value for each label.

A label k which is near the root node in a label hierarchy tends to have a higher occurrence $\vec{C}_k$ value in augmented label vectors. Asserting the belongingness of a label which is in proximity to the root node to an instance is less likely to be fallible. Therefore, labels with high occurrence values make themselves more supportive in similarity estimation. By summing up the occurrence of each label in all the augmented label vectors, labels close to the root node in the hierarchy are frequently augmented, thus have higher occurrence values $\vec{C}_k$.

However, using the occurrence value to estimate the support value can be very inaccurate because although the label predictions are collected from multiple information sources, the occurrences of many labels near the leaf nodes in a label hierarchy only share a very small portion over the sum of occurrences, even after label augmentation. This leads to very small occurrence values for all those labels.

In this work, we model the occurrence of a label in an augmented label vector with a confidence interval. The occurrence of a label within all augmented label vectors can be considered as it is sampled from a subset of a population of labels. The occurrence information will be more accurate when we observe this label more frequently among all the augmented label vectors, which leads to a narrow confidence bound. Otherwise, if we rarely observe the occurrence of a label, the resulting confidence bound will be wide and it will be riskier to incorporate this piece of occurrence information into the support value calculation. By incorporating confidence intervals, the occurrence value itself shows how uncertain we are about the occurrence value of a label.

We use the occurrence value $\vec{C}_k$ of label k over the number of instances N as the proportion. Since the root node will be activated in all the augmented label vectors, the root node will have the highest proportion as 1. One label is either activated or not in an augmented label vector, therefore the binomial probability distribution is used. The resulting confidence interval can be presented in an alternate formulation that uses quantiles from the beta distribution [10]:

$$B\left(\frac{\alpha}{2}; \vec{C}_k, N - \vec{C}_k + 1\right) < \theta_k < B\left(1 - \frac{\alpha}{2}; \vec{C}_k, N - \vec{C}_k + 1\right), \tag{8}$$

where B is the Beta distribution and α is the significance level, which usually has the value 0.05 (5%). θ_k is the probability of a label k being activated in an augmented label vector. $\vec{C}_k$ is the occurrence value of label k over all augmented label vectors.

The Equation 8 has an appealing property that the less frequent a label k being sampled, the wider confidence interval it will end up with. A narrow confidence bound indicates a stronger certainty during the support value calculation. Therefore the lower bound value of the confidence interval is used to calculate the support value for each label:

$$\vec{S}_k = B\left(\frac{\alpha}{2}; \vec{C}_k, N - \vec{C}_k + 1\right) \tag{9}$$

Once we calculate the support value for each label with confidence, the instance similarity matrix $\mathbf{W}$ in Equation 7 can be calculated with the support label vector $\vec{S}$ learned from the label hierarchy. Hence, $\mathbf{W}$ is called a hierarchical instance similarity matrix.

4. CONSOLIDATING HIERARCHICAL LABELS

4.1 The MHPC Algorithm

Although we provide a closed-form solution to find the global minimum for the consensus cost when the hierarchical instance similarity matrix $\mathbf{W}$ is given, it is still hard to estimate both $\hat{\mathbf{Y}}$ that associates with a minimized consensus cost $J(\hat{\mathbf{Y}})$ and the hierarchical instance similarity matrix $\mathbf{W}$ at the same time. Hence, we propose a two-phase iterative algorithm, namely the multi-source hierarchical prediction consolidation (MHPC) algorithm, which naturally decouples the computation within each iteration.

The MHPC algorithm has two phases within each iteration: estimating the hierarchical similarity (Section 3.2) and minimizing the consensus cost (Section 3.1). The MHPC algorithm starts at iteration t_0 with an initial estimation for hierarchical instance similarity matrix $(\mathbf{W}_{ij})_{t_0}$ and the consolidation result $\left(\hat{\mathbf{Y}}\right)_{t_0}$. $(\mathbf{W}_{ij})_{t_0}$ is initialized by the following equation:

$$(\mathbf{W}_{ij})_{t_0} = \exp\left(-\frac{1}{\sigma}\sqrt{\sum_{k=1}^{K} \vec{S}_k(\bar{\mathbf{Y}}^k_{(i)} - \bar{\mathbf{Y}}^k_{(j)})^2}\right), \tag{10}$$

where $\bar{\mathbf{Y}}^k_{(i)}$ is the simple averaging result on the k-th label of the instance i from all M sources, calculated by $\bar{\mathbf{Y}}^k_{(i)} = \frac{1}{M}\sum_{m=1}^{M} \mathbf{Y}^k_{m(i)}$. Note that support values in $\vec{S}$ and the occurrence values in $\vec{C}$ are derived from all the multi-source label predictions we obtained, which we only initialize once in the entire algorithm, regardless of iterations. $(\hat{\mathbf{Y}})_{t_0}$ is initialized using the Equation 6.

Once we obtain an initial value for $(\mathbf{W}_{ij})_{t_0}$ and $(\hat{\mathbf{Y}})_{t_0}$, each iteration afterwards follows the following updating rules.

Estimating the hierarchical similarity:

$$(\mathbf{W}_{ij})_{t_x+1} = \exp\left(-\frac{1}{\sigma}\sqrt{\sum_{k=1}^{K} \vec{S}_k\left(\left(\hat{\mathbf{Y}}^k_{(i)}\right)_{t_x} - \left(\hat{\mathbf{Y}}^k_{(j)}\right)_{t_x}\right)^2}\right), \tag{11}$$

where the hierarchical instance similarity $(\mathbf{W}_{ij})_{t_x+1}$ is calculated by the most up-to-date consolidation result $\left(\hat{\mathbf{Y}}\right)_{t_x}$.

Minimizing the consensus cost:

$$\left(\hat{\mathbf{Y}}\right)_{t_x+1} = \left(1 + \lambda \cdot (\mathbf{L})_{t_x}\right)^{-1}\left(\hat{\mathbf{Y}}\right)_{t_x}, \tag{12}$$

where the laplacian matrix $(\mathbf{L})_{t_x}$ is calculated by the most up-to-date $(\mathbf{W})_{t_x}$ value using Equation 3. Note that in Equation 12, the consolidation result in the latest iteration $(\hat{\mathbf{Y}})_{t_x}$ is used for updating, rather than $\bar{\mathbf{Y}}$ as shown in Equation 6. With this updating function, the consolidation result can accumulate the consolidation progresses from previous iterations. Otherwise, if $(\bar{\mathbf{Y}})_{t_x}$ is used in Equation 12, we simply ignore the consolidation results from all the previous iterations, and $\mathbf{L}_{t_x}$ is the only factor we can rely on to guide the consolidation process toward a final consensus. The algorithm terminates whenever the updates on the consolidation result $(\hat{\mathbf{Y}})_{t_x+1}$ is no longer significant after an iteration.

5. EXPERIMENTS

In this section, the yeast data sets, the real-world medical data sets and their label hierarchies are briefly introduced. After that, the performance of the MHPC algorithm is compared with other alternatives on both data sets. Experiments on yeast data sets illustrate the ability of the proposed method in overcoming the various degree of label vagueness and noise from multiple information sources. While the real-world medical data set emphasizes more on the label sparsity because in real-world medical consultation, we can't ensure that all the information sources provide labels to all instances. Due to page limitation, experiment details such as detailed data description, convergence analysis on the proposed algorithm as well as parameter estimation can be found in [11].

5.1 Data description and data preprocessing

5.1.1 Yeast Data Sets

The yeast data sets has ten subsets, each annotates yeast genome from different aspects. Each yeast genome is annotated with hierarchical-structured labels in the Functional Catalogue (FunCat) [12]. For example, a yeast genome can be associated with three functionalities: {20/01/03/01 (sugar transport), 20/03/02/02/01 (proton driven symporter), 20/09/18 (cellular import)}. The annotation scheme follows the protein functional description of each genome instance, with up to 6 levels of label taxonomy. On average, each instance has 8.8 labels.

Based on the ground truth multi-label label predictions, we introduce vague labels, as well as noisy labels to the yeast data sets to model real-world cases where imperfect predictive models or inexperienced human annotators are involved in MHPC problems. The algorithm for generating the synthetic datasets can be found in [11].

5.1.2 Medical Data Sets

The medical data set and the disease label hierarchy are obtained from an online medical consultation website xywy.com[1], where patients post their healthcare related questions and multiple medical professionals give online suggestions or general advice as answers.

Given certain symptoms, each doctor is considered as an individual information source that provides disease names as labels. Ground truth disease labels are obtained by a medical knowledge base in Baidu Baike[2](an online encyclopedia of Baidu) where registered doctors provide knowledge about certain disease names that closely associate with some symptoms. The disease label hierarchy is organized in an anatomical structure, with up to three levels of labels(e.g. disease - otorhinolaryngology - rhinitis). Usually, a doctor provides around 2.5 labels to an instance on average, which leads to a low label coverage over all labels in a hierarchy: not all doctors provide labels for each instance; not all instances get label predictions from every doctor. Only 0.011506% of labels are activated among label predictions over all instances from all the information sources we obtained.

5.2 Comparison Methods

To show the advantages of the MHPC algorithm in solving multi-source hierarchical prediction consolidation problem, we compare the MHPC method with many baseline methods. Considering that no known multi-source hierarchical prediction consolidation methods are available, averaging methods as well as other model-level ensemble learning methods are introduced, which can be divided into three categories:

Averaging Methods

- SA: The simple averaging method. The SA method simply takes the average of multi-source label predictions. In [13], the authors observe that the simple averaging method is competitive with a variety of adaptive algorithms under the quadratic loss criterion.
- WA: The weighted averaging method. Besides the simple averaging method which considers an equal contribution of each label to the consolidation result, the WA weights labels by support values learned in Section 3.2.

[1]http://club.xyxy.com

[2]http://baike.baidu.com

Consensus Maximization Methods

- MLCM: The multi-label consensus maximization method is introduced in [6]. The MLCM learns a consolidation result from both label predictions and cluster predictions of the same instance from multiple information sources. By ignoring the cluster predictions, the MLCM adapts to the problem setting of MHPC. However, the label hierarchy is not explored in MLCM.

Multi-source Prediction Consolidation Methods

- MPC-U: The multi-source prediction aggregation method that minimizes the consensus cost as mentioned in Section 3.1, but uses a uniform support label vector $\vec{S}$ during instance similarity estimation.
- MHPC: The proposed method which minimizes the consensus cost by optimization and incorporates the label hierarchy in estimating hierarchical instance similarities. The support value of each label is estimated based on the lower bound confidence interval of the proportion of occurrence based on all the augmented label vectors we obtained.

5.3 Experimental results

5.3.1 Yeast Data Sets

For yeast data sets, two parameters (α_{vague} on x-axis and α_{noise} on y-axis) are varied from 0.1 to 1 to test how sensitive vague and noisy labels will affect the model performance. The performance on three evaluation metrics (Ranking loss, micro-AUC [14] and coverage error [15] on z-axes) of the MHPC method and other alternatives are compared on each combination of α_{vague} and α_{noise}. For each model, the performance on all combinations of α_{vague} and α_{noise} values are connected as a surface. Due to space limitation, only the result on church, one of the ten yeast data sets, is reported with $\lambda = 10$. Multi-source label predictions from four information sources are used.

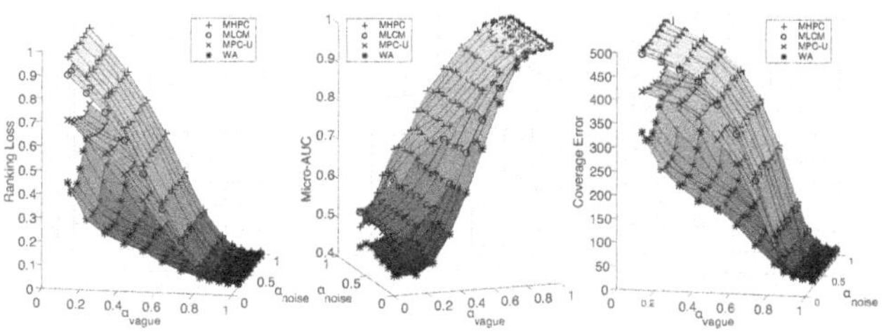

Figure 3: Performance with varying degrees of vagueness and noises on church, one of the yeast data sets.

Figure 3 shows the performance comparison results. We observe that the MPHC (the surface with the "+" sign) outperforms other alternatives consistently. When the vagueness level α_{noise} increases, the performance deteriorates for all the methods. However, the MHPC performs relatively better than others. On the other hand, when the noise level increases and α_{vague} is fixed, WA and MPC-U methods are more easily affected by the noisy label, which leads to fluctuations on the performance surfaces. While MHPC has a relative stable performance when we varies α_{noise} from 0.1 to 1 on almost all the values α_{vauge} can take. Note that the performance of SA is similar with WA, so the performance of SA is not presented in this figure.

5.3.2 *Medical Data Sets*

The medical data sets come with multi-source label predictions inherently when multiple doctors gives suggestions to each patient. The medical date sets consist of six subsets (MED.1 to MED.6) and we randomly sampled 500 instances from each data set. The label predictions associate with those instances are used for prediction consolidation. Table 1 shows the performance of MHPC with other baseline methods, from which we can see the superior performance of MHPC method in real-world scenarios.

Datasets	Methods	Evaluation Metrics		
		Ranking Loss	Micro-AUC	Coverage Error
MED.1	SA	0.520 (5)	0.620 (5)	213.175 (5)
	WA	0.518 (4)	0.621 (3)	212.844 (4)
	MPC-U	0.304 (3)	0.547 (5)	125.108 (3)
	MLCM	0.262 (2)	0.643 (2)	108.146 (1)
	MHPC	0.196 (1)	0.754 (1)	125.107 (2)
MED.2	SA	0.358 (5)	0.603 (4)	75.544 (5)
	WA	0.357 (4)	0.604 (3)	75.416 (4)
	MPC-U	0.200 (2)	0.539 (5)	42.630 (3)
	MLCM	0.268 (3)	0.680 (2)	31.221 (1)
	MHPC	0.166 (1)	0.715 (1)	35.336 (2)
MED.3	SA	0.067 (4)	0.706 (2)	3.400 (4)
	WA	0.065 (3)	0.704 (3)	3.314 (3)
	MPC-U	0.069 (5)	0.432 (5)	3.543 (5)
	MLCM	0.064 (2)	0.542 (4)	3.288 (2)
	MHPC	0.038 (1)	0.847 (1)	2.000 (1)
MED.4	SA	0.301 (5)	0.601 (4)	38.325 (5)
	WA	0.300 (4)	0.602 (3)	38.275 (4)
	MPC-U	0.173 (2)	0.460 (5)	22.242 (3)
	MLCM	0.225 (3)	0.617 (2)	19.325 (2)
	MHPC	0.118 (1)	0.707 (1)	15.233 (1)
MED.5	SA	0.355 (5)	0.563 (4)	67.534 (5)
	WA	0.353 (4)	0.564 (3)	67.170 (4)
	MPC-U	0.189 (1)	0.549 (5)	36.080 (2)
	MLCM	0.276 (3)	0.565 (2)	52.523 (3)
	MHPC	0.232 (2)	0.572 (1)	32.648 (1)
MED.6	SA	0.365 (5)	0.598 (3)	47.175 (5)
	WA	0.363 (4)	0.599 (2)	46.991 (4)
	MPC-U	0.236 (3)	0.491 (5)	30.632 (3)
	MLCM	0.190 (1)	0.632 (1)	24.798 (2)
	MHPC	0.203 (2)	0.594 (4)	22.633 (1)

Table 1: Performance on medical data sets.

6. CONCLUSIONS

As information explodes, we are able to obtain an increasing number of label predictions from a large population of information sources at the same time. Due to privacy concerns or storage limitations, the raw features of instances are usually discarded or withheld. The labels we collect from multiple information sources bring not only diversity of labels, but also vagueness and noises. In this work, we studied the multi-source hierarchical prediction consolidation (MHPC) problem. Traditional model-level ensemble learning problems deal with multi-source information but they simply ignore the hierarchical structure of labels. On the other hand, hierarchical multi-label learning problems try to bring the label hierarchy into varies single-source learning tasks such as classification. The MHPC problem effectively incorporates the existing label hierarchy to resolve vagueness and noise originate from multiple information sources, where very few work has been done. We formulate the MHPC problem as an optimization task with a closed-form solution. Two phases, namely minimizing the consensus cost and estimating the hierarchical similarity, are performed in an iterative fashion to learn a consolidation result while preserving the structures of the label hierarchy. Experiments conducted on both synthetic and real-world data sets show the advantages of the proposed method over other alternatives.

7. ACKNOWLEDGMENTS

This work is supported in part by NSF through grants III-1526499. We would like to thank the anonymous reviewers for helpful comments. We gratefully acknowledge the support of NVIDIA Corporation with the donation of the Titan X GPU used for this research.

8. REFERENCES

[1] J Ross Quinlan. Bagging, boosting, and C4. 5. In *AAAI/IAAI, Vol. 1*, 1996.

[2] Chi-Hoon Lee. Learning to combine discriminative classifiers: confidence based. In *KDD*, 2010.

[3] Lijuan Cai and Thomas Hofmann. Hierarchical document categorization with support vector machines. In *CIKM*, pages 78–87, 2004.

[4] Wei Bi and James T Kwok. Mandatory leaf node prediction in hierarchical multilabel classification. In *NIPS*, pages 153–161, 2012.

[5] Jing Gao, Feng Liang, Wei Fan, Yizhou Sun, and Jiawei Han. Graph-based consensus maximization among multiple supervised and unsupervised models. In *NIPS*, pages 585–593. 2009.

[6] Sihong Xie, Xiangnan Kong, Jing Gao, Wei Fan, and Philip S. Yu. Multilabel consensus classification. In *ICDM*, pages 1241–1246, 2013.

[7] Bowen Dong, Sihong Xie, Jing Gao, Wei Fan, and Philip S. Yu. OnlineCM: Real-time consensus maximization with missing values. In *SDM*, 2014.

[8] Bojan Mohar, Y Alavi, G Chartrand, and OR Oellermann. The laplacian spectrum of graphs. *Graph theory, combinatorics, and applications*, 2(871-898):12, 1991.

[9] A Ravindran, Gintaras Victor Reklaitis, and Kenneth Martin Ragsdell. *Engineering optimization: methods and applications*. John Wiley & Sons, 2006.

[10] Lawrence D Brown, T Tony Cai, and Anirban DasGupta. Interval estimation for a binomial proportion. *Statistical science*, pages 101–117, 2001.

[11] Chenwei Zhang, Sihong Xie, Yaliang Li, Jing Gao, Wei Fan, and Philip S. Yu. Multi-source Hierarchical Prediction Consolidation. *ArXiv e-prints arXiv: 1608.03344*, 2016.

[12] Andreas Ruepp, Alfred Zollner, Dieter Maier, Kaj Albermann, Jean Hani, Mokrejs, et al. The funcat, a functional annotation scheme for systematic classification of proteins from whole genomes. *Nucleic acids research*, 32(18):5539–5545, 2004.

[13] Varsha Dani, Omid Madani, David Pennock, and Sumit Sanghai. An empirical comparison of algorithms for aggregating expert predictions. In *UAI*, 2006.

[14] Corinna Cortes and Mehryar Mohri. Auc optimization vs. error rate minimization. *NIPS*, 16(16), 2004.

[15] Grigorios Tsoumakas, Ioannis Katakis, and Ioannis Vlahavas. Mining multi-label data. In *Data mining and knowledge discovery handbook*, pages 667–685. Springer, 2009.

Probabilistic Knowledge Graph Construction: Compositional and Incremental Approaches

Dongwoo Kim
ANU
Australia
dongwoo.kim@anu.edu.au

Lexing Xie
ANU & Data to Decision CRC
Australia
lexing.xie@anu.edu.au

Cheng Soon Ong
Data61 & ANU
Australia
chengsoon.ong@anu.edu.au

ABSTRACT

Knowledge graph construction consists of two tasks: extracting information from external resources (knowledge population) and inferring missing information through a statistical analysis on the extracted information (knowledge completion). In many cases, insufficient external resources in the knowledge population hinder the subsequent statistical inference. The gap between these two processes can be reduced by an incremental population approach. We propose a new probabilistic knowledge graph factorisation method that benefits from the path structure of existing knowledge (e.g. syllogism) and enables a common modelling approach to be used for both incremental population and knowledge completion tasks. More specifically, the probabilistic formulation allows us to develop an incremental population algorithm that trades off exploitation-exploration. Experiments on three benchmark datasets show that the balanced exploitation-exploration helps the incremental population, and the additional path structure helps to predict missing information in knowledge completion.

Keywords

Knowledge graph, active learning, Thompson sampling

1. INTRODUCTION

Relational knowledge graphs formalise our understanding about the world. This in turn helps us reason and infer in a wide range of tasks such as information retrieval, question answering, and semantic parsing [4, 8, 11]. The construction of a knowledge graph is an active research area with many important and challenging research questions. The early stage of knowledge graph construction relies on the **knowledge population** task where the goal is to maximise the number of discovered facts in the form of `(entity1, relation, entity2)` triples. External sources such as Wikipedia are used to extract the triples [7], or human experts encode a prior knowledge manually [2]. Despite efforts towards a comprehensive knowledge graph, even the largest commercial knowledge graph is still far from complete [5]. The **knowledge completion** task has emerged as a complement of the knowledge population task to scale up the knowledge graph construction. Unlike the knowledge population task, the goal of knowledge completion is to correctly predict unknown triples based on a statistical analysis of the known triples [14, 18].

An obstacle to knowledge graph construction is a gap between knowledge population and completion. The more a knowledge graph is populated, the better a statistical model predict the unknown triples. In many cases, however, there is insufficient external resource to extract knowledge, and thus the construction relies solely on the incremental population by human experts, which can be slow and costly. We need an active way of selecting triples to be labelled, in order to maximise the performance of the following knowledge completion. A recent attempt at active incremental population [9] has had difficulties simultaneously achieving a high population and faithful reconstruction.

We propose a statistical relational model, providing a probabilistic framework for both knowledge completion and knowledge population. We formulate bilinear tensor factorisation [18] in a probabilistic way, where entities and relations are embedded into a latent feature space. We propose an extension to the tensor factorisation model that incorporates the path structure of a knowledge graph into the factorisation. The probabilistic formulation provides a natural way of exploiting uncertainty of triples, allowing us to develop an active triple selection for the incremental population. We employ Thompson sampling [21] to find an optimal trade-off between exploration and exploitation during the active selection.

Based on experiments with three benchmark datasets, we find that the additional path structure helps predict unobserved triples, while the model without the path structure is more helpful in the incremental population. This apparent contradiction in results can be explained by the different requirements on the latent structure. For knowledge completion, it is important to find good latent structures, For incremental population, however, it is more important to accurately estimate uncertainty such that we can explore the latent space efficiently over time. To the best of our knowledge, this is the first study that explicitly investigates the contrasting effects of path structure in knowledge completion and incremental population.

Related work The literature on data factorisation and vector space models for relational data is vast. We give a brief overview of related work along three design choices:

CIKM'16, October 24-28, 2016, Indianapolis, IN, USA

DOI: http://dx.doi.org/10.1145/2983323.2983677

Table 1: The categorisation of factorisation problems with respect to three design considerations (see main text for details).

Pr/N-Pr	P/A	M/T/C	References
N-Pr	P	M	[15]
N-Pr	A	M	[19]
N-Pr	P	T	[18][13]
N-Pr	A	T	[9]
N-Pr	P	C	[17][6]
N-Pr	A	C	–
Pr	P	M	[16]
Pr	A	M	[10][22]
Pr	P	T	*, [24][20]
Pr	A	T	*
Pr	P	C	*
Pr	A	C	*

the method, the learning strategy, and the data representation. In Table 1, we summarise related work along all combinations in each dimension. Our work address the uncovered combination of three design choices in the probabilistic method, indicated by an asterisk.

Probabilistic (Pr) / Non-Probabilistic (N-Pr) This refers to two broad classes of model formulation, whether an obtained model has a probabilistic interpretation.

Passive (P) / Active (A) This refers to two different learning strategies, of passively learning a model given labeled data points, or actively requesting data points to be labelled.

Matrix (M) / Tensor (T) / Composition (C) This refers to three data representations. Matrix represents single relational data such as `(user, item)`. Tensor represents multiple relational data such as `(entity, relation, entity2)`. Composition includes more complex structures of multiple relational data such as `(entity1 - relation1 - entity2 - relation2 - entity3)`.

Model details and additional results can be found in the online appendix [12].

2. PROBABILISTIC RESCAL

A relational knowledge graph consists of a set triples in the form of (i, k, j) where i, j are entities, and k is a relation. A triple can be distinguished in a valid triple and invalid triple based on a semantic meaning of the triple. An example of the valid triple in Freebase is `(BarackObama, PresidentOf, U.S.)`, and an example of the invalid triple is `(BarackObama, PresidentOf, U.K.)`. A knowledge graph can be represented in a three-way binary tensor $\mathcal{X} \in \{0,1\}^{N\times K\times N}$, where K is a number of relations, N is a number of entities, and $x_{ikj} \in \{0, 1\}$ indicates whether the triple is valid.

We model the entity i as vectors e_i and the relation k as matrix R_k with an appropriately chosen latent dimension D. This follows a popular model for statistical relational learning, which is to factorise the tensor into a set of latent vector representations, such as the bilinear model RESCAL [18]. RESCAL aims to factorise each relational slice $\mathcal{X}_{:k:}$ into a set of rank-D latent features as follows:

$$\mathcal{X}_{:k:} \approx E R_k E^\top, \qquad \text{for } k = 1, \ldots, K$$

Here, $E \in \mathbb{R}^{N\times D}$ contains the latent features of the entities $e_1, \ldots, e_N$ and $R_k \in \mathbb{R}^{D\times D}$ models the interaction of the latent features between entities in relation k.

We propose a probabilistic framework that directly generalises RESCAL (PRESCAL) by placing priors over the latent features. For each entity i, the latent feature of an entity $e_i \in \mathbb{R}^D$ is drawn from an isotropic multivariate-normal distribution with variance σ_e^2,

$$e_i \sim N(\mathbf{0}, \sigma_e^2 I_D). \tag{1}$$

For each relation k, we draw matrix R_k from a zero-mean isotropic matrix normal distribution with variance σ_r^2,

$$R_k \sim \mathcal{MN}_{D\times D}(\mathbf{0}, \sigma_r I_D, \sigma_r I_D) \tag{2}$$

$$\text{or equivalently } r_k = \text{vec}(R_k) \sim N(\mathbf{0}, \sigma_r^2 I_{D^2})$$

where $\text{vec}(R_k)$ denotes the flattening of the matrix.

PNORMAL We consider two observation models for x_{ikj}: real or binary variables. By placing a normal distribution over x_{ikj},

$$x_{ikj}|e_i, e_j, R_k \sim \mathcal{N}(e_i^\top R_k e_j, \sigma_x^2), \tag{3}$$

we model the value of triple as a real variable. This is not a natural choice since the triple is a binary variable, however, we can control the confidence on different observations through the variance parameter σ_x^2. We develop a Gibbs sampler to perform the posterior inference for the normally distributed observation model. The conditional distribution of each latent variable is given by:

$$p(e_i|E_{-i}, \mathcal{R}, \mathcal{X}^t, \sigma_e, \sigma_x) = \mathcal{N}(e_i|\mu_i, \Lambda_i^{-1}) \tag{4}$$

$$p(R_k|E, \mathcal{X}, \sigma_r, \sigma_x) = \mathcal{N}(\text{vec}(R_k)|\mu_k, \Lambda_k^{-1}) \tag{5}$$

where the negative subscript $-i$ indicates the every other entity variables except entity i. Exact forms of the posterior means and precision matrices are listed in Table 2, where we have used the identity $e_i^\top R_k e_j = r_k^\top e_i \otimes e_j$.

PLOGIT One may want to model the binary observation more precisely. Here, we model x_{ikj} as a Bernoulli random variable whose probability is determined by logistic regression:

$$p(x_{ikj} = 1) = \sigma(e_i^\top R_k e_j), \tag{6}$$

where σ is a sigmoid function. We approximate the conditional posterior of E and R by the Laplace approximation [1] through an alternative sampling. The detailed derivations are provided in Appendix A.

Thompson Sampling The probabilistic framework allows us to quantify the uncertainty of predictive distribution, which is then used to formulate an active learning algorithm. Specifically, we adopt Thompson sampling for active learning, which finds an optimal trade off between exploitation and exploration during active learning. Thompson sampling provides a model based query selection process [3, 21]. Let $x_{1:t}$ be a sequence of observed triples up to time t, and θ is an underlying parameter governing the rewards r. Thompson sampling chooses the next action a (triple to label), according to its probability of having high reward:

$$\arg\max_a \int \mathbb{I}\left[\mathbb{E}(r|a, \theta) = \max_{a'} \mathbb{E}(r|a', \theta)\right] p(\theta|x_{1:t-1}) d\theta,$$

where $\mathbb{I}$ is an indicator function. Note that it is sufficient to draw a random sample from the posterior instead of computing the integral.

Table 2: Parameters for Gibbs updates. The conditional of e_i and R_k follows the normal distribution with mean μ and precision matrix Λ. $\otimes$ is the Kronecker product.

var	μ	Λ	ξ
e_i	$\frac{1}{\sigma_x^2}\Lambda_i^{-1}\xi_i$	$\frac{1}{\sigma_x^2}\sum_{jk:x_{ikj}\in\mathcal{X}^t}(R_k e_j)(R_k e_j)^\top$	$\sum_{jk:x_{ikj}\in\mathcal{X}^t} x_{ikj}R_k e_j + \sum_{jk:x_{jki}\in\mathcal{X}^t} x_{jki}R_k^\top e_j$.
$vec(R_k)$	$\frac{1}{\sigma_x^2}\Lambda_k^{-1}\xi_k$	$\frac{1}{\sigma_x^2}\sum_{ij:x_{ikj}\in\mathcal{X}^t}(e_i\otimes e_j)(e_i\otimes e_j)^\top + \frac{1}{\sigma_r^2}I_{D^2}$	$\sum_{ij:x_{ikj}\in\mathcal{X}^t} x_{ikj}(e_i\otimes e_j)$.

We generalise the idea of a particle Thompson sampling originally proposed in [10] for a matrix factorisation to the tensor factorisation. The detailed algorithm is provided in Appendix B.

3. COMPOSITIONAL RELATIONS

In this section, we propose a compositional relation model that exploits the compositional structure of knowledge graphs to capture the latent semantic structure of the entities and relations. A very recent study shows the benefit of using compositionality in the vector space model [6]. Here, we further extend their framework in a probabilistic way.

The compositionality represents a semantic meaning of a path over a knowledge graph that corresponds to a sequence of composable triples. For example, given two triples, "Barack Obama is a 44th president of U.S." (`BarackObama, PresidentOf, U.S`) and "Joe Biden was a running mate of Barack Obama" (`JoeBiden, RunningMateOf, BarackObama`), one can naturally deduce that the "Joe Biden is a vice president of U.S." (`JoeBiden, VicePresidentOf, U.S.`). Here the composition of two relations, president of, and running mate of, yields a compositional relation, vice president of. More formally, if there is a sequence of triples where the target entity of a former triple is a source entity of a latter triple in a consecutive pair of triples in the sequence, then we can form a compositional triple as follows. Given the sequence of n triples (i_1, k_1, j_1), (i_2, k_2, j_2), (i_3, k_3, j_3) ... (i_n, k_n, j_n), where $j_k = i_{k+1}$ for all k, we form a compositional triple $(i_1, c(k_1, k_2, \dots, k_n), j_n)$, where c denotes the compositional relation of the sequence of relations.

Let $\mathcal{C}^L$ be a set of all possible compositions whose length is up to L, $c \in \mathcal{C}$ be a sequence of relations, $c(i)$ be ith index of a relation in sequence c and $|c|$ be the length of the sequence. With set of compositions $\mathcal{C}^L$, we can expand set of observed triples $\mathcal{X}$ to set of compositional triples $\mathcal{X}^{\mathcal{C}^L}$ in which compositional triple x_{icj} is an indicator variable that show the existence of the path from entity i to entity j through sequence of relations c in $\mathcal{X}$. Note that the compositional relation c is an abstract relation, and there might be a multiple possible paths from entity i to j.

With these extended compositional triples, we again model x_{icj} with a bilinear Gaussian distribution,

$$x_{(i,c(k_1,k_2,\dots,k_n),j)} \sim \mathcal{N}(e_i^\top R_{c(k_1,k_2,\dots,k_n)} e_j, \sigma_c^2), \quad (7)$$

where $R_{c(k_1,k_2)} \in \mathbb{R}^{D\times D}$ is a latent matrix of compositional relation c, and σ_c^2 is a covariance of the compositional triples. Again the entity vectors are shared across the compositional and non-compositional triples. With the compositions of relations, the PRESCAL may place a new relation matrix R_c for each composition c. However the number of required matrices increases exponentially with respect to the length of composition. Consequently, the computational cost will also increase exponentially. To limit the required number of parameters, we propose two different ways of modelling the compositional relation R_c.

3.1 Additive Compositionality

We define an additive compositional relation R_c as a normalised sum over the sequence of relation matrices in composition c, i.e., $R_c = \frac{1}{|c|}(R_{c(1)} + R_{c(2)} + \cdots + R_{c(|c|)})$, then compositional triple x_{icj} is modelled as

$$\begin{aligned} x_{(i,c,j)} &\sim \mathcal{N}(e_i^\top R_c e_j, \sigma_c^2) \quad (8)\\ &= \mathcal{N}(e_i^\top \frac{1}{|c|}(R_{c(1)} + R_{c(2)} + \cdots + R_{c(|c|)}) e_j, \sigma_c^2). \end{aligned}$$

This treats the relations as vectors, finding the average of a sequence of composed relations. The conditional distribution of e_i and R_k given the rest can be obtained in the same way used for the posterior distribution of PRESCAL. Parameter estimation is shown in Appendix C.1.

3.2 Multiplicative Compositionality

Second, we define an multiplicative compositional relation R_c as a sequence of multiplication over relations in composition c, i.e. $R_c = R_{c(1)}R_{c(2)}\dots R_{c(|c|)}$, and the compositional triple as a bilinear Gaussian distribution with the compositional relation R_c,

$$x_{(i,c,j)} \sim \mathcal{N}(e_i^\top R_{c(1)} R_{c(2)} \dots R_{c(|c|-1)} R_{c(|c|)} e_j, \sigma_c^2) \quad (9)$$

The multiplicative compositionality can be understood as a sequence of linear transformation from the original entity i with the compositional relations, and the inner product between the transformed entity and target entity forms a value of the compositional triple. Again, the details of the parameter estimators are shown in Appendix C.2.

In contrast with the additive model, the multiplicative model preserves the ordering in a compositional relation, and hence the different orderings of relations result different relations in the compositional model.

4. KNOWLEDGE COMPLETION

We first evaluate our model for the knowledge completion task to measure the predictive performance of PRESCAL with all non compositional and compositional variants. We evaluate the models on three benchmark datasets: KINSHIP, UMLS, and NATION, and compare performances with the original RESCAL. Detailed description of each dataset is shown in Table 3.

Table 3: Description of datasets. Sparsity denotes the ratio of valid triples to invalid triples.

Dataset	# rel	# entities	# triples	sparsity
Kinship	26	104	10,790	0.038
UMLS	49	135	6,752	0.008
Nation	56	14	2,024	0.184

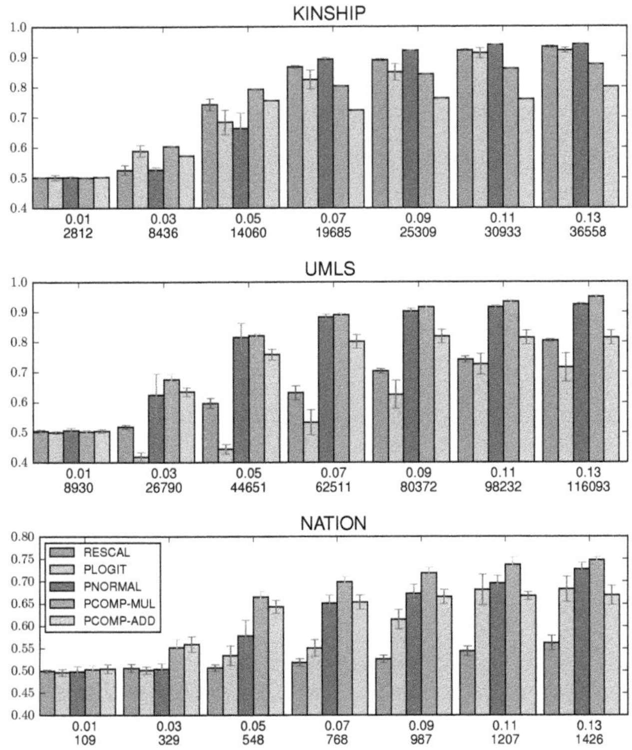

Figure 1: ROC-AUC scores of compositional models. The x-axis denotes the proportion and total number of triples used for training. Error bars denote one standard deviation.

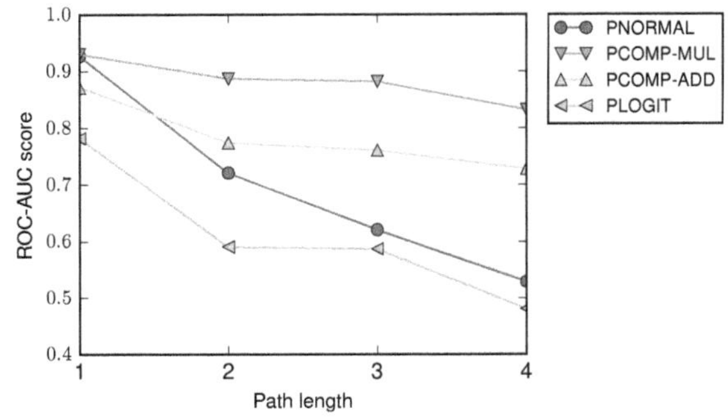

Figure 2: Path prediction result with UMLS. The performances of both compositional models remain consistent whereas those of the non-compositional models drop sharply as the length increases.

We set the compositional length L to two, split the dataset into 20% for validation and 30% for testing. We vary the proportion of training triples from 1% to 13% of datasets. For RESCAL, we use the original implementation[1], and measure performance over 10 runs with random initialisations. For PRESCAL and all the variants, we sample triples x_{ikj} from its posterior, and measure performance over 10 different samples. The performances of models are measured by the ROC-AUC score on the test set ranked according to a posterior mean: $\frac{1}{|\mathcal{X}_p||\mathcal{X}_n|}\sum_{\{i,k,j\}\in\mathcal{X}_p,\{i',k',j'\}\in\mathcal{X}_n}\mathbb{I}[\bar{x}_{ikj} > \bar{x}_{ikj}]$, where $\mathcal{X}_p$ and $\mathcal{X}_n$ are the set of positive and negative triples in the test set, respectively, and $\bar{x}$ is a reconstructed triple.

Figure 1 shows the ROC-AUC scores of the compositional models with the various baseline models. The PRESCAL with the normal output (PNORMAL) or logistic output (PLOGIT) generally outperform RESCAL, and PNORMAL outperforms PLOGIT. We conjecture that an additional flexibility of controlling the variance of triples makes PNORMAL to perform better than PLOGIT. We compare the compositional model with the original RESCAL, PNORMAL, and PLOGIT. In general, the multiplicative compositional model (PCOMP-MUL) outperforms the additive compositional model (PCOMP-ADD), and performs better than the other baseline models when the training set is small. For UMLS and NATION, PCOMP-MUL has the best performance across the all training proportions. For KINSHIP, however, PCOMP-MUL performs better when the training proportion is less than 7%.

The goal of the compositional models is to factorise triples along with the graph structure as a whole. The triple prediction task tells us a trained model is capable of triple prediction, but does not tell whether the features can recover the graph structure. If the model factorises the graph structure properly, then the trained model can predict not only triples but the graph structure as well. To validate the model assumption, we evaluate a path prediction task. For this task, we use 10% of UMLS dataset for training. We compute an expected value of an unobserved path given a trained model. The non-compositional models may not be able to compute the expected value. In such a case, we approximate paths with the multiplicative model assumption in Equation 9. We vary the path length from 1 (triple) to 4, and measure ROC-AUC scores on the reconstructed compositional triples. Figure 2 shows the result of the path prediction task. Both compositional models show consistent performance regardless of the path length. However, the performance of the non-compositional models drops sharply as the length increases. The results show the compositional models preserve graph structure in the embedded space. It is worth emphasising that although the compositional length for training is 2, the compositional models show consistent results on predicting paths of length 3 and 4.

Table 4 shows an example of the path prediction result starting from entity `Mental-or-Behavioral (MB) Dysfunction` followed by two relations `Affects` and `Produces` in the UMLS dataset. Both compositional and non-compositional models predict triples well. For length-2 path prediction, only the compositional models can capture correct entities on top 5. We also visualise the multi-dimensional entities inferred by PNORMAL and PCOMP-MUL into a two-dimensional space using spectral clustering [23] in Appendix D.

5. KNOWLEDGE POPULATION

In this section, we show results of incremental knowledge population task using Thomson sampling on the three datasets. Additional verification on the Thompson sampling with synthetic datasets is also provided in Appendix E.

Experimental settings: We compare the Thompson sampling models with AMDC models, and PRESCAL for passive learning. AMDC model has been proposed to achieve two different active learning goals, constructing a predictive model and maximising the valid triples in a knowledge base, with two different querying strategies [9]. AMDC-PRED is a

[1]https://github.com/mnick/rescal.py

Table 4: Example of path prediction from UMLS data. We predict top 5 entities in compositional triples starting from entity `Mental-or-Behavioral (MB) Dysfunction` followed by two relations `Affects` and `Produces`. Correct entities are bolded.

(a) Triple prediction: `(MB Dysfunction, Affects, -)`

Model	Top 1	Top 2	Top 3	Top 4	Top 5
PNORMAL	**Invertebrate**	**Reptile**	**Archaeon**	**Bird**	**Phy.-Function**
PLOGIT	**Cell-Function**	**Disease-or-Syndrome**	**Cell-or-Molecular-Dysf.**	**Exp.-Model-of-Disease**	**Mental-Process**
PCOMP-MUL	**Archaeon**	**Fish**	**Fungus**	**Invertebrate**	**Human**
PCOMP-ADD	**Path.-Function**	**Bird**	**Cell-or-Molecular-Dysf.**	Drug-Delivery-Device	Congenital-Abnormality

(b) Length-2 path prediction: `(MB Dysfunction, Affects, Produces, -)`

Model	Top 1	Top 2	Top 3	Top 4	Top 5
PNORMAL	Clinical-Drug	Sign-or-Symptom	Org.-Attribute	Drug-Delivery-Device	Clinical-Attr.
PLOGIT	Amphibian	Gov.-or-Reg.-Activity	Food	Biologic-Func.	Classification
PCOMP-MUL	**Enzyme**	**Body-Substance**	**Biogenic-Amine**	Carbohydrate	**Immunologic-Factor**
PCOMP-ADD	**Immunologic-Factor**	**Body-Substance**	Molecular-Biology-Research-Technique	Clinical-Drug	Chemical-Viewed-Structurally

predictive model construction strategy and chooses a triple which is the most ambiguous (close to the decision boundary) at each time t. AMDC-POP is a population strategy which aims to maximise the number of valid triples in a knowledge base, choosing a triple with the highest expected value at each time. To train all models we only use the observed triples up to the current time. For the passive learning with PRESCAL, we generate a random sample at each time period. For the particle Thompson sampling models, we set variance parameter σ_e and σ_r to 1, σ_x to 0.1, and vary σ_c from 1 to 100.

We leave 30 % of triples as a test set to measure test error. At each time period, each model chooses one triple to query, if the selected triple is in the test set then we choose the next highest expected triple that is not in the test set. All models start from zero observation. After every query, a model obtains a label of the queried triple from an oracle, then the model updates the parameters.

Evaluation metric: We use two different evaluation metrics, the cumulative gain and ROC-AUC score, for the performance comparison. The goal of the Thompson sampling is to maximise the knowledge population through the balanced querying strategy between exploration and exploitation. To measure how many triples are obtained through the querying stage, we compute the cumulative gain which is the number of valid triple obtained up to time t. Additionally, we compute the ROC-AUC score on the test set to understand how this balanced querying strategy results in making a predictive model.

Exploitation and exploration: Figure 3 shows the cumulative gains and ROC-AUC scores of the Thompson sampling on three real datasets. The model names with suffix -TS represent the models adopting the Thompson sampling strategy. PNORMAL-TS performs better than other baseline models for the cumulative gain, and shows comparable result for the ROC-AUC scores. Both compositional models perform worse than PNORMAL-TS across all datasets.

In the original AMDC [9], AMDC-POP model obtains more valid triples than AMDC-PRED, and AMDC-PRED shows high ROC-AUC scores than AMDC-POP. In our experiment, however, AMDC-POP shows comparable cumulative gain to AMDC-PRED and even worse than AMDC-PRED for the UMLS. We conjecture the initial observation and query size results in the different performances: in the original experiment, the model starts from a small set of training data, and the query size was 1,000 for KINSHIP and UMLS. With larger query size, the model focuses on exploit and takes advantages, whereas in our experiment, we start from zero observation and query one triple at each time, which makes the model hard to exploit. This result shows the importance of balancing between exploitation and exploration.

We note that the compositional model performs worse than the non-compositional models, especially than PNORMAL-TS. This is counter-intuitive to our general understanding where the model that performs well in the predictive task also shows a better performance in the active learning.

6. CONCLUSION

Throughout the paper, we have considered the two knowledge base construction tasks: knowledge population and knowledge completion. Based on a probabilistic framework, we propose new knowledge base factorisation methods where the latent factorisation reflects the graph structure of a knowledge graph. The probabilistic formulation allows us to quantify the uncertainty of predictive distributions, which is then used for the knowledge population task. The experiments of two tasks on three datasets show that the compositional model benefits graph structure for knowledge completion, and the probabilistic formulation helps to explore the latent space efficiently for knowledge population.

Acknowledgments This work is supported in part by the Australian Research Council via the Discovery Project program DP140102185. The work has been supported by the Data to Decisions Cooperative Research Centre whose activities are funded by the Australian Commonwealth Government's Cooperative Research Centres Programme.

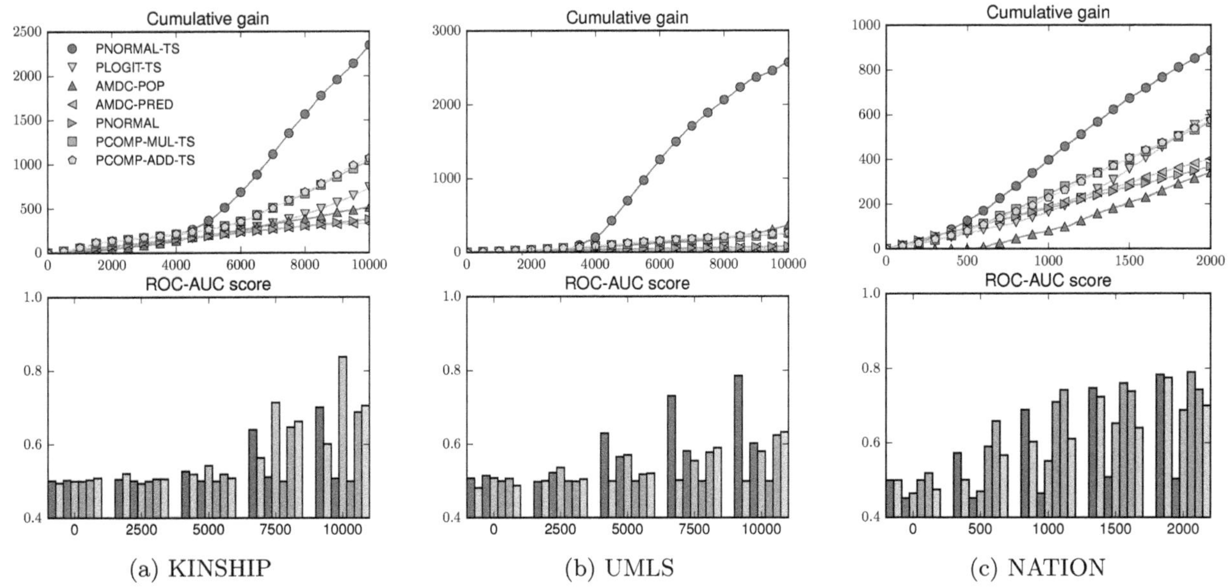

Figure 3: The cumulative gain and ROC-AUC score of the Thompson sampling with passive learning and AMDC models. Thompson sampling with PRESCAL (PNORMAL-TS) model achieves the highest cumulative gain to compare with the other models and shows comparable performance on ROC-AUC scores.

7. REFERENCES

[1] C. M. Bishop. Pattern recognition. *Machine Learning*, 2006.

[2] K. Bollacker, C. Evans, P. Paritosh, T. Sturge, and J. Taylor. Freebase: a collaboratively created graph database for structuring human knowledge. In *SIGMOD*. ACM, 2008.

[3] O. Chapelle and L. Li. An empirical evaluation of thompson sampling. In *NIPS*, 2011.

[4] L. Dong, F. Wei, M. Zhou, and K. Xu. Question Answering over Freebase with Multi-Column Convolutional Neural Networks. In *ACL*, 2015.

[5] X. Dong, E. Gabrilovich, G. Heitz, W. Horn, N. Lao, K. Murphy, T. Strohmann, S. Sun, and W. Zhang. Knowledge vault: A web-scale approach to probabilistic knowledge fusion. In *KDD*. ACM, 2014.

[6] K. Guu, J. Miller, and P. Liang. Traversing knowledge graphs in vector space. In *EMNLP*, 2015.

[7] J. Hoffart, F. M. Suchanek, K. Berberich, and G. Weikum. Yago2: A spatially and temporally enhanced knowledge base from wikipedia. *Artificial Intelligence*, 194, 2013.

[8] J.-Y. Jiang, J. Liu, C.-Y. Lin, and P.-J. Cheng. Improving ranking consistency for web search by leveraging a knowledge base and search logs. In *CIKM*. ACM, 2015.

[9] H. Kajino, A. Kishimoto, A. Botea, E. Daly, and S. Kotoulas. Active learning for multi-relational data construction. In *WWW*, 2015.

[10] J. Kawale, H. H. Bui, B. Kveton, L. Tran-Thanh, and S. Chawla. Efficient thompson sampling for online matrix-factorization recommendation. In *NIPS*, 2015.

[11] D. Kim, H. Wang, and A. Oh. Context-dependent conceptualization. *IJCAI*, 2013.

[12] D. Kim, L. Xie, and C. S. Ong. Probabilistic knowledge graph construction - supplemental material. *arXiv preprint arXiv:1608.05921*, 2016.

[13] T. G. Kolda and B. W. Bader. Tensor decompositions and applications. *SIAM review*, 51(3), 2009.

[14] N. Lao and W. Cohen. Relational retrieval using a combination of path-constrained random walks. *Machine learning*, 2010.

[15] D. D. Lee and H. S. Seung. Learning the parts of objects by non-negative matrix factorization. *Nature*, 401(6755), 1999.

[16] A. Mnih and R. Salakhutdinov. Probabilistic matrix factorization. In *NIPS*, 2007.

[17] A. Neelakantan, B. Roth, and A. McCallum. Compositional Vector Space Models for Knowledge Base Completion. In *ACL*, 2015.

[18] M. Nickel, V. Tresp, and H.-P. Kriegel. A three-way model for collective learning on multi-relational data. In *ICML*, 2011.

[19] N. Ruchansky, M. Crovella, and E. Terzi. Matrix completion with queries. In *KDD*. ACM, 2015.

[20] M. N. Schmidt and S. Mohamed. Probabilistic non-negative tensor factorization using markov chain monte carlo. In *Signal Processing*. IEEE, 2009.

[21] S. L. Scott. A modern bayesian look at the multi-armed bandit. *Applied Stochastic Models in Business and Industry*, 26, 2010.

[22] D. J. Sutherland, B. Póczos, and J. Schneider. Active learning and search on low-rank matrices. In *KDD*. ACM, 2013.

[23] U. Von Luxburg. A tutorial on spectral clustering. *Statistics and computing*, 17(4), 2007.

[24] L. Xiong, X. Chen, T.-K. Huang, J. G. Schneider, and J. G. Carbonell. Temporal collaborative filtering with bayesian probabilistic tensor factorization. In *ICDM*, volume 10. SIAM, 2010.

Explaining Sentiment Spikes in Twitter

Anastasia Giachanou, Ida Mele and Fabio Crestani
Faculty of Informatics, Università della Svizzera italiana
Lugano, Switzerland
{anastasia.giachanou, ida.mele, fabio.crestani}@usi.ch

ABSTRACT

Tracking public opinion in social media provides important information to enterprises or governments during a decision making process. In addition, identifying and extracting the causes of sentiment spikes allows interested parties to redesign and adjust strategies with the aim to attract more positive sentiments. In this paper, we focus on the problem of tracking sentiment towards different entities, detecting sentiment spikes and on the problem of extracting and ranking the causes of a sentiment spike. Our approach combines LDA topic model with Relative Entropy. The former is used for extracting the topics discussed in the time window before the sentiment spike. The latter allows to rank the detected topics based on their contribution to the sentiment spike.

Keywords

Tracking sentiment; sentiment spikes; Twitter.

1. INTRODUCTION

Recent years have witnessed a rapid growth of social media platforms, such as Twitter and Facebook, where millions of people share their thoughts and opinions on several topics. The increasing popularity of social media has transformed the web into a vast repository of opinions towards various topics. Hence, understanding users' opinions is very important in the decision-making process.

Public opinion changes over time, therefore tracking opinion and sentiment evolution is very critical for the interested parties. The analysis of sentiment evolution gives the opportunity to identify sudden changes of sentiment and, more importantly, to get insights on what has caused these sentiment spikes. Detecting sentiment spikes allows to take quick reactions in response to user sentiments (especially a negative one), whereas understanding the reasons that likely caused a sentiment spike provides valuable information for governments and companies to be proactive and improve their tactics. For example, suppose that the negative sentiment towards a political person increases during the electoral campaign, then the respective Press Office can extract the causes for such increase and avoid, in future, those situations that may have caused the negative sentiment. Another example is related to movie production companies that may want to better understand what people think of the actors that participate in their movies.

Extracting causes of sentiment spikes is very challenging since they can be also caused by external factors that are very difficult to capture. Previous work by Montero et al. [10] focused on identifying the likely causes of emotion spikes using the most popular keyphrases. Tan et al. [13] proposed an extension of LDA to rank the extracted foreground topics according to their popularity within the sentiment variation period. Although using the popularity of the topics seems sensible, we believe that it is intuitive and its effectiveness requires deeper analysis.

In this paper, we focus on the problem of tracking sentiment evolution towards different entities, we identify sentiment spikes and we extract and rank the causes behind those spikes. In our study, we firstly apply an outlier-detection approach to identify the sentiment spikes [6]. Then, we present an approach that combines LDA topic model with Relative Entropy for ranking the possible causes of a sentiment spike. The former allows to extract the topics discussed in the time window right before the sentiment spike and the latter to detect the topics which probably caused the sudden change. To the best of our knowledge, our work is the first that tries to rank the extracted causes of a sentiment spike based on the extent of the sentiment change they caused.

2. RELATED WORK

Sentiment analysis has attracted much attention in the research community. In its most typical scenario, sentiment analysis aims to detect the sentiment polarity of a given text. Recently, researchers applied sentiment analysis on Twitter that is one of the most popular microblogging services. The majority of the proposed approaches applied methods from machine learning field to classify a tweet as positive or negative [7, 8]. Other researchers proposed lexicon-based approaches that do not require any training data. One of the most well-known lexicon-based algorithms is SentiStrength [14] that can effectively identify the sentiment strength of informal text using a human-coded lexicon. Besides the sentiment lexicon, SentiStrength uses a list of emoticons, negations and boosting words. A thorough review on opinion retrieval and sentiment analysis can be found in a survey by Pang and Lee [11] whereas a survey focused on Twitter sentiment analysis can be found in [5].

CIKM'16, October 24-28, 2016, Indianapolis, IN, USA
© 2016 ACM. ISBN 978-1-4503-4073-1/16/10...$15.00
DOI: http://dx.doi.org/10.1145/2983323.2983678

Sentiment dynamics has also attracted much attention. Bollen et al. [4] used a psychometric instrument called Profile of Mood States (POMS) to extract and analyze different moods (tension, depression, anger, vigor, fatigue, confusion) detected in tweets. They found that the mood level in Twitter posts was correlated with cultural, political and other world global events. An et al. [1] combined classical sentiment analysis algorithms, data mining techniques and time series methods with the aim to detect and track sentiment regarding climate change from Twitter feeds.

Other researchers tried to identify the causes behind sentiment spikes. Balog et al. [2] used LiveJournal posts which mention the user mood and they extracted unusually common words in order to find the causes of the identified mood changes. These words were then used to search the related events in a news dataset. Tan et al. [13] analyzed sentiment variations and extracted possible causes of such variations. They proposed the Foreground and Background LDA model to extract the foreground topics and the Reason Candidate and Background LDA model to rank the extracted foreground topics according to their popularity within the sentiment variation period.

A similar work is the one conducted by Montero et al. [10] who tried to identify the likely causes of emotion spikes of influential users. They used empirical heuristics to identify the emotional spikes and keyphrases to extract the causes of the spikes. Differently from their approach, which is based on a simple linguistic and statistical analysis for the extraction of keyphrases, we present a more sophisticated approach which allows to extract the causes of a sentiment spike by comparing the sentiment distributions behind the tweets.

3. METHODOLOGY

The problem of tracking sentiment evolution towards an entity and extracting and ranking the causes of a sentiment spike can be viewed as a four-step approach. First, we need to observe the sentiment evolution towards the entity of interest. Given this sentiment evolution, we have to identify the most important sentiment spikes. Next, we need to extract the topics that were discussed when the sentiment spike occurred. The last step is to rank the extracted topics based on their contribution to the sentiment spike.

3.1 Sentiment Evolution & Sentiment Spikes

Here, we describe the approach we use to track the sentiment evolution towards a specific entity. To address this problem, we have to estimate the overall sentiment towards the entity on a given time point. Therefore, we need to quantify the sentiment rather than to measure the absolute sentiment values of individual documents[1].

To better describe the approach, we introduce some notation. Let $X = (x_1, x_2, ..., x_n)$ be a set of data observed at consecutive and equal time partitions denoted as $\{t_1, t_2, ..., t_n\}$. Based on this, we can use the frequency of tweets to observe how the popularity towards an entity e changes over time, denoted as $N_t(e)$.

The popularity of an entity does not reflect the sentiment evolution. For determining the sentiment evolution, we need to focus on the ratio of tweets that express a specific sentiment. Let $N_t(e, s)$ be the number of tweets, posted during a particular time period t, which express a sentiment s towards a specific entity e, and let $N_t(e)$ be the number of total tweets posted towards e at t, then we can define the ratio of tweets that share a common sentiment s as:

$$r_t(e, s) = \frac{N_t(e, s)}{N_t(e)}$$

In this study we only consider positive, neutral, and negative sentiments. However, our approach can be also applied for tracking emotions such as love, anger, sadness etc.

To identify sentiment spikes, we use an outlier detection approach adopted from the field of time series and which was first applied on the problem of detecting sentiment spikes by [6]. The outliers are visually depicted as sudden peaks and in most of the cases are caused by some important events that not only influence the popularity of an entity but also the public sentiment towards the entity. In order to identify the outliers we calculate the difference: $e_i = x_i - x'_i$ where x_i is the observation i and x'_i is the prediction of the observation i. In other words, this equation calculates the ordinary residuals for each observation. We use *LOESS* that is also known as the locally weighted polynomial regression model and interquartile range to detect the residuals. Let Q_1 and Q_3 be the lower and upper quartiles, respectively, then the outliers are the observations that are outside the range:

$$[Q_1 - k * (Q_3 - Q_1), Q_3 + k * (Q_3 - Q_1)]$$

where k represents the span of the range, and it is usually set between 1.5 and 3.0.

3.2 LDA & KL-divergence Approach

As explained before, our ultimate aim is, given a sentiment spike, to get a ranked list of topics that can reflect their contribution in having caused the specific spike. More formally, let $P_{e,s}$ (for peak) be a sentiment spike that is related to an entity e and a sentiment s. The first step is to decide the time window that we need to focus. The starting point of the time window can be the point when the sentiment s had started increasing. This time point is denoted as t_{start}. As an ending point of the time window, we consider the time point when the spike occurred and this is denoted as t_{prev}. Figure 1 shows the phases of the sentiment spike from the point when the sentiment started increasing to the one when the sentiment has become prevalent.

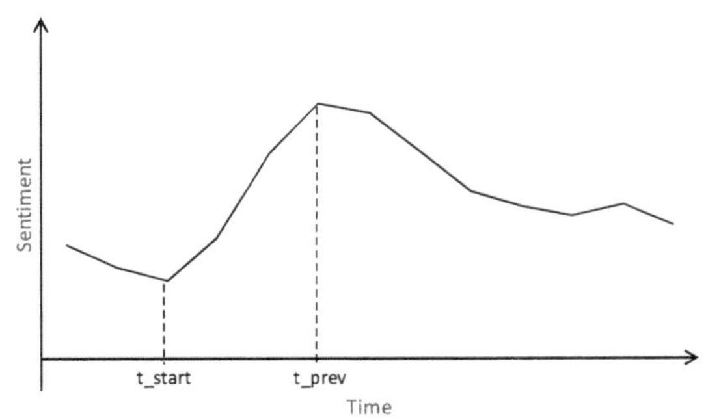

Figure 1: Starting and prevalent time point of a sentiment spike

[1]The terms *document* and *tweet* are used interchangeably in this paper.

We believe that the topics discussed within the time window $[t_{start}, t_{prev}]$ represent the topics that contributed to the sentiment spike. Hence, we apply the Latent Dirichlet Allocation (LDA) topic model [3] to all the tweets within the time window $[t_{start}, t_{prev}]$ to extract the topics discussed within this window. LDA that is one of the most well-known topic models is based on a "bag of words" approach and treats each document as a vector of word counts.

The next step is to rank the extracted topics according to their contribution to the sentiment spike. For this problem we use Kullback-Leibler divergence (KL-divergence) [9] that is a measure of the difference between two probability distributions, where one typically represents the actual distribution of observations and the other one is an approximation of it. For this reason, KL-divergence is usually applied to measure the information lost between one distribution and its approximation. Although the KL-divergence is not a true metric, it is often interpreted as a way of measuring the distance between two probability distributions. Inspired by this, we show how it is possible to use the KL-divergence to determine the causes of a sentiment spike in Twitter.

In particular, we present an approach based on computing the total distribution of the sentiment towards an entity and compare it against another distribution of the sentiment towards the same entity, which is obtained by removing tweets belonging to a specific topic. The intuition is that if a sentiment has changed for a specific reason, such reason can be captured by the tweets that are about a related topic. We can quantify this by using the difference between the distribution of the sentiment using all tweets and the distribution of sentiment computed using all the tweets except for those belonging to a specific topic. This can be done for all topics, namely, considering one topic at a time we remove the tweets corresponding to it and compare the obtained distribution against the original one. As a result, we can determine for which topic the two distributions are more different and rank the topics accordingly. The final ranking should reflect the contribution of the topics to the sentiment spike.

Let S_e be the distribution of the sentiment s over time towards an entity e, and $T = (T_1, ..., T_z, ..., T_{|T|})$ be the topics extracted after applying LDA on the tweets' collection D. For the distribution we use the sentiment ratio as explained in Section 3.1. Also, the collection D is made of the tweets that are related to the sentiment spike $P_{e,s}$ and which were actually posted within the time window $[t_{start}, t_{prev}]$.

In addition, let $D_{T_z} = (d_1, ..., d_t)$ be the tweets assigned to the topic T_z. Then, for each topic T_z we define a new distribution that we denote as $S^*_{e,T_z} = S_e - S_{e,T_z}$ and which is calculated based on the sentiment and after removing the tweets that belong to D_{T_z}. Based on this, we calculate the KL-divergence between the distribution S_e and S^*_{e,T_z} as:

$$KL(S_e, S^*_{e,T_z}) = \sum_i S_e(i) \log \frac{S_e(i)}{S^*_{e,T_z}(i)}$$

Finally the topics are ranked based on their KL-divergence value. The highest the value, the highest the contribution of the specific topic to the sentiment spike. For example, if we track the negative sentiment towards an entity, then the topic with the highest KL-divergence value is considered to be the most responsible to the sentiment spike. Figure 2 shows an example of one initial distribution and of three different distributions related to three topics. In this example,

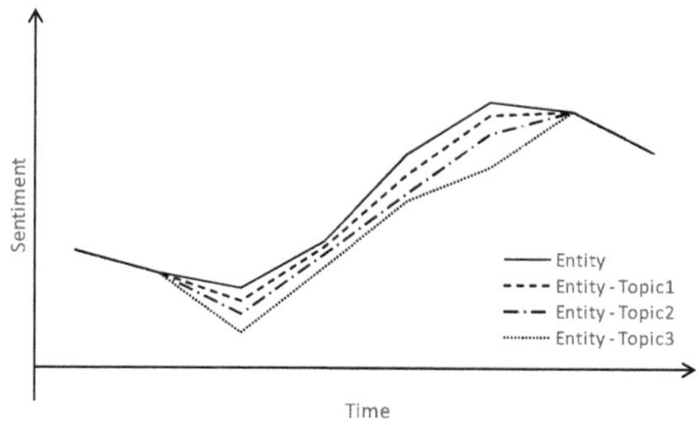

Figure 2: Example of the distributions of three topics compared to the entity's distribution

Topic3 has the largest contribution to the sentiment spike, because removing it makes the difference between the two distributions bigger compared to the other two topics.

4. EXPERIMENTAL DESIGN

To the best of our knowledge, there is no available dataset for the tasks of tracking and extracting causes of sentiment spike. Therefore, we used Twitter API over a period of time to collect our data. Our collection spans from the 10th of April to the 31st of December 2015. We used a list of 70 entities from different domains including politics, cities, products etc. In this study, we focus on three entities that are well known personalities: *Michelle Obama* (1,076,732 tweets), *Angela Merkel* (1,369,756 tweets) and *Angelina Jolie* (1,265,001 tweets). To collect the ground truth we used CrowdFlower. Although we cannot describe the annotation process here due to space limitation, we plan to do so in a future work. The collection and the ground truth we collected are publicly available[2].

To identify the sentiment of a tweet we used SentiStrength that has been shown to be effective in different social media platforms [14]. Although SentiStrength can also apply a sentiment score to each tweet, in this study we only considered the three following classes: *positive, neutral,* and *negative.* For the entities *Michelle Obama* and *Angela Merkel* we focused on negative spikes, whereas for the entity *Angelina Jolie* we focused on positive spikes.

To identify the topics discussed before and after a sentiment spike, we applied the LDA [3] topic model on the tweets posted between the date that the spike started increasing and the actual date of the spike. We considered each tweet to be a document, and we extracted 10 topics for each spike. Before applying LDA, we removed from the set of tweets all the occurrences of terms that were referring to the entity (e.g., for the entity *Michelle Obama* we removed all the occurrences of the terms "Michelle" and "Obama" as well as their variations). For the analysis, we applied Gibbs sampling for the LDA model parameter estimation and we set the number of iterations to 2,000.

We compare our approach with one baseline that is based on the number of tweets assigned to each extracted topic. To compare the two different rankings we use *Spearman* (Sp.) correlation. We use the average ranking given by the anno-

[2]Please contact the first author

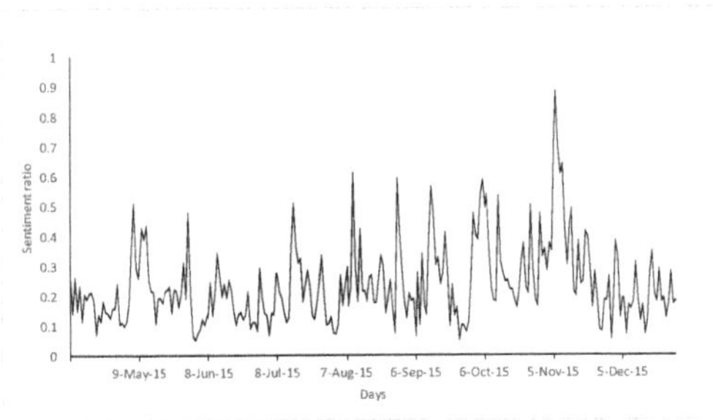

Figure 3: Ratio of negative tweets about "Michelle Obama" per day

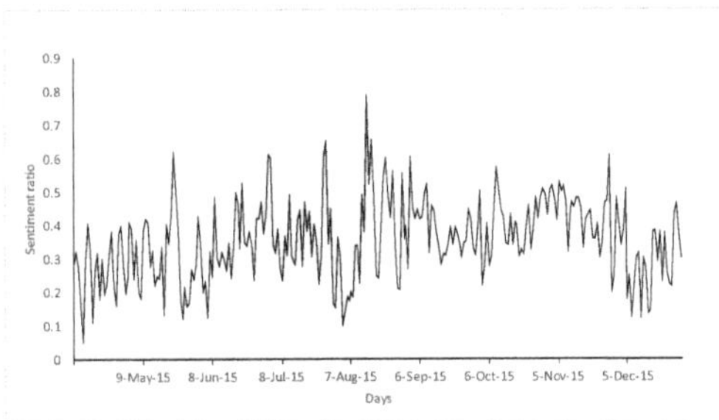

Figure 4: Ratio of negative tweets about "Angela Merkel" per day

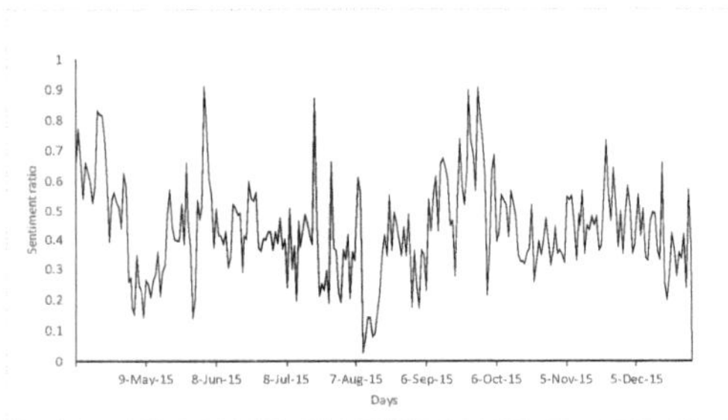

Figure 5: Ratio of positive tweets about "Angelina Jolie" per day

tators as ground truth and we compare this ranking with the one generated by the baseline and the LDA & KL-divergence approach. To measure the correlation of the rankings using the average values we use *Pearson* (Pear.) correlation. Finally, we report *Precision* and *Mean Average Precision* (MAP).

5. RESULTS AND DISCUSSION

First, we present the results on sentiment tracking and outlier detection. Figures 3 and 4 show the ratio of negative tweets published per day for the entities *Michelle Obama* and *Angela Merkel*, respectively. In Figure 5 we show the ratio of positive tweets published per day for *Angelina Jolie*. These figures are very useful for understanding how the sentiment changes over time for a specific entity. Also, we can observe if there were any sudden sentiment spikes towards the specific entity and when these occurred.

Table 1 summarizes the most important statistics of the sentiment spikes. To understand the causes of a sentiment spike, we need to look through the tweets that were published not only on the specific day but also a bit before. As a starting point, we considered the day when the number of tweets with the same sentiment had started increasing, that is, the most recent day before the sentiment spike which presented the lowest number of tweets with the same sentiment. For each entity we took into account 5 different spikes. Hence, we have 5 different time windows per entity.

Table 1: Statistics for the different sentiment spikes

	Start date	Date of spike	Number of tweets
Michelle Obama	03 May 2015	07 May 2015	20,839
	30 May 2015	31 May 2015	7,496
	13 July 2015	16 July 2015	12,521
	10 Aug. 2015	12 Aug. 2015	4,890
	06 Nov. 2015	08 Nov. 2015	29,214
Angela Merkel	21 May 2015	23 May 2015	10,264
	01 July 2015	03 July 2015	31,454
	26 July 2015	29 July 2015	8,627
	15 Aug. 2015	16 Aug. 2015	2,507
	25 Nov. 2015	29 Nov. 2015	28,578
Angelina Jolie	17 Apr. 2015	19 Apr. 2015	9,357
	02 June 2015	04 June 2015	18,360
	20 July 2015	21 July 2015	7,099
	24 Sep. 2015	26 Sep. 2015	12,220
	29 Sep. 2015	30 Sep. 2015	9,654

We applied LDA [3] to extract the topics discussed when each sentiment spike occurred. Table 2 shows the extracted topics of each spike and for each of the three entities. We observe that LDA managed to group terms that were about the same topic together. Also, some of those topics are related to important news (i.e. the topic detected for *Angela Merkel* on the 23rd of May that is about a political scandal) whereas other are about less important events (i.e. the topic on the 4th of June that is about wishing happy birthday to *Angelina Jolie*). This is a consequence of the informal style of Twitter in which users frequently retweet a message that does not refer to an important event but the users may find the topic interesting or funny.

Table 3 shows the results on the task of ranking the causes of sentiment spikes using the baseline and the LDA & KL-

Table 2: Sample of extracted topics from different sentiment spikes

	Michelle Obama
07 May 2015	ruined lunch cookies college signing
31 May 2015	grieving tonight bidens beau death
16 July 2015	mayor gorilla resign face racist
12 Aug. 2015	stand years feminist attacks miss
08 Nov. 2015	kids drag fam roast mom
	Merkel
23 May 2015	scandal political crisis spy germany
03 July 2015	debt unsustainable greek wikileaks phone
29 July 2015	girl palestinian cry caused abolish
16 Aug. 2015	bigger challenge migrants crisis european
29 Nov. 2015	syria military french downing aircraft
	Angelina Jolie
19 Apr. 2015	life structure cheekbones appreciation amazing
04 June 2015	birthday happy beautiful women inspirational
21 July 2015	blood imagine veins donate celebrities
26 Sep. 2015	awards academy flaws bones kardashians
30 Sep. 2015	pitt brad smith movie amazing

Table 3: Performance results for the entities *Michelle Obama*, *Angela Merkel* and *Angelina Jolie*. A tick mark (✓) means that there is a correlation whereas a x mark (✗) means that there is no correlation compared to the ground truth

		Baseline						LDA & KL-divergence					
		Sp.	Pear.	MAP@5	MAP	P@3	P@5	Sp.	Pear.	MAP@5	MAP	P@3	P@5
Michelle Obama	07 May 2015	✗	✗	0.353	0.574	0.667	0.600	✓	✓	0.493	0.692	0.667	0.800
	31 May 2015	✗	✗	0.040	0.410	0.000	0.200	✗	✗	0.247	0.521	0.333	0.400
	16 July 2015	✗	✗	0.040	0.418	0.000	0.200	✓	✓	0.793	0.815	0.667	0.800
	12 Aug. 2015	✗	✗	0.170	0.487	0.000	0.600	✗	✗	0.180	0.475	0.000	0.400
	08 Nov. 2015	✗	✗	0.237	0.504	0.333	0.600	✗	✗	0.337	0.597	0.333	0.600
Angela Merkel	23 May 2015	✗	✗	0.287	0.529	0.333	0.600	✗	✗	0.537	0.670	0.333	0.600
	03 July 2015	✗	✗	0.130	0.467	0.000	0.400	✗	✗	0.387	0.564	0.333	0.600
	29 July 2015	✗	✗	0.337	0.583	0.333	0.600	✗	✗	0.287	0.583	0.333	0.600
	16 Aug. 2015	✗	✗	0.130	0.463	0.000	0.400	✗	✓	0.327	0.620	0.333	0.800
	29 Nov. 2015	✗	✗	0.327	0.578	0.333	0.800	✗	✗	0.220	0.526	0.000	0.600
Angelina Jolie	19 Apr. 2015	✗	✗	0.693	0.763	0.667	0.800	✓	✓	0.743	0.828	0.667	0.800
	04 June 2015	✗	✗	0.413	0.648	0.667	0.400	✓	✓	0.643	0.805	0.667	0.800
	21 July 2015	✗	✗	0.197	0.507	0.333	0.400	✗	✗	0.080	0.454	0.667	0.400
	26 Sep. 2015	✗	✗	0.503	0.668	0.667	0.600	✓	✓	0.593	0.756	0.667	0.800
	30 Sep. 2015	✗	✗	0.703	0.759	0.667	0.600	✓	✗	0.753	0.817	0.667	0.600

divergence approach. In case of *Michelle Obama* we observe that on some days the LDA & KL-divergence approach managed to obtain a similar ranking compared to the ground truth. Also, we observe that the LDA & KL-divergence approach performs better on all the sentiment spikes compared to baseline. For the entity *Angela Merkel* the rankings generated from the LDA & KL-divergence approach are very different compared to the ground truth. On the contrary, in case of *Angelina Jolie* the LDA & KL-divergence approach was effective for most of the spikes. We now analyze and discuss the results for each entity.

Table 4: The three most negative topics based on human judgments for two sentiment spikes (*07 May 2015* and *16 July 2015*) of the entity *Michelle Obama*

07 May 2015
Topic 4: school museums lunches ruined people
Topic 6: trip ski cost taxpayers aspen daughters
Topic 3: don't hey feel care barack wrong anymore
16 July 2015
Topic 7: mayor gorilla resign face racist won't admitting
Topic 9: sailors fried food ban navy blame lady
Topic 8: calls monkey gorilla mayor face barack man

To get a better understanding, we analyze the results on the sentiment spikes of *Michelle Obama* for which the LDA & KL-divergence method returned a ranking similar to the ground truth. Table 4 shows the three topics that were ranked as the most negative by human annotators for the spikes observed on *May 7* and *July 16, 2015.* As we see from the keywords, the tweets belonging to those topics express negative sentiment. Then, we manually checked the set of tweets to examine if they truly express a negative sentiment. One example is *"Topic 4: school, museums, lunches, ruined, people"* that was ranked as the most negative according to human annotators for the spike on *May 7.* This topic contains a great amount of tweets saying: *"Michelle Obama ruined our lunch".* Looking in the web, it is easy to find out that this is related to the fact that Michele Obama changed schools' lunch program, but the students did not like the change and so they started complaining on Twitter. Note that this topic was ranked as the second most negative by the LDA & KL-divergence approach.

However, for some other sentiment spikes the ranking generated from the LDA & KL-divergence approach is different from the ground truth. More specifically, on the spikes occurred on *May 31, Aug. 12,* and *Nov. 08, 2015* there is no correlation between the two rankings. To get a deeper understanding, we manually looked and compared the results on these spikes. First, we analyzed the spike on *May 31, 2015.* To this end, we measured the absolute difference between the rankings per each topic. From the results we observe that the biggest difference is on the *Topic 4* whereas the second largest is for the *Topic 1* and *Topic 2.* More specifically, our method ranked *Topic 4* as the second most positive topic, whereas annotators considered that it is the second most negative topic. Looking through the topic's tweets, we could see that they are about a picture that was edited by photoshop and the majority of the tweets are ironic towards *Michelle Obama.* For example, most of them are retweets of the message *"So I found this picture of Michelle Obama playing tennis"*, and it is obvious that the picture is not real. Irony is very difficult to be detected automatically [11]. There are a few studies focused on irony detection on Twitter [12] but we believe that this problem is still under explored. As expected, annotators managed to detect the irony whereas our approach could not.

We also noticed a difference in *Topic 1* and *Topic 2* that were ranked as negative by the LDA & KL-divergence approach whereas annotators did not consider that they express negative sentiment. The tweets that belong to these topics are about the death of Beau Biden (i.e., *"Michelle and*

Table 5: Performance results for the entity *Angela Merkel* after considering tweets that refer to news. A tick mark (✓) means that there is a correlation whereas a x mark (✗) means that there is no correlation compared to the ground truth

	Angela Merkel					
	LDA & KL-divergence					
	Sp.	Pear.	MAP@5	MAP	P@3	P@5
23 May 2015	✗	✗	0.587	0.695	0.333	0.600
03 July 2015	✗	✗	0.287	0.541	0.333	0.600
29 July 2015	✓	✓	0.743	0.797	0.666	0.800
16 Aug. 2015	✓	✓	0.393	0.671	0.667	0.800
29 Nov. 2015	✓	✗	0.443	0.667	0.667	0.800

I are grieving tonight. Beau Biden was a friend of ours."). Even the annotators were asked to take also into account negative emotions, still they did not consider the content of such tweets as negative, since if one is grieving for having lost a person, this can be seen as a positive sentiment towards the person who passed away. In general, the interpretation of emotions is very personal and sometimes it is difficult to obtain a full agreement.

For the entity *Angela Merkel* we observe from Table 3 that for most of the days the rankings generated from the LDA & KL-divergence approach are very different compared to the ground truth. One example is the sentiment spike on the *July 3, 2015*. In this case, the majority of topics are about Greece: the Greek debt and the Greek referendum that took place on the 5th of July 2015. This case is a typical example that highlights the risk of attracting biased annotations due to the subjectivity of the task. In an effort to understand this disagreement we observed that in the entity *Angela Merkel* there are a lot of tweets that are retweets of news and which do not express any sentiment. For example, the tweet *"BREAKING: German Chancellor Angela Merkel briefly collapsed while attending an event in Bayreuth - local media"* is considered by SentiStrength as negative, probably due to the word *"collapsed"*. However, human annotators considered this tweet as neutral, probably because it is reported in the news.

To have a better understanding on the effect of the false polarity detection of the tweets with news, we generated a new ranking. The new ranking considered that tweets containing news are neutral. We used the following set of news channels and keywords: *abcnews, ajenglish, ap, bbc, breaking, channel4news, cnn, nbcnews, reuters, rt_com, skynews, telegraph*. Tweets that were posted from these channels, and their plain retweets were considered as neutral. Table 5 shows the results after considering tweets that express news. We observe that in most of the spikes, there is a big improvement. More importantly, the new ranking seems to be similar compared to the human annotators for three sentiment spikes; *July 29, Aug. 16,* and *Nov. 29, 2015*.

Finally, in case of *Angelina Jolie* the LDA & KL-divergence approach was effective for most of the spikes. We believe that one reason is that positive sentiment is clearly expressed and is more likely that humans will agree on a positive sentiment compared to a negative. One example is the sentiment spike on the *June 4, 2015* related to *Angelina Jolie*. In this case, there are three topics that all the annotators considered positive and in particular the 80% of the annotators considered them very positive (score of *+3*). We believe that topics with positive sentiment are less controversial and therefore it is easier to be ranked with an automatic approach. However, to validate this we need to perform further analysis which we cannot report here due to space limitations.

6. CONCLUSIONS AND FUTURE WORK

In this paper, we analyzed a large collection of tweets to get a better understanding of sentiment evolution towards different entities and the causes of sentiment spikes. We applied an outlier detection approach to identify the sentiment spikes and we proposed the LDA & KL-divergence approach that combines LDA and Relative Entropy to extract the topics that are discussed on the sentiment spikes and to rank those topics according to their contribution to the sentiment spike. Our results showed that the LDA & KL-divergence approach can effectively be used to extract and rank the topics identified on sentiment spikes.

In future, we plan to track the sentiment evolution on more entities such as products and movies. Finally, we plan to examine if the extracted causes and in particular those that are highly ranked are related to any event from news.

Acknowledgement

This research was partially funded by the Swiss National Science Foundation (SNSF) under the project OpiTrack.

7. REFERENCES

[1] X. An, R. A. Ganguly, Y. Fang, B. S. Scyphers, M. A. Hunter, and G. J. Dy. Tracking Climate Change Opinions from Twitter Data. In *KDD'14: Workshop on Data Science for Social Good*, 2014.

[2] K. Balog, G. Mishne, and M. de Rijke. Why are they excited?: Identifying and explaining spikes in blog mood levels. In *EACL '06: Posters Demonstrations*, pages 207–210, 2006.

[3] D. Blei, A. Ng, and M. Jordan. Latent dirichlet allocation. *Journal of Machine Learning Research*, 3:993–1022, 2003.

[4] J. Bollen, A. Pepe, and H. Mao. Modeling Public Mood and Emotion : Twitter Sentiment and Socio-Economic Phenomena. In *ICWSM'11*, pages 450–453, 2011.

[5] A. Giachanou and F. Crestani. Like it or not: A survey of twitter sentiment analysis methods. *ACM Computing Surveys (CSUR)*, 49(2):28, 2016.

[6] A. Giachanou and F. Crestani. Tracking sentiment by time series analysis. In *SIGIR '16*, pages 1037–1040, 2016.

[7] A. Go, R. Bhayani, and L. Huang. Technical report, Standford, 2009.

[8] E. Kouloumpis, T. Wilson, and J. Moore. Twitter sentiment analysis: The good the bad and the omg! In *ICWSM'11*, pages 538–541, 2011.

[9] S. Kullback and R. A. Leibler. On information and sufficiency. *The Annals of Mathematical Statistics*, 22(1):79–86, 03 1951.

[10] C. S. Montero, H. Haddad, M. Mozgovoy, and C. B. Ali. Detecting the likely causes behind the emotion spikes of influential twitter users. In *CICLing'16*, 2016.

[11] B. Pang and L. Lee. Opinion mining and sentiment analysis. *Foundations and Trends in Information Retrieval*, 2(1-2):1–135, 2008.

[12] A. Reyes, P. Rosso, and T. Veale. A multidimensional approach for detecting irony in twitter. *Language Resources and Evaluation*, 47(1):239–268, 2013.

[13] S. Tan, Y. Li, H. Sun, Z. Guan, X. Yan, J. Bu, C. Chen, and X. He. Interpreting the public sentiment variations on twitter. *IEEE Transactions on Knowledge and Data Engineering*, 26(5):1158–1170, 2014.

[14] M. Thelwall, K. Buckley, G. Paltoglou, D. Cai, and A. Kappas. Sentiment strength detection in short informal text. *Journal of the American Society for Information Science and Technology*, 61(12):2544–2558, 2010.

Qualitative Cleaning of Uncertain Data

Henning Köhler
School of Engineering & Advanced Technology
Massey University, New Zealand
H.Koehler@massey.ac.nz

Sebastian Link
Department of Computer Science
The University of Auckland, New Zealand
S.Link@auckland.ac.nz

ABSTRACT

We propose a new view on data cleaning: Not data itself but the degrees of uncertainty attributed to data are dirty. Applying possibility theory, tuples are assigned degrees of possibility with which they occur, and constraints are assigned degrees of certainty that say to which tuples they apply. Classical data cleaning modifies some minimal set of tuples. Instead, we marginally reduce their degrees of possibility. This reduction leads to a new qualitative version of the vertex cover problem. Qualitative vertex cover can be mapped to a linear-weighted constraint satisfaction problem. However, any off-the-shelf solver cannot solve the problem more efficiently than classical vertex cover. Instead, we utilize the degrees of possibility and certainty to develop a dedicated algorithm that is fixed parameter tractable in the size of the qualitative vertex cover. Experiments show that our algorithm is faster than solvers for the classical vertex cover problem by several orders of magnitude, and performance improves with higher numbers of uncertainty degrees.

CCS Concepts

•Information systems → **Uncertainty; Data cleaning;** **•Mathematics of computing** → *Graph algorithms;* **•Theory of computation** → *Fixed parameter tractability;*

Keywords

Database repair; Possibility theory; Vertex cover

1. INTRODUCTION

Background. Dirty data is costly and the main inhibitor for deriving insight.Integrity constraints can detect inconsistent information and help obtain clean(er) data. A classical approach to cleaning data is to remove tuples which violate some given constraint. A repair is a minimal set of tuples, which constitute the dirty data, whose removal results in a maximal subset of the given tuples that satisfy the given constraints. For important constraints, such as keys, the data cleaning problem is equivalent to the vertex cover problem. We illustrate the classical approach in Figure 1. We

CIKM'16 , October 24–28, 2016, Indianapolis, IN, USA

ISBN 978-1-4503-4073-1/16/10 . . . $15.00

DOI: http://dx.doi.org/10.1145/2983323.2983679

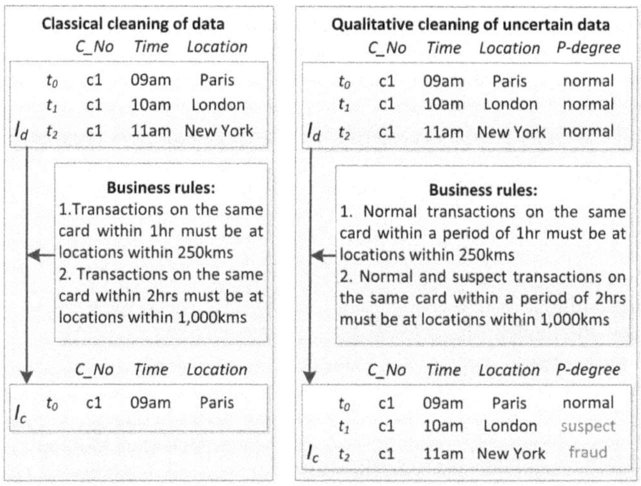

Figure 1: Classical vs. qualitative data cleaning

record the *time* and *location* of physical transactions on credit cards with a unique *C_No*. Some constraints aim at detecting fraud: σ_1 denotes the differential dependency [30] that any two transactions on the same card within 1hr occur within 250kms; and σ_2 denotes that any two transactions on the same card within 2hrs occur within 1,000kms. The instance I_d is dirty as t_0, t_1 violate σ_1, t_0, t_3 and t_2, t_3 violate σ_2. Classical cleaning via vertex cover may result in the clean data set I_c at the bottom left of Figure 1, removing t_2 and t_3. Here, uncertainty is not modeled, data is changed, and all constraints target all tuples.

Motivation. Data-driven decision making is a competitive imperative today, improving how organizations market to, sell to, and service customers. The veracity and poor quality of data motivates a qualitative framework for cleaning uncertain data, illustrated in Figure 1. We model the uncertainty of transactions by associating a degree of possibility (p-degree) with them. P-degrees increase the expressivity of classical constraints, such as keys and our dependencies σ_1 and σ_2 above. We can stipulate that σ_1 holds only for transactions with *normal* p-degree; and that σ_2 holds only for transactions with *normal* or *suspect* p-degree. Instead of removing transactions, we lower the p-degrees of conflicting tuples. Figure 1 shows that the cleaned data set I_c still contains all transactions, but the p-degree of t_1 is *suspect* and that of t_2 is *fraud*. This motivates our qualitative framework, particularly for applications in which probabilities are unavailable, undesirable, or too costly to maintain.

Contributions. 1. After distinguishing our work in Section 2, we propose possibilistic data cleaning in Section 3. Tuples are assigned p-degrees and constraints are assigned degrees of certainty (c-degrees). **2.** We combine the classical metric (removing fewer tuples is better) with the new qualitative metric (removing tuples of low p-degree is better). This makes it unnecessary to remove tuples. **3.** Possibilistic data cleaning is reduced to a new, qualitative, variant of vertex cover, which is NP-complete. We establish an algorithm that is FPT in the size of the qualitative vertex cover in Section 4. **4.** Experiments with benchmark and real-world data show in Section 5 that our algorithm is very fast, outperforms the classical algorithm, and performance improves with more p-degrees. We conclude in Section 6.

2. RELATED WORK

For strong economic reasons data cleaning receives more and more attention [2, 4, 27, 28, 31], with surveys [5, 13]. We depart from viewing data itself as dirty, but view their p-degrees as dirty: i) we do not modify data, but simply lower the p-degrees of tuples until conflicts with constraints are resolved, and ii) the c-degree of our constraints provide a scope to which tuples they apply.

Probabilistic approaches are quantitative, require real probabilities and high computational complexities in managing them [29]. Possibilistic approaches can offer a qualitative approach with less precise outcomes, but the acquisition and computation of possibilities/certainties is simpler [10]. We follow the second line motivated by qualitative applications (eg. fraud detection) where probabilities are hard to attain, to deal with, or undesirable. While work on possibilistic modeling is extensive [9], there is no work on data cleaning. Our possibilistic model from [15, 19, 26] assigns p-degrees to data and c-degrees to constraints, while others associate attribute values with possibility distributions, or c-degrees to data.

We borrow ideas from consistency preservation (maintaining c-degrees) and belief revision (minimally change the p-degrees) [14]. Lowering p-degrees in response to c-degree violations is closely related to the bipolar form of belief revision [11]. Here, a negative part states what is impossible (our c-degrees), and a positive part states what is possible (our p-degrees). Cleaning modifies the degrees of either the positive or the negative part. We modify the positive part as the constraints are given rules. The alternative is future work. The complexity of belief revision is well-studied [12, 25], but not at all for bipolar revision.

Possibilistic vertex cover can be mapped to a linear-weighted CSP [6], by assigning graph-specific weights to vertices based on p-degrees that ensure optimality w.r.t. lexicographical order. However, this would hide the strict separation by degree, so any off-the-shelf solver will not solve possibilistic vertex cover more efficiently than classical vertex cover. Instead, our dedicated solver is faster by several orders of magnitude.

Consistent query answering [1, 24] only returns tuples consistent with all repairs. In future work we will integrate our framework with this approach by 1) considering the repairs obtained via possibilistic data cleaning, and 2) returning tuples with the minimal c-degree ensured by all repairs. In Figure 1, no tuples form a consistent answer to a `SELECT *` query as each singleton constitutes a repair. Due to the two possibilistic repairs $\{(t_0, \textit{normal}), (t_1, \textit{suspect}), (t_2, \textit{fraud})\}$ and $\{(t_0, \textit{suspect}), (t_1, \textit{normal}), (t_2, \textit{fraud})\}$, our framework returns $\{(t_0, \textit{suspect}), (t_1, \textit{suspect}), (t_2, \textit{fraud})\}$.

[7] clean probabilistic data by updating the probabilities of worlds proportionally to the weight of constraints they satisfy or violate. In contrast, tuples that violate our constraints move to less possible worlds.

[3] compute repairs to data as well as constraints, using multiple minimal pairs of (data, constraint) repairs for varying levels of relative trust. We associate trust (uncertainty) with individual tuples and constraints rather than all data or all constraints as a whole, uncertain constraints apply only to subsets of data and are not repaired, and our data cleaning only changes meta-data.

Finally, our cleaning approach reduces to a possibilistic version of vertex cover. We do not aim to compete with other vertex cover algorithms [32], but instead show how the classical vertex cover algorithm [8] can be adapted to solve possibilistic vertex cover.

3. POSSIBILISTIC DATA CLEANING

One central classical idea is as follows: Whenever two tuples violate a constraint, at least one of them is removed. Hence, given a relation r and set Σ of constraints, inducing conflicts between tuple pairs (e.g. differential dependencies), *classical data cleaning* refers to finding a subset $r' \subseteq r$ of maximal cardinality so that Σ holds on r'.

In a possibilistic database, we associate a p-degree with each tuple in the database, and a c-degree with each constraint (e.g. differential dependency). We denote the *degrees of possibility* by $\alpha_1 > \ldots > \alpha_{k+1}$ where α_{k+1} means "not possible" and is only used for tuples not in our database. In our example we associate each transaction with some p-degree from *normal* > *suspect* > *fraud* > *not possible*. We denote the *c-degrees* by $\beta_1 > \ldots > \beta_k$. In our example we associate differential dependencies with some c-degree from *certain* > *likely* > *selective* > *not certain at all*, for instance $(\sigma_1, \textit{selective})$ and $(\sigma_2, \textit{likely})$. A possibilistic relation (p-relation) r *satisfies* a possibilistic constraint with certainty β_{k+1-i} iff the subtable $r_i := \{t \mid Poss_r(t) \geq \alpha_i\}$ satisfies the constraint. In Figure 1, I_d violates $(\sigma_1, \textit{selective})$ and $(\sigma_2, \textit{likely})$, but I_c satisfies both. This calls for a now notion of a subset. Given two possibilistic sets r, r', we say that r' is a *possibilistic subset* of r, denoted as $r' \subseteq_p r$, iff $r'_i \subseteq r_i$ for $i = 1 \ldots k$. For example, when $r = I_d$ and $r' = I_c$ in the right of Figure 1, then $r' \subseteq_p r$ since $r'_1 = \{t_0\} \subseteq r_1 = \{t_0, t_1, t_2\}$, $r'_2 = \{t_0, t_1\} \subseteq r_2 = r_1$ and $r'_3 = r_3 = r_1$.

The *possibilistic cardinality* (p-cardinality) of a p-relation r is the mapping $card(r) := \alpha_i \mapsto |r_i|$ for $i = 1 \ldots k$. When we talk about a maximal cardinality, we must decide on some ordering. While many linearizations of the natural partial order between p-cardinalities are possible, lexicographical order is of particular interest. Here we maintain as many tuples of high p-degree as possible since a high p-degree expresses confidence that a tuple is correct. Furthermore, lexicographical ordering unlocks important optimizations when designing algorithms for the possibilistic data cleaning problem, which is known to be NP-hard already in the non-possibilistic case [18]. This motivates the comparison of p-cardinalities $\mathcal{C}_1, \mathcal{C}_2$ w.r.t. the lexicographical order $\mathcal{C}_1 <_L \mathcal{C}_2 :\Leftrightarrow \exists \alpha_i (\mathcal{C}_1(\alpha_i) < \mathcal{C}_2(\alpha_i) \wedge \forall \alpha_j > \alpha_i (\mathcal{C}_1(\alpha_j) = \mathcal{C}_2(\alpha_j)))$. Given a p-relation r and set Σ of possibilistic keys and/or differential dependencies, *possibilistic data cleaning* refers to finding a possibilistic subset $r' \subseteq_p r$ of maximal p-cardinality such that Σ holds on r'. On the right of Figure 1, $I_c \subseteq_p I_d$ is of maximal p-cardinality $\mathcal{C}_{I_c} = \{\alpha_1 \mapsto 1, \alpha_2 \mapsto 2, \alpha_3 \mapsto 3\}$ such that $(\sigma_1, \textit{selective})$ and $(\sigma_2, \textit{likely})$ hold. The constraints also hold on $I = \{(t_0, \textit{suspect}), (t_1, \textit{suspect}), (t_2, \textit{fraud})\} \subseteq_p I_d$, but the p-cardinality $\mathcal{C}_I = \{\alpha_1 \mapsto 0, \alpha_2 \mapsto 2, \alpha_3 \mapsto 3\}$ is not maximal with respect to $<_L$.

Vertex Cover. Classical data cleaning reduces to an instance of Vertex Cover, with tuples as nodes and edges where tuple pairs violate constraints. The resulting graph is called the *conflict graph* of a relation (tuples not in conflict can be omitted). Similarly, possibilistic data cleaning reduces to an extension of Vertex Cover. Here the p-degree of tuples is preserved, while a violated constraint with c-degree β_{k+1-i} induces an edge with p-degree α_i. A *possi-*

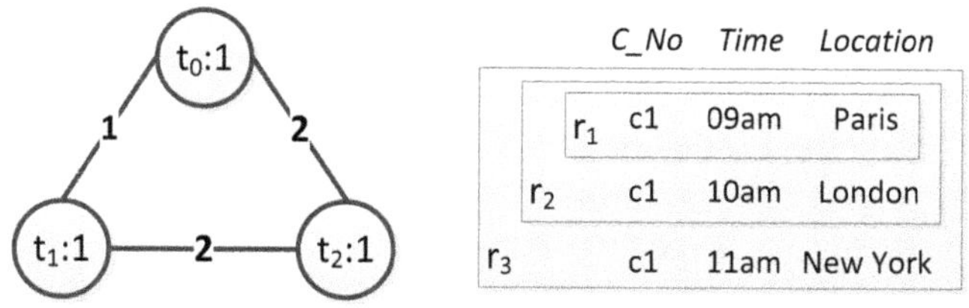

Figure 2: Conflict graph and worlds of p-vertex cover I_c

bilistic graph $G = (V, E)$ consists of a set of vertices V, a set of edges E over V, and associated functions P_V, P_E assigning p-degrees to vertices and edges in V, E. In our running example, consider the p-relation $r = I_d$ from the top right of Figure 1, where $r_1 = r_2 = r_3 = \{t_0, t_1, t_2\}$ ($\alpha_1 \equiv$ normal, $\alpha_2 \equiv$ suspect, $\alpha_3 \equiv$ fraud), and possibilistic differential dependencies (σ_1, β_3) and (σ_2, β_2) which hold on sub-relations r_1 and r_2, respectively ($k = 3$). The resulting possibilistic conflict graph is on the left of Figure 2.

The term "vertex cover" is traditionally used to describe the difference between vertex sets. We extend this notion to the possibilistic case. Let V', V be possibilistic sets with $V' \subseteq_p V$. Their *difference* is the partial mapping assigning new possibilities to elements that changed:

$$V - V' := \left\{ \begin{array}{c} v \mapsto (P_V(v) \mapsto P_{V'}(v)) \\ \mid v \in V \wedge P_V(v) \neq P_{V'}(v) \end{array} \right\}$$

We say that a partial mapping D is a *difference from* V iff there exists $V' \subseteq_p V$ such that $D = V - V'$. We denote a vertex v with its possibility $Poss(v) = \alpha_i$ short as $v : i$. We write an element of a difference mapping $v \mapsto (\alpha_i \mapsto \alpha_j)$ short as $v : i \mapsto j$. The cardinality of D is the difference between the cardinalities of V and V': $card(D) := card(V) - card(V') = \{ \alpha_i \mapsto |V_i| - |V_i'|\}$ where V_i is defined as $V_i := \{v \in V \mid P_V(v) \geq \alpha_i\}$ (compare r_i for relations). Given a difference D from V, we denote the unique set V' with $D = V - V'$ as $V \setminus D$. A cardinality mapping $\{\alpha_i \mapsto c_i\}$ is denoted as $[c_1, \ldots, c_k]$.

In the right of Figure 1, $D = \{t_1 : 1 \mapsto 2, t_2 : 1 \mapsto 3\}$ is a difference from I_d, since $I_c \subseteq_p I_d$ such that $D = I_d - I_c$ holds. The cardinality of D is $card(D) = [2, 1, 0]$. Moreover, $D' = \{t_0 : 1 \mapsto 2, t_1 : 1 \mapsto 2, t_2 : 1 \mapsto 3\}$ is a difference from I_d, since $I \subseteq_p I_d$ such that $D' = I_d - I$ holds. The cardinality of D' is $card(D') = [3, 1, 0]$.

Given a possibilistic graph $G = (V, E)$, a *vertex cover* of G is a difference $D = V - V'$ from V such that $G' = (V', E)$ contains no edge e with $P_E(e) \leq P_{V'}(v)$ for all $v \in e$. The *possibilistic vertex cover problem* is now to find a vertex cover of minimal cardinality. We shall call a possibilistic vertex cover *L-minimal* if it is minimal w.r.t. $\leq_L$.

In the right of Figure 1, $D = \{t_1 : 1 \mapsto 2, t_2 : 1 \mapsto 3\}$ is an L-minimal possibilistic vertex cover of I_d, which translates into the clean relation $r = I_c$ whose worlds are shown on the right of Figure 2. On the other hand, $D' = \{t_0 : 1 \mapsto 2, t_1 : 1 \mapsto 2, t_2 : 1 \mapsto 3\}$ is also a possibilistic vertex cover of I_d, which translates into the clean relation I above, but its cardinality $card(D') = [3, 1, 0]$ is not L-minimal since $card(D) = [2, 1, 0] <_L [3, 1, 0] = card(D)$. The only other L-minimal possibilistic vertex cover of I_d is $\{t_0 : 1 \mapsto 2, t_2 : 1 \mapsto 3\}$, also with cardinality $[2, 1, 0]$, which translates into the clean relation $s = \{(t_1, \textit{normal}), (t_0, \textit{suspect}), (t_2, \textit{fraud})\}$.

The example highlights the advantages of our possibilistic data-cleaning approach. Firstly, L-minimal vertex covers incorporate our confidence in the correctness of tuples. There are several alternative non-possibilistic covers, namely $\{t_1\}$, $\{t_2\}$, and $\{t_3\}$, which cannot help with fraud detection. Secondly, tuples are not necessarily discarded entirely, but instead preserved with a lower p-degree. This makes it possible to exploit our qualitative framework in many applications, for example the detection of different fraud scenarios.

4. POSSIBILISTIC VERTEX COVER

As vertex cover is a special case of possibilistic vertex cover, finding a minimal possibilistic vertex cover is NP-hard. However, vertex cover is fixed parameter tractable (FPT) in the size of a minimal vertex cover, making exact solutions computationally feasible in many cases. We will develop an algorithm for finding a minimal possibilistic vertex cover in exponential time, based on the classical bounded search tree algorithm [8], and show that it is also FPT in the size of a minimal possibilistic vertex cover. Similar extensions of more advanced vertex cover algorithms are possible, but outside our scope.

For finding a minimal possibilistic vertex cover w.r.t. lexicographical order, we first find minimal vertex covers for the *vertices* in G with possibility degree α_1, reducing vertices of degree α_1 to degree α_2 or less, then extend these to minimal vertex covers for vertices of lower degree, one degree at a time. This ensures that any extension of a partial vertex cover will not increase the cardinality for previously considered degrees, so after each "round" we will already know the cardinality values of the final minimal vertex cover (which we do not know yet), up to the current degree. This is useful for pruning the search space, as done in Algorithm 1.

Before going into more detail, we need some additional concepts. The α_i-vertices/edges of a graph are those with degree exactly α_i. The α_i-neighbours of a vertex are those which are neighbours w.r.t. α_i-edges. Removal of a difference $D = V - V'$ from a graph $G = (V, E)$ results in $G \setminus D := (V', E)$. When solving the possibilistic vertex cover problem, we further want to eliminate edges containing vertices of lower degree, as these are already covered, and isolated vertices, as these need not be reduced. Given a possibilistic graph $G = (V, E, P_V, P_E)$ we define

$$E^* := \{e \in E \mid \forall v \in e.\ P_E(e) \leq P_V(v)\}$$
$$V^* := \{v \in V \mid \exists e \in E^*.\ v \in e\}$$

We denote the reduced graph (V^*, E^*) by $vcr(G)$, standing for **v**ertex **c**over **r**eduction. This graph reduction performs just a simple "cleanup", comparable to the removal of isolated vertices in the non-possibilistic case.

Classical vertex cover prunes a search branch when the size of a (partial) vertex cover exceeds a given bound. In the possibilistic case the notion of size becomes more complex. A *partial (possibilistic) cardinality* is a partial mapping from $\{\alpha_1, \ldots, \alpha_k\}$ to non-negative integers. Given partial cardinalities $\mathcal{C}_1, \mathcal{C}_2$, $\mathcal{C}_1 \leq_p \mathcal{C}_2$ iff for every α_i where $\mathcal{C}_2$ is defined, $\mathcal{C}_1$ is defined as well and $\mathcal{C}_1(\alpha_i) \leq \mathcal{C}_2(\alpha_i)$. The sum (or difference) between partial cardinalities maps those α_i where both are defined to be the sum (or difference) of their values. We denote unmapped values by "-", so e.g. $[1, 2, -]$ denotes $\{\alpha_1 \mapsto 1, \alpha_2 \mapsto 2\}$. Partial cardinalities are used to prune the search space for a minimal possibilistic vertex cover.

The cardinality of a vertex cover is thus a partial cardinality where every α_i is mapped, and the partial cardinalities for the partial vertex covers we compute are simply the projections of the cardinality of the final minimal vertex cover onto the p-degrees "handled" so far. The central difference lies in the ordering w.r.t. which we compare. The $\leq_L$ ordering is linear, and defines when a vertex cover is minimal. The ordering $\leq_p$, used for comparing partial cardinalities, is only partial (e.g. $[0,1]$ and $[1,0]$ are incomparable w.r.t. $\leq_p$). Hence, the search space can be pruned more efficiently since we will prune all branches where the current cardinality is not $\leq_p \mathcal{C}$ for some partial cardinality $\mathcal{C}$ from the previous round. This includes cases were cardinalities are incomparable w.r.t $\leq_p$. When minimizing w.r.t $\leq_L$, we start with vertices of degree α_1 and work our way down.

An α_i-L-cover of a graph is a difference set D that covers all vertices of degree α_i or above, meaning that $vcr(G \setminus D)$ contains no adjacent vertices of degree α_i or above. We call a graph G α_i-L-trivial if $\emptyset$ is an α_i-L-cover of G.

With this definition we may now state that we search for minimal α_i-L-covers, for $i = 1 \dots k$. Each round the α_{i-1}-L-covers are recalculated as in the previous round and extended to α_i-L-covers. Instead of removing vertices as in the classical case, we lower their p-degrees.

In the basic vertex cover algorithm, the allowed size for a vertex cover is increased until a vertex cover is found. This admits early pruning while progressing in a depth-first manner, requiring less memory than a breadth-first approach. For possibilistic vertex covers, this corresponds to slowly increasing the allowed p-cardinality. Thus, when searching for minimal α_i-L-covers, we slowly increase the maximal α_i-cardinality. The maximal cardinalities for α_j values with $j < i$ is already known from the previous round. Our possibilistic vertex cover algorithm, using lexicographical ordering, is detailed in Algorithm 1.

Algorithm 1 Possibilistic Vertex Cover ($\leq_L$)

Input: Possibilistic graph $G = (V, E)$
Output: Minimal (w.r.t. $\leq_L$) vertex cover VC of G.
$G := vcr(G)$
$\mathcal{C} := [-, \dots, -]$ ▷ empty partial cardinality
for $i = 1 \dots k$ **do**
  $VC := \bot$, n := -1
  while $VC = \bot$ **do**
    n += 1
    $VC :=$ Find-PVC$(G, \mathcal{C} \cup \{\alpha_i \mapsto n\}, i, 1)$
  $\mathcal{C} := \mathcal{C} \cup \{\alpha_i \mapsto n\}$
return VC

Subroutine Find-PVC$(G, \mathcal{C}, i, j)$
Input: Graph $G = (V, E)$, partial cardinality $\mathcal{C}$, $i \geq j$;
  G must be vcr-reduced and α_{j-1}-L-trivial
Output: α_i-L-cover of G of size $\leq \mathcal{C}$, $\bot$ if none exists
if $\mathcal{C} \not\geq_p [0, \dots, 0]$ **then return** $\bot$
while G is α_j-L-trivial **do**
  if $j = i$ **then return** $\emptyset$
  else $j := j + 1$
pick $v \in V$ of degree α_j
  {Case 1: $v \in$ VC}
if v has neighbour(s) of degree α_j **then**
  {otherwise Case 2 leads to $\leq_L$-smaller VC}
  $e_{\max} := \max\{P_E(v, n) \mid n \text{ is } \alpha_j\text{-neighbour of } v\}$
  $D_v := \{v : P_V(v) \mapsto e_{\max} + 1\}$
  $VC :=$ Find-PVC$(vcr(G \setminus D_v), \mathcal{C} - card(D_v), i, j)$
  if $VC \neq \bot$ **then**
    return $VC \cup D_v$
  {Case 2: $v \notin$ VC}
$N :=$ neighbours of v in G
$D_N := \{n : P_V(n) \mapsto \alpha_{d+1} \mid n \in N, d := P_E(v, n)\}$
$VC :=$ Find-PVC$(vcr(G \setminus D_N), \mathcal{C} - card(D_N), i, j)$
if $VC \neq \bot$ **then**
  return $VC \cup D_N$
return $\bot$

Complexity. As a vertex that had its degree lowered is effectively isolated for subsequent higher-degree vertex cover calculations, this gives us fixed parameter tractability w.r.t. the size of the possibilistic vertex cover, as defined next. Let $D = V - V'$ be a difference from V. We define the *size* of D as the sum of its cardinality values, denoted as $|D|$. Note that all minimal vertex covers have the same cardinality, and thus the same size. When talking about the size of a graph, we mean the sum of its edges and vertices.

THEOREM 1. *Let G be a possibilistic graph, and VC a minimal possibilistic vertex cover of G w.r.t. $\leq_L$. Then Algorithm 1 finds a minimal possibilistic vertex cover of G w.r.t. $\leq_L$ in time $O\left(2^{|VC|} \cdot |G|\right)$.*

Indeed, for each recursive call of function Find-PVC, at least one vertex is reduced, so that the height of our search tree is bounded by the size of $\mathcal{C}$. Since our search tree is binary, this limits the number of recursive calls to $2^{|\mathcal{C}|}$. All calculations within a single call of Find-PVC can be performed in time $O(|G|)$. Hence any call to Find-PVC from the main loop with bound $\mathcal{C}$ will be completed in time $O(2^{|\mathcal{C}|} \cdot |G|)$. Finally, the number of calls made to Find-PVC from the main loop is limited by $|VC|$, with the size of the parameter $\mathcal{C}$ iterating over $1 \dots |VC|$. This gives an overall runtime bounded by $O(\sum_{|\mathcal{C}|=1}^{|VC|} 2^{|\mathcal{C}|} \cdot |G|) = O(2^{|VC|} \cdot |G|)$.

When running our algorithms, we applied some additional optimizations. First, we partition a graph into maximal connected component, solving the vertex cover problem for each individually. Second, we employed two kernelization rules.

RULE 1 (DEGREE 1). *If a vertex $v \in G$ has only a single neighbour n and $P_V(v) \geq P_V(n)$ then add $n : P_V(n) \mapsto P_E(v, n) + 1$ to the vertex cover.*

RULE 2 (DEGREE 2). *If a vertex $v \in G$ has exactly two neighbours n_1, n_2, these are connected by an edge, and*

i) $P_V(v) \geq \max(P_V(n_1), P_V(n_1))$

ii) $P_E(n_1, n_2) \leq \max(P_E(v, n_1), P_E(v, n_2))$

then add the following to the vertex cover: $\{n_1 : P_V(n_1) \mapsto P_E(v, n_1) + 1, n_2 : P_V(n_1) \mapsto P_E(v, n_2) + 1\}$.

5. EXPERIMENTS AND WEB INTERFACE

We tested our possibilistic data cleaning approach on several (non-possibilistic) real world databases, all of which are publicly available. As in our example, we assigned all tuples the initial p-degree α_1, and mined the given relations for so-called near-keys [20, 22, 23]. A *near-key of order n* is an expression of the form $K_n\langle X\rangle$, where n is a positive integer and $X \subseteq T$ is a set of attributes. We say that $K_n\langle X\rangle$ holds on I iff there do not exist $n+1$ distinct tuples $t_1, \dots, t_{n+1} \in I$ with $t_1(X) = \dots = t_{n+1}(X)$. For our experiments, we re-interpreted a mined near-key of order n as a possibilistic key (p-key) with c-degree β_n. In particular, a classical key (i.e. a near-key of order 1) is a p-key with c-degree β_1. During near-key mining we performed some filtering where we removed any near-keys which were violated by too many tuples ($> \sqrt{|I|}$), and columns unlikely to participate in any real-world keys - this eliminated some false positives which were due to table structure.

Table 1: Experiment Summary

Measure	Median	75%-quantile	Max
Time(key mining)	1.1s	51s	837s
Time(conflict graph)	0.5s	11s	243s
Time(p-VC)	4ms	60ms	42s
minimal keys	4	8	973
Conflict graph (V)	45	628	45247
Conflict graph (E)	27	409	22703
MCC (V)	2	3	4732
MCC (E)	1	3	6012
α_1-Card(p-VC)	24	326	22650
α_2-Card(p-VC)	7	39	7843

We chose the following datasets for our experiments primarily because they are publicly available in their original format (many published data sets have been carefully curated and often merged into a single table): i) GO-termdb (Gene Ontology) at geneontology.org/, ii) IPI (International Protein Index) at ebi.ac.uk/IPI, iii) PFAM (protein families) at pfam.sanger.ac.uk/, and iv) RFAM (RNA families) at rfam.sanger.ac.uk/. For each table in these data sets, we first mined all minimal near-keys up to order 3. Our analysis was restricted to the first 5 million tuples to ensure they would fit into main memory as required by our prototype implementation.

Among the remaining 92 tables, 44 had near-keys of order 2 or 3 which suggest dirty data and lead to non-empty conflict graphs. These near-keys were interpreted as p-keys, and used to clean the table they were mined from. Table 1 shows the computation time for near-key mining, construction of the conflict graph and possibilistic vertex cover, number of minimal near-keys, size of the conflict graph and its largest connected component, as well as cardinality for the minimal vertex cover found.

Experiments were run on a 4.0GHz AMD FX8350 machine with 8GB memory, and a single-threaded python implementation.

Evidently, the computation of possibilistic vertex cover is extremely fast, primarily due to the structure of our conflict graphs. While they can be fairly large, they are sparse and highly disconnected, so that the graphs, remaining after partitioning and kernelization, are very small. This is perhaps not surprising, since one would not expect a large number of tuples to violate a key in the same way. This highlights the advantage of using uncertainty information during cleaning, as for conflicts between only 2 tuples, the choice which one of the two to remove is arbitrary in the classical approach.

We also computed possibilistic vertex cover over random graphs. This allows us to put the conflict graphs obtained during possibilistic cleaning into context, and to compare possibilistic and non-possibilistic vertex cover, as used in classical data cleaning, in terms of computational difficulty.

Computation times for varying graph size (mean degree of 4) and density (on 100 vertices) are shown in Figures 3 and 4, for different values of k. Graphs were constructed uniformly at random, and for each parameter configuration (number of edges and vertices) we constructed 100 graphs and report median values. For p-degrees, vertex degrees were assigned first (uniformly at random between α_1 and α_k), then edge-degrees were assigned uniformly between the minimum degree of the adjacent vertices and α_k. In all cases, classical vertex cover performs slower than Algorithm 1 for possibilistic vertex cover by several orders of magnitude, and performance improves with increasing values of k. This behaviour

Figure 3: Computation time by size

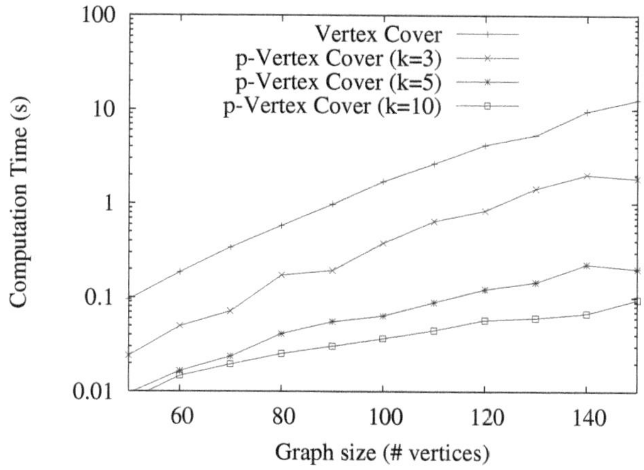

Figure 4: Computation time by density

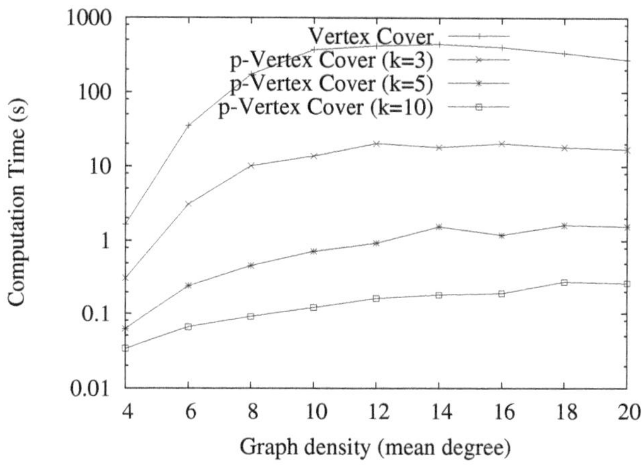

can be explained as follows: During each iteration of Algorithm 1, we consider only vertices of a particular p-degree. Hence, we solve the vertex cover problem on a much smaller graph, inversely proportional to k. For $k = 1$, the classical vertex cover algorithm becomes essentially identical to Algorithm 1. Another observation is that for conflict graphs constructed from real-world databases, running times are much lower than they are for random graphs of the same size. This is primarily due to the highly disconnected nature of conflict graphs. Together with the problem simplification incurred by having p-degrees, this should ensure that solving the possibilistic vertex cover problem does not become a bottleneck. Table 1 confirm this, at least for the data sets considered.

Web Interface and Final Example. Figure 5 shows a public web interface, where users can apply our approach to their own data sets in a step-by-step manner. The figure contains an example in which we record the *time* at which Grizzly bears appear in *zone*s of their habitat. The bears are identified by a unique *RFID* tag. Multiple sensors record the data and the p-degrees represent the highest quality of any sensor with that reading ($k = 3$ here). The application requirements stipulate that the key {*Time*, *RFID*} holds with c-degree β_2, and the key {*Zone*, *Time*} has c-degree β_3. The conflict graph is

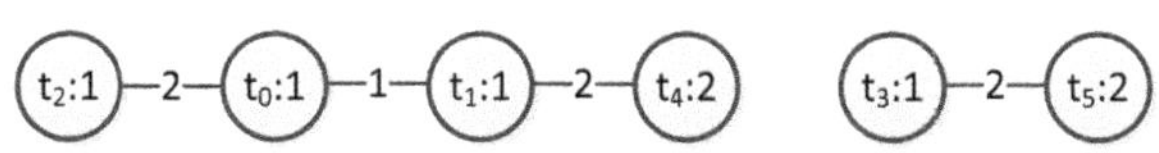

Figure 5: Prototype Web Interface

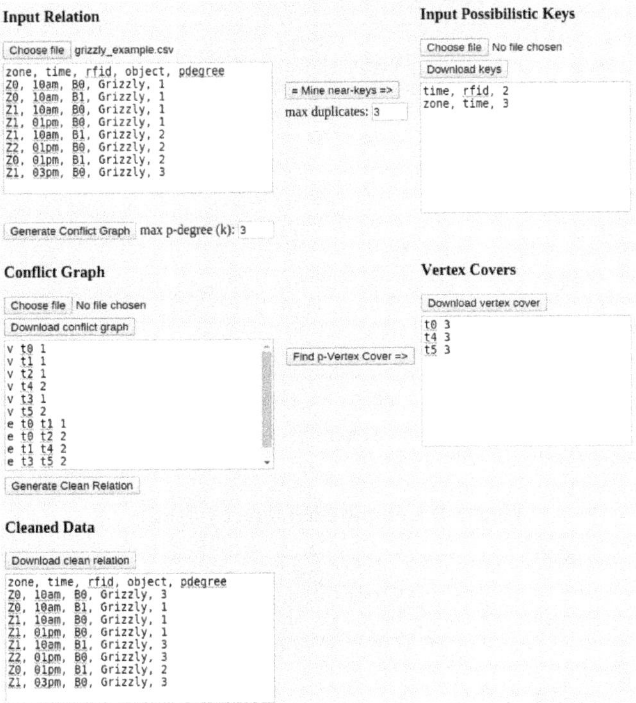

where the eight given tuples from top to bottom are denoted by $t_0, \ldots, t_7$. The unique L-minimal vertex cover is $\{t_0 : 1 \mapsto 3, t_4 : 2 \mapsto 3, t_5 : 2 \mapsto 3\}$, which translates into the bottom relation of Figure 5. Specifically, t_0, t_4, t_5 are not removed, enabling the discovery of insight not possible with the classical approach: at 10am, grizzly B1 had likely been close to zone Z1, possibly mating with B0.

6. CONCLUSION AND FUTURE WORK

We presented a new approach to qualitative cleaning of uncertain data by eliminating conflicts detected as constraint violations. Exploiting uncertainty information we 1) achieve better results for identifying the correct tuples to clean, and 2) reduce loss of information. Our framework leads to a possibilistic vertex cover problem, for which we developed a fixed parameter tractable algorithm. Though more complex than classical vertex cover, it appears to be easier to solve, as shown by our experiments. We conclude that our framework outperforms the classical data cleaning approach both in terms of quality of results and performance, assuming uncertainty information is available. To deal with cases where constraints are unknown, we developed an approach for mining them.

For future work, we plan to extend our approach to other types of constraints, in particular to independence atoms [16, 17] and functional dependencies [21], and to investigate query answering over uncertain data within a possibilistic framework.

7. REFERENCES

[1] M. Arenas, L. E. Bertossi, and J. Chomicki. Consistent query answers in inconsistent databases. In *SIGMOD*, pages 68–79, 1999.

[2] L. E. Bertossi, S. Kolahi, and L. V. S. Lakshmanan. Data cleaning and query answering with matching dependencies and matching functions. *Theory Comput. Syst.*, 52(3):441–482, 2013.

[3] G. Beskales, I. F. Ilyas, L. Golab, and A. Galiullin. On the relative trust between inconsistent data and inaccurate constraints. In *ICDE*, pages 541–552, 2013.

[4] A. Chalamalla, I. F. Ilyas, M. Ouzzani, and P. Papotti. Descriptive and prescriptive data cleaning. In *SIGMOD*, pages 445–456, 2014.

[5] X. Chu, I. F. Ilyas, S. Krishnan, and J. Wang. Data cleaning: Overview and emerging challenges. In *SIGMOD*, pages 2201–2206, 2016.

[6] M. C. Cooper, S. de Givry, M. Sanchez, T. Schiex, M. Zytnicki, and T. Werner. Soft arc consistency revisited. *Artif. Intell.*, 174(7-8):449–478, 2010.

[7] P. Domingos and D. Lowd. *Markov Logic: An Interface Layer for Artificial Intelligence*. Morgan & Claypool Publishers, 2009.

[8] R. G. Downey and M. R. Fellows. *Fundamentals of Parameterized Complexity*. Springer, 2013.

[9] D. Dubois and H. Prade. Fuzzy set and possibility theory-based methods in artificial intelligence. *Artif. Intell.*, 148(1-2):1–9, 2003.

[10] D. Dubois and H. Prade. Practical methods for constructing possibility distributions. *Int. J. Intell. Syst.*, 31(3):215–239, 2016.

[11] D. Dubois, H. Prade, and P. Smets. "not impossible" vs. "guaranteed possible" in fusion and revision. In *ECSQARU*, pages 522–531, 2001.

[12] T. Eiter and G. Gottlob. On the complexity of propositional knowledge base revision, updates, and counterfactuals. *Artif. Intell.*, 57(2-3):227–270, 1992.

[13] V. Ganti and A. D. Sarma. *Data Cleaning: A Practical Perspective*. Morgan & Claypool Publishers, 2013.

[14] P. Gärdenfors and H. Rott. Belief revision. In *Handbook of Logic in Artificial Intelligence and Logic Programming*, volume 4, page 35Ú132. Oxford University Press, 1995.

[15] N. Hall, H. Köhler, S. Link, H. Prade, and X. Zhou. Cardinality constraints on qualitatively uncertain data. *Data Knowl. Eng.*, 99:126–150, 2015.

[16] M. Hannula, J. Kontinen, and S. Link. On independence atoms and keys. In *CIKM*, pages 1229–1238, 2014.

[17] M. Hannula, J. Kontinen, and S. Link. On the finite and general implication problems of independence atoms and keys. *J. Comput. Syst. Sci.*, 82(5):856–877, 2016.

[18] R. M. Karp. Reducibility among combinatorial problems. In *Complexity of Computer Computations*, pages 85–103, 1972.

[19] H. Köhler, U. Leck, S. Link, and H. Prade. Logical foundations of possibilistic keys. In *JELIA*, pages 181–195, 2014.

[20] H. Köhler, U. Leck, S. Link, and X. Zhou. Possible and certain keys for SQL. *VLDB J.*, 25(4):571–596, 2016.

[21] H. Köhler and S. Link. SQL schema design: Foundations, normal forms, and normalization. In *SIGMOD*, pages 267–279, 2016.

[22] H. Köhler, S. Link, and X. Zhou. Possible and certain SQL keys. *PVLDB*, 8(11):1118–1129, 2015.

[23] H. Köhler, S. Link, and X. Zhou. Discovering meaningful certain keys from incomplete and inconsistent relations. *IEEE Data Eng. Bull.*, 39(2):21–37, 2016.

[24] P. Koutris and J. Wijsen. Consistent query answering for primary keys. *SIGMOD Record*, 45(1):15–22, 2016.

[25] P. Liberatore. The complexity of belief update. *Artif. Intell.*, 119(1-2):141–190, 2000.

[26] S. Link and H. Prade. Possibilistic functional dependencies and their relationship to possibility theory. *IEEE Trans. Fuzzy Systems*, 24(3):757–763, 2016.

[27] L. Mo, R. Cheng, X. Li, D. W. Cheung, and X. S. Yang. Cleaning uncertain data for top-k queries. In *ICDE*, pages 134–145, 2013.

[28] N. Prokoshyna, J. Szlichta, F. Chiang, R. J. Miller, and D. Srivastava. Combining quantitative and logical data cleaning. *PVLDB*, 9(4):300–311, 2015.

[29] D. Suciu, D. Olteanu, C. Ré, and C. Koch. *Probabilistic Databases*. Morgan & Claypool Publishers, 2011.

[30] M. W. Vincent, J. Liu, H. Liu, and S. Link. Technical correspondence: "Differential dependencies: Reasoning and discovery" revisited. *ACM Trans. Database Syst.*, 40(2):14, 2015.

[31] J. Wang and N. Tang. Towards dependable data repairing with fixing rules. In *SIGMOD*, pages 457–468, 2014.

[32] G. J. Woeginger. Exact algorithms for NP-hard problems: A survey. In *Combinatorial Optimization*, pages 185–208, 2001.

APAM: Adaptive Eager-Lazy Hybrid Evaluation of Event Patterns for Low Latency

Ilyeop Yi[†] Jae-Gil Lee[‡*] Kyu-Young Whang[†*]
[†]School of Computing, KAIST, Daejeon, Korea
[‡]Graduate School of Knowledge Service Engineering, KAIST, Daejeon, Korea
{iyyi, kywhang}@mozart.kaist.ac.kr jaegil@kaist.ac.kr

ABSTRACT

Event pattern detection refers to identifying combinations of events matched to a user-specified query event pattern from a real-time event stream. *Latency* is an important measure of the performance of an event pattern detection system. Existing methods can be classified into the eager evaluation method and the lazy evaluation method depending on when each event arrival is evaluated. These methods have advantages and disadvantages in terms of latency depending on the event arrival rate. In this paper, we propose a *hybrid eager-lazy* evaluation method that combines the advantages of both methods. For each event type, the hybrid method, which we call *APAM* (*Adaptive Partitioning-And-Merging*), determines which method to use: eager or lazy. We also propose a formal cost model to estimate the latency and propose a method of finding the optimal partition based on the cost model. Finally, we show through experiments that our method can improve the latency by up to 361.48 times over the eager evaluation method and 27.94 times over the lazy evaluation method using a synthetic data set.

1. INTRODUCTION

Event pattern detection refers to finding combinations of events (called *pattern instances*) matched to a user-specified event pattern from a real-time event stream [8]. Throughput and latency are the major measures of the performance of event pattern detection. *Throughput* refers to the number of events processed per unit time [11], and *latency* the time elapsed between the arrival of the last event of a pattern instance matched to a query event pattern and the point at which the system identifies that the pattern instance is matched [12]. While both measures are important, latency is highly significant for mission-critical or time-critical applications. However, most existing studies assume that the event arrival rate is extremely fast, and thus, only focus on improving the throughput [1, 2, 4, 5, 10, 11, 13, 14].

Existing event pattern detection methods can be classified into the eager evaluation method and the lazy evaluation method depending on when each arriving event is evaluated. Each method has its advantages and disadvantages in terms of latency depending on the event arrival rate.

- The *eager evaluation method* evaluates all events immediately when they arrive. Thus, events are always evaluated in the order in which they arrive. An advantage of the eager evaluation method is that latency is low when the event arrival rate is slow. The slower the event arrival rate is, the more idle time there will be. The eager evaluation method utilizes this idle time to evaluate arriving events immediately. Because most events of a pattern instance have been detected prior to the arrival of the last event of that pattern instance, the eager evaluation method can detect the pattern instance as soon as the last event arrives. However, a disadvantage of the eager evaluation method is that latency may be high when the event arrival rate is fast. The faster the event arrival rate is, the less idle time there will be. Hence, events may *not* be evaluated immediately when they arrive, and these evaluations may be delayed. In this case, latency is significantly affected (i.e., gets higher) by lower throughput, which decreases because the order in which events are evaluated may not be optimal in eager evaluation.
- The *lazy evaluation method* defers evaluations of arriving events and evaluate them in batch later. Thus, events can be evaluated in any order. An advantage of the lazy evaluation method is that latency is low when the event arrival rate is fast. As mentioned above, when the event arrival rate is fast, the latency is heavily dependent on the throughput. Given that events can always be evaluated in the optimal order, the throughput is high and latency is low. However, a disadvantage of the lazy evaluation method is that the latency is high when the event arrival rate is slow. Even when there is sufficient idle time, the lazy evaluation method defers all evaluations of arriving events until the batch evaluation starts. When the last event of a pattern instance arrives, all the events that arrived prior to the last event must be evaluated in batch. Hence, the time taken to detect the pattern instance in this case is delayed.

In this paper, we propose a *hybrid eager-lazy evaluation method*, which combines the advantages of both methods providing low latency at any event arrival rate. For each event type, the proposed method determines which method to use: eager or lazy. At slower event arrival rate, more event types are evaluated by the eager evaluation method in order to fully utilize the idle time. At faster event arrival rate, more event types are evaluated by the lazy evaluation method in order to evaluate more events in the optimal order.

Toward this goal, we first propose a hybrid method **APAM** (meaning *Adaptive Partitioning-And-Merging*). **APAM** partitions event types into an eager evaluation group and a lazy evaluation group, and merges the results of evaluations of the eager evaluation group with the deferred events of the lazy evaluation group to construct

*Jae-Gil Lee and Kyu-Young Whang are the co-corresponding authors

CIKM'16, October 24-28, 2016, Indianapolis, IN, USA
© 2016 ACM. ISBN 978-1-4503-4073-1/16/10...$15.00
DOI: http://dx.doi.org/10.1145/2983323.2983680

the pattern instances. Second, we propose a method of selecting the optimal plan. **APAM** is able to use various plans according to how event types are partitioned. The proposed method estimates the latency of each plan and selects the plan with the lowest latency. We define a cost model to estimate the latency. Finally, we empirically validate the performance of our optimal plan selection method and show that **APAM** achieves the lower-bound of latency of both existing methods at any event arrival rate.

2. PRELIMINARIES

An *event* is a tuple that represents an instantaneous and atomic occurrence of interest at a point in time [3, 8]. Each event has a set of attributes according to the schema defined for the type of that event. Essentially, an event has the name of the type of that event and the time of the event associated with (when the event occurred) as attributes. For ease of explanation, an event type is denoted by an upper-case letter (e.g., A), and an event by a lower-case letter with its timestamp value subscripted (e.g., a_1). *Event stream* is a linearly ordered sequence of events [8, 11] and is the input to the event pattern detection system. An event stream may contain events of heterogeneous types. In the event stream, events are assumed to be sorted by their timestamp values.

The query language of an event pattern detection system specifies the event pattern to be detected. We use a declarative query language [1, 10, 11, 14]. A query event pattern consists of the following three clauses:

PATTERN	*Event Pattern*
WHERE	*Predicates on the Event Attributes*
WITHIN	*Time Window*

A PATTERN clause specifies an event pattern by using event types and event operators that represent the correlations among event types. A sequence operator (;) is the primary event operator focused on by the event pattern detection area [7, 10, 11], and thus, we concentrate on the event patterns specified by sequence operators. $A; B$ indicates that an event of type B occurs after an event of type A has occurred. All the combinations of events (a_x, b_y), where $x < y$, are matched to the event pattern $A; B$.

WHERE and WITHIN clauses specify the predicate and the time conditions that the events matched to the event pattern satisfy. A WHERE clause specifies the predicates on event attributes. There are two types of predicates: a simple and a parameterized predicate. A simple predicate is a predicate on an attribute of one event type (e.g., $A.attr1 > 10$). A parameterized predicate is a predicate between attributes of different event types (e.g., $A.attr1 = B.attr1$). A WITHIN clause specifies a time window that represents the time period within which events matched must occur.

3. OVERVIEW OF APAM

In **APAM**, event types are partitioned into two groups: the *eager evaluation group (EEG)* and the *lazy evaluation group (LEG)*. Events in the *EEG* are evaluated immediately when they arrive, and evaluations of events in the *LEG* are deferred until the last event of a pattern instance, called the *final event* [10], arrives. Whenever the final event arrives, events whose evaluations are deferred and the results of the eager evaluations are merged to construct pattern instances. Parameterized predicates are also partitioned into two groups along with the event types. Predicates involving the event types of the *EEG* are grouped into the *EEG*, and other predicates (those involving the event types of the *LEG* and those involving the event types of both groups) are grouped into the *LEG*. Predicates are evaluated when events of the same group are evaluated.

Figure 1 shows the architecture of an event pattern detection system that uses **APAM**. For simplicity, we assume that events whose types are not specified in the query event pattern and who do not satisfy the simple predicate are filtered out beforehand. As shown in the figure, the system consists of four modules.

- The *Partitioner* determines the evaluation method of each arriving event according to the plan selected by the *Plan Optimizer*. The *Plan Optimizer* selects the plan that minimizes the latency according to the event arrival rate, which will be explained in Section 4. In addition, it maintains the statistics needed to select the optimal plan. Statistics are calculated using simple windowed averages based on sampling [10].
- The *Eager Evaluator* evaluates the *EEG* events immediately. As a result, pattern instances matched to the partial query event pattern consisting of the event types in the *EEG* are constructed and stored in the eager evaluation result buffer.
- The *Lazy Evaluator* stores the *LEG* events into deferred event buffers allocated per event type. Evaluations of these events are deferred until the final event arrives.
- The *Merger* constructs pattern instances matched to the query event pattern using the results of eager evaluations and the events whose evaluations are deferred. In Section 5, we explain merging in more detail.

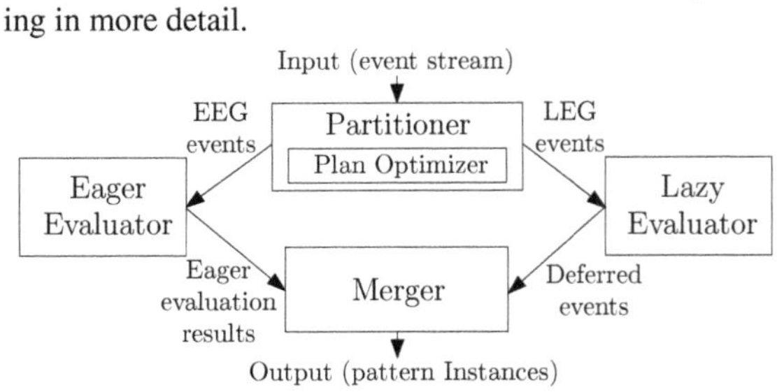

Figure 1: The architecture of APAM.

4. OPTIMAL PLAN SELECTION

In this section, we explain the optimal plan selection method reducing the latency of **APAM**. Before proceeding, we summarize the notation used in the following sections in Table 1. For an event pattern whose length is l, the number of possible plans is $\sum_{i=0}^{l} \binom{l}{i}$. To reduce the search space, we fix the matching order to the optimal matching order. A *matching order* is an order by which the events matched are detected, and the *optimal matching order* corresponds to the optimal join order [6]. Here, we use a heuristic method to find the optimal order processing more selective matching earlier. Thus, we consider $l+1$ evaluation plans resulting from binary partitioning of event types sorted by the optimal matching order as candidate plans. We then estimate the latency of each candidate plan. The candidate plan with the lowest estimated latency is selected as the optimal plan. For example, $/BCAD$, B/CAD, BC/AD, ABC/D, and $ABCD/$ are the candidate plans of $A; B; C; D$, whose optimal matching order is B, C, A, D. Here, BC/AD represents the evaluation plan where B and C are grouped into the *EEG*, A and D are grouped into the *LEG*, and the matching order is B, C, A, D. Notice that the plan resulting from binary partitioning where three event types are grouped into the *EEG* is ABC/D rather than BCA/D. This is because the matching order of the *EEG* is fixed to the order specified in the query event pattern.

4.1 Queueing model

To estimate the latency of the evaluation plan, we model **APAM** using an M/G/1 queue. Characteristics of the M/G/1 queue is summarized as follows [9]:

- M: Events arrive at the input queue of the system at a rate λ according to a Poisson process.

Table 1: Summary of the notation used in Sections 4.1 ~ 6.

Notation	Description
λ	event arrival rate (the number of events arriving per unit time)
λ_E	arrival rate of events of type E
μ	event service rate (the number of events served per unit time)
ρ	system utilization ($= \frac{\lambda}{\mu}$ [9])
QWT	queue waiting time (time spent by an event waiting in the input queue)
ST	service time (time taken to serve an event)
ST_E	service time of the event of type E
c_{ST}	coefficient of variance of ST ($= \mu\sigma_{ST}$, where σ_{ST} is the standard deviation of ST [9])
T_M	time taken to execute the merging
T_{PE}	time taken to evaluate one predicate (measured by experiments)
T_{RC}	time taken to construct (i.e., concatenate two partial pattern instances) one result (measured by experiments)
T_{BI}	time taken to insert one event into the buffer (measured by experiments)
Q	query event pattern
W	time window of Q
NP_{E_i,E_j} / $NP_{E_i;E_j}$	the number of parameterized/sequence predicates between event types E_i and E_j
SP_{E_i,E_j} / $SP_{E_i;E_j}$	total selectivity of parameterized/sequence predicates between event types E_i and E_j
$PI_{E_1;\ldots;E_n}$	set of pattern instances matched to partial pattern $E_1;\ldots;E_n$ from events arriving within W
$\lvert PI_{E_1;\ldots;E_n}\rvert$	cardinality of $PI_{E_1;\ldots;E_n}$ ($= \prod_{i=1}^{n}(\lambda_{E_i} \times W) \times \prod_{i=1}^{n-1}\prod_{j=i+1}^{n}(SP_{E_i,E_j} \times SP_{E_i;E_j})$)

- *G*: ST has a general distribution ($\mu = \frac{1}{E[ST]}$).
- *1*: A single server serves events one at a time according to a first-come, first-served discipline.

A *service* of an event is defined differently according to the event type. A service of an event of EEG is to eager-evaluate it, and that of LEG is to defer the evaluation. If the event is a final event, constructing pattern instances by merging is included in the service.

The output of the system is a set of pattern instances matched to Q. Such an output exists only when a *true final event*, which is defined in Definition 1, is served.

Definition 1. A final event is a *true final event* if there exists any pattern instance that contains the final event. Otherwise, the final event is called a *false final event*.

In this model, the expected latency $E[L]$ is as shown in Eq.(1). $E[L]$ is the average elapsed time from the point at which a final event arrives to the point at which all pattern instances that contain the final event are detected. $E[QWT_{TFE}]$ is the expected queue waiting time of a true final event. This time is caused by the events that arrive before the true final event arrives and the services for them. This time increases as ρ becomes higher and μ becomes slower [9]. $E[ST_{TFE}]$ is the expected service time of a true final event. Since this time includes the merging time, it increases as more event types are grouped into the LEG.

$$E[L] = E[QWT_{TFE}] + E[ST_{TFE}] \tag{1}$$

4.2 Latency estimation

We estimate $E[L]$ as shown in Eq.(2). We use the expected queue waiting time $E[QWT]$ instead of $E[QWT_{TFE}]$ in Eq.(1), and the expected service time of a final event $E[ST_{FE}]$ instead of $E[ST_{TFE}]$ in Eq.(1). While $E[QWT]$ and $E[ST_{FE}]$ are simpler to estimate, they have the same tendency as that of the $E[QWT_{TFE}]$ and $E[ST_{TFE}]$: $E[QWT]$ increases as ρ becomes higher and μ becomes slower [9], and $E[ST_{FE}]$ increases as more event types are grouped into the LEG.

$$E[L] = E[QWT] + E[ST_{FE}] \tag{2}$$

$E[QWT]$ can be calculated as shown in Eq.(3) [9]. We estimate μ, which is the inverse of $E[ST]$ as shown in Eq.(4). We estimate σ_{ST} which is the component of c_{ST} as shown in Eq.(5).

$$E[QWT] = \frac{\rho}{2\mu(1-\rho)}(1 + c_{ST}{}^2), \text{ where } \rho < 1 \tag{3}$$

$$E[ST] = \sum_{\forall E_i \text{ of } Q} \frac{\lambda_{E_i}}{\lambda} \times E[ST_{E_i}] \tag{4}$$

$$\sigma_{ST} = \sum_{\forall E_i \text{ of } Q} \sqrt{\frac{\lambda_{E_i}}{\lambda} \times (E[ST_{E_i}] - E[ST])^2} \tag{5}$$

$E[ST_{E_i}]$ in Eqs.(4) and (5) differs depending on which of *EEG* or *LEG* E_i belongs to. Suppose that the evaluation plan is $E_{E_1}E_{E_2}\ldots E_{E_{|EEG|}}/E_{L_1}E_{L_2}\ldots E_{L_{|LEG|}}$ where $|EEG|$ (or $|LEG|$) is the number of event types in EEG (or LEG). Then, $E[ST_{E_i}]$ is estimated as in Eqs.(6) ~ (8).

$$E[ST_{E_{E_i}}] = \underbrace{(|PI_{E_{E_1};\ldots;E_{E_{i-1}}}| \times \sum_{j=1}^{i-1} NP_{E_{E_i},E_{E_j}} \times T_{PE})}_{\text{the total number of predicate evaluations}} + \underbrace{(|PI_{E_{E_1};\ldots;E_{E_{i-1}}}| \times \prod_{j=1}^{i-1} SP_{E_{E_i},E_{E_j}} \times T_{RC})}_{\text{the total number of results constructed}} \tag{6}$$

$$E[ST_{E_{L_i}}] = T_{BI} \tag{7}$$

$$E[ST_{FE}] = (E[ST_{E_{E_i}}] \text{ or } E[ST_{E_{L_i}}]) + T_M \tag{8}$$

If E is not the final event type, $E[ST_E]$ is estimated using either Eq.(6) or Eq.(7). If E is in the *EEG*, $E[ST_E]$ is estimated using Eq.(6). The first term estimates the time taken to evaluate parameterized predicates. The second term estimates the time taken to construct the result when all of the predicates are satisfied. If E is in the *LEG*, $E[ST_E]$ is equal to the time taken to insert the event into the buffer as shown in Eq.(7).

If E is the final event type, where E is in either the *EEG* or the *LEG*, $E[ST_E]$ is estimated using Eq.(8). The first term estimates the service time of the final event itself, which differs depending on the group to which the final event type belongs. The second term estimates the time taken by merging. T_M is estimated as the sum of the time taken to perform the join operations composing the merging. The time taken to perform each join operation is estimated using Eq.(9). The first term is the time taken to evaluate join conditions, and the second term is the time taken to construct the results of join operations when all of the join conditions are satisfied.

$$T_{E_i \bowtie E_j} = \underbrace{(|PI_{E_i}| \times |PI_{E_j}| \times (NP_{E_i,E_j} + NP_{E_i;E_j}) \times T_{PE})}_{\text{the total number of predicate evaluations}} + \underbrace{(|PI_{E_i}| \times |PI_{E_j}| \times SP_{E_i,E_j} \times SP_{E_i;E_j} \times T_{RC})}_{\text{the total number of results constructed}} \tag{9}$$

As shown in Eq.(3), $E[QWT]$ is stable and can be calculated only if $\rho < 1$ [9]. If ρ of a candidate plan is greater than or equal to one, we consider the $E[QWT]$ of that plan infinite, and thus, $E[L]$ of that plan is estimated to be infinite. If $E[L]$'s of all candidate plans are estimated to be infinite, we select the plan in which μ is the fastest. This is because the latency is heavily dependent on the throughput (i.e., μ) when $\rho \geq 1$, as noted in Section 1.

4.3 Heuristic intuition

Among the candidate plans, $E[ST_{FE}]$ decreases while $E[QWT]$ increases as the *eager evaluation ratio* (defined in Definition 2) of the candidate plan gets higher. $E[ST_{FE}]$ decreases because the cost of the merging decreases since more events are immediately evaluated even before the final event arrives. $E[QWT]$ increases because $E[ST]$ increases given that the matching order differs from the optimal order. On the other hand, $E[ST_{FE}]$ increases while $E[QWT]$ decreases as the *lazy evaluation ratio* (defined in Definition 2) of the candidate plan gets higher.

Definition 2. The *eager* (or *lazy*) *evaluation ratio* of an evaluation plan is the ratio of the number of event types in *EEG* (or *LEG*) to those in Q. An *eager* (or *lazy*) *evaluation plan* refers to the one whose eager (or lazy) evaluation ratio is 1.

Given the characteristics above, we state the heuristic intuition to select the optimal plan according to λ as follows, which will be used for sanity check of our proposed cost-based plan selection method in Section 6.

- Case 1: λ is slow ($\rho < \theta_{lower}$). It is best to use the eager evaluation plan. Because there is sufficient idle time, most events are evaluated using the idle time. In this case, the increase in $E[QWT]$ is shorter than the decrease in $E[ST_{FE}]$. Thus, the latency can be reduced by reducing $E[ST_{FE}]$.
- Case 2: λ is fast ($\rho > \theta_{upper}$). It is best to use the lazy evaluation plan. Because there is little idle time, most evaluations of events are delayed. In this case, the increase in $E[QWT]$ is longer than the decrease in $E[ST_{FE}]$. Thus, the latency can be reduced by reducing $E[QWT]$. If a prefix of the optimal matching order is same as the order specified in Q, it is better to group the event types of the prefix into the EEG because $E[ST_{FE}]$ decreases while $E[QWT]$ stays the same (ρ is the same) since the matching order does not change (i.e., stays the same as the optimal matching order).
- Case 3: λ is in the middle ($\theta_{lower} < \rho < \theta_{upper}$). The optimal evaluation ratio can be found by considering the trade-off between $E[QWT]$ and $E[ST_{FE}]$. An event type is grouped into the *EEG*, if grouped it reduces the latency since the increase in $E[QWT]$ is shorter than the decrease in $E[ST_{FE}]$. The lazy evaluation ratio of the optimal plan will become higher as λ becomes faster.

5. INTERMEDIATE RESULT MERGING

Whenever a final event arrives, the pattern instances matched to Q are constructed using partial pattern instances stored in the eager evaluation result buffer and events stored in deferred event buffers. Here, only those partial pattern instances and events within W are used to satisfy the time window condition of Q. We refer to this process as merging, which is formally defined in Definition 4.

Definition 3. Consider $E_1; E_2; ...; E_n$. For E_i and E_j (where $i < j$), a *sequence predicate* is $E_i.timestamp < E_j.timestamp$.

Definition 4. Suppose that the evaluation plan is $E_{E_1}E_{E_2}...E_{E_{|EEG|}}/E_{L_1}E_{L_2}...E_{L_{|LEG|}}$. *Merging* is $PI_{E_{E_1};...;E_{E_{|EEG|}}} \bowtie PI_{E_{L_1}} \bowtie ... \bowtie PI_{E_{L_{|LEG|}}}$ using the conjunction of the following predicates as a join condition:

- parameterized predicates grouped into *LEG*
- sequence predicates between an event type in *EEG* and the one in *LEG*
- sequence predicates among event types in *LEG*

Example 1. Figure 2(c) shows an example of merging detecting the query event pattern in Figure 2(a). The figure shows the state right after the event stream in Figure 2(b) arrived completely and the merging initiated by d_{15} is finished. In the join tree shown in the figure, leaf nodes represent the eager evaluation result buffer (green colored) and deferred event buffers (yellow colored), and internal nodes represent buffers into which the intermediate join results are materialized. First, the time window condition is evaluated prior to the start of the merging. (1) In this figure, a_1 and a_5, which are outside of the time window based on d_{15}, are discarded. When the merging starts, two-way join operations are performed repeatedly according to the predetermined join order. In this figure, the join order $((EERB_{BC} \bowtie DEB_D) \bowtie DEB_A)$ is used, in which the most selective join operation is performed first. Initially, (2) the partial pattern instances in $EERB_{BC}$ and DEB_D are joined, with the results being inserted into BCD. Next, (3) the results of prior join and pattern instances in DEB_A are joined, with the results being inserted into $ABCD$.

```
PATTERN A(attr1); B(attr1); C(attr1, attr2); D(attr1, attr2)
WHERE A.attr1 < D.attr1
AND B.attr1 = C.attr1
AND C.attr2 = D.attr2
WITHIN 10
```

(a) Query event pattern

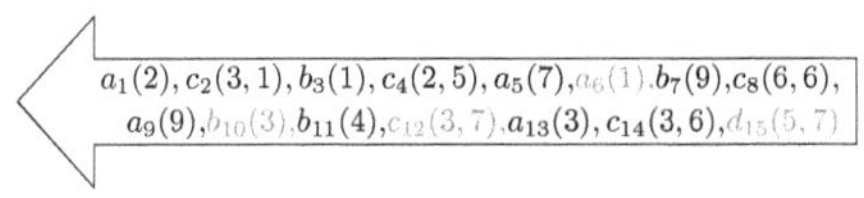

(b) Event stream

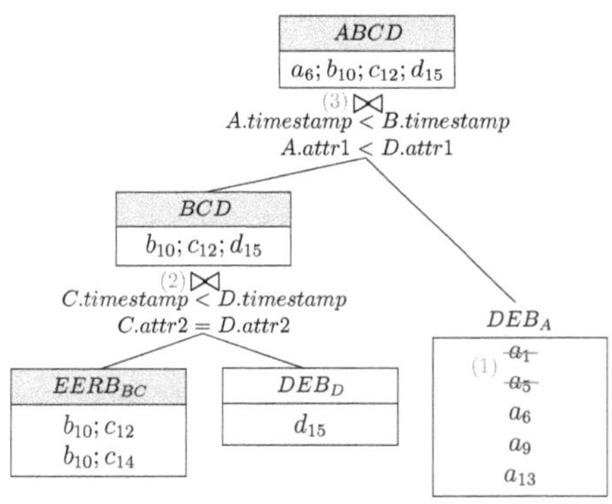

(c) Merging

Figure 2: An example of the merging.

6. PERFORMANCE EVALUATION

In this section, we test the performance of **APAM**. We validate the proposed optimal plan selection method, and show that **APAM** achieves the lower bound of latency of the eager and lazy evaluation methods at any arrival rates.

6.1 Experimental setting

We conduct three experiments in which the optimal matching orders differ, as shown in Table 2. Next, we compare the performance of **APAM** with those of existing methods, i.e., the eager evaluation method and the lazy evaluation method. As the representative existing methods, we use SASE [1, 11, 13, 14] for the eager evaluation method and ZStream [10] for the lazy evaluation method. SASE acts as **APAM** that uses an eager evaluation plan does, and ZStream as **APAM** that uses a lazy evaluation plan does.

Table 2: Three cases of experiments conducted.

No.	Description
1	The optimal matching order ($EDCBA$) is the reverse order of that specified in Q ($ABCDE$)
2	The optimal matching order ($ABCDE$) is identical to the order specified in Q ($ABCDE$)
3	Part of the optimal matching order ($BCDAE$) is identical to part of the order specified in Q ($ABCDE$)

The performance metric is latency. We measure the average elapsed time from the point at which each final event arrives to the point at which all pattern instances that contain the final event are detected. We conduct each experiment five times and use the average value.

For each experiment, we generate a synthetic event stream that consists of 100,000 events (50,000 for warm-up and 50,000 for measuring the performance). Events arrive into the system at arrival rate λ according to a Poisson process. For each experiment, we vary λ from 100 to 4500 events/sec. The event stream is a heterogeneous event stream that consists of five types of events. The distribution of event types follows a uniform distribution. The event schema is shown in Figure 3(a).

Figure 3(b) shows the query event pattern used in the experiments. The optimal matching order of each experiment in Table 2 is determined by selectivities of the parameterized predicates of this query event pattern. In the first experiment, the selectivities are 0.008, 0.006, 0.004, and 0.002. In the second experiment, they are 0.002, 0.004, 0.006, and 0.008, respectively. In the third experiment, the corresponding selectivities are 0.006, 0.002, 0.004, and 0.008. The selectivity of each parameterized predicate can be varied by varying the domain of the relevant event attribute.

eID (integer)
$type$ (integer, [0, 4])
$timestamp$ (long)
$attr1 \sim 9$ (integer)

(a) Event schema

PATTERN $A; B; C; D; E$
WHERE $A.attr1 < B.attr1$
AND $B.attr2 < C.attr2$
AND $C.attr3 < D.attr3$
AND $D.attr4 < E.attr4$
WITHIN 2000 events

(b) Query

Figure 3: The event schema and the query.

All experiments are conducted on a Linux machine equipped with an Intel Core i7 4790 CPU and 8 GB of main memory. We use SASE provided as an open-source software and implement ZStream as described in Mei, Y. et al. [10] These are implemented in Java.

6.2 Experimental results

6.2.1 Experiment 1

Figure 4 shows the results of the measurements of the latency of candidate plans for No. 1 in Table 2 while varying the event arrival rate. Figure 4 also shows QWT_{TFE} and ST_{TFE}, which are the time components of the latency. The x-axis represents the candidate plans, where the optimal plan selected by the proposed method is underlined.

As shown in Figure 4(a), when the event arrival rate is slow (where $\rho < 0.1$), the optimal plan selection method proposed in Section 4 selects the eager evaluation plan so as to utilize the idle time to the greatest extent possible. On the other hand, as shown in Figure 4(d), when the event arrival rate is fast (where $\rho > 1$), it selects the plan that uses the optimal matching order so as to increase the service rate. Here, the matching order of the plan selected is $DECBA$, which is another optimal matching order since selectivity of matching E after matching D is the same as that of matching D after matching E. As shown in Figures 4(b) and 4(c), when the event arrival rate is in the middle, the proposed method selects the plan that maximizes using the idle time provided that the queueing delay does not cancel the benefit. This result also conforms to the heuristic intuition in Section 4.3.

When the event arrival rate is 1500 event/sec, the proposed method selects the second optimal plan, but there is only a slight difference (1.30 times higher) between the latency of the selected plan and that of the optimal plan. In all cases, the latency of **APAM** which uses the plan selected is lower than or equal to the latency of the existing methods. When the event arrival rate is 100 events/sec, the latency of the proposed method is equal to the latency of SASE and is 27.94 times lower than that of ZStream. When the event arrival rate is 1500~4500 event/sec, the latency of the proposed method is 15.73~361.48 times lower than that of SASE and is 1.04~1.17 times lower than that of ZStream.

6.2.2 Experiment 2

Figure 5 shows the results for No. 2 in Table 2. In this result, the proposed method selects the eager evaluation plan for all event arrival rate. Since the optimal matching order is identical to the order specified in Q, increasing eager evaluation ratio makes ST_{TFE} decrease while not affecting QWT_{TFE}. Thus, a plan with a higher eager evaluation ratio achieves a lower latency regardless of the event arrival rate. This result also conforms to the heuristic intuition. In all cases, the latency of **APAM** is lower than or equal to the latency of the existing methods. As the eager evaluation plan is selected for all event arrival rate, the latency of **APAM** is same with that of SASE, and 1.25~5.71 times lower than that of ZStream.

6.2.3 Experiment 3

Figure 6 shows the results for No. 3 in Table 2. As shown in Figure 6(a), when the event arrival rate is slow, the proposed method selects the eager evaluation plan. On the other hand, as shown in Figure 6(d), when the event arrival rate is fast, it selects the plan that uses the optimal matching order. As shown in Figures 6(b) and 6(c), when the event arrival rate is in the middle, the proposed method selects the plan that maximizes using the idle time provided that the queueing delay does not cancel the benefit. This result also conforms to the heuristic intuition.

When the event arrival rate is 4500 event/sec, the proposed method selects the third optimal plan, but there is only a slight difference (1.05 times higher) between the latency of the selected plan and that of the optimal plan. In all cases, the latency of **APAM** which uses the plan selected is lower than or equal to the latency of the existing methods. When the event arrival rate is 100 events/sec, the latency of the proposed method is equal to the latency of SASE and is 5.51 times lower than the latency of ZStream. For the rest of the case, the latency of the proposed method is 3.32~60.09 times lower than that of SASE and is similar to or up to 1.61 times lower than the latency of ZStream.

7. CONCLUSION

In this paper, we propose a hybrid eager-lazy evaluation method, called **APAM**, for low-latency event pattern detection. In **APAM**, event types and parameterized predicates of the query event pattern are partitioned into an eager evaluation group and a lazy evaluation group. When the final event arrives, pattern instances are constructed by merging partial pattern instances constructed from the eager evaluation group and events whose evaluations have been deferred in the lazy evaluation group. **APAM** can act as the eager evaluation method, the lazy evaluation method, or as a hybrid

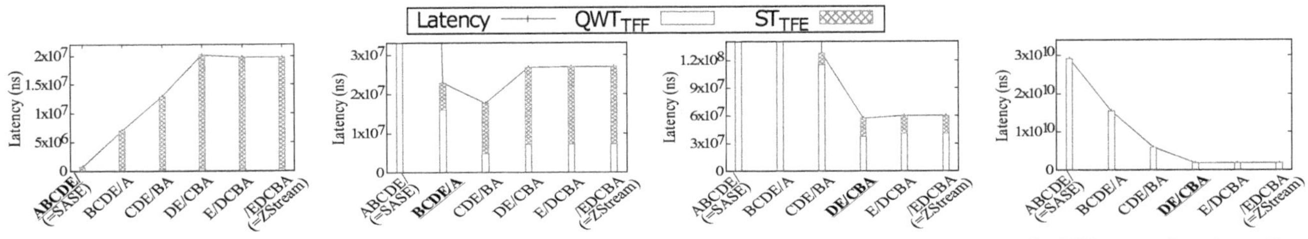

(a) 100 events/sec ($\rho < 0.1$) (b) 1500 events/sec (c) 3000 events/sec (d) 4500 events/sec ($\rho > 1$)

Figure 4: Latency of candidate plans with varying arrival rates in Experiment 1.

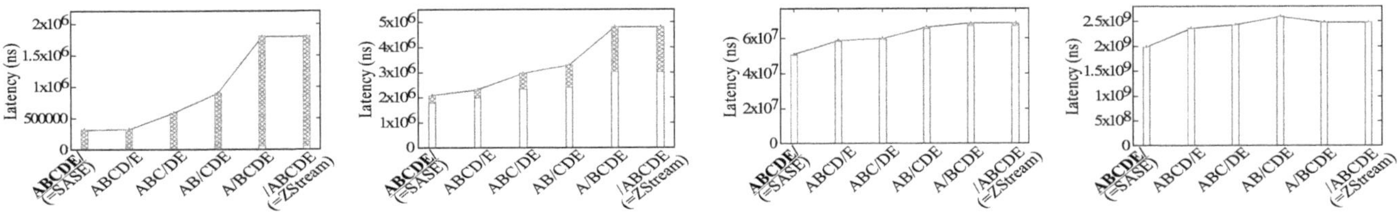

(a) 100 events/sec ($\rho < 0.1$) (b) 1500 events/sec (c) 3000 events/sec (d) 4500 events/sec ($\rho > 1$)

Figure 5: Latency of candidate plans with varying arrival rates in Experiment 2.

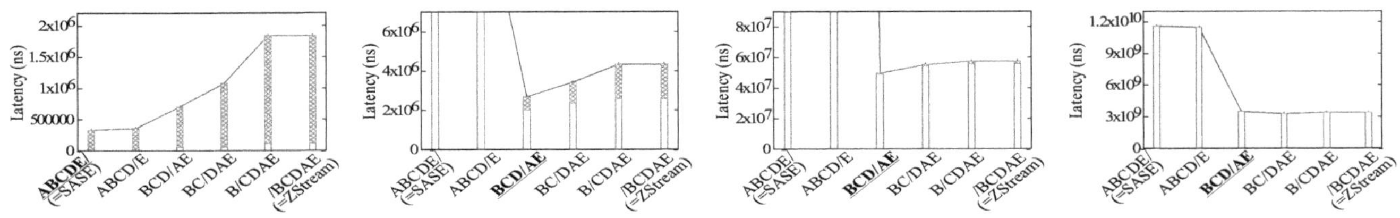

(a) 100 events/sec ($\rho < 0.1$) (b) 1500 events/sec (c) 3000 events/sec (d) 4500 events/sec ($\rho > 1$)

Figure 6: Latency of candidate plans with varying arrival rates in Experiment 3.

evaluation method according to the evaluation plan. By using the optimal evaluation plan, **APAM** can provide a lower-bound latency of those of existing methods at any event arrival rate. To find the optimal evaluation plan, we propose a cost model for estimating the latency of an evaluation plan. Based on the cost model, we propose a method that selects the optimal evaluation plan. Experimental results show that this method selects the optimal or near-optimal evaluation plan at varying arrival rates, which constitutes a lower-bound latency of existing methods. The results also show that **APAM** under the optimal evaluation plan can improve the latency by up to 361.48 times over the eager evaluation method and 27.94 times over the lazy evaluation method.

8. ACKNOWLEDGMENTS

This work was supported by the National Research Foundation of Korea(NRF) grant funded by Korean Government (MSIP) (No. 2016R1A2B4015929).

9. REFERENCES

[1] J. Agrawal, Y. Diao, D. Gyllstrom, and N. Immerman. Efficient pattern matching over event streams. In *Proc. ACM SIGMOD*, pages 147–160, 2008.

[2] B. Cadonna, J. Gamper, and M. H. Böhlen. Efficient event pattern matching with match windows. In *Proc. ACM SIGKDD*, pages 471–479, 2012.

[3] S. Chakravarthy, V. Krishnaprasad, E. Anwar, and S.-K. Kim. Composite events for active databases: Semantics, contexts and detection. In *Proc. VLDB*, pages 606–617, 1994.

[4] Q. Chen, Z. Li, and H. Liu. Optimizing complex event processing over rfid data streams. In *Proc. IEEE ICDE*, pages 1442–1444, 2008.

[5] A. Demers, J. Gehrke, M. Hong, M. Riedewald, and W. White. Towards expressive publish/subscribe systems. In *Proc. EDBT*, pages 627–644, 2006.

[6] R. Elmasri and S. Navathe. *Database Systems: Models, Languages, Design, and Application Programming*. Pearson, 2011.

[7] I. Kolchinsky, I. Sharfman, and A. Schuster. Lazy evaluation methods for detecting complex events. In *Proc. ACM DEBS*, pages 34–45, 2015.

[8] D. Luckham, W. R. Schulte, J. Adkins, P. Bizarro, H.-A. Jacobsen, A. Mavashev, B. M. Michelson, P. Niblett, and D. Tucker. *Event Processing Glossary – Version 2.0*. Event Processing Technical Society, 2011.

[9] J. Medhi. *Stochastic Models in Queueing Theory (2nd Edition)*. Academic Press, 2003.

[10] Y. Mei and S. Madden. Zstream: A cost-based query processor for adaptively detecting composite events. In *Proc. ACM SIGMOD*, pages 193–206, 2009.

[11] E. Wu, Y. Diao, and S. Rizvi. High-performance complex event processing over streams. In *Proc. ACM SIGMOD*, pages 407–418, 2006.

[12] Y. Yan, J. Zhang, and M.-C. Shan. Scheduling for fast response multi-pattern matching over streaming events. In *Proc. IEEE ICDE*, pages 89–100, 2010.

[13] H. Zhang, Y. Diao, and N. Immerman. Recognizing patterns in streams with imprecise timestamps. *VLDB Endowment*, 3(1-2):244–255, 2010.

[14] H. Zhang, Y. Diao, and N. Immerman. On complexity and optimization of expensive queries in complex event processing. In *Proc. ACM SIGMOD*, pages 217–228, 2014.

OrientStream: A Framework for Dynamic Resource Allocation in Distributed Data Stream Management Systems

Chunkai Wang[1] Xiaofeng Meng[1] Qi Guo[2] Zujian Weng[1] Chen Yang[1]

[1]School of Information, Renmin University, Beijing, China
[2]Institute of Computing Technology, Chinese Academy of Sciences, Beijing, China

[1]{wangchunkai,xfmeng,zjweng,yang_chen}@ruc.edu.cn [2]guoqi@ict.ac.cn

ABSTRACT

Distributed data stream management systems (DDSMS) are usually composed of upper layer relational query systems (RQS) and lower layer stream processing systems (SPS). When users submit new queries to RQS, a query planner needs to be converted into a directed acyclic graph (DAG) consisting of tasks which are running on SPS. Based on different query requests and data stream properties, SPS need to configure different deployments strategies. However, how to dynamically predict deployment configurations of SPS to ensure the processing throughput and low resource usage is a great challenge. This article presents OrientStream, a framework for dynamic resource allocation in DDSMS using incremental machine learning techniques. By introducing the data-level, query plan-level, operator-level and cluster-level's four-level feature extraction mechanism, we firstly use the different query workloads as training sets to predict the resource usage of DDSMS and then select the optimal resource configuration from candidate settings based on the current query requests and stream properties. Finally, we validate our approach on the open source SPS–Storm. Experiments show that OrientStream can reduce CPU usage of 8%-15% and memory usage of 38%-48% respectively.

CCS Concepts

•**Information systems → Database query processing; Stream management;**

Keywords

Stream Processing System, Relational Query System, Incremental Learning, Modeling and Prediction

CIKM '16, October 24–28, 2016, Indianapolis, IN, USA

© 2016 ACM. ISBN 978-1-4503-4073-1/16/10...$15.00

DOI: http://dx.doi.org/10.1145/2983323.2983681

1. INTRODUCTION

Nowadays, many modern applications require large-scale continuous queries and analysis, such as analytic over microblogs in social networks, monitoring of high frequency trading in financial fields, real-time recommendation in electronic business and so on. Therefore, there have been many open source SPS, such as S4 [15] and Storm [20]. For enhancing the ease of use and processing capability of them, some RQS that contain query languages have been developed, such as Squall [1].

For completing the query requests given by users within the specified latency, DDSMS need to guarantee the high throughput and low latency of stream processing. This often requires users to set the relevant configurations in advance, such as the operator parallelism and the memory usage of processes. However, according to data stream properties (e.g., arrival rate and value distribution) and the difference of query tasks, the reasonable setting of configurations for ensuring both processing in real-time and low resource usage is a very challenging problem.

Motivating Example. Consider an application which analyzes the traffic GPS data collected from taxes and buses in real time. We take traffic-monitoring (TM) system as a query example, and Storm as a SPS example.

Traffic-monitoring needs to process and analyze the traffic GPS data collected from taxes and buses in real-time. The scenario is a typical application of streaming execution. We use GeoLife GPS Trajectories [21] for this workload that contains GPS trajectory data collected by 182 users in a period of over five years, and simulate a traffic-monitoring system. It contains a map matching processing logic which accepts trajectories data of a GPS-loggers or GPS-phones including altitude, latitude, and longitude, and determines the location of this object in terms of a road ID. The speed calculate processing logic accepts the road ID result from the matching processing logic and calculate the average speed according to the road ID.

The execution tasks in Storm can be expressed as a DAG (called *topology*), where nodes are data sources (called *spouts*) or processing logic (called *bolts*) which run in different processes (called *workers*), and edges indicate the flow of data between nodes. For real-time computation, the topology should be created at first. Then, before the deployment of the topology to the Storm cluster, the user should specify various topology parameters (e.g., the number of workers, spout parallelism, and bolt parallelism, etc.) according to either experience or machine configurations. Finally, the Storm cluster receives continuous data stream and processes them in a real-time fashion.

However, the topology parameters are not aware of dynamic data stream. For example, as shown in Figure 1.a, due to the fixed parameters, some processing delays are beyond the user's threshold (e.g., 1 second) with the change of data stream rate. Meanwhile, it also leads to the higher cluster resources usage. As shown in Figure 1.b, the average usage of CPU is about 40%, and the average usage of memory (the user specifies the maximum memory usage of each worker) is more than 90%. As DDSMS are always deployed in the cloud environment, the problem of fixed configurations not only leads to high resource usage, reduces the user's return-on-investment (ROI), and even causes the system bottleneck.

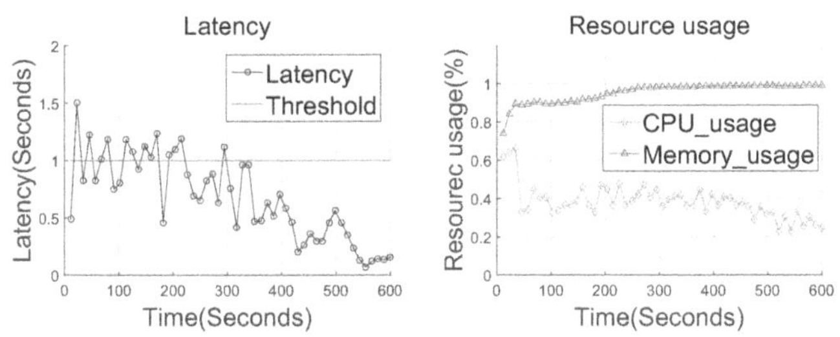

(a) Latency (b) Resource Usage

Figure 1: Traffic-Monitoring Example

So, in this paper, we present the design of OrientStream that implements dynamic resource allocation for Storm. The contributions of our work are summarized as follows:

1. We construct initial training sets by using the different workloads for meeting the characteristics of RQS, divide queries in four different levels to predict CPU and memory usage, and use incremental learning technique to build prediction models in real time.

2. According to the related independent of different regression models, we give the algorithm of Ensemble Different kinds of Regressions (EDKR) to integrate different models for enhancing the prediction accuracy.

3. We introduce the outlier execution detection mechanism to monitor the anomalous executions. So as to further improve the prediction accuracy.

The rest of the paper is organized as follows. Section 2 surveys the related work. Then, there is the problem definition in section 3. And, in Section 4, we give the architecture of OrientStream. Next, we describe the prediction process in Section 5. Section 6 gives the results of our experiment evaluation. Finally, Section 7 concludes this paper.

2. RELATED WORK

To meet users' different query requests, DDSMS needs to build a complete operator library in RQS and dynamically set up the parallelism of processing nodes of SPS based on different query requests. There are roughly three lines of related work as below.

Dynamic Load Scheduling. Aeolus [19] is an optimizer to set up the parallel degree and the batch size of intra-node dataflow programs. It defined a cost model based on four measurements of processing tuple time, including shipping time, queuing time, pure processing time and actual processing time. According to the model, Aeolus can get the best configuration scheme for the parallel degree of operators and batch size. DRS [10] is a dynamic resource scheduler for cloud-based DDSMS. It designed an accurate performance model that can get the setting of optimal parallel degree of operators. Aniello et al. [7] proposed two scheduling algorithms by using topology-based static scheduling strategy and traffic-based dynamic scheduling strategy for reducing the latency of processing tuples and inter-node traffic between multiple topologies.

Machine Learning Techniques. Khoshkbarforoushha et al. [12] proposed a model based on the Mixture Density Network [8] for resource usage estimation of data stream processing workloads. This model can help users to make a decision about whether to register a new query or not. ALOJA [17] project presented an open, vendor neutral repository, featuring over Hadoop executions. It can predict query time and abnormal detection by using machine learning techniques to interpret Hadoop benchmark performance data and performance tuning.

Resource Estimation for RQS. Li et al. [14] set up two kinds of mechanisms of feature extractions: coarse-grained global features and fine-grained operator-specific features for different queries over Microsoft SQL Server. Akdere et al. [6] built three models for predicting query performance based on different query plans: query plan-level model, operator-level model and hybrid model for nested query.

OrientStream is orthogonal to the above works since we focus on constructing training sets for the data stream properties and the parameter configurations of different levels, predicting resource usage by online machine learning techniques, and dynamically tuning the related parameter configurations of DDSMS.

3. PROBLEM DEFINITION

Query requests always need to set different parameter configurations by user's experience. Whether the parameter configurations are reasonable directly affects the throughput and the latency of DDSMS, as well as the resource usage. With the change of data stream rate, we should dynamically adjust parameter configurations to meet user's needs of the throughput and latency thresholds. But, SPS are often not allowed to adjust parameters arbitrarily.

So, we need to predict the resource usage, the throughput and latency for any candidate configurations. Based on the predicted results, the optimal configuration is defined as the one using minimal CPU and memory resource while the throughput and the latency requirements are still guaranteed under the thresholds set by users. Thus, the problem can be modeled as a resource usage optimization problem as we discuss next.

Let $N = (n_1, n_2, n_3, ...)$ be the set of all nodes in a cluster. The CPU usage U_{CPU} and memory usage U_{Memory} of each node n_i can be defined as follows.

$$T(n_i) = \alpha * U_{CPU}(n_i) + \beta * U_{Memory}(n_i) \qquad (\alpha + \beta = 1) \quad (1)$$

where, α and β are the weight of the CPU and memory usage respectively, which set as 50% by default.

Then, for the entire cluster, the optimization problem is

$$
\begin{aligned}
&Minimize \sum_{n_i \in \mathcal{N}} T(n_i) \\
&s.t. \quad R(latency) < T(latency), \\
&and \quad R(throughput) > T(throughput).
\end{aligned} \tag{2}
$$

where, $R(latency)$ and $R(throughput)$ are the processing latency and throughput of query requests. $T(latency)$ and $T(throughput)$ are the thresholds set by users.

4. ORIENTSTREAM ARCHITECTURE

This section gives the overview of OrientStream and working principles of each step.

OrientStream Overview. Figure 2 illustrates the overall architecture of OrientStream, by extending the original Storm and Kafka [13] cluster. It is mainly divided into two parts: the left part is the hierarchical feature extractions, and the right part is the query monitor that is responsible for collecting the feature data and predicting the resource usage by incremental learning models.

In the left part, according to the characteristics of DDSMS and clusters, we divide feature extractions into four levels. There are data-level features of the data source, plan-level features of RQS, operator-level features of SPS and cluster-level features of the hardware platform (see section 5.1 for details). Each data source collects and transmits data stream using the Kafka message queue. In the right part, we analyze the real-time collected feature data and build the incremental learning models, and predict the resource usage of DDSMS using model-based methods.

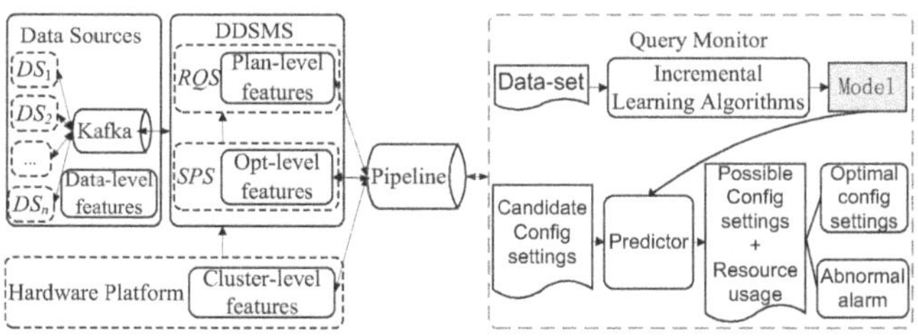

Figure 2: OrientStream architecture

Model Construction. During the incremental learning phrase, we collect the feature data dynamically to generate OrientStream data-set, use the data set to predict the accuracy of the each model and use the prediction results to re-train the model by incremental learning. According to the characteristics of the data-set, we choose different incremental learning algorithms to build models based on MOA [2] and Weka [3] toolkits.

Resource Prediction. *Query Monitor* is responsible for building incremental learning models and generating the *Predictor* by collecting the feature data. Then, We can use the *Predictor* to predict the candidate configuration settings, select the optimal configuration setting for using the least resource, and alarm the abnormal setting for using resource too much or the throughput/latency in excess of thresholds.

Dynamic Tuning. During model deployment, the constructed models are used for determining the optimal configuration setting for the current data rate, so as to minimize the resource usage while still preserving real-time property. Due to the limitations of the re-balance mechanism of Storm, we propose to deactivate the old topology and then switch to a new topology with the optimal configuration. To maintain the streaming behavior of the old topology, before deactivating it, the behavior data should be stored into Kafka. After deploying the new topology, the behavior data should be read from Kafka to recover the final state of the old topology. This process of switching to a new topology will last for about 1 minute. So, the application scenarios of OrientStream need to meet the following two requirements: (1) the monitor cycle of data stream is longer; (2) the data fluctuation is not frequent and far lower than the switching time.

5. MODELING RESOURCE PREDICTION

This section focuses on the implementation details, including features extraction, model building and integration, abnormal detection mechanism and applications.

5.1 Data-set Features

In this section, we will describe the features that use as the input OrientStream data-set to the learning model for predicting resource usage. For this purpose, we need to specify the level of input features for learning models. According to a series of experiments and specific domain knowledge, we choose features from the following four aspects:

Data-Level Features. We control the rate of input data stream as DATA_RATE by changing the spout parallelism. Also, the number of Kafka brokers and the number of topics' partitions are also taken into account. In addition, because the change of DATA_RATE could influence the rate of subsequent operators, we need to calculate the rate of relevant operators dynamically (e.g., map matching bolt rate and speed calculate bolt rate in the TM workload).

Query Plan-Level Features. The continuous query can generate DAG-style topology by using the query plan. The amount of data waiting to be processed and the window sliding step can be controlled by WINDOW_SIZE and SLIDING_STEP. Moreover, we count the number of input and output tuples in a window to predict the average selectivity, and count the number of different types of operators.

Operator-Level Features. We can monitor resource usage by adjusting the operator parallelism in different windows. If the same operator appears more than once, we take the average value as the criterion of feature extraction. Meanwhile, we need to involve the number of workers about Storm as the feature that can influence the processing efficiency of operators.

Cluster-Level Features. We defines cluster-level features including the number of worker nodes, CPU cores, memory capacity and network transmission rate.

5.2 Algorithms

According to analyzing the prediction results by using models to support incremental learning in MOA and Weka toolkits, we select four models with the highest prediction accuracy:

Bayes model: we use the Naive Bayes (NB) from the MOA toolkit. Bayes [11] algorithm updates internal counters with each new instance and uses the counter to assign a class in a probabilistic fashion to a new item in the stream.

Hoeffding trees model: we use the HoeffdingTree (HT), also from the MOA toolkit. A hoeffding tree or VFDT [9] is an incremental decision tree that is capable of learning from massive data stream. It exploits the fact that a small sample can often be enough to choose an optimal splitting attribute.

Online bagging model: we use the OzaBagging (Oza) [16] from the MOA toolkit and use hoeffding tree as the base learner. Oza and Russell proposed the online bagging algorithm that gives each instance a weight for re-sampling according to the Poisson distribution of λ equal to 1.

Nearest neighbors model: we use the IBk [5] from the Weka toolkit, through introducing updateable classifier method to achieve incremental learning characteristics.

5.3 EDKR Model

As we know, ensemble learning is one of the most effective methods to improve the accuracy of the regression algorithm, which is considered as one of the most effective learning ideas. Its contribution is to improve regression accuracy by aggregating multiple base models. However, it only ensembles the same regression model. As discussed in section 5.2, four models has no contact and the prediction is independent of each other. Therefore, we combine these four models and propose a regression model EDKR (Ensemble Different Kind of Regression).

In the process of prediction, firstly, EDKR lets each base regression model to make prediction; then, according to the relative absolute error (RAE) value of the each base regression model, EDKR calculates the voting weights respectively; finally, it determine the regression value of the sample with a weighted vote. Among them, RAE and the objective function of EDKR are defined as below:

Let N be the set of training samples in each regression model and n be the nth sample to be predicted. P_n is the prediction value of the regression model to the sample n. T_n is the true value of the sample n. AVG_N is the mean of N samples. Then,

$$RAE_n = \sum_{i=1}^{N} |P_{in} - T_i| \,/\, \sum_{j=1}^{N} |T_j - AVG_N| \tag{3}$$

where, RAE_n is the RAE of the nth sample using specified base regression model.

So, based on the K base regression models, the objective function of EDKR to predict the sample n is,

$$F_n = \sum_{i=1}^{K} (1 - RAE_{in})/(K - \sum_{j=1}^{K} RAE_{jn}) * P_{in} \tag{4}$$

where, F_n is the RAE of the nth sample using EDKR model, and P_{in} is the prediction value of the nth sample using the ith base regression model.

5.4 Abnormal Detection Mechanism

Due to the abnormal execution of the cluster (e.g., the cluster load is not balanced, network transmission is not stable), or the observation does not fit into the model, it results in some abnormal training data. Based on the difference between the predicted value and the observed value (e.g., resource usage), we divide the training data into three types:

- *Normal.* Detected data can be predicted correctly by learning models.
- *Warning.* Detected data is mis-predicted, and more than a half of nearest neighbors to the data are mis-predicted too.
- *Outlier.* Detected data is mis-predicted, but more than a half of nearest neighbors to the data are predicted correctly.

We can improve the prediction accuracy by discarding abnormal training data and not getting it into the incremental learning model. Besides using this method to test new observations, we can re-train our models by subtracting observations marked as outlier. Algorithm 1 gives the detailed description of the detection procedure. For each detected data, firstly, we select the normal data based on the error threshold T_e (Algorithm 1 line 1-2). Then, for each abnormal test data, we compute the k_{NN} tuples that are nearest to the test data. Line 4-6 in Algorithm 2 depicts this process. Next, we count the number of warning or outlier of these k_{NN} tuples by the definition of warning or outlier category (Algorithm 1 line 7-13). Finally, we judge whether the test data is warning or outlier (Algorithm 1 line 14-18).

Algorithm 1 Abnormal detection algorithm.

Require:
Prediction Error Threshold T_e;
The number of tuples to nearest tag tuple k_{NN};
The regression file F contains predicted value and true value;
Ensure:
The type of detected tuple t;

```
1:  if (|t.PredictedValue − t.TrueValue| < T_e) then
2:    t is Normal;
3:  else
4:    for (i = 1; i < Number_of_TestDataSet; i++) do
5:      Computing the k_NN tuples nearest to t;
6:    end for
7:    for (j = 1; j < k_NN; j++) do
8:      if (|t_k.PredictedValue − t_k.TrueValue| > T_e) then
9:        N_warning + 1;
10:     else
11:       N_outlier + 1;
12:     end if
13:   end for
14:   if (N_warning > N_outlier) then
15:     t is Warning;
16:   else
17:     t is Outlier;
18:   end if
19: end if
```

6. EVALUATION

This section presents three workloads of each test scenario and gives the result of prediction of resource usage with different learning models. We take the prediction of CPU usage as an example to verify the effect of anomaly detection mechanism and verify the resource save situation through using the dynamic tuning mechanism.

The testbed is established on a cluster of ten nodes connected by a 1Gbit Ethernet switch. Five nodes are used to transmit data source through kafka. One node serves as the nimbus of Storm, and the remaining four nodes act as supervisor nodes. Each data source node and the nimbus node have a Intel E5-2620 2.00GHz four-core CPU and 4GB of DDR3 RAM. Each supervisor node has two Intel E5-2620 2.00GHz twelve-core CPU and 64G of DDR3 RAM. We implement comprehensive evaluations of our prototype on Storm-0.9.5 and Ubuntu-14.04.3.

In order to cover the different query characteristics, we choose three different workloads as below.

Traffic Monitoring (TM). This workload has been introduced in detail in Section 1.

Word Count (WC). Word count represents word frequency statistics of different sentences. It is composed of a bolt for splitting sentences into words and another one for counting the number of occurrences for each word in a hashmap. We use the word count data-set from HiBench [4]. There are about 3 million sentences and more than 30 million words for testing.

TPC-H (Q3). TPC-H is a decision support benchmark. The queries and the data populating the database have been chosen to have broad industry-wide relevance. In order to verify the query processing of multiple data streams, we choose Q3 as the workload that includes three data sources and use 15 million tuples for each data source for this workload. It contains three filter bolts to filter data source, two join bolts to make equi-join for the three data sources, a group bolt to group the result of join bolts, and a order bolt to order the result of the group bolt.

The sink bolt is used to merge the output results. For simplicity, we only use sink as the count statistics of received results. The topologies of three workloads are shown in Figure 3. Our workloads cover two aspects: (1) various topology structural complexity, from single chain topology of one data source to complex DAG topology of multiple data sources. (2) different runtime characteristics, such as memory intensive of TM workload, communication intensive of WC workload and compute intensive of Q3 workload.

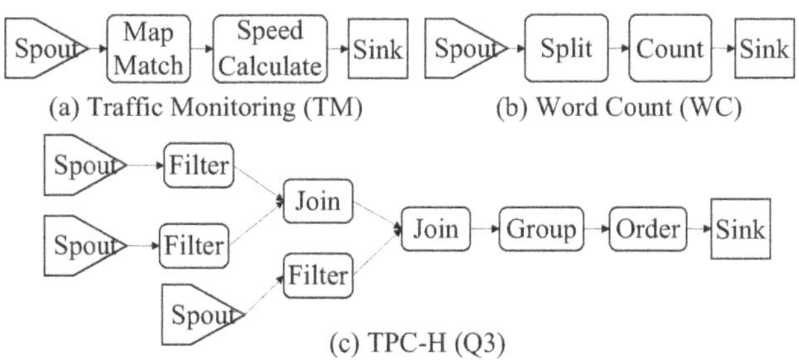

Figure 3: Topology of three different workloads

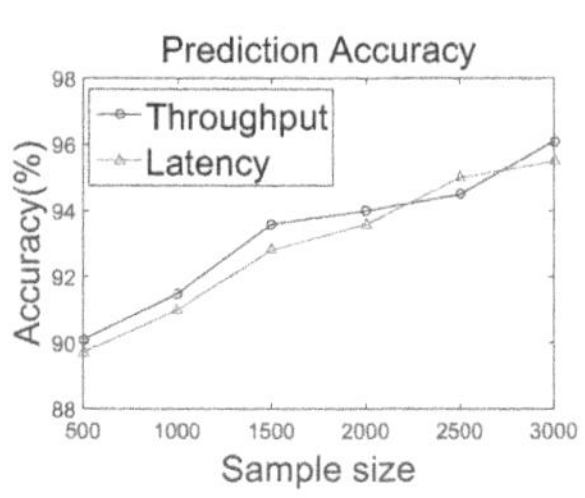

Figure 4: Accuracy

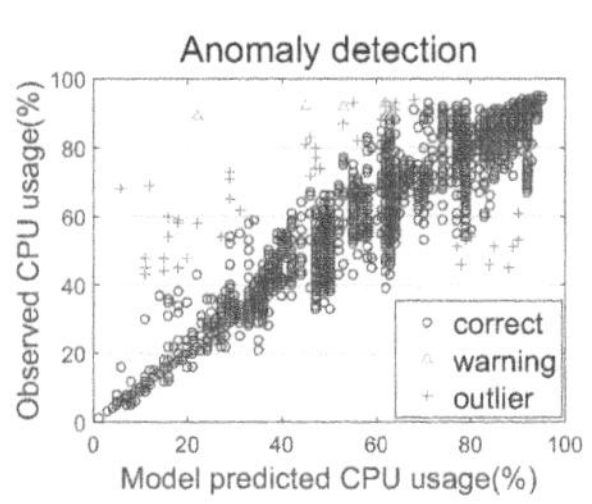

Figure 5: Anomaly Detection

6.1 Online Resource Prediction

In order to improve the prediction accuracy, we collect a training sample in every 3 minutes, and calculate the mean of CPU usage, memory usage, throughput and latency as the prediction targets. For each workload, we respectively collect 3000 samples by setting data rate and window sizes randomly.

According to $T(throughput)$ and $T(latency)$ set by users, we build two binary classification models and use J48 in Weka to classify. J48 is an open source java implementation of C4.5 [18] algorithm. The classification accuracy of the throughput and latency about three different workloads is shown in Figure 4.

The accuracy of predicting the throughput and latency is maintained at about 90% to 96% with increasing samples(from 500 to 3000). This provides a high security for the next step in predicting the resource usage.

For the regression prediction of resource usage, we use different learning models mentioned in section 5.2 and 5.3. Table 1 and 2 show the test results of the mean absolute error (MAE) and RAE per method based on different workloads. The experimental results show that:

(1) The average RAE of prediction memory usage is lower than that of prediction CPU usage, because of the fluctuation of memory usage is lower than that of CPU usage.

(2) EDKR is better than the best model in the four models. For prediction of CPU usage in different workloads, MAE can reduce 0.65-0.67, and RAE can reduce 3.5%-6.2%. For prediction of memory usage in different workloads, MAE can reduce 0.41-0.55 and RAE can reduce 2.55%-3.1%.

Models	TM		WC		Q3	
	MAE	RAE	MAE	RAE	MAE	RAE
NB	4.8633	0.2478	4.7251	0.2297	5.5328	0.2871
HT	5.3241	0.2687	5.1275	0.2503	5.5936	0.2971
Oza	4.7925	0.2365	4.5238	0.2156	5.1350	0.2665
IBk	5.6412	0.2825	5.5179	0.2655	5.8911	0.3059
EDKR	4.1325	0.2018	3.8729	0.1537	4.4655	0.2317

Table 1: MAE and RAE of CPU usage prediction

Models	TM		WC		Q3	
	MAE	RAE	MAE	RAE	MAE	RAE
NB	4.3926	0.2538	4.0158	0.2246	4.8593	0.2883
HT	4.8726	0.2955	4.4715	0.2643	5.1827	0.3390
Oza	4.6528	0.2511	0.3271	4.2819	5.0001	0.2871
IBk	2.7612	0.1285	2.5463	0.1157	2.8739	0.1305
EDKR	2.2109	0.0975	2.1035	0.0902	2.4639	0.1028

Table 2: MAE and RAE of memory usage prediction

6.2 Abnormal Filter Prediction

In this section, we take 3000 data samples of the CPU usage of TM workload as an example, use the EDKR as the prediction model, and set the prediction error threshold T_e to one standard deviation, set the number of tuples to nearest target to 5. As shown in Figure 5, there are 55 outlier records and 8 warning records in the data set. We subtract the outlier records in the data samples, and use to re-learn the prediction model. We predict MAE from 4.1325 to 3.8563, RAE from 0.2018 to 0.1765.

6.3 Dynamic Tuning

As shown in Figure 6.a and 6.b, by monitoring the whole running process of different workloads, we can find that OrientStream can save 8%-15% CPU usage and 38%-48% memory usage respectively. Among them, TM can save 8% of the CPU usage and 48% of the memory usage due to its memory intensive characteristic. WC save 12% of the CPU usage and 38% of the memory usage due to its communication intensive characteristic. Q3 can save 15% of the CPU usage and 45% of the memory usage due to its compute intensive characteristic. Note that we ignore the time overhead of switching to a new topology.

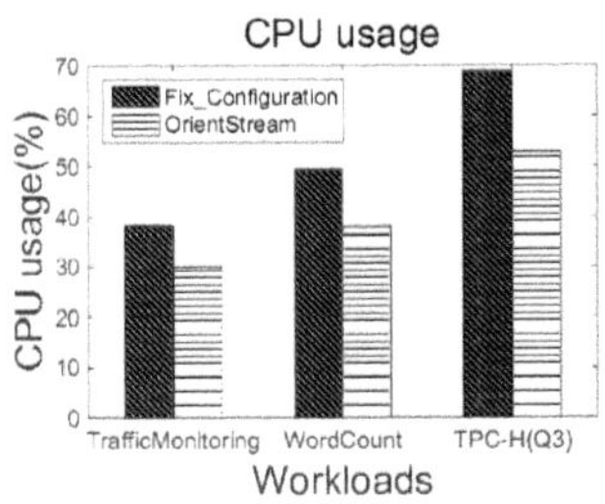

(a) CPU Usage

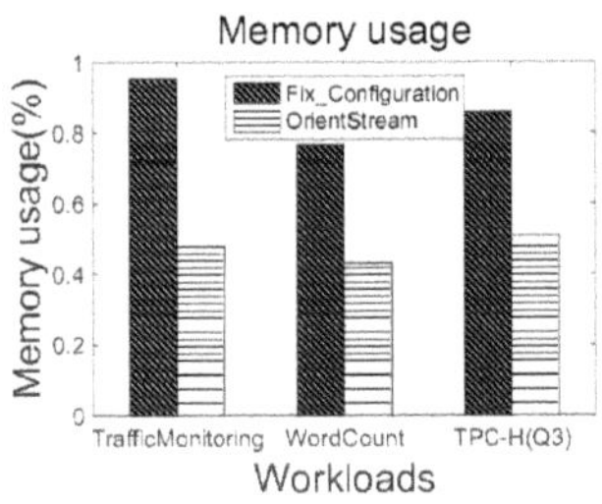

(b) Memory Usage

Figure 6: Resource Usage

7. CONCLUSIONS AND FUTURE WORK

In this paper. we propose OrientStream to predict the resource usage of DDSMS by using incremental learning techniques, develop the learning tool that can be implemented data acquisition automatically based on the different workloads. Our approach uses MOA and Weka toolkits to build real-time prediction model by defining four-level features extraction mechanism. In addition, we introduce the EDKR algorithm and the outlier execution detection mechanism for improving the prediction accuracy, and verify the validity of our methods. In the future, we plan to build up the state operator for saving the state information at run time. In this case, we can achieve the arbitrary adjustment of different configurations without building a new topology.

8. ACKNOWLEDGMENTS

This research was partially supported by the grants from the Natural Science Foundation of China (No. 61532016, 61532010, 61379050, 91224008); the National Key R&D Program (No. 2016YFB1000602, 2016YFB1000603); Specialized Research Fund for the Doctoral Program of Higher Education (No. 20130004130001), and the Fundamental Research Funds for the Central Universities, the Research Funds of Renmin University (No. 11XNL010).

9. REFERENCES

[1] https://github.com/epfldata/squall/.

[2] http://moa.cs.waikato.ac.nz/.

[3] http://www.cs.waikato.ac.nz/ml/weka/.

[4] https://github.com/intel-hadoop/HiBench.

[5] D. W. Aha, D. Kibler, and M. K. Albert. Instance-based learning algorithms. *Machine Learning*, 6(1):37–66, 1991.

[6] M. Akdere, U. C?Etintemel, M. Riondato, E. Upfal, and S. B. Zdonik. Learning-based query performance modeling and prediction. In *Data Engineering (ICDE), 2012 IEEE 28th International Conference on*, pages 390–401, 2012.

[7] L. Aniello, R. Baldoni, and L. Querzoni. Adaptive online scheduling in storm. In *ACM International Conference on Distributed Event-Based Systems*, pages 207–218, 2013.

[8] C. Bishop. *Mixture Density Networks.* 1994.

[9] P. Domingos and G. Hulten. Mining high-speed data streams. In *ACM SIGKDD International Conference on Knowledge Discovery & Data Mining*, pages 71–80, 2000.

[10] T. Z. J. Fu, J. Ding, R. T. B. Ma, M. Winslett, Y. Yang, and Z. Zhang. Drs: Dynamic resource scheduling for real-time analytics over fast streams. *Computer Science*, 690(1):411–420, 2015.

[11] G. H. John and P. Langley. Estimating continuous distributions in bayesian classifiers. In *Proceedings of the Eleventh conference on Uncertainty in artificial intelligence*, pages 338–345, 2013.

[12] A. Khoshkbarforoushha, R. Ranjan, R. Gaire, P. P. Jayaraman, J. Hosking, and E. Abbasnejad. Resource usage estimation of data stream processing workloads in datacenter clouds. *Computer Science*, 2015.

[13] J. Kreps, L. Corp, N. Narkhede, J. Rao, and L. Corp. Kafka: a distributed messaging system for log processing. netdbąŕ11. *Proceedings of the Netdb*, 2011.

[14] J. Li, A. C. Nig, V. Narasayya, and S. Chaudhuri. Robust estimation of resource consumption for sql queries using statistical techniques. *Eprint Arxiv*, 5(11):1555–1566, 2012.

[15] L. Neumeyer, B. Robbins, A. Nair, and A. Kesari. S4: Distributed stream computing platform. In *Icdmw 2010, the IEEE International Conference on Data Mining Workshops, Sydney, Australia, 14 December*, pages 170–177, 2010.

[16] N. C. Oza and S. Russell. Experimental comparisons of online and batch versions of bagging and boosting. *Carcinogenesis*, 22(3):515–517(3), 2001.

[17] N. Poggi, D. Carrera, A. Call, and S. Mendoza. Aloja: A systematic study of hadoop deployment variables to enable automated characterization of cost-effectiveness. In *IEEE International Conference on Big Data*, pages 905–913, 2015.

[18] J. R. Quinlan. *C4.5: programs for machine learning.* Morgan Kaufmann Publishers Inc., 2014.

[19] M. J. Sax, M. Castellanos, Q. Chen, and M. Hsu. Aeolus: An optimizer for distributed intra-node-parallel streaming systems. In *IEEE International Conference on Data Engineering*, pages 1280–1283, 2013.

[20] A. Toshniwal, S. Taneja, A. Shukla, K. Ramasamy, J. M. Patel, S. Kulkarni, J. Jackson, K. Gade, M. Fu, and J. Donham. Storm@twitter. 2014.

[21] Y. Zheng, L. Zhang, X. Xie, and W. Y. Ma. Mining interesting locations and travel sequences from gps trajectories. In *International Conference on World Wide Web*, pages 791–800, 2009.

Tag2Word: Using Tags to Generate Words for Content Based Tag Recommendation

Yong Wu
State Key Laboratory for Novel Software Technology, Nanjing University, China
wy@smail.nju.edu.cn

Yuan Yao
State Key Laboratory for Novel Software Technology, Nanjing University, China
y.yao@nju.edu.cn

Feng Xu
State Key Laboratory for Novel Software Technology, Nanjing University, China
xf@nju.edu.cn

Hanghang Tong
Arizona State University, USA
hanghang.tong@asu.edu

Jian Lu
State Key Laboratory for Novel Software Technology, Nanjing University, China
lj@nju.edu.cn

ABSTRACT

Tag recommendation is helpful for the categorization and searching of online content. Existing tag recommendation methods can be divided into collaborative filtering methods and content based methods. In this paper, we put our focus on the content based tag recommendation due to its wider applicability. Our key observation is the *tag-content co-occurrence*, i.e., many tags have appeared multiple times in the corresponding content. Based on this observation, we propose a generative model (Tag2Word), where we generate the words based on the tag-word distribution as well as the tag itself. Experimental evaluations on real data sets demonstrate that the proposed method outperforms several existing methods in terms of recommendation accuracy, while enjoying linear scalability.

Keywords

tag recommendation; tag-content co-occurrence; generative model

1. INTRODUCTION

Tags usually indicate the keywords that help people to describe the online content, and therefore allow better information organization and retrieval. However, over 50% online content lacks tag information or even does not have tags at all [13]. Additionally, it is often painstaking for users (even the content creators) to manually tag the online content, especially under many situations where the users are not certain about what the appropriate tags are. Therefore, tag recommendation is necessary to automatically provide suitable tags for online content.

CIKM '16, October 24–28, 2016, Indianapolis, IN, USA.

DOI: http://dx.doi.org/10.1145/2983323.2983682

Roughly, existing tag recommendation methods can be divided into collaborative filtering methods and content based methods. Collaborative filtering methods aim to provide subjective tag recommendations based on users' historical behavior. On the other hand, content based methods take the content as input, and therefore have a wider applicability (see Section 5 for a review).

In this work, we put our focus on the content based tag recommendation. Our key observation is the *tag-content co-occurrence* phenomenon that widely exists in many online content sites. Figure 1 gives several examples from different websites. As we can see from the figures, many tags have appeared multiple times in the corresponding content. However, such co-occurrence is largely ignored by existing work.

In this paper, we propose a model Tag2Word to leverage the tag-content co-occurrence phenomenon. We take a generative view by generating the content words based on the tag-word distribution[1] and the tag itself. In other words, when generating a word, we directly use the tag as the word with a probability (which can be learned for different domains), and sample the word from the tag-word distribution otherwise.

The main contributions of this paper include:

- A generative model for content based tag recommendation. The model makes use the tag-content co-occurrence observation. Typically, we use the title and the body of a post as the content (Tag2Word). To speed up, we can simply use the title as content (Tag2Word_0).

- Experimental evaluations on the two data sets demonstrating the effectiveness and efficiency of our proposed methods. For example, compared with the existing best competitors, the proposed methods can lead up to 15.0% improvement in terms of prediction accuracy, while enjoying linear scalability.

The rest of the paper is organized as follows. Section 2 presents the problem definition. Section 3 describes the proposed method. Section 4 presents the experimental eval-

[1]The tag-word distribution or the topic-word distribution can be learned by topic models.

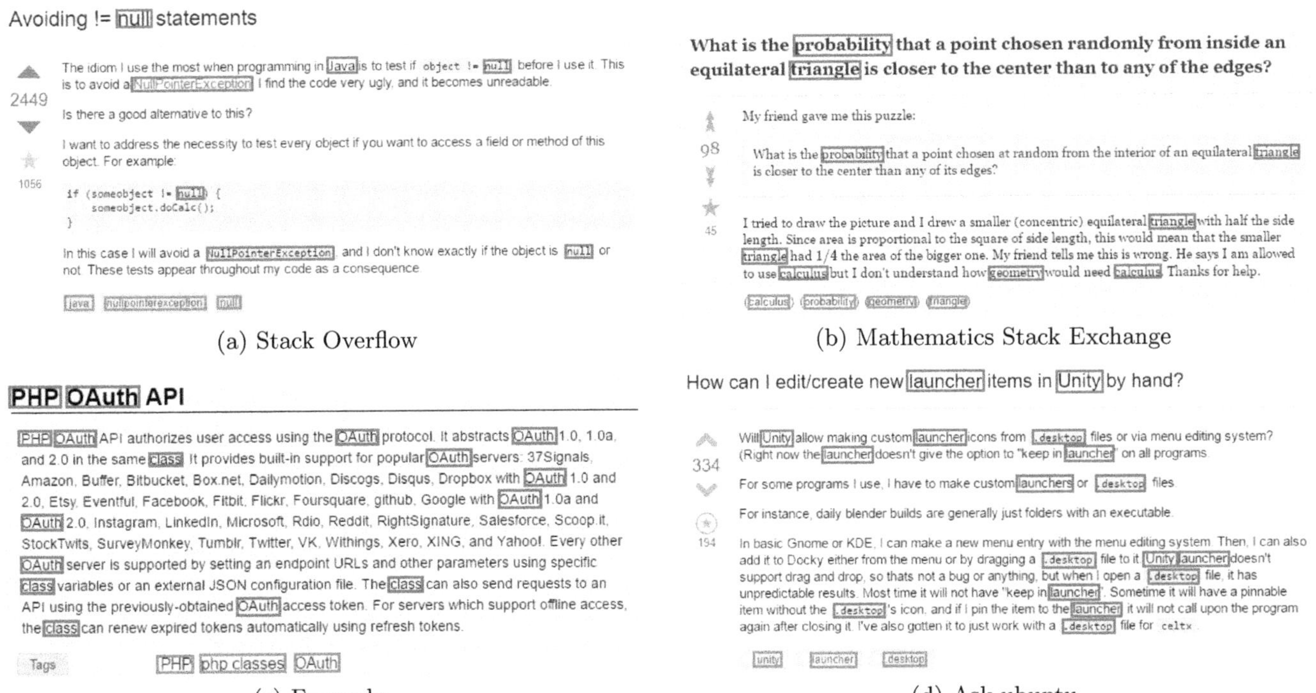

(a) Stack Overflow

(b) Mathematics Stack Exchange

(c) Freecode

(d) Ask ubuntu

Figure 1: Tag-content co-occurrence examples on different websites.

Table 1: Symbols.

Symbol	Definition and Description
D	Collection of documents
V	Vocabulary
T	Tag space
M	Total number of documents
K	Total number of latent topics
$\overrightarrow{W}_d$	List of words in document d
$\overrightarrow{\Lambda}_d$	List of tags in document d
N_d	Number of words in document d

uations. Section 5 reviews related work, and Section 6 concludes the paper.

2. PROBLEM DEFINITION

In this section, we present the problem statement. Table 1 lists the main symbols used throughout this paper. We use D to stand for a collection of input documents[2]. Each document d contains a list of words $\overrightarrow{W}_d$ and a list of tags $\overrightarrow{\Lambda}_d$. All the words form the vocabulary V, and all the tags form the tag space T. We denote K as the total number of latent topics in the input documents.

With these notations, we define the tag recommendation problem as

PROBLEM 1. *Tag Recommendation Problem*

Given: *(1) a collection of documents D, where each document $d \in D$ has its own words $\overrightarrow{W}_d$ and tags $\overrightarrow{\Lambda}_d$, and*

(2) a new document $d_{new} \notin D$ which only contains words $\overrightarrow{W}_{d_{new}}$;

Find: *the estimated list of tags for the new document d_{new}.*

[2]In this paper, we interchangeably use 'document' and 'post' as both of them indicate the online content that we aim to recommend tags for.

In the above problem definition, although not explicitly stated, words in $\overrightarrow{\Lambda}_d$ may have appeared multiple times in $\overrightarrow{W}_d$ for a given document d. In addition, the observation holds when we only use the words in the title as the content. Identifying and exploiting such co-occurrence is the main difference between our work and the existing work on this problem.

3. THE TAG2WORD MODEL

In this section, we present the proposed Tag2Word model for Problem 1. We use generative models to incorporate the tag-content co-occurrence, as it is a more natural way compared to the discriminative models. Figure 2 shows the graphical representation for Tag2Word.

As we can see from the figure, there are three parts in Tag2Word:

- First, Tag2Word builds on the LDA model [2] to generate words for documents. For each document, LDA assumes that it has several latent topics (θ). Words are generated from a specific topic (z) and the topic-word distributions (Φ).

- Second, following the LLDA model [17], we assume that the tags Λ determine the latent topics during the generative process, and constrain that tag and latent topic are one-one correspondent. That is, each tag is

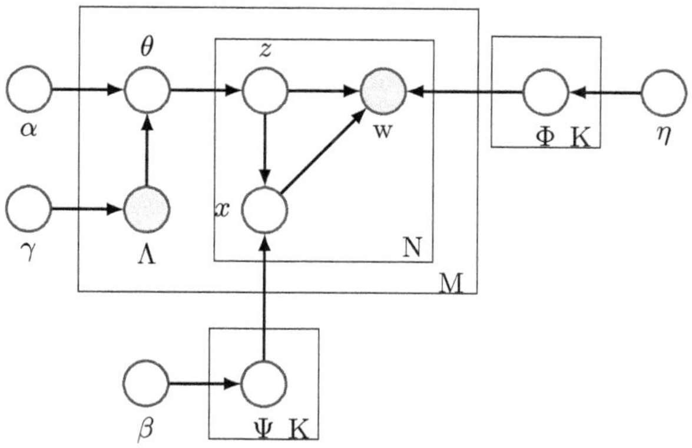

Figure 2: Graphical representation for Tag2Word.

Table 2: Generative process of Tag2Word.

1	*For each topic* $k \in [1, K]$
2	*Generate* $\overrightarrow{\Phi}_k \sim Dir(\overrightarrow{\eta})$
3	*Generate* $\Psi_k \sim Beta(\overrightarrow{\beta})$
4	*For each document* $d \in [1, M]$
5	*For each topic* $k \in [1, K]$
6	*Generate* $\Lambda_{d,k} \in \{0, 1\} \sim Bernoulli(\gamma_k)$
7	*Generate* $\overrightarrow{\alpha}_d = \overrightarrow{\Lambda}_d \circ \overrightarrow{\alpha}$
8	*Generate* $\overrightarrow{\theta}_d \sim Dir(\overrightarrow{\alpha}_d)$
9	*For each word* $i \in [1, N_d]$
10	*Generate* $z_i \sim Mult(\overrightarrow{\theta}_d)$
11	*Generate* $x_i \in \{0, 1\} \sim Bernoulli(\Psi_{z_i})$
12	*if* $x_i = 1$
13	*Generate* $w_i \sim Identity(z_i)$
14	*else*
15	*Generate* $w_i \sim Mult(\overrightarrow{\Phi}_{z_i})$

associated with one topic, and the topic number of a document is the same with its tag number[3].

- Third, to make use of the tag-content co-occurrence, we further add a latent variable x to indicate the probability that the word w is generated by the tag itself (z) or by the tag-word distribution (Φ). The latent variable x is sampled from a Bernoulli distribution (Ψ), and it is dependent on the specific topic (z), i.e., different topics may have different probabilities.

The generative process for our model is summarized in Table 2. For each topic k, Step 2 draws a multinomial topic-word distribution $\overrightarrow{\Phi}_k$ from a Dirichlet prior $\overrightarrow{\eta}$, and Step 3 draws a Bernoulli distribution Ψ_k from a Beta prior $\overrightarrow{\beta}$. Here, Ψ_k indicates the probability to directly use the tag as the generated word for tag/topic k. For each document d, a multinomial distribution $\overrightarrow{\theta}_d$ is drawn over restricted topics that correspond to its tags $\overrightarrow{\Lambda}_d$[4] (Steps 5-8). In Step 7, we compute the Hardamard product between $\overrightarrow{\Lambda}_d$ and $\overrightarrow{\alpha}$, so that the topic assignment z_i for each word in document d is limited within its own tags. For each word i, we use a latent variable x_i to determine where it is generated from. When x_i equals 1, the word is directly generated using the tag z_i (Steps 12-13). Otherwise, if x_i equals 0, the word is generated from the multinomial distributions $\overrightarrow{\Phi}_{z_i}$ for the topic/tag (Steps 14-15).

To solve the model, we can develop a Gibbs sampling algorithm to train the parameters. However, Gibbs sampling is inherently stochastic and unstable when iterations are not enough. On the other hand, it is noticed that the CVB0 learning algorithm [1] converges faster and more stable than the Gibbs sampling algorithm [16]. Therefore, we choose to build our learning algorithm based on CVB0 approximation algorithm. The details are omitted for brevity.

[3]The total number of topics is the same with the total number of tags, i.e., $K = |T|$.

[4]The tags $\overrightarrow{\Lambda}_d$ in document d are observed variables in the model, and the prior γ is unused. We include it for completeness.

4. EXPERIMENTS

In this section, we present our experimental evaluations. The experiments are designed to answer the following questions:

- *Effectiveness*: How accurate is the proposed algorithm for tag recommendation?
- *Efficiency*: How scalable is the proposed algorithm?

4.1 Experimental Setup

We study two data sets of Stack Overflow (SO) and Mathematics Stack Exchange (Math). Both data sets are officially published and publicly available[5]. For each data set, it contains question posts and their corresponding tags. Each question post contains a title and a body. We need some preprocessing on the data sets. For the posts, we remove the stopwords and some low frequency words to reduce noise. We deliberately keep those words that are tags (e.g., C or VB). All the remaining words are then stemmed. For the tags, we remove some low frequency tags as they are seldom used. Table 3 shows the statistics of the two preprocessed data sets.

For these two data sets, we randomly select 90% posts as training data and use the rest as test data. Since some compared methods are computationally prohibitive on the whole SO data, we also randomly sample subsets (SO-10K and SO-100K) of the whole SO data to compare their effectiveness results. For the three hyper-parameters, we fix α, η, and β to $50/K$, 0.01, and 0.1, respectively.

As to evaluation metrics, we adopt Recall@n for effectiveness comparison. The reason is that finding all the useful tags in the recommendation list is important for tag recommendation tasks [19]. As to the list size n, we choose $n = 5$ and $n = 10$ as such choices will not cause many burdens to the users. Recall@n is defined as follows

$$Recall@n = \frac{1}{M} \sum_{i=1}^{M} \frac{hit(n)_i}{tag_i} \quad (1)$$

where M is the number of posts in the data, $hit(n)_i$ is the number of tags that have been successfully recommended in the top-n ranked list, and tag_i is the number of actual tags of the ith post.

For efficiency, we simply report the wall-clock time of the proposed algorithm. All the experiments were run on a machine with eight 3.4GHz Intel Cores and 32GB memory.

[5]http://blog.stackoverflow.com/tags/cc-wiki-dump/

Table 3: **Statistics of the Datasets**

Dataset	# of posts	Post vocabulary size	# of tags	# of average words per post
Math	19950	7705	461	54
SO	3350978	9357	1035	81

Table 4: Effective Comparisons on SO-10K data. Higher is better. Tag2Word outperforms all the compared methods.

Methods	Recall@5	Recall@10
LLDA	0.47805	0.58870
Link-LDA	0.33651	0.43010
MATAR	0.48988	0.55168
Snaff	0.38248	0.48103
Maxide	0.38995	0.46815
Tag2Word	0.56330	0.67707
Tag2Word_0	0.58538	0.65870

Table 5: Effective Comparisons on SO-100K data. Higher is better. Tag2Word outperforms all the compared methods.

Methods	Recall@5	Recall@10
LLDA	0.54254	0.64804
Link-LDA	0.32907	0.42514
MATAR	0.53774	0.59125
Snaff	0.45165	0.54921
Maxide	0.50998	0.62361
Tag2Word	0.60939	0.70339
Tag2Word_0	0.63607	0.71477

4.2 Experiemental Results

Next, we present the experimental results.

4.2.1 Empirical Study

We first empirically study the tag-content co-occurrence in the two data sets. We find that more than 70% tags have appeared in the content of the SO data, while only less than 30% tags have appeared in the content of the Math data. Moreover, there are over 30% posts in the SO data that have all tags appeared in the content. We also study the degree of tag-content co-occurrence when only the title of the post is used as content. We found that 65.3% posts in SO data and 15.4% posts in Math data have at least one tag appeared in the title.

Overall, we find that the tag-content co-occurrence exists in both data sets, although the co-occurrence degree may be different in different domains. Additionally, tags may appear in both the title and the body of the content.

4.2.2 Effectiveness Results

For effectiveness, we compare the proposed Tag2Word with several existing methods including LLDA [17], Link-LDA [3], MATAR [9], Snaff [10], and Maxide [31]. In the compared methods, LLDA and Link-LDA are topic models, MATAR and Maxide are multi-label learning methods, and Snaff is a hybrid method. The results are shown in Table 4 - 7. In the tables, we show the results of both Tag2Word and Tag2Word_0, where Tag2Word takes both title and body as content and Tag2Word_0 takes only title as content. On the whole SO data, we do not show the results of Maxide and MATAR as they are computationally prohibitive (e.g., cannot return results in 24 hours).

There are several observations from the tables. First, Tag2Word outperforms all the compared existing methods on all the data sets. For example, on SO-10K data, Tag2Word improves its best competitors (MATAR and LLDA, respectively) by 14.9% wrt Recall@5 and by 15.0% wrt Recall@10. On Math data, Tag2Word is 3.7% and 4.1% better than the best competitor LLDA for Recall@5 and Recall@10, respectively. This result indicates that the tag-content co-occurrence indeed can help improve the recommendation accuracy, especially considering that LLDA can be a special

Table 6: Effective Comparisons on whole SO data. Higher is better. Tag2Word outperforms all the compared methods.

Methods	Recall@5	Recall@10
LLDA	0.55660	0.66422
Link-LDA	0.33847	0.43429
MATAR	-	-
Snaff	0.46402	0.58363
Maxide	-	-
Tag2Word	0.62169	0.71036
Tag2Word_0	0.64548	0.72682

case of Tag2Word if we delete the tag-content co-occurrence considerations in the model. Second, we find that the improvement of Tag2Word is more significant on the SO data than the Math data. This is probably due to the fact that the tag-content co-occurrence degree is higher on SO than that on Math. Third, comparing the results on three SO data, we can find that the recommendation accuracy improves as the training data size increases. Finally, Tag2Word_0 can already achieve better results than the existing methods on the SO data. Tag2Word_0 can even outperform Tag2Word in some cases. This is due to the fact that even when only the title is considered, the tag-content co-occurrence degree is already very high on the SO data. This means that we can recommend tags solely based on the title of the content, if there are plenty tags appeared in the title of the content.

4.2.3 Efficiency Results

Next, we study the scalability of the proposed algorithm in the training stage. We vary the size of the training data on the SO data, and report the results of wall-clock time in Figure 3. Similar results are observed on Math data, and we omit the figures for brevity.

As we can see from the figure, both Tag2Word and Tag2Word_0 scale linearly wrt the size of training data (the number of posts), which is also consistent with our algorithm analysis in Section 4.2. Additionally, Tag2Word_0 runs much faster than Tag2Word (around 9x faster), as it only involves the title as input.

We also compare the prediction time for a new post at the

Table 7: **Effective Comparisons on Math data. Higher is better. Tag2Word outperforms all the compared methods.**

Methods	Recall@5	Recall@10
LLDA	0.58859	0.68992
Link-LDA	0.43850	0.58259
MATAR	0.55271	0.65750
Snaff	0.48833	0.57042
Maxide	0.52436	0.64942
Tag2Word	0.61057	0.71797
Tag2Word_0	0.59352	0.68529

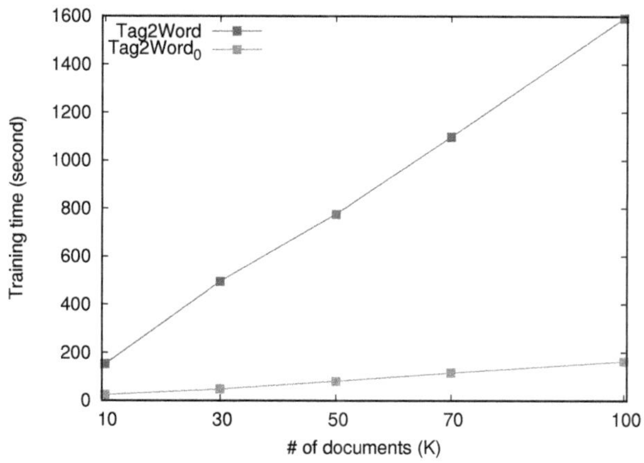

Figure 3: Scalability of the proposed algorithm2. Both Tag2Word and Tag2Word_0 scale linearly wrt the data size.

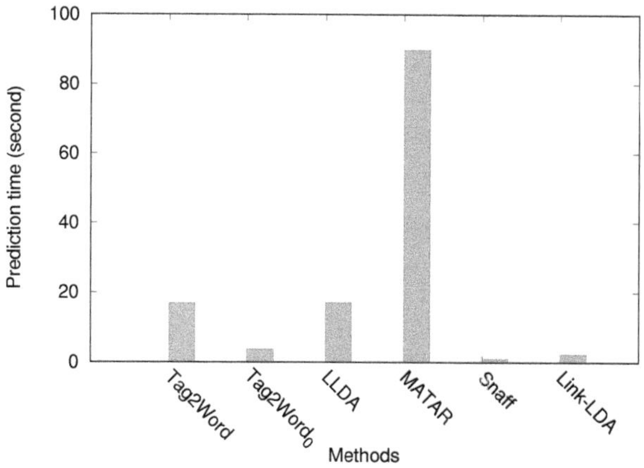

Figure 4: Response time comparison. Tag2Word_0 has a favorable response speed.

response stage of different methods. The results on Math data are showed in Figure 4. Similar results are observed on the SO data. As we can see, both Tag2Word and Tag2Word_0 can make predictions within 20 seconds. Tag2Word and LLDA have comparable response speed. The response time of MATAR is long as it adopts the lazy strategy. Snaff and Link-LDA are faster, andTag2Word_0 can have close response time with them.

5. RELATED WORK

In this section, we briefly review the related work. We roughly divide existing tag recommendation methods into collaborative filtering method and content-based method.

The key insight of collaborative filtering method is to employ the tagging histories (i.e., user-item-tag tuples). For example, Symeonidis et al. [26] model users, items, and tags into 3-order tensors and use high-order singular value decomposition to recommend tags; Rendle et al. [19, 20] further model the pairwise rankings into tensor factorization; Fang et al. [4] propose a non-linear tensor factorization method via Gaussian kernel; Feng et al. [5] model a social tagging system as a multi-type graph, and recommend tag by learning the weights of nodes and edges in the graph. Other examples in this category include [7, 23, 24, 6]. Methods in this class are more suitable to recommend a list of personalized tags for a fixed set of items, and they are not able to recommend tags for new content.

In contrast to collaborative filtering method, content based method takes the content as input, and therefore could be used to recommend tags for new content. For example, Sood et al. [25] and Mishne [14] leverage previous tags associated with similar content to recommend tags for new content. Murfi et al. [15] first use keyword extraction to filter candidate tags and then apply non-negative matrix factorization for tag recommendation; Wang et al. [28] also extract keywords, and then apply association rules to recommend tags. Erosheva et al. [3] extends LDA by mixing the generation of tags and words; Ramage et al. [17] also extends LDA by constraining the one-one correspondence between tags and latent topics. Other examples include [8, 18, 21, 29, 22]. Our method falls into this category of content based method. Different from the above work, our main observation is from the tag-content co-occurrence.

Recently, there are also some other lines of research about tag recommendation. For example, Lops et al. [12] design a hybrid tag recommender that combines the collaborative filtering and content based methods. Liu et al. [11] explore locations to recommend tags for photos. Xia et al. [30] combine several components for software information sites. Wang et al. [27] adopt a deep learning model and combine probabilistic matrix factorization to find effective and compact content representation for tag recommendation.

6. CONCLUSIONS

In this paper, we have proposed a content based tag recommendation model Tag2Word as well as its variant Tag2Word_0. Our key observation is that the tags usually appear as regular words in the content. Then, the proposed model takes a generative view to incorporate such observation to improve the recommendation accuracy. Experimental evaluations on two real data sets show that the proposed methods can lead up to 15.0% improvement over the best competitors in terms of prediction accuracy, while enjoying linear scalability in the training stage.

7. ACKNOWLEDGMENTS

This work is supported by the National Basic Research Program of China (No. 2015CB352202) and the National Natural Science Foundation of China (No. 91318301). This work is partially supported by the National Science Foundation under Grant No. IIS1017415, by DTRA under the grant number HDTRA1-16-0017, by Army Research Office under the contract number W911NF-16-1-0168, by National Institutes of Health under the grant number R01LM011986, Region II University Transportation Center under the project number 49997-33 25 and a Baidu gift.

8. REFERENCES

[1] A. Asuncion, M. Welling, P. Smyth, and Y. W. Teh. On smoothing and inference for topic models. In *UAI*, pages 27–34, 2009.

[2] D. M. Blei, A. Y. Ng, and M. I. Jordan. Latent dirichlet allocation. *the Journal of machine Learning research*, 3:993–1022, 2003.

[3] E. Erosheva, S. Fienberg, and J. Lafferty. Mixed-membership models of scientific publications. *Proceedings of the National Academy of Sciences*, 101(suppl 1):5220–5227, 2004.

[4] X. Fang, R. Pan, G. Cao, X. He, and W. Dai. Personalized tag recommendation through nonlinear tensor factorization using gaussian kernel. In *AAAO*, 2015.

[5] W. Feng and J. Wang. Incorporating heterogeneous information for personalized tag recommendation in social tagging systems. In *KDD*, pages 1276–1284, 2012.

[6] S. Hamouda and N. Wanas. Put-tag: personalized user-centric tag recommendation for social bookmarking systems. *Social network analysis and mining*, 1(4):377–385, 2011.

[7] R. Jäschke, L. Marinho, A. Hotho, L. Schmidt-Thieme, and G. Stumme. Tag recommendations in social bookmarking systems. *AI Communications*, 21(4):231–247, 2008.

[8] R. Krestel, P. Fankhauser, and W. Nejdl. Latent dirichlet allocation for tag recommendation. In *RecSys*, pages 61–68, 2009.

[9] L. Li, Y. Yao, F. Xu, and J. Lu. Matar: Keywords enhanced multi-label learning for tag recommendation. In *APWeb*, pages 268–279, 2015.

[10] M. Lipczak and E. Milios. Learning in efficient tag recommendation. In *RecSys*, pages 167–174, 2010.

[11] J. Liu, Z. Li, J. Tang, Y. Jiang, and H. Lu. Personalized geo-specific tag recommendation for photos on social websites. *IEEE Transactions on Multimedia*, 16(3):588–600, 2014.

[12] P. Lops, M. De Gemmis, G. Semeraro, C. Musto, and F. Narducci. Content-based and collaborative techniques for tag recommendation: an empirical evaluation. *Journal of Intelligent Information Systems*, 40(1):41–61, 2013.

[13] Y.-T. Lu, S.-I. Yu, T.-C. Chang, and J. Y.-j. Hsu. A content-based method to enhance tag recommendation. In *IJCAI*, volume 9, pages 2064–2069, 2009.

[14] G. Mishne. Autotag: a collaborative approach to automated tag assignment for weblog posts. In *WWW*, pages 953–954, 2006.

[15] H. Murfi and K. Obermayer. A two-level learning hierarchy of concept based keyword extraction for tag recommendations. *ECML PKDD discovery challenge*, pages 201–214, 2009.

[16] I. Porteous, D. Newman, A. Ihler, A. Asuncion, P. Smyth, and M. Welling. Fast collapsed gibbs sampling for latent dirichlet allocation. In *KDD*, pages 569–577, 2008.

[17] D. Ramage, D. Hall, R. Nallapati, and C. D. Manning. Labeled lda: A supervised topic model for credit attribution in multi-labeled corpora. In *EMNLP*, pages 248–256, 2009.

[18] D. Ramage, C. D. Manning, and S. Dumais. Partially labeled topic models for interpretable text mining. In *KDD*, pages 457–465, 2011.

[19] S. Rendle, L. Balby Marinho, A. Nanopoulos, and L. Schmidt-Thieme. Learning optimal ranking with tensor factorization for tag recommendation. In *KDD*, pages 727–736, 2009.

[20] S. Rendle and L. Schmidt-Thieme. Pairwise interaction tensor factorization for personalized tag recommendation. In *WSDM*, pages 81–90, 2010.

[21] A. K. Saha, R. K. Saha, and K. A. Schneider. A discriminative model approach for suggesting tags automatically for stack overflow questions. In *Proceedings of the 10th Working Conference on Mining Software Repositories*, pages 73–76. IEEE Press, 2013.

[22] P. Seitlinger, D. Kowald, C. Trattner, and T. Ley. Recommending tags with a model of human categorization. In *CIKM*, pages 2381–2386, 2013.

[23] B. Sigurbjörnsson and R. Van Zwol. Flickr tag recommendation based on collective knowledge. In *WWW*, pages 327–336, 2008.

[24] Y. Song, L. Zhang, and C. L. Giles. Automatic tag recommendation algorithms for social recommender systems. *ACM Transactions on the Web (TWEB)*, 5(1):4, 2011.

[25] S. Sood, S. Owsley, K. J. Hammond, and L. Birnbaum. Tagassist: Automatic tag suggestion for blog posts. In *ICWSM*, 2007.

[26] P. Symeonidis, A. Nanopoulos, and Y. Manolopoulos. Tag recommendations based on tensor dimensionality reduction. In *RecSys*, pages 43–50, 2008.

[27] H. Wang, X. Shi, and D.-Y. Yeung. Relational stacked denoising autoencoder for tag recommendation. In *AAAI*, pages 3052–3058, 2015.

[28] J. Wang, L. Hong, and B. D. Davison. Tag recommendation using keywords and association rules. In *KDD*, 2009.

[29] T. Wang, H. Wang, G. Yin, C. X. Ling, X. Li, and P. Zou. Tag recommendation for open source software. *Frontiers of Computer Science*, 8(1):69–82, 2014.

[30] X. Xia, D. Lo, X. Wang, and B. Zhou. Tag recommendation in software information sites. In *Proceedings of the 10th Working Conference on Mining Software Repositories*, pages 287–296. IEEE Press, 2013.

[31] M. Xu, R. Jin, and Z.-H. Zhou. Speedup matrix completion with side information: Application to multi-label learning. In *NIPS*, pages 2301–2309, 2013.

Digesting Multilingual Reader Comments via Latent Discussion Topics with Commonality and Specificity*

Bei Shi[1], Wai Lam[1], Lidong Bing[2] and Yinqing Xu[1]
[1]Department of Systems Engineering and Engineering Management, The Chinese University of Hong Kong
[2]Machine Learning Department, Carnegie Mellon University
[1]{bshi,wlam,yqxu}@se.cuhk.edu.hk
[2]lbing@cs.cmu.edu

ABSTRACT

Many news websites from different regions in the world allow readers to write comments in their own languages about an event. Digesting such enormous amount of comments in different languages is difficult. One elegant way to digest and organize these comments is to detect latent discussion topics with the consideration of language attributes. Some discussion topics are common topics shared between languages whereas some topics are specifically dominated by a particular language. To tackle this task of discovering discussion topics that exhibit commonality or specificity from news reader comments written in different languages, we propose a new model called TDCS based on graphical models, which can cope with the language gap and detect language-common and language-specific latent discussion topics simultaneously. Our TDCS model also exploits comment-oriented clues via a scalable Dirichlet Multinomial Regression method. To learn the model parameters, we develop an inference method which alternates between EM and Gibbs sampling. Experimental results show that our proposed TDCS model can provide an effective way to digest multilingual news reader comments.

Keywords

multilingual news reader comments; commonality and specificity; latent discussion topics

1. INTRODUCTION

The volume of comments under news websites from different continents in the world reporting the same significant events is often enormous especially for popular events. For instance, on March 25 2015, Lee Kuan Yew, the first Prime President of Singapore, died at the Singapore General Hospital. Upon the happening of this event, many news articles around the world reported it and many readers from different continents commented on this event. We observe that there were more than 8000 English and more than 5000 Chinese reader comments from *Yahoo!* News[1] and *Sina* News[2] respectively. Obviously, it is difficult to digest all the reader comments manually. One elegant way is to organize the comments via discussion topics which are not known in advance. For example, when analyzing the comments manually, we find that many comments are related to a topic about expressing R.I.P. This discussion topic is not previously known and can only be identified after analyzing the content of reader comments. We also observe that readers from a particular region tend to write comments in their own preferred languages. Despite different backgrounds, readers may use their own languages to talk about similar topics. We can attribute such commonality to the widespread adoption of social networks connecting people in different languages [7]. In this paper, such common topics are called **language-common** discussion topics. For example, the discussion topic of expressing R.I.P mentioned above is a language-common topic because it is commonly found in both English and Chinese reader comments. Language-common discussion topics indicate some common concerns or interests of readers from regions with different languages. On the other hand, readers in different languages, express not only common discussion topics but also specific discussion topics with respect to their own languages. For example, referring to the event about the death of Lee Kuan Yew mentioned above, we also observe from the news reader comments that many English-speaking readers gave critical remarks to President Obama based on the comparison with Lee Kuan Yew. On the other hand, many Chinese-speaking readers remarked on the topic about the support of President Xi to Singapore. Naturally, readers originated from different language backgrounds, would discuss some different topics specific to their own characteristics such as cultures or customs. In this paper, such topics specifically dominated by a particular language are called **language-specific** discussion topics. Detecting language-specific discussion topics can provide insight for global market and international business [12]. With awareness of customers' characteristics associated with languages, better and more suitable advertising strategy can be adopted.

To support the automation of the reader comment analysis mentioned above, we investigate the task of detecting discussion topics with commonality and specificity from multilingual news reader comments. The main goal of this task is to discover specifically language-common and language-specific latent discussion topics from raw multilingual news reader comments for a news event. Figure 2 depicts some sample discussion topics discovered by our proposed model for the event of the death of Lee Kuan Yew. Both

*The work described in this paper is substantially supported by grants from the Research Grant Council of the Hong Kong Special Administrative Region, China (Project Code: 14203414). This work is also affiliated with the CUHK MoE-Microsoft Key Laboratory of Human-centric Computing and Interface Technologies.

CIKM'16, October 24-28, 2016, Indianapolis, IN, USA

DOI: http://dx.doi.org/10.1145/2983323.2983683

[1]http://news.yahoo.com
[2]http://news.sina.com.cn/world/

kinds of discussion topics, namely, language-common and language-specific discussion topics mentioned above can be detected. Such technology can be deployed to build a reader comment digest system that can organize comments by language-common and language-specific discussion topics, and then rank the topics by popularity. This provides a functionality for analyzing characteristics associated with languages of readers on a particular event.

There are several challenges in the task. The first challenge is that the discussion topics are not known in advance. We need to discover latent discussion topics from the content of comments automatically. The second challenge is to deal with the language gap, which refers to the observation that the words of reader comments in different languages typically do not co-occur in a piece of comment. The third challenge is to capture the commonality and specificity of discussion topics simultaneously. For reader comments in different languages, language-common topics should capture common semantics from multilingual news reader comments. On the other hand, language-specific topics should reveal specific semantics reflected from the corresponding language. Traditional word matching based methods can only select comment pairs which share words in different languages but cannot capture the commonality or specificity on the topic level.

Recently, there are some research works dealing with news reader comments. Prasojo et al. [10] proposed to organize news reader comments around entities and aspects discussed by readers. Das et al. [3] detected news reader comments which are specific to a particular sentence in the news article. However, these models cannot identify latent discussion topics with commonality and specificity and cannot handle the multilingual setting. Some cross-lingual topic models, such as Muto [2], can extract common topics from multilingual documents. Their model outputs cross-lingual topics of matching word pairs, which focus on finding one-to-one correspondence at the vocabulary level. The PCLSA model proposed by [14], which uses a mixture of English words and Chinese words to represent common topics, is able to detect language-common topics. PCLSA incorporates bilingual constraints into the Probabilistic Latent Semantic Analysis (PLSA) model [5] and assumes that word pairs in the dictionary share the same probability in a common topic. One limitation of both of the above models is that they just identify common topics from multilingual documents without considering the specificity of discussion topics with respect to each language. Moreover, these models do not consider comment-oriented clues, such as the thread relationship among the comments.

To tackle the task, we propose a new model called TDCS based on graphical models, which is able to detect latent discussion topics with commonality and specificity from multilingual news reader comments. In this paper, we focus on dealing with two languages, namely, English and Chinese news reader comments. Our model is able to cope with the language gap and detect both language-common and language-specific discussion topics simultaneously. Our TDCS model also considers comment-oriented clues. One such clue is the consideration of thread relationship among the comments. It can be observed that reader comments originated from the same thread very likely belong to the same discussion topic. Another comment-oriented clue is association relationship between comments and news documents. Our model incorporates comment-oriented clues via a scalable Dirichlet Multinomial Regression (DMR) [8] method. To learn the model parameters in our proposed TDCS model, we develop an inference method which alternates between EM and Gibbs sampling. In the EM phase, we evaluate the prior topic parameters considering comment-oriented clues from the given topic assignments. In the Gibbs sampling phase, we develop a partially collapsed Gibbs sampler which decouples the inference of topic distribution and word distribution. In the sampling procedure, we incorporate bilingual translation relationship, derived from a bilingual dictionary and sample the assignment of language-common and language-specific topics from the current prior topic distribution.

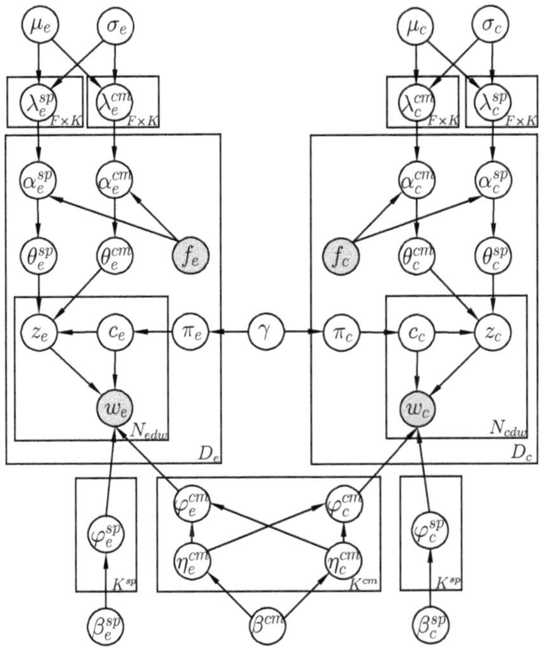

Figure 1: Our proposed graphical model TDCS

In order to evaluate our model, we have prepared a corpus by collecting English and Chinese reader comments from different regions for some events. We perform extensive experiments and the experimental results demonstrate that our model can detect discussion topics with commonality and specificity more effectively than the state-of-the-art model.

2. OUR METHODOLOGY

For a particular event, the input consists of multilingual news reader comments. In this paper, we focus on English and Chinese news reader comments collected from different regions. Each event is processed independently. Formally, given an event, the set of English comments is denoted by $\mathcal{E}$ and the set of Chinese comments is denoted by $\mathcal{C}$. The goal of the task is to discover language-common topics $k^{cm} \in \{1, 2, \ldots, K^{cm}\}$ and language-specific topics $k^{sp} \in \{1, 2, \ldots, K^{sp}\}$ from $\mathcal{E} \cup \mathcal{C}$. We develop a probabilistic graphical model, called **T**opic **D**etection with **C**ommonality and **S**pecificity from multilingual reader comments (TDCS) to tackle the task. The set of multilingual news reader comments of each event are processed independently. Figure 1 shows the graphical model of TDCS. The bottom middle plate represents language-common topics. Each language-common topic k^{cm} is represented by an English word distribution φ_{ek}^{cm} over English vocabulary Λ_e and a Chinese word distribution φ_{ck}^{cm} over Chinese vocabulary Λ_c. We make use of a bilingual dictionary, which is composed of many-to-many word translations among English and Chinese words. To capture common semantics of multilingual news reader comments, we design two auxiliary distributions η_{ek}^{cm}, with dimension $|\Lambda_e|$, and η_{ck}^{cm}, with dimension $|\Lambda_c|$, to help the generation of φ_{ek}^{cm} and φ_{ck}^{cm}. We draw φ_{ek}^{cm} from the mixture of η_{ek}^{cm} and the translation of

η_{ck}^{cm}. It is formulated as:

$$\varphi_{ek}^{cm} \propto \rho(\eta_{ck}^{cm})^T M_{c\to e} + (1-\rho)\eta_{ek}^{cm} \quad \text{where} \quad \eta_{ek}^{cm}, \eta_{ck}^{cm} \sim Dir(\beta^{cm}) \tag{1}$$

where $\rho \in (0,1)$ is a parameter which balances the nature of original topics and transferred information from the other language. $M_{c\to e}$ is a mapping $|\Lambda^c| \times |\Lambda^e|$ matrix from Λ^c to Λ^e. Each element $M_{ij,c\to e}$ is the mapping occurrence probability of the English term w_{ej} given the Chinese term w_{ci} in the set of news reader comments. This probability is calculated as:

$$M_{ij,c\to e} = \frac{C(w_{ej})+1}{|T(w_{ci})| + \sum_{w\in T(w_{ci})} C(w)} \tag{2}$$

where $C(w_{ej})$ is the count of w_{ej} in all news reader comments and $T(w_{ci})$ is the set of English translations of w_{ci} found in the bilingual dictionary. The "add-one" smoothing is adopted. Using the same principle, we can derive the Chinese word distribution φ_{ck}^{cm}. As a result, η_{ek}^{cm} and η_{ck}^{cm} encourage word distribution φ_{ek}^{cm} and φ_{ck}^{cm} to share common semantic components of reader comments in different languages.

The bottom left plate represents latent discussion topics which are specific with English. Each English language-specific topic k_e^{sp} is represented by a word distribution φ_{ek}^{sp} over the English vocabulary Λ_e. We sample φ_{ek}^{sp} from a Dirichlet prior distribution $Dir(\beta_e^{sp} \cdot \mathbf{1}_{|\Lambda_e|})$.

The left largest plate denotes English reader comments and D_e denotes the number of English reader comments. Each English news reader comment d_e is characterized by a K^{cm}-dimensional language-common topic membership θ_e^{cm} and a K^{sp}-dimensional language-specific topic membership θ_e^{sp}. The mixture coefficient of these two kinds of topic membership is denoted by a Bernoulli distribution $Bern(\pi_e)$ and we sample it from a Beta prior distribution $Beta(\gamma)$. We sample θ_e^{cm} and θ_e^{sp} from the prior Dirichlet distributions $Dir(\alpha_e^{cm} \cdot \mathbf{1}_{\mathbf{K^{cm}}})$ and $Dir(\alpha_e^{sp} \cdot \mathbf{1}_{\mathbf{K^{sp}}})$ respectively.

The inner plate denotes a word w_{en} in a comment d_e. N_{edw} denotes the number of words in d_e. For each English word w_{en}, z_{en} denotes the corresponding discussion topic of w_{en}. c_{en} represents a binary switch variable which indicates the commonality or specificity of w_{en}. We sample c_{en} from the corresponding mixture coefficient distribution $Bern(\pi_e)$. If $c_{en} = sp$, we generate w_{en} from the language-specific route, which samples z_{en} from $Multi(\theta_e^{sp})$ and generates w_{en} from $Multi(\varphi_e^{sp})$ according to the assignment of z_{en}. Otherwise, we sample the discussion topic z_{en} from $Multi(\theta_e^{cm})$ and generate w_{en} as a language-common word sampled from $Multi(\varphi_e^{cm})$. Using the similar principle, we can generate Chinese words w_{cn} in each Chinese reader comment.

Our TDCS model also exploits comment-oriented clues for identifying latent discussion topics. The first comment-oriented clue is related to the discussion thread structure. It can be observed that news reader comments originated from the same discussion thread very likely belong to the same discussion topic. The second comment-oriented clue is whether the comments have the same corresponding news article. Typically, the comments provided under a particular news article usually talk about more coherent discussion topics related to the news. To capture the comment-oriented clue information, we design a vector encoding the information. For each English news reader comment, f_e is a vector encoding comment-oriented clue values. Each dimension of f_e refers to a particular thread or an associated news. f_e will take on the value of 1 to indicate positive membership between the comment and a particular thread or a particular news. Otherwise its value is 0. Similar representation f_c is designed for Chinese comments. We integrate the vector into our model via Dirichlet-Multinomial Regression (DMR) method [8]. For each document d_e, the prior parameters of topic distribution α_{ed}^{sp} and α_{ed}^{cm} are specific with f_e. Specifically, for each topic k regardless of commonality and specificity, we have $\alpha_{ek} = \exp(f_e^T \lambda_{\mathbf{ek}})$, where $\lambda_{\mathbf{ek}}$ is a $|f_e|$-dimensional weight vector and it is sampled from a Gaussian distribution $\mathcal{N}(\mu_e, \sigma_e^2 I)$.

3. POSTERIOR INFERENCE

We train our TDCS model using a stochastic EM sampling scheme. In this scheme, we alternate between Gibbs sampling [4] and EM. In our TDCS model, we have two sets of latent variables, c and z. For the Gibbs sampling part, we draw each (c_{ei}, z_{ei}) pair as a block from English reader comments, conditioned on all other variables. We have:

$$\begin{aligned} &P(c_{ei} = cm, z_{ei} = k^{cm} | \mathbf{c}_{e,\neg i}, \mathbf{z}_{e,\neg i}, W_e, \alpha_{ed}^{cm}, \varphi_{ek}^{cm}) \propto \\ &\frac{N_{ed,\neg i}^{cm} + \gamma}{N_{ed,\neg i} + 2\gamma} \times \frac{N_{edk,\neg i}^{cm} + \alpha_{ed}^{cm}}{\sum_{k'} N_{edk',\neg i}^{cm} + \sum_{k'} \alpha_{edk'}^{cm}} \times \varphi_{ekw_i}^{cm} \\ &P(c_{ei} = sp, z_{ei} = k^{sp} | \mathbf{c}_{e,\neg i}, \mathbf{z}_{e,\neg i}, W_e, \alpha_{ed}^{sp}, \varphi_{ek}^{sp}) \propto \\ &\frac{N_{ed,\neg i}^{sp} + \gamma}{N_{ed,\neg i} + 2\gamma} \times \frac{N_{edk,\neg i}^{sp} + \alpha_{ed}^{sp}}{\sum_{k'} N_{edk',\neg i}^{sp} + \sum_{k'} \alpha_{edk'}^{sp}} \times \varphi_{ekw_i}^{sp} \end{aligned} \tag{3}$$

where $\mathbf{c}_{e,\neg i}$ denotes the assignment of commonality or specificity label except the ith word. $\mathbf{z}_{e,\neg i}$ denotes the topic assignments except the assignment of the ith word. N_{ed} is the number of the words in the English document d. N_{ed}^{cm} denotes the number of words in the English comment d_e whose switch variables are assigned to cm. N_{edk}^{cm} is the number of words in English document d^e whose c_{ei} are assigned to cm and topics are assigned to k. $\varphi_{ekw_i}^{cm}$ denotes the word probability of w_i in the language-common discussion topic k. For Chinese reader comments, we can sample the assignment of (c_{ci}, z_{ci}) similarly.

Given the assignment of commonality or specificity and the topic assignments of each English and Chinese word, the probability of language-common words set can be:

$$p(W^{cm} | \mathbf{z}, \varphi_{ek}^{cm}, \varphi_{ck}^{cm}) = \prod_{w\in\Lambda_e} (\varphi_{ekw}^{cm})^{N_{ekw}^{cm}} \times \prod_{w\in\Lambda_c} (\varphi_{ckw}^{cm})^{N_{ckw}^{cm}} \tag{4}$$

where N_{ekw}^{cm} is the number of w in English news reader comments assigned to the language-common discussion topic k and N_{ckw}^{cm} is the number of words w in Chinese news reader comments assigned to the language-common topic k.

Using Eq.4, we can obtain the posterior likelihood related to η_{ek}^{cm} and η_{ck}^{cm}. We optimize the likelihood under the constraints of $\sum_{w_i\in\Lambda_e} \eta_{ekw_i}^{cm} = 1$ and $\sum_{w_i\in\Lambda_c} \eta_{ckw_i}^{cm} = 1$. Using the fixed-point method, we obtain the update equations of $\eta_{ekw_t}^{cm}$ and $\eta_{ckw_t}^{cm}$ shown in Eq.5.

$$\begin{aligned} \eta_{ekw_t}^{cm} \propto [&\frac{(1-\rho)N_{ekw_t}^{cm}}{\rho\sum_{w_j\in\Lambda_c} M_{jt,c\to e}\eta_{ckw_j}^{cm} + (1-\rho)\eta_{ekw_t}^{cm}} + \\ &\sum_{w_i\in\Lambda_c} \frac{\rho N_{ckw_i}^{cm} M_{ti,e\to c}}{\rho\sum_{w_j\in\Lambda_e} M_{ji,e\to c}\eta_{ekw_j}^{cm} + (1-\rho)\eta_{ckw_i}^{cm}}]\eta_{ekw_t}^{cm} + \beta^{cm} \\ \eta_{ckw_t}^{cm} \propto [&\frac{(1-\rho)N_{ckw_t}^{cm}}{\rho\sum_{w_j\in\Lambda^e} M_{jt,e\to c}\eta_{ekw_j}^{cm} + (1-\rho)\eta_{ckw_t}^{cm}} + \\ &\sum_{w_i\in\Lambda_e} \frac{\rho N_{ekw_i}^{cm} M_{ti,c\to e}}{\rho\sum_{w_j\in\Lambda_c} M_{ji,c\to e}\eta_{ckw_j}^{cm} + (1-\rho)\eta_{ekw_i}^{cm}}]\eta_{ckw_t}^{cm} + \beta^{cm} \end{aligned} \tag{5}$$

Moreover, the posterior estimates for the language-specific word distribution φ_{ek}^{sp} and φ_{ck}^{sp} can be computed as follows.

$$\varphi_{ek}^{sp} \sim Dir(N_{ekw_1}^{sp} + \beta_e^{sp}, N_{ekw_2}^{sp} + \beta_e^{sp}, \cdots) \tag{6}$$

$$\varphi_{ck}^{sp} \sim Dir(N_{ckw_1}^{sp} + \beta_c^{sp}, N_{ckw_2}^{sp} + \beta_c^{sp}, \cdots) \quad (7)$$

In the EM phase, we update the value of λ_e^{cm}, λ_e^{sp}, λ_c^{cm} and λ_c^{sp}. Then we can let $\alpha_{dk} = exp(f^T \lambda_k)$ for each language.

Considering the update of λ_e^{sp}, we can construct the log likelihood for the portion of the English language-specific topics. The derivative of the logarithm function with respect to the parameter λ_{ekt}^{sp} for a given topic k and the feature t is:

$$\begin{aligned}\frac{\partial l}{\partial \lambda_{ekt}^{sp}} &= \sum_{d_e \in \mathcal{D}_e} f_{dt} \exp(f_{ed}^T \lambda_k) \\ &[\Psi(\sum_{k \in \mathcal{K}^{sp}} \exp(f_{ed}^T \lambda_k)) - \Psi(\sum_{k \in \mathcal{K}^{sp}} \exp(f_{ed}^T \lambda_k) + N_{ed}) + \\ &\Psi(\exp(f_{ed}^T \lambda_k) + N_{edk}) - \Psi(\exp(f_{ed}^T \lambda_k))] - \frac{\lambda_{ekt}}{\sigma^2}\end{aligned} \quad (8)$$

Then we use L-BFGS algorithm [6] to maxmize the logarithm. Similary, we can get the corresponding update equations of λ_{ekf}^{cm}, λ_{ckf}^{sp} and λ_{ckf}^{cm}.

4. EXPERIMENT

4.1 Corpus and Preprocessing

To evaluate our model, we have prepared a corpus by collecting English and Chinese comments from different news websites for some significant events. The English reader comments are collected from Yahoo[3] and the Chinese reader comments are collected from Sina News[4]. Table 1 depicts the statistics of the corpus. For text preprocessing, we first remove news reader comments whose length is less than 5 words. We remove the punctuations and stop words using the NLTK[5] package. We utilize an English-Chinese dictionary from MDBG[6] in our method.

Table 1: The statistics for the corpus

Event	Title	#English comments	#Chinese comments
1	MH370 flight accident	8608	5223
2	ISIS in Iraq	6341	3263
3	Ebola occurs	2974	1622
4	Taiwan crashed plane	6780	2648
5	iPhone6 publish	5837	4352
6	Shooting of Michael Brown	17547	3693
7	Charlie Hebdo shooting	1845	551
8	Shanghai stampede	3824	3175
9	Lee Kuan Yew death	2418	1534
10	AIIB foundation	7221	3198

4.2 Comparative Methods

One comparative model used in the experiment is derived from the popular LDA model [1]. The standard LDA method merely discovers latent discussion topics from monolingual documents. We first run LDA model for each language separately and discover K topics respectively. K is the sum of K^{cm} and K^{sp}. In order to discover language-common and language-specific topics, the next step is to align the output topics across different languages. To compute the KL-divergence between topics in different languages, we design a cross-language symmetric KL-divergence function between two topics in different languages, denoted as CsymKL(p, q), for the distribution p and q in two different languages as follows:

$$\text{CsymKL}(p, q) = \frac{\textbf{symKL}(p||T(q)) + \textbf{symKL}(q||T(p))}{2} \quad (9)$$

where symKL$(T_1||T_2)$ denotes the standard symmetric KL-divergence between T_1 and T_2 and $T(k)$ is the distribution after the translation of words in the topic k. The lower the CsymKL, the more similar the topics in different languages. We compute the CsymKL value for all possible pairs of English topics and Chinese topics. Finally, we select top K^{cm} topic pairs for the lowest CsymKL measure, as the language-common latent discussion topics. The rest of K^{sp} English topics and K^{sp} Chinese topics are regarded as language-specific. This method is called Aligned-LDA in this paper.

The second comparative model is called PCLSA model proposed by Zhang et al.[14], which can detect latent language-common topics from multilingual text documents. We implemented PCLSA for comparison in our experiments.

4.3 Experiment Settings

In our experiment, we repeated the runs five times. As a result, we have five runs for our method as well as comparative methods. We make use of the data of one event, namely, the event "MH370 Flight Accident", to estimate the number of language-common topics K^{cm}, the number of language-specific topics K^{sp}, and ρ in Eq.1 for our model. We set $K^{cm} = 10$, $K^{sp} = 50$, and $\rho = 0.5$ after tuning. For hyper-parameters, we set $\gamma = 0.5$, $\beta^{cm} = \beta_e^{sp} = \beta_c^{sp} = 0.01$. We optimize the prior of the topic distributions α for our baselines using stochastic EM as described in [13]. When performing our EM sampling algorithm, we set the maximum iteration number as 1000, and the burn-in sweeps as 100.

4.4 Latent Discussion Topic Quality Evaluation

We conduct quantitative experiments to evaluate how well our TDCS model can discover latent discussion topics with language characteristics.

4.4.1 Evaluation Metrics

We use two metrics to evaluate the topic quality. The first metric is the cross-collection likelihood measure denoted as *CCL* which is also adopted in the experiments presented in the paper for the PCLSA model [14]. The *CCL* metric can measure the quality of topic models detecting common topics across different languages with respect to the collection of the original documents. To take the specific topics into consideration, we calculate *CCL* via two steps: *1)* For each language-common topic $k^{cm} \in \mathcal{K}^{cm}$, we translate φ_{ek}^{cm} into Chinese word distribution $T(\varphi_{ek}^{cm})$ and translate φ_{ck}^{cm} into English word distribution $T(\varphi_{ck}^{cm})$. To translate φ_{ek}^{cm} and φ_{ck}^{cm}, we look up the bilingual dictionary and conduct word-to-word translation. If one word has several translations, we distribute its probability mass equally to each English translation. *2)* We use $T(\varphi_{ek}^{cm})$ and φ_{ck}^{sp} to fit the held-out Chinese comments $\mathcal{C}$. And we also use $T(\varphi_{ck}^{cm})$ and φ_{ek}^{sp} to fit the held-out English comments $\mathcal{E}$. The *CCL* of latent topics with good commonality and specificity should be higher than those language-common topics which are not shared by the English and Chinese reader comments or language-specific topics which cannot capture the specific semantics in the corresponding language. The higher the *CCL* value, the better is the performance of topics on the fitness of held-out comments.

Since the *CCL* metric requires a held-out data set, for each event, we partitioned the comments into a subset of 90% for the graphical model parameter estimation. The remaining 10% is used as a held-out data for the evaluation of *CCL*.

[3]http://news.yahoo.com

[4]http://news.sina.com.cn/world/

[5]http://www.nltk.org/

[6]http://www.mdbg.net/chindict/chindict.php?page=cc-cedict

4.4.2 Experimental Results

Table 2: The left and right tables show *CCL* (in 1.0E+06) and *CSD* of the three models respectively. The higher the value, the better is the performance.

Event	Aligned-LDA	PCLSA	TDCS
1	-2.73	-2.82	-2.66
2	-2.84	-2.88	-2.75
3	-1.14	-1.17	-1.09
4	-3.16	-3.26	-3.15
5	-2.05	-2.12	-1.96
6	-4.36	-4.43	-4.24
7	-1.03	-1.05	-1.03
8	-2.52	-2.65	-2.42
9	-1.49	-1.54	-1.43
10	-2.92	-2.83	-2.71
avg.	-2.42	−2.48	**−2.34**

Table 2 shows the average *CCL* values (in 1.0E+06). Our TDCS model achieves the best performance compared with PCLSA and Aligned-LDA. Both TDCS and Aligned-LDA achieve a better *CCL* than PCLSA because they consider not only language-common latent discussion topics but also language-specific topics. Compared with Aligned-LDA, our TDCS model demonstrates a 5.9% improvement. Our TDCS model provides a better characterization of the collections. One reason is that our TDCS model discovers language-common topics using auxiliary distributions which can capture common semantics better. Moreover, our TDCS model utilizes comment-oriented clues to detect latent discussion topics, which benefits the determination of the topic distribution of each English and Chinese comment.

4.5 Topic Coherence Evaluation

We also evaluate the coherence of topics reflecting the interpretability of topics. We use a common metric called pointwise mutual information (PMI) score which is also used in previous works such as [9]. We compute the average PMI score of top 20 topic word pairs. Newman et al. [9] observed that it is desirable to use an external data set to evaluate PMI. Therefore, we use a 20-word sliding window in Wikipedia [11] to identify the co-occurrence of word pairs.

The experimental results are shown in Table 3. We can see that our TDCS model generally improves the coherence of the learned topics. One reason is that the word-to-word bilingual constraints in PCLSA are not as effective. On the other hand, our TDCS model considering language characteristics and comment-oriented clues can discover more coherent latent discussion topics.

5. CASE STUDY

Under each event, the system can digest and organize reader comments into latent discussion topics with commonality and specificity which can capture not only common concerns of readers in different languages but also the discussion topics specific to the language background of readers. For each discussion topic, we can extract top ranked words and corresponding reader comments according to θ^{cm}_{ek}, θ^{sp}_{ek}, θ^{cm}_{ck} and θ^{sp}_{ck}. We present a case study showing some examples of detected latent discussion topics of some events in Figure 2. Considering the event "AIIB foundation", it shows some samples of detected language-common and language-specific topics. The sample language-common topic is related to the economic organizations such as World Bank and IMF. The sample English language-specific topic indicates the effect of "AIIB foundation" on the U.S. On the other hand, the sample Chinese language-specific topic is related to the opposition of Chinese readers about Japan's joining in AIIB. For the sample language-common topic about the economic organizations, we can see that the topic contains both English words and Chinese words which are very relevant and share common semantics of "bank" and "organization". Moreover, both of the associated English and Chinese reader comments, mention some economic organizations such as "World Bank" or "IMF". For the sample English language-specific topic, from the top words and the comments, we can see that English readers consider that U.S. is losing its leadership in the world. On the other hand, for the sample Chinese language-specific topic, the top words and related Chinese comments indicate that Chinese readers strongly oppose Japan's joining in AIIB. Interesting discussion topics are also detected for the event "the death of Lee Kuan Yew" whose topics are mentioned in Section 1.

Table 3: Topic coherence evaluation. The higher the value, the better is the coherence.

Event	Aligned-LDA	PCLSA	TDCS
1	0.124	0.117	0.136
2	0.142	0.116	0.156
3	0.106	0.110	0.120
4	0.137	0.121	0.163
5	0.131	0.101	0.150
6	0.135	0.122	0.151
7	0.092	0.113	0.113
8	0.108	0.088	0.124
9	0.083	0.098	0.101
10	0.125	0.122	0.152
avg.	0.118	0.110	**0.136**

6. CONCLUSIONS

In this paper, we investigate the task of detecting discussion topic with commonality across different languages and specificity for each language from multilingual news reader comments. We propose a new model called TDCS which can cope with the language gap and detect language-common and language-specific latent discussion topics simultaneously. To learn the model parameters, we develop an inference method which alternates between EM and Gibbs sampling. Experimental results show that our proposed TDCS model can provide an effective way to digest multilingual news reader comments and outperform the state-of-the-art method.

7. REFERENCES

[1] D. M. Blei, A. Y. Ng, and M. I. Jordan. Latent dirichlet allocation. *the Journal of Machine Learning Research*, 3:993–1022, 2003.

[2] J. Boyd-Graber and D. M. Blei. Multilingual topic models for unaligned text. In *Proceedings of the 25th Conference on Uncertainty in Artificial Intelligence*, pages 75–82, 2009.

[3] M. K. Das, T. Bansal, and C. Bhattacharyya. Going beyond corr-lda for detecting specific comments on news & blogs. In *Proceedings of the 7th ACM International Conference on Web Search and Data Mining*, pages 483–492, 2014.

[4] T. L. Griffiths and M. Steyvers. Finding scientific topics. *Proceedings of the National Academy of Sciences*, 101(suppl 1):5228–5235, 2004.

[5] T. Hofmann. Unsupervised learning by probabilistic latent semantic analysis. *Machine learning*, 42(1-2):177–196, 2001.

[6] D. C. Liu and J. Nocedal. On the limited memory bfgs method for large scale optimization. *Mathematical*

Event: AIIB Foundation		
class	Topic Terms	Reader Comments
language-common	bank aiib world imf asian develop investment institution infrastructure member 银行(bank) 金融(finance) 世界银行(The World Bank) 世行(The World Bank) 金融机构(Finance institution) 亚洲开发银行(Asian Development Bank) 成员(member) 国际货币基金组织(IMF) 国际(International) 世界(world)	Looks like all the rats are jumping off the sinking world bank and IMF ship. America has pushed their bulling ways long enough and people are...
		The Federal Reserve, the World Bank, The IMF, and the BIS are failed, self-serving institutions. One can only hope that ...
		Bank shopping !!! No more stranglehold by the IMF and World Bank. If Ukraine had only waited another year. Too bad.
		把米国和日本排除在亚投行之外，让他们自己单独经营亚洲开发银行和世界银行！[哈哈]
		欧洲国家被美国坑惨了，世界银行、国际货币基金的钱都在为美国服务，反过来美国又利用乌克兰危机打压欧元，如今欧洲国家看明白了，还是中国靠普。
		世界银行和亚洲开发银行都对亚投行表示欢迎，明显有些言不由衷。信他才怪
		⋮
English language-specific	us obama world american change congress policy bush become leader come	No question the U.S. got egg in its face in regard to the AIIB. But it is the trend going forward that is most alarming to the U.S. Leadership in global trade and is now leaning toward China. China has a great balance sheet, offers trade and loans, doesn't bring armies or navies. The U.S. is drowning in a quagmire of petty domestic issues, a lack of sound leadership...
		America still sticks to its obsolet cold war mindsets, from thinktanks, congress to WH. Obi has been an aggressive but stupid warrmonger all over, force regime change in Ukraine and Syria and bombing Libya.The results are: USA has lost its world leadership.
		US lost its leadership quality since JFK was murdered - suspectedly by ' we know but dare not say it?. Eisenhower warned Americans about MIC hijacking American Democracy.According analyst, Eisenhower would be shock how accurate is ...
		⋮
Chinese language-specific	日本(Japan) 二战(World War II) 侵略(aggression) 历史(history) 抵制(resist) 道歉(apologize) 加入(join) 禁止(prohibit) 旅游(travel) 反省(introspection)	日本是最固的之一...更也是最任性国家侵略史.美是最固的用事行的国家, 者有,有兵任性的霸家.美日本始不加入AIIB, 面上法取中国, 意挑起地事突南及洲迎好加入AIIB.
		日本归根结底是一个没有主权的国家。这一点暂时无法改变，谁让他犯下了侵略罪行，而战败后又想投靠美国崛起，，现在是日本付出代价的时候。。
		中国应该明确拒绝日本加入亚投行，应该重申：日本加入的前提是对二战侵略历史进行反省并道歉！
		安倍又借机攻击中国！日本在没有端正其对二战侵略的认识、没有对南京大屠杀罪行的认罪、没有对强征慰安妇的认罪和赔偿、没有对强征及迫害中国劳工的赔偿、没有撤销对钓鱼岛所谓的"国有化"之前，坚决不许日本加入亚投行！
		日本必须全面彻底履行二战战败投降国义务、清除一切侵略战争罪恶遗迹之后才能提交申请加入亚投行！
		⋮
⋮		

Event: The Death of Lee Kuan Yew		
class	Topic Terms	Reader Comments
language-common	lee mr yew kuan Singapore thank rest rip respect peace minister 李光耀(lee kuan yew) 先生(mr) 新加坡(Singapore) 新加坡人(Singapore) 安息(R.I.P) 哀悼(mourn) 感谢(thank) 致哀(respect) 国父(father) 沉痛(sad)	Have been to Singapore dozen of times. I'm crying! R.I.P. Honorable Lee Kuan Yew, the founder of modern Singapore!!!
		I recently found out that Mr Lee, in the 1970s, warned Australia that if they don't reform, they will become the "poor White trash of Asia". LOL! I respect someone who dares speak the truth, especially to powerful people. R.I.P.
		Salute. R.I.P Sir.
		一位伟大的领导人，拯救了新加坡，逝者安息
		李光耀先生以卓越政治才能建立一个繁新加坡新，加坡的成就有目共睹，李光耀值得新人民永尊敬和怀念！
		一个领导人，只要他为这个国家奉献一生，就让人值得尊敬!一路走好！！！！！
		⋮
English language-specific	better best obama problem think suggestion question nothing accept America	Not perfect butt Definitely better than Obama, anytime.
		Nothing to do with Obama. I lived in SG - 2008 to 2011 and it is clean efficient and very safe especially when compared to it's neighbors. I think that has a lot to do with LKY and the decisions he made.
		America could learn alot from Lee Kuan Yew. Especially after the damage Obama has done to America.
		Say what you will, he transformed Singapore into a great place to live and work ! Unlike Obama has done in the past 6+ years....
		⋮
Chinese language-specific	愿(hope) 希望(hope) 习(Xi) 支持(support) 主席(chairman) 美好(happy) 辛苦(work hard) 发展(develop) 祖国(country) 国家(country)	习大大把人民放在心中最高位置，始终与人民心心相印、与人民同甘共苦、与人民团结奋斗
		习大大 赞一个 在您的领导下 祖国会越来越好.
		当一个国家领导人多不容易啊，事事都要周全。习大大辛苦了，相信在您带领下，中国会越来越好。
		执政为民国家领导者，肩负国家稳健和高效运行的使命与责任。为习主席点赞！
		⋮
⋮		

Figure 2: Sample language-common and language-specific discussion topics of some events.

Programming, 45(1-3):503–528, 1989.

[7] S. Melluish. Globalization, culture and psychology. *International Review of Psychiatry*, 26(5):538–543, 2014.

[8] D. Mimno and A. McCallum. Topic models conditioned on arbitrary features with dirichlet-multinomial regression. *arXiv preprint arXiv:1206.3278*, 2012.

[9] D. Newman, J. H. Lau, K. Grieser, and T. Baldwin. Automatic evaluation of topic coherence. In *Proceedings of the Annual Conference of the North American Chapter of the Association for Computational Linguistics*, pages 100–108, 2010.

[10] R. E. Prasojo, M. Kacimi, and W. Nutt. Entity and aspect extraction for organizing news comments. In *Proceedings of the 24th ACM International on Conference on Information and Knowledge Management*, pages 233–242, 2015.

[11] C. Shaoul. The westbury lab wikipedia corpus. *Edmonton, AB: University of Alberta*, 2010.

[12] C. Tamer, K. Gary, and R. Riesenberger John. International business: Strategy, management and the new realities, 2010.

[13] H. M. Wallach. Topic modeling: beyond bag-of-words. In *Proceedings of the 23rd International Conference on Machine Learning*, pages 977–984, 2006.

[14] D. Zhang, Q. Mei, and C. Zhai. Cross-lingual latent topic extraction. In *Proceedings of the 48th Annual Meeting of the Association for Computational Linguistics*, pages 1128–1137, 2010.

Digesting News Reader Comments via Fine-Grained Associations with Event Facets and News Contents*

Bei Shi, Wai Lam
Department of Systems Engineering and Engineering Management,
The Chinese University of Hong Kong.
{bshi, wlam}@se.cuhk.edu.hk

ABSTRACT

News articles from different sources reporting the same event are often associated with an enormous amount of reader comments resulting in difficulty in digesting the comments manually. Some of these comments, despite coming from different sources, discuss about a certain facet of the event. On the other hand, some comments discuss on the specific topic of the corresponding news article. We propose a framework that can digest reader comments automatically via fine-grained associations with event facets and news. We propose an unsupervised model called DRC, based on collective matrix factorization and develop a multiplicative-update method to infer the parameters. Experimental results show that our proposed DRC model can provide an effective way to digest news reader comments.

Keywords

news comments; event facets; matrix factorization

1. INTRODUCTION

Everyday large amounts of news websites in the world report the same significant event sometimes from different angles. These websites also allow news readers to express and share their comments. Through digesting these news reader comments from different sources for the same event, we can gain some insights into the reactions, opinions, or personal experiences of news readers. For instance, on July 2014, Ebola, the terrible lethal disease, got out of control in West Africa. Upon the happening of this event, many news articles from different sources reported it and many readers commented on this event. Figure 1 demonstrates two of these articles, namely, News1 from CBC News and News2 from Guardian, as well as the corresponding reader comments associated with each piece of the news. Considering an event composed of tens of news articles, there are typically some event facets found in the content of majority news articles of the event. For example, the facet about easy transmission of Ebola is mentioned in many news articles. Additionally, it can be observed that the associated reader comments for News1 and News2 are enormous ranging from hundreds to thousands. Such large volume makes it impossible to effectively digest the reader comments manually. Some reader comments, despite coming from different sources, express information or viewpoints about a certain facet of the event. On the other hand, some comments discuss on the specific topic of the corresponding news article. Analyzing and digesting the discussion topics or concerns of all reader comments from different sources manually is impractical.

There is a growing interest in mining news reader comments [21, 17, 7, 19, 12, 4]. Bansal et al. [1] detected valuable reader comments and proposed a graphical model to recommend comments-worthy news articles. Rizos et al. [16] exploited the comment tree and user graph to predict several news story popularity indicators and a measure of controversiality. However, the above works cannot digest reader comments via fine-grained associations with event facets and news.

To cope with the problem mentioned above, we propose a framework that can analyze and digest reader comments automatically via fine-grained associations with event facets and news. Consider the news and comments about the event of Ebola in Figure 1 mentioned above, Figure 2 depicts the result of digesting the comments by our framework. The topmost panel contains groups of comments that discuss certain event facets. We call the comments related to an event facet as **event facet oriented comments**. Event facets are defined as an aspect content found in majority news of the event. One challenge is that event facets are not previously known. The identification of event facet oriented comments can help us understand the concerns of readers on the event-level issues. For example, the comments under Event_Facet1 in Figure 2 talk about the event facet regarding easy transmission of Ebola. Some examples of the comments are New1_Comment55 "I think ebola is very hard to transmit, only through someone vomiting or bleeding on..." and News2_Comment34 "It also easy to transmit but only if the proper precautions aren't taken, it spread through bodily fluids ...". Note that comments belonging to the same facet may be originated from different news sources.

*The work described in this paper is substantially supported by grants from the Research Grant Council of the Hong Kong Special Administrative Region, China (Project Code: 14203414). This work is also affiliated with the CUHK MoE-Microsoft Key Laboratory of Human-centric Computing and Interface Technologies.

CIKM'16 , October 24-28, 2016, Indianapolis, IN, USA
© 2016 ACM. ISBN 978-1-4503-4073-1/16/10...$15.00
DOI: http://dx.doi.org/10.1145/2983323.2983684

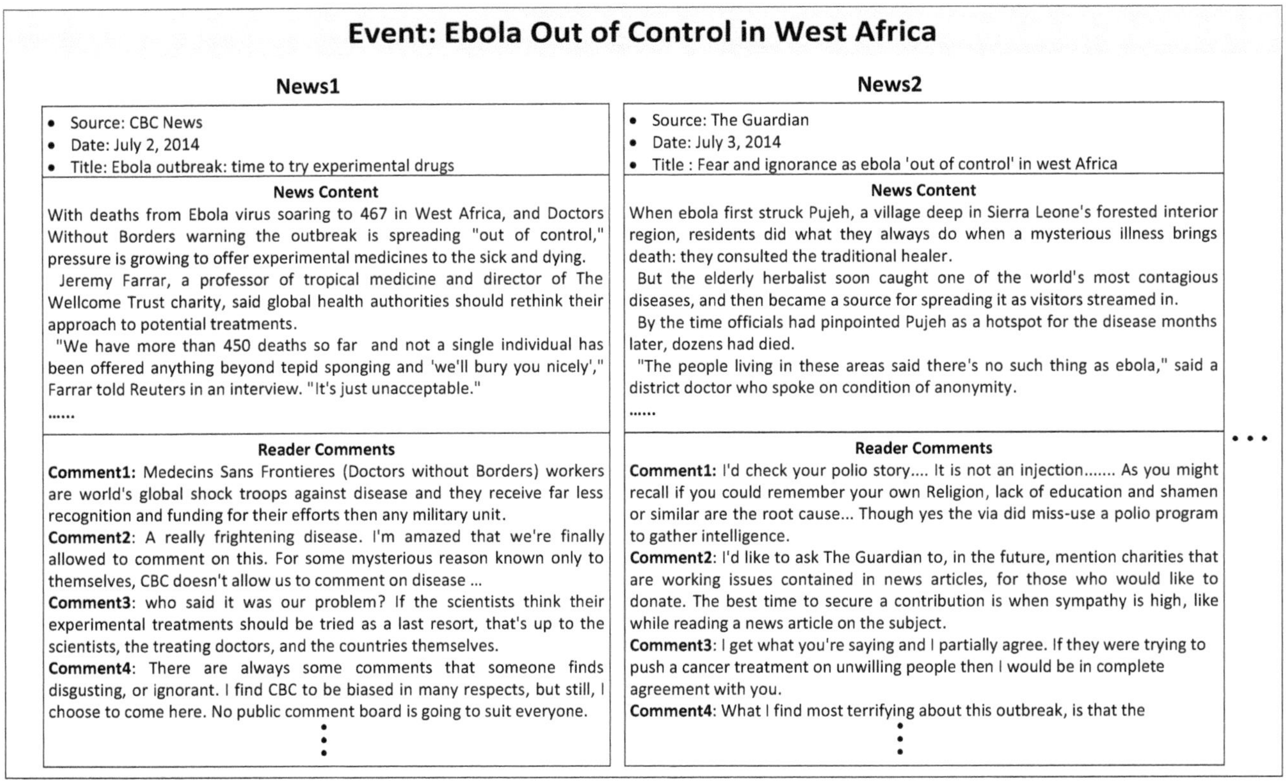

Figure 1: News articles and reader comments about the event "Ebola out of control in West Africa"

Besides event facet oriented comments, we observe that some comments talk about the specific topic of the corresponding news article. We call such comments as **news oriented comments**. Different from event facets, the specific topic is mentioned in just a single corresponding news article. For example, the panel entitled as News Oriented Comments in Figure 2 depicts some examples of news oriented comments. The news article News1 talks about the specific topic of the use of experimental drugs. Comment17 "If they give the drugs out and something goes wrong they get..." discusses about the result of using experimental drugs which is related to the specific topic of News1.

We investigate the technical challenges in this task of digesting reader comments mentioned above. First, the facets of each event are not known in advance. Second, fine-grained associations considering event facets and news are complicated. Third, generally there is very low overlap of terms between comments and the corresponding news content leading to the vocabulary gap issue. Consequently, keyword match based approaches are not effective.

We propose an unsupervised model called DRC based on matrix factorization which can digest news reader comments considering fine-grained associations with event facets and news mentioned above. To cope with the intricate associations among events, news, and comments, we employ the Collective Matrix Factorization (CMF) method which exploits common components between factorizations. Matrix factorization and its variants have been widely used in text mining applications [18, 11, 13, 2, 3, 6]. The collective matrix factorization (CMF) method which shares common variable across factorizations can connect two modalities. Vaca et al. [22] exploited CMF to learn jointly the topics evolution and their time dependencies. Kalyanam et al. [8] proposed a CMF based topic model to incorporate both the textual information and social context information. Our model makes use of the CMF method to depict fine-grained associations of comments with event facets and news contents. To infer the parameters, we develop an effective multiplicative-update method. In order to evaluate our model, we have prepared a corpus by collecting news articles and comments from different sources. The experimental results demonstrate that our model can digest these news reader comments more effectively than the state-of-the-art model.

2. OUR APPROACH

We present the problem definition of the task of digesting news reader comments. A particular event e often has a set of news articles, denoted as $\mathcal{D}$, from various sources. For each news article $d \in \mathcal{D}$, there exists a set of reader comments, denoted as $\mathcal{C}_d$, associated with it. The goal of the task is to discover event facet oriented comments $\mathcal{C}_d^e$ and news oriented comments $\mathcal{C}_d^n$ from $\mathcal{C}_d$.

We propose a model called **D**igest **R**eader **C**omments (DRC) which is based on matrix factorization to tackle the task. In our DRC model, we decompose the event, the news articles, and reader comments using non-negative matrix factorization [10] with shared components matrices [20]. The event facets and news oriented topics are modeled as latent factors

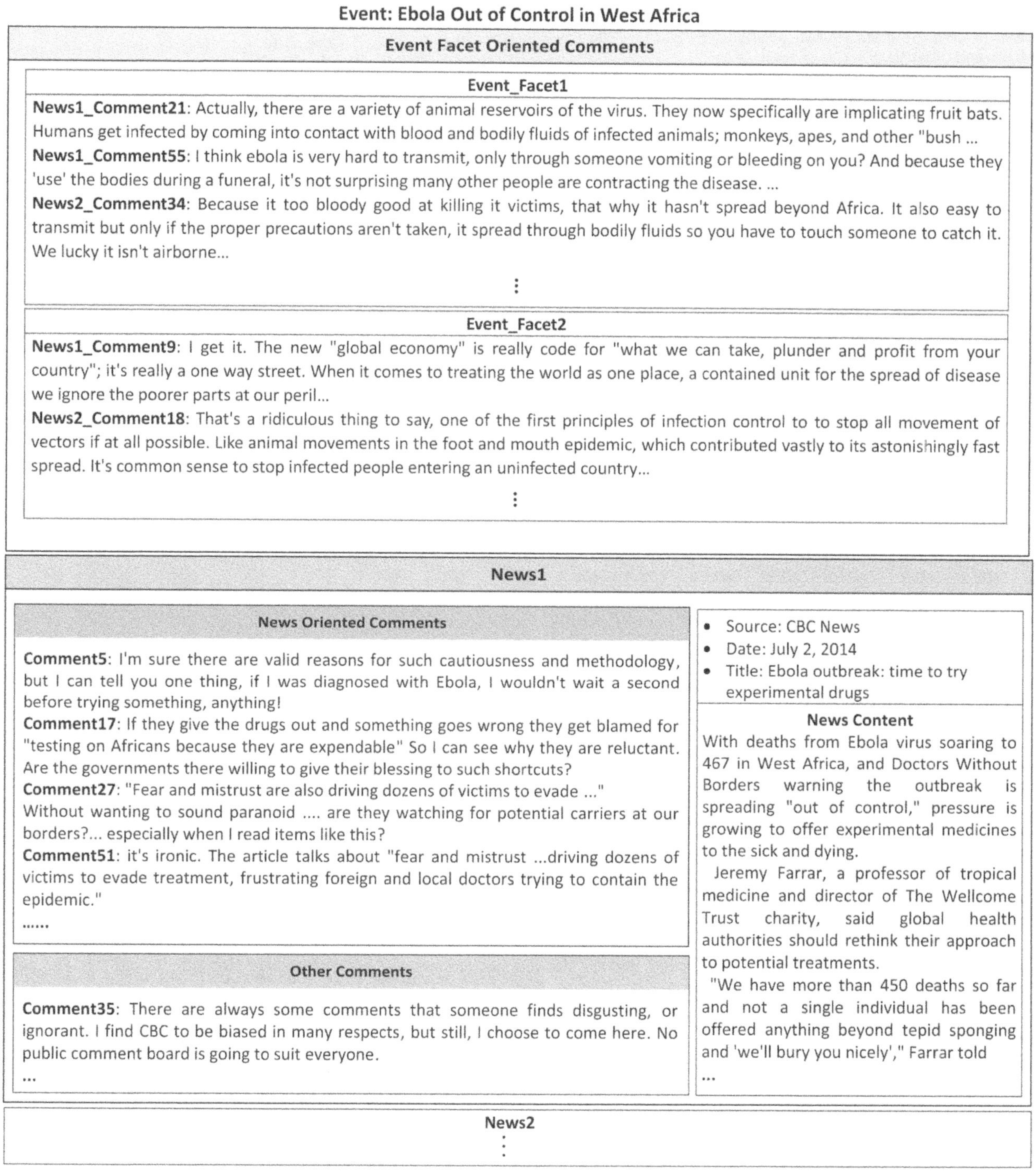

Figure 2: The result of news comment digest and analysis for the event "Ebola out of control in West Africa".

which are shared in the decomposition to depict the fine-grained associations with event facets and news contents.

Let $\mathbf{X}_e$ be a $N_d \times |V|$ matrix, where N_d denotes the number of news articles in e and $|V|$ is the size of the vocabulary. Each item x_{dw} in $\mathbf{X}_e$ is the term weight of the term w in d.

To identify event facets from $\mathbf{X}_e$, we employ non-negative matrix factorization to decompose $\mathbf{X}_e$. Therefore, we have:

$$\mathbf{X}_e \approx \mathbf{W}_e \mathbf{H}_e \quad \text{where} \quad \mathbf{W}_e \geq 0, \mathbf{H}_e \geq 0 \tag{1}$$

where $\mathbf{H}_e$ is a $K_e \times |V|$ event facets matrix and K_e is the number of event facets. Each row in $\mathbf{H}_e$ represents an event facet. $\mathbf{W}_e$ represents how each news article is decomposed in terms of events facets in $\mathbf{H}_e$. The unit in $\mathbf{W}_e$ and $\mathbf{H}_e$ should be non-negative.

For a news article d, we wish to analyze the content by considering various local contexts modeled by a window size of consecutive sentences. $\mathbf{X}_d$ is a matrix including the single sentence or the windows of adjacent sentences. Let T denote the maximum of the window width. The dimension of $\mathbf{X}_d$ is a $(N_s + N_{s\times s} + \cdots + N_{\underbrace{s \times \cdots \times s}_{T}}) \times |V|$ matrix. N_s denotes the number of sentences and $N_{s\times s}$ is the number of windows of two adjacent sentences. Each row of $\mathbf{X}_d$ denotes a sentence or a slide window of sentences in d. Similarly, each item x_{sw} is the term weight of the term w in the sentence or the window s. Therefore, $\mathbf{X}_d$ depicts text features of d locally. To identify news oriented topics in d, we decompose $\mathbf{X}_d$ with non-negative matrices as:

$$\mathbf{X}_d \approx \mathbf{W}_d\mathbf{H}_d \quad \text{where} \quad \mathbf{W}_d \geq 0, \mathbf{H}_d \geq 0 \tag{2}$$

Assuming the number of news oriented topics is K_d, $\mathbf{H}_d$ is a $K_d \times |V|$ topic matrix and $\mathbf{W}_d$ is the encoding matrix in terms of news oriented topics.

For reader comments $\mathcal{C}_d$ of d, $\mathbf{X}_c$ is a $N_c \times |V|$ matrix. N_c is the number of reader comments. Similarly, each item x_{cw} is the term weight of the term w in the reader comment c. As mentioned in Section 1, reader comments include event facet oriented comments, news oriented comments (including news general and news specific), and irrelevant comments. Therefore, $\mathbf{X}_c$ can be decomposed as follows:

$$\begin{aligned} \mathbf{X}_c \approx \mathbf{W}_{ce}\mathbf{H}_e + \mathbf{W}_{cd}\mathbf{H}_d + \mathbf{W}_c\mathbf{H}_c \\ \text{where} \quad \mathbf{W}_{ce}, \mathbf{W}_{cd}, \mathbf{W}_c, \mathbf{H}_c \geq 0 \end{aligned} \tag{3}$$

In Eq. 3, we have the common decomposition matrix $\mathbf{H}_e$ from Eq. 1. The rationale is that event facet oriented comments share event facets $\mathbf{H}_e$ commonly found in $\mathbf{X}_e$. Similarly, the decompositions of $\mathbf{X}_c$ and $\mathbf{X}_d$ share the same news oriented topics $\mathbf{H}_d$. Hence, the shared $\mathbf{H}_e$ and $\mathbf{H}_d$ depict fine-grained associations among events, news articles, and comments. $\mathbf{W}_{ce}$ and $\mathbf{W}_{cd}$ are the encoding matrices, which measure the weight of $\mathbf{X_c}$ in terms of events and news respectively. The weight matrix $\mathbf{W}_c$ and the topic matrix $\mathbf{H}_c$ model irrelevant reader comments in $\mathbf{X}_c$.

By putting Eq. 1 through Eq. 3 together, our loss function is formulated as follows:

$$\begin{aligned} & L = L_e + L_d + L_c + \lambda R \\ & L_e = \frac{1}{2}||\mathbf{X}_e - \mathbf{W}_e\mathbf{H}_e||_F^2 \quad L_d = \frac{1}{2}||\mathbf{X}_d - \mathbf{W}_d\mathbf{H}_d||_F^2 \\ & L_c = \frac{1}{2}||\mathbf{X}_c - \mathbf{W}_{ce}\mathbf{H}_e - \mathbf{W}_{cd}\mathbf{H}_d - \mathbf{W}_c\mathbf{H}_c||_F^2 \end{aligned} \tag{4}$$

Where λ is the balance parameter. $||\cdot||_F$ is the Frobenius-norm of a matrix. L_e, L_d, and L_c are the event, news articles, and reader comments part of the objective function respectively. To encourage sparsity, R denotes l_1 regularization on all the matrices. We formulate R as follows:

$$\begin{aligned} R = & ||\mathbf{W}_e||_1 + ||\mathbf{H}_e||_1 + ||\mathbf{W}_d||_1 + ||\mathbf{H}_d||_1 + ||\mathbf{W}_{ce}||_1 + \\ & ||\mathbf{W}_{cd}||_1 + ||\mathbf{W}_c||_1 + ||\mathbf{H}_c||_1 \end{aligned} \tag{5}$$

Where $||\cdot||_1$ is the l_1 norm.

The optimization of the loss function L can be formalized as:

$$\begin{aligned} \{\mathbf{W}_e^*, \mathbf{H}_e^*, \mathbf{W}_d^*, \mathbf{H}_d^*, \mathbf{W}_{ce}^*, \mathbf{W}_{cd}^*, \mathbf{W}_c^*, \mathbf{H}_c^*\} = \\ \underset{\mathbf{W}_e,\mathbf{H}_e,\mathbf{W}_d,\mathbf{H}_d,\mathbf{W}_{ce},\mathbf{W}_{cd},\mathbf{W}_c,\mathbf{H}_c}{\arg\min} L \end{aligned} \tag{6}$$

The optimization problem in Eq. 6 is not convex in all the parameters simultaneously. We use multiplicative iterations as in [9]. From the Karush Kuhn Tucker (KKT) first order conditions, the complementary slackness is as follows:

$$\nabla_{\mathbf{Q}} L \odot \mathbf{Q} = \mathbf{0} \tag{7}$$

where $\odot$ is the element-wise product and $\nabla_{\mathbf{Q}} L$ is the gradient of the loss function with respect to $\mathbf{Q}$. $\mathbf{Q}$ is each variable matrix. By substituting the gradients into Eq. 7 and employing the fixed point method, the update equations are as follows:

$$\begin{aligned} & N = \mathbf{W}_{ce}\mathbf{H}_e + \mathbf{W}_{cd}\mathbf{H}_d + \mathbf{W}_c\mathbf{H}_c \\ & \mathbf{W}_e \leftarrow \frac{\mathbf{W}_e \odot \mathbf{X}_e\mathbf{H}_e^T}{\mathbf{W}_e\mathbf{H}_e\mathbf{H}_e^T + \lambda} \quad \mathbf{W}_d \leftarrow \frac{\mathbf{W}_d \odot \mathbf{X}_d\mathbf{H}_d^T}{\mathbf{W}_d\mathbf{H}_d\mathbf{H}_d^T + \lambda} \\ & \mathbf{H}_e \leftarrow \mathbf{H}_e \odot \frac{\mathbf{W}_e^T\mathbf{X}_e + \mathbf{W}_{ce}^T\mathbf{X}_c}{N_e} \\ & \text{where} \quad N_e = \mathbf{W}_e^T\mathbf{W}_e\mathbf{H}_e + \mathbf{W}_{ce}^T N + \lambda \\ & \mathbf{H}_d \leftarrow \mathbf{H}_d \odot \frac{\mathbf{W}_d^T\mathbf{X}_d + \mathbf{W}_{cd}^T\mathbf{X}_c}{N_d} \\ & \text{where} \quad N_d = \mathbf{W}_d^T\mathbf{W}_d\mathbf{H}_d + \mathbf{W}_{cd}^T N + \lambda \end{aligned} \tag{8}$$

$$\begin{aligned} & \mathbf{W}_{cd} \leftarrow \frac{\mathbf{W}_{cd} \odot \mathbf{X}_c\mathbf{H}_d^T}{N\mathbf{H}_d^T + \lambda} \quad \mathbf{W}_{ce} \leftarrow \frac{\mathbf{W}_{ce} \odot \mathbf{X}_c\mathbf{H}_e^T}{N\mathbf{H}_e^T + \lambda} \\ & \mathbf{W}_c \leftarrow \frac{\mathbf{W}_c \odot \mathbf{X}_c\mathbf{H}_c^T}{N\mathbf{H}_c^T + \lambda} \quad \mathbf{H}_c \leftarrow \mathbf{H}_c \odot \frac{\mathbf{W}_c^T\mathbf{X}_c}{N_c} \\ & \text{where} \quad N_c = \mathbf{W}_c^T N + \lambda \end{aligned} \tag{9}$$

Note that $\frac{[\cdot]}{[\cdot]}$ denotes element-wise division.

THEOREM 1. *The loss function L in Eq. 4 is non-increasing under the update rules in Eq. 8. The loss function L is invariant under these updates if and only if* $\mathbf{W}_e$, $\mathbf{H}_e$, $\mathbf{W}_d$, $\mathbf{H}_d$, $\mathbf{W}_{ce}$, $\mathbf{W}_{cd}$, $\mathbf{W}_c$, $\mathbf{H}_c$ *are at a stationary point of the function.*

The details of proof can be analyzed using the auxiliary function approach presented in Lee and Seung [10] and Vaca et al. [22].

After the estimation of the parameters, we can use $\mathbf{W}_{ce}$, $\mathbf{W}_{cd}$, $\mathbf{H}_e$ and $\mathbf{H}_d$ to identify event facet oriented and news oriented reader comments. To identify event fact oriented reader comments, for each comment $c \in \mathcal{C}_d$, we propose an event facet score function denoted by EFS as follows:

$$\text{EFS}(c) = ||w_{ce}||_2 \tag{10}$$

where w_{ce} are the corresponding row vector of c in $\mathbf{W}_{ce}$. $||\cdot||_2$ is the Euclidean length of the vector. The larger EFS(c), the more likely that c talks about an event facet.

Similarly we propose a news oriented score function (NOS) to identify news oriented reader comments. The NOS of c can be formulated as:

$$\text{NOS}(c) = ||w_{cd}||_2 \tag{11}$$

To detect event facet oriented and news oriented reader comments, we rank all the comments according to EFS and

NOS respectively and select top $N \times \rho$ comments from the ranking lists, where N is the total number of comments and ρ is a threshold.

3. EXPERIMENT

3.1 Data Set and Evaluation Metric

Table 1: The list of the events

Event ID	Title
1	Sochi terrorist attack
2	Malaysia Airlines disappearance
3	Kunming station massacre
4	New South Wales bush fires
5	Taiwan police evict student protesters
6	UK Cameron calls for action on superbug threat
7	Africa ebola out of control in West Africa

We have prepared a data set by collecting news articles and corresponding comments from different sources. Our data set contains 7 events as depicted in Table 1. Each event contains 10 related news articles and at least 100 reader comments.

We wish to obtain the ground truth of the associations of comments with event facets or news contents. Therefore, we hired some undergraduates majoring in journalism to conduct manual annotations. The annotation process consists of two main stages. In the first stage, the aim is to determine the facets of each event. In the second stage, the aim is to determine the comment label together with the associations of comments with facets or news content.

For the determination of event facets in the first stage, we asked the annotators to refer to the facet categories such as "what happened", "when", "why happened", etc, which can guide the extraction of facets from the set of news articles in the event. Such facet categories have also been considered when preparing manual summaries for events in the evaluation forum TAC 2010[1] which investigates multi-document summarization for an event (events and facet categories are referred to as topics and aspects respectively in TAC). The detailed steps for facet extraction are as follows. Consider a particular event, we first asked the annotators to read and digest all news articles under the event. Next, for each facet category, the annotators identified some specific facets by extracting clauses or sentences concerning the facets in each news article. One requirement for a valid facet is that it should be mentioned in more than half of the number of news articles in the event. This can ensure that the facet is important at the event level. For each facet, before the extraction of the corresponding clauses or sentences from the news content, we asked the annotators to write one sentence describing the facet facilitating accurate facet understanding and validation among annotators. It is possible that there are more than one facets extracted for each facet category.

For the second stage of annotation, the aim is to determine comment labels indicating the associations of comments with facets or news content. For each reader comment associated with a particular news article, the annotators determine a label, namely, "event facet oriented", "news oriented", or "others". This annotation stage consists of two phases. In the first phase, the annotators read and digest each comment carefully and identify whether each comment can be classified as "event facet oriented". Next, the aim is to determine the label for the remaining comments which will be analyzed in the second phase. Specifically, for each remaining reader comment of a particular news, the annotators should judge whether there are associations between the comment and the corresponding news content. If related, it will be annotated as "news oriented". After the two phases, the comments without any labels will be labeled as "others". To estimate the annotation challenge and quality, we calculate the inter-annotator agreement. The average Cohen's Kappa was 0.7, which is considered as a good agreement [5].

In total, 702 comments have been annotated. The number of event facet oriented and news oriented reader comments are 157 and 206 respectively.

After obtaining the ground truth, we can measure the performance using the information retrieval related metrics: Mean Average Precision (MAP) and Normalized Discounted Cumulative Gain (NDCG) [14]. Our model as well as comparative methods will output a ranked list of comments for each kind of labels, namely, event facet oriented and news oriented. Then we compare the ground truth label of the comments in the ranked list and give a judgment of true or false. Finally, the metrics of MAP and NDCG can be calculated.

3.2 Comparative Method

The comparative model used in the experiment is derived from the standard non-negative matrix factorization model [10] and we refer it as NGM in this paper. In order to identify all kinds of reader comments via NGM, we concatenate $\mathbf{X}_e$, $\mathbf{X}_d$, and $\mathbf{X}_c$, and get $\mathbf{X} = [\mathbf{X}_e\ \mathbf{X}_d\ \mathbf{X}_c]^T$. We decompose $\mathbf{X}$ to get the corresponding weight matrices $[\mathbf{W}'_e\ \mathbf{W}'_d\ \mathbf{W}'_c]^T$ and the topic matrix $\mathbf{H}'$. To identify event facet oriented comments, we rank the reader comments according to the sum of the cosine similarity between $\mathbf{W}'_c$ and $\mathbf{W}'_e$. Similarly we detect news oriented comments using the cosine similarity between $\mathbf{W}'_c$ and $\mathbf{W}'_d$. The obvious difference between NGM and our DRC method is that NGM projects the event matrix, the news matrix, and the comments under one common topic space $\mathbf{H}'$. In contrast, our DRC method can factorize $\mathbf{X}_e$, $\mathbf{X}_d$, and $\mathbf{X}_c$ into topics with different specificity, i.e., $\mathbf{H}_e$, $\mathbf{H}_d$ and $\mathbf{H}_c$ respectively.

3.3 Experiment Settings

For text preprocessing, we first remove news reader comments whose length is less than 5 words. We remove punctuations and stop words. We also stem each word to its root form using Porter Stemmer [15].

In our experiment, considering $\mathbf{X}_d$, we set the maximum width of windows to 3. When performing the multiplicative-update algorithm, we set the maximum iteration number as 1000 and the threshold of stopping iterations as 0.001.

We tune the parameters using the event "Sochi terrorist attack". We obtained $\lambda = 0.1$ after tuning. We set $K_e = 10$, $K_d = 5$, and $K_c = 10$ empirically. For the comparative model NGM, we set the number of latent factors as the sum of K_e, K_d, and K_c, i.e, 25.

3.4 Experimental Result

Table 2 depicts the performance of our DRC model and the comparative method NGM. Our DRC model achieves

[1]http://www.nist.gov/tac/2010/Summarization/Guided-Summ.2010.guidelines.html

Table 2: **The performance of our model DRC and the comparative method NGM**

	NGM		DRC	
	MAP	NDCG	MAP	NDCG
event facet oriented	0.12	0.16	0.15	0.20
news oriented	0.17	0.22	0.21	0.25
Avg.	0.14	0.19	**0.18**	**0.22**

the best performance compared with NGM. Compared with NGM, our DRC model demonstrates an improvement over both event facet oriented and news oriented reader comments because our DRC model provides a better characterization of fine-grained associations among events, news articles, and reader comments via collective matrix factorization. In contrast, NGM models the topics of news and comments in a common space, which is not effective for distinguishing the associations among events, news articles, and reader comments.

4. CONCLUSIONS

We investigate the task of digesting news reader comments considering event facets and news contents. We propose an unsupervised model called DRC, which is based on collective matrix factorization and develop a multiplicative-update method to infer the parameters. Experimental results show that our proposed DRC model can provide an effective way to digest news reader comments.

5. REFERENCES

[1] T. Bansal, M. Das, and C. Bhattacharyya. Content driven user profiling for comment-worthy recommendations of news and blog articles. In *Proceedings of the 9th ACM Conference on Recommender Systems*, pages 195–202, 2015.

[2] M. W. Berry, M. Browne, A. N. Langville, V. P. Pauca, and R. J. Plemmons. Algorithms and applications for approximate nonnegative matrix factorization. *Computational Statistics & Data Analysis*, 52(1):155–173, 2007.

[3] G. Bouchard, D. Yin, and S. Guo. Convex collective matrix factorization. In *Proceedings of the 16th International Conference on Artificial Intelligence and Statistics*, pages 144–152, 2013.

[4] M. K. Das, T. Bansal, and C. Bhattacharyya. Going beyond corr-lda for detecting specific comments on news & blogs. In *7th International Conference on Web Search and Data Mining*, pages 483–492, 2014.

[5] J. L. Fleiss, B. Levin, and M. C. Paik. *Statistical Methods for Rates and Proportions*. John Wiley & Sons, 2013.

[6] P. O. Hoyer. Non-negative matrix factorization with sparseness constraints. *Journal of Machine Learning Research*, 5:1457–1469, 2004.

[7] M. Hu, A. Sun, and E.-P. Lim. Comments-oriented blog summarization by sentence extraction. In *Proceedings of the 16th ACM Conference on Conference on Information and Knowledge Management*, pages 901–904, 2007.

[8] J. Kalyanam, A. Mantrach, D. Saez-Trumper, H. Vahabi, and G. Lanckriet. Leveraging social context for modeling topic evolution. In *Proceedings of the 21th ACM SIGKDD International Conference on Knowledge Discovery and Data Mining*, pages 517–526, 2015.

[9] D. D. Lee and H. S. Seung. Learning the parts of objects by non-negative matrix factorization. *Nature*, 401(6755):788–791, 1999.

[10] D. D. Lee and H. S. Seung. Algorithms for non-negative matrix factorization. In *Advances in Neural Information Processing Systems*, pages 556–562, 2001.

[11] C.-J. Lin. Projected gradient methods for nonnegative matrix factorization. *Neural Computation*, 19(10):2756–2779, 2007.

[12] Z. Ma, A. Sun, Q. Yuan, and G. Cong. Topic-driven reader comments summarization. In *Proceedings of the 21st International Conference on Information and Knowledge Management*, pages 265–274, 2012.

[13] J. Mairal, F. Bach, J. Ponce, and G. Sapiro. Online learning for matrix factorization and sparse coding. *Journal of Machine Learning Research*, 11:19–60, 2010.

[14] C. D. Manning, P. Raghavan, H. Schütze, et al. *Introduction to Information Retrieval*. Cambridge university press Cambridge, 2008.

[15] M. F. Porter. An algorithm for suffix stripping. *Program*, 14(3):130–137, 1980.

[16] G. Rizos, S. Papadopoulos, and Y. Kompatsiaris. Predicting news popularity by mining online discussions. In *Proceedings of the 25th International Conference on World Wide Web, WWW 2016, Companion Volume*, pages 737–742, 2016.

[17] A. Schuth, M. Marx, and M. de Rijke. Extracting the discussion structure in comments on news-articles. In *Proceedings of the 9th Annual ACM International Workshop on Web Information and Data Management*, pages 97–104, 2007.

[18] F. Shahnaz, M. W. Berry, V. P. Pauca, and R. J. Plemmons. Document clustering using nonnegative matrix factorization. *Information Processing & Management*, 42(2):373–386, 2006.

[19] D. K. Sil, S. H. Sengamedu, and C. Bhattacharyya. Supervised matching of comments with news article segments. In *Proceedings of the 20th Conference on Information and Knowledge Management*, pages 2125–2128, 2011.

[20] A. P. Singh and G. J. Gordon. Relational learning via collective matrix factorization. In *Proceedings of the 14th International Conference on Knowledge Discovery and Data mining*, pages 650–658, 2008.

[21] M. Tsagkias, W. Weerkamp, and M. De Rijke. News comments: Exploring, modeling, and online prediction. In *Proceedings of the 32nd European Conference on IR Research*, pages 191–203. 2010.

[22] C. K. Vaca, A. Mantrach, A. Jaimes, and M. Saerens. A time-based collective factorization for topic discovery and monitoring in news. In *Proceedings of the 23rd International Conference on World Wide Web*, pages 527–538, 2014.

Efficient Algorithms for the Two Locus Problem in Genome-Wide Association Study

Sanguthevar Rajasekaran*
Department of Computer Science and Engineering
University of Connecticut, Storrs, CT
rajasek@engr.uconn.edu

Subrata Saha
Department of Computer Science and Engineering
University of Connecticut, Storrs, CT
subrata.saha@engr.uconn.edu

ABSTRACT

Advances made in sequencing technology have resulted in the sequencing of thousands of genomes. Novel analysis tools are needed to process these data and extract useful information. Such tools could aid in personalized medicine. As an example, we could identify the causes for a disease by comparing the genomes of people who have the disease and those who do not have this disease. Given that human variability happens due to single nucleotide polymorphisms (SNPs), we could focus our attention on these SNPs. Investigations that try to understand human variability using SNPs fall under genome-wide association study (GWAS). A crucial step in GWAS is the identification of the correlation between genotypes (SNPs) and phenotypes (i.e., characteristics such as the presence of a disease). This step can be modeled as the k-locus problem (where k is any integer). A number of algorithms have been proposed in the literature for this problem when $k = 2$. In this paper we present an algorithm for solving the 2-locus problem that is up to two orders of magnitude faster than the previous best known algorithms.

Keywords

Genome-wide association study; Two-locus problem; String correlations

1. INTRODUCTION

There are a number of ways in which any two human genomes can differ. Variations are largely due to the single nucleotide polymorphisms (SNPs in short) as well as deletions, insertions and copy number variations [6]. Any of these variations may result in alterations in an individual's traits, or phenotypes. A phenotype of interest can be anything from a disease risk to physical properties such as height. In genetic epidemiology, a genome-wide association study (GWA study, or GWAS), also known as whole genome association study (WGA study, or WGAS), is an examination of many common genetic variants in different individuals to observe if any variant is associated with a trait. GWAS plays a major role in personalized medicine.

A lot of effort has been spent to identify mappings between phenotypical traits and genomic data. Due to the advent of next generation high throughput sequencing technologies, nowadays it is possible to study the genomic structure of individuals in detail. In GWAS, two different problems have been focused on. In single locus association study, researchers try to find out the association between phenotypical traits and individual SNPs. In two locus association study, the goal is to figure out the association between pairs of SNPs and phenotypical traits. A major task in this study is that of identifying the most correlated pair of SNPs. Two locus associations are also known as gene-gene interactions. Such interactions are believed to be major factors responsible for many complex phenotypical traits [10, 2, 5, 7, 8, 14]. It is a proven fact that such gene-gene interactions are the major actors to express many complex traits such as various human diseases. A generalization of this problem is that of identifying the k most important loci responsible for a specific phenotype. This is known as the k-locus problem.

Given that the number of SNPs found in humans is 10^5 to 10^7, a brute force way of scanning through every possible pair of SNPs to identify the most correlated pair is not feasible in practice. A number of algorithms for the two locus problem can be found in the literature. For instance, genetic algorithms are used in [11] and [13]. The algorithms proposed in [15] and [16] take $O(n^2m + nm^2)$ time, where n is the number of SNPs and m is the number of subjects. This algorithm is called FastANOVA. An algorithm with an expected run time of $O(n^{1+\epsilon} \log^2 n)$, where $0 < \epsilon < 1$ is a constant, has been presented in [1]. This algorithm exploits an algorithm known for the Light Bulb Problem [12] and Locality Sensitive Hashing (LSH) [3]. In this paper we present an algorithm for the two locus problem whose expected run time is $O(n^{1+\epsilon} \log n)$ (where $0 < \epsilon < 1$ is a constant). Our algorithm is asymptotically better than that of [1] by a logarithmic factor. Moreover, we have employed a number of innovations at the coding level and hence the improvement is indeed by more than a logarithmic factor. Our algorithm is up to two orders of magnitude faster than prior algorithms (specifically FastANOVA [16] and the algorithm of [1]) on various benchmark datasets.

The rest of this paper is organized as follows. In Section 2 we provide some notations. In Section 3 we present

*Corresponding Author

CIKM'16, October 24-28, 2016, Indianapolis, IN, USA

DOI: http://dx.doi.org/10.1145/2983323.2983685

some preliminaries needed for solving the two locus problem. Specifically, we consider the problems of finding the largest correlated pair of strings (from out of n given strings) and the problem of finding the least correlated pair of strings. We present novel algorithms for solving these problems and compare them with prior best known algorithms for solving these. In Section 4 we describe our algorithm (called TLA) for solving the two locus problem and in Section 5 we compare our algorithm with prior best algorithms. Some concluding remarks are given in Section 6.

2. NOTATIONS AND DEFINITIONS

Let $T = a_1, a_2, \ldots, a_n$ be a sequence of real numbers (or characters from a finite alphabet). An ℓ-mer of T is nothing but a subsequence of T of ℓ contiguous elements of T. The ℓ-mers of T are $T_i = a_i, a_{i+1}, \ldots, a_{i+\ell-1}$, for $1 \leq i \leq (n-\ell+1)$.

If the elements of T are real numbers, then the Euclidean distance between T_i and T_j, denoted as $d(T_i, T_j)$, is $\sqrt{\sum_{k=0}^{\ell-1}(a_{i+k} - a_{j+k})^2}$.

If the elements of T are characters from an alphabet Σ, then the Hamming distance between T_i and T_j, denoted as $d(T_i, T_j)$, is $\sum_{k=0}^{\ell-1} \delta(a_{i+k}, a_{j+k})$ where $\delta(a,b) = 1$ if $a \neq b$ and $\delta(a,b) = 0$ if $a = b$ (for any $a, b \in \Sigma$). A sequence of characters can be thought of as a string of characters, since we can obtain a string from the sequence by concatenating the characters. Thus we'll use the terms 'a sequence of characters' and 'a string of characters' interchangeably.

Let $A = a_1, a_2, \ldots, a_n$ and $B = b_1, b_2, \ldots, b_n$ be two sequences of characters. Also, let the Hamming distance between A and B be d. Then, by the *number of matches* between A and B we mean $n-d$. Also, the *correlation* between A and B is defined to be $\frac{n-d}{n}$.

3. SOME PRELIMINARIES

In this section we provide some preliminary ideas and techniques that will be useful for solving the two locus problem. Specifically, in this section we consider the following problems: finding the most similar pair of character strings, and finding the least similar pair of character strings, where the similarity is in terms of the Hamming distance between strings.

3.1 Finding the most correlated pair of strings

For this problem we are given n Boolean vectors $\hat{b}_1, \hat{b}_2, \ldots, \hat{b}_n$ each of length t. The problem is to find the pair of vectors that are the most similar (i.e., the Hamming distance between them is the smallest). Note that, given two vectors, we can find the Hamming distance between them in $O(t)$ time. A straight forward algorithm to identify the most correlated pair of vectors takes $O(n^2 t)$ time. This algorithm computes the Hamming distance between every pair of vectors. We can achieve a better run time using randomization. We say that the correlation between a pair of strings is p if the Hamming distance between them is $t(1-p)$. Let p_1 be the correlation between the most correlated pair of strings and p_2 be the correlation between the second most correlated pair of strings.

Consider a matrix M of size $n \times t$, such that the ith row of M is $\hat{b}_i$, for $1 \leq i \leq n$. The idea of our algorithm is to iteratively collect pairs of strings that are candidates to be the most correlated. Once we collect enough pairs, we compute the distance between each pair in this collection and output the closest. In each iteration we pick q columns randomly. For any vector (or string), the values in these columns can be concatenated to get a q-bit integer. We hash the vectors based this integer value. Subsequently, we generate pairs as follows: Consider any bucket in the hash table. If there are m vectors in this bucket, then each pair of vectors in this bucket is added as a candidate to a list C. There are $O\left(n^{\frac{\log p_1}{\log p_2}} \log n\right)$ iterations in the algorithm.

We can show that after $O\left(n^{\frac{\log p_1}{\log p_2}} \log n\right)$ iterations, C will have the most correlated pair of bulbs with high probability (i.e., with a probability of $1 - n^{-\Omega(1)}$). This algorithm is similar to the algorithm given in [12] but faster (by more than a logarithmic factor). We can generalize the above algorithm to arbitrary alphabets and get the following

Theorem 3.1. *Let M be a matrix of size $n \times t$. Each entry in this matrix is an element from some set Σ of cardinality σ. We can find the most correlated pair of rows of M in an expected $O\left(n^{1+\frac{\log p_1}{\log p_2}} \log n\right)$ time where p_1 is the correlation between the most correlated pair of rows, p_2 is the correlation between the second most correlated pair of rows. (Here correlation is based on Hamming distance. For example, p_1 is the largest fraction of columns in which any two rows agree).*

Proof: Probability that the most correlated pair of strings falls into the same bucket is p_1^q. (Note that each row is a string). Probability that this pair does not fall into the same bucket in a given iteration is $(1-p_1^q)$. Thus, the probability that this pair does not fall into the same bucket in z successive iterations is $(1-p_1^q)^z$. This probability is $\leq \exp(-zp_1^q)$ using the fact that $(1-x)^{1/x} \leq 1/e$ for any $0 < x < 1$. In turn, this probability will be $\leq n^{-\alpha}$ if $z \geq \frac{\alpha \log n}{p_1^q}$.

To ensure that the run time is as small as possible, we want to ensure that the size of C is not too large. Since we spend a linear time in each iteration of the algorithm, an optimal strategy will be to make sure that the number of candidate pairs generated in each iteration is also $O(n)$. If p_2 is the second largest correlation, the probability that any pair other than the largest correlated falls into the same bucket in any iteration is $\leq p_2^q$. If this probability is $\leq \frac{1}{n}$, then the expected number pairs generated in any iteration will be $\leq n$. This happens if $q = \frac{\log n}{\log(1/p_2)}$. For this value of q, the value of z becomes $\alpha \log n \; n^{\log p_1/\log p_2}$.

Given that the expected time we spend in hashing in each iteration and the time for generating the pairs is $O(n)$, it follows that the expected run time of the algorithm is $O\left(n^{1+\frac{\log p_1}{\log p_2}} \log n\right)$. □

Note: The run time of MCP is better than that of the light bulb algorithm presented in [12] by more than a logarithmic factor.

Let the above general algorithm be called MCP.

The case of random data. To get an idea of how large $\frac{\log p_1}{\log p_2}$ could get consider the case where all the strings are random (i.e., each character of any string is randomly chosen to be 0 or 1 with equal probability). Consider a collection of n random strings of length t each. Let A and B be any two of these vectors. The expected correlation between A and B is $1/2$, i.e., the expected number of positions in which they match is $t/2$. We can use Chernoff bounds to get high probability estimates on p_1 and p_2.

Chernoff bounds: If X is the sum of t independent Bernoulli trials with a probability p of success each, then the following are true, for any $0 < \delta < 1$ [9]:

$$Prob.[X < ((1-\delta)\mu] < \exp(-\mu\delta^2/2).$$

Here $\mu = tp$. Also, if $p \geq 1/2$, then, for any $x > 0$,

$$Prob.[X > tp + x] < \exp\left(\frac{-x^2}{2tp(1-p)}\right).$$

Using the above bounds, it follows that the probability that the correlation between A and B is more than $\frac{t}{2} + x$ is $\leq \exp(-2x^2/t)$. Thus the probability that there exists at least one pair whose correlation is $> \frac{t}{2} + x$ is $\leq n^2 \exp(-2x^2/t)$. As a result, we infer that the correlation between any pair is $\leq \frac{1}{2} + \sqrt{\frac{2\ln n - \ln u}{t}}$ with probability $\geq (1-u)$, for any $0 < u < 1$. Similarly, the probability that none of the pairs has a correlation less than $\frac{1}{2} - \sqrt{\frac{2\ln n - \ln u}{t}}$ is $\geq (1-u)$. Thus a high probability upper bound on p_1 is $\hat{p}_1 = \frac{1}{2} + \sqrt{\frac{2\ln n - \ln u}{t}}$ and a high probability lower bound on p_2 is $\check{p}_2 = \frac{1}{2} - \sqrt{\frac{2\ln n - ln u}{t}}$.

Table 1 displays these estimates for different values of n. For this table, the value of t has been chosen to be 200 and that of u is 0.01. It also shows the corresponding values of $\frac{\log \hat{p}_1}{\log \check{p}_2}$. From this table we see that for a fixed value of t when the value of n increases, the value of $\frac{\log \hat{p}_1}{\log \check{p}_2}$ decreases.

Table 1: Correlation estimates for the case of random data.

n	$\hat{p}_1$	$\check{p}_2$	$\frac{\log \hat{p}_1}{\log \check{p}_2}$
10,000	0.8393	0.1607	0.0958
50,000	0.8622	0.1378	0.0748
100,000	0.8717	0.1283	0.0669

3.2 An experimental comparison of MK and MCP

An algorithm called MK for solving the Time Series Motif Mining (TSMM) problem has been given in [4]. MK can be used to solve the problem of finding the most correlated pair of strings as well, since both of these problems are special cases of the well studied closest pair problem. The algorithm of [4] for approximate TSMM partitions the input time series data T based on a window of size w (for an appropriate value of w), computes the mean of every window, and discretizes the mean into four possible values. As a result, the time series data is transformed into a string T' of characters form the alphabet $\{1,2,3,4\}$. It then uses any (ℓ, d)-motif finding algorithm to find the motifs in T'. However, all the exact algorithms for finding (ℓ, d)-motifs take time that is exponential on ℓ and d. Note that the last step of finding (ℓ, d) motifs can be replaced with a problem of finding time series motifs in T' which is nothing but the closest pair problem in the domain of strings of characters, the motif length being ℓ.

One could employ MK to solve the problem of finding the most correlated pair of strings. The only difference is that we have to replace Euclidean distance with Hamming distance. We have implemented this algorithm. It turns out that MK does not perform well for the case of binary strings. To be fair, the authors of MK have not tested MK for this case. We have compared MK with MCP and the results are shown in Table 2. As this Table reveals, MCP has a much better performance than MK. Please, see Figure 1 for visual details. It is also clear that if we employ MCP in place of (l, d)-motif finding algorithms, the performance of the approximate TSMM algorithm given in [4] will improve significantly.

When n is very large, we *inject* pairs with known correlations. As an example, consider the problem of finding the largest correlated pair of rows in a $m \times n$ matrix M. Say we generate each row by picking each element to be either 0 or 1 with equal probability. For any two rows, clearly, the expected correlation is $\frac{1}{2}$. We can perform a probabilistic analysis to get a high probability bound on the largest correlation between any two rows (see Table 1). For example, for $n = 10,000$, we generated several random data sets and computed the largest correlation in each and calculated an average. Let p be this value. To inject a pair with a correlation of p' where p' is $> p$ we generate a row a with all ones and another row b with $p'm$ ones and $m(1-p')$ zeros. We then replace (any) two rows of M with a and b. Clearly, the correlation between a and b is p'. The expected correlation between a and any other row of M (other than b) is $\frac{1}{2}$. Similarly, the expected correlation between b and any other row of M (other than a) is $\frac{1}{2}$. Thus the pair (a, b) is likely to be the winner with high probability. We have picked a value for p' that is only slightly larger than p so as to get an accurate estimate on the run time. We have used a similar technique to inject pairs to find most correlated pairs as well. We stop our algorithm MCP after a fixed number of runs i.e., 50. We are always able to find the most correlated pair we injected within the fixed number of runs. In Table 3 we show the results for our algorithm. As evident from Table 3 MCP finds the injected pair within a very short period of time. As an example consider the dataset D3.8. It consists of 16 million timeseries, the motif length being 1024. It processed 249.02×10^8 pairs only in 37 minutes to find the most correlated pair. Please, see Figure 1. Note that all the experiments were done on an Intel Haswell compute node with 48 GB of RAM. The operating system running was Red Hat Enterprise Linux Server release 5.7 (Tikanga).

3.3 Identification of the Least Correlated Pair of Strings

The MCP algorithm identifies the closest pair of strings, from out of n given binary strings. An interesting question is if we can use the same algorithm to identify the **furthest** pair of strings. This problem has relevance in many problems including the two locus problem in GWAS. The authors of [1] present an elegant adaptation of the light bulb algorithm of [12] to solve this problem when the strings are binary. In this section we show how to adapt MCP to solve this problem. Our experimental comparison shows that our algorithm has a significantly better run time than that of [1].

3.3.1 *Some notations*

Let $m(x, y)$ stand for the number of matches between two strings (of equal length) x and y. For instance, if $x = 10010$ and $y = 00111$, then $m(x, y) = 2$ (since they match in posi-

Table 2: Number of pairs and runtime comparisons in Hamming space on binary strings. CPU times are given in seconds.

		MK		MCP		Gain	Speed up
Dataset	Size	Processed Pairs	CPU Time	Processed Pairs	CPU Time	Processed Pairs	Time
D2.1	2×10^3	976,520	2.34	1,515	0.27	644.57	8.82
D2.2	4×10^3	3,437,171	9.09	6,099	0.44	563.56	20.81
D2.3	6×10^3	5,958,494	17.50	13,889	0.51	429.01	33.99
D2.4	8×10^3	7,513,580	22.51	24,308	0.80	309.10	28.29
D2.5	10×10^3	20,788,832	60.59	38,076	0.81	545.98	74.69
D2.6	12×10^3	29,722,565	90.28	54,707	0.95	543.30	94.87
D2.7	14×10^3	35,408,500	110.38	75,058	1.09	471.75	101.08
D2.8	16×10^3	42,735,676	130.22	97,934	1.26	436.37	103.06
D2.9	18×10^3	48,137,187	157.73	124,126	1.37	387.81	114.90
D2.10	20×10^3	119,362,627	381.11	152,837	1.51	780.98	251.86

Table 3: Number of pairs and runtime of MCP in Hamming space on binary strings. CPU times are given in minutes.

		Brute-force	MCP		Gain
Dataset	Size	Processed Pairs	Processed Pairs	CPU Time	Processed Pairs
D3.1	2×10^6	2×10^{12}	3.89×10^8	2.22	5,140.10
D3.2	4×10^6	8×10^{12}	15.56×10^8	5.21	5,139.87
D3.3	6×10^6	18×10^{12}	35.02×10^8	9.38	5,140.06
D3.4	8×10^6	32×10^{12}	74.46×10^8	16.07	4,297.45
D3.5	10×10^6	50×10^{12}	97.27×10^8	18.80	5,140.10
D3.6	12×10^6	72×10^{12}	140.08×10^8	24.42	5,140.02
D3.7	14×10^6	98×10^{12}	190.66×10^8	30.91	5,140.03
D3.8	16×10^6	128×10^{12}	249.02×10^8	37.98	5,140.09

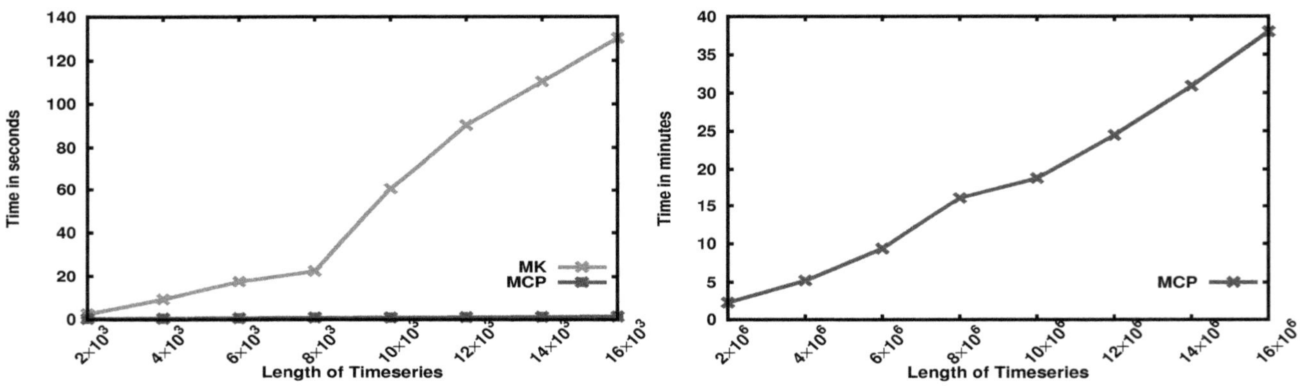

(a) CPU times consumed by MK and MCP methods

(b) CPU times consumed by MCP method

Figure 1: Performance evaluations between MK and MCP methods.

tions 2 and 4). Let $X = x_1, x_2, \ldots, x_q$ and $Y = y_1, y_2, \ldots, y_q$ be two sequences of strings (each string having the same length). We define $M(X,Y)$ to be $\sum_{i=1}^{q} m(x_i, y_i)$.

Consider the sequences $A_i = a_1^i, a_2^i, \ldots, a_k^i$, for $1 \le i \le n$, where each a_j^i is 0, or 1 (for $1 \le j \le k$). Note that each A_i is a sequence of strings where each string is of length 1. Let $M(A_i, A_j) = u_{ij}$.

Each A_i can be thought of as a binary string. In the application of GWAS, we can let A_i correspond to the SNP i, for $1 \le i \le n$. Specifically, a_j^i is the value of the ith SNP in subject j, for $1 \le j \le k$. If we are interested in finding the two most correlated SNPs, then we can use MCP to identify this pair (as shown in Section 3.1). On the other hand, if our goal is to identify the least correlated pair, then, it is not clear how to do this using MCP. To solve the two locus GWAS problem, we have to identify not only the most correlated pair of strings but also the least correlated pair.

3.3.2 *Finding the least correlated pair*

The authors of [1] present an elegant solution for this problem. The idea is to construct a matrix D of size $k \times 2n$ where each column of D corresponds to either a light bulb or its 'complement'. (A light bulb can be thought of as a string or a SNP). Specifically, the first n columns correspond to the bulbs and the next n columns correspond to the complements of the bulbs. In other words, $D[j,i] = a_j^i$, for $1 \le i \le n, 1 \le j \le k$ and $D[j,i] = \bar{a}_j^i$ for $1 \le j \le k, (n+1) \le i \le 2n$. Here, if x is any bit, then, $\bar{x}$ denotes its complement. Let $D_1 = \{q : 1 \le q \le n\}$ and $D_2 = \{q : (n+1) \le q \le 2n\}$. The algorithm of [1] for finding the least correlated pair works as follows. Consider all the pairs of columns (a, b) such that

$a \in D_1$ and $b \in D_2$. From out of these pairs, identify the pair (a', b') of columns with the maximum number of matches. If $a' = i$ and $b' = n + j$, then (i, j) is the least correlated pair of bulbs. Finding such a pair (a', b') can be done using the light bulb algorithm of [12]. The correctness of this algorithm follows from the fact that if the two bulbs i and j have the least number of matches, then, column i and the complement of column j will have the most number of matches. In this approach we can replace the light bulb algorithm with MCP to drastically improve the run time (by more than a logarithmic factor).

4. TWO LOCUS ASSOCIATION PROBLEM

The two locus association problem is defined as follows. Input is a matrix M of size $(m_1 + m_2) \times n$ where $m_1 + m_2$ is the number of patients (subjects) each with n SNPs. Here m_1 is the number of cases and m_2 is the number of controls. The cases are of phenotype 1 and the controls are of phenotype 0. Rows 1 through m_1 of M correspond to cases. Let this submatrix be called A. Rows $m_1 + 1$ through $m_1 + m_2$ of M correspond to controls and let this submatrix be called B. Each column of M corresponds to an SNP. The two locus association problem is to identify the pair of SNPs whose statistical correlation with phenotype is maximally different between cases and controls. As mentioned in [1], the goal is to identify the pair:

$$\arg\max_{i,j} |P_A(i,j) - P_B(i,j)|.$$

If Q is any matrix, then, $P_Q(i,j)$ stands for the correlation between the columns i and j of Q.

The algorithm of [1] exploits the light bulb algorithm of [12] and locality sensitive hashing (LSH) [3]. They use LSH to transform matrices A and B to A' and B', respectively. In particular, each column c_i of A is converted to a column c_i' of zeros and ones. The size of c_i is $1 \times m_1$ and the size of c_i' is chosen to be $u = \max\{m_1, m_2\}$. The matrix B is also transformed into B' in a similar manner using LSH. Followed by this, the pair of interest is identified.

To be precise, using A' and B', the matrix D is formed where

$$D = \begin{bmatrix} A' & A' \\ B' & \bar{B}' \end{bmatrix}$$

where $\bar{B}'$ is obtained from B' by complementing every element of B'. Note that D is of size $2u \times 2n$. Let $D_1 = \{1, 2, \ldots, n\}$ and $D_2 = \{n+1, n+2, \ldots, 2n\}$. Consider all the pairs of columns (i, j) such that $i \in D_1$ and $j \in D_2$. From out of these pairs, identify the pair (i', j') of columns with the maximum number of matches. If $i' = a$ and $j' = n + b$, then (a, b) is the pair of interest. The authors of [1] find this pair using the light bulb algorithm of [12].

We can use MCP instead of the light bulb algorithm to get the following theorem. In this case the run time will improve by more than a logarithmic factor.

Theorem 4.1. *We can find the pair (i, j) of SNPs that maximizes $|P_A(i,j) - P_B(i,j)|$ in an expected time of $O\left(n^{1+\frac{\log p_1}{\log p_2}} \log n\right)$, where p_1 and p_2 are the smallest and the next smallest values of $|P_A(i,j) - P_B(i,j)|$, respectively, over all possible pairs (i, j) of SNPs.*

Proof: Similar to that of Theorem 3.1 and hence omitted. We call our algorithm for the two locus problem TLA.

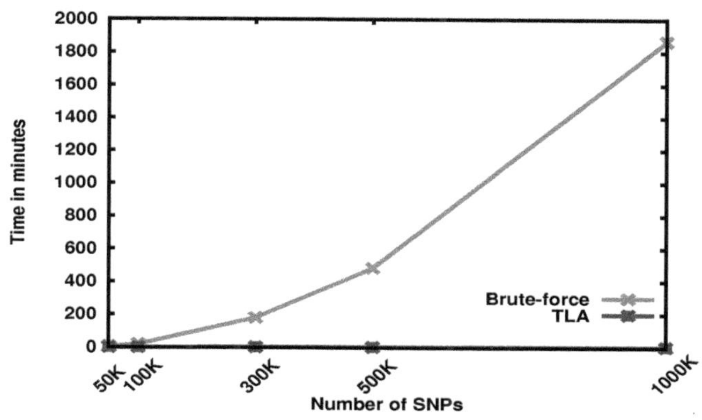

Figure 2: Performance evaluations between Brute-force and TLA methods.

5. AN EXPERIMENTAL COMPARISON

The notion of similarity (between two SNPs) used in [1] is Pearson's correlation coefficient. In this paper the similarity we use is based on the Hamming distance. We believe that the Hamming distance is a better measure since it can be used to derive other measures. In terms of run times, these two measures do not have a significant difference. Specifically, the complement of the Hamming distance is the measure of similarity we employ. The authors of [1] have tested their algorithms on different data sets (including random data). Since we do not have access to either these data sets or their algorithms, the only comparison we can do was on the random data. As explained in [1], we have also generated SNPs randomly. In particular, for each subject, the value of each SNP is chosen uniformly randomly to be either 0 or 1 with equal probability. This dataset is called NOISE Data in [1] (c.f. Table 4 in [1]). The authors of [1] note that random data are the hadest instances for the identification of the most (and least) correlated pair as well as the two locus problem. We have generated data of sizes 50K, 100K, 300K, 500K and 1,000K with 50 cases and 50 controls to demonstrate how effective our algorithm is. For example FastANOVA [16] took almost 1000 seconds for 42K SNPs. On the other hand for 50K SNPs our algorithm took only 7.8 seconds. All the experiments were done on an Intel Haswell compute node with 48 GB of RAM. The operating system running was Red Hat Enterprise Linux Server release 5.7 (Tikanga).

We have also compared the performance of our algorithm with the algorithm reported in [1]. Our results are shown in Table 4. The recall rates for us are much better than those of [1] (see Table 6 in [1]). Recall rates refer to the accuracy of the different algorithms in terms of how many of the top q correlated pairs were identified by these algorithms (for different values of q). For example, for 50K SNPs, the top 10 recall rate of [1] is 0.2, whereas it is 0.74 for our algorithm. As another example, for 100K SNPs, the top 10 recall rate of [1] is 0 whereas it is 0.74 for our algorithm.

In terms of run times we can only do an estimation of the speedup since they [1] do not report any actual run times. They report that the brute force algorithm takes several days using 1,000 processors (for less than 1,000K SNPs). To give

Table 4: Number of pairs and runtime comparisons in Hamming space on NOISE datasets. CPU times are given in minutes.

	Brute-force		TLA				Gain	Speed up
# SNPs	Processed Pairs	CPU Time	Processed Pairs	CPU Time	Top 10	Top 100	Processed Pairs	Time
5×10^4	25×10^8	4.97	715,553	0.13	0.74	0.87	3,493.80	39.29
1×10^5	10×10^9	19.00	2,861,457	0.22	0.74	0.92	3,494.72	84.85
3×10^5	90×10^9	178.23	25,749,044	0.87	0.80	0.94	3,495.28	203.96
5×10^5	25×10^{10}	482.30	71,529,899	1.35	0.88	0.83	3,495.04	356.09
1×10^6	10×10^{11}	1,867.05	286,110,791	3.48	0.80	0.75	3,495.15	536.00

the benefit of doubt, we take the time as 2 days. This means that for 100K SNPs, the brute force algorithm took 20 days on a single processor. For 100K SNPs, in Table 6 (of [1]) they indicate that their algorithm achieves a speedup of 184 over the brute force. This means that their algorithm took more than 156 minutes. Also they have used 400 subjects whereas we have used 100 subjects. This means that on 100 subjects and 100K SNPs, their algorithm will take 39 minutes. Our run time for 100K SNPs and 100 subjects is 0.22 minutes. This means that our algorithm is more than 177 times faster. Note that this is only a very conservative estimate. Also note that the improvement our algorithm achieves is quite significant since the typical processing times reported in the literature for the two locus problem are quite high. The improvement we achieve is not only due to the novel algorithm but also due to a number of techniques we have used at the implementation level. We have used bit operations as much as possible. This also reduces the memory used. Any improvement in the run time achieved for solving the two locus problem could make a noticeable difference in GWAS. Please, see Figure 2 for visual details.

6. CONCLUSIONS

In this paper we have presented a novel algorithm for the two locus problem that plays a central role in GWAS. Our algorithm is two orders of magnitude faster than previous algorithms. We also offer algorithms for the finding the most and least correlated pairs of strings. In summary, we improve the results presented in many prior papers including [16] and [1].

Funding

This work has been supported in part by the following grants: NIH R01-LM010101 and NSF 1447711.

7. REFERENCES

[1] P. Achlioptas, B. Schölkopf and K. Borgwardt, Two-locus association mapping in subquadratic runtime, ACM SIGKDD international conference on Knowledge discovery and data mining (KDD) 2011.

[2] C.E. Aston, D.A. Ralph, D.P. Lalo, S. Manjeshwar, B.A. Gramling, D.C. DeFreese, A.D. West, D.E. Branam, L.F. Thompson, M.A. Craft, D.S. Mitchell, C.D. Shimasaki, J.J. Mulvihill, and E.R. Jupe, Oligogenic combinations associated with breast cancer risk in women under 53 years of age, *Human Genetics*, 116(3):208-221, Feb. 2005.

[3] M. S. Charikar. Similarity estimation techniques from rounding algorithms, *Proc. ACM Symposium on Theory of Computing* (STOC), 2002.

[4] B. Chiu, E. Keogh, and S. Lonardi, Probabilistic discovery of time series motifs, *Proc. of the 9th International Conference on Knowledge Discovery and Data mining* (KDD), pp. 493-498, 2003.

[5] J.H. Cho, D.L. Nicolae, L.H. Gold, C.T. Fields, et al., Identification of novel susceptibility loci for inflammatory bowel disease on chromosomes 1p, 3q, and 4q: evidence for epistasis between 1p and IBD1, *Proceedings of the National Academy of Sciences of the United States of America*, 95(13):7502-7507, June 1998.

[6] T. H. Consortium, A second generation human haplotype map of over 3.1 million SNPs, *Nature*, 449(7164):851-61, Oct. 2007.

[7] H. J. Cordell, Detecting gene-gene interactions that underlie human diseases, *Nat Rev Genet*, 10(6):392-404, June 2009.

[8] N.J. Cox, M. Frigge, D.L. Nicolae, P. Concannon, C.L. Hanis, G.I. Bell, and A. Kong, Loci on chromosomes 2 (NIDDM1) and 15 interact to increase susceptibility to diabetes in mexican americans, *Nature Genetics*, 21(2):213-215, Feb. 1999.

[9] R. Motwani and P. Raghavan, *Randomized Algorithms*, Cambridge University Press, 1995.

[10] S. K. Musani, D. Shriner, N. Liu, R. Feng, et al., Detection of gene x gene interactions in genome-wide association studies of human population data, *Human Heredity*, 63(2):67-84, 2007.

[11] R. Nakamichi, Y. Ukai, and H. Kishino, Detection of closely linked multiple quantitative trait loci using a genetic algorithm, *Genetics*, 158(1):463-475, May 2001.

[12] R. Paturi, S. Rajasekaran, and J. Reif. The light bulb problem, *Information and Computation* 117, 1995, pp. 187-192.

[13] Y. Wang, X. Liu, K. Robbins, and R. Rekaya, AntEpiSeeker: detecting epistatic interactions for case-control studies using a two-stage ant colony optimization algorithm, *BMC Bioinformatics*, 3:117-117, 2010.

[14] J. Xu, C.D. Langefeld, S.L. Zheng, E.M. Gillanders, et al., Interaction effect of PTEN and CDKN1B chromosomal regions on prostate cancer linkage, *Human Genetics*, 115(3):255-262, Aug. 2004.

[15] X. Zhang, S. Huang, F. Zou, and W. Wang, TEAM: efficient two-locus epistasis tests in human genome-wide association study, *Bioinformatics* (Oxford, England), 26(12):i217-227, June 2010.

[16] X. Zhang, F. Zou, and W. Wang, Fastanova: an efficient algorithm for genome-wide association study, *Proc. 14th ACM SIGKDD international conference on Knowledge discovery and data mining* (KDD), pages 821-829, Las Vegas, Nevada, USA, 2008.

FolkTrails: Interpreting Navigation Behavior in a Social Tagging System

Thomas Niebler, Martin Becker, Daniel Zoller
DMIR Group, University of Würzburg, Germany
{niebler,becker,zoller}@informatik.uni-wuerzburg.de

Stephan Doerfel
KDE Group, University of Kassel, Germany
doerfel@cs.uni-kassel.de

Andreas Hotho
DMIR Group, University of Würzburg and L3S Research Center, Germany
hotho@informatik.uni-wuerzburg.de

ABSTRACT

Social tagging systems have established themselves as a quick and easy way to organize information by annotating resources with tags. In recent work, user behavior in social tagging systems was studied, that is, how users assign tags, and consume content. However, it is still unclear how users make use of the navigation options they are given. Understanding their behavior and differences in behavior of different user groups is an important step towards assessing the effectiveness of a navigational concept and improving it to better suit the users' needs. In this work, we investigate navigation trails in the popular scholarly social tagging system BibSonomy from six years of log data. We discuss dynamic browsing behavior of the general user population and show that different navigational subgroups exhibit different navigational traits. Furthermore, we provide strong evidence that the semantic nature of the underlying folksonomy is an essential factor for explaining navigation.

1. INTRODUCTION

With the advent of social media and the Web 2.0, it became very easy to contribute and arrange content on web platforms, even for technical laymen, for example in wikis, social networks or social tagging systems. As a direct consequence, not only providing, but browsing and consuming content accounts for a big part of user interaction in today's Web. Among those various platforms, social tagging systems have established themselves as a quick and easy way to organize and store information, such as websites[1] and publications[2]. In such systems, users can post resources and freely annotate them with keywords (called *tags*), for example, for means of later retrieval by themselves and by other users. The emerging structure over users, tags, and resources and their connections is called a *folksonomy* and serves as the main navigational concept in social tagging systems, providing links between co-occurring entities. Through those links, folksonomies possess an inherently semantic nature. However, it is still largely unclear how users make use of the navigation options they are given. Understanding their behavior and its differences between various user groups is an important step towards assessing the effectiveness of a navigational concept and of improving it to better suit the users' needs. This task has attracted broad interest in the research community and previous work has focused on the navigation within one particular website [20, 7] or on the Web in general [6, 14]. Also, studying the navigation behavior of users in social tagging systems is of great interest, especially because of these systems' inherent semantic structure. Consequently, different studies have addressed this issue: [9] conducted a user survey on usage motivation in social tagging systems and [7] used log files to study actual navigation behavior of the overall user population through request counts. While these findings give a first insight into the behavioral properties of user navigation, they focus on the overall population of users and their *global* request counts.

Problem Setting and Approach: Although the above mentioned works give first insights into behavioral properties of user navigation, there exist several competing ideas and hypotheses about how users browse within a social tagging system based on *local* transition probabilities. Up to this point, such hypotheses were not objectively compared on actual navigation data. To address this issue, we utilize log files of BibSonomy, which provide a unique opportunity to study the navigational trails of user groups in a folksonomy. In particular, we formulate several navigation hypotheses and compare them using HypTrails [17], a method for comparing hypotheses about human movement on the Web. We also study how the performance of explaining navigation behavior differs on different data subsets, such as navigation grouped by gender, tagging behavior, or long-term experience. In the process, we revisit the aspects described in [7], and extend on their work, providing additional explanations for user intentions during navigation and their comparison. Furthermore, because tags and their inherent semantic information exert a great influence on social tagging systems, it is a logical assumption that navigating those systems is influenced by the semantic content. Thus, we explicitly search for a signal of the influence of tags on navigation, that is, a semantic component.

Contributions: The contributions in this paper are threefold: 1. We study different hypotheses about the navigational user behavior in a tagging system. 2. We provide evidence for the existence of a semantic influence on navigation. 3. We show that users with different tagging behavior also exhibit different navigational traits.

Overall, we contribute to a better understanding of navigation in tagging systems and the role of the folksonomy structure. We support the claims from [7] and shed light on general as well as subgroup specific behavior. We expect our results to be relevant not only for researchers interested in understanding human behavior and social tagging, or operators of any system utilizing tags (e.g., Twitter), but also for the whole Semantic Web community.

[1] e.g., Delicious (http://www.delicious.com)

[2] e.g., BibSonomy (http://www.bibsonomy.org)

CIKM'16 , October 24 - 28, 2016, Indianapolis, IN, USA

ISBN 978-1-4503-4073-1/16/10...$15.00

DOI: http://dx.doi.org/10.1145/2983323.2983686

2. RELATED WORK

In the following, we cover related work on research about the analysis of user navigation in web systems, as well as, research covering folksonomies and social tagging systems.

Navigation Analysis: Understanding human trails on the Web and the underlying generative processes is an open and complex challenge for the research community. However, a lot of previous work addresses these problems. In [20], click paths from a navigation game on Wikipedia have been examined to find way-finding patterns. A promising approach to model human navigation is provided by Markov models, which have been previously used for click-stream data in [4]. [18] noted that while Markov chains of higher order are too complex and inefficient to actually be useful, the memoryless first-order Markov model does account well for navigation on the Web. [17] presented the HypTrails method which is used to compare different hypotheses about user navigation in both web [1] and real-life contexts [2].

Folksonomies: The term *folksonomy* was first mentioned by Vander Wal in 2004 on his personal blog.[3] He used this term to describe the underlying structure connecting users, tags, and annotated resources in social tagging systems. While [13] hypothesized that tag distributions follow a power law distribution, thus possibly causing semantic stabilization, [8] showed that after a certain time span, regularities in user activity, tag frequencies and relative frequency proportions could be observed. In turn, this motivated further investigations of tagging systems, especially about the effective extraction of semantically stable content [5] and motivation of tag usage [12]. [9] conducted a user survey on the users' motivation for using social tagging systems, that is, whether users store resources for their own retrieval or social sharing purposes. While there exists a large amount of literature on tagging systems, to the best of our knowledge, there exists only a small amount of work utilizing and analyzing log data from a tagging system. [15] investigated user logs of the social tagging system Dogear, which is internally used at IBM and thus not publicly available, as opposed to BibSonomy. They could find strong evidence for social navigation, that is, users are looking at posts from other people instead of mainly their own. In [7], a thorough study of user behavior in BibSonomy was presented. In the study at hand, we extend these findings, focusing on the actual navigation behavior of users.

3. BACKGROUND

Before we describe and evaluate the hypotheses on navigation in social tagging systems, we recall social tagging systems as well as the formal model of their underlying structure, the so-called folksonomy and briefly introduce our use case BibSonomy. Then, we explain the HypTrails method used for comparing the hypotheses.

3.1 Folksonomies and Tagging

Social tagging systems have established themselves as popular means for organizing and managing digital resources on the Web. The basic idea of a tagging system is that each user can post resources and annotate these resources with freely chosen keywords (tags). By allowing users to assign arbitrary keywords to a resource, they form a powerful alternative to more traditional resource directories or catalogs with fixed taxonomies.

The structure emerging from tagging activities is called a *folksonomy*. [10] models a folksonomy as a quadruple $\mathbb{F} := (U, T, R, Y)$, where U, T, and R are the finite sets of all users, tags, and resources, respectively. The set of *tag assignments* $Y \subseteq U \times T \times R$ is a ternary relation between these sets. Hereby, $(u, t, r) \in Y$ means that user u has annotated resource r with tag t. A *post* from a user u with a posted resource r and the annotated set of tags T_{ur} is defined as a set $P_{u,r} = \{(u, t, r) | t \in T_{ur}\} \subseteq Y$. This also implies that users cannot assign the same tag to a resource twice.

An example for a folksonomy is BibSonomy, a social tagging system for bookmarks and scientific publications (cf. [3]). Note that next to the navigation structure described above, real world implementations often introduce additional navigational features such as showing *related* tags on tag pages or a menu with links to a logged-in user's own pages. Because of this, navigation does not always strictly follow the folksonomy-induced link structure.

3.2 The HypTrails Method

HypTrails [17] is an approach utilizing first-order Markov chain models (MC) and Bayesian inference for expressing and comparing hypotheses about human trails. In our case, the states of the MC are pages in a social tagging system and hypotheses represent ideas about how users navigate these pages. Specifically, hypotheses are formulated as transition probabilities. That is, given a page $s_i \in S$, we define the probability to choose any other page $s_j \in S$: $P(s_j|s_i)$. We introduce several such hypotheses in Section 4. There, we use transition functions $\bar{P}$ to represent hypotheses, which can be converted into the required probability distributions by normalizing the values for each source state s_i.

To obtain insights into the relative plausibility of a set of hypotheses $\mathbf{H} = \{H_1, \ldots, H_n\}$ given data D, HypTrails resorts to the Bayes factor, which compares the marginal likelihoods $P(D|H_i) = \int P(D|\theta)P(\theta|H_i)d\theta$, also called *evidences*, of the different hypotheses H_i. Generally, a hypothesis H_i is more "plausible" than another hypothesis H_j if its marginal likelihood $P(D|H_i)$ is greater.[4] Hypotheses are encoded into the marginal likelihood via the prior $P(\theta|H_i)$ by eliciting the parameters of a Dirichlet distribution from the corresponding transition probabilities of hypothesis H_i and a concentration factor K. The higher we set K, the more we believe in a given hypothesis. This means that the higher K, the stronger we believe in the actual transition probability distribution specified by the hypothesis. With lower values of K, the Dirichlet prior also assigns probability mass to other probability distributions similar to the original one, thus, we give the hypothesis some "tolerance". To understand the difference of our hypotheses in detail, we compare hypotheses based on different values of K. In this work, we express evidences on a log scale. We present corresponding results in Section 6. Note that, while HypTrails gives significant results regarding the ordering of the plausibility of different hypotheses, it is not an absolute measure. We can thus only give a qualified statement regarding the qualitative, not the quantitative difference in performance between the evidence of two hypotheses.

4. HYPOTHESES ON NAVIGATION IN SOCIAL TAGGING SYSTEMS

To be able to compare abstract ideas about how users navigate social tagging systems, we formulate them as transition hypotheses, so we can calculate their evidence with the HypTrails method.

4.1 Basic Hypotheses

First, we formulate basic hypotheses, each representing only a basic aspect of navigation.

Uniform Hypothesis: The uniform hypothesis serves as the baseline for all other hypotheses. It models the assumption that users randomly choose an arbitrary page to visit next, without regard for

[3]http://vanderwal.net/random/category.php?cat=153

[4]According to the reference table in [11], all differences reported in this work are decisive.

the underlying link structure (also called teleportation). Formally, this is expressed as $\bar{P}_{\text{uniform}}(s_j|s_i) = 1$. Since this hypothesis does not require any additional information, it can be considered the least informative one. We expect that any "real" hypothesis capturing a structurally interesting aspect of user behavior, will exhibit a higher evidence than this simple hypothesis.

Page Consistent Hypothesis: Results found by [7] motivate the idea that users often make a transition from a page to itself. This might be accounted for by various reasons, for example to follow pagination, that is, showing the next n elements in a truncated list. This hypothesis is formalized as $\bar{P}_{\text{page}}(s_j|s_i) = \sigma_{id}(s_i, s_j)$.[5]

Category Consistent Hypothesis: [7] found that transitions between two pages often occur between pages of the same category, i.e., after a user has visited a *tag* page, the next page is likely to be a *tag* page again. The same holds for *resource* and *user* pages. The classification of pages into one of these categories is described in Section 5. Thus, the hypothesis states that users stick to the same category. It is defined as $\bar{P}_{\text{cat}}(s_j|s_i) = \sigma_{id}(cat(s_i), cat(s_j))$, where $cat(s_k)$ denotes the category of page s_k.

User Consistent Hypothesis: Similarly to the category consistent hypothesis, this hypothesis assumes that a transition's target and source page belong to the same user. The motivating intuition for this hypothesis is that visitors, who are interested in the work of a specific user, will not only read one, but several of her articles and try to further explore her personomy (i.e., the subset of the folksonomy that only contains the user and her posted resources and tags). It is defined as $\bar{P}_{\text{user}}(s_j|s_i) = \sigma_{id}(user(s_i), user(s_j))$, where $user(s_k)$ denotes the user associated with page s_k.

Folksonomy Consistent Hypothesis: Social tagging systems map links of the underlying folksonomy to actual hyperlinks of the system. For example, the page of a resource contains hyperlinks leading to the page of the resource's owner as well as to the pages of the assigned tags. For that reason, this hypothesis assumes that users navigate only to pages which are reachable in the folksonomy structure and related-tags relations. To calculate reachability, we construct the page graph from the tag-assignments in the folksonomy dataset and (since they are an integral part of the BibSonomy user interface) we add tag-to-tag relations, when tags occur together at the same post. Formally, we define: $\bar{P}_{\text{folk}}(s_j|s_i) = 1$, if s_j is directly reachable in the folksonomy from s_i, 0 otherwise.

Semantic Navigation Hypothesis: Because the folksonomy structure can be used to extract emergent semantics, we aim to investigate the influence of a potential semantic component in navigation behavior. To compute the similarities between two pages, a page is treated as a document. The set of tags which appear on that page with respective frequencies (see Section 5) is treated as the document's "text", represented as the TF-IDF vector v_k. The similarity of two pages is then calculated with the cosine measure $cossim(v_i, v_j) = \langle \hat{v}_i, \hat{v}_j \rangle$, where $\hat{v}_k$ denotes the normalized vector of v_k. The hypothesis is defined as $\bar{P}_{\text{tfidf}}(s_j|s_i) = cossim(v_i, v_j)$.

4.2 Combining Hypotheses

In order to investigate possible mutual influences between hypotheses, it is also possible to combine them. In the following, we motivate and describe certain combinations.

Folksonomy Consistent & Semantic Navigation Hypothesis: As described earlier, it is a natural assumption that users utilize the folksonomy structure when navigating a social bookmarking system. If the folksonomy does indeed exhibit notable semantic properties, we should be able to see that adding a semantic component to folksonomic navigation improves the evidence of this hypothesis compared to the bare folksonomy navigation hypothesis. We define the hypothesis as $\bar{P}_{\text{folk-tfidf}}(s_j|s_i) := \bar{P}_{\text{folk}}(s_j|s_i) \cdot \bar{P}_{\text{tfidf}}(s_j|s_i)$.

User Consistent & Semantic Navigation Hypothesis: A similar motivation as with folksonomic and semantic navigation arises when we combine user consistent and semantic navigation. Users are usually thematically restricted in their research interests and can thus serve as a good selector for a limited field of topics. Navigation in the user's personomy is expected to show a strong semantic component. This hypothesis is defined as $\bar{P}_{\text{user-tfidf}}(s_j|s_i) := \bar{P}_{\text{user}}(s_j|s_i) \cdot \bar{P}_{\text{tfidf}}(s_j|s_i)$.

User Consistent & Folksonomy Navigation Hypothesis: The intuition behind combining user consistent and folksonomic navigation is that if navigation is mostly user consistent and partially follows folksonomy-induced links, folksonomic navigation on pages from the same user should yield a good model of navigation. We define this hypothesis as $\bar{P}_{\text{folk-user}}(s_j|s_i) := \bar{P}_{\text{user}}(s_j|s_i) \cdot \bar{P}_{\text{folk}}(s_j|s_i)$.

5. DATASETS

The datasets used in this paper are based on web server logs and database contents of BibSonomy. Since in 2012 the login mechanism was modified, which introduced significant changes to the logging infrastructure, we restrict the datasets to data created between the start of BibSonomy in 2006 and the end of 2011. Anonymized datasets of logs and posts are made available to researchers by the BibSonomy team.[6] Because BibSonomy is a popular target for users who bookmark advertisements, the system uses a learning classifier as well as manual classification by the system's administrators to detect spam. In all experiments, we only use data of users that have been classified as nonspammers.

User and Content Dataset: We use the folksonomy data (all nonspammers with their respective resources and tags) from the BibSonomy database. In the considered time frame, 17,932 users were explicitly classified as nonspammers. They created 456,777 bookmark posts and 2,410,844 publication posts using 204,309 distinct tags. Since we need semantic similarity scores between pages for the semantic navigation hypothesis, we consider all tags which have been used at least twice in order to receive more meaningful results by avoiding typos or rarely used words. With this pruning step, we end up with 65,228 distinct tags.

Request Log Dataset: The BibSonomy log files include all HTTP requests to the system (caching is disabled), including common request attributes like IP address, date and referer, as well as a session identifier and a cookie containing the name of the logged-in user. We only considered direct (i.e., no redirected) valid requests, which have been generated by logged-in nonspammers. Both the referer and the target page of a request must be a retrieval page, that is a page that is used to retrieve information (e.g., a resource or a list of resources; we discuss each considered retrieval page type in the next subsection). For the semantic navigation hypothesis, we had to extract the tag cloud representation of each page. Because a successful request does not imply that the requested page contains any content (e.g., a user tried to filter her collection by a tag that she had not used), we only consider requests that yield a non-empty set of tags using the procedure described in the last subsection. The remaining dataset contains 103,415 distinct visited pages. We recorded 327,060 transitions between these pages. 123,452 transitions were self-transitions (i.e., transitions from a page to itself) and 261,300 were own-transitions (i.e., transitions, where the logged in user owns both the source and the target page). One factor responsible for the large number of self-transitions are pagination effects.

[5] $\sigma_{id}(x, y) = 1$ if x is equal to y, 0 otherwise.

[6] http://www.kde.cs.uni-kassel.de/bibsonomy/dumps/

Page Types and Categories: The pages we consider after filtering the request logs can be assigned to exactly one of six page types. These page types can be grouped into three categories, matching the three folksonomic entity types *tag*, *resource*, and *user*. The six page types (with their corresponding categories) are:[7]

- **`/user/USER`** lists all posts of the requested user `USER` (*user*).
- **`/user/USER/TAG`** shows all posts which were tagged with tag `TAG` by user `USER` (*tag*).
- **`/tag/TAG`** lists all resources with the tag `TAG` (*tag*).
- **`/url/RESOURCE_IDENTIFIER`**[8] describes pages of bookmarked web links to the same web page (*resource*).
- **`/bibtex/RESOURCE_IDENTIFIER`** describes pages that show all publication posts, with the same resource contributed by different users (*resource*). Similar to the previous page type.
- **`/bibtex/RESOURCE_IDENTIFIER/USER`** shows all information that the user `USER` added for a specific publication (*resource*).

A details page for bookmarks is not available, clicking a bookmarked link leads to the bookmarked page (which is outside BibSonomy, thus, these requests are not tracked in the log files).

Tag Clouds as Semantic Page Representations: Since each retrieval page in BibSonomy shows a set of posts, we can define a *tag cloud* for each page. Given a page s_k, its tag cloud is defined as the set of tags with their respective frequencies, which are assigned to the posts of this page. For example, the tag cloud of a page showing two posts, one resource tagged with $social$ and web and another resource tagged with $social$, $concept$ and web, would be $tagcloud(s_k) := \{(social, 2), (concept, 1), (web, 2)\}$. The corresponding document-term vector v_k for the page s_k with the above mentioned tags as features would thus yield $v_k := (2, 1, 2)$, which can used to represent the page s_k.

6. RESULTS

In this section, we evaluate hypotheses about how users navigate on BibSonomy. We first compare our hypotheses (cf. Section 4) on the overall request log dataset. Then we analyze behavioral characteristics of different subsets of the data.

6.1 Overall Request Log Dataset

In this section, we first evaluate the basic hypotheses (cf. Section 4.1) and then the combined hypotheses (cf. Section 4.2) on the overall log dataset (cf. Section 5). Figure 1 shows the results.

Basic Hypotheses: All of the basic hypotheses explain the observed transitions better than the baseline (the uniform hyp.) to varying degrees. This indicates that they all introduce at least some structural properties which help to explain the observed transitions.

Besides this fact, there is a clear order of hypotheses: the user consistent hypothesis works best, the semantic and the folksonomy hypotheses are somewhat similarly plausible, followed by the page consistent and the category consistent hypotheses. Many of the observed effects are explainable by the large number of self-transitions in the dataset caused, for example, by pagination (cf. Section 5): 1. The page consistent hypothesis strongly improves on the uniform hypothesis. 2. The category consistent hypothesis is more plausible than the the uniform hypothesis, even though it directly contradicts navigation as induced by a folksonomy structure. 3. The user consistent hypothesis as well as semantically induced hypotheses are strongly favored because of self-transitions.

[7]Both `/url/RESOURCE_IDENTIFIER` and `/bibtex/RESOURCE_IDENTIFIER` have been restructured and redesigned in mid 2016. They now show combined information about the web page or the publication instead of a list of the same resource.

[8]BibSonomy calculates an identifier for each resource (URL or publication). See http://www.bibsonomy.org/help_en/InterIntraHash for details.

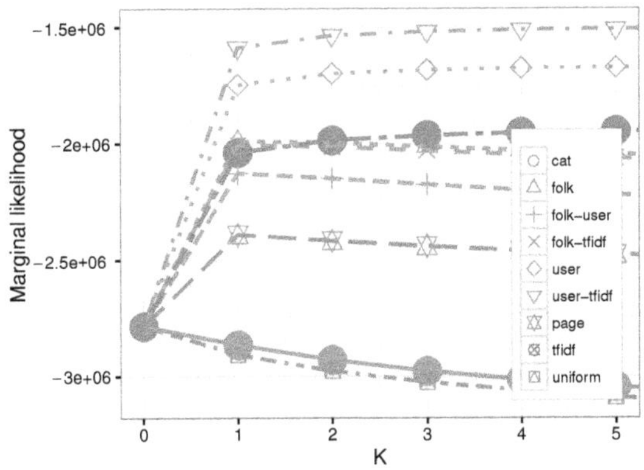

Figure 1: Evidence chart for our hypotheses on the complete request log dataset. Of the basic hypotheses, the user consistent hypothesis explains the data best, followed by the semantic and the folksonomy hypotheses. When combining the user consistent hypothesis with a semantic bias, the evidence improves. This indicates that users are actually semantically biased while navigating through resources. In contrast, combining other hypotheses with the folksonomy hypothesis does not yield better explanations for the observed navigation.

Nevertheless, the user consistent as well as semantically induced hypotheses are also more plausible than the page consistent hypothesis, indicating that their structural properties cover further important factors. That is, the superiority of the user consistent hypothesis indicates that users indeed navigate mostly on their own resources (cf. Section 5). The good performance of the semantic hypotheses indicates that semantic similarity of pages (with regard to tags) is a strong explaining factor for navigation on our dataset.

Finally, we consider the *folksonomy hypothesis* which models the navigation we expect in a folksonomy (see Section 4.1). It performs similarly well as the semantic hypotheses. We observe that the corresponding evidence curve crosses the semantic hypothesis (TF-IDF) for increasing believe factors K. This indicates that the folksonomy hypothesis covers an important factor of the navigation, but fails to model certain transitions, which are covered by the semantic hypothesis. The fact that the folksonomy hypothesis cannot cover certain transitions is due to navigation outside the folksonomy structure as elaborated in Section 5.

Combined Hypotheses: Overall, the combination of the user consistent and the semantic hypotheses performs best, indicating that navigation on BibSonomy can mainly be explained by semantic navigation within the resources of a specific user.

In contrast, combining the folksonomy hypothesis with the semantic hypothesis decreases the observed evidence slightly. Also, combining the folksonomy hypothesis with the user consistent hypothesis decreases the observed evidence dramatically. Both observations indicate that users excessively take advantage of additional navigation features provided by BibSonomy (see Section 3.1) when navigating on their own resources. Interestingly, in Section 6.2 we see that this does not hold when users navigate outside their own scope, that is, on resources exclusively from other users.

6.2 Request Log Subsets

We expect that there are subsets of the data where some hypotheses perform differently than on the overall dataset. Thus, in this section, we investigate different data subsets as listed in Table 1.

Table 1: Statistics of the request log subsets.

type	source states	links	counts
overall	55,129	149,542	327,060
inside	37,244	105,222	261,300
outside	14,757	28,760	42,193
male	23,090	61,616	130,988
female	5,598	14,413	29,705
neutral	28,726	73,575	161,830
lower_trr	30,368	83,268	176,755
upper_trr	7,084	15,474	32,517
lower_ten	3,459	6,959	15,451
upper_ten	51,542	140,844	307,072
shortterm	10,285	21,912	48,221
longterm	45,535	126,453	274,302

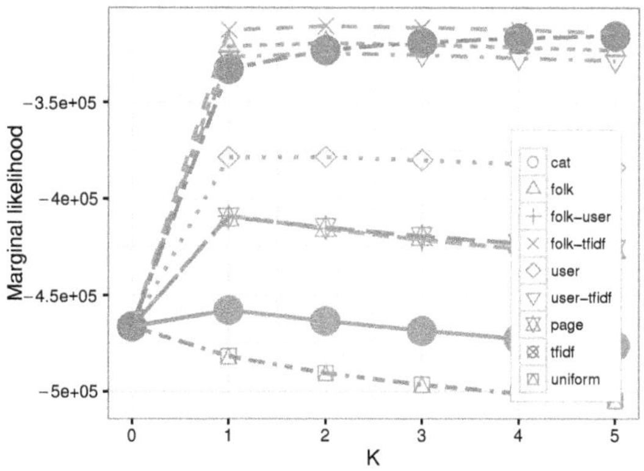

Figure 2: Evidence curves for navigation outside of the user's resources. In contrast to the overall dataset we observe that outside navigation can be explained best by a hypothesis assuming semantic behavior on the folksonomy structure (cf. *folk-tfidf*).

Inside and Outside Navigation: Motivated by the fact that users often navigate on their own pages (cf. Section 5), we investigate whether users behave differently when they are browsing the folksonomy *outside* of their own resources. In particular, we study the transitions where the source as well as the target state do not belong to the browsing user. The results can be seen in Figure 2. Here, the best explanation for the observed navigation is the *folk-tfidf* hypothesis which considers semantic behavior in combination with the structural properties of the folksonomy. This allows us to conclude that while users do not use the folksonomy structure when accessing their own resources (because they most likely explicitly access known publications), they fall back to the folksonomy structure when browsing resources outside of their scope. Furthermore, the evidence for the user consistent hypothesis drops strongly compared to the other hypotheses, because it is restricted to user consistent navigation *outside* of the browsing user's resources. This leads us to believe that browsing outside of the own resources is a process aimed at the discovery of new resources which in turn is not bound to the ownership of resources. Additionally, the fact that the plain user consistent hypothesis performs similarly well as the self-transition hypothesis indicates that the observed user-consistent outside navigation is mostly due to pagination effects.

User Gender: Since gender bias in online systems is an active research area [19], we also investigate the navigation for different genders. In BibSonomy, users can set their gender explicitly. If no gender was set, we assign the label *neutral*, otherwise, we can distinguish between *male* and *female*.

We hardly observe any difference between the genders, thus, to save space, we do not show specific plots. There is only a slight difference when considering the semantic hypotheses compared to the folksonomy hypothesis. It seems that the navigation behavior of male users shows a tendency towards following the folksonomy structure whereas the navigation behavior of female and especially neutral users can be better explained using the semantic hypothesis.

Usage Continuity: Since we expect users to adapt to systems they are using, we investigate if their navigation behavior changes over time. We divide users into *short-term* and *long-term users*, according to the temporal difference of their first and last request. If the difference is less than half a year, we classify a user as a *short-term user* and as a *long-term user* otherwise. In Figure 3, we report the results for short-term users. The results for long-term users are very similar to the results of the overall dataset (cf. Section 4.1).

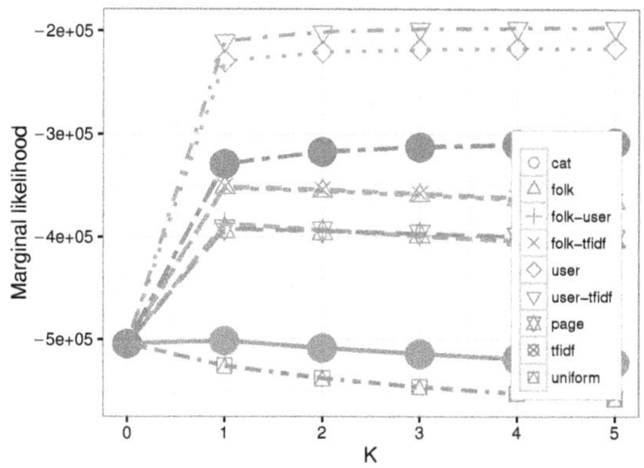

Figure 3: Evidence charts for short-term users ($\leq$ half a year according to their first and last request). We observe a stronger performance of the semantic hypothesis compared to the folksonomy hypothesis and see that the self and folk-user hypotheses perform equally well in explaining navigation. We attribute this to the increased browsing aspect of new users.

When comparing against the overall dataset (or, equivalently, the long-term user group), we observe two conspicuous differences for short-term users. First, the semantic hypothesis performs significantly better when compared to the folksonomy hypothesis. Second, the page-consistent and the folk-user hypotheses are explaining navigation equally well. The former may be explained by the fact that new users are not as tuned to the folksonomy structure as long-term users. Thus, we may actually observe a learning process: the longer users work with the folksonomy, the more they exploit the folksonomy structure in order to navigate their own resources or to discover new ones. The similar evidence curves for the page-consistent and the folk-user hypotheses can be explained by increased pagination effects while exploring the system in combination with the lack of transitions on resources owned by the browsing user. In contrast to outside navigation, here, the lack of transitions on own resources can be explained by the fact that new users have no or a lot less own resources than long-term users.

Tagger Classes: In [12] and [16], different types of folksonomy users were characterized by their tagging behavior. [12] define *categorizers and describers* and [16] identify *generalists and specialists*. Categorizers and describers are classified by their *tag-resource-ratio* (or short *trr*). That is, while categorizers use a small set of different tags for a large number of resources, indicating elaborate category systems, describers use many different tags, indicating a very descriptive approach when tagging. Generalists and specialists are classified using *tag entropy* (or short *ten*), where generalists have a high tag entropy, indicating a wide variety of tagged topics with regard to their resources, while specialists have a low entropy indicating a very specialized set of topics. For both classes we order users according to their *trr* and *ten* values separately and select the upper and lower 30%, respectively. We observe that categorizers and generalists show very similar evidence curves when compared to the overall navigation dataset. For the describers and specialists the curves are very similar to those of short-term users, thus, to save space, we refrain from depicting them.

For both, describers and specialists, we see the same tendency as for short-term users: the semantic hypothesis works better compared to the folk hypothesis and the user-consistent hypothesis has a tendency to perform equally well as the folk-user hypothesis.

The tendency towards semantic navigation over structural navigation on the folksonomy structure can most likely be explained by the nature of the tagging types: Specialists can be considered to be interested in rather few abstract topics, implying a more directed browsing behavior than generalists (whose interests are more varied). Consequently, their navigation is expected to also be more semantically influenced, because of their use of a small, but highly specialized tag subset. As for describers, resources are tagged with more keywords. Thus, for the semantic measure based on TFIDF, calculating the similarity may simply be easier than on the very sparse tagging structures induced by a categorizer's tagging habits.

In general, both types, specialists and describers, can be considered to be of a more explorative nature, as can be seen by the relative performance drop of the folk-user hypothesis and/or the increase of evidence for the self-transition hypothesis.

7. CONCLUSION

Understanding human navigation in web systems is an important step towards improving the design and usability of web pages. In this work, we analyzed navigational behavior of users in a social tagging system. We presented several hypotheses on navigational patterns and evaluated them on a large weblog dataset of the social tagging system BibSonomy.

Beyond confirming the results from [7], that is, that users mainly navigate on their own resources, we were able to show that within these resources, navigation follows a semantic bias (cf. Section 6.1). Also, the semantic hypothesis performs well in general, confirming the semantic component in navigation behavior on BibSonomy.

Furthermore, we studied different navigation subsets and were able to find significant differences in behavior. This includes that even though semantic, user consistent navigation represents a major aspect of the navigational characteristics of BibSonomy, users fall back to the folksonomy structure when browsing outside of their own pages (cf. Section 6.2). Also while different genders did not exhibit interesting behavioral deviations, short-term users, as well as different tagging types, follow certain behavioral patterns matching their individual characteristics. In particular, while it was only hypothesized in prior work [12] that categorizers and describers (as well as generalists and specialists) differ in navigation behavior, we have found specific components of their behavior which differ significantly, thus, indicating that navigation behavior and tagging pragmatics are indeed connected.

Overall, we were able to gain new insights into the underlying processes of navigation in tagging systems, which can be extended and leveraged in the future, for example, by considering new hypotheses, improving navigation experience or extracting semantics.

Acknowledgements: This work was partially funded by the DFG German Science Fund research project "PoSTs II".

8. REFERENCES

[1] Becker, M., Borchert, K., Hirth, M., Mewes, H., Hotho, A., Tran-Gia, P.: MicroTrails: comparing hypotheses about task selection on a crowd sourcing platform. In: Proc. of the 15th iKNOW Conf. (2015)

[2] Becker, M., Singer, P., Lemmerich, F., Hotho, A., Helic, D., Strohmaier, M.: Photowalking the city: comparing hypotheses about urban photo trails on Flickr. In: Proc. of the 7th SocInfo Conf. (2015)

[3] Benz, D., Hotho, A., Jäschke, R., Krause, B., Mitzlaff, F., Schmitz, C., Stumme, G.: The social bookmark and publication management system BibSonomy. VLDB Journal 19 (2010)

[4] Bollen, J., Van de Sompel, H., Hagberg, A., Bettencourt, L., Chute, R., Rodriguez, M.A., Balakireva, L.: Clickstream data yields high-resolution maps of science. PLoS One (2009)

[5] Cattuto, C., Benz, D., Hotho, A., Stumme, G.: Semantic Grounding of Tag Relatedness in Social Bookmarking Systems. In: Proc. of the 7th ISWC (2008)

[6] Chi, E.H., Pirolli, P., Chen, K., Pitkow, J.: Using information scent to model user information needs and actions and the web. In: Proc. of the SIGCHI Conf. on Human Factors in Computing Systems (2001)

[7] Doerfel, S., Zoller, D., Singer, P., Niebler, T., Hotho, A., Strohmaier, M.: What users actually do in a social tagging system: A study of user behavior in BibSonomy. ACM Transactions on the Web 10(2) (2016)

[8] Golder, S.A., Huberman, B.A.: Usage patterns of collaborative tagging systems. JIS 32 (2006)

[9] Heckner, M., Heilemann, M., Wolff, C.: Personal information management vs. resource sharing: Towards a model of information behaviour in social tagging systems. In: Proc. of the 3rd ICWSM (2009)

[10] Hotho, A., Jäschke, R., Schmitz, C., Stumme, G.: Information Retrieval in Folksonomies: Search and Ranking. In: The Semantic Web: Research and Applications (2006)

[11] Kass, R.E., Raftery, A.E.: Bayes factors. Journal of the American Statistical Association (1995)

[12] Körner, C., Benz, D., Strohmaier, M., Hotho, A., Stumme, G.: Stop Thinking, start Tagging - Tag Semantics emerge from Collaborative Verbosity. In: Proc. of the 19th WWW Conf. (2010)

[13] Mathes, A.: Folksonomies - Cooperative Classification and Communication Through Shared Metadata (2004)

[14] Meiss, M., Menczer, F., Fortunato, S., Flammini, A., Vespignani, A.: Ranking web sites with real user traffic. In: Proc of the 1st WSDM (2008)

[15] Millen, D.R., Feinberg, J.: Using social tagging to improve social navigation. In: Workshop on the Social Navigation and Community based Adaptation Technologies (2006)

[16] Niebler, T., Singer, P., Benz, D., Körner, C., Strohmaier, M., Hotho, A.: How tagging pragmatics influence tag sense discovery in social annotation systems. In: Advances in Information Retrieval. Springer Berlin Heidelberg (2013)

[17] Singer, P., Helic, D., Hotho, A., Strohmaier, M.: HypTrails: A bayesian approach for comparing hypotheses about human trails on the Web. In: Proc. of the 24th WWW Conf. (2015)

[18] Singer, P., Helic, D., Taraghi, B., Strohmaier, M.: Detecting Memory and Structure in Human Navigation Patterns Using Markov Chain Models of Varying Order. PLoS ONE 9 (2014)

[19] Wagner, C., Garcia, D., Jadidi, M., Strohmaier, M.: It's a Man's Wikipedia? Assessing Gender Inequality in an Online Encyclopedia (2015)

[20] West, R., Leskovec, J.: Human wayfinding in information networks. In: Proc. of the 21st WWW Conf. (2012)

Memory-Optimized Distributed Graph Processing through Novel Compression Techniques*

Panagiotis Liakos
University of Athens
Athens, Greece
p.liakos@di.uoa.gr

Katia Papakonstantinopoulou
University of Athens
Athens, Greece
katia@di.uoa.gr

Alex Delis
University of Athens
Athens, Greece
ad@di.uoa.gr

ABSTRACT

A multitude of contemporary applications now involve graph data whose size continuously grows and this trend shows no signs of subsiding. This has caused the emergence of many distributed graph processing systems including **Pregel** and **Apache Giraph**. However, the unprecedented scale now reached by real-world graphs hardens the task of graph processing even in distributed environments and the current memory usage patterns rapidly become a primary concern for such contemporary graph processing systems. We seek to address this challenge by exploiting empirically-observed properties demonstrated by graphs that are generated by human activity. In this paper, we propose three space-efficient adjacency list representations that can be applied to any distributed graph processing system. Our suggested compact representations reduce respective memory requirements for accommodating the graph elements up to 5 times if compared with state-of-the-art methods. At the same time, our memory-optimized methods retain the efficiency of uncompressed structures and enable the execution of algorithms for large scale graphs in settings where contemporary alternative structures fail due to memory errors.

Keywords

Graph compression; Pregel; distributed computing.

1. INTRODUCTION

The proliferation of WWW-based applications, the explosive growth of social networks, as well as the continually-expanding WWW-space, have collectively led to systems whose operations routinely deal with voluminous data that are modeled as graphs. The active users of Facebook are more than 1 billion [11] and Google indexes over 1 trillion unique URLs [2]. This ever-increasing requirement in terms of graph vertices has given rise to a number of distributed graph-processing systems [1, 18, 21, 22] that efficiently handle large-scale graphs using commodity hardware [13].

*This work has been partially supported by the University of Athens Special Account of Research Grants № 13233.

CIKM'16, October 24-28, 2016, Indianapolis, IN, USA
© 2016 ACM. ISBN 978-1-4503-4073-1/16/10... $15.00
DOI: http://dx.doi.org/10.1145/2983323.2983687

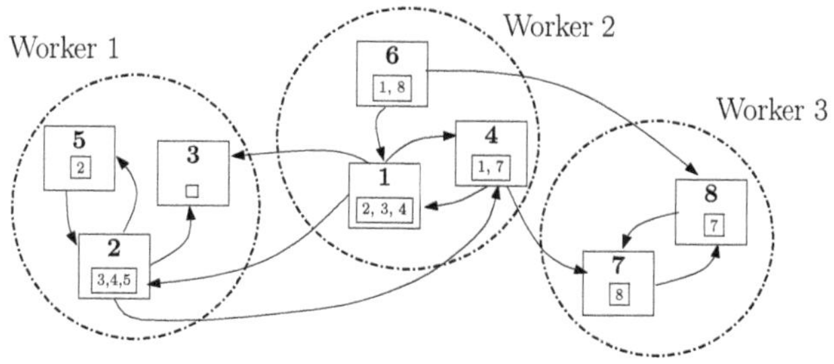

Figure 1: A graph partitioned on a vertex basis in a distributed environment. Each vertex maintains a list of its out-edges.

Most of these approaches parallelize the execution of algorithms by dividing graphs into partitions and assigning vertices to workers (i.e., machines) following the "*think like a vertex*" programming paradigm introduced with **Pregel** [19]. However, recent studies [9, 13] point out that the proposed frameworks fail to handle the unprecedented scale of real-world graphs due to ineffective memory usage [13]. Thus, memory optimization has become critical when dealing with graphs of such magnitude even in a distributed environment.

Figure 1 illustrates a graph partitioned over three workers. Every vertex is assigned to a *single* machine and maintains a list of its out-edges. This partitioning hardens the task of compression, as related research efforts have focused on a centralized machine environment and exploit similarities exhibited between vertices [3, 5, 8, 10, 16, 17]. However, this is infeasible when graphs are partitioned on a vertex basis. A major step towards memory optimization was contributed to **Apache Giraph** [1] by Facebook [11]. However, improvements focused entirely on a more careful implementation for the representation of the out-edges of a vertex; the redundancy exhibited in real-world graphs was not exploited.

In this paper, we follow the **Pregel** paradigm and partition the graph vertices among the nodes of a distributed computing environment. In this context, we present three novel techniques that 1) offer space efficient-representations of the out-edges of vertices, 2) allow fast mining (in-situ) of the graph elements without the need of decompression, 3) enable the execution of graph algorithms in memory-constrained settings, and 4) ease the task of memory management, thus allowing faster execution. The vertex placement policy that **Pregel**-like systems follow forces us to store the out-edges of each vertex independently as Figure 1 depicts. This preserves the *locality of reference* property, known to be exhibited in real-world graphs [4, 20], and enables us to exploit patterns that arise among the out-edges of a *single* vertex.

Our first technique, termed **BVEdges**, applies all methods of [5] that are appropriate for the vertex placement policy of **Pregel**. **BVEdges** primarily focuses on identifying intervals of consecutive out-edges of a vertex and employs universal codings to efficiently represent them. To facilitate access without imposing the significant computing overheads of **BVEdges**, we propose **IntervalResidualEdges**, which holds the corresponding values of intervals in a non-encoded format. Additionally, we propose **IndexedBitArrayEdges**, a novel technique that considers the out-edges of each vertex as a row in the adjacency matrix of the graph and indexes only the areas holding edges using byte sized bit-arrays.

Our experimental results show significant improvements on space-efficiency for all proposed techniques. We manage to reduce memory requirements up to 5 times in comparison with currently applied techniques. This eases the task of scaling to billions of vertices and allows us to load much larger graphs than was ever possible before. In settings where earlier approaches were also able to execute graph algorithms, we achieve significant performance improvements in terms of time of up to 31% due to memory optimization, as less time is spent for garbage collection. These findings establish our structures as the undisputed preferable option for web graphs, which offer compression-friendly orderings, or any other type of graph, after the application of a reordering that favors its compressibility.

2. RELATED WORK

Our work lies in the intersection of distributed graph processing and compressed graph representations. In this regard, we outline here pertinent aspects of these two areas.

Google's proprietary **Pregel** [19] is a graph processing system that enables scalable batch execution of iterative graph algorithms. As the source code of **Pregel** is not publicly available, a number of graph processing systems that follow the same data flow paradigm have emerged. **Apache Giraph** [1] is such an open-source **Java** implementation with contributions from Yahoo! and Facebook, that operates on top of **HDFS**. Our work focuses on **Pregel**-like systems and extends **Giraph**'s implementation. **GPS** [21] is a similar **Java** open-source system that proposes the large adjacency list partitioning technique for high-degree vertices. **Pregel+** [22] is implemented in **C++** and uses **MPI** processes as workers to achieve high efficiency. Unlike the aforementioned systems, **GraphLab** [18] does not follow the **Pregel** paradigm but rather supports asynchronous execution and adopts a data-pull model with a shared memory abstraction. Our work is orthogonal to these approaches as our compressed representations can be readily applied to all above systems.

The field of graph compression has yielded significant research results after the work presented in [20]. Randall et al. exploit the *locality of reference* as well as the *similarity property* that is unveiled in web graphs when their links are ordered lexicographically. The seminal work on web graph compression is that of Boldi and Vigna [5], who introduce a number of sophisticated techniques to further reduce the bits per link ratio. Following efforts present improved results with regard to space [3], study the compressibility characteristics of social graphs [10], and employ adjacency matrix representations to reduce access time of the graph's elements [8, 16, 17]. All the above approaches focus on providing a compact representation of a graph to be loaded in the memory of a *single* machine. Hence, they exploit the presence of all edges in a centralized computing node, which is not suitable for **Pregel**-like systems offering distributed execution.

To the best of our knowledge, **GBASE** [14] is the only approach that considers compressed graph representations in a distributed environment. Kang et al. consider the case of a graph stored over **HDFS**. **GBASE** uses block compression to efficiently store graphs by splitting the respective adjacency matrices into regions. The latter are compressed using several methods including *Gzip* and *Gap Elias'-γ* encoding. We should note, however, that **GBASE** does not follow the vertex-centric model we have adopted in this work.

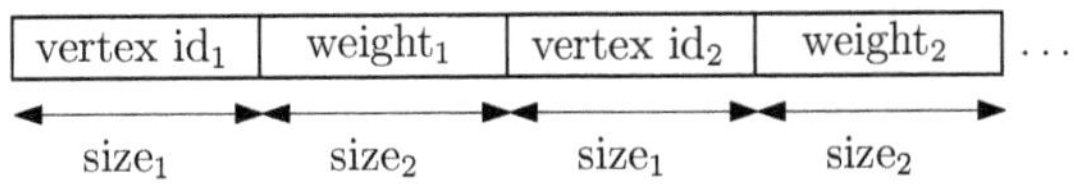

Figure 2: **Giraph**'s *ByteArrayEdges* representation.

3. BACKGROUND

In this section we outline **Pregel** and **Apache Giraph**, and offer definitions for the encodings that we use for our suggested compression techniques.

3.1 Pregel & Apache Giraph

Pregel [19] is a computational model suitable for large scale graph processing, inspired by the *Bulk Synchronous Parallel* programming model. **Pregel** encourages programmers to *"think like a vertex"* by following a vertex-centric approach. The input to a **Pregel** algorithm is a directed graph whose vertices, along with their respective out-edges, are distributed among the machines of a computing cluster. **Pregel** algorithms are executed as a sequence of iterations, termed *supersteps*. During a *superstep*, every vertex independently computes a user-defined list of actions and sends messages to vertices that are to be used during the following *superstep*. A synchronization barrier between *supersteps* is used to ensure that all messages are delivered at the beginning of the next *superstep*. A vertex may vote to halt at any *superstep* and will be reactivated upon receiving a message. The algorithm terminates when all vertices are halted and there are no messages in transit. **Pregel** loads the input graph and performs all associated computations in-memory. Thereby, **Pregel** only supports graphs whose edges entirely fit in main-memory.

Apache Giraph [1] is an open-source implementation of **Pregel**. The default **Giraph** structure for holding the out-edges of a vertex is that of **ByteArrayEdges** [11]. This representation is realized as a byte array, in which target vertex ids and their respective weights are held consecutively, as Figure 2 illustrates. The bytes required per out-edge are determined by the data type used for its id and weight; for integer numbers $4+4=8$ bytes are required. **ByteArrayEdges** are impractical for algorithms involving mutations as they deserialize all out-edges to perform a removal.

3.2 Codings for Graph Compression

Over the last two decades studies of real-world graphs have revealed the presence of common properties [5, 15, 20].

In this work we exploit two of these properties, namely the *heavy-tailed degrees' distribution* and the *locality of reference*, to achieve effective compression. The former property implies the sparsity of such graphs, while due to the latter, the majority of the edges of a graph link vertices that are close to each other in the order. The locality of reference is evident in web graphs whose vertices are ordered lexicographically, and can be surfaced in other types of graphs by applying the reordering algorithm of [4].

In order to compress the data in our structure, we can use various encoding approaches; below, we provide the definitions of *Elias' γ* and ζ codings that we employ in Section 4.1.1. We also furnish the definitions of unary and minimal binary coding that help define the first two codings. Let x denote a positive integer, b its binary representation and l its length. The aforementioned codings are defined as follows:

1. *Unary coding*: the unary coding of x consists of $x-1$ 0s followed by a 1.
2. *Minimal binary coding* over an interval: consider the interval $[0, z-1]$ and let $s = \lceil \log z \rceil$. If $x < 2^s - z$ then x is coded using the x-th binary word of length $s-1$ (in lexicographical order), otherwise, x is coded using the $(x - z + 2^s)$-th binary word of length s.
3. *Elias' γ coding* [12]: the γ coding of x consists of l in unary, followed by the last $l-1$ digits of b.
4. *ζ coding* with parameter k [6]: given a fixed positive integer k, if $x \in [2^{hk}, 2^{(h+1)k} - 1]$, its ζ_k-coding consists of $h+1$ in unary, followed by a minimal binary coding of $x - 2^{hk}$ in the interval $[0, 2^{(h+1)k} - 2^{hk} - 1]$.

In the context of graph compression, Elias' γ coding is preferred for the representation of rather small values of x, whereas ζ coding is more proper for potentially large values.

4. OVERVIEW OF OUR APPROACH

In this section we detail our compressed data structures for the representation of a vertex's neighbors in a graph.

4.1 Representations based on intervals

The *locality of reference* property is evident through the adjacency lists of the graphs of our dataset, all of which tend to have a lot of neighbors with *consecutive* ids. We can exploit this property by applying a technique similar to the one introduced in [5]. In particular, [5] distinguishes between the neighbors whose ids form some *interval* of consecutive ids, and the rest. To reconstruct all the edges of the *intervals* only the leftmost neighbor id and the length of the *interval* needs to be kept. This information is further compressed using gap *Elias' γ coding*. The rest of the edges, termed *residuals*, are compressed using *ζ coding*. We build on these ideas and introduce two vertex-centric representations that exploit *locality of reference* in a similar fashion.

4.1.1 BVEdges

Our first representation, namely `BVEdges`, focuses solely on compressing the neighbors of a vertex, at the cost of computing overheads. Therefore, we simply adjust the method of Boldi and Vigna [5] to the requirements imposed by `Pregel`'s model. The compressed data structure discussed in [5] considers the whole graph and exploits the current vertex's id during compression. However, this information is not available in the level where adjacency lists are kept in the `Pregel` model. To overcome this issue, we use the first neighbor id we store in our structure as a reference to proceed with

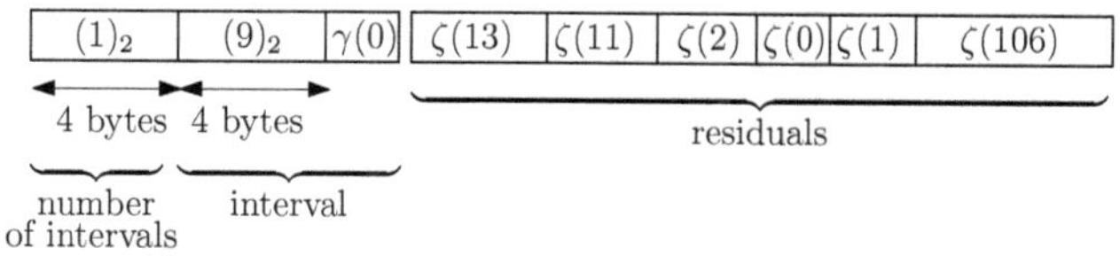

Figure 3: The storage of neighbors in **BVEdges**, detailed in Example 1. $\gamma(x)$ and $\zeta(x)$ denote the γ and ζ encodings of x respectively.

gap encoding. We use *Elias' γ coding* for *intervals*, and *ζ coding* for *residuals*. *Elias' γ coding* is most preferable for *intervals* of at least 4 elements [5]; shorter *intervals* are more compactly stored as *residuals*.

Definition 1 (`BVEdges`): *Given a list l of a node's neighbors, `BVEdges` is a sequence of bits holding consecutively: the number of intervals in l of length at least 4; for each such interval, the smallest neighbor id in it and the γ-coded difference of the interval length minus 4; a ζ coding for each of the remaining neighbors, its argument being either the difference x between the current node's id and the previous node id which was encoded to be stored in the sequence minus 1, or, in case $x < 0$, the quantity $2|x| - 1$.*

Example 1: *Consider the following sequence of neighbors to be represented:* (2, 9, 10, 11, 12, 14, 17, 18, 20, 127). *We employ `BVEdges` as illustrated in Figure 3. Here, there is only one* interval *of length at least equal to* 4: [9 .. 12]. *We first store the number of* intervals *in unencoded binary form. Then, we store the leftmost id of the* interval, *i.e.,* 9, *again using its unencoded binary representation. We proceed with storing a representation of the length of the* interval *to enable the recovery of the remaining elements. In particular, we store the* γ coding *of the difference of the* interval *length minus the minimum* interval *length, which is* $4 - 4 = 0$ *in our case. Then, we append a representation for the* residual *neighbors. For each* residual, *we store the* ζ coding *of the difference of its id with the id of the last node stored, minus* 1 *(as each id appears at most once in the neighbors' list). The* residual *id 2 is smaller than the smallest id of the first* interval, *so we store the* residual *neighbor* 2 *as* $\zeta(13)$, *since* $2|2-9| - 1 = 13$, *and the* residual 14 *as* $\zeta(11)$, *since* $14 - 2 - 1 = 11$. *Similarly, we store* 17, 18, 20 *and* 127 *as* $\zeta(2), \zeta(0), \zeta(1)$ *and* $\zeta(106)$, *respectively.*

The respective values computed in each step are written using a bit stream. This, combined with the fact that values have to be encoded, renders the operation costly. We also investigated the idea of treating all neighbors as *residuals* to examine if the re-construction of *intervals* was more expensive. However, we experimentally found that the resulting larger bit stream offered worse access time. Accessing the out-edges of a vertex requires the following procedure: first, we decode the *intervals* and create an iterator using them. After this iterator returns all its elements, we create a second one that decodes the *residuals* one by one.

4.1.2 IntervalResidualEdges

Our second representation, namely `IntervalResidualEdges`, also incorporates the idea of using *intervals* and *residuals*. However, to avoid costly bit stream writes and reads, we propose a different structure. In particular, we opt to keep the value of the leftmost id of an *interval* unencoded, along with a byte that is able to index up to 256 consecutive neighbors. *Residuals* are then also kept unencoded. Clearly,

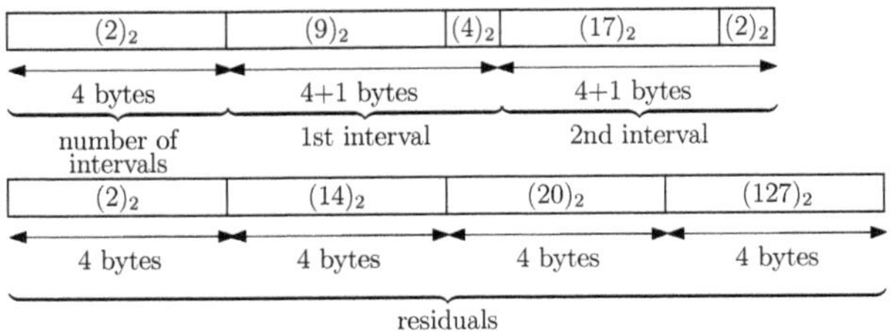

Figure 4: The storage of neighbors in `IntervalResidualEdges`, detailed in Example 2. $(x)_2$ is the binary representation of x.

any consecutive neighbors of length at least equal to 2 are represented more efficiently using an *interval* rather than two or more *residuals*. Therefore we set the minimum interval length with `IntervalResidualEdges` equal to 2. Due to the *locality of reference* property, this one byte allows us to compress the adjacency list significantly, while also avoiding the use of expensive encodings and bit streams. We note here that all ids are stored in binary form.

Definition 2 (`IntervalResidualEdges`)**:** *Given a list l of a node's neighbors,* ***`IntervalResidualEdges`*** *is a sequence of bits holding consecutively: the number of intervals in l; the smallest neighbor id and the length of each such interval; the id of each of the remaining neighbors.*

Example 2: *The representation of the aforementioned sequence of neighbors* (2, 9, 10, 11, 12, 14, 17, 18, 20, 127) *using* ***`IntervalResidualEdges`*** *is illustrated in Figure 4. In this case there are two* intervals *of at least 2 consecutive neighbors, namely* [9 .. 12] *and* [17, 18]*. We first store the number of* intervals, *and then use one 5-byte element for each* interval, *consisting of a 4-byte representation of the smallest neighbor id in it (i.e.,* 9 *and* 17*), plus a byte holding the number of neighbors in this* interval *(*4 *and* 2 *respectively). Finally we append a 4-byte representation for each* residual *neighbor.*

This representation delivers its elements through the following procedure: while there are still unread *intervals*, the procedure reads 5-bytes, i.e., the leftmost element of the *interval* and its length, and produces one by one the elements of the *interval*. When all *intervals* are processed, the procedure reads in the *residuals* directly as integers.

4.2 IndexedBitArrayEdges

Our first two representations exploit the *consecutivity* exhibited among the neighbors of a vertex. Here we propose `IndexedBitArrayEdges`, which takes advantage of the *concentration* of edges in *specific areas* of the adjacency matrix, regardless of whether these edges are in fact consecutive. `IndexedBitArrayEdges` uses a single byte to depict eight possible out-edges. Using a byte array, we construct a data structure of 5-byte elements, one for each interval of neighbor ids having the same quotient by 8. The first 4 bytes of each element represent the quotient, while the last one serves as a set of 8 flags indicating whether each possible edge in this interval exists. As the neighbor ids of each node tend to concentrate within a few areas, the number of intervals is small and the compression achieved is exceptional.

Definition 3 (`IndexedBitArrayEdges`)**:** *Given a bit-array r representing a list of a node's neighbors,* ***`IndexedBitArrayEdges`*** *is a sequence of 5-byte elements, each one holding an octet of r that contains at least one 1: the first 4 bytes hold the distance in r of the first bit of the octet from the beginning of r; the last one holds the octet.*

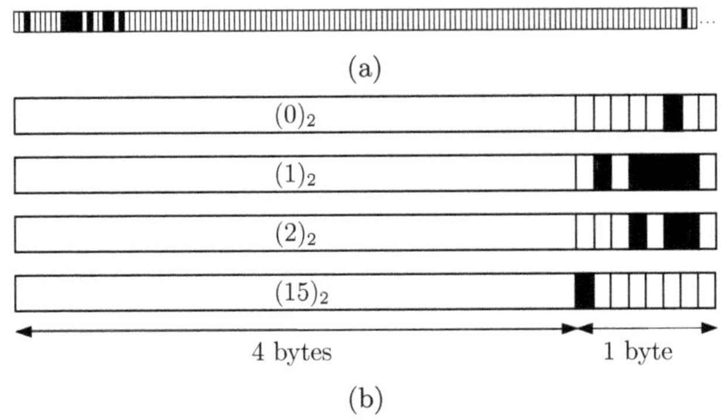

Figure 5: A bit-array representation of an adjacency list (a) and the storage of these neighbors in `IndexedBitArrayEdges (b), detailed in Example 3`. $(x)_2$ denotes the binary representation of x.

Example 3: *The representation of the aforementioned sequence of neighbors* (2, 9, 10, 11, 12, 14, 17, 18, 20, 127) *using* ***`IndexedBitArrayEdges`*** *is illustrated in Figure 5. The bit-array representation of this adjacency list is shown in Figure 5(a). The quotient and remainder of each node id divided by* 8 *give us the approximate position (octet) and the exact position, respectively, of the node in the bit-array; hence, as depicted in Figure 5(b), the neighbors are grouped in four sets:* $\{2\}$, $\{9, 10, 11, 12, 14\}$, $\{17, 18, 20\}$, $\{127\}$. *All ids in each set share the same quotient when divided by* 8, *which will be referred as* index number *henceforth. For instance, the index number of the third set is* 2, *and is stored in binary form, denoted by* $(2)_2$, *in the first part of the third element. Moreover, the remainders of the ids* 17, 18 *and* 20 *divided by* 8 *are* 1, 2, *and* 4 *respectively, and so the* 2*nd,* 3*rd and* 5*th flags from the right side of the same element are set to* 1 *to depict these neighbors.*

Accessing the out-edges of a vertex requires the following procedure: first, we read a 5-byte element. Then, we recover out-edges from the flags of its last byte and reconstruct the neighbor ids using the first 4 bytes. After we examine all flags of the last byte, we proceed by reading the next 5-byte element and repeat until we retrieve all out-edges.

5. EXPERIMENTAL EVALUATION

We implemented[1] our techniques using `Java` and compared their performance against `ByteArrayEdges` using a number of well-studied web and social network graphs [4, 5], reaching up to 2 billion edges. We first present the dataset and detail the specifications of the machines used in our experiments. Then, we proceed with the evaluation of our out-edge representations by answering the following questions: (i) How much more space-efficient is each of our three compressed out-edge representations compared to `ByteArrayEdges`? (ii) Are our techniques competitive speed-wise when memory is not a concern? (iii) How much more efficient are our compressed representations when the available memory is constrained? (iv) Can we execute algorithms for large graphs in settings where it was not possible before?

[1] https://goo.gl/TSWcyO

graph	vertices	edges	ByteArrayEdges	BVEdges	IntervalResidualEdges	IndexedBitArrayEdges
uk-2007-05@100000	100,000	3,050,615	22.61MB	6.41MB	7.92MB	8.91MB
uk-2007-05@1000000	1,000,000	41,247,159	279.16MB	67.36MB	82.7MB	97.79MB
indochina-2004	7,414,866	194,109,311	1,511.67MB	442.34MB	646.03MB	554.23MB
hollywood-2011	2,180,759	228,985,632	1,381.91MB	287.53MB	613.52MB	676.88MB
uk-2002	18,520,486	298,113,762	2,733.6MB	1,092.82MB	1,224.07MB	1,255.67MB
arabic-2005	22,744,080	639,999,458	4,820.09MB	1,428.97MB	1,674.75MB	1,849.83MB
uk-2005	39,459,925	936,364,282	7,401.88MB	2,383.54MB	2,728.74MB	2,928.81MB
sk-2005	50,636,154	1,949,412,601	14,829.64MB	4,889.85MB	5,657.79MB	6,354.17MB

Table 1: Memory requirements for the small and large-scale graphs of our dataset.

5.1 Experimental Setting

Our dataset consists of 8 web and social network graphs, whose properties are detailed in Table 1. We run our experiments on a cluster that comprises 8 virtual machines with 13GB of virtual RAM each, running on a Dell PowerEdge R630 with an Intel® Xeon® E5-2630 v3, 2.40 GHz with 8 cores and 128GB of RAM. We set up Apache Hadoop 1.0.2 with 1 master and 8 slave nodes and a maximum per machine JVM heap size of 10GB. Lastly, we used Giraph 1.1.0.

5.2 Space Efficiency Comparison

We present here our results regarding space efficiency for the web and social network graphs of our dataset. We compare our methods involving compression with Giraph's default representation, namely ByteArrayEdges.

Table 1 lists the memory required by all four representations in MB. We observe that our techniques require significantly less memory compared to ByteArrayEdges. BVEdges outperforms all representations, as expected. In particular, BVEdges always needs less than 40% of the requirements of ByteArrayEdges, and reaches much smaller figures in certain cases, e.g., 20.08% for *hollywood-2011*. However, we see that our novel IntervalResidualEdges, that does not impose any computing overheads, also manages to achieve equivalent space-efficiency, with its requirements ranging from 29% to 44% compared to those of ByteArrayEdges. Finally, the results of our IndexedBitArrayEdges are impressive as well, as its requirements are usually less than 40% and always below 50% of those of ByteArrayEdges.

5.3 Execution Time Comparison

In this section, we present results regarding the execution time of the PageRank [7] algorithm.[2] We expect that any Pregel algorithm not involving mutations would exhibit similar behavior for the different representations, as it would feature the same set of actions regarding out-edges, i.e., initialization and retrieval. Reported timings are averages of multiple executions. We do not consider the initialization time as it is negligible compared to the execution time.

5.3.1 Comparison using small-scale graphs

We begin by investigating the performance of the different out-edge representations in settings where memory is sufficient. Figure 6 depicts the total time needed for each of the four techniques when executing the PageRank algorithm on setups of 2, 4, and 8 workers for the graph *indochina-2004*.

We observe that IndexedBitArrayEdges and IntervalResidualEdges do not impose any latency in the process. In particular, using either of our two novel representations we achieve execution times that are slightly better than those of ByteArrayEdges for all three setups. BVEdges is inferior speed-wise due to the computationally expensive access of the out-edges offered through this structure which requires decoding *Elias-γ* and *ζ-coding* values. Thus, the computing overheads imposed by the techniques of [5] are not negligible and simply adopting them proves to be inefficient.

[2]https://goo.gl/CEbvOX

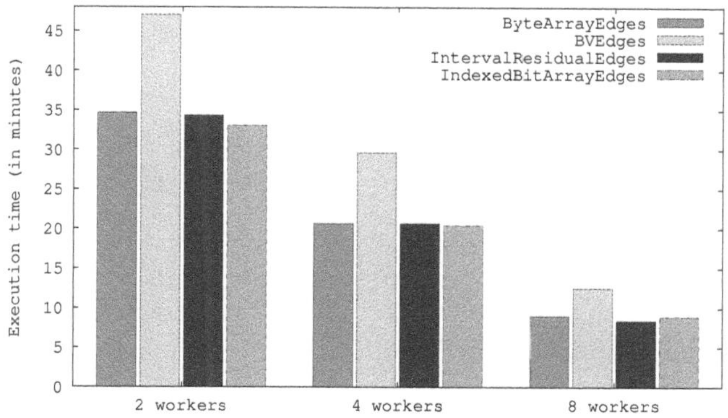

Figure 6: Execution time of PageRank algorithm for the graph *indochina-2004* using 2, 4, and 8 workers.

For graphs which are equivalent to or smaller than *indochina-2004* the performance was similar. In particular, for all three setups IndexedBitArrayEdges and IntervalResidualEdges managed to execute the PageRank algorithm in slightly less time than that of ByteArrayEdges. On the contrary, BVEdges required more time for each *superstep*.

5.3.2 Comparison using large-scale graphs

We further examine the performance of our representations using setups where memory does not suffice for the needs of the execution of PageRank. Figure 7 depicts the time needed for each *superstep* of the execution of PageRank for the *uk-2005* graph for all four out-edge representations. We see that BVEdges requires significantly more time than our two other representations for every *superstep*, as was the case with small-scale graphs. We also see, however, that in this setup the execution with ByteArrayEdges tends to fluctuate in performance, and occasionally performs worse than BVEdges. The increased memory requirements of Giraph's default implementation, result in an unstable pace during the execution of PageRank, as it needs to perform garbage collection very frequently to accommodate the memory objects required in every *superstep*. ByteArrayEdges still manages to outperform BVEdges requiring an average of 4.8 minutes per *superstep* as opposed to 5.08 minutes per *superstep*. However, both IndexedBitArrayEdges and IntervalResidualEdges greatly outperformed ByteArrayEdges, requiring 3.15 and 3.56 minutes per *superstep*, respectively.

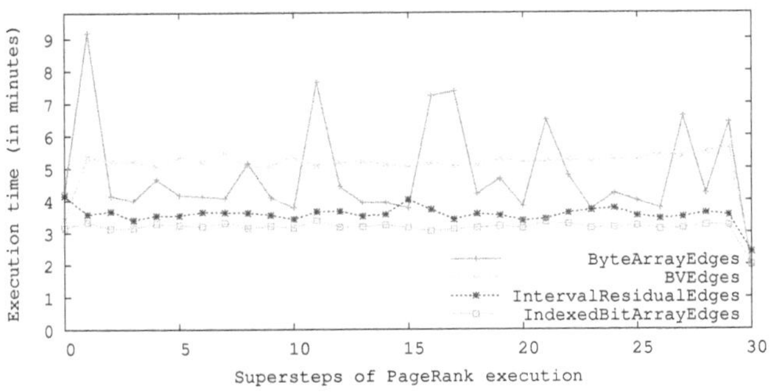

Figure 7: Execution time for each *superstep* of PageRank for the graph *uk-2005* using 5 workers.

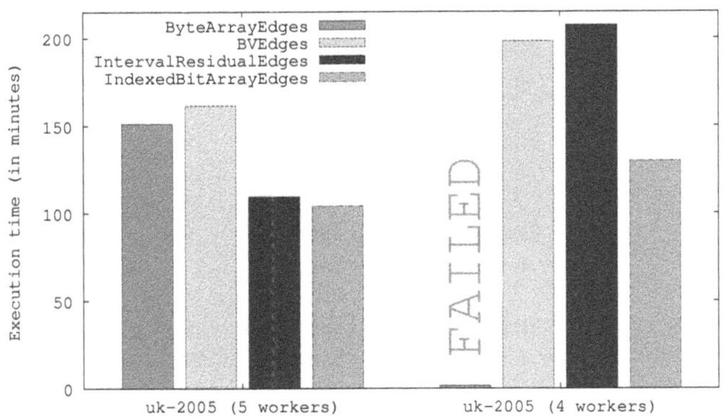

Figure 8: Execution time of the PageRank algorithm for the graph *uk-2005* using 5 and 4 workers.

The performance difference of the four representations with regard to the total execution time of PageRank is evident in Figure 8 (left). The executions using **IndexedBitArrayEdges** and **IntervalResidualEdges** are faster by 31.1% and 27.54% than the one with **ByteArrayEdges**, respectively.

We repeat the same experiment using 4 workers and illustrate the respective results in Figure 8 (right). The execution with **ByteArrayEdges** on this setup fails as the garbage collection overhead limit is exceeded, i.e., more than 98% of the total time is spent doing garbage collection. Our proposed implementations, however, are able to execute PageRank for the *uk-2005* graph despite the limited resources. We observe that under these settings **IntervalResidualEdges** performs worse than both **BVEdges** and **IndexedBitArrayEdges**. As we can see in Table 1, the latter requires more memory than **IntervalResidualEdges** to represent the out-edges of *uk-2005*. However, the retrieval of out-edges using **IndexedBitArrayEdges** is more memory-efficient than that of **IntervalResidualEdges**. Therefore, execution spends much less time performing garbage collection with **IndexedBitArrayEdges** which results in it being 37.42% faster than **IntervalResidualEdges** under these settings.

6. CONCLUSIONS

In this paper, we propose and implement three compressed out-edge representations for distributed graph processing, termed **BVEdges**, **IntervalResidualEdges**, and **IndexedBitArrayEdges**. We focus on the vertex-centric model that all **Pregel**-like graph processing systems follow and examine the efficiency of our structures by extending one such system, namely **Apache Giraph**. Our techniques build on empirically-observed properties of real-world graphs and offer significant memory optimizations that are applicable to any distributed graph compressing system that follows the **Pregel** paradigm. Our **IntervalResidualEdges** and **IndexedBitArrayEdges** representations outperform **Giraph**'s default representation, namely **ByteArrayEdges**, and are able to execute algorithms over large-scale graphs under very modest settings. Furthermore, our representations are clearly superior than **ByteArrayEdges** when memory is an issue, and are capable of successfully performing executions in settings where **Giraph** fails due to memory requirements.

7. REFERENCES

[1] Apache Giraph. http://giraph.apache.org/.

[2] We knew the web was big.... https://goo.gl/ugjWuI.

[3] A. Apostolico and G. Drovandi. Graph compression by BFS. *Algorithms*, 2(3):1031–1044, 2009.

[4] P. Boldi, M. Rosa, M. Santini, and S. Vigna. Layered Label Propagation: A Multiresolution Coordinate-Free Ordering for Compressing Social Networks. In *WWW*, 2011.

[5] P. Boldi and S. Vigna. The Webgraph Framework I: Compression Techniques. In *WWW*, 2004.

[6] P. Boldi and S. Vigna. The WebGraph Framework II: Codes For The World-Wide Web. In *DCC*, 2004.

[7] S. Brin and L. Page. The Anatomy of a Large-Scale Hypertextual Web Search Engine. *Computer Networks*, 30(1-7):107–117, 1998.

[8] N. Brisaboa, S. Ladra, and G. Navarro. k2-Trees for Compact Web Graph Representation. In *SPIRE*. 2009.

[9] Z. Cai, Z. J. Gao, S. Luo, L. L. Perez, Z. Vagena, and C. M. Jermaine. A Comparison of Platforms for Implementing and Running Very Large Scale Machine Learning Algorithms. In *ACM SIGMOD*, 2014.

[10] F. Chierichetti, R. Kumar, S. Lattanzi, M. Mitzenmacher, A. Panconesi, and P. Raghavan. On Compressing Social Networks. In *KDD*, 2009.

[11] A. Ching, S. Edunov, M. Kabiljo, D. Logothetis, and S. Muthukrishnan. One Trillion Edges: Graph Processing at Facebook-Scale. *Proc. of the VLDB Endowment*, 8(12):1804–1815, 2015.

[12] P. Elias. Universal codeword sets and representations of the integers. *IEEE Transactions on Information Theory*, 21(2):194–203, 1975.

[13] M. Han, K. Daudjee, K. Ammar, M. T. Özsu, X. Wang, and T. Jin. An Experimental Comparison of Pregel-like Graph Processing Systems. *Proc. of the VLDB Endowment*, 7(12):1047–1058, 2014.

[14] U. Kang, H. Tong, J. Sun, C. Lin, and C. Faloutsos. GBASE: an efficient analysis platform for large graphs. *VLDB J.*, 21(5):637–650, 2012.

[15] J. Leskovec, J. M. Kleinberg, and C. Faloutsos. Graphs over Time: Densification Laws, Shrinking Diameters and Possible Explanations. In *KDD*, 2005.

[16] P. Liakos, K. Papakonstantinopoulou, and M. Sioutis. On the Effect of Locality in Compressing Social Networks. In *ECIR*, 2014.

[17] P. Liakos, K. Papakonstantinopoulou, and M. Sioutis. Pushing the Envelope in Graph Compression. In *CIKM*, 2014.

[18] Y. Low, J. Gonzalez, A. Kyrola, D. Bickson, C. Guestrin, and J. M. Hellerstein. Distributed GraphLab: A Framework for Machine Learning in the Cloud. *Proc. of the VLDB Endowment*, 5(8):716–727, 2012.

[19] G. Malewicz, M. H. Austern, A. J. C. Bik, J. C. Dehnert, I. Horn, N. Leiser, and G. Czajkowski. Pregel: A System for Large-Scale Graph Processing. In *ACM SIGMOD*, 2010.

[20] K. H. Randall, R. Stata, J. L. Wiener, and R. Wickremesinghe. The Link Database: Fast Access to Graphs of the Web. In *DCC*, 2002.

[21] S. Salihoglu and J. Widom. GPS: A Graph Processing System. In *SSDBM*, 2013.

[22] D. Yan, J. Cheng, Y. Lu, and W. Ng. Effective Techniques for Message Reduction and Load Balancing in Distributed Graph Computation. In *WWW*, 2015.

Tracking the Evolution of Congestion in Dynamic Urban Road Networks

Tarique Anwar[†*1], Chengfei Liu[†2], Hai L. Vu[†3] and Md. Saiful Islam[#4]
[†]Swinburne University of Technology, Melbourne, Australia
[*]Data61, CSIRO, Melbourne, Australia
[#]La Trobe University, Melbourne, Australia
{[1]tanwar, [2]cliu, [3]hvu}@swin.edu.au, [4]m.islam5@latrobe.edu.au

ABSTRACT

The congestion scenario on a road network is often represented by a set of differently congested partitions having homogeneous level of congestion inside. Due to the changing traffic, these partitions evolve with time. In this paper, we propose a two-layer method to incrementally update the differently congested partitions from those at the previous time point in an efficient manner, and thus track their evolution. The physical layer performs low-level computations to incrementally update a set of small-sized road network building blocks, and the logical layer provides an interface to query the physical layer about the congested partitions. At each time point, the unstable road segments are identified and moved to their most suitable building blocks. Our experimental results on different datasets show that the proposed method is much efficient than the existing re-partitioning methods without significant sacrifice in accuracy.

Keywords

Road network motif, Incremental partitioning, Tracking congestion evolution, Urban road networks

1. INTRODUCTION

The roads of different localities usually experience specific traffic flow patterns based on their *spatiotemporal* significance. In the spatial perspective, roads inside the city center or an area having popular venues like a stadium or hospital, usually remain more congested than others without such significance. It leads to the fact that the different small sub-networks (of small areas like suburbs) of a large urban road network experience distinctive traffic flow within them. Previous works have applied congestion based partitioning of road networks to identify such sub-networks called *spatial partitions* or simply *partitions* [2]. In the temporal perspective, the roads usually remain busier during the peak times than the off-peak times. It reflects the dynamic nature of congestion in the spatial partitions. These spatiotemporal behaviors altogether lead to the evolution of traffic congestion on urban road networks. For example, during the morning office-opening hours, the congestion generally starts developing in the outer suburbs and the roads connecting them to the city center, mostly occur inside the city during the day, and starts moving outwards again during the office-closing hours. The congestion can be simply understood as a congested partition that keeps on changing its structure, location, and level of congestion. The maintenance and tracking of the differently congested partitions can potentially aid traffic management systems [4] and traffic visualization platforms like `Google Traffic` [3]. A naive way to track the change in partitions is to perform spatial partitioning of the road network at each time point, and analyze the change. But a complete re-partitioning is a computationally expensive task. Generally in successive time points, the traffic does not change abruptly, rather it is a gradual process. A logically better way is to incrementally update the previously obtained set of partitions by processing only the sections of probable change. It heavily reduces the computations, while may sacrifice the quality of partitions marginally. There exist works on the complete partitioning of road networks [4, 2], and some other related problems, including spatiotemporal propagation of congestion [5], identification of important road segments having high influence in propagating congestion [1], and incremental clustering of spatial data streams collected from sensors [7]. [3] identifies the congested partitions, and performs an experimental analysis by updating the partitions simply based on similarity in the traffic.

In this paper, we propose a two-layer method to incrementally compute the differently-congested partitions of a road network and use them to track the evolution of congestion. The physical layer performs low-level computations for the incremental update, whereas the logical layer presents the required congestion related information to the user after a light makeover. Our method in the physical layer starts with a set of *building blocks* (defined in Section 3.2) of the road network at the beginning time point. At each new time point, the unstable road segments are identified using a *stability measure*, indexed as a heap tree, and moved to their most suitable building blocks using the concepts of *road network motifs*.

CIKM'16, October 24-28, 2016, Indianapolis, IN, USA
© 2016 ACM. ISBN 978-1-4503-4073-1/16/10...$15.00
DOI: http://dx.doi.org/10.1145/2983323.2983688

2. PROBLEM DEFINITION

DEFINITION 1: (**Road Network**) An urban road network is defined as $\mathcal{N} = (\mathcal{I}, \mathcal{R})$ comprising a set of intersection points $\mathcal{I} = \{\iota_1, \iota_2, \ldots, \iota_{n_\iota}\}$ as nodes, which are connected among themselves by a set of directed road segments

$\mathcal{R} = \{r_1, r_2, \ldots, r_{n_r}\}$ as links, where each road segment r_i associates a measure of traffic density $r_i.d$ with itself. ■

DEFINITION 2: (**Road Graph**) Given a road network $\mathcal{N}$, the corresponding road graph $\mathcal{G} = (\mathcal{V}, \mathcal{E})$ is constructed by representing each road segment $r_i \in \mathcal{N}$ as a node v_i, and establishing an undirected link e_i between each possible node pair (v_j, v_k) if there exists at least one intersection point ι_l which is a common intersection for the roads r_j and r_k, and the traffic can flow either from r_j to r_k or vice versa. Each node v_i ($node(r_i)$) $\in \mathcal{V}$ associates with it a feature value $v_i.f$, which is the road traffic density $r_i.d$. ■

DEFINITION 3: (**Partition**) A given road network $\mathcal{N}$ can be partitioned into multiple segments, each of whom is called a partition $\mathcal{P}_i$ of $\mathcal{N}$. All the different segments form a set of partitions $\mathcal{P} = \{\mathcal{P}_1, \mathcal{P}_2, \ldots, \mathcal{P}_k\}$, such that *i)* $\bigcup_{i=1}^{k} \mathcal{P}_i = \mathcal{R}$ and $\mathcal{P}_i \bigcap \mathcal{P}_j = \emptyset$ for all $i \neq j$, and *ii)* each $\mathcal{P}_i$ is connected inside and all adjacency relations, except the cross-partition relations (inter-partition links), are maintained as in $\mathcal{N}$. A partition of a road network can be transformed to that of a road graph by following Definition 2, and vice versa. ■

DEFINITION 4: (**Inter-Partition Associativity**) For a given set of partitions $\mathcal{P}$, the inter-partition associativity is defined as the aggregation of the traffic similarity between all possible pairs (r_i, r_j) for which r_i and r_j lie in different partitions. ■

DEFINITION 5: (**Intra-Partition Associativity**) For a given set of partitions $\mathcal{P}$, intra-partition associativity is defined as the aggregation of the traffic similarity between all possible linked pairs (r_i, r_j) for which r_i and r_j lie in the same partition. ■

Problem: Let us suppose, we are given a set of road network partitions $\mathcal{P}^{i-1} = \{\mathcal{P}_1^{i-1}, \mathcal{P}_2^{i-1}, \ldots, \mathcal{P}_k^{i-1}\}$ based on the traffic at time t_{i-1}, such that $\mathcal{P}^{i-1}$ has a minimum possible inter-partition associativity and a maximum possible intra-partition associativity. Our objective is to incrementally update $\mathcal{P}^{i-1}$ to $\mathcal{P}^{i} = \{\mathcal{P}_1^{i}, \mathcal{P}_2^{i}, \ldots, \mathcal{P}_k^{i}\}$ at each new time point t_i based on the respective traffic data, without re-partitioning the whole network, in such a way that the properties of inter-partition and intra-partition associativities are maintained.

3. PROPOSED METHOD

The proposed method tracks the evolution of traffic congestion over a period of time. Instead of incrementally maintaining the partitions directly, we embed the functionalities in two different layers. The *logical layer* gets the query to identify the congested partitions at a time point from the user, passes it to the physical layer, lightly processes the returned data, and returns the results to the user, whereas the *physical layer* incrementally updates a large number of small-sized building blocks at each new time point.

3.1 Logical Layer

From the user end, the logical layer provides the service to get the congested/non-congested partitions at any point of time. It is based on a set of so-called building blocks that are maintained up-to-date by the physical layer. After getting a query from the user, this layer transforms the granularity of the query from partitions to the building blocks, and passes to to the physical layer. For example, a query to fetch k *differently congested partitions* of the network at the current time is transformed to fetch the building blocks of the current time. The physical layer returns the result as $\mathcal{B} = \{\mathcal{B}_1, \mathcal{B}_2, \ldots, \mathcal{B}_{n_b}\}$. The logical layer constructs a building block graph $\mathcal{G}^b = (\mathcal{V}^b, \mathcal{E}^b)$, where each building block forms a node $\varsigma_i \in \mathcal{V}^b$ and all pairs of *neighboring* (defined later) building blocks or nodes $\{\varsigma_i, \varsigma_j\} \in \mathcal{V}^b$ are connected by links $\varepsilon_l \in \mathcal{E}^b$. The number of nodes in this graph is much smaller than that in the road graph ($|\mathcal{V}^b| = n_b << n_r$). The nodes are first assigned their feature values $\varsigma_i.f$ as the mean of the corresponding building block. The links ε_l between nodes ς_i and ς_j are weighted by the similarity between $\varsigma_i.f$ and $\varsigma_j.f$ as in [2]. Then a partitioning is performed on $\mathcal{G}^b$ to obtain a set of k differently congested partitions, utilizing any existing method. For example, α-Cut [2] is one such algorithm to do this task. Those with high means are considered as congested, and those with low means are considered as non-congested. Using this information the user query is responded accordingly.

The physical layer always keeps itself up-to-date with the building blocks that are to be served to the logical layer, and the logical layer partitions a small graph of building blocks, which takes fractions of a second. Thus the method is able to produce the results immediately for any query. Below we will focus on the development of the physical layer and the algorithms to maintain the building blocks.

3.2 Physical Layer

The traffic congestion has the property to form and gradually grow from small regions to spread into other parts via the linked road segments. It is also very natural to have multiple blocks of independent congestions at the same time, which sometimes even merge with others. Considering both the congested and non-congested blocks of road segments, we propose the concept of *building blocks* in road networks, as the most fundamental constituents maintained in the physical layer.

DEFINITION 6: (**Building Block**) Given a road graph $\mathcal{G}$, a building block $\mathcal{B}_i = (\mathcal{V}_i^b, \mathcal{E}_i^b)$ is defined as a subgraph that forms one of the n_b fundamental constituents $\mathcal{B} = \{\mathcal{B}_1, \mathcal{B}_2, \ldots, \mathcal{B}_{n_b}\}$ in the physical layer at a time point, such that $\bigcup_{i=0}^{n_b} \mathcal{V}_i^b = \mathcal{V}$ and $\mathcal{V}_i^b \bigcap \mathcal{V}_j^b = \emptyset$ for all $i \neq j$. ■

The building blocks[1] are small constituents that represent the differently congested blocks of the spatial road network at a point of time in a fine granularity. Two blocks $\mathcal{B}_p$ and $\mathcal{B}_q$ are called *neighbors*, if there exist nodes v_i and v_j such that $\langle v_i, v_j \rangle \in \mathcal{E}$ and $v_i \in \mathcal{B}_p \wedge v_j \in \mathcal{B}_q$. A node $v_i \in \mathcal{B}_p$ is called a *boundary node*, if there exists another node v_j such that $\langle v_i, v_j \rangle \in \mathcal{E}$ and $v_j \notin \mathcal{B}_p$. Each block has a set of spatially linked blocks as *neighbors* and a set of *boundary nodes*. The continuously changing traffic conditions affect their structure in terms of size, shape and location. For example, in the day time the traffic generally remains varied in the different regions, and thus require blocks in fine granularity to effectively represent the traffic condition. At each subsequent time point their structure keeps changing, as much as the variation in network traffic, and the congestion hotspots keep evolving. A *quality* building block $\mathcal{B}_i$ is characterized by two properties: high homogeneity (in terms of their feature values) amongst the nodes inside, and a stable structure that tends to change the least with time. We capture the evolution of network congestion by tracking the evolution of blocks in a low level. The blocks for the beginning time point are mined by partitioning the network based

[1] *Building block* and *block* are used synonymously hereafter.

on historical traffic data, and the proposed method in this paper starts tracking from this initial set.

The physical layer is the backbone of the proposed tracking method. It continuously maintains the evolving building blocks by incrementally updating them based on the most recent traffic data. To efficiently perform the incremental update, we start with an off-line preprocessing step to mine the road network building blocks. In the illustration examples of this paper, we will partition the road network based on the historical traffic data using α-Cut [2], and consider the obtained partitions as the building blocks for the starting point. At each new time point, the most recent traffic data is fetched, based on which these blocks are incrementally updated by identifying and processing the *unstable* road segments. For any query being passed from the logical layer, it returns back the results instantly.

4. BUILDING BLOCK EVOLUTION

We start this section with some fundamental concepts, and then explain the algorithm working in the physical layer to incrementally update the building blocks.

4.1 Stability

During the 24 hours of a day, the traffic load on an urban road network varies from time to time. For example, in early morning the roads are mostly free, and as peak hour draws near, they become busy quite rapidly. The period of time during which the traffic changes from free to congested (or vice versa) is very short for some roads, depending on their spatial importance, which makes the vicinity unstable. After sometime, the traffic gradually approaches towards being stable. Thus *stability* is an important feature of road networks that leads to a better understanding of the spatiotemporal aspects of traffic congestion.

DEFINITION 7: (**Node Stability**) If a node v_i belongs to block $\mathcal{B}_j$ at time t_{r-1}, then the stability $stab^r(v_i)$ is defined as the likelihood of v_i to remain in the same block $\mathcal{B}_j$ at time t_r. ■

We consider two different kinds of node stability, *i*) *spatial* stability, which looks into how well the feature values of v_i match with those of the rest in $\mathcal{B}_j$ at the current time t_r; and *ii*) *temporal* stability, which looks into how much stable was v_i in the previous time points. Equation 1 shows the formulation to compute its measure, where μ_j^r denotes the mean feature value inside $\mathcal{B}_j$ at time t_r. The formula is an average of two quantities – the first one $stab^{(r-1)}(v_i)$, which is its stability measure from the previous time point t_{r-1}, stands for the temporal stability, and the second quantity, which is from the current time point t_r, stands for the spatial stability. The second quantity firstly gets the normalized distance of the node from the centroid of its block, and then subtracts it from 1 to get the closeness, which determines the spatial stability. Its value ($\in [0,1]$) becomes 1 when the node feature value is exactly the same as the block mean value. A low value of this measure indicates that the node is less suitable for being part of the corresponding block.

$$stab^{(r)}(v_i) = \frac{\left(stab^{(r-1)}(v_i) + \left(1 - \text{abs}\left(\frac{v_i.f - \mu_j^r}{factor}\right)\right)\right)}{2} \quad (1)$$

$$factor = \max\{(\mu_j^r - v_j^{min}), (v_j^{max} - \mu_j^r)\} \quad (2)$$

Stability Tree: The blocks have one set of nodes lying on the boundaries (boundary nodes) and another set lying in the interior. As the boundary nodes are directly linked to nodes of a neighboring block, they are more likely to undergo a change (change in the block to which a node belongs) than the internal nodes in the next time point. Even among the boundary nodes, they all differ in their likelihood of change, which is captured by our stability measure. We use this measure to prioritize the boundary adjustment of nodes with high unstablity using a min-heap tree called *stability tree* (denoted by ST).

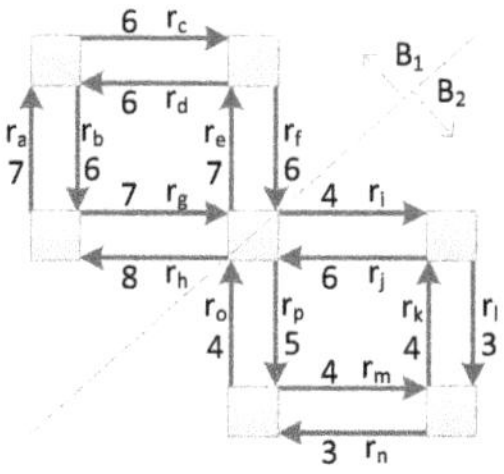

(a) A road sub-network

$\mathbf{B}_1$	$\mathbf{B}_2$
r_a-r_c-r_f-r_h	r_i-r_l-r_n-r_o
r_a-r_c-r_d-r_b	r_i-r_l-r_k-r_j
r_a-r_b-r_g-r_h	r_i-r_j-r_p-r_o
r_b-r_g-r_e-r_d	r_j-r_p-r_m-r_k
r_c-r_f-r_e-r_d	r_k-r_l-r_n-r_m
r_e-r_f-r_h-r_g	r_m-r_n-r_o-r_p
r_e-r_f-r_i-r_j	

(b) 2-bounded-4-roadcycles

Figure 1: Example of γ-*bounded*-l-*roadcycles*

4.2 Road Network Motifs

Similar to general graph motifs, road networks too have small connected structures that are commonly found all over the network. Generally the intersection points connect four different roads, each of which have their own traffic in the two opposite directions. This kind of intersections lead to the formation of directed cycles of length 4 (4-cycle or rectangle), 6 (6-cycles), and other cycles of higher *even* length in the road network. Triangles, 5-cycles, and other cycles of higher odd length are found only in rare situations. Based on the concepts of graph motifs, we define the following motif concepts in road networks.

DEFINITION 8: (**Road Cycle**) Given a road network $\mathcal{N} = (\mathcal{I}, \mathcal{R})$, a path $p = (r_1, r_2, \ldots, r_l)$ comprising l different road segments is said to be an *l-roadcycle* if there exists a path $p' = (r_1, r_2, \ldots, r_l, r_{l+1})$ such that $r_1 = r_{l+1}$ and the traffic flow is directed as $r_1 \rightarrow r_2 \rightarrow \cdots \rightarrow r_l \rightarrow r_{l+1}$. ■

DEFINITION 9: (**Bounded Road Cycle**) Given a road network $\mathcal{N} = (\mathcal{I}, \mathcal{R})$, a path $p = (r_1, r_2, \ldots, r_l)$ is said to be a γ-*bounded*-l-*roadcycle* if it is an l-*roadcycle* and the Euclidean distance between each r_i and r_{i+1} in p is less than or equal to γ. ■

A bounded road cycle ensures that it is a tightly bound road cycle where all the participating road segments have similar traffic measures up to a certain extent. All such cycles are transformed into paths of the road graph $\mathcal{G}$ as $p = (v_1, v_2, \ldots, v_l)$ where each v_i refers to the node in $\mathcal{V}$ corresponding to road segment r_i in $\mathcal{R}$. Due to the static structure of the road networks, the road cycles remain the same throughout, but the dynamic traffic keeps the set of bounded road cycles open to change at any point of time.

The blocks maintained by our method have the properties of high homogeneity and high connectivity inside them. Figure 1 shows an example of a small road sub-network and the list of all γ-bounded-l-roadcycles where γ and l are set to 2 and 4 respectively. The network in Figure 1(a) is divided by a dashed line into blocks B_1 and B_2, in which both the blocks have homogeneous traffic measures inside them, with B_1 having higher measures than B_2. Figure 1(b) shows all the 2-bounded-4-roadcycles. It is found that out of the total of 13 road cycles, 6 lie completely inside B_1, the same amount being inside B_2, and only one cycle shown at the

Algorithm 1: IncrementalUpdate(Block Set $\mathcal{B}$, Short cycle index SCI)

```
1  Compute stability of boundary nodes at t_i;
2  Stability tree ST ← Create a max-heap tree of boundary
   nodes;
3  Node v_root ← Delete root of ST;
4  while stablity(v_root) ≤ ε_stab do
5      Block bcurrent ← Current block of v_root in B;
6      sctree ← SCI[v_root];
7      Block bnext ← IdentifyMSB(B, sctree);
8      if bnext ≠ bcurrent then
9          bcurrent ← bcurrent\{v_root};
10         bnext ← bnext ∪ {v_root};
11         Update ST ←
           AddRemoveSTNodes(B, ST, v_root, bcurrent, bnext);
12     Node v_root ← Delete root of ST;
13 return B;
```

bottom is shared between the two blocks. This observation leads to the fact that the number of occurrences of bounded road cycles inside each block is significantly higher than those across different blocks. These bounded cycles thus give information about the block structure and can be used to locate their suitable boundaries. The lengthy cycles are mostly composed of short cycles (e.g., rectangles). Therefore, instead of all the possible cycles, we consider only the short-length bounded cycles to give an indication about the block structures.

Short Cycle Index: We pre-compute all the possible *road cycles* of path length smaller than or equal to ϵ_{path} in the road graph as an offline task and index them as follows. Firstly a sorted set of all nodes in $\mathcal{V}$ is created based on their id. For each node $v_i \in \mathcal{V}$, all the cycles that involve this node in the path are computed. Let us suppose $\{(v_i, v_a, v_b, v_i), (v_i, v_a, v_c, v_i), (v_i, v_d, v_e, v_i), (v_i, v_d, v_f, v_i)\}$ is the set of road cycles involving v_i. A trie tree is created having v_i as the root node, v_a and v_d as the children of v_i, v_b and v_c as the children of v_b, and v_e and v_f as the children of v_d. Then the end-marker leaf nodes having the information of their depth in the tree are added as children of v_b, v_c, v_e, and v_f. In this way the trie trees corresponding to all $v_i \in \mathcal{V}$ are created and attached to the sorted set. This structure is called *short cycle index* (denoted by SCI).

4.3 Incremental Update

The incremental update algorithm looks into all the unstable nodes and moves them to the most suitable blocks at each time point. Let us suppose we have a given set of blocks $\mathcal{B}$ at time t_{i-1} and the short cycle index SCI. The complete algorithm to incrementally compute the blocks at time t_i is shown in Algorithm 1. It starts with computing the stability measures from the traffic data at t_i for all the boundary nodes and creating the stability tree ST (lines 1-2). The iterative steps of computing the most suitable block for the most unstable boundary node and updating $\mathcal{B}$ are carried out until all the boundary nodes having their stability measure less than the threshold ϵ_{stab} have been processed (lines 3-12). After getting the most unstable node v_{root} by deleting the root of ST (line 3), its current block $bcurrent(\in \mathcal{B})$ and the short cycle tree *sctree* (from SCI) are accessed (lines 5-6). The most suitable block *bnext* ($\in \mathcal{B}$) is computed using the function `IdentifyMSB(.)` described later in Algorithm 2 (line 7). This computation is based on the new traffic data at t_i in contrast to the current block *bcurrent* based on the data at t_{i-1}. If the new block is different than the existing one (line 8), then v is deleted from *bcurrent* (line 9) and inserted into *bnext* (line 10). It completes the update of $\mathcal{B}$ for v_{root}. The stability tree ST is then updated by inserting all the newly created boundary nodes and deleting those nodes which no more lie on the boundary using `AddRemoveSTNodes(.)` (line 11). This function first gets all the nodes u linked to v_{root} in the road graph. If the block of u is same as the block of v_{root} before the update (*bcurrent*), it means that u is a boundary node. If this u does not exist in ST, being a new boundary node it is added to the tree. If the block of u is same as the block of v_{root} after the update (*bnext*), it means that u may not be a boundary node anymore. If this u exists in ST and does not lie on the boundary, being a new internal node it is removed from the tree. After completing the processing of v_{root}, the next most unstable node is extracted from ST (line 12) and the same process (lines 4-12) is carried out repeatedly until all the unstable nodes have been processed.

4.4 Computing the most suitable block

As mentioned earlier in Section 4.2, the short length bounded road cycles are likely to be found in significantly large numbers within the blocks rather than crossing multiple of them. A naive way to find the most suitable block for a node v at time t_i is to select the one having the highest number of bounded road cycles with all the nodes lying in the same block. But often there are cycles passing through multiple blocks, where most part of the cycle lie within the most suitable block leaving some fractions in neighboring blocks. The naive method ignores these fractions. Our main idea here is to identify the block that is involved in most part of the bounded road cycles of node v. For this, we consider all the road cycles of path length shorter than or equal to ϵ_{path}, making the range as $[3, \epsilon_{path}]$. Each block is quantified by a weight function $W(.)$ that considers the total of fractions from all the cycles lying in the respective block. For this quantification, all cycles account for a weight of 1, which is equally divided among all the cycle nodes other than v. For longer cycles the value being divided among more nodes gives lesser power to each. Therefore, the shorter the cycle, the bigger the impact of its nodes.

Formulated in Equation 3, $W(v, \mathcal{B}_j)$ computes the weight assigned to block $\mathcal{B}_j$ to identify the most suitable block for v, where $RCycles(v)$ gives all the γ-bounded short road cycles involving v, and u is another node that is involved in the same cycle and belongs to $\mathcal{B}_j$ at time t_i.

$$W(v, \mathcal{B}_i) = \sum_{\substack{\forall C \in RCycles(v) \\ (u \in C) \wedge (u \in \mathcal{B}_i)}} \frac{1}{pathlength(C) - 1} \tag{3}$$

In other words, each road cycle C that involves v is traversed, and for each node u in that cycle, if it belongs to block $\mathcal{B}_j$, the weight for $\mathcal{B}_j$ is incremented by $\frac{1}{pathlength(C)-1}$. For example, if there is a cycle $\{v_1(\in \mathcal{B}_1), v_2(\in \mathcal{B}_2), v_3(\in \mathcal{B}_1), v_4(\in \mathcal{B}_1)\}$, each node (except the one for which the weight is being computed) will have the power to make an affect by $\frac{1}{3}$, which in total equals to 1. To compute $W(v_1, \mathcal{B}_1)$, v_3 and v_4 both belonging to $\mathcal{B}_1$ adds up to $\frac{2}{3}$, and the weight $\frac{1}{3}$ of $v_2 \in \mathcal{B}_2$ is added to $W(v_1, \mathcal{B}_2)$. In this manner, the weights for all the blocks are computed

Algorithm 2: IdentifyMSB(Block Set $\mathcal{B}$, Short cycle tree *sctree*)

```
1  s1, s2, s3 ← initialize new stack;
2  Node nparent ← sctree(root);
3  forall the Node nchild ∈ sctree(root).child do
4      if nchild ≠ φ AND dist(nparent, nchild) ≤ γ then
5          Push nchild into s1;
6  repeat
7      Node nparent ← pop out from s1;
8      Push nparent into s2;
9      count = 0;
10     forall the Node nchild ∈ ctree(nparent).child do
11         if nchild ≠ φ AND dist(nparent, nchild) ≤ γ then
12             Push nchild into s1;
13             count ← count + 1;
14     Push count into s3;
15 until s1 ≠ empty;
16 s1 ← re-initialize stack;
17 wblock[ ] ← initialize an array of values of size n_b;
18 repeat
19     Node node ← pop out from s2;
20     countchild ← pop out from s3;
21     if countchild = 0 then
22         Value weight = 1/depth(node);
23     else
24         Value weight ← initialize with 0;
25         for i ← 1 to countchild do
26             Value childweight ← pop out from s1;
27             weight ← weight + childweight;
28     Push weight into s1;
29     wblock[Block of node] ← Increment by weight;
30 until s2 ≠ empty;
31 wmax ← maximum value in wblock[ ];
32 msb ← block corresponding to wmax;
33 return msb;
```

by adding the values from all the different cycles, and the one with the highest weight is selected as the most suitable block. However, as the number of road cycles is usually large, traversing all of them individually to compute the weight for the blocks in this way adds a lot of computations, and affects the running time.

In most of the road cycles in which a node v is involved, there exists an overlapping of some parts of the complete path of multiple cycles. For example, the cycles $C_1 = \{v, v_1, v_2, v_3\}$ and $C_2 = \{v, v_1, v_2, v_4\}$ of v have three overlapping nodes (v, v_1 and v_2). Computing the weights by traversing through C_1 and C_2 independently, repeats the computations done for v, v_1 and v_2. We make use of these overlappings in computing the block weights, thereby avoid redundant computations. This is done by our **multi-stack based algorithm** (shown in Algorithm 2) with the help of our short cycle index SCI that keeps the cycles indexed as a tree, having no repeating nodes even for the overlapping cycles. It accesses the set of blocks $\mathcal{B}$ and the short cycle tree *sctree* from SCI, and computes the most suitable block ($\in \mathcal{B}$) for the root node of *sctree* at time t_i. The stacks used in the algorithm explore the cycles in *sctree* and keep part of the computed information saved for its reuse later for the overlapping cycles.

The algorithm starts with pushing all the children of root node of *sctree* to the stack $s1$, if the Euclidean distance between the parent and the child $dist(nparent, nchild)$ is less than or equal to γ (lines 1-5). The $dist(.)$ function ensures that only the γ-bounded road cycles are explored. It is followed by iterative steps of popping out a node from $s1$ (line 7), pushing it into the stack $s2$ (line 8), pushing all its children back into $s1$ if the parent-child satisfies the γ distance condition (lines 10-13), and pushing the count of these children into the stack $s3$ (line 14). These steps are repeated until $s1$ becomes empty (line 15). They compute the number of children of each node and keep them saved in the stacks for computing the block weights later. Thereafter an array of values is initialized to store the weights $W(.)$ computed for each block in order to select the most suitable one (line 17). Each value in the array correspond to a block in $\mathcal{B}$ at time t_i. Then the nodes are popped out from $s2$ one after another (line 19), the count of their children are popped out from $s3$ (line 20), followed by a set of steps to compute the weights. A value of 0 as the count of children indicates that it is the last node in the branch and its *depth* gives the path length of the cycle. Hence the weight of $\frac{1}{pathlength(C)-1}$ that is carried by each node in the cycle C is computed as $\frac{1}{depth(node)}$ (line 22) and pushed into $s1$ (line 28) to be used later to compute weights for its parents. The depth of the node is found from its leaf node child in *sctree* that contains the depth information. If the count of children is non-zero, the weight is computed by adding the weights of all its children obtained by popping up $s1$ as many times as the count (lines 23-27), which is again pushed back into $s1$ (line 28). In addition to pushing the weight of nodes into $s1$, the weight for the blocks in the array *wblock*[ ] is updated by adding *weight* to the array element corresponding to the block of *node* in $\mathcal{B}$ (line 29). These steps of popping out from $s2$ and $s3$ and computing the values of *wblock*[ ] using $s1$ (lines 19-29) are repeated until $s2$ becomes empty (lines 18,30), which marks the completion of processing of all the bounded short road cycles. At last we select the most suitable block *msb* for the current time t_i by getting the block corresponding to the maximum weight in *wblock*[ ] (lines 31-33).

5. EXPERIMENTS

Our datasets, shown in Table 1, include one real (M_s) and two semi-synthetic (M_1, and M_2) datasets. M_s is recorded by the Sydney Coordinated Adaptive Traffic System (SCATS) from the Melbourne road network provided to us by VicRoads[2]. M_1, and M_2 are synthetically generated on the real road network of Melbourne using a web-based[3] random road traffic generator MNTG [6].

Table 1: Dataset statistics

Dataset	Place	Area(sq ml)	Road seg	Inter pts
M_s(*real*)	Melbourne	627.5	7245	2928
M_1	CBD Melbourne	6.6	17,206	10,096
M_2	CBD(+) Melbourne	31.5	53,494	28,465

The incremental partitioning results are evaluated by using the metric ANS (derived from Silhouette) that looks into the inter-partition heterogeneity and intra-partition homogeneity to quantify the overall quality of the obtained partitions [4, 2]. A value less than 1 for this measure indicates a good partitioning, and lower values indicate better partitioning.

Quality of incremental results: We start the experiments by firstly mining a set of blocks that are to be main-

[2]https://www.vicroads.vic.gov.au/

[3]It can be accessed through http://mntg.cs.umn.edu/tg/

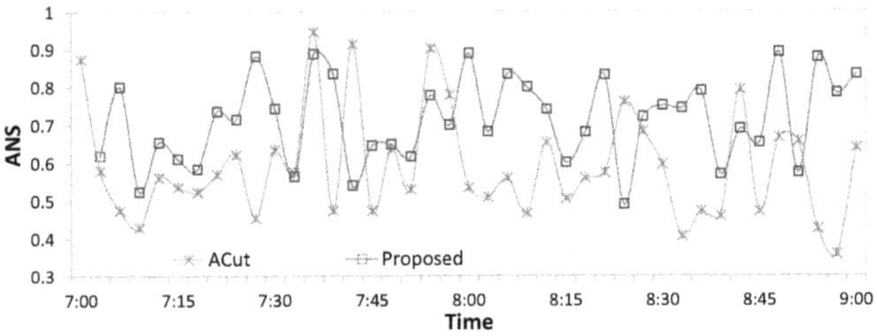

(a) ANS on Ms

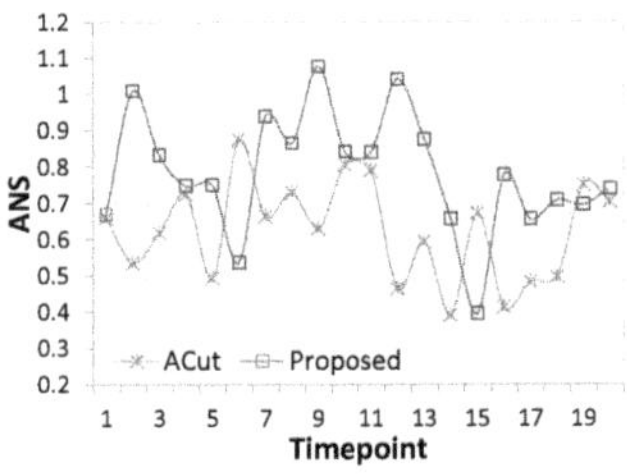

(b) ANS on M1

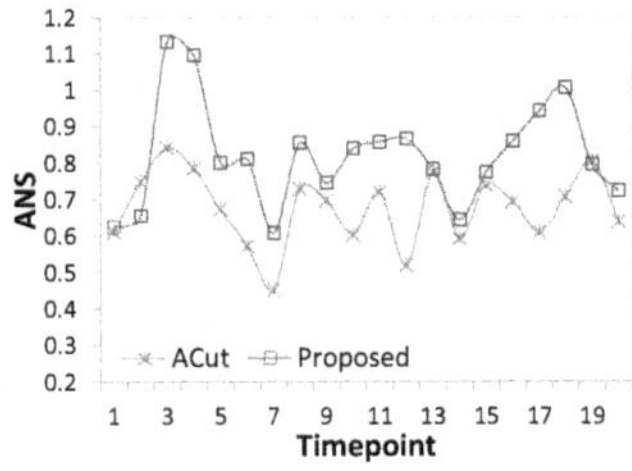

(c) ANS on M2

Figure 2: Partitioning quality

tained in the physical layer. For this, we partition the road network into a relatively large number of small sized partitions and consider them as the blocks for the beginning time point. As a preprocessing step, all the short road cycles are computed and indexed in SCI. We evaluate the quality of our results by comparing them with the partitions obtained by directly applying the α-Cut algorithm [2]. Figure 2 shows this comparison on `Ms`, `M1` and `M2` datasets in terms of *ANS*. The measure for the proposed method is computed by incrementally maintaining a set of 200 blocks in the physical layer and obtaining a set of 10 partitions from the logical layer at each of the shown time points. The results shown on the `Ms` dataset refer to the real scats traffic data on 03-12-2012 (Monday). We observe that the curve of the proposed method is most of the time higher but close to that of the α-Cut, which means that the incrementally obtained partitions by the proposed method are not significantly inferior than those obtained by partitioning the road network directly using α-Cut. Also, the ANS measure is always less than 1 for the real `Ms` dataset and most of the times less than 1 for the `M1` and `M2` datasets, which indicates that our results are still considerably good in quality. The main objective of the proposed method is to maintain the partitions efficiently, which lacks in α-Cut or any other road network (or graph) partitioning algorithm.

Efficiency of incremental computations: As the proposed method continuously operates to incrementally update the blocks in real-time, its efficiency is of great importance. Table 2 shows the average running time[4] of the logical layer for producing partitions from the blocks and that of the physical layer for incrementally updating the blocks at each time point. Its shows the running time by varying the number of maintained blocks, in comparison to [2]. We observe that the lower the number of maintained blocks, the faster is the method. The logical layer performs faster because it has to partition a smaller graph where the number of nodes is the number of maintained blocks, and the physical layer is faster because of lesser overhead. When there is a large number of blocks, it creates a large number of unstable and noisy road segments lying on the boundaries, which too often shift themselves from one block to another, leading to an overhead. Therefore selecting the right number of blocks for an application environment is important for the method to have stable blocks and partitions. The longest running time for the real dataset `Ms` is just a few seconds (for 1000 blocks), which shows its applicability for the real urban road networks. It can also be performed in fractions of a second by maintaining less number of blocks. We observe in the table that even our longest running time for any dataset is significantly lower than that of the existing re-partitioning method [2]. It suggests that our method can be effectively used with any real traffic management systems by properly setting its parameters.

[4]On a Core i5 computer with 8GB RAM

Table 2: Running time (in seconds)

Number of maintained building blocks		Dataset Ms	M1	M2
100	Logical layer	<1	<1	<1
	Physical layer	<1	1	72
400	Logical layer	<1	<1	1
	Physical layer	<1	1	96
800	Logical layer	3	3	5
	Physical layer	1	1	145
1000	Logical layer	10	12	15
	Physical layer	1	6	173
[2] (α-Cut)		98	129	1905

6. CONCLUSION

In this paper, we proposed a two-layer method to incrementally update the differently congested partitions of a road network in an efficient manner, in order to track the evolution of traffic congestion. The physical layer maintains and incrementally updates a set of small-sized building blocks of the network, and the logical layer provides an interface to query the physical layer about the congested partitions. We conducted extensive experiments on real and synthetic datasets to demonstrate the efficacy of our method. Our method can effectively serve real traffic management systems for a continuous tracking of the evolution of congestion and aid in smart transportation services.

Acknowledgment

This research was supported by the Data61 (formerly NICTA), ARC Discovery Projects DP140103499 and DP160102412, and Future Fellowship grant FT120100723.

7. REFERENCES

[1] T. Anwar, C. Liu, H. L. Vu, and M. S. Islam. Roadrank: Traffic diffusion and influence estimation in dynamic urban road networks. In *Proc. of the CIKM*, pages 1671–1674, 2015.

[2] T. Anwar, C. Liu, H. L. Vu, and C. Leckie. Spatial partitioning of large urban road networks. In *EDBT*, pages 343–354, 2014.

[3] T. Anwar, H. L. Vu, C. Liu, and S. P. Hoogendoorn. Temporal tracking of congested partitions in dynamic urban road networks. In *Proc. of the TRB Annual Meeting*, 2016.

[4] Y. Ji and N. Geroliminis. On the spatial partitioning of urban transportation networks. *Transp. Res. Part B: Methodological*, 46(10):1639–1656, 2012.

[5] Y. Ji, J. Luo, and N. Geroliminis. Empirical observations of congestion propagation and dynamic partitioning with probe data for large-scale systems. *Transportation Research Record*, 2422:1–11, 2014.

[6] M. F. Mokbel, L. Alarabi, J. Bao, A. Eldawy, A. Magdy, M. Sarwat, E. Waytas, and S. Yackel. Mntg: an extensible web-based traffic generator. In *SSTD*, pages 38–55, 2013.

[7] L.-Y. Wei and W.-C. Peng. An incremental algorithm for clustering spatial data streams: exploring temporal locality. *Knowledge and Information Systems*, 37(2):453–483, 2013.

The Rich and the Poor: A Markov Decision Process Approach to Optimizing Taxi Driver Revenue Efficiency

Huigui Rong[1]*, Xun Zhou[2]†, Chang Yang[1], Zubair Shafiq[3], Alex Liu[4]
[1]College of Computer Science and Electronic Engineering, Hunan University, Changsha, HN 410082
[2]Department of Management Sciences, [3]Department of Computer Science
University of Iowa, Iowa City, IA 52242
[4]Department of Computer Science and Engineering, Michigan State University, East Lansing, MI 48824
{ronghg, yangchangchn}@hnu.edu.cn, {xun-zhou, zubair-shafiq}@uiowa.edu
alexliu@cse.msu.edu

ABSTRACT

Taxi services play an important role in the public transportation system of large cities. Improving taxi business efficiency is an important societal problem since it could improve the income of the drivers and reduce gas emissions and fuel consumption. The recent research on seeking strategies may not be optimal for the overall revenue over an extended period of time as they ignored the important impact of passengers' destinations on future passenger seeking. To address these issues, this paper investigates how to increase the revenue efficiency (revenue per unit time) of taxi drivers, and models the passenger seeking process as a Markov Decision Process (MDP). For each one-hour time slot, we learn a different set of parameters for the MDP from data and find the best move for a vacant taxi to maximize the total revenue in that time slot. A case study and several experimental evaluations on a real dataset from a major city in China show that our proposed approach improves the revenue efficiency of inexperienced drivers by up to 15% and outperforms a baseline method in all the time slots.

Keywords

Taxi Driver, Markov Decision Process, Revenue Efficiency

1. INTRODUCTION

Taxi services are playing an important role in the public transportation system in modern cities. Taxi drivers are a big social group in many major cities in the world, and improving the business efficiency helps increase taxi drivers' annual income and thus contributes to the development of urban economy. Also, higher efficiency means less driving time and cruising distance needed, and thus leads to lower gas emission and fuel consumption.

*Co-first author
†Co-first author and corresponding author.

CIKM '16, October 24–28, 2016, Indianapolis, IN, USA.

DOI: http://dx.doi.org/10.1145/2983323.2983689

Recent research [1–3, 8, 11] have focused on developing recommendation systems for taxi drivers. These work usually learn knowledge about passenger demand distribution from data and recommend the best route or location for a driver to optimize one or more of the following measures: the profit margins for the next trip [1, 8], the chance of finding the next passenger [4, 7], or energy consumption before finding the next passenger [3]. Some other work learns knowledge from taxi data for other types of recommendation scenarios such as fast routing, ride-sharing, or fair-recommendation [9, 10, 13, 14], which is not directly related with our topic.

The above work, although effective in improving the proposed measures, still have some limitations. First of all, some of the above work (e.g., [3, 8, 12]) simply aggregated the historical data over the entire study period and ignored the temporal variation of the passenger distribution. This may lead to inaccuracy in the recommendations. More importantly, all of the existing work focus on optimizing the measures for the immediate next trip. However, they do not consider the impact of the driver's move on the overall revenue in the next few trips.

To address the limitations of the related work, this paper investigates how to learn business strategies from historical data to increase the revenue efficiency (revenue per unit time) of taxi drivers. This paper models the passenger-seeking process as a Markov Decision Process (MDP). The study area is partitioned into grids. Each state in MDP is a combination of current grid, time, and the driving direction. For each state, a vacant taxi may choose to travel to a subset of its neighboring grids and cruise through that grid. At a probability p_{seek}, the driver may find a passenger during the cruising, and the destination of the passenger may follow another probability distribution p_{dest}.We learn the necessary MDP parameters (e.g., p_{seek}, p_{dest}) for each time slot from historical data. The MDP optimization problem is solved by a dynamic programming algorithm. The output, which contains the best action to take for each state, will be recommended to taxi drivers.

The major contributions of this paper are summarized as follows: (1) We perform a detailed analysis to quantify taxi business efficiency and identify the key strategic differences between the most successful and the least successful drivers. (2) We model the passenger-seeking process as a Markov Decision Process (MDP). For each time slot, we learn a different set of input parameters for MDP from historical data. A dynamic programming approach is employed to solve the MDP.(3) We propose a recommendation mechanism based on our MDP solution in each time slot. Computer simulations show that our solution can improve the revenue efficiency of drivers by up to 15% in real data and up to 8.4% over a baseline method.

2. PROBLEM FORMULATION

In this section we present our data analysis to quantify the success of a driver and identify the more (less) successful drivers. Then we identify the most important factors for drivers to improve their business. Based on these analysis we formulate the problem as an optimal decision problem. The dataset we are using in this study contains taxi operation record for a whole year from the capital city of a central province in China. There are approximately 19 million taxi trip records (53,000 per day), where each record has the latitude-longitude coordinates and timestamps of the pick-up and drop-off events, along with total traveled distance and the fare of the corresponding trip. There are totally about 1400 taxi cabs in the data.

2.1 Who Are More Successful?

We first calculate the total business time of each taxi cab to better estimate the drivers' time commitment. The total business time (denoted as T_{bus}) is the sum of two parts, the total operating time (T_{drive}) and the total seeking time (T_{seek}) as shown in Eq. 1. The total operating time T_{drive} is the sum of all the trip duration of a taxi. Calculating total seeking time is tricky since the gap between two consecutive trips vary and some drivers may choose to take a rest between trips. We considered all the gaps between consecutive trips in the dataset and call these gaps "seeking trips". Figure 2 shows the distribution of the length of all the seeking trips. As can be observed, 90% of the gaps are shorter than 25 minutes, so, we thus use 25 minutes as the threshold.

$$T_{bus} = T_{drive} + T_{seek} \quad (1)$$

Revenue Efficiency. An obvious way to increase revenue is by driving taxi for longer time duration. However, given time constraints, it makes sense to maximize revenue per unit of time. To this end, we define a revenue efficiency (E_{rev}) metric: revenue earned divided by total taxi driver's business time. Formally it can be expressed as follows:

$$E_{rev} = \frac{M}{T_{bus}} = \frac{M}{T_{drive} + T_{seek}} \quad (2)$$

where M denotes the total money earned by the taxi driver. The revenue efficiency measure could be calculated for an hour, a day, or a whole year.

Identifying Top and Bottom Drivers. Based on the above proposed measure, we first rank all the day-time drivers and find the top and bottom ones. Figure 1 plots the histogram of overall revenue efficiency for all taxi drivers in our data set. About 80% drivers have a revenue efficiency between 0.72 and 0.80. We find the top 10% and bottom 10% drivers as successful and not-so-successful drivers.

We also further zoom into each time slot to show the difference in efficiency between the top and bottom drivers. We calculate the average revenue efficiency of the top 10% and bottom 10% drivers in each time slot. Figure 3(a) shows the average revenue efficiency of the top 10% drivers (yellow

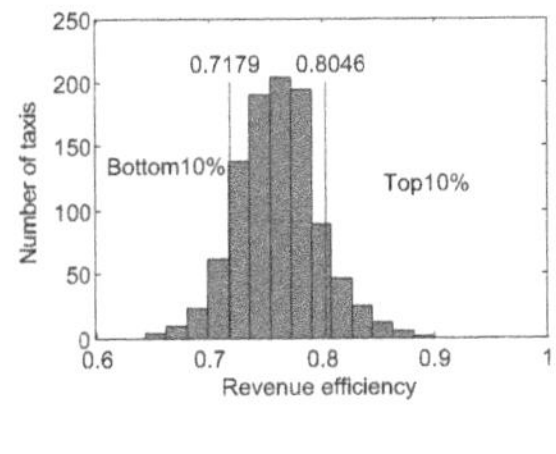

Figure 1: Distribution of Revenue Efficiency for all the day-time drivers

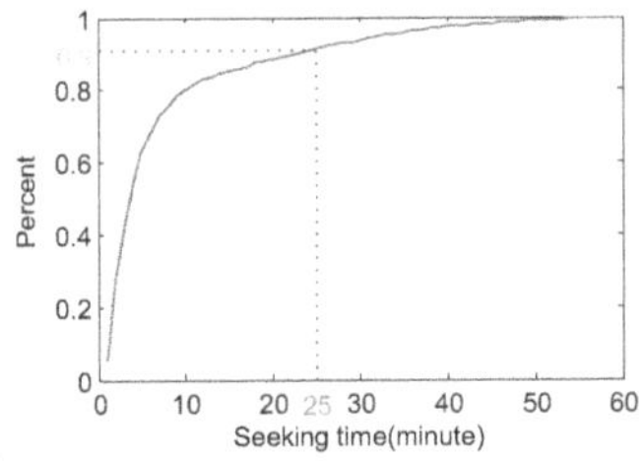

Figure 2: Distribution of seeking time

bar) and the bottom 10% drivers (red bar) during different time slots of a day. As can be seen, there is a 15%-20% difference between the two groups.

2.2 Why Are the Top Drivers Successful?

As noted previously, the total business time includes driving time (occupied taxi) and seeking time (vacant taxi). A taxi driver has positive money income when driving with passenger but no income while seeking. The revenue efficiency of a driver depends on (1) how much money a driver can make while driving for one minute, i.e., driving efficiency, and (2) how quickly can one driver find the next passenger (seeking efficiency). Taking slower routes, running into traffic congestions will be likely to lower his/her driving efficiency and revenue efficiency. First we define driving efficiency E_{drive} as follows:

$$E_{drive} = \frac{M}{T_{drive}} \quad (3)$$

The best way to improve the revenue efficiency is to increase E_{drive} while reducing the total seeking time. Figure 3(b) shows the comparison of driving efficiency between the top and bottom drivers. The difference is about 10% to 13%, which is smaller compared to the difference in the overall revenue efficiency (approximately 17% difference).

We also compare the average seeking time of the top 10% and bottom 10% drivers. Figure 3(c) shows the average seeking time (the time gap between consecutive trips that are less than 25 minutes) of the top (yellow bar) and bottom drivers (red bar) in each time slot. Results show that top drivers on average save up to 25% to 35% time between trips, respectively.

2.3 What is the Optimal Strategy?

A number of related work have used taxi data to calculate the chance of finding a passenger in each region or along each road segment. Based on this probability and the current location of a driver, one can choose the route or destination with the highest probability to find the next passenger. So where passengers want to go is also a key issue to drivers. However, drivers don't have much freedom in choosing where to go after they have found a passenger. In China, most cities will fine taxi drivers who refuse to take a passenger. Taking this issue into consideration, we believe that the driver's decision on where to find the next passenger is very important, not only because it determines the seeking time of this iteration, but also to some degree the next few trips and the overall revenue efficiency. To this end, we formulate the best taxi seeking strategy as follows:

Given the historical passenger trips and seeking trips for each time slot, the current status of an vacant taxi, we aim to **find** the next movement for the driver. **The objective**

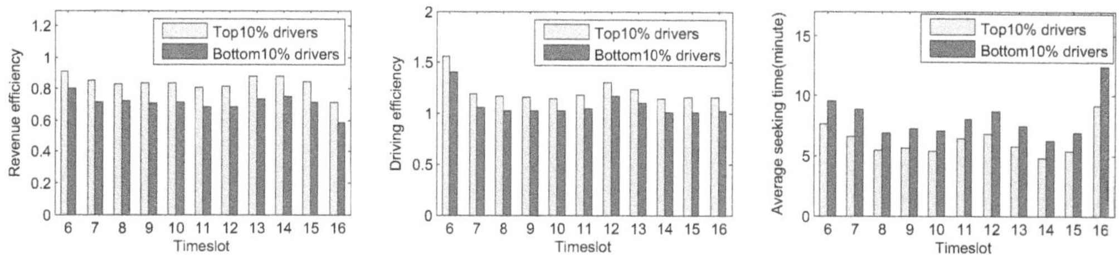

(a) Average Revenue efficiency (b) Average Driving efficiency (c) Average Seeking time

Figure 3: Comparison between top 10% and bottom 10% drivers on (a) Revenue efficiency (b) Driving Efficiency and (c) Average seeking time

Table 1: Major variables in this paper

Variable	Meaning
l, L	The current location and the location set
t	Number of minutes into a time slot
d,D	Incoming direction to the current grid and the set of all the possible directions
s	A state of the MDP model, $s = (l, t, d)$
S	The collection of all the states. $s \in S$
a	An action taken by a vacant taxi
A	The set of all the possible actions, $a \in A$
$A_{allowed}(s)$	The allowed actions for state s
$\pi(s)$	the optimal action for state s
$t_{seek}(j)$	The time needed for a taxi to cruise grid j
$t_{drive}(i,j)$	The time needed to drive from grid i to j
$P_{dest}(j,k)$	The probability a passenger picked up in grid j wishes to go to grid k
$P_{find}(j)$	The probability that a passenger can be found in grid j during the vacant cruise
$r(i,j)$	The expected reward (trip fare) from grid i to j
E_{drive}	Driving efficiency (Yuan per minute while occupied)

is to maximize the total expected revenue for this taxi in the rest time of the current time slot.

3. A MARKOV DECISION PROCESS APPROACH

A Markov Decision Process (MDP) [5] is a stochastic decision process with a set of states (S) and a set of possible actions (A) that transfer the states from one to another. A MDP must have the Markov property, which requires that the next state of the process only depends on the current state and the action, but not any previous state or action. Each action will transfer the process from the current state to a new state at a probability (P) with a corresponding reward (R). Usually the optimal action for each state (often denoted as "policy") is desired, which maximizes the total reward over a finite or infinite number of steps.

We model the passenger seeking strategy of a taxi as a Markov Decision Process. Solving this MDP model will give us the best seeking strategy for a taxi at each different state. Table 1 shows all the parameters we use in the MDP model.

3.1 System States

It is obvious that the best seeking strategy of a taxi is dependent on the current location and the remaining time of the business time window. In our model, each state of a vacant taxi is described by three parameters: current location (grid cell number)$l \in L = \{1, 2, ..., 128 \times 128\}$, current time (minutes into the time slot) $t \in T = \{1, 2, ..., 60\}$, and the direction from which the taxi arrived at the current location $d \in D$, where $D = \{\emptyset, \nearrow, \uparrow, \nwarrow, \leftarrow, \circlearrowleft, \rightarrow, \searrow, \downarrow, \swarrow\}$.

The "incoming direction" is needed for each state to ensure that the taxi does not fall into a infinite loop among a small number of grid cells or staying in the same grid forever. The set of arrival directions for a location includes the eight possible directions from the queen-connectivity neighbors, plus from the grid itself. We also include a NULL direction $\emptyset$ in the set, which indicates that the taxi just dropped off a passenger and does not have any arriving direction. We use ten numbers (0-9) to index these directions, which is illustrated in Figure 4(a). 0 is for the NULL direction and 5 is for the direction to the current grid itself. Formally, a state in our MDP model can be represented as $s = (l, t, d)$. The maximum number of states in our problem setting is $|L| \times |T| \times |D| = 16384 \times 60 \times 10 = 9830400$. However, the actual number of states is much smaller than this.

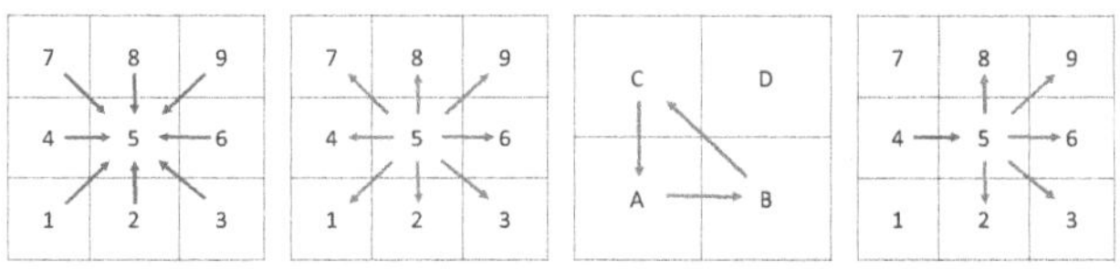

(a) Arrival Direction (b) Possible Actions (c) Unallowable actions (d) Allowable actions

Figure 4: An illustration of the direction of MDP model

3.2 Actions

In our model, each vacant taxi at one of the states has nine possible actions to choose. Each action (a) is to move from the current grid to one of the eight neighbors or stay in the current grid. Formally, it can be expressed as: $a \in A$, $A = \{\swarrow \downarrow, \searrow, \rightarrow, \circlearrowleft, \leftarrow, \nwarrow, \uparrow, \nearrow\}$. Similar to D, we also use numbers (1-9) to index the directions. Figure 4(b) illustrates the mapping of the directions. The arrow directions are the opposite compared to the mapping of the d parameter in the states. The same direction in D and A are indexed with different numbers.

For each grid cell i, we examine all the seeking trips that origin from i and end at each of i's eight neighbors. For each of i's neighbors j, we calculate how many percent of these seeking trips are between i and j. If the percentage of such trips between i and j is lower than a minimum threshold then we could conclude that there is no road connecting these grids. In this case, we do not allow the taxi to move from i to j. Taken into account the precision errors of GPS signal, the threshold is set to 5%.

Finally, we also need to prevent a taxi from cruising the

same grid or a small number of grids in a loop. Figure 4(c) illustrate such a scenario. To this end, we require that in a state s, a taxi may only choose actions from a subset of A, denoted as the allowed action set $A_{allowed}(s)$. For a taxi that just dropped off a passenger, the incoming direction is 0 (no direction). The taxi may choose any action.After the taxi searched the current grid, it must leave the current grid.Also a taxi must follow approximately the same direction and should not make a very sharp turn. Specifically, if the taxi came to the current grid l at time t from direction d, then $A_{allowed}(l,t,d)$ should be within the range of $[-90°, 90°]$ of d. Figure 4(d) illustrates an example. A taxi coming to the current state from left (4) can only go to the top, top-right, right, bottom-right, or bottom grid (2,3,6,8,9).

3.3 State Transition and Objective Function

Assuming the current state of the taxi is $s = (i,t,d)$. An action a is taken to move the taxi from grid i to its neighbor j. As a result, the taxi will cruise to the next destination j and cruise the entire grid j in $t_{seek}(j)$ minutes. There will be two possible consequences.

(1) The taxi successfully finds a passenger in grid j after cruising the grid for $t_{seek}(j)$ minutes. In this case, the passenger may choose to go to one of the grid cells as destination (denoted as k) at a probability $p_{dest}(j,k)$. We will discuss how to obtain this probability later. Upon finishing this trip, the taxi will arrive at location k. We use $t_{drive}(j,k)$ to represent the total time needed to travel from j to k. The driver will receive a fare of $r(j,k)$ Yuan, where $r(j,k)$ represents the expected fare between grids j and k. The taxi will start seeking from k again. The state of the taxi is thus transitioned to $s' = (k, t + t_{seek}(j) + t_{drive}(j,k), 0)$.

(2) The taxi did not find any passenger after $t_{seek}(j)$ minutes in j. Then the taxi must leave the current grid and move to the next one. Assume the taxi took action $a = 6$ $(\rightarrow)$. Then the taxi will end up in the next state $s' = (j, t + t_{seek}(j), 4)$ (from the left grid, $\rightarrow$).

In the above process, an important parameter needed is the probability that the taxi can find a passenger during the cruising in grid j, denoted as $P_{find}(j)$. We will discuss how we estimate this parameter in the next subsection.

To summarize, a vacant taxi in any state $s_0 = (i,t,d)$, $s_0 \in S$ may take one of the possible actions $a \in A_{allowed}(s_0)$ to cruise to a nearby grid j. With the probability $1 - P_{find}(j)$ the taxi will transition to state $s_1 = (j, t + t_{seek}(j), 10 - a)$ with no reward. With the probability of $P_{find}(j) \times P_{dest}(j,k)$, $(k = 1, 2, ..., |L|)$, the taxi will end up in the next state $s_2 = (k, t + t_{seek}(j) + t_{drive}(j,k), 0)$ and receive a reward of $r(j,k)$ Yuan. The state transition diagram of the proposed MDP model is shown in Figure 5. Each circle represents a state with the three parameters listed beside it.

The objective of the MDP model is to maximize the total expected reward (taxi fare) in the current time slot. The MDP has a set of terminal states with $t = 60$. Once the system reaches these states, no more actions can be taken.

For every a, the $V^*(s,a)$ function represents the maximal expected revenue in the current time slot if action a is taken at state s. $V(s)$ is the maximum expected revenue for state s. Formally the objective can be expressed as follows:

$$V^*(s,a) = (1 - P_{find}(l)) \times V(l_a, t + t_{seek}(l_a), 10 - a) + \Sigma_{k=1}^{|L|} P_{find}(j) \times P_{dest}(j,k) \times (r(j,k) + V(k, t + t_{seek}(j) + t_{drive}(j,k), 0)) \quad (4)$$

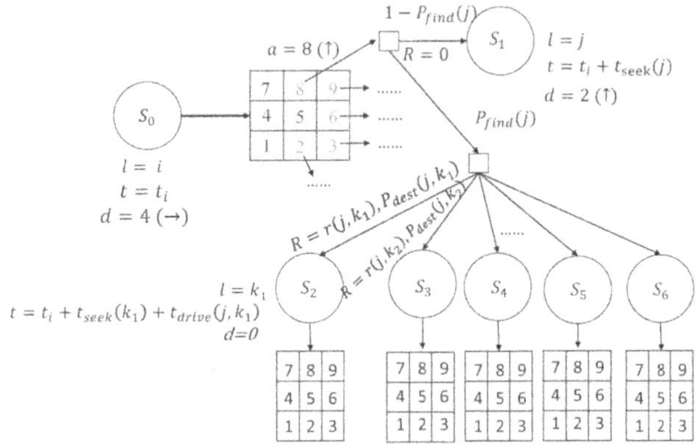

Figure 5: An illustration of the MDP model

where $s = (l,t,d)$ is a state and a is an action that moves the taxi from l to l_a. The optimal policy (π) is defined as follows:

$$\pi(s) = arg\max\{V^*(s,a)\} \quad (5)$$
$$V(s) = V^*(s, \pi(s)) \quad (6)$$

3.4 Learning Parameters for MDP

Now we discuss how to decide the necessary parameters for the MDP. All the parameters are learned from our historical passenger trips and seeking trips.

Learning the passenger pickup probability P_{find}. First we estimate the probability that a vacant taxi successfully picks up a passenger during its cruise in each grid. For each of the time slots, we calculate a 128×128 matrix P_{find} with the pick up probability of each grid.

The basic idea is: the probability of picking up a passenger in grid i can be approximated by dividing the number of successful pickups in i by the total number of times this grid is visited by a vacant taxi. Since the data only contains the origin and destination of each trip, we have to estimate the route taken by each taxi when seeking for a passenger. For each "seeking trip", we use the API provided by Baidu Map to calculate the shortest path between the origin (the previous drop-off) and the destination (the next pick-up). Then we map each estimated seeking trip obtained to corresponding grids and count how many times each grid is passed by a vacant taxi during each time slot (denoted as n_{seek}). We also calculate the pickup counts n_{pickup} in each grid. The pick up probability is thus calculated as follows:

$$P_{find}(i) = \frac{n_{find}(i)}{n_{find}(i) + n_{pickup}(i)} \quad (7)$$

Learning passenger destination probability P_{dest}
To estimate the destination probability for a time slot, we calculate the number of trips between each pair of source and destination in that time slot and get a 128 by 128 matrix W. Each value W_{ij} represents the total number of trips from i to j in the corresponding time slot. We normalize the data in each row (each value divided by the sum of the entire row, except for zero sums). In the resulting matrix P_{dest}, each row i has the empirical probability distribution of a passenger choosing destination j when picked-up in grid i.

Estimating the reward function $r(i,j)$. In our model, the reward (r) is the fare income for a trip. We simply calculate the average fare of trips between each pair of source and destinations in the same time slot as the expected fare.

Estimating the driving time t_{drive}. Here we consider the average driving efficiency of top 10% and bottom 10% drivers. Specifically, we calculate the total fare income of the two groups of drivers and divide them by the total driving time, respectively. The driving efficiency of top 10% and bottom 10% drivers are 1.3061 and 1.1648. Using the driving efficiency, we estimate the travel time for a trip by dividing the estimated fare by the corresponding driving efficiency. Formally we have $t_{drive}(i,j) = r(i,j)/E_{drive}$

Seeking time for each grid t_{seek}. We calculated the average speed of seeking trips and find it is about 300m/min. Since the grid size in our analysis is fairly small, we set the seeking time t_{seek} to 1 minute for every grid.

3.5 Solving MDP

For each time slot, we build a MDP with parameters learned from our data. Now we solve the MDP to find the optimal policy. For each state in the MDP model, the result is the best action to take for that state to maximize total expected rewards in the remaining time of the time slot. The MDP does not have a fixed number of steps. Instead, there are a few terminal states. Once the system reaches a state with t=60 the system terminates. The MDP can be solved by employing a dynamic programming approach.

The pseudo code of the algorithm is presented in Algorithm 1.The algorithm starts from the states with $t = 60$ and find out the maximum expected reward for them. Then the algorithm traces back along time to $t = 1$. For each state s, the algorithm examines all the possible actions and calculates the maximum expected reward for each of them (Lines 2-4). The total expected reward of state s after taking action a, $V^*(s,a)$, is calculated using Equation 4 (Line 5). Here $V(l_a, t+t_{seek}(l_a), 10-a)$ and $V(k, t+t_{seek}(j)+t_{drive}(j,k), 0)$ must have been calculated already since they have larger t value than s. Then the action with the maximum V^* for s (denoted as a_{max}) is selected (Line 6). The maximum expected reward of s is thus set to $V^*(s, a_{max})$ (Line 7). The output of this algorithm is one action for each state.

The algorithm has time complexity of $O(|T| \times |D| \times |L| \times |A|)$. Since $|D|$ and $|A|$ are small constant numbers, the complexity can be simplified to $O(|T| \cdot |L|)$. Similarly, the space complexity is $O(|T| \cdot |L|)$.

Algorithm 1 Solving MDP using Dynamic Programming

Input: $L, A, D, T, P_{find}, P_{dest}, R, t_{seek}$
Output: The best policy π
1: V is a $|L| \times |T|$ matrix; $V \leftarrow 0$
2: **for** $t = |T|$ to 1 **do**
3:     **for** $l = 1$ To $|L|$ **do**
4:         **for** d in D **do** $\triangleright\ s = (l, t, d)$
5:             $a_{max} \leftarrow a$ that maximizes $V^*(s, a)$
6:             $\pi(s) \leftarrow a_{max}$
7:             $V(s) \leftarrow V^*(s, a_{max})$
8: Return π

4. EVALUATION

In this section, we perform a number of experiments to evaluate the quality of our result. Specifically, we hope to answer the following questions: (1) How much more revenue can be generated if a driver uses our strategy? (2) Is our proposed method better than methods in related work?

4.1 Revenue Improvement

In order to verify the effectiveness of our recommendation, We carry out a simulation based on our MDP model, and compare our revenue efficiency of simulated results with that of the top 10% and bottom 10% drivers.

Figure 6 (a)-(b) show the revenue efficiency distribution of the top 10% drivers (left, yellow) and our simulated results using the top 10% drivers' driving efficiency (right, red) for time slot 12-13. The average revenue efficiency is improved from 0.828 yuan/min to 0.89 yuan/min, yielding a 7.6% improvement. Figure 6 (c)-(d) show the revenue efficiency distribution of the bottom 10% drivers (left, green) and our simulated results using the bottom 10% drivers' driving efficiency (right, red) for the same time slot. The average revenue efficiency is improved from 0.75 yuan/min to 0.82 yuan/min, yielding a 9.8% improvement. We also perform the same simulations for all the day-time slots. Figure 7 (a) show the average revenue efficiency of the top drivers in reality compared to the simulated revenue efficiency using the bottom 10% drivers' driving efficiency for all the day-time slots. The improvement is between 3.6% and 12%. Figure 7 (b) shows the comparison of revenue efficiency between the bottom drivers and the simulated results using the bottom 10% drivers' driving efficiency for the day-time slots. The corresponding improvement are between 4.2% and 15.5%. As can be observed, our approach has more improvements during morning and evening rush hours because there are more data records and our parameters learned from the data are more accurate.

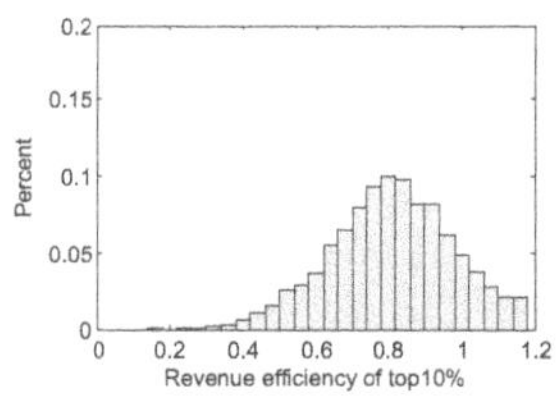

(a) Distribution of revenue efficiency of top10% drivers for 12-13

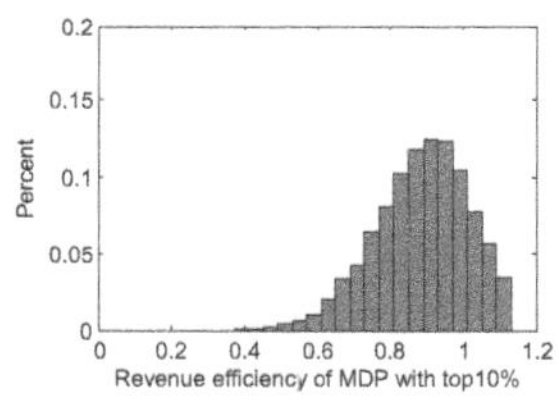

(b) Distribution of simulated revenue efficiency baed on top 10% drivers

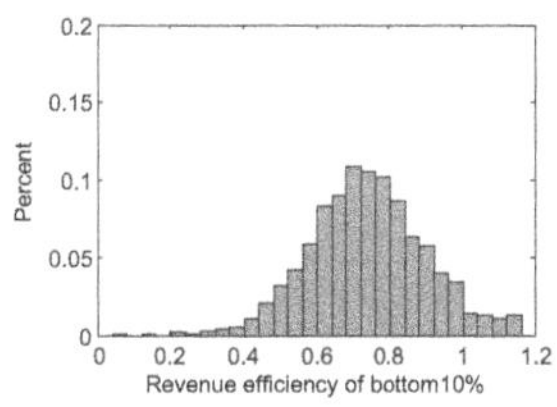

(c) Distribution of revenue efficiency of bottom10% drivers

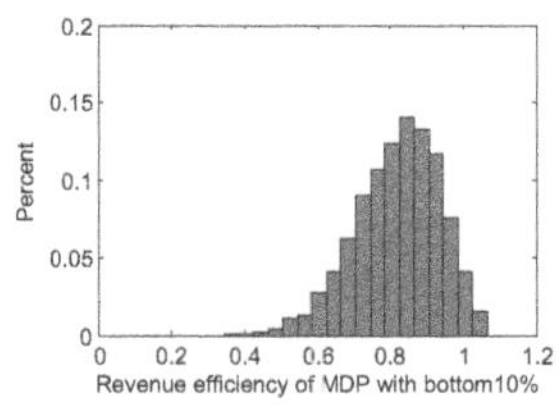

(d) Distribution of simulated revenue efficiency based on bottom 10% drivers

Figure 6: Comparison between simulated and real revenue efficiency in time slot 12-13

Figure 7 (c) shows the simulated revenue efficiency (red line) is higher than the top 10% drivers' revenue efficiency for almost all the time slots. This result validates the effectiveness of our proposed method: the bottom drivers with limited driving efficiency can still make the same amount of money as the top drivers if they follow our driving strategy.

4.2 Comparison with Baseline Method

Next we compare the output of our method with a baseline

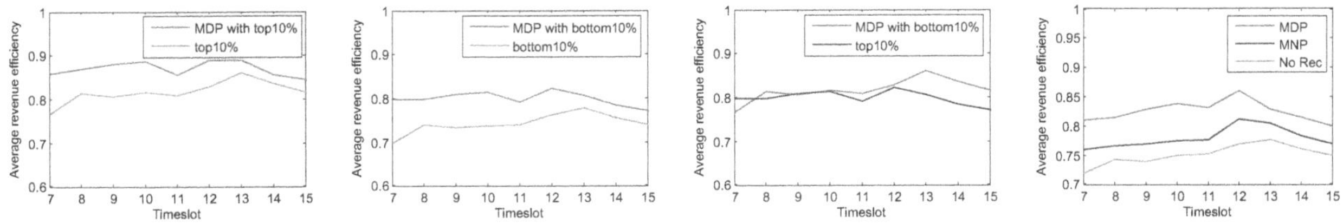

(a) Simulated MDP vs. real revenue efficiency with top 10% drivers' driving efficiency

(b) Simulated MDP vs. real revenue efficiency with bottom 10% drivers' driving efficiency

(c) Simulated MDP revenue efficiency using bottom 10% drivers' driving efficiency vs. real top10% drivers

(d) Simulated revenue efficiency of MDP vs. baseline and real data (all drivers)

Figure 7: Revenue efficiency comparison between our method, real data, and a baseline method (best viewed in color).

algorithm called MNP algorithm in related work [8], which is the most relevant and similar to ours. Given the current location of a taxi, the baseline method MNP recommends the next five road segments to seek passengers. The objective of the MNP algorithm is to maximize the total expected net profit along the seeking trip. If no passenger is found, the algorithm will recommend another five road segments based on the new location of the taxi.

Here we use grids to replace road segments to make a fair comparison. The experiment settings are the same as described in 4.1. We calculate the average simulated revenue of all the 6000 taxis in each of the one-hour time slots based on the two methods, respectively. Figure 7(d) shows the average revenue in the simulated results. Our method (red curve) outperformed the baseline method (blue curve) in average revenue efficiency (Yuan per minute) in all the time slots. The maximum improvement is about 8.4%.

5. CONCLUSION AND FUTURE WORK

This paper investigated how to learn the best taxi seeking strategy from historical data to improve taxi drivers' business efficiency over an extended period of time. This problem is of great societal importance.This paper proposed to model the passenger-seeking process as a Markov Decision Process (MDP)to get the best move for a vacant taxi at any state. Case study and experiment results showed that our approach effectively improved the revenue efficiency of inexperienced drivers by up to 15% and outperformed a baseline by up to 8.4%.

For future work, we plan to improve our MDP model to incorporate the total revenue and driving time covering the taxi shift time, and recommend the best strategy to improve the overall revenue efficiency. Finally, we plan to include other attributes such weather condition and traffic conditions to improve the results of our method.

6. ACKNOWLEDGMENTS

Xun Zhou is supported in part by the National Science Foundation under Grant No.1566386. Huigui Rong and Chang Yang are supported in part by the National Natural Science Foundation of China under Grant No.61672221, No.61273232 and No.61304184. Alex Liu is partially supported by the National Science Foundation under Grant Numbers CNS-1318563, CNS-1524698, and CNS-1421407, and the National Natural Science Foundation of China under Grant Numbers 61472184 and 61321491, and the Jiangsu High-level Innovation and Entrepreneurship (Shuangchuang) Program.

7. REFERENCES

[1] J. Yuan, Y. Zheng, L. Zhang, X. Xie, and G. Sun. Where to find my next passenger. The 13th international conference on Ubiquitous computing (UbiComp), pp. 109-118, ACM, 2011.

[2] Y. Zheng, J. Yuan, W. Xie, X. Xie, and G. Sun. Drive smartly as a taxi driver. The 7th International Conference on Ubiquitous Intelligence & Computing (UIC), pp. 484-486, IEEE, 2010.

[3] Y. Ge, H. Xiong, A.Tuzhilin, K. Xiao, M. Gruteser, An energy-efficient mobile recommender system. the 16th International Conference on Knowledge Discovery and Data Mining (SIGKDD), pp. 899-908, ACM, 2010.

[4] D. Ziebart, L. Maas, K. Dey, and J. Bagnell. Navigate like a cabbie: probabilistic reasoning from observed context-aware behavior. The 10th international conference on Ubiquitous computing (UbiComp), pp. 322-331, Springer Berlin Heidelberg,2008.

[5] Bellman, Richard. A Markovian decision process. No. P-1066. RAND CORP SANTA MONICA CA, 1957.

[6] Lee J, Shin I, Park G L. Analysis of the passenger pick-up pattern for taxi location recommendation. The 4th International Conference on Networked Computing and Advanced Information Management (NCM), pp. 199-204, IEEE, 2008.

[7] Y. Ge, C. Liu, et al. A Taxi Business Intelligence System. The 17th International Conference on Knowledge Discovery and Data Mining, pp. 735-738, ACM, 2011.

[8] M. Qu, H. Zhu et al. A Cost-Effective Recommender System for Taxi Drivers. The 20th international conference on Knowledge discovery and data mining (SIGKDD), pp. 45-54, ACM, 2014.

[9] Castro P S, Zhang D, Li S. Urban traffic modelling and prediction using large scale taxi GPS traces. The 10th International Conference on Ubiquitous Computing (UbicomP), pp. 57-72, Springer Berlin Heidelberg, 2012.

[10] Chawla S, Zheng Y, Hu J. Inferring the Root Cause in Road Traffic Anomalies. The 12th International conference on Data Mining, pp. 141-150, IEEE, 2012.

[11] D. Zhang, L. Sun, B. Li, C. Chen. Understanding Taxi Service Strategies from Taxi GPS Traces. IEEE Transactions on Intelligent Transportation Systems, 2015,16(1): 123-135.

[12] J. Huang, X. Huangfu, H. Sun, H. Li. Backward path growth for efficient mobile sequential recommendation. IEEE Transactions on Knowledge and Data Engineering (TKDE), 2015, 27(1):46-60.

[13] S. Ma, Y. Zheng, Wolfson, O. T-share: A large-scale dynamic taxi ridesharing service. The 29th International Conference on Data Engineering (ICDE), pp. 410-421, IEEE, 2013.

[14] S. Qian, J. Cao, et al. A Sharing Considered Route Assignment Mechanism for Fair Taxi Route Recommendations. The 21th Iinternational conference on SIGKDD, pp. 955-964, ACM, 2015.

Ensemble of Anchor Adapters for Transfer Learning

Fuzhen Zhuang[1], Ping Luo[1], Sinno Jialin Pan[2], Hui Xiong[3] and Qing He[1]

[1]Key Lab of Intelligent Information Processing of Chinese Academy of Sciences (CAS), Institute of Computing Technology, CAS, Beijing 100190, zhuangfz@ics.ict.ac.cn, luop@ict.ac.cn,heq@ics.ict.ac.cn

[2]Nanyang Technological University, Singapore, sinnopan@ntu.edu.sg

[3]MSIS Department, Rutgers University, hxiong@rutgers.edu

ABSTRACT

In the past decade, there have been a large number of transfer learning algorithms proposed for various real-world applications. However, most of them are vulnerable to *negative transfer*[1] since their performance is even worse than traditional supervised models. Aiming at more robust transfer learning models, we propose an ENsemble framework of *anCHOR adapters* (ENCHOR for short), in which an *anchor adapter* adapts the features of instances based on their similarities to a specif c *anchor* (i.e., a selected instance). Specif cally, the more similar to the anchor instance, the higher degree of the original feature of an instance remains unchanged in the adapted representation, and vice versa. This adapted representation for the data actually expresses the local structure around the corresponding anchor, and then any transfer learning method can be applied to this adapted representation for a prediction model, which focuses more on the neighborhood of the anchor. Next, based on multiple anchors, multiple anchor adapters can be built and combined into an ensemble for f nal output. Additionally, we develop an effective measure to select the anchors for ensemble building to achieve further performance improvement. Extensive experiments on hundreds of text classif cation tasks are conducted to demonstrate the effectiveness of ENCHOR. The results show that: when traditional supervised models perform poorly, ENCHOR (based on only 8 selected anchors) achieves $6\% - 13\%$ increase in terms of average accuracy compared with the state-of-the-art methods, and it greatly alleviates negative transfer.

Categories and Subject Descriptors

I.2.6 [**Artif cial Intelligence**]: Learning–Machine Learning

1. INTRODUCTION

Traditional classif cation algorithms often fail to obtain satisfactory performances, since the assumption that the training data from source domain and test data from target domain are drawn from the same distribution does not always hold in real-world applications. Transfer learning focuses on adapting the common knowledge from related source domain to improve the learning performance in target domain with distribution mismatch, and has attracted vast amount of research studies in the past decade [1].

Generally, the proposed transfer learning algorithms can be grouped into two types, i.e., single model [2, 3, 4] learning and ensemble learning [5, 6, 7, 8]. For the f rst type, Liao et al. [2] f rst estimated the degree of mismatch of each instance in the source domain with the whole target domain, and then presented an active learning approach for selecting the labeled examples in target domain. Finally they incorporated this information into logistic regression for transfer learning. Chen et al. [4] tried to learn robust data representations by reconstruction, recovering original features from data that are artif cially corrupted with noise for transfer learning. All the above methods are only based on single model learning, which may not achieve stable and robust results. In this paper, we try to ensemble the outputs on multi-model level, which considers the local structure of source and target domains simultaneously for each local model. For the second type, there are several transfer learning methods, which focus on learning from multiple source domains [5, 6] and assigning different weights to models [7, 8]. Gao et al. [7] proposed a locally weighted ensemble framework to combine multiple models for transfer learning, where the weights are dynamically assigned according to a model's predictive power on each test example. However, most of these methods do not explicitly exploit the local structures of source and target domain simultaneously.

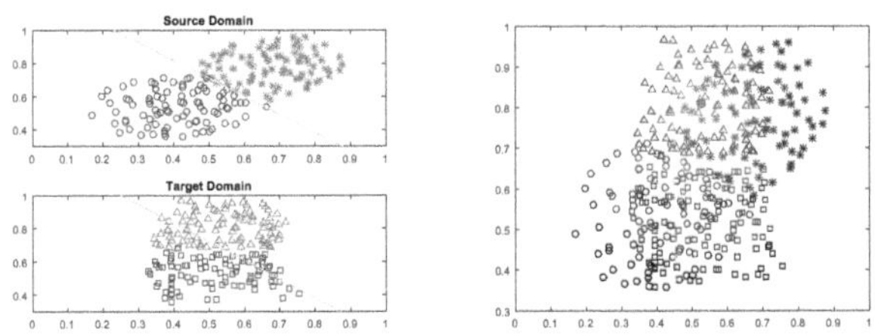

(a) Source Domain and Target Domain (b) The Selected Anchor and Its Similarity to Other Samples

Figure 1: The Intuitive Example of Why Selecting Anchor

It is often observed that the source and target domains may not be closely related over all the data. However, it is possible to make safe transfer if the training performs only in the same local neighborhood areas of the source and target domains. The intuitive example is shown in Figure 1. In this example, we show a toy data set with two dimensions, and the source domain and target domain data are plotted in Figure 1(a), where red "$*$" and "$\triangle$" denote positive instances and blue "$\circ$" and "$\square$" denote negative ones. Obviously, we can f nd that the source domain and target domain have different distributions, and the classif er trained from the source domain may not give satisfying predictions on target domain. If we can select the data points from source and target domains that located

[1]Here we say the "negative transfer" occurs when the accuracy from transfer learning algorithm is lower than the one of supervised learning algorithm, i.e., Logistic Regression (LR) in this paper.

CIKM'16 , October 24-28, 2016, Indianapolis, IN, USA

© 2016 ACM. ISBN 978-1-4503-4073-1/16/10. . . $15.00

DOI: http://dx.doi.org/10.1145/2983323.2983690

in the same local neighborhood area, then the classifcation performance would be better. In Figure 1(b), for given anchor red solid "o", we calculate the similarities between the anchor and the rest data points, then we plot all data points with different colors (i.e., indicating different degree of similarities with the anchor.). Note that, cosine distance is used to compute the similarity of two data points. In this fgure, red data points mean the similar ones with the anchor, while the black ones are dissimilar with the anchor. We can fnd that the data points located in the same local neighborhood area can be selected, and based on them the classifcation performance may be much better. Motivated by this observations, we propose an ENsemble framework of *anCHOR adapters* (ENCHOR for short) for transfer learning, in which each *anchor adapter* adapts the features of instances (from both source and target domains) based on their similarities to a specifc *anchor* (an instance selected from source or target domains). Specifcally, the more similar to the anchor instance, the higher degree of the original feature of an instance remains unchanged in the adapted representation, and vice versa. In other words, the instances from both source and target domains are more likely to be unchanged if they are more similar to the selected anchor. Thus, the data distributions after adaption for both source and target domains are more likely to be similar, and the models learned over the adapted data may achieve better performance (at least in the corresponding local area). Then, based on multiple anchors, multiple anchor adapters can be built and combined into an ensemble for fnal output. Additionally, we develop an effective measure to select the anchors for ensemble building to achieve further performance improvement. Extensive experiments on hundreds of text classifcation tasks are conducted to demonstrate the effectiveness of ENCHOR. The results show that: when traditional supervised models perform poorly, ENCHOR (based on only 8 selected anchors) achieves $6\% - 13\%$ increase in terms of average accuracy compared with the state-of-the-art methods, and it greatly alleviates negative transfer.

The remainder of this paper is organized as follows. We introduce the proposed framework in Section 2, and then propose the anchor selection strategy in Section 3. In Section 4, we conduct extensive experiments on text classifcation problems to demonstrate the effectiveness of the proposed algorithm. Related work is summarized in Section 5. Finally, Section 6 concludes the paper.

2. ENSEMBLE OF ANCHOR ADAPTERS

Next, we propose an ensemble of anchor adapters for transfer learning. Note that, bold letters, such as $\boldsymbol{u}$ and $\boldsymbol{v}$, are used to represent vectors. Data matrices are written in bold upper case, such as $\boldsymbol{X}$ and $\boldsymbol{Y}$. Also, $\boldsymbol{X}_{(i,j)}$ indicates the i-th row and j-th column element of matrix $\boldsymbol{X}$. Calligraphic letters, such as $\mathcal{A}$ and $\mathcal{D}$, are used to represent sets. Finally, we use $\mathbb{R}$ and $\mathbb{R}_+$ to denote the sets of real numbers and nonnegative real numbers. Without specifcal illustration, all the vectors are column vectors.

2.1 Anchor-based Adapter

Given the source domain with labeled data $\mathcal{D}_s = \{\boldsymbol{x}_i^{(s)}, y_i^{(s)}\}|_{i=1}^{n_s}$ and target domain with unlabeled data $\mathcal{D}_t = \{\boldsymbol{x}_i^{(t)}\}|_{i=1}^{n_t}$, and their corresponding word-document co-occurrence matrices are $\boldsymbol{X}_s \in \mathbb{R}_+^{m\times n_s}$ and $\boldsymbol{X}_t \in \mathbb{R}_+^{m\times n_t}$, where m is the number of features and n_s, n_t are respectively the numbers of instances in source domain and target domain. First, we randomly select q anchors $(\boldsymbol{a}_1, \boldsymbol{a}_2, \cdots, \boldsymbol{a}_q)$ (i.e., an anchor is an instance) from source or target domain, then compute the similarities between each anchor and the source (target) domain data. To compute the similarity, we can use the Gaussian distance function or cosine distance function. In this paper, we adopt the cosine function $\cos(\boldsymbol{a}, \boldsymbol{x}) = \frac{\boldsymbol{a}^\top \boldsymbol{x}}{\sqrt{\boldsymbol{a}^\top \boldsymbol{a}}\cdot\sqrt{\boldsymbol{x}^\top \boldsymbol{x}}}$. Then for the τ-th anchor, we can adapt the data matrices of $\boldsymbol{X}_s$ and $\boldsymbol{X}_t$ from source and target domains to new data matrices $\hat{\boldsymbol{X}}_s^{(\tau)}$ and $\hat{\boldsymbol{X}}_t^{(\tau)}$, called anchor-adapted matrices in this paper. The computations of $\hat{\boldsymbol{X}}_s^{(\tau)}$ and $\hat{\boldsymbol{X}}_t^{(\tau)}$ are as follows,

$$\begin{aligned} \hat{\boldsymbol{X}}_s^{(\tau)} &= (\cos(\boldsymbol{a}_\tau, \boldsymbol{x}_1^{(s)}) \cdot \boldsymbol{x}_1^{(s)}, \cdots, \cos(\boldsymbol{a}_\tau, \boldsymbol{x}_{n_s}^{(s)}) \cdot \boldsymbol{x}_{n_s}^{(s)}), \\ \hat{\boldsymbol{X}}_t^{(\tau)} &= (\cos(\boldsymbol{a}_\tau, \boldsymbol{x}_1^{(t)}) \cdot \boldsymbol{x}_1^{(t)}, \cdots, \cos(\boldsymbol{a}_\tau, \boldsymbol{x}_{n_t}^{(t)}) \cdot \boldsymbol{x}_{n_t}^{(t)}). \end{aligned} \quad (1)$$

By the anchor-based adapter, the high similar instances with anchor from source and target domains are retained, while the importance of the instances with low similarities to anchor are degraded.

There are several advantages can be benefted from the proposed framework, 1) For each anchor, only the similar instances from source and target domains are selected according to the similarities, then the new constructed source domain and target domain become more similar and their distribution difference is decreased. 2) Since the distributions of the new constructed data matrices are similar, we believe the better prediction results can be achieved. 3) The proposed framework ENCHOR is very easy to parallelize, since the anchors are independent of each other.

2.2 Ensemble of Anchor Adapters

Given q randomly selected anchors $(\boldsymbol{a}_1, \boldsymbol{a}_2, \cdots, \boldsymbol{a}_q)$ and according to the anchor-based adapter, we can obtain q pairs of new source and target domains $((\hat{\boldsymbol{X}}_s^{(1)}, \hat{\boldsymbol{X}}_t^{(1)}), (\hat{\boldsymbol{X}}_s^{(2)}, \hat{\boldsymbol{X}}_t^{(2)}), \cdots, (\hat{\boldsymbol{X}}_s^{(q)}, \hat{\boldsymbol{X}}_t^{(q)}))$. We can perform any transfer learning algorithm on each pair of new source domain and target domain, and the output predictions on target domain data can be obtained. For the selected q anchors, we can fnally get q predictions $(\hat{\boldsymbol{G}}_t^{(1)}, \hat{\boldsymbol{G}}_t^{(2)}, \cdots, \hat{\boldsymbol{G}}_t^{(q)})$ for target domain, where $\hat{\boldsymbol{G}}_t^{(\tau)} \in \mathbb{R}_+^{n_t\times c}$ ($\tau \in \{1, \cdots, q\}$, c is the number of instance classes.). Each row of $\hat{\boldsymbol{G}}_t$ denotes the prediction vector of an instance yielding to $\sum_j^c \hat{\boldsymbol{G}}_{t(i,j)} = 1$, and $\hat{\boldsymbol{G}}_{t(i,j)}$ is the prediction probability of instance $\boldsymbol{x}_i^{(t)}$ belonging to class j.

In the proposed framework ENCHOR, all the output predictions can be combined in two ways, one is in weighted manner and the other with simply average predictions,

$$\bar{\boldsymbol{G}}_{t(i,\cdot)}^{w} = \frac{\sum_{\tau=1}^{q} \cos(\boldsymbol{a}_\tau, \boldsymbol{x}_i^{(t)}) \cdot \hat{\boldsymbol{G}}_{t(i,\cdot)}^{(\tau)}}{\sum_{\tau'=1}^{q} \cos(\boldsymbol{a}_{\tau'}, \boldsymbol{x}_i^{(t)})}, \bar{\boldsymbol{G}}_{t(i,\cdot)}^{a} = \frac{\sum_{\tau=1}^{q} \hat{\boldsymbol{G}}_{t(i,\cdot)}^{(\tau)}}{q}. \quad (2)$$

Actually, these two ways achieve very similar results in our experiments, so we will only list the weighted version in the experimental section. Our framework ENCHOR is a general framework, which can be adapted to any transfer learning with probabilistic outputs. In this paper, we implement ENCHOR based on non-negative matrix tri-factorization for transfer learning [9].

3. SELECTION STRATEGY FOR ANCHORS

As you have noted in Section 2, the anchors are randomly selected. Actually, the randomly selected anchors may lead to poor performance, since they may be outliers or located in low density area. How to select the effective anchors is very important and challenging to obtain outstanding transfer learning performance. To the best of our knowledge, there has not yet previous work devoting to this task. Next, we will propose our strategy and some baseline strategies for selecting anchors.

3.1 The Proposed Strategy

Given the q anchors $(\boldsymbol{a}_1, \boldsymbol{a}_2, \cdots, \boldsymbol{a}_q)$ and the corresponding output predictions $(\hat{\boldsymbol{G}}_t^{(1)}, \hat{\boldsymbol{G}}_t^{(2)}, \cdots, \hat{\boldsymbol{G}}_t^{(q)})$ by the iterating algorithm, we propose an effective measure to select the high-quality anchors. We require the measure have the following properties, 1) the value range of the measure to be [0,1]; 2) larger value of the measure indicates the better of the anchor. Therefore, we will only select the top ℓ anchors with the largest values of the proposed measure for f nal ensemble of anchor adapters.

Along this line, we f rst introduce two criterions based on Shannon Entropy to measure the conf dence and class ratio when performing prediction. For each test instance, we hope the classif ers trained on the anchor-adapted data sets can predict the instance to some class with the highest conf dence. Take the binary classif cation problem as an example, if an instance $\boldsymbol{x}$ belongs to the f rst class, then we think the prediction vector (1, 0) is better than the one (0.6, 0.4), since the classif er assigns $\boldsymbol{x}$ with the label of f rst class with 100% conf dence in the f rst vector. Following, we give the def nition of conf dence criterion on the i-th instance in target domain as

$$E_{c(i)} = \sum_{j=1}^{c} \hat{\boldsymbol{G}}_{t(i,j)} \log_c \hat{\boldsymbol{G}}_{t(i,j)}, \tag{3}$$

where $\log_c$ is a base-c logarithm, which can ensure $E_{c(i)} \in [-1, 0]$, and c is the number of instance classes. Large value of $E_{c(i)}$ indicates the classif er can predict the instance $\boldsymbol{x}_i$ into some class with high conf dence. Since $E_{c(i)} \in [-1, 0]$, so we make a slight amendment to let $\hat{E}_{c(i)} = E_{c(i)} + 1 \in [0, 1]$, then the conf dence criterion over all target domain data is def ned,

$$E_c = \frac{1}{n_t} \sum_{i=1}^{n_t} \hat{E}_{c(i)}, \; E_c \in [0, 1]. \tag{4}$$

Obviously, when the classif er predicts all the instances from target domain with 100% conf dence, E_c gets the largest value 1.

For the class ratio criterion, we assume that it would be better if the classif er can give the predictions with the true class ratio of target domain. Assuming that the true class distribution of target domain is $\boldsymbol{p} = (p_1, p_2, \cdots, p_c)$, $\sum_i^c p_i = 1$, and the predicted class distribution is $\hat{\boldsymbol{p}} = (\hat{p}_1, \hat{p}_2, \cdots, \hat{p}_c)$, $\sum_i^c \hat{p}_i = 1$, where $n_t^{(j)}$ be the number of instances belonging to class j and the label of $\boldsymbol{x}_i^{(t)}$ is computed as $\max_j \hat{\boldsymbol{G}}_{t(i,j)}$, then the class ratio criterion is def ned as

$$E_r = \sum_{j=1}^{c} \frac{\hat{p}_i}{p_i \cdot N} \log_c \frac{p_i \cdot N}{\hat{p}_i}, \; E_r \in [0, 1], \tag{5}$$

where $N = \sum_{j=1}^{c} \frac{\hat{p}_i}{p_i}$ is the normalization factor. When the predicted class distribution is the same as the true class distribution, i.e., $\hat{p}_c = p_c$, E_r gets the largest value 1.

Based on the above two criterions, we f nally come to the proposed measure for selecting high-quality anchors,

$$E_{cr} = E_c \times E_r, \; E_{cr} \in [0, 1]. \tag{6}$$

In this measure, we simultaneously consider the conf dence criterion and class ratio criterion. In other word, we hope the classif er not only can predict the instances with high conf dence, but also the predicted class distribution can be the same as the true one. However, in real-world applications, we always do not know the true class distribution of target domain. In this case, we simple set $\boldsymbol{p} = (\frac{1}{c}, \frac{1}{c}, \cdots, \frac{1}{c})$ when computing our measure. Fortunately, the experimental results in Section 4 show that the proposed measure can also work well even when the true class distribution is unknown.

After sorting the q values of E_{cr} (each anchor corresponding to a value of E_{cr}), we select the top ℓ anchors with the largest values of E_{cr}. Then, the f nal output is

$$\tilde{\boldsymbol{G}}^{*w}_{t(i,\cdot)} = \frac{\sum_{\tau=1}^{\ell} \boldsymbol{w}_{t(i)}^{(\tau)} \cdot \hat{\boldsymbol{G}}_{t(i,\cdot)}^{(\tau)}}{\sum_{\tau'=1}^{\ell} \boldsymbol{w}_{t(i)}^{(\tau')}}. \tag{7}$$

The proposed framework with and without selection strategy are denoted as ENCHOR* and ENCHOR, respectively.

3.2 Some Baseline Strategies

To validate the effectiveness of our strategy, we also introduce some baseline strategies to select anchors. Kullback-Leibler (KL) divergence [10] and Maximum Mean Discrepancy (MMD) [11] are used to measure the distribution difference between different domains, and some works [12, 13] have adopted them for transfer learning. Smaller values of KL divergence and MMD can usually lead to better transfer learning performance, so we also adapt them to anchor selection.

4. EXPERIMENTAL EVALUATION

In this section, we construct hundreds of classif cation problems to validate the effectiveness of the proposed framework ENCHOR. Note that we only focus on binary classif cation problems, while obviously our algorithm can handle multi-class classif cation problems.

4.1 Data Preparation

We adopt the widely use data set *20Newsgroups*[2], which is one of the benchmark data sets for evaluating transfer learning algorithms [1, 7, 14, 3]. This corpus has approximately 20,000 newsgroup documents, which are evenly divided into 20 subcategories. Some similar subcategories are grouped into a top category, e.g., the four subcategories *sci.crypt*, *sci.electronics*, *sci.med* and *sci.space* belong to the top category *sci*. We select three top categories, i.e., *rec*, *sci* and *talk*, to construct the classif cation problems. The top categories are used for classif cation, e.g., in the combination *rec vs. sci*, the data from *rec* are positive instances, while the data from *sci* are negative ones.

To construct the transfer learning tasks, we follow the approach in [9]. For the combination *rec vs. sci*, we randomly select a subcategory from *rec* as positive class and a subcategory from *sci* as negative class to produce the source domain. The target domain is similarly constructed, thus in totally 144 ($P_4^2 \cdot P_4^2$) classif cation tasks are generated for this combination. We have three combinations for the three top categories *rec*, *sci* and *talk*, i.e., *rec vs. sci*, *rec vs. talk* and *sci vs. talk*, and in totally 432 (144 $\times$ 3) classif cation problems are constructed.

For the above constructed classif cation tasks, they almost have balanced class distribution. To validate our algorithm can also perform well when the classes are unbalanced, we change the ratios of positive instances and negative instances in target domain on 144 problems of the combination *rec vs. sci*. Specif cally, we only randomly sample 50%, 40%, 30%, 20% and 10% negative instances for each task, then the corresponding ratios are 2:1, 2.5:1, 3.3:1, 5:1 and 10:1. The average results are reported on three independent trials.

4.2 Experimental Settings

4.2.1 Baselines

we compare our algorithm ENCHOR with the following state-of-the-art baselines, including

- The supervised algorithm: Logistic Regression (LR) [15];
- The transfer learning methods:
  - Transfer learning based on non-negative matrix tri-factorization

[2]http://people.csail.mit.edu/jrennie/20Newsgroups/.

(MTrick) [9], which does not consider the local transfer and anchor selection strategy;
– Locally weighted Ensemble (LWE) [7], in which the classif cation models are assigned with different weights according to the local structure of each test instance;
– Marginalized Stacked Denoising Autoencoders (mSDA) [4], which learns robust features for transfer learning;

- We also compare our anchor selection strategy E_{cr} with the following four strategies, conf dence Criterion (E_c) in Eq. (4), class ratio criterion (E_r) in Eq. (5), Kullback-Leibler (KL) divergence [10] and Maximum Mean Discrepancy (MMD) [11].

4.2.2 Parameter Settings

In ENCHOR, the parameters of the number of word clusters k, trade-off factor β, error threshold ε and the maximal number of iterations T are set following the suggestion of MTrick [9], $k = 50$, $\beta = 1$, $\varepsilon = 10^{-11}$, $T = 100$. After some preliminary test, the parameters of q and ℓ are set as 50 and 8 for all selection strategies. The parameters of the baselines are set according to the suggestions of their original papers.

The variables $\hat{\boldsymbol{F}}_s$, $\hat{\boldsymbol{F}}_t$ and $\hat{\boldsymbol{G}}_t$ are initialized as the feature clustering results by PLSA [16] on the whole data set of the source and target domain. We adopt the Matlab implementation of PLSA[3] in the experiments. $\hat{\boldsymbol{G}}_s$ is initialized as the true class information in the source-domain, and $\hat{\boldsymbol{G}}_t$ is initialized as the predicted results of any supervised classif er, which is trained based on the source domain data. In this experiment Logistic Regression is adopted to give these initial results.

4.3 Results on Classif cation Problems with Balanced Classes

4.3.1 Comparison among ENCHOR, MTrick, LWE, mSDA and LR

Indeed, the anchors can be randomly selected from source domain or target domain, and there are different explanations for these two ways. If we select the anchors from source domain, then each time we choose the similar instances from target domain to predict; while if the anchors selected from target domain, each time the similar instances from source domain are chosen for training. In these two ways, the propose algorithms are denoted as ENCHOR$_s$, ENCHOR$_s^*$ for selecting anchors from source domain, and ENCHOR$_t$, ENCHOR$_t^*$ for selecting anchors from target domain. ENCHOR$_s^*$ and ENCHOR$_t^*$ are output by the proposed anchor selection strategy. The detailed results on *rec vs. sci* of all compared algorithms are shown in Figure 2 (The results on the other two combinations are very similar with *rec vs. sci*), and the average accuracies are reported in Table 1. In Figure 2, the classif cation problems are sorted with the increasing order by the accuracies of LR. Thus, the x-axes in these f gures can also indicate the degree of diff culty in knowledge transferring. To clearly validate the superiority of our algorithms, the 144 problems are divided into two parts in Table 1. The f rst part includes the problems with accuracies from MTrick lower than 90%, on which we think MTrick could not perform well. The other part contains the ones whose accuracies are greater than or equivalent to 90%, on which MTrick can achieve satisfying performance. In Table 1, the third column indicates the number of problems whose accuracies from MTrick $< 90\%$ or $\geq 90\%$. The number in the parentheses denotes how many problems suffering from negative transfer for the compared algorithms.

From the results in Figure 2 and Table 1, we have the following insightful observations:

[3] http://www.kyb.tuebingen.mpg.de/bs/people/pgehler/code/index.html

- In Figure 2(a) and Table 1, we f nd that 1) both ENCHOR$_t^*$ and ENCHOR$_s^*$ are signif cantly better than ENCHOR$_t$ and ENCHOR$_s$, which indicates the effectiveness of the proposed selection strategy E_{cr}, and the randomly selected anchors maybe outliers or located in low dense area; 2) from a general view, the results of selecting anchors from target domain are very similar with the ones of selecting anchors from source domain. Therefore, in Figure 2(b) and the following sections, we only list the results of ENCHOR$_t^*$.
- Overall, all the transfer learning algorithms are better than LR, which implies that the traditional learning algorithm may be not suitable for transfer learning tasks.
- ENCHOR$_t^*$ and MTrick dramatically outperform LWE and mSDA. MTrick achieves unstable performance in Figure 2(b), especially when the accuracy of LR is low, which indicates that MTrick can not perform well on diff cult transfer learning problems. Overall, our algorithm ENCHOR$_t^*$ obtains the best results.
- To clear validate the robustness of ENCHOR$_t^*$ and ENCHOR$_s^*$, it can be observed from Table 1 that ENCHOR$_t^*$ and ENCHOR$_s^*$ perform signif cantly better than all the baselines when the accuracy of MTrick is lower than 90%.
- Except ENCHOR$_t^*$ and ENCHOR$_s^*$, all the compared algorithms suffer from negative transfer learning, which again shows the robustness and effectiveness of the proposed anchor selection strategy.

In a word, all the results demonstrate the superiority of the proposed algorithms ENCHOR$_t^*$ and ENCHOR$_s^*$.

4.3.2 Comparison of Anchor Selection Strategies

To investigate the effectiveness of the proposed anchor selection strategy E_{cr}, we compare it with the other four strategies, i.e., E_c, E_r, KL and MMD. T average accuracies over 144 problems are list in Table 2. From these results, we can f nd that the selection strategies E_{cr} and E_r are signif cantly better than the other three strategies MMD, KL and E_c, and E_c obtains the worst results. It is also observed that, all the selection strategies outperform LR with respect to the average accuracies in Table 2. Though E_r performs very similar with E_{cr}, these results are based on the conditions that the problems are with balanced class distributions. In Section 4.4, we will show that the results of E_{cr} is better than E_r when the tasks are with unbalanced classes.

Table 2: Average results (%) on Three Combinations for Selection Strategy Comparison

Combination	E_{cr}	E_r	MMD	KL	E_c	LR
rec vs. sci	94.77	95.10	90.69	90.69	78.93	65.57
rec vs. talk	94.43	95.47	92.58	91.81	86.35	72.46
sci vs. talk	91.88	91.85	88.65	86.63	76.54	70.65

Note that, the result of E_{cr} is the same as the one of ANCHOR$_t^*$.

4.4 Results on Classif cation Problems with Unbalanced Classes

In this section, we want to show that our algorithm can also perform well under the unbalanced class condition. We intentionally change the ratio of positive and negative instances in the target domain of 144 problems on *rec vs. sci*, and the ratios includes 2:1, 2.5:1, 3.3:1, 5:1 and 10:1. The strategy E_r can achieve good results when the classes are balanced in Section 4.3.2, therefore we compare ENCHOR$_t^*$ with MTrick, E_r and LR here. The detailed results are shown in Table 3. Sometimes, the class ratio maybe unknown and can not be estimated, so in this case we simply set $\boldsymbol{p} = (\frac{1}{c}, \cdots, \frac{1}{c})$, i.e., the uniform class distribution. We denote

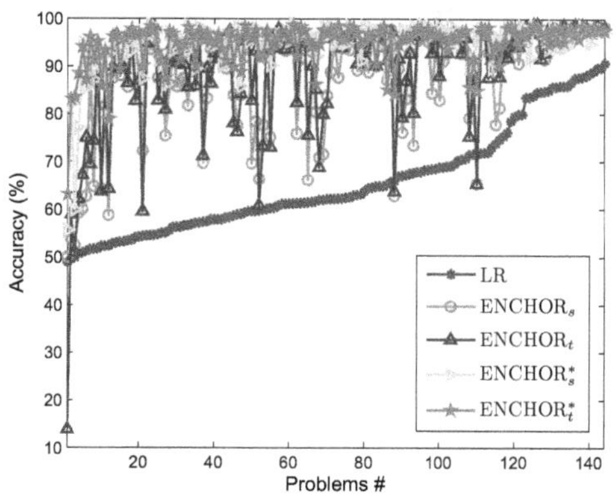

(a) Comparison among ENCHOR$^*_t$, ENCHOR$^*_s$, ENCHOR$_t$, ENCHOR$_s$ and LR

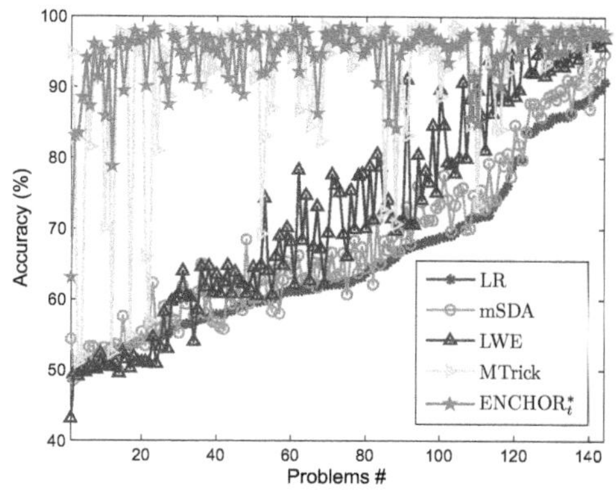

(b) Comparison among ENCHOR$^*_t$, MTrick, LWE, mSDA and LR

Figure 2: The Performance Comparison among ENCHOR, MTrick, LWE, mSDA and LR on *rec vs. sci*

Table 1: Average Results (%) on Three Combinations for the Comparison of ENCHOR, MTrick, LWE, mSDA and LR

Combination		Problems #	ENCHOR$^*_t$	ENCHOR$^*_s$	ENCHOR$_t$	ENCHOR$_s$	MTrick	LWE	mSDA	LR
	< 90	31	90.84(0)	91.34(0)	75.16(2)	77.01(2)	77.61(0)	67.16(10)	63.01(5)	61.22
rec vs. sci	≥ 90	113	95.85(0)	95.49(0)	91.47(0)	92.24(1)	96.19(0)	73.59(14)	69.22(20)	66.76
	Total		94.77(0)	94.59(0)	87.96(2)	88.96(3)	92.19(0)	72.20(24)	67.88(25)	65.57
	< 90	13	92.56(0)	95.88(0)	83.09(2)	84.32(2)	86.89(0)	83.86(0)	77.13(0)	70.75
rec vs. talk	≥ 90	131	94.61(0)	95.64(0)	92.93(3)	93.66(3)	96.23(0)	78.11(20)	77.86(0)	72.63
	Total		94.43(0)	95.66(0)	92.04(5)	92.82(5)	95.39(0)	78.63(20)	77.79(0)	72.46
	< 90	27	87.45(0)	84.55(0)	77.17(2)	75.55(4)	80.99(2)	69.42(4)	65.81(2)	62.15
sci vs. talk	≥ 90	117	92.90(0)	93.55(0)	89.68(2)	90.38(2)	94.61(0)	82.78(1)	75.75(13)	72.61
	Total		91.88(0)	91.86(0)	87.33(4)	87.60(6)	92.06(2)	80.27(5)	73.89(15)	70.65

Table 3: Average Results (%) on *rec vs. sci* for Unbalanced Class Classif cation

Ratio		Problems #	ENCHOR$^{*(u)}_t$	$E^{(u)}_r$	ENCHOR$^*_t$	E_r	MTrick	LR
	< 90	51	87.13	80.32	89.60	83.20	68.50	57.86
2:1	≥ 90	93	93.72	87.56	94.58	89.34	95.48	66.60
	Total		91.38	85.00	92.81	87.16	85.92	63.51
	< 90	71	85.38	77.82	89.30	83.87	68.21	59.59
2.5:1	≥ 90	73	92.04	85.10	94.11	88.49	95.51	66.09
	Total		88.76	81.51	91.74	86.21	82.05	62.89
	< 90	91	77.77	71.59	86.80	81.38	64.10	59.09
3.3:1	≥ 90	53	88.11	81.04	93.35	88.91	95.19	67.50
	Total		81.58	75.07	89.21	84.15	75.54	62.19
	< 90	114	68.34	66.77	83.92	81.37	61.31	58.13
5:1	≥ 90	30	82.53	75.84	91.25	88.22	93.26	73.88
	Total		71.29	68.66	85.45	82.79	67.97	61.41
	< 90	131	61.29	59.22	78.40	77.38	54.13	58.60
10:1	≥ 90	13	75.64	68.94	88.53	88.98	93.89	79.12
	Total		62.58	60.10	79.32	78.43	57.72	60.45

our algorithms and E_r as ENCHOR$^{*(u)}_t$ and $E^{(u)}_r$ in Table 3 when the true class distribution of target domain is unknown.

From these results, we f nd that 1) ENCHOR$^*_t$ outperforms all the baselines under different ratios for unbalanced class classif cation; 2) with the increasing values of ratio, the accuracies from all algorithms decrease and the number of problems whose accuracies from MTrick lower than 90% increases; 3) ENCHOR$^{*(u)}_t$ also performs better than all baselines, which indicates that all the baselines are signif cantly inf uenced by the class imbalance. In summary, these results again validate the effectiveness of our algorithm.

5. RELATED WORKS

Transfer learning has provoked suff cient attention in recent years, and there are many algorithms are proposed following different pipelines. Here, we group them into two types, namely learning from single source domain and learning multiple source domains for transfer learning.

For the works of learning from single source domain, Dai et al. [17] proposed a novel transfer-learning algorithm based on an EM-based Naive Bayes classif ers, which f rst estimated the initial probabilities under a distribution of source domain data and then used an EM algorithm to revise the model for the distribution of target domain data. Si et al. [18] proposed a transfer subspace learning framework, which includes two items. The f rst one is the general subspace learning framework, while the second one is to minimize the Bregman divergence between the distribution of source and target domains in the selected subspace. There are also several works based on matrix factorization. Zhuang et al. [9]

first argued the associations between word clusters and document classes maybe stable across different domains, and then proposed a new transfer learning algorithm based on non-negative matrix factorization. Pan et al.[19] proposed transfer component analysis to learn some transfer components across domains in a reproducing kernel Hilbert space using maximum mean discrepancy. However, these methods do not make full use of the neighbourhood structures of source and target domains. It is excited that the proposed framework can be easily adapted to these matrix factorization based method to improve performance.

Along the second pipeline, Duan et al. [20] proposed to learn a robust decision function for the target domain data by leveraging a set of auxiliary/source classifiers from multiple source domains. Mansour et al. [21] presented a theoretical analysis of the problem of domain adaptation with multiple sources, and remarked that for any fixed target function, there exists a distribution weighted combining rule that has a loss of at most ϵ with respect to any target mixture of the source distributions. Dredze at al. [8] developed a new multi-domain online learning framework based on parameter combination from multiple classifiers to a new target domain, based on an online learning algorithm for linear classifiers that incorporates confidence about each parameter into the update. Ge et al. [22] proposed a novel two-phase framework to effectively transfer knowledge from multiple sources. However, all the above algorithms need multiple source domains. Our method focuses on one source domains, and through elaborately selecting the anchors, the final prediction is the weighted sum of outputs of anchor adapters.

6. CONCLUSIONS

In this paper, we argue that the transfer learning algorithms performing on the original source and target domains may not obtain stable performance due to the large gap of distribution difference. Then along this line, we propose a transfer learning framework, called ensemble of anchor adapters, and implement it based on non-negative matrix tri-factorization. Specifically, the anchors are first selected from source domain or target domain, and then only the similar instances from both domains are chosen to form anchor-adapted matrices, between which the distribution difference can be reduced. Moreover, we design an entropy based strategy to select high-quality anchors, leading to the outstanding and robust results. Finally, extensive experiments on text classification demonstrate the effectiveness and robustness of the proposed method.

7. ACKNOWLEDGMENTS

This work was supported by the National Natural Science Foundation of China (No. 9154610306, 61573335, 61473273), Guangdong provincial science and technology plan projects (No. 2015 B010109005).

8. REFERENCES

[1] Sinno Jialin Pan and Qiang Yang. A survey on transfer learning. *IEEE TKDE*, pages 1345–1359, 2010.

[2] Xuejun Liao, Ya Xue, and Lawrence Carin. Logistic regression with an auxiliary data source. In *Proceedings of the 22nd ICML*, pages 505–512, 2005.

[3] Wenyuan Dai, Qiang Yang, Gui-Rong Xue, and Yong Yu. Boosting for transfer learning. In *Proceedings of the 24th ICML*, pages 193–200, 2007.

[4] Minmin Chen, Zhixiang Eddie Xu, Kilian Q. Weinberger, and Fei Sha. Marginalized denoising autoencoders for domain adaptation. In *Proceedings of the 29th ICML*, 2012.

[5] Ping Luo, Fuzhen Zhuang, Hui Xiong, Yuhong Xiong, and Qing He. Transfer learning from multiple source domains via consensus regularization. In *Proceedings of the 17th ACM CIKM*, pages 103–112, 2008.

[6] Lixin Duan, Dong Xu, and Shih-Fu Chang. Exploiting web images for event recognition in consumer videos: A multiple source domain adaptation approach. In *IEEE CVPR*, pages 1338–1345, 2012.

[7] Jing Gao, Wei Fan, Jing Jiang, and Jiawei Han. Knowledge transfer via multiple model local structure mapping. In *Proceedings of the 14th ACM SIGKDD*, 2008.

[8] Mark Dredze, Alex Kulesza, and Koby Crammer. Multi-domain learning by confidence-weighted parameter combination. *Machine Learning*, pages 123–149, 2010.

[9] Fuzhen Zhuang, Ping Luo, Hui Xiong, Qing He, Yuhong Xiong, and Zhongzhi Shi. Exploiting associations between word clusters and document classes for cross-domain text categorization. *Statistical Analysis and Data Mining*, pages 100–114, 2011.

[10] Solomon Kullback. Letter to the editor: the kullback-leibler distance. *AMERICAN STATISTICIAN*, 1987.

[11] Karsten M Borgwardt, Arthur Gretton, Malte J Rasch, Hans-Peter Kriegel, Bernhard Schölkopf, and Alex J Smola. Integrating structured biological data by kernel maximum mean discrepancy. *Bioinformatics*, pages e49–e57, 2006.

[12] Wenyuan Dai, Gui-Rong Xue, Qiang Yang, and Yong Yu. Co-clustering based classification for out-of-domain documents. In *Proceedings of the 13th ACM SIGKDD*, pages 210–219, 2007.

[13] Sinno Jialin Pan, James T Kwok, and Qiang Yang. Transfer learning via dimensionality reduction. In *AAAI*, pages 677–682, 2008.

[14] Fuzhen Zhuang, Ping Luo, Hui Xiong, Yuhong Xiong, Qing He, and Zhongzhi Shi. Cross-domain learning from multiple sources: a consensus regularization perspective. *IEEE TKDE*, pages 1664–1678, 2010.

[15] David Hosmer and Stanley Lemeshow. *Applied Logistic Regression*. Wiley, New York, 2000.

[16] Thomas Hofmann. Unsupervised learning by probabilistic latent semantic analysis. *Machine learning*, pages 177–196, 2001.

[17] Wenyuan Dai, Gui-Rong Xue, Qiang Yang, and Yong Yu. Transferring naive bayes classifiers for text classification. In *AAAI*, pages 540–545, 2007.

[18] Si Si, Dacheng Tao, and Bo Geng. Bregman divergence-based regularization for transfer subspace learning. *IEEE TKDE*, pages 929–942, 2010.

[19] Sinno Jialin Pan, Ivor W Tsang, James T Kwok, Qiang Yang, et al. Domain adaptation via transfer component analysis. *IEEE TNN*, pages 199–210, 2011.

[20] Lixin Duan, Ivor W Tsang, Dong Xu, and Tat-Seng Chua. Domain adaptation from multiple sources via auxiliary classifiers. In *Proceedings of the 26th ICML*, pages 289–296, 2009.

[21] Yishay Mansour, Mehryar Mohri, and Afshin Rostamizadeh. Domain adaptation with multiple sources. In *NIPS*, pages 1041–1048, 2009.

[22] Liang Ge, Jing Gao, Hung Ngo, Kang Li, and Aidong Zhang. On handling negative transfer and imbalanced distributions in multiple source transfer learning. *Statistical Analysis and Data Mining: The ASA Data Science Journal*, pages 254–271, 2014.

Incremental Mining of High Utility Sequential Patterns in Incremental Databases

Jun-Zhe Wang
Department of Computer Science
National Chiao Tung University
Hsinchu, Taiwan
jzwang@cs.nctu.edu.tw

Jiun-Long Huang
Department of Computer Science
National Chiao Tung University
Hsinchu, Taiwan
jlhuang@cs.nctu.edu.tw

ABSTRACT

High utility sequential pattern (HUSP) mining is an emerging topic in pattern mining, and only a few algorithms have been proposed to address it. In practice, most sequence databases usually grow over time, and it is inefficient for existing algorithms to mine HUSPs from scratch when databases grow with a small portion of updates. In view of this, we propose the IncUSP-Miner algorithm to mine HUSPs incrementally. Specifically, to avoid redundant computations, we propose a tighter upper bound of the utility of a sequence, called TSU, and then design a novel data structure, called the candidate pattern tree, to maintain the sequences whose TSU values are greater than or equal to the minimum utility threshold. Accordingly, to avoid keeping a huge amount of utility information for each sequence, a set of auxiliary utility information is designed to be stored in each tree node. Moreover, for those nodes whose utilities have to be updated, a strategy is also proposed to reduce the amount of computation, thereby improving the mining efficiency. Experimental results on three real datasets show that IncUSP-Miner is able to efficiently mine HUSPs incrementally.

Keywords

High utility sequential pattern mining; incremental mining; incremental high utility sequential pattern mining

1. INTRODUCTION

Some recent studies have incorporated the concept of utility into classic sequential pattern mining, leading to the emergence of *high utility sequential pattern* (HUSP) mining [5, 14, 13, 15, 10]. In HUSP mining, the utility of a sequence represents its importance, which may be measured in terms of profit or other information valuable for users. Only a few algorithms [5, 14, 13, 10] have been proposed to mine HUSPs, and HUSP mining has been applied to analyze web-access log [4] and mobile commerce data [12].

However, in practice, a sequence database (SDB) is *incrementally* updated over time. For example, in a retail database, a series of transactions made by a new customer will make a new sequence *inserted* into the database, and those made by an existing customer will make a sequence *appended* to the corresponding sequence already in the SDB. When an SDB D is updated to D', a low utility sequence in D may become high utility in D'. In such cases, applying existing algorithms to mine HUSPs from scratch is obviously inefficient each time when the SDB is updated. Moreover, some challenges posed by the incremental HUSP mining are listed as below.

First, the utility of a sequence is not downward closed, meaning that the incremental frequent sequential pattern mining algorithms [9, 11, 8] cannot be directly applied to find HUSPs. Although some algorithms have been proposed to incrementally mine high utility itemsets (HUIs) [6, 16], they cannot be applied to this problem either since the HUSP mining is intrinsically more complex than HUI mining (e.g., the case of sequence appending is not considered in incremental HUI mining).

Second, a tree structure can be used to buffer the previous mining results and other information to avoid redundant computation when an SDB is updated. However, the tree structure will consume a lot of memory due to the huge number of generated tree nodes. Furthermore, a sequence may have multiple instances in one of its supersequences and each instance has its own utility. When the SDB is updated, updating the utility of a buffered sequence by obtaining its utilities from all its new instances and those existing instances in the tree structure is time-consuming, thereby resulting in poor mining efficiency. Therefore, how to design a tighter upper bound of sequence utility for better tree node pruning and a concise tree node structure for efficient utility update is important.

In this paper, we address both of the above challenges by proposing a new incremental HUSP mining algorithm named IncUSP-Miner. The major contributions of this paper are summarized as follows:

(1) We propose a tight utility upper bound of a sequence, called TSU, to improve mining efficiency by eliminating more sequences not able to be high utility compared with existing HUSP mining algorithms.

(2) To facilitate incremental HUSP mining, we propose a novel data structure, called the *candidate pattern tree*, to maintain each sequence whose TSU is greater than or equal to the minimum utility threshold. Specifically, we design an efficient and compact tree node structure storing some auxiliary information of the corresponding sequence, so that the auxiliary information such as TSU and utility of the sequence can be quickly obtained without recomputation.

(3) Based on the proposed candidate pattern tree, one strategy is proposed to reduce the amount of computation when a node has to be updated to further improve mining efficiency.

(4) We then propose algorithm IncUSP-Miner to incrementally

CIKM'16, October 24-28, 2016, Indianapolis, IN, USA

DOI: http://dx.doi.org/10.1145/2983323.2983691

mine HUSPs based on TSU, the candidate pattern tree and the proposed strategy.

(5) Experiments on three real datasets are conducted to evaluate the performance of IncUSP-Miner. The experimental results show that IncUSP-Miner outperforms the state-of-the-art HUSP mining algorithms in incremental databases.

The rest of this paper is organized as follows. Section 2 gives the problem definitions. Section 3 shows the preliminary concept while Section 4 presents the details of algorithm IncUSP-Miner. Section 5 shows the experimental results, and finally, Section 6 concludes this paper.

2. PROBLEM DEFINITION

Let $I = \{i_1, i_2, \ldots, i_n\}$ be a set of distinct items. A nonempty subset $X \subseteq I$ is called an itemset. In this paper, X is denoted as $[x_1, x_2, \ldots, x_k]$, where $x_j \in I$, for $1 \le j \le k$. For brevity, the brackets are omitted if an itemset contains only one item. Without loss of generality, all items within an itemset are assumed to be arranged lexicographically. A sequence $\langle E_1 E_2 \ldots E_m \rangle$ is an ordered list of itemsets, where $E_i \subseteq I$, $\forall\, i = 1, \ldots, m$. The *length* of sequence $\langle E_1 E_2 \ldots E_m \rangle$, denoted as l, is defined as $l \equiv \Sigma_{i=1}^{m} |E_i|$, and a sequence with length l is called an l-sequence. Sequence $t = \langle X_1 X_2 \ldots X_k \rangle$ is called a subsequence of another sequence $s = \langle Y_1 Y_2 \ldots Y_m \rangle$, denoted as $t \sqsubseteq s$, if there exists k integers $1 \le j_1 < j_2 < \cdots < j_k \le m$ such that $X_1 \subseteq Y_{j_1}$, $X_2 \subseteq Y_{j_2}$, ..., $X_k \subseteq Y_{j_k}$, and we say that s has an *instance* of t at position $\langle j_1, j_2, \ldots, j_k \rangle$. A sequence database D is a set of tuples (*sid*, *s*), where *sid* is the ID of sequence s. Each item i of the j-th itemset Y_j in a sequence s is associated with a positive real number $q(i, j, s)$, which is called the *internal utility* or quantity of item i in sequence s. In the example SDB shown in Table 1(a), the internal utility of item a within the second itemset in s_2 (i.e., $q(a, 2, s_2)$) is 4. The *external utility* of item i, denoted as $p(i)$, is a positive real number which represents the unit profit or importance of i. The external utility of each item $i \in I$ is recorded in a profit table. Table 1(b) shows the corresponding profit table of the SDB shown in Table 1(a).

Definition 1. The utility of item i within the j-th itemset of sequence s is defined as $u(i, j, s) = p(i) \times q(i, j, s)$. The utility of itemset X contained in the j-th itemset of sequence s is defined as $u(X, j, s) = \Sigma_{\forall i \in X \wedge X \subseteq Y_j} u(i, j, s)$. If s has an *instance* of t at position $\langle j_1, j_2, \ldots, j_k \rangle$, the utility of the instance is defined as
$u(t, \langle j_1, j_2, \ldots, j_k \rangle, s) = \Sigma_{i=1}^{k} u(X_i, j_i, s)$, where $X_i \subseteq Y_{j_i}$. For example, $u(\langle a, c \rangle, \langle 1, 2 \rangle, s_2) = u(a, 1, s_2) + u(c, 2, s_2) = 3 + 6 = 9$.

Definition 2. The *utility* of sequence t in sequence s, denoted as $u(t, s)$, is defined as the *maximum* of the utilities of all instances of t in s. That is,

$$u(t, s) = \max\{u(t, \langle j_1, j_2, \ldots, j_k \rangle, s) | \; \forall \langle j_1, j_2, \ldots, j_k \rangle : t \sqsubseteq \langle Y_{j_1} Y_{j_2} \ldots Y_{j_k} \rangle\}. \quad (1)$$

The utility of a sequence t in D, denoted as $u_D(t)$, is defined as $u_D(t) = \Sigma_{\forall s \in D \wedge t \sqsubseteq s} u(t, s)$.

A sequence t is called a *high utility sequential pattern* in a sequence database D if $u_D(t) \ge min\_util$, where *min_util* is a user-specified minimum utility threshold.

For example, we have $u(\langle a, c \rangle, s_2) = \max\{u(\langle a, c \rangle, \langle 1, 2 \rangle, s_2), u(\langle a, c \rangle, \langle 1, 3 \rangle, s_2), u(\langle a, c \rangle, \langle 2, 3 \rangle, s_2)\} = \max\{9, 5, 14\} = 14$, and $u_D(\langle a, c \rangle) = u(\langle a, c \rangle, s_2) + u(\langle a, c \rangle, s_5) = 14 + 4 = 18$. Given $min\_util = 20$, $\langle a, c \rangle$ is not a *high utility sequential pattern* in D since $u_D(\langle a, c \rangle) = 18 < 20$.

For an original sequence database D, the following two types of operations: 1) sequence insertion or 2) sequence appending will update D. To facilitate the following discussions, we have the following definitions.

Definition 3. (*Updated Sequence*) When a new sequence s is inserted into D, s is called an *inserted sequence* of D. Given two sequences $s = \langle Y_1\; Y_2 \ldots Y_m \rangle$ and $s_a = \langle Z_1 Z_2 \ldots Z_k \rangle$ *s.t.* $m > 0$ and $k > 0$, sequence $s \cdot s_a$ is defined as $\langle Y_1 Y_2 \ldots Y_m Z_1 Z_2 \ldots Z_k \rangle$, meaning that $s \cdot s_a$ is formed by appending s_a to the end of s. When $s \in D$, s' is called an *appended sequence* of D if $s' = s \cdot s_a$. A sequence s is called an *updated sequence* of D if s is either an inserted sequence or an appended sequence of D. In the example shown in Table 1(a), sequence $s_6 = \langle f, b, e, d, c \rangle$ is an inserted sequence in the SDB, and appending a sequence $\langle [c, d] f [a, e] \rangle$ to sequence $s_4 = \langle e, c \rangle$ updates sequence s_4 to $s'_4 = \langle e, c [c, d] f [a, e] \rangle$.

Definition 4. (*Incremental Part*) The incremental part, denoted as Δdb, of D is the set of the sequences where each sequence, say s_a, in Δdb satisfies one of the following two criteria: (1) s_a is an inserted sequence of D, or (2) there exists a sequence, say s, in D where $s \cdot s_a$ is an appended sequence of D. Considering the example in Table 1(a), the left column represents the original database D and the right column is the incremental part Δdb. After D is updated by Δdb, the updated database is denoted as D'.

For a sequence t, its utility may increase due to database updates (i.e., $u_D(t) \ne u_{D'}(t)$), and the possible cases of utility increase are as below. **(1)** Given an inserted sequence s' in D' and $t \sqsubseteq s'$, it is obvious that the insertion of s' will make t's utility increase by $u(t, s')$. Considering the inserted sequence s_6 in Table 1(a), since $\langle b, d \rangle \sqsubseteq s_6$, s_6 will make the utility of $\langle b, d \rangle$ increase by $u(\langle b, d \rangle, s_6) = 8$. **(2)** Given an appended sequence $s' \in D'$ where $s' = s \cdot s_a$ and $s \in D$, if $t \not\sqsubseteq s$ but $t \sqsubseteq s'$, the update of s will make t's utility increase by $u(t, s')$. In the example shown in Table 1(a), since sequence $\langle f \rangle \not\sqsubseteq s_4$ in D but $\langle f \rangle \sqsubseteq s'_4$ in D', the update of s_4 will make the utility of $\langle f \rangle$ increase by $u(\langle f \rangle, s'_4) = 10$. **(3)** Given an appended sequence $s' \in D'$ where $s' = s \cdot s_a$ and $s \in D$, if $t \sqsubseteq s$ and s' has at least one new instance of t at position $\langle j_1, j_2, \ldots, j_k \rangle$ and $u(t, \langle j_1, j_2, \ldots, j_k \rangle, s') > u(t, s)$, $u(t, s')$ is greater than $u(t, s)$ and the update of s will make t's utility increase by $u(t, s') - u(t, s)$. For example, sequence s'_5 has two new instances of sequence $\langle a, c \rangle$ at positions $\langle 1, 3 \rangle$ and $\langle 2, 3 \rangle$ whose utilities are 4 and 16, respectively. Since $\max\{u(\langle a, c \rangle, \langle 1, 3 \rangle, s'_5), u(\langle a, c \rangle, \langle 2, 3 \rangle, s'_5)\} = 16 > u_D(\langle a, c \rangle, s_5) = 4$, the update of s'_5 will make the utility of $\langle a, c \rangle$ increase by $16 - 4 = 12$.

It is obvious that some sequences of insufficient utility in D may become of high utility sequences in D'. Thus, the problem of incremental HUSP mining can be formulated as below.

Problem Statement. Given an original SDB D, an increment SDB Δdb, an external utility table, the minimum utility threshold *min_util*, and the set of high utility sequential patterns in D, the problem of *incremental high utility sequential pattern mining* is to identify all high utility sequential patterns in the updated SDB D' without mining the whole D' from scratch.

3. PRELIMINARY CONCEPT

3.1 Sequence Extension

Similar to [7, 14, 13], the search space of the HUSP mining problem can be represented as a lexicographic tree. In a lexicographic tree, a child node, say t', of a node t is called an *extension sequence* of t and t is called the *parent sequence* of t'. Consider an l-sequence t and let the last item within t's last itemset be i_e. An extension sequence of t, say t', is an $(l+1)$-sequence which should belong to one of the following two types. (1) t' is called an i-extension

Table 1: A Sequence Database and Its External Utility Table

(a) A Sequence Database

SID	Original Database (D)	Incremental Part (Δdb)
s_1	$[(a,5)(b,3)][(d,1)][(b,6)]$	
s_2	$[(a,1)(c,1)][(a,4)(c,6)][(c,2)][(e,1)][(d,2)]$	
s_3	$[(c,2)][(b,5)][(d,4)][(a,2)]$	
s_4	$[(e,5)][(c,2)]$	$[(c,2)(d,6)][(f,5)][(a,2)(e,5)]$
s_5	$[(a,1)(c,1)][(a,5)(c,1)(e,1)]$	$[(a,5)(c,1)(e,1)][(d,1)(e,2)]$
s_6		$[(f,2)][(b,1)][(e,4)][(d,2)][(c,1)]$

(b) An External Utility Table

Item	External Utility
a	3
b	4
c	1
d	2
e	1
f	2

sequence of t if it is formed by inserting an item, which is lexicographically greater than i_e, into the last itemset of t. (2) t' is called an s-extension sequence of t if t' is generated by appending a new itemset consisting of a single item to the end of t. Furthermore, if a sequence t_d can be formed by a series of extensions from another sequence t, t_d is called a *descendant sequence* of t.

To facilitate the following discussions, we give the definitions of *maximum utility* and *remaining utility* as below.

Definition 5. If $s = \langle Y_1 Y_2 \ldots Y_m \rangle$ has an instance of t at position $\langle j_1, j_2, \ldots, j_k \rangle$, the last item within the last itemset in t, say item i, is called the *extension item* of t, and j_k is called an *extension position* of t in s. For example, item c is the extension item of sequence $\langle a, c \rangle$, while 2 and 3 are the extension positions of $\langle a, c \rangle$ in sequence s_2.

The *maximum utility* of t at extension position p in s, denoted as $u(t, p, s)$, is defined as

$$u(t,p,s) = \max\{u(t, \langle j_1, j_2, \ldots, p \rangle, s) \mid \forall 1 \le j_1 < j_2 < \cdots < p \le m : t \sqsubseteq \langle Y_{j_1} Y_{j_2} \ldots Y_p \rangle\}, \quad (2)$$

which is the maximum of the utilities of all instances of t whose extension position is p. For example, $u(\langle a,c \rangle, 3, s_2) = \max\{u(\langle a,c \rangle, \langle 1,3 \rangle, s_2), u(\langle a,c \rangle, \langle 2,3 \rangle, s_2)\} = \max\{5, 14\} = 14$.

Definition 6. Given a sequence s, the *remaining utility* of the item i within the j_k*-th* itemset in s is denoted as $ru(i, j_k, s)$ [14, 13]. In the example shown in Table 1(a), the remaining utility $ru(a, 2, s_2)$ is $u(c,2,s_2) + u(c,3,s_2) + u(e,4,s_2) + u(d,5,s_2) = 13$.

3.2 Utility Upper Bounds

Two utility upper bounds, Prefix-Extension Utility (abbreviated as PEU) and Reduced Sequence Utility (abbreviated as RSU) are proposed in [13] to facilitate efficient mining of HUSPs. To better mining efficiency, we propose in this subsection a new utility upper bound, named Tight Sequence Utility (abbreviated as TSU), which is tighter than RSU, and use PEU and TSU to design our incremental HUSP mining algorithm, IncUSP-Miner, in Section 4.

3.2.1 The Tight Sequence Utility

In this subsection, a novel upper bound of the utility of a sequence, named TSU, is defined as follows to facilitate the design of our incremental HUSP mining algorithm.

Definition 7. (*TSU for 1-sequences*) Consider a sequence $s \in D$ and a 1-sequence t whose extension item is i. Let p_1 be the smallest extension position of t in s. The TSU of t in sequence s, denoted as $TSU(t, s)$, is defined as:

$$TSU(t,s) = u(i, p_1, s) + ru(i, p_1, s) \quad (3)$$

Considering the example in Table 1(a), sequence $\langle c \rangle$ has three extension positions in s_2, which are 1, 2, and 3, respectively. By Definition 7, $TSU(\langle c \rangle, s_2) = u(c, 1, s_2) + ru(c, 1, s_2) = 1 + (12 + 6 + 2 + 1 + 4) = 26$.

Definition 8. (*TSU for l-sequences where $l \geq 2$*) Consider an l-sequence t whose extension item is item i. Suppose t is an extension sequence of an $(l-1)$-sequence α. For a sequence $s \in D$ and $t \sqsubseteq s$, let p_1 be the smallest extension position of t in s and ap_1 be the smallest extension position of α in s. The TSU of t in sequence s, denoted as $TSU(t, s)$, is defined as:

$$TSU(t,s) = \begin{cases} u(\alpha, ap_1, s) + u(i, p_1, s) + ru(i, p_1, s) & \text{if } u(\alpha, s) = u(\alpha, ap_1, s) \\ PEU(\alpha, s) & \text{otherwise.} \end{cases} \quad (4)$$

For example, sequence $\langle [a,c]c \rangle$ is a subsequence of s_2. The smallest extension position of its parent sequence, $\langle [a,c] \rangle$, in s_2 is 1. Since $u(\langle [a,c] \rangle, s_2) = 18$ is not equal to $u(\langle [a,c] \rangle, 1, s_2) = 4$, by definition, we have $TSU(\langle [a,c]c \rangle, s_2) = PEU(\langle [a,c] \rangle, s_2) = 29$. Consider another sequence $\langle a, d \rangle$ contained in s_1. Since the extension positions of all the instances of $\langle a \rangle$ are 1, it is obvious that $u(\langle a \rangle, s_1) = u(\langle a \rangle, 1, s_1) = 15$. By definition, we have $TSU(\langle a, d \rangle, s_1) = u(\langle a \rangle, 1, s_1) + u(d, 2, s_1) + ru(d, 2, s_1) = 15 + 2 + 24 = 41$.

Definition 9. The TSU of a sequence t in the sequence database D, denoted as $TSU_D(t)$, is defined as:

$$TSU_D(t) = \sum_{\forall s \in D \wedge t \sqsubseteq s} TSU(t, s). \quad (5)$$

Consider the SDB shown in Table 1(a). Since $\langle [a,c]c \rangle$ has instances only in s_2 and s_5, we have $TSU_D(\langle [a,c]c \rangle) = TSU(\langle [a,c]c \rangle, s_2) + TSU(\langle [a,c]c \rangle, s_5) = 29 + 21 = 50$.

THEOREM 1. *Given a sequence t and a sequence database D, $u_D(t) \le TSU_D(t) \le RSU_D(t) \le SWU_D(t)$ holds. In addition, for each descendant sequence t' of t, $u_D(t') \le TSU_D(t)$ also holds.*

According to Theorem 1, we conclude that TSU is a tighter upper bound of the sequence utility than RSU, and we will use TSU and PEU to design algorithm IncUSP-Miner in Section 4.

4. THE PROPOSED APPROACH

4.1 Overview

Figure 1 shows the architecture of the proposed incremental HUSP mining approach. Our approach consists of two phases, the initial phase and the incremental phase. In the initial phase, we propose algorithm USP-Miner to use TSU and PEU to mine HUSPs in the origin database D and keep the HUSPs in the list *HUSP*. To facilitate better performance in the incremental phase, we propose the concept of the *candidate pattern tree* and in addition to HUSPs, USP-Miner will construct a candidate pattern tree T as well.

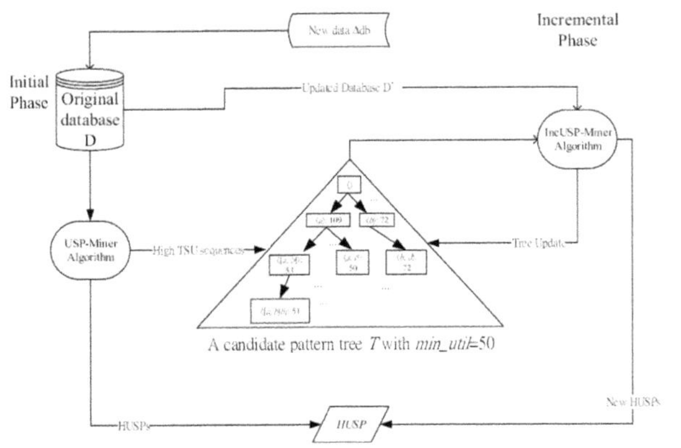

Figure 1: Architecture of the Proposed Approach

After Δdb is inserted into D, algorithm IncUSP-Miner is employed to incrementally mine the new HUSPs in D' based on the tree T in the incremental phase. The basic idea of IncUSP-Miner is to traverse each node in T from the root in a depth-first manner and skip those nodes not appearing in the updated sequences. Since some sequences of insufficient utility in D may become of high utility in D', IncUSP-Miner needs to adjust T to get correct mining results.

The details of algorithm USP-Miner are described in Section 4.2, while the details of algorithm IncUSP-Miner are given in Section 4.3.

4.2 Initial Phase

4.2.1 *Efficient Utility Calculation*

Considering two sequences s and t where $t \sqsubseteq s$, it is possible that s contains multiple instances of t at different positions. A naive way to obtain the utility of t in s is to find the positions of all instances of t in s, compute the utility of each instance, and obtain the maximum of the utilities of all instances. It is obvious that such a naive way is inefficient. This motivates us to design an efficient way to calculate the maximum utility of t in s.

LEMMA 1. *Given two sequences s and t where $t \sqsubseteq s$, suppose that s has multiple instances of t and let the set of the distinct extension positions of sequence t in s be $P = \{p_1, p_2, \ldots, p_q\}$. The utility of t in s (i.e., $u(t,s)$) equals to* $\max\{u(t,p_i,s) | \forall p_i \in P\}$.

THEOREM 2. *Given a sequence t, one t's i-extension sequence t', and a sequence s in D where $t' \sqsubseteq s$, the maximum utility of t' in s at extension position p (i.e., $u(t',p,s)$) can be derived by $u(t',p,s) = u(t,p,s) + u(i',p,s)$ where item i' is the extension item of t'.*

THEOREM 3. *Given a sequence t, one t's s-extension sequence t', and a sequence s in D where $t' \sqsubseteq s$, let item i' be the extension item of t' and p be an extension position of t'. Also let $P = \{p_1, p_2, \ldots p_q\}$ be the set of extension positions of t in s. The maximum utility of t' in s at extension position p can be derived from $u(t',p,s) = \max\{u(t,p_i,s) | \forall\ p_i \in P \text{ and } p_i < p\} + u(i',p,s)$.*

According to Theorems 2 and 3, the maximum utility of an i- or s-extension sequence t' of sequence t in s at extension position p (i.e., $u(t',p,s)$) can be efficiently derived from the maximum utility of t at each extension position p_i (i.e., $u(t,p_i,s)$) and $u(i',p,s)$. Moreover, according to Lemma 1, it is efficient to derive the utility of t' in s (i.e., $u(t',s)$) from the maximum utilities of t' in s at each extension position p (i.e., $u(t',p,s)$) without finding all instances of t' in s.

Seq	PEU(t)	TSU(t)	u(t)	IsHUSP
$\langle a \rangle$	103	109	48	false
sid	**PEU(t,s)**	**u(t, s)**	**{⟨p, u(t,p,s)⟩}**	
1	53	15	⟨1, 15⟩	
2	29	12	⟨1, 3⟩	⟨2, 12⟩
3	0	6	⟨4, 6⟩	
5	21	15	⟨1, 3⟩	⟨2, 15⟩

Figure 2: The Compact Node Structure of Sequence $\langle a \rangle$

Algorithm 1: USP-Miner(t)

Input: A sequence database D, the minimum utility threshold ξ, an empty set $HUSP$, and a sequence t in T
Output: $HUSP$: the set of HUSPs

```
if PEU(t) < min_util then
    return;
scan t-projected DB once to put i- and s-extension items into ilist and
    slist, respectively;
delete low TSU items from ilist and slist;
foreach item i ∈ ilist and slist do
    if i ∈ ilist then
        t' ← I − Extension(t, i);
    if i ∈ slist then
        t' ← S − Extension(t, i);
    BuildNode(t') and add t' to T as t's child;
    if u(t') ≥ min_util then
        insert t' into HUSP;
    USP-Miner(t');
```

4.2.2 *Buffering Sequences in the Candidate Pattern Tree*

A candidate pattern tree is an extension of the lexicographic tree buffering a set of sequences in D for incremental HUSP mining. According to Theorem 1, TSU is a tighter upper bound of the utilities of t and all t's descendant sequences. Hence, we use TSU to guide the construction of the candidate pattern tree T in the initial phase. A sequence t is called a *high TSU sequence* in D when $TSU_D(t) \geq min\_util$. Otherwise, t is called a *low TSU sequence* in D. Since a high utility sequential pattern is also a high TSU sequence, all high TSU sequences are buffered in the candidate pattern tree T for better mining efficiency in the incremental phase. Based on the discussion in Section 4.2.1, we design a compact node structure storing auxiliary information to speedup utility calculation in the incremental phase. In Figure 2, we use sequence $\langle a \rangle$ with $min\_util = 50$ as an example to illustrate our design.

4.2.3 *USP-Miner Algorithm*

As shown in Algorithm 1, algorithm USP-Miner is designed to build all tree nodes of the candidate pattern tree and extract HUSPs from the root in a DFS manner. For each node t, if PEU(t)< min_util, USP-Miner can safely skip t without expansion [13]. Otherwise, USP-Miner scans the t-projected database in D to collect all t's high TSU extension sequences. For each t's high TSU extension sequence t', USP-Miner builds the corresponding node structure as a child node of t, inserts t' into $HUSP$ if it is, and expands t' by recursively calling USP-Miner with t' as the input.

4.3 Incremental Phase

Definition 10. The updated database D' can be partitioned into two disjoint parts. (1) *LDB*: the set of updated sequences (i.e., inserted and appended sequences) in D'. (2) *NDB*: the set of sequences not in *LDB*. In other words, *NDB* is the set of the sequences in D and unchanged in D'. In the example shown in Table 1(a), $NDB = \{s_1, s_2, s_3\}$ and $LDB = \{s_4, s_5, s_6\}$.

After D is updated to D', we have to find new HUSPs and adjust the candidate pattern tree T in order to support multiple database updates. Since an HUSP is also a high TSU sequence, keeping the tree T storing all high TSU sequences in D' and keeping the auxiliary information stored in the tree T up-to-date are crucial to incremental HUSP mining. For each sequence t, we have to consider the following cases after database update.

- *Case 1*: t is a high TSU sequence in D and D'.
- *Case 2*: t is a low TSU sequence in D and becomes a high TSU sequence in D'.

The rationales to handle the above cases are as follows.

Handling Case (1): Since t is already in the tree T, if t is contained by some sequence(s) in *LDB*, keeping t's auxiliary information stored in T up-to-date is necessary. The proposed method to update the auxiliary information stored in tree nodes is described in Section 4.3.1. On the other hand, if t is not contained by any sequence in *LDB*, we can skip all tree nodes in the subtree rooted by t without updating the auxiliary information in these tree nodes. The proposed method to skip these tree nodes is given in Section 4.3.2.

Handling Case (2): Let s be the longest prefix of t where the tree node of s is already in the tree T. If such s exists, to add the tree node of t to the tree T, algorithm USP-Miner can be recursively applied on s and each node of the subtree rooted by s. Thus, the tree node of t will be eventually added to the tree T. Otherwise, USP-Miner can be applied on root and thus the node of t will be added to T.

Based on above discussions, we devise algorithm IncUSP-Miner to incrementally mine HUSPs in an incremental database, and the details of the IncUSP-Miner algorithm are described in Section 4.3.3.

4.3.1 Tree Node Update

Generally, when the utility of a sequence t buffered in the tree T has to be updated, to obtain the up-to-date utility of t (i.e., $u_{D'}(t)$), scanning Δdb is enough to find its maximum utility $u(t,p,s')$ at each new extension position p for each updated sequence s' containing t in *LDB* based on the efficient utility calculation method described in Section 4.2.1. After each new extension position p with $u(t,p,s')$ for each s' in *LDB* is obtained, because $|D'|$ is usually much larger than $|LDB|$, the following equation can be used to calculate $u_{D'}(t)$ efficiently with the aid of $u_D(t)$ and $u_D(t,s)$ kept in the proposed tree node structure:

$$u_{D'}(t) = u_D(t) + \sum_{\forall s' \in LDB \wedge t \sqsubseteq s'} \left(u(t,s') - u_D(t,s) \right), \qquad (6)$$

where $u_D(t,s) = 0$ if s' is an *inserted sequence*, or s' is an *appended sequence* of s in D but $t \not\sqsubseteq s$.

Other auxiliary information of t such as TSU and PEU can be efficiently calculated in a similar manner.

4.3.2 Node Skipping Strategy

After an SDB is updated, tree nodes in the tree T and without any instance in any one of the sequences in *LDB* can be safely skipped without updating. In other words, we can skip a tree node t and its subtree when t does not have any instance in *LDB*. In addition, it is obvious that all t's descendant sequences will have no instance in *LDB* when the t-projected DB of *LDB* is empty or contains only $\langle\rangle$. Therefore, we propose the following node skipping strategy for better mining efficiency.

STRATEGY 1. *For a sequence t in the tree T, all t's descendant sequences can be safely skipped without updating if the t-projected DB of LDB is empty or contains only* $\langle\rangle$.

4.3.3 IncUSP-Miner Algorithm

After an SDB is updated, IncUSP-Miner is executed with input $\langle\rangle$ (i.e., the root of T) to mine the HUSPs of D' incrementally. IncUSP-Miner is a recursive algorithm and the behavior of IncUSP-Miner with input t is as follows. If all sequences in the t-projected DB of *LDB* (i.e. $LDB|_t$) are empty sequences, IncUSP-Miner skips t without further processing according to Strategy 1. Otherwise, IncUSP-Miner scans $D'|_t$ to calculate the TSU of each extension sequence of t in D'. For each t's high TSU extension sequence, say t', having instances in *LDB*, if t' is also in T (Case 1), IncUSP-Miner updates the node of t', inserts t' into *HUSP* if it is a new HUSP, and recursively calls IncUSP-Miner with t' as the input to process the subtree rooted by t'. Otherwise (Case 2), IncUSP-Miner builds the node of t', inserts t' into *HUSP* if it is, and expands t' by recursively calling USP-Miner with t' as the input. Finally, the algorithmic form of IncUSP-Miner is shown in Algorithm 2.

Algorithm 2: IncUSP-Miner (t)

Input: A sequence database D', *min_util*, a candidate pattern tree T, *HUSP* (the set of HUSPs in D), and a sequence t in T.
Output: *HUSP*: the set of HUSPs in D'

```
D'|_t ← t-projected DB of D';
if all sequences in LDB|_t are empty sequences then // Strategy 1
    return;
if PEU_D'(t) < min_util then
    return;
scan D'|_t to calculate the TSU of all t's extension sequences;
foreach t's extension sequence t' ∈ D' do
    if TSU_D'(t') ≥ min_util then
        if t' ∈ LDB then
            if t' ∈ T then // case (1)
                UpdateNode(t');
                if u(t') ≥ min_util ∧ ¬t'.IsHUSP then
                    t'.IsHUSP ← True and insert t' into HUSP;
                IncUSP-Miner(t');
            else // case (2)
                BuildNode(t') and add t' to T;
                if u(t') ≥ min_util then
                    t'.IsHUSP ← True and insert t' into HUSP;
                USP-Miner(t');
        else
            Skip Node t';
```

Table 2: Characteristics of Datasets

Dataset	Foodmart [2]	Tafeng [3]	Music[1] [1]
Number of sequences ($|D'|$)	8842	32266	32778
Average Length per sequence	30.5	25.34	4.55
Number of distinct items	1559	23812	100
Updated Ratio ($\frac{|\Delta db|}{|D|}$)	0.05	0.05	0.05

5. PERFORMANCE EVALUATION

In this section, the performance of algorithm IncUSP-Miner is evaluated. Two state-of-the-art algorithms for mining HUSPs from

[1]This SDB is composed of the 100 most popular music products in the original dataset.

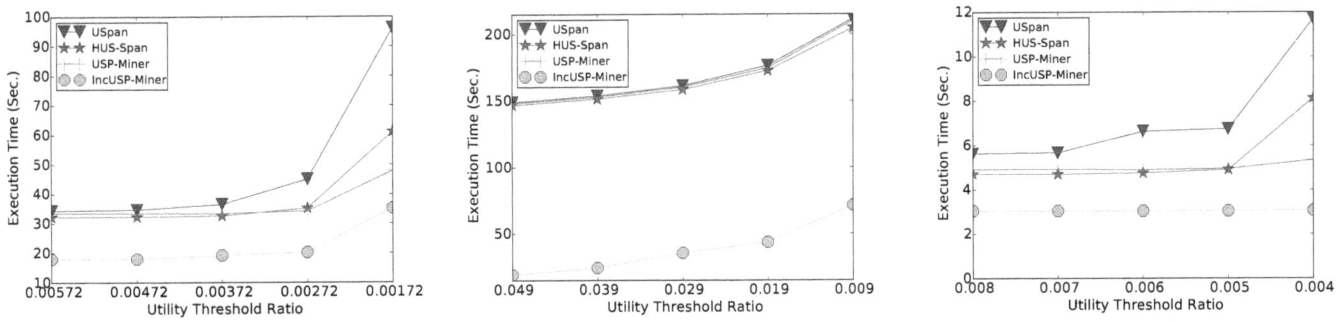

(a) Foodmart (b) Tafeng (c) Music

Figure 3: Effect of Utility Threshold

scratch, algorithms USpan [14] and HUS-Span [13], are also implemented for comparison purposes. All algorithms are implemented in C++ using Mingw-w64 compiler with -O3 optimization. Experiments were performed on a computer with a 3.4 GHz Intel Core i7 CPU, 12 GB memory, and running on Windows 7 x64 operating system. Three real datasets are used in experiments and their characteristics are summarized in Table 2.

5.1 Effect of Utility Threshold

This subsection shows the experimental results of all the above algorithms on each dataset under varied utility thresholds. The minimum utility threshold *min_util* is set as a threshold ratio (ξ) times the utility of the original database (i.e., $min\_util = \xi \times \sum_{\forall s \in D} u_D(s)$).

Figure 3 shows the execution time on each dataset under varied utility threshold ratio ξ. Generally, for each dataset, IncUSP-Miner outperforms all algorithms for mining HUSPs from scratch. The reason is that the candidate pattern tree is helpful for efficiently calculating utilities and the proposed node skipping strategy is able to skip some nodes not necessary to be visited. It is interesting that although adopting an upper bound of sequence utility (i.e., TSU) tighter than HUS-Span, USP-Miner is not as efficient as HUS-Span on dataset Tafeng. It is because in addition to mining HUSPs, USP-Miner has an extra job for building the candidate pattern tree, resulting in more computation overhead. Fortunately, USP-Miner outperforms HUS-Span and USpan in most cases, showing the advantage of TSU.

6. CONCLUSIONS

In this paper, we addressed the problem of incremental mining of HUSPs. Specifically, we introduced the concept of TSU, which is a tight upper bound of sequence utility, and the candidate pattern tree, which is an extension of the lexicographic tree storing high TSU sequences, to facilitate incremental HUSP mining. Accordingly, the node structure on the candidate pattern tree is designed to keep concise auxiliary information to eliminate redundant computation. We then proposed algorithm IncUSP-Miner to incrementally mine HUSPs with the aid of the candidate pattern tree. Experimental results show that IncUSP-Miner outperforms the state-of-the-art HUSP mining algorithms in incremental databases in terms of mining efficiency.

Acknowledgement

This work was supported in part by Ministry of Science and Technology, Taiwan, under contracts 103-2221-E-009-126-MY2, 104-2218-E-009-029, 105-2221-E-009-160 and 105-2218-E-009-003.

7. REFERENCES

[1] Amazon reviews. http://snap.stanford.edu/data/web-Amazon.html.

[2] Microsoft sql server 2008 analysis services unleashed. http://www.informit.com/store/microsoft-sql-server-2008-analysis-services-unleashed-9780672330018.

[3] Ta-feng datasets. http://aiia.iis.sinica.edu.tw/index.php?option=com_frontpage&Itemid=1.

[4] C. F. Ahmed, S. K. Tanbeer, and J. Byeong-Soo. A framework for mining high utility web access sequences. *IETE Technical Review*, 28(1):3–16, 2011.

[5] C. F. Ahmed, S. K. Tanbeer, and B.-S. Jeong. A novel approach for mining high-utility sequential patterns in sequence databases. *ETRI Journal*, 32(5):676–686, 2010.

[6] C. F. Ahmed, S. K. Tanbeer, B.-S. Jeong, and Y.-K. Lee. Efficient tree structures for high utility pattern mining in incremental databases. *IEEE TKDE*, 21(12):1708–1721, 2009.

[7] J. Ayres, J. Gehrke, T. Yiu, and J. Flannick. Sequential pattern mining using a bitmap representation. In *KDD*, 2002.

[8] Y. Chen, J. Guo, Y. Wang, Y. Xiong, and Y. Zhu. Incremental mining of sequential patterns using prefix tree. In *PAKDD*, 2007.

[9] H. Cheng, X. Yan, and J. Han. Incspan: Incremental mining of sequential patterns in large database. In *KDD*, 2004.

[10] G.-C. Lan, T.-P. Hong, V. S. Tseng, and S.-L. Wang. Applying the maximum utility measure in high utility sequential pattern mining. *Expert Systems with Applications*, 41(11):5071 – 5081, 2014.

[11] S. Nguyen, X. Sun, and M. Orlowska. Improvements of incspan: Incremental mining of sequential patterns in large database. In *PAKDD*, 2005.

[12] B.-E. Shie, H.-F. Hsiao, V. S. Tseng, and P. S. Yu. Mining high utility mobile sequential patterns in mobile commerce environments. In *DASFAA*, 2011.

[13] J.-Z. Wang, J.-L. Huang, and Y.-C. Chen. On efficiently mining high utility sequential patterns. *KAIS*, to be published.

[14] J. Yin, Z. Zheng, and L. Cao. Uspan: an efficient algorithm for mining high utility sequential patterns. In *KDD*, 2012.

[15] J. Yin, Z. Zheng, L. Cao, Y. Song, and W. Wei. Efficiently mining top-k high utility sequential patterns. In *ICDM*, 2013.

[16] U. Yun and H. Ryang. Incremental high utility pattern mining with static and dynamic databases. *Applied Intelligence*, 42(2):323–352, 2015.

Understanding Stability of Noisy Networks through Centrality Measures and Local Connections

Vladimir Ufimtsev
Dept. of CS
Univ. of Nebraska at Omaha
NE 68182, USA
vufimtsev@unomaha.edu

Soumya Sarkar
Dept. of CSE
IIT Kharagpur, India – 721302
soumya015@iitkgp.ac.in

Animesh Mukherjee
Dept. of CSE
IIT Kharagpur, India – 721302
animeshm@cse.iitkgp.ernet.in

Sanjukta Bhowmick
Dept. of CS
Univ. of Nebraska at Omaha
NE 68182, USA
sbhowmick@unomaha.edu

ABSTRACT

Networks created from real-world data contain some inaccuracies or noise, manifested as small changes in the network structure. An important question is whether these small changes can significantly affect the analysis results.

In this paper, we study the effect of noise in *changing ranks of the high centrality vertices.* We compare, using the Jaccard Index (JI), how many of the top-k high centrality nodes from the original network are also part of the top-k ranked nodes from the noisy network. We deem a network as stable if the JI value is high.

We observe two features that affect the stability. First, *the stability is dependent on the number of top-ranked vertices considered.* When the vertices are ordered according to their centrality values, they group into clusters. Perturbations to the network can change the relative ranking within the cluster, but vertices rarely move from one cluster to another. Second, *the stability is dependent on the local connections of the high ranking vertices.* The network is highly stable if the high ranking vertices are connected to each other.

Our findings show that the stability of a network is affected by the local properties of high centrality vertices, rather than the global properties of the entire network. Based on these local properties we can identify the stability of a network, without explicitly applying a noise model.

CCS Concepts

•Networks → Network reliability; •Theory of computation → *Graph algorithms analysis; Random networks;*

Keywords

betweenness; closeness; stability; noise; rich-club

CIKM'16 , October 24 - 28, 2016, Indianapolis, IN, USA

ISBN 123-4567-24-567/08/06...$15.00

DOI: http://dx.doi.org/10.1145/2983323.2983692

1. INTRODUCTION

Network analysis is a very efficient tool for understanding complex systems of interacting entities that arise in diverse applications. Analysis of the network models provide insights to the properties of the underlying systems.

However, measurements of real-world systems is influenced by the experimental setup. Modeling of this data as networks is also affected by subjective choices. Given these uncertainties in data collection, any network created from real-world data will contain some inaccuracy (or noise). Noise in networks is manifested in the form of extra or missing edges.

Measuring the effect of noise: In recent studies, researchers perturb the network by adding/deleting a specified percentage of edges (noise level). Then they observe by how much the properties of the network alter and correlate this change in the properties with the noise level. A network is deemed stable if the noise does not affect the properties. Most of these studies focus on vertex-based measurements including centrality metrics and core numbers [1, 3, 9, 5, 8].

Despite these studies, there is yet no definite answer to this key question – *how can we identify whether a network would be stable under noise?* Although studies such as [9] claim that the stability is affected by global properties, we see in the experiments reported here, that these correlations do not always hold. Instead, our observations lead us to the conclusion that it is the *local structure around the high centrality vertices, that significantly affect the stability.*

Noise model: We consider an additive model, where a percentage of edges, selected from the complementary graph at random, are added to the existing network. We focus only on edge addition because missing edges can be predicted using link prediction algorithms. Therefore understanding the effect of extraneous edges is the more critical problem.

Key observations and contributions: We observe that two important factors affect the stability of the networks. First, *the stability of the rankings depend on the value of* k. The top-k ranked vertices arrange themselves into clusters. Within a cluster, the centrality values are very similar. However, the difference in values between the last vertex of a cluster and the first vertex of the next cluster is large. This phenomena makes the distribution of the high centrality values look like a step function. If the value of k falls at the end of a cluster, the results are stable, otherwise they become unstable. Second, we observe that *the stability of a network depends on the density of the subgraph induced by high centrality vertices, i.e., a rich-club.* This is because the centrality metrics are more affected by changes to their immediate neighbors than to nodes at a larger distance.

These observations highlight that network stability is dependent on localized subgraphs induced by the top-k high centrality vertices, and not the global topology. Our findings allow users to identify stable networks with respect to a centrality metric without applying the noise model on the network. **Our main contributions** are as follows;

- Demonstrating that stability is dependent on the value of k and that stability over successive k is non-monotonic.
- Demonstrating that stability of networks is high if the subgraph induced by the high centrality vertices is dense.
- Providing a template to identify highly stable networks.

2. EXPERIMENTS AND OBSERVATIONS

Here we describe our experimental setup and report the behavior of the results under the perturbations. We used the following centrality metrics as defined in [7].

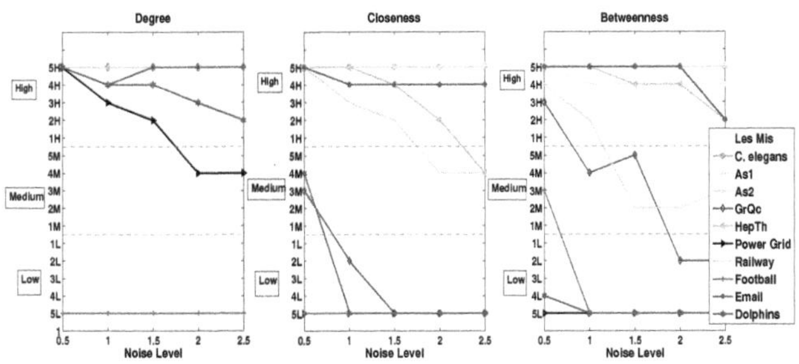

Figure 1: **Changes in dominant stability of centrality metrics over different noise levels.** Left: Degree Centrality, Middle: Closeness Centrality , Right: Betweenness Centrality. X-axis: Noise Levels. Y-axis: Number of times the stability value fell in the high (H), medium (M) or low (L) range. **The dominant stability decreases with increased noise level, but the rate of decrease depends on the centrality metric.**

Degree centrality, $D(v)$ of a vertex v measures the number of its neighbors. *Closeness centrality*, of a vertex v is computed as $CC(v) = \frac{1}{\sum\limits_{s \neq v \in V} dis(v,s)}$, where $dis(v,s)$ is the length of a shortest path between v and s. *Betweenness centrality* of a vertex v is defined as $BC(v) = \sum\limits_{s \neq v \neq t \in V} \frac{\sigma_{st}(v)}{\sigma_{st}}$,where σ_{st} is the total number of shortest paths between s and t, and $\sigma_{st}(v)$ is the total number of shortest paths between s and t that pass through v. We used the real-world networks listed in Table 1 from [6, 2, 4].

Noise model: Our noise model is as follows. Of all the possible edges in a graph with $|V|$ vertices we pick an edge with probability $\frac{\epsilon}{|V|}$; $\epsilon, 0 \leq \epsilon \leq |V|$. If the edge is not part of the network it is added to the network.

If the degree of a vertex is d, then it has $n-1-d$ nodes that can get added due to perturbation. Therefore the expected number of edges added to it will be $\frac{\epsilon}{|V|}(n-1-d)$. Thus vertices with higher degree will have fewer edge additions.

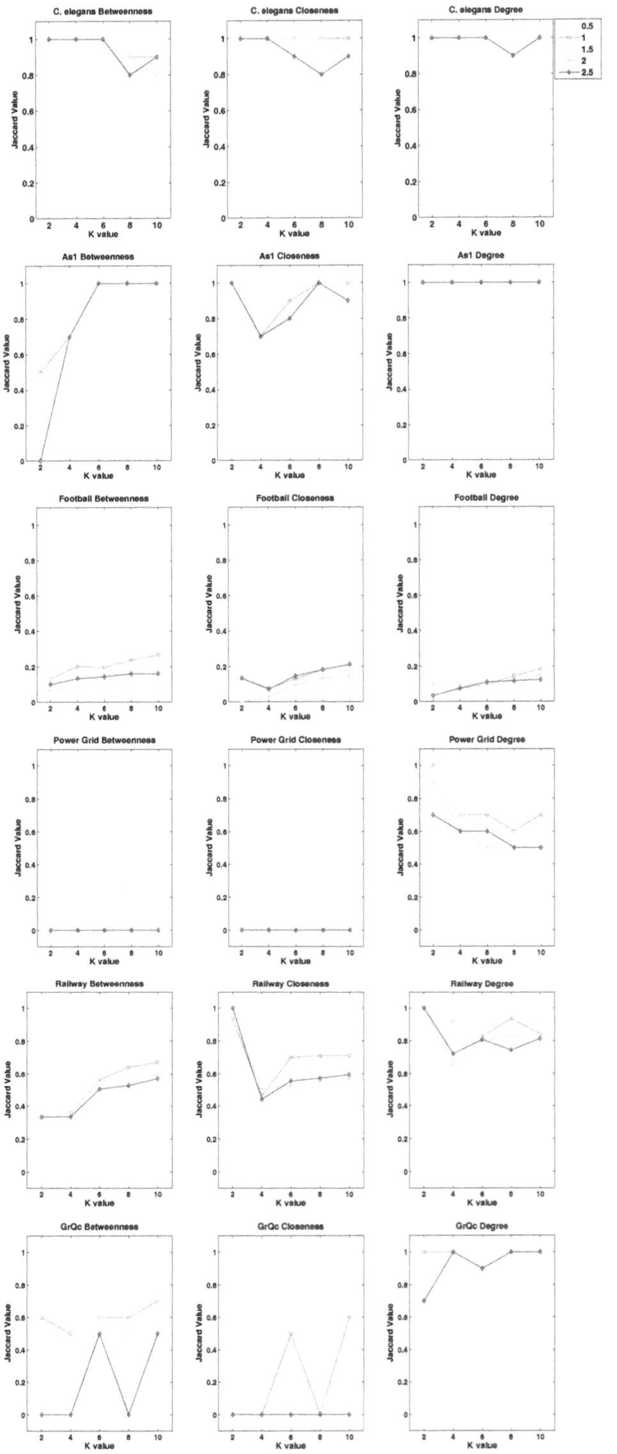

Figure 2: **Change in centrality values for different k, over different noise levels.** Left: Betweenness, Middle: Closeness, Right: Degree. Y-axis: Jaccard Index. X-axis: The number of top vertices (k). First two rows, networks with **high stability**, Middle two rows, networks with **low stability**, Last two rows, networks whose betwenness and closeness stability **changes from high to low and back. The choice of k can significantly affect the JI value.**

Table 1: **Test suite of real-world networks**

Name	Nodes	Edges	CC	α
AS2	6474	13895	0.39	1.49
AS1	3570	7750	0.31	1.57
C. elegans	453	2025	0.65	1.65
Les Mis.	77	254	0.73	3.05
GrQc	5242	14496	0.68	1.78
HepTh	9877	25998	0.59	1.66
Power Grid	4941	6594	0.10	1.45
Railway	301	1224	0.74	6.68
Football	115	613	0.40	1.57
Email	1133	5451	0.25	2.75
Dolphins	62	159	0.30	5.53

Measuring stability: For a given network and a given centrality metric we compute the stability as follows: We apply the noise model to the network with levels (i.e. ϵ) of values $.5, 1, 1.5, 2, 2.5$. For each network we compute the centrality values. We then compute the Jaccard Index (JI) to see how many of the top k vertices in the original network are also among the top k vertices in the perturbed network. For two sets A and B, $JI = \frac{A \cap B}{A \cup B}$. The highest value of JI is 1 (two sets have exactly the same elements) and the lowest value is 0 (sets have no elements in common).

We conducted these experiments for each network over 10 perturbed networks per noise level. The JI presented in the results is the mean over the 10 networks. We classified the stability into three groups ; *High Stability* (JI $\geq .7$); *Medium Stability* ($.4 \leq$ JI $< .7$) and *Low Stability* ($.4 >$JI ≥ 0).

Results: In Figure 1, each line represents a network. The X-axis represents the noise levels (ϵ). For ease of visualization we plot only for the even values of k from 2 to 10. Y-axis measures the *dominant stability*, i.e. the longest consecutively occurring stability range for that noise level. For example, 5H denotes that at that noise level, for all the five values of k the stability was high. 3M denotes that for three consecutive values of k the stability was in the middle range.

Figure 2 shows the changes for the individual networks, per value of k, not just the dominant stability. We have included two networks that were consistently in the high range (AS1 and C. elegans), two that were consistently in the low range (Power Grid and Football) and two that changed their stability values according to the centrality metric and noise level (GrQc and Railway). The results show that the stability value can change depending on the value of k.

Observations: The results show that even a small amount of noise (average edges added per vertex is 2.5) can significantly change the analysis results. However, the behavior of the three centrality metrics varies as follows:
Degree: The dominant stability decreases monotonically for *degree centrality.* With the exception of Power Grid (has some middle level stability) and Football (all stabilities are low) all other networks show high stability.
Closeness: Several networks that show predominantly low dominant stability (Power Grid, Football, GrQc and Dolphins). Networks HepTh and Railway start as high stability, but their stability decreases with higher noise levels.
Betweenness: Here, Power Grid, Football and Dolphins have low dominant stability. GrQc goes from high, to medium to low. Railway also starts from high and ends at low.

To summarize, our **main observations** are as follows;

- The dominant stability decreases with increasing levels of noise. However, the individual stability changes non- monotonically with the values of k.
- Among the centrality metrics, degree is most stable, closeness has a clearer separation between the high and low stability networks and in betweeness the separation is not as clear. The same network (e.g. GrQc at noise level 1.5) can have high (degree), low (closeness) and medium (betwenness) stability based on the centrality metrics.
- The global topology of the network is not a deciding factor. In Table 1, the clustering coefficients are very diverse and α is between 1.5 and 3. Neither of these parameters seem to strongly correlate with the stability values.

3. FACTORS AFFECTING STABILITY

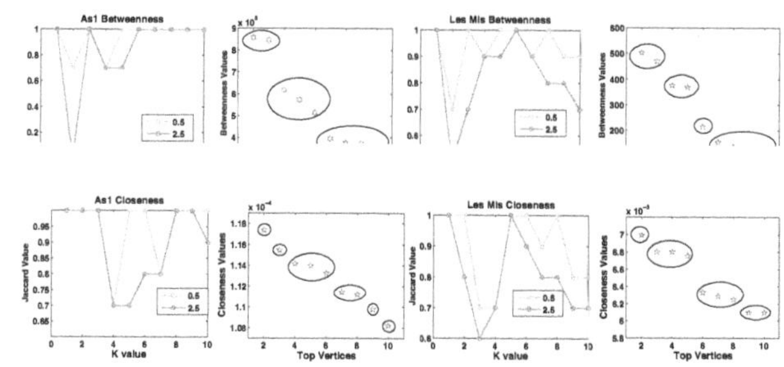

Figure 3: **Stable clusters of centrality values** Top: Betweenness Centrality. Bottom: Closeness Centrality. **Line Graphs:** X-axis plots k, the number of top centrality vertices. Y-axis plots the Jaccard Index. **Scattered Plot:** X-axis plots vertex id for the top 10 centrality vertices. Y-axis plots the centrality values. The vertices are clustered based on the relative difference of their centrality values. **Stability increases when k is in the beginning of a cluster and decreases when k falls within a cluster**

This section contains our *main contribution*, where we explain how properties of the network affect the stability.

Stability of centrality metrics: Consider two nodes v_1 and v_2, whose values for a centrality metric, are $X(v_1)$ and $X(v_2)$ respectively. In the original network, $X(v_1) > X(v_2)$, thus v_1 has a higher rank than v_2 [1]. After applying perturbation p, the centrality values become $X_p(v_1)$ and $X_p(v_2)$.

Our goal is to identify the lower bound on the difference between $X(v_1)$ and $X(v_2)$, such that after perturbation $X_p(v_1)$ will remain greater than $X_p(v_2)$. We consider the most optimal situation for $X_p(v_2)$ to become larger than $X_p(v_1)$. We assume that $X(v_1)$ has the maximum decrease after perturbation and $X(v_2)$ has the maximum increase, given that on average ϵ edges are added per vertex. Our computations for each centrality values are as follows;
Degree centrality: The degree of a vertex will either increase or remain the same. Thus the maximum decrease of v_1 is zero. The value of $X_p(v_2) = X(v_2) + \epsilon$. Therefore, if $X(v_1) - X(v_2) > \epsilon$, then the ranking will not change.

For most networks the difference between the higher ranked vertices is larger than the maximum ϵ we set for our experiments, so the ranking of the vertices remain relatively stable.

[1]We consider ranking from 1 (high) to n (low). The vertex with highest centrality value is ranked 1

Closeness centrality: For simplicity, we consider $X(v)$ to be the inverse of closeness centrality, i.e. $X(v) = \sum_{s \neq v \in V} dis(v, s)$

Since we are adding edges, this value will either increase or remain the same. The change in $X(v_2)$ will depend on where the edges are added.

Assume, due to perturbations, v_2 is added to a vertex v_x, which is at distance d_x from v_2. Therefore, v_x, and other vertices whose shortest paths to v_2 passed through v_x will have their distance to v_2 reduced by $d_x - 1$. The maximum decrease is $X_p(v_2) = X(v_2) - \sum_{t \in E_{add}} (d_t - 1)R_t$, where E_{add} is the set of nodes that are added to v_2, d_t is distance of t from v_2 in the original graph and R_t is the number of vertices whose shortest path to v_2 passes through t. Thus the following has to hold: $X(v_2) - X(v_1) > \sum_{t \in E_{add}} (d_t - 1)R_t$ for the ordering between these two vertices to be stable. R_t will increase with ϵ. The values of d_t depends on the depth of the BFS tree originating from v_2.

Betweenness Centrality: By adding edges the betweenness centrality of a vertex can increase if it gets connected to another high centrality vertex. It can also decrease, if new edges lead to alternate or smaller shortest paths.

Assume due to addition of edges to a vertex v, there are R new pairs of vertices whose shortest paths pass through v. Also due to addition of edges in other parts of the network, there are P pairs of vertices whose shortest paths used to pass through v in the original network, but do not in the perturbed network. There are also Q pairs of edges, whose length of shortest path does not change, but after perturbation there are new shortest paths between them.

We assume that v_1 sees only decrease in its BC value and v_2 sees only increase. Therefore $X_p(v_1) = X(v_1) - \sum_{s_p \neq v \neq t_p \in P} \frac{\sigma_{s_p t_p}(v_1)}{\sigma_{s_p t_p}} - \sum_{s_q \neq v_1 \neq t_q \in Q} \frac{q_x(\sigma_{s_q t_q}(v_1))}{(\sigma_{s_q t_q} + q_x)\sigma_{s_q t_q}}$, where q_x is the number of new shortest paths for the vertex pair s_q and t_q and $X_p(v_2) = X(v_2) + \sum_{s_r \neq v_2 \neq t_r \in R} \frac{\sigma_{s_r t_r}(v_2)}{\sigma_{s_r t_r}}$. Therefore, the difference between $X(v_1) - X(v_2)$, must be larger than $\sum_{s_p \neq v \neq t_p \in P} \frac{\sigma_{s_p t_p}(v_1)}{\sigma_{s_p t_p}} + \sum_{s_q \neq v_1 \neq t_q \in Q} \frac{q_x(\sigma_{s_q t_q}(v_1))}{(\sigma_{s_q t_q} + q_x)\sigma_{s_q t_q}}$
$+ \sum_{s_r \neq v_2 \neq t_r \in R} \frac{\sigma_{s_r t_r}(v_2)}{\sigma_{s_r t_r}}$

The number of elements in R will increase as ϵ increases. The number of elements in P and Q depend on the length of the shortest paths. If the length of most of the shortest paths through v_1 is already low, then there is less chance that they will become even shorter or alternate paths will be found with addition of new edges. Based on these formulas we observe that the **stability decreases with higher ϵ.** For closeness and betweeness centrality, the increase (if any) also depends on network structure.

Stability based on centrality values: We observe that the relative differences of consecutive centrality values can indicate whether the ordering will be maintained. Figure 3 plots the change in stability as the noise levels remain constant, and the value of k changes (line-graphs) and the values of the top-10 high centrality vertices (scattered plots).[2] The vertices can be grouped into clusters, where within the clusters the values are relatively close to each other, and across the clusters there is a large difference between the last vertex in the previous cluster and the first vertex in the next cluster. The stability increases when k is at the beginning of a cluster ($k = 4$ for AS1 Betweenness) and decreases when k is within the cluster ($k = 3$ for AS1 Betweenness).

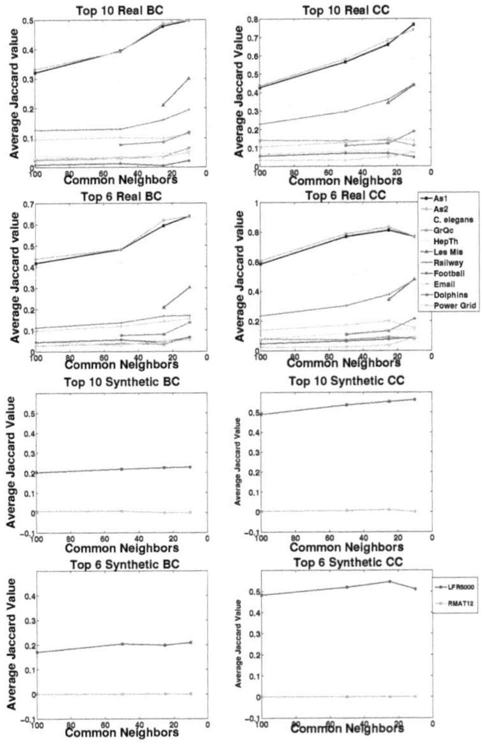

Figure 4: **High ranked common neighbors of the top-k ranked vertices**. X-axis is the number of high ranked neighbors. Y-axis is the average JI. For the high stability networks, the slope is increasing. This indicates that **in stable networks, the most of the common neighbors of high ranked vertices are other high-ranked vertices.**

Stable clusters: This phenomena occurs because it is difficult to reverse the ranking between two vertices if they have a large difference in their values. However if the values are very close then slight perturbation can change the rankings.

Therefore, we can use the relative difference between consecutively ranked vertices to group similarly valued vertices into **stable clusters**. If the value of k falls within the cluster, the Jaccard Index is likely to change. On the other hand, if k is selected such that it falls at the beginning of the cluster, then the ranking becomes more stable due to the large relative difference. This is borne out in Figure 3.

Identifying stable clusters: To identify the stable groups we compare the difference between the centrality values of the consecutively ordered vertices. The breaks into clusters occurs between the two vertices that have the high relative difference. We continue dividing the vertices into clusters until the difference is lower than a certain threshold. Identifying these stable clusters allows us to have an improved understanding of how the network will behave under various levels of noise. **Networks where the clusters are small in size and the clusters have high difference between them should have high stability.**

Stability based on network structure: We now see

[2]Rank 1 node is not shown due its high value. By plotting it, the relative difference between the other vertices cannot be visualized well.

Table 2: **Comparing Stability and Local Connections of Networks Network Stability** gives the mean of the stability over the noise levels at the specified k. **Subgraph Density** gives the density of the subgraph induced by the top k vertices. **Common Top Neighbors** reports whether the corresponding line in Figure 4 was in high, medium or low range. **Networks with dense (sparse) clusters of high ranking nodes have high (low) stability.**

Network	Network Stability		Subgraph Density		Common Top Neighbors	
	Closeness	**Betweenness**	**Closeness**	**Betweenness**	**Closeness**	**Betweenness**
Top 10 High Ranked Vertices						
Dense Cluster and High Stability Networks						
AS20000101	High (.96)	High (1)	.97	.71	High	High
AS20000102	High (1)	High (.78)	.95	.71	High	High
C. elegans	High (.94)	High (.76)	.82	.66	High	High
Les Mis	High (.8)	High (.76)	.66	.46	Medium	Medium
Sparse Cluster and Low Stability Networks						
GrQc	Low (.26)	Medium (.64)	.26	.11	Low	Low
Dolphin	Low (.1)	Low (.1)	.36	.24	Low	Low
Football	Low (0)	Low (0)	.16	.09	Low	Low
Power Grid	Low (0)	Low (0)	.24	.15	Low	Low
Outlier Networks						
Email	High (.98)	High (.96)	.31	.24	Low	Low
Railway	Medium (.68)	Medium (.68)	.67	.38	Medium	Low
HepTh	Medium (.68)	High (.72)	.17	.13	Low	Low
Synthetic Networks						
LFR5000	High (.78)	High (1)	.77	.44	High	Medium
RMAT12	Medium (.58)	Medium (.48)	.04	.04	Low	Low
Top 6 High Ranked Vertices						
Dense Cluster and High Stability Networks						
AS20000101	High (.86)	High (1)	1	.93	High	High
AS20000102	High (.8)	High (.96)	1	.93	High	High
C. elegans	High (.96)	High (1)	1	.87	High	High
Les Mis	High (.90)	High(1)	.87	.60	Medium	Medium
Sparse Cluster and Low Stability Networks						
GrQc	Low (.22)	Medium (.60)	.20	.13	Low	Low
Dolphin	Low (.12)	Low (0)	.47	.40	Low	Low
Football	Low (0)	Low (.10)	.27	.07	Low	Low
Power Grid	Low (0)	Low (0)	.27	.13	Low	Low
Outlier Networks						
Email	High (.90)	High (.76)	.33	.27	Low	Low
Railway	Medium (.68)	Medium (.62)	.73	.40	Medium	Low
HepTh	Medium (.66)	High (1)	.27	.13	Low	Low
Synthetic Networks						
LFR5000	High (.72)	High (.84)	.73	.4	High	Medium
RMAT12	Medium (.64)	Medium (.6)	.07	.07	Low	Low

how the network structure affects its stability. The slope of the degree distributions (α) for most of the networks in our test suite are from 1.5 to 3, their average local clustering coefficient is very varied, and neither of these correlate to the stability of the networks. Therefore, as seen from the earlier equations that the **stability seems to be dependent on the local structure of the high centrality vertices.**

High ranked common neighbors: We investigated whether the common neighbors of the top k nodes also have high rank. For each pair of nodes within the top k (k=10 and k=6) set (for a given centrality metric) we calculated the Jaccard Index between their connections to the top 100, 50, 25, and 10 high ranking nodes, and computed the average JI for each set of neighbors (top 100, top 50, etc.).

As the range of high ranked neighbors decreases (from 100 down to 10), the average JI value increases (Figure 4). This indicates that the **top-k high rank nodes have more common neighbors among the high-ranked nodes.** The curves divide into three regions. The top networks are the ones with high stability (e.g., C. elegans), the networks in the middle have not so high stability (e.g., Email) and the ones at the bottom show low stability (e.g., Football).

Subgraph induced by high ranked vertices: For each metric, we identified the top k high ranked vertices and then computed the density of the induced subgraphs from the vertices in this set. **Networks that achieve more instances of high stability have more dense subgraphs** (Figure 5)

Summary: Table 2 summarizes the results for $k = 10$ and $k = 6$. The density of a subgraph is the ratio of the total number of edges in the subgraph by the total possible edges.

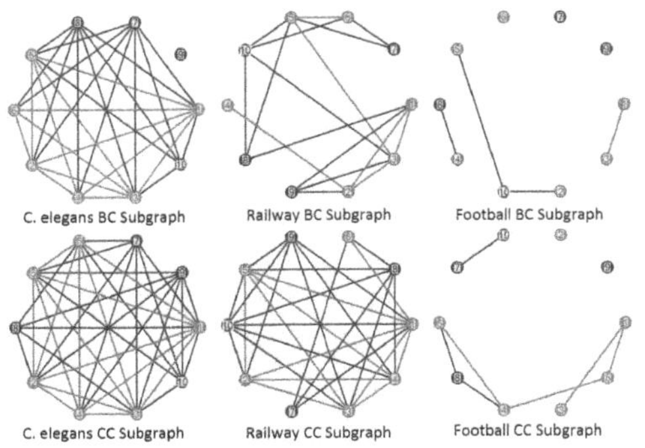

Figure 5: **Subgraphs for high betwenness (top) and high closeness (bottom) centrality vertices**. Left: C. elegans (high stability). Middle: Railway (medium stability). Right: Football (low stability). The red (blue) vertices and edges show the subgraph for the top 6 (10) vertices. **High stability networks have dense subgraphs and low stability networks have very sparse subgraphs.**

If the networks have high stability for the top-k vertices, then the subgraph induced by those vertices is also dense ($\geq$ .60). Conversely, if the network has low stability, then the corresponding subgraphs are sparse ($\leq$ .40, with Dolphin being the exception). This pattern is also observed when comparing their common neighbors. For high (low) stability networks, the corresponding line in Figure 4 is in the high (low) range. The results are similar for $k = 10$ and $k = 6$.

The exceptions are listed under Outliers. For example, Email and HepTh have high stability but low subgraph density. In these cases, a smaller subgroup of the high centrality vertices form a dense cluster, and the remaining high centrality vertices connect to that cluster. Another case is Railway with medium, tending to high stability for BC. Here, the subgraph for betwenness consists of two smaller clusters connected to each other (see Figure 5). Similar characteristics appear for Les Mis and GrQc (high BC, low density)

Table 2, also shows the results of two synthetic networks, RMAT12 (random network created using RMAT generator) and LFR5000 (scale free network created using LFR generator with μ=.1). The subgraph density of RMAT12 is constant for both centralities. LFR5000 however, shows strong subgraphs for closeness and a strong cluster over a subset of vertices for betweenness centrality. Therefore **compared to random graphs, scale-free networks with strong communities are more stable.**

Template to detect high stability networks: Based on our observations, we propose a template to identify stable networks as follows; 1. Identify the top-k centrality nodes and their values 2. *Stability Condition 1:* Identify the lower bound between the differences of the centrality values that will maintain the ordering. If the difference in the high centrality nodes is greater than the lower bound, then the network is stable for that range of k.

3. *Stability Condition 2:* Find stable clusters based on the values of high centrality nodes. If k falls at the beginning of the cluster, then the network is stable for that range of k.

4. *Stability Condition 3:* Find the subgraph induced by the top-k nodes. If the subgraphs are dense and the number of common high ranked neighbors is high, then the network is stable for that range of k.

If all these conditions are satisfied, the network should be highly stable. Conversely, if none of these conditions are satisfied the network should have low stability. Note that our method does not require the user to actually perturb the network to estimate its stability.

4. DISCUSSION

Our experiments demonstrate two extremely important findings which have so far never been observed. The first is that networks where the high centrality vertices are very well-connected, i.e., they form a "rich-club", are more stable. The second is that the stability of the rankings of nodes depends on the number of top ranked nodes (k) being investigated. The top nodes seem to arrange themselves into groups; if the value of k is such that it does not split a group then the results are stable, otherwise they are unstable.

Based on these conditions of stability, users can evaluate the stability of their networks, without applying the noise model. They can also use these conditions to improve the stability of their data collection methods.

In future, we plan to extend this study to other forms of noise models and other varieties of network properties. We also plan to develop methods to determine the thresholds automatically. A final direction would be to analyze the performance of the stability detection algorithm for other networks and other application areas.

5. ACKNOWLEDGEMENTS

SB and VU thank NSF Award Number 1533881 for funding this project.

6. REFERENCES

[1] A. Adiga and A. K. Vullikanti. How robust is the core of a network? In *Proceedings of the European Conference on Machine Learning and Knowledge Discovery in Databases - Volume 8188*, ECML PKDD 2013, pages 541–556, 2013.

[2] D. A. Bader, H. Meyerhenke, P. Sanders, and D. Wagner. Graph partitioning and graph clustering. 10th dimacs implementation challenge. http://www.cc.gatech.edu/dimacs10/archive/clustering.shtml, 2012.

[3] S. P. Borgatti, K. M. Carley, and D. Krackhardt. On the robustness of centrality measures under conditions of imperfect data. *Social networks*, 28(2):124–136, 2006.

[4] S. Ghosh, A. Banerjee, N. Sharma, S. Agarwal, and N. Ganguly. Statistical analysis of the indian railway network: a complex network approach. *Acta Physica Polonica B Proceedings Supplement*, 4:123–137, 2011.

[5] M. Herland, P. Pastran, and X. Zhu. An empirical study of robustness of network centrality scores in various networks and conditions. In *Tools with Artificial Intelligence (ICTAI), 2013 IEEE 25th International Conference on*, pages 221–228. IEEE, 2013.

[6] J. Leskovec and A. Krevl. SNAP Datasets: Stanford large network dataset collection. http://snap.stanford.edu/data, June 2014.

[7] M. Newman. *Networks: an introduction.* Oxford, 2010.

[8] S. Tsugawa and H. Ohsaki. Analysis of the robustness of degree centrality against random errors in graphs. In *Complex Networks VI*, pages 25–36. Springer, 2015.

[9] D. J. Wang, X. Shi, D. A. McFarland, and J. Leskovec. Measurement error in network data: A re-classification. *Social Networks*, 34(4):396–409, 2012.

Online Adaptive Topic Focused Tweet Acquisition

Mehdi Sadri Sharad Mehrotra Yaming Yu
University of California, Irvine
{msadri, sharad, yamingy}@ics.uci.edu

ABSTRACT

Twitter provides a public streaming API that is strictly limited, making it difficult to simultaneously achieve good coverage and relevance when monitoring tweets for a specific topic of interest. In this paper, we address the tweet acquisition challenge to enhance monitoring of tweets based on the client/application needs in an online adaptive manner such that the quality and quantity of the results improves over time. We propose a Tweet Acquisition System (TAS), that iteratively selects phrases to track based on an explore-exploit strategy. Our experimental studies show that TAS significantly improves recall of relevant tweets and the performance improves when the topics are more specific.

1. INTRODUCTION

The past decade has witnessed emergence of wide variety of applications to tap into live Twitter data to gain awareness about events, opinions and sentiments of the community about diverse topics of interest. For instance, Sakaki *et al.* [17] created an emergency management system to track earthquake instantly through Twitter. Other examples include predicting the stock market [7] and elections [20] based on the Twitter mood. A vital task, common across Twitter applications, is that of *acquiring content relevant to the topic of interest to the application.* Such data may then be subjected to diverse types of analysis. Typically, applications require acquired data to be both relevant, as well as, to provide good coverage of the topic of interest (i.e., support high recall). Such a data acquisition task over social media has proven to be difficult.

Many current systems [17, 21] use a fixed manual strategy for data acquisition in which the client selects a set of phrases that they believe when used as a query would provide simultaneously good coverage, as well as, maintain high relevance amongst the tweets retrieved. A fixed strategy has several drawbacks. The manually specified phrases may be too limited to provide good coverage. While a larger set of potential phrases could be generated (using appropriate knowledge bases), one further needs a mechanism to select a subset of them [8]. For instance, given a "US Presidential Debate" as the topic of interest, phrases such as "GOP Nominee" and "Republican Nominee" could be generated as potentially important. However, it is not obvious which one would generate better coverage if one needs to choose one of the two based on the limits imposed by the Twitter interface.

In order to overcome disadvantages of the fixed approach, prior research has explored adaptive strategies for Twitter data acquisition [6, 11, 8, 12]. Boanjak [6] proposes a focused crawler, which crawls topic related tweets from heuristically selected users. Joseph *et al.* [8] propose an approach based on natural language aspects (e.g., alternative spellings) to uncover relevant keywords in tracking tweets contributing to situational awareness. In [15, 14, 19] authors propose approaches to detect events in order to collect tweets. Chang *et al.* [11] propose an iterative process that in each iteration takes a sample of the Twitter stream to extract patterns relevant to the topic of interest. It then chooses from relevant patterns to probe Twitter to collect more relevant tweets.

While the experiments in [11] show that the adaptive approach performs better compared to the fixed approaches, it still has several disadvantages. *First,* while the approach of [11] works well for popular topics, if the topic of interest is not of broad interest (e.g., a news article in a local newspaper or an event in a small town), the random sample may not have enough relevant tweets for the approach to learn the set of important phrases resulting in poor performance. *Second,* it is limited to where the system can be provided with a classifier that, given a tweet, could determine whether the tweet is relevant to the topic or not. *Third,* since the approach of [11] does not support a feedback procedure, there is no way to detect if a phrase does not result in collecting relevant tweets and avoid it in consecutive iterations. *Finally,* since it processes a large number of sample tweets, its computational overhead is high.

In this paper, strategy we have designed in building a *Tweet Acquisition System (TAS)* [16]. TAS starts with an initial set of phrases of relevance to the topic of interest. Such phrases could either be specified by the user and/or learnt through knowledge bases or topical content from other sources (e.g., news stories). At any instance, TAS maintains an estimate of the relative degree of importance for each phrase and uses such a model to dynamically ascertain the relevance of the incoming tweets collected to the topic of interest. The relevance measure incorporates also features about the tweeter (i.e., the person who posted the tweet), as well as, the statistics of pattern co-occurrences.

CIKM'16, October 24-28, 2016, Indianapolis, IN, USA

DOI: http://dx.doi.org/10.1145/2983323.2983693

TAS follows an iterative process with the objective of maximizing the recall by automatically changing the query and updating the set of phrases representing the topic of interest. The basic intuition is that the "current" patterns trending in relevant tweets can help retrieve more relevant tweets in the "near" future and furthermore "repetitive co-occurrence" of terms can help identify additional patterns that may empower the acquisition system. TAS uses a reinforcement learning algorithm to adaptively select a set of phrases that strike a balance between exploring the importance of different phrases and that of exploiting the phrases it has determined to be of high retrieval quality.

2. OVERVIEW OF TAS

In TAS, the client defines interest I by providing a cohesive set of phrases $I.P$ with a subtext of the topic of interest. A phrase p_i in TAS is a triple (k, w, l), where $p_i.k$ is a set of terms, $p_i.l$ is a nullable location bounding box and $p_i.w$ is the weight that gives a comparative measure of how distinctive p_i is for the corresponding interest. Table 1 illustrates an example for an interest in "US Presidential Debate". The last phrase, states that a tweet from California having both keywords "clinton" and "drought" in its text has a 90% chance of being relevant to the topic of interest of the client.

Table 1: Example Phrases of an Interest

Terms(k)	Weight(w)	Location(l)
"presidential debate"	0.8	
"republicans debate"	0.7	
"democrats debate"	0.6	
"clinton drought"	0.9	33.71,-117.89,33.57,-117.78

In TAS we define a tweet t as a tuple: (k, u, τ, l), where $t.k$ is the textual vector of t, $t.u$ is the embedded information of the Twitter user who posted the tweet, $t.\tau$ is the timestamp of t and $t.l$ is the nullable location information where the tweet has been posted from.

Match: Tweet t matches phrase p_i if all the terms in $p_i.k$ are present in $t.k$, regardless of order and ignoring the case. It matches a set of phrases $\{p_1, ...p_j\}$ if it matches *ALL* the phrases $\{p_1, ...p_j\}$, also it matches the interest I if there is *At Least One* phrase $p_i \in I.P$ that t matches p_i.

Relevance: Not every matching tweet is relevant. TAS uses a dynamic relevance model based on the representation of the topic of interest, phrase level correlated patterns and the history of the tweeter in posting relevant tweets to determine relevance of a tweet to the interest.

TAS Iterations: TAS follows an iterative process with two iterations nested inside each other. Each inner iteration δ_i begins by selecting a set of phrases to query Twitter and lasts as long as TAS collects $|\delta|$ number of relevant tweets. An outer iteration Δ_j, consists of $|\Delta|$ number of internal iterations. The set of tweets captured in Δ_j is used by TAS to dynamically adapt the representation of the topic of interest before starting Δ_{j+1}.

The overall flow of TAS is shown in Algorithm 1. It initiates by generating a query *(line 6)* and collecting tweets based on the filter endpoint of the Twitter's streaming API. The filter endpoint allows a limited number of track phrases to monitor the live stream of tweets [9]. Then TAS receives tweets matching the query *(line 7)*.

Query Generation: At the beginning of each δ_i, the `Query Generator` generates q_j by selecting a set of phrases $q_j.P \subseteq I.P$ such that $|q_j.P| \leq B_p$ where B_p is the phrase budget.

Algorithm 1: High-Level Flow of TAS

```
   input : an interest I, the budget B_p,
   output: a set of collected tweets
1  if |I.P| ≤ B_p then
2      return;
3  j = 0 //index of the outer iteration
4  while Acquisition.IsRunning do
5      for i = 1 to |Δ| do
6          q ← GenerateQuery(I, B_p)[Sec. 3];
7          δ_i ← Acquisition.StartListening(q);
8          for t ∈ δ_i do
9              t.rel ← CheckRelevance(t, I)[Sec. 4];
10         Store(δ_i);
11         Acquisition.UpdateStatistics(δ_i, I);
12         Δ_j ← Δ_j + δ_i;
13     I ← MaintainTopic(I, Δ_j);
14     j = j + 1
```

Topic Maintenance: By the end of each outer iteration, TAS may dynamically add new phrases with new patterns after logging repetitive concurrences of patterns in relevant tweets in the coarser iteration of the system or drop/modify existing phrases in $I.P$ *(line 13)*.

Updating Statistics In order to choose the set of phrases during query generation and/or phrases during topic maintenance, TAS maintains statistics about the tweets it captures during its iterations. In particular, for each phrase $p_i \in I.P$, two pieces of information are maintained:

- **Tweet Rate:** $f(p_i)$ represents the rate of tweets matching p_i in *tweets/sec*.
- **Probability of Relevance:** $p(R|p_i)$ represents the probability that a tweet matching p_i being relevant to the topic of interest.

In addition to the above, TAS maintains similar statistics for a set of phrases $\{p_1, ..., p_j\}$. For instance, $f(p_1, ..., p_j)$ represents the rate of tweets matching the set of phrases $\{p_1, ..., p_j\}$ in *tweets/sec*. When TAS starts, it initializes the probability of relevance of single phrases with their initial weights and sets all single phrase tweet rates equal to 1 ($\forall p_i \in I.P, \quad p(R|p_i) = p_i.w, \quad f(p_i) = 1$). For pairs of phrases $\forall p_i, p_j \in I.P \land p_i \neq p_j$, TAS initializes its statistics as $\quad p(R|p_i, p_j) = max(p_i.w, p_j.w), \quad f(p_i, p_j) = 1$. We adopt a Bayesian approach to update statistics in TAS as more information becomes available but due to space reasons, we omit details here.

This paper focusses on Query Generation and details about Topic Maintenance/Updating Statistics can be found in a longer version of the paper [16].

3. QUERY GENERATION

At the beginning of each iteration, due to limitations by Twitter, TAS selects a subset from the set of potential phrases. We refer to this process as *Query Generation*. TAS is designed as a multi-client system, in which Twitter imposed phrase budget is split amongst clients. We will limit the phrase budget in our experiments to a portion of the imposed limit by Twitter.

3.1 Probabilistic Query Coverage

The goal of the query generation is to select phrases to maximize the number of relevant tweets collected. We formalize the goal by defining the concept of query coverage.

Query Coverage: Assume that we are given a phrase set $I.P$ and let q_i be a query such that $q_i.P \subseteq I.P$. The coverage of q_i, denoted as $Cov(q_i.P, I.P)$, and defined in Eq. 1, reflects the proportion of the target tweets covered by q_i.

$$Cov(q_i.P, I.P) = \frac{|\bigcup_{p_j \in q_i.P} R(T(p_j), I)|}{|\bigcup_{p_k \in I.P} R(T(p_k), I)|} \quad (1)$$

In Eq. 1, $T(p_j)$ represents the set of tweets matching phrase p_j over the next iteration and $R(T(p_j), I)$ represents the subset of relevant tweets to the topic of interest I from $T(p_j)$. Intuitively, the numerator of Eq. 1 reflects the number of relevant tweets covered by q_i, while the denominator reflects the total number of relevant tweets covered by $I.P$. Since we do not know $\forall p_j \in I.P, R(T(p_j), I)$, apriori, we cannot directly compute the coverage of all possible query selections and choose the one that maximizes coverage. We, thus, define a probabilistic version of the query coverage which we can estimate using phrase level statistics gathered by TAS.

Probabilistic Query Coverage: We estimate the coverage of a query using the *Inclusion-Exclusion* principle having estimates for effectiveness of phrase in $I.P$ as:

$$\hat{Cov}(Q, I.P) = \frac{\sum_{k=1}^{|Q|} (-1)^{K-1} \sum_{\substack{\forall S \subseteq Q \\ |S|=k \\ S=\{p_{i1},\ldots,p_{ik}\}}} f(p_{i_1}, \ldots, p_{i_k}) p(R|p_{i_1}, \ldots, p_{i_k})}{\sum_{l=1}^{|I.P|} (-1)^{l-1} \sum_{\substack{\forall R \subseteq I.P \\ |R|=l \\ R=\{p_{j1},\ldots,p_{jl}\}}} f(p_{j_1}, \ldots, p_{j_l}) p(R|p_{j_1}, \ldots, p_{j_l})} \quad (2)$$

where the denominator in Eq. 2 is a constant for all possible queries at each instance of query generation. Without loss of generality, we remove the constant denominator from the Eq. 2 and we refer to $\hat{Cov}(Q, I.P)$ as $Cov(Q, I.P)$ in the remaining of this paper.

3.2 Query Generation

Having defined the concept of query coverage, we can now define the goal of query generation more formally.

Definition 1. *(Query Generation). Let $I.P = \{p_1, \ldots, p_{|I.P|}\}$ be a set of phrases for the topic of interest I. Given a positive number $B_p \in N^+$, where $B_p \leq |I.P|$, the goal of the query generation is to find a set $Q \subseteq I.P$ of size $|Q| \leq B_p$, such that $Cov(Q, I.P)$ is maximized.*

In other words, the goal is to find the optimal query Q^* such that $Q^* = \arg\max_{Q \subseteq I.P, |Q| \leq B_p} Cov(Q, I.P)$. The query generation leads to the following challenges:

(a) How should we estimate the rate and probability of relevance for a (set of) phrases? As the iterations proceed, we obtain more statistics about the phrases that have been selected so far. We can, therefore, update our initial belief to come up with more accurate assessment of these parameters.

(b) A query selection mechanism can easily fall into a local trap. First, the probabilities and rates we determine are only estimates. If a phrase p_i is better compared to p_j, and we always select it, the system may improve the estimate for p_i, but will never update the probability and rate for p_j. This is further a problem since twitter is dynamic and as a function of time a phrase's value may change. So we need an adaptive mechanism that allows us to learn statistics of all phrases so that we do not lose an important phrase.

(c) Query coverage, just like most max coverage problems studied in the literature [18, 3], is NP-hard. We need efficient ways to solve the query coverage problem.

For (a) we use incremental updates based on bayesian analysis [16]. We address (b) using a *Reinforcement Learning* approach by mapping our problem to a *Multi-armed Bandit (MAB)* problem and (c) in Sec. 3.4.

3.3 Combinatorial MAB Framework

TAS achieves adaptive acquisition by using an explore-exploit strategy for query generation. In particular, it uses a Multi-armed Bandit (MAB) [5, 22] approach. The query generation problem can be viewed as an instance of *Combinatorial MAB (CMAB)* [2], where the gambler is allowed to select a subset of k arms (a.k.a, super arms). In query generation, each phrase in $I.P$ can be viewed as a simple arm associated with a set of i.i.d. random outcomes with an unknown expectation μ_i. Thus, $\mu = (\mu_1, \mu_2, \ldots, \mu_{|I.P|})$ is the vector of expectations of all phrases. We view the queries $Q \subseteq 2^{[|I.P|]}$, where $|Q| \leq B_p$ as super arms. We denote the expected reward for Q as $r_\mu(Q) = \mathbf{E}[R_t(Q)]$ where $R_t(Q)$ is a non-negative random variable denoting the reward of round t when super arm Q is played. The most common performance measure for bandit algorithms is the total expected regret defined as the gap between the expected reward achieved by the algorithm and that achieved by an algorithm always selecting the best arm. In CMAB, bound on rate of growth of the regret is $O(\log n)$.

Algorithm 2: Combinatorial UCB

input : an interest I, the budget B_p,
output: a set of selected phrases for the topic of interest I as Q

For each phrase p_i, maintain: (1) variable T_i as the total number of times p_i is queried so far, initially 0; (2) variable $\hat{\mu}_i$ as the latest outcome $Cov(\{p_i\}, I.P)$ of phrase p_i, initially 1.
$t \leftarrow 0$
while *Acquisition.IsRunning* **do**
  $t \leftarrow t + 1$
  for *each phrase* $p_i \in I.P$ **do**
    set $\bar{\mu}_i = min(\hat{\mu}_i + \sqrt{\frac{3 ln t}{2T_i}}, 1)$
  $Q = Oracle(\bar{\mu}_1, \bar{\mu}_2, \ldots, \bar{\mu}_{|I.P|})$
  Query Q, observe outcomes of phrases in the Q, update all T_i's and $\hat{\mu}_i$'s.
return Q;

Algorithm 2 shows the Combinatorial UCB (CUCB) algorithm. After each iteration, CUCB maintains an empirical mean $\hat{\mu}_i$ for each p_i. More precisely, the value of $\hat{\mu}_i$ after updating phrase statistics is $Cov(\{p_i\}, I.P)$. The actual expectation vector $\bar{\mu}$ given to the oracle contains an adjustment term for each $\hat{\mu}_i$, which depends on the round number t and the number of times phrase p_i has been queried (stored in variable T_i). Then CUCB plays the super arm (query) returned by the oracle and update variables T_i's and $\hat{\mu}_i$'s accordingly. Note that in our model all phrases have bounded support on $[0, 1]$, but with the adjustment $\bar{\mu}_i$ may exceed 1. If such $\bar{\mu}_i$ is illegal to the oracle, we simply replace it with 1. Since replacing any value larger than 1 with 1 does not violate monotonicity and bounded smoothness of the reward function we directly use the original $\bar{\mu}_i$ and the bound on the regret is not affected.

Oracle: The *oracle* in algorithm 2 is a mechanism to efficiently solve the optimization problem of the probabilistic coverage model in Def.(1). We propose an algorithm for efficiently computing the maximum coverage.

3.4 Computing Query Coverage

Identifying a subset of phrases to maximize coverage defined in Eq.(2), requires TAS to enumerate all subset of phrases in $I.P$ which is exponential [1]. In this section we propose a greedy algorithm that has an approximation bound for computing probabilistic coverage that achieves the same goal, but can be computed efficiently.

3.4.1 Greedy Approximation Bound

To develop the greedy algorithm with approximation bound, we first show the submodularity of the *coverage* model.

Definition 2. *(Submodularity). Given a finite set $I.P$, a set function $f : 2^{|I.P|} \rightarrow \mathbb{R}$ is submodular iff for any two sets $Q \subseteq Q' \subseteq I.P$ and $p \in Q' \setminus I.P$ it holds that $f(Q \cup \{p\}) - f(Q) \geq f(Q' \cup \{p\}) - f(Q')$*

That is, for a submodular f, adding p to a smaller subset of a set will have larger incremental impact on f than adding p to the set itself. The connection between submodulaity and coverage of a query is very intuitive: adding an phrase to a small query will have larger incremental impact compared to that of the same query with many more phrases added.

Lemma 1. *$Cov(., I.P)$ is a non-decreasing submodular set function.* ***Proof.*** *See [16].*

In the context of non-decreasing submodular set function f where $f(\varnothing) = 0$, it has been proven in [13] that the greedy algorithm that always selects the object whose addition maximizes the function f produces a solution with approximation ratio $(1 - 1/e)$, where e is the base of the natural logarithm. That is, the algorithm yields a solution that is at least $(1 - 1/e)$ fraction of the optimal solution.

3.4.2 Greedy Algorithm

The outline of the algorithm is shown in Algorithm 3. It starts with an empty query Q. At every step of the process, the algorithm traverses the remaining phrases in $I.P \setminus Q$ and adds into Q the phrase p^* whose addition will lead to maximum coverage of $I.P$ by the resulting set $Q \cup \{p^*\}$.

Algorithm 3: Greedy Phrase Selection

```
input : an interest I, the budget B_p,
output: a set of selected phrases for I as Q
Q ← ∅
while |Q| ≤ B_p do
    p* ← arg max_{p∈I.P\Q} Cov(Q ∪ {p}, I.P)
    Q ← Q ∪ {p*}
return Q
```

In order to make the computation of coverage $Cov(Q \cup \{p^*\}, I.P)$ even more efficient, one approach is to incrementaly update it as:

$$Cov(Q \cup \{p^*\}, I.P) =$$
$$Cov(Q, I.P) + f(p^*)p(R|p^*) - \sum_{i=1}^{|Q|} f(p^*, p_i)p(R|p^*, p_i).$$

[1]It can be proven by a reduction from the Maximum Coverage problem that maximizing $Cov(Q, I.P)$ is NP-Hard [18].

4. CHECKING FOR RELEVANCE

In TAS, we measure relevance of incoming tweets to the interest in order to select phrases during query generation (Sec. 3). Difficulty in determining relevance arises due to:

- The short and ill-structured nature of text in tweets.
- The dynamic nature of Twitter where the terms used to refer to the topic shift quickly.

The relevance of a tweet t to the topic I, denoted by $R(t, I)$ is measured using a combination of three factors: phrase based relevance (R_t), the relevance based on the proximity of the textual vector of the tweet to the clusters of acquired relevant tweets to the interest I (R_c) and the history of the tweeter who posted the tweet in posting relevant tweets to the topic of interest in the past (R_u). The overall relevance is computed as a combination of the three factors as $R(t, I) = w_t.R_t + w_c.R_c + w_u.R_u$ where w_t, w_c and w_u are weights specifying the importance of each factor in determining the relevance of incoming tweet t to I. These weights, assigned by the client, can be different based on the characteristics of the topic of interest.

Phrase Based Relevance (R_t): Given a tweet t containing terms $t.k$, we define the phrase-based relevance of t to the interest I with a set of phrases $I.P = \{p_1, ...p_{|I.P|}\}$, denoted $R_t(t, I)$ by first defining relevance of a tweet to a given phrase p_i (denoted as $R_p(t, p_i)$) as defined below:

$$R_p(t, p_i) = \begin{cases} p(R|p_i)|p_i.k \cap t.k|/|p_i.k| & p_i.l = null \\ p(R|p_i)(\alpha.|p_i.k \cap t.k|/|p_i.k| + \\ \quad (1-\alpha)LP(t, p_i)) & \text{otherwise} \end{cases}$$

The function $LP(t, p_i)$ shows the proximity of t to $p_i.l$ with a number in $[0, 1]$, where $LP(t, p_i) = 1$ means a location matches with strong evidence (e.g. geo-tag point of t being in the location bounding box of p_i). Essentially, $R_p(t, p_i)$ is a product of the probability of relevance of p_i to the interest times the degree of match between t and p_i. We compute $R_t(t, I)$ based on all the phrases in I as follows:

$$R_t(t, I) = \max_{p_i \in I.P} R_p(t, p_i) +$$
$$(\sum_{p_i \in I.P} R_p(t, p) - \max_{p_i \in I.P} R_p(t, p_i))/(|I.P|-1)(1 - \max_{p_i \in I.P} R_p(t, p_i))$$

In the computation above, $R_t(t, I)$ is computed as sum of the relevance based on the best matching phrase as well as partial relevance of other phrases in $P.I$.

Clue Relevance (R_c): We also compute relevance based on the observed frequent patterns in relevant tweets that match other phrases in $I.P$. For each phrase $p_i \in I.P$, TAS maintains a set of frequent patterns (extracted using Apriori algorithm [4]) $FP(p_i)$ such that the patterns have a given level of support. For a tweet t retrieved due to a match to phrase p_i, we compute if it contains any of these frequent patterns associated with other phrases. If the number of such patterns contained in t is more than a threshold γ, we associate a clue-relevance measure R_c to 1. That is,

$$|\bigcup_{p_j \in (I.P - \{p_i\})} \{s \in FP(p_j) | s \subset t.k \wedge s \notin I.P\}| > \gamma$$

User History (R_u): A tweet t has a higher chance to be relevant to a topic of interest, if the Twitter user $t.u$ who posted t, had posted relevant tweets in the past. The user relevance $R_u(t)$ is equal to the maximum of the average relevance of all the past tweets by $t.u$ and the average relevance of tweets posted by $t.u$ in the latest iteration.

5. EXPERIMENTAL EVALUATION

In this section, we study the performance of TAS in the online **Twitter Stream** setting. We conduct experiments for the TAS and the baselines all starting at the same time on different machines assuming the returning results are all from the same sample of the Twitter stream.

Tweet Normalization: We focus on English tweets using a simple classifier based on a given dictionary. We also remove stop words (e.g. "the") and common special Twitter terms (e.g. "rt") from the text of the incoming tweet.

Topic of Interest: In order to show that TAS works for any topic of interest, we evaluated TAS with different topics based on news articles that were being discussed during the experimentation period [1]. We manually chose news articles from a wide range of topics with different popularities on Twitter (broadness) to show the effectiveness of TAS on *broad as well as more specific topics* from *different topical categories.* We obtain the initial representation for each news article by parsing the corresponding web page and extracting the most important phrases from it. In order to identify the most important phrases from a web page, we have considered the structural information of the web page (e.g., title, headings, formatting) as well as the textual content itself. We believe the important phrases in a news article are distinguishing to identify relevant content elsewhere. We approximate the comparative broadness of a topic of interest considering number of tweets mentioning the topic of corresponding news article. We categorize them in three levels of broadness: narrow, semi-broad and broad and then we select from different levels of broadness. In order to cover a general set of topics, we choose news articles from Crisis, Entertainment, Politics, News and Sport categories based on their posted categories on original websites (e.g., CNN).

Baseline Methods: We compared the performance of TAS to the following baselines:

- **BaseM** captures target tweets for a topic of interest using a static list of B_p most important phrases from the initial representation of the topic of interest.
- **ATM** is the state of the art in topic focused Twitter monitoring based on a given classifier [11].

TAS Parameters: TAS uses a relatively large number of parameters in its various components/sub-algorithms (e.g., English language classifer, stop word remover, relevance model, size of iterations, etc.). While it would be interesting to explore which of these parameters, if any, could be learnt automatically, such an exploration is beyond the scope of our current paper. In TAS, the parameters have been set manually by considering performance over a large number of example queries to keep the evaluation unbiased. In our experiments, the following values are used for the system parameters: $|\Delta| = 5$, $\tau = 0.5$, $\eta = 1$, $w_t = 0.5$, $w_c = 0.3$, $w_u = 0.2$, $\alpha = 0.7$ in $R_p(t, p_i)$, $\gamma = 2$ in Clue Relevance.

Evaluation Criteria: The ultimate goal of TAS is to maximize the number of collected target tweets (viz. "recall" in IR). We note that because of the sample nature of the Twitter API's output, to be able to maximize the recall, the system should improve precision as well. Since we do not have access to all the tweets, we can not compute the real recall of different techniques. Similar to search engine evaluation [10] where there is no access to all the possible results, we report relative recall. Relative recall is the proportion of tweets that any specific technique retrieves of the total or relevant tweets retrieved by all systems.

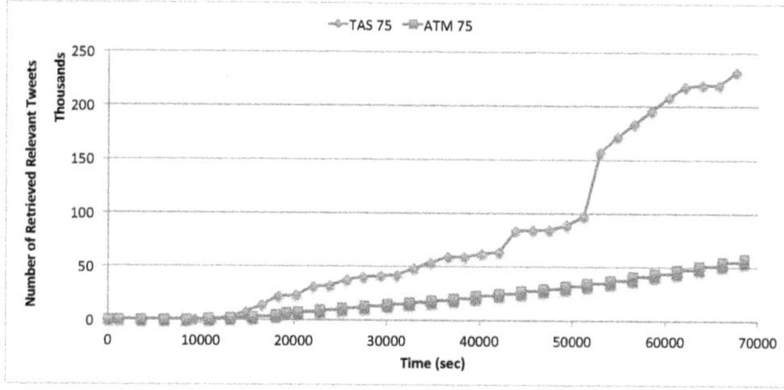

Figure 1: TAS vs. ATM: Topic 75

5.1 Experimental Results

We empirically confirm that TAS outperforms other methods in acquiring relevant tweets to the interest of client on the stream of tweets. We conducted experiments to compare TAS with each baseline separately on collecting relevant tweets for 20 selected news articles. Due to the limited space, we report detailed results for a few of topics shown in Table 2. We also report the overall results for all the topics.

Table 2: Streaming Topics of Interest

ID	Category	Topic	Source	Broadness
75	Crisis	Porter Ranch Gas Leak	LATimes	Narrow
85	Entertainment	Star Wars	CNN	Broad
95	Politics	Malia Obama	CNN	Semibroad
105	News	Birth on Plane	CNN	Narrow
115	Politics	White House Dinner	CNN	Broad

Each experiment is based on a concurrent execution of TAS with baselines simultaneously. Since Twitter has some restrictions on number of concurrent connections from an IP address, for our experiments on live Twitter stream, we use separate machines with different registered application keys. We use the same configuration (e.g. B_p) on all the systems. In these experiments, $B_p = 50$ and the size of each inner iteration is 1000 for broad, 500 for semi-broad and 200 for narrow topics. The duration of acquisition is different for different topics in the range of 12 to 24 hours.

Classifiers: Since ATM works based on a given classifier, in order to compare it with TAS we train classifiers as discussed in [11]. We obtain a classifier of a topic in the following steps. First, we define different types of features including textual features and other additional features (e.g., whether a tweet is from a news agent). Then, we manually label a set of tweets for training (selected from the initial output of the BaseM results), and train classifiers with different models (Naive Bayes and Support Vector Machine). Finally, we select the best one to use. For example, we created training sets of size 200 and 1000 manually labeled tweets for topics 75 and 85 respectively. Here, we emphasize that our focus is not designing classifiers and we train classifiers just for the purpose of fairly comparing TAS with ATM.

Table 3: Streaming Experiment Summary

Method	Topic 75			Topic 85			Topic 95			Topic 105			Topic 115			Overall		
	P	RR	F1	P	RR	F1	P	RR	F1	P	RR	F1	P	RR	F1	P	RR	F1
TAS	0.48	**0.95**	**0.64**	0.58	0.66	**0.61**	0.33	**0.84**	0.47	0.6	0.75	**0.67**	0.37	**0.81**	0.51	0.43	**0.82**	**0.57**
ATM	0.06	0.24	0.09	0.17	0.73	0.28	0.08	0.50	0.14	0.19	0.33	0.24	0.22	0.83	0.35	0.3	0.49	0.35
BaseM	0.81	0.1	0.17	0.88	0.12	0.22	0.72	0.21	0.31	0.93	0.24	0.38	0.79	0.17	0.28	0.81	0.14	0.28

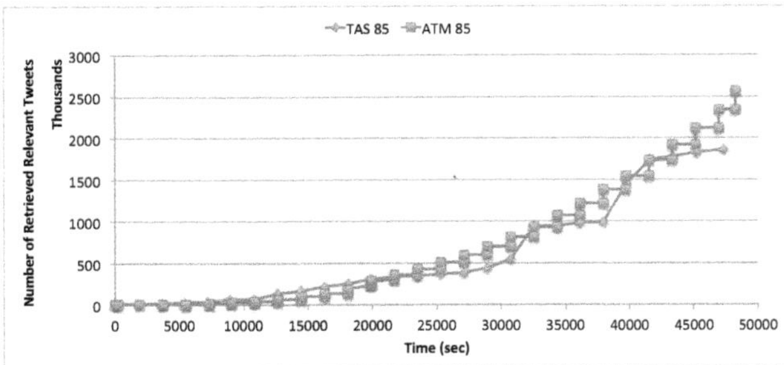

Figure 2: TAS vs. ATM: Topic 85

Figures 1, 2 show the tweet acquisition trend over time for topics 75 and 85 respectively. As expected, Figure 1 clearly shows the effectiveness of TAS in capturing more relevant tweets compared to ATM for the finer topic of interest 75. Figure 2 illustrates the comparable effectiveness of TAS in acquiring relevant tweets to coarser topics such as 85. Also, ATM resulted in capturing a huge number of irrelevant tweets that shows the need for post processing. Computational complexity is not an important factor since all approaches collect tweets with the speed of stream.

Since we are using classifiers, we could measure the precision (P) and the Relative Recall (RR) of TAS and the baselines. We also report the F1-Score (computed as $F1 = 2 \times \frac{P \times RR}{P + RR}$) of each method. Table 3 clearly shows significant improvements in overall performance (based on RR and F1 score) of TAS over the baselines. As expected, the performance gap increases when the topics are more specific (e.g., topics 75, 105).

6. CONCLUSIONS AND FUTURE WORK

In this paper, we study the task of adaptive collection of target tweets for a topic of interest with Twitter APIs. We make the following contributions: We propose TAS that enables collecting target tweets in an online adaptive way. The cornerstone of our approach is the phrase selection strategy that uses reinforcement learning to iterative find a set of phrases to provide consistent good coverage. In addition, we develop a tweet relevance model, which enables checking the relevance of collected tweets to the interest. Finally, we conduct extensive experiments to evaluate TAS and demonstrate that it greatly improves the baseline methods.

7. ACKNOWLEDGMENTS

This work was supported in part by NSF grants CNS-1527536, CNS-1545071, CNS-1450768, CNS-1450768, CNS-1059436, CNS-1118114.

8. REFERENCES

[1] List of tas experimental topics. http://www.uci311.ics.uci.edu/sodas/tas.html.

[2] W. C. 0013, Y. Wang, and Y. Yuan. Combinatorial multi-armed bandit: General framework and applications. In *ICML*, volume 28 of *JMLR Proceedings*, pages 151–159. JMLR.org, 2013.

[3] R. Agrawal, S. Gollapudi, A. Halverson, and S. Ieong. Diversifying search results. In *WSDM*, WSDM, pages 5–14, New York, NY, USA, 2009. ACM.

[4] R. Agrawal and R. Srikant. Fast algorithms for mining association rules in large databases. VLDB, pages 487–499, San Francisco, CA, USA, 1994. Morgan Kaufmann Publishers Inc.

[5] P. Auer, N. Cesa-Bianchi, and P. Fischer. Finite-time analysis of the multiarmed bandit problem. *Mach. Learn.*, 47(2-3):235–256, May 2002.

[6] M. Boanjak, E. Oliveira, J. Martins, E. Mendes Rodrigues, and L. Sarmento. Twitterecho: A distributed focused crawler to support open research with twitter data. WWW, pages 1233–1240, New York, NY, USA, 2012. ACM.

[7] J. Bollen, H. Mao, and X. Zeng. Twitter mood predicts the stock market. *Journal of Computational Science*, 2(1):1–8, 2011.

[8] K. Joseph, P. L. Landwehr, and K. M. Carley. An approach to selecting keywords to track on twitter during a disaster. In *ISCRAM*, State College, PA, 2014.

[9] K. Joseph, P. M. Landwehr, and K. M. Carley. Two 1% s dont make a whole: Comparing simultaneous samples from twitters streaming api. In *Social Computing, Behavioral-Cultural Modeling and Prediction*, pages 75–83. Springer, 2014.

[10] B. S. Kumar and J. Prakash. Precision and relative recall of search engines: A comparative study of google and yahoo. *Singapore Journal of Library & Information Management*, 38(1):124–137, 2009.

[11] R. Li, S. Wang, and K. C. Chang. Towards social data platform: Automatic topic-focused monitor for twitter stream. *PVLDB*, 6(14):1966–1977, 2013.

[12] W. Magdy and T. Elsayed. Adaptive method for following dynamic topics on twitter. In *ICWSM*, 2014.

[13] G. Nemhauser, L. Wolsey, and M. Fisher. An analysis of approximations for maximizing submodular set functions–i. *Mathematical Programming*, 14(1):265–294, 1978.

[14] M. Osborne, S. Moran, R. McCreadie, A. von Lunen, M. Sykora, E. Cano, N. Ireson, C. Macdonald, I. Ounis, Y. He, T. Jackson, F. Ciravegna, and A. O'Brien. *Real-time detection, tracking, and monitoring of automatically discovered events in social media.* 2014.

[15] S. Petrović, M. Osborne, and V. Lavrenko. Streaming first story detection with application to twitter. HLT, pages 181–189, Stroudsburg, PA, USA, 2010. Association for Computational Linguistics.

[16] M. Sadri, S. Mehrotra, and Y. Yu. Online adaptive topic focused tweet acquisition. Technical report, University of California, Irvine, 2016.

[17] T. Sakaki, M. Okazaki, and Y. Matsuo. Earthquake shakes twitter users: Real-time event detection by social sensors. WWW, pages 851–860, New York, NY, USA, 2010. ACM.

[18] Proof of probabilistic maximum coverage being np-hard. http://www.ics.uci.edu/dvk/pub/sigmod14ext.pdf.

[19] Real-time filtering task. https://github.com/lintool/twitter-tools/wiki/TREC-2015-Track-Guidelines.

[20] A. Tumasjan, T. Sprenger, P. Sandner, and I. Welpe. Predicting elections with twitter: What 140 characters reveal about political sentiment. In *ICWSM*, pages 178–185, 2010.

[21] X. Wang, F. Wei, X. Liu, M. Zhou, and M. Zhang. Topic sentiment analysis in twitter: A graph-based hashtag sentiment classification approach. CIKM, pages 1031–1040, New York, NY, USA, 2011. ACM.

[22] Y. Yue and T. Joachims. Interactively optimizing information retrieval systems as a dueling bandits problem. ICML, pages 1201–1208, New York, NY, USA, 2009. ACM.

Optimizing Nugget Annotations with Active Learning

Gaurav Baruah[1], Haotian Zhang[1], Rakesh Guttikonda[1],
Jimmy Lin[1], Mark D. Smucker[2], Olga Vechtomova[2]

[1] David R. Cheriton School of Computer Science
[2] Department of Management Sciences
University of Waterloo

{gbaruah, haotian.zhang, rguttiko, jimmylin, mark.smucker, ovechtomova}@uwaterloo.ca

ABSTRACT

Nugget-based evaluations, such as those deployed in the TREC Temporal Summarization and Question Answering tracks, require human assessors to determine whether a nugget is present in a given piece of text. This process, known as nugget annotation, is labor-intensive. In this paper, we present two active learning techniques that prioritize the sequence in which candidate nugget/sentence pairs are presented to an assessor, based on the likelihood that the sentence contains a nugget. Our approach builds on the recognition that nugget annotation is similar to high-recall retrieval, and we adapt proven existing solutions. Simulation experiments with four existing TREC test collections show that our techniques yield far more matches for a given level of effort than baselines that are typically deployed in previous nugget-based evaluations.

1. INTRODUCTION

In the context of the Cranfield Paradigm [11], we have witnessed the evolution toward more fine-grained batch evaluation methodologies for assessing system outputs. Examples include passage retrieval [1], aspect retrieval [20], and the nugget evaluation methodology [19, 3]. This paper focuses on the nugget annotation phase of the nugget evaluation methodology, where assessors determine if a piece of text contains a particular nugget.

Nuggets represent atomic facts relevant to users' information needs, usually expressed as short natural language phrases. Given a set of nuggets, which can be viewed as an "answer key", assessors must read all system outputs and determine which (if any) nuggets are present—this is called nugget annotation. Once the nuggets have been identified, it is straightforward to compute a final metric based on the matches. It bears emphasizing that the nuggets represent concepts, and thus the nugget matching process requires understanding the *semantics* of the system output—taking into account synonyms, paraphrasing, and other linguistic phenomena. For example, the nugget "the train crashed at the buffer stop" might manifest in system responses as "slammed into the end of the line", "smash into a barrier", and "hit the barrier at the end of the platform". A baseline evaluation workflow, and indeed one that is typically deployed in existing implementations of nugget evaluation methodologies, requires assessors to exhaustively consider all system outputs with respect to all nuggets.

The insight behind our work is the recognition that the process of nugget annotation can be viewed as a high-recall retrieval task, where system outputs represent the "document collection" and the nuggets represent the "topics". Thus, we can exploit recently-developed active learning techniques that have been validated for high-recall retrieval to the nugget annotation problem. The additional wrinkle, however, is that each topic contains multiple nuggets that all (eventually) need to be found. Thus, the question is—in what order shall we "search" for the nuggets? Our answer is to let the active learning technique (the learner) itself tell us where to look next.

The main contribution of this paper is the novel adaptation of a state-of-the-art active learning technique for high-recall retrieval to the problem of nugget annotation. We developed two different matching strategies for letting the learner guide the assessor as to which system output to examine next and what nuggets are likely to be found there: in the greedy approach, the learner simply proposes the system output most likely to contain a nugget (i.e., a nugget-sentence pair is presented as a candidate match for annotation); in an alternative approach, we attempt to maximize the likely number of candidate matches presented to the user. We apply our proposed techniques to simulate the nugget annotation process using four large-scale evaluations from TREC, the QA tracks from 2004–2005 and the Temporal Summarization tracks from 2013–2014. Experimental results show that our techniques yield far more matches for a given level of effort than baselines that are typically deployed in existing nugget-based evaluations.

2. BACKGROUND AND RELATED WORK

2.1 Nugget-Based Evaluations

We begin with a more precise formulation of the problem. In nugget-based evaluations, for a particular information need (i.e., a topic), we have an "answer key" comprising $|N|$ nuggets (expressed as short natural language phrases). We assume that system outputs are discretized into some unit of text (in our case, sentences), and there are $|D|$ such units across all the system outputs we are trying to evaluate.

CIKM'16, October 24 - 28, 2016, Indianapolis, IN, USA

ISBN 978-1-4503-4073-1/16/10...$15.00

DOI: http://dx.doi.org/10.1145/2983323.2983694

test collection	# topics	#identified nuggets |N|	#pooled sentences |D|	match matrix |N| x |D|	avg. #ngts / topic	avg. #upds / topic	#confirmed matches	avg. #conf. matches/topic	uniq. #ngts in matches
TS13	9	1,077	9,113	1,283,298	119.7	1,012.6	4,850	538.9	484
TS14	15	1,394	14,651	1,407,448	92.9	976.7	13,635	909.0	837
QA04	64	580	61,642	471,881	9.1	963.2	3,840	60.0	545
QA05	75	758	496,535	4,981,989	10.1	6,620.5	4,159	55.5	687

Table 1: Statistics of the four TREC test collections used in this study. For confirmed matches, exact duplicates were removed from the judged set of sentences.

The nugget annotation process is to complete an $|N| \times |D|$ matrix with boolean values: true if the nugget is contained in the text and false if not. As discussed above, this matching requires considering the meaning of the system output. Evaluation results are then straightforwardly computed as a function of this match matrix, although for the purposes of this work, the actual metrics are not important, and therefore it is not necessary to keep track of which $d \in D$ was produced by which system. We make the additional simplifying assumption that the cost of nugget matching is a constant, even though the unit of system output (sentences) might vary in length and judging some nuggets may require more cognitive load than others.

Note that for exhaustive evaluation, we must fill the entire match matrix. It would, however, make sense to prioritize the examination of match candidates based on the likelihood that it contains a nugget. This is especially valuable in a scenario where resources are constrained, as it would represent a more efficient use of assessor effort. We do exactly this, guided by active learning techniques.

Four large-scale implementations of the nugget evaluation methodology include the TREC Question Answering (QA) tracks in 2004–2005 [18, 19] and the TREC Temporal Summarization (TS) tracks in 2013–2014 [2, 3]. For the TS tracks, systems were required to return sentences that are relevant and timely with respect to specified newsworthy events (topics). The QA tracks required systems to return responses (sentences) to questions regarding events or entities. For both, the relevance of returned sentences was measured in terms of nuggets contained in them. We used data from all these evaluations to validate our work. To quantify the amount of effort involved in the nugget annotation process, Table 1 lists the number of nuggets identified by assessors for the various tracks. For example, in TS13, there was an average of 119.7 nuggets and 1012.6 sentences per topic with $|N| \times |D| = 1,283,298$ total matches across all topics. For TS13, assessors took on average 15 hours per topic to perform the matching [10].

For the TS tracks, the annotation process was aided by an assistive user interface [2] that lists all sentences to be judged and all nuggets, in two columns. For each relevant sentence, an assessor annotated parts of the sentence that match the corresponding nugget. A nugget can match more than one sentence and a sentence can contain more than one nugget. For QA evaluations, assessors took a similar approach.

We note that researchers have developed automatic techniques for matching nuggets against system outputs based on n-gram overlap, e.g., POURPRE [13] and Nuggeteer [14] in the context of QA. These techniques are useful for rapid formative evaluations, but we believe that human review is still necessary for summative evaluations such as TREC.

To be clear, our work tackles only the nugget annotation process and assumes the existence of a nugget "answer key". These nuggets, however, must come from somewhere: in TREC QA, the nuggets were identified during topic development as well as derived manually from the pooled system outputs by assessors [18], which was a labor-intensive process. Pavlu et al. [15] manually extracted nuggets from returned documents and used features of identified nuggets to prioritize assessment of additional documents. Rajput et al. [16] utilized an active learning feedback loop where "nuggetization" and assessments are interleaved by automatically weighting sentences within documents as candidate nuggets. In this work we tackle the more established workflow where the creation of the nuggets is distinct from the nugget annotation process itself; e.g., in TREC TS, the nuggets were first extracted from Wikipedia articles corresponding to news events that comprised the topics [3].

2.2 Technology-Assisted Review

Technology-assisted review (TAR) applies iterative retrieval to help reviewers identify as many relevant documents as possible from a collection in the context of electronic discovery (eDiscovery). Cormack and Grossman [9] developed an autonomous TAR (AutoTAR) protocol by extending continuous active learning (CAL) for TAR. In CAL, the most likely relevant documents identified using a machine learning method are interactively presented to reviewers for assessment. Application of CAL for TAR maximizes recall while requiring less review effort than comparable methods [8].

AutoTAR was implemented as the baseline model implementation (BMI) for the TREC 2015 Total Recall Track [17]. It initially ranks all documents in the collection with a classifier trained on an initial query (treated as a pseudo-document) and 100 randomly selected documents, which are assumed to be non-relevant. The user is asked to assess the most relevant (i.e., highest scoring) document, and then the classifier is retrained on this new assessment along with the query and 100 new random (assumed non-relevant) documents. In an ideal situation, AutoTAR would repeat this process, selecting the top document for assessment and then retraining on all available assessments. Since this is not computationally practical, AutoTAR requests assessments in exponentially increasing batches, starting with a batch size of one and increasing the batch size by $\text{MAX}(1, 0.1 \cdot$ `batch_size`$)$ each iteration.

The TREC 2015 Total Recall overview paper [17] indicates that the BMI was hard to beat, i.e., no automatic or manual run performed consistently better than the BMI. Given the similarities between identifying relevant documents in a collection and identifying matching nuggets in system responses (both of which require high recall), we adapted AutoTAR to our problem, described next.

3. NUGGET ANNOTATION STRATEGIES

For matching sentences with nuggets, we envision an assistive user interface that presents the assessor with *match*

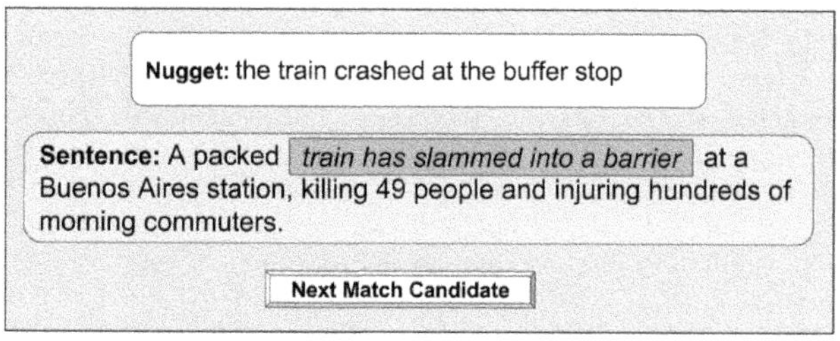

Figure 1: Simulated assessment interface for nugget annotation. An assessor reads the sentence and the nugget, annotates the substring that represents the nugget (if there is a match), and moves on to the next match candidate.

candidates—a nugget and a sentence that is likely to contain the nugget (see Figure 1). The assessor judges whether the sentence indeed contains the nugget and appropriately *annotates* the match (i.e., records a representation of the nugget in the sentence), or rejects the match. The assessor then moves on to the next match candidate. This is repeated until all matches are found or some stopping criterion is met (e.g., the assessor runs out of time or the evaluation runs out of resources). We present a number of nugget annotation strategies that select the next match candidate for presentation.

3.1 Baselines

Let us consider the match matrix (Section 2) as having rows that represent nuggets and columns that represent sentences. One obvious nugget annotation strategy is to consider each sentence in turn and look to see if each nugget is found in it; this strategy can be described as a *column-by-column* (CBC) matching strategy. A converse strategy is to present a nugget at a time to the assessor and match all sentences against the nugget. Here, the item under scrutiny is the nugget and the matches are made *row-by-row* (RBR). The choice of sentence or nugget to be assessed next is arbitrary. Thus, RBR and CBC represent baselines, and indeed quite close to the approaches that have been deployed by previous large-scale evaluations.

3.2 Proposed Techniques

Although the total number of valid matches is the same across strategies, depending on the matching algorithm, as well as the assessment interface, the effort required for complete assessment may vary. Given the various combinations possible, we describe a nugget annotation strategy as the combination of an assistive user interface along with a specific active learning algorithm for matching. We develop two matching strategies and compare them with the CBC and RBR baselines. Each matching strategy takes as input the set D sentences pooled for a topic and the set N nuggets that were identified for the topic. Both strategies follow the general outline of the AutoTAR BMI deployed for the TREC Total Recall track, described in Section 2.2, with one key difference: we train one classifier for each nugget instead of one classifier for the entire topic.

Most Likely Candidate (MLC). The Most Likely Candidate matching strategy presents to the assessor the match candidate (sentence s_i, nugget n_k) that is most likely to result in a positive match, i.e., the likelihood of nugget n_k being present in sentence s_i is the highest across *all* possible match candidate pairs. Initially, a separate classifier is constructed for each nugget in a given topic using the nugget's features. Then, all sentences in D are classified according to each nugget's classifier and the scores are recorded, i.e., a classification score is produced for each element in the match matrix. The (s_i, n_k) pair with the highest global classification score is presented to the assessor for review. The classifier for n_k is retrained after the assessor either confirms (annotates the nugget representation in the sentence) or rejects the match. Once assessed, the match candidate pair (s_i, n_k) is never presented again for assessment. When five match candidates have been assessed, all sentences are rescored against the newly-trained classifiers for each nugget. Since we have multiple classifiers for each topic, we do not retrain the classifiers in increasing batch sizes as in the BMI; instead, we retrain immediately but we recompute sentence scores periodically after a set number of assessments (per above). The process is repeated until a sufficient number of matches are identified or until some specified stopping criterion is met.

Cover Maximum Candidates (CMC). The Cover Maximum Candidates (CMC) matching strategy tries to prioritize sentences that are likely to have multiple matching nuggets for assessment. That is, CMC selects sentences that potentially match multiple nuggets. We extend the assessment interface envisioned in Figure 1 to display M nuggets that are likely to match the sentence.

As in MLC, a classifier is trained for each nugget in a topic. Then, classification scores are computed for the entire match matrix. The sentence s_i that likely matches the most number of nuggets (with classification scores greater than a threshold ϵ) is chosen for assessment. First, all candidate matches that score above the threshold ϵ are shortlisted from the match matrix. Then, from the shortlisted candidate matches, the sentence s_i that is likely to match the most nuggets is selected. Finally, sentence s_i and its top M likely matching nuggets are presented to the assessor for review. The assessor either confirms or rejects each of the M match candidates and the respective nuggets' classifiers are accordingly retrained. All sentences are rescored against the newly-trained classifiers for each nugget after M match candidates are assessed. The process is repeated until a sufficient number of valid matches are found. If there are no scores above ϵ in the match matrix, then we fall back to MLC.

Although the choice of M for CMC is arbitrary, presenting a relatively small number of nuggets at a time serves two purposes: (i) the assessor deals with minimal information overload, and (ii) the match candidates can be displayed on the screen without the need to scroll. In our simulation experiment, one sentence along with at most $M = 5$ nuggets are putatively displayed in the assessment interface. As the probability of presenting non-matching candidates increases in later stages of the assessment process, assessment effort may increase accordingly. We therefore set a global threshold ϵ for filtering the likely match candidates. Without this threshold ϵ or the presentation limit M, we risk falling back to CBC from CMC, since TS topics routinely contain upwards of 50 nuggets. Presenting a large number of nuggets may cause errors as assessment fatigue sets in over time. For our experiments we use logistic regression classifiers for AutoTAR (see Section 5) and through manual observation of the match candidates' classification scores, we set a threshold of $\epsilon = 1$ (corresponding to a match probability of 0.73).

We found that scores above this setting were more likely to be valid matches across all test collections.

Another advantage of using a threshold and presentation limit is that secondary assessors (who are not topic originators) may benefit by having limited information presented to them at any given time. It is possible to tune ϵ and M dynamically according to the status of the classifiers at various stages of assessment, and set optimal values via cross-validation for each test collection. We leave these improvements for future work.

4. EVALUATION METHODOLOGY

Evaluation effort can be measured in a variety of ways, for example, in terms of time or mental energy spent to perform a particular evaluation task (e.g., to judge a document). In nugget annotations, not only do assessors have to judge if a sentence is relevant (i.e., contains a nugget), but they must also provide support by annotating the text content corresponding to the nugget. It is therefore necessary to quantify the effort for various components of the assessment process explicitly. The amount and types of user interactions with the nugget annotation interface differ across matching strategies, but in general, the total effort of using an assessment interface to perform an evaluation can be estimated as the sum of the effort of each interaction [12, 4]. For simplicity, we model effort in abstract units instead of real-world quantities such as time. Of course, the actual effort may be estimated by observing assessor behavior or by utilizing available information about the reading speed of users [6].

We designed our assessment interface (Section 3) to incur negligible memory load on the assessor by explicitly presenting all information needed to reach a decision. In the case of CBC, RBR, and MLC, the assessor considers only a nugget and a sentence at a time. In the case of CMC, the interface eliminates scrolling by presenting a small, fixed number of nuggets to the assessor.

Our basic effort model has the following components:

1. The effort of reading the sentence, λ_{read};
2. The effort of rendering a judgment about the match, λ_{match} (which includes annotating the nugget representation in the sentence if necessary).

Given the effort associated with these actions, we can compute the cost of making a single match as:

$$\text{effort} = \lambda_{read} + \lambda_{match} \quad (1)$$

The total cost of the CBC, RBR, and MLC strategies is the sum of the effort required for each match candidate. For simplicity, we assume unit cost, i.e., $\lambda_{read} = \lambda_{match} = 1$.

For CMC, we need a slightly different effort model. Here as well, reading the sentence incurs effort λ_{read}. Then, considering the first matching nugget incurs effort λ_{match}, as before. However, considering additional nuggets may not incur the full matching effort. This is because after considering the first match, the assessor already has the semantic content of the sentence in short-term working memory, and so considering additional nuggets might not take as much effort. Let us call the effort associated with each subsequent match $\lambda_{match'}$. We currently lack empirical evidence as to what the proper setting of this effort should be, but for these experiments we consider the values $\lambda_{match'} = \{0, 0.25, 0.5, 0.75, 1\}$. In the first case, subsequent matches are "free" (i.e., zero effort), and in the last case, each additional match is just as expensive as the first. These seem like reasonable bounds for effort in practice. Thus, for CMC, we arrive at the following (where $M = 5$):

$$\text{effort} = \lambda_{read} + \lambda_{match} + (M - 1) \cdot \lambda_{match'} \quad (2)$$

Note that in this model for CMC, we assume that each subsequent nugget match has constant cost.

5. EXPERIMENTS AND RESULTS

Our experiments were conducted using the nugget-based test collections from the TREC QA04, QA05, TS13, and TS14 tracks. Each track provides, for each topic, (i) a set of nuggets, (ii) a pool of sentences from system outputs, and (iii) a mapping of nuggets to the assessed sentences (i.e., qrels). It is therefore possible to use these data to evaluate our nugget annotation strategies via simulation, based on the qrels. Table 1 presents statistics for each dataset. Note that since matches were not found by NIST for every nugget, we restricted our experiments to only those that have at least one confirmed match in the system outputs (Table 1; column 10). Also, we observed many duplicate sentences in the judged set for each track. Although adding duplicates of judged sentences for evaluation does not significantly affect the relative effectiveness of systems [5], for our experiments, we removed all exact duplicates and keep only one copy to reduce assessment effort. Finally, we note that QA05 is substantially larger than the other collections in terms of the number of pooled sentences.

Following the AutoTAR process, our implementations use tf-idf Porter-stemmed word features and the Sofia-ML logistic regression classifier.[1] We retained digits as features since numbers are heavily used in nuggets. We removed terms with a document frequency of one due to their sparsity in order to prune the feature space. For our simulation, a given sentence is matched with a particular nugget only once.

5.1 Detailed Topic Analysis

We begin with a detailed analysis of a single topic (topic 10 from TS13) to give the reader an illustration of the behavior of our techniques. This particular topic has 521 unique (non-duplicate) sentences and 27 nuggets, with a total of 349 matches.

Figure 2 shows the matches vs. effort plot comparing MLC to the CBC and RBR baselines. For each curve, each point represents a nugget match and color is used to identify individual nuggets (i.e., all points with the same color represent the same nugget). The slope of the curves can be interpreted as the rate at which we're finding matches—i.e., the steeper the slope, the more nuggets we're finding given a unit of effort. The RBR matching strategy considers each nugget in turn, and cycles through all sentences (with an arbitrary ordering of the nuggets). The CBC matching strategy considers each sentence in turn, and cycles through all nuggets. We see that the MLC strategy switches between nuggets since it proposes the most promising candidate each time—for example, the long run of nugget matches in brown for RBR near the end is prioritized much earlier because it represents a sequence of "easier" and more likely matches.

[1]https://code.google.com/archive/p/sofia-ml/

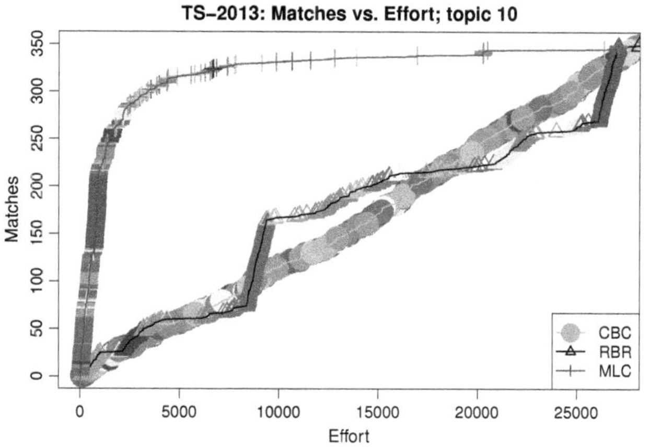

Figure 2: Illustration of how MLC switches between different nuggets, based on the most likely match.

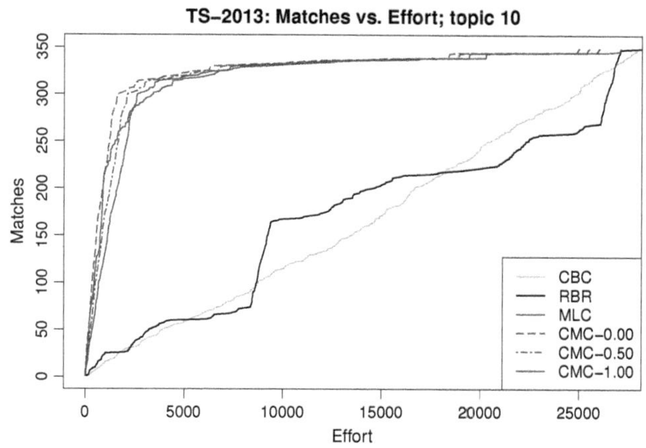

Figure 3: Comparison of CMC, MLC, and the baselines (CBC and RBR) for TS13 topic 10.

Overall, we clearly see that for a given level of effort (x-axis), the MLC strategy finds more matches.

Figure 3 shows the performance of the CMC strategy in comparison with the MLC, CBC and RBR strategies on the same topic (we now remove the point markers for clarity). Recall that CMC presents multiple nuggets that are likely to be contained in the same sentence for assessment (Section 3.2). Matching the first nugget to the sentence incurs full effort. However, as we discussed, consideration of subsequent nuggets may not require full effort, since the assessor already holds the sentence in working memory (Section 4). Unsurprisingly, if we model the effort of matching additional nuggets as zero, $\lambda_{match'} = 0$ in the curve CMC–0.00, then we see that it is the most efficient of all strategies. On the other hand, if matching additional nuggets incurs the full cost of the first match, $\lambda_{match'} = 1$ in the curve CMC–1.00, then the strategy is less efficient than MLC, at least in the initial stages of the simulation. For the intermediate values, $\lambda_{match'} = \{0.25, 0.75\}$, the curves lie between those of $\lambda_{match'} = \{0.0, 1.0\}$, and therefore are not shown for brevity. For this particular topic, the relative performance of MLC vs. CMC depends on the level of effort and the setting of $\lambda_{match'}$, but the overall differences are relatively minor.

5.2 Aggregate Performance

To gauge the performance of a matching strategy across multiple topics in a test collection, we first normalize, for each topic, the effort required for finding all matches using RBR to the range [0,1]. The amount of effort required by the other strategies are then scaled relative to the total RBR effort; note that total CBC effort is the same as the RBR effort. The number of matches is similarly scaled to the range [0,1], which can be interpreted as recall. We then perform a 101-point interpolation (at 1% increments) to plot the match-recall vs. effort for each strategy. The results are shown in Figure 4 for each test collection: TREC QA from 2004 and 2005 (top row), and TREC TS from 2013 and 2014 (bottom row). Note that all figures have the same scales, with the exception of QA05, which has substantially more pooled sentences than the rest (see Table 1).

We find that MLC performs slightly better than CMC on average when $\lambda_{match'} = 1$, i.e., the CMC–1.00 curve, at least in the early stages of the simulation. We might consider this an upper bound on effort, as matching additional nuggets is likely to be cheaper in practice. On the other hand, $\lambda_{match'} = 0$, i.e., the CMC–0.00 curve, should be considered a lower bound on effort, as it makes an unrealistic assumption about assessment effort. We suspect that the real answer lies somewhere between these two curves, but note that there is no appreciable difference between the various strategies across all test collections. However, it is clear that MLC and CMC are much more efficient in finding nugget matches than the RBR and CBC baselines.

6. FUTURE WORK AND CONCLUSIONS

The starting point of this paper is the observation that nugget annotations can be viewed as a high-recall retrieval problem, where system outputs are the "documents" and the nuggets represent the "topics". We have successfully adapted AutoTAR, a highly-effective baseline from the TREC Total Recall tracks, to tackle this problem. We show that by training a separate classifier for each nugget in a topic, we can let active learning techniques guide the assessment process. Although simulation experiments show that our proposed variants are virtually indistinguishable in terms of performance, they are both much more efficient than existing baselines.

There are, however, a number of limitations to our study. We currently use a crude effort model measured in abstract units: actual effort in practice should be measured in terms of physical units such as time, and depends on many additional factors we have not accounted for such as assessor expertise. A more accurate model must also take into account assessor fatigue and learning effects, as our effort parameters are unlikely to remain constant throughout a real evaluation. Calibration against observations of actual human behavior is necessary to further validate our model.

Another issue we have yet to address is the question of when to stop. One simple answer would be to stop when a pre-allocated amount of effort has been expended, but it might be desirable to stop when the assessment process reaches the point of diminishing returns (i.e., it might not be worthwhile to find the "tail" nugget matches that take disproportionate effort). For this, we might also look at solutions developed for high-recall retrieval [7].

Nevertheless, despite these shortcomings, we note that refinements and improvements to our techniques are unlikely to alter the finding that active learning techniques can re-

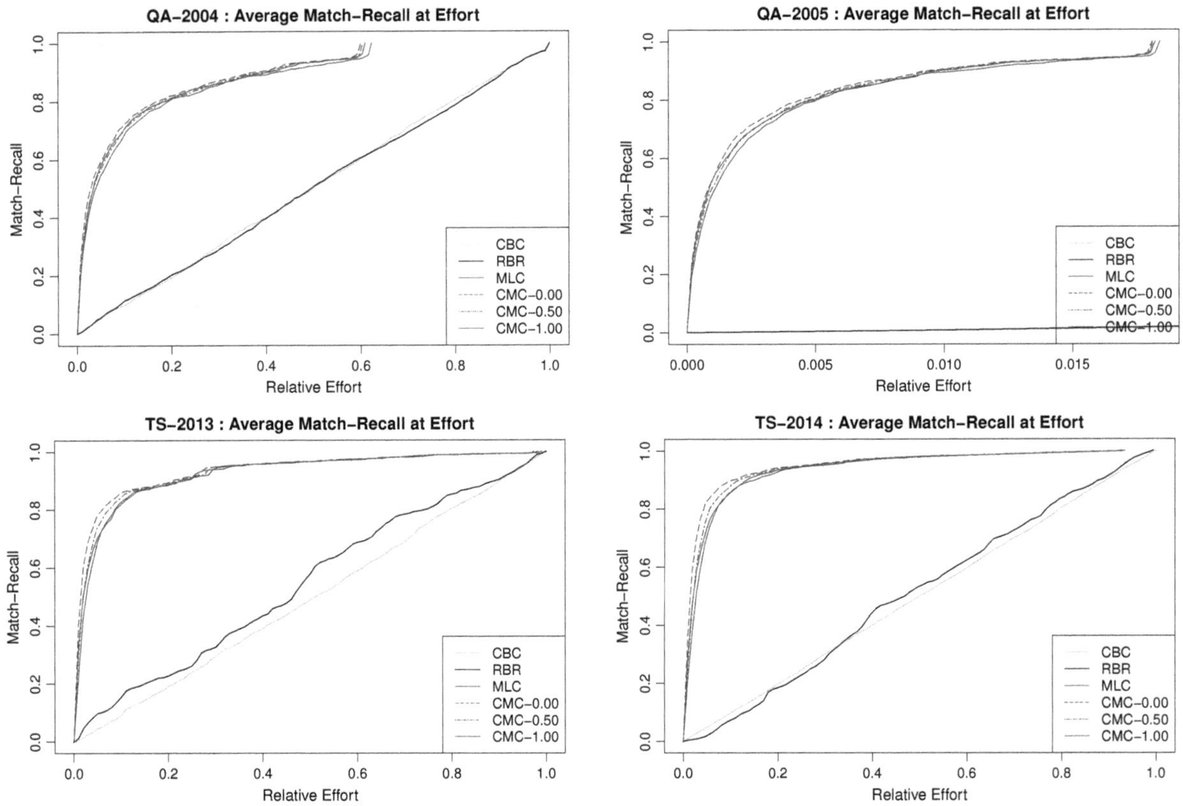

Figure 4: Average interpolated results: QA04 (top, left), QA05 (top, right), TS13 (bottom, left), and TS14 (bottom, right). Note that all graphs are on the same scale except for QA05.

duce the effort associated with nugget annotations. Future nugget-based evaluations should consider deploying the types of techniques that we propose here.

7. ACKNOWLEDGMENTS

We would like to thank Leif Azzopardi for helpful discussions and Adam Roegiest for comments on earlier drafts of this paper. This work was made possible by the facilities of SHARCNET (www.sharcnet.ca) and Compute Canada, and was supported in part by NSERC, in part by a Google Founders Grant, and in part by the University of Waterloo.

8. REFERENCES

[1] J. Allan. HARD Track Overview in TREC 2004 High Accuracy Retrieval from Documents. *TREC*, 2004.
[2] J. A. Aslam, M. Ekstrand-Abueg, V. Pavlu, F. Diaz, and T. Sakai. TREC 2013 Temporal Summarization. *TREC*, 2013.
[3] J. A. Aslam, M. Ekstrand-Abueg, V. Pavlu, F. Diaz, and T. Sakai. TREC 2014 Temporal Summarization. *TREC*, 2014.
[4] L. Azzopardi and G. Zuccon. Building and Using Models of Information Seeking Search and Retrieval: Full Day Tutorial. *SIGIR*, 2015.
[5] G. Baruah, A. Roegiest, and M. D. Smucker. The Effect of Expanding Relevance Judgements with Duplicates. *SIGIR*, 2014.
[6] C. L. A. Clarke and M. D. Smucker. Time Well Spent. *IIiX*, 2014.
[7] G. Cormack and M. Grossman. Engineering Quality and Reliability in Technology-Assisted Review. *SIGIR*, 2016.
[8] G. V. Cormack and M. R. Grossman. Evaluation of Machine-Learning Protocols for Technology-Assisted Review in Electronic Discovery. *SIGIR*, 2014.
[9] G. V. Cormack and M. R. Grossman. Autonomy and Reliability of Continuous Active Learning for Technology-Assisted Review. *CoRR*, abs/1504.06868, 2015.
[10] M. Ekstrand-Abueg. Personal Communication. 2014
[11] D. Harman. Information Retrieval Evaluation. *Synthesis Lectures on Information Concepts, Retrieval, and Services*, 3(2), 2011.
[12] J. He, M. Bron, A. de Vries, L. Azzopardi, and M. de Rijke. Untangling Result List Refinement and Ranking Quality: A Framework for Evaluation and Prediction. *SIGIR*, 2015.
[13] J. Lin and D. Demner-Fushman. Automatically Evaluating Answers to Definition Questions. *NAACL-HLT*, 2005.
[14] G. Marton and A. Radul. Nuggeteer: Automatic Nugget-Based Evaluation using Descriptions and Judgements. *NAACL-HLT*, 2006.
[15] V. Pavlu, S. Rajput, P. B. Golbus, and J. A. Aslam. IR System Evaluation using Nugget-based Test Collections. *WSDM*, 2012.
[16] S. Rajput, M. Ekstrand-Abueg, V. Pavlu, and J. A. Aslam. Constructing Test Collections by Inferring Document Relevance via Extracted Relevant Information. *CIKM*, 2012.
[17] A. Roegiest, G. Cormack, M. Grossman, and C. Clarke. TREC 2015 Total Recall Track Overview. *TREC*, 2015.
[18] E. M. Voorhees. Overview of the TREC 2004 Question Answering Track. *TREC*, 2004.
[19] E. M. Voorhees. Overview of the TREC 2005 Question Answering Track. *TREC*, 2005.
[20] E. M. Voorhees and D. K. Harman. *TREC: Experiment and Evaluation in Information Retrieval*, MIT press Cambridge, 2005.

Uncovering Fake Likers in Online Social Networks

Prudhvi Ratna Badri Satya[†] Kyumin Lee[†] Dongwon Lee[§]
Thanh Tran[†] Jason (Jiasheng) Zhang[§]

[†] Department of Computer Science, Utah State University, UT, USA
[§] College of Information Sciences and Technology, The Pennsylvania State University, PA, USA

{prudhvibadri|thanh.tran}@aggiemail.usu.edu kyumin.lee@usu.edu {dongwon|jpz5181}@psu.edu

ABSTRACT

As the commercial implications of *Likes* in online social networks multiply, the number of *fake Likes* also increase rapidly. To maintain a healthy ecosystem, however, it is critically important to prevent and detect such *fake Likes*. Toward this goal, in this paper, we investigate the problem of detecting the so-called *"fake likers"* who frequently make *fake Likes* for illegitimate reasons. To uncover *fake Likes* in online social networks, we: (1) first collect a substantial number of profiles of both fake and legitimate *Likers* using linkage and honeypot approaches, (2) analyze the characteristics of both types of *Likers*, (3) identify effective features exploiting the learned characteristics and apply them in supervised learning models, and (4) thoroughly evaluate their performances against three baseline methods and under two attack models. Our experimental results show that our proposed methods with effective features significantly outperformed baseline methods, with accuracy = 0.871, false positive rate = 0.1, and false negative rate = 0.14.

Keywords: Fake Likers; Fiverr; Microworkers; Online Social Networks; Facebook

1. INTRODUCTION

Everyday billions of people actively use online social networks (OSNs) such as Facebook, Twitter, and Instagram. They share information regarding their daily lives, engage with friends and followers, and express their opinions through reviews, votes, and *Likes* in OSNs. Similarly, businesses promote and attempt to increase positive images of their services and products in OSNs. In such OSNs, in recent years, the commercial implications of *Likes* have multiplied. For instance, the *Like* function can be a good marketing tool since businesses can recognize interested users and the accumulated *Likes* help promote businesses in various searches. Similarly, *Likes* help understand users better in OSNs [8].

To benefit from the increased importance of *Likes*, however, a set of new markets to buy and sell illegitimate *Likes* also have emerged in OSNs. In such markets, for instance, by paying $5, it is fairly easy to buy thousands of *Likes*. Note that such paid liking activities are strictly prohibited in OSNs (e.g., on Facebook[1]). In this paper, we refer to such illegitimate *Likes* as **fake Likes**. As such artificially manipulated fake *Likes* hurt the healthy ecosystem in OSNs, it is important to actively prevent, deter, detect, and respond to them. In particular, in this paper, we focus on the problem of "detecting fake *Likes*". Similar problems including detecting fake reviews, spammers/sybils, fake followers, or manipulated keyword searches have been reported in literature (e.g., [12, 13, 14, 16, 18]).

While related, however, we believe that the problem of detecting *fake Likes* is more challenging because: (1) information available in a *Like* is much more limited than fake reviews or sybils, and (2) the difference between fake and legitimate *Likes* is often unclear for 3rd party to judge. Therefore, as a way to detect *fake Likes*, we propose to first detect "fake likers" who have performed at least k *fake Likes* in OSNs. As k increases, the likelihood of one being a *fake Liker* increases but the number of *fake Likers* in a dataset decreases. As such, to maintain a proper data size for our experiments, k is set to 2. Formally, we solve the following problem:

Problem 1 (Fake Liker Detection Problem) Consider a user class with binary types C={`fake-liker`, `legit-liker`}. Then, for a user u, given a set of u's features $f \in F$, and a training set S of users labeled with C, learn a classifier γ such that: $\gamma : u \rightarrow C$. ■

Recently, researchers (e.g., [1, 3, 17]) have studied the related problem. Despite promising results, however, their approaches are limited to some extent as they require: (1) expensive features such as temporal data of *Likes*, and (2) an array of input parameters with tuning. In complementing these prior works and improving shortfalls therein, in this paper, we make the following contributions: (1) Collecting over 13,000 fake and legitimate *Likers* in Facebook from two types of sources–Fiverr and Microworkers–using both linkage and honeypot methods, we present comprehensive analysis to understand both types of *Likers* better; (2) Based on the learned characteristics of both types of *Likers*, then, we identify five types of effective and cost-effective features and apply them to build supervised learning models; and (3) Against three baseline methods under individual and coordinated attack models, finally, we empirically validate the

CIKM'16, October 24-28, 2016, Indianapolis, IN, USA

DOI: http://dx.doi.org/10.1145/2983323.2983695

[1] https://www.facebook.com/10152309368645766/

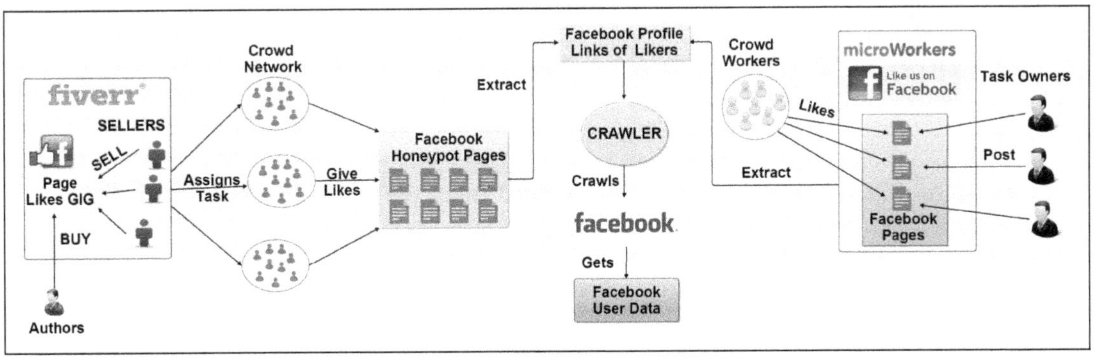

Figure 1: Collecting *fake Likers* from Fiverr and Microworkers.

effectiveness of our proposed solutions with high accuracies and low false positive rates.

2. RELATED WORK

Researchers [9, 15] deployed honeypots to uncover spammers on Twitter and Facebook, and developed machine learning based classification models to detect spammers. Lee et al. [11] performed comprehensive analysis of Fiverr to reveal the existence of crowdturfing tasks therein, and developed a crowdturfing task detection method to remove such tasks.

De Cristofaro et al. [5] presented a comparative study of Facebook ads and *Likes* farms by analyzing demographic, temporal, and social characteristics of likers but did not investigate the detection of *fake Likers* accounts. Viswanath et al. [17] used the principal component analysis technique to detect anomalous accounts on Facebook. While showing good performance, this work lacks comprehensive analysis on the differences between the users of various *Like* platforms, and temporal features that they used are expensive to obtain. In our work, however, we aim to achieve the accurate detection without expensive temporal features.

CopyCatch [1] detected undesirable accounts making *fake Likes* by extracting near bipartite cores from users and Facebook pages based on *Likes* and liked time. SynchroTrap [3] detected groups of malicious accounts by running hierarchical clustering based on their liking similarity during the same time interval. However, in our study, we found that Facebook security system that reportedly uses both methods did not detect *fake Likes* (that we detected), and did not remove their accounts even two months later.

3. DATA COLLECTION

To build an accurate classification model, the first challenge is to obtain a good size of labeled training data. As it is virtually impossible for 3rd party to tell if a *Like* is "fake" or not, instead, we actively solicit *fake Likes* in two crowdsourcing platforms (e.g., Fiverr and Microworkers), and collect the Facebook users who gave at least k *fake Likes*–thus by definition *fake Likers*. Recent research [10, 11] reported that some users in Fiverr and Microworkers have performed malicious tasks (e.g., fake liking or following). Figure 1 illustrates our data collection process. Next, as positive samples, we also collected two legitimate user sets – conference groups and a random pool. In total, we constructed two fake and two legitimate users sets with 6,895 faker liker profiles and 6,252 legitimate liker profiles, as summarized in Table 1. We describe further details in data collection below.

Figure 2: A Facebook *Like* ad by a seller in Fiverr.

Types	|Likers|	|pages|	|posts|	|friends|
Fake (Fiverr)	3,207	1.86M	0.21M	0.82M
Fake (Microworkers)	3,688	1.63M	0.33M	1.54M
Legit (Conference)	2,552	0.57M	0.17M	0.87M
Legit (Random)	3,700	0.60M	0.28M	2.24M
Total	13,147	4.66M	0.99M	5.47M

Table 1: Sizes of labeled datasets.

Fake Likers in Fiverr. Fiverr is a seller-driven marketplace. As shown in Figure 2, for instance, a seller advertises to sell hundreds of *fake Likes* for a fee. Such a seller often acts as a broker, who in turn hires hundreds of other *fake Likers* to actually make *fake Likes*. We contacted ten sellers in Fiverr to purchase *fake Likes* to our honeypot Facebook pages. To avoid receiving legitimate *Likes* from other Facebook users, our honeypot pages clearly displayed a message "This is a fake page. Please do not like this" and had no other contents. Then, at each hour for next 10 days, a crawler attempted to collect all user related information who "liked" the honeypot pages. At the end, out of 3,916 *Likes* made to the honeypot pages, 3,207 *fake Likers* had no privacy setting. Then, we collected 3,207 profiles of those *fake Likers* including a total of 1.86 million pages that they liked, 0.21 million posts, and 0.82 million friends information in Facebook.

Fake Likers in Microworkers. In contrast to Fiverr, Microworkers is a buyer-driven platform where a buyer creates an ad (e.g., "I'll pay $0.01 if you *Like* a Facebook page XYZ"). First, we selected 353 tasks in Microworkers, whose titles contained "Facebook Like" and extracted targeted Facebook page URLs therein. Then, we extracted a list of users who liked the targeted pages. These are potential *fake Likers*. Then, we selected 3,688 users who liked at least $k = 2$

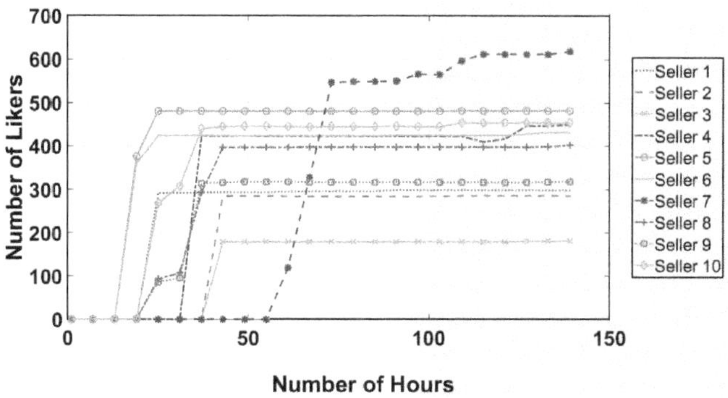

Figure 3: Temporal change of # of *fake Likes*.

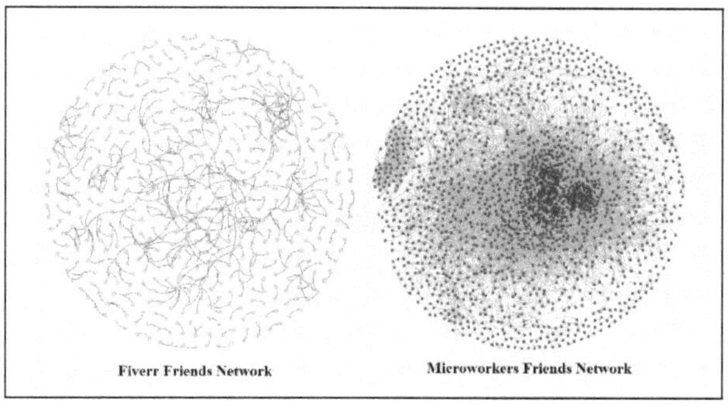

Figure 4: The 2-hop (mutual) friendship relations in Fiverr and Microworkers communities.

pages among 353 target pages and did not have any privacy setting, and collected their profiles including a total of 1.63 million pages that they liked, 0.33 million posts, and 1.54 million friends information in Facebook.

Legitimate Likers from Conferences. As the first heuristic to collect legitimate *Likers*, we borrowed the idea from [17], and collected 2,552 user profiles from 13 CS conference groups on Facebook. As in [17], we also assumed that these technically savvy users were less likely to be infected by malware or other attacks, and unlike to perform fake liking activity. In addition, we sampled 1,000 out of the 2,552 user profiles, checked whether they were suspicious accounts or not, and found none. These users liked 0.57 million pages, posted 0.17 million posts, and had 0.87 million friends.

Legitimate Likers from a Random Pool. Finally, from 20 random seed users who live in different countries, we crawled their 2-hop friends network using the breadth first search (BFS) technique. From the 28,200 users in the network, to further randomize, we randomly selected 5,700 users. Out of 5,700 random users, 3,779 users did not have any privacy setting. Then, two labelers conducted manual labeling process for the 3,779 user profiles, investigating each user's posts and timeline information. They achieved 99.7% agreement with Kappa coefficient of 0.78. Selecting only users agreed by both labelers, at the end, we kept 3,700 legitimate users who liked 0.6 million pages, posted 0.28 million posts, and had 2.24 million friends. Note that almost 2% accounts on Facebook are undesirable accounts according to Facebook SEC filing report [6].

Download. Our dataset is publicly available at:

http://digital.cs.usu.edu/~kyumin/data.html

4. UNDERSTANDING LIKERS

In this section, we analyze the characteristics of both fake and legitimate *Likers*.

Who are Fake Likers? First, we analyzed how quickly each Fiverr seller delivered *fake Likes*. Figure 3 illustrates the temporal change of the number of *Likes* by ten sellers. Note that most of *fake Likes* were delivered within three days in a bursty fashion, that is consistent with the finding in [5].

Next, we analyzed the demographics of *fake Likers* associated with Fiverr sellers. Since we created honeypot pages on Facebook, we were able to access the demographic information of the *fake Likers*. 73% of all *fake Likers* were from 10 countries–Egypt, Iraq, Tunisia, Algeria, Morocco, Philippines, Brazil, Jordan, Saudi Arabia, UK–which are all developing countries except UK. We also observed most *fake Likers* were in the range of 18-34 years old, regardless of sellers whom they were associated with. Surprisingly, some *fake Likers* were teenagers, and overall, there were more male than female *fake Likers*.

Another interesting question is if *fake Likers* unliked our honeypot pages a certain period later (e.g., a week or a month)? Researchers observed such behavior on Twitter that spammers often followed and unfollowed users [9]. In our study, however, only 10% of *fake Likers* unliked our pages when we checked the status after 3 months.

Fiverr vs. Microworkers Fake Likers. First, we analyzed how *fake Likers* from Fiverr and Microworkers were connected via Facebook friendship network and observed no direct friendship connections among *fake Likers* in Fiverr. However, *fake Likers* in Microworkers were densely connected. For instance, on average, 1,099 out of 3,688 *fake Likers* (i.e., nodes) in Microworkers were connected via 5,239 friendship connections (i.e., edges) with 9.5 degree and 0.446 clustering coefficient on average.

In Figure 4, a node indicates a *fake Liker* and if a pair of *fake Likers* within a community has at least one common friend (i.e., 2-hop friend), we added an edge between them. *fake Likers* in Fiverr were sparsely connected whereas *fake Likers* in Microworkers were densely connected. In particular, 570 *fake Likers* in Fiverr were connected via 578 friendship connections with 2.0 degree and 0.233 clustering coefficient on average while 1,802 *fake Likers* in Microworkers were connected via 48,173 friendship connections with 53.4 degree and 0.612 clustering coefficient on average. In addition, we found no direct friendship relations between *fake Likers* of Fiverr and Microworkers. However, there were 672 mutual friends between *fake Likers* from Fiverr and Microworkers.

Next, we computed pair-wise similarities of pages liked by *fake Likers* to find out any cross-workers between Fiverr and Microworkers who performed tasks in both sites. We observed only a negligible similarity due to verified pages a.k.a authentic pages (e.g., Amazon, Disney). This implies that there were few cross-workers. However, a pairwise similarity of pages liked by *fake Likers* from each site/community was much larger.

Next, we analyzed what URLs *fake Likers* frequently shared or posted on Facebook. Table 2 presents top 5 URLs in each platform. For instance, *fake Likers* in Fiverr posted URLs related to Facebook apps and games while those in Microwork-

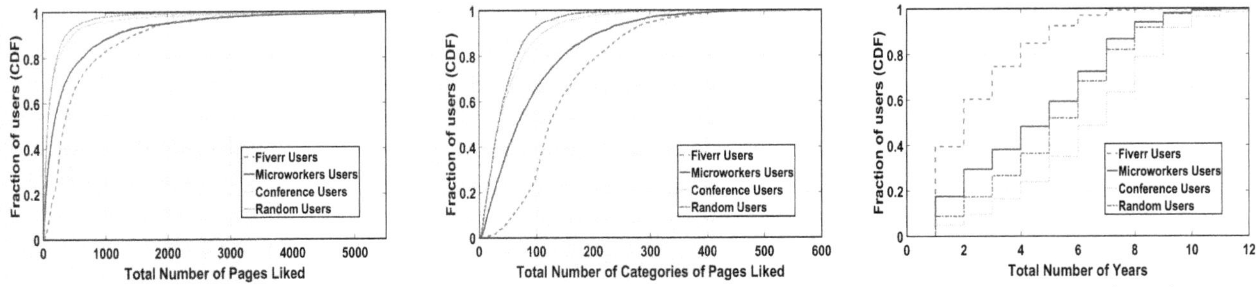

(a) Number of liked pages.

(b) Number of liked page categories.

(c) Longevity (years).

Figure 5: The CDFs of fake and legitimate *Likers*.

Platform	Top 5 URLs	# of Likers
Fiverr	https://www.facebook.com/facebook/	215
	http://apps.facebook.com/monsterlegends	89
	http://apps.facebook.com/dragoncity	38
	http://apps.facebook.com/stick_run	37
	http://apps.facebook.com/topeleven	31
Microworkers	https://www.krowdster.co	537
	http://www.indiegogo.com/projects/1240265	412
	https://www.indiegogo.com/projects/1528609	312
	http://www.fitneszszakuzlet.hu	276
	https://www.mykomms.com/	197

Table 2: Top 5 URLs shared or posted by *fake Likers*, and corresponding # of *Likers*.

ers posted URLs related to advertisements of crowdfunding projects and other websites. This may indicate that Microworkers workers used their Facebook accounts for not only fake liking activities, but also other crowdturfing tasks.

Based on the analysis, we conclude that *fake Likers* in Fiverr are distinctively different from those in Microworkers in terms of direct relationship, mutual friends, job tasks that they performed, and URL sharing patterns.

Fake vs. Legitimate Likers. Next, we contrasted fake and legitimate *Likers*. Figure 5(a) clearly shows that *fake Likers* from Fiverr and Microworkers performed more page liking activities than legitimate likers. In particular, 90% of random and conference legitimate users liked at most 369 and 481 pages, respectively, whereas 90% of *fake Likers* from Fiverr and Microworkers liked at most 1,481 and 1,137 pages, respectively. In addition, Figure 5(b) presents the number of categories associated with Facebook pages liked by fake and legitimate *Likers*. Note that *fake Likers* liked pages with more diverse categories than legitimate *Likers*. In particular, Fiverr's *fake Likers* liked pages with the most diverse categories. This may reflect the lack of personal interests of *fake Likers* in liking pages as they would like any pages for a fee. Finally, Figure 5(c) shows that the accounts of legitimate *Likers* were created earlier than those of *fake Likers*. In particular, we note that conference users created their accounts earlier than other users, and Fiverr's accounts were created recently (i.e., 80% of them were created within four years).

5. FEATURE ENGINEERING

Based on our findings from Section 4, now, we present four sets of features effective to detect *fake Likers* as follows:

1. **Profile Features**: # of lines in *About* section; longevity of an account; # of friends.
2. **Posting Activity Features**: These include two types of posts by a user u–u's own posts (i.e., posts created by u) and shared posts (i.e., posts created by other user but shared by u). Posts include photos, pages, videos, text messages, etc. We extracted following features: average # of posts per day; total # of posts created by u; proportion of shared photos, posts or pages out of total # of posts; maximum # of posts in a day; average # of URLs per post; and skewness of daily posted posts.
3. **Page Liking Features**: We extracted two features: (1) category entropy: A larger category entropy indicates that a user randomly liked pages under various categories. Given a list of Facebook categories $C = c_1, c_2, c_3, \ldots, c_k$ and corresponding number of pages in each category liked by a user u, the user's category entropy is calculated as follows: $CatEntropy(u) = -\sum_{i=1}^{k} \frac{p_i}{N} \log \frac{p_i}{N}$, where N is the total # of pages liked by u, and p_i is # of liked pages under a category i; and (2) proportion of verified pages out of total # of pages liked by a user.
4. **Social Attention Features**: average # of *Likes* (selected by other users) per post; average # of comments per post; and average # of shared per post.

In addition, for us to implement three state-of-the-art approaches (i.e., PCA [17], SynchroTrap [3] and CopyCatch [1]) for comparison, we also extracted temporal features. We collected temporal snapshot data of 1,400 *Likers* (i.e., 700 fake and 700 legitimate *Likers*) and extracted following two features: (1) A change rate of # of liked pages during 30 days: We extracted 30 values, each of which was # of liked pages by a user of the day. Then, we measured a standard deviation of those 30 values; and (2) A change rate of category entropies during 30 days: We measured a category entropy per day and computed a standard deviation of those 30 category entropies.

To avoid the features that are too similar or correlated, we measured Pearson correlation and computed Chi-square values for the four feature sets. Note that we did the same process for all feature sets including temporal features in a small dataset containing temporal data, but showed Pearson correlation results for the four feature sets in the entire dataset in this paper. The largest correlation score was less than 0.5, so we kept all the features.

Finally, we computed the Chi-square values [20] to rank features in the order of the largest distinguishing power. The larger Chi-square value a feature has, the larger distinguish-

Features	F. Likers	L. Likers
Category entropy	6.35	4.47
Longevity	3.62	5.53
Average # of posts per day	0.31	0.12
# of lines in *About* section	4.02	4.08
Proportion of verified pages	0.23	0.26

Table 3: Top 5 features and average feature values.

ing power it has. Table 3 shows top-5 results, and average feature values of fake and legitimate *Likers*.

6. EMPIRICAL VALIDATION

In this section, we conduct three experiments: (1) we build *fake Liker* classifiers in a small dataset with temporal data to evaluate against three baseline methods (i.e., PCA [17], SynchroTrap [3] and CopyCatch [1]); (2) we build *fake Liker* classifiers in the entire dataset without temporal data, and compare the classifiers with the three baseline methods; and (3) we measure how robust our classification models are under two attack scenarios–individual attack model and coordinated attack model.

For evaluation, we measured accuracy, false positive rate (FPR), and false negative rate (FNR). In our context, a false positive indicates a legitimate user misclassified as *fake Liker*, while a false negative is a *fake Liker* misclassified as a legitimate user. Note that it is critical for our solutions to yield few false positives even if they yield some false negatives.

Detecting Fake Likers in a Small Dataset. First, out of 13,147 Facebook *Likers* in our dataset in Table 1, we further collected temporal data of 1,400 (i.e., 700 fake and 700 legitimate *Likers*) for 30 days between Dec 1 and Dec 30, 2015 because the PCA based approach in [17] required temporal features. Then, we split this small dataset to training and test sets. The training set consisted of 1,000 *Likers* (i.e., 500 *fake Likers* and 500 legitimate *Likers*), and the test set consisted of 400 *Likers* (i.e., 200 *fake Likers* and 200 legitimate *Likers*).

In our classification approach, we built classifiers based on 30+ machine learning algorithms (e.g., LogitBoost [7], Random Forest [2], XGBoost [4], SVM) using our proposed features to check which classifier produced the best result.

For PCA based approach [17], we extracted 30 temporal, 1,079 spatial/categorical and 30 spatio-temporal/category-temporal feature values from each *Liker*'s profile in both training and test sets as the authors did. We determined principal components and observed 95% variance in the top 400 principal components. We computed the L2 norm [19] and set the squared prediction error (SPE) as a threshold to find *fake Likers*. If a user exceeds the SPE value, then the user is likely to be a *fake Liker*. For determining the SPE, we changed a threshold value from 1% to 99% by increasing 1% each time in the training set. We found the optimal threshold, and applied the threshold value to the test set.

SynchroTrap [3] measures page liking similarity of each pair of users, and runs single-linkage hierarchical clustering. The output of the algorithm is a dendrogram structure, and the algorithm requires a cutoff threshold (i.e., similarity threshold) and a minimum size of a cluster to determine clusters of malicious accounts. Again, we found the best cutoff and size values from the training set and applied to the test set.

Approach	Accuracy	FPR	FNR
PCA	0.690	0.30	0.32
SynchroTrap	0.505	0	0.99
CopyCatch	0.565	0.85	0.02
PCA - Test	0.690	0.30	0.32
SynchroTrap - Test	0.635	0	0.73
CopyCatch - Test	0.655	0.46	0.23
our LogitBoost	0.875	0.11	0.13
our Random Forest	0.885	0.09	0.13
our XGBoost	**0.897**	0.08	0.11

Table 4: Experimental results in a small dataset containing temporal data.

Approach	Accuracy	FPR	FNR
PCA	0.563	0.49	0.38
SynchroTrap	0.521	0	0.91
CopyCatch	0.601	0.80	0.04
PCA - Test	0.576	0.28	0.54
SynchroTrap - Test	0.620	0.01	0.71
CopyCatch - Test	0.669	0.09	0.55
our LogitBoost	0.856	0.16	0.12
our Random Forest	0.865	0.15	0.11
our XGBoost	**0.871**	0.10	0.14

Table 5: Experiment results in the entire dataset. The improvement of XGBoost over the baseline methods is significant at the 0.01 level using the Wilcoxon directional test.

CopyCatch [1] discovers groups of *fake Likers* by measuring page liking similarity of the groups in a specific time range, and outputs near bipartite cores/graphs which can be considered as malicious accounts. This method needs three input parameters: (1) minimum number of users in a near bipartite core; (2) minimum number of pages in a near bipartite core; and (3) how densely users are connected to pages (e.g., each user in a near bipartite core should like 90% pages). We varied these parameter values and found the best values from the training set and applied them to the test set.

Table 4 presents experimental results of the three baseline methods and our three most effective classifiers. XGBoost classifier achieved 0.897 accuracy, 0.08 FPR and 0.11 FNR, improving up to 0.392 (= 0.897 - 0.505) accuracy compared with the baseline methods. PCA, SynchroTrap and CopyCatch achieved 0.690, 0.505 and 0.565 accuracy, respectively. Their upper bound results (i.e., PCA - Test, SynchroTrap - Test and CopyCatch - Test which found optimal threshold/parameter values within the test set) achieved 0.690, 0.635 and 0.655 accuracy, respectively. These two different results show that a weakness of the baseline methods is hard to find optimal threshold or input parameter values. Second, even though we found the upper bound, they were still less effective than our classification models. Interestingly, SynchroTrap achieved 0 FPR but only identified 1% of *fake Likers* (i.e., 0.01 recall).

Detecting Fake Likers in the Wild. Now we turn to detect *fake Likers* in the entire dataset containing the profiles of 13,147 users without using expensive temporal data/features. In this experiment, we conducted 10-fold cross-validation, creating 10 pairs of training and test sets. All three baselines were applied to proposed 16 features excluding temporal features. Similar to what we did in the previous experiment, PCA, CopyCatch and SynchroTrap found an optimal

Features	Accuracy	FPR	FNR
Social attention features (3 feat.)	0.861	0.12	0.15
Profile features (3 feat.)	0.842	0.13	0.17
Posting activity features (8 feat.)	0.841	0.13	0.17
Page liking features (2 feat.)	0.824	0.17	0.17

Table 6: Our classification results under the coordinated attack model.

threshold in each training set and applied it to each test set. In addition, we measured the upper bound of the three baseline methods.

Table 5 show experimental results in the entire dataset. Again, XGBoost based classifier outperformed PCA, SynchroTrap and CopyCatch, achieving 0.871 accuracy, 0.1 FPR and 0.14 FNR. We further focused on misclassification cases of XGBoost. Out of 1,013 false negatives, 56 *fake Likers* were from Fiverr and the remaining 957 were from Microworkers. This shows Microworkers workers used their own personal facebook accounts for fake-liking activity unlike Fiverr. In false positive cases, some legitimate *Likers* had similar behaviors with *fake Likers* by posting many posts in a single day and having higher proportion of shared pages out of the total number of posts.

We also evaluated the performance of our approach in an unbalanced dataset consisting of 2% *fake Likers* [6] and 98% legitimate *Likers*. Our approach consistently outperformed the three baseline methods.

Robustness of Our Approach. To measure the robustness of our approaches, next, we simulated two attack models: (1) individual attack model; and (2) coordinated (group) attack model.

In the individual attack model, we assumed that each *fake Liker* *independently* selects one of our features, and then change its value to a legitimate *Liker*'s feature value. Specifically, given a range of feature values of legitimate *Likers*, the simulator randomly choose a value which is used for a *fake Liker*. We conducted 10-fold cross-validation and ran the simulation 10 times. Our XGBoost based classifier achieved 0.855 accuracy, 0.157 FPR and 0.133 FNR, decreasing 0.016 accuracy compared with our approach (0.871 accuracy).

In the coordinated attack model, we assumed that all *fake Likers* choose the *same* feature or features, and change its value or their values to a legitimate *Liker*'s feature value or values. Compared with the individual attack model, these *fake Likers* already know which feature/features they are going to manipulate. We tested changing one feature to multiple features. Again, we conducted 10-fold cross-validation and ran 10 times.

Table 6 show experimental results under the coordinate attack model. The coordinated attack for single feature decreased accuracy to between 0.834 and 0.870. When the fake likers targeted all features in one of four feature sets, accuracy decreased to between 0.824 and 0.861. The coordinated attack model slightly affected the performance of our approach (0.871 accuracy).

7. CONCLUSION

In this paper, we conducted a comprehensive analysis of *fake Likers* on Facebook collected from Fiverr and Microworkers by using the linkage and honeypot approaches. We compared how *fake Likers* from two different sources were different. In the comparison between *fake Likers* and legitimate *Likers*, we found that *fake Likers* were different from legitimate *Likers* with respect to liking behaviors, longevity, etc. Based on the analysis, we proposed 4 types of feature sets toward building accurate classification models. Experimental results show that our models significantly outperformed the baseline methods (i.e., PCA, SynchroTrap and CopyCatch) with accuracy = 0.871, false positive rate = 0.1, and false negative rate = 0.14. Under individual and simulated attack models, our approach consistently achieved over 0.82 of accuracy.

Acknowledgment. This work was supported in part by NSF grants CNS-1422215, CNS-1553035, and IUSE-1525601. Any opinions, findings and conclusions or recommendations expressed in this material are the author(s) and do not necessarily reflect those of the sponsors.

8. REFERENCES

[1] A. Beutel, W. Xu, V. Guruswami, C. Palow, and C. Faloutsos. Copycatch: stopping group attacks by spotting lockstep behavior in social networks. In *WWW*, 2013.

[2] L. Breiman. Random forests. *Machine learning*, 45(1):5–32, 2001.

[3] Q. Cao, X. Yang, J. Yu, and C. Palow. Uncovering large groups of active malicious accounts in online social networks. In *CCS*, 2014.

[4] T. Chen and T. He. xgboost: extreme gradient boosting. 2015.

[5] E. De Cristofaro, A. Friedman, G. Jourjon, M. A. Kaafar, and M. Z. Shafiq. Paying for likes?: Understanding facebook like fraud using honeypots. In *IMC*, 2014.

[6] Facebook. SEC filings form 10-Q. http://tinyurl.com/zgnx9b6, 2016.

[7] J. Friedman, T. Hastie, R. Tibshirani, et al. Additive logistic regression: a statistical view of boosting (with discussion and a rejoinder by the authors). *The annals of statistics*, 28(2):337–407, 2000.

[8] J. Y. Jang, K. Han, P. C. Shih, and D. Lee. "Generation Like: Comparative characteristics in instagram. In *CHI*, 2015.

[9] K. Lee, B. D. Eoff, and J. Caverlee. Seven Months with the Devils: A Long-Term Study of Content Polluters on Twitter. In *ICWSM*, 2011.

[10] K. Lee, P. Tamilarasan, and J. Caverlee. Crowdturfers, campaigns, and social media: Tracking and revealing crowdsourced manipulation of social media. In *ICWSM*, 2013.

[11] K. Lee, S. Webb, and H. Ge. The dark side of micro-task marketplaces: Characterizing fiverr and automatically detecting crowdturfing. *ICWSM*, 2014.

[12] Y. Liu, Y. Liu, M. Zhang, and M. Shaoping. Pay me and i'll follow you: Detection of crowdturfing following activities in microblog environment. In *IJCAI*, 2016.

[13] M. Motoyama, D. McCoy, K. Levchenko, S. Savage, and G. M. Voelker. Dirty jobs: The role of freelance labor in web service abuse. In *USENIX Conference on Security*, 2011.

[14] G. Stringhini, M. Egele, C. Kruegel, and G. Vigna. Poultry markets: On the underground economy of twitter followers. In *Workshop on Online Social Networks*, 2012.

[15] G. Stringhini, C. Kruegel, and G. Vigna. Detecting spammers on social networks. In *ACSAC*, 2010.

[16] K. Thomas, D. McCoy, C. Grier, A. Kolcz, and V. Paxson. Trafficking fraudulent accounts: The role of the underground market in twitter spam and abuse. In *USENIX Conference on Security*, 2013.

[17] B. Viswanath, M. A. Bashir, M. Crovella, S. Guha, K. P. Gummadi, B. Krishnamurthy, and A. Mislove. Towards detecting anomalous user behavior in online social networks. In *USENIX Conference on Security*, 2014.

[18] G. Wang, C. Wilson, X. Zhao, Y. Zhu, M. Mohanlal, H. Zheng, and B. Y. Zhao. Serf and turf: crowdturfing for fun and profit. In *WWW*, 2012.

[19] I. Wolfram Research. L2 norm. http://mathworld.wolfram.com/L2-Norm.html, 2016.

[20] Y. Yang and J. O. Pedersen. A comparative study on feature selection in text categorization. In *ICML*, 1997.

Where to Place Your Next Restaurant? Optimal Restaurant Placement via Leveraging User-Generated Reviews

Feng Wang
Department of Computer Science
Hong Kong Baptist University
Hong Kong, China
fwang@comp.hkbu.edu.hk

Li Chen
Department of Computer Science
Hong Kong Baptist University
Hong Kong, China
lichen@comp.hkbu.edu.hk

Weike Pan
College of Computer Science and Software Engineering
Shenzhen University
Shenzhen, China
panweike@szu.edu.cn

ABSTRACT

When opening a new restaurant, *geographical placement* is of prime importance in determining whether it will thrive. Although some methods have been developed to assess the attractiveness of *candidate* locations for a restaurant, the accuracy is limited as they mainly rely on traditional data sources, such as demographic studies or consumer surveys. With the advent of abundant user-generated restaurant reviews, there is a potential to leverage these reviews to gain some insights into users' preferences for restaurants. In this paper, we particularly take advantage of user-generated reviews to construct predictive features for assessing the attractiveness of candidate locations to expand a restaurant. Specifically, we investigate three types of features: review-based *market attractiveness*, review-based *market competitiveness* and *geographic characteristics* of a location under consideration for a prospective restaurant. We devise the three sets of features and incorporate them into a regression model to predict the number of check-ins that a prospective restaurant at a candidate location would be likely to attract. We then conduct an experiment with real-world restaurant data, which demonstrates the predictive power of features we constructed in this paper. Moreover, our experimental results suggest that market attractiveness and market competitiveness features mined solely from user-generated restaurant reviews are more predictive than geographic features.

CCS Concepts

•Information systems → Data mining;

Keywords

Optimal restaurant placement; User-generated reviews; Market attractiveness features; Market competitiveness features; Geographic features

CIKM'16, October 24-28, 2016, Indianapolis, IN, USA
© 2016 ACM. ISBN 978-1-4503-4073-1/16/10... $15.00
DOI: http://dx.doi.org/10.1145/2983323.2983696

1. INTRODUCTION

When a restaurant thrives in one geographic location (location refers to a general area within a city), the temptation can be great to expand it to new locations. Each location specifically has its own advantages and disadvantages with regard to different types of restaurants [10]. For example, access, visibility, population demographics, traffic patterns, and the presence of complementary businesses including other restaurants have been recognised as major factors affecting a restaurant's success or failure [9]. Thus, business success in one location does not necessarily guarantee success in another location.

In related work, the restaurant location selection mainly relies on data obtained from demographic studies, consumer surveys and the like [4, 16], which, however, are usually very expensive to acquire. Recently, some studies have attempted to automatically assess location quality based on the analysis of spatial distribution [12], but they require access to datasets that are not usually publicly available. Hence, the issue of how to identify the right location for a restaurant in an accurate and timely fashion, particularly by using publicly accessible data, remains a challenging problem that requires extensive study.

In this work, we are engaged in the problem of selecting an optimal new place to expand an existing restaurant. The priority when we are planing the expansion of a restaurant to a new location is to profile the restaurant's existing *customers'* preference. When we understand the preference of customers a restaurant attracts, we may then identify proper locations that have high concentrations of users with similar preferences (i.e., potential customers). The primary novelty of our work lies in leveraging a particular form of user-generated content, restaurant reviews, which are publicly available in local directory services such as *Yelp.com*. Usually, the customers often write reviews to express detailed opinions about multi-faceted aspects of a restaurant, as illustrated in Figure 1. The descriptive reviews of restaurants contributed by customers provide a valuable opportunity to understand why a restaurant in a particular location is attractive or not. We can hence discover the cultural idiosyncrasies of that area and gain insight into the preferences of restaurant customers. Specifically, given a collection of restaurant reviews, we can apply aspect-based opinion mining techniques [14] to extract the aspects of a restaurant (e.g., food, price and service), as well as inferring sentiment polarity for each aspect. With the results of aspect-based opinion mining, we can first infer how often

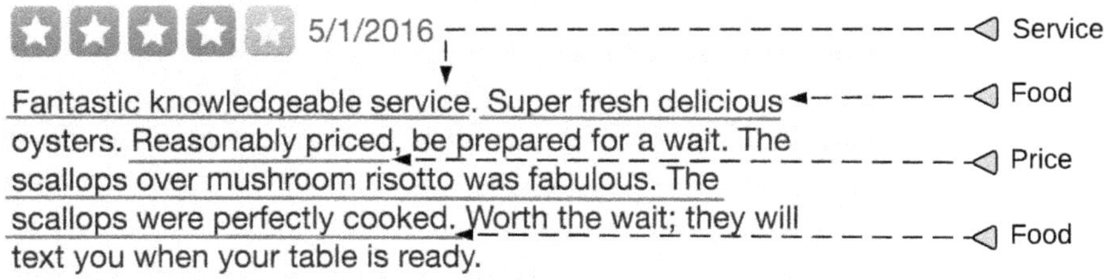

Figure 1: An example of a restaurant review that expresses *positive* opinions about the restaurant's food, price and service.

an aspect is commented in reviews of a restaurant. If its customers often commented an aspect, it implies that the customers have high interest in that aspect. Hence, such aspect distribution can be used to profile the preference of customers for a restaurant. Meanwhile, we can summarize the sentiment polarities of aspects into sentiment scores for that restaurant, which can be used to represent how satisfied the customers are with that restaurant.

As the major contribution of this paper, we investigate two types of geographic dependency features between locations and restaurants, which are mined solely from restaurant reviews: 1) *market attractiveness* features which measure whether a restaurant would be attractive to customers who may visit its located place; 2) *market competitiveness* features which measure whether a restaurant would offer competitive quality in comparison with competitors located in the same place. Besides the above two types of review-based features, we also consider the *geographic* features which can be mined from publicly accessible data source to encode the spatial properties (e.g., the number of restaurants) of a location. In our work, we mainly focus on the case of expanding a chain restaurant to a new location. For individual who wants to identify a good location for a new restaurant, the locations of other similar and successful restaurants can provide important guidelines.

2. OPTIMAL RESTAURANT PLACEMENT

In this section, we formalize the optimal restaurant placement problem as a dyadic predictive task for predicting the number of *check-ins* a prospective restaurant will receive if it is placed in a candidate location.

2.1 Problem Statement

Formally, there is a set of candidate locations $\mathcal{L}$ from which a location $\ell \in \mathcal{L}$ can be chosen for the next place a restaurant is expanded to. As previously noted, our goal is to identify the *optimal* restaurant location ℓ^* that will potentially attract the largest number of visits. Location ℓ can be formally defined by its longitude and latitude coordinates and radius r, as illustrated in Figure 2. Unless otherwise specified, in our experiment, r is set to 200 metres, as that radius is estimated to be the optimal size of a neighbourhood [13]. Our problem can be defined as a dyadic prediction problem in which the dyad is a restaurant-location pair, and concretely described by a set of features.

To solve this problem, we seek to exploit the mined features from reviews to predict the number of visits. The valuable information contained in reviews provides a unique opportunity to arrive at a more holistic understanding of customers, restaurants and locations. For a prospective restaurant, the location that obtains the highest predicted number of visits will be identified as the optimal location. As the starting time varies across restaurants, it is better to use the average number of check-ins *per* month rather than the total number of check-ins to assess the popularity of a restaurant.

Figure 2: The demonstration of a location, which refers to an area with a radius of $r = 200m$ around a particular point in New York.

2.2 Features

In this section, we first introduce the two types of features: *market attractiveness* features and *market competitiveness* features, which are referred as *review-based* features, as they are mined solely from the review texts and expected to reveal the attractiveness and competitiveness of a location for a specific restaurant. Then, we introduce the third type of features, *geographic* features, to describe the spatial properties of a candidate location.

2.2.1 Review-based Market Attractiveness Features (MAF)

We attempt to construct *market attractiveness* features to measure whether a restaurant would be attractive to customers who may visit its located place. Specifically, to estimate the *market attractiveness* of a restaurant in a new location, the preference of the restaurant's target customers could be a valuable source of information. As one of the highlights in our work, we are engaged to infer how often each aspect is commented in the restaurant's reviews to represent its customers' preference. With this goal, we adopt a LDA-based topic model [5] to identify aspects[1] from restaurant reviews, by following the assumption used in [18], which states the words in one sentence of a review can be referred to the same aspect.

[1]For the sake of simplicity, the terms "topic" and "aspect" are exchangeable through this paper, unless otherwise specified.

Formally, to profile the customers' preference of a given restaurant, we treat the reviews associated with a restaurant $v \in V$ as a single document d_v (where V is the set of restaurants included in the dataset). Following the idea of LDA model, let $t_{vk} = p(k|v)$ be the probability of document d_v belonging to aspect k, and $\beta_{kw} = p(w|k)$ be the probability that aspect k generates word w, then the likelihood of observing the whole review document corpus is defined as:

$$L(\mathbf{W}|\mathbf{\Theta}, \boldsymbol{\beta}) = \prod_v \prod_w (\sum_{k=1}^{K} t_{vk}\beta_{kw})^{n(v,w)} \quad (1)$$

where $\mathbf{W}$ is the document-word count matrix, $n(v,w)$ is the occurrence count of word w in document d_v, and $\mathbf{\Theta} = \{\boldsymbol{\theta}_v\}_{v=1}^{V}$ and $\boldsymbol{\beta} = \{\boldsymbol{\beta}_k\}_{k=1}^{K}$ are the parameters to be estimated by maximizing the likelihood function $L(\mathbf{W}|\mathbf{\Theta}, \boldsymbol{\beta})$. Then, the preference of the restaurant v's customers can be represented as the aspect distribution in document d_v, such as $\boldsymbol{\theta}_v = \{t_{v1}, \ldots, t_{vK} | 0 \leq t_{vk} \leq 1 \text{ and } \sum_{k=1}^{K} t_{vk} = 1\}$.

Furthermore, for a location $\ell \in \mathcal{L}$, its customers' preference $\boldsymbol{\theta}_\ell \in \mathbb{R}^K$ can be taken as the aggregation of all restaurants in location l. Concretely, each aspect probability $t_{\ell k}$ ($k \in [1, K]$) can be defined as

$$t_{\ell k} = \frac{1}{Z} \sum_{v \in A(\ell, r)} \log(N(v) + 1) t_{vk} \quad (2)$$

where $N(v)$ is the number of reviews of restaurant v, $v \in A(\ell, r)$ indicates that restaurant v is located in location ℓ with radius r, and $Z = \sum_{v \in A(\ell,r)} \log(N(v) + 1)$ is the normaliser ensuring that $\boldsymbol{\theta}_\ell$ lies on a $(K-1)$ dimensional simplex. Note that this aggregation formula gives higher weight to restaurants with more reviews.

Once the preferences of customers from restaurant v and ℓ are respectively represented as aspect distributions as mentioned above, we define two attractiveness features to reveal the attractiveness of a location for a specific restaurant, which are described as follows.

- *Affinity* attractiveness feature:

$$x_{v\ell} = \{t_{vk} \times t_{\ell k}, 1 \leq k \leq K\} \quad (3)$$

  where each entity $t_{vk} \times t_{\ell k}$ is used to indicate the preference affinity between customers of restaurant v and those of location ℓ.

- *Complementary* attractiveness feature:

$$x_{v\ell} = \{t_{vk} \times (1 - t_{\ell k}), 1 \leq k \leq K\} \quad (4)$$

  where each entity $t_{vk} \times (1 - t_{\ell k})$ indicates the preference complementary between customers of restaurant v and those of location ℓ.

In particular, as chain restaurants share a brand name (e.g., McDonald's), and often have common menu items, services and advertising, it is reasonable to merge the reviews of different restaurants belonging to the same chain into a single document. Doing so allows preference of customers from restaurants belonging to the same chain to be represented by the same aspect distribution.

2.2.2 *Review-based Market Competitiveness Feature (MCF)*

In this section, we attempt to construct the *market competitiveness* features to measure whether a restaurant could offer competitive quality relative to restaurants (i.e., competitors) located in the same place. To estimate the *market competitiveness* of a prospective restaurant if it will be located in a new location, we attempt to summarize the sentiment scores over multiple aspects based on opinions expressed in its reviews, to reveal the restaurant's quality.

For this purpose, we apply SentiWordNet [6] to assign each word w with a triple of polarity scores (i.e., positivity $s_+(w)$, negativity $s_-(w)$ and objectivity $s_o(w)$, each in range [0,1], and $s_+(w) + s_-(w) + s_o(w) = 1$). Specifically, for review r, the sentiment score of an aspect k is defined as the average positivity score of all related words:

$$s_{rk} = \frac{\sum_{w \in W(r,k)} s_+(w)}{|W(r,k)|} \quad (5)$$

where $W(r,k)$ denotes the set of words which is related to aspect k included in review r as identified by topic LDA model. Then, for restaurant v, the sentiment score of aspect k is defined as

$$s_{vk} = \frac{\sum_{r \in R(v,k)} s_{rk}}{|R(v,k)|} \quad (6)$$

where $R(v,k)$ denotes the set of reviews of restaurant v, which all commented on aspect k.

Finally, the restaurant v's quality can be represented as the sentiment scores over aspects, such as $\mathbf{s}_v = \{s_{v1}, \ldots, s_{vK} | 0 \leq s_{vk} \leq 1\}$. The market competitiveness feature of a restaurant if it is located in a candidate location is accordingly defined as:

$$x_{v\ell} = \{rank_k(v, \ell), 1 \leq k \leq K\} \quad (7)$$

where $rank_k(v, \ell)$ represents the rank value of restaurant v if it is ranked together with all existing restaurants within location ℓ in the decreasing order of sentiment scores on aspect k.

2.2.3 *Geographic Features (GeoF)*

To represent the geographic characteristics of a location, we also consider three specific geographic features inspired by [11]. In our work, we extract these features from the venue information via the public API of Foursquare.com, in which each venue is associated with a geographic coordinate and categories (e.g., *sub way*, *school* and *residential*).

Density refers to the number of restaurants $A(\ell, r)$ located in location ℓ with radius r:

$$x_{v\ell} = |\{v \in A(\ell, r)\}| \quad (8)$$

Intuitively, a dense area implies a greater likelihood of opportunistic visits to the restaurants located there.

Neighbourhood Entropy is an entropy measure of the frequency of restaurant categories, assessing the heterogeneity of restaurants located in location ℓ [11], which can be calculated by:

$$x_{v\ell} = -\sum_{\gamma \in \Gamma} \frac{N_\gamma(\ell, r)}{N(\ell, r)} \times \log \frac{N_\gamma(\ell, r)}{N(\ell, r)} \quad (9)$$

where Γ is the set of all restaurant categories in the entire dataset, $N_\gamma(\ell, r)$ denotes the number of restaurants of category γ in location ℓ with radius r, and $N(\ell, r)$ is the total number of restaurants in location ℓ with radius r. A location with higher entropy value is expected to be more diverse in terms of restaurant categories, whereas low entropy implies that the location is biased towards some specific types of restaurant.

Competitiveness measures the proportion of nearby restaurants with the same type of restaurant that is under consideration with respect to the total number of restaurants located in location ℓ:

$$x_{v\ell} = -\frac{N_{\gamma_v}(\ell, r)}{N(\ell, r)} \tag{10}$$

where γ_v denotes the type of restaurant v. In general, the area with large competitiveness score implies many of restaurants with the same type (i.e., competitors) would share the potential customers.

Jensen Quality measures the spatial interactions between restaurants and venues. In contrast to [11], we treat the Jensen Quality of each venue category as a feature value, rather than simply aggregating Jensen Quality values over all venue categories as a single feature value. Formally, given a restaurant v, for each venue category $\hat{\gamma} \in \hat{\Gamma}$ (where $\hat{\Gamma}$ is the set of all venue categories), the Jensen Quality of venue category $\hat{\gamma}$ for restaurant v is defined as:

$$x_{v\ell}(\hat{\gamma} \to v) = \frac{\sum_{\gamma \in \Gamma(v)} \log(\kappa_{\hat{\gamma}\to\gamma}) \times (N_{\hat{\gamma}}(\ell, r) - \overline{N_{\hat{\gamma}}(\ell, r)})}{|\Gamma(v)|} \tag{11}$$

where $\Gamma(v)$ is the set of categories to which restaurant v belongs, $N_{\hat{\gamma}}(\ell, r)$ denotes the number of venues of category $\hat{\gamma} \in \hat{\Gamma}$ in location ℓ with radius r, $\overline{N_{\hat{\gamma}}(\ell, r)}$ denotes how many venues of category $\hat{\gamma}$ are observed on average around the restaurant of category γ_v, and $\kappa_{\hat{\gamma}\to\gamma_v}$ denotes the inter-type attractiveness coefficients, which are defined as

$$\kappa_{\hat{\gamma}\to\gamma} = \frac{N - N_{\hat{\gamma}}}{N_{\hat{\gamma}} \times N_{\gamma}} \sum_{\ell \in \mathcal{L}} \frac{N_{\gamma}(\ell, r)}{N(\ell, r) - N_{\hat{\gamma}}(\ell, r)} \tag{12}$$

where N, N_{γ} and $N_{\hat{\gamma}}$ denote the number of venues, the number of restaurants of category γ_v and the number of venues of type $\hat{\gamma}$ respectively.

In summary, *density* and *neighbourhood entropy* geographic features are restaurant-independent, but *competitiveness* and *Jensen Quality* features depend on the location and the restaurant's categories. It is obvious that these geographic features can reflect only the general area properties of the locations without considering the restaurant's detailed properties, e.g., food, service and so on.

2.3 Methodology

We formulate the problem of predicting the visit number of a given restaurant as a regression problem. Given a set of input features $\mathbf{x}_{v\ell}$ and a target variable $y_{v\ell}$ (the number of check-ins received *per* month), we exploit different regression methods to predict the target variable. In order to make the variable better fit the assumptions underlying regression As the distribution of target variable $y_{v\ell}$ is strongly positively skewed, we use the logarithm of $y_{v\ell}$ to make the variable better fit the assumptions underling regression[2]. In our experiment, we exploit three different regression algorithms: Ridge regression, support vector regression (SVR) [17], and Gradient Boosted Regression Trees (GBRT) [7], in order to minimize the error between actual and predicted target variables.

To open a new restaurant $\hat{v}$, we first construct the features $\mathbf{x}_{\hat{v}\ell}$ (as defined in Section 2.2) across different candidate locations $\ell \in \mathcal{L}$. Subsequently, we rank the candidate locations based on the predicted values resulting from the trained regression model by applying the constructed features.

[2]For simplicity, in the following, the logarithm of target variable $y_{v\ell}$ is also denoted as $y_{v\ell}$ unless otherwise specified.

3. EXPERIMENT

3.1 Dataset Description

We collected a set of restaurant reviews in New York City across 260 different categories that were posted on Yelp.com from October 2012 to June 2014. In the experiment, we only consider restaurants that received at least 50 reviews to ensure that the features extracted from the reviews are reliable. As shown in Table 1, the resulting restaurant dataset comprises 1,094,717 reviews to 5,220 restaurants. As noted in the introduction, we emphasize selecting the optimal location for a new branch of a restaurant. Therefore, we use chain restaurants in the dataset as the testing set that contains 93 chain brands and a total of 389 restaurants. The other restaurants are treated as the training set.

The number of check-ins, geographic features (as described in Section 2.2.3) and venue information in New York were obtained from the public API of Foursquare.com. The total number of venues is 147,307, covering 588 different categories (see Table 1).

	Statistics
Yelp restaurant dataset	
# Restaurants	5,220
# Reviews	1,094,717
# Avg. reviews	209.72
# Restaurant categories	260
Foursquare venue dataset	
# Venues	147,307
# Venue categories	588

Table 1: Statistical summary of the *restaurant* dataset from Yelp.com and the *venue* dataset from Foursquare.com

To obtain the candidate locations $\mathcal{L}$, we use a density-based spatial clustering method (OPTICS) [1] to segment a city into cells, each of which is treated as a candidate location. As a result, in our experiment, the New York city is segmented into 995 cells.

3.2 Testing Procedure & Evaluation Metrics

Given a set of candidate locations $\mathcal{L}$, our goal is to select the optimal location ℓ^* for a prospective restaurant v. For each candidate location $\ell \in \mathcal{L}$, we first construct features $\mathbf{x}_{v\ell}$ using the method described in Section 2.2. They are then fed into the trained regression model to predict the number of check-ins that restaurant v will receive during a month.

Firstly, we use Rooted Mean Square Error ($RMSE$) to test whether our model can predict the number of visits (i.e., check-ins) precisely:

$$RMSE = \sqrt{\frac{1}{|T|} \sum_{(v,\ell)\in T} (\hat{y}_{v\ell} - y_{v\ell})^2} \tag{13}$$

in which T is the testing dataset containing pairs of chain restaurant and its location, and $\hat{y}_{v\ell}$ and $y_{v\ell}$ are the predicted and ground-truth numbers of check-ins restaurant v receives in location ℓ respectively.

Secondly, we use the Spearman's rank correlation coefficient (ρ) [15] to measure how well the predicted number of check-ins can preserve the relative order of ground-truth check-ins, defined as:

$$\rho = \frac{1}{|B|}\sum_{b\in B}\left(1 - \frac{6\sum_{(v,\ell)\in T_b}\left(r(\hat{y}_{v\ell}) - r(y_{v\ell})\right)^2}{|T_b|\left(|T_b|^2 - 1\right)}\right) \quad (14)$$

where B represents the set of restaurant brands, T_b represents the set of restaurants belonging to brand b, and $r(\hat{y}_{v\ell})$ and $r(y_{v\ell})$ represent the rank variables based on predicted and ground-truth check-ins respectively.

Thirdly, we treat each chain restaurant brand as a query, and the locations where the chain restaurants are placed as the relevant locations, in order to test whether these relevant locations could be ranked on the top according to the predicted number of check-ins. In this evaluation, we use Mean Average Precision to evaluate the model's ranking accuracy of relevant locations:

$$MAP = \frac{1}{|Q|}\sum_{q\in Q}\frac{\sum_{n=1}^{|\mathcal{L}|}(P@n * rel(n))}{\#\text{ relevant locations for query q}} \quad (15)$$

where Q is the set of queries (i.e., chain restaurant brands) and $P@n$ indicates the precision at n:

$$P@n = \frac{\#\text{ relevant locations in the top } n \text{ results}}{n} \quad (16)$$

and $rel(n) = 1$ if the n-th location is relevant, otherwise 0.

3.3 Results and Discussion

3.3.1 Impact of Parameter K

In our work, the review-based features (i.e., market attractiveness and market competitiveness features) are extracted from LDA topic model. Hence, the choice of aspect number, K, will affect the prediction accuracy. To determine the optimal number of aspects for constructing the review-based features, we tune parameter K in the range of $[5, 25]$ with a tuning step of 5.

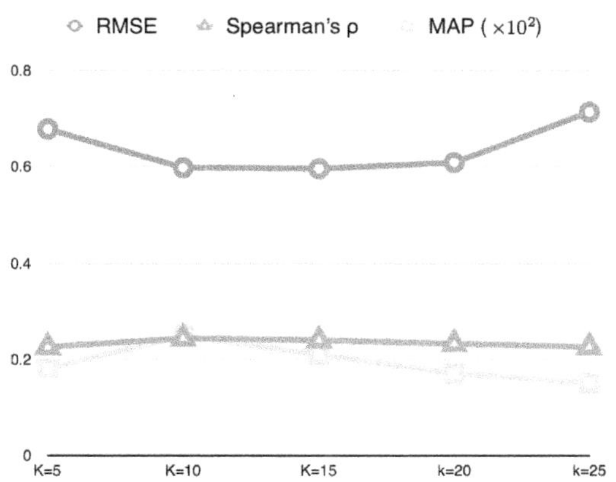

Figure 3: Performance comparison with the review-based features in GBRT algorithm for different aspect numbers K.

Figure 3 shows the changes in terms of $RMSE$, Spearman's ρ and MAP for GBRT algorithm when the aspect number K varies. We can see that the $RMSE$ score reaches the lowest point when $K = 10$, then increases with an increasing number of aspects K. We can also observe that the highest Spearman's ρ (0.244) and MAP (0.0025) are achieved when $K = 10$. For the other two prediction algorithms (i.e., Ridge regression and SVR), the best performance is also achieved when $K = 10$. Hence, we select $K = 10$ as the optimal number of aspects in our experiment.

3.3.2 Algorithm Performance

To evaluate the performance of different prediction algorithms, we conducted a comparison experiment. Table 2 presents the performance results with different features applied to the prediction algorithms. Specifically, in addition to the three types of features we introduced in Section 2.2, we also consider the combination of market attractiveness and market competitiveness features (at $K = 10$) as *review-based* features, and the combination of all the three different types of features (i.e., market attractiveness features, market competitiveness features and geographic features). From Table 2, we can see that SVR algorithm achieves slight improvement against Ridge regression. For example, in terms of Spearman's ρ, SVR algorithm obtains 0.5% improvement with geographic features and 1.5% improvement with review-based features. In addition, we can observe that GBRT algorithm performs better than Ridge regression and SVR algorithms with respect to all features. For example, when only considering the review-based features, GBRT algorithm achieves 6.4% improvement relative to SVR algorithm ($RMSE = 0.597$ versus $RMSE = 0.638$).

	RMSE	Spearman's ρ	MAP
Geographic Features (GeoF)			
Ridge	0.795	0.187	0.0011
SVR	0.793	0.188	0.0014
GBRT	**0.761**	**0.192**	**0.0017**
Market Attractiveness Features (MAF)			
Ridge	0.657	0.215	0.0023
SVR	0.642	0.223	0.0021
GBRT	**0.604**	**0.241**	**0.0025**
Market Competitiveness Features (MCF)			
Ridge	0.772	0.200	0.0015
SVR	0.768	0.203	0.0015
GBRT	**0.760**	**0.205**	**0.0016**
Review-based Features (MAF & MCF)			
Ridge	0.646	0.221	0.0024
SVR	0.638	0.235	0.0021
GBRT	**0.597**	**0.244**	**0.0025**
Combined Features (GeoF & MAF & MCF)			
Ridge	0.631	0.236	0.0026
SVR	0.620	0.251	0.0028
GBRT	**0.586**	**0.308**	**0.0031**

Table 2: Overall performance comparison of different prediction algorithms in terms of $RMSE$, Spearman's ρ and MAP.

3.3.3 Feature Performance

From Table 2, we can also observe that the predictions based on features mined from reviews are more accurate than those based on geographic features. For example, by using the GBRT algorithm, the market attractiveness features achieve 20.6%, 25.5% and 47.0% improvements relative to geographic features in terms of RMSE, Spearman's ρ and MAP respectively. What's more, the market attractiveness features obtain better results than the market competitiveness features across all measures. It can also be seen that the combination of market attractiveness features and market competitiveness features (i.e., review-based features) performs better than geographic features in terms of all measures. Moreover, the combination of all features achieves better results than taking geographic and review-based features alone with regard to $RMSE$, Spearman's ρ and $MAP@10$.

4. RELATED WORK

The optimal placement problem, which is also called the site selection problem [16], has attracted research attention in recent years. A common approach to assessing location is to first develop a checklist to ensure that all relevant factors are considered [2]. However, some of the factors may be quite subjective, and the acquisition of them typically depends on certain local demographics, such as transportation links, and the ease of ingress and egress in the area, which are expensive and time-consuming to acquire.

There are several spatial interaction approaches that draw on the assumptions that the intensity of between-location interactions decreases with distance and the quality of a retail store location increases with the intensity of use and proximity of complementary locations [3, 12]. However, these approaches are applicable only to the selection of agglomeration locations, such as for large shopping centres.

Some researchers have proposed approaches based on analysis of the spatial distribution of commercial activities [8, 11, 19]. For example, in [11], the human mobility trace (check-ins) data in location-based social networks (LBSN) are used to mine certain features in order to provide insights into the quality of an area for opening a new restaurant. However, the limitation of this work is that only three chain restaurants are evaluated (Starbucks, Dunkin' Donuts and McDonald's). Its applicability to other restaurant chains is unclear. In our work, we particularly investigate whether the information embedded in user-generated reviews can be helpful for solving the optimal placement problem. To our knowledge, this is one of the first efforts to tackle the problem by leveraging the publicly available user-generated reviews.

5. CONCLUSIONS AND FUTURE WORK

In this paper, we study the problem of optimal restaurant placement, by taking advantage of online user-generated reviews. We design three sets of features, namely, review-based *market attractiveness* features, review-based *market competitiveness* features, and *geographic* features, which are then exploited to predict the potential number of visits for a prospective restaurant in a given location. We also conducted an experiment with real-world restaurant data to investigate the predictive power of our constructed features. In the experiment, we evaluated each set of features separately, and found that the market attractiveness and market competitiveness features have greater predictive value than geographic features. The prediction accuracy is further increased when both geographic and review-based features are considered. We can hence conclude that the information embedded in user-generated reviews can be helpful to tackle the optimal restaurant placement problem.

In the future, we plan to: (i) exploit additional types of features to improve prediction accuracy (e.g., traffic conditions); (ii) evaluate the effectiveness of our method with other datasets; (iii) show some real case study in our experiments; and (iv) develop algorithm to identify the optimal location for a new restaurant.

Acknowledgement

We thank Hong Kong RGC and China NSFC for sponsoring the described research work (under projects RGC/HKBU12200415 and NSFC/61272365).

6. REFERENCES

[1] M. Ankerst, M. M. Breunig, H.-P. Kriegel, and J. Sander. Optics: Ordering points to identify the clustering structure. In *Proc. 25th SIGMOD*, pages 49–60. ACM, 1999.

[2] W. Applebaum. Can store location research be a science? *Economic Geography*, pages 234–237, 1965.

[3] A. Athiyaman. Location decision making: The case of retail service development in a closed population. *Academy of Marketing Studies*, 15(1):13, 2010.

[4] O. Berman and D. Krass. The generalized maximal covering location problem. *Computers & Operations Research*, 29(6):563–581, 2002.

[5] D. M. Blei, A. Y. Ng, and M. I. Jordan. Latent dirichlet allocation. *JMLR*, 3:993–1022, 2003.

[6] A. Esuli and F. Sebastiani. Sentiwordnet: A publicly available lexical resource for opinion mining. In *Proc. 5th LREC*, pages 417–422. 2006.

[7] J. H. Friedman. Stochastic gradient boosting. *Computational Statistics & Data Analysis*, 38(4):367–378, 2002.

[8] A. S. Furtado, R. Fileto, and C. Renso. Assessing the attractiveness of places with movement data. *Journal of Information and Data Management*, 4(2):124, 2013.

[9] N. Hing. Franchisee satisfaction: Contributors and consequences. *Journal of Small Business Management*, 33(2):12, 1995.

[10] C. H. Hsu, T. F. Powers, and T. F. Powers. *Marketing Hospitality*. John Wiley & Sons, 2002.

[11] D. Karamshuk, A. Noulas, S. Scellato, V. Nicosia, and C. Mascolo. Geo-spotting: Mining online location-based services for optimal retail store placement. In *Proc. 19th KDD*, pages 793–801. ACM, 2013.

[12] A. Kubis and M. Hartmann. Analysis of location of large-area shopping centres. a probabilistic gravity model for the halle–leipzig area. *Jahrbuch für Regionalwissenschaft*, 27(1):43–57, 2007.

[13] M. Mehaffy, S. Porta, Y. Rofè, and N. Salingaros. Urban nuclei and the geometry of streets: The 'emergent neighborhoods' model. *Urban Design International*, 15(1):22–46, 2010.

[14] S. Moghaddam and M. Ester. On the design of LDA models for aspect-based opinion mining. In *Proc. 21st CIKM*, pages 803–812. ACM, 2012.

[15] J. L. Myers, A. Well, and R. F. Lorch. *Research Design and Statistical Analysis*. Routledge, 2010.

[16] T. R. Rex and K. S. Walls. Site selection factors vary widely by economic cluster. *Arizona Business*, pages 6–8, 2000.

[17] A. Smola and V. Vapnik. Support vector regression machines. *Advances in NIPS*, 9:155–161, 1997.

[18] I. Titov and R. McDonald. Modeling online reviews with multi-grain topic models. In *Proc. 17th WWW*, pages 111–120. ACM, 2008.

[19] M. Xu, T. Wang, Z. Wu, J. Zhou, J. Li, and H. Wu. Store location selection via mining search query logs of baidu maps. *arXiv preprint arXiv:1606.03662*, 2016.

Leveraging the Implicit Structure within Social Media for Emergent Rumor Detection

Justin Sampson, Fred Morstatter, Liang Wu, Huan Liu
School of Computing, Informatics, and Decision Systems Engineering
Arizona State University
699 S. Mill Ave.
Tempe, AZ 85287-8809

ABSTRACT

The automatic and early detection of rumors is of paramount importance as the spread of information with questionable veracity can have devastating consequences. This became starkly apparent when, in early 2013, a compromised Associated Press account issued a tweet claiming that there had been an explosion at the White House. This tweet resulted in a significant drop for the Dow Jones Industrial Average. Most existing work in rumor detection leverages conversation statistics and propagation patterns, however, such patterns tend to emerge slowly requiring a conversation to have a significant number of interactions in order to become eligible for classification. In this work, we propose a method for classifying conversations within their formative stages as well as improving accuracy within mature conversations through the discovery of implicit linkages between conversation fragments. In our experiments, we show that current state-of-the-art rumor classification methods can leverage implicit links to significantly improve the ability to properly classify emergent conversations when very little conversation data is available. Adopting this technique allows rumor detection methods to continue to provide a high degree of classification accuracy on emergent conversations with as few as a single tweet. This improvement virtually eliminates the delay of conversation growth inherent in current rumor classification methods while significantly increasing the number of conversations considered viable for classification.

1. INTRODUCTION

Social media is an expansive and varied source of social conversation and interaction data. As social media continues to pervade our culture, it has become an attractive platform to facilitate the spread of information to a large group of people. This is an invaluable feature for the communication of important and time-sensitive information, commercial advertising, and the creation and maintenance of communities. Unfortunately, these properties, combined with the potential for automation, allow for the rapid creation and dissemination of rumors. Rumors spread through social media have the ability to create wide-reaching confusion, distrust, and chaos. Additionally, they are easily spread through the social network. For example, a rumor spread by a compromised Associated Press account on Twitter resulted in an estimated \$136.5 billion drop on the Dow Jones Industrial Average[1]. Unfortunately, while this is an example of a particularly well crafted attack using rumors, this situation is far from isolated. To complicate the problem, repairing damage may not be as simple as refuting the information through a reputable source. In addition, if a rumor gains enough attention to become viral it may also become more difficult to derail. Therefore, it is necessary to identify a rumor as early as possible to provide the best possible chance for countermeasures.

The ability to detect viral rumors in their formative stages is imperative in order to take early action. However, current state-of-the-art detection methods employ a pruning process where conversations with less than a certain threshold of tweets are removed from the dataset. Unfortunately, pruning is a necessary step for several reasons. First, graph propagation methods and time series-based methods cannot be effectively employed on emergent conversations as there is not enough usable network and statistical data generated until several posts have been made. Second, small conversations suffer from data sparsity issues that add noise to otherwise effectively classifiable data. Therefore, a significant problem exists where it is important to perform classification early enough to allow for timely detection while reducing the noise inherent to early conversation data. Fortunately, conversations do not exist in a vacuum. Disjointed conversations, those without explicit links created through reply chains, that share similar topics of discussion may contain important context and propagation data. These can be leveraged in order to provide proper classification of smaller conversations as well as improving the discriminative quality of the features of larger conversations.

We formulate the problem as follows: given a conversation M with m_i messages such that $i \in \{1, ..., |M|\}$ in chronological order and some classification function, $F(M_t) = \alpha$, where t is a detection deadline and α is the resulting classification accuracy, it is understood that $F(M_1) < F(M_t) < F(M_{|M|})$. Now, suppose we can find some related conversation N with the same properties and $N_i < M_1$. Is it possible to leverage the additional information in N such that $F(N_i + M_t) > F(M_t)$? Additionally, it is important to know at what point,

[1]http://www.cnbc.com/id/100646197

CIKM'16, October 24-28, 2016, Indianapolis, IN, USA

DOI: http://dx.doi.org/10.1145/2983323.2983697

if any, is $F(M_{|M|}) > F(N_i + M_t)$ as intuitively the approximation $N_i + M_t$ may not perform as well as M_M. In line with explicit links, those that are explicitly created as a function of conversation responses, we define implicit links as links that join conversation structures based on some similarity but are not inherent to the social media structure. Implicit links can be used to reduce the noise inherent to emergent conversation structure by employing additional information from related conversations which can significantly improve the rate at which new rumor conversations are detectable. Related conversation statistics can also be used to improve discriminative features within established rumors for additional classification accuracy. However, this is also a challenging proposition as it is not trivial to decide what data should be connected, what augmenting data source should be applied, what steps should be taken to reduce cross contamination between classes, and what types of links provide the best discriminating features. The main contributions of this paper are:

- We design a conversation-centric approach to the gathering of rumor data along with curated ground truth;
- We identify and analyze implied links, their distributions, and their impact upon detecting rumors within their emergent stages; and
- We propose two methods for the discovery of implicit links including: Hashtag Linkage and Web Linkage.

2. DATA SETS AND DATA COLLECTION

We study the problem of emergent rumor detection using two credibility-based datasets. The first was initially created by Castillo et al. [3] in order to discover features that could be used to classify the credibility of news and has since become a benchmark dataset for rumor detection. This dataset is made up of 280 separate groups of tweets created by using a set of keywords tailored to gather tweets related to individual news events. Keyword-based search methods result in a dataset which has characteristics such as failing to incorporate either conversation structure or important contextual information that would be found within reply tweets, an exaggerated conversation lifecycle of 29.57 hours, and low content variability within discovered tweets. These characteristics are optimal for studying the feasibility of various methods of rumor detection upon heavily duplicated news data. Though the tweets in each group are loosely associated, to avoid confusion between datasets we will refer to all groups of tweets associated with a specific label as a conversation.

Keyword-based news datasets provide a basis for credibility assessment based on viral data but are unable to provide valuable insight useful for credibility assessment at the conversation level. Studying the effects of conversation structure, reply content, and user engagement is necessary for early detection of rumors as the lag time inherent to news reporting can slow detection speed. To combat this, we propose a new dataset that automatically captures conversation trees related to rumors. Snopes[2] provides a professional rumor repository and verification services. While professional annotation is not applicable to real-time rumor detection applications due to the significant investigation time required for each rumor, known and suspected rumors can be leveraged to discover active rumor-based conversation threads. Often on Twitter, when it is difficult to verify the truthfulness of a conversation, users will mention Snopes in an effort to ask for help, implore other users to verify their statements, or provide known facts related to a rumor. We use this Snopes mentioning trait to gather rumor conversations from the twitter search stream using keywords: snopes, #snopes, snopes.com, and @snopes. Each Snopes mention acts as a 'seed' tweet that is used to reconstruct the conversation structure using Twitter Search API functionality. Dataset statistics can be seen in Table 1.

[2]http://www.snopes.com

Table 1: Statistics of the Datasets

Statistic	Castillo	Snopes
Users	48,224	39,535
Tweets	53,147	90,779
Conversations	280	19,397
Rumors	133	9,397
Non-Rumors	147	10,000
Avg. Conversation Time	29.57 hrs	18.33 hrs
Avg. Duplication	54.3%	9.5%
Conversation Length $\geq$ 10	76.7%	4.5%

3. DETECTING EMERGENT RUMORS

For each given tweet in a conversation, we extract a feature vector, $\hat{t}$, using the set of features proposed by Ma et. al [9]. Conversation feature vectors, used for classification, can then be built using z-score normalized average of the tweet features with links within a given conversation,

$$\theta_i = \frac{t_i - \mu_{t_i}}{\sigma_{t_i}}, \quad (1)$$

where θ_i is the ith feature in the aggregate conversation feature set θ, t_i is the average of the ith feature for all conversations, μ_{t_i} is the mean, and σ_{t_i} is the standard deviation. Therefore, we can group all conversation vectors into the set, R. In order to improve discriminative quality, we create several types of implicit links which we define as underlying contextual clues, or similarities, between otherwise unconnected conversations. For example, if conversation A is discussing event C and we can determine that conversation B is also discussing event C then we can claim that there is an implicit link between these conversations. This is beneficial as the additional user and content information help to reduce noise that is caused by outlier discussions that have too few connected responses. To accomplish this, we need an appropriate transformation that can accommodate various types of implicit links. We express this as follows:

$$R' = \{\theta \in R | \frac{1}{N}(\theta + \sum_{\theta \in R} \mathbb{1}_\theta(I)\theta) > 0\}, \quad (2)$$

where I is any defined implicit link discovery formula, N is the number of discovered links, and $\mathbb{1}_\theta$ is an indicator function defining whether the implicit link I exists in θ. Additional constraints to the set provide filtering that reduces those conversations without any sloping feature values. In effect, this transformation discards any conversations which will not show change over time and are also unable to be linked to other gathered conversations.

3.1 Implicit Links

Implicit links are any form of similarity that can be discovered between otherwise unlinked conversations.

3.1.1 Hashtag Linkage

The use of hashtags has become very prevalent within social media communication. Since hashtags are a general abstraction, it is simple to find links within tweets. As a result, it is difficult to determine the extent to which an implicit link formed using hashtags should impact the extracted conversation features.

3.1.2 Web Linkage

Implicit links formed with web links are rare but with much stronger evidence for similarity. In this case, a conversation link is formed when two unlinked conversations use the same web link. This is a very strict requirement which enforces similarity down to the individual page level of a web domain. Intuitively, this requirement could be loosened to allow links to form between conversations who provide links to the same domain, or link to similar web content types. However, we adhere to a strict web linking policy in order to quantify the impact of the extreme accuracy of exact web links at the expense of additional general link discovery.

4. RESULTS

In order to verify the efficacy of implicit linking techniques, we examine the problem through three distinct experiments. The first experiment involves performing classification using the proposed linking methods on both datasets without performing pruning. This allows us to study how linking methods relate to standard classification methods. The second experiment involves the use of a detection deadline to determine the implications of the addition of external data and at what point, if any, the algorithm will obtain optimal performance. The third experiment involves classification of pruned datasets with several classifiers to understand the relation between linking methods, separability, and classification performance.

4.1 Zero Pruning Classification

In contrast to standard rumor detection, a prime advantage of implicit linking to support rumor detection is the ability to classify datasets without removing data that would otherwise contribute an undue amount of noise. To show this, we perform classification using a linear Support Vector Machine (SVM) and 10-fold cross validation. The experiment was run ten times for each method and the results were averaged. We report accuracy, precision, recall, and F1 score for each method. First, all 280 conversations were classified within the Castillo dataset. As can be seen in Figure 1, standard classification fails to capture discriminating patterns when a pruning strategy is not employed. However, with the addition of implicit links our classification measurements rise using all three methods. In particular, hashtag linking shows an averaged 30% improvement in all metrics when compared to unlinked performance. Web linking was also able to achieve a small improvement in discriminative performance. However, this is acceptable as the extremely duplicated nature of the Castillo news dataset contains very low variability within conversations, resulting in very few web link matches. The same procedure was repeated for all 19,397 conversations within the Snopes dataset. Following the same pattern as the Castillo data, unpruned classification again fails when implicit linking is not used to mitigate the problem. In addition, the larger dataset results in a severe drop in recall. Fortunately, both linking methods provide ample improvement in classification performance.

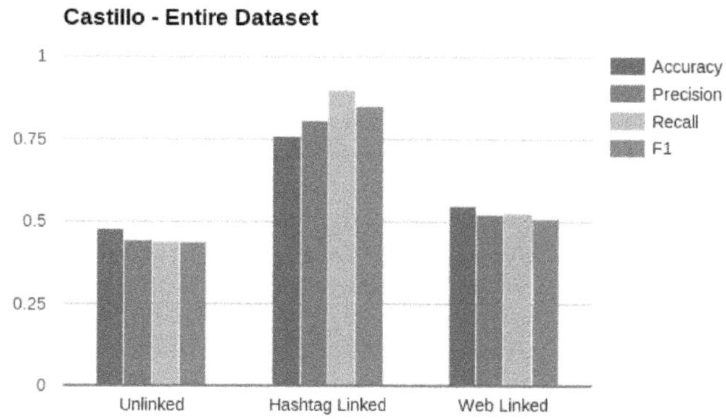

Figure 1: Classification on the Castillo dataset without the removal of small conversations results in near-random classification performance. Hashtag linking performs well while Web linking improves performance but is hampered by difficulty in finding links within the dataset.

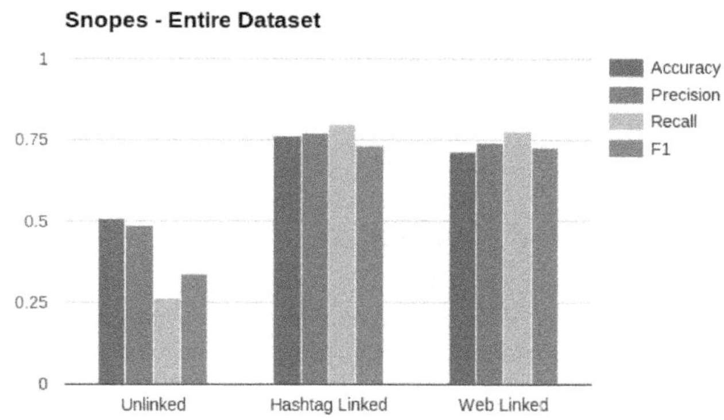

Figure 2: Similarly to the Castillo dataset, classification on the Snopes dataset performs poorly pruning. All linking methods perform well due to the wide range of variability with real conversation data.

4.2 Early Detection and Detection Deadline

By the problem formulation given in Section 1.1, the previous experiment was able to show that the addition of conversation data from conversation N into M was able to achieve significantly improved performance. In order to determine the extent of improvement over time, we perform classification with the addition of a detection deadline. In the initial state, the detection deadline, t, begins at hour 0, the first tweet is exposed for classification. Therefore at time $t = 0$ classification is performed using $F(N_t + M_1)$ where N is any implicitly linkable conversation with tweet timestamps $t \leq M_1$ if using implicit linkage and M_1 other-

Table 2: Classification without Linkage

Castillo Dataset **215 Convs | 45% Rumors**	Accuracy	Precision	Recall	F1
DT	0.5471	0.5253	0.5318	0.5230
DSTS	0.5351	0.5189	0.4964	0.5014
Hybrid SVM	0.5897	0.5852	0.5055	0.5360
RBF	**0.6617**	**0.6633**	**0.5518**	**0.5857**
Snopes Dataset **848 Convs | 55% Rumors**				
DT	0.8197	0.8282	**0.8514**	0.8389
DSTS	0.6995	0.7105	0.7758	0.7403
Hybrid SVM	0.7895	0.7950	0.8387	0.8148
RBF	**0.8428**	**0.8646**	0.8492	**0.8562**

Table 3: Classification with Hashtag Linkage

Castillo Dataset **231 Convs | 45% Rumors**	Accuracy	Precision	Recall	F1
DT	0.7785	0.7823	0.7427	0.7607
DSTS	0.7923	**0.7994**	0.7536	0.7722
Hybrid SVM	**0.7967**	0.7927	**0.7809**	**0.7814**
RBF	0.7876	0.7820	0.7800	0.7765
Snopes Dataset **3,323 Convs | 41% Rumors**				
DT	**0.9416**	**0.9250**	**0.9325**	**0.9284**
DSTS	0.9224	0.8993	0.9118	0.9052
Hybrid SVM	0.9311	0.9111	0.9206	0.9156
RBF	0.9260	0.8938	0.9280	0.9103

Table 4: Classification with Web Linkage

Snopes Dataset **5,947 Convs | 93% Rumors**	Accuracy	Precision	Recall	F1
DT	**0.9825**	**0.9889**	0.9924	**0.9907**
DSTS	0.9650	0.9728	0.9903	0.9814
Hybrid SVM	0.9724	0.9801	0.9906	0.9853
RBF	0.9815	0.9877	**0.9926**	0.9901

wise. At each successive hour deadline, all tweets in M_t and N_t may be used for classification such that all timestamps are less than t.

Following this procedure, at the initial detection deadline the unlinked Snopes dataset was able to correctly classify about 350 tweets while the implicitly linked data performed twice as well at 700 tweets. Likewise, the Castillo implicitly linked data outperformed unlinked classification but with a smaller margin. However, as the detection deadline increased and additional data was able to be incorporated into N, the number of correctly classifiable instances grows significantly for the initial six hours for both implicitly linked datasets. Additionally, counter to intuition, while the improvement gain becomes negligible as time increases, degradation of performance due to incorporation of estimated conversation data does not take place within the first ten hours. This indicates that as a conversation grows, the performance gain from estimated data is not completely removed while the error introduced becomes negligible. While counter-intuitive, this result can be explained by the classification process using averaged aggregate statistics. This also suggests that, using a principled matching process, data from external conversations can improve classification results in the general case.

4.3 Pruned Classification

Optimally, implicit linking should be applied without performing pruning. However, it is necessary to perform classification using current state-of-the-art methods to allow for comparison with previous work. Classification was performed using several state-of-the-art rumor classification methods including a decision tree (DT), Dynamic Series-Time Structure (DSTS) [9], Hybrid DSTS with SVM classifier, and RBF kernel method. Following previous work, only conversations with 10 or more tweets were used and classification was performed using 10-fold cross validation. First, both datasets were classified without applying any form of implicit linking. This gave us a classification accuracy of 66.2% and 84.3% using the RBF kernel for the Castillo and Snopes datasets respectively as shown in Table 2. For both datasets, the RBF kernel is capable of providing improved discrimination between classes by projecting the feature vectors into a high dimensional space. When compared to the simpler models, it is clear that the gap in performance on unlinked data can be attributed to features that cannot be linearly separated.

With the application of implicit hashtag link discovery, classification accuracy saw an improvement of 13.5% and 9.9% for the Castillo and Snopes datasets respectively. Classification results using pruned hashtag linking is shown in Table 3. At the same time, the volume of classifiable conversations was improved for both datasets. The largest gain was within the significantly pruned Snopes dataset - an improvement of over three times as many classifiable instances. Additionally, the gap in classification performance that was caused by difficulty in separability as seen on the unlinked data vanishes.

In both datasets, the discriminative quality of the features was improved to the point where a high level of accuracy was obtainable with simpler, less time consuming classifiers that do not rely on projecting the features into a higher dimensional space. Web linking was performed on the Snopes dataset, however, a low number of classifiable instances and highly redundant data of the Castillo dataset did not allow for the discovery of a suitable number of links. Classification results for web linking can be seen in Table 4. Web linking improved classification accuracy for several of the under-performing methods by 2-3% while also having a positive impact on recall.

5. RELATED WORK

The study of rumor spread and detection has been approached from several angles. The impact, spread, and perception of rumors within social media was examined in order to propose strategies for increasing credibility within social search [10, 6, 13]. These works provide insights into the spread of rumor ideas which can be leveraged by automatic rumor detection models. Such automated methods can be classified into three general types: Epidemic Models, User and Message-based Classification, and Propagation-enhanced Classification.

5.1 Epidemic Models

The spread of information and rumors within social media share many characteristics in common with epidemics. Several studies have employed epidemic models on network and information flow [1, 11]. Jin et al. proposed an extension which specifically targets rumors [7]. Their model, the SEIZ (susceptible, exposed, infected, skeptic) enhanced epidemic model, accurately captures the spread of both news and rumors through the inclusion of an additional state which helps to model exposure delay caused by preheld views as well

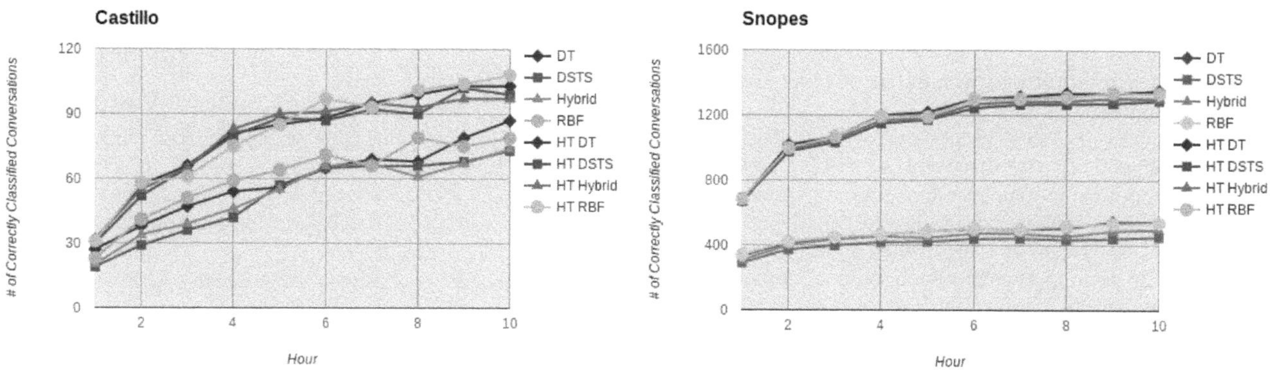

(a) Castillo Dataset

(b) Snopes Dataset

Figure 3: The number of correctly classified rumors as time progresses. With the addition of implicit links, the number of correctly classifiable instances for both rumor and non-rumor conversations see a large increase. This is a combined result of the reduction of noise due to additional tweet statistics as well as an improvement in classification accuracy for conversations that were previously too small for classification.

as other potential factors [7]. Additionally, Takayasu et al. leveraged the SIR model to study the impact of corrective tweets upon rumors during crisis events [15]. While these methods are useful for understanding and generalizing the underlying rumor spreading mechanics, they do not easily allow for prediction or classification which are cornerstone tasks that enable response and preemption.

5.2 User and Message-Based Classification

In order to allow for rapid response, several studies have employed machine learning techniques with the intent of creating classifiers that can, with a high degree of accuracy, decide whether a conversation is credible. Castillo et al. proposed a classifier capable of differentiating news from chatter while also providing initial credibility assessment of conversations [3]. A large body of work has proposed classifier improvements and alternative features to improve the performance of the information credibility task [2, 4, 5, 12, 14, 17]. Other diverging works employ rumor detection through discovery of enquiry content [20]. This has lead to several systems that attempt to automatically detect and verify or debunk rumor conversations [8, 19]. These works provide a strong basis for rumor detection but are severly hampered by datasets that often contain only a few hundred labeled rumor instances. Additionally, all of these previous works perform some form of data pruning method to reduce noise within their data and provide an improvement in classification accuracy. While this usually a reasonable tradeoff when early detection of rumors is not a factor, the practice has become prevalent within works specifically designed to provide early results. This leads to misleading results without real applicability. Fortunately, our work provides a major stepping stone for rumor detection methods which will allow most recent work to function without the need to prune data by leveraging related data.

5.3 Propagation-Enhanced Classification

More recently, conversation propagation statistics have been shown to be an effective source of information in order to detect rumors. Wu et al. [16] employed a random walk kernel in order to measure the similarity in the underlying conversation networks. This form of structural information was shown to be nearly as effective as the combination of all other classification features. In conjunction with additional features this form of detection achieved a 6% gain over other methods. While this reliance on network structure can achieve particularly impressive results, the highest level of accuracy is only seen after the conversation structure has been allowed to develop for more than 24 hours. Other work [18, 9] proposes a timeseries-based method that captures the change of standard statistics as a conversation progresses. While our contribution focuses primarily on early detection, we do propose a modification to these methods which allow rumors to be accurately classified regardless of initial volume of statistics, overcoming one of the few significant problems inherent to timeseries modeling.

6. CONCLUSION AND FUTURE WORK

In this paper, we analyzed how the implicit structure within social media conversations can be leveraged to allow for the detection of emergent rumors. We find that implicit linkage can significantly improve the ability to classify rumors within their formative stages by leveraging information within related conversations. Through the use of implicit links, it was shown that rumor classification can be augmented by historical data in order to achieve state-of-the-art results with computationally cheap classification models. This discovery paves the way for rumor detection methods to progress beyond pruning methods while maintaining a high degree of accuracy on as few as a single tweet.

We discussed the implicit linkage capabilities of hashtags, web links, and content similarity. We discovered that with the addition of implicit structure, not only can rumor detection on a single tweet be significantly improved, but the gain in performance achieved by addition estimated data does not erode performance as the conversation grows. We find that hashtag-based linkage provided the strongest improvement with a gain of up to 30% over unlinked classification on an unpruned dataset. Additionally, we discovered that under-performing classification methods saw improvement from the remaining implicit link types. Further analysis showed that the use of implicit links must be tempered with caution as an over-abundance of external conversation statistics may harm detection accuracy. Our experimental results suggest that consistent accuracy gains through linking can be obtained by limiting the number of links formed to between five and ten.

This work has many possible extensions. While hashtags were greatly beneficial for the discovery of similar conversations, the hashtag graph structure between conversations revealed usage patterns that may provide additional clues for early rumor detection. Likewise, the affinity of certain types of implicit links to be found within each type of conversation could be harnessed as a detection feature. Finally, there are many other forms of potential implied links such as content similarity through document embedding which could provide new insights into the information veracity problem.

Though not explicitly explored in this work, the creation of a multi-label dataset allows for many exciting avenues of exploration. For example, implicit link distribution may vary by type of rumor as it does for non-rumors. This may allow for the discovery of additional characteristics related to the veracity of a rumor that can be harnessed for implicit link creation as well as improved veracity inference.

7. ACKNOWLEDGEMENTS

This work is sponsored, in part, by Office of Naval Research grants N00014-16-1-2257 and N00014131083.

8. REFERENCES

[1] L. M. Bettencourt, A. Cintrón-Arias, D. I. Kaiser, and C. Castillo-Chávez. The power of a good idea: Quantitative modeling of the spread of ideas from epidemiological models. *Physica A: Statistical Mechanics and its Applications*, 364:513–536, 2006.

[2] C. Boididou, S. Papadopoulos, Y. Kompatsiaris, S. Schifferes, and N. Newman. Challenges of computational verification in social multimedia. In *Proceedings of the companion publication of the 23rd international conference on World wide web companion*, pages 743–748. International World Wide Web Conferences Steering Committee, 2014.

[3] C. Castillo, M. Mendoza, and B. Poblete. Information credibility on twitter. In *Proceedings of the 20th international conference on World wide web*, pages 675–684. ACM, 2011.

[4] C. Castillo, M. Mendoza, and B. Poblete. Predicting information credibility in time-sensitive social media. *Internet Research*, 23(5):560–588, 2013.

[5] A. Gupta and P. Kumaraguru. Credibility ranking of tweets during high impact events. In *Proceedings of the 1st Workshop on Privacy and Security in Online Social Media*, page 2. ACM, 2012.

[6] M. Indrawan-Santiago, M. Miyabe, A. Nadamoto, and E. Aramaki. How do rumors spread during a crisis? analysis of rumor expansion and disaffirmation on twitter after 3.11 in japan. *International Journal of Web Information Systems*, 10(4):394–412, 2014.

[7] F. Jin, E. Dougherty, P. Saraf, Y. Cao, and N. Ramakrishnan. Epidemiological modeling of news and rumors on twitter. In *Proceedings of the 7th Workshop on Social Network Mining and Analysis*, page 8. ACM, 2013.

[8] X. Liu, A. Nourbakhsh, Q. Li, R. Fang, and S. Shah. Real-time rumor debunking on twitter. In *Proceedings of the 24th ACM International on Conference on Information and Knowledge Management*, pages 1867–1870. ACM, 2015.

[9] J. Ma, W. Gao, Z. Wei, Y. Lu, and K.-F. Wong. Detect rumors using time series of social context information on microblogging websites. In *Proceedings of the 24th ACM International on Conference on Information and Knowledge Management*, pages 1751–1754. ACM, 2015.

[10] M. R. Morris, S. Counts, A. Roseway, A. Hoff, and J. Schwarz. Tweeting is believing?: understanding microblog credibility perceptions. In *Proceedings of the ACM 2012 conference on Computer Supported Cooperative Work*, pages 441–450. ACM, 2012.

[11] M. E. Newman. Spread of epidemic disease on networks. *Physical review E*, 66(1):016128, 2002.

[12] V. Qazvinian, E. Rosengren, D. R. Radev, and Q. Mei. Rumor has it: Identifying misinformation in microblogs. In *Proceedings of the Conference on Empirical Methods in Natural Language Processing*, pages 1589–1599. Association for Computational Linguistics, 2011.

[13] J. Ratkiewicz, M. Conover, M. Meiss, B. Gonçalves, S. Patil, A. Flammini, and F. Menczer. Truthy: mapping the spread of astroturf in microblog streams. In *Proceedings of the 20th international conference companion on World wide web*, pages 249–252. ACM, 2011.

[14] T. Takahashi and N. Igata. Rumor detection on twitter. In *Soft Computing and Intelligent Systems (SCIS) and 13th International Symposium on Advanced Intelligent Systems (ISIS), 2012 Joint 6th International Conference on*, pages 452–457. IEEE, 2012.

[15] M. Takayasu, K. Sato, Y. Sano, K. Yamada, W. Miura, and H. Takayasu. Rumor diffusion and convergence during the 3.11 earthquake: a twitter case study. *PLoS one*, 10:e0121443–e0121443, 2015.

[16] K. Wu, S. Yang, and K. Q. Zhu. False rumors detection on sina weibo by propagation structures. In *IEEE International Conference on Data Engineering, ICDE*, 2015.

[17] F. Yang, Y. Liu, X. Yu, and M. Yang. Automatic detection of rumor on sina weibo. In *Proceedings of the ACM SIGKDD Workshop on Mining Data Semantics*, page 13. ACM, 2012.

[18] Y. Yang, K. Niu, and Z. He. Exploiting the topology property of social network for rumor detection. In *Computer Science and Software Engineering (JCSSE), 2015 12th International Joint Conference on*, pages 41–46. IEEE, 2015.

[19] Q. Zhang, S. Zhang, J. Dong, J. Xiong, and X. Cheng. Automatic detection of rumor on social network. In *Natural Language Processing and Chinese Computing*, pages 113–122. Springer, 2015.

[20] Z. Zhao, P. Resnick, and Q. Mei. Enquiring minds: Early detection of rumors in social media from enquiry posts. In *Proceedings of the 24th International Conference on World Wide Web*, pages 1395–1405, 2015.

Automatical Storyline Generation with Help from Twitter

Ting Hua
Dept. of Computer Science
Virginia Tech
tingh88@vt.edu

Xuchao Zhang
Dept. of Computer Science
Virginia Tech
xuczhang@vt.edu

Wei Wang
Dept. of Computer Science
Virginia Tech
wwang15@vt.edu

Chang-Tien Lu
Dept. of Computer Science
Virginia Tech
ctlu@vt.edu

Naren Ramakrishnan
Dept. of Computer Science
Virginia Tech
naren@cs.vt.edu

ABSTRACT

Storyline detection aims to connect seemly irrelevant single documents into meaningful chains, which provides opportunities for understanding how events evolve over time and what triggers such evolutions. Most previous work generated the storylines through unsupervised methods that can hardly reveal underlying factors driving the evolution process. This paper introduces a Bayesian model to generate storylines from massive documents and infer the corresponding hidden relations and topics. In addition, our model is the first attempt that utilizes Twitter data as human input to "supervise" the generation of storylines. Through extensive experiments, we demonstrate our proposed model can achieve significant improvement over baseline methods and can be used to discover interesting patterns for real world cases.

1. INTRODUCTION

Many philosophers such as Nietzsche believe that: nothing exists in isolation – all things are interrelated and interdependent. In the era of information explosion, although searching engines such as Google can help users reach the information of a specific event, there is still a lack of technics that can help ordinary users identify the underlying relationships between "isolated" incidents. Storyline generation is one of such technologies that give people useful insights toward better understanding of the world.

Organizing massive documents into the form of storylines can provide users with structured summaries for given subjects, showing the evolution process of relevant events. Unfortunately, detecting storylines is never an easy task. Some researchers have tried generating storylines from unorganized documents, but most of these studies were based on unsupervised clustering techniques [14, 18]. These methods can separate irrelevant storylines easily (e.g., "Sports" and "Earthquake"), however, they perform poorly in distinguishing storylines with overlapped events. As shown in Figure 1, an "Earthquake" storyline may share many common factors with a "Terrorism" storyline. For instance, both of the two storylines may involve aspects such as how many people died or injured (casualties) and how to save more lives (rescue). Previous approaches often fail to differentiate these overlapped storylines since they merely connect documents based on similarity metrics, without capturing knowledge of the hidden events and topics within the storylines.

Bayesian models such as LDA [2] are proved to be effective in learning hidden factors. Compared to clustering based approaches, few studies have been conducted in storyline generation with Bayesian networks. And the existing work often ignore the structure of storylines [4], or fail to model the hidden relations properly [20]. In this paper, we propose a hierarchical Bayesian model for Automatical Storyline Generation (ASG). As shown in Figure 1, ASG is the first storyline model with the three-level structure: storylines are root nodes, event types lie in the second-level, and the finest granularity is topic. In ASG model, different storylines can share common event types, and events can be viewed as various combinations of topics. For instance, both the storylines shown in Figure 1 include event types "Rescue" and "Casualties", and both these event types incorporate words from Topic 2 and Topic 3. ASG model also captures the relationships across the layers through two specially designed matrices. This is the first scheme by now that can quantitatively measure the hidden relations between storyline and its hidden factors.

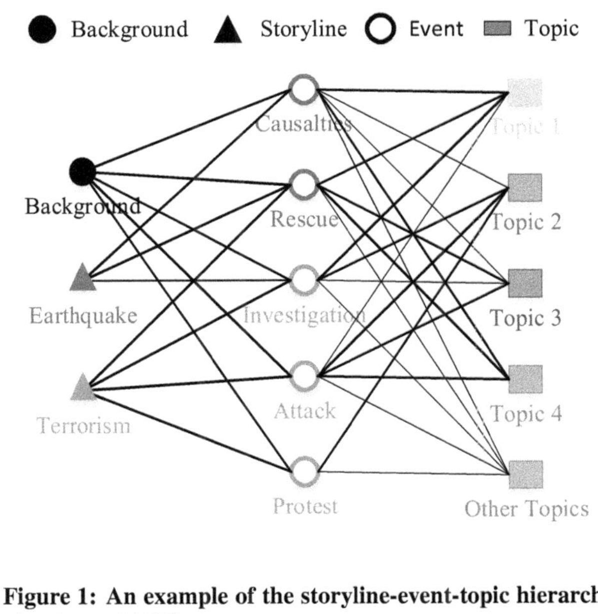

Figure 1: An example of the storyline-event-topic hierarchical structure of ASG.

CIKM '16, October 24–28, 2016, Indianapolis, IN, USA.
© 2016 ACM. ISBN 978-1-4503-4073-1/16/10... $15.00
DOI: http://dx.doi.org/10.1145/2983323.2983698

To further improve performance, ASG model uses the Twitter hashtags created by users as labels to "supervise" story generation in long news reports. Nowadays, "sharing to Twitter/Facebook" options are embedded into each news article posted on the web sites of major news media, such as CNN and BBC. When Twitter users share these articles from the original web site or retweet related tweets from their friends, they create special terms that start with #, the so-called "hashtag", to denote the topics/trends of their posts. Although Twitter data is so noisy that most existing storyline generation tools are unable to cope with it adequately [10, 15], these user self-created hashtags effectively provide human annotations for long articles. The major contributions of this paper are summarized as follows:

- **A novel Bayesian model is proposed to capture the features of real world events.** ASG model represents storyline as a three-layer structure, and provides solutions to measure hidden relations among storylines, events, and topics.

- **Human input is incorporated into the storyline generation process.** The rich up-to-date Twitter data provide the "cheapest" human made labels (hashtags), since they are publicly accessible. And ASG easily improves its performance by using these user-created Twitter hashtags to filter redundant event types.

- **An efficient Gibbs sampling inference is provided for the proposed ASG model.** Gibbs sampling was chosen for the inference and parameter estimation of ASG model for its high accuracy in estimations for LDA-like graphical model.

- **The effectiveness of the proposed ASG model is demonstrated through the comparison with existing state-of-the-art algorithms.** ASG model was tested on large datasets associated with real world events. With extensively quantitative and qualitative results, ASG model showed significant improvements over baseline methods.

2. RELATED WORK

To the best of our knowledge, this is the first attempt to generate storylines for long articles utilizing knowledge from social media, but there are several lines of related research such as topic tracking, news & Twitter modeling, and storyline discovery.

Topic tracking methods aim to identify hidden topics and track topical changes across time. Most of the earlier work in this area, for example DTM [1], estimated current topic distribution through parameters learned from the previous epoch. In addition to methods based on Markov assumptions, there has been some work modeling the evolution of topics using time stamps generated from continuous distribution [17]. TAM model [6] is a hybrid of these two approaches, which captures changes via a property dubbed a "trend class"–a latent variable with distributions over topic, words, and time. However, the granularity of "epoch" or "trend" in topic tracking approaches is inherently too fine to be suitable for the storyline discovery task.

Twitter is a newly emerging platform for news spreading [7], which covers almost all domains of newswire events [11]. Approaches that combine news and social media data in one joint model have been proposed to improve Twitter topic modeling performance, by "transferring" knowledge learned from long articles such as those in Wikipedia, blogs, news reports to short tweets [3, 5]. It is generally agreed that Twitter data is inherently noisy [19]. Therefore, few previous studies have sought to reversely use knowledge provided by social media users to label or organize long articles. Unlike these methods, our proposed ASG model only used "hashtags" from tweets, and omitted the rest of noisy content.

Storyline discovery is the closest research branch to our work. Shahaf et al. [14] proposed a metro-map format story generation framework, which first detected community clusters in each time window, and then grouped these communities into the stories. Yan et al. tracked the evolution trajectory along the timeline by emphasizing relevance, coverage, coherence and diversity of themes [18]. Mei et al. [12] proposed a HMM style probabilistic method to discover and summarize the evolutionary patterns of themes in text streams. Lappas et al. [8] designed a term burstness model to discover the temporal trend of terms in news article streams. Taking user queries as input, [10] first extracted relevant tweets and then generated storylines through graph optimization. Lin et al. [9] built a HDP (Hierarchical Dirichlet Process) model for each time epoch and then selected sentences for the storyline by considering multiple aspects such as topic relevance and coherence. Huang et al. identified local/global aspects of documents and organized these components into a storyline via optimization [4], while Zhou et al. modeled storylines as distributions over topics and named entities [20]. None of the above work jointly considered social media and news data, and all of them failed to provide a complete storyline-event-topic structure such as the one proposed in this paper.

3. MODEL

The graphical model and generative process of ASG are shown in Figure 2 and Algorithm 1 respectively. Each document d_m is a news article embed in tweet URL, associated with tweet hashtags $\mathbf{\Lambda_m}$. Storyline s is a multinational variable indicating which storyline document d_m belonging to, generated from multinomial distribution π_s. Each storyline has one multinomial distribution ψ_s over events. Variable e denotes a document's event label drawn from E-dimensional distribution ψ_s. Each event e has a multinomial distribution ϕ_e over K topics. As we will discuss in detail later, matrix ψ_s and matrix ϕ_e can reflect the relations among storyline s, event e, and topic z.

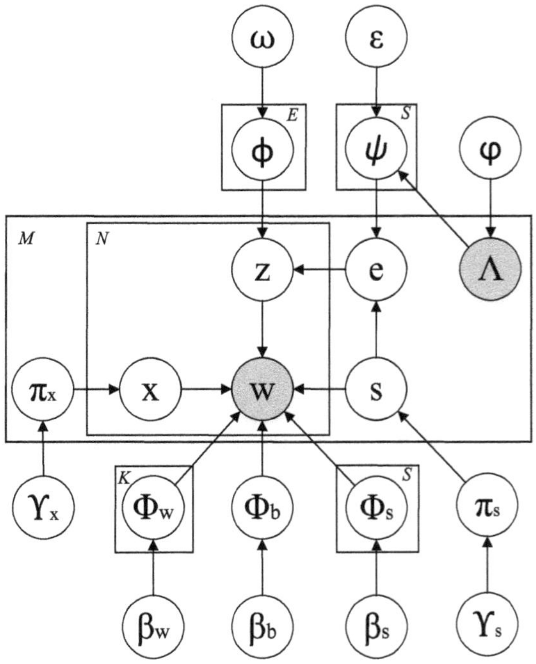

Figure 2: Graphical model for ASG.

Each word w in document d_m is associated with two labels: switching variable x and topic indicator z. $x = 0$ means the word w is generated from background distribution Φ_b, $x = 1$ shows the word is generated from storyline distribution Φ_s, and $x = 2$ denotes the word is generated via topic distribution Φ_w. Also, in the case of x taking value 2, topic z is sampled from K-dimension multinomial distribution ϕ_e. Under this strategy, ASG model can explain words in three different ways, from topics, from storylines, and from a background word distribution. The whole dataset has only one background word distribution Φ_b, while there are S different storyline-words distributions Φ_s and K different Φ_w topic distributions. This matches the intuition that a document is a mixture of background words (e.g., stop words), storyline words, and a set of aspect topics (e.g., locations).

Algorithm 1 Generation Process of ASG model

1: Draw $\pi_s \sim Dir(\gamma_s)$
2: Draw $\Phi_b \sim Dir(\beta_b)$
3: **for** each storyline $s = 1, 2, ..., S$ **do**
4:     Draw $\Phi_s^{(s)} \sim Dir(\beta_s)$
5: **for** each event $e = 1, 2, ..., E$ **do**
6:     Draw $\phi^{(e)} \sim Dir(\omega)$
7: **for** each topic $z = 1, 2, ..., K$ **do**
8:     Draw $\Phi_w^{(z)} \sim Dir(\beta_w)$
9: **for** each document $m = 1, 2, ..., M$ **do**
10:     **for** each event $e = 1, 2, ..., E$ **do**
11:         Draw $\Lambda_m^{(e)} \sim Bernoulli(\cdot|\varphi_e)$
12:     Draw $s \sim Multi(\pi_s)$
13:     Generate $\varepsilon_m = diag(\Lambda_m) \times \varepsilon$
14:     Draw $\psi_s^{(s)} \sim Dir(\varepsilon_m)$
15:     Draw $e \sim Multi(\psi_s^{(s)})$
16:     Draw $\pi_x \sim Dir(\gamma_x)$
17:     **for** each word w in document m **do**
18:         Draw $x \sim Multi(\pi_x)$
19:         Draw $z \sim Multi(\phi^{(e)})$
20:         **if** x=0 **then** Draw $w \sim \Phi_b$
21:         **if** x=1 **then** Draw $w \sim \Phi_s^{(s)}$
22:         **if** x=2 **then** Draw $w \sim \Phi_w^{(z)}$

Twitter users often create hashtags to emphasize the key points of their posts. For example, a tweet about president election may contain hashtags such as #Hillary or #Trump. As a kind of human made labels, hashtags can be used to simplify search, indexing, and topic discovery [13]. To enable modeling of context associated with hashtags, we restrict storyline-event distribution ψ_s to be filtered by its hashtags Λ_m. Namely, the choices of events for each document are restricted to its set of hashtags. Towards this goal, we set E to be the number of hashtags contained in the whole dataset. The dependency of ψ_s on both ε and Λ is shown as directed edges connecting them in Figure 2. Each element $\Lambda_m^{(e)}$ of hashtag labels Λ_m is generated through Bernoulli distribution with prior probability φ_e. As shown in Line 13 and Line 14 of Algorithm 1, storyline-event vector ψ_s is then drawn from a Dirichlet distribution with parameters $diag(\Lambda_m) \times \varepsilon$. Suppose there are 5 important hashtags in the datasets, then the value of E is 5 and Λ_m is a 5-dimension vector, within which each element is either 0 or 1. For a document associated with 2 hashtags, such as the president election tweet mentioned above, ψ_s is sampled with prior $\varepsilon_m = diag(\Lambda_m) \times \varepsilon = (0, 0, \varepsilon_3, \varepsilon_4, 0)^T$.

4. MODEL INFERENCE AND LEARNING

In this section, we first describe the inference process of collapsed Gibbs sampler for ASG mdoel, and then discuss the training and testing operations for the proposed model.

4.1 Model Inference

The prior parameter φ is d-separated from the rest of ASG model, when the hashtag labels Λ_m of document m are observed. The key to the inference is to estimate posterior distributions of hidden variables: (1) multinomial switch variable $\mathbf{x}_{mn}$ for word w_{mn}; (2) topic assignment variable $\mathbf{z}_{mn}$ for word w_{mn} when the corresponding switch variable $\mathbf{x}_{mn}$ equals to 2; (3) event assignment variable $\mathbf{e}_m$ for document m; (4) storyline assignment variable $\mathbf{s}_m$ for document m.

Gibbs sampling is chosen for the inference. First, the posterior of $\mathbf{s}_m$ is calculated through Equation (1). Due to space limitations, we only present the result here.

$$p(\mathbf{s}_m|\mathbf{w}, \mathbf{z}, \mathbf{s}_{\neg m}, \mathbf{e}, \mathbf{x}) = \prod_{v=1}^{V} \left(\frac{n_s^v + \beta_s}{\sum_{v=1}^{V} (n_s^v + \beta_s)} \right)^{n_{ms}^v} \cdot \frac{n_{se}^e + \omega}{\sum_{i=1}^{E} (n_{se}^i + \omega)} \cdot \frac{n_{ss}^i + \gamma_s}{\sum_{i=1}^{S} (n_{ss}^i + \gamma_s)} \quad (1)$$

In the above equation, V is the size of the vocabulary, E is the number of events, and S is the number of storylines. n_s^v is the number of term v choosing storyline s (when its $x = 1$), n_{ms}^v is the number of term v choosing storyline s in the scope of document m. n_{se}^i is number of document choosing event e within storyline s, and n_{ss}^i is the number of documents choosing storyline i.

The inference of $\mathbf{e}_m$ is slightly different from that of $\mathbf{s}_m$. Each storyline s has a distribution ψ_s over events. Given storyline s, document chooses corresponding event e from ψ_s:

$$p(\mathbf{e}_m|\mathbf{w}, \mathbf{z}, \mathbf{s}, \mathbf{e}_{\neg m}, \mathbf{x}) = \prod_{z=1}^{K} \left(\frac{n_e^z + \omega}{\sum_{z=1}^{K} (n_e^z + \omega)} \right)^{n_{em}^z} \frac{n_{se}^e + \varepsilon}{\sum_{i=1}^{E} (n_{se}^i + \varepsilon)}, \quad (2)$$

where K is the number of topics, n_e^z is the counts of words choosing topic z under event e, and n_{em}^z is the number of words in document m choosing topic z.

In word-level, word w_{mn} first decides its value x: (1) when $x_{mn} = 0$, word w_{mn} is sampled from background words distribution Φ_b; (2) when $x_{mn} = 1$, word w_{mn} is chosen from storyline words distribution Φ_s, where s is the choice of document m; (3) when $x_{mn} = 2$, word w_{mn} is drawn from topic distribution $\Phi_w^{(z)}$, where z is chosen beforehand by the word:

$$p(\mathbf{x}|\mathbf{w}, \mathbf{z}, \mathbf{s}, \mathbf{e}, \mathbf{x}_{\neg \mathbf{i}}) = \begin{cases} \frac{n_b^v + \beta_b}{\sum_{v=1}^{V} (n_b^v + \beta_b)} \frac{n_{xm}^0 + \gamma_x}{\sum_{i=0}^{2} (n_{xm}^i + \gamma_x)}, x = 0 \\ \frac{n_s^v + \beta_s}{\sum_{v=1}^{V} (n_s^v + \beta_s)} \frac{n_{xm}^1 + \gamma_x}{\sum_{i=0}^{2} (n_{xm}^i + \gamma_x)}, x = 1 \\ \frac{n_z^v + \beta_w}{\sum_{v=1}^{V} (n_z^v + \beta_w)} \frac{n_{xm}^2 + \gamma_x}{\sum_{i=0}^{2} (n_{xm}^i + \gamma_x)}, x = 2. \end{cases} \quad (3)$$

When $x_{mn} = 2$, topic assignment z_{mn} needs to be decided first. Similar to storyline-event relationship, each event has a distribution over topics. Given event e, topics are chosen from multinomial distribution ϕ_e:

$$p(\mathbf{z}_i|\mathbf{w},\mathbf{z}_{\neg i},\mathbf{s},\mathbf{e},\mathbf{x}) = \frac{n_k^v+\beta_w}{\sum_{v=1}^{V}(n_k^v+\beta_w)}\frac{n_e^k+\omega}{\sum_{z=1}^{K}(n_e^z+\omega)}, \quad (4)$$

where n_z^v is the number of term v choosing topic z in the scope of the whole corpus.

4.2 Learning Operations

ASG can be treated as a semi-supervised model because the hidden variables are learned under the supervision of human made hashtags. In the training process, ASG model is fed with pre-given storyline labels. That is, the storyline labels of documents can be seen by the model, while event labels, topic assignments, and switch variables are inferred to maximize the likelihood of observed words and storyline labels. With trained model $\mathcal{M}$, ASG model can be used to estimate the posterior distributions of switch variables $\tilde{\mathbf{x}}$, topics $\tilde{\mathbf{z}}$, events $\tilde{\mathbf{e}}$, and storyline labels $\tilde{\mathbf{s}}$ for new coming documents, without any pre-given labels. In order to achieve this goal, we follow the approach introduced in [16] to run the inference process on the new documents exclusively. Inference for this testing process corresponds to Equation (1)~(4) with the difference that: current Gibbs sampler is run with estimated parameters Φ_b, Φ_s, Φ_w, ϕ, ψ, and fixed hyperparameters.

Taking the inference of switch variable x for example. In the initial stage, the algorithm randomly assigns switch variables to words. Then a number of Gibbs sampling updates are conduct to estimate the posterior. Similar to switch variable $\tilde{x}$, the estimations of storyline label $\tilde{s}$, event label $\tilde{e}$, and topic assignment $\tilde{z}$ can be calculated according to Equation (1), (2), and (4).

5. EXPERIMENT

In this section, we first describe our evaluation datasets, and then compare our proposed ASG model with existing state of the-art algorithms. Finally, extensive discovery results are presented by exploring the outputs of ASG model.

5.1 Datasets and Experiment Settings

To evaluate our proposed model and other storyline generation methods, we conducted our experiments on datasets containing 110, 347 tweets and 27, 308 news articles of 6 event subjects. These events were chosen due to their great social influence and high evolution complexity. Specifically, the datasets were collected via the following steps: 1) For each event, filter Twitter data through Twitter REST API using event-relevant keywords and hashtags provided by domain experts. 2) Extract URL links embedded in the tweets, download documents associated with these links. 3) Conduct stemming and lemmatization. Note that, we didn't remove stop words in the preprocessing step, since our proposed ASG model could treat these words as background words. Table 1 lists the statistical information about evaluation datasets.

We asked human annotators to create labels for these documents: 1) select storyline label from the six event subjects for each document, and 2) assign event label from 21 event types provided by domain experts for each document. One document is associated to one storyline label and one event label. We divided the whole dataset evenly into 4 parts and assigned to 4 groups of annotators. Within each group, a label will be included in the groud-truth only if it is chosen by at least 2 out of the 3 annotators.

In our evaluation, we used weak symmetric priors for all Dirichlet parameters: $\gamma_s = 0.1$, $\gamma_x = 0.3$, $\beta_s = 0.0001$, $\beta_w = \beta_b = 0.001$, $\varepsilon = \omega = 0.01$. The number of topics K is 50, the number of

Dataset	#Tweets	#News	Country
World Cup	11K	3352	Brazil
President Election	9K	2491	Colombia
Security Protests	12K	3787	Venezuela
Education March	14K	4841	Chile
Iguala Kidnap	25K	5853	Mexico
Paris Attack	37K	6984	France

Table 1: Detailed information of datasets

events is decided by the total number of hashtags contained in the datasets, and the storyline number is set to be 6. The Gibbs sampler is run for 500 iterations with the first 100 iterations as built-in period. We compared our ASG model with the following methods. 1) Random: The random method selects documents randomly for storylines and events. 2) K-means: This method identifies storylines and events by K-means clustering. The number of clusters is set to be 6 (number of ground truth storylines). 3) LSA: LSA is a method of analyzing relationships between a set of documents and terms they contain, which uses SVD to reduce the dimension of features with high similarity. In our experiment, the number of clusters is set to be 6. 4) LDA: This method applies standard LDA twice to discovery storylines and events. First, topics found in the first run are treated as storylines ($K_1 = 6$). Then, within each obtained topic, another LDA is run to distinguish the events ($K_2 = 50$). 5) ASGH: This approach is a variant of ASG that ASGH model doesn't use Twitter hashtags for generation of events. 6) ASGB: This method is another variant of ASG that ASGB model excludes the background distribution Φ_b and has a symmetric beta prior $\gamma_x = 0.5$.

5.2 Experiment Results

Table 2 reports the ACC and NMI results for seven methods. ACC denotes the performance on storyline-level, and NMI can better evaluate the results on event-level. Random selection is the worst performer that its ratio of correct guess on storylines (ACC) is around 1/6, and the probability of successful guess in event-level (NMI) is almost equal to 0. Our ASG model outperforms the baseline methods in most of the fields, except on "World Cup", where ASGB achieves the best outcome.

Two interesting observations can be made from Table 2. First, Bayesian models perform better than clustering methods. Two clustering methods K-means and LSA are much better than random selection method, however, significantly poorer than Bayesian models LDA, ASGH, ASGB, and ASG. This is because these methods are simply built on word similarities, without further knowledge on relationship between words (hidden topics). Second, "Hashtag" factor is more important than "background words" factor. Compared to ASGH model, ASGB model obtain the performance closer to ASG model, which indicates utilization of hashtags indeed improve performance significantly. As later shown in Table 3, the scheme of background distribution can remove stop words and commonly used words, which therefore benefit the overall performance of ASG model.

Table 3 lists top 15 terms of background, storyline, and topic words learned by ASG model. In general, the ration of words assigned to background distribution, storyline distributions, and topic distributions are 33%, 27%, and 38% respectively.

We discuss the three types of words as follows. 1) **Background words**. There is only one background word distribution over the whole corpus. Most of the top ranked background words are stop words such as "en"(Spanish), "the", "de"(Spanish), or common used words such as "video", "http", "com". 2) **Storyline words**. Storyline words are not used as commonly as background words,

Table 2: Performance comparison among storyline detection methods (ACC, NMI)

	World Cup		President Election		Security Protests		Education March	
	Acc	NMI	Acc	NMI	Acc	NMI	Acc	NMI
Random	0.14411	2.84E-05	0.153098	0.000515	0.156086	0.00158	0.17796	0.000962
K-means	0.342921	0.02507	0.302279	0.024265	0.354775	0.16668	0.323172	0.117916
LSA	0.426756	0.000448	0.40866	0.009094	0.36727	0.117569	0.378563	0.00213
LDA	0.498904	0.280061	0.457191	0.141977	0.461266	0.271075	0.482378	0.243714
ASGH	0.512481	0.319418	0.484782	0.152756	0.517365	0.313238	0.495184	0.248761
ASGB	**0.623336**	**0.399913**	0.585973	0.181412	0.597942	0.394318	0.505529	0.268152
ASG	0.598904	0.380061	**0.622446**	**0.210056**	**0.617287**	**0.415664**	**0.528883**	**0.290283**

Table 3: Example of background/storyline/topic words learned by ASG model.

Background		Storyline 1		Storyline 2		Topic 16		Topic 21	
la	0.0093	paris	0.0104	presidente	0.0058	office	0.0076	pineda	0.0030
el	0.0087	help	0.0057	estudiante	0.0055	view	0.0074	esporte	0.0026
en	0.0058	theater	0.0049	EPN	0.0054	gobierno	0.0072	abarca	0.0025
the	0.0057	http	0.0043	news	0.0053	police	0.0061	right	0.0023
video	0.0053	shoot	0.0039	mar	0.0051	time	0.0037	zuluaga	0.0023
com	0.0051	news	0.0034	mexico	0.0049	comment	0.0034	dilma	0.0022
de	0.0038	hurt	0.0032	home	0.0047	city	0.0032	trial	0.0019
www	0.0038	hall	0.0030	iguala	0.0041	voice	0.0029	hecha	0.0018
marzo	0.0037	kill	0.0029	youtube	0.0037	new	0.0027	santos	0.0017
Twitter	0.0036	world	0.0029	gobierno	0.0035	report	0.0027	vaga	0.0016
filter	0.0034	police	0.0029	toda	0.0035	tudo	0.0027	jamariro	0.0016
apply	0.0034	terrorist	0.0026	nacional	0.0035	medium	0.0026	soho	0.0014
email	0.0033	people	0.0026	poltica	0.0035	share	0.0025	bio	0.0012
http	0.0031	maduro	0.0026	kidnap	0.0030	arrest	0.0024	bundchen	0.0011
da	0.0031	gun	0.0025	secuestrado	0.0030	agosto	0.0023	lula	0.0011

but still across a broad range of documents within the storyline. Storyline 1 seems to be related to "Paris attack", since it contains word "paris" and some other event words such as "theather", "hurt", and "shoot". Similarly, Storyline 2 is about kidnap in Mexico, which is consisted of words such as "mexico", "secuestrado" (Spanish of kidnap), and "estudiante"(Spanish of student). 3) **Topic words**. Compared to storyline words and background words, topic words are narrowed to more specifical context. For example, Topic 16 is a set of words describing government, with words such as "office", "police", and "gobierno" (Spanish of government), while Topic 21 is about people names, which includes words such as "dilma" (Brazilian president), "santos" (Colombian president), and "zuluaga" (a Colombian economist).

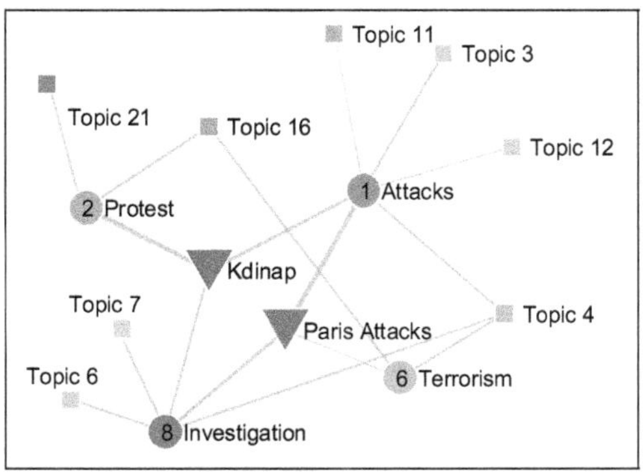

Figure 3: Relations among storyline, event type, and topics. The triangles are symbols for storylines, the circles denote event type, and the squares indicate topics.

One of the major contributions of ASG model is that: ASG is the first storyline generation model that can quantitatively measure the relations among storylines, events, and topics. In practice, these knowledge are learned from storyline-event matrix ψ and event-topic matrix ϕ. Figure 3 illustrates the usage of these matrices. Corresponding to Figure 1 in the introduction section, here triangles in the central parts denote storylines, the circles around the triangles represent event types, and the outermost squares stand for topics. The thickness of the edge between a triangle (storyline s) and a circle (event e) is proportional to the corresponding value of ψ_{se}, and similarly, the thickness of the edge between a circle (event e) and a square (topic z) is corresponding to the value of ϕ_{ez}. By correlating Table 3 with Figure 3, some interesting patterns can be obtained. 1) **Mapping ground-truth labels**. By referring to the storyline words distribution in Table 3, we mapped the storylines to real cases: the blue triangle should be the "Kidnap" storyline, with storyline words such as "mexico" and "students"; the red triangle is the "Paris attack", because words such as "terrorist" and "Paris" are top ranked in the storyline-words list. Also, as mentioned above in Table 3, topic 16 is related to "government", and topic 21 is related to "people names". 2) **Relations between topics and event types**. By referring to the values of matrix ϕ_{ez}, the result event types can be inferred through their connected topics. For example, in Figure 3, event 2 is connected to topic 16 (government) and topic 21 (people names). Among the 21 event types, the combination of the two topics is closest to event type "investigation". Similarly, event 1 is recognized as "attack", event 6 means "protest", and event 8 denotes "terrorism". 3) **Relations between storylines and event types**. The impact of event type factors to storylines can be analyzed through values of matrix ψ_{se}. As can be seen from Figure 3, both the storyline "Paris attack" and "Kidnap" are connected to event "investigation" and "attack", the difference is that: "Paris attack" storyline has a stronger connection on event "attack" over event "investigation", while storyline "Kidnap" has balanced weights on the two events. Besides the common shared events, "Paris attack" owns a private event type "terrorism", and storyline "Kidnap" has one exclusive event type "protest".

These above mentioned observations match the real world truth well, and therefore directly implies ASG model is a useful tool to identify and interpret the hidden factors that driving the evolution of events.

6. CONCLUSION

In this paper, we proposed a hierarchical Bayesian model named ASG to detect storylines. ASG is the only model with three-layer structure for the task of storyline generation. It ignores the noisy context of tweets and utilizes their promising labels made by Twitter users (hashtags) to improve the performance. Besides, through special designed data structures, ASG is capable to measure the hidden relations among storylines, events, and topics. We present the results of applying ASG model to real-word events and show its effectiveness over non-trivial baselines. Based on the outputs of ASG model, further analysis can be made to understand the underlying factors inside the documents, which can lead to a broad spectrum of future research.

7. ACKNOWLEDGEMENT

This work is supported by the Intelligence Advanced Research Projects Activity (IARPA) via Department of Interior National Business Center (DoI/NBC) contract D12PC00337. The views and conclusions contained herein are those of the authors and should not be interpreted as necessarily representing the official policies or endorsements, either expressed or implied, of IARPA, DoI/NBC, or the US government.

8. REFERENCES

[1] David M Blei and John D Lafferty. Dynamic topic models. In *Proceedings of the 23rd international conference on Machine learning*, pages 113–120. ACM, 2006.

[2] David M Blei, Andrew Y Ng, and Michael I Jordan. Latent dirichlet allocation. In *The Journal of Machine Learning Research*, volume 3, pages 993–1022. MIT Press, 2003.

[3] Ting Hua, Ning Yue, Feng Chen, Chang-Tien Lu, and Naren Ramakrishnan. Topical analysis of interactions between news and social media. In *Proceedings of the 30th AAAI Conference on Artificial Intelligence*, pages 2964–2971, 2016.

[4] Lifu Huang and Lian'en Huang. Optimized event storyline generation based on mixture-event-aspect model. In *Proceedings of the 12th Conference on Empirical Methods in Natural Language Processing*, pages 726–735, 2013.

[5] Ou Jin, Nathan N Liu, Kai Zhao, Yong Yu, and Qiang Yang. Transferring topical knowledge from auxiliary long texts for short text clustering. In *Proceedings of the 20th ACM international conference on Information and knowledge management*, pages 775–784. ACM, 2011.

[6] Noriaki Kawamae. Trend analysis model: trend consists of temporal words, topics, and timestamps. In *Proceedings of the 4th ACM international conference on Web search and data mining*, pages 317–326. ACM, 2011.

[7] Haewoon Kwak, Changhyun Lee, Hosung Park, and Sue Moon. What is twitter, a social network or a news media? In *Proceedings of the 19th international conference on World wide web*, pages 591–600. ACM, 2010.

[8] Theodoros Lappas, Benjamin Arai, Manolis Platakis, Dimitrios Kotsakos, and Dimitrios Gunopulos. On burstiness-aware search for document sequences. In *Proceedings of the 15th ACM SIGKDD International Conference on Knowledge Discovery and Data Mining*, pages 477–486. ACM, 2009.

[9] Jiwei Li and Sujian Li. Evolutionary hierarchical dirichlet process for timeline summarization. In *Proceedings of the 51st Annual Meeting of the Association for Computational Linguistics*, pages 556–560, 2013.

[10] Chen Lin, Chun Lin, Jingxuan Li, Dingding Wang, Yang Chen, and Tao Li. Generating event storylines from microblogs. In *Proceedings of the 21st ACM international conference on Information and knowledge management*, pages 175–184. ACM, 2012.

[11] Craig Macdonald, Richard McCreadie, Miles Osborne, Iadh Ounis, Saša Petrovic, and Luke Shrimpton. Can twitter replace newswire for breaking news. In *Proceedings of the 7th International AAAI Conference on Weblogs and Social Media*, 2013.

[12] Qiaozhu Mei and ChengXiang Zhai. Discovering evolutionary theme patterns from text: An exploration of temporal text mining. In *Proceedings of the 11th ACM SIGKDD International Conference on Knowledge Discovery in Data Mining*, pages 198–207. ACM, 2005.

[13] Daniel Ramage, Susan T Dumais, and Daniel J Liebling. Characterizing microblogs with topic models. In *Proceedings of the 4th International AAAI Conference on Weblogs and Social Media*, pages 130–137, 2010.

[14] Dafna Shahaf, Jaewon Yang, Caroline Suen, Jeff Jacobs, Heidi Wang, and Jure Leskovec. Information cartography: creating zoomable, large-scale maps of information. In *Proceedings of the 19th ACM SIGKDD international conference on Knowledge discovery and data mining*, pages 1097–1105. ACM, 2013.

[15] Lidan Shou, Zhenhua Wang, Ke Chen, and Gang Chen. Sumblr: continuous summarization of evolving tweet streams. In *Proceedings of the 36th international ACM SIGIR conference on Research and development in information retrieval*, pages 533–542. ACM, 2013.

[16] Mark Steyvers, Padhraic Smyth, Michal Rosen-Zvi, and Thomas Griffiths. Probabilistic author-topic models for information discovery. In *Proceedings of the 10th ACM SIGKDD international conference on Knowledge discovery and data mining*, pages 306–315. ACM, 2004.

[17] Xuerui Wang and Andrew McCallum. Topics over time: a non-markov continuous-time model of topical trends. In *Proceedings of the 12th ACM SIGKDD international conference on Knowledge discovery and data mining*, pages 424–433. ACM, 2006.

[18] Rui Yan, Xiaojun Wan, Jahna Otterbacher, Liang Kong, Xiaoming Li, and Yan Zhang. Evolutionary timeline summarization: a balanced optimization framework via iterative substitution. In *Proceedings of the 34th international ACM SIGIR conference on Research and development in Information Retrieval*, pages 745–754. ACM, 2011.

[19] Shuang-Hong Yang, Alek Kolcz, Andy Schlaikjer, and Pankaj Gupta. Large-scale high-precision topic modeling on twitter. In *Proceedings of the 20th ACM SIGKDD international conference on Knowledge discovery and data mining*, pages 1907–1916. ACM, 2014.

[20] Deyu Zhou, Haiyang Xu, and Yulan He. An unsupervised bayesian modelling approach to storyline detection from news articles. In *Proceedings of the 14th Conference on Empirical Methods in Natural Language Processing*, pages 1943–1948, 2015.

A Comparative Study of Query-biased and Non-redundant Snippets for Structured Search on Mobile Devices

Nikita Spirin[1], Alexander Kotov[2], Karrie Karahalios[1], Vassil Mladenov[1], Pavel Izhutov[3]
[1]UIUC, Urbana, IL; [2]Wayne State University, Detroit, MI; [3]Stanford University[3], Stanford, CA
Department of Computer Science[1,2] and Graduate School of Business[3]
{spirin2,kkarahal,mladeno2}@illinois.edu, kotov@wayne.edu, izhutov@stanford.edu

ABSTRACT

To investigate what kind of snippets are better suited for structured search on mobile devices, we built an experimental mobile search application and conducted a task-oriented interactive user study with 36 participants. Four different versions of a search engine result page (SERP) were compared by varying the snippet type (query-biased vs. non-redundant) and the snippet length (two vs. four lines per result). We adopted a within-subjects experiment design and made each participant do four realistic search tasks using different versions of the application. During the study sessions, we collected search logs, "think-aloud" comments, and post-task surveys. Each session was finalized with an interview. We found that with non-redundant snippets the participants were able to complete the tasks faster and find more relevant results. Most participants preferred non-redundant snippets and wanted to see more information about each result on the SERP for any snippet type. Yet, the participants felt that the version with query-biased snippets was easier to use. We conclude with a set of practical design recommendations.

Keywords

Mobile Search; Structured Search; Snippet; User Study

1. INTRODUCTION

The ideal search system presents the best results at the top. However, due to complexities of the natural language existing systems cannot guarantee perfect retrieval results. Therefore, relevant results might appear in any position on a SERP. To address this issue, search engines "cooperate" with their users via intelligent search user interfaces (SUI). On the SERP, each result is represented as a title/name and accompanied by a snippet, which summarizes the key information about the result and helps users assess relevance.

The de facto method to generate search snippets is based on the extraction of sentences or attributes containing query terms [8, 17, 19–21]. Such query-biased snippets signal relevance by letting users see the usage of the query terms in context. Initially introduced for full-text search [17], this method is used nowadays for all sorts of search applications.

However, this approach has limitations when both queries and documents are structured and the matching is exact rather than probabilistic (e.g. structured/faceted search [18] provided by e-commerce or social networking sites). In this case, query-biased snippets don't provide any new information as they merely repeat the constraints on attribute values expressed in the query. Therefore, all results on the SERP look the same and a user might have a hard time deciding which results to view/click on. We illustrate this limitation in Figure 1. On the left, there is a SERP for structured search in LinkedIn's Android mobile app, which provides non-discriminative snippets and exhibits high query-snippet redundancy. On the right, there is the same SERP with the redundant information removed. As we can see, the original seemingly information-rich interface on the left actually contains a very minimal amount of new information as indicated by the blank areas on the right. Moreover, in the case of structured search, we observe a query-snippet duality, i.e. *the longer the query, the more redundant and uninformative are the snippets.* This might demotivate users from submitting longer queries, which are shown to be more effective [1].

Thus, researchers proposed multiple approaches to generate non-redundant snippets for structured search. The main idea behind these approaches is that we can utilize space on the SERP more effectively by showing information that helps differentiate the results, and, hence, complementary to the query. For example, there are methods to generate informative [3, 4] and diverse [10, 12] snippets for database tuples, for XML documents [8], and for job postings [14].

To sum up, there is a disconnect between the theory and practice. On the one hand, there are powerful methods to generate non-redundant, informative, and discriminative snippets for structured documents [3, 4, 8, 10, 12, 14]. On the other hand, query-biased snippets have shown its utility for full-text search [17, 20, 21] and are used ubiquitously (e.g. Figure 1 and http://imgur.com/a/aEqEq). We formulated two research questions to resolve this disconnect.

- **RQ1:** Which snippets do users prefer in the case of structured search on mobile devices? (subjective)
- **RQ2:** Which snippets make users more productive and effective when performing structured search on mobile devices? (objective)

We created an experimental mobile search application (Section 2) and conducted a task-oriented interactive user study (Section 3) to answer these questions and determine the best

CIKM'16 , October 24-28, 2016, Indianapolis, IN, USA
 ISBN 978-1-4503-4073-1/16/10. . . $15.00
DOI: http://dx.doi.org/10.1145/2983323.2983699

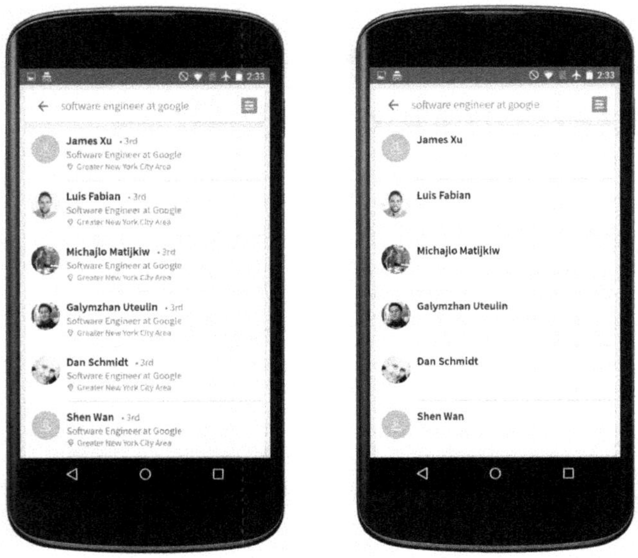

Figure 1: LinkedIn's Android mobile app SERP for the query *"Software Engineer at Google; Location: Greater New York City Area; Degree: 3+"*: (Left) the original SERP; (Right) the same SERP with the redundant information removed from the snippets.

snippet version *from the users' perspective.* Among many different search verticals (e.g. *e-commerce*, *travel*, etc.), we focused on *people* search since it is the most popular vertical on social networking sites [15], which contain a lot of structured data on people. Moreover, people search is by nature an exploratory task [6, 11], and, therefore, it was interesting to investigate whether users benefit from having extra non-redundant information in the snippets. We focused on mobile search because mobile devices have smaller screens and, again, it is crucial to understand whether redundant query-biased snippets are really necessary. The experimental results are presented in Sections 4 and 5. We discuss the results and present our SUI design recommendations in Section 6. We conclude and highlight future work in Section 7.

2. EXPERIMENTAL SYSTEM

2.1 Experimental Collection

As the collection, we used Indeed's Resume Search production index, which contains over 21,000,000 real resumes. Our application programmatically interacted with Indeed by sending carefully tuned HTTP requests and parsing the responses. For example, to retrieve only resumes from *"New York"*, we appended the `in-New-York-NY?co=US` parameter string to the URL, got the HTML version of a SERP from Indeed, and post-processed it to generate our own SERP.

2.2 Structured Search User Interface

Our app consisted of four different pages. The *Settings Page* (where users could enter their anonymized userID, select the task type and the version of the SERP), the *Filters Page* (where users could specify search criteria), and the *Details Page* (where the detailed information about the particular search result was shown) were the same in all versions of the experimental system. However, our app had four different versions of the SERP shown in Figures 2(a-d):

- **QB2**, which showed **query-biased** snippets with **two attribute lines** per result (Figure 2(a));
- **NR2**, which showed **non-redundant** snippets with **two attribute lines** per result (Figure 2(b));
- **QB4**, which showed **query-biased** snippets with **four attribute lines** per result (Figure 2(c));
- **NR4**, which showed **non-redundant** snippets with **four attribute lines** per result (Figure 2(d)).

To submit a new query, a user had to open the *Filters Page* and set constraints/filters on the attribute values using drop-down menus. Then, the user could either submit a modified query or go back to the original SERP keeping the previous query. The user could filter results by using eight different attributes: *Job Title*, *Company*, *University*, *Degree*, *Location*, *Skills*, *Years of Experience*, and *Major*. The SUI was designed in such a way that only one attribute value could be selected at a time. We decided to adopt this strategy to get the maximum control over the collected experimental data. Finally, there was a special *Favorites* filter, which overrides all other filters and returns only "starred" results (added to favorites). The search criteria (query constraints) were always shown as tags/"breadcrumbs" [7] in the navigation bar. The navigation bar stayed at the top of the SERP as users scrolled down. For query-biased snippets it merely showed the current query, while for non-redundant snippets it had a more important role — it served as a part of the snippet shared across all results (in the exact match scenario all results share a subset of attribute values).

Query-biased snippets were generated as follows. First, we took all the attributes specified in a query and sorted them by priority (a global score for attribute importance that could be derived based on the frequency of filters usage or a user study). Then, we appended all attributes that weren't mentioned in the query also sorted by priority. Finally, we took as many attributes from the top of this concatenated attribute list as there were lines in a specific snippet version. For non-redundant snippets we did the same but considered only the attributes not used in the query.

3. USER STUDY METHODOLOGY

We used a simulated work task situation approach [2, 9], i.e. we analyzed the behavior of participants seeking to accomplish real tasks by interacting with the experimental search application. The study consisted of two stages.

In the first stage (12 participants), we compared four different versions of the SERP by varying the snippet type and the snippet length. Adopting a within-subjects study design, we made each participant perform four different search tasks using four different versions of the system. Each participant performed only one randomly assigned task using each version. The task/version order was randomized following the Greek-Latin square experiment design [16] to account for fatigue, task difficulty, and learning effects. The goal was to quickly eliminate two least favorable versions.

In the second stage (24 participants), we compared only the best two versions from the first stage. This time, each participant performed two out of four tasks using each version. It allowed us to increase the number of measurements

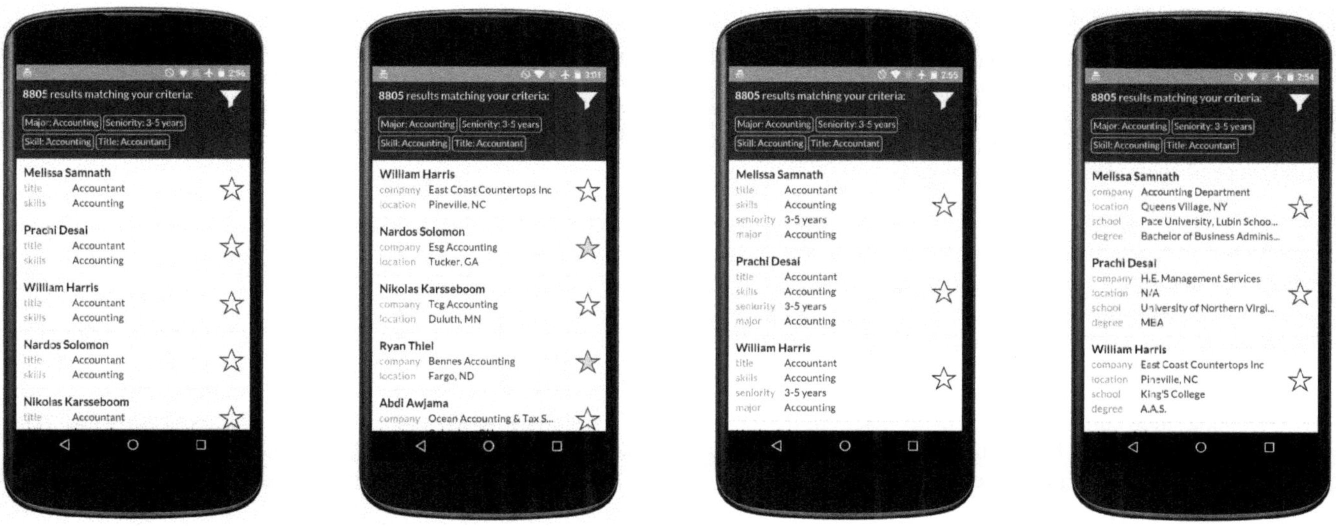

(a) QB2 (b) NR2 (c) QB4 (d) NR4

Figure 2: Four different experimental versions of the SERP corresponding to four different snippet versions.

per participant-version combination to two and make the analysis more rigorous. The goal of the second stage was to actually answer our research questions and collect extensive data to make valid conclusions. Again, we used the Greek-Latin square design as a randomization protocol.

3.1 Participants

The participants were required to be at least 18 years old, use a social networking site at least once a week, search for people online at least once a month, and have a mobile device. Of the 36 participants that we recruited, 32 were UIUC students with diverse majors (e.g. Computer Science, Business, Linguistics, etc.) and four were working professionals. 20 participants were female. More than 80% of the participants searched for people online at least once a week and more than 30% did it every day. All participants were active Facebook (log in at least a few times per week) and LinkedIn (60% log in at least once a week) users.

3.2 Tasks

We designed four people search tasks simulating a real need: (1) find a person to ask for career advice, (2) find a keynote speaker for a conference, (3) help a recruiter find candidates to hire, (4) find a collaborator for a project. For instance, the wording for Task 2 was *"Suppose you are a part of the organizing committee for a conference on ________ and your task is to find a keynote speaker. You understand that people are busy and not everyone will agree/have time to accept your invitation. Your strategy is to find five candidates, message them, and hope that one of them will accept the invitation. A search tool is provided to assist you in this task. You are also required to rank and evaluate the selected candidates after you finish the task."*. The participants needed to fill the gaps in the task templates based on their background. We did it to further increase relevance of the tasks to the participants and make them as realistic as possible. We asked the participants to pick a different topic for each task to avoid carry-over effects across tasks. According to our post-task surveys (Table 3, Q8), the participants found the tasks as realistic (4.06 on a 5-point Likert scale).

3.3 Experimental Procedure

Each participant in our user study was asked to work on four tasks using different versions of the experimental search system. We allocated 10 minutes per task, which is typically enough for users to carefully explore the results [6,21]. The participants were asked to "think-aloud" as they worked on the tasks, and the experimenter took the detailed notes.

After each task, a participant was asked to complete a short post-task survey to capture her/his subjective satisfaction with the specific version of the system, which s/he just tested. The survey contained nine multiple choice questions (eight 5-point Likert scales [13] and one 5-point semantic differential). We also asked each participant to evaluate the quality of selected search results on a 5-point Likert scale. Each result was judged independently, and, hence, more than one result could receive the same relevance score.

All tasks were completed using our app with no interventions by the experimenter. The study was conducted in the same room to decrease the influence of external factors on study results. Since we interacted with the live search index, we grouped all user study sessions as close as possible timewise (12 days starting March 24th, 2016) to ensure minimal influence of changes in Indeed's index on the study results.

At the end of each study session, we conducted a 15-20 minute semi-structured interview by asking open-ended questions motivating the participants to express their thoughts about four (two, during Stage 2 of the study) versions of the SERP. The participants could see all four (two) versions and provide suggestions on how to improve the application.

To understand the way participants interacted with the search system, we logged all possible actions performed by them, such as page views, clicks on the search results, additions/removals from favorites, and page scrolls. For each event, we always logged the following metadata: task type, snippet type, timestamp, current query (combination of constraints on attribute values), and anonymized userID, which allowed us to measure system effectiveness and efficiency. We describe the metrics/dimensions that we used to compare different system versions in Section 5.

4. USER STUDY RESULTS: STAGE ONE

The key conclusion from 12 user study sessions in Stage 1 is that the participants mostly noticed the difference in the snippet length and not in the snippet type and favored longer snippets (11 out of 12 participants). Eight out of 12 participants placed NR4 in either first or second place; three placed QR4 in either first or second place. When scored on a scale from 1 to 4 (lower is better), shorter snippets obtained mean scores of 3.5 (QB2) and 2.8 (NR2), whereas longer snippets obtained mean scores of 2.2 (QB4) and 1.5 (NR4).

Surprisingly, we found that the extra scrolling cost caused by longer snippets didn't have a negative impact on participants' preferences. Many participants said that they either didn't notice it or preferred to have more information on the SERP to make more informed click decisions, like in [22].

It is also worth noting from this stage of the study that most of the participants preferred non-redundant snippets over query-biased snippets given the fixed snippet length.

5. USER STUDY RESULTS: STAGE TWO

Based on the results from Stage 1, we limited the number of snippet versions to two and only kept the ones that were more favored by the participants, i.e. in Stage 2 we compared query-biased snippets spanning 4 lines (QB4) and non-redundant snippets spanning 4 lines (NR4). Both objective and subjective data was used to compare these versions. The objective evaluation was based on search user interaction logs, and the subjective evaluation was based on user post-task survey responses and post-study interviews.

5.1 Subjective System Preference

At the end of each session, we asked the participants *"Which version do you like most?"*. The majority (17 out of 24) preferred NR4, which is statistically significant according to the exact two-tailed binomial test ($p = 0.0433$).

Next, we probed the participants further and asked them to explain the reasons behind their decision (*"Why do you like this version more? What makes it better than the other version?"*). In responding to these open-ended questions, the participants provided many rich and diverse opinions.

The participants who preferred NR4 said that it: (a) shows new non-redundant information (15 out of 17 participants); (b) helps discriminate results (11 out of 17 participants); (c) shows more relevant attributes (6 out of 17 participants); (d) helps accomplish a task faster (3 out of 17 participants); (e) requires less scrolling (3 out of 17 participants); (f) returns more relevant results (1 out of 17 participants).

The participants who preferred QB4 paid more attention to other aspects of the SERP. They liked the version with query-biased snippets because it: (a) has a more regular layout (6 out of 7 participants); (b) shows more relevant attributes (5 out of 7 participants); (c) is more predictable and reassuring (5 out of 7 participants); (d) demands less cognitive load/effort (5 out of 7 participants); (e) provides a good balance of selected and new information (2 out of 7 participants); (f) works faster (2 out of 7 participants); (g) returns more relevant results (1 out of 7 participants); (h) forces to check individual profiles (1 out of 7 participants).

To summarize, almost everyone who preferred NR4 noted the lack of redundancy. On the other hand, rather than focusing on SERP informativeness, the participants who favored QB4 liked the consistent layout of the SERP.

This key finding is also supported by numerous other subjective data that we collected during the study (Table 3). For example, in the post-task surveys, people gave slightly higher scores to NR4 (Q6) but felt that QB4 was easier to use (Q1) and that the search process was less stressful (Q9).

5.2 System Effectiveness

Rather than using predefined topics typical for information retrieval system evaluation [9], we used templatized tasks to closer simulate real life situations and motivate participants to engage in exploratory search, where the objective is usually subtle and might evolve during the search session [11]. Therefore, only the participants themselves could evaluate the quality of selected candidates. To this end, after each task we asked the participants to provide independent relevance judgments to the selected candidates on a scale from 1 to 5 (5 is the highest), like in [6, 22]. Then, we computed the average relevance score over the five selected candidates. We also computed the average relevance score for the candidates selected at a specific position in the session, i.e. if some candidate was the first discovered candidate among five selected candidates, then his/her relevance score was aggregated under the *First* group. The results are presented in a global comparative Table 3.

From the second part of Table 3, it follows that NR4 helps people find more relevant candidates than QB4. The data also suggests that candidates discovered at a specific position in the session have a higher relevance in the case of NR4.

The post-task survey responses also indicate that NR4 helps find more relevant results. The participants rated NR4 as more helpful for deciding who to contact (Q3), felt that the information on the SERP was more useful (Q5 and Q7), and, overall, rated NR4 slightly higher (Q6).

5.3 System Efficiency

In addition to the analysis of system effectiveness, we also used query log data and subjective post-task responses to compare the efficiency of different systems. The primary measure to assess the efficiency of different systems was time. In particular, we computed the average time required by each participant to finish a task and found that NR4 led to faster task completion times in seconds ($\mu = 389.04$; $\sigma = 118.30$) than QB4 ($\mu = 414.77$; $\sigma = 122.10$).

We performed further analysis to understand why the participants were able to complete the tasks faster with NR4. We discovered that the average time between consecutive queries within a session was smaller for NR4 ($\mu = 56.77$; $\sigma = 34.88$) than for QB4 ($\mu = 63.80$; $\sigma = 39.59$) and that the average number of queries per session was also smaller for NR4 ($\mu = 4.96$; $\sigma = 3.90$) than for QB4 ($\mu = 5.91$; $\sigma = 5.60$). We continued our investigation to understand why the time between queries was shorter and why the participants submitted less queries when using NR4. We discovered that the participants made less clicks on the SERP (visited fewer number of detailed profiles) in the case of NR4 ($\mu = 16.00$; $\sigma = 4.60$) than in the case of QB4 ($\mu = 18.51$; $\sigma = 5.80$). This difference is statistically significant according to the non-parametric two-tailed Mann-Whitney test ($p = 0.0368$). However, time to the first SERP click was longer for NR4 ($\mu = 13.17$; $\sigma = 6.96$) compared to QB4 ($\mu = 11.36$; $\sigma = 4.71$), which suggests that the participants engaged more with the SERP and made more informed decisions by looking at the snippets. There are several other

Metric \ Snippet Version	Query-biased, 4	Non-redundant, 4
Part I: Post-task Subjective Survey Responses		
Q1: The system is easy to use	**4.06 ± 0.59**	3.91 ± 0.79
Q2: The system provides me relevant candidates	3.98 ± 0.98	3.98 ± 0.86
Q3: The system helps me decide who to contact	3.92 ± 0.71	**4.13 ± 0.64**
Q4: The system helps me find relevant candidates efficiently	3.65 ± 0.93	**3.69 ± 0.88**
Q5: The display of each profile on the SERP is useful	3.96 ± 0.92	**4.04 ± 0.77**
Q6: Overall, I am satisfied with the system in this task	3.71 ± 0.68	**3.73 ± 0.68**
Q7: Summaries/attributes presented for each result on the SERP are useful	3.94 ± 0.93	**4.08 ± 0.82**
Q8: I can see myself doing this task in the real world	4.06 ± 0.81	4.06 ± 0.78
Q9: The search process is (stressful / relaxing)	**3.40 ± 0.87**	3.35 ± 0.93
Part II: Post-task Subjective Result Relevance Judgments		
Selected result relevance	4.00 ± 0.96	**4.07 ± 0.92**
First selected result relevance	4.23 ± 0.81	4.23 ± 0.93
Second selected result relevance	4.02 ± 0.93	**4.04 ± 0.82**
Third selected result relevance	3.81 ± 0.87	**3.88 ± 1.10**
Fourth selected result relevance	3.83 ± 1.17	**3.90 ± 0.99**
Fifth selected result relevance	4.10 ± 0.97	**4.31 ± 0.69**
Part III: Query Log Data		
Query length	3.03 ± 0.97	**3.14± 0.95**
# of queries per task session	**5.91 ± 5.60**	4.96 ± 3.90
Time between consecutive queries within a task session (seconds)	**63.80 ± 39.59**	56.77 ± 34.88
Time to complete a task (seconds)	**414.77 ± 122.10**	389.04 ± 118.30
Time to the first SERP click after submitting a query (seconds)	11.36 ± 4.71	**13.17 ± 6.96**
# of SERP clicks (profile views) per task session***	**18.51 ± 5.80**	16.00 ± 4.60
# of profiles *added* to favorites per task session (*SERP*)	1.00 ± 2.13	**1.44 ± 2.77**
# of profiles *removed* from favorites per task session (*SERP*)	0.43 ± 1.11	**0.65 ± 1.40**
# of profiles *added* to favorites per task session (*detailed profile page*)	**4.85 ± 2.11**	4.48 ± 2.03
# of profiles *removed* from favorites per task session (*detailed profile page*)	**0.45 ± 0.78**	0.39 ± 0.74
Part IV: Post-study Subjective Preference (Interview Data)		
Percentage of participants favoring a specific version (out of 24)***	29.2% (7/24)	**70.8% (17/24)**

Table 1: Metrics for two versions of the experimental application used in the formal study (Stage 2): query-biased snippets with four lines per result and non-redundant snippets with four lines per result. We use * to mark statistically significant differences according to the two-tailed Mann-Whitney test ($p < 0.05$).**

findings supporting the hypothesis that the participants engaged with the SERP more in the case of NR4. While not statistically significant, the participants added ($\mu = 1.44$; $\sigma = 2.77$) and removed ($\mu = 0.65$; $\sigma = 1.40$) from favorites on the SERP more often when using NR4 than they added ($\mu = 1.00$; $\sigma = 2.13$) and removed ($\mu = 0.43$; $\sigma = 1.11$) when using QB4. In the surveys, the utility of NR4 was also rated higher (Q5, Q7) compared to QB4.

6. DISCUSSION AND IMPLICATIONS

In this section, we discuss the implications from our findings for the design of more useful future structured SUIs.

6.1 Eliminate Redundancy

Our key finding is that users do notice redundancy in the search user interface and prefer non-redundant snippets. At the same time, non-redundant snippets cannot be used when users specify multiple constraints per attribute (e.g. *"Uber or Lyft or YellowCabNYCTaxi"*) or when an attribute has an array type (e.g. skills *"Java, Scala, Hadoop, Spark"*) because attribute values will vary from one result to another. Therefore, we suggest using non-redundant snippets when the query formulation interface doesn't allow people to specify multiple constraints per attribute (e.g. Zappos mobile app) or when only one value per facet is selected. Query-biased snippets should be used when the query implies that the attribute values might vary from one result to another.

We also discovered that users mostly add people to favorites from the detailed profile page and, hence, the stars that occupy a significant part of the SERP space could be eliminated, too. We propose allowing users to (un)bookmark candidates by swiping to the left/right rather than by clicking on stars. Since the swipe is an interaction pattern, no space on the SERP is required to provide this functionality.

The freed space might be used to show some additional information to help users make more informed click decisions. From the interviews, we learned that in the case of people search the searchers not only try to assess candidates based on their relevance to the query/task but also use other factors such as social similarity, status, approachability, seniority. Therefore, to simplify this process for the users, search engines might explicitly show on the SERP the similarity score between a searcher and a candidate result or a simple data visualization with the scores along several dimensions [6]. Plus, these scores can be made more interpretable by showing explanatory comments next to each number, e.g. *"87% (both you and John Smith went to MIT)"*.

From Stage 1, we concluded that users don't notice the scrolling cost and prefer having more information about each result on the SERP. Therefore, we suggest using long non-redundant snippets. At the same time, we warn the readers that there must be at least a few results per page to enable comparison. This is because several of our participants explicitly mentioned that they used the results above and below the result in question to decide whether to "star" it.

6.2 Provide More Control

Many participants mentioned that they would love to have more control over the search process, e.g. the ability to specify what attributes to show on the SERP or set importance weights for attributes to manipulate result ranking, like in [6]. The participants also mentioned that, despite having a good ranking algorithm, they would prefer to have more ranking algorithm transparency and be able to resort the attributes based on well-defined criteria, e.g. years of work experience and age. Therefore, we suggest exposing the seams and providing more control, which might be especially beneficial for advanced users. Interestingly, some of the participants even wanted to reorder the sections of the resume depending on the task. The algorithmic transparency might lead to many positive outcomes for the users [5] and establish a higher level of trust between the users and the systems.

From the study, we also learned that some users prefer to have input confirmation, while others seek more information per pixel. We think that a balanced solution might be designed. One idea is to mix non-redundant and query-biased snippets by always showing one query-biased attribute and filling in the rest of the lines with non-redundant information. Alternatively, this decision might be "delegated" to the users such that they could select a snippet type in the search settings. Finally, one can predict the user type algorithmically based on search interaction data and show the snippets which are more appropriate for them, e.g. the elderly users might benefit from a less dynamic interface with query-biased snippets, while the younger users actively using digital products and searching online might see a more information-rich SERP with non-redundant snippets.

7. CONCLUSIONS AND FUTURE WORK

This work serves as the first real evidence discovered via an interactive user-centric study that structured search engines should eliminate SUI redundancy. We found that the participants liked non-redundant snippets more when performing structured search on mobile devices. Our qualitative and quantitative data indicates that the system with non-redundant snippets was more effective and efficient. Non-redundant snippets led to faster task completion times, helped find more relevant results, and made the participants do more informed SERP click decisions. The participants engaged with the SERP more when using the system with non-redundant snippets. On the other hand, the participants who favored query-biased snippets paid more attention to the visual features of the SUI and felt that the system was easier to use. We also learned that the participants favored longer snippets without respect to the snippet type.

Despite our efforts to design a rigorous study, it still has several limitations. First, we focused on *people* search, and that's why our findings are limited only to this search vertical. In the future, we will examine other structured search verticals, such as *travel*, *e-commerce*, or *jobs*. Second, the majority of our participants were students. We plan to expand the pool of participants and investigate whether there is some interaction between a snippet type and a level of professional experience. Third, we used subjective judgments to evaluate system effectiveness since there was no ground-truth labels. A live A/B test should help understand what kind of snippet leads to better search outcomes for end-users.

8. ACKNOWLEDGEMENTS

We thank Nick Craswell, Susan Dumais, Jiawei Han, Dawid Hawking, Daniel Tunkelang, ChengXiang Zhai, all participants of the WSDM2016 DC, and anonymous CIKM reviewers for thoughtful discussions and critical comments.

9. REFERENCES

[1] N. J. Belkin, D. Kelly, G. Kim, J.-Y. Kim, H.-J. Lee, G. Muresan, M.-C. Tang, X.-J. Yuan, and C. Cool. Query length in interactive information retrieval. SIGIR '03, 2003.

[2] P. Borlund. Experimental components for the evaluation of interactive information retrieval systems. *Journal of documentation*, 56(1):71–90, 2000.

[3] G. Das, V. Hristidis, N. Kapoor, and S. Sudarshan. Ordering the attributes of query results. SIGMOD '06.

[4] M. Das, H. Rahman, G. Das, and V. Hristidis. Generating informative snippet to maximize item visibility. CIKM '13.

[5] M. Eslami, A. Rickman, K. Vaccaro, A. Aleyasen, A. Vuong, K. Karahalios, K. Hamilton, and C. Sandvig. "i always assumed that i wasn't really that close to [her]": Reasoning about invisible algorithms in news feed. CHI '15.

[6] S. Han, D. He, J. Jiang, and Z. Yue. Supporting exploratory people search: A study of factor transparency and user control. CIKM '13, 2013.

[7] M. A. Hearst. *Search User Interfaces*. Cambridge University Press, New York, NY, USA, 1st edition, 2009.

[8] Y. Huang, Z. Liu, and Y. Chen. eXtract: A snippet generation system for XML search. *Proc. of VLDB*, 2008.

[9] D. Kelly. Methods for evaluating interactive information retrieval systems with users. *Foundations and Trends in Information Retrieval*, 3(1–2):1–224, 2009.

[10] Z. Liu, P. Sun, and Y. Chen. Structured search result differentiation. *Proc. VLDB Endow.*, 2009.

[11] G. Marchionini. Exploratory search: From finding to understanding. *Communications of ACM*, April 2006.

[12] M. Miah, G. Das, V. Hristidis, and H. Mannila. Standing out in a crowd: Selecting attributes for maximum visibility. In *Proc. of ICDE 2008*, pages 356–365.

[13] J. Preece, Y. Rogers, H. Sharp, D. Benyon, S. Holland, and T. Carey. *Human-Computer Interaction*. Addison-Wesley Longman Ltd., Essex, UK, UK, 1994.

[14] N. Spirin and K. Karahalios. Unsupervised approach to generate informative structured snippets for job search engines. WWW '13 Companion, 2013.

[15] N. V. Spirin, J. He, M. Develin, K. G. Karahalios, and M. Boucher. People search within an online social network: Large scale analysis of facebook graph search query logs. In *Proceedings of CIKM '14*, 2014.

[16] J. Tague-Sutcliffe. The pragmatics of information retrieval experimentation, revisited. *IPM*, 28(4):467–490, 1992.

[17] A. Tombros and M. Sanderson. Advantages of query biased summaries in information retrieval. SIGIR '98, 1998.

[18] D. Tunkelang. *Faceted Search*. Morgan and Claypool, 2009.

[19] R. Varadarajan and V. Hristidis. A system for query-specific document summarization. CIKM '06, 2006.

[20] C. Wang, F. Jing, L. Zhang, and H.-J. Zhang. Learning query-biased web page summarization. CIKM '07, 2007.

[21] R. W. White, J. M. Jose, and I. Ruthven. A task-oriented study on the influencing effects of query-biased summarisation in web searching. *IPM*, 39(5):707–733, 2003.

[22] S. Yarosh, T. Matthews, and M. Zhou. Asking the right person: Supporting expertise selection in the enterprise. In *Proceedings of CHI '12*, 2012.

Content-Agnostic Malware Detection in Heterogeneous Malicious Distribution Graph *

Ibrahim Alabdulmohsin
King Abdullah University of Science & Technology
ibrahim.alabdulmohsin@kaust.edu.sa

Yufei HAN
Symantec Research Labs
yufei_han@symantec.com

Yun Shen
Symantec Research Labs
yun_shen@symantec.com

Xiangliang Zhang
King Abdullah University of Science & Technology
xiangliang.zhang@kaust.edu.sa

ABSTRACT

Malware detection has been widely studied by analysing either file dropping relationships or characteristics of the file distribution network. This paper, for the first time, studies a global heterogeneous malware delivery graph fusing file dropping relationship and the topology of the file distribution network. The integration offers a unique ability of structuring the end-to-end distribution relationship. However, it brings large heterogeneous graphs to analysis. In our study, an average daily generated graph has more than 4 million edges and 2.7 million nodes that differ in type, such as IPs, URLs, and files. We propose a novel Bayesian label propagation model to unify the multi-source information, including content-agnostic features of different node types and topological information of the heterogeneous network. Our approach does not need to examine the source codes nor inspect the dynamic behaviours of a binary. Instead, it estimates the maliciousness of a given file through a semi-supervised label propagation procedure, which has a linear time complexity w.r.t. the number of nodes and edges. The evaluation on 567 million real-world download events validates that our proposed approach efficiently detects malware with a high accuracy.

1. INTRODUCTION

Modern cyber criminals employ various sophisticated mechanisms to drop malicious files such as adware, ransomware, and rouge antivirus. They can set up short lived websites (e.g., using domain fluxing), hire a third party (e.g., pay-per-install), or utilise exploit kits (e.g., drive-by download) to deliver the payloads. In recent years, malware delivered to the endpoints uses various antivirus evasion techniques to avoid detection. These include environment awareness, timing-based evasion, repackaging internal data obfuscation and so on.

*All authors contributed equally and are ordered alphabetically.

CIKM'16 , October 24 - 28, 2016, Indianapolis, IN, USA

ISBN 978-1-4503-4073-1/16/10... $15.00

DOI: http://dx.doi.org/10.1145/2983323.2983700

Despite all the previous efforts [5, 18, 10, 4, 14, 9, 15, 6, 3, 7, 8], how to quickly identify if a new binary is malicious or benign remains a crucial problem yet to be satisfactorily solved. Naturally, binary analysis techniques are effective solutions to this problem as static [15] and dynamic analysis [3, 8] can offer deep insights of a binary via thorough low-level examinations. However, such techniques need considerable amount of computational resources to carry out the inspection. The sheer volume of suspicious binaries, together with the repackaging and obfuscation techniques used by cyber criminals make the task of timely analysing binary files nearly impossible. Even though recent research efforts in large-scale malware analysis (e.g., [6], [7]) are proven effective in uncovering clusters of malware that share known low-level similarity, they are less effective and computationally costly in identifying unknown malware or threats.

On the other hand, content-agnostic approaches have advantages in coping with the large and heterogeneous space of malicious binaries by avoiding content inspection, hence becoming more popular in recent years to compliment binary analysis approaches. Previous work in this direction detects malware from various perspectives, e.g., understanding the characteristics of malware delivery infrastructures [2, 14], identifying topological relations among hosts and IPs in the malicious Web infrastructure used by cyber criminals [18, 10, 5], proactively and efficiently crawling potential malicious hosting sites [4], mining file co-occurrence relationship [16], getting insights from downloader-payload relationship of executable files on an endpoint [9], and so on.

It is interesting to note that the aforementioned work either focuses on analysing network characteristics of malware distribution [2, 14, 18, 10, 5] or centres the analysis on file dropping relationships from the endpoints [9]. It makes more sense to fuse the aforementioned file dropping graph and file distribution network to form a global view of end-to-end distribution network instead of evaluating whether a given file is malicious or benign from either perspective. This global view offers the integral ability of structuring the relationship in a scalable manner and handling heterogeneous sources of information. However, it brings a couple of intriguing challenges. It requires a method capable of working with the heterogeneous graph and, at the same time, the method should be computationally efficient to handle large scale graphs while offering a high accuracy.

The contributions of this paper are summarised as follows.

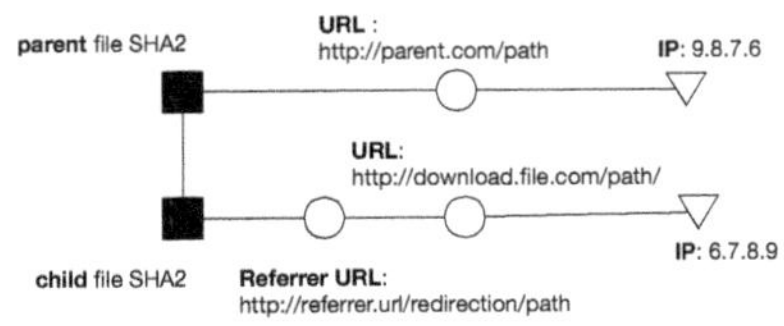

Figure 1: Abstract model of malware distribution graph.

- We provide a global heterogeneous malware delivery graph fusing file dropping relationship and the topology of the file distribution network.
- We unify topological information of heterogeneous network and content-agnostic features of different node types using a novel Bayesian label propagation model.
- We demonstrate our method is efficient and effective in identifying malicious files from over 567 million real-world download events.

Comparing to the state-of-the-art research work, our proposed approach has the following advantages:

- It only requires a small amount of labelled data to achieve high detection precision, thanks to its novel approach of combining topological information with content-agnostic features in a unified manner using Bayesian label propagation.
- The proposed approach is computationally efficient. It doesn't need to examine the source codes, nor inspect the dynamic behaviours of a binary. It estimates the maliciousness of a given file through a semi-supervised label propagation procedure. The proposed method's time complexity is $O((|E|+|V|)\times T)$, where $|V|$ is the number of nodes in the graph, $|E|$ is the number of edges in the graph, and T is the number of iterations.

2. METHODOLOGY

As mentioned earlier, the primary objective of this work is to be able to detect malware reliably in a content-agnostic manner. This has the advantage of yielding a computationally efficient solution, since signature-based low-level inspection of binary files is avoided, as well as providing a more robust solution to obfuscation techniques, such as polymorphism and metamorphism. In order to accomplish the desired goal, we propose to utilise both topological information, such as the dropping relationship of files, as well as content-agnostic features, such as lexical tokens in URLs and file names. Clearly, topological information and content-agnostic features are quite different in nature. Yet, we will show that they can be seamlessly combined in a *unified* manner using Bayesian label propagation. In brief terms, supervised classification via the content-agnostic features will form the *prior* to the Bayesian label propagation algorithm. Later, we will demonstrate experimentally that such a unified approach indeed outperforms label propagation and supervised classification when they are implemented separately.

2.1 Preliminary

To describe the malware detection problems in formal terms, suppose we have $\{(x_1,z_1,y_1)...(x_l,z_l,y_l)\}$ instance-type-label tuples, which are assumed to be drawn i.i.d. from some fixed unknown probability distribution $\mathcal{D}$ over the product space $\mathcal{X}\times\mathcal{Z}\times\{+1,-1\}$. Here, a positive label $y_i=+1$ implies that the instance $x_i\in\mathcal{X}$ whose type is z_i is malicious. The instance types are the types of nodes available in the malware distribution network (MDN), which, in our case, includes files, URLs, and IP addresses. In addition to the labeled data, we also have *unlabelled* instances $\{(x_{l+1},z_{l+1}),\dots,(x_{l+u},z_{l+u})\}$, whose underlying (unknown) true class labels are denoted $\{y_{l+1},...,y_{l+u}\}$. The goal is to use the labeled data $\{(x_1,z_1,y_1),...,(x_l,z_l,y_l)\}$ and the unlabelled instances $\{(x_{l+1},z_{l+1}),\dots,(x_{l+u},z_{l+u})\}$ to predict the unknown labels $\{y_{l+1},...,y_{l+u}\}$. In other words, we operate in the *transductive* learning setting, as opposed to the *inductive* learning setting. Operating in the transductive learning setting is more appropriate for malware detection since malware distribution networks change over time, with new URLs, IPs, and files being created on a regular basis.

In our implementation, we classify node types into the following three categories (see Section 2.2 for a more detailed descriptions of the features used for each node type):

1. *Files*: Some of its features include the file size and average reputation scores of the workstations that downloaded the file.
2. *URLs*: Its features are mostly lexical in nature, which has been demonstrated in some recent work to be quite effective for URL classification [11]. Such lexical features include the URL length, the number of tokens in the fully-qualified domain name (FQDN), the number of common phishing words, such as `ebayisapi` and `webscr`, as well as a the presence or absence of explicit port numbers in the URL.
3. *IP Addresses*: Some of its features include the number of unique top-level domain names hosted by the IP address and the total number of files downloaded from the given IP address.

These three node types are clearly related to each other. Consequently, in addition to the content-agnostic features, we also assume that the relationships between nodes are captured in a graph. Hence, we have content-agnostic features as well as graph-based topological information that both aid the malware detection task.

The proposed approach is to first implement supervised classification for each node type separately. These classifiers output probabilistic scores, which, in turn, are used as priors to the label propagation algorithm carried out over the graph. We describe each stage of the process in details next.

2.2 Supervised Classification

The first stage of the proposed algorithm is to implement a binary classifier for each node type in the graph using its content-agnostic features. The goal of the classifier is to output a probability score if the given node is malicious or benign, i.e. $P(y_i=+1|x_i,z_i)$. These probability scores can be obtained, for example, using logistic regression, the naïve Bayes classifier, or support vector machine (SVM) with the Platt scaling [13]. The classification algorithm used in our

Table 1: Features for file, URL and IP classification.

Category	Features	Feature Description
Features for file classification	in/out degree	The number of landing pages to the file and files dropped by the file
	src/trgt reputation	The average reputation score of droppers/payloads (if any)
	src/trgt prevalence	The average prevalence score of droppers/payloas
	size	The size of the file in kilobytes (KB)
Features for URL classification	url len	The number of characters in the URL
	cnt. of dom and path token	The number of tokens in FQDN and in the path
	avg. of dom and path token	The average token length in the domain and in the path
	domain is ip	A binary indicator if an IP address is used directly, instead of a FQDN
	has port	A binary indicator if a port is present in the URL
	len. dom. token	The length of longest token in FQDN
	num of dots and hyph	The number of '.' and '-' in the URL
	has phish	The number of phishing words in the list `'webscr'`, `'secure'`, `'banking'`, `'ebayisapi'`, `'account'`, `'confirm'`, `'login'`, `'signing'`
	brand present	The name of a Fortune 500 company is present in the URL
	num of subd.	The number of subdomains given in the URL
Features for IP classification	size	The size of the subgraph rooted on the IP address
	num urls / rurls	The number of URLs/referrer URLs in the subgraph rooted on the IP address
	num files	The number of files in the subgraph
	uniq url tlds/subd	The number of unique top level domains/subdomains hosted by the IP address
	avg url/rurl hfiles	The average number of files hosted per URL / referred by a referrer URL
	rurl file cover	The total number of files referred by referrer URLs in the subgraph
	uniq rurl tlds / uniq rurl subd	The total number of files directly hosted in the URLs / unique subdomains
	avg/max/min url priori	The average/max/min score of URL priori in the subgraph
	avg/max/min file priori	The average/max/min score of file priori in the subgraph

implementation is 200-tree random forest for file, URL and IP, which is implemented using scikit-learn 0.17.1. The full list of features used is shown in Table 1.

2.3 Bayesian Label Propagation

Having obtained a binary classifier for each node type, the next stage is to use the predicted score as a prior to the label propagation algorithm. The basic idea of label propagation is to model the relations between instances using an undirected unweighted graph $G = (\mathcal{V}, \mathcal{E})$ and to use the adjacency matrix to infer the labels [1, 19, 17]. Each node $v_i \in \mathcal{V}$ corresponds to a single training instance-type pair (x_i, z_i). Each edge $e_{i,j} \in \mathcal{E}$ represents the relation between node v_i and v_j. As mentioned earlier, we have three node types in our implementation: files, URLs, and IP addresses, where the set of edges $\mathcal{E}$ indicate the file delivery relation. For example, if one file A is downloaded from URL B and the URL is hosted by the IP address C, the corresponding nodes should be linked in the graph G to encode this delivery relation. These relations are illustrated in Figure 1.

To derive a Bayesian version of label propagation, we closely follow the proof steps of the SocNL algorithm proposed in [17]. We will show how the supervised classifier can be incorporated as well in the form of a prior.

First, suppose that for every node in the graph $v_i \in \mathcal{V}$, there exists a Bernoulli parameter θ_i such that $P(y_i = +1) = \theta_i$. Also, suppose that the neighbours N_i of node v_i are labeled. The goal of label propagation is to compute $f_i = P(y_i = +1 \mid N_i)$. In line with the Bayesian spirit, we will achieve this by first computing:

$$P(\theta_i \mid N_i) = \frac{P(\theta_i) \cdot P(N_i \mid \theta_i)}{P(N_i)} \quad (1)$$

Next, as is used in the derivation of the SocNL algorithm [17], we impose a *smoothness* constrain on the graph. In particular, we assume that $\theta_i \approx \theta_j$ for all $v_j \in N_i$. With this approximation, we obtain:

$$P(N_i \mid \theta_i) = \prod_{v_j \in N_i} \theta_i^{\delta(y_j=+1)} \cdot (1-\theta_i)^{\delta(y_j=-1)} \quad (2)$$

Next, we use the beta distribution as a prior $P(\theta_i)$ since it is conjugate to the Bernoulli distribution. So, we write:

$$P(\theta_i) \propto \theta_i^{\alpha_i - 1} \cdot (1-\theta_i)^{\beta_i - 1}, \quad (3)$$

with shape parameters $\alpha_i, \beta_i > 0$. As a result, we obtain:

$$P(\theta_i \mid N_i) \propto \theta_i^{|N_i^+| + \alpha_i - 1} \cdot (1-\theta_i)^{|N_i^-| + \beta_i - 1}, \quad (4)$$

where $|N_i^+|$ and $|N_i^-|$ is the number of positive and negative neighbors respectively to node v_i. Finally, as shown in [17], we predict using marginalisation:

$$\begin{aligned} f_i &= P(y_i = +1 | N_i, \alpha_i, \beta_i) \\ &= \int_{\theta_i} P(y_i = +1 | \theta_i) \cdot P(\theta_i | N_i, \alpha_i, \beta_i) \, d\theta_i \\ &= \frac{|N_i^+| + \alpha_i}{|N_i| + \alpha_i + \beta_i} \end{aligned} \quad (5)$$

Intuitively, the prediction rule in Eq. (5) states that the probability $P(y_i = +1 | N_i)$ is estimated by counting the fraction of positively-labeled neighbours to node v_i, where the prior parameters α_i, β_i play the role of a bias.

Our next goal is to let the classifier determine the values of the hyper-parameters α_i and β_i. The output of the classifier, denoted $\hat{y}_i$, can be interpreted as the *mean* of θ_i. Since the marginal distribution of θ_i is a beta distribution, whose mean is $\alpha_i/(\alpha_i + \beta_i)$, we write $\gamma = \alpha_i + \beta_i$ and $\alpha_i = \gamma \, \hat{y}_i$. Note that $E[\theta_i] = \hat{y}_i$, which is the probability score predicted by the classifier. Therefore, the prediction rule reduces to:

$$f_i = P(y_i = +1|N_i, \alpha_i, \beta_i) = \frac{|N_i^+| + \gamma \hat{y}_i}{|N_i| + \gamma} \quad (6)$$

Of course, this rule assumes that all of the neighbours of node v_i are labeled. However, it can be shown (see for instance Section 4.2 in [17]) that the rule above can be translated into an iterative label propagation rule of the form:

$$f_i = \frac{\sum_{v_j \in N_i} f_j \ + \ \gamma \hat{y}_i}{\sum_{v_j \in N_i} f_j \ + \ \gamma} \quad (7)$$

This is the label propagation algorithm used in our implementation. The LP update rules in Eq. (7) are guaranteed to converge as long as $\gamma > 0$ [17].

As we can see, the estimated label of an unlabelled instance is decided by the weighted average of label probability of its neighbours in addition to the probability estimate predicted by the supervised classifier. In this way, information about class membership is recursively propagated from labelled instances to unlabelled ones through the connected paths inside the graph G until convergence is achieved. Label propagation has advantages in terms of time complexity. The propagation procedure is conducted by simple and fast local linear weighted averaging operations, as shown in Eq. (7), which runs in $O((|E| + |V|) \times T)$ time, where $|V|$ is the number of nodes in the graph, $|E|$ is the number of edges in the graph, and T is the number of iterations.

3. DATASETS

3.1 Study Dataset and Ground Truth

Study Dataset. We use the user *download activity data* provided by Symantec. This dataset is collected from users who opt in for data sharing program, and client identifiers are anonymised. It is not possible to link back the collected data to the client from which the requests originated. The download activity data provide meta-information about all download activities on the endpoints. The dataset is further enriched using *binary reputation* to include metadata about reputation band and prevalence of the downloaded files. We extract over 567 million download events from 17th March to 11th April 2016 to form our study dataset.

Additional Datasets. We collect benign URLs and malicious URLs from various sources to build a training dataset for the URL node classifier (see Section 2). For benign URLs, we use the top 10,000 of 2015 most popular search words and get the top 6 URLs of each word from Google search results. We also get a list of benign URLs (whitelisted) from the security vendor's internal database. In total we have 87,974 benign URLs. For malicious URLs, we obtain these URLs from publicly available sources - cybercrime tracker, phishtank, and malc0de[1]. We also get a list of known malicious URLs from the security vendor's internal database. In total we have 36,036 malicious URLs.

Ground Truth. We query VirusTotal (a free online service that aggregates files and URLs scanning outputs from different antivirus engines) for each file SHA2 to obtain its *first seen* timestamp, the number of AV products (and associated vendor names) that flagged the file as malicious, and the total number of AV products that scanned the file. We consider a file malicious if *at least one* of the top five AV vendors (w.r.t. market share) and *a minimum of two other* AV vendors detect it as malicious [12]. We also obtained additional ground truth about files from the same major security company. The verdicts come from the company's static and dynamic binary analysis platform. In total, our ground truth consists of 4,868,770 benign and 1,544,215 malicious files. We summarise our datasets in Table 2.

[1]Respectively at http://cybercrime-tracker.net, https://www.phishtank.com, http://malc0de.com/database

Table 2: Graph data size (on average between 17th March and 11th April 2016), and URLs for priori classifiers training

Graph (Avg. per day)	No. of nodes			No. of edges
	file	URL	IP	
	1,648,458	892,394	155,533	4,047,741
Ground Truth files (Total)	4,868,770 benign, 1,544,215 malicious			
URL	87,974 benign, 36,036 malicious (external)			

4. EXPERIMENTAL ANALYSIS

4.1 Experimental setup

Our experiments are organised in two parts. In the first part, we aim to verify the benefits of the proposed method and compare its performance against both standard label propagation [19] and the Bayesian inference based variation of LP, named SocNL [17]. Note that we neither compare to NAZCA, due to its scalability issue in large graphs, nor other malware detection techniques as they have only partial information regarding malware distribution network. We traverse different sampling ratios of benign files and malicious files to identify potential malware with different numbers of initially labelled file nodes in the graph. Both Area Under ROC Curve (AUC) and F1-score of all three algorithms are used to evaluate detection performances quantitatively. The second part demonstrates how our method can identify malware with a real-world case study.

The datasets used to conduct the experimental study were summarised in Section 3. To conduct malware detection on day t, we use the features of benign files and malicious files that have been identified before day $t-1$ as the training set to build the file node classifiers. URL node specific classifier is trained independently using additional exteriorly labelled malicious and benign URL samples (see Section 3). To construct the IP-specific node classifier, we borrow the idea from self-training technology [1] and build the initial training set using March 16th data. That is, we run the proposed method on the March 16th graph with non-informative priors for IP nodes. Once the inference finishes, we set up a threshold on the derived probabilistic labels of the IP nodes. IP nodes with the probabilistic score larger/smaller than the threshold are recognised as a potential malicious/benign IP. We then extract features from these IP nodes and train the node classifier accordingly.

To choose the optimal setting of the regularisation parameter γ in Eq. (7), we carry out a grid search in the set {0.1, 0.01, 0.001, 0.0001} using cross validation, and report the results with the best detection performance.

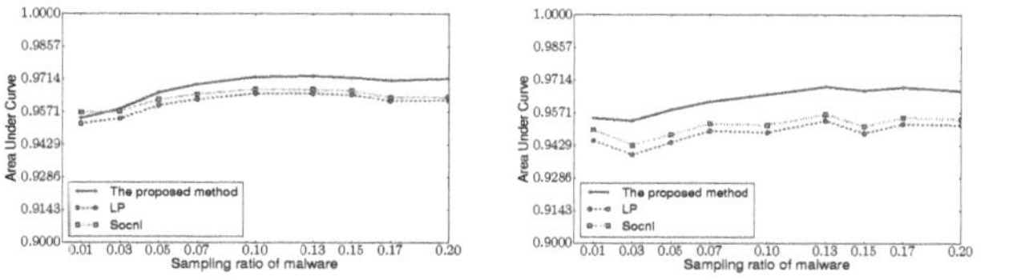

(a) Benign sampling rate = 0.3 (b) Benign sampling rate = 0.5

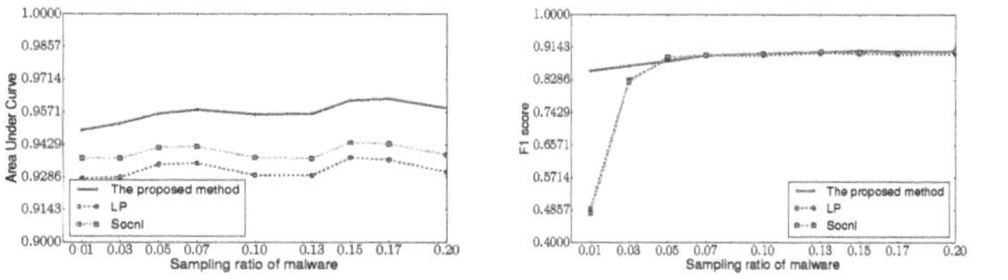

(c) Benign sampling rate = 0.7 (d) Benign sampling rate = 0.3

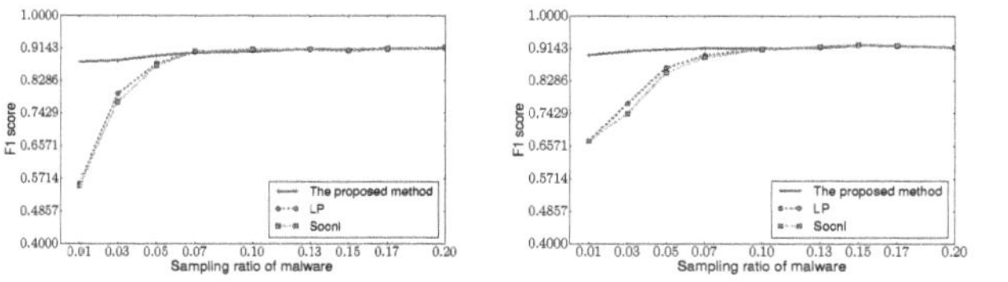

(e) Benign sampling rate = 0.5 (f) Benign sampling rate = 0.7

Figure 2: Average AUC and F1 scores with different number of initially labelled nodes.

Table 3: Comparison of F1 scores between file classifier and the proposed method

Date	File classifier	The proposed method
March 30	0.833	0.910
March 31	0.834	0.896
April 1	0.826	0.902
April 2	0.838	0.884

4.2 Comparative Study

To investigate how the proposed method performs given different numbers of initially labelled file nodes, we vary the benign file sampling ratio as 0.3, 0.5 and 0.7. For each level of benign file sampling ratio, we further choose 9 different malware sampling ratios, respectively 0.01, 0.03, 0.05, 0.07, 0.09, 0.11, 0.13, 0.15, 0.17, and 0.19. The ranges of the two sampling ratios are selected to reflect the real world scenario; there are plenty of benign files available while the number of malware samples is limited.

We use the settings of sampling initially labelled nodes for all three algorithms involved in the comparison and run all the algorithms three times on each day. Given a specific benign file sampling ratio and a fixed malware sampling ratio, AUC values and F1 scores derived from all 26 days are then averaged. The mean AUC and F1 score of each algorithm evaluate its overall malware detection performance under the given level of the sampling rates. Figure 2a, Figure 2b and Figure 2c show the mean AUC value derived by fixing the benign sampling rate and increasing gradually the malware sampling rate. Figure 2d, Figure 2e and Figure 2f shows the mean F1 scores following the same setting.

As shown in the figures, the proposed method provides *superior* detection accuracy over the other two algorithms when the number of sampled malware is limited, e.g., malware sampling rate less than 0.07, no matter how large the benign file sampling rate is. In terms of average AUC and F1 scores, the proposed method yields a more distinctive improvement of detection accuracy with increasingly larger benign file sampling rate. This observation is consistent with the target of the algorithmic design. Given limited number of initially labelled malware samples and imbalance between benign and malware samples, the node classifiers built on the heterogeneous MDN graph provide a discriminative prior over the class label of graph nodes. This node prior estimate provides a complementary supervised information to the label propagation procedure, which reduces the impact of the imbalance issue and lack of labelled malware samples. Such a property of the proposed method makes it well suited for solving challenging malware detection problems.

We measure also the average F1 score of the content-agnostic file-specific classifier with each level of malware sampling rate. Across different malware and benign file sampling rates, the average F1 score of the file-specific classifier is less than 0.83, distinctively lower than all the label propagation based methods in the comparison. In Table 3, we illustrate an example by comparing the F1 scores of the file specific classifier with those of the proposed method from March 30th to April 2nd, given benign file sampling rate as 0.5 and malware sampling rate as 0.05. These results indicate that the file specific classifier is unable to achieve a satisfying detection accuracy by itself. However, the probabilistic output of the classifier does produce complementary prior information to improve the detection accuracy of label propagation. Increasing the sampling rate of benign file over 0.5 results in a slight decrease in the AUC scores for all three algorithms. It is caused by the imbalanced issue of the training data, which increases slightly the type II error.

We run daily malware detection on the MDN graph, in order to simulate real-world malware filtering applications. The MDN graph generated per day has on average 1,648,458 file nodes, 892,394 URL node and 155,533 IP nodes, as summarised in Table 2. Average running time for malware detection on the large-scale MDN graph is 11 minutes, with 8 minutes for building the priori classifiers and 3 minutes for conducting label propagation concatenated with the priori information on the graph. Furthermore, as we observed in our experimental study, the running time of the whole malware detection increases linearly with the graph size. In practice, fast computing of the proposed method makes it possible to conduct semi-real time, e.g. hourly, malware detection on large-scale file collections.

4.3 Real-World Case Study

In this section, we provide a detailed case study showing how our proposed method is able to identify malicious files in a real-world malware distribution network excerpted from our March 17th graph. For the sake of simplicity, we use a tuple $(1 - f_i, f_i)$ in the figures to denote the label inference score of each node, where $f_i = P(y_i = +1 \mid N_i)$ and $f_i \in [0, 1]$ (see Section 2.3 for details). From our training data, node 1 is identified as information stealer malware 'limitail' $(0, 1)$ and node 3 is a legitimate windows 'calculator' application $(1, 0)$. Note that both files are hosted in the same site. This is a common strategy taken by cybercriminals to target different platforms; depending on various criteria set by these cybercriminals, either a benign file or malicious binary could be dropped. However, such strategy brings issues to graph-based inference methods. Take SocNL

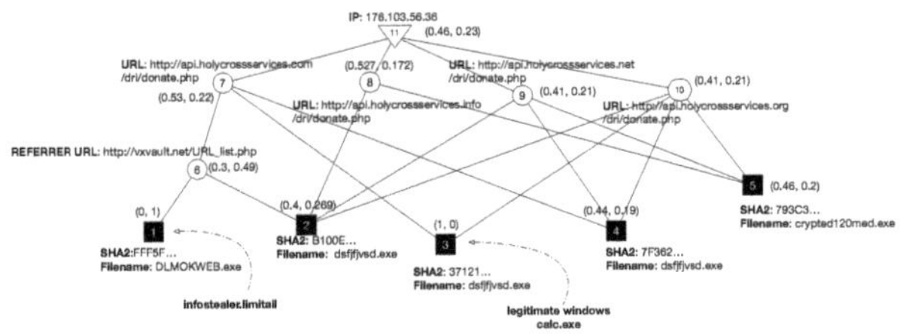

Figure 3: Real-world malware delivery network example: SocNL inference result.

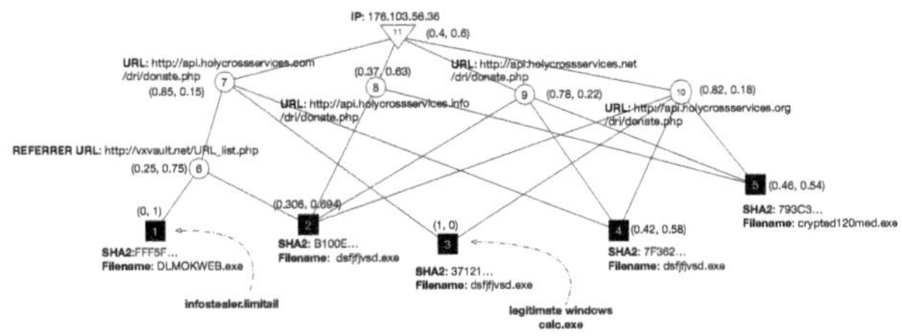

Figure 4: Real-world malware delivery network example: inference result by the proposed method.

for example, without a node priori information, SocNL can only use node 1 and node 3's initial labels leaving the rest of the nodes unlabelled. As we can see in Figure 3, SocNL is inclined to infer node 2, 4, and 5 as benign with high confidence scores. Thanks to the node classifiers (see Section 2 for details), our method is able to give each node *a priori* bias before label propagation begins. As we can observe in Figure 4, the proposed method is able to convict node 2, 4, and 5 as malicious. All three nodes are later confirmed in VirusTotal as 'Dridex' malware. Additionally, the proposed method is also able to convict node 8 as malicious. However, this graph connects to the whole malware distribution graph via a single node (node 1). This creates a propagation bottleneck and the proposed method is thus not able to convict the rest of the nodes.

5. CONCLUSION

In this paper, we propose a content-agnostic approach to detect malware by constructing a heterogeneous file distribution graph and leveraging semi-supervised learning on the built graph. Our work avoids the time-consuming binary analysis of malicious binaries and, at the same time, has the advantages of detecting malicious files accurately. It integrates exterior node classifiers for different node types (e.g., files, URLs and IP addresses) to reduce uncertainty during the inference process. The proposed approach is computationally scalable and can be easily parallelised for large-scale malware detection applications. We intend to measure the performance of the proposed method in dynamic networks where temporal factor is considered.

6. REFERENCES

[1] Y. Bengio, O. Delalleau, and N. L. Roux. *Label Propagation and Quadratic Criterion*, pages 193–216. MIT Press, 2006.

[2] J. Caballero, C. Grier, C. Kreibich, and V. Paxson. Measuring pay-per-install: The commoditization of malware distribution. In *USENIX Conference on Security*, 2011.

[3] M. Egele, T. Scholte, E. Kirda, and C. Kruegel. A survey on automated dynamic malware-analysis techniques and tools. *ACM Comput. Surv.*, 44(2), 2012.

[4] L. Invernizzi and P. M. Comparetti. Evilseed: A guided approach to finding malicious web pages. In *IEEE Security and Privacy*, 2012.

[5] L. Invernizzi, S. Miskovic, R. Torres, C. Kruegel, S. Saha, G. Vigna, S. Lee, and M. Mellia. NAZCA: Detecting malware distribution in large-scale networks. In *NDSS*, 2014.

[6] J. Jang, D. Brumley, and S. Venkataraman. Bitshred: Feature hashing malware for scalable triage and semantic analysis. In *ACM CCS*, pages 309–320, 2011.

[7] A. Kapravelos, Y. Shoshitaishvili, M. Cova, C. Kruegel, and G. Vigna. Revolver: An automated approach to the detection of evasive web-based malware. In *USENIX Security*, 2013.

[8] D. Kirat, G. Vigna, and C. Kruegel. Barecloud: bare-metal analysis-based evasive malware detection. In *USENIX Security*, 2014.

[9] B. J. Kwon, J. Mondal, J. Jang, L. Bilge, and T. Dumitras. The dropper effect: Insights into malware distribution with downloader graph analytics. In *ACM CCS*, pages 1118–1129, 2015.

[10] Z. Li, S. Alrwais, Y. Xie, F. Yu, and X. Wang. Finding the linchpins of the dark web: A study on topologically dedicated hosts on malicious web infrastructures. In *IEEE Security and Privacy*, 2013.

[11] J. Ma, L. K. Saul, S. Savage, and G. M. Voelker. Identifying suspicious urls: An application of large-scale online learning. In *ICML*, 2009.

[12] T. Nelms, R. Perdisci, M. Antonakakis, and M. Ahamad. Webwitness: Investigating, categorizing, and mitigating malware download paths. In *USENIX Security*, 2015.

[13] J. Platt. Probabilistic outputs for support vector machines and comparisons to regularized likelihood methods. *NIPS*, 10(3):61–74, 1999.

[14] C. Rossow, C. Dietrich, and H. Bos. Large-scale analysis of malware downloaders. In *DIMVA*. 2013.

[15] D. Song, D. Brumley, H. Yin, J. Caballero, I. Jager, M. G. Kang, Z. Liang, J. Newsome, P. Poosankam, and P. Saxena. Bitblaze: A new approach to computer security via binary analysis. In *Information systems security*. 2008.

[16] A. Tamersoy, K. Roundy, and D. H. Chau. Guilt by association: Large scale malware detection by mining file-relation graphs. In *SIGKDD*, 2014.

[17] Y. Yamaguchi, C. Faloutsos, and H. Kitagawa. Socnl: Bayesian label propagation with confidence. In *PAKDD*, 2015.

[18] J. Zhang, C. Seifert, J. W. Stokes, and W. Lee. Arrow: Generating signatures to detect drive-by downloads. In *WWW*, 2011.

[19] X. Zhu, Z. Ghahramani, and J. Lafferty. Semi-supervised learning using gaussian fields and harmonic functions. In *ICML*, pages 912–919, 2003.

Improving Advertisement Recommendation by Enriching User Browser Cookie Attributes

Liang Wang, Kuang-chih Lee, Quan Lu
Yahoo! Inc.
701 First Avenue
Sunnyvale, CA, US
{wlliang@, kclee@, qlu@}yahoo-inc.com

ABSTRACT

User attributes including online behavior history and demographic information are the keys to decide whether a user is the right audience for an advertisement. When a user visits a website, the website generally plugs a browser cookie string ('bcookie' for short). The bcookie is then used as an identifier to collect the user's online behavior, as well as the joint key to link user profile attributes, such as demographic information and browsing history. However, the same users can have different bcookies across different browsers and devices. Moreover, bcookies can expire after some period, be cleared by browsers or users. This situation of bcookie discounting typically introduces both performance and delivery problems in online advertising since advertisers are hard to find the most receptive audiences based on the user profile information. In this paper, we try to tackle this problem by using an 'assistant identifier' to find the linkage between different bcookies. For most of the Internet company, in addition to the bcookie information, there are always other identifiers such as IP address, user agent, OS type and version , *etc.*, stored in the serving log data. Therefore, we propose an unified framework to link different bcookies from the same users according to those assistant identifiers. Specifically, our proposed method first constructs a bipartite graph with linkages between the assistant identifiers and the bcookies. Next all attributes associated with each bcookie are propagated along the graph using the state-of-the-art random walk model. Offline comparative experimental studies are conducted to confirm that by enriching the bcookie attributes we can recover 20% more online users whose bcookie information is lost, which is greatly helpful to delivery more budget spending with a little loss in precision of predicting converted users. On-product evaluation further confirms the effectiveness of the proposed method.

Keywords

Advertisement recommendation; user attribute enrichment; probability mass propagation

CIKM'16 , October 24-28, 2016, Indianapolis, IN, USA

DOI: http://dx.doi.org/10.1145/2983323.2983374

1. INTRODUCTION

After many years of exploration, online advertising has become more mature with very large market shares. In 2014, spendings on online advertising approached more than 50 billion dollars in the whole world [5]. Different from traditional media advertising like TV and newspaper, the online advertising systems know more about the users' attributes including their demography information and propensities in products, which are noted by some registration information and user online behaviors. Thus the online advertising is capable of serving more proper advertisement to the users, and meanwhile yields more returns for the advertiser by the predictable user response. Therefore the key to the success of online advertising is the completeness of the user attributes.

To simultaneously protect the privacy of users and collect the users' attributes from their registration information and behavior history, the online users' browsers are assigned a browser cookie ('bcookie' for short) by a website when they first visit this website. The website then track the users's activity until the bcookies expires or deleted by the users. However, as studied in literature [3][8], users may frequently clear their cookies (so called 'cookie churn' problem), and one user may associate with multiple bcookies when they are working with multiple browsers or multiple devices. As a result, most of the bcookies we are dealing with typically have fragmented user attributes or even no user attribute at all.

To provide a better personalized advertisement serving experience, one essential step is to identify the underlying real user behind the bcookies so that we can link the fragmented user information among a set of bcookies together to form a complete user profile. In [8], the author provided a thorough study of whether using a single user identifier (including IP address, user agent, bcookie) or the combination of user identifiers can correctly identify a user client host. The study shows that bcookie is the best user uniqueness identifier except the registrated user ids and the major reason for the bcookie mismatch is the cookie churn problem. However, this task is difficult due to the lack of real user level identification information.

In the literature, there are several studies [3][2][9] that focus on linking the bcookies together according to whether they belong to the same browser or device. In [3], the authors propose a graph coloring method to cluster the bcookies with no lifetime overlap (since they belong to the same browser) and similar in their behavior patterns including visiting webpage categories and IP used. They use the Yahoo toolbar id as the ground truth to measure the performance of their method. The method has limited applications due to the fact that all bcookies form the same users needs to be stored in the same browsers; however, since users may switch to different browsers or different devices frequently nowadays, this method is less applicable to mobile related advertising business. Yen *et al.* in [9] studied the problem of assigning the search queries to multiple users working on a single machine. Comparing to the bcookie grouping task, this problem assumes there are fixed machine identifiers so the problem is simplified. In summary, most of the existing approaches only concern the correctness of the bcookie grouping (into one host client or browser), and less studies have been made on whether clustering the users to enrich the bcookie attributes really improves the performance of applications like advertisement recommendation.

In this paper, we propose the solution to a more general problem of enriching bcookie attributes from a set of the bcookies which are likely to arise from the same underlying user. Based on the enriched user attributes, we also study the performance improvements on the advertisement recommendation problem. Our study is conducted on Yahoo advertising serving logs. For each raw log, the user is not only identified by bcookie, but also other identifiers like IP address, user agent, device type, *etc.* We build a bipartite graph by linking the bcookies to another identifier (let's call it 'assistant identifier' in the following sections) according to the logs, and enrich the attributes associated with each bcookie by the propagation method that executes the state-of-the-art random walk algorithm with an iterative updated transition probability on the graph, so that the bcookies can transmit their attributes to the ones which are strongly linked to them by the assistant identifier. The intuition behind this method is that bcookies that shares similar assistant identifiers are likely to be raised from the same underlying user or the closely connected group of persons (like the family members). Since we are dealing with large scale data with billions of bcookies every week, the proposed method is designed to support parallel computing. We also study the performance of the proposed enrichment method by the application of finding potential customers in advertisement recommendation. Experimental results confirm that, by enriching the attributes of the bcookies, we are capable of discovering more potential customers for online advertising even for bcookies without any history.

1.1 Organization

The rest of this paper is organized as follows. The proposed algorithm to enrich the bcookies' attributes are detailed in Section 2. The performance study of enriching the bcookies' attributes for finding potential customers in advertisement recommendation is presented in Section 3. We conclude the proposed method in Section 4.

2. ENRICH THE BCOOKIES' ATTRIBUTES BY ATTRIBUTE PROPAGATION

To enrich bcookies' attributes by graph propagation between 'linked' bcookies, we need to solve two key issues: (1) find the linkage and the strength of the linkage between different users; (2) since we are working on large scale internet company level data, the computational algorithm should be scalable well. Specifically, we conduct our study on Yahoo's display advertising platform.

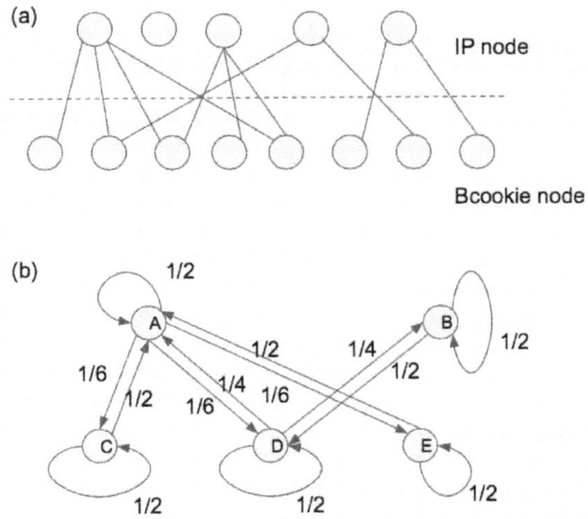

Figure 1: (a) Illustration of building the linkage between bcookies by the assistant identifier (IP address), when a bcookie and an IP appeared together in a log, we link them by an edge; (b) demonstration of the method to compute the transition probability between nodes for random walk.

2.1 Find linkage between bcookies

In the advertising logs, besides the bcookie, the user in each serving log is also indexed by other user identifiers including the IP address, user agent, device type *etc.* Although the bcookies themselves are independent to each other, some of them may have the same IP addresses, user agents, *etc.* We use these identifiers as 'assistant identifiers' to link different bcookies. According to our data analysis, among these assistant identifiers, the IP address is the most informative one compare to others and is more robust with the smallest missing rate in logs. In this paper, we carry out our study by using IP address as assistant identifier.

As illustrated in Fig. 1 (a), we build a bipartite graph to represent the connection between IPs and bcookies. A link between an IP node and a bcookie node is formed only when they appeared in one serving log together. In reality, there are some commercial IPs shared thousands of users, and there are also fraudulent bcookies fake their traffic as coming from hundreds of IPs. These connections will bring noises to the graph. Hence, we deploy the following pre-filtering strategies before propagation to remove the suspicious bcookie-IP pairs.

1. Abnormal impression volume rule: filter out bcookies with number of impressions larger than $threshold_1$
2. Abnormal IP address association pattern: filter out bcookies associated with more than $threshold_2$ of IPs
3. Commercial IP address rule: filter out IPs associated with more than $threshold_3$ of bcookies

In our experiment, we analyze the data for one month and set the thresholds as $threshold_1 = 10000$, $threshold_2 = 50$ and $threshold_3 = 100$. These rules may filter out the significantly suspicious bcookie-IP pairs but leave the nonsignificant ones still in the graph. As we will present in the following sections, we use edge weighting method to minimize the impact of these noisy pairs.

2.2 Propagate bcookie attributes by random walk

We propose the following two assumptions when designing the propagation algorithm on the bipartite graph: (1) when two bcookie nodes shares many IP addresses, they are likely to belong to the same underlying users or a closely connected groups of people (like family members); (2) the more outer links a node (IP or bcookie) has, the more likely the node would be some fraudulent IPs/bcookies or commercial IPs, and we are less confident in transmitting their attributes to their linkages. Regarding to criterion (1), we define the transition probability between nodes according to markov chain formulation [4]. Starting from a node v_s, the probability of arriving at v_e in t step is:

$$P^t(v_b, v_e) = \begin{cases} w(v_b, v_e) & \text{if } t = 1 \\ \sum_k w(v_k, v_e) \cdot P^{t-1}(v_b, v_k) & \text{if } t > 1 \end{cases} \quad (1)$$

where $w(v_i, v_j)$ represents the transition probability from v_i to v_j, and is equal to 0 when there is no edge between them. By defining the transition probability this way, when two bcookies share more IP nodes in common, they transmit their attributes to each other with higher probability.

Considering the criterion (2), we design the edge weight (transition probability) from node u to v in the bi-direct graph according to the random walk model [6], *i.e.*

$$w_{u,v} = \begin{cases} 1/2 & \text{if } u = v \\ 1/(2 * d(u)) & \text{if u and v are linked} \end{cases} \quad (2)$$

where $d(u)$ is the outer degree of node u. In this way, the edge weights between nodes are asymmetrically defined and the more outer links a node has, the less confident it can transmit its attributes out to other nodes. An example to compute the transition probability between nodes is shown in Fig. 1 (b). For the node A, its out-degree is 3, such that its transition probability to each outer links (to node C, D and E) are 1/6, and 1/2 to itself.

According to this design, for each attribute associated with a bcookie, we set its initial weight to be 1, then, we transmit the attribute with the transition probability defined in the graph and set its weight in the target bcookie (or IP) according to Eq. 1. The final attribute set associated with a node can be determined by thresholding the weights of these attributes.

Since the markov chain propagation process can be performed by matrix multiplication [4], and in our case, most items in the transition matrix defined on Eq. 2 is 0. We employ the distributed sparse matrix multiplication method in [1] to compute propagation probability between nodes as Eq. 1 to compute the final attributes associated with each nodes and their weights. There is a debate between the number of iterations we should perform. On the one hand, when we run more iterations of attribute propagations, we can have more information for the bcookies, however, these informations is more likely to contain noise; on the other hand, when we iterate less, we are more confident in the final bcookie attributes, but we will still face the lacking of information phenomenon. In Fig. 2, we show the result of the enrichment performance changes when using different numbers of iterations. It can be seen, after 3 iterations, the number of bcookies being enriched does not increase too much under more iterations. Hence, we only perform 3 iterations as our experimental protocol.

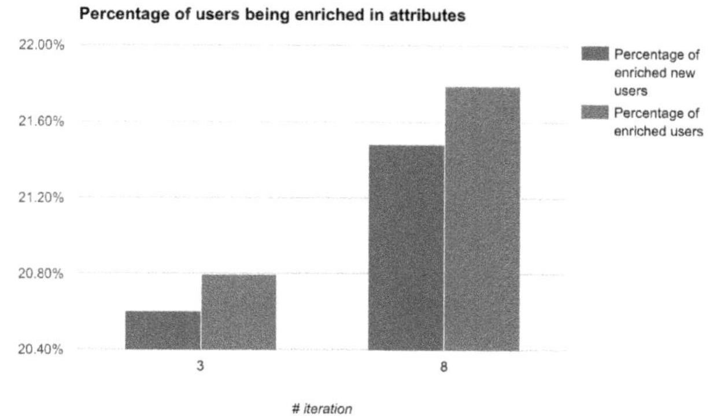

Figure 2: Illustration of the enrichment performance changes using different number of iterations.

Table 1: Performance in bcookie attributes enrichment. Here, 'new' means the user has no attributes in our logs and 'old' means the users are associated with certain attributes

Method	percentage of new users being enriched	percentage of old users being enriched
IP grouping	20.5%	19.7%
Propagation	20.6%	20.8%

3. EXPERIMENTS

We conduct extensive offline and online evaluation of the proposed method on Yahoo's display advertising platform which serves billions of bid request per-day. Since most of the existing works [3][2][9] try to group the users according to their underlying real-world users, we use the user grouping method as a benchmark for comparison purpose. The benchmark method proceeds as follows: first, we apply the same pre-filtering rules as in Section 2 to remove the fraudulent/commercial IP addresses and bcookies from the data. Then, we compute the number of impressions (the number of log items) $N_{bcookie,IP}$ for each $< bcookie, IP >$ pair, and assign the bcookie to the IP with the largest number of $N_{bcookie,IP}$. Finally, the attributes sets of all the bcookies in the same IP group are shared to each other to enrich their attribute set.

Nowadays, the advertisers begin to concern more about the conversion rate of their advertisement, *i.e.*, the number of bcookies found by our system can finally purchase the products related to the recommended advertisements. In this paper, we use the purchase history as the attributes for bcookies to study the performance changes. However, the proposed method can be applied to any attributes for bcookies.

We collect one month's advertisement serving log data to perform the attribute enrichment experiment. There are more than one billion of unique bcookies appeared in the logs. The enrichment impact is illustrated in Table 1. We can see that both the propagation method and the grouping method enriched about 20% of bcookies previously recorded with no purchase history, this is a large contribution to solve

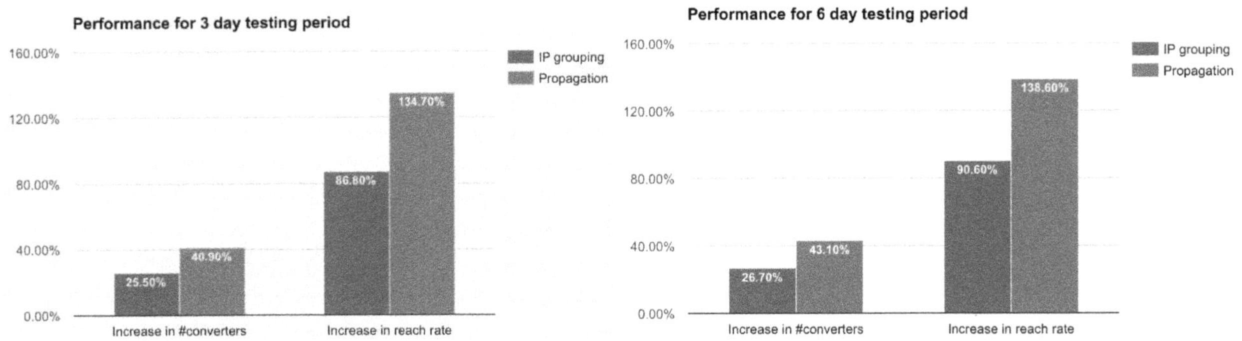

Figure 3: Illustration of the performance changes in advertisement recommendation when applying the enrichment methods.

the cold start problem of our system. Since we are more interested in the quality of the enrichment process, we conduct experiments on advertisement recommendation performance improvements. Specifically, we focused on the purchase prediction improvement brought by the enrichment methods. We use the item-based collaborative filtering algorithm [7] to predict the potential purchased products of the bcookies and recommend them with the advertisements related to these products. In the experiment, we select the top 50 recommendations with score larger than 0 from the output the collaborative filtering algorithm.

We use the enrichment results above, and the following M ($M = 3$, 6) days' bcookie advertisement serving history and purchase history as the ground truth to evaluate the performance. Fig. 3 provides the performance changes brought by the attribute enrichment methods. As can be observed from the result, the propagation based method is capable of discovering more converters (the bcookies purchase the products related to recommended advertisements) and reaching more online users than the grouping based approaches. Since in the online serving, there are competition between different advertisements and different advertisement bidding systems, larger reach rate gives the system more chance to win the recommended bcookies for certain advertisements.

3.1 On production test

We put the propagation based enrichment method for online test on two campaigns for two days. The online system runs by combining a set of recommendation modules in a comparative manner. To simplify the implementation, we directly recommend an IP list for each campaign associated with the recommended bcookies. The results are presented in Tab. 2. Compare with the performance of the previous two days (the same weekdays as the testing days), we see the improvement in both the revenue (which is related to the number of advertisements impressions we served) and the conversion rate.

Table 2: On production performance.

Increase in revenue	Increase in conversion rate
1.86%	1.92%

4. CONCLUSION

In this paper, we try to solve the fundamental problem of cookie loss, which leads to the result that user information becomes fragment. This problem is important because it introduces significant performance and delivery drop for online advertising business. In this paper, we propose to link the bcookies through the 'assistant identifiers' which are logged together with the bcookies in advertising serving logs. The attributes of the bcookies are then enriched based on the linkage. Instead of finding ground truth data for validating the correctness of the attribute enrichment, we evaluate both the online and offline advertising recommendation to proof the effectiveness of the proposed methods. As future work, we would like to incorporate more user attributes to improve the performance of our proposed method.

5. REFERENCES

[1] A. Buluc, J. Fineman, M. Frigo, J. Gilbert, and C. Leiserson. Parallel sparse matrix-vector and matrix-transpose-vector multiplication using compressed sparse blocks. In *Symposium on Parallelism in algorithms and architectures*, pages 233–244, 2009.

[2] D. Coey and M. Bailey. People and cookies: Imperfect treatment assignment in online experiments. In *to appear in WWW'16*, 2016.

[3] A. Dasgupta, M. Gurevich, L. Zhang, B. Tseng, and A. Thomas. Overcoming browser cookie churn with clustering. In *WWW'12*, pages 83–92, 2012.

[4] F. Fouss, A. Pirotte, J. Renders, and M. Saerens. Random-walk computation of similarities between nodes of a graph with application to collaborative recommendation. *IEEE Transaction KDE*, 19(3):355–369, 2007.

[5] K. Olmstead and K. Lu. Digital news - revenue: Fact sheet. *State of The Media*, 2015.

[6] K. Pearson. The problem of the random walk. *Nature*, 72(294), 1905.

[7] B. Sarwar, G. Karypis, J. Konstan, and J. Riedl. Item-based collaborative filtering recommendation algorithms. In *WWW'01*, pages 285–295, 2001.

[8] R. White, A. Hassan, A. Singla, and E. Horvitz. From devices to people: Attribution of search activity in multi-user settings. In *WWW'14*, pages 431–442, 2014.

[9] T. Yen, Y. Xie, F. Yu, R. Yu, and M. Abadi. Host fingerprinting and tracking on the web: Privacy and security implications. In *NDSS'12*, 2012.

Balanced Supervised Non-Negative Matrix Factorization for Childhood Leukaemia Patients

Ali Braytee[†], Daniel R. Catchpoole[‡], Paul J. Kennedy[†], Wei Liu[∓]
[†] Quantum Computation and Intelligent Systems, University of Technology Sydney, Australia
[‡] The Tumour Bank, Children's Cancer Research Unit, The Children's Hospital at Westmead
[∓] Advanced Analytics Institute, University of Technology Sydney, Australia
{Ali.Braytee, Paul.Kennedy, Wei.Liu}@uts.edu.au,
Daniel.Catchpoole@health.nsw.gov.au

ABSTRACT

Supervised feature extraction methods have received considerable attention in the data mining community due to their capability to improve the classification performance of the unsupervised dimensionality reduction methods. With increasing dimensionality, several methods based on supervised feature extraction are proposed to achieve a feature ranking especially on microarray gene expression data. This paper proposes a method with twofold objectives: it implements a balanced supervised non-negative matrix factorization (BSNMF) to handle the class imbalance problem in supervised non-negative matrix factorization techniques. Furthermore, it proposes an accurate gene ranking method based on our proposed BSNMF for microarray gene expression datasets. To the best of our knowledge, this is the first work to handle the class imbalance problem in supervised feature extraction methods. This work is part of a Human Genome project at The Children's Hospital at Westmead (TB-CHW), Australia. Our experiments indicate that the factorized components using supervised feature extraction approach have more classification capability than the unsupervised one, but it drastically fails at the presence of class imbalance problem. Our proposed method outperforms the state-of-the-art methods and shows promise in overcoming this concern.

Keywords

Supervised feature extraction; Imbalance class problem; Non-negative matrix factorization; Gene selection

1. INTRODUCTION

The Tumour Bank of The Children's Hospital at Westmead (TB-CHW), Australia, is a biobanking facility that collects and stores paediatric biospecimens such as bone marrow, fresh frozen tumor, biopsies, and others to support the research projects in the hospital [8]. The Human Genome project goals are: to facilitate research on the collected tissue samples of the most common malignancy cancer of children *Acute Lymphoblastic Leukaemia (ALL)*, to detect relevant genes able to improve the classification performance for paediatric cancer patients, and to enhance the interdependence between genomic researchers and clinical practitioners. The causes of ALL disease are still unknown, but some results assume from genetic mutations. The major risk of ALL patients is suffering from a relapse; that means the cancer recurs after initial therapy, yet approximately 20 % of children relapsed. Therefore, building an accurate classification model to predict whether patients will suffer a relapse or not is considered a crucial step in successful treatment.

The complexities and challenges of paediatric cancer as rare diseases are reflected in the generated childhood leukaemia gene expression dataset which is collected from the TB-CHW centre. The dataset in this project comprises several open challenges in data mining, including high dimensionality, high class-imbalance with low number of samples. The total number of genes is 22678 with only 20% "Relapse" and the rest are "Non-Relapse". Moreover, the total number of patients is only 60.

Supervised feature extraction methods are proposed to enhance the classification of the factorized matrices by utilizing class labels [4]. The most popular methods in supervised feature extraction are Supervised PCA [2], Supervised NMF [4], and Discriminant Non-Negative Matrix Factorization (DNMF) [5]. Although these methods are useful in dimensionality reduction, they are not appropriate for application to imbalanced datasets because the factorized components are biased to predict the majority class samples that lead to poor performance on classification, and the class imbalance problem is exacerbated when dealing with high-dimensional data. Moreover, the resulting principal components of PCA and Supervised PCA [2] suffer from a lack of intuitive meaning. In contrast NMF, because of the non-negativity constraint on its entries, provides an elegant interpretation of the data decomposition in many fields. For instance, after applying NMF, the non-negative coefficients of the decomposed basis matrix in microarray gene expression are considered as the contribution of the genes [3].

In this paper, we propose a Balanced Supervised NMF (BSNMF) method which aims to exploit the class labels to lessen the inherent bias of the extracted components to the majority class. Then, we use the proposed BSNMF to achieve the gene ranking. In fact, we are unaware of any pre-

CIKM'16, October 24-November 28, 2016, Indianapolis, IN, USA

DOI: http://dx.doi.org/10.1145/2983323.2983375

vious studies that address the imbalanced class problem in the supervised feature extraction approaches. Specifically, **the contributions** of this paper are:

1. We propose a balanced supervised NMF (BSNMF) method to extract non-biased factorized components.
2. We propose a feature selection model able to identify the most relevant genes to predict the relapsed leukemia childhood patients.
3. We provide comprehensive evaluations of our method on several imbalanced microarray gene expression datasets which show the advantages of our method.

2. A BRIEF REVIEW OF NMF

Lee and Sueng [6] introduce NMF as an unsupervised dimension reduction paradigm. Mathematically, given a data matrix $X \in \mathbb{R}^{M\times N}$, where the columns of the matrix represent the sample vectors x_i, and the rows represent the features or dimensions, NMF seeks to find two matrices U and V whose product can approximate the original matrix X as described below:

$$X \approx UV^T \tag{1}$$

where $U \in \mathbb{R}^{M\times K}$,$V \in \mathbb{R}^{N\times K} \geq 0$ and $K < min(N, M)$. To evaluate the quality of reconstructing the original matrix X by multiplying U and V, the square Euclidean distance is proposed as a cost function to quantify the difference between two matrices:

$$\mathbf{O} = \left\| X - UV^T \right\|^2 = \sum_{i,j} \left[X_{ij} - (UV)_{ij} \right]^2 \tag{2}$$

The objective function $\mathbf{O}$ in Eq. 2 is to minimize the residual sum of squares of the matrices. A good approximation of the feature vectors in U will assist in discovering the structure of the data. NMF is a parts-based local representation of data, which means that combining the parts will lead to forming the whole [6].

3. BALANCED SUPERVISED NMF (BSNMF)

NMF is an unsupervised matrix factorization which suffers from the lack of classification capability. It is designed for reconstruction, not for classification. Several approaches have been proposed as shown in section 1 to improve NMF by constructing more descriptive features for classification. These approaches utilize the existence of the class labels to improve the recognition capability of the constructed features. However, the current supervised NMF methods in the literature fail to handle the imbalance problem of the data, because the extracted features are biased to predict the majority class samples that lead to poor performance on classification. In this section, we introduce our Balanced Supervised NMF which avoids this limitation by considering the imbalance class ratio.

3.1 NMF with Coupled Matrix Factorization

Coupled matrix factorization aims to capture the sparse factors of jointly analysed multiple matrices with one mode in common. This approach has previously been used in several data fusion studies [7]. Without any loss of generality, assume matrices $Y \in \mathbb{R}^{N\times M}$ and $Z \in \mathbb{R}^{N\times L}$ have the first mode in common. The objective from the coupled matrix factorization is to find three matrices $A \in \mathbb{R}^{N\times R}$, $B \in \mathbb{R}^{M\times R}$ and $C \in \mathbb{R}^{L\times R}$ by minimizing the cost function below:

$$F(A, B, C) = \left\| Y - AB^T \right\|^2 + \left\| Z - AC^T \right\|^2$$

where matrix A is the common factorized matrix between Y and Z, and $\|.\|$ denotes the Frobenius norm for matrices.

In this paper, we use the idea of coupled matrix factorization to handle the imbalance problem in supervised non-negative matrix factorization. Our approach aims to enhance the classification capability of the NMF on the imbalanced datasets. In the binary case, we exploit the existence of the class labels to extract the shared mode (basis matrix U) from the positive and negative matrices, X^+andX^- respectively by using the idea of coupled matrix factorization.

Given a data matrix $X = [x_{ij}] \in \mathbb{R}^{M\times N}$, where M and N represent the dimensions and samples of the matrix respectively. We decompose the original matrix X into two matrices as follows:

$$\begin{cases} X_i^-, & \textbf{If } y_i = -1, \text{(Negative class)} \\ X_i^+, & \textbf{If } y_i = +1, \text{(Positive class)} \end{cases}$$

where X^- corresponds to a features by negative class samples matrix and X^+ corresponds to a features by positive class samples matrix. Our BSNMF method aims to find the shared feature matrix U and the other two matrices V^+ and V^- by minimizing the objective function below:

$$\mathbf{O}\left(U, V^-, V^+\right) = \left\| X^- - U(V^-)^T \right\|^2 + \left\| X^+ - U(V^+)^T \right\|^2 \quad s.t.\ U, V^-, V^+ \geq 0 \tag{3}$$

However, in the imbalance class problem, the magnitude of the error of the negative samples (the first part of Eq. 3) dominates the magnitude error of positive samples. Obviously, this is because the number of negative samples is bigger than the positive ones. Therefore, we propose to discount the objective function in Eq. 3 with the class ratio of the samples. The objective function is changed to be as follows:

$$\mathbf{O}\left(U, V^-, V^+\right) = \sigma^- \left\| X^- - U(V^-)^T \right\|^2 + \sigma^+ \left\| X^+ - U(V^+)^T \right\|^2 \tag{4}$$

where $\sigma^- = \frac{N}{N^-}$, $\sigma^+ = \frac{N}{N^+}$, N is total number of samples, N^- and N^+ denote the total number of negative and positive samples respectively.

The objective function $\mathbf{O}$ in Eq. 4 is convex in U, V^- and V^+ separately. Therefore, we introduce three iterative procedures which are able to find the local minima.

By expanding Eq. (4), the objective function is written as:

$$\begin{aligned} \mathbf{O}\left[U, V^-, V^+\right] = {} & \sigma^- \left[X^-(X^-)^T - 2X^-V^-U + U(V^-)^T V^- U^T\right] \\ & + \sigma^+ \left[X^+(X^+)^T - 2X^+V^+U + U(V^+)^T V^+ U^T\right] \end{aligned} \tag{5}$$

The three factor matrices U, V^-, V^+ are initialized to non-negative values and then refined by means of gradient descent approaches. So, we propose Lagrange multipliers ψ, ϕ and ε for constraint U, V^-, V^+. Therefore the Lagrange form is:

$$\begin{aligned} \mathbf{L} = {} & \sigma^- \left[X^-(X^-)^T - 2X^-V^-U + U(V^-)^T V^- U^T\right] \\ & + \sigma^+ \left[X^+(X^+)^T - 2X^+V^+U + U(V^+)^T V^+ U^T\right] \\ & + \psi U + \phi V^- + \varepsilon V^+ \end{aligned} \tag{6}$$

The partial derivatives of $\mathbf{L}$ with respect to U, V^- and V^+ are:

$$\begin{aligned} \frac{\partial \mathbf{L}}{\partial U} = & - 2\sigma^- X^-(V^-)^T + 2\sigma^- U(V^-)^T V^- \\ & - 2\sigma^+ X^+(V^+)^T + 2\sigma^+ U(V^+)^T V^+ + \psi \end{aligned} \tag{7}$$

$$\frac{\partial \mathbf{L}}{\partial V^-} = -2\sigma^- X^- U^T + 2\sigma^- V^- U U^T + \phi \tag{8}$$

$$\frac{\partial \mathbf{L}}{\partial V^+} = -2\sigma^+ X^+ U^T + 2\sigma^+ V^+ U U^T + \varepsilon \tag{9}$$

We formulate the below equations based on Karush-Kuhn-Tucker conditions where $\psi_{ik} u_{ik} = 0$, $\phi_{jk} vm_{jk} = 0$ and $\varepsilon_{mk} vp_{mk} = 0$,

$$\begin{aligned} &-\left[\sigma^- X^- (V^-)^T\right]_{ik} u_{ik} + \left[\sigma^- U (V^-)^T V^-\right]_{ik} u_{ik} \\ &-\left[\sigma^+ X^+ (V^+)^T\right]_{ik} u_{ik} + \left[\sigma^+ U (V^+)^T V^+\right]_{ik} u_{ik} = 0 \end{aligned} \tag{10}$$

$$-\left[\sigma^- X^- U^T\right]_{jk} vm_{jk} + \left[\sigma^- V^- U U^T\right]_{jk} vm_{jk} = 0 \tag{11}$$

$$-\left[\sigma^+ X^+ U^T\right]_{mk} vp_{mk} + \left[\sigma^+ V^+ U U^T\right]_{mk} vp_{mk} = 0 \tag{12}$$

These equations lead to three updating rules denoted below:

$$u_{ik} \leftarrow u_{ik} \frac{\left[\sigma^- X^- (V^-)^T\right]_{ik} + \left[\sigma^+ X^+ (V^+)^T\right]_{ik}}{[\sigma^- U V^- (V^-)^T]_{ik} + [\sigma^+ U V^+ (V^+)^T]_{ik}} \tag{13}$$

$$vm_{jk} \leftarrow vm_{jk} \frac{\left[X^- U^T\right]_{jk}}{[V^- U U^T]_{jk}} \tag{14}$$

$$vp_{mk} \leftarrow vp_{mk} \frac{\left[X^+ U^T\right]_{mk}}{[V^+ U U^T]_{mk}} \tag{15}$$

The convergence analysis and proving that objective function $\mathbf{O}$ is non-increasing under the updating rules in Eq. 13, 14 and 15 is described in Appendix file [1].

4. BSNMF GENE SELECTION

NMF has been applied recently to computational biology such as molecular pattern discovery, disease prediction, and others. It has been successfully used for gene ranking analysis in microarray gene expression data [3]. However, the unsupervised NMF method has limits in identifying the relevant genes which have a classification capability due to the non-exploiting the sample label information. Furthermore, as we showed in section 1, the supervised NMF methods such as Supervised NMF [4] and DNMF [5] are not able to handle the class imbalance problem in the generated components.

This section uses the common shared basis matrix U generated from BSNMF rank genes. The samples in coefficient matrices V^- and V^+ are more predictive than those generated by unbalanced NMF methods. Our method provides a more efficient and flexible approach to gene ranking, and is computationally similar to NMF methods.

BSNMF gene ranking is described as follows. Given a gene expression matrix of M genes and N samples decomposed using BSNMF, a sparse shared basis matrix U is obtained which carries the original gene contributions in its entries. Differentially expressed features can be recognized using U, which can be expressed as

$$U = \begin{bmatrix} u_{11} & u_{12} & \cdots & u_{1K} \\ \vdots & \vdots & \vdots & \vdots \\ u_{m1} & u_{m2} & \cdots & u_{MK} \end{bmatrix}$$

[1] Appendix online at https://drive.google.com/open?id=0B3vYeJ3OoqO8SUx1YTktbk5kSmc

Dataset	#Attributes	#Instances	#IR	Source
Childhood Leukaemia	22277	60	2.85	TB-CHW
Colon cancer	2000	60	1.81	[1]
Lung cancer	12533	181	4.8	[1]
Global Cancer Map	16064	281	2.11	[1]
Lymphoma Outcome	7130	78	3.05	[1]
ALL/AML	7129	73	2.92	[1]
Breast cancer	4869	77	1.33	[1]
DLBCL	5470	77	3.05	[1]

Table 1: Datasets, column #IR is the imbalance ratio (Neg/Pos)

The columns of the shared basis matrix U represent the contribution of each original gene in the factors V^- and V^+. The values of the basis matrix U are called gene values and define the gene ranks. To discover differentially expressed genes we first compute the rank of the original genes by summing rows of the shared basis matrix U

$$Score_j = \left[\sum_{k=1}^{K} u_{1k} \cdots\cdots \sum_{k=1}^{K} u_{mk}\right]^T \tag{16}$$

where K is desired rank, $m = 1, \cdots, M$ is the number of features in U. As $Score_j \to 0$, feature j is considered less important. Secondly, the score list obtained in Eq. 16 is sorted in descending order. Finally, without loss of generality, the most differentially expressed genes are identified from the sorted list with a threshold on *Score* list entries.

Here, we estimate the significance of the gene scores in BSNMF. A permutation test is defined based on a test proposed by Wang [5]. We set a null hypothesis to check if the summed columns of U is non-discriminative to the sample classification. Elements of U are randomly shuffled and the permutated $Score^{ob}$ is computed for every iteration B, where $B = 1000$ times. The P-value (p) for an observed $Score^{ob}$ vector will be

$$p = \frac{1}{MB} \sum_{b=1}^{B} \sum_{j=1}^{M} I\left(\left|Score^{ob}\right| < \left|Score_j^b\right|\right) \tag{17}$$

where M is the number of features, $Score_j^b$ is the permutated feature score and $I(.)$ is an indicator function giving 1 if true and 0 otherwise.

5. EXPERIMENTS

Our code is available for experimental reproducibility[2]. We conducted experiments on eight high-dimensional imbalanced microarray datasets. Dataset characteristics are summarised in Table 1. The main dataset used is an Affymetrix childhood leukaemia dataset, collected on the U133A platform at The Children's Hospital at Westmead. It is important to note that the main purpose of these experiments is to show the strength of BSNMF in finding non-biased informative genes that are closely correlated with relapse.

Performance of BSNMF is compared with standard NMF and supervised DNMF [5]. Without loss of generality, we use a linear SVM with soft margin loss function for learning and AUC as an evaluation metric. AUC estimates were averaged over Leave-One-Out cross-validation. Moreover, dataset entries are normalized to [0,1].

We conduct t-tests between BSNMF (Base) against the compared methods under the null hypothesis that the AUC of used methods is not significantly different. P-values in Table 2 reject the null hypothesis, as most values of BSNMF

[2] BSNMF code at https://drive.google.com/open?id=0B3vYeJ3OoqO8S21rMjdBZ1pNZDA

Dataset	Rank (K)	NMF AUC|FS	DNMF AUC|FS	BSNMF AUC|FS
Childhood Leukaemia (Children's Hospital dataset)	2	.75|14	.50|15	**.85|15**
	4	.75|37	-	**.90|56**
	6	.55|37	-	**.80|6**
	8	.75|22	-	.75|**31**
	10	.65|16	-	**.90|15**
Colon cancer	2	.75|10	.90|37	**.85|14**
	4	.85|34	-	**.85|28**
	6	.81|4	-	**.90|9**
	8	.85|39	-	**.95|45**
	10	.85|24	-	**.90|7**
Lung cancer	2	.88|33	.50|20	**.89|17**
	4	.79|45	-	**.99|27**
	6	.91|36	-	**.98|10**
	8	.98|47	-	**.93|43**
	10	.95|37	-	**.97|5**
Global Cancer Map	2	.77|42	.60|31	**.78|52**
	4	.73|44	-	**.87|25**
	6	.84|80	-	**.79|34**
	8	.81|92	-	**.85|38**
	10	.79|72	-	**.86|43**
Lymphoma Outcome	2	.84|79	.50|22	**.97|18**
	4	.81|11	-	**.84|43**
	6	.91|27	-	**.86|28**
	8	.81|9	-	**.86|9**
	10	.78|66	-	**.83|22**
ALL/AML	2	.77|60	.50|32	**.80|63**
	4	.78|15	-	**.99|28**
	6	.89|13	-	**.92|27**
	8	.72|5	-	**.88|49**
	10	.96|76	-	**.97|15**
Breast cancer	2	.51|19	.61|22	**.73|4**
	4	.60|12	-	**.63|14**
	6	.63|26	-	**.80|50**
	8	.70|7	-	**.70|2**
	10	.70|30	-	**.76**|12
Diffuse large b-cell lymphomas (DLBCL)	2	.84|16	.75|31	**.88|23**
	4	.81|37	-	**.87|35**
	6	.94|17	-	**.95|12**
	8	.81|31	-	**.90|43**
	10	.81|41	-	**.94|17**
t-test	2	.01	.003	Base
	4	.009	-	Base
	6	.01	-	Base
	8	.07	-	Base
	10	.02	-	Base

Table 2: AUC Evaluation results on imbalanced datasets. Values are on the test sets. FS: is the number of the selected genes

are lower than 0.05. Obtained results in Table 2 show that the performance of the SVM classifier is substantially improved by using BSNMF and it outperformed the state-of-the-art. Furthermore, our method selected important genes in the childhood leukaemia dataset which are able to predict relapse. These genes will be analysed in future to identify pathways for cancer relapse. Results also indicate that the skewed data are exacerbated for high-dimensional data. BSNMF addresses the class imbalance in supervised NMF without needing to change the data distribution or modifying existing classifiers. Gene ranking in DNMF [5] is designed to work only on rank equal to 2.

6. CONCLUSIONS

Supervised feature extraction is a growing research area in data mining. Several supervised feature extraction methods have been suggested to enhance classification of constructed features. NMF attracted the attention due to the intuitive interpretation of its data decomposition in many fields. This paper introduces a balanced supervised non-negative matrix factorization (BSNMF) based on the theory of coupling matrix factorization to extract the common balanced basis matrix between positive and negative samples. Our method exploits the class labels to lessen the inherent bias of the extracted components to the majority class. We use BSNMF algorithm to achieve feature selection in high dimensional data. Experiments show that our method outperforms NMF and DNMF methods especially in the project's dataset. In future we will analyse the selected genes to identify pathways associated with paediatric cancer.

7. ACKNOWLEDGMENTS

We acknowledge the support of the 2015 Cancer Institute NSW Big Data Big Impact award for this research work.

8. REFERENCES

[1] GenePattern Database. http://broadinstitute.org/cgi-bin/cancer/datasets.cgi.

[2] X. Chen, L. Wang, J. D. Smith, and B. Zhang. Supervised principal component analysis for gene set enrichment of microarray data with continuous or survival outcomes. *Bioinformatics*, 24(21):2474–2481, 2008.

[3] K. Devarajan. Nonnegative matrix factorization: an analytical and interpretive tool in computational biology. *PLoS Comput Biol*, 4(7):e1000029, 2008.

[4] S.-i. Huh, M. D. Gupta, and J. Xiao. Supervised nonnegative matrix factorization, Aug. 20 2013. US Patent 8,515,879.

[5] Z. Jia, X. Zhang, et al. Gene ranking of RNA-Seq data via discriminant non-negative matrix factorization. *PLoS ONE*, 10(9):e0137782, 2015.

[6] D. D. Lee and H. S. Seung. Algorithms for non-negative matrix factorization. In *Advances in neural information processing systems*, pages 556–562, 2001.

[7] N. Yokoya, T. Yairi, et al. Coupled nonnegative matrix factorization unmixing for hyperspectral and multispectral data fusion. *IEEE Trans. on Geoscience and Remote Sensing*, 50(2):528–537, 2012.

[8] L. Zhou, N. Nath, et al. The Tumour Bank of The Children's Hospital at Westmead. *Biopreservation and biobanking*, 13(2):147–148, 2015.

SoLSCSum: A Linked Sentence-Comment Dataset for Social Context Summarization

Minh-Tien Nguyen* , Chien-Xuan Tran, Duc-Vu Tran, and Minh-Le Nguyen
School of Information Science,
Japan Advanced Institute of Science and Technology (JAIST).
1-1, Asahidai, Nomi, Ishikawa, 923-1292, Japan.
{tiennm, chien-tran, vu.tran, nguyenml}@jaist.ac.jp

ABSTRACT

This paper presents a dataset named *SoLSCSum* for social context summarization. The dataset includes 157 open-domain articles along with their comments collected from Yahoo News. The articles and their comments were manually annotated by two annotators to extract standard summaries. The inter-annotator agreement is 74.5% and Cohen's Kappa is 0.5845. To illustrate the potential use of our dataset, a learning to rank model was trained by using a set of local and cross features. Experimental results demonstrate that: (1) our model trained by Ranking SVM obtains significant improvements from 5.5% to 14.8% of ROUGE-1 over state-of-the-art baselines in document summarization and (2) our dataset can be used to train summary methods such as SVM.

Keywords

Dataset, Information Retrieval, Learning to Rank, Text Summarization, Social Context Summarization, NLP.

1. INTRODUCTION

User-generated content such as comments from readers in Yahoo News[1] can be combined with a news article to provide a perspective viewpoint regarding an event. For example, after reading a web document mentioning the Yemen capital bombing, readers can write their comments on the event on the web interface. These messages, one form of social information [18, 23, 22, 24], not only reflect the content of a document and describe facts of an event but also reveal the opinions of readers. This observation inspires a novel summary task which utilizes the social information of a web document to support sentences for generating a high-quality summarization.

Given a web document d containing S sentences and C comments, social context summarization (called social summarization) is a task which extracts important sentences and representative comments as the summarization [5, 24, 22, 18]. This task has been studied by using topic modeling [5, 13]; clustering [21, 8]; graphical model [7, 6]; ranking [9, 23, 18], or supervised methods [24, 22].

The bottleneck of social context summarization is that released datasets do not contain both annotation and social information because annotating data is usually labor-intensive and time-consuming. For example, DUC (2001, 2003, and 2004)[2] has been used as a standard dataset to evaluate summary systems. The data contains news articles and standard summaries generated by human in both extractive and abstractive aspect. This data, however, do not contain social information. This challenges evaluation in which summarization systems which consider both sentences and social messages. In social context summarization, Yang et al. created a dataset containing news articles and tweets by using a crowdsourcing system [24]. However, this dataset is now unavailable for downloading. Other datasets which contain web documents and tweets were also released [5, 22, 1]. These datasets, however, have three issues. Firstly, they were collected without annotation, e.g. 0 and 1; therefore, this challenges for training supervised methods, e.g. SVM. Secondly, tweets are short messages (maximal 140 characters) and usually written in informal form; thus, they may not be efficient enough to reflect the content of a document. Finally, summarization systems need a lot of effort to remove unnecessary information of tweets, e.g. noise. The statistics of five datasets in Table 1 indicate that: (1) DUC datasets can not be used in social context summarization and (2) TGSum and WG challenge supervised methods, e.g. SVM, due to the lack of annotated data.

Table 1: The statistics of five datasets

Dataset	# docs	# sents	# refs	# coms	label
DUC 01	309	10.639	60	0	Yes
DUC 02	567	15.188	116	0	Yes
DUC 04	500	13.129	200	0	Yes
TGSum [1]	1114	33.968	4.658	—	No
WG [22]	121	6.413	455	78.419	No

This paper addresses the three issues by presenting a new open-domain dataset that bridges the information from comments to supports sentences in generating the summarization. The dataset was collected from Yahoo News and annotated by two annotators. The inter-annotator agreement is 75.4% and Cohen's Kappa is 0.5845 showing that the agreement is moderate. A summary model was trained by using Ranking SVM[3] [10] on our dataset. Experimental results show that our summary model significantly outperforms baselines. The dataset can be publicly accessed[4].

*Hung Yen University of Technology and Education (UTEHY), Hung Yen, Vietnam.
[1]http://news.yahoo.com

[2]http://duc.nist.gov/data.html
[3]https://www.cs.cornell.edu/people/tj/svm_light/svm_rank.html
[4]Download at: http://150.65.242.101:9292/yahoo-news.zip

CIKM'16, October 24–28, 2016, Indianapolis, USA.
© 2016 ACM. ISBN 978-1-4503-4073-1/16/10. . . $15.00
DOI: http://dx.doi.org/10.1145/2983323.2983376

2. SOLSCSUM FOR SUMMARIZATION

2.1 Data Collection

A new open-domain dataset was created by crawling up-to-date news articles from Yahoo News in May 2015. Yahoo News was chosen because comments are more formal than tweets from Twitter[5]. The collection was conducted in two steps: (1) crawling web page URLs and (2) parsing. In the first step, we monitored the web page of Yahoo News and collected up-to-date URLs. In the second step, with each URL, we retrieved a web content including HTML tags and parsed the web page to achieve the content of a news article. Sentences and comments in the content were also divided into single ones. Unnecessary information, e.g. links in comments was also ignored.

The dataset contains 157 open-domain articles along with 3,462 sentences, 5,858 extracted sentences as summaries and 25,633 comments. The extracted sentences also include comments.

Table 2: Statistical observation; *s*: sentences, *c*: comments.

# Docs	Sentences	Summaries	Comments
157	3,462	5,858	25,633
# Tokens	78,634	116,845	375,836
# Avg-sents/article	22.05	37.31	163.26
# Avg-tokens/article	500.85	744.23	2,393.85
# Avg-tokens/sent	22.71	19.94	14.66
% positive examples	47.75	—	15.78
% Tok-overlapping	s/c: 13.26	—	c/s: 42.05
% Tok-overlapping (stopword removal)	s/c: 8.90	—	c/s: 31.21

2.2 Data Annotation

Since annotation is labor-expensive, two annotators were asked to annotate this dataset in two rounds: data annotation and cross validation. In the annotation, each annotator read a complete article and selected important sentences. After that, the annotator read all comments and picked up representative comments. The important sentences and representative comments (called instances) are sentences which mainly reflect the content of a web document. A selected sentence or comment would become a standard summary if the two annotators agree yes; otherwise, it is an unimportant sentence. The number of instances is no less than six for documents and 15 for comments. The maximal extracted sentences (combining both sentences and comments) are less than 40 for each document.

In the cross validation, the annotated data was cross-checked to show inter-annotator agreement between two annotators. Each annotator was asked to vote the extracted data of the other. In voting, given an annotated sentence, if an annotator agrees with the prior label, this sentence was also labeled by 1 and called by completely matched; otherwise, it was labeled 0. Finally, the inter-annotator agreement was computed by dividing completely matched sentences by total extracted sentences. Formally, the inter-annotator agreement is defined by Eq. (1).

$$\text{inter-agreement} = \frac{\#matched\ sentences}{\#extracted\ sentences} * 100 \quad (1)$$

where: $\#matched\ sentences$ are the number of matched sentences which two annotators agree with label 1; # *extracted sentences* are the number of extracted sentences of each annotator. The inter-annotator agreement is 74.5%. The agreement of two annotators was also computed by using Cohen's Kappa[6] which is 0.5845. The inter-agreement and Cohen's Kappa indicate that the agreement is moderate. The annotation was conducted in 75 days.

2.3 Data Observation

Table 2 shows two important points: (1) there exists common words or phrases between sentences and comments, and (2) readers tend to use words or phrases appearing in sentences to create their comments (31.21% of word overlapping).

The literature review and data observation suggest four hypothesis: (1) *representation*: important sentences in a web document contain informative information of the document; (2) *reflection*: comments written by readers after reading a web document usually reflect the content of the document; (3) *generation*: readers tend to use important words appearing in sentences to create their comments; and (4) *common topics*: sentences and comments in a web document share common topics through common words.

2.4 Summary Generation

The summarization was formulated in the form of learning to rank suggested by [22]. To train a learning to rank model (L2R), Ranking SVM [10] was applied. Ranking SVM applies the characteristics of SVM to perform pairwise classification. Given n training queries $\{q_i\}_{i=1}^{n}$, their associated document pairs $(x_u^{(i)}, x_v^{(i)})$ and corresponding ground truth label $y_(u,v)^{(i)}$, Ranking SVM optimizes the objective function shown in Eq. (2):

$$\min \frac{1}{2}\|w\|^2 + \lambda \sum_{i=1}^{n} \sum_{u,v:y_{u,v}^{(i)}} \xi_{u,v}^{(i)} \quad (2)$$

$$\text{s.t. } w^T(x_u^i - x_v^{(i)}) \geqslant 1 - \xi_{u,v}^{(i)}, \text{ if } y_{u,v}^{(i)} = 1 \quad (3)$$

$$\xi_{u,v}^{(i)} \geqslant 0, i = 1, ..., n \quad (4)$$

where $f(x) = w^T x$ is a linear scoring function, (x_u, x_v) is a pairwise and $\xi_{u,v}^{(i)}$ is the loss. The document pair-wise is sentence-sentence or comment-comment and the pair-wise order is determined by the salient score between a sentence or comment and ground-truth summary sentences [22]. Given $E = \{e_1, e_2, ..., e_k\}$ is a set of extracted standard sentences, the salient score of a sentence or comment was computed by Eq. (5)

$$score(I_i) = max\{RF(I_i, e_j)\}, j \in \{1, k\} \quad (5)$$

where: $RF()$ returns ROUGE-1 F-score between I_i and e_j.

A set of features in [22] were used to train the summary model in which the social information in comments supports sentences. For example, a sentence was represented by a vector which contains local features, e.g. sentence length and cross features, e.g. maximal ROUGE-1 F-score of the sentence and comments. Similarly, sentences were deemed as social information when modeling a sentence. Two models were separately trained with $C = 3.0$ and *linear* kernel for documents and their comments. After training and ranking, top *m* ranked sentences and comments were selected as the summarization.

3. RESULTS AND DISCUSSION

3.1 Experimental Setup

Comments with less than five tokens were removed because they are quite short for summarization. 10-fold cross validation with

[5]https://twitter.com

[6]http://graphpad.com/quickcalcs/kappa1.cfm

$m = 6$ (less than 30% average sentences, see Table 2) was used; stop words and links were removed; and summary sentences an comments were also stemmed[7] [20].

Support Vector Machines (SVM)[8] [2] was selected for the classification. *Word2Vec* was obtained by SkipGram model[9] [15], dimension = 300, data from Google 1 billion words. Uni-gram and bi-gram taken from KenLM[10] were used as language models for learning to rank (L2R).

3.2 Summary Systems

- **Random**: selects sentences and comments randomly.
- **SentenceLead:** chooses the first x sentences as the summarization [16].
- **SociVote**: selects sentences based on the voting of Cosine similarity suggested in [23]; the threshold = 0.65.
- **LexRank:** algorithm[11] [3]; tokenization and stemming[12] were used.
- **cc-TAM**: built a cross-collection topic-aspect modeling (cc-TAM) as a preliminary step to generate a bipartite graph for co-ranking algorithm [5].
- **L2R**: was utilized by [22] using RankBoost [4] with 300 iterations and ERR metric score. Unnecessary features i.e., hashtags, URLs or quality depend were ignored.
- **SVM:** was used in [24, 11, 19, 25]. RBF kernel was used with scaling in [-1, 1]. Due to imbalance data in comments (see Tab. 2), positive examples were weighted by 85%.
- **SoRTESum:** was proposed by [18] using a set of RTE similarity features [17].

3.3 Evaluation Metric

Standard summaries were used for evaluation by using F-1 of ROUGE-N[13] (N=1, 2) [12] with stemming and stopword removal.

3.4 Results

Table 3 shows the results of summary methods on our dataset. The results indicate that: (1) our dataset benefits summarization methods in the social context summarization task and (2) the social information supports sentences to generate summaries.

SVM ranking with local and social features obtains the best results on our dataset except for ROUGE-2 in document summarization. This is because, firstly, SVMRank inherits nice properties of SVM. For example, it can create correct margins for classification based on the help of margin maximization. In training, these properties help SVMRank to avoid overfitting problem, which can appear in other methods, e.g. AdaBoost or RankBoost. The results of L2R using RankBoost in Table 3 support this statement. Secondly, SVMRank integrates social information leading significant improvements compared to SVM which uses local features, e.g. sentence length, sentence position. Finally, formulating the summarization in the form of learning to rank may be more appropriate than sentence classification, i.e. SVM. This also shows the efficiency of local and cross features proposed in [22].

Table 3: Summary performance on SoDBSum dataset. * is supervised methods; **bold** is the best and *italic* is second best results.

System	Document		Comment	
	F-1 R-1	F-1 R-2	F-1 R-1	F-1 R-2
Random	0.272	0.201	0.103	0.045
SentenceLead	*0.365*	**0.322**	—	—
LexRank	0.328	0.257	*0.244*	*0.140*
SoviVote	0.328	0.276	0.155	0.095
cc-TAM	0.321	0.268	0.166	0.088
L2R* Local features	0.353	0.307	0.205	0.098
L2R* Cross features	0.363	*0.321*	0.217	0.111
SVM*	0.293	0.239	0.141	0.074
SoRTESum Inter Wing	0.357	0.299	0.237	0.135
SoRTESum Dual Wing	0.362	0.302	0.206	0.113
SVMRank*	**0.420**	0.317	**0.365**	**0.154**

Interestingly, SVM obtains poor results in document and comment summarization. In document summarization, low quality of classification (0.6 of F-score with around 3.100 training examples) eliminates several important sentences; hence, the performance of summarization is limited. In comment summarization, the performance of classification even raises (0.74 F-score with around 22.000 sentences), SVM still achieves lower performance compared to other methods. This suggests a careful feature combination should be considered.

L2R methods were also investigated on our dataset by running RankBoost [4] (iteration = 300, metric is ERR10) and Coordinate Ascent [14] (random restart = 2, iteration = 25, tolerance = 0.001 with non-regularization) implemented in RankLib[14]. Results in Table 4 show that SVMRank is the best and RankBoost and Coordinate Ascent are competitive compared to the methods in Table 3.

Table 4: The performance of learning to rank methods

L2R Method	Document		Comment	
	F-1 R-1	F-1 R-2	F-1 R-1	F-1 R-2
RankBoost	0.363	**0.321**	0.217	0.111
Coordinate Ascent	0.358	0.294	0.324	0.133
SVMRank	**0.420**	0.317	**0.365**	**0.154**

Table 3 also shows that Sentence Lead is a strong baseline [16]. LexRank also is a strong method for comment summarization due to the sharing common words among comments(see Table 2). cc-TAM obtains quite poor results because cc-TAM is designed for multi-document summarization whereas our dataset is collected for single-document summarization. SoRTESum achieves competitive results showing the efficiency of RTE features for generating the summarization.

3.5 Sentence Position Observation

From Figure 1, we observed that most important sentences are located within top 15 sentences on document side and 100 comments on comment side. There are also some outlier points, e.g. 57th in Figure 1a and 250th in Figure 1b because some documents contains a larger number of sentences and comments.

Considering the data observation from Table 2, we conclude that: (1) important sentences appear in the first part of a web document (usually in top 10 sentences) supporting the results of Sentence Lead method in Table 3, (2) Figure 1b indicates that representative comments appear in a wider range compared to document; therefore, Sentence Lead is inefficient to summarize comments.

[7] http://snowball.tartarus.org/algorithms/porter/stemmer.html
[8] http://www.csie.ntu.edu.tw/~cjlin/libsvm/
[9] https://code.google.com/p/word2vec/
[10] https://kheafield.com/code/kenlm/
[11] https://code.google.com/p/louie-nlp/source/browse/trunk/louie-ml/src/main/java/org/louie/ml/lexrank/?r=10
[12] http://nlp.stanford.edu/software/corenlp.shtml
[13] http://kavita-ganesan.com/content/rouge-2.0-documentation
[14] http://people.cs.umass.edu/~vdang/ranklib.html

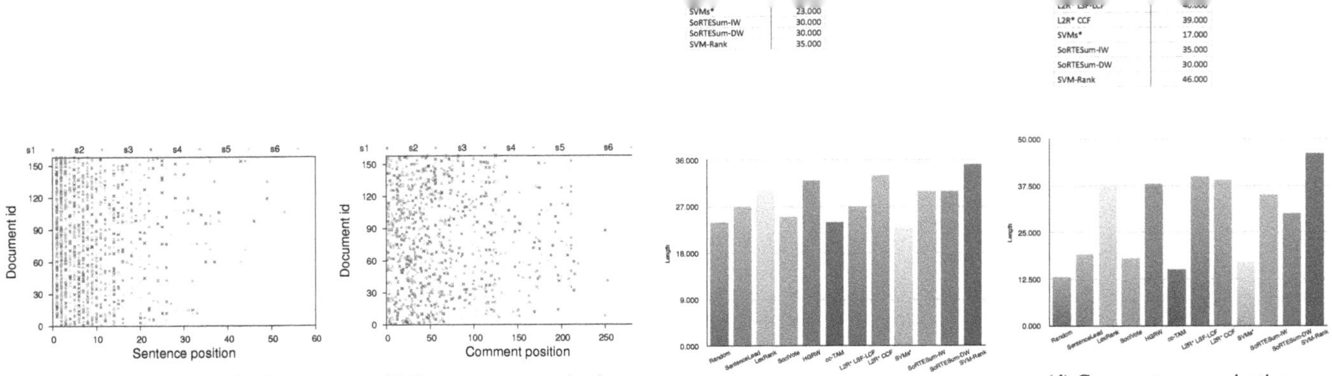

(a) Document summarization (b) Comment summarization (d) Comment summarization

Figure 1: The sentence position and length of extracted summaries

3.6 Sentence Length Observation

Figures 1c and 1d indicate that longer sentences belong to the best models, i.e. Sentence Lead and L2R CCF. SVMRank generates the longest sentences, i.e. 35 in document summarization and 46 in comment summarization supporting results in Table 3. Other models obtain similar sentence length, e.g. LexRank, SoRTESum, and L2R while poor models achieve shorter length, i.e. cc-TAM, SVM. This trend is similar in Figure 1d.

4. CONCLUSION

This paper presents *SoLSCSum*, a linked sentence-comment dataset for social context summarization. Data is collected from Yahoo News and annotated by two annotators. The inter-annotator agreement is 74.5% and Cohen's Kappa is 0.5845 indicating that the agreement is moderate. SoLSCSum has two important characteristics: (1) it contains comments which are utilized to support sentences to generate high-quality summaries and (2) sentences and comments are manually labeled; therefore, our dataset can be used to train supervised methods for generating the summarization. This paper also makes two main contributions: (1) releasing a new dataset of a novel task and (2) comparing the performance of state-of-the-art methods in social context summarization.

Our dataset should be annotated by a larger number of annotators to reduce human errors. Other social sources, e.g. tweets from Twitter should also be combined with the current dataset.

Acknowledgments

We deeply thank Wei Gao and Peng Li for sharing the code of [5]. This work was supported by JSPS KAKENHI Grant number 3050941, JSPS KAKENHI Grant Number JP15K12094, and CREST, JST.

5. REFERENCES

[1] Z. Cao, C. Chen, W. Li, S. Li, F. Wei, and M. Zhou. Tgsum: Build tweet guided multi-document summarization dataset. In *arXiv preprint arXiv:1511.08417*, 2015.

[2] C. Cortes and V. Vapnik. Support-vector networks. *Machine Learning 20(3): 273-297*, 1995.

[3] G. Erkan and D. R. Radev. Lexrank: Graph-based lexical centrality as salience in text summarization. *Journal of Artificial Intelligence Research: 457-479*, 2004.

[4] Y. Freund, R. D. Lyeryer, R. E. Schapire, and Y. Singer. An efficient boosting algorithm for combining preferences. *Journal of Machine Learning Research 4: 933-969*, 2003.

[5] W. Gao, P. Li, and K. Darwish. Joint topic modeling for event summarization across news and social media streams. In *CIKM:1173-1182*, 2012.

[6] M. Hu, A. Sun, and E.-P. Lim. Comments-oriented blog summarization by sentence extraction. In *CIKM: 901-904*, 2007.

[7] M. Hu, A. Sun, and E.-P. Lim. Comments-oriented document summarization: Understanding document with readers' feedback. In *SIGIR: 291-298*, 2008.

[8] P. Hu, C. Sun, L. Wu, D.-H. Ji, and C. Teng. Social summarization via automatically discovered social context. In *IJCNLP: 483-490*, 2011.

[9] L. Huang, H. Li, and L. Huang. Comments-oriented document summarization based on multi-aspect co-feedback ranking. In *WAIM: 363-374*, 2013.

[10] T. Joachims. Training linear svms in linear time. In *KDD: 217-226*, 2006.

[11] J. Kupiec, J. O. Pedersen, and F. Chen. A trainable document summarizer. In *SIGIR: 68-73*, 1995.

[12] C.-Y. Lin and E. H. Hovy. Automatic evaluation of summaries using n-gram co-occurrence statistics. In *HLT-NAACL: 71-78*, 2003.

[13] Y. Lu, C. Zhai, and N. Sundaresan. Rated aspect summarization of short comments. In *WWW: 131-140*, 2009.

[14] D. Metzler and W. B. Croft. Linear feature-based models for information retrieval. *Inf. Retr. 10(3): 257-274*, 2007.

[15] T. Mikolov, I. Sutskever, K. Chen, G. Corrado, and J. Dean. Distributed representations of words and phrases and their compositionality. In *NIPS: 3111-3119*, 2013.

[16] A. Nenkova. Automatic text summarization of newswire: lessons learned from the document understanding conference. In *AAAI: 1436-1441*, 2005.

[17] M.-T. Nguyen, Q.-T. Ha, T.-D. Nguyen, T.-T. Nguyen, and L.-M. Nguyen. Recognizing textual entailment in vietnamese text: An experimental study. In *KSE: 108-113*, 2015.

[18] M.-T. Nguyen and M.-L. Nguyen. Sortesum: A social context framework for single-document summarization. In *ECIR: 3-14*, 2016.

[19] M. Osborne. Using maximum entropy for sentence extraction. In *ACL Workshop on Automatic Summarization: 1-8*, 2002.

[20] M. F. Porter. Snowball: A language for stemming algorithms. 2011.

[21] X. Wan and J. Yang. Multi-document summarization using cluster-based link analysis. In *SIGIR: 299-306*, 2008.

[22] Z. Wei and W. Gao. Utilizing microblogs for automatic news highlights extraction. In *COLING: 872-883*, 2014.

[23] Z. Wei and W. Gao. Gibberish, assistant, or master?: Using tweets linking to news for extractive single-document summarization. In *SIGIR: 1003-1006*, 2015.

[24] Z. Yang, K. Cai, J. Tang, L. Zhang, Z. Su, and J. Li. Social context summarization. In *SIGIR: 255-264*, 2011.

[25] J.-Y. Yeh, H.-R. Ke, W.-P. Yang, and I.-H. Meng. Text summarization using a trainable summarizer and latent semantic analysis. *Inf. Process. Manage. 41(1): 75-95*, 2005.

Distributed Deep Learning for Question Answering

Minwei Feng
IBM Watson, Yorktown Heights, NY, USA, 10598
mfeng@us.ibm.com

Bing Xiang
IBM Watson, Yorktown Heights, NY, USA, 10598
bingxia@us.ibm.com

Bowen Zhou
IBM Watson, Yorktown Heights, NY, USA, 10598
zhou@us.ibm.com

ABSTRACT

This paper is an empirical study of the distributed deep learning for question answering subtasks: answer selection and question classification. Comparison studies of SGD, MSGD, ADADELTA, ADAGRAD, ADAM/ADAMAX, RMSPROP, DOWNPOUR and EASGD/EAMSGD algorithms have been presented. Experimental results show that the distributed framework based on the message passing interface can accelerate the convergence speed at a sublinear scale. This paper demonstrates the importance of distributed training. For example, with 48 workers, a 24x speedup is achievable for the answer selection task and running time is decreased from 138.2 hours to 5.81 hours, which will increase the productivity significantly.

Keywords

distributed training; deep learning; question answering

1. INTRODUCTION

Deep Learning technology [9] has been widely adopted in various AI tasks and has achieved the state-of-the-art performance. One practical challenge of Deep Learning is the highly time consuming training procedure. It is not unusual to see the reported training time in the magnitude of days or even weeks in research papers. However, this is rarely acceptable for practical commercial usage (e.g. training as a service on the cloud) where short turn around time is expected by customers. Even for research environment the long time computation could stop scientists from running as many experiments as needed and slow down the R&D cycle. Hence the distributed training has become a crucial research direction along with the advancement of deep learning itself on the algorithm side.

Various infrastructures and experimental results have been published recently. Most of the published results are on computer vision benchmark tasks like CIFAR10 or ImageNet. On the other hand, distributed training study on natural language processing (NLP) tasks are rarely reported. In this paper, we focus on the question answering (QA) which is an important field of NLP. We study two subtasks of QA: answer selection and question classification. It is trivial to observe the epoch speed (training data processing speed) increased after more computing resources have been adopted. However, this does not necessarily guarantee that the convergence speed is also improved. The ultimate goal is to have convergence speedup as users will expect models with equal accuracy to be trained faster when the cost is increased for more computing resources. Many optimization algorithms are available but their performances have not been compared under the distributed training mode. The motivation of this paper is to conduct comparison study for distributed training algorithms and demonstrate the sublinear scalability of the distributed training on convergence speed. We have compared the latest technologies, including SGD [1] , MSGD [11] , RMSPROP [6], ADADELTA [13], ADAGRAD [4], ADAM/ADAMAX [8], DOWNPOUR [3] and EASGD/EAMSGD [14]. To our best knowledge, it is the first time that such results of distributed training algorithms have been reported on the QA subtasks.

The rest of the paper is organized as follows: section 2 is the summary of related work; section 3 will describe the answer selection benchmark task; section 4 summarizes the question classification task; we demonstrate the MPI-based infrastructure in section 5 and the review of the distributed training algorithms is given in section 6 . Experimental results are reported in section 7 and finally conclusions are drawn in section 8 .

CIKM'16 , October 24-October 28, 2016, Indianapolis, IN, USA

ISBN 978-1-4503-4073-1/16/10... $15.00

DOI: http://dx.doi.org/10.1145/2983323.2983377

2. RELATED WORK

Various systems have been proposed for distributed deep learning. One of the pioneering work is Google's Distbelief system [3] in which DOWNPOUR has been proposed. The system has multiple parameter servers and clients. Most of other work follow the same spirit of DOWNPOUR. The system Adam [2] is another similar framework which has many engineering features like reduced memory copies and mitigating the impact of slow machines. IBM's Rudra system [7] is a master-client based distributed framework where the servers are organized as a tree structure to save communication overhead. A parameter server framework is proposed in [10] that supports flexible consistency models, elastic scalability and continuous fault tolerance. [10] provides the APIs so that other framework like MXNet[1] can utilize it. The platform Petuum [12] supports a synchronization

[1]https://github.com/dmlc/mxnet

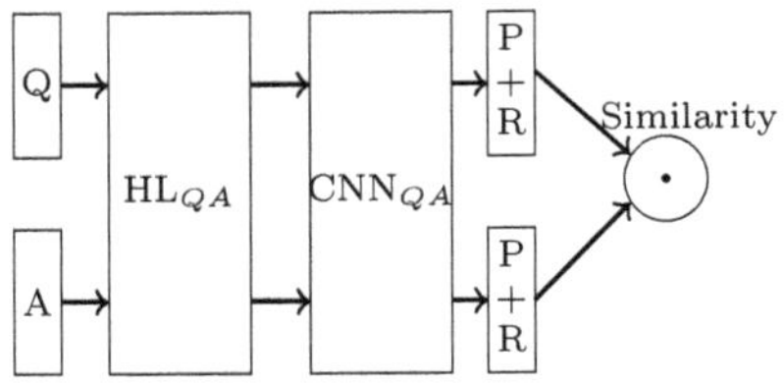

Figure 1: Architecture for answer selection. HL is the hidden layer with *Tanh* activation function. CNN is the convolutional neural networks. P stands for maxpooling and R stands for the *ReLU* activation function. QA means the weights of corresponding layer are shared by Q and A.

model with bounded staleness. Compared to the previous work, the main contribution of this paper is that we study a different task, answer selection, and focus on the comparison of state-of-the-art algorithms.

3. ANSWER SELECTION TASK

Different from many previous work, we study a QA task: answer selection. The paper [5] created an open task (including the released corpus) which serves as a benchmark for comparison purpose. For the detailed description of the data and task please refer to [5]. A summary is given here to make the paper self-contained. Given a question q and an answer candidate pool $\{a_1, a_2, ..., a_s\}$ for that question (s is the pool size), the goal is to find the best answer candidate a_k, $1 \leq k \leq s$. If the selected answer a_k is inside the ground truth set of q (questions could have multiple correct answers), the question q is considered correct. In this paper the best architecture (Figure 1) from [5] has been used. The idea is to learn a vector representation of a given question and its answer candidates and then use a similarity metric to measure the matching degree. The similarity metric is Geometric mean of Euclidean and Sigmoid Dot product (GESD) $k(x,y) = \frac{1}{1+\|x-y\|} \cdot \frac{1}{1+exp(-(x^\intercal y+1))}$. x and y are the vector representations of Q and A. The training is computational expensive due to the usage of the hinge loss: for each training question Q there is a positive answer A^+(the ground truth). A training instance is then constructed by pairing this A^+ with a negative answer A^-(a wrong answer) sampled from the whole answer space. The forward pass calculation generates vector representations for the question and the two candidates: V_Q , V_{A^+} and V_{A^-} . The similarities $GESD(V_Q, V_{A^+})$ and $GESD(V_Q, V_{A^-})$ are calculated and their difference is compared to a margin m: $GESD(V_Q, V_{A^+}) - GESD(V_Q, V_{A^-}) < m$. If this condition is not satisfied, there is no update to the model and a new negative example is sampled until the margin is less than m (this repetitive negative sampling procedure is time-consuming and to reduce running time we set maximum sampling times to be 100).

4. QUESTION CLASSIFICATION TASK

The second QA subtask we study in this paper is question classification. For certain application scenario (e.g. online customer service), the set of possible answers for all incoming questions is limited and predefined. Hence we can convert the QA into a question classification problem, where each question's label represents the specific answer in the predefined set. Usually there is a *noAnswer* label in

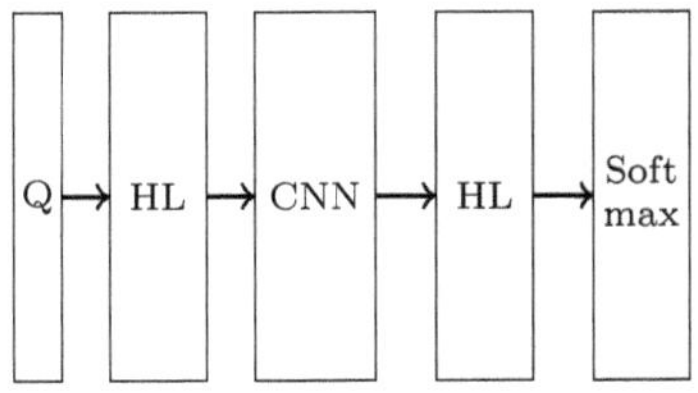

Figure 2: Architecture for question classification. HL is the hidden layer with *Tanh* activation function. CNN is the convolutional neural networks.

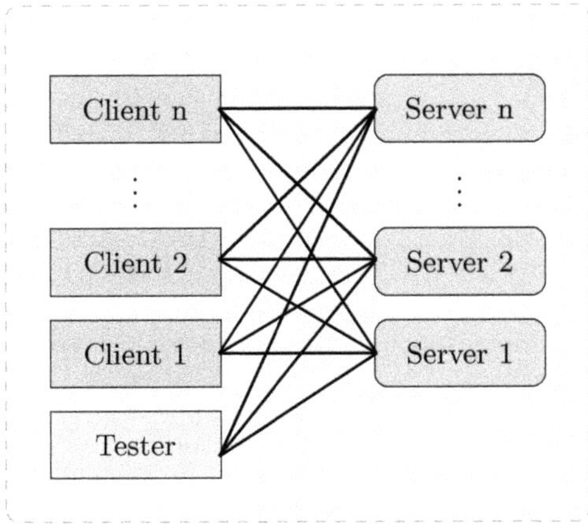

Figure 3: MPI framework

the set for chit-chat questions. The data we used for this task is a customer corpus in financial domain. There are 78566 questions and the answer set size is 6763 (6763 different labels for the classifier). We further randomly split the data into train/valid/test parts with the question size 74566/2000/2000. We use a convolutional neural networks based model (Figure 2) to tackle this task. The last layer is *Softmax* since this is a classification task. Please note that this general model can be applied to many natural language classification tasks such as relation classification, intent classification and sentiment analysis.

5. MPI-BASED FRAMEWORK

Figure 3 demonstrates the Message Passing Interface (MPI) framework. There are three types of process: worker, parameter server and tester. Those processes are allocated across the high performance computing clusters. The worker will conduct the forward pass/backward pass calculations and send the update messages to servers. The servers hold a central model. They receive the messages from workers and update the central model and send the latest model back to the workers. A tester will only receive the latest model from the servers and run testing over the test corpus periodically. For MPI the non-blocking communication (`MPI_ISend`/`MPI_IRecv`) is used to increase the overall speed. To reduce the communication overhead, we split the model into partitions and set up multiple servers. Each server is responsible for the storage and update of one model partition. The amount of worker and server is set to be equal. We use the popular MPI toolkit MPICH.

Method	Peak Accuracy(%)	Time (hour)	Comment
SGD	64.61	145.98	61.50@50.95
MSGD	65.50	138.20	61.50@54.07
RMSPROP	64.89	99.06	61.50@37.03
ADADELTA	61.50	49.83	
ADAGRAD	58.50	126.52	
ADAM	54.06	140.00	
ADAMAX	52.06	145.55	

Table 1: Answer selection task: single worker training results. Accuracy is the peak accuracy of test corpus within 6 days. Time is the wall clock time of the peak accuracy.

Method	Peak Accuracy(%)	Time (hour)	Comment
DOWNPOUR	64.61	5.26	
EASGD	66.11	8.57	65.50@8.23
EAMSGD	67.50	11.09	65.50@5.81
RMSPROP	64.44	5.30	
ADADELTA	61.39	6.34	
ADAGRAD	59.50	8.73	58.50@3.75
ADAM	55.28	9.95	54.28@5.82

Table 2: Answer selection task: distributed training results with 48 workers. Accuracy is the peak accuracy of test corpus within 12 hours. Time is the wall clock time of the peak accuracy.

Method	Peak Accuracy(%)	Time (hour)	Comment
SGD	98.60	39.02	98.50@33.30
MSGD	98.50	38.30	
RMSPROP	98.70	40.97	98.50@29.15
ADADELTA	93.10	70.84	
ADAGRAD	98.50	37.57	
ADAM	91.90	57.06	
ADAMAX	82.70	60.53	

Table 3: Question classification task: single worker training results. Accuracy is the peak accuracy of test corpus within 3 days. Time is the wall clock time of the peak accuracy.

Method	Peak Accuracy(%)	Time (hour)	Comment
DOWNPOUR	98.55	5.20	
EASGD	97.65	10.06	
EAMSGD	98.35	4.80	
RMSPROP	98.30	4.87	
ADADELTA	97.40	5.42	
ADAGRAD	82.65	11.61	
ADAM	88.45	2.82	

Table 4: Question classification task: distributed training results with 48 workers. Accuracy is the peak accuracy of test corpus within 12 hours. Time is the wall clock time of the peak accuracy.

6. DISTRIBUTED TRAINING ALGORITHMS

We have compared state-of-the-art algorithms: stochastic gradient descent (SGD) [1] , momentum stochastic gradient descent (MSGD) [11], RMSPROP (implemented same as section 4.2 of [6]), ADADELTA [13], ADAGRAD [4], ADAM/ADAMAX [8], DOWNPOUR [3] , elastic averaging stochastic gradient descent (EASGD) and its variation momentum EASGD (EAMSGD) [14] .

7. EXPERIMENTAL RESULTS

Table 1 demonstrates the results of conventional optimization algorithms which use only one worker for the answer selection task. Table 2 demonstrates the results of distributed optimization algorithms for the answer selection task. Similarly, the results of the question classification task are shown in Table 3 and Table 4. Each method has its own hyper parameters. We have conducted extensive tuning experiments and only the best results of each method are presented in all tables. The strategy of hyper parameter tuning is two steps of grid search. In the first step, a coarse-grained grid selection of hyper parameters is conducted to find the rough range of the best hyper parameters. Then in the second step, a fine-grained grid selection of hyper parameters is conducted within the range that are discovered in the first step. All the results reported in this paper are conducted with staleness off mode(the worker always communicates with the server after finishing each minibatch). Communication overhead will be reduced if the staleness mode is on since the worker will do more work before it can synchronize with the server. But it will also incur accuracy loss. In this work, both the server and client processes run on CPUs. For the answer selection task, **Peak Accuracy** is the top accuracy score on the test1 corpus of the released corpus from [5] within the whole running period. For the question classification task, **Peak Accuracy** is the top accuracy score on the test corpus within the whole running period. **Time** is the wall clock time (unit is hour) when the accuracy reaches that peak value. In **Comment**, 65.50@8.23 means the accuracy climbs up to 65.50% at wall clock time 8.23 hours. For the answer selection task, we let the single worker training methods keep running for 150 hours (approximately 6 days); for the question classification task, the single worker training methods are set to keep running for 3 days. For distributed methods the running time limit is set to 12 hours for both tasks. This is to save the computing resources so that more experiments can be scheduled. Also in practice it is much less meaningful if the running time is still prohibitive when large amount of computing resources are used. Finally, from previous study we notice that: for the answer selection task, the highest accuracy scores of test1 corpus are around 65%; for the question classification task, the model accuracy on test corpus should be around 98.5%.

7.1 Results of Answer Selection Task

In Table 1, we observe the following facts from the single worker experiments: (1) in terms of peak accuracy, SGD, MSGD and RMSPROP have scores around 65% which is same with the highest number reported in [5]; (2) ADADELTA and ADAGRAD lose several points of accuracy; (3) ADAM and ADAMAX perform significantly worse than other methods; (4) if a top accuracy is the goal, the best method is MSGD; (5) if for some practical applications where light accuracy loss is acceptable(e.g. 61.50% is fine), then RMSPROP is preferable as it converges faster.

Since ADAMAX does not work well and is similar to ADAM, we did not conduct experiments using distributed versions of ADAMAX algorithm. Also notice the algorithms EASGD/EAMSGD are only designed for the distributed training. In Table 2, we observe the following facts from the 48-worker experiments: (1) overall distributed training does not incur accuracy loss; (2) EASGD/EAMSGD achieve higher peak accuracy than the best score 65.50% from single worker results; (3) overall distributed training speeds up the training; (4) for EAMSGD it takes 5.81 hours to reach 65.50% and compared to single worker MSGD where it takes 138.20 hours to climb up to 65.50% , a 24x speed up is achievable by using distributed training.

7.2 Results of Question Classification Task

In Table 3, we observe the following facts from the single worker experiments: (1) in terms of peak accuracy, SGD, MSGD, RMSPROP and ADAGRAD have scores around 98.50% which is the expected accuracy score from previous study; (2) ADADELTA and ADAM lose several points of accuracy; (3) ADAMAX performs significantly worse than other methods.

In Table 4, we observe the following facts from the 48-worker experiments: (1) in terms of accuracy DOWNPOUR, EASGD, ADADELTA, EAMSGD and RMSPROP perform well; (2) ADAGRAD performs poorly under the distributed scenario where large accuracy loss is incurred; (3) considering both accuracy and convergence speed, DOWNPOUR, EAMSGD and RMSPROP are outstanding. Overall the training time has been decreased from 29.15 hours to 5.2 hours. The improvement is less compared to the answer selection task but it is still a significant productivity boost in practice.

8. CONCLUSIONS

We have conducted an empirical study of the distributed training for the answer selection task and question classification task which are crucial components of QA. We build the framework with MPI. The state-of-the-art algorithms have been compared, including SGD, MSGD, RMSPROP, ADADELTA, ADAGRAD, ADAM, ADAMAX, DOWNPOUR and EASGD/EAMSGD. To our best knowledge, it is the first time that the experimental results for distributed training have been reported on QA subtasks. This work proves the significance of the distributed training and a proper algorithm selection is crucial. E.g., for the answer selection task, a 24x speedup is achievable with the deployment of 48 workers and running time is decreased from 138.2 hours to 5.81 hours which is a huge gain for practical productivity. We realize that due to the lack of a solid mathematical foundation, the distributed training is still a trial-and-error procedure. Our experiences show that the hyper parameter tuning (especially the learning rate) can play a crucial role for the performance. On the other hand, the task itself could change the performance. For example, in [8] the ADAM demonstrates superior performance for image classification tasks while in our study the performance of ADAM/ADAMAX is relatively weak. From the four tables we can reach the conclusion that DOWNPOUR, EAMSGD and RMSPROP are the most attractive distributed training methods as they significantly increase the convergence speed while maintain the accuracy. The code in this paper has been written based on the Torch7 framework and our source code have been released in the mpiT package of Torch7. For future work we plan to study an algorithm combination strategy so that different distributed training methods could benefit from each other and further improvement could be achieved.

9. REFERENCES

[1] L. Bottou. Online learning in neural networks. chapter Online Learning and Stochastic Approximations. Cambridge University Press, New York, NY, USA, 1998.

[2] T. Chilimbi, Y. Suzue, J. Apacible, and K. Kalyanaraman. Project adam: Building an efficient and scalable deep learning training system. In *Proceedings of the 11th USENIX Symposium on Operating Systems Design and Implementation (OSDI 14)*, pages 571–582, Broomfield, CO, 2014.

[3] J. Dean, G. Corrado, R. Monga, K. Chen, M. Devin, Q. V. Le, M. Z. Mao, M. A. Ranzato, A. W. Senior, P. A. Tucker, K. Yang, and A. Y. Ng. Large scale distributed deep networks. In *Advances in Neural Information Processing Systems 25: 26th Annual Conference on Neural Information Processing Systems 2012.*, pages 1232–1240, 2012.

[4] J. Duchi, E. Hazan, and Y. Singer. Adaptive subgradient methods for online learning and stochastic optimization. *J. Mach. Learn. Res.*, 12:2121–2159, July 2011.

[5] M. Feng, B. Xiang, M. R. Glass, L. Wang, and B. Zhou. Applying deep learning to answer selection: A study and an open task. In *Proceedings of the 2015 IEEE Automatic Speech Recognition and Understanding Workshop (ASRU 2015)*, Scottsdale, Arizona, 2015.

[6] A. Graves. Generating sequences with recurrent neural networks. *CoRR*, abs/1308.0850, 2013.

[7] S. Gupta, W. Zhang, and J. Milthorpe. Model Accuracy and Runtime Tradeoff in Distributed Deep Learning. *ArXiv e-prints*, September 2015.

[8] D. P. Kingma and J. Ba. Adam: A method for stochastic optimization. *CoRR*, abs/1412.6980, 2014.

[9] Y. LeCun, Y. Bengio, and G. Hinton. Deep learning. *Nature*, 521:436–444, May 2015.

[10] M. Li, D. G. Andersen, J. W. Park, A. J. Smola, A. Ahmed, V. Josifovski, J. Long, E. J. Shekita, and B. Su. Scaling distributed machine learning with the parameter server. In *11th USENIX Symposium on Operating Systems Design and Implementation (OSDI 14)*, pages 583–598, Broomfield, CO, Oct. 2014. USENIX Association.

[11] I. Sutskever, J. Martens, G. E. Dahl, and G. E. Hinton. On the importance of initialization and momentum in deep learning. In *Proceedings of the 30th International Conference on Machine Learning (ICML-13)*, volume 28, pages 1139–1147. JMLR Workshop and Conference Proceedings, May 2013.

[12] E. P. Xing, Q. Ho, W. Dai, J. Kim, J. Wei, S. Lee, X. Zheng, P. Xie, A. Kumar, and Y. Yu. Petuum: A new platform for distributed machine learning on big data. In *Proceedings of the 21th ACM SIGKDD International Conference on Knowledge Discovery and Data Mining*, KDD '15, pages 1335–1344, 2015.

[13] M. D. Zeiler. ADADELTA: an adaptive learning rate method. *CoRR*, abs/1212.5701, 2012.

[14] S. Zhang, A. Choromanska, and Y. LeCun. Deep learning with elastic averaging SGD. In *Proceedings of the 2015 Conference on Neural Information Processing Systems. (NIPS 2015)*, 2015.

Bus Routes Design and Optimization via Taxi Data Analytics

Seong Ping Chuah, Huayu Wu, Yu Lu, Liang Yu
Institute for Infocomm Research
1 Fusionopolis Way, Singapore 138632
{chuahsp,huwu,luyu,yul}@i2r.a-star.edu.sg

Stephane Bressan
School of Computing,
National University of Singapore
13 Computing Drive, Singapore 117417
steph@nus.edu.sg

ABSTRACT

Public bus services are often planned in the context of urban planning. For a city with efficient and extensive network of public transportation system like Singapore, enhancing the existing coverage of bus service to meet the dynamic mobility needs of the population requires data mining approach. Specifically, frequent taxi rides between two locations at a period of time may suggest possible poor coverage of public transport service, if not lacking of the public transport service. In this paper, we describe a proof of concept effort to discover this weakness and its improvement in public transportation system via mining of taxi ride dataset. We cluster taxi rides dataset to determine some popular taxi rides in Singapore. From the clustered taxi rides, we filter and select only the clusters whose commuting via existing public transport are tortuous if not unreachable door-to-door. Based on the discovered travel pattern, we propose new bus routes that serve the passengers of these clusters. We formulate the bus planning problem as an optimization of directed cycle graph, and present it's preliminary solution and results. We showcase our idea in the case of Singapore.

Keywords

Taxi Rides, Clustering, Bus Route Design & Optimization

1. INTRODUCTION

Singapore is well known for its high quality and efficient public transport service. Millions of people rely on its high quality, efficient, and extensive network of public bus and mass rapid transit (MRT) to move around everyday. Despite its efficiency, there are 28,286 strong of taxi fleet as of March 2016 [1], and 519,645 private cars on road in 2015 [2]. The figure is compared to just 17,740 buses (all types) in 2015 [2].

[1] www.lta.gov.sg/content/dam/ltaweb/corp/PublicationsResearch/files /FactsandFigures/taxi_info_2016.pdf

[2] www.lta.gov.sg/content/dam/ltaweb/corp/PublicationsResearch/files /FactsandFigures/MVP01-1_MVP_by_type.pdf

CIKM '16, October 24–28, 2016, Indianapolis, IN, USA.
© 2016 ACM. ISBN 978-1-4503-4073-1/16/10...$15.00
DOI: http://dx.doi.org/10.1145/2983323.2983378

Public bus service can be extended to offer more efficient solutions to the mobility needs of the population. Traditionally, public bus services are often planned in the context of urban planning [2] and operation research [3]. For a city with efficient and extensive network of public transportation system, enhancing the existing coverage of bus service requires data mining approach. Specifically, frequent taxi rides between two locations at a particular period of time may suggest possible poor/lacking of bus route services in the existing transportation network at that particular period of time. An extreme situation is usually found after midnight, where MRT lines and bus services cease to operate while taxis becomes the only public transport. Currently, Singapore has 14 routes of night bus operating from 12am to 2am of Friday, Saturday, and eve of public holiday. However, these bus routes are designated to transport party-goers from downtown city center returning to various suburban residential areas before 2am rather than the transportation needs of the nightlife-goers throughout midnight.

On the other hand, improving the efficiency of the existing public transportation system of Singapore is non-trivial, given its current level of efficiency. We seek to improve the efficiency of public transportation system by determining new bus route solutions for a specific period of time. Travel patterns of these passengers are not available in the trip records of the public transportation system. A natural way is to refer to the statistics of taxi rides. Mining the taxi rides data provides insights to the travel patterns of not only these taxi takers, but also potentially the private car owners whose lifestyle and consumer behaviours are likely similar.

In this paper, we showcase a proof of concept effort in improving the public transportation network via mining of taxi ride dataset. We mine the most popular origin-destiny of taxi ride within a specific period of time from a dataset of taxi rides. Based on the clusters of trajectory, we determine the popular origins and destinies where people would take taxi. We filter out the clusters whose journeys can be commuted easily (within a single trip ride) by the existing public transportation system. We study the remaining clusters whose commuting via public transports are tortuous if not unreachable door-to-door. Based on these taxi ride clusters and travel patterns, we propose new bus routes for the specific time windows that serve the passengers of these clusters by minimizing the distance the buses travel without passengers, while ensuring quality of service such as travelling time and bus load.

The paper is organized as follows. We discuss the mining of taxi rides data in Section 2. In Section 3, we discuss the planning problem of new bus routes, and formulate its optimization problem and solution. We showcase a case study in Section 4. The paper is concluded in Section 5

2. CLUSTERING OF TAXI RIDES

Taxi service provides the most flexible transportation service in a city. In a modern city with extensive coverage of public buses and MRT, frequent taxi rides from one location to another indicate high demand of travelling on the route that is not covered by the public transportations. In this section, we discuss the mining of these frequent taxi rides to discover potential new bus routes.

2.1 DBSCAN Clustering

We aim to discover these travel patterns of frequent taxi ride from the taxi ride data, which contains GPS data and time stamp of the origin and destiny of each taxi ride. We perform clustering on the data of taxi rides within a period of time. Taxi pick-up and drop-off locations are usually along roadsides, their geographical distributions are non-globular. Thus, we deploy density-based method, DBSCAN for clustering of taxi rides. DBSCAN [4] has the advantages of robustness to noise and capability to handle clusters in arbitrary shape of road. As each taxi ride consists of a pair of pick-up and a drop-off point, each data sample input to DBSCAN is a four-dimensional coordinates (coordinate-X and coordinate-Y for both points).

2.2 Clusters Filtering

DBSCAN clustering returns clusters of frequent taxi rides. However, despite their high number of ridership, not every cluster suggests potential new routes of bus service. Some clusters should be filtered out based on several factors as in the following discussions. After filtering out these unsuitable clusters, clusters with the higher number of point (taxi ride) are selected for new bus route planning and optimization.

2.2.1 *Availability of Public Transport*

From the clustering, we may get many clusters of taxi rides which is covered by the existing public buses or MRT service. These clusters represent the group of passenger who is willing to pay a bit more for easier, faster, and more convenient way to reach home. These clusters are often found in suburban residential areas of Singapore. A suburban residential area usually has an MRT station, a bus interchange and shopping malls co-located as the hub to the residential area. People take a short range taxi ride from the hub to their apartment, despite frequent community buses plying the neighbourhood of the residential area from the hub. For these clusters, there is no new bus route to be proposed.

2.2.2 *Airport Traffic*

Many people travel by air for business and vacation purposes in Singapore. From the clustering result, we may get many clusters which have the airport either its origin or destiny. While there are buses and MRT service connecting the airport, taxi is still a popular choice for passenger with luggages. Departure passengers take taxi to reduce the risk of running late, while the arrival passengers take taxi to reach home/hotel faster after tiring flight. Thus, these clusters do not suggest any lack of coverage of public bus plying to and from the airport.

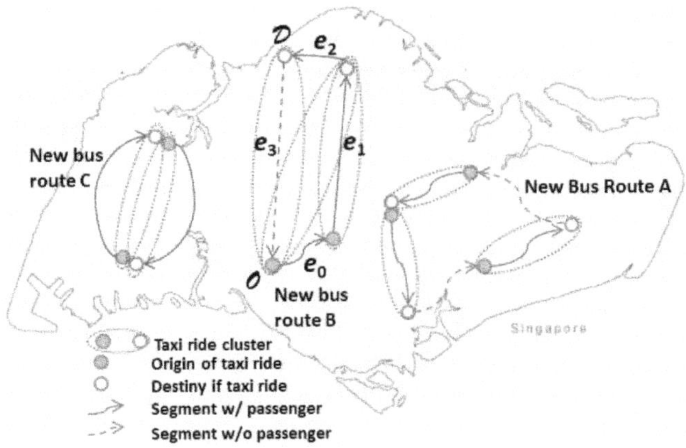

Figure 1: Linking the origins and destinies of all clusters with directed cycle graphs.

3. NEW BUS ROUTES OPTIMIZATION

Based on the clusters of taxi rides obtained from the clustering, we plan new bus routes for the travelling needs of these clusters. Given sets of taxi rides with an origin and a destiny for each cluster, we optimize the bus routes to transport the passengers of these clusters in the most efficient way. In this section, we present the routing problem of the new buses, and some preliminary solution to the problem.

3.1 The Bus Routing Problem

The bus routing problem for several clusters is illustrated in Fig.1. The bus routing problem bears some resemblance to the travelling salesman problem (TSP)[1] where the salesman needs to visit all cities in a single trip. But unlike TSP where the salesman is free to visit the cities in any order, the new bus should visit the origin before the destiny of each cluster. That limits the search space of the next location the bus should visit in the combinatorial optimization. Besides, the bus routing problem is not limited to just one bus route to serve all clusters. To sustain the dispatching of buses over a long period of time, a new bus route that passes through the cluster(s) should form a directed cycle graph.

Fig.1 shows three types of new bus routes identified based on the taxi ride clusters. In practice, a new bus route can be a combination of these three types. An origin (green filled circle) and a destiny (green unfilled circle) form a taxi ride cluster (circled by red dotted line). Solid blue lines are the segments of bus route that carries passenger from their origins to destinies, while dash blue lines are the segments of bus route whereby the bus travel to the next taxi ride origin to pick up the passenger.

It can be seen that all new bus routes in Fig.1 form directed cycles. To reduce operating cost, it is desired that the blue dash line be minimized, since empty bus receives no bus fare. Thus, New Bus Route A is the least preferable case where significant fraction of the bus route are travelled without passenger load. Conversely, New Bus Route C is the most preferable case where shuttle buses plying both locations serve two clusters with opposite travelling directions. In New Bus Route B, two clusters (generalized to N clusters) are merged into a route travelling to a same direction before returning to the origin with empty load. Merging more clusters into New Bus Route B results in less operating cost, but degrade quality of service for some passengers. It discourages them from switching to public bus from the existing taxi rides. Under New Bus Route B, the path from origin $\mathcal{O}$ to destiny $\mathcal{D}$ is actually $\{e_0 \rightarrow e_1 \rightarrow e_2\}$ rather than the direct opposite direction of e_3. Thus, the travelling time for this cluster ($\mathcal{O}$-$\mathcal{D}$ pair) under New Bus Route B is longer than that of separate bus route for both clusters. Besides, buses travelling on e_1 may be overcrowded due to the merging of two clusters in a service route.

3.2 Optimization Formulation

We formulate the bus routing problem as an optimization problem of directed cycle graphs. Let $\mathcal{C}_n$ be the taxi ride cluster in the set $n \in \mathcal{N}$ to be served by new bus routes. Each cluster consists of a pair of origin ($\mathcal{C}_n.\mathcal{O} \in \mathcal{V}$) and destiny ($\mathcal{C}_n.\mathcal{D} \in \mathcal{V}$) serving as vertices in set $\mathcal{V}$. These clusters are served by set of proposed bus routes $\mathcal{R}_m, m \in \mathcal{M}$ which is directed cycle graph $\mathcal{R}_m = \{e_m(\mathcal{C}_n.\mathcal{O}, *), \cdots, e_m(*, \mathcal{C}_n.\mathcal{D}), \cdots, \tilde{e}_m(*, \mathcal{C}_n.\mathcal{O})\}$ comprising a series of directed edges e_m with passenger load, and directed edges with empty load $\tilde{e}_m$. $e(a, b)$ is an edge that travels from vertex a to vertex b. $\{e_m(\mathcal{C}_n.\mathcal{O}, *), \cdots, e_m(*, \mathcal{C}_n.\mathcal{D})\}$ represents that bus route m picks up passengers of $\mathcal{C}_n$ at $\mathcal{C}_n.\mathcal{O}$, and drops them at $\mathcal{C}_n.\mathcal{D}$ after passing through some other vertices/edges. Similar notation for $\tilde{e}_m$.

We optimize the bus routes such that the travel distances of empty buses $\tilde{e}_m(*, *).dist$ are minimized while all clusters are served with some quality of service. The optimization problem can be formulated as

$$\min_{\mathcal{R}_m} \quad \textstyle\sum_{m \in \mathcal{M}} \sum_{dist} \tilde{e}_m(*, *).dist \tag{1}$$

$$\text{s.t.} \quad \mathcal{R}_m.arg(\mathcal{C}_n.\mathcal{O}) < \mathcal{R}_m.arg(\mathcal{C}_n.\mathcal{D}) \;\; \forall\, m, n \tag{2}$$

$$\mathcal{R}_m = \{e_m(\mathcal{C}_n.\mathcal{O}, *), \cdots, \tilde{e}_m(*, \mathcal{C}_n.\mathcal{O})\} \;\; \forall\, m \tag{3}$$

$$\mathcal{R}_m.time(\mathcal{C}_n) \leq \alpha \cdot \mathcal{C}_n.time \;\; \forall\, m, n \tag{4}$$

$$e_m(*, *).load \leq \text{max\_load} \;\; \forall\, m \tag{5}$$

where (2) ensures that the origins of all clusters are visited before its destinies in all bus routes; (3) ensures that all bus routes are directed cycle graphs; (4) and (5) ensure the quality of bus service. (4) requires that the travelling time for all clusters in all bus routes should be less than a factor (α) of the mean travelling times ($\mathcal{C}_n.time$) of taxi rides of their corresponding cluster. $\alpha > 1$ is acceptable since taxi rides are usually faster. (5) ensures no overcrowding at all edges in all bus routes.

3.3 Solution Method

The formulated problem (1)-(5) is a combinatorial optimization which is NP-hard in general. To determine new bus routes, we develop a heuristic method to obtain a preliminary solution. Specifically, we aim to merge as many clusters as possible subject to the constraints of (4)-(5). We exploit constraint (2) to reduce the search space of the next vertex to visit, where candidates of the next vertex comprise

1. the departing vertex of the route, ie the origin of the first cluster it visited
2. destinies of all clusters visited by the route before
3. the origins of clusters not served by any bus route

Point 1 ensures that the route ends at the departing vertex, thus forming a cycle graph. We deploy a greedy approach to select the shortest distance among the candidate vertices which satisfy the load and time constraints in (4)-(5). Both constraints impose a limit to the merging of clusters to avoid overcrowding of buses and long travelling time. When no origin of other clusters can be admitted into the candidate vertices (due to constraints (4)-(5)), and destinies of all clusters has been visited, the route end in the departing vertex of the route. The bus routing algorithm is run to determine another new bus route until all taxi ride clusters are served by bus routes. Algorithm 1 summarizes all.

Algorithm 1 Algorithm for discovering new bus routes

```
Initialize m = 0
while |N| > 0 do
  Initialize a new route R_m
  x_cur = C_n.O // Initialize an origin as the current vertex
  Initialize V = C_n.D ⋃ {C_n.O, ∀ n ∈ N} // All origins
  in N + destiny of the current vertex
  while |V| > 0 do
    x* = arg min_{x∈V} e_m(x_cur, x).dist s.t. (4)-(5)
    x_cur = x*
    if (x* == O) // if the next vertex is an origin then
      V = V ⋃ arg(x*).D // include its destiny in the
      set of candidate vertices
    else
      N = N \ arg(x*) // the cluster is served, so re-
      moved the corresponding cluster from N
    end if
  end while
  m = m + 1
end while
```

4. CASE STUDY

We showcase a case study to identify new bus routes using historical dataset of taxi rides in Singapore. The entire taxi rides dataset comprises roughly 7.1 millions taxi rides recorded by 15028 taxis in Singapore. The dataset contains the GPS records and the time stamps of pick-up and drop-off locations of each taxi ride. We first clean the dataset by removing negligible number (around 20 out of roughly 7.1 millions records) of erroneous records of GPS data.

In metropolitan Singapore, travel pattern of its population depends largely on the work week. In particular, Friday evening is among the busiest periods on Singapore's roads. We mine the taxi rides dataset and discover that Friday evening, from 5pm till 12am midnight to be the period of time where clusters of taxi rides link business areas to shopping/entertainments/restaurants/chill out areas not directly accessible via public transportation network. DBSCAN clustering of the taxi rides and filtering of the clusters are as described in Section 2.

We obtain $|\mathcal{N}| = 8$ suitable clusters of most popular taxi rides. Fig.2 and Fig.3 show the locations of these clusters. Table 1 shows the origins and destinies, and the traffic volume of each cluster. Using Algorithm 1 where $\alpha = 2$ and max_load $= 70$, we obtain $|\mathcal{M}| = 3$ new bus routes where each route serves the following clusters: $\mathcal{R}_1 = \{\mathcal{C}_4, \mathcal{C}_6, \mathcal{C}_7, \mathcal{C}_8\}$, $\mathcal{R}_2 = \{\mathcal{C}_1, \mathcal{C}_3, \mathcal{C}_5\}$, $\mathcal{R}_3 = \{\mathcal{C}_2\}$. Paths of the bus routes are given in Table 2 where

$$\tilde{d}_m \triangleq \sum_{dist} \tilde{e}_m(*, *).dist \;, \;\; d_m \triangleq \tilde{d}_m + \sum_{dist} e_m(*, *).dist \tag{6}$$

Figure 2: Clusters of taxi ride origins

Figure 3: Clusters of taxi ride destinies

All these routes takes long time to commute and transit via existing public transport, are not reachable via MRT or any single bus ride. From the table, $\mathcal{R}_2$ is the most efficient route as it has the shortest distance (and fraction) of path without passenger load, while $\mathcal{R}_3$ has the highest fraction of path without passenger load as it only serves $\mathcal{C}_2$. $\mathcal{R}_1$ has the longest distance of path without passenger load. Table 3 compares the mean travelling time of taking taxi ($\mathcal{C}_n.time$) with expected travelling time taking the new bus routes ($\mathcal{R}_m.time(\mathcal{C}_n)$). We deploy the API of Singapore Journey Planner [5] developed at Institute for Infocomm Research to obtain the route and expected travelling time. The expected travelling times for all clusters under the proposed new bus routes are within twice of the mean travelling time of taxi rides. Note that taking bus is usually much cheaper than taxi in Singapore. Fare analyses of both transportation modes are left out due to page limit.

5. CONCLUSIONS

We present in this paper a proof of concept in planning new routes of public bus service via data mining approach. Through the mining of taxi dataset, we identify some leaks of coverage of public transportation network at a specific time windows within a week. Based on the travel patterns of taxi rides clusters, we show that the efficiency and quality of service of the public transport can be improved by proposing new feasible bus routes for a specific time windows. We illustrate our proof of concept in a case study of Singapore. For future works, passengers' travel patterns in public transports can be mined to jointly optimize the routings of existing and newly proposed bus routes. Besides GPS data, fare data of passengers of both transport modes can be factored in to improve the competitiveness of public transports. Finally, the framework can be extended to cater for dynamic demand of mobility needs in a work week.

Table 1: Clusters of taxi rides

Cluster	Origin	Destiny	Vol. (taxi/hour)
$\mathcal{C}_1$	Harbour Front	Civic District	13.5
$\mathcal{C}_2$	CBD	Holland Village	9.7
$\mathcal{C}_3$	Geylang	Orchard Rd.	7.6
$\mathcal{C}_4$	Civic District	Marine Parade	7.6
$\mathcal{C}_5$	Chinatown	Geyland	6.7
$\mathcal{C}_6$	Civic District	East Coast	5.7
$\mathcal{C}_7$	CBD	East Coast	4.5
$\mathcal{C}_8$	CBD	Marine Parade	4.0

Table 2: Proposed new bus routes

Route	Path	$\tilde{d}_m$ / d_m (km)
$\mathcal{R}_1$	CBD → Civic District → Marine Parade → East Coast → CBD	13.9 / 31.8
$\mathcal{R}_2$	Harbour Front → Chinatown → Civic District → Geylang → Orchard Rd. → Harbour Front	7.5 / 27.0
$\mathcal{R}_3$	CBD → Holland Village → CBD	8.7 / 19.3

Table 3: Comparison of travelling times

Cluster	$\mathcal{C}_n.time$ (min)	$\mathcal{R}_m.time(\mathcal{C}_n)$ (min)
$\mathcal{C}_1$	17.8	22
$\mathcal{C}_2$	18.7	27
$\mathcal{C}_3$	16.1	25
$\mathcal{C}_4$	19.1	33
$\mathcal{C}_5$	16.6	24
$\mathcal{C}_6$	18.6	24
$\mathcal{C}_7$	18.9	37
$\mathcal{C}_8$	19.4	28

6. ACKNOWLEDGMENTS

This research is partially supported by the National Research Foundation, Prime Minister's Office, Singapore under its Campus for Research Excellence and Technological Enterprise (CREATE) programme. NUS Ref: R-702-005-101-281.

7. REFERENCES

[1] D. Applegate, R. Bixby, V. Chvátal, and W. Cook. *The Traveling Salesman Problem: A Computational Study*. Princeton Series in Applied Mathematics. Princeton University Press, 2011.

[2] C. Daraio, M. Diana, F. D. Costa, C. Leporelli, G. Matteucci, and A. Nastasi. Efficiency and effectiveness in the urban public transport sector: A critical review with directions for future research. *Eur. J. of Operational Research*, 248(1):1 – 20, 2016.

[3] V. Schmid. Hybrid large neighborhood search for the bus rapid transit route design problem. *Eur. J. of Operational Research*, 238(2):427 – 437, 2014.

[4] P.-N. Tan, M. Steinbach, and V. Kumar. *Introduction to Data Mining, (First Edition)*. Addison-Wesley Longman Publishing Co., Inc., Boston, MA, USA, 2005.

[5] L. Yu, D. Shao, and H. Wu. Next generation of journey planner in a smart city. In *2015 IEEE International Conference on Data Mining Workshop (ICDMW)*, pages 422–429, Nov 2015.

Routing an Autonomous Taxi with Reinforcement Learning

Miyoung Han
Télécom ParisTech, Paris
IPAL, I2R, A*STAR, Singapore

Pierre Senellart
Télécom ParisTech, Paris
IPAL, NUS, Singapore

Stéphane Bressan
IPAL, NUS, Singapore

Huayu Wu
I2R, A*STAR, Singapore

ABSTRACT

Singapore's vision of a Smart Nation encompasses the development of effective and efficient means of transportation. The government's target is to leverage new technologies to create services for a demand-driven intelligent transportation model including personal vehicles, public transport, and taxis. Singapore's government is strongly encouraging and supporting research and development of technologies for autonomous vehicles in general and autonomous taxis in particular. The design and implementation of intelligent routing algorithms is one of the keys to the deployment of autonomous taxis. In this paper we demonstrate that a reinforcement learning algorithm of the Q-learning family, based on a customized exploration and exploitation strategy, is able to learn optimal actions for the routing autonomous taxis in a real scenario at the scale of the city of Singapore with pick-up and drop-off events for a fleet of one thousand taxis.

1. INTRODUCTION

Singapore's Prime Minister Office outlines its vision of a Smart Nation as the harnessing of information and communication technologies "to support better living, create more opportunities, and support stronger communities"[1]. The vision encompasses the development of effective and efficient means of transportation and aims at the development of a demand-driven intelligent transportation model including personal vehicles, public transports, and taxis. In particular, Singapore's government is strongly encouraging and supporting research and development of technologies for autonomous vehicles (AV). Its agencies, together with academia and industry, are involved in learning and understanding opportunities and challenges for autonomous vehicle technologies and autonomous taxis. For example, the Land Transport Authority of Singapore [9] has been working with A*STAR's Institute for Infocomm Research to evaluate their AV Proof-of-Concept on-road trials[2] since last year. "Unlike autonomous vehicle trials elsewhere, Singapore is focusing on applying the technology to public buses, freight carriers, autonomous taxis and utility operations such as road sweepers." [8]. Self-driving riders have already been experienced by the public at Gardens by the Bay last December[3].

The design and implementation of intelligent routing algorithms is one of the keys to the deployment of autonomous taxis. While prior studies have explored reinforcement learning approaches to taxi routing, they have mostly done so with synthetic models and data in small and static state spaces. In this paper we demonstrate that a reinforcement learning algorithm is able to progressively, adaptively, efficiently, and effectively learn optimal actions for the routing to passenger pick-up points of an autonomous taxi in a real scenario at the scale of the city of Singapore.

We present a solution based on a customized exploration and exploitation strategy for an algorithm of the *Q-learning* family [10]. Q-learning is an approach to solve *reinforcement learning* [7] problems. Reinforcement learning is used for learning an optimal policy in a dynamic environment: an agent takes an action in a state, receives a reward, moves to some next state, and repeats this procedure. Initially, the agent has no knowledge of which action has to be taken in a given state. The algorithm has the choice between *exploiting* its knowledge by choosing the action with highest estimated value and *exploring* its environment by taking any other action. The trade-off between exploration and exploitation is crucial. We devise an exploration strategy that follows an almost-greedy policy. The strategy first selects a set of candidate actions with long-term reward above a given threshold and then selects, among candidates, the action with the highest probability of finding a passenger.

We evaluate how Q-learning progressively learns and how to balance exploration and exploitation. We quantify the influence of the parameters. We propose an original selection strategy. The evaluation uses a dataset of taxi pickups and drop-offs for a fleet of 1000 taxis for one month in Singapore.

2. BACKGROUND AND RELATED WORK

Most studies addressing the taxi routing problem focus on providing the fastest route and a sequence of pick-up points [6] by mining historical data [6,11–13]. Yuan et al. [11]

[1]http://www.pmo.gov.sg/smartnation

CIKM'16, October 24 - 28, 2016, Indianapolis, IN, USA

ISBN 978-1-4503-4073-1/16/10... $15.00

DOI: http://dx.doi.org/10.1145/2983323.2983379

[2]http://www.lta.gov.sg/apps/news/page.aspx?c=2&id=7dac9bd2-e6d1-448f-ba0e-f31fd13a8c3e

[3]http://www.opengovasia.com/articles/6792-asias-first-fully-operational-autonomous-vehicle-running-at-gardens-by-the-bay-singapore

cluster road segments and travel time to build a landmark graph of traffic patterns and time-dependent fastest routes. They then present in [12] a recommendation system for taxi drivers and passengers by clustering road segments extracted from GPS trajectories. The system recommends a parking place and road segments to taxi drivers and passengers. Qu et al. [6] propose a method to recommend a route. They develop a graph representation of a road network by mining the historical taxi GPS traces and generate an optimal route for finding passengers. Those models rely on the availability of accurate historical data and trajectories. They might not be relevant in dynamic environments such as an autonomous taxi looking for optimal passenger pick-up points.

Reinforcement learning [7] has the potential to continuously and adaptively learn from interaction with the environment. The algorithm discovers which actions produce the greatest reward by experience and estimates how good it is to take a certain action in a given state. Yet reinforcement learning aims to maximize cumulated reward. The notion of *Markov Decision Process (MDP)* underlies much of the work on reinforcement learning, and is at the basis of our work.

Q-learning [10] is widely used because of its computational simplicity. In Q-learning, one does not require a model of transition functions and reward functions but learns directly from observed experience. This is an advantage as learning a model often requires exhaustive exploration that is not suitable for a large state space. Thus, Q-learning seems suitable for taxi routing in a city of the scale of Singapore.

While taxi routing has often been used as the example application for reinforcement learning algorithms, it often remained relegated to toy or small scale examples, as it is the case of the seminal 5×5 grid introduced by the authors of [1] and used for experimental purposes by the authors of [2–5]. Learning pick-up points is a somewhat new application of reinforcement learning.

3. Q-LEARNING FOR TAXI ROUTING

We consider an autonomous taxi completely relying on reinforcement learning. The algorithm decides where the autonomous taxi should go in order to pick up passengers by learning the existence probability of passengers from its gathered experience. Reinforcement learning models an agent taking an action a in state s, receiving a reward r, and moving to the next state s'. With Q-learning, the estimated value of taking action a in state s, denoted $Q(s, a)$, is updated as: $Q(s,a) := Q(s,a) + \alpha\,[r + \gamma \max_{a'} Q(s',a') - Q(s,a)]$.

Here, α is a positive fraction such that $0 < \alpha \leqslant 1$, the step-size parameter that influences the rate of learning. When $\alpha = 1$, the agent considers only the most recent information for learning. If α is properly reduced over time, the function converges [7]. The discount rate γ ($0 \leqslant \gamma < 1$) determines the present value of future rewards. If $\gamma = 0$, the agent is only concerned with the immediate reward. The agent's action influences only the current reward. If γ approaches 1, the agent considers future rewards more strongly.

To maximize total reward, the agent must select the action with highest value (exploitation), but to discover such action it has to try actions not selected before (exploration). The ε-greedy method works as follows: most of the time, select an action with the highest estimated value, but with small probability ε select an action uniformly at random. This exploration enables to experience other actions not taken before and it may increase the greater total reward in the long run because we would discover better actions.

Algorithm 1 Taxi Routing for Learning Pick-up Points

1: Initialize $Q(s,a)$, existence probability of passengers p
2: **repeat**
3:   **repeat**
4:     **if** greedy **then**
5:       $V := \{ a \in A \mid Q(s,a) \geqslant \max_{a'} Q(s,a') - \eta \}$
6:       **if** $|V| > 1$ **then**
7:         Select action a with highest probability p
8:     **else** /* not greedy */
9:       Select action a uniformly at random
10:     Take action a, obtain reward r, observe next state s'
11:     $Q(s,a) := Q(s,a) + \alpha\,[r + \gamma \max_{a'} Q(s',a') - Q(s,a)]$
12:     Increment visit count on s'
13:     Update existence passenger probability $p(s')$
14:     **if** passenger found in s' **then**
15:       Increment found count on s'
16:       s becomes the end of the passenger route from s'
17:     **else**
18:       $s := s'$
19:   **until** a passenger is found
20: **until** algorithm converges

We call an episode the movement of a taxi to an actual pick-up point. For the first episode, the taxi located at a random position moves according to the initial oblivious learning policy. The episode ends when the taxi finds a passenger. Then, it moves to the passenger's destination and starts a new episode. As the taxi moves it receives rewards and updates its action-value and the existence probability. The road network is discretized and the movements correspond to steps in the discretized network. At each step, the taxi learns where passengers are likely to be located.

The Taxi Routing algorithm for learning pick-up points is outlined in Algorithm 1. According to the ε-greedy policy, an action a is selected in a given state s.

The action selection rule selects the action with the maximum estimated action value (greedy action). However, with this rule, the algorithm ignores other actions that, although they have slightly lesser value, may lead to a state having a higher chance to pick a passenger up. Hence, instead of selecting one greedy action, we loosen the selection condition by setting a lower bound below the maximum value in order to choose from more potentially valuable candidate actions (Line 5). The candidate actions are compared with existence probabilities of passengers in their corresponding states (Line 7). We later refer to the algorithm with this selection strategy as *Q-learning using LB/Proba*.

After taking an action, we update the Q-value in the current state s with reward r and next state s'. As we visit a new state s', the visit and found counts are incremented and the existence probability of passengers is also recalculated. We repeat this procedure until we find a passenger.

4. PERFORMANCE EVALUATION

For the sake of simplicity, in this paper, we present the results for a map discretized into cells of 0.01 degree longitude × 0.01 degree latitude (about 1.1km × 1.1km) forming a 38 × 20 grid. At each cell of the grid, eight actions are possible: up, down, right, left, and diagonally. A step is the movement from one cell to an adjacent one. Although such a representation does not capture several natural constraints on the traffic, it is sufficient, with limited loss of generality, to evaluate the effectiveness of the algorithm.

Since popular pick-up points generally depend on the time of the day, we run the experiments for selected time intervals. Here, we present the results for two off-peak hours (12h to 13h and 14h to 15h), but we obtain comparable results for other time slots. At each episode we select 300 passengers according to actual geographical distribution in the given time interval in a dataset of taxi pickups and drop-offs for a fleet of one thousand taxis for one month in Singapore.

We first look into the impact of the step-size parameter α, the discount rate γ, and the probability of exploration ε. We evaluate how these parameters influence the learning performance with ordinary Q-learning. We compare the average number of steps. The average steps are calculated at every 100 episode by dividing the total steps from the first episode to the last by the total number of episodes.

Figures 1a–1b show the average number of steps with different step-size parameter α values for different time intervals. We compare four different α with a fixed γ $(= 0.5)$ and ε $(= 0.3)$. For all the time intervals, as the α is smaller, the average number of steps also decreases. Lower step-size values perform better. This indicates that accumulated experience affects value estimation more significant than recent experience, i.e., that the problem is indeed stochastic.

For the discount rate γ experiment, we fixed α $(= 0.5)$ and ε $(= 0.3)$ and changed the γ. The average number of steps with different γ values for different time intervals are shown in Figures 1c–1d. In Figure 1d, the lowest γ $(= 0.25)$ perform better. This means that immediate rewards are more important than future rewards. In Figure 1c, as episodes continue, a higher γ $(= 0.75)$ is slightly better. In 1c, relatively longer step counts than those of the other time intervals are needed to achieve a goal. In this case, future rewards are more significant than current rewards.

Figures 1e–1f show the average number of steps with different ε values for different time intervals, given $\alpha = 0.5$ and $\gamma = 0.5$. The average number of steps first decreases dramatically and then converges gradually. For all time intervals, when ε is 0.1, the average number of steps is higher than the other cases in early episodes but it dominates after about 30,000 episodes. At the beginning, exploration is more effective and relatively inexpensive. Eventually, sufficient knowledge is accumulated and exploitation is worthy.

We now compare Q-learning using LB/Proba (our algorithm) with ordinary Q-learning. For experiments, we select three parameter values shown in the previous section. The step-size parameter α is set to 0.25 because low learning rate is appropriate to our problem. The probability of exploration ε is set to 0.1. Since loosened selection for maximum action has the effect of exploration, high ε is not needed. We take $\eta = 0.01$ to set the lower bound on the maximum action value per state. Two algorithms are compared by varying the discount rate γ value.

In Figures 1g–1j, when $\gamma = 0.75$ or 0.5, Q-learning using LB/Proba converges faster than Q-learning. On the other hand, when γ is 0.25 (Figures 1k–1l), Q-learning performs similary well or slightly better than Q-learning using LB/Proba. These experiments show that when the learning rate α is low and the discount rate γ approaches 1, Q-learning using LB/Proba outperforms Q-learning. In other words, it has to accumulate much experience for value prediction and it considers future rewards more strongly. The reason is that Q-learning using LB/Proba depends on existence probability of passengers that requires enough experience and that is more related to long-term high rewards.

5. CONCLUSIONS AND FUTURE WORK

A*STAR's Institute for Infocomm Research, with its academic partners, is contributing to Singapore's Land Transport Authority's efforts to evaluate the viability of autonomous vehicles. We explored the use of reinforcement learning for autonomous taxi routing. The evaluation results provide empirical support of the effectiveness of reinforcement learning for the task at hand. We are planning more extensive studies as soon as extensive on-road trials are carried out and more data is available to us. We are also currently extending this work to consider a more dynamic environment. We are considering a multi-agent approach to scale to larger and more complex state spaces. We also investigate hierarchies, factored representations, and other extended methods that can improve adaptiveness, effectiveness and efficiency of learning.

Acknowledgment. This research was supported in part by the Télécom ParisTech Chair on Big Data & Market Insights, and in part by the National Research Foundation, Prime Minister's Office, Singapore under the CREATE program, NUS ref. R-702-005-101-281.

6. REFERENCES

[1] T. G. Dietterich. The MAXQ method for hierarchical reinforcement learning. In *ICML*, 1998.

[2] C. Diuk, A. L. Strehl, and M. L. Littman. A hierarchical approach to efficient reinforcement learning in deterministic domains. In *AAMAS*, 2006.

[3] M. Ghavamzadeh and S. Mahadevan. A multiagent reinforcement learning algorithm by dynamically merging Markov decision processes. In *AAMAS*, 2002.

[4] M. Ghavamzadeh and S. Mahadevan. Learning to communicate and act using hierarchical reinforcement learning. In *AAMAS*, 2004.

[5] T. Hester and P. Stone. Generalized model learning for reinforcement learning in factored domains. In *AAMAS*, 2009.

[6] M. Qu, H. Zhu, J. Liu, G. Liu, and H. Xiong. A cost-effective recommender system for taxi drivers. In *KDD*, 2014.

[7] R. S. Sutton and A. G. Barto. *Introduction to Reinforcement Learning*. MIT Press, 1998.

[8] C. Tan. Driverless vehicles hit the road in trials around singapore. *Straits Times*, 2015. http://www.straitstimes.com/singapore/transport/driverless-vehicles-hit-the-road-in-trials-around-singapore.

[9] T. K. S. TAN Cheon Kheong. Autonomous vehicles, next stop: Singapore. *Journeys*, 2014.

[10] C. J. C. H. Watkins and P. Dayan. Technical note: Q-learning. *Mach. Learn.*, 8(3-4), 1992.

[11] J. Yuan, Y. Zheng, X. Xie, and G. Sun. T-drive: Enhancing driving directions with taxi drivers' intelligence. *TKDE*, 25(1), 2013.

[12] N. J. Yuan, Y. Zheng, L. Zhang, and X. Xie. T-finder: A recommender system for finding passengers and vacant taxis. *TKDE*, 25(10), 2013.

[13] Y. Zheng. Trajectory data mining: An overview. *ACM Trans. Intell. Syst. Technol.*, 6(3), 2015.

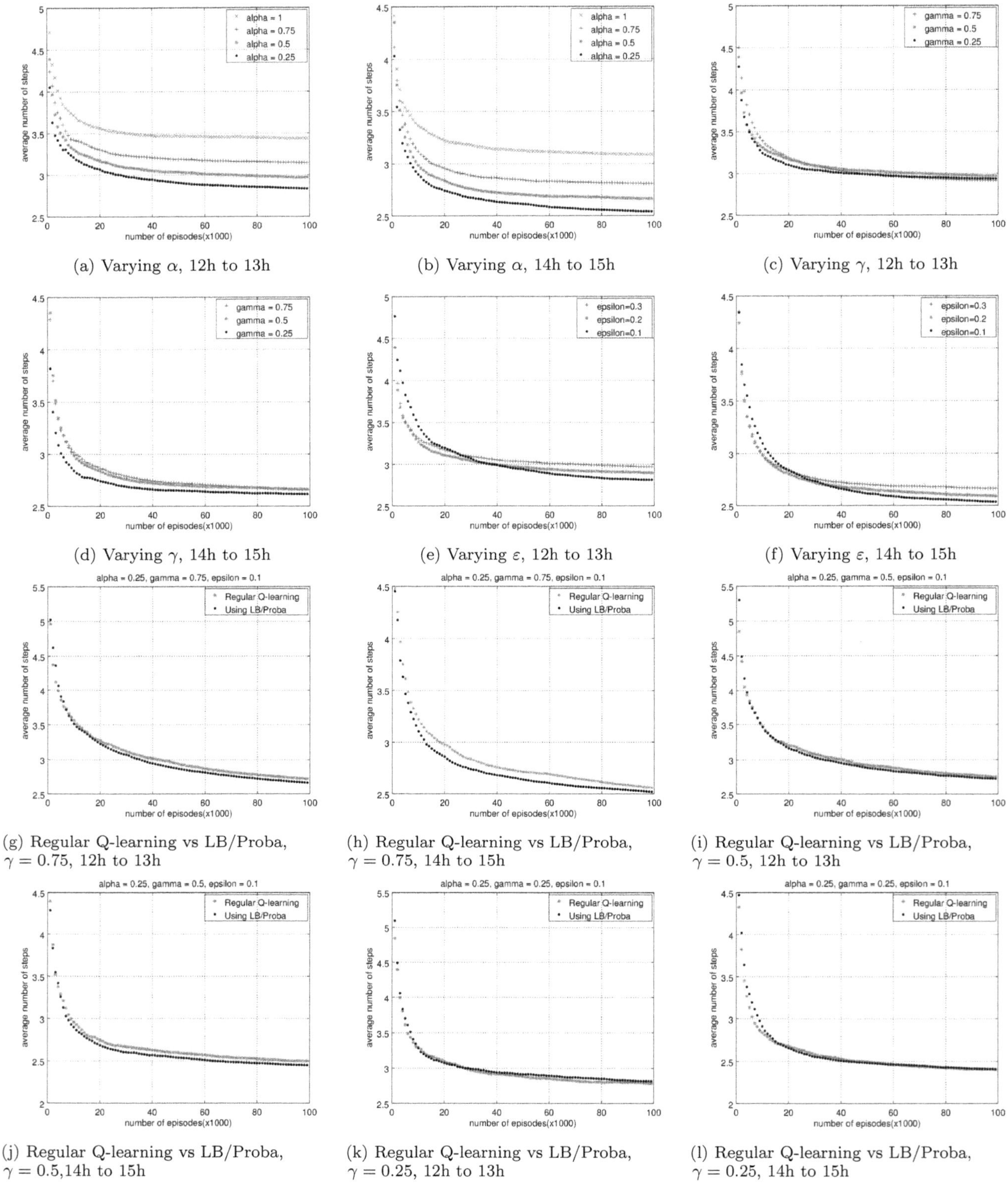

(a) Varying α, 12h to 13h

(b) Varying α, 14h to 15h

(c) Varying γ, 12h to 13h

(d) Varying γ, 14h to 15h

(e) Varying ε, 12h to 13h

(f) Varying ε, 14h to 15h

(g) Regular Q-learning vs LB/Proba, $\gamma = 0.75$, 12h to 13h

(h) Regular Q-learning vs LB/Proba, $\gamma = 0.75$, 14h to 15h

(i) Regular Q-learning vs LB/Proba, $\gamma = 0.5$, 12h to 13h

(j) Regular Q-learning vs LB/Proba, $\gamma = 0.5$,14h to 15h

(k) Regular Q-learning vs LB/Proba, $\gamma = 0.25$, 12h to 13h

(l) Regular Q-learning vs LB/Proba, $\gamma = 0.25$, 14h to 15h

Figure 1: Average number of steps as the number of episodes increases.

XKnowSearch! Exploiting Knowledge Bases for Entity-based Cross-lingual Information Retrieval

Lei Zhang
Karlsruhe Institute of Technology (KIT)
76128 Karlsruhe, Germany
l.zhang@kit.edu

Michael Färber
Karlsruhe Institute of Technology (KIT)
76128 Karlsruhe, Germany
michael.faerber@kit.edu

Achim Rettinger
Karlsruhe Institute of Technology (KIT)
76128 Karlsruhe, Germany
rettinger@kit.edu

ABSTRACT

In recent years, the amount of entities in large knowledge bases available on the Web has been increasing rapidly, making it possible to propose new ways of intelligent information access. Within the context of globalization, there is a clear need for techniques and systems that can enable multilingual and cross-lingual information access. In this paper, we present XKnowSearch!, a novel entity-based system for multilingual and cross-lingual information retrieval, which supports keyword search and also allows users to influence the search process according to their search intents. By leveraging the multilingual knowledge base on the Web, keyword queries and documents can be represented in their semantic forms, which can facilitate query disambiguation and expansion, and can also overcome the language barrier between queries and documents in different languages.

1. INTRODUCTION

The Web has radically altered the way that information is shared by lowering the barrier to publishing and accessing documents. With more than one trillion pages, the Web has become a *global document repository*, which encompasses practically almost every topic of human interest. As the founding language, English has always dominated the Web, where it is estimated that more than half of all Web content is in English. However, the share of English Web pages decreases and that of other languages increases rapidly, which ensures the multilingual viability of the Web.

Accessing Web documents can be efficient when the information needs of users are expressed as keywords. However, both documents and keyword queries are usually treated as plain text by current search engines, i.e., term-based matching algorithms are used to retrieve the relevant documents according to a given information need. Due to the problem for ambiguous terms, there exists a *semantic gap* between unstructured text and its actual meaning.

As a consequence of the ability to understand more than one language, many Web users are interested in relevant information in multiple languages, especially when relevant documents on the Web are scare in their native language. With the goal that users from different countries have access to the same information on the Web, there exists a *language barrier* for cross-lingual access to information originally produced for a different culture and language.

On the other hand, the Semantic Web has come a long way with the goal of extending the existing Web by bringing semantics to its content. There has been an increasing effort in which the Semantic Web community has envisioned how semantics and the Web can be combined. Linked Open Data (LOD)[1] is such a way of publishing semantic data on the Web that gives humans and machines direct access to such structured data [1]. It is important to note that many LOD sources are generally in multiple languages. As an example, DBpedia[2], staying in the center of the LOD cloud, is a crowd-sourced community effort to extract structured knowledge from multilingual Wikipedia, resulting in localized versions of DBpedia in more than 100 languages, and to make this information available on the Web [5].

The ever-increasing quantities of semantic data in large knowledge bases (KBs) on the Web, such as DBpedia, Freebase and YAGO, pose new challenges but at the same time open up new opportunities of intelligent information access. These knowledge bases contain a vast amount of entities and the knowledge about them such that the Web also serves as a *global knowledge repository* of entities. Due to an increasing portion of queries involving entities for Web search [6], the exploitation of *entities and their knowledge* beyond the term-based paradigm for information retrieval (IR) has become an area of particular interest.

In this paper, we present XKnowSearch!, a novel system for multilingual and cross-lingual IR by exploiting entities and their relations in the KB with the goal of addressing the following challenges that traditional keyword search systems mainly suffer from:

Inflexibility. Keyword search has proven to be a simple and intuitive paradigm for expressing the information needs. However, traditional keyword search systems do not allow users to be involved in the search process to perform query refinement according to their search intents.

Ambiguity. Keyword queries are naturally ambiguous due to the fact that keywords could refer to different things in different contexts. This problem is more serious in the multilingual and cross-lingual setting, because the same keywords could have different meanings in different languages.

Incompleteness. Keyword queries are often incomplete in the sense that only the aliases, acronyms and misspellings

CIKM '16, October 24–28, 2016, Indianapolis, IN, USA.

ACM ISBN 978-1-4503-4073-1/16/10..

DOI: http://dx.doi.org/10.1145/2983323.2983324

[1]http://lod-cloud.net/
[2]http://dbpedia.org/

are usually given in the queries. In addition, keyword queries might contain concept names, e.g., *"online companies of US"*, which could refer to a set of entities.

Cross-linguality. Multilingual users probably formulate their information needs using native language, but they are interested in relevant information in any language that they can understand. Moreover, specifying the query language should not be the burden of users and they could even issue queries consisting of keywords in multiple languages.

Concerned with these challenges, XKnowSearch! supports keyword search on Web documents by representing the information needs of users as entity graphs in the KB to avoid the semantic ambiguity of keyword queries. Based on various query interpretations, it allows users to explore entity relations in the KB to further refine the queries and also enables automatic query expansion. In order to bridge the language barrier between queries and documents, we leverage the multilingual KB, namely DBpedia, to construct semantic representations of queries and documents in different languages and use them to develop a more effective way of modeling the document relevance on the basis of entity knowledge for satisfying the information needs of users.

2. LIMITATIONS OF EXISTING SYSTEMS

In this section, we review the existing entity-based search systems and discuss their limitations, which serve as the motivation of our XKnowSearch! system.

EntEXPO [4] provides entity-based query expansion by finding a list of related entities of a single query entity and it allows users to manually adjust the weight of each related entity. However, there is no discussion about how to resolve the ambiguity of the query keywords and it does not concern with the queries containing concept names or multiple entities. EntEXPO seems to support search only in English.

Kuphi [2] employs semantic annotations of documents to enhance the performance of document retrieval. It allows interactive query reformulation by selecting the intended entity and adjusting the weights of related entities. However, the system assumes that a keyword query is a single entity name such that it cannot handle queries containing more than one entity name or concept names.

STICS [3] has been proposed to support users in searching for terms, entities and categories. However, users have to specify the query entities and categories explicitly such that the ambiguity of queries can only be resolved by users. Moreover, it supports neither query expansion with related entities nor interactive query formulation / refinement. Finally, STICS also does not support cross-lingual search.

Recently, almost every major commercial Web search engine has announced their work on incorporating entity information from knowledge bases into its search process, including Google's Knowledge Graph, Yahoo!'s Web of Objects and Microsoft's Satori Graph / Bing Snapshots. However, there are still some limitations. Firstly, most search engines take into account only the most prominent entities matching the keyword query. Secondly, they can only understand individual entities, but cannot deal with a set of entities expressed by a concept name. For example, given the keyword query "Internet companies of US", they do not suggest the expected entities, such as Google and Yahoo!, and the retrieved documents are mostly only matched against the query keywords, such as "Internet companies" and "US". Finally, they do not support cross-lingual search. For example, given the Chinese query "马云" denoting Jack_Ma, the founder of Alibaba_Group, they rarely retrieve any relevant English documents about Jack_Ma or Alibaba_Group.

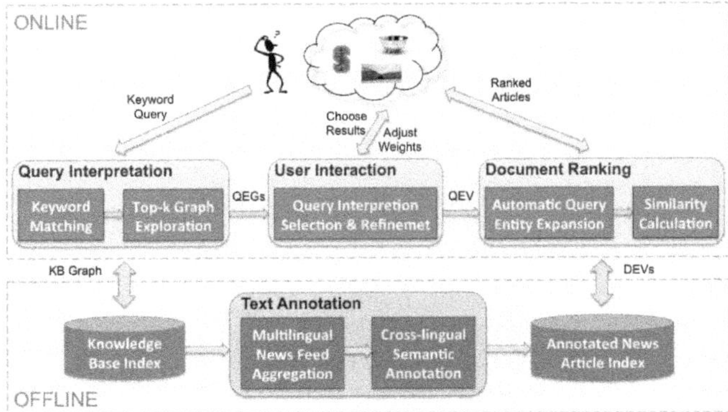

Figure 1: The System Architecture of XKnowSearch!.

In summary, existing entity-based search systems cannot well address the challenges of *inflexibility*, *ambiguity* and *incompleteness*. More importantly, all of them do not support *cross-lingual search*. For example, EntEXPO seems to support only English and STICS supports both English and German, but neither of them can handle cross-lingual search. Although Kuphi enables users to search documents in one language by using queries in another language, users have to specify the input language of the query, which can only be a single entity name. To the best of our knowledge, XKnowSearch! is the first entity-based system to multilingual and cross-lingual IR with the goal of addressing these challenges, where users can issue keyword queries in any language, which can even contain keywords in multiple languages, for retrieving multilingual documents, especially in any other languages. In order to avoid the users' burden of specifying the query languages, XKnowSearch! does not assume any input language given by users.

3. SYSTEM ARCHITECTURE

The system architecture of XKnowSearch!, as shown in Fig. 1, consists of a set of components. While *text annotation* is performed offline, *query interpretation*, *user interaction* and *document ranking* are handled online. In this section, we briefly introduce these components.

Text Annotation. For offline processing, we first employ a *news feed aggregator*[3] to acquire a multilingual real-time stream of news articles on the Web across the world. The collected articles are in various languages, such as English (50% of all articles), German (10%) and Chinese (5%).

Then *cross-lingual semantic annotation* is performed to enrich the collected news articles in different languages with entities in the KB. More specifically, the KB we use, namely DBpedia, contains a formal representation of entities and semantic relations between them. In addition, it is multilingual, i.e., there are multiple language versions containing entities grounded in different languages. Based on that, we employ our cross-lingual semantic annotation system[4] to annotate the multilingual documents with entities grounded in one or more hub languages [8]. It helps to bridge the ambiguity of natural language text and precise formal semantics captured by the KB as well as to transform documents in different languages into a unified representation. The result-

[3]http://newsfeed.ijs.si

[4]http://km.aifb.kit.edu/sites/xlisa/

ing annotated documents are stored in an inverted index to make them searchable with KB entities.

Query Interpretation. The online process starts with a keyword query in any language (even with keywords in multiple languages). Instead of retrieving documents directly by keywords, XKnowSearch! first finds the *query entity graphs* (*QEGs*) matching the keyword query by exploring the semantic graph of the KB[5] with nodes representing entities and edges describing their relations.

The first step of *query interpretation* is *keyword matching*. To address the challenge of matching query keywords in different languages to entities, we constructed a cross-lingual lexica[6] by exploiting multilingual Wikipedia to extract the cross-lingual groundings of entities [7]. After obtaining the matching entities, the *top-k graph exploration* is then performed on the graph of the KB for finding the top-k optimal QEGs. The resulting QEGs represent different semantic interpretations of the keyword query. Thus it can help users to refine the query and influence document ranking according to the search intents. More details about our approach to query interpretation can be found in [9].

User Interaction. Different interpretations of the keyword query, i.e., the generated QEGs, are then presented to users for *selecting* the one that fulfills their search intents. The selected QEG can be further *refined*. From an entity in the QEG, users can navigate its description and the connected entities through their relations in the KB, such that they can add additional entities into the QEG or delete unnecessary ones. After that, the entities in the refined QEG constitute the *query entity vector* (*QEV*), where each entry contains the weight of the corresponding entity, which is calculated by the top-k graph exploration algorithm [9] and can also be adjusted by users. These weights will be leveraged for document ranking in the next component.

We consider *user interaction* as beneficial because it enables the interactive query disambiguation and expansion according to users' search intents. Although refinement can be made more precisely on QEGs than on keywords, user interaction is optional in our system. Users can also search the documents directly without interactive query refinement. In this case, the QEG with highest score obtained by the query interpretation component is selected to generate the QEV.

Document Ranking. For document retrieval, the entities in the QEV are used to find relevant documents. However, the documents without the entities in the QEV could also be relevant when they contain entities that are related to the ones in the QEV. Therefore, integrating the related entities into the query can help to cover more complementary information and thus improve the performance of document retrieval. Based on the above observation, we first construct the *expanded query entity vector* (*EQEV*) by *automatically expanding* the QEV with additional related entities.

For each document, we construct the *document entity vector* (*DEV*), where the entries contain the confidence scores of the annotations (i.e., the linked entities of the document), which are generated by our semantic annotation system and stored in the index. It is noted that all the entities in both EQEV and DEV are grounded in the same hub languages such that they serve as the bridge to overcome the language barrier between keyword queries and documents. The semantic similarity between the EQEV and each DEV can be

[5]The language of the KB to be explored and thus the entities in QEGs grounded in can also be selected by users.
[6]http://km.aifb.kit.edu/sites/xlid-lexica/

(a) (b) (c)

Figure 2: Examples of QEGs for queries (a) *"WM Götze"*, (b) *"online companies of US NDX"* and (c) *"Google 百度"*.

calculated based on standard similarity measures, such as cosine similarity, which is then used for *document ranking*.

4. DEMONSTRATION

In this section, we demonstrate four major features of XKnowSearch!. A screencast of the demonstration is available at http://km.aifb.kit.edu/sites/XKnowSearch and the online prototype of XKnowSearch! can be accessed at http://km.aifb.kit.edu/services/XKnowSearch.

Query Flexibility. XKnowSearch! supports two search modes: *direct search* and *indirect search*. The direct search mode takes a keyword query and retrieves the relevant documents directly without user involvement in the search process. The indirect search mode provides the opportunity for users to understand the meaning of the query entities and the underlying semantic relations between them yielded by query interpretation, such that users are able to refine and extend the information needs. While the direct search enables users to search in a familiar and convenient manner, the indirect search provides users a *more flexible way* to influence the search process according to their search intents.

Query Disambiguation. Query disambiguation can be performed both automatically and manually. On the one hand, XKnowSearch! *automatically eliminates the ambiguity* of keyword queries by taking advantage of the context, i.e., all candidate query entities, and exploiting the semantic graph of the KB to generate the top-k QEGs. On the other hand, users can also *disambiguate the query manually* by selecting the most appropriate QEG and further refining it. As query interpretations, QEGs are more informative and expressive than keywords such that users can obtain information about not only entities but also relations between them. Consider the keyword query "*WM Götze*", where we assume that the input languages of the keywords are unknown. As shown in Fig. 2 (a), the keyword "*WM*", which could refer to the entity Windows_Mobile in English and FIFA_World_Cup in German[7], has been disambiguated as FIFA_World_Cup based on the relation to Mario_Götze referred to by "*Götze*".

Query Expansion. XKnowSearch! supports keyword search using keywords that match either entities or concepts in their *incomplete* forms, such as aliases, acronyms and misspellings instead of the full names. In addition, the matching concept is automatically expanded into a set of individual entities. Given the keyword query "*online companies of US NDX*" and the top-ranked QEG shown in Fig. 2 (b), it is observed that the alias "*online companies of US*" referring to the concept Internet_companies_of_the_United_States has been resolved to the entity Google, which is listed in NASDAQ-100 referred to by the acronym "*NDX*". Besides

[7]*WM* is the abbreviation of *Weltmeisterschaft* in German, which means *World Cup*.

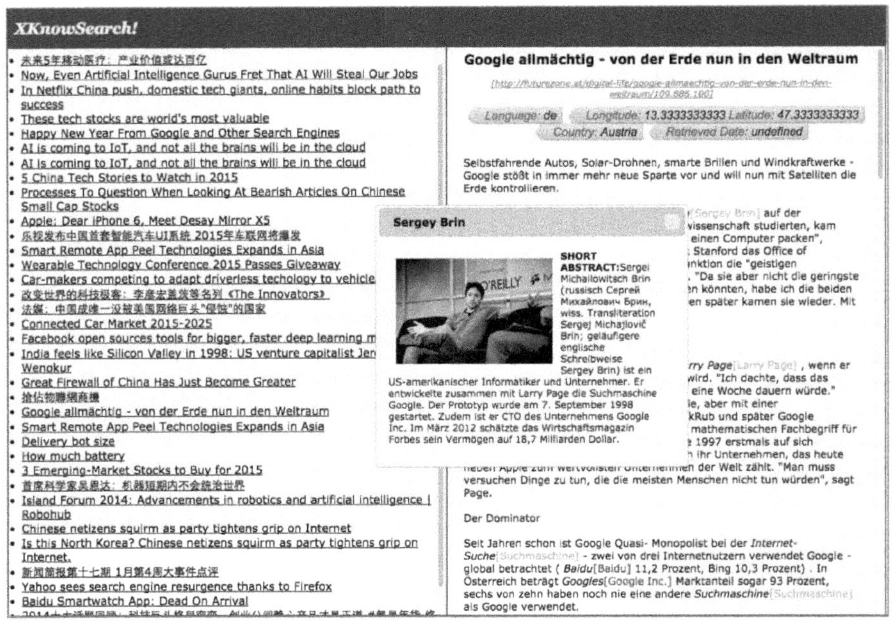

Figure 3: Examples of the retrieved news articles in different languages for *"Google 百度"* and a selected German article.

the role as query interpretation, the resulting QEGs can help users to *manually expand* the query by navigating the KB through entity relations and adding more intended entities that are then used for document retrieval.

Cross-lingual Search. XKnowSearch! enables cross-lingual search in the sense that users can use keyword queries in any language (even in multiple languages) to retrieve multilingual documents, especially in any other languages. The recent progress in cross-lingual technologies is largely due to the increased availability of multilingual data sources on the Web. In this regard, we exploit entities in DBpedia, a multilingual KB, which serve as an interlingua to connect keyword queries and documents across languages. Fig. 2 (c) shows one example of the QEGs generated by our system for the multilingual keyword query "*Google 百度*". Based on that, Fig. 3 illustrates some examples of the retrieved news articles in different languages, where both the query entities (e.g., Google_Inc.) and the additional related entities (e.g., Sergey_Brin), which affect document ranking, are highlighted and linkable to the corresponding resources in the KB.

5. CONCLUSIONS

In this paper, we present XKnowSearch!, a novel entity-based system for multilingual and cross-lingual IR, with the goal of addressing the challenges that traditional keyword search systems mainly suffer from. By leveraging the multilingual KB, namely DBpedia, keyword queries and documents in different languages can be captured on the semantic level to avoid the ambiguity of terms and to bridge the language barriers between queries and documents, where user interaction can also be involved to influence the search process according to the search intents of users.

We believe that this work could complement the term-based document retrieval models and open up new research directions on cross-lingual and entity-based IR. Firstly, it would be interesting to further explore the possibilities of cross-lingual search with the recent initiatives like Wikidata, which tried to make the knowledge bases less language dependent to allow cross-lingual or language independent knowledge access. Secondly, it would be beneficial to query interpretation by also taking into account entity relations expressed in the queries to construct the QEGs. Finally, predicting what type of queries can benefit from the entity-based approach and combining both term-based and entity-based approaches would be a promising direction to pursue.

Acknowledgments.

The research leading to these results has received funding from the European Union Seventh Framework Programme (FP7/2007-2013) under grant agreement no. 611346.

6. REFERENCES

[1] C. Bizer, T. Heath, and T. Berners-Lee. Linked Data - The Story So Far. *Int. J. Semantic Web Inf. Syst.*, 5(3):1–22, 2009.

[2] M. Färber, L. Zhang, and A. Rettinger. Kuphi - an investigation tool for searching for and via semantic relations. In *ESWC*, pages 349–354, 2014.

[3] J. Hoffart, D. Milchevski, and G. Weikum. STICS: searching with strings, things, and cats. In *SIGIR*, pages 1247–1248, 2014.

[4] X. Liu, P. Yang, and H. Fang. Entexpo: An interactive search system for entity-bearing queries. In *ECIR*, pages 784–788, 2014.

[5] P. N. Mendes, M. Jakob, and C. Bizer. DBpedia: A Multilingual Cross-domain Knowledge Base. In *LREC*, pages 1813–1817, 2012.

[6] J. Pound, P. Mika, and H. Zaragoza. Ad-hoc object retrieval in the web of data. In *WWW*, pages 771–780, 2010.

[7] L. Zhang, M. Färber, and A. Rettinger. xlid-lexica: Cross-lingual linked data lexica. In *LREC*, pages 2101–2105, 2014.

[8] L. Zhang and A. Rettinger. X-lisa: Cross-lingual semantic annotation. *PVLDB*, 7(13):1693–1696, 2014.

[9] L. Zhang, A. Rettinger, and J. Zhang. A knowledge base approach to cross-lingual keyword query interpretation. In *ISWC*, 2016.

TweetSift: Tweet Topic Classification Based on Entity Knowledge Base and Topic Enhanced Word Embedding

Quanzhi Li, Sameena Shah, Xiaomo Liu, Armineh Nourbakhsh, Rui Fang
Research and Development
Thomson Reuters
3 Times Square, NYC, NY 10036
{quanzhi.li, sameena.shah, xiaomo.liu, armineh.nourbakhsh, rui.fang}@thomsonreuters.com

ABSTRACT

Classifying tweets into topic categories is necessary and important for many applications, since tweets are about a variety of topics and users are only interested in certain topical areas. Many tweet classification approaches fail to achieve high accuracy due to data sparseness issue. Tweet, as a special type of short text, in additional to its text, also has other metadata that can be used to enrich its context, such as user name, mention, hashtag and embedded link. In this demonstration, we present TweetSift, an efficient and effective real time tweet topic classifier. TweetSift exploits external tweet-specific entity knowledge to provide more topical context for a tweet, and integrates them with topic enhanced word embeddings for topic classification. The demonstration will show how TweetSift works and how it is incorporated with our social media event detection system.

Keywords

Tweet topic classification; entity knowledge base; topic enhanced word embedding; twitter

1. INTRODUCTION

Different tweets may talk about different topics. Users and applications are usually only interested in tweets belonging to certain types of topics. Therefore, identifying exactly which tweet is about which topic is important and necessary. Classifying tweets poses a set of new challenges, because they are short, noisy, and less topic-focused. They do not provide enough shared context necessary for most content similarity measures.

Previous studies have attempted to overcome the data sparseness problem by exploiting external knowledge. One option is to use search engines to enrich or expand the data context [5, 11, 13]. Another option is to use the embedded URL to get the linked web pages [12], and use them to enrich the tweet data. Some studies have also tried to utilize social network structure to obtain more information [9]. All these methods have long latency, and are not suitable for real-time applications. Using concepts and categories defined in online repositories, such as Wikipedia, is another way to expand the context of short text. However, this approach only exploits the concepts in tweets and its performance is not satisfactory [1].

CIKM'16 , October 24-28, 2016, Indianapolis, IN, USA
ACM 978-1-4503-4073-1/16/10.
http://dx.doi.org/10.1145/2983323.2983325

In addition to its text, a tweet also provides a set of metadata that we can use to enrich its topical context. For example, there are mentions, URLs, hashtags, named entities, user handle, user name, and profile description. TweetSift makes use of these data by trying to find complete or partial matches between these entities and entries in an entity knowledge base (Entity KB) built from knowledge sources specific for social media. The Entity KB contains popular entities, such as sports stars, popular Twitter handles and their corresponding domains. Compared to previous studies utilizing online repositories, this KB provides more data types, and is specifically for social media. And it is easier to build.

Another challenge for text categorization is the word mismatch problem. This problem is more serious for short text, due to its limited context. This issue can be solved partially by using word embedding instead of the traditional bag of words. A word embedding is a dense, low-dimensional and real-valued vector for a word. The embeddings of a word capture both the syntactic and semantics of the word. Traditional bag-of-words and bag-of-n-grams hardly capture the semantics of words, or the distances between words. The embeddings help learning algorithms achieve better performance in NLP tasks by grouping similar words together, and have been used in many applications. However, most word embedding models assume only one vector for each word, which ignores polysemy and therefore may affect the performance of applications. In order to enhance discriminativeness, one approach is to exploit latent topic models to assign topics for each word, and learn topic enhanced word embeddings (TEWE) based on both words and their topics. The basic idea is that we allow each word to have different embeddings under different latent topics.

These two types of information, Entity KB and TEWE, complement each other to some degree. TweetSift classifies tweets by integrating features generated from both of them. In this demonstration, we will show how TweetSift works.

2. RELATED STUDIES

Word embedding and their variations have been researched in previous studies [2, 8, 6, 7]. C&W model [2] and word2vec [8] are two popular ones. TEWE is an extension of word2vec with topic information incorporated.

Many learning algorithms, such as Rocchio classifier, SVM, KNN, naive Bayes, and maximum entropy, have been used in lots of text classification problems, and achieved good results. But usually those texts are long enough for a classifier to generate features. Several studies have attempted to overcome the short text data sparseness problem by exploiting external knowledge [5, 11, 13, 12, 9], but they are not suitable for real-time applications. Many topic modeling studies on tweet topic analysis are based on LDA related technologies, such as [3, 4]. These approaches are effective in clustering documents into a predefined number of clusters, but cannot be directly used in our case, in which there is a list of pre-defined topic categories. But we can generate LDA topics for tweets and uses them as features to do classification, which is one of the baseline methods in our experiment.

3. TweetSift: INCORPORATING TEWE and ENTITY KB

Table 1 presents the 11 topics used in TweetSift. These topics are defined by journalists and they reflect the requirements of users from our real-time tweet event detection system. Although the experiments were conducted on these topics, we believe that the approach used in TweetSift may be applied, directly or with some adjustment, to other applications with different topics.

Figure 1 shows the overall workflow for Entity KB & TEWE generation and the TweetSift classifier build process. Figure 2 shows the workflow of classifying tweets by TweetSift. The following sections describe more details about TEWE, Entity KB, and the classifier training and evaluation process.

Table 1. Topics used in TweetSift

Topics	BUSINESS/FINANCE, TECHNOLOGY/SCIENCE, POLITICS, SPORTS, ENTERTAINMENT, HEALTH/MEDICAL, CRISIS (WAR/DISASTER), WEATHER, LAW/CRIME, LIFE/SOCIETY, OTHER

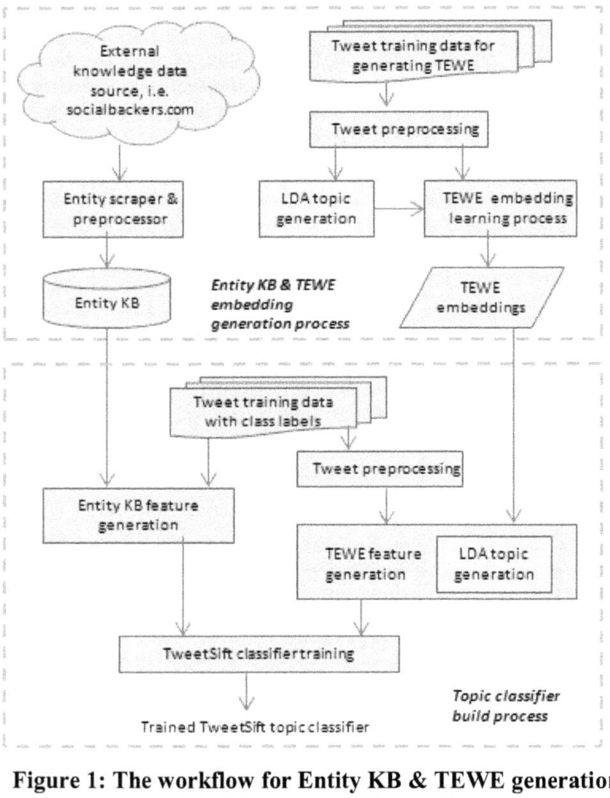

Figure 1: The workflow for Entity KB & TEWE generation and building TweetSift classifier

3.1 Topic Enhanced Word Embedding

TEWE tries to exploit latent topic models to assign topics for each word, and learn topic enhanced word embeddings based on both words and their topics, so that the same word in different contexts with different meanings will have different embeddings.

To generate TEWE embeddings for TweetSift, a multi-thread version of LDA and Gibbs sampling are used to iteratively assign latent topics for each word. After all, each word w_i will be discriminated into a specific topic t_i, forming a word-topic pair (w_i, t_i), which can be used to learn TEWE embeddings. The Skip-Gram word embedding model [8, 7] is extended to implement the TEWE model. For each target word w_i with its topic t_i, the objective is to maximize the following average log probability:

$$L(D) = \frac{1}{M}\sum_{i=1}^{M} \sum_{-k\leq c\leq k, c\neq 0} \log \Pr(w_{i+c} \mid w_i) + \log \Pr(w_{i+c} \mid t_i)$$

where M is the number of words and k is the context size of the target word. Compared to only using the target word w_i to predict context words in Skip-Gram, TEWE also uses the topic t_i of target word to predict the context words. Here we consider each topic as a pseudo word that occurs in all the positions of words assigned with this topic. The topic vector will represent the collective semantics of words under this topic. In the training process, the general word embeddings are first learned using Skip-Gram. Then, each topic vector is initialized with the average over all words assigned to this topic, and topic embeddings are learned while the word embeddings keep unchanged. A word's TEWE embedding is the concatenation of its word embedding and topic embedding.

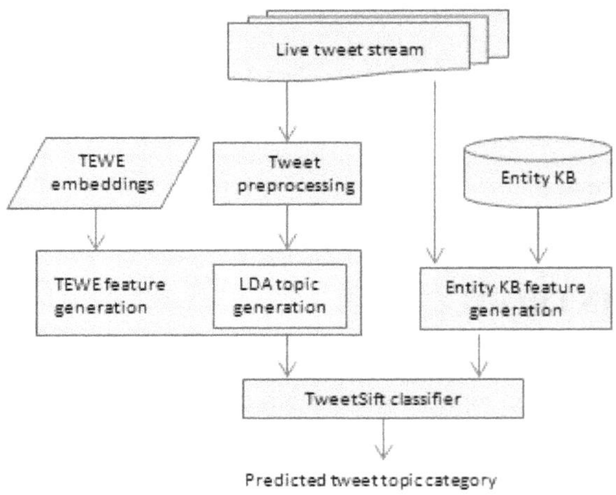

Figure 2: TweetSift topic prediction workflow

The training tweets are collected from Twitter's 1% public streaming API and Decahose data (10% of Twitter's streaming data). Only English tweets are not used. Totally, there are about 500 million tweets, and 7.5 billion words.

Tweet preprocessing: Each tweet used in the training process is preprocessed to get a clean version by the following steps:

- All URLs are removed
- All mentions are removed
- Dates and years are converted to two symbols
- All numbers are normalized to a special symbol
- All special characters, except #, are removed

Stop words are not removed for building embedding model, since they provide important context in which other words are used.

Model setting: for generating embeddings, the term frequency threshold is set as 8 (tokens less than 8 occurrences in the training data set are discarded). The number of topics is set as 200. Both the word embedding size and topic embedding size are 300. So a TEWE embedding size is 600. These numbers are chosen based on our preliminary experiments.

Tweet representation: A tweet has multiple words, and its length varies. There are different ways to obtain tweet representation from word embeddings. We explored four types of convolutional layers: min, average (ave), max, and the concatenation of max, min and ave. Our experiment shows that the concatenation approach gives the best result, and so it is used in TweetSift.

3.2 Entity Knowledge Base

The Entity KB is created by automatically scraping social data provider websites, which is Socialbakers in this study (http://www.socialbakers.com/). One can increase the entity coverage by scraping more sources. Table 2 shows the number of entities. This KB contains three types of entities:

- Popular Twitter handles and their corresponding domains. For example, *ESPN*'s handle *@espn* and its domain, *Sports*. The domain may be one other than the 11 topic categories, e.g. the domain of *@cnn* is *Media*. Their relevance to the topic categories will be learned in the classifier training process, which is also true for the next two entity types.
- Popular entity names (named entities) and their domains. Entities include person, company, brand name and location.
- Important concepts and their domains, e.g. the concept *cancer* and its domain *Health*.

Table 2. Entity KB information

Entity Type	Count	Example
user handles	1,964	@espn – SPORTS, @FBI- LAW
named entities	1,930	Justin Bieber - ENTERTAINMENT
domain concepts	210	cancer – HEALTH

Features based on Entity KB are generated at two levels, tweet level and user level. On the tweet level, features are generated based on complete or partial matches between KB entities and mentions, URLs, hashtags, named entities in this tweet. On the user level, we examine user handle, user name and profile description.

3.3 TweetSift Classifier

Building classifier: TweetSift classifier integrates features generated from TEWE and Entity KB. These two types of information complement each other to some degree. For example, if the user handle of a tweet is @espn, or @espn is mentioned in this tweet, it is very possible that this tweet is about Sports. This type of information is not learned in the TEWE embeddings. 26,300 tweets were collected as training data. They were labeled by six domain experts, in terms of their topic category. Each tweet was labeled by two experts, and a third person decided its label if the two annotators disagreed. Finally we got 25, 964 tweets that at least two annotators agreed upon their labels. They were split into training, validation and test sets. We applied several classification algorithms, such as LibLinear, SMO, Random Forest and Logistic, to see which algorithm performs the best. SMO, a sequential minimal optimization algorithm for training a support vector classifier, performed the best and is the algorithm used in TweetSift.

Performance evaluation: we compare TweetSift classifier to three baselines: OpenCalais, the LDA approach, and the method using TEWE only. OpenCalais (http://www.opencalais.com/) uses a set of 16 topics to categorize text. Theses 16 categories are mapped to the 11 categories by journalists, so that we can directly compare its result to TweetSift. LDA has been used in previous studies for text classification, mainly for short text. It uses topics to represent a tweet. Another baseline method is the classifier using just TEWE without Entity KB. Figure 3 shows the results based on F-measure. It shows that TweetSift outperforms all the three baselines.

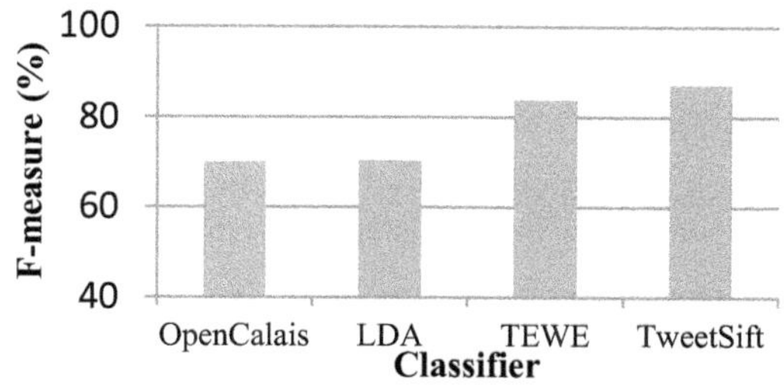

Figure 3. classifier performance

4. DEMONSTRATION

TweetSift can be used as a standalone tool, and also in applications that need classifying tweets into different topic categories. For example, our event detection system, Reuters' Tracer, uses TweetSift to classify tweets at real time. To make the demo more interesting, we demonstrate how TweetSift is used in the context of Tracer. In Tracer, TweetSift processes Twitter's public data stream at real time and classify them into one of the 11 topic domains. On average, each tweet is processed by TweetSift within 5 milliseconds. The appendix presents a screenshot to show how TweetSift works in Tracer.

REFERENCES

[1] S. Banerjee, K. Ramanathan, and A. Gupta. Clustering short texts using Wikipedia. *Proc. ACM SIGIR*, 2007.

[2] R. Collobert, J. Weston, L. Bottou, M. Karlen, K. Kavukcuoglu, and P. Kuksa. Natural language processing (almost) from scratch. *Journal of Machine Learning Research*, 2011

[3] Blei, D., Ng, A. and Jordan, M., Latent Dirichlet Allocation. *Journal of Machine Learning Research*, 3:993–1022, 2003

[4] Blei, D., Probabilistic topic models. *Communication of ACM*, 55(4):77-84, 2012

[5] Bollegala, D., Y. Matsuo, and M. Ishizuka, Measuring semantic similarity between words using Web search engines. *WWW* 2007

[6] P. Liu, X. Qiu and X. Huang, Learning Context-Sensitive Word Embeddings with Neural Tensor Skip-Gram Model, *IJCAI 2015*

[7] Y. Liu, Z. Liu, T. Chua and M. Sun, Topical Word Embeddings, *AAAI 2015*

[8] Mikolov, T.; Chen, K.; Corrado, G. and Dean J., Efficient Estimation of Word Representations in Vector Space. *Workshop at ICLR, 2013*

[9] A. Pal nad S. Counts, Identifying Topical Authorities in Microblogs, *WSDM 2011*

[10] Owoputi, O.; Connor, B.; Dyer, C., Gimpel, K., Schneider, N., and Smith, N., Improved part-of-speech tagging for online conversational text with word clusters. *NAACL 2013*.

[11] Sahami, M. & Heilman. T., A Web based kernel function for measuring the similarity of short text snippets. *WWW* 2006.

[12] Yang, S., Kolcz, A., Schlaikjer, A., and Gupta, P., Large-scale high-precision topic modeling on Twitter, *KDD 2014*

[13] W. Yih and C. Meek. Improving similarity measures for short segments of text. *AAAI 2007*

Appendix. Screenshot of how TweetSift is used in our event detection system, Reuters Tracer

- Tracer is a real time news event detection system that is based on Twitter's public data stream.
- Tracer has multiple subsystems (components), and TweetSift is one of them. Here we focus only on TweetSift, not other components, such as grouping tweets into clusters.
- For an incoming tweet, TweetSift classify it into one of the 11 topics at real time. All information displayed in the UI is updated dynamically at real time.
- Users can setup multiple channels, which are shown as separate panels in the screenshot.
- There are three channels (panels) in this screenshot. The one on the left displays tweets/events from all the 11 topics. The one at the center shows the Topic dropdown list, and users can choose a topic to see tweets classified into that category. The one on the right is an example for Health/Medical category.
- The Topic dropdown list is marked with RED ellipse
- Each event/cluster, consisting of multiple similar tweets, has a topic type identified by TweetSift (marked with BLUE ellipse).
- The number in the green small circle (e.g., 3 and 9) is the amount of tweets similar to the displayed one. They form a cluster. Users can click on it to see all the tweets in that cluster.

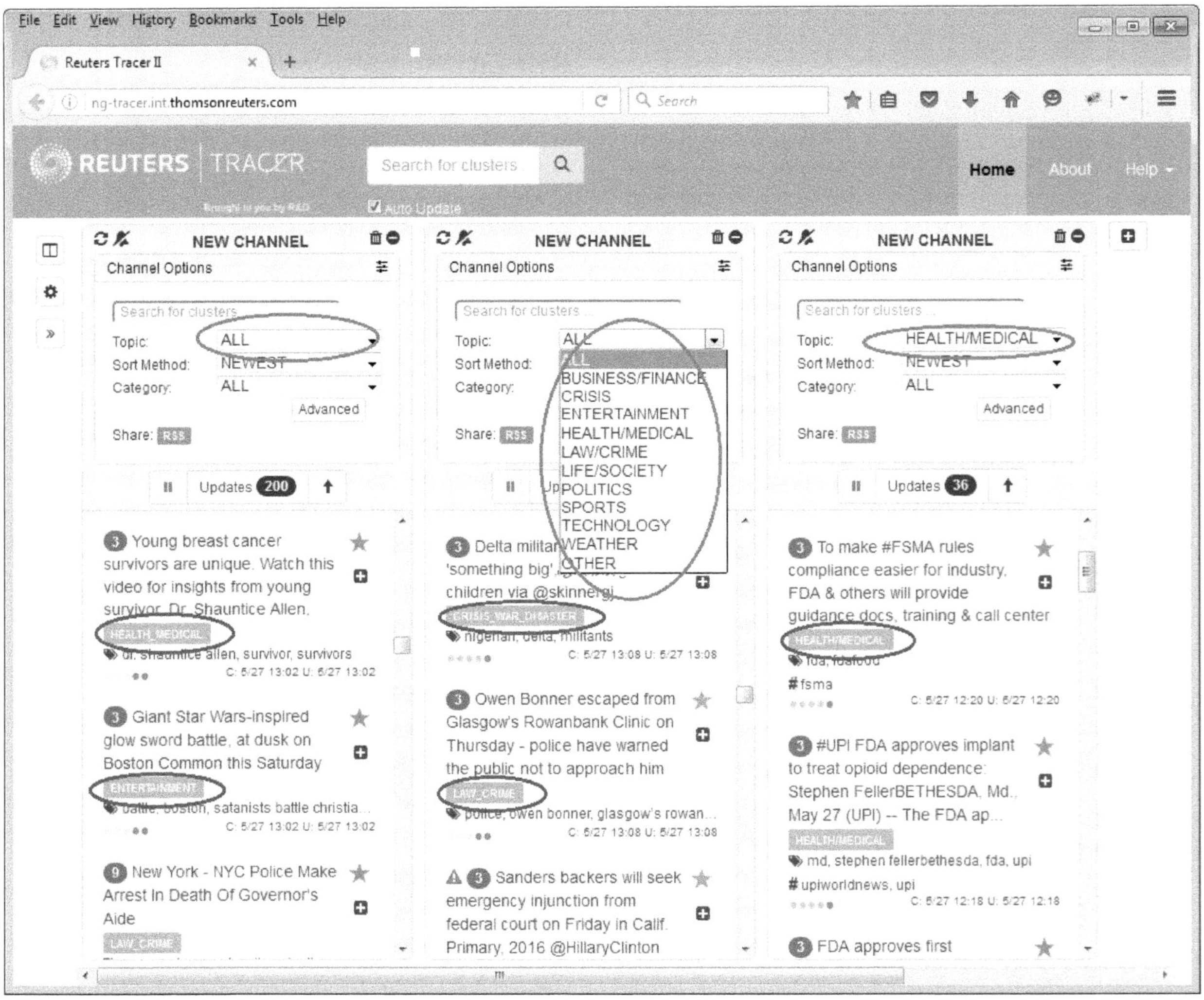

PARC: Privacy-Aware Data Cleaning

Dejun Huang, Dhruv Gairola, Yu Huang, Zheng Zheng, Fei Chiang
Department of Computing and Software
McMaster University
{huangd27, gairold, huang223, zhengz13, fchiang}@mcmaster.ca

ABSTRACT

Poor data quality has become a persistent challenge for organizations as data continues to grow in complexity and size. Existing data cleaning solutions focus on identifying repairs to the data to minimize either a cost function or the number of updates. These techniques, however, fail to consider underlying data privacy requirements that exist in many real data sets containing sensitive and personal information. In this demonstration, we present PARC, a Privacy-AwaRe data Cleaning system that corrects data inconsistencies w.r.t. a set of FDs, and limits the disclosure of sensitive values during the cleaning process. The system core contains modules that evaluate three key metrics during the repair search, and solves a multi-objective optimization problem to identify repairs that balance the privacy vs. utility tradeoff. This demonstration will enable users to understand: (1) the characteristics of a privacy-preserving data repair; (2) how to customize data cleaning and data privacy requirements using two real datasets; and (3) the distinctions among the repair recommendations via visualization summaries.

Categories and Subject Descriptors

H.4 [**Information Systems**]: Data cleaning

Keywords

data quality; constraint based cleaning; information disclosure

1. INTRODUCTION

As data continues to grow in complexity and size, data cleaning has become essential to achieve consistent and accurate information. Real data often contains erroneous, duplicated and missing values. Recent studies have reported that by 2017, 33% of the largest global companies will experience a data quality crisis due to their inability to trust and govern their enterprise information [8].

In constraint based data cleaning, data dependencies are used to specify data quality requirements. Data that is inconsistent with respect to the dependencies are identified as erroneous. Recent work has focused on identifying updates to the data (also referred to as *repairs*) that correct these inconsistencies by minimizing either the cost or the number of repairs [4, 9], identifying the most necessary repairs [3], or by interactively soliciting user feedback [10]. Extensions have included techniques that consider master data, and assuming portions of the data are trusted and immutable [7, 4].

All these techniques recommend data repairs that re-align the data as closely as possible with the constraints, and assume that all data values are fully accessible with no privacy nor confidentiality limitations. That is, to correct the data inconsistencies, a repair algorithm searches for a set of candidate repairs. During the evaluation of candidate repairs, all attribute values are assumed to be accessible to all data cleaning participants, and can be disclosed to a user without penalty. However, this underlying assumption does not hold in all data cleaning situations. Organizations often have proprietary data that contain varying degrees of sensitivity where particular attributes have more stringent privacy requirements than other attributes. Consider two examples. First, a medical database containing patient records describing name, illness, and drug treatments would be considered more sensitive than the city where the patient lives. Secondly, an organization (with dirty data values) needs to coordinate with a trusted master data source to clean its data accurately. Consider the example below.

Table 1: Master data: hospital patient records.

ID	Illness	Symptom	Drug	Age	Dosage
m1	flu	sneezing	Benadryl	[12, 30]	20 mg
m2	cold	sore throat	Diphen	[0, 6]	6 mg
m3	cold	runny nose	Banophen	[12, 30]	40 mg
m4	cold	sore throat	Diphen	[12, 30]	25 mg
m5	cold	sore throat	Diphen	[55, 70]	35 mg
m6	insomnia	can't sleep	Ambien	[30, 60]	5 mg

Table 2: Target data: pharmacy patient records.

ID	Illness	Symptom	Drug	Age	Dosage
t1	flu	sneezing	Benadryl	[30, 60]	30 mg
t2	cold	sore throat	Diphen	[12, 30]	25 mg
t3	cold	sore throat	Banophen	[12, 30]	40 mg
t4	cold	sore throat	Diphen	[12, 30]	15 mg

EXAMPLE 1. *Tables 1 and 2 show patient medical records from a hospital, and a local pharmacy database, respectively. Consider two functional dependencies:* F_1*: [Illness, Symptom]* $\rightarrow$ *[Drug], and* F_2*: [Drug, Age]* $\rightarrow$ *[Dosage]. We observe that in Table 2, records* $t_2 - t_4$ *violate* F_1*, and* t_2 *and* t_4 *violate* F_2*. If the pharmacy wishes to clean its data (Table 2), consulting with a trusted, master data source (such as Table 1) will ensure that the values are correct and accurate. However, in this case, the hospital is unlikely*

CIKM'16 October 24 - October 28, 2016, Indianapolis, IN, USA

ACM ISBN 978-1-4503-4073-1/16/10...$15.00

DOI: http://dx.doi.org/10.1145/2983323.2983326

to disclose all its sensitive patient medical records to the pharmacy. Under these circumstances, a data cleaning protocol must be developed to allow the local pharmacy and the hospital to exchange information that allows the pharmacy to correct its data errors while minimizing the amount of information the hospital must disclose.

We consider a protocol that first involves matching records from the master data source against records in the target data source that satisfy a minimum similarity threshold τ. For F_1 and $\tau = 0.6$, we have two potential matches: (i) records $t_2 - t_4$ match m_2, m_4, m_5, and we update t_3[Drug] to 'Diphen'; (ii) t_3 matches m_3, and we update t_3[Symptom] to 'runny nose'. If our objective is to minimize the number of updates to the data, then selecting either repair option (both involve a single update to t_3) would suffice.

However, we observe that repair option (i) resolves the inconsistency w.r.t. F_1 but introduces a further inconsistency in t_3 (in addition to records t_2, t_4) w.r.t. F_2. In option (ii), we resolve all errors w.r.t. F_1 and do not introduce further errors. However, if the hospital considers particular attributes, such as 'Symptom', as more sensitive, then revealing this information will be undesirable. This can lead us to select option (i) as the preferred repair choice.

In option (i), revealing 'Drug' details may lead to inadvertent disclosure of other attribute values. For example, a patient's drug prescription(s) provides information on their symptoms and illness. The decision of selecting the best repair to correct the errors requires an analysis that captures all these requirements and must consider the tradeoff among minimizing the number of changes to the data, data disclosure limitations, and maximizing data utility.

Key Techniques. Existing data cleaning solutions assume that the data values are fully viewable to all parties with equal information disclosure. In this demo, we showcase *PARC*, a Privacy AwaRe data Cleaning system that removes this assumption to consider data privacy requirements. The system cleans a target dataset by referring to a (trusted) master data source. While existing repair algorithms have focused on minimizing the number or necessary changes to the data, PARC considers the additional parameter of *information disclosure*. Not all values in the master data source contain an equal amount of information, and restrictions may exist to limit the disclosure of particular values. PARC aims to disclose values with the smallest information content. Furthermore, revealing a value v can indirectly reveal information about a related value u. We provide a privacy parameter that considers this dependency among data values. Users can specify how much data disclosure is permitted, ranging from full to minimal disclosure, and can customize their privacy settings to application requirements. Existing systems do not provide this option during the data cleaning process.

Our declarative approach uses functional dependencies (FDs) to define the conditions that both the target and master data must satisfy. We assume all parties are semi-honest. A record matching between the target and master data records is performed to generate a space of possible repairs. Our repair algorithm aims to find the repairs that optimize the conflicting requirements of minimizing the number of repairs, maximizing data utility (i.e., minimizing the number of errors), and minimizing the amount of information disclosed by the master.

Demonstration Objectives. Demonstration participants will have the opportunity to explore and compare different repair solutions from four different optimization functions. Beginning with a few sample datasets, we will show users how to first specify their requirements to balance the tradeoff between minimizing information disclosure and maximizing data utility. We will compare the set of repairs produced by the optimizations functions by providing visualization summaries across three metrics. Our demonstration will help to answer questions such as:

- *How do I find the best repairs to clean a dirty dataset?*
- *How can a user customize their data privacy vs. data utility preferences?*
- *How does PARC identify the best repair(s)?*
- *How do the repair recommendations differ among the optimization functions? Are there guidelines of when to use a particular optimization function for a data cleaning task?*

2. SYSTEM ARCHITECTURE

Figure 1 illustrates the system architecture consisting of: an input *target* data source, *master* data source, and the *repair generation* engine. The system accepts a target dataset containing inconsistent records w.r.t. a set of FDs. After identifying the violating records, the target data source is cleaned by referring to records from the master dataset. We assume that the master data source aims to disclose as little information as possible, and we record the amount of information in each of the (master) data values. To start the cleaning process, the repair generation module first identifies master records that are similar to the inconsistent (target) records according to a given similarity threshold. A set of candidate repairs are generated based on these record matches, which are each evaluated by optimizing a set of three objective metrics. A configuration panel allows users to customize the relative weight of these metrics according to four possible objective functions. A final set of repair recommendations and visualizations summaries are provided to the user. In the following, we discuss each component in detail.

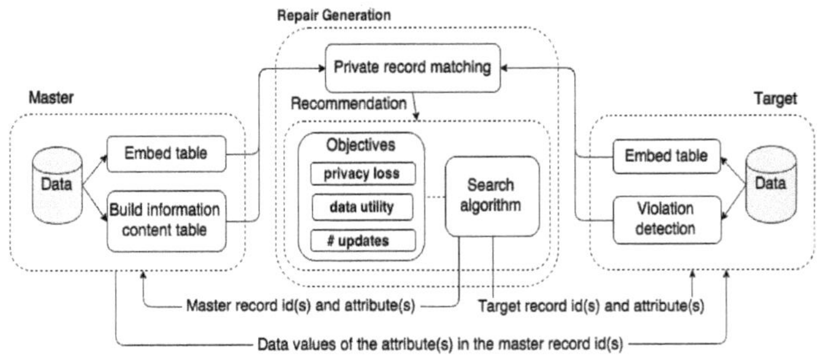

Figure 1: System Architecture

2.1 Target and Master Data Sources

2.1.1 Target

A user uploads the target dataset, T, and defines a set of FDs Σ over T. The *violation detection* module identifies all tuples $t \in T$ that are inconsistent w.r.t. Σ. The goal is to correct as many inconsistencies as possible with the help of a master data set.

2.1.2 Master

A user provides a clean master dataset, M, w.r.t. Σ. To clean T with the help of M, we assume that the data values between M and T are not fully shared and disclosed to both parties. Specifically, M aims to disclose as little information as possible to T (via the repair generation module). Hence, we build an information content table that tracks the amount of information in each value of M.

To ensure that information is conveyed securely between M and T, the repair generation module serves as a third-party. The three parties are assumed to be semi-honest, i.e., the parties follow the algorithm but may try to deduce additional information. Both M and T embed their respective datasets such that the repair generation module only works with embedded data. We apply the SparseMap method, which is a particular instance of Lipschitz embeddings [5].

2.2 Repair Generation

The repair generation module consists of three main components: *private record matching*, optimizing a set of *objective metrics*, and the *search algorithm.*

2.2.1 *Private Record Matching*

For each tuple $t \in T$ that is inconsistent w.r.t. Σ, we identify matching tuples in M that satisfy a similarity threshold. The record matching module performs the comparison using embedded vectors (each vector represents a tuple from M or T), and uses Euclidean distance to evaluate the distance between the two vectors. Since there can be more than one matching tuple $m \in M$ with t, there are multiple candidate repairs to correct the errors in t.

2.2.2 *Objective Metrics*

Each candidate repair is evaluated using three metrics: (i) privacy loss (pvt); (ii) data utility ($util$); and (iii) the number of updates to T (upd). Our goal is to minimize privacy loss, maximize data utility, and minimize the number of updates to T.

Privacy loss. Each time M discloses a value $v \in M$ to clean T, there is some privacy loss incurred with v. To quantify this loss, we apply a similar idea as Arenas et al. and use the concept of entropy to measure the information content of each cell in M [2]. We compute the information content by hypothesizing if we lose the value in a given cell, and then the value is restored (to either the original value or some other value). For example in Table 1, if we lose the value in m_5[Drug], the information content (gained) is zero if the value is restored, since we know from the other tuples w.r.t. F_1, the value should be 'Diphen'. We also consider the impact of disclosing v on other attribute values u, by computing the entropy $H(u) - H(u|v)$ (the amount of information revealed about u).

Data utility. We measure $util$ according to the degree of consistency that T satisfies Σ. We use an information-theoretic measure that quantifies the amount of uncertainty (entropy) for an $F \in \Sigma$, $F : X \rightarrow Y$, as $util = 1 - (H(X \cup Y) - H(X))$, where $H()$ is the entropy function [6]. When $util = 1$, T satisfies F.

Number of updates. We seek data repairs that are *cardinality minimal*, i.e., to correct the inconsistencies, we want to minimize the number of updates to T.

2.2.3 *Search Algorithm*

Given the space of possible repairs generated from the target-master record matching, PARC solves a multi-objective optimization problem that optimizes privacy loss, data utility and the number of data updates. PARC utilizes a simulated annealing approach to traverse the space of repairs, and provides four optimization functions that allow a user to specify relative weights among the metrics, and to configure thresholds to narrow the search.

3. DEMONSTRATION OVERVIEW

In this demonstration, we highlight PARC's features: (1) how to prepare the input datasets and define the FDs; (2) how users can customize the search and optimization parameters; (3) how visualization summaries provide a user with comparative views among the different repairs and optimization functions; and (4) how to interpret repair details to understand its impact on the data.

We use two real datasets: (1) the *medical trials* dataset contains over 60,000 worldwide clinical trials with 18 attributes describing patient illnesses, symptoms, outcomes, and medications [1]; and (2) the *consumer expenditures* data consists of 20 attributes describing consumer spending habits (e.g., address, occupation, methods of payment, purchase amounts, spending categories) from data.gov. PARC is available online at http://milford.cas.mcmaster.ca/parc/.

(1) User Customization. Users define the target and master datasets either via a new data upload or retrieving a saved version. Users define FDs to model attribute relationships representing industry regulations and domain specific rules (e.g., in the medical domain, qualifying symptoms and illnesses to prescribed medications). PARC allows users to customize the simulated annealing search parameters (e.g., temperature settings controlling the extensiveness of the search, how neighbours are visited), and the relative weights of the three objective metrics (Figure 2). The relative weights should sum to 1, where a higher weight indicates a greater influence (preference) during the multi-objective optimization.

(2) Visualization Summaries. Visualization summaries allow a user to compare the repair recommendations along the three objective metrics. Figure 3 displays normalized scores for each metric, for each recommended repair. The goal is to maximize data utility (maximum score of 1), minimize privacy loss, and the number of data updates. The repairs are sorted according to the user configured relative weights. Figure 4 shows the actual (raw) scores for each metric that provide a comparative analysis across the repairs. Participants will also be able to compare the repairs across four different optimization functions: weighted, constrained, dynamic, and hierarchical, and observe the influence of how the threshold values and relative weights, and evaluation order among the metrics, influence the final recommendation. We will provide guidelines advising when particular optimization functions are best applied.

(3) Detailed Repair Information. For each of the summary graphs, users can drill down to view the details of a repair (Figure 5). The updates are sorted in descending order according to the expected number of repaired tuples. For example, Figure 5 shows the first update to attribute 'drug_name', the dirty and recommended (clean) values, and 60 tuples will be corrected.

Summary. This demonstration showcases, PARC, a Privacy-AwaRe data Cleaning system, that (as far as we know) is the first to consider data privacy alongside data cleaning. We focus on limiting the amount of information disclosed by a master dataset towards achieving consistency in a target dataset with a minimal number of updates. This demo highlights how a user can interact with PARC to: configure the system to achieve desired cleaning objectives, compare repair solutions using the visualization summaries, and drill down to identify the most relevant repairs.

4. REFERENCES

[1] Linkedct database: linkedct.org.

[2] M. Arenas and L. Libkin. Information-theoretic approach to normal forms for relational and xml data. *J. ACM*, 52(2):246–283, 2005.

[3] G. Beskales, I. F. Ilyas, and L. Golab. Sampling the repairs of functional dependency violations under hard constraints. In *PVLDB*, pages 197–207, 2010.

[4] G. Beskales, I. F. Ilyas, L. Golab, and A. Galiullin. On the relative trust between inconsistent data and inaccurate constraints. In *ICDE*, pages 541–552, 2013.

[5] J. Bourgain. On lipschitz embedding of finite metric spaces in hilbert space. *Israel Journal of Mathematics*, 52(1-2):46–52, 1985.

[6] M. Dalkilic and E. Robertson. Information dependencies. *PODS*, pages 245–253, 2000.

[7] W. Fan, J. Li, S. Ma, N. Tang, and W. Yu. Towards certain fixes with editing rules and master data. *PVLDB*, 3(1):173–184, 2010.

[8] S. Judah and T. Friedman. Twelve ways to improve your data quality. *Gartner Research Report*, 2014.

[9] M. Volkovs, F. Chiang, J. Szchilta, and R. J. Miller. Continuous data cleaning. In *ICDE*, pages 244–255, 2014.

[10] M. Yakout, A. K. Elmagarmid, J. Neville, M. Ouzzani, and I. F. Ilyas. Guided data repair. *PVLDB*, 4(5):279–289, 2011.

APPENDIX

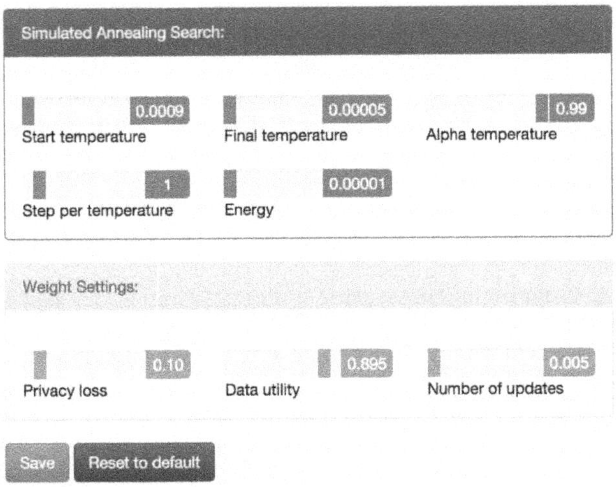

Figure 2: Parameter configuration

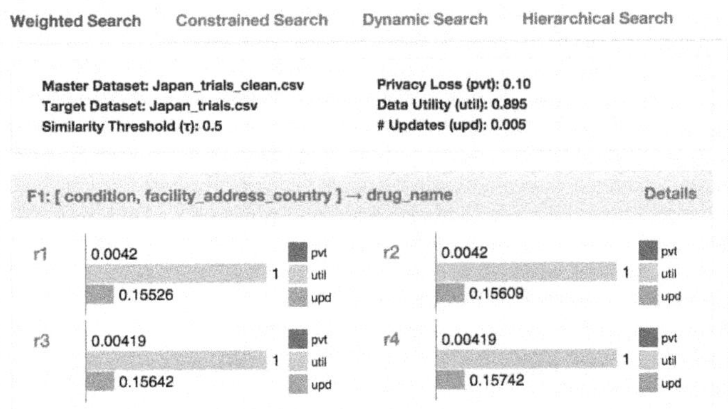

Figure 3: Recommended repairs

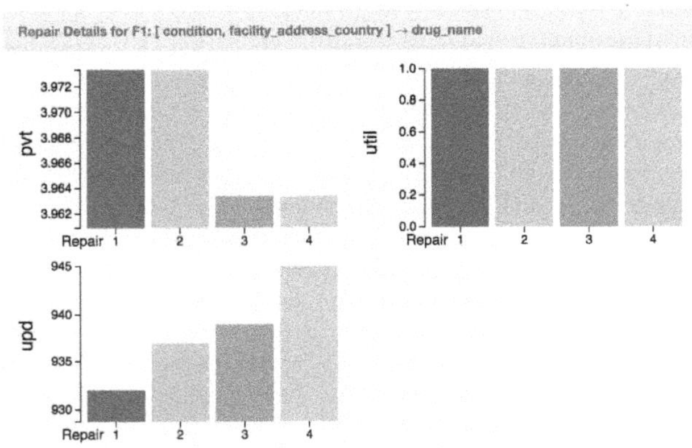

Figure 4: Actual scores across the repair recommendations.

Repair Details for r1 F1: [condition, facility_address_country] → drug_name

Attribute	Original Value	Recommended Value	# Repaired Records
drug_name	Cetuximab	Letrozole	60
condition	Rheumatoid Arthritis	Crohn's Disease	59
condition	Breast Neoplasms	Prostatic Neoplasms	46
condition	Prostate Cancer	Duodenal Cancer	43

Figure 5: Attribute updates belonging to a repair.

Ease the Process of Machine Learning with Dataflow

Tianyou Guo, Jun Xu,* Xiaohui Yan,† Jianpeng Hou,
Ping Li, Zhaohui Li, Jiafeng Guo, Xueqi Cheng
CAS Key Lab of Network Data Science and Technology, Institute of Computing Technology,
Chinese Academy of Sciences
{guotianyou, houjianpeng, liping, lizhaohui}@software.ict.ac.cn,
{junxu, yanxiaohui, guojiafeng, cxq}@ict.ac.cn

ABSTRACT

Machine learning algorithms have become the key components in many big data applications. However, the full potential of machine learning is still far from been realized because using machine learning algorithms is hard, especially on distributed platforms such as Hadoop and Spark [8]. The key barriers come from not only the implementation of the algorithms themselves, but also the processing for applying them to real applications which often involve multiple steps and different algorithms. In this demo we present a general-purpose dataflow-based system for easing the process of applying machine learning algorithms to real world tasks. In the system, a learning task is formulated as a directed acyclic graph (DAG) in which each node represents an operation (e.g., a machine learning algorithm), and each edge represents the flow of the data from one node to its descendants. Graphical user interface is implemented for making users to create, configure, submit, and monitor a task in a drag-and-drop manner. Advantages of the system include 1) lowering the barriers of defining and executing machine learning tasks; 2) sharing and re-using the implementations of the algorithms, the task dataflow DAGs, and the (intermediate) experimental results; 3) seamlessly integrating the stand-alone algorithms as well as the distributed algorithms in one task. The system has been deployed as a machine learning service and can be access from the Internet.

Keywords

Machine learning process; dataflow; directed acyclic graph

1. INTRODUCTION

Machine learning has become the core of many big data applications such as information retrieval, question answering, and recommender system etc. To fulfill the increasing requirements on machine learning algorithms, a number of scalable machine learning libraries, including Apache Mahout [3] and Spark MLlib [4], have been developed and widely used. Despite the widespread impacts of the machine learning libraries, it is still difficult for ordinary users to use the machine learning in their applications. The barrier mainly comes from the complex process of using machine learning algorithms to solve a real-world task. A machine learning task usually consists of multiple steps including data preparation, feature extraction, model training, testing, and performance evaluation etc. The process could become more complicated if multiple learning algorithms and datasets are involved. For example, the user may want to use the topics as features in the task of document categorization. Thus, the process need to first train a topic model based on some dataset, and then feed the learned topics to a classification model. It has been widely recognized that constructing an appropriate process is crucial for the success of applying machine learning to real world application. Therefore, a platform that can help to ease the machine learning process will be of great help to users.

In this demo, we present a general-purpose machine learning system for lowering the barrier to applying machine learning algorithms. In the system, we consider the process of applying machine learning algorithms from the viewpoint of dataflow. Thus, the process can be formulated as a directed acyclic graph (DAG) in which the source data flow into the root nodes. Each node makes operations on the data, generates new data, and sends the generated data to its descendant nodes for conducting further operations. Finally, the results flow out from the leaf nodes.

The system consists of three major components: 1) A distributed machine learning library which implements popular machine learning algorithms as well as the algorithms for data pre/post-processing, format transformation, feature generation, performance evaluation etc. 2) A GUI-based machine learning studio which enable users to create, configure, submit, monitor, and share their machine learning process in a drag-and-drop manner. The algorithms in the machine learning library can be accessed in the studio. 3) A cloud service for executing the tasks. We build the service based on the open source big data platform of Hadoop and Spark. After receiving a task DAG from the GUI, each node will be automatically scheduled to run when all of its dependent data sources are ready.

The system offers several distinct advantages for applying machine learning to real tasks: 1) The dataflow formulation of machine learning tasks is quite intuitive and easy to understand. The GUI hides the unnecessary technical

*Corresponding author: Jun Xu
†Current affiliation: DiDi Research, Beijing

CIKM'16 October 24-28, 2016, Indianapolis, IN, USA

ACM ISBN 978-1-4503-4073-1/16/10.

DOI: http://dx.doi.org/10.1145/2983323.2983327

details of the algorithms (e.g., the complex command line) and helps user to focus on building the task process; 2) Users can upload and share their own data, algorithms, and tasks to other users; 3) It has the ability to use the stand-alone, Spark, and Map-Reduce algorithms in one DAG.

Several similar systems have been developed and released in enterprise and open source community. Mahout [3] and MLlib [4] are two distributed machine learning libraries developed with Hadoop Map-Reduce and Spark, respectively. A number of popular machine learning algorithms have been implemented in the libraries. To make these algorithms working together, people considers the application of machine learning as a workflow and several workflow schedulers have been developed, including the open source systems of Oozie [7], HUE [1], and Azkaban [2] etc. However, compare with the dataflow, the workflow cannot specify data dependencies between nodes, which increases the complexity of configuration. Microsoft has released Azure machine learning [5] in which a machine learning process is formalized as a dataflow.

2. MACHINE LEARNING PROCESS AS A DATAFLOW DAG

A typical application of the machine learning algorithms consists of several steps include gathering and preprocessing the data, extracting features, applying the training algorithm, and testing the performances of the trained model. From the viewpoint of data, the whole process can be viewed as the raw data flow into the processing pipeline. After a number of step-by-step operations on the data, the result data flow out the pipeline. The process could be more complex if multiple machine learning algorithms are involved.

Our system formulates the complex process of applying machine learning algorithms as a DAG of dataflow in which the data flow in the graph according to the directed edges. The data will be processed by the nodes it flows through. Each node consists of several input ports, output ports, and an operation. Each input port corresponds to an flow in data file and each output port corresponds to a data file that flows out. The operation is a (stand-alone or distributed) program that reads the input ports and writes the results to output ports. In our system, the operation of each node is implemented as a command line. A dataflow DAG may also contain some data nodes which represent the input data sources. Please note that a data node only have one output port. Figure 1 shows a typical dataflow DAG of applying logistic regression for identifying the SMS spam. Different colors are used to show the different status of the nodes: green for success, yellow for under executing, gray for waiting, and red for failed.

3. SYSTEM OVERVIEW

Figure 2 shows the architecture of the our system. The whole system consists of three parts: big data infrastructure for providing the foundation services, machine learning library for providing the core building blocks of the machine learning tasks, and machine learning studio for providing user-friendly GUI to lower the barrier of using machine learning.

- **Big data infrastructure**

Our system is built upon the open source big data system of Hadoop and Spark. All the data, machine learning algorithms, and other dependent information are stored in the distributed file system HDFS and data management system of Hive. A relational database system of MySQL is used for storing the metadata. Our system also depend on the distributed computational framework of Map-Reduce [6] and Spark [8]. All of the computational resources are managed with Yarn. Each of the submitted machine learning task (a dataflow DAG) is first converted to a workflow DAG and scheduled with the workflow scheduler system Oozie.

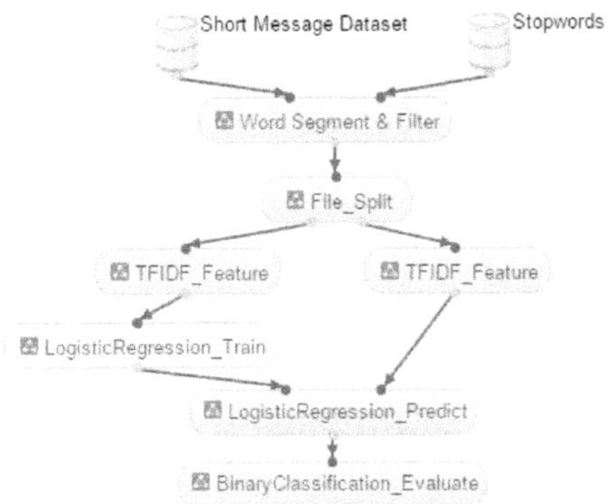

Figure 1: An example dataflow DAG.

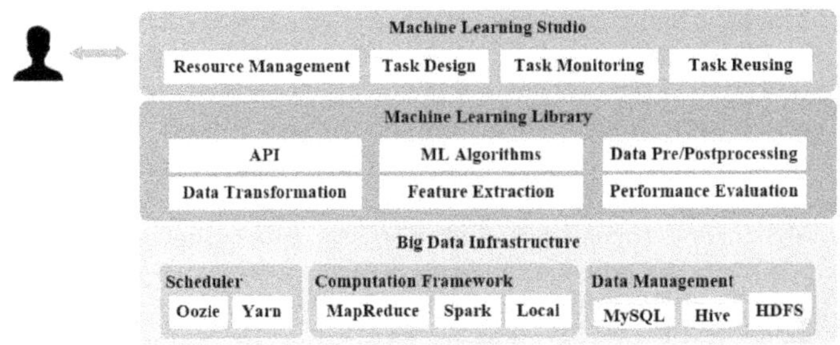

Figure 2: An overview of system architecture.

- **Machine learning library**

The machine learning library implements a number of popular machine learning algorithms (e.g., classification, topic modeling, graph processing, and information recommendation etc). For each algorithm, we implemented the distributed version on Spark as well as the standalone version because the standalone versions are usually more efficient than the distributed versions if the datasets are not big enough. Besides the core algorithms, the library also implements necessary modules for supporting the core algorithms including data pre/post-processing, data format transformation, feature extraction, and performance evaluation etc. All of the algorithms and modules can be called via both the command line and Java API. These algorithms constitute the core building blocks for users to define their machine learning tasks.

- **Machine learning studio**

The main goal of the machine learning studio is to provide a user-friendly GUI so that ordinary users can use the machine learning algorithms to solve their own problems easily. The machine learning studio is implemented as a web service and can be accessed via web browsers. It provides the follow main features:

(1) **Resource management**: All algorithms implemented in the machine learning library can be accessed from the

studio system. The system also provide a a number of data and tasks for showing how to use the algorithms to solve a problem. To construct a machine learning task, users may directly use the algorithms and data in the system. They can also upload their own data and algorithm packages. To upload an algorithm package, the user need to specify the format of the command line pattern string for running the algorithm. The string defines the program name, the input ports, the output ports, and the parameters settings. In this way, an uploaded algorithm can be run with different parameter settings. In a specified task dataflow DAG, the algorithm can be scheduled to run according to the command line pattern. After a machine learning task is submitted, it will be assigned a unique ID and stored in the task repository. Users can check and reuse the task in the future. They can also share the task to other users.

(2) **Task design**: To construct a machine learning task, a user may drag the algorithms and data sets (nodes) to the work panel, connect these nodes as a dataflow DAG, and set the parameters of all the nodes. If the users can find a similar task in our repository (in most cases), they can directly clone an existing task and make necessary modifications (add/remove nodes and edges, change parameters). By selecting a node in the work panel, the parameter setting panel will be shown in the right part of the page, which enables the users to set the specific parameter values for the corresponding algorithm in the task. After submitting a machine learning task, the studio will check the correctness of the dataflow DAG, generate the file paths of the temporal files, convert dataflow DAG to a work-flow DAG, and finally submit the work-flow DAG to Oozie for execution.

(3) **Task monitoring**: Users can monitor the progresses of a submitted task through the studio. During the execution of a task, different colors are used to indicate the status of the nodes: green for completed successfully, yellow for under running, red for completed with errors, and gray for waiting to execute. The results of a success node can be checked and downloaded via right clicking the corresponding output ports. The information printed to the standard out and standard error consoles can also be checked by right clicking the corresponding nodes. Through this way, users can know the status of a task and debug their algorithms and tasks if any error occurs.

(4) **Task Reusing**: An existing task can not only be used as templates for designing new tasks but also be reused for saving the execution time and system resource. Users may directly modify a completed task (e.g., modify the parameters of the nodes, add nodes and edges, or delete nodes and edges etc.) and resubmit the task. In the newly submitted task, only the influenced nodes are scheduled to execute and the results outputted by the uninfluenced nodes will be reused directly. For solving a real task, users usually need to tune their task dataflow DAG and parameters of the algorithms over and over. Task re-usage provides an effective mechanism to save the user's waiting time and resources.

4. ADVANTAGES

Our system offers the following advantages.

1) It is an easy-to-use and quite powerful system. The dataflow DAG formulation of the machine learning task is intuitive and easy to understand for ordinary users. Many unnecessary details are hidden. On the other hand, it still provides a lot of details (e.g., the parameters settings, the input/output ports etc.) for expert users.

2) The system seamlessly integrates the heterogeneous programs in one task. Since we used the HDFS for exchanging the information across different nodes, we have very few restriction on the form of the programs for the DAG nodes. The program corresponds to a node could be executed in stand-alone or distributed manner. It could be written with the programming language of C++, Java, Python, Perl or even the shell language.

3) The data, algorithms, and tasks in the system are highly reusable. Users can make use of the data and algorithms developed our library for constructing different machine learning tasks. The can also make use of the data and algorithms uploaded/shared by other users. A task can be cloned to construct similar tasks. Moreover, the intermediate results of an existing task can be reused by modifying and appending the task directly.

5. DEMO PLAN

We will present our system in the following aspects: (1) We will use a poster to give an overview of system architecture and briefly show the dataflow DAG formulation of the machine learning tasks and the system components. (2) We will show the audience how to use the system to complete a example machine learning task, including creating, configuring, submitting, and monitoring a task. (3) We will show the algorithms and datasets in the system. We will also show advanced functions of the system such as uploading new algorithms and datasets, sharing and reusing existing tasks etc. The audience will gain a deeper understanding on the system. (4) We will share our thoughts on the strengths and weakness of the system, and further discuss future work.

6. ACKNOWLEDGMENTS

This work was funded by the 973 Program of China under Grant No. 2014CB340401 and 2013CB329606, the 863 Program of China under Grant No. 2014AA015204, the National Natural Science Foundation of China (NSFC) under Grant No. 61502447, 61232010, 61425016, 61472401, and 61203298, and the Youth Innovation Promotion Association CAS under Grant No. 20144310 and 2016102.

7. REFERENCES

[1] http://gethue.com/.

[2] https://azkaban.github.io/.

[3] https://mahout.apache.org/.

[4] http://spark.apache.org/mllib/.

[5] R. Barga, V. Fontama, and W. H. Tok. *Predictive Analytics with Microsoft Azure Machine Learning: Build and Deploy Actionable Solutions in Minutes*, chapter Introducing Microsoft Azure Machine Learning, pages 21–42. Apress, Berkeley, CA, 2014.

[6] J. Dean and S. Ghemawat. Mapreduce: simplified data processing on large clusters. *Operating Systems Design and Implementation*, 2004.

[7] M. Islam, A. K. Huang, M. Battisha, M. Chiang, S. Srinivasan, C. Peters, A. Neumann, and A. Abdelnur. Oozie: Towards a scalable workflow management system for hadoop. In *In SIGMOD Workshop on SWEET*, SWEET '12.

[8] M. Zaharia, M. Chowdhury, M. J. Franklin, S. Shenker, and I. Stoica. Spark: Cluster computing with working sets. In *In 2nd USENIX Conference on Hot Topics in Cloud Computing*, HotCloud'10, 2010.

APPENDIX

Our system can be accessed via http://159.226.40.104:18080/studio/ with a test account "**bdaict@hotmail.com**" and password "**bdaict**". For the best user experience, it is recommended to use Chrome.

As shown in the following figure, the users can create a machine learning task (a dataflow DAG) with the algorithms and data sets listed in the left panel of the page. They can choose to click the algorithms and data sets listed in the "Program" and "Data" panels. They can also click the "Job" panel, select an existing task, clone it, and make necessary modifications. The users can configure the task information and parameter values of each node in the right panel. The nodes in the task could corresponds to either a stand-alone Linux program or a distributed program running on Spark or Hadoop Map-Reduce.

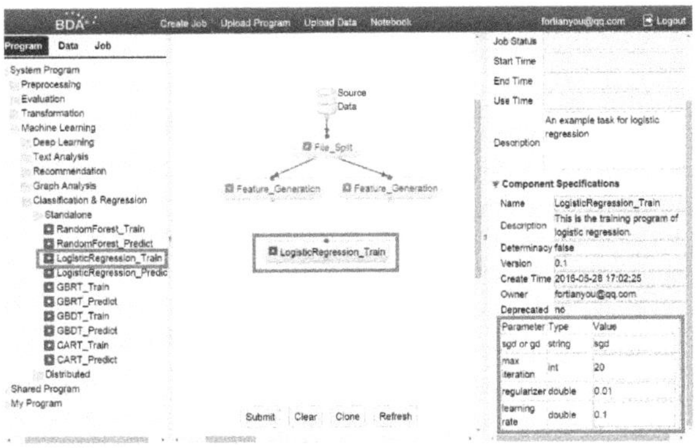

The task is submitted to run on the cloud after clicking the "submit" button. The status of each node is indicated with different colors, as shown in the following figure.

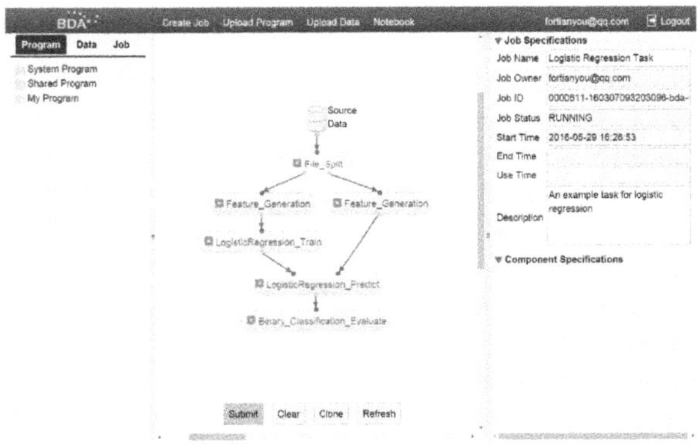

The users may check the outputs of a node by right clicking the corresponding output ports. The standard output and standard error information printed during the execution can be checked through right clicking the corresponding nodes and selects the menu "Show STDOUT" and "Show STDERR".

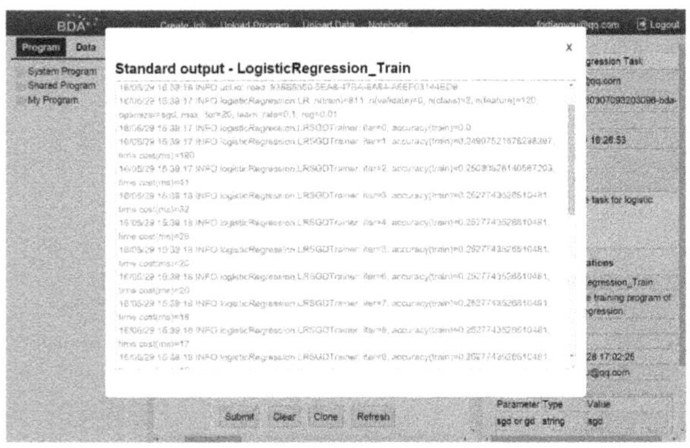

A finished (either success or not) task can be further modified and resubmitted to run, as shown in the following figure. Our system will only schedule the influenced nodes to run. The outputs of uninfluenced nodes are directly reused to save the running time and system resources.

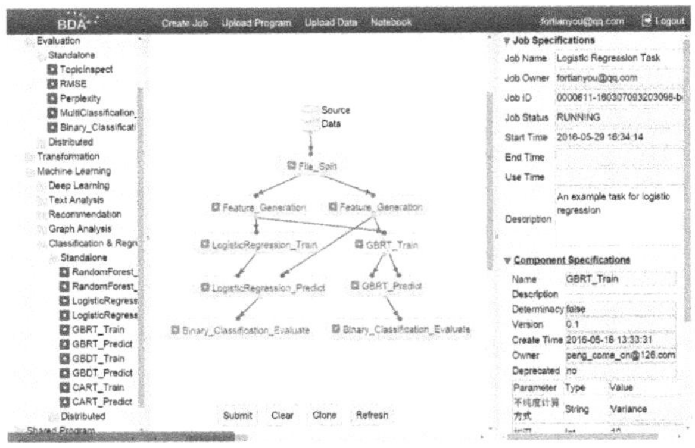

The users can upload their own algorithm packages and data sets for creating their own tasks or shared with other users. By clicking the "upload program" button, the popup window allows the users to specify the necessary information of the algorithm package, including the name, the category, the description, and the command line pattern string etc, as shown in the following figure. The most important thing is to write the command line pattern string with the predefined format. It defined the input ports, output ports, and parameter settings of a node. We developed a tool in the panel for helping users to write the command line string patterns. By clicking the "upload data" button, users can upload a data set in the similar way as that of uploading a algorithms package.

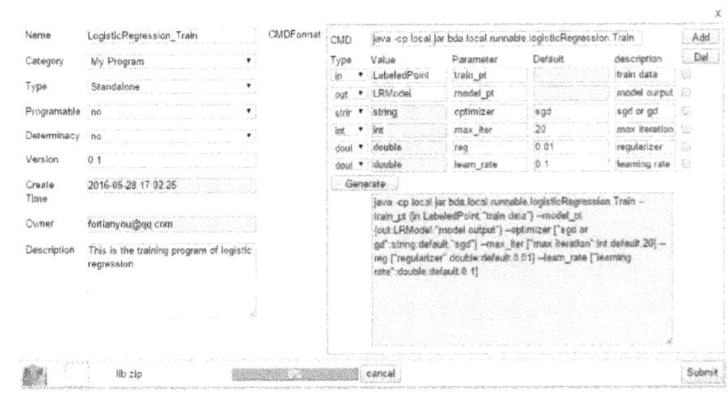

All the algorithms in the machine learning library can also be called via Java API. The details can be found via http://159.226.40.104:18080/api/#package and the following figure shows the snippet.

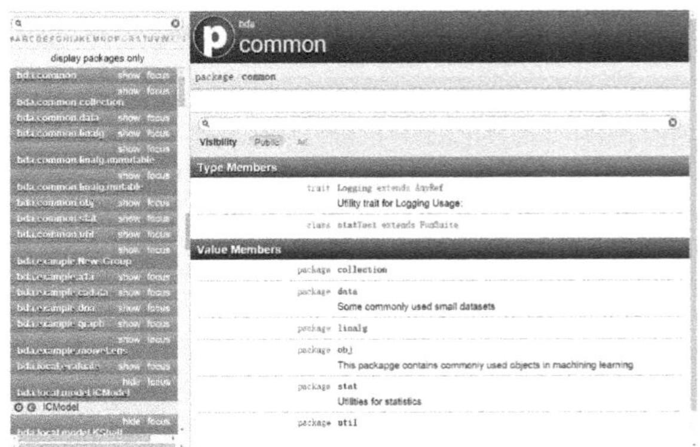

FIN10K: A Web-based Information System for Financial Report Analysis and Visualization

Yu-Wen Liu*, Liang-Chih Liu†, Chuan-Ju Wang‡, and Ming-Feng Tsai*
*Department of Computer Science, National Chengchi University, Taipei, Taiwan
†Institute of Finance, National Chiao Tung University, Hsinchu, Taiwan
‡Research Center for Information Technology Innovation, Academia Sinica, Taipei, Taiwan
g10435@cs.nccu.edu.tw, tony919kimo@gmail.com, cjwang@citi.sinica.edu.tw, mftsai@nccu.edu.tw

ABSTRACT

In this demonstration, we present FIN10K, a web-based information system that facilitates the analysis of textual information in financial reports. The proposed system has three main components: (1) a 10-K Corpus, including an inverted index of financial reports on Form 10-K, several numerical finance measures, and pre-trained word embeddings; (2) an information retrieval system; and (3) two data visualizations of the analyzed results. The system can be of great help in revealing valuable insights within large amounts of textual information. The system is now online available at http://clip.csie.org/10K/.

Keywords

web-based system; text mining; data visualization

1. INTRODUCTION

In the past few decades, a great deal of textual information in financial markets has accumulated, including financial reports and investor message boards. This textual information contains copious signals that significantly affect observable economic numbers such as stock prices and the corresponding trading volumes. Due to this close relationship between textual information and financial numerical measures, a growing body of accounting and finance research has adopted techniques from natural language processing such as sentiment analysis to deal with the textual information in finance [6, 10, 3, 4, 9]. For example, academics have investigated how financial sentiment keywords in annual SEC-mandated financial reports influence investor expectations about a company's future stock prices and potential risk [5, 7].[1] Practitioners such as fund managers utilize these sentiment keywords to offer prospects for companies and design their own investment strategies. However, when analyzing financial textual information, academics and practitioners both encounter a major hurdle — the findings are usually insignificant and biased because most finance keywords are context-sensitive. Therefore, it is essential to construct an information system to assist people to discover meaningful insights within large amounts of textual information in finance.

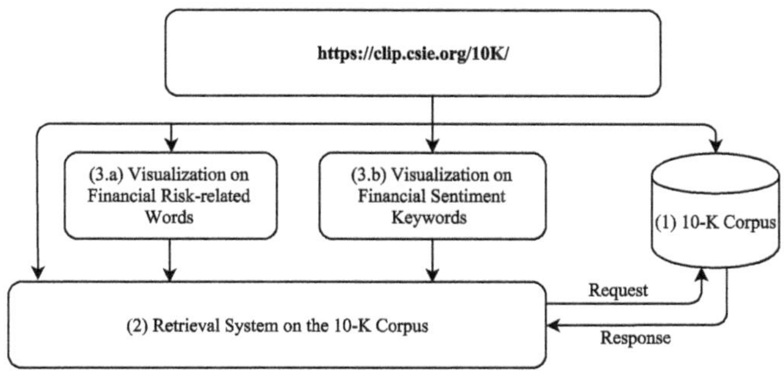

Figure 1: System architecture.

In this demonstration, we present FIN10K, a web-based information system for financial report analysis and visualization which aims to bridge the gap between technical results and useful interpretations. The system has three main parts: (1) a 10-K Corpus, including an inverted index of financial reports on Form 10-K, some numerical finance measures, and pre-trained word embedding vectors,[2] (2) an information retrieval system, and (3) two data visualizations of the analyzed results. First, the 10-K corpus contains 40,708 financial reports from years 1996 to 2013 along with three financial measures and word embedding vectors trained using a continuous bag-of-words (CBOW) model [8].[3] Second, a retrieval system is provided that quickly locates and highlights target keywords in the original texts of specified financial reports for companies. In addition, in the retrieval system, we also provide the annualized stock return volatility and the relative risk level for corresponding companies, both of which can be treated as proxies for financial risk. Third, in our system, two data visualizations are provided to showcase interesting results. The first part visualizes high-risk and low-risk words learned via the ranking models proposed in [11]. The visualization shows the correlation between words and financial risk and provides quantitative values for the words, which are plotted as bouncy balls of varying sizes, representing the intensity of their correlation with financial risk. Moreover, the second part visualizes the words in the six financial sentiment lexicons from [7] based on our learned word representations via the CBOW models. Each word representation is a 200-dimensional real-valued vector and is transformed

[1] SEC indicates Securities and Exchange Commission. One of the SEC-mandated financial reports is the 10-K report.

[2] The data is available at http://clip.csie.org/10K/data.

[3] We used the word2vec toolkit: https://code.google.com/p/word2vec/.

CIKM'16 October 24-28, 2016, Indianapolis, IN, USA

ACM ISBN 978-1-4503-4073-1/16/10.
DOI: http://dx.doi.org/10.1145/2983323.2983328

into two-dimensional space using t-distributed stochastic neighbor embedding (t-SNE), a technique for dimensionality reduction that is particularly well suited for the visualization of high-dimensional data [13]. The visualization results drive our other work related to financial keyword expansion published in [12]. Note that for both visualizations, the selected words can be fed back to the retrieval system, which is of great help in extracting relevant texts and further analyzing the relationships among multiple words.

The remainder of this paper is arranged as follows. In Section 2 we describe our platform in detail. We then provide two case studies in Section 3. Section 4 concludes the paper.

2. SYSTEM DESCRIPTION

The proposed FIN10K system consists of three main components (see Figure 1). In the following subsections, we provide detailed descriptions for each component of the system.

2.1 The 10-K Corpus

Our collected corpus is composed of three types of data: financial reports on Form 10-K, three financial measures, and pre-trained word embedding vectors. There are in total 40,708 SEC financial reports from publicly traded U.S. companies with release dates in the period from 1996 to 2013; for each report, we provide the original form 10-K, the Management Discussion and Analysis (MD&A), and the tokenized MD&A section. In addition to this textual information, we also calculate three financial measures: abnormal trading volumes, and stock return volatilities measured in the twelve-month period before and after each report. Finally, we publish pre-trained vectors via word2vec trained on the collected financial reports. The models (with and without syntactic information) contain 200-dimensional vectors for each word. For details on incorporating syntactic information, please see [12].

2.2 The Retrieval System for 10-K Corpus

Figure A.1 illustrates the interface of the retrieval system and search results for the example query word "forbear*" and metadata "data:[2002 to 2003]." First, a user can either enter a keyword in the search bar (1) or select the pre-defined negative words (4) and positive words (5) from the financial sentiment lexicons. In addition, the user can conduct a meta search for the reports from a specific year or a specified period via the dropdown selector (2) and the text field (3), respectively. Then, the user activates the retrieval by clicking the GO! button (6). After the retrieval, the system returns the relevant snippets with the corresponding release dates, company names, stock return volatilities measured in the twelve-month period after each report (i.e., $\sigma^{+}(+12)$), and their relative risk levels (7). We split the volatilities into five relative risk levels; see [11] for detailed calculations. In addition, the user can obtain the original MD&A section via button (8).

The retrieval system was developed using Bottle, a Python Web Framework, and the front-end framework Bootstrap. In addition, the 10-K corpus is indexed using an open source pure-Python text indexing library.

2.3 Visualization

The FIN10K system also presents interactive SVG graphs with D3.js to help users quickly understand not only the relation between stock volatility [11] and textual information but also the syntactic and contextual information among financial sentiment words [7].

Figure A.2 is a visualization of high-risk and low-risk words trained via the ranking models proposed in [11]. First, a user can specify the words learned from 5-year period reports via the dropdown selector (1). We categorize risk-associated words into two types: low-risk words (i.e., words with negative weights) and high-risk words (those with positive weights). In the figure, the left panel (2) exhibits the low-risk words, and the right one (3) plots the high-risk words; note that the circle area is proportional to the absolute value of the learned weight for each word.[4] Low-risk words such as "unsecur" (4) and "merger" are associated with low future stock volatilities; in contrast, high-risk words such as "forbear" (5) and "lender" are related to high future stock volatilities. For example, as observed in Figure 1, the future risks (measured by stock volatilities) of the top-3 retrieved companies are rather high (i.e., RR4 or RR5) for the query "forbear*." Additionally, by clicking on the bubble, the corresponding word is fed back to the retrieval system, which retrieves the relevant financial reports; thus the user can further analyze the contextual information of each learned word.

Figure A.3 shows a screenshot of the scatter plot for the words in the six financial sentiment lexicons based on the learned word representations. The six lexicons are *litigious*, *negative*, *positive*, *strong*, *uncertainty*, and *weak*, each of which is assigned a specific color (1). When a user hovers the mouse over a particular node (2), the word is shown with its POS tag and the corresponding sentiment lexicon. Also, each node is clickable; the word on it can be fed back to the retrieval system. Since our proposed approach in [12] also incorporates syntactic information into the CBOW model to learn the continuous word vector representations, each word in the figure is associated with a POS tag; the tag mappings are listed in the right panel (3).

3. CASE STUDY

3.1 Case 1: Ranking risk levels of companies via keywords in financial reports

Via the ranking models learned in [11], we draw attention to some strong and interesting correlations between texts and financial risk. With the presented visualization and retrieval system, users can more easily understand the results and thus gain greater insight and understanding into the usefulness of textual information in financial reports.

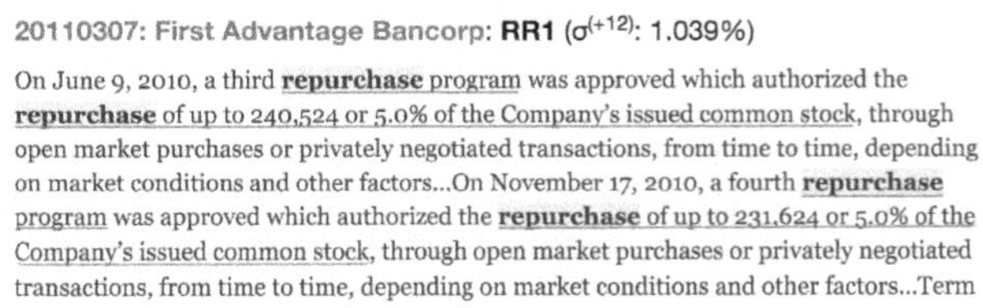
20110307: First Advantage Bancorp: **RR1** ($\sigma^{(+12)}$: 1.039%)

On June 9, 2010, a third **repurchase** program was approved which authorized the **repurchase** of up to 240,524 or 5.0% of the Company's issued common stock, through open market purchases or privately negotiated transactions, from time to time, depending on market conditions and other factors...On November 17, 2010, a fourth **repurchase** program was approved which authorized the **repurchase** of up to 231,624 or 5.0% of the Company's issued common stock, through open market purchases or privately negotiated transactions, from time to time, depending on market conditions and other factors...Term

Figure 2: Low-risk word "repurchase."

Among the retrieved results, stemmed low-risk keywords such as "repurchas" and "unsecur" have negative weights and thus negative relations to the magnitude of future stock volatility. Figure 2 shows that the stemmed word "repurchas" is mostly in the context of "share repurchases" or "repurchase program." Companies announcing share repurchase programs signal undervaluation of their prior stock return and further reveal information about their positive perspective on future profitability [2]. Thus, "repurchas" is in general negatively correlated with financial risk and hence lends a negative weight to volatility. On the other, "unsecur" is mostly in the context of "unsecured term loan" and "unsecured line of credit." Companies allowed to provide unsecured loans by banks are usually regarded as

[4]The Porter stemmer was used to generate the stemmed forms of the risk-associated words in the system.

financially healthier borrowers than those that are required to pledge part of their assets as collateral [1]. Therefore, "unsecur" is also negatively correlated with financial risk.

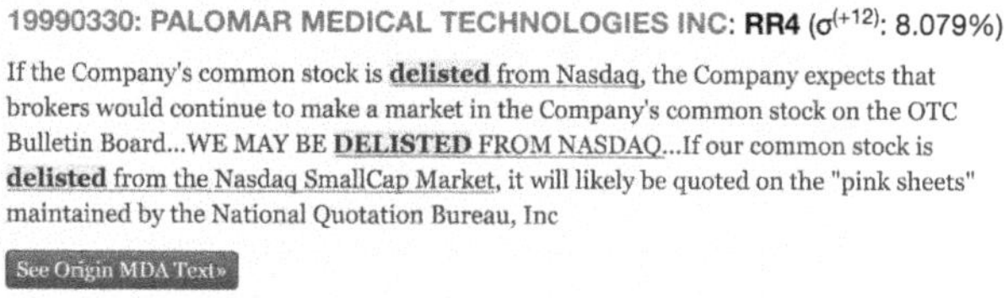

Figure 3: High-risk word "delist."

In contrast to low-risk words, the retrieved high-risk keyword "deficit" implies a negative perspective on future profitability and is thus positively correlated with financial risk and volatility of stock returns. However, it could be difficult to explain why the word "nasdaq" is associated with high financial risk. With our retrieval system, though, it can be easily found that the high-risk words "delist," "nasdaq," and "smallcap" are found mostly in the context of the sentence "delist from the Nasdaq smallcap market," as shown in Figure 3.

3.2 Case 2: Visualization of six financial sentiment lexicons

As illustrated in Figure A.3, words in the same financial sentiment lexicon generally belong to one or two groups. In addition, Figure A.4 shows that the positive and negative words are for the most part distanced from each other; Figure A.5 indicates that the group of litigious words overlaps substantially with the negative group, which could be due to the fact that in finance litigious words usually carry negative implications. From the 2-D visualization, we observe that words with similar meanings in finance are usually close to each other, based on the learned word representations; for instance, achiev v.s. accomplish and default v.s. bankruptcy (see Figures A.4 and A.5). The visualization facilitates the discovery of highly-correlated words and makes it possible to expand sentiment keywords in financial reports.

4. CONCLUSIONS AND FUTURE WORK

In this paper we have introduced a new web-based information system that can be used to retrieve relevant financial reports for a query and to visualize the analyzed results. In its current form, it conducts both full-text and meta search and displays the relevant snippets of financial reports with their corresponding release dates, company names, stock return volatilities measured in the twelve-month period after each report, and their relative risk levels. Additionally, it visualizes high- and low-risk words learned via the ranking models, as well as the syntactic and contextual information among financial sentiment words. The web demo effectively bridges the gap between technical analyzed results and useful interpretations and give a first impression for academics and practitioners interested in understanding and inspecting valuable insights into large amounts of financial textual information.

We continue to develop and extend the system, with emphasis on incorporating several type of statistics into the retrieval system. The goal of this extension is equip users with a better understanding of the corresponding financial measures of the retrieved financial reports, for instance by aggregating the risk levels and displaying their statistics for a given query. On the other hand, enhancing the interactiveness of our system will be one of the future work; for this enhancement, we may consider the techniques adopted in *Tweet Sentiment Visualization App* (https://www.csc.ncsu.edu/faculty/healey/tweet_viz/).

Acknowledgments

This work has been partially supported by the Ministry of Science and Technology in Taiwan under the grants MOST 102-2221-E-845-002-MY3 and MOST 104-2221-E-004-010.

5. REFERENCES

[1] M. T. Billett, M. J. Flannery, and J. A. Garfinkel. The effect of lender identity on a borrowing firm's equity return. *The Journal of Finance*, 50(2):699–718, 1995.

[2] A. K. Dittmar. Why do firms repurchase stock*. *The Journal of Business*, 73(3):331–355, 2000.

[3] R. Feldman. Techniques and applications for sentiment analysis. *Communications of the ACM*, 56(4):82–89, 2013.

[4] D. Garcia. Sentiment during recessions. *The Journal of Finance*, 68(3):1267–1300, 2013.

[5] S. Kogan, D. Levin, B. R. Routledge, J. S. Sagi, and N. A. Smith. Predicting risk from financial reports with regression. In *Proceedings of Human Language Technologies: The 2009 Annual Conference of the North American Chapter of the Association for Computational Linguistics*, NAACL '09, pages 272–280, 2009.

[6] M.-C. Lin, A. J. T. Lee, R.-T. Kao, and K.-T. Chen. Stock price movement prediction using representative prototypes of financial reports. *ACM Transactions on Management Information Systems*, 2(3):19:1–19:18, 2008.

[7] T. Loughran and B. McDonald. When is a liability not a liability? textual analysis, dictionaries, and 10-ks. *The Journal of Finance*, 66(1):35–65, 2011.

[8] T. Mikolov, W.-t. Yih, and G. Zweig. Linguistic regularities in continuous space word representations. In *Proceedings of the 2013 Conference of the North American Chapter of the Association for Computational Linguistics: Human Language Technologies*, NAACL-HLT '13, pages 746–751, 2013.

[9] T. H. Nguyen and K. Shirai. Topic modeling based sentiment analysis on social media for stock market prediction. In *Proceedings of the 53rd Annual Meeting of the Association for Computational Linguistics and the 7th International Joint Conference on Natural Language Processing*, ACL '15, pages 1354–1364, 2015.

[10] S. M. Price, J. S. Doran, D. R. Peterson, and B. A. Bliss. Earnings conference calls and stock returns: The incremental informativeness of textual tone. *Journal of Banking & Finance*, 36(4):992–1011, 2012.

[11] M.-F. Tsai and C.-J. Wang. *Advances in Information Retrieval: 35th European Conference on IR Research (ECIR 2013)*, chapter Risk Ranking from Financial Reports, pages 804–807. 2013.

[12] M.-F. Tsai and C.-J. Wang. Financial keyword expansion via continuous word vector representations. In *Proceedings of the 2014 Conference on Empirical Methods in Natural Language Processing*, EMNLP '14, pages 1453–1458, 2014.

[13] L. Van Der Maaten. Accelerating t-sne using tree-based algorithms. *The Journal of Machine Learning Research*, 15(1):3221–3245, 2014.

APPENDIX

A. THE SCREENSHOTS OF THE SYSTEM

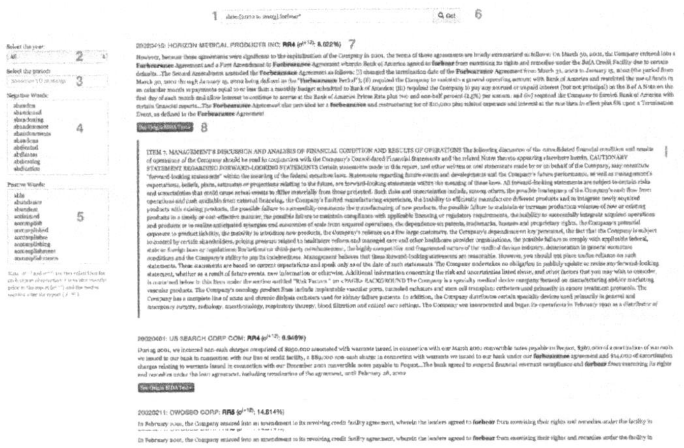

Figure A.1: The Retrieval System for 10-K Corpus.

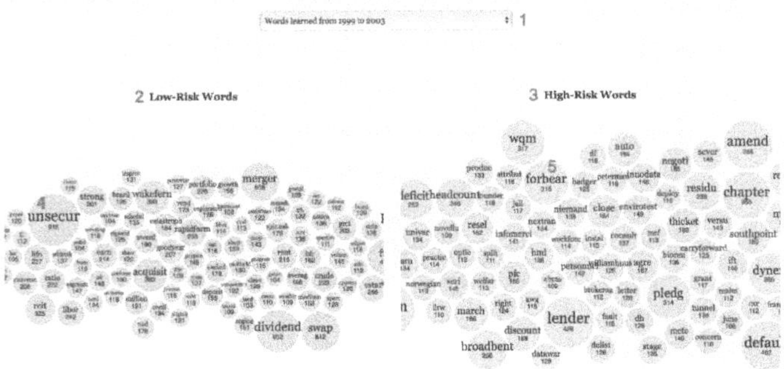

Figure A.2: Visualization of high-risk and low-risk words.

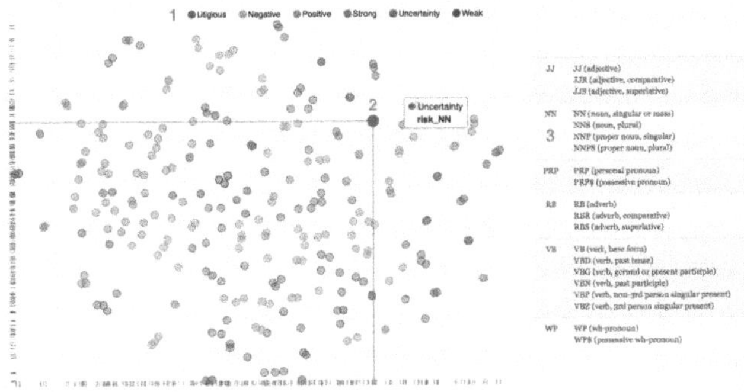

Figure A.3: Visualization of the six financial sentiment lexicons based on the learned word representations.

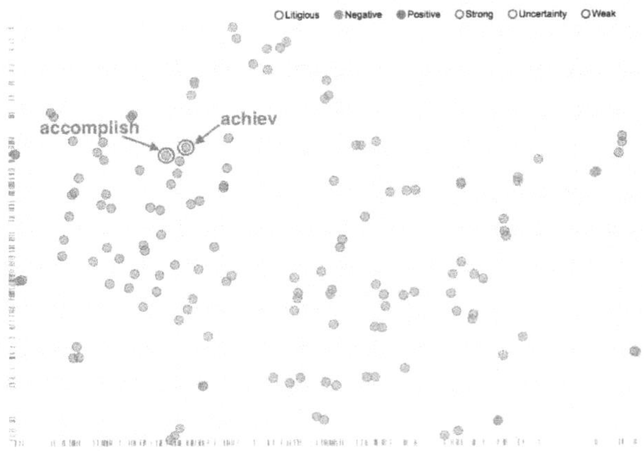

Figure A.4: Positive and negative words.

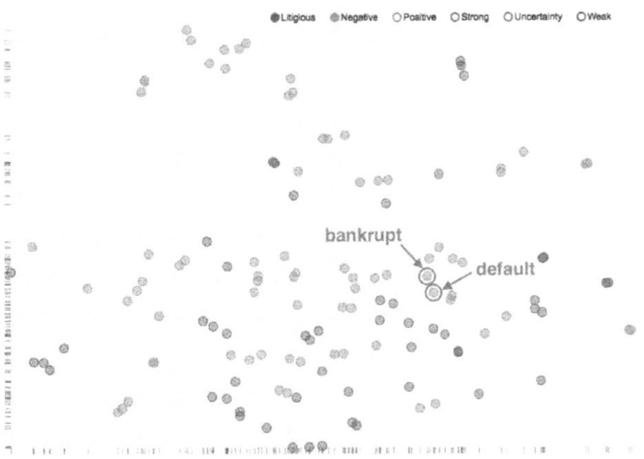

Figure A.5: Negative and litigious words.

FeatureMiner: A Tool for Interactive Feature Selection

Kewei Cheng, Jundong Li and Huan Liu
Computer Science and Engineering,
Arizona State University, Tempe, AZ 85281, USA
{Kewei.Cheng, jundong.li, huan.liu}@asu.edu

ABSTRACT

The recent popularity of big data has brought immense quantities of high-dimensional data, which presents challenges to traditional data mining tasks due to curse of dimensionality. Feature selection has shown to be effective to prepare these high dimensional data for a variety of learning tasks. To provide easy access to feature selection algorithms, we provide an interactive feature selection tool *FeatureMiner* based on our recently released feature selection repository *scikit-feature*[1]. *FeatureMiner* eases the process of performing feature selection for practitioners by providing an interactive user interface. Meanwhile, it also gives users some practical guidance in finding a suitable feature selection algorithm among many given a specific dataset. In this demonstration, we show (1) How to conduct data preprocessing after loading a dataset; (2) How to apply feature selection algorithms; (3) How to choose a suitable algorithm by visualized performance evaluation.

Keywords

Data Mining; Feature Selection; Interactive User Interface

1. INTRODUCTION

We are now in the era of big data, massive amounts of high-dimensional data are generated at an unprecedented rate. For example, 2.5 quintillion bytes of data are created every day and 90% of data in the world today was produced within the last two years[2]. These massive amount of high-dimensional data (e.g., social media data, images, videos) presents challenges to data mining techniques due to the curse of dimensionality. As a traditional and effective approach to prepare high-dimensional data, feature selection [5] aims to select a subset of relevant features to build a comprehensible learning model with good predictive performance.

In the past few decades, a large number of feature selection algorithms have been developed [3, 4]. These algorithms are designed to serve different purposes and have their own advantages and disadvantages. With so many feature selection algorithms in literature, there is a urgent need for a system to collect some widely used feature selection algorithms that have been developed to serve as a platform for facilitating their application, comparison and joint study [8, 9]. Recently, we release a open-source feature selection repository *scikit-feature* which includes around 40 representative feature selection algorithms. However, this repository is initially built for experienced users and programmers with some background knowledge of feature selection. It would be better for users to have some prior knowledge about these algorithms since different feature selection algorithms may require different inputs and provide different outputs. In this work, in order to provide easy access to these feature selection algorithms, we present a system *FeatureMiner*, which facilitates the use of these feature selection algorithms in practical usage by providing an interactive user interface.

2. FEATURE SELECTION

According to the availability of label information, feature selection algorithms can be either supervised [2] or unsupervised [1]. Supervised feature selection algorithms take advantage of the class labels to evaluate feature relevance by its ability to distinguish instances from different classes. A general framework of supervised feature selection is illustrated in Figure 1. It consists of two phases - the training phase and the prediction phase. In the training phase, supervised feature selection algorithms first select subset of highly discriminant features. With training data represented by these selected features, classifiers are trained under the guidance of label information. In the prediction phase, the trained classifier predicts class labels of testing data on the selected features.

However, due to the lack of label information, unsupervised feature selection exploits alternative criteria instead of class labels to define the relevance of features which include data similarity, local discriminative information and data reconstruction error. A general framework of unsupervised feature selection is illustrated in Figure 2. Different from supervised feature selection, unsupervised feature selection usually uses all instances in the feature selection phase then outputs the cluster structure of all data samples on the selected features by using a typical clustering algorithm.

[1]http://featureselection.asu.edu/
[2]http://www-01.ibm.com/software/data/bigdata/what-is-big-data.html

CIKM'16 October 24-28, 2016, Indianapolis, IN, USA

ACM ISBN 978-1-4503-4073-1/16/10.
DOI: http://dx.doi.org/10.1145/2983323.2983329

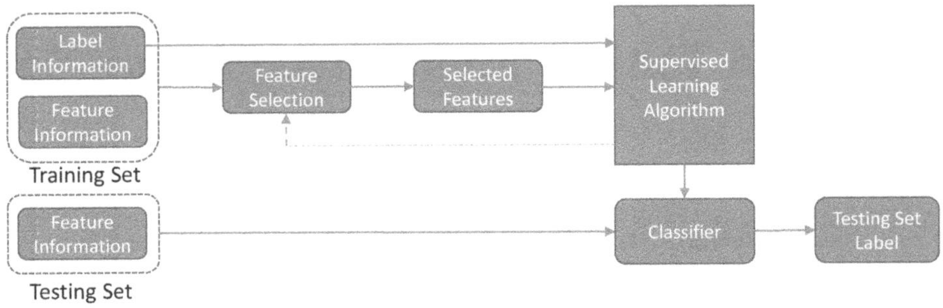

Figure 1: A general framework of supervised feature selection.

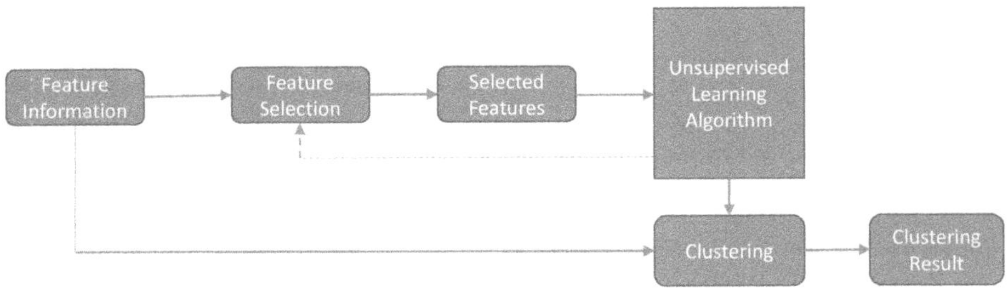

Figure 2: A general framework of unsupervised feature selection.

3. SYSTEM DESIGN

We develop the interactive feature selection tool *FeatureMiner* on the basis of our recently released feature selection repository *scikit-feature*, which consists of most the popular supervised and unsupervised feature selection algorithms. The tool is designed to simplify the usage of these feature selection algorithms for users without much experience of feature selection. The workflow of *FeatureMiner* is shown in Figure 3. As shown in Figure 3, *FeatureMiner* is a hierarchically-organized tool, with the low-level procedures at the bottom of the hierarchy as loading data and conducting data preprocessing. These low-level procedures are assembled into higher-level feature selection algorithms. As the highest-level procedures, the selected features are used to build a learning model for performance evaluation. There are three tabs in *FeatureMiner*, with the first allowing data preprocessing, the second providing access to supervised feature selection algorithms with performance evaluation and the third is designed for unsupervised feature selection and its performance evaluation. In the following subsections, we will introduce our interactive tool in detail. For more information on our tool, please visit the demo webpage[3].

3.1 Data Preprocessing

As shown in Figure 4, on the *preprocess* tab, users can obtain some basic information of dataset and prepare the dataset for certain types of feature selection algorithms. It currently support two kinds of formats: Matlab data format and CSV file format. Once the dataset has been loaded, some basic information of the dataset is presented to users, including the number of instances, the number of features, and the number of classes. To give users an overview of data distribution, *FeatureMiner* also offers a bar graph to show the class distribution of the dataset. It also supports other data preprocessing. Functions supported in data preprocessor are shown as follows:

(1) data normalization: It transforms features by scaling each feature to the range of $(0, 1)$.

(2) data discretization: With the number of bins as input, it partitions continuous values of features into a smaller number of bins.

3.2 Performing Feature Selection

As discussed in Section 2, unsupervised feature selection algorithms are distinct with supervised feature selection algorithms in both algorithm design and performance evaluation. Thus, we separate supervised feature selection and unsupervised feature selection into two tabs, *supervised* tab as shown Figure 5 and *unsupervised* tab as shown Figure 6.

For supervised feature selection, users can select a supervised feature selection algorithm from drop down list with its parameters and number of selected features as input. It should be noted that different feature selection algorithms may have different requirements for datasets. For example, some supervised feature selection algorithms can only tackle binary-class classification problems while others can tackle multi-class classification problems. Some methods can only deal with discrete feature values while others can also deal with continuous feature values. To ensure that the dataset is well prepared for a chosen algorithm, *FeatureMiner* checks dataset before conducting the feature selection. If the dataset is not well prepared, it reminds users to conduct corresponding preprocessing on the dataset first. As mentioned above, it is a difficult task to choose a suitable feature selection algorithm for a particular application [6]. To give users further guidance, we divide supervised feature selection algorithms into five categories: (1) information theoretical based methods [7] are proposed to maximize feature rele-

[3]http://featureselection.asu.edu/featureminer.php

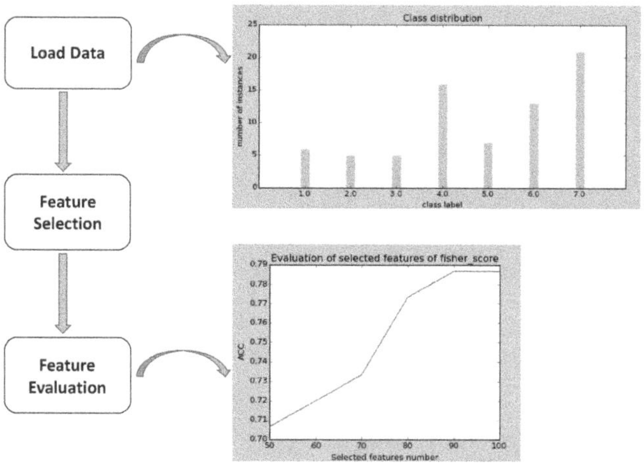

Figure 3: Overview of the *FeatureMiner* for interactive feature selection.

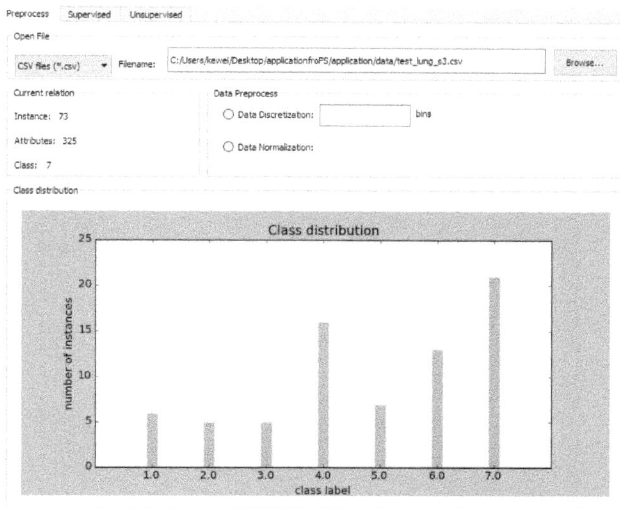

Figure 4: The preprocess tab of *FeatureMiner* showing example of loading lung cancer dataset.

vance and minimize feature redundancy (i.e., CIFE, CMIM, DISR, FCBF, ICAP, IGFS, JMI, MIFS, MIM, MRMR); (2) similarity based methods select features based on their ability to preserve data similarity (i.e., Fisher Score, ReliefF, Trace Ratio); (3) sparse learning based methods aim to minimize the fitting error with sparse regularization terms (i.e., RFS, Least square loss, Logistic loss); (4) statistical based methods evaluate importance of features based on different statistical measures (i.e., T-score, F-score, Chi-square, Gini Index) and (5) wrapper methods measure features by their predictive accuracy of a predetermined learning algorithm (i.e., Decision Tree based backward elimination, Decision Tree based forward selection, SVM based backward elimination, SVM based forward selection). To choose a suitable algorithm for a loaded dataset, user can first find a best category and then conduct deeper analysis with visualized performance evaluation.

Similar to supervised feature selection, to conduct unsupervised feature selection, users first choose an unsupervised feature selection algorithm from drop down list then specify its parameters and the number of selected features. Feature selection methods supported in *unsupervised* tab include: (1) similarity based methods (i.e., SPEC, Laplacian Score); and (2) sparse learning based methods (i.e., MCFS, NDFS, UDFS).

3.3 Evaluation

After we obtain the selected features as illustrated in Section 3.2, we evaluate these feature selection algorithms. There are some differences between evaluation of supervised and unsupervised feature selection algorithms.

As shown in Figure 1, to test performance of the supervised feature selection algorithms, the whole dataset is usually divided into two parts including the training set and testing set. With guidance of label information, feature selection algorithms will be first applied on the training set to select a subset of relevant features; then the testing set on the selected features are regarded as input to a classification model for the performance evaluation purpose. The predicted labels are compared with the label information of testing set by different classification evaluation metrics. In the system, the evaluation results will be visually plotted, which enables users to have a clear sense about how classification performance vary with respect to the number of selected features. The visual plots are very useful since users can determine the optimal value for the number of selected features. Besides, for the request of users, the system can also save the evaluation results to a file with the classification performance and the indexes of selected features.

A user can specify evaluation setting for supervised feature selection algorithms including: (1) classification models (e.g., Linear SVM, Nearest Neighbors, Decision Tree); (2) number of runs for the classification evaluation; (3) percentage of training/test data; and (4) classification evaluation metrics (e.g., classification accuracy and F1 score).

As shown in Figure 2, for performance evaluation of unsupervised feature selection algorithms, there is no need to divide the whole dataset into the training set and testing set. The label information(ground truth) is only used for the evaluation purpose. Each feature selection algorithm is first applied on the whole dataset to select features, then clustering models are performed based on the selected features. We repeat the clustering algorithm 10 times and report the average clustering results visually in the same way as the line chart for performance evaluation of supervised feature selection. Similarly, it can also save results to a file including the clustering performance and the indexes of selected features for the request of users.

A user can specify evaluation setting for unsupervised feature selection including: (1) clustering models (e.g., K-Means, spectral clustering); and (2) clustering evaluation metrics(e.g., clustering accuracy (ACC), normalized mutual information (NMI) and adjusted rand Index (ARI)).

4. DEMO SCENARIOS

During the demonstration, we will apply several feature selection algorithms to different kinds of datasets with various types of settings and show users: (1) How to conduct

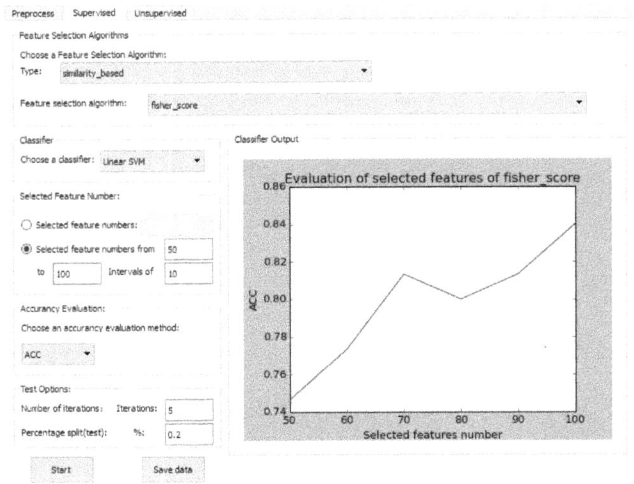

Figure 5: The supervised tab of *FeatureMiner* showing example of conducting fisher score algorithm.

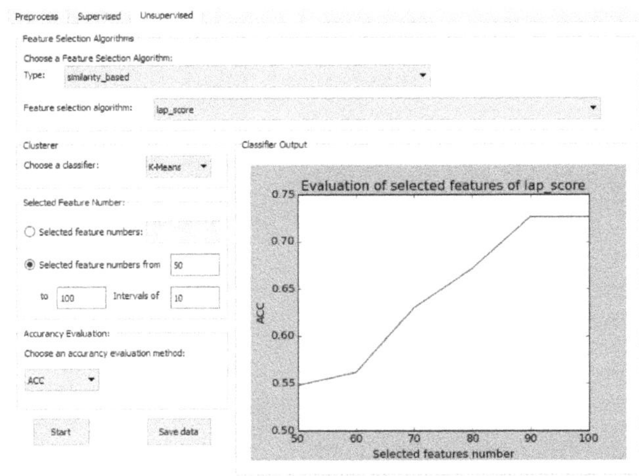

Figure 6: The unsupervised tab of *FeatureMiner* showing example of conducting laplacian score algorithm.

data preprocessing after loading a dataset; (2) How to apply feature selection algorithms; (3) How to choose a suitable algorithm by visualized performance evaluation. We have an example to demonstrate how to find a suitable feature selection algorithm for lung cancer dataset[4]. To find the most suitable supervised feature selection algorithm for this dataset, first we randomly choose an algorithm from each of the five categories mentioned in Section 3.2 and set the number of selected feature to the same range then apply these algorithms to the lung cancer dataset. After comparing the classification performance of these algorithms, the category of that shows the best classification performance is considered as the best algorithm category for this dataset. Then we apply each algorithms in this category to lung cancer dataset in order to find out the most suitable feature selection algorithm. Similarly, we use the same method to find a most suitable unsupervised feature selection algorithm for this dataset.

5. CONCLUSIONS AND FUTURE WORK

In this work we have built a user interactive feature selection tool *FeatureMiner* which provides easy access to different feature selection algorithms. The tool is built upon our recently released open-source feature selection repository *scikit-feature*. It facilitates the use of feature selection algorithms for users with limited background knowledge and gives them some practical guidance in finding a suitable feature selection algorithm among many given a specific dataset.

In the future, to expand the functionality of *FeatureMiner*, we would like to automatically recommend the most suitable algorithms to users based on the experimental results of similar datasets. Besides, *FeatureMiner* currently only provides users access to traditional feature selection algorithms. Due to the prevalence of heterogeneous data sources such as social media data, we would like to integrate some feature selection algorithms for heterogeneous data into our system.

[4]http://penglab.janelia.org/proj/mRMR/index.htm#data

Acknowledgments

This material is, in part, supported by the National Science Foundation (NSF) under grant number IIS-1217466.

6. REFERENCES

[1] S. Alelyani, J. Tang, and H. Liu. Feature selection for clustering: A review. *Data Clustering: Algorithms and Applications*, 29, 2013.

[2] M. Dash and H. Liu. Feature selection for classification. *Intelligent data analysis*, 1(3):131–156, 1997.

[3] J. Li, K. Cheng, S. Wang, F. Morstatter, R. Trevino, J. Tang, and H. Liu. Feature selection: A data perspective. 2016.

[4] J. Li and H. Liu. Challenges of feature selection for big data analytics. *IEEE Intelligent Systems*, 2016.

[5] H. Liu and H. Motoda. *Computational methods of feature selection*. CRC Press, 2007.

[6] H. Liu and L. Yu. Toward integrating feature selection algorithms for classification and clustering. *Knowledge and Data Engineering, IEEE Transactions on*, 17(4):491–502, 2005.

[7] H. Peng, F. Long, and C. Ding. Feature selection based on mutual information criteria of max-dependency, max-relevance, and min-redundancy. *IEEE Transactions on pattern analysis and machine intelligence*, 27(8):1226–1238, 2005.

[8] P. Somol and P. Pudil. Feature selection toolbox. *Pattern Recognition*, 35(12):2749–2759, 2002.

[9] Z. Zhao, F. Morstatter, S. Sharma, S. Alelyani, A. Anand, and H. Liu. Advancing feature selection research. *ASU feature selection repository*, pages 1–28, 2010.

Deola: A System for Linking Author Entities in Web Document with DBLP

Yinan Liu, Wei Shen*, Xiaojie Yuan
College of Computer and Control Engineering, Nankai University, Tianjin 300071, China
2120150391@mail.nankai.edu.cn, shenwei@nankai.edu.cn, yuanxj@nankai.edu.cn

ABSTRACT

In this paper, we present Deola, an Online system for Author Entity Linking with DBLP. Unlike most existing entity linking systems which focus on linking entities with Wikipedia and depend largely on the special features associated with Wikipedia (e.g., Wikipedia articles), Deola links author names appearing in the web document which belongs to the domain of computer science with their corresponding entities existing in the DBLP network. This task is helpful for the enrichment of the DBLP network and the understanding of the domain-specific document. This task is challenging due to name ambiguity and limited knowledge existing in DBLP. Given a fragment of domain-specific web document belonging to the domain of computer science, Deola can return the mapping entity in DBLP for each author name appearing in the input document.

CCS Concepts

•**Information systems** → **Data mining;** *Data cleaning;*

Keywords

Entity linking; Author name disambiguation; Domain-specific entity linking

1. INTRODUCTION

Motivation. Real-world, multi-type objects are often interconnected, forming diverse heterogeneous information networks. The DBLP bibliographic network[1] contains five types of objects: papers (P), authors (A), publication venues (V), title terms (T), and publication years (Y). Links exist between authors and papers by the relations *write* and $write^{-1}$, between publication venues and papers by *publish* and $publish^{-1}$, between papers and title terms by *contain* and $contain^{-1}$, and between papers and publication years by *publishedIn* and $publishedIn^{-1}$. However, author names in DBLP may be potentially ambiguous: the same author name may refer to many different author entities. As the example shown in Figure 1, in the DBLP network, the author name "Lei Wang" may refer to 27 different authors, including "Lei Wang" at University of Connecticut, "Lei Wang" at Louisiana State University, "Lei Wang" at University of Wollongong, NSW, Australia. The task of linking author names in the domain-specific document with their corresponding entities in DBLP is beneficial for document understanding and DBLP enrichment. For example, we could annotate the document in Figure 1 with some related knowledge about the linked author entity "Lei Wang" mined from the DBLP network (e.g., publication records, similar authors, research areas, etc.) after linking it with "Lei Wang" at University of Wollongong, NSW, Australia in DBLP.

Our Task (author entity linking with DBLP). Given an author name set M detected from a domain-specific web document d belonging to the domain of computer science, the goal is to identify the mapping entity e in DBLP for each author name $m \in M$.

Most traditional entity linking approaches work on linking entities with Wikipedia or Wikipedia-derived knowledge bases (e.g., YAGO[8]) [2, 3, 4, 7]. They depend largely on the context information embedded in the Wikipedia article [2, 4], Wikipedia-based semantic relatedness measures [3, 4], and some special structures in Wikipedia [2, 4] (e.g., disambiguation page and hyperlink in the Wikipedia article). Since the DBLP network does not have these specific features, these traditional entity linking approaches cannot be applied to our task. For example, these previous approaches [2, 3, 4] are all based on some context similarity measures between the document where the entity appears and the Wikipedia article associated with the candidate entity. However, for each author entity in DBLP, we do not have her descriptive article and cannot calculate the context similarity.

Our Approach. In this demo, we develop an online linking system Deola based on the SHINE model [6]. The SHINE model consists of two parts: the entity popularity model and the entity object model. The entity popularity model captures the popularity of an entity and it is context independent. For example, a famous professor named "Lei Wang" who has published a large number of papers is usually more popular than an undergraduate who is also named "Lei Wang" and has published very few papers.

The entity object model captures the probability of multi-type objects appearing in the document context of an entity.

---

*Corresponding author
[1]http://www.informatik.uni-trier.de/~ley/db/

CIKM'16, October 24–28, 2016, Indianapolis, IN, USA

ACM ISBN 978-1-4503-4073-1/16/10..
DOI: http://dx.doi.org/10.1145/2983323.2983330

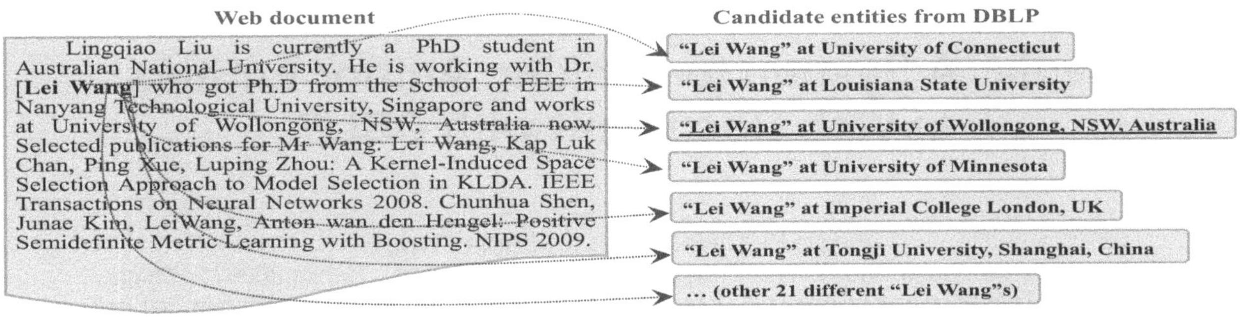

Figure 1: An illustration for the task. Author entity detected from the web document is in bold face; candidate entities from DBLP for this entity are shown on the right; true mapping entity is underlined.

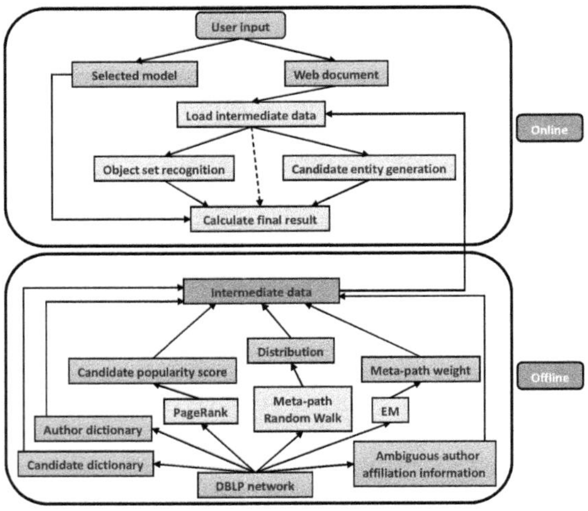

Figure 2: System Architecture.

In the DBLP network, multi-type objects are connected via different types of relations or sequences of relations, forming a set of meta-paths [9]. Different meta-paths imply distinct semantic meanings, which may lead to diverse distributions over objects. For example, A-P-Y is a meta-path denoting a relation between an author and a year when her paper is published, whereas A-P-T denotes a relation between an author and a title term which her paper contains. Random walks starting from one author along the meta-path A-P-Y may generate a different distribution compared with the meta-path A-P-T. SHINE assigns different weights to each meta-path based on the expectation-maximization (EM) algorithm without requiring any training data. About the SHINE model you can refer to the paper [6] for more details.

2. SYSTEM ARCHITECTURE

Deola consists of two parts shown in Figure 2. As an online entity linking system, Deola needs to do a real-time linking for each user input. To save the runtime, we calculate and store the author dictionary, the candidate dictionary, the ambiguous author affiliation information, the candidate popularity score, the distribution over objects and the meta-path weight as the intermediate data offline. In the online procedure, Deola only needs to load a small part of the intermediate data into memory and calculate the final result according to the selected model and the input web document.

2.1 Off ine Procedure

Generate the author dictionary. For all author entities in DBLP, Deola stores their names as a dictionary.

Generate the candidate dictionary. For ambiguous author names, Deola stores all candidates for each of them as a dictionary.

Extract the ambiguous author affiliation information. In order to give a better user experience, the affiliation information for all ambiguous author entities in DBLP is extracted from the raw data set and stored ahead.

Generate the candidate popularity score. The entity popularity model uses PageRank algorithm [1] to calculate the popularity of entity. Deola computes the candidate popularity score $\mathbf{P}(e)$ of each ambiguous author entity e in the DBLP network offline and stores them in a file.

Generate the distribution. Deola generates the distribution $\mathbf{P_e}(v|p)$ of observing object v given ambiguous author entity e and meta-path p. Deola utilizes meta-path constrained random walks [5] to estimate the distribution based on the DBLP network and stores all distributions in files offline.

Generate the meta-path weight. As different kinds of meta-paths may lead to diverse distributions over objects and further lead to different entity linking results, it is desirable to learn the relative importance for each meta-path. For the sake of efficiency, Deola selects four length-2 meta-paths (i.e., A-P-A, A-P-V, A-P-T and A-P-Y) in the entity object model. Deola learns the weight w_p for each meta-path p using the EM algorithm based on a large web document set. We show the learned meta-path weight in Table 1.

Table 1: The learned meta-path weight

Meta-path	Weight	Meta-path	Weight
A-P-A	0.16412	A-P-V	0.11967
A-P-T	0.51133	A-P-Y	0.24086

2.2 Online Procedure

Deola system requires users to specify the author names that need to be linked in their input document explicitly by using surrounded square brackets (e.g., "[Lei Wang]" in the web document of Figure 1). In the online procedure, given a fragment of domain-specific web document, Deola firstly recognizes the square bracketed author name in the document. Then Deola judges whether there exists the same textual name in DBLP by leveraging the author dictionary. If it exists, Deola will generate the candidate entity, recognize the object set and calculate the final result.

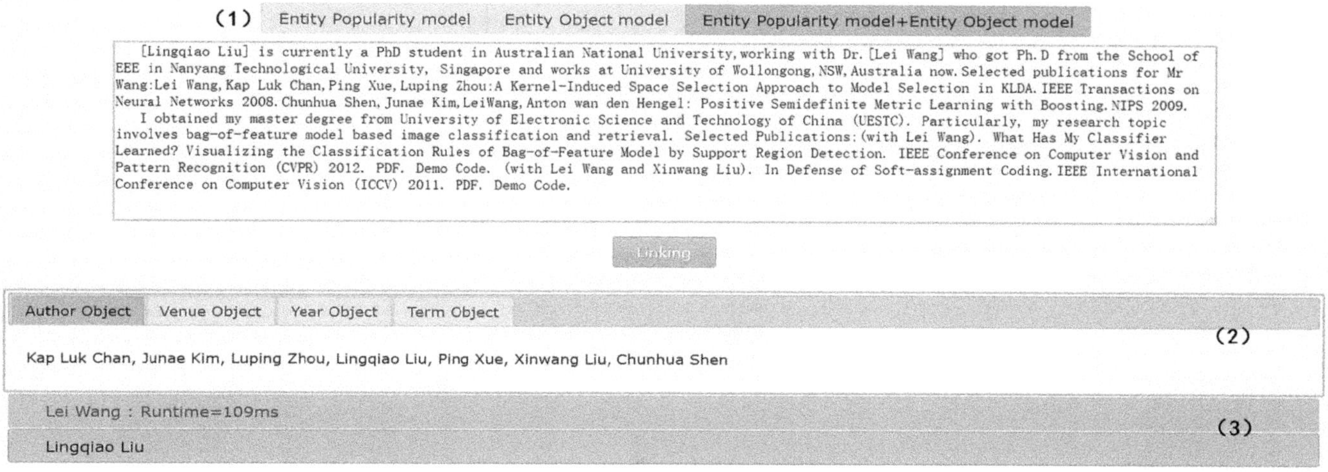

Figure 3: User Interface of Deola.

Load intermediate data. Deola needs to read a small part of the intermediate data into memory according to the user input as follows:

- The candidate dictionary.
- The author affiliation information set.
- The candidate popularity score.
- The distribution.
- The meta-path weight.

Candidate entity generation. Given an author name specified by the user that needs to be linked, Deola needs to generate the candidate entities for the author name by searching the candidate dictionary.

Object set recognition. After loading the intermediate data, Deola recognizes four types of object sets in the input web document, namely author set, venue set, year set, and term set based on the candidate dictionary and the distribution using the string matching method.

Calculate final result. After candidate entity generation and object set recognition, Deola calculates the final result according to the selected model. Deola constructs the entity popularity model by obtaining the popularity score $\mathbf{P}(e)$ for each candidate. Deola constructs the entity object model $\mathbf{P}(d|e)$ that captures the probability of multi-type objects appearing in the document context of the author entity based on the meta-path weight w_p and the distribution $\mathbf{P_e}(v|p)$ as follows:

$$\mathbf{P_e}(v) = \sum_{p} w_p \mathbf{P_e}(v|p) \tag{1}$$

$$\mathbf{P}(d|e) = \prod_{v \in d} (\theta \cdot \mathbf{P_e}(v) + (1-\theta) \cdot \mathbf{P_g}(v)) \tag{2}$$

In real application, we set $\theta = 0.3$, $\mathbf{P_g}(v) = 0.0013$ for simplicity. Then Deola computes the most likely mapping entity e given an input web document d as follows:

$$\arg\max_{e \in E} \mathbf{P}(e)\mathbf{P}(d|e) \tag{3}$$

where E is the set of candidate entities for the ambiguous author name that needs to be linked.

3. DEMONSTRATION

Deola provides a concise and friendly interface for the user, which consists of three parts: (1)the input part consists of three radio buttons for model selection and a text field for user input; (2)the intermediate result part displays four tabs and their panels for displaying the detected four types of object sets; (3)the final result part shows an accordion for each author name that needs to be linked. A screenshot of the graphical user interface is shown in Figure 3.

1. Interaction with Deola is simple. Deola provides three linking model (i.e., the entity popularity model, the entity object model, and the combination of them that is the SHINE model). The default model is the SHINE model. User only needs to input a piece of domain-specific document belonging to the domain of computer science, and select a model by clicking the button at the top. The clicked button will turn blue. Deola system requires that there is at least one square bracketed author name in the input web document. In addition, Deola can only deal with the English language.

2. When clicking the orange linking button, user can see the intermediate result part immediately. The intermediate results contain four types of object sets that are identified from the web document, namely author set, venue set, year set, and term set. Clicking the tab, the selected tab will turn blue and its panel will show the corresponding recognized objects.

3. For each ambiguous author name, user can click its blue header of the accordion and see the probability of each candidate entity from the drop-down list (see Figure 4). The candidate entities are sorted according to their probabilities in descending order. To give a better user experience, we show the affiliation information for each candidate entity. When the user clicks a candidate entity, it will jump to the corresponding webpage in DBLP for that candidate entity. In the example shown in Figure 4, Deola outputs Lei Wang at University of Wollongong, NSW, Australia as the most likely mapping author entity for the author name "Lei Wang". The runtime for this linking is 109ms which is

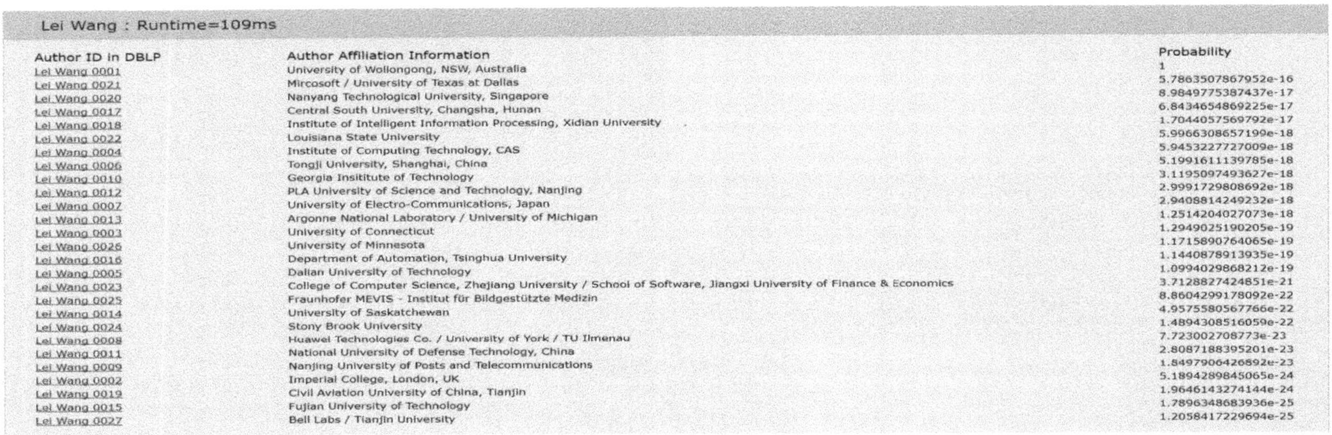

Lei Wang : Runtime=109ms

Author ID in DBLP	Author Affiliation Information	Probability
Lei Wang 0001	University of Wollongong, NSW, Australia	1
Lei Wang 0021	Mircosoft / University of Texas at Dallas	5.7863507867952e-16
Lei Wang 0020	Nanyang Technological University, Singapore	8.9849775387437e-17
Lei Wang 0017	Central South University, Changsha, Hunan	6.8434654869225e-17
Lei Wang 0018	Institute of Intelligent Information Processing, Xidian University	1.7044057569792e-17
Lei Wang 0022	Louisiana State University	5.9966308657199e-18
Lei Wang 0004	Institute of Computing Technology, CAS	5.9453227727009e-18
Lei Wang 0006	Tongji University, Shanghai, China	5.1991611139785e-18
Lei Wang 0010	Georgia Insititute of Technology	3.1195097493627e-18
Lei Wang 0012	PLA University of Science and Technology, Nanjing	2.9991729808692e-18
Lei Wang 0007	University of Electro-Communications, Japan	2.9408814249232e-18
Lei Wang 0013	Argonne National Laboratory / University of Michigan	1.2514204027073e-18
Lei Wang 0003	University of Connecticut	1.2949025190205e-19
Lei Wang 0026	University of Minnesota	1.1715890764065e-19
Lei Wang 0016	Department of Automation, Tsinghua University	1.1440878913935e-19
Lei Wang 0005	Dalian University of Technology	1.0994029868212e-19
Lei Wang 0023	College of Computer Science, Zhejiang University / School of Software, Jiangxi University of Finance & Economics	3.7128827424851e-21
Lei Wang 0025	Fraunhofer MEVIS - Institut für Bildgestützte Medizin	8.8604299178092e-22
Lei Wang 0014	University of Saskatchewan	4.9575580567766e-22
Lei Wang 0024	Stony Brook University	1.4894308516059e-22
Lei Wang 0008	Huawei Technologies Co. / University of York / TU Ilmenau	7.723002708773e-23
Lei Wang 0011	National University of Defense Technology, China	2.8087188395201e-23
Lei Wang 0009	Nanjing University of Posts and Telecommunications	1.8497906426892e-23
Lei Wang 0002	Imperial College, London, UK	5.1894289845065e-24
Lei Wang 0019	Civil Aviation University of China, Tianjin	1.9646143274144e-24
Lei Wang 0015	Fujian University of Technology	1.7896348683936e-25
Lei Wang 0027	Bell Labs / Tianjin University	1.2058417229694e-25

Figure 4: Result for ambiguous author name.

Figure 5: Result for unambiguous author name.

shown in the blue header. For each unambiguous author name, Deola outputs that the author name has no ambiguity and shows the corresponding webpage link in DBLP for that author directly (see Figure 5). The linking results Deola outputs for the two author names in the example are correct according to the analysis of the input document.

4. SYSTEM IMPLEMENTATION

Deola is a browser-server architecture system. We use Apache HTTP server. The system is implemented using LAJP-10.05[2] frame which can bridge the socket communication between JAVA and PHP. The back-end module is written in JAVA. The front-end module is written in PHP and jQuery. All the programs are implemented on a computer (four 3.6GHz CPU cores, 8GB memory) with 64-bit Windows 10. We downloaded the November 2015 version of DBLP as our raw data set. This DBLP contains over 1,689,081 authors and 2,941,533 papers.

5. CONCLUSION

Our Deola system provides a friendly and concise interface that helps users link the author entity in web document belonging to the domain of computer science with DBLP. To the best of our knowledge, our Deola is the first system that addresses the task of author entity linking with DBLP. We are currently working on supporting other kinds of data (such as tables and tweets) to enhance our system functionality.

6. ACKNOWLEDGMENTS

This work was supported in part by National Natural Science Foundation of China under Grant No. 61502253, National 863 Program of China under Grant No. 2015AA015401 and the Fundamental Research Funds for the Central Universities.

[2]https://code.google.com/p/lajp/

7. REFERENCES

[1] S. Brin and L. Page. The anatomy of a large-scale hypertextual web search engine. In *WWW*, pages 107–117, 1998.

[2] S. Cucerzan. Large-Scale Named Entity Disambiguation Based on Wikipedia Data. In *EMNLP-CoNLL*, pages 708–716, 2007.

[3] J. Hoffart, M. A. Yosef, I. Bordino, H. Fürstenau, M. Pinkal, M. Spaniol, B. Taneva, S. Thater, and G. Weikum. Robust disambiguation of named entities in text. In *EMNLP*, pages 782–792, 2011.

[4] S. Kulkarni, A. Singh, G. Ramakrishnan, and S. Chakrabarti. Collective annotation of wikipedia entities in web text. In *SIGKDD*, pages 457–466, 2009.

[5] N. Lao and W. W. Cohen. Relational retrieval using a combination of path-constrained random walks. *Mach. Learn.*, 81(1):53–67, Oct. 2010.

[6] W. Shen, J. Han, and J. Wang. A probabilistic model for linking named entities in web text with heterogeneous information networks. In *SIGMOD*, pages 1199–1210, 2014.

[7] W. Shen, J. Wang, and J. Han. Entity linking with a knowledge base: Issues, techniques, and solutions. *IEEE Transactions on Knowledge and Data Engineering*, 27(2):443–460, Feb. 2015.

[8] F. Suchanek, G. Kasneci, and G. Weikum. Yago: A core of semantic knowledge unifying wordnet and wikipedia. In *WWW*, pages 697–706, 2007.

[9] Y. Sun, J. Han, X. Yan, P. S. Yu, and T. Wu. Pathsim: Meta path-based top-k similarity search in heterogeneous information networks. In *VLDB*, pages 992 – 1003, 2011.

ConHub: A Metadata Management System for Docker Containers

Chris Xing Tian
National University of Singapore
tianxing@comp.nus.edu.sg

Aditya Pan
Amity University
aditya.pan@student.amity.edu

Y.C. Tay
National University of Singapore
dcstayyc@nus.edu.sg

ABSTRACT

For many years now, enterprises and cloud providers have been using virtualization to run their workloads. Until recently, this means running an application in a virtual machine (hardware virtualization). However, virtual machines are increasingly replaced by containers (operating system virtualization), as evidenced by the rapid rise of Docker. A containerized software environment can generate a large amount of metadata. If properly managed, these metadata can greatly facilitate the management of containers themselves.

This demonstration introduces ConHub, a PostgreSQL-based container metadata management system. Visitors will see that (1) ConHub has a language CQL that supports Docker commands; (2) it has a user-friendly interface for querying and visualizing container relationships; and (3) they can use CQL to formulate sophisticated queries to facilitate container management.

A video of the demonstration can be found at

`https://youtu.be/aWPgbeo_79g`

Keywords

OS Virtualization; Container Metadata; Relational Database

1. INTRODUCTION

Datacenters and cloud providers largely rely on virtualization to run enterprise workloads and user applications. Until recently, this means hardware virtualization, where execution happens in virtual machines (VMs).

Previously, a user process would run on a bare-metal machine that consists of a physical machine and an operating system (OS). Now, the user process and the **guest** OS that it calls are contained in a VM (another process) that runs on a hypervisor that takes on the role of a **host** OS. The hardware is thus virtualized.

The guest OS becomes largely redundant if it shares the same kernel as the host OS. In this case, the VM can be replaced by a **container** that consists of the application, and the files, libraries and binaries that it needs. Two containers on the same bare-metal may have different OS versions, distributions (libraries, tools, window system, etc.) or namespaces (file system, process identifiers, etc.). The OS is thus virtualized.

CIKM'16, October 24 – November 28, 2016, Indianapolis, IN, USA
ACM 978-1-4503-4073-1/16/10.
DOI: http://dx.doi.org/10.1145/2983323.2983331

Interest in container-based virtualization is rising rapidly, as evidenced by the viral adoption of the Docker engine [1] for containers, replacing the hypervisor for VMs. In fact, even before the rise of Docker, Google [1] and Facebook[2] have both been using containerized infrastructures for some years. There are 2 main reasons for the surging interest in containerization:

C1: A container **image** is generated by scripts that specify dependencies, thus facilitating code development, debugging and deployment; the container is a running instance of the image (like a process is a running instance of its code).

C2: The removal of the guest OS makes these images much smaller, so a physical machine can host many more containers than VMs, and spawning containers (in response to a flash crowd, say) is also much faster than booting VMs.

A containerized system has a lot of metadata that can facilitate code development and debugging (**C1**): which OS version does image *X* use? who is the developer for *X*? when was *X* last modified? which containers are running *X*? Etc.

There are also a lot of metadata that can facilitate container deployment (**C2**): how much free memory is there on a particular node? which hosts are running replicas of a container? which containers can be collocated without performance interference? which containers are using a particular port? Etc.

While there are already systems for managing containers, there is none so far for managing metadata for images and containers. This demonstration introduces such a system, namely **ConHub**.

1.1 Related Work

Examples of OS virtualization include HP-UX[3], BSD jails [2], Solaris Zones [3] and Linux containers (LXC[4]), which were recently extended by Docker. Queries on the Docker metadata for images and containers can only be expressed as keyword search.

Docker Datacenter[5] and Kubernetes[6] are systems for managing Docker containers in a cluster environment; other container management systems include Huawei CCE[7] and Netease Hive[8].

---

[1] http://www.docker.com/

[2] http://www.slideshare.net/Docker/aravindnarayanan-facebook140613153626phpapp02-37588997

[3] http://www.hpl.hp.com/hpjournal/pdfs/IssuePDFs/1985-10.pdf

[4] https://linuxcontainers.org

[5] https://www.docker.com/products/docker-datacenter

[6] http://kubernetes.io/

[7] http://console.hwclouds.com/cce

[8] http://c.163.com

These systems dynamically generate a lot of metadata for container deployment (failures, replication, resource allocation etc.). The dynamic setting in a datacenter calls for a powerful metadata management system to support container management.

We designed ConHub to fill this need. ConHub is built on PostgreSQL[9], so it brings to bear well-developed, industrial-strength relational database technology on the management and querying of metadata for images and containers.

2. CONHUB ARCHITECTURE

ConHub has 3 key components: (1) **ConSQL,** a metadata management system. (2) A query processor that supports **CQL**, a language for querying and generating metadata for images and containers; it includes a set of APIs for developers to implement third-party applications that suit their purpose. (3) An ecosystem of applications, built on the APIs, for queries and visualization.

These components are illustrated in Figure 1, and described below:

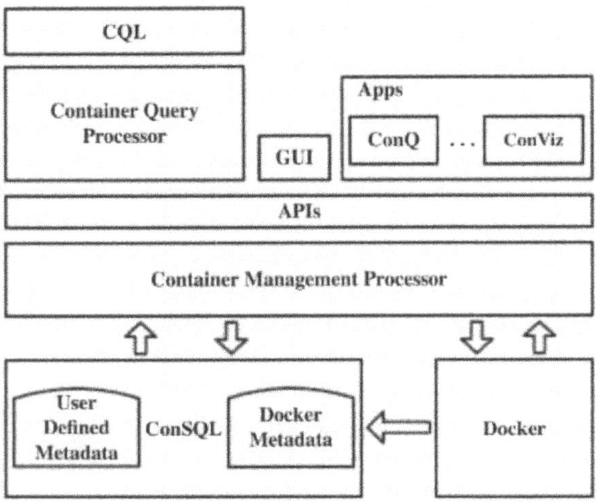

Figure 1. ConHub Architecture

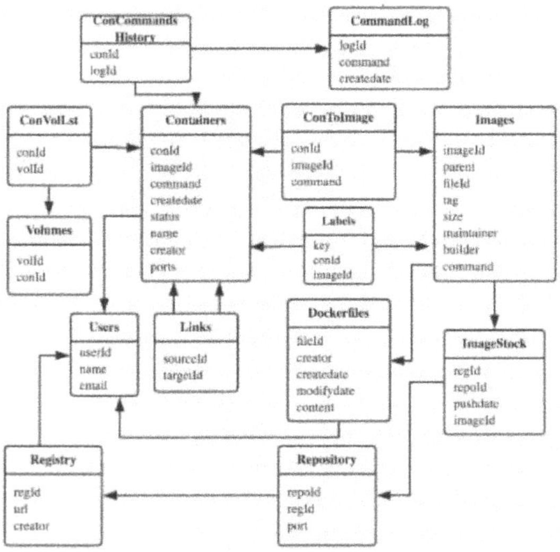

Figure 2. ConSchema has 9 tables for entities and 5 tables for relationships (arrows point from primary key to foreign key).

(1) **ConSQL**
ConSQL is a database system implemented with PostgreSQL. We have designed a relational schema called ConSchema, shown in Figure 2, to model the metadata underlying a container system. ConSchema has 9 tables for entities (Images, Containers, Users, Dockerfiles, etc.) and 5 relationship tables (ConToImage, Labels, etc.).

Much of these metadata are extracted from the JSON files generated by Docker. Users can also generate metadata, via Docker labels or CQL **tags**. If integrated with a container management system like Docker Datacenter or Kubernetes, ConSQL can also manage metadata from that system.

(2) **CQL**
CQL is an extension of SQL, the standard language for managing relational data. CQL thus inherits the power of SQL in the declarative formulation of semantically rich queries, like those illustrated in the Introduction for provenance (**C1**) and management (**C2**). This is a tremendous improvement over the simple keyword search provided by current container systems.

The CQL extension of SQL consists of the following APIs:

- **TAG** (Set objects, String label): Tags a set of objects with the specified label.
- **INTERSECTION** (id1, id2): Returns the lowest common ancestor that two images or containers share.
- **CHILD** (imageId): Returns all the child images that derived from the specified image in the form of a Set.
- **IMAGE**(conId): Returns the id of the image that generated the specified container.
- **CONTAINER**(imageId): Returns the containers generated from the specified image.
- **DISTANCE**(id1, id2): Returns the distance between two images in the version chain; returns –1 if they are unrelated.

(3) **Application Ecosystem**
The APIs accessible from CQL can also be used to build applications for image and container management. So far, we have implemented the following applications:

ConQ: A tool for formulating CQL queries by manipulating ConSchema tables using a graphical user interface. We designed this tool to help the Docker user who is unfamiliar with SQL syntax and semantics.

ConViz: A tool for visualizing the provenance relationship among images and containers. For example, a user can specify two containers, and ConViz will display the image paths that lead from the containers to their common ancestor image (if any).

ConRecovery: A tool to facilitate recovery from a container failure (using a reported incident[10] as a guide). Suppose there is a code change to an image *X*, and the container *CX* spawned from *X* crashes a service. A user can use ConRecovery to find a previous, safe image version *Y*, spawn a new container *CY* to replace *CX*, and notify the developer that made the change to *X*.

---

9 http://www.postgresql.org/

10 http://blog.flux7.com/blogs/docker/docker-saves-the-day-at-flux7

3. DEMONSTRATION SCENARIOS

Our demonstration of ConHub will proceed in 3 stages:

Stage I: Docker

Visitors at the conference who are familiar with Docker can verify that ConHub is an extension of Docker: they can query the ConHub repository (preloaded), create new images, and label, spawn or shutdown containers, like they can with a Docker client. For visitors who are unfamiliar with Docker, we will demonstrate how these can be done with Docker commands.

Stage II: ConQ and ConViz

In Stage II, the visitors can use ConQ's table manipulation interface (see Fig.2) to formulate queries of the metadata stored in ConSchema, including those for any new images or containers created in Stage I. They can also use ConViz to visualize the version tree for an image, or the provenance among images and containers (see Fig.3).

Stage III: ConRecovery and CQL

Finally, we use ConRecovery to demonstrate the scenario described above for recovering from a container failure (see Fig.4).

We will also demonstrate how the power of CQL can help a development team deal with bugs. Suppose the team identifies two containers, *conIdX* and *conIdY*, with similar faulty behavior; they believe the fault is inherited from some common image *Z* that both are based on, and want to find all containers and images derived from *Z* and label them "*hazard*". This can be done with a CQL statement:

***TAG ((SELECT** C.conId, I.imageId*
***FROM** Containers C, Images I **WHERE** I.imageId*
***IN CHILD(INTERSECTION**(conIdX, conIdY))*
***AND** C.imageId= I.imageId) , "hazard")*

The team suspects that *Z* has a virus that came from an infected IDE downloaded by a developer when creating *Z*. They decide to identify all developers of "*hazard*" images and label the images and containers they produced as "*potential hazard*", using the CQL statement:

***TAG((SELECT** C.conId, I2.imageId*
***FROM** Containers C, Images I1, Images I2, Labels L*
***WHERE** L.key="hazard" **AND** I1.imageId=L.imageId*
***AND** I1.maintainer = I2.maintainer*
***AND** C.imageId = I2.imageId) , "potential hazard")*

Note the use of APIs ***TAG***, ***CHILD*** and ***INTERSECTION***. Also, the second CQL statement uses four joins; it will be hard to do the same thing with just keyword search.

We will encourage visitors to suggest queries so we can demonstrate how they can be formulated with CQL.

4. FUTURE WORK

A video of the demonstration can be found at

`https://youtu.be/aWPgbeo_79g`

The metadata in this demonstration are generated by the user and a Docker client. We plan to integrate ConHub with a container management system, like Docker Datacenter or Kubernetes. That will require expansion of ConSchema and addition of APIs, so the application ecosystem can host more tools for facilitating container deployment in a datacenter.

5. REFERENCES

[1] A. Verma, L. Pedrosa, M. Korupolu, D. Oppenheimer, E. Tune, and J. Wilkes. Large-scale cluster management at Google with Borg. In Proc. EuroSys, page 18, April 2015.

[2] P.-H. Kamp and R.N. Watson. Jails: Confining the omnipotent root. In Proc SANE, vol.43, 2000.

[3] J. Beck, D. Comay, Ozgur L., D. Price, Andy T., Andrew G., and Blaise S. Virtualization and namespace isolation in the Solaris operating system (psarc/2002/174), 2006.

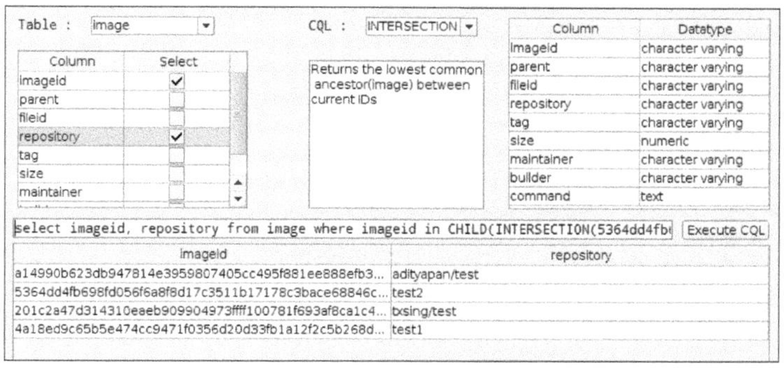

Figure 2. ConQ: graphical interface for query formulation.

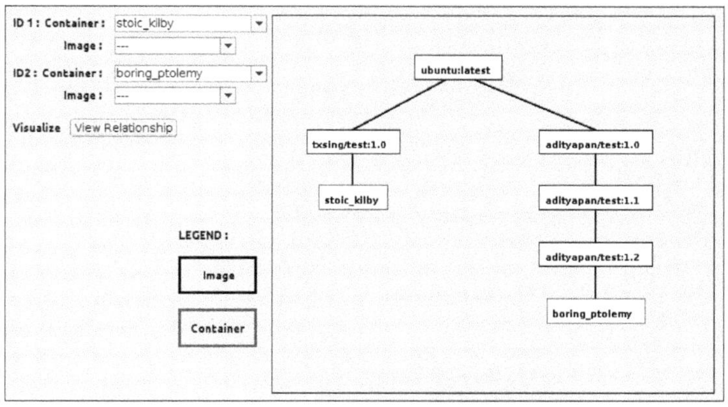

Figure 3. ConViz: visualizing provenance.

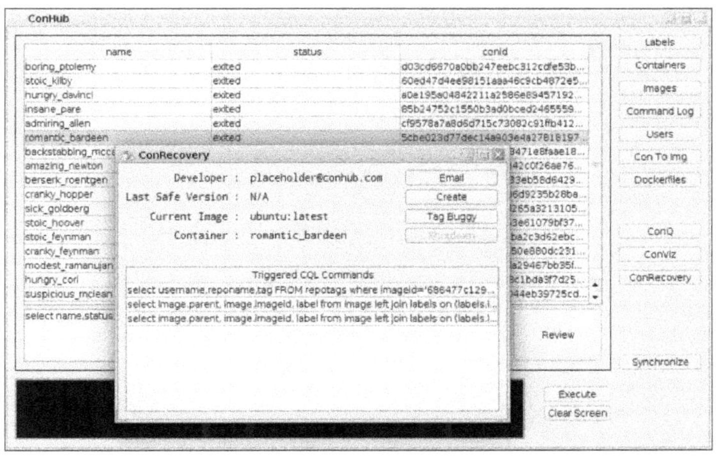

Figure 4. ConRecovery: a tool for recovering from container failure.

BIGtensor: Mining Billion-Scale Tensor Made Easy

Namyong Park*
Seoul National University
namyong.park@snu.ac.kr

Byungsoo Jeon*
Seoul National University
jbsimdicd@gmail.com

Jungwoo Lee
Seoul National University
ljw9111@snu.ac.kr

U Kang
Seoul National University
ukang@snu.ac.kr

ABSTRACT

Many real-world data are naturally represented as tensors, or multi-dimensional arrays. Tensor decomposition is an important tool to analyze tensors for various applications such as latent concept discovery, trend analysis, clustering, and anomaly detection. However, existing tools for tensor analysis do not scale well for billion-scale tensors or offer limited functionalities.

In this paper, we propose BIGtensor, a large-scale tensor mining library that tackles both of the above problems. Carefully designed for scalability, BIGtensor decomposes at least 100× larger tensors than the current state of the art. Furthermore, BIGtensor provides a variety of distributed tensor operations and tensor generation methods. We demonstrate how BIGtensor can help users discover hidden concepts and analyze trends from large-scale tensors that are hard to be processed by existing tensor tools.

Keywords

Tensor, Tensor Decompositions, Distributed Computing

1. INTRODUCTION

Many real-world data with multiple attributes are naturally represented as tensors, or multi-dimensional arrays. Examples include movie rating data (movie, user, time, rating) and network intrusion logs (source IP, destination IP, port number, time), to name a few.

Tensor decomposition is a crucial tool that allows us to analyze such data for various applications including latent concept discovery, trend analysis, clustering, and anomaly detection [11]. PARAFAC and Tucker are two widely-used tensor decomposition methods [9]. Each method comes with two different versions: the unconstrained and the nonnegativity-constrained. The nonnegative tensor decomposition enforces all elements in the factors to be nonnegative. Sometimes we have supplementary information coupled with certain modes of the tensor data. For example, for the (movie, user, time, rating) tensor, we may have a (movie, genre) matrix. Coupled Matrix-Tensor Factorization (CMTF) [1] is the standard tool to jointly analyze coupled matrix-tensor data.

Although there exist several tools for analyzing tensors [3, 2, 4, 13, 1], they suffer from either or both of the following limitations:

1. Limited scalability. They run on a single machine, and thus cannot handle large tensors that exceed the capacity of a single machine. While distributed tools also exist (e.g. [4]), their scalability is still limited for truly large tensors [5].
2. Limited functionality. They do not provide a unified framework to handle tensors and tensor decompositions. They support only a couple of tensor algorithms, requiring the user to assemble several different tools to process tensors. Table 1 shows a comparison between BIGtensor and two other state-of-the-art tensor tools.

In this paper, we present BIGtensor, a large-scale tensor mining library running on the Hadoop platform. As a unified framework to handle tensor and tensor decompositions, BIGtensor provides four different sets of functionalities:

- **Tensor Decomposition.** PARAFAC, Nonnegative PARAFAC, Tucker, Nonnegative Tucker, CMTF.
- **Tensor Generation.** FromFactors (from factor matrices and core tensor), Random (tensor values are set randomly), etc.
- **Tensor-Tensor Operation.** BinaryOps (and, or, xor),

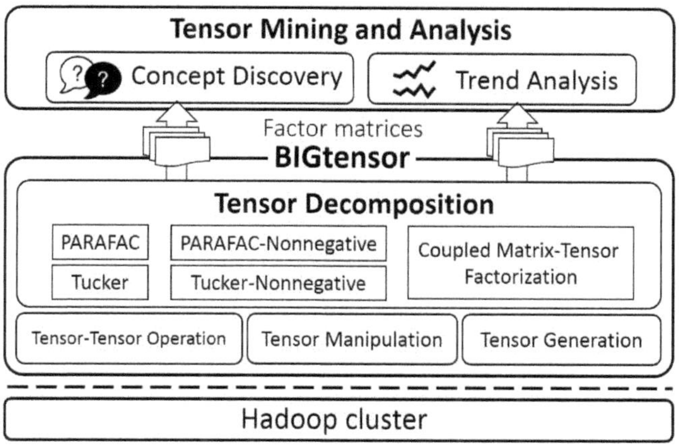

Figure 1: Overview of the system which consists of two parts: BIGtensor is a suite of large-scale algorithms running on the Hadoop platform to handle tensor and tensor decomposition; the tensor mining and analysis module allows the user to discover concepts and analyze trends from the factor matrices, which are the results of tensor decomposition.

*These authors contributed equally to this work.

CIKM '16, October 24–28, 2016, Indianapolis, IN, USA.

ACM ISBN 978-1-4503-4073-1/16/10...$15.00
DOI: http://dx.doi.org/10.1145/2983323.2983332

ArithmeticOps (+, −, ×, ÷), NModeProduct (n-mode product of two tensors), etc.

- **Tensor Manipulation.** Matricization (unfolding a tensor into a certain mode), Convert2Binary (converting a tensor into a binary tensor), etc.

Carefully designed for scalability, BIGtensor decomposes at least 100× larger tensors than the current state of the art.

For our demonstration, we apply BIGtensor to large real-world tensors that lie beyond the ability of existing tools. We will show how we can employ BIGtensor for tensor decomposition and analysis, and invite the audience to uncover latent concepts and trends from real-world tensor data on their own by interactively exploring the factor matrices decomposed from the Microsoft academic graph, NELL, DARPA, MovieLens, YELP, and PhoneCall tensor data (see Table 3 for details on these tensors). The web site for this paper is located at http://datalab.snu.ac.kr/bigtensordemo.

Table 1: Comparison of functionalities provided by BIGtensor and other state-of-the-art tensor tools. P: PARAFAC, T: Tucker, PN: PARAFAC-Nonnegative, TN: Tucker-Nonnegative, C: CMTF.

Functionality	BIGtensor	Tensor Toolbox	Flexi-FaCT
Tensor Decomposition	**P, PN, T, TN, C**	P, PN, T	P, PN, C
Tensor Generation	**Yes**	Yes	No
Tensor-Tensor Operation	**Yes**	Yes	No
Tensor Manipulation	**Yes**	Yes	No
Distributed	**Yes**	No	Yes

2. SYSTEM OVERVIEW

Our system consists of two parts: 1) BIGtensor and 2) the tensor mining and analysis module. As illustrated in Figure 1, our system relies on BIGtensor for the decomposition of large-scale tensors, and uses the tensor mining and analysis module to discover concepts and analyze trends from the resulting factor matrices. In the following subsections, we give an overview of our system.

2.1 Distributed Tensor Decomposition

BIGtensor supports both tensor decomposition and coupled matrix-tensor decomposition (CMTF) methods. A common challenge shared by both types of decompositions is to scale up to large tensors with millions or billions of elements in each dimension, that are becoming more common in real-world settings. The most important issue is the 'intermediate data explosion' problem [8] where the amount of space required for the materialization of intermediate matrices is too large for a single machine, or even for a cluster.

BIGtensor is carefully designed for massive scalability. The main ideas [8, 7, 6, 5] employed by BIGtensor are as follows: 1) BIGtensor solves the intermediate data explosion problem by (a) exploiting the sparsity of real-world tensors, (b) decoupling the steps involved in n-mode vector product, (c) reusing intermediate data, and (d) using optimizations for MapReduce such as parallel outer products and distributed cache multiplication. 2) BIGtensor minimizes floating point operations through careful ordering of computations to update tensor factors. 3) BIGtensor significantly reduces the number of jobs and disk accesses by integrating redundant MapReduce jobs. Due to the lack of space, we refer the reader to [8, 7, 6, 5] for more details on these ideas.

Scalability. We demonstrate the scalability of tensor decomposition using BIGtensor by comparing BIGtensor against the two state-of-the-art tools, the Tensor Toolbox [3] and FlexiFaCT [4], in terms of tensor size. We run BIGtensor and FlexiFaCT on a Hadoop cluster with 40 machines, each of which has a quad-core Intel Xeon E3-1230v3 CPU and 32GB RAM. The Tensor Toolbox runs on a single machine in the cluster. In all experiments, the rank size for PARAFAC is set to 10, and the core tensor size for Tucker is set to 10×10×10.

Table 2: Scalability of BIGtensor and other tools. We report the mode length and the density of the largest data each tool processes using two representative tensor decomposition algorithms, PARAFAC and Tucker. BIGtensor decomposes 100× larger data in terms of mode length than both of the tools, and also decomposes 100× denser data than the Tensor Toolbox.

Scalability	Method	BIG tensor	Tensor Toolbox	Flexi-FaCT
Mode Length & Nonzeros	PARAFAC	$\geq 10^9$	$\leq 10^7$	$\leq 10^7$
	Tucker	$\geq 10^9$	$\leq 10^7$	–
Density	PARAFAC	$\geq 10^{-5}$	$\leq 10^{-7}$	$\geq 10^{-5}$
	Tucker	$\geq 10^{-5}$	$\leq 10^{-7}$	–

We measure the scalability of each tool on synthetic random tensors in the following two aspects. (a) *Mode Length and Number of Nonzeros.* We increase the length $I = J = K$ of each mode from 10^3 to 10^9, and set the number of nonzeros to $I \times 10$. In Table 2, we report the size of the largest data each tool processes using two representative decomposition algorithms, PARAFAC and Tucker. While BIGtensor processes 10^9 scale tensor, both the Tensor Toolbox and FlexiFaCT run out of memory when the mode length goes beyond 10^7. (b) *Density.* We increase the tensor density from 10^{-9} to 10^{-5}, while fixing the mode length $I = J = K$ to 10^5. Table 2 shows that BIGtensor processes 100× denser data than the Tensor Toolbox. For both of the above aspects, nonnegative PARAFAC and Tucker, and CMTF also show a similar performance.

2.2 Tensor Mining and Analysis

Tensor decomposition enables us to analyze the original tensor data from multiple perspectives. By analyzing factor matrices, which are the output of tensor decomposition, we discover latent concepts, anomalies, and trends.

However, for large-scale tensors, two challenges exist with this process. First, it is infeasible to investigate all elements of factor matrices since the number of elements in each factor matrix is the same as that of the huge input tensor. For example, for NELL data, the minimum number of elements to explore in each factor matrix is 26 million. To handle this issue, we consider only the top-k highest valued elements in each factor matrix. Second, even after this top-k filtering, there are often elements that appear in most columns of the factor matrix. Although their values are high, they do not add much information. Therefore, we calculate new scores for the top-k elements to reflect the specificity of elements that appear in only a few columns. New scoring function based on IDF score is $(1 + \alpha \log(R/col)) \times val$, where α is a predefined constant, R is the number of columns in the factor matrix, col is the number of columns the element appears in, and val is the value of the element. We set α to 2.0. Then, we sort the elements in the descending order of these new scores.

Concept Discovery. Columns of the factor matrices can be roughly regarded as the soft-clustering of the tensor data. Examining each preprocessed factor matrix and seeing what kind of elements form each column reveals the nature of concepts hidden in the data. For instance, we discover 'Comedy' and 'Horror' concepts from MovieLens data as in Figure 4. Furthermore, elements whose values are distinct from those of other elements in the same concept represent anomalies. Figure 5 shows that we find an attacker whose value is the highest in the first concept. To facilitate the finding of concepts, we can also use additional information for each attribute, such as the user demographics. Visualizing additional information for the selected concept shows its various features at a single glance.

Trend Analysis. For tensors with a timestamp attribute, we can discover temporal trends from the time factor matrix. Since vectors for the n-th concept from different factor matrices are related, a temporal pattern indicates a temporal characteristic of the associated factors. For example, we find from MovieLens data that the 'Horror' concept experiences seasonal spikes as shown in Figure 4. For trend analysis, we visualize the temporal values of each concept over time, and look for interesting patterns and temporal correlations between concepts.

3. DEMONSTRATION PLAN

Demonstration Detail. In our demonstration, the audience will be invited to apply PARAFAC and Tucker to several real-world datasets, and analyze them using our system. We will prepare three ways for the users to learn about our system. First, we will prepare a poster to give an overview of the system. Second, we will give a guided tour in which we show the process of how we arrived at our discoveries from the data. Third, we will let our audience to mine the data and make their own discoveries with our system.

Users will be given the options to select (1) the tensor data, (2) the tensor decomposition method among PARAFAC and Tucker, (3) the rank size for PARAFAC or the core tensor size for Tucker, and (4) the analysis mode between concept discovery and trend analysis.

For concept discovery, we provide an overview mode and a detail mode. In the overview mode, users will be able to see all vectors in a specific factor they choose, such as the movie factor, and their top-k elements in a tabular form. More details on each element will appear when the user moves the mouse over it. In the detail mode (Figure 2), they will have a more comprehensive look at each vector of a particular factor matrix. Users will be presented highly ranked elements of the chosen vector. Additional information for each element, such as the movie genres and its statistics, will also be displayed when available to help with the discovery process of the audience. Since vectors for the n-th concept from different factor matrices are closely related with each other, we also show the other vectors of the n-th concept from other factor matrices on the side for a better understanding of the characteristics of the n-th concept in general.

In the trend analysis mode (Figure 3), we visualize the values of temporal elements (e.g. 'year-month' elements) over time so that the user can find meaningful patterns. The tool supports overlapping multiple graphs; users can choose to visualize several concepts at the same time, and look for temporal relationships among them. The graph is zoomable; users can zoom into a shorter time frame, for example, to observe the pattern of a concept over the course of a day, or they can zoom out to month or year level to have a broader view. Moreover, our tool displays those vectors from other factor matrices, which correspond to the concepts selected by the user. This makes it convenient to associate the temporal characteristic with the linked dimension at a glance.

Datasets. For the demonstration, we will use the following real-world tensors: Microsoft academic graph, NELL, DARPA, MovieLens, YELP, and PhoneCall (see Table 3).

4. RELATED WORK

Several scalable algorithms for tensor analysis have been developed. GigaTensor [8] is the first work on large-scale PARAFAC decomposition running on MapReduce. HaTen2 [7, 6] improves upon GigaTensor, and combines Tucker and PARAFAC decompositions into a general framework. Jeon et al. [5] propose SCouT for scalable coupled matrix-tensor factorization. BIGtensor unifies tensor decomposition methods proposed by [8, 7, 5] in a single library, and further improves PARAFAC and Tucker decomposition algorithms from [8, 7] by adopting the ideas from [5] with code optimization. As a tensor mining library, BIGtensor also provides various tensor operations and tensor generation methods. Shin et al. [12] propose PARAFAC-based distributed tensor decomposition methods for partially observable tensors. In [4], Beutel et al. propose FlexiFaCT, a scalable MapReduce algorithm for decomposing matrix, tensor, and coupled matrix-tensor through distributed stochastic gradient descent. ParCube [10] is a parallelizable PARAFAC decomposition method that leverages random sampling techniques.

5. ACKNOWLEDGMENTS

This work was supported by the Basic Science Research Program through the National Research Foundation of Korea funded by the Ministry of Science, ICT and Future Planning (grant No. 2013R1A1A1064409). This work was also supported by ICT R&D program of MSIP/IITP. [R0101-15-0176, Development of Core Technology for Human-like Self-taught Learning based on Symbolic Approach]

6. REFERENCES

[1] E. Acar, T. G. Kolda, and D. M. Dunlavy. All-at-once optimization for coupled matrix and tensor factorizations. *CoRR*, abs/1105.3422, 2011.

[2] C. A. Andersson and R. Bro. The n-way toolbox for matlab. *Chemometrics and Intelligent Laboratory Systems*, 52(1):1–4.

[3] B. W. Bader, T. G. Kolda, et al. Matlab tensor toolbox version 2.6. Available online, February 2015.

[4] A. Beutel, P. P. Talukdar, A. Kumar, C. Faloutsos, E. E. Papalexakis, and E. P. Xing. Flexifact: Scalable flexible factorization of coupled tensors on hadoop. In *SDM*, 2014.

[5] B. Jeon, I. Jeon, S. Lee, and U. Kang. Scout: Scalable coupled matrix-tensor factorization-algorithms and discoveries. In *ICDE*, 2016.

[6] I. Jeon, E. E. Papalexakis, C. Faloutsos, L. Sael, and U. Kang. Mining billion-scale tensors: algorithms and discoveries. *The VLDB Journal*, 25(4):519–544, 2016.

[7] I. Jeon, E. E. Papalexakis, U. Kang, and C. Faloutsos. Haten2: Billion-scale tensor decompositions. In *ICDE*, 2015.

[8] U. Kang, E. E. Papalexakis, A. Harpale, and C. Faloutsos. Gigatensor: scaling tensor analysis up by 100 times - algorithms and discoveries. In *KDD*, pages 316–324, 2012.

[9] T. G. Kolda and B. W. Bader. Tensor decompositions and applications. *SIAM Review*, 51(3):455–500, 2009.

[10] E. E. Papalexakis, C. Faloutsos, and N. D. Sidiropoulos. Parcube: Sparse parallelizable tensor decompositions. In *ECML-PKDD*, pages 521–536, 2012.

[11] L. Sael, I. Jeon, and U. Kang. Scalable tensor mining. *Big Data Research*, 2(2):82 – 86, 2015. Visions on Big Data.

[12] K. Shin and U. Kang. Distributed methods for high-dimensional and large-scale tensor factorization. In *ICDM*, 2014.

[13] J. O. Yoo, A. Ramanathan, and C. J. Langmead. Pytensor: A python based tensor library. Technical Report CMU-CS-10-102, Carnegie Mellon University, 2010.

APPENDIX

A. SCREENSHOTS

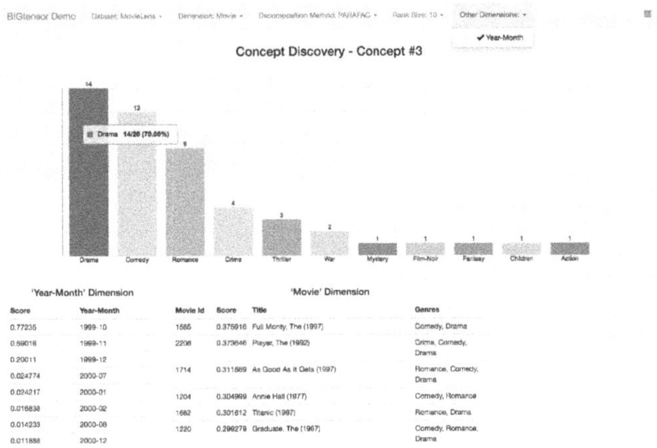

Figure 2: Detail mode for concept discovery using PARAFAC on MovieLens dataset. The detail mode shows highly ranked elements of the selected concept with additional information such as the movie genres. It also shows a bar chart for the genre occurrences in the chosen concept to help with the discovery process of the audience. Further, the tool displays other vectors of the current concept from other factor matrices on the side.

Figure 3: Trend analysis mode using PARAFAC on MovieLens dataset, in which the values of temporal elements of the selected concepts are visualized. (1) The tool supports overlapping multiple graphs. (2) The graph is zoomable; users can zoom into a shorter time frame, or zoom out to month or year level. (3) The tool displays those vectors from other factor matrices, which correspond to the concepts the user selects near the top of the tool.

B. OMITTED MATERIAL

Table 3: Summary of the tensor data used for the experiments and the demonstration. More details on each dataset can be found at http://datalab.snu.ac.kr/bigtensordemo. B: billion, M: million, K: thousand.

Name	Mode			Nonzeros
Microsoft Academic Graph	Paper	Author	Affiliation	325 M
	123 M	123 M	2.7 M	
NELL	Noun phrase 1	Noun phrase 2	Context	144 M
	26 M	26 M	48 M	
DARPA	Source IP	Dest IP	Time	28 M
	22 K	22 K	24 M	
MovieLens	User	Movie	YearMonth	10 M
	72 K	11 K	157	
YELP	User	Business	YearMonth	334 K
	71 K	16 K	108	
PhoneCall	Source	Dest	Date	1 B
	30 M	30 M	62	
Random	I	J	K	10 K∼10 B
	1 K∼1 B	1 K∼1 B	1 K∼1 B	

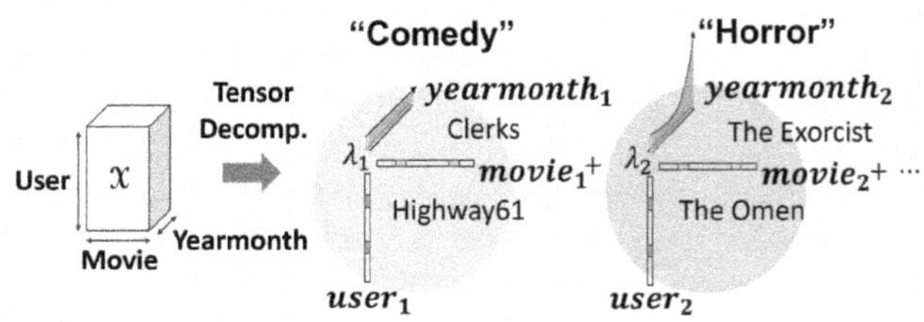

Figure 4: Overview of concept discovery and trend analysis on MovieLens dataset. We find from the movie factor matrix that movies in the same genre are clustered into the same concept, for example, comedy and horror. In the yearmonth factor matrix, we see that the demand for horror movies suddenly increases at a certain period, while the demand for comedy movies is almost constant.

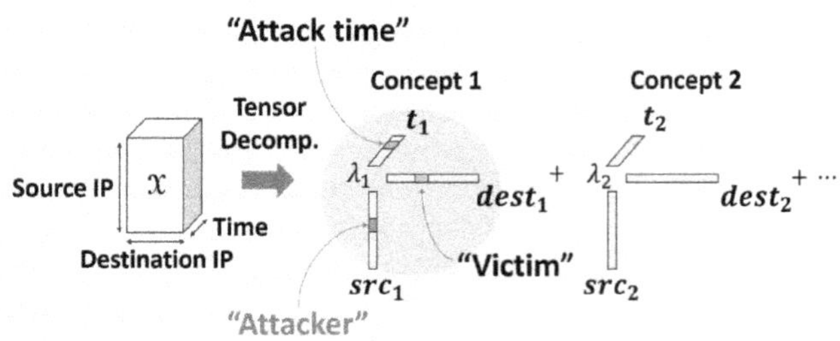

Figure 5: Overview of anomaly detection on DARPA dataset. Concept 1 shows an example of network attacks. The highest values of each vector in concept 1 indicate an attacker, a victim, and the attack time, respectively.

eGraphSearch: Effective Keyword Search in Graphs

Mehdi Kargar*, Lukasz Golab#, Jaroslaw Szlichta$
*University of Windsor, Windsor, Canada
#University of Waterloo, Waterloo, Canada
$University of Ontario Institute of Technology, Oshawa, Canada
mkargar@uwindsor.ca, lgolab@uwaterloo.ca, jaroslaw.szlichta@uoit.ca

ABSTRACT

In a node-labeled graph, keyword search finds subtrees of the graph whose nodes contain all of the query keywords. This provides a way to query graph databases that neither requires mastery of a query language such as SPARQL, nor a deep knowledge of the database schema. We demonstrate eGraphSearch, a new system for effective keyword search in graph databases. Previous work ranks answer trees using combinations of structural and content-based metrics, such as path length between keywords or relevance of the labels in the answer tree to the query keywords. However, different nodes in the graph might have different importance, which affects the utility of the answer. In the proposed system, we implemented two new ways to rank keyword search results over graphs: the first one takes node importance into account while the second one is a bi-objective optimization of edge weights and node importance. In the demonstration, participants will execute keyword queries against several popular graph datasets.

1. INTRODUCTION

Many datasets, e.g., Web and social data, describe connections and relationships, and can be naturally represented as graphs. Graph databases have recently been proposed to natively manage such data, with SPARQL being a popular query language. However, users who are not familiar with the query language or the database schema risk being locked out of valuable data. This is where keyword search comes in: as an intuitive way to explore graphs whose nodes are associated with text, without having deep knowledge of query languages or the database schema. While the keyword search approach certainly has merit, a technical challenge is to extract *semantically meaningful* subsets of the data that contain the specified keywords. Given the limitations of existing tools, we present the novel eGraphSearch system that allows non-technical users to effectively search for answers in graph databases.

Given a set of query keywords, the problem that eGraphSearch solves is to find a subtree of the graph that contains all the keywords. An answer tree consists of a *root node*, *content nodes* at the leaves, which contain the query keywords, and *middle nodes* that connect the content nodes together through the root node. By convention, the root node is also considered to be a middle node.

CIKM'16 October 24–November 28, 2016, Indianapolis, IN, USA.

ACM ISBN 978-1-4503-4073-1/16/10.
DOI: http://dx.doi.org/10.1145/2983323.2983333

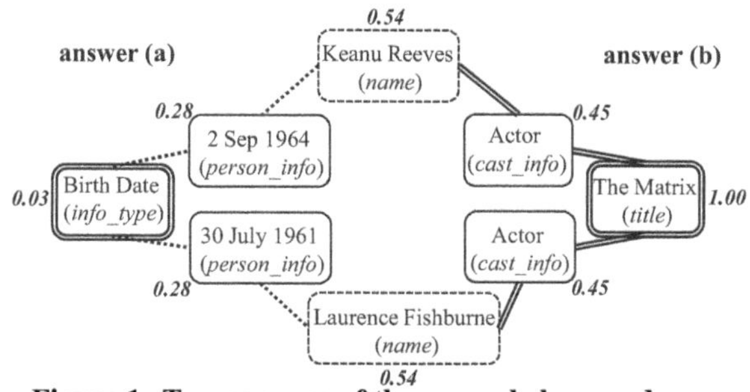

Figure 1: Two answers of the example keyword query.

Previous work ranks answer trees using combinations of structural and content-based metrics, such as the sum of edge weights (shorter weighted paths from the root to the content nodes are better), and IR metrics corresponding to the relevance of the text in the answer tree to the query keywords [2, 3]. However, different nodes in the graph may have different semantic importance to the answer. Following on our recent work in keyword search in databases [4], we have implemented eGraphSearch, a system for effective keyword search over graph databases, that takes node importance, including the middle nodes, into account.

To motivate our approach and illustrate the shortcomings of existing techniques, consider a graph obtained from the Internet Movie Database (IMDb) by converting *foreign keys* in the database schema to undirected equally-weighted edges as shown in Figure 1. For each node, the name of its table in the database is also shown (e.g., The Matrix movie appeared in the *title* table). In total, IMDb[1] has 21 tables associated with 21 different node types in the graph. Suppose we issue the keyword query [*"Keanu Reeves" "Laurence Fishburne"*] to find the relationship(s) between these two actors. Two answers, labeled (a) (rooted at Birth Date and using dotted edges) and (b) (rooted at The Matrix and using double edges), are shown in Figure 1. Answer (a) suggests that Reeves and Fishburne are connected because they both have an *info_type* called Birth Date in the *person_info* table, though their actual birth dates are different. Answer (b) reveals that these two actors both starred in the movie The Matrix. Clearly, answer (b) is more meaningful. However, previous work cannot distinguish between these two answers because their content nodes have the same keywords (i.e., the same IR score) and they both have the same number of edges. The difference is in the middle nodes: as shown in Figure 1, The Matrix (*title*) and Actor (*cast_info*) nodes have higher weights than

[1]We computed the node importance values in Figure 1 from the importance of the corresponding tables in the IMDb database, which in turn we computed using our algorithm from [4]. In general, node importance is application-specific; e.g., social credibility of people in a social graph or PageRank scores in the WWW graph.

info_type and *person_info* nodes because acting in the same movie is a strong relationship.

The eGraphSearch system builds on our foundations developed in [4, 5]. Our contributions and demonstration goals are as follows.

1. We demonstrate eGraphSearch, a system for effective keyword search in graphs. The system provides two new ways to rank the results: the first one takes node importance into account whereas the second one is a bi-objective optimization of edge weights and node importance (Section 2). Since both of these problems are NP-hard [5], eGraphSearch implements two greedy solutions to rank answers (Section 3).
2. We ensure the efficiency of our ranking algorithms by implementing a 2-hop cover index that returns the shortest path distance between any two nodes. We propose several optimizations that significantly improve performance and scalability without compromising the precision (Section 3).
3. The eGraphSearch system provides new relevance measures for the importance of nodes and edges based on our prior work on keyword search over databases [4].
4. We demonstrate eGraphSearch using popular graph datasets from different application domains, including DBLP, IMDb and Twitter (details in Section 4). In addition to the two ranking methods that we propose, we have also implemented two methods from previous work. Thus, participants will be able to interactively explore the effect of a wide variety of different ranking strategies and different measures to assign edge and node weights in the input graph.

2. PROBLEM STATEMENT

Given a node-labeled graph with application-supplied node and edge weights, as well as a query consisting of a set of keywords, we want to find and rank a set of ***trees*** that contain all the query keywords. Each leaf node in the tree must be a content node (i.e., minimality property). Assuming that edge weights denote semantic distance between nodes, effective answer trees should have a small sum of edge weights and a large sum of node (importance) weights.

Definition 1. **Edge Weight Objective (EW):** Suppose that the edges of an answer tree T are denoted as $\{e_1, e_2, \dots, e_m\}$. The edge weight of the answer is defined as $EW(T) = \sum_{i=1}^{m} w(e_i)$, where $w(e_i)$ is the weight of edge e_i.

Minimizing the edge weight objective is NP-hard [2]. Now, assume that $imp(n_i)$ is the importance of node n_i and let $imp'(n_i) = \frac{1}{imp(n_i)}$. We use the inverse of node importance to convert the maximization problem into a minimization problem.

Definition 2. **Node Importance Objective (NI):** Suppose that the nodes (content and middle) of an answer tree T are denoted as $\{n_1, n_2, \dots, n_k\}$. The node importance of the answer tree is defined as $NI(T) = \sum_{i=1}^{k} imp'(n_i)$.

Given a graph G and a set of query keywords, our problem is to find a minimal tree T in G that covers the keywords and minimizes the node importance objective $NI(T)$. We proved in [5] by a reduction to *group Steiner tree* that this is an NP-hard problem. Additionally, we are interested in the bi-criteria optimization problem of minimizing both the edge weight and the (inverse of) node importance objectives. One way to solve a bi-criteria optimization problem is to convert it into a single objective problem by combining the two objective functions into one. We define a single objective that combines edge weights and node importance with a tradeoff parameter λ as follows (λ varies from 0 to 1).

Definition 3. **Combined Objective (C):** Given an answer tree T from graph G for a given set of input keywords and a tradeoff parameter λ between the edge weights and the node importance, where $0 \leq \lambda \leq 1$, the combined objective of T is defined as $C(T) = \lambda.NI(T) + (1 - \lambda).EW(T)$.

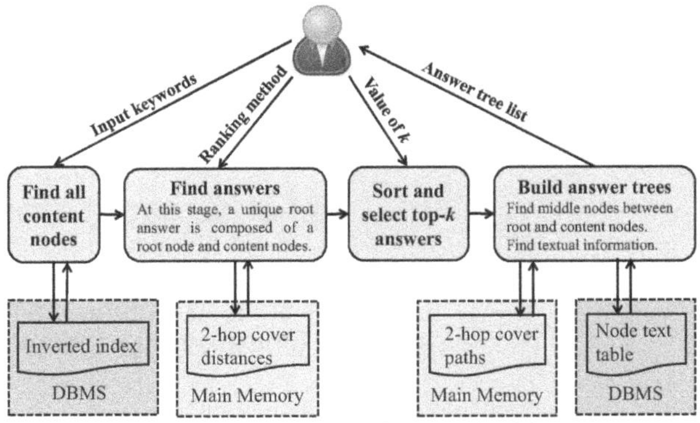

Figure 2: eGraphSearch System Architecture.

Since $EW(T)$ and $NI(T)$ may have different scales, they should first be normalized. Using the combined cost objective, we define the following problem. Given a graph G, a set of input keywords and a tradeoff λ between the edge weight and node importance objectives, find a minimal tree T in G that covers the input keywords and minimizes the combined objective $C(T)$. We showed in [5] that optimizing this problem is also NP-hard. Since λ is application-dependent, we leverage user and domain expert feedback to set and update it over time. Incorporating user feedback is a vital component towards achieving high search precision.

3. SYSTEM DESCRIPTION

The eGraphSearch system builds on our fundamentals presented in [4, 5]. Figure 2 shows the system architecture of eGraphSearch. For each query keyword, the system finds the IDs of the (content) nodes that contain the keyword using an inverted index. These node IDs are stored in a map in which the key is the keyword and the value is a set of node IDs that contain the keyword. This map is passed to the procedure for finding unique answer trees. First, potential root nodes are selected using an index of shortest distances between nodes. At this stage, each answer contains a root node and a set of content nodes. These are passed to the next step to sort and select top-k answers. For each answer in the top-k list, the last functional component completes the answer tree by finding the middle nodes from the path index and the textual information from the node text table. At the end, the list of top-k answer trees are shown to the user.

3.1 Search and Ranking Algorithms

Since minimizing the node importance and combined objectives is NP-hard, we propose two greedy algorithms to solve them [5]. The first algorithm is based on converting the input graph into a new graph with importance/weights only on the edges. The new graph G' has the same set of nodes as the original graph G, but the node importance in G is moved onto the edges in G'. Assume that the edge weight between nodes n_i and n_j in G is denoted by $w(n_i, n_j)$. In G', the edge weight between nodes n_i and n_j is defined as $w'(n_i, n_j) = \lambda.(imp'(n_i) + imp'(n_j)) + 2.(1 - \lambda).w(n_i, n_j)$. When λ is set to 1, this algorithm only minimizes the node importance objective.

For finding answers, we adapt the unique root semantics [2]. Each node n_r in the graph could be a potential root for an answer tree. To build a tree around n_r, for each given keyword k_i, we assign the closest node n_{k_i} in G' that contains k_i to a tree rooted at n_r. The tree with the lowest sum of the new edge weights is the best answer. Since we use the unique root semantics, and we run this polynomial operation on every node (i.e., potential root) of the graph once, the total runtime of the algorithm is also polynomial.

To further improve efficiency, we introduce the second algorithm, which does not require separate indexes for different values of λ and therefore saves space. Here, we build a new graph G'' with the same set of nodes as G. In G'', the edge weight between nodes n_i and n_j is defined as $w''(n_i, n_j) = imp'(n_i) + imp'(n_j)$. This is similar to G' when $\lambda = 1$. From the query keywords, we choose the one with the smallest set of content nodes. Call this keyword k and its set of content nodes S_k. Then, for each node $n_i \in S_k$ and for the remaining query keywords, we select the content node closest to n_i in G''. A tree rooted at n_i is formed and its $C(T)$ is calculated. Then, for each query keyword other than k, we replace the content node of that keyword with the second closest content node to n_i in G''. If this improves the value of $C(T)$, this operation is applied permanently. This process is repeated for a limited number of times or until the replace operation does not decrease $C(T)$ by more than a pre-defined threshold δ. Among the trees rooted at the content nodes of S_k, the one with the lowest $C(T)$ is chosen as the best answer.

We found in [5] by conducting a user study that ranking answers using our node importance and combined objectives returns more meaningful results than previous methods. In Figure 1, both of the proposed algorithms return answer (b) as the best answer (with λ set to 0.25, 0.5, 0.75 or 1).

3.2 Indexing and Data Storage

For an input graph G, we build the following four data structures to facilitate the search process: 1) An *Inverted Index* that stores, for each keyword in the input graph, the IDs of the nodes that contain the keyword; 2) A *2-Hop Cover Distance Index* to find the shortest distance between two nodes; 3) A *2-Hop Cover Path Index* to find the shortest path from the root to each of the content nodes; and 4) A *Node Text Table* to store the textual information contained in each node (e.g., the names of the actors).

A distance query returns the shortest distance between two nodes in the input graph G. We frequently need to find the distance between a potential root and the content nodes. However, computing distance on-the-fly is too slow to be interactive, while precomputing the distances between all pairs of nodes takes too much space ($O(N^2)$ for a graph with N nodes; thus, for big graphs, it quickly runs out of memory). In eGraphSearch, we use *distance labeling*, or *2-hop cover* [1], which is a practical middle ground between the two extremes mentioned above. For each node n_i in graph G, a label $L(n_i)$ is computed and stored. $L(n_i)$ is a set of pairs $(n_j, d(n_j, n_i))$ where n_j is a node in G and $d(n_j, n_i)$ is the shortest distance between n_j and n_i. The set of labels $\{L(n_i)\}|n_i \in N_G\}$ is called the 2-hop cover index (N_G is the set of all nodes in G) and is used to answer distance queries between any pair of nodes n_s and n_t (details in [5]).

To produce the 2-hop cover list, we use a modification of the algorithm in [1] to improve efficiency. We are only interested in answers in which the content nodes are reasonably close to each other. Therefore, we only keep the distances up to a threshold D_{max}. Our experiments show that the 2-hop cover index controlled by the D_{max} parameter scales well for large graph databases. The index can be stored in main memory or in an SSD. This optimization turns to be an effective approach for building a scalable system without sacrificing the quality of answers.

3.3 Edge and Node Weights

The system includes three ways of assigning weights to edges: 1) equal weights, 2) logarithmic weights, in which the weight of an edge between two nodes n_i and n_j is $(\log_2(1 + deg_{n_i}) + \log_2(1 + deg_{n_j}))/2$, where deg_n is the degree of node n, and 3), application-dependent semantic weights, in which the weight of an edge is related to the semantic relation between the two end nodes of the edge. For example, in the IMDb dataset, we use the weight of the associated foreign keys between two tuples in the relational database as the semantic weights between the associated nodes in the input graph, computed using the algorithm from [4]. Node weights are application-dependent. For IMDb, we calculate node importance using the algorithm from [4]. In DBLP, we will provide several ways of computing node importance, e.g., the number of publications for an author node or the number of citations for a paper node. The importance of a user node in Twitter will be for instance, the number of followers that the user has.

4. DEMONSTRATION OUTLINE

The eGraphSearch system features a Java web-based browsing interface to support interactive keyword search in graphs. In the front page of the system (see Appendix A for the screen screenshot), users specify the query keywords, the method for calculating edge weights (recall Section 3.3), the ranking algorithm (Combined, Edge Weight, Node Importance and IR-based ranking methods), the number of answer trees to be shown (i.e., top-k), and the value of λ for the combined optimization objective (λ values are 0.25, 0.5 and 0.75). Then, the ranked list of answer trees, based on the selected ranking method, is shown. Our graphical presentation is based on *GraphViz Google Charts* which is suitable for displaying different trees.

The main objective of the demonstration is to allow users to interactively experiment with a wide variety of ranking algorithms and parameters, edge and node weight functions, relative importance of edge versus node weights, and different datasets (including DBLP, IMDb and Twitter). Participants will be able to examine and rank the search results, and gain a better understanding of the factors affecting search results in various datasets. Furthermore, demonstrating eGraphSearch will allow us to collect feedback from the participants about our ranking algorithms and about improving the search experience in various application domains.

We will also provide specific examples of keyword queries where different ranking methods give very different answers (see an example in Appendix B). Finally, to show the benefits of a graph keyword search system such as eGraphSearch, we will provide alternative manual tools, e.g., using a query language such as SPARQL. Participants will be able to compare the features of an automatic system such as eGraphSearch against these other tools, and experience the benefits, especially when dealing with large and complex datasets such as IMDb. In particular, our user study in [5] revealed that eGraphSearch substantially reduced the end-to-end time to find answers compared to SPARQL, even for expert users.

5. REFERENCES

[1] T. Akiba, Y. Iwata, and Y. Yoshida. Fast exact shortest-path distance queries on large networks by pruned landmark labeling. In *SIGMOD*, 2013.

[2] H. He, H. Wang, J. Yang, and P. S. Yu. Blinks: Ranked keyword searches on graphs. In *SIGMOD*, 2007.

[3] M. Kargar and A. An. Efficient top-k keyword search in graphs with polynomial delay. In *ICDE*, 2012.

[4] M. Kargar, A. An, N. Cercone, P. Godfrey, J. Szlichta, and X. Yu. Meaningful keyword search in relational databases with large and complex schema. In *ICDE*, 2015.

[5] M. Kargar, L. Golab, and J. Szlichta. Effective keyword search in graphs. *CoRR abs/1512.06395, Technical Report available at http://arxiv.org/abs/1512.06395*, 2015.

Appendix

Appendix A Graphical Interface

The front page of eGraphSearch is shown in Figure 3. As mentioned before, users can specify the query keywords, the method for calculating edge weights, the ranking algorithm, the number of answers (i.e., top-k), and the value of λ for the combined optimization objective. The possible values of λ are 0.25, 0.5 and 0.75.

Figure 3: Front page of eGraphSearch.

Appendix B Demonstration Example

During the demonstration, we will provide examples of keyword queries in which different ranking methods produce different answers. For instance, using the IMDb dataset and assuming that edges have equal weights, the top answer returned by edge-weight ranking and IR-based ranking for the query ["Morgan Freeman" "Tim Robbins" "Keanu Reeves"] is shown in Figure 4 (a). The top answer returned by our node-importance method is shown in Figure 4 (b).

Answer (a) suggests that all three of these actors are connected merely because they are actors. Answer (b) reveals that Morgan Freeman starred in the same movie with Tim Robbins (Boffo! Tinseltown's). Furthermore, it shows that Morgan Freeman and Keanu Reeves played in the same movie (Chain Reaction). We argue that answer (b) is more interesting than answer (a) and reveals a deeper connection between the content nodes that may not have been known to a user who is unfamiliar with the dataset.

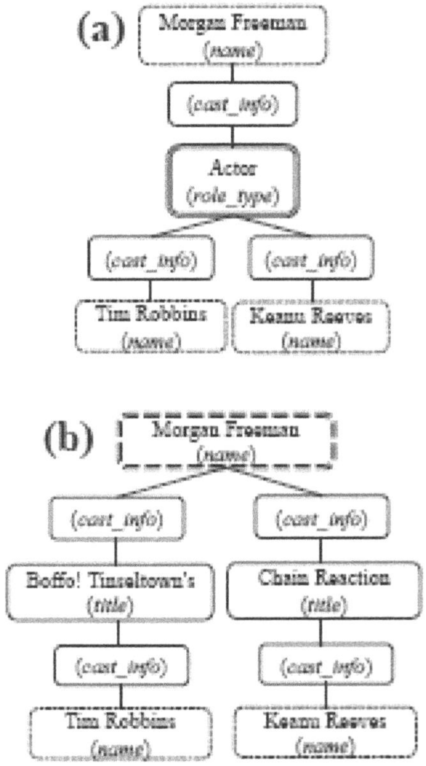

Figure 4: Two top answers returned by different ranking strategies. Content nodes are shown in dotted boxes. Root nodes are shown in double lines.

EnerQuery: Energy-Aware Query Processing

Amine Roukh
University of Mostaganem
Mostaganem, Algeria
roukh.amine@univ-mosta.dz

Ladjel Bellatreche
LIAS/ISAE-ENSMA
Poitiers, France
bellatreche@ensma.fr

Carlos Ordonez
University of Houston
Houston, USA
ordonez@cs.uh.edu

ABSTRACT

Energy consumption is increasingly more important in large-scale query processing. This problem requires revisiting traditional query processing in actual DBMSs to identify the potential of energy saving, and to study the trade-offs between energy consumption and performance. In this paper, we propose *EnerQuery*, a tool built on top of a traditional DBMS to capitalize the efforts invested in building energy-aware query optimizers, which have the lion's share in energy consumption. Energy consumption is estimated on all query plan steps and integrated into a mathematical linear cost model used to select the best query plans. To increase end users' energy awareness, *EnerQuery* features a diagnostic GUI to visualize energy consumption per step and its savings when tuning key parameters during query execution.

Keywords

Database Design; Query Processing; Energy Efficiency

1. INTRODUCTION

Nowadays, with the deluge of data, emerging hardware technologies and the query efficiency requirements of developers and users of database applications, data centers are in the line of sight, because they increase the greenhouse gas emissions. In a typical data center, DBMS is one of the most avid consumers in terms of computational resources among other software deployed [2]. As researchers working in the database field, we must propose an initiative that integrates energy management into DBMS functionalities and gives developers and end users the possibility to see the energy consumption when executing their queries. In this demonstration, we only focus on the query optimizer which is one of the main DBMS components. A past work [5] argues that optimizing for performance always leads to a high energy efficiency. However, in their study the authors considered the idle power of the system under test, which limits the potential for active power savings. Moreover, recent studies have shown that there exist opportunities for an energy efficient query optimization in current DBMSs [2, 3]; this is also proven in our finding.

In this paper, we propose an energy-aware query optimizer framework, called EnerQuery[1], which leverages the PostgreSQL query optimizer by integrating the energy dimension (we use the terms energy and power interchangeably). To ensure this integration, we fix three main objectives: **(i)** the identification energy-sensitive layers of the query optimizer, **(ii)** the definition of mathematical cost models estimating the energy consumption of SQL queries, and **(iii)** the development of a graphical user interface that plays the role of a diagnostic tool for end users, developers and DBA to increase their energy awareness and pushing them to save it. These three objectives will be discussed in the next sections.

2. ENERGY-AWARE QUERY PROCESSING

The process of executing a given query passes through four main steps: **(i)** parsing, **(ii)** rewriting, **(iii)** planning & optimizing, and **(iv)** executing. The *parser* checks the query string for valid syntax using a set of grammar rules, then translates the query into an equivalent relational algebra expression. The output is the *query tree*. The *rewriter* processes and rewrites the tree using a set of rules. In our demonstration, the energy cost of query parser and rewrite is negligible. The *planner & optimizer* creates an optimal execution plan. A given SQL query can be executed in different ways while producing the same results. The optimizer's task is to estimate the cost of executing each plan using a mathematical cost model and to find out the fast one. In *EnerQuery*, the optimizer evaluates a query plan by considering two metrics: the query processing time and the energy consumption. The cost model is composed of functions for each basic SQL operator. Generally, the cost formula used to estimate the cost of an operation *op* is: $Cost_{op} = \alpha \times I/O \oplus \beta \times CPU \oplus \gamma \times Net$. Where I/O, CPU, and Net are respectively the estimated page numbers, tuple numbers, and communication messages required to execute *op*. They are usually computed using database statistics and selectivity formulas. The coefficients α, β and γ are used to convert estimations into the desired unit (e.g., time, energy). $\oplus$ represents the relationship between the parameters (linear, non-linear). The coefficient parameters and the relationship can be obtained using various techniques such as calibration, regression, and statistics. The *executor* takes

[1] *EnerQuery* can be found at: http://www.lias-lab.fr/forge/projects/ecoprod A video demonstration of its features is available at: https://youtu.be/cWK5rf4MBNQ

CIKM'16 October 24 - 28, 2016, Indianapolis, IN, USA

ACM ISBN 978-1-4503-4073-1/16/10...$15.00

DOI: http://dx.doi.org/10.1145/2983323.2983334

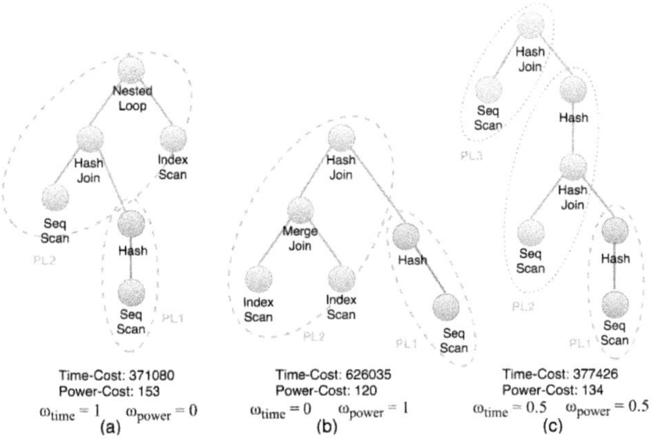

Figure 1: Segmented plans of query *Q3* associated with trade-off values.

the plan created by the planner & optimizer and processes it recursively to extract the required set of rows. This is essentially a demand-pull *pipeline* (PL) mechanism (called *iterator* or *GetNext* model in [1]).

To illustrate this mechanism supported by our *EnerQuery*, we consider the execution of the query *Q3* of the TPC-H benchmark[2]. Figure 1 gives three possible execution plans of *Q3* returned by *EnerQuery* based on the trade-off values assigned to the query response time and the energy consumption. Note that the time and power costs are different and impacted by the *model of pipelined execution* used by the DBMS [3]. Usually, this model segments each query plan into a set of PLs. In Figure 1, the plans **(a)** and **(b)** both have two PLs, whereas the plan **(c)** has three PLs. The execution of PLs is enforced by their terminal blocking operators (e.g., PL3 cannot begin until PL2 is complete).

EnerQuery is guided by a PL-based power cost model which delivers a high estimation accuracy. The end user *is free to guide* the process of evaluating execution plans of a given query by setting up the trade-off between the query response time and the energy consumption. *EnerQuery* is associated with a graphical user interface that offers the possibility to interact with the DBMS, to calibrate parameters of the cost model, and to identify the energy consumption of each part of the query being executed.

3. SYSTEM ARCHITECTURE

In this section, we describe the architecture of *EnerQuery*. It is composed of two parts, the backend and a GUI (Graphical User Interface). The backend contains the DBMS with the new power cost model and the evaluation model. It is responsible for executing queries with the desired trade-off and returning results to end users. In our study, we based on PostgreSQL, mostly because it is open source. However, our techniques can be integrated into any other DBMS. The GUI part helps to manipulate *EnerQuery*, to set parameters and to show in real-time their impact on the power consumption. The framework architecture of our demonstration is described in Figure 2. In the following sections, we will briefly present our underlying models. Full details can be found in [4].

[2]http://www.tpc.org/tpch/

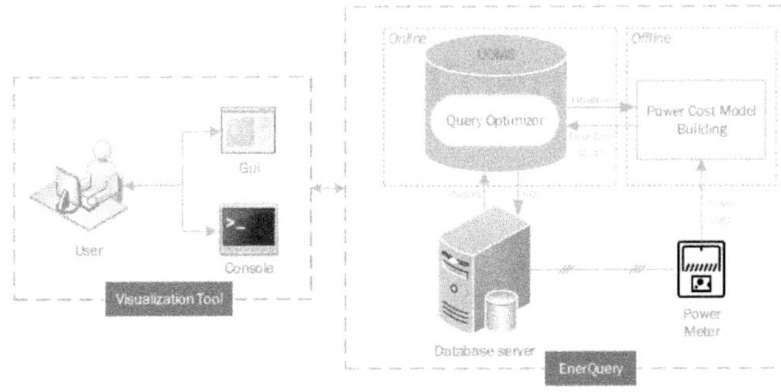

Figure 2: *EnerQuery* system architecture.

3.1 Power Consumption Linear Cost Model

The characteristics of our model dedicated to estimating queries power include: **(i)** the segmentation of an execution plan into a set of PLs, **(ii)** the utilization of the PL cost to build the regression model (*off-line*), and **(iii)** the estimation of the power of future PL based on PL cost and the regression equation (*on-line*).

3.1.1 Pipeline Segmentation

A physical operator of a query execution plan can be either *blocking* or *nonblocking*. An operator is blocking if it cannot produce any output tuple without reading as least one of its inputs (e.g., sort operator) [1]. Based on this, we decompose a plan in a set of PLs delimited by blocking operators. Thus, a PL consists of a set of concurrently running operators, as showed in Figure 1.

3.1.2 Model Parameters

Our strategy for PL modeling is to leverage the PostgreSQL cost models by integrating energy. To process a query, each operator in a PL needs to perform CPU and/or I/O tasks. The cost of these tasks is the active power to be consumed in order to finish them. More formally, the power cost $Power(Q)$ of the query Q composed of p pipelines is: $Power(Q) = \frac{\sum_{i=1}^{p} Power(PL_i) * Time(PL_i)}{Time(Q)}$. The *time* variable represents the PLs and the query estimated time to finish the execution. These informations are available directly from the DBMS. The power cost $Power(PL_i)$ of the pipeline PL_i composed of n algebraic operations is the summation of CPU and I/O costs of all its operators: $Power(PL_i) = \beta_{cpu} \times \sum_{j=1}^{n_i} CPU\_COST_j + \beta_{io} \times \sum_{j=1}^{n_i} IO\_COST_j$, where β_{cpu} and β_{io} are the model parameters (i.e., unit power costs) for the PLs. These parameters are computed using multiple polynomial regression techniques, which describes perfectly the behavior of PLs power consumption on the hardware components (disk and CPU) of our platform [3]. The β parameters are estimated during the learning phase from a training data, by finding the least-squares solution.

3.2 Query Plans Comparison

Adding energy criterion to the query optimizer, we must adjust the comparison functions to reflect the trade-offs between energy cost and processing time. In order to give a solution with the desired trade-off, we use the weighted sum of the cost functions method to aggregate criteria and to have an equivalent single criterion to be minimized. This method is defined as follows: minimize $y = f(x) = \sum_{i=1}^{k} \omega_i \cdot f_i(\vec{x})$ such that $\sum_{i=1}^{k} \omega_i = 1$, where ω_i are the weighting

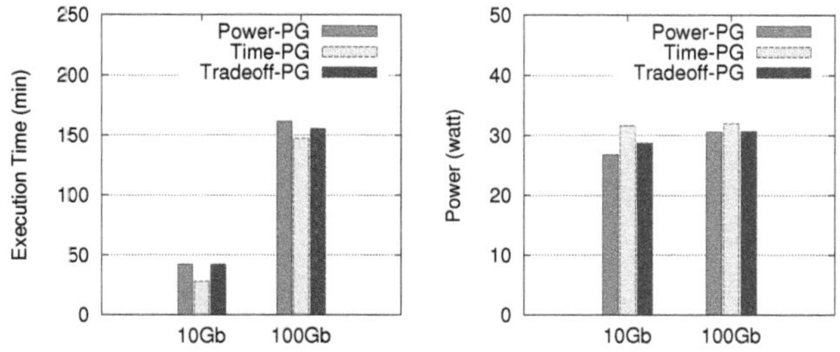

Figure 3: Performance and power saving of *EnerQuery* with different configurations using TPC-H.

coefficients representing the relative importance of the k cost functions. $f_i(x)$ represents power and performance cost functions. We implemented these two coefficients as an external parameter in *EnerQuery*, so the DBA or users can change them on-the-fly either by the GUI or the console.

4. DEMONSTRATION SCENARIO

In our demonstration, we will use a "Watts UP? Pro ES" power meter to measure the laptop power, which acts like a server and sets up the *EnerQuery* framework. We will use the TPC-H benchmark datasets and queries, and the SSB benchmark by varying their size. During the demonstration, we will highlight the role of *EnerQuery* in evaluating the effectiveness and efficiency of our proposal in several prominent scenarios. In practice, we study the effect of **(i)** varying the optimization goal of the query planner, **(ii)** varying dataset and queries, and **(iii)** showing the estimation and actual power consumption. Moreover, in each scenario, we will visualize the actual power consumption of the system and show the total energy consumption, as well as the query performance. Based on these scenarios, we can study and compare query operators behavior on power and performance results. We will also use the *EnerQuery* GUI interfaces to allow the user manipulating the framework settings and seeing their impact on the system.

The interface is implemented using C++ programming language and Qt library, which provides a better integration with the DBMS. Figure 1 illustrates a scenario where different query plans of the same query generated by *EnerQuery*: **(a)** is performance-oriented, **(b)** is power-oriented, and **(c)** is a trade-off. Users can analyze the costs of each operator using *EnerQuery* GUI, they can realize that the joins have a major impact on the nature of query plan. Figure 3 represents a scenario of the previous experiment extended to the overall TPC-H query workload (details can be found in [4]). The main GUI component modules are listed below.

4.1 Power Monitoring Configuration

This module is responsible for the connection establishment with the DBMS server. Users can also specify the path for the power meter driver in order to capture real-time power consumption. The most important part here is the power/performance settings, which parametrize the optimization goals: performance or power or trade-off. Users can also change the query planner configuration parameters by forcing the optimizer to evaluate other plans (see screenshot ①), as Oracle *hints* do. These parameters cover the following optimization modes: *sequential*, *index*, *index-only*, *bitmap*, and *TIDs* scan types, *hash*, *merge*, and *nested loop* join types, *sort* and *hash aggregate*. *EnerQuery* offers end users the possibility to quantify the consumed power of a given query by varying the optimization modes.

4.2 SQL Queries Workload

In this module, users can give either a single SQL query or a workload to be executed. Queries supported vary from simple transactional operations to more complex reporting operations involving several large size tables. The workload is composed of queries generated from the benchmarks tools and can be run concurrently at a predefined multi-programming level. The execution is done in a separate thread for each query and the results are displayed in a tree table widget. An example of query that users can introduce is *Q7* of TPC-H, which is a nested query of two levels that joins 7 tables; it also contains a complex ordering and grouping operations.

4.3 Power Consumption Timeline

When the user executes a query, we will dynamically display the real-time power consumption via the power meter. When the query finishes executing, we will compute and show the total energy that has been consumed. This can give users a real observation of the energy that has been saved using the desired trade-off parameters. For example, in Figure 1 (c), for a 1.7% performance degradation, we get 12.4% of power saving. Also, users can compare the estimated and the real values to check the accuracy of mathematical models or further refine their parameters.

4.4 Execution Plan

When the user submits a query, the query optimizer selects its best execution plan relative to the pre-defined trade-off. We will show this execution plan with various information, such as estimated cost, power consumption, I/O and CPU costs for every physical operator through mouse-hovering events. Users can identify which operator consumes more power, for instance, we will show that CPU intensive operators such as sort and aggregate are power hungry in traditional servers. Moreover, we will highlight in which case I/O intensive operators lead to high power consumption. Also, the pipeline notation will be demonstrated as shown in Figure 1, the pipeline trees are grouped with the *same color*. We will show how the trade-off parameters affect the generated plans. This helps interpreting runtime optimizations and different pipelines.

5. REFERENCES

[1] S. Chaudhuri, V. Narasayya, and R. Ramamurthy. Estimating Progress of Execution for SQL Queries. In *SIGMOD*, pages 803–814. 2004.

[2] W. Lang, R. Kandhan, and J. M. Patel. Rethinking Query Processing for Energy Efficiency: Slowing Down to Win the Race. *IEEE Data Eng. Bull.*, 12–23. 2011.

[3] A. Roukh and L. Bellatreche. Eco-Processing of OLAP Complex Queries. In *DaWaK*, pages 229–242. 2015.

[4] A. Roukh, L. Bellatreche, A. Boukorca, and S. Bouarar. Eco-DMW: Eco-Design Methodology for Data warehouses. In *DOLAP*, pages 1–10. 2015.

[5] D. Tsirogiannis, S. Harizopoulos, and M. A. Shah. Analyzing the Energy Efficiency of a Database Server. In *SIGMOD*, pages 231–242. 2010.

APPENDIX

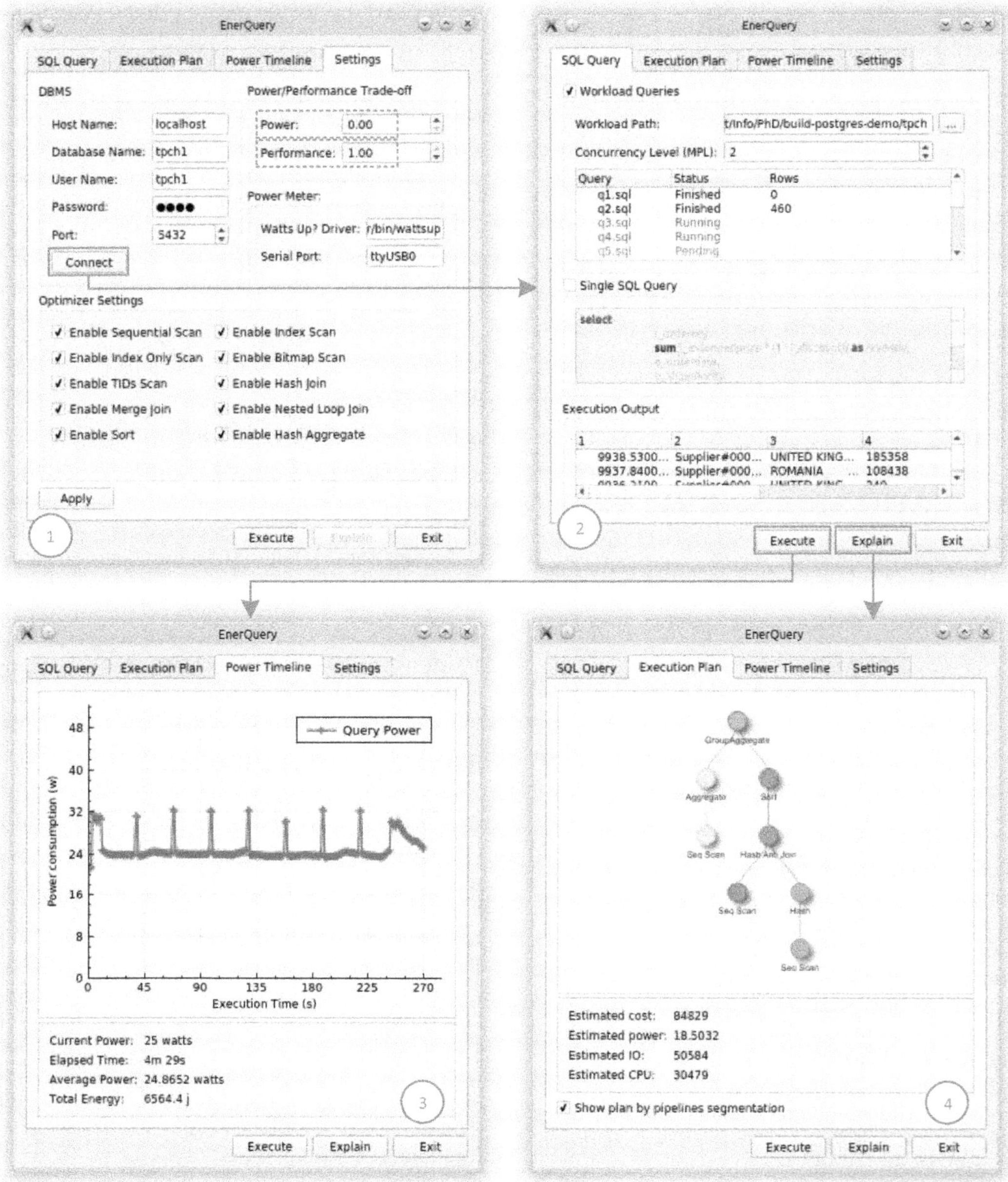

Figure 4: *EnerQuery* main GUI and its component module panels.

TGraph: A Temporal Graph Data Management System

Haixing Huang Jinghe Song Xuelian Lin Shuai Ma* Jinpeng Huai
SKLSDE Lab, Beihang University, China
Beijing Advanced Innovation Center for Big Data and Brain Computing, Beijing, China
{huanghx, songjh, linxl}@act.buaa.edu.cn {mashuai, huaijp}@buaa.edu.cn

ABSTRACT

Temporal graphs are a class of graphs whose nodes and edges, together with the associated properties, continuously change over time. Recently, systems have been developed to support snapshot queries over temporal graphs. However, these systems barely support aggregate time range queries. Moreover, these systems cannot guarantee ACID transactions, an important feature for data management systems as long as concurrent processing is involved. To solve these issues, we design and develop TGraph, a temporal graph data management system, that assures the ACID transaction feature, and supports fast temporal graph queries.

1. INTRODUCTION

Graph databases have attracted attention from both academia and industry. Numerous applications, from social media analysis and traffic navigation to recommendation systems, handle a vast collection of entities with their relationships [5], which can be naturally represented by graphs. Some commercialized graph database products, such as Neo4j [6] and Titan [9], have also been developed to manage graph data and to support graph-oriented applications, which usually provide update and read operations over the latest state of graphs, and support ACID transactions, a key feature of traditional DBMS [8].

Temporal graphs (see a recent survey [2]) are a class of graphs whose nodes, edges and their properties continuously change over time. For example, traffic conditions in a road network vary from morning to evening, friendships between people in a social network evolve with time. Temporal graph databases manage temporal graph data by storing all snapshots of graphs, as user queries may focus on historical states and changing patterns of graphs.

Temporal data management started from the 80's of last century, which mainly focused on the temporal query language on temporal relational databases [7]. Temporal graph data management has recently been initiated, and several temporal graph management systems have been developed. DeltaGraph [3] stores temporal graphs using a log-based storage approach and provides snapshot queries; And G* [4] provides a distributed storage of temporal graph data. Further, how to analyze temporal graphs is also a hot research topic in database and data mining fields [10].

However, these existing temporal graph data management systems have certain limitations. First, most of them mainly support snapshot queries. For a temporal range query, DeltaGraph needs to load all the relevant data falling into the time interval from all snapshots, which makes it very inefficient. Indeed, this is typically unnecessary as many such queries only need a small part of nodes and relationships (edges). Second, these systems cannot guarantee the ACID transaction feature, which potentially leads the systems to inconsistent states when concurrent data processing is involved. Finally, we find that there is an important type of temporal graphs in real-life, whose nodes and relationships barely change while the properties of nodes and relationships change frequently. For example, roads are associated with certain properties, such as the length and the direction of the roads, and a road network topology keeps static for a long time, but the traffic condition changes frequently.

Contributions. To this end, we develop TGraph for managing temporal graphs, whose structures barely change, but associated properties change frequently. To the best of our knowledge, this is among the first temporal graph management system that is able to handle such temporal graphs and to support ACID transactions.

(1) We develop a fast and effective storage called DPS designed to maintain the frequent changing properties of nodes/relationships in temporal graph data.

(2) We also provide a transaction manager to ensure the ACID transaction feature of temporal graph data.

(3) We finally build a prototype temporal graph data management system that supports various temporal queries.

Organization. We first describe the data model in Section 2. We then introduce the architecture and key mechanism of TGraph in Section 3. Finally, we demonstrate TGraph with an experiment study and two use cases in Section 4.

2. TEMPORAL GRAPH MODEL

A temporal graph is $G = (V, E)$, where V is a set of nodes, and E is a set of relationships. A node $v = (id, P, DynP) \in V$, where id is the identity of v in V, P is a set of static properties, and $DynP$ is a set of dynamic properties.

A static property (a concept borrowed from Neo4j) is $p = (name, value) \in P$, where $name$ is the unique name of p, and $value$ is the value of p, respectively.

CIKM'16 October 24 - November 28, 2016, Indianapolis, IN, USA

ACM ISBN 978-1-4503-4073-1/16/10.
DOI: http://dx.doi.org/10.1145/2983323.2983335

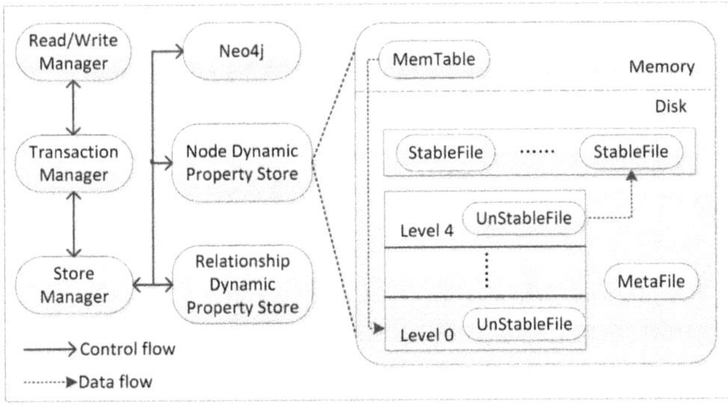

Figure 1: TGraph architecture.

A dynamic property is $dp = (name, vlist) \in DynP$, where *vlist* is a list of $(t, value)$, which means that value v is valid from time t. A $vlist=\langle(t_1, value_1), (t_2, value_2), (t_3, value_3), \ldots, (t_n, value_n)\rangle$, satisfying $t_i < t_{i+1}$ for $1 \leq i < n$. A tuple $(t_i, value_i)$ represents that the value of dp in $[t_i, t_{i+1})$ is $value_i$. For the last tuple $(t_n, value_n)$, its value of dp from t_n to *now* is $value_n$.

A relationship is $e = (id, vs, ve, ty, P, DynP) \in E$, where id is the identity of e, vs and ve are the start node and end node of e, and ty is the type of e, respectively.

3. ARCHITECTURE

TGraph is an extension of Neo4j [6], a popular, open source graph database. TGraph uses Neo4j to store nodes, relationships and static properties of nodes/relatinships, while dynamic properties of nodes/relationships is stored in another component, referred to as DPS (Dynamic Properties Storage). TGraph integrates Neo4j and DPS together to provide a complete temporal graph data management system, and its architecture is shown in Figure 1.

The Read/Write Manager detects read and write requests, and passes them to the Transaction Manager with the ACID transaction feature. The Store Manager manages the storage of nodes, relationships, static and dynamic properties, and the node and relationship dynamic properties are separately stored as two different DPS instances. We next explain the details of DPS and the transaction manager.

3.1 Dynamic Property Storage

In DPS (right side of Fig. 1), all data is first written into an in-memory data structure MemTable. It is dumped to disks when MemTable is full. DPS has three types of local files: UnStableFile, StableFile and MetaFile. Both UnStableFile and StableFile are data files to store dynamic properties. MetaFile stores the metadata of DPS, including the names of data files, and the valid time ranges of data files, which is loaded into memory when the system is started.

UnStableFiles are used to save the most recent data. When a MemTable is dumped to disks, a level 0 UnStableFile is created. Then they can be merged into a level 1 UnStableFile, and so on. Level 4 UnStableFiles can be merged into a StableFile. Each StableFile/UnStableFile covers a valid time interval. Any two valid time intervals of StableFiles/UnStableFiles have no overlaps with each other. Dynamic properties stored in a file have their time fall into the time interval of the file. The MetaFile is used to maintain the name and valid time interval of each data file.

Data Format. StableFile and UnStableFile files have the same format, and are divided into data and index segments.

(1) The data segment has a number of data blocks whose sizes are set to 4KB by default, and are configurable. All data of dynamic properties is stored in data blocks. The system allocates a *proid* for a dynamic property when it is created, to identify the dynamic property within a node or a relationship. Logically, dynamic property data is stored in a list of records. A record is a tuple (*id*, *proid*, *t*, *value*), where *id* is the id of a node or a relationship, *t* is the valid time and *value* is the value. Each record uses (*id*, *proid*, *t*) as its key. As all records are stored in the ascending order of their keys, each data block is associated with a range of record keys. (2) The index segment stores the indexing information of all data blocks.

Writes and Reads on Dynamic Properties. All write operations (create, update and delete) must be logged in the MemTable first. When the MemTable is full, its data is dumped to disks, and TGraph decides whether to write a data record into a newly created UnStableFile, or to insert it into an existing StableFile or an UnStableFile, depending on the valid time of the data record.

(1) The insert operation could cost lots of IOs as records are ordered by their keys in a data file. Consider there is an insertion to a StableFile sf. To reduce the insertion IO cost, the system allocates a Buffer in memory for sf, and all subsequent insertions to sf are inserted into the Buffer. When the Buffer reaches 4MB (configurable), the system merges it with sf. When an UnStableFile is merged with another UnStableFile, their Buffers is merged as well. The system also creates a BufferFile for each Buffer as its backup in case the system crashes.

(2) For the update operation, consider a record to be updated in MemTable. The system updates it in MemTable directly. However, if it is in disks, the system transforms it into an insert operation, and adds it to MemTable. When MemTable is dumped to disks, it is added to the Buffer of the target file, and the corresponding record is finally updated during the merging process.

(3) The delete operation is similar to the update operation. The system does not delete the target record directly, but labels the record with a deletion mark and adds it to the Buffer of the target file, and the records with deletion marks in the Buffer do not participate in any merging process.

(4) All user queries first read from MemTable, then from a StableFile (or an UnStableFile) and its Buffer, and the system itself chooses and returns the right answers.

3.2 Transaction Manager

TGraph uses Neo4j's mechanism to ensure ACID guarantee with one major improvement. First, Neo4j ensures the ACID feature by the following. (1) Binding a transaction with a thread and making uncommitted data as a private member of the thread so that uncommitted data cannot be accessed by other transactions. (2) Using read-write locks on nodes/relationships to control concurrent accesses. So writes on the same data are serialized. (3) Writing all the modified data to the disk only at the commit stage of a transaction. So there will not be half-committed transaction. (4) Using the write–ahead logging technique [8] to record all operations in a transaction in case crash occurs.

Second, TGraph extends the resource lock of Neo4j to two types of resource locks: one for nodes, relationships and static properties, and the other for dynamic properties. The former is the common read-write lock that uses a node or relationship as the unit of a lock. The latter uses a dynamic property as the unit of a lock. Unlike common read-write locks, not all read operations are blocked by the write lock on the same resource. For example, if a transaction updates a dynamic property p at time t and holds a write lock of p, and another transaction needs to read the value of p at time t', then the read transaction is not blocked if $t' < t$.

4. DEMONSTRATION

We demonstrate TGraph by comparing its performance with Neo4j and by introducing two use cases with details in the Appendix. We use a *real-life traffic dataset* recording the traffic of Beijing road network's conditions within a period of six months. The data contains nearly 110,000 roads such that joints of roads are graph nodes, and roads are relationships between nodes, which have four dynamic properties (travel time, vehicle count, traffic condition, jammed segment count) whose values are updated every 5 minutes and some static properties such as length and direction.

All experiments were conducted on a machine with 2 Intel Xeon E5-2630 2.4GHz CPUs and 64 GB of Memory, running a 64 bit Windows 7 Ultimate system.

(1) Performance Evaluation. We compare the performance between TGraph and Neo4j to show the advantages of TGraph's performance in Figure 2. The reasons why we chose Neo4j are its popularity and support of ACID transactions, while other temporal graph management systems rarely do. In Neo4j, we encode a dynamic property into an integer array whose size is around 5MB, and store it as a static property of a relationship since Neo4j supports the array as the value type of a property.

Figure 2(a) shows the result of write operations. TGraph makes 52,551 write operations per second on average, which is 20 times faster than Neo4j (2,621/s). The write speed of TGraph does not slow down as the write operation continues while Neo4j decreases significantly.

Figures 2(b) and 2(c) show the results of time point and time range queries. TGraph can finish more read operations than Neo4j (12,500/s vs. 439/s and 10,858/s vs. 403/s for time point and time range queries, respectively). That is because Neo4j needs to load the entire array from disks for any query covering this property. Note that the length of an array becomes very large when the value of the dynamic property changes frequently. However TGraph stores dynamic properties in DPS which is designed for storing frequent changing properties.

Figure 2(d) shows the result of concurrent capacities. We use a different number of threads to read or write randomly from/to both systems. Every transaction only contains a single operation, either read or write. We let each transaction sleep for 10ms to replace the cost of system IO to see the improvement of the transaction manager in TGraph without the disturbance of the differences between the storage methods of the two systems. The concurrent capacity of TGraph transaction manager is 1.13 times better than the one of Neo4j, mainly because the resources lock of TGraph is optimized for read/write operations of temporal graphs.

(2) Use Cases. We further demonstrate TGraph by building a traffic data management system on top of TGraph, by making use of TGraph APIs. The system supports historical traffic condition queries, historical traffic condition aggregate queries, and temporal shortest path queries. All these capacities are supported by TGraph's time point and time range query abilities. The interface of TGraph is shown in the Appendix, with an example on how to use its APIs.

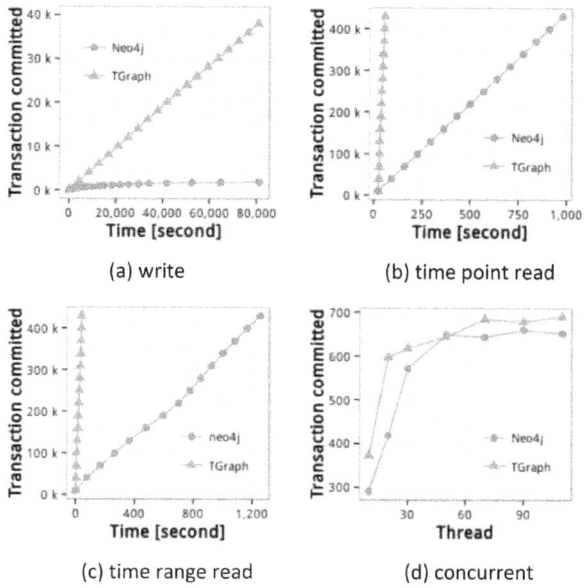

Figure 2: Performance comparison: TGraph vs. Neo4j.

5. CONCLUSIONS

We have introduced TGraph for managing temporal graphs whose structures barely change, but the associated properties change frequently. TGraph has been equipped with DPS, a fast and effective storage to maintain the dynamic properties of temporal graph data, and a transaction manager to ensure the ACID transaction feature for temporal graph data. Experiments on real traffic data have shown that TGraph is more suitable to manage temporal graph data than Neo4j, and, moreover, we have also illustrated use cases on how to utilize TGraph to develop applications.

Acknowledgment This work is supported in part by 973 program (2014CB340300), NSFC (61322207&61421003), Special Funds of Beijing Municipal Science & Technology Commission, and MSRA Collaborative Research Program. For any correspondence, please refer to Shuai Ma.

6. REFERENCES

[1] S. E. Dreyfus. An appraisal of some shortest-path algorithms. *Operations Research*, 17(3):395–412, 1969.

[2] P. Holme and J. Saramäki. Temporal networks. *Physics reports*, 519(3):97–125, 2012.

[3] U. Khurana and A. Deshpande. Efficient snapshot retrieval over historical graph data. In *ICDE*, 2013.

[4] A. G. Labouseur, P. W. Olsen, and J.-H. Hwang. Scalable and robust management of dynamic graph data. In *BD3@VLDB*, 2013.

[5] S. Ma, J. Li, C. Hu, X. Lin, and J. Huai. Big graph search: challenges and techniques. *FCS*, 10(3):387–397, 2016.

[6] Neo4j. http://neo4j.com/.

[7] G. Özsoyoğlu and R. T. Snodgrass. Temporal and real-time databases: A survey. *TKDE*, 7(4):513–532, 1995.

[8] R. Ramakrishnan and J. Gehrke. *Database management systems*. Osborne/McGraw-Hill, 2000.

[9] Titan. http://thinkaurelius.github.io/titan/.

[10] H. Wu, J. Cheng, S. Huang, Y. Ke, Y. Lu, and Y. Xu. Path problems in temporal graphs. *PVLDB*, 7(9):721–732, 2014.

APPENDIX

A. TRAFFIC DATA MANAGEMENT SYSTEM

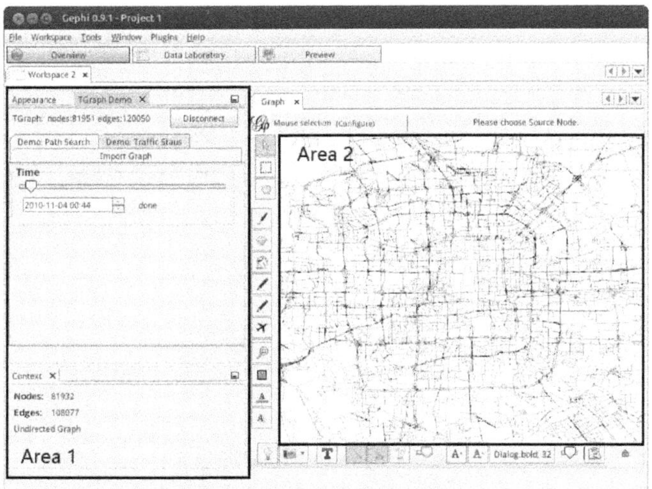

Figure 3: User interface of a traffic data management system

An Example Program of TGraph

```
1. GraphService service = new GraphService(...);
2. Transaction tx = service.beginTx();
3. Node tom = service.getNodes("name", "tom").get(0);
4. tom.setDynProperty("work place",
                      "2016/1/01", "Google");
5. tom.setDynProperty("salary", "2016/1/01", 20000);
6. tx.sucess();
7. tx.close();
8. ···
9. tx = service.beginTx();
10. tom.getDynProperty("work place", "2016/1/01");
11. tom.getDynPropertyMax("salary",
                      "2016/1/01", "2016/6/01");
12. tx.success();
13. tx.close().
```

Table 1: An Example Program of TGraph

Figure 3 is the user interface of traffic data management system built on top of TGraph, based on Gephi (https://gephi.org). It has two major areas. (1) Area 1 is the control panel from where users choose the type of queries, and set the conditions of queries, and (2) road network topologies and query answers are shown at area 2, which supports zoomIn and zoomOut commands to present different levels of network details.

If a user wants to query the traffic situation at a history time point, the user needs to set the time point at area 1 and to trigger the query. The system then sends the query to TGraph and shows the corresponding results returned from TGraph on the road network.

If a user wants to find a temporal shortest path between two nodes, the user needs to select a start node and an end node by clicking them at area 2, and sets a departure time at area 1. The system runs a time-dependent *generalized Dijkstra* algorithm [1] to compute a path with the earliest arrival time, and highlights the resulting path at area 2.

Figure 4 is an example that tells the temporal shortest pathes between two nodes at different departure time. Figure 4(a) illustrates the path, departed at 1:05 am, recommended by TGraph, which is indeed the same as the shortest distance path since all traffic conditions are smooth during that time; Figure 4(b) illustrates the recommended path departed at 8:05 am in the traffic peak time, and the system returns a different path that avoids jammed roads.

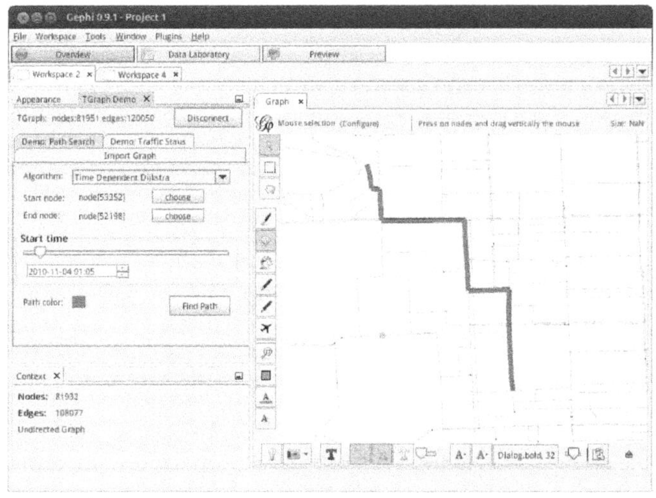

(a) Temporal shortest path departing at 1:05 am

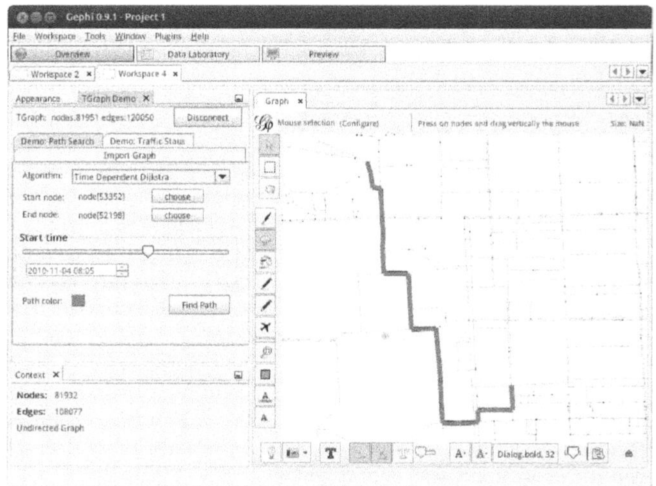

(b) Temporal shortest path departing at 8:05 am

Figure 4: Temporal shortest path queries: given the same two nodes with the different departure time, return two different pathes.

B. PROGRAMMING WITH TGRAPH APIS

TGraph provides a full package of operations to write and query both static and dynamic graph data, and to assure ACID transactions.

An example program is provided in Table 1. The program first initializes the TGraph service (line 1), and starts a transaction to find the first node whose "name" property is "tom" (lines 2, 3). Then it sets the property "work place" of the node "tom" to "Google" on date "2016/1/01", and the salary of "tom" to "20000" on date "2016/1/01" (lines 4, 5). After that, it closes the transaction (lines 6, 7). (3) Finally, it starts a new transaction to query information from those modifications (line 9). It finds the "work place" of "tom" on date "2016/1/01" (line 10), and the max salary of "tom" from dates "2016/1/01" to "2016/6/01" (line 11).

Analyzing Data Relevance and Access Patterns of Live Production Database Systems

Martin Boissier, Carsten Meyer, Timo Djürken, Jan Lindemann, Kathrin Mao, Pascal Reinhardt, Tim Specht, Tim Zimmermann, Matthias Uflacker
Hasso Plattner Institute, University of Potsdam, Germany
{firstname.lastname}@hpi.de

ABSTRACT

Access to real-world database systems and their workloads is an invaluable source of information for database researchers. However, usually such full access is not possible due to tracing overheads, data protection, or legal reasons. In this paper, we present a tool set to analyze and compare synthetic and real-world database workloads, their characteristics, and access patterns. This tool set processes SQL workload traces and collects fine-grained access information without requiring direct read access to the production system. To gain insights into large real-world systems, we traced a live production enterprise system of a Global 2000 company and compare it with the synthetic benchmarks TPC-C and TPC-E.

Keywords

Mixed Workloads; OLxP; Data Smartist; Data Relevance; Data Tiering; Access Patterns; ERP; Production Systems

1. INTRODUCTION

Database researchers regularly face the problem of how to evaluate new ideas or algorithms. Synthetic benchmarks do not accurately reflect the properties of real-world systems [2]. To understand why some research projects provide only limited benefits in realistic scenarios, access to production systems is required. An example for the mismatch between real-world systems and benchmarks is the often employed partitioning along the warehouse identifier in TPC-C with an almost perfect distribution of both data and workload. A scenario barely found in real-world systems.

Insights from real-world applications help to make better and more profound assumptions. In some cases, it is possible to access the data of a system or the database plan cache (i.e., cached storage of execution plans without predicate bindings). But neither facilitates the ability to answer questions, such as "Which queries join tables X and Y and return data older than three years?" or evaluate different partitioning schemas. For those questions, access to both – data as well as the full SQL workload trace – is needed.

We present a tool set that answers such questions by parsing SQL workload traces and obtaining access information without the need of direct read access to the production database system and thus without access to business-critical information. With this tool set, we can analyze access patterns and quantify the relevance of data down to the level of accesses per tuple.

CIKM'16 October 24–28, 2016, Indianapolis, IN, USA

ACM ISBN 978-1-4503-4073-1/16/10.

DOI: http://dx.doi.org/10.1145/2983323.2983336

1.1 Motivation

Mixed workloads (OLxP) and in-memory databases are two of the major trends in enterprise systems computing. Both led to a dramatic shift in the workload modern database systems are expected to handle. This change has vast implications for research topics such as data aging/tiering or partitioning. For data aging, the classification of relevant/hot data is comparatively straightforward for classical OLTP systems with single tuple-focused accesses. But modern applications with OLxP characteristics – such as complex joins and aggregations – exhibit completely different access patterns [1]. Hence, data relevance questions cannot be studied using OLTP-oriented benchmarks as TPC-C/-E.

In this project, we want to provide profound insights into real-world enterprise resource planning (ERP) systems by analyzing both, single tuple accesses as well as complex analytical queries in order to quantify data relevance down to the finest level of granularity based on production database workloads.

1.2 Analyzed Workloads

Krueger et al. have analyzed ERP systems and shown that synthetic benchmarks as TPC-C do not reflect the properties found in real-world enterprise applications accurately [2]. This was our major motivation to focus on complete SQL workload traces of production systems instead of synthetic benchmarks or plan cache exports. Using SQL workload traces allows the analysis of topics as partitioning and query pruning, which is not possible using solely the database plan cache. Hence, we think it is crucial to look at 1) real-world data instead of synthetically created data and 2) real-world workloads to analyze and evaluate database systems.

Besides synthetic benchmarks, we have analyzed real-world systems, i.a., the following *live production SAP-based Enterprise Resource Planning (ERP) system of a Global 2000 company*:

- Over seven terabytes of uncompressed data
- Handles ~1.5 billion queries each day
- Sampled SQL workload traces of the financial and controlling modules over several days, resulting in ~50M queries
- One of the most recent versions of an SAP ERP system including operational reporting on transactional data (i.e., OLxP)
- Plan cache exports over a time span of several weeks

2. WORKFLOW

In short, the workflow of our analyses looks as follows: First, the logging functionality of the traced database is activated to log all queries. Depending on the system load, the tracing can be iteratively activated for short intervals. The resulting query logs are copied to another system, which runs the analyses to keep the load on the production system as low as possible. On the analysis system, the query logs are parsed to extract relevant information (e.g., selections, predicates, projections, join partners, et cetera).

In case it is possible to access a snapshot of the database – directly or indirectly – a SQL log replay on a mirrored source system is performed to obtain tuple access information (Section 3). The results of the analyses are visualized in an HTML-based front end.

3. SQL LOG REPLAY

Having the complete SQL workload trace of a live production system is already a tremendous source of information. However, to discuss issues such as data aging/tiering, data relevance, and partitioning, further analyses are necessary. We replay SQL workload traces on a database snapshot with which we can determine for every tuple, which queries have accessed it, when, and how often.

Indirect Snapshot Access. Our research focuses on production ERP systems. Consequently, getting direct access to a snapshot of the enterprise system for the replay is hardly possible as it contains business-critical financial data. Therefore, we implemented the replay process in a way that the process can be run by the owner of the ERP system and will output only statistical data (i.e., *indirect access*). This data includes database meta data as table sizes, existing indices et cetera. But more importantly, we exported the internal tuple identifiers (i.e., the row identifier) of each replayed query. We use the tuple identifiers of the result set of each query to answer questions as "Which data is actually relevant and regularly accessed?". To obtain the tuple identifiers for returned tuples, we replace the projected columns by the internal system column (e.g., `$ROW_ID$` for SAP HANA) storing tuple identifiers.

```
-- original query
SELECT CUSTOMER_NAME, PRODUCT_ID, AMOUNT, CURRENCY
FROM CUSTOMER_ORDERS_VIEW
WHERE CUSTOMER_ID=17
GROUP BY CUSTOMER_ID;
-- rewriting to access base tables and obtain tuple
-- identifiers instead of the actual projection
SELECT REWR_VIEW.ORDERS_ROWID, REWR_VIEW.CUSTOMERS_ROWID
FROM (SELECT O.CUST_ID, O.$ROW_ID$ AS "ORDERS_ROWID",
        C.$ROW_ID$ AS "CUSTOMERS_ROWID"
  FROM ORDERS__TIMESLOT_004 AS O JOIN CUSTOMERS AS C
    ON O.CUSTOMER_ID=C.CUSTOMER_ID
) AS REWR_VIEW WHERE REWR_VIEW.CUSTOMER_ID=17;
```

Listing 1: Rewriting of queries using views.

3.1 Data Growth

Another issue is missing information about data growth when only a single database snapshot is available. Due to data protection, the obtained traces include full `SELECT` statements but only masked `INSERT/UPDATE` statements (i.e., no values) as they potentially include business data. If we now replay the SQL workload traces that have been traced over a long period, queries such as 'SELECT * FROM ORDERS WHERE CUSTOMER_ID = 3 ORDER BY DATE DESC LIMIT 0, 10' would always return the same set of tuples even though the data might have changed in the meanwhile.

To deal with that issue we recorded the maximum and minimum tuple identifiers of each traced table each time the SQL workload trace was started or stopped (i.e., twice every ten minutes in the case of the ERP system). This information is used to create a logical view on top of the base table of the static snapshot, limiting the

	SELECT	(joining[1])	UPDATE	INSERT	DELETE
SAP ERP	97.10%	(21.20%)	0.25%	2.65%	0.00%
TPC-C	69.48%	(2.52%)	18.57%	9.76%	2.20%
TPC-E	88.14%	(15.91%)	6.66%	4.79%	0.4%

Table 1: Distribution of reading and modifying statements.

size of the table to an approximation its size at the traced point of time. For each traced table, a view accessing the original table is created that selects on the tuple identifier column to limit the table to the corresponding table size at that point in time.

3.2 Views

Plattner [4] discussed modern enterprise applications that make increasing use of logical database views as they ease the transition to new systems. Most interestingly, most complex OLxP queries including aggregations and joins are written using views. We found views in the financial module that join up to five tables and reference other views themselves (up to six layers of views). In order to obtain all accesses on a particular table for our analyses, we rewrite queries on views to directly access the actual base tables. There are several issues to consider when rewriting views as handing down tuple identifiers from the base tables up to the top level projection, including resolving potential attribute name collisions and more. An exemplary rewrite of a query on a view to directly access the base tables and project tuple identifiers is shown in Listing 1.

4. REPLAY PERFORMANCE

The performance of the query replay is crucial since there are hard time constraints whenever the ERP system owner has to provide a system copy (e.g., a standby system). Besides obvious measures as proper parallelization and efficient storing of results, our focus is on the reduction of queries (e.g., recognition of semantic duplicates), which are to be executed.

In short, the replay works as follows:

1. To group queries, the interval length is defined. As a lower bound, the interval length depends on the granularity of which the table size information is exported (e.g., every ten minutes for 90 seconds). Shorter intervals improve accuracy but in parallel impede performance (cf. Step 2).
2. Per time slot the following steps are taken:
   (a) For each query, we sort search arguments lexically by attribute name and replace projections by `$ROW_ID$`.
   (b) A mapping between distinct replay queries and their initial trace instances is created. For the replay, only distinct replay queries have to be executed, because the initial queries that map to that replay query yield the same tuple accesses anyways.
3. The queries of each time slot are executed in parallel. The eventually executed query projects its own query identifier to allow for later identification and the tuple identifiers.
4. After the replay, tuple accesses are again mapped to the original query trace instances and stored.

5. DEMONSTRATION

Our demonstration allows to browse through our HTML-based workload analyses and investigate the differences between synthetic workloads and a traced production SAP ERP system. We provide

[1]Percentage of `SELECT` queries that join tables.

guided access to both our visualization for easy browsing and to the database storing the trace information to answer more detailed questions from the audience.

The following two sections present the two main analyses of the front end that the audience, amongst others, can walk through.

5.1 Partitioning Evaluation

Effective partitioning is crucial for analytical applications, which usually access data without indices and hence profit from effective pruning. We provide a tool that allows evaluating different partitioning schemas interactively. With the help of that tool, we were also able to evaluate several published automated partitioning approaches, e.g., *aggressive data skipping* [6] or *PREF* [7].

5.2 Workload Characteristics

We revisited the numbers of Krueger et al. [2] who compared TPC-C with a production ERP system. For the ERP system, we calculated workload fractions for tables corresponding to the TPC-C benchmark. As listed in Table 1, the examined part of the ERP system is even more read-dominated than expected and executes joins significantly more often than TPC-C. Comparing TPC-C and TPC-E solely by these numbers, TPC-E does a better job reflecting production ERP systems. To further ease the comparison of workloads, we visualize the distribution of queries over time, query selections and their particular value distributions (Fig. 1), and the ratios of query types per table. Such analyses of read/write ratios and the composition of expensive queries are of particular interest for OLxP-optimized databases, which deploy read-optimized (columnar) data structures [1, 3, 5].

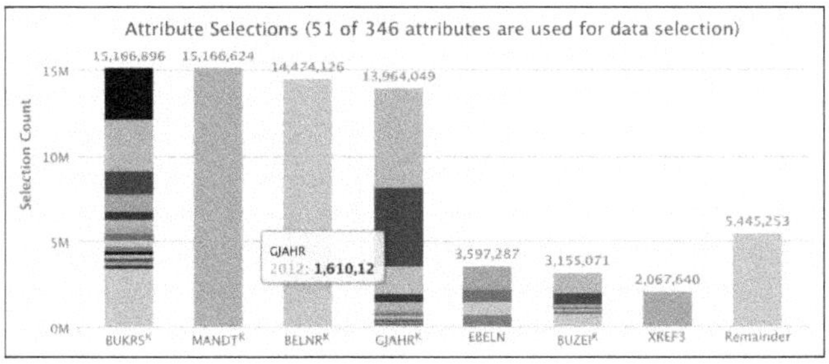

Figure 1: Demo screen showing which columns of SAP ERP's main accounting table *BSEG* have been selected with which values.

Time-Correlation of Data Accesses. Apart from calculating access frequencies, access skew, et cetera, we tried to visualize data access patterns, which we have obtained from the workload replay. We decided to combine time series and heat maps to visualize decreasing relevance of transactional data over time.

Fig. 2 shows a heat map visualizing accesses to a table storing customer master data. For this particular example, it can be seen that recent data is not accessed at a significantly higher frequency than less recent data. In contrast, transactional data (e.g., TPC-C's `ORDER` or SAP EPR's `BSEG` table) exhibit more time-correlated patterns where recent data is accessed at a much higher frequency while accesses decrease over time as tuples age.

However, comparing the heat maps of the traced ERP system and synthetic workloads shows a significant difference in the number of accesses to non-recent data. One reason is the increasing analytical load of such OLxP systems. More interestingly, another reason is the removal of materialized aggregates in favor of on-the-fly aggregations in modern enterprise systems [4]. Without ma-

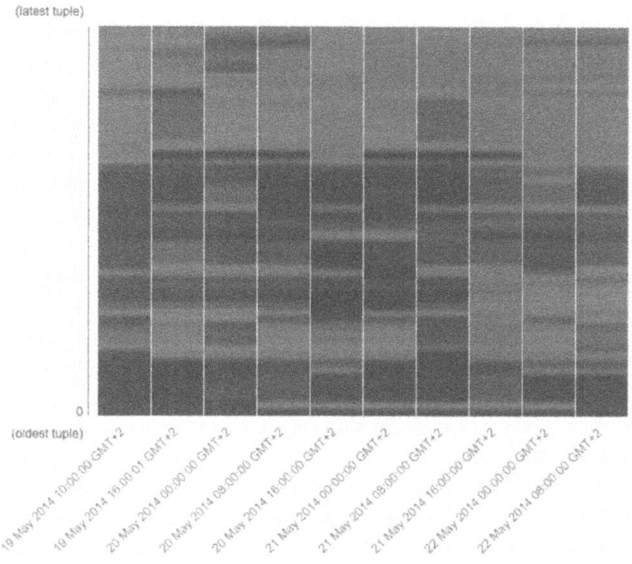

Figure 2: *Heat map visualization* of tuple accesses for an SAP ERP master data table. Each column shows the accesses to the table for an 8h long time slot.

terialized aggregates, the fraction of frequently accessed tuples is much larger, because aggregations are not longer lookups to recently modified tuples (thus probably cached) but complex scans and joins of large sets of data. This development can be nicely observed and compared using the heat maps and is particularly interesting for research areas as buffer management or data tiering.

6. CONCLUSION

The presented tool set analyzes large SQL workload traces and gathers access information down to the finest level of granularity without the need of direct access to the production system. It visualizes various aspects that allow exploring and comparing workload characteristics and thus enable thorough evaluations in a realistic OLxP scenario.

Our analyses show that both TPC-C and TPC-E fall short of representing production systems accurately. The demo provides valuable insights for the audience to spur research towards *real-world-optimized* database systems, especially for upcoming enterprise systems without materialized aggregates and OLxP workloads. We will include the audience's feedback into a publication, which analyses and quantifies the differences between synthetic and realistic systems in detail.

7. REFERENCES

[1] F. Funke, A. Kemper, and T. Neumann. Compacting transactional data in hybrid OLTP & OLAP databases. *PVLDB*, 5(11):1424–1435, 2012.

[2] J. Krueger et al. Fast updates on read-optimized databases using multi-core CPUs. *PVLDB*, 5(1):61–72, 2011.

[3] J. Lee et al. High-performance transaction processing in SAP HANA. *IEEE Data Eng. Bull.*, 36(2):28–33, 2013.

[4] H. Plattner. The impact of columnar in-memory databases on enterprise systems. *PVLDB*, 7(13):1722–1729, 2014.

[5] V. Raman et al. DB2 with BLU acceleration: So much more than just a column store. *PVLDB*, 6(11):1080–1091, 2013.

[6] L. Sun et al. Fine-grained partitioning for aggressive data skipping. In *Proc. ACM SIGMOD*, pages 1115–1126, 2014.

[7] E. Zamanian et al. Locality-aware partitioning in parallel database systems. In *Proc. ACM SIGMOD*, pages 17–30, 2015.

Thymeflow, A Personal Knowledge Base with Spatio-temporal Data

David Montoya
Engie Ineo & ENS Cachan & INRIA
david.montoya@inria.fr

Thomas Pellissier Tanon
ENS Lyon
thomas.tanon@ens-lyon.fr

Serge Abiteboul
INRIA & ENS Cachan
serge.abiteboul@inria.fr

Fabian M. Suchanek
Télécom ParisTech
suchanek@enst.fr

ABSTRACT

The typical Internet user has data spread over several devices and across several online systems. We demonstrate an open-source system for integrating user's data from different sources into a single Knowledge Base. Our system integrates data of different kinds into a coherent whole, starting with email messages, calendar, contacts, and location history. It is able to detect event periods in the user's location data and align them with calendar events. We will demonstrate how to query the system within and across different dimensions, and perform analytics over emails, events, and locations.

Keywords

personal information; data integration; querying; open-source

1. INTRODUCTION

Today, typical Internet users have their data spread over several devices and services. This includes emails, contact lists, calendars, location histories, and many other types of data. However, commercial systems often function as data traps, where it is easy to check in information and difficult to query it. This problem becomes all the more important as more and more of our lives happens in the digital sphere.

With this paper, we propose to demonstrate a fully functional personal knowledge management system, called Thymeflow. Our system integrates personal information from different sources into a single knowledge base (KB). The system runs locally on the users' machine, and thus gives them complete control over their data. Thymeflow replicates data from outside services (such as email, calendar, contacts, location services, etc.), and thus acts as a digital home for personal data. This provides users with a high-level global view of that data, which they can use for querying and analysis.

Our demonstration will illustrate the features of Thymeflow, the connection to external services, and its capacity to answer to questions such as "Where did I have lunch with Alice last week?". We will present the architecture of Thymeflow and illustrate its main functionalities. In particular, we will show how an incremental change in a data source leads to changes in the KB and its enrichment. We will also illustrate the management of location data (such as GPS traces). We believe that such location data becomes useful only if it is semantically enriched with events and people in the user's personal space – which is what Thymeflow achieves. We will demo alignments based on time (a meeting in calendar and a GPS location) and on space (an address in contacts and a GPS location). Finally, we released the code under an open-source software license[1].

This paper is structured as follows: Section 2 describes our system, its model, data sources and knowledge enrichment processes. Section 3 discusses our demonstration setting and Section 4 the related work.

2. THE SYSTEM

Our system is a Scala program that the user installs locally. The user provides the system with a list of data sources (such as email accounts, calendars, or address books), together with authorizations to access them (such as tokens or passwords). The system accesses the data sources (as the user would), and pulls in the data. All code runs locally on the user's machine. Thus, the user remains in complete control of her data. The system uses adapters to access the sources, and to transform their data into RDF. We store the data in a Sesame based triple store [2]. Since the KB is persistent, we can restart the system at any time without losing information.

Architecture. One of the main challenges in the creation of a personal KB is that data sources may change, and these updates have to be reflected in the KB. To address this dynamics, our system uses software modules called *loaders* and *enrichers*. Figure 1 shows the loaders $L_1, \ldots, L_n$ on the left, and the enrichers $E_1, \ldots, E_p$ in the center. Loaders are responsible for accessing the data sources. Enrichers are responsible for inferring new statements, such as alignments between entities obtained by entity resolution. Loaders are triggered by updates in the data sources (e.g., calendar entries) and insertion of new pieces of information in the KB triggers the execution of a pipeline of enricher modules, as shown in Figure 1.

[1]https://github.com/thymeflow/thymeflow

CIKM'16 October 24-28, 2016, Indianapolis, IN, USA

ACM ISBN 978-1-4503-4073-1/16/10.

DOI: http://dx.doi.org/10.1145/2983323.2983337

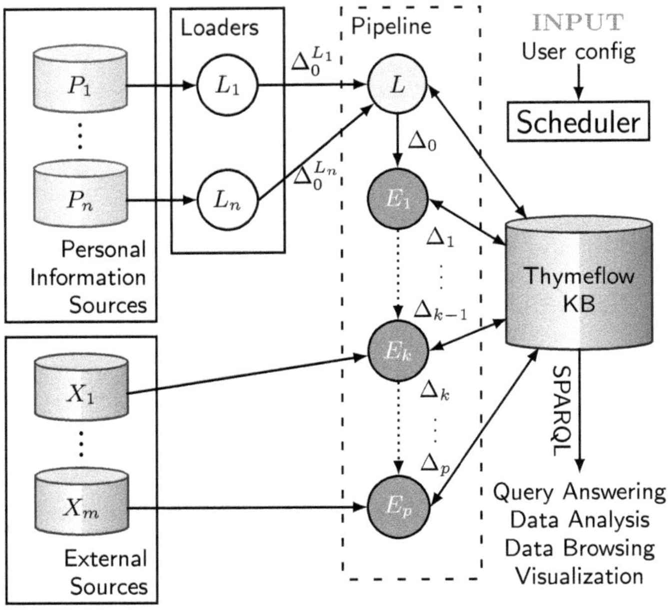

Figure 1: System architecture

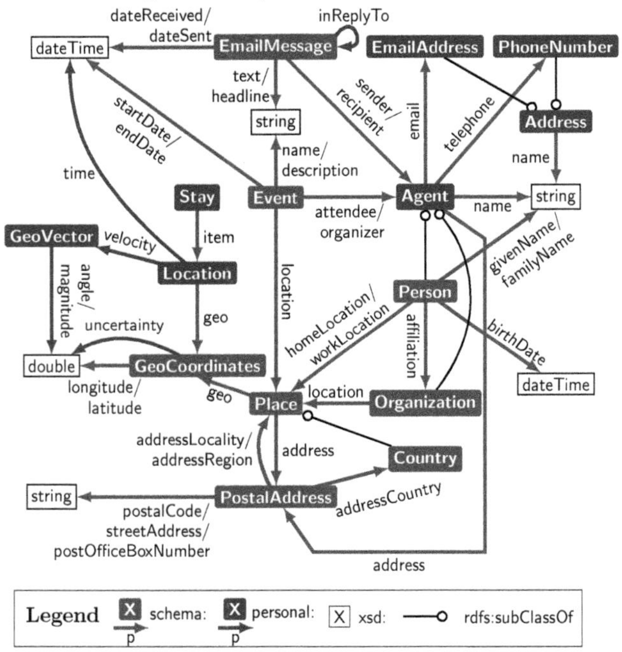

Figure 2: Personal Data Model

Data model. We use the RDF standard [7] for knowledge representation inside of the knowledge base. Figure 2 illustrates a part of our schema. Nodes represent classes, rounded ones are non-literal classes, and an arrow edge with label p from X to Y means that the property p links instances of type X to instances of type Y.

Loading. The loader modules are responsible for retrieving new data from a data source. We have designed adapters that transform items from the data source into our schema. For each data source that has been updated, the adapter for that particular source transforms the source updates since last synchronization into a Δ, a set of insertions/deletions in RDF. We have implemented loaders for the following protocols:

- CardDav [8] provides contacts encoded in the vCard format [15]. They are represented as instances of type `personal:Agent`.
- CalDav [9] provides calendar events and todos in the iCalendar format [10]. We consider only events for now and we extract a new `schema:Event` for each of them. The location of an event is typically given as a postal address, and we will discuss later how to associate it to geo-coordinates and richer place semantics.
- IMAP [5] provides emails in the RFC 822 format [6]. We represent senders and receivers as instances of `personal:Agent`. We will discuss later how to map these agents to the ones extracted from other sources.
- Location data in the Google Location History format. This format provides the user's location history as points with a timestamp and geo coordinates, which we represent as instances of `personal:Location`. Competing formats for location data include GPX and KML, but no standardized protocol exists for managing a location history (i.e. with synchronization capabilities).

Enrichers. After a loading phase, the enricher modules perform inference tasks such as entity resolution, event geolocation, and other knowledge enrichment tasks. Such an enricher takes as input the current state of the KB, and some collection Δ_i of changes that have happened recently. It computes a new collection Δ_{i+1} of enrichments. Intuitively, this allows reacting to changes of a data source. When some Δ_0 is detected (typically by some adapter), the system runs a pipeline of enrichers to take these new changes into consideration. For instance, when a new entry is entered in the calendar with an address, a geocoding enricher is called to attempt to locate it. Another enricher will later try to match it with a position in the location history. We have for instance implemented the following enrichers:

- An enricher that detects that two `personal:Agents` are about the same real world agent. Agents are matched based on similar attributes such as email addresses or names. The enricher can thus link emails to contacts.
- An enricher that analyzes the location history to detect places where the user stayed for a prolonged period of time. The enricher uses an algorithm similar to the time-based clustering algorithm in [13].
- An enricher that matches the stays extracted by the previous enricher with events in the calendar. This enricher works by detecting shared periods of time.
- A geocoder that links each calendar event with one or more real world places (street addresses, landmarks, etc.). This module uses both the location stated by the calendar and the coordinates the previous enricher associates to events.

3. DEMONSTRATION SETTING

Our system is equipped with a SPARQL 1.1 compliant engine [12] with optional full-text search capabilities based on Apache Lucene. This allows users to launch SPARQL queries on their personal data. Since the KB unites different data sources, queries span different types of data.

During the demonstration we will present the system as seen by a particular user, say Mr. S. Our user will first launch the system, and connect it to his Google account (Figure 3). The system will then begin to load the data contained in his account, including emails, contacts, calendar, and location history. (For the interested, we will show the loading progress.) Once his data loaded, Mr. S. can execute SPARQL queries on it. This allows him to see, e.g.,

- what are the telephone numbers of his birthday party guests? (So he can send them a last-minute message.)
- what are the latest emails sent by any participant of the "Financial Restructuring" meetings?
- what are the places he visited during his previous trip to London? (So he does not go there a second time.)

Mr. S. can also perform analytics, e.g.,

- who does he most frequently communicate with?
- what are the places where he usually meets one particular person (based on his calendar)?
- how much time does it usually take to get an email answer from that particular person?

Figure 4 shows a sample query, which asks for emails sent by the organizer of an event during the month of the event.

We will show how users can verify that the enrichments proposed by the algorithm are correct, and possibly manually correct some of the knowledge. For this, the system keeps track, if necessary, of overwrites made to source data within the KB, ensuring that they are not overridden by the next incremental update. Finally, we will also present the results of some experiments we performed with real users and real data to illustrate the quality of the enrichers.

4. RELATED WORK

This work is motivated by the general concept of personal information management, see e.g. [1].

Personal Knowledge Bases. The problem of building a knowledge base for querying and managing personal information is not new. Among the first projects in this direction were IRIS [3] and NEPOMUK [11]. They used Semantic Web technologies to exchange data between different applications within a single desktop computer. They also provided semantic search facilities for desktop data. Our work is different from these projects: We do not tackle personal information management by reinventing the user experience for reading/writing emails, managing a calendar, organizing files, etc. We embrace personal information as being fundamentally distributed and focusing on the need of providing integration on top for creating completely new services (complex query answering, analytics).

Information Integration. Data matching (also known as record linkage, entity resolution, information integration, or object matching) is extensively utilized in data mining projects and in large-scale information systems by business, public bodies and governments [4]. Example application areas include national census, the health sector, etc. Recently, contact managers from known vendors have started providing de-duplication tools for finding duplicate contacts and merging them in bulk. However, these tools restrict themselves to contacts present in the user's address book.

Location History and Calendar. A lot of studies have already been done related around user location data. Few of them, however, have exploited the user's calendar and other available user data for creating richer and more semantic activity histories. Recently, a study has recognized the importance of fusing location histories with location data for improving the representation of information contained in the user's calendar: e.g. for distinguishing genuine real-world events from reminders [14].

Commercial Solutions. Some commercial providers, such as Gmail and Apple, have arguably come quite close to our vision of a personal knowledge base. They integrate calendars, emails, and address books, and allow smart exchanges between them. Google Now even pro-actively interacts with the user. However, these are closed-source. They do not allow the scientific community to build on their technology.

5. CONCLUSION

We propose to demonstrate a fully functional open-source personal knowledge management system. Our system integrates data from emails, calendars, address books, and the location history. Users can query the system for people, locations and events, or for any combination of these entities.

References

[1] S. Abiteboul, B. André, and D. Kaplan. "Managing your digital life". *Communications of the ACM* (2015).

[2] J. Broekstra, A. Kampman, and F. Van Harmelen. "Sesame: A generic architecture for storing and querying RDF and RDF schema". In: *ISWC '02*. Springer, 2002.

[3] A. Cheyer, J. Park, and R. Giuli. *IRIS: Integrate, Relate. Infer. Share.* Tech. rep. DTIC Document, 2005.

[4] P. Christen. *Data matching: concepts and techniques for record linkage, entity resolution, and duplicate detection.* Springer Science & Business Media, 2012.

[5] M. Crispin. *Internet Message Access protocol - version 4rev1.* RFC 3501. IETF, Mar. 2003.

[6] D. H. Crocker. *Standard for the format of ARPA Internet text messages.* RFC 822. IETF, Aug. 1982.

[7] R. Cyganiak, D. Wood, and M. Lanthaler. *RDF 1.1 Concepts and Abstract Syntax.* W3C, Feb. 2014.

[8] C. Daboo. *CardDAV: vCard Extensions to Web Distributed Authoring and Versioning (WebDAV).* RFC 6352. IETF, Aug. 2011.

[9] C. Daboo, B. Desruisseaux, and L. Dusseault. *Calendaring Extensions to WebDAV (CalDAV).* RFC 4791. IETF, Mar. 2007.

[10] B. Desruisseaux. *Internet Calendaring and Scheduling Core Object Specification (iCalendar).* RFC 5545. IETF, Sept. 2009.

[11] S. Handschuh, K. Möller, and T. Groza. "The NEPOMUK project-on the way to the social semantic desktop". In: *I-SEMANTICS '07.* 2007.

[12] S. Harris, A. Seaborne, and E. Prud'hommeaux. *SPARQL 1.1 Query Language.* W3C, Mar. 2013.

[13] J. H. Kang, W. Welbourne, B. Stewart, and G. Borriello. "Extracting Places from Traces of Locations". In: *WMASH '04.* 2004.

[14] T. Lovett, E. O'Neill, J. Irwin, and D. Pollington. "The calendar as a sensor: analysis and improvement using data fusion with social networks and location". In: *UbiComp '10.* 2010.

[15] S. Perreault. *vCard Format Specification.* RFC 6350. IETF, Aug. 2011.

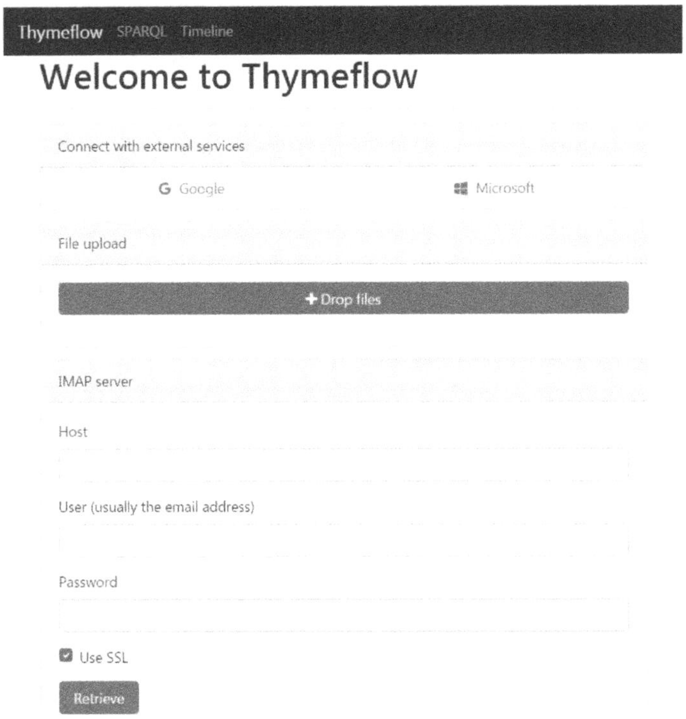

Figure 3: Thymeflow's user interface home page, which allows one to connect with external data sources.

Figure 4: Thymeflow's user interface query capabilities – a query that retrieves the subject of all emails sent by the organizer of the "OPW mentors meeting" event during the month of the event.

Inferring Traffic Incident Start Time with Loop Sensor Data

Mingxuan Yue
Computer Science Department
University of Southern California, Los Angeles, CA
mingxuay@usc.edu

Liyue Fan
Integrated Media Systems Center
University of Southern California, Los Angeles, CA
liyuefan@usc.edu

Cyrus Shahabi
Integrated Media Systems Center
University of Southern California, Los Angeles, CA
shahabi@usc.edu

ABSTRACT

Traffic incidents and their impacts have been largely studied to improve road safety and to reduce incurred life and economic losses. However, the inaccuracy of incident data collected from transportation agencies, especially the start time, poses a great challenge to traffic incident research. We present INFIT, a system that infers the incident start time utilizing traffic data collected by loop sensors. The core of INFIT is IIG, our newly developed inference algorithm. The key idea is that IIG considers the traffic speed at multiple upstream locations, to mitigate the randomness in traffic data and to distinguish among multiple impact factors. INFIT includes an interactive interface with real-world incident datasets. We demonstrate INFIT with three exploratory use cases and show the usefulness of our inference algorithms.

Keywords

Impact Propagation; Traffic Data; Traffic Incidents

1. INTRODUCTION

According to National Safety Council [4], nearly 19,000 people died and 2.2 million were seriously injured in traffic incidents across the U.S. during the first six months of 2015, resulting a total cost of $152 billion. To reduce the life and economic losses, the impact of traffic incidents has been studied in various disciplines including transportation, civil engineering, policy, and operation research (e.g., [7, 5]).

In our previous study [3], we built ADMS, a large-scale database to maintain real-time and historical traffic data including incident data reported by transportation agencies in Southern California. We further studied in [5] the impact propagation of traffic incidents with ADMS. However, we find the agency-reported incident *start time* is often inaccurate, containing up to 15-minute error based on our estimation. In general, the agency reported incident time is derived from human estimate or the 911 call record, which may be the cause of errors as people must ensure their safety first after an incident happens.

CIKM'16 October 24–28, 2016, Indianapolis, IN, USA.

ACM ISBN 978-1-4503-4073-1/16/10. . . $15.00

DOI: http://dx.doi.org/10.1145/2983323.2983339

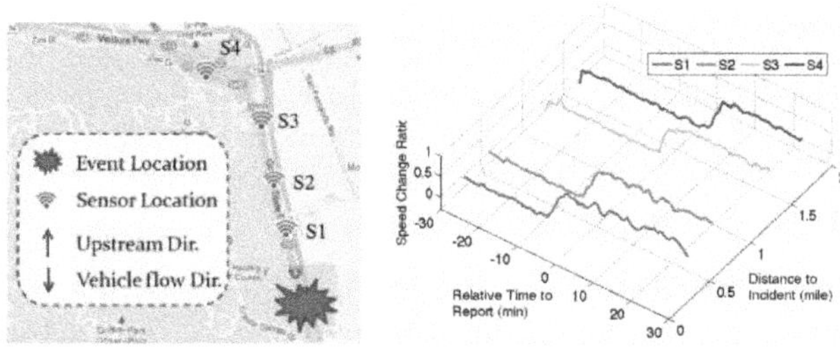

(a) Sample Incident [5] (b) Upstream Speed Change

Figure 1: Example of Traffic Incident Impact Propagation

For a reported incident in Figure 1a, we identify 4 upstream loop sensors, i.e., $S1$-$S4$, and retrieve the traffic speed measured 30 minutes before and after the reported time. We observe that the upstream traffic speed at $S1$ is significantly affected 10 minutes *before* the reported incident time, i.e., speed change ratio (defined in Section 2) exceeds 40%. This effect is present at other upstream locations consistently. Therefore, we estimate that the "actual" incident start time is around 10 minutes *before* the reported time.

Since the accuracy of incident data is essential to all incident related research, the goal of our study is to infer the start time of agency-reported traffic incidents using traffic data detected by loop sensors. Two major *challenges* arise when analyzing the traffic data: the first challenge is that the traffic data contains sensor noise and frequent fluctuations, which creates *lags* and *gaps* when performing temporal analysis; the second challenge is the co-existence of multiple incidents or external factors, such as weather or construction, the impact of which may *overlap* in time and space and thus is difficult to distinguish.

In this paper, we present INFIT, a system for inferring the start time of traffic incidents using loop sensor traffic data. INFIT visualizes the agency-reported incidents on a map and illustrates the inaccuracy of the reported incident time with upstream traffic speed data. It also demonstrates the effectiveness our newly developed inference algorithm, which recognizes the propagation of speed change through *multiple* upstream locations. The inferred time can be used for data cleansing in the ADMS database and to enable various research studies on incident impact.

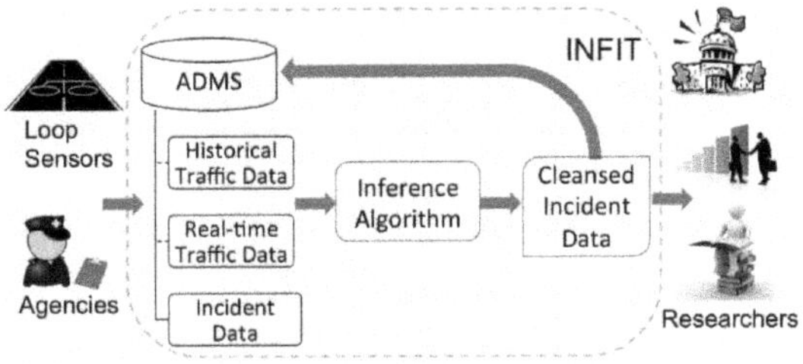

Figure 2: INFIT Framework

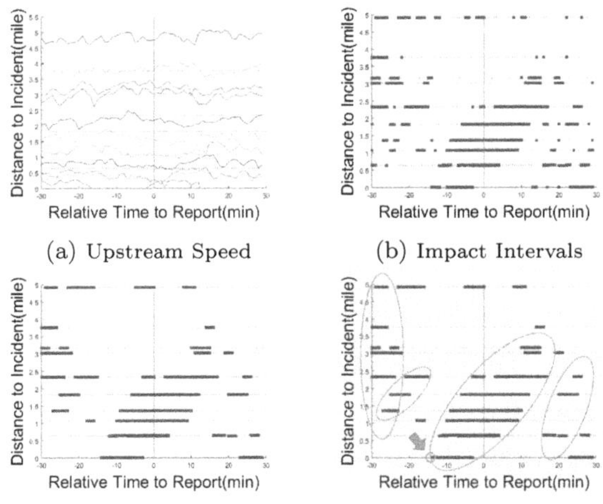

(a) Upstream Speed (b) Impact Intervals (c) Smoothing (d) Interval Groups

Figure 3: Illustration of IIG Algorithm

2. INFIT OVERVIEW

The framework of INFIT is presented in Figure 2. We have access to the ADMS database [3] that collects incident reports from transportation agencies and high-resolution traffic data from loop sensors. Our newly developed inference algorithm will generate accurate estimates of incident start time, which will be used to cleanse the noisy incident reports and to enable other traffic studies.

2.1 Datasets

We will utilize two of our in-house datasets collected from LA County highways and arterial streets. **Incident Data.** The incident dataset [1] is collected in real-time from various reporting agencies including California Highway Patrol, LA Department of Transportation, CalTrans. For each incident, 43 attributes are reported including time, location, type of incident, direction, etc. The type of incident various from traffic collision to road construction, and we only consider collisions in this paper.

Traffic Data. We also have access to historical and real-time traffic data collected from around 4,230 loop sensors in OC and LA County covering nearly 5000 miles [5]. The sensors report speed, volume, and occupancy values every 30 seconds. We only consider traffic speed in this paper. One-minute aggregation is performed to fill missing values.

2.2 Inference Algorithms

Existing Approach - Bayesian: The majority of previous studies [6, 8] addressed the automatic detection of traffic incidents by considering traffic data *only*, as they may not have access to the agency-reported incident data. In our case, we can utilize both traffic data and incident data, yielding 0% false positive rate. Singliar and Hauskrecht [9] studied the *supervised* realignment of incident time given the inaccurate reported time with Bayesian probabilistic models. However, they only considered traffic data, i.e., features, at the nearest loop sensor, and the inferred time is often a local optimum due to sensor noise and random fluctuations. Nonetheless, we adapted the Bayesian [9] algorithm to our datasets and implemented them for comparison in Section 3.

IIG Algorithm: We design an *unsupervised* approach, i.e., Impact Interval Grouping (IIG) algorithm, to infer the start time of a traffic incident by recognizing a series of *impact intervals* at multiple upstream locations.

For each sensor location, an *impact interval* is a consecutive time period during which the speed change ratio, compared to historical data, exceeds a predefined threshold λ. Specifically, for each loop sensor, we generate its historical average speed over a month as in [5] for each minute of the day. Given a reported incident, we retrieve the traffic speed $v[t]$ at each upstream location during a 60-minute window centered at the reported time, as shown in Figure 3a. We then compare the real-time speed with the historical average $\bar{v}[t]$ to obtain the impacted time t, i.e., $\frac{|v[t]-\bar{v}[t]|}{\bar{v}[t]} \geq \lambda$. The raw impact intervals, i.e., solid blue lines, are shown in Figure 3b, and they are relatively short due to sensor noise and fluctuations in traffic speed. Smoothing can be adopted, such as Moving Average and concatenation, to eliminate the noise and randomness (Figure 3c).

Another challenge is that *multiple* impact intervals are present at each upstream location within the time window, e.g., two significant impact intervals at the nearest upstream sensor in Figure 3c. By the nearest sensor alone, we may not correctly identify the interval impacted by the specified incident. Therefore, we propose to group the impact intervals throughout multiple upstream sensors that conform to the impact propagation behavior discovered in [5]. For simplicity, we adopt two heuristics, i.e., maximum overlap and nearest center, to identify the impact interval potentially resulted from that of the preceding sensor. Furthermore, the impact of *multiple* incident or external factors may coexist in the same time window, i.e., several impact interval groups circled by orange lines in Figure 3d. We preserve the nearest group to the report time and its start time is used to estimate the actual incident time (arrow in Figure 3d).

Hybrid Solution: Since the IIG algorithm depends on the predefined impact threshold λ, lower λ values allow for more sensitivity to *minor* incidents but incur more noisy intervals, and vice versa. Therefore we design a hybrid approach that combines IIG with Bayesian [9] to eliminate the inference bias by λ. We first apply IIG with a fixed λ value and identify a shorter time window, e.g., 20 minutes centered at the estimated time, and then apply Bayesian in the new window for more accurate inference.

3. DEMONSTRATION PLANS

We built INFIT with Django framework and utilized Google Maps API as well as a back-end SQLite database. INFIT incorporates our newly developed IIG algorithm in Python and the project source code is available for download [2]. We will demonstrate three interactive use cases: (1) exploring incidents and real-time traffic data at upstream lo-

Table 1: Average Error of IIG in Minutes

λ	Grouping Heuristic	AvgErr (mins)
20%	Nearest Center	4.71
20%	Maximum Overlap	4.71
40%	Nearest Center	3.92
40%	Maximum Overlap	4.03
60%	Nearest Center	6.55
60%	Maximum Overlap	7.02

cations; (2) exploring the IIG inference algorithm; (3) comparing the accuracy of the aforementioned algorithms.

Exploring Incident and Traffic Data: The main purpose of this scenario is to allow the audience to interact with the incident data provided by the ADMS database. They will observe the inaccuracy of the agency-reported incident time by looking at traffic data at upstream locations given the selected incident. On the main frame of INFIT as in Figure 4, the audience will find an interactive map showing the locations of reported incidents. The audience can then click on any incident and observe on the right its attributes retrieved from our database. Below the map, we will show the time series of traffic speed detected by multiple upstream loop sensors, for 30 minutes before and after the reported incident time. The audience can observe significant speed decrease at various upstream locations before the agency reported incident time, indicating the report may be inaccurate. On the bottom right, we include a 3D plot showing the spatiotemporal impact propagation of the selected incident.

Exploring IIG Algorithm: Once an incident is selected, the audience can navigate to "IIG: Under-the-Hood" page as in Figure 5 to explore our algorithm. The audience can specify IIG parameters and heuristics, such as λ and grouping heuristics, and observe intermediate as well as final results. The IIG demo will present the major steps to the audience, similar to Figure 3, given the specified incident: (1) the speed series of upstream locations, where each horizontal curve represents the speed series at one upstream location in the 60-minute window; (2) the raw impact intervals calculated using the real-time speed series and historical speed according to the specified the impact threshold λ; (3) the smoothed impact intervals, depending on the specified smoothing techniques, i.e., moving average or concatenation; (4) the interval groups, depending on the specified grouping heuristics, i.e., nearest start, nearest center, or maximum overlap; (5) the start time of the chosen interval group will be highlighted, identifying the estimated incident start time.

We studied the sensitivity of our IIG algorithm for 183 incidents from the dataset used in [5] with manually labeled incident start time. As can be seen in Table 1, the inferred time is less accurate when the impact threshold λ is either too high or too low. When λ is set to 40%, the algorithm achieves a trade-off between robustness and early detection. As for the grouping heuristics, we found that the "Maximum Overlap" heuristic is slightly better.

Comparison of Inference Algorithms: Once an incident is selected on the main frame, the audience can navigate to the "Inference Comparisons" page, as in Figure 6, to observe the difference between several inference algorithms, including Bayesian, IIG, and Hybrid. We show that the Bayesian algorithm considers the speed time series of the nearest sensor location only and as a result is largely affected by noise in the data. The IIG algorithm considers traffic speed at multiple upstream locations as input data. Therefore the inferred start time is more accurate and aligned well with observation by eye in the 3D plot. The Hybrid approach which benefits from both IIG and Bayesian generates the most accurate inference. We also conducted a comparative evaluation with the three algorithms and the results (omitted for brevity) confirmed the superiority of the Hybrid solution.

4. CONCLUSIONS

In this demo, we presented the INFIT system, which infers the incident start time using traffic speed data from loop sensors. We described the IIG algorithm, i.e., the INFIT core, for accurate incident time inference by identifying the traffic impact throughout multiple upstream locations of a given incident. IIG provides robust performance in the presence of noise in the traffic data and accurate inference even when multiple impact factors are present at the same time. Our interactive, graphical interface provided an exploratory experience to the audience with real-world incident datasets. We visualized the IIG internal procedures and demonstrated the usefulness compared to the existing solution.

Future work may include: (1) the integration of INFIT to TransDec [3] for data cleansing; (2) the improvement of IIG by considering the "severity" of impact, in addition to time and space. The severity can be evaluated by generating impact intervals with a range of impact thresholds for each sensor. It may improve the grouping of impact intervals and eliminate the algorithm's dependency on the threshold λ.

5. ACKNOWLEDGMENTS

This research has been funded in part by NSF grant IIS-1115153, METRANS Transportation Center under grant from Caltrans DTRT12-G-UTC57, the USC Integrated Media Systems Center (IMSC), and unrestricted cash gifts from Oracle. Any opinions, findings, and conclusions or recommendations expressed in this material are those of the authors and do not necessarily reflect the views of any of the sponsors.

6. REFERENCES

[1] ADMS incident dataset. http://imsc.usc.edu/AccidentMonitoring.

[2] INFIT repository. http://www-scf.usc.edu/ mingxuay/INFIT/project/.

[3] U. Demiryurek, F. Banaei-Kashani, and C. Shahabi. Transdec:a spatiotemporal query processing framework for transportation systems. In *ICDE '10,2010*, pages 1197–1200, March 2010.

[4] National Safety Council. U.S. on pace for deadliest driving year since 2007, says national safety council. http://www.nsc.org/Connect/NSCNewsReleases/Lists/Posts/Post.aspx?ID=64, 2015. [Online; accessed 5-January-2016].

[5] B. Pan, U. Demiryurek, C. Gupta, and C. Shahabi. Forecasting spatiotemporal impact of traffic incidents for next-generation navigation systems. *Knowl. Inf. Syst.*, 45(1):75–104, 2015.

[6] H. Payne, E. Helfenbein, and H. Knobel. Development and testing of incident detection algorithms. Technical report, FHWA, 1976.

[7] C. Quiroga, E. Kraus, R. Pina, K. Hamad, and E. S. Park. Incident characteristics and impact on freeway traffic. Technical report, 2004. http://d2dtl5nnlpfr0r.cloudfront.net/tti.tamu.edu/documents/0-4745-1.pdf.

[8] S. Sadek, A. Al-Hamadi, B. Michaelis, and U. Sayed. A statistical framework for real-time traffic accident recognition. *J Signal Inf. Proc.*, 1(1):77–81, 2010.

[9] T. Singliar and M. Hauskrecht. Learning to detect incidents from noisily labeled data. *Machine Learning*, 79(3):335–354, September 2009.

APPENDIX

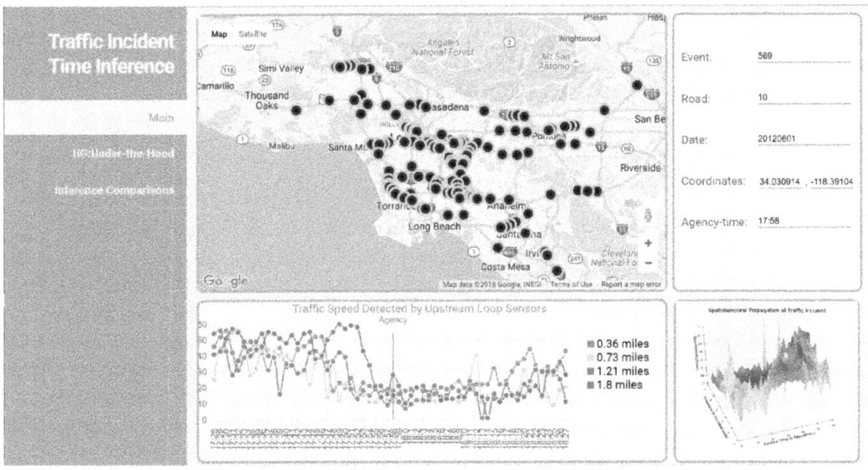

Figure 4: INFIT Main Frame

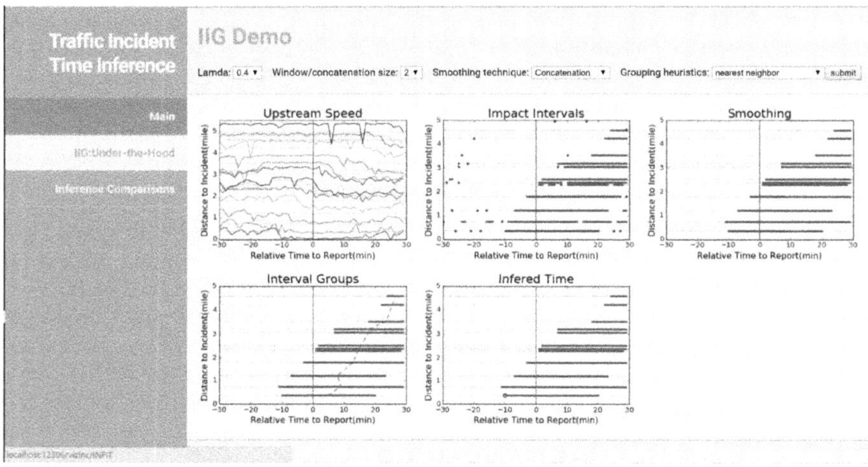

Figure 5: IIG Demonstration

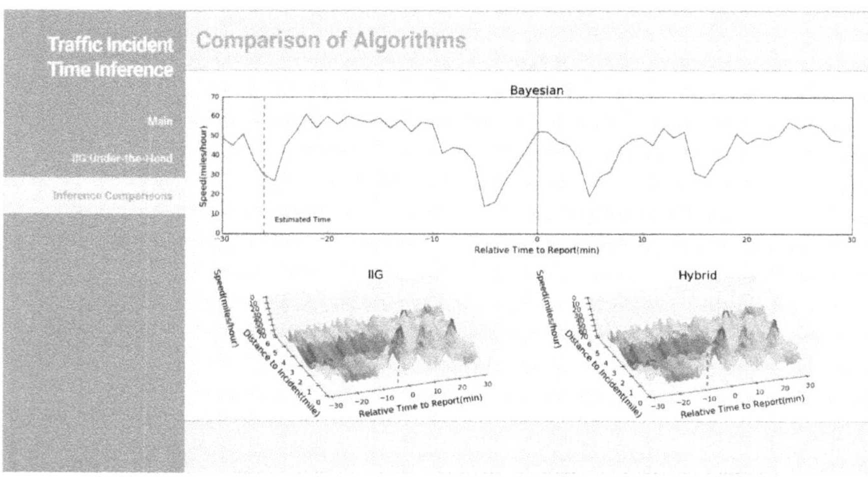

Figure 6: Comparison of Inference Algorithms

TEAMOPT: Interactive Team Optimization in Big Networks

Liangyue Li
Arizona State University
liangyue@asu.edu

Hanghang Tong
Arizona State University
hanghang.tong@asu.edu

Nan Cao
NYU Shanghai
nan.cao@nyu.edu

Kate Ehrlich
IBM Research
katee@us.ibm.com

Yu-Ru Lin
University of Pittsburgh
yurulin@pitt.edu

Norbou Buchler
US Army Research Laboratory
norbou.buchler.civ@mail.mil

ABSTRACT

The science of team science is a rapidly emerging research field that studies strategies to understand and enhance the process and outcomes of collaborative, team-based research. An interesting research question we address in this work is how to maintain and optimize the team performance should certain changes happen to the team. In particular, we take the network approach to understanding the teams and consider optimizing the teams with several operations (e.g., replacement, expansion, shrinkage).

We develop TEAMOPT, a system to assist users in optimizing the team performance interactively to support the changes to a team. TEAMOPT takes as input a large network of individuals (e.g., co-author network of researchers) and is able to assist users in assembling a team with specific requirements and optimizing the team in response to the changes made to the team. It is effective in finding the best candidates, and interactive with users' feedback in the loop. The system is developed using HTML5, JavaScript, D3.js (front-end) and Python CGI (back-end). A prototype system is already deployed. We will invite the audience to experiment with our TEAMOPT in terms of its effectiveness, efficiency and applicability to various scenarios.

1. INTRODUCTION

The science of team science is a rapidly emerging research field that "encompasses both conceptual and methodological strategies aimed at understanding and enhancing the process and outcomes of collaborative, team-based research" [6]. Both internal and external environments can drive the changes of a team, e.g., the churn of a team member, team expansion, team shrinkage. An interesting research question is how to maintain and optimize the team performance under such circumstances.

The network approach to understanding the teams places the individuals in their social context and treats a team as a subgraph embedded in a larger social network. In this work, we consider optimizing the team performance interactively in a large network and specifically address a family of problems under the scope of Team Enhancement, including (1) Team Replacement [4], i.e., to find a best candidate to replace a team member who is leaving; (2) Team Refinement, i.e., to refine the team by editing the skills and connectivity among the members; (3) Team Expansion, i.e., to find a best candidate to join the team; (4) Team Shrinkage, i.e., to find a proper team member to leave the team; and (5) Team Conflict Resolution, i.e., to resolve the conflict between two or more team members.

We develop TEAMOPT (http://team-net-work.org/), a system to assist users in optimizing the team performance interactively to support the changes to a team. TEAMOPT takes as input a large network of individuals (e.g., co-author network of researchers) and is able to assist users in assembling a team with specific requirements and optimizing the team in response to the changes made to the team. To the best of our knowledge, this is the first system specializing in forming and optimizing teams with the following key features. First (*effectiveness*), we carefully identify our design objectives and develop effective algorithms with the key technique of graph kernels. Compared with other competitors, our algorithm can achieve the highest precision and recall in finding the best team member candidate. Second (*interaction*), we design fast solutions to our algorithms, enabling an interactive user experience with users' feedback in the loop. Third (*deployment*), we build our system with HTML5, Javascript, D3.js (front-end) and Python CGI (back-end).

The rest of the paper is organized as follows. Section 2 demonstrates the main functionality of TEAMOPT. Section 3 presents the technical details behind the scene. Section 4 reviews the related works and Section 5 concludes the paper.

2. FUNCTIONALITY DEMONSTRATION

In this section, we demonstrate the main functionalities of TEAMOPT. Figure 1 shows the user interface of the system, where Figure 1(1) is the main component allowing the user to explore the network dataset, form a team and perform a series of operations (e.g., replacement, refinement, expansion) to optimize the team in terms of performance/output. Figure 1(2) visualizes the hierarchical clusters in an icicle tree view [2], exhibiting the overall hierarchy structure in the network. Figure 1(3) provides the overview of the parent cluster of the current one in the hierarchy and Figure 1(4) visualizes the candidate teams to support the team optimization operations. We detail the functionalities next.

Team Formation: the system provides users with three ways of forming a team to suit their different needs. (1)

CIKM'16 October 24 - November 28, 2016, Indianapolis, IN, USA

ACM ISBN 978-1-4503-4073-1/16/10.
DOI: http://dx.doi.org/10.1145/2983323.2983340

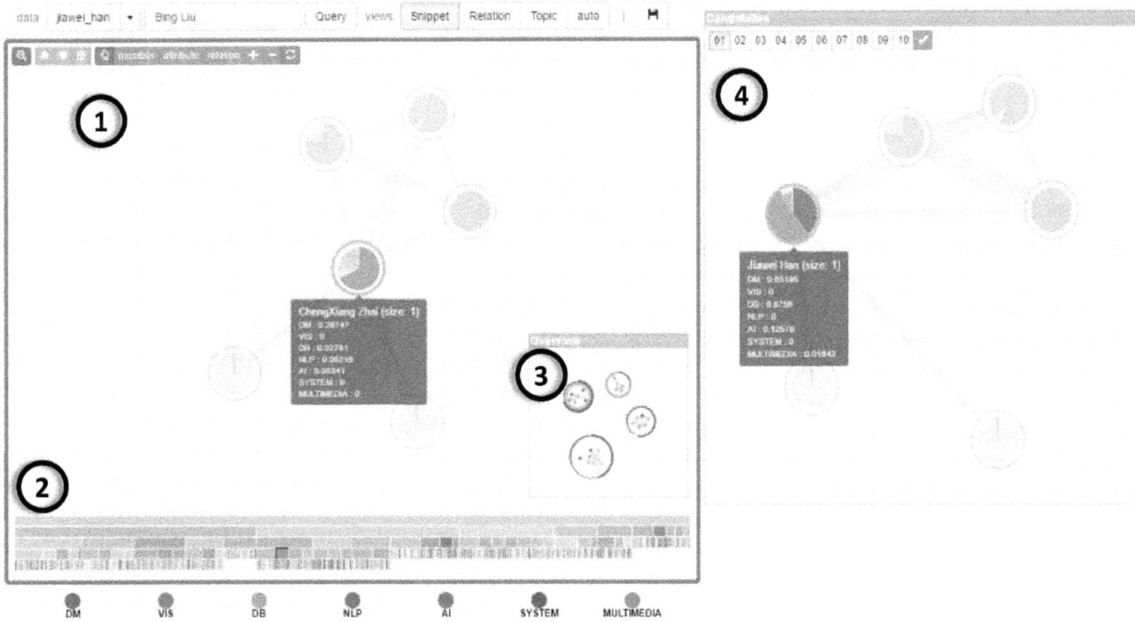

Figure 1: An illustrative example of using our TEAMOPT to find a candidate (e.g., Jiawei Han) to replace one team member (e.g., ChengXiang Zhai) when the member has to leave the team.

Skill coverage: the user specifies a subset of skills required to perform a task and the system will output a set of individuals with the minimum communication cost that can cover these skills [3]. (2) *Template matching:* the user has a specific configuration of the team in terms of the skills each team member has as well as how the team members are connected to each other. The system would then return a set of team members from the network dataset that best matches the user-input configuration. (3) *Ego network:* the user is interested in having a particular person on the team and s/he can query the system with the member's name. The system would locate the member in the dataset and show the member's ego network, including the connections among the member's immediate neighbors.

Team Replacement: the churn of team members is a common phenomenon across a wide variety of application domains, including sports, business, entertainment, etc. Figure 1 shows an example of the system in assisting the user find a best candidate that can replace the member who is leaving. The user only needs to select the member that is leaving and the system would recommend a list of candidates with the new teams visualized for an easy visual comparison.

Team Refinement: most often than not, the user might not be satisfied with the initial team formed. In this case, the user can refine the team by further editing the skills of the members and/or connections between them. The system would then recommend a list of candidate teams that best fulfill the new requirements.

Team Expansion: sometimes a new team member is needed to ramp up the team's capacity. The user can indicate the skills the new member should have as well as the connections s/he has to the current team members. The system would then recommend a list of candidates that best suit the user's requirement.

Team Shrinkage: on the contrary to the team expansion, in team shrinkage, the size of a team needs to be reduced in response to new challenges such as a shortage of the available resources. In this case, the system would recommend a list of candidates to leave the team without exerting too much negative effect on the team performance.

Team Conflict Resolution: it happens that two or multiple team members have conflict of interest with each other, in which case, the system can resolve such conflict by either replacing one conflicting member or asking s/he to leave the team.

The system is developed using HTML5, JavaScript, D3.js (front-end) and Python CGI (back-end). A prototype system is deployed at http://team-net-work.org/.

3. TECHNICAL DETAILS

In this section, we first present the algorithm that enables the team optimization operations in TEAMOPT, followed by some evaluation results.

3.1 Algorithm Details

We first show the solution for Team Replacement and later point out that other operations (e.g., Team Refinement, Team Expansion) can be solved in a strategically similar way. The churn of a member might adversely affect the performance of a team for several reasons, including loss of certain skills, change of the network connectivity, and dissolution of certain critical skill configurations (e.g., the *triangle offense* created by *the center, the forward,* and *the guard* in NBA teams sustains as a classic tactic). As a result, our goal in finding the best candidate for the replacement is to minimize such negative disruptions and maintain the stability of the team as an organic system of skills and network connectivities. Realizing this, we devote ourselves to finding the candidates that are as similar to the member leaving as possible and propose the concept of *team context aware similarity* to measure the similarity of the two members in the context of the team. Such similarity is able to capture the following three aspects:

- *skill matching:* the new member should have a similar

skill set to the person leaving to preserve the skill set of the whole team.

- *structural matching:* the new member should have a similar network connectivity to the rest of the team members.
- *skill configurations matching:* the new member should have similar skill configurations among the sub-groups in the team required by certain sub-tasks of the team.

Mathematically, the *team context aware similarity* can be instantiated by the attributed graph kernel defined on the current and new teams. Formally, the best candidate for Team Replacement can be described by the following objective:

$$q = \arg\max_{j \notin \mathcal{T}} \text{Ker}(G(\mathcal{T}), G(\mathcal{T}_{p \to j})), \quad (1)$$

where the individual q is to replace the member p, $\mathcal{T}$ is used to index the members of a team, $G(\mathcal{T})$ is the induced subgraph by the current team members from the attributed network, and $G(\mathcal{T}_{p \to j})$ is the subgraph induced after the team member p is replaced by another individual j in the network. The function $\text{Ker}(\cdot)$ is the kernel between the two attributed subgraphs. The basic idea behind graph kernels is to aggregate the similarities between the subgraphs in the two graphs, which corresponds to skill configurations among the sub-groups in the two teams. As such, the graph kernel can naturally encode the three aspects required by the *team context aware similarity*. We adopt the random walk based graph kernel [5] in the system implementation for its mathematical elegance and superior empirical performance. The solution to other operations are similar, with the key idea of having a new team (e.g., the team after expansion, refinement, and shrinkage) most similar to the original team. The similarity is still measured using graph kernels.

To enable an interactive user experience, we need to address the computational challenges brought up by the large-scale networks. To scale up, we first design an efficient pruning strategy to filter out those unpromising candidates, i.e., those who do not have any connections to any of the rest team members. We then speed up each graph kernel computation by exploring the smoothness and correspondences between the existing and the new teams.

3.2 Evaluations

We perform a user study with 20 people aged from 22 to 35. We choose 10 papers from various fields, replace one author of each paper, run our method and the two comparison methods, and each of them recommends five candidates. We then mix the 15 recommendations and ask the users to (a) mark exactly one best replacement; and (b) mark all the good replacements. The result is shown in Figure 2 and our method is the best in terms of both precision and recall.

4. RELATED WORK

In data mining community, the pioneering work in assembling a team of experts in social networks requires the members in the team not only meet the skill requirements of the task, but also have the minimum communication cost [3]. Going beyond team formation, a recent work [4] designs fast algorithms for team member recommendation in response to the churn of a team member. An interactive system called

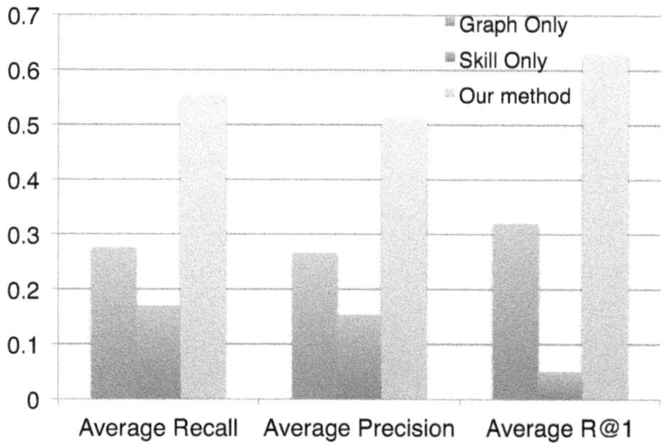

Figure 2: The comparison result of the user study.

"g-Miner" [1] is developed for mining groups with complex criteria.

5. CONCLUSIONS

In this work, we address the problem of maintaining and optimizing the team performance in response to certain changes made to the team. In particular, we treat a team as a subgraph embedded in a larger social network. We develop TEAMOPT, a system to assist users in optimizing the team performance interactively to support the changes to a team. TEAMOPT takes as input a large network of individuals (e.g., co-author network of researchers) and is able to assist users in assembling a team with specific requirements and optimizing the team in response to the changes. The system is effective in recommending the best candidates, and efficient to support interactive user experience. A prototype system is already deployed and we will invite the audience to play with the system for various application scenarios.

6. ACKNOWLEDGMENTS

This work is partially supported by the National Science Foundation under Grant No. IIS1017415, by DTRA under the grant number HDTRA1-16-0017, by Army Research Office under the contract number W911NF-16-1-0168, by National Institutes of Health under the grant number R01LM011986, Region II University Transportation Center under the project number 49997-33 25 and a Baidu gift.

7. REFERENCES

[1] N. Cao, Y. Lin, L. Li, and H. Tong. g-miner: Interactive visual group mining on multivariate graphs. In *CHI*, pages 279–288, 2015.

[2] J. B. Kruskal and J. M. Landwehr. Icicle plots: Better displays for hierarchical clustering. *The American Statistician*, 37(2):162–168, 1983.

[3] T. Lappas, K. Liu, and E. Terzi. Finding a team of experts in social networks. In *KDD*, pages 467–476. ACM, 2009.

[4] L. Li, H. Tong, N. Cao, K. Ehrlich, Y. Lin, and N. Buchler. Replacing the irreplaceable: Fast algorithms for team member recommendation. In *WWW*, pages 636–646, 2015.

[5] S. V. N. Vishwanathan, N. N. Schraudolph, R. Kondor, and K. M. Borgwardt. Graph kernels. *The Journal of Machine Learning Research*, 11:1201–1242, 2010.

[6] Wikipedia. Science of team science. https://en.wikipedia.org/wiki/Science_of_team_science.

GStreamMiner: A GPU-accelerated Data Stream Mining Framework

Chandima HewaNadungodage, Yuni Xia
Department of Computer & Information Science
Purdue School of Science
IUPUI
Indianapolis, IN, USA
chewanad@iupui.edu, yuxia@iupui.edu

John Jaehwan Lee
Department of Electrical & Computer Engineering
Purdue School of Engineering & Technology
IUPUI
Indianapolis, IN, USA
johnlee@iupui.edu

ABSTRACT
Due to the continuous, unbounded, and dynamic characteristics of the streaming data, mining data streams becomes a very challenging task. When analyzing online data streams, it is necessary to produce accurate results in a very short amount of time. The parallel processing power of Graphics Processing Units (GPUs) can be used to accelerate the processing and produce results in a timely manner. In this paper, we present *GStreamMiner*, a GPU-accelerated data stream mining framework and demonstrate its application using outlier detection over continuous streaming data as a case study. The demo software provides a visual interface which is continuously get updated with new results as the data stream progresses. It also facilitates the users to compare the performance of the GPU and CPU versions of the outlier detection algorithm.

Keywords
Data stream mining; GPU; outlier detection.

1. INTRODUCTION
The recent advances in technology have enabled the capture of different measurements of data in a wide range of fields. These data are generated continuously and in a very rapid rate, which makes it more appropriate to model them as transient data streams as opposed to static persistent datasets [1]. With the emergence of network and sensor technology in recent times, there is a growing need of management and mining techniques for collecting, querying, and analyzing data streams in real time. Various research areas have been emerged in streaming data such as stock market applications, network traffic analysis, power consumption measurements, and environmental monitoring.

Due to the huge volume and high input rates of streaming data, storing entire set of data tuples is not possible. Scanning the data multiple times is also not an option due to real time processing requirements. Since data streams are continuous, it is impossible to wait for the entire dataset to be collected; therefore, data stream algorithms have to incrementally revise the underlying model as the new data streams in. Segmentation-based or window-based approaches are preferred in data stream analysis [2]. Usually, data streams are subjected to *concept-drifts*; therefore, the characteristics of the underlying data model may change over time. In order to make time-critical predictions, the model learned from the streaming data must be able to capture up-to-date trends and transient patterns in the data stream. Therefore, it is required to gradually discard the obsolete information and incorporate new information as the data stream progresses. Because of these requirements, maintaining an up-to-date model that accurately represents the characteristics of a data stream under real time processing constraints is a challenging task.

Graphics Processing Units (GPUs) are designed to handle highly parallel workloads and can execute thousands of concurrent threads. To address the real time processing requirements of high speed data streams, we have used the parallel processing power of GPUs to accelerate the computations and produce results in timely manner.

Outlier detection is applied in numerous applications, such as network intrusion detection, fraud detection, manufacturing, and environmental monitoring. In this paper we demonstrate our GPU-accelerated data stream mining framework, using data stream outlier detection as a case study.

2. GStreamMiner FRAMEWORK

2.1 Related Work
During the past decade GPU computing became more and more popular in accelerating large-scale data mining applications, few examples are [3-5]. However, most of these work focus on static, persistent data. There is limited research conducted using GPUs for data stream analysis. Cazalas and Guha [6] proposed a GPU based algorithm for the evaluation of continuous spatio-temporal proximity area queries over spatio-temporal data streams. Verner et al [7] proposed a scheduling approach for multiple data streams with real-time deadlines on heterogeneous CPU-GPU system for data encryption application. Both of these work are application specific and cannot be considered as a general purpose data stream mining system. The GStream system proposed by Zhang and Mueller [8] can be considered as the most relevant existing work related to our topic. GStream is a general purpose data streaming framework on GPU Clusters. However it does not provide any scheduling mechanism for streaming operators. In our work we have implemented a scheduling scheme to further enhance parallel execution of the streaming operators and achieve more speedup.

2.2 GStreamMiner Framework Design
A typical data streaming algorithm can be modeled using the boxes and arrows model as shown in Figure 1 [9]. Boxes represents the *operators* or data processing units and arrows represents the *channels* or data links that connect the operators. Operators read data from one or more input channels and write results to one or more output channels. *Source* operators collect data from (input) client applications and *Sink* operators send the results back to (output) client applications.

CIKM'16, October 24–28, 2016, Indianapolis, IN, USA.
ACM ISBN 978-1-4503-4073-1/16/10.
DOI: http://dx.doi.org/10.1145/2983323.2983341

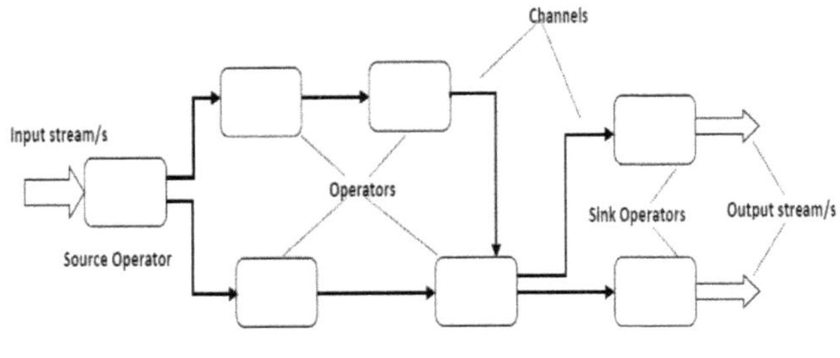

Figure 1. Boxes and arrows representation of a data stream algorithm.

Streaming algorithm execution depends on the availability of input data, as the data continue to arrive, the system uses *push-based* model to invoke the necessary computational units, system keeps repeating the algorithm as new batches of data arrives. Therefore, opposed to one-time algorithms executed on static data, streaming algorithms are continuous (i.e. consume continuous input and produce continuous output).

Each operator in the query graph is mapped to a GPU kernel. The CPU will serve as the central control unit which handles splitting the continuous data stream to batches and keep repeatedly invoking the GPU kernels as new data arrives. Each operator has an output data buffer assigned to its output channel which resides in GPU global memory. Only the source operators have input data buffers, for other operators their upstream operators' output buffer will be their input buffer. One output channel can be shared by multiple downstream operators.

2.3 Operator Scheduling

In CPU-based systems, the processing order of individual operators are decided by an operator scheduling unit. In GPUs the assigning a kernel process to the available GPU cores is handled by hardware and cannot be explicitly controlled by the software. However, using CUDA streams we can hint the hardware scheduler the possible opportunities for concurrent processing. For example in the diagram given in Figure 2, operators O2 and O3 are independent from the operators O4 and O5, thus assigning them to two separate CUDA streams allows the concurrent execution of those operators. Therefore, in our GStreamMiner framework, the task of the operator scheduling unit is to efficiently assign the operators to concurrent CUDA streams.

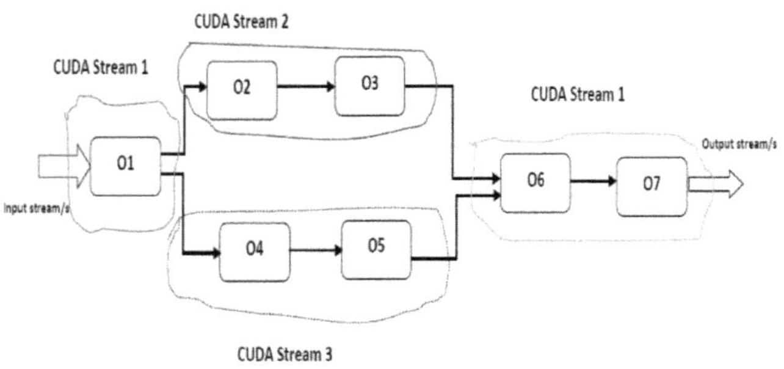

Figure 2. Assigning operators to CUDA streams.

Each CUDA stream can consists of one or more query operators (or GPU kernels). When the user specify the operator diagram for a particular data mining task (or an algorithm), the system allocates the data channels and assign the operators to appropriate CUDA streams. When assigning the operators, the scheduling algorithm considers the memory requirements of the operators and also the interdependencies. If the operators have dependencies and need to be executed in sequence they will be assigned to the same CUDA stream, otherwise they will be assigned to different CUDA streams to maximize concurrency.

3. CASE STUDY – DATA STREAM OUTLIER DETECTION DEMO

3.1 Data Stream Outlier Detection

An outlier in a dataset can be defined as an observation that is considerably different from the remainder as if it is generated by a different mechanism. Outlier detection is applied in numerous applications, such as network intrusion detection, fraud detection, manufacturing, and environmental monitoring.

When detecting outliers in a streaming environment, it is not accurate to simply conclude that a data point is an outlier only considering the statistics of the current window, because, it can be a non-outlier when the recent history is considered. Similarly, a set of points that appear to be non-outliers in the current window can be outliers when the entire dataset is considered. To address the above issue, in our previous work, we proposed a GPU-based streaming outlier detection algorithm (SOD_GPU) [10] which considers a global view of the data, only using a single pass over the dataset. SOD_GPU is a kernel-density based outlier detection algorithms for streaming data. As it is impossible to store the entire set of input tuples, SOD_GPU maintains a statistical synopsis of the data stream seen so far using data bins. Using this synopsis and the current portion of the data available, it applies Gaussian kernel-density estimation to detect outliers based on a cumulative picture of the data stream. Due to the large number of nearest neighbor calculations required, this is a compute intensive task; therefore, to address the real-time processing requirements of streaming data, GPUs are used to accelerate the computation and produce results in a timely manner. Technical details of the SOD_GPU algorithm can be found in [10].

In [10] operator scheduling of the SOD_GPU algorithm and data transfer between CPU and GPU were required to be built in to the algorithm code. In this paper we utilize the GStreamMiner framework to automatically schedule the operators and maximize the concurrency of the SOD_GPU algorithm. Also the framework will take care of the data transfer between CPU and GPU, so the algorithm developer does not have to worry about it.

3.2 SOD_GPU Algorithm Demonstration using GStreamMiner Framework

In this section we present the online outlier detection application built on top of the GStreamMiner framework. The visual interface continuously gets updated with new data and new results as the data stream progresses. The client GUI facilitates the users to interact with the system to get more information on the detected outliers. The users can evaluate the runtime and speedup of the GPU implementation by comparing it with the CPU implementation.

3.2.1 Setting up the algorithms and input

Figures 3 shows the GStreamMiner user interface. User can add a new data mining algorithm to the framework or execute an already saved algorithm. When adding a new algorithm user should provide an xml file which describes the operator diagram and input parameters. The location of the CUDA source code files related to the operators and the client program to display the output should also be provided. If no client program specified results will be saved to a text file. Once added to the system, the new algorithm will be available in "Run Existing Algorithm" tab and can be executed whenever necessary.

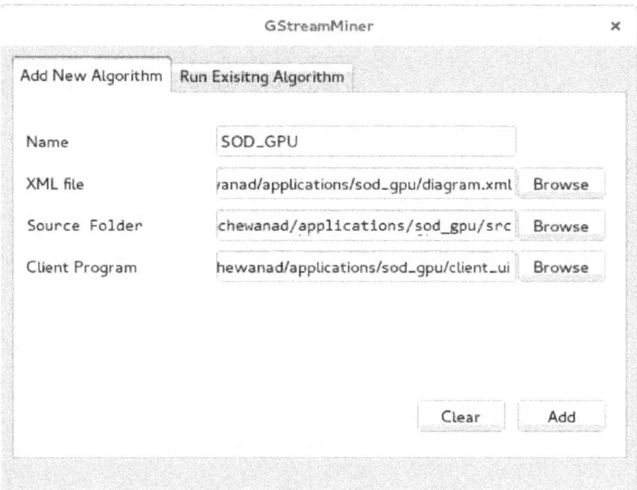

Figure 3. GStreamMiner GUI

When running an existing algorithm, users can use the already saved parameters (these values are populated using the xml file) or adjust them as necessary. Users can configure the input source, batch size, and algorithm specific parameters if there are any. Please see appendix Screenshots 1 and 2 for an illustration of the interface. Currently the system supports two possible modes of input, 1) Data file or 2) Synthetic data stream. If the first mode is chosen, the GStreamMiner framework will read data from the specified input file and feed it to the algorithm as a data stream at a specified data rate (see Appendix Screenshot 3). In our experiments, we simulated data streams using real-world datasets downloaded from the UCI machine learning repository[1]. If the second mode is chosen, the framework will generate a synthetic data stream according to the specified parameter values; currently the system can generate a synthetic 2D normal distribution with random noise, we are working on adding more synthetic distributions. Also, as future work we plan to support directly collecting input data from live data streams through the network.

The framework will parse the xml file and assign the operators to appropriate GPU kernels and CUDA streams. It also automatically transfer the necessary input data from CPU to GPU and output results from GPU to CPU. To minimize the data transfer overhead the framework will try to overlap the data transfers with kernel execution as much as possible.

3.2.2 Client interface and Output

SOD_GPU client interface provides options to view and analyze the outlier detection results (see Appendix Screenshot 4, 5). Currently the system only supports 2D visualization, if the data consists of more than two attributes users can select which attributes to be plotted in the chart area. Screenshot 5 shows a snapshot of the SOD_GPU client interface while the algorithm execution is in progress. The chart area at the bottom left displays the data points; normal data points are displayed in blue color and outlier points are displayed in red color. The text panel at bottom right lists outlier points. Users can select an outlier point to view more information on that point such as attribute values, outlier score, and outlier rank. The status bar displays the average processing time for the current batch.
The results will be saved to an output file and can be re-examined if necessary. In the "Setup" tab, users have the option to select "GPU mode", "CPU mode", or both. If both modes are selected, we provide a runtime and speedup analysis of the GPU and CPU versions in the "Analyze" tab (see Appendix Screenshot 6).

4. Conclusion

In this demo we present GStreamMiner: a GPU-accelerated framework for mining streaming data and demonstrate its application using data stream outlier detection as a case study. We used binned kernel density estimation to detect outliers and GStreamMiner framework was used to maximize the concurrency and accelerate the computation. Our demo system presents the output of the algorithm in a 2D graphical interface and facilitates to explore the outlier points in detail. It also provides the facility to compare the GPU and CPU implementations of the SOD_GPU algorithm.

5. REFERENCES

[1] Babcock B., Babu S., Datar M., Motwani R., and Widom J. "Models and Issues in Data Stream Systems," *In proc. of ACM SIGMOD-SIGACT-SIGART symposium on Principles of database systems*, 2002, pp. 1-16.

[2] Datar M., Gionis A., Indyk P., and Motwani R. "Maintaining Stream Statistics over Sliding Windows," *In Proc. of ACM-SIAM Symposium on Discrete Algorithms*, 2002, pp. 1794-1813.

[3] Garcia V., Debreuve E., and Barlaud M. "Fast k nearest neighbor search using GPU," *In Proc. of IEEE Computer Vision and Pattern Recognition Workshops*, 2008, pp. 1–6.

[4] Farivar R., Rebolledo D., Chan E., and Campbell R., "A parallel implementation of k-means clustering on GPUs," *In Proc. of International Conference on Parallel and Distributed Processing Techniques and Applications*, 2008, pp. 340–345.

[5] HewaNadungodage, C., Xia, Y., Lee, J.J., Lee, M. and Park, C.S. "GPU accelerated item-based collaborative filtering for big-data applications," *In Proc. of IEEE International Conference on BigData*, 2013, pp. 175-180.

[6] Cazalas, J. and Guha, R. "GEDS: GPU execution of continuous queries on spatio-temporal data streams," *In Proc. of IEEE/IFIP International Conference on Embedded and Ubiquitous Computing*, 2010, pp. 112-119.

[7] Verner, U., Schuster, A., Silberstein, M., Mendelson, A. "Scheduling processing of real-time data streams on heterogeneous multi-GPU systems," *In Proc. of the International Systems and Storage Conference*, 2012, pp. 8.

[8] Zhang, Y., Mueller, F. "GStream: A General-Purpose Data Streaming Framework on GPU Clusters," *In Proc. of IEEE International Conference on Parallel Processing*, 2011, pp. 245-254.

[9] Abadi, D. J., Carney, D., Çetintemel, U., Cherniack, M., Convey, C., Lee, S., Zdonik, S. "Aurora: a new model and architecture for data stream management," *The International Journal on Very Large Data Bases*, 2003, 12(2), pp. 120-139.

[10] HewaNadungodage C., Xia Y., Lee J.J. "GPU-accelerated Outlier Detection for Continuous Data Streams," *In Proc. of International Parallel and Distributed Processing Symposium,* 2016. pp. 1133-1142.

[1] https://archive.ics.uci.edu/ml/index.html

APPENDIX

The GStreamMiner GUI and SOD_GPU client GUI is developed using the QT Creator, a cross-platform application and UI framework for C++. GPU programming is done using CUDA 7.0. All the experiments were carried out in a server running 64-bit Fedora 21, equipped with two Intel Xeon 3.3GHz quad-core CPUs and 64GB memory, and an NVIDIA GTX TITAN GPU card with 6GB memory.

GStreamMiner GUI

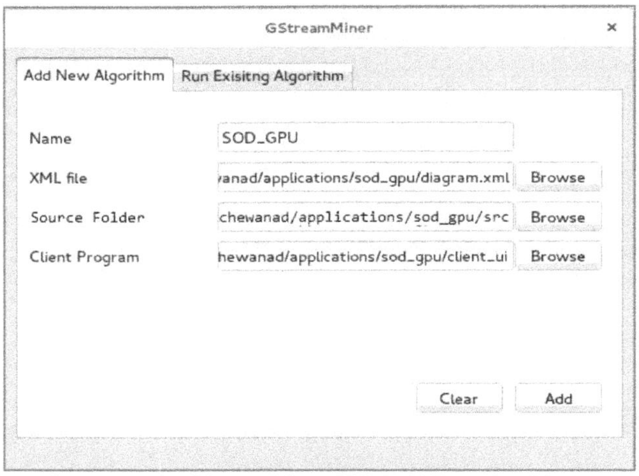

Screenshot 1 - GStreamMiner GUI (Add New Algorithm).

Screenshot 2 - GStreamMiner GUI (Run Existing Algorithm).

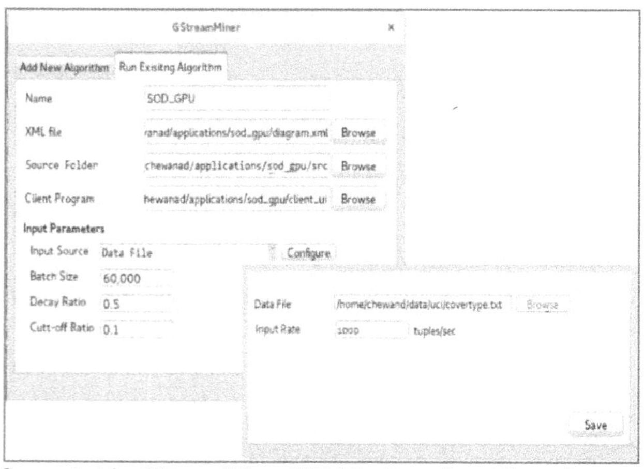

Screenshot 3 - GStreamMiner GUI (Configure Input Source).

SOD_GPU Client GUI

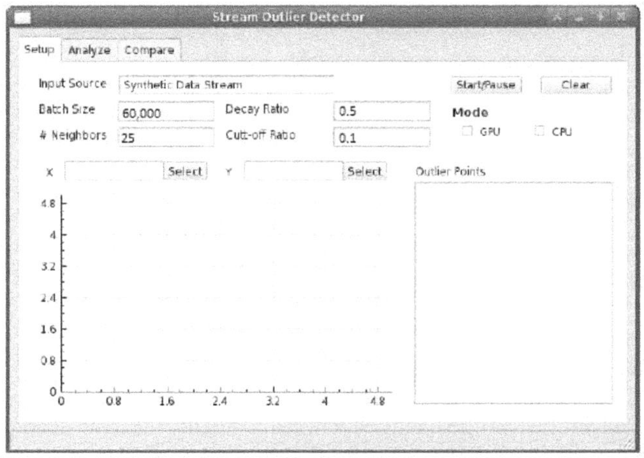

Screenshot 4 - SOD_GPU Client GUI (Output Panel).

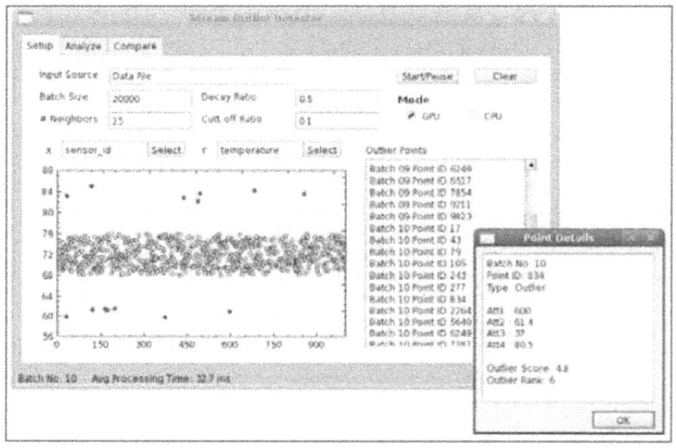

Screenshot 5 - SOD_GPU Client GUI (Visualizing Outlier Points).

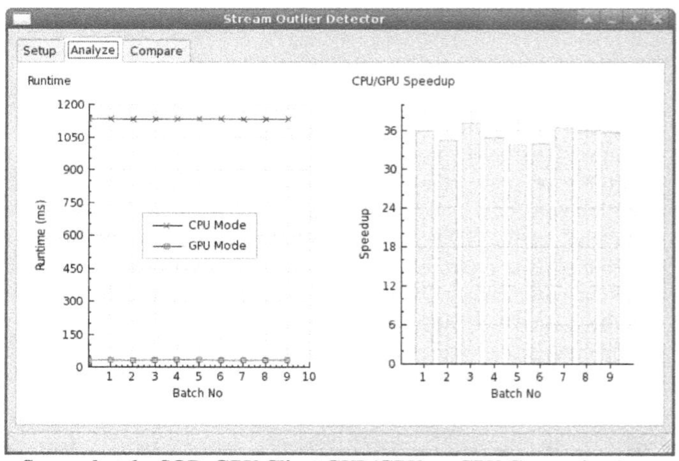

Screenshot 6 – SOD_GPU Client GUI (GPU vs. CPU Comparison)

QART: A Tool for Quality Assurance in Real-Time in Contact Centers

Ragunathan Mariappan, Balaji Peddamuthu, Preethi R Raajaratnam, Sandipan Dandapat, Neeta Pande, Shourya Roy
Xerox Research Centre India, Bangalore, INDIA
{firstname.lastname@xerox.com}

ABSTRACT

In this paper, we describe an automatic real-time quality assurance system QA^{RT} (pronounced *cart*) for contact center chats. QA^{RT} performs multi-faceted analysis on dialogue utterances, as they happen, using sophisticated statistical and rule-based natural language processing (NLP) techniques. It covers various aspects inspired by today's Quality Assurance and Customer Satisfaction Scoring(C-Sat) practices as well as introduces novel components such as incremental dialogue summarization capability. QA^{RT} front-end is an interactive dashboard providing views of ongoing dialogues at different granularity, enabling contact center supervisors to monitor and take corrective actions as needed. It is developed on state of the art stream computing platform Apache Spark Streaming with HBase datastore and Python Flask front end.

Keywords

Contact Center Automation; Real-time Quality Assurance; Customer Behavior; Dialogue summarization;

1. INTRODUCTION

Contact centers generate huge volume dialog data (chat and speech) from support sessions addressing customer requests, grievances and queries. Providing highest quality of service leading to satisfied customers is a key objective of contact centers. Popular manual practices towards ensuring the same are *Quality Assurance* (QA) and *Customer Satisfaction analysis* (C-Sat). Broadly speaking, QA process entails assessment of agents on a variety of metrics to measure how compliant and effective they have been, whereas C-Sat is about analyzing customers' post-interaction feedback to identify drivers for (dis)satisfaction. By design, today both QA and C-Sat reveal outcomes of their analysis and associated reasons, always in hindsight. Secondly, owing to their different focus of analysis - customers' post-interaction feedback in C-Sat versus best practices mandated by the organization in QA, it is not uncommon to have conflicting outcome from these two processes. Thirdly, only a small number of contact center workforce are responsible for QA and C-Sat [1] processes, hence they can analyze only a small fraction (typically $< 5\%$) of total interactions thereby missing out on the most.

We demonstrate QA^{RT}, a system for quality assurance in real-time for contact center dialogs. It analyzes customer and agent dialogue utterances, in real time, bringing together several aspects of QA and C-Sat. Various aggregate and fine-grained features are extracted using state of the art and novel machine learning and natural language processing techniques. Additionally, an incremental dialogue summarizer generates actionable summaries in real-time for supervisors to quickly gather context and possibly intercept a dialogue faster. Finally, it provides an interactive dashboard showing real-time status of ongoing dialogues at various granularity. An example dialogue from a telecommunication contact center and associated issues identified by QA^{RT} can be seen in Table 1.

12:24:29	AGENT:	Hi there, thanks for contacting Mobile Product Support. My name is AGENT, how can I assist you today?
12:25:05	CUST:	i just swapped my MODEL-1 phone for a MODEL-2. how do i get to my voicemail.
12:26:48	CUST:	is anyone there **(Customer Behavior: Customer is unhappy)**
12:29:09	AGENT:	You can access your voicemail by pressing and holding on the 1 key **(Conversational characteristic: Agent's delayed/unusual response time)**
12:29:44	CUST:	i did that and it said that it wasnt set up
12:29:59	AGENT:	Are you using the same carrier? **(Organizational compliance: Agent didn't apologize)**
12:30:19	CUST:	no i switched from PROVIDER-1 to PROVIDER-2
...	...	...

Table 1: An example dialogue from our dataset

QA^{RT} overcomes the shortcomings of today's QA and C-Sat process by automating the analysis and producing results in real-time. It enables new features such as efficient real-time intervention using incremental summarizer. We are currently in the process of discussion with multiple contact centers for operational deployment and pilot study.A common challenge we encounter in such discussions was about building trust so that QART can be adopted over manual QA.Due to space constraint we refer the reader to our prior work [2] for the experimental results supporting QART's effectiveness over a human and details on the related work in this space.

2. FACETS AND FEATURES

In this section, we describe the key backend modules of QA^{RT} which is a conglomeration of novel features designed

CIKM'16 October 24-28, 2016, Indianapolis, IN, USA

ACM ISBN 978-1-4503-4073-1/16/10.
DOI: http://dx.doi.org/10.1145/2983323.2983342

based on a rich domain knowledge gained through our customer engagements and techniques in natural language processing (NLP) and built on the state-of-the-art machine learning to extract relevant information from utterances. We acknowledge this section is brief owing to space constraint. Please refer our prior work [2] for details.

Customer Behavior.

In a contact center dialogue, experience of a customer can be best understood and potentially measured by her expressed views and opinions as well as her feelings expressed during a dialogue. *Customer Behaviour* is designed to identify emotions (such as *sad*, *apologetic* or *angry*) of customers from their utterances and obtain sentiment categories (such as *positive*, *negative*) as a by-product. We created a contact center specific 8-class emotion tag-set viz. *Happiness* (Ha), *Assurance* (As), *Agreement* (Ag), *Courteousness* (Co), *Apology* (Ap), *Unhappiness* (Uh), *Disagreement* (Di) and *No-Emotion* (Ne). The technique consists of two main components - (i) splitting an utterance turn into parts which are homogeneous with respect to emotion and (ii) assigning emotion categories to turns. For (i), we implemented a boundary detection module based on simple heuristics which identified sentence boundaries. We modeled (ii) as a sequential labeling problem and applied Conditional Random Field (CRF) where the conditional dependency between consecutive turns are defined through different content-based attributes such as count of words with positive/negative orientations, emoticons etc. as well as meta attributes such as time difference between consecutive turns, turn length etc.

Organizational Compliance.

Contact centers employ certain best practices towards ensuring uniform, courteous and effective interaction style across all agents. We folded in this process as an automatic module in QA^{RT} and thereby enabling compliance checking for agent utterances in real-time. From a list of about 30 organizational guidelines provided to us by domain experts, we noted that most can be validated by applying regular expression like rules on agent utterances. For example, the rule for standard greeting for one of the clients was captured by the following rule: $t.isFirstTurn(Agent) \wedge t.startsWith$ ("$Welcome\ to\ WeCare\ helpdesk.$").

Dialogue Summarization.

While QA^{RT} provides a number of aggregated statistics in real-time, to understand context of the same, supervisors would need to go through long transcripts. To enable supervisors to obtain context at-a-glance, we introduced a novel task-oriented, incremental dialogue summarization module. Dialogue summaries consist of two parts – (i) an information template and (ii) dialogue excerpts in support of extracted information. We have designed a template to present this information which gets incrementally filled up as conversations proceed. We use a combination of dictionary lookups (for device names) and Random Forest classifiers with Bag-of-Word features (Problem Type and Problem Resolution Type) for information extraction from dialogues. The other part of the summarizer excerpts key phrases from dialogues in support of template entries. Manually analyzing tens of dialogues we observed that Parts Of Speech (POS) tags of such key phrases have some commonalities. $< VBZ >< VB.* >$ and $< VP >< IN > *$ are two such

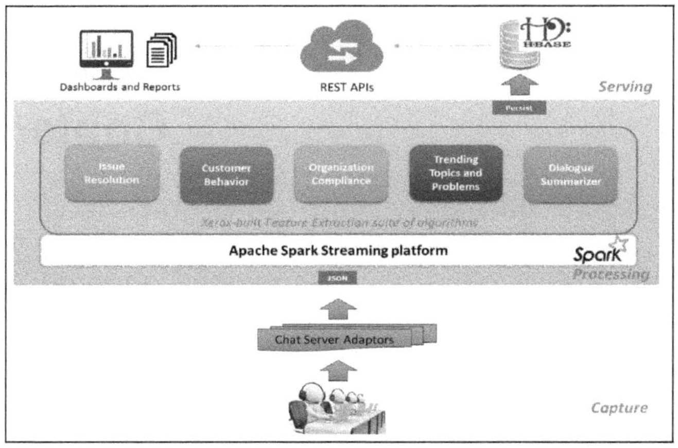

Figure 1: QA^{RT} architecture block diagram

POS patterns.[1] We extracted actual phrases corresponding to these patterns and annotated as 1 or 0 indicating whether or not they were key phrases. A classifier is then trained to predict whether a phrase could be summary excerpt or not.

3. SYSTEM OVERVIEW

QA^{RT} backend is developed in Python and powered by the Apache Spark Streaming platform[2], along with a rich visualization dashboard developed in Python, HTML5, CSS3, Bootstrap and D3 (Figure 1). The system was designed to be able to interface with potentially any chat technology in the market and extensible to call centers of any domain. The backend engine comprises three major modules, namely *Data Capture*, *Data Processing* and *Data Serving*.

Data Capture.

This module connects to the call center chat infrastructure to ingest utterances from hundreds of ongoing chats and converts to an internal JSON format. This module is decoupled from the different chat servers, data formats and protocols, and communicates with external systems over the network via custom software adapters.

Data Processing.

The Data Processing module is the heart of QA^{RT} backend running different feature and facet extraction algorithms. It is composed of several state-of-the-art machine learning and natural language techniques as described in Section 2. As this is the most computationally intensive module of QA^{RT} and is expected to process chats arriving at high velocity and volume in real-time, we developed it on the scalable Spark Streaming platform. In order to provide high concurrency and low latency, extracted information is stored in Apache HBase[3]. Some of the feature-extraction algorithms depend on the client domain for organizational guidelines and conversation protocols, but we have ensured that the algorithms remain independent of such domain knowledge and can be configured easily using rules for different clients.

[1]Penn Treebank POS tags : http://bit.ly/1gwbird
[2]http://spark.apache.org/streaming/
[3]https://hbase.apache.org/

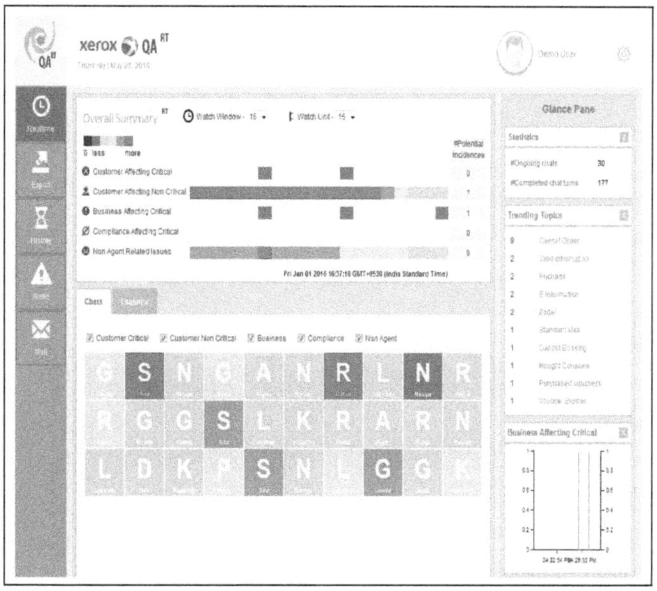

Figure 2: Homescreen of QA^{RT} dashboard (best viewed in color and at high zoom level)

Data Serving.

The Data Serving module caters to both real-time and offline requirements from QA^{RT} frontend dashboard through representational state transfer (REST) APIs. The *Streaming APIs* serve various aggregated and raw features extracted from dialogue utterances in real-time. The *offline APIs* generate analytics, such as computing agent performance metrics over a period of time. In addition, the module exposes REST APIs to look up a chat using a unique identifier.

4. DEMONSTRATION

Contact center supervisors interact with QA^{RT} through a rich interactive dashboard, designed based on concepts from visualization and interaction design theory. It provides real-time interactive visualization of the analysis outcomes at various granularities (landing screen of the dashboard is shown in Figure 2) to enable them for effective monitoring and regulation. While QA^{RT} is designed to interface with commercial chat systems such as LivePerson[4], in this demonstration, we will use simulated streaming environment with few tens of chats, to explain key features. With a 16-CPU and 64GB driver and four 8-CPU and 32GB worker machines of standard configurations, one can support 200 concurrent chats in QA^{RT}. A video demonstration of QA^{RT} with different use-cases illustrated can be found at URL[5].

Effective monitoring.

The top 'overall summary' panel of the dashboard provides a facet level summary view in all of the ongoing chat sessions. It provides a heatmap of the potential incidences for a given watch window of watch units, where a watch unit is a time period for which the potential incidences are computed. The 'chats' tab in the bottom panel provides a glanceable binary view of the ongoing chats. Each box corresponds to an ongoing chat session identified by the initial of the agent handling it. The colour of the box indicates whether the supervisor should pay attention to a particular session - red indicating presence of potential issues and blue otherwise. It further provides an option to *filter* based on facets. In Figure 2, there are 30 ongoing chats, of which about five chats with stronger red tinge are potentially problematic at a glance. Clicking on any of these boxes will lead to the single chat view (Figure 3b). This view would help a supervisor to read and monitor a single support session as it is ongoing and provides an option to take over the chat if the need be. Additionally the view also provides the supervisor with indicators (as icons on the top right) for the potential issues across facets.

Exploratory analysis and regulation.

Besides 'chats' tab, the other 'features' tab (Figure 3a) is designed for supervisors to perform exploratory analysis to track down problematic chats among all of the ongoing chats.[6]. This view shows in real-time issues pertaining to different features and facets such as organizational noncompliance, customer negative emotions with various customizable charts.

Usability features.

The facets and features described in Section 2 are useful to identify issues (e.g. angry emotion, unusual delay by agent) in contact center dialogues efficiently. However in practice, to understand context of these issues and potentially take over, supervisors would need to go through long transcripts. To enable supervisors to obtain context at-a-glance, we introduce a novel task-oriented incremental dialogue summarization module (Figure 3d). These summaries consist of two parts: (i) a template-based abstract containing the key entities extracted from the support session and (ii) dialogue excerpts in support of extracted information. The summary is available in the chat view to obtain easy correspondence with the full chat. Additionally, QA^{RT} provides options where contact center supervisors can configure various alerts based on types and frequencies of issues observed in chats (Figure 3c). The configuration involves selecting one or more facets and the threshold of the potential incidences, crossing which the notification flashes on their desktops. Finally, QA^{RT} provides an option to export the real-time QA metrics for reporting, offline analysis and easy archival.

5. REFERENCES

[1] S. Godbole and S. Roy. Text to intelligence: Building and deploying a text mining solution in the services industry for customer satisfaction analysis. In *Services Computing, 2008.*, volume 2, pages 441–448. IEEE, 2008.

[2] S. Roy, R. Mariappan, S. Dandapat, S. Srivastava, S. Galhotra, and B. Peddamuthu. Qart: A system for real-time holistic quality assurance for contact center dialogues. In D. Schuurmans and M. P. Wellman, editors, *AAAI*, pages 3768–3775. AAAI Press, 2016.

[4]https://www.liveperson.com/

[5]https://goo.gl/qfWvpW

[6]For this and the following scenario, screenshots are given in the Appendix (Figure 3) owing to lack of space.

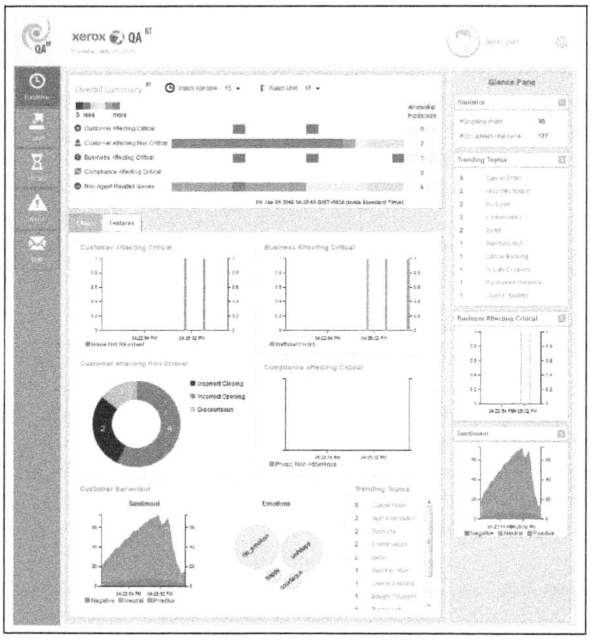

a: Features view of QA^{RT} dashboard

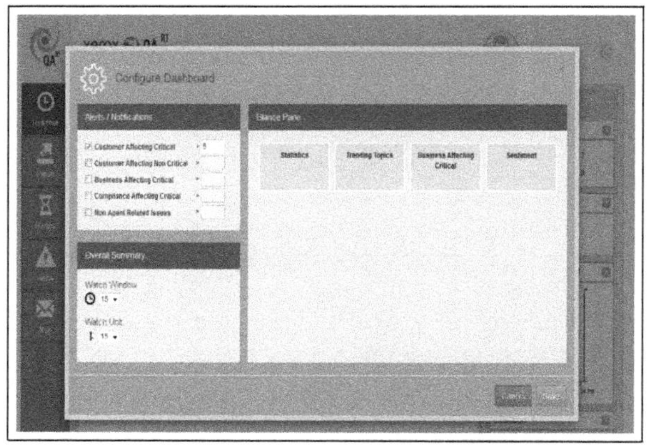

c: Configuring alerts in QA^{RT} dashboard

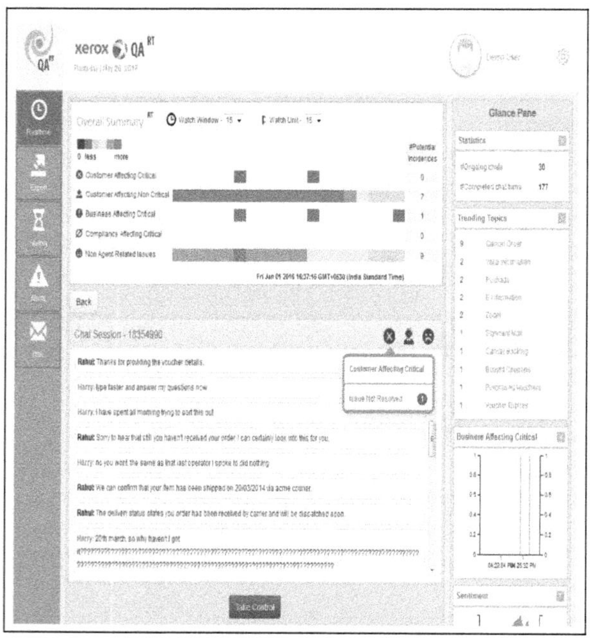

b: Single chat view of QA^{RT} dashboard

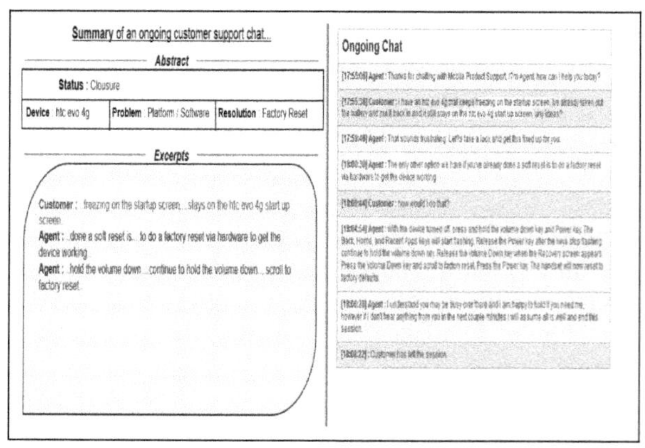

d: Summary view of QA^{RT} dashboard

Figure 3: Appendix - screenshots to help reader understand the various scenarios explained in the Demonstration section

A Fatigue Strength Predictor for Steels Using Ensemble Data Mining

Ankit Agrawal and Alok Choudhary
Electrical Engineering and Computer Science
Northwestern University
Evanston IL 60201

ABSTRACT

Fatigue strength is one of the most important mechanical properties of steel. High cost and time for fatigue testing, and potentially disastrous consequences of fatigue failures motivates the development of predictive models for this property. We have developed advanced data-driven ensemble predictive models for this purpose with an extremely high cross-validated accuracy of >98%, and have deployed these models in a user-friendly online web-tool, which can make very fast predictions of fatigue strength for a given steel represented by its composition and processing information. Such a tool with fast and accurate models is expected to be a very useful resource for the materials science researchers and practitioners to assist in their search for new and improved quality steels. The web-tool is available at http://info.eecs.northwestern.edu/SteelFatigueStrengthPredictor

1. INTRODUCTION

Deciphering the processing-structure-property-performance (PSPP) relationships in materials is the key to understand the science of materials, and subsequently engineer and design new improved materials. The Materials Genome Initiative (MGI) was launched by the US government in 2011 [1] to realize the vision of development of advanced materials necessary for economic security and human well-being. The MGI Strategic Plan released in 2014 [2] also identifies data analytics as one of the key objectives as part of integrating experiments, computation, and theory, in order to realize the vision of MGI. The increasing applications of data analytics in this domain has made the new field of materials informatics very popular [4].

It is in the spirit and pursuit of the vision and approach of MGI that we discuss and present in this demonstration paper, an online data informatics tool deploying forward PSPP models to predict the fatigue strength of a given steel alloy, given its composition and processing. Fatigue strength of steel is a crucial property to know, given the high cost and time of fatigue testing, and potentially disastrous consequences of fatigue failures. It is the most important information required for design and failure analysis of mechanical components. Fatigue is estimated to account for over 90% of all mechanical failures of structural components, and hence, fatigue strength prediction is of critical importance. The predictive models deployed in the tool are a result of the application of supervised learning techniques on an experimental fatigue dataset from Japan National Institute of Materials Science MatNavi database [3], which is freely accessible online. This dataset has been previously used to perform similar predictive modeling [6, 5], but the resulting models had not been deployed. Following are the contributions of this study:

- Comparison of 40 supervised modeling configurations on the NIMS steel fatigue dataset, including ensemble modeling techniques, resulting in more accurate predictive models than prior works on the same data.
- Using data-driven feature selection techniques to identify a reduced set of non-redundant attributes for the purpose of building a predictive model using fewer input features while still having a satisfactory predictive accuracy.
- Deployment of the most accurate "forward" PSPP models using both the full and reduced set of attributes in a publicly accessible web-tool.

2. DATASET

The overall data-driven analytics process is depicted as a block diagram in Figure 1. Rotating bending fatigue testing data was obtained from the publicly available NIMS MatNavi database [3]. This NIMS data has 437 experimental observations of steel, with 9 composition attributes (%C, %Si, %Mn, %P, %S, %Ni, %Cr, %Cu, and %Mo (remaining is Fe)), 16 processing attributes (normalization temperature, through hardening temperature, through hardening time, cooling rate for through hardening, carburization temperature, carburization time, diffusion temperature, diffusion time, quenching media temperature, tempering temperature, tempering time, cooling rate for tempering, reduction ratio, area proportion of inclusions deformed by plastic work, those occurring in discontinuous array, and the isolated ones), and 1 mechanical property (rotating bending fatigue strength @10^7 cycles.) The work in [5] preprocessed this data to make a coherent database with all key processes included (for cases where a process did not take place, the time was set to zero and temperature to austenization temperature or average of rest of the data). This data was made

CIKM'16 October 24-28, 2016, Indianapolis, IN, USA

ACM ISBN 978-1-4503-4073-1/16/10.
DOI: http://dx.doi.org/10.1145/2983323.2983343

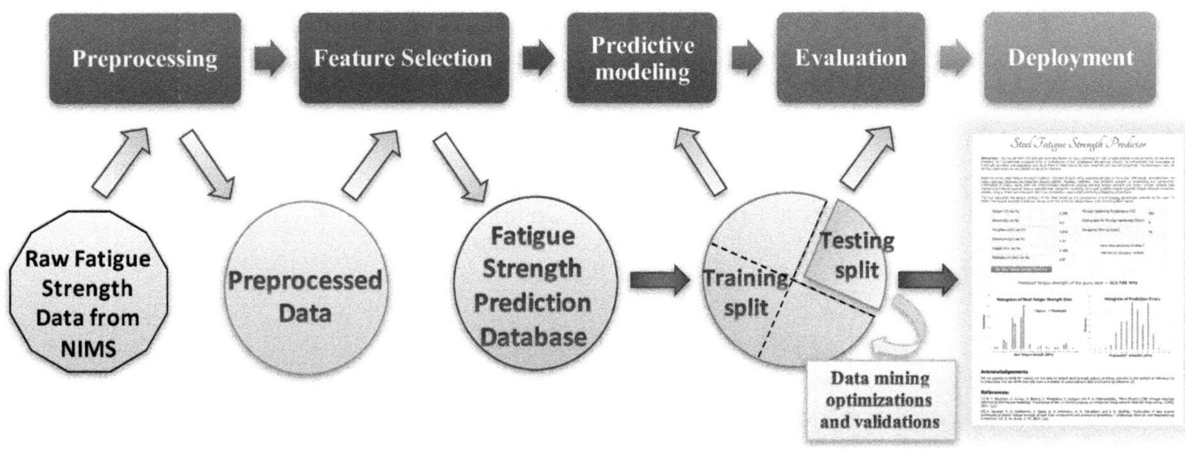

Figure 1: The data mining workflow used in this work.

available as supplementary data of [5], and is the starting point of the current study.

3. EXPERIMENTS AND RESULTS

We used 40 regression schemes in this study listed in Table 1, including both direct application of regression techniques and constructing their ensembles using various ensembling techniques (compatible combinations). The correlation feature selection (CFS) method was used for feature selection. It is used to identify a subset of features highly correlated with the class variable and weakly correlated amongst them. CFS was used in conjunction with a best first search to find a subset with best average merit. WEKA software [7] version 3.7.13 was used for all analytics with default parameters, unless otherwise stated. Quantitative assessments of the degree to how close the models could predict the experimental fatigue strength are used to evaluate the models' predictive performance. The metrics used for this purpose include the coefficient of correlation (R), explained variance (R^2), Mean Absolute Error (MAE), Root Mean Squared Error ($RMSE$), Relative Absolute Error (RAE), and Root Relative Squared Error ($RRSE$).

Table 2 presents the comparison of the top 10 modeling techniques used in this work with respect to the different metrics mentioned earlier. All results are based on 10 independent runs of 10-fold cross-validation to facilitate statistical significance testing. In addition, the training and testing times for each model, and the model size is also listed. The top four models from Table 2 are subsequently combined using the Voting modeling scheme to obtain the final model ($R^2 = 0.9819, MAE = 17.67MPa, RMSE = 25.08MPa$), whose performance was found to be significantly better than all the four constituent models, as well as better than the modeling techniques used previously in [5], at p=0.05. Visual inspection of the scatter plots (Figure 2) also reveal that the current model is able to make more accurate predictions for carbon and low alloy steels, where the best model in [5] had failed.

The application of CFS technique to composition attributes identified a subset of six composition attributes: C, Si, P, Cr, Cu, and Mo. The same analysis on processing attributes

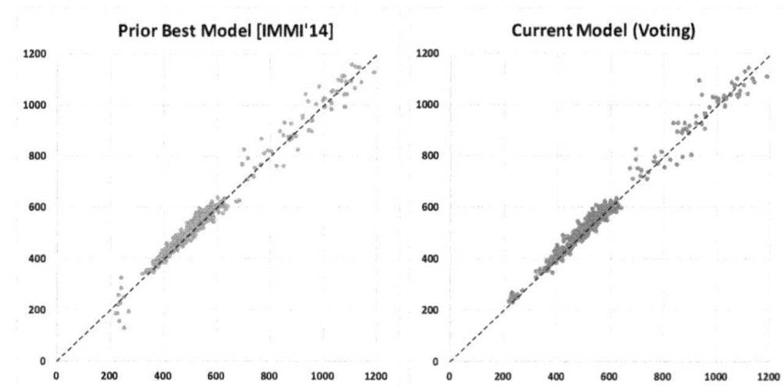

Figure 2: Scatter plots comparing the best model from [5] and the final model from the current study based on Voting scheme. The new model can be seen to perform significantly better in the low fatigue strength region of the plot where the old model had failed.

identified a subset of three processing attributes: THT (through hardening temperature), THQCr (cooling rate for through hardening), and Tt (tempering time). Subsequently we redid the modeling using the reduced set of nine attributes. Three best models were found to have statistically indistinguishable accuracy, and were thus combined using the Voting scheme, resulting in the following accuracy numbers: $R^2 = 0.9440, MAE = 36.41MPa, RMSE = 44.14MPa$.

Typically, data-driven predictive models are not simple equations and require the use of specialized software to make predictions. To make the forward predictive models developed in this work readily accessible for use by the materials science and engineering community, we have created an online steel fatigue strength predictor that can take as input the values of the reduced set of 9 attributes, and generate predictions of fatigue strength for a given steel. The reduced set of attributes was chosen for the tool so that the user does not have to enter too many attributes and still gets satisfactory accuracy, but the option of using the full calculator with all 25 attributes is also available. The screenshot of the calculator is depicted in the Appendix, and it is available online at http://info.eecs.northwestern.edu/SteelFatigueStrengthPredictor.

Table 1: Predictive modeling algorithms explored in this work

Modeling Technique	*Brief description*
Linear regression	A linear least-squares fit of the data with respect to the input features
Nearest-neighbor (IBk)	Uses the most similar instance in the training data for making predictions
Nearest-neighbor (KStar)	Uses entropy based function for distance instead of Euclidean distance
Artificial neural networks (MLP)	Uses hidden layer(s) of neurons to connect inputs and outputs, edge weights learnt using back propagation
Gaussian process	Generates data following multivariate Gaussian distribution to make predictions
Support vector machines	Based on the Structural Risk Minimization, constructs hyperplanes multidimensional feature space
Decision table	Constructs rules involving different combinations of attributes
Decision stump	A weak tree-based machine learning model consisting of a single-level decision tree
M5 model tree	A tree with linear regression function at the leaves
Random tree	Considers a randomly chosen subset of attributes
Reduced error pruning tree	Builds a tree using information gain/variance and prunes it using reduced-error pruning to avoid over-fitting
Random forest	An ensemble of multiple random trees
Additive regression	Enhances performance of a base regressor by fitting a model to the residuals left in previous iteration
Bagging	Builds multiple models on bootstrapped subsets of data to improve model stability by reducing variance
Random committee	Ensemble of randomizable base models run with different seeds and individual predictions averaged
Random subspace	Constructs multiple trees systematically by pseudo-randomly selecting subsets of features
Rotation Forest	Generates model ensembles based on feature extraction followed by axis rotations
Voting	Combines predictions from multiple models by taking average, maximum, minimum, median, etc.

Table 2: Top 10 modeling techniques (10-fold cross-validation results, best statistically indistinguishable results at p=0.05, and the techniques used in final Voting model are boldfaced)

Modeling Scheme	*R*	R^2	*MAE (MPa)*	*RMSE (MPa)*	*RAE (%)*	*RRSE (%)*	*TrainTime (s)*	*TestTime (s)*	*ModelSize (bytes)*
RotationForest_M5	**0.9900**	**0.9801**	**18.74**	**26.50**	**14.76**	**14.44**	1.1058	0.0094	716215
RotationForest_MLP	**0.9894**	**0.9789**	**18.97**	**27.00**	**15.00**	**14.76**	3.4866	0.0102	664851
Bagging_MLP	**0.9895**	**0.9791**	**18.97**	**27.03**	**14.99**	**14.78**	3.0486	0.0009	99700
AdditiveRegression_M5	**0.9897**	**0.9795**	**19.05**	**26.66**	**15.01**	**14.54**	0.3996	0.0003	44210
Bagging_M5	0.9890	0.9781	19.36	27.96	15.23	15.21	0.8039	0.0008	264058
M5 ModelTrees	0.9893	0.9787	19.64	27.46	15.45	14.94	0.0885	0.0001	19684
NeuralNetworks (MLP)	0.9881	0.9763	19.89	28.41	15.72	15.56	0.3652	0.0002	13616
RandomCommittee_MLP	0.9877	0.9756	20.37	29.14	16.05	15.84	3.0811	0.0010	99424
AdditiveRegression_MLP	0.9851	0.9704	20.94	32.27	16.49	17.56	3.5265	0.0009	99476
RandomCommittee_REPTree	0.9874	0.9750	21.39	29.48	16.86	16.09	0.0637	0.0003	83087

4. CONCLUSION AND FUTURE WORK

In this demonstration paper, we compared 40 different modeling configurations for predicting fatigue strength of steel alloys using a publicly available experimental database from NIMS, and obtained significantly more accurate models than prior models. The most accurate forward models both on the full dataset and on a reduced set of attributes were deployed in a publicly accessible online web-tool. The primary advantage of such a tool is ready access to *fast* and *accurate* forward models of PSPP relationships without having to do experiments/simulations, which can help identify promising candidates for further exploration. The presented workflow can be readily applied on other experimental and computational materials science data.

5. ACKNOWLEDGEMENTS

We are grateful to NIMS for making the MatNavi database [3] publicly available, and also to the authors of reference [6] for preprocessing the raw NIMS data and making it publicly available as supplementary data accompanying reference [5]. This work was performed under the following financial assistance award 70NANB14H012 from U.S. Department of Commerce, National Institute of Standards and Technology as part of the Center for Hierarchical Materials Design (CHiMaD). The authors also acknowledge partial support from AFOSR award FA9550-12-1-0458.

6. REFERENCES

[1] Materials Genome Initiative for Global Competitiveness, June 2011; OSTP 2011.

[2] Materials Genome Initiative Strategic Plan, National Science and Technology Council Committee on Technology Subcommittee on the Materials Genome Initiative, June 2014.

[3] URL: National Institute of Materials Science, http://smds.nims.go.jp/fatigue/index_en.html, Accessed: March 31, 2016.

[4] A. Agrawal and A. Choudhary. Perspective: Materials informatics and big data: Realization of the "fourth paradigm" of science in materials science. *APL Materials*, 4(053208):1–10, 2016.

[5] A. Agrawal, P. D. Deshpande, A. Cecen, G. P. Basavarsu, A. N. Choudhary, and S. R. Kalidindi. Exploration of data science techniques to predict fatigue strength of steel from composition and processing parameters. *Integrating Materials and Manufacturing Innovation*, 3(8):1–19, 2014.

[6] B. P. Gautham, R. Kumar, S. Bothra, G. Mohapatra, N. Kulkarni, and K. A. Padmanabhan. *More Efficient ICME through Materials Informatics and Process Modeling*, pages 35–42. John Wiley & Sons, Inc., 2011.

[7] M. Hall, E. Frank, et al. The weka data mining software: An update. *SIGKDD Explorations*, 11(1), 2009.

Steel Fatigue Strength Predictor

Disclaimer: The results from this tool are estimates based on data consisting of a set of experimental measurements. All results are provided for informational purposes only, in furtherance of the developers' educational mission, to complement the knowledge of materials scientists and engineers, and assist them in their search for new materials with desired properties. The developers may not be held responsible for any decisions based on this tool.

Welcome to the steel fatigue strength predictor. This tool is built using experimental data of more than 400 steels, available from the Japan National Institute for Materials Science (NIMS) MatNavi database. This database consists of processing and composition information of steels, along with the experimentally measured rotating bending fatigue strength (10 million cycles). Various data analytics techniques such as feature selection and regression modeling were used to obtain highly accurate fatigue strength prediction models using a small non-redundant set of six composition parameters and three processing parameters.

The tool estimates the fatigue strength of the steel based on the composition and processing parameters entered by the user. To obtain the fatigue strength prediction, please enter the attribute values below, and click the submit button.

Carbon (C) (wt %)	0.388	Through Hardening Temperature (°C)	850
Silicon (Si) (wt %)	0.3	Cooling Rate for Through Hardening (°C/hr)	8
Phosphorus (P) (wt %)	0.016	Tempering Time (minutes)	60
Chromium (Cr) (wt %)	0.57		
Copper (Cu) (wt %)	0.068		
Molybdenum (Mo) (wt %)	0.07		

Have more attributes to enter?

Use the full calculator instead!

Get Steel Fatigue Strength Prediction

Predicted fatigue strength of the given steel = **512.788 MPa**

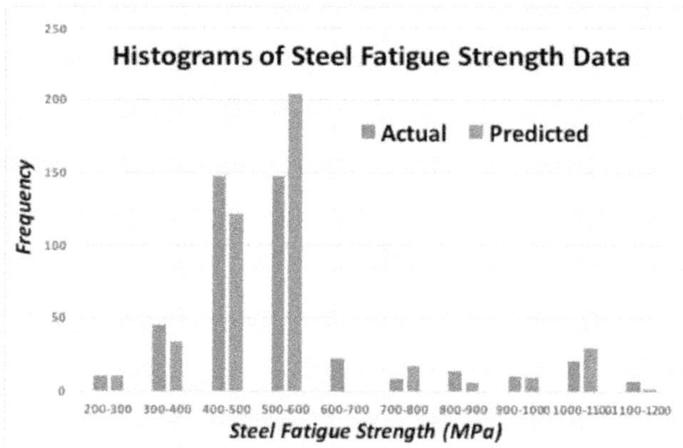

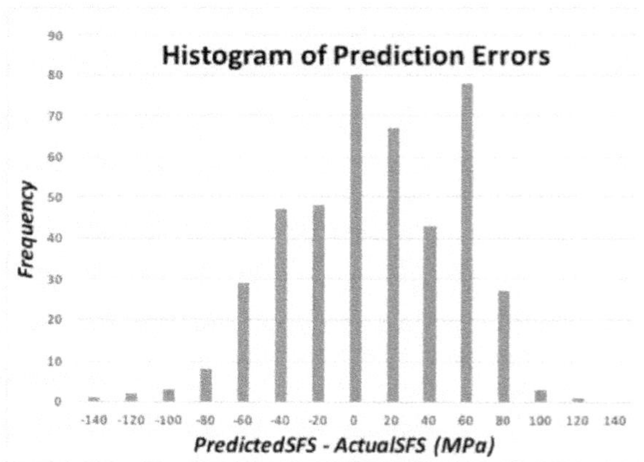

Acknowledgements

We are grateful to NIMS for making the raw data on fatigue steel strength publicly available, and also to the authors of reference [1] to preprocess the raw NIMS data and make it available as supplementary data accompanying reference [2].

References:

[1] B. P. Gautham, R. Kumar, S. Bothra, G. Mohapatra, N. Kulkarni and K. A. Padmanabhan, "More Efficient ICME through Materials Informatics and Process Modeling," Proceedings of the 1st World Congress on Integrated Computational Materials Engineering (ICME), 2011. [url]

[2] A. Agrawal, P. D. Deshpande, A. Cecen, G. P. Basavarsu, A. N. Choudhary, and S. R. Kalidindi, "Exploration of data science techniques to predict fatigue strength of steel from composition and processing parameters," Integrating Materials and Manufacturing Innovation, vol. 3, no. 8, pp. 1–19, 2014. [url]

Figure 3: A screenshot of the deployed steel fatigue strength predictor.

CyberSafety 2016: The First International Workshop on Computational Methods for CyberSafety

Shivakant Mishra[1], Qin Lv[1], Richard Han[1], Jeremy Blackburn[2]

[1] University of Colorado Boulder, USA [2] Telefonica Research, Spain
mishras@cs.colorado.edu, qin.lv@colorado.edu,
richard.han@colorado.edu, jeremy.blackburn@telefonica.com

ABSTRACT

The goal of this inaugural workshop on cybersafety is to bring together researchers and practitioners from academia, industry, government and research labs working in the area of cybersafety to discuss the unique challenges in addressing various cybersafety issues and to share experiences, solutions, tools and techniques. Examples of cybersafety issues include cyberbullying, cyberthreats, recruiting minors via Internet services for nefarious purposes, using deceptive means to dupe vulnerable populations, exhibiting misbehaving behaviors such as using profanity or flashing in online video chats, and many others. The focus of the CyberSafety workshop is on the detection, prevention and mitigation of various cybersafety issues, as well as education and promoting safe practices.

CyberSafety 2016 will be a one-day workshop, held on October 28, 2016 in conjunction with ACM CIKM 2016 in Indianapolis, IN, USA.

CCS Concepts

•**Information systems** → **Web applications;**

Keywords

CyberSafety; computational methods

1. INTRODUCTION

The theme of cybersafety is an important emerging research topic on the Internet that manifests itself daily as users navigate the Web and networked applications. Examples of cybersafety issues include cyberbullying, cyberthreats, recruiting minors via Internet services for nefarious purposes, using deceptive means to dupe vulnerable populations, exhibiting misbehaving behaviors such as using profanity or flashing in online video chats, and many others. These issues have a direct negative impact on the social, psychological and in some cases physical well-being of the end users. An important characteristic of these issues is that they fall in a grey legal area, where perpetrators may claim freedom of speech or rights to free expression despite causing harm.

CIKM'16 October 24-28, 2016, Indianapolis, IN, USA

ACM ISBN 978-1-4503-4073-1/16/10.

DOI: http://dx.doi.org/10.1145/2983323.2988541

2. TOPICS OF INTEREST

Topics of interest include but are not limited to the following:

- Cyberbullying in social media
- Cyberthreats, coercion, and undue social pressure
- Misbehaving users in online video chat services
- Trolls in chat rooms, discussion boards and other social media
- Deception to shape opinion, such as spinning
- Deceptive techniques targeted at vulnerable populations such as the elderly and K-12 minors
- Bad actors in social media
- Online exposure of inappropriate material to minors
- Education and promoting safe practices
- Remedies for preventing or thwarting cybersafety issues

3. PROGRAM

We have an exciting program covering diverse cybersafety topics such as bad actors in social media, hoaxes on the Internet, extensive coverage of cyberbullying, and detecting advertising strategies. More details of the workshop and program can be found at http://cybersafety2016.github.io/.

Session 1

- Invited Keynote Speech
  Bad Actors in Social Media
  Francesca Spezzano (Boise State University)

Session 2

- **Hoaxes in the Internet**
  Srijan Kumar (University of Maryland)
- **Survey of Computational Methods in Cyberbullying Research**
  Homa Hosseinmardi (Danaher Labs)

3.1 Session 3

- **Informing Cyberbullying Research with Social/ Psychological Insights**
  Jeremy Blackburn (Telefonica Research)
- **Catching Social Media Advertisers with Strategy Analysis**
  Meng Jiang (University of Illinois at Urbana-Champaign)
- **Detecting Cyberbullying using Latent Semantic Indexing**
  Jacob L. Bigelow, April Edwards Kontostathis, Lynne Edwards (Ursinus College)

Session 4

- **A Weakly Supervised Approach for Adaptive Detection of Cyberbullying Roles**
  Bert Huang (Virginia Tech)
- Panel Discussion
  Future directions, community growth, and industry partnership in Cybersafety research

4. ORGANIZING COMMITTEE

4.1 General Chairs

- Shivakant Mishra (University of Colorado Boulder, USA)
- Qin Lv (University of Colorado Boulder, USA)

4.2 Program Committee Chairs

- Richard Han (University of Colorado Boulder, USA)
- Jeremy Blackburn (Telefonica Research Boulder, Spain)

4.3 Program Committee

- Emiliano De Cristofaro, University College London, UK
- Homa Hosseinmardi, Danaher Labs, USA
- Bert Huang, Virginia Tech, USA
- Haewoon Kwak, Qatar Computing Research Institute, Qatar
- Qin Lv, University of Colorado Boulder, USA
- Shivakant Mishra, University of Colorado Boulder, USA
- Gianluca Stringhini, University College London, UK
- Yi Zhang, University of California Santa Cruz, USA
- Srijan Kumar, University of Maryland, College Park, USA

4.4 Webmaster

- Rahat Ibn Rafiq (University of Colorado, USA)

The Fourth International Workshop on Social Web for Disaster Management (SWDM 2016)

Carlos Castillo
EURECAT
Barcelona, Spain
chato@acm.org

Fernando Diaz
Microsoft Research
New York, NY, USA
fdiaz@microsoft.com

Yu-Ru Lin
University of Pittsburgh
Pittsburgh, PA, USA
yurulin@pitt.edu

Jie Yin
CSIRO
Epping, Australia
jie.yin@csiro.au

ABSTRACT

The proliferation of social media platforms together with the wide adoption of smartphone devices has transformed how we communicate and share news. During large-scale emergencies, such as natural disasters or armed attacks, victims, responders, and volunteers increasingly use social media to post situation updates and to request and offer help. The use of social media for emergency and disaster response has been a prominent application of information and knowledge management techniques in recent years.

There are a number of challenges associated with near real-time processing of vast volumes of information in a way that makes sense for people directly affected, for volunteer organizations, and for official emergency response agencies. As massive amount of messages posted by users are transformed into semi-structured records via information extraction and natural language processing techniques, there is a growing need for developing advanced techniques to aggregate this large-scale data to gain an understanding of the "big picture" of an emergency, and to detect and predict how a disaster could develop.

This workshop seeks to provide a platform for the exchange of ideas, identification of important problems, and discovery of possible synergies. It will enable interesting discussions and encouraged collaboration between various disciplines, and information and knowledge management approaches is the core of this workshop.

Keywords

social media, emergency management, disaster relief

1. INTRODUCTION

The SWDM workshop series, now in its fourth edition, has been a meeting point for computer scientists, government officials, emergency agencies, and other interested participants to discuss issues and challenges in the understanding of large-scale social media data during mass emergencies. The workshop seeks to provide a platform for the exchange of ideas, identification of important problems, and discovery of possible synergies. It has enabled and will continue to enable interesting discussions and encouraged collaboration between various disciplines. Information and knowledge management of time-critical information is at the core of this workshop.

CIKM'16 October 24-28, 2016, Indianapolis, IN, USA

ACM ISBN 978-1-4503-4073-1/16/10... $15.00

DOI: http://dx.doi.org/10.1145/2983323.2988535

2. TOPICS

The focal point of this workshop is disaster-related information and knowledge management challenges and solutions. How can we extract credible information from heterogeneous, fragmented, biased sources? How can we build scalable systems, accommodating increasingly large volumes of social media data, and supporting growing volunteer crowds? How can we derive actionable insights to better support decision-making?

This workshop welcomes submissions on various research topics within the contexts of emergency and crisis informatics and management. Each submission is evaluated by at least 3 program committee members.

As in previous years, the workshop offers several alternatives for submissions, including research papers, position papers, and practice and experience reports, as well as demo proposals describing a software prototype or real-world system.

3. PROGRAM COMMITTEE

The following researchers have agreed to serve in the Program Committee (PC) in the 2016 edition:

- Harith Alani, Open University, UK.
- James Caverlee, Texas A&M University, USA.
- Kyumin Lee, Utah State University, USA.
- Richard Mccreadie, University of Glasgow, UK.
- Muhammad Imran, Qatar Computing Research Institute, Qatar.
- Hemant Purohit, George Mason University, USA.
- Melanie Roberts, IBM, USA.
- Emma Spiro, University of Washington, USA
- Kentaro Torisawa, NICT, Japan.

4. KEYNOTE SPEAKERS

As in previous years, we have invited renowned speakers to offer a keynote at the workshop.

Dr. Huan Liu, Arizona State University

Some Challenges in Using Social Media Data for Disaster Response

Abstract: The popularity of social media and its ease of use make social media a new source in disaster response and relief. Social media data is mainly user-generated with geospatial, pictorial, temporal, and social information. Social media users can play a key role in disaster response and relief to share, offer, and disseminate disaster related information anytime anywhere. Given the nature of social media, social media data can be steeped with dis-, fake, or genuine information. Indiscriminate use of social media data in a disaster context may cause wasteful delays, wrong dispatches, and missed opportunities for disaster response, exacerbating the catastrophic impact of a disaster. We use some examples to illustrate challenges in using social media data for disaster response and opportunities for collaborative research in mining big social media data.

Bio Sketch: Dr. Huan Liu is a professor of Computer Science and Engineering at Arizona State University. He obtained his Ph.D. in Computer Science at University of Southern California. He was recognized for excellence in teaching and research in Computer Science and Engineering at Arizona State University. His research interests are in data mining, machine learning, social computing, and artificial intelligence, investigating problems that arise in real-world applications with high-dimensional data of disparate forms. His well-cited publications include books, book chapters, encyclopedia entries as well as conference and journal papers. He serves on journal editorial/advisory boards and numerous conference program committees. He is a Fellow of IEEE and a member of several professional societies.

Dr. Amanda Lee Hughes, Utah State University

Supporting Emergency Manager Social Media Needs with Human-Centered Methods

Abstract: Social media have recently transformed the ways in which emergency responders can create, collect, and share crisis information with support for more timely, direct, and widespread interaction with the public. In this talk, I present findings from several empirical studies that examine how social media and the forms of public participation enabled by it are changing the role of emergency responders. I then describe the exploration of solutions for emergency responders through human-centered methods that include these responders in the technology design and development process. With the aim of improving emergency response efforts, this research demonstrates how empirically-based understandings of emergency management work can inform technology design, practice, and policy.

Bio Sketch: Dr. Amanda Lee Hughes is an Assistant Professor of Computer Science at Utah State University. Her research interests span human-computer interaction, computer-supported cooperative work, social computing, software engineering, and disaster studies. She grounds her work in the empirical analysis of social relationships and work practices, after which she designs, prototypes, tests, and implements digital solutions that support this analysis. Her current work investigates the use of information communication technology (ICT) during crises and mass emergencies with particular attention to how social media affect emergency response organizations. Amanda completed a Bachelor's degree in Computer Science from Brigham Young University and a Master's and PhD degree in Computer Science from the University of Colorado Boulder.

5. ORGANIZATION

Workshop Organizers:

- Carlos Castillo, Eurecat, Spain.
- Fernando Diaz, Microsoft Research, USA.
- Yu-Ru Lin, University of Pittsburgh, USA.
- Jie Yin, CSIRO, Australia.

Series co-founder/advisor:

- Maja Vukovic, IBM Research, USA.

6. PREVIOUS EDITIONS

- First workshop, in conjunction with WWW 2012: https://swdmwww12.wordpress.com/
- Second workshop, in conjunction with WWW 2013: https://sites.google.com/site/swdmwww13/
- Third workshop, in conjunction with WWW 2015: https://sites.google.com/site/swdmwww15/

7. WEBPAGE OF SWDM 2016

The workshop's webpage is available at:
https://sites.google.com/site/swdm2016/

BigNet 2016: First Workshop on Big Network Analytics

Jie Tang[1], Keke Cai[2], Zhong Su[2], Hanghang Tong[3], Michalis Vazirgiannis[4], Yang Yang[5]
[1]Tsinghua University; [2]IBM, China Research Lab; [3]Arizona State University;
[4]Ecole Polytechnique; [5]Zhejiang University
jietang@tsinghua.edu.cn, {caikeke, suzhong}@cn.ibm.com, {hanghang.tong, michalis.vazirgiannis, sherlockbourne}@gmail.com

ABSTRACT

The first ACM international workshop on big network analytics is held in Indianapolis, Indiana, USA on October 24, 2016 and co-located with the ACM 25th Conference on Information and Knowledge Management (CIKM). The main objective of the workshop is to provide a forum for presenting the most recent advances in mining big networks to unearth rich knowledge. It is related to information retrieval, Web mining, social network analysis, and computational advertising. The anticipated outcome includes a fruitful discussion about the emerging challenges in this field, the development of novel theories for mining big networks, and motivating the interesting applications. The broader anticipated outcome includes: fostering future research directions, publishing high quality papers, attracting new researchers to this field, and concrete solutions to the existing problems.

Categories and Subject Descriptors

A. [**General Literature**]

Keywords

Big network

1. INTRODUCTION

Our world is networked: people are closer to each other through online social network services or mobile communication networks, while information is capable to be exchanged faster by World Wide Web or email networks. The network is a treasure trove of user experiences and knowledge that presents great opportunities to understand the fundamental science of our world. On the other hand, the network, with huge amount of data, and multiple types of entities (e.g., users, documents, organizations, etc.), user behaviors, and relations between entities, has become so large and complex that traditional methodologies are inadequate.

This workshop aims to provide a forum for presenting the most recent advances in mining big networks to unearth rich knowledge. It is related to information retrieval, Web mining, social network analysis, and computational advertising. In particular, topics of interest include but are not limited to:

- Novel algorithms for handling large-scaled networks;
- Data integration from multiple networks;
- Graph based recommendations;
- Large-scaled link prediction algorithms;
- User influence analysis algorithms or information diffusion models;
- Clustering and community detection in big networks;
- Events detection and evolution analysis;
- Personalized based ranking methods for recommendations, marketing, or advertising;
- Visualization and exploration for big network data;
- Distributed algorithms on graph;
- Privacy and security concerns on networks;
- Graph embedding;
- Graph mining on text data;
- Applications and platforms for social network.

2. WORKSHOP OBJECTIVES

The anticipated outcome includes a fruitful discussion about the emerging challenges in this field, the development of novel theories for mining big networks, and motivating the interesting applications. The broader anticipated outcome includes: fostering future research directions, publishing high quality papers, attracting new researchers to this field, and concrete solutions to the existing problems.

3. WORKSHOP PROGRAM FORMAT

The workshop is a one-day workshop. We invite several keynotes to talk about state-of-the-art research processing on big network analytics. We also accept ten research papers to be presented in the workshop. Each submitted paper has been evaluated by at least three reviewers from the aspects of novelty, significance, technical soundness, experimental evaluation, and presentation. Only papers that are deemed to be satisfactorily novel and technically sound by the program committee will be accepted. The presentations will be grouped based on topics.

CIKM'16 October 24-28, 2016, Indianapolis, IN, USA

ACM ISBN 978-1-4503-4073-1/16/10.

DOI: http://dx.doi.org/10.1145/2983323.2988536

4. CONCLUSION

This workshop aims to provide a forum for presenting the most recent advances in mining big networks to unearth rich knowledge. We have constructed an exciting program of refereed papers and invited talks that will give participants a full dose of emerging research.

5. WORKSHOP ORGANIZERS

Keke Cai (PC co-chairs) is a research staff member at Information Analysis and Search department, IBM Research-China. She joined IBM in 2007 after receiving her Ph.D. degree in Computer Science from Zhejiang University. Her research interests lie primarily in web/social mining, text analytics, cognitive computing and natural language analysis.

Zhong Su (general co-chairs) is a Senior Technical Staff Member (STSM) at the IBM Research - China and manages the deep learning and natural language processing team. He joined CRL after receiving his Ph.D. degree in computer science at Tsinghua University in 2002. He has been involved in many projects including text analytics, cognitive computing, enterprise search, metadata management and information integration. Zhong Su has published more than 30 journal and conference papers on WWW, CIMK, ACL and KDD. Zhong Su was selected as an IBM Master Inventor for his excellent patent application records and great contribution to IBMs global leadership on patents creation. Zhong Su totally owns more than 50 US / international patent applications.

Jie Tang (general co-chairs) is an associate professor at Tsinghua University. He received the PhD degree in Computer Science from Tsinghua University in 2006. His research interests include social network mining and semantic web. He has published 60+ conference/journal papers and three book chapters, and filed seven patents. He has served as a PC member of 40+ conferences including WWW, SIGKDD, SIGIR, and ACL and as a reviewer of TKDE, TKDD, TNN, TALIP, and TSMC.
HP: http://keg.cs.tsinghua.edu.cn/persons/tj/

Hanghang Tong (PC co-chairs) is currently an assistant professor at School of Computing, Informatics, and Decision Systems Engineering (CIDSE), Arizona State University since August 2014. He received his M.Sc and Ph.D. degree from Carnegie Mellon University in 2008 and 2009, both majored in Machine Learning. His research interest is in large scale data mining for graphs and multimedia. He has received several awards, including one test of time award (ICDM 10-Year highest impact paper award), four best paper awards and four best of conference. He has published over 100 referred articles and more than 20 patents.
HP: http://tonghanghang.org

Michalis Vazirgiannis (general co-chairs) is a Professor at LIX, Ecole Polytechnique in France. He has conducted research in GMD-IPSI, Max Planck MPI (Germany), in INRIA/FUTURS (Paris). He has been a teaching in AUEB (Greece), Ecole Polytechnique, Telecom-Paristech, ENS (France), Tsinghua (China) and in Deusto University (Spain).

His current research interests are on machine learning and combinatorial methods for Graph analysis (including community detection, graph clustering and embeddings, influence maximization), Text mining including Graph of Words, word embeddings with applications to web advertising and marketing, event detection and summarization. Also distributed machine learning algorithms, distributed dimensionality reduction, distributed resource management. He has active cooperation with industrial partners in the area of data analytics and machine learning for large scale data repositories in different application domains such as Web advertising and recommendations, social networks, medical data, aircraft logs, insurance data. He has supervised fourteen completed PhD theses several of the supported by industrial funding including Google and Airbus.

On the publication frontier, he has contributed chapters in books and encyclopedias, published three books and more than a hundred forty papers in international refereed journals and conferences. He is also co-author of three patents. He has received the ERCIM and the Marie Curie EU fellowships and lead a DIGITEO chair grant. Since 2015 M. Vazirgiannis leads the AXA Data Science chair.

Yang Yang is an assistant professor in the College of Computer Science, Zhejiang University. Before this, Yang received his Ph.D. degree in Computer Science and Technology from Tsinghua University. His research interests include information diffusion, social influence and probabilistic graphical models. He has been visiting in Cornell University and Leuven University. He has served as the PC member of ICDM 2016 and ASONAM 2015.
HP: http://yangy.org

6. ACKNOWLEDGMENT

We would like to acknowledge all authors who submitted contributions and the program committee members for their excellent work to review the papers. We are also very grateful for the invited keynote speakers for their presentations in the workshop.

DDTA 2016 – The Workshop on Data-Driven Talent Acquisition

Yi Fang
Santa Clara University
Santa Clara, CA, USA
yfang@scu.edu

Maarten de Rijke
University of Amsterdam
Amsterdam, The Netherlands
derijke@uva.nl

Huangming Xie
LinkedIn
Mountain View, CA, USA
hxie@linkedin.com

ABSTRACT

Expertise search is a well-established field in information retrieval. In recent years, the increasing availability of data enables accumulation of evidence of talent and expertise from a wide range of domains. The availability of big data significantly benefits employers and recruiters. By analyzing the massive amounts of structured and unstructured data, organizations may be able to find the exact skill sets and talent they need to grow their business. The aim of this workshop is to provide a forum for industry and academia to discuss the recent progress in talent search and management, and how the use of big data and data-driven decision making can advance talent acquisition and human resource management.

CCS Concepts

•Information systems → Expert search; Business intelligence; Enterprise search;

Keywords

Talent Acquisition; Human Resource Management; Expertise Retrieval; Data-driven

1. INTRODUCTION

Employees are one of the greatest assets of a company. Recruiting the right people and retaining the best are crucial for many organizations. Talent acquisition and management in many businesses have traditionally revolved around personal relationships or decision making based on experience rather than deep quantitative analysis. Big data analytics enables huge opportunities to improve workforce planning, development and productivity, including to identify potential talents and experts, to predict hiring needs, and to optimize hiring performance. According to [3], a leading healthcare organization, has used data analytics techniques to generate more than 100 million dollars in savings while simultaneously improving the engagement of its workforce. Another company reduced its retention bonuses by 20 million dollars and employee attrition by half, due to the use of predictive behavioral analytics.

On the other hand, expert search is a well-established field in information retrieval [1]. With the TREC Enterprise Track in 2005 [2], there was an early focus on the enterprise setting. In recent years, the increasing availability of data enables accumulation of evidence of talent and expertise from a wide range of domains beyond the enterprise. The availability of big data significantly benefits employers and recruiters. By analyzing the massive amounts of structured and unstructured data, organizations may be able to find the exact skill sets and talent they need to grow their business. The aim of this workshop is to provide a forum for industry and academia to discuss the recent progress in talent search and how the use of big data and data-driven decision making can advance talent acquisition and management.

CIKM'16 October 24-28, 2016, Indianapolis, IN, USA

ACM ISBN 978-1-4503-4073-1/16/10.

DOI: http://dx.doi.org/10.1145/2983323.2988538

2. WORKSHOP TOPICS

The workshop seeks to uncover the next research frontiers in talent acquisition and management by exploiting the abundance of data. Examples of topic of interest include (but are not limited to):

- Talent and expertise related data in heterogeneous media: enterprise, Web, user generated content (social media sites, weblogs, microblogs, wikis), Linked Open Data, etc.
- Integration of expertise data from multiple sources
- Expertise retrieval
- Expert profiling
- Data analytics for human resource management
- Prediction of hiring needs and optimization of hiring performance
- Personalized job search
- Recommender systems for talent acquisition (e.g., job recommendation)
- Behavior modelling of job seekers
- Data-driven marketing for talent acquisition
- Test collections and evaluation methodology
- Interfaces, case studies, and applications

3. PROGRAM

The workshop called for two types of submissions: 1) papers including research results, position papers, and practice and experience reports, having 4-8 pages (regular), or 2-4 pages (short); 2) demo proposals describing a prototype of system, up to a maximum of 2 pages. All submissions must be formatted according to the ACM SIG proceedings format. The reviewing process is double-blind, so submissions need to be anonymous. At least one author of each accepted paper is required to present their work at the workshop. The list of accepted contributions, corresponding resources, and all other outcomes of the workshop are available at https://sites.google.com/site/ddta2016cikm.

4. WORKSHOP ORGANIZERS

- **Yi Fang** is assistant professor in Santa Clara University. He received his PhD in Computer Science from Purdue University, West Lafayette. He has published in reputable conferences and journals including SIGIR, CIKM, WSDM, AAAI, FnTIR, and IRJ. He is the program committee member for a number of conferences including SIGIR, CIKM, IJCAI, AAAI, ECIR, ICDM, AIRS, etc. He served as the Tutorial Chair for IEEE BigData 2016 and the Senior Program Committee member for CIKM 2016. He also served as Local Chair for CIKM 2013 and received the Outstanding Service Award for his service.
- **Maarten de Rijke** is full professor of Information Processing and Internet in the Informatics Institute at the University of Amsterdam. He holds MSc degrees in Philosophy and Mathematics (both cum laude), and a PhD in Theoretical Computer Science. He is editor-in-chief of ACM Transactions on Information Systems, co-editor-in-chief of Foundations and Trends in Information Retrieval and of Springer's Information Retrieval book series, (associate) editor for various journals and book series, and a current and former coordinator of retrieval evaluation tracks at TREC, CLEF and INEX. He was co-chair for SIGIR 2013, general chair for ECIR 2014, co-chair "web search systems and applications" for WWW 2015, short paper co-chair for SIGIR 2015, and program co-chair for information retrieval for CIKM 2015. He is also general co-chair of ICTIR 2017 and WSDM 2017.
- **Huangming Xie** is the Staff Data Scientist and Tech Lead at LinkedIn. He received his PhD in Computation and System Biology from Massachusetts Institute of Technology (MIT) and was a Postdoctoral Research Fellow at Harvard Medical School. He worked as Senior Data Scientist at Simply Hired, one of the largest job search engines in the world, by exploring big data analytics to improve job search relevancy and match the right candidate for the right job. At LinkedIn, He spearheaded a cross-team initiative to build the member value action framework, creating leverage for multiple analytics and machine learning projects across the company. He is leading data science for Search & Discovery team at LinkedIn to improve personalized search for people, jobs, content, companies and more across desktop and mobile.

5. REFERENCES

[1] K. Balog, Y. Fang, M. de Rijke, P. Serdyukov, and L. Si. Expertise retrieval. *Foundations and Trends in Information Retrieval*, 6(2–3):127–256, 2012.

[2] N. Craswell, A. P. de Vries, and I. Soboroff. Overview of the trec 2005 enterprise track. In *Trec*, volume 5, pages 199–205, 2005.

[3] B. Fecheyr-Lippens, B. Schaninger, and K. Tanner. Power to the new people analytics. *McKinsey Quarterly*, 51(1):61–63, 2015.

ACM DAVA'16: 2nd International Workshop on DAta mining meets Visual Analytics at Big Data Era

Lei Shi
Chinese Academy of Sciences
shijim@gmail.com

Hanghang Tong
Arizona State University
hanghang.tong@gmail.com

Chaoli Wang
University of Notre Dame
chaoli.wang@nd.edu

Leman Akoglu
Stony Brook University
leman@cs.stonybrook.edu

ABSTRACT

The world is awash with big data now - we are generating ten exabytes of data in a variety of different forms every day. In this wave, there is a trend to integrate the data mining methods with interactive visualizations to advance the so-called visual analytics (VA) technology. The VA technique enjoys the joint advantage of the human intelligence and the machineąŕs computational power. Various aspects of the data mining method need to be inspected, justified, organized and evaluated for a successful VA system. The challenges include but not limited to the data reduction, integration, governance and knowledge representation. Exploring all these directions for joining the data analysis with visualization and finally delivering values to users is a problem of vital importance and requires a lot of efforts from different parties where information management researchers from both data mining and visualization play major roles. This makes the workshop highly relevant to CIKM, the premier international conference on topics at the confluence of information retrieval, databases, and knowledge management.

Moreover, the National Science Foundation of United States sets up a continuous program on the foundation of data and visual analytics, the FODAVA, which makes this workshop an in-time event for people to share their opinions and experiences on this topic.

The DAVA'16 workshop includes 3 invited keynote talks, 2 paper sessions and some posters. Authors of accepted oral papers give 20-minute presentation on their papers. Three keynote speakers from both data mining and visualization give invited talks in this workshop (40-minute each). The DAVA'16 organization committee selects one paper of the highest quality to receive the DAVA'16 best paper award. An extended version of the selected papers will be recommended to Chinese of Journal Electronics (SCI-indexed) or International Journal of Software and Informatics (IJSI) as a special issue on visual analytics.

Keywords

Visual Analytics; Data Mining; Big Data

CIKM'16 October 24-28, 2016, Indianapolis, IN, USA

ACM ISBN 978-1-4503-4073-1/16/10.

DOI: http://dx.doi.org/10.1145/2983323.2988539

DTMBIO 2016: The Tenth International Workshop on Data and Text Mining in Biomedical Informatics

Sangwoo Kim
Severance Biomedical Science Institute, Yonsei Univeristy College of Medicine, Korea
swkim@yuhs.ac

Jake Chen
Department of Genetics, University of Alabama at Birmingham, USA
jakechen@uab.edu

Vincenzo Cutello
Department of Mathematics and Computer Science, University of Catania, Italy
cutello@dmi.unict.it

Doheon Lee
Department of Bio and Brain Engineering, KAIST, Korea
dhlee@kaist.ac.kr

ABSTRACT

Started in 2006 as a specialized workshop in the field of text mining applied to biomedical informatics, DTMBIO (ACM international workshop on Data and Text Mining in Biomedical Informatics) has been held annually in conjunction with one of the largest data management conferences, CIKM, bringing together researchers working on computer science and bioinformatics area. The purpose of DTMBIO is to foster discussions regarding the state-of-the-art applications of data and text mining on biomedical research problems. DTMBIO 2016 will help scientists navigate emerging trends and opportunities in the evolving area of informatics related techniques and problems in the context of biomedical research.

1. INTRODUCTION

As biomedical "big-data" are rapidly growing in quantity and quality, computational techniques to handle, store and analyze such information to acquire more valuable knowledge is now essential for relevant researchers. Along with the traditional medical records including electronic medical records (EMR), clinical test results and environmental records, high-throughput observations upon biological entities such as genes, transcripts, proteins and metabolites are coupled with individual phenotype information to infer elements that are associated with a specific phenomenon of our interest. This also requires an exploration of previously reported knowledge that exists in a form of canonical database and literature, to build a hypothesis and confirm the consistency. Accordingly, it is doubtless that application of cutting-edge techniques in data and text mining is a key for efficient biomedical knowledge generation in this "big-data" era.

Since its inaugural meeting in 2006, started as the Text-mining in bioinformatics (TMBIO), DTMBIO has been continuously bringing together multidisciplinary pioneers from computer and biomedical communities. Over 100 high-quality studies have been presented in the past DTMBIO workshops, many of which are finally published as full paper in scientific journals. Although highly diverse in terms of methods, information sources and target phenotypes (diseases), DTMBIO 2016 holds two major tracks, as in the past workshops: (1) method development and improvement for data and text mining in bioinformatics that forms a basis for more efficient and accurate analyses, and (2) novel biomedical discoveries from high-throughput data based upon data and text mining techniques. We regard the balanced combination between pure computer science and biology as the primary factor for being successful in holding a creative and innovative workshop for both groups.

The call for papers attracted 26 submissions from all over the world. The selection process was highly competitive. Each paper went through a rigorous double-blinded peer review by at least 3 members of the Program Committee. Based on the referee reports, the papers were ranked according to their original contribution, and the program committee accepted 7 papers and 4 short papers (which will be invited to a supplement issue of BMC Decision Making and Medical Informatics) that cover a variety of topics, including novel information extraction techniques, ontologies, and application to large biomedical data. In addition, the program includes a keynote speech by Vincenzo Cutello at University of Catania. We hope that these proceedings will serve as a valuable reference for researchers and developers who are interested in applying Text Mining to Medical Informatics.

2. PAPER SUMMARY

Track 1 presents research pertinent to various data and text mining techniques in the biomedical domain. Heo *et al* [1] analyzed the field of bioinformatics with time-series data to understand the topical trends and their characteristics over the time. They applied ACT models to consider key phrases, authors, and journals simultaneously, and deduced interesting and informative results for the changing trends of bioinformatics. Alamri *et al* [2] introduced an approach to automatically annotating contradictory facts that are reported in biomedical research literature, by a database of semantic predications extracted from MEDLINE (SemMedDB). We anticipate that the constructed corpus have the potential to be used by bioinformatics researchers. Preiss *et al* [3] describe a novel Literature-based discovery (LBD) method that extracts hidden connections between well-known knowledge, from published biological articles. As a data mining method, this new LBD system automatically detect relationships between pairs of terms. They also suggested the possibility of connecting terms that have no direct link, with chain of multiple links. Tran *et al* [4] developed a tool to explore evidence networks to better interpret and evaluate potential drug-mediator pairs. It allows the researchers get access to those evidences in a more efficient

CIKM'16 , October 24-28, 2016, Indianapolis, IN, USA
ACM 978-1-4503-4073-1/16/10.
http://dx.doi.org/10.1145/2983323.2988540

manner through an interactive web-portal for evidence networks. Kim et al [5] defined the biomedical verb, and constructed the list of biomedical verbs using the PKDE4J tool. They attempted to construct the verb list with relation type classified by their characteristics and a nominalization form of extracted verbs for usability. Moreover, they established the actual list of biomedical verb and constructed the linguistic source out of the entire PubMed records.

Track 2 presents research in the area of text mining in the biomedical informatics field, especially in analyzing bio "big-data" considering a practical use. Kim *et al* [6] proposed a new way of predicting toxicity of various chemicals to liver using molecular fingerprinting. They present an interesting approach of constructing feature vectors by assigning weights (log ratios) only in a subset of fingerprint features. The method showed a better performance in predicting DILI with their weighting approach, and they also presented important fingerprint features used in the prediction. Kimothi *et al* [7] proposed a distributed representation framework so called 'seq2vec' for sequence comparison and classification, and showed the performance of their framework for classifying proteins. Based on 'doc2vec' which is the improved model of word2vec, authors applied this principle to biological sequence classification. Kim *et al* [8] addressed an efficient way of epidemic parameter searching strategy based on the new measure, the value of recovered on turning point, VRTP. Unlike the previous studies that focused on the effect of different global network structure in epidemics, this study focused on the more realistic network setting, scale-free network. Kim *et al* [9] attempted to identify molecular properties of proteins for their drug targetability. They examined additional attributes (features), as well as feature selection, to improve machine learning classification performance in an existing task, a task to identify drug target proteins. Jung *et al* [10] proposed a new method to predict therapeutic targets for muscle atrophy. A Petri-net based approach on a phosphorylation network was used to identify potential targets that when inhibited can restore a atrophic state to the normal state. Tsutsui *et al* [11] proposed an approach for enhancing understanding about a specific domain by extracting knowledge from literature. In this study, Alzheimer's disease (AD) was selected for the target domain. They first generated topics related to AD using the LDA approach and then manually created questions based on words included in the topics. Then, the questions in the form of triplet were answered using Open IE approach. Several interesting questions about AD were presented in the paper, showing benefits of the proposed approach.

3. CONCLUSION

This workshop continues the line of DTMBIO workshops organized in conjunction with CIKM in 2006, 2008, 2009, 2010, 2011, 2012, 2013, 2014 and 2015. We invite researchers and practitioners from a variety of backgrounds such as computer science, information system, information science, bioinformatics, medical informatics, and medical sciences. The main objective of the workshop will be to strengthen the cooperation within the growing community in medical data and text mining research, allowing lively exchange of ideas and foster new collaborations.

4. REFERENCES

[1] Heo, G.E., Kang, K.Y., and Song M. 2016. Examining the Field of Bioinformatics by the Multi-faceted Informetric Approach. In *DTMBIO 2016*.

[2] Alamri, A., Stetvenson, M. 2016. Introducing a New Methodology to Construct a Potentially Contradictory Corpus from Biomedical Domain. In *DTMBIO 2016*.

[3] Preiss, J., and Stevenson, M. 2016 Quantifying and Filtering Knowledge Generated by Literature Based Discovery. In *DTMBIO 2016*.

[4] Tran, H., Kiefer, J., and Kim, S. 2016. Contextualization of Drug-Mediator Relations Using Public Knowledge-bases. In *DTMBIO 2016*.

[5] Kim, Y., Beak, and Song, M. 2016. Constructing Linguistic Verb Source for Relation Extraction. In *DTMBIO 2016*.

[6] Kim, E., and Nam, H. 2016. Prediction models for drug-induced hepatotoxicity by using weighted molecular fingerprints. In *DTMBIO 2016*.

[7] Kimothi, D., Soni, A., Biyani, P., and Hogan, J. 2016. Distributed Representations for Biological Sequence Analysis. In *DTMBIO 2016*.

[8] Kim, K., Lee, S., Lee, K.H., and Lee, D. 2016. The coupling effect on VRTP of SIR epidemics in Scale-Free Networks. In *DTMBIO 2016*.

[9] Kim, B., Jo, J., Han, J., Park, C., and Lee, H. 2016. In silico re-identification of properties of drug target proteins. In *DTMBIO 2016*.

[10] Jung, J., Kwon, M., Bae, S., Yim, S., Kim, S., and Lee, D. 2016. Therapeutic target prediction for muscle atrophy by using Petri-net simulation on phosphorylation networks. In *DTMBIO 2016*.

[11] Tsutsui, S., Ding, Y., and Meng, G. 2016. Machine Reading Approach to Understand Alzheimer's Disease Literature. In *DTMBIO 2016*.

Author Index

www.ingramcontent.com/pod-product-compliance
Ingram Content Group UK Ltd.
Pitfield, Milton Keynes, MK11 3LW, UK
UKHW051419290926
15471UKWH00009B/1680

9 781450 347198